## FORMULAS/EQUATIONS

**Distance Formula**  The distance from $(x_1, y_1)$ to $(x_2, y_2)$ is $\sqrt{(x_2 - }$

**Midpoint Formula**  The midpoint of the line segment with endpoints $(x_1, y_1)$ and $(x_2, y_2)$ is $\left( \dfrac{x_1 + x_2}{2}, \dfrac{y_1 + y_2}{2} \right)$.

**Standard Equation of a Circle**  The standard equation of a circle of radius $r$ with center at $(h, k)$ is
$$(x - h)^2 + (y - k)^2 = r^2$$

**Slope Formula**  The slope $m$ of the line containing the points $(x_1, y_1)$ and $(x_2, y_2)$ is
$$\text{slope } (m) = \frac{\text{change in } y}{\text{change in } x} = \frac{y_2 - y_1}{x_2 - x_1} \quad (x_1 \neq x_2)$$
$m$ is undefined if $x_1 = x_2$

**Slope-Intercept Equation of a Line**  The equation of a line with slope $m$ and $y$-intercept $(0, b)$ is $y = mx + b$

**Point-Slope Equation of a Line**  The equation of a line with slope $m$ containing the point $(x_1, y_1)$ is $y - y_1 = m(x - x_1)$

**Quadratic Formula**  The solutions of the equation $ax^2 + bx + c = 0$, $a \neq 0$, are $x = \dfrac{-b \pm \sqrt{b^2 - 4ac}}{2a}$

If $b^2 - 4ac > 0$, there are two distinct real solutions.
If $b^2 - 4ac = 0$, there is a repeated real solution.
If $b^2 - 4ac < 0$, there are two complex solutions (complex conjugates).

## GEOMETRY FORMULAS

**Circle**   $r$ = Radius, $A$ = Area, $C$ = Circumference
$$A = \pi r^2 \quad C = 2\pi r$$

**Triangle** 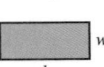  $b$ = Base, $h$ = Height (Altitude), $A$ = area
$$A = \tfrac{1}{2}bh$$

**Rectangle** 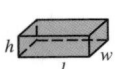  $l$ = Length, $w$ = Width, $A$ = area, $P$ = perimeter
$$A = lw \quad P = 2l + 2w$$

**Rectangular Box**   $l$ = Length, $w$ = Width, $h$ = Height, $V$ = Volume, $S$ = Surface area
$$V = lwh \quad S = 2lw + 2lh + 2wh$$

**Sphere**   $r$ = Radius, $V$ = Volume, $S$ = Surface area
$$V = \tfrac{4}{3}\pi r^3 \quad S = 4\pi r^2$$

**Right Circular Cylinder**  $r$ = Radius, $h$ = Height, $V$ = Volume, $S$ = Surface area
$$V = \pi r^2 h \quad S = 2\pi r^2 + 2\pi rh$$

## CONVERSION TABLE

| | | |
|---|---|---|
| 1 centimeter ≈ 0.394 inch | 1 joule ≈ 0.738 foot-pound | 1 mile ≈ 1.609 kilometers |
| 1 meter ≈ 39.370 inches | 1 gram ≈ 0.035 ounce | 1 gallon ≈ 3.785 liters |
| ≈ 3.281 feet | 1 kilogram ≈ 2.205 pounds | 1 pound ≈ 4.448 newtons |
| 1 kilometer ≈ 0.621 mile | 1 inch ≈ 2.540 centimeters | 1 foot-lb ≈ 1.356 Joules |
| 1 liter ≈ 0.264 gallon | 1 foot ≈ 30.480 centimeters | 1 ounce ≈ 28.350 grams |
| 1 newton ≈ 0.225 pound | ≈ 0.305 meter | 1 pound ≈ 0.454 kilogram |

## FUNCTIONS

| | |
|---|---|
| **Constant Function** | $f(x) = b$ |
| **Linear Function** | $f(x) = mx + b$, where $m$ is the slope and $b$ is the $y$-intercept |
| **Quadratic Function** | $f(x) = ax^2 + bx + c$, $a \neq 0$ or $f(x) = a(x - h)^2 + k$ parabola vertex $(h, k)$ |
| **Polynomial Function** | $f(x) = a_n x^n + a_{n-1} x^{n-1} + \cdots + a_1 x + a_0$ |
| **Rational Function** | $R(x) = \dfrac{n(x)}{d(x)} = \dfrac{a_n x^n + a_{n-1} x^{n-1} + \cdots + a_1 x + a_0}{b_m x^m + a_{m-1} x^{m-1} + \cdots + b_1 x + b_0}$ |
| **Exponential Function** | $f(x) = b^x, b > 0, b \neq 1$ |
| **Logarithmic Function** | $f(x) = \log_b x, b > 0, b \neq 1$ |

## GRAPHS OF COMMON FUNCTIONS

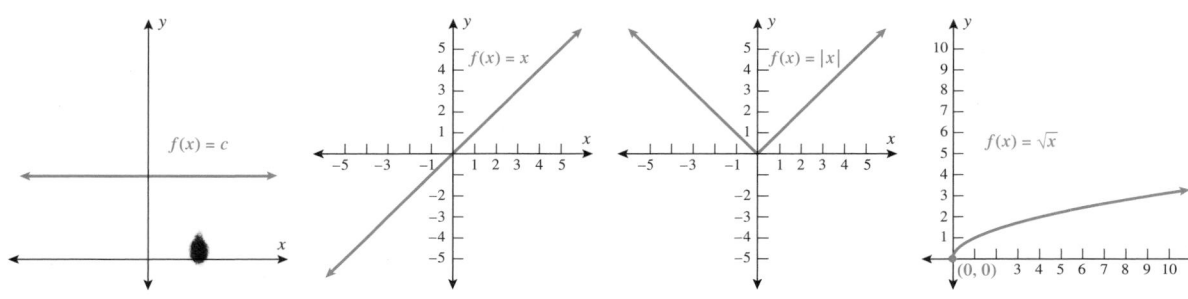

| Constant Function | Identity Function | Absolute Value Function | Square Root Function |
|---|---|---|---|

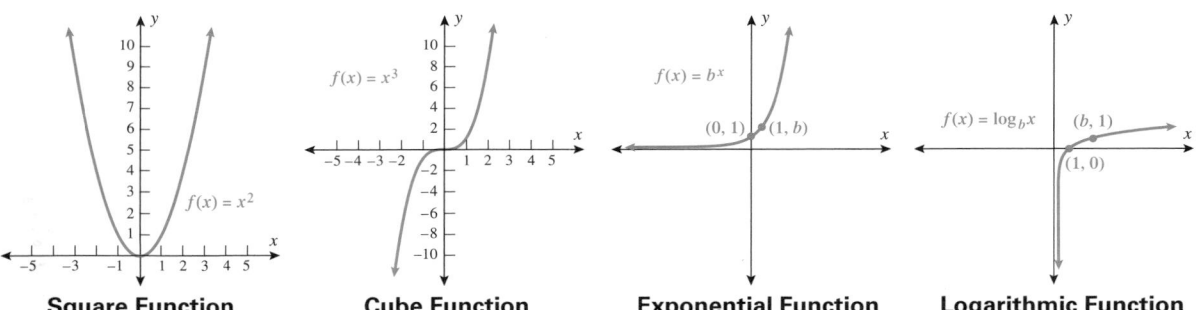

| Square Function | Cube Function | Exponential Function | Logarithmic Function |
|---|---|---|---|

## TRANSFORMATIONS

In each case, $c$ represents a positive real number.

| Function | | Draw the graph of $f$ and: |
|---|---|---|
| Vertical translations | $\begin{cases} y = f(x) + c \\ y = f(x) - c \end{cases}$ | Shift $f$ upward $c$ units. <br> Shift $f$ downward $c$ units. |
| Horizontal translations | $\begin{cases} y = f(x - c) \\ y = f(x + c) \end{cases}$ | Shift $f$ to the right $c$ units. <br> Shift $f$ to the left $c$ units. |
| Reflections | $\begin{cases} y = -f(x) \\ y = f(-x) \end{cases}$ | Reflect $f$ about the $x$-axis. <br> Reflect $f$ about the $y$-axis. |

## HERON'S FORMULA FOR AREA

If the semiperimeter, $s$, of a triangle is

$$s = \frac{a + b + c}{2}$$

then the area of that triangle is

$$A = \sqrt{s(s - a)(s - b)(s - c)}$$

# Precalculus

**Second Edition**

**CYNTHIA Y. YOUNG** | *Professor of Mathematics*
UNIVERSITY OF CENTRAL FLORIDA

**WILEY**

| | |
|---|---|
| PUBLISHER | Laurie Rosatone |
| ACQUISITIONS EDITOR | Joanna Dingle |
| PROJECT EDITOR | Jennifer Brady |
| ASSISTANT CONTENT EDITOR | Jacqueline Sinacori |
| EDITORIAL ASSISTANT | Courtney Welsh |
| MARKETING MANAGER | Kimberly Kanakes |
| CONTENT MANAGER | Karoline Luciano |
| SENIOR PRODUCTION EDITOR | Ken Santor |
| DESIGNER | Madelyn Lesure |
| OPERATIONS MANAGER | Melissa Edwards |
| PHOTO EDITOR | Kathleen Pepper |
| COVER DESIGN | Madelyn Lesure |
| COVER PHOTO | Front Cover: Combined image: Ty Milford/Masterfile and Leslie Banks/iStockphoto |
| | Back Cover: Rustem Gurler/iStockphoto |

"Modeling Our World" image: © David Woodfall/Getty Images

This book was set in 10/12 Times by MPS Limited, and printed and bound by Quad/Graphics, Inc.
The cover was printed by Quad/Graphics, Inc.

This book is printed on acid free paper. ∞

Founded in 1807, John Wiley & Sons, Inc. has been a valued source of knowledge and understanding for more than 200 years, helping people around the world meet their needs and fulfill their aspirations. Our company is built on a foundation of principles that include responsibility to the communities we serve and where we live and work. In 2008, we launched a Corporate Citizenship Initiative, a global effort to address the environmental, social, economic, and ethical challenges we face in our business. Among the issues we are addressing are carbon impact, paper specifications and procurement, ethical conduct within our business and among our vendors, and community and charitable support. For more information, please visit our website: www.wiley.com/go/citizenship.

ISBN: 978-0-470-90413-8
BRV ISBN: 978-1-118-69247-9
*Precalculus with Limits* 2e HSE: 978-1-118-85027-5

**Library of Congress Cataloging-in-Publication Data**

Young, Cynthia Y.
    Precalculus / Cynthia Y. Young. -- Second edition.
        pages cm
    Includes indexes.
    ISBN   978-0-470-90413-8   (cloth)
    1.    Precalculus--Textbooks.    I. Title.
    QA39.3.Y68 2013
    510--dc23

                                                        2013033552

Printed in the United States of America

10 9 8 7 6 5 4 3 2

*For Christopher and Caroline*

Cynthia Y. Young is a native of Tampa, Florida. She currently is a Professor of Mathematics at the University of Central Florida (UCF) and the author of *College Algebra*, *Trigonometry*, *Algebra and Trigonometry*, and *Precalculus*. She holds a B.A. degree in Secondary Mathematics Education from the University of North Carolina (Chapel Hill), an M.S. degree in Mathematical Sciences from UCF, and both an M.S. in Electrical Engineering and a Ph.D in Applied Mathematics from the University of Washington. She has taught high school in North Carolina and Florida, developmental mathematics at Shoreline Community College in Washington, and undergraduate and graduate students at UCF. Dr. Young's two main research interests are laser propagation through random media and improving student learning in STEM. She has authored or co-authored over 60 books and articles and been involved in over $2.5M in external funding. Her atmospheric propagation research was recognized by the Office of Naval Research Young Investigator award, and in 2007 she was selected as a Fellow of the International Society for Optical Engineers. She is currently the co-director of UCF's EXCEL program whose goal is to improve the retention of STEM majors.

Although Dr. Young excels in research, she considers teaching her true calling. She has been the recipient of the UCF Excellence in Undergraduate Teaching Award, the UCF Scholarship of Teaching and Learning Award, and a two-time recipient of the UCF Teaching Incentive Program. Dr. Young is committed to improving student learning in mathematics and has shared her techniques and experiences with colleagues around the country through talks at colleges, universities, and conferences.

Dr. Young and her husband, Dr. Christopher Parkinson, enjoy spending time outdoors and competing in Field Trials with their Labrador Retrievers. *Laird's Cynful Wisdom* (call name "*Wiley*") is titled in Canada and currently pursuing her U.S. title. *Laird's Cynful Ellegance* (call name "*Ellie*") was a finalist in the Canadian National in 2009 and is retired (relaxing at home).

Dr. Young is pictured here with Ellie's 2011 litter of puppies!

Bonnie Farris

# Preface

As a mathematics professor I would hear my students say, "I understand you in class, but when I get home I am lost." When I would probe further, students would continue with "I can't read the book." As a mathematician I always found mathematics textbooks quite easy to read—and then it dawned on me: don't look at this book through a mathematician's eyes; look at it through the eyes of students who might not view mathematics the same way that I do. What I found was that the books were not at all like my class. Students understood me in class, but when they got home they couldn't understand the book. It was then that the folks at Wiley lured me into writing. My goal was to write a book that is seamless with how we teach and is an ally (not an adversary) to student learning. I wanted to give students a book they could read without sacrificing the rigor needed for conceptual understanding. The following quote comes from a reviewer of this third edition when asked about the rigor of the book:

> *I would say that this text comes across as a little less rigorous than other texts, but I think that stems from how easy it is to read and how clear the author is. When one actually looks closely at the material, the level of rigor is high.*

## Distinguishing Features

Four key features distinguish this book from others, and they came directly from my classroom.

### PARALLEL WORDS AND MATH

Have you ever looked at your students' notes? I found that my students were only scribbling down the mathematics that I would write—never the words that I would say in class. I started passing out handouts that had two columns: one column for math and one column for words. Each Example would have one or the other; either the words were there and students had to fill in the math, or the math was there and students had to fill in the words. If you look at the Examples in this book, you will see that the words (your voice) are on the left and the mathematics is on the right. In most math books, when the author illustrates an Example, the mathematics is usually down the center of the page, and if the students don't know what mathematical operation was performed, they will look to the right for some brief statement of help. That's not how we teach; we don't write out an Example on the board and then say, "Class, guess what I just did!" Instead we lead our students, telling them what step is coming and then performing that mathematical step *together*—and reading naturally from left to right. Student reviewers have said that the Examples in this book are easy to read; that's because *your* voice is right there with them, working through problems *together*.

---

**EXAMPLE 1** **Graphing a Quadratic Function Given in Standard Form**

Graph the quadratic function $f(x) = (x - 3)^2 - 1$.

**Solution:**

STEP 1 The parabola opens up. $\quad a = 1,$ so $a > 0$

STEP 2 Determine the vertex. $\quad (h, k) = (3, -1)$

STEP 3 Find the $y$-intercept. $\quad f(0) = (-3)^2 - 1 = 8$
$(0, 8)$ corresponds to the $y$-intercept

---

## SKILLS AND CONCEPTS (LEARNING OBJECTIVES AND EXERCISES)

In my experience as a mathematics teacher/instructor/professor, I find skills to be on the micro level and concepts on the macro level of understanding mathematics. I believe that too often skills are emphasized at the expense of conceptual understanding.

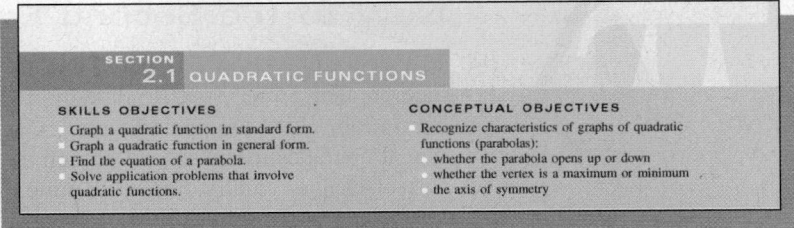

I have purposely separated *learning objectives* at the beginning of every section into two categories: *skills objectives*—what students should be able to do; and *conceptual objectives*—what students should understand. At the beginning of every class I discuss the learning objectives for the day—both skills and concepts. These are reinforced with both skills exercises and conceptual exercises.

## CATCH THE MISTAKE

Have you ever made a mistake (or had a student bring you his or her homework with a mistake) and you go over it and over it and can't find the mistake? It's often easier to simply take out a new sheet of paper and solve it from scratch again than it is to actually find the mistake. Finding the mistake demonstrates a higher level of understanding. I include a few *Catch the Mistake* exercises in each section that demonstrate a common mistake that I have seen in my experience. I use these in class (either as a whole or often in groups), which leads to student discussion and offers an opportunity for formative assessment in real time.

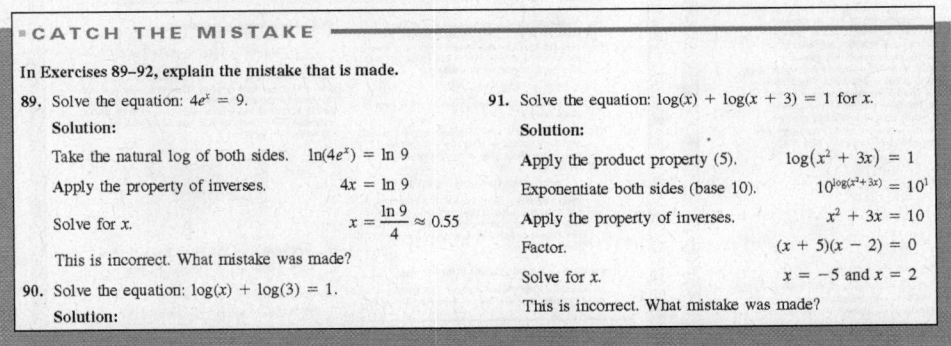

## LECTURE VIDEOS BY THE AUTHOR

To ensure consistency in the students' learning experiences, I authored the videos myself. Throughout the book wherever a student sees the video icon, that indicates a video. These videos provide a mini lecture in that the chapter openers and chapter summaries are more like class discussion and selected Examples. Your Turns throughout the book also have an accompanying video of me working out that exact problem.

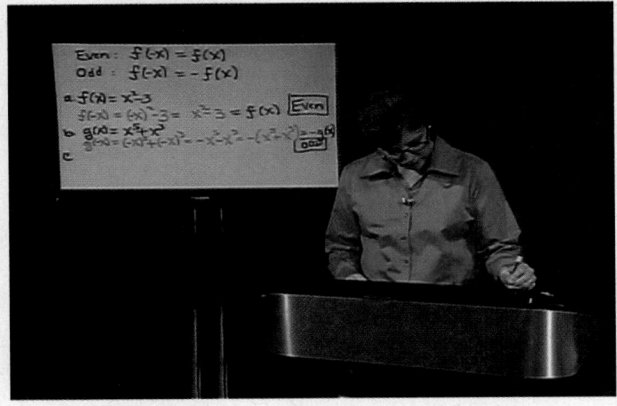

# New to the Second Edition

The first edition was *our* book, and this second edition is *our even better* book. I've incorporated some specific line-by-line suggestions from reviewers throughout the exposition, added some new Examples, and added over 200 new Exercises. The three main global upgrades to the second edition are a new Chapter Map with Learning Objectives, End-of-chapter Inquiry-Based Learning Projects, and additional Applications Exercises in areas such as Business, Economics, Life Sciences, Health Sciences, and Medicine. A section (0.8*) on Linear Regression was added, as well as some technology exercises on Quadratic, Exponential, and Logarithmic Regression.

## LEARNING OBJECTIVES

> **LEARNING OBJECTIVES**
>
> - Evaluate exponential functions for particular values and understand the characteristics of the graph of an exponential function.
> - Evaluate logarithmic functions for particular values and understand the characteristics of the graph of a logarithmic function.
> - Understand that logarithmic functions are inverses of exponential functions and derive the properties of logarithms.
> - Solve exponential and logarithmic equations.
> - Use the exponential growth, exponential decay, logarithmic, logistic growth, and Gaussian distribution models to represent real-world phenomena.

## INQUIRY-BASED LEARNING PROJECTS

## APPLICATIONS TO BUSINESS, ECONOMICS, HEALTH SCIENCES, AND MEDICINE

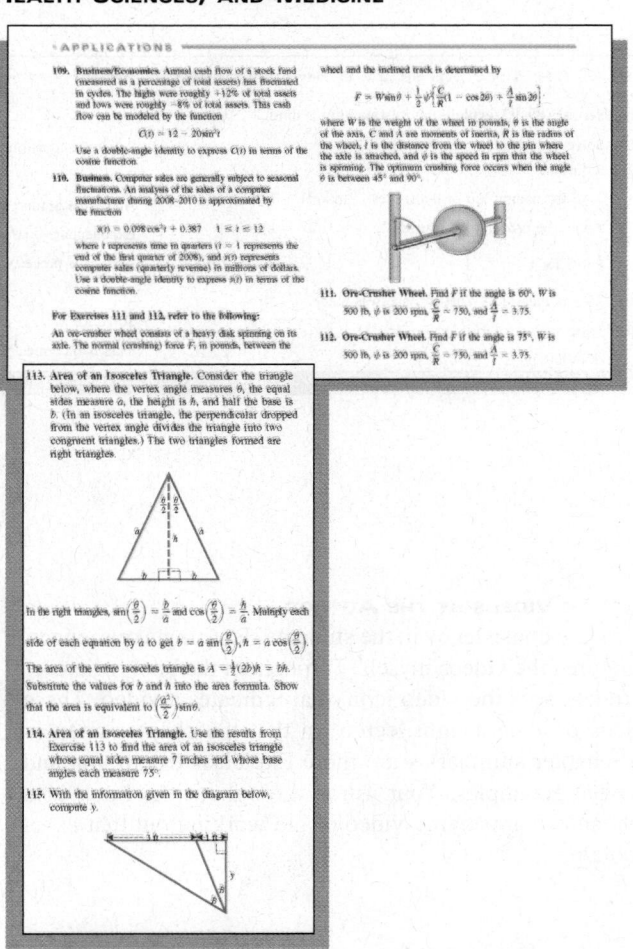

| FEATURE | BENEFIT TO STUDENT |
|---|---|
| **Chapter Opening Vignette** | Piques the student's interest with a real-world application of material presented in the chapter. Later in the chapter, the same concept from the vignette is reinforced. |
| **Chapter Overview, Flowchart, and Learning Objectives** | Students see the big picture of how topics relate and overarching learning objectives are presented. |
| **Skills and Conceptual Objectives** | Skills objectives represent what students should be able to do. Conceptual objectives emphasize a higher level global perspective of concepts. |
| **Clear, Concise, and Inviting Writing Style, Tone, and Layout** | Students are able to *read* this book, which reduces math anxiety and promotes student success. |
| **Parallel Words and Math** | Increases students' ability to read and understand examples with a seamless representation of their instructor's class (instructor's voice and what they would write on the board). |
| **Common Mistakes** | Addresses a different learning style: teaching by counter-example. Demonstrates common mistakes so that students understand why a step is incorrect and reinforces the correct mathematics. |
| **Color for Pedagogical Reasons** | Particularly helpful for visual learners when they see a function written in red and then its corresponding graph in red or a function written in blue and then its corresponding graph in blue. |
| **Study Tips** | Reinforces specific notes that you would want to emphasize in class. |
| **Author Videos** | Gives students a mini class of several examples worked by the author. |
| **Your Turn** | Engages students during class, builds student confidence, and assists instructor in real-time assessment. |
| **Catch the Mistake Exercises** | Encourages students to assume the role of teacher—demonstrating a higher mastery level. |
| **Conceptual Exercises** | Teaches students to think more globally about a topic. |
| **Inquiry-Based Learning Project** | Lets students *discover* a mathematical identify, formula, etc. that is derived in the book. |
| **Modeling OUR World** | Engages students in a modeling project of a timely subject: global climate change. |
| **Chapter Review** | Key ideas and formulas are presented section by section in a chart. Improves study skills. |
| **Chapter Review Exercises** | Improves study skills. |
| **Chapter Practice Test** | Offers self-assessment and improves study skills. |
| **Cumulative Test** | Improves retention. |

# Supplements

## Instructor Supplements

### INSTRUCTOR'S SOLUTIONS MANUAL (ISBN VOL. 1: 9781118640678; VOL. 2: 9781118777909)
- Contains worked out solutions to all exercises in the text.

### INSTRUCTOR'S MANUAL
Authored by Cynthia Young, the manual provides practical advice on teaching with the text, including:
- sample lesson plans and homework assignments
- suggestions for the effective utilization of additional resources and supplements
- sample syllabi
- Cynthia Young's Top 10 Teaching Tips & Tricks
- online component featuring the author presenting these Tips & Tricks

### ANNOTATED INSTRUCTOR'S EDITION (ISBN: 9781118693087)
- Displays answers to all exercise questions, which can be found in the back of the book.
- Provides additional classroom examples within the standard difficulty range of the in-text exercises, as well as challenge problems to assess your students mastery of the material.

### POWERPOINT SLIDES
- For each section of the book, a corresponding set of lecture notes and worked out examples are presented as PowerPoint slides, available on the Book Companion Site (www.wiley.com/college/young) and WileyPLUS.

### TEST BANK (ISBN: 9781118172346)
Contains approximately 900 questions and answers from every section of the text.

### COMPUTERIZED TEST BANK
Electonically enhanced version of the Test Bank that
- contains approximately 900 algorithmically-generated questions.
- allows instructors to freely edit, randomize, and create questions.
- allows instructors to create and print different versions of a quiz or exam.
- recognizes symbolic notation.
- allows for partial credit if used within WileyPLUS.

### BOOK COMPANION WEBSITE (WWW.WILEY.COM/COLLEGE/YOUNG)
- Contains all instructor supplements listed plus a selection of personal response system questions.

## Student Supplements

### STUDENT SOLUTIONS MANUAL (ISBN: 9781118640746)
- Includes worked out solutions for all odd problems in the text.

### BOOK COMPANION WEBSITE (WWW.WILEY.COM/COLLEGE/YOUNG)
- Provides additional resources for students, including web quizzes, video clips, and audio clips.

# What Do Students Receive with *WileyPLUS?*

### A RESEARCH-BASED DESIGN

*WileyPLUS* provides an online environment that integrates relevant resources, including the entire digital textbook, in an easy-to-navigate framework that helps students study more effectively.

- *WileyPLUS* adds structure by organizing textbook content into smaller, more manageable "chunks."
- Related media, examples, and sample practice items reinforce the learning objectives.
- Innovative features such as visual progress tracking, and self-evaluation tools improve time management and strengthen areas of weakness.

### ONE-ON-ONE ENGAGEMENT

With *WileyPLUS*, students receive 24/7 access to resources that promote positive learning outcomes. Students engage with related examples (in various media) and sample practice items, including:

- Self-Study Quizzes
- Video Quizzes
- Proficiency Exams
- Guided Online (GO) Tutorial Problems
- Concept Questions
- Lecture Videos by Cynthia Young, including chapter introductions, chapter summaries, and selected video examples.

### MEASURABLE OUTCOMES

Throughout each study session, students can assess their progress and gain immediate feedback. *WileyPLUS* provides precise reporting of strengths and weaknesses, as well as individualized quizzes, so that students are confident they are spending their time on the right things. With *WileyPLUS*, students always know the exact outcome of their efforts.

# What Do Instructors Receive with *WileyPLUS?*

*WileyPLUS* provides reliable, customizable resources that reinforce course goals inside and outside of the classroom, as well as visibility into individual student progress. Pre-created materials and activities help instructors optimize their time.

### CUSTOMIZABLE COURSE PLAN

*WileyPLUS* comes with a pre-created Course Plan designed by a subject matter expert uniquely for this course.

### PRE-CREATED ACTIVITY TYPES INCLUDE:

- Questions
- Readings and Resources
- Print Tests

### COURSE MATERIALS AND ASSESSMENT CONTENT

- Lecture Notes PowerPoint Slides
- Instructor's Manual
- Question Assignments (all end-of-chapter problems coded algorithmically with hints, links to text, whiteboard/show work feature, and instructor controlled problem solving help)

### GRADEBOOK

*WileyPLUS* provides instant access to reports on trends in class performance, student use of course materials, and progress toward learning objectives, helping inform decisions and drive classroom discussions.

## Acknowledgments

I want to express my sincerest gratitude to the entire Wiley team. I've said this before, and I will say it again: Wiley is the right partner for me. There is a reason that my dog is named Wiley—she's smart, competitive, a team player, and most of all, a joy to be around. There are several people within Wiley to whom I feel the need to express my appreciation: first and foremost to Laurie Rosatone who convinced Wiley Higher Ed to invest in a young assistant professor's vision for a series and who has been unwavering in her commitment to student learning. To my editor Joanna Dingle whose judgment I trust in both editorial and preschool decisions; thank you for surpassing my greatest expectations for an editor. To the rest of the ladies on the math editorial team (Jen Brady, Liz Baird, and Courtney Welsh), you are all first class! This revision was planned and executed exceptionally well thanks to you three. To the math marketing manager, Kimberly Kanakes, thank you for helping reps tell my story. To Ken Santor, thank you for your attention to detail. And finally, I'd like to thank all of the Wiley reps: thank you for your commitment to my series and your tremendous efforts to get professors to adopt this book for their students.

I would also like to thank all of the contributors who helped us make this *our even better book*. I'd first like to thank Mark McKibben. He is known as the author of the solutions manuals that accompany this series, but he is much more than that. Mark, thank you for making this series a priority, for being so responsive, and most of all for being my "go-to" person to think through ideas. I'd also like to especially thank Jodi B.A. McKibben who is a statistician and teamed with Mark to develop the new regression material. I'd like to thank Steve Davis who was the inspiration for the Inquiry-Based Learning Projects and a huge thanks to Lyn Riverstone who developed all of the IBLPs. Special thanks to Laura Watkins for finding applications that are real and timely and to Ricki Alexander for updating all of the Technology Tips. I'd also like to thank Becky Schantz for her environmental problems (I now use AusPens because of Becky).

I'd also like to thank the following reviewers whose input helped make this book even better.

Seongchun Kwon, *Union College*
Catherine Stevens, *Lone Star College*
Kathryn Pearson, *Hudson Valley Community College*
Teresa Adams, *Centralia College*
Shane Brewer, *Utah State University*
Valerie Miller, *Georgia State University*
Dave Bregenzer, *Utah State University*
Draga Vidakovic, *Georgia State University*
Ginny Powell, *Georgia Perimeter College*
Doug Furman, *SUNY Ulster*
Sharon Welker, *Wake Technical Community College*

Sarah Bergmann, *Alamance Community College*
Thomas O'Brien, *Keene State College*
Nicholas Horne, *Community College of Rhode Island*
Sonja Goerdt, *St. Cloud State University*
Faith John, *J. Sargeant Reynolds Community College*
Jason Geary, *Harper College*
Maureen Nicholson, *Ulster Community College*
Minhua Liu, *Harper College*
Sunil Koswatta, *Harper College*
Piotr Runge, *Utah State University*

# Table of Contents

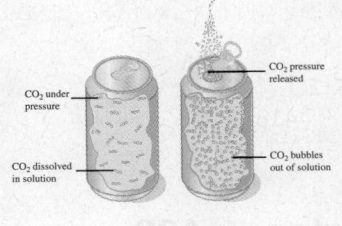
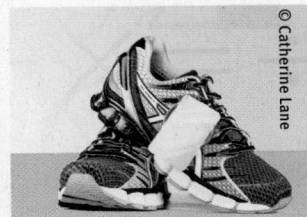
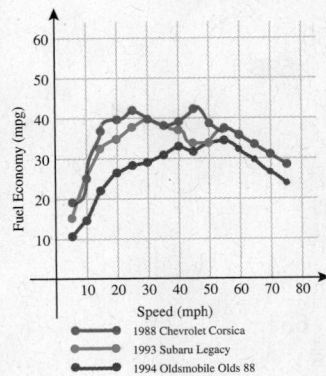

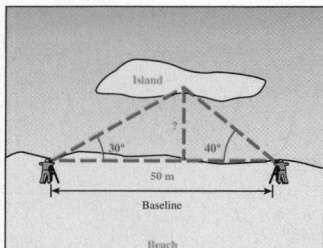

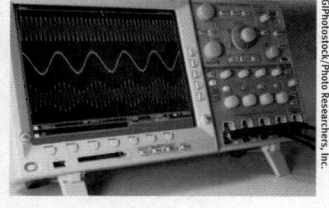

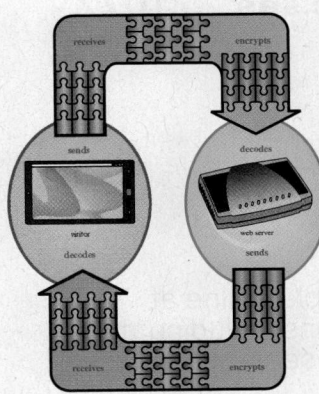

Jamirae/iStockphoto

© Photodisc/Age Fotostock America, Inc.

Gaillardia Flower (55), Kenneth M. Highfil/Photo Researchers, Inc.;
Michaelmas Daisy (89), Maxine Adcock/Photo Researchers, Inc.;
Yellow Iris (3), Edward Kinsman/Photo Researchers, Inc.;
Blue Columbine (5), Jeffrey Lepore/Photo Researchers, Inc.;
Gerbera Daisy (34), Bonnie Sue Rauch/Photo Researchers, Inc.;
Erect Dayflower (2), Michael Lustbader/Photo Researchers, Inc.;
Calla Lilies (1), Adam Jones/Photo Researchers, Inc.; Cosmos Flower (8),
Maria Mosolova/Photo Researchers, Inc.; Lemon Symphony (21),
Bonnie Sue Rauch/Photo Researchers, Inc.; Black-Eyed Susan (13),
Rod Planck/Photo Researchers, Inc.

Chapter 11 Limits and the Appendix are available online at
www.wiley.com/college/young. For print options including this
material, please contact your local Wiley representative.

# A Note from the Author to the Student

I wrote this text with careful attention to ways in which to make your learning experience more successful. If you take full advantage of the unique features and elements of this textbook, I believe your experience will be fulfilling and enjoyable. Let's walk through some of the special book features that will help you in your study of algebra and trigonometry.

## Prerequisites and Review (Chapter 0)

A comprehensive review of prerequisite knowledge (intermediate algebra topics) in Chapter 0 provides a brush up on knowledge and skills necessary for success in the course.

## Clear, Concise, and Inviting Writing

Special attention has been made to present an engaging, clear, precise narrative in a layout that is easy to use and designed to reduce any math anxiety you may have.

**0**

### Review: Equations and Inequalities

Have you ever noticed when you open a can of soda that more messy fizz (carbonation) seems to be released if the soda is warm than if it has been refrigerated? Boyle's law in chemistry says that the pressure of a gas (cans of carbonated beverages contain carbon dioxide) is directly proportional to the temperature of the gas and inversely proportional to the volume of that gas. For example, if the volume stays the same (container of soda), and the temperature of the soda increases, the pressure also increases (more carbonation).*

*See Section 0.7 Exercise 53.

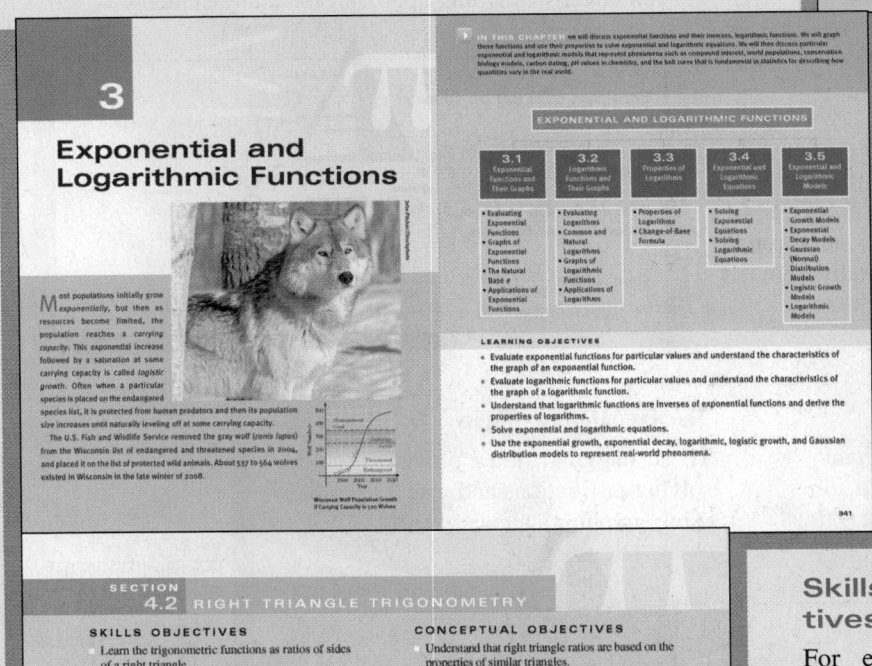

## Chapter Introduction, Flow Chart, Section Headings, and Objectives

An opening vignette, flow chart, list of chapter sections, and chapter learning objectives give you an overview of the chapter.

## Skills and Conceptual Objectives

For every section, objectives are further divided by skills *and* concepts so you can see the difference between solving problems and truly understanding concepts.

## Examples

Examples pose a specific problem using concepts already presented and then work through the solution. These serve to enhance your understanding of the subject matter.

## Your Turn

Immediately following many examples, you are given a similar problem to reinforce and check your understanding. This helps build confidence as you progress in the chapter. These are ideal for in-class activity or for preparing for homework later. Answers are provided in the margin for a quick check of your work.

**EXAMPLE 9   Using the Change-of-Base Formula**

Use the change-of-base formula to evaluate $\log_4 17$. Round to four decimal places.

**Solution:**

We will illustrate this in two ways (choosing common and natural logarithms) using a scientific calculator.

**Common Logarithms**

Use the change-of-base formula with base 10.   $\log_4 17 = \dfrac{\log 17}{\log 4}$

Approximate with a calculator.   $\approx 2.043731421$

$\approx \boxed{2.0437}$

**Natural Logarithms**

Use the change-of-base formula with base $e$.   $\log_4 17 = \dfrac{\ln 17}{\ln 4}$

Approximate with a calculator.   $\approx 2.043731421$

$\approx \boxed{2.0437}$

■ **YOUR TURN**  Use the change-of-base formula to approximate $\log_7 34$. Round to four decimal places.

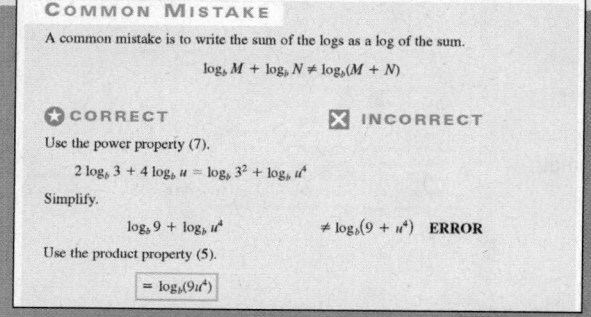

**COMMON MISTAKE**

A common mistake is to write the sum of the logs as a log of the sum.

$$\log_b M + \log_b N \neq \log_b(M + N)$$

⭐ CORRECT                    ❌ INCORRECT

Use the power property (7).

$2 \log_b 3 + 4 \log_b u = \log_b 3^2 + \log_b u^4$

Simplify.

$\log_b 9 + \log_b u^4$          $\neq \log_b(9 + u^4)$  **ERROR**

Use the product property (5).

$= \log_b(9u^4)$

## Common Mistake/ Correct vs. Incorrect

In addition to standard examples, some problems are worked out both correctly and incorrectly to highlight common errors students make. Counter examples like these are often an effective learning approach for many students.

## Parallel Words and Math

This text reverses the common textbook presentation of examples by placing the explanation in words *on the left* and the mathematics in parallel *on the right*. This makes it easier for students to read through examples as the material flows more naturally from left to right and as commonly presented in class.

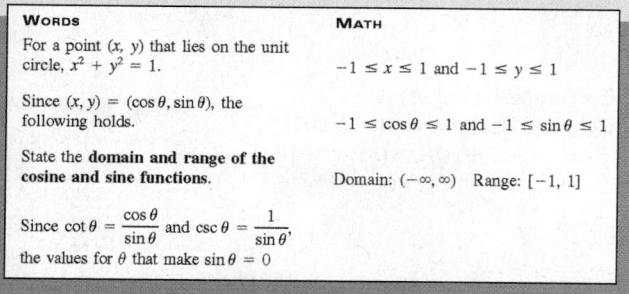

| WORDS | MATH |
|---|---|
| For a point $(x, y)$ that lies on the unit circle, $x^2 + y^2 = 1$. | $-1 \leq x \leq 1$ and $-1 \leq y \leq 1$ |
| Since $(x, y) = (\cos\theta, \sin\theta)$, the following holds. | $-1 \leq \cos\theta \leq 1$ and $-1 \leq \sin\theta \leq 1$ |
| State the **domain and range of the cosine and sine functions.** | Domain: $(-\infty, \infty)$   Range: $[-1, 1]$ |
| Since $\cot\theta = \dfrac{\cos\theta}{\sin\theta}$ and $\csc\theta = \dfrac{1}{\sin\theta}$, the values for $\theta$ that make $\sin\theta = 0$ | |

## Study Tips and Caution Notes

These marginal reminders call out important hints or warnings to be aware of related to the topic or problem.

## Technology Tips

These marginal notes provide problem solving instructions and visual examples using graphing calculators.

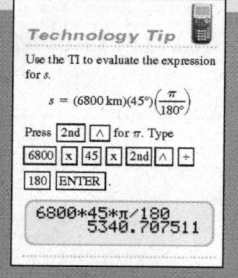

**Technology Tip**

Use the TI to evaluate the expression for $s$.

$$s = (6800 \text{ km})(45°)\left(\frac{\pi}{180°}\right)$$

Press 2nd ∧ for $\pi$. Type
6800 × 45 × 2nd ∧ ÷
180 ENTER.

6800*45*π/180
        5340.707511

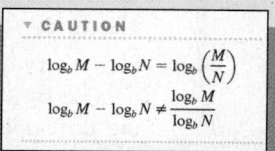

**Study Tip**

Both the initial side (initial ray) and the terminal side (terminal ray) of an angle are rays.

▼ **CAUTION**

$$\log_b M - \log_b N = \log_b\left(\frac{M}{N}\right)$$

$$\log_b M - \log_b N \neq \frac{\log_b M}{\log_b N}$$

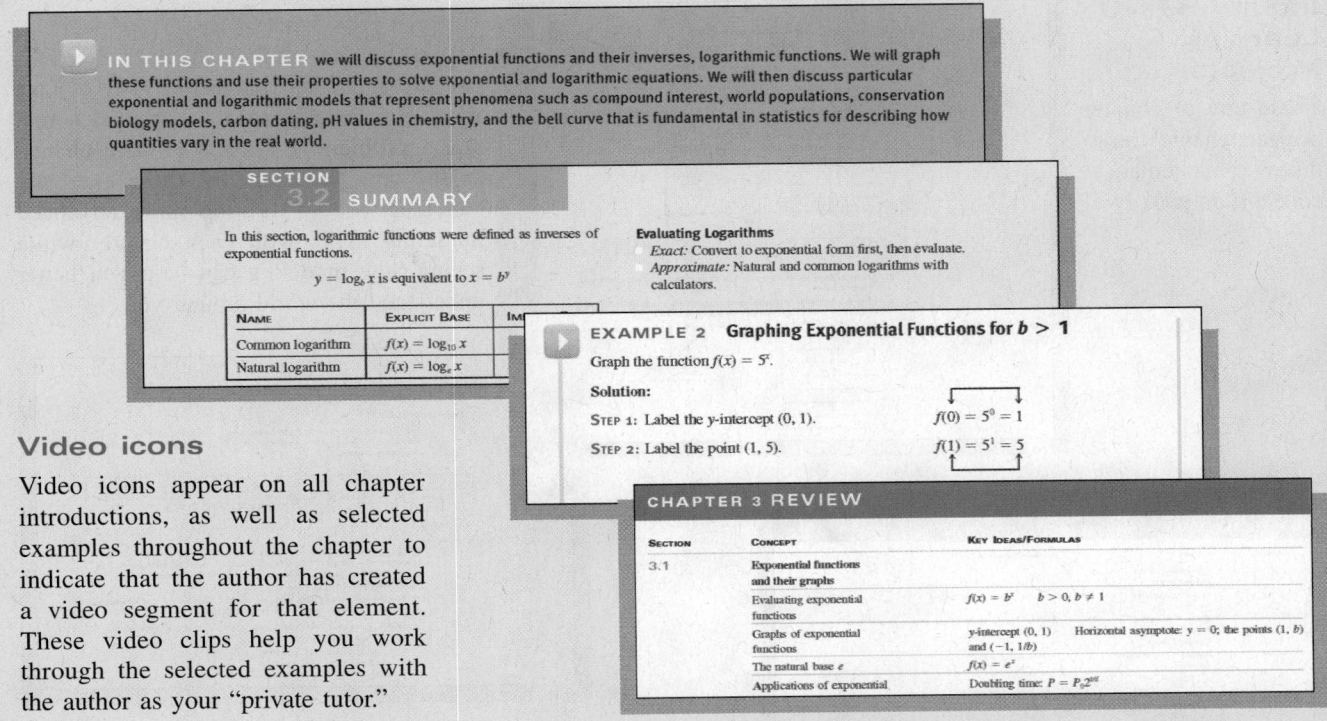

**IN THIS CHAPTER** we will discuss exponential functions and their inverses, logarithmic functions. We will graph these functions and use their properties to solve exponential and logarithmic equations. We will then discuss particular exponential and logarithmic models that represent phenomena such as compound interest, world populations, conservation biology models, carbon dating, pH values in chemistry, and the bell curve that is fundamental in statistics for describing how quantities vary in the real world.

### SECTION 3.2 SUMMARY

In this section, logarithmic functions were defined as inverses of exponential functions.

$$y = \log_b x \text{ is equivalent to } x = b^y$$

**Evaluating Logarithms**
- *Exact:* Convert to exponential form first, then evaluate.
- *Approximate:* Natural and common logarithms with calculators.

| NAME | EXPLICIT BASE | IM... |
|------|---------------|-------|
| Common logarithm | $f(x) = \log_{10} x$ | |
| Natural logarithm | $f(x) = \log_e x$ | |

### EXAMPLE 2   Graphing Exponential Functions for $b > 1$

Graph the function $f(x) = 5^x$.

**Solution:**

STEP 1: Label the y-intercept $(0, 1)$.          $f(0) = 5^0 = 1$

STEP 2: Label the point $(1, 5)$.                $f(1) = 5^1 = 5$

### CHAPTER 3 REVIEW

| SECTION | CONCEPT | KEY IDEAS/FORMULAS |
|---------|---------|--------------------|
| 3.1 | Exponential functions and their graphs | |
| | Evaluating exponential functions | $f(x) = b^x$   $b > 0, b \neq 1$ |
| | Graphs of exponential functions | y-intercept $(0, 1)$   Horizontal asymptote: $y = 0$; the points $(1, b)$ and $(-1, 1/b)$ |
| | The natural base $e$ | $f(x) = e^x$ |
| | Applications of exponential | Doubling time: $P = P_0 2^{t/d}$ |

## Video icons

Video icons appear on all chapter introductions, as well as selected examples throughout the chapter to indicate that the author has created a video segment for that element. These video clips help you work through the selected examples with the author as your "private tutor."

## Six Different Types of Exercises

Every text section ends with **Skills, Applications, Catch the Mistake, Conceptual, Challenge, and Technology** exercises. The exercises gradually increase in difficulty and vary in skill and conceptual emphasis. Catch the Mistake exercises increase the depth of understanding and reinforce what you have learned. Conceptual and Challenge exercises specifically focus on assessing conceptual understanding. Technology exercises enhance your understanding and ability using scientific and graphing calculators.

### SECTION 3.5 EXERCISES

**• SKILLS**

In Exercises 1–6, match the function with the graph (a to f) and the model name (i to v).

1. $f(t) = 5e^{2t}$
2. $N(t) = 28e^{-t/2}$
3. $T(x) = 4e^{-(x-80)^2/10}$
4. $P(t) = \dfrac{200}{1 + 5e^{-0.4t}}$
5. $D(x) = 4 + \log(x - 1)$
6. $h(t) = 2 + \ln(t + 3)$

**Model Name**
i. Logarithmic

**Graphs**

**• APPLICATIONS**

47. **Population Doubling Time.** In 2002 there were 7.1 million people living in London, England. If the population is expected to double by 2090, what is the expected population in London in 2050?

48. **Population Doubling Time.** In 2004 the population in Morganton, Georgia, was 43,000. The population in Morganton doubled by 2010. If the growth rate remains the same, what is the expected population in Morganton in 2020?

49. **Investments.** Suppose ... area for $1500 an acre ... at $3000 an acre ... $6000. Write a func... that area, assuming ... would the expected ...

55. **Depreciation of Furniture.** A couple buy a new bedroom set for $8000 and 10 years later sell it for $4000. If the depreciation continues at the same rate, how much would the bedroom set be worth in 4 more years?

56. **Depreciation of a Computer.** A student buys a new laptop for $1500 when she arrives as a freshman. A year later, the computer is worth approximately $750. If the depreciation continues at the same rate, how much would she expect to ... the laptop for when the graduates 4 years after she ...

**• CATCH THE MISTAKE**

In Exercises 105–108, explain the mistake that is made.

105. Evaluate the logarithm $\log_2 4$.

**Solution:**

Set the logarithm equal to $x$.          $\log_2 4 = x$

Write the logarithm in exponential form.   $x = 2^4$

Simplify.

Answer:

This is incorrect. ...
What went wrong? ...

106. Evaluate the logarithm $\log_{100} 10$.

**Solution:**

Set the logarithm equal to $x$.          $\log_{100} 10 = x$

Express the equation in exponential form.   $10^x = 100$

Solve for ...                             $x = 2$

**• CONCEPTUAL**

In Exercises 73–76, determine whether each statement is true or false.

73. The function $f(x) = -e^{-x}$ has the y-intercept $(0, 1)$.

74. The function $f(x) = -e^{-x}$ has a horizontal asymptote along the x-axis.

75. The functions $y = 3^{-x}$ and $y = \left(\frac{1}{3}\right)^x$ have the same graphs.

76. $e = 2.718$.

77. Plot $f(x)$ ...

79. Graph ...

**• CHALLENGE**

113. State the domain, range, and x-intercept of the function $f(x) = -\ln(x - a) + b$ for $a$ and $b$ real positive numbers.

114. State the domain, range, and x-intercept of the function $f(x) = \log(a - x) - b$ for $a$ and $b$ real positive numbers.

115. Graph the function $f(x) = \begin{cases} \ln(-x) & x < 0 \\ \ln(x) & x > 0 \end{cases}$

116. Graph the function $f(x) = \begin{cases} -\ln(-x) & x < 0 \\ -\ln(x) & x > 0 \end{cases}$

**• TECHNOLOGY**

117. Apply a graphing utility to graph $y = e^x$ and $y = \ln x$ in the same viewing screen. What line are these two graphs symmetric about?

118. Apply a graphing utility to graph $y = 10^x$ and $y = \log x$ in the same viewing screen. What line are these two graphs symmetric about?

119. Apply a graphing utility to graph $y = \log x$ and $y = \ln x$ in the same viewing screen. What are the two common characteristics?

120. Using a graphing utility, graph $y = \ln|x|$. Is the function defined everywhere?

## Inquiry-Based Learning Projects

These end of chapter projects enable you to discover mathematical concepts on your own!

## Modeling Our World

These unique end-of-chapter exercises provide a fun and interesting way to take what you have learned and model a real world problem. By using climate change as the continuous theme, these exercises can help you to develop more advanced modeling skills with each chapter while seeing how modeling can help you better understand the world around you.

## Chapter Review, Review Exercises, Practice Test, Cumulative Test

At the end of every chapter, a summary review chart organizes the key learning concepts in an easy to use one or two-page layout. This feature includes key ideas and formulas, as well as indicating relevant pages and review exercises so that you can quickly summarize a chapter and study smarter. Review Exercises, arranged by section heading, are provided for extra study and practice. A Practice Test, without section headings, offers even more self-practice before moving on. A new Cumulative Test feature offers study questions based on all previous chapters' content, thus helping you build upon previously learned concepts.

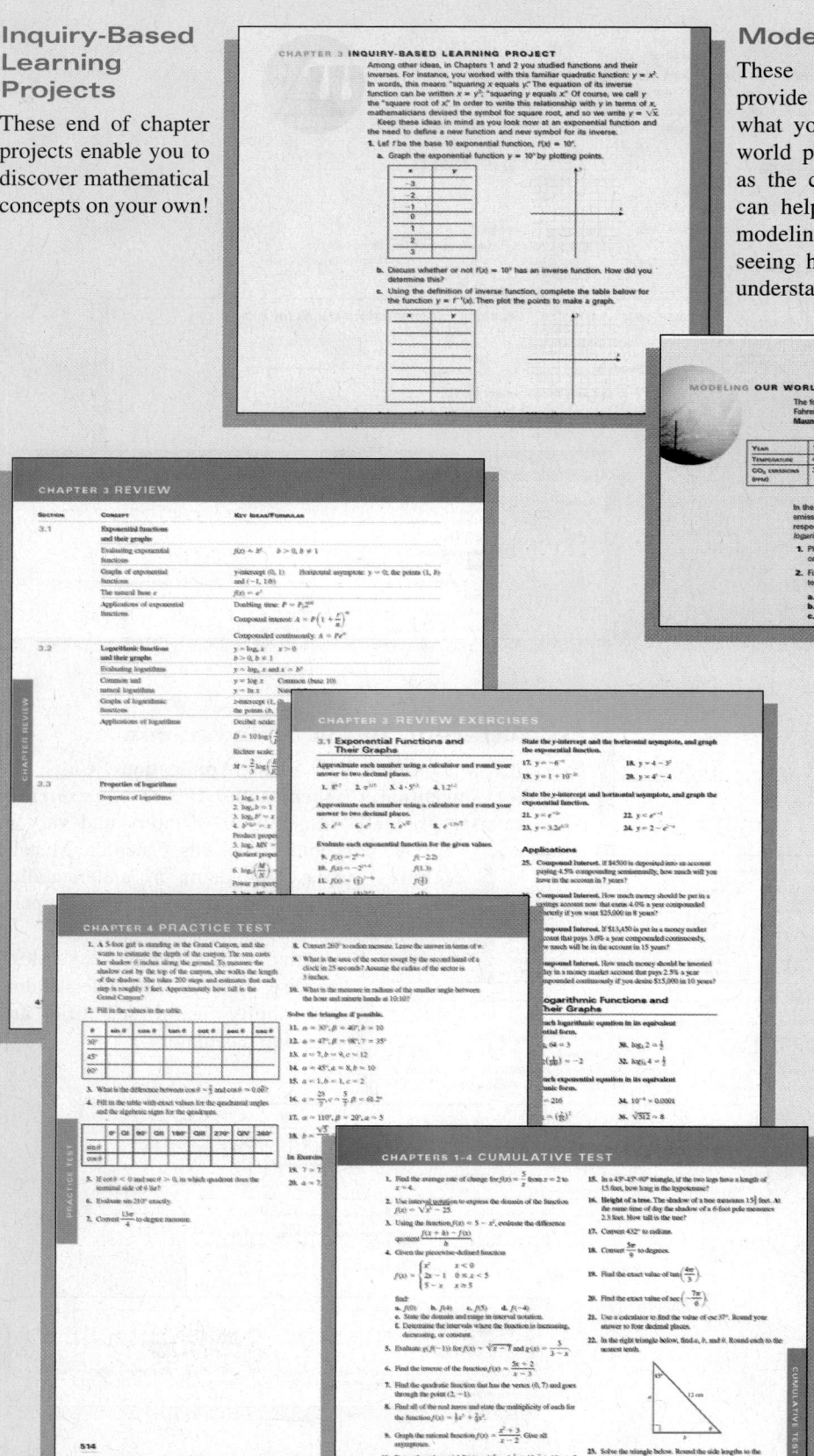

# WileyPLUS

## WileyPLUS is a research-based online environment for effective teaching and learning.

*WileyPLUS* builds students' confidence because it takes the guesswork out of studying by providing students with a clear roadmap:

- **what to do**
- **how to do it**
- **if they did it right**

It offers interactive resources along with a complete digital textbook that help students learn more. With *WileyPLUS*, students take more initiative so you'll have greater impact on their achievement in the classroom and beyond.

# WileyPLUS

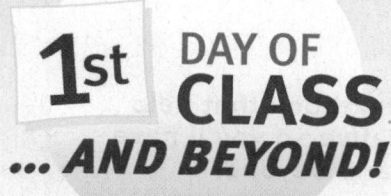

# Precalculus

**Second Edition**

**CYNTHIA Y. YOUNG** | *Professor of Mathematics*
UNIVERSITY OF CENTRAL FLORIDA

**WILEY**

# 0

# Review: Equations and Inequalities

Have you ever noticed when you open a can of soda that more messy fizz (carbonation) seems to be released if the soda is warm than if it has been refrigerated? Boyle's law in chemistry says that the pressure of a gas (cans of carbonated beverages contain carbon

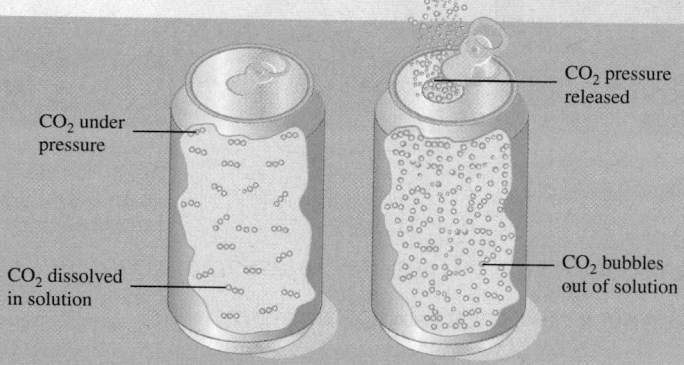

CO₂ under pressure

CO₂ dissolved in solution

CO₂ pressure released

CO₂ bubbles out of solution

dioxide) is directly proportional to the temperature of the gas and inversely proportional to the volume of that gas. For example, if the volume stays the same (container of soda), and the temperature of the soda increases, the pressure also increases (more carbonation).*

*See Section 0.7 Exercise 53.

**IN THIS CHAPTER** we will review solving equations in one variable. We will start with linear and quadratic equations and then move on to other types of equations. We will review solving linear, polynomial, rational, and absolute value inequalities in one variable. We will discuss how to graph equations in two variables in the Cartesian plane and specifically discuss circles. Lastly, we will use equations to model variation.

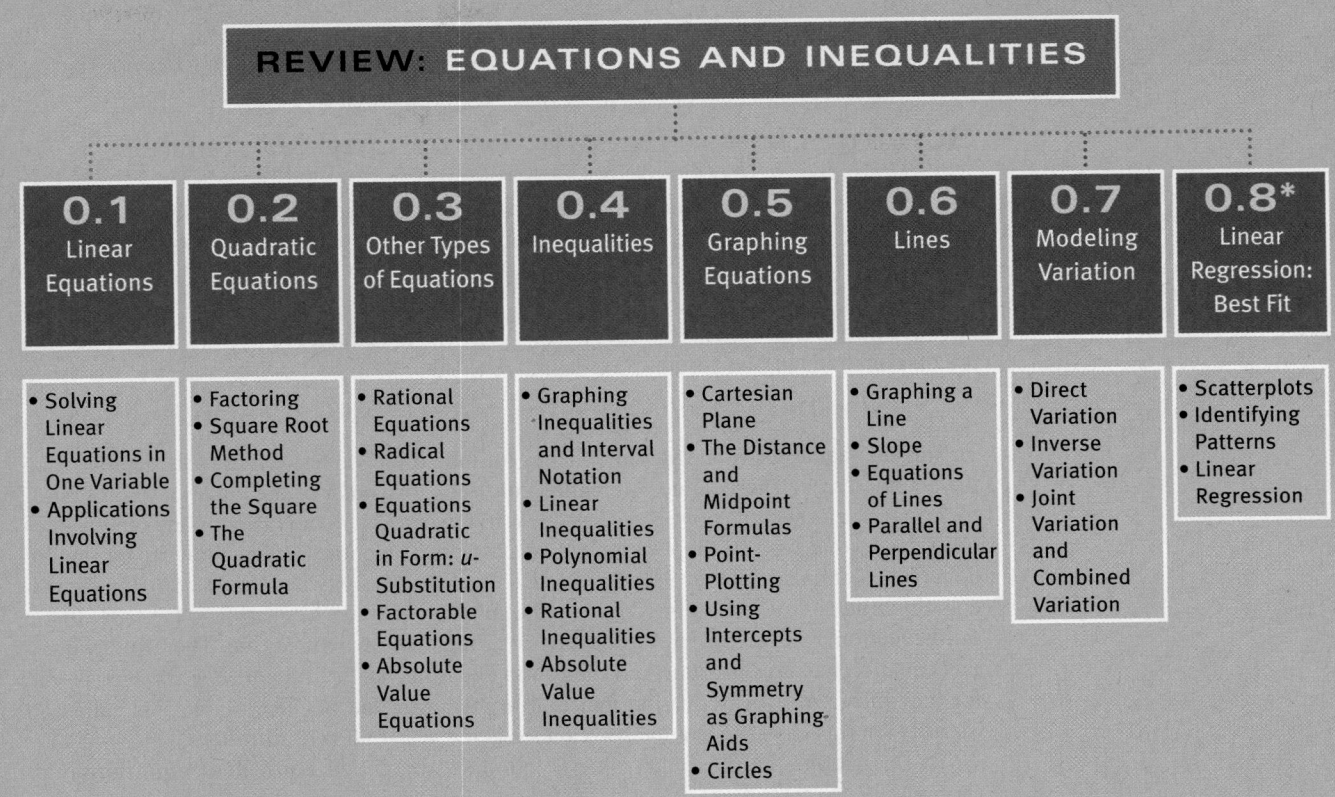

## REVIEW: EQUATIONS AND INEQUALITIES

| 0.1 Linear Equations | 0.2 Quadratic Equations | 0.3 Other Types of Equations | 0.4 Inequalities | 0.5 Graphing Equations | 0.6 Lines | 0.7 Modeling Variation | 0.8* Linear Regression: Best Fit |
|---|---|---|---|---|---|---|---|
| • Solving Linear Equations in One Variable<br>• Applications Involving Linear Equations | • Factoring<br>• Square Root Method<br>• Completing the Square<br>• The Quadratic Formula | • Rational Equations<br>• Radical Equations<br>• Equations Quadratic in Form: *u*-Substitution<br>• Factorable Equations<br>• Absolute Value Equations | • Graphing Inequalities and Interval Notation<br>• Linear Inequalities<br>• Polynomial Inequalities<br>• Rational Inequalities<br>• Absolute Value Inequalities | • Cartesian Plane<br>• The Distance and Midpoint Formulas<br>• Point-Plotting<br>• Using Intercepts and Symmetry as Graphing Aids<br>• Circles | • Graphing a Line<br>• Slope<br>• Equations of Lines<br>• Parallel and Perpendicular Lines | • Direct Variation<br>• Inverse Variation<br>• Joint Variation and Combined Variation | • Scatterplots<br>• Identifying Patterns<br>• Linear Regression |

## LEARNING OBJECTIVES

- Solve linear equations in one variable.
- Solve quadratic equations in one variable.
- Solve other types of equations that can be transformed into linear or quadratic equations.
- Solve inequalities in one variable.
- Graph equations in two variables in the Cartesian plane.
- Find the equation of a line.
- Use equations to model variation.
- Find the line of best fit for a given data set.*

---

*Optional Technology Required Section.

**SKILLS OBJECTIVES**
- Solve linear equations in one variable.
- Solve application problems involving linear equations.

**CONCEPTUAL OBJECTIVE**
- Understand the mathematical modeling process.

## Solving Linear Equations in One Variable

An **algebraic expression** (see Appendix) consists of one or more terms that are combined through basic operations such as addition, subtraction, multiplication, or division; for example,

$$3x + 2 \qquad 5 - 2y \qquad x + y$$

An **equation** is a statement that says two expressions are equal. For example, the following are all equations in one variable, $x$:

$$x + 7 = 11 \qquad x^2 = 9 \qquad 7 - 3x = 2 - 3x \qquad 4x + 7 = x + 2 + 3x + 5$$

To **solve** an equation in one variable means to find all the values of that variable that make the equation true. These values are called **solutions**, or **roots**, of the equation. The first of these statements shown above, $x + 7 = 11$, is true when $x = 4$ and false for any other values of $x$. We say that $x = 4$ is the solution to the equation. Sometimes an equation can have more than one solution, as in $x^2 = 9$. In this case, there are actually two values of $x$ that make this equation true, $x = -3$ and $x = 3$. We say the **solution set** of this equation is $\{-3, 3\}$. In the third equation, $7 - 3x = 2 - 3x$, no values of $x$ make the statement true. Therefore, we say this equation has **no solution**. And the fourth equation, $4x + 7 = x + 2 + 3x + 5$, is true for any values of $x$. An equation that is true for any value of the variable $x$ is called an **identity**. In this case, we say the solution set is the **set of all real numbers**.

Two equations that have the same solution set are called **equivalent equations**. For example,

$$3x + 7 = 13 \qquad 3x = 6 \qquad x = 2$$

are all equivalent equations because each of them has the solution set $\{2\}$. Note that $x^2 = 4$ is not equivalent to these three equations because it has the solution set $\{-2, 2\}$.

When solving equations, it helps to find a simpler equivalent equation in which the variable is isolated (alone). The following table summarizes the procedures for generating equivalent equations.

### Generating Equivalent Equations

| ORIGINAL EQUATION | DESCRIPTION | EQUIVALENT EQUATION |
|---|---|---|
| $3(x - 6) = 6x - x$ | ■ Eliminate the parentheses.<br>■ Combine like terms on one or both sides of the equation. | $3x - 18 = 5x$ |
| $7x + 8 = 29$ | Add (or subtract) the same quantity to (from) *both* sides of the equation.<br>$7x + 8 - \mathbf{8} = 29 - \mathbf{8}$ | $7x = 21$ |
| $5x = 15$ | Multiply (or divide) both sides of the equation by the same nonzero quantity: $\dfrac{5x}{5} = \dfrac{15}{5}$. | $x = 3$ |
| $-7 = x$ | Interchange the two sides of the equation. | $x = -7$ |

You probably already know how to solve simple linear equations. Solving a linear equation in one variable is done by finding an equivalent equation. In generating an equivalent equation, remember that whatever operation is performed on one side of an equation must also be performed on the other side of the equation.

### EXAMPLE 1   Solving a Linear Equation

Solve the equation $3x + 4 = 16$.

**Solution:**

Subtract 4 from both sides of the equation.

$$3x + 4 = 16$$
$$\underline{\phantom{3x}\; -4 \;\; -4}$$
$$3x \;\;\;\; = 12$$

Divide both sides by 3.

$$\frac{3x}{3} = \frac{12}{3}$$

The solution is $x = 4$.

$$\boxed{x = 4}$$

The solution set is {4}.

■ **YOUR TURN** Solve the equation $2x + 3 = 9$.

**Technology Tip**

Use a graphing utility to display graphs of $y_1 = 3x + 4$ and $y_2 = 16$.

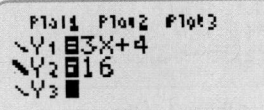

The $x$-coordinate of the point of intersection is the solution to the equation $3x + 4 = 16$.

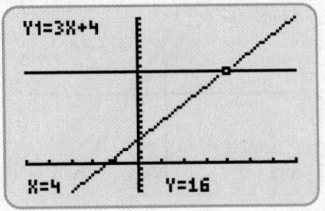

■ **Answer:** The solution is $x = 3$. The solution set is {3}.

Example 1 illustrates solving linear equations in one variable. What is a linear equation in one variable?

### DEFINITION   Linear Equation

A **linear equation in one variable**, $x$, can be written in the form

$$ax + b = 0$$

where $a$ and $b$ are real numbers and $a \neq 0$.

What makes this equation linear is that $x$ is raised to the first power. We can also classify a linear equation as a **first-degree** equation.

| Equation | Degree | General Name |
|---|---|---|
| $x - 7 = 0$ | First | Linear |
| $x^2 - 6x - 9 = 0$ | Second | Quadratic |
| $x^3 + 3x^2 - 8 = 0$ | Third | Cubic |

### EXAMPLE 2    Solving a Linear Equation

Solve the equation $5x - (7x - 4) - 2 = 5 - (3x + 2)$.

**Solution:**

## Technology Tip

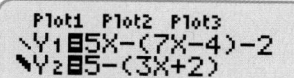

Use a graphing utility to display graphs of $y_1 = 5x - (7x - 4) - 2$ and $y_2 = 5 - (3x + 2)$.

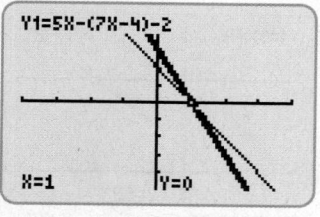

```
Plot1 Plot2 Plot3
\Y1日5X-(7X-4)-2
\Y2日5-(3X+2)
```

The $x$-coordinate of the point of intersection is the solution to the equation $5x - (7x - 4) - 2 = 5 - (3x + 2)$.

```
Y1=5X-(7X-4)-2
```

```
X=1        Y=0
```

■ **Answer:** The solution is $x = 2$.
The solution set is $\{2\}$.

Eliminate the parentheses.

Don't forget to distribute the negative sign through *both* terms inside the parentheses.

$$5x - (7x - 4) - 2 = 5 - (3x + 2)$$

$$5x - 7x + 4 - 2 = 5 - 3x - 2$$

Combine like terms on each side.

$$-2x + 2 = 3 - 3x$$

Add $3x$ to both sides.

$$\begin{array}{r} +3x \qquad\qquad + 3x \\ \hline x + 2 = 3 \end{array}$$

Subtract 2 from both sides.

$$\begin{array}{r} -2 \quad -2 \\ \hline x = 1 \end{array}$$

Check to verify that $x = 1$ is a solution to the original equation.

$$5 \cdot 1 - (7 \cdot 1 - 4) - 2 = 5 - (3 \cdot 1 + 2)$$
$$5 - (7 - 4) - 2 = 5 - (3 + 2)$$
$$5 - (3) - 2 = 5 - (5)$$
$$0 = 0$$

Since the solution $x = 1$ makes the equation true, the solution set is $\{1\}$.

■ **YOUR TURN** Solve the equation $4(x - 1) - 2 = x - 3(x - 2)$.

---

To solve a linear equation involving fractions, find the least common denominator (LCD) of all terms and multiply both sides of the equation by the LCD. We will first review how to find the LCD.

To add the fractions $\frac{1}{2} + \frac{1}{6} + \frac{2}{5}$, we must first find a common denominator. Some people are taught to find the lowest number that 2, 6, and 5 all divide evenly into. Others prefer a more systematic approach in terms of prime factors.

## Study Tip

$$\begin{array}{r} \text{Prime Factors} \\ 2 = 2 \\ 6 = 2 \cdot 3 \\ 5 = \qquad \cdot 5 \\ \hline \text{LCD} = 2 \cdot 3 \cdot 5 = 30 \end{array}$$

## Technology Tip

Use a graphing utility to display graphs of $y_1 = \frac{1}{2}p - 5$ and $y_2 = \frac{3}{4}p$.

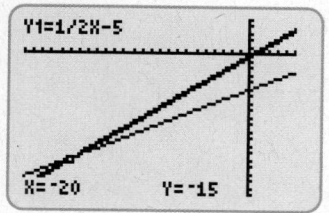

```
Plot1 Plot2 Plot3
\Y1日1/2X-5
\Y2日3/4X
```

The $x$-coordinate of the point of intersection is the solution.

```
Y1=1/2X-5
```

```
X=-20      Y=-15
```

■ **Answer:** The solution is $m = -18$.
The solution set is $\{-18\}$.

### EXAMPLE 3    Solving a Linear Equation Involving Fractions

Solve the equation $\frac{1}{2}p - 5 = \frac{3}{4}p$.

**Solution:**

Write the equation.

$$\frac{1}{2}p - 5 = \frac{3}{4}p$$

Multiply each term in the equation by the LCD, 4.

$$(4)\frac{1}{2}p - (4)5 = (4)\frac{3}{4}p$$

The result is a linear equation with no fractions.

$$2p - 20 = 3p$$

Subtract $2p$ from both sides.

$$\begin{array}{r} -2p \qquad -2p \\ \hline -20 = p \end{array}$$

$$\boxed{p = -20}$$

Since $p = -20$ satisfies the original equation, the solution set is $\{-20\}$.

■ **YOUR TURN** Solve the equation $\frac{1}{4}m = \frac{1}{12}m - 3$.

## Solving a Linear Equation in One Variable

| STEP | DESCRIPTION | EXAMPLE |
|---|---|---|
| 1 | Simplify the algebraic expressions on both sides of the equation. | $-3(x-2)+5 = 7(x-4)-1$<br>$-3x+6+5 = 7x-28-1$<br>$-3x+11 = 7x-29$ |
| 2 | Gather all variable terms on one side of the equation and all constant terms on the other side. | $\begin{aligned} -3x+11 &= 7x-29 \\ +3x \qquad & \quad +3x \\ \hline 11 &= 10x-29 \\ +29 & \qquad +29 \\ \hline 40 &= 10x \end{aligned}$ |
| 3 | Isolate the variable. | $10x = 40$<br>$\boxed{x = 4}$ |

# Applications Involving Linear Equations

We now use linear equations to solve problems that occur in our day-to-day lives. You typically will read the problem in words, develop a mathematical model (equation) for the problem, solve the equation, and write the answer in words.

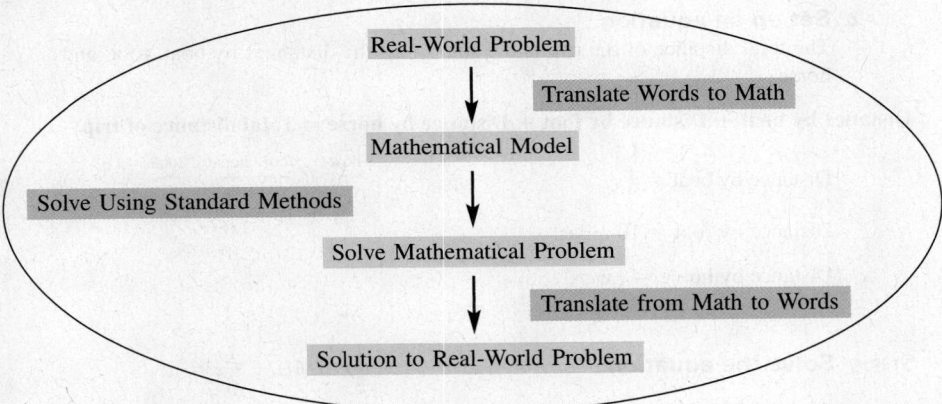

You will have to come up with a unique formula to solve each kind of word problem, but there is a universal *procedure* for approaching all word problems.

### PROCEDURE FOR SOLVING WORD PROBLEMS

**Step 1: Identify the question.** Read the problem *one* time and note what you are asked to find.

**Step 2: Make notes.** Read until you can note something (an amount, a picture, anything). Continue reading and making notes until you have read the problem a second* time.

**Step 3: Assign a variable to whatever is being asked for.** If there are two choices, then let it be the smaller of the two.

**Step 4: Set up an equation.** Assign a variable to represent what you are asked to find.

**Step 5: Solve the equation.**

**Step 6: Check the solution.** Substitute the solution for the variable in the equation, and also run the solution past the "common sense department" using estimation.

*Step 2 often requires multiple readings of the problem.

**EXAMPLE 4    How Long Was the Trip?**

During a camping trip in North Bay, Ontario, a couple went one-third of the way by boat, 10 miles by foot, and one-sixth of the way by horse. How long was the trip?

**Solution:**

STEP 1    **Identify the question.**

How many miles was the trip?

STEP 2    **Make notes.**

| Read | Write |
|------|-------|
| ... one-third of the way by boat | BOAT: $\frac{1}{3}$ of the trip |
| ... 10 miles by foot | FOOT: 10 miles |
| ... one-sixth of the way by horse | HORSE: $\frac{1}{6}$ of the trip |

STEP 3    **Assign a variable.**

Distance of total trip in miles $= x$

STEP 4    **Set up an equation.**

The total distance of the trip is the sum of all the distances by boat, foot, and horse.

**Distance by boat + Distance by foot + Distance by horse = Total distance of trip**

Distance by boat $= \frac{1}{3}x$

Distance by foot $= 10$ miles

Distance by horse $= \frac{1}{6}x$

$$\overbrace{\frac{1}{3}x}^{\text{boat}} + \overbrace{10}^{\text{foot}} + \overbrace{\frac{1}{6}x}^{\text{horse}} = \overbrace{x}^{\text{total}}$$

STEP 5    **Solve the equation.**

$$\frac{1}{3}x + 10 + \frac{1}{6}x = x$$

Multiply by the LCD, 6.  $\qquad 2x + 60 + x = 6x$

Collect $x$ terms on the right.  $\qquad 60 = 3x$

Divide by 3.  $\qquad 20 = x$

The trip was 20 miles.  $\qquad x = 20$

STEP 6    **Check the solution.**

*Estimate:* The boating distance, $\frac{1}{3}$ of 20 miles, is approximately 7 miles; the riding distance on horse, $\frac{1}{6}$ of 20 miles, is approximately 3 miles. Adding these two distances to the 10 miles by foot gives a trip distance of 20 miles.

■ **Answer:** The distance from their car to the gate is 1.5 miles.

■ **YOUR TURN** A family arrives at the Walt Disney World parking lot. To get from their car in the parking lot to the gate at the Magic Kingdom, they walk $\frac{1}{4}$ mile, take a tram for $\frac{1}{3}$ of their total distance, and take a monorail for $\frac{1}{2}$ of their total distance. How far is it from their car to the gate of the Magic Kingdom?

## Geometry Problems

Some problems require geometric formulas in order to be solved.

---

**EXAMPLE 5   Geometry**

A rectangle 24 meters long has the same area as a square with 12-meter sides. What are the dimensions of the rectangle?

**Solution:**

**STEP 1  Identify the question.**
What are the dimensions (length and width) of the rectangle?

**STEP 2  Make notes.**

| Read | Write/Draw |
|------|------------|

A rectangle 24 meters long

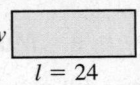

$l = 24$

area of rectangle $= 1 \cdot w = 24w$

A square with 12-meter sides

$144 \text{ m}^2$  12 m

12 m

area of square $= 12 \cdot 12 = 144$

**STEP 3  Assign a variable.**      Let $w$ = width of the rectangle.

**STEP 4  Set up an equation.**
The area of the rectangle is
equal to the area of the square.        rectangle area = square area

Substitute in known quantities.              $24w = 144$

**STEP 5  Solve the equation.**

Divide by 24.                       $w = \dfrac{144}{24} = 6$

> The rectangle is 24 meters long and 6 meters wide.

**STEP 6  Check the solution.**
A 24 meter by 6 meter rectangle has an area of 144 square meters.

---

■ **YOUR TURN**  A rectangle 3 inches wide has the same area as a square with 9-inch sides. What are the dimensions of the rectangle?

■ **Answer:** The rectangle is 27 in. long and 3 in. wide.

## Interest Problems

In our personal or business financial planning, a particular concern we have is interest. **Interest** is money paid for the use of money; it is the cost of borrowing money. The total amount borrowed is called the **principal**. The principal can be the price of our new car; we pay the bank interest for loaning us money to buy the car. The principal can also be the amount we keep in a CD or money market account; the bank uses this money and pays us interest. Typically, interest rate, expressed as a percentage, is the amount charged for the use of the principal for a given time, usually in years.

*Simple interest* is interest that is paid only on the principal during a period of time. Later we will discuss *compound interest*, which is interest paid on both the principal and the interest accrued over a period of time.

**DEFINITION** **Simple Interest**

If a principal of $P$ dollars is borrowed for a period of $t$ years at an annual interest rate $r$ (expressed in decimal form), the interest $I$ charged is

$$I = Prt$$

This is the formula for **simple interest**.

**EXAMPLE 6** **Multiple Investments**

Theresa earns a full athletic scholarship for college. Her parents give her the $20,000 they had saved to pay for her college tuition. She decides to invest that money with an overall goal of earning 11% interest. She wants to put some of the money in a low-risk investment that has been earning 8% a year and the rest of the money in a medium-risk investment that typically earns 12% a year. How much money should she put in each investment to reach her goal?

**Solution:**

STEP 1 **Identify the question.**

How much money is invested in each (the 8% and the 12%) account?

STEP 2 **Make notes.**

| Read | Write/Draw |
|---|---|
| Theresa has $20,000 to invest. | |
| If part is invested at 8% and the rest at 12%, how much should be invested at each rate to yield 11% on the total amount invested? | |

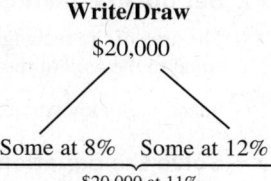

STEP 3 **Assign a variable.**

If we let $x$ represent the amount Theresa puts into the 8% investment, how much of the $20,000 is left for her to put in the 12% investment?

Amount in the 8% investment: $x$

Amount in the 12% investment: $20,000 - x$

STEP 4 **Set up an equation.**

Simple interest formula: $I = Prt$

| INVESTMENT | PRINCIPAL | RATE | TIME (YR) | INTEREST |
|---|---|---|---|---|
| 8% Account | $x$ | 0.08 | 1 | $0.08x$ |
| 12% Account | $20,000 - x$ | 0.12 | 1 | $0.12(20,000 - x)$ |
| Total | 20,000 | 0.11 | 1 | $0.11(20,000)$ |

Adding the interest earned in the 8% investment to the interest earned in the 12% investment should earn an average of 11% on the total investment.

$$0.08x + 0.12(20,000 - x) = 0.11(20,000)$$

STEP 5  **Solve the equation.**

Eliminate the parentheses.                         $0.08x + 2400 - 0.12x = 2200$

Collect $x$ terms on the left,
constants on the right.                            $-0.04x = -200$

Divide by $-0.04$.                                 $x = \boxed{5000}$

Calculate the amount at 12%.         $20,000 - 5000 = \boxed{15,000}$

$\boxed{\text{Theresa should invest \$5000 at 8\% and \$15,000 at 12\% to reach her goal.}}$

STEP 6  **Check the solution.**

If money is invested at 8% and 12% with a goal of averaging 11%, our intuition
tells us that more should be invested at 12% than 8%, which is what we found.
The exact check is as follows:

$$0.08(5000) + 0.12(15,000) = 0.11(20,000)$$
$$400 + 1800 = 2200$$
$$2200 = 2200$$

■ **YOUR TURN**  You win $24,000 and you decide to invest the money in two different
investments: one paying 18% and the other paying 12%. A year later you
have $27,480 total. How much did you originally invest in each account?

## Mixture Problems

Mixtures are something we come across every day. Different candies that sell for different
prices may make up a movie snack. New blends of coffees are developed by coffee
connoisseurs. Chemists mix different concentrations of acids in their labs. Whenever two or
more distinct ingredients are combined, the result is a **mixture**.

Our choice at a gas station is typically 87, 89, and 93 octane. The octane number is the
number that represents the percentage of iso-octane in fuel. 89 octane is significantly
overpriced. Therefore, if your car requires 89 octane, it would be more cost-effective to
mix 87 and 93 octane.

 **EXAMPLE 7    Mixture Problem**

The manual for your new car suggests using gasoline that is 89 octane. In order to save money,
you decide to use some 87 octane and some 93 octane in combination with the 89 octane
currently in your tank in order to have an approximate 89 octane mixture. Assuming you have
1 gallon of 89 octane remaining in your tank (your tank capacity is 16 gallons), how many
gallons of 87 and 93 octane should be used to fill up your tank to achieve a mixture of
89 octane?

**Solution:**

STEP 1  **Identify the question.**

How many gallons of 87 octane and how many gallons of 93 octane should be used?

STEP 2  **Make notes.**

| Read | Write/Draw |
|---|---|
| Assuming you have 1 gallon of 89 octane remaining in your tank (your tank capacity is 16 gallons), how many gallons of 87 and 93 octane should you add? | 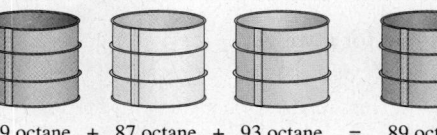 |

89 octane  +  87 octane  +  93 octane  =  89 octane
[1 gallon]      [? gallons]      [? gallons]        [16 gallons]

STEP 3 **Assign variables.**

$$x = \text{gallons of 87 octane gasoline added at the pump}$$

$$15 - x = \text{gallons of 93 octane gasoline added at the pump}$$

$$1 = \text{gallons of 89 octane gasoline already in the tank}$$

STEP 4 **Set up an equation.**

$$0.89(1) + 0.87x + 0.93(15 - x) = 0.89(16)$$

STEP 5 **Solve the equation.**                    $0.89(1) + 0.87x + 0.93(15 - x) = 0.89(16)$

Eliminate the parentheses.                    $0.89 + 0.87x + 13.95 - 0.93x = 14.24$

Collect $x$ terms on the left side.                    $-0.06x + 14.84 = 14.24$

Subtract 14.84 from both sides
of the equation.                    $-0.06x = -0.6$

Divide both sides by $-0.06$.                    $x = 10$

Calculate the amount of 93 octane.                    $15 - 10 = 5$

> Add 10 gallons of 87 octane and 5 gallons of 93 octane.

STEP 6 **Check the solution.**

*Estimate:* Our intuition tells us that if the desired mixture is 89 octane, then we should add approximately 1 part 93 octane and 2 parts 87 octane. The solution we found, 10 gallons of 87 octane and 5 gallons of 93 octane, agrees with this.

■ **Answer:** 40 ml of 5% HCl and 60 ml of 15% HCl

■ **YOUR TURN**  For a certain experiment, a student requires 100 ml of a solution that is 11% HCl (hydrochloric acid). The storeroom has only solutions that are 5% HCl and 15% HCl. How many milliliters of each available solution should be mixed to get 100 ml of 11% HCl?

## Distance–Rate–Time Problems

The next example deals with distance, rate, and time. On a road trip, you see a sign that says your destination is 90 miles away, and your speedometer reads 60 miles per hour. Dividing 90 miles by 60 miles per hour tells you that if you continue at this speed, your arrival will be in 1.5 hours. Here is how you know.

If the rate, or speed, is assumed to be constant, then the equation that relates distance ($d$), rate ($r$), and time ($t$) is given by $d = r \cdot t$. In the above driving example,

$$d = 90 \text{ miles} \qquad r = 60 \frac{\text{miles}}{\text{hour}}$$

Substituting these into
$d = r \cdot t$, we arrive at                    $90 \text{ miles} = \left[ 60 \frac{\text{miles}}{\text{hour}} \right] \cdot t$

Solving for $t$, we get                    $t = \dfrac{90 \text{ miles}}{60 \frac{\text{miles}}{\text{hour}}} = 1.5 \text{ hours}$

**EXAMPLE 8    Distance–Rate–Time**

It takes 8 hours to fly from Orlando to London and 9.5 hours to return. If an airplane averages 550 miles per hour (mph) in still air, what is the average rate of the wind blowing in the direction from Orlando to London? Assume the wind speed is constant for both legs of the trip. Round your answer to the nearest mph.

**Solution:**

STEP 1  **Identify the question.**
At what rate in miles per hour is the wind blowing?

STEP 2  **Make notes.**

| Read | Write/Draw |
|---|---|
| It takes 8 hours to fly from Orlando to London and 9.5 hours to return. | 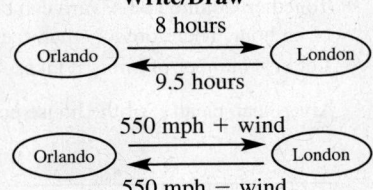 |
| If the airplane averages 550 mph in still air ... | |

STEP 3  **Assign a variable.**
$w$ = wind speed

STEP 4  **Set up an equation.**
The formula relating distance, rate, and time is $d = r \cdot t$. The distance $d$ of each flight is the same. On the Orlando to London flight, the time is 8 hours due to an increased speed from a tailwind. On the London to Orlando flight, the time is 9.5 hours and the speed is decreased due to the headwind.

Orlando to London:          $d = (550 + w)8$

London to Orlando:          $d = (550 - w)9.5$

These distances are the same, so set them equal to each other:

$$(550 + w)8 = (550 - w)9.5$$

STEP 5  **Solve the equation.**
Eliminate the parentheses.                    $4400 + 8w = 5225 - 9.5w$

Collect $w$ terms on the left, constants on the right.          $17.5w = 825$

Divide by 17.5.                    $w = 47.1429 \approx 47$

The wind is blowing approximately ⟨ 47 mph ⟩ in the direction from Orlando to London.

STEP 6  **Check the solution.**
*Estimate:* Going from Orlando to London, the tailwind is approximately 50 mph, which when added to the plane's 550 mph speed yields a ground speed of 600 mph. The Orlando to London route took 8 hours. The distance of that flight is (600 mph) (8 hr), which is 4800 miles. The return trip experienced a headwind of approximately 50 mph, so subtracting the 50 from 550 gives an average speed of 500 mph. That route took 9.5 hours, so the distance of the London to Orlando flight was (500 mph)(9.5 hr), which is 4750 miles. Note that the estimates of 4800 and 4750 miles are close.

■ **YOUR TURN**  A Cessna 150 averages 150 mph in still air. With a tailwind it is able to make a trip in $2\frac{1}{3}$ hours. Because of the headwind, it is only able to make the return trip in $3\frac{1}{2}$ hours. What is the average wind speed?

■ **Answer:** The wind is blowing 30 mph.

▶ **EXAMPLE 9 Work**

Connie can clean her house in 2 hours. If Alvaro helps her, together they can clean the house in 1 hour and 15 minutes. How long would it take Alvaro to clean the house by himself?

**Solution:**

STEP 1 **Identify the question.**

How long does it take Alvaro to clean the house?

STEP 2 **Make notes.**

- Connie can clean her house in 2 hours, so Connie can clean $\frac{1}{2}$ of the house per hour.
- Together Connie and Alvaro can clean the house in 1 hour and 15 minutes, or $\frac{5}{4}$ of an hour. Therefore together, they can clean $\frac{1}{5/4} = \frac{4}{5}$ of the house per hour.
- Let $x$ = number of hours it takes Alvaro to clean the house by himself. So Alvaro can clean $\frac{1}{x}$ of the house per hour.

|  | AMOUNT OF TIME TO DO ONE JOB | AMOUNT OF JOB DONE PER UNIT OF TIME |
|---|---|---|
| Connie | 2 | $\frac{1}{2}$ |
| Alvaro | $x$ | $\frac{1}{x}$ |
| Together | $\frac{5}{4}$ | $\frac{4}{5}$ |

STEP 3 **Set up an equation.**

$$\underbrace{\frac{1}{2}}_{\substack{\text{Amount of house Connie}\\\text{can clean per hour}}} + \underbrace{\frac{1}{x}}_{\substack{\text{Amount of house Alvaro}\\\text{can clean per hour}}} = \underbrace{\frac{4}{5}}_{\substack{\text{Amount of house they can clean per}\\\text{hour if they work together}}}$$

STEP 4 **Solve the equation.**

Multiply by the LCD, $10x$.  $5x + 10 = 8x$

Solve for $x$.  $x = \dfrac{10}{3} = 3\dfrac{1}{3}$

It takes Alvaro ⬚ 3 hours and 20 minutes ⬚ to clean the house by himself.

STEP 5 **Check the solution.**

*Estimate:* Since Connie can clean the house in 2 hours and together with Alvaro it takes 1.25 hours, we know it takes Alvaro longer than 2 hours to clean the house himself.

To solve a linear equation

1. Simplify the algebraic expressions on both sides of the equation.
2. Gather all variable terms on one side of the equation and all constant terms on the other side.
3. Isolate the variable.

In the real world, many kinds of application problems can be solved through modeling with linear equations. Some problems require the development of a mathematical model, while others rely on common formulas. The following procedure will guide you:

1. Identify the question.
2. Make notes.
3. Assign a variable.
4. Set up an equation.
5. Solve the equation.
6. Check the solution against your intuition.

■ SKILLS

**In Exercises 1–26, solve for the indicated variable.**

**1.** $9m - 7 = 11$

**2.** $2x + 4 = 5$

**3.** $5t + 11 = 18$

**4.** $7x + 4 = 21 + 24x$

**5.** $3x - 5 = 25 + 6x$

**6.** $5x + 10 = 25 + 2x$

**7.** $20n - 30 = 20 - 5n$

**8.** $14c + 15 = 43 + 7c$

**9.** $4(x - 3) = 2(x + 6)$

**10.** $5(2y - 1) = 2(4y - 3)$

**11.** $-3(4t - 5) = 5(6 - 2t)$

**12.** $2(3n + 4) = -(n + 2)$

**13.** $2(x - 1) + 3 = x - 3(x + 1)$

**14.** $4(y + 6) - 8 = 2y - 4(y + 2)$

**15.** $5p + 6(p + 7) = 3(p + 2)$

**16.** $3(z + 5) - 5 = 4z + 7(z - 2)$

**17.** $7x - (2x + 3) = x - 2$

**18.** $3x - (4x + 2) = x - 5$

**19.** $2 - (4x + 1) = 3 - (2x - 1)$

**20.** $5 - (2x - 3) = 7 - (3x + 5)$

**21.** $2a - 9 (a + 6) = 6(a + 3) - 4a$

**22.** $25 - [2 + 5y - 3(y + 2)] = -3(2y - 5) - [5(y - 1) - 3y + 3]$

**23.** $32 - [4 + 6x - 5(x + 4)] = 4(3x + 4) - [6(3x - 4) + 7 - 4x]$

**24.** $12 - [3 + 4m - 6(3m - 2)] = -7(2m - 8) - 3[(m - 2) + 3m - 5]$

**25.** $20 - 4[c - 3 - 6(2c + 3)] = 5(3c - 2) - [2(7c - 8) - 4c + 7]$

**26.** $46 - [7 - 8y + 9(6y - 2)] = -7(4y - 7) - 2[6(2y - 3) - 4 + 6y]$

**Exercises 27–38 involve fractions. Clear the fractions by first multiplying by the least common denominator, and then solve the resulting linear equation.**

**27.** $\dfrac{1}{5}m = \dfrac{1}{60}m + 1$

**28.** $\dfrac{1}{12}z = \dfrac{1}{24}z + 3$

**29.** $\dfrac{x}{7} = \dfrac{2x}{63} + 4$

**30.** $\dfrac{a}{11} = \dfrac{a}{22} + 9$

**31.** $\dfrac{1}{3}p = 3 - \dfrac{1}{24}p$

**32.** $\dfrac{3x}{5} - x = \dfrac{x}{10} - \dfrac{5}{2}$

**33.** $\dfrac{5y}{3} - 2y = \dfrac{2y}{84} + \dfrac{5}{7}$

**34.** $2m - \dfrac{5m}{8} = \dfrac{3m}{72} + \dfrac{4}{3}$

**35.** $p + \dfrac{p}{4} = \dfrac{5}{2}$

**36.** $\dfrac{c}{4} - 2c = \dfrac{5}{4} - \dfrac{c}{2}$

**37.** $\dfrac{x - 3}{3} - \dfrac{x - 4}{2} = 1 - \dfrac{x - 6}{6}$

**38.** $1 - \dfrac{x - 5}{3} = \dfrac{x + 2}{5} - \dfrac{6x - 1}{15}$

■ **APPLICATIONS** ━━━━━━━━━━━━━━━━━━━━━━━━━

**39. Puzzle.** Angela is on her way from home in Jersey City to New York City for dinner. She walks 1 mile to the train station, takes the train $\frac{3}{4}$ of the way, and takes a taxi $\frac{1}{6}$ of the way to the restaurant. How far does Angela live from the restaurant?

**40. Puzzle.** An employee at Kennedy Space Center (KSC) lives in Daytona Beach and works in the vehicle assembly building (VAB). She carpools to work with a colleague. On the days that her colleague drives the car pool, she drives 7 miles to the park-and-ride, continues with her colleague to the KSC headquarters building, and then takes the KSC shuttle from the headquarters building to the VAB. The drive from the park-and-ride to the headquarters building is $\frac{5}{6}$ of her total trip and the shuttle ride is $\frac{1}{20}$ of her total trip. How many miles does she travel from her house to the VAB on days when her colleague drives?

**41. Budget.** A company has a total of $20,000 allocated for monthly costs. Fixed costs are $15,000 per month and variable costs are $18.50 per unit. How many units can be manufactured in a month?

**42. Budget.** A woman decides to start a small business making monogrammed cocktail napkins. She can set aside $1870 for monthly costs. Fixed costs are $1329.50 per month and variable costs are $3.70 per set of napkins. How many sets of napkins can she afford to make per month?

**43. Geometry.** Consider two circles, a smaller one and a larger one. If the larger one has a radius that is 3 feet larger than that of the smaller circle and the ratio of the circumferences is 2:1, what are the radii of the two circles?

**44. Geometry.** The length of a rectangle is 2 more than 3 times the width, and the perimeter is 28 inches. What are the dimensions of the rectangle?

**45. Biology: Alligators.** It is common to see alligators in ponds, lakes, and rivers in Florida. The ratio of head size (back of the head to the end of the snout) to the full body length of an alligator is typically constant. If a $3\frac{1}{2}$-foot alligator has a head length of 6 inches, how long would you expect an alligator to be whose head length is 9 inches?

**46. Biology: Snakes.** In the African rainforest there is a snake called a Gaboon viper. The fang size of this snake is proportional to the length of the snake. A 3-foot snake typically has 2-inch fangs. If a herpetologist finds Gaboon viper fangs that are 2.6 inches long, how big a snake would she expect to find?

**47. Investing.** Ashley has $120,000 to invest and decides to put some in a CD that earns 4% interest per year and the rest in a low-risk stock that earns 7%. How much did she invest in each to earn $7800 interest in the first year?

**48. Investing.** You inherit $13,000 and you decide to invest the money in two different investments: one paying 10% and the other paying 14%. A year later your investments are worth $14,580. How much did you originally invest in each account?

**49. Investing.** Wendy was awarded a volleyball scholarship to the University of Michigan, so on graduation her parents gave her the $14,000 they had saved for her college tuition. She opted to invest some money in a privately held company that pays 10% per year and evenly split the remaining money between a money market account yielding 2% and a high-risk stock that yielded 40%. At the end of the first year she had $16,610 total. How much did she invest in each of the three?

**50. Interest.** A high school student was able to save $5000 by working a part-time job every summer. He invested half the money in a money market account and half the money in a stock that paid three times as much interest as the money market account. After a year he earned $150 in interest. What were the interest rates of the money market account and the stock?

**51. Chemistry.** For a certain experiment, a student requires 100 ml of a solution that is 8% HCl (hydrochloric acid). The storeroom has only solutions that are 5% HCl and 15% HCl. How many milliliters of each available solution should be mixed to get 100 ml of 8% HCl?

**52. Chemistry.** How many gallons of pure alcohol must be mixed with 5 gallons of a solution that is 20% alcohol to make a solution that is 50% alcohol?

**53. Communications.** The speed of light is approximately $3.0 \times 10^8$ meters per second (670,616,629 miles per hour). The distance from Earth to Mars varies because their orbits around the Sun are independent. On average, Mars is 100 million miles from Earth. If we use laser communication systems, what will be the delay between Houston and NASA astronauts on Mars?

**54. Speed of Sound.** The speed of sound is approximately 760 miles per hour in air. If a gun is fired $\frac{1}{2}$ mile away, how long will it take the sound to reach you?

**55. Business.** During the month of February 2011, the average price of gasoline rose 4.7% in the United States. If the average price of gasoline at the end of February 2011 was $3.21 per gallon, what was the price of gasoline at the beginning of February?

**56. Business.** During the Christmas shopping season of 2010, the average price of a flat screen television fell by 40%. A shopper purchased a 42-inch flat screen television for $299 in late November 2010. How much would the shopper have paid, to the nearest dollar, for the same television if it was purchased in September 2010?

**57. Medicine.** A patient requires an IV of 0.9% saline solution, also known as normal saline solution. How much distilled water, to the nearest milliliter, must be added to 100 milliliters of a 3% saline solution to produce normal saline?

**58. Medicine.** A patient requires an IV of D5W, a 5% solution of Dextrose (sugar) in water. To the nearest milliliter, how much D20W, a 20% solution of Dextrose in water, must be added to 100 milliliters of distilled water to produce a D5W solution?

**59. Boating.** A motorboat can maintain a constant speed of 16 miles per hour relative to the water. The boat makes a trip upstream to a marina in 20 minutes. The return trip takes 15 minutes. What is the speed of the current?

**60. Aviation.** A Cessna 175 can average 130 miles per hour. If a trip takes 2 hours one way and the return takes 1 hour and 15 minutes, find the wind speed, assuming it is constant.

**61. Distance–Rate–Time.** A jogger and a walker cover the same distance. The jogger finishes in 40 minutes. The walker takes an hour. How fast is each exerciser moving if the jogger runs 2 miles per hour faster than the walker?

**62. Distance–Rate–Time.** A high school student in Seattle, Washington, attended the University of Central Florida. On the way to UCF he took a southern route. After graduation he returned to Seattle via a northern trip. On both trips he had the same average speed. If the southern trek took 45 hours and the northern trek took 50 hours, and the northern trek was 300 miles longer, how long was each trip?

**63. Distance–Rate–Time.** College roommates leave for their first class in the same building. One walks at 2 miles per hour and the other rides his bike at a slow 6 miles per hour pace. How long will it take each to get to class if the walker takes 12 minutes longer to get to class and they travel on the same path?

**64. Distance–Rate–Time.** A long-distance delivery service sends out a truck with a package at 7 A.M. At 7:30 the manager realizes there was another package going to the same location. He sends out a car to catch the truck. If the truck travels at an average speed of 50 miles per hour and the car travels at 70 miles per hour, how long will it take the car to catch the truck?

**65. Work.** Christopher can paint the interior of his house in 15 hours. If he hires Cynthia to help him, together they can do the same job in 9 hours. If he lets Cynthia work alone, how long will it take her to paint the interior of his house?

**66. Work.** Jay and Morgan work in the summer for a landscaper. It takes Jay 3 hours to complete the company's largest yard alone. If Morgan helps him, it takes only 1 hour. How much time would it take Morgan alone?

**67. Work.** Tracey and Robin deliver Coke products to local convenience stores. Tracey can complete the deliveries in 4 hours alone. Robin can do it in 6 hours alone. If they decide to work together on a Saturday, how long will it take?

**68. Work.** Joshua can deliver his newspapers in 30 minutes. It takes Amber 20 minutes to do the same route. How long would it take them to deliver the newspapers if they worked together?

**69. Sports.** In Super Bowl XXXVII, the Tampa Bay Buccaneers scored a total of 48 points. All of their points came from field goals and touchdowns. Field goals are worth 3 points and each touchdown was worth 7 points (Martin Gramatica was successful in every extra point attempt). They scored a total of 8 times. How many field goals and touchdowns were scored?

**70. Sports.** A tight end can run the 100-yard dash in 12 seconds. A defensive back can do it in 10 seconds. The tight end catches a pass at his own 20 yard line with the defensive back at the 15 yard line. If no other players are nearby, at what yard line will the defensive back catch up to the tight end?

**71. Recreation.** How do two children of different weights balance on a seesaw? The heavier child sits closer to the center and the lighter child sits further away. When the product of the weight of the child and the distance from the center is equal on both sides, the seesaw should be horizontal to the ground. Suppose Max weighs 42 pounds and Maria weighs 60 pounds. If Max sits 5 feet from the center, how far should Maria sit from the center in order to balance the seesaw horizontal to the ground?

**72. Recreation.** Refer to Exercise 71. Suppose Martin, who weighs 33 pounds, sits on the side of the seesaw with Max. If their average distance to the center is 4 feet, how far should Maria sit from the center in order to balance the seesaw horizontal to the ground?

**73. Recreation.** If a seesaw has an adjustable bench, then the board can be positioned over the fulcrum. Maria and Max in Exercise 71 decide to sit on the very edge of the board on each side. Where should the fulcrum be placed along the board in order to balance the seesaw horizontally to the ground? Give the answer in terms of the distance from each child's end.

**74. Recreation.** Add Martin (Exercise 72) to Max's side of the seesaw and recalculate Exercise 73.

# ■ CATCH THE MISTAKE

**In Exercises 75–76, explain the mistake that is made.**

**75.** Solve the equation $4x + 3 = 6x - 7$.

**Solution:**

Subtract $4x$ and add 7 to the equation.      $3 = 6x$

Divide by 3.      $x = 2$

This is incorrect. What mistake was made?

**76.** Solve the equation $3(x + 1) + 2 = x - 3(x - 1)$.

**Solution:**
$$3x + 3 + 2 = x - 3x - 3$$
$$3x + 5 = -2x - 3$$
$$5x = -8$$
$$x = -\frac{8}{5}$$

This is incorrect. What mistake was made?

# ■ CONCEPTUAL

**77.** Solve for $x$, given that $a$, $b$, and $c$ are real numbers and $a \neq 0$:
$$ax + b = c$$

**78.** Find the number $a$ for which $y = 2$ is a solution of the equation $y - a = y + 5 - 3ay$.

**In Exercises 79–86, solve each formula for the specified variable.**

**79.** $P = 2l + 2w$ for $w$

**80.** $P = 2l + 2w$ for $l$

**81.** $A = \frac{1}{2}bh$ for $h$

**82.** $C = 2\pi r$ for $r$

**83.** $A = lw$ for $w$

**84.** $d = rt$ for $t$

**85.** $V = lwh$ for $h$

**86.** $V = \pi r^2 h$ for $h$

# ■ CHALLENGE

**87.** Tricia and Janine are roommates and leave Houston on Interstate 10 at the same time to visit their families for a long weekend. Tricia travels west and Janine travels east. If Tricia's average speed is 12 miles per hour faster than Janine's, find the speed of each if they are 320 miles apart in 2 hours and 30 minutes.

**88.** Rick and Mike are roommates and leave Gainesville on Interstate 75 at the same time to visit their girlfriends for a long weekend. Rick travels north and Mike travels south. If Mike's average speed is 8 miles per hour faster than Rick's, find the speed of each if they are 210 miles apart in 1 hour and 30 minutes.

# ■ TECHNOLOGY

**In Exercises 89–92, graph the function represented by each side of the equation in the same viewing rectangle and solve for $x$.**

**89.** $3(x + 2) - 5x = 3x - 4$

**90.** $-5(x - 1) - 7 = 10 - 9x$

**91.** $2x + 6 = 4x - 2x + 8 - 2$

**92.** $10 - 20x = 10x - 30x + 20 - 10$

**93.** Suppose you bought a house for $132,500 and sold it 3 years later for $168,190. Plot these points using a graphing utility. Assuming a linear relationship, how much could you have sold the house for had you waited 2 additional years?

**94.** Suppose you bought a house for $132,500 and sold it 3 years later for $168,190. Plot these points using a graphing utility. Assuming a linear relationship, how much could you have sold the house for had you sold it 1 year after buying it?

**95.** A golf club membership has two options. Option A is a $300 monthly fee plus $15 cart fee every time you play. Option B has a $150 monthly fee and a $42 fee every time you play. Write a mathematical model for monthly costs for each plan and graph both in the same viewing rectangle using a graphing utility. Explain when Option A is the better deal and when Option B is the better deal.

**96.** A phone provider offers two calling plans. Plan A has a $30 monthly charge and a $0.10 per minute charge on every call. Plan B has a $50 monthly charge and a $0.03 per minute charge on every call. Explain when Plan A is the better deal and when Plan B is the better deal.

**SKILLS OBJECTIVES**

- Solve quadratic equations by factoring.
- Use the square root method to solve quadratic equations.
- Solve quadratic equations by completing the square.
- Use the quadratic formula to solve quadratic equations.

**CONCEPTUAL OBJECTIVES**

- Choose appropriate methods for solving quadratic equations.
- Interpret different types of solution sets (real, imaginary, complex conjugates, repeated roots).
- Derive the quadratic formula.

# Factoring

In a linear equation, the variable is raised only to the first power in any term where it occurs. In a *quadratic equation*, the variable is raised to the second power in at least one term. Examples of *quadratic equations*, also called second-degree equations, are

$$x^2 + 3 = 7 \qquad 5x^2 + 4x - 7 = 0 \qquad x^2 - 3 = 0$$

**DEFINITION** **Quadratic Equation**

A **quadratic equation** in $x$ is an equation that can be written in the **standard form**

$$ax^2 + bx + c = 0$$

where $a$, $b$, and $c$ are real numbers and $a \neq 0$.

**Study Tip**

In a quadratic equation the variable is raised to the power of 2, which is the highest power present in the equation.

There are several methods for solving quadratic equations: *factoring*, the *square root method*, *completing the square*, and the *quadratic formula*.

**FACTORING METHOD**

The **factoring method** applies the **zero product property**:

| **WORDS** | **MATH** |
|---|---|
| If a product is zero, then at least one of its factors has to be zero. | If $B \cdot C = 0$, then $B = 0$ or $C = 0$ or both. |

Consider $(x - 3)(x + 2) = 0$. The zero product property says that $x - 3 = 0$ or $x + 2 = 0$, which leads to $x = -2$ or $x = 3$. The solution set is $\{-2, 3\}$.

When a quadratic equation is written in the standard form $ax^2 + bx + c = 0$, it may be possible to factor the left side of the equation as a product of two first-degree polynomials. We use the zero product property and set each linear factor equal to zero. We solve the resulting two linear equations to obtain the solutions of the quadratic equation.

**EXAMPLE 1** **Solving a Quadratic Equation by Factoring**

Solve the equation $x^2 - 6x - 16 = 0$.

**Solution:**

The quadratic equation is already in
standard form.

$$x^2 - 6x - 16 = 0$$

Factor the left side into a product of two
linear factors.

$$(x - 8)(x + 2) = 0$$

If a product equals zero, one of its factors
has to be equal to zero.

$$x - 8 = 0 \quad \text{or} \quad x + 2 = 0$$

Solve both linear equations.

$$\boxed{x = 8 \quad \text{or} \quad x = -2}$$

The solution set is $\boxed{\{-2, 8\}}$.

■ **Answer:** The solution is $x = -5, 4$.
The solution set is $\{-5, 4\}$.

■ **YOUR TURN** Solve the quadratic equation $x^2 + x - 20 = 0$ by factoring.

▼ **CAUTION**

Do not divide by a variable (because
the value of that variable may be
zero). Bring all terms to one side first
and then factor.

 **EXAMPLE 2** **Solving a Quadratic Equation by Factoring**

Solve the equation $2x^2 = 3x$.

**COMMON MISTAKE**

The common mistake here is dividing both sides by $x$, which is not allowed because $x$
might be 0.

 **CORRECT**

Write the equation in standard form by
subtracting $3x$.

$$2x^2 - 3x = 0$$

Factor the left side.

$$x(2x - 3) = 0$$

Use the zero product property and set
each factor equal to zero.

$$x = 0 \quad \text{or} \quad 2x - 3 = 0$$

Solve each linear equation.

$$\boxed{x = 0 \quad \text{or} \quad x = \frac{3}{2}}$$

The solution set is $\boxed{\left\{0, \frac{3}{2}\right\}}$.

**INCORRECT**

Write the original equation.

$$2x^2 = 3x$$

The **error** occurs here when both sides
are divided by $x$.

$$2x = 3$$

*Technology Tip*

Use a graphing utility to display
graphs of $y_1 = 2x^2$ and $y_2 = 3x$.

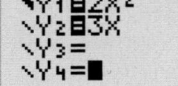

The $x$-coordinates of the points of
intersection are the solutions to
this equation.

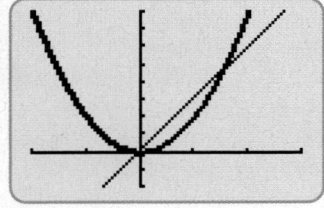

In Example 2, the root $x = 0$ is lost when the original quadratic equation is divided by $x$.
Remember to put the equation in standard form first and then factor.

# Square Root Method

The square root of 16, $\sqrt{16}$, is 4, *not* $\pm 4$. In the Appendix, the **principal square root** is discussed. The solutions to $x^2 = 16$, however, are $x = -4$ and $x = 4$. Let us now investigate quadratic equations that do not have a first-degree term. They have the form

$$ax^2 + c = 0 \quad a \neq 0$$

The method we use to solve such equations uses the square root property.

**SQUARE ROOT PROPERTY**

| **WORDS** | **MATH** |
|---|---|
| If an expression squared is equal to a constant, then that expression is equal to the positive or negative square root of the constant. | If $x^2 = P$, then $x = \pm\sqrt{P}$. |

*Note:* The variable squared must be isolated first (coefficient equal to 1).

**EXAMPLE 3  Using the Square Root Property**

Solve the equation $3x^2 - 27 = 0$.

**Solution:**

| | |
|---|---|
| Add 27 to both sides. | $3x^2 = 27$ |
| Divide both sides by 3. | $x^2 = 9$ |
| Apply the square root property. | $x = \pm\sqrt{9} = \pm 3$ |

The solution set is $\boxed{\{-3, 3\}}$.

If we alter Example 3 by changing subtraction to addition, we see in Example 4 that we get imaginary roots, as opposed to real roots which is reviewed in the Appendix.

**EXAMPLE 4  Using the Square Root Property**

Solve the equation $3x^2 + 27 = 0$.

**Solution:**

| | |
|---|---|
| Subtract 27 from both sides. | $3x^2 = -27$ |
| Divide by 3. | $x^2 = -9$ |
| Apply the square root property. | $x = \pm\sqrt{-9}$ |
| Simplify. | $x = \pm i\sqrt{9} = \pm 3i$ |

The solution set is $\boxed{\{-3i, 3i\}}$.

■ **YOUR TURN** Solve the equations:

**a.** $y^2 - 147 = 0$   **b.** $v^2 + 64 = 0$

■ **Answer:**
**a.** The solution is $y = \pm 7\sqrt{3}$. The solution set is $\{-7\sqrt{3}, 7\sqrt{3}\}$.
**b.** The solution is $v = \pm 8i$. The solution set is $\{-8i, 8i\}$.

**EXAMPLE 5** **Using the Square Root Property**

Solve the equation $(x - 2)^2 = 16$.

**Solution:**

**Approach 1:** If an expression squared is 16, then the expression equals $\pm\sqrt{16}$.

$$(x - 2) = \pm\sqrt{16}$$

Separate into two equations.

$$x - 2 = \sqrt{16} \quad \text{or} \quad x - 2 = -\sqrt{16}$$

$$x - 2 = 4 \qquad\qquad x - 2 = -4$$

$$x = 6 \qquad\qquad x = -2$$

The solution set is $\boxed{\{-2, 6\}}$.

**Approach 2:** It is acceptable notation to keep the equations together.

$$(x - 2) = \pm\sqrt{16}$$

$$x - 2 = \pm 4$$

$$x = 2 \pm 4$$

$$\boxed{x = -2, 6}$$

## Completing the Square

Factoring and the square root method are two efficient, quick procedures for solving many quadratic equations. However, some equations, such as $x^2 - 10x - 3 = 0$, cannot be solved directly by these methods. A more general procedure to solve this kind of equation is called **completing the square**. The idea behind completing the square is to transform any standard quadratic equation $ax^2 + bx + c = 0$ into the form $(x + A)^2 = B$, where $A$ and $B$ are constants and the left side, $(x + A)^2$, has the form of a **perfect square**. This last equation can then be solved by the square root method. How do we transform the first equation into the second equation?

Note that the above-mentioned example, $x^2 - 10x - 3 = 0$, cannot be factored into expressions in which all numbers are integers (or even rational numbers). We can, however, transform this quadratic equation into a form that contains a perfect square.

| WORDS | MATH |
|---|---|
| Write the original equation. | $x^2 - 10x - 3 = 0$ |
| Add 3 to both sides. | $x^2 - 10x = 3$ |
| Add 25 to both sides.* | $x^2 - 10x + 25 = 3 + 25$ |
| The left side can be written as a perfect square. | $(x - 5)^2 = 28$ |
| Apply the square root method. | $x - 5 = \pm\sqrt{28}$ |
| Add 5 to both sides. | $x = 5 \pm 2\sqrt{7}$ |

*Why did we add 25 to both sides? Recall that $(x - c)^2 = x^2 - 2xc + c^2$. In this case $c = 5$ in order for $-2xc = -10x$. Therefore, the desired perfect square $(x - 5)^2$ results in $x^2 - 10x + 25$. Applying this product, we see that $+25$ is needed.

If the coefficient of $x^2$ is 1, a systematic approach is to take the coefficient of the first degree term of $x^2 - 10x - 3 = 0$, which is $-10$. Divide $-10$ by 2 to get $-5$; then square $-5$ to get 25.

### SOLVING A QUADRATIC EQUATION BY COMPLETING THE SQUARE

| WORDS | MATH |
|---|---|
| Express the quadratic equation in the following form. | $x^2 + bx = c$ |
| Divide $b$ by 2 and square the result, then add the square to both sides. | $x^2 + bx + \left(\dfrac{b}{2}\right)^2 = c + \left(\dfrac{b}{2}\right)^2$ |
| Write the left side of the equation as a perfect square. | $\left(x + \dfrac{b}{2}\right)^2 = c + \left(\dfrac{b}{2}\right)^2$ |
| Solve using the square root method. | |

### EXAMPLE 6   Completing the Square

Solve the quadratic equation $x^2 + 8x - 3 = 0$ by completing the square.

**Solution:**

Add 3 to both sides.

$$x^2 + 8x = 3$$

Add $\left(\frac{1}{2} \cdot 8\right)^2 = 4^2$ to both sides.

$$x^2 + 8x + 4^2 = 3 + 4^2$$

Write the left side as a perfect square and simplify the right side.

$$(x + 4)^2 = 19$$

Apply the square root method to solve.

$$x + 4 = \pm\sqrt{19}$$

Subtract 4 from both sides.

$$\boxed{x = -4 \pm \sqrt{19}}$$

The solution set is $\boxed{\left\{-4 - \sqrt{19},\ -4 + \sqrt{19}\right\}}$.

***Technology Tip***

Graph $y_1 = x^2 + 8x - 3$.

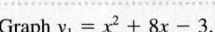

The $x$-intercepts are the solutions to this equation.

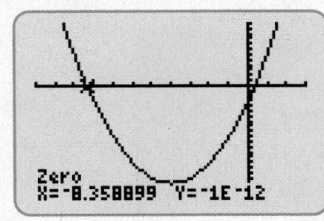

In Example 6, the leading coefficient (the coefficient of the $x^2$ term) is 1. When the leading coefficient is not 1, start by first dividing the equation by that leading coefficient.

***Study Tip***

When the leading coefficient is not 1, start by first dividing the equation by that leading coefficient.

## Technology Tip

Graph $y_1 = 3x^2 - 12x + 13$.

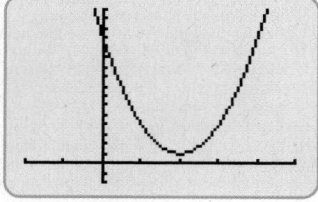

The graph does not cross the x-axis, so there is no real solution to this equation.

**EXAMPLE 7    Completing the Square When the Leading Coefficient Is Not Equal to 1**

Solve the equation $3x^2 - 12x + 13 = 0$ by completing the square.

**Solution:**

| | |
|---|---|
| Divide by the leading coefficient, 3. | $x^2 - 4x + \dfrac{13}{3} = 0$ |
| Collect the variables to one side of the equation and constants to the other side. | $x^2 - 4x = -\dfrac{13}{3}$ |
| Add $\left(-\dfrac{4}{2}\right)^2 = 4$ to both sides. | $x^2 - 4x + 4 = -\dfrac{13}{3} + 4$ |
| Write the left side of the equation as a perfect square and simplify the right side. | $(x - 2)^2 = -\dfrac{1}{3}$ |
| Solve using the square root method. | $x - 2 = \pm\sqrt{-\dfrac{1}{3}}$ |
| Simplify. | $x = 2 \pm i\sqrt{\dfrac{1}{3}}$ |
| Rationalize the denominator (Appendix). | $x = 2 \pm \dfrac{i}{\sqrt{3}} \cdot \dfrac{\sqrt{3}}{\sqrt{3}}$ |
| Simplify. | $x = 2 \pm \dfrac{i\sqrt{3}}{3}$ |

$$x = 2 - \frac{i\sqrt{3}}{3}, \quad x = 2 + \frac{i\sqrt{3}}{3}$$

The solution set is $\left\{ 2 - \dfrac{i\sqrt{3}}{3}, 2 + \dfrac{i\sqrt{3}}{3} \right\}$.

■ **Answer:** The solution is $x = 1 \pm \dfrac{i\sqrt{2}}{2}$. The solution set is $\left\{ 1 - \dfrac{i\sqrt{2}}{2}, 1 + \dfrac{i\sqrt{2}}{2} \right\}$.

■ **YOUR TURN** Solve the equation $2x^2 - 4x + 3 = 0$ by completing the square.

# The Quadratic Formula

Let us now consider the most general quadratic equation:

$$ax^2 + bx + c = 0 \quad a \neq 0$$

We can solve this equation by completing the square.

| WORDS | MATH |
|---|---|
| Divide the equation by the leading coefficient $a$. | $x^2 + \dfrac{b}{a}x + \dfrac{c}{a} = 0$ |
| Subtract $\dfrac{c}{a}$ from both sides. | $x^2 + \dfrac{b}{a}x = -\dfrac{c}{a}$ |
| Square half of $\dfrac{b}{a}$ and add the result $\left(\dfrac{b}{2a}\right)^2$ to both sides. | $x^2 + \dfrac{b}{a}x + \left(\dfrac{b}{2a}\right)^2 = \left(\dfrac{b}{2a}\right)^2 - \dfrac{c}{a}$ |
| Write the left side of the equation as a perfect square and the right side as a single fraction. | $\left(x + \dfrac{b}{2a}\right)^2 = \dfrac{b^2 - 4ac}{4a^2}$ |
| Solve using the square root method. | $x + \dfrac{b}{2a} = \pm\sqrt{\dfrac{b^2 - 4ac}{4a^2}}$ |
| Subtract $\dfrac{b}{2a}$ from both sides and simplify the radical. | $x = -\dfrac{b}{2a} \pm \dfrac{\sqrt{b^2 - 4ac}}{2a}$ |
| Write as a single fraction. | $x = \dfrac{-b \pm \sqrt{b^2 - 4ac}}{2a}$ |

We have derived the **quadratic formula**.

## THE QUADRATIC FORMULA

If $ax^2 + bx + c = 0$, $a \neq 0$, then the solution is

$$x = \frac{-b \pm \sqrt{b^2 - 4ac}}{2a}$$

*Note:* The quadratic equation must be in standard form ($ax^2 + bx + c = 0$) in order to identify the parameters:

$a$—coefficient of $x^2$     $b$—coefficient of $x$     $c$—constant

**Study Tip**

$$x = \frac{-b \pm \sqrt{b^2 - 4ac}}{2a}$$

Read as "negative $b$ plus or minus the square root of the quantity $b$ squared minus 4ac all over 2a."

We read this formula as *negative b plus or minus the square root of the quantity b squared minus 4ac all over 2a.* It is important to note that negative $b$ could be positive (if $b$ is negative). For this reason, an alternate form is "opposite $b$. . . ." The quadratic formula should be memorized and used when simpler methods (factoring and the square root method) cannot be used. The quadratic formula works for *any* quadratic equation.

**Study Tip**

The quadratic formula works for *any* quadratic equation.

## Study Tip

Using parentheses as placeholders helps avoid $\pm$ errors.

$$x = \frac{-b \pm \sqrt{b^2 - 4ac}}{2a}$$

$$x = \frac{-(\square) \pm \sqrt{(\square)^2 - 4(\square)(\square)}}{2(\square)}$$

### EXAMPLE 8  Using the Quadratic Formula and Finding Two Distinct Real Roots

Use the quadratic formula to solve the quadratic equation $x^2 - 4x - 1 = 0$.

**Solution:**

For this problem, $a = 1$, $b = -4$, and $c = -1$.

Write the quadratic formula.

$$x = \frac{-b \pm \sqrt{b^2 - 4ac}}{2a}$$

Use parentheses to avoid losing a minus sign.

$$x = \frac{-(\square) \pm \sqrt{(\square)^2 - 4(\square)(\square)}}{2(\square)}$$

Substitute values for $a$, $b$, and $c$ into the parentheses.

$$x = \frac{-(-4) \pm \sqrt{(-4)^2 - 4(1)(-1)}}{2(1)}$$

Simplify.

$$x = \frac{4 \pm \sqrt{16 + 4}}{2} = \frac{4 \pm \sqrt{20}}{2} = \frac{4 \pm 2\sqrt{5}}{2} = \frac{4}{2} \pm \frac{2\sqrt{5}}{2} = \boxed{2 \pm \sqrt{5}}$$

The solution set $\boxed{\{2 - \sqrt{5}, 2 + \sqrt{5}\}}$ contains two distinct real numbers.

■ **Answer:** The solution is $x = -3 \pm \sqrt{11}$. The solution set is $\{-3 - \sqrt{11}, -3 + \sqrt{11}\}$.

■ **YOUR TURN**  Use the quadratic formula to solve the quadratic equation $x^2 + 6x - 2 = 0$.

### EXAMPLE 9  Using the Quadratic Formula and Finding Two Complex Roots

Use the quadratic formula to solve the quadratic equation $x^2 + 8 = 4x$.

**Solution:**

Write this equation in standard form $x^2 - 4x + 8 = 0$ in order to identify $a = 1$, $b = -4$, and $c = 8$.

Write the quadratic formula.

$$x = \frac{-b \pm \sqrt{b^2 - 4ac}}{2a}$$

Use parentheses to avoid overlooking a minus sign.

$$x = \frac{-(\square) \pm \sqrt{(\square)^2 - 4(\square)(\square)}}{2(\square)}$$

Substitute the values for $a$, $b$, and $c$ into the parentheses.

$$x = \frac{-(-4) \pm \sqrt{(-4)^2 - 4(1)(8)}}{2(1)}$$

Simplify.

$$x = \frac{4 \pm \sqrt{16 - 32}}{2} = \frac{4 \pm \sqrt{-16}}{2} = \frac{4 \pm 4i}{2} = \frac{4}{2} \pm \frac{4i}{2} = \boxed{2 \pm 2i}$$

The solution set $\boxed{\{2 - 2i, 2 + 2i\}}$ contains two complex numbers. Note that they are complex conjugates of each other.

■ **Answer:** The solution set is $\{1 - i, 1 + i\}$.

■ **YOUR TURN**  Use the quadratic formula to solve the quadratic equation $x^2 + 2 = 2x$.

**EXAMPLE 10** **Using the Quadratic Formula and Finding One Repeated Real Root**

Use the quadratic formula to solve the quadratic equation $4x^2 - 4x + 1 = 0$.

**Solution:**

Identify $a$, $b$, and $c$.
$$a = 4, b = -4, c = 1$$

Write the quadratic formula.
$$x = \frac{-b \pm \sqrt{b^2 - 4ac}}{2a}$$

Use parentheses to avoid losing a minus sign.
$$x = \frac{-(\Box) \pm \sqrt{(\Box)^2 - 4(\Box)(\Box)}}{2(\Box)}$$

Substitute values $a = 4$, $b = -4$, $c = 1$.
$$x = \frac{-(-4) \pm \sqrt{(-4)^2 - 4(4)(1)}}{2(4)}$$

Simplify.
$$x = \frac{4 \pm \sqrt{16 - 16}}{8} = \frac{4 \pm 0}{8} = \frac{1}{2}$$

The solution set is a repeated real root $\boxed{\left\{\frac{1}{2}\right\}}$.

*Note:* This quadratic also could have been solved by factoring: $(2x - 1)^2 = 0$.

■ **YOUR TURN** Use the quadratic formula to solve the quadratic equation $9x^2 - 6x + 1 = 0$.

■ **Answer:** $\left\{\frac{1}{3}\right\}$

## TYPES OF SOLUTIONS

The expression inside the radical, $b^2 - 4ac$, is called the **discriminant**. The discriminant gives important information about the corresponding solutions or roots of $ax^2 + bx + c = 0$, where $a$, $b$, and $c$ are real numbers.

| $b^2 - 4ac$ | SOLUTIONS (ROOTS) |
|---|---|
| Positive | Two distinct real roots |
| 0 | One real root (a double or repeated root) |
| Negative | Two complex roots (complex conjugates) |

In Example 8, the discriminant is positive and the solution has two distinct real roots. In Example 9, the discriminant is negative and the solution has two complex (conjugate) roots. In Example 10, the discriminant is zero and the solution has one repeated real root.

## Applications Involving Quadratic Equations

In Section 0.1, we developed a procedure for solving word problems involving linear equations. The procedure is the same for applications involving quadratic equations. The only difference is that the mathematical equations will be quadratic, as opposed to linear.

## EXAMPLE 11   Stock Value

From 1999 to 2001 the price of Abercrombie & Fitch's (ANF) stock was approximately given by $P = 0.2t^2 - 5.6t + 50.2$, where $P$ is the price of stock in dollars, $t$ is in months, and $t = 1$ corresponds to January 1999. When was the value of the stock worth $30?

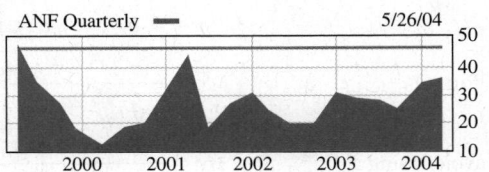

ANF Quarterly ▬      5/26/04

### Technology Tip

The graphing utility screen for

$$\frac{-(-5.6) \pm \sqrt{(-5.6)^2 - 4(0.2)(20.2)}}{2(0.2)}$$

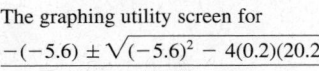

```
(-(-5.6)-√((-5.6
)²-4*.2*20.2))/(
2*.2)
          4.253205655
```

```
(-(-5.6)+√((-5.6
)²-4*.2*20.2))/(
2*.2)
          23.74679434
■
```

### Study Tip

Dimensions such as length and width are distances, which are defined as positive quantities. Although the mathematics may yield both positive and negative values, the negative values are excluded.

### Solution:

**STEP 1  Identify the question.**

When is the price of the stock equal to $30?

**STEP 2  Make notes.**

Stock price:

$$P = 0.2t^2 - 5.6t + 50.2$$
$$P = 30$$

**STEP 3  Set up an equation.**      $0.2t^2 - 5.6t + 50.2 = 30$

**STEP 4  Solve the equation.**

Subtract 30 from both sides.      $0.2t^2 - 5.6t + 20.2 = 0$

Solve for $t$ using the quadratic formula.

$$t = \frac{-(-5.6) \pm \sqrt{(-5.6)^2 - 4(0.2)(20.2)}}{2(0.2)}$$

Simplify.      $t \approx \dfrac{5.6 \pm 3.9}{0.4} \approx 4.25,\ 23.75$

Rounding these two numbers, we find that $t \approx 4$ and $t \approx 24$. Since $t = 1$ corresponds to January 1999, these two solutions correspond to   April 1999 and December 2000 .

**STEP 5  Check the solution.**

Look at the figure. The horizontal axis represents the year (2000 corresponds to January 2000), and the vertical axis represents the stock price. Estimating when the stock price is approximately $30, we find April 1999 and December 2000.

---

## SECTION
## 0.2  SUMMARY

The four methods for solving quadratic equations,

$$ax^2 + bx + c = 0 \qquad a \neq 0$$

are *factoring,* the *square root method, completing the square,* and the *quadratic formula.* Factoring and the square root method are the quickest and easiest but cannot always be used. The quadratic formula and completing the square work for all quadratic equations.

Quadratic Formula:      $x = \dfrac{-b \pm \sqrt{b^2 - 4ac}}{2a}$

A quadratic equation can have three types of solutions: two distinct real roots, one real root (repeated), or two complex roots (conjugates of each other).

**SECTION**
**0.2** EXERCISES

■ **SKILLS**

**In Exercises 1–22, solve by factoring.**

**1.** $x^2 - 5x + 6 = 0$    **2.** $v^2 + 7v + 6 = 0$    **3.** $p^2 - 8p + 15 = 0$    **4.** $u^2 - 2u - 24 = 0$

**5.** $x^2 = 12 - x$    **6.** $11x = 2x^2 + 12$    **7.** $16x^2 + 8x = -1$    **8.** $3x^2 + 10x - 8 = 0$

**9.** $9y^2 + 1 = 6y$    **10.** $4x = 4x^2 + 1$    **11.** $8y^2 = 16y$    **12.** $3A^2 = -12A$

**13.** $9p^2 = 12p - 4$    **14.** $4u^2 = 20u - 25$    **15.** $x^2 - 9 = 0$    **16.** $16v^2 - 25 = 0$

**17.** $x(x + 4) = 12$    **18.** $3t^2 - 48 = 0$    **19.** $2p^2 - 50 = 0$    **20.** $5y^2 - 45 = 0$

**21.** $3x^2 = 12$    **22.** $7v^2 = 28$

**In Exercises 23–34, solve using the square root method.**

**23.** $p^2 - 8 = 0$    **24.** $y^2 - 72 = 0$    **25.** $x^2 + 9 = 0$    **26.** $v^2 + 16 = 0$

**27.** $(x - 3)^2 = 36$    **28.** $(x - 1)^2 = 25$    **29.** $(2x + 3)^2 = -4$    **30.** $(4x - 1)^2 = -16$

**31.** $(5x - 2)^2 = 27$    **32.** $(3x + 8)^2 = 12$    **33.** $(1 - x)^2 = 9$    **34.** $(1 - x)^2 = -9$

**In Exercises 35–46, solve by completing the square.**

**35.** $x^2 + 2x = 3$    **36.** $y^2 + 8y - 2 = 0$    **37.** $t^2 - 6t = -5$    **38.** $x^2 + 10x = -21$

**39.** $y^2 - 4y + 3 = 0$    **40.** $x^2 - 7x + 12 = 0$    **41.** $2p^2 + 8p = -3$    **42.** $2x^2 - 4x + 3 = 0$

**43.** $2x^2 - 7x + 3 = 0$    **44.** $3x^2 - 5x - 10 = 0$    **45.** $\dfrac{x^2}{2} - 2x = \dfrac{1}{4}$    **46.** $\dfrac{t^2}{3} + \dfrac{2t}{3} + \dfrac{5}{6} = 0$

**In Exercises 47–58, solve using the quadratic formula.**

**47.** $t^2 + 3t - 1 = 0$    **48.** $t^2 + 2t = 1$    **49.** $s^2 + s + 1 = 0$    **50.** $2s^2 + 5s = -2$

**51.** $3x^2 - 3x - 4 = 0$    **52.** $4x^2 - 2x = 7$    **53.** $x^2 - 2x + 17 = 0$    **54.** $4m^2 + 7m + 8 = 0$

**55.** $5x^2 + 7x = 3$    **56.** $3x^2 + 5x = -11$    **57.** $\frac{1}{4}x^2 + \frac{2}{3}x - \frac{1}{2} = 0$    **58.** $\frac{1}{4}x^2 - \frac{2}{3}x - \frac{1}{3} = 0$

**In Exercises 59–74, solve using any method.**

**59.** $v^2 - 8v = 20$    **60.** $v^2 - 8v = -20$    **61.** $t^2 + 5t - 6 = 0$    **62.** $t^2 + 5t + 6 = 0$

**63.** $(x + 3)^2 = 16$    **64.** $(x + 3)^2 = -16$    **65.** $(p - 2)^2 = 4p$    **66.** $(u + 5)^2 = 16u$

**67.** $8w^2 + 2w + 21 = 0$    **68.** $8w^2 + 2w - 21 = 0$    **69.** $3p^2 - 9p + 1 = 0$    **70.** $3p^2 - 9p - 1 = 0$

**71.** $\frac{2}{3}t^2 - \frac{4}{3}t = \frac{1}{5}$    **72.** $\frac{1}{2}x^2 + \frac{2}{3}x = \frac{2}{5}$    **73.** $x^2 - 0.1x = 0.12$    **74.** $y^2 - 0.5y = -0.06$

■ **APPLICATIONS**

**75. Stock Value.** From June 2003 until April 2004 JetBlue airlines stock (JBLU) was approximately worth $P = -4t^2 + 80t - 360$, where $P$ denotes the price of the stock in dollars and $t$ corresponds to months, with $t = 1$ corresponding to January 2003. During what months was the stock equal to $24?

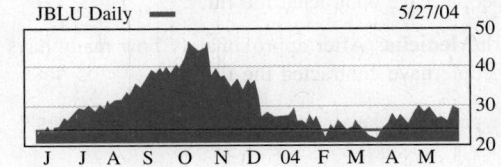

**76. Stock Value.** From November 2003 until March 2004 Wal-Mart Stock (WMT) was approximately worth $P = 2t^2 - 12t + 70$, where $P$ denotes the price of the stock in dollars and $t$ corresponds to months, with $t = 1$ corresponding to November 2003. During what months was the stock equal to $60?

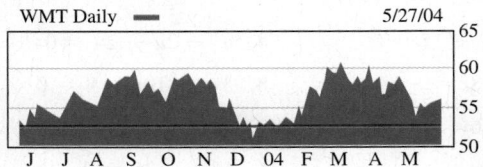

**In Exercises 77 and 78 refer to the following:**

Research indicates that monthly profit for Widgets R Us is modeled by the function

$$P = -100 + (0.2q - 3)q$$

where $P$ is profit measured in millions of dollars and $q$ is the quantity of widgets produced measured in thousands.

**77. Business.** Find the break-even point for a month to the nearest unit.

**78. Business.** Find the production level that produces a monthly profit of $40 million.

**In Exercises 79 and 80 refer to the following:**

In response to economic conditions, a local business explores the effect of a price increase on weekly profit. The function

$$P = -5(x + 3)(x - 24)$$

models the effect that a price increase of $x$ dollars on a bottle of wine will have on the profit $P$ measured in dollars.

**79. Business/Economics.** What is the smallest price increase that will produce a weekly profit of $460?

**80. Business/Economics.** What is the smallest price increase that will produce a weekly profit of $630?

**In Exercises 81 and 82 refer to the following:**

An epidemiological study of the spread of the flu in a small city finds that the total number $P$ of people who contracted the flu $t$ days into an outbreak is modeled by the function

$$P = -t^2 + 13t + 130 \quad 1 \le t \le 6$$

**81. Health/Medicine.** After approximately how many days will 160 people have contracted the flu?

**82. Health/Medicine.** After approximately how many days will 172 people have contracted the flu?

**83. Environment: Reduce Your Margins, Save a Tree.** Let's define the *usable area* of an 8.5-inch by 11-inch piece of paper as the rectangular space between the margins of that piece of paper. Assume the default margins in a word processor in a college's computer lab are set up to be 1.25 inches wide (top and bottom) and 1 inch wide (left and right). Answer the following questions using this information.

  **a.** Determine the amount of usable space, in square inches, on one side of an 8.5-inch by 11-inch piece of paper with the default margins of 1.25 inch and 1 inch.

  **b.** The Green Falcons, a campus environmental club, has convinced their college's computer lab to reduce the default margins in their word-processing software by $x$ inches. Create and simplify the quadratic expression that represents the new usable area, in square inches, of one side of an 8.5-inch by 11-inch piece of paper if the default margins at the computer lab are each reduced by $x$ inches.

  **c.** Subtract the usable space in part (a) from the expression in part (b). Explain what this difference represents.

  **d.** If 10 pages are printed using the new margins and as a result the computer lab saved one whole sheet of paper, then by how much did the computer lab reduce the margins? Round to the nearest tenth of an inch.

**84. Environment: Reduce Your Margins, Save a Tree.** Repeat Exercise 83 assuming the computer lab's default margins are 1 inch all the way around (left, right, top, and bottom). If 15 pages are printed using the new margins and as a result the computer lab saved one whole sheet of paper, then by how much did the computer lab reduce the margins? Round to the nearest tenth of an inch.

**85. Television.** A standard 32-inch television has a 32 inch diagonal and a 25 inch width. What is the height of the 32-inch television?

**86. Television.** A 42-inch LCD television has a 42 inch diagonal and a 20 inch height. What is the width of the 42-inch LCD television?

**87. Numbers.** Find two consecutive numbers such that their product is 306.

**88. Numbers.** Find two consecutive odd integers such that their product is 143.

**89. Geometry.** The area of a rectangle is 135 square feet. The width is 6 feet less than the length. Find the dimensions of the rectangle.

**90. Geometry.** A rectangle has an area of 31.5 square meters. If the length is 2 meters more than twice the width, find the dimensions of the rectangle.

**91. Geometry.** A triangle has a height that is 2 more than 3 times the base and an area of 60 square units. Find the base and height.

**92. Geometry.** A square's side is increased by 3 yards, which corresponds to an increase in the area by 69 square yards. How many yards is the side of the initial square?

**93. Falling Objects.** If a person drops a water balloon off the rooftop of a 100-foot building, the height of the water balloon is given by the equation $h = -16t^2 + 100$, where $t$ is in seconds. When will the water balloon hit the ground?

**94. Falling Objects.** If the person in Exercise 85 throws the water balloon downward with a speed of 5 feet per second, the height of the water balloon is given by the equation $h = -16t^2 - 5t + 100$, where $t$ is in seconds. When will the water balloon hit the ground?

**95. Gardening.** A square garden has an area of 900 square feet. If a sprinkler (with a circular pattern) is placed in the center of the garden, what is the minimum radius of spray the sprinkler would need in order to water all of the garden?

**96. Sports.** A baseball diamond is a square. The distance from base to base is 90 feet. What is the distance from home plate to second base?

**97. Volume.** A flat square piece of cardboard is used to construct an open box. Cutting a 1 foot by 1 foot square off of each corner and folding up the edges will yield an open box (assuming these edges are taped together). If the desired volume of the box is 9 cubic feet, what are the dimensions of the original square piece of cardboard?

**98. Volume.** A rectangular piece of cardboard whose length is twice its width is used to construct an open box. Cutting a 1 foot by 1 foot square off of each corner and folding up the edges will yield an open box. If the desired volume is 12 cubic feet, what are the dimensions of the original rectangular piece of cardboard?

**99. Gardening.** A landscaper has planted a rectangular garden that measures 8 feet by 5 feet. He has ordered 1 cubic yard (27 cubic feet) of stones for a border along the outside of the garden. If the border needs to be 4 inches deep and he wants to use all of the stones, how wide should the border be?

**100. Gardening.** A gardener has planted a semicircular rose garden with a radius of 6 feet, and 2 cubic yards of mulch (1 cu yd = 27 cu ft) is being delivered. Assuming she uses all of the mulch, how deep will the layer of mulch be?

**101. Work.** Lindsay and Kimmie, working together, can balance the financials for the Kappa Kappa Gamma sorority in 6 days. Lindsay by herself can complete the job in 5 days less than Kimmie. How long will it take Lindsay to complete the job by herself?

**102. Work.** When Jack cleans the house, it takes him 4 hours. When Ryan cleans the house, it takes him 6 hours. How long would it take both of them if they worked together?

## ▪ CATCH THE MISTAKE

**In Exercises 103–106, explain the mistake that is made.**

**103.** 
$$t^2 - 5t - 6 = 0$$
$$(t - 3)(t - 2) = 0$$
$$t = 2, 3$$

**104.** 
$$(2y - 3)^2 = 25$$
$$2y - 3 = 5$$
$$2y = 8$$
$$y = 4$$

**105.** 
$$16a^2 + 9 = 0$$
$$16a^2 = -9$$
$$a^2 = -\frac{9}{16}$$
$$a = \pm\sqrt{\frac{9}{16}}$$
$$a = \pm\frac{3}{4}$$

**106.** 
$$2x^2 - 4x = 3$$
$$2(x^2 - 2x) = 3$$
$$2(x^2 - 2x + 1) = 3 + 1$$
$$2(x - 1)^2 = 4$$
$$(x - 1)^2 = 2$$
$$x - 1 = \pm\sqrt{2}$$
$$x = 1 \pm \sqrt{2}$$

## ▪ CONCEPTUAL

**In Exercises 107–110, determine whether the following statements are true or false.**

**107.** The equation $(3x + 1)^2 = 16$ has the same solution set as the equation $3x + 1 = 4$.

**108.** The quadratic equation $ax^2 + bx + c = 0$ can be solved by the square root method only if $b = 0$.

**109.** All quadratic equations can be solved exactly.

**110.** The quadratic formula can be used to solve any quadratic equation.

**111.** Write a quadratic equation in standard form that has $x = a$ as a repeated real root. Alternate solutions are possible.

**112.** Write a quadratic equation in standard form that has $x = bi$ as a root. Alternate solutions are possible.

**113.** Write a quadratic equation in standard form that has the solution set {2, 5}. Alternate solutions are possible.

**114.** Write a quadratic equation in standard form that has the solution set {−3, 0}. Alternate solutions are possible.

**In Exercises 115–118, solve for the indicated variable in terms of other variables.**

**115.** Solve $s = \frac{1}{2}gt^2$ for $t$.

**116.** Solve $A = P(1 + r)^2$ for $r$.

**117.** Solve $a^2 + b^2 = c^2$ for $c$.

**118.** Solve $P = EI - RI^2$ for $I$.

**119.** Solve the equation by factoring: $x^4 - 4x^2 = 0$.

**120.** Solve the equation by factoring: $3x - 6x^2 = 0$.

**121.** Solve the equation using factoring by grouping:
$x^3 + x^2 - 4x - 4 = 0$.

**122.** Solve the equation using factoring by grouping:
$x^3 + 2x^2 - x - 2 = 0$.

## ▪ CHALLENGE

**123.** Show that the sum of the roots of a quadratic equation is equal to $-\dfrac{b}{a}$.

**124.** Show that the product of the roots of a quadratic equation is equal to $\dfrac{c}{a}$.

**125.** Write a quadratic equation in standard form whose solution set is $\{3 - \sqrt{5}, 3 + \sqrt{5}\}$. Alternate solutions are possible.

**126.** Write a quadratic equation in standard form whose solution set is $\{2 - i, 2 + i\}$. Alternate solutions are possible.

**127.** **Aviation.** An airplane takes 1 hour longer to go a distance of 600 miles flying against a headwind than on the return trip with a tailwind. If the speed of the wind is a constant 50 miles per hour for both legs of the trip, find the speed of the plane in still air.

**128.** **Boating.** A speedboat takes 1 hour longer to go 24 miles up a river than to return. If the boat cruises at 10 miles per hour in still water, what is the rate of the current?

**129.** Find a quadratic equation whose two distinct real roots are the negatives of the two distinct real roots of the equation $ax^2 + bx + c = 0$.

**130.** Find a quadratic equation whose two distinct real roots are the reciprocals of the two distinct real roots of the equation $ax^2 + bx + c = 0$.

**131.** A small jet and a 757 leave Atlanta at 1 P.M. The small jet is traveling due west. The 757 is traveling due south. The speed of the 757 is 100 miles per hour faster than that of the small jet. At 3 P.M. the planes are 1000 miles apart. Find the average speed of each plane. (Assume there is no wind.)

**132.** Two boats leave Key West at noon. The smaller boat is traveling due west. The larger boat is traveling due south. The speed of the larger boat is 10 miles per hour faster than that of the smaller boat. At 3 P.M. the boats are 150 miles apart. Find the average speed of each boat. (Assume there is no current.)

## ▪ TECHNOLOGY

**133.** Solve the equation $x^2 - x = 2$ by first writing in standard form and then factoring. Now plot both sides of the equation in the same viewing screen ($y_1 = x^2 - x$ and $y_2 = 2$). At what $x$-values do these two graphs intersect? Do those points agree with the solution set you found?

**134.** Solve the equation $x^2 - 2x = -2$ by first writing in standard form and then using the quadratic formula. Now plot both sides of the equation in the same viewing screen ($y_1 = x^2 - 2x$ and $y_2 = -2$). Do these graphs intersect? Does this agree with the solution set you found?

**135. a.** Solve the equation $x^2 - 2x = b$, $b = 8$ by first writing in standard form. Now plot both sides of the equation in the same viewing screen ($y_1 = x^2 - 2x$ and $y_2 = b$). At what $x$-values do these two graphs intersect? Do those points agree with the solution set you found?

**b.** Repeat (a) for $b = -3, -1, 0$, and 5.

**136. a.** Solve the equation $x^2 + 2x = b$, $b = 8$ by first writing in standard form. Now plot both sides of the equation in the same viewing screen ($y_1 = x^2 + 2x$ and $y_2 = b$). At what $x$-values do these two graphs intersect? Do those points agree with the solution set you found?

**b.** Repeat (a) for $b = -3, -1, 0$, and 5.

**SKILLS OBJECTIVES**

- Solve rational equations.
- Solve radical equations.
- Solve equations that are quadratic in form.
- Solve equations that are factorable.
- Solve absolute value equations.

**CONCEPTUAL OBJECTIVES**

- Transform a difficult equation into a simpler linear or quadratic equation.
- Recognize the need to check solutions when the transformation process may produce extraneous solutions.
- Realize that not all polynomial equations are factorable.

## Rational Equations

A **rational equation** is an equation that contains one or more rational expressions (Appendix). Some rational equations can be transformed into linear or quadratic equations that you can then solve, but as you will see momentarily, you must be certain that the solution to the resulting linear or quadratic equation also satisfies the original rational equation.

**EXAMPLE 1  Solving a Rational Equation That Can Be Reduced to a Linear Equation**

Solve the equation $\dfrac{2}{3x} + \dfrac{1}{2} = \dfrac{4}{x} + \dfrac{4}{3}$.

**Solution:**

State the excluded values (those which make any denominator equal 0).

$$\frac{2}{3x} + \frac{1}{2} = \frac{4}{x} + \frac{4}{3} \qquad x \neq 0$$

Multiply *each term* by the LCD, $6x$.

$$6x\left(\frac{2}{3x}\right) + 6x\left(\frac{1}{2}\right) = 6x\left(\frac{4}{x}\right) + 6x\left(\frac{4}{3}\right)$$

Simplify both sides.

$$4 + 3x = 24 + 8x$$

Subtract 4.

$$\begin{array}{r} -4 \qquad\qquad -4 \\ \hline 3x = 20 + 8x \end{array}$$

Subtract $8x$.

$$\begin{array}{r} -8x \qquad\quad -8x \\ \hline -5x = 20 \end{array}$$

Divide by $-5$.

$$\boxed{x = -4}$$

Since $x = -4$ satisfies the original equation, the solution set is $\{-4\}$.

**■ YOUR TURN**  Solve the equation $\dfrac{3}{y} + 2 = \dfrac{7}{2y}$.

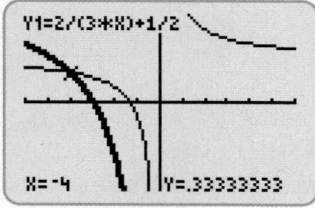
■ **Answer:** The solution is $y = \frac{1}{4}$. The solution set is $\{\frac{1}{4}\}$.

Use a graphing utility to display

graphs of $y_1 = \dfrac{3x}{x-1} + 2$ and

$y_2 = \dfrac{3}{x-1}$.

```
Plot1  Plot2  Plot3
\Y1∎3X/(X-1)+2
\Y2∎3/(X-1)
\Y3∎
```

The $x$-coordinate of the point of
intersection is the solution to the

equation $\dfrac{3x}{x-1} + 2 = \dfrac{3}{x-1}$.

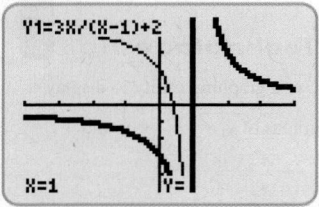

```
Y1=3X/(X-1)+2
```

```
X=1        Y=
```

No intersection implies no solution.

- **Answer:** no solution

---

### EXAMPLE 2  Solving Rational Equations: Eliminating Extraneous Solutions

Solve the equation $\dfrac{3x}{x-1} + 2 = \dfrac{3}{x-1}$.

**Solution:**

State the excluded values (those which make any denominator equal 0).

$$\dfrac{3x}{x-1} + 2 = \dfrac{3}{x-1} \qquad x \neq 1$$

Eliminate the fractions by multiplying each term by the LCD, $x - 1$.

$$\dfrac{3x}{x-1} \cdot (x-1) + 2 \cdot (x-1) = \dfrac{3}{x-1} \cdot (x-1)$$

Simplify.

$$\dfrac{3x}{x-1} \cdot (x-1) + 2 \cdot (x-1) = \dfrac{3}{x-1} \cdot (x-1)$$

$$3x + 2(x-1) = 3$$

Distribute the 2. $\qquad 3x + 2x - 2 = 3$

Combine $x$ terms on the left. $\qquad 5x - 2 = 3$

Add 2 to both sides. $\qquad 5x = 5$

Divide both sides by 5. $\qquad x = 1$

It may seem that $x = 1$ is the solution. However, the original equation had the restriction $x \neq 1$. Therefore, $x = 1$ is an extraneous solution and must be eliminated as a possible solution.

Thus, the equation $\dfrac{3x}{x-1} + 2 = \dfrac{3}{x-1}$ has $\boxed{\text{no solution}}$.

- **YOUR TURN**  Solve the equation $\dfrac{2x}{x-2} - 3 = \dfrac{4}{x-2}$.

---

When a variable is in the denominator of a fraction, the LCD will contain the variable. This sometimes results in an extraneous solution.

In order to find a *least* common denominator of more complicated expressions, it is useful to first factor the denominators to identify common multiples.

Rational equation: $\qquad \dfrac{1}{3x-3} + \dfrac{1}{2x-2} = \dfrac{1}{x^2-x}$

Factor the denominators: $\qquad \dfrac{1}{3(x-1)} + \dfrac{1}{2(x-1)} = \dfrac{1}{x(x-1)}$

LCD: $\qquad 6x(x-1)$

**EXAMPLE 3   Solving Rational Equations**

Solve the equation $\dfrac{1}{3x + 18} - \dfrac{1}{2x + 12} = \dfrac{1}{x^2 + 6x}$.

**Solution:**

Factor the denominators.

$$\frac{1}{3(x + 6)} - \frac{1}{2(x + 6)} = \frac{1}{x(x + 6)}$$

State the excluded values.

$$x \neq 0, -6$$

Multiply the equation by the LCD, $6x(x + 6)$.

$$6x(x + 6) \cdot \frac{1}{3(x + 6)} - 6x(x + 6) \cdot \frac{1}{2(x + 6)} = 6x(x + 6) \cdot \frac{1}{x(x + 6)}$$

Divide out the common factors.

$$6x\cancel{(x + 6)} \cdot \frac{1}{3\cancel{(x + 6)}} - 6x\cancel{(x + 6)} \cdot \frac{1}{2\cancel{(x + 6)}} = 6\cancel{x(x + 6)} \cdot \frac{1}{\cancel{x(x + 6)}}$$

Simplify.

$$2x - 3x = 6$$

Solve the linear equation.

$$x = -6$$

Since one of the excluded values is $x \neq -6$, we say that $x = -6$ is an extraneous solution. Therefore, this rational equation has   no solution  .

∎ **YOUR TURN**   Solve the equation $\dfrac{2}{x} + \dfrac{1}{x + 1} = -\dfrac{1}{x(x + 1)}$.

■ **Answer:**  no solution

**EXAMPLE 4   Solving a Rational Equation That Can Be Reduced to a Quadratic Equation**

Solve the equation $1 + \dfrac{3}{x^2 - 2x} = \dfrac{2}{x - 2}$.

**Solution:**

Factor the denominators.

$$1 + \frac{3}{x(x - 2)} = \frac{2}{x - 2}$$

State the excluded values (those which make any denominator equal to 0).

$$x \neq 0, 2$$

Multiply each term by the LCD, $x(x - 2)$.

$$1 \cdot x(x - 2) + \frac{3}{x(x - 2)} \cdot x(x - 2) = \frac{2}{(x - 2)} \cdot x(x - 2)$$

Divide out the common factors.

$$x(x - 2) + \frac{3}{\cancel{x(x - 2)}}\cancel{x(x - 2)} = \frac{2}{\cancel{(x - 2)}}x\cancel{(x - 2)}$$

Simplify.

$$x(x - 2) + 3 = 2x$$

Eliminate the parentheses.

$$x^2 - 2x + 3 = 2x$$

Write the quadratic equation in standard form.

$$x^2 - 4x + 3 = 0$$

Factor.

$$(x - 3)(x - 1) = 0$$

Apply the zero product property.

$$x = 3 \quad \text{or} \quad x = 1$$

Since $x = 3$ or $x = 1$ both satisfy the original equation, the solution set is $\{1, 3\}$.

## Radical Equations

**Radical equations** are equations in which the variable is inside a radical (that is, under a square root, cube root, or higher root). Examples of radical equations follow:

$$\sqrt{x-3} = 2 \qquad \sqrt{2x+3} = x \qquad \sqrt{x+2} + \sqrt{7x+2} = 6$$

Often you can transform a radical equation into a simple linear or quadratic equation. Sometimes the transformation process yields **extraneous solutions,** or apparent solutions that may solve the transformed problem but are not solutions of the original radical equation. Therefore, it is very important to check your answers in the original equation.

### EXAMPLE 5  Solving an Equation Involving a Radical

Solve the equation $\sqrt{x-3} = 2$.

**Solution:**

*Square* both sides of the equation. $\qquad\qquad\qquad \left(\sqrt{x-3}\right)^2 = 2^2$

Simplify. $\qquad\qquad\qquad\qquad\qquad\qquad\qquad x - 3 = 4$

Solve the resulting linear equation. $\qquad\qquad\qquad \boxed{x = 7}$

The solution set is {7}.

*Check:* $\sqrt{7-3} = \sqrt{4} = 2$

■ **YOUR TURN** Solve the equation $\sqrt{3p+4} = 5$.

### EXAMPLE 6  Solving an Equation Involving a Radical

Solve the equation $\sqrt{2x+3} = x$.

**Solution:**

*Square* both sides of the equation. $\qquad\qquad\qquad \left(\sqrt{2x+3}\right)^2 = x^2$

Simplify. $\qquad\qquad\qquad\qquad\qquad\qquad\qquad 2x + 3 = x^2$

Write the quadratic equation in standard form. $\qquad x^2 - 2x - 3 = 0$

Factor. $\qquad\qquad\qquad\qquad\qquad\qquad\qquad (x-3)(x+1) = 0$

Use the zero product property. $\qquad\qquad\qquad x = 3 \quad \text{or} \quad x = -1$

Check these values to see whether they *both* make the original equation statement true.

$$x = 3: \ \sqrt{2(3)+3} = 3 \Rightarrow \sqrt{6+3} = 3 \Rightarrow \sqrt{9} = 3 \Rightarrow 3 = 3 \ \checkmark$$
$$x = -1: \sqrt{2(-1)+3} = -1 \Rightarrow \sqrt{-2+3} = -1 \Rightarrow \sqrt{1} = -1 \Rightarrow 1 \neq -1 \ \bm{\times}$$

The solution is $\boxed{x = 3}$. The solution set is {3}.

■ **YOUR TURN** Solve the equation $\sqrt{12+t} = t$.

■ **YOUR TURN** Solve the equation $\sqrt{2x+6} = x + 3$.

---

### Study Tip

Extraneous solutions are common when we deal with radical equations, so remember to check your answers.

■ **Answer:** $p = 7$ or {7}

### Technology Tip

Use a graphing utility to display graphs of $y_1 = \sqrt{2x+3}$ and $y_2 = x$.

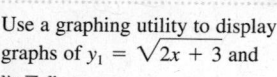

The *x*-coordinate of the point of intersection is the solution to the equation $\sqrt{2x+3} = x$.

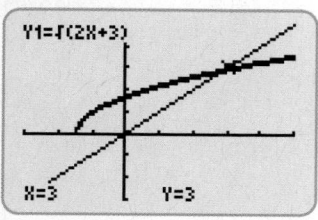

■ **Answer:** $t = 4$ or {4}

■ **Answer:** $x = -1$ and $x = -3$ or {−3, −1}

Examples 5 and 6 contained only one radical each. We transformed the radical equation into a linear (Example 5) or quadratic (Example 6) equation with one step. The next example contains two radicals. Our technique will be to isolate one radical on one side of the equation with the other radical on the other side of the equation.

| ★ CORRECT | ✖ INCORRECT |
|---|---|
| Square the expression. | Square the expression. |
| $$\left(3 + \sqrt{x + 2}\right)^2$$ | $$\left(3 + \sqrt{x + 2}\right)^2$$ |
| Write the square as a product of two factors. | The **error** occurs here when only individual terms are squared. |
| $$\left(3 + \sqrt{x + 2}\right)\left(3 + \sqrt{x + 2}\right)$$ | $$\neq 9 + (x + 2)$$ |
| Use the FOIL method. | |
| $$9 + 6\sqrt{x + 2} + (x + 2)$$ | |

▶ **EXAMPLE 7** **Solving an Equation with More Than One Radical**

Solve the equation $\sqrt{x + 2} + \sqrt{7x + 2} = 6$.

**Solution:**

Subtract $\sqrt{x + 2}$ from both sides.
$$\sqrt{7x + 2} = 6 - \sqrt{x + 2}$$

Square both sides.
$$\left(\sqrt{7x + 2}\right)^2 = \left(6 - \sqrt{x + 2}\right)^2$$

Simplify.
$$7x + 2 = \left(6 - \sqrt{x + 2}\right)\left(6 - \sqrt{x + 2}\right)$$

Multiply the expressions on the right side of the equation.
$$7x + 2 = 36 - 12\sqrt{x + 2} + (x + 2)$$

Isolate the term with the radical on the left side.
$$12\sqrt{x + 2} = 36 + x + 2 - 7x - 2$$

Combine like terms on the right side.
$$12\sqrt{x + 2} = 36 - 6x$$

Divide by 6.
$$2\sqrt{x + 2} = 6 - x$$

Square both sides.
$$4(x + 2) = (6 - x)^2$$

Simplify.
$$4x + 8 = 36 - 12x + x^2$$

Rewrite the quadratic equation in standard form.
$$x^2 - 16x + 28 = 0$$

Factor.
$$(x - 14)(x - 2) = 0$$

Solve.
$$x = 14 \quad \text{and} \quad x = 2$$

The apparent solutions are 2 and 14. Note that $x = 14$ does not satisfy the original equation; therefore, it is extraneous. The solution is $\boxed{x = 2}$. The solution set is {2}.

▪ **YOUR TURN** Solve the equation $\sqrt{x - 4} = 5 - \sqrt{x + 1}$.

*Technology Tip*

Use a graphing utility to display graphs of
$$y_1 = \sqrt{x + 2} + \sqrt{7x + 2}$$
and $y_2 = 6$.

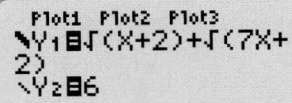

The $x$-coordinate of the point of intersection is the solution to the equation
$$\sqrt{x + 2} + \sqrt{7x + 2} = 6.$$

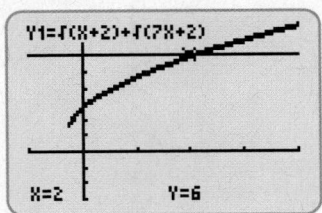

▪ **Answer:** $x = 8$ or {8}

## PROCEDURE FOR SOLVING RADICAL EQUATIONS

**Step 1:** Isolate the term with a radical on one side.

**Step 2:** Raise both (*entire*) sides of the equation to the power that will eliminate this radical, and simplify the equation.

**Step 3:** If a radical remains, repeat Steps 1 and 2.

**Step 4:** Solve the resulting linear or quadratic equation.

**Step 5:** Check the solutions and eliminate any extraneous solutions.

*Note:* If there is more than one radical in the equation, it does not matter which radical is isolated first.

# Equations Quadratic in Form: *u*-Substitution

Equations that are higher order or that have fractional powers often can be transformed into a quadratic equation by introducing a *u*-substitution. When this is the case, we say that equations are **quadratic in form**. In the table below, the two original equations are quadratic in form because they can be transformed into a quadratic equation given the correct substitution.

| ORIGINAL EQUATION | SUBSTITUTION | NEW EQUATION |
|---|---|---|
| $x^4 - 3x^2 - 4 = 0$ | $u = x^2$ | $u^2 - 3u - 4 = 0$ |
| $t^{2/3} + 2t^{1/3} + 1 = 0$ | $u = t^{1/3}$ | $u^2 + 2u + 1 = 0$ |
| $\dfrac{2}{y} - \dfrac{1}{\sqrt{y}} + 1 = 0$ | $u = y^{-1/2}$ | $2u^2 - u + 1 = 0$ |

For example, the equation $x^4 - 3x^2 - 4 = 0$ is a fourth-degree equation in $x$. How did we know that $u = x^2$ would transform the original equation into a quadratic equation? If we rewrite the original equation as $(x^2)^2 - 3(x^2) - 4 = 0$, the expression in parentheses is the *u*-substitution.

Let us introduce the substitution $u = x^2$. Note that squaring both sides implies $u^2 = x^4$. We then replace $x^2$ in the original equation with $u$, and $x^4$ in the original equation with $u^2$, which leads to a quadratic equation in $u$: $u^2 - 3u - 4 = 0$.

| WORDS | MATH |
|---|---|
| Solve for $x$. | $x^4 - 3x^2 - 4 = 0$ |
| Introduce *u*-substitution. | $u = x^2$ (Note that $u^2 = x^4$.) |
| Write the quadratic equation in $u$. | $u^2 - 3u - 4 = 0$ |
| Factor. | $(u - 4)(u + 1) = 0$ |
| Solve for $u$. | $u = 4$  or  $u = -1$ |
| Transform back to $x$, $u = x^2$. | $x^2 = 4$  or  $x^2 = -1$ |
| Solve for $x$. | $\boxed{x = \pm 2 \quad \text{or} \quad x = \pm i}$ |

The solution set is $\{\pm 2, \pm i\}$.

It is important to correctly determine the appropriate substitution in order to arrive at an equation quadratic in form. For example, $t^{2/3} + 2t^{1/3} + 1 = 0$ is an original equation given in the above table. If we rewrite this equation as $\left(t^{1/3}\right)^2 + 2\left(t^{1/3}\right) + 1 = 0$, then it becomes apparent that the correct substitution is $u = t^{1/3}$, which transforms the equation in $t$ into a quadratic equation in $u$: $u^2 + 2u + 1 = 0$.

### PROCEDURE FOR SOLVING EQUATIONS QUADRATIC IN FORM

**Step 1:** Identify the substitution.
**Step 2:** Transform the equation into a quadratic equation.
**Step 3:** Solve the quadratic equation.
**Step 4:** Apply the substitution to rewrite the solution in terms of the original variable.
**Step 5:** Solve the resulting equation.
**Step 6:** Check the solutions in the original equation.

**EXAMPLE 8** **Solving an Equation Quadratic in Form with Negative Exponents**

Find the solutions to the equation $x^{-2} - x^{-1} - 12 = 0$.

**Solution:**

Rewrite the original equation.

$$\left(x^{-1}\right)^2 - \left(x^{-1}\right) - 12 = 0$$

Determine the $u$-substitution.

$$u = x^{-1} \text{ (Note that } u^2 = x^{-2}.\text{)}$$

The original equation in $x$ corresponds to a quadratic equation in $u$.

$$u^2 - u - 12 = 0$$

Factor.

$$(u - 4)(u + 3) = 0$$

Solve for $u$.

$$u = 4 \quad \text{or} \quad u = -3$$

**The most common mistake is forgetting to transform back to $x$.**

Transform back to $x$. Let $u = x^{-1}$.

$$x^{-1} = 4 \quad \text{or} \quad x^{-1} = -3$$

Write $x^{-1}$ as $\dfrac{1}{x}$.

$$\frac{1}{x} = 4 \quad \text{or} \quad \frac{1}{x} = -3$$

Solve for $x$.

$$\boxed{x = \frac{1}{4}} \quad \text{or} \quad \boxed{x = -\frac{1}{3}}$$

The solution set is $\left\{-\dfrac{1}{3}, \dfrac{1}{4}\right\}$.

■ **YOUR TURN** Find the solutions to the equation $x^{-2} - x^{-1} - 6 = 0$.

**Technology Tip**

Use a graphing utility to graph $y_1 = x^{-2} - x^{-1} - 12$.

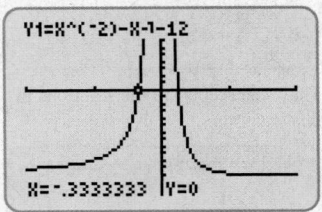

```
Plot1 Plot2 Plot3
\Y1■X^(-2)-X-1-12
\Y2=■
```

The $x$-intercepts are the solutions to this equation.

```
Y1=X^(-2)-X-1-12
X=-.3333333  Y=0
```

**Study Tip**

Remember to transform back to the original variable.

■ **Answer:** The solution is $x = -\frac{1}{2}$ or $x = \frac{1}{3}$. The solution set is $\left\{-\frac{1}{2}, \frac{1}{3}\right\}$.

**EXAMPLE 9** **Solving an Equation Quadratic in Form with Fractional Exponents**

Find the solutions to the equation $x^{2/3} - 3x^{1/3} - 10 = 0$.

**Solution:**

| | |
|---|---|
| Rewrite the original equation. | $\left(x^{1/3}\right)^2 - 3x^{1/3} - 10 = 0$ |
| Identify the substitution as $u = x^{1/3}$. | $u^2 - 3u - 10 = 0$ |
| Factor. | $(u - 5)(u + 2) = 0$ |
| Solve for $u$. | $u = 5$ or $u = -2$ |
| Let $u = x^{1/3}$ again. | $x^{1/3} = 5$ $x^{1/3} = -2$ |
| Cube both sides of the equations. | $\left(x^{1/3}\right)^3 = (5)^3$ $\left(x^{1/3}\right)^3 = (-2)^3$ |
| Simplify. | $\boxed{x = 125}$ $\boxed{x = -8}$ |

The solution set is $\boxed{\{-8, 125\}}$, which a check will confirm.

■ **Answer:** $t = 9$ or $\{9\}$

■ **YOUR TURN** Find the solution to the equation $2t - 5t^{1/2} - 3 = 0$.

## Factorable Equations

Some equations (both polynomial and with rational exponents) that are factorable can be solved using the zero product property.

**Technology Tip**

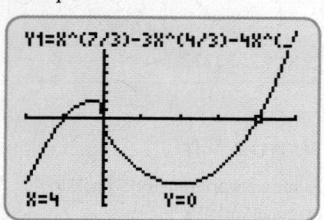

Use a graphing utility to graph $y_1 = x^{7/3} - 3x^{4/3} - 4x^{1/3}$.

```
Plot1 Plot2 Plot3
\Y1▤X^(7/3)-3X^(
4/3)-4X^(1/3)
```

The $x$-intercepts are the solutions to this equation.

```
Y1=X^(7/3)-3X^(4/3)-4X^(
X=4        Y=0
```

**EXAMPLE 10** **Solving an Equation with Rational Exponents by Factoring**

Solve the equation $x^{7/3} - 3x^{4/3} - 4x^{1/3} = 0$.

**Solution:**

| | |
|---|---|
| Factor the left side of the equation. | $x^{1/3}\left(x^2 - 3x - 4\right) = 0$ |
| Factor the quadratic expression. | $x^{1/3}(x - 4)(x + 1) = 0$ |
| Apply the zero product property. | $x^{1/3} = 0$ or $x - 4 = 0$ or $x + 1 = 0$ |
| Solve for $x$. | $\boxed{x = 0}$ or $\boxed{x = 4}$ or $\boxed{x = -1}$ |

The solution set is $\{-1, 0, 4\}$.

**EXAMPLE 11**   **Solving a Polynomial Equation Using Factoring by Grouping**

Solve the equation $x^3 + 2x^2 - x - 2 = 0$.

**Solution:**

| | |
|---|---|
| Factor by grouping (Appendix). | $(x^3 - x) + (2x^2 - 2) = 0$ |
| Identify the common factors. | $x(x^2 - 1) + 2(x^2 - 1) = 0$ |
| Factor. | $(x + 2)(x^2 - 1) = 0$ |
| Factor the quadratic expression. | $(x + 2)(x - 1)(x + 1) = 0$ |
| Apply the zero product property. | $x + 2 = 0$   or   $x - 1 = 0$   or   $x + 1 = 0$ |
| Solve for $x$. | $\boxed{x = -2}$   or   $\boxed{x = 1}$   or   $\boxed{x = -1}$ |

The solution set is $\{-2, -1, 1\}$.

■ **YOUR TURN**   Solve the equation $x^3 + x^2 - 4x - 4 = 0$.

■ **Answer:** $x = -1$ or $x = \pm 2$ or $\{-2, -1, 2\}$

## Absolute Value Equations

The **absolute value** of a real number can be interpreted algebraically and graphically.

**DEFINITION**   **Absolute Value**

The **absolute value** of a real number $a$, denoted by the symbol $|a|$, is defined by

$$|a| = \begin{cases} a, & \text{if } a \geq 0 \\ -a, & \text{if } a < 0 \end{cases}$$

*Study Tip*

Algebraically: $|x| = 5$ implies $x = -5$ or $x = 5$.
Graphically: $-5$ and $5$ are five units from 0.

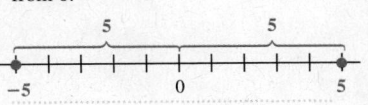

When absolute value is involved in algebraic equations, we interpret the definition of absolute value as follows.

**DEFINITION**   **Absolute Value Equation**

If $|x| = a$, then $x = -a$ or $x = a$, where $a \geq 0$.

In words, "If the absolute value of a number is $a$, then that number equals $-a$ or $a$." For example, the equation $|x| = 7$ is true if $x = -7$ or $x = 7$. We say the equation $|x| = 7$ has the solution set $\{-7, 7\}$. *Note:* $|x| = -3$ does not have a solution because there is no value of $x$ such that its absolute value is $-3$.

Use a graphing utility to display graphs of $y_1 = |x - 3|$ and $y_2 = 8$.

The $x$-coordinates of the points of intersection are the solutions to $|x - 3| = 8$.

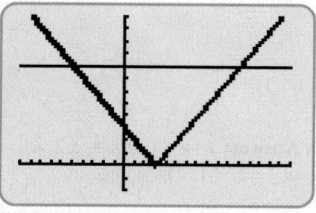

■ **Answer:** $x = 2$ or $x = -12$. The solution set is $\{-12, 2\}$.

**EXAMPLE 12   Solving an Absolute Value Equation**

Solve the equation $|x - 3| = 8$ algebraically and graphically.

**Solution:**

Using the absolute value equation definition, we see that if the absolute value of an expression is 8, then that expression is either $-8$ or 8. Rewrite as two equations:

$$x - 3 = -8 \qquad \text{or} \qquad x - 3 = 8$$
$$x = -5 \qquad\qquad\qquad x = 11$$

The solution set is $\boxed{\{-5, 11\}}$.

Graph: The absolute value equation $|x - 3| = 8$ is interpreted as "What numbers are eight units away from 3 on the number line?" We find that eight units to the right of 3 is 11 and eight units to the left of 3 is $-5$.

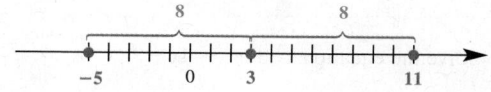

■ **YOUR TURN** Solve the equation $|x + 5| = 7$.

**EXAMPLE 13   Solving an Absolute Value Equation**

Solve the equation $2 - 3|x - 1| = -4|x - 1| + 7$.

**Solution:**

Isolate the absolute value expressions to one side.

Add $4|x - 1|$ to both sides. $\qquad\qquad\qquad\qquad\qquad 2 + |x - 1| = 7$

Subtract 2 from both sides. $\qquad\qquad\qquad\qquad\qquad\qquad |x - 1| = 5$

If the absolute value of an expression is equal to 5, then the expression is equal to either $-5$ or 5.

$$x - 1 = -5 \quad \text{or} \quad x - 1 = 5$$
$$x = -4 \qquad\qquad\quad x = 6$$

The solution set is $\boxed{\{-4, 6\}}$.

■ **Answer:** $x = -4$ or $x = 12$. The solution set is $\{-4, 12\}$.

■ **YOUR TURN** Solve the equation $3 - 2|x - 4| = -3|x - 4| + 11$.

## EXAMPLE 14   Solving a Quadratic Absolute Value Equation

Solve the equation $|5 - x^2| = 1$.

**Solution:**

If the absolute value of an expression is 1, that expression is either $-1$ or 1, which leads to two equations.

$$5 - x^2 = -1 \quad \text{or} \quad 5 - x^2 = 1$$
$$-x^2 = -6 \qquad\qquad -x^2 = -4$$
$$x^2 = 6 \qquad\qquad x^2 = 4$$
$$x = \pm\sqrt{6} \qquad\qquad x = \pm\sqrt{4} = \pm 2$$

The solution set is $\boxed{\{\pm 2, \pm\sqrt{6}\}}$.

■ **YOUR TURN**   Solve the equation $|7 - x^2| = 2$.

■ **Answer:** $x = \pm\sqrt{5}$ or $x = \pm 3$.
The solution set is $\{\pm\sqrt{5}, \pm 3\}$.

---

## SECTION 0.3   SUMMARY

Rational equations, radical equations, equations quadratic in form, factorable equations, and absolute value equations can often be solved by transforming them into simpler linear or quadratic equations.

■ **Rational Equations:** Multiply the entire equation by the LCD. Solve the resulting equation (if it is linear or quadratic). Check for extraneous solutions.

■ **Radical Equations:** Isolate the term containing a radical and raise it to the appropriate power that will eliminate the radical. If there is more than one radical, it does not matter which

radical is isolated first. Raising radical equations to powers may cause extraneous solutions, so check each solution.

■ **Equations Quadratic in Form:** Identify the $u$-substitution that transforms the equation into a quadratic equation. Solve the quadratic equation and then remember to transform back to the original variable.

■ **Factorable Equations:** Look for a factor common to all terms or factor by grouping.

■ **Absolute Value Equations:** Transform the absolute value equation into two equations that do not involve absolute value.

---

## SECTION 0.3   EXERCISES

■ **SKILLS**

**In Exercises 1–20, specify any values that must be excluded from the solution set and then solve the rational equation.**

1. $\dfrac{x}{x - 2} + 5 = \dfrac{2}{x - 2}$

2. $\dfrac{n}{n - 5} + 2 = \dfrac{n}{n - 5}$

3. $\dfrac{2p}{p - 1} = 3 + \dfrac{2}{p - 1}$

4. $\dfrac{4t}{t + 2} = 3 - \dfrac{8}{t + 2}$

5. $\dfrac{3x}{x + 2} - 4 = \dfrac{2}{x + 2}$

6. $\dfrac{5y}{2y - 1} - 3 = \dfrac{12}{2y - 1}$

7. $\dfrac{1}{n} + \dfrac{1}{n + 1} = \dfrac{-1}{n(n + 1)}$

8. $\dfrac{1}{x} + \dfrac{1}{x - 1} = \dfrac{1}{x(x - 1)}$

9. $\dfrac{3}{a} - \dfrac{2}{a + 3} = \dfrac{9}{a(a + 3)}$

10. $\dfrac{1}{c - 2} + \dfrac{1}{c} = \dfrac{2}{c(c - 2)}$

11. $\dfrac{n - 5}{6n - 6} = \dfrac{1}{9} - \dfrac{n - 3}{4n - 4}$

12. $\dfrac{5}{m} + \dfrac{3}{m - 2} = \dfrac{6}{m(m - 2)}$

**13.** $\dfrac{2}{5x + 1} = \dfrac{1}{2x - 1}$

**14.** $\dfrac{3}{4n - 1} = \dfrac{2}{2n - 5}$

**15.** $\dfrac{t - 1}{1 - t} = \dfrac{3}{2}$

**16.** $\dfrac{2 - x}{x - 2} = \dfrac{3}{4}$

**17.** $x + \dfrac{12}{x} = 7$

**18.** $x - \dfrac{10}{x} = -3$

**19.** $\dfrac{4(x - 2)}{x - 3} + \dfrac{3}{x} = \dfrac{-3}{x(x - 3)}$

**20.** $\dfrac{5}{y + 4} = 4 + \dfrac{3}{y - 2}$

**In Exercises 21–60, solve the radical equation for the given variable.**

**21.** $\sqrt{u + 1} = -4$

**22.** $-\sqrt{3 - 2u} = 9$

**23.** $\sqrt[3]{5x + 2} = 3$

**24.** $\sqrt[3]{1 - x} = -2$

**25.** $(4y + 1)^{1/3} = -1$

**26.** $(5x - 1)^{1/3} = 4$

**27.** $(x + 3)^{5/3} = 32$

**28.** $(x + 2)^{4/3} = 16$

**29.** $(x + 1)^{2/3} = 4$

**30.** $(x - 7)^{4/3} = 81$

**31.** $\sqrt{12 + x} = x$

**32.** $x = \sqrt{56 - x}$

**33.** $y = 5\sqrt{y}$

**34.** $\sqrt{y} = \dfrac{y}{4}$

**35.** $s = 3\sqrt{s - 2}$

**36.** $-2s = \sqrt{3 - s}$

**37.** $\sqrt{2x + 6} = x + 3$

**38.** $\sqrt{8 - 2x} = 2x - 2$

**39.** $\sqrt{1 - 3x} = x + 1$

**40.** $\sqrt{2 - x} = x - 2$

**41.** $3x - 6\sqrt{x - 1} = 3$

**42.** $5x - 10\sqrt{x + 2} = -10$

**43.** $3x - 6\sqrt{x + 2} = 3$

**44.** $2x - 4\sqrt{x + 1} = 4$

**45.** $3\sqrt{x + 4} - 2x = 9$

**46.** $2\sqrt{x + 1} - 3x = -5$

**47.** $\sqrt{x^2 - 4} = x - 1$

**48.** $\sqrt{25 - x^2} = x + 1$

**49.** $\sqrt{x^2 - 2x - 5} = x + 1$

**50.** $\sqrt{2x^2 - 8x + 1} = x - 3$

**51.** $\sqrt{3x + 1} - \sqrt{6x - 5} = 1$

**52.** $\sqrt{2 - x} + \sqrt{6 - 5x} = 6$

**53.** $\sqrt{x + 12} + \sqrt{8 - x} = 6$

**54.** $\sqrt{5 - x} + \sqrt{3x + 1} = 4$

**55.** $\sqrt{2x - 1} - \sqrt{x - 1} = 1$

**56.** $\sqrt{8 - x} = 2 + \sqrt{2x + 3}$

**57.** $\sqrt{3x - 5} = 7 - \sqrt{x + 2}$

**58.** $\sqrt{x + 5} = 1 + \sqrt{x - 2}$

**59.** $\sqrt{2 + \sqrt{x}} = \sqrt{x}$

**60.** $\sqrt{2 - \sqrt{x}} = \sqrt{x}$

**In Exercises 61–80, solve the equations by introducing a substitution that transforms these equations to quadratic form.**

**61.** $x^{2/3} + 2x^{1/3} = 0$

**62.** $x^{1/2} - 2x^{1/4} = 0$

**63.** $x^4 - 3x^2 + 2 = 0$

**64.** $x^4 - 8x^2 + 16 = 0$

**65.** $2x^4 + 7x^2 + 6 = 0$

**66.** $x^8 - 17x^4 + 16 = 0$

**67.** $4(t - 1)^2 - 9(t - 1) = -2$

**68.** $2(1 - y)^2 + 5(1 - y) - 12 = 0$

**69.** $x^{-8} - 17x^{-4} + 16 = 0$

**70.** $2u^{-2} + 5u^{-1} - 12 = 0$

**71.** $3y^{-2} + y^{-1} - 4 = 0$

**72.** $5a^{-2} + 11a^{-1} + 2 = 0$

**73.** $z^{2/5} - 2z^{1/5} + 1 = 0$

**74.** $2x^{1/2} + x^{1/4} - 1 = 0$

**75.** $6t^{-2/3} - t^{-1/3} - 1 = 0$

**76.** $t^{-2/3} - t^{-1/3} - 6 = 0$

**77.** $3 = \dfrac{1}{(x + 1)^2} + \dfrac{2}{(x + 1)}$

**78.** $\dfrac{1}{(x + 1)^2} + \dfrac{4}{(x + 1)} + 4 = 0$

**79.** $u^{4/3} - 5u^{2/3} = -4$

**80.** $u^{4/3} + 5u^{2/3} = -4$

**In Exercises 81–96, solve by factoring.**

**81.** $x^3 - x^2 - 12x = 0$

**82.** $2y^3 - 11y^2 + 12y = 0$

**83.** $4p^3 - 9p = 0$

**84.** $25x^3 = 4x$

**85.** $u^5 - 16u = 0$

**86.** $t^5 - 81t = 0$

**87.** $x^3 - 5x^2 - 9x + 45 = 0$

**88.** $2p^3 - 3p^2 - 8p + 12 = 0$

**89.** $y(y - 5)^3 - 14(y - 5)^2 = 0$

**90.** $v(v + 3)^3 - 40(v + 3)^2 = 0$

**91.** $x^{9/4} - 2x^{5/4} - 3x^{1/4} = 0$

**92.** $u^{7/3} + u^{4/3} - 20u^{1/3} = 0$

**93.** $t^{5/3} - 25t^{-1/3} = 0$

**94.** $4x^{9/5} - 9x^{-1/5} = 0$

**95.** $y^{3/2} - 5y^{1/2} + 6y^{-1/2} = 0$

**96.** $4p^{5/3} - 5p^{2/3} - 6p^{-1/3} = 0$

**In Exercises 97–118, solve the absolute value equation.**

**97.** $|p - 7| = 3$      **98.** $|p + 7| = 3$      **99.** $|4 - y| = 1$      **100.** $|2 - y| = 11$

**101.** $|3t - 9| = 3$      **102.** $|4t + 2| = 2$      **103.** $|7 - 2x| = 9$      **104.** $|6 - 3y| = 12$

**105.** $|1 - 3y| = 1$      **106.** $|5 - x| = 2$      **107.** $\left|\frac{2}{3}x - \frac{4}{7}\right| = \frac{5}{3}$      **108.** $\left|\frac{1}{2}x + \frac{3}{4}\right| = \frac{1}{16}$

**109.** $|x - 5| + 4 = 12$      **110.** $|x + 3| - 9 = 2$      **111.** $2|p + 3| - 15 = 5$      **112.** $8 - 3|p - 4| = 2$

**113.** $5|y - 2| - 10 = 4|y - 2| - 3$      **114.** $3 - |y + 9| = 11 - 3|y + 9|$      **115.** $|4 - x^2| = 1$

**116.** $|7 - x^2| = 3$      **117.** $|x^2 + 1| = 5$      **118.** $|x^2 - 1| = 5$

## ▪ APPLICATIONS

**In Exercises 119 and 120 refer to the following:**

An analysis of sales indicates that demand for a product during a calendar year is modeled by

$$d = 3\sqrt{t + 1} - 0.75t$$

where $d$ is demand in millions of units and $t$ is the month of the year where $t = 0$ represents January.

**119. Economics.** During which month(s) is demand 3 million units?

**120. Economics.** During which month(s) is demand 4 million units?

**In Exercises 121 and 122 refer to the following:**

Body Surface Area (BSA) is used in physiology and medicine for many clinical purposes. BSA can be modeled by the function

$$BSA = \sqrt{\frac{wh}{3600}}$$

where $w$ is weight in kilograms and $h$ is height in centimeters.

**121. Health.** The BSA of a 72-kilogram female is 1.8. Find the height of the female to the nearest centimeter.

**122. Health.** The BSA of a 177-centimeter tall-male is 2.1. Find the weight of the male to the nearest kilogram.

**For Exercises 123–126, refer to this lens law.**

The position of the image is found using the thin lens equation

$$\frac{1}{f} = \frac{1}{d_o} + \frac{1}{d_i}$$

where $d_o$ is the distance from the object to the lens, $d_i$ is the distance from the lens to the image, and $f$ is the focal length of the lens.

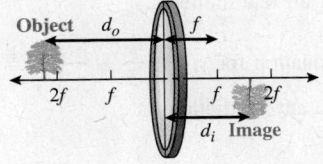

**123. Optics.** If the focal length of a lens is 3 centimeters and the image distance is 5 centimeters from the lens, what is the distance from the object to the lens?

**124. Optics.** If the focal length of the lens is 8 centimeters and the image distance is 2 centimeters from the lens, what is the distance from the object to the lens? *Note:* A negative $d_i$ implies that the image is behind the lens.

**125. Optics.** The focal length of a lens is 2 centimeters. If the image distance from the lens is half the distance from the object to the lens, find the object distance.

**126. Optics.** The focal length of a lens is 8 centimeters. If the image distance from the lens is half the distance from the object to the lens, find the object distance.

**127. Speed of Sound.** A man buys a house with an old well but does not know how deep the well is. To get an estimate, he decides to drop a rock at the opening of the well and count how long it takes until he hears the splash. The total elapsed time $T$ given by $T = t_1 + t_2$, is the sum of the time it takes for the rock to reach the water, $t_1$, and the time it takes for the sound of the splash to travel to the top of the well, $t_2$. The time (seconds) that it takes for the rock to reach the water is given by $t_1 = \frac{\sqrt{d}}{4}$, where $d$ is the depth of the well in feet. Since the speed of sound is 1100 feet per second, the time (seconds) it takes for the sound to reach the top of the well is $t_2 = \frac{d}{1100}$. If the splash is heard after 3 seconds, how deep is the well?

**128. Speed of Sound.** If the owner of the house in Exercise 127 forgot to account for the speed of sound $\left( T = t_1 = \frac{\sqrt{d}}{4} \right)$, what would he have calculated the depth of the well to be?

**129. Physics: Pendulum.** The period $(T)$ of a pendulum is related to the length $(L)$ of the pendulum and acceleration due to gravity $(g)$ by the formula $T = 2\pi\sqrt{\frac{L}{g}}$. If gravity is 9.8 m/s² and the period is 1 second, find the approximate length of the pendulum. Round to the nearest centimeter. *Note:* 100 cm = 1 m.

**130. Physics: Pendulum.** The period ($T$) of a pendulum is related to the length ($L$) of the pendulum and acceleration due to gravity ($g$) by the formula $T = 2\pi\sqrt{\dfrac{L}{g}}$. If gravity is 32 ft/s$^2$ and the period is 1 second, find the approximate length of the pendulum. Round to the nearest inch. *Note:* 12 in. = 1 ft.

**For Exercises 131 and 132, refer to the following:**

Einstein's special theory of relativity states that time is relative: Time speeds up or slows down, depending on how fast one object is moving with respect to another. For example, a space probe traveling at a velocity $v$ near the speed of light $c$ will have "clocked" a time $t$ hours, but for a stationary observer on Earth that corresponds to a time $t_0$. The formula governing this relativity is given by

$$t = t_0\sqrt{1 - \frac{v^2}{c^2}}$$

**131. Physics: Special Theory of Relativity.** If the time elapsed on a space probe mission is 18 years but the time elapsed on Earth during that mission is 30 years, how fast is the space probe traveling? Give your answer relative to the speed of light.

**132. Physics: Special Theory of Relativity.** If the time elapsed on a space probe mission is 5 years but the time elapsed on Earth during that mission is 30 years, how fast is the space probe traveling? Give your answer relative to the speed of light.

### ▪ CATCH THE MISTAKE

**In Exercises 133–136, explain the mistake that is made.**

**133.** Solve the equation $\sqrt{3t + 1} = -4$.

**Solution:**

$$3t + 1 = 16$$
$$3t = 15$$
$$t = 5$$

This is incorrect. What mistake was made?

**135.** Solve the equation $\dfrac{4}{p} - 3 = \dfrac{2}{5p}$.

**Solution:**

Cross multiply.

$$(p - 3)2 = 4(5p)$$
$$2p - 6 = 20p$$
$$-6 = 18p$$
$$p = -\frac{6}{18}$$
$$p = -\frac{1}{3}$$

This is incorrect. What mistake was made?

**134.** Solve the equation $x = \sqrt{x + 2}$.

**Solution:**

$$x^2 = x + 2$$
$$x^2 - x - 2 = 0$$
$$(x - 2)(x + 1) = 0$$
$$x = -1, x = 2$$

This is incorrect. What mistake was made?

**136.** Solve the equation $\dfrac{1}{x} + \dfrac{1}{x - 1} = \dfrac{1}{x(x - 1)}$.

**Solution:**

Multiply by the LCD, $x(x - 1)$.

$$\frac{x(x - 1)}{x} + \frac{x(x - 1)}{x - 1} = \frac{x(x - 1)}{x(x - 1)}$$

Simplify.

$$(x - 1) + x = 1$$
$$x - 1 + x = 1$$
$$2x = 2$$
$$x = 1$$

This is incorrect. What mistake was made?

### ▪ CONCEPTUAL

**In Exercises 137–138, determine whether each statement is true or false.**

**137.** The solution to the equation $x = \dfrac{1}{1/x}$ is the set of all real numbers.

**138.** The solution to the equation $\dfrac{1}{(x - 1)(x + 2)} = \dfrac{1}{x^2 + x - 2}$ is the set of all real numbers.

**139.** Solve for $x$, given that $a$, $b$, and $c$ are real numbers and $c \neq 0$.

$$\frac{a}{x} - \frac{b}{x} = c$$

**140.** Solve the equation for $y$: $\dfrac{1}{y - a} + \dfrac{1}{y + a} = \dfrac{2}{y - 1}$.

Does $y$ have any restrictions?

2

## ■ CHALLENGE

**141.** Solve the equation $\sqrt{x+6} + \sqrt{11+x} = 5\sqrt{3+x}$.

**142.** Solve the equation $3x^{7/12} - x^{5/6} - 2x^{1/3} = 0$.

**143.** Solve the equation for $x$ in terms of $y$: $y = \dfrac{a}{1 + \dfrac{b}{x} + c}$.

**144.** Solve for $t$: $\dfrac{t + \dfrac{1}{t}}{\dfrac{1}{t} - 1} = 1$.

## ■ TECHNOLOGY

**145.** Solve the equation $\sqrt{x-3} = 4 - \sqrt{x+2}$. Plot both sides of the equation in the same viewing screen, $y_1 = \sqrt{x-3}$ and $y_2 = 4 - \sqrt{x+2}$, and zoom in on the $x$-coordinate of the point of intersection. Does the graph agree with your solution?

**146.** Solve the equation $2\sqrt{x+1} = 1 + \sqrt{3-x}$. Plot both sides of the equation in the same viewing screen, $y_1 = 2\sqrt{x+1}$ and $y_2 = 1 + \sqrt{3-x}$, and zoom in on the $x$-coordinate of the points of intersection. Does the graph agree with your solution

**147.** Solve the equation $x^{1/2} = -4x^{1/4} + 21$. Plot both sides of the equation in the same viewing screen, $y_1 = x^{1/2}$ and $y_2 = -4x^{1/4} + 21$. Does the point(s) of intersection agree with your solution?

**148.** Solve the equation $x^{-1} = 3x^{-2} - 10$. Plot both sides of the equation in the same viewing screen, $y_1 = x^{-1}$ and $y_2 = 3x^{-2} - 10$. Does the point(s) of intersection agree with your solution?

<br>

**SECTION 0.4 INEQUALITIES**

**SKILLS OBJECTIVES**

- Use interval notation.
- Solve linear inequalities.
- Solve polynomial inequalities.
- Solve rational inequalities.
- Solve absolute value inequalities.

**CONCEPTUAL OBJECTIVES**

- Apply intersection and union concepts.
- Understand that inequalities may have one solution, no solution, or an interval solution.
- Understand zeros and test intervals.
- Realize that a rational inequality has an implied domain restriction on the variable.

# Graphing Inequalities and Interval Notation

We will express solutions to inequalities four ways: an inequality, a solution set, an interval, and a graph. The following are ways of expressing all real numbers greater than or equal to $a$ and less than $b$:

| Inequality Notation | Solution Set | Interval Notation | Graph/Number Line |
|---|---|---|---|
| $a \le x < b$ | $\{x \mid a \le x < b\}$ | $[a, b)$ | |

In this example, $a$ is referred to as the **left endpoint** and $b$ is referred to as the **right endpoint**. If an inequality is a strict inequality ($<$ or $>$), then the graph and interval notation use *parentheses*. If it includes an endpoint ($\ge$ or $\le$), then the graph and interval notation use *brackets*. Number lines are drawn with either closed/open circles or brackets/parentheses. In this text the brackets/parentheses notation will be used. Intervals are classified as follows:

Open ( , )     Closed [ , ]     Half open ( , ] or [ , )

**LET $x$ BE A REAL NUMBER.**

| $x$ IS... | INEQUALITY | SET NOTATION | INTERVAL | GRAPH |
|---|---|---|---|---|
| greater than $a$ and less than $b$ | $a < x < b$ | $\{x \mid a < x < b\}$ | $(a, b)$ | |
| greater than or equal to $a$ and less than $b$ | $a \leq x < b$ | $\{x \mid a \leq x < b\}$ | $[a, b)$ | |
| greater than $a$ and less than or equal to $b$ | $a < x \leq b$ | $\{x \mid a < x \leq b\}$ | $(a, b]$ | |
| greater than or equal to $a$ and less than or equal to $b$ | $a \leq x \leq b$ | $\{x \mid a \leq x \leq b\}$ | $[a, b]$ | |
| less than $a$ | $x < a$ | $\{x \mid x < a\}$ | $(-\infty, a)$ | |
| less than or equal to $a$ | $x \leq a$ | $\{x \mid x \leq a\}$ | $(-\infty, a]$ | |
| greater than $b$ | $x > b$ | $\{x \mid x > b\}$ | $(b, \infty)$ | |
| greater than or equal to $b$ | $x \geq b$ | $\{x \mid x \geq b\}$ | $[b, \infty)$ | |
| all real numbers | $\mathbb{R}$ | $\mathbb{R}$ | $(-\infty, \infty)$ | |

1. *Infinity* ($\infty$) is not a number. It is a symbol that means continuing indefinitely to the right on the number line. Similarly, *negative infinity* ($-\infty$) means continuing indefinitely to the left on the number line. Since both are unbounded, we use a parenthesis, never a bracket.

2. In interval notation, the lower number is always written to the left.

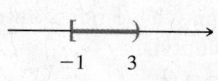

Write the inequality in interval notation: $-1 \leq x < 3$.

⭐ **CORRECT**     $[-1, 3)$          ❎ **INCORRECT**     $(3, -1]$

---

**EXAMPLE 1   Expressing Inequalities Using Interval Notation and a Graph**

Express the following as an inequality, an interval, and a graph:

**a.** $x$ is greater than $-3$.
**b.** $x$ is less than or equal to 5.
**c.** $x$ is greater than or equal to $-1$ and less than 4.
**d.** $x$ is greater than or equal to 0 and less than or equal to 4.

**Solution:**

| | Inequality | Interval | Graph |
|---|---|---|---|
| **a.** | $x > -3$ | $(-3, \infty)$ | |
| **b.** | $x \leq 5$ | $(-\infty, 5]$ | |
| **c.** | $-1 \leq x < 4$ | $[-1, 4)$ | |
| **d.** | $0 \leq x \leq 4$ | $[0, 4]$ | |

Since the solutions to inequalities are sets of real numbers, it is useful to discuss two operations on sets called **intersection** and **union**.

---

**DEFINITION** **Union and Intersection**

The **union** of sets $A$ and $B$, denoted $A \cup B$, is the set formed by combining all the elements in $A$ with all the elements in $B$.

$$A \cup B = \{x \mid x \text{ is in } A \textbf{ or } B \textbf{ or } \text{both}\}$$

The **intersection** of sets $A$ and $B$, denoted $A \cap B$, is the set formed by the elements that are in both $A$ and $B$.

$$A \cap B = \{x \mid x \text{ is in } A \textbf{ and } B\}$$

The notation "$x \mid x$ is in" is read "all $x$ such that $x$ is in." The vertical line represents "such that."

---

**EXAMPLE 2** **Determining Unions and Intersections: Intervals and Graphs**

If $A = [-3, 2]$ and $B = (1, 7)$, determine $A \cup B$ and $A \cap B$. Write these sets in interval notation, and graph.

**Solution:**

| Set | Interval notation | Graph |
|-----|-------------------|-------|
| $A$ | $[-3, 2]$ | |
| $B$ | $(1, 7)$ | |
| $A \cup B$ | $[-3, 7)$ | |
| $A \cap B$ | $(1, 2]$ | |

**■ YOUR TURN** If $C = [-3, 3)$ and $D = (0, 5]$, find $C \cup D$ and $C \cap D$. Express the intersection and union in interval notation, and graph.

**■ Answer:**
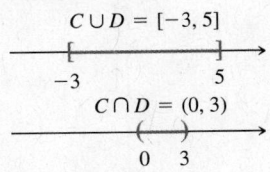
$$C \cup D = [-3, 5]$$

$$C \cap D = (0, 3)$$

# Linear Inequalities

If we were to solve the linear equation $3x - 2 = 7$, we would add 2 to both sides, divide by 3, and find that $x = 3$ is the solution, the *only* value that makes the equation true. If we were to solve the *linear inequality* $3x - 2 \leq 7$, we would follow the same procedure: Add 2 to both sides, divide by 3, and find that $x \leq 3$, which is an *interval* or *range* of numbers that make the inequality true.

In solving linear inequalities, we follow the same procedures that we used in solving linear equations with one general exception: *If you multiply or divide an inequality by a negative number, then you must change the direction of the inequality sign.*

*Study Tip*

If you multiply or divide an inequality by a negative number, remember to change the direction of the inequality sign.

**INEQUALITY PROPERTIES**

**Procedures That Do Not Change the Inequality Sign**

| | |
|---|---|
| 1. Simplifying by eliminating parentheses and collecting like terms. | $3(x - 6) < 6x - x$ <br> $3x - 18 < 5x$ |
| 2. Adding or subtracting the same quantity on both sides. | $7x + 8 \geq 29$ <br> $7x \geq 21$ |
| 3. Multiplying or dividing by the same *positive* real number. | $5x \leq 15$ <br> $x \leq 3$ |

**Procedures That Change (Reverse) the Inequality Sign**

| | |
|---|---|
| 1. Interchanging the two sides of the inequality. | $x \leq 4$ is equivalent to $4 \geq x$ |
| 2. Multiplying or dividing by the same *negative* real number. | $-5x \leq 15$ is equivalent to $x \geq -3$ |

**Technology Tip**

Use a graphing utility to display graphs of $y_1 = 5 - 3x$ and $y_2 = 23$.

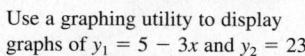

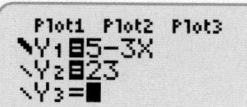

The solutions are the *x*-values such that the graph of $y_1 = 5 - 3x$ is below that of $y_2 = 23$.

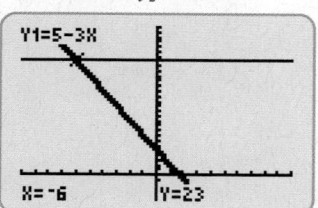

■ **Answer:** Solution set: $\{x \mid x \leq -1\}$
Interval notation: $(-\infty, -1]$
Graph: ⟵———|———⟶
$\qquad\qquad -1$

**EXAMPLE 3   Solving a Linear Inequality**

Solve and graph the inequality $5 - 3x < 23$.

**Solution:**

| | |
|---|---|
| Write the original inequality. | $5 - 3x < 23$ |
| Subtract 5 from both sides. | $-3x < 18$ |
| Divide both sides by $-3$ and reverse the inequality sign. | $\dfrac{-3x}{-3} > \dfrac{18}{-3}$ |
| Simplify. | $x > -6$ |

Solution set: $\boxed{\{x \mid x > -6\}}$    Interval notation: $\boxed{(-6, \infty)}$    Graph: ⟵(———⟶
$\qquad\qquad\qquad\qquad\qquad\qquad\qquad\qquad\qquad -6$

■ **YOUR TURN** Solve the inequality $5 \leq 3 - 2x$. Express the solution in set and interval notation, and graph.

**EXAMPLE 4   Solving a Double Linear Inequality**

Solve the inequality $-2 < 3x + 4 \leq 16$.

**Solution:**

| | |
|---|---|
| This double inequality can be written as two inequalities. | $\overbrace{-2 < 3x + 4} \leq 16$ |
| Both inequalities must be satisfied. | $-2 < 3x + 4$ and $3x + 4 \leq 16$ |
| Subtract 4 from both sides of each inequality. | $-6 < 3x$ and $3x \leq 12$ |
| Divide each inequality by 3. | $-2 < x$ and $x \leq 4$ |

Combining these two inequalities gives us $-2 < x \leq 4$ in inequality notation; in interval notation we have $(-2, \infty) \cap (-\infty, 4)$ or $(-2, 4]$.

Notice that the steps we took in solving these inequalities individually were identical. This leads us to a **shortcut method** in which we solve them together:

| | |
|---|---|
| Write the combined inequality. | $-2 < 3x + 4 \leq 16$ |
| Subtract 4 from each part. | $-6 < 3x \leq 12$ |
| Divide each part by 3. | $-2 < x \leq 4$ |

Interval notation: $\boxed{(-2, 4]}$

## Technology Tip

Use a graphing utility to display graphs of $y_1 = -2$, $y_2 = 3x + 4$, and $y_3 = 16$.

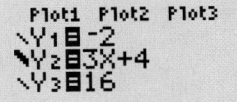

The solutions are the $x$-values such that the graph of $y_2 = 3x + 4$ is between the graphs of $y_1 = -2$ and $y_3 = 16$ and overlaps that of $y_3 = 16$.

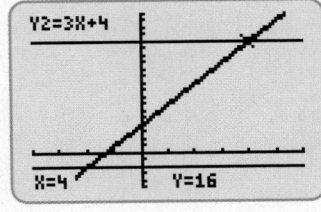

### EXAMPLE 5  Comparative Shopping

Two car rental companies have advertised weekly specials on full-size cars. Hertz is advertising an $80 rental fee plus an additional $0.10 per mile. Thrifty is advertising $60 and $0.20 per mile. How many miles must you drive for the rental car from Hertz to be the better deal?

**Solution:**

Let $x$ = number of miles driven during the week.

| | |
|---|---|
| Write the cost for the Hertz rental. | $80 + 0.1x$ |
| Write the cost for the Thrifty rental. | $60 + 0.2x$ |
| Write the inequality if Hertz is less than Thrifty. | $80 + 0.1x < 60 + 0.2x$ |
| Subtract $0.1x$ from both sides. | $80 < 60 + 0.1x$ |
| Subtract 60 from both sides. | $20 < 0.1x$ |
| Divide both sides by 0.1. | $200 < x$ |

You must drive more than 200 miles for Hertz to be the better deal.

## Polynomial Inequalities

A polynomial must pass through zero before its value changes from positive to negative or from negative to positive. **Zeros** of a polynomial are the values of $x$ that make the polynomial equal to zero. These zeros divide the real number line into **test intervals** where the value of the polynomial is either positive or negative. For $x^2 + x - 2 < 0$, if we set the polynomial equal to zero and solve:

$$x^2 + x - 2 = 0$$
$$(x + 2)(x - 1) = 0$$
$$x = -2 \quad \text{or} \quad x = 1$$

we find that $x = -2$ and $x = 1$ are the zeros. These zeros divide the real number line into three test intervals: $(-\infty, -2)$, $(-2, 1)$, and $(1, \infty)$.

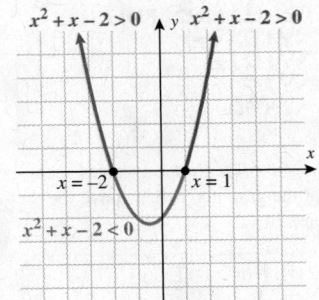

Since the polynomial is equal to zero at $x = -2$ and $x = 1$, we select one real number that lies in each of the three intervals and test to see whether the value of the polynomial at each point is either positive or negative. In this example, we select the real numbers $x = -3$, $x = 0$, and $x = 2$. At this point, there are two ways we can determine whether the value of the polynomial is positive or negative on the interval. One approach is to substitute each of the test points into the polynomial $x^2 + x - 2$.

| | | |
|---|---|---|
| $x = -3$: | $(-3)^2 + (-3) - 2 = 9 - 3 - 2 = 4$ | Positive |
| $x = 0$: | $(0)^2 + (0) - 2 = 0 - 0 - 2 = -2$ | Negative |
| $x = 2$: | $(2)^2 + (2) - 2 = 4 + 2 - 2 = 4$ | Positive |

The second approach is to simply determine the sign of the result as opposed to actually calculating the exact number. This alternate approach is often used when the expressions or test points get more complicated to evaluate. The polynomial is written as the product $(x + 2)(x - 1)$; therefore, we simply look for the sign in each set of parentheses.

$$(x + 2)(x - 1)$$

$$x = -3: \quad (-3 + 2)(-3 - 1) = (-1)(-4) \rightarrow (-)(-) = (+)$$

$$x = \quad : \quad (0 + 2)(0 - 1) = (2)(-1) \rightarrow (+)(-) = (-)$$

$$x = 2: \quad (2 + 2)(2 - 1) = (4)(1) \rightarrow (+)(+) = (+)$$

$$(-)(-) = (+) \qquad (+)(-) = (-) \qquad (+)(+) = (+)$$

$$\overset{\displaystyle\longleftarrow}{\underset{-3 \quad -2 \qquad 0 \qquad 1 \quad 2}{\vert \qquad \vert \qquad \vert \qquad \vert \quad \vert}}\longrightarrow$$

In this second approach we find the same result: $(-\infty, -2)$ and $(1, \infty)$ correspond to a positive value of the polynomial, and $(-2, 1)$ corresponds to a negative value of the polynomial.

In this example, the statement $x^2 + x - 2 < 0$ is true when the value of the polynomial (in factored form), $(x + 2)(x - 1)$, is negative. In the interval $(-2, 1)$, the value of the polynomial is negative. Thus, the solution to the inequality $x^2 + x - 2 < 0$ is $(-2, 1)$. To check the solution, select any number in the interval and substitute it into the original inequality to make sure it makes the statement true. The value $x = -1$ lies in the interval $(-2, 1)$. Upon substituting into the original inequality, we find that $x = -1$ satisfies the inequality $(-1)^2 + (-1) - 2 = -2 < 0$.

**PROCEDURE FOR SOLVING POLYNOMIAL INEQUALITIES**

**Step 1:** Write the inequality in *standard form*.
**Step 2:** Identify zeros of the polynomial.
**Step 3:** Draw the number line with zeros labeled.
**Step 4:** Determine the sign of the polynomial in each interval.
**Step 5:** Identify which interval(s) make the inequality true.
**Step 6:** Write the solution in interval notation.

**Technology Tip**

Use a graphing utility to display graphs of $y_1 = x^2 - x$ and $y_2 = 12$.

```
Plot1 Plot2 Plot3
\Y1▤X²-X
\Y2▤12
\Y3=
\Y4=■
```

The solutions are the $x$-values such that the graph of $y_1$ lies above the graph of $y_2$.

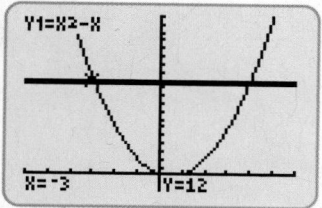

```
Y1=X2-X
X=-3        Y=12
```

*Note:* Be careful in Step 5. If the original polynomial is $<0$, then the interval(s) that correspond(s) to the value of the polynomial being negative should be selected. If the original polynomial is $>0$, then the interval(s) that correspond(s) to the value of the polynomial being positive should be selected.

 **EXAMPLE 6  Solving a Quadratic Inequality**

Solve the inequality $x^2 - x > 12$.

**Solution:**

STEP 1: Write the inequality in standard form. $\qquad\qquad x^2 - x - 12 > 0$

Factor the left side. $\qquad\qquad (x + 3)(x - 4) > 0$

STEP 2: Identify the zeros. $\qquad\qquad (x + 3)(x - 4) = 0$

$$x = -3 \quad \text{or} \quad x = 4$$

**STEP 3:** Draw the number line with the zeros labeled.

**STEP 4:** Determine the sign of $(x + 3)(x - 4)$ in each interval.

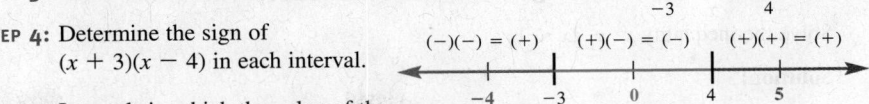

**STEP 5:** Intervals in which the value of the polynomial is *positive* make this inequality true.

$(-\infty, -3)$ or $(4, \infty)$

**STEP 6:** Write the solution in interval notation.

$(-\infty, -3) \cup (4, \infty)$

■ **YOUR TURN** Solve the inequality $x^2 - 5x \leq 6$ and express the solution in interval notation.

■ **Answer:** $[-1, 6]$

The inequality in Example 6, $x^2 - x > 12$, is a strict inequality, so we use parentheses when we express the solution in interval notation $(-\infty, -3) \cup (4, \infty)$. It is important to note that if we change the inequality sign from $>$ to $\geq$, then the zeros $x = -3$ and $x = 4$ also make the inequality true. Therefore, the solution to $x^2 - x \geq 12$ is $(-\infty, -3] \cup [4, \infty)$.

### EXAMPLE 7    Solving a Quadratic Inequality

Solve the inequality $x^2 > -5x$.

## COMMON MISTAKE

A common mistake is to divide by $x$. Never divide by a variable, because the value of the variable might be zero. Always start by writing the inequality in standard form and then factor to determine the zeros.

**★ CORRECT**

**STEP 1:** Write the inequality in standard form.

$$x^2 + 5x > 0$$

Factor.

$$x(x + 5) > 0$$

**STEP 2:** Identify the zeros.

$$x = 0, x = -5$$

**STEP 3:** Draw the number line with the zeros labeled.

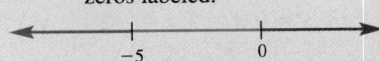

**STEP 4:** Determine the sign of $x(x + 5)$ in each interval.

$(-)(-) = (+)$ $(-)(+) = (-)$ $(+)(+) = (+)$

$-6$  $-5$  $-1$  $0$  $1$

**STEP 5:** Intervals in which the value of the polynomial is *positive* satisfy the inequality.

$(-\infty, -5)$ and $(0, \infty)$

**STEP 6:** Express the solution in interval notation.

$(-\infty, -5) \cup (0, \infty)$

**☒ INCORRECT**

Write the original inequality.

$$x^2 > -5x$$

**ERROR:**
Divide both sides by $x$.

$$x > -5$$

Dividing by $x$ is the mistake. If $x$ is negative, the inequality sign must be reversed. What if $x$ is zero?

*Technology Tip*

Using a graphing utility, graph $y_1 = x^2 + 2x$ and $y_2 = 1$.

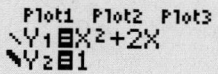

The solutions are the $x$-values such that the graph of $y_1$ lies below the graph of $y_2$.

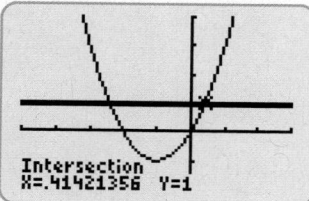

Note that

$$-1-\sqrt{(2)}$$
$$\phantom{-1}-2.414213562$$
$$-1+\sqrt{(2)}$$
$$\phantom{-1+}.4142135624$$
■

■ **Answer:**
$(-\infty, 1-\sqrt{2}\,] \cup [1+\sqrt{2}, \infty)$

### EXAMPLE 8  Solving a Quadratic Inequality

Solve the inequality $x^2 + 2x < 1$.

**Solution:**

Write the inequality in standard form. $\qquad x^2 + 2x - 1 < 0$

Identify the zeros. $\qquad\qquad\qquad\qquad x^2 + 2x - 1 = 0$

Apply the quadratic formula. $\qquad\qquad x = \dfrac{-2 \pm \sqrt{2^2 - 4(1)(-1)}}{2(1)}$

Simplify. $\qquad\qquad x = \dfrac{-2 \pm \sqrt{8}}{2} = \dfrac{-2 \pm 2\sqrt{2}}{2} = -1 \pm \sqrt{2}$

Draw the number line with the intervals labeled.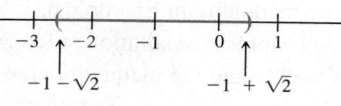
*Note:* $-1 - \sqrt{2} \approx -2.41$
$\phantom{Note:} -1 + \sqrt{2} \approx 0.41$

Test each interval.

| | | |
|---|---|---|
| $(-\infty, -1 - \sqrt{2})$ | $x = -3:$ | $(-3)^2 + 2(-3) - 1 = 2 > 0$ |
| $(-1 - \sqrt{2}, -1 + \sqrt{2})$ | $x = 0:$ | $(0)^2 + 2(0) - 1 = -1 < 0$ |
| $(-1 + \sqrt{2}, \infty)$ | $x = 1:$ | $(1)^2 + 2(1) - 1 = 2 > 0$ |

Intervals in which the value of the polynomial is *negative* make this inequality true. $\boxed{(-1 - \sqrt{2}, -1 + \sqrt{2})}$

■ **YOUR TURN** Solve the inequality $x^2 - 2x \geq 1$.

### EXAMPLE 9  Solving a Polynomial Inequality

Solve the inequality $x^3 - 3x^2 \geq 10x$.

**Solution:**

Write the inequality in standard form. $\qquad\qquad x^3 - 3x^2 - 10x \geq 0$

Factor. $\qquad\qquad\qquad\qquad\qquad\qquad x(x - 5)(x + 2) \geq 0$

Identify the zeros. $\qquad\qquad\qquad\qquad x = 0, x = 5, x = -2$

Draw the number line with the zeros (intervals) labeled.

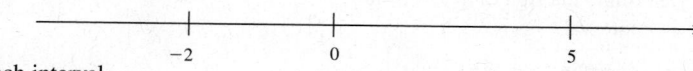

Test each interval.

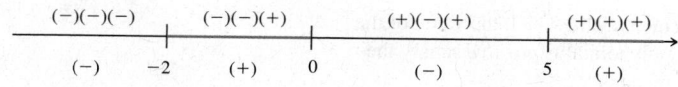

Intervals in which the value of the polynomial is *positive* make this inequality true. $\boxed{[-2, 0] \cup [5, \infty)}$

■ **Answer:** $(-\infty, -2) \cup (0, 3)$

■ **YOUR TURN** Solve the inequality $x^3 - x^2 - 6x < 0$.

# Rational Inequalities

A rational expression can change signs if either the numerator or denominator changes signs. In order to go from positive to negative or vice versa, you must pass through zero. To *solve* rational inequalities such as $\dfrac{x-3}{x^2-4} \geq 0$, we use a similar procedure to the one used for solving polynomial inequalities, with one exception. You must eliminate from the solution set values for $x$ that make the denominator equal to zero. In this example, we must eliminate $x = -2$ and $x = 2$ because these values make the denominator equal to zero. Rational inequalities have implied domains. In this example, $x \neq \pm 2$ is a domain restriction and these values ($x = -2$ and $x = 2$) must be eliminated from a possible solution.

We will proceed with a similar procedure involving zeros and test intervals that was outlined for polynomial inequalities. However, in rational inequalities once expressions are combined into a single fraction, any values that make *either* the numerator *or* the denominator equal to zero divide the number line into intervals.

**Study Tip**

Values that make the denominator equal to zero are always excluded.

## EXAMPLE 10  Solving a Rational Inequality

Solve the inequality $\dfrac{x-3}{x^2-4} \geq 0$.

**Solution:**

Factor the denominator.                                              $\dfrac{(x-3)}{(x-2)(x+2)} \geq 0$

State the domain restrictions on the variable.                       $x \neq 2,\ x \neq -2$

Identify the zeros of numerator and denominator.                     $x = -2,\ x = 2,\ x = 3$

Draw the number line and divide into intervals.

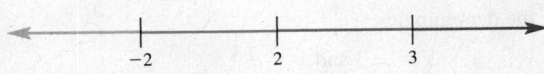

Test the intervals.

$$\frac{(x-3)}{(x-2)(x+2)}$$

Intervals in which the value of the rational expression          $(-2, 2)$ and $(3, \infty)$
is *positive* satisfy this inequality.

Since this inequality is greater than or equal to, we include $x = 3$ in our solution because it satisfies the inequality. However, $x = -2$ and $x = 2$ are not included in the solution because they make the denominator equal to zero.

The solution is  $\boxed{(-2, 2) \cup [3, \infty)}$.

**Technology Tip**

Use a graphing utility to display the graph of $y_1 = \dfrac{x-3}{x^2-4}$.

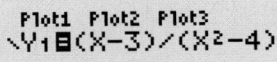

The solutions are the $x$-values such that the graph of $y_1$ lies on top and above the $x$-axis, excluding $x = \pm 2$.

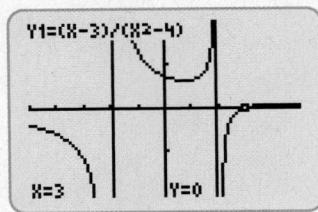

■ **YOUR TURN**  Solve the inequality $\dfrac{x+2}{x-1} \leq 0$.

■ **Answer:** $[-2, 1)$

**EXAMPLE 11   Solving a Rational Inequality**

Solve the inequality $\dfrac{x}{x+2} \le 3$.

## COMMON MISTAKE

Do not cross multiply. The LCD or expression by which you are multiplying might be negative for some values of $x$, and that would require the direction of the inequality sign to be reversed.

⭐ **CORRECT**

Subtract 3 from both sides.

$$\frac{x}{x+2} - 3 \le 0$$

Write as a single rational expression.

$$\frac{x - 3(x+2)}{x+2} \le 0$$

Eliminate the parentheses.

$$\frac{x - 3x - 6}{x+2} \le 0$$

Simplify the numerator.

$$\frac{-2x - 6}{x+2} \le 0$$

Factor the numerator.

$$\frac{-2(x+3)}{x+2} \le 0$$

Identify the zeros of the numerator and the denominator.

$$x = -3 \text{ and } x = -2$$

Draw the number line and test the intervals.

$$\frac{-2(x+3)}{x+2} \le 0$$

$$\frac{(-)(-)}{(-)} = (-) \quad \frac{(-)(+)}{(-)} = (+) \quad \frac{(-)(+)}{(+)} = (-)$$

$$\overset{\displaystyle \longleftarrow \;\;\;\; \overset{|}{-3} \;\;\;\;\;\; \overset{|}{-2} \;\;\;\; \longrightarrow}{}$$

Intervals in which the value of the rational expression is *negative* satisfy the inequality. $(-\infty, -3]$ and $(-2, \infty)$. Note that $x = -2$ is not included in the solution because it makes the denominator zero, and $x = -3$ is included because it satisfies the inequality.
  The solution is

$$\boxed{(-\infty, -3] \cup (-2, \infty)}$$

❌ **INCORRECT**

**ERROR:**
Do not cross multiply.

$$x \le 3(x+2)$$

# Absolute Value Inequalities

To solve the inequality $|x| < 3$, look for all real numbers that make this statement true. If we interpret this inequality as distance, we ask *what numbers are less than three units from the origin?* We can represent the solution in the following ways:

Inequality notation:   $-3 < x < 3$

Interval notation:     $(-3, 3)$

Graph:

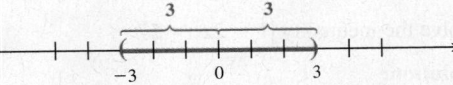

Similarly, to solve the inequality $|x| \geq 3$, look for all real numbers that make the statement true. If we interpret this inequality as a distance, we ask *what numbers are at least three units from the origin?* We can represent the solution in the following three ways:

Inequality notation:   $x \leq -3$ or $x \geq 3$

Interval notation:     $(-\infty, -3] \cup [3, \infty)$

Graph:

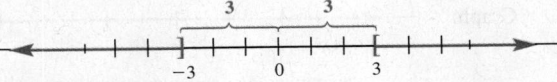

This discussion leads us to the following equivalence relations.

## PROPERTIES OF ABSOLUTE VALUE INEQUALITIES

**1.** $|x| < a$    is equivalent to    $-a < x < a$

**2.** $|x| \leq a$    is equivalent to    $-a \leq x \leq a$

**3.** $|x| > a$    is equivalent to    $x < -a$ or $x > a$

**4.** $|x| \geq a$    is equivalent to    $x \leq -a$ or $x \geq a$

It is important to realize that in the above four properties, the variable $x$ can be any algebraic expression.

### EXAMPLE 12   Solving an Inequality Involving an Absolute Value

Solve the inequality $|3x - 2| \leq 7$.

**Solution:**

We apply property (2) and squeeze the absolute value expression between $-7$ and $7$.

$$-7 \leq 3x - 2 \leq 7$$

Add 2 to all three parts.

$$-5 \leq 3x \leq 9$$

Divide all three parts by 3.

$$-\frac{5}{3} \leq x \leq 3$$

The solution in interval notation is $\boxed{\left[-\frac{5}{3}, 3\right]}$.

Graph:

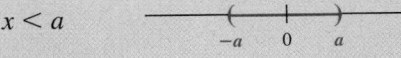

■ **YOUR TURN**   Solve the inequality $|2x + 1| < 11$.

**Technology Tip**

Use a graphing utility to display graphs of $y_1 = |3x - 2|$ and $y_2 = 7$.

```
Plot1 Plot2 Plot3
\Y1◻abs(3X-2)
\Y2◻7
```

The values of $x$ where the graph of $y_1$ lies on top and below the graph of $y_2$ are the solutions to this inequality.

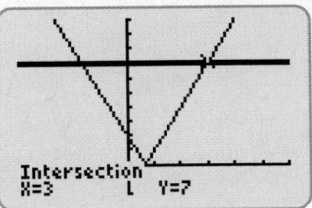

■ **Answer:**
Inequality notation: $-6 < x < 5$
Interval notation: $(-6, 5)$

It is often helpful to note that for absolute value inequalities,

- *less than* inequalities can be written as a single statement (see Example 12).
- *greater than* inequalities must be written as two statements (see Example 13).

**EXAMPLE 13** **Solving an Inequality Involving an Absolute Value**

Solve the inequality $|1 - 2x| > 5$.

**Solution:**

| | |
|---|---|
| Apply property (3). | $1 - 2x < -5$    or    $1 - 2x > 5$ |
| Subtract 1 from all expressions. | $-2x < -6$       $-2x > 4$ |
| Divide by $-2$ and reverse the inequality sign. | $x > 3$       $x < -2$ |
| Express the solution in interval notation. | $(-\infty, -2) \cup (3, \infty)$ |

Graph:
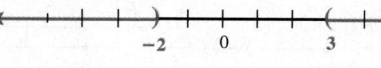

 **Answer:**
Inequality notation: $x \le 2$ or $x \ge 3$
Interval notation: $(-\infty, 2] \cup [3, \infty)$

■ **YOUR TURN** Solve the inequality $|5 - 2x| \ge 1$.

Notice that if we change the problem in Example 13 to $|1 - 2x| > -5$, the answer is all real numbers because **the absolute value of any expression is greater than or equal to zero**. Similarly, $|1 - 2x| < -5$ would have no solution because **the absolute value of an expression can never be negative**.

**EXAMPLE 14** **Solving an Inequality Involving an Absolute Value**

Solve the inequality $2 - |3x| < 1$.

**Solution:**

| | |
|---|---|
| Subtract 2 from both sides. | $-|3x| < -1$ |
| Multiply by $(-1)$ and reverse the inequality sign. | $|3x| > 1$ |
| Apply property (3). | $3x < -1$    or    $3x > 1$ |
| Divide both inequalities by 3. | $x < -\dfrac{1}{3}$   or   $x > \dfrac{1}{3}$ |
| Express in interval notation. | $\left(-\infty, -\dfrac{1}{3}\right) \cup \left(\dfrac{1}{3}, \infty\right)$ |

Graph.
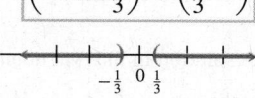

# SECTION
## 0.4 SUMMARY

In this section, we used interval notation to represent the solution to inequalities.

- **Linear Inequalities:** Solve linear inequalities similarly to how we solve linear equations with one exception—when you multiply or divide by a negative number, you must reverse the inequality sign.

- **Polynomial Inequalities:** First write the inequality in standard form (zero on one side). Determine the zeros, draw the number line, test the intervals, select the intervals according to the sign of the inequality, and write the solution in interval notation.

- **Rational Inequalities:** Write as a single fraction and then proceed with a similar approach as used in ploynomial inequalities—only the test intervals are determined by finding the zeros of either the numerator or the denominator. Exclude any values from the solution that result in the denominator being equal to zero.

- **Absolute Value Inequalities:** Write an absolute value inequality in terms of two inequalities that do not involve absolute value:
  - $|x| < A$ is equivalent to $-A < x < A$.
  - $|x| > A$ is equivalent to $x < -A$ or $x > A$.

# SECTION
## 0.4 EXERCISES

### ▪ SKILLS

**In Exercises 1–10, rewrite in interval notation and graph.**

1. $-2 \leq x < 3$
2. $-4 \leq x \leq -1$
3. $-3 < x \leq 5$
4. $0 < x < 6$
5. $x \leq 6$ and $x \geq 4$
6. $x > -3$ and $x \leq 2$
7. $x \leq -6$ and $x \geq -8$
8. $x < 8$ and $x < 2$
9. $x > 4$ and $x \leq -2$
10. $x \geq -5$ and $x < -6$

**In Exercises 11–20, graph the indicated set and write as a single interval, if possible.**

11. $(-\infty, 4) \cap [1, \infty)$
12. $(-3, \infty) \cap [-5, \infty)$
13. $[-5, 2) \cap [-1, 3]$
14. $[-4, 5) \cap [-2, 7)$
15. $(-\infty, 4) \cup (4, \infty)$
16. $(-\infty, -3] \cup [-3, \infty)$
17. $(-\infty, -3] \cup [3, \infty)$
18. $(-2, 2) \cap [-3, 1]$
19. $(-\infty, \infty) \cap (-3, 2]$
20. $(-\infty, \infty) \cup (-4, 7)$

**In Exercises 21–36, solve each linear inequality and express the solution set in interval notation.**

21. $3(t + 1) > 2t$
22. $2(y + 5) \leq 3(y - 4)$
23. $7 - 2(1 - x) > 5 + 3(x - 2)$
24. $4 - 3(2 + x) < 5$
25. $\frac{2}{3}y - \frac{1}{2}(5 - y) < \frac{5y}{3} - (2 + y)$
26. $\frac{s}{2} - \frac{(s - 3)}{3} > \frac{s}{4} - \frac{1}{12}$
27. $-1.8x + 2.5 > 3.4$
28. $2.7x - 1.3 < 6.8$
29. $-3 < 1 - x \leq 9$
30. $3 \leq -2 - 5x \leq 13$
31. $0 < 2 - \frac{1}{3}y < 4$
32. $3 < \frac{1}{2}A - 3 < 7$
33. $\frac{1}{2} \leq \frac{1 + y}{3} \leq \frac{3}{4}$
34. $-1 < \frac{2 - z}{4} \leq \frac{1}{5}$
35. $-0.7 \leq 0.4x + 1.1 \leq 1.3$
36. $7.1 > 4.7 - 1.2x > 1.1$

**In Exercises 37–54, solve each polynomial inequality and express the solution set in interval notation.**

37. $2t^2 - 3 \leq t$
38. $3t^2 \geq -5t + 2$
39. $5v - 1 > 6v^2$
40. $12t^2 < 37t + 10$
41. $2s^2 - 5s \geq 3$
42. $8s + 12 \leq -s^2$
43. $y^2 + 2y \geq 4$
44. $y^2 + 3y \leq 1$
45. $x^2 - 4x < 6$
46. $x^2 - 2x > 5$
47. $u^2 \geq 3u$
48. $u^2 \leq -4u$
49. $x^2 > 9$
50. $t^2 \leq 49$
51. $x^3 + x^2 - 2x \leq 0$
52. $x^3 + 2x^2 - 3x > 0$
53. $x^3 + x > 2x^2$
54. $x^3 + 4x \leq 4x^2$

**In Exercises 55–70, solve each rational inequality and express the solution set in interval notation.**

**55.** $\dfrac{s+1}{4-s^2} \geq 0$

**56.** $\dfrac{s+5}{4-s^2} \leq 0$

**57.** $\dfrac{3t^2}{t+2} \geq 5t$

**58.** $\dfrac{-2t-t^2}{4-t} \geq t$

**59.** $\dfrac{3p-2p^2}{4-p^2} < \dfrac{3+p}{2-p}$

**60.** $-\dfrac{7p}{p^2-100} \leq \dfrac{p+2}{p+10}$

**61.** $\dfrac{x^2+10}{x^2+16} > 0$

**62.** $-\dfrac{x^2+2}{x^2+4} < 0$

**63.** $\dfrac{v^2-9}{v-3} \geq 0$

**64.** $\dfrac{v^2-1}{v+1} \leq 0$

**65.** $\dfrac{2}{t-3} + \dfrac{1}{t+3} \geq 0$

**66.** $\dfrac{1}{t-2} + \dfrac{1}{t+2} \leq 0$

**67.** $\dfrac{3}{x+4} - \dfrac{1}{x-2} \leq 0$

**68.** $\dfrac{2}{x-5} - \dfrac{1}{x-1} \geq 0$

**69.** $\dfrac{1}{p-2} - \dfrac{1}{p+2} \geq \dfrac{3}{p^2-4}$

**70.** $\dfrac{2}{2p-3} - \dfrac{1}{p+1} \leq \dfrac{1}{2p^2-p-3}$

**In Exercises 71–86, solve the absolute value inequality and express the solution set in interval notation.**

**71.** $|x-4| > 2$

**72.** $|x-1| < 3$

**73.** $|4-x| \leq 1$

**74.** $|1-y| < 3$

**75.** $|2x| > -3$

**76.** $|2x| < -3$

**77.** $|7-2y| \geq 3$

**78.** $|6-5y| \leq 1$

**79.** $|4-3x| \geq 0$

**80.** $|4-3x| \geq 1$

**81.** $2|4x| - 9 \geq 3$

**82.** $5|x-1| + 2 \leq 7$

**83.** $9 - |2x| < 3$

**84.** $4 - |x+1| > 1$

**85.** $|x^2-1| \leq 8$

**86.** $|x^2+4| \geq 29$

## ▪ APPLICATIONS

**87. Lasers.** A circular laser beam with a radius $r_T$ is transmitted from one tower to another tower. If the received beam radius $r_R$ fluctuates 10% from the transmitted beam radius due to atmospheric turbulence, write an inequality representing the received beam radius.

**88. Electronics: Communications.** Communication systems are often evaluated based on their signal-to-noise ratio (SNR), which is the ratio of the average power of received signal, $S$, to average power of noise, $N$, in the system. If the SNR is required to be at least 2 at all times, write an inequality representing the received signal power if the noise can fluctuate 10%.

**The following table is the 2007 Federal Tax Rate Schedule for people filing as *single*:**

| TAX BRACKET # | IF TAXABLE INCOME IS OVER– | BUT NOT OVER– | THE TAX IS: |
|---|---|---|---|
| I | $0 | $7,825 | 10% of the amount over $0 |
| II | $7,825 | $31,850 | $782.50 plus 15% of the amount over $7,825 |
| III | $31,850 | $77,100 | $4,386.25 plus 25% of the amount over $31,850 |
| IV | $77,100 | $160,850 | $15,698.75 plus 28% of the amount over $77,100 |
| V | $160,850 | $349,700 | $39,148.75 plus 33% of the amount over $160,850 |
| VI | $349,700 | No limit | $101,469.25 plus 35% of the amount over $349,700 |

**89. Federal Income Tax.** What was the range of federal income taxes a person in tax bracket III would pay the IRS?

**90. Federal Income Tax.** What was the range of federal income taxes a person in tax bracket IV would pay the IRS?

**In Exercises 91 and 92 refer to the following:**

The annual revenue for a small company is modeled by

$$R = 5000 + 1.75x$$

where $x$ is hundreds of units sold and $R$ is revenue in thousands of dollars.

**91. Business.** Find the number of units (to the nearest 100) that must be sold to generate at least $10 million in revenue.

**92. Business.** Find the number of units (to the nearest 100) that must be sold to generate at least $7.5 million in revenue.

**In Exercises 93 and 94 refer to the following:**

The Target or Training Heart Rate (THR) is a range of heart rate (measured in beats per minute) that enables a person's heart and lungs to benefit the most from an aerobic workout. THR can be modeled by the formula

$$THR = (HR_{\max} - HR_{\text{rest}}) \times I + HR_{\text{rest}}$$

where $HR_{\max}$ is the maximum heart rate that is deemed safe for the individual, $HR_{\text{rest}}$ is the resting heart rate, and $I$ is the intensity of the workout that is reported as a percentage.

**93. Health.** A female with a resting heart rate of 65 beats per minute has a maximum safe heart rate of 170 beats per minute. If her target heart rate is between 100 and 140 beats per minute, what percent intensities of workout can she consider?

**94. Health.** A male with a resting heart rate of 75 beats per minute has a maximum safe heart rate of 175 beats per minute. If his target heart rate is between 110 and 150 beats per minute, what percent intensities of workout can he consider?

**95. Profit.** A Web-based embroidery company makes monogrammed napkins. The profit associated with producing $x$ orders of napkins is governed by the equation

$$P(x) = -x^2 + 130x - 3000$$

Determine the range of orders the company should accept in order to make a profit.

**96. Profit.** Repeat Exercise 95 using $P(x) = x^2 - 130x + 3600$.

**97. Car Value.** The term "upside down" on car payments refers to owing more than a car is worth. Assume you buy a new car and finance 100% over 5 years. The difference between the value of the car and what is owed on the car is governed by the expression $\dfrac{t}{t-3}$, where $t$ is age (in years) of the car. Determine the time period when the car is worth more than you owe $\left(\dfrac{t}{t-3} > 0\right)$. When do you owe more than it's worth $\left(\dfrac{t}{t-3} < 0\right)$?

**98. Car Value.** Repeat Exercise 97 using the expression $-\dfrac{2-t}{4-t}$.

**99. Bullet Speed.** A .22 caliber gun fires a bullet at a speed of 1200 feet per second. If a .22 caliber gun is fired straight upward into the sky, the height of the bullet in feet is given by the equation $h = -16t^2 + 1200t$, where $t$ is the time in seconds with $t = 0$ corresponding to the instant the gun is fired. How long is the bullet in the air?

**100. Bullet Speed.** A .38 caliber gun fires a bullet at a speed of 600 feet per second. If a .38 caliber gun is fired straight upward into the sky, the height of the bullet in feet is given by the equation $h = -16t^2 + 600t$. How many seconds is the bullet in the air?

**In Exercises 101 and 102 refer to the following:**

In response to economic conditions, a local business explores the effect of a price increase on weekly profit. The function

$$P = -5(x + 3)(x - 24)$$

models the effect that a price increase of $x$ dollars on a bottle of wine will have on the profit $P$ measured in dollars.

**101. Economics.** What price increase will lead to a weekly profit of less than $460?

**102. Economics.** What price increases will lead to a weekly profit of more than $550?

**103. Sports.** Two women tee off of a par-3 hole on a golf course. They are playing "closest to the pin." If the first woman tees off and lands exactly 4 feet from the hole, write an inequality that describes where the second woman lands to the hole in order to win the hole. What equation would suggest a tie? Let $d =$ the distance from where the second woman lands to the tee.

**104. Electronics.** A band-pass filter in electronics allows certain frequencies within a range (or band) to pass through to the receiver and eliminates all other frequencies. Write an absolute value inequality that allows any frequency $f$ within 15 hertz of the carrier frequency $f_c$ to pass.

**In Exercises 105 and 106 refer to the following:**

A company is reviewing revenue for the prior sales year. The model for projected revenue and the model for actual revenue are

$$R_{projected} = 200 + 5x$$

$$R_{actual} = 210 + 4.8x$$

where $x$ represents the number of units sold and $R$ represents the revenue in thousands of dollars. Since the two revenue models are not identical, an error in projected revenue occurred. This error is represented by

$$E = |R_{projected} - R_{actual}|$$

**105. Business.** For what number of units sold was the error in projected revenue less than $5000?

**106. Business.** For what number of units sold was the error in projected revenue less than $3000?

## ▪ CATCH THE MISTAKE

**In Exercises 107–110, explain the mistake that is made.**

**107.** Solve the inequality $2 - 3p \le -4$ and express the solution in interval notation.

**Solution:**
$$\begin{aligned} 2 - 3p &\le -4 \\ -3p &\le -6 \\ p &\le 2 \\ (-\infty, 2] \end{aligned}$$

This is incorrect. What mistake was made?

**108.** Solve the inequality $u^2 < 25$.

**Solution:**

Take the square root of both sides.    $u < -5$

Write the solution in interval notation.    $(-\infty, -5)$

This is incorrect. What mistake was made?

**109.** Solve the inequality $3x < x^2$.

**Solution:**

Divide by $x$.          $3 < x$

Write the solution in interval notation.     $(3, \infty)$

This is incorrect. What mistake was made?

**110.** Solve the inequality $\dfrac{x+4}{x} < -\dfrac{1}{3}$.

**Solution:**

Cross multiply.          $3(x+4) < -1(x)$

Eliminate the parentheses.     $3x + 12 < -x$

Combine like terms.         $4x < -12$

Divide both sides by 4.       $x < -3$

This is incorrect. What mistake was made?

## ▪ CONCEPTUAL

**In Exercises 111–114, determine whether each statement is true or false. Assume that $a$ is a positive real number.**

**111.** If $x < a$, then $a > x$.

**112.** If $-x \geq a$, then $x \geq -a$.

**113.** If $x < a^2$, then the solution is $(-\infty, a)$.

**114.** If $x \geq a^2$, then the solution is $[a, \infty)$.

## ▪ CHALLENGE

**In Exercises 115 and 116, solve for $x$ given that $a$ and $b$ are both positive real numbers.**

**115.** $\dfrac{x^2 + a^2}{x^2 + b^2} \geq 0$

**116.** $\dfrac{x^2 - b^2}{x + b} < 0$

**117.** For what values of $x$ does the absolute value equation $|x+1| = 4 + |x-2|$ hold?

**118.** Solve the inequality $|3x^2 - 7x + 2| > 8$.

## ▪ TECHNOLOGY

**119. a.** Solve the inequality $x - 3 < 2x - 1 < x + 4$.
    **b.** Graph all three expressions of the inequality in the same viewing screen. Find the range of $x$-values when the graph of the middle expression lies above the graph of the left side and below the graph of the right side.
    **c.** Do (a) and (b) agree?

**120. a.** Solve the inequality $x - 2 < 3x + 4 \leq 2x + 6$.
    **b.** Graph all three expressions of the inequality in the same viewing screen. Find the range of $x$-values when the graph of the middle expression lies above the graph of the left side and on top of and below the graph of the right side.
    **c.** Do (a) and (b) agree?

**121.** Solve the inequality $\left| \dfrac{x}{x+1} \right| < 1$ by graphing both sides of the inequality, and identify which $x$-values make this statement true.

**122.** Solve the inequality $\left| \dfrac{x}{x+1} \right| < 2$ by graphing both sides of the inequality, and identify which $x$-values make this statement true.

**SKILLS OBJECTIVES**

- Calculate the distance between two points and the midpoint of a line segment joining two points.
- Graph equations in two variables by point-plotting.
- Use intercepts and symmetry as graphing aids.
- Graph circles.

**CONCEPTUAL OBJECTIVES**

- Expand the concept of a one-dimensional number line to a two-dimensional plane.
- Relate symmetry graphically and algebraically.

## Cartesian Plane

HIV infection rates, stock prices, and temperature conversions are all examples of relationships between two quantities that can be expressed in a two-dimensional graph. Because it is two-dimensional, such a graph lies in a **plane**.

Two perpendicular real number lines, known as the **axes** in the plane, intersect at a point we call the **origin**. Typically, the horizontal axis is called the *x*-axis and the vertical axis is denoted as the *y*-axis. The axes divide the plane into four **quadrants**, numbered by Roman numerals and ordered counterclockwise.

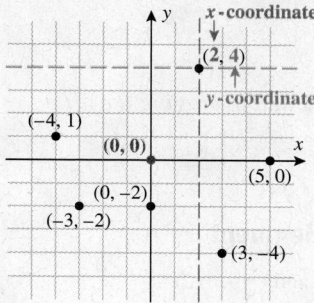

Points in the plane are represented by **ordered pairs**, denoted (*x*, *y*). The first number of the ordered pair indicates the position in the horizontal direction and is often called the *x*-**coordinate** or **abscissa**. The second number indicates the position in the vertical direction and is often called the *y*-**coordinate** or **ordinate**. The origin is denoted (**0, 0**).

Examples of other coordinates are given on the graph to the left.

The point (**2, 4**) lies in quadrant I. To **plot** this point, start at the origin (**0, 0**) and move to the right two units and up four units.

All points in quadrant I have positive coordinates, and all points in quadrant III have negative coordinates. Quadrant II has negative *x*-coordinates and positive *y*-coordinates; quadrant IV has positive *x*-coordinates and negative *y*-coordinates.

This representation is called the **rectangular coordinate system** or **Cartesian coordinate system**, named after the French mathematician René Descartes.

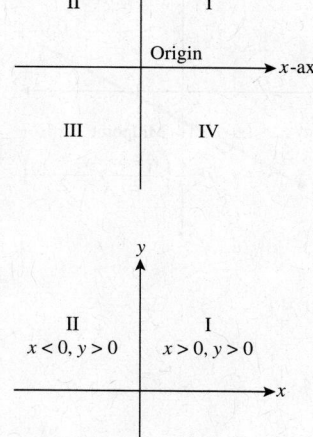

## The Distance and Midpoint Formulas

**DEFINITION** **Distance Formula**

The **distance** *d* between two points $P_1 = (x_1, y_1)$ and $P_2 = (x_2, y_2)$ is given by

$$d = \sqrt{(x_2 - x_1)^2 + (y_2 - y_1)^2}$$

*The distance between two points is the square root of the sum of the square of the difference between the x-coordinates and the square of the difference between the y-coordinates.*

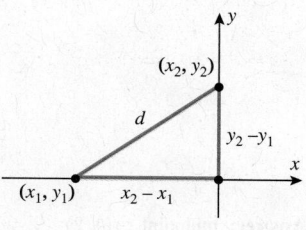

**63**

**EXAMPLE 1** **Using the Distance Formula to Find the Distance Between Two Points**

Find the distance between $(-3, 7)$ and $(5, -2)$.

**Solution:**

Write the distance formula.          $d = \sqrt{[x_2 - x_1]^2 + [y_2 - y_1]^2}$

Substitute $(x_1, y_1) = (-3, 7)$
and $(x_2, y_2) = (5, -2)$.          $d = \sqrt{[5 - (-3)]^2 + [-2 - 7]^2}$

Simplify.          $d = \sqrt{[5 + 3]^2 + [-2 - 7]^2}$

$d = \sqrt{8^2 + (-9)^2} = \sqrt{64 + 81} = \sqrt{145}$

Solve for $d$.          $\boxed{d = \sqrt{145}}$

■ **Answer:** $d = \sqrt{58}$

■ **YOUR TURN** Find the distance between $(4, -5)$ and $(-3, -2)$.

**DEFINITION**    **Midpoint Formula**

The **midpoint**, $(x_m, y_m)$, of the line segment with endpoints $(x_1, y_1)$ and $(x_2, y_2)$ is given by

$$(x_m, y_m) = \left(\frac{x_1 + x_2}{2}, \frac{y_1 + y_2}{2}\right)$$

*The midpoint can be found by averaging the x-coordinates and averaging the y-coordinates.*

 **EXAMPLE 2** **Finding the Midpoint of a Line Segment**

Find the midpoint of the line segment joining the points $(2, 6)$ and $(-4, -2)$.

**Solution:**

Write the midpoint formula.          $(x_m, y_m) = \left(\frac{x_1 + x_2}{2}, \frac{y_1 + y_2}{2}\right)$

Substitute $(x_1, y_1) = (2, 6)$
and $(x_2, y_2) = (-4, -2)$.          $(x_m, y_m) = \left(\frac{2 + (-4)}{2}, \frac{6 + (-2)}{2}\right)$

Simplify.          $\boxed{(x_m, y_m) = (-1, 2)}$

One way to verify your answer is to plot the given points and the midpoint to make sure your answer looks reasonable.

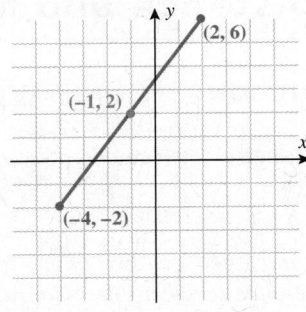

■ **Answer:** midpoint = $(4, 2)$

■ **YOUR TURN** Find the midpoint of the line segment joining the points $(3, -4)$ and $(5, 8)$.

# Point-Plotting

The **graph of an equation** in two variables, $x$ and $y$, consists of all the points in the $xy$-plane whose coordinates $(x, y)$ satisfy the equation. A procedure for plotting the graphs of equations is outlined below and is illustrated with the example $y = x^2$.

**WORDS**

**Step 1:** In a table, list several pairs of coordinates that make the equation true.

**MATH**

| $x$ | $y = x^2$ | $(x, y)$ |
|-----|-----------|----------|
| 0   | 0         | (0, 0)   |
| −1  | 1         | (−1, 1)  |
| 1   | 1         | (1, 1)   |
| −2  | 4         | (−2, 4)  |
| 2   | 4         | (2, 4)   |

**Step 2:** Plot these points on a graph and connect the points with a smooth curve. Use arrows to indicate that the graph continues.

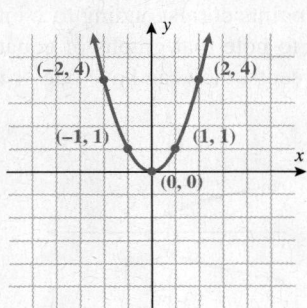

In graphing an equation, first select arbitrary values for $x$ and then use the equation to find the corresponding value of $y$, or vice versa.

## EXAMPLE 3 Graphing an Equation by Plotting Points

Graph the equation $y = x^3$.

**Solution:**

**STEP 1** In a table, list several pairs of coordinates that satisfy the equation.

| $x$ | $y = x^3$ | $(x, y)$  |
|-----|-----------|-----------|
| 0   | 0         | (0, 0)    |
| −1  | −1        | (−1, −1)  |
| 1   | 1         | (1, 1)    |
| −2  | −8        | (−2, −8)  |
| 2   | 8         | (2, 8)    |

**STEP 2** Plot these points on a graph and connect the points with a smooth curve, indicating with arrows that the curve continues in both the positive and negative directions.

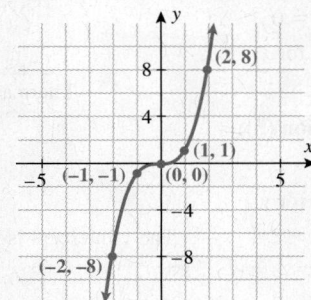

# Using Intercepts and Symmetry as Graphing Aids

## Intercepts

When point-plotting graphs of equations, which points should be selected? Points where a graph crosses (or touches) either the *x*-axis or *y*-axis are called **intercepts** and identifying these points helps define the graph unmistakably.

An ***x*-intercept** of a graph is a point where the graph intersects the *x*-axis. Specifically, an *x*-intercept is the *x*-coordinate of such a point. For example, if a graph intersects the *x*-axis at the point (3, 0), then we say that 3 is the *x*-intercept. Since the value for *y* along the *x*-axis is zero, all points corresponding to *x*-intercepts have the form (*a*, 0).

A ***y*-intercept** of a graph is a point where the graph intersects the *y*-axis. Specifically, a *y*-intercept is the *y*-coordinate of such a point. For example, if a graph intersects the *y*-axis at the point (0, 2), then we say that 2 is the *y*-intercept. Since the value for *x* along the *y*-axis is zero, all points corresponding to *y*-intercepts have the form (0, *b*).

It is important to note that graphs of equations do not have to have intercepts, and if they do have intercepts, they can have one or more of each type.

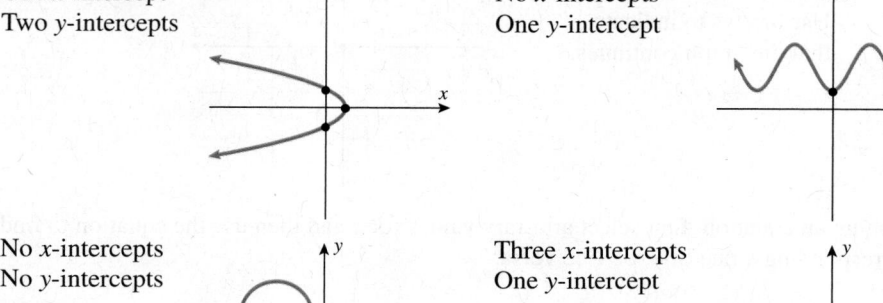

One *x*-intercept
Two *y*-intercepts

No *x*-intercepts
One *y*-intercept

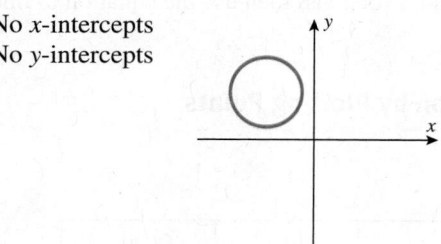

No *x*-intercepts
No *y*-intercepts

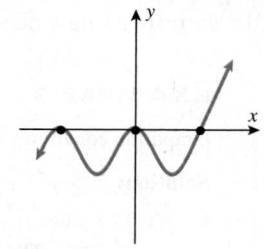

Three *x*-intercepts
One *y*-intercept

*Note:* The origin (0, 0) corresponds to both an *x*-intercept and a *y*-intercept.

### EXAMPLE 4  Finding Intercepts from an Equation

Given the equation $y = x^2 + 1$, find the indicated intercepts of its graph, if any.

**a.** *x*-intercept(s)  **b.** *y*-intercept(s)

**Solution (a):**

Let $y = 0$.  $0 = x^2 + 1$

Solve for *x*.  $x^2 = -1$  no real solution

There are no *x*-intercepts.

**Solution (b):**

Let $x = 0$.  $y = 0^2 + 1$

Solve for *y*.  $y = 1$

The *y*-intercept is located at the point (0, 1).

**Answer:**
**a.** *x*-intercepts: −2 and 2
**b.** *y*-intercept: −4

**YOUR TURN** For the equation $y = x^2 - 4$
**a.** find the *x*-intercept(s), if any.  **b.** find the *y*-intercept(s), if any.

# Symmetry

The word **symmetry** conveys balance. Suppose you have two pictures to hang on a wall. If you space them equally apart on the wall, then you prefer a symmetric décor. This is an example of symmetry about a line. The word (water) written in the margin is identical if you rotate the word 180 degrees (or turn the page upside down). This is an example of symmetry about a point. Symmetric graphs have the characteristic that their mirror image can be obtained about a reference, typically a line or a point.

Symmetry aids in graphing by giving information "for free." For example, if a graph is symmetric about the y-axis, then once the graph to the right of the y-axis is found, the left side of the graph is the mirror image of that. If a graph is symmetric about the origin, then once the graph is known in quadrant I, the graph in quadrant III is found by rotating the known graph 180 degrees.

It would be beneficial to know whether a graph of an equation is symmetric about a line or point before the graph of the equation is sketched. Although a graph can be symmetric about any line or point, we will discuss only symmetry about the x-axis, y-axis, and origin. These types of symmetry and the algebraic procedures for testing for symmetry are outlined below.

## Types and Tests for Symmetry

| TYPE OF SYMMETRY | GRAPH | IF THE POINT (**a, b**) IS ON THE GRAPH, THEN THE POINT . . . | ALGEBRAIC TEST FOR SYMMETRY |
|---|---|---|---|
| Symmetric with respect to the x-axis | | $(a, -b)$ is on the graph. | Replacing y with $-y$ leaves the equation unchanged. |
| Symmetric with respect to the y-axis | | $(-a, b)$ is on the graph. | Replacing x with $-x$ leaves the equation unchanged. |
| Symmetric with respect to the origin | | $(-a, -b)$ is on the graph. | Replacing x with $-x$ and y with $-y$ leaves the equation unchanged. |

**Study Tip**

Symmetry gives us information about the graph "for free."

**Study Tip**

When testing for symmetry about the $x$-axis, $y$-axis, and origin, there are *five* possibilities:

- No symmetry.
- Symmetry with respect to the $x$-axis
- Symmetry with respect to the $y$-axis
- Symmetry with respect to the origin
- Symmetry with respect to the $x$-axis, $y$-axis, and origin

**Technology Tip**

Graph of $y_1 = x^2 + 1$ is shown.

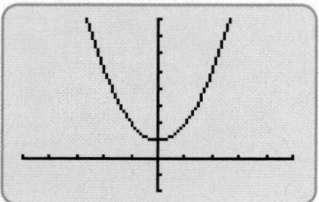

Graph of $y_1 = x^3 + 1$ is shown.

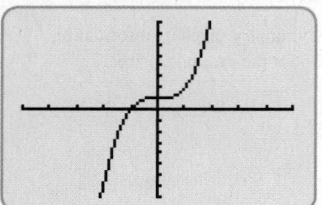

■ **Answer:** The graph of the equation is symmetric with respect to the $x$-axis.

 **EXAMPLE 5**   **Testing for Symmetry**

Determine what type of symmetry (if any) the graphs of the equations exhibit.

**a.**   $y = x^2 + 1$     **b.** $y = x^3 + 1$

**Solution (a):**

Replace $x$ with $-x$.                                              $y = (-x)^2 + 1$

Simplify.                                                                $y = x^2 + 1$

The resulting equation is equivalent to the original equation, so the graph of the equation $y = x^2 + 1$ is **symmetric with respect to the $y$-axis**.

Replace $y$ with $-y$.                                             $(-y) = x^2 + 1$

Simplify.                                                               $y = -x^2 - 1$

The resulting equation $y = -x^2 - 1$ is not equivalent to the original equation $y = x^2 + 1$, so the graph of the equation $y = x^2 + 1$ is **not symmetric with respect to the $x$-axis**.

Replace $x$ with $-x$ and $y$ with $-y$.           $(-y) = (-x)^2 + 1$

Simplify.                                                               $-y = x^2 + 1$

                                                                          $y = -x^2 - 1$

The resulting equation $y = -x^2 - 1$ is not equivalent to the original equation $y = x^2 + 1$, so the graph of the equation $y = x^2 + 1$ is **not symmetric with respect to the origin**.

> The graph of the equation $y = x^2 + 1$ is **symmetric with respect to the $y$-axis**.

**Solution (b):**

Replace $x$ with $-x$.                                              $y = (-x)^3 + 1$

Simplify.                                                                $y = -x^3 + 1$

The resulting equation $y = -x^3 + 1$ is not equivalent to the original equation $y = x^3 + 1$. Therefore, the graph of the equation $y = x^3 + 1$ is **not symmetric with respect to the $y$-axis**.

Replace $y$ with $-y$.                                             $(-y) = x^3 + 1$

Simplify.                                                               $y = -x^3 - 1$

The resulting equation $y = -x^3 - 1$ is not equivalent to the original equation $y = x^3 + 1$. Therefore, the graph of the equation $y = x^3 + 1$ is **not symmetric with respect to the $x$-axis**.

Replace $x$ with $-x$ and $y$ with $-y$.           $(-y) = (-x)^3 + 1$

Simplify.                                                               $-y = -x^3 + 1$

                                                                          $y = x^3 - 1$

The resulting equation $y = x^3 - 1$ is not equivalent to the original equation $y = x^3 + 1$. Therefore, the graph of the equation $y = x^3 + 1$ is **not symmetric with respect to the origin**.

> The graph of the equation $y = x^3 + 1$ exhibits **no symmetry**.

■ **YOUR TURN** Determine the symmetry (if any) for $x = y^2 - 1$.

### EXAMPLE 6   Using Intercepts and Symmetry as Graphing Aids

For the equation $x^2 + y^2 = 25$, use intercepts and symmetry to help you graph the equation using the point-plotting technique.

**Solution:**

STEP 1 **Find the intercepts.**

For the $x$-intercepts, let $y = 0$.          $x^2 + 0^2 = 25$

Solve for $x$.          $x = \pm 5$

The two $x$-intercepts correspond to the points $(-5, 0)$ and $(5, 0)$.

For the $y$-intercepts, let $x = 0$.          $0^2 + y^2 = 25$

Solve for $y$.          $y = \pm 5$

The two $y$-intercepts correspond to the points $(0, -5)$ and $(0, 5)$.

STEP 2 **Identify the points on the graph corresponding to the intercepts.**

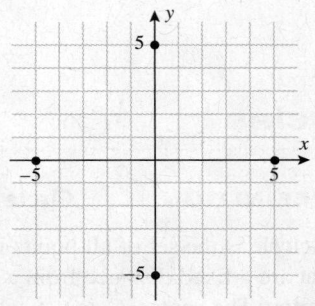

STEP 3 **Test for symmetry with respect to the $y$-axis, $x$-axis, and origin.**

Test for symmetry with respect to the $y$-axis.

Replace $x$ with $-x$.          $(-x)^2 + y^2 = 25$

Simplify.          $x^2 + y^2 = 25$

The resulting equation is equivalent to the original, so the graph of $x^2 + y^2 = 25$ is **symmetric with respect to the $y$-axis.**

Test for symmetry with respect to the $x$-axis.

Replace $y$ with $-y$.          $x^2 + (-y)^2 = 25$

Simplify.          $x^2 + y^2 = 25$

The resulting equation is equivalent to the original, so the graph of $x^2 + y^2 = 25$ is **symmetric with respect to the $x$-axis.**

Test for symmetry with respect to the **origin.**

Replace $x$ with $-x$ and $y$ with $-y$.          $(-x)^2 + (-y)^2 = 25$

Simplify.          $x^2 + y^2 = 25$

The resulting equation is equivalent to the original, so the graph of $x^2 + y^2 = 25$ is **symmetric with respect to the origin.**

*Technology Tip*

To enter the graph of $x^2 + y^2 = 25$, solve for $y$ first. The graphs of
$y_1 = \sqrt{25 - x^2}$ and
$y_2 = -\sqrt{25 - x^2}$ are shown.

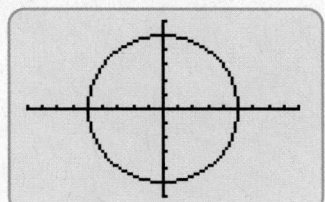

We need to determine solutions to the equation on only the positive $x$- and $y$-axes and in quadrant I because of the following symmetries:

- **Symmetry with respect to the $y$-axis gives the solutions in quadrant II.**
- **Symmetry with respect to the origin gives the solutions in quadrant III.**
- **Symmetry with respect to the $x$-axis yields solutions in quadrant IV.**

Solutions to $x^2 + y^2 = 25$.

Quadrant I: (3, 4), (4, 3)

Additional points due to symmetry:

**Quadrant II: $(-3, 4)$, $(-4, 3)$**

**Quadrant III: $(-3, -4)$, $(-4, -3)$**

**Quadrant IV: $(3, -4)$, $(4, -3)$**

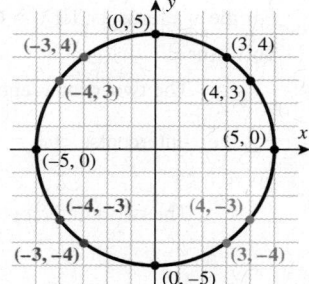

# Circles

**DEFINITION**    **Circle**

A **circle** is the set of all points in a plane that are a fixed distance from a point, the **center**. The center, $C$, is typically denoted by $(h, k)$, and the fixed distance, or **radius**, is denoted by $r$.

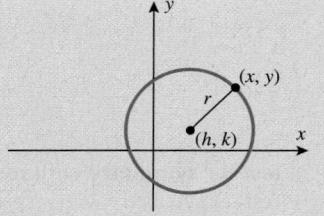

**EQUATION OF A CIRCLE**

The standard form of the equation of a **circle** with **radius** $r$ and **center** $(h, k)$ is

$$(x - h)^2 + (y - k)^2 = r^2$$

For the special case of a circle with center at the origin (0, 0), the equation simplifies to $x^2 + y^2 = r^2$.

**UNIT CIRCLE**

A circle with radius 1 and center (0, 0) is called the **unit circle**:

$$x^2 + y^2 = 1$$

The unit circle plays an important role in the study of trigonometry. Note that if $x^2 + y^2 = 0$, the radius is 0, so the "circle" is just a point.

**EXAMPLE 7   Finding the Center and Radius of a Circle**

Identify the center and radius of the given circle and graph.

$$(x - 2)^2 + (y + 1)^2 = 4$$

**Solution:**

Rewrite this equation in standard form.    $[x - 2]^2 + [y - (-1)]^2 = 2^2$

Identify $h$, $k$, and $r$ by comparing this equation with
the standard form of a circle: $(x - h)^2 + (y - k)^2 = r^2$.    $h = 2$, $k = -1$, and $r = 2$

Center $(2, -1)$ and $r = 2$

To draw the circle, label the center $(2, -1)$. Label
four additional points 2 units (the radius) away from
the center: $(4, -1)$, $(0, -1)$, $(2, 1)$, and $(2, -3)$.

Note that the easiest four points to get are those
obtained by going out from the center both
horizontally and vertically. Connect those four
points with a smooth curve.

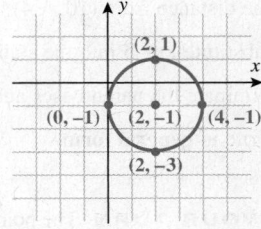

To enter the graph of
$(x - 2)^2 + (y + 1)^2 = 4$, solve for $y$
first. The graphs of

$y_1 = \sqrt{4 - (x - 2)^2} - 1$ and

$y_2 = -\sqrt{4 - (x - 2)^2} - 1$ are shown.

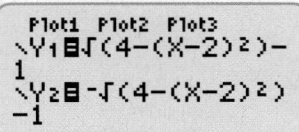

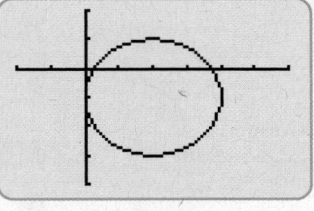

■ **YOUR TURN** Identify the center and radius of the given circle and graph.

$$(x + 1)^2 + (y + 2)^2 = 9$$

■ **Answer:** Center: $(-1, -2)$
Radius: 3

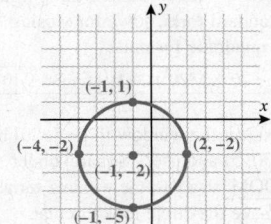

Let's change the look of the equation given in Example 7.

In Example 7, the equation of the circle was given as    $(x - 2)^2 + (y + 1)^2 = 4$

Eliminate the parentheses.    $x^2 - 4x + 4 + y^2 + 2y + 1 = 4$

Group like terms and subtract 4 from both sides.    $x^2 + y^2 - 4x + 2y + 1 = 0$

We have written the *general form* of the equation of the circle in Example 7.

> The **general form** of the **equation of a circle** is
> $$x^2 + y^2 + ax + by + c = 0$$

Suppose you are given a point that lies on a circle and the center of the circle. Can you find
the equation of the circle?

**EXAMPLE 8** **Finding the Equation of a Circle Given Its Center and One Point**

The point $(10, -4)$ lies on a circle centered at $(7, -8)$. Find the equation of the circle in general form.

**Solution:**

This circle is centered at $(7, -8)$, so its standard equation is $(x - 7)^2 + (y + 8)^2 = r^2$.

Since the point $(10, -4)$ lies on the circle, it must satisfy the equation of the circle.

Substitute $(x, y) = (10, -4)$. $\qquad\qquad\qquad (10 - 7)^2 + (-4 + 8)^2 = r^2$

Simplify. $\qquad\qquad\qquad\qquad\qquad\qquad\qquad\qquad 3^2 + 4^2 = r^2$

The distance from $(10, -4)$ to $(7, -8)$ is 5 units. $\qquad\qquad r = 5$

Substitute $r = 5$ into the standard equation. $\qquad (x - 7)^2 + (y + 8)^2 = 5^2$

Eliminate the parentheses and simplify. $\quad x^2 - 14x + 49 + y^2 + 16y + 64 = 25$

Write in **general form**. $\qquad\qquad\qquad\boxed{x^2 + y^2 - 14x + 16y + 88 = 0}$

■ **YOUR TURN** The point $(1, 11)$ lies on a circle centered at $(-5, 3)$. Find the equation of the circle in general form.

If the equation of a circle is given in general form, it must be rewritten in standard form in order to identify its center and radius. To transform equations of circles from general to standard form, complete the square on both the $x$- and $y$-variables.

 **Technology Tip**

To graph $x^2 - 8x + y^2 + 20y + 107 = 0$ without transforming it into a standard form, solve for $y$ using the quadratic formula:

$$y = \frac{-20 \pm \sqrt{20^2 - 4(1)(x^2 - 8x + 107)}}{2}$$

Next, set the window to $[-5, 30]$ by $[-30, 5]$ and use ZSquare under ZOOM to adjust the window variable to make the circle look circular. The graphs of

$$y_1 = \frac{-20 + \sqrt{20^2 - 4(x^2 - 8x + 107)}}{2}$$

and

$$y_2 = \frac{-20 - \sqrt{20^2 - 4(x^2 - 8x + 107)}}{2}$$

are shown.

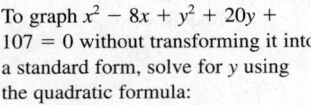

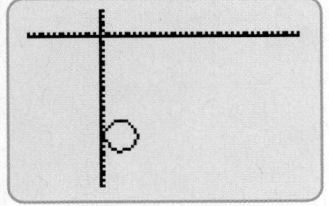

 **EXAMPLE 9** **Finding the Center and Radius of a Circle by Completing the Square**

Find the center and radius of the circle with the equation:

$$x^2 - 8x + y^2 + 20y + 107 = 0$$

**Solution:**

Our goal is to transform this equation into standard form. $\qquad (x - h)^2 + (y - k)^2 = r^2$

Group $x$ and $y$ terms, respectively, on the left side of the equation; move constants to the right side. $\qquad (x^2 - 8x) + (y^2 + 20y) = -107$

Complete the square on both the $x$ and $y$ expressions. $\qquad (x^2 - 8x + \square) + (y^2 + 20y + \square) = -107$

Add $\left(-\frac{8}{2}\right)^2 = 16$ and $\left(\frac{20}{2}\right)^2 = 100$ to both sides.

$$(x^2 - 8x + 16) + (y^2 + 20y + 100) = -107 + 16 + 100$$

Factor the perfect squares on the left side and simplify the right side. $\qquad (x - 4)^2 + (y + 10)^2 = 9$

Write in standard form. $\qquad (x - 4)^2 + [y - (-10)]^2 = 3^2$

$\boxed{\text{The center is } (4, -10) \text{ and the radius is } 3.}$

■ **YOUR TURN** Find the center and radius of the circle with the equation:

$$x^2 + y^2 + 4x - 6y - 12 = 0$$

## SECTION 0.5 SUMMARY

Distance between two points

$$d = \sqrt{(x_2 - x_1)^2 + (y_2 - y_1)^2}$$

Midpoint of segment joining two points

$$(x_m, y_m) = \left(\frac{x_1 + x_2}{2}, \frac{y_1 + y_2}{2}\right)$$

**Intercepts**

- $x$-intercept: Let $y = 0$ and solve for $x$.
- $y$-intercept: Let $x = 0$ and solve for $y$.

**Symmetry**

- About the $x$-axis: Replace $y$ with $-y$ and the resulting equation is the same.
- About the $y$-axis: Replace $x$ with $-x$ and the resulting equation is the same.
- About the origin: Replace $x$ with $-x$ and $y$ with $-y$ and the resulting equation is the same.

**Circles**

$$(x - h)^2 + (y - k)^2 = r^2 \quad \text{center } (h, k) \text{ and radius } r$$

## SECTION 0.5 EXERCISES

### ▪ SKILLS

**In Exercises 1–12, calculate the distance between the given points, and find the midpoint of the segment joining them.**

1. $(1, 3)$ and $(5, 3)$
2. $(-2, 4)$ and $(-2, -4)$
3. $(-1, 4)$ and $(3, 0)$
4. $(-3, -1)$ and $(1, 3)$
5. $(-10, 8)$ and $(-7, -1)$
6. $(-2, 12)$ and $(7, 15)$
7. $(-3, -1)$ and $(-7, 2)$
8. $(-4, 5)$ and $(-9, -7)$
9. $(-6, -4)$ and $(-2, -8)$
10. $(0, -7)$ and $(-4, -5)$
11. $\left(-\frac{1}{2}, \frac{1}{3}\right)$ and $\left(\frac{7}{2}, \frac{10}{3}\right)$
12. $\left(\frac{1}{5}, \frac{7}{3}\right)$ and $\left(\frac{9}{5}, -\frac{2}{3}\right)$

**In Exercises 13–18, graph the equation by plotting points.**

13. $y = -3x + 2$
14. $y = 4 - x$
15. $y = x^2 - x - 2$
16. $y = x^2 - 2x + 1$
17. $x = y^2 - 1$
18. $x = |y + 1| + 2$

**In Exercises 19–24, find the $x$-intercept(s) and $y$-intercepts(s) (if any) of the graphs of the given equations.**

19. $2x - y = 6$
20. $y = 4x^2 - 1$
21. $y = \sqrt{x - 4}$
22. $y = \dfrac{x^2 - x - 12}{x}$
23. $4x^2 + y^2 = 16$
24. $x^2 - y^2 = 9$

**In Exercises 25–30, test algebraically to determine whether the equation's graph is symmetric with respect to the $x$-axis, $y$-axis, or origin.**

25. $x = y^2 + 4$
26. $y = x^5 + 1$
27. $x = |y|$
28. $x^2 + 2y^2 = 30$
29. $y = x^{2/3}$
30. $xy = 1$

**In Exercises 31–36, plot the graph of the given equation.**

31. $y = x^2 - 1$
32. $x = y^2 + 1$
33. $y = \dfrac{1}{x}$
34. $|x| = |y|$
35. $x^2 - y^2 = 16$
36. $\dfrac{x^2}{4} + \dfrac{y^2}{9} = 1$

**In Exercises 37–44, write the equation of the circle in standard form.**

**37.** Center $(5, 7)$
$r = 9$

**38.** Center $(2, 8)$
$r = 6$

**39.** Center $(-11, 12)$
$r = 13$

**40.** Center $(6, -7)$
$r = 8$

**41.** Center $(5, -3)$
$r = 2\sqrt{3}$

**42.** Center $(-4, -1)$
$r = 3\sqrt{5}$

**43.** Center $\left(\frac{2}{3}, -\frac{3}{5}\right)$
$r = \frac{1}{4}$

**44.** Center $\left(-\frac{1}{3}, -\frac{2}{7}\right)$
$r = \frac{2}{5}$

**In Exercises 45–50, state the center and radius of the circle with the given equations.**

**45.** $(x - 2)^2 + (y + 5)^2 = 49$

**46.** $(x + 3)^2 + (y - 7)^2 = 81$

**47.** $(x - 4)^2 + (y - 9)^2 = 20$

**48.** $(x + 1)^2 + (y + 2)^2 = 8$

**49.** $\left(x - \frac{2}{5}\right)^2 + \left(y - \frac{1}{7}\right)^2 = \frac{4}{9}$

**50.** $\left(x - \frac{1}{2}\right)^2 + \left(y - \frac{1}{3}\right)^2 = \frac{9}{25}$

**In Exercises 51–60, find the center and radius of each circle.**

**51.** $x^2 + y^2 - 10x - 14y - 7 = 0$

**52.** $x^2 + y^2 - 4x - 16y + 32 = 0$

**53.** $x^2 + y^2 - 2x - 6y + 1 = 0$

**54.** $x^2 + y^2 - 8x - 6y + 21 = 0$

**55.** $x^2 + y^2 - 10x + 6y + 22 = 0$

**56.** $x^2 + y^2 + 8x + 2y - 28 = 0$

**57.** $x^2 + y^2 - 6x - 4y + 1 = 0$

**58.** $x^2 + y^2 - 2x - 10y + 2 = 0$

**59.** $x^2 + y^2 - x + y + \frac{1}{4} = 0$

**60.** $x^2 + y^2 - \frac{x}{2} - \frac{3y}{2} + \frac{3}{8} = 0$

■ **APPLICATIONS**

**In Exercises 61–62, refer to the following:**

It is often useful to display data in visual form by plotting the data as a set of points. This provides a graphical display between the two variables. The following table contains data on the average monthly price of gasoline.

**U.S. All Grades Conventional Retail Gasoline Prices, 1994–2010 (Dollars per Gallon)**

| YEAR | JAN | FEB | MAR | APR | MAY | JUN | JUL | AUG | SEP | OCT | NOV | DEC |
|------|------|------|------|------|------|------|------|------|------|------|------|------|
| 1994 |      |      |      |      |      |      |      |      |      |      | 1.175 | 1.112 |
| 1995 | 1.107 | 1.099 | 1.099 | 1.143 | 1.213 | 1.226 | 1.189 | 1.161 | 1.148 | 1.122 | 1.098 | 1.105 |
| 1996 | 1.123 | 1.121 | 1.169 | 1.259 | 1.302 | 1.282 | 1.254 | 1.238 | 1.238 | 1.243 | 1.273 | 1.273 |
| 1997 | 1.270 | 1.263 | 1.237 | 1.228 | 1.229 | 1.227 | 1.206 | 1.250 | 1.254 | 1.222 | 1.198 | 1.159 |
| 1998 | 1.115 | 1.082 | 1.055 | 1.064 | 1.088 | 1.086 | 1.078 | 1.049 | 1.033 | 1.045 | 1.020 | 0.964 |
| 1999 | 0.957 | 0.940 | 1.000 | 1.137 | 1.143 | 1.134 | 1.177 | 1.237 | 1.279 | 1.271 | 1.280 | 1.302 |
| 2000 | 1.319 | 1.409 | 1.538 | 1.476 | 1.496 | 1.645 | 1.568 | 1.480 | 1.562 | 1.546 | 1.533 | 1.458 |
| 2001 | 1.467 | 1.471 | 1.423 | 1.557 | 1.689 | 1.586 | 1.381 | 1.422 | 1.539 | 1.312 | 1.177 | 1.111 |
| 2002 | 1.134 | 1.129 | 1.259 | 1.402 | 1.394 | 1.380 | 1.402 | 1.398 | 1.403 | 1.466 | 1.424 | 1.389 |
| 2003 | 1.164 | 1.622 | 1.675 | 1.557 | 1.477 | 1.489 | 1.519 | 1.625 | 1.654 | 1.551 | 1.512 | 1.488 |
| 2004 | 1.595 | 1.654 | 1.728 | 1.794 | 1.981 | 1.950 | 1.902 | 1.880 | 1.880 | 1.993 | 1.973 | 1.843 |
| 2005 | 1.852 | 1.927 | 2.102 | 2.251 | 2.155 | 2.162 | 2.287 | 2.489 | 2.907 | 2.736 | 2.265 | 2.216 |
| 2006 | 2.343 | 2.293 | 2.454 | 2.762 | 2.873 | 2.849 | 2.964 | 2.952 | 2.548 | 2.258 | 2.254 | 2.328 |
| 2007 | 2.237 | 2.276 | 2.546 | 2.831 | 3.157 | 3.067 | 2.989 | 2.821 | 2.858 | 2.838 | 3.110 | 3.032 |
| 2008 | 3.068 | 3.064 | 3.263 | 3.468 | 3.783 | 4.038 | 4.051 | 3.789 | 3.760 | 3.065 | 2.153 | 1.721 |
| 2009 | 1.821 | 1.942 | 1.987 | 2.071 | 2.289 | 2.645 | 2.530 | 2.613 | 2.530 | 2.549 | 2.665 | 2.620 |
| 2010 | 2.730 | 2.657 | 2.793 | 2.867 | 2.847 | 2.733 | 2.728 | 2.733 | 2.727 | 2.816 | 2.866 | 3.004 |

*Source:* http://www.eia.doe.gov/dnav/pet/hist/LeafHandler.ashx?n=PET&s=EMM_EPM0U_PTE_NUS_DPG&f=M

The following graph displays the data for the year 2000.

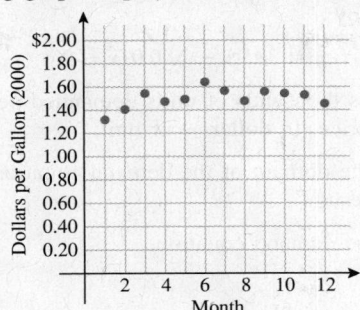

**61. Economics.** Create a graph displaying the price of gasoline for the year 2008.

**62. Economics.** Create a graph displaying the price of gasoline for the year 2009.

**63. Travel.** A retired couple who live in Columbia, South Carolina, decide to take their motor home and visit their two children who live in Atlanta and in Savannah, Georgia. Savannah is 160 miles south of Columbia and Atlanta is 215 miles west of Columbia. How far apart do the children live from each other?

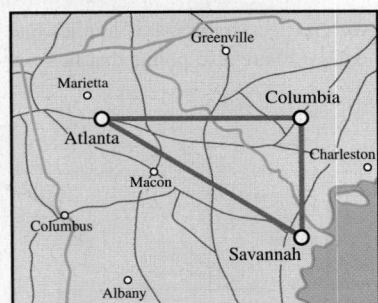

**64. Sports.** In the 1984 Orange Bowl, Doug Flutie, the 5 foot 9 inch quarterback for Boston College, shocked the world as he threw a "hail Mary" pass that was caught in the end zone with no time left on the clock, defeating the Miami Hurricanes 47–45. Although the record books have it listed as a 48-yard pass, what was the actual distance the ball was thrown? The following illustration depicts the path of the ball.

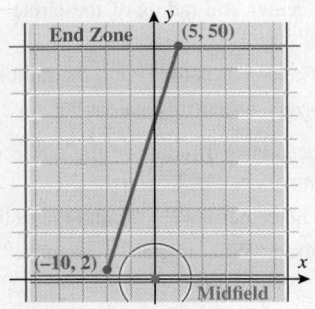

**65. NASCAR Revenue.** Action Performance, Inc., the leading seller of NASCAR merchandise, recorded $260 million in revenue in 2002 and $400 million in revenue in 2004. Calculate the midpoint to estimate the revenue Action Performance, Inc. recorded in 2003. Assume the horizontal axis represents the year and the vertical axis represents the revenue in millions.

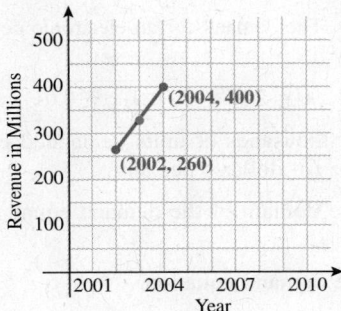

**66. Ticket Price.** In 1993 the average Miami Dolphins ticket price was $28 and in 2001 the average price was $56. Find the midpoint of the segment joining these two points to estimate the ticket price in 1997.

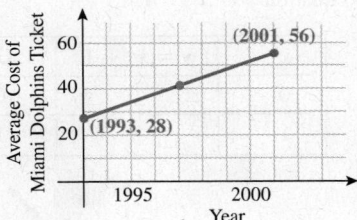

**67. Design.** A university designs its campus with a master plan of two concentric circles. All of the academic buildings are within the inner circle (so that students can get between classes in less than 10 minutes), and the outer circle contains all the dormitories, the Greek park, cafeterias, the gymnasium, and intramural fields. Assuming the center of campus is the origin, write an equation for the inner circle if the diameter is 3000 feet.

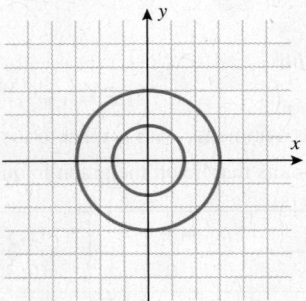

**68. Design.** Repeat Exercise 67 for the outer circle with a diameter of 6000 feet.

**69. Cell Phones.** A cellular phone tower has a reception radius of 200 miles. Assuming the tower is located at the origin, write the equation of the circle that represents the reception area.

**70. Environment.** In a state park, a fire has spread in the form of a circle. If the radius is 2 miles, write an equation for the circle.

**71. Economics.** The demand for an electronic device is modeled by

$$p = 2.95 - \sqrt{0.01x - 0.01}$$

where $x$ is thousands of units demanded per day and $p$ is the price (in dollars) per unit.

**a.** Find the domain of the demand equation. Interpret your result.

**b.** Plot the demand equation.

**72. Economics.** The demand for a new electronic game is modeled by

$$p = 39.95 - \sqrt{0.01x - 0.4}$$

where $x$ is thousands of units demanded per day and $p$ is the price (in dollars) per unit.

**a.** Find the domain of the demand equation. Interpret your result.

**b.** Plot the demand equation.

## ▪CATCH THE MISTAKE

**In Exercises 73–76, explain the mistake that is made.**

**73.** Graph the equation $y = x^2 + 1$.

**Solution:**

| $x$ | $y = x^2 + 1$ | $(x, y)$ |
|-----|-----|-----|
| 0 | 1 | (0, 1) |
| 1 | 2 | (1, 2) |

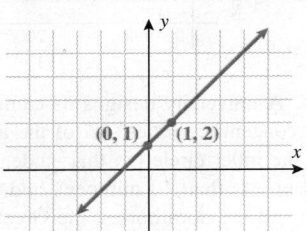

This is incorrect. What mistake was made?

**74.** Use symmetry to help you graph $x^2 = y - 1$.

**Solution:**

Replace $x$ with $-x$.          $(-x)^2 = y - 1$

Simplify.          $x^2 = y - 1$

$x^2 = y - 1$ is symmetric with respect to the $x$-axis.

Determine points that lie on the graph in quadrant I.

| $y$ | $x^2 = y - 1$ | $(x, y)$ |
|-----|-----|-----|
| 1 | 0 | (0, 1) |
| 2 | 1 | (1, 2) |
| 5 | 2 | (2, 5) |

Symmetry with respect to the $x$-axis implies that $(0, -1)$, $(1, -2)$, and $(2, -5)$ are also points that lie on the graph.

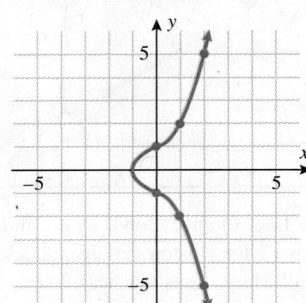

This is incorrect. What mistake was made?

**75.** Identify the center and radius of the circle with equation $(x - 4)^2 + (y + 3)^2 = 25$.

**Solution:** The center is (4, 3) and the radius is 5.

This is incorrect. What mistake was made?

**76.** Identify the center and radius of the circle with equation $(x - 2)^2 + (y + 3)^2 = 2$.

**Solution:** The center is (2, −3) and the radius is 2.

This is incorrect. What mistake was made?

■ **CONCEPTUAL**

**In Exercises 77–80, determine whether each statement is true or false.**

77. If the point $(a, b)$ lies on a graph that is symmetric about the $x$-axis, then the point $(-a, b)$ also must lie on the graph.

78. If the point $(a, b)$ lies on a graph that is symmetric about the $y$-axis, then the point $(-a, b)$ also must lie on the graph.

79. If the point $(a, -b)$ lies on a graph that is symmetric about the $x$-axis, $y$-axis, and origin, then the points $(a, b)$, $(-a, -b)$, and $(-a, b)$ must also lie on the graph.

80. Two points are all that is needed to plot the graph of an equation.

81. Describe the graph (if it exists) of
$$x^2 + y^2 + 10x - 6y + 34 = 0$$

82. Describe the graph (if it exists) of
$$x^2 + y^2 - 4x + 6y + 49 = 0$$

■ **CHALLENGE**

83. Determine whether the graph of $y = \dfrac{ax^2 + b}{cx^3}$ has any symmetry, where $a$, $b$, and $c$ are real numbers.

84. Find the intercepts of $y = (x - a)^2 - b^2$, where $a$ and $b$ are real numbers.

85. Find the equation of a circle that has a diameter with endpoints $(5, 2)$ and $(1, -6)$.

86. Find the equation of a circle that has a diameter with endpoints $(3, 0)$ and $(-1, -4)$.

87. For the equation $x^2 + y^2 + ax + by + c = 0$, specify conditions on $a$, $b$, and $c$ so that the graph is a single point.

88. For the equation $x^2 + y^2 + ax + by + c = 0$, specify conditions on $a$, $b$, and $c$ so that there is no corresponding graph.

■ **TECHNOLOGY**

**In Exercises 89–90, graph the equation using a graphing utility and state whether there is any symmetry.**

89. $y = 16.7x^4 - 3.3x^2 + 7.1$

90. $y = 0.4x^5 + 8.2x^3 - 1.3x$

**In Exercises 91 and 92, (a) with the equation of the circle in standard form, state the center and radius, and graph; (b) use the quadratic formula to solve for $y$; and (c) use a graphing utility to graph each equation found in (b). Does the graph in (a) agree with the graphs in (c)?**

91. $x^2 + y^2 - 11x + 3y - 7.19 = 0$

92. $x^2 + y^2 + 1.2x - 3.2y + 2.11 = 0$

**SKILLS OBJECTIVE**

- Graph a line.
- Calculate the slope of a line.
- Find the equation of a line using slope–intercept form.
- Find the equation of a line using point–slope form.
- Find the equation of a line that is parallel or perpendicular to a given line.

**CONCEPTUAL OBJECTIVES**

- Classify lines as increasing, decreasing, horizontal, or vertical.
- Understand slope as a rate of change.

## Graphing a Line

First-degree equations such as

$$y = -2x + 4 \qquad 3x + y = 6 \qquad y = 2 \qquad x = -3$$

have graphs that are straight lines. The first two equations given represent inclined or "slant" lines, whereas $y = 2$ represents a horizontal line and $x = -3$ represents a vertical line. One way of writing an equation of a straight line is called *general form.*

### EQUATION OF A STRAIGHT LINE: GENERAL* FORM

If $A$, $B$, and $C$ are constants and $x$ and $y$ are variables, then the equation

$$Ax + By = C$$

is in **general form** and its graph is a straight line.

*Note:* $A$ or $B$ (but not both) can be zero.

The equation $2x - y = -2$ is a first-degree equation, so its graph is a straight line. To graph this line, find the two intercepts, plot those points, and use a straight edge to draw the line.

$$2x - y = -2$$

| Intercept | $x$ | $y$ | $(x, y)$ |
|-----------|-----|-----|----------|
| $x$-intercept | $-1$ | $0$ | $(-1, 0)$ |
| $y$-intercept | $0$ | $2$ | $(0, 2)$ |

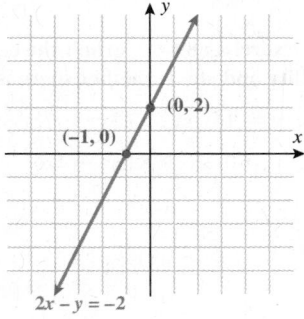

## Slope

If the graph of $2x - y = -2$ represented an incline that you were about to walk on, would you classify that incline as steep? In the language of mathematics, we use the word **slope** as a measure of steepness. Slope is the ratio of the change in $y$ over the change in $x$. An easy way to remember this is *rise over run.*

---

*Some books refer to this as standard form.

## SLOPE OF A LINE

A nonvertical line passing through two points $(x_1, y_1)$ and $(x_2, y_2)$ has slope $m$ given by the formula

$$m = \frac{y_2 - y_1}{x_2 - x_1}, \text{ where } x_1 \neq x_2 \text{ or}$$

$$m = \frac{\text{rise}}{\text{run}} = \frac{\text{vertical change}}{\text{horizontal change}}$$

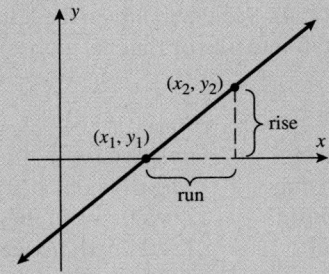

*Note:* Always start with the same point for both the *x*-coordinates and the *y*-coordinates.

**Study Tip**

To get the correct sign (±) for the slope, remember to start with the same point for both *x* and *y*.

Let's find the slope of our graph $2x - y = -2$. We'll let $(x_1, y_1) = (-2, -2)$ and $(x_2, y_2) = (1, 4)$ in the slope formula:

$$m = \frac{y_2 - y_1}{x_2 - x_1} = \frac{[4 - (-2)]}{[1 - (-2)]} = \frac{6}{3} = 2$$

Notice that if we had chosen the two intercepts $(x_1, y_1) = (0, 2)$ and $(x_2, y_2) = (-1, 0)$ instead, we still would have found the slope to be $m = 2$.

## COMMON MISTAKE

The most common mistake in calculating slope is writing the coordinates in the wrong order, which results in the slope being opposite in sign.

Find the slope of the line containing the two points $(1, 2)$ and $(3, 4)$.

**▼ CAUTION**

Interchanging the coordinates will result in a sign error in a nonzero slope.

### ✪ CORRECT

Label the points.

$$(x_1, y_1) = (1, 2)$$
$$(x_2, y_2) = (3, 4)$$

Write the slope formula.

$$m = \frac{y_2 - y_1}{x_2 - x_1}$$

Substitute the coordinates.

$$m = \frac{4 - 2}{3 - 1}$$

Simplify. $m = \frac{2}{2} = \boxed{1}$

### ✖ INCORRECT

The **ERROR** is interchanging the coordinates of the first and second points.

$$m = \frac{4 - 2}{1 - 3}$$

The calculated slope is **INCORRECT** by a negative sign.

$$m = \frac{2}{-2} = -1$$

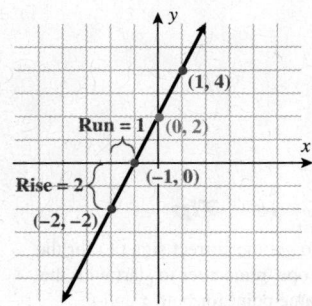

When interpreting slope, always read the graph from *left to right*. Since we have determined the slope to be 2, or $\frac{2}{1}$, we can interpret this as rising two units and running (to the right) one unit. If we start at the point $(-2, -2)$ and move two units up and one unit to the right, we end up at the $x$-intercept, $(-1, 0)$. Again, moving two units up and one unit to the right put us at the $y$-intercept, $(0, 2)$. Another rise of 2 and run of 1 take us to the point $(1, 4)$. See the figure on the left.

Lines fall into one of four categories: increasing, decreasing, horizontal, or vertical.

| Line | Slope |
|------|-------|
| **Increasing** | **Positive ($m > 0$)** |
| **Decreasing** | **Negative ($m < 0$)** |
| **Horizontal** | **Zero ($m = 0$), hence $y = b$** |
| **Vertical** | **Undefined, hence $x = a$** |

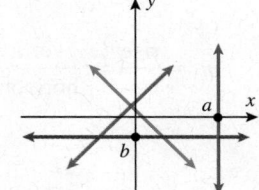

The slope of a horizontal line is 0 because the $y$-coordinates of any two points are the same. The change in $y$ in the slope formula's numerator is 0, hence $m = 0$. The slope of a vertical line is undefined because the $x$-coordinates of any two points are the same. The change in $x$ in the slope formula's denominator is zero; hence $m$ is undefined.

**EXAMPLE 1   Graph, Classify the Line, and Determine the Slope**

Sketch a line through each pair of points, classify the line as increasing, decreasing, vertical, or horizontal, and determine its slope.

**a.** $(-1, -3)$ and $(1, 1)$     **b.** $(-3, 3)$ and $(3, 1)$
**c.** $(-1, -2)$ and $(3, -2)$     **d.** $(1, -4)$ and $(1, 3)$

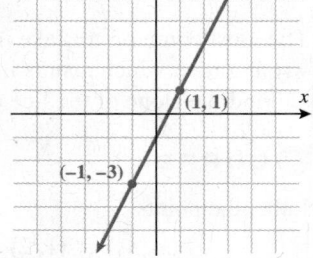

**Solution (a):**   $(-1, -3)$ and $(1, 1)$

This line is **increasing**, so its slope is positive.

$$m = \frac{1 - (-3)}{1 - (-1)} = \frac{4}{2} = \frac{2}{1} = 2.$$

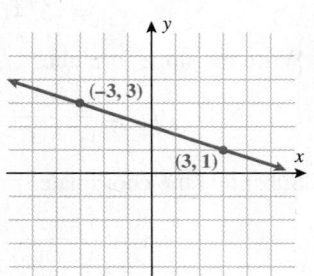

**Solution (b):**   $(-3, 3)$ and $(3, 1)$

This line is **decreasing**, so its slope is negative.

$$m = \frac{3 - 1}{-3 - 3} = -\frac{2}{6} = -\frac{1}{3}.$$

**Solution (c):**   $(-1, -2)$ and $(3, -2)$

This is a **horizontal** line, so its slope is zero.

$$m = \frac{-2 - (-2)}{3 - (-1)} = \frac{0}{4} = 0.$$

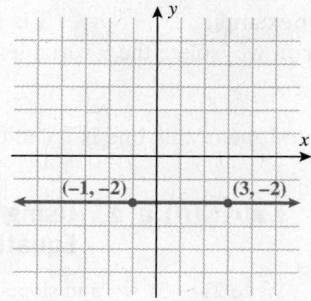

**Solution (d):**   $(1, -4)$ and $(1, 3)$

This is a **vertical** line, so its slope is undefined.

$$m = \frac{3 - (-4)}{1 - 1} = \frac{7}{0}, \text{ which is undefined.}$$

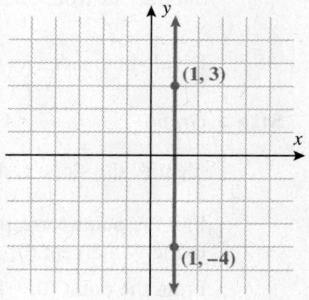

■ **YOUR TURN**   For each pair of points, classify the line that passes through them as increasing, decreasing, vertical, or horizontal, and determine its slope. Do not graph.

a. $(2, 0)$ and $(1, 5)$        b. $(-2, -3)$ and $(2, 5)$

c. $(-3, -1)$ and $(-3, 4)$     d. $(-1, 2)$ and $(3, 2)$

■ **Answer:**
a. $m = -5$, increasing
b. $m = 2$, decreasing
c. slope is undefined, vertical
d. $m = 0$, horizontal

# Equations of Lines

## Slope–Intercept Form

As mentioned earlier, the general form for an equation of a line is $Ax + By = C$. A more standard way to write an equation of a line is in slope–intercept form, because it identifies the slope and the $y$-intercept.

**EQUATION OF A STRAIGHT LINE:**
**SLOPE–INTERCEPT FORM**

The **slope–intercept form** for the equation of a nonvertical line is

$$y = mx + b$$

Its graph has slope $m$ and $y$-intercept $b$.

**Technology Tip**

To graph the equation $2x - 3y = 15$, solve for $y$ first. The graph of $y_1 = \frac{2}{3}x - 5$ is shown.

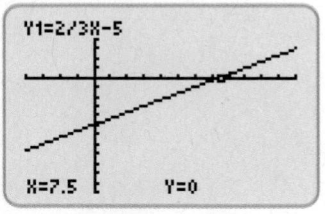

■ **Answer:** $y = \frac{3}{2}x - 6$

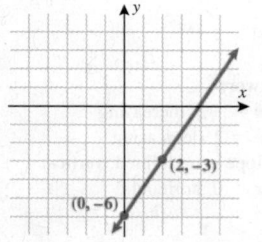

■ **Answer:** $y = -\frac{3}{2}x + 2$

For example, $2x - y = -3$ is in general form. To write this equation in **slope–intercept form**, we isolate the $y$ variable:

$$y = 2x + 3$$

The **slope** of this line is **2** and the **y-intercept** is **3**.

**EXAMPLE 2    Using Slope–Intercept Form to Graph an Equation of a Line**

Write $2x - 3y = 15$ in slope–intercept form and graph it.

**Solution:**

STEP 1 *Write in slope–intercept form.*

Subtract $2x$ from both sides.         $-3y = -2x + 15$

Divide both sides by $-3$.         $y = \frac{2}{3}x - 5$

STEP 2 *Graph.*

Identify the slope and $y$-intercept.         Slope: $m = \frac{2}{3}$   $y$-intercept: $b = -5$

Plot the point corresponding to the $y$-intercept $(0, -5)$.

From the point $(0, -5)$, rise two units and run (to the right) three units, which corresponds to the point $(3, -3)$.

Draw the line passing through the two points.

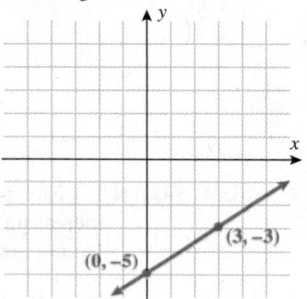

■ **YOUR TURN** Write $3x - 2y = 12$ in slope–intercept form and graph it.

Instead of starting with equations of lines and characterizing them, let us now start with particular features of a line and derive its governing equation. Suppose that you are given the $y$-intercept and the slope of a line. Using the slope–intercept form of an equation of a line, $y = mx + b$, you could find its equation.

**EXAMPLE 3    Using Slope–Intercept Form to Find the Equation of a Line**

Find the equation of a line that has slope $\frac{2}{3}$ and $y$-intercept $(0, 1)$.

**Solution:**

Write the slope–intercept form of an equation of a line.         $y = mx + b$

Label the slope.         $m = \frac{2}{3}$

Label the $y$-intercept.         $b = 1$

The equation of the line in slope–intercept form is $y = \frac{2}{3}x + 1$.

■ **YOUR TURN** Find the equation of the line that has slope $-\frac{3}{2}$ and $y$-intercept $(0, 2)$.

# Point–Slope Form

Now, suppose that the two pieces of information you are given about an equation are its slope and one point that lies on its graph. You still have enough information to write an equation of the line. Recall the formula for slope:

$$m = \frac{y_2 - y_1}{x_2 - x_1}, \quad \text{where } x_2 \neq x_1$$

We are given the slope $m$, and we know a particular point that lies on the line $(x_1, y_1)$. We refer to all other points that lie on the line as $(x, y)$. Substituting these values into the slope formula gives us

$$m = \frac{y - y_1}{x - x_1}$$

Cross multiplying yields

$$y - y_1 = m(x - x_1)$$

This is called the *point–slope form* of an equation of a line.

---

### EQUATION OF A STRAIGHT LINE: POINT-SLOPE FORM

The **point–slope form** for the equation of a line is

$$y - y_1 = m(x - x_1)$$

Its graph passes through the point $(x_1, y_1)$, and its slope is $m$.

*Note:* This formula does not hold for vertical lines since their slope is undefined.

---

### EXAMPLE 4   Using Point–Slope Form to Find the Equation of a Line

Find the equation of the line that has slope $-\frac{1}{2}$ and passes through the point $(-1, 2)$.

**Solution:**

Write the point–slope form of an equation of a line.     $y - y_1 = m(x - x_1)$

Substitute the values $m = -\frac{1}{2}$ and $(x_1, y_1) = (-1, 2)$.     $y - 2 = -\frac{1}{2}[x - (-1)]$

Distribute.     $y - 2 = -\frac{1}{2}x - \frac{1}{2}$

Isolate $y$.     $y = -\frac{1}{2}x + \frac{3}{2}$

We can also express the equation in general form $\boxed{x + 2y = 3}$.

---

■ **YOUR TURN** Find the equation of the line that has slope $\frac{1}{4}$ and passes through the point $\left(1, -\frac{1}{2}\right)$.

■ **Answer:** $y = \frac{1}{4}x - \frac{3}{4}$  or  $-x + 4y = -3$

## Finding the Equation of a Line Given Two Points

Suppose the slope of a line is not given at all. Instead, two points that lie on the line are given. If we know two points that lie on the line, then we can calculate the slope. Then, using the slope and *either* of the two points, we can derive the equation of the line.

▶ **EXAMPLE 5   Finding the Equation of a Line Given Two Points**

Find the equation of the line that passes through the points $(-2, -1)$ and $(3, 2)$.

**Solution:**

Write the equation of a line.

$$y = mx + b$$

Calculate the slope.

$$m = \frac{y_2 - y_1}{x_2 - x_1}$$

Substitute $(x_1, y_1) = (-2, -1)$ and $(x_2, y_2) = (3, 2)$.

$$m = \frac{2 - (-1)}{3 - (-2)} = \frac{3}{5}$$

Proceed using either *slope–intercept* or *point–slope* form (see Study Tip).

Substitute $\frac{3}{5}$ for the slope.

$$y = \frac{3}{5}x + b$$

Let $(x, y) = (3, 2)$. (Either point satisfies the equation.)

$$2 = \frac{3}{5}(3) + b$$

Solve for $b$.

$$b = \frac{1}{5}$$

Write the equation in slope–intercept form.

$$y = \frac{3}{5}x + \frac{1}{5}$$

Write the equation in general form.

$$\boxed{-3x + 5y = 1}$$

■ **YOUR TURN**  Find the equation of the line that passes through the points $(-1, 3)$ and $(2, -4)$.

**Study Tip**

When two points that lie on a line are given, first calculate the slope of the line, then use either point and the slope–intercept form (shown in Example 5) or the point–slope form:

$$m = \tfrac{3}{5}, (3, 2)$$
$$y - y_1 = m(x - x_1)$$
$$y - 2 = \tfrac{3}{5}(x - 3)$$
$$5y - 10 = 3(x - 3)$$
$$5y - 10 = 3x - 9$$
$$\boxed{-3x + 5y = 1}$$

■ **Answer:** $y = -\frac{7}{3}x + \frac{2}{3}$  or  $7x + 3y = 2$

## Parallel and Perpendicular Lines

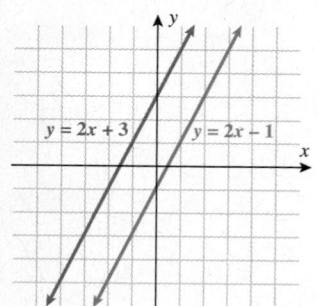

Two distinct nonintersecting lines in a plane are *parallel*. How can we tell whether the two lines in the graph on the left are parallel? Parallel lines must have the same steepness. In other words, parallel lines must have the same slope. The two lines shown on the left are parallel because they have the same slope, 2.

$y = 2x + 3$     $y = 2x - 1$

**DEFINITION**     **Parallel Lines**

Two distinct lines in a plane are **parallel** if and only if their slopes are equal.

In other words, if two lines in a plane are parallel, then their slopes are equal, and if the slopes of two lines in a plane are equal, then the lines are parallel.

| WORDS | MATH |
|---|---|
| Lines $L_1$ and $L_2$ are parallel. | $L_1 \parallel L_2$ |
| Two parallel lines have the same slope. | $m_1 = m_2$ |

### EXAMPLE 6   Finding an Equation of a Parallel Line

Find the equation of the line that passes through the point (1, 1) and is parallel to the line $y = 3x + 1$.

**Solution:**

| | |
|---|---|
| Write the slope–intercept equation of a line. | $y = mx + b$ |
| Parallel lines have equal slope. | $m = 3$ |
| Substitute the slope into the equation of the line. | $y = 3x + b$ |
| Since the line passes through (1, 1), this point must satisfy the equation. | $1 = 3(1) + b$ |
| Solve for $b$. | $b = -2$ |

The equation of the line is $\boxed{y = 3x - 2}$ .

■ **YOUR TURN**  Find the equation of the line parallel to $y = 2x - 1$ that passes through the point $(-1, 3)$.

■ **Answer:** $y = 2x + 5$

Two *perpendicular* lines form a right angle at their point of intersection. Notice the slopes of the two perpendicular lines in the figure to the right. They are $-\frac{1}{2}$ and 2, negative reciprocals of each other. It turns out that almost all perpendicular lines share this property. Horizontal ($m = 0$) and vertical ($m$ undefined) lines do not share this property.

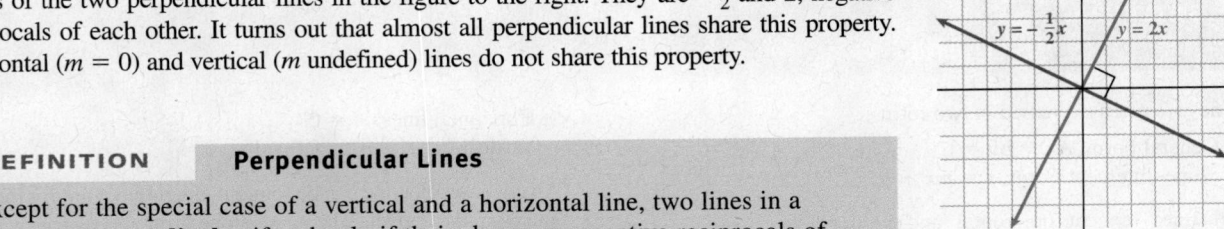

### DEFINITION   Perpendicular Lines

Except for the special case of a vertical and a horizontal line, two lines in a plane are **perpendicular** if and only if their slopes are negative reciprocals of each other.

In other words, if two lines in a plane are perpendicular, their slopes are negative reciprocals, provided their slopes are defined. Similarly, if the slopes of two lines in a plane are negative reciprocals, then the lines are perpendicular.

| WORDS | MATH |
|---|---|
| Lines $L_1$ and $L_2$ are perpendicular. | $L_1 \perp L_2$ |
| Two perpendicular lines have negative reciprocal slopes. | $m_1 = -\dfrac{1}{m_2}$   $m_1 \neq 0, m_2 \neq 0$ |

*Study Tip*

If a line has slope equal to 3, then a line perpendicular to it has slope $-\frac{1}{3}$.

**EXAMPLE 7 Finding an Equation of a Line That Is Perpendicular to Another Line**

Find the equation of the line that passes through the point $(3, 0)$ and is perpendicular to the line $y = 3x + 1$.

**Solution:**

Identify the slope of the given line $y = 3x + 1$. $\qquad m_1 = 3$

The slope of a line perpendicular to the given line is the negative reciprocal of the slope of the given line. $\qquad m_2 = -\dfrac{1}{m_1} = -\dfrac{1}{3}$

Write the equation of the line we are looking for in slope–intercept form. $\qquad y = m_2 x + b$

Substitute $m_2 = -\frac{1}{3}$ into $y = m_2 x + b$. $\qquad y = -\dfrac{1}{3}x + b$

Since the desired line passes through $(3, 0)$, this point must satisfy the equation. $\qquad 0 = -\dfrac{1}{3}(3) + b$

$$0 = -1 + b$$

Solve for $b$. $\qquad b = 1$

The equation of the line is $\boxed{y = -\frac{1}{3}x + 1}$.

■ **Answer:** $y = 2x - 7$

■ **YOUR TURN** Find the equation of the line that passes through the point $(1, -5)$ and is perpendicular to the line $y = -\frac{1}{2}x + 4$.

---

**SECTION**
# 0.6 SUMMARY

Lines are often expressed in two forms:

  General Form: $Ax + By = C$
  Slope–Intercept Form: $y = mx + b$

All lines (except horizontal and vertical) have exactly one $x$-intercept and exactly one $y$-intercept. The slope of a line is a measure of steepness.

  Slope of a line passing through $(x_1, y_1)$ and $(x_2, y_2)$:

$$m = \frac{y_2 - y_1}{x_2 - x_1} = \frac{\text{rise}}{\text{run}} \qquad x_1 \neq x_2$$

  Horizontal lines: $m = 0$
  Vertical lines: $m$ is undefined

An equation of a line can be found if either two points or the slope and a point are given. The point–slope form $y - y_1 = m(x - x_1)$ is useful when the slope and a point are given. Parallel lines have the same slope. Perpendicular lines have negative reciprocal (opposite) slopes, provided their slopes are defined.

■ SKILLS

In Exercises 1–10, find the slope of the line that passes through the given points.

**1.** (1, 3) and (2, 6)  **2.** (2, 1) and (4, 9)  **3.** (−2, 5) and (2, −3)  **4.** (−1, −4) and (4, 6)

**5.** (−7, 9) and (3, −10)  **6.** (11, −3) and (−2, 6)  **7.** (0.2, −1.7) and (3.1, 5.2)  **8.** (−2.4, 1.7) and (−5.6, −2.3)

**9.** $\left(\frac{2}{3}, -\frac{1}{4}\right)$ and $\left(\frac{5}{6}, -\frac{3}{4}\right)$  **10.** $\left(\frac{1}{2}, \frac{3}{5}\right)$ and $\left(-\frac{3}{4}, \frac{7}{5}\right)$

For each graph in Exercises 11–16, identify (by inspection) the $x$- and $y$-intercepts and slope if they exist, and classify the line as increasing, decreasing, horizontal, or vertical.

**11.**

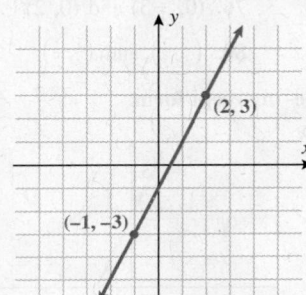

**12.**

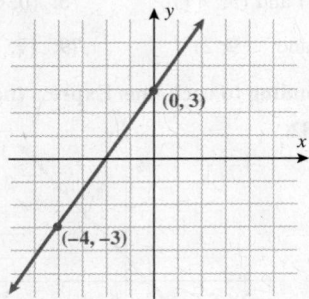

**13.**

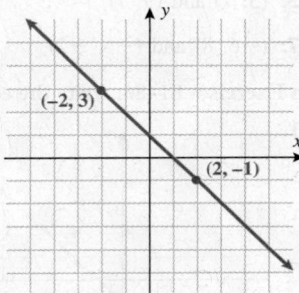

**14.**

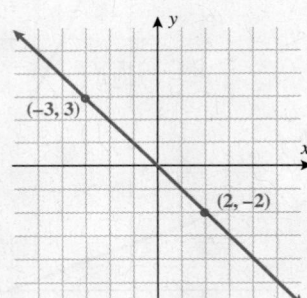

**15.**

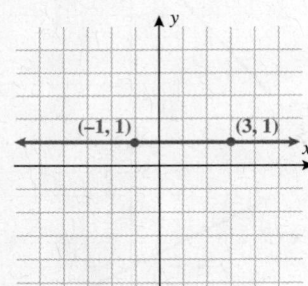

**16.**

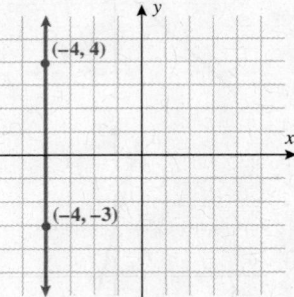

In Exercises 17–30, find the $x$- and $y$-intercepts if they exist and graph the corresponding line.

**17.** $y = 2x - 3$  **18.** $y = -3x + 2$  **19.** $y = -\frac{1}{2}x + 2$  **20.** $y = \frac{1}{3}x - 1$  **21.** $2x - 3y = 4$

**22.** $-x + y = -1$  **23.** $\frac{1}{2}x + \frac{1}{2}y = -1$  **24.** $\frac{1}{3}x - \frac{1}{4}y = \frac{1}{12}$  **25.** $x = -1$  **26.** $y = -3$

**27.** $y = 1.5$  **28.** $x = -7.5$  **29.** $x = -\frac{7}{2}$  **30.** $y = \frac{5}{3}$

In Exercises 31–42, write the equation in slope–intercept form. Identify the slope and the $y$-intercept.

**31.** $2x - 5y = 10$  **32.** $3x - 4y = 12$  **33.** $x + 3y = 6$  **34.** $x + 2y = 8$

**35.** $4x - y = 3$  **36.** $x - y = 5$  **37.** $12 = 6x + 3y$  **38.** $4 = 2x - 8y$

**39.** $0.2x - 0.3y = 0.6$  **40.** $0.4x + 0.1y = 0.3$  **41.** $\frac{1}{2}x + \frac{2}{3}y = 4$  **42.** $\frac{1}{4}x + \frac{2}{5}y = 2$

In Exercises 43–50, write the equation of the line, given the slope and intercept.

**43.** Slope: $m = 2$
 $y$-intercept: (0, 3)

**44.** Slope: $m = -2$
 $y$-intercept: (0, 1)

**45.** Slope: $m = -\frac{1}{3}$
 $y$-intercept: (0, 0)

**46.** Slope: $m = \frac{1}{2}$
 $y$-intercept: (0, −3)

**47.** Slope: $m = 0$
 $y$-intercept: (0, 2)

**48.** Slope: $m = 0$
 $y$-intercept: (0, −1.5)

**49.** Slope: undefined
 $x$-intercept: $\left(\frac{3}{2}, 0\right)$

**50.** Slope: undefined
 $x$-intercept: (−3.5, 0)

In Exercises 51–60, write an equation of the line in slope–intercept form, if possible, given the slope and a point that lies on the line.

**51.** Slope: $m = 5$
$(-1, -3)$

**52.** Slope: $m = 2$
$(1, -1)$

**53.** Slope: $m = -3$
$(-2, 2)$

**54.** Slope: $m = -1$
$(3, -4)$

**55.** Slope: $m = \frac{3}{4}$
$(1, -1)$

**56.** Slope: $m = -\frac{1}{7}$
$(-5, 3)$

**57.** Slope: $m = 0$
$(-2, 4)$

**58.** Slope: $m = 0$
$(3, -3)$

**59.** Slope: undefined
$(-1, 4)$

**60.** Slope: undefined
$(4, -1)$

In Exercises 61–80, write the equation of the line that passes through the given points. Express the equation in slope–intercept form or in the form $x = a$ or $y = b$.

**61.** $(-2, -1)$ and $(3, 2)$

**62.** $(-4, -3)$ and $(5, 1)$

**63.** $(-3, -1)$ and $(-2, -6)$

**64.** $(-5, -8)$ and $(7, -2)$

**65.** $(20, -37)$ and $(-10, -42)$

**66.** $(-8, 12)$ and $(-20, -12)$

**67.** $(-1, 4)$ and $(2, -5)$

**68.** $(-2, 3)$ and $(2, -3)$

**69.** $\left(\frac{1}{2}, \frac{3}{4}\right)$ and $\left(\frac{3}{2}, \frac{9}{4}\right)$

**70.** $\left(-\frac{2}{3}, -\frac{1}{2}\right)$ and $\left(\frac{7}{3}, \frac{1}{2}\right)$

**71.** $(3, 5)$ and $(3, -7)$

**72.** $(-5, -2)$ and $(-5, 4)$

**73.** $(3, 7)$ and $(9, 7)$

**74.** $(-2, -1)$ and $(3, -1)$

**75.** $(0, 6)$ and $(-5, 0)$

**76.** $(0, -3)$ and $(0, 2)$

**77.** $(-6, 8)$ and $(-6, -2)$

**78.** $(-9, 0)$ and $(-9, 2)$

**79.** $\left(\frac{2}{5}, -\frac{3}{4}\right)$ and $\left(\frac{2}{5}, \frac{1}{2}\right)$

**80.** $\left(\frac{1}{3}, \frac{2}{5}\right)$ and $\left(\frac{1}{3}, \frac{1}{2}\right)$

In Exercises 81–86, write the equation corresponding to each line. Express the equation in slope–intercept form.

**81.**
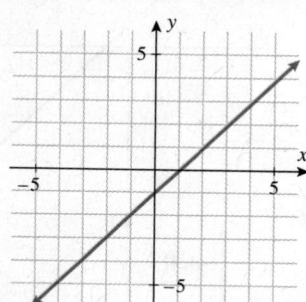

**82.**
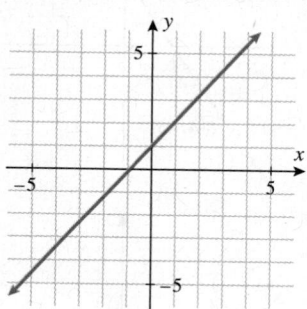

**83.**
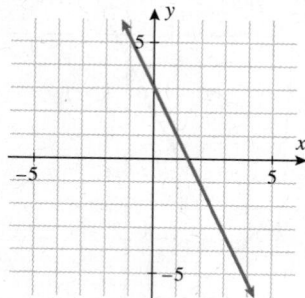

**84.**
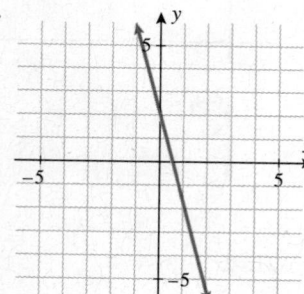

**85.**
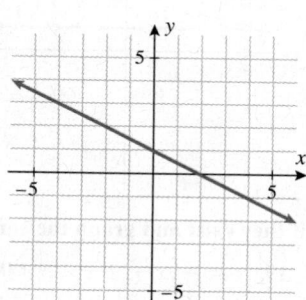

**86.**
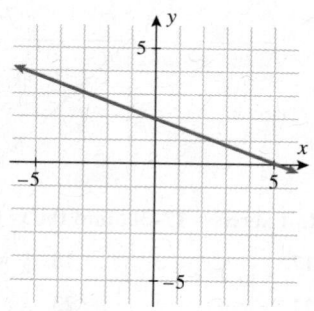

In Exercises 87–96, find the equation of the line that passes through the given point and also satisfies the additional piece of information. Express your answer in slope–intercept form, if possible.

**87.** $(-3, 1)$; parallel to the line $y = 2x - 1$

**88.** $(1, 3)$; parallel to the line $y = -x + 2$

**89.** $(0, 0)$; perpendicular to the line $2x + 3y = 12$

**90.** $(0, 6)$; perpendicular to the line $x - y = 7$

**91.** $(3, 5)$; parallel to the x-axis

**92.** $(3, 5)$; parallel to the y-axis

**93.** $(-1, 2)$; perpendicular to the y-axis

**94.** $(-1, 2)$; perpendicular to the x-axis

**95.** $(-2, -7)$; parallel to the line $\frac{1}{2}x - \frac{1}{3}y = 5$

**96.** $(1, 4)$; perpendicular to the line $-\frac{2}{3}x + \frac{3}{2}y = -2$

**97.** $\left(-\frac{2}{3}, \frac{2}{3}\right)$; perpendicular to the line $8x + 10y = -45$

**98.** $\left(\frac{6}{5}, 3\right)$; perpendicular to the line $6x + 14y = 7$

**99.** $\left(\frac{7}{2}, 4\right)$; parallel to the line $-15x + 35y = 7$

**100.** $\left(-\frac{1}{4}, -\frac{13}{9}\right)$; parallel to the line $10x + 45y = -9$

■ **APPLICATIONS**

**101. Budget: Home Improvement.** The cost of having your bathroom remodeled is the combination of material costs and labor costs. The materials (tile, grout, toilet, fixtures, etc.) cost is $1200 and the labor cost is $25 per hour. Write an equation that models the total cost $C$ of having your bathroom remodeled as a function of hours $h$. How much will the job cost if the worker estimates 32 hours?

**102. Budget: Rental Car.** The cost of a one-day car rental is the sum of the rental fee, $50, plus $0.39 per mile. Write an equation that models the total cost associated with the car rental.

**103. Budget: Monthly Driving Costs.** The monthly costs associated with driving a new Honda Accord are the monthly loan payment plus $25 every time you fill up with gasoline. If you fill up 5 times in a month, your total monthly cost is $500. How much is your loan payment?

**104. Budget: Monthly Driving Costs.** The monthly costs associated with driving a Ford Explorer are the monthly loan payment plus the cost of filling up your tank with gasoline. If you fill up 3 times in a month, your total monthly cost is $520. If you fill up 5 times in a month, your total monthly cost is $600. How much is your monthly loan, and how much does it cost every time you fill up with gasoline?

**105. Business.** The operating costs for a local business are a fixed amount of $1300 plus $3.50 per unit sold, while revenue is $7.25 per unit sold. How many units does the business have to sell in order to break even?

**106. Business.** The operating costs for a local business are a fixed amount of $12,000 plus $13.50 per unit sold, while revenue is $27.25 per unit sold. How many units does the business have to sell in order to break even?

**107. Weather: Temperature.** The National Oceanic and Atmospheric Administration (NOAA) has an online conversion chart that relates degrees Fahrenheit, °F, to degrees Celsius, °C. 77°F is equivalent to 25°C, and 68°F is equivalent to 20°C. Assuming the relationship is linear, write the equation relating degrees Celsius to degrees Fahrenheit. What temperature is the same in both degrees Celsius and degrees Fahrenheit?

**108. Weather: Temperature.** According to NOAA, a "standard day" is 15°C at sea level, and every 500-feet elevation above sea level corresponds to a 1°C temperature drop. Assuming the relationship between temperature and elevation is linear, write an equation that models this relationship. What is the expected temperature at 2500 feet on a "standard day"?

**109. Life Sciences: Height.** The average height of a man has increased over the last century. What is the rate of change in inches per year of the average height of men?

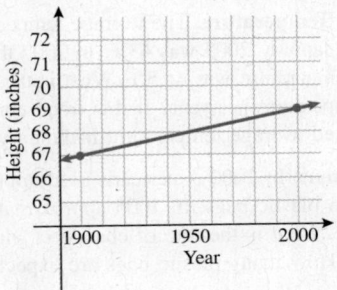

**110. Life Sciences: Height.** The average height of a woman has increased over the last century. What is the rate of change in inches per year of the average height of women?

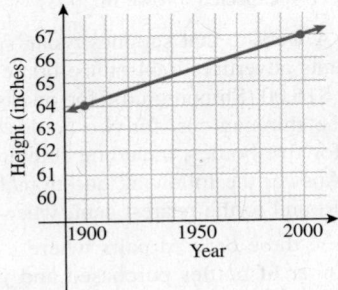

**111. Life Sciences: Weight.** The average weight of a baby born in 1900 was 6 pounds 4 ounces. In 2000 the average weight of a newborn was 6 pounds 10 ounces. What is the rate of change of birth weight in ounces per year? What do we expect babies to weigh at birth in 2040?

**112. Sports.** The fastest a man could run a mile in 1906 was 4 minutes and 30 seconds. In 1957 Don Bowden became the first American to break the 4-minute mile. Calculate the rate of change in mile speed per year.

**113. Monthly Phone Costs.** Mike's home phone plan charges a flat monthly fee plus a charge of $0.05 per minute for long-distance calls. The total monthly charge is represented by $y = 0.05x + 35$, $x \geq 0$, where $y$ is the total monthly charge and $x$ is the number of long-distance minutes used. Interpret the meaning of the $y$-intercept.

**114. Cost: Automobile.** The value of a Daewoo car is given by $y = 11,100 - 1850x$, $x \geq 0$, where $y$ is the value of the car and $x$ is the age of the car in years. Find the $x$-intercept and $y$-intercept and interpret the meaning of each.

**115. Weather: Rainfall.** The average rainfall in Norfolk, Virginia, for July was 5.2 inches in 2003. The average July rainfall for Norfolk was 3.8 inches in 2007. What is the rate of change of rainfall in inches per year? If this trend continues, what is the expected average rainfall in 2010?

**116. Weather: Temperature.** The average temperature for Boston in January 2005 was 43°F. In 2007 the average January temperature was 44.5°F. What is the rate of change of the temperature per year? If this trend continues, what is the expected average temperature in January 2010?

**117. Environment.** In 2000 Americans used approximately 380 billion plastic bags. In 2005 approximately 392 billion were used. What is the rate of change of plastic bags used per year? How many plastic bags are expected to be used in 2010?

**118. Finance: Debt.** According to the Federal Reserve, Americans individually owed $744 in revolving credit in 2004. In 2006 they owed approximately $788. What is the rate of change of the amount of revolving credit owed per year? How much were Americans expected to owe in 2008?

**119. Business.** A website that supplies Asian specialty foods to restaurants advertises a 64-ounce bottle of Hoisin Sauce for $16.00. Shipping cost for one bottle is $15.93. The shipping cost for two bottles is $19.18. The cost for five bottles, including shipping, is $111.83. Answer the following questions based on this scenario. Round to the nearest cent, when necessary.

    **a.** Write the three ordered pairs where $x$ represents the number of bottles purchased and $y$ represents the total cost (including shipping) for one, two, or five bottles purchased.

    **b.** Calculate the slope between the origin and the ordered pair that represents the purchase of one bottle of Hoisin Sauce. Explain what this amount means in terms of the sauce purchase.

    **c.** Calculate the slope between the origin and the ordered pair that represents the purchase of two bottles of Hoisin (including shipping). Explain what this amount means in terms of the sauce purchase.

    **d.** Calculate the slope between the origin and the ordered pair that represents the purchase of five bottles of Hoisin (including shipping). Explain what this amount means in terms of the sauce purchase.

**120. Business.** A website that supplies Asian specialty foods to restaurants advertises an 8-ounce bottle of Plum Sauce for $4.00, but shipping for one bottle is $14.27. The shipping cost for two bottles is $14.77. The cost for five bottles, including shipping, is $35.93. Answer the following questions based on this scenario. Round to the nearest cent, when necessary.

    **a.** Write the three ordered pairs where $x$ represents the number of bottles purchased and $y$ represents the total cost, including shipping for one, two, or five bottles purchased.

    **b.** Calculate the slope between the origin and the ordered pair that represents the purchase of one bottle of Plum Sauce. Explain what this amount means in terms of the sauce purchase.

    **c.** Calculate the slope between the origin and the ordered pair that represents the purchase of two bottles of Plum sauce (including shipping). Explain what this amount means in terms of the sauce purchase.

    **d.** Calculate the slope between the origin and the ordered pair that represents the purchase of five bottles of Plum sauce (including shipping). Explain what this amount means in terms of the sauce purchase.

# ■ CATCH THE MISTAKE

**In Exercises 121–124, explain the mistake that is made.**

**121.** Find the $x$- and $y$-intercepts of the line with equation $2x - 3y = 6$.

**Solution:**

$x$-intercept: set $x = 0$ and solve for $y$.      $-3y = 6$
$$y = -2$$

The $x$-intercept is $(0, -2)$.

$y$-intercept: set $y = 0$ and solve for $x$.      $2x = 6$
$$x = 3$$

The $y$-intercept is $(3, 0)$.

This is incorrect. What mistake was made?

**122.** Find the slope of the line that passes through the points $(-2, 3)$ and $(4, 1)$.

**Solution:**

Write the slope formula.      $m = \dfrac{y_2 - y_1}{x_2 - x_1}$

Substitute $(-2, 3)$ and $(4, 1)$.      $m = \dfrac{1 - 3}{-2 - 4} = \dfrac{-2}{-6} = \dfrac{1}{3}$

This is incorrect. What mistake was made?

**123.** Find the slope of the line that passes through the points $(-3, 4)$ and $(-3, 7)$.

**Solution:**

Write the slope formula. $m = \dfrac{y_2 - y_1}{x_2 - x_1}$

Substitute $(-3, 4)$ and $(-3, 7)$. $m = \dfrac{-3 - (-3)}{4 - 7} = 0$

This is incorrect. What mistake was made?

**124.** Given the slope, classify the line as increasing, decreasing, horizontal, or vertical.

**a.** $m = 0$  **b.** $m$ undefined

**c.** $m = 2$  **d.** $m = -1$

**Solution:**

**a.** vertical line  **b.** horizontal line

**c.** increasing  **d.** decreasing

These are incorrect. What mistakes were made?

**CONCEPTUAL**

In Exercises 125–130, determine whether each statement is true or false.

**125.** A nonhorizontal line can have at most one $x$-intercept.

**126.** A line must have at least one $y$-intercept.

**127.** If the slopes of two lines are $-\frac{1}{5}$ and 5, then the lines are parallel.

**128.** If the slopes of two lines are $-1$ and 1, then the lines are perpendicular.

**129.** If a line has slope equal to zero, describe a line that is perpendicular to it.

**130.** If a line has no slope (undefined slope), describe a line that is parallel to it.

**CHALLENGE**

**131.** Find an equation of a line that passes through the point $(-B, A + 1)$ and is parallel to the line $Ax + By = C$. Assume that $B$ is not equal to zero.

**132.** Find an equation of a line that passes through the point $(B, A - 1)$ and is parallel to the line $Ax + By = C$. Assume that $B$ is not equal to zero.

**133.** Find an equation of a line that passes through the point $(-A, B - 1)$ and is perpendicular to the line $Ax + By = C$. Assume that $A$ and $B$ are both nonzero.

**134.** Find an equation of a line that passes through the point $(A, B + 1)$ and is perpendicular to the line $Ax + By = C$.

**135.** Show that two lines with equal slopes and different $y$-intercepts have no point in common. *Hint:* Let $y_1 = mx + b_1$ and $y_2 = mx + b_2$ with $b_1 \neq b_2$. What equation must be true for there to be a point of intersection? Show that this leads to a contradiction.

**136.** Let $y_1 = m_1 x + b_1$ and $y_2 = m_2 x + b_2$ be two nonparallel lines ($m_1 \neq m_2$). What is the $x$-coordinate of the point where they intersect?

**TECHNOLOGY**

In Exercises 137–142, determine whether the lines are parallel, perpendicular, or neither, and then graph both lines in the same viewing screen using a graphing utility to confirm your answer.

**137.** $y_1 = 17x + 22$
$y_2 = -\frac{1}{17}x - 13$

**138.** $y_1 = 0.35x + 2.7$
$y_2 = 0.35x - 1.2$

**139.** $y_1 = 0.25x + 3.3$
$y_2 = -4x + 2$

**140.** $y_1 = \frac{1}{2}x + 5$
$y_2 = 2x - 3$

**141.** $y_1 = 0.16x + 2.7$
$y_2 = 6.25x - 1.4$

**142.** $y_1 = -3.75x + 8.2$
$y_2 = \frac{4}{15}x + \frac{5}{6}$

**SKILLS OBJECTIVES**

- Develop mathematical models using direct variation.
- Develop mathematical models using inverse variation.
- Develop mathematical models using combined variation.
- Develop mathematical models using joint variation.

**CONCEPTUAL OBJECTIVES**

- Understand the difference between direct variation and inverse variation.
- Understand the difference between combined variation and joint variation.

In this section, we discuss mathematical models for different applications. Two quantities in the real world often *vary* with respect to one another. Sometimes, they vary *directly*. For example, the more money we make, the more total dollars of federal income tax we expect to pay. Sometimes, quantities vary *inversely*. For example, when interest rates on mortgages decrease, we expect the number of homes purchased to increase, because a buyer can afford "more house" with the same mortgage payment when rates are lower. In this section, we discuss quantities varying *directly*, *inversely*, or *jointly*.

## Direct Variation

When one quantity is a constant multiple of another quantity, we say that the quantities are *directly proportional* to one another.

### DIRECT VARIATION

Let $x$ and $y$ represent two quantities. The following are equivalent statements:

- $y = kx$, where $k$ is a nonzero constant.
- $y$ **varies directly** with $x$.
- $y$ is **directly proportional** to $x$.

The constant $k$ is called the **constant of variation** or the **constant of proportionality**.

In 2005 the national average cost of residential electricity was 9.53 ¢/kWh (cents per kilowatt-hour). For example, if a residence used 3400 kWh, then the bill would be $324, and if a residence used 2500 kWh, then the bill would be $238.25.

## EXAMPLE 1    Finding the Constant of Variation

In the United States, the cost of electricity is directly proportional to the number of kilowatt · hours (kWh) used. If a household in Tennessee on average used 3098 kWh per month and had an average monthly electric bill of $179.99, find a mathematical model that gives the cost of electricity in Tennessee in terms of the number of kilowatt · hours used.

**Solution:**

Write the direct variation model.

$$y = kx$$

Label the variables and constant.

$x$ = number of kWh
$y$ = cost (dollars)
$k$ = cost per kWh

Substitute the given data $x = 3098$ kWh
and $y = \$179.99$ into $y = kx$.

$$179.99 = 3098k$$

Solve for $k$.

$$k = \frac{179.99}{3098} \approx 0.05810$$

$$y = 0.0581x$$

In Tennessee the cost of electricity is $\boxed{5.81 \text{ ¢/kWh}}$.

■ **YOUR TURN**   Find a mathematical model that describes the cost of electricity in California if the cost is directly proportional to the number of kWh used and a residence that consumes 4000 kWh is billed $480.

■ **Answer:** $y = 0.12x$; the cost of electricity in California is 12 ¢/kWh.

Not all variation we see in nature is direct variation. Isometric growth, where the various parts of an organism grow in direct proportion to each other, is rare in living organisms. If organisms grew isometrically, young children would look just like adults, only smaller. In contrast, most organisms grow nonisometrically; the various parts of organisms do not increase in size in a one-to-one ratio. The relative proportions of a human body change dramatically as the human grows. Children have proportionately larger heads and shorter legs than adults. *Allometric growth* is the pattern of growth whereby different parts of the body grow at different rates with respect to each other. Some human body characteristics vary directly, and others can be mathematically modeled by *direct variation with powers*.

## DIRECT VARIATION WITH POWERS

Let $x$ and $y$ represent two quantities. The following are equivalent statements:

■ $y = kx^n$, where $k$ is a nonzero constant.
■ $y$ **varies directly with the *n*th power** of $x$.
■ $y$ **is directly proportional to the *n*th power** of $x$.

One example of direct variation with powers is height and weight of humans. Statistics show that weight (in pounds) is directly proportional to the cube of height (feet):

$$W = kH^3$$

### EXAMPLE 2  Direct Variation with Powers

The following is a personal ad:

*Single professional male (6 ft/194 lb) seeks single professional female for long-term relationship. Must be athletic, smart, like the movies and dogs, and have height and weight similarly proportioned to mine.*

Find a mathematical equation that describes the height and weight of the male who wrote the ad. How much would a 5 feet 6 inches woman weigh who has the same proportionality as the male?

**Solution:**

Write the direct variation (cube) model for height versus weight.

$$W = kH^3$$

Substitute the given data $W = 194$ and $H = 6$ into $W = kH^3$.

$$194 = k(6)^3$$

Solve for $k$.

$$k = \frac{194}{216} = 0.898148 \approx 0.90$$

$$W = 0.9H^3$$

Let $H = 5.5$ ft.

$$W = 0.9(5.5)^3 \approx 149.73$$

A woman 5 feet 6 inches tall with the same height and weight proportionality as the male would weigh approximately $\boxed{150 \text{ pounds}}$.

■**Answer:** ≈ 200 pounds

■ **YOUR TURN**  A brother and sister both have weight (pounds) that varies as the cube of height (feet) and they share the same proportionality constant. The sister is 6 feet tall and weighs 170 pounds. Her brother is 6 feet 4 inches. How much does he weigh?

# Inverse Variation

Two fundamental topics covered in economics are supply and demand. Supply is the quantity that producers are willing to sell at a given price. For example, an artist may be willing to paint and sell 5 portraits if each sells for $50, but that same artist may be willing to sell 100 portraits if each sells for $10,000. Demand is the quantity of a good that consumers are not only willing to purchase but also have the capacity to buy at a given price. For example, consumers may purchase 1 billion Big Macs from McDonald's every year, but perhaps only 1 million filets mignons are sold at Outback. There may be 1 billion people who want to buy the filet mignon but don't have the financial means to do so. Economists study the equilibrium between supply and demand.

Demand can be modeled with an *inverse variation* of price: When the price increases, demand decreases, and vice versa.

### INVERSE VARIATION

Let $x$ and $y$ represent two quantities. The following are equivalent statements:

- $y = \dfrac{k}{x}$, where $k$ is a nonzero constant.
- $y$ **varies inversely** with $x$.
- $y$ is **inversely proportional** to $x$.

The constant $k$ is called the **constant of variation** or the **constant of proportionality**.

**EXAMPLE 3   Inverse Variation**

The number of potential buyers of a house decreases as the price of the house increases (see graph on the right). If the number of potential buyers of a house in a particular city is inversely proportional to the price of the house, find a mathematical equation that describes the demand for houses as it relates to price. How many potential buyers will there be for a $2 million house?

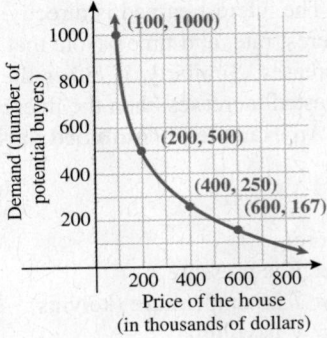

**Solution:**

| | |
|---|---|
| Write the inverse variation model. | $y = \dfrac{k}{x}$ |
| Label the variables and constant. | $x$ = price of house in thousands of dollars<br>$y$ = number of buyers |
| Select *any* point that lies on the curve. | (200, 500) |
| Substitute the given data $x = 200$ and $y = 500$ into $y = \dfrac{k}{x}$. | $500 = \dfrac{k}{200}$ |
| Solve for $k$. | $k = 200 \cdot 500 = 100{,}000$ |
| | $y = \dfrac{100{,}000}{x}$ |
| Let $x = 2000$. | $y = \dfrac{100{,}000}{2000} = 50$ |

There are only 50 potential buyers for a $2 million house in this city.

■ **YOUR TURN**   In New York City, the number of potential buyers in the housing market is inversely proportional to the price of a house. If there are 12,500 potential buyers for a $2 million condominium, how many potential buyers are there for a $5 million condominium?

■ **Answer:** 5000

Two quantities can vary inversely with the $n$th power of $x$.

> If $x$ and $y$ are related by the equation $y = \dfrac{k}{x^n}$, then we say that $y$ varies **inversely**
> with the **$n$th power of $x$**, or $y$ is inversely **proportional to the $n$th power of $x$**.

## Joint Variation and Combined Variation

We now discuss combinations of variations. When one quantity is directly proportional to the product of two or more other quantities, the variation is called **joint variation**. When direct variation and inverse variation occur at the same time, the variation is called **combined variation**.

An example of a **joint variation** is simple interest (Section 0.1), which is defined as

$$I = Prt$$

where
- $I$ is the interest in dollars.
- $P$ is the principal (initial) in dollars.
- $r$ is the interest rate (expressed in decimal form).
- $t$ is time in years.

The interest earned is directly proportional to the product of three quantities (principal, interest rate, and time). Note that if the interest rate increases, then the interest earned also increases. Similarly, if either the initial investment (principal) or the time the money is invested increases, then the interest earned also increases.

An example of **combined variation** is the combined gas law in chemistry:

$$P = k\frac{T}{V}$$

where

- $P$ is pressure.
- $T$ is temperature (kelvins).
- $V$ is volume.
- $k$ is a gas constant.

This relation states that the pressure of a gas is directly proportional to the temperature and inversely proportional to the volume containing the gas. For example, as the temperature increases, the pressure increases, but when the volume decreases, pressure increases.

As an example, the gas in the headspace of a soda bottle has a fixed volume. Therefore, as temperature increases, the pressure increases. Compare the different pressures of opening a twist-off cap on a bottle of soda that is cold versus one that is hot. The hot one feels as though it "releases more pressure."

 **EXAMPLE 4   Combined Variation**

The gas in the headspace of a soda bottle has a volume of 9.0 milliliters, pressure of 2 atm (atmospheres), and a temperature of 298 K (standard room temperature of 77°F). If the soda bottle is stored in a refrigerator, the temperature drops to approximately 279 K (42°F). What is the pressure of the gas in the headspace once the bottle is chilled?

**Solution:**

Write the combined gas law.

$$P = k\frac{T}{V}$$

Let $P = 2$ atm, $T = 298$ K, and $V = 9.0$ ml.

$$2 = k\frac{298}{9}$$

Solve for $k$.

$$k = \frac{18}{298}$$

Let $k = \frac{18}{298}$, $T = 279$, and $V = 9.0$ in $P = k\frac{T}{V}$.

$$P = \frac{18}{298} \cdot \frac{279}{9} \approx 1.87$$

Since we used the same physical units for both the chilled and room-temperature soda bottles, the pressure is in atmospheres.

$$\boxed{P = 1.87 \text{ atm}}$$

# SECTION 0.7 SUMMARY

Direct, inverse, joint, and combined variation can be used to model the relationship between two quantities. For two quantities $x$ and $y$, we say that

- $y$ is directly proportional to $x$ if $y = kx$.
- $y$ is inversely proportional to $x$ if $y = \frac{k}{x}$.

Joint variation occurs when one quantity is directly proportional to two or more quantities. Combined variation occurs when one quantity is directly proportional to one or more quantities and inversely proportional to one or more other quantities.

## SECTION 0.7 EXERCISES

■ SKILLS

In Exercises 1–16, write an equation that describes each variation. Use $k$ as the constant of variation.

1. $y$ varies directly with $x$.

2. $s$ varies directly with $t$.

3. $V$ varies directly with $x^3$.

4. $A$ varies directly with $x^2$.

5. $z$ varies directly with $m$.

6. $h$ varies directly with $\sqrt{t}$.

7. $f$ varies inversely with $\lambda$.

8. $P$ varies inversely with $r^2$.

9. $F$ varies directly with $w$ and inversely with $L$.

10. $V$ varies directly with $T$ and inversely with $P$.

11. $v$ varies directly with both $g$ and $t$.

12. $S$ varies directly with both $t$ and $d$.

13. $R$ varies inversely with both $P$ and $T$.

14. $y$ varies inversely with both $x$ and $z$.

15. $y$ is directly proportional to the square root of $x$.

16. $y$ is inversely proportional to the cube of $t$.

In Exercises 17–36, write an equation that describes each variation.

17. $d$ is directly proportional to $t$; $d = r$ when $t = 1$.

18. $F$ is directly proportional to $m$; $F = a$ when $m = 1$.

19. $V$ is directly proportional to both $l$ and $w$; $V = 6h$ when $w = 3$ and $l = 2$.

20. $A$ is directly proportional to both $b$ and $h$; $A = 10$ when $b = 5$ and $h = 4$.

21. $A$ varies directly with the square of $r$; $A = 9\pi$ when $r = 3$.

22. $V$ varies directly with the cube of $r$; $V = 36\pi$ when $r = 3$.

23. $V$ varies directly with both $h$ and $r^2$; $V = 1$ when $r = 2$ and $h = \dfrac{4}{\pi}$.

24. $W$ is directly proportional to both $R$ and the square of $I$; $W = 4$ when $R = 100$ and $I = 0.25$.

25. $V$ varies inversely with $P$; $V = 1000$ when $P = 400$.

26. $I$ varies inversely with the square of $d$; $I = 42$ when $d = 16$.

27. $F$ varies inversely with both $\lambda$ and $L$; $F = 20\pi$ when $\lambda = 1$ $\mu$m (micrometers or microns) and $L = 100$ km.

28. $y$ varies inversely with both $x$ and $z$; $y = 32$ when $x = 4$ and $z = 0.05$.

29. $t$ varies inversely with $s$; $t = 2.4$ when $s = 8$.

30. $W$ varies inversely with the square of $d$; $W = 180$ when $d = 0.2$.

31. $R$ varies inversely with the square of $I$; $R = 0.4$ when $I = 3.5$.

32. $y$ varies inversely with both $x$ and the square root of $z$; $y = 12$ when $x = 0.2$ and $z = 4$.

33. $R$ varies directly with $L$ and inversely with $A$; $R = 0.5$ when $L = 20$ and $A = 0.4$.

34. $F$ varies directly with $m$ and inversely with $d$; $F = 32$ when $m = 20$ and $d = 8$.

35. $F$ varies directly with both $m_1$ and $m_2$ and inversely with the square of $d$; $F = 20$ when $m_1 = 8$, $m_2 = 16$, and $d = 0.4$.

36. $w$ varies directly with the square root of $g$ and inversely with the square of $t$; $w = 20$ when $g = 16$ and $t = 0.5$.

■ APPLICATIONS

37. **Wages.** Jason and Valerie both work at Panera Bread and have the following paycheck information for a certain week. Find an equation that shows their wages $W$ varying directly with the number of hours worked $H$.

| EMPLOYEE | HOURS WORKED | WAGES |
|---|---|---|
| Jason | 23 | $172.50 |
| Valerie | 32 | $240.00 |

**38. Sales Tax.** The sales tax in Orange and Seminole Counties in Florida differs by only 0.5%. A new resident knows this but doesn't know which of the counties has the higher tax. The resident lives near the border of the counties and is in the market for a new plasma television and wants to purchase it in the county with the lower tax. If the tax on a pair of $40 sneakers is $2.60 in Orange County and the tax on a $12 T-shirt is $0.84 in Seminole County, write two equations: one for each county that describes the tax $T$, which is directly proportional to the purchase price $P$.

**For Exercises 39 and 40, refer to the following:**

The ratio of the speed of an object to the speed of sound determines the Mach number. Aircraft traveling at a subsonic speed (less than the speed of sound) have a Mach number less than 1. In other words, the speed of an aircraft is directly proportional to its Mach number. Aircraft traveling at a supersonic speed (greater than the speed of sound) have a Mach number greater than 1. The speed of sound at sea level is approximately 760 miles per hour.

**39. Military.** The U.S. Navy Blue Angels fly F-18 Hornets that are capable of Mach 1.7. How fast can F-18 Hornets fly at sea level?

**40. Military.** The U.S. Air Force's newest fighter aircraft is the F-22A Raptor, which is capable of Mach 1.5. How fast can a F-22A Raptor fly at sea level?

**Exercises 41 and 42 are examples of the golden ratio, or phi, a proportionality constant that appears in nature. The numerical approximate value of phi is 1.618 (from www.goldenratio.net).**

**41. Human Anatomy.** The length of your forearm $F$ (wrist to elbow) is directly proportional to the length of your hand $H$ (length from wrist to tip of middle finger). Write the equation that describes this relationship if the length of your forearm is 11 inches and the length of your hand is 6.8 inches.

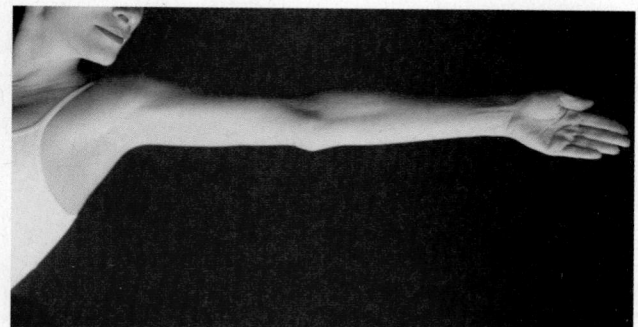

Kim Steele/Getty Images, Inc.

**42. Human Anatomy.** Each section of your index finger, from the tip to the base of the wrist, is larger than the preceding one by about the golden (Fibonacci) ratio. Find an equation that represents the ratio of each section of your finger related to the previous one if one section is eight units long and the next section is five units long.

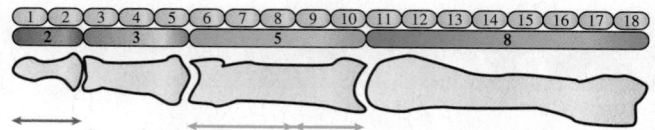

**For Exercises 43 and 44, refer to the following:**

Hooke's law in physics states that if a spring at rest (equilibrium position) has a weight attached to it, then the distance the spring stretches is directly proportional to the force (weight), according to the formula:

$$F = kx$$

where $F$ is the force in Newtons (N), $x$ is the distance stretched in meters (m), and $k$ is the spring constant (N/m).

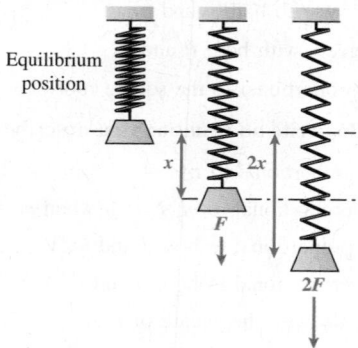

**43. Physics.** A force of 30 N will stretch the spring 10 centimeters. How far will a force of 72 N stretch the spring?

**44. Physics.** A force of 30 N will stretch the spring 10 centimeters. How much force is required to stretch the spring 18 centimeters?

**45. Business.** A cell phone company develops a pay-as-you-go cell phone plan in which the monthly cost varies directly as the number of minutes used. If the company charges $17.70 in a month when 236 minutes are used, what should the company charge for a month in which 500 minutes are used?

**46. Economics.** Demand for a product varies inversely with the price per unit of the product. Demand for the product is 10,000 units when the price is $5.75 per unit. Find the demand for the product (to the nearest hundred units) when the price is $6.50.

**47. Sales.** Levi's makes jeans in a variety of price ranges for juniors. The Flare 519 jeans sell for about $20, whereas the 646 Vintage Flare jeans sell for $300. The demand for Levi's jeans is inversely proportional to the price. If 300,000 pairs of the 519 jeans were bought, approximately how many of the Vintage Flare jeans were bought?

**48. Sales.** Levi's makes jeans in a variety of price ranges for men. The Silver Tab Baggy jeans sell for about $30, whereas the Offender jeans sell for about $160. The demand for Levi's jeans is inversely proportional to the price. If 400,000 pairs of the Silver Tab Baggy jeans were bought, approximately how many of the Offender jeans were bought?

**For Exercises 49 and 50, refer to the following:**

In physics, the inverse square law states that any physical force or energy flow is inversely proportional to the square of the distance from the source of that physical quantity. In particular, the intensity of light radiating from a point source is inversely proportional to the square of the distance from the source. Below is a table of average distances from the Sun:

| PLANET | DISTANCE TO THE SUN |
| --- | --- |
| Mercury | 58,000 km |
| Earth | 150,000 km |
| Mars | 228,000 km |

49. **Solar Radiation.** The solar radiation on Earth is approximately 1400 watts per square meter ($W/m^2$). How much solar radiation is there on Mars? Round to the nearest hundred watts per square meter.

50. **Solar Radiation.** The solar radiation on Earth is approximately 1400 watts per square meter. How much solar radiation is there on Mercury? Round to the nearest hundred watts per square meter.

51. **Investments.** Marilyn receives a $25,000 bonus from her company and decides to put the money toward a new car that she will need in 2 years. Simple interest is directly proportional to the principal and the time invested. She compares two different banks' rates on money market accounts. If she goes with Bank of America, she will earn $750 in interest, but if she goes with the Navy Federal Credit Union, she will earn $1500. What is the interest rate on money market accounts at both banks?

52. **Investments.** Connie and Alvaro sell their house and buy a fixer-upper house. They made $130,000 on the sale of their previous home. They know it will take 6 months before the general contractor can start their renovation, and they want to take advantage of a 6-month CD that pays simple interest. What is the rate of the 6-month CD if they will make $3250 in interest?

53. **Chemistry.** A gas contained in a 4-milliliter container at a temperature of 300 K has a pressure of 1 atm. If the temperature decreases to 275 K, what is the resulting pressure?

54. **Chemistry.** A gas contained in a 4-milliliter container at a temperature of 300 K has a pressure of 1 atm. If the container changes to a volume of 3 milliliters, what is the resulting pressure?

## ■ CATCH THE MISTAKE

**In Exercises 55 and 56, explain the mistake that is made.**

55. $y$ varies directly with $t$ and inversely with $x$. When $x = 4$ and $t = 2$, then $y = 1$. Find an equation that describes this variation.

**Solution:**

Write the variation equation.     $y = ktx$

Let $x = 4$, $t = 2$, and $y = 1$.     $1 = k(2)(4)$

Solve for $k$.     $k = \dfrac{1}{8}$

Substitute $k = \frac{1}{8}$ into $y = ktx$.     $y = \dfrac{1}{8}tx$

This is incorrect. What mistake was made?

56. $y$ varies directly with $t$ and the square of $x$. When $x = 4$ and $t = 1$, then $y = 8$. Find an equation that describes this variation.

**Solution:**

Write the variation equation.     $y = kt\sqrt{x}$

Let $x = 4$, $t = 1$, and $y = 8$.     $8 = k(1)\sqrt{4}$

Solve for $k$.     $k = 4$

Substitute $k = 4$ into $y = kt\sqrt{x}$.     $y = 4t\sqrt{x}$

This is incorrect. What mistake was made?

## ■ CONCEPTUAL

**In Exercises 57 and 58, determine whether each statement is true or false.**

57. The area of a triangle is directly proportional to both the base and the height of the triangle (joint variation).

58. Average speed is directly proportional to both distance and time (joint variation).

**In Exercises 59 and 60, match the variation with the graph.**

59. Inverse variation

60. Direct variation

a.

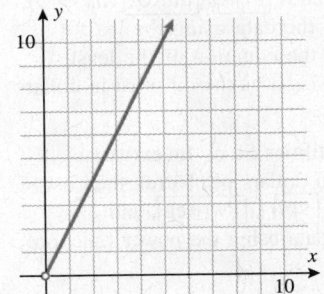

b.

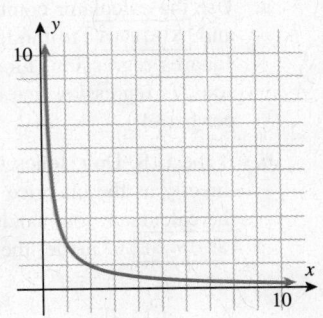

■ **CHALLENGE**

**Exercises 61 and 62 involve the theory governing laser propagation through Earth's atmosphere.**

The three parameters that help classify the strength of optical turbulence are the following:

- $C_n^2$, index of refraction structure parameter
- $k$, wave number of the laser, which is inversely proportional to the wavelength $\lambda$ of the laser:

$$k = \frac{2\pi}{\lambda}$$

- $L$, propagation distance

The variance of the irradiance of a laser, $\sigma^2$, is directly proportional to $C_n^2$, $k^{7/6}$, and $L^{11/16}$.

**61.** When $C_n^2 = 1.0 \times 10^{-13}\,\mathrm{m}^{-2/3}$, $L = 2$ km, and $\lambda = 1.55\ \mu$m, the variance of irradiance for a plane wave $\sigma_{pl}^2$ is 7.1. Find the equation that describes this variation.

**62.** When $C_n^2 = 1.0 \times 10^{-13}\,\mathrm{m}^{-2/3}$, $L = 2$ km, and $\lambda = 1.55\ \mu$m, the variance of irradiance for a spherical wave $\sigma_{sp}^2$ is 2.3. Find the equation that describes this variation.

■ **TECHNOLOGY**

**For Exercises 63–66, refer to the following:**

Data from 1995 to 2006 for oil prices in dollars per barrel, the U.S. Dow Jones Utilities Stock Index, New Privately Owned Housing, and 5-year Treasury Constant Maturity Rate are given in the table below. (These data are from Forecast Center's Historical Economic and Market Home Page at www.neatideas.com/djutil.htm.)

Use the calculator STAT EDIT commands to enter the table with $L_1$ as the oil price, $L_2$ as the utilities stock index, $L_3$ as number of housing units, and $L_4$ as the 5-year maturity rate.

| JANUARY OF EACH YEAR | OIL PRICE, $ PER BARREL | U.S. DOW JONES UTILITIES STOCK INDEX | NEW, PRIVATELY OWNED HOUSING UNITS | 5-YEAR TREASURY CONSTANT MATURITY RATE |
|---|---|---|---|---|
| 1995 | 17.99 | 193.12 | 1407 | 7.76 |
| 1996 | 18.88 | 230.85 | 1467 | 5.36 |
| 1997 | 25.17 | 232.53 | 1355 | 6.33 |
| 1998 | 16.71 | 263.29 | 1525 | 5.42 |
| 1999 | 12.47 | 302.80 | 1748 | 4.60 |
| 2000 | 27.18 | 315.14 | 1636 | 6.58 |
| 2001 | 29.58 | 372.32 | 1600 | 4.86 |
| 2002 | 19.67 | 285.71 | 1698 | 4.34 |
| 2003 | 32.94 | 207.75 | 1853 | 3.05 |
| 2004 | 32.27 | 271.94 | 1911 | 3.12 |
| 2005 | 46.84 | 343.46 | 2137 | 3.71 |
| 2006 | 65.51 | 413.84 | 2265 | 4.35 |

**63.** An increase in oil price in dollars per barrel will drive the U.S. Dow Jones Utilities Stock Index to soar.

  **a.** Use the calculator commands STAT, linReg $(ax + b)$, and STATPLOT to model the data using the least squares regression. Find the equation of the least squares regression line using $x$ as the oil price in dollars per barrel.

  **b.** If the U.S. Dow Jones Utilities Stock Index varies directly as the oil price in dollars per barrel, then use the calculator commands STAT, PwrReg, and STATPLOT to model the data using the power function.

Find the variation constant and equation of variation using $x$ as the oil price in dollars per barrel.

  **c.** Use the equations you found in (a) and (b) to calculate the stock index when the oil price hit $72.70 per barrel in September 2006. Which answer is closer to the actual stock index of 417? Round all answers to the nearest whole number.

**64.** An increase in oil price in dollars per barrel will affect the interest rates across the board—in particular, the 5-year Treasury constant maturity rate.

**a.** Use the calculator commands STAT, linReg $(ax + b)$, and STATPLOT to model the data using the least squares regression. Find the equation of the least squares regression line using $x$ as the oil price in dollars per barrel.

**b.** If the 5-year Treasury constant maturity rate varies inversely as the oil price in dollars per barrel, then use the calculator commands STAT, PwrReg, and STATPLOT to model the data using the power function. Find the variation constant and equation of variation using $x$ as the oil price in dollars per barrel.

**c.** Use the equations you found in (a) and (b) to calculate the maturity rate when the oil price hit $72.70 per barrel in September 2006. Which answer is closer to the actual maturity rate at 5.02%? Round all answers to two decimal places.

**65.** An increase in interest rates—in particular, the 5-year Treasury constant maturity rate—will affect the number of new, privately owned housing units.

**a.** Use the calculator commands STAT, linReg $(ax + b)$, and STATPLOT to model the data using the least squares regression. Find the equation of the least squares regression line using $x$ as the 5-year rate.

**b.** If the number of new privately owned housing units varies inversely as the 5-year Treasury constant maturity rate, then use the calculator commands STAT, PwrReg,

and STATPLOT to model the data using the power function. Find the variation constant and equation of variation using $x$ as the 5-year rate.

**c.** Use the equations you found in (a) and (b) to calculate the number of housing units when the maturity rate was 5.02% in September 2006. Which answer is closer to the actual number of new, privately owned housing units of 1861? Round all answers to the nearest unit.

**66.** An increase in the number of new, privately owned housing units will affect the U.S. Dow Jones Utilities Stock Index.

**a.** Use the calculator commands STAT, linReg $(ax + b)$, and STATPLOT to model the data using the least squares regression. Find the equation of the least squares regression line using $x$ as the number of housing units.

**b.** If the U.S. Dow Jones Utilities Stock Index varies directly as the number of new, privately owned housing units, then use the calculator commands STAT, PwrReg, and STATPLOT to model the data using the power function. Find the variation constant and equation of variation using $x$ as the number of housing units.

**c.** Use the equations you found in (a) and (b) to find the utilities stock index if there were 1861 new, privately owned housing units in September 2006. Which answer is closer to the actual stock index of 417? Round all answers to the nearest whole number.

**For Exercises 67 and 68, refer to the following:**

From March 2000 to March 2008, data for retail gasoline price in dollars per gallon are given in the table below. (These data are from Energy Information Administration, Official Energy Statistics from the U.S. Government at http://tonto.eia.doe.gov/oog/info/gdu/gaspump.html.) Use the calculator STAT EDIT command to enter the table below with $L_1$ as the year ($x = 1$ for year 2000) and $L_2$ as the gasoline price in dollars per gallon.

| MARCH OF EACH YEAR | 2000 | 2001 | 2002 | 2003 | 2004 | 2005 | 2006 | 2007 | 2008 |
|---|---|---|---|---|---|---|---|---|---|
| RETAIL GASOLINE PRICE $ PER GALLON | 1.517 | 1.409 | 1.249 | 1.693 | 1.736 | 2.079 | 2.425 | 2.563 | 3.244 |

**67. a.** Use the calculator commands STAT LinReg to model the data using the least squares regression. Find the equation of the least squares regression line using $x$ as the year ($x = 1$ for year 2000) and $y$ as the gasoline price in dollars per gallon. Round all answers to three decimal places.

**b.** Use the equation to determine the gasoline price in March 2006. Round all answers to three decimal places. Is the answer close to the actual price?

**c.** Use the equation to find the gasoline price in March 2009. Round all answers to three decimal places.

**68. a.** Use the calculator commands STAT PwrReg to model the data using the power function. Find the variation constant and equation of variation using $x$ as the year ($x = 1$ for year 2000) and $y$ as the gasoline price in dollars per gallon. Round all answers to three decimal places.

**b.** Use the equation to find the gasoline price in March 2006. Round all answers to three decimal places. Is the answer close to the actual price?

**c.** Use the equation to determine the gasoline price in March 2009. Round all answers to three decimal places.

**SKILLS OBJECTIVES**

- Draw a scatterplot.
- Use linear regression to determine the line of best fit associated with some data.
- Use the line of best fit to predict values of one variable from the values of another.

**CONCEPTUAL OBJECTIVES**

- Recognize positive or negative association.
- Recognize linear or nonlinear association.
- Understand what "best fit" means.

## Scatterplots

An important aspect of applied research across disciplines is to discover and understand relationships between variables, and often how to use such a relationship to predict values of one variable in terms of another. You have likely encountered such issues while watching TV, reading a magazine or newspaper, or simply talking with friends. Some *questions* include

- Is age predictive of texting speed?
- Is the level of pollution in a country related to the prevalence of asthma in that country?
- Do the ratings of car reliability necessarily increase with the price of the car?

In this section we focus on situations involving relationships between two variables $x$ and $y$, so that the experimental data gathered consists of ordered pairs $(x_1, y_1), \ldots, (x_n, y_n)$.

A first step in understanding a data set of the form $\{(x_1, y_1), \ldots, (x_n, y_n)\}$ is to create a pictorial representation of it. Identifying the first coordinates of these ordered pairs as values of an **independent variable** (or **predictor variable**) $x$ and the second coordinates as the values of a **dependent variable** (or **response variable**) $y$, we simply plot them all on a single $xy$-plane. The resulting picture is called a **scatterplot**.

### EXAMPLE 1  Drawing a Scatterplot of Olympic Decathlon Data

The 2004 Men's Olympic Decathlon consisted of the following 10 events: 100 meter, long jump, shot put, high jump, 400 meter, 110 meter hurdles, discus, pole vault, javelin throw, and 1500 meter. Actual scores are converted to a point system where points are assigned to each of these events based on performance. Events are equally weighted when converting to points. These points are then summed to obtain total scores, and, in turn, medals are assigned based on these total scores.

It would be interesting to know if certain events are more predictive of the total scores than are others. If someone does exceedingly well in the javelin throw, for example, is that person more likely to do well across all events and therefore obtain a large total points score?

Data from the Men's 2004 Olympic Decathlon are presented on the next page and were retrieved from the following Web source: **http://rss.acs.unt.edu/Rdoc/library/FactoMineR/html/decathlon.html**.

Let's consider the paired data set $\{(x, y)\}$ where $x$ = score on the 400 m and $y$ = total score.

---

*Optional Technology Required Section.

One scatterplot using the 400 m and total points information from this data set is shown in the following graph.

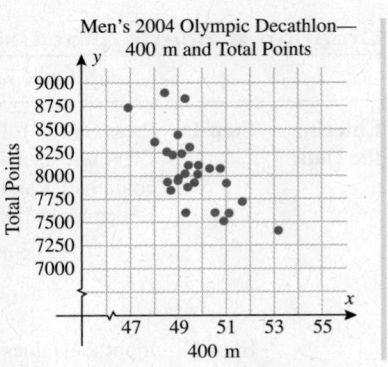

Men's 2004 Olympic Decathlon—
400 m and Total Points

Several natural questions arise: How are different pairs of these data related? Are there any discernible patterns present, and if so, how strong are they? Is there a single curve that can be used to describe the general trend present in the data? We shall answer these questions one by one in this section.

| Olympians | X100m | Long Jump | Shot-put | High Jump | X400m | X110m Hurdle | Discus | Pole Vault | Javelin | X1500m | Rank | Total Score |
|---|---|---|---|---|---|---|---|---|---|---|---|---|
| Sebrle | 10.85 | 7.84 | 16.36 | 2.12 | 48.36 | 14.05 | 48.72 | 5.00 | 70.52 | 280.01 | 1 | 8893 |
| Clay | 10.44 | 7.96 | 15.23 | 2.06 | 49.19 | 14.13 | 50.11 | 4.90 | 69.71 | 282.00 | 2 | 8820 |
| Karpov | 10.50 | 7.81 | 15.93 | 2.09 | 46.81 | 13.97 | 51.65 | 4.60 | 55.54 | 278.11 | 3 | 8725 |
| Macey | 10.89 | 7.47 | 15.73 | 2.15 | 48.97 | 14.56 | 48.34 | 4.40 | 58.46 | 265.42 | 4 | 8414 |
| Warners | 10.62 | 7.74 | 14.48 | 1.97 | 47.97 | 14.01 | 43.73 | 4.90 | 55.39 | 278.05 | 5 | 8343 |
| Zsivoczky | 10.91 | 7.14 | 15.31 | 2.12 | 49.40 | 14.95 | 45.62 | 4.70 | 63.45 | 269.54 | 6 | 8287 |
| Hernu | 10.97 | 7.19 | 14.65 | 2.03 | 48.73 | 14.25 | 44.72 | 4.80 | 57.76 | 264.35 | 7 | 8237 |
| Nool | 10.80 | 7.53 | 14.26 | 1.88 | 48.81 | 14.80 | 42.05 | 5.40 | 61.33 | 276.33 | 8 | 8235 |
| Bernard | 10.69 | 7.48 | 14.80 | 2.12 | 49.13 | 14.17 | 44.75 | 4.40 | 55.27 | 276.31 | 9 | 8225 |
| Schwarzl | 10.98 | 7.49 | 14.01 | 1.94 | 49.76 | 14.25 | 42.43 | 5.10 | 56.32 | 273.56 | 10 | 8102 |
| Pogorelov | 10.95 | 7.31 | 15.10 | 2.06 | 50.79 | 14.21 | 44.60 | 5.00 | 53.45 | 287.63 | 11 | 8084 |
| Schoenbeck | 10.90 | 7.30 | 14.77 | 1.88 | 50.30 | 14.34 | 44.41 | 5.00 | 60.89 | 278.82 | 12 | 8077 |
| Barras | 11.14 | 6.99 | 14.91 | 1.94 | 49.41 | 14.37 | 44.83 | 4.60 | 64.55 | 267.09 | 13 | 8067 |
| Smith | 10.85 | 6.81 | 15.24 | 1.91 | 49.27 | 14.01 | 49.02 | 4.20 | 61.52 | 272.74 | 14 | 8023 |
| Averyanov | 10.55 | 7.34 | 14.44 | 1.94 | 49.72 | 14.39 | 39.88 | 4.80 | 54.51 | 271.02 | 15 | 8021 |
| Ojaniemi | 10.68 | 7.50 | 14.97 | 1.94 | 49.12 | 15.01 | 40.35 | 4.60 | 59.26 | 275.71 | 16 | 8006 |
| Smirnov | 10.89 | 7.07 | 13.88 | 1.94 | 49.11 | 14.77 | 42.47 | 4.70 | 60.88 | 263.31 | 17 | 7993 |
| Qi | 11.06 | 7.34 | 13.55 | 1.97 | 49.65 | 14.78 | 45.13 | 4.50 | 60.79 | 272.63 | 18 | 7934 |
| Drews | 10.87 | 7.38 | 13.07 | 1.88 | 48.51 | 14.01 | 40.11 | 5.00 | 51.53 | 274.21 | 19 | 7926 |
| Parkhomenko | 11.14 | 6.61 | 15.69 | 2.03 | 51.04 | 14.88 | 41.90 | 4.80 | 65.82 | 277.94 | 20 | 7918 |
| Terek | 10.92 | 6.94 | 15.15 | 1.94 | 49.56 | 15.12 | 45.62 | 5.30 | 50.62 | 290.36 | 21 | 7893 |
| Gomez | 11.08 | 7.26 | 14.57 | 1.85 | 48.61 | 14.41 | 40.95 | 4.40 | 60.71 | 269.70 | 22 | 7865 |
| Turi | 11.08 | 6.91 | 13.62 | 2.03 | 51.67 | 14.26 | 39.83 | 4.80 | 59.34 | 290.01 | 23 | 7708 |
| Lorenzo | 11.10 | 7.03 | 13.22 | 1.85 | 49.34 | 15.38 | 40.22 | 4.50 | 58.36 | 263.08 | 24 | 7592 |
| Karlivans | 11.33 | 7.26 | 13.30 | 1.97 | 50.54 | 14.98 | 43.34 | 4.50 | 52.92 | 278.67 | 25 | 7583 |
| Korkizoglou | 10.86 | 7.07 | 14.81 | 1.94 | 51.16 | 14.96 | 46.07 | 4.70 | 53.05 | 317.00 | 26 | 7573 |
| Uldal | 11.23 | 6.99 | 13.53 | 1.85 | 50.95 | 15.09 | 43.01 | 4.50 | 60.00 | 281.70 | 27 | 7495 |
| Casarsa | 11.36 | 6.68 | 14.92 | 1.94 | 53.20 | 15.39 | 48.66 | 4.40 | 58.62 | 296.12 | 28 | 7404 |

Creating a scatterplot by hand can be tedious, especially for large data sets. You can also very easily lose precision and detail. Using technology to create a scatterplot is very appropriate and quite easy. Below are the procedures for how you would create the scatterplot shown in Example 1 using the TI-83+ (or TI-84) and *Excel* 2007.

## Creating a Scatterplot Using the TI-83+ (or TI-84)

| | | INSTRUCTION | SCREENSHOT |
|---|---|---|---|
| **Entering the Data** | **Step 1** | Press **STAT**, followed by **1:Edit**. . . . Clear any data already present in columns L1 and L2 so that the screen looks like the one to the right. | 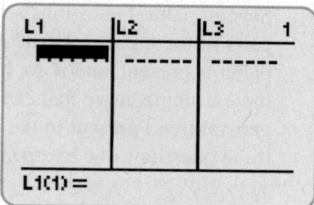 |
| | **Step 2** | Input the values of the *x*-variable (first entries in the ordered pairs) in column L1, pressing **ENTER** after each entry. Then, right arrow over to column L2 and input the values of the *y*-variable. The screen (starting from the beginning of the data set) should look like the one to the right when you are done. | 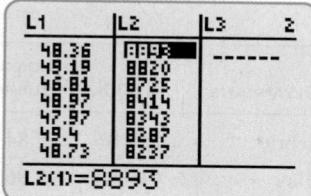 |
| **Plotting the Data** | **Step 3** | Press **Y=** and then select **Plot1** in the top row of the screen. If either **Plot2** or **Plot3** is darkened, move the cursor onto it and press **ENTER** to undarken it. The screen should look like the one to the right when you are done. | 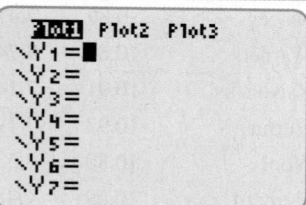 |
| | **Step 4** | Press **2nd**, followed by **Y=** (for **StatPlot**). Select 1: and modify the entries to make the screen look like the one to the right. |  |
| | **Step 5** | Press **2nd**, followed by **Y=** and make certain that both **Plot2** and **Plot3** are OFF. The screen should look like the one to the right. | 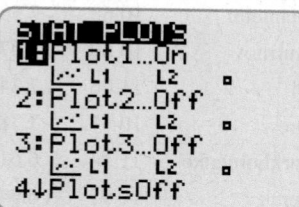 |
| | **Step 6** | Make certain the ranges for the *x* and *y* values are appropriate for the given data set. Here, we use the window shown to the right. | 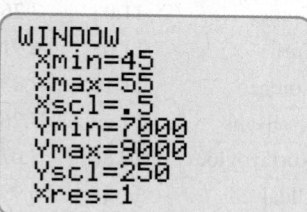 |
| | **Step 7** | Press **GRAPH** and you should get the scatterplot shown to the right. | 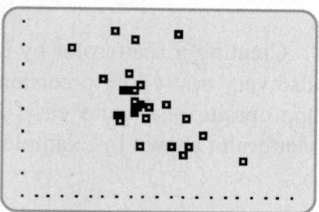 |

## Creating a Scatterplot Using *Excel* 2007

| | INSTRUCTION | SCREENSHOT |
|---|---|---|

**Entering the Data**

**Step 1**  Open a new *Excel* spreadsheet. Input the values of the *x*-variable (first entries in the ordered pairs) in column A, starting with cell 1A. Then, input the values of the *y*-variable in column B, starting with cell 1B. The screen should look like the one to the right when you are done.

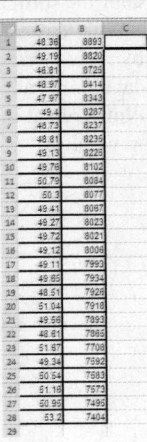

**Plotting the Data**

**Step 2**  Highlight the data. The screen should look like the one to the right when you are done.

**Step 3**  Go to the **Insert** tab and select the icon labeled **Scatter**. A window list of five possible choices pops up.

Step 2

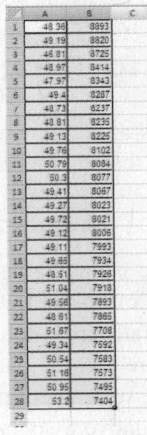

Step 3

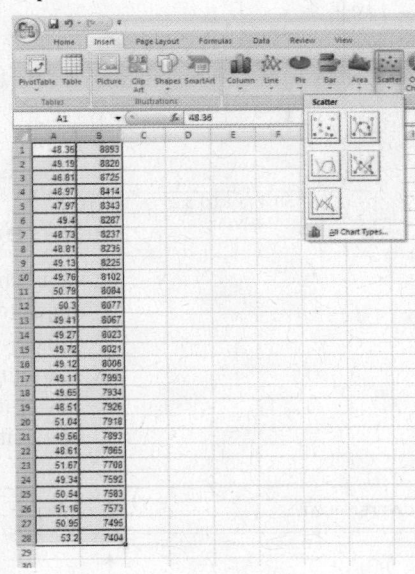

**Step 4**  Select the leftmost choice in the top row. Press **ENTER**. The scatterplot shown to the right should appear on the screen.

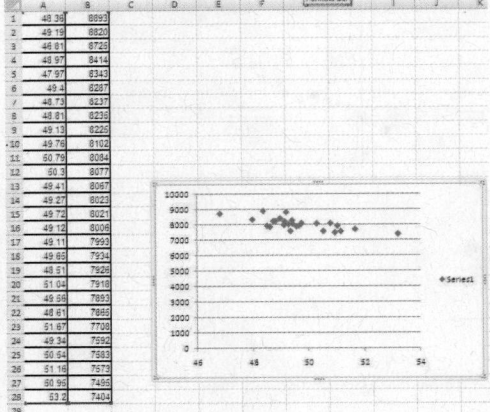

| INSTRUCTION | SCREENSHOT |
|---|---|

**Step 5** You can alter the format of the scatterplot with various bells and whistles by *right-clicking* anywhere near the data points and then selecting **Format Plot Area** at the bottom of the pop-up window.

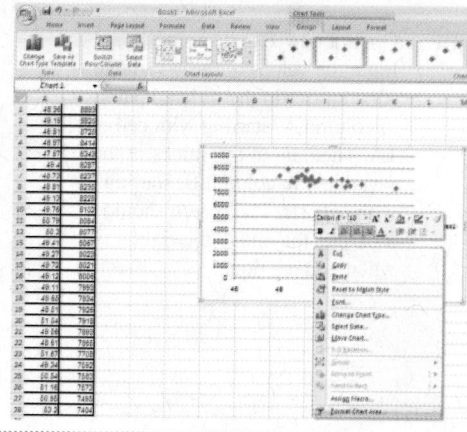

**■Answer:**

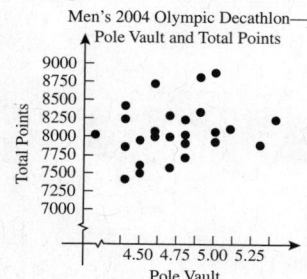

Men's 2004 Olympic Decathlon— Pole Vault and Total Points

**■ YOUR TURN** Using the data in Example 1, identify $x$ = *score on the pole vault* and $z$ = *total score*. Use technology to create a scatterplot for the data set consisting of the ordered pairs $(x, z)$.

# Identifying Patterns

While scatterplots are comprised merely of clusters of ordered pairs, patterns of various types can emerge that can provide insight into how the variables $x$ and $y$ are related.

## Direction of Association

This characteristic is analogous to the concept of slope of a line. If the cluster of points tends to rise from left to right, we say that $x$ and $y$ are **positively associated**, whereas if the cluster of points falls from left to right, we say that $x$ and $y$ are **negatively associated**. Certainly, the more closely packed together the points are to an identifiable curve, the easier it is to make such a determination. Some examples of scatterplots of varying degrees of positive and negative association are shown in the following table.

| SCATTERPLOT | DIRECTION OF ASSOCIATION | VERBAL DESCRIPTION |
|---|---|---|
| 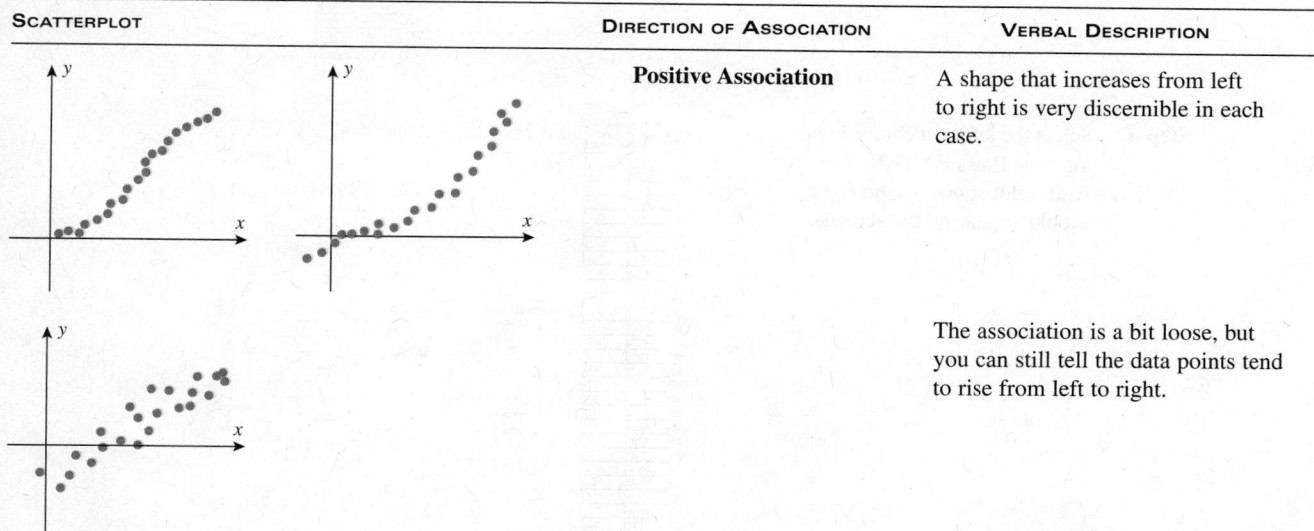 | **Positive Association** | A shape that increases from left to right is very discernible in each case. |
| | | The association is a bit loose, but you can still tell the data points tend to rise from left to right. |

| SCATTERPLOT | DIRECTION OF ASSOCIATION | VERBAL DESCRIPTION |
|---|---|---|
| | **No Association** | Haphazard scattering of points suggests neither positive nor negative association. |
| | **Negative Association** | The association is a bit loose, but you can still tell the data points tend to fall from left to right. |
| | **Negative Association** | A shape that decreases from left to right is very discernible in each case. |

## Linearity

Depending on the phenomena being studied and the actual sample being used, the data points comprising a scatterplot can conform very closely to an actual curve. If the curve is a line, we say that the relationship between $x$ and $y$ is **linear**; otherwise, we say the relationship is **nonlinear**. Some illustrative examples follow.

| SCATTERPLOT | LINEARITY | VERBAL DESCRIPTION |
|---|---|---|
| | **Linear** | Perfect linear relationship; positive association |
| | **Linear** | Perfect linear relationship; negative association |

| SCATTERPLOT | LINEARITY | VERBAL DESCRIPTION |
|---|---|---|
| 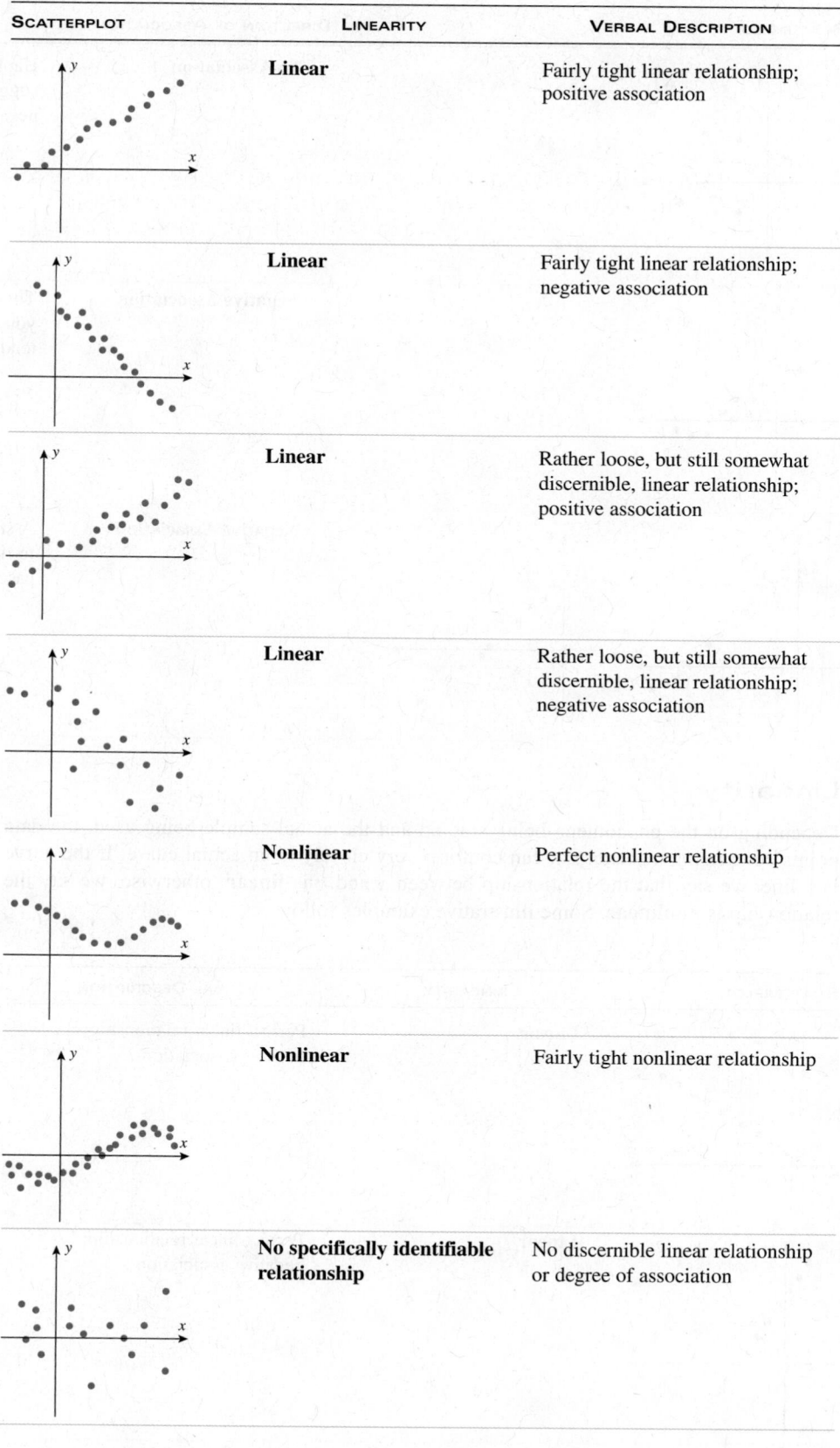 | **Linear** | Fairly tight linear relationship; positive association |
| | **Linear** | Fairly tight linear relationship; negative association |
| | **Linear** | Rather loose, but still somewhat discernible, linear relationship; positive association |
| | **Linear** | Rather loose, but still somewhat discernible, linear relationship; negative association |
| | **Nonlinear** | Perfect nonlinear relationship |
| | **Nonlinear** | Fairly tight nonlinear relationship |
| | **No specifically identifiable relationship** | No discernible linear relationship or degree of association |

### EXAMPLE 2  Describing Patterns in a Data Set

Describe the patterns present in the paired data set $(x, y)$ considered in Example 1, where $x = $ *points on the 400 m* and $y = $ *total score*. Is this intuitive?

**Solution:**

We can surmise that the variable *score on the 400 m* has a relatively strong linear, negative association with the variable *total score*. This means that as the 400 m score decreases, the total score tends to increase. A negative relationship makes sense here in that 400 m scores reflect how much time it took to complete this race. So, lower scores (less time) reflect better performance and therefore more total points.

........................................................................

■ **YOUR TURN**  Using the data in Example 1, identify $x = $ *score on the pole vault* and $z = $ *total score*. Comment on the degree of association and linearity of the scatterplot consisting of the ordered pairs $(x, z)$. Is this intuitive?

■ **Answer:** The variable *score the pole vault* has a rather weak linear, positive association with the variable *total score*. This means that as the pole vault score increases, the total score tends to increase. In this case, a positive relationship makes sense in that pole vault scores reflect the height achieved. So, higher scores (greater height) reflect better performance and therefore more total points.

## Strength of Linear Relationship

The variability in the data can render it difficult to determine if there is a linear relationship between two variables. As such, it is useful to have a way of measuring how tightly a paired data set conforms to a linear shape. This measure is called the **correlation coefficient**, $r$, and is defined by the following formula:

**DEFINITION**

For a paired data set $\{(x_1, y_1), \ldots, (x_n, y_n)\}$, the *correlation coefficient*, $r$, is defined by

$$r = \frac{n\sum xy - (\sum x)(\sum y)}{\sqrt{n\sum x^2 - (\sum x)^2} \cdot \sqrt{n\sum y^2 - (\sum y)^2}}$$

The symbol $\sum z$ is a shorthand way of writing $z_1 + \cdots + z_n$. So, for instance,

$$\sum x^2 = x_1^2 + \cdots + x_n^2.$$

This is tedious to calculate by hand but is easily computed using technology. Below are the procedures for how you would compute the correlation coefficient for the data set introduced in Example 1 using the TI-83+ (or TI-84) and *Excel* 2007.

## Computing a Correlation Coefficient Using the TI-83+ (or TI-84)

| INSTRUCTION | SCREENSHOT |
|---|---|
| **Step 1**  **Enter the data** following the procedure outlined earlier in this section. The screen should look like the one to the right. |  |

| INSTRUCTION | SCREENSHOT |
|---|---|
| **Step 2** | **Set up what will display!** In order for the desired output to display once we execute the commands to follow, we must tell the calculator to do so. As such, do the following:<br><br>i. Press **2nd**, followed by 0 to get **CATALOG**.<br>ii. Scroll down until you get to **DiagnosticOn**. Press **ENTER**. Then, this command will appear on the home screen. Press **ENTER** again. The resulting screen should look like the one to the right. | DiagnosticOn<br>　　　　　Done<br>■ |
| **Step 3** | Press **STAT**, followed by **CALC**, and then by **4:LinReg**(ax+b). The resulting screen should look like the one to the right. Press **ENTER**. | EDIT **CALC** TESTS<br>1:1-Var Stats<br>2:2-Var Stats<br>3:Med-Med<br>**4:**LinReg(ax+b)<br>5:QuadReg<br>6:CubicReg<br>7↓QuartReg |
| **Step 4** | Press **ENTER** again. After a brief moment, your screen should look like the one to the right. The value we want is in the bottom row of the screen, about $r = -0.7045$. | LinReg<br>y=ax+b<br>a=-206.9238808<br>b=18317.02944<br>r²=.4963043621<br>r=-.7044887239 |

*Note:* The other information provided will be pertinent once we define the *best fit line* in the next subsection.

## Computing a Correlation Coefficient Using *Excel* 2007

| INSTRUCTION | SCREENSHOT |
|---|---|
| **Step 1** | **Enter the data** following the procedure outlined earlier in this section. The screen should look like the one to the right. |
| **Step 2** | Select the **Formulas** tab at the top of the screen and then choose the **More Functions** within the *Function Library* grouping (on the left). The pull-down menu should be as shown to the right. |

| INSTRUCTION | SCREENSHOT |
|---|---|

**Step 3**    From here, select **Statistical**, and then from this list, scroll down and choose **CORREL**. A pop-up window should appear, as shown to the right.

**Step 4**    Enter **A1:A28** in Array 1 and **B1:B28** in Array 2, as shown to the right. Press **OK**. You will notice that the correlation coefficient appears directly beneath Array 2. In this case, $r$ is about $-0.7045$.

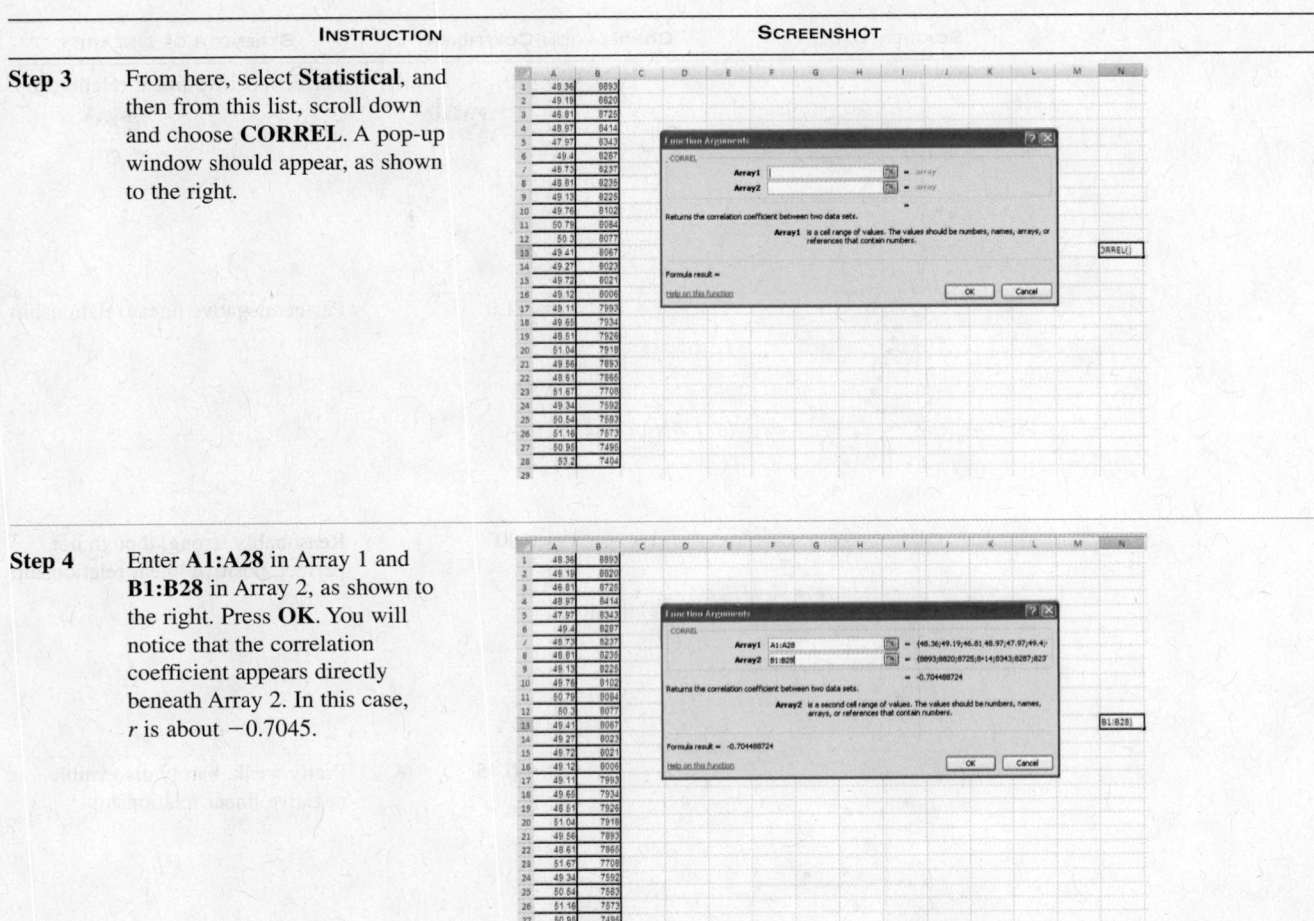

The square of the correlation coefficient is interpreted as a signed percentage of the variability among the $y$-values that is actually explained by the linear relationship, where the sign corresponds to the direction of the association. For instance, an $r$-value of $+1$ means that 100% of the variability among the $y$-values is explained by a line with positive slope; in such a case, all of the points in the data set actually lie on a single line. An $r$-value of $-1$ means the same thing, but the line has a negative slope. As the $r$-values get closer to zero, the more dispersed the points become from a line describing the pattern, so that an $r$-value very close to zero suggests no linear relationship whatsoever is discernible. The following sample of scatterplots with the associated correlation coefficients should provide you with a feel for the strength of linearity suggested by various values of $r$.

| SCATTERPLOT | CORRELATION COEFFICIENT $r$ | STRENGTH OF LINEARITY |
|---|---|---|
| | $r = 1.0$ | Perfect positive linear relationship |
| | $r = -1.0$ | Perfect negative linear relationship |
| | $r = 0.80$ | Reasonably strong, though not perfect, positive linear relationship |
| | $r = -0.45$ | Pretty weak, barely discernible, negative linear relationship |
| | $r = 0.10$ | Essentially no discernible linear relationship whatsoever |

**EXAMPLE 3  Calculating the Correlation Coefficient Associated with a Data Set**

Use technology to calculate the correlation coefficient $r$ for the paired data set $(x, y)$ considered in Example 1, where $x = points$ $on$ $the$ $400$ $m$ and $y = total$ $score$. Interpret the strength of the linear relationship.

**Solution:**

We see that using either form of technology yields $r = -0.7045$. This suggests that the data follow a relatively strong negative (i.e., negative slope) linear pattern.

■ **Answer:** The correlation coefficient is approximately $r = 0.28$. This suggests that while the data follow a positive (i.e., positive slope) pattern, the degree to which an actual line describes the trend in the data is rather weak.

■ **YOUR TURN** Using the data in Example 1, identify $x = score$ $on$ $the$ $pole$ $vault$ and $z = total$ $score$, and calculate the correlation coefficient for the data set consisting of the ordered pairs $(x, z)$ using technology. Interpret the strength of the linear relationship.

# Linear Regression

## Determining the "Best Fit" Line

Assuming that a data set follows a reasonably strong linear pattern, it is natural to ask which *single straight line* best describes this pattern. Having such a line would enable us to not only describe the relationship between the two variables $x$ and $y$ precisely, but it would also enable us to predict values of $y$ from values of $x$ not present among the points of the data set.

Consider the paired data set $(x, y)$ from Example 1, where $x = $ *points on the 400 m* and $y = $ *total score*. You learned in Section 0.6 that between any two points there is a unique line whose equation can be determined. Three such lines passing through various pairs of points in the data set are illustrated below.

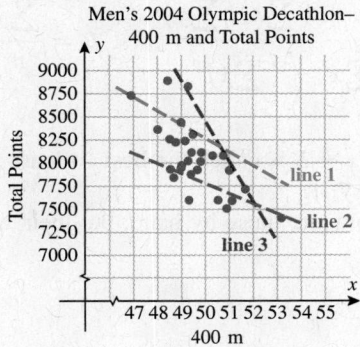

The unavoidable shortcoming of all of these lines, however, is that not all of the data points lie on a single one of them. Each has a negative slope, which *is* characteristic of the data set, and each of the lines is close to some of the data points, but not close to others. In fact, we could draw infinitely many such lines and make a similar assessment. But which one *best fits* the data?

The answer to this question depends on how you define "best." Reasonably, for the line that *best fits* the data, the error incurred in using it to describe *all* of the points in the data set should be as small as possible. The conventional approach is to define this error by summing the $n$ distances $d_i$ between the $y$-coordinates of the data points and the corresponding $y$-value on the line $y = Mx + B$ (that is, the $y$-value of the point on the line corresponding to the same $x$-value). These distances are, in effect, the error in making the approximation. This is illustrated below:

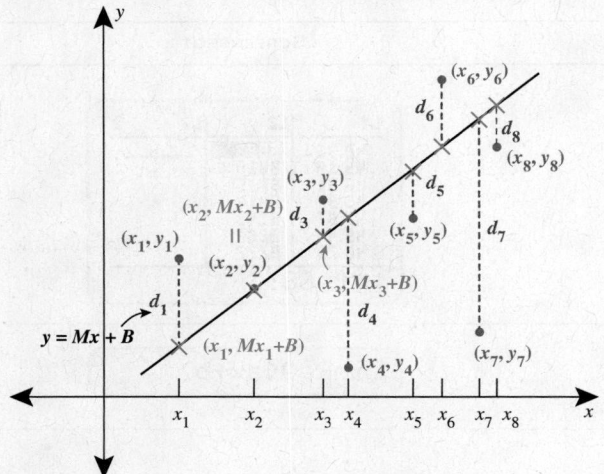

Using the distance formula, we find that

$$d_i = \sqrt{(x_i - x_i)^2 + (y_i - (Mx_i + B))^2} = |y_i - (Mx_i + B)|.$$

Note that $d_i = 0$ precisely when the data point $(x_i, y_i)$ lies directly on the line $y = Mx + B$, and that the closer $d_i$ is to 0, the closer the point $(x_i, y_i)$ is to the line $y = Mx + B$. As such, the goal is to determine the values of the slope $M$ and $y$-intercept $B$ for which the sum $d_1 + \cdots + d_n$ is as small as possible. Then, the resulting straight line $y = Mx + B$ best fits the data set $\{(x_1, y_1), \ldots, (x_n, y_n)\}$.

This is fine, in theory, but it turns out to be inconvenient to work with a sum of absolute value expressions. It is actually much more convenient to work with the *squared distances* $d_i^2$. The values of $M$ and $B$ that minimize $d_1 + \cdots + d_n$ are precisely the same as those that minimize $d_1^2 + \cdots + d_n^2$. Using calculus, it can be shown that the formulas for $M$ and $B$ are as follows:

$$M = \frac{n\sum xy - (\sum x)(\sum y)}{n\sum x^2 - (\sum x)^2}, \qquad B = \frac{\sum y}{n} - M\frac{\sum x}{n}$$

The resulting line $y = Mx + B$ is called the **best fit least-squares regression line** for the data set $\{(x_1, y_1), \ldots, (x_n, y_n)\}$.

Again, it is tedious to compute these by hand, but their values are actually produced easily using technology.

## EXAMPLE 4 Finding the Line of Best Fit by Linear Regression

Find the line of best fit (best fit least-squares regression line) for the paired data set $(x, y)$ from Example 1, where $x = $ *points on the 400 m* and $y = $ *total score,* using (a) the TI-83+ (or TI-84) and (b) *Excel* 2007.

**Solution (a):**

Determining the Best Fit Least-Squares Regression Line Using the TI-83+ (or TI-84).

| INSTRUCTION | SCREENSHOT |
|---|---|
| **STEP 1 Enter the data** following the procedure outlined earlier in this section. The screen should look like the one to the right. | L1: 48.36, 49.19, 46.81, 48.97, 47.97, 49.4, 48.73; L2: 8893, 8820, 8725, 8414, 8343, 8287, 8237; L2(1)=8893 |
| **STEP 2** Press **STAT**, followed by **CALC**, and then by **4:LinReg(ax+b)**. The resulting screen should look like the one to the right. | LinReg(ax+b) |

| INSTRUCTION | SCREENSHOT |
|---|---|

**STEP 3** For this example, the data is stored in lists L1 and L2. And, since we will want to graph our best fit line on the scatterplot, it will need to be stored as a function of *x*, say as Y1. In order to do this, proceed as follows:

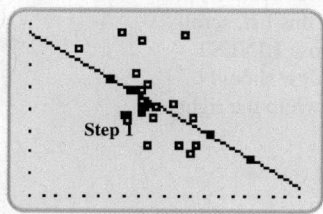

Directly next to **LinReg(ax+b)** on the home screen, we need to type the following: **L1, L2, Y1**.

Use the following key strokes: **2nd, 1, ⬚, 2nd, 2, ⬚, VARS, Y-VARS, 1:FUNCTION, Y1** The resulting screen should look like the one to the right.

---

**STEP 4** Press **ENTER**. The equation of the best fit least-squares line with the slope (labeled as *a*) and the *y*-intercept (labeled as *b*) appears on the screen as shown to the right.

```
LinReg
 y=ax+b
 a=-206.9238808
 b=18317.02944
 r²=.4963043621
 r=-.7044887239
```

So, the equation of the best fit least-squares regression line is approximately
$y = -206.9x + 18317.03$.

---

**STEP 5** In order to obtain a graph of the scatterplot *with* the best fit line from Step 4 superimposed on it, press **ZOOM**, then **9:ZoomStat**. The resulting screen should look like the one to the right.

**Solution (b):**

Determining the Best Fit Least-Squares Regression Line Using *Excel* 2007.

| INSTRUCTION | SCREENSHOT |
|---|---|

**STEP 1** **Enter the data** following the procedure outlined earlier in this section. The screen should look like the one to the right.

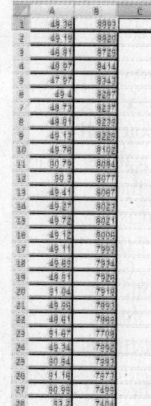

| INSTRUCTION | SCREENSHOT |
|---|---|

**STEP 2** Select the **Formulas** tab at the top of the screen and then choose the **More Functions** within the *Function Library* grouping (on the left). The pull-down menu should be as shown to the right.

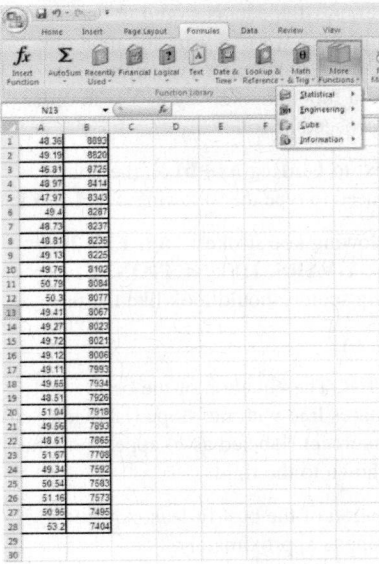

**STEP 3** From here, select **Statistical**, and then from this list, scroll down and choose **LINEST**. A pop-up window should appear, as shown to the right.

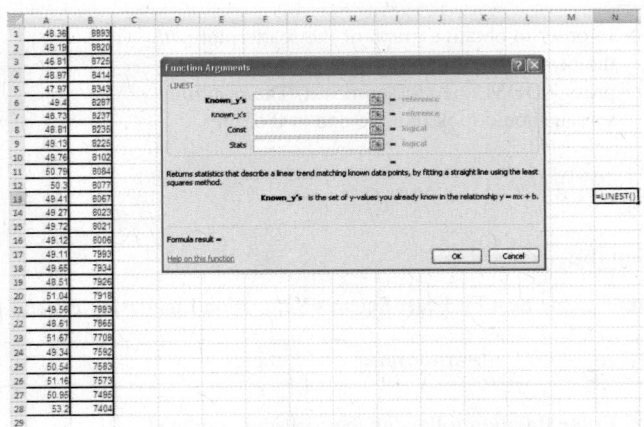

**STEP 4** Enter **B1:B28** in **Known_y's** and **A1:A28** in **Known_x's**, as shown to the right. You will notice that a set of two values occurs directly beneath the entry boxes—the output is about { −206.92, 18,317.03 }.

The first value is the slope *M*, and the second value is the *y*-intercept *B* of the best fit line.

So, the equation of the best fit least-squares regression line is approximately
$y = -206.92x + 18{,}317.03.$

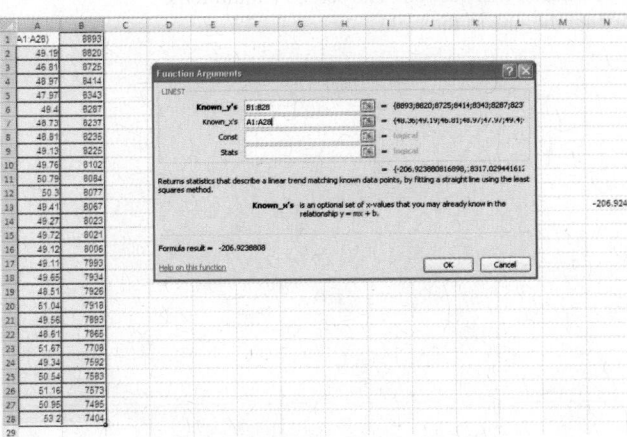

| INSTRUCTION | SCREENSHOT |
|---|---|
| **STEP 5** In order to obtain a graph of the scatterplot *with* the best fit line from Step 4 superimposed on it, construct the scatterplot as before, right-click on the scatterplot near the data points, choose **Add Trendline**, and press **ENTER**. | 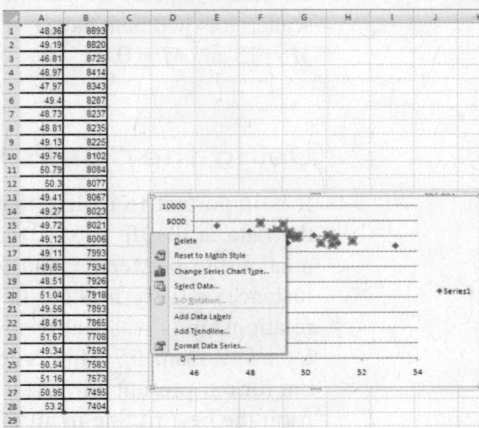 |
| **STEP 6** The best fit line will appear on the scatterplot, along with a pop-up window allowing you to change the format of the line/ curve that is displayed. | 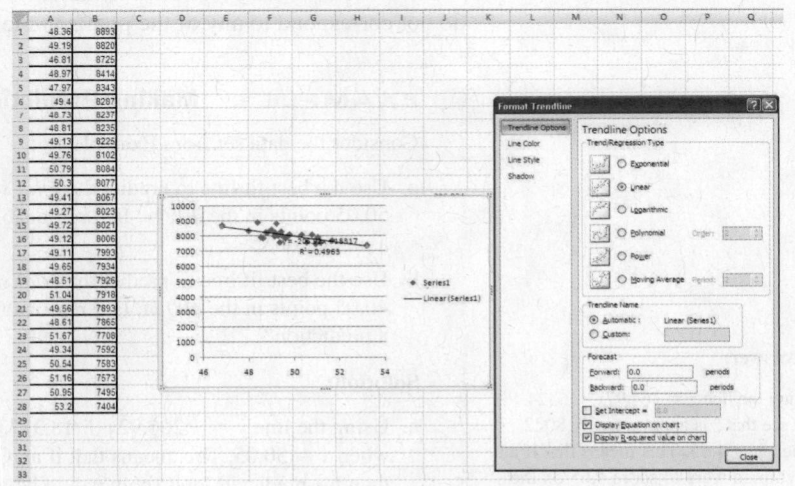 |

■ **YOUR TURN** Using the data in Example 1, identify $x$ = *score on the pole vault* and $z$ = *total score*, and determine the best fit least-squares regression line for the data set consisting of the ordered pairs $(x, z)$. Superimpose the graph of this line on the scatterplot.

■ **Answer:**

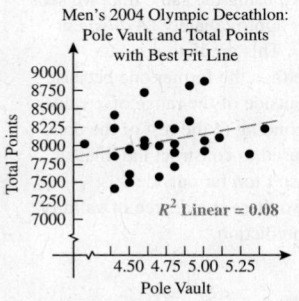

Men's 2004 Olympic Decathlon: Pole Vault and Total Points with Best Fit Line

Here, the best fit line displays a positive relationship, and its equation is $z = 364.97x + 6324.46$.

It is important to realize that the correlation coefficient is NOT equal, or even related to, the actual slope of the best fit line. In fact, two distinct perfectly linear, positively associated scatterplots will both have $r = 1$, even though the actual lines that fit the data might have slope $M = 15$ and $M = 0.04$.

## Using the "Best Fit" Line for Prediction

It is important to realize that for any scatterplot, no matter how haphazardly dispersed the data, a best fit least-squares regression line can be created. This is true even when the relationship between $x$ and $y$ is *non*linear. However, the utility of such a line in these instances is very limited. In fact, a best fit line should only be created when the linear relationship is reasonably strong, which means the correlation coefficient is "reasonably far away from 0." This criterion can be made more precise using statistical methods, but for our present purposes, we shall make the blanket assumption that it makes sense to form the best fit line in all of the scenarios we present.

Once we have the best fit line in hand, we can use it to predict $y$-values for values of $x$ that do not correspond to any of the points in the data set. For instance, consider the following:

### EXAMPLE 5  Making Predictions Using the Line of Best Fit

Consider the data set from Example 1.

**a.** Use the best fit line to predict the *total score* given that an Olympian scored 50.05 points in the *400 m*. Is it reasonable to use the best fit line to make such a prediction?

**b.** Use the best fit line to predict the *total score* given that an Olympian scored 40.05 points in the *400 m*. Is it reasonable to use the best fit line to make such a prediction?

**Solution:**

**a.** Using the line $y = -206.92x + 18{,}317.03$, we see that $y$ is approximately 7961 when $x = 50.05$. This means that if an Olympian were to score 50.05 on the *400 m*, then his predicted *total score* would be approximately 7961. Using the best fit line to predict the total score in this case is reasonable because the value 50.05 is well within the range of $x$-values already present in the data set.

**b.** Using the line $y = -206.92x + 18{,}317.03$, we see that $y$ is approximately 10,030 when $x = 40.05$. This means that if an Olympian were to score 40.05 on the *400 m*, then his predicted *total score* would be approximately 10,030. This prediction is questionable because the $x$-value at which you are using the best fit line to predict $y$ is sufficiently far away from the rest of the data points that were used to construct the line. As such, there is no reason to believe that the line is valid for such $x$-values.

■ **YOUR TURN** Using the data in Example 1, identify $x = $ *score on the pole vault* and $z = $ *total score*, and use the best fit line to predict the *total score* given that an Olympian scored 4.65 points on the *pole vault* and then, given that an Olympian scored 5.9 points on the *pole vault*. Comment on the validity of these predictions.

■ **Answer:**

Using the line $z = 364.97x + 6324.46$, we see that $z$ is approximately 8022 when $x = 4.65$. This means that if an Olympian were to score 4.65 on the *pole vault*, then his predicted *total score* would be approximately 8022. Using the best fit line to predict the total score in this case is reasonable because the value 4.65 is well within the range of $x$-values already present in the data set.

Next, using the same line, we see that $z$ is approximately 8478 when $x = 5.9$. This prediction is less reliable than the former one because 5.9 is outside of the range of $x$-values corresponding to the rest of the data points used to construct the line. But it isn't too far outside this range, so there is a degree of validity to the prediction.

## EXAMPLE 6   The Power of TV Advertisement

Video Board Tests, Inc., an advertising testing agency, collected data based on 4000 adult participants of a survey. The participants (who were regular product users) were asked to recall a commercial that they had viewed for a given product category in the previous week. The goal was to examine the relationship between retained impressions of commercials and the corresponding TV advertising budget for a given product. The data were published in the *Wall Street Journal* in March 1984.

The following is an adaptation of the original data set (**TV Ad Yields was obtained from the following Web source: http://lib.stat.cmu.edu/DASL/Datafiles/tvadsdat.html**), but contains three modifications made for illustrative purposes. Specifically, ATT/BELL, FORD, and MCDONALD'S have been replaced with DIALTONE USA, CARZ, and HAPPY BURGERS, respectively. These changes have been highlighted in green.

| COMPANY | TV ADVERTISING BUDGET, 1983 ($ MILLIONS) | MILLIONS RETAINED IMPRESSIONS PER WEEK |
|---|---|---|
| MILLER_LITE | 50.1 | 32.1 |
| PEPSI | 74.1 | 99.6 |
| STROH'S | 19.3 | 11.7 |
| FEDERAL_EXPRESS | 22.9 | 21.9 |
| BURGER_KING | 82.4 | 60.8 |
| COCA-COLA | 40.1 | 78.6 |
| HAPPY_BURGERS | 165.0 | 10.0 |
| MCI | 26.9 | 50.7 |
| DIET_COLA | 20.4 | 21.4 |
| CARZ | 165.0 | 50.0 |
| LEVI'S | 27.0 | 40.8 |
| BUD_LITE | 45.6 | 10.4 |
| DIALTONE_USA | 70.0 | 88.9 |
| CALVIN_KLEIN | 5.0 | 12.0 |
| WENDY'S | 49.7 | 29.2 |
| POLAROID | 26.9 | 38.0 |
| SHASTA | 5.7 | 10.0 |
| MEOW_MIX | 7.6 | 12.3 |
| OSCAR_MEYER | 9.2 | 23.4 |
| CREST | 32.4 | 71.1 |
| KIBBLES_'N_BITS | 6.1 | 4.4 |

First, a scatterplot for this data set (formed using PASW Statistics 18) is shown below. The approximate regression line is $y = 0.18x + 29.04$ and $r = 0.28$.

It appears that there *might* be a relationship between the budget and the retained impressions. Both CARZ and HAPPY_BURGERS are pretty far away from the bulk of the data and might be skewing an otherwise tighter relationship between $x$ and $y$; such points are potential *outliers*. What would happen to the regression line if we removed each of these points, one at a time? Would the new line be dramatically different from the original one, or might there be very little change?

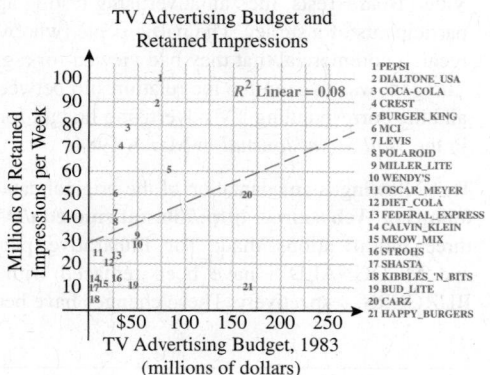

Let's start by removing CARZ. The resulting regression line is $y = 0.21x + 27.96$. We observe only a small change in both the slope and intercept. Next, let's put CARZ back into the data set and remove HAPPY_BURGERS instead. In this case, the best fit regression line is $y = 0.40x + 22.61$. This time, we have a slightly larger change in the $y$-intercept, but more importantly, the slope is more than double the slope of the regression line from the original data set. The resulting best fit regression line is displayed to the right.

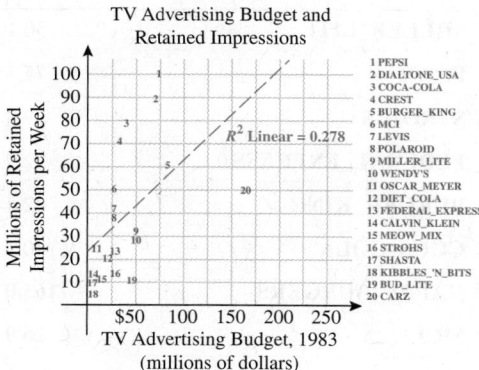

Clearly, HAPPY_BURGERS was a very influential data point since removing it dramatically changed the slope between the budget and retained impressions, thereby considerably changing the mathematical description of the relationship between these two variables. But why did this happen?

There was a large distance between it and both the $x$- and $y$-directions from the bulk of the data set. When a potential outlier is distant in only one of the two directions ($x$ or $y$), as was the case with CARZ, it is far less likely to be influential.

## SECTION
## 0.8* SUMMARY

Two variables $x$ and $y$ can be related in different ways. A paired data set $\{(x_1, y_1), \ldots, (x_n, y_n)\}$ obtained experimentally can be illustrated using a *scatterplot*. Patterns concerning the direction of association and linearity can be used to describe the relationship between $x$ and $y$, and the strength of the linear relationship can be measured using the correlation coefficient $r$. If $r$ is sufficiently far from 0, a *best fit least-squares regression line* can be formed to precisely describe the linear relationship and used for reasonable prediction purposes.

## SECTION
## 0.8* EXERCISES

■ SKILLS

**In Exercises 1–4, for each of the following scatterplots, identify the pattern as**

**a.** having a positive association, negative association, or no identifiable association.

**b.** being linear or nonlinear.

**1.**
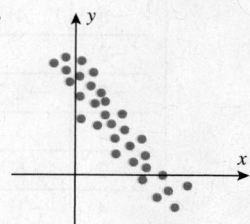

**2.**
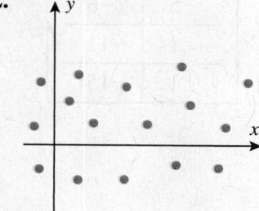

**3.**
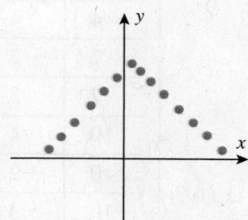

**4.**
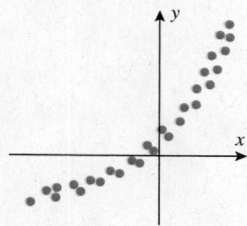

**In Exercises 5–8, match the following scatterplots with the following correlation coefficients.**

**a.** $r = -0.90$     **c.** $r = -0.68$

**b.** $r = 0.80$     **d.** $r = 0.20$

**5.**
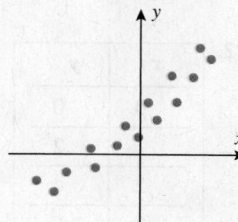

**6.**
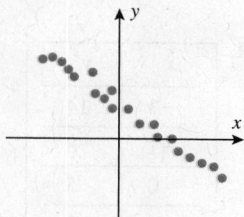

**7.**
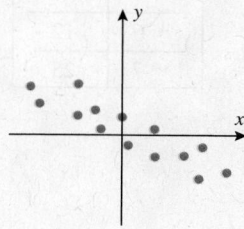

**8.**
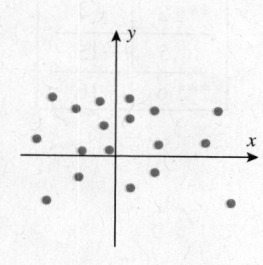

**For each of the following data sets,**

**a.** create a scatterplot.

**b.** guess the value of the correlation coefficient $r$.

**c.** use technology to determine the equation of the best fit line and to calculate $r$.

**d.** give a verbal description of the relationship between $x$ and $y$.

**9.**

| $x$ | $y$ |
|---|---|
| $-3$ | 14 |
| $-1$ | 8 |
| 0 | 5 |
| 1 | 2 |
| 3 | $-4$ |
| 5 | $-10$ |

**10.**

| $x$ | $y$ |
|---|---|
| $-8$ | $-16$ |
| $-6$ | $-12$ |
| $-4$ | $-8$ |
| $-2$ | $-4$ |
| 1 | 2 |
| 3 | 6 |

**11.**

| $x$ | $y$ |
|---|---|
| $-10$ | 1 |
| $-6$ | 0 |
| 0 | $-2$ |
| 8 | $-10$ |
| 14 | $-11$ |
| 20 | $-16$ |

**12.**

| $x$ | $y$ |
|---|---|
| $-1$ | $-17$ |
| $-1/2$ | $-11$ |
| $-1/4$ | $-5$ |
| $-1/10$ | 0 |
| 0 | 1 |
| 1/10 | 1 |
| 1/5 | 8 |
| 1 | 12 |

**13.**

| $x$ | $y$ |
|---|---|
| $-3$ | $-6$ |
| $-2$ | 3 |
| $-1$ | 1 |
| 0 | 1 |
| 1 | 5 |
| 2 | $-1$ |
| 4 | 1 |

**14.**

| $x$ | $y$ |
|---|---|
| $-6$ | $-1$ |
| $-3$ | 4 |
| $-1$ | 3 |
| 1 | 0 |
| 2 | $-6$ |
| 5 | $-4$ |
| 8 | 1 |

**In Exercises 15–18, for each of the data sets,**

a. use technology to create a scatterplot, to determine the best fit line, and to compute $r$.

b. indicate whether or not the best fit line can be used for predictive purposes for the following $x$-values. For those for which it can be used, give the predicted value of $y$:

  i. $x = 0$        iii. $x = 12$

  ii. $x = -6$       iv. $x = -15$

c. Using the best fit line, at what $x$-value would you expect $y$ to be equal to 2?

**15.**

| x | y |
|---|---|
| −5 | −8 |
| −3 | 0 |
| −2 | 0 |
| 2 | 1.5 |
| 5 | 4 |
| 7. | 2 |
| 10 | 8 |

**16.**

| x | y |
|---|---|
| 5 | 0 |
| 5 | 3 |
| 6 | 3 |
| 7 | 6 |
| 7 | 9 |
| 8 | 9 |
| 8 | 15 |
| 9 | 9 |
| 9 | 15 |
| 10 | 15 |
| 10 | 18 |

**17.**

| x | y |
|---|---|
| −20 | 15 |
| −18 | 10 |
| −14 | 3 |
| −14 | 8 |
| −13 | 3 |
| −8 | 0 |
| −8 | −3 |
| −5 | −6 |
| 1 | −11 |
| 1 | −15 |

**18.**

| x | y |
|---|---|
| −15 | 4 |
| −15 | 12 |
| −15 | 16 |
| −13 | 3 |
| −10 | 4 |
| −10 | 8 |
| −10 | 12 |
| −5 | 4 |
| −2 | 3 |
| −2 | −2 |
| 2 | 3 |
| 2 | 6 |
| 4 | −1 |
| 4 | 0 |
| 4 | 4 |
| 7 | −2 |
| 7 | 3 |
| 10 | −4 |
| 10 | −2 |
| 10 | 3 |

**For Exercises 19–22,**

a. use technology to create a scatterplot, to determine the best fit line, and to compute $r$ for the *entire* data set.

b. repeat (a), but with the data set obtained by removing the *starred* (***) data points.

c. compare the $r$-values from (a) and (b), as well as the slopes of the best fit lines. Comment on any differences, whether they are substantive, and why this seems reasonable.

**19.**

| x | y |
|---|---|
| −3 | 14 |
| −1 | 8 |
| 0 | 5 |
| 1 | 2 |
| 3 | −4 |
| *** 5 | −10 |

**20.**

| x | y |
|---|---|
| −10 | 1 |
| −6 | 0 |
| 0 | −2 |
| 8 | −10 |
| 14 | −11 |
| *** 20 | −16 |

**21.**

| x | y |
|---|---|
| −3 | 14 |
| −1 | 8 |
| 0 | 5 |
| 1 | 2 |
| *** 3 | −4 |
| 5 | −15 |
| *** 6 | −16 |

**22.**

| x | y |
|---|---|
| 0 | 0 |
| 1 | 2 |
| 2 | 4 |
| 3 | 6 |
| 4 | 8 |
| 6 | 12 |
| *** 7 | 25 |

■ **CONCEPTUAL**

**23.** Consider the data set from Exercise 17.

   **a.** Reverse the roles of $x$ and $y$ so that now $y$ is the *explanatory* variable and $x$ is the *response* variable. Create a scatterplot for the ordered pairs of the form $(y, x)$ using this data set.

   **b.** Compute $r$. How does it compare to the $r$-value from Exercise 17? Why does this make sense?

   **c.** The best fit line for the scatterplot in (a) will be of the form $x = my + b$. Determine this line.

   **d.** Using the line from (c), find the predicted $x$-value for the following $y$-values, if appropriate. If it is not appropriate, tell why.

     **i.** $y = 23$      **ii.** $y = 2$      **iii.** $y = -16$

**24.** Consider the data set from Exercise 16. Redo the parts in Exercise 23.

**25.** Consider the following data set.

| $x$ | $y$ |
|-----|-----|
| 3 | 0 |
| 3 | 1 |
| 3 | -1 |
| 3 | -2 |
| 3 | 4 |
| 3 | 15 |
| 3 | -6 |
| 3 | 8 |
| 3 | 10 |

Guess the values of $r$ and the best fit line. Then, check your answers using technology. What happens? Can you reason why this is the case?

**26.** Consider the following data set.

| $x$ | $y$ |
|-----|-----|
| -5 | -2 |
| -4 | -2 |
| -1 | -2 |
| 0 | -2 |
| 1 | -2 |
| 3 | -2 |
| 8 | -2 |
| 17 | -2 |

Guess the values of $r$ and the best fit line. Then, check your answers using technology. What happens? Can you reason why this is the case?

■ **CATCH THE MISTAKE**

**27.** The following screenshot was taken when using the TI-83+ to determine the equation of the best fit line for paired data $(x, y)$:

```
LinReg
 y=ax+b
 a=5.175
 b=1.257142857
 r²=.9960156546
 r=.998005839
■
```

Using the regression line, we observe that there is a strong positive linear association between $x$ and $y$, and that for every unit increase in $x$, the $y$-value increases by about 1.257 units.

**28.** The following scatterplot was produced using the TI-83+ for paired data $(x, y)$.

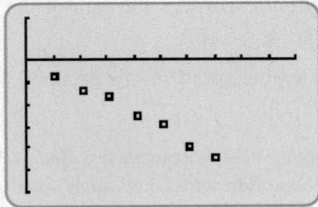

The equation of the best fit line was reported to be $y = -3.207x + 0.971$ with $r^2 = 0.9827$. Thus, the correlation coefficient is given by $r = 0.9913$, which indicates a strong linear association between $x$ and $y$.

## ■ APPLICATIONS

**For Exercises 29 and 30, refer to the data set in Example 1.**

**29. a.** Examine the relationship between each of the decathlon events and the total points by computing the correlation coefficient in each case.

   **b.** Using the information from part (a), which event has the strongest relationship to the total points?

   **c.** What is the equation of the best fit line that describes the relationship between the event from part (b) and the total points?

   **d.** Using the best fit line, if you had a score of 40 for this event, what would the predicted total points score be?

**30. a.** Using the information from part (a), which event has the second strongest relationship to the total points?

   **b.** What is the equation of the best fit line that describes the relationship between the event in part (b) and the total points?

   **c.** Is it reasonable to expect the best fit line from part (c) to produce accurate predictions of total points using this event?

   **d.** Using the best fit line, if you had a score of 40 for this event, what would the total points score be?

**For Exercises 31 and 32, refer to the following scenario:** *Texting Speed.*

According to the CTIA—The Wireless Association, as of December 2010, 187.7 billion messages were sent per month or 2.1 trillion messages in that year.[1] According to a 2010 Pew Internet survey, 72% of all teens—or 88% of teen cell phone users—are text-messagers. Teens make and receive far fewer phone calls than text messages on their cell phones.

A number of competitions regarding texting speed have taken place worldwide. According to the Guinness World Records, "The fastest completion of a prescribed 160-character text message is 34.65 seconds and was achieved by Frode Ness (Norway) at the Norwegian SMS championships held at the Oslo City shopping centre in Oslo, Østlandet, Norway, on 13 November 2010."[2]

The data set regarding texting speed on the next page was provided by AP Central. (**http://apcentral.collegeboard.com/apc/public/courses/teachers_corner/195435.html**)

In the data given, the *A total score* is the amount of time (in seconds) it took to text the following message, "Statistics students are above average." The *B total score* is the amount of time (in seconds) to type, "Meet me at my car after school today." The *Total both scores* is the sum of the *A total score* and *B total score*.

What influences texting speed in this group? Let's consider thumb length.

**31.** What is the relationship between the variables *left thumb length* and *total both scores*?

   **a.** Create a scatterplot to show the relationship between *left thumb length* and *total both scores*.

   **b.** What is the correlation coefficient between *left thumb length* and *total both scores*?

   **c.** Describe the strength of the relationship between *left thumb length* and *total both scores*.

   **d.** What is the equation of the best fit line that describes the relationship between *left thumb length* and *total both scores*?

   **e.** Could you use the best fit line to produce accurate predictions of *total both scores* using *left thumb length*?

**32.** Repeat Exercise 31 for *right thumb length* and *total both scores*.

[1] http://www.cita.org/advocacy/research/index.cfm/aid/10323

[2] http://www.guinnessworldrecords.com/Search/Details/Fastest-text-message/57979.htm

| Gender | Texting Style | Left Thumb Length | Right Thumb Length | A Total Score | B Total Score | Total Both Scores | A Minus B | Avg Thumb | Diff Thumb |
|---|---|---|---|---|---|---|---|---|---|
| Male | Char | 6.5 | 6.5 | 35 | 25 | 60 | 10 | 6.5 | 0 |
| Female | Char | 5 | 5 | 61 | 57 | 118 | 4 | 5 | 0 |
| Female | Word | 6 | 6 | 24 | 20 | 44 | 4 | 6 | 0 |
| Male | Word | 7 | 7 | 43 | 60 | 103 | −17 | 7 | 0 |
| Female | Word | 6 | 6 | 14 | 19 | 33 | −5 | 6 | 0 |
| Male | Word | 7 | 6 | 15 | 18 | 33 | −3 | 6.5 | −1 |
| Female | Word | 6 | 6 | 13 | 14 | 27 | −1 | 6 | 0 |
| Female | Word | 6 | 6 | 22 | 10 | 22 | 12 | 6 | 0 |
| Male | Word | 6.5 | 6 | 13 | 15 | 28 | −2 | 6.25 | −0.5 |
| Female | Word | 5.5 | 5.5 | 16 | 16 | 32 | 0 | 5.5 | 0 |
| Male | Char | 6 | 5 | 85 | 78 | 163 | 7 | 5.5 | −1 |
| Male | Char | 6 | 6 | 126 | 120 | 246 | 6 | 6 | 0 |
| Male | Word | 7.5 | 6.5 | 67 | 69 | 136 | −2 | 7 | −1 |
| Female | Char | 5.5 | 5.5 | 11 | 7 | 18 | 4 | 5.5 | 0 |
| Female | Word | 5.5 | 5.7 | 14 | 17 | 31 | −3 | 5.6 | 0.2 |
| Female | Word | 6 | 6 | 17 | 14 | 31 | 3 | 6 | 0 |
| Female | Word | 5 | 5 | 20 | 15 | 35 | 5 | 5 | 0 |
| Male | Word | 6.5 | 6.5 | 15 | 13 | 28 | 2 | 6.5 | 0 |
| Male | Word | 7 | 7 | 30 | 31 | 61 | −1 | 7 | 0 |
| Male | Word | 6 | 6.1 | 120 | 117 | 237 | 3 | 6.05 | 0.1 |
| Male | Word | 6 | 6 | 74 | 25 | 99 | 49 | 6 | 0 |
| Male | Word | 6.3 | 6 | 23 | 21 | 44 | 2 | 6.15 | −0.3 |
| Male | Char | 6 | 5.9 | 45 | 50 | 95 | −5 | 5.95 | −0.1 |
| Male | Word | 6 | 6.1 | 86 | 100 | 186 | −14 | 6.05 | 0.1 |
| Male | Char | 6 | 6 | 25 | 23 | 48 | 2 | 6 | 0 |
| Male | Char | 6.3 | 6.3 | 81 | 57 | 138 | 24 | 6.3 | 0 |
| Female | Char | 5.5 | 5.5 | 88 | 66 | 154 | 22 | 5.5 | 0 |
| Female | Word | 7 | 6.8 | 10 | 9 | 19 | 1 | 6.9 | −0.2 |
| Male | Char | 6.5 | 7 | 21 | 18 | 39 | 3 | 6.75 | 0.5 |
| Female | Char | 5.4 | 5.2 | 72 | 48 | 121 | 24 | 5.3 | −0.2 |
| Female | Char | 8 | 8 | 36 | 23 | 59 | 13 | 8 | 0 |
| Male | Char | 7 | 6.5 | 46 | 45 | 91 | 1 | 6.75 | −0.5 |
| Female | Char | 6 | 6.8 | 48 | 39 | 87 | 9 | 6.4 | 0.8 |
| Female | Char | 7.1 | 7.1 | 84 | 57 | 141 | 27 | 7.1 | 0 |
| Female | Word | 5.9 | 5.5 | 25 | 23 | 48 | 2 | 5.7 | −0.4 |
| Female | Char | 7.6 | 7.2 | 32 | 45 | 77 | −13 | 7.4 | −0.4 |
| Male | Word | 6.9 | 7 | 23 | 28 | 51 | −5 | 6.95 | 0.1 |
| Female | Char | 7.7 | 7.5 | 18 | 15 | 33 | 3 | 7.6 | −0.2 |
| Male | Char | 8.6 | (cast) | 22 | 20 | 42 | 2 | N/A | N/A |
| Male | Char | 7.3 | 7.1 | 54 | 50 | 104 | 4 | 7.2 | −0.2 |

**For Exercises 33 and 34, refer to the following data set: *Herd Immunity*.**

According to the U.S. Department of Health and Human Services, herd immunity is defined as "a concept of protecting a community against certain diseases by having a high percentage of the community's population immunized. Even if a few members of the community are unable to be immunized, the entire community will be indirectly protected because the disease has little opportunity for an outbreak. However, with a low percentage of population immunity, the disease would have great opportunity for an outbreak."[3]

Suppose a study is conducted in the year 2016 looking at the outbreak of *Haemophilus influenzae type b* in the winter of 2015 across 22 nursing homes. We might look at the percentage of residents in each of the nursing homes that were immunized and the percentage of residents who were infected with this type of influenza.

The fictional data set is as follows.

| NURSING HOME | % RESIDENTS IMMUNIZED | % RESIDENTS WITH INFLUENZA |
|---|---|---|
| 1 | 70 | 11 |
| 2 | 68 | 9 |
| 3 | 80 | 8 |
| 4 | 10 | 34 |
| 5 | 12 | 30 |
| 6 | 18 | 31 |
| 7 | 27 | 22 |
| 8 | 64 | 18 |
| 9 | 73 | 6 |
| 10 | 9 | 31 |
| 11 | 35 | 19 |
| 12 | 56 | 16 |
| 13 | 57 | 22 |
| 14 | 83 | 10 |
| 15 | 74 | 13 |
| 16 | 64 | 15 |
| 17 | 16 | 28 |
| 18 | 23 | 25 |
| 19 | 29 | 24 |
| 20 | 33 | 20 |
| 21 | 82 | 28 |
| 22 | 67 | 9 |

**33.** What is the relationship between the variables **% residents immunized** and **% residents with influenza**?

   **a.** Create a scatterplot to illustrate the relationship between **% residents immunized** and **% residents with influenza**.

   **b.** What is the correlation coefficient between **% residents immunized** and **% residents with influenza**?

   **c.** Describe the strength of the relationship between **% residents immunized** and **% residents with influenza**.

   **d.** What is the equation of the best fit line that describes the relationship between **% residents immunized** and **% residents with influenza**?

   **e.** Could you use the best fit line to produce accurate predictions of **% residents with influenza** using **% residents immunized**?

**34.** What is the impact of the outlier(s) on this data set?

   **a.** Identify the outlier in this data set. What is the nursing home number for this outlier?

   **b.** Remove the outlier and re-create the scatterplot to show the relationship between **% residents immunized** and **% residents with influenza**.

   **c.** What is the revised correlation coefficient between **% residents immunized** and **% residents with influenza**?

   **d.** By removing the outlier is the strength of the relationship between **% residents immunized** and **% residents with influenza** increased or decreased?

   **e.** What is the revised equation of the best fit line that describes the relationship between **% residents immunized** and **% residents with influenza**?

**For Exercises 35–38, refer to the following data set: *Amusement Park Rides*.**

According to the International Association of Amusement Parks and Attractions (IAAPA), "There are more than 400 amusement parks and traditional attractions in the United States alone. In 2008, amusement parks in the United States entertained 300 million visitors who safely enjoyed more than 1.7 billion rides."[4] Despite the popularity of amusement parks, the wait times, especially for the most popular rides, are not so highly regarded. There are different approaches and tactics that people take to get the most rides in their visit to the park. Now, there are even apps for the iPhone and Android to track waiting times at various amusement parks.

One might ask, "Are the wait times worth it? Are the rides with the longest wait times, the most enjoyable?"

Consider the following fictional data.

---

[3] http://www.hhs.gov/nvpo/glossary1.htm

[4] http://www.iaapa.org/pressroom/Amusement_Park_Industry_Statistics.asp

| Ride ID | Ride Name | Avg Wait Time | Avg Enjoyment Rating | Park | Park Location |
|---------|-----------|---------------|----------------------|------|---------------|
| 1 | Xoom | 45 | 58 | 1 | Florida |
| 2 | Accentuator | 35 | 40 | 1 | Florida |
| 3 | Wobbler | 15 | 15 | 1 | Florida |
| 4 | Arctic_Attack | 75 | 75 | 1 | Florida |
| 5 | Gusher | 60 | 70 | 1 | Florida |
| 6 | Alley_Cats | 5 | 60 | 1 | Florida |
| 7 | Moon_Swing | 10 | 15 | 1 | Florida |
| 8 | Speedster | 70 | 50 | 1 | Florida |
| 9 | Hailstorm | 80 | 90 | 1 | Florida |
| 10 | DragonFire | 70 | 88 | 1 | Florida |
| 1 | Xoom | 50 | 10 | 2 | California |
| 2 | Accentuator | 35 | 40 | 2 | California |
| 3 | Wobbler | 20 | 75 | 2 | California |
| 4 | Arctic_Attack | 70 | 60 | 2 | California |
| 5 | Gusher | 70 | 80 | 2 | California |
| 6 | Alley_Cats | 10 | 18 | 2 | California |
| 7 | Moon_Swing | 15 | 80 | 2 | California |
| 8 | Speedster | 80 | 35 | 2 | California |
| 9 | Hailstorm | 95 | 40 | 2 | California |
| 10 | DragonFire | 55 | 60 | 2 | California |

The data shows 10 popular rides in two sister parks located in Florida and California. For each ride in each park, average wait times (in minutes) in the summer of 2010 and the average rating of ride enjoyment (on a scale of 1–100) are provided.

35. What is the relationship between the variables *average wait times* and *average rating of enjoyment*?

   a. Create a scatterplot to show the relationship between *average wait times* and *average rating of enjoyment*.

   b. What is the correlation coefficient between *average wait times* and *average rating of enjoyment*?

   c. Describe the strength of the relationship between *average wait times* and *average rating of enjoyment*.

   d. What is the equation of the best fit line that describes the relationship between *average wait times* and *average rating of enjoyment*?

   e. Could you use the best fit line to produce accurate predictions of *average wait times* using *average rating of enjoyment*?

36. Examine the relationship between *average wait times* and *average rating of enjoyment* for *Park 1* in *Florida* by repeating Exercise 35 for only *Park 1*.

37. Examine the relationship between *average wait times* and *average rating of enjoyment* for *Park 2* in *California* repeating Exercise 35 for only *Park 2*.

38. Compare the relationship between *average wait times* and *average rating of enjoyment* for *Park 1 in Florida* versus *Park 2 in California*.

■ CHALLENGE

**For Exercises 39–42, refer to the following:**

*Exploring other types of best-fit curves*

When describing the patterns that emerge in paired data sets, there are many more possibilities other than best fit *lines*. Indeed, once you have drawn a scatterplot and are ready to identify the curve that *best fits* the data, there is a substantive collection of other curves that might more accurately describe the data. The following are listed among those in **STATS/CALC** on the TI-83+, along with some comments:

| Name of Regression Curve | Form of the Curve | Comments |
|--------------------------|-------------------|----------|
| 5: QuadReg | $y = ax^2 + bx + c$ | The data set must have at least 3 points to be able to select this option. |
| 6: CubicReg | $y = ax^3 + bx^2 + cx + d$ | The data set must have at least 4 points to be able to select this option. |
| 7: QuartReg | $y = ax^4 + bx^3 + cx^2 + dx + e$ | The data set must have at least 5 points to be able to select this option. |
| 9: LnReg | $y = a + b \ln x$ | The data set must have at least 2 points to be able to select this option, and $x$ cannot take on negative values. |
| 0: ExpReg | $y = a * b^x$ | The data set must have at least 2 points to be able to select this option, and $y$ cannot take on the value of 0. |
| A: PwrReg | $y = a * x^b$ | The data set must have at least 2 points to be able to select this option. |

**For each of the following data sets,**

a. Create a scatterplot.

b. Use **LinReg(ax+b)** to determine the best fit *line* and r. Does the line seem to accurately describe the pattern in the data?

c. For each of the different choices listed in the above chart, find the equation of the best fit curve and its associated $r^2$ value. Of all of the curves, which seems to provide the best fit?

*Note:* The $r^2$-value reported in each case is NOT the *linear* correlation coefficient reported when running LinReg(ax+B). Rather, the value will typically change depending on the curve. The reason why is that each time, the $r^2$-value is measuring how accurate the fit is between the data and *that type of curve*. A value of $r^2$ close to 1 still corresponds to a good fit with whichever curve you are fitting to the data.

**41.**

| x | y |
|-----|------|
| 1 | 0.2 |
| 1.5 | 0.93 |
| 2 | 1.46 |
| 3 | 2.25 |
| 10 | 4.51 |
| 15 | 5.50 |

**42.**

| x | y |
|---|--------|
| 1 | 32.3 |
| 2 | 8.12 |
| 3 | −16.89 |
| 5 | −45.2 |
| 6 | 0.89 |
| 8 | 62.1 |

**39.**

| x | y |
|---|------|
| 1 | 16.2 |
| 2 | 21 |
| 3 | 23.7 |
| 4 | 24.8 |
| 5 | 23.9 |
| 6 | 20.7 |
| 7 | 15.8 |
| 8 | 9.1 |
| 9 | 0.3 |

**40.**

| x | y |
|-----|-------|
| 0.5 | 1.20 |
| 1.0 | 0.760 |
| 1.5 | 0.412 |
| 2.1 | 0.196 |
| 2.9 | 0.131 |
| 3.3 | 0.071 |

### Equivalent Equations and Extraneous Solutions

A general strategy for solving all the various types of equations you encountered in this chapter can be summarized as follows: From a given equation, perform algebraic operations on both sides in order to generate equivalent equations. Remember, *equivalent equations* have the same solution set.

**1.** Consider first a linear equation: $3x - 1 = 5$.

    **a.** Use a graphing utility to show $y_1 = 3x - 1$ and $y_2 = 5$ and determine the point of intersection. Make a sketch and label it.

    **b.** How does the graph in part (a) relate to the solution set of the equation $3x - 1 = 5$?

    **c.** To solve the equation $3x - 1 = 5$ algebraically, the first step is to add 1 to both sides of the equation, as follows:

$$
\begin{array}{rcl}
3x - 1 &=& 5 \\
+\,1 & & +1 \\
\hline
3x &=& 6
\end{array}
$$

    Use a graphing utility to show $y_1 = 3x$ and $y_2 = 6$, and determine the point of intersection. Make a sketch and label it. How does this graph relate to the equation $3x = 6$?

    **d.** The final algebraic step to solve the equation is to divide both sides of the equation by 3.

$$
\frac{3x}{3} = \frac{6}{3}
$$
$$
x = 2
$$

    Use a graphing utility to show $y_1 = x$ and $y_2 = 2$, and determine the point of intersection. Make a sketch and label it. How does this graph relate to the equation $x = 2$?

    **e.** The algebraic steps to solve the equation $3x - 1 = 5$ produce two equations: $3x = 6$ and $x = 2$. How do the graphs you sketched above represent the fact that these equations are equivalent to the original?

**2.** Next consider the equation $x - 2 = \sqrt{4 - x}$

**a.** Use a graphing utility to show $y_1 = x - 2$ and $y_2 = \sqrt{4 - x}$ and determine any points of intersection. What do you learn about the solution set of the equation $x - 2 = \sqrt{4 - x}$? Make a sketch to explain.

**b.** The algebraic steps to solve this equation are as follows:

| | |
|---|---|
| $x - 2 = \sqrt{4 - x}$ | |
| $(x - 2)^2 = (\sqrt{4 - x})^2$ | Square both sides. |
| $x^2 - 4x + 4 = 4 - x$ | Simplify. |
| $x^2 - 3x = 0$ | Write the quadratic equation in standard form. |
| $x(x - 3) = 0$ | Factor. |
| $x = 0$ or $x = 3$ | Use the zero product property. |

Use a graphing utility to show the first step above: $y_1 = (x - 2)^2$ and $y_2 = (\sqrt{4 - x})^2$. What do you learn about the solution set of $(x - 2)^2 = (\sqrt{4 - x})^2$?

**c.** Discuss whether $x - 2 = \sqrt{4 - x}$ and $(x - 2)^2 = (\sqrt{4 - x})^2$ are equivalent equations.

**d.** The algebraic process of squaring both sides introduced an *extraneous solution*. What do you think that means?

**e.** Why is it important to always check the solutions you obtain when solving equations?

**3.** Consider $x^4 - x^2 = 0$

**a.** A fellow student suggests dividing both sides of the equation by $x^2$. What will be the resulting equation?

**b.** Is the equation you wrote in part (a) equivalent to the original equation? How can you use a graphing utility to illustrate this?

**c.** Show the algebraic steps you should take to solve $x^4 - x^2 = 0$.

# CHAPTER 0 INQUIRY-BASED LEARNING PROJECT (2)

The following table shows U.S. population estimates for the years 1991 to 2002, along with the number of tons of municipal waste generated (in 100 million tons) and the percentage that was recycled in the United States during those years.

| YEAR | U.S. POPULATION ESTIMATE (100 MILLION PEOPLE) | MUNICIPAL WASTE GENERATED (100 MILLION TONS) | PERCENTAGE RECYCLED |
|---|---|---|---|
| 1991 | 2.46 | 2.69 | 8% |
| 1992 | 2.49 | 2.93 | 11.5% |
| 1993 | 2.52 | 2.80 | 14% |
| 1994 | 2.55 | 2.91 | 17% |
| 1995 | 2.58 | 3.06 | 19% |
| 1996 | 2.60 | 3.22 | 23% |
| 1997 | 2.63 | 3.26 | 27% |
| 1998 | 2.65 | 3.27 | 28% |
| 1999 | 2.68 | 3.40 | 30% |
| 2000 | 2.73 | 3.74 | 31.5% |
| 2001 | 2.80 | 3.82 | 33% |
| 2002 | 2.86 | 4.09 | 32% |

*Adapted from: A Yearly Snapshot of U.S. (Municipal) Waste and Recycling* (Data Source: BIOCYCLE/Table & Conversion: ZWA http://www.zerowasteamerica.org/statistics.htm)

1. For parts (a)–(f), consider the columns for U.S. Population Estimate, *x*, and Municipal Waste Generated, *y*.

   a. Write the equation (in slope–intercept form) of the line that passes through the points (2.60, 3.22) and (2.80, 3.82).

   b. How can you interpret the slope of the line in part (a)?

   c. Now choose two other data points and write the equation of the line that passes through your chosen points. How can you interpret the slope of this line?

   d. How does the slope of this line compare to the line in part (a)?

   e. Sketch a graph of the two lines. What do you notice about their *y*-intercepts?

   f. Finally, plot all the other ordered points (Population, Waste Generated).

The graph of all the data points is called a **scatterplot.** Since the data fall in approximately a straight line, each of the lines you graphed above is an approximation of the data. Section 0.8 presented methods for finding the line that *best* fits a set of data points, called the least-squares regression line.

**2.** For parts (a)–(c) below, consider the columns U.S. Population Estimate, $x$, and Percentage Recycled, $y$.

   **a.** Graph the scatterplot for this data.

   **b.** Sketch the graph of a line that contains two data points. Choose a line you think fits the data well.

   **c.** Write the equation of the line.

   **d.** How can you interpret the slope of this line?

The Intergovernmental Panel on Climate Change (IPCC) claims that carbon dioxide ($CO_2$) production from industrial activity (such as fossil fuel burning and other human activities) has increased the $CO_2$ concentrations in the atmosphere. Because it is a greenhouse gas, elevated $CO_2$ levels will increase global mean (average) temperature. In this section, we will examine the increasing rate of carbon emissions on Earth.

In 1955 there were (globally) 2 billion tons of carbon emitted per year. In 2005 the carbon emissions more than tripled to reach approximately 7 billion tons of carbon emitted per year. Currently, we are on the path to doubling our current carbon emissions in the next 50 years.

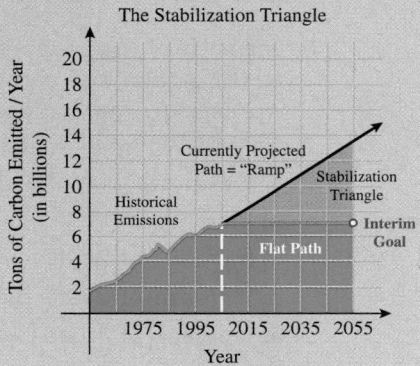

Two Princeton professors* (Stephen Pacala and Rob Socolow) introduced the Climate Carbon Wedge concept. A "wedge" is a strategy to reduce carbon emissions over a 50-year time period from zero to 1.0 GtC/yr (gigatons of carbon per year).

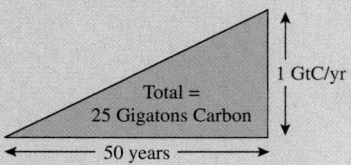

1. Draw the Cartesian plane. Label the vertical axis $C$, where $C$ represents the number of gigatons (billions of tons) of carbon emitted, and label the horizontal axis $t$, where $t$ is the number of years. Let $t = 0$ correspond to 2005.

---

*S. Pacala and R. Socolow, "Stabilization Wedges: Solving the Climate Problem for the Next 50 Years with Current Technologies," *Science*, Vol. 305 (2004).

**2.** Find the equations of the flat path and the seven lines corresponding to the seven wedges.

   **a.** Flat path (no increase) over 50 years (2005 to 2055)

   **b.** Increase of 1 GtC over 50 years (2005 to 2055)

   **c.** Increase of 2 GtC over 50 years (2005 to 2055)

   **d.** Increase of 3 GtC over 50 years (2005 to 2055)

   **e.** Increase of 4 GtC over 50 years (2005 to 2055)

   **f.** Increase of 5 GtC over 50 years (2005 to 2055)

   **g.** Increase of 6 GtC over 50 years (2005 to 2055)

   **h.** Increase of 7 GtC over 50 years (2005 to 2055) [projected path]

**3.** For each of the seven wedges and the flat path, determine how many **total** gigatons of carbon will be reduced over a 50-year period. In other words, how many gigatons of carbon would the world have to reduce in each of the eight cases?

   **a.** Flat path

   **b.** Increase of 1 GtC over 50 years

   **c.** Increase of 2 GtC over 50 years

   **d.** Increase of 3 GtC over 50 years

   **e.** Increase of 4 GtC over 50 years

   **f.** Increase of 5 GtC over 50 years

   **g.** Increase of 6 GtC over 50 years

   **h.** Increase of 7 GtC over 50 years (projected path)

**4.** Research the "climate carbon wedge" concept and discuss the types of changes (transportation efficiency, transportation conservation, building efficiency, efficiency in electricity production, alternate energies, etc.) the world would have to make that would correspond to each of the seven wedges and the flat path.

   **a.** Flat path

   **b.** Wedge 1

   **c.** Wedge 2

   **d.** Wedge 3

   **e.** Wedge 4

   **f.** Wedge 5

   **g.** Wedge 6

| SECTION | CONCEPT | KEY IDEAS/FORMULAS |
|---------|---------|--------------------|
| 0.1 | **Linear equations** | $ax + b = 0$ |
| | Solving linear equations in one variable | Isolate variable on one side and constants on the other side. |
| | Applications involving linear equations | Six-step procedure:<br>Step 1: Identify the question.  Step 4: Set up an equation.<br>Step 2: Make notes.  Step 5: Solve the equation.<br>Step 3: Assign a variable.  Step 6: Check the solution.<br>**Geometry problems:** Formulas for rectangles, triangles, and circles<br>**Interest problems:** Simple interest: $I = Prt$<br>**Mixture problems:** Whenever two *distinct* quantities are mixed, the result is a mixture.<br>**Distance–rate–time problems:** $d = r \cdot t$ |
| 0.2 | **Quadratic equations** | $ax^2 + bx + c = 0$ |
| | Factoring | If $(x - h)(x - k) = 0$, then $x = h$ or $x = k$. |
| | Square root method | If $x^2 = P$, then $x = \pm\sqrt{P}$. |
| | Completing the square | Find half of $b$; square that quantity; add the result to both sides. |
| | The quadratic formula | $x = \dfrac{-b \pm \sqrt{b^2 - 4ac}}{2a}$ |
| 0.3 | **Other types of equations** | |
| | Rational equations | Eliminate any values that make the denominator equal to 0. |
| | Radical equations | Check solutions to avoid extraneous solutions. |
| | Equations quadratic in form: $u$-substitution | Use a $u$-substitution to write the equation in quadratic form. |
| | Factorable equations | Extract common factor or factor by grouping. |
| | Absolute value equations | If $|x| = a$, then $x = -a$ or $x = a$. |
| 0.4 | **Inequalities** | Solutions are a range of real numbers. |
| | Graphing inequalities and interval notation | ■ $a < x < b$ is equivalent to $(a, b)$.<br>■ $x \leq a$ is equivalent to $(-\infty, a]$.<br>■ $x > a$ is equivalent to $(a, \infty)$. |
| | Linear inequalities | If an inequality is multiplied or divided by a *negative* number, the inequality sign must be reversed. |
| | Polynomial inequalities | Zeros are values that make the polynomial equal to 0. |
| | Rational inequalities | The number line is divided into intervals. The endpoints of these intervals are values that make either the numerator or denominator equal to 0. Always exclude values that make the denominator equal to 0. |
| | Absolute value inequalities | ■ $|x| \leq a$ is equivalent to $-a \leq x \leq a$.<br>■ $|x| > a$ is equivalent to $x < -a$ or $x > a$. |

**CHAPTER REVIEW**

| SECTION | CONCEPT | KEY IDEAS/FORMULAS |
| --- | --- | --- |
| **0.5** | **Graphing equations** | |
| | Cartesian plane | 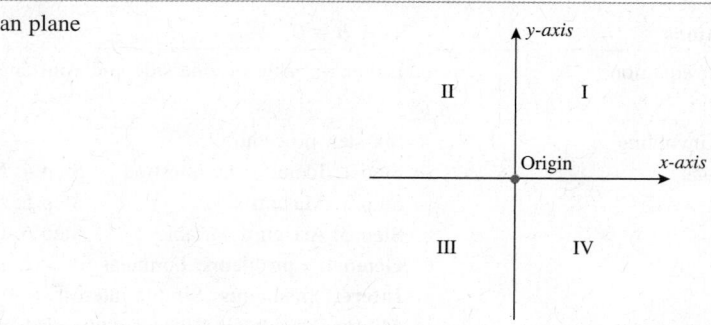 |
| | The distance and midpoint formulas | $d = \sqrt{(x_2 - x_1)^2 + (y_2 - y_1)^2}$<br><br>$(x_m, y_m) = \left( \dfrac{x_1 + x_2}{2}, \dfrac{y_1 + y_2}{2} \right)$ |
| | Point-plotting | List a table with several coordinates that are solutions to the equation; plot and connect. |
| | Using intercepts and symmetry as graphing aids | If $(a, b)$ is on the graph of the equation, then $(-a, b)$ is on the graph if symmetric about the $y$-axis, $(a, -b)$ is on the graph if symmetric about the $x$-axis, and $(-a, -b)$ is on the graph if symmetric about the origin.<br><br>**Intercepts:** $x$-intercept: let $y = 0$.<br>$y$-intercept: let $x = 0$.<br><br>**Symmetry:** The graph of an equation can be symmetric about the $x$-axis, $y$-axis, or origin. |
| | Circles | Standard equation of a circle with center $(h, k)$ and radius $r$.<br>$$(x - h)^2 + (y - k)^2 = r^2$$<br>General form: $x^2 + y^2 + ax + by + c = 0$<br>Transform equations of circles to the standard form by completing the square |
| **0.6** | **Lines** | General form: $Ax + By = C$ |
| | Graphing a line | Vertical: $x = a$      Slant: $Ax + By = C$, where $A \neq 0$ and $B \neq 0$<br>Horizontal: $y = b$ |
| | Slope | $m = \dfrac{y_2 - y_1}{x_2 - x_1}$, where $x_1 \neq x_2$    $\dfrac{\text{"rise"}}{\text{"run"}}$ |
| | Equations of lines | **Slope–intercept form:**<br>$y = mx + b$<br>$m$ is the slope and $b$ is the $y$-intercept.<br>**Point–slope form:** $y - y_1 = m(x - x_1)$ |
| | Parallel and perpendicular lines | $L_1 \parallel L_2$ if and only if $m_1 = m_2$ (slopes are equal).<br><br>$L_1 \perp L_2$ if and only if $m_1 = -\dfrac{1}{m_2} \begin{cases} m_1 \neq 0 \\ m_2 \neq 0 \end{cases}$<br>(slopes are negative reciprocals). |

| SECTION | CONCEPT | KEY IDEAS/FORMULAS |
|---------|---------|--------------------|
| 0.7 | **Modeling variation** | |
| | Direct variation | $y = kx$ |
| | Inverse variation | $y = \dfrac{k}{x}$ |
| | Joint variation and combined variation | Joint: One quantity is directly proportional to the product of two or more other quantities. |
| | | Combined: Direct variation and inverse variation occur at the same time. |
| 0.8* | **Linear regression: Best fit** | Fitting data with a line |
| | Scatterplots | Creating a scatterplot: <br> ■ Using Microsoft Excel   ■ Using a Graphing Calculator |
| | Identifying patterns | Association: Positive or Negative    Linearity: Linear or Nonlinear <br> Correlation coefficient, $r$ |
| | Linear regression | ■ Determine the "best fit" line <br> ■ Making predictions |

## 0.1 Linear Equations

**Solve for the variable.**

1. $7x - 4 = 12$

2. $13d + 12 = 7d + 6$

3. $20p + 14 = 6 - 5p$

4. $4(x - 7) - 4 = 4$

5. $3(x + 7) - 2 = 4(x - 2)$

6. $7c + 3(c - 5) = 2(c + 3) - 14$

7. $14 - [-3(y - 4) + 9] = [4(2y + 3) - 6] + 4$

8. $[6 - 4x + 2(x - 7)] - 52 = 3(2x - 4) + 6[3(2x - 3) + 6]$

9. $\dfrac{12}{b} - 3 = \dfrac{6}{b} + 4$

10. $\dfrac{g}{3} + g = \dfrac{7}{9}$

11. $\dfrac{13x}{7} - x = \dfrac{x}{4} - \dfrac{3}{14}$

12. $5b + \dfrac{b}{6} = \dfrac{b}{3} - \dfrac{29}{6}$

13. **Investments.** You win $25,000 and you decide to invest the money in two different investments: one paying 20% and the other paying 8%. A year later you have $27,600 total. How much did you originally invest in each account?

14. **Investments.** A college student on summer vacation was able to make $5000 by working a full-time job every summer. He invested half the money in a mutual fund and half the money in a stock that yielded four times as much interest as the mutual fund. After a year he earned $250 in interest. What were the interest rates of the mutual fund and the stock?

15. **Chemistry.** For an experiment, a student requires 150 milliliters of a solution that is 8% NaCl (sodium chloride). The storeroom has only solutions that are 10% NaCl and 5% NaCl. How many milliliters of each available solution should be mixed to get 150 milliliters of 8% NaCl?

16. **Chemistry.** A mixture containing 8% salt is to be mixed with 4 ounces of a mixture that is 20% salt, in order to obtain a solution that is 12% salt. How much of the first solution must be used?

## 0.2 Quadratic Equations

**Solve by factoring.**

17. $b^2 = 4b + 21$

18. $x(x - 3) = 54$

19. $x^2 = 8x$

20. $6y^2 - 7y - 5 = 0$

**Solve by the square root method.**

21. $q^2 - 169 = 0$

22. $c^2 + 36 = 0$

23. $(2x - 4)^2 = -64$

24. $(d + 7)^2 - 4 = 0$

**Solve by completing the square.**

25. $x^2 - 4x - 12 = 0$

26. $2x^2 - 5x - 7 = 0$

27. $\dfrac{x^2}{2} = 4 + \dfrac{x}{2}$

28. $8m = m^2 + 15$

**Solve by the quadratic formula.**

29. $3t^2 - 4t = 7$

30. $4x^2 + 5x + 7 = 0$

31. $8f^2 - \frac{1}{3}f = \frac{7}{6}$

32. $x^2 = -6x + 6$

**Solve by any method.**

33. $5q^2 - 3q - 3 = 0$

34. $(x - 7)^2 = -12$

35. $2x^2 - 3x - 5 = 0$

36. $(g - 2)(g + 5) = -7$

37. $7x^2 = -19x + 6$

38. $7 = (2b^2 + 1)$

39. **Geometry.** Find the base and height of a triangle with an area of 2 square feet if its base is 3 feet longer than its height.

40. **Falling Objects.** A man is standing on top of a building 500 feet tall. If he drops a penny off the roof, the height of the penny is given by $h = -16t^2 + 500$, where $t$ is in seconds. Determine how many seconds it takes until the penny hits the ground.

## 0.3 Other Types of Equations

**Specify any values that must be excluded from the solution set and then solve the rational equation.**

41. $\dfrac{1}{x} - 4 = 3(x - 7) + 5$

42. $\dfrac{4}{x + 1} - \dfrac{8}{x - 1} = 3$

43. $\dfrac{2}{t + 4} - \dfrac{7}{t} = \dfrac{6}{t(t + 4)}$

44. $\dfrac{3}{2x - 7} = \dfrac{-2}{3x + 1}$

45. $\dfrac{3}{2x} - \dfrac{6}{x} = 9$

46. $\dfrac{3 - 5/m}{2 + 5/m} = 1$

**Solve the radical equation for the given variable.**

47. $\sqrt[3]{2x - 4} = 2$

48. $\sqrt{x - 2} = -4$

49. $(2x - 7)^{1/5} = 3$

50. $x = \sqrt{7x - 10}$

51. $x - 4 = \sqrt{x^2 + 5x + 6}$

52. $\sqrt{2x - 7} = \sqrt{x + 3}$

53. $\sqrt{x + 3} = 2 - \sqrt{3x + 2}$

54. $4 + \sqrt{x - 3} = \sqrt{x - 5}$

**Solve the equation by introducing a substitution that transforms the equation to quadratic form.**

55. $y^{-2} - 5y^{-1} + 4 = 0$

56. $p^{-2} + 4p^{-1} = 12$

57. $3x^{1/3} + 2x^{2/3} = 5$

58. $2x^{2/3} - 3x^{1/3} - 5 = 0$

59. $x^{-2/3} + 3x^{-1/3} + 2 = 0$

**60.** $y^{-1/2} - 2y^{-1/4} + 1 = 0$

**61.** $x^4 + 5x^2 = 36$

**62.** $3 - 4x^{-1/2} + x^{-1} = 0$

**Solve the equation by factoring.**

**63.** $x^3 + 4x^2 - 32x = 0$

**64.** $9t^3 - 25t = 0$

**65.** $p^3 - 3p^2 - 4p + 12 = 0$

**66.** $4x^3 - 9x^2 + 4x - 9 = 0$

**67.** $p(2p - 5)^2 - 3(2p - 5) = 0$

**68.** $2(t^2 - 9)^3 - 20(t^2 - 9)^2 = 0$

**69.** $y - 81y^{-1} = 0$

**70.** $9x^{3/2} - 37x^{1/2} + 4x^{-1/2} = 0$

**Solve the absolute value equation.**

**71.** $|x - 3| = -4$

**72.** $|2 + x| = 5$

**73.** $|3x - 4| = 1.1$

**74.** $|x^2 - 6| = 3$

## 0.4 Inequalities

**Graph the indicated set and write as a single interval, if possible.**

**75.** $(4, 6] \cup [5, \infty)$

**76.** $(-\infty, -3) \cup [-7, 2]$

**77.** $(3, 12] \cap [8, \infty)$

**78.** $(-\infty, -2) \cap [-2, 9)$

**Solve the linear inequality and express the solution set in interval notation.**

**79.** $2x < 5 - x$

**80.** $6x + 4 \le 2$

**81.** $4(x - 1) > 2x - 7$

**82.** $\dfrac{x + 3}{3} \ge 6$

**83.** $6 < 2 + x \le 11$

**84.** $-6 \le 1 - 4(x + 2) \le 16$

**85.** $\dfrac{2}{3} \le \dfrac{1 + x}{6} \le \dfrac{3}{4}$

**86.** $\dfrac{x}{3} + \dfrac{x + 4}{9} > \dfrac{x}{6} - \dfrac{1}{3}$

**Solve the polynomial inequality and express the solution set using interval notation.**

**87.** $x^2 \le 36$

**88.** $6x^2 - 7x < 20$

**89.** $4x \le x^2$

**90.** $-x^2 \ge 9x + 14$

**91.** $4x^2 - 12 > 13x$

**92.** $3x \le x^2 + 2$

**Solve the rational inequality and express the solution set using interval notation.**

**93.** $\dfrac{x}{x - 3} < 0$

**94.** $\dfrac{x - 1}{x - 4} > 0$

**95.** $\dfrac{x^2 - 3x}{3} \ge 18$

**96.** $\dfrac{x^2 - 49}{x - 7} \ge 0$

**97.** $\dfrac{3}{x - 2} - \dfrac{1}{x - 4} \le 0$

**98.** $\dfrac{4}{x - 1} \le \dfrac{2}{x + 3}$

**Solve the absolute value inequality and express the solution set using interval notation.**

**99.** $|x + 4| > 7$

**100.** $|-7 + y| \le 4$

**101.** $|2x| > 6$

**102.** $\left| \dfrac{4 + 2x}{3} \right| \ge \dfrac{1}{7}$

**103.** $|2 + 5x| \ge 0$

**104.** $|1 - 2x| \le 4$

## 0.5 Graphing Equations

**Calculate the distance between the two points.**

**105.** $(-2, 0)$ and $(4, 3)$

**106.** $(1, 4)$ and $(4, 4)$

**107.** $(-4, -6)$ and $(2, 7)$

**108.** $\left( \frac{1}{4}, \frac{1}{12} \right)$ and $\left( \frac{1}{3}, -\frac{7}{3} \right)$

**Calculate the midpoint of the segment joining the two points.**

**109.** $(2, 4)$ and $(3, 8)$

**110.** $(-2, 6)$ and $(5, 7)$

**111.** $(2.3, 3.4)$ and $(5.4, 7.2)$

**112.** $(-a, 2)$ and $(a, 4)$

**Find the $x$-intercept(s) and $y$-intercept(s) if any.**

**113.** $x^2 + 4y^2 = 4$

**114.** $y = x^2 - x + 2$

**115.** $y = \sqrt{x^2 - 9}$

**116.** $y = \dfrac{x^2 - x - 12}{x - 12}$

**Use algebraic tests to determine symmetry with respect to the $x$-axis, $y$-axis, or origin.**

**117.** $x^2 + y^3 = 4$

**118.** $y = x^2 - 2$

**119.** $xy = 4$

**120.** $y^2 = 5 + x$

**Use symmetry as a graphing aid and point-plot the given equations.**

**121.** $y = x^2 - 3$  **122.** $y = |x| - 4$  **123.** $y = \sqrt[3]{x}$

**124.** $x = y^2 - 2$  **125.** $y = x\sqrt{9 - x^2}$  **126.** $x^2 + y^2 = 36$

**Find the center and the radius of the circle given by the equation.**

**127.** $(x + 2)^2 + (y + 3)^2 = 81$

**128.** $(x - 4)^2 + (y + 2)^2 = 32$

**129.** $x^2 + y^2 + 2y - 4x + 11 = 0$

**130.** $3x^2 + 3y^2 - 6x - 7 = 0$

## 0.6 Lines

**Write an equation of the line, given the slope and a point that lies on the line.**

**131.** $m = -2$  $(-3, 4)$

**132.** $m = \frac{3}{4}$  $(2, 16)$

**133.** $m = 0$  $(-4, 6)$

**134.** $m$ is undefined  $(2, -5)$

Write the equation of the line that passes through the given points. Express the equation in slope–intercept form or in the form of $x = a$ or $y = b$.

**135.** $(-4, -2)$ and $(2, 3)$

**136.** $(-1, 4)$ and $(-2, 5)$

**137.** $\left(-\frac{3}{4}, \frac{1}{2}\right)$ and $\left(-\frac{7}{4}, \frac{5}{2}\right)$

**138.** $(3, -2)$ and $(-9, 2)$

Find the equation of the line that passes through the given point and also satisfies the additional piece of information.

**139.** $(-2, -1)$      parallel to the line $2x - 3y = 6$

**140.** $(5, 6)$      perpendicular to the line $5x - 3y = 0$

## 0.7 Modeling Variation

Write an equation that describes each variation.

**141.** $C$ is directly proportional to $r$; $C = 2\pi$ when $r = 1$.

**142.** $V$ is directly proportional to both $l$ and $w$; $V = 12h$ when $w = 6$ and $l = 2$.

**143.** $A$ varies directly with the square of $r$; $A = 25\pi$ when $r = 5$.

**144.** $F$ varies inversely with both $\lambda$ and $L$; $F = 20\pi$ when $\lambda = 10\ \mu$m and $L = 10$ km.

# CHAPTER 0 PRACTICE TEST

**Solve the equation.**

1. $4p - 7 = 6p - 1$

2. $-2(z - 1) + 3 = -3z + 3(z - 1)$

3. $3t = t^2 - 28$

4. $8x^2 - 13x = 6$

5. $6x^2 - 13x = 8$

6. $\dfrac{3}{x - 1} = \dfrac{5}{x + 2}$

7. $\dfrac{5}{y - 3} + 1 = \dfrac{30}{y^2 - 9}$

8. $x^4 - 5x^2 - 36 = 0$

9. $\sqrt{2x + 1} + x = 7$

10. $2x^{2/3} + 3x^{1/3} - 2 = 0$

11. $\sqrt{3y - 2} = 3 - \sqrt{3y + 1}$

12. $x(3x - 5)^3 - 2(3x - 5)^2 = 0$

13. $x^{7/3} - 8x^{4/3} + 12x^{1/3} = 0$

14. Solve for $x$: $\left|\frac{1}{5}x + \frac{2}{3}\right| = \frac{7}{15}$.

**Solve the inequality and express the solution in interval notation.**

15. $3x + 19 \geq 5(x - 3)$

16. $-1 \leq 3x + 5 < 26$

17. $\dfrac{2}{5} < \dfrac{x + 8}{4} \leq \dfrac{1}{2}$

18. $3x \geq 2x^2$

19. $3p^2 \geq p + 4$

20. $|5 - 2x| > 1$

21. $\dfrac{x - 3}{2x + 1} \leq 0$

22. $\dfrac{x + 4}{x^2 - 9} \geq 0$

23. Find the distance between the points $(-7, -3)$ and $(2, -2)$.

24. Find the midpoint between $(-3, 5)$ and $(5, -1)$.

**In Exercises 25 and 26, graph the equations.**

25. $2x^2 + y^2 = 8$

26. $y = \dfrac{4}{x^2 + 1}$

27. Find the $x$-intercept and the $y$-intercept of the line $x - 3y = 6$.

28. Find the $x$-intercept(s) and the $y$-intercept(s), if any: $4x^2 - 9y^2 = 36$.

29. Express the line in slope–intercept form: $\frac{2}{3}x - \frac{1}{4}y = 2$.

30. Express the line in slope–intercept form: $4x - 6y = 12$.

**Find the equation of the line that is characterized by the given information. Graph the line.**

31. Passes through the points $(-3, 2)$ and $(4, 9)$

32. Parallel to the line $y = 4x + 3$ and passes through the point $(1, 7)$

33. Perpendicular to the line $2x - 4y = 5$ and passes through the point $(1, 1)$

34. Determine the center and radius of the circle $x^2 + y^2 - 10x + 6y + 22 = 0$.

**In Exercises 35 and 36, use variation to find a model for the given problem.**

35. $F$ varies directly with $m$ and inversely with $p$; $F = 20$ when $m = 2$ and $p = 3$.

36. $y$ varies directly with the square of $x$; $y = 8$ when $x = 5$.

# Functions and Their Graphs

You are buying a pair of running shoes. Their original price was $100, but they have been discounted 30% as part of a weekend sale. Because you arrived early, you can take advantage of door-buster savings: an additional 20% off the sale price. Naïve shoppers might be lured into thinking these shoes will cost $50 because they add the 20% and 30% to get 50% off, but they will end up paying more than that. Experienced shoppers know that the store will first take 30% off of $100, which results in a price of $70, and then it will take an additional 20% off of the sale price, $70, which results in a final discounted price of $56. Experienced shoppers already understand the concept of a function—taking an input (original price) and mapping it to an output (sale price).

A composition of functions can be thought of as a function of a function. One function takes an input (original price, $100) and maps it to an output (sale price, $70), and then another function takes that output as its input (sale price, $70) and maps that to an output (checkout price, $56).

## FUNCTIONS AND THEIR GRAPHS

| **1.1** Functions | **1.2** Graphs of Functions | **1.3** Graphing Techniques: Transformations | **1.4** Combining Functions | **1.5** One-to-One Functions and Inverse Functions |
|---|---|---|---|---|
| • Definition of a Function <br> • Functions Defined by Equations <br> • Function Notation <br> • Domain of a Function | • Recognizing and Classifying Functions <br> • Increasing and Decreasing Functions <br> • Average Rate of Change <br> • Piecewise-Defined Functions | • Horizontal and Vertical Shifts <br> • Reflection About the Axes <br> • Stretching and Compressing | • Adding, Subtracting, Multiplying, and Dividing Functions <br> • Composition of Functions | • One-to-One Functions <br> • Inverse Functions <br> • Graphical Interpretation of Inverse Functions <br> • Finding the Inverse Function |

## LEARNING OBJECTIVES

- Evaluate a function for any argument using placeholder notation.
- Determine characteristics of graphs: even or odd, increasing or decreasing, and the average rate of change.
- Graph functions that are transformations of common functions.
- Find composite functions and their domains.
- Find inverse functions and their domains and ranges.

**SKILLS OBJECTIVES**

- Determine whether a relation is a function.
- Determine whether an equation represents a function.
- Use function notation.
- Find the value of a function.
- Determine the domain and range of a function.

**CONCEPTUAL OBJECTIVES**

- Think of function notation as a placeholder or mapping.
- Understand that all functions are relations but not all relations are functions.

## Definition of a Function

What do the following pairs have in common?

- Every person has a blood type.
- Temperature is some typical value at a particular time of day.
- Every working household phone in the United States has a 10-digit phone number.
- First-class postage rates correspond to the weight of a letter.
- Certain times of the day are start times for sporting events at a university.

They all describe a particular correspondence between two groups. A **relation** is a correspondence between two sets. The first set is called the **domain** and the corresponding second set is called the **range**. Members of these sets are called **elements**.

---

**DEFINITION**  **Relation**

A **relation** is a correspondence between two sets where each element in the first set, called the **domain**, corresponds to *at least* one element in the second set, called the **range**.

---

A relation is a set of ordered pairs. The domain is the set of all the first components of the ordered pairs, and the range is the set of all the second components of the ordered pairs.

| PERSON | BLOOD TYPE | ORDERED PAIR |
|---|---|---|
| Michael | A | (Michael, A) |
| Tania | A | (Tania, A) |
| Dylan | AB | (Dylan, AB) |
| Trevor | O | (Trevor, O) |
| Megan | O | (Megan, O) |

| WORDS | MATH |
|---|---|
| The domain is the set of all the first components. | {Michael, Tania, Dylan, Trevor, Megan} |
| The range is the set of all the second components. | {A, AB, O} |

A relation in which each element in the domain corresponds to exactly one element in the range is a **function**.

## DEFINITION   Function

A **function** is a correspondence between two sets where each element in the first set, called the **domain**, corresponds to *exactly* one element in the second set, called the **range**.

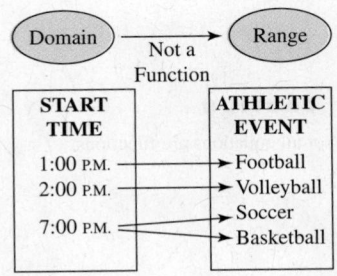

Note that the definition of a function is more restrictive than the definition of a relation. For a relation, each input corresponds to *at least* one output, whereas, for a function, each input corresponds to *exactly* one output. The blood-type example given is both a relation and a function.

Also note that the range (set of values to which the elements of the domain correspond) is a subset of the set of all blood types. Although all functions are relations, not all relations are functions.

For example, at a university, four primary sports typically overlap in the late fall: football, volleyball, soccer, and basketball. On a given Saturday, the table to the right indicates the start times for the competitions.

| TIME OF DAY | COMPETITION |
|---|---|
| 1:00 P.M. | Football |
| 2:00 P.M. | Volleyball |
| 7:00 P.M. | Soccer |
| 7:00 P.M. | Basketball |

**WORDS**

The 1:00 start time corresponds to exactly one event, Football.

The 2:00 start time corresponds to exactly one event, Volleyball.

The 7:00 start time corresponds to two events, Soccer and Basketball.

**MATH**

(1:00 P.M., Football)

(2:00 P.M., Volleyball)

(7:00 P.M., Soccer)
(7:00 P.M., Basketball)

Because an element in the domain, 7:00 P.M., corresponds to more than one element in the range, Soccer and Basketball, this is not a function. It is, however, a relation.

### EXAMPLE 1   Determining Whether a Relation Is a Function

Determine whether the following relations are functions:

**a.** {(−3, 4), (2, 4), (3, 5), (6, 4)}
**b.** {(−3, 4), (2, 4), (3, 5), (2, 2)}
**c.** Domain = Set of all items for sale in a grocery store;  Range = Price

**Solution:**

**a.** No *x*-value is repeated. Therefore, each *x*-value corresponds to exactly one *y*-value.

> This relation is a function.

**b.** The value $x = 2$ corresponds to *both* $y = 2$ and $y = 4$.   This relation is not a function.

**c.** Each item in the grocery store corresponds to exactly one price.   This relation is a function.

**■ YOUR TURN** Determine whether the following relations are functions:

  **a.** {(1, 2), (3, 2), (5, 6), (7, 6)}
  **b.** {(1, 2), (1, 3), (5, 6), (7, 8)}
  **c.** {(11:00 A.M., 83°F), (2:00 P.M., 89°F), (6:00 P.M., 85°F)}

*Study Tip*

All functions are relations but not all relations are functions.

■ **Answer: a.** function
        **b.** not a function
        **c.** function

All of the examples we have discussed thus far are **discrete** sets in that they represent a countable set of distinct pairs of $(x, y)$. A function can also be defined algebraically by an equation.

## Functions Defined by Equations

Let's start with the equation $y = x^2 - 3x$, where $x$ can be any real number. This equation assigns to each $x$-value exactly one corresponding $y$-value. For example,

| $x$ | $y = x^2 - 3x$ | $y$ |
|---|---|---|
| 1 | $y = (1)^2 - 3(1)$ | $-2$ |
| 5 | $y = (5)^2 - 3(5)$ | 10 |
| $-\frac{2}{3}$ | $y = \left(-\frac{2}{3}\right)^2 - 3\left(-\frac{2}{3}\right)$ | $\frac{22}{9}$ |
| 1.2 | $y = (1.2)^2 - 3(1.2)$ | $-2.16$ |

Since the variable $y$ *depends* on what value of $x$ is selected, we denote $y$ as the **dependent variable**. The variable $x$ can be any number in the domain; therefore, we denote $x$ as the **independent variable**.

Although functions are defined by equations, it is important to recognize that *not all equations define functions*. The requirement for an equation to define a function is that each element in the domain corresponds to exactly one element in the range. Throughout the ensuing discussion, we assume $x$ to be the independent variable and $y$ to be the dependent variable.

▼ CAUTION

Not all equations are functions.

**Equations that represent functions of $x$:**   $y = x^2$   $y = |x|$   $y = x^3$

**Equations that do not represent functions of $x$:**   $x = y^2$   $x^2 + y^2 = 1$   $x = |y|$

*Study Tip*

We say that $x = y^2$ is not a function of $x$. However, if we reverse the independent and dependent variables, then $x = y^2$ is a function of $y$.

In the "equations that represent functions of $x$," every $x$-value corresponds to exactly one $y$-value. Some ordered pairs that correspond to these functions are

$$y = x^2: \quad (-1, 1)\ (0, 0)\ (1, 1)$$
$$y = |x|: \quad (-1, 1)\ (0, 0)\ (1, 1)$$
$$y = x^3: \quad (-1, -1)\ (0, 0)\ (1, 1)$$

The fact that $x = -1$ and $x = 1$ both correspond to $y = 1$ in the first two examples does not violate the definition of a function.

In the "equations that do not represent functions of $x$," some $x$-values correspond to *more than one* $y$-value. Some ordered pairs that correspond to these equations are given in the two right-hand columns of the table below.

| RELATION | SOLVE RELATION FOR $y$ | POINTS THAT LIE ON GRAPH | |
|---|---|---|---|
| $x = y^2$ | $y = \pm\sqrt{x}$ | $(1, -1)\ (0, 0)\ (1, 1)$ | $x = 1$ maps to **both** $y = -1$ and $y = 1$ |
| $x^2 + y^2 = 1$ | $y = \pm\sqrt{1 - x^2}$ | $(0, -1)\ (0, 1)\ (-1, 0)\ (1, 0)$ | $x = 0$ maps to **both** $y = -1$ and $y = 1$ |
| $x = |y|$ | $y = \pm x$ | $(1, -1)\ (0, 0)\ (1, 1)$ | $x = 1$ maps to **both** $y = -1$ and $y = 1$ |

Let's look at the graphs of the three **functions of $x$**:

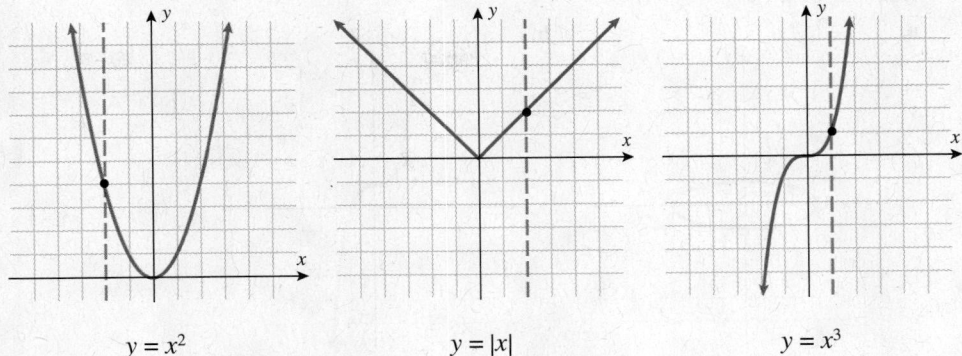

$$y = x^2 \qquad\qquad y = |x| \qquad\qquad y = x^3$$

Let's take any value for $x$, say, $x = a$. The graph of $x = a$ corresponds to a vertical line. A function of $x$ maps each $x$-value to exactly one $y$-value; therefore, there should be at most one point of intersection with any vertical line. We see in the three graphs of the functions above that if a vertical line is drawn at any value of $x$ on any of the three graphs, the vertical line only intersects the graph in one place. Look at the graphs of the three equations that do **not** represent **functions of $x$**.

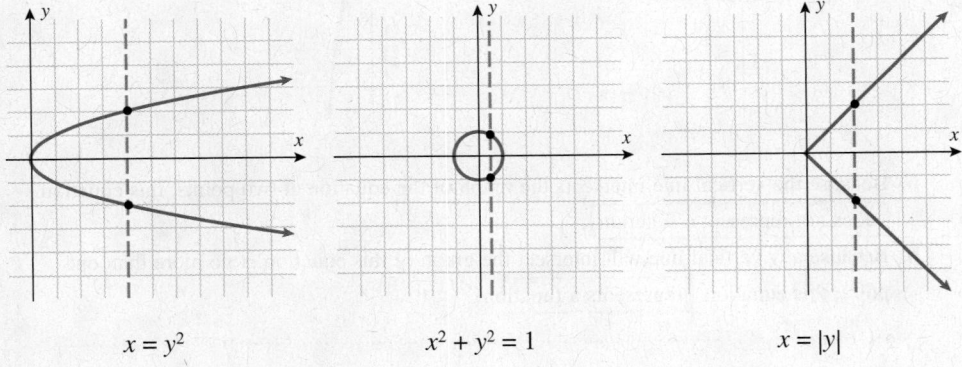

$$x = y^2 \qquad\qquad x^2 + y^2 = 1 \qquad\qquad x = |y|$$

A vertical line can be drawn on any of the three graphs such that the vertical line will intersect each of these graphs at two points. Thus, there is more than one $y$-value that corresponds to some $x$-value in the domain, which is why these equations do not define $y$ as functions of $x$.

**DEFINITION    Vertical Line Test**

Given the graph of an equation, if any vertical line that can be drawn intersects the graph at no more than one point, the equation defines $y$ as a function of $x$. This test is called the **vertical line test**.

**Study Tip**

If any $x$-value corresponds to more than one $y$-value, then $y$ is **not** a function of $x$.

EXAMPLE 2   **Using the Vertical Line Test**

Use the vertical line test to determine whether the graphs of equations define
functions of $x$.

**a.**                                                    **b.**

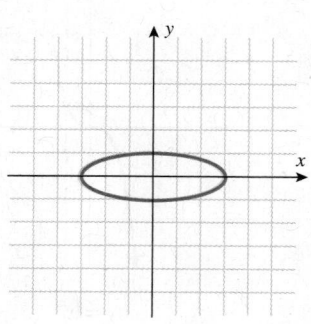                    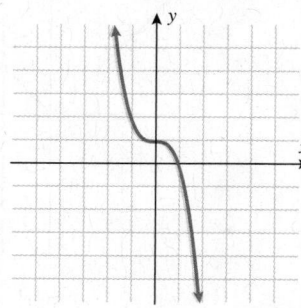

**Solution:**

Apply the vertical line test.

**a.**                                                    **b.**

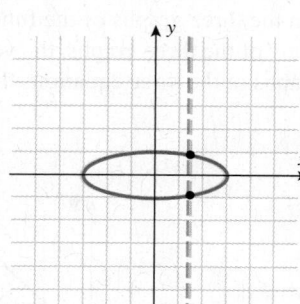                    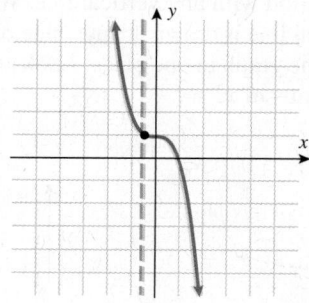

**a.** Because the vertical line intersects the graph of the equation at two points, this equation
  does not represent a function .

**b.** Because any vertical line will intersect the graph of this equation at no more than one
  point, this equation   represents a function .

∎ **Answer:** The graph of the equation
is a circle, which does not pass the
vertical line test. Therefore, the
equation does not define a function.

■ **YOUR TURN**   Determine whether the equation $(x - 3)^2 + (y + 2)^2 = 16$ is a
function of $x$.

To recap, a function can be expressed one of four ways: verbally, numerically, algebraically,
and graphically. This is sometimes called the Rule of 4.

## Expressing a Function

| VERBALLY | NUMERICALLY | ALGEBRAICALLY | GRAPHICALLY |
|---|---|---|---|
| Every real number has a corresponding absolute value. | $\{(-3, 3), (-1, 1), (0, 0), (1, 1), (5, 5)\}$ | $y = \|x\|$ | |

# Function Notation

We know that the equation $y = 2x + 5$ defines $y$ as a function of $x$ because its graph is a nonvertical line and thus passes the vertical line test. We can select $x$-values (input) and determine unique corresponding $y$-values (output). The output is found by taking 2 times the input and then adding 5. If we give the function a name, say, "$f$", then we can use **function notation**:

$$f(x) = 2x + 5$$

**DEFINITION**  **Function Notation**

The symbol $f(x)$ is read "$f$ evaluated at $x$" or "$f$ of $x$" and represents the $y$-value that corresponds to a particular $x$-value. In other words, $y = f(x)$.

| INPUT | FUNCTION | OUTPUT | EQUATION |
|-------|----------|--------|----------|
| $x$ | $f$ | $f(x)$ | $f(x) = 2x + 5$ |
| Independent variable | Mapping | Dependent variable | Mathematical rule |

It is important to note that $f$ is the function name, whereas $f(x)$ is the value of the function. In other words, the function $f$ maps some value $x$ in the domain to some value $f(x)$ in the range.

| $x$ | $f(x) = 2x + 5$ | $f(x)$ |
|-----|-----------------|--------|
| 0 | $f(0) = 2(0) + 5$ | $f(0) = 5$ |
| 1 | $f(1) = 2(1) + 5$ | $f(1) = 7$ |
| 2 | $f(2) = 2(2) + 5$ | $f(2) = 9$ |

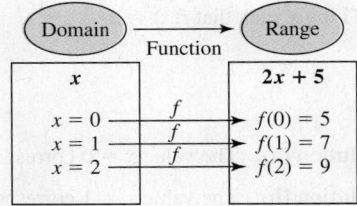

The independent variable is also referred to as the **argument** of a function. To evaluate functions, it is often useful to think of the independent variable or argument as a placeholder. For example, $f(x) = x^2 - 3x$ can be thought of as

$$f(\square) = (\square)^2 - 3(\square)$$

In other words, "$f$ of the argument is equal to the argument squared minus 3 times the argument." Any expression can be substituted for the argument:

$$f(1) = (1)^2 - 3(1)$$
$$f(x + 1) = (x + 1)^2 - 3(x + 1)$$
$$f(-x) = (-x)^2 - 3(-x)$$

It is important to note:

- $f(x)$ does *not* mean $f$ times $x$.
- The most common function names are $f$ and $F$ since the word function begins with an "f". Other common function names are $g$ and $G$, but any letter can be used.
- The letter most commonly used for the independent variable is $x$. The letter $t$ is also common because in real-world applications it represents time, but any letter can be used.
- Although we can think of $y$ and $f(x)$ as interchangeable, the function notation is useful when we want to consider two or more functions of the same independent variable or when we want to evaluate a function at more than one argument.

*Study Tip*

It is important to note that $f(x)$ does not mean $f$ times $x$.

**EXAMPLE 3    Evaluating Functions by Substitution**

Given the function $f(x) = 2x^3 - 3x^2 + 6$, find $f(-1)$.

**Solution:**

Consider the independent variable $x$ to be a placeholder.

$$f(\square) = 2(\square)^3 - 3(\square)^2 + 6$$

To find $f(-1)$, substitute $x = -1$ into the function.

$$f(-1) = 2(-1)^3 - 3(-1)^2 + 6$$

Evaluate the right side.

$$f(-1) = -2 - 3 + 6$$

Simplify.

$$\boxed{f(-1) = 1}$$

**EXAMPLE 4    Finding Function Values from the Graph of a Function**

The graph of $f$ is given on the right.

a. Find $f(0)$.
b. Find $f(1)$.
c. Find $f(2)$.
d. Find $4f(3)$.
e. Find $x$ such that $f(x) = 10$.
f. Find $x$ such that $f(x) = 2$.

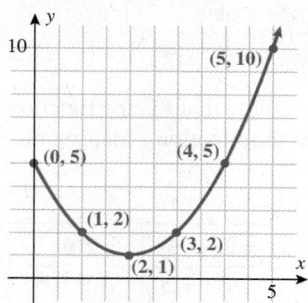

**Solution (a):**  The value $x = 0$ corresponds to the value $y = 5$.  $\boxed{f(0) = 5}$

**Solution (b):**  The value $x = 1$ corresponds to the value $y = 2$.  $\boxed{f(1) = 2}$

**Solution (c):**  The value $x = 2$ corresponds to the value $y = 1$.  $\boxed{f(2) = 1}$

**Solution (d):**  The value $x = 3$ corresponds to the value $y = 2$.   $4f(3) = 4 \cdot 2 = \boxed{8}$

**Solution (e):**  The value $y = 10$ corresponds to the value  $\boxed{x = 5}$ .

**Solution (f):**  The value $y = 2$ corresponds to the values  $\boxed{x = 1}$  and  $\boxed{x = 3}$ .

■ **Answer: a.** $f(-1) = 2$
     **b.** $f(0) = 1$
     **c.** $3f(2) = -21$
     **d.** $x = 1$

■ **YOUR TURN**  For the following graph of a function, find

    **a.** $f(-1)$    **b.** $f(0)$    **c.** $3f(2)$
    **d.** the value of $x$ that corresponds to $f(x) = 0$

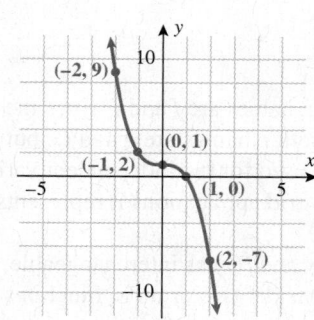

**EXAMPLE 5**  **Evaluating Functions with Variable Arguments (Inputs)**

For the given function $f(x) = x^2 - 3x$, evaluate $f(x + 1)$ and simplify if possible.

## COMMON MISTAKE

A common misunderstanding is to interpret the notation $f(x + 1)$ as a sum: $f(x + 1) \neq f(x) + f(1)$.

### ★ CORRECT

Write the original function.

$$f(x) = x^2 - 3x$$

Replace the argument $x$ with a placeholder.

$$f(\square) = (\square)^2 - 3(\square)$$

Substitute $x + 1$ for the argument.

$$f(x + 1) = (x + 1)^2 - 3(x + 1)$$

Eliminate the parentheses.

$$f(x + 1) = x^2 + 2x + 1 - 3x - 3$$

Combine like terms.

$$\boxed{f(x + 1) = x^2 - x - 2}$$

### ✖ INCORRECT

The **ERROR** is in interpreting the notation as a sum.

$$f(x + 1) \neq f(x) + f(1)$$
$$f(x + 1) \neq x^2 - 3x - 2$$

▼ **CAUTION**

$f(x + 1) \neq f(x) + f(1)$

■ **YOUR TURN** For the given function $g(x) = x^2 - 2x + 3$, evaluate $g(x - 1)$.

■ **Answer:** $g(x - 1) = x^2 - 4x + 6$

---

**EXAMPLE 6**  **Evaluating Functions: Sums**

For the given function $H(x) = x^2 + 2x$, evaluate

**a.** $H(x + 1)$     **b.** $H(x) + H(1)$

**Solution (a):**

Write the function $H$ in placeholder notation.  $H(\square) = (\square)^2 + 2(\square)$

Substitute $x + 1$ for the argument of $H$.  $H(x + 1) = (x + 1)^2 + 2(x + 1)$

Eliminate the parentheses on the right side.  $H(x + 1) = x^2 + 2x + 1 + 2x + 2$

Combine like terms on the right side.  $\boxed{H(x + 1) = x^2 + 4x + 3}$

**Solution (b):**

Write $H(x)$.  $H(x) = x^2 + 2x$

Evaluate $H$ at $x = 1$.  $H(1) = (1)^2 + 2(1) = 3$

Evaluate the sum $H(x) + H(1)$.  $H(x) + H(1) = x^2 + 2x + 3$

$\boxed{H(x) + H(1) = x^2 + 2x + 3}$

*Note:* Comparing the results of part (a) and part (b), we see that

$$H(x + 1) \neq H(x) + H(1).$$

**Technology Tip**

Use a graphing utility to display graphs of
$y_1 = H(x + 1) = (x + 1)^2 + 2(x + 1)$
and $y_2 = H(x) + H(1) = x^2 + 2x + 3$.

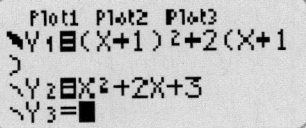

The graphs are not the same.

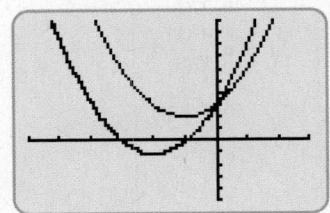

Use a graphing utility to display graphs of $y_1 = G(-x) = (-x)^2 - (-x)$ and $y_2 = -G(x) = -(x^2 - x)$.

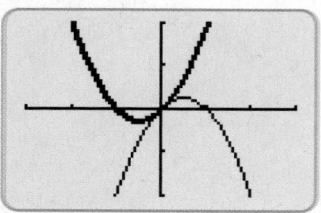

The graphs are not the same.

### EXAMPLE 7 Evaluating Functions: Negatives

For the given function $G(t) = t^2 - t$, evaluate

**a.** $G(-t)$    **b.** $-G(t)$

**Solution (a):**

| | |
|---|---|
| Write the function $G$ in placeholder notation. | $G(\square) = (\square)^2 - (\square)$ |
| Substitute $-t$ for the argument of $G$. | $G(-t) = (-t)^2 - (-t)$ |
| Eliminate the parentheses on the right side. | $\boxed{G(-t) = t^2 + t}$ |

**Solution (b):**

| | |
|---|---|
| Write $G(t)$. | $G(t) = t^2 - t$ |
| Multiply by $-1$. | $-G(t) = -(t^2 - t)$ |
| Eliminate the parentheses on the right side. | $\boxed{-G(t) = -t^2 + t}$ |

*Note:* Comparing the results of part (a) and part (b), we see that $G(-t) \neq -G(t)$. If $G(t)$ was an odd function, then $G(-t) = -G(t)$, but in general this is not true.

### EXAMPLE 8 Evaluating Functions: Quotients

For the given function $F(x) = 3x + 5$, evaluate

**a.** $F\left(\dfrac{1}{2}\right)$    **b.** $\dfrac{F(1)}{F(2)}$

**Solution (a):**

| | |
|---|---|
| Write $F$ in placeholder notation. | $F(\square) = 3(\square) + 5$ |
| Replace the argument with $\frac{1}{2}$. | $F\left(\dfrac{1}{2}\right) = 3\left(\dfrac{1}{2}\right) + 5$ |
| Simplify the right side. | $\boxed{F\left(\dfrac{1}{2}\right) = \dfrac{13}{2}}$ |

**Solution (b):**

| | |
|---|---|
| Evaluate $F(1)$. | $F(1) = 3(1) + 5 = 8$ |
| Evaluate $F(2)$. | $F(2) = 3(2) + 5 = 11$ |
| Divide $F(1)$ by $F(2)$. | $\boxed{\dfrac{F(1)}{F(2)} = \dfrac{8}{11}}$ |

*Note:* Comparing the results of part (a) and part (b), we see that $F\left(\dfrac{1}{2}\right) \neq \dfrac{F(1)}{F(2)}$.

■ **Answer:** **a.** $G(t - 2) = 3t - 10$
     **b.** $G(t) - G(2) = 3t - 6$
     **c.** $\dfrac{G(1)}{G(3)} = -\dfrac{1}{5}$
     **d.** $G\left(\dfrac{1}{3}\right) = -3$

■ **YOUR TURN**   Given the function $G(t) = 3t - 4$, evaluate

     **a.** $G(t - 2)$    **b.** $G(t) - G(2)$    **c.** $\dfrac{G(1)}{G(3)}$    **d.** $G\left(\dfrac{1}{3}\right)$

Examples 6–8 illustrate the following in general:

$$f(a + b) \neq f(a) + f(b) \qquad f(-t) \neq -f(t) \qquad f\left(\frac{a}{b}\right) \neq \frac{f(a)}{f(b)}$$

# Domain of a Function

Sometimes the domain of a function is stated *explicitly*. For example,

$$f(x) = |x| \qquad \underbrace{x < 0}_{\text{domain}}$$

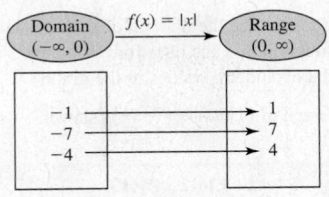

Here, the **explicit domain** is the set of all negative real numbers, $(-\infty, 0)$. Every negative real number in the domain is mapped to a positive real number in the range through the absolute value function.

If the expression that defines the function is given but the domain is not stated explicitly, then the domain is implied. The **implicit domain** is the largest set of real numbers for which the function is defined and the output value $f(x)$ is a real number. For example,

$$f(x) = \sqrt{x}$$

does not have the domain explicitly stated. There is, however, an implicit domain. Note that if the argument is negative, that is, if $x < 0$, then the result is an imaginary number. In order for the output of the function, $f(x)$, to be a real number, we must restrict the domain to nonnegative numbers, that is, if $x \geq 0$.

| FUNCTION | IMPLICIT DOMAIN |
|---|---|
| $f(x) = \sqrt{x}$ | $[0, \infty)$ |

In general, we ask the question, "What can $x$ be?" The implicit domain of a function excludes values that cause a function to be undefined or have outputs that are not real numbers.

| EXPRESSION THAT DEFINES THE FUNCTION | EXCLUDED x-VALUES | EXAMPLE | IMPLICIT DOMAIN |
|---|---|---|---|
| Polynomial | None | $f(x) = x^3 - 4x^2$ | All real numbers |
| Rational | x-values that make the denominator equal to 0 | $g(x) = \dfrac{2}{x^2 - 9}$ | $x \neq \pm 3$ or $(-\infty, -3) \cup (-3, 3) \cup (3, \infty)$ |
| Radical | x-values that result in a square (even) root of a negative number | $h(x) = \sqrt{x - 5}$ | $x \geq 5$ or $[5, \infty)$ |

## EXAMPLE 9   Determining the Domain of a Function

State the domain of the given functions.

**a.** $F(x) = \dfrac{3}{x^2 - 25}$     **b.** $H(x) = \sqrt[4]{9 - 2x}$     **c.** $G(x) = \sqrt[3]{x - 1}$

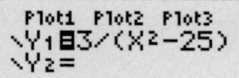
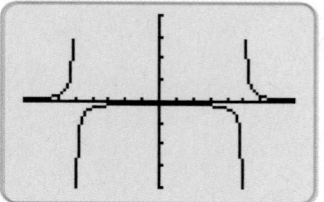

**Solution (a):**

| | |
|---|---|
| Write the original equation. | $F(x) = \dfrac{3}{x^2 - 25}$ |
| Determine any restrictions on the values of $x$. | $x^2 - 25 \neq 0$ |
| Solve the restriction equation. | $x^2 \neq 25$ or $x \neq \pm\sqrt{25} = \pm 5$ |
| State the domain restrictions. | $x \neq \pm 5$ |
| Write the domain in interval notation. | $\boxed{(-\infty, -5) \cup (-5, 5) \cup (5, \infty)}$ |

**Solution (b):**

| | |
|---|---|
| Write the original equation. | $H(x) = \sqrt[4]{9 - 2x}$ |
| Determine any restrictions on the values of $x$. | $9 - 2x \geq 0$ |
| Solve the restriction equation. | $9 \geq 2x$ |
| State the domain restrictions. | $x \leq \dfrac{9}{2}$ |
| Write the domain in interval notation. | $\boxed{\left(-\infty, \dfrac{9}{2}\right]}$ |

**Solution (c):**

| | |
|---|---|
| Write the original equation. | $G(x) = \sqrt[3]{x - 1}$ |
| Determine any restrictions on the values of $x$. | no restrictions |
| State the domain. | $\mathbb{R}$ |
| Write the domain in interval notation. | $\boxed{(-\infty, \infty)}$ |

■ **YOUR TURN**   State the domain of the given functions.

**a.** $f(x) = \sqrt{x - 3}$     **b.** $g(x) = \dfrac{1}{x^2 - 4}$

■ **Answer:**

**a.** $x \geq 3$ or $[3, \infty)$

**b.** $x \neq \pm 2$ or $(-\infty, -2) \cup (-2, 2) \cup (2, \infty)$

## Applications

Functions that are used in applications often have restrictions on the domains due to physical constraints. For example, the volume of a cube is given by the function $V(x) = x^3$, where $x$ is the length of a side. The function $f(x) = x^3$ has no restrictions on $x$, and therefore, the domain is the set of all real numbers. However, the volume of any cube has the restriction that the length of a side can never be negative or zero.

### EXAMPLE 10   The Dimensions of a Pool

Express the volume of a 30 foot by 10 foot rectangular swimming pool as a function of its depth.

**Solution:**

The volume of any rectangular box is $V = lwh$, where $V$ is the volume, $l$ is the length, $w$ is the width, and $h$ is the height. In this example, the length is 30 feet, the width is 10 feet, and the height represents the depth $d$ of the pool.

| | |
|---|---|
| Write the volume as a function of depth $d$. | $V(d) = (30)(10)d$ |
| Simplify. | $\boxed{V(d) = 300d}$ |
| Determine any restrictions on the domain. | $d > 0$ |

SECTION
1.1 SUMMARY

**Relations and Functions (Let $x$ represent the independent variable and $y$ the dependent variable.)**

| TYPE | MAPPING/CORRESPONDENCE | EQUATION | GRAPH |
|---|---|---|---|
| Relation | Every $x$-value in the domain maps to **at least one** $y$-value in the range. | $x = y^2$ | |
| Function | Every $x$-value in the domain maps to **exactly one** $y$-value in the range. | $y = x^2$ | Passes vertical line test |

All functions are relations, but not all relations are functions. Functions can be represented by equations. In the following table, each column illustrates an alternative notation.

| INPUT | CORRESPONDENCE | OUTPUT | EQUATION |
|---|---|---|---|
| $x$ | Function | $y$ | $y = 2x + 5$ |
| Independent variable | Mapping | Dependent variable | Mathematical rule |
| Argument | $f$ | $f(x)$ | $f(x) = 2x + 5$ |

The **domain** is the set of all inputs ($x$-values) and the **range** is the set of all corresponding outputs ($y$-values). Placeholder notation is useful when evaluating functions.

$$f(x) = 3x^2 + 2x$$

$$f(\square) = 3(\square)^2 + 2(\square)$$

An **explicit domain** is stated, whereas an **implicit domain** is found by *excluding* $x$-values that

- make the function undefined (denominator $= 0$).
- result in a nonreal output (even roots of negative real numbers).

SECTION
1.1 EXERCISES

▪ SKILLS

In Exercises 1–18, determine whether each relation is a function. Assume that the coordinate pair $(x, y)$ represents the independent variable $x$ and the dependent variable $y$.

**1.** $\{(0, -3), (0, 3), (-3, 0), (3, 0)\}$

**2.** $\{(2, -2), (2, 2), (5, -5), (5, 5)\}$

**3.** $\{(0, 0), (9, -3), (4, -2), (4, 2), (9, 3)\}$

**4.** $\{(0, 0), (-1, -1), (-2, -8), (1, 1), (2, 8)\}$

**5.** {(0, 1), (1, 0), (2, 1), (−2, 1), (5, 4), (−3, 4)}    **6.** {(0, 1), (1, 1), (2, 1), (3, 1)}

**7.** $x^2 + y^2 = 9$    **8.** $x = |y|$    **9.** $x = y^2$

**10.** $y = x^3$    **11.** $y = |x − 1|$    **12.** $y = 3$

**13.**
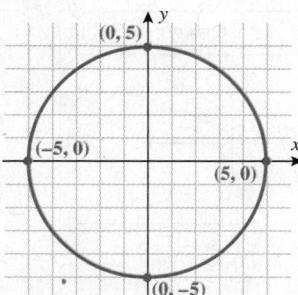

**14.**
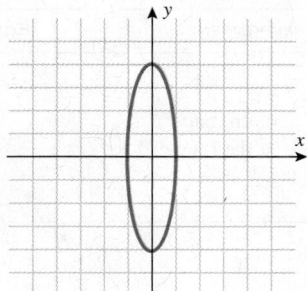

**15.**
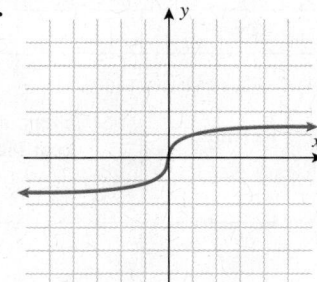

**16.**
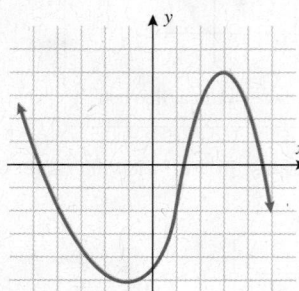

**17.**
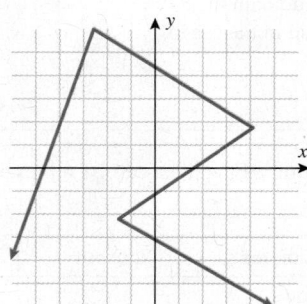

**18.**
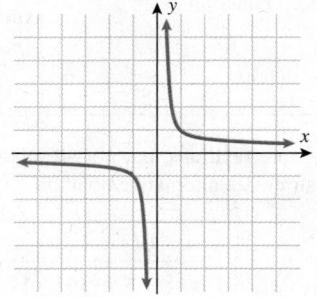

**In Exercises 19–26, use the given graphs to evaluate the functions.**

**19.** $y = f(x)$
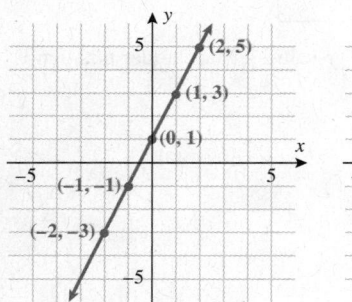

a. $f(2)$  b. $f(0)$  c. $f(−2)$

**20.** $y = g(x)$
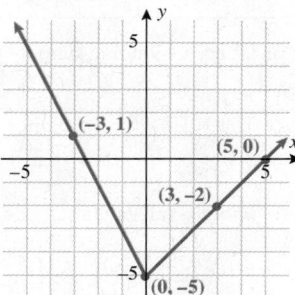

a. $g(−3)$  b. $g(0)$  c. $g(5)$

**21.** $y = p(x)$
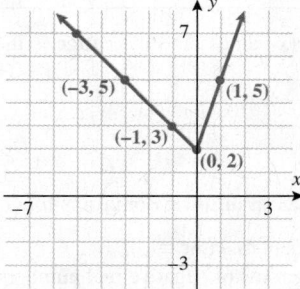

a. $p(−1)$  b. $p(0)$  c. $p(1)$

**22.** $y = r(x)$
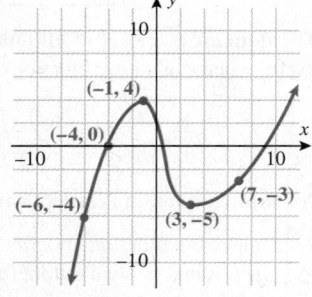

a. $r(−4)$  b. $r(−1)$  c. $r(3)$

**23.** $y = C(x)$
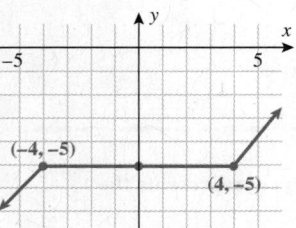

a. $C(2)$  b. $C(0)$  c. $C(−2)$

**24.** $y = q(x)$

a. $q(−4)$  b. $q(0)$  c. $q(2)$

**25.** $y = S(x)$

a. $S(−3)$  b. $S(0)$  c. $S(2)$

**26.** $y = T(x)$

a. $T(−5)$  b. $T(−2)$  c. $T(4)$

**27.** Find $x$ if $f(x) = 3$ in Exercise 19.   **28.** Find $x$ if $g(x) = -2$ in Exercise 20.   **29.** Find $x$ if $p(x) = 5$ in Exercise 21.

**30.** Find $x$ if $C(x) = -7$ in Exercise 22.   **31.** Find $x$ if $C(x) = -5$ in Exercise 23.   **32.** Find $x$ if $q(x) = -2$ in Exercise 24.

**33.** Find $x$ if $S(x) = 1$ in Exercise 25.   **34.** Find $x$ if $T(x) = 4$ in Exercise 26.

**In Exercises 35–50, evaluate the given quantities applying the following four functions:**

$$f(x) = 2x - 3 \qquad F(t) = 4 - t^2 \qquad g(t) = 5 + t \qquad G(x) = x^2 + 2x - 7$$

**35.** $f(-2)$   **36.** $G(-3)$   **37.** $g(1)$   **38.** $F(-1)$

**39.** $f(-2) + g(1)$   **40.** $G(-3) - F(-1)$   **41.** $3f(-2) - 2g(1)$   **42.** $2F(-1) - 2G(-3)$

**43.** $\dfrac{f(-2)}{g(1)}$   **44.** $\dfrac{G(-3)}{F(-1)}$   **45.** $\dfrac{f(0) - f(-2)}{g(1)}$   **46.** $\dfrac{G(0) - G(-3)}{F(-1)}$

**47.** $f(x + 1) - f(x - 1)$   **48.** $F(t + 1) - F(t - 1)$   **49.** $g(x + a) - f(x + a)$   **50.** $G(x + b) + F(b)$

**In Exercises 51–82, find the domain of the given function. Express the domain in interval notation.**

**51.** $f(x) = 2x - 5$   **52.** $f(x) = -2x - 5$   **53.** $g(t) = t^2 + 3t$   **54.** $h(x) = 3x^4 - 1$

**55.** $P(x) = \dfrac{x + 5}{x - 5}$   **56.** $Q(t) = \dfrac{2 - t^2}{t + 3}$   **57.** $T(x) = \dfrac{2}{x^2 - 4}$   **58.** $R(x) = \dfrac{1}{x^2 - 1}$

**59.** $F(x) = \dfrac{1}{x^2 + 1}$   **60.** $G(t) = \dfrac{2}{t^2 + 4}$   **61.** $q(x) = \sqrt{7 - x}$   **62.** $k(t) = \sqrt{t - 7}$

**63.** $f(x) = \sqrt{2x + 5}$   **64.** $g(x) = \sqrt{5 - 2x}$   **65.** $G(t) = \sqrt{t^2 - 4}$   **66.** $F(x) = \sqrt{x^2 - 25}$

**67.** $F(x) = \dfrac{1}{\sqrt{x - 3}}$   **68.** $G(x) = \dfrac{2}{\sqrt{5 - x}}$   **69.** $f(x) = \sqrt[3]{1 - 2x}$   **70.** $g(x) = \sqrt[5]{7 - 5x}$

**71.** $P(x) = \dfrac{1}{\sqrt[5]{x + 4}}$   **72.** $Q(x) = \dfrac{x}{\sqrt[3]{x^2 - 9}}$   **73.** $R(x) = \dfrac{x + 1}{\sqrt[4]{3 - 2x}}$   **74.** $p(x) = \dfrac{x^2}{\sqrt{25 - x^2}}$

**75.** $H(t) = \dfrac{t}{\sqrt{t^2 - t - 6}}$   **76.** $f(t) = \dfrac{t - 3}{\sqrt[4]{t^2 + 9}}$   **77.** $f(x) = (x^2 - 16)^{1/2}$   **78.** $g(x) = (2x - 5)^{1/3}$

**79.** $r(x) = x^2(3 - 2x)^{-1/2}$   **80.** $p(x) = (x - 1)^2 (x^2 - 9)^{-3/5}$   **81.** $f(x) = \frac{2}{5}x - \frac{2}{4}$   **82.** $g(x) = \frac{2}{3}x^2 - \frac{1}{6}x - \frac{3}{4}$

**83.** Let $g(x) = x^2 - 2x - 5$ and find the values of $x$ that correspond to $g(x) = 3$.

**84.** Let $g(x) = \frac{5}{6}x - \frac{3}{4}$ and find the value of $x$ that corresponds to $g(x) = \frac{2}{3}$.

**85.** Let $f(x) = 2x(x - 5)^3 - 12(x - 5)^2$ and find the values of $x$ that correspond to $f(x) = 0$.

**86.** Let $f(x) = 3x(x + 3)^2 - 6(x + 3)^3$ and find the values of $x$ that correspond to $f(x) = 0$.

# ▪ APPLICATIONS

**87. Temperature.** The average temperature in Tampa, Florida in the springtime is given by the function $T(x) = -0.7x^2 + 16.8x - 10.8$, where $T$ is the temperature in degrees Fahrenheit and $x$ is the time of day in military time and is restricted to $6 \leq x \leq 18$ (sunrise to sunset). What is the temperature at 6 A.M.? What is the temperature at noon?

**88. Temperature.** The average temperature in Orlando, Florida in the summertime is given by the function $T(x) = -0.5x^2 + 14.2x - 2.8$, where $T$ is the temperature in degrees Fahrenheit and $x$ is the time of the day in military time and is restricted to $7 \leq x \leq 20$ (sunrise to sunset). What is the temperature at 9 A.M.? What is the temperature at 3 P.M.?

**89. Falling Objects: Baseballs.** A baseball is hit and its height is a function of time, $h(t) = -16t^2 + 45t + 1$, where $h$ is the height in feet and $t$ is the time in seconds, with $t = 0$ corresponding to the instant the ball is hit. What is the height after 2 seconds? What is the domain of this function?

**90. Falling Objects: Firecrackers.** A firecracker is launched straight up, and its height is a function of time, $h(t) = -16t^2 + 128t$, where $h$ is the height in feet and $t$ is the time in seconds, with $t = 0$ corresponding to the instant it launches. What is the height 4 seconds after launch? What is the domain of this function?

**91. Volume.** An open box is constructed from a square 10-inch piece of cardboard by cutting squares of length $x$ inches out of each corner and folding the sides up. Express the volume of the box as a function of $x$, and state the domain.

**92. Volume.** A cylindrical water basin will be built to harvest rainwater. The basin is limited in that the largest radius it can have is 10 feet. Write a function representing the volume of water $V$ as a function of height $h$. How many additional gallons of water will be collected if you increase the height by 2 feet? *Hint:* 1 cu ft = 7.48 gal.

**For Exercises 93–94, refer to the following:**

The weekly exchange rate of the U.S. dollar to the Japanese yen is shown in the graph as varying over an 8-week period. Assume the exchange rate $E(t)$ is a function of time (week); let $E(1)$ be the exchange rate during Week 1.

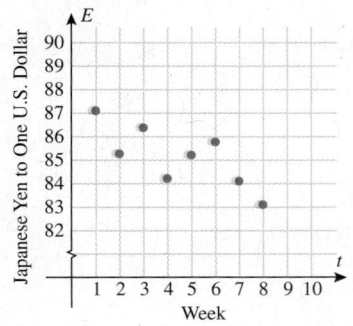

**93. Economics.** Approximate the exchange rates of the U.S. dollar to the nearest yen during Weeks 4, 7, and 8.

**94. Economics.** Find the increase or decrease in the number of Japanese yen to the U.S. dollar exchange rate, to the nearest yen, from (a) Week 2 to Week 3 and (b) Week 6 to Week 7.

**For Exercises 95–96, refer to the following:**

An epidemiological study of the spread of malaria in a rural area finds that the total number $P$ of people who contracted malaria $t$ days into an outbreak is modeled by the function

$$P(t) = -\frac{1}{4}t^2 + 7t + 180 \qquad 1 \leq t \leq 14$$

**95. Medicine/Health.** How many people have contracted malaria 14 days into the outbreak?

**96. Medicine/Health.** How many people have contracted malaria 6 days into the outbreak?

**97. Environment: Tossing the Envelopes.** The average American adult receives 24 pieces of mail per week, usually of some combination of ads and envelopes with windows. Suppose each of these adults throws away a dozen envelopes per week.

a. The width of the window of an envelope is 3.375 inches less than its length $x$. Create the function $A(x)$ that represents the area of the window in square inches. Simplify, if possible.

b. Evaluate $A(4.5)$ and explain what this value represents.

c. Assume the dimensions of the envelope are 8 inches by 4 inches. Evaluate $A(8.5)$. Is this possible for this particular envelope? Explain.

**98. Environment: Tossing the Envelopes.** Each month, Jack receives his bank statement in a 9.5 inch by 6 inch envelope. Each month, he throws away the envelope after removing the statement.

a. The width of the window of the envelope is 2.875 inches less than its length $x$. Create the function $A(x)$ that represents the area of the window in square inches. Simplify, if possible.

b. Evaluate $A(5.25)$ and explain what this value represents.

c. Evaluate $A(10)$. Is this possible for this particular envelope? Explain.

**For Exercises 99 and 100, refer to the table below. It illustrates the average federal funds rate for the month of January (2000 to 2008).**

99. **Finance.** Is the relation whose domain is the year and whose range is the average federal funds rate for the month of January a function? Explain.

100. **Finance.** Write five ordered pairs whose domain is the set of even years from 2000 to 2008 and whose range is the set of corresponding average federal funds rate for the month of January.

| YEAR | FED. RATE |
|------|-----------|
| 2000 | 5.45 |
| 2001 | 5.98 |
| 2002 | 1.73 |
| 2003 | 1.24 |
| 2004 | 1.00 |
| 2005 | 2.25 |
| 2006 | 4.50 |
| 2007 | 5.25 |
| 2008 | 3.50 |

**For Exercises 101 and 102, use the following figure:**

Employer-Provided Health Insurance Premiums for Family Plans (1988–2005, adjusted for inflation)

■ Employee Share
■ Employer Share

*Source:* Kaiser Family Foundation Health Research and Education Trust. *Note:* The following years were interpolated: 1989–1992; 1994–1995; 1997–1998.

101. **Health-Care Costs:** Fill in the following table. Round dollars to the nearest $1000.

| YEAR | TOTAL HEALTH-CARE COST FOR FAMILY PLANS |
|------|------------------------------------------|
| 1989 | |
| 1993 | |
| 1997 | |
| 2001 | |
| 2005 | |

Write the five ordered pairs resulting from the table.

102. **Health-Care Costs.** Using the table found in Exercise 101, let the years correspond to the domain and the total costs correspond to the range. Is this relation a function? Explain.

**For Exercises 103 and 104, use the following information:**

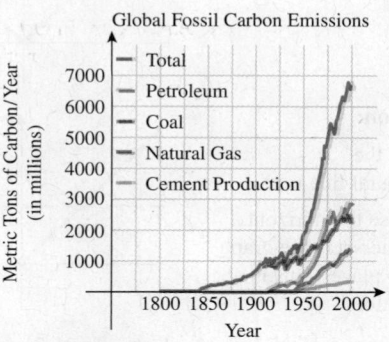

*Source:* http://www.naftc.wvu.edu

Let the functions $f$, $F$, $g$, $G$, and $H$ represent the number of tons of carbon emitted per year as a function of year corresponding to cement production, natural gas, coal, petroleum, and the total amount, respectively. Let $t$ represent the year, with $t = 0$ corresponding to 1900.

103. **Environment: Global Climate Change.** Estimate (to the nearest thousand) the value of

   a. $F(50)$     b. $g(50)$     c. $H(50)$

104. **Environment: Global Climate Change.** Explain what the sum $F(100) + g(100) + G(100)$ represents.

■ **CATCH THE MISTAKE**

**In Exercises 105–110, explain the mistake that is made.**

**105.** Determine whether the relationship is a function.

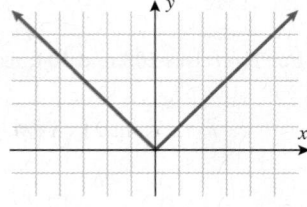

**Solution:**

Apply the horizontal line test.

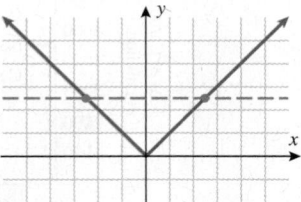

Because the horizontal line intersects the graph in two places, this is not a function.

This is incorrect. What mistake was made?

**106.** Given the function $H(x) = 3x - 2$, evaluate the quantity $H(3) - H(-1)$.

**Solution:** $H(3) - H(-1) = H(3) + H(1) = 7 + 1 = 8$

This is incorrect. What mistake was made?

**107.** Given the function $f(x) = x^2 - x$, evaluate the quantity $f(x + 1)$.

**Solution:** $f(x + 1) = f(x) + f(1) = x^2 - x + 0$
$$f(x + 1) = x^2 - x$$

This is incorrect. What mistake was made?

**108.** Determine the domain of the function $g(t) = \sqrt{3 - t}$ and express it in interval notation.

**Solution:**

What can $t$ be? Any nonnegative real number.
$$3 - t > 0$$
$$3 > t \quad \text{or} \quad t < 3$$
Domain: $(-\infty, 3)$

This is incorrect. What mistake was made?

**109.** Given the function $G(x) = x^2$, evaluate
$$\frac{G(-1 + h) - G(-1)}{h}.$$

**Solution:**
$$\frac{G(-1 + h) - G(-1)}{h} = \frac{G(-1) + G(h) - G(-1)}{h}$$

$$= \frac{G(h)}{h} = \frac{h^2}{h} = h$$

This is incorrect. What mistake was made?

**110.** Given the functions $f(x) = |x - A| - 1$ and $f(1) = -1$, find $A$.

**Solution:**

Since $f(1) = -1$, the point $(-1, 1)$ must satisfy the function. $\quad -1 = |-1 - A| - 1$

Add 1 to both sides of the equation. $\quad |-1 - A| = 0$

The absolute value of zero is zero, so there is no need for the absolute value signs: $-1 - A = 0 \Rightarrow A = -1$.

This is incorrect. What mistake was made?

■ **CONCEPTUAL**

**In Exercises 111–116, determine whether each statement is true or false.**

**111.** If a vertical line does not intersect the graph of an equation, then that equation does not represent a function.

**112.** If a horizontal line intersects a graph of an equation more than once, the equation does not represent a function.

**113.** For $x = y^2$, $x$ is a function of $y$.

**114.** For $y = x^2$, $y$ is a function of $x$.

**115.** If $f(x) = Ax^2 - 3x$ and $f(1) = -1$, find $A$.

**116.** If $g(x) = \dfrac{1}{b - x}$ and $g(3)$ is undefined, find $b$.

■ **CHALLENGE**

**117.** If $F(x) = \dfrac{C - x}{D - x}$, $F(-2)$ is undefined, and $F(-1) = 4$, find $C$ and $D$.

**118.** Construct a function that is undefined at $x = 5$ and whose graph passes through the point $(1, -1)$.

**In Exercises 119 and 120, find the domain of each function, where $a$ is any positive real number.**

**119.** $f(x) = \dfrac{-100}{x^2 - a^2}$

**120.** $f(x) = -5\sqrt{x^2 - a^2}$

■ TECHNOLOGY

**121.** Using a graphing utility, graph the temperature function in Exercise 87. What time of day is it the warmest? What is the temperature? Looking at this function, explain why this model for Tampa, Florida, is valid only from sunrise to sunset (6 to 18).

**122.** Using a graphing utility, graph the height of the firecracker in Exercise 90. How long after liftoff is the firecracker airborne? What is the maximum height that the firecracker attains? Explain why this height model is valid only for the first 8 seconds.

**123.** Let $f(x) = x^2 + 1$. Graph $y_1 = f(x)$ and $y_2 = f(x - 2)$ in the same viewing window. Describe how the graph of $y_2$ can be obtained from the graph of $y_1$.

**124.** Let $f(x) = 4 - x^2$. Graph $y_1 = f(x)$ and $y_2 = f(x + 2)$ in the same viewing window. Describe how the graph of $y_2$ can be obtained from the graph of $y_1$.

■ PREVIEW TO CALCULUS

**For Exercises 125–128, refer to the following:**

In calculus, the difference quotient $\dfrac{f(x + h) - f(x)}{h}$ of a function $f$ is used to find a new function $f'$, called the *derivative* of $f$. To find $f'$, we let $h$ approach 0, $h \to 0$, in the difference quotient. For example, if $f(x) = x^2$, $\dfrac{f(x + h) - f(x)}{h} = 2x + h$, and allowing $h = 0$, we have $f'(x) = 2x$.

**125.** Given $f(x) = x^3 + x$, find $f'(x)$.

**126.** Given $f(x) = 6x + \sqrt{x}$, find $f'(x)$.

**127.** Given $f(x) = \dfrac{x - 5}{x + 3}$, find $f'(x)$.

**128.** Given $f(x) = \sqrt{\dfrac{x + 7}{5 - x}}$, find $f'(x)$.

**SECTION**

# 1.2   GRAPHS OF FUNCTIONS

### SKILLS OBJECTIVES

- Classify functions as even, odd, or neither.
- Determine whether functions are increasing, decreasing, or constant.
- Calculate the average rate of change of a function.
- Evaluate the difference quotient for a function.
- Graph piecewise-defined functions.

### CONCEPTUAL OBJECTIVES

- Identify common functions.
- Develop and graph piecewise-defined functions.
  - Identify and graph points of discontinuity.
  - State the domain and range.
- Understand that even functions have graphs that are symmetric about the $y$-axis and odd functions have graphs that are symmetric about the origin.
- Understand that the difference quotient is an average rate of change.

# Recognizing and Classifying Functions

## Common Functions

The nine main functions you will read about in this section will constitute a "library" of functions that you should commit to memory. We will draw on this library of functions in the next section when graphing transformations are discussed.

In Section 0.6, we discussed equations and graphs of lines. All lines (with the exception of vertical lines) pass the vertical line test, and hence are classified as functions. Instead of the traditional notation of a line, $y = mx + b$, we use function notation and classify a function whose graph is a *line* as a *linear* function.

### LINEAR FUNCTION

$$f(x) = mx + b \qquad \text{$m$ and $b$ are real numbers.}$$

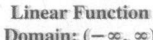

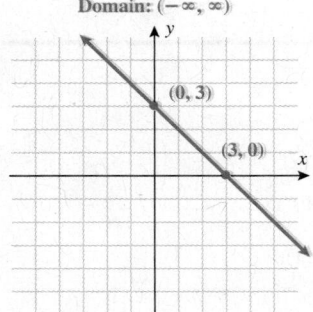

**Linear Function**
**Domain: $(-\infty, \infty)$**

The domain of a linear function $f(x) = mx + b$ is the set of all real numbers $\mathbb{R}$. The graph of this function has slope $m$ and $y$-intercept $b$.

| LINEAR FUNCTION: $f(x) = mx + b$ | SLOPE: $m$ | $y$-INTERCEPT: $b$ |
|---|---|---|
| $f(x) = 2x - 7$ | $m = 2$ | $b = -7$ |
| $f(x) = -x + 3$ | $m = -1$ | $b = 3$ |
| $f(x) = x$ | $m = 1$ | $b = 0$ |
| $f(x) = 5$ | $m = 0$ | $b = 5$ |

One special case of the linear function is the *constant function* ($m = 0$).

### CONSTANT FUNCTION

$$f(x) = b \qquad \text{$b$ is any real number.}$$

The graph of a constant function $f(x) = b$ is a horizontal line. The $y$-intercept corresponds to the point $(0, b)$. The domain of a constant function is the set of all real numbers $\mathbb{R}$. The range, however, is a single value $b$. In other words, all $x$-values correspond to a single $y$-value.

Points that lie on the graph of a constant function $f(x) = b$ are

$(-5, b)$

$(-1, b)$

$(0, b)$

$(2, b)$

$(4, b)$

$\cdots$

$(x, b)$

Domain: $(-\infty, \infty)$   Range: $[b, b]$ or $\{b\}$

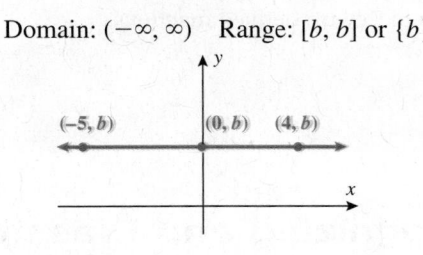

Another specific example of a linear function is the function having a slope of one ($m = 1$) and a $y$-intercept of zero ($b = 0$). This special case is called the *identity function*.

## IDENTITY FUNCTION

$$f(x) = x$$

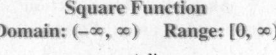

Identity Function
Domain: $(-\infty, \infty)$  Range: $(-\infty, \infty)$

The graph of the identity function has the following properties: it passes through the origin, and every point that lies on the line has equal $x$- and $y$-coordinates. Both the domain and the range of the identity function are the set of all real numbers $\mathbb{R}$.

A function that squares the input is called the *square function.*

## SQUARE FUNCTION

$$f(x) = x^2$$

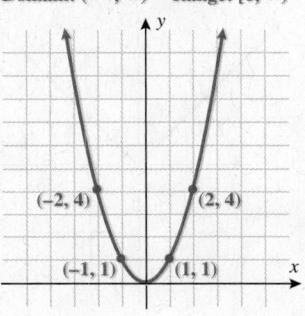

Square Function
Domain: $(-\infty, \infty)$  Range: $[0, \infty)$

The graph of the square function is called a parabola and will be discussed in further detail in Chapter 9. The domain of the square function is the set of all real numbers $\mathbb{R}$. Because squaring a real number always yields a positive number or zero, the range of the square function is the set of all nonnegative numbers. Note that the only intercept is the origin and the square function is symmetric about the $y$-axis. This graph is contained in quadrants I and II.

A function that cubes the input is called the *cube function.*

## CUBE FUNCTION

$$f(x) = x^3$$

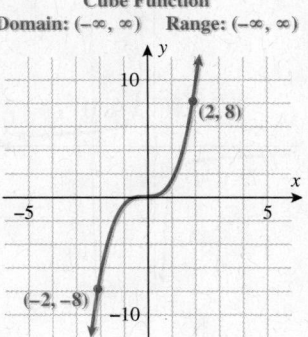

Cube Function
Domain: $(-\infty, \infty)$  Range: $(-\infty, \infty)$

The domain of the cube function is the set of all real numbers $\mathbb{R}$. Because cubing a negative number yields a negative number, cubing a positive number yields a positive number, and cubing 0 yields 0, the range of the cube function is also the set of all real numbers $\mathbb{R}$. Note that the only intercept is the origin and the cube function is symmetric about the origin. This graph extends only into quadrants I and III.

The next two functions are counterparts of the previous two functions: square root and cube root. When a function takes the square root of the input or the cube root of the input, the function is called the *square root function* or the *cube root function,* respectively.

## SQUARE ROOT FUNCTION

$$f(x) = \sqrt{x} \quad \text{or} \quad f(x) = x^{1/2}$$

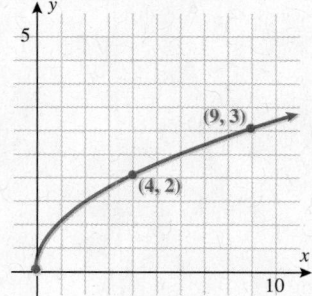

Square Root Function
Domain: $[0, \infty)$  Range: $[0, \infty)$

In Section 1.1, we found the domain to be $[0, \infty)$. The output of the function will be all real numbers greater than or equal to zero. Therefore, the range of the square root function is $[0, \infty)$. The graph of this function will be contained in quadrant I.

**Cube Root Function**
Domain: $(-\infty, \infty)$   Range: $(-\infty, \infty)$

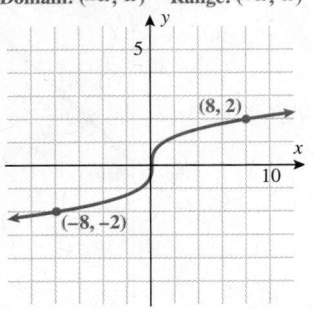

## CUBE ROOT FUNCTION

$$f(x) = \sqrt[3]{x} \quad \text{or} \quad f(x) = x^{1/3}$$

In Section 1.1, we stated the domain of the cube root function to be $(-\infty, \infty)$. We see by the graph that the range is also $(-\infty, \infty)$. This graph is contained in quadrants I and III and passes through the origin. This function is symmetric about the origin.

In Sections 0.3 and 0.4, absolute value equations and inequalities were reviewed. Now we shift our focus to the graph of the *absolute value function*.

**Absolute Value Function**
Domain: $(-\infty, \infty)$   Range: $[0, \infty)$

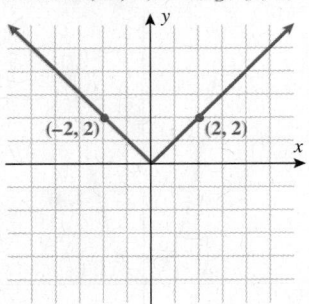

## ABSOLUTE VALUE FUNCTION

$$f(x) = |x|$$

Some points that are on the graph of the absolute value function are $(-1, 1)$, $(0, 0)$, and $(1, 1)$. The domain of the absolute value function is the set of all real numbers $\mathbb{R}$, yet the range is the set of nonnegative real numbers. The graph of this function is symmetric with respect to the $y$-axis and is contained in quadrants I and II.

A function whose output is the reciprocal of its input is called the *reciprocal function*.

**Reciprocal Function**
Domain: $(-\infty, 0) \cup (0, \infty)$
Range: $(-\infty, 0) \cup (0, \infty)$

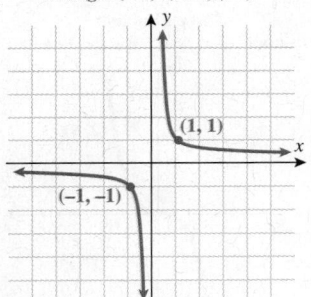

## RECIPROCAL FUNCTION

$$f(x) = \frac{1}{x} \quad x \neq 0$$

The only restriction on the domain of the reciprocal function is that $x \neq 0$. Therefore, we say the domain is the set of all real numbers excluding zero. The graph of the reciprocal function illustrates that its range is also the set of all real numbers except zero. Note that the reciprocal function is symmetric with respect to the origin and is contained in quadrants I and III.

## Even and Odd Functions

Of the nine functions discussed above, several have similar properties of symmetry. The constant function, square function, and absolute value function are all symmetric with respect to the $y$-axis. The identity function, cube function, cube root function, and reciprocal function are all symmetric with respect to the origin. The term **even** is used to describe functions that are symmetric with respect to the $y$-axis, or vertical axis, and the term **odd** is used to describe functions that are symmetric with respect to the origin. Recall from Section 0.5 that symmetry can be determined both graphically and algebraically. The box below summarizes the graphic and algebraic characteristics of even and odd functions.

### EVEN AND ODD FUNCTIONS

| Function | Symmetric with Respect to | On Replacing $x$ with $-x$ |
|---|---|---|
| Even | $y$-axis or vertical axis | $f(-x) = f(x)$ |
| Odd | origin | $f(-x) = -f(x)$ |

The algebraic method for determining symmetry with respect to the $y$-axis, or vertical axis, is to substitute in $-x$ for $x$. If the result is an equivalent equation, the function is symmetric with respect to the $y$-axis. Some examples of even functions are $f(x) = b$, $f(x) = x^2$, $f(x) = x^4$, and $f(x) = |x|$. In any of these equations, if $-x$ is substituted for $x$, the result is the same, that is, $f(-x) = f(x)$. Also note that, with the exception of the absolute value function, these examples are all even-degree polynomial equations. All constant functions are degree zero and are even functions.

The algebraic method for determining symmetry with respect to the origin is to substitute $-x$ for $x$. If the result is the negative of the original function, that is, if $f(-x) = -f(x)$, then the function is symmetric with respect to the origin and, hence, classified as an odd function. Examples of odd functions are $f(x) = x$, $f(x) = x^3$, $f(x) = x^5$, and $f(x) = x^{1/3}$. In any of these functions, if $-x$ is substituted for $x$, the result is the negative of the original function. Note that with the exception of the cube root function, these equations are odd-degree polynomials.

Be careful, though, because functions that are combinations of even- and odd-degree polynomials can turn out to be neither even nor odd, as we will see in Example 1.

**EXAMPLE 1**   **Determining Whether a Function Is Even, Odd, or Neither**

Determine whether the functions are even, odd, or neither.

**a.** $f(x) = x^2 - 3$    **b.** $g(x) = x^5 + x^3$    **c.** $h(x) = x^2 - x$

**Solution (a):**

| | |
|---|---|
| Original function. | $f(x) = x^2 - 3$ |
| Replace $x$ with $-x$. | $f(-x) = (-x)^2 - 3$ |
| Simplify. | $f(-x) = x^2 - 3 = f(x)$ |

Because $f(-x) = f(x)$, we say that $\boxed{f(x) \text{ is an } even \text{ function}}$.

**Solution (b):**

| | |
|---|---|
| Original function. | $g(x) = x^5 + x^3$ |
| Replace $x$ with $-x$. | $g(-x) = (-x)^5 + (-x)^3$ |
| Simplify. | $g(-x) = -x^5 - x^3 = -(x^5 + x^3) = -g(x)$ |

Because $g(-x) = -g(x)$, we say that $\boxed{g(x) \text{ is an } odd \text{ function}}$.

**Solution (c):**

| | |
|---|---|
| Original function. | $h(x) = x^2 - x$ |
| Replace $x$ with $-x$. | $h(-x) = (-x)^2 - (-x)$ |
| Simplify. | $h(-x) = x^2 + x$ |

$h(-x)$ **is neither** $-h(x)$ **nor** $h(x)$; therefore, the function $h(x)$ is $\boxed{\text{neither even nor odd}}$.

In parts (a), (b), and (c), we classified these functions as either even, odd, or neither, using the algebraic test. Look back at them now and reflect on whether these classifications agree with your intuition. In part (a), we combined two functions: the square function and the constant function. Both of these functions are even, and adding even functions yields another even function. In part (b), we combined two odd functions: the fifth-power function and the cube function. Both of these functions are odd, and adding two odd functions yields another odd function. In part (c), we combined two functions: the square function and the identity function. The square function is even, and the identity function is odd. In this part, combining an even function with an odd function yields a function that is neither even nor odd and, hence, has no symmetry with respect to the vertical axis or the origin.

■ **YOUR TURN** Classify the functions as even, odd, or neither.

**a.** $f(x) = |x| + 4$    **b.** $f(x) = x^3 - 1$

*Technology Tip*

**a.** Graph $y_1 = f(x) = x^2 - 3$.

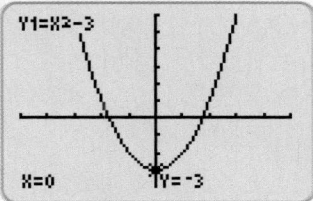

Even; symmetric with respect to the $y$-axis.

**b.** Graph $y_1 = g(x) = x^5 + x^3$.

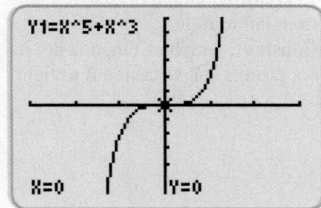

Odd; symmetric with respect to origin.

**c.** Graph $y_1 = h(x) = x^2 - x$.

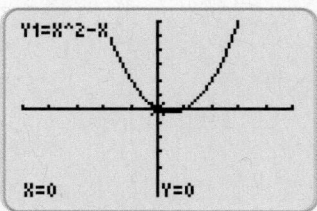

No symmetry with respect to $y$-axis or origin.

■ **Answer: a.** even    **b.** neither

# Increasing and Decreasing Functions

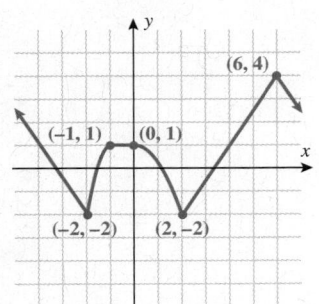

Look at the figure on the left. Graphs are read from *left to right*. If we start at the left side of the graph and trace the red curve, we see that the function values (values in the vertical direction) are decreasing until arriving at the point $(-2, -2)$. Then, the function values increase until arriving at the point $(-1, 1)$. The values then remain constant ($y = 1$) between the points $(-1, 1)$ and $(0, 1)$. Proceeding beyond the point $(0, 1)$, the function values decrease again until the point $(2, -2)$. Beyond the point $(2, -2)$, the function values increase again until the point $(6, 4)$. Finally, the function values decrease and continue to do so.

When specifying a function as increasing, decreasing, or constant, the *intervals are classified according to the x-coordinate.* For instance, in this graph, we say the function is increasing when $x$ is between $x = -2$ and $x = -1$ and again when $x$ is between $x = 2$ and $x = 6$. The graph is classified as decreasing when $x$ is less than $-2$ and again when $x$ is between 0 and 2 and again when $x$ is greater than 6. The graph is classified as constant when $x$ is between $-1$ and 0. In interval notation, this is summarized as

| Decreasing | Increasing | Constant |
|:---:|:---:|:---:|
| $(-\infty, -2) \cup (0, 2) \cup (6, \infty)$ | $(-2, -1) \cup (2, 6)$ | $(-1, 0)$ |

An algebraic test for determining whether a function is increasing, decreasing, or constant is to compare the value $f(x)$ of the function for particular points in the intervals.

**INCREASING, DECREASING, AND CONSTANT FUNCTIONS**

1. A function $f$ is **increasing** on an open interval $I$ if for any $x_1$ and $x_2$ in $I$, where $x_1 < x_2$, then $f(x_1) < f(x_2)$.
2. A function $f$ is **decreasing** on an open interval $I$ if for any $x_1$ and $x_2$ in $I$, where $x_1 < x_2$, then $f(x_1) > f(x_2)$.
3. A function $f$ is **constant** on an open interval $I$ if for any $x_1$ and $x_2$ in $I$, then $f(x_1) = f(x_2)$.

In addition to classifying a function as increasing, decreasing, or constant, we can also determine the domain and range of a function by inspecting its graph from left to right:

■ The domain is the set of all *x*-values where the function is defined.
■ The range is the set of all *y*-values that the graph of the function corresponds to.
■ A solid dot on the left or right end of a graph indicates that the graph terminates there and the point is included in the graph.
■ An open dot indicates that the graph terminates there and the point is not included in the graph.
■ Unless a dot is present, it is assumed that a graph continues indefinitely in the same direction. (An arrow is used in some books to indicate direction.)

**EXAMPLE 2    Finding Intervals When a Function Is
Increasing or Decreasing**

Given the graph of a function:

**a.** State the domain and range of the
function.

**b.** Find the intervals when the function is
increasing, decreasing, or constant.

**Solution:**

Domain: $[-5, \infty)$

Range: $[0, \infty)$

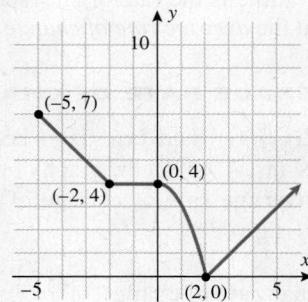

Reading the graph from **left to right**, we see that
the graph

- decreases from the point $(-5, 7)$ to the
point $(-2, 4)$.

- is constant from the point $(-2, 4)$ to the
point $(0, 4)$.

- decreases from the point $(0, 4)$ to the
point $(2, 0)$.

- increases from the point $(2, 0)$ on.

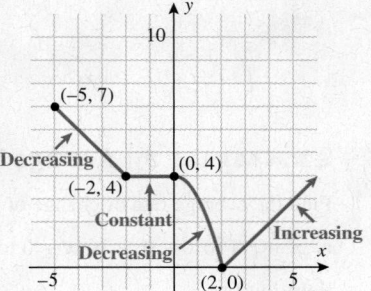

The intervals of increasing and decreasing
correspond to the **x-coordinates**.

We say that this function is

- increasing on the interval $(2, \infty)$.

- decreasing on the interval $(-5, -2) \cup (0, 2)$.

- constant on the interval $(-2, 0)$.

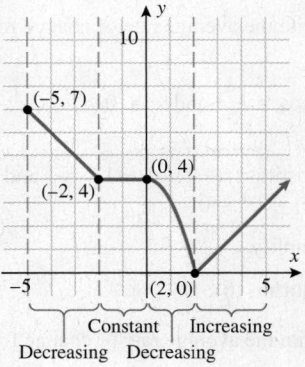

*Note:* The intervals of increasing or decreasing are defined on *open* intervals. This
should not be confused with the domain. For example, the point $x = -5$ is included in
the domain of the function but not in the interval where the function is classified as
decreasing.

# Average Rate of Change

How do we know *how much* a function is increasing or decreasing? For example, is the
price of a stock slightly increasing or is it doubling every week? One way we determine
how much a function is increasing or decreasing is by calculating its *average rate of
change.*

Let $(x_1, y_1)$ and $(x_2, y_2)$ be two points that lie on the graph of a function $f$. Draw the line
that passes through these two points $(x_1, y_1)$ and $(x_2, y_2)$. This line is called a **secant line.**

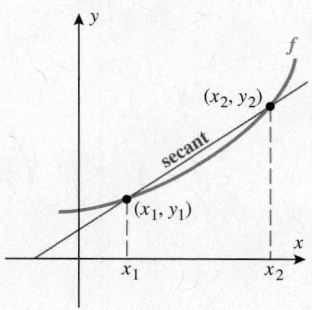

Note that the slope of the secant line is given by $m = \dfrac{y_2 - y_1}{x_2 - x_1}$, and recall that the slope of a line is the rate of change of that line. The **slope of the secant line** is used to represent the *average rate of change* of the function.

**AVERAGE RATE OF CHANGE**

Let $(x_1, f(x_1))$ and $(x_2, f(x_2))$ be two distinct points, $(x_1 \neq x_2)$, on the graph of the function $f$. The **average rate of change** of $f$ between $x_1$ and $x_2$ is given by

$$\text{Average rate of change} = \frac{f(x_2) - f(x_1)}{x_2 - x_1}$$

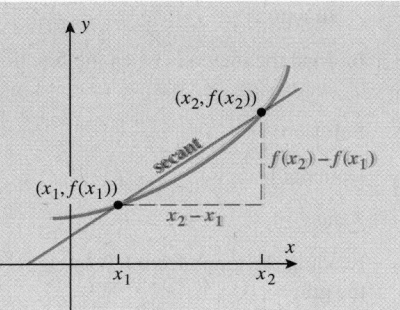

**EXAMPLE 3   Average Rate of Change**

Find the average rate of change of $f(x) = x^4$ from

**a.** $x = -1$ to $x = 0$    **b.** $x = 0$ to $x = 1$    **c.** $x = 1$ to $x = 2$

**Solution (a):**

Write the average rate of change formula.
$$\frac{f(x_2) - f(x_1)}{x_2 - x_1}$$

Let $x_1 = -1$ and $x_2 = 0$.
$$= \frac{f(0) - f(-1)}{0 - (-1)}$$

Substitute $f(-1) = (-1)^4 = 1$ and $f(0) = 0^4 = 0$.
$$= \frac{0 - 1}{0 - (-1)}$$

Simplify.
$$= \boxed{-1}$$

**Solution (b):**

Write the average rate of change formula.
$$\frac{f(x_2) - f(x_1)}{x_2 - x_1}$$

Let $x_1 = 0$ and $x_2 = 1$.
$$= \frac{f(1) - f(0)}{1 - 0}$$

Substitute $f(0) = 0^4 = 0$ and $f(1) = (1)^4 = 1$.
$$= \frac{1 - 0}{1 - 0}$$

Simplify.
$$= \boxed{1}$$

**Solution (c):**

Write the average rate of change formula.
$$\frac{f(x_2) - f(x_1)}{x_2 - x_1}$$

Let $x_1 = 1$ and $x_2 = 2$.
$$= \frac{f(2) - f(1)}{2 - 1}$$

Substitute $f(1) = 1^4 = 1$ and $f(2) = (2)^4 = 16$.
$$= \frac{16 - 1}{2 - 1}$$

Simplify.
$$= \boxed{15}$$

## Graphical Interpretation: Slope of the Secant Line

**a.** Between $(-1, 1)$ and $(0, 0)$, this function is decreasing at a rate of 1.

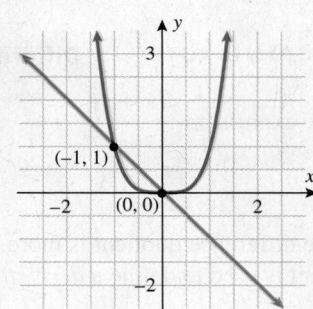

**b.** Between $(0, 0)$ and $(1, 1)$, this function is increasing at a rate of 1.

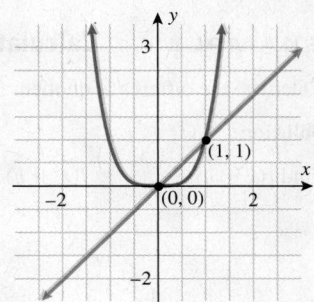

**c.** Between $(1, 1)$ and $(2, 16)$, this function is increasing at a rate of 15.

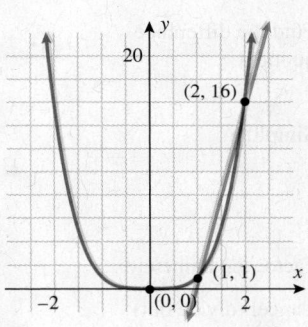

■ **YOUR TURN** Find the average rate of change of $f(x) = x^2$ from

**a.** $x = -2$ to $x = 0$     **b.** $x = 0$ to $x = 2$

■ **Answer: a.** $-2$   **b.** 2

---

The average rate of change can also be written in terms of the *difference quotient.*

| WORDS | MATH |
|---|---|
| Let the distance between $x_1$ and $x_2$ be $h$. | $x_2 - x_1 = h$ |
| Solve for $x_2$. | $x_2 = x_1 + h$ |
| Substitute $x_2 - x_1 = h$ into the denominator and $x_2 = x_1 + h$ into the numerator of the average rate of change. | Average rate of change $= \dfrac{f(x_2) - f(x_1)}{x_2 - x_1}$ |
| | $= \dfrac{f(x_1 + h) - f(x_1)}{h}$ |
| Let $x_1 = x$. | $\boxed{= \dfrac{f(x + h) - f(x)}{h}}$ |

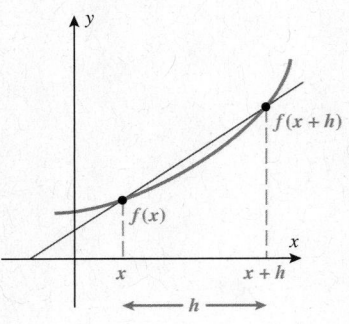

When written in this form, the average rate of change is called the **difference quotient**.

### DEFINITION    Difference Quotient

The expression $\dfrac{f(x + h) - f(x)}{h}$, where $h \neq 0$, is called the **difference quotient**.

The difference quotient is more meaningful when $h$ is small. In calculus the difference quotient is used to define a *derivative*.

**Study Tip**

Use brackets or parentheses around $f(x)$ to avoid forgetting to distribute the negative sign:

$$\frac{f(x + h) - [f(x)]}{h}$$

### EXAMPLE 4    Calculating the Difference Quotient

Calculate the difference quotient for the function $f(x) = 2x^2 + 1$.

**Solution:**

Find $f(x + h)$.

$$f(x + h) = 2(x + h)^2 + 1$$
$$= 2(x^2 + 2xh + h^2) + 1$$
$$= 2x^2 + 4xh + 2h^2 + 1$$

Find the difference quotient.

$$\frac{f(x + h) - f(x)}{h} = \frac{\overbrace{2x^2 + 4xh + 2h^2 + 1}^{f(x+h)} - \overbrace{(2x^2 + 1)}^{f(x)}}{h}$$

Simplify.

$$= \frac{2x^2 + 4xh + 2h^2 + 1 - 2x^2 - 1}{h}$$

$$= \frac{4xh + 2h^2}{h}$$

Factor the numerator.

$$= \frac{h(4x + 2h)}{h}$$

Cancel (divide out) the common $h$.

$$= \boxed{4x + 2h} \qquad h \neq 0$$

■ **Answer:**

$$\frac{f(x + h) - f(x)}{h} = -2x - h$$

■ **YOUR TURN** Calculate the difference quotient for the function $f(x) = -x^2 + 2$.

### EXAMPLE 5    Evaluating the Difference Quotient

For the function $f(x) = x^2 - x$, find $\dfrac{f(x + h) - f(x)}{h}$.

**Solution:**

Use placeholder notation for the function $f(x) = x^2 - x$.

$$f(\square) = (\square)^2 - (\square)$$

Calculate $f(x + h)$.

$$f(x + h) = (x + h)^2 - (x + h)$$

Write the difference quotient.

$$\frac{f(x + h) - f(x)}{h}$$

Let $f(x + h) = (x + h)^2 - (x + h)$ and $f(x) = x^2 - x$.

$$\frac{f(x + h) - f(x)}{h} = \frac{\overbrace{\left[(x + h)^2 - (x + h)\right]}^{f(x+h)} - \overbrace{\left[x^2 - x\right]}^{f(x)}}{h} \qquad h \neq 0$$

Eliminate the parentheses inside the first set of brackets.

$$= \frac{[x^2 + 2xh + h^2 - x - h] - [x^2 - x]}{h}$$

Eliminate the brackets in the numerator.

$$= \frac{x^2 + 2xh + h^2 - x - h - x^2 + x}{h}$$

Combine like terms.

$$= \frac{2xh + h^2 - h}{h}$$

Factor the numerator.

$$= \frac{h(2x + h - 1)}{h}$$

Divide out the common factor, $h$.

$$= \boxed{2x + h - 1} \qquad h \neq 0$$

▪ **YOUR TURN**   Evaluate the difference quotient for $f(x) = x^2 - 1$.

▪**Answer:** $2x + h$

# Piecewise-Defined Functions

Most of the functions that we have seen in this text are functions defined by polynomials. Sometimes the need arises to define functions in terms of *pieces*. For example, most plumbers charge a flat fee for a house call and then an additional hourly rate for the job. For instance, if a particular plumber charges $100 to drive out to your house and work for 1 hour and then $25 an hour for every additional hour he or she works on your job, we would define this function in pieces. If we let $h$ be the number of hours worked, then the charge is defined as

$$\text{Plumbing charge} = \begin{cases} 100 & 0 < h \leq 1 \\ 100 + 25(h - 1) & h > 1 \end{cases}$$

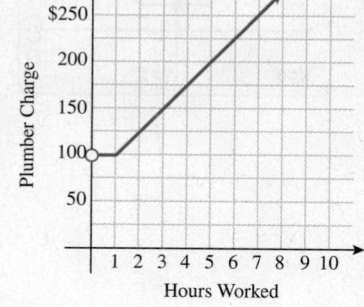

We can see in the graph of this function that there is 1 hour that is constant and after that the function continually increases.

The next example is a piecewise-defined function given in terms of pieces of functions from our "library of functions." Because the function is defined in terms of pieces of other functions, we draw the graph of each individual function and, then, for each function darken the piece corresponding to its part of the domain.

*Technology Tip*

Plot a piecewise-defined function using the $\boxed{\text{TEST}}$ menu operations to define the inequalities in the function. Press:

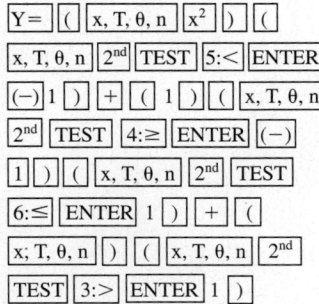

Set the viewing rectangle as $[-4, 4]$ by $[-2, 5]$; then press $\boxed{\text{GRAPH}}$.

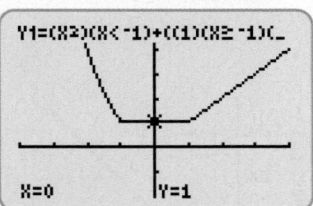

## EXAMPLE 6   Graphing Piecewise-Defined Functions

Graph the piecewise-defined function, and state the domain, range, and intervals when the function is increasing, decreasing, or constant.

$$G(x) = \begin{cases} x^2 & x < -1 \\ 1 & -1 \leq x \leq 1 \\ x & x > 1 \end{cases}$$

**Solution:**

Graph each of the functions on the same plane.

**Square function:**
$$f(x) = x^2$$

**Constant function:**
$$f(x) = 1$$

**Identity function:**
$$f(x) = x$$

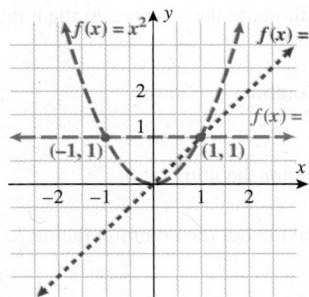

The points to focus on in particular are the $x$-values where the pieces change over—that is, $x = -1$ and $x = 1$.

Let's now investigate each piece. When $x < -1$, this function is defined by the square function, $f(x) = x^2$, so darken that particular function to the left of $x = -1$. When $-1 \leq x \leq 1$, the function is defined by the constant function, $f(x) = 1$, so darken that particular function between the $x$-values of $-1$ and 1. When $x > 1$, the function is defined by the identity function, $f(x) = x$, so darken that function to the right of $x = 1$. Erase everything that is not darkened, and the resulting graph of the piecewise-defined function is given on the right.

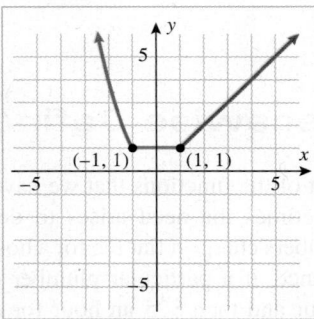

This function is defined for all real values of $x$, so the domain of this function is the set of all real numbers. The values that this function yields in the vertical direction are all real numbers greater than or equal to 1. Hence, the range of this function is $[1, \infty)$. The intervals of increasing, decreasing, and constant are as follows:

Decreasing: $(-\infty, -1)$

Constant: $(-1, 1)$

Increasing: $(1, \infty)$

The term **continuous** implies that there are no holes or jumps and that the graph can be drawn without picking up your pencil. A function that does have holes or jumps and cannot be drawn in one motion without picking up your pencil is classified as **discontinuous**, and the points where the holes or jumps occur are called *points of discontinuity*.

The previous example illustrates a *continuous* piecewise-defined function. At the $x = -1$ junction, the square function and constant function both pass through the point $(-1, 1)$. At the $x = 1$ junction, the constant function and the identity function both pass through the point $(1, 1)$. Since the graph of this piecewise-defined function has no holes or jumps, we classify it as a continuous function.

The next example illustrates a *discontinuous* piecewise-defined function.

### EXAMPLE 7    Graphing a Discontinuous Piecewise-Defined Function

Graph the piecewise-defined function, and state the intervals where the function is increasing, decreasing, or constant, along with the domain and range.

$$f(x) = \begin{cases} 1 - x & x < 0 \\ x & 0 \le x < 2 \\ -1 & x > 2 \end{cases}$$

**Solution:**

Graph these functions on the same plane.

> **Linear function:**
> $f(x) = 1 - x$
>
> **Identity function:**
> $f(x) = x$
>
> **Constant function:**
> $f(x) = -1$

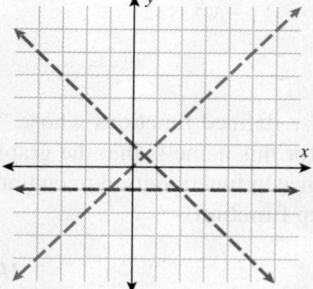

Darken the piecewise-defined function on the graph. For all values less than zero $(x < 0)$, the function is defined by the **linear function**. Note the use of an open circle, indicating up to but not including $x = 0$. For values $0 \le x < 2$, the function is defined by the **identity function**.

The circle is filled in at the left endpoint, $x = 0$. An open circle is used at $x = 2$. For all values greater than 2, $x > 2$, the function is defined by the **constant function**. Because this interval does not include the point $x = 2$, an open circle is used.

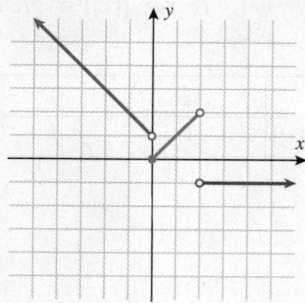

At what intervals is the function increasing, decreasing, or constant? Remember that the intervals correspond to the $x$-values.

Decreasing: $(-\infty, 0)$      Increasing: $(0, 2)$      Constant: $(2, \infty)$

**Technology Tip**

Plot a piecewise-defined function using the TEST menu operations to define the inequalities in the function. Press:

Y= ( ( 1 − X, T, θ, n ) ) ( (
X, T, θ, n 2nd MATH 5 <
0 ) + ( ( X, T, θ, n ) ) ( (
X, T, θ, n 2nd MATH 4 ≥
0 ) ) ( ( X, T, θ, n ) 2nd MATH
5 < 2 ) ) + ( ( (−) 1 ) ) ( (
X, T, θ, n 2nd MATH 3 >
2 ) )

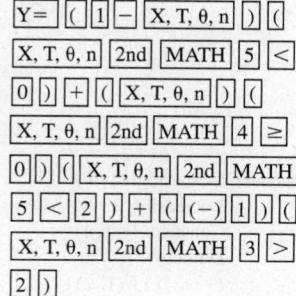

To avoid connecting graphs of the pieces, press MODE and Dot. Set the viewing rectangle as $[-3, 4]$ by $[-2, 5]$; then press GRAPH.

Be sure to include the open circle and closed circle at the appropriate endpoints of each piece in the function.

The table of values supports the graph, except at $x = 2$. The function is not defined at $x = 2$.

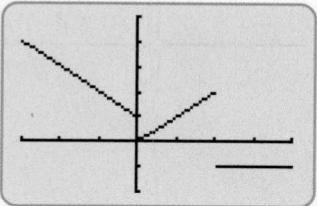

The function is defined for all values of $x$ except $x = 2$.

$$\text{Domain:} \quad (-\infty, 2) \cup (2, \infty)$$

The output of this function (vertical direction) takes on the $y$-values $y \geq 0$ and the additional single value $y = -1$.

$$\text{Range:} \quad [-1, -1] \cup [0, \infty) \text{ or } \{-1\} \cup [0, \infty)$$

We mentioned earlier that a discontinuous function has a graph that exhibits holes or jumps. In Example 6, the point $x = 0$ corresponds to a jump, because you would have to pick up your pencil to continue drawing the graph. The point $x = 2$ corresponds to both a hole and a jump. The hole indicates that the function is not defined at that point, and there is still a jump because the identity function and the constant function do not meet at the same $y$-value at $x = 2$.

■ **Answer:** Increasing: $(1, \infty)$
Decreasing: $(-\infty, -1)$
Constant: $(-1, 1)$
Domain:
$(-\infty, 1) \cup (1, \infty)$
Range: $[1, \infty)$

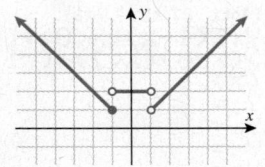

■ **YOUR TURN** Graph the piecewise-defined function, and state the intervals where the function is increasing, decreasing, or constant, along with the domain and range.

$$f(x) = \begin{cases} -x & x \leq -1 \\ 2 & -1 < x < 1 \\ x & x > 1 \end{cases}$$

Piecewise-defined functions whose "pieces" are constants are called **step functions**. The reason for this name is that the graph of a step function looks like steps of a staircase. A common step function used in engineering is the **Heaviside step function** (also called the **unit step function**):

$$H(t) = \begin{cases} 0 & t < 0 \\ 1 & t \geq 0 \end{cases}$$

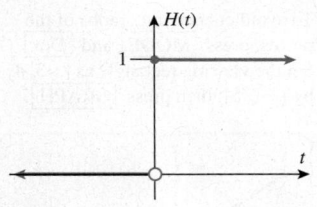

This function is used in signal processing to represent a signal that turns on at some time and stays on indefinitely.

A common step function used in business applications is the *greatest integer function*.

## GREATEST INTEGER FUNCTION

$$f(x) = [[x]] = \text{greatest integer less than or equal to } x$$

| $x$ | 1.0 | 1.3 | 1.5 | 1.7 | 1.9 | 2.0 |
|---|---|---|---|---|---|---|
| $f(x) = [[x]]$ | 1 | 1 | 1 | 1 | 1 | 2 |

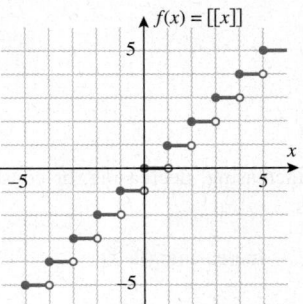

**SECTION**
**1.2 SUMMARY**

| NAME | FUNCTION | DOMAIN | RANGE | GRAPH | EVEN/ODD |
|------|----------|--------|-------|-------|----------|
| Linear | $f(x) = mx + b, m \neq 0$ | $(-\infty, \infty)$ | $(-\infty, \infty)$ | | Neither (unless $y = x$) |
| Constant | $f(x) = c$ | $(-\infty, \infty)$ | $[c, c]$ or $\{c\}$ | | Even |
| Identity | $f(x) = x$ | $(-\infty, \infty)$ | $(-\infty, \infty)$ | | Odd |
| Square | $f(x) = x^2$ | $(-\infty, \infty)$ | $[0, \infty)$ | | Even |
| Cube | $f(x) = x^3$ | $(-\infty, \infty)$ | $(-\infty, \infty)$ | | Odd |
| Square Root | $f(x) = \sqrt{x}$ | $[0, \infty)$ | $[0, \infty)$ | | Neither |
| Cube Root | $f(x) = \sqrt[3]{x}$ | $(-\infty, \infty)$ | $(-\infty, \infty)$ | | Odd |
| Absolute Value | $f(x) = |x|$ | $(-\infty, \infty)$ | $[0, \infty)$ | | Even |
| Reciprocal | $f(x) = \dfrac{1}{x}$ | $(-\infty, 0) \cup (0, \infty)$ | $(-\infty, 0) \cup (0, \infty)$ | | Odd |

## Domain and Range of a Function

- **Implied Domain:** Exclude any values that lead to the function being undefined (dividing by zero) or imaginary outputs (square root of a negative real number).

- Inspect the graph to determine the set of all inputs (domain) and the set of all outputs (range).

**Finding Intervals Where a Function Is Increasing, Decreasing, or Constant**

- **Increasing:** Graph of function rises from left to right.
- **Decreasing:** Graph of function falls from left to right.
- **Constant:** Graph of function does not change height from left to right.

**Average Rate of Change**   $\dfrac{f(x_2) - f(x_1)}{x_2 - x_1}$   $x_1 \neq x_2$

**Difference Quotient**   $\dfrac{f(x + h) - f(x)}{h}$   $h \neq 0$

**Piecewise-Defined Functions**

- **Continuous:** You can draw the graph of a function without picking up the pencil.
- **Discontinuous:** Graph has holes and/or jumps.

## SECTION 1.2 EXERCISES

### ■ SKILLS

In Exercises 1–16, determine whether the function is even, odd, or neither.

**1.** $h(x) = x^2 + 2x$

**2.** $G(x) = 2x^4 + 3x^3$

**3.** $h(x) = x^{1/3} - x$

**4.** $g(x) = x^{-1} + x$

**5.** $f(x) = |x| + 5$

**6.** $f(x) = |x| + x^2$

**7.** $f(x) = |x|$

**8.** $f(x) = |x^3|$

**9.** $G(t) = |t - 3|$

**10.** $g(t) = |t + 2|$

**11.** $G(t) = \sqrt{t - 3}$

**12.** $f(x) = \sqrt{2 - x}$

**13.** $g(x) = \sqrt{x^2 + x}$

**14.** $f(x) = \sqrt{x^2 + 2}$

**15.** $h(x) = \dfrac{1}{x} + 3$

**16.** $h(x) = \dfrac{1}{x} - 2x$

In Exercises 17–28, state the (a) domain, (b) range, and (c) *x*-interval(s) where the function is increasing, decreasing, or constant. Find the values of (d) $f(0)$, (e) $f(-2)$, and (f) $f(2)$.

**17.**
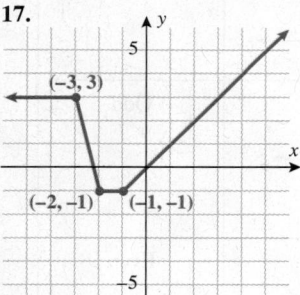

**18.**
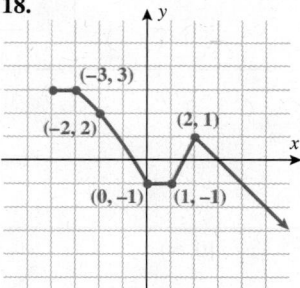

**19.**
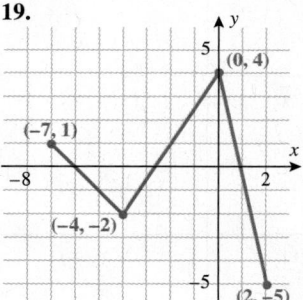

**20.**
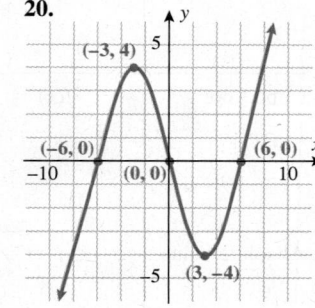

**21.**
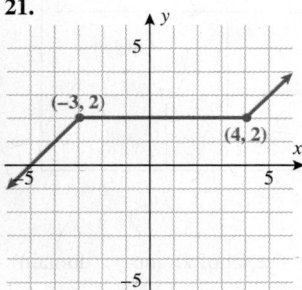

**22.**
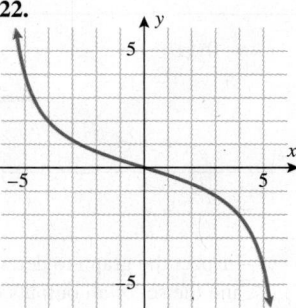

**23.**
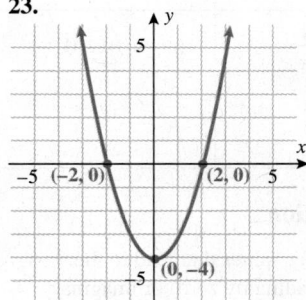

**24.**
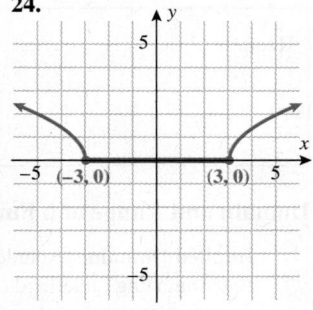

**25.** 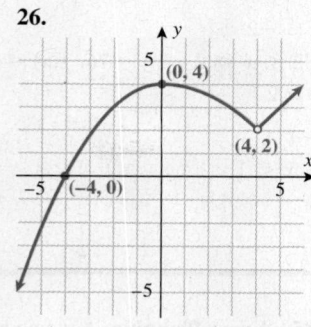  **26.**  **27.** 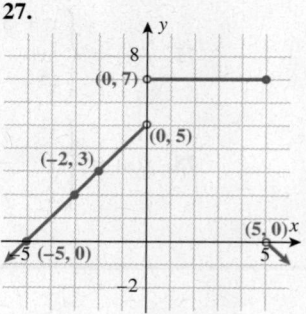  **28.**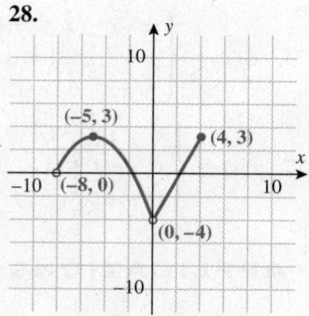

In Exercises 29–44, find the difference quotient $\dfrac{f(x+h)-f(x)}{h}$ for each function.

**29.** $f(x) = x^2 - x$

**30.** $f(x) = x^2 + 2x$

**31.** $f(x) = 3x + x^2$

**32.** $f(x) = 5x - x^2$

**33.** $f(x) = x^2 - 3x + 2$

**34.** $f(x) = x^2 - 2x + 5$

**35.** $f(x) = -3x^2 + 5x - 4$

**36.** $f(x) = -4x^2 + 2x - 3$

**37.** $f(x) = x^3 + x^2$

**38.** $f(x) = (x-1)^4$

**39.** $f(x) = \dfrac{2}{x-2}$

**40.** $f(x) = \dfrac{x+5}{x-7}$

**41.** $f(x) = \sqrt{1-2x}$

**42.** $f(x) = \sqrt{x^2 + x + 1}$

**43.** $f(x) = \dfrac{4}{\sqrt{x}}$

**44.** $f(x) = \sqrt{\dfrac{x}{x+1}}$

In Exercises 45–52, find the average rate of change of the function from $x = 1$ to $x = 3$.

**45.** $f(x) = x^3$

**46.** $f(x) = \dfrac{1}{x}$

**47.** $f(x) = |x|$

**48.** $f(x) = 2x$

**49.** $f(x) = 1 - 2x$

**50.** $f(x) = 9 - x^2$

**51.** $f(x) = |5 - 2x|$

**52.** $f(x) = \sqrt{x^2 - 1}$

In Exercises 53–78, graph the piecewise-defined functions. State the domain and range in interval notation. Determine the intervals where the function is increasing, decreasing, or constant.

**53.** $f(x) = \begin{cases} x & x < 2 \\ 2 & x \ge 2 \end{cases}$

**54.** $f(x) = \begin{cases} -x & x < -1 \\ -1 & x \ge -1 \end{cases}$

**55.** $f(x) = \begin{cases} 1 & x < -1 \\ x^2 & x \ge -1 \end{cases}$

**56.** $f(x) = \begin{cases} x^2 & x < 2 \\ 4 & x \ge 2 \end{cases}$

**57.** $f(x) = \begin{cases} x & x < 0 \\ x^2 & x \ge 0 \end{cases}$

**58.** $f(x) = \begin{cases} -x & x \le 0 \\ x^2 & x > 0 \end{cases}$

**59.** $f(x) = \begin{cases} -x + 2 & x < 1 \\ x^2 & x \ge 1 \end{cases}$

**60.** $f(x) = \begin{cases} 2 + x & x \le -1 \\ x^2 & x > -1 \end{cases}$

**61.** $f(x) = \begin{cases} 5 - 2x & x < 2 \\ 3x - 2 & x > 2 \end{cases}$

**62.** $f(x) = \begin{cases} 3 - \dfrac{1}{2}x & x < -2 \\ 4 + \dfrac{3}{2}x & x > -2 \end{cases}$

**63.** $G(x) = \begin{cases} -1 & x < -1 \\ x & -1 \le x \le 3 \\ 3 & x > 3 \end{cases}$

**64.** $G(x) = \begin{cases} -1 & x < -1 \\ x & -1 < x < 3 \\ 3 & x > 3 \end{cases}$

**65.** $G(t) = \begin{cases} 1 & t < 1 \\ t^2 & 1 \le t \le 2 \\ 4 & t > 2 \end{cases}$

**66.** $G(t) = \begin{cases} 1 & t < 1 \\ t^2 & 1 < t < 2 \\ 4 & t > 2 \end{cases}$

**67.** $f(x) = \begin{cases} -x - 1 & x < -2 \\ x + 1 & -2 < x < 1 \\ -x + 1 & x \ge 1 \end{cases}$

**68.** $f(x) = \begin{cases} -x - 1 & x \le -2 \\ x + 1 & -2 < x < 1 \\ -x + 1 & x > 1 \end{cases}$

**69.** $G(x) = \begin{cases} 0 & x < 0 \\ \sqrt{x} & x \ge 0 \end{cases}$

**70.** $G(x) = \begin{cases} 1 & x < 1 \\ \sqrt[3]{x} & x > 1 \end{cases}$

**71.** $G(x) = \begin{cases} 0 & x = 0 \\ \dfrac{1}{x} & x \ne 0 \end{cases}$

**72.** $G(x) = \begin{cases} 0 & x = 0 \\ -\dfrac{1}{x} & x \ne 0 \end{cases}$

**73.** $G(x) = \begin{cases} -\sqrt[3]{x} & x \le -1 \\ x & -1 < x < 1 \\ -\sqrt{x} & x > 1 \end{cases}$

**74.** $G(x) = \begin{cases} -\sqrt[3]{x} & x < -1 \\ x & -1 \le x < 1 \\ \sqrt{x} & x > 1 \end{cases}$

**75.** $f(x) = \begin{cases} x + 3 & x \le -2 \\ |x| & -2 < x < 2 \\ x^2 & x \ge 2 \end{cases}$

**76.** $f(x) = \begin{cases} |x| & x < -1 \\ 1 & -1 < x < 1 \\ |x| & x > 1 \end{cases}$

**77.** $f(x) = \begin{cases} x & x \le -1 \\ x^3 & -1 < x < 1 \\ x^2 & x > 1 \end{cases}$

**78.** $f(x) = \begin{cases} x^2 & x \le -1 \\ x^3 & -1 < x < 1 \\ x & x \ge 1 \end{cases}$

## ▪ APPLICATIONS

**For Exercises 79 and 80, refer to the following:**

A manufacturer determines that his *profit* and *cost* functions over one year are represented by the following graphs.

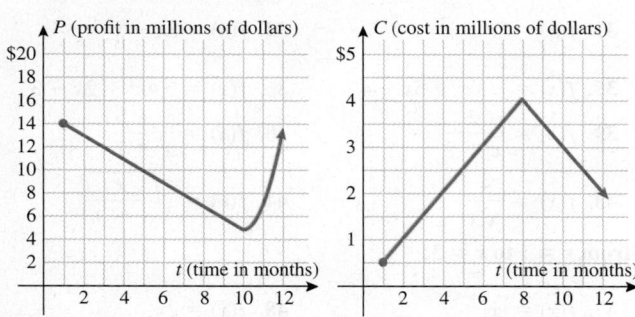

**79. Business.** Find the intervals on which profit is increasing, decreasing, and constant.

**80. Business.** Find the intervals on which cost is increasing, decreasing, and constant.

**81. Budget: Costs.** The Kappa Kappa Gamma sorority decides to order custom-made T-shirts for its *Kappa Krush* mixer with the Sigma Alpha Epsilon fraternity. If the sorority orders 50 or fewer T-shirts, the cost is $10 per shirt. If it orders more than 50 but fewer than 100, the cost is $9 per shirt. If it orders 100 or more the cost is $8 per shirt. Find the cost function $C(x)$ as a function of the number of T-shirts $x$ ordered.

**82. Budget: Costs.** The marching band at a university is ordering some additional uniforms to replace existing uniforms that are worn out. If the band orders 50 or fewer, the cost is $176.12 per uniform. If it orders more than 50 but fewer than 100, the cost is $159.73 per uniform. Find the cost function $C(x)$ as a function of the number of new uniforms $x$ ordered.

**83. Budget: Costs.** The Richmond rowing club is planning to enter the *Head of the Charles* race in Boston and is trying to figure out how much money to raise. The entry fee is $250 per boat for the first 10 boats and $175 for each additional boat. Find the cost function $C(x)$ as a function of the number of boats $x$ the club enters.

**84. Phone Cost: Long-Distance Calling.** A phone company charges $0.39 per minute for the first 10 minutes of an international long-distance phone call and $0.12 per minute every minute after that. Find the cost function $C(x)$ as a function of the length of the phone call $x$ in minutes.

**85. Event Planning.** A young couple are planning their wedding reception at a yacht club. The yacht club charges a flat rate of $1000 to reserve the dining room for a private party. The cost of food is $35 per person for the first 100 people and $25 per person for every additional person beyond the first 100. Write the cost function $C(x)$ as a function of the number of people $x$ attending the reception.

**86. Home Improvement.** An irrigation company gives you an estimate for an eight-zone sprinkler system. The parts are $1400, and the labor is $25 per hour. Write a function $C(x)$ that determines the cost of a new sprinkler system if you choose this irrigation company.

**87. Sales.** A famous author negotiates with her publisher the monies she will receive for her next suspense novel. She will receive $50,000 up front and a 15% royalty rate on the first 100,000 books sold, and 20% on any books sold beyond that. If the book sells for $20 and royalties are based on the selling price, write a royalties function $R(x)$ as a function of total number $x$ of books sold.

**88. Sales.** Rework Exercise 87 if the author receives $35,000 up front, 15% for the first 100,000 books sold, and 25% on any books sold beyond that.

**89. Profit.** A group of artists are trying to decide whether they will make a profit if they set up a Web-based business to market and sell stained glass that they make. The costs associated with this business are $100 per month for the website and $700 per month for the studio they rent. The materials cost $35 for each work in stained glass, and the artists charge $100 for each unit they sell. Write the monthly profit as a function of the number of stained-glass units they sell.

**90. Profit.** Philip decides to host a shrimp boil at his house as a fund-raiser for his daughter's AAU basketball team. He orders gulf shrimp to be flown in from New Orleans. The shrimp costs $5 per pound. The shipping costs $30. If he charges $10 per person, write a function $F(x)$ that represents either his loss or profit as a function of the number of people $x$ that attend. Assume that each person will eat 1 pound of shrimp.

91. **Postage Rates.** The following table corresponds to first-class postage rates for the U.S. Postal Service. Write a piecewise-defined function in terms of the greatest integer function that models this cost of mailing flat envelopes first class.

| WEIGHT LESS THAN (OUNCES) | FIRST-CLASS RATE (LARGE ENVELOPES) |
|---|---|
| 1 | $0.88 |
| 2 | $1.05 |
| 3 | $1.22 |
| 4 | $1.39 |
| 5 | $1.56 |
| 6 | $1.73 |
| 7 | $1.90 |
| 8 | $2.07 |
| 9 | $2.24 |
| 10 | $2.41 |
| 11 | $2.58 |
| 12 | $2.75 |
| 13 | $2.92 |

92. **Postage Rates.** The following table corresponds to first-class postage rates for the U.S. Postal Service. Write a piecewise-defined function in terms of the greatest integer function that models this cost of mailing parcels first class.

| WEIGHT LESS THAN (OUNCES) | FIRST-CLASS RATE (PACKAGES) |
|---|---|
| 1 | $1.22 |
| 2 | $1.39 |
| 3 | $1.56 |
| 4 | $1.73 |
| 5 | $1.90 |
| 6 | $2.07 |
| 7 | $2.24 |
| 8 | $2.41 |
| 9 | $2.58 |
| 10 | $2.75 |
| 11 | $2.92 |
| 12 | $3.09 |
| 13 | $3.26 |

**For Exercises 93 and 94, refer to the following:**

A square wave is a waveform used in electronic circuit testing and signal processing. A square wave alternates regularly and instantaneously between two levels.

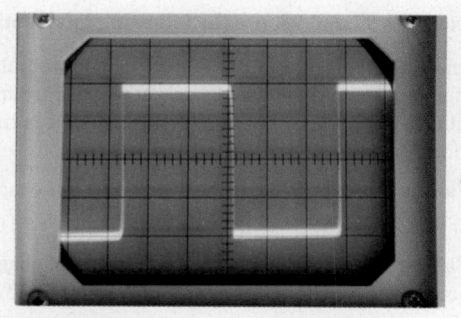

93. **Electronics: Signals.** Write a step function $f(t)$ that represents the following square wave:

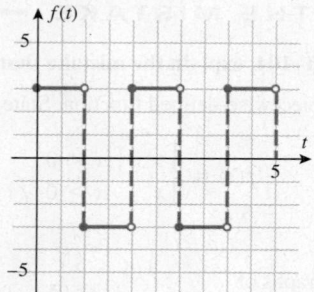

94. **Electronics: Signals.** Write a step function $f(x)$ that represents the following square wave, where $x$ represents frequency in Hz:

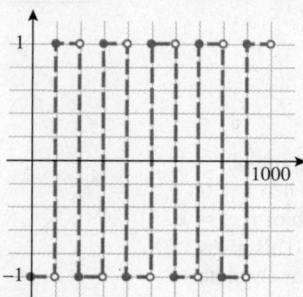

**For Exercises 95 and 96, refer to the following table:**

**Global Carbon Emissions from Fossil Fuel Burning**

| YEAR | MILLIONS OF TONS OF CARBON |
|---|---|
| 1900 | 500 |
| 1925 | 1000 |
| 1950 | 1500 |
| 1975 | 5000 |
| 2000 | 7000 |

95. **Climate Change: Global Warming.** What is the average rate of change in global carbon emissions from fossil fuel burning from
   **a.** 1900 to 1950?          **b.** 1950 to 2000?

96. **Climate Change: Global Warming.** What is the average rate of change in global carbon emissions from fossil fuel burning from
   **a.** 1950 to 1975?          **b.** 1975 to 2000?

**For Exercises 97 and 98, use the following information:**

The height (in feet) of a falling object with an initial velocity of 48 feet per second launched straight upward from the ground is given by $h(t) = -16t^2 + 48t$, where $t$ is time (in seconds).

**97. Falling Objects.** What is the average rate of change of the height as a function of time from $t = 1$ to $t = 2$?

**98. Falling Objects.** What is the average rate of change of the height as a function of time from $t = 1$ to $t = 3$?

**For Exercises 99 and 100, refer to the following:**

An analysis of sales indicates that demand for a product during a calendar year (no leap year) is modeled by

$$d(t) = 3\sqrt{t^2 + 1} - 2.75t$$

where $d$ is demand in thousands of units and $t$ is the day of the year and $t = 1$ represents January 1.

**99. Economics.** Find the average rate of change of the demand of the product over the first quarter.

**100. Economics.** Find the average rate of change of the demand of the product over the fourth quarter.

■**CATCH THE MISTAKE**

**In Exercises 101–104, explain the mistake that is made.**

**101.** Graph the piecewise-defined function. State the domain and range.

$$f(x) = \begin{cases} -x & x < 0 \\ x & x > 0 \end{cases}$$

**Solution:**

Draw the graphs of $f(x) = -x$ and $f(x) = x$.

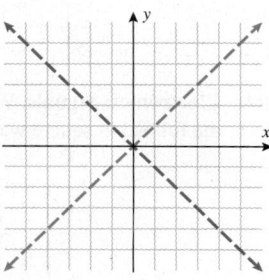

Darken the graph of $f(x) = -x$ when $x < 0$ and the graph of $f(x) = x$ when $x > 0$. This gives us the familiar absolute value graph.

Domain: $(-\infty, \infty)$ or $\mathbb{R}$
Range: $[0, \infty)$

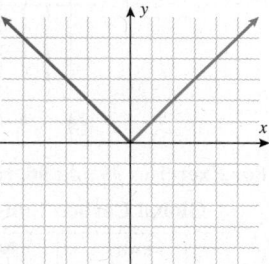

This is incorrect. What mistake was made?

**102.** Graph the piecewise-defined function. State the domain and range.

$$f(x) = \begin{cases} -x & x \le 1 \\ x & x > 1 \end{cases}$$

**Solution:**

Draw the graphs of $f(x) = -x$ and $f(x) = x$.

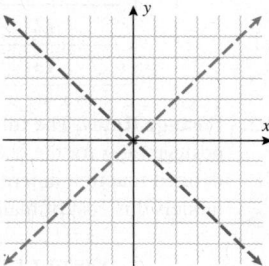

Darken the graph of $f(x) = -x$ when $x < 1$ and the graph of $f(x) = x$ when $x > 1$.

The resulting graph is as shown.

Domain: $(-\infty, \infty)$ or $\mathbb{R}$
Range: $(-1, \infty)$

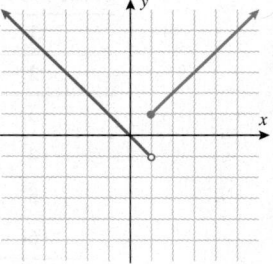

This is incorrect. What mistake was made?

**103.** The cost of airport Internet access is $15 for the first 30 minutes and $1 per minute for each additional minute. Write a function describing the cost of the service as a function of minutes used online.

**Solution:** $C(x) = \begin{cases} 15 & x \le 30 \\ 15 + x & x > 30 \end{cases}$

This is incorrect. What mistake was made?

**104.** Most money market accounts pay a higher interest with a higher principal. If the credit union is offering 2% on accounts with less than or equal to $10,000 and 4% on the additional money over $10,000, write the interest function $I(x)$ that represents the interest earned on an account as a function of dollars in the account.

**Solution:** $I(x) = \begin{cases} 0.02x & x \le 10{,}000 \\ 0.02(10{,}000) + 0.04x & x > 10{,}000 \end{cases}$

This is incorrect. What mistake was made?

## ▪ CONCEPTUAL

**In Exercises 105 and 106, determine whether each statement is true or false.**

**105.** If an odd function has an interval where the function is increasing, then it also has to have an interval where the function is decreasing.

**106.** If an even function has an interval where the function is increasing, then it also has to have an interval where the function is decreasing.

**In Exercises 107 and 108, for $a$ and $b$ real numbers, can the function given ever be a continuous function? If so, specify the value for $a$ and $b$ that would make it so.**

**107.** $f(x) = \begin{cases} ax & x \le 2 \\ bx^2 & x > 2 \end{cases}$    **108.** $f(x) = \begin{cases} -\dfrac{1}{x} & x < a \\ \dfrac{1}{x} & x \ge a \end{cases}$

## ▪ CHALLENGE

**In Exercises 109 and 110, find the values of $a$ and $b$ that make $f$ continuous.**

**109.** $f(x) = \begin{cases} -x^2 - 10x - 13 & x \le -2 \\ ax + b & -2 < x < 1 \\ \sqrt{x - 1} - 9 & x \ge 1 \end{cases}$

**110.** $f(x) = \begin{cases} -2x - a + 2b & x \le -2 \\ \sqrt{x + a} & -2 < x \le 2 \\ x^2 - 4x + a + 4 & x > 2 \end{cases}$

## ▪ TECHNOLOGY

**111.** In trigonometry you will learn about the sine function, $\sin x$. Plot the function $f(x) = \sin x$, using a graphing utility. It should look like the graph on the right. Is the sine function even, odd, or neither?

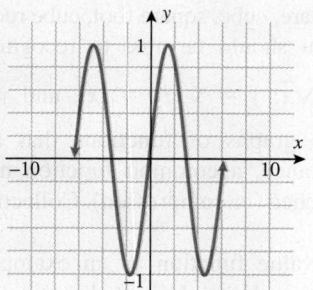

**112.** In trigonometry you will learn about the cosine function, $\cos x$. Plot the function $f(x) = \cos x$, using a graphing utility. It should look like the graph on the right. Is the cosine function even, odd, or neither?

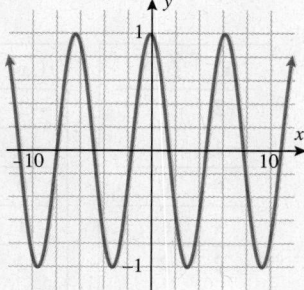

**113.** In trigonometry you will learn about the tangent function, $\tan x$. Plot the function $f(x) = \tan x$, using a graphing utility. If you restrict the values of $x$ so that $-\dfrac{\pi}{2} < x < \dfrac{\pi}{2}$, the graph should resemble the graph below. Is the tangent function even, odd, or neither?

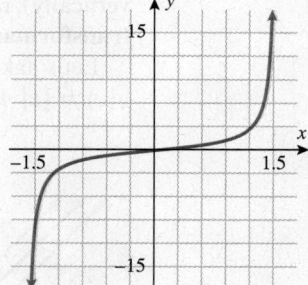

**114.** Plot the function $f(x) = \dfrac{\sin x}{\cos x}$. What function is this?

**115.** Graph the function $f(x) = [[3x]]$ using a graphing utility. State the domain and range.

**116.** Graph the function $f(x) = \left[\left[\tfrac{1}{3}x\right]\right]$ using a graphing utility. State the domain and range.

## ▪ PREVIEW TO CALCULUS

**For Exercises 117–120, refer to the following:**

In calculus, the difference quotient $\dfrac{f(x + h) - f(x)}{h}$ of a function $f$ is used to find the derivative $f'$ of $f$, by allowing $h$ to approach zero, $h \to 0$. Find the derivative of the following functions.

**117.** $f(x) = k$, where $k$ is a constant

**118.** $f(x) = mx + b$, where $m$ and $b$ are constants, $m \ne 0$

**119.** $f(x) = ax^2 + bx + c$, where $a$, $b$, and $c$ are constants, $a \ne 0$

**120.** $f(x) = \begin{cases} 7 & x < 0 \\ 2 - 3x & 0 < x < 4 \\ x^2 + 4x - 6 & x > 4 \end{cases}$

**SKILLS OBJECTIVES**

- Sketch the graph of a function using horizontal and vertical shifting of common functions.
- Sketch the graph of a function by reflecting a common function about the *x*-axis or *y*-axis.
- Sketch the graph of a function by stretching or compressing a common function.
- Sketch the graph of a function using a sequence of transformations.

**CONCEPTUAL OBJECTIVES**

- Identify the common functions by their graphs.
- Apply multiple transformations of common functions to obtain graphs of functions.
- Understand that domain and range also are transformed.

## Horizontal and Vertical Shifts

The focus of the previous section was to learn the graphs that correspond to particular functions such as identity, square, cube, square root, cube root, absolute value, and reciprocal. Therefore, at this point, you should be able to recognize and generate the graphs of

$$y = x, y = x^2, y = x^3, y = \sqrt{x}, \ y = \sqrt[3]{x}, y = |x|, \text{ and } y = \frac{1}{x}.$$ In this section, we will

discuss how to sketch the graphs of functions that are very simple modifications of these functions. For instance, a common function may be shifted (horizontally or vertically), reflected, or stretched (or compressed). Collectively, these techniques are called **transformations**.

Let's take the absolute value function as an example. The graphs of $f(x) = |x|$, $g(x) = |x| + 2$, and $h(x) = |x - 1|$ are shown below.

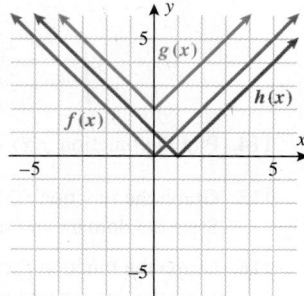

| $x$ | $f(x)$ |
|-----|--------|
| $-2$ | 2 |
| $-1$ | 1 |
| 0 | 0 |
| 1 | 1 |
| 2 | 2 |

| $x$ | $g(x)$ |
|-----|--------|
| $-2$ | 4 |
| $-1$ | 3 |
| 0 | 2 |
| 1 | 3 |
| 2 | 4 |

| $x$ | $h(x)$ |
|-----|--------|
| $-2$ | 3 |
| $-1$ | 2 |
| 0 | 1 |
| 1 | 0 |
| 2 | 1 |

Notice that the graph of $g(x) = |x| + 2$ is the graph of $f(x) = |x|$ shifted *up* two units. Similarly, the graph of $h(x) = |x - 1|$ is the graph of $f(x) = |x|$ shifted to the *right* one unit. In both cases, the base or starting function is $f(x) = |x|$.

Note that we could rewrite the functions $g(x)$ and $h(x)$ in terms of $f(x)$:

$$g(x) = |x| + 2 = f(x) + 2$$

$$h(x) = |x - 1| = f(x - 1)$$

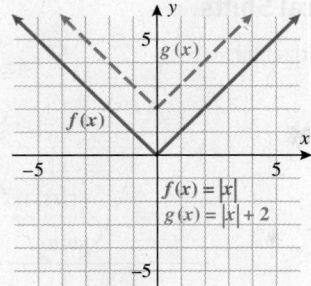
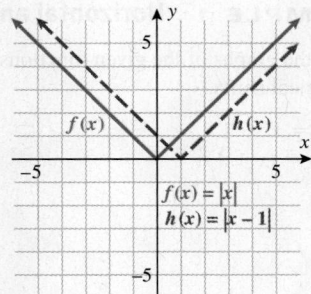

In the case of $g(x)$, the shift $(+2)$ occurs "outside" the function—that is, outside the parentheses showing the argument. Therefore, the output for $g(x)$ is 2 more than the typical output for $f(x)$. Because the output corresponds to the vertical axis, this results in a shift *upward* of two units. In general, shifts that occur *outside* the function correspond to a *vertical* shift corresponding to the sign of the shift. For instance, had the function been $G(x) = |x| - 2$, this graph would have started with the graph of the function $f(x)$ and shifted down two units.

In the case of $h(x)$, the shift occurs "inside" the function—that is, inside the parentheses showing the argument. Note that the point $(0, 0)$ that lies on the graph of $f(x)$ was shifted to the point $(1, 0)$ on the graph of the function $h(x)$. The $y$-value remained the same, but the $x$-value shifted to the right one unit. Similarly, the points $(-1, 1)$ and $(1, 1)$ were shifted to the points $(0, 1)$ and $(2, 1)$, respectively. In general, shifts that occur *inside* the function correspond to a *horizontal* shift opposite the sign. In this case, the graph of the function $h(x) = |x - 1|$ shifted the graph of the function $f(x)$ to the right one unit. If, instead, we had the function $H(x) = |x + 1|$, this graph would have started with the graph of the function $f(x)$ and shifted to the left one unit.

## VERTICAL SHIFTS

Assuming that $c$ is a positive constant,

| To Graph | Shift the Graph of $f(x)$ |
|---|---|
| $f(x) + c$ | $c$ units upward |
| $f(x) - c$ | $c$ units downward |

Adding or subtracting a constant **outside** the function corresponds to a **vertical** shift that goes **with the sign**.

## HORIZONTAL SHIFTS

Assuming that $c$ is a positive constant,

| To Graph | Shift the Graph of $f(x)$ |
|---|---|
| $f(x + c)$ | $c$ units to the left |
| $f(x - c)$ | $c$ units to the right |

Adding or subtracting a constant **inside** the function corresponds to a **horizontal** shift that goes **opposite the sign**.

**Study Tip**

- Shifts *outside* the function are *vertical* shifts with the sign.
- Shifts *inside* the function are *horizontal* shifts opposite the sign.

*Technology Tip*

**a.** Graphs of $y_1 = x^2$ and $y_2 = g(x) = x^2 - 1$ are shown.

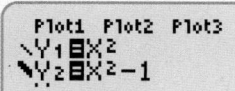

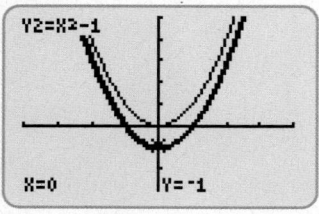

**b.** Graphs of $y_1 = x^2$ and $y_2 = H(x) = (x + 1)^2$ are shown.

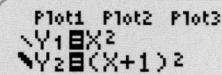

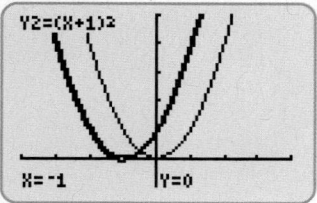

■ **Answer:**

**a.**

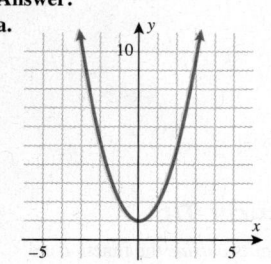

**b.**

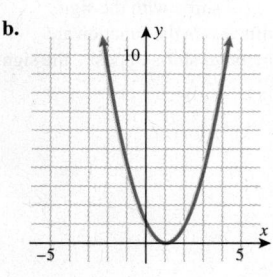

**EXAMPLE 1    Horizontal and Vertical Shifts**

Sketch the graphs of the given functions using horizontal and vertical shifts.

**a.** $g(x) = x^2 - 1$

**b.** $H(x) = (x + 1)^2$

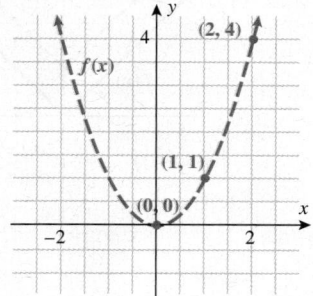

**Solution:**

In both cases, the function to start with is $f(x) = x^2$.

**a.** $g(x) = x^2 - 1$ can be rewritten as $g(x) = f(x) - 1$.

1. The shift (one unit) occurs *outside* of the function. Therefore, we expect a vertical shift that goes with the sign.

2. Since the sign is *negative*, this corresponds to a *downward* shift.

3. Shifting the graph of the function $f(x) = x^2$ down one unit yields the graph of $g(x) = x^2 - 1$.

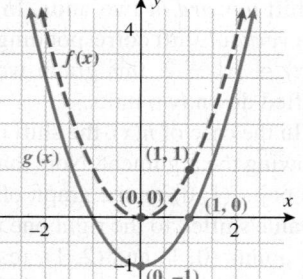

**b.** $H(x) = (x + 1)^2$ can be rewritten as $H(x) = f(x + 1)$.

1. The shift (one unit) occurs *inside* of the function. Therefore, we expect a horizontal shift that goes *opposite* the sign.

2. Since the sign is *positive*, this corresponds to a shift to the *left*.

3. Shifting the graph of the function $f(x) = x^2$ to the left one unit yields the graph of $H(x) = (x + 1)^2$.

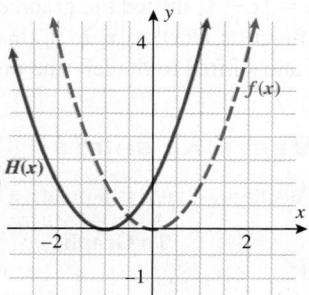

■ **YOUR TURN** Sketch the graphs of the given functions using horizontal and vertical shifts.

**a.** $g(x) = x^2 + 1$    **b.** $H(x) = (x - 1)^2$

It is important to note that the domain and range of the resulting function can be thought of as also being shifted. Shifts in the domain correspond to horizontal shifts, and shifts in the range correspond to vertical shifts.

**EXAMPLE 2   Horizontal and Vertical Shifts and Changes in the Domain and Range**

Graph the functions using translations and state the domain and range of each function.

**a.** $g(x) = \sqrt{x + 1}$

**b.** $G(x) = \sqrt{x} - 2$

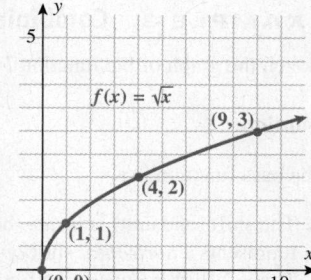

**Solution:**

In both cases the function to start with is $f(x) = \sqrt{x}$.

$$\text{Domain:} \quad [0, \infty)$$

$$\text{Range:} \quad [0, \infty)$$

**a.** $g(x) = \sqrt{x + 1}$ can be rewritten as $g(x) = f(x + 1)$.

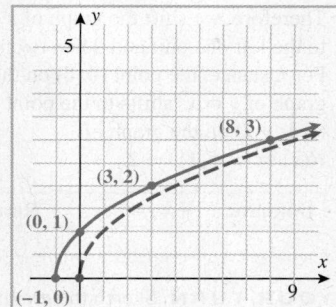

1. The shift (one unit) is *inside* the function, which corresponds to a *horizontal* shift *opposite the sign*.

2. Shifting the graph of $f(x) = \sqrt{x}$ to the *left* one unit yields the graph of $g(x) = \sqrt{x + 1}$. Notice that the point $(0, 0)$, which lies on the graph of $f(x)$, gets shifted to the point $(-1, 0)$ on the graph of $g(x)$.

Although the original function $f(x) = \sqrt{x}$ had an implicit restriction on the domain $[0, \infty)$, the function $g(x) = \sqrt{x + 1}$ has the implicit restriction that $x \geq -1$. We see that the output or range of $g(x)$ is the same as the output of the original function $f(x)$.

$$\boxed{\text{Domain:} \quad [-1, \infty) \qquad \text{Range:} \quad [0, \infty)}$$

**b.** $G(x) = \sqrt{x} - 2$ can be rewritten as $G(x) = f(x) - 2$.

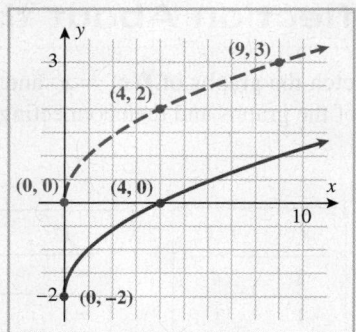

1. The shift (two units) is *outside* the function, which corresponds to a *vertical* shift *with the sign*.

2. The graph of $G(x) = \sqrt{x} - 2$ is found by shifting $f(x) = \sqrt{x}$ down two units. Note that the point $(0, 0)$, which lies on the graph of $f(x)$, gets shifted to the point $(0, -2)$ on the graph of $G(x)$.

The original function $f(x) = \sqrt{x}$ has an implicit restriction on the domain: $[0, \infty)$. The function $G(x) = \sqrt{x} - 2$ also has the implicit restriction that $x \geq 0$. The output or range of $G(x)$ is always two units less than the output of the original function $f(x)$.

$$\boxed{\text{Domain:} \quad [0, \infty) \qquad \text{Range:} \quad [-2, \infty)}$$

**■ YOUR TURN** Sketch the graph of the functions using shifts and state the domain and range.

**a.** $G(x) = \sqrt{x - 2}$   **b.** $h(x) = |x| + 1$

**■ Answer:**

**a.** $G(x) = \sqrt{x - 2}$

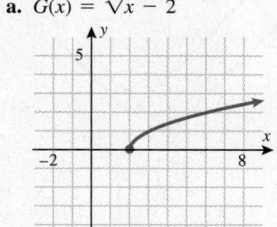

Domain: $[2, \infty)$   Range: $[0, \infty)$

**b.** $h(x) = |x| + 1$

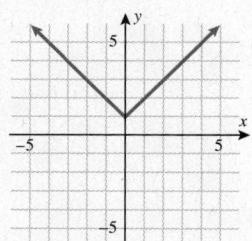

Domain: $(-\infty, \infty)$   Range: $[1, \infty)$

The previous examples have involved graphing functions by shifting a known function either in the horizontal or vertical direction. Let us now look at combinations of horizontal and vertical shifts.

### EXAMPLE 3  Combining Horizontal and Vertical Shifts

**Technology Tip**

Graphs of $y_1 = x^2$, $y_2 = (x + 1)^2$, and $y_3 = F(x) = (x + 1)^2 - 2$ are shown.

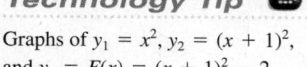

Sketch the graph of the function $F(x) = (x + 1)^2 - 2$. State the domain and range of $F$.

**Solution:**

The base function is $y = x^2$.

1. The shift (one unit) is *inside* the function, so it represents a *horizontal* shift *opposite the sign*.
2. The $-2$ shift is *outside* the function, which represents a *vertical* shift *with the sign*.
3. Therefore, we shift the graph of $y = x^2$ to the left one unit and down two units. For instance, the point $(0, 0)$ on the graph of $y = x^2$ shifts to the point $(-1, -2)$ on the graph of $F(x) = (x + 1)^2 - 2$.

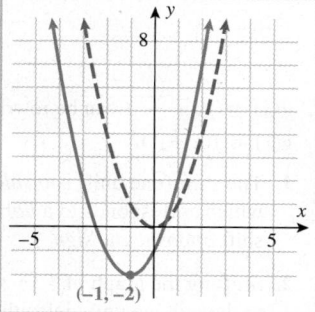

| Domain: $(-\infty, \infty)$ | Range: $[-2, \infty)$ |

**Answer:**
$f(x) = |x - 2| + 1$
$f(x) = |x|$
Domain: $(-\infty, \infty)$
Range: $[1, \infty)$

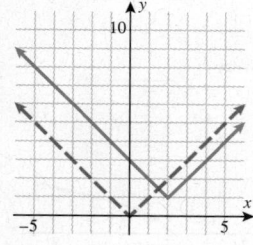

■ **YOUR TURN** Sketch the graph of the function $f(x) = |x - 2| + 1$. State the domain and range of $f$.

All of the previous transformation examples involve starting with a common function and shifting the function in either the horizontal or the vertical direction (or a combination of both). Now, let's investigate *reflections* of functions about the $x$-axis or $y$-axis.

## Reflection About the Axes

To sketch the graphs of $f(x) = x^2$ and $g(x) = -x^2$, start by first listing points that are on each of the graphs and then connecting the points with smooth curves.

| $x$ | $f(x)$ |
|-----|--------|
| $-2$ | 4 |
| $-1$ | 1 |
| 0 | 0 |
| 1 | 1 |
| 2 | 4 |

| $x$ | $g(x)$ |
|-----|--------|
| $-2$ | $-4$ |
| $-1$ | $-1$ |
| 0 | 0 |
| 1 | $-1$ |
| 2 | $-4$ |

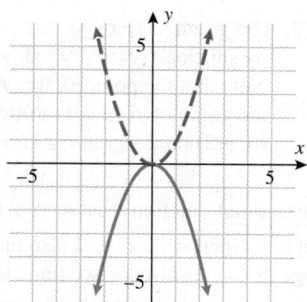

Note that if the graph of $f(x) = x^2$ is reflected about the $x$-axis, the result is the graph of $g(x) = -x^2$. Also note that the function $g(x)$ can be written as the negative of the function $f(x)$; that is $g(x) = -f(x)$. In general, **reflection about the $x$-axis** is produced by multiplying a function by $-1$.

Let's now investigate reflection about the $y$-axis. To sketch the graphs of $f(x) = \sqrt{x}$ and $g(x) = \sqrt{-x}$, start by listing points that are on each of the graphs and then connecting the points with smooth curves.

| $x$ | $f(x)$ |
|-----|--------|
| 0 | 0 |
| 1 | 1 |
| 4 | 2 |
| 9 | 3 |

| $x$ | $g(x)$ |
|-----|--------|
| −9 | 3 |
| −4 | 2 |
| −1 | 1 |
| 0 | 0 |

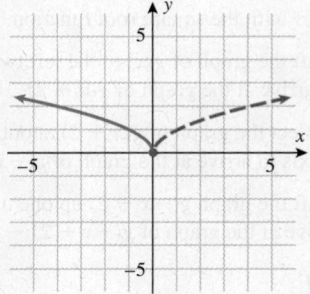

Note that if the graph of $f(x) = \sqrt{x}$ is reflected about the $y$-axis, the result is the graph of $g(x) = \sqrt{-x}$. Also note that the function $g(x)$ can be written as $g(x) = f(-x)$. In general, **reflection about the $y$-axis** is produced by replacing $x$ with $-x$ in the function. Notice that the domain of $f$ is $[0, \infty)$, whereas the domain of $g$ is $(-\infty, 0]$.

## REFLECTION ABOUT THE AXES

The graph of $-f(x)$ is obtained by reflecting the graph of $f(x)$ about the $x$-axis.
The graph of $f(-x)$ is obtained by reflecting the graph of $f(x)$ about the $y$-axis.

### EXAMPLE 4   Sketching the Graph of a Function Using Both Shifts and Reflections

Sketch the graph of the function $G(x) = -\sqrt{x + 1}$.

**Solution:**

Start with the square root function.

$$f(x) = \sqrt{x}$$

Shift the graph of $f(x)$ to the left one unit to arrive at the graph of $f(x + 1)$.

$$f(x + 1) = \sqrt{x + 1}$$

Reflect the graph of $f(x + 1)$ about the $x$-axis to arrive at the graph of $-f(x + 1)$.

$$-f(x + 1) = -\sqrt{x + 1}$$

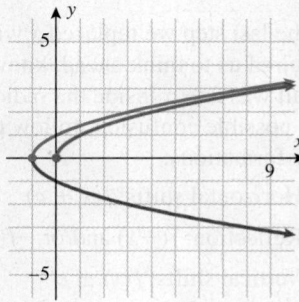

## Technology Tip

Graphs of $y_1 = \sqrt{x}$, $y_2 = \sqrt{x+2}$, $y_3 = \sqrt{-x+2}$, and $y_4 = f(x) = \sqrt{2-x} + 1$ are shown.

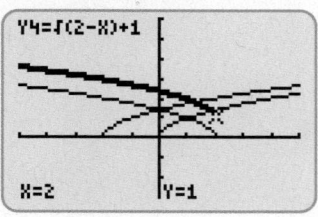

■ **Answer:**
Domain: $[1, \infty)$
Range: $(-\infty, 2]$

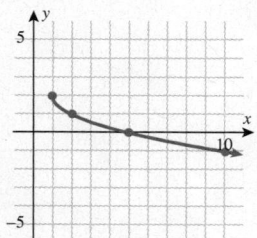

**EXAMPLE 5** **Sketching the Graph of a Function Using Both Shifts and Reflections**

Sketch the graph of the function $f(x) = \sqrt{2-x} + 1$.

**Solution:**

Start with the square root function. $g(x) = \sqrt{x}$

Shift the graph of $g(x)$ to the left two units to arrive at the graph of $g(x+2)$. $g(x+2) = \sqrt{x+2}$

Reflect the graph of $g(x+2)$ about the $y$-axis to arrive at the graph of $g(-x+2)$. $g(-x+2) = \sqrt{-x+2}$

Shift the graph $g(-x+2)$ up one unit to arrive at the graph of $g(-x+2) + 1$. $g(-x+2) + 1 = \sqrt{2-x} + 1$

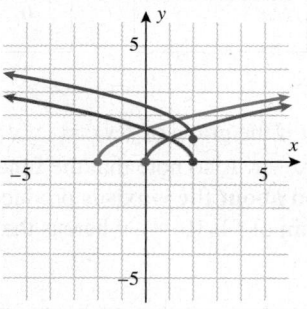

■ **YOUR TURN** Use shifts and reflections to sketch the graph of the function $f(x) = -\sqrt{x-1} + 2$. State the domain and range of $f(x)$.

Look back at the order in which transformations were performed in Example 5: horizontal shift, reflection, and then vertical shift. Let us consider an alternate order of transformations.

**WORDS** **MATH**

Start with the square root function. $g(x) = \sqrt{x}$

Shift the graph of $g(x)$ up one unit to arrive at the graph of $g(x) + 1$. $g(x) + 1 = \sqrt{x} + 1$

Reflect the graph of $g(x) + 1$ about the $y$-axis to arrive at the graph of $g(-x) + 1$. $g(-x) + 1 = \sqrt{-x} + 1$

Replace $x$ with $x - 2$, which corresponds to a shift of the graph of $g(-x) + 1$ to the right two units to arrive at the graph of $g[-(x-2)] + 1$. $g(-x+2) + 1 = \sqrt{2-x} + 1$

In the last step we replaced $x$ with $x - 2$, which required us to think ahead, knowing the desired result was $2 - x$ inside the radical. To avoid any possible confusion, follow this order of transformations:

1. Horizontal shifts: $f(x \pm c)$
2. Reflection: $f(-x)$ and/or $-f(x)$
3. Vertical shifts: $f(x) \pm c$

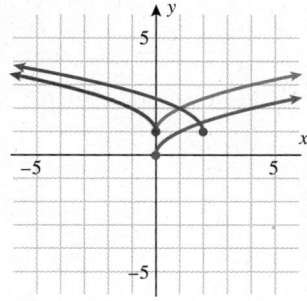

# Stretching and Compressing

Horizontal shifts, vertical shifts, and reflections change only the position of the graph in the Cartesian plane, leaving the basic shape of the graph unchanged. These transformations (shifts and reflections) are called **rigid transformations** because they alter only the *position.* **Nonrigid transformations**, on the other hand, distort the *shape* of the original graph. We now consider *stretching* and *compressing* of graphs in both the vertical and the horizontal direction.

A vertical stretch or compression of a graph occurs when the function is multiplied by a positive constant. For example, the graphs of the functions $f(x) = x^2$, $g(x) = 2f(x) = 2x^2$, and $h(x) = \frac{1}{2}f(x) = \frac{1}{2}x^2$ are illustrated below. Depending on if the constant is larger than 1 or smaller than 1 will determine whether it corresponds to a stretch (expansion) or compression (contraction) in the vertical direction.

| $x$ | $f(x)$ |
|-----|--------|
| $-2$ | 4 |
| $-1$ | 1 |
| 0 | 0 |
| 1 | 1 |
| 2 | 4 |

| $x$ | $g(x)$ |
|-----|--------|
| $-2$ | 8 |
| $-1$ | 2 |
| 0 | 0 |
| 1 | 2 |
| 2 | 8 |

| $x$ | $h(x)$ |
|-----|--------|
| $-2$ | 2 |
| $-1$ | $\frac{1}{2}$ |
| 0 | 0 |
| 1 | $\frac{1}{2}$ |
| 2 | 2 |

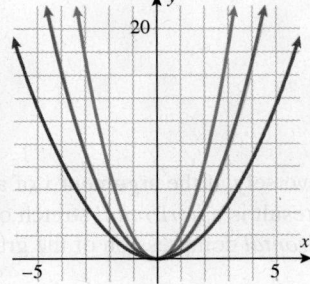

Note that when the function $f(x) = x^2$ is multiplied by 2, so that $g(x) = 2f(x) = 2x^2$, the result is a graph stretched in the vertical direction. When the function $f(x) = x^2$ is multiplied by $\frac{1}{2}$, so that $h(x) = \frac{1}{2}f(x) = \frac{1}{2}x^2$, the result is a graph that is compressed in the vertical direction.

## VERTICAL STRETCHING AND VERTICAL COMPRESSING OF GRAPHS

The graph of $cf(x)$ is found by:

- **Vertically stretching** the graph of $f(x)$     if $c > 1$
- **Vertically compressing** the graph of $f(x)$     if $0 < c < 1$

*Note: c* is any positive real number.

**EXAMPLE 6    Vertically Stretching and Compressing Graphs**

Graph the function $h(x) = \frac{1}{4}x^3$.

**Solution:**

1. Start with the cube function.

$$f(x) = x^3$$

2. Vertical compression is expected because $\frac{1}{4}$ is less than 1.

$$h(x) = \frac{1}{4}x^3$$

3. Determine a few points that lie on the graph of $h$.

$$(0, 0) \quad (2, 2) \quad (-2, -2)$$

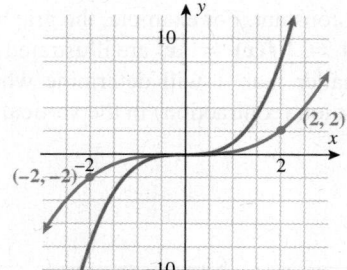

Conversely, if the argument $x$ of a function $f$ is multiplied by a positive real number $c$, then the result is a *horizontal* stretch of the graph of $f$ if $0 < c < 1$. If $c > 1$, then the result is a *horizontal* compression of the graph of $f$.

**HORIZONTAL STRETCHING AND HORIZONTAL COMPRESSING OF GRAPHS**

The graph of $f(cx)$ is found by:

- **Horizontally stretching** the graph of $f(x)$      if $0 < c < 1$
- **Horizontally compressing** the graph of $f(x)$      if $c > 1$

*Note: c* is any positive real number.

**EXAMPLE 7    Vertically Stretching and Horizontally Compressing Graphs**

Given the graph of $f(x)$, graph

**a.** $2f(x)$      **b.** $f(2x)$

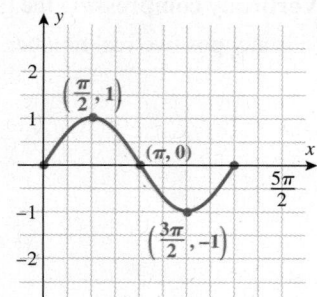

**Solution (a):**

Since the function is multiplied (on the outside) by 2, the result is that each **y-value** of $f(x)$ is *multiplied* by **2**, which corresponds to vertical stretching.

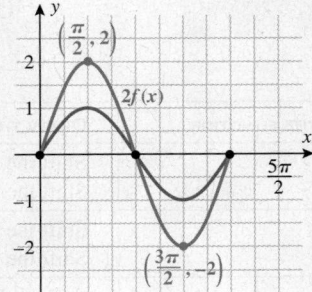

**Solution (b):**

Since the argument of the function is multiplied (on the inside) by 2, the result is that each **x-value** of $f(x)$ is **divided by 2**, which corresponds to horizontal compression.

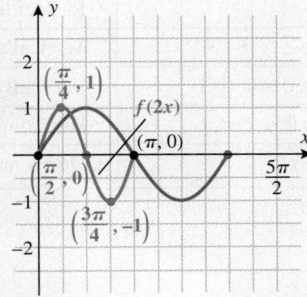

■ **YOUR TURN** Graph the function $g(x) = 4x^3$.

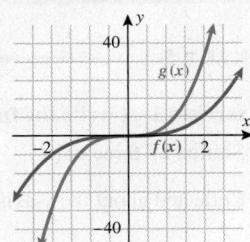

**EXAMPLE 8**  **Sketching the Graph of a Function Using Multiple Transformations**

Sketch the graph of the function $H(x) = -2(x - 3)^2$.

**Solution:**

| | |
|---|---|
| Start with the square function. | $f(x) = x^2$ |
| Shift the graph of $f(x)$ to the right three units to arrive at the graph of $f(x - 3)$. | $f(x - 3) = (x - 3)^2$ |
| Vertically stretch the graph of $f(x - 3)$ by a factor of 2 to arrive at the graph of $2f(x - 3)$. | $2f(x - 3) = 2(x - 3)^2$ |
| Reflect the graph $2f(x - 3)$ about the $x$-axis to arrive at the graph of $-2f(x - 3)$. | $-2f(x - 3) = -2(x - 3)^2$ |

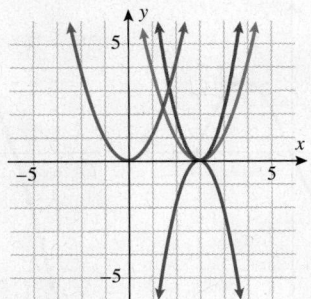

*Technology Tip*

Graphs of $y_1 = x^2$, $y_2 = (x - 3)^2$, $y_3 = 2(x - 3)^2$, and $y_4 = H(x) = -2(x - 3)^2$ are shown.

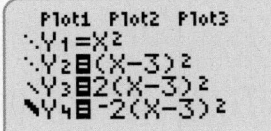

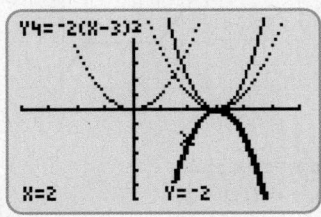

In Example 8 we followed the same "inside out" approach with the functions to determine the order for the transformations: horizontal shift, vertical stretch, and reflection.

## SECTION 1.3 SUMMARY

| TRANSFORMATION | TO GRAPH THE FUNCTION... | DRAW THE GRAPH OF $f$ AND THEN... | DESCRIPTION |
|---|---|---|---|
| Horizontal shifts ($c > 0$) | $f(x + c)$<br>$f(x - c)$ | Shift the graph of $f$ to the left $c$ units.<br>Shift the graph of $f$ to the right $c$ units. | Replace $x$ by $x + c$.<br>Replace $x$ by $x - c$. |
| Vertical shifts ($c > 0$) | $f(x) + c$<br>$f(x) - c$ | Shift the graph of $f$ up $c$ units.<br>Shift the graph of $f$ down $c$ units. | Add $c$ to $f(x)$.<br>Subtract $c$ from $f(x)$. |
| Reflection about the $x$-axis | $-f(x)$ | Reflect the graph of $f$ about the $x$-axis. | Multiply $f(x)$ by $-1$. |
| Reflection about the $y$-axis | $f(-x)$ | Reflect the graph of $f$ about the $y$-axis. | Replace $x$ by $-x$. |
| Vertical stretch | $cf(x)$, where $c > 1$ | Vertically stretch the graph of $f$. | Multiply $f(x)$ by $c$. |
| Vertical compression | $cf(x)$, where $0 < c < 1$ | Vertically compress the graph of $f$. | Multiply $f(x)$ by $c$. |
| Horizontal stretch | $f(cx)$, where $0 < c < 1$ | Horizontally stretch the graph of $f$. | Replace $x$ by $cx$. |
| Horizontal compression | $f(cx)$, where $c > 1$ | Horizontally compress the graph of $f$. | Replace $x$ by $cx$. |

## SECTION 1.3 EXERCISES

### ▪ SKILLS

**In Exercises 1–6, write the function whose graph is the graph of $y = |x|$, but is transformed accordingly.**

**1.** Shifted up three units

**2.** Shifted to the left four units

**3.** Reflected about the $y$-axis

**4.** Reflected about the $x$-axis

**5.** Vertically stretched by a factor of 3

**6.** Vertically compressed by a factor of 3

**In Exercises 7–12, write the function whose graph is the graph of $y = x^3$, but is transformed accordingly.**

**7.** Shifted down four units

**8.** Shifted to the right three units

**9.** Shifted up three units and to the left one unit

**10.** Reflected about the $x$-axis

**11.** Reflected about the $y$-axis

**12.** Reflected about both the $x$-axis and the $y$-axis

**In Exercises 13–36, use the given graph to sketch the graph of the indicated functions.**

**13.**

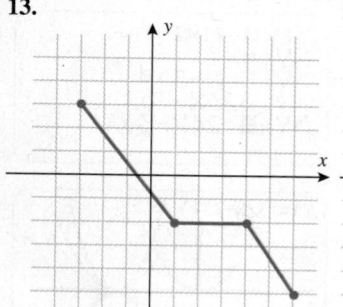

**a.** $y = f(x - 2)$
**b.** $y = f(x) - 2$

**14.**

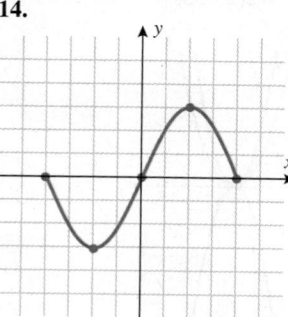

**a.** $y = f(x + 2)$
**b.** $y = f(x) + 2$

**15.**

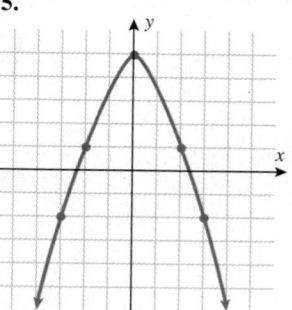

**a.** $y = f(x) - 3$
**b.** $y = f(x - 3)$

**16.**

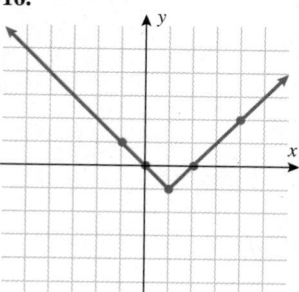

**a.** $y = f(x) + 3$
**b.** $y = f(x + 3)$

**17.**
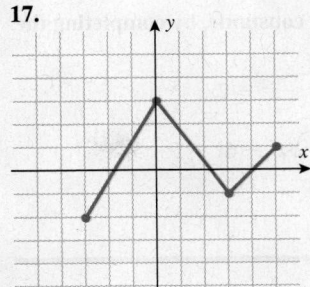

a. $y = -f(x)$
b. $y = f(-x)$

**18.**
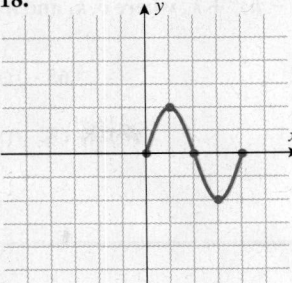

a. $y = -f(x)$
b. $y = f(-x)$

**19.**
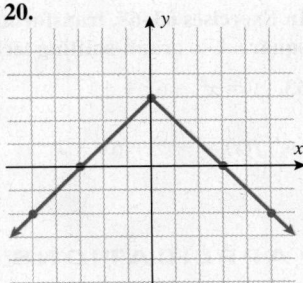

a. $y = 2f(x)$
b. $y = f(2x)$

**20.**
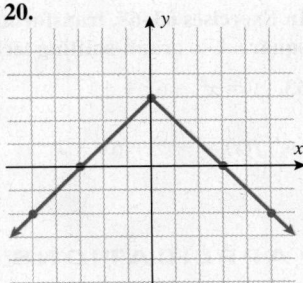

a. $y = 2f(x)$
b. $y = f(2x)$

**21.** $y = f(x - 2) - 3$

**22.** $y = f(x + 1) - 2$

**23.** $y = -f(x - 1) + 2$

**24.** $y = -2f(x) + 1$

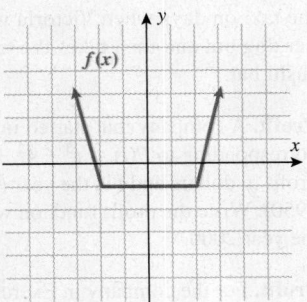

**25.** $y = -\frac{1}{2}g(x)$

**26.** $y = \frac{1}{4}g(-x)$

**27.** $y = -g(2x)$

**28.** $y = g\left(\frac{1}{2}x\right)$

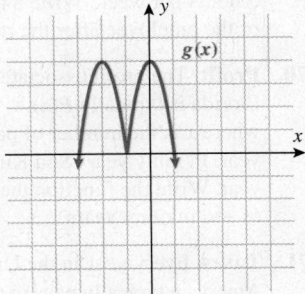

**29.** $y = \frac{1}{2}F(x - 1) + 2$

**30.** $y = \frac{1}{2}F(-x)$

**31.** $y = -F(1 - x)$

**32.** $y = -F(x - 2) - 1$

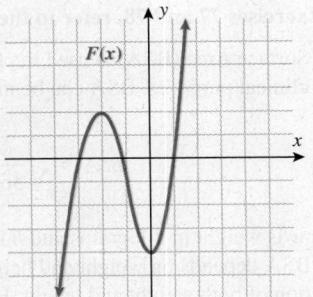

**33.** $y = 2G(x + 1) - 4$

**34.** $y = 2G(-x) + 1$

**35.** $y = -2G(x - 1) + 3$

**36.** $y = -G(x - 2) - 1$

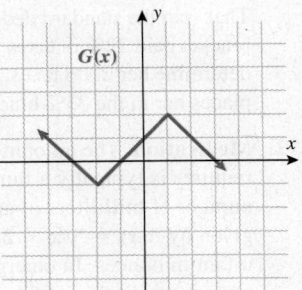

**In Exercises 37–62, graph the function using transformations.**

**37.** $y = x^2 - 2$

**38.** $y = x^2 + 3$

**39.** $y = (x + 1)^2$

**40.** $y = (x - 2)^2$

**41.** $y = (x - 3)^2 + 2$

**42.** $y = (x + 2)^2 + 1$

**43.** $y = -(1 - x)^2$

**44.** $y = -(x + 2)^2$

**45.** $y = |-x|$

**46.** $y = -|x|$

**47.** $y = -|x + 2| - 1$

**48.** $y = |1 - x| + 2$

**49.** $y = 2x^2 + 1$

**50.** $y = 2|x| + 1$

**51.** $y = -\sqrt{x - 2}$

**52.** $y = \sqrt{2 - x}$

**53.** $y = -\sqrt{2 + x} - 1$

**54.** $y = \sqrt{2 - x} + 3$

**55.** $y = \sqrt[3]{x - 1} + 2$

**56.** $y = \sqrt[3]{x + 2} - 1$

**57.** $y = \dfrac{1}{x + 3} + 2$

**58.** $y = \dfrac{1}{3 - x}$

**59.** $y = 2 - \dfrac{1}{x + 2}$

**60.** $y = 2 - \dfrac{1}{1 - x}$

**61.** $y = 5\sqrt{-x}$

**62.** $y = -\frac{1}{5}\sqrt{x}$

**In Exercises 63–68, transform the function into the form** $f(x) = c(x - h)^2 + k$, **where** $c, k,$ **and** $h$ **are constants, by completing the square. Use graph-shifting techniques to graph the function.**

**63.** $y = x^2 - 6x + 11$

**64.** $f(x) = x^2 + 2x - 2$

**65.** $f(x) = -x^2 - 2x$

**66.** $f(x) = -x^2 + 6x - 7$

**67.** $f(x) = 2x^2 - 8x + 3$

**68.** $f(x) = 3x^2 - 6x + 5$

## ▪ APPLICATIONS

**69. Salary.** A manager hires an employee at a rate of $10 per hour. Write the function that describes the current salary of the employee as a function of the number of hours worked per week, $x$. After a year, the manager decides to award the employee a raise equivalent to paying him for an additional 5 hours per week. Write a function that describes the salary of the employee after the raise.

**70. Profit.** The profit associated with St. Augustine sod in Florida is typically $P(x) = -x^2 + 14,000x - 48,700,000$, where $x$ is the number of pallets sold per year in a normal year. In rainy years Sod King gives away 10 free pallets per year. Write the function that describes the profit of $x$ pallets of sod in rainy years.

**71. Taxes.** Every year in the United States each working American typically pays in taxes a percentage of his or her earnings (minus the standard deduction). Karen's 2005 taxes were calculated based on the formula $T(x) = 0.22(x - 6500)$. That year the standard deduction was $6500 and her tax bracket paid 22% in taxes. Write the function that will determine her 2006 taxes, assuming she receives a raise that places her in the 33% bracket.

**72. Medication.** The amount of medication that an infant requires is typically a function of the baby's weight. The number of milliliters of an antiseizure medication $A$ is given by $A(x) = \sqrt{x} + 2$, where $x$ is the weight of the infant in ounces. In emergencies there is often not enough time to weigh the infant, so nurses have to estimate the baby's weight. What is the function that represents the actual amount of medication the infant is given if his weight is overestimated by 3 ounces?

**73. Taxi Rates.** Victoria lives in a condo on Peachtree Street in downtown Atlanta and works at the Federal Reserve Bank of Atlanta, which is 1 mile north of her condo on Peachtree Street. She often eats lunch at Nava Restaurant in Buckhead that is $x$ miles north of the Federal Reserve Bank on Peachtree Street. A taxi in downtown Atlanta costs $7.00 for the first mile and $0.30 for every mile after that. Write a function that shows the cost of traveling from Victoria's office to Nava for lunch. Then rewrite the same function to show the cost of the taxi on days when Victoria walks home first to let her dog out and then takes the taxi from her condo to the Nava Restaurant.

**74. Taxi Rates.** Victoria (in Exercise 73) also likes to eat lunch at a sushi bar $x$ miles south of the Federal Reserve Bank on Peachtree Street. Write a function that shows the cost of traveling from Victoria's office to the sushi bar for lunch. Then rewrite the same function to show the cost of the taxi on days when Victoria walks home first to let her dog out and then takes the taxi from her condo to the sushi bar.

**75. Profit.** A company that started in 1900 has made a profit corresponding to $P(t) = t^3 - t^2 + t - 1$, where $P$ is the profit in dollars and $t$ is the year (with $t = 0$ corresponding to 1950). Write the profit function with $t = 0$ corresponding to the year 2000.

**76. Profit.** For the company in Exercise 75, write the profit function with $t = 0$ corresponding to the year 2010.

**For Exercises 77 and 78, refer to the following:**

Body Surface Area (BSA) is used in physiology and medicine for many clinical purposes. BSA can be modeled by the function

$$BSA = \sqrt{\frac{wh}{3600}}$$

where $w$ is weight in kilograms and $h$ is height in centimeters. Since BSA depends on weight and height, it is often thought of as a function of both weight and height. However, for an individual adult height is generally considered constant; thus BSA can be thought of as a function of weight alone.

**77. Health/Medicine.** (a) If an adult female is 162 centimeters tall, find her BSA as a function of weight. (b) If she loses 3 kilograms, find a function that represents her new BSA.

**78. Health/Medicine.** (a) If an adult male is 180 centimeters tall, find his BSA as a function of weight. (b) If he gains 5 kilograms, find a function that represents his new BSA.

■ **CATCH THE MISTAKE**

**In Exercises 79–82, explain the mistake that is made.**

79. Describe a procedure for graphing the function
$f(x) = \sqrt{x-3} + 2$.

**Solution:**
a. Start with the function $f(x) = \sqrt{x}$.
b. Shift the function to the left three units.
c. Shift the function up two units.

This is incorrect. What mistake was made?

80. Describe a procedure for graphing the function
$f(x) = -\sqrt{x+2} - 3$.

**Solution:**
a. Start with the function $f(x) = \sqrt{x}$.
b. Shift the function to the left two units.
c. Reflect the function about the $y$-axis.
d. Shift the function down three units.

This is incorrect. What mistake was made?

81. Describe a procedure for graphing the function
$f(x) = |3 - x| + 1$.

**Solution:**
a. Start with the function $f(x) = |x|$.
b. Reflect the function about the $y$-axis.
c. Shift the function to the left three units.
d. Shift the function up one unit.

This is incorrect. What mistake was made?

82. Describe a procedure for graphing the function
$f(x) = -2x^2 + 1$.

**Solution:**
a. Start with the function $f(x) = x^2$.
b. Reflect the function about the $y$-axis.
c. Shift the function up one unit.
d. Expand in the vertical direction by a factor of 2.

This is incorrect. What mistake was made?

■ **CONCEPTUAL**

**In Exercises 83–88, determine whether each statement is true or false.**

83. The graph of $y = |-x|$ is the same as the graph of $y = |x|$.

84. The graph of $y = \sqrt{-x}$ is the same as the graph of $y = \sqrt{x}$.

85. If the graph of an odd function is reflected around the $x$-axis and then the $y$-axis, the result is the graph of the original odd function.

86. If the graph of $y = \dfrac{1}{x}$ is reflected around the $x$-axis, it produces the same graph as if it had been reflected about the $y$-axis.

87. If $f$ is a function and $c > 1$ is a constant, then the graph of $-cf$ is a reflection about the $x$-axis of a vertical stretch of the graph of $f$.

88. If $a$ and $b$ are positive constants and $f$ is a function, then the graph of $f(x + a) + b$ is obtained by shifting the graph of $f$ to the right $a$ units and then shifting this graph up $b$ units.

■ **CHALLENGE**

89. The point $(a, b)$ lies on the graph of the function $y = f(x)$. What point is guaranteed to lie on the graph of $f(x - 3) + 2$?

90. The point $(a, b)$ lies on the graph of the function $y = f(x)$. What point is guaranteed to lie on the graph of $-f(-x) + 1$?

91. The point $(a, b)$ lies on the graph of the function $y = f(x)$. What point is guaranteed to lie on the graph of $2f(x + 1) - 1$?

92. The point $(a, b)$ lies on the graph of the function $y = f(x)$. What point is guaranteed to lie on the graph of $-2f(x - 3) + 4$?

■ **TECHNOLOGY**

93. Use a graphing utility to graph
a. $y = x^2 - 2$ and $y = |x^2 - 2|$
b. $y = x^3 - 1$ and $y = |x^3 - 1|$

What is the relationship between $f(x)$ and $|f(x)|$?

94. Use a graphing utility to graph
a. $y = x^2 - 2$ and $y = |x|^2 - 2$
b. $y = x^3 + 1$ and $y = |x|^3 + 1$

What is the relationship between $f(x)$ and $f(|x|)$?

95. Use a graphing utility to graph
a. $y = \sqrt{x}$ and $y = \sqrt{0.1x}$
b. $y = \sqrt{x}$ and $y = \sqrt{10x}$

What is the relationship between $f(x)$ and $f(ax)$, assuming that $a$ is positive?

96. Use a graphing utility to graph
a. $y = \sqrt{x}$ and $y = 0.1\sqrt{x}$
b. $y = \sqrt{x}$ and $y = 10\sqrt{x}$

What is the relationship between $f(x)$ and $af(x)$, assuming that $a$ is positive?

**97.** Use a graphing utility to graph $y = f(x) = [[0.5x]] + 1$. Use transformations to describe the relationship between $f(x)$ and $y = [[x]]$.

**98.** Use a graphing utility to graph $y = g(x) = 0.5 [[x]] + 1$. Use transformations to describe the relationship between $g(x)$ and $y = [[x]]$.

**■ PREVIEW TO CALCULUS** ────────────────

**For Exercises 99–102, refer to the following:**

In calculus, the difference quotient $\dfrac{f(x + h) - f(x)}{h}$ of a function $f$ is used to find the derivative $f'$ of $f$, by letting $h$ approach $0$, $h \to 0$. Find the derivatives of $f$ and $g$.

**99. Horizontal Shift.** $f(x) = x^2$, $g(x) = (x - 1)^2$. How are the graphs of $g'$ and $f'$ related?

**100. Horizontal Shift.** $f(x) = \sqrt{x}$, $g(x) = \sqrt{x + 5}$. How are the graphs of $g'$ and $f'$ related?

**101. Vertical Shift.** $f(x) = 2x$, $g(x) = 2x + 7$. How are the graphs of $g'$ and $f'$ related?

**102. Vertical Shift.** $f(x) = x^3$, $g(x) = x^3 - 4$. How are the graphs of $g'$ and $f'$ related?

## SECTION
## 1.4 COMBINING FUNCTIONS

### SKILLS OBJECTIVES

- Add, subtract, multiply, and divide functions.
- Evaluate composite functions.
- Determine domain of functions resulting from operations on and composition of functions.

### CONCEPTUAL OBJECTIVES

- Understand domain restrictions when dividing functions.
- Realize that the domain of a composition of functions excludes values that are not in the domain of the inside function.

## Adding, Subtracting, Multiplying, and Dividing Functions

Two functions can be added, subtracted, and multiplied. The domain of the resulting function is the intersection of the domains of the two functions. However, for division, any value of $x$ (input) that makes the denominator equal to zero must be eliminated from the domain.

| Function | Notation | Domain |
|---|---|---|
| Sum | $(f + g)(x) = f(x) + g(x)$ | {domain of $f$} ∩ {domain of $g$} |
| Difference | $(f - g)(x) = f(x) - g(x)$ | {domain of $f$} ∩ {domain of $g$} |
| Product | $(f \cdot g)(x) = f(x) \cdot g(x)$ | {domain of $f$} ∩ {domain of $g$} |
| Quotient | $\left(\dfrac{f}{g}\right)(x) = \dfrac{f(x)}{g(x)}$ | {domain of $f$} ∩ {domain of $g$} ∩ {$g(x) \neq 0$} |

We can think of this in the following way: Any number that is in the domain of *both* the functions is in the domain of the combined function. The exception to this is the quotient function, which also eliminates values that make the denominator equal to zero.

**EXAMPLE 1** **Operations on Functions: Determining Domains of New Functions**

For the functions $f(x) = \sqrt{x - 1}$ and $g(x) = \sqrt{4 - x}$, determine the sum function, difference function, product function, and quotient function. State the domain of these four new functions.

**Solution:**

Sum function: $\quad f(x) + g(x) = \sqrt{x - 1} + \sqrt{4 - x}$

Difference function: $\quad f(x) - g(x) = \sqrt{x - 1} - \sqrt{4 - x}$

Product function: $\quad f(x) \cdot g(x) = \sqrt{x - 1} \cdot \sqrt{4 - x}$

$$= \sqrt{(x - 1)(4 - x)} = \sqrt{-x^2 + 5x - 4}$$

Quotient function: $\quad \dfrac{f(x)}{g(x)} = \dfrac{\sqrt{x - 1}}{\sqrt{4 - x}} = \sqrt{\dfrac{x - 1}{4 - x}}$

The domain of the square root function is determined by setting the argument under the radical greater than or equal to zero.

Domain of $f(x)$: $\quad [1, \infty)$

Domain of $g(x)$: $\quad (-\infty, 4]$

The domain of the sum, difference, and product functions is

$$[1, \infty) \cap (-\infty, 4] = [1, 4]$$

The quotient function has the additional constraint that the denominator cannot be zero. This implies that $x \neq 4$, so the domain of the quotient function is $[1, 4)$.

- - - - - - - - - - - - - - - - - - - - - - - - - - - - - - - - - - - - - -

■ **YOUR TURN** Given the function $f(x) = \sqrt{x + 3}$ and $g(x) = \sqrt{1 - x}$, find $(f + g)(x)$ and state its domain.

■ **Answer:**
$(f + g)(x) = \sqrt{x + 3} + \sqrt{1 - x}$
Domain: $[-3, 1]$

**EXAMPLE 2** **Quotient Function and Domain Restrictions**

Given the functions $F(x) = \sqrt{x}$ and $G(x) = |x - 3|$, find the quotient function, $\left(\dfrac{F}{G}\right)(x)$, and state its domain.

**Solution:**

The quotient function is written as

$$\left(\frac{F}{G}\right)(x) = \frac{F(x)}{G(x)} = \frac{\sqrt{x}}{|x - 3|}$$

Domain of $F(x)$: $[0, \infty)$ $\quad$ Domain of $G(x)$: $(-\infty, \infty)$

The real numbers that are in both the domain for $F(x)$ and the domain for $G(x)$ are represented by the intersection $[0, \infty) \cap (-\infty, \infty) = [0, \infty)$. Also, the denominator of the quotient function is equal to zero when $x = 3$, so we must eliminate this value from the domain.

$$\boxed{\text{Domain of } \left(\frac{F}{G}\right)(x): [0, 3) \cup (3, \infty)}$$

- - - - - - - - - - - - - - - - - - - - - - - - - - - - - - - - - - - - - -

■ **YOUR TURN** For the functions given in Example 2, determine the quotient function $\left(\dfrac{G}{F}\right)(x)$, and state its domain.

**Technology Tip**

The graphs of $y_1 = F(x) = \sqrt{x}$, $y_2 = G(x) = |x - 3|$, and $y_3 = \dfrac{F(x)}{G(x)} = \dfrac{\sqrt{x}}{|x - 3|}$ are shown.

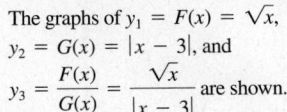

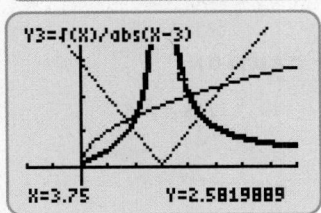

■ **Answer:**
$\left(\dfrac{G}{F}\right)(x) = \dfrac{G(x)}{F(x)} = \dfrac{|x - 3|}{\sqrt{x}}$
Domain: $(0, \infty)$

## Composition of Functions

Recall that a function maps every element in the domain to exactly one corresponding element in the range as shown in the figure below.

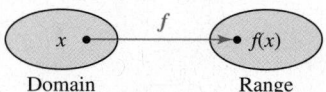

Suppose there is a sales rack of clothes in a department store. Let $x$ correspond to the original price of each item on the rack. These clothes have recently been marked down 20%. Therefore, the function $g(x) = 0.80x$ represents the current sale price of each item. You have been invited to a special sale that lets you take 10% off the current sale price and an additional \$5 off every item at checkout. The function $f(g(x)) = 0.90g(x) - 5$ determines the checkout price. Note that the output of the function $g$ is the input of the function $f$ as shown in the figure below.

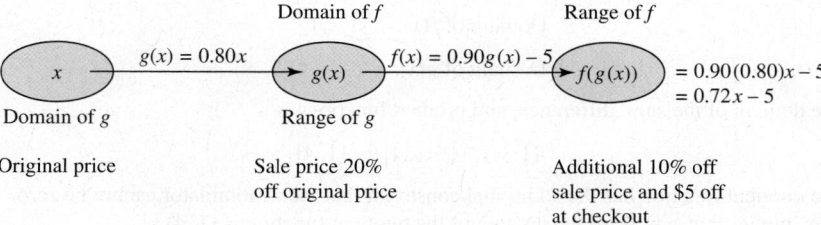

The "checkout" price is found by taking 28% off the original price and subtracting an additional \$5.

This is an example of a **composition of functions**, when the output of one function is the input of another function. It is commonly referred to as a function of a function.

An algebraic example of this is the function $y = \sqrt{x^2 - 2}$. Suppose we let $g(x) = x^2 - 2$ and $f(x) = \sqrt{x}$. Recall that the independent variable in function notation is a placeholder. Since $f(\square) = \sqrt{(\square)}$, then $f(g(x)) = \sqrt{(g(x))}$. Substituting the expression for $g(x)$, we find $f(g(x)) = \sqrt{x^2 - 2}$. The function $y = \sqrt{x^2 - 2}$ is said to be a composite function, $y = f(g(x))$.

Note that the domain of $g(x)$ is the set of all real numbers, and the domain of $f(x)$ is the set of all nonnegative numbers. The domain of a composite function is the set of all $x$ such that $g(x)$ is in the domain of $f$. For instance, in the composite function $y = f(g(x))$, we know that the allowable inputs into $f$ are all numbers greater than or equal to zero. Therefore, we restrict the outputs of $g(x) \geq 0$ and find the corresponding $x$-values. Those $x$-values are the only allowable inputs and constitute the domain of the composite function $y = f(g(x))$.

▼ **CAUTION**

$f \circ g \neq f \cdot g$

The symbol that represents composition of functions is a small open circle; thus $(f \circ g)(x) = f(g(x))$ and is read aloud as "f of g." It is important not to confuse this with the multiplication sign: $(f \cdot g)(x) = f(x)g(x)$.

## COMPOSITION OF FUNCTIONS

Given two functions $f$ and $g$, there are two **composite functions** that can be formed.

| NOTATION | WORDS | DEFINITION | DOMAIN |
|---|---|---|---|
| $f \circ g$ | $f$ composed with $g$ | $f(g(x))$ | The set of all real numbers $x$ in the domain of $g$ such that $g(x)$ is also in the domain of $f$. |
| $g \circ f$ | $g$ composed with $f$ | $g(f(x))$ | The set of all real numbers $x$ in the domain of $f$ such that $f(x)$ is also in the domain of $g$. |

It is important to realize that there are two "filters" that allow certain values of $x$ into the domain. The first filter is $g(x)$. If $x$ is not in the domain of $g(x)$, it cannot be in the domain of $(f \circ g)(x) = f(g(x))$. Of those values for $x$ that are in the domain of $g(x)$, only some pass through, because we restrict the output of $g(x)$ to values that are allowable as input into $f$. This adds an additional filter.

The domain of $f \circ g$ is always a subset of the domain of $g$, and the range of $f \circ g$ is always a subset of the range of $f$.

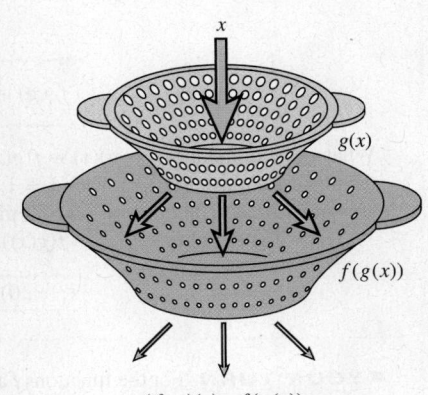

$(f \circ g)(x) = f(g(x))$

**Study Tip**

Order is important:

$$(f \circ g)(x) = f(g(x))$$
$$(g \circ f)(x) = g(f(x))$$

**Study Tip**

The domain of $f \circ g$ is always a subset of the domain of $g$, and the range of $f \circ g$ is always a subset of the range of $f$.

---

### EXAMPLE 3    Finding a Composite Function

Given the functions $f(x) = x^2 + 1$ and $g(x) = x - 3$, find $(f \circ g)(x)$.

**Solution:**

Write $f(x)$ using placeholder notation.          $f(\square) = (\square)^2 + 1$

Express the composite function $f \circ g$.          $f(g(x)) = (g(x))^2 + 1$

Substitute $g(x) = x - 3$ into $f$.          $f(g(x)) = (x - 3)^2 + 1$

Eliminate the parentheses on the right side.          $f(g(x)) = x^2 - 6x + 10$

$$\boxed{(f \circ g)(x) = f(g(x)) = x^2 - 6x + 10}$$

▪ **YOUR TURN**  Given the functions in Example 3, find $(g \circ f)(x)$.

▪**Answer:** $g \circ f = g(f(x)) = x^2 - 2$

**EXAMPLE 4**   **Determining the Domain of a Composite Function**

Given the functions $f(x) = \dfrac{1}{x-1}$ and $g(x) = \dfrac{1}{x}$, determine $f \circ g$, and state its domain.

**Solution:**

Write $f(x)$ using placeholder notation.

$$f(\square) = \frac{1}{(\square) - 1}$$

Express the composite function $f \circ g$.

$$f(g(x)) = \frac{1}{g(x) - 1}$$

Substitute $g(x) = \dfrac{1}{x}$ into $f$.

$$f(g(x)) = \frac{1}{\dfrac{1}{x} - 1}$$

Multiply the right side by $\dfrac{x}{x}$.

$$f(g(x)) = \frac{1}{\dfrac{1}{x} - 1} \cdot \frac{x}{x} = \frac{x}{1-x}$$

$$\boxed{(f \circ g) = f(g(x)) = \frac{x}{1-x}}$$

What is the domain of $(f \circ g)(x) = f(g(x))$? By inspecting the final result of $f(g(x))$, we see that the denominator is zero when $x = 1$. Therefore, $x \neq 1$. Are there any other values for $x$ that are not allowed? The function $g(x)$ has the domain $x \neq 0$; therefore, we must also exclude zero. The domain of $(f \circ g)(x) = f(g(x))$ excludes $x = 0$ and $x = 1$ or, in interval notation,

$$\boxed{(-\infty, 0) \cup (0, 1) \cup (1, \infty)}$$

■ **YOUR TURN**   For the functions $f$ and $g$ given in Example 4, determine the composite function $g \circ f$ and state its domain.

The domain of the composite function cannot always be determined by examining the final form of $f \circ g$, as illustrated in Example 4.

**EXAMPLE 5**   **Determining the Domain of a Composite Function (Without Finding the Composite Function)**

Let $f(x) = \dfrac{1}{x-2}$ and $g(x) = \sqrt{x+3}$. Find the domain of $f(g(x))$. Do not find the composite function.

**Solution:**

Find the domain of $g$. $\qquad\qquad\qquad\qquad\qquad\qquad$ $[-3, \infty)$

Find the range of $g$. $\qquad\qquad\qquad\qquad\qquad\qquad$ $[0, \infty)$

In $f(g(x))$, the output of $g$ becomes the input for $f$. Since the domain of $f$ is the set of all real numbers except 2, we eliminate any values of $x$ in the domain of $g$ that correspond to $g(x) = 2$.

Let $g(x) = 2$. $\qquad\qquad\qquad$ $\sqrt{x+3} = 2$

Square both sides. $\qquad\qquad\qquad$ $x + 3 = 4$

Solve for $x$. $\qquad\qquad\qquad\qquad$ $x = 1$

Eliminate $x = 1$ from the domain of $g$, $[-3, \infty)$.

State the domain of $f(g(x))$. $\qquad\qquad$ $\boxed{[-3, 1) \cup (1, \infty)}$

**EXAMPLE 6    Evaluating a Composite Function**

Given the functions $f(x) = x^2 - 7$ and $g(x) = 5 - x^2$, evaluate

**a.** $f(g(1))$    **b.** $f(g(-2))$    **c.** $g(f(3))$    **d.** $g(f(-4))$

**Solution:**

One way of evaluating these composite functions is to calculate the two individual composites in terms of $x$: $f(g(x))$ and $g(f(x))$. Once those functions are known, the values can be substituted for $x$ and evaluated.

Another way of proceeding is as follows:

**a.** Write the desired quantity.                          $f(g(1))$
    Find the value of the inner function $g$.        $g(1) = 5 - 1^2 = 4$
    Substitute $g(1) = 4$ into $f$.                  $f(g(1)) = f(4)$
    Evaluate $f(4)$.                                 $f(4) = 4^2 - 7 = 9$

$$\boxed{f(g(1)) = 9}$$

**b.** Write the desired quantity.                          $f(g(-2))$
    Find the value of the inner function $g$.        $g(-2) = 5 - (-2)^2 = 1$
    Substitute $g(-2) = 1$ into $f$.                 $f(g(-2)) = f(1)$
    Evaluate $f(1)$.                                 $f(1) = 1^2 - 7 = -6$

$$\boxed{f(g(-2)) = -6}$$

**c.** Write the desired quantity.                          $g(f(3))$
    Find the value of the inner function $f$.        $f(3) = 3^2 - 7 = 2$
    Substitute $f(3) = 2$ into $g$.                  $g(f(3)) = g(2)$
    Evaluate $g(2)$.                                 $g(2) = 5 - 2^2 = 1$

$$\boxed{g(f(3)) = 1}$$

**d.** Write the desired quantity.                          $g(f(-4))$
    Find the value of the inner function $f$.        $f(-4) = (-4)^2 - 7 = 9$
    Substitute $f(-4) = 9$ into $g$.                 $g(f(-4)) = g(9)$
    Evaluate $g(9)$.                                 $g(9) = 5 - 9^2 = -76$

$$\boxed{g(f(-4)) = -76}$$

■ **YOUR TURN**  Given the functions $f(x) = x^3 - 3$ and $g(x) = 1 + x^3$, evaluate $f(g(1))$ and $g(f(1))$.

■ **Answer:** $f(g(1)) = 5$
              $g(f(1)) = -7$

## Application Problems

Recall the example at the beginning of this section regarding the clothes that are on sale. Often, real-world applications are modeled with composite functions. In the clothes example, $x$ is the original price of each item. The first function maps its input (original price) to an output (sale price). The second function maps its input (sale price) to an output (checkout price). Example 7 is another real-world application of composite functions.

Three temperature scales are commonly used:

■ The degree Celsius (°C) scale
   ● This scale was devised by dividing the range between the freezing (0°C) and boiling (100°C) points of pure water at sea level into 100 equal parts. This scale is used in science and is one of the standards of the "metric" (SI) system of measurements.

■ The Kelvin (K) temperature scale
  ● This scale shifts the Celsius scale down so that the zero point is equal to absolute zero (about $-273.15°C$), a hypothetical temperature at which there is a complete absence of heat energy.
  ● Temperatures on this scale are called **kelvins**, *not* degrees kelvin, and kelvin is not capitalized. The symbol for the kelvin is K.

■ The degree Fahrenheit (°F) scale
  ● This scale evolved over time and is still widely used mainly in the United States, although Celsius is the preferred "metric" scale.
  ● With respect to pure water at sea level, the **degrees Fahrenheit** are gauged by the spread from 32°F (freezing) to 212°F (boiling).

The equations that relate these temperature scales are

$$F = \frac{9}{5}C + 32 \qquad C = K - 273.15$$

### EXAMPLE 7   Applications Involving Composite Functions

Determine degrees Fahrenheit as a function of kelvins.

**Solution:**

Degrees Fahrenheit is a function of degrees Celsius.

$$F = \frac{9}{5}C + 32$$

Now substitute $C = K - 273.15$ into the equation for $F$.

$$F = \frac{9}{5}(K - 273.15) + 32$$

Simplify.

$$F = \frac{9}{5}K - 491.67 + 32$$

$$\boxed{F = \frac{9}{5}K - 459.67}$$

## SECTION 1.4  SUMMARY

### Operations on Functions

| Function | Notation |
|---|---|
| Sum | $(f + g)(x) = f(x) + g(x)$ |
| Difference | $(f - g)(x) = f(x) - g(x)$ |
| Product | $(f \cdot g)(x) = f(x) \cdot g(x)$ |
| Quotient | $\left(\dfrac{f}{g}\right)(x) = \dfrac{f(x)}{g(x)} \qquad g(x) \neq 0$ |

The domain of the sum, difference, and product functions is the intersection of the domains, or common domain shared by both $f$ and $g$. The domain of the quotient function is also the intersection of the domain shared by both $f$ and $g$ with an additional restriction that $g(x) \neq 0$.

### Composition of Functions

$$(f \circ g)(x) = f(g(x))$$

The domain restrictions cannot always be determined simply by inspecting the final form of $f(g(x))$. Rather, the domain of the composite function is a subset of the domain of $g(x)$. Values of $x$ must be eliminated if their corresponding values of $g(x)$ are not in the domain of $f$.

## SECTION
## 1.4 EXERCISES

### ■ SKILLS

In Exercises 1–10, given the functions $f$ and $g$, find $f + g$, $f - g$, $f \cdot g$, and $\dfrac{f}{g}$, and state the domain of each.

**1.** $f(x) = 2x + 1$    **2.** $f(x) = 3x + 2$    **3.** $f(x) = 2x^2 - x$    **4.** $f(x) = 3x + 2$    **5.** $f(x) = \dfrac{1}{x}$

$g(x) = 1 - x$    $g(x) = 2x - 4$    $g(x) = x^2 - 4$    $g(x) = x^2 - 25$    $g(x) = x$

**6.** $f(x) = \dfrac{2x + 3}{x - 4}$    **7.** $f(x) = \sqrt{x}$    **8.** $f(x) = \sqrt{x - 1}$    **9.** $f(x) = \sqrt{4 - x}$    **10.** $f(x) = \sqrt{1 - 2x}$

$g(x) = \dfrac{x - 4}{3x + 2}$    $g(x) = 2\sqrt{x}$    $g(x) = 2x^2$    $g(x) = \sqrt{x + 3}$    $g(x) = \dfrac{1}{x}$

In Exercises 11–20, for the given functions $f$ and $g$, find the composite functions $f \circ g$ and $g \circ f$, and state their domains.

**11.** $f(x) = 2x + 1$    **12.** $f(x) = x^2 - 1$    **13.** $f(x) = \dfrac{1}{x - 1}$    **14.** $f(x) = \dfrac{2}{x - 3}$    **15.** $f(x) = |x|$

$g(x) = x^2 - 3$    $g(x) = 2 - x$    $g(x) = x + 2$    $g(x) = 2 + x$    $g(x) = \dfrac{1}{x - 1}$

**16.** $f(x) = |x - 1|$    **17.** $f(x) = \sqrt{x - 1}$    **18.** $f(x) = \sqrt{2 - x}$    **19.** $f(x) = x^3 + 4$    **20.** $f(x) = \sqrt[3]{x^2 - 1}$

$g(x) = \dfrac{1}{x}$    $g(x) = x + 5$    $g(x) = x^2 + 2$    $g(x) = (x - 4)^{1/3}$    $g(x) = x^{2/3} + 1$

In Exercises 21–38, evaluate the functions for the specified values, if possible.

$$f(x) = x^2 + 10 \qquad g(x) = \sqrt{x - 1}$$

**21.** $(f + g)(2)$    **22.** $(f + g)(10)$    **23.** $(f - g)(2)$    **24.** $(f - g)(5)$    **25.** $(f \cdot g)(4)$    **26.** $(f \cdot g)(5)$

**27.** $\left(\dfrac{f}{g}\right)(10)$    **28.** $\left(\dfrac{f}{g}\right)(2)$    **29.** $f(g(2))$    **30.** $f(g(1))$    **31.** $g(f(-3))$    **32.** $g(f(4))$

**33.** $f(g(0))$    **34.** $g(f(0))$    **35.** $f(g(-3))$    **36.** $g(f(\sqrt{7}))$    **37.** $(f \circ g)(4)$    **38.** $(g \circ f)(-3)$

In Exercises 39–50, evaluate $f(g(1))$ and $g(f(2))$, if possible.

**39.** $f(x) = \dfrac{1}{x}$, $g(x) = 2x + 1$    **40.** $f(x) = x^2 + 1$, $g(x) = \dfrac{1}{2 - x}$    **41.** $f(x) = \sqrt{1 - x}$, $g(x) = x^2 + 2$

**42.** $f(x) = \sqrt{3 - x}$, $g(x) = x^2 + 1$    **43.** $f(x) = \dfrac{1}{|x - 1|}$, $g(x) = x + 3$    **44.** $f(x) = \dfrac{1}{x}$, $g(x) = |2x - 3|$

**45.** $f(x) = \sqrt{x - 1}$, $g(x) = x^2 + 5$    **46.** $f(x) = \sqrt[3]{x - 3}$, $g(x) = \dfrac{1}{x - 3}$    **47.** $f(x) = \dfrac{1}{x^2 - 3}$, $g(x) = \sqrt{x - 3}$

**48.** $f(x) = \dfrac{x}{2 - x}$, $g(x) = 4 - x^2$    **49.** $f(x) = (x - 1)^{1/3}$, $g(x) = x^2 + 2x + 1$    **50.** $f(x) = (1 - x^2)^{1/2}$, $g(x) = (x - 3)^{1/3}$

**In Exercises 51–60, show that** $f(g(x)) = x$ **and** $g(f(x)) = x$.

**51.** $f(x) = 2x + 1, \quad g(x) = \dfrac{x - 1}{2}$

**52.** $f(x) = \dfrac{x - 2}{3}, \quad g(x) = 3x + 2$

**53.** $f(x) = \sqrt{x - 1}, \quad g(x) = x^2 + 1$ for $x \geq 1$

**54.** $f(x) = 2 - x^2, \quad g(x) = \sqrt{2 - x}$ for $x \leq 2$

**55.** $f(x) = \dfrac{1}{x}, \quad g(x) = \dfrac{1}{x}$ for $x \neq 0$

**56.** $f(x) = (5 - x)^{1/3}, \quad g(x) = 5 - x^3$

**57.** $f(x) = 4x^2 - 9, \quad g(x) = \dfrac{\sqrt{x + 9}}{2}$ for $x \geq 0$

**58.** $f(x) = \sqrt[3]{8x - 1}, \quad g(x) = \dfrac{x^3 + 1}{8}$

**59.** $f(x) = \dfrac{1}{x - 1}, \quad g(x) = \dfrac{x + 1}{x}$ for $x \neq 0, x \neq 1$

**60.** $f(x) = \sqrt{25 - x^2}, \quad g(x) = \sqrt{25 - x^2}$ for $0 \leq x \leq 5$

**In Exercises 61–66, write the function as a composite of two functions** $f$ **and** $g$. **(More than one answer is correct.)**

**61.** $f(g(x)) = 2(3x - 1)^2 + 5(3x - 1)$

**62.** $f(g(x)) = \dfrac{1}{1 + x^2}$

**63.** $f(g(x)) = \dfrac{2}{|x - 3|}$

**64.** $f(g(x)) = \sqrt{1 - x^2}$

**65.** $f(g(x)) = \dfrac{3}{\sqrt{x + 1} - 2}$

**66.** $f(g(x)) = \dfrac{\sqrt{x}}{3\sqrt{x} + 2}$

## ▪ APPLICATIONS

**Exercises 67 and 68 depend on the relationship between degrees Fahrenheit, degrees Celsius, and kelvins:**

$$F = \frac{9}{5}C + 32 \qquad C = K - 273.15$$

**67. Temperature.** Write a composite function that converts kelvins into degrees Fahrenheit.

**68. Temperature.** Convert the following degrees Fahrenheit to kelvins: 32°F and 212°F.

**69. Dog Run.** Suppose that you want to build a *square* fenced-in area for your dog. Fencing is purchased in linear feet.

a. Write a composite function that determines the area of your dog pen as a function of how many linear feet are purchased.

b. If you purchase 100 linear feet, what is the area of your dog pen?

c. If you purchase 200 linear feet, what is the area of your dog pen?

**70. Dog Run.** Suppose that you want to build a *circular* fenced-in area for your dog. Fencing is purchased in linear feet.

a. Write a composite function that determines the area of your dog pen as a function of how many linear feet are purchased.

b. If you purchase 100 linear feet, what is the area of your dog pen?

c. If you purchase 200 linear feet, what is the area of your dog pen?

**71. Market Price.** Typical supply and demand relationships state that as the number of units for sale increases, the market price decreases. Assume that the market price $p$ and the number of units for sale $x$ are related by the demand equation:

$$p = 3000 - \frac{1}{2}x$$

Assume that the cost $C(x)$ of producing $x$ items is governed by the equation

$$C(x) = 2000 + 10x$$

and the revenue $R(x)$ generated by selling $x$ units is governed by

$$R(x) = 100x$$

a. Write the cost as a function of price $p$.

b. Write the revenue as a function of price $p$.

c. Write the profit as a function of price $p$.

**72. Market Price.** Typical supply and demand relationships state that as the number of units for sale increases, the market price decreases. Assume that the market price $p$ and the number of units for sale $x$ are related by the demand equation:

$$p = 10{,}000 - \frac{1}{4}x$$

Assume that the cost $C(x)$ of producing $x$ items is governed by the equation

$$C(x) = 30{,}000 + 5x$$

and the revenue $R(x)$ generated by selling $x$ units is governed by

$$R(x) = 1000x$$

a. Write the cost as a function of price $p$.

b. Write the revenue as a function of price $p$.

c. Write the profit as a function of price $p$.

**In Exercises 73 and 74, refer to the following:**

The cost of manufacturing a product is a function of the number of hours $t$ the assembly line is running per day. The number of products manufactured $n$ is a function of the number of hours $t$ the assembly line is operating and is given by the function $n(t)$. The cost of manufacturing the product $C$ measured in thousands of dollars is a function of the quantity manufactured, that is, the function $C(n)$.

**73. Business.** If the quantity of a product manufactured during a day is given by

$$n(t) = 50t - t^2$$

and the cost of manufacturing the product is given by

$$C(n) = 10n + 1375$$

a. Find a function that gives the cost of manufacturing the product in terms of the number of hours $t$ the assembly line was functioning, $C(n(t))$.
b. Find the cost of production on a day when the assembly line was running for 16 hours. Interpret your answer.

**74. Business.** If the quantity of a product manufactured during a day is given by

$$n(t) = 100t - 4t^2$$

and the cost of manufacturing the product is given by

$$C(n) = 8n + 2375$$

a. Find a function that gives the cost of manufacturing the product in terms of the number of hours $t$ the assembly line was functioning, $C(n(t))$.
b. Find the cost of production on a day when the assembly line was running for 24 hours. Interpret your answer.

**In Exercises 75 and 76, refer to the following:**

Surveys performed immediately following an accidental oil spill at sea indicate the oil moved outward from the source of the spill in a nearly circular pattern. The radius of the oil spill $r$ measured in miles is a function of time $t$ measured in days from the start of the spill, while the area of the oil spill is a function of radius, that is, the function $A(r)$.

**75. Environment: Oil Spill.** If the radius of the oil spill is given by

$$r(t) = 10t - 0.2t^2$$

and the area of the oil spill is given by

$$A(r) = \pi r^2$$

a. Find a function that gives the area of the oil spill in terms of the number of days since the start of the spill, $A(r(t))$.
b. Find the area of the oil spill to the nearest square mile 7 days after the start of the spill.

**76. Environment: Oil Spill.** If the radius of the oil spill is given by

$$r(t) = 8t - 0.1t^2$$

and the area of the oil spill is given by

$$A(r) = \pi r^2$$

a. Find a function that gives the area of the oil spill in terms of the number of days since the start of the spill, $A(r(t))$.
b. Find the area of the oil spill to the nearest square mile 5 days after the start of the spill.

**77. Environment: Oil Spill.** An oil spill makes a circular pattern around a ship such that the radius in feet grows as a function of time in hours $r(t) = 150\sqrt{t}$. Find the area of the spill as a function of time.

**78. Pool Volume.** A 20 foot by 10 foot rectangular pool has been built. If 50 cubic feet of water is pumped into the pool per hour, write the water-level height (feet) as a function of time (hours).

**79. Fireworks.** A family is watching a fireworks display. If the family is 2 miles from where the fireworks are being launched and the fireworks travel vertically, what is the distance between the family and the fireworks as a function of height above ground?

**80. Real Estate.** A couple are about to put their house up for sale. They bought the house for $172,000 a few years ago; if they list it with a realtor, they will pay a 6% commission. Write a function that represents the amount of money they will make on their home as a function of the asking price $p$.

## ■ CATCH THE MISTAKE

**In Exercises 81–85, for the functions $f(x) = x + 2$ and $g(x) = x^2 - 4$, find the indicated function and state its domain. Explain the mistake that is made in each problem.**

**81.** $\dfrac{g}{f}$

Solution:
$$\frac{g(x)}{f(x)} = \frac{x^2 - 4}{x + 2}$$
$$= \frac{(x - 2)(x + 2)}{x + 2} = x - 2$$

Domain: $(-\infty, \infty)$

This is incorrect. What mistake was made?

**82.** $\dfrac{f}{g}$

Solution:
$$\frac{f(x)}{g(x)} = \frac{x + 2}{x^2 - 4}$$
$$= \frac{x + 2}{(x - 2)(x + 2)} = \frac{1}{x - 2} = \frac{1}{x - 2}$$

Domain: $(-\infty, 2) \cup (2, \infty)$

This is incorrect. What mistake was made?

**83.** $f \circ g$

Solution:
$$f \circ g = f(x)g(x)$$
$$= (x + 2)(x^2 - 4)$$
$$= x^3 + 2x^2 - 4x - 8$$

Domain: $(-\infty, \infty)$

This is incorrect. What mistake was made?

**85.** $(f + g)(2) = (x + 2 + x^2 - 4)(2)$
$$= (x^2 + x - 2)(2)$$
$$= 2x^2 + 2x - 4$$

Domain: $(-\infty, \infty)$

This is incorrect. What mistake was made?

**84.** $f(x) - g(x) = x + 2 - x^2 - 4$
$$= -x^2 + x - 2$$

Domain: $(-\infty, \infty)$

This is incorrect. What mistake was made?

**86.** Given the function $f(x) = x^2 + 7$ and $g(x) = \sqrt{x - 3}$, find $f \circ g$, and state the domain.

Solution:  $f \circ g = f(g(x)) = \left(\sqrt{x - 3}\right)^2 + 7$
$$= f(g(x)) = x - 3 + 7$$
$$= x - 4$$

Domain: $(-\infty, \infty)$

This is incorrect. What mistake was made?

## ▪CONCEPTUAL

**In Exercises 87–90, determine whether each statement is true or false.**

**87.** When adding, subtracting, multiplying, or dividing two functions, the domain of the resulting function is the union of the domains of the individual functions.

**88.** For any functions $f$ and $g$, $f(g(x)) = g(f(x))$ for all values of $x$ that are in the domain of both $f$ and $g$.

**89.** For any functions $f$ and $g$, $(f \circ g)(x)$ exists for all values of $x$ that are in the domain of $g(x)$, provided the range of $g$ is a subset of the domain of $f$.

**90.** The domain of a composite function can be found by inspection, without knowledge of the domain of the individual functions.

## ▪CHALLENGE

**91.** For the functions $f(x) = x + a$ and $g(x) = \dfrac{1}{x - a}$, find $g \circ f$ and state its domain.

**92.** For the functions $f(x) = ax^2 + bx + c$ and $g(x) = \dfrac{1}{x - c}$, find $g \circ f$ and state its domain.

**93.** For the functions $f(x) = \sqrt{x + a}$ and $g(x) = x^2 - a$ find $g \circ f$ and state its domain.

**94.** For the functions $f(x) = \dfrac{1}{x^a}$ and $g(x) = \dfrac{1}{x^b}$, find $g \circ f$ and state its domain. Assume $a > 1$ and $b > 1$.

## ▪TECHNOLOGY

**95.** Using a graphing utility, plot $y_1 = \sqrt{x + 7}$ and $y_2 = \sqrt{9 - x}$. Plot $y_3 = y_1 + y_2$. What is the domain of $y_3$?

**96.** Using a graphing utility, plot $y_1 = \sqrt[3]{x + 5}$, $y_2 = \dfrac{1}{\sqrt{3 - x}}$, and $y_3 = \dfrac{y_1}{y_2}$. What is the domain of $y_3$?

**97.** Using a graphing utility, plot $y_1 = \sqrt{x^2 - 3x - 4}$, $y_2 = \dfrac{1}{x^2 - 14}$, and $y_3 = \dfrac{1}{y_1^2 - 14}$. If $y_1$ represents a function $f$ and $y_2$ represents a function $g$, then $y_3$ represents the composite function $g \circ f$. The graph of $y_3$ is only defined for the domain of $g \circ f$. State the domain of $g \circ f$.

**98.** Using a graphing utility, plot $y_1 = \sqrt{1 - x}$, $y_2 = x^2 + 2$, and $y_3 = y_1^2 + 2$. If $y_1$ represents a function $f$ and $y_2$ represents a function $g$, then $y_3$ represents the composite function $g \circ f$. The graph of $y_3$ is only defined for the domain of $g \circ f$. State the domain of $g \circ f$.

**■ PREVIEW TO CALCULUS**

**For Exercises 99–102, refer to the following:**

In calculus, the difference quotient $\dfrac{f(x + h) - f(x)}{h}$ of a function $f$ is used to find the derivative $f'$ of $f$ by letting $h$ approach $0$, $h \to 0$.

**99. Addition.** Find the derivatives of $F(x) = x$, $G(x) = x^2$, and $H(x) = (F + G)(x) = x + x^2$. What do you observe?

**100. Subtraction.** Find the derivatives of $F(x) = \sqrt{x}$, $G(x) = x^3 + 1$, and $H(x) = (F - G)(x) = \sqrt{x} - x^3 - 1$. What do you observe?

**101. Multiplication.** Find the derivatives of $F(x) = 5$, $G(x) = \sqrt{x - 1}$, and $H(x) = (FG)(x) = 5\sqrt{x - 1}$. What do you observe?

**102. Division.** Find the derivatives of $F(x) = x$, $G(x) = \sqrt{x + 1}$, and $H(x) = \left(\dfrac{F}{G}\right)(x) = \dfrac{x}{\sqrt{x + 1}}$. What do you observe?

---

**SECTION**

# 1.5

# ONE-TO-ONE FUNCTIONS AND INVERSE FUNCTIONS

**SKILLS OBJECTIVES**

- Determine algebraically and graphically whether a function is a one-to-one function.
- Verify that two functions are inverses of one another.
- Graph the inverse function given the graph of the function.
- Find the inverse of a function.

**CONCEPTUAL OBJECTIVES**

- Visualize the relationships between domain and range of a function and the domain and range of its inverse.
- Understand why functions and their inverses are symmetric about $y = x$.

## One-to-One Functions

Every human being has a blood type, and every human being has a DNA sequence. These are examples of functions, where a person is the input and the output is blood type or DNA sequence. These relationships are classified as functions because each person can have one and only one blood type or DNA strand. The difference between these functions is that many people have the same blood type, but DNA is unique to each individual. Can we map backwards? For instance, if you know the blood type, do you know specifically which person it came from? No, but, if you know the DNA sequence, you know that the sequence belongs to only one person. When a function has a one-to-one correspondence, like the DNA example, then mapping backwards is possible. The map back is called the *inverse function*.

In Section 1.1, we defined a function as a relationship that maps an input (contained in the domain) to exactly one output (found in the range). Algebraically, each value for $x$ can correspond to only a single value for $y$. Recall the square, identity, absolute value, and reciprocal functions from our library of functions in Section 1.3.

All of the graphs of these functions satisfy the vertical line test. Although the square function and the absolute value function map each value of $x$ to exactly one value for $y$, these two functions map two values of $x$ to the same value for $y$. For example, $(-1, 1)$ and $(1, 1)$ lie on both graphs. The identity and reciprocal functions, on the other hand, map each $x$ to a single value for $y$, and no two $x$-values map to the same $y$-value. These two functions are examples of *one-to-one functions*.

---

**DEFINITION**     **One-to-One Function**

A function $f(x)$ is **one-to-one** if no two elements in the domain correspond to the same element in the range; that is,

$$\text{if } x_1 \neq x_2, \text{then } f(x_1) \neq f(x_2).$$

---

In other words, it is one-to-one if no two inputs map to the same output.

**EXAMPLE 1**    **Determining Whether a Function Defined as a Set of Points Is a One-to-One Function**

For each of the three relations, determine whether the relation is a function. If it is a function, determine whether it is a one-to-one function.

$$f = \{(0, 0), (1, 2), (1, 3)\}$$
$$g = \{(2, 1), (0, 0), (3, 1)\}$$
$$h = \{(-1, -1), (0, 0), (1, 1)\}$$

**Solution:**

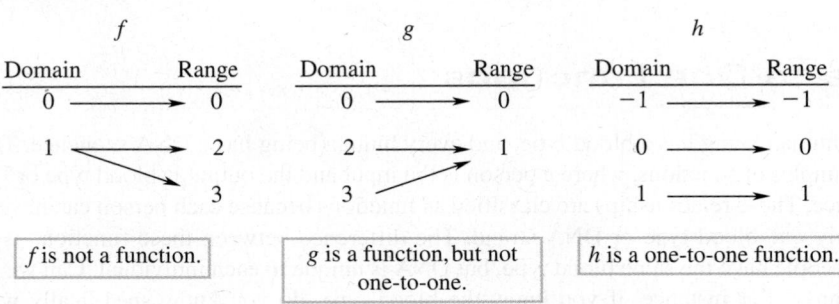

Just as there is a graphical test for functions, the vertical line test, there is a graphical test for one-to-one functions, the *horizontal line test*. Note that a horizontal line can be drawn on the square and absolute value functions so that it intersects the graph of each function at two points. The identity and reciprocal functions, however, will intersect a horizontal line in at most only one point. This leads us to the horizontal line test for one-to-one functions.

**DEFINITION**  **Horizontal Line Test**

If every horizontal line intersects the graph of a function in at most one point, then the function is classified as a one-to-one function.

**EXAMPLE 2**  **Using the Horizontal Line Test to Determine Whether a Function Is One-to-One**

For each of the three relations, determine whether the relation is a function. If it is a function, determine whether it is a one-to-one function. Assume that $x$ is the independent variable and $y$ is the dependent variable.

$$x = y^2 \qquad y = x^2 \qquad y = x^3$$

**Solution:**

$$x = y^2 \qquad\qquad y = x^2 \qquad\qquad y = x^3$$

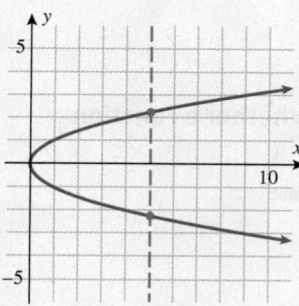 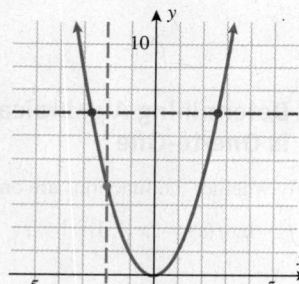 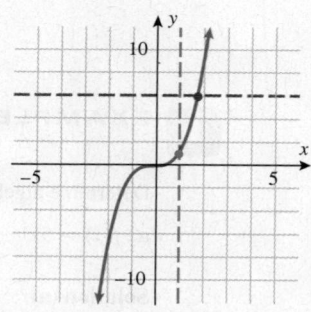

| Not a function | Function, but not one-to-one | One-to-one function |
| :---: | :---: | :---: |
| (fails vertical line test) | (passes vertical line test, but fails horizontal line test) | (passes both vertical and horizontal line tests) |

■ **YOUR TURN**  Determine whether each of the functions is a one-to-one function.

　　**a.** $f(x) = x + 2$　　**b.** $f(x) = x^2 + 1$

■ **Answer:**
**a.** yes　**b.** no

Another way of writing the definition of a one-to-one function is

$$\text{If } f(x_1) = f(x_2), \text{ then } x_1 = x_2.$$

In the Your Turn following Example 2, we found (using the horizontal line test) that $f(x) = x + 2$ is a one-to-one function, but that $f(x) = x^2 + 1$ is not a one-to-one function. We can also use this alternative definition to determine algebraically whether a function is one-to-one.

| WORDS | MATH |
|---|---|
| State the function. | $f(x) = x + 2$ |
| Let there be two real numbers, $x_1$ and $x_2$, such that $f(x_1) = f(x_2)$. | $x_1 + 2 = x_2 + 2$ |
| Subtract 2 from both sides of the equation. | $x_1 = x_2$ |

$f(x) = x + 2$ is a one-to-one function.

| WORDS | MATH |
|---|---|
| State the function. | $f(x) = x^2 + 1$ |
| Let there be two real numbers, $x_1$ and $x_2$, such that $f(x_1) = f(x_2)$. | $x_1^2 + 1 = x_2^2 + 1$ |
| Subtract 1 from both sides of the equation. | $x_1^2 = x_2^2$ |
| Solve for $x_1$. | $x_1 = \pm x_2$ |

$f(x) = x^2 + 2$ is *not* a one-to-one function.

**EXAMPLE 3**   **Determining Algebraically Whether a Function Is One-to-One**

Determine algebraically whether the functions are one-to-one.

**a.** $f(x) = 5x^3 - 2$      **b.** $f(x) = |x + 1|$

**Solution (a):**

| | |
|---|---|
| Find $f(x_1)$ and $f(x_2)$. | $f(x_1) = 5x_1^3 - 2$ and $f(x_2) = 5x_2^3 - 2$ |
| Let $f(x_1) = f(x_2)$. | $5x_1^3 - 2 = 5x_2^3 - 2$ |
| Add 2 to both sides of the equation. | $5x_1^3 = 5x_2^3$ |
| Divide both sides of the equation by 5. | $x_1^3 = x_2^3$ |
| Take the cube root of both sides of the equation. | $\left(x_1^3\right)^{1/3} = \left(x_2^3\right)^{1/3}$ |
| Simplify. | $x_1 = x_2$ |

$f(x) = 5x^3 - 2$ is a one-to-one function.

**Solution (b):**

| | |
|---|---|
| Find $f(x_1)$ and $f(x_2)$. | $f(x_1) = |x_1 + 1|$ and $f(x_2) = |x_2 + 1|$ |
| Let $f(x_1) = f(x_2)$. | $|x_1 + 1| = |x_2 + 1|$ |
| Solve the absolute value equation. | $(x_1 + 1) = (x_2 + 1)$ or $(x_1 + 1) = -(x_2 + 1)$ |
| | $x_1 = x_2$ or $x_1 = -x_2 - 2$ |

$f(x) = |x + 1|$ is **not** a one-to-one function.

# Inverse Functions

If a function is one-to-one, then the function maps each $x$ to exactly one $y$, and no two $x$-values map to the same $y$-value. This implies that there is a one-to-one correspondence between the inputs (domain) and outputs (range) of a one-to-one function $f(x)$. In the special case of a one-to-one function, it would be possible to map from the output (range of $f$) back to the input (domain of $f$), and this mapping would also be a function. The function that maps the output back to the input of a function $f$ is called the **inverse function** and is denoted $f^{-1}(x)$.

A one-to-one function $f$ maps every $x$ in the domain to a unique and distinct corresponding $y$ in the range. Therefore, the inverse function $f^{-1}$ maps every $y$ back to a unique and distinct $x$.

The function notations $f(x) = y$ and $f^{-1}(y) = x$ indicate that if the point $(x, y)$ satisfies the function, then the point $(y, x)$ satisfies the inverse function.

For example, let the function $h(x) = \{(-1, 0), (1, 2), (3, 4)\}$.

$$h = \{(-1, 0), (1, 2), (3, 4)\}$$

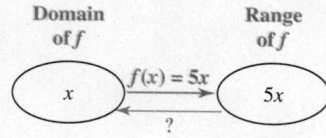

Domain     Range

$-1 \rightleftarrows 0$

$1 \rightleftarrows 2$     $h$ is a one-to-one function

$3 \rightleftarrows 4$

Range     Domain

$$h^{-1} = \{(0, -1), (2, 1), (4, 3)\}$$

The inverse function undoes whatever the function does. For example, if $f(x) = 5x$, then the function $f$ maps any value $x$ in the domain to a value $5x$ in the range. If we want to map backwards or undo the $5x$, we develop a function called the inverse function that takes $5x$ as input and maps back to $x$ as output. The inverse function is $f^{-1}(x) = \frac{1}{5}x$. Note that if we input $5x$ into the inverse function, the output is $x$: $f^{-1}(5x) = \frac{1}{5}(5x) = x$.

**DEFINITION**     **Inverse Function**

If $f$ and $g$ denote two one-to-one functions such that

$$f(g(x)) = x \text{ for every } x \text{ in the domain of } g$$

and

$$g(f(x)) = x \text{ for every } x \text{ in the domain of } f,$$

then $g$ is the **inverse** of the function $f$. The function $g$ is denoted by $f^{-1}$ (read "f-inverse").

*Note:* $f^{-1}$ is used to denote the inverse of $f$. The superscript $-1$ is not used as an exponent and, therefore, does not represent the reciprocal of $f$: $\dfrac{1}{f}$.

Two properties hold true relating one-to-one functions to their inverses: (1) The range of the function is the domain of the inverse, and the range of the inverse is the domain of the function, and (2) the composite function that results with a function and its inverse (and vice versa) is the identity function $x$.

**Domain of $f$**     **Range of $f$**

$x \xrightarrow{\quad f \quad} y$

Range of $f^{-1}$    $f^{-1}$    Domain of $f^{-1}$

**Domain of $f$**     **Range of $f$**

$x \xrightarrow{\ f(x) = 5x\ } 5x$

$\xleftarrow{\quad ? \quad}$

$x \xrightarrow{\ f(x) = 5x\ } 5x$

$f^{-1}(5x) = x$

▼ **CAUTION**

$$f^{-1} \neq \frac{1}{f}$$

$$\text{Domain of } f = \text{range of } f^{-1} \text{ and range of } f = \text{domain of } f^{-1}$$
$$f^{-1}(f(x)) = x \quad \text{and} \quad f(f^{-1}(x)) = x$$

## EXAMPLE 4   Verifying Inverse Functions

Verify that $f^{-1}(x) = \frac{1}{2}x - 2$ is the inverse of $f(x) = 2x + 4$.

**Solution:**

Show that $f^{-1}(f(x)) = x$ and $f(f^{-1}(x)) = x$.

Write $f^{-1}$ using placeholder notation.        $f^{-1}(\square) = \frac{1}{2}(\square) - 2$

Substitute $f(x) = 2x + 4$ into $f^{-1}$.        $f^{-1}(f(x)) = \frac{1}{2}(2x + 4) - 2$

Simplify.        $f^{-1}(f(x)) = x + 2 - 2 = x$
        $f^{-1}(f(x)) = x$

Write $f$ using placeholder notation.        $f(\square) = 2(\square) + 4$

Substitute $f^{-1}(x) = \frac{1}{2}x - 2$ into $f$.        $f(f^{-1}(x)) = 2\left(\frac{1}{2}x - 2\right) + 4$

Simplify.        $f(f^{-1}(x)) = x - 4 + 4 = x$
        $f(f^{-1}(x)) = x$

Note the relationship between the domain and range of $f$ and $f^{-1}$.

|  | DOMAIN | RANGE |
|---|---|---|
| $f(x) = 2x + 4$ | $(-\infty, \infty)$ | $(-\infty, \infty)$ |
| $f^{-1}(x) = \frac{1}{2}x - 2$ | $(-\infty, \infty)$ | $(-\infty, \infty)$ |

## EXAMPLE 5   Verifying Inverse Functions with Domain Restrictions

Verify that $f^{-1}(x) = x^2$, for $x \geq 0$, is the inverse of $f(x) = \sqrt{x}$.

**Solution:**

Show that $f^{-1}(f(x)) = x$ and $f(f^{-1}(x)) = x$.

Write $f^{-1}$ using placeholder notation.        $f^{-1}(\square) = (\square)^2$
Substitute $f(x) = \sqrt{x}$ into $f^{-1}$.        $f^{-1}(f(x)) = (\sqrt{x})^2 = x$
        $f^{-1}(f(x)) = x \text{ for } x \geq 0$

Write $f$ using placeholder notation.        $f(\square) = \sqrt{(\square)}$

Substitute $f^{-1}(x) = x^2, x \geq 0$ into $f$.        $f(f^{-1}(x)) = \sqrt{x^2} = x, x \geq 0$
        $f(f^{-1}(x)) = x \text{ for } x \geq 0$

|  | DOMAIN | RANGE |
|---|---|---|
| $f(x) = \sqrt{x}$ | $[0, \infty)$ | $[0, \infty)$ |
| $f^{-1}(x) = x^2, x \geq 0$ | $[0, \infty)$ | $[0, \infty)$ |

# Graphical Interpretation of Inverse Functions

In Example 4, we showed that $f^{-1}(x) = \frac{1}{2}x - 2$ is the inverse of $f(x) = 2x + 4$. Let's now investigate the graphs that correspond to the function $f$ and its inverse $f^{-1}$.

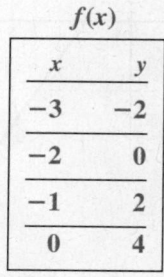

$f(x)$

| $x$ | $y$ |
|-----|-----|
| $-3$ | $-2$ |
| $-2$ | $0$ |
| $-1$ | $2$ |
| $0$ | $4$ |

$f^{-1}(x)$

| $x$ | $y$ |
|-----|-----|
| $-2$ | $-3$ |
| $0$ | $-2$ |
| $2$ | $-1$ |
| $4$ | $0$ |

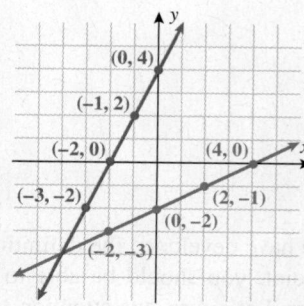

Note that the point $(-3, -2)$ lies on the function and the point $(-2, -3)$ lies on the inverse. In fact, every point $(a, b)$ that lies on the function corresponds to a point $(b, a)$ that lies on the inverse.

Draw the line $y = x$ on the graph. In general, the point $(b, a)$ on the inverse $f^{-1}(x)$ is the reflection (about $y = x$) of the point $(a, b)$ on the function $f(x)$.

In general, if the point $(a, b)$ is on the graph of a function, then the point $(b, a)$ is on the graph of its inverse.

 **EXAMPLE 6** **Graphing the Inverse Function**

Given the graph of the function $f(x)$, plot the graph of its inverse $f^{-1}(x)$.

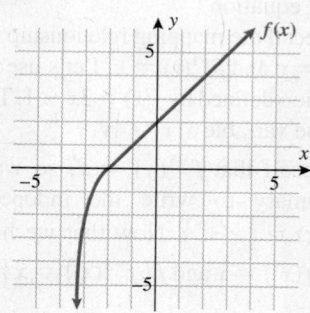

**Solution:**

Because the points $(-3, -2)$, $(-2, 0)$, $(0, 2)$, and $(2, 4)$ lie on the graph of $f$, then the points $(-2, -3)$, $(0, -2)$, $(2, 0)$, and $(4, 2)$ lie on the graph of $f^{-1}$.

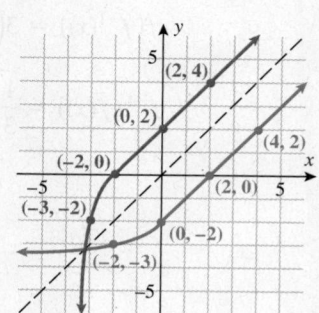

■ **Answer:**

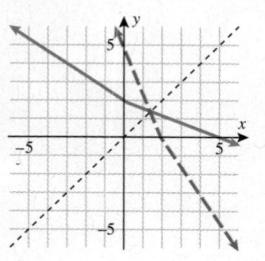

■ **YOUR TURN** Given the graph of a function $f$, plot the inverse function.

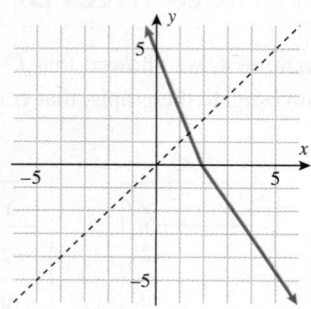

We have developed the definition of an inverse function, and properties of inverses. At this point, you should be able to determine whether two functions are inverses of one another. Let's turn our attention to another problem: How do you find the inverse of a function?

## Finding the Inverse Function

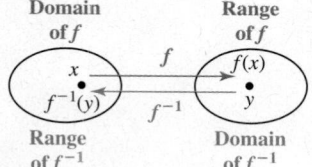

If the point $(a, b)$ lies on the graph of a function, then the point $(b, a)$ lies on the graph of the inverse function. The symmetry about the line $y = x$ tells us that the roles of $x$ and $y$ interchange. Therefore, if we start with every point $(x, y)$ that lies on the graph of a function, then every point $(y, x)$ lies on the graph of its inverse. Algebraically, this corresponds to interchanging $x$ and $y$. Finding the inverse of a finite set of ordered pairs is easy: Simply interchange the $x$- and $y$-coordinates. Earlier, we found that if $h(x) = \{(-1, 0), (1, 2), (3, 4)\}$, then $h^{-1}(x) = \{(0, -1), (2, 1), (4, 3)\}$. But how do we find the inverse of a function defined by an equation?

Recall the mapping relationship if $f$ is a one-to-one function. This relationship implies that $f(x) = y$ and $f^{-1}(y) = x$. Let's use these two identities to find the inverse. Now consider the function defined by $f(x) = 3x - 1$. To find $f^{-1}$, we let $f(x) = y$, which yields $y = 3x - 1$. Solve for the variable $x$: $x = \frac{1}{3}y + \frac{1}{3}$.

Recall that $f^{-1}(y) = x$, so we have found the inverse to be $f^{-1}(y) = \frac{1}{3}y + \frac{1}{3}$. It is customary to write the independent variable as $x$, so we write the inverse as $f^{-1}(x) = \frac{1}{3}x + \frac{1}{3}$. Now that we have found the inverse, let's confirm that the properties $f^{-1}(f(x)) = x$ and $f(f^{-1}(x)) = x$ hold.

$$f(f^{-1}(x)) = 3\left(\frac{1}{3}x + \frac{1}{3}\right) - 1 = x + 1 - 1 = x$$

$$f^{-1}(f(x)) = \frac{1}{3}(3x - 1) + \frac{1}{3} = x - \frac{1}{3} + \frac{1}{3} = x$$

## FINDING THE INVERSE OF A FUNCTION

Let $f$ be a one-to-one function, then the following procedure can be used to find the inverse function $f^{-1}$ if the inverse exists.

| STEP | PROCEDURE | EXAMPLE |
|------|-----------|---------|
| 1 | Let $y = f(x)$. | $f(x) = -3x + 5$ <br> $y = -3x + 5$ |
| 2 | Solve the resulting equation for $x$ in terms of $y$ (if possible). | $3x = -y + 5$ <br> $x = -\frac{1}{3}y + \frac{5}{3}$ |
| 3 | Let $x = f^{-1}(y)$. | $f^{-1}(y) = -\frac{1}{3}y + \frac{5}{3}$ |
| 4 | Let $y = x$ (interchange $x$ and $y$). | $f^{-1}(x) = -\frac{1}{3}x + \frac{5}{3}$ |

The same result is found if we first interchange $x$ and $y$ and then solve for $y$ in terms of $x$.

| STEP | PROCEDURE | EXAMPLE |
|------|-----------|---------|
| 1 | Let $y = f(x)$. | $f(x) = -3x + 5$ <br> $y = -3x + 5$ |
| 2 | Interchange $x$ and $y$. | $x = -3y + 5$ |
| 3 | Solve for $y$ in terms of $x$. | $3y = -x + 5$ <br> $y = -\frac{1}{3}x + \frac{5}{3}$ |
| 4 | Let $y = f^{-1}(x)$ | $f^{-1}(x) = -\frac{1}{3}x + \frac{5}{3}$ |

Note the following:

- Verify first that a function is one-to-one prior to finding an inverse (if it is not one-to-one, then the inverse does not exist).
- State the domain restrictions on the inverse function. The domain of $f$ is the range of $f^{-1}$ and vice versa.
- To verify that you have found the inverse, show that $f\big(f^{-1}(x)\big) = x$ for all $x$ in the domain of $f^{-1}$ and $f^{-1}(f(x)) = x$ for all $x$ in the domain of $f$.

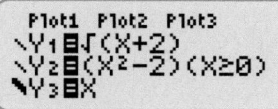
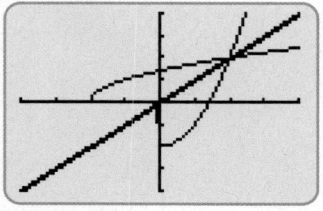
### Study Tip

Had we ignored the domain and range in Example 7, we would have found the inverse function to be the square function $f(x) = x^2 - 2$, which is not a one-to-one function. It is only when we restrict the domain of the square function that we get a one-to-one function.

## EXAMPLE 7   The Inverse of a Square Root Function

Find the inverse of the function $f(x) = \sqrt{x + 2}$ and state the domain and range of both $f$ and $f^{-1}$.

**Solution:**

$f(x)$ is a one-to-one function because it passes the horizontal line test.

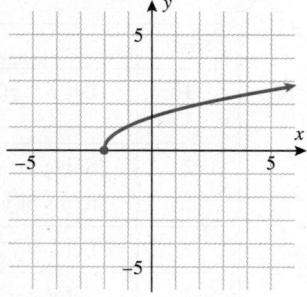

**STEP 1**  Let $y = f(x)$.                                   $y = \sqrt{x + 2}$

**STEP 2**  Interchange $x$ and $y$.                          $x = \sqrt{y + 2}$

**STEP 3**  Solve for $y$.

  Square both sides of the equation.                          $x^2 = y + 2$

  Subtract 2 from both sides.                                 $x^2 - 2 = y$ or $y = x^2 - 2$

**STEP 4**  Let $y = f^{-1}(x)$.                              $f^{-1}(x) = x^2 - 2$

**Note any domain restrictions.** (State the domain and range of both $f$ and $f^{-1}$.)

|  |  |  |
|---|---|---|
| $f$: | Domain: $[-2, \infty)$ | Range: $[0, \infty)$ |
| $f^{-1}$: | Domain: $[0, \infty)$ | Range: $[-2, \infty)$ |

The inverse of $f(x) = \sqrt{x + 2}$ is $\boxed{f^{-1}(x) = x^2 - 2 \text{ for } x \geq 0}$.

**Check.**

$f^{-1}(f(x)) = x$ for all $x$ in the domain of $f$.

$$f^{-1}(f(x)) = \left(\sqrt{x + 2}\right)^2 - 2$$
$$= x + 2 - 2 \text{ for } x \geq -2$$
$$= x$$

$f(f^{-1}(x)) = x$ for all $x$ in the domain of $f^{-1}$.

$$f(f^{-1}(x)) = \sqrt{(x^2 - 2) + 2}$$
$$= \sqrt{x^2} \text{ for } x \geq 0$$
$$= x$$

Note that the function $f(x) = \sqrt{x + 2}$ and its inverse $f^{-1}(x) = x^2 - 2$ for $x \geq 0$ are symmetric about the line $y = x$.

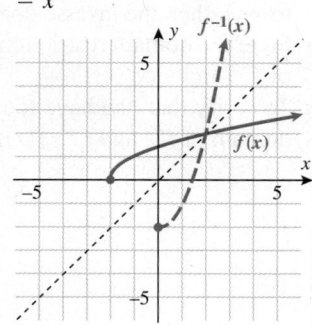

■ **Answers:**

**a.** $f^{-1}(x) = \dfrac{x + 3}{7}$, Domain: $(-\infty, \infty)$, Range: $(-\infty, \infty)$

**b.** $g^{-1}(x) = x^2 + 1$, Domain: $[0, \infty)$, Range: $[1, \infty)$

■ **YOUR TURN**  Find the inverse of the given function and state the domain and range of the inverse function.

  **a.** $f(x) = 7x - 3$          **b.** $g(x) = \sqrt{x - 1}$

### EXAMPLE 8   A Function That Does Not Have an Inverse Function

Find the inverse of the function $f(x) = |x|$ if it exists.

**Solution:**

The function $f(x) = |x|$ fails the horizontal line test and therefore is not a one-to-one function. Because $f$ is not a one-to-one function, its inverse function does not exist.

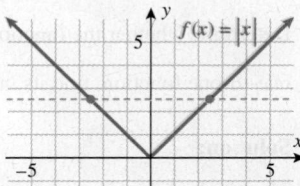

### EXAMPLE 9   Finding the Inverse Function

The function $f(x) = \dfrac{2}{x+3}$, $x \ne -3$, is a one-to-one function. Find its inverse.

**Solution:**

**STEP 1**  Let $y = f(x)$.

$$y = \frac{2}{x+3}$$

**STEP 2**  Interchange $x$ and $y$.

$$x = \frac{2}{y+3}$$

**STEP 3**  Solve for $y$.
Multiply the equation by $(y + 3)$.

$$x(y+3) = 2$$

Eliminate the parentheses.

$$xy + 3x = 2$$

Subtract $3x$ from both sides.

$$xy = -3x + 2$$

Divide the equation by $x$.

$$y = \frac{-3x+2}{x} = -3 + \frac{2}{x}$$

**STEP 4**  Let $y = f^{-1}(x)$.

$$f^{-1}(x) = -3 + \frac{2}{x}$$

**Note any domain restrictions on $f^{-1}(x)$.**

$$x \ne 0$$

The inverse of the function $f(x) = \dfrac{2}{x+3}$, $x \ne -3$, is $\boxed{f^{-1}(x) = -3 + \dfrac{2}{x},\ x \ne 0}$.

**Check.**

$$f^{-1}(f(x)) = -3 + \frac{2}{\left(\dfrac{2}{x+3}\right)} = -3 + (x+3) = x,\ x \ne -3$$

$$f(f^{-1}(x)) = \frac{2}{\left(-3 + \dfrac{2}{x}\right) + 3} = \frac{2}{\left(\dfrac{2}{x}\right)} = x,\ x \ne 0$$

■ **YOUR TURN**  The function $f(x) = \dfrac{4}{x-1}$, $x \ne 1$, is a one-to-one function. Find its inverse.

*Technology Tip*

The graphs of $y_1 = f(x) = \dfrac{2}{x+3}$, $x \ne -3$, and $y_2 = f^{-1}(x) = -3 + \dfrac{2}{x}$, $x \ne 0$, are shown.

Note that the graphs of the function $f(x)$ and its inverse $f^{-1}(x)$ are symmetric about the line $y = x$.

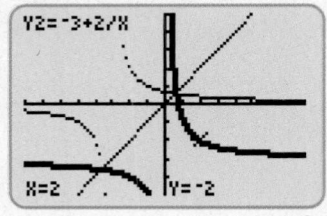

*Study Tip*

The range of the function is equal to the domain of its inverse function.

■ **Answer:** $f^{-1}(x) = 1 + \dfrac{4}{x},\ x \ne 0$

Note in Example 9 that the domain of $f$ is $(-\infty, -3) \cup (-3, \infty)$ and the domain of $f^{-1}$ is $(-\infty, 0) \cup (0, \infty)$. Therefore, we know that the range of $f$ is $(-\infty, 0) \cup (0, \infty)$, and the range of $f^{-1}$ is $(-\infty, -3) \cup (-3, \infty)$.

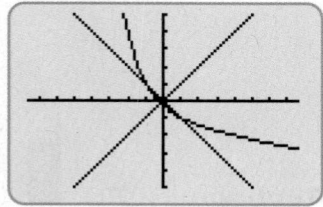
**EXAMPLE 10  Finding the Inverse of a Piecewise-Defined Function**

Determine whether the function $f(x) = \begin{cases} x^2 & x < 0 \\ -x & x \geq 0 \end{cases}$ is a one-to-one function. If it is a one-to-one function, find its inverse.

**Solution:**

The graph of the function $f$ passes the horizontal line test and therefore $f$ is a one-to-one function.

**STEP 1**   Let $y = f(x)$.

Let $y_1 = x_1^2$ for $x_1 < 0$ and $y_2 = -x_2$ for $x_2 \geq 0$ represent the two pieces of $f$. Note the domain and range for each piece.

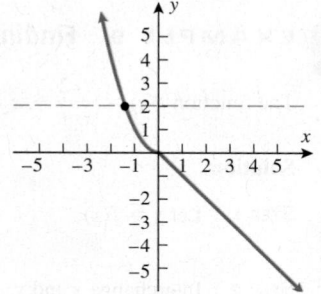

| EQUATION | DOMAIN | RANGE |
|----------|--------|-------|
| $y_1 = x_1^2$ | $x_1 < 0$ | $y_1 > 0$ |
| $y_2 = -x_2$ | $x_2 \geq 0$ | $y_2 \leq 0$ |

**STEP 2**   Solve for $x$ in terms of $y$.

Solve for $x_1$.                                    $x_1 = \pm\sqrt{y_1}$

Select the negative root since $x_1 < 0$.    $x_1 = -\sqrt{y_1}$

Solve for $x_2$.                                    $x_2 = -y_2$

**STEP 3**   Let $x = f^{-1}(y)$.

| | | |
|----------|--------|-------|
| $x_1 = f^{-1}(y_1) = -\sqrt{y_1}$ | $x_1 < 0$ | $y_1 > 0$ |
| $x_2 = f^{-1}(y_2) = -y_2$ | $x_2 \geq 0$ | $y_2 \leq 0$ |

Express the two "pieces" in terms of a piecewise-defined function.

$$f^{-1}(y) = \begin{cases} -\sqrt{y} & y > 0 \\ -y & y \leq 0 \end{cases}$$

**STEP 4**   Let $y = x$ (interchange $x$ and $y$).

$$f^{-1}(x) = \begin{cases} -\sqrt{x} & x > 0 \\ -x & x \leq 0 \end{cases}$$

## SECTION
## 1.5 SUMMARY

### One-to-One Functions

Each input in the domain corresponds to exactly one output in the range, and no two inputs map to the same output. There are three ways to test a function to determine whether it is a one-to-one function.

1. **Discrete points:** For the set of all points $(a, b)$, verify that no $y$-values are repeated.
2. **Algebraic equations:** Let $f(x_1) = f(x_2)$; if it can be shown that $x_1 = x_2$, then the function is one-to-one.
3. **Graphs:** Use the horizontal line test; if any horizontal line intersects the graph of the function in more than one point, then the function is not one-to-one.

### Properties of Inverse Functions

1. If $f$ is a one-to-one function, then $f^{-1}$ exists.
2. Domain and range
   - Domain of $f$ = range of $f^{-1}$
   - Domain of $f^{-1}$ = range of $f$
3. Composition of inverse functions
   - $f^{-1}(f(x)) = x$ for all $x$ in the domain of $f$
   - $f(f^{-1}(x)) = x$ for all $x$ in the domain of $f^{-1}$
4. The graphs of $f$ and $f^{-1}$ are symmetric with respect to the line $y = x$.

### Procedure for Finding the Inverse of a Function

1. Let $y = f(x)$.
2. Interchange $x$ and $y$.
3. Solve for $y$.
4. Let $y = f^{-1}(x)$.

## SECTION
## 1.5 EXERCISES

### ▪ SKILLS

**In Exercises 1–10, determine whether the given relation is a function. If it is a function, determine whether it is a one-to-one function.**

1. $\{(0, 0), (9, -3), (4, -2), (4, 2), (9, 3)\}$
2. $\{(0, 1), (1, 1), (2, 1), (3, 1)\}$
3. $\{(0, 1), (1, 0), (2, 1), (-2, 1), (5, 4), (-3, 4)\}$
4. $\{(0, 0), (-1, -1), (-2, -8), (1, 1), (2, 8)\}$

5.
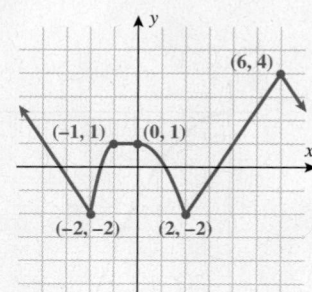

6.
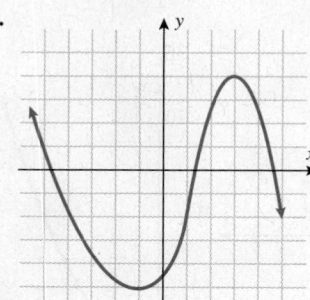

7.
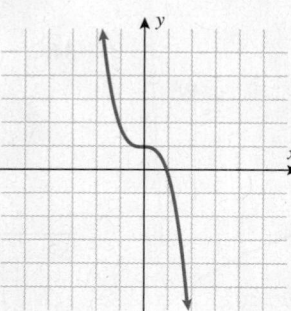

8.
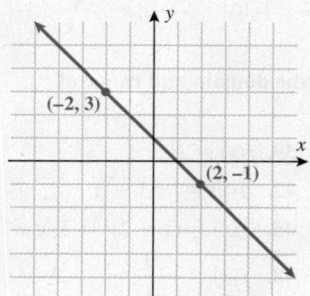

9.
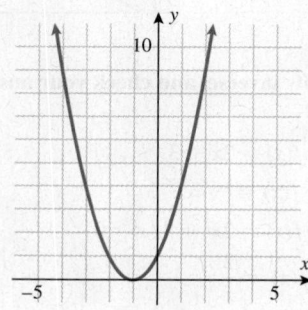

10.
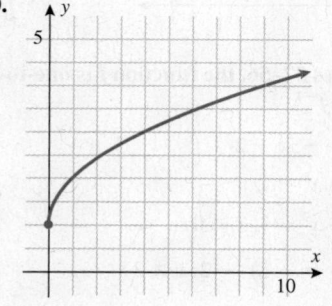

In Exercises 11–18, determine algebraically and graphically whether the function is one-to-one.

**11.** $f(x) = |x - 3|$

**12.** $f(x) = (x - 2)^2 + 1$

**13.** $f(x) = \dfrac{1}{x - 1}$

**14.** $f(x) = \sqrt[3]{x}$

**15.** $f(x) = x^2 - 4$

**16.** $f(x) = \sqrt{x + 1}$

**17.** $f(x) = x^3 - 1$

**18.** $f(x) = \dfrac{1}{x + 2}$

In Exercises 19–28, verify that the function $f^{-1}(x)$ is the inverse of $f(x)$ by showing that $f(f^{-1}(x)) = x$ and $f^{-1}(f(x)) = x$. Graph $f(x)$ and $f^{-1}(x)$ on the same axes to show the symmetry about the line $y = x$.

**19.** $f(x) = 2x + 1$; $f^{-1}(x) = \dfrac{x - 1}{2}$

**20.** $f(x) = \dfrac{x - 2}{3}$; $f^{-1}(x) = 3x + 2$

**21.** $f(x) = \sqrt{x - 1}, x \geq 1$; $f^{-1}(x) = x^2 + 1, x \geq 0$

**22.** $f(x) = 2 - x^2, x \geq 0$; $f^{-1}(x) = \sqrt{2 - x}, x \leq 2$

**23.** $f(x) = \dfrac{1}{x}$; $f^{-1}(x) = \dfrac{1}{x}, x \neq 0$

**24.** $f(x) = (5 - x)^{1/3}$; $f^{-1}(x) = 5 - x^3$

**25.** $f(x) = \dfrac{1}{2x + 6}, x \neq -3$; $f^{-1}(x) = \dfrac{1}{2x} - 3, x \neq 0$

**26.** $f(x) = \dfrac{3}{4 - x}, x \neq 4$; $f^{-1}(x) = 4 - \dfrac{3}{x}, x \neq 0$

**27.** $f(x) = \dfrac{x + 3}{x + 4}, x \neq -4$; $f^{-1}(x) = \dfrac{3 - 4x}{x - 1}, x \neq 1$

**28.** $f(x) = \dfrac{x - 5}{3 - x}, x \neq 3$; $f^{-1}(x) = \dfrac{3x + 5}{x + 1}, x \neq -1$

In Exercises 29–36, graph the inverse of the one-to-one function that is given.

**29.**

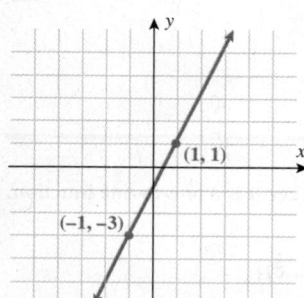

**30.**

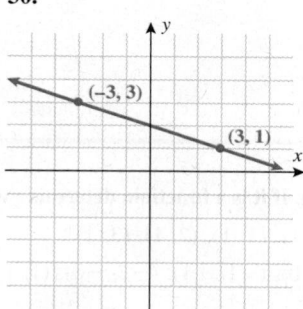

**31.**

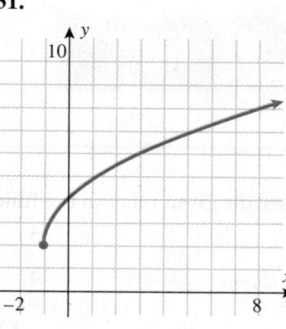

**32.**

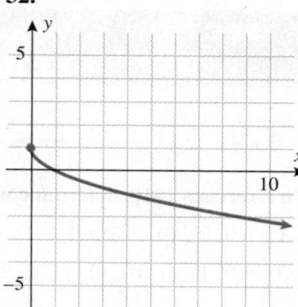

**33.**

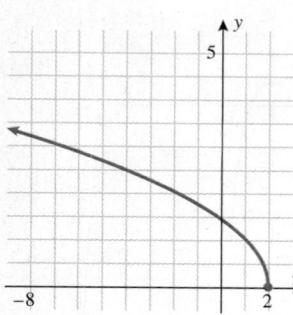

**34.**

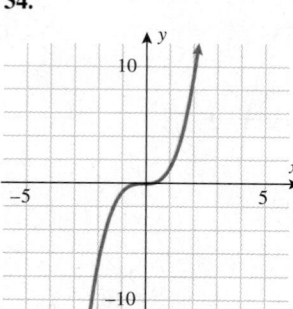

**35.**

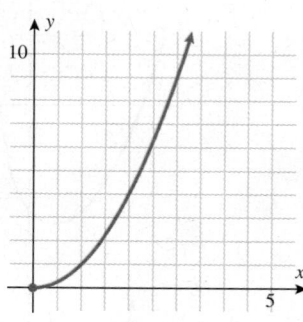

**36.**

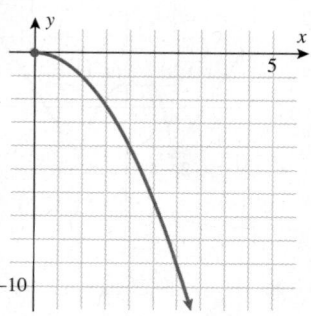

In Exercises 37–56, the function $f$ is one-to-one. Find its inverse, and check your answer. State the domain and range of both $f$ and $f^{-1}$.

**37.** $f(x) = -3x + 2$

**38.** $f(x) = 2x + 3$

**39.** $f(x) = x^3 + 1$

**40.** $f(x) = x^3 - 1$

**41.** $f(x) = \sqrt{x - 3}$

**42.** $f(x) = \sqrt{3 - x}$

**43.** $f(x) = x^2 - 1, x \geq 0$

**44.** $f(x) = 2x^2 + 1, x \geq 0$

**45.** $f(x) = (x + 2)^2 - 3, x \geq -2$

**46.** $f(x) = (x - 3)^2 - 2, x \geq 3$

**47.** $f(x) = \dfrac{2}{x}$

**48.** $f(x) = -\dfrac{3}{x}$

**49.** $f(x) = \dfrac{2}{3 - x}$

**50.** $f(x) = \dfrac{7}{x + 2}$

**51.** $f(x) = \dfrac{7x + 1}{5 - x}$

**52.** $f(x) = \dfrac{2x + 5}{7 + x}$

**53.** $f(x) = \dfrac{1}{\sqrt{x}}$

**54.** $f(x) = \dfrac{x}{\sqrt{x + 1}}$

**55.** $f(x) = \sqrt{\dfrac{x + 1}{x - 2}}$

**56.** $f(x) = \sqrt{x^2 - 1}, x \geq 1$

In Exercises 57–62, graph the piecewise-defined function to determine whether it is a one-to-one function. If it is a one-to-one function, find its inverse.

**57.** $G(x) = \begin{cases} 0 & x < 0 \\ \sqrt{x} & x \geq 0 \end{cases}$

**58.** $G(x) = \begin{cases} \dfrac{1}{x} & x < 0 \\ \sqrt{x} & x \geq 0 \end{cases}$

**59.** $f(x) = \begin{cases} \sqrt[3]{x} & x \leq -1 \\ x^2 + 2x & -1 < x \leq 1 \\ \sqrt{x} + 2 & x > 1 \end{cases}$

**60.** $f(x) = \begin{cases} -x & x < -2 \\ \sqrt{4 - x^2} & -2 \leq x \leq 0 \\ -\dfrac{1}{x} & x > 0 \end{cases}$

**61.** $f(x) = \begin{cases} x & x \leq -1 \\ x^3 & -1 < x < 1 \\ x & x \geq 1 \end{cases}$

**62.** $f(x) = \begin{cases} x + 3 & x \leq -2 \\ |x| & -2 < x < 2 \\ x^2 & x \geq 2 \end{cases}$

■ **APPLICATIONS**

**63. Temperature.** The equation used to convert from degrees Celsius to degrees Fahrenheit is $f(x) = \frac{9}{5}x + 32$. Determine the inverse function $f^{-1}(x)$. What does the inverse function represent?

**64. Temperature.** The equation used to convert from degrees Fahrenheit to degrees Celsius is $C(x) = \frac{5}{9}(x - 32)$. Determine the inverse function $C^{-1}(x)$. What does the inverse function represent?

**65. Budget.** The Richmond rowing club is planning to enter the Head of the Charles race in Boston and is trying to figure out how much money to raise. The entry fee is $250 per boat for the first 10 boats and $175 for each additional boat. Find the cost function $C(x)$ as a function of the number of boats $x$ the club enters. Find the inverse function that will yield how many boats the club can enter as a function of how much money it will raise.

**66. Long-Distance Calling Plans.** A phone company charges $0.39 per minute for the first 10 minutes of a long-distance phone call and $0.12 per minute every minute after that. Find the cost function $C(x)$ as a function of length $x$ of the phone call in minutes. Suppose you buy a "prepaid" phone card that is planned for a single call. Find the inverse function that determines how many minutes you can talk as a function of how much you prepaid.

**67. Salary.** A student works at Target making $7 per hour and the weekly number of hours worked per week $x$ varies. If Target withholds 25% of his earnings for taxes and Social Security, write a function $E(x)$ that expresses the student's take-home pay each week. Find the inverse function $E^{-1}(x)$. What does the inverse function tell you?

**68. Salary.** A grocery store pays you $8 per hour for the first 40 hours per week and time and a half for overtime. Write a piecewise-defined function that represents your weekly earnings $E(x)$ as a function of the number of hours worked $x$. Find the inverse function $E^{-1}(x)$. What does the inverse function tell you?

In Exercises 69–72, refer to the following:

By analyzing available empirical data it was determined that during an illness a patient's body temperature fluctuated during one 24-hour period according to the function

$$T(t) = 0.0003(t - 24)^3 + 101.70$$

where $T$ represents that patient's temperature in degrees Fahrenheit and $t$ represents the time of day in hours measured from 12:00 A.M. (midnight).

**69. Health/Medicine.** Find the domain and range of the function $T(t)$.

**70. Health/Medicine.** Find time as a function of temperature, that is, the inverse function $t(T)$.

**71. Health/Medicine.** Find the domain and range of the function $t(T)$ found in Exercise 70.

**72. Health/Medicine.** At what time, to the nearest hour, was the patient's temperature 99.5°F?

**73. ATM Charges.** A bank charges $0.60 each time that a client uses an ATM machine for the first 15 transactions of the month, and $0.90 for every additional transaction. Find a function $M(x)$ as a function of the number of monthly transactions that describes the amount charged by the bank. Find the inverse function that will yield how many transactions per month a client can do as a function of the client's budget.

**74. Truck Renting.** For renting a truck, a company charges $19.95 per day plus $0.80 per mile plus 10% in taxes. Find the cost of renting a truck for two days as a function of the miles driven $x$. Find the inverse function that determines how many miles you can drive as a function of the money you have available.

**75. Depreciation.** The value of a family car decreases $600 per year for the first 5 years; after that it depreciates $900 per year. Find the resale value function $V(x)$, where $x$ is the number of years the family has owned the car whose original price was $20,000. Find the inverse function $V^{-1}(x)$. What does the inverse function tell you?

**76. Production.** The number of pounds of strawberries produced per square yard in a strawberry field depends on the number of plants per square yard. When $x < 25$ plants are planted per square yard, each square yard produces $\dfrac{50 - x}{5}$ pounds. Find a function $P$ as a function of the number of plants $x$ per square yard. Find the inverse function $P^{-1}$. What does the inverse function tell you?

## ▪CATCH THE MISTAKE

**In Exercises 77–80, explain the mistake that is made.**

**77.** Is $x = y^2$ a one-to-one function?

**Solution:**

Yes, this graph represents a one-to-one function because it passes the horizontal line test.

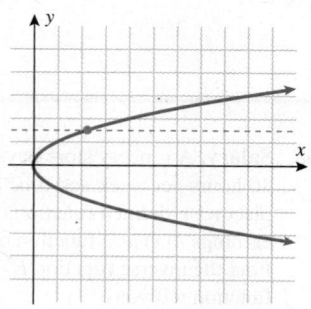

This is incorrect. What mistake was made?

**78.** A linear one-to-one function is graphed below. Draw its inverse.

**Solution:**

Note that the points $(3, 3)$ and $(0, -4)$ lie on the graph of the function.

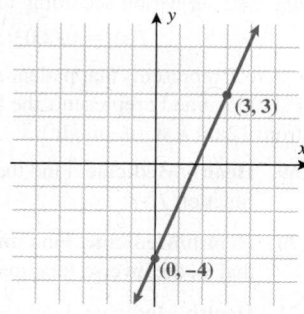

By symmetry, the points $(-3, -3)$ and $(0, 4)$ lie on the graph of the inverse.

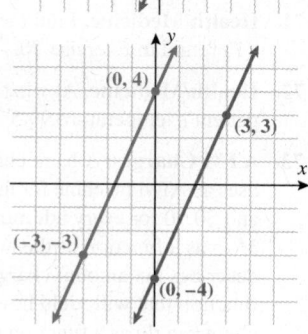

This is incorrect. What mistake was made?

**79.** Given the function $f(x) = x^2$, find the inverse function $f^{-1}(x)$.

**Solution:**

**Step 1:** Let $y = f(x)$. $\qquad\qquad y = x^2$

**Step 2:** Solve for $x$. $\qquad\qquad x = \sqrt{y}$

**Step 3:** Interchange $x$ and $y$. $\qquad y = \sqrt{x}$

**Step 4:** Let $y = f^{-1}(x)$. $\qquad f^{-1}(x) = \sqrt{x}$

Check: $f\left(f^{-1}(x)\right) = \left(\sqrt{x}\right)^2 = x$ and $f^{-1}(f(x)) = \sqrt{x^2} = x$.

The inverse of $f(x) = x^2$ is $f^{-1}(x) = \sqrt{x}$.

This is incorrect. What mistake was made?

**80.** Given the function $f(x) = \sqrt{x - 2}$, find the inverse function $f^{-1}(x)$, and state the domain restrictions on $f^{-1}(x)$.

**Solution:**

**Step 1:** Let $y = f(x)$. $\qquad\qquad y = \sqrt{x - 2}$

**Step 2:** Interchange $x$ and $y$. $\qquad x = \sqrt{y - 2}$

**Step 3:** Solve for $y$. $\qquad\qquad y = x^2 + 2$

**Step 4:** Let $f^{-1}(x) = y$. $\qquad f^{-1}(x) = x^2 + 2$

**Step 5:** Domain restrictions $f(x) = \sqrt{x - 2}$ has the domain restriction that $x \geq 2$.

The inverse of $f(x) = \sqrt{x - 2}$ is $f^{-1}(x) = x^2 + 2$.

The domain of $f^{-1}(x)$ is $x \geq 2$.

This is incorrect. What mistake was made?

## ■ CONCEPTUAL

**In Exercises 81–84, determine whether each statement is true or false.**

**81.** Every even function is a one-to-one function.

**82.** Every odd function is a one-to-one function.

**83.** It is not possible that $f = f^{-1}$.

**84.** A function $f$ has an inverse. If the function lies in quadrant II, then its inverse lies in quadrant IV.

**85.** If $(0, b)$ is the $y$-intercept of a one-to-one function $f$, what is the $x$-intercept of the inverse $f^{-1}$?

**86.** If $(a, 0)$ is the $x$-intercept of a one-to-one function $f$, what is the $y$-intercept of the inverse $f^{-1}$?

## ■ CHALLENGE

**87.** The unit circle is not a function. If we restrict ourselves to the semicircle that lies in quadrants I and II, the graph represents a function, but it is not a one-to-one function. If we further restrict ourselves to the quarter circle lying in quadrant I, the graph does represent a one-to-one function. Determine the equations of both the one-to-one function and its inverse. State the domain and range of both.

**88.** Find the inverse of $f(x) = \dfrac{c}{x}, c \neq 0$.

**89.** Under what conditions is the linear function $f(x) = mx + b$ a one-to-one function?

**90.** Assuming that the conditions found in Exercise 89 are met, determine the inverse of the linear function.

**91.** Determine the value of $a$ that makes $f(x) = \dfrac{x - 2}{x^2 - a}$ a one-to-one function. Determine $f^{-1}(x)$ and its domain.

**92.** The point $(a, b)$ lies on the graph of the one-to-one function $y = f(x)$. What other points are guaranteed to lie on the graph of $y = f^{-1}(x)$?

## ■ TECHNOLOGY

**In Exercises 93–96, graph the following functions and determine whether they are one-to-one.**

**93.** $f(x) = |4 - x^2|$

**94.** $f(x) = \dfrac{3}{x^3 + 2}$

**95.** $f(x) = x^{1/3} - x^5$

**96.** $f(x) = \dfrac{1}{x^{1/2}}$

**In Exercises 97–100, graph the functions $f$ and $g$ and the line $y = x$ in the same screen. Do the two functions appear to be inverses of each other?**

**97.** $f(x) = \sqrt{3x - 5}; \quad g(x) = \dfrac{x^2}{3} + \dfrac{5}{3}$

**98.** $f(x) = \sqrt{4 - 3x}; \quad g(x) = \dfrac{4}{3} - \dfrac{x^2}{3}, x \geq 0$

**99.** $f(x) = (x - 7)^{1/3} + 2; \quad g(x) = x^3 - 6x^2 + 12x - 1$

**100.** $f(x) = \sqrt[3]{x + 3} - 2; \quad g(x) = x^3 + 6x^2 + 12x + 6$

## ■ PREVIEW TO CALCULUS

**For Exercises 101–104, refer to the following:**

In calculus, the difference quotient $\dfrac{f(x + h) - f(x)}{h}$ of a function $f$ is used to find the derivative $f'$ of $f$, by allowing $h$ to approach zero, $h \to 0$. The derivative of the inverse function $\left(f^{-1}\right)'$ can be found using the formula

$$\left(f^{-1}\right)'(x) = \dfrac{1}{f'\left(f^{-1}(x)\right)}$$

provided that the denominator is not 0 and both $f$ and $f^{-1}$ are differentiable. For the following one-to-one function, find (a) $f^{-1}$, (b) $f'$, (c) $\left(f^{-1}\right)'$, and (d) verify the formula above. For (b) and (c), use the difference quotient.

**101.** $f(x) = 2x + 1$

**102.** $f(x) = x^2, x > 0$

**103.** $f(x) = \sqrt{x + 2}, x > -2$

**104.** $f(x) = \dfrac{1}{x + 1}, x > -1$

*Transformations of Functions*

Being a creature of habit, Dylan usually sets out each morning at 7 A.M. from his house for a jog. Figure 1 shows the graph of a function, $y = d(t)$, that represents Dylan's jog on Friday.

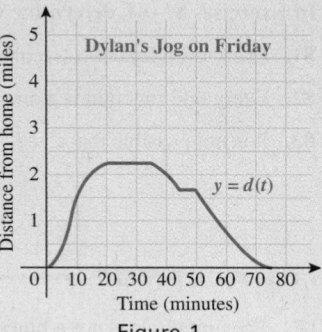

Figure 1

**a.** Use the graph in Figure 1 to fill in the table below.

| $t$ | | | | | | | | | |
|---|---|---|---|---|---|---|---|---|---|
| $y = d(t)$ | | | | | | | | | |

Describe a jogging scenario that fits the graph and table above.

**b.** The graph shown in Figure 2 represents Dylan's jog on Saturday. It is a transformation of the function $y = d(t)$ shown in Figure 1.

Complete the table of values below for this transformation. You may find it helpful to refer to the table in part (a).

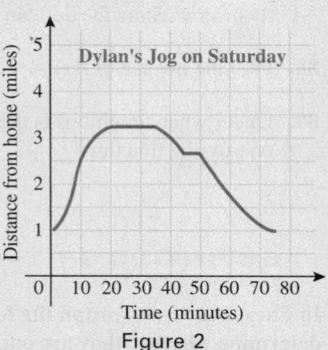

Figure 2

| $t$ | | | | | | | | | |
|---|---|---|---|---|---|---|---|---|---|
| $y$ | | | | | | | | | |

What is the real-world meaning of this transformation? How is Dylan's jog on Saturday different from his usual jog? How is it the same?

The original function (in Figure 1) is represented by the equation $y = d(t)$. Write an equation, in terms of $d(t)$, that represents the function graphed in Figure 2. Explain.

**c.** The graph shown in Figure 3 represents Dylan's jog on Sunday. It is a transformation of the function $y = d(t)$ shown in Figure 1.

Complete the table of values below for this transformation.

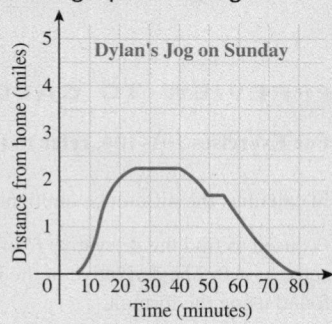

Figure 3

| $t$ | | | | | | | | | |
|---|---|---|---|---|---|---|---|---|---|
| $y$ | | | | | | | | | |

What is the real-world meaning of this transformation? How is Dylan's jog on Sunday different from his usual jog?

The original function (in Figure 1) is represented by the equation $y = d(t)$. Use function notation to represent the function graphed in Figure 3. Explain.

**d.** Suppose Dylan's jog on Monday can be represented by the equation $y = \frac{1}{2}d(t)$.

Complete the table of values below and sketch a graph at the right for this transformation.

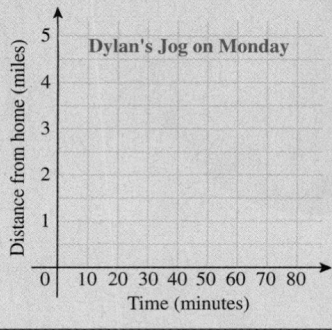

| $t$ | | | | | | | | | | | | |
|---|---|---|---|---|---|---|---|---|---|---|---|---|
| $y$ | | | | | | | | | | | | |

What is the real-world meaning of this transformation? How does Dylan's jog on Monday differ from his usual jog? How is it the same?

**e.** Suppose Dylan has a goal of cutting his usual jogging time in half, while covering the same distance. Represent this scenario as a transformation of $y = d(t)$ shown in Figure 1. Complete the table, sketch a graph, and write an equation in function notation. Explain why your equation makes sense. Finally, discuss whether you think Dylan's goal is realistic.

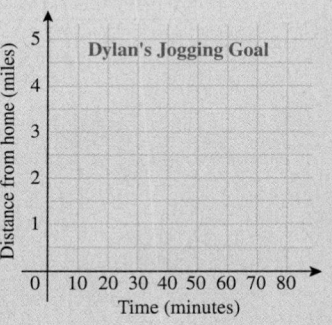

$y = $ _____

| $t$ | | | | | | | | | | | | |
|---|---|---|---|---|---|---|---|---|---|---|---|---|
| $y$ | | | | | | | | | | | | |

The U.S. National Oceanic and Atmospheric Association (NOAA) monitors temperature and carbon emissions at its observatory in Mauna Loa, Hawaii. NOAA's goal is to help foster an informed society that uses a comprehensive understanding of the role of the oceans, coasts, and atmosphere in the global ecosystem to make the best social and economic decisions. The data presented in this chapter are from the Mauna Loa Observatory, where historical atmospheric measurements have been recorded for the last 50 years. You will develop linear models based on this data to predict temperature and carbon emissions in the future.

The following table summarizes average yearly temperature in degrees Fahrenheit °F and carbon dioxide emissions in parts per million (ppm) for **Mauna Loa, Hawaii**.

| Year | 1960 | 1965 | 1970 | 1975 | 1980 | 1985 | 1990 | 1995 | 2000 | 2005 |
|---|---|---|---|---|---|---|---|---|---|---|
| Temperature (°F) | 44.45 | 43.29 | 43.61 | 43.35 | 46.66 | 45.71 | 45.53 | 47.53 | 45.86 | 46.23 |
| $CO_2$ Emissions (ppm) | 316.9 | 320.0 | 325.7 | 331.1 | 338.7 | 345.9 | 354.2 | 360.6 | 369.4 | 379.7 |

1. Plot the temperature data with time on the horizontal axis and temperature on the vertical axis. Let $t = 0$ correspond to 1960.

2. Find a *linear function* that models the temperature in Mauna Loa.
   a. Use data from 1965 and 1995.
   b. Use data from 1960 and 1990.
   c. Use linear regression and all data given.

3. Predict what the temperature will be in Mauna Loa in 2020.
   a. Apply the line found in Exercise 2(a).
   b. Apply the line found in Exercise 2(b).
   c. Apply the line found in Exercise 2(c).

4. Predict what the temperature will be in Mauna Loa in 2100.
   a. Apply the line found in Exercise 2(a).
   b. Apply the line found in Exercise 2(b).
   c. Apply the line found in Exercise 2(c).

5. Do you think your models support the claim of "global warming"? Explain.

6. Plot the carbon dioxide emissions data with time on the horizontal axis and carbon dioxide emissions on the vertical axis. Let $t = 0$ correspond to 1960.

7. Find a *linear function* that models the $CO_2$ emissions (ppm) in Mauna Loa.
   a. Use data from 1965 and 1995.
   b. Use data from 1960 and 1990.
   c. Use linear regression and all data given.

**8.** Predict the expected $CO_2$ emissions in Mauna Loa in 2020.

    **a.** Apply the line found in Exercise 7(a).
    **b.** Apply the line found in Exercise 7(b).
    **c.** Apply the line found in Exercise 7(c).

**9.** Predict the expected $CO_2$ emissions in Mauna Loa in 2100.

    **a.** Apply the line found in Exercise 7(a).
    **b.** Apply the line found in Exercise 7(b).
    **c.** Apply the line found in Exercise 7(c).

**10.** Do you think your models support the claim of the "greenhouse effect"? Explain.

| Section | Concept | Key Ideas/Formulas |
|---|---|---|
| 1.1 | **Functions** | |
| | Definition of a function | All functions are relations but not all relations are functions. |
| | Functions defined by equations | A vertical line can intersect a function in at most one point. |
| | Function notation | Placeholder notation<br><br>Difference quotient: $\dfrac{f(x+h) - f(x)}{h}, h \neq 0$ |
| | Domain of a function | Are there any restrictions on $x$? |
| 1.2 | **Graphs of functions** | |
| | Recognizing and classifying functions | **Common functions**<br>$f(x) = mx + b, f(x) = x, f(x) = x^2,$<br>$f(x) = x^3, \ f(x) = \sqrt{x}, \ f(x) = \sqrt[3]{x},$<br>$f(x) = \lvert x \rvert, \ f(x) = \dfrac{1}{x}$<br><br>**Even and odd functions:**<br>*Even:* $f(-x) = f(x)$ Symmetry about $y$-axis<br>*Odd:* $f(-x) = -f(x)$ Symmetry about origin |
| | Increasing and decreasing functions | ▪ Increasing: rises (left to right)<br>▪ Decreasing: falls (left to right) |
| | Average rate of change | $\dfrac{f(x_2) - f(x_1)}{x_2 - x_1} \quad x_1 \neq x_2$ |
| | Piecewise-defined functions | Points of discontinuity |
| 1.3 | **Graphing techniques: Transformations** | Shift the graph of $f(x)$. |
| | Horizontal and vertical shifts | $f(x + c)$    $c$ units to the left    where $c > 0$<br>$f(x - c)$    $c$ units to the right    where $c > 0$<br>$f(x) + c$    $c$ units upward    where $c > 0$<br>$f(x) - c$    $c$ units downward    where $c > 0$ |
| | Reflection about the axes | $-f(x)$    Reflection about the $x$-axis<br>$f(-x)$    Reflection about the $y$-axis |
| | Stretching and compressing | $cf(x)$ if $c > 1$    stretch vertically<br>$cf(x)$ if $0 < c < 1$    compress vertically<br>$f(cx)$ if $c > 1$    compress horizontally<br>$f(cx)$ if $0 < c < 1$    stretch horizontally |

| SECTION | CONCEPT | KEY IDEAS/FORMULAS |
|---------|---------|---------------------|
| 1.4 | **Combining functions** | |
| | Adding, subtracting, multiplying, and dividing functions | $(f + g)(x) = f(x) + g(x)$<br>$(f - g)(x) = f(x) - g(x)$<br>$(f \cdot g)(x) = f(x) \cdot g(x)$<br>Domain of the resulting function is the intersection of the individual domains.<br>$\left(\dfrac{f}{g}\right)(x) = \dfrac{f(x)}{g(x)}, \; g(x) \neq 0$<br>Domain of the quotient is the intersection of the domains of $f$ and $g$, and any points when $g(x) = 0$ must be eliminated. |
| | Composition of functions | $(f \circ g)(x) = f(g(x))$<br>The domain of the composite function is a subset of the domain of $g(x)$. Values for $x$ must be eliminated if their corresponding values $g(x)$ are not in the domain of $f$. |

$$(f \circ g)(x) = f(g(x))$$

| SECTION | CONCEPT | KEY IDEAS/FORMULAS |
|---------|---------|---------------------|
| 1.5 | **One-to-one functions and inverse functions** | |
| | One-to-one functions | ■ No two $x$-values map to the same $y$-value. If $f(x_1) = f(x_2)$, then $x_1 = x_2$.<br>■ A horizontal line may intersect a one-to-one function in at most one point. |
| | Inverse functions | ■ Only one-to-one functions have inverses.<br>■ $f^{-1}(f(x)) = x$ for all $x$ in the domain of $f$.<br>■ $f(f^{-1}(x)) = x$ for all $x$ in the domain of $f^{-1}$.<br>■ Domain of $f$ = range of $f^{-1}$.<br>  Range of $f$ = domain of $f^{-1}$. |
| | Graphical interpretation of inverse functions | ■ The graph of a function and its inverse are symmetric about the line $y = x$.<br>■ If the point $(a, b)$ lies on the graph of a function, then the point $(b, a)$ lies on the graph of its inverse. |
| | Finding the inverse function | 1. Let $y = f(x)$.<br>2. Interchange $x$ and $y$.<br>3. Solve for $y$.<br>4. Let $y = f^{-1}(x)$. |

## 1.1 Functions

**Determine whether each relation is a function. Assume that the coordinate pair $(x, y)$ represents independent variable $x$ and dependent variable $y$.**

1. $\{(-2, 3), (1, -3), (0, 4), (2, 6)\}$

2. $\{(4, 7), (2, 6), (3, 8), (1, 7)\}$

3. $x^2 + y^2 = 36$      4. $x = 4$

5. $y = |x + 2|$      6. $y = \sqrt{x}$

7.

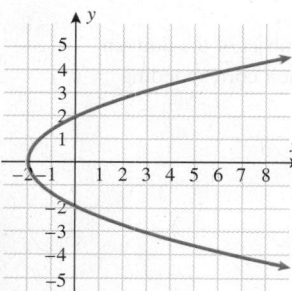

8.

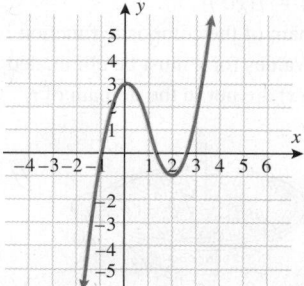

**Use the graphs of the functions to find:**

9.

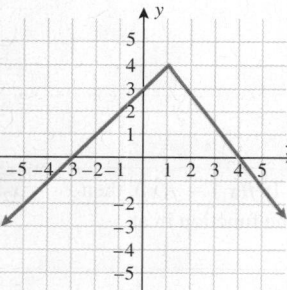

10.

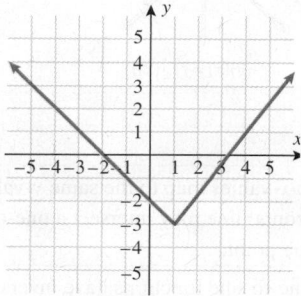

a. $f(-1)$    b. $f(1)$

c. $x$, where $f(x) = 0$

a. $f(-4)$    b. $f(0)$

c. $x$, where $f(x) = 0$

11.

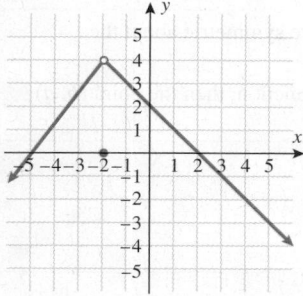

12.

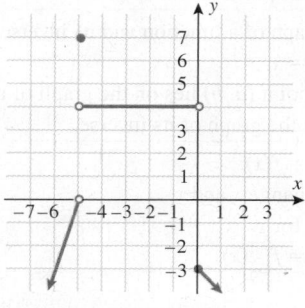

a. $f(-2)$    b. $f(4)$

c. $x$, where $f(x) = 0$

a. $f(-5)$    b. $f(0)$

c. $x$, where $f(x) = 0$

**Evaluate the given quantities using the following three functions:**

$$f(x) = 4x - 7 \qquad F(t) = t^2 + 4t - 3 \qquad g(x) = |x^2 + 2x + 4|$$

13. $f(3)$     14. $F(4)$     15. $f(-7) \cdot g(3)$

16. $\dfrac{F(0)}{g(0)}$     17. $\dfrac{f(2) - F(2)}{g(0)}$     18. $f(3 + h)$

19. $\dfrac{f(3 + h) - f(3)}{h}$     20. $\dfrac{F(t + h) - F(t)}{h}$

**Find the domain of the given function. Express the domain in interval notation.**

21. $f(x) = -3x - 4$     22. $g(x) = x^2 - 2x + 6$

23. $h(x) = \dfrac{1}{x + 4}$     24. $F(x) = \dfrac{7}{x^2 + 3}$

25. $G(x) = \sqrt{x - 4}$     26. $H(x) = \dfrac{1}{\sqrt{2x - 6}}$

### Challenge

27. If $f(x) = \dfrac{D}{x^2 - 16}$, $f(4)$ and $f(-4)$ are undefined, and $f(5) = 2$, find $D$.

28. Construct a function that is undefined at $x = -3$ and $x = 2$ such that the point $(0, -4)$ lies on the graph of the function.

## 1.2 Graphs of Functions

**Determine whether the function is even, odd, or neither.**

29. $h(x) = x^3 - 7x$     30. $f(x) = x^4 + 3x^2$

31. $f(x) = \dfrac{1}{x^3} + 3x$     32. $f(x) = \dfrac{1}{x^2} + 3x^4 + |x|$

**In Exercises 33–36, state the (a) domain, (b) range, and (c) $x$-interval(s), where the function is increasing, decreasing, or constant. Find the values of (d) $f(0)$, (e) $f(-3)$, and (f) $f(3)$.**

33.

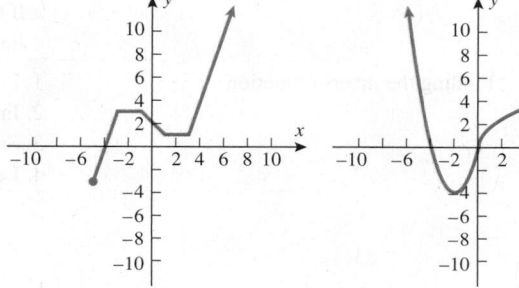

34.

**35.** **36.**

In Exercises 37–40, find the difference quotient $\dfrac{f(x+h)-f(x)}{h}$

for each function.

**37.** $f(x) = x^3 - 1$

**38.** $f(x) = \dfrac{x-1}{x+2}$

**39.** $f(x) = x + \dfrac{1}{x}$

**40.** $f(x) = \sqrt{\dfrac{x}{x+1}}$

**41.** Find the average rate of change of $f(x) = 4 - x^2$ from $x = 0$ to $x = 2$.

**42.** Find the average rate of change of $f(x) = |2x - 1|$ from $x = 1$ to $x = 5$.

**Graph the piecewise-defined function. State the domain and range in interval notation.**

**43.** $F(x) = \begin{cases} x^2 & x < 0 \\ 2 & x \geq 0 \end{cases}$

**44.** $f(x) = \begin{cases} -2x - 3 & x \leq 0 \\ 4 & 0 < x \leq 1 \\ x^2 + 4 & x > 1 \end{cases}$

**45.** $f(x) = \begin{cases} x^2 & x \leq 0 \\ -\sqrt{x} & 0 < x \leq 1 \\ |x + 2| & x > 1 \end{cases}$

**46.** $F(x) = \begin{cases} x^2 & x < 0 \\ x^3 & 0 < x < 1 \\ -|x| - 1 & x \geq 1 \end{cases}$

## Applications

**47. Housing Cost.** In 2001 the market value of a house was $135,000; in 2006 the market price of the same house was $280,000. What is the average rate of the market price as a function of the time, where $t = 0$ corresponds to 2001.

**48. Digital TV Conversion.** A newspaper reported that by February 2009, only 38% of the urban population was ready for the conversion to digital TV. Ten weeks later, the newspaper reported that 64% of the population was prepared for the broadcasting change. Find the average rate of change of the population percent as a function of the time (in weeks).

## 1.3 Graphing Techniques: Transformations

**Graph the following functions using graphing aids:**

**49.** $y = -(x - 2)^2 + 4$

**50.** $y = |-x + 5| - 7$

**51.** $y = \sqrt[3]{x - 3} + 2$

**52.** $y = \dfrac{1}{x - 2} - 4$

**53.** $y = -\frac{1}{2}x^3$

**54.** $y = 2x^2 + 3$

**Use the given graph to graph the following:**

**55.** **56.**

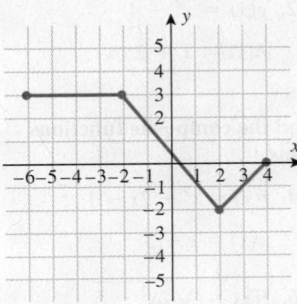 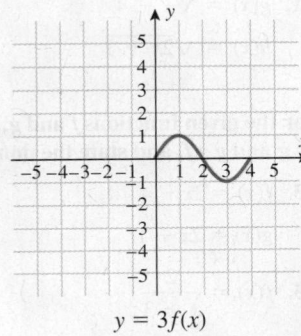

$y = f(x - 2)$         $y = 3f(x)$

**57.** **58.**

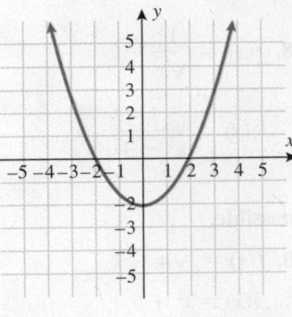 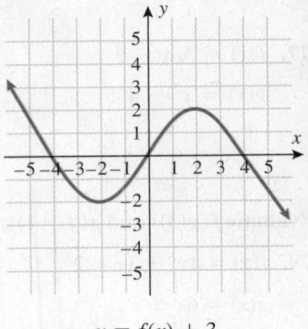

$y = -2f(x)$         $y = f(x) + 3$

**Write the function whose graph is the graph of $y = \sqrt{x}$, but is transformed accordingly, and state the domain of the resulting function.**

**59.** Shifted to the left three units

**60.** Shifted down four units

**61.** Shifted to the right two units and up three units

**62.** Reflected about the $y$-axis

**63.** Stretched by a factor of 5 and shifted vertically down six units

**64.** Compressed by a factor of 2 and shifted vertically up three units

**Transform the function into the form $f(x) = c(x - h)^2 + k$ by completing the square and graph the resulting function using transformations.**

**65.** $y = x^2 + 4x - 8$

**66.** $y = 2x^2 + 6x - 5$

## 1.4 Combining Functions

Given the functions $g$ and $h$, find $g + h$, $g - h$, $g \cdot h$, and $\dfrac{g}{h}$, and state the domain.

**67.** $g(x) = -3x - 4$

$h(x) = x - 3$

**68.** $g(x) = 2x + 3$

$h(x) = x^2 + 6$

**69.** $g(x) = \dfrac{1}{x^2}$

$h(x) = \sqrt{x}$

**70.** $g(x) = \dfrac{x + 3}{2x - 4}$

$h(x) = \dfrac{3x - 1}{x - 2}$

**71.** $g(x) = \sqrt{x - 4}$

$h(x) = \sqrt{2x + 1}$

**72.** $g(x) = x^2 - 4$

$h(x) = x + 2$

For the given functions $f$ and $g$, find the composite functions $f \circ g$ and $g \circ f$, and state the domains.

**73.** $f(x) = 3x - 4$

$g(x) = 2x + 1$

**74.** $f(x) = x^3 + 2x - 1$

$g(x) = x + 3$

**75.** $f(x) = \dfrac{2}{x + 3}$

$g(x) = \dfrac{1}{4 - x}$

**76.** $f(x) = \sqrt{2x^2 - 5}$

$g(x) = \sqrt{x + 6}$

**77.** $f(x) = \sqrt{x - 5}$

$g(x) = x^2 - 4$

**78.** $f(x) = \dfrac{1}{\sqrt{x}}$

$g(x) = \dfrac{1}{x^2 - 4}$

Evaluate $f(g(3))$ and $g(f(-1))$, if possible.

**79.** $f(x) = 4x^2 - 3x + 2$

$g(x) = 6x - 3$

**80.** $f(x) = \sqrt{4 - x}$

$g(x) = x^2 + 5$

**81.** $f(x) = \dfrac{x}{|2x - 3|}$

$g(x) = |5x + 2|$

**82.** $f(x) = \dfrac{1}{x - 1}$

$g(x) = x^2 - 1$

**83.** $f(x) = x^2 - x + 10$

$g(x) = \sqrt[3]{x - 4}$

**84.** $f(x) = \dfrac{4}{x^2 - 2}$

$g(x) = \dfrac{1}{x^2 - 9}$

Write the function as a composite $f(g(x))$ of two functions $f$ and $g$.

**85.** $h(x) = 3(x - 2)^2 + 4(x - 2) + 7$

**86.** $h(x) = \dfrac{\sqrt[3]{x}}{1 - \sqrt[3]{x}}$

**87.** $h(x) = \dfrac{1}{\sqrt{x^2 + 7}}$

**88.** $h(x) = \sqrt{|3x + 4|}$

## Applications

**89. Rain.** A rain drop hitting a lake makes a circular ripple. If the radius, in inches, grows as a function of time, in minutes, $r(t) = 25\sqrt{t + 2}$, find the area of the ripple as a function of time.

**90. Geometry.** Let the area of a rectangle be given by $42 = l \cdot w$, and let the perimeter be $36 = 2 \cdot l + 2 \cdot w$. Express the perimeter in terms of $w$.

## 1.5 One-to-One Functions and Inverse Functions

Determine whether the given function is a one-to-one function.

**91.** $\{(-2, 0), (4, 5), (3, 7)\}$

**92.** $\{(-8, -6), (-4, 2), (0, 3), (2, -8), (7, 4)\}$

**93.** $y = \sqrt{x}$    **94.** $y = x^2$    **95.** $f(x) = x^3$    **96.** $f(x) = \dfrac{1}{x^2}$

In Exercises 97–100, determine whether the function is one-to-one.

**97.**

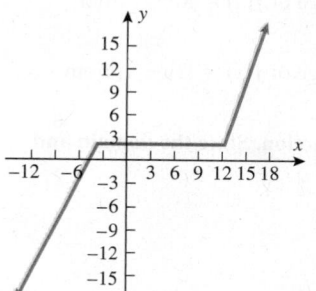

**98.**

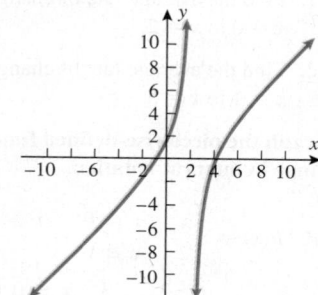

**99.**

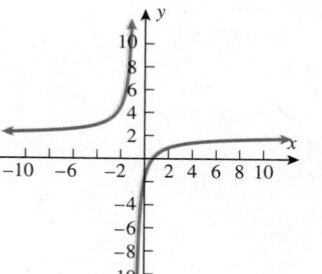

**100.**

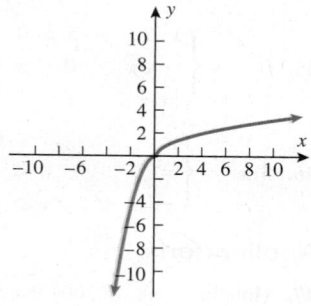

Verify that the function $f^{-1}(x)$ is the inverse of $f(x)$ by showing that $f(f^{-1}(x)) = x$. Graph $f(x)$ and $f^{-1}(x)$ on the same graph and show the symmetry about the line $y = x$.

**101.** $f(x) = 3x + 4$; $f^{-1}(x) = \dfrac{x - 4}{3}$

**102.** $f(x) = \dfrac{1}{4x - 7}$; $f^{-1}(x) = \dfrac{1 + 7x}{4x}$

103. $f(x) = \sqrt{x+4}; f^{-1}(x) = x^2 - 4 \quad x \geq 0$

104. $f(x) = \dfrac{x+2}{x-7}; f^{-1}(x) = \dfrac{7x+2}{x-1}$

**The function $f$ is one-to-one. Find its inverse and check your answer. State the domain and range of both $f$ and $f^{-1}$.**

105. $f(x) = 2x + 1$

106. $f(x) = x^5 + 2$

107. $f(x) = \sqrt{x+4}$

108. $f(x) = (x+4)^2 + 3 \quad x \geq -4$

109. $f(x) = \dfrac{x+6}{x+3}$

110. $f(x) = 2\sqrt[3]{x-5} - 8$

## Applications

111. **Salary.** A pharmaceutical salesperson makes \$22,000 base salary a year plus 8% of the total products sold. Write a function $S(x)$ that represents her yearly salary as a function of the total dollars $x$ worth of products sold. Find $S^{-1}(x)$. What does this inverse function tell you?

112. **Volume.** Express the volume $V$ of a rectangular box that has a square base of length $s$ and is 3 feet high as a function of the square length. Find $V^{-1}$. If a certain volume is desired, what does the inverse tell you?

## Technology Exercises

### Section 1.1

113. Use a graphing utility to graph the function and find the domain. Express the domain in interval notation.

$$f(x) = \dfrac{1}{\sqrt{x^2 - 2x - 3}}$$

114. Use a graphing utility to graph the function and find the domain. Express the domain in interval notation.

$$f(x) = \dfrac{x^2 - 4x - 5}{x^2 - 9}$$

### Section 1.2

115. Use a graphing utility to graph the function. State the (a) domain, (b) range, and (c) $x$ intervals where the function is increasing, decreasing, and constant.

$$f(x) = \begin{cases} 1 - x & x < -1 \\ [[x]] & -1 \leq x < 2 \\ x + 1 & x > 2 \end{cases}$$

116. Use a graphing utility to graph the function. State the (a) domain, (b) range, and (c) $x$ intervals where the function is increasing, decreasing, and constant.

$$f(x) = \begin{cases} |x^2 - 1| & -2 < x < 2 \\ \sqrt{x-2} + 4 & x > 2 \end{cases}$$

### Section 1.3

117. Use a graphing utility to graph $f(x) = x^2 - x - 6$ and $g(x) = x^2 - 5x$. Use transforms to describe the relationship between $f(x)$ and $g(x)$?

118. Use a graphing utility to graph $f(x) = 2x^2 - 3x - 5$ and $g(x) = -2x^2 - x + 6$. Use transforms to describe the relationship between $f(x)$ and $g(x)$?

### Section 1.4

119. Using a graphing utility, plot $y_1 = \sqrt{2x+3}$, $y_2 = \sqrt{4-x}$, and $y_3 = \dfrac{y_1}{y_2}$. What is the domain of $y_3$?

120. Using a graphing utility, plot $y_1 = \sqrt{x^2 - 4}$, $y_2 = x^2 - 5$, and $y_3 = y_1^2 - 5$. If $y_1$ represents a function $f$ and $y_2$ represents a function $g$, then $y_3$ represents the composite function $g \circ f$. The graph of $y_3$ is only defined for the domain of $g \circ f$. State the domain of $g \circ f$.

### Section 1.5

121. Use a graphing utility to graph the function and determine whether it is one-to-one.

$$f(x) = \dfrac{6}{\sqrt[5]{x^3 - 1}}$$

122. Use a graphing utility to graph the functions $f$ and $g$ and the line $y = x$ in the same screen. Are the two functions inverses of each other?

$$f(x) = \sqrt[4]{x-3} + 1, \, g(x) = x^4 - 4x^3 + 6x^2 - 4x + 3$$

**Assuming that $x$ represents the independent variable and $y$ represents the dependent variable, classify the relationships as:**

  a.  not a function
  b.  a function, but not one-to-one
  c.  a one-to-one function

**1.** $f(x) = |2x + 3|$     **2.** $x = y^2 + 2$     **3.** $y = \sqrt[3]{x + 1}$

**Use $f(x) = \sqrt{x - 2}$ and $g(x) = x^2 + 11$, and determine the desired quantity or expression. In the case of an expression, state the domain.**

**4.** $f(11) - 2g(-1)$     **5.** $\left(\dfrac{f}{g}\right)(x)$

**6.** $\left(\dfrac{g}{f}\right)(x)$     **7.** $g(f(x))$

**8.** $(f + g)(6)$     **9.** $f(g(\sqrt{7}))$

**Determine whether the function is odd, even, or neither.**

**10.** $f(x) = |x| - x^2$

**11.** $f(x) = 9x^3 + 5x - 3$

**12.** $f(x) = \dfrac{2}{x}$

**Graph the functions. State the domain and range of each function.**

**13.** $f(x) = -\sqrt{x - 3} + 2$

**14.** $f(x) = -2(x - 1)^2$

**15.** $f(x) = \begin{cases} -x & x < -1 \\ 1 & -1 < x < 2 \\ x^2 & x \geq 2 \end{cases}$

**Use the graphs of the function to find:**

**16.**

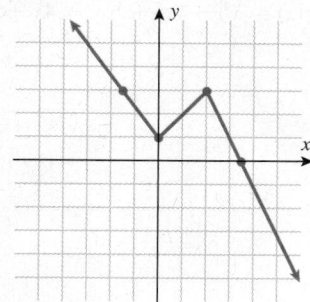
$$y = f(x)$$

  **a.** $f(3)$     **b.** $f(0)$     **c.** $f(-4)$
  **d.** $x$, where $f(x) = 3$     **e.** $x$, where $f(x) = 0$

**17.**

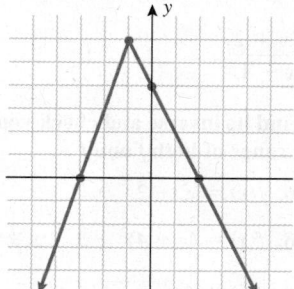
$$y = g(x)$$

  **a.** $g(3)$     **b.** $g(0)$     **c.** $g(-4)$
  **d.** $x$, where $g(x) = 0$

**18.**

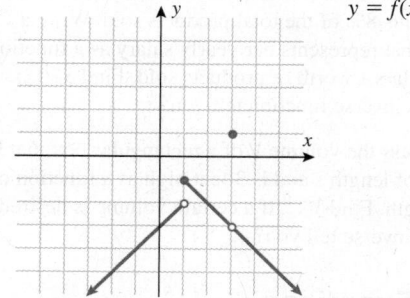
$$y = f(x)$$

  **a.** $p(0)$     **b.** $x$, where $p(x) = 0$
  **c.** $p(1)$     **d.** $p(3)$

**Find the difference equation, $\dfrac{f(x + h) - f(x)}{h}$, for:**

**19.** $f(x) = 3x^2 - 4x + 1$     **20.** $f(x) = x^3 - \dfrac{1}{\sqrt{x}}$

**Find the average rate of change of the given functions.**

**21.** $f(x) = 64 - 16x^2$ for $x = 0$ to $x = 2$

**22.** $f(x) = \sqrt{x - 1}$ for $x = 2$ to $x = 10$

**In Exercises 23–26, given the function $f$, find the inverse if it exists. State the domain and range of both $f$ and $f^{-1}$.**

**23.** $f(x) = \sqrt{x - 5}$     **24.** $f(x) = x^2 + 5$

**25.** $f(x) = \dfrac{2x + 1}{5 - x}$     **26.** $f(x) = \begin{cases} -x & x \leq 0 \\ -x^2 & x > 0 \end{cases}$

27. What domain restriction can be made so that $f(x) = x^2$ has an inverse?

28. If the point $(-2, 5)$ lies on the graph of a function, what point lies on the graph of its inverse function?

29. **Pressure.** A mini-submarine descends at a rate of 5 feet per second. The pressure on the submarine structure is a linear function of the depth; when the submarine is on the surface, the pressure is 10 pounds per square inch, and when 100 feet underwater, the pressure is 28 pounds per square inch. Write a function that describes the pressure $P$ as a function of the time $t$ in seconds.

30. **Geometry.** Both the volume $V$ and surface area $S$ of a sphere are functions of the radius $R$. Write the volume as a function of the surface area.

31. **Circles.** If a quarter circle is drawn by tracing the unit circle in quadrant III, what does the inverse of that function look like? Where is it located?

32. **Sprinkler.** A sprinkler head malfunctions at midfield in an NFL football field. The puddle of water forms a circular pattern around the sprinkler head with a radius in yards that grows as a function of time, in hours: $r(t) = 10\sqrt{t}$. When will the puddle reach the sidelines? (A football field is 30 yards from sideline to sideline.)

33. **Internet.** The cost of airport Internet access is $15 for the first 30 minutes and $1 per minute for each minute after that. Write a function describing the cost of the service as a function of minutes used.

34. **Temperature and $CO_2$ Emissions.** The following table shows average yearly temperature in degrees Fahrenheit °F and carbon dioxide emissions in parts per million (ppm) for Mauna Loa, Hawaii. Scientists discovered that both temperature and $CO_2$ emissions are linear functions of the time. Write a function that describes the temperature $T$ as a function of the $CO_2$ emissions $x$. Use this function to determine the temperature when the $CO_2$ reaches the level of 375 ppm.

| Year | 2000 | 2005 |
|---|---|---|
| Temperature (°F) | 45.86 | 46.23 |
| $CO_2$ emissions (ppm) | 369.4 | 379.7 |

# 2

# Polynomial and Rational Functions

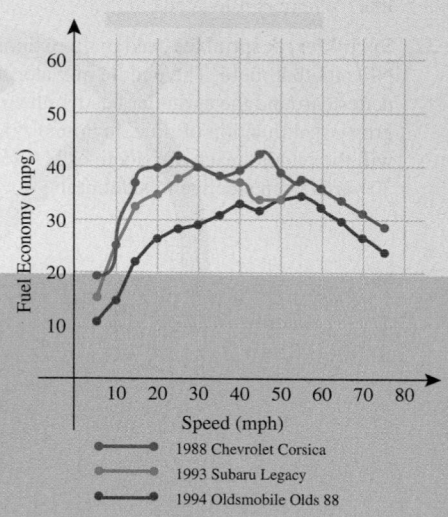

1988 Chevrolet Corsica
1993 Subaru Legacy
1994 Oldsmobile Olds 88

The gas mileage you achieve (in whatever vehicle you drive) is a function of speed, which can be modeled by a *polynomial function*. The number of turning points in the graph of a polynomial function is related to the degree of that polynomial.

We can approximate the above trends with a simple second-degree polynomial function, called a *quadratic function*, whose graph is a parabola. We see from the graph why hypermilers do not drive above posted speed limits (and often drive below them).

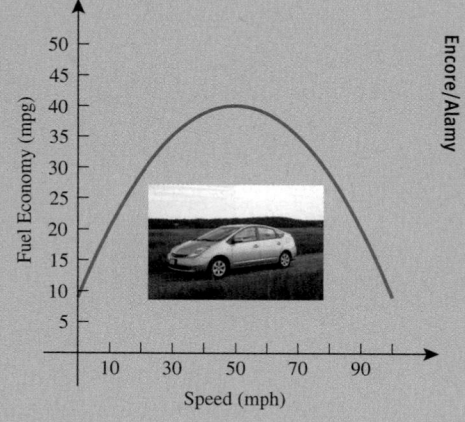

IN THIS CHAPTER we will start by discussing quadratic functions (polynomial functions of degree 2), whose graphs are parabolas. We will find the vertex, which is the maximum or minimum point on the graph. Then we will expand our discussion to higher degree polynomial functions. We will discuss techniques to find zeros of polynomial functions and strategies for graphing polynomial functions. Lastly, we will discuss rational functions, which are ratios of polynomial functions.

# POLYNOMIAL AND RATIONAL FUNCTIONS

| 2.1 Quadratic Functions | 2.2 Polynomial Functions of Higher Degree | 2.3 Dividing Polynomials | 2.4 The Real Zeros of a Polynomial Function | 2.5 Complex Zeros: The Fundamental Theorem of Algebra | 2.6 Rational Functions |
|---|---|---|---|---|---|
| • Graphs of Quadratic Functions: Parabolas<br>• Finding the Equation of a Parabola | • Identifying Polynomial Functions<br>• Graphing Polynomial Functions Using Transformations of Power Functions<br>• Real Zeros of a Polynomial Function<br>• Graphing General Polynomial Functions | • Long Division of Polynomials<br>• Synthetic Division of Polynomials | • The Remainder Theorem and the Factor Theorem<br>• The Rational Zero Theorem and Descartes' Rule of Signs<br>• Factoring Polynomials<br>• The Intermediate Value Theorem<br>• Graphing Polynomial Functions | • Complex Zeros<br>• Factoring Polynomials | • Domain of Rational Functions<br>• Vertical, Horizontal, and Slant Asymptotes<br>• Graphing Rational Functions |

## LEARNING OBJECTIVES

- Given a quadratic function in either standard or general form, find its vertex and sketch its graph.
- Use multiplicity of zeros and end behavior as guides in sketching the graph of a polynomial function.
- Divide polynomials using long division and understand when synthetic division can be used.
- Find all real zeros of a polynomial function (x-intercepts) and use these as guides in sketching the graph of a polynomial function.
- Factor a polynomial function completely over the set of complex numbers.
- Use asymptotes and intercepts as guides in graphing rational functions.

SKILLS OBJECTIVES

- Graph a quadratic function in standard form.
- Graph a quadratic function in general form.
- Find the equation of a parabola.
- Solve application problems that involve quadratic functions.

CONCEPTUAL OBJECTIVES

- Recognize characteristics of graphs of quadratic functions (parabolas):
  - whether the parabola opens up or down
  - whether the vertex is a maximum or minimum
  - the axis of symmetry

## Graphs of Quadratic Functions: Parabolas

In Chapter 1, we studied functions in general. In this chapter, we will learn about a special group of functions called *polynomial functions*. Polynomial functions are simple functions; often, more complicated functions are approximated by polynomial functions. Polynomial functions model many real-world applications such as the stock market, football punts, business costs, revenues and profits, and the flight path of NASA's "vomit comet." Let's start by defining a polynomial function.

**DEFINITION**    **Polynomial Function**

Let $n$ be a nonnegative integer, and let $a_n, a_{n-1}, \ldots, a_2, a_1, a_0$ be real numbers with $a_n \neq 0$. The function

$$f(x) = a_n x^n + a_{n-1} x^{n-1} + \cdots + a_2 x^2 + a_1 x + a_0$$

is called a **polynomial function of $x$ with degree $n$**. The coefficient $a_n$ is called the **leading coefficient**, and $a_0$ is the constant.

Polynomials of particular degrees have special names. In Chapter 1, the library of functions included the constant function $f(x) = b$, which is a horizontal line; the linear function $f(x) = mx + b$, which is a line with slope $m$ and $y$-intercept $(0, b)$; the square function $f(x) = x^2$; and the cube function $f(x) = x^3$. These are all special cases of a polynomial function.

In Section 1.3, we graphed functions using transformation techniques such as $F(x) = (x + 1)^2 - 2$, which can be graphed by starting with the square function $y = x^2$ and shifting one unit to the left and down two units. See the graph on the left.

Note that if we eliminate the parentheses in $F(x) = (x + 1)^2 - 2$ to get

$$F(x) = x^2 + 2x + 1 - 2$$
$$= x^2 + 2x - 1$$

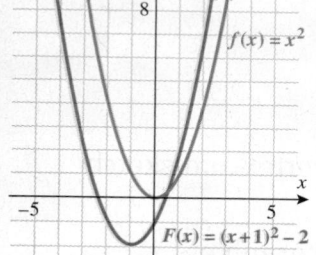

the result is a function defined by a second-degree polynomial (a polynomial with $x^2$ as the highest degree term), which is also called a *quadratic function*.

**DEFINITION**    **Quadratic Function**

Let $a$, $b$, and $c$ be real numbers with $a \neq 0$. The function

$$f(x) = ax^2 + bx + c$$

is called a **quadratic function**.

The graph of any quadratic function is a **parabola**. If the leading coefficient $a$ is *positive*, then the parabola opens *upward*. If the leading coefficient $a$ is *negative*, then the parabola opens *downward*. The **vertex** (or turning point) is the *minimum* point, or low point, on the graph if the parabola opens upward, whereas it is the *maximum* point, or high point, on the graph if the parabola opens downward. The vertical line that intersects the parabola at the vertex is called the **axis of symmetry**.

The axis of symmetry is the line $x = h$, and the vertex is located at the point $(h, k)$, as shown in the following two figures:

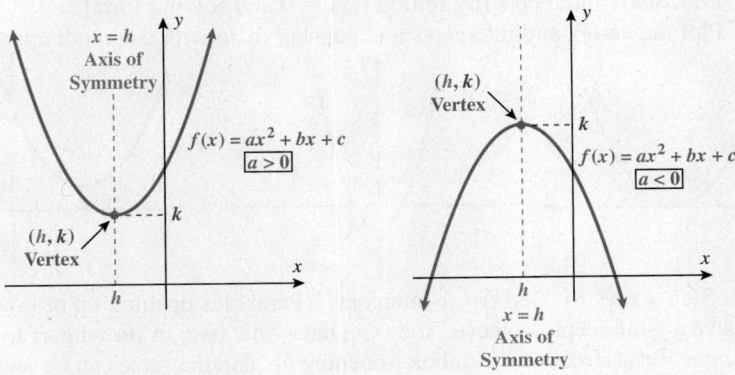

## Graphing Quadratic Functions in Standard Form

In general, writing a quadratic function in the form

$$f(x) = a(x - h)^2 + k$$

allows the vertex $(h, k)$ and the axis of symmetry $x = h$ to be determined by inspection. This form is a convenient way to express a quadratic function in order to quickly determine its corresponding graph. Hence, this form is called *standard form*.

**QUADRATIC FUNCTION: STANDARD FORM**

The quadratic function

$$f(x) = a(x - h)^2 + k$$

is in **standard form**. The graph of $f$ is a parabola whose vertex is the point $(h, k)$. The parabola is symmetric with respect to the line $x = h$. If $a > 0$, the parabola opens up. If $a < 0$, the parabola opens down.

Recall that graphing linear functions requires finding two points on the line, or a point and the slope of the line. However, for a quadratic function, simply knowing two points that lie on its graph is no longer sufficient. Below is a general step-by-step procedure for graphing quadratic functions given in standard form.

### GRAPHING QUADRATIC FUNCTIONS

To graph $f(x) = a(x - h)^2 + k$

**Step 1:** Determine whether the parabola opens up or down.

$$a > 0 \quad \text{up}$$
$$a < 0 \quad \text{down}$$

**Step 2:** Determine the vertex $(h, k)$.
**Step 3:** Find the $y$-intercept (by setting $x = 0$).
**Step 4:** Find any $x$-intercepts [by setting $f(x) = 0$ and solving for $x$].
**Step 5:** Plot the vertex and intercepts and connect them with a smooth curve.

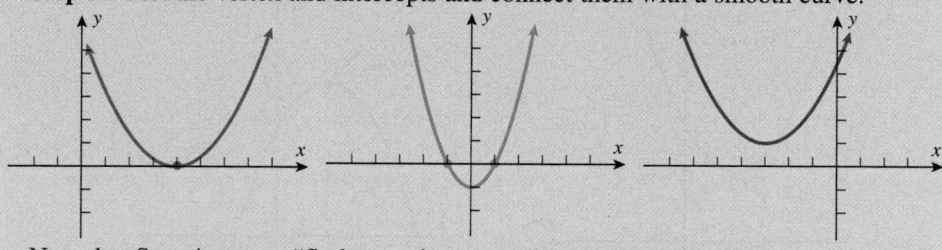

Note that Step 4 says to "find any $x$-intercepts." Parabolas opening up or down will always have a $y$-intercept. However, they can have **one, two,** or **no** $x$-intercepts. The figures above illustrate this for parabolas opening up, and the same can be said about parabolas opening down.

**EXAMPLE 1** **Graphing a Quadratic Function Given in Standard Form**

Graph the quadratic function $f(x) = (x - 3)^2 - 1$.

**Solution:**

STEP 1 The parabola opens up.     $a = 1$, so $a > 0$

STEP 2 Determine the vertex.     $(h, k) = (3, -1)$

STEP 3 Find the $y$-intercept.     $f(0) = (-3)^2 - 1 = 8$
     $(0, 8)$ corresponds to the $y$-intercept

STEP 4 Find any $x$-intercepts.     $f(x) = (x - 3)^2 - 1 = 0$
     $(x - 3)^2 = 1$

Use the square root method.     $x - 3 = \pm 1$

Solve.     $x = 2$ or $x = 4$
     $(2, 0)$ and $(4, 0)$ correspond to the $x$-intercepts

STEP 5 Plot the vertex and intercepts $(3, -1), (0, 8), (2, 0), (4, 0)$.

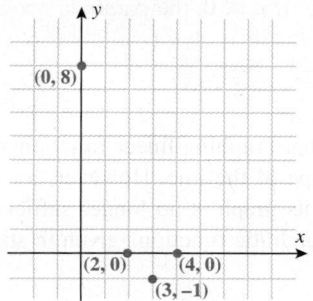

Connect the points with a smooth curve opening up.

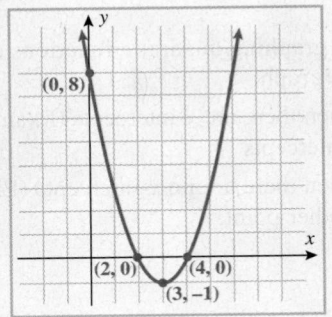

The graph in Example 1 could also have been found by shifting the square function to the right three units and down one unit.

■ **YOUR TURN** Graph the quadratic function $f(x) = (x - 1)^2 - 4$.

■ **Answer:**

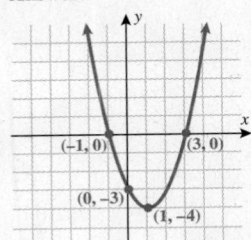

▶ **EXAMPLE 2** **Graphing a Quadratic Function Given in Standard Form with a Negative Leading Coefficient**

Graph the quadratic function $f(x) = -2(x - 1)^2 - 3$.

**Solution:**

STEP 1 The parabola opens down.  $\quad a = -2$, so $a < 0$

STEP 2 Determine the vertex.  $\quad (h, k) = (1, -3)$

STEP 3 Find the $y$-intercept.
$$f(0) = -2(-1)^2 - 3 = -2 - 3 = -5$$
$(0, -5)$ corresponds to the $y$-intercept

STEP 4 Find any $x$-intercepts.
$$f(x) = -2(x - 1)^2 - 3 = 0$$
$$-2(x - 1)^2 = 3$$
$$(x - 1)^2 = -\frac{3}{2}$$

A real quantity squared cannot be negative so there are no real solutions. There are no $x$-intercepts.

STEP 5 Plot the vertex $(1, -3)$ and $y$-intercept $(0, -5)$. Connect the points with a smooth curve.

Note that the axis of symmetry is $x = 1$. Because the point $(0, -5)$ lies on the parabola, then by symmetry with respect to $x = 1$, the point $(2, -5)$ also lies on the graph.

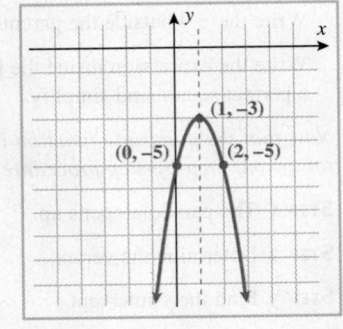

■ **Answer:**

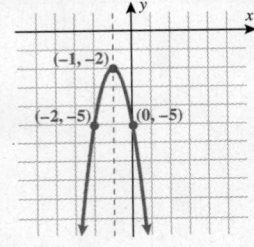

■ **YOUR TURN** Graph the quadratic function $f(x) = -3(x + 1)^2 - 2$.

When graphing quadratic functions (parabolas), have *at least three points* labeled on the graph.

- When there are *x*-intercepts (Example 1), label the vertex, *y*-intercept, and *x*-intercepts.

- When there are no *x*-intercepts (Example 2), label the vertex, *y*-intercept, and another point.

## Graphing Quadratic Functions in General Form

A quadratic function is often written in one of two forms:

$$\text{Standard form: } f(x) = a(x - h)^2 + k$$
$$\text{General form: } f(x) = ax^2 + bx + c$$

When the quadratic function is expressed in standard form, the graph is easily obtained by identifying the vertex $(h, k)$ and the intercepts and drawing a smooth curve that opens either up or down, depending on the sign of $a$.

Typically, quadratic functions are expressed in general form and a graph is the ultimate goal, so we must first express the quadratic function in standard form. One technique for transforming a quadratic function from general form to standard form was reviewed in Section 0.2 and is called *completing the square*.

**EXAMPLE 3** **Graphing a Quadratic Function Given in General Form**

Write the quadratic function $f(x) = x^2 - 6x + 4$ in standard form and graph $f$.

**Solution:**

*Express the quadratic function in standard form by completing the square.*

| | |
|---|---|
| Write the original function. | $f(x) = x^2 - 6x + 4$ |
| Group the variable terms together. | $= (x^2 - 6x) + 4$ |

Complete the square.

Half of $-6$ is $-3$; $-3$ squared is 9.

| Add and subtract 9 within the parentheses. | $= (x^2 - 6x + 9 - 9) + 4$ |
|---|---|
| Write the $-9$ outside the parentheses. | $= (x^2 - 6x + 9) - 9 + 4$ |
| Write the expression inside the parentheses as a perfect square and simplify. | $= (x - 3)^2 - 5$ |

*Now that the quadratic function is written in standard form, $f(x) = (x - 3)^2 - 5$, we follow our step-by-step procedure for graphing a quadratic function in standard form.*

**STEP 1** The parabola opens up.   $a = 1$, so $a > 0$

**STEP 2** Determine the vertex.   $(h, k) = (3, -5)$

**STEP 3** Find the *y*-intercept.

$$f(x) = x^2 - 6x + 4$$
$$f(0) = (0)^2 - 6(0) + 4 = 4$$

$(0, 4)$ corresponds to the *y*-intercept

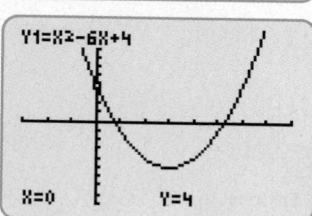

STEP 4 Find any $x$-intercepts.

$$f(x) = 0$$

**Using the standard form:**

$$f(x) = (x - 3)^2 - 5 = 0$$
$$(x - 3)^2 = 5$$
$$x - 3 = \pm\sqrt{5}$$
$$x = 3 \pm \sqrt{5}$$

**Using the general form:**

$$f(x) = x - 6x + 4 = 0$$
$$x = \frac{-(-6) \pm \sqrt{(-6)^2 - 4(1)(4)}}{2(1)}$$
$$x = 3 \pm \sqrt{5}$$

$(3 + \sqrt{5}, 0)$ and $(3 - \sqrt{5}, 0)$ correspond to the $x$-intercepts.

STEP 5 Plot the vertex and intercepts $(3, -5)$, $(0, 4)$, $(3 + \sqrt{5}, 0)$, and $(3 - \sqrt{5}, 0)$.

Connect the points with a smooth parabolic curve.

*Note:* $3 + \sqrt{5} \approx 5.24$ and $3 - \sqrt{5} \approx 0.76$.

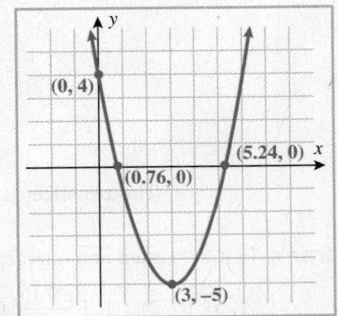

**Study Tip**

Although either form (standard or general) can be used to find the intercepts, it is often more convenient to use the general form when finding the $y$-intercept and the standard form when finding the $x$-intercept.

■ **Answer:**

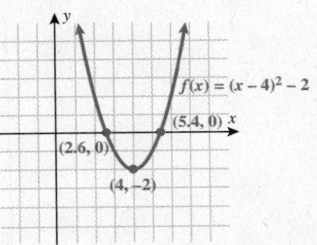

■ **YOUR TURN** Write the quadratic function $f(x) = x^2 - 8x + 14$ in standard form and graph $f$.

When the leading coefficient of a quadratic function is not equal to 1, the leading coefficient must be factored out before completing the square.

**Technology Tip**

Use a graphing utility to graph the function $f(x) = -3x^2 + 6x + 2$ as $y_1$.

### EXAMPLE 4 Graphing a Quadratic Function Given in General Form with a Negative Leading Coefficient

Graph the quadratic function $f(x) = -3x^2 + 6x + 2$.

**Solution:**

*Express the function in standard form by completing the square.*

| | |
|---|---|
| Write the original function. | $f(x) = -3x^2 + 6x + 2$ |
| Group the variable terms together. | $= (-3x^2 + 6x) + 2$ |
| Factor out $-3$ in order to make the coefficient of $x^2$ equal to 1 inside the parentheses. | $= -3(x^2 - 2x) + 2$ |
| Add and subtract 1 inside the parentheses to create a perfect square. | $= -3(x^2 - 2x + 1 - 1) + 2$ |
| Regroup the terms. | $= -3(x^2 - 2x + 1) - 3(-1) + 2$ |
| Write the expression inside the parentheses as a perfect square and simplify. | $= -3(x - 1)^2 + 5$ |

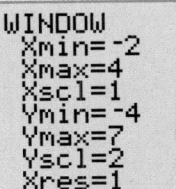

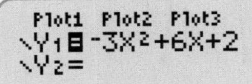

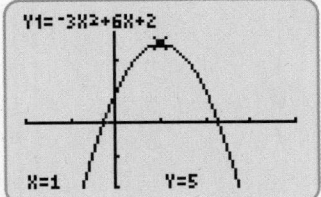

*Now that the quadratic function is written in standard form,* $f(x) = -3(x - 1)^2 + 5$, *we follow our step-by-step procedure for graphing a quadratic function in standard form.*

**STEP 1** The parabola opens down.          $a = -3$; therefore, $a < 0$

**STEP 2** Determine the vertex.          $(h, k) = (1, 5)$

**STEP 3** Find the *y*-intercept using          $f(0) = -3(0)^2 + 6(0) + 2 = 2$
the general form.          $(0, 2)$ corresponds to the *y*-intercept

**STEP 4** Find any *x*-intercepts using
the standard form.

$$f(x) = -3(x - 1)^2 + 5 = 0$$
$$-3(x - 1)^2 = -5$$
$$(x - 1)^2 = \frac{5}{3}$$
$$x - 1 = \pm\sqrt{\frac{5}{3}}$$
$$x = 1 \pm \sqrt{\frac{5}{3}}$$
$$= 1 \pm \frac{\sqrt{15}}{3}$$

The *x*-intercepts are $\left(1 + \frac{\sqrt{15}}{3}, 0\right)$ and $\left(1 - \frac{\sqrt{15}}{3}, 0\right)$.

**STEP 5** Plot the vertex and intercepts

$(1, 5)$, $(0, 2)$, $\left(1 + \frac{\sqrt{15}}{3}, 0\right)$, and

$\left(1 - \frac{\sqrt{15}}{3}, 0\right)$.

Connect the points with a smooth curve.

*Note:* $1 + \frac{\sqrt{15}}{3} \approx 2.3$ and

$1 - \frac{\sqrt{15}}{3} \approx -0.3$.

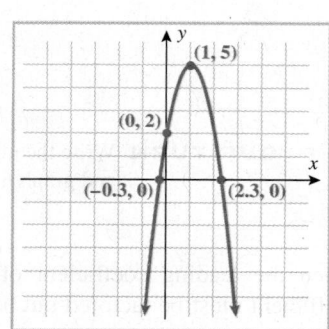

■**Answer:**

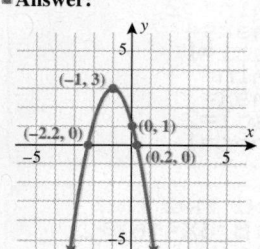

■ **YOUR TURN** Graph the quadratic function $f(x) = -2x^2 - 4x + 1$.

In Examples 3 and 4, the quadratic functions were given in general form and they were transformed into standard form by completing the square. It can be shown (by completing the square) that the vertex of a quadratic function in general form, $f(x) = ax^2 + bx + c$, is located at $x = -\frac{b}{2a}$.

Another approach to sketching the graphs of quadratic functions is to first find the vertex and then find additional points through point-plotting.

**VERTEX OF A PARABOLA**

The graph of a quadratic function $f(x) = ax^2 + bx + c$ is a parabola with the **vertex** located at the point

$$\left(-\frac{b}{2a}, f\left(-\frac{b}{2a}\right)\right)$$

### GRAPHING A QUADRATIC FUNCTION IN GENERAL FORM

**Step 1:** Find the vertex.

**Step 2:** Determine whether the parabola opens up or down.

■ If $a > 0$, the parabola opens up.

■ If $a < 0$, the parabola opens down.

**Step 3:** Find additional points near the vertex.

**Step 4:** Sketch the graph with a parabolic curve.

**EXAMPLE 5    Graphing a Quadratic Function Given in General Form**

Sketch the graph of $f(x) = -2x^2 + 4x + 5$.

**Solution:** Let $a = -2$, $b = 4$, and $c = 5$.

STEP 1 Find the vertex.

$$x = -\frac{b}{2a} = -\frac{4}{2(-2)} = 1$$

$$f(1) = -2(1)^2 + 4(1) + 5 = 7$$

Vertex: $(1, 7)$

STEP 2 The parabola opens down.

$$a = -2$$

STEP 3 Find additional points near the vertex.

| $x$ | $-1$ | $0$ | $1$ | $2$ | $3$ |
|---|---|---|---|---|---|
| $f(x)$ | $f(-1) = -1$ | $f(0) = 5$ | $f(1) = 7$ | $f(2) = 5$ | $f(3) = -1$ |

STEP 4 Label the vertex and additional
points then sketch the graph.

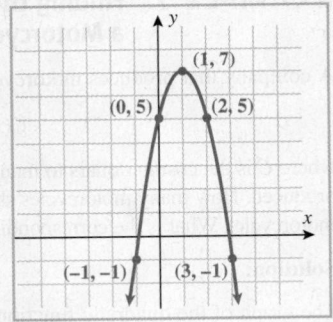

■ **YOUR TURN** Sketch the graph of $f(x) = 3x^2 - 6x + 4$.

■ **Answer:**

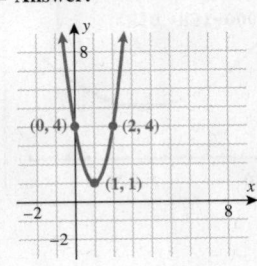

# Finding the Equation of a Parabola

It is important to understand that the equation $y = x^2$ is equivalent to the quadratic function $f(x) = x^2$. Both have the same parabolic graph. Thus far, we have been given the function and then asked to find characteristics (vertex and intercepts) in order to graph. We now turn our attention to the problem of determining the function, given certain characteristics.

**EXAMPLE 6    Finding the Quadratic Function Given the Vertex
and a Point That Lies on Its Graph**

Find the quadratic function whose graph has a vertex at $(3, 4)$ and which passes through the point $(2, 3)$. Express the quadratic function in both standard and general forms.

**Solution:**

Write the standard form of a quadratic function.        $f(x) = a(x - h)^2 + k$

Substitute the coordinates of the vertex $(h, k) = (3, 4)$.        $f(x) = a(x - 3)^2 + 4$

Use the point $(2, 3)$ to find $a$.

The point $(2, 3)$ implies $f(2) = 3$.

$$f(2) = a(2 - 3)^2 + 4 = 3$$

Solve for $a$.

$$a(2 - 3)^2 + 4 = 3$$
$$a(-1)^2 + 4 = 3$$
$$a + 4 = 3$$
$$a = -1$$

Write both forms of the quadratic function.

Standard form: $\boxed{f(x) = -(x - 3)^2 + 4}$   General form: $\boxed{f(x) = -x^2 + 6x - 5}$

■ **Answer:** Standard form:
$$f(x) = (x + 3)^2 - 5$$

■ **YOUR TURN** Find the standard form of the equation of a parabola whose graph has a vertex at $(-3, -5)$ and which passes through the point $(-2, -4)$.

As we have seen in Example 6, once the vertex is known, the leading coefficient $a$ can be found from any point that lies on the parabola.

## Application Problems That Involve Quadratic Functions

Because the vertex of a parabola represents either the minimum or maximum value of the quadratic function, in application problems it often suffices simply to find the vertex.

### Technology Tip

Use a graphing utility to graph the cost function
$C(x) = 2000 - 15x + 0.05x^2$ as $y_1$.

```
WINDOW
 Xmin=-50
 Xmax=300
 Xscl=25
 Ymin=-500
 Ymax=2500
 Yscl=250
 Xres=1
```

```
Plot1  Plot2  Plot3
\Y₁■2000-15X+.05
X²
\Y₂=■
```

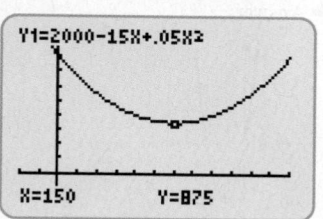

```
Y1=2000-15X+.05X²
X=150        Y=875
```

■ **Answer:** 250,000 bottles

**EXAMPLE 7   Finding the Minimum Cost of Manufacturing a Motorcycle**

A company that produces motorcycles has a per unit production cost of

$$C(x) = 2000 - 15x + 0.05x^2$$

where $C$ is the cost in dollars to manufacture a motorcycle and $x$ is the number of motorcycles produced. How many motorcycles should be produced in order to minimize the cost of each motorcycle? What is the corresponding minimum cost?

**Solution:**

The graph of the quadratic function is a parabola.

Rewrite the quadratic function in general form.   $C(x) = 0.05x^2 - 15x + 2000$

The parabola opens up, because $a$ is positive.   $a = 0.05 > 0$

Because the parabola opens up, the vertex of the parabola is a *minimum*.

Find the $x$-coordinate of the vertex.   $x = -\dfrac{b}{2a} = -\dfrac{(-15)}{2(0.05)} = 150$

*The company keeps per unit cost to a minimum when 150 motorcycles are produced.*

The minimum cost is $875 per motorcycle.   $C(150) = 875$

■ **YOUR TURN** The revenue associated with selling vitamins is

$$R(x) = 500x - 0.001x^2$$

where $R$ is the revenue in dollars and $x$ is the number of bottles of vitamins sold. Determine how many bottles of vitamins should be sold to maximize the revenue.

**EXAMPLE 8** **Finding the Dimensions That Yield a Maximum Area**

*Technology Tip*

You have just bought a puppy and want to fence in an area in the backyard for her. You buy 100 linear feet of fence from Home Depot and have decided to make a rectangular fenced-in area using the back of your house as one side. Determine the dimensions of the rectangular pen that will maximize the area in which your puppy may roam. What is the maximum area of the rectangular pen?

Use a graphing utility to graph the area function $A(x) = -2x^2 + 100x$.

**Solution:**

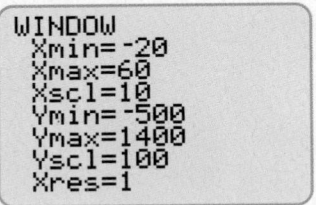

**STEP 1 Identify the question.**

Find the dimensions of the rectangular pen.

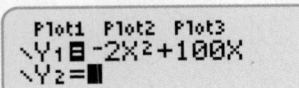

**STEP 2 Draw a picture.**

Pen

House

The maximum occurs when $x = 25$. The maximum area is $y = 1250$ sq ft.

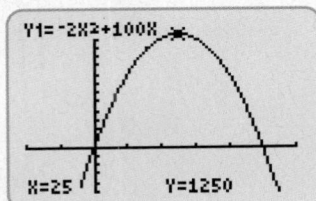

**STEP 3 Set up a function.**

If we let $x$ represent the length of one side of the rectangle, then the opposite side is also of length $x$. Because there are 100 feet of fence, the remaining fence left for the side opposite the house is $100 - 2x$.

The area of a rectangle is equal to length times width:

$$A(x) = x(100 - 2x)$$

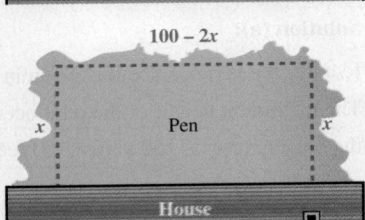

$100 - 2x$

$x$ Pen $x$

House

A table of values supports the solution.

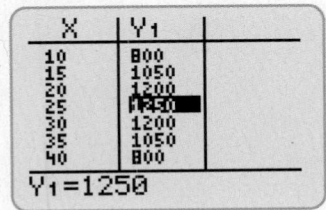

**STEP 4 Find the maximum value of the function.**

$$A(x) = x(100 - 2x) = -2x^2 + 100x$$

Find the maximum of the parabola that corresponds to the quadratic function for area $A(x) = -2x^2 + 100x$.

$a = -2$ and $b = 100$; therefore, the maximum occurs when

$$x = -\frac{b}{2a} = -\frac{100}{2(-2)} = 25$$

Replacing $x$ with 25 in our original diagram:

The dimensions of the rectangle are

25 feet by 50 feet .

The maximum area $A(25) = 1250$ is

1250 square feet .

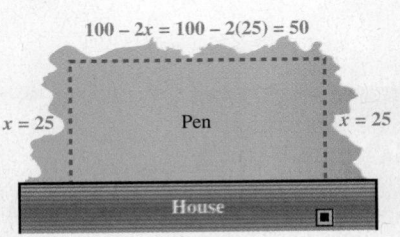

$100 - 2x = 100 - 2(25) = 50$

$x = 25$ Pen $x = 25$

House

**STEP 5 Check the solution.**

Two sides are 25 feet and one side is 50 feet, and together they account for all 100 feet of fence.

■ **YOUR TURN** Suppose you have 200 linear feet of fence to enclose a rectangular garden. Determine the dimensions of the rectangle that will yield the greatest area.

■ **Answer:** 50 ft by 50 ft

### EXAMPLE 9  Path of a Punted Football

The path of a particular punt follows the quadratic function: $h(x) = -\frac{1}{8}(x-5)^2 + 50$, where $h(x)$ is the height of the ball in yards and $x$ corresponds to the horizontal distance in yards. Assume $x = 0$ corresponds to midfield (the 50 yard line). For example, $x = -20$ corresponds to the punter's own 30 yard line, whereas $x = 20$ corresponds to the other team's 30 yard line.

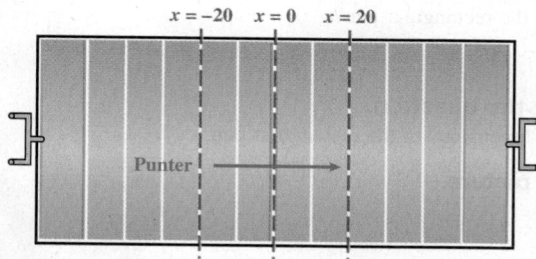

**a.** Find the maximum height the ball achieves.
**b.** Find the horizontal distance the ball covers. Assume the height is zero when the ball is kicked and when the ball is caught.

**Solution (a):**

Identify the vertex since it is given in standard form.        $(h, k) = (5, 50)$

The maximum height of the punt occurs at the other team's 45 yard line, and the height the ball achieves is $\boxed{50 \text{ yards (150 feet)}}$.

**Solution (b):**

The height when the ball is kicked
or caught is zero.

$$h(x) = -\frac{1}{8}(x-5)^2 + 50 = 0$$

Solve for $x$.

$$\frac{1}{8}(x-5)^2 = 50$$
$$(x-5)^2 = 400$$
$$(x-5) = \pm\sqrt{400}$$
$$x = 5 \pm 20$$
$$x = -15 \quad \text{and} \quad x = 25$$

The horizontal distance is the distance between these two points: $|25 - (-15)| = \boxed{40 \text{ yd}}$.

---

### SECTION 2.1  SUMMARY

All quadratic functions $f(x) = ax^2 + bx + c$ or $f(x) = a(x-h)^2 + k$ have graphs that are parabolas:

- If $a > 0$, the parabola opens up.
- If $a < 0$, the parabola opens down.
- The vertex is at the point

$$(h, k) = \left(-\frac{b}{2a}, f\left(-\frac{b}{2a}\right)\right) = \left(-\frac{b}{2a}, \frac{4ac - b^2}{4a}\right)$$

- When the quadratic function is given in general form, completing the square can be used to rewrite the function in standard form.
- At least three points are needed to graph a quadratic function:
  - vertex
  - $y$-intercept
  - $x$-intercept(s) or other point(s)

## SECTION 2.1 EXERCISES

### ▪ SKILLS

In Exercises 1–4, match the quadratic function with its graph.

**1.** $f(x) = 3(x + 2)^2 - 5$     **2.** $f(x) = 2(x - 1)^2 + 3$     **3.** $f(x) = -\frac{1}{2}(x + 3)^2 + 2$     **4.** $f(x) = -\frac{1}{3}(x - 2)^2 + 3$

a.
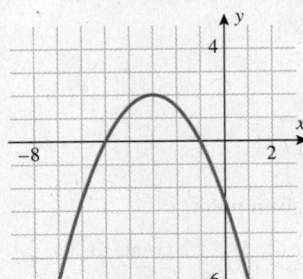

b.
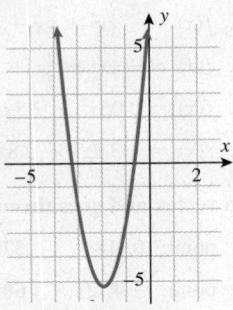

c.
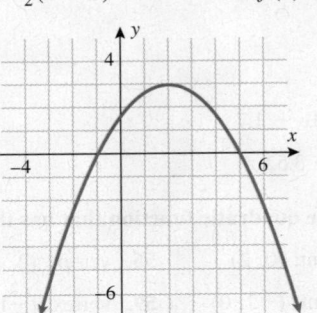

d.
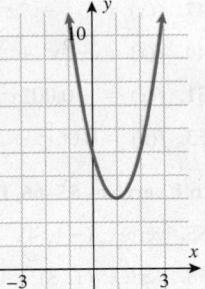

In Exercises 5–8, match the quadratic function with its graph.

**5.** $f(x) = 3x^2 + 5x - 2$     **6.** $f(x) = 3x^2 - x - 2$     **7.** $f(x) = -x^2 + 2x - 1$     **8.** $f(x) = -2x^2 - x + 3$

a.
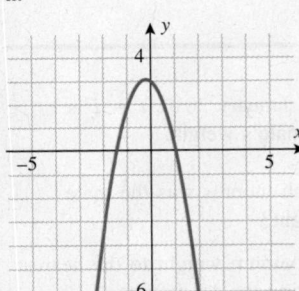

b.
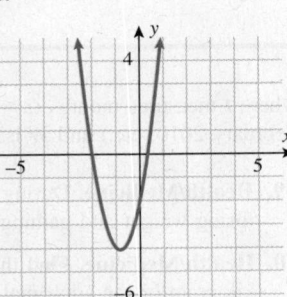

c.
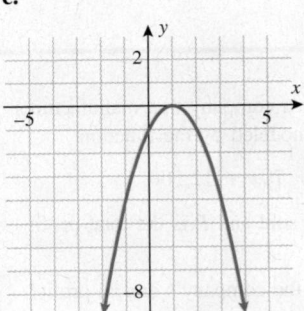

d.
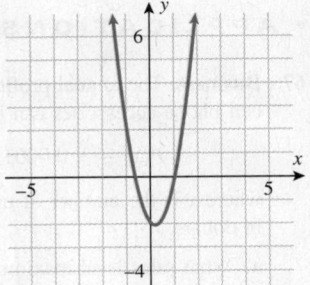

In Exercises 9–22, graph the quadratic function, which is given in standard form.

**9.** $f(x) = (x + 1)^2 - 2$

**10.** $f(x) = (x + 2)^2 - 1$

**11.** $f(x) = (x - 2)^2 - 3$

**12.** $f(x) = (x - 4)^2 + 2$

**13.** $f(x) = -(x - 3)^2 + 9$

**14.** $f(x) = -(x - 5)^2 - 4$

**15.** $f(x) = -(x + 1)^2 - 3$

**16.** $f(x) = -(x - 2)^2 + 6$

**17.** $f(x) = 2(x - 2)^2 + 2$

**18.** $f(x) = -3(x + 2)^2 - 15$

**19.** $f(x) = \left(x - \frac{1}{3}\right)^2 + \frac{1}{9}$

**20.** $f(x) = \left(x + \frac{1}{4}\right)^2 - \frac{1}{2}$

**21.** $f(x) = -0.5(x - 0.25)^2 + 0.75$

**22.** $f(x) = -0.2(x + 0.6)^2 + 0.8$

In Exercises 23–34, rewrite the quadratic function in standard form by completing the square.

**23.** $f(x) = x^2 + 6x - 3$

**24.** $f(x) = x^2 + 8x + 2$

**25.** $f(x) = -x^2 - 10x + 3$

**26.** $f(x) = -x^2 - 12x + 6$

**27.** $f(x) = 2x^2 + 8x - 2$

**28.** $f(x) = 3x^2 - 9x + 11$

**29.** $f(x) = -4x^2 + 16x - 7$

**30.** $f(x) = -5x^2 + 100x - 36$

**31.** $f(x) = x^2 + 10x$

**32.** $f(x) = -4x^2 + 12x - 2$

**33.** $f(x) = \frac{1}{2}x^2 - 4x + 3$

**34.** $f(x) = -\frac{1}{3}x^2 + 6x + 4$

**In Exercises 35–44, graph the quadratic function.**

**35.** $f(x) = x^2 + 6x - 7$     **36.** $f(x) = x^2 - 3x + 10$     **37.** $f(x) = -x^2 - 5x + 6$     **38.** $f(x) = -x^2 + 3x + 4$

**39.** $f(x) = 4x^2 - 5x + 10$     **40.** $f(x) = 3x^2 + 9x - 1$     **41.** $f(x) = -2x^2 - 12x - 16$     **42.** $f(x) = -3x^2 + 12x - 12$

**43.** $f(x) = \frac{1}{2}x^2 - \frac{1}{2}$     **44.** $f(x) = -\frac{1}{3}x^2 + \frac{4}{3}$

**In Exercises 45–54, find the vertex of the parabola associated with each quadratic function.**

**45.** $f(x) = 33x^2 - 2x + 15$                    **46.** $f(x) = 17x^2 + 4x - 3$

**47.** $f(x) = \frac{1}{2}x^2 - 7x + 5$                    **48.** $f(x) = -\frac{1}{3}x^2 + \frac{2}{5}x + 4$

**49.** $f(x) = -\frac{2}{5}x^2 + \frac{3}{7}x + 2$                    **50.** $f(x) = -\frac{1}{7}x^2 - \frac{2}{3}x + \frac{1}{9}$

**51.** $f(x) = -0.002x^2 - 0.3x + 1.7$                    **52.** $f(x) = 0.05x^2 + 2.5x - 1.5$

**53.** $f(x) = 0.06x^2 - 2.6x + 3.52$                    **54.** $f(x) = -3.2x^2 + 0.8x - 0.14$

**In Exercises 55–66, find the quadratic function that has the given vertex and goes through the given point.**

**55.** vertex: $(-1, 4)$     point: $(0, 2)$     **56.** vertex: $(2, -3)$     point: $(0, 1)$     **57.** vertex: $(2, 5)$     point: $(3, 0)$

**58.** vertex: $(1, 3)$     point: $(-2, 0)$     **59.** vertex: $(-1, -3)$     point: $(-4, 2)$     **60.** vertex: $(0, -2)$     point: $(3, 10)$

**61.** vertex: $(-2, -4)$     point: $(-1, 6)$     **62.** vertex: $(5, 4)$     point: $(2, -5)$     **63.** vertex: $\left(\frac{1}{2}, -\frac{3}{4}\right)$     point: $\left(\frac{3}{4}, 0\right)$

**64.** vertex: $\left(-\frac{5}{6}, \frac{2}{3}\right)$     point: $(0, 0)$     **65.** vertex: $(2.5, -3.5)$     point: $(4.5, 1.5)$     **66.** vertex: $(1.8, 2.7)$     point: $(-2.2, -2.1)$

## ▪ APPLICATIONS

**67. Business.** The annual profit for a company that manufactures cell phone accessories can be modeled by the function

$$P(x) = -0.0001x^2 + 70x + 12{,}500$$

where $x$ is the number of units sold and $P$ is the total profit in dollars.

**a.** What sales level maximizes the company's annual profit?

**b.** Find the maximum annual profit for the company.

**68. Business.** A manufacturer of office supplies has daily production costs of

$$C(x) = 0.5x^2 - 20x + 1600$$

where $x$ is the number of units produced measured in thousands and $C$ is cost in hundreds of dollars.

**a.** What production level will minimize the manufacturer's daily production costs?

**b.** Find the minimum daily production costs for the manufacturer.

**For Exercises 69 and 70, refer to the following:**

An adult male's weight, in kilograms, can be modeled by the function

$$W(t) = -\frac{2}{3}t^2 + \frac{13}{5}t + \frac{433}{5}; \quad 1 \leq t \leq 18$$

where $t$ measures months ($t = 1$ is January 2010, $t = 2$ is February 2010, etc.) and $W$ is the male's weight.

**69. Health/Medicine.** During which months was the male losing weight and gaining weight?

**70. Health/Medicine.** Find the maximum weight to the nearest kilogram of the adult male during the 18 months.

**Exercises 71 and 72 concern the path of a punted football. Refer to the diagram in Example 9.**

**71. Sports.** The path of a particular punt follows the quadratic function

$$h(x) = -\frac{8}{125}(x + 5)^2 + 40$$

where $h(x)$ is the height of the ball in yards and $x$ corresponds to the horizontal distance in yards. Assume $x = 0$ corresponds to midfield (the 50 yard line). For example, $x = -20$ corresponds to the punter's own 30 yard line, whereas $x = 20$ corresponds to the other team's 30 yard line.

**a.** Find the maximum height the ball achieves.

**b.** Find the horizontal distance the ball covers. Assume the height is zero when the ball is kicked and when the ball is caught.

**72. Sports.** The path of a particular punt follows the quadratic function

$$h(x) = -\frac{5}{40}(x - 30)^2 + 50$$

where $h(x)$ is the height of the ball in yards and $x$ corresponds to the horizontal distance in yards. Assume $x = 0$ corresponds to midfield (the 50 yard line). For example, $x = -20$ corresponds to the punter's own 30 yard line, whereas $x = 20$ corresponds to the other team's 30 yard line.

**a.** Find the maximum height the ball achieves.

**b.** Find the horizontal distance the ball covers. Assume the height is zero when the ball is kicked and when the ball is caught.

**73. Ranching.** A rancher has 10,000 linear feet of fencing and wants to enclose a rectangular field and then divide it into two equal pastures with an internal fence parallel to one of the rectangular sides. What is the maximum area of each pasture? Round to the nearest square foot.

**74. Ranching.** A rancher has 30,000 linear feet of fencing and wants to enclose a rectangular field and then divide it into four equal pastures with three internal fences parallel to one of the rectangular sides. What is the maximum area of each pasture?

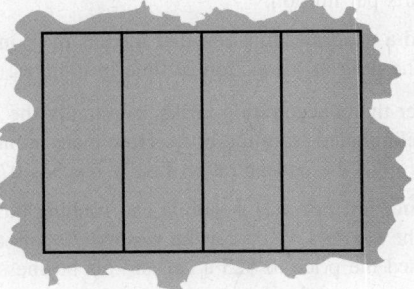

**75. Gravity.** A person standing near the edge of a cliff 100 feet above a lake throws a rock upward with an initial speed of 32 feet per second. The height of the rock above the lake at the bottom of the cliff is a function of time and is described by

$$h(t) = -16t^2 + 32t + 100$$

**a.** How many seconds will it take until the rock reaches its maximum height? What is that height?

**b.** At what time will the rock hit the water?

**c.** Over what time interval is the rock higher than the cliff?

100 feet

**76. Gravity.** A person holds a pistol straight upward and fires. The initial velocity of most bullets is around 1200 feet per second. The height of the bullet is a function of time and is described by

$$h(t) = -16t^2 + 1200t$$

How long, after the gun is fired, does the person have to get out of the way of the bullet falling from the sky?

**77. Zero Gravity.** As part of their training, astronauts ride the "vomit comet," NASA's reduced gravity KC 135A aircraft that performs parabolic flights to simulate weightlessness. The plane starts at an altitude of 20,000 feet and makes a steep climb at 52° with the horizon for 20–25 seconds and then dives at that same angle back down, repeatedly. The equation governing the altitude of the flight is

$$A(x) = -0.0003x^2 + 9.3x - 46{,}075$$

where $A(x)$ is altitude and $x$ is horizontal distance in feet.

**a.** What is the maximum altitude the plane attains?

**b.** Over what horizontal distance is the entire maneuver performed? (Assume the starting and ending altitude is 20,000 feet.)

NASA's "Vomit Comet"

**78. Sports.** A soccer ball is kicked from the ground at a 45° angle with an initial velocity of 40 feet per second. The height of the soccer ball above the ground is given by $H(x) = -0.0128x^2 + x$, where $x$ is the horizontal distance the ball travels.

   **a.** What is the maximum height the ball reaches?

   **b.** What is the horizontal distance the ball travels?

**79. Profit.** A small company in Virginia Beach manufactures handcrafted surfboards. The profit of selling $x$ boards is given by

$$P(x) = 20,000 + 80x - 0.4x^2$$

   **a.** How many boards should be made to maximize the profit?

   **b.** What is the maximum profit?

**80. Environment: Fuel Economy.** Gas mileage (miles per gallon, mpg) can be approximated by a quadratic function of speed. For a particular automobile, assume the vertex occurs when the speed is 50 miles per hour (the mpg will be 30).

   **a.** Write a quadratic function that models this relationship, assuming 70 miles per hour corresponds to 25 mpg.

   **b.** What gas mileage would you expect for this car driving 90 miles per hour?

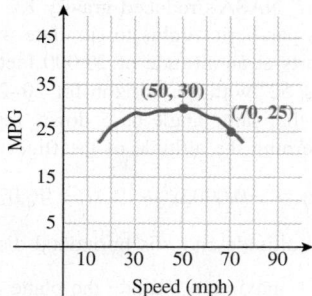

**For Exercises 81 and 82, use the following information:**

One function of particular interest in economics is the **profit function**. We denote this function by $P(x)$. It is defined to be the difference between revenue $R(x)$ and cost $C(x)$ so that

$$P(x) = R(x) - C(x)$$

The total revenue received from the sale of $x$ goods at price $p$ is given by

$$R(x) = px$$

The total cost function relates the cost of production to the level of output $x$. This includes both fixed costs $C_f$ and variable costs $C_v$ (costs per unit produced). The total cost in producing $x$ goods is given by

$$C(x) = C_f + C_v x$$

Thus, the profit function is

$$P(x) = px - C_f - C_v x$$

Assume fixed costs are \$1000, variable costs per unit are \$20, and the demand function is

$$p = 100 - x$$

**81. Profit.** How many units should the company produce to break even?

**82. Profit.** What is the maximum profit?

**83. Cell Phones.** The number of cell phones in the United States can be approximated by a quadratic function. In 1996 there were approximately 16 million cell phones, and in 2005 there were approximately 100 million. Let $t$ be the number of years since 1996. The number of cell phones in 1996 is represented by (0, 16), and the number in 2005 is (9, 100). Let (0, 16) be the vertex.

   **a.** Find a quadratic function that represents the number of cell phones.

   **b.** Based on this model, how many cell phones will be in use in 2010?

**84. Underage Smoking.** The number of underage cigarette smokers (ages 10–17) has declined in the United States. The peak percent was in 1998 at 49%. In 2006 this had dropped to 36%. Let $t$ be time in years after 1998 ($t = 0$ corresponds to 1998).

   **a.** Find a quadratic function that models the percent of underage smokers as a function of time. Let (0, 49) be the vertex.

   **b.** Now that you have the model, predict the percent of underage smokers in 2010.

**85. Drug Concentration.** The concentration of a drug in the bloodstream, measured in parts per million, can be modeled with a quadratic function. In 50 minutes the concentration is 93.75 parts per million. The maximum concentration of the drug in the bloodstream occurs in 225 minutes and is 400 parts per million.

   **a.** Find a quadratic function that models the concentration of the drug as a function of time in minutes.

   **b.** After the concentration peaks, eventually the drug will be eliminated from the body. How many minutes will it take until the concentration finally reaches 0?

**86. Revenue.** Jeff operates a mobile car washing business. When he charged \$20 a car, he washed 70 cars a month. He raised the price to \$25 a car and his business dropped to 50 cars a month.

   **a.** Find a linear function that represents the demand equation (the price per car as a function of the number of cars washed).

   **b.** Find the revenue function $R(x) = xp$.

   **c.** How many cars should he wash to maximize the revenue?

   **d.** What price should he charge to maximize revenue?

# ▪CATCH THE MISTAKE

**In Exercises 87–90, explain the mistake that is made. There may be a single mistake or there may be more than one mistake.**

**87.** Plot the quadratic function $f(x) = (x + 3)^2 - 1$.

**Solution:**

**Step 1:** The parabola opens up because $a = 1 > 0$.

**Step 2:** The vertex is $(3, -1)$.

**Step 3:** The $y$-intercept is $(0, 8)$.

**Step 4:** The $x$-intercepts are $(2, 0)$ and $(4, 0)$.

**Step 5:** Plot the vertex and intercepts, and connect the points with a smooth curve.

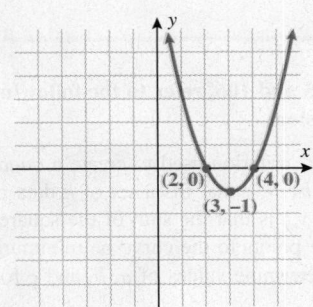

This is incorrect. What mistake(s) was made?

**88.** Determine the vertex of the quadratic function $f(x) = 2x^2 - 6x - 18$.

**Solution:**

**Step 1:** The vertex is given by $(h, k) = \left(-\dfrac{b}{2a}, f\left(-\dfrac{b}{2a}\right)\right)$.

In this case, $a = 2$ and $b = 6$.

**Step 2:** The $x$-coordinate of the vertex is

$$x = -\frac{6}{2(2)} = -\frac{6}{4} = -\frac{3}{2}$$

**Step 3:** The $y$-coordinate of the vertex is

$$f\left(-\frac{3}{2}\right) = -2\left(-\frac{3}{2}\right)^2 + 6\left(-\frac{3}{2}\right) - 18$$

$$= -2\left(\frac{9}{4}\right) - \frac{18}{2} - 18$$

$$= -\frac{9}{2} - 9 - 18$$

$$= -\frac{63}{2}$$

This is incorrect. What mistake(s) was made?

**89.** Rewrite the following quadratic function in standard form:

$$f(x) = -x^2 + 2x + 3$$

**Solution:**

**Step 1:** Group the variables together. $(-x^2 + 2x) + 3$

**Step 2:** Factor out a negative. $-(x^2 + 2x) + 3$

**Step 3:** Add and subtract 1 inside the parentheses. $-(x^2 + 2x + 1 - 1) + 3$

**Step 4:** Factor out the $-1$. $-(x^2 + 2x + 1) + 1 + 3$

**Step 5:** Simplify. $-(x + 1)^2 + 4$

This is incorrect. What mistake(s) was made?

**90.** Find the quadratic function whose vertex is $(2, -3)$ and whose graph passes through the point $(9, 0)$.

**Solution:**

**Step 1:** Write the quadratic function in standard form. $f(x) = a(x - h)^2 + k$

**Step 2:** Substitute $(h, k) = (2, -3)$. $f(x) = a(x - 2)^2 - 3$

**Step 3:** Substitute the point $(9, 0)$ and solve for $a$.
$f(0) = a(0 - 2)^2 - 3 = 9$
$4a - 3 = 9$
$4a = 12$
$a = 3$

The quadratic function sought is $f(x) = 3(x - 2)^2 - 3$.

This is incorrect. What mistake(s) was made?

# ▪CONCEPTUAL

**In Exercises 91–94, determine whether each statement is true or false.**

**91.** A quadratic function must have a $y$-intercept.

**92.** A quadratic function must have an $x$-intercept.

**93.** A quadratic function may have more than one $y$-intercept.

**94.** A quadratic function may have more than one $x$-intercept.

**95.** For the general quadratic equation, $f(x) = ax^2 + bx + c$, show that the vertex is $(h, k) = \left(-\dfrac{b}{2a}, f\left(-\dfrac{b}{2a}\right)\right)$.

**96.** Given the quadratic function $f(x) = a(x - h)^2 + k$, determine the $x$- and $y$-intercepts in terms of $a$, $h$, and $k$.

■ CHALLENGE

**97.** A rancher has 1000 feet of fence to enclose a pasture.

    **a.** Determine the maximum area if a rectangular fence is used.

    **b.** Determine the maximum area if a circular fence is used.

**98.** A 600-room hotel in Orlando is filled to capacity every night when the rate is \$90 per night. For every \$5 increase in the rate, 10 fewer rooms are filled. How much should the hotel charge to produce the maximum income? What is its maximum income?

**99.** The speed of the river current is $\dfrac{1}{x + 4}$ mph. In quiet waters, the speed of a swimmer is $\dfrac{1}{x + 11}$ mph. When the swimmer swims down the river, her speed is $\frac{25}{144}$ mph. What is the value of $x$?

**100.** When a rectangle is reduced 25% (length and width each reduced by 25%), the new length equals the original width. Find the dimensions of the original rectangle given that the area of the reduced rectangle is 36 sq ft.

■ TECHNOLOGY

**101.** On a graphing calculator, plot the quadratic function $f(x) = -0.002x^2 + 5.7x - 23$.

    **a.** Identify the vertex of this parabola.

    **b.** Identify the $y$-intercept.

    **c.** Identify the $x$-intercepts (if any).

    **d.** What is the axis of symmetry?

**102.** Determine the quadratic function whose vertex is $(-0.5, 1.7)$ and whose graph passes through the point $(0, 4)$.

    **a.** Write the quadratic function in general form.

    **b.** Plot this quadratic function with a graphing calculator.

    **c.** Zoom in on the vertex and $y$-intercept. Do they agree with the given values?

In Exercises 103 and 104, (a) use the calculator commands  STAT   QuadReg  to model the data using a quadratic function; (b) write the quadratic function in standard form and identify the vertex; (c) plot this quadratic function with a graphing calculator and use the  TRACE  key to highlight the given points. Do they agree with the given values?

**103.**

| $x$ | $-2$ | $2$ | $5$ |
|---|---|---|---|
| $y$ | $-29.28$ | $21.92$ | $18.32$ |

**104.**

| $x$ | $-9$ | $-2$ | $4$ |
|---|---|---|---|
| $y$ | $-2.72$ | $-16.18$ | $6.62$ |

**For Exercises 105 and 106, refer to the following discussion of quadratic regression:**

The "least-squares" criterion used to create a *quadratic regression* curve $y = ax^2 + bx + c$ that fits a set of $n$ data points $(x_1, y_1)$, $(x_2, y_2), \ldots, (x_n, y_n)$ is that the sum of the squares of the vertical distances from the points to the curve be minimum. This means that we need to determine values of $a$, $b$, and $c$ for which

$$\sum_{i=1}^{n}(y_i - (ax_i^2 + bx_i + c))^2 \text{ is as small as possible. Calculus can}$$

be used to determine formulas for $a$, $b$, and $c$ that do the job, but computing them by hand is tedious and unnecessary because the TI-83+ has a built-in program called *QuadReg* that does this. In fact, this was introduced in Section 2.5, Problems 15–48. The following are application problems that involve experimental data for which the best fit curve is a parabola.

*Projectile Motion*
It is well known that the trajectory of an object thrown with initial velocity $v_0$ from an initial height $s_0$ is described by the quadratic function $s(t) = -16t^2 + v_0 t + s_0$. If we have data points obtained in such a context, we can apply the procedure outlined in Section 2.5 with *QuadReg* in place of *LinReg(ax+b)* to find a best fit *parabola* of the form $y = ax^2 + bx + c$.

    Each year during Halloween season, it is tradition to hold the Pumpkin Launching Contest where students literally hurl their pumpkins in the hope of throwing them the farthest horizontal distance. Ben claims that it is better to use a steeper trajectory since it will have more air time, while Rick believes in throwing the pumpkin with all of his might, but with less inclination. The following data points that describe the pumpkin's horizontal $x$ and vertical $y$ distances (measured in feet) are collected during the flights of their pumpkins:

| BEN'S DATA | | RICK'S DATA | |
|---|---|---|---|
| $x$ | $y$ | $x$ | $y$ |
| 0 | 4 | 0 | 4 |
| 1 | 14.2 | 1 | 8.5 |
| 2 | 28.4 | 2 | 10.6 |
| 3 | 30.1 | 3 | 13.3 |
| 4 | 35.9 | 4 | 16.2 |
| 5 | 37.8 | 5 | 17.3 |
| 6 | 41.1 | 6 | 19.3 |
| 7 | 38.2 | 7 | 19.5 |

**105.** **a.** Form a scatterplot for Ben's data.

**b.** Determine the equation of the best fit parabola and report the value of the associated correlation coefficient.

**c.** Use the best fit curve from (b) to answer the following:

   **i.** What is the initial height of the pumpkin's trajectory and with what initial velocity was it thrown?

   **ii.** What is the maximum height of Ben's pumpkin's trajectory?

   **iii.** How much horizontal distance has the pumpkin traveled by the time it lands?

**106.** Repeat Exercise 105 for Rick's data.

# ■PREVIEW TO CALCULUS

Parabolas, ellipses, and hyperbolas form a family of curves called conic sections. These curves are studied later in Chapter 9 and in calculus. The general equation of each curve is given below:

Parabola: $(x - h)^2 = 4p(y - k)$

Ellipse: $\dfrac{(x - h)^2}{a^2} + \dfrac{(y - k)^2}{b^2} = 1$

Hyperbola: $\dfrac{(x - h)^2}{a^2} - \dfrac{(y - k)^2}{b^2} = 1$

In Exercises 107–110, write the general equation of each conic section and identify the curve.

**107.** $4x^2 + 9y^2 = 36y$     **108.** $x^2 + 16y = 4y^2 + 2x + 19$     **109.** $x^2 + 6x - 20y + 5 = 0$     **110.** $x^2 + 105 = 6x - 40y + 4y^2$

**SKILLS OBJECTIVES**

- Graph polynomial functions using transformations.
- Identify real zeros of a polynomial function and their multiplicities.
- Determine the end behavior of a polynomial function.
- Sketch graphs of polynomial functions using intercepts and end behavior.

**CONCEPTUAL OBJECTIVES**

- Understand that real zeros of polynomial functions correspond to $x$-intercepts.
- Understand the intermediate value theorem and how it assists in graphing polynomial functions.
- Realize that end behavior is a result of the leading term dominating.

## Identifying Polynomial Functions

**DEFINITION** **Polynomial Function**

Let $n$ be a nonnegative integer and let $a_n, a_{n-1}, \ldots, a_2, a_1, a_0$ be real numbers with $a_n \neq 0$. The function

$$f(x) = a_n x^n + a_{n-1} x^{n-1} + \cdots + a_2 x^2 + a_1 x + a_0$$

is called a **polynomial function of $x$ with degree $n$**. The coefficient $a_n$ is called the leading coefficient.

**EXAMPLE 1** **Identifying Polynomials and Their Degree**

For each of the functions given, determine whether the function is a polynomial function. If it is a polynomial function, then state the degree of the polynomial. If it is not a polynomial function, justify your answer.

**a.** $f(x) = 3 - 2x^5$  **b.** $F(x) = \sqrt{x} + 1$  **c.** $g(x) = 2$

**d.** $h(x) = 3x^2 - 2x + 5$  **e.** $H(x) = 4x^5(2x - 3)^2$  **f.** $G(x) = 2x^4 - 5x^3 - 4x^{-2}$

**Solution:**

**a.** $f(x)$ is a polynomial function of degree 5.

**b.** $F(x)$ is not a polynomial function. The variable $x$ is raised to the power of $\frac{1}{2}$, which is not an integer.

**c.** $g(x)$ is a polynomial function of degree zero, also known as a constant function. Note that $g(x) = 2$ can also be written as $g(x) = 2x^0$ (assuming $x \neq 0$).

**d.** $h(x)$ is a polynomial function of degree 2. A polynomial function of degree 2 is called a quadratic function.

**e.** $H(x)$ is a polynomial function of degree 7. *Note:* $4x^5(4x^2 - 12x + 9) = 16x^7 - 48x^6 + 36x^5$.

**f.** $G(x)$ is not a polynomial function. $-4x^{-2}$ has an exponent that is negative.

■ **Answer:**
**a.** $f(x)$ is not a polynomial because $x$ is raised to the power of $-1$, which is a negative integer.
**b.** $g(x)$ is a polynomial of degree 13.

■ **YOUR TURN** For each of the functions given, determine whether the function is a polynomial function. If it is a polynomial function, then state the degree of the polynomial. If it is not a polynomial function, justify your answer.

**a.** $f(x) = \dfrac{1}{x} + 2$  **b.** $g(x) = 3x^8(x - 2)^2(x + 1)^3$

Whenever we have discussed a particular polynomial function of degree 0, 1, or 2, we have graphed it too. These functions are summarized in the table below.

| POLYNOMIAL | DEGREE | SPECIAL NAME | GRAPH |
|---|---|---|---|
| $f(x) = c$ | 0 | Constant function | Horizontal line |
| $f(x) = mx + b$ | 1 | Linear function | Line<br>• Slope $= m$<br>• $y$-intercept: $(0, b)$ |
| $f(x) = ax^2 + bx + c$ | 2 | Quadratic function | Parabola<br>• Opens up if $a > 0$.<br>• Opens down if $a < 0$. |

How do we graph polynomial functions that are of degree 3 or higher, and why do we care? Polynomial functions model real-world applications. One example is the percentage of fat in our bodies as we age. We can model the weight of a baby after it comes home from the hospital as a function of time. When a baby comes home from the hospital, it usually experiences weight loss. Then typically there is an increase in the percent of body fat when the baby is nursing. When infants start to walk, the increase in exercise is associated with a drop in the percentage of fat. Growth spurts in children are examples of the percent of body fat increasing and decreasing. Later in life, our metabolism slows down, and typically, the percent of body fat increases. We will model this with a polynomial function. Other examples are stock prices, the federal funds rate, and yo-yo dieting as functions of time.

Graphs of all polynomial functions are both *continuous* and *smooth*. A **continuous** graph is one you can draw completely without picking up your pencil (the graph has no jumps or holes). A **smooth** graph has no sharp corners. The following graphs illustrate what it means to be smooth (no sharp corners or cusps) and continuous (no holes or jumps).

The graph is *not continuous*.

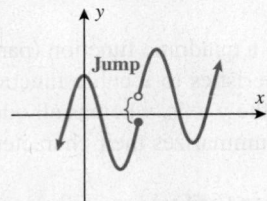

The graph is *not continuous*.

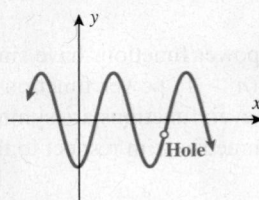

The graph is *continuous* but *not smooth*.

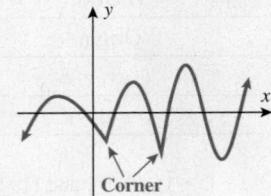

The graph is *continuous* and *smooth*.

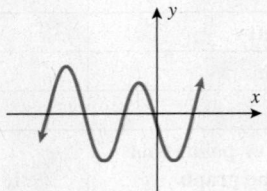

# Graphing Polynomial Functions Using Transformations of Power Functions

Recall from Chapter 1 that graphs of functions can be drawn by hand using graphing aids such as intercepts and symmetry. The graphs of polynomial functions can be graphed using these same aids. Let's start with the simplest types of polynomial functions, called

**power functions**. Power functions are monomial functions (Appendix) of the form $f(x) = x^n$, where $n$ is a positive integer.

---

**DEFINITION**    **Power Function**

Let $n$ be a positive integer and the coefficient $a \neq 0$ be a real number. The function

$$f(x) = ax^n$$

is called a **power function of degree $n$**.

---

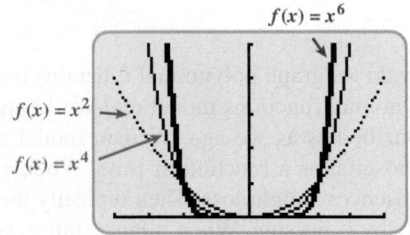

Power functions with *even* powers look similar to the square function.

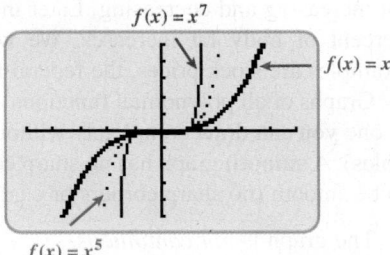

Power functions with *odd* powers (other than $n = 1$) look similar to the cube function.

All even power functions have similar characteristics to a quadratic function (parabola), and all odd ($n > 1$) power functions have similar characteristics to a cubic function. For example, all even functions are symmetric with respect to the $y$-axis, whereas all odd functions are symmetric with respect to the origin. This table summarizes their characteristics.

**CHARACTERISTICS OF POWER FUNCTIONS: $f(x) = x^n$**

|  | *n* Even | *n* Odd |
|---|---|---|
| **Symmetry** | $y$-axis | Origin |
| **Domain** | $(-\infty, \infty)$ | $(-\infty, \infty)$ |
| **Range** | $[0, \infty)$ | $(-\infty, \infty)$ |
| **Some key points that lie on the graph** | $(-1, 1)$, $(0, 0)$, and $(1, 1)$ | $(-1, -1)$, $(0, 0)$, and $(1, 1)$ |
| **Increasing** | $(0, \infty)$ | $(-\infty, \infty)$ |
| **Decreasing** | $(-\infty, 0)$ | Nowhere |

We now have the tools to graph polynomial functions that are transformations of power functions. We will use the power functions combined with our graphing techniques such as horizontal and vertical shifting and reflection (Section 1.3).

**EXAMPLE 2    Graphing Transformations of Power Functions**

Graph the function $f(x) = (x - 1)^3$.

**Solution:**

STEP 1   Start with the graph of $y = x^3$.

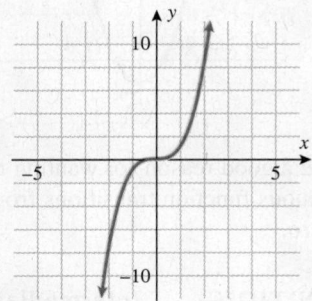

STEP 2   Shift $y = x^3$ to the right one unit to yield the graph of $f(x) = (x - 1)^3$.

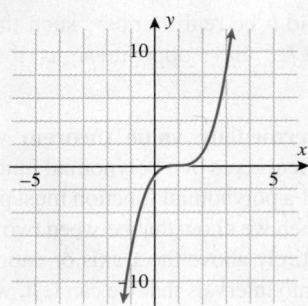

■ **YOUR TURN**   Graph the function $f(x) = 1 - x^4$.

■ **Answer:** $f(x) = 1 - x^4$

# Real Zeros of a Polynomial Function

How do we graph general polynomial functions of degree greater than or equal to 3 if they cannot be written as transformations of power functions? We start by identifying the $x$-intercepts of the polynomial function. Recall that we determine the $x$-intercepts by setting the function equal to *zero* and solving for $x$. Therefore, an alternative name for an $x$-intercept of a function is a *zero* of the function. In our experience, to set a quadratic function equal to zero, the first step is to factor the quadratic expression into linear factors and then set each factor equal to zero. Therefore, there are four equivalent relationships that are summarized in the following box.

**REAL ZEROS OF POLYNOMIAL FUNCTIONS**

If $f(x)$ is a polynomial function and $a$ is a *real* number, then the following statements are equivalent.

- $x = a$ is a **solution**, or **root**, of the equation $f(x) = 0$.
- $(a, 0)$ is an **x-intercept** of the graph of $f(x)$.
- $x = a$ is a **zero** of the function $f(x)$.
- $(x - a)$ is a **factor** of $f(x)$.

*Study Tip*

Real zeros correspond to $x$-intercepts.

Let's use a simple polynomial function to illustrate these four relationships. We'll focus on the quadratic function $f(x) = x^2 - 1$. The graph of this function is a parabola that opens up and has as its vertex the point $(0, -1)$.

| SOLUTION | X-INTERCEPT | | ZERO | FACTOR |
|---|---|---|---|---|
| $x = -1$ and $x = 1$ are solutions, or roots, of the equation $x^2 - 1 = 0$. | The $x$-intercepts correspond to the points $(-1, 0)$ and $(1, 0)$. | | $f(-1) = 0$ $f(1) = 0$ | $f(x) = (x - 1)(x + 1)$ |

We have a good reason for wanting to know the $x$-intercepts, or zeros. When the value of a continuous function transitions from negative to positive and vice versa, it must pass through zero.

### *Technology Tip*

Graph $y_1 = x^3 + x^2 - 2x$.

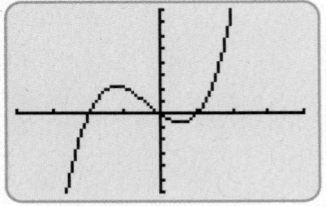

The zeros of the function $-2, 0,$ and $1$ correspond to the $x$-intercepts $(-2, 0), (0, 0),$ and $(1, 0)$.

The table supports the real zeros shown by the graph.

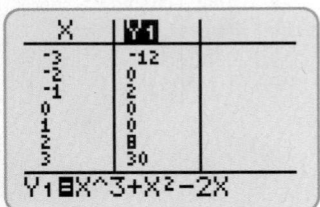

#### DEFINITION     Intermediate Value Theorem

Let $a$ and $b$ be real numbers such that $a < b$ and let $f$ be a polynomial function. If $f(a)$ and $f(b)$ have opposite signs, then there is at least one zero between $a$ and $b$.

The **intermediate value theorem** will be used later in this chapter to assist us in finding the real zeros of a polynomial function. For now, it tells us that in order to change signs, the graph of a polynomial function must pass through the $x$-axis. In other words, once we know the zeros, then we know that between two consecutive zeros the graph of a polynomial function is either entirely above the $x$-axis or entirely below the $x$-axis. This enables us to break down the $x$-axis into intervals that we can test, which will assist us in graphing polynomial functions. Keep in mind, though, that the existence of a zero does not imply that the function will change signs—as you will see in the subsection on graphing general polynomial functions.

#### EXAMPLE 3   Identifying the Real Zeros of a Polynomial Function

Find the zeros of the polynomial function $f(x) = x^3 + x^2 - 2x$.

**Solution:**

Set the function equal to zero. $\qquad\qquad\qquad x^3 + x^2 - 2x = 0$

Factor out an $x$ common to all three terms. $\qquad x(x^2 + x - 2) = 0$

Factor the quadratic expression inside the parentheses. $\qquad\qquad\qquad x(x + 2)(x - 1) = 0$

Apply the zero product property. $\qquad x = 0$ or $(x + 2) = 0$ or $(x - 1) = 0$

Solve. $\qquad\qquad\qquad\qquad\qquad x = -2, x = 0,$ and $x = 1$

The zeros are $\boxed{-2, 0, \text{ and } 1}$.

■ **Answer:** The zeros are 0, 3, and 4.

■ **YOUR TURN** Find the zeros of the polynomial function $f(x) = x^3 - 7x^2 + 12x$.

When factoring a quadratic equation, if the factor is raised to a power greater than 1, the corresponding root, or zero, is repeated. For example, the quadratic equation $x^2 - 2x + 1 = 0$ when factored is written as $(x - 1)^2 = 0$. The solution, or root, in this case is $x = 1$, and we say that it is a **repeated** root. Similarly, when determining zeros of higher order polynomial functions, if a factor is repeated, we say that the zero is a repeated, or **multiple**, zero of the function. The number of times that a zero repeats is called its *multiplicity*.

---

**DEFINITION**    **Multiplicity of a Zero**

If $(x - a)^n$ is a factor of a polynomial $f$, then $a$ is called a **zero of multiplicity $n$** of $f$.

---

**EXAMPLE 4    Finding the Multiplicities of Zeros of a Polynomial Function**

Find the zeros, and state their multiplicities, of the polynomial function
$g(x) = (x - 1)^2\left(x + \frac{3}{5}\right)^7(x + 5)$.

**Solution:**

> 1 is a zero of multiplicity 2.
>
> $-\frac{3}{5}$ is a zero of multiplicity 7.
>
> $-5$ is a zero of multiplicity 1.

*Note:* Adding the multiplicities yields the degree of the polynomial. The polynomial $g(x)$ is of degree 10, since $2 + 7 + 1 = 10$.

................................................................

■ **YOUR TURN**    For the polynomial $h(x)$, determine the zeros and state their multiplicities.

$$h(x) = x^2(x - 2)^3\left(x + \frac{1}{2}\right)^5$$

■ **Answer:**
  0 is a zero of multiplicity 2.
  2 is a zero of multiplicity 3.
  $-\frac{1}{2}$ is a zero of multiplicity 5.

**EXAMPLE 5    Finding a Polynomial from Its Zeros**

Find a polynomial of degree 7 whose zeros are

$\qquad -2$ (multiplicity 2)$\qquad$ 0 (multiplicity 4)$\qquad$ 1 (multiplicity 1)

**Solution:**

If $x = a$ is a zero, then $(x - a)$ is a factor.$\qquad f(x) = (x + 2)^2(x - 0)^4(x - 1)^1$

Simplify.$\qquad\qquad\qquad\qquad\qquad\qquad\quad = x^4(x + 2)^2(x - 1)$

Square the binomial.$\qquad\qquad\qquad\qquad = x^4(x^2 + 4x + 4)(x - 1)$

Multiply the two polynomials.$\qquad\qquad = x^4\left(x^3 + 3x^2 - 4\right)$

Distribute $x^4$.$\qquad\qquad\qquad\qquad\qquad = \boxed{x^7 + 3x^6 - 4x^4}$

# Graphing General Polynomial Functions

Let's develop a strategy for sketching an approximate graph of any polynomial function. First, we determine the $x$- and $y$-intercepts. Then we use the $x$-intercepts, or zeros, to divide the domain into intervals where the value of the polynomial is positive or negative so that we can find points in those intervals to assist in sketching a smooth and continuous graph. *Note:* It is not always possible to find $x$-intercepts. Some even degree polynomial functions have no $x$-intercepts on their graph.

**Study Tip**

It is not always possible to find $x$-intercepts. Sometimes there are no $x$-intercepts (for some even degree polynomial functions).

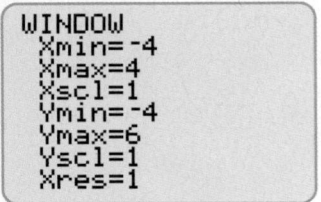
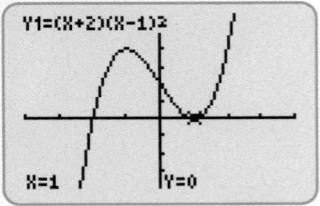
### EXAMPLE 6  Using a Strategy for Sketching the Graph of a Polynomial Function

Sketch the graph of $f(x) = (x + 2)(x - 1)^2$.

**Solution:**

STEP 1  Find the $y$-intercept.         $f(0) = (2)(-1)^2 = 2$
(Let $x = 0$.)               $(0, 2)$ is the $y$-intercept

STEP 2  Find any $x$-intercepts.       $f(x) = (x + 2)(x - 1)^2 = 0$
(Set $f(x) = 0$.)           $x = -2$   or   $x = 1$
                            $(-2, 0)$ and $(1, 0)$ are the $x$-intercepts

STEP 3  Plot the intercepts.

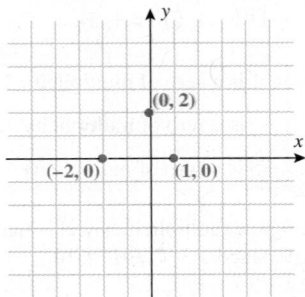

STEP 4  Divide the $x$-axis into intervals:      $(-\infty, -2), (-2, 1),$ and $(1, \infty)$

STEP 5  Select a number in each interval and test each interval. The function $f(x)$ either *crosses* the $x$-axis at an $x$-intercept or *touches* the $x$-axis at an $x$-intercept. Therefore, we need to check each of these intervals to determine whether the function is positive (above the $x$-axis) or negative (below the $x$-axis). We do so by selecting numbers in the intervals and determining the value of the function at the corresponding points.

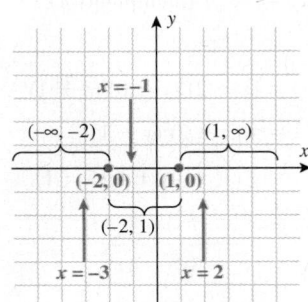

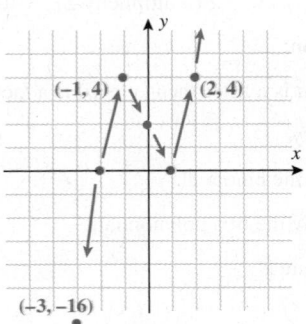

| Interval | $(-\infty, -2)$ | $(-2, 1)$ | $(1, \infty)$ |
|---|---|---|---|
| **Number Selected in Interval** | $-3$ | $-1$ | $2$ |
| **Value of Function** | $f(-3) = -16$ | $f(-1) = 4$ | $f(2) = 4$ |
| **Point on Graph** | $(-3, -16)$ | $(-1, 4)$ | $(2, 4)$ |
| **Interval Relation to $x$-Axis** | Below $x$-axis | Above $x$-axis | Above $x$-axis |

From the table, we find three additional points on the graph: $(-3, -16)$, $(-1, 4)$, and $(2, 4)$. The point $(-2, 0)$ is an intercept where the function *crosses* the $x$-axis, because it is below the $x$-axis to the left of $-2$ and above the $x$-axis to the right of $-2$. The point $(1, 0)$ is an intercept where the function *touches* the $x$-axis, because it is above the $x$-axis on both sides of $x = 1$. Connecting these points with a smooth curve yields the graph.

**STEP 6** Sketch a plot of the function.

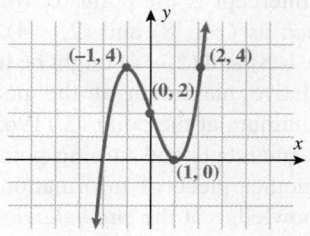

■ **YOUR TURN** Sketch the graph of $f(x) = x^2(x + 3)^2$.

■ **Answer:**

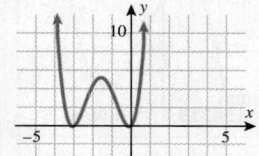

In Example 6, we found that the function crosses the $x$-axis at the point $(-2, 0)$. Note that $-2$ is a zero of multiplicity 1. We also found that the function touches the $x$-axis at the point $(1, 0)$. Note that 1 is a zero of multiplicity 2. In general, zeros with even multiplicity correspond to intercepts where the function touches the $x$-axis, and zeros with odd multiplicity correspond to intercepts where the function crosses the $x$-axis.

## MULTIPLICITY OF A ZERO AND RELATION TO THE GRAPH OF A POLYNOMIAL FUNCTION

If $a$ is a zero of $f(x)$, then

| MULTIPLICITY OF $a$ | $f(x)$ ON EITHER SIDE OF $x = a$ | GRAPH OF FUNCTION AT THE INTERCEPT |
|---|---|---|
| Even | Does not change sign | Touches the $x$-axis (turns around) at point $(a, 0)$ |
| Odd | Changes sign | Crosses the $x$-axis at point $(a, 0)$ |

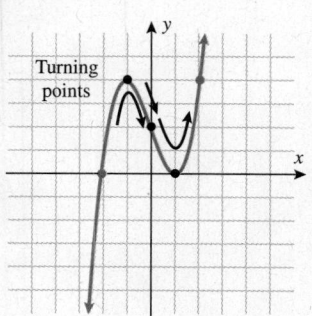

Also in Example 6, we know that somewhere in the interval $(-2, 1)$ the function must reach a relative or local maximum and then turn back toward the $x$-axis, because both points $(-2, 0)$ and $(1, 0)$ correspond to $x$-intercepts. When we sketch the graph, it "appears" that the point $(-1, 4)$ is a *turning point*. The point $(1, 0)$ also corresponds to a turning point. In general, if $f$ is a polynomial of degree $n$, then the graph of $f$ has at most $n - 1$ turning points.

The point $(-1, 4)$, which we call a turning point, is also a relative or local "high point" on the graph in the vicinity of the point $(-1, 4)$. Also note that the point $(1, 0)$, which we call a turning point, is a relative or local "low point" on the graph in the vicinity of the point $(1, 0)$. We call a "high point" on a graph a **local (relative) maximum** and a "low point" on a graph a **local (relative) minimum**. For quadratic functions we can find the maximum or minimum point by finding the vertex. However, for higher degree polynomial functions, we rely on

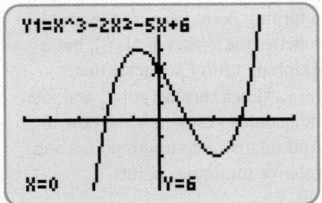
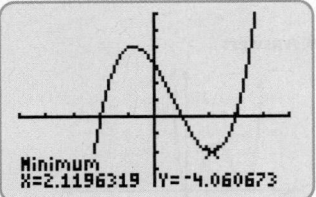
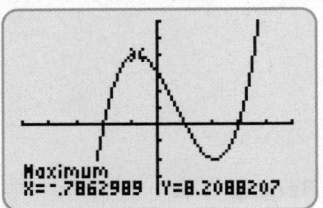
graphing utilities to assist us in locating such points. Later in calculus, techniques will be developed for finding such points exactly. For now, we use the [zoom] and [trace] features to locate such points on a graph, and we can use the [table] feature of a graphing utility to approximate relative minima or maxima.

Let us take the polynomial $f(x) = x^3 - 2x^2 - 5x + 6$. Using methods discussed thus far we can find that the $x$-intercepts of its graph are $(-2, 0)$, $(1, 0)$, and $(3, 0)$ and the $y$-intercept is the point $(0, 6)$. We can also find additional points that lie on the graph such as $(-1, 8)$ and $(2, -4)$. Plotting these points, we might "think" that the points $(-1, 8)$ and $(2, -4)$ might be turning points, but a graphing utility reveals an approximate relative maximum at the point $(-0.7863, 8.2088207)$ and an approximate relative minimum at the point $(2.1196331, -4.060673)$.

Intercepts and turning points assist us in sketching graphs of polynomial functions. Another piece of information that will assist us in graphing polynomial functions is knowledge of the *end behavior*. All polynomials eventually rise or fall without bound as $x$ gets large in both the positive $(x \to \infty)$ and negative $(x \to -\infty)$ directions. The highest degree monomial within the polynomial dominates the *end behavior*. In other words, the highest power term is eventually going to overwhelm the other terms as $x$ grows without bound.

### END BEHAVIOR

As $x$ gets large in the positive $(x \to \infty)$ and negative $(x \to -\infty)$ directions, the graph of the polynomial

$$f(x) = a_n x^n + a_{n-1} x^{n-1} + \cdots + a_2 x^2 + a_1 x + a_0$$

has the same behavior as the power function

$$y = a_n x^n$$

Power functions behave much like a quadratic function (parabola) for even-degree polynomial functions and much like a cubic function for odd-degree polynomial functions. There are four possibilities because the leading coefficient can be positive or negative with either an odd or even power.

Let $y = a_n x^n$; then

| $n$ | Even | Even | Odd | Odd |
|---|---|---|---|---|
| $a_n$ | Positive | Negative | Negative | Positive |
| $x \to -\infty$ (Left) | The graph of the function *rises*. | The graph of the function *falls*. | The graph of the function *rises*. | The graph of the function *falls*. |
| $x \to \infty$ (Right) | The graph of the function *rises*. | The graph of the function *falls*. | The graph of the function *falls*. | The graph of the function *rises*. |
| Graph | $a_n > 0$ | $a_n < 0$ | $a_n < 0$ | $a_n > 0$ |

**EXAMPLE 7    Graphing a Polynomial Function**

Sketch a graph of the polynomial function $f(x) = 2x^4 - 8x^2$.

**Solution:**

The graph of $f(x) = (x + 2)(x - 1)^2$ is shown.

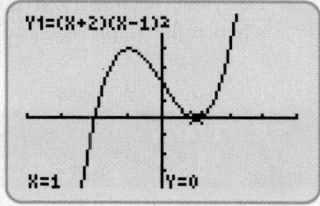

**STEP 1**   Determine the $y$-intercept: $(x = 0)$.          $f(0) = 0$

The $y$-intercept corresponds to the point $(0, 0)$.

**STEP 2**   Find the zeros of the polynomial.          $f(x) = 2x^4 - 8x^2$

Factor out the common $2x^2$.          $= 2x^2(x^2 - 4)$

Factor the quadratic binomial.          $= 2x^2(x - 2)(x + 2)$

Set $f(x) = 0$.          $= 2x^2(x - 2)(x + 2) = 0$

**0 is a zero of multiplicity 2.** The graph will *touch* the $x$-axis.

**2 is a zero of multiplicity 1.** The graph will *cross* the $x$-axis.

**−2 is a zero of multiplicity 1.** The graph will *cross* the $x$-axis.

**STEP 3**   Determine the end behavior.          $f(x) = 2x^4 - 8x^2$ behaves like $y = 2x^4$.

$y = 2x^4$ is of even degree, and the leading coefficient is positive, so the graph rises without bound as $x$ gets large in both the positive and negative directions.

**STEP 4**   Sketch the intercepts and end behavior.

*Note:* The graph crosses the $x$-axis at the point $x = -2$ and touches the $x$-axis at the point $x = 1$. A table of values supports the graph.

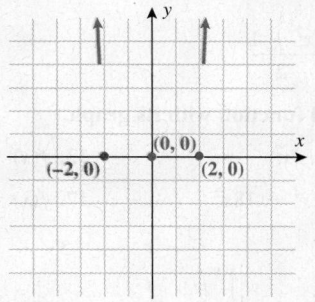

| X | Y1 |
|---|---|
| -3 | -16 |
| -2 | 0 |
| -1 | 4 |
| 0 | 2 |
| 1 | 0 |
| 2 | 4 |
| 3 | 20 |

Y1=(X+2)(X−1)²

**STEP 5**   Find additional points.

| $x$ | $-1$ | $-\frac{1}{2}$ | $\frac{1}{2}$ | $1$ |
|---|---|---|---|---|
| $f(x)$ | $-6$ | $-\frac{15}{8}$ | $-\frac{15}{8}$ | $-6$ |

**STEP 6**   Sketch the graph.

■ estimate additional points

■ connect with a smooth curve

Note the symmetry about the $y$-axis. This function is an even function: $f(-x) = f(x)$.

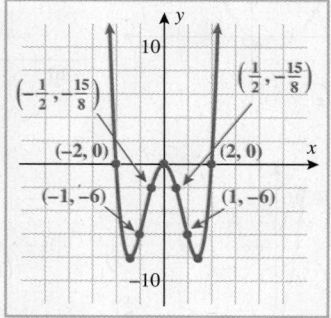

It is important to note that the absolute minimum occurs when $x = \pm\sqrt{2} \approx \pm 1.14$, but at this time can only be illustrated using a graphing utility.

■ **Answer:**

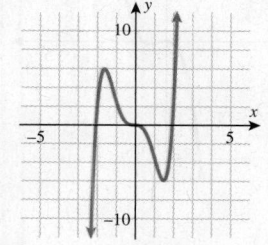

■ **YOUR TURN**   Sketch a graph of the polynomial function $f(x) = x^5 - 4x^3$.

## SECTION 2.2 SUMMARY

In general, polynomials can be graphed in one of two ways:

- Use graph-shifting techniques with power functions.
- General polynomial function.
  1. Identify intercepts.
  2. Determine each real zero and its multiplicity, and ascertain whether the graph crosses or touches the $x$-axis there.

3. $x$-intercepts (real zeros) divide the $x$-axis into intervals. Test points in the intervals to determine whether the graph is above or below the $x$-axis.
4. Determine the end behavior by investigating the end behavior of the highest degree monomial.
5. Sketch the graph with a smooth curve.

## SECTION 2.2 EXERCISES

### ▪ SKILLS

In Exercises 1–10, determine which functions are polynomials, and for those that are, state their degree.

**1.** $g(x) = (x + 2)^3 \left(x - \frac{3}{5}\right)^2$   **2.** $g(x) = \left(x - \frac{1}{4}\right)^4 \left(x + \sqrt{7}\right)^2$   **3.** $g(x) = x^5(x + 2)(x - 6.4)$   **4.** $g(x) = x^4(x - 1)^2(x + 2.5)^3$

**5.** $h(x) = \sqrt{x} + 1$            **6.** $h(x) = (x - 1)^{1/2} + 5x$      **7.** $F(x) = x^{1/3} + 7x^2 - 2$     **8.** $F(x) = 3x^2 + 7x - \dfrac{2}{3x}$

**9.** $G(x) = \dfrac{x + 1}{x^2}$       **10.** $H(x) = \dfrac{x^2 + 1}{2}$

In Exercises 11–18, match the polynomial function with its graph.

**11.** $f(x) = -3x + 1$        **12.** $f(x) = -3x^2 - x$       **13.** $f(x) = x^2 + x$         **14.** $f(x) = -2x^3 + 4x^2 - 6x$

**15.** $f(x) = x^3 - x^2$        **16.** $f(x) = 2x^4 - 18x^2$      **17.** $f(x) = -x^4 + 5x^3$      **18.** $f(x) = x^5 - 5x^3 + 4x$

**a.**

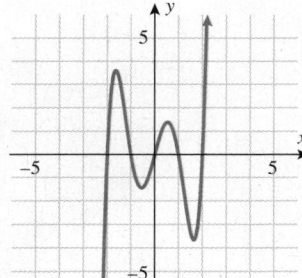

**b.**

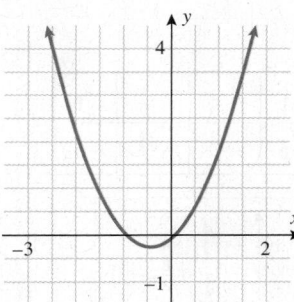

**c.**

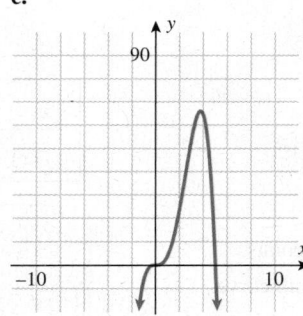

**d.**

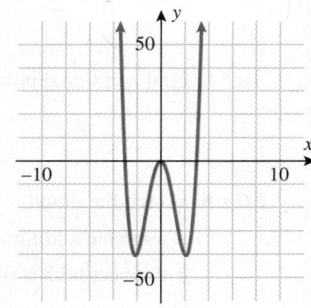

**e.**

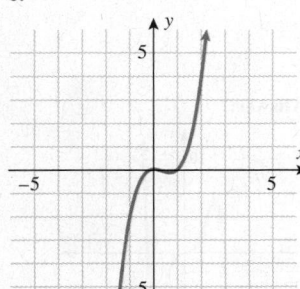

**f.**

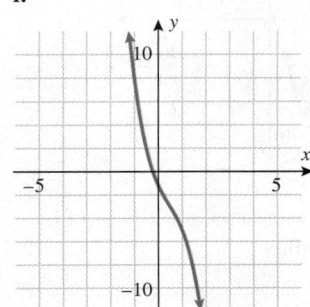

**g.**

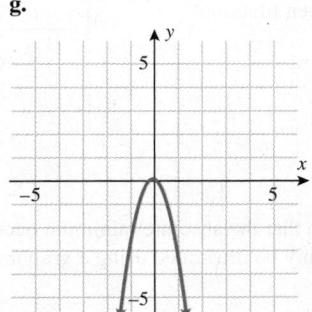

**h.**

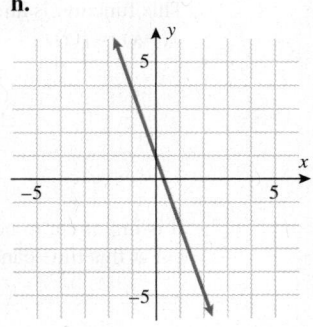

In Exercises 19–24, graph each function by transforming a power function $y = x^n$.

**19.** $f(x) = (x - 2)^4$

**20.** $f(x) = (x + 2)^5$

**21.** $f(x) = x^5 + 3$

**22.** $f(x) = -x^4 - 3$

**23.** $f(x) = 3 - (x + 1)^4$

**24.** $f(x) = (x - 3)^5 - 2$

In Exercises 25–36, find all the real zeros (and state their multiplicities) of each polynomial function.

**25.** $f(x) = 2(x - 3)(x + 4)^3$

**26.** $f(x) = -3(x + 2)^3(x - 1)^2$

**27.** $f(x) = 4x^2(x - 7)^2(x + 4)$

**28.** $f(x) = 5x^3(x + 1)^4(x - 6)$

**29.** $f(x) = 4x^2(x - 1)^2(x^2 + 4)$

**30.** $f(x) = 4x^2(x^2 - 1)(x^2 + 9)$

**31.** $f(x) = 8x^3 + 6x^2 - 27x$

**32.** $f(x) = 2x^4 + 5x^3 - 3x^2$

**33.** $f(x) = -2.7x^3 - 8.1x^2$

**34.** $f(x) = 1.2x^6 - 4.6x^4$

**35.** $f(x) = \frac{1}{3}x^6 + \frac{2}{5}x^4$

**36.** $f(x) = \frac{2}{7}x^5 - \frac{3}{4}x^4 + \frac{1}{2}x^3$ ,

In Exercises 37–50, find a polynomial (there are many) of minimum degree that has the given zeros.

**37.** $-3, 0, 1, 2$

**38.** $-2, 0, 2$

**39.** $-5, -3, 0, 2, 6$

**40.** $0, 1, 3, 5, 10$

**41.** $-\frac{1}{2}, \frac{2}{3}, \frac{3}{4}$

**42.** $-\frac{3}{4}, -\frac{1}{3}, 0, \frac{1}{2}$

**43.** $1 - \sqrt{2}, 1 + \sqrt{2}$

**44.** $1 - \sqrt{3}, 1 + \sqrt{3}$

**45.** $-2$ (multiplicity 3), $0$ (multiplicity 2)

**46.** $-4$ (multiplicity 2), $5$ (multiplicity 3)

**47.** $-3$ (multiplicity 2), $7$ (multiplicity 5)

**48.** $0$ (multiplicity 1), $10$ (multiplicity 3)

**49.** $-\sqrt{3}$ (multiplicity 2), $-1$ (multiplicity 1), $0$ (multiplicity 2), $\sqrt{3}$ (multiplicity 2)

**50.** $-\sqrt{5}$ (multiplicity 2), $0$ (multiplicity 1), $1$ (multiplicity 2), $\sqrt{5}$ (multiplicity 2)

In Exercises 51–68, for each polynomial function given: (a) list each real zero and its multiplicity; (b) determine whether the graph touches or crosses at each $x$-intercept; (c) find the $y$-intercept and a few points on the graph; (d) determine the end behavior; and (e) sketch the graph.

**51.** $f(x) = (x - 2)^3$

**52.** $f(x) = -(x + 3)^3$

**53.** $f(x) = x^3 - 9x$

**54.** $f(x) = -x^3 + 4x^2$

**55.** $f(x) = -x^3 + x^2 + 2x$

**56.** $f(x) = x^3 - 6x^2 + 9x$

**57.** $f(x) = -x^4 - 3x^3$

**58.** $f(x) = x^5 - x^3$

**59.** $f(x) = 12x^6 - 36x^5 - 48x^4$

**60.** $f(x) = 7x^5 - 14x^4 - 21x^3$

**61.** $f(x) = 2x^5 - 6x^4 - 8x^3$

**62.** $f(x) = -5x^4 + 10x^3 - 5x^2$

**63.** $f(x) = x^3 - x^2 - 4x + 4$

**64.** $f(x) = x^3 - x^2 - x + 1$

**65.** $f(x) = -(x + 2)^2(x - 1)^2$

**66.** $f(x) = (x - 2)^3(x + 1)^3$

**67.** $f(x) = x^2(x - 2)^3(x + 3)^2$

**68.** $f(x) = -x^3(x - 4)^2(x + 2)^2$

In Exercises 69–72, for each graph given: (a) list each real zero and its smallest possible multiplicity; (b) determine whether the degree of the polynomial is even or odd; (c) determine whether the leading coefficient of the polynomial is positive or negative; (d) find the $y$-intercept; and (e) write an equation for the polynomial function (assume the least degree possible).

**69.**

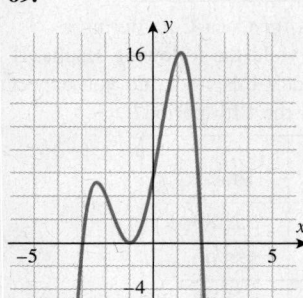

**70.**

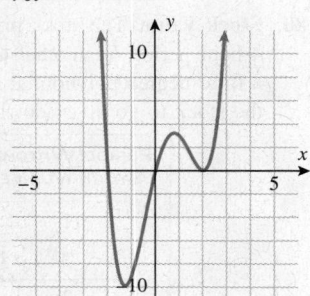

**71.**

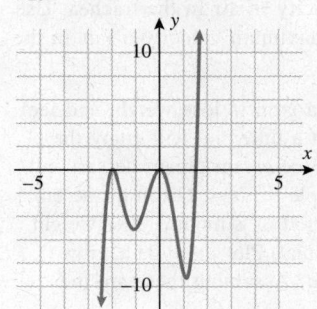

**72.**

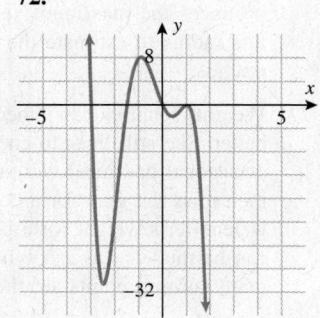

## ▪ APPLICATIONS

**For Exercises 73 and 74, refer to the following:**

The relationship between a company's total revenue $R$ (in millions of dollars) is related to its advertising costs $x$ (in thousands of dollars). The relationship between revenue $R$ and advertising costs $x$ is illustrated in the graph.

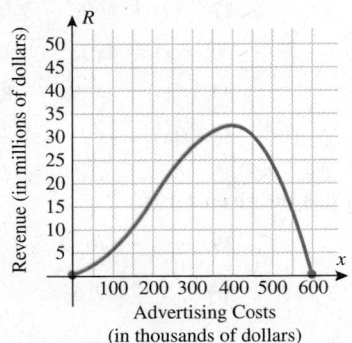

**73. Business.** Analyze the graph of the revenue function.

    **a.** Determine the intervals on which revenue is increasing and decreasing.

    **b.** Identify the zeros of the function. Interpret the meaning of zeros for this function.

**74. Business.** Use the graph to identify the maximum revenue for the company and the corresponding advertising costs that produce maximum revenue.

**For Exercises 75 and 76, refer to the following:**

During a cough, the velocity $v$ (in meters per second) of air in the trachea may be modeled by the function

$$v(r) = -120r^3 + 80r^2$$

where $r$ is the radius of the trachea (in centimeters) during the cough.

**75. Health/Medicine.** Graph the velocity function and estimate the intervals on which the velocity of air in the trachea is increasing and decreasing.

**76. Health/Medicine.** Estimate the radius of the trachea that produces the maximum velocity of air in the trachea. Use this radius to estimate the maximum velocity of air in the trachea.

**77. Weight.** Jennifer has joined a gym to lose weight and feel better. She still likes to cheat a little and will enjoy the occasional bad meal with an ice cream dream dessert and then miss the gym for a couple of days. Given in the table is Jennifer's weight for a period of 8 months. Her weight can be modeled as a polynomial. Plot these data. How many turning points are there? Assuming these are the minimum number of turning points, what is the lowest degree polynomial that can represent Jennifer's weight?

| MONTH | WEIGHT |
|-------|--------|
| 1 | 169 |
| 2 | 158 |
| 3 | 150 |
| 4 | 161 |
| 5 | 154 |
| 6 | 159 |
| 7 | 148 |
| 8 | 153 |

**78. Stock Value.** A day trader checks the stock price of Coca-Cola during a 4-hour period (given below). The price of Coca-Cola stock during this 4-hour period can be modeled as a polynomial function. Plot these data. How many turning points are there? Assuming these are the minimum number of turning points, what is the lowest degree polynomial that can represent the Coca-Cola stock price?

| PERIOD WATCHING STOCK MARKET | PRICE |
|------------------------------|-------|
| 1 | $53.00 |
| 2 | $56.00 |
| 3 | $52.70 |
| 4 | $51.50 |

**79. Stock Value.** The price of Tommy Hilfiger stock during a 4-hour period is given below. If a third-degree polynomial models this stock, do you expect the stock to go up or down in the fifth period?

| PERIOD WATCHING STOCK MARKET | PRICE |
|------------------------------|-------|
| 1 | $15.10 |
| 2 | $14.76 |
| 3 | $15.50 |
| 4 | $14.85 |

**80. Stock Value.** The stock prices for Coca-Cola during a 4-hour period on another day yield the following results. If a third-degree polynomial models this stock, do you expect the stock to go up or down in the fifth period?

| PERIOD WATCHING STOCK MARKET | PRICE |
|------------------------------|-------|
| 1 | $52.80 |
| 2 | $53.00 |
| 3 | $56.00 |
| 4 | $52.70 |

For Exercises 81 and 82, the following table graph illustrates the average federal funds rate in the month of January (2000 to 2008):

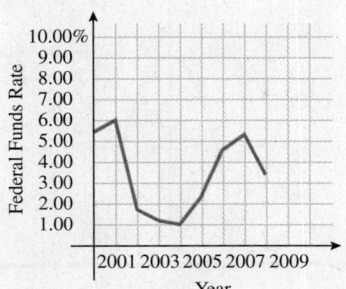

81. **Finance.** If a polynomial function is used to model the federal funds rate data shown in the graph, determine the degree of the lowest degree polynomial that can be used to model those data.

82. **Finance.** Should the leading coefficient in the polynomial found in Exercise 81 be positive or negative? Explain.

83. **Air Travel.** An airline has a daily flight Chicago–Miami. The number of passengers per flight is given in the table below. Which would be the minimum degree of a polynomial that models the number of passengers of the airline?

| DAY | PASSENGERS |
|---|---|
| Monday | 180 |
| Tuesday | 150 |
| Wednesday | 175 |
| Thursday | 160 |
| Friday | 100 |
| Saturday | 98 |
| Sunday | 120 |

84. **Air Travel.** The airline in Exercise 83 discovered that the information about the number of passengers corresponding to Monday and Sunday was mixed. On Sunday, they have 180 passengers, while on Monday, they have 120 passengers. Determine the degree of the lowest degree polynomial that can be used to model those data.

85. **Temperature.** The weather report indicates that the daily highest temperatures for next week can be described as a cubic polynomial function. The forecasting for Tuesday, Wednesday, and Thursday is 39°, 42°, and 35°, respectively. Thursday will be the coolest day of the week. What can you say about Monday's temperature $T$?

86. **Sports.** A basketball player scored more than 20 points on each of the past 9 games.

| GAME | 1 | 2 | 3 | 4 | 5 | 6 | 7 | 8 | 9 |
|---|---|---|---|---|---|---|---|---|---|
| POINTS | 25 | 27 | 30 | 28 | 25 | 24 | 26 | 27 | 25 |

a. If he scores 24 points in the next game, what is the degree of the polynomial function describing this data?

b. If he scores 26 points in the next game, what is the degree of the polynomial function describing this data?

## ■CATCH THE MISTAKE

In Exercises 87–90, explain the mistake that is made.

87. Find a fourth-degree polynomial function with zeros $-2$, $-1$, 3, 4.

**Solution:**        $f(x) = (x - 2)(x - 1)(x + 3)(x + 4)$

This is incorrect. What mistake was made?

88. Determine the end behavior of the polynomial function $f(x) = x(x - 2)^3$.

**Solution:**

This polynomial has similar end behavior to the graph of $y = x^3$.

End behavior falls to the left and rises to the right.

This is incorrect. What mistake was made?

89. Graph the polynomial function $f(x) = (x - 1)^2(x + 2)^3$.

**Solution:**

The zeros are $-2$ and 1, and therefore, the $x$-intercepts are $(-2, 0)$ and $(1, 0)$.

The $y$-intercept is $(0, 8)$.

Plotting these points and connecting with a smooth curve yield the graph on the right.

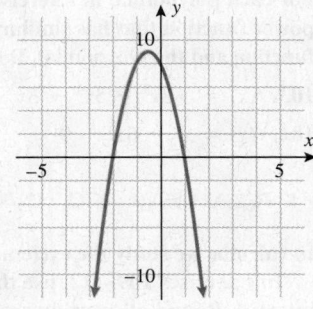

This graph is incorrect. What did we forget to do?

**90.** Graph the polynomial function $f(x) = (x + 1)^2(x - 1)^2$.

**Solution:**

The zeros are $-1$ and $1$, so the $x$-intercepts are $(-1, 0)$ and $(1, 0)$.

The $y$-intercept is $(0, 1)$.

Plotting these points and connecting with a smooth curve yield the graph on the right.

This graph is incorrect. What did we forget to do?

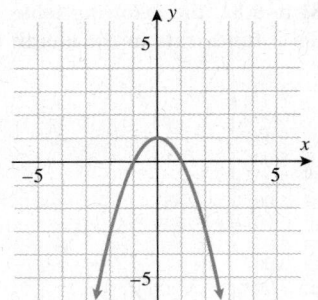

■ **CONCEPTUAL**

**In Exercises 91–94, determine whether each statement is true or false.**

**91.** The graph of a polynomial function might not have any $y$-intercepts.

**92.** The graph of a polynomial function might not have any $x$-intercepts.

**93.** The domain of all polynomial functions is $(-\infty, \infty)$.

**94.** The range of all polynomial functions is $(-\infty, \infty)$.

**95.** What is the maximum number of zeros that a polynomial of degree $n$ can have?

**96.** What is the maximum number of turning points a graph of an $n$th-degree polynomial can have?

■ **CHALLENGE**

**97.** Find a seventh-degree polynomial that has the following graph characteristics: The graph touches the $x$-axis at $x = -1$, and the graph crosses the $x$-axis at $x = 3$. Plot this polynomial function.

**98.** Find a fifth-degree polynomial that has the following graph characteristics: The graph touches the $x$-axis at $x = 0$ and crosses the $x$-axis at $x = 4$. Plot the polynomial function.

**99.** Determine the zeros of the polynomial $f(x) = x^3 + (b - a)x^2 - abx$ for the positive real numbers $a$ and $b$.

**100.** Graph the function $f(x) = x^2(x - a)^2(x - b)^2$ for the positive real numbers $a$, $b$, where $b > a$.

■ **TECHNOLOGY**

**In Exercises 101 and 102, use a graphing calculator or computer to graph each polynomial. From that graph, estimate the $x$-intercepts (if any). Set the function equal to zero, and solve for the zeros of the polynomial. Compare the zeros with the $x$-intercepts.**

**101.** $f(x) = x^4 + 2x^2 + 1$

**102.** $f(x) = 1.1x^3 - 2.4x^2 + 5.2x$

**For each polynomial in Exercises 103 and 104, determine the power function that has similar end behavior. Plot this power function and the polynomial. Do they have similar end behavior?**

**103.** $f(x) = -2x^5 - 5x^4 - 3x^3$

**104.** $f(x) = x^4 - 6x^2 + 9$

**In Exercises 105 and 106, use a graphing calculator or a computer to graph each polynomial. From the graph, estimate the $x$-intercepts and state the zeros of the function and their multiplicities.**

**105.** $f(x) = x^4 - 15.9x^3 + 1.31x^2 + 292.905x + 445.7025$

**106.** $f(x) = -x^5 + 2.2x^4 + 18.49x^3 - 29.878x^2 - 76.5x + 100.8$

**In Exercises 107 and 108, use a graphing calculator or a computer to graph each polynomial. From the graph, estimate the coordinates of the relative maximum and minimum points. Round your answers to two decimal places.**

**107.** $f(x) = 2x^4 + 5x^3 - 10x^2 - 15x + 8$

**108.** $f(x) = 2x^5 - 4x^4 - 12x^3 + 18x^2 + 16x - 7$

■ **PREVIEW TO CALCULUS**

**In calculus we study the extreme values of functions; in order to find these values we need to solve different types of equations.**

**In Exercises 109–112, use the Intermediate Value Theorem to find all the zeros of the polynomial functions in the given interval. Round all your answers to three decimal places.**

**109.** $x^3 + 3x - 5 = 0$, $[0, 2]$

**110.** $x^5 - x + 0.5 = 0$, $[0, 1]$

**111.** $x^4 - 3x^3 + 6x^2 - 7 = 0$, $[-2, 2]$

**112.** $x^3 + x^2 - 2x - 2 = 0$, $[1, 2]$

**SKILLS OBJECTIVES**

- Divide polynomials with long division.
- Divide polynomials with synthetic division.

**CONCEPTUAL OBJECTIVES**

- Extend long division of real numbers to polynomials.
- Understand *when* synthetic division can be used.

## Long Division of Polynomials

Let's start with an example whose answer we already know. We know that a quadratic expression can be factored into the product of two linear factors: $x^2 + 4x - 5 = (x + 5)(x - 1)$. Therefore, if we divide both sides of the equation by $(x - 1)$, we get

$$\frac{x^2 + 4x - 5}{x - 1} = x + 5$$

We can state this by saying $x^2 + 4x - 5$ divided by $x - 1$ is equal to $x + 5$. Confirm this statement by long division:

$$x - 1 \overline{)x^2 + 4x - 5}$$

Note that although this is standard division notation, the **dividend**, $x^2 + 4x - 5$, and the **divisor**, $x - 1$, are both polynomials that consist of multiple terms. The *leading* terms of each algebraic expression will guide us.

**Technology Tip**

Using the graphs of the two functions, a graphing utility can be used to confirm that $(x^2 - 5x + 6)(2x + 1) = 2x^3 - 9x^2 + 7x + 6$.

| **WORDS** | **MATH** |
|---|---|
| Q: $x$ times what quantity gives $x^2$? <br> A: $x$ | $\boxed{x}$ <br> $\boxed{x} - 1 \overline{)\boxed{x^2} + 4x - 5}$ |
| Multiply $x(x - 1) = x^2 - x.$ | $x$ <br> $x - 1 \overline{)x^2 + 4x - 5}$ <br> $x^2 - \ \ x$ |
| Subtract $(x^2 - x)$ from $x^2 + 4x - 5$. <br> *Note:* $-(x^2 - x) = -x^2 + x$. <br> Bring down the $-5$. | $x$ <br> $x - 1 \overline{)x^2 + 4x - 5}$ <br> $\underline{-x^2 + \ \ x}$ <br> $\qquad 5x - 5$ |
| Q: $x$ times what quantity is $5x$? <br> A: 5 <br> Multiply $5(x - 1) = 5x - 5$. | $x + \boxed{5}$ <br> $\boxed{x} - 1 \overline{)x^2 + 4x - 5}$ <br> $\underline{-x^2 + \ \ x}$ <br> $\qquad \boxed{5x} - 5$ |
| | $x + 5$ <br> $x - 1 \overline{)x^2 + 4x - 5}$ <br> $\underline{-x^2 + \ \ x}$ <br> $\qquad 5x - 5$ |
| Subtract $(5x - 5)$. <br> *Note:* $-(5x - 5) = -5x + 5$. | $\underline{-5x + 5}$ <br> $\qquad \qquad 0$ |

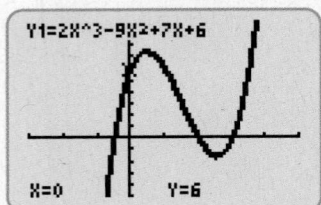

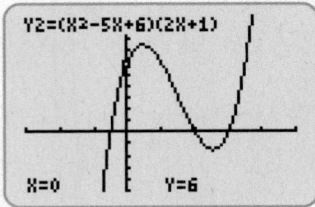

Notice that the graphs are the same.

The **quotient** is $x + 5$, and as expected, the **remainder** is 0. By long division we have shown that

$$\frac{x^2 + 4x - 5}{x - 1} = x + 5$$

*Check:* Multiplying the equation by $x - 1$ yields $x^2 + 4x - 5 = (x + 5)(x - 1)$, which we knew to be true.

▶ **EXAMPLE 1    Dividing Polynomials Using Long Division; Zero Remainder**

Divide $2x^3 - 9x^2 + 7x + 6$ by $2x + 1$.

**Solution:**

$$
\require{enclose}
\begin{array}{r}
x^2 - 5x + 6 \phantom{000} \\
2x + 1 \enclose{longdiv}{2x^3 - 9x^2 + 7x + 6} \\
\end{array}
$$

Multiply: $x^2(2x + 1)$.

$\qquad\qquad\qquad -(2x^3 + x^2)$

Subtract: Bring down the $7x$.

$\qquad\qquad\qquad -10x^2 + 7x$

Multiply: $-5x(2x + 1)$.

$\qquad\qquad\qquad -(-10x^2 - 5x)$

Subtract: Bring down the 6.

$\qquad\qquad\qquad\qquad\quad 12x + 6$

Multiply: $6(2x + 1)$.

$\qquad\qquad\qquad\qquad\quad -(12x + 6)$

Subtract.

$\qquad\qquad\qquad\qquad\qquad\quad 0$

Quotient:

$\boxed{x^2 - 5x + 6}$

Check: $(2x + 1)(x^2 - 5x + 6) = 2x^3 - 9x^2 + 7x + 6$.

*Note:* The divisor cannot be equal to zero, $2x + 1 \neq 0$, so we say $x \neq -\frac{1}{2}$.

■ **Answer:** $x^2 + 2x - 3$, remainder 0.

■ **YOUR TURN**  Divide $4x^3 + 13x^2 - 2x - 15$ by $4x + 5$.

Why are we interested in dividing polynomials? Because it helps us find zeros of polynomials. In Example 1, using long division, we found that

$$2x^3 - 9x^2 + 7x + 6 = (2x + 1)(x^2 - 5x + 6)$$

Factoring the quadratic expression enables us to write the cubic polynomial as a product of three linear factors:

$$2x^3 - 9x^2 + 7x + 6 = (2x + 1)(x^2 - 5x + 6) = (2x + 1)(x - 3)(x - 2)$$

Set the value of the polynomial equal to zero, $(2x + 1)(x - 3)(x - 2) = 0$, and solve for $x$. The zeros of the polynomial are $-\frac{1}{2}$, 2, and 3. In Example 1 and in the Your Turn, the remainder was 0. Sometimes there is a nonzero remainder (Example 2).

**EXAMPLE 2**   **Dividing Polynomials Using Long Division; Nonzero Remainder**

Divide $6x^2 - x - 2$ by $x + 1$.

**Solution:**

$$
\begin{array}{r}
6x - 7 \\
x + 1 \overline{)6x^2 - x - 2} \\
-(6x^2 + 6x) \\
\hline
-7x - 2 \\
-(-7x - 7) \\
\hline
+ 5
\end{array}
$$

Multiply $6x(x + 1)$.

Subtract and bring down $-2$.

Multiply $-7(x + 1)$.

Subtract and identify the remainder.

$$
\underbrace{\dfrac{6x^2 - x - 2}{x + 1}}_{\text{Dividend} \atop \text{Divisor}} = \underbrace{6x - 7}_{\text{Quotient}} + \underbrace{\dfrac{5}{x + 1}}_{\text{Remainder} \atop \text{Divisor}} \qquad \boxed{x \neq -1}
$$

*Check:* Multiply equation by $x + 1$.

$$6x^2 - x - 2 = (6x - 7)(x + 1) + \frac{5}{(x + 1)} \cdot (x + 1)$$

$$= 6x^2 - x - 7 + 5$$

$$= 6x^2 - x - 2 \checkmark$$

▪ **YOUR TURN**   Divide $2x^3 + x^2 - 4x - 3$ by $x - 1$.

▪ **Answer:** $2x^2 + 3x - 1 \ R: -4$ or
$$2x^2 + 3x - 1 - \frac{4}{x - 1}$$

In general, when a polynomial is divided by another polynomial, we express the result in the following form:

$$\frac{P(x)}{d(x)} = Q(x) + \frac{r(x)}{d(x)}$$

where $P(x)$ is the **dividend**, $d(x) \neq 0$ is the **divisor**, $Q(x)$ is the **quotient**, and $r(x)$ is the **remainder**. Multiplying this equation by the divisor $d(x)$ leads us to the division algorithm.

**THE DIVISION ALGORITHM**

If $P(x)$ and $d(x)$ are polynomials with $d(x) \neq 0$, and if the degree of $P(x)$ is greater than or equal to the degree of $d(x)$, then unique polynomials $Q(x)$ and $r(x)$ exist such that

$$P(x) = d(x) \cdot Q(x) + r(x)$$

If the remainder $r(x) = 0$, then we say that $d(x)$ divides $P(x)$ and that $d(x)$ and $Q(x)$ are factors of $P(x)$.

**EXAMPLE 3** **Long Division of Polynomials with "Missing" Terms**

Divide $3x^4 + 2x^3 + x^2 + 4$ by $x^2 + 1$.

**Solution:**

Insert $0x$ as a placeholder in both the divisor and the dividend.

Multiply $3x^2(x^2 + 0x + 1)$.

Subtract and bring down $0x$.

Multiply $2x(x^2 + 0x + 1)$.

Subtract and bring down 4.

Multiply $-2(x^2 - 2x + 1)$.

Subtract and get remainder $-2x + 6$.

$$
\begin{array}{r}
3x^2 + 2x - 2 \\
x^2 + 0x + 1 \overline{\smash{)}\ 3x^4 + 2x^3 + x^2 + 0x + 4} \\
-(3x^4 + 0x^3 + 3x^2) \\
\hline
2x^3 - 2x^2 + 0x \\
-(2x^3 + 0x^2 + 2x) \\
\hline
-2x^2 - 2x + 4 \\
-(-2x^2 + 0x - 2) \\
\hline
-2x + 6
\end{array}
$$

$$\boxed{\dfrac{3x^4 + 2x^3 + x^2 + 4}{x^2 + 1} = 3x^2 + 2x - 2 + \dfrac{-2x + 6}{x^2 + 1}}$$

**Answer:**
$$2x^2 + 6 + \dfrac{11x^2 + 18x + 36}{x^3 - 3x - 4}$$

**YOUR TURN** Divide $2x^5 + 3x^2 + 12$ by $x^3 - 3x - 4$.

**EXAMPLE 4** **Long Division of Polynomials Resulting in Quotients with Rational Coefficients**

Divide $8x^4 - 5x^3 + 7x - 2$ by $2x^2 + 1$.

**Solution:**

Insert $0x^2$ as a placeholder in the dividend and $0x$ as a placeholder in the divisor.

Multiply $4x^2(2x^2 + 0x + 1)$.

Subtract and bring down remaining terms.

Multiply $-\frac{5}{2}x(2x^2 + 0x + 1)$.

Subtract and bring down remaining terms.

Multiply $-2(2x^2 + 0x + 1)$.

Subtract and bring down the remainder $\frac{19}{2}x$.

$$
\begin{array}{r}
4x^2 - \frac{5}{2}x - 2 \\
2x^2 + 0x + 1 \overline{\smash{)}\ 8x^4 - 5x^3 + 0x^2 + 7x - 2} \\
-(8x^4 + 0x^3 + 4x^2) \\
\hline
-5x^3 - 4x^2 + 7x \\
-(-5x^3 + 0x^2 - \frac{5}{2}x) \\
\hline
-4x^2 + \frac{19}{2}x - 2 \\
-(-4x^2 + 0x - 2) \\
\hline
\frac{19}{2}x
\end{array}
$$

$$\dfrac{8x^4 - 5x^3 + 7x - 2}{2x^2 + 1} = 4x^2 - \dfrac{5}{2}x - 2 + \dfrac{\frac{19}{2}x}{2x^2 + 1}$$

**Answer:**
$$5x^2 - \tfrac{3}{2}x + \tfrac{5}{2} + \dfrac{\frac{7}{2}x - \frac{3}{2}}{2x^2 - 1}$$

**YOUR TURN** Divide $10x^4 - 3x^3 + 5x - 4$ by $2x^2 - 1$.

# Synthetic Division of Polynomials

In the special case when the *divisor is a linear factor* of the form $x - a$ or $x + a$, there is another, more efficient way to divide polynomials. This method is called **synthetic division**. It is called synthetic because it is a contrived shorthand way of dividing a polynomial by a linear factor. A detailed step-by-step procedure is given below for synthetic division. Let's divide $x^4 - x^3 - 2x + 2$ by $x + 1$ using synthetic division.

**Step 1:** Write the division in synthetic form.
- List the coefficients of the dividend. **Remember to use 0 for a placeholder**.
- The divisor is $x + 1$, so $x = -1$ is used.

Coefficients of Dividend

$-1$ | $1 \quad -1 \quad 0 \quad -2 \quad 2$

**Study Tip**

If $(x - a)$ is a divisor, then $a$ is the number used in synthetic division.

**Step 2:** *Bring down* the first term (**1**) in the dividend.

$-1$ | $1 \quad -1 \quad 0 \quad -2 \quad 2$

Bring down the 1

$1$

**Step 3:** *Multiply* the $-1$ by this leading coefficient (**1**), and place the product up and to the right in the second column.

$-1$ | $1 \quad -1 \quad 0 \quad -2 \quad 2$

$-1$

$1$

**Step 4:** *Add* the values in the second column.

$-1$ | $1 \quad -1 \quad 0 \quad -2 \quad 2$

$-1$ ADD

$1 \quad -2$

**Step 5:** Repeat Steps 3 and 4 until all columns are filled.

$-1$ | $1 \quad -1 \quad 0 \quad -2 \quad 2$

$-1 \quad 2\downarrow \quad -2\downarrow \quad 4\downarrow$

$1 \quad -2 \quad 2 \quad -4 \quad 6$

**Study Tip**

Synthetic division can only be used when the divisor is of the form $x - a$. Realize that $a$ may be negative, as in the divisor $x + 2$.

**Step 6:** Identify the **quotient** by assigning powers of $x$ in descending order, beginning with $x^{n-1} = x^{4-1} = x^3$. The last term is the **remainder**.

$-1$ | $1 \quad -1 \quad 0 \quad -2 \quad 2$

$-1 \quad 2 \quad -2 \quad 4$

$\underbrace{1 \quad -2 \quad 2 \quad -4}_{\text{Quotient Coefficients}} \quad \overset{\text{Remainder}}{6}$

$x^3 - 2x^2 + 2x - 4$

We know that the degree of the first term of the quotient is 3, because a fourth-degree polynomial was divided by a first-degree polynomial. Let's compare dividing $x^4 - x^3 - 2x + 2$ by $x + 1$ using both long division and synthetic division.

**Long Division**

$$x + 1 \overline{) x^4 - x^3 + 0x^2 - 2x + 2}$$

Quotient: $x^3 - 2x^2 + 2x - 4$

$$\begin{array}{r} x^4 + x^3 \\ \hline -2x^3 + 0x^2 \\ -(-2x^3 - 2x^2) \\ \hline 2x^2 - 2x \\ -(2x^2 + 2x) \\ \hline -4x + 2 \\ -(-4x - 4) \\ \hline + 6 \end{array}$$

**Synthetic Division**

$$\begin{array}{r|rrrrr} -1 & 1 & -1 & 0 & -2 & 2 \\ & & -1 & 2 & -2 & 4 \\ \hline & 1 & -2 & 2 & -4 & 6 \end{array}$$

$$x^3 - 2x^2 + 2x - 4$$

Both long division and synthetic division yield the same answer.

$$\frac{x^4 - x^3 - 2x + 2}{x + 1} = x^3 - 2x^2 + 2x - 4 + \frac{6}{x + 1}$$

 **EXAMPLE 5  Synthetic Division**

Use synthetic division to divide $3x^5 - 2x^3 + x^2 - 7$ by $x + 2$.

**Solution:**

STEP 1  Write the division in synthetic form.
- List the coefficients of the dividend. Remember to use **0** for a placeholder.
- The divisor of the original problem is $x + 2$. If we set $x + 2 = 0$, we find that $x = -2$, so $-2$ is the divisor for synthetic division.

$$\begin{array}{r|rrrrrr} -2 & 3 & 0 & -2 & 1 & 0 & -7 \end{array}$$

STEP 2  Perform the synthetic division steps.

$$\begin{array}{r|rrrrrr} -2 & 3 & 0 & -2 & 1 & 0 & -7 \\ & & -6 & 12 & -20 & 38 & -76 \\ \hline & 3 & -6 & 10 & -19 & 38 & -83 \end{array}$$

STEP 3  Identify the quotient and remainder.

$$\begin{array}{r|rrrrrr} -2 & 3 & 0 & -2 & 1 & 0 & -7 \\ & & -6 & 12 & -20 & 38 & -76 \\ \hline & 3 & -6 & 10 & -19 & 38 & \boxed{-83} \end{array}$$

$$3x^4 - 6x^3 + 10x^2 - 19x + 38$$

$$\frac{3x^5 - 2x^3 + x^2 - 7}{x + 2} = 3x^4 - 6x^3 + 10x^2 - 19x + 38 - \frac{83}{x + 2}$$

■ **Answer:** $2x^2 + 2x + 1 + \dfrac{4}{x - 1}$

■ **YOUR TURN**  Use synthetic division to divide $2x^3 - x + 3$ by $x - 1$.

## SECTION 2.3 SUMMARY

### Division of Polynomials

- Long division can always be used.
- Synthetic division is restricted to when the divisor is of the form $x - a$ or $x + a$.

### Expressing Results

- $\dfrac{\text{Dividend}}{\text{Divisor}} = \text{quotient} + \dfrac{\text{remainder}}{\text{divisor}}$
- Dividend = (quotient)(divisor) + remainder

### When Remainder Is Zero

- Dividend = (quotient)(divisor)
- Quotient and divisor are factors of the dividend.

## SECTION 2.3 EXERCISES

### ■ SKILLS

In Exercises 1–26, divide the polynomials using long division. Use exact values and express the answer in the form $Q(x) = $ ?, $r(x) = $ ?.

1. $(3x^2 - 9x - 5) \div (x - 2)$
2. $(x^2 + 4x - 3) \div (x - 1)$
3. $(3x^2 - 13x - 10) \div (x + 5)$
4. $(3x^2 - 13x - 10) \div (x + 5)$
5. $(x^2 - 4) \div (x + 4)$
6. $(x^2 - 9) \div (x - 2)$
7. $(9x^2 - 25) \div (3x - 5)$
8. $(5x^2 - 3) \div (x + 1)$
9. $(4x^2 - 9) \div (2x + 3)$
10. $(8x^3 + 27) \div (2x + 3)$
11. $(11x + 20x^2 + 12x^3 + 2) \div (3x + 2)$
12. $(12x^3 + 2 + 11x + 20x^2) \div (2x + 1)$
13. $(4x^3 - 2x + 7) \div (2x + 1)$
14. $(6x^4 - 2x^2 + 5) \div (-3x + 2)$
15. $(4x^3 - 12x^2 - x + 3) \div (x - \frac{1}{2})$
16. $(12x^3 + 1 + 7x + 16x^2) \div (x + \frac{1}{3})$
17. $(-2x^5 + 3x^4 - 2x^2) \div (x^3 - 3x^2 + 1)$
18. $(-9x^6 + 7x^4 - 2x^3 + 5) \div (3x^4 - 2x + 1)$
19. $\dfrac{x^4 - 1}{x^2 - 1}$
20. $\dfrac{x^4 - 9}{x^2 + 3}$
21. $\dfrac{40 - 22x + 7x^3 + 6x^4}{6x^2 + x - 2}$
22. $\dfrac{-13x^2 + 4x^4 + 9}{4x^2 - 9}$
23. $\dfrac{-3x^4 + 7x^3 - 2x + 1}{x - 0.6}$
24. $\dfrac{2x^5 - 4x^3 + 3x^2 + 5}{x - 0.9}$
25. $(x^4 + 0.8x^3 - 0.26x^2 - 0.168x + 0.0441) \div (x^2 + 1.4x + 0.49)$
26. $(x^5 + 2.8x^4 + 1.34x^3 - 0.688x^2 - 0.2919x + 0.0882) \div (x^2 - 0.6x + 0.09)$

In Exercises 27–46, divide the polynomial by the linear factor with synthetic division. Indicate the quotient $Q(x)$ and the remainder $r(x)$.

27. $(3x^2 + 7x + 2) \div (x + 2)$
28. $(2x^2 + 7x - 15) \div (x + 5)$
29. $(7x^2 - 3x + 5) \div (x + 1)$
30. $(4x^2 + x + 1) \div (x - 2)$
31. $(3x^2 + 4x - x^4 - 2x^3 - 4) \div (x + 2)$
32. $(3x^2 - 4 + x^3) \div (x - 1)$
33. $(x^4 + 1) \div (x + 1)$
34. $(x^4 + 9) \div (x + 3)$
35. $(x^4 - 16) \div (x + 2)$
36. $(x^4 - 81) \div (x - 3)$
37. $(2x^3 - 5x^2 - x + 1) \div (x + \frac{1}{2})$
38. $(3x^3 - 8x^2 + 1) \div (x + \frac{1}{3})$
39. $(2x^4 - 3x^3 + 7x^2 - 4) \div (x - \frac{2}{3})$
40. $(3x^4 + x^3 + 2x - 3) \div (x - \frac{3}{4})$
41. $(2x^4 + 9x^3 - 9x^2 - 81x - 81) \div (x + 1.5)$
42. $(5x^3 - x^2 + 6x + 8) \div (x + 0.8)$
43. $\dfrac{x^7 - 8x^4 + 3x^2 + 1}{x - 1}$
44. $\dfrac{x^6 + 4x^5 - 2x^3 + 7}{x + 1}$
45. $(x^6 - 49x^4 - 25x^2 + 1225) \div (x - \sqrt{5})$
46. $(x^6 - 4x^4 - 9x^2 + 36) \div (x - \sqrt{3})$

**In Exercises 47–60, divide the polynomials by either long division or synthetic division.**

**47.** $(6x^2 - 23x + 7) \div (3x - 1)$

**48.** $(6x^2 + x - 2) \div (2x - 1)$

**49.** $(x^3 - x^2 - 9x + 9) \div (x - 1)$

**50.** $(x^3 + 2x^2 - 6x - 12) \div (x + 2)$

**51.** $(x^3 + 6x^2 - 2x - 5) \div (x^2 - 1)$

**52.** $(3x^5 - x^3 + 2x^2 - 1) \div (x^3 + x^2 - x + 1)$

**53.** $(x^6 - 2x^5 + x^4 - 6x^3 + 7x^2 - 4x + 7) \div (x^2 + 1)$

**54.** $(x^6 - 1) \div (x^2 + x + 1)$

**55.** $(x^5 + 4x^3 + 2x^2 - 1) \div (x - 2)$

**56.** $(x^4 - x^2 + 3x - 10) \div (x + 5)$

**57.** $(x^4 - 25) \div (x^2 - 1)$

**58.** $(x^3 - 8) \div (x^2 - 2)$

**59.** $(x^7 - 1) \div (x - 1)$

**60.** $(x^6 - 27) \div (x - 3)$

## ▪ APPLICATIONS

**61. Geometry.** The area of a rectangle is $6x^4 + 4x^3 - x^2 - 2x - 1$ square feet. If the length of the rectangle is $2x^2 - 1$ feet, what is the width of the rectangle?

**62. Geometry.** If the rectangle in Exercise 61 is the base of a rectangular box with volume $18x^5 + 18x^4 + x^3 - 7x^2 - 5x - 1$ cubic feet, what is the height of the box?

**63. Travel.** If a car travels a distance of $x^3 + 60x^2 + x + 60$ miles at an average speed of $x + 60$ miles per hour, how long does the trip take?

**64. Sports.** If a quarterback throws a ball $-x^2 - 5x + 50$ yards in $5 - x$ seconds, how fast is the football traveling?

## ▪ CATCH THE MISTAKE

**In Exercises 65–68, explain the mistake that is made.**

**65.** Divide $x^3 - 4x^2 + x + 6$ by $x^2 + x + 1$.

**Solution:**

$$
\begin{array}{r}
x - 3 \\
x^2 + x + 1 \overline{\smash{)}\, x^3 - 4x^2 + \phantom{.}x + 6} \\
\underline{x^3 + \phantom{4}x^2 + \phantom{.}x} \\
-3x^2 + 2x + 6 \\
\underline{-3x^2 - 3x - 3} \\
-x + 3
\end{array}
$$

This is incorrect. What mistake was made?

**66.** Divide $x^4 - 3x^2 + 5x + 2$ by $x - 2$.

**Solution:**

$$
\begin{array}{r|rrrr}
-2 & 1 & -3 & 5 & 2 \\
   &   & -2 & 10 & -30 \\
\hline
   & 1 & -5 & 15 & \boxed{-28}
\end{array}
$$

$$\underbrace{\phantom{1 \quad -5 \quad 15}}_{x^2 - 5x + 15}$$

This is incorrect. What mistake was made?

**67.** Divide $x^3 + 4x - 12$ by $x - 3$.

**Solution:**

$$
\begin{array}{r|rrr}
3 & 1 & 4 & -12 \\
  &   & 3 & 21 \\
\hline
  & 1 & 7 & \boxed{9}
\end{array}
$$

$$\underbrace{\phantom{1 \qquad 7}}_{x + 7}$$

This is incorrect. What mistake was made?

**68.** Divide $x^3 + 3x^2 - 2x + 1$ by $x^2 + 1$.

**Solution:**

$$
\begin{array}{r|rrrr}
-1 & 1 & 3 & -2 & 1 \\
   &   & -1 & -2 & 4 \\
\hline
   & 1 & 2 & -4 & \boxed{5}
\end{array}
$$

$$\underbrace{\phantom{1 \quad 2 \quad -4}}_{x^2 - 2x - 4}$$

This is incorrect. What mistake was made?

■ **CONCEPTUAL**

In Exercises 69–74, determine whether each statement is true or false.

**69.** A fifth-degree polynomial divided by a third-degree polynomial will yield a quadratic quotient.

**70.** A third-degree polynomial divided by a linear polynomial will yield a linear quotient.

**71.** Synthetic division can be used whenever the degree of the dividend is exactly one more than the degree of the divisor.

**72.** When the remainder is zero, the divisor is a factor of the dividend.

**73.** When both the dividend and the divisor have the same degree, the quotient equals one.

**74.** Long division must be used whenever the degree of the divisor is greater than one.

■ **CHALLENGE**

**75.** Is $x + b$ a factor of $x^3 + (2b - a)x^2 + (b^2 - 2ab)x - ab^2$?

**76.** Is $x + b$ a factor of $x^4 + (b^2 - a^2)x^2 - a^2b^2$?

**77.** Divide $x^{3n} + x^{2n} - x^n - 1$ by $x^n - 1$.

**78.** Divide $x^{3n} + 5x^{2n} + 8x^n + 4$ by $x^n + 1$.

■ **TECHNOLOGY**

**79.** Plot $\dfrac{2x^3 - x^2 + 10x - 5}{x^2 + 5}$. What type of function is it? Perform this division using long division, and confirm that the graph corresponds to the quotient.

**80.** Plot $\dfrac{x^3 - 3x^2 + 4x - 12}{x - 3}$. What type of function is it? Perform this division using synthetic division, and confirm that the graph corresponds to the quotient.

**81.** Plot $\dfrac{x^4 + 2x^3 - x - 2}{x + 2}$. What type of function is it? Perform this division using synthetic division, and confirm that the graph corresponds to the quotient.

**82.** Plot $\dfrac{x^5 - 9x^4 + 18x^3 + 2x^2 - 5x - 3}{x^4 - 6x^3 + 2x + 1}$. What type of function is it? Perform this division using long division, and confirm that the graph corresponds to the quotient.

**83.** Plot $\dfrac{-6x^3 + 7x^2 + 14x - 15}{2x + 3}$. What type of function is it? Perform this division using long division, and confirm that the graph corresponds to the quotient.

**84.** Plot $\dfrac{-3x^5 - 4x^4 + 29x^3 + 36x^2 - 18x}{3x^2 + 4x - 2}$. What type of function is it? Perform this division using long division, and confirm that the graph corresponds to the quotient.

■ **PREVIEW TO CALCULUS**

For some of the operations in calculus it is convenient to write rational fractions $\dfrac{P(x)}{d(x)}$ in the form $Q(x) + \dfrac{r(x)}{d(x)}$, where

$$\frac{P(x)}{d(x)} = Q(x) + \frac{r(x)}{d(x)}.$$

In Exercises 85–88, write each rational function $\dfrac{P(x)}{d(x)}$ in the form $Q(x) + \dfrac{r(x)}{d(x)}$.

**85.** $\dfrac{2x^2 - x}{x + 2}$

**86.** $\dfrac{5x^3 + 2x^2 - 3x}{x - 3}$

**87.** $\dfrac{2x^4 + 3x^2 + 6}{x^2 + x + 1}$

**88.** $\dfrac{3x^5 - 2x^3 + x^2 + x - 6}{x^2 + x + 5}$

### SKILLS OBJECTIVES

- Apply the remainder theorem to evaluate a polynomial function.
- Apply the factor theorem.
- Use the rational zero (root) theorem to list possible rational zeros.
- Apply Descartes' rule of signs to determine the possible combination of positive and negative real zeros.
- Utilize the upper and lower bound theorems to narrow the search for real zeros.
- Find the real zeros of a polynomial function.
- Factor a polynomial function.
- Employ the intermediate value theorem to approximate a real zero.

### CONCEPTUAL OBJECTIVES

- Understand that a polynomial of degree $n$ has at most $n$ real zeros.
- Understand that a real zero can be either rational or irrational and that irrational zeros will not be listed as possible zeros through the rational zero test.
- Realize that rational zeros can be found exactly, whereas irrational zeros must be approximated.

## The Remainder Theorem and the Factor Theorem

The zeros of a polynomial function assist us in finding the $x$-intercepts of the graph of a polynomial function. How do we find the zeros of a polynomial function if we cannot factor them easily? For polynomial functions of degree 2, we have the quadratic formula, which allows us to find the two zeros. For polynomial functions whose degree is greater than 2, much more work is required.* In this section, we focus our attention on finding the *real* zeros of a polynomial function. Later, in Section 2.5, we expand our discussion to *complex* zeros of polynomial functions.

In this section, we start by listing possible rational zeros. As you will see, there are sometimes many possibilities. We can then narrow the search using Descartes' rule of signs, which tells us possible combinations of positive and negative real zeros. We can narrow the search even further with the upper and lower bound rules. Once we have tested possible values and determined a zero, we will employ synthetic division to divide the polynomial by the linear factor associated with the zero. We will continue the process until we have factored the polynomial function into a product of either linear factors or irreducible quadratic factors. Last, we will discuss how to find irrational real zeros using the intermediate value theorem.

If we divide the polynomial function $f(x) = x^3 - 2x^2 + x - 3$ by $x - 2$ using synthetic division, we find the remainder is $-1$.

$$
\begin{array}{r|rrrr}
2 & 1 & -2 & 1 & -3 \\
  &   & 2 & 0 & 2 \\
\hline
  & 1 & 0 & 1 & -1
\end{array}
$$

Notice that if we evaluate the function at $x = 2$, the result is $-1$. $\qquad f(2) = -1$

---

*There are complicated formulas for finding the zeros of polynomial functions of degree 3 and 4, but there are no such formulas for degree 5 and higher polynomials (according to the Abel–Ruffini theorem).

| WORDS | MATH |
|---|---|
| Recall the Division Algorithm. | $P(x) = d(x) \cdot Q(x) + r(x)$ |
| Let $d(x) = x - a$ for any real number $a$. The degree of the remainder is always less than the degree of the divisor; therefore the remainder must be a constant (Call it $r$, $r(x) = r$). | $P(x) = (x - a) \cdot Q(x) + r(x)$ |
| | $P(x) = (x - a) \cdot Q(x) + r$ |
| Let $x = a$. | $P(a) = \underbrace{(a - a)}_{0} \cdot Q(x) + r$ |
| Simplify. | $\boxed{P(a) = r}$ |

This leads us to the *remainder theorem*.

## REMAINDER THEOREM

If a polynomial $P(x)$ is divided by $x - a$, then the remainder is $r = P(a)$.

The remainder theorem tells you that polynomial division can be used to evaluate a polynomial function at a particular point.

### EXAMPLE 1    Two Methods for Evaluating Polynomials

Let $P(x) = 4x^5 - 3x^4 + 2x^3 - 7x^2 + 9x - 5$ and evaluate $P(2)$ by

**a.** evaluating $P(2)$ directly.
**b.** the remainder theorem and synthetic division.

**Solution:**

**a.**  $P(2) = 4(2)^5 - 3(2)^4 + 2(2)^3 - 7(2)^2 + 9(2) - 5$
$= 4(32) - 3(16) + 2(8) - 7(4) + 9(2) - 5$
$= 128 - 48 + 16 - 28 + 18 - 5$
$= \boxed{81}$

**b.**
$$
\begin{array}{r|rrrrrr}
2 & 4 & -3 & 2 & -7 & 9 & -5 \\
  &   & 8 & 10 & 24 & 34 & 86 \\
\hline
  & 4 & 5 & 12 & 17 & 43 & \boxed{81}
\end{array}
$$

■ **YOUR TURN** Let $P(x) = -x^3 + 2x^2 - 5x + 2$ and evaluate $P(-2)$ using the remainder theorem and synthetic division.

Recall that when a polynomial is divided by $x - a$, if the remainder is zero, we say that $x - a$ is a factor of the polynomial. Through the remainder theorem, we now know that the remainder is related to evaluation of the polynomial at the point $x = a$. We are then led to the *factor theorem*.

### FACTOR THEOREM

If $P(a) = 0$, then $x - a$ is a factor of $P(x)$. Conversely, if $x - a$ is a factor of $P(x)$, then $P(a) = 0$.

## Technology Tip

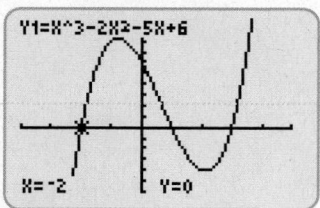

The three zeros of the function give the three factors $x + 2$, $x - 1$, and $x - 3$. A table of values supports the zeros of the graph.

| X | Y1 |
|---|---|
| -3 | -24 |
| -2 | 0 |
| -1 | 8 |
| 0 | 6 |
| 1 | 0 |
| 2 | -4 |
| 3 | 0 |

Y1■X^3-2X²-5X+6

■ **Answer:** $(x - 1)$ is a factor; $P(x) = (x - 5)(x - 1)(x + 2)$

### EXAMPLE 2    Using the Factor Theorem to Factor a Polynomial

Determine whether $x + 2$ is a factor of $P(x) = x^3 - 2x^2 - 5x + 6$. If so, factor $P(x)$ completely.

**Solution:**

STEP 1 Divide $P(x) = x^3 - 2x^2 - 5x + 6$ by $x + 2$ using synthetic division.

$$
\begin{array}{r|rrrr}
-2 & 1 & -2 & -5 & 6 \\
   &   & -2 & 8 & -6 \\
\hline
   & 1 & -4 & 3 & \boxed{0} \\
\end{array}
$$
$$x^2 - 4x + 3$$

Since the remainder is zero, $P(-2) = 0$, $\boxed{x + 2 \text{ is a factor}}$ of $P(x) = x^3 - 2x^2 - 5x + 6$.

STEP 2 Write $P(x)$ as a product.        $P(x) = (x + 2)(x^2 - 4x + 3)$

STEP 3 Factor the quadratic polynomial.        $\boxed{P(x) = (x + 2)(x - 3)(x - 1)}$

■ **YOUR TURN** Determine whether $x - 1$ is a factor of $P(x) = x^3 - 4x^2 - 7x + 10$. If so, factor $P(x)$ completely.

### EXAMPLE 3   Using the Factor Theorem to Factor a Polynomial

Determine whether $x - 3$ and $x + 2$ are factors of $P(x) = x^4 - 13x^2 + 36$. If so, factor $P(x)$ completely.

**Solution:**

STEP 1  With synthetic division, divide $P(x) = x^4 - 13x^2 + 36$ by $x - 3$.

$$\begin{array}{r|rrrrr} 3 & 1 & 0 & -13 & 0 & 36 \\ & & 3 & 9 & -12 & -36 \\ \hline & 1 & 3 & -4 & -12 & \boxed{0} \end{array}$$

$$\underbrace{}_{x^3 + 3x^2 - 4x - 12}$$

Because the remainder is 0, $\boxed{x - 3 \text{ is a factor}}$, and we can write the polynomial as

$$P(x) = (x - 3)(x^3 + 3x^2 - 4x - 12)$$

STEP 2  With synthetic division, divide the remaining cubic polynomial $(x^3 + 3x^2 - 4x - 12)$ by $x + 2$.

$$\begin{array}{r|rrrr} -2 & 1 & 3 & -4 & -12 \\ & & -2 & -2 & 12 \\ \hline & 1 & 1 & -6 & \boxed{0} \end{array}$$

$$\underbrace{}_{x^2 + x - 6}$$

Because the remainder is 0, $\boxed{x + 2 \text{ is a factor}}$, and we can now write the polynomial as

$$P(x) = (x - 3)(x + 2)(x^2 + x - 6)$$

STEP 3  Factor the quadratic polynomial: $x^2 + x - 6 = (x + 3)(x - 2)$.

STEP 4  Write $P(x)$ as a product of linear factors:

$$\boxed{P(x) = (x - 3)(x - 2)(x + 2)(x + 3)}$$

■ YOUR TURN   Determine whether $x - 3$ and $x + 2$ are factors of $P(x) = x^4 - x^3 - 7x^2 + x + 6$. If so, factor $P(x)$ completely.

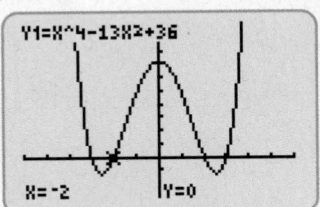

■ **Answer:**
$(x - 3)$ and $(x + 2)$ are factors;
$P(x) = (x - 3)(x + 2)(x - 1)(x + 1)$

## The Search for Real Zeros

In all of the examples thus far, the polynomial function and one or more real zeros (or linear factors) were given. Now, we will not be given any real zeros to start with. Instead, we will develop methods to search for them.

Each real zero corresponds to a linear factor and each linear factor is of degree 1. Therefore, the largest number of real zeros a polynomial function can have is equal to the degree of the polynomial.

### THE NUMBER OF REAL ZEROS

A polynomial function cannot have more real zeros than its degree.

***Study Tip***

The largest number of zeros a polynomial can have is equal to the degree of the polynomial.

The following functions illustrate that a polynomial function of degree $n$ can have at most $n$ real zeros:

| POLYNOMIAL FUNCTION | DEGREE | REAL ZEROS | COMMENTS |
|---|---|---|---|
| $f(x) = x^2 - 9$ | 2 | $x = \pm 3$ | **Two** real zeros |
| $f(x) = x^2 + 4$ | 2 | None | **No** real zeros |
| $f(x) = x^3 - 1$ | 3 | $x = 1$ | **One** real zero |
| $f(x) = x^3 - x^2 - 6x$ | 3 | $x = -2, 0, 3$ | **Three** real zeros |

Now that we know the *maximum* number of real zeros a polynomial function can have, let us discuss how to find these zeros.

## The Rational Zero Theorem and Descartes' Rule of Signs

When the coefficients of a polynomial are integers, then the *rational zero theorem* (*rational root test*) gives us a list of possible rational zeros. We can then test these possible values to determine whether they really do correspond to actual zeros. *Descartes' rule of signs* tells us the possible combinations of *positive* real zeros and *negative* real zeros. Using Descartes' rule of signs will assist us in narrowing down the large list of possible zeros generated through the rational zero theorem to a (hopefully) shorter list of possible zeros. First, let's look at the rational zero theorem; then we'll turn to Descartes' rule of signs.

### THE RATIONAL ZERO THEOREM (RATIONAL ROOT TEST)

If the polynomial function $P(x) = a_n x^n + a_{n-1} x^{n-1} + \cdots + a_2 x^2 + a_1 x + a_0$ has *integer* coefficients, then every rational zero of $P(x)$ has the form

$$\text{Rational zero} = \frac{\text{integer factors of } a_0}{\text{integer factors of } a_n} = \frac{\text{integer factors of constant term}}{\text{integer factors of leading coefficient}}$$

$$= \pm \frac{\text{positive integer factors of constant term}}{\text{positive integer factors of leading coefficient}}$$

To use this theorem, simply list all combinations of integer factors of both the constant term $a_0$ and the leading coefficient term $a_n$ and take all appropriate combinations of ratios. This procedure is illustrated in Example 4. Notice that when the leading coefficient is 1, then the possible rational zeros will simply be the possible integer factors of the constant term.

### EXAMPLE 4   Using the Rational Zero Theorem

Determine possible rational zeros for the polynomial $P(x) = x^4 - x^3 - 5x^2 - x - 6$ by the rational zero theorem. Test each one to find all rational zeros.

**Solution:**

STEP 1  List factors of the constant and leading coefficient terms.  $\quad a_0 = -6 \qquad \pm 1, \pm 2, \pm 3, \pm 6$
$\quad a_n = 1 \qquad \pm 1$

STEP 2  List possible rational zeros $\frac{a_0}{a_n}$.  $\quad \frac{\pm 1}{\pm 1}, \frac{\pm 2}{\pm 1}, \frac{\pm 3}{\pm 1}, \frac{\pm 6}{\pm 1} = \pm 1, \pm 2, \pm 3, \pm 6$

There are three ways to test whether any of these are zeros: Substitute these values into the polynomial to see which ones yield zero, or use either polynomial division or synthetic division to divide the polynomial by these possible zeros, and look for a zero remainder.

**STEP 3** Test possible zeros by looking for zero remainders.

$$1 \text{ is not a zero:} \quad P(1) = (1)^4 - (1)^3 - 5(1)^2 - (1) - 6 = -12$$

$$-1 \text{ is not a zero:} \quad P(-1) = (-1)^4 - (-1)^3 - 5(-1)^2 - (-1) - 6 = -8$$

We could continue testing with direct substitution, but let us now use synthetic division as an alternative.

2 is not a zero:

```
2 | 1   -1   -5   -1   -6
  |      2    2   -6  -14
  ---------------------------
    1    1   -3   -7  |-20|
```

−2 is a zero:

```
-2 | 1   -1   -5   -1   -6
   |     -2    6   -2    6
   ---------------------------
     1   -3    1   -3   | 0 |
```

Since $-2$ is a zero, then $x + 2$ is a factor of $P(x)$, and the remaining quotient is $x^3 - 3x^2 + x - 3$. Therefore, if there are any other real roots remaining, we can now use the simpler $x^3 - 3x^2 + x - 3$ for the dividend. Also note that the rational zero theorem can be applied to the new dividend and possibly shorten the list of possible rational zeros. In this case, the possible rational zeros of $F(x) = x^3 - 3x^2 + x - 3$ are $\pm 1$ and $\pm 3$.

3 is a zero:

```
3 | 1   -3    1   -3
  |      3    0    3
  -----------------------
    1    0    1   | 0 |
```

We now know that $\boxed{-2}$ and $\boxed{3}$ are confirmed zeros. If we continue testing, we will find that the other possible zeros fail. This is a fourth-degree polynomial, and we have found two rational real zeros. We see in the graph on the right that these two real zeros correspond to the $x$-intercepts.

**Study Tip**

The remainder can be found by evaluating the function or synthetic division. For simple values like $x = \pm 1$, it is easier to evaluate the polynomial function. For other values, it is often easier to use synthetic division.

**Study Tip**

Notice in Step 3 that the polynomial $F(x) = x^3 - 3x^2 + x - 3$ can be factored by grouping: $F(x) = (x - 3)(x^2 + 1)$.

■ **YOUR TURN** List the possible rational zeros of the polynomial
$$P(x) = x^4 + 2x^3 - 2x^2 + 2x - 3,$$ and determine rational real zeros.

■ **Answer:** Possible rational zeros: $\pm 1$ and $\pm 3$. Rational real zeros: 1 and $-3$.

Notice in Example 4 that the polynomial function $P(x) = x^4 - x^3 - 5x^2 - x - 6$ had two rational real zeros, $-2$ and 3. This implies that $x + 2$ and $x - 3$ are factors of $P(x)$. Also note in the last step when we divided by the zero 3, the quotient was $x^2 + 1$. Therefore, we can write the polynomial in factored form as

$$P(x) = \underbrace{(x + 2)}_{\substack{\text{linear} \\ \text{factor}}} \underbrace{(x - 3)}_{\substack{\text{linear} \\ \text{factor}}} \underbrace{(x^2 + 1)}_{\substack{\text{irreducible} \\ \text{quadratic} \\ \text{factor}}}$$

Notice that the first two factors are of degree 1, so we call them **linear factors**. The third expression, $x^2 + 1$, is of degree 2 and cannot be factored in terms of real numbers.

We will discuss complex zeros in the next section. For now, we say that a quadratic expression, $ax^2 + bx + c$, is called **irreducible** if it cannot be factored over the real numbers.

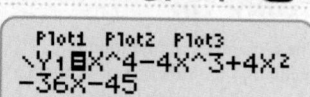
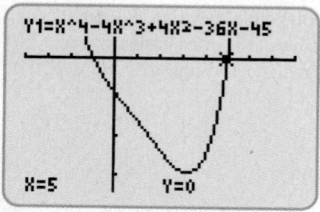
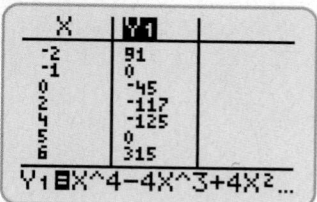
### EXAMPLE 5    Factoring a Polynomial Function

Write the following polynomial function as a product of linear and/or irreducible quadratic factors:

$$P(x) = x^4 - 4x^3 + 4x^2 - 36x - 45$$

**Solution:**

Use the rational zero theorem to list possible rational roots.

$$x = \pm 1, \pm 3, \pm 5, \pm 9, \pm 15, \pm 45$$

Test possible zeros by evaluating the function or by utilizing synthetic division.

$x = 1$ is not a zero.       $P(1) = -80$

$x = -1$ is a zero.       $P(-1) = 0$

Divide $P(x)$ by $x + 1$.

$$
\begin{array}{r|rrrr}
-1 & 1 & -4 & 4 & -36 & -45 \\
   &   & -1 & 5 & -9  & 45 \\
\hline
   & 1 & -5 & 9 & -45 & \boxed{0}
\end{array}
$$

$x = 5$ is a zero.

$$
\begin{array}{r|rrrr}
5 & 1 & -5 & 9 & -45 \\
  &   & 5  & 0 & 45 \\
\hline
  & 1 & 0  & 9 & \boxed{0}
\end{array}
$$
$$\underbrace{\phantom{1 \quad 0 \quad 9}}_{x^2 + 9}$$

The factor $x^2 + 9$ is irreducible.

Write the polynomial as a product of linear and/or irreducible quadratic factors.

$$\boxed{P(x) = (x - 5)(x + 1)(x^2 + 9)}$$

Notice that the graph of this polynomial function has $x$-intercepts at $x = -1$ and $x = 5$.

■ **Answer:**
$P(x) = (x + 1)(x - 3)(x^2 + 2)$

■ **YOUR TURN**   Write the following polynomial function as a product of linear and/or irreducible quadratic factors:

$$P(x) = x^4 - 2x^3 - x^2 - 4x - 6$$

The rational zero theorem lists possible zeros. It would be helpful if we could narrow that list. Descartes' rule of signs determines the possible combinations of positive real zeros and negative real zeros through variations of sign. A *variation in sign* is a sign difference seen between consecutive coefficients.

$$P(x) = 2x^6 - 5x^5 - 3x^4 + 2x^3 - x^2 - x - 1$$

Sign Change − to +

Sign Change + to −

Sign Change + to −

This polynomial experiences three sign changes or variations in sign.

## DESCARTES' RULE OF SIGNS

If the polynomial function $P(x) = a_n x^n + a_{n-1} x^{n-1} + \cdots + a_2 x^2 + a_1 x + a_0$ has real coefficients and $a_0 \neq 0$, then:

- The number of **positive** real zeros of the polynomial is either equal to the number of variations of sign of $P(x)$ or less than that number by an even integer.
- The number of **negative** real zeros of the polynomial is either equal to the number of variations of sign of $P(-x)$ or less than that number by an even integer.

Descartes' rule of signs narrows our search for real zeros, because we don't have to test all of the possible rational zeros. For example, if we know there is one positive real zero, then if we find a positive rational zero, we no longer need to continue to test possible positive zeros.

**EXAMPLE 6  Using Descartes' Rule of Signs to Find Possible Combinations of Real Zeros**

Determine the possible combinations of real zeros for

$$P(x) = x^4 - 2x^3 + x^2 + 2x - 2$$

**Solution:**

$P(x)$ has three variations in sign.

**Sign Change**

$$P(x) = x^4 - 2x^3 + x^2 + 2x - 2$$

**Sign Change**     **Sign Change**

Apply Descartes' rule of signs.     $P(x)$ has *either* three or one **positive** real zero.

Find $P(-x)$.     $P(-x) = (-x)^4 - 2(-x)^3 + (-x)^2 + 2(-x) - 2$

$$= x^4 + 2x^3 + x^2 - 2x - 2$$

$P(-x)$ has one variation in sign.     $P(-x) = x^4 + 2x^3 + x^2 - 2x - 2$

**Sign Change**

Apply Descartes' rule of signs.     $P(x)$ has one **negative** real zero.

Since $P(x) = x^4 - 2x^3 + x^2 + 2x - 2$ is a *fourth*-degree polynomial, there are at most four real zeros. One zero is a negative real number.

> $P(x)$ has one negative real zero and could have three positive real zeros or one positive real zero.

Look at the graph in the Technology Tip to confirm one negative real zero and one positive real zero.

■ **YOUR TURN** Determine the possible combinations of zeros for

$$P(x) = x^4 + 2x^3 + x^2 + 8x - 12$$

*Technology Tip*

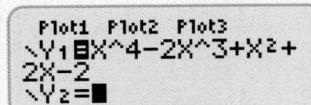

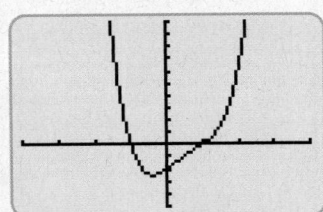

There are one negative real zero and one positive real zero.

The number of negative real zero is 1 and the number of positive real zero is 1. So, it has two complex conjugate zeros.

A table of values supports the zeros of the function.

■ **Answer:** Positive real zeros: 1
Negative real zeros: 3 or 1

## Factoring Polynomials

Now let's draw on the tests discussed in this section thus far to help us in finding all real zeros of a polynomial function. Doing so will enable us to factor polynomials.

### EXAMPLE 7 Factoring a Polynomial

Write the polynomial $P(x) = x^5 + 2x^4 - x - 2$ as a product of linear and/or irreducible quadratic factors.

**Solution:**

**STEP 1** Determine variations in sign.

$P(x)$ has one sign change.         $P(x) = x^5 + 2x^4 - x - 2$

$P(-x)$ has two sign changes.     $P(-x) = -x^5 + 2x^4 + x - 2$

**STEP 2** Apply Descartes' rule of signs.

Positive Real Zeros:     1

Negative Real Zeros:     2 or 0

**STEP 3** Use the rational zero theorem to determine the possible rational zeros.     $\pm 1, \pm 2$

We know (Step 2) that there is one positive real zero, so test the possible positive rational zeros first.

**STEP 4** Test possible rational zeros.

$$
\begin{array}{r|rrrrrr}
1 & 1 & 2 & 0 & 0 & -1 & -2 \\
  &   & 1 & 3 & 3 & 3  & 2 \\
\hline
  & 1 & 3 & 3 & 3 & 2 & \boxed{0}
\end{array}
$$

1 is a zero:

Now that we have found *the* positive zero, we can test the other two possible negative zeros—because either they both are zeros or neither is a zero (or one is a double root).

$$
\begin{array}{r|rrrrr}
-1 & 1 & 3 & 3 & 3 & 2 \\
   &   & -1 & -2 & -1 & -2 \\
\hline
   & 1 & 2 & 1 & 2 & \boxed{0}
\end{array}
$$

−1 is a zero:

Let's now try the other possible negative zero, −2.

$$
\begin{array}{r|rrrr}
-2 & 1 & 2 & 1 & 2 \\
   &   & -2 & 0 & -2 \\
\hline
   & 1 & 0 & 1 & \boxed{0} \\
   & & x^2 + 1
\end{array}
$$

−2 is a zero:

**STEP 5** Three of the five have been found to be zeros: −1, −2, and 1.

**STEP 6** Write the fifth-degree polynomial as a product of three linear factors and an irreducible quadratic factor.

$$\boxed{P(x) = (x - 1)(x + 1)(x + 2)(x^2 + 1)}$$

■ **Answer:** $P(x) =$
$(x - 2)(x + 1)(x - 1)(x^2 + 2)$

■ **YOUR TURN** Write the polynomial $P(x) = x^5 - 2x^4 + x^3 - 2x^2 - 2x + 4$ as a product of linear and/or irreducible quadratic factors.

## EXAMPLE 8  Factoring a Polynomial

Write the polynomial $P(x) = 2x^4 + 3x^3 - 12x^2 - 7x + 6$ as a product of linear and/or irreducible quadratic factors.

**Solution:**

STEP 1  Determine variations in sign.

$P(x)$ has two sign changes.

$P(-x)$ has two sign changes.

$P(x) = 2x^4 + 3x^3 - 12x^2 - 7x + 6$

$P(-x) = 2x^4 - 3x^3 - 12x^2 + 7x + 6$

STEP 2  Apply Descartes' rule of signs.

Positive Real Zeros:　　2 or 0

Negative Real Zeros:　　2 or 0

STEP 3  Use the rational zero theorem to determine the possible rational zeros.

$\pm 1, \pm 2, \pm 3, \pm 6, \pm \dfrac{1}{2}, \pm \dfrac{3}{2}$

STEP 4  Test possible rational zeros.

$$
\begin{array}{r|rrrrr}
-1 & 2 & 3 & -12 & -7 & 6 \\
   &   & -2 & -1 & 13 & -6 \\
\hline
   & 2 & 1 & -13 & 6 & \boxed{0}
\end{array}
$$

$-1$ is a zero:

Since there are either two or no negative real zeros and we have found one of the negative zeros, try the other negative real zeros.

$-3$ is a zero:

$$
\begin{array}{r|rrrr}
-3 & 2 & 1 & -13 & 6 \\
   &   & -6 & 15 & -6 \\
\hline
   & 2 & -5 & +2 & \boxed{0}
\end{array}
$$

$$2x^2 - 5x + 2$$

Factor $2x^2 - 5x + 2$ to find the remaining two zeros.

$$(2x - 1)(x - 2)$$

STEP 5  Write the fourth-degree polynomial as a product of four linear factors.

$$\boxed{P(x) = (2x - 1)(x - 2)(x + 3)(x + 1)}$$

- - - - - - - - - - - - - - - - - - - - - - - - - - - - - - - - - - - -

■ **YOUR TURN**  Write the polynomial $P(x) = 3x^4 - 5x^3 - 17x^2 + 13x + 6$ as a product of linear and/or irreducible quadratic factors.

■ **Answer:** $P(x) = (3x + 1)(x - 1)(x + 2)(x - 3)$

The rational zero theorem gives us possible rational zeros of a polynomial, and Descartes' rule of signs gives us possible combinations of positive and negative real zeros. Additional aids that help eliminate possible zeros are the *upper* and *lower bound rules*. These rules can give you an upper and lower bound on the real zeros of a polynomial function. If $f(x)$ has a common monomial factor, you should factor it out first, and then follow the upper and lower bound rules.

**Study Tip**

If $f(x)$ has a common monomial factor, it should be canceled first before applying the bound rules.

UPPER AND LOWER BOUND RULES

Let $f(x)$ be a polynomial with real coefficients and a positive leading coefficient. Suppose $f(x)$ is divided by $x - c$ using synthetic division.

1. If $c > 0$ and each number in the bottom row is either positive or zero, $c$ is an **upper bound** for the real zeros of $f$.
2. If $c < 0$ and the numbers in the bottom row are alternately positive and negative (zero entries count as either positive or negative), $c$ is a **lower bound** for the real zeros of $f$.

**EXAMPLE 9** **Using Upper and Lower Bounds to Eliminate Possible Zeros**

Find the real zeros of $f(x) = 4x^3 - x^2 + 36x - 9$.

**Solution:**

STEP 1 The rational zero theorem gives possible rational zeros.

$$\frac{\text{Factors of } 9}{\text{Factors of } 4} = \frac{\pm 1, \ \pm 3, \ \pm 9}{\pm 1, \ \pm 2, \ \pm 4}$$

$$= \pm 1, \ \pm \frac{1}{2}, \ \pm \frac{1}{4}, \ \pm \frac{3}{4}, \ \pm \frac{3}{2}, \ \pm \frac{9}{4}, \ \pm 3, \ \pm \frac{9}{2}, \ \pm 9$$

STEP 2 Apply Descartes' rule of signs:

$f(x)$ has three sign variations.

$f(-x)$ has no sign variations.

three or one positive real zeros

no negative real zeros

STEP 3 Try $x = 1$.

$$
\begin{array}{r|rrrr}
1 & 4 & -1 & 36 & -9 \\
  &   & 4  & 3  & 39 \\
\hline
  & 4 & 3  & 39 & 30
\end{array}
$$

$x = 1$ is not a zero, but because the last row contains all positive entries, $x = 1$ is an *upper* bound. Since we know there are no negative real zeros, we restrict our search to between 0 and 1.

STEP 4 Try $x = \frac{1}{4}$.

$$
\begin{array}{r|rrrr}
\frac{1}{4} & 4 & -1 & 36 & -9 \\
            &   & 1  & 0  & 9 \\
\hline
            & 4 & 0  & 36 & 0
\end{array}
$$

$\frac{1}{4}$ is a zero and the quotient $4x^2 + 36$ has all positive coefficients; therefore, $\frac{1}{4}$ is an upper bound, so $\boxed{\frac{1}{4} \text{ is the only real zero}}$.

*Note:* If $f(x)$ has a common monomial factor, it should be factored out first before applying the bound rules.

**Study Tip**

In Example 9, Steps 3 and 4 long division can be used as well as evaluating the function at $x = 1$ and $x = \frac{1}{4}$ to determine if these are zeros.

# The Intermediate Value Theorem

In our search for zeros, we sometimes encounter irrational zeros, as in, for example, the polynomial

$$f(x) = x^5 - x^4 - 1$$

Descartes' rule of signs tells us there is exactly one real positive zero. However, the rational zero test yields only $x = \pm 1$, neither of which is a zero. So if we know there is a real positive zero and we know it's not rational, it must be irrational. Notice that $f(1) = -1$ and $f(2) = 15$. Since polynomial functions are continuous and the function goes from negative to positive between $x = 1$ and $x = 2$, we expect a zero somewhere in that interval. Generating a graph with a graphing utility, we find that there is a zero around $x = 1.3$.

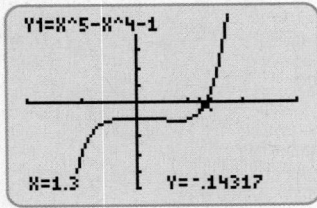

The *intermediate value theorem* is based on the fact that polynomial functions are continuous.

### INTERMEDIATE VALUE THEOREM

Let $a$ and $b$ be real numbers such that $a < b$ and $f(x)$ is a polynomial function. If $f(a)$ and $f(b)$ have opposite signs, then there is at least one real zero between $a$ and $b$.

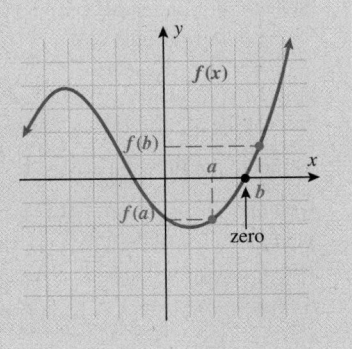

If the intermediate value theorem tells us that there is a real zero in the interval $(a, b)$, how do we approximate that zero? The **bisection method**\* is a root-finding algorithm that approximates the solution to the equation $f(x) = 0$. In the bisection method the interval is divided in half and then the subinterval that contains the zero is selected. This is repeated until the bisection method converges to an approximate root of $f$.

---

\*In calculus you will learn Newton's method, which is a more efficient approximation technique for finding zeros.

**EXAMPLE 10  Approximating Real Zeros of a Polynomial Function**

Approximate the real zero of $f(x) = x^5 - x^4 - 1$.

*Note:* Descartes' rule of signs tells us that there are no real negative zeros and there is exactly one real positive zero.

**Solution:**

Find two consecutive integer values
for $x$ that have corresponding function
values opposite in sign.

| $x$ | $f(x)$ |
|---|---|
| 1 | $-1$ |
| 2 | 15 |

Note that a graphing utility would have shown an $x$-intercept between $x = 1$ and $x = 2$.

*Apply the bisection method,* with
$a = 1$ and $b = 2$.

$$c = \frac{a+b}{2} = \frac{1+2}{2} = \frac{3}{2}$$

Evaluate the function at $x = c$.

$f(1.5) \approx 1.53$

Compare the values of $f$ at the
endpoints and midpoint.

$f(1) = -1, f(1.5) \approx 1.53, f(2) = 15$

Select the subinterval corresponding
to the *opposite* signs of $f$.

$(1, 1.5)$

*Apply the bisection method again*
(repeat the algorithm).

$$\frac{1+1.5}{2} = 1.25$$

Evaluate the function at $x = 1.25$.

$f(1.25) \approx -0.38965$

Compare the values of $f$ at the
endpoints and midpoint.

$f(1) = -1, f(1.25) \approx -0.38965, f(1.5) \approx 1.53$

Select the subinterval corresponding
to the *opposite* signs of $f$.

$(1.25, 1.5)$

*Apply the bisection method again*
(repeat the algorithm).

$$\frac{1.25+1.5}{2} = 1.375$$

Evaluate the function at $x = 1.375$.

$f(1.375) \approx 0.3404$

Compare the values of $f$ at the
endpoints and midpoint.

$f(1.25) \approx -0.38965, f(1.375) \approx 0.3404, f(1.5) \approx 1.53$

Select the subinterval corresponding
to the *opposite* signs of $f$.

$(1.25, 1.375)$

We can continue this procedure (*applying the bisection method*) to find that the zero is somewhere between $x = 1.32$ and $x = 1.33$, since $f(1.32) \approx -0.285$ and $f(1.33) \approx 0.0326$.

We find that, to three significant digits, $\boxed{1.32}$ is an approximation to the real zero.

The graph of $f(x) = x^5 - x^4 - 1$ is
shown. To find the zero of the function,
press

$\boxed{\text{2nd}}$ $\boxed{\text{TRACE}}$ $\boxed{2}$ $\boxed{\text{Zero}}$ $\boxed{1}$ $\boxed{\text{ENTER}}$

$\boxed{2}$ $\boxed{\text{ENTER}}$ $\boxed{\text{ENTER}}$

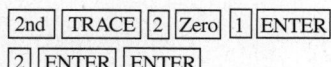

A table of values supports this zero of
the function.

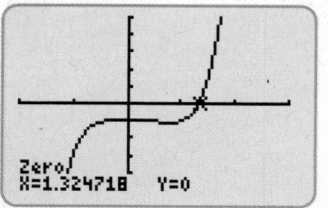

# Graphing Polynomial Functions

In Section 2.2, we graphed simple polynomial functions that were easily factored. Now that we have procedures for finding real zeros of polynomial functions (rational zero theorem, Descartes' rule of signs, and upper and lower bound rules for rational zeros, and the intermediate value theorem and the bisection method for irrational zeros), let us return to the topic of graphing polynomial functions. Since a real zero of a polynomial function corresponds to an $x$-intercept of its graph, we now have methods for finding (or estimating) any $x$-intercepts of the graph of any polynomial function.

**EXAMPLE 11   Graphing a Polynomial Function**

Graph the function $f(x) = 2x^4 - 2x^3 + 5x^2 + 17x - 22$.

**Solution:**

**STEP 1   Find the $y$-intercept.**           $f(0) = -22$

**STEP 2   Find any $x$-intercepts (real zeros).**

*Apply Descartes' rule of signs.*

Three sign changes correspond to three or one positive real zeros.           $f(x) = 2x^4 - 2x^3 + 5x^2 + 17x - 22$

One sign change corresponds to one negative real zero.           $f(-x) = 2x^4 + 2x^3 + 5x^2 - 17x - 22$

*Apply the rational zero theorem.*

Let $a_0 = -22$ and $a_n = 2$.           $\dfrac{\text{Factors of } a_0}{\text{Factors of } a_n} = \pm\dfrac{1}{2}, \pm1, \pm2, \pm\dfrac{11}{2}, \pm11, \pm22$

*Test the possible zeros.*

$x = 1$ is a zero.           $f(1) = 0$

There are no other rational zeros.

*Apply the upper bound rule.*

$$
\begin{array}{r|rrrr}
1 & 2 & -2 & 5 & 17 & -22 \\
  &   & 2 & 0 & 5 & 22 \\
\hline
  & 2 & 0 & 5 & 22 & \boxed{0}
\end{array}
$$

Since $x = 1$ is positive and all of the numbers in the bottom row are positive (or zero), $x = 1$ is an upper bound for the real zeros. We know there is exactly one negative real zero, but none of the possible zeros from the rational zero theorem is a zero. Therefore, the negative real zero is irrational.

*Apply the intermediate value theorem and the bisection method.*

$f$ is positive at $x = -2$.           $f(-2) = 12$

$f$ is negative at $x = -1$.           $f(-1) = -30$

Use the bisection method to find the negative real zero between $-2$ and $-1$.           $x \approx -1.85$

**STEP 3   Determine the end behavior.**           $y = 2x^4$

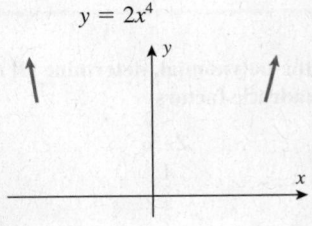

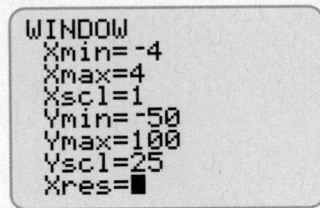

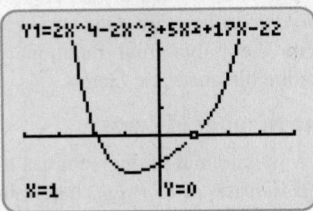
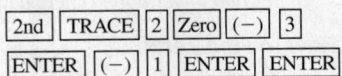
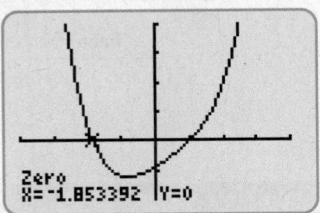
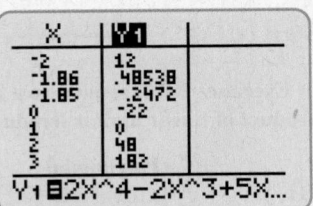

STEP 4 **Find additional points.**

| $x$ | $-2$ | $-1.85$ | $-1$ | $0$ | $1$ | $2$ |
|------|------|---------|------|-----|-----|-----|
| $f(x)$ | 12 | 0 | $-30$ | $-22$ | 0 | 48 |
| Point | $(-2, 12)$ | $(-1.85, 0)$ | $(-1, -30)$ | $(0, -22)$ | $(1, 0)$ | $(2, 48)$ |

STEP 5 **Sketch the graph.**

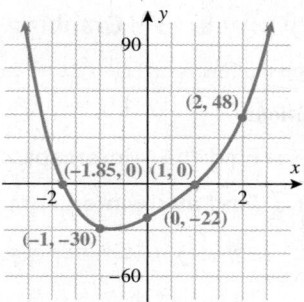

# SECTION 2.4 SUMMARY

In this section, we discussed how to find the real zeros of a polynomial function. Once real zeros are known, it is possible to write the polynomial function as a product of linear and/or irreducible quadratic factors.

## The Number of Zeros

- A polynomial of degree $n$ has *at most n* real zeros.
- *Descartes' rule of signs* determines the possible combinations of positive and negative real zeros.
- *Upper and lower bounds* help narrow the search for zeros.

## How to Find Zeros

- *Rational zero theorem:* List possible rational zeros:

$$\frac{\text{Factors of constant, } a_0}{\text{Factors of leading coefficient, } a_n}$$

- *Irrational zeros:* Approximate zeros by determining when the polynomial function changes sign (intermediate value theorem).

## Procedure for Factoring a Polynomial Function

- List possible rational zeros (rational zero theorem).
- List possible combinations of positive and negative real zeros (Descartes' rule of signs).
- Test possible values until a zero is found.*
- Once a real zero is found, repeat testing on the quotient until linear and/or irreducible quadratic factors remain.
- If there is a real zero but all possible rational roots have failed, then approximate the zero using the *intermediate value theorem* and the *bisection method*.

*Depending on the form of the quotient, upper and lower bounds may eliminate possible zeros.

# SECTION 2.4 EXERCISES

■ SKILLS

In Exercises 1–10, given a real zero of the polynomial, determine all other real zeros, and write the polynomial in terms of a product of linear and/or irreducible quadratic factors.

| Polynomial | Zero | Polynomial | Zero |
|------------|------|------------|------|
| **1.** $P(x) = x^3 - 13x + 12$ | 1 | **2.** $P(x) = x^3 + 3x^2 - 10x - 24$ | 3 |
| **3.** $P(x) = 2x^3 + x^2 - 13x + 6$ | $\frac{1}{2}$ | **4.** $P(x) = 3x^3 - 14x^2 + 7x + 4$ | $-\frac{1}{3}$ |

| **Polynomial** | **Zero** | **Polynomial** | **Zero** |
|---|---|---|---|
| **5.** $P(x) = x^4 - 2x^3 - 11x^2 - 8x - 60$ | $-3, 5$ | **6.** $P(x) = x^4 - x^3 + 7x^2 - 9x - 18$ | $-1, 2$ |
| **7.** $P(x) = x^4 - 5x^2 + 10x - 6$ | $1, -3$ | **8.** $P(x) = x^4 - 4x^3 + x^2 + 6x - 40$ | $4, -2$ |
| **9.** $P(x) = x^4 + 6x^3 + 13x^2 + 12x + 4$ | $-2$ (multiplicity 2) | **10.** $P(x) = x^4 + 4x^3 - 2x^2 - 12x + 9$ | 1 (multiplicity 2) |

In Exercises 11–18, use the rational zero theorem to list the *possible* rational zeros.

**11.** $P(x) = x^4 + 3x^2 - 8x + 4$

**12.** $P(x) = -x^4 + 2x^3 - 5x + 4$

**13.** $P(x) = x^5 - 14x^3 + x^2 - 15x + 12$

**14.** $P(x) = x^5 - x^3 - x^2 + 4x + 9$

**15.** $P(x) = 2x^6 - 7x^4 + x^3 - 2x + 8$

**16.** $P(x) = 3x^5 + 2x^4 - 5x^3 + x - 10$

**17.** $P(x) = 5x^5 + 3x^4 + x^3 - x - 20$

**18.** $P(x) = 4x^6 - 7x^4 + 4x^3 + x - 21$

In Exercises 19–22, list the possible rational zeros, and test to determine all rational zeros.

**19.** $P(x) = x^4 + 2x^3 - 9x^2 - 2x + 8$

**20.** $P(x) = x^4 + 2x^3 - 4x^2 - 2x + 3$

**21.** $P(x) = 2x^3 - 9x^2 + 10x - 3$

**22.** $P(x) = 3x^3 - 5x^2 - 26x - 8$

In Exercises 23–34, use Descartes' rule of signs to determine the possible number of positive real zeros and negative real zeros.

**23.** $P(x) = x^4 - 32$

**24.** $P(x) = x^4 + 32$

**25.** $P(x) = x^5 - 1$

**26.** $P(x) = x^5 + 1$

**27.** $P(x) = x^5 - 3x^3 - x + 2$

**28.** $P(x) = x^4 + 2x^2 - 9$

**29.** $P(x) = 9x^7 + 2x^5 - x^3 - x$

**30.** $P(x) = 16x^7 - 3x^4 + 2x - 1$

**31.** $P(x) = x^6 - 16x^4 + 2x^2 + 7$

**32.** $P(x) = -7x^6 - 5x^4 - x^2 + 2x + 1$

**33.** $P(x) = -3x^4 + 2x^3 - 4x^2 + x - 11$

**34.** $P(x) = 2x^4 - 3x^3 + 7x^2 + 3x + 2$

For each polynomial in Exercises 35–52: (a) use Descartes' rule of signs to determine the possible combinations of positive real zeros and negative real zeros; (b) use the rational zero test to determine possible rational zeros; (c) test for rational zeros; and (d) factor as a product of linear and/or irreducible quadratic factors.

**35.** $P(x) = x^3 + 6x^2 + 11x + 6$

**36.** $P(x) = x^3 - 6x^2 + 11x - 6$

**37.** $P(x) = x^3 - 7x^2 - x + 7$

**38.** $P(x) = x^3 - 5x^2 - 4x + 20$

**39.** $P(x) = x^4 + 6x^3 + 3x^2 - 10x$

**40.** $P(x) = x^4 - x^3 - 14x^2 + 24x$

**41.** $P(x) = x^4 - 7x^3 + 27x^2 - 47x + 26$

**42.** $P(x) = x^4 - 5x^3 + 5x^2 + 25x - 26$

**43.** $P(x) = 10x^3 - 7x^2 - 4x + 1$

**44.** $P(x) = 12x^3 - 13x^2 + 2x - 1$

**45.** $P(x) = 6x^3 + 17x^2 + x - 10$

**46.** $P(x) = 6x^3 + x^2 - 5x - 2$

**47.** $P(x) = x^4 - 2x^3 + 5x^2 - 8x + 4$

**48.** $P(x) = x^4 + 2x^3 + 10x^2 + 18x + 9$

**49.** $P(x) = x^6 + 12x^4 + 23x^2 - 36$

**50.** $P(x) = x^4 - x^2 - 16x^2 + 16$

**51.** $P(x) = 4x^4 - 20x^3 + 37x^2 - 24x + 5$

**52.** $P(x) = 4x^4 - 8x^3 + 7x^2 + 30x + 50$

In Exercises 53–56, use the information found in Exercises 37, 41, 45, and 51 to assist in sketching a graph of each polynomial function.

**53.** Exercise 37

**54.** Exercise 41

**55.** Exercise 45

**56.** Exercise 51

In Exercises 57–64, use the intermediate value theorem and the bisection method to approximate the real zero in the indicated interval. Approximate to two decimal places.

**57.** $f(x) = x^4 - 3x^3 + 4$    $[1, 2]$

**58.** $f(x) = x^5 - 3x^3 + 1$    $[0, 1]$

**59.** $f(x) = 7x^5 - 2x^2 + 5x - 1$    $[0, 1]$

**60.** $f(x) = -2x^3 + 3x^2 + 6x - 7$    $[-2, -1]$

**61.** $f(x) = x^3 - 2x^2 - 8x - 3$    $[-1, 0]$

**62.** $f(x) = x^4 + 4x^2 - 7x - 13$    $[-2, -1]$

**63.** $f(x) = x^5 + 2x^4 - 6x^3 - 25x^2 + 8x - 10$    $[2, 3]$

**64.** $f(x) = \frac{1}{2}x^6 + x^4 - 2x^2 - x + 1$    $[1, 2]$

■ **APPLICATIONS**

**65. Geometry.** The distances (in inches) from one vertex of a rectangle to the other three vertices are $x$, $x + 2$, and $x + 4$. Find the dimensions of the rectangle.

**66. Geometry.** A box is constructed to contain a volume of 97.5 cubic inches. The length of the base is 3.5 inches larger than the width, and the height is 0.5 inch larger than the length. Find the dimensions of the box.

**67. Agriculture.** The weekly volume (in liters) of milk produced in a farm is given by $v(x) = x^3 + 21x^2 - 1480x$, where $x$ is the number of cows. Find the number of cows that corresponds to a total production of 1500 liters of milk in a week.

**68. Profit.** A bakery uses the formula $f(x) = 2x^4 - 7x^3 + 3x^2 + 8x$ to determine the profit of selling $x$ loaves of bread. How many loaves of bread must be sold to have a profit of \$4? Assume $x \geq 1$.

**For Exercises 69 and 70, refer to the following:**

The demand function for a product is

$$p(x) = 28 - 0.0002x$$

where $p$ is the unit price (in dollars) of the product and $x$ is the number of units produced and sold. The cost function for the product is

$$C(x) = 20x + 1500$$

where $C$ is the total cost (in dollars) and $x$ is the number of units produced. The total profit obtained by producing and selling $x$ units is

$$P(x) = xp(x) - C(x)$$

**69. Business.** Find the total profit function when $x$ units are produced and sold. Use Descartes' rule of signs to determine possible combinations of positive zeros for the profit function.

**70. Business.** Find the break-even point(s) for the product to the nearest unit. Discuss the significance of the break-even point(s) for the product.

**71. Health/Medicine.** During the course of treatment of an illness the concentration of a dose of a drug (in mcg/mL) in the bloodstream fluctuates according to the model

$$C(t) = 15.4 - 0.05t^2$$

where $t = 0$ is when the drug was administered. Assuming a single dose of the drug is administered, in how many hours (to the nearest hour) after being administered will the drug be eliminated from the bloodstream?

**72. Health/Medicine.** During the course of treatment of an illness, the concentration of a dose of a drug (in mcg/mL) in the bloodstream fluctuates according to the model

$$C(t) = 60 - 0.75t^2$$

where $t = 0$ is when the drug was administered. Assuming a single dose of the drug is administered, in how many hours (to the nearest hour) after being administered will the drug be eliminated from the bloodstream?

■ **CATCH THE MISTAKE**

**In Exercises 73 and 74, explain the mistake that is made.**

**73.** Use Descartes' rule of signs to determine the possible combinations of zeros of

$$P(x) = 2x^5 + 7x^4 + 9x^3 + 9x^2 + 7x + 2$$

**Solution:**

No sign changes, so no positive real zeros.

$$P(x) = 2x^5 + 7x^4 + 9x^3 + 9x^2 + 7x + 2$$

Five sign changes, so five negative real zeros.

$$P(-x) = -2x^5 + 7x^4 - 9x^3 + 9x^2 - 7x + 2$$

This is incorrect. What mistake was made?

**74.** Determine whether $x - 2$ is a factor of

$$P(x) = x^3 - 2x^2 - 5x + 6$$

**Solution:**

$$
\begin{array}{r|rrrr}
-2 & 1 & -2 & -5 & 6 \\
   &   & -2 & 8 & -6 \\
\hline
   & 1 & -4 & 3 & \boxed{0}
\end{array}
$$

Yes, $x - 2$ is a factor of $P(x)$.

This is incorrect. What mistake was made?

■ **CONCEPTUAL**

**In Exercises 75–80, determine whether each statement is true or false.**

**75.** All real zeros of a polynomial correspond to $x$-intercepts.

**76.** A polynomial of degree $n$, $n > 0$, must have at least one zero.

**77.** A polynomial of degree $n$, $n > 0$, can be written as a product of $n$ linear factors over real numbers.

**78.** The number of sign changes in a polynomial is equal to the number of positive real zeros of that polynomial.

**79.** A polynomial of degree $n$, $n > 0$, must have exactly $n$ $x$-intercepts.

**80.** A polynomial with an odd number of zeros must have odd degree.

■ **CHALLENGE**

**81.** Given that $x = a$ is a zero of
$P(x) = x^3 - (a + b + c)x^2 + (ab + ac + bc)x - abc$,
find the other two zeros, given that $a$, $b$, and $c$ are real numbers and $a > b > c$.

**82.** Given that $x = a$ is a zero of
$p(x) = x^3 + (-a + b - c)x^2 - (ab + bc - ac)x + abc$,
find the other two real zeros, given that $a$, $b$, and $c$ are real positive numbers.

**83.** Given that $b$ is a zero of
$P(x) = x^4 - (a + b)x^3 + (ab - c^2)x^2 + (a + b)c^2x - abc^2$,
find the other three real zeros, given that $a$, $b$, and $c$ are real positive numbers.

**84.** Given that $a$ is a zero of $P(x) =$
$x^4 + 2(b - a)x^3 + (a^2 - 4ab + b^2)x^2 + 2ab(a - b)x + a^2b^2$,
find the other three real zeros, given that $a$ and $b$ are real positive numbers.

■ **TECHNOLOGY**

**In Exercises 85 and 86, determine all possible rational zeros of the polynomial. There are many possibilities. Instead of trying them all, use a graphing calculator or software to graph $P(x)$ to help find a zero to test.**

**85.** $P(x) = x^3 - 2x^2 + 16x - 32$

**86.** $P(x) = x^3 - 3x^2 + 16x - 48$

**In Exercises 87 and 88: (a) determine all possible rational zeros of the polynomial, using a graphing calculator or software to graph $P(x)$ to help find the zeros; and (b) factor as a product of linear and/or irreducible quadratic factors.**

**87.** $P(x) = 12x^4 + 25x^3 + 56x^2 - 7x - 30$

**88.** $P(x) = -3x^3 - x^2 - 7x - 49$

■ **PREVIEW TO CALCULUS**

In calculus we use the zeros of the derivative $f'$ of a function $f$ to determine whether the function $f$ is increasing or decreasing around the zeros.
   In Exercises 89–92, find the zeros of each polynomial function and determine the intervals over which $f(x) > 0$.

**89.** $f(x) = x^3 - 4x^2 - 7x + 10$

**90.** $f(x) = 6x^3 - 13x^2 - 11x + 8$

**91.** $f(x) = -2x^4 + 5x^3 + 7x^2 - 10x - 6$

**92.** $f(x) = -3x^4 + 14x^3 - 11x^2 + 14x - 8$

**SKILLS OBJECTIVES**

- Find the complex zeros of a polynomial function.
- Use the complex conjugate zeros theorem.
- Factor polynomial functions over the complex numbers.

**CONCEPTUAL OBJECTIVES**

- Extend the domain of polynomial functions to complex numbers.
- Understand how the fundamental theorem of algebra guarantees at least one zero.
- Understand why complex zeros occur in conjugate pairs.

## Complex Zeros

In Section 2.4, we found the *real* zeros of a polynomial function. In this section, we find the *complex* zeros of a polynomial function. The domain of polynomial functions thus far has been the set of all real numbers. Now, we consider a more general case, where the domain of a polynomial function is the set of *complex numbers*. Note that the set of real numbers is a subset of the complex numbers. (Choose the imaginary part to be zero.)

It is important to note, however, that when we are discussing *graphs* of polynomial functions, we restrict the domain to the set of real numbers.

A *zero* of a polynomial $P(x)$ is the *solution* or *root* of the equation $P(x) = 0$. The *zeros of a polynomial can be complex numbers.* However, since the axes of the $xy$-plane represent real numbers, we interpret zeros as $x$-intercepts only when the zeros are real numbers.

We can illustrate the relationship between real and complex zeros of polynomial functions and their graphs with two similar examples. Let's take the two quadratic functions $f(x) = x^2 - 4$ and $g(x) = x^2 + 4$. The graphs of these two functions are parabolas that open upward with $f(x)$ shifted down four units and $g(x)$ shifted up four units as shown on the left. Setting each function equal to zero and solving for $x$, we find that the zeros for $f(x)$ are $-2$ and $2$ and the zeros for $g(x)$ are $-2i$ and $2i$. Notice that the $x$-intercepts for $f(x)$ are $(-2, 0)$ and $(2, 0)$ and $g(x)$ has **no** $x$-intercepts.

*Study Tip*

The zeros of a polynomial can be complex numbers. Only when the zeros are real numbers do we interpret zeros as $x$-intercepts.

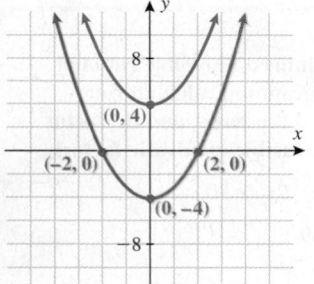

## The Fundamental Theorem of Algebra

In Section 2.4, we were able to write a polynomial function as a product of linear and/or irreducible quadratic factors. Now, we consider factors over complex numbers. Therefore, what were irreducible quadratic factors over real numbers will now be a product of two linear factors over the complex numbers.

What are the minimum and maximum number of zeros a polynomial can have? Every polynomial has *at least one zero* (provided the degree is greater than zero). The largest number of zeros a polynomial can have is equal to the degree of the polynomial.

*Study Tip*

The largest number of zeros a polynomial can have is equal to the degree of the polynomial.

**THE FUNDAMENTAL THEOREM OF ALGEBRA**

Every polynomial $P(x)$ of degree $n > 0$ has *at least one zero* in the complex number system.

The fundamental theorem of algebra and the factor theorem are used to prove the following $n$ zeros theorem.

**$n$ ZEROS THEOREM**

Every polynomial $P(x)$ of degree $n > 0$ can be expressed as the product of $n$ linear factors in the complex number system. Hence, $P(x)$ has exactly $n$ zeros, not necessarily distinct.

These two theorems are illustrated with five polynomials below:

**a.** The **first**-degree polynomial $f(x) = x + 3$ has exactly **one** zero: $x = -3$.

**b.** The **second**-degree polynomial $f(x) = x^2 + 10x + 25 = (x + 5)(x + 5)$ has exactly **two** zeros: $x = -5$ and $x = -5$. It is customary to write this as a single zero of multiplicity 2 or refer to it as a repeated root.

**c.** The **third**-degree polynomial $f(x) = x^3 + 16x = x(x^2 + 16) = x(x + 4i)(x - 4i)$ has exactly **three** zeros: $x = 0$, $x = -4i$, and $x = 4i$.

**d.** The **fourth**-degree polynomial $f(x) = x^4 - 1 = (x^2 - 1)(x^2 + 1)$ $= (x - 1)(x + 1)(x - i)(x + i)$ has exactly **four** zeros: $x = 1$, $x = -1$, $x = i$, and $x = -i$.

**e.** The **fifth**-degree polynomial $f(x) = x^5 = x \cdot x \cdot x \cdot x \cdot x$ has exactly **five** zeros: $x = 0$, which has multiplicity 5.

The fundamental theorem of algebra and the $n$ zeros theorem only tell you that the zeros *exist*—not how to find them. We must rely on techniques discussed in Section 2.4 and additional strategies discussed in this section to determine the zeros.

## Complex Conjugate Pairs

Often, at a grocery store or a drugstore, we see signs for special offers—"buy one, get one free." A similar phenomenon occurs for complex zeros of a polynomial function with real coefficients. If we restrict the coefficients of a polynomial to real numbers, complex zeros always come in conjugate pairs. In other words, if a zero of a polynomial function is a complex number, then another zero will always be its complex conjugate. Look at the third-degree polynomial in the above illustration, part (c), where two of the zeros were $-4i$ and $4i$, and in part (d), where two of the zeros were $i$ and $-i$. In general, if we restrict the coefficients of a polynomial to real numbers, complex zeros always come in conjugate pairs.

**COMPLEX CONJUGATE ZEROS THEOREM**

If a polynomial $P(x)$ has real coefficients, and if $a + bi$ is a zero of $P(x)$, then its complex conjugate $a - bi$ is also a zero of $P(x)$.

We use the complex zeros theorem to assist us in factoring a higher degree polynomial.

**Technology Tip**

The graph of
$P(x) = x^4 - x^3 - 5x^2 - x - 6$
is shown.

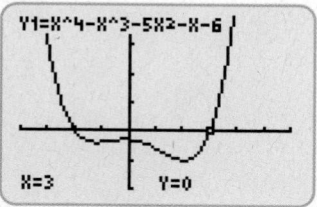

The real zeros of the function at
$x = -2$ and $x = 3$ give the factors of
$x + 2$ and $x - 3$. Use the synthetic
division to find the other factors.

A table of values supports the real zeros
of the function and its factors.

**EXAMPLE 1   Factoring a Polynomial with Complex Zeros**

Factor the polynomial $P(x) = x^4 - x^3 - 5x^2 - x - 6$ given that $i$ is a zero of $P(x)$.

Since $P(x)$ is a *fourth*-degree polynomial, we expect *four* zeros. The goal in this problem is to write $P(x)$ as a product of four linear factors: $P(x) = (x - a)(x - b)(x - c)(x - d)$, where $a$, $b$, $c$, and $d$ are complex numbers and represent the zeros of the polynomial.

**Solution:**

Write known zeros and linear factors.

Since $i$ is a zero, we know that $-i$ is a zero.          $x = i$ and $x = -i$

We now know two linear factors of $P(x)$.          $(x - i)$ and $(x + i)$

Write $P(x)$ as a product of four factors.          $P(x) = (x - i)(x + i)(x - c)(x - d)$

Multiply the two known factors.
$$(x + i)(x - i) = x^2 - i^2$$
$$= x^2 - (-1)$$
$$= x^2 + 1$$

Rewrite the polynomial.          $P(x) = (x^2 + 1)(x - c)(x - d)$

Divide both sides of the equation by $x^2 + 1$.          $\dfrac{P(x)}{x^2 + 1} = (x - c)(x - d)$

Divide $P(x)$ by $x^2 + 1$ using long division.

$$
\require{enclose}
\begin{array}{r}
x^2 - x - 6 \\
x^2 + 0x + 1 \enclose{longdiv}{x^4 - x^3 - 5x^2 - x - 6} \\
\underline{-(x^4 + 0x^3 + x^2)} \\
-x^3 - 6x^2 - x \\
\underline{-(-x^3 + 0x^2 - x)} \\
-6x^2 + 0x - 6 \\
\underline{-(-6x^2 + 0x - 6)} \\
0
\end{array}
$$

Since the remainder is 0, $x^2 - x - 6$
is a factor.          $P(x) = (x^2 + 1)(x^2 - x - 6)$

Factor the quotient $x^2 - x - 6$.          $x^2 - x - 6 = (x - 3)(x + 2)$

Write $P(x)$ as a product of four linear factors.     $\boxed{P(x) = (x - i)(x + i)(x - 3)(x + 2)}$

Check: $P(x)$ is a *fourth*-degree polynomial and we found *four* zeros, two of which are complex conjugates.

■**Answer:** $P(x) =$
$(x - 2i)(x + 2i)(x - 1)(x - 2)$
*Note:* The zeros of $P(x)$ are 1, 2,
$2i$, and $-2i$.

■ **YOUR TURN** Factor the polynomial $P(x) = x^4 - 3x^3 + 6x^2 - 12x + 8$ given that $x - 2i$ is a factor.

**EXAMPLE 2   Factoring a Polynomial with Complex Zeros**

Factor the polynomial $P(x) = x^4 - 2x^3 + x^2 + 2x - 2$ given that $1 + i$ is a zero of $P(x)$.

Since $P(x)$ is a *fourth*-degree polynomial, we expect *four* zeros. The goal in this problem is to write $P(x)$ as a product of four linear factors: $P(x) = (x - a)(x - b)(x - c)(x - d)$, where $a$, $b$, $c$, and $d$ are complex numbers and represent the zeros of the polynomial.

**Solution:**

STEP 1   Write known zeros and linear factors.

Since $1 + i$ is a zero, we know that $1 - i$ is a zero.                     $x = 1 + i$ and $x = 1 - i$

We now know two linear factors of $P(x)$.                     $[x - (1 + i)]$ and $[x - (1 - i)]$

STEP 2   Write $P(x)$ as a product of four factors.     $P(x) = [x - (1 + i)][x - (1 - i)](x - c)(x - d)$

STEP 3   Multiply the first two terms.                     $[x - (1 + i)][x - (1 - i)]$

First regroup the expressions in each bracket.                     $[(x - 1) - i][(x - 1) + i]$

Use the special product $(a - b)(a + b) = a^2 - b^2$, where $a$ is $(x - 1)$ and $b$ is $i$.
$$(x - 1)^2 - i^2$$
$$(x^2 - 2x + 1) - (-1)$$
$$x^2 - 2x + 2$$

STEP 4   Rewrite the polynomial.                     $P(x) = (x^2 - 2x + 2)(x - c)(x - d)$

STEP 5   Divide both sides of the equation by $x^2 - 2x + 2$, and substitute in the original polynomial $P(x) = x^4 - 2x^3 + x^2 + 2x - 2$.
$$\frac{x^4 - 2x^3 + x^2 + 2x - 2}{x^2 - 2x + 2} = (x - c)(x - d)$$

STEP 6   Divide the left side of the equation using long division.
$$\frac{x^4 - 2x^3 + x^2 + 2x - 2}{x^2 - 2x + 2} = x^2 - 1$$

STEP 7   Factor $x^2 - 1$.                     $(x - 1)(x + 1)$

STEP 8   Write $P(x)$ as a product of four linear factors.

$$\boxed{P(x) = [x - (1 + i)][x - (1 - i)][x - 1][x + 1]}$$

or

$$\boxed{P(x) = (x - 1 - i)(x - 1 + i)(x - 1)(x + 1)}$$

■ **YOUR TURN**   Factor the polynomial $P(x) = x^4 - 2x^2 + 16x - 15$ given that $1 + 2i$ is a zero.

■ **Answer:** $P(x) = [x - (1 + 2i)] \cdot [x - (1 - 2i)](x - 1)(x + 3)$
*Note:* The zeros of $P(x)$ are $1$, $-3$, $1 + 2i$, and $1 - 2i$.

Because an $n$-degree polynomial function has exactly $n$ zeros and since complex zeros always come in conjugate pairs, if the degree of the polynomial is **odd**, there is guaranteed to be **at least one zero that is a real number**. If the degree of the polynomial is even, there is no guarantee that a zero will be real—all the zeros could be complex.

*Study Tip*

Odd-degree polynomials have at least one real zero.

### EXAMPLE 3 Finding Possible Combinations of Real and Complex Zeros

List the possible combinations of real and complex zeros for the given polynomials.

**a.** $17x^5 + 2x^4 - 3x^3 + x^2 - 5$    **b.** $5x^4 + 2x^3 - x + 2$

**Solution:**

**a.** Since this is a *fifth*-degree polynomial, there are *five* zeros. Because complex zeros come in conjugate pairs, the table describes the possible five zeros.

| REAL ZEROS | COMPLEX ZEROS |
|---|---|
| 1 | 4 |
| 3 | 2 |
| 5 | 0 |

Applying Descartes' rule of signs, we find that there are three or one positive real zeros and two or no negative real zeros.

| POSITIVE REAL ZEROS | NEGATIVE REAL ZEROS | COMPLEX ZEROS |
|---|---|---|
| 1 | 0 | 4 |
| 3 | 0 | 2 |
| 1 | 2 | 2 |
| 3 | 2 | 0 |

**b.** Because this is a *fourth*-degree polynomial, there are *four* zeros. Since complex zeros come in conjugate pairs, the table describes the possible four zeros.

| REAL ZEROS | COMPLEX ZEROS |
|---|---|
| 0 | 4 |
| 2 | 2 |
| 4 | 0 |

Applying Descartes' rule of signs, we find that there are two or no positive real zeros and two or no negative real zeros.

| POSITIVE REAL ZEROS | NEGATIVE REAL ZEROS | COMPLEX ZEROS |
|---|---|---|
| 0 | 0 | 4 |
| 2 | 0 | 2 |
| 0 | 2 | 2 |
| 2 | 2 | 0 |

■ **Answer:**

| REAL ZEROS | COMPLEX ZEROS |
|---|---|
| 0 | 6 |
| 2 | 4 |
| 4 | 2 |
| 6 | 0 |

■ **YOUR TURN** List the possible combinations of real and complex zeros for

$$P(x) = x^6 - 7x^5 + 8x^3 - 2x + 1$$

## Factoring Polynomials

Now let's draw on the tests discussed in this chapter to help us find all the zeros of a polynomial. Doing so will enable us to write polynomials as a product of linear factors. Before reading Example 4, reread Section 2.4, Example 7.

# EXAMPLE 4   Factoring a Polynomial

Factor the polynomial $P(x) = x^5 + 2x^4 - x - 2$.

**Solution:**

**STEP 1** Determine variations in sign.

$P(x)$ has one sign change.        $P(x) = x^5 + 2x^4 - x - 2$

$P(-x)$ has two sign changes.      $P(-x) = -x^5 + 2x^4 + x - 2$

**STEP 2** Apply Descartes' rule of signs and summarize the results in a table.

| POSITIVE REAL ZEROS | NEGATIVE REAL ZEROS | COMPLEX ZEROS |
|:---:|:---:|:---:|
| 1 | 2 | 2 |
| 1 | 0 | 4 |

**STEP 3** Utilize the rational zero theorem to determine the possible rational zeros.     $\pm 1, \pm 2$

**STEP 4** Test possible rational zeros.

1 is a zero:

$$\begin{array}{r|rrrrrr} 1 & 1 & 2 & 0 & 0 & -1 & -2 \\ & & 1 & 3 & 3 & 3 & 2 \\ \hline & 1 & 3 & 3 & 3 & 2 & \boxed{0} \end{array}$$

$-1$ is a zero:

$$\begin{array}{r|rrrrr} -1 & 1 & 3 & 3 & 3 & 2 \\ & & -1 & -2 & -1 & -2 \\ \hline & 1 & 2 & 1 & 2 & \boxed{0} \end{array}$$

$-2$ is a zero:

$$\begin{array}{r|rrrr} -2 & 1 & 2 & 1 & 2 \\ & & -2 & 0 & -2 \\ \hline & 1 & 0 & 1 & \boxed{0} \end{array}$$

$\underbrace{x^2 + 1}\ = (x - i)(x + i)$

**STEP 5** Write $P(x)$ as a product of linear factors.

$$\boxed{P(x) = (x - 1)(x + 1)(x + 2)(x - i)(x + i)}$$

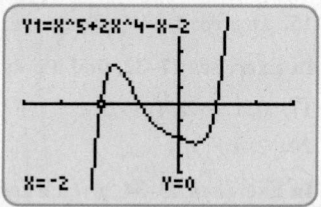
---

## SECTION
## 2.5 SUMMARY

In this section, we discussed **complex zeros** of polynomial functions. A polynomial function $P(x)$ of degree $n$ with real coefficients has the following properties:

- $P(x)$ has at least one zero (if $n > 0$) and no more than $n$ zeros.
- If $a + bi$ is a zero, then $a - bi$ is also a zero.
- The polynomial can be written as a product of linear factors, not necessarily distinct.

▪ **SKILLS**

In Exercises 1–8, find all zeros (real and complex). Factor the polynomial as a product of linear factors.

**1.** $P(x) = x^2 + 4$   **2.** $P(x) = x^2 + 9$   **3.** $P(x) = x^2 - 2x + 2$   **4.** $P(x) = x^2 - 4x + 5$

**5.** $P(x) = x^4 - 16$   **6.** $P(x) = x^4 - 81$   **7.** $P(x) = x^4 - 25$   **8.** $P(x) = x^4 - 9$

In Exercises 9–16, a polynomial function is described. Find all remaining zeros.

**9.** Degree: 3   Zeros: $-1, i$   **10.** Degree: 3   Zeros: $1, -i$

**11.** Degree: 4   Zeros: $2i, 3 - i$   **12.** Degree: 4   Zeros: $3i, 2 + i$

**13.** Degree: 6   Zeros: 2 (multiplicity 2), $1 - 3i, 2 + 5i$   **14.** Degree: 6   Zeros: $-2$ (multiplicity 2), $1 - 5i, 2 + 3i$

**15.** Degree: 6   Zeros: $-i, 1 - i$ (multiplicity 2)   **16.** Degree: 6   Zeros: $2i, 1 + i$ (multiplicity 2)

In Exercises 17–22, find a polynomial of minimum degree that has the given zeros.

**17.** $0, 1 - 2i, 1 + 2i$   **18.** $0, 2 - i, 2 + i$   **19.** $1, 1 - 5i, 1 + 5i$

**20.** $2, 4 - i, 4 + i$   **21.** $1 - i, 1 + i, -3i, 3i$   **22.** $-i, i, 1 - 2i, 1 + 2i$

In Exercises 23–34, given a zero of the polynomial, determine all other zeros (real and complex) and write the polynomial in terms of a product of linear factors.

| Polynomial | Zero | Polynomial | Zero |
|---|---|---|---|
| **23.** $P(x) = x^4 - 2x^3 - 11x^2 - 8x - 60$ | $-2i$ | **24.** $P(x) = x^4 - x^3 + 7x^2 - 9x - 18$ | $3i$ |
| **25.** $P(x) = x^4 - 4x^3 + 4x^2 - 4x + 3$ | $i$ | **26.** $P(x) = x^4 - x^3 + 2x^2 - 4x - 8$ | $-2i$ |
| **27.** $P(x) = x^4 - 2x^3 + 10x^2 - 18x + 9$ | $-3i$ | **28.** $P(x) = x^4 - 3x^3 + 21x^2 - 75x - 100$ | $5i$ |
| **29.** $P(x) = x^4 - 9x^2 + 18x - 14$ | $1 + i$ | **30.** $P(x) = x^4 - 4x^3 + x^2 + 6x - 40$ | $1 - 2i$ |
| **31.** $P(x) = x^4 - 6x^3 + 6x^2 + 24x - 40$ | $3 - i$ | **32.** $P(x) = x^4 - 4x^3 + 4x^2 + 4x - 5$ | $2 + i$ |
| **33.** $P(x) = x^4 - 9x^3 + 29x^2 - 41x + 20$ | $2 - i$ | **34.** $P(x) = x^4 - 7x^3 + 14x^2 + 2x - 20$ | $3 + i$ |

In Exercises 35–58, factor each polynomial as a product of linear factors.

**35.** $P(x) = x^3 - x^2 + 9x - 9$   **36.** $P(x) = x^3 - 2x^2 + 4x - 8$   **37.** $P(x) = x^3 - 5x^2 + x - 5$

**38.** $P(x) = x^3 - 7x^2 + x - 7$   **39.** $P(x) = x^3 + x^2 + 4x + 4$   **40.** $P(x) = x^3 + x^2 - 2$

**41.** $P(x) = x^3 - x^2 - 18$   **42.** $P(x) = x^4 - 2x^3 - 2x^2 - 2x - 3$   **43.** $P(x) = x^4 - 2x^3 - 11x^2 - 8x - 60$

**44.** $P(x) = x^4 - x^3 + 7x^2 - 9x - 18$   **45.** $P(x) = x^4 - 4x^3 - x^2 - 16x - 20$   **46.** $P(x) = x^4 - 3x^3 + 11x^2 - 27x + 18$

**47.** $P(x) = x^4 - 7x^3 + 27x^2 - 47x + 26$   **48.** $P(x) = x^4 - 5x^3 + 5x^2 + 25x - 26$   **49.** $P(x) = -x^4 - 3x^3 + x^2 + 13x + 10$

**50.** $P(x) = -x^4 - x^3 + 12x^2 + 26x + 24$   **51.** $P(x) = x^4 - 2x^3 + 5x^2 - 8x + 4$   **52.** $P(x) = x^4 + 2x^3 + 10x^2 + 18x + 9$

**53.** $P(x) = x^6 + 12x^4 + 23x^2 - 36$   **54.** $P(x) = x^6 - 2x^5 + 9x^4 - 16x^3 + 24x^2 - 32x + 16$

**55.** $P(x) = 4x^4 - 20x^3 + 37x^2 - 24x + 5$   **56.** $P(x) = 4x^4 - 44x^3 + 145x^2 - 114x + 26$

**57.** $P(x) = 3x^5 - 2x^4 + 9x^3 - 6x^2 - 12x + 8$   **58.** $P(x) = 2x^5 - 5x^4 + 4x^3 - 26x^2 + 50x - 25$

▪ **APPLICATIONS**

In Exercises 59–62, assume the profit model is given by a polynomial function $P(x)$, where $x$ is the number of units sold by the company per year.

**59. Profit.** If the profit function of a given company has all imaginary zeros and the leading coefficient is positive, would you invest in this company? Explain.

**60. Profit.** If the profit function of a given company has all imaginary zeros and the leading coefficient is negative, would you invest in this company? Explain.

**61. Profit.** If the profit function of a company is modeled by a third-degree polynomial with a negative leading coefficient and this polynomial has two complex conjugates as zeros and one positive real zero, would you invest in this company? Explain.

**62. Profit.** If the profit function of a company is modeled by a third-degree polynomial with a positive leading coefficient and this polynomial has two complex conjugates as zeros and one positive real zero, would you invest in this company? Explain.

**For Exercises 63 and 64, refer to the following:**

The following graph models the profit $P$ of a company where $t$ is months and $t \geq 0$.

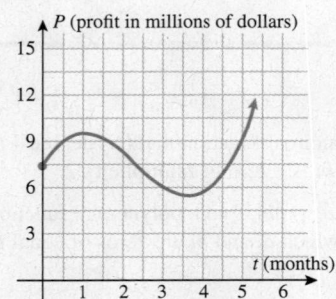

**63. Business.** If the profit function pictured is a third-degree polynomial, how many real and how many complex zeros does the function have? Discuss the implications of these zeros.

**64. Business.** If the profit function pictured is a fourth-degree polynomial with a negative leading coefficient, how many real and how many complex zeros does the function have? Discuss the implications of these zeros.

**For Exercises 65 and 66, refer to the following:**

The following graph models the concentration, $C$ (in $\mu$g/mL) of a drug in the bloodstream; and $t$ is time in hours after the drug is administered where $t \geq 0$.

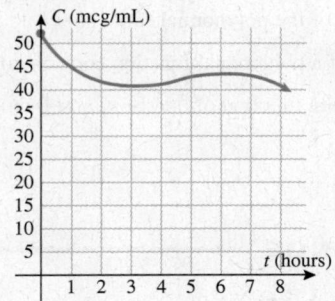

**65. Health/Medicine.** If the concentration function pictured is a third-degree polynomial, how many real and how many complex zeros does the function have? Discuss the implications of these zeros.

**66. Health/Medicine.** If the concentration function pictured is a fourth-degree polynomial with a negative leading coefficient, how many real and how many complex zeros does the function have? Discuss the implications of these zeros.

## ■ CATCH THE MISTAKE

**In Exercises 67 and 68, explain the mistake that is made.**

**67.** Given that 1 is a zero of $P(x) = x^3 - 2x^2 + 7x - 6$, find all other zeros.

**Solution:**

**Step 1:** $P(x)$ is a third-degree polynomial, so we expect three zeros.

**Step 2:** Because 1 is a zero, $-1$ is a zero, so two linear factors are $(x - 1)$ and $(x + 1)$.

**Step 3:** Write the polynomial as a product of three linear factors.

$$P(x) = (x - 1)(x + 1)(x - c)$$
$$P(x) = (x^2 - 1)(x - c)$$

**Step 4:** To find the remaining linear factor, we divide $P(x)$ by $x^2 - 1$.

$$\frac{x^3 - 2x^2 + 7x - 6}{x^2 - 1} = x - 2 + \frac{6x - 8}{x^2 - 1}$$

Which has a nonzero remainder? What went wrong?

**68.** Factor the polynomial $P(x) = 2x^3 + x^2 + 2x + 1$.

**Solution:**

**Step 1:** Since $P(x)$ is an odd-degree polynomial, we are guaranteed one real zero (since complex zeros come in conjugate pairs).

**Step 2:** Apply the rational zero test to develop a list of potential rational zeros.

Possible zeros: $\pm 1$

**Step 3:** Test possible zeros.

1 is not a zero: $P(x) = 2(1)^3 + (1)^2 + 2(1) + 1$
$$= 6$$

$-1$ is not a zero: $P(x) = 2(-1)^3 + (-1)^2 + 2(-1) + 1$
$$= -2$$

*Note:* $-\frac{1}{2}$ is the real zero. Why did we not find it?

### ▪ CONCEPTUAL

**In Exercises 69–72, determine whether each statement is true or false.**

**69.** If $x = 1$ is a zero of a polynomial function, then $x = -1$ is also a zero of the polynomial function.

**70.** All zeros of a polynomial function correspond to $x$-intercepts.

**71.** A polynomial function of degree $n$, $n > 0$ must have at least one zero.

**72.** A polynomial function of degree $n$, $n > 0$ can be written as a product of $n$ linear factors.

**73.** Is it possible for an odd-degree polynomial to have all imaginary complex zeros? Explain.

**74.** Is it possible for an even-degree polynomial to have all imaginary zeros? Explain.

### ▪ CHALLENGE

**In Exercises 75 and 76, assume $a$ and $b$ are nonzero real numbers.**

**75.** Find a polynomial function that has degree 6 and for which $bi$ is a zero of multiplicity 3.

**76.** Find a polynomial function that has degree 4 and for which $a + bi$ is a zero of multiplicity 2.

**77.** Find a polynomial function that has degree 6 and for which $ai$ and $bi$ are zeros, where $ai$ has multiplicity 2. Assume $|a| \neq |b|$.

**78.** Assuming $|a| \neq |b|$, find a polynomial function of lowest degree for which $ai$ and $bi$ are zeros of equal multiplicity.

### ▪ TECHNOLOGY

**For Exercises 79 and 80, determine possible combinations of real and complex zeros. Plot $P(x)$ and identify any real zeros with a graphing calculator or software. Does this agree with your list?**

**79.** $P(x) = x^4 + 13x^2 + 36$

**80.** $P(x) = x^6 + 2x^4 + 7x^2 - 130x - 288$

**For Exercises 81 and 82, find all zeros (real and complex). Factor the polynomial as a product of linear factors.**

**81.** $P(x) = -5x^5 + 3x^4 - 25x^3 + 15x^2 - 20x + 12$

**82.** $P(x) = x^5 + 2.1x^4 - 5x^3 - 5.592x^2 + 9.792x - 3.456$

### ▪ PREVIEW TO CALCULUS

**In Exercises 83–86, refer to the following:**

In calculus we study the integration of rational functions by partial fractions.

**a.** Factor each polynomial into linear factors. Use complex numbers when necessary.

**b.** Factor each polynomial using only real numbers.

**83.** $f(x) = x^3 + x^2 + x + 1$

**84.** $f(x) = x^3 - 6x^2 + 21x - 26$

**85.** $f(x) = x^4 + 5x^2 + 4$

**86.** $f(x) = x^4 - 2x^3 - 7x^2 + 18x - 18$

**SKILLS OBJECTIVES**

▪ Find the domain of a rational function.
▪ Determine vertical, horizontal, and slant asymptotes of rational functions.
▪ Graph rational functions.

**CONCEPTUAL OBJECTIVE**

▪ Interpret the behavior of the graph of a rational function approaching an asymptote.

## Domain of Rational Functions

So far in this chapter, we have discussed polynomial functions. We now turn our attention to *rational functions*, which are *ratios* of polynomial functions. Ratios of integers are called *rational numbers*. Similarly, ratios of polynomial functions are called *rational functions*.

**DEFINITION**     **Rational Function**

A function $f(x)$ is a **rational function** if

$$f(x) = \frac{n(x)}{d(x)} \qquad d(x) \neq 0$$

where the numerator $n(x)$ and the denominator $d(x)$ are polynomial functions. The domain of $f(x)$ is the set of all real numbers $x$ such that $d(x) \neq 0$.

*Note:* If $d(x)$ is a constant, then $f(x)$ is a polynomial function.

The domain of any polynomial function is the set of all real numbers. When we divide two polynomial functions, the result is a *rational function*, and we must exclude any values of $x$ that make the denominator equal to zero.

**EXAMPLE 1**     **Finding the Domain of a Rational Function**

Find the domain of the rational function $f(x) = \dfrac{x + 1}{x^2 - x - 6}$. Express the domain in interval notation.

**Solution:**

| | |
|---|---|
| Set the denominator equal to zero. | $x^2 - x - 6 = 0$ |
| Factor. | $(x + 2)(x - 3) = 0$ |
| Solve for $x$. | $x = -2 \quad \text{or} \quad x = 3$ |
| Eliminate these values from the domain. | $x \neq -2 \quad \text{or} \quad x \neq 3$ |
| State the domain in interval notation. | $\boxed{(-\infty, -2) \cup (-2, 3) \cup (3, \infty)}$ |

▪ **YOUR TURN** Find the domain of the rational function $f(x) = \dfrac{x - 2}{x^2 - 3x - 4}$. Express the domain in interval notation.

▪ **Answer:** The domain is the set of all real numbers such that $x \neq -1$ or $x \neq 4$. Interval notation: $(-\infty, -1) \cup (-1, 4) \cup (4, \infty)$

It is important to note that there are not always restrictions on the domain. For example, if the denominator is never equal to zero, the domain is the set of all real numbers.

**307**

**EXAMPLE 2    When the Domain of a Rational Function Is the Set of All Real Numbers**

Find the domain of the rational function $g(x) = \dfrac{3x}{x^2 + 9}$. Express the domain in interval notation.

**Solution:**

| | |
|---|---|
| Set the denominator equal to zero. | $x^2 + 9 = 0$ |
| Subtract 9 from both sides. | $x^2 = -9$ |
| Solve for $x$. | $x = -3i \quad \text{or} \quad x = 3i$ |
| There are no *real* solutions; therefore, the domain has no restrictions. | $\mathbb{R}$, the set of all real numbers |
| State the domain in interval notation. | $\boxed{(-\infty, \infty)}$ |

■ **Answer:** The domain is the set of all real numbers. Interval notation: $(-\infty, \infty)$

■ **YOUR TURN**  Find the domain of the rational function $g(x) = \dfrac{5x}{x^2 + 4}$. Express the domain in interval notation.

It is important to note that $f(x) = \dfrac{x^2 - 4}{x + 2}$, where $x \neq -2$, and $g(x) = x - 2$ are *not* the same function. Although $f(x)$ can be written in the factored form $f(x) = \dfrac{(x - 2)(x + 2)}{x + 2} = x - 2$, its domain is different. The domain of $g(x)$ is the set of all real numbers, whereas the domain of $f(x)$ is the set of all real numbers such that $x \neq -2$. If we were to plot $f(x)$ and $g(x)$, they would both look like the line $y = x - 2$. However, $f(x)$ would have a hole, or discontinuity, at the point $x = -2$.

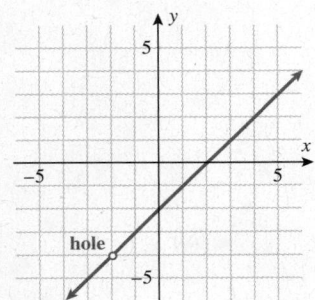

## Vertical, Horizontal, and Slant Asymptotes

If a function is not defined at a point, then it is still useful to know how the function behaves near that point. Let's start with a simple rational function, the reciprocal function $f(x) = \dfrac{1}{x}$. This function is defined everywhere except at $x = 0$.

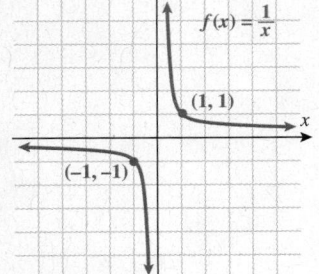

| $x$ | $-\dfrac{1}{10}$ | $-\dfrac{1}{100}$ | $-\dfrac{1}{1000}$ | $0$ | $\dfrac{1}{1000}$ | $\dfrac{1}{100}$ | $\dfrac{1}{10}$ |
|---|---|---|---|---|---|---|---|
| $f(x) = \dfrac{1}{x}$ | $-10$ | $-100$ | $-1000$ | undefined | $1000$ | $100$ | $10$ |

$x$ approaching 0 from the left      $x$ approaching 0 from the right

| $x$ | $f(x) = \dfrac{1}{x}$ |
|---|---|
| $-10$ | $-\dfrac{1}{10}$ |
| $-1$ | $-1$ |
| $1$ | $1$ |
| $10$ | $\dfrac{1}{10}$ |

We cannot let $x = 0$, because that point is not in the domain of the function. We should, however, ask the question, "How does $f(x)$ behave as $x$ *approaches* zero?" Let us take values that get closer and closer to $x = 0$, such as $\frac{1}{10}, \frac{1}{100}, \frac{1}{1000}, \ldots$ (See the table above.) We use an *arrow* to represent the word *approach*, a *positive* superscript to represent from the *right*, and a *negative* superscript to represent from the *left*. A plot of this function can be generated using point-plotting techniques. The following are observations of the graph $f(x) = \dfrac{1}{x}$.

| WORDS | MATH | |
|---|---|---|

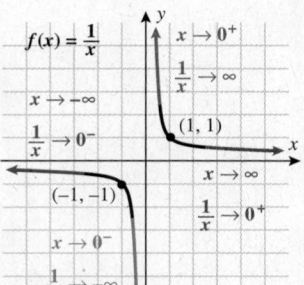

| WORDS | MATH |
|---|---|
| As $x$ approaches zero from the *right*, the function $f(x)$ increases without bound. | $x \to 0^+$ <br> $\dfrac{1}{x} \to \infty$ |
| As $x$ approaches zero from the *left*, the function $f(x)$ decreases without bound. | $x \to 0^-$ <br> $\dfrac{1}{x} \to -\infty$ |
| As $x$ approaches infinity (increases without bound), the function $f(x)$ approaches zero from *above*. | $x \to \infty$ <br> $\dfrac{1}{x} \to 0^+$ |
| As $x$ approaches negative infinity (decreases without bound), the function $f(x)$ approaches zero from *below*. | $x \to -\infty$ <br> $\dfrac{1}{x} \to 0^-$ |

The symbol $\infty$ does not represent an actual real number. This symbol represents growing without bound.

1. Notice that the function is not defined at $x = 0$. The $y$-axis, or the vertical line $x = 0$, represents the *vertical asymptote*.
2. Notice that the value of the function is never equal to zero. The $x$-axis is approached but not actually reached by the function. The $x$-axis, or $y = 0$, is a *horizontal asymptote*.

**Asymptotes** are lines that the graph of a function approaches. Suppose a football team's defense is its own 8 yard line and the team gets an "offsides" penalty that results in loss of "half the distance to the goal." Then the offense would get the ball on the 4 yard line. Suppose the defense gets another penalty on the next play that results in "half the distance to the goal." The offense would then get the ball on the 2 yard line. If the defense received 10 more penalties all resulting in "half the distance to the goal," would the referees *give* the offense a touchdown? No, because although the offense may appear to be snapping the ball from the goal line, technically it has not actually reached the goal line. Asymptotes utilize the same concept.

We will start with *vertical asymptotes*. Although the function $f(x) = \dfrac{1}{x}$ had one vertical asymptote, in general, rational functions can have *none*, *one*, or *several* vertical asymptotes. We will first formally define what a vertical asymptote is and then discuss how to find it.

**DEFINITION** **Vertical Asymptotes**

The line $x = a$ is a **vertical asymptote** for the graph of a function if $f(x)$ either increases or decreases without bound as $x$ approaches $a$ from either the left or the right.

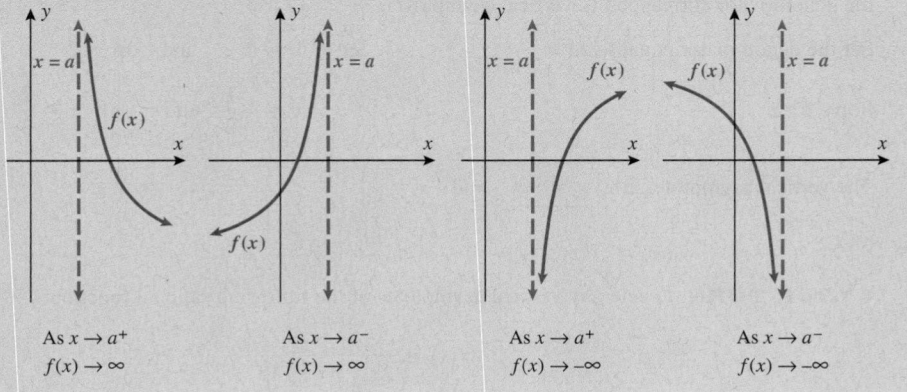

| As $x \to a^+$ <br> $f(x) \to \infty$ | As $x \to a^-$ <br> $f(x) \to \infty$ | As $x \to a^+$ <br> $f(x) \to -\infty$ | As $x \to a^-$ <br> $f(x) \to -\infty$ |
|---|---|---|---|

Vertical asymptotes assist us in graphing rational functions since they essentially "steer" the function in the vertical direction. How do we locate the vertical asymptotes of a rational function? Set the denominator equal to zero. If the numerator and denominator have no common factors, then any numbers that are excluded from the domain of a rational function locate vertical asymptotes.

A rational function $f(x) = \dfrac{n(x)}{d(x)}$ is said to be in **lowest terms** if the numerator $n(x)$ and denominator $d(x)$ have no common factors. Let $f(x) = \dfrac{n(x)}{d(x)}$ be a rational function in lowest terms; then any zeros of the numerator $n(x)$ correspond to x-intercepts of the graph of $f$, and any zeros of the denominator $d(x)$ correspond to vertical asymptotes of the graph of $f$. If a rational function does have a common factor (is not in lowest terms), then the common factor(s) should be canceled, resulting in an equivalent rational function $R(x)$ in lowest terms. If $(x - a)^p$ is a factor of the numerator and $(x - a)^q$ is a factor of the denominator, then there is a *hole* in the graph at $x = a$ provided $p \geq q$ and $x = a$ is a vertical asymptote if $p < q$.

### LOCATING VERTICAL ASYMPTOTES

Let $f(x) = \dfrac{n(x)}{d(x)}$ be a rational function in lowest terms [that is, assume $n(x)$ and $d(x)$ are polynomials with no common factors]; then the graph of $f$ has a vertical asymptote at any real zero of the denominator $d(x)$. That is, if $d(a) = 0$, then $x = a$ corresponds to a vertical asymptote on the graph of $f$.

*Note:* If $f$ is a rational function that is not in lowest terms, then divide out the common factors, resulting in a rational function $R$ that is in lowest terms. Any common factor $x - a$ of the function $f$ corresponds to a hole in the graph of $f$ at $x = a$ provided the multiplicity of $a$ in the numerator is greater than or equal to the multiplicity of $a$ in the denominator.

**EXAMPLE 3  Determining Vertical Asymptotes**

Locate any vertical asymptotes of the rational function $f(x) = \dfrac{5x + 2}{6x^2 - x - 2}$.

**Solution:**

Factor the denominator.
$$f(x) = \frac{5x + 2}{(2x + 1)(3x - 2)}$$

The numerator and denominator have no common factors, which means that all zeros of the denominator correspond to vertical asymptotes.

Set the denominator equal to zero.
$$2x + 1 = 0 \quad \text{and} \quad 3x - 2 = 0$$

Solve for $x$.
$$x = -\frac{1}{2} \quad \text{and} \quad x = \frac{2}{3}$$

The vertical asymptotes are $\boxed{x = -\frac{1}{2}}$ and $\boxed{x = \frac{2}{3}}$.

**■ Answer:** $x = -\frac{5}{2}$ and $x = 3$

**■ YOUR TURN** Locate any vertical asymptotes of the following rational function:
$$f(x) = \frac{3x - 1}{2x^2 - x - 15}$$

**EXAMPLE 4   Determining Vertical Asymptotes When the Rational Function Is Not in Lowest Terms**

Locate any vertical asymptotes of the rational function $f(x) = \dfrac{x + 2}{x^3 - 3x^2 - 10x}$.

**Solution:**

Factor the denominator.

$$\begin{aligned} x^3 - 3x^2 - 10x &= x\left(x^2 - 3x - 10\right) \\ &= x(x - 5)(x + 2) \end{aligned}$$

Write the rational function in factored form.

$$f(x) = \frac{(x + 2)}{x(x - 5)(x + 2)}$$

Cancel (divide out) the common factor $(x + 2)$.

$$R(x) = \frac{1}{x(x - 5)} \quad x \neq -2$$

Find the values when the denominator of $R$ is equal to zero.

$$x = 0 \quad \text{and} \quad x = 5$$

The vertical asymptotes are $\boxed{x = 0}$ and $\boxed{x = 5}$.

*Note:* $x = -2$ is not in the domain of $f(x)$, even though there is no vertical asymptote there. There is a "hole" in the graph at $x = -2$. Graphing calculators do not always show such "holes."

■ **YOUR TURN** Locate any vertical asymptotes of the following rational function:

$$f(x) = \frac{x^2 - 4x}{x^2 - 7x + 12}$$

■ **Answer:** $x = 3$

We now turn our attention to *horizontal asymptotes*. As we have seen, rational functions can have several vertical asymptotes. However, rational functions can have *at most* one horizontal asymptote. Horizontal asymptotes imply that a function approaches a constant value as $x$ becomes large in the positive or negative direction. Another difference between vertical and horizontal asymptotes is that the graph of a function never touches a vertical asymptote but, as you will see in the next box, the graph of a function may cross a horizontal asymptote, just not at the "ends" $(x \rightarrow \pm\infty)$.

**DEFINITION**   **Horizontal Asymptote**

The line $y = b$ is a **horizontal asymptote** of the graph of a function if $f(x)$ approaches $b$ as $x$ increases or decreases without bound. The following are three examples:

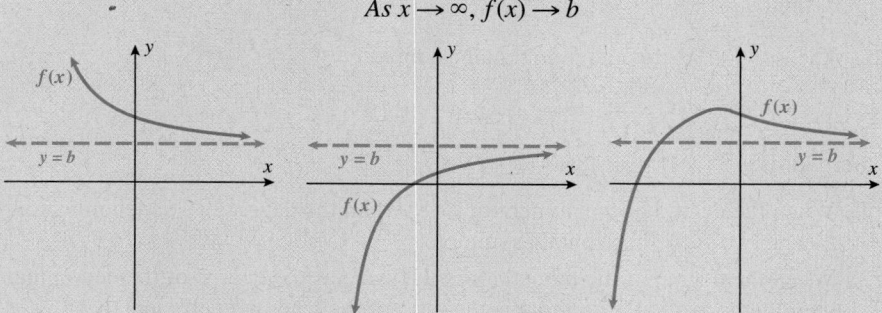

As $x \rightarrow \infty$, $f(x) \rightarrow b$

*Note:* A horizontal asymptote steers a function as $x$ gets large. Therefore, when $x$ is not large, the function may cross the asymptote.

How do we determine whether a horizontal asymptote exists? And, if it does, how do we locate it? We investigate the value of the rational function as $x \to \infty$ or as $x \to -\infty$. One of two things will happen: Either the rational function will increase or decrease without bound or the rational function will approach a constant value.

We say that a rational function is **proper** if the degree of the numerator is less than the degree of the denominator. Proper rational functions, like $f(x) = \dfrac{1}{x}$, approach zero as $x$ gets large. Therefore, all proper rational functions have the specific horizontal asymptote, $y = 0$ (see Example 5a).

We say that a rational function is **improper** if the degree of the numerator is greater than or equal to the degree of the denominator. In this case, we can divide the numerator by the denominator and determine how the quotient behaves as $x$ increases without bound.

- If the quotient is a constant (resulting when the degrees of the numerator and denominator are equal), then as $x \to \infty$ or as $x \to -\infty$, the rational function approaches the constant quotient (see Example 5b).
- If the quotient is a polynomial function of degree 1 or higher, then the quotient depends on $x$ and does not approach a constant value as $x$ increases (see Example 5c). In this case, we say that there is no horizontal asymptote.

We find horizontal asymptotes by comparing the degree of the numerator and the degree of the denominator. There are three cases to consider:

1. The degree of the numerator is less than the degree of the denominator.
2. The degree of the numerator is equal to the degree of the denominator.
3. The degree of the numerator is greater than the degree of the denominator.

### LOCATING HORIZONTAL ASYMPTOTES

Let $f$ be a rational function given by

$$f(x) = \frac{n(x)}{d(x)} = \frac{a_n x^n + a_{n-1} x^{n-1} + \cdots + a_1 x + a_0}{b_m x^m + b_{m-1} x^{m-1} + \cdots + b_1 x + b_0}$$

where $n(x)$ and $d(x)$ are polynomials.

1. When $n < m$, the $x$-axis ($y = 0$) is the horizontal asymptote.

2. When $n = m$, the line $y = \dfrac{a_n}{b_m}$ (ratio of leading coefficients) is the horizontal asymptote.

3. When $n > m$, there is no horizontal asymptote.

In other words:

1. When the degree of the numerator is less than the degree of the denominator, then $y = 0$ is the horizontal asymptote.
2. When the degree of the numerator is the same as the degree of the denominator, then the horizontal asymptote is the ratio of the leading coefficients.
3. If the degree of the numerator is greater than the degree of the denominator, then there is no horizontal asymptote.

## EXAMPLE 5   Finding Horizontal Asymptotes

Determine whether a horizontal asymptote exists for the graph of each of the given rational functions. If it does, locate the horizontal asymptote.

**a.** $f(x) = \dfrac{8x + 3}{4x^2 + 1}$      **b.** $g(x) = \dfrac{8x^2 + 3}{4x^2 + 1}$      **c.** $h(x) = \dfrac{8x^3 + 3}{4x^2 + 1}$

**Solution (a):**

The degree of the numerator $8x + 3$ is 1.      $n = 1$

The degree of the denominator $4x^2 + 1$ is 2.      $m = 2$

The degree of the numerator is less than the
degree of the denominator.      $n < m$

The $x$-axis is the horizontal asymptote for the graph of $f(x)$.      $y = 0$

The line $\boxed{y = 0}$ is the horizontal asymptote for the graph of $f(x)$.

**Solution (b):**

The degree of the numerator $8x^2 + 3$ is 2.      $n = 2$

The degree of the denominator $4x^2 + 1$ is 2.      $m = 2$

The degree of the numerator is equal to the
degree of the denominator.      $n = m$

The ratio of the leading coefficients is the
horizontal asymptote for the graph of $g(x)$.      $y = \dfrac{8}{4} = 2$

The line $\boxed{y = 2}$ is the horizontal asymptote for the graph of $g(x)$.

If we divide the numerator by the denominator,
the resulting quotient is the constant 2.      $g(x) = \dfrac{8x^2 + 3}{4x^2 + 1} = 2 + \dfrac{1}{4x^2 + 1}$

**Solution (c):**

The degree of the numerator $8x^3 + 3$ is 3.      $n = 3$

The degree of the denominator $4x^2 + 1$ is 2.      $m = 2$

The degree of the numerator is greater than
the degree of the denominator.      $n > m$

The graph of the rational function $h(x)$ has $\boxed{\text{no horizontal asymptote}}$.

If we divide the numerator by the denominator,
the resulting quotient is a linear function and
corresponds to the slant asymptote $y = 2x$.      $h(x) = \dfrac{8x^3 + 3}{4x^2 + 1} = 2x + \dfrac{-2x + 3}{4x^2 + 1}$

■ **YOUR TURN** Find the horizontal asymptote (if one exists) for the graph of the rational function $f(x) = \dfrac{7x^3 + x - 2}{-4x^3 + 1}$.

There are three types of lines: horizontal (slope is zero), vertical (slope is undefined), and slant (nonzero slope). Similarly, there are three types of linear asymptotes: horizontal, vertical, and *slant*.

*Technology Tip*

The following graphs correspond to the rational functions given in Example 5. The horizontal asymptotes are apparent, but are not drawn in the graph.

**a.** Graph $f(x) = \dfrac{8x + 3}{4x^2 + 1}$.

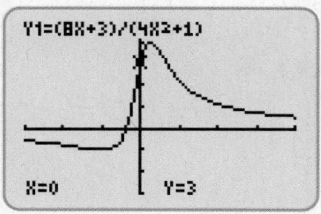

**b.** Graph $g(x) = \dfrac{8x^2 + 3}{4x^2 + 1}$.

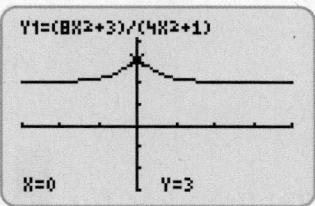

**c.** Graph $h(x) = \dfrac{8x^3 + 3}{4x^2 + 1}$.

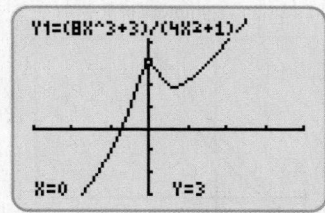

■ **Answer:** $y = -\dfrac{7}{4}$ is the horizontal asymptote.

*Study Tip*

There are three types of linear asymptotes: horizontal, vertical, and *slant*.

Recall that in dividing polynomials, the degree of the quotient is always the difference between the degree of the numerator and the degree of the denominator. For example, a cubic (third-degree) polynomial divided by a quadratic (second-degree) polynomial results in a linear (first-degree) polynomial. A fifth-degree polynomial divided by a fourth-degree polynomial results in a first-degree (linear) polynomial. When the degree of the numerator is exactly one more than the degree of the denominator, the quotient is linear and represents a *slant asymptote*.

### SLANT ASYMPTOTES

Let $f$ be a rational function given by $f(x) = \dfrac{n(x)}{d(x)}$, where $n(x)$ and $d(x)$ are polynomials and the degree of $n(x)$ is *one more than* the degree of $d(x)$. On dividing $n(x)$ by $d(x)$, the rational function can be expressed as

$$f(x) = mx + b + \frac{r(x)}{d(x)}$$

where the degree of the remainder $r(x)$ is less than the degree of $d(x)$ and the line $y = mx + b$ is a **slant asymptote** for the graph of $f$.

Note that as $x \rightarrow -\infty$ or $x \rightarrow \infty$, $f(x) \rightarrow mx + b$.

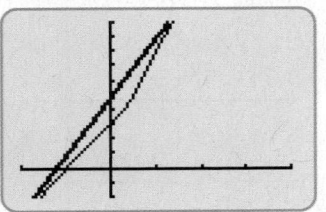
### EXAMPLE 6  Finding Slant Asymptotes

Determine the slant asymptote of the rational function $f(x) = \dfrac{4x^3 + x^2 + 3}{x^2 - x + 1}$.

**Solution:**

Divide the numerator by the denominator with long division.

$$
\begin{array}{r}
4x + 5 \phantom{xxxxxx} \\
x^2 - x + 1 \overline{\smash{)}\, 4x^3 + x^2 + 0x + 3} \\
\underline{-(4x^3 - 4x^2 + 4x)} \phantom{xx} \\
5x^2 - 4x + 3 \\
\underline{-(5x^2 - 5x + 5)} \\
x - 2
\end{array}
$$

Note that as $x \rightarrow \pm\infty$, the rational expression approaches 0.

$$f(x) = 4x + 5 + \underbrace{\frac{x - 2}{x^2 - x + 1}}_{\substack{\rightarrow 0 \text{ as} \\ x \rightarrow \pm\infty}}$$

The quotient is the slant asymptote.

$$\boxed{y = 4x + 5}$$

■ **YOUR TURN** Find the slant asymptote of the rational function $f(x) = \dfrac{x^2 + 3x + 2}{x - 2}$.

## Graphing Rational Functions

We can now graph rational functions using asymptotes as graphing aids. The following box summarizes the six-step procedure for graphing rational functions.

## GRAPHING RATIONAL FUNCTIONS

Let $f$ be a rational function given by $f(x) = \dfrac{n(x)}{d(x)}$.

**Step 1:** Find the domain of the rational function $f$.

**Step 2:** Find the **intercept(s)**.
- $y$-intercept: evaluate $f(0)$.
- $x$-intercept: solve the equation $n(x) = 0$ for $x$ in the domain of $f$.

**Step 3:** Find any **holes**.
- Factor the numerator and denominator.
- Divide out common factors.
- A common factor $x - a$ corresponds to a hole in the graph of $f$ at $x = a$ if the multiplicity of $a$ in the numerator is greater than or equal to the multiplicity of $a$ in the denominator.
- The result is an equivalent rational function $R(x) = \dfrac{p(x)}{q(x)}$ in lowest terms.

**Step 4:** Find any **asymptotes**.
- Vertical asymptotes: solve $q(x) = 0$.
- Compare the degree of the numerator and the degree of the denominator to determine whether either a horizontal or slant asymptote exists. If one exists, find it.

**Step 5:** Find **additional points** on the graph of $f$—particularly near asymptotes.

**Step 6:** **Sketch** the graph; draw the asymptotes, label the intercept(s) and additional points, and complete the graph with a smooth curve between and beyond the vertical asymptotes.

***Study Tip***

Any real number excluded from the domain of a rational function corresponds to either a vertical asymptote or a hole on its graph.

It is important to note that any real number eliminated from the domain of a rational function corresponds to either a vertical asymptote or a hole on its graph.

### EXAMPLE 7   Graphing a Rational Function

Graph the rational function $f(x) = \dfrac{x}{x^2 - 4}$.

**Solution:**

**STEP 1** Find the **domain**.

| | |
|---|---|
| Set the denominator equal to zero. | $x^2 - 4 = 0$ |
| Solve for $x$. | $x = \pm 2$ |
| State the domain. | $(-\infty, -2) \cup (-2, 2) \cup (2, \infty)$ |

**STEP 2** Find the **intercepts**.

$y$-intercept: $\qquad\qquad\qquad f(0) = \dfrac{0}{-4} = 0 \qquad y = 0$

$x$-intercepts: $\qquad\qquad\quad f(x) = \dfrac{x}{x^2 - 4} = 0 \qquad x = 0$

The only intercept is at the point $\boxed{(0, 0)}$.

**STEP 3** Find any holes.

$$f(x) = \frac{x}{(x+2)(x-2)}$$

There are no common factors, so $f$ is in lowest terms.
Since there are no common factors, there are no holes on the graph of $f$.

**STEP 4** Find any **asymptotes**.

Vertical asymptotes:

$$d(x) = (x+2)(x-2) = 0$$

$\boxed{x = -2}$ and $\boxed{x = 2}$

Horizontal asymptote:

$$\frac{\text{Degree of numerator}}{\text{Degree of denominator}} = \frac{1}{2}$$

Degree of numerator < Degree of denominator $\boxed{y = 0}$

**STEP 5** Find **additional points** on the graph.

| $x$ | $-3$ | $-1$ | $1$ | $3$ |
|---|---|---|---|---|
| $f(x)$ | $-\frac{3}{5}$ | $\frac{1}{3}$ | $-\frac{1}{3}$ | $\frac{3}{5}$ |

**STEP 6** **Sketch** the graph; label the intercepts, asymptotes, and additional points and complete with a smooth curve approaching the asymptotes.

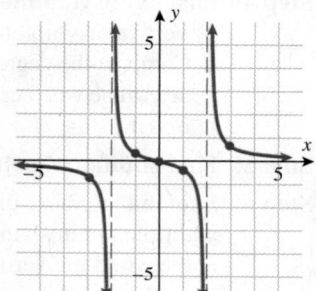

■ **Answer:**

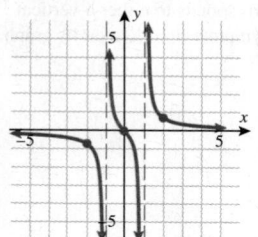

■ **YOUR TURN** Graph the rational function $f(x) = \dfrac{x}{x^2 - 1}$.

*Technology Tip*

The behavior of each function as $x$ approaches $\infty$ or $-\infty$ can be shown using tables of values.

Graph $f(x) = \dfrac{x^4 - x^3 - 6x^2}{x^2 - 1}$.

```
WINDOW
 Xmin=-4
 Xmax=5
 Xscl=1
 Ymin=-8
 Ymax=8
 Yscl=1
 Xres=1
```

```
Plot1 Plot2 Plot3
\Y1■(X^4-X^3-6X²
)/(X²-1)
\Y2=■
```

**EXAMPLE 8**  **Graphing a Rational Function with No Horizontal or Slant Asymptotes**

State the asymptotes (if there are any) and graph the rational function $f(x) = \dfrac{x^4 - x^3 - 6x^2}{x^2 - 1}$.

**Solution:**

**STEP 1** Find the domain.

Set the denominator equal to zero.      $x^2 - 1 = 0$

Solve for $x$.      $x = \pm 1$

State the domain.      $(-\infty, -1) \cup (-1, 1) \cup (1, \infty)$

**STEP 2** Find the **intercepts**.

$y$-intercept:      $f(0) = \dfrac{0}{-1} = 0$

$x$-intercepts:      $n(x) = x^4 - x^3 - 6x^2 = 0$

Factor.      $x^2(x - 3)(x + 2) = 0$

Solve.      $x = 0, x = 3,$ and $x = -2$

The **intercepts** are the points **(0, 0)**, **(3, 0)**, and **(−2, 0)**.

**STEP 3** Find any **holes**.

$$f(x) = \frac{x^2(x-3)(x+2)}{(x-1)(x+1)}$$

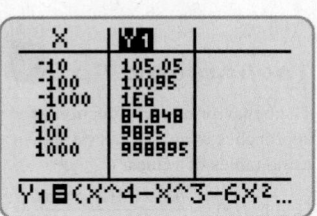

There are no common factors, so $f$ is in lowest terms.
Since there are no common factors, there are no holes on the graph of $f$.

The graph of $f(x)$ shows that the vertical asymptotes are at $x = \pm 1$ and there is no horizontal asymptote or slant asymptote.

**STEP 4** Find the **asymptotes**.

Vertical asymptote: $\qquad\qquad\qquad\qquad d(x) = x^2 - 1 = 0$

Factor. $\qquad\qquad\qquad\qquad\qquad (x+1)(x-1) = 0$

Solve. $\qquad\qquad\qquad\qquad\qquad x = -1 \text{ and } x = 1$

No horizontal asymptote: degree of $n(x) >$ degree of $d(x)$ $\qquad [4 > 2]$

No slant asymptote: degree of $n(x) -$ degree of $d(x) > 1$ $\qquad [4 - 2 = 2 > 1]$

The **asymptotes** are $x = -1$ and $x = 1$.

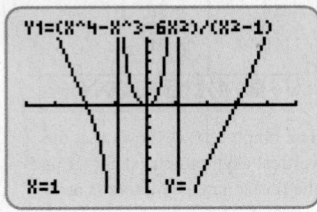

**STEP 5** Find **additional points** on the graph.

| $x$ | $-3$ | $-0.5$ | $0.5$ | $2$ | $4$ |
|---|---|---|---|---|---|
| $f(x)$ | $6.75$ | $1.75$ | $2.08$ | $-5.33$ | $6.4$ |

**STEP 6** **Sketch** the graph; label the **intercepts** and **asymptotes**, and complete with a smooth curve between and beyond the vertical asymptote.

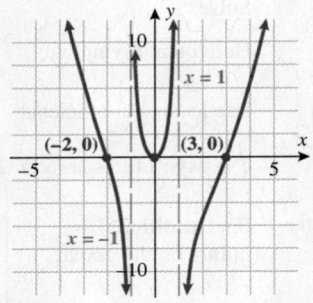

★ **YOUR TURN** State the asymptotes (if there are any) and graph the rational function:

$$f(x) = \frac{x^3 - 2x^2 - 3x}{x+2}$$

■ **Answer:** Vertical asymptote: $x = -2$. No horizontal or slant asymptotes.

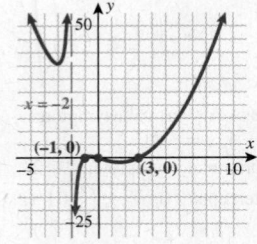

**EXAMPLE 9** **Graphing a Rational Function with a Horizontal Asymptote**

State the asymptotes (if there are any) and graph the rational function

$$f(x) = \frac{4x^3 + 10x^2 - 6x}{8 - x^3}$$

**Solution:**

**STEP 1** Find the **domain**.

Set the denominator equal to zero. $\qquad 8 - x^3 = 0$

Solve for $x$. $\qquad\qquad\qquad\qquad\qquad x = 2$

State the domain. $\qquad\qquad\qquad\qquad (-\infty, 2) \cup (2, \infty)$

## Technology Tip

The behavior of each function as $x$ approaches $\infty$ or $-\infty$ can be shown using tables of values.

Graph $f(x) = \dfrac{4x^3 - 10x^2 - 6x}{8 - x^3}$.

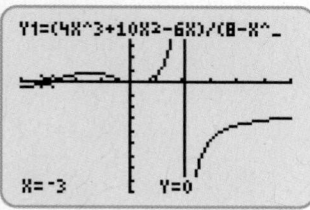

The graph of $f(x)$ shows that the vertical asymptote is at $x = 1$ and the horizontal asymptote is at $y = -4$.

**STEP 2** Find the **intercepts**.

$y$-intercept: $\qquad\qquad\qquad\qquad\qquad f(0) = \dfrac{0}{8} = 0$

$x$-intercepts: $\qquad\qquad\qquad\qquad n(x) = 4x^3 + 10x^2 - 6x = 0$

Factor. $\qquad\qquad\qquad\qquad\qquad 2x(2x - 1)(x + 3) = 0$

Solve. $\qquad\qquad\qquad\qquad\qquad x = 0, x = \dfrac{1}{2}, \text{ and } x = -3$

The **intercepts** are the points $(0, 0), \left(\frac{1}{2}, 0\right)$, and $(-3, 0)$.

**STEP 3** Find the **holes**. $\qquad\qquad\qquad f(x) = \dfrac{2x(2x - 1)(x + 3)}{(2 - x)(x^2 + 2x + 4)}$

There are no common factors, so $f$ is in lowest terms (no holes).

**STEP 4** Find the **asymptotes**.

Vertical asymptote: $\qquad\qquad\qquad d(x) = 8 - x^3 = 0$

Solve. $\qquad\qquad\qquad\qquad\qquad x = 2$

Horizontal asymptote: $\qquad\qquad$ degree of $n(x) =$ degree of $d(x)$

Use leading coefficients. $\qquad\qquad y = \dfrac{4}{-1} = -4$

The **asymptotes** are $x = 2$ and $y = -4$.

**STEP 5** Find **additional points** on the graph.

| $x$ | $-4$ | $-1$ | $\frac{1}{4}$ | $1$ | $3$ |
|---|---|---|---|---|---|
| $f(x)$ | $-1$ | $1.33$ | $-0.10$ | $1.14$ | $-9.47$ |

**STEP 6** **Sketch** the graph; label the intercepts and asymptotes and complete with a smooth curve.

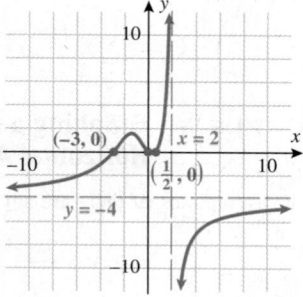

**Answer:** Vertical asymptotes: $x = 4, x = -1$

Horizontal asymptote: $y = 2$

Intercepts: $\left(0, -\frac{3}{2}\right), \left(\frac{3}{2}, 0\right), (2, 0)$

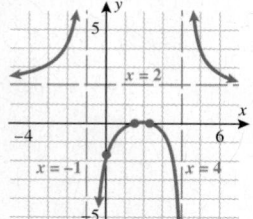

■ **YOUR TURN** Graph the rational function $f(x) = \dfrac{2x^2 - 7x + 6}{x^2 - 3x - 4}$. Give equations of the vertical and horizontal asymptotes and state the intercepts.

**EXAMPLE 10   Graphing a Rational Function with a Slant Asymptote**

Graph the rational function $f(x) = \dfrac{x^2 - 3x - 4}{x + 2}$.

**Solution:**

**STEP 1** Find the **domain**.

| | |
|---|---|
| Set the denominator equal to zero. | $x + 2 = 0$ |
| Solve for $x$. | $x = -2$ |
| State the domain. | $(-\infty, -2) \cup (-2, \infty)$ |

**STEP 2** Find the **intercepts**.

$y$-intercept:  $f(0) = -\dfrac{4}{2} = -2$

$x$-intercepts:  $n(x) = x^2 - 3x - 4 = 0$

Factor.  $(x + 1)(x - 4) = 0$

Solve.  $x = -1$ and $x = 4$

The **intercepts** are the points $(0, -2)$, $(-1, 0)$, and $(4, 0)$.

**STEP 3** Find any **holes**.  $f(x) = \dfrac{(x - 4)(x + 1)}{(x + 2)}$

There are no common factors, so $f$ is in lowest terms.
Since there are no common factors, there are no holes on the graph of $f$.

**STEP 4** Find the **asymptotes**.

| | |
|---|---|
| Vertical asymptote: | $d(x) = x + 2 = 0$ |
| Solve. | $x = -2$ |
| Slant asymptote: | degree of $n(x)$ − degree of $d(x) = 1$ |

Divide $n(x)$ by $d(x)$.  $f(x) = \dfrac{x^2 - 3x - 4}{x + 2} = x - 5 + \dfrac{6}{x + 2}$

Write the equation of the asymptote.  $y = x - 5$

The **asymptotes** are $x = -2$ and $y = x - 5$.

**STEP 5** Find **additional points** on the graph.

| $x$ | $-6$ | $-5$ | $-3$ | $5$ | $6$ |
|---|---|---|---|---|---|
| $f(x)$ | $-12.5$ | $-12$ | $-14$ | $0.86$ | $1.75$ |

**STEP 6 Sketch** the graph; label the intercepts and asymptotes, and complete with a smooth curve between and beyond the vertical asymptote.

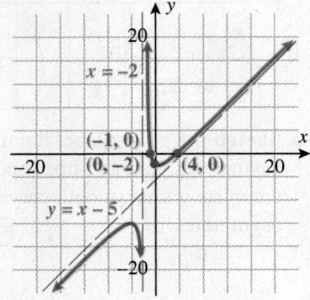

■ **YOUR TURN** For the function $f(x) = \dfrac{x^2 + x - 2}{x - 3}$, state the asymptotes (if any exist) and graph the function.

*Technology Tip*

The behavior of each function as $x$ approaches $\infty$ or $-\infty$ can be shown using tables of values.

Graph $f(x) = \dfrac{x^2 - 3x - 4}{x + 2}$.

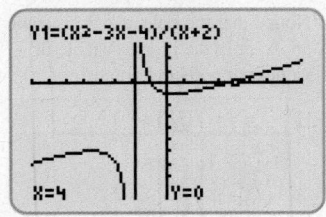

The graph of $f(x)$ shows that the vertical asymptote is at $x = -2$ and the slant asymptote is at $y = x - 5$.

■ **Answer:**
Vertical asymptote: $x = 3$
Slant asymptote: $y = x + 4$

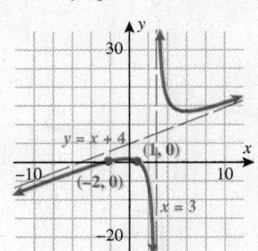

## Technology Tip

The behavior of each function as $x$ approaches $\infty$ or $-\infty$ can be shown using tables of values.

Graph $f(x) = \dfrac{x^2 + x - 6}{x^2 - x - 2}$.

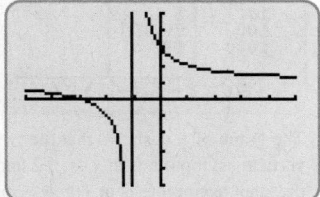

The graph of $f(x)$ shows that the vertical asymptote is at $x = -1$ and the horizontal asymptote is at $y = 1$.

Notice that the hole at $x = 2$ is not apparent in the graph. A table of values supports the graph.

■ **Answer:**

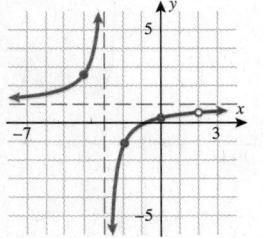

### EXAMPLE 11 Graphing a Rational Function with a Hole in the Graph

Graph the rational function $f(x) = \dfrac{x^2 + x - 6}{x^2 - x - 2}$.

**Solution:**

**STEP 1** Find the **domain**.

Set the denominator equal to zero. $\qquad\qquad x^2 - x - 2 = 0$

Solve for $x$. $\qquad\qquad\qquad\qquad\qquad (x - 2)(x + 1) = 0$

$$x = -1 \quad \text{or} \quad x = 2$$

State the domain. $\qquad\qquad\qquad (-\infty, -1) \cup (-1, 2) \cup (2, \infty)$

**STEP 2** Find the **intercepts**.

$y$-intercept: $\qquad\qquad\qquad\qquad f(0) = \dfrac{-6}{-2} = 3 \qquad y = 3$

$x$-intercepts: $\qquad\qquad\qquad\qquad n(x) = x^2 + x - 6 = 0$

$$(x + 3)(x - 2) = 0$$

$$x = -3 \quad \text{or} \quad x = 2$$

The intercepts correspond to the points $\boxed{(0, 3)}$ and $\boxed{(-3, 0)}$. The point $(2, 0)$ appears to be an $x$-intercept; however, $x = 2$ is not in the domain of the function.

**STEP 3** Find any **holes**. $\qquad\qquad\qquad f(x) = \dfrac{(x - 2)(x + 3)}{(x - 2)(x + 1)}$

Since $x - 2$ is a common factor, there is a *hole* in the graph of $f$ at $x = 2$.

Dividing out the common factor generates an equivalent rational function in lowest terms. $\qquad R(x) = \dfrac{(x + 3)}{(x + 1)}$

**STEP 4** Find the **asymptotes**.

Vertical asymptotes: $\qquad\qquad\qquad x + 1 = 0$

$$\boxed{x = -1}$$

Horizontal asymptote: $\qquad \dfrac{\text{Degree of numerator}}{\text{Degree of denominator}} = \dfrac{\overset{f}{2}}{2} = \dfrac{\overset{R}{1}}{1}$

Since the degree of the numerator equals the degree of the denominator, use the leading coefficients. $\qquad \boxed{y = \dfrac{1}{1} = 1}$

**STEP 5** Find **additional points** on the graph.

| $x$ | $-4$ | $-2$ | $-\frac{1}{2}$ | $1$ | $3$ |
|---|---|---|---|---|---|
| $f(x)$ or $R(x)$ | $\frac{1}{3}$ | $-1$ | $5$ | $2$ | $\frac{3}{2}$ |

**STEP 6** **Sketch** the graph; label the intercepts, asymptotes, and additional points and complete with a smooth curve approaching asymptotes.

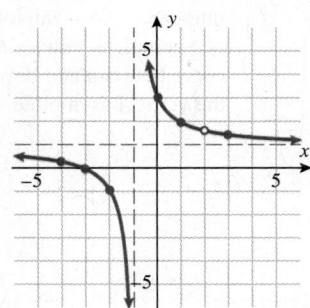

■ **YOUR TURN** Graph the rational function $f(x) = \dfrac{x^2 - x - 2}{x^2 + x - 6}$.

## SECTION
### 2.6 SUMMARY

In this section, rational functions were discussed.

$$f(x) = \frac{n(x)}{d(x)}$$

- **Domain:** All real numbers except the $x$-values that make the denominator equal to zero, $d(x) = 0$.
- **Vertical Asymptotes:** Vertical lines, $x = a$, where $d(a) = 0$, after all common factors have been divided out. Vertical asymptotes steer the graph and are never touched.
- **Horizontal Asymptote:** Horizontal line, $y = b$, that steers the graph as $x \rightarrow \pm\infty$.
  1. If degree of the numerator $<$ degree of the denominator, then $y = 0$ is a horizontal asymptote.
  2. If degree of the numerator $=$ degree of the denominator, then $y = c$ is a horizontal asymptote, where $c$ is the ratio of the leading coefficients of the numerator and denominator, respectively.
  3. If degree of the numerator $>$ degree of the denominator, then there is no horizontal asymptote.
- **Slant Asymptote:** Slant line, $y = mx + b$, that steers the graph as $x \rightarrow \pm\infty$.

1. If degree of the numerator $-$ degree of the denominator $= 1$, then there is a slant asymptote.
2. Divide the numerator by the denominator. The quotient corresponds to the equation of the line (slant asymptote).

### Procedure for Graphing Rational Functions
1. Find the domain of the function.
2. Find the intercept(s).
   - $y$-intercept (does not exist if $x = 0$ is a vertical asymptote)
   - $x$-intercepts (if any)
3. Find any holes.
   - If $x - a$ is a common factor of the numerator and denominator, then $x = a$ corresponds to a hole in the graph of the rational function if the multiplicity of $a$ in the numerator is greater than or equal to the multiplicity of $a$ in the denominator. The result after the common factor is canceled is an equivalent rational function in lowest terms (no common factor).
4. Find any asymptotes.
   - Vertical asymptotes
   - Horizontal/slant asymptotes
5. Find additional points on the graph.
6. Sketch the graph: Draw the asymptotes and label the intercepts and points and connect with a smooth curve.

## SECTION
### 2.6 EXERCISES

■ **SKILLS**

**In Exercises 1–8, find the domain of each rational function.**

**1.** $f(x) = \dfrac{x + 4}{x^2 + x - 12}$

**2.** $f(x) = \dfrac{x - 1}{x^2 + 2x - 3}$

**3.** $f(x) = \dfrac{x - 2}{x^2 - 4}$

**4.** $f(x) = \dfrac{x + 7}{2(x^2 - 49)}$

**5.** $f(x) = \dfrac{7x}{x^2 + 16}$

**6.** $f(x) = -\dfrac{2x}{x^2 + 9}$

**7.** $f(x) = -\dfrac{3(x^2 + x - 2)}{2(x^2 - x - 6)}$

**8.** $f(x) = \dfrac{5(x^2 - 2x - 3)}{(x^2 - x - 6)}$

**In Exercises 9–16, find all vertical asymptotes and horizontal asymptotes (if there are any).**

**9.** $f(x) = \dfrac{1}{x + 2}$

**10.** $f(x) = \dfrac{1}{5 - x}$

**11.** $f(x) = \dfrac{7x^3 + 1}{x + 5}$

**12.** $f(x) = \dfrac{2 - x^3}{2x - 7}$

**13.** $f(x) = \dfrac{6x^5 - 4x^2 + 5}{6x^2 + 5x - 4}$

**14.** $f(x) = \dfrac{6x^2 + 3x + 1}{3x^2 - 5x - 2}$

**15.** $f(x) = \dfrac{\frac{1}{3}x^2 + \frac{1}{3}x - \frac{1}{4}}{x^2 + \frac{1}{9}}$

**16.** $f(x) = \dfrac{\frac{1}{10}(x^2 - 2x + \frac{3}{10})}{2x - 1}$

**In Exercises 17–22, find the slant asymptote corresponding to the graph of each rational function.**

**17.** $f(x) = \dfrac{x^2 + 10x + 25}{x + 4}$

**18.** $f(x) = \dfrac{x^2 + 9x + 20}{x - 3}$

**19.** $f(x) = \dfrac{2x^2 + 14x + 7}{x - 5}$

**20.** $f(x) = \dfrac{3x^3 + 4x^2 - 6x + 1}{x^2 - x - 30}$

**21.** $f(x) = \dfrac{8x^4 + 7x^3 + 2x - 5}{2x^3 - x^2 + 3x - 1}$

**22.** $f(x) = \dfrac{2x^6 + 1}{x^5 - 1}$

**In Exercises 23–28, match the function to the graph.**

**23.** $f(x) = \dfrac{3}{x - 4}$

**24.** $f(x) = \dfrac{3x}{x - 4}$

**25.** $f(x) = \dfrac{3x^2}{x^2 - 4}$

**26.** $f(x) = -\dfrac{3x^2}{x^2 + 4}$

**27.** $f(x) = \dfrac{3x^2}{4 - x^2}$

**28.** $f(x) = \dfrac{3x^2}{x + 4}$

**a.**
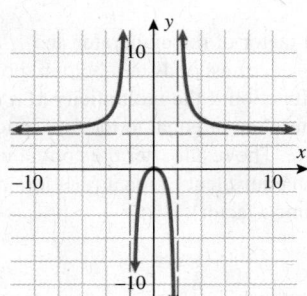

**b.**
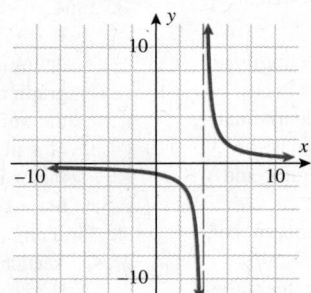

**c.**
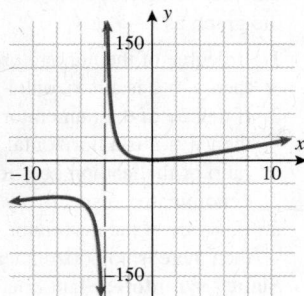

**d.**
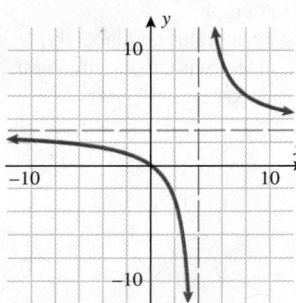

**e.**
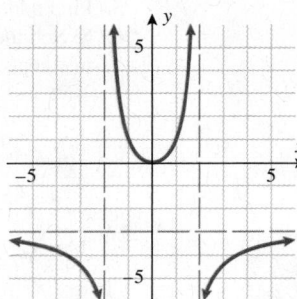

**f.**
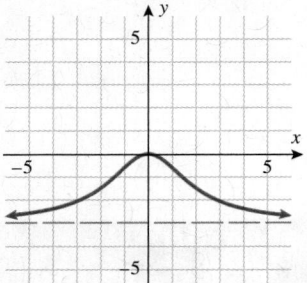

**In Exercises 29–56, graph the rational functions. Locate any asymptotes on the graph.**

**29.** $f(x) = \dfrac{2}{x + 1}$

**30.** $f(x) = \dfrac{4}{x - 2}$

**31.** $f(x) = \dfrac{2x}{x - 1}$

**32.** $f(x) = \dfrac{4x}{x + 2}$

**33.** $f(x) = \dfrac{x - 1}{x}$

**34.** $f(x) = \dfrac{2 + x}{x - 1}$

**35.** $f(x) = \dfrac{2(x^2 - 2x - 3)}{x^2 + 2x}$

**36.** $f(x) = \dfrac{3(x^2 - 1)}{x^2 - 3x}$

**37.** $f(x) = \dfrac{x^2}{x + 1}$

**38.** $f(x) = \dfrac{x^2 - 9}{x + 2}$

**39.** $f(x) = \dfrac{2x^3 - x^2 - x}{x^2 - 4}$

**40.** $f(x) = \dfrac{3x^3 + 5x^2 - 2x}{x^2 + 4}$

**41.** $f(x) = \dfrac{x^2 + 1}{x^2 - 1}$

**42.** $f(x) = \dfrac{1 - x^2}{x^2 + 1}$

**43.** $f(x) = \dfrac{7x^2}{(2x + 1)^2}$

**44.** $f(x) = \dfrac{12x^4}{(3x + 1)^4}$

**45.** $f(x) = \dfrac{1 - 9x^2}{(1 - 4x^2)^3}$

**46.** $f(x) = \dfrac{25x^2 - 1}{(16x^2 - 1)^2}$

**47.** $f(x) = 3x + \dfrac{4}{x}$

**48.** $f(x) = x - \dfrac{4}{x}$

**49.** $f(x) = \dfrac{(x - 1)^2}{(x^2 - 1)}$

**50.** $f(x) = \dfrac{(x + 1)^2}{(x^2 - 1)}$

**51.** $f(x) = \dfrac{(x - 1)(x^2 - 4)}{(x - 2)(x^2 + 1)}$

**52.** $f(x) = \dfrac{(x - 1)(x^2 - 9)}{(x - 3)(x^2 + 1)}$

**53.** $f(x) = \dfrac{3x(x - 1)}{x(x^2 - 4)}$

**54.** $f(x) = \dfrac{-2x(x - 3)}{x(x^2 + 1)}$

**55.** $f(x) = \dfrac{x^2(x + 5)}{2x(x^2 + 3)}$

**56.** $f(x) = \dfrac{4x(x - 1)(x + 2)}{x^2(x^2 - 4)}$

In Exercises 57–60, for each graph of the rational function given determine: (a) all intercepts, (b) all asymptotes, and (c) an equation of the rational function.

**57.**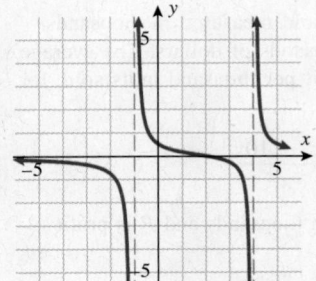

**58.**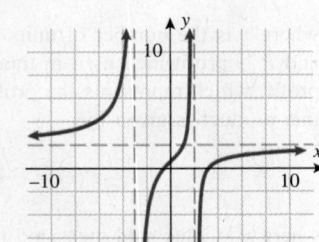

**59.**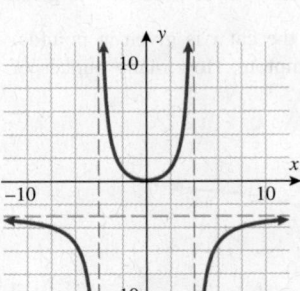

**60.**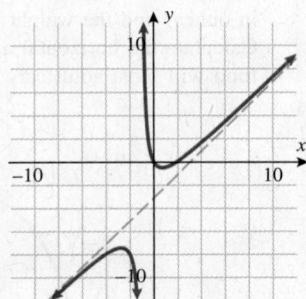

■ **APPLICATIONS**

**61. Epidemiology.** Suppose the number of individuals infected by a virus can be determined by the formula

$$n(t) = \frac{9500t - 2000}{4 + t}$$

where $t > 0$ is the time in months.

**a.** Find the number of infected people by the end of the fourth month.

**b.** After how many months are there 5500 infected people?

**c.** What happens with the number of infected people if the trend continues?

**62. Investment.** A financial institution offers to its investors a variable annual interest rate using the formula

$$r(x) = \frac{4x^2}{x^2 + 2x + 5}$$

where $x$ is the amount invested in thousands of dollars.

**a.** What is the annual interest rate for an investment of $8000?

**b.** What is the annual interest rate for an investment of $20,000?

**c.** What is the maximum annual interest rate offered by them?

**63. Medicine.** The concentration $C$ of a particular drug in a person's bloodstream $t$ minutes after injection is given by

$$C(t) = \frac{2t}{t^2 + 100}$$

**a.** What is the concentration in the bloodstream after 1 minute?

**b.** What is the concentration in the bloodstream after 1 hour?

**c.** What is the concentration in the bloodstream after 5 hours?

**d.** Find the horizontal asymptote of $C(t)$. What do you expect the concentration to be after several days?

**64. Medicine.** The concentration $C$ of aspirin in the bloodstream $t$ hours after consumption is given by $C(t) = \dfrac{t}{t^2 + 40}$.

**a.** What is the concentration in the bloodstream after $\frac{1}{2}$ hour?

**b.** What is the concentration in the bloodstream after 1 hour?

**c.** What is the concentration in the bloodstream after 4 hours?

**d.** Find the horizontal asymptote for $C(t)$. What do you expect the concentration to be after several days?

**65. Typing.** An administrative assistant is hired after graduating from high school and learns to type on the job. The number of words he can type per minute is given by

$$N(t) = \frac{130t + 260}{t + 5} \quad t \geq 0$$

where $t$ is the number of months he has been on the job.

**a.** How many words per minute can he type the day he starts?

**b.** How many words per minute can he type after 12 months?

**c.** How many words per minute can he type after 3 years?

**d.** How many words per minute would you expect him to type if he worked there until he retired?

**66. Memorization.** A professor teaching a large lecture course tries to learn students' names. The number of names she can remember $N(t)$ increases with each week in the semester $t$ and is given by the rational function

$$N(t) = \frac{600t}{t + 20}$$

How many students' names does she know by the third week in the semester? How many students' names should she know by the end of the semester (16 weeks)? According to this function, what are the most names she can remember?

67. **Food.** The amount of food that cats typically eat increases as their weight increases. A rational function that describes this is $F(x) = \dfrac{10x^2}{x^2 + 4}$, where the amount of food $F(x)$ is given in ounces and the weight of the cat $x$ is given in pounds. Calculate the horizontal asymptote. How many ounces of food will most adult cats eat?

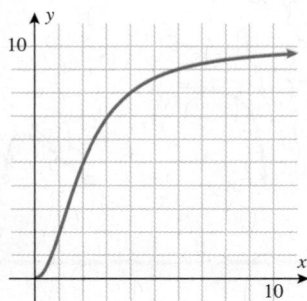

68. **Memorization.** The *Guinness Book of World Records, 2004* states that Dominic O'Brien (England) memorized on a single sighting a random sequence of 54 separate packs of cards all shuffled together (2808 cards in total) at Simpson's-In-The-Strand, London, England, on May 1, 2002. He memorized the cards in 11 hours 42 minutes, and then recited them in exact sequence in a time of 3 hours 30 minutes. With only a 0.5% margin of error allowed (no more than 14 errors), he broke the record with just 8 errors. If we let $x$ represent the time (hours) it takes to memorize the cards and $y$ represent the number of cards memorized, then a rational function that models this event is given by $y = \dfrac{2800x^2 + x}{x^2 + 2}$. According to this model, how many cards could be memorized in an hour? What is the greatest number of cards that can be memorized?

69. **Gardening.** A 500-square-foot rectangular garden will be enclosed with fencing. Write a rational function that describes how many linear feet of fence will be needed to enclose the garden as a function of the width of the garden $w$.

70. **Geometry.** A rectangular picture has an area of 414 square inches. A border (matting) is used when framing. If the top and bottom borders are each 4 inches and the side borders are 3.5 inches, write a function that represents the area $A(l)$ of the entire frame as a function of the length of the picture $l$.

**For Exercises 71 and 72, refer to the following:**

The monthly profit function for a product is given by

$$P(x) = -x^3 + 10x^2$$

where $x$ is the number of units sold measured in thousands and $P$ is profit measured in thousands of dollars. The average profit, which represents the profit per thousand units sold, for this product is given by

$$P(x) = \frac{-x^3 + 10x^2}{x}$$

where $x$ is units sold measured in thousands and $P$ is profit measured in thousands of dollars.

71. **Business.** Find the number of units that must be sold to produce an average profit of $16,000 per thousand units. Convert the answer to average profit in dollars per unit.

72. **Business.** Find the number of units that must be sold to produce an average profit of $25,000 per thousand units. Convert the answer to average profit in dollars per unit.

**For Exercises 73 and 74, refer to the following:**

Some medications, such as Synthroid, are prescribed as a maintenance drug because they are taken regularly for an ongoing condition, such as hypothyroidism. Maintenance drugs function by maintaining a therapeutic drug level in the bloodstream over time. The concentration of a maintenance drug over a 24-hour period is modeled by the function

$$C(t) = \frac{22(t - 1)}{t^2 + 1} + 24$$

where $t$ is time in hours after the dose was administered and $C$ is the concentration of the drug in the bloodstream measured in $\mu$g/mL. This medication is designed to maintain a consistent concentration in the bloodstream of approximately 25 $\mu$g/mL. *Note:* This drug will become inert; that is, the concentration will drop to 0 $\mu$g/mL, during the 25th hour after taking the medication.

73. **Health/Medicine.** Find the concentration of the drug, to the nearest tenth of $\mu$g/mL, in the bloodstream 15 hours after the dose is administered. Is this the only time this concentration of the drug is found in the bloodstream? At what other times is this concentration reached? Round to the nearest hour. Discuss the significance of this answer.

74. **Health/Medicine.** Find the time, after the first hour and a half, at which the concentration of the drug in the bloodstream has dropped to 25 $\mu$g/mL. Find the concentration of the drug 24 hours after taking a dose to the nearest tenth of a $\mu$g/mL. Discuss the importance of taking the medication every 24 hours rather than every day.

## ■CATCH THE MISTAKE

**In Exercises 75–78, explain the mistake that is made.**

**75.** Determine the vertical asymptotes of the function

$$f(x) = \frac{x-1}{x^2-1}.$$

**Solution:**

Set the denominator equal to zero.     $x^2 - 1 = 0$

Solve for $x$.     $x = \pm 1$

The vertical asymptotes are $x = -1$ and $x = 1$.

The following is a correct graph of the function:

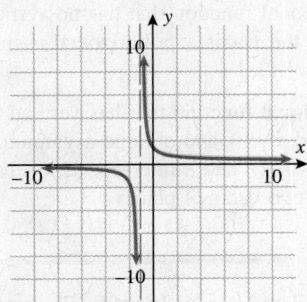

Note that only $x = -1$ is an asymptote. What went wrong?

**76.** Determine the vertical asymptotes of $f(x) = \dfrac{2x}{x^2+1}.$

**Solution:**

Set the denominator equal to zero.     $x^2 + 1 = 0$

Solve for $x$.     $x = \pm 1$

The vertical asymptotes are $x = -1$ and $x = 1$.

The following is a correct graph of the function:

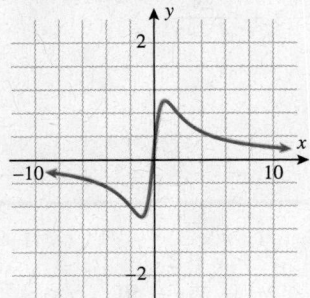

Note that there are no vertical asymptotes. What went wrong?

**77.** Determine whether a horizontal or a slant asymptote exists for the function $f(x) = \dfrac{9-x^2}{x^2-1}.$ If one does, find it.

**Solution:**

**Step 1:** The degree of the numerator equals the degree of the denominator, so there is a horizontal asymptote.

**Step 2:** The horizontal asymptote is the ratio of the lead coefficients: $y = \frac{9}{1} = 9.$

The horizontal asymptote is $y = 9$.

The following is a correct graph of the function.

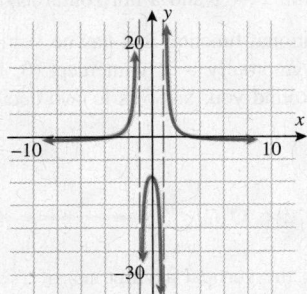

Note that there is no horizontal asymptote at $y = 9$. What went wrong?

**78.** Determine whether a horizontal or a slant asymptote exists for the function $f(x) = \dfrac{x^2+2x-1}{3x^3-2x^2-1}.$ If one does, find it.

**Solution:**

**Step 1:** The degree of the denominator is exactly one more than the degree of the numerator, so there is a slant asymptote.

**Step 2:** Divide.

$$
\begin{array}{r}
3x - 8 \\
x^2 + 2x - 1 \overline{)3x^3 - 2x^2 + 0x - 1} \\
\underline{3x^3 + 6x^2 - 3x\phantom{00}} \\
-8x^2 + 3x - 1 \\
\underline{8x^2 - 16x + 8} \\
19x - 9
\end{array}
$$

The slant asymptote is $y = 3x - 8$.

The following is the correct graph of the function.

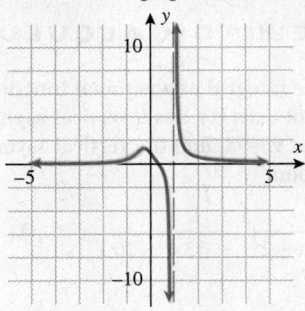

Note that $y = 3x - 8$ is not an asymptote. What went wrong?

■ **CONCEPTUAL**

**For Exercises 79–82, determine whether each statement is true or false.**

**79.** A rational function can have either a horizontal asymptote or an oblique asymptote, but not both.

**80.** A rational function can have at most one vertical asymptote.

**82.** A rational function can cross a horizontal or an oblique asymptote.

**81.** A rational function can cross a vertical asymptote.

**83.** Determine the asymptotes of the rational function
$$f(x) = \frac{(x-a)(x+b)}{(x-c)(x+d)}.$$

**84.** Determine the asymptotes of the rational function
$$f(x) = \frac{3x^2 + b^2}{x^2 + a^2}.$$

■ **CHALLENGE**

**85.** Write a rational function that has vertical asymptotes at $x = -3$ and $x = 1$ and a horizontal asymptote at $y = 4$.

**86.** Write a rational function that has no vertical asymptotes, approaches the x-axis as a horizontal asymptote, and has an x-intercept of $(3, 0)$.

**87.** Write a rational function that has no vertical asymptotes and oblique asymptote $y = x$, y-intercept $(0, 1)$, and x-intercept $(-1, 0)$. Round your answers to two decimal places.

**88.** Write a rational function that has vertical asymptotes at $x = -3$ and $x = 1$ and oblique asymptote $y = 3x$, y-intercept $(0, 2)$, and x-intercept $(2, 0)$. Round your answers to two decimal places.

■ **TECHNOLOGY**

**89.** Determine the vertical asymptotes of $f(x) = \frac{x-4}{x^2 - 2x - 8}$. Graph this function utilizing a graphing utility. Does the graph confirm the asymptotes?

**90.** Determine the vertical asymptotes of $f(x) = \frac{2x+1}{6x^2 + x - 1}$. Graph this function utilizing a graphing utility. Does the graph confirm the asymptotes?

**91.** Find the asymptotes and intercepts of the rational function $f(x) = \frac{1}{3x+1} - \frac{2}{x}$. (*Note:* Combine the two expressions into a single rational expression.) Graph this function utilizing a graphing utility. Does the graph confirm what you found?

**92.** Find the asymptotes and intercepts of the rational function $f(x) = -\frac{1}{x^2+1} + \frac{1}{x}$. (*Note:* Combine the two expressions into a single rational expression.) Graph this function utilizing a graphing utility. Does the graph confirm what you found?

**For Exercises 93 and 94: (a) Identify all asymptotes for each function. (b) Plot $f(x)$ and $g(x)$ in the same window. How does the end behavior of the function $f$ differ from that of $g$? (c) Plot $g(x)$ and $h(x)$ in the same window. How does the end behavior of $g$ differ from that of $h$? (d) Combine the two expressions into a single rational expression for the functions $g$ and $h$. Does the strategy of finding horizontal and slant asymptotes agree with your findings in (b) and (c)?**

**93.** $f(x) = \frac{1}{x-3}$, $g(x) = 2 + \frac{1}{x-3}$, and
$$h(x) = -3 + \frac{1}{x-3}$$

**94.** $f(x) = \frac{2x}{x^2-1}$, $g(x) = x + \frac{2x}{x^2-1}$, and
$$h(x) = x - 3 + \frac{2x}{x^2-1}$$

■ **PREVIEW TO CALCULUS**

In calculus the integral of a rational function $f$ on an interval $[a, b]$ might not exist if $f$ has a vertical asymptote in $[a, b]$.
    In Exercises 95–98, find the vertical asymptotes of each rational function.

**95.** $f(x) = \frac{x-1}{x^3 - 2x^2 - 13x - 10}$    $[0, 3]$

**96.** $f(x) = \frac{x^2 + x + 2}{x^3 + 2x^2 - 25x - 50}$    $[-3, 2]$

**97.** $f(x) = \frac{5x+2}{6x^2 - x - 2}$    $[-2, 0]$

**98.** $f(x) = \frac{6x - 2x^2}{x^3 + x}$    $[-1, 1]$

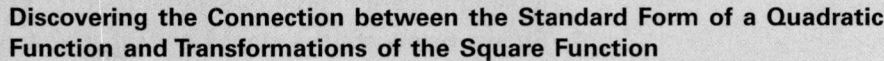

**Discovering the Connection between the Standard Form of a Quadratic Function and Transformations of the Square Function**

In Chapter 1, you saw that if you are familiar with the graphs of a small library of common functions, you can sketch the graphs of many related functions using transformation techniques. These ideas will help you here as you discover the relationship between the standard form of a quadratic function and its graph.

Let $G$ and $H$ be functions with:

$$G(x) = F(x - 1) + 3 \quad \text{and} \quad H(x) = -F(x + 2) - 4$$

where $F(x) = x^2$.

**1.** For this part, consider the function $G$.

    **a.** List the transformation you'd use to sketch the graph of $G$ from the graph of $F$.

    **b.** Write an equation for $G(x)$ in the form $G(x) = a(x - h)^2 + k$. This is called the **standard form** of a quadratic function. What are the values of $a$, $h$, and $k$?

    **c.** The **vertex**, or turning point, of the graph of $F(x) = x^2$ is $(0, 0)$. How can you use the transformations you listed in part (a) to determine the coordinates of the vertex of the graph of $G$?

    **d.** The vertical line that passes through the vertex of a parabola is called its **axis of symmetry**. The axis of symmetry of the graph of $F(x) = x^2$ is the y-axis, or the vertical line with equation $x = 0$. How can you determine the axis of symmetry of the graph of $G$? Write the equation of this line.

    **e.** Sketch graphs of $F$ and $G$.

**2.** Next consider the function $H$ given above.

    **a.** List the transformations that will produce the graph of $H$ from the graph of $F$.

    **b.** Write an equation for $H(x)$ in standard form. What are the values of $a$, $h$, and $k$?

    **c.** What are the coordinates of the vertex of the graph of $H$? How do the transformations you listed in part (a) help you determine this?

    **d.** Determine the equation of the axis of symmetry of the graph of $H$.

    **e.** Sketch graphs of $F$ and $H$.

**3. a.** What do you know about the graph of a quadratic function just by looking at its equation in standard form, $f(x) = a(x - h)^2 + k$?

**b.** Shown below are the graphs of $F(x) = x^2$ and another quadratic function, $y = K(x)$. Write the equation of $K$ in standard form. *Hint:* Think about the transformations.

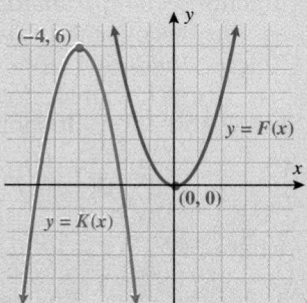

# MODELING OUR WORLD

The following table summarizes average yearly temperature in degrees Fahrenheit (°F) and carbon dioxide emissions in parts per million (ppm) for **Mauna Loa, Hawaii**.

| YEAR | 1960 | 1965 | 1970 | 1975 | 1980 | 1985 | 1990 | 1995 | 2000 | 2005 |
|---|---|---|---|---|---|---|---|---|---|---|
| TEMPERATURE | 44.45 | 43.29 | 43.61 | 43.35 | 46.66 | 45.71 | 45.53 | 47.53 | 45.86 | 46.23 |
| CO₂ EMISSIONS (ppm) | 316.9 | 320.0 | 325.7 | 331.1 | 338.7 | 345.9 | 354.2 | 360.6 | 369.4 | 379.7 |

In the Modeling Our World in Chapter 0, the temperature and carbon emissions were modeled with *linear functions*. Now, let us model these same data using *polynomial functions*.

1. Plot the temperature data with time on the horizontal axis and temperature on the vertical axis. Let $t = 0$ correspond to 1960. Adjust the vertical range of the graph to (43, 48). How many turning points (local maxima and minima) do these data exhibit? What is the lowest degree polynomial function whose graph can pass through these data?

2. Find a *polynomial function* that models the temperature in Mauna Loa.
   a. Find a quadratic function: Let the data from 1995 correspond to the vertex of the graph and apply the 2005 data to determine the function.
   b. Find a quadratic function: Let the data from 2000 correspond to the vertex of the graph and apply the 2005 data to determine the function.
   c. Utilize regression and all data given to find a polynomial function whose degree is found in 1.

3. Predict what the temperature will be in Mauna Loa in 2020.
   a. Use the line found in Exercise 2(a).
   b. Use the line found in Exercise 2(b).
   c. Use the line found in Exercise 2(c).

4. Predict what the temperature will be in Mauna Loa in 2100.
   a. Use the line found in Exercise 2(a).
   b. Use the line found in Exercise 2(b).
   c. Use the line found in Exercise 2(c).

5. Do your models support the claim of "global warming"? Explain.

6. Plot the carbon dioxide emissions data with time on the horizontal axis and carbon dioxide emissions on the vertical axis. Let $t = 0$ correspond to 1960. Adjust the vertical range of the graph to (315, 380).

**7.** Find a *quadratic function* that models the $CO_2$ emissions (ppm) in Mauna Loa.

    **a.** Let the data from 1960 correspond to the vertex of the graph and apply the 2005 data to determine the function.

    **b.** Let the data from 1980 correspond to the vertex of the graph and apply the 2005 data to determine the function.

    **c.** Utilize regression and all data given.

**8.** Predict the expected $CO_2$ levels in Mauna Loa in 2020.

    **a.** Use the line found in Exercise 7(a).

    **b.** Use the line found in Exercise 7(b).

    **c.** Use the line found in Exercise 7(c).

**9.** Predict the expected $CO_2$ levels in Mauna Loa in 2100.

    **a.** Use the line found in Exercise 7(a).

    **b.** Use the line found in Exercise 7(b).

    **c.** Use the line found in Exercise 7(c).

**10.** Do your models support the claim of "global warming"? Explain. Do these models give similar predictions to the linear models found in Chapter 0?

**11.** Discuss differences in models and predictions found in parts (a), (b), and (c) and also discuss difference in linear and polynomial functions.

| SECTION | CONCEPT | KEY IDEAS/FORMULAS |
|---------|---------|--------------------|
| 2.1 | **Quadratic functions** | |
| | Graphs of quadratic functions: parabolas | **Graphing quadratic functions in standard form**<br>$f(x) = a(x - h)^2 + k$<br>■ Vertex: $(h, k)$<br>■ Opens up: $a > 0$<br>■ Opens down: $a < 0$<br><br>**Graphing quadratic functions in general form**<br>$f(x) = ax^2 + bx + c$, vertex is $(h, k) = \left(-\dfrac{b}{2a}, f\left(-\dfrac{b}{2a}\right)\right)$ |
| | Finding the equation of a parabola | Applications |
| 2.2 | **Polynomial functions of higher degree** | |
| | Identifying polynomial functions | $P(x) = a_n x^n + a_{n-1} x^{n-1} + \cdots + a_2 x^2 + a_1 x + a_0$<br>is a polynomial of degree $n$. |
| | Graphing polynomial functions using transformations of power functions | $y = x^n$ behave similar to<br>■ $y = x^2$, when $n$ is even.<br>■ $y = x^3$, when $n$ is odd. |
| | Real zeros of a polynomial function | $P(x) = (x - a)(x - b)^n = 0$<br>■ $a$ is a zero of multiplicity 1.<br>■ $b$ is a zero of multiplicity $n$. |
| | Graphing general polynomial functions | Intercepts; zeros and multiplicities; end behavior |
| 2.3 | **Dividing polynomials** | Use zero placeholders for missing terms. |
| | Long division of polynomials | Can be used for all polynomial division. |
| | Synthetic division of polynomials | Can only be used when dividing by $(x \pm a)$. |
| 2.4 | **The real zeros of a polynomial function** | $P(x) = a_n x^n + a_{n-1} x^{n-1} + \cdots + a_2 x^2 + a_1 x + a_0$<br>If $P(c) = 0$, then $c$ is a zero of $P(x)$. |
| | The remainder theorem and the factor theorem | If $P(x)$ is divided by $x - a$, then the remainder $r$ is $r = P(a)$. |
| | The rational zero theorem and Descartes' rule of signs | Possible zeros $= \dfrac{\text{Factors of } a_0}{\text{Factors of } a_n}$<br><br>Number of positive or negative real zeros is related to the number of sign variations in $P(x)$ or $P(-x)$. |

| SECTION | CONCEPT | KEY IDEAS/FORMULAS |
|---------|---------|--------------------|
| | Factoring polynomials | 1. List possible rational zeros (rational zero theorem). |
| | | 2. List possible combinations of positive and negative real zeros (Descartes' rule of signs). |
| | | 3. Test possible values until a zero is found. |
| | | 4. Once a real zero is found, use synthetic division. Then repeat testing on the quotient until linear and/or irreducible quadratic factors are reached. |
| | | 5. If there is a real zero but all possible rational roots have failed, then approximate the real zero using the intermediate value theorem/bisection method. |
| | The intermediate value theorem | Intermediate value theorem and the bisection method are used to approximate irrational zeros. |
| | Graphing polynomial functions | 1. Find the intercepts. |
| | | 2. Determine end behavior. |
| | | 3. Find additional points. |
| | | 4. Sketch a smooth curve. |
| **2.5** | **Complex zeros: The fundamental theorem of algebra** | $P(x) = a_n x^n + a_{n-1} x^{n-1} + \cdots + a_2 x^2 + a_1 x + a_0$ <br> $P(x) = \underbrace{(x - c_1)(x - c_2) \cdots (x - c_n)}_{n \text{ factors}}$ <br> where the $c$'s represent complex (not necessarily distinct) zeros. |
| | Complex zeros | **The fundamental theorem of algebra** <br> $P(x)$ of degree $n$ has at least one zero and at most $n$ zeros. |
| | Complex conjugate pairs | If $a + bi$ is a zero of $P(x)$, then $a - bi$ is also a zero. |
| | Factoring polynomials | The polynomial can be written as a product of linear factors, not necessarily distinct. |
| **2.6** | **Rational functions** | $f(x) = \dfrac{n(x)}{d(x)} \qquad d(x) \neq 0$ |
| | Domain of rational functions | **Domain:** All real numbers except $x$-values that make the denominator equal to zero; that is, $d(x) = 0$. <br><br> A rational function $f(x) = \dfrac{n(x)}{d(x)}$ is said to be in *lowest terms* if $n(x)$ and $d(x)$ have no common factors. |
| | Vertical, horizontal, and slant asymptotes | A rational function that has a common factor $x - a$ in both the numerator and denominator has a hole at $x = a$ in its graph if the multiplicity of $a$ in the numerator is greater than or equal to the multiplicity of $a$ in the denominator. <br><br> *Vertical Asymptotes* <br> A rational function in lowest terms has a vertical asymptote corresponding to any $x$-values that make the denominator equal to zero. |

| SECTION | CONCEPT | KEY IDEAS/FORMULAS |
|---------|---------|---------------------|
| | | *Horizontal Asymptote* |
| | | ■ $y = 0$ if degree of $n(x)$ < degree of $d(x)$. |
| | | ■ No horizontal asymptote if degree of $n(x)$ > degree of $d(x)$. |
| | | ■ $y = \dfrac{\text{Leading coefficient of } n(x)}{\text{Leading coefficient of } d(x)}$ if degree of $n(x)$ = degree of $d(x)$. |
| | | *Slant Asymptote* |
| | | If degree of $n(x)$ − degree of $d(x) = 1$. |
| | | Divide $n(x)$ by $d(x)$ and the quotient determines the slant asymptote; that is, $y$ = quotient. |
| | Graphing rational functions | 1. Find the domain of the function. |
| | | 2. Find the intercept(s). |
| | | 3. Find any holes. |
| | | 4. Find any asymptote. |
| | | 5. Find additional points on the graph. |
| | | 6. *Sketch the graph:* Draw the asymptotes and label the intercepts and points and connect with a smooth curve. |

## 2.1 Quadratic Functions

**Match the quadratic function with its graph.**

1. $f(x) = -2(x + 6)^2 + 3$     2. $f(x) = \frac{1}{4}(x - 4)^2 + 2$

3. $f(x) = x^2 + x - 6$     4. $f(x) = -3x^2 - 10x + 8$

**a.**

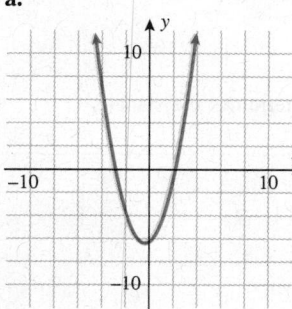

**b.**

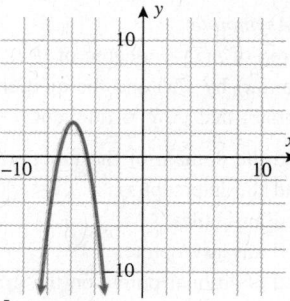

**c.**

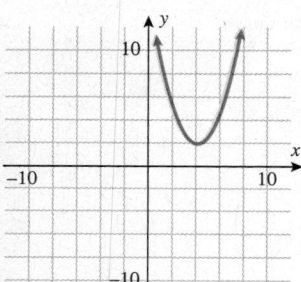

**d.**

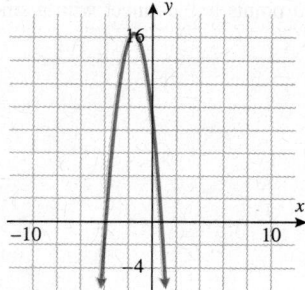

**Graph the quadratic function given in standard form.**

5. $f(x) = -(x - 7)^2 + 4$     6. $f(x) = (x + 3)^2 - 5$

7. $f(x) = -\frac{1}{2}\left(x - \frac{1}{3}\right)^2 + \frac{2}{5}$     8. $f(x) = 0.6(x - 0.75)^2 + 0.5$

**Rewrite the quadratic function in standard form by completing the square.**

9. $f(x) = x^2 - 3x - 10$     10. $f(x) = x^2 - 2x - 24$

11. $f(x) = 4x^2 + 8x - 7$     12. $f(x) = -\frac{1}{4}x^2 + 2x - 4$

**Graph the quadratic function given in general form.**

13. $f(x) = x^2 - 3x + 5$

14. $f(x) = -x^2 + 4x + 2$

15. $f(x) = -4x^2 + 2x + 3$

16. $f(x) = -0.75x^2 + 2.5$

**Find the vertex of the parabola associated with each quadratic function.**

17. $f(x) = 13x^2 - 5x + 12$

18. $f(x) = \frac{2}{5}x^2 - 4x + 3$

19. $f(x) = -0.45x^2 - 0.12x + 3.6$

20. $f(x) = -\frac{3}{4}x^2 + \frac{2}{5}x + 4$

**Find the quadratic function that has the given vertex and goes through the given point.**

21. vertex: $(-2, 3)$     point: $(1, 4)$

22. vertex: $(4, 7)$     point: $(-3, 1)$

23. vertex: $(2.7, 3.4)$     point: $(3.2, 4.8)$

24. vertex: $\left(-\frac{5}{2}, \frac{7}{4}\right)$     point: $\left(\frac{1}{2}, \frac{3}{5}\right)$

## Applications

25. **Profit.** The revenue and the cost of a local business are given below as functions of the number of units $x$ in thousands produced and sold. Use the cost and the revenue to answer the questions that follow.

$$C(x) = \frac{1}{3}x + 2 \quad \text{and} \quad R(x) = -2x^2 + 12x - 12$$

   a. Determine the profit function.

   b. State the break-even points.

   c. Graph the profit function.

   d. What is the range of units to make and sell that will correspond to a profit?

26. **Geometry.** Given the length of a rectangle is $2x - 4$ and the width is $x + 7$, find the area of the rectangle. What dimensions correspond to the largest area?

27. **Geometry.** A triangle has a base of $x + 2$ units and a height of $4 - x$ units. Determine the area of the triangle. What dimensions correspond to the largest area?

28. **Geometry.** A person standing at a ridge in the Grand Canyon throws a penny upward and toward the pit of the canyon. The height of the penny is given by the function:

$$h(t) = -12t^2 + 80t$$

   a. What is the maximum height that the penny will reach?

   b. How many seconds will it take the penny to hit the ground below?

## 2.2 Polynomial Functions of Higher Degree

**Determine which functions are polynomials, and for those, state their degree.**

29. $f(x) = x^6 - 2x^5 + 3x^2 + 9x - 42$

30. $f(x) = (3x - 4)^3(x + 6)^2$

31. $f(x) = 3x^4 - x^3 + x^2 + \sqrt[4]{x} + 5$

32. $f(x) = 5x^3 - 2x^2 + \dfrac{4x}{7} - 3$

**Match the polynomial function with its graph.**

**33.** $f(x) = 2x - 5$

**34.** $f(x) = -3x^2 + x - 4$

**35.** $f(x) = x^4 - 2x^3 + x^2 - 6$

**36.** $f(x) = x^7 - x^5 + 3x^4 + 3x + 7$

**a.**

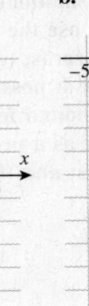

**b.**

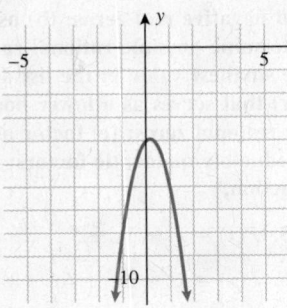

**c.**

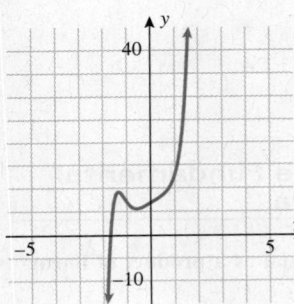

**d.**

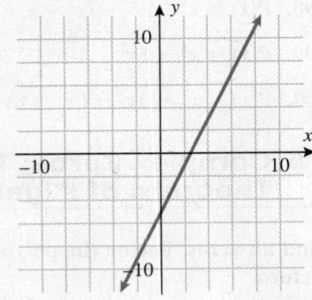

**Graph each function by transforming a power function $y = x^n$.**

**37.** $f(x) = -x^7$

**38.** $f(x) = (x - 3)^3$

**39.** $f(x) = x^4 - 2$

**40.** $f(x) = -6 - (x + 7)^5$

**Find all the real zeros of each polynomial function, and state their multiplicities.**

**41.** $f(x) = 3(x + 4)^2(x - 6)^5$

**42.** $f(x) = 7x(2x - 4)^3(x + 5)$

**43.** $f(x) = x^5 - 13x^3 + 36x$

**44.** $f(x) = 4.2x^4 - 2.6x^2$

**Find a polynomial of minimum degree that has the given zeros.**

**45.** $-3, 0, 4$

**46.** $2, 4, 6, -8$

**47.** $-\frac{2}{5}, \frac{3}{4}, 0$

**48.** $2 - \sqrt{5}, 2 + \sqrt{5}$

**49.** $-2$ (multiplicity of 2), 3 (multiplicity of 2)

**50.** 3 (multiplicity of 2), $-1$ (multiplicity of 2), 0 (multiplicity of 3)

**For each polynomial function given: (a) list each real zero and its multiplicity; (b) determine whether the graph touches or crosses at each $x$-intercept; (c) find the $y$-intercept and a few points on the graph; (d) determine the end behavior; and (e) sketch the graph.**

**51.** $f(x) = x^2 - 5x - 14$

**52.** $f(x) = -(x - 5)^5$

**53.** $f(x) = 6x^7 + 3x^5 - x^2 + x - 4$

**54.** $f(x) = -x^4(3x + 6)^3(x - 7)^3$

## Applications

**55. Salary.** Tiffany has started tutoring students $x$ hours per week. The tutoring job corresponds to the following additional income:

$$f(x) = (x - 1)(x - 3)(x - 7)$$

**a.** Graph the polynomial function.

**b.** Give any real zeros that occur.

**c.** How many hours of tutoring are financially beneficial to Tiffany?

**56. Profit.** The following function is the profit for Walt Disney World, where $P(x)$ represents profit in millions of dollars and $x$ represents the month ($x = 1$ corresponds to January):

$$P(x) = 3(x - 2)^2(x - 5)^2(x - 10)^2 \quad 1 \le x \le 12$$

Graph the polynomial. When are the peak seasons?

## 2.3 Dividing Polynomials

**Divide the polynomials with long division. If you choose to use a calculator, do not round off. Keep the exact values instead. Express the answer in the form $Q(x) = ?, \quad r(x) = ?$.**

**57.** $(x^2 + 2x - 6) \div (x - 2)$

**58.** $(2x^2 - 5x - 1) \div (2x - 3)$

**59.** $(4x^4 - 16x^3 + x - 9 + 12x^2) \div (2x - 4)$

**60.** $(6x^2 + 2x^3 - 4x^4 + 2 - x) \div (2x^2 + x - 4)$

**Use synthetic division to divide the polynomial by the linear factor. Indicate the quotient $Q(x)$ and the remainder $r(x)$.**

**61.** $(x^4 + 4x^3 + 5x^2 - 2x - 8) \div (x + 2)$

**62.** $(x^3 - 10x + 3) \div (2 + x)$

**63.** $(x^6 - 64) \div (x + 8)$

**64.** $(2x^5 + 4x^4 - 2x^3 + 7x + 5) \div (x - \frac{3}{4})$

**Divide the polynomials with either long division or synthetic division.**

**65.** $(5x^3 + 8x^2 - 22x + 1) \div (5x^2 - 7x + 3)$

**66.** $(x^4 + 2x^3 - 5x^2 + 4x + 2) \div (x - 3)$

**67.** $(x^3 - 4x^2 + 2x - 8) \div (x + 1)$

**68.** $(x^3 - 5x^2 + 4x - 20) \div (x^2 + 4)$

## Applications

**69. Geometry.** The area of a rectangle is given by the polynomial $6x^4 - 8x^3 - 10x^2 + 12x - 16$. If the width is $2x - 4$, what is the length of the rectangle?

**70. Volume.** A 10 inch by 15 inch rectangular piece of cardboard is used to make a box. Square pieces $x$ inches on a side are cut out from the corners of the cardboard and then the sides are folded up. Find the volume of the box.

## 2.4 The Real Zeros of a Polynomial Function

Find the following values by applying synthetic division. Check by substituting the value into the function.

$$f(x) = 6x^5 + x^4 - 7x^2 + x - 1 \qquad g(x) = x^3 + 2x^2 - 3$$

**71.** $f(-2)$   **72.** $f(1)$   **73.** $g(1)$   **74.** $g(-1)$

Determine whether the number given is a zero of the polynomial.

**75.** $-3, P(x) = x^3 - 5x^2 + 4x + 2$

**76.** 2 and $-2, P(x) = x^4 - 16$

**77.** $1, P(x) = 2x^4 - 2x$

**78.** $4, P(x) = x^4 - 2x^3 - 8x$

Given a zero of the polynomial, determine all other real zeros, and write the polynomial in terms of a product of linear or irreducible factors.

| Polynomial | Zero |
|---|---|
| **79.** $P(x) = x^4 - 6x^3 + 32x$ | $-2$ |
| **80.** $P(x) = x^3 - 7x^2 + 36$ | 3 |
| **81.** $P(x) = x^5 - x^4 - 8x^3 + 12x^2$ | 0 |
| **82.** $P(x) = x^4 - 32x^2 - 144$ | 6 |

Use Descartes' rule of signs to determine the possible number of positive real zeros and negative real zeros.

**83.** $P(x) = x^4 + 3x^3 - 16$

**84.** $P(x) = x^5 + 6x^3 - 4x - 2$

**85.** $P(x) = x^9 - 2x^7 + x^4 - 3x^3 + 2x - 1$

**86.** $P(x) = 2x^5 - 4x^3 + 2x^2 - 7$

Use the rational zero theorem to list the possible rational zeros.

**87.** $P(x) = x^3 - 2x^2 + 4x + 6$

**88.** $P(x) = x^5 - 4x^3 + 2x^2 - 4x - 8$

**89.** $P(x) = 2x^4 + 2x^3 - 36x^2 - 32x + 64$

**90.** $P(x) = -4x^5 - 5x^3 + 4x + 2$

List the possible rational zeros, and test to determine all rational zeros.

**91.** $P(x) = 2x^3 - 5x^2 + 1$

**92.** $P(x) = 12x^3 + 8x^2 - 13x + 3$

**93.** $P(x) = x^4 - 5x^3 + 20x - 16$

**94.** $P(x) = 24x^4 - 4x^3 - 10x^2 + 3x - 2$

For each polynomial: (a) use Descartes' rule of signs to determine the possible combinations of positive real zeros and negative real zeros; (b) use the rational zero test to determine possible rational zeros; (c) determine, if possible, the smallest value in the list of possible rational zeros for $P(x)$ that serves as a lower bound for all real zeros; (d) test for rational zeros; (e) factor as a product of linear and/or irreducible quadratic factors; and (f) graph the polynomial function.

**95.** $P(x) = x^3 + 3x - 5$

**96.** $P(x) = x^3 + 3x^2 - 6x - 8$

**97.** $P(x) = x^3 - 9x^2 + 20x - 12$

**98.** $P(x) = x^4 - x^3 - 7x^2 + x + 6$

**99.** $P(x) = x^4 - 5x^3 - 10x^2 + 20x + 24$

**100.** $P(x) = x^5 - 3x^3 - 6x^2 + 8x$

## 2.5 Complex Zeros: The Fundamental Theorem of Algebra

Find all zeros. Factor the polynomial as a product of linear factors.

**101.** $P(x) = x^2 + 25$   **102.** $P(x) = x^2 + 16$

**103.** $P(x) = x^2 - 2x + 5$   **104.** $P(x) = x^2 + 4x + 5$

A polynomial function is described. Find all remaining zeros.

**105.** Degree: 4   Zeros: $-2i, 3 + i$

**106.** Degree: 4   Zeros: $3i, 2 - i$

**107.** Degree: 6   Zeros: $i, 2 - i$ (multiplicity 2)

**108.** Degree: 6   Zeros: $2i, 1 - i$ (multiplicity 2)

Given a zero of the polynomial, determine all other zeros (real and complex) and write the polynomial in terms of a product of linear factors.

| Polynomial | Zero |
|---|---|
| **109.** $P(x) = x^4 - 3x^3 - 3x^2 - 3x - 4$ | $i$ |
| **110.** $P(x) = x^4 - 4x^3 + x^2 + 16x - 20$ | $2 - i$ |
| **111.** $P(x) = x^4 - 2x^3 + 11x^2 - 18x + 18$ | $-3i$ |
| **112.** $P(x) = x^4 - 5x^2 + 10x - 6$ | $1 + i$ |

**Factor each polynomial as a product of linear factors.**

113. $P(x) = x^4 - 81$

114. $P(x) = x^3 - 6x^2 + 12x$

115. $P(x) = x^3 - x^2 + 4x - 4$

116. $P(x) = x^4 - 5x^3 + 12x^2 - 2x - 20$

## 2.6 Rational Functions

**Determine the vertical, horizontal, or slant asymptotes (if they exist) for the following rational functions.**

117. $f(x) = \dfrac{7 - x}{x + 2}$

118. $f(x) = \dfrac{2 - x^2}{(x - 1)^3}$

119. $f(x) = \dfrac{4x^2}{x + 1}$

120. $f(x) = \dfrac{3x^2}{x^2 + 9}$

121. $f(x) = \dfrac{2x^2 - 3x + 1}{x^2 + 4}$

122. $f(x) = \dfrac{-2x^2 + 3x + 5}{x + 5}$

**Graph the rational functions.**

123. $f(x) = -\dfrac{2}{x - 3}$

124. $f(x) = \dfrac{5}{x + 1}$

125. $f(x) = \dfrac{x^2}{x^2 + 4}$

126. $f(x) = \dfrac{x^2 - 36}{x^2 + 25}$

127. $f(x) = \dfrac{x^2 - 49}{x + 7}$

128. $f(x) = \dfrac{2x^2 - 3x - 2}{2x^2 - 5x - 3}$

## Technology Exercises

### Section 2.1

129. On a graphing calculator, plot the quadratic function:

$$f(x) = 0.005x^2 - 4.8x - 59$$

  a. Identify the vertex of this parabola.

  b. Identify the $y$-intercept.

  c. Identify the $x$-intercepts (if any).

  d. What is the axis of symmetry?

130. Determine the quadratic function whose vertex is $(2.4, -3.1)$ and passes through the point $(0, 5.54)$.

  a. Write the quadratic function in general form.

  b. Plot this quadratic function with a graphing calculator.

  c. Zoom in on the vertex and $y$-intercept. Do they agree with the given values?

### Section 2.2

**Use a graphing calculator or a computer to graph each polynomial. From the graph, estimate the $x$-intercepts and state the zeros of the function and their multiplicities.**

131. $f(x) = 5x^3 - 11x^2 - 10.4x + 5.6$

132. $f(x) = -x^3 - 0.9x^2 + 2.16x - 2.16$

### Section 2.3

133. Plot $\dfrac{15x^3 - 47x^2 + 38x - 8}{3x^2 - 7x + 2}$. What type of function is it?

   Perform this division using long division, and confirm that the graph corresponds to the quotient.

134. Plot $\dfrac{-4x^3 + 14x^2 - x - 15}{x - 3}$. What type of function is it?

   Perform this division using synthetic division, and confirm that the graph corresponds to the quotient.

### Section 2.4

**(a) Determine all possible rational zeros of the polynomial. Use a graphing calculator or software to graph $P(x)$ to help find the zeros. (b) Factor as a product of linear and/or irreducible quadratic factors.**

135. $P(x) = x^4 - 3x^3 - 12x^2 + 20x + 48$

136. $P(x) = -5x^5 - 18x^4 - 32x^3 - 24x^2 + x + 6$

### Section 2.5

**Find all zeros (real and complex). Factor the polynomial as a product of linear factors.**

137. $P(x) = 2x^3 + x^2 - 2x - 91$

138. $P(x) = -2x^4 + 5x^3 + 37x^2 - 160x + 150$

### Section 2.6

**(a) Graph the function $f(x)$ utilizing a graphing utility to determine whether it is a one-to-one function. (b) If it is, find its inverse. (c) Graph both functions in the same viewing window.**

139. $f(x) = \dfrac{2x - 3}{x + 1}$

140. $f(x) = \dfrac{4x + 7}{x - 2}$

REVIEW EXERCISES

1. Graph the quadratic function $f(x) = -(x-4)^2 + 1$.

2. Write the quadratic function in standard form $f(x) = -x^2 + 4x - 1$.

3. Find the vertex of the parabola $f(x) = -\frac{1}{2}x^2 + 3x - 4$.

4. Find a quadratic function whose graph has a vertex at $(-3, -1)$ and whose graph passes through the point $(-4, 1)$.

5. Find a sixth-degree polynomial function with the given zeros:

   2 of multiplicity 3   1 of multiplicity 2   0 of multiplicity 1

6. For the polynomial function $f(x) = x^4 + 6x^3 - 7x$:

   a. List each real zero and its multiplicity.

   b. Determine whether the graph touches or crosses at each $x$-intercept.

   c. Find the $y$-intercept and a few points on the graph.

   d. Determine the end behavior.

   e. Sketch the graph.

7. Divide $-4x^4 + 2x^3 - 7x^2 + 5x - 2$ by $2x^2 - 3x + 1$.

8. Divide $17x^5 - 4x^3 + 2x - 10$ by $x + 2$.

9. Is $x - 3$ a factor of $x^4 + x^3 - 13x^2 - x + 12$?

10. Determine whether $-1$ is a zero of $P(x) = x^{21} - 2x^{18} + 5x^{12} + 7x^3 + 3x^2 + 2$.

11. Given that $x - 7$ is a factor of $P(x) = x^3 - 6x^2 - 9x + 14$, factor the polynomial in terms of linear factors.

12. Given that $3i$ is a zero of $P(x) = x^4 - 3x^3 + 19x^2 - 27x + 90$, find all other zeros.

13. Can a polynomial have zeros that are not $x$-intercepts? Explain.

14. Apply Descartes' rule of signs to determine the possible combinations of positive real zeros, negative real zeros, and complex zeros of $P(x) = 3x^5 + 2x^4 - 3x^3 + 2x^2 - x + 1$.

15. From the rational zero test, list all possible rational zeros of $P(x) = 3x^4 - 7x^2 + 3x + 12$.

**In Exercises 16–18, determine all zeros of the polynomial function and graph.**

16. $P(x) = -x^3 + 4x$

17. $P(x) = 2x^3 - 3x^2 + 8x - 12$

18. $P(x) = x^4 - 6x^3 + 10x^2 - 6x + 9$

19. **Sports.** A football player shows up in August at 300 pounds. After 2 weeks of practice in the hot sun, he is down to 285 pounds. Ten weeks into the season he is up to 315 pounds because of weight training. In the spring he does not work out, and he is back to 300 pounds by the next August. Plot these points on a graph. What degree polynomial could this be?

20. **Profit.** The profit of a company is governed by the polynomial $P(x) = x^3 - 13x^2 + 47x - 35$, where $x$ is the number of units sold in thousands. How many units does the company have to sell to break even?

21. **Interest Rate.** The interest rate for a 30-year fixed mortgage fluctuates with the economy. In 1970 the mortgage interest rate was 8%, and in 1988 it peaked at 13%. In 2002 it dipped down to 4%, and in 2005 it was up to 6%. What is the lowest degree polynomial that can represent this function?

**In Exercises 22–25, determine (if any) the:**

   a. $x$- and $y$-intercepts

   b. vertical asymptotes

   c. horizontal asymptotes

   d. slant asymptotes

   e. graph

22. $f(x) = \dfrac{2x - 9}{x + 3}$

23. $g(x) = \dfrac{x}{x^2 - 4}$

24. $h(x) = \dfrac{3x^3 - 3}{x^2 - 4}$

25. $F(x) = \dfrac{x - 3}{x^2 - 2x - 8}$

26. **Food.** After a sugary snack, the glucose level of the average body almost doubles. The percentage increase in glucose level $y$ can be approximated by the rational function $y = \dfrac{25x}{x^2 + 50}$, where $x$ represents the number of minutes after eating the snack. Graph the function.

27. a. Use the calculator commands $\boxed{\text{STAT}}$ $\boxed{\text{QuadReg}}$ to model the data using a quadratic function.

   b. Write the quadratic function in standard form and identify the vertex.

   c. Find the $x$-intercepts.

   d. Plot this quadratic function with a graphing calculator. Do they agree with the given values?

| $x$ | $-3$ | $2.2$ | $7.5$ |
|---|---|---|---|
| $y$ | $10.01$ | $-9.75$ | $25.76$ |

28. Find the asymptotes and intercepts of the rational function $f(x) = \dfrac{x(2x - 3)}{x^2 - 3x} + 1$. (*Note:* Combine the two expressions into a single rational expression.) Graph this function utilizing a graphing utility. Does the graph confirm what you found?

1. If $f(x) = 4x - \dfrac{1}{\sqrt{x+2}}$, find $f(2), f(-1), f(1+h)$, and $f(-x)$.

2. If $f(x) = (x-1)^4 - \sqrt{2x+3}$, $f(1), f(3)$, and $f(x+h)$.

3. If $f(x) = \dfrac{3x-5}{2-x-x^2}$, find $f(-3), f(0), f(1)$, and $f(4)$.

4. If $f(x) = 4x^3 - 3x^2 + 5$, evaluate the difference quotient $\dfrac{f(x+h) - f(x)}{h}$.

5. If $f(x) = \sqrt{x} - \dfrac{1}{x^2}$, evaluate the difference quotient $\dfrac{f(x+h) - f(x)}{h}$.

6. If $f(x) = \begin{cases} 0 & x < 0 \\ 3x + x^2 & 0 \le x \le 4 \\ |2x - x^3| & x > 4 \end{cases}$

   find $f(-5), f(0), f(3), f(4)$, and $f(5)$.

**In Exercises 7 and 8, (a) Graph the piecewise-defined functions. (b) State the domain and range in interval notation. (c) Determine the intervals where the function is increasing, decreasing, or constant.**

7. $f(x) = \begin{cases} |6 - 2x| & x \le 8 \\ 10 & 8 < x < 10 \\ \dfrac{1}{x-10} & x > 10 \end{cases}$

8. $f(x) = \begin{cases} (x+5)^2 - 6 & x < -2 \\ \sqrt{x-1} + 3 & -2 \le x < 10 \\ 26 - 2x & 10 \le x \le 14 \end{cases}$

9. The position of a particle is described by the curve $y = \dfrac{2t}{t^2 + 3}$, where $t$ is time (in seconds). What is the average rate of change of the position as a function of time from $t = 5$ to $t = 9$?

10. Express the domain of the function $f(x) = \sqrt{6x - 7}$ with interval notation.

11. Determine whether the function $g(x) = \sqrt{x + 10}$ is even, odd, or neither.

12. For the function $y = -(x+1)^2 + 2$, identify all of the transformations of $y = x^2$.

13. Sketch the graph of $y = \sqrt{x-1} + 3$ and identify all transformations.

14. Find the composite function $f \circ g$ and state the domain for $f(x) = x^2 - 3$ and $g(x) = \sqrt{x+2}$.

15. Evaluate $g(f(-1))$ for $f(x) = 7 - 2x^2$ and $g(x) = 2x - 10$.

16. Find the inverse of the function $f(x) = (x-4)^2 + 2$, where $x \ge 4$.

17. Find a quadratic function whose graph has a vertex at $(-2, 3)$ and passes through the point $(-1, 4)$.

18. Find all of the real zeros and state the multiplicity of the function $f(x) = -3.7x^4 - 14.8x^3$.

19. Use long division to find the quotient $Q(x)$ and the remainder $r(x)$ of $\left(-20x^3 - 8x^2 + 7x - 5\right) \div (-5x + 3)$.

20. Use synthetic division to find the quotient $Q(x)$ and the remainder $r(x)$ of $\left(2x^3 + 3x^2 - 11x + 6\right) \div (x - 3)$.

21. List the possible rational zeros, and test to determine all rational zeros for $P(x) = 12x^3 + 29x^2 + 7x - 6$.

22. Given the real zero $x = 5$ of the polynomial $P(x) = 2x^3 - 3x^2 - 32x - 15$, determine all the other zeros and write the polynomial in terms of a product of linear factors.

23. Factor the polynomial $P(x) = x^3 - 5x^2 + 2x + 8$ completely.

24. Factor the polynomial $P(x) = x^5 + 7x^4 + 15x^3 + 5x^2 - 16x - 12$ completely.

25. Find all vertical and horizontal asymptotes of $f(x) = \dfrac{3x - 5}{x^2 - 4}$.

26. Graph the function $f(x) = \dfrac{2x^3 - x^2 - x}{x^2 - 1}$.

27. Find the asymptotes and intercepts of the rational function $f(x) = \dfrac{5}{2x - 3} - \dfrac{1}{x}$. (*Note:* Combine the two expressions into a single rational expression.) Graph this function utilizing a graphing utility. Does the graph confirm what you found?

28. Find the asymptotes and intercepts of the rational function $f(x) = \dfrac{6x}{3x + 1} - \dfrac{6x}{4x - 1}$. (*Note:* Combine the two expressions into a single rational expression.) Graph this function utilizing a graphing utility. Does the graph confirm what you found?

# 3

# Exponential and Logarithmic Functions

Most populations initially grow *exponentially*, but then as resources become limited, the population reaches a *carrying capacity*. This exponential increase followed by a saturation at some carrying capacity is called *logistic growth*. Often when a particular species is placed on the endangered species list, it is protected from human predators and then its population size increases until naturally leveling off at some carrying capacity.

The U.S. Fish and Wildlife Service removed the gray wolf (*canis lupus*) from the Wisconsin list of endangered and threatened species in 2004, and placed it on the list of protected wild animals. About 537 to 564 wolves existed in Wisconsin in the late winter of 2008.

Wisconsin Wolf Population Growth
if Carrying Capacity is 500 Wolves

**IN THIS CHAPTER** we will discuss exponential functions and their inverses, logarithmic functions. We will graph these functions and use their properties to solve exponential and logarithmic equations. We will then discuss particular exponential and logarithmic models that represent phenomena such as compound interest, world populations, conservation biology models, carbon dating, pH values in chemistry, and the bell curve that is fundamental in statistics for describing how quantities vary in the real world.

## EXPONENTIAL AND LOGARITHMIC FUNCTIONS

| 3.1 Exponential Functions and Their Graphs | 3.2 Logarithmic Functions and Their Graphs | 3.3 Properties of Logarithms | 3.4 Exponential and Logarithmic Equations | 3.5 Exponential and Logarithmic Models |
|---|---|---|---|---|
| • Evaluating Exponential Functions<br>• Graphs of Exponential Functions<br>• The Natural Base *e*<br>• Applications of Exponential Functions | • Evaluating Logarithms<br>• Common and Natural Logarithms<br>• Graphs of Logarithmic Functions<br>• Applications of Logarithms | • Properties of Logarithms<br>• Change-of-Base Formula | • Solving Exponential Equations<br>• Solving Logarithmic Equations | • Exponential Growth Models<br>• Exponential Decay Models<br>• Gaussian (Normal) Distribution Models<br>• Logistic Growth Models<br>• Logarithmic Models |

### LEARNING OBJECTIVES

- Evaluate exponential functions for particular values and understand the characteristics of the graph of an exponential function.
- Evaluate logarithmic functions for particular values and understand the characteristics of the graph of a logarithmic function.
- Understand that logarithmic functions are inverses of exponential functions and derive the properties of logarithms.
- Solve exponential and logarithmic equations.
- Use the exponential growth, exponential decay, logarithmic, logistic growth, and Gaussian distribution models to represent real-world phenomena.

**SKILLS OBJECTIVES**

- Evaluate exponential functions.
- Graph exponential functions.
- Find the domain and range of exponential functions.
- Define the number $e$.
- Solve real-world problems using exponential functions.

**CONCEPTUAL OBJECTIVES**

- Understand the difference between algebraic and exponential functions.
- Understand that irrational exponents lead to approximations.

## Evaluating Exponential Functions

Most of the functions (polynomial, rational, radical, etc.) we have studied thus far have been **algebraic functions**. Algebraic functions involve basic operations, powers, and roots. In this chapter, we discuss *exponential functions* and *logarithmic functions*. The following table illustrates the difference between algebraic functions and *exponential functions*:

| FUNCTION | VARIABLE IS IN THE | CONSTANT IS IN THE | EXAMPLE | EXAMPLE |
|---|---|---|---|---|
| **Algebraic** | Base | Exponent | $f(x) = x^2$ | $g(x) = x^{1/3}$ |
| **Exponential** | Exponent | Base | $F(x) = 2^x$ | $G(x) = \left(\dfrac{1}{3}\right)^x$ |

**DEFINITION**　　**Exponential Function**

An **exponential function** with **base $b$** is denoted by

$$f(x) = b^x$$

where $b$ and $x$ are any real numbers such that $b > 0$ and $b \neq 1$.

Note:

- We eliminate $b = 1$ as a value for the base because it merely yields the constant function $f(x) = 1^x = 1$.
- We eliminate negative values for $b$ because they would give nonreal-number values such as $(-9)^{1/2} = \sqrt{-9} = 3i$.
- We eliminate $b = 0$ because $0^x$ corresponds to an undefined value when $x$ is negative.

Our experience with integer exponents has implied a constant multiplication:

$$2^5 = 2 \cdot 2 \cdot 2 \cdot 2 \cdot 2 = 32$$

We can now think of $f(x) = 2^x$ as a continuous function that for positive integers will result in a constant multiplication.

Sometimes the value of an exponential function for a specific argument can be found by inspection as an *exact* number.

| $x$ | $-3$ | $-1$ | $0$ | $1$ | $3$ |
|---|---|---|---|---|---|
| $F(x) = 2^x$ | $2^{-3} = \dfrac{1}{2^3} = \dfrac{1}{8}$ | $2^{-1} = \dfrac{1}{2^1} = \dfrac{1}{2}$ | $2^0 = 1$ | $2^1 = 2$ | $2^3 = 8$ |

If an exponential function cannot be evaluated exactly, then we find the decimal *approximation* using a calculator.

| $x$ | $-2.7$ | $-\frac{4}{5}$ | $\frac{5}{7}$ | $2.7$ |
|---|---|---|---|---|
| $F(x) = 2^x$ | $2^{-2.7} \approx 0.154$ | $2^{-4/5} \approx 0.574$ | $2^{5/7} \approx 1.641$ | $2^{2.7} \approx 6.498$ |

The domain of exponential functions, $f(x) = b^x$, is the set of all real numbers. All of the arguments discussed in the first two tables have been rational numbers. What happens if $x$ is irrational? We can approximate the irrational number with a decimal approximation such as $b^\pi \approx b^{3.14}$ or $b^{\sqrt{2}} \approx b^{1.41}$.

Consider $7^{\sqrt{3}}$, and realize that the irrational number $\sqrt{3}$ is a decimal that never terminates or repeats: $\sqrt{3} \approx 1.7320508$. We can show in advanced mathematics that there is a number $7^{\sqrt{3}}$, and although we cannot write it exactly, we can approximate the number. In fact, the closer the exponent is to $\sqrt{3}$, the closer the approximation is to $7^{\sqrt{3}}$.

It is important to note that the properties of exponents (Appendix) hold when the exponent is any real number (rational or irrational).

$7^{1.7} \approx 27.3317$

$7^{1.73} \approx 28.9747$

$7^{1.732} \approx 29.0877$

$\ldots$

$7^{\sqrt{3}} \approx 29.0906$

## EXAMPLE 1   Evaluating Exponential Functions

Let $f(x) = 3^x$, $g(x) = \left(\frac{1}{4}\right)^x$ and $h(x) = 10^{x-2}$. Find the following values:

**a.** $f(2)$   **b.** $f(\pi)$   **c.** $g\left(-\frac{3}{2}\right)$   **d.** $h(2.3)$   **e.** $f(0)$   **f.** $g(0)$

If an approximation is required, approximate to four decimal places.

**Solution:**

**a.** $f(2) = 3^2 = \boxed{9}$

**b.** $f(\pi) = 3^\pi \approx \boxed{31.5443}$ *

**c.** $g\left(-\frac{3}{2}\right) = \left(\frac{1}{4}\right)^{-3/2} = 4^{3/2} = \left(\sqrt{4}\right)^3 = 2^3 = \boxed{8}$

**d.** $h(2.3) = 10^{2.3-2} = 10^{0.3} \approx \boxed{1.9953}$

**e.** $f(0) = 3^0 = \boxed{1}$

**f.** $g(0) = \left(\frac{1}{4}\right)^0 = \boxed{1}$

Notice that parts (a) and (c) were evaluated exactly, whereas parts (b) and (d) required approximation using a calculator.

■ **YOUR TURN** Let $f(x) = 2^x$ and $g(x) = \left(\frac{1}{9}\right)^x$ and $h(x) = 5^{x-2}$. Find the following values:

**a.** $f(4)$   **b.** $f(\pi)$   **c.** $g\left(-\frac{3}{2}\right)$   **d.** $h(2.9)$

Evaluate exactly when possible, and round to four decimal places when a calculator is needed.

■ **Answer: a.** 16   **b.** 8.8250
**c.** 27   **d.** 4.2567

---

*In part (b), the $\pi$ button on the calculator is selected. If we instead approximate $\pi$ by 3.14, we get a slightly different approximation for the function value:

$$f(\pi) = 3^\pi \approx 3^{3.14} \approx 31.4891$$

# Graphs of Exponential Functions

Let's graph two exponential functions, $y = 2^x$ and $y = 2^{-x} = \left(\frac{1}{2}\right)^x$, by plotting points.

| $x$ | $y = 2^x$ | $(x, y)$ |
|---|---|---|
| $-2$ | $2^{-2} = \dfrac{1}{2^2} = \dfrac{1}{4}$ | $\left(-2, \dfrac{1}{4}\right)$ |
| $-1$ | $2^{-1} = \dfrac{1}{2^1} = \dfrac{1}{2}$ | $\left(-1, \dfrac{1}{2}\right)$ |
| $0$ | $2^0 = 1$ | $(0, 1)$ |
| $1$ | $2^1 = 2$ | $(1, 2)$ |
| $2$ | $2^2 = 4$ | $(2, 4)$ |
| $3$ | $2^3 = 8$ | $(3, 8)$ |

| $x$ | $y = 2^{-x}$ | $(x, y)$ |
|---|---|---|
| $-3$ | $2^{-(-3)} = 2^3 = 8$ | $(-3, 8)$ |
| $-2$ | $2^{-(-2)} = 2^2 = 4$ | $(-2, 4)$ |
| $-1$ | $2^{-(-1)} = 2^1 = 2$ | $(-1, 2)$ |
| $0$ | $2^0 = 1$ | $(0, 1)$ |
| $1$ | $2^{-1} = \dfrac{1}{2^1} = \dfrac{1}{2}$ | $\left(1, \dfrac{1}{2}\right)$ |
| $2$ | $2^{-2} = \dfrac{1}{2^2} = \dfrac{1}{4}$ | $\left(2, \dfrac{1}{4}\right)$ |

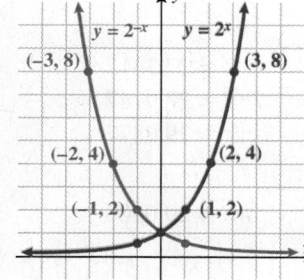

Notice that both graphs' $y$-intercept is $(0, 1)$ (as shown to the left) and neither graph has an $x$-intercept. The $x$-axis is a horizontal asymptote for both graphs. The following box summarizes general characteristics of the graphs of exponential functions.

## CHARACTERISTICS OF GRAPHS OF EXPONENTIAL FUNCTIONS

$$f(x) = b^x, \qquad b > 0, \qquad b \neq 1$$

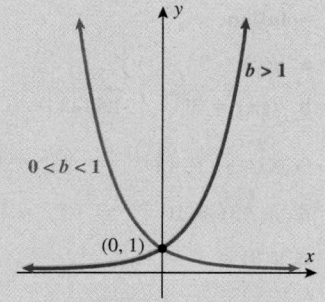

- Domain: $(-\infty, \infty)$
- Range: $(0, \infty)$
- $x$-intercepts: none
- $y$-intercept: $(0, 1)$
- Horizontal asymptote: $x$-axis
- The graph passes through $(1, b)$ and $\left(-1, \dfrac{1}{b}\right)$.
- As $x$ increases, $f(x)$ increases if $b > 1$ and decreases if $0 < b < 1$.
- The function $f$ is one-to-one.

Since exponential functions, $f(x) = b^x$, all go through the point $(0, 1)$ and have the $x$-axis as a horizontal asymptote, we can find the graph by finding two additional points as outlined in the following procedure.

## PROCEDURE FOR GRAPHING $f(x) = b^x$

**Step 1:** Label the point $(0, 1)$ corresponding to the $y$-intercept $f(0)$.

**Step 2:** Find and label two additional points corresponding to $f(-1)$ and $f(1)$.

**Step 3:** Connect the three points with a *smooth* curve with the $x$-axis as the horizontal asymptote.

**EXAMPLE 2**   **Graphing Exponential Functions for $b > 1$**

Graph the function $f(x) = 5^x$.

**Solution:**

*Technology Tip*

The graph of $f(x) = 5^x$ is shown.

**STEP 1:** Label the $y$-intercept $(0, 1)$.             $f(0) = 5^0 = 1$

**STEP 2:** Label the point $(1, 5)$.                        $f(1) = 5^1 = 5$

Label the point $(-1, 0.2)$.                $f(-1) = 5^{-1} = \dfrac{1}{5} = 0.2$

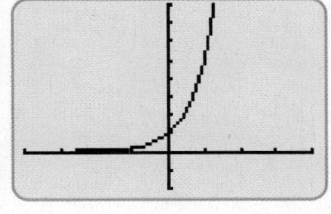

**STEP 3:** Sketch a smooth curve through the three points with the $x$-axis as a horizontal asymptote.

Domain: $(-\infty, \infty)$

Range: $(0, \infty)$

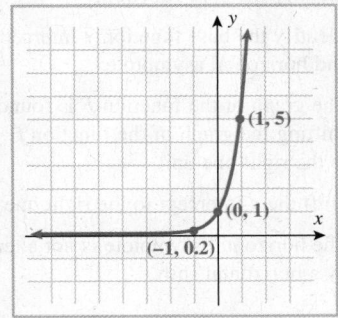

**YOUR TURN** Graph the function $f(x) = 5^{-x}$.

**Answer:**

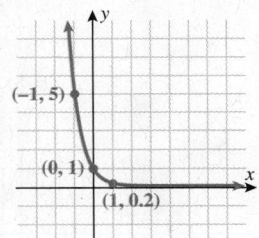

**EXAMPLE 3**   **Graphing Exponential Functions for $b < 1$**

Graph the function $f(x) = \left(\dfrac{2}{5}\right)^x$.

**Solution:**

**STEP 1:** Label the $y$-intercept $(0, 1)$.             $f(0) = \left(\dfrac{2}{5}\right)^0 = 1$

**STEP 2:** Label the point $(-1, 2.5)$.              $f(-1) = \left(\dfrac{2}{5}\right)^{-1} = \dfrac{5}{2} = 2.5$

Label the point $(1, 0.4)$.                 $f(1) = \left(\dfrac{2}{5}\right)^1 = \dfrac{2}{5} = 0.4$

**STEP 3:** Sketch a smooth curve through the three points with the $x$-axis as a horizontal asymptote.

Domain: $(-\infty, \infty)$

Range: $(0, \infty)$

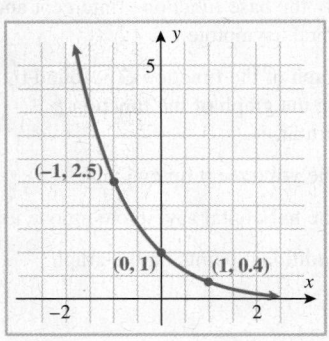

Exponential functions, like all functions, can be graphed by point-plotting. We can also use transformations (horizontal and vertical shifting and reflection; Section 1.3) to graph exponential functions.

**EXAMPLE 4  Graphing Exponential Functions Using a Horizontal or Vertical Shift**

**a.** Graph the function $F(x) = 2^{x-1}$. State the domain and range of $F$.
**b.** Graph the function $G(x) = 2^x + 1$. State the domain and range of $G$.

**Solution (a):**

| | |
|---|---|
| Identify the base function. | $f(x) = 2^x$ |
| Identify the base function $y$-intercept and horizontal asymptote. | $(0, 1)$ and $y = 0$ |
| The graph of the function $F$ is found by shifting the graph of the function $f$ to the right one unit. | $F(x) = f(x - 1)$ |
| Shift the $y$-intercept to the right one unit. | $(0, 1)$ shifts to $(1, 1)$ |
| The horizontal asymptote is not altered by a horizontal shift. | $y = 0$ |
| Find additional points on the graph. | $F(0) = 2^{0-1} = 2^{-1} = \dfrac{1}{2}$ |

$$y\text{-intercept: } \left(0, \frac{1}{2}\right)$$

$$F(2) = 2^{2-1} = 2^1 = 2$$

Sketch the graph of $F(x) = 2^{x-1}$ with a *smooth* curve.

Domain: $(-\infty, \infty)$
Range: $(0, \infty)$

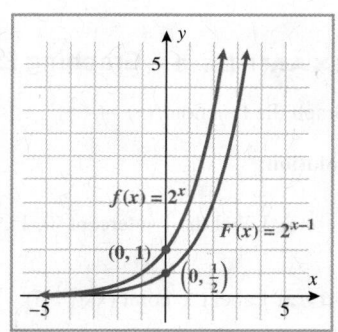

**Solution (b):**

| | |
|---|---|
| Identify the base function. | $f(x) = 2^x$ |
| Identify the base function $y$-intercept and horizontal asymptote. | $(0, 1)$ and $y = 0$ |
| The graph of the function $G$ is found by shifting the graph of the function $f$ up one unit. | $G(x) = f(x) + 1$ |
| Shift the $y$-intercept up one unit. | $(0, 1)$ shifts to $(0, 2)$ |
| Shift the horizontal asymptote up one unit. | $y = 0$ shifts to $y = 1$ |
| Find additional points on the graph. | $G(1) = 2^1 + 1 = 2 + 1 = 3$ |

$$G(-1) = 2^{-1} + 1 = \frac{1}{2} + 1 = \frac{3}{2}$$

Sketch the graph of $G(x) = 2^x + 1$
with a *smooth* curve.

Domain: $(-\infty, \infty)$
Range: $(1, \infty)$

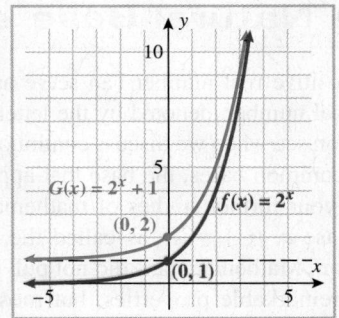

## EXAMPLE 5    Graphing Exponential Functions Using Both Horizontal and Vertical Shifts

Graph the function $F(x) = 3^{x+1} - 2$. State the domain and range of $F$.

**Solution:**

Identify the base function.

$f(x) = 3^x$

Identify the base function $y$-intercept
and horizontal asymptote.

$(0, 1)$ and $y = 0$

The graph of the function $F$ is found by
shifting the graph of the function $f$ to
the left one unit and down two units.

$F(x) = f(x + 1) - 2$

Shift the $y$-intercept to the left one unit
and down two units.

$(0, 1)$ shifts to $(-1, -1)$

Shift the horizontal asymptote down
two units.

$y = 0$ shifts to $y = -2$

Find additional points on the graph.

$F(0) = 3^{0+1} - 2 = 3 - 2 = 1$

$F(1) = 3^{1+1} - 2 = 9 - 2 = 7$

Sketch the graph of $F(x) = 3^{x+1} - 2$ with
a *smooth* curve.

Domain: $(-\infty, \infty)$
Range: $(-2, \infty)$

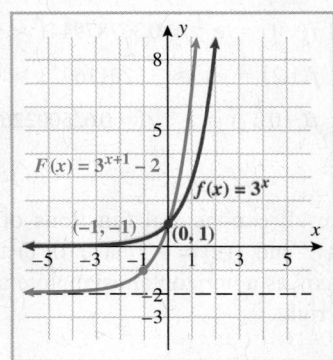

*Technology Tip*

The graph of $f(x) = 3^{x+1} - 2$ is
shown.

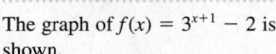

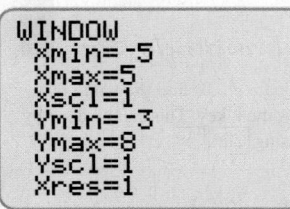

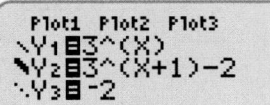

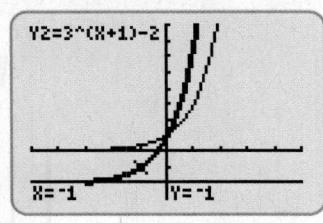

■ **Answer:** Domain: $(-\infty, \infty)$
Range: $(-1, \infty)$

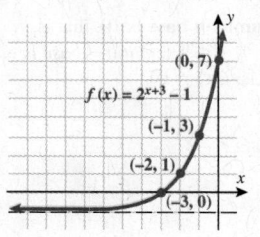

$f(x) = 2^{x+3} - 1$

(0, 7)

(-1, 3)

(-2, 1)

(-3, 0)

■ **YOUR TURN**   Graph $f(x) = 2^{x+3} - 1$. State the domain and range of $f$.

# The Natural Base e

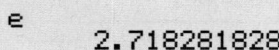

Any positive real number can serve as the base for an exponential function. A particular irrational number, denoted by the letter $e$, appears as the base in many applications, as you will soon see when we discuss continuous compounded interest. Although you will see 2 and 10 as common bases, the base that appears most often is $e$, because $e$, as you will come to see in your further studies of mathematics, is the **natural base**. The exponential function with base $e$, $f(x) = e^x$, is called the **exponential function** or the **natural exponential function**. Mathematicians did not pull this irrational number out of a hat. The number $e$ has many remarkable properties, but most simply, it comes from evaluating the expression $\left(1 + \dfrac{1}{m}\right)^m$ as $m$ gets large (increases without bound).

| $m$ | $\left(1 + \dfrac{1}{m}\right)^m$ |
|---|---|
| 1 | 2 |
| 10 | 2.59374 |
| 100 | 2.70481 |
| 1000 | 2.71692 |
| 10,000 | 2.71815 |
| 100,000 | 2.71827 |
| 1,000,000 | **2.71828** |

$e \approx 2.71828$

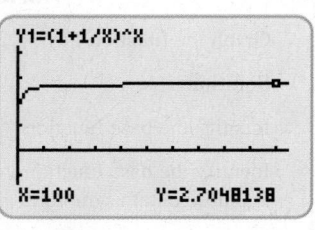

Calculators have an $\boxed{e^x}$ button for approximating the natural exponential function.

▶ **EXAMPLE 6** **Evaluating the Natural Exponential Function**

Evaluate $f(x) = e^x$ for the given $x$-values. Round your answers to four decimal places.

**a.** $x = 1$    **b.** $x = -1$    **c.** $x = 1.2$    **d.** $x = -0.47$

**Solution:**

**a.** $f(1) = e^1 \approx 2.718281828 \approx \boxed{2.7183}$

**b.** $f(-1) = e^{-1} \approx 0.367879441 \approx \boxed{0.3679}$

**c.** $f(1.2) = e^{1.2} \approx 3.320116923 \approx \boxed{3.3201}$

**d.** $f(-0.47) = e^{-0.47} \approx 0.625002268 \approx \boxed{0.6250}$

Like all exponential functions of the form $f(x) = b^x$, $f(x) = e^x$ and $f(x) = e^{-x}$ have $(0, 1)$ as their $y$-intercept and the $x$-axis as a horizontal asymptote as shown in the figure on the right.

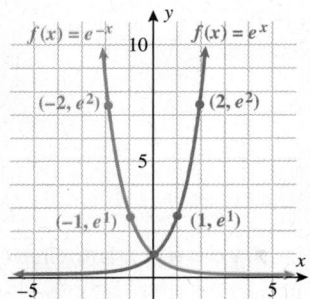

**EXAMPLE 7** **Graphing Exponential Functions with Base *e***

Graph the function $f(x) = 3 + e^{2x}$.

**Solution:**

**Technology Tip**

The graph of $y_1 = 3 + e^{2x}$ is shown. To setup the split screen, press MODE G-T ENTER GRAPH.

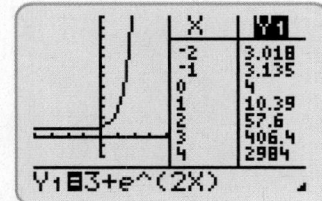

| $x$ | $f(x) = 3 + e^{2x}$ | $(x, y)$ |
|-----|-----|-----|
| $-2$ | 3.02 | $(-2, 3.02)$ |
| $-1$ | 3.14 | $(1, 3.14)$ |
| 0 | 4 | $(0, 4)$ |
| 1 | 10.39 | $(1, 10.39)$ |
| 2 | 57.60 | $(2, 57.60)$ |

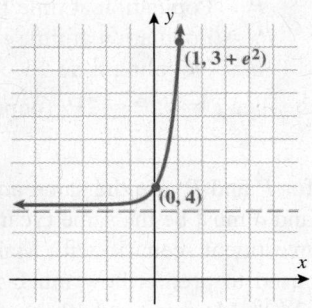

*Note:* The $y$-intercept is $(0, 4)$, and the line $y = 3$ is the horizontal asymptote.

■ **YOUR TURN** Graph the function $f(x) = e^{x+1} - 2$.

■**Answer:**

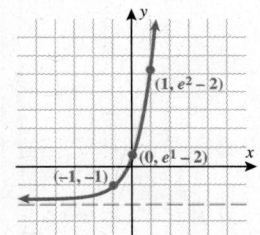

# Applications of Exponential Functions

Exponential functions describe either *growth* or *decay*. Populations and investments are often modeled with exponential growth functions, while the declining value of a used car and the radioactive decay of isotopes are often modeled with exponential decay functions. In Section 3.5, various exponential models will be discussed. In this section, we discuss doubling time, half-life, and compound interest.

A successful investment program, growing at about 7.2% per year, will double in size every 10 years. Let's assume that you will retire at the age of 65. There is a saying: *It's not the first time your money doubles, it's the last time that makes such a difference.* As you may already know or as you will soon find, it is important to start investing early.

Suppose Maria invests $5000 at age 25 and David invests $5000 at age 35. Let's calculate how much will accrue from the initial $5000 investment by the time they each retire, assuming their money doubles every 10 years and that they both retire at age 65.

| AGE | MARIA | DAVID |
|-----|-----|-----|
| 25 | $5,000 | |
| 35 | $10,000 | $5,000 |
| 45 | $20,000 | $10,000 |
| 55 | $40,000 | $20,000 |
| **65** | **$80,000** | **$40,000** |

They each made a one-time investment of $5000. By investing 10 years sooner, Maria made twice what David made.

A measure of growth rate is the *doubling time*, the time it takes for something to double. Often doubling time is used to describe populations.

### DOUBLING TIME GROWTH MODEL

The doubling time growth model is given by

$$P = P_0 2^{t/d}$$

where
$P$ = Population at time $t$
$P_0$ = Population at time $t = 0$
$d$ = Doubling time

Note that when $t = d$, $P = 2P_0$ (population is equal to twice the original).

The units for $P$ and $P_0$ are the same and can be any quantity (people, dollars, etc.). The units for $t$ and $d$ must be the same (years, weeks, days, hours, seconds, etc.).

In the investment scenario with Maria and David, $P_0 = \$5000$ and $d = 10$ years, so the model used to predict how much money the original $5000 investment yielded is $P = 5000(2)^{t/10}$. Maria retired 40 years after the original investment, $t = 40$, and David retired 30 years after the original investment, $t = 30$.

Maria: $P = 5000(2)^{40/10} = 5000(2)^4 = 5000(16) = 80,000$
David: $P = 5000(2)^{30/10} = 5000(2)^3 = 5000(8) = 40,000$

### EXAMPLE 8 Doubling Time of Populations

In 2004 the population in Kazakhstan, a country in Asia, reached 15 million. It is estimated that the population doubles in 30 years. If the population continues to grow at the same rate, what will the population be in 2024? Round to the nearest million.

**Solution:**

Write the doubling model. $\qquad P = P_0 2^{t/d}$

Substitute $P_0 = 15$ million,
$d = 30$ years, and $t = 20$ years. $\qquad P = 15(2)^{20/30}$

Simplify. $\qquad P = 15(2)^{2/3} \approx 23.8110$

In 2024, there will be approximately 24 million people in Kazakhstan.

■ **Answer:** 38 million

■ **YOUR TURN** What will the approximate population in Kazakhstan be in 2044? Round to the nearest million.

We now turn our attention from exponential growth to exponential decay, or negative growth. Suppose you buy a brand-new car from a dealership for $24,000. The value of a car decreases over time according to an exponential decay function. The **half-life** of this particular car, or the time it takes for the car to depreciate 50%, is approximately 3 years. The exponential decay is described by

$$A = A_0\left(\frac{1}{2}\right)^{t/h}$$

where $A_0$ is the amount the car is worth (in dollars) when new (that is, when $t = 0$), $A$ is the amount the car is worth (in dollars) after $t$ years, and $h$ is the half-life in years. In our car scenario, $A_0 = 24,000$ and $h = 3$:

$$A = 24,000\left(\frac{1}{2}\right)^{t/3}$$

How much is the car worth after three years? Six years? Nine years? Twenty-four years?

$$t = 3: \quad A = 24{,}000\left(\frac{1}{2}\right)^{3/3} = 24{,}000\left(\frac{1}{2}\right) = 12{,}000$$

$$t = 6: \quad A = 24{,}000\left(\frac{1}{2}\right)^{6/3} = 24{,}000\left(\frac{1}{2}\right)^{2} = 6000$$

$$t = 9: \quad A = 24{,}000\left(\frac{1}{2}\right)^{9/3} = 24{,}000\left(\frac{1}{2}\right)^{3} = 3000$$

$$t = 24: \quad A = 24{,}000\left(\frac{1}{2}\right)^{24/3} = 24{,}000\left(\frac{1}{2}\right)^{8} = 93.75 \approx 100$$

The car that was worth \$24,000 new is worth \$12,000 in 3 years, \$6000 in 6 years, \$3000 in 9 years, and about \$100 in the junkyard in 24 years.

### EXAMPLE 9   Radioactive Decay

The radioactive isotope of potassium $^{42}K$, which is used in the diagnosis of brain tumors, has a half-life of 12.36 hours. If 500 milligrams of potassium 42 are taken, how many milligrams will remain after 24 hours? Round to the nearest milligram.

**Solution:**

Write the half-life formula.

$$A = A_0\left(\frac{1}{2}\right)^{t/h}$$

Substitute $A_0 = 500$ mg, $h = 12.36$ hours, $t = 24$ hours.

$$A = 500\left(\frac{1}{2}\right)^{24/12.36}$$

Simplify.

$$A \approx 500(0.2603) \approx 130.15$$

After 24 hours, there are approximately $\boxed{130\ \text{milligrams}}$ of potassium 42 left.

■ **YOUR TURN** How many milligrams of potassium 42 are expected to be left in the body after 1 week?

■ **Answer:** 0.04 mg (less than 1 mg)

In Section 0.1, *simple interest* was defined where the interest $I$ is calculated based on the principal $P$, the annual interest rate $r$, and the time $t$ in years, using the formula $I = Prt$.

If the interest earned in a period is then reinvested at the same rate, future interest is earned on both the principal and the reinvested interest during the next period. Interest paid on both the principal and interest is called *compound interest*.

### COMPOUND INTEREST

If a **principal $P$** is invested at an annual **rate $r$ compounded** $n$ times a year, then the **amount $A$** in the account at the end of $t$ years is given by

$$A = P\left(1 + \frac{r}{n}\right)^{nt}$$

The annual interest rate $r$ is expressed as a decimal.

The following list shows the typical number of times interest is compounded:

| | | | |
|---|---|---|---|
| Annually | $n = 1$ | Monthly | $n = 12$ |
| Semiannually | $n = 2$ | Weekly | $n = 52$ |
| Quarterly | $n = 4$ | Daily | $n = 365$ |

**Answer:** $6312.38

### EXAMPLE 10   Compound Interest

If $3000 is deposited in an account paying 3% compounded quarterly, how much will you have in the account in 7 years?

**Solution:**

| | |
|---|---|
| Write the compound interest formula. | $A = P\left(1 + \dfrac{r}{n}\right)^{nt}$ |
| Substitute $P = 3000$, $r = 0.03$, $n = 4$, and $t = 7$. | $A = 3000\left(1 + \dfrac{0.03}{4}\right)^{(4)(7)}$ |
| Simplify. | $A = 3000(1.0075)^{28} \approx 3698.14$ |

You will have $\boxed{\$3698.14}$ in the account.

■ **YOUR TURN**  If $5000 is deposited in an account paying 6% compounded annually, how much will you have in the account in 4 years?

Notice in the compound interest formula that as $n$ increases the amount $A$ also increases. In other words, the more times the interest is compounded per year, the more money you make. Ideally, your bank will compound your interest infinitely many times. This is called *compounding continuously*. We will now show the development of the continuous compounding formula, $A = Pe^{rt}$.

| WORDS | MATH |
|---|---|
| Write the compound interest formula. | $A = P\left(1 + \dfrac{r}{n}\right)^{nt}$ |
| Note that $\dfrac{r}{n} = \dfrac{1}{n/r}$ and $nt = \left(\dfrac{n}{r}\right)rt$. | $A = P\left(1 + \dfrac{1}{n/r}\right)^{(n/r)rt}$ |
| Let $m = \dfrac{n}{r}$. | $A = P\left(1 + \dfrac{1}{m}\right)^{mrt}$ |
| Use the exponential property: $x^{mrt} = (x^m)^{rt}$. | $A = P\left[\left(1 + \dfrac{1}{m}\right)^{m}\right]^{rt}$ |

Recall that as $m$ increases, $\left(1 + \dfrac{1}{m}\right)^{m}$ approaches $e$. Therefore, as the number of times the interest is compounded approaches infinity, or as $n \to \infty$, the amount in an account $A = P\left(1 + \dfrac{r}{n}\right)^{nt}$ approaches $A = Pe^{rt}$.

### CONTINUOUS COMPOUND INTEREST

If a **principal $P$** is invested at an annual **rate $r$ compounded continuously**, then the **amount $A$** in the account at the end of $t$ years is given by

$$A = Pe^{rt}$$

The annual interest rate $r$ is expressed as a decimal.

It is important to note that for a given interest rate, the highest return you can earn is by compounding continuously.

## EXAMPLE 11   Continuously Compounded Interest

If $3000 is deposited in a savings account paying 3% a year compounded continuously, how much will you have in the account in 7 years?

**Technology Tip**

Enter $3000e^{(0.03)(7)}$ into the graphing calculator.

```
3000e^(0.03*7)
          3701.03418
```

**Solution:**

Write the continuous compound interest formula.   $A = Pe^{rt}$

Substitute $P = 3000$, $r = 0.03$, and $t = 7$.   $A = 3000e^{(0.03)(7)}$

Simplify.   $A \approx 3701.034$

There will be   $3701.03   in the account in 7 years.

*Note:* In Example 10, we worked this same problem compounding *quarterly,* and the result was $3698.14.

If the number of times per year interest is compounded increases, then the total interest earned that year also increases.

**Study Tip**

If the number of times per year interest is compounded increases, then the total interest earned that year also increases.

■ **YOUR TURN**  If $5000 is deposited in an account paying 6% compounded continuously, how much will be in the account in 4 years?

■ **Answer:** $6356.25

---

## SECTION
## 3.1   SUMMARY

In this section, we discussed exponential functions (constant base, variable exponent).

**General Exponential Functions:**  $f(x) = b^x$, $b \neq 1$, and $b > 0$

1. Evaluating exponential functions
   - Exact (by inspection): $f(x) = 2^x$   $f(3) = 2^3 = 8$.
   - Approximate (with the aid of a calculator): $f(x) = 2^x$
     $f(\sqrt{3}) = 2^{\sqrt{3}} \approx 3.322$
2. Graphs of exponential functions
   - Domain: $(-\infty, \infty)$ and range: $(0, \infty)$.
   - The point $(0, 1)$ corresponds to the $y$-intercept.
   - The graph passes through the points $(1, b)$ and $\left(-1, \dfrac{1}{b}\right)$.
   - The $x$-axis is a horizontal asymptote.
   - The function $f$ is one-to-one.

$$f(x) = b^x, \qquad b > 0, \qquad b \neq 1$$

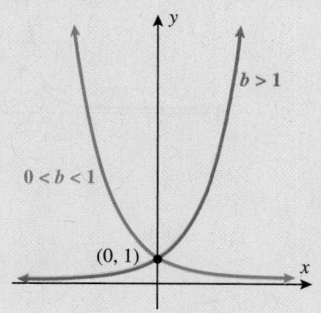

**Procedure for Graphing:**  $f(x) = b^x$

**Step 1:** Label the point $(0, 1)$ corresponding to the $y$-intercept $f(0)$.

**Step 2:** Find and label two additional points corresponding to $f(-1)$ and $f(1)$.

**Step 3:** Connect the three points with a smooth curve with the $x$-axis as the horizontal asymptote.

**The Natural Exponential Function:**  $f(x) = e^x$
   - The irrational number $e$ is called the natural base.
   - $e = \left(1 + \dfrac{1}{m}\right)^m$ as $m \rightarrow \infty$
   - $e \approx 2.71828$

**Applications of Exponential Functions (all variables expressed in consistent units)**

1. Doubling time: $P = P_0 2^{t/d}$
   - $d$ is doubling time.
   - $P$ is population at time $t$.
   - $P_0$ is population at time $t = 0$.
2. Half-life: $A = A_0 \left(\frac{1}{2}\right)^{t/h}$
   - $h$ is the half-life.
   - $A$ is amount at time $t$.
   - $A_0$ is amount at time $t = 0$.
3. Compound interest ($P$ = principal, $A$ = amount after $t$ years, $r$ = interest rate)
   - Compounded $n$ times a year: $A = P\left(1 + \dfrac{r}{n}\right)^{nt}$
   - Compounded continuously: $A = Pe^{rt}$

## SECTION
## 3.1 EXERCISES

■ **SKILLS**

**In Exercises 1–6, evaluate *exactly* (without using a calculator). For rational exponents, consider converting to radical form first.**

**1.** $5^{-2}$      **2.** $4^{-3}$      **3.** $8^{2/3}$      **4.** $27^{2/3}$      **5.** $\left(\frac{1}{9}\right)^{-3/2}$      **6.** $\left(\frac{1}{16}\right)^{-3/2}$

**In Exercises 7–12, approximate with a calculator. Round your answer to four decimal places.**

**7.** $5^{\sqrt{2}}$      **8.** $6^{\sqrt{3}}$      **9.** $e^2$      **10.** $e^{1/2}$      **11.** $e^{-\pi}$      **12.** $e^{-\sqrt{2}}$

**In Exercises 13–20, for the functions $f(x) = 3^x$, $g(x) = \left(\frac{1}{16}\right)^x$, and $h(x) = 10^{x+1}$, find the function value at the indicated points.**

**13.** $f(3)$      **14.** $h(1)$      **15.** $g(-1)$      **16.** $f(-2)$

**17.** $g\left(-\frac{1}{2}\right)$      **18.** $g\left(-\frac{3}{2}\right)$      **19.** $f(e)$      **20.** $g(\pi)$

**In Exercises 21–26, match the graph with the function.**

**21.** $y = 5^{x-1}$      **22.** $y = 5^{1-x}$      **23.** $y = -5^x$

**24.** $y = -5^{-x}$      **25.** $y = 1 - 5^{-x}$      **26.** $y = 5^x - 1$

**a.**

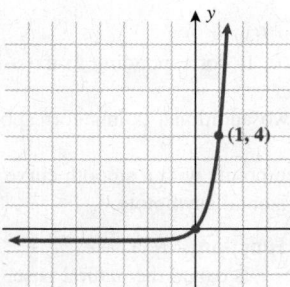

**b.**

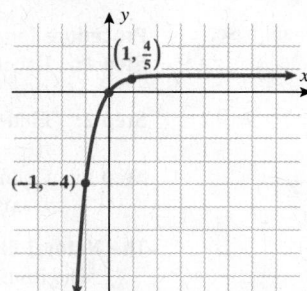

**c.**

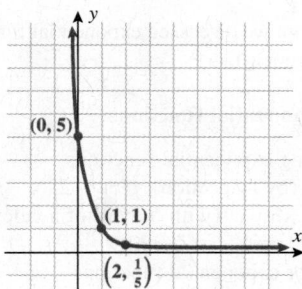

**d.**

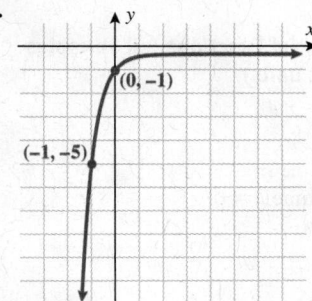

**e.**

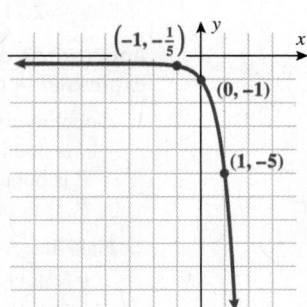

**f.**

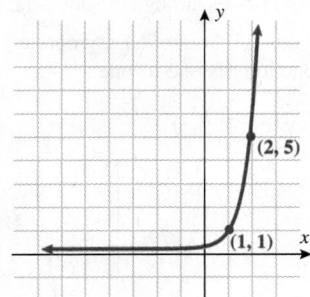

In Exercises 27–46, graph the exponential function using transformations. State the $y$-intercept, two additional points, the domain, the range, and the horizontal asymptote.

**27.** $f(x) = 6^x$

**28.** $f(x) = 7^x$

**29.** $f(x) = 10^{-x}$

**30.** $f(x) = 4^{-x}$

**31.** $f(x) = e^x$

**32.** $f(x) = -e^{-x}$

**33.** $f(x) = e^{-x}$

**34.** $f(x) = -e^x$

**35.** $f(x) = 2^x - 1$

**36.** $f(x) = 3^x - 1$

**37.** $f(x) = 2 - e^x$

**38.** $f(x) = 1 + e^{-x}$

**39.** $f(x) = 5 + 4^{-x}$

**40.** $f(x) = 5^x - 2$

**41.** $f(x) = e^{x+1} - 4$

**42.** $f(x) = e^{x-1} + 2$

**43.** $f(x) = 3e^{x/2}$

**44.** $f(x) = 2e^{-x}$

**45.** $f(x) = 1 + \left(\frac{1}{2}\right)^{x-2}$

**46.** $f(x) = 2 - \left(\frac{1}{3}\right)^{x+1}$

## ▪ APPLICATIONS

**47. Population Doubling Time.** In 2002 there were 7.1 million people living in London, England. If the population is expected to double by 2090, what is the expected population in London in 2050?

**48. Population Doubling Time.** In 2004 the population in Morganton, Georgia, was 43,000. The population in Morganton doubled by 2010. If the growth rate remains the same, what is the expected population in Morganton in 2020?

**49. Investments.** Suppose an investor buys land in a rural area for $1500 an acre and sells some of it 5 years later at $3000 an acre and the rest of it 10 years later at $6000. Write a function that models the value of land in that area, assuming the growth rate stays the same. What would the expected cost per acre be 30 years after the initial investment of $1500?

**50. Salaries.** Twin brothers, Collin and Cameron, get jobs immediately after graduating from college at the age of 22. Collin opts for the higher starting salary, $55,000, and stays with the same company until he retires at 65. His salary doubles every 15 years. Cameron opts for a lower starting salary, $35,000, but moves to a new job every 5 years; he doubles his salary every 10 years until he retires at 65. What is the annual salary of each brother upon retirement?

**51. Radioactive Decay.** A radioactive isotope of selenium, $^{75}$Se, which is used in medical imaging of the pancreas, has a half-life of 119.77 days. If 200 milligrams are given to a patient, how many milligrams are left after 30 days?

**52. Radioactive Decay.** The radioactive isotope indium-111 ($^{111}$In), used as a diagnostic tool for locating tumors associated with prostate cancer, has a half-life of 2.807 days. If 300 milligrams are given to a patient, how many milligrams will be left after a week?

**53. Radioactive Decay.** A radioactive isotope of beryllium-11 decays to borom-11 with a half-life of 13.81 seconds. Beryllium is given to patients that suffer Chronic Beryllium Disease (CBD). If 800 milligrams are given to a CBD patient, how much beryllium is present after 2 minutes? Round your answer to the nearest milligram.

**54. Radioactive Decay.** If the CBD patient in Exercise 53 is given 1000 milligrams, how much beryllium is present after 1 minute? Round your answer to the nearest milligram.

**55. Depreciation of Furniture.** A couple buy a new bedroom set for $8000 and 10 years later sell it for $4000. If the depreciation continues at the same rate, how much would the bedroom set be worth in 4 more years?

**56. Depreciation of a Computer.** A student buys a new laptop for $1500 when she arrives as a freshman. A year later, the computer is worth approximately $750. If the depreciation continues at the same rate, how much would she expect to sell her laptop for when she graduates 4 years after she bought it?

**57. Compound Interest.** If you put $3200 in a savings account that earns 2.5% interest per year compounded quarterly, how much would you expect to have in that account in 3 years?

**58. Compound Interest.** If you put $10,000 in a savings account that earns 3.5% interest per year compounded annually, how much would you expect to have in that account in 5 years?

**59. Compound Interest.** How much money should you put in a savings account now that earns 5% a year compounded daily if you want to have $32,000 in 18 years?

**60. Compound Interest.** How much money should you put in a savings account now that earns 3.0% a year compounded weekly if you want to have $80,000 in 15 years?

**61. Compound Interest.** If you put $3200 in a savings account that pays 2% a year compounded continuously, how much will you have in the account in 15 years?

**62. Compound Interest.** If you put $7000 in a money market account that pays 4.3% a year compounded continuously, how much will you have in the account in 10 years?

**63. Compound Interest.** How much money should you deposit into a money market account that pays 5% a year compounded continuously to have $38,000 in the account in 20 years?

**64. Compound Interest.** How much money should you deposit into a certificate of deposit that pays 6% a year compounded continuously to have $80,000 in the account in 18 years?

**For Exercises 65 and 66, refer to the following:**

Exponential functions can be used to model the concentration of a drug in a patient's body. Suppose the concentration of Drug X in a patient's bloodstream is modeled by

$$C(t) = C_0 e^{-rt}$$

where $C(t)$ represents the concentration at time $t$ (in hours), $C_0$ is the concentration of the drug in the blood immediately after injection, and $r > 0$ is a constant indicating the removal of the drug by the body through metabolism and/or excretion. The rate constant $r$ has units of 1/time (1/hr). It is important to note that this model assumes that the blood concentration of the drug $C_0$ peaks immediately when the drug is injected.

65. **Health/Medicine.** After an injection of Drug Y, the concentration of the drug in the bloodstream drops at the rate of 0.020 1/hr. Find the concentration, to the nearest tenth, of the drug 20 hours after receiving an injection with initial concentration of 5.0 mg/L.

66. **Health/Medicine.** After an injection of Drug Y, the concentration of the drug in the bloodstream drops at the rate of 0.009 1/hr. Find the concentration, to the nearest tenth, of the drug 4 hours after receiving an injection with initial concentration of 4.0 mg/L.

**For Exercises 67 and 68, refer to the following:**

The demand for a product, in thousands of units, can be expressed by the exponential demand function

$$D(p) = 2300(0.85)^p$$

where $p$ is the price per unit.

67. **Economics.** Find the demand for the product by completing the following table.

| P (PRICE PER UNIT) | D(P)–DEMAND FOR PRODUCT IN UNITS |
|---|---|
| 1.00 | |
| 5.00 | |
| 10.00 | |
| 20.00 | |
| 40.00 | |
| 60.00 | |
| 80.00 | |
| 90.00 | |

68. **Economics.** Evaluate $D(91)$ and interpret what this means in terms of demand.

**■CATCH THE MISTAKE**

**In Exercises 69–72, explain the mistake that is made.**

69. Evaluate the expression $4^{-1/2}$.

   **Solution:** $\qquad 4^{-1/2} = 4^2 = 16$

   The correct value is $\frac{1}{2}$. What mistake was made?

70. Evaluate the function for the given $x$: $f(x) = 4^x$ for $x = \frac{3}{2}$.

   **Solution:** $\qquad f\left(\frac{3}{2}\right) = 4^{3/2}$

   $$= \frac{4^3}{4^2} = \frac{64}{16} = 4$$

   The correct value is 8. What mistake was made?

71. If \$2000 is invested in a savings account that earns 2.5% interest compounding continuously, how much will be in the account in one year?

   **Solution:**

   Write the compound continuous interest formula. $\qquad A = Pe^{rt}$

   Substitute $P = 2000$, $r = 2.5$, and $t = 1$. $\quad A = 2000e^{(2.5)(1)}$

   Simplify. $\qquad A = 24{,}364.99$

   This is incorrect. What mistake was made?

72. If \$5000 is invested in a savings account that earns 3% interest compounding continuously, how much will be in the account in 6 months?

   **Solution:**

   Write the compound continuous interest formula. $\qquad A = Pe^{rt}$

   Substitute $P = 5000$, $r = 0.03$, and $t = 6$. $\quad A = 5000e^{(0.03)(6)}$

   Simplify. $\qquad A = 5986.09$

   This is incorrect. What mistake was made?

■ CONCEPTUAL

**In Exercises 73–76, determine whether each statement is true or false.**

**73.** The function $f(x) = -e^{-x}$ has the $y$-intercept $(0, 1)$.

**74.** The function $f(x) = -e^{-x}$ has a horizontal asymptote along the $x$-axis.

**75.** The functions $y = 3^{-x}$ and $y = \left(\frac{1}{3}\right)^x$ have the same graphs.

**76.** $e = 2.718$.

**77.** Plot $f(x) = 3^x$ and its inverse on the same graph.

**78.** Plot $f(x) = e^x$ and its inverse on the same graph.

**79.** Graph $f(x) = e^{|x|}$.

**80.** Graph $f(x) = e^{-|x|}$.

■ CHALLENGE

**81.** Find the $y$-intercept and horizontal asymptote of $f(x) = be^{-x+1} - a$.

**82.** Find the $y$-intercept and horizontal asymptote of $f(x) = a + be^{x+1}$.

**83.** Graph $f(x) = b^{|x|}$, $b > 1$, and state the domain.

**84.** Graph the function $f(x) = \begin{cases} a^x & x < 0 \\ a^{-x} & x \geq 0 \end{cases}$ where $a > 1$.

**85.** Graph the function
$$f(x) = \begin{cases} -a^x & x < 0 \\ -a^{-x} & x \geq 0 \end{cases} \quad \text{where } 0 < a < 1.$$

**86.** Find the $y$-intercept and horizontal asymptote(s) of $f(x) = 2^x + 3^x$.

■ TECHNOLOGY

**87.** Plot the function $y = \left(1 + \frac{1}{x}\right)^x$. What is the horizontal asymptote as $x$ increases?

**88.** Plot the functions $y = 2^x$, $y = e^x$, and $y = 3^x$ in the same viewing screen. Explain why $y = e^x$ lies between the other two graphs.

**89.** Plot $y_1 = e^x$ and $y_2 = 1 + x + \frac{x^2}{2} + \frac{x^3}{6} + \frac{x^4}{24}$ in the same viewing screen. What do you notice?

**90.** Plot $y_1 = e^{-x}$ and $y_2 = 1 - x + \frac{x^2}{2} - \frac{x^3}{6} + \frac{x^4}{24}$ in the same viewing screen. What do you notice?

**91.** Plot the functions $f(x) = \left(1 + \frac{1}{x}\right)^x$, $g(x) = \left(1 + \frac{2}{x}\right)^x$, and $h(x) = \left(1 + \frac{2}{x}\right)^{2x}$ in the same viewing screen. Compare their horizontal asymptotes as $x$ increases. What can you say about the function values of $f$, $g$, and $h$ in terms of the powers of $e$ as $x$ increases?

**92.** Plot the functions $f(x) = \left(1 + \frac{1}{x}\right)^x$, $g(x) = \left(1 - \frac{1}{x}\right)^x$, and $h(x) = \left(1 - \frac{2}{x}\right)^x$ in the same viewing screen. Compare their horizontal asymptotes as $x$ increases. What can you say about the function values of $f$, $g$, and $h$ in terms of the powers of $e$ as $x$ increases?

**For Exercises 93 and 94, refer to the following:**

**Newton's Law of Heating and Cooling:** Have you ever heated soup in a microwave and, upon taking it out, have it seem to cool considerably in the matter of minutes? Or has your ice-cold soda become tepid in just moments while outside on a hot summer's day? This phenomenon is based on the so-called *Newton's Law of Heating and Cooling*. Eventually, the soup will cool so that its temperature is the same as the temperature of the room in which it is being kept, and the soda will warm until its temperature is the same as the outside temperature.

**93.** Consider the following data:

| TIME (IN MINUTES) | 1.0 | 1.5 | 2.0 | 2.5 | 3.0 | 3.5 | 4.0 | 4.5 |
|---|---|---|---|---|---|---|---|---|
| TEMPERATURE OF SOUP (IN DEGREES FAHRENHEIT) | 203 | 200 | 195 | 188 | 180 | 171 | 160 | 151 |

a. Form a scatterplot for this data.
b. Use *ExpReg* to find the best fit exponential function for this data set, and superimpose its graph on the scatterplot. How good is the fit?
c. Use the best fit exponential curve from (b) to answer the following:
   i. What will the predicted temperature of the soup be at 6 minutes?
   ii. What was the temperature of the soup the moment it was taken out of the microwave?
d. Assume the temperature of the house is 72°F. According to Newton's Law of Heating and Cooling, the temperature of the soup should approach 72°. In light of this, comment on the shortcomings of the best fit exponential curve.

**94.** Consider the following data:

| TIME (IN MINUTES) | 1 | 2 | 3 | 4 | 5 | 6 | 7 | 8 |
|---|---|---|---|---|---|---|---|---|
| TEMPERATURE OF SODA (IN DEGREES FAHRENHEIT) | 45 | 48 | 49 | 53 | 57 | 61 | 68 | 75 |

a. Form a scatterplot for this data.
b. Use *ExpReg* to find the best fit exponential function for this data set, and superimpose its graph on the scatterplot. How good is the fit?

c. Use the best fit exponential curve from (b) to answer the following:
   i.  What will the predicted temperature of the soda be at 10 minutes?
   ii. What was the temperature of the soda the moment it was taken out of the refrigerator?
d. Assume the temperature of the house is 90°F. According to Newton's Law of Heating and Cooling, the temperature of the soda should approach 90°. In light of this, comment on the shortcomings of the best fit exponential curve.

■ PREVIEW TO CALCULUS

**In calculus the following two functions are studied:**

$$\sinh x = \frac{e^x - e^{-x}}{2} \quad \text{and} \quad \cosh x = \frac{e^x + e^{-x}}{2}$$

**95.** Determine whether $f(x) = \sinh x$ is an even function or an odd function.

**96.** Determine whether $f(x) = \cosh x$ is an even function or an odd function.

**97.** Show that $\cosh^2 x - \sinh^2 x = 1$.

**98.** Show that $\cosh x + \sinh x = e^x$.

LOGARITHMIC FUNCTIONS
AND THEIR GRAPHS

**SKILLS OBJECTIVES**

- Convert exponential expressions to logarithmic expressions.
- Convert logarithmic expressions to exponential expressions.
- Evaluate logarithmic expressions exactly by inspection.
- Approximate common and natural logarithms using a calculator.
- Graph logarithmic functions.
- Determine domain restrictions on logarithmic functions.

**CONCEPTUAL OBJECTIVES**

- Interpret logarithmic functions as inverses of exponential functions.
- Understand that logarithmic functions allow very large ranges of numbers in science and engineering applications to be represented on a smaller scale.

## Evaluating Logarithms

In Section 3.1, we found that the graph of an exponential function, $f(x) = b^x$, passes through the point $(0, 1)$, with the $x$-axis as a horizontal asymptote. The graph passes both the vertical line test (for a function) and the horizontal line test (for a one-to-one function), and therefore an inverse exists. We will now apply the technique outlined in Section 1.5 to find the inverse of $f(x) = b^x$:

| WORDS | MATH |
|---|---|
| Let $y = f(x)$. | $y = b^x$ |
| Interchange $x$ and $y$. | $x = b^y$ |
| Solve for $y$. | $y = ?$ |

**DEFINITION**    **Logarithmic Function**

For $x > 0$, $b > 0$, and $b \neq 1$, the **logarithmic function with base $b$** is denoted $f(x) = \log_b x$, where

$$y = \log_b x \quad \text{if and only if} \quad x = b^y$$

We read $\log_b x$ as "log base $b$ of $x$."

**Study Tip**

- $\log_b x = y$ is equivalent to $b^y = x$.
- The exponent $y$ is called a logarithm (or "log" for short).

This definition says that $x = b^y$ (**exponential form**) and $y = \log_b x$ (**logarithmic form**) are equivalent. One way to remember this relationship is by adding arrows to the logarithmic form:

$$\log_b x = y \Leftrightarrow b^y = x$$

**EXAMPLE 1    Changing from Logarithmic Form to Exponential Form**

Express each equation in its equivalent exponential form.

**a.** $\log_2 8 = 3$    **b.** $\log_9 3 = \frac{1}{2}$    **c.** $\log_5\left(\frac{1}{25}\right) = -2$

**Solution:**

**a.** $\log_2 8 = 3$          is equivalent to       $\boxed{2^3 = 8}$

**b.** $\log_9 3 = \frac{1}{2}$          is equivalent to       $\boxed{9^{1/2} = 3}$

**c.** $\log_5\left(\frac{1}{25}\right) = -2$       is equivalent to       $\boxed{5^{-2} = \frac{1}{25}}$

■ **Answer: a.** $9 = 3^2$
       **b.** $4 = 16^{1/2}$
       **c.** $\frac{1}{8} = 2^{-3}$

■ **YOUR TURN** Write each equation in its equivalent exponential form.

   **a.** $\log_3 9 = 2$    **b.** $\log_{16} 4 = \frac{1}{2}$    **c.** $\log_2\left(\frac{1}{8}\right) = -3$

**EXAMPLE 2    Changing from Exponential Form to Logarithmic Form**

Write each equation in its equivalent logarithmic form.

**a.** $16 = 2^4$    **b.** $9 = \sqrt{81}$    **c.** $\frac{1}{9} = 3^{-2}$    **d.** $x^a = z$

**Solution:**

**a.** $16 = 2^4$              is equivalent to       $\boxed{\log_2 16 = 4}$

**b.** $9 = \sqrt{81} = 81^{1/2}$       is equivalent to       $\boxed{\log_{81} 9 = \frac{1}{2}}$

**c.** $\frac{1}{9} = 3^{-2}$            is equivalent to       $\boxed{\log_3\left(\frac{1}{9}\right) = -2}$

**d.** $x^a = z$              is equivalent to       $\boxed{\log_x z = a \quad \text{for } x > 0}$

■ **Answer: a.** $\log_9 81 = 2$
       **b.** $\log_{144} 12 = \frac{1}{2}$
       **c.** $\log_7\left(\frac{1}{49}\right) = -2$
       **d.** $\log_y w = b \quad \text{for } y > 0$

■ **YOUR TURN** Write each equation in its equivalent logarithmic form.

   **a.** $81 = 9^2$    **b.** $12 = \sqrt{144}$    **c.** $\frac{1}{49} = 7^{-2}$    **d.** $y^b = w$

Some logarithms can be found exactly, while others must be approximated. Example 3 illustrates how to find the exact value of a logarithm. Example 4 illustrates approximating values of logarithms with a calculator.

**EXAMPLE 3   Finding the Exact Value of a Logarithm**

Find the exact value of

**a.** $\log_3 81$      **b.** $\log_{169} 13$      **c.** $\log_5\left(\frac{1}{5}\right)$

**Solution (a):**

| | |
|---|---|
| The logarithm has some value. Let's call it $x$. | $\log_3 81 = x$ |
| Change from logarithmic to exponential form. | $3^x = 81$ |
| 3 raised to what power is 81? | $3^4 = 81$   $x = 4$ |
| Change from exponential to logarithmic form. | $\boxed{\log_3 81 = 4}$ |

**Solution (b):**

| | |
|---|---|
| The logarithm has some value. Let's call it $x$. | $\log_{169} 13 = x$ |
| Change from logarithmic to exponential form. | $169^x = 13$ |
| 169 raised to what power is 13? | $169^{1/2} = \sqrt{169} = 13$   $x = \dfrac{1}{2}$ |
| Change from exponential to logarithmic form. | $\boxed{\log_{169} 13 = \dfrac{1}{2}}$ |

**Solution (c):**

| | |
|---|---|
| The logarithm has some value. Let's call it $x$. | $\log_5\left(\dfrac{1}{5}\right) = x$ |
| Change from logarithmic to exponential form. | $5^x = \dfrac{1}{5}$ |
| 5 raised to what power is $\frac{1}{5}$? | $5^{-1} = \dfrac{1}{5}$   $x = -1$ |
| Change from exponential to logarithmic form. | $\boxed{\log_5\left(\dfrac{1}{5}\right) = -1}$ |

■ **YOUR TURN** Evaluate the given logarithms exactly.

      **a.** $\log_2 \frac{1}{2}$      **b.** $\log_{100} 10$      **c.** $\log_{10} 1000$

■ **Answer: a.** $\log_2 \frac{1}{2} = -1$
      **b.** $\log_{100} 10 = \frac{1}{2}$
      **c.** $\log_{10} 1000 = 3$

## Common and Natural Logarithms

Two logarithmic bases that arise frequently are base 10 and base $e$. The logarithmic function of base 10 is called the **common logarithmic function**. Since it is common, $f(x) = \log_{10} x$ is often expressed as $f(x) = \log x$. Thus, if no explicit base is indicated, base 10 is implied. The logarithmic function of base $e$ is called the **natural logarithmic function**. The natural logarithmic function $f(x) = \log_e x$ is often expressed as $f(x) = \ln x$. Both the LOG and LN buttons appear on scientific and graphing calculators. For the *logarithms* (not the functions), we say "the log" (for base 10) and "the natural log" (for base $e$).

Earlier in this section, we evaluated logarithms exactly by converting to exponential form and identifying the exponent. For example, to evaluate $\log_{10} 100$, we ask the question, 10 raised to what power is 100? The answer is 2.

Calculators enable us to approximate logarithms. For example, evaluate $\log_{10} 233$. We are unable to evaluate this exactly by asking the question, 10 raised to what power is 233? Since $10^2 < 10^x < 10^3$, we know the answer $x$ must lie between 2 and 3. Instead, we use a calculator to find an approximate value 2.367.

*Study Tip*

• $\log_{10} x = \log x$. No explicit base implies base 10.
• $\log_e x = \ln x$

**EXAMPLE 4** **Using a Calculator to Evaluate Common and Natural Logarithms**

Use a calculator to evaluate the common and natural logarithms. Round your answers to four decimal places.

**a.** log 415    **b.** ln 415    **c.** log 1    **d.** ln 1    **e.** log(−2)    **f.** ln(−2)

**Solution:**

**a.** $\log(415) \approx 2.618048097 \approx \boxed{2.6180}$    **b.** $\ln(415) \approx 6.02827852 \approx \boxed{6.0283}$

**c.** $\log(1) = \boxed{0}$    **d.** $\ln(1) = \boxed{0}$

**e.** $\log(-2)$    $\boxed{\text{undefined}}$    **f.** $\ln(-2)$    $\boxed{\text{undefined}}$

*Study Tip*

Logarithms can only be evaluated for positive arguments.

Parts (c) and (d) in Example 4 illustrate that all logarithmic functions pass through the point $(1, 0)$. Parts (e) and (f) in Example 4 illustrate that the domains of logarithmic functions are positive real numbers.

## Graphs of Logarithmic Functions

The general logarithmic function $y = \log_b x$ is defined as the inverse of the exponential function $y = b^x$. Therefore, when these two functions are plotted on the same graph, they are symmetric about the line $y = x$. Notice the symmetry about the line $y = x$ when $y = b^x$ and $y = \log_b x$ are plotted on the same graph.

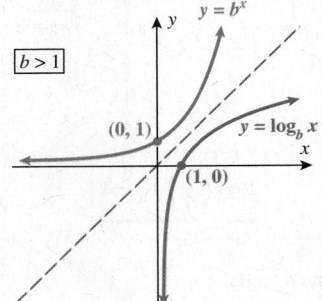
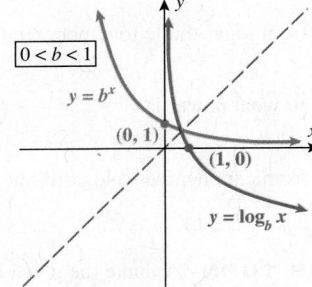

## Comparison of Inverse Functions:
$f(x) = \log_b x$ and $f^{-1}(x) = b^x$

| EXPONENTIAL FUNCTION | LOGARITHMIC FUNCTION |
|---|---|
| $y = b^x$ | $y = \log_b x$ |
| $y$-intercept $(0, 1)$ | $x$-intercept $(1, 0)$ |
| Domain $(-\infty, \infty)$ | Domain $(0, \infty)$ |
| Range $(0, \infty)$ | Range $(-\infty, \infty)$ |
| Horizontal asymptote: $x$-axis | Vertical asymptote: $y$-axis |

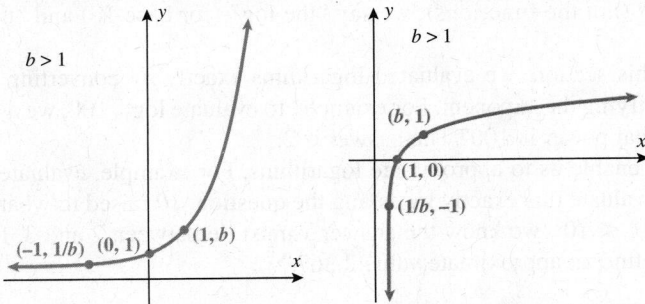

Additionally, the domain of one function is the range of the other, and vice versa. When dealing with logarithmic functions, special attention must be paid to the domain of the function. The domain of $y = \log_b x$ is $(0, \infty)$. In other words, you can only take the log of a positive real number, $x > 0$.

### EXAMPLE 5    Finding the Domain of a Shifted Logarithmic Function

Find the domain of each of the given logarithmic functions.

**a.** $f(x) = \log_b(x - 4)$      **b.** $g(x) = \log_b(5 - 2x)$

**Solution (a):**

| | |
|---|---|
| Set the argument greater than zero. | $x - 4 > 0$ |
| Solve the inequality. | $x > 4$ |
| Write the domain in interval notation. | $\boxed{(4, \infty)}$ |

**Solution (b):**

| | |
|---|---|
| Set the argument greater than zero. | $5 - 2x > 0$ |
| Solve the inequality. | $-2x > -5$ |
| | $2x < 5$ |
| | $x < \dfrac{5}{2}$ |
| Write the domain in interval notation. | $\boxed{\left(-\infty, \dfrac{5}{2}\right)}$ |

**■ YOUR TURN** Find the domain of the given logarithmic functions.

**a.** $f(x) = \log_b(x + 2)$      **b.** $g(x) = \log_b(3 - 5x)$

■ **Answer: a.** $(-2, \infty)$
      **b.** $\left(-\infty, \frac{3}{5}\right)$

It is important to note that when finding the domain of a logarithmic function, we set the argument strictly greater than zero and solve.

### Study Tip

Review solving inequalities in Section 0.4.

### EXAMPLE 6    Finding the Domain of a Logarithmic Function with a Complicated Argument

Find the domain of each of the given logarithmic functions.

**a.** $\ln(x^2 - 9)$      **b.** $\log(|x + 1|)$

**Solution (a):**

| | |
|---|---|
| Set the argument greater than zero | $x^2 - 9 > 0$ |
| Solve the inequality. | $\boxed{(-\infty, -3) \cup (3, \infty)}$ |

**Solution (b):**

| | |
|---|---|
| Set the argument greater than zero | $|x + 1| > 0$ |
| Solve the inequality. | $x \neq -1$ |
| Write the domain in interval notation. | $\boxed{(-\infty, -1) \cup (-1, \infty)}$ |

**■ YOUR TURN** Find the domain of each of the given logarithmic functions.

**a.** $\ln(x^2 - 4)$      **b.** $\log(|x - 3|)$

■ **Answer: a.** $(-\infty, -2) \cup (2, \infty)$
      **b.** $(-\infty, 3) \cup (3, \infty)$

Recall from Section 1.3 that a technique for graphing general functions is transformations of known functions. For example, to graph $f(x) = (x - 3)^2 + 1$, we start with the known parabola $y = x^2$, whose vertex is at $(0, 0)$, and we shift that graph to the right three units and up one unit. We use the same techniques for graphing logarithmic functions. To graph $y = \log_b(x + 2) - 1$, we start with the graph of $y = \log_b(x)$ and shift the graph to the left two units and down one unit.

### EXAMPLE 7 Graphing Logarithmic Functions Using Horizontal and Vertical Shifts

Graph the functions, and state the domain and range of each.

**a.** $y = \log_2(x - 3)$ **b.** $\log_2 x - 3$

**Solution:**

Identify the base function.

Label key features of $y = \log_2 x$.

$x$-intercept: $(1, 0)$

Vertical asymptote: $x = 0$

Additional points: $(2, 1), (4, 2)$

$y = \log_2 x$

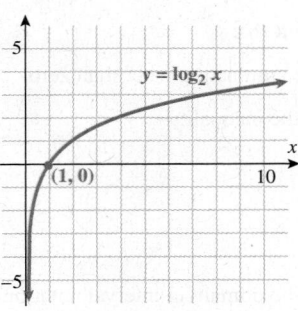

**a.** Shift base function to the *right* three units.

$x$-intercept: $(4, 0)$

Vertical asymptote: $x = 3$

Additional points: $(5, 1), (7, 2)$

Domain: $(3, \infty)$ Range: $(-\infty, \infty)$

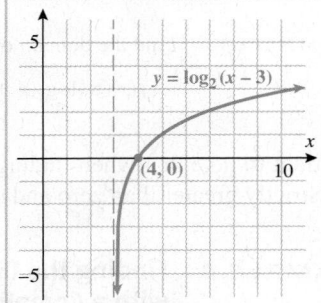

**b.** Shift base function *down* three units.

$x$-intercept: $(1, -3)$

Vertical asymptote: $x = 0$

Additional points: $(2, -2), (4, -1)$

Domain: $(0, \infty)$ Range: $(-\infty, \infty)$

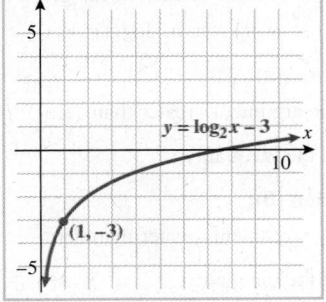

■ **Answer:**
**a.** Domain: $(0, \infty)$ Range: $(-\infty, \infty)$
**b.** Domain: $(-3, \infty)$ Range: $(-\infty, \infty)$
**c.** Domain: $(0, \infty)$ Range: $(-\infty, \infty)$

■ **YOUR TURN** Graph the functions and state the domain and range of each.

**a.** $y = \log_3 x$ **b.** $y = \log_3(x + 3)$ **c.** $\log_3 x + 1$

All of the transformation techniques (shifting, reflection, and compression) discussed in Chapter 1 also apply to logarithmic functions. For example, the graphs of $-\log_2 x$ and $\log_2(-x)$ are found by reflecting the graph of $y = \log_2 x$ about the $x$-axis and $y$-axis, respectively.

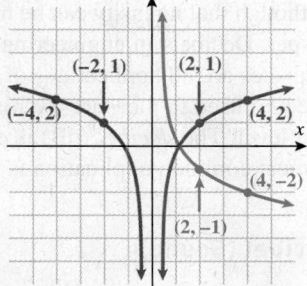

 **EXAMPLE 8 Graphing Logarithmic Functions Using Transformations**

Graph the function $f(x) = -\log_2(x - 3)$ and state its domain and range.

**Solution:**

Graph $y = \log_2 x$.

$x$-intercept: $(1, 0)$

Vertical asymptote: $x = 0$

Additional points: $(2, 1)$, $(4, 2)$

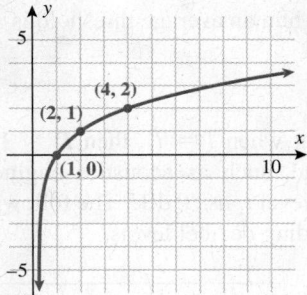

Graph $y = \log_2(x - 3)$ by shifting $y = \log_2 x$ to the *right* three units.

$x$-intercept: $(4, 0)$

Vertical asymptote: $x = 3$

Additional points: $(5, 1)$, $(7, 2)$

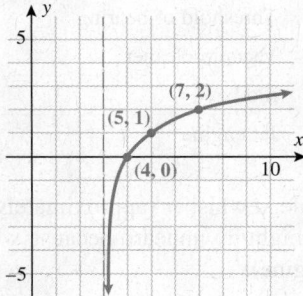

Graph $y = -\log_2(x - 3)$ by reflecting $y = \log_2(x - 3)$ about the $x$-axis.

$x$-intercept: $(4, 0)$

Vertical asymptote: $x = 3$

Additional points: $(5, -1)$, $(7, -2)$

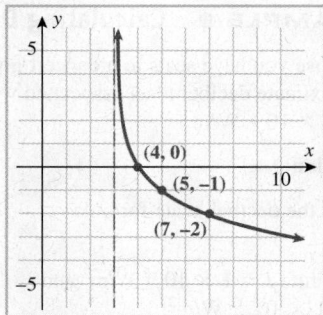

Domain: $(3, \infty)$     Range: $(-\infty, \infty)$

## Applications of Logarithms

Logarithms are used to make a large range of numbers manageable. For example, to create a scale to measure a human's ability to hear, we must have a way to measure the sound intensity of an explosion, even though that intensity can be more than a trillion $(10^{12})$ times greater than that of a soft whisper. Decibels in engineering and physics, pH in chemistry, and the Richter scale for earthquakes are all applications of logarithmic functions.

The **decibel** is a logarithmic unit used to measure the magnitude of a physical quantity relative to a specified reference level. The *decibel* (dB) is employed in many engineering and science applications. The most common application is the intensity of sound.

---

**DEFINITION**    Decibel (Sound)

The **decibel** is defined as
$$D = 10 \log\left(\frac{I}{I_T}\right)$$

where $D$ is the decibel level (dB), $I$ is the intensity of the sound measured in watts per square meter, and $I_T$ is the intensity threshold of the least audible sound a human can hear.

The human average threshold is $I_T = 1 \times 10^{-12}$ W/m².

---

Notice that when $I = I_T$, then $D = 10 \overbrace{\log 1}^{0} = 0$ dB. People who work professionally with sound, such as acoustics engineers or medical hearing specialists, refer to this threshold level $I_T$ as "0 dB." The following table illustrates typical sounds we hear and their corresponding decibel levels.

| SOUND SOURCE | SOUND INTENSITY (W/m²) | DECIBELS (dB) |
|---|---|---|
| Threshold of hearing | $1.0 \times 10^{-12}$ | 0 |
| Vacuum cleaner | $1.0 \times 10^{-4}$ | 80 |
| iPod | $1.0 \times 10^{-2}$ | 100 |
| Jet engine | $1.0 \times 10^{3}$ | 150 |

For example, a whisper (approximately 0 dB) from someone standing next to a jet engine (150 dB) might go unheard because when these are added, we get approximately 150 dB (the jet engine).

---

**EXAMPLE 9**    Calculating Decibels of Sounds

Suppose you have seats to a concert given by your favorite musical artist. Calculate the approximate decibel level associated with the typical sound intensity, given $I = 1 \times 10^{-2}$ W/m².

**Solution:**

Write the decibel-scale formula.

$$D = 10 \log\left(\frac{I}{I_T}\right)$$

Substitute $I = 1 \times 10^{-2}$ W/m² and $I_T = 1 \times 10^{-12}$ W/m².

$$D = 10 \log\left(\frac{1 \times 10^{-2}}{1 \times 10^{-12}}\right)$$

Simplify. $\qquad$ $D = 10 \log(10^{10})$

Recall that the implied base for log is 10. $\qquad$ $D = 10 \log_{10}(10^{10})$

Evaluate the right side. $\left[\log_{10}(10^{10}) = 10\right]$ $\qquad$ $D = 10 \cdot 10$

$$D = 100$$

The typical sound level in the front row of a rock concert is $\boxed{100 \text{ dB}}$ .

■ **YOUR TURN** Calculate the approximate decibels associated with a sound so loud it will cause instant perforation of the eardrums, $I = 1 \times 10^4 \text{ W/m}^2$.

■ **Answer:** 160 dB

The Richter scale (earthquakes) is another application of logarithms.

> **DEFINITION** **Richter Scale**
>
> The magnitude $M$ of an earthquake is measured using the **Richter scale**
>
> $$M = \frac{2}{3} \log\left(\frac{E}{E_0}\right)$$
>
> where
>
>     $M$ is the magnitude
>     $E$ is the seismic energy released by the earthquake (in joules)
>     $E_0$ is the energy released by a reference earthquake $E_0 = 10^{4.4}$ joules

### EXAMPLE 10    Calculating the Magnitude of an Earthquake

On October 17, 1989, just moments before game 3 of the World Series between the Oakland A's and the San Francisco Giants was about to start—with 60,000 fans in Candlestick Park—a devastating earthquake erupted. Parts of interstates and bridges collapsed, and President George H. W. Bush declared the area a disaster zone. The earthquake released approximately $1.12 \times 10^{15}$ joules. Calculate the magnitude of the earthquake using the Richter scale.

**Technology Tip**

Enter the number $1.12 \times 10^{15}$ using the scientific notation key $\boxed{\text{EXP}}$ or $\boxed{\text{EE}}$.

```
2/3log(1.12E15/1
0^4.4)
       7.099478682
```

**Solution:**

Write the Richter scale formula. $\qquad$ $M = \frac{2}{3} \log\left(\frac{E}{E_0}\right)$

Substitute $E = 1.12 \times 10^{15}$ and $E_0 = 10^{4.4}$. $\qquad$ $M = \frac{2}{3} \log\left(\frac{1.12 \times 10^{15}}{10^{4.4}}\right)$

Simplify. $\qquad$ $M = \frac{2}{3} \log\left(1.12 \times 10^{10.6}\right)$

Approximate the logarithm using a calculator. $\qquad$ $M \approx \frac{2}{3}(10.65) \approx 7.1$

The 1989 earthquake in California measured $\boxed{7.1}$ on the Richter scale.

■ **YOUR TURN** On May 3, 1996, Seattle experienced a moderate earthquake. The energy that the earthquake released was approximately $1.12 \times 10^{12}$ joules. Calculate the magnitude of the 1996 Seattle earthquake using the Richter scale.

■ **Answer:** 5.1

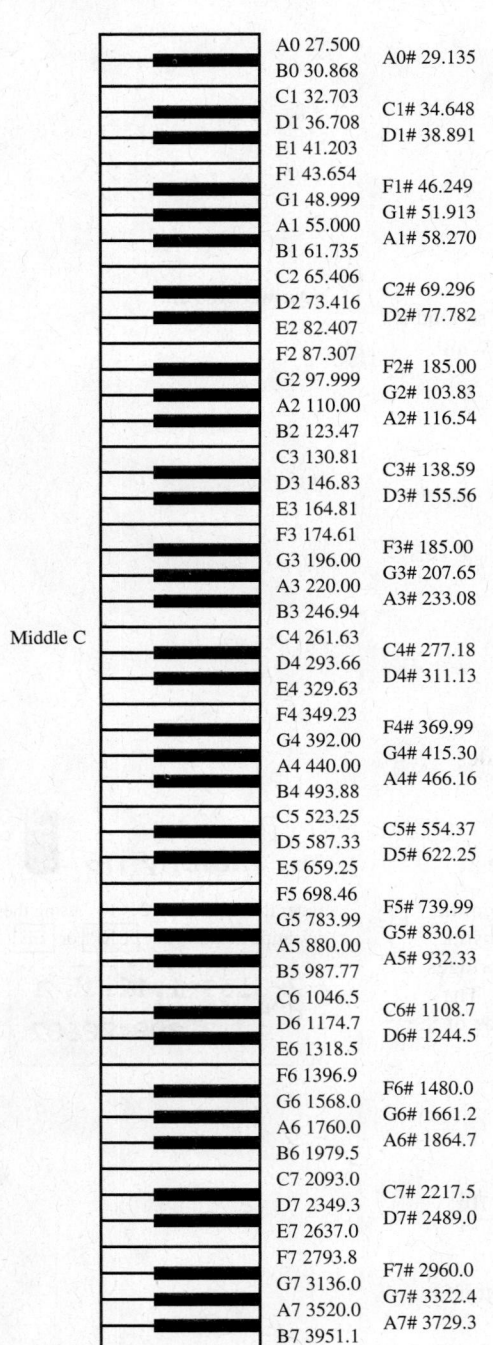

Middle C

| | | |
|---|---|---|
| A0 27.500 | | |
| B0 30.868 | A0# 29.135 | |
| C1 32.703 | | |
| D1 36.708 | C1# 34.648 | |
| E1 41.203 | D1# 38.891 | |
| F1 43.654 | | |
| G1 48.999 | F1# 46.249 | |
| A1 55.000 | G1# 51.913 | |
| B1 61.735 | A1# 58.270 | |
| C2 65.406 | | |
| D2 73.416 | C2# 69.296 | |
| E2 82.407 | D2# 77.782 | |
| F2 87.307 | | |
| G2 97.999 | F2# 185.00 | |
| A2 110.00 | G2# 103.83 | |
| B2 123.47 | A2# 116.54 | |
| C3 130.81 | | |
| D3 146.83 | C3# 138.59 | |
| E3 164.81 | D3# 155.56 | |
| F3 174.61 | | |
| G3 196.00 | F3# 185.00 | |
| A3 220.00 | G3# 207.65 | |
| B3 246.94 | A3# 233.08 | |
| C4 261.63 | | |
| D4 293.66 | C4# 277.18 | |
| E4 329.63 | D4# 311.13 | |
| F4 349.23 | | |
| G4 392.00 | F4# 369.99 | |
| A4 440.00 | G4# 415.30 | |
| B4 493.88 | A4# 466.16 | |
| C5 523.25 | | |
| D5 587.33 | C5# 554.37 | |
| E5 659.25 | D5# 622.25 | |
| F5 698.46 | | |
| G5 783.99 | F5# 739.99 | |
| A5 880.00 | G5# 830.61 | |
| B5 987.77 | A5# 932.33 | |
| C6 1046.5 | | |
| D6 1174.7 | C6# 1108.7 | |
| E6 1318.5 | D6# 1244.5 | |
| F6 1396.9 | | |
| G6 1568.0 | F6# 1480.0 | |
| A6 1760.0 | G6# 1661.2 | |
| B6 1979.5 | A6# 1864.7 | |
| C7 2093.0 | | |
| D7 2349.3 | C7# 2217.5 | |
| E7 2637.0 | D7# 2489.0 | |
| F7 2793.8 | | |
| G7 3136.0 | F7# 2960.0 | |
| A7 3520.0 | G7# 3322.4 | |
| B7 3951.1 | A7# 3729.3 | |
| C8 4186.0 | | |

A **logarithmic scale** expresses the logarithm of a physical quantity instead of the quantity itself. In music, the pitch is the perceived fundamental frequency of sound. The note A above middle C on a piano has the pitch associated with a pure tone of 440 hertz. An octave is the interval between one musical pitch and another with either double or half its frequency. For example, if a note has a frequency of 440 hertz, then the note an octave above it has a frequency of 880 hertz, and the note an octave below it has a frequency of 220 hertz. Therefore, the ratio of two notes an octave apart is 2:1.

The following table lists the frequencies associated with A notes.

| NOTE | $A_1$ | $A_2$ | $A_3$ | $A_4$ | $A_5$ | $A_6$ | $A_7$ |
|---|---|---|---|---|---|---|---|
| Frequency (Hz) | 55 | 110 | 220 | 440 | 880 | 1760 | 3520 |
| Octave with respect to $A_4$ | −3 | −2 | −1 | 0 | +1 | +2 | +3 |

We can graph $\dfrac{\text{Frequency of note}}{440 \text{ Hz}}$ on the horizontal axis and the octave (with respect to $A_4$) on the vertical axis.

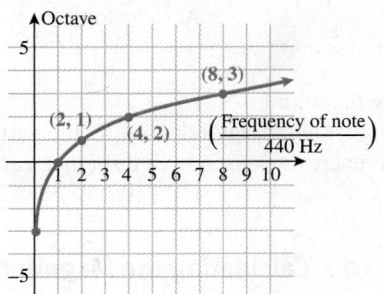

If we instead graph the logarithm of this quantity, $\log\left[\dfrac{\text{Frequency of note}}{440 \text{ Hz}}\right]$, we see that using a logarithmic scale expresses octaves linearly (up or down an octave). In other words, an "octave" is a purely logarithmic concept.

When a logarithmic scale is used we typically classify a graph one of two ways:

- Log-log plot (both the horizontal and vertical axes use logarithmic scales)
- Semilog plot (one of the axes uses a logarithmic scale)

The second graph with octaves on the vertical axis and the log of the ratio of frequencies on the horizontal axis is called a semilog plot.

**Semilog Plot**

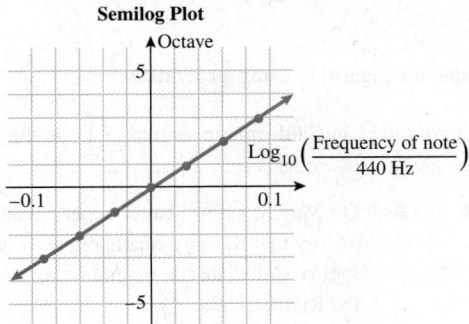

## EXAMPLE 11   Graphing Using a Logarithmic Scale

Frequency is inversely proportional to the wavelength: In a vacuum $f = \dfrac{c}{\lambda}$, where $f$ is the frequency (in hertz), $c = 3.0 \times 10^8$ m/s is the speed of light in a vacuum, and $\lambda$ is the wavelength in meters. Graph frequency versus wavelength using a log-log plot.

### Solution:

Let wavelength range from microns ($10^{-6}$) to hundreds of meters ($10^2$) by powers of 10 along the horizontal axis.

| $\lambda$ | $f = \dfrac{3.0 \times 10^8}{\lambda}$ | |
|---|---|---|
| $10^{-6}$ | $3.0 \times 10^{14}$ | |
| $10^{-5}$ | $3.0 \times 10^{13}$ | |
| $10^{-4}$ | $3.0 \times 10^{12}$ | (TeraHertz: THz) |
| $10^{-3}$ | $3.0 \times 10^{11}$ | |
| $10^{-2}$ | $3.0 \times 10^{10}$ | |
| $10^{-1}$ | $3.0 \times 10^{9}$ | (GigaHertz: GHz) |
| $10^{0}$ | $3.0 \times 10^{8}$ | |
| $10^{1}$ | $3.0 \times 10^{7}$ | |
| $10^{2}$ | $3.0 \times 10^{6}$ | (MegaHertz: MHz) |

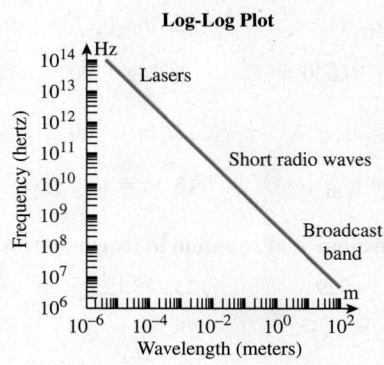

The logarithmic scales allow us to represent a large range of numbers. In this graph, the $x$-axis ranges from microns, $10^{-6}$ meters, to hundreds of meters, and the $y$-axis ranges from megahertz (MHz), $10^6$ hertz, to hundreds of terahertz (THz), $10^{12}$ hertz.

## SECTION
## 3.2   SUMMARY

In this section, logarithmic functions were defined as inverses of exponential functions.

$$y = \log_b x \text{ is equivalent to } x = b^y$$

| NAME | EXPLICIT BASE | IMPLICIT BASE |
|---|---|---|
| Common logarithm | $f(x) = \log_{10} x$ | $f(x) = \log x$ |
| Natural logarithm | $f(x) = \log_e x$ | $f(x) = \ln x$ |

### Evaluating Logarithms
- *Exact:* Convert to exponential form first, then evaluate.
- *Approximate:* Natural and common logarithms with calculators.

### Graphs of Logarithmic Functions

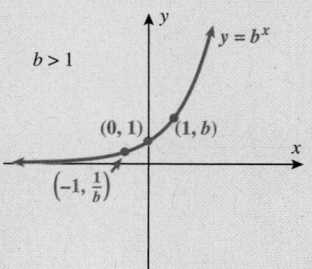

| EXPONENTIAL FUNCTION | LOGARITHMIC FUNCTION |
|---|---|
| $y = b^x$ | $y = \log_b x$ |
| $y$-intercept: $(0, 1)$ | $x$-intercept: $(1, 0)$ |
| Domain: $(-\infty, \infty)$ | Domain: $(0, \infty)$ |
| Range: $(0, \infty)$ | Range: $(-\infty, \infty)$ |
| Horizontal asymptote: $x$-axis | Vertical asymptote: $y$-axis |

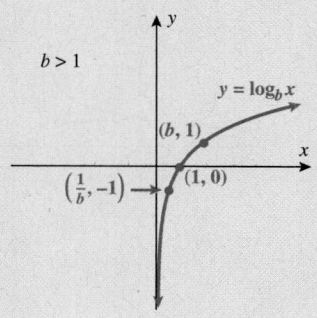

■ SKILLS

**In Exercises 1–20, write each logarithmic equation in its equivalent exponential form.**

**1.** $\log_{81} 3 = \frac{1}{4}$   **2.** $\log_{121} 11 = \frac{1}{2}$   **3.** $\log_2\left(\frac{1}{32}\right) = -5$   **4.** $\log_3\left(\frac{1}{81}\right) = -4$   **5.** $\log 0.01 = -2$

**6.** $\log 0.0001 = -4$   **7.** $\log 10{,}000 = 4$   **8.** $\log 1000 = 3$   **9.** $\log_{1/4}(64) = -3$   **10.** $\log_{1/6}(36) = -2$

**11.** $-1 = \ln\left(\frac{1}{e}\right)$   **12.** $1 = \ln e$   **13.** $\ln 1 = 0$   **14.** $\log 1 = 0$   **15.** $\ln 5 = x$

**16.** $\ln 4 = y$   **17.** $z = \log_x y$   **18.** $y = \log_x z$   **19.** $x = \log_y(x + y)$   **20.** $z = \ln x^y$

**In Exercises 21–34, write each exponential equation in its equivalent logarithmic form.**

**21.** $0.00001 = 10^{-5}$   **22.** $3^6 = 729$   **23.** $78{,}125 = 5^7$   **24.** $100{,}000 = 10^5$   **25.** $15 = \sqrt{225}$

**26.** $7 = \sqrt[3]{343}$   **27.** $\frac{8}{125} = \left(\frac{2}{5}\right)^3$   **28.** $\frac{8}{27} = \left(\frac{2}{3}\right)^3$   **29.** $3 = \left(\frac{1}{27}\right)^{-1/3}$   **30.** $4 = \left(\frac{1}{1024}\right)^{-1/5}$

**31.** $e^x = 6$   **32.** $e^{-x} = 4$   **33.** $x = y^z$   **34.** $z = y^x$

**In Exercises 35–46, evaluate the logarithms exactly (if possible).**

**35.** $\log_2 1$   **36.** $\log_5 1$   **37.** $\log_5 3125$   **38.** $\log_3 729$

**39.** $\log 10^7$   **40.** $\log 10^{-2}$   **41.** $\log_{1/4} 4096$   **42.** $\log_{1/7} 2401$

**43.** $\log 0$   **44.** $\ln 0$   **45.** $\log(-100)$   **46.** $\ln(-1)$

**In Exercises 47–54, approximate (if possible) the common and natural logarithms using a calculator. Round to two decimal places.**

**47.** $\log 29$   **48.** $\ln 29$   **49.** $\ln 380$   **50.** $\log 380$

**51.** $\log 0$   **52.** $\ln 0$   **53.** $\ln 0.0003$   **54.** $\log 0.0003$

**In Exercises 55–66, state the domain of the logarithmic function in interval notation.**

**55.** $f(x) = \log_2(x + 5)$   **56.** $f(x) = \log_2(4x - 1)$   **57.** $f(x) = \log_3(5 - 2x)$   **58.** $f(x) = \log_3(5 - x)$

**59.** $f(x) = \ln(7 - 2x)$   **60.** $f(x) = \ln(3 - x)$   **61.** $f(x) = \log|x|$   **62.** $f(x) = \log|x + 1|$

**63.** $f(x) = \log(x^2 + 1)$   **64.** $f(x) = \log(1 - x^2)$   **65.** $f(x) = \log(10 + 3x - x^2)$   **66.** $f(x) = \log_3(x^3 - 3x^2 + 3x - 1)$

**In Exercises 67–72, match the graph with the function.**

**67.** $y = \log_5 x$   **68.** $y = \log_5(-x)$   **69.** $y = -\log_5(-x)$

**70.** $y = \log_5(x + 3) - 1$   **71.** $y = \log_5(1 - x) - 2$   **72.** $y = -\log_5(3 - x) + 2$

**a.**

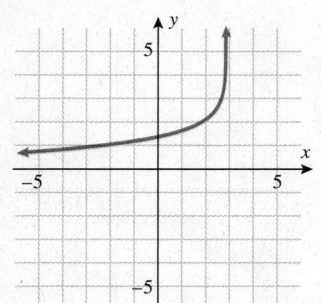

**b.**

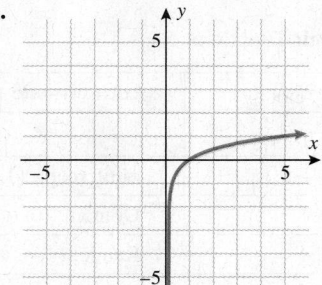

**c.**

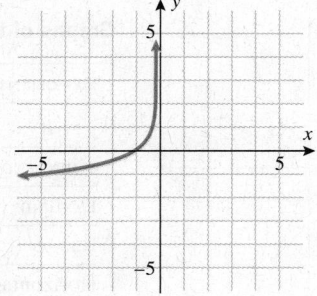

**d.**

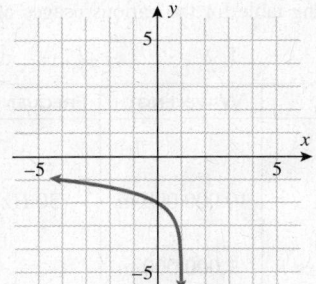

**e.**

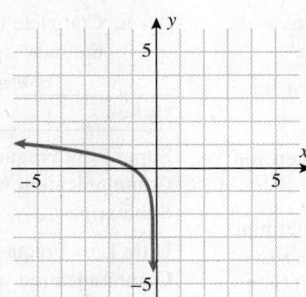

**f.**

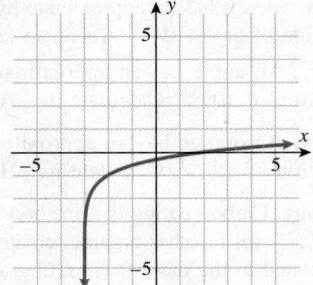

**In Exercises 73–84, graph the logarithmic function using transformation techniques. State the domain and range of $f$.**

**73.** $f(x) = \log(x - 1)$
**74.** $f(x) = \log(x + 2)$
**75.** $\ln(x + 2)$
**76.** $\ln(x - 1)$

**77.** $f(x) = \log_3(x + 2) - 1$
**78.** $f(x) = \log_3(x + 1) - 2$
**79.** $f(x) = -\log(x) + 1$
**80.** $f(x) = \log(-x) + 2$

**81.** $f(x) = \ln(x + 4)$
**82.** $f(x) = \ln(4 - x)$
**83.** $f(x) = \log(2x)$
**84.** $f(x) = 2\ln(-x)$

## ▪ APPLICATIONS

**For Exercises 85–88, refer to the following:**

$$\text{Decibel: } D = 10 \log\left(\frac{I}{I_T}\right) \qquad I_T = 1 \times 10^{-12} \text{ W/m}^2$$

**85. Sound.** Calculate the decibels associated with *normal conversation* if the intensity is $I = 1 \times 10^{-6}$ W/m$^2$.

**86. Sound.** Calculate the decibels associated with the *onset of pain* if the intensity is $I = 1 \times 10^{1}$ W/m$^2$.

**87. Sound.** Calculate the decibels associated with attending *a football game in a loud college stadium* if the intensity is $I = 1 \times 10^{-0.3}$ W/m$^2$.

**88. Sound.** Calculate the decibels associated with a *doorbell* if the intensity is $I = 1 \times 10^{-4.5}$ W/m$^2$.

**For Exercises 89–92, refer to the following:**

$$\text{Richter scale: } M = \frac{2}{3} \log\left(\frac{E}{E_0}\right) \qquad E_0 = 10^{4.4} \text{ joules}$$

**89. Earthquakes.** On Good Friday 1964, one of the most severe North American earthquakes ever recorded struck Alaska. The energy released measured $1.41 \times 10^{17}$ joules. Calculate the magnitude of the 1964 Alaska earthquake using the Richter scale.

**90. Earthquakes.** On January 22, 2003, Colima, Mexico, experienced a major earthquake. The energy released measured $6.31 \times 10^{15}$ joules. Calculate the magnitude of the 2003 Mexican earthquake using the Richter scale.

**91. Earthquakes.** On December 26, 2003, a major earthquake rocked southeastern Iran. In Bam, 30,000 people were killed, and 85% of buildings were damaged or destroyed. The energy released measured $2 \times 10^{14}$ joules. Calculate the magnitude of the 2003 Iran earthquake with the Richter scale.

**92. Earthquakes.** On November 1, 1755, Lisbon was destroyed by an earthquake, which killed 90,000 people and destroyed 85% of the city. It was one of the most destructive earthquakes in history. The energy released measured $8 \times 10^{17}$ joules. Calculate the magnitude of the 1755 Lisbon earthquake with the Richter scale.

**For Exercises 93–98, refer to the following:**

The pH of a solution is a measure of the molar concentration of hydrogen ions, $H^+$, in moles per liter, in the solution, which means that it is a measure of the acidity or basicity of the solution. The letters pH stand for "power of hydrogen," and the numerical value is defined as

$$\text{pH} = -\log_{10}\left[H^+\right]$$

Very acid corresponds to pH values near 1, neutral corresponds to a pH near 7 (pure water), and very basic corresponds to values near 14. In the next six exercises you will be asked to calculate the pH value of wine, Pepto-Bismol, normal rainwater, bleach, and fruit. List these six liquids and use your intuition to classify them as neutral, acidic, very acidic, basic, or very basic before you calculate their actual pH values.

**93. Chemistry.** If wine has an approximate hydrogen ion concentration of $5.01 \times 10^{-4}$, calculate its pH value.

**94. Chemistry.** Pepto-Bismol has a hydrogen ion concentration of about $5.01 \times 10^{-11}$. Calculate its pH value.

**95. Chemistry.** Normal rainwater is slightly acidic and has an approximate hydrogen ion concentration of $10^{-5.6}$. Calculate its pH value. Acid rain and tomato juice have similar approximate hydrogen ion concentrations of $10^{-4}$. Calculate the pH value of acid rain and tomato juice.

**96. Chemistry.** Bleach has an approximate hydrogen ion concentration of $5.0 \times 10^{-13}$. Calculate its pH value.

**97. Chemistry.** An apple has an approximate hydrogen ion concentration of $10^{-3.6}$. Calculate its pH value.

**98. Chemistry.** An orange has an approximate hydrogen ion concentration of $10^{-4.2}$. Calculate its pH value.

**99. Archaeology.** Carbon dating is a method used to determine the age of a fossil or other organic remains. The age $t$ in years is related to the mass $C$ (in milligrams) of carbon 14 through a logarithmic equation:

$$t = -\frac{\ln\left(\dfrac{C}{500}\right)}{0.0001216}$$

How old is a fossil that contains 100 milligrams of carbon 14?

**100. Archaeology.** Repeat Exercise 99, only now the fossil contains 40 milligrams of carbon 14.

**101. Broadcasting.** Decibels are used to quantify losses associated with atmospheric interference in a communication system. The ratio of the power (watts) received to the power transmitted (watts) is often compared. Often, *watts* are transmitted, but losses due to the atmosphere typically correspond to *milliwatts* being received:

$$dB = 10 \log\left(\frac{\text{Power received}}{\text{Power transmitted}}\right)$$

If 1 watt of power is transmitted and 3 megawatts is received, calculate the power loss in decibels.

**102. Broadcasting.** Repeat Exercise 101, assuming 3 watts of power is transmitted and 0.2 megawatt is received.

**For Exercises 103 and 104, refer to the following:**

The range of all possible frequencies of electromagnetic radiation is called the electromagnetic spectrum. In a vacuum the frequency of electromagnetic radiation is modeled by

$$f = \frac{c}{\lambda}$$

where $c$ is $3.0 \times 10^8$ m/s and $\lambda$ is wavelength in meters.

**103. Physics/Electromagnetic Spectrum.** The *radio spectrum* is the portion of the electromagnetic spectrum that corresponds to radio frequencies. The radio spectrum is used for various transmission technologies and is government regulated. Ranges of the radio spectrum are often allocated based on usage; for example, AM radio, cell phones, and television. (Source: http://en.wikipedia.org/wiki/Radio_spectrum)

**a.** Complete the following table for the various usages of the radio spectrum.

| USAGE | WAVELENGTH | FREQUENCY |
|---|---|---|
| Super Low Frequency—Communication with Submarines | 10,000,000 m | 30 Hz |
| Ultra Low Frequency—Communication within Mines | 1,000,000 m | |
| Very Low Frequency—Avalanche Beacons | 100,000 m | |
| Low Frequency—Navigation, AM Long-wave Broadcasting | 10,000 m | |
| Medium Frequency—AM Broadcasts, Amateur Radio | 1000 m | |
| High Frequency—Shortwave broadcasts, Citizens Band Radio | 100 m | |
| Very High Frequency—FM Radio, Television | 10 m | |
| Ultra High Frequency—Television, Mobile Phones | 0.050 m | |

**b.** Graph the frequency within the radio spectrum (in hertz) as a function of wavelength (in meters).

**104. Physics/Electromagnetic Spectrum.** The *visible spectrum* is the portion of the electromagnetic spectrum that is visible to the human eye. Typically, the human eye can see wavelengths between 390 and 750 nm (nanometers or $10^{-9}$ m).

**a.** Complete the following table for the following colors of the visible spectrum.

| COLOR | WAVELENGTH | FREQUENCY |
|---|---|---|
| Violet | 400 nm | $750 \times 10^{12}$ Hz |
| Cyan | 470 nm | |
| Green | 480 nm | |
| Yellow | 580 nm | |
| Orange | 610 nm | |
| Red | 630 nm | |

**b.** Graph the frequency (in hertz) of the colors as a function of wavelength (in meters) on a log-log plot.

■ **CATCH THE MISTAKE**

**In Exercises 105–108, explain the mistake that is made.**

**105.** Evaluate the logarithm $\log_2 4$.

**Solution:**

Set the logarithm equal to $x$.  $\log_2 4 = x$

Write the logarithm in exponential form.  $x = 2^4$

Simplify.  $x = 16$

Answer:  $\log_2 4 = 16$

This is incorrect. The correct answer is $\log_2 4 = 2$. What went wrong?

**106.** Evaluate the logarithm $\log_{100} 10$.

**Solution:**

Set the logarithm equal to $x$.  $\log_{100} 10 = x$

Express the equation in exponential form.  $10^x = 100$

Solve for $x$.  $x = 2$

Answer:  $\log_{100} 10 = 2$

This is incorrect. The correct answer is $\log_{100} 10 = \frac{1}{2}$. What went wrong?

**107.** State the domain of the logarithmic function $f(x) = \log_2(x + 5)$ in interval notation.

**Solution:**

The domain of all logarithmic functions is $x > 0$.

Interval notation: $(0, \infty)$

This is incorrect. What went wrong?

**108.** State the domain of the logarithmic function $f(x) = \ln|x|$ in interval notation.

**Solution:**

Since the absolute value eliminates all negative numbers, the domain is the set of all real numbers.

Interval notation: $(-\infty, \infty)$

This is incorrect. What went wrong?

■ **CONCEPTUAL**

**In Exercises 109–112, determine whether each statement is true or false.**

**109.** The domain of the standard logarithmic function, $y = \ln x$, is the set of nonnegative real numbers.

**110.** The horizontal axis is the horizontal asymptote of the graph of $y = \ln x$.

**111.** The graphs of $y = \log x$ and $y = \ln x$ have the same $x$-intercept $(1, 0)$.

**112.** The graphs of $y = \log x$ and $y = \ln x$ have the same vertical asymptote, $x = 0$.

■ **CHALLENGE**

**113.** State the domain, range, and $x$-intercept of the function $f(x) = -\ln(x - a) + b$ for $a$ and $b$ real positive numbers.

**114.** State the domain, range, and $x$-intercept of the function $f(x) = \log(a - x) - b$ for $a$ and $b$ real positive numbers.

**115.** Graph the function $f(x) = \begin{cases} \ln(-x) & x < 0 \\ \ln(x) & x > 0 \end{cases}$.

**116.** Graph the function $f(x) = \begin{cases} -\ln(-x) & x < 0 \\ -\ln(x) & x > 0 \end{cases}$.

■ **TECHNOLOGY**

**117.** Apply a graphing utility to graph $y = e^x$ and $y = \ln x$ in the same viewing screen. What line are these two graphs symmetric about?

**118.** Apply a graphing utility to graph $y = 10^x$ and $y = \log x$ in the same viewing screen. What line are these two graphs symmetric about?

**119.** Apply a graphing utility to graph $y = \log x$ and $y = \ln x$ in the same viewing screen. What are the two common characteristics?

**120.** Using a graphing utility, graph $y = \ln|x|$. Is the function defined everywhere?

**121.** Apply a graphing utility to graph $f(x) = \ln(3x)$, $g(x) = \ln 3 + \ln x$, and $h(x) = (\ln 3)(\ln x)$ in the same viewing screen. Determine which two functions give the same graph, then state the domain of the function.

**122.** Apply a graphing utility to graph $f(x) = \ln(x^2 - 4)$, $g(x) = \ln(x + 2) + \ln(x - 2)$, and $h(x) = \ln(x + 2)\ln(x - 2)$ in the same viewing screen. Determine the domain where two functions give the same graph.

**For Exercises 123 and 124, refer to the following:**

Experimental data is collected all the time in biology and chemistry labs as scientists seek to understand natural phenomena. In biochemistry, the *Michaelis–Menten* kinetics law describes the rates of enzyme reactions using the relationship between the rate of the reaction and the concentration of the substrate involved.

The following data has been collected, where the velocity $v$ is measured in $\mu$mol/min of the enzyme reaction and the substrate level [S] is measured in mol/L.

| [S] (IN MOL/L) | V (IN $\mu$MOL/MIN) |
|---|---|
| $4.0 \times 10^{-4}$ | 130 |
| $2.0 \times 10^{-4}$ | 110 |
| $1.0 \times 10^{-4}$ | 89 |
| $5.0 \times 10^{-5}$ | 62 |
| $4.0 \times 10^{-5}$ | 52 |
| $2.5 \times 10^{-5}$ | 38 |
| $2.0 \times 10^{-5}$ | 32 |

**123. a.** Create a scatterplot of this data by identifying [S] with the x-axis and $v$ with the y-axis.
   **b.** The graph *seems* to be leveling off. Give an estimate of the maximum value the velocity might achieve. Call this estimate $V_{max}$.
   **c.** Another constant of importance in describing the relationship between $v$ and [S] is $K_m$. This is the value of [S] that results in the velocity being half its maximum value. Estimate this value.
   *Note:* $K_m$ measures the affinity level of a particular enzyme to a particular substrate. The lower the value of $K_m$, the higher the affinity. The higher the value of $K_m$, the lower the affinity.
   **d.** The actual equation that governs the relationship between $v$ and [S] is $v = \dfrac{V_{max}}{1 + K_m/[S]}$, which is NOT linear. This is the *simple Michaelis–Menten kinetics equation.*

   **i.** Use *LnReg* to get a best fit logarithmic curve for this data. Although the relationship between $v$ and [S] is not logarithmic (rather, it is logistic), the best fit logarithmic curve does not grow very quickly and so it serves as a reasonably good fit.
   **ii.** At what [S] value, approximately, is the velocity 100 $\mu$mol/min?

**124.** The Michaelis–Menten equation can be arranged into various other forms that give a straight line (rather than a logistic curve) when one variable is plotted against another. One such rearrangement is the *double-reciprocal Lineweaver–Burk equation*. This equation plots the data values of the reciprocal of velocity (1/v) versus the reciprocal of the substrate level (1/[S]). The equation is as follows:

$$\frac{1}{v} = \frac{K_m}{V_{max}} \frac{1}{[S]} + \frac{1}{V_{max}}$$

Think of $y$ as $\dfrac{1}{v}$ and $x$ as $\dfrac{1}{[S]}$.

**a.** What is the slope of the "line"? How about its y-intercept?
**b.** Using the data from Exercise 123, we create two new columns for 1/v and 1/[S] to obtain the following data set:

| [S] (MOL/L) | 1/[S] | V ($\mu$MOL/MIN) | 1/v |
|---|---|---|---|
| 4.00E−04 | 2.50E+03 | 130 | 0.00769231 |
| 2.00E−04 | 5.00E+03 | 110 | 0.00909091 |
| 1.00E−04 | 1.00E+04 | 89 | 0.01123596 |
| 5.00E−05 | 2.00E+04 | 62 | 0.01612903 |
| 4.00E−05 | 2.50E+04 | 53 | 0.01886792 |
| 2.50E−05 | 4.00E+04 | 38 | 0.02631579 |
| 2.00E−05 | 5.00E+04 | 32 | 0.03125 |

Create a scatterplot for the new data, treating $x$ as 1/[S] and $y$ as 1/v.
**c.** Determine the best fit line and value of $r$.
**d.** Use the equation of the best fit line in (c) to calculate $V_{max}$.
**e.** Use the above information to determine $K_m$.

■ **PREVIEW TO CALCULUS**

**In Exercises 125–126, refer to the following:**

Recall that the derivative of $f$ can be found by letting $h \to 0$ in the difference quotient $\dfrac{f(x+h)-f(x)}{h}$. In calculus we prove that $\dfrac{e^h-1}{h}=1$, when $h$ approaches 0; that is, for really small values of $h$, $\dfrac{e^h-1}{h}$ gets very close to 1.

**125.** Use this information to find the derivative of $f(x)=e^x$.

**126.** Use this information to find the derivative of $f(x)=e^{2x}$. *Hint:* $e^{2h}-1=(e^h-1)(e^h+1)$

We also prove in calculus that the derivative of the inverse function $f^{-1}$ is given by $(f^{-1})'(x) = \dfrac{1}{f'(f^{-1}(x))}$.

**127.** Given $f(x)=e^x$, find
  **a.** $f^{-1}(x)$   **b.** $(f^{-1})'(x)$

**128.** Given $f(x)=e^{2x}$, find
  **a.** $f^{-1}(x)$   **b.** $(f^{-1})'(x)$

## SECTION 3.3 PROPERTIES OF LOGARITHMS

**SKILLS OBJECTIVES**

- Write a single logarithm as a sum or difference of logarithms.
- Write a logarithmic expression as a single logarithm.
- Evaluate logarithms of a general base (other than base 10 or $e$).

**CONCEPTUAL OBJECTIVES**

- Derive the seven basic logarithmic properties.
- Derive the change-of-base formula.

## Properties of Logarithms

Since exponential functions and logarithmic functions are inverses of one another, properties of exponents are related to properties of logarithms. We will start by reviewing properties of exponents (Appendix), and then proceed to properties of logarithms.

**PROPERTIES OF EXPONENTS**

Let $a$, $b$, $m$, and $n$ be any real numbers and $m>0$, $n>0$, and $b \neq 0$; then the following are true:

**1.** $b^m \cdot b^n = b^{m+n}$

**2.** $b^{-m} = \dfrac{1}{b^m} = \left(\dfrac{1}{b}\right)^m$

**3.** $\dfrac{b^m}{b^n} = b^{m-n}$

**4.** $(b^m)^n = b^{mn}$

**5.** $(ab)^m = a^m \cdot b^m$

**6.** $b^0 = 1$

**7.** $b^1 = b$

From these properties of exponents, we can develop similar properties for logarithms. We list seven basic properties.

**PROPERTIES OF LOGARITHMS**

If $b$, $M$, and $N$ are positive real numbers, where $b \neq 1$, and $p$ and $x$ are real numbers, then the following are true:

**1.** $\log_b 1 = 0$

**2.** $\log_b b = 1$

**3.** $\log_b b^x = x$

**4.** $b^{\log_b x} = x \quad x > 0$

**5.** $\log_b MN = \log_b M + \log_b N$ — *Product rule:* Log of a product is the sum of the logs.

**6.** $\log_b \left( \dfrac{M}{N} \right) = \log_b M - \log_b N$ — *Quotient rule:* Log of a quotient is the difference of the logs.

**7.** $\log_b M^p = p \log_b M$ — *Power rule:* Log of a number raised to an exponent is the exponent times the log of the number.

We will devote this section to proving and illustrating these seven properties.

The first two properties follow directly from the definition of a logarithmic function and properties of exponentials.

$$\text{Property (1):} \quad \log_b 1 = 0 \text{ since } b^0 = 1$$

$$\text{Property (2):} \quad \log_b b = 1 \text{ since } b^1 = b$$

The third and fourth properties follow from the fact that exponential functions and logarithmic functions are inverses of one another. Recall that inverse functions satisfy the relationship that $f^{-1}(f(x)) = x$ for all $x$ in the domain of $f(x)$, and $f(f^{-1}(x)) = x$ for all $x$ in the domain of $f^{-1}$. Let $f(x) = b^x$ and $f^{-1}(x) = \log_b x$.

Property (3):

Write the inverse identity. $\qquad\qquad f^{-1}(f(x)) = x$

Substitute $f^{-1}(x) = \log_b x$. $\qquad\quad \log_b(f(x)) = x$

Substitute $f(x) = b^x$. $\qquad\qquad\quad \log_b b^x = x$

Property (4):

Write the inverse identity. $\qquad\qquad f(f^{-1}(x)) = x$

Substitute $f(x) = b^x$. $\qquad\qquad\quad b^{f^{-1}(x)} = x$

Substitute $f^{-1}(x) = \log_b x \quad x > 0$. $\qquad b^{\log_b x} = x$

The first four properties are summarized below for common and natural logarithms:

**COMMON AND NATURAL LOGARITHM PROPERTIES**

| Common Logarithm (base 10) | Natural Logarithm (base $e$) |
|---|---|
| **1.** $\log 1 = 0$ | **1.** $\ln 1 = 0$ |
| **2.** $\log 10 = 1$ | **2.** $\ln e = 1$ |
| **3.** $\log 10^x = x$ | **3.** $\ln e^x = x$ |
| **4.** $10^{\log x} = x \quad x > 0$ | **4.** $e^{\ln x} = x \quad x > 0$ |

## EXAMPLE 1   Using Logarithmic Properties

Use properties (1)–(4) to simplify the expressions.

**a.** $\log_{10} 10$     **b.** $\ln 1$     **c.** $10^{\log(x+8)}$

**d.** $e^{\ln(2x+5)}$     **e.** $\log 10^{x^2}$     **f.** $\ln e^{x+3}$

**Solution:**

**a.** Use property (2).                $\log_{10} 10 = \boxed{1}$

**b.** Use property (1).                $\ln 1 = \boxed{0}$

**c.** Use property (4).                $10^{\log(x+8)} = \boxed{x+8}$     $x > -8$

**d.** Use property (4).                $e^{\ln(2x+5)} = \boxed{2x+5}$     $x > -\frac{5}{2}$

**e.** Use property (3).                $\log 10^{x^2} = \boxed{x^2}$

**f.** Use property (3).                $\ln e^{x+3} = \boxed{x+3}$

The fifth through seventh properties follow from the properties of exponents and the definition of logarithms. We will prove the product rule and leave the proofs of the quotient and power rules for the exercises.

$$\text{Property (5):} \quad \log_b MN = \log_b M + \log_b N$$

| WORDS | MATH |
|---|---|
| Assume two logs that have the same base. | Let $u = \log_b M$ and $v = \log_b N$ $M > 0, N > 0$ |
| Change to equivalent exponential forms. | $b^u = M$ and $b^v = N$ |
| Write the log of a product. | $\log_b MN$ |
| Substitute $M = b^u$ and $N = b^v$. | $= \log_b(b^u\, b^v)$ |
| Use properties of exponents. | $= \log_b(b^{u+v})$ |
| Apply property (3). | $= u + v$ |
| Substitute $u = \log_b M$, $v = \log_b N$. | $= \log_b M + \log_b N$ |

$$\boxed{\log_b MN = \log_b M + \log_b N}$$

In other words, the log of a product is the sum of the logs. Let us illustrate this property with a simple example.

$$\overbrace{\log_2 8}^{3} + \overbrace{\log_2 4}^{2} = \overbrace{\log_2 32}^{5}$$

Notice that $\log_2 8 + \log_2 4 \neq \log_2 12$.

**EXAMPLE 2** **Writing a Logarithmic Expression as a Sum of Logarithms**

Use the logarithmic properties to write the expression $\log_b\left(u^2\sqrt{v}\right)$ as a sum of simpler logarithms.

**Solution:**

Convert the radical to exponential form.
$$\log_b\left(u^2\sqrt{v}\right) = \log_b\left(u^2 v^{1/2}\right)$$

Use the product property (5).
$$= \log_b u^2 + \log_b v^{1/2}$$

Use the power property (7).
$$= \boxed{2\log_b u + \tfrac{1}{2}\log_b v}$$

■ **Answer:**
$\log_b\left(x^4\sqrt[3]{y}\right) = 4\log_b x + \tfrac{1}{3}\log_b y$

■ **YOUR TURN** Use the logarithmic properties to write the expression $\log_b\left(x^4\sqrt[3]{y}\right)$ as a sum of simpler logarithms.

**EXAMPLE 3** **Writing a Sum of Logarithms as a Single Logarithmic Expression: The Right Way and the Wrong Way**

Use properties of logarithms to write the expression $2\log_b 3 + 4\log_b u$ as a single logarithmic expression.

**COMMON MISTAKE**

A common mistake is to write the sum of the logs as a log of the sum.

$$\log_b M + \log_b N \neq \log_b(M + N)$$

▼ **CAUTION**

$\log_b M + \log_b N = \log_b(MN)$

$\log_b M + \log_b N \neq \log_b(M + N)$

⭐ **CORRECT**

Use the power property (7).

$2\log_b 3 + 4\log_b u = \log_b 3^2 + \log_b u^4$

Simplify.

$\log_b 9 + \log_b u^4$

Use the product property (5).

$\boxed{= \log_b(9u^4)}$

❌ **INCORRECT**

$\neq \log_b(9 + u^4)$   **ERROR**

■ **Answer:** $\ln(x^2 y^3)$

■ **YOUR TURN** Express $2\ln x + 3\ln y$ as a single logarithm.

**EXAMPLE 4** **Writing a Logarithmic Expression as a Difference of Logarithms**

Write the expression $\ln\left(\dfrac{x^3}{y^2}\right)$ as a difference of logarithms.

**Solution:**

Apply the quotient property (6).
$$\ln\left(\frac{x^3}{y^2}\right) = \ln(x^3) - \ln(y^2)$$

Apply the power property (7).
$$= \boxed{3\ln x - 2\ln y}$$

■ **Answer:** $4\log a - 5\log b$

■ **YOUR TURN** Write the expression $\log\left(\dfrac{a^4}{b^5}\right)$ as a difference of logarithms.

Another common mistake is misinterpreting the quotient rule.

**EXAMPLE 5** **Writing the Difference of Logarithms as a Logarithm of a Quotient**

Write the expression $\frac{2}{3}\ln x - \frac{1}{2}\ln y$ as a logarithm of a quotient.

### COMMON MISTAKE

$$\log_b M - \log_b N \neq \frac{\log_b M}{\log_b N}$$

⭐ **CORRECT**

Use the power property (7).

$$\frac{2}{3}\ln x - \frac{1}{2}\ln y = \ln x^{2/3} - \ln y^{1/2}$$

Use the quotient property (6).

$$\ln\left(\frac{x^{2/3}}{y^{1/2}}\right)$$

❌ **INCORRECT**

$$\frac{\ln x^{2/3}}{\ln y^{1/2}} \quad \textbf{ERROR}$$

■ **YOUR TURN** Write the expression $\frac{1}{2}\log a - 3\log b$ as a single logarithm.

■ **Answer:** $\log\left(\dfrac{a^{1/2}}{b^3}\right)$

**EXAMPLE 6** **Combining Logarithmic Expressions into a Single Logarithm**

Write the expression $3\log_b x + \log_b(2x + 1) - 2\log_b 4$ as a single logarithm.

**Solution:**

Use the power property (7) on the first and third terms.

$$= \log_b x^3 + \log_b(2x + 1) - \log_b 4^2$$

Use the product property (5) on the first two terms.

$$= \log_b\left[x^3(2x + 1)\right] - \log_b 16$$

Use the quotient property (6).

$$= \log_b\left[\frac{x^3(2x + 1)}{16}\right]$$

■ **YOUR TURN** Write the expression $2\ln x - \ln(3y) + 3\ln z$ as a single logarithm.

■ **Answer:** $\ln\left(\dfrac{x^2 z^3}{3y}\right)$

**EXAMPLE 7** **Expanding a Logarithmic Expression into a Sum or Difference of Logarithms**

Write $\ln\left(\dfrac{x^2 - x - 6}{x^2 + 7x + 6}\right)$ as a sum or difference of logarithms.

**Solution:**

Factor the numerator and denominator.

$$= \ln\left[\frac{(x - 3)(x + 2)}{(x + 6)(x + 1)}\right]$$

Use the quotient property (6).

$$= \ln[(x - 3)(x + 2)] - \ln[(x + 6)(x + 1)]$$

Use the product property (5).

$$= \ln(x - 3) + \ln(x + 2) - [\ln(x + 6) + \ln(x + 1)]$$

Eliminate brackets.

$$= \ln(x - 3) + \ln(x + 2) - \ln(x + 6) - \ln(x + 1)$$

## Change-of-Base Formula

Recall that in the last section, we were able to evaluate logarithms two ways: (1) exactly by writing the logarithm in exponential form and identifying the exponent and (2) using a calculator if the logarithms were base 10 or $e$. How do we evaluate a logarithm of general base if we cannot identify the exponent? We use the *change-of-base formula*.

> **EXAMPLE 8** **Using Properties of Logarithms to Change the Base to Evaluate a General Logarithm**
>
> Evaluate $\log_3 8$. Round the answer to four decimal places.
>
> **Solution:**
>
> | | |
> |---|---|
> | Let $y = \log_3 8$. | $y = \log_3 8$ |
> | Write the logarithm in exponential form. | $3^y = 8$ |
> | Take the log of both sides. | $\log 3^y = \log 8$ |
> | Use the power property (7). | $y \log 3 = \log 8$ |
> | Divide both sides by $\log 3$. | $y = \dfrac{\log 8}{\log 3}$ |
> | Let $y = \log_3 8$. | $\boxed{\log_3 8 = \dfrac{\log 8}{\log 3}}$ |

Example 8 illustrated our ability to use properties of logarithms to change from base 3 to base 10, which our calculators can handle. This leads to the general change-of-base formula.

### CHANGE-OF-BASE FORMULA

For any logarithmic bases $a$ and $b$ and any positive number $M$, the change-of-base formula says that

$$\log_b M = \frac{\log_a M}{\log_a b}$$

In the special case when $a$ is either 10 or $e$, this relationship becomes

**Common Logarithms**

$$\log_b M = \frac{\log M}{\log b}$$

or

**Natural Logarithms**

$$\log_b M = \frac{\ln M}{\ln b}$$

It does not matter what base we select (10, $e$, or any other base); the ratio will be the same.

## Proof of Change-of-Base Formula

| WORDS | MATH |
|---|---|
| Let $y$ be the logarithm we want to evaluate. | $y = \log_b M$ |
| Write $y = \log_b M$ in exponential form. | $b^y = M$ |
| Let $a$ be any positive real number (where $a \neq 1$). | |
| Take the log of base $a$ of both sides of the equation. | $\log_a b^y = \log_a M$ |
| Use the power rule on the left side of the equation. | $y \log_a b = \log_a M$ |
| Divide both sides of the equation by $\log_a b$. | $y = \dfrac{\log_a M}{\log_a b}$ |

## EXAMPLE 9    Using the Change-of-Base Formula

Use the change-of-base formula to evaluate $\log_4 17$. Round to four decimal places.

**Solution:**

We will illustrate this in two ways (choosing common and natural logarithms) using a scientific calculator.

### Common Logarithms

Use the change-of-base formula with base 10.    $\log_4 17 = \dfrac{\log 17}{\log 4}$

Approximate with a calculator.    $\approx 2.043731421$

$\approx \boxed{2.0437}$

### Natural Logarithms

Use the change-of-base formula with base $e$.    $\log_4 17 = \dfrac{\ln 17}{\ln 4}$

Approximate with a calculator.    $\approx 2.043731421$

$\approx \boxed{2.0437}$

▪ **YOUR TURN**  Use the change-of-base formula to approximate $\log_7 34$. Round to four decimal places.

▪ **Answer:** $\log_7 34 \approx 1.8122$

---

## SECTION 3.3  SUMMARY

### Properties of Logarithms

If $b$, $M$, and $N$ are positive real numbers, where $b \neq 1$, and $p$ and $x$ are real numbers, then the following are true:

▪ Product Property:    $\log_b MN = \log_b M + \log_b N$

▪ Quotient Property:    $\log_b\left(\dfrac{M}{N}\right) = \log_b M - \log_b N$

▪ Power Property:    $\log_b M^p = p \log_b M$

| GENERAL LOGARITHM | COMMON LOGARITHM | NATURAL LOGARITHM |
|---|---|---|
| $\log_b 1 = 0$ | $\log 1 = 0$ | $\ln 1 = 0$ |
| $\log_b b = 1$ | $\log 10 = 1$ | $\ln e = 1$ |
| $\log_b b^x = x$ | $\log 10^x = x$ | $\ln e^x = x$ |
| $b^{\log_b x} = x \quad x > 0$ | $10^{\log x} = x \quad x > 0$ | $e^{\ln x} = x \quad x > 0$ |
| $\log_b M = \dfrac{\log_a M}{\log_a b}$ | $\log_b M = \dfrac{\log M}{\log b}$ | $\log_b M = \dfrac{\ln M}{\ln b}$ |

**SECTION**
**3.3** EXERCISES

■ SKILLS

**In Exercises 1–20, apply the properties of logarithms to simplify each expression. Do not use a calculator.**

**1.** $\log_9 1$      **2.** $\log_{69} 1$      **3.** $\log_{1/2}\left(\frac{1}{2}\right)$      **4.** $\log_{3.3} 3.3$      **5.** $\log_{10} 10^8$

**6.** $\ln e^3$      **7.** $\log_{10} 0.001$      **8.** $\log_3 3^7$      **9.** $\log_2 \sqrt{8}$      **10.** $\log_5 \sqrt[3]{5}$

**11.** $8^{\log_8 5}$      **12.** $2^{\log_2 5}$      **13.** $e^{\ln(x+5)}$      **14.** $10^{\log(3x^2+2x+1)}$      **15.** $5^{3\log_5 2}$

**16.** $7^{2\log_7 5}$      **17.** $7^{-2\log_7 3}$      **18.** $e^{-2\ln 10}$      **19.** $7e^{-3\ln x}$      **20.** $-19e^{-2\ln x^2}$

**In Exercises 21–36, write each expression as a sum or difference of logarithms.**

Example: $\log(m^2 n^5) = 2\log m + 5\log n$

**21.** $\log_b(x^3 y^5)$      **22.** $\log_b(x^{-3} y^{-5})$      **23.** $\log_b(x^{1/2} y^{1/3})$      **24.** $\log_b(\sqrt{r}\,\sqrt[3]{t})$

**25.** $\log_b\left(\frac{r^{1/3}}{s^{1/2}}\right)$      **26.** $\log_b\left(\frac{r^4}{s^2}\right)$      **27.** $\log_b\left(\frac{x}{yz}\right)$      **28.** $\log_b\left(\frac{xy}{z}\right)$

**29.** $\log(x^2\sqrt{x+5})$      **30.** $\log[(x-3)(x+2)]$      **31.** $\ln\left[\frac{x^3(x-2)^2}{\sqrt{x^2+5}}\right]$      **32.** $\ln\left[\frac{\sqrt{x+3}\,\sqrt[3]{x-4}}{(x+1)^4}\right]$

**33.** $\log\left(\frac{x^2-2x+1}{x^2-9}\right)$      **34.** $\log\left(\frac{x^2-x-2}{x^2+3x-4}\right)$      **35.** $\ln\sqrt{\frac{x^2+3x-10}{x^2-3x+2}}$      **36.** $\ln\left[\frac{\sqrt[3]{x-1}(3x-2)^4}{(x+1)\sqrt{x-1}}\right]^2$

**In Exercises 37–48, write each expression as a single logarithm.**

Example: $2\log m + 5\log n = \log(m^2 n^5)$

**37.** $3\log_b x + 5\log_b y$      **38.** $2\log_b u + 3\log_b v$      **39.** $5\log_b u - 2\log_b v$      **40.** $3\log_b x - \log_b y$

**41.** $\frac{1}{2}\log_b x + \frac{2}{3}\log_b y$      **42.** $\frac{1}{2}\log_b x - \frac{2}{3}\log_b y$      **43.** $2\log u - 3\log v - 2\log z$      **44.** $3\log u - \log 2v - \log z$

**45.** $\ln(x+1) + \ln(x-1) - 2\ln(x^2+3)$      **46.** $\ln\sqrt{x-1} + \ln\sqrt{x+1} - 2\ln(x^2-1)$

**47.** $\frac{1}{2}\ln(x+3) - \frac{1}{3}\ln(x+2) - \ln(x)$      **48.** $\frac{1}{3}\ln(x^2+4) - \frac{1}{2}\ln(x^2-3) - \ln(x-1)$

**In Exercises 49–58, evaluate the logarithms using the change-of-base formula. Round to four decimal places.**

**49.** $\log_5 7$      **50.** $\log_4 19$      **51.** $\log_{1/2} 5$      **52.** $\log_5 \frac{1}{2}$      **53.** $\log_{2.7} 5.2$

**54.** $\log_{7.2} 2.5$      **55.** $\log_\pi 10$      **56.** $\log_\pi 2.7$      **57.** $\log_{\sqrt{3}} 8$      **58.** $\log_{\sqrt{2}} 9$

■ APPLICATIONS

**59. Sound.** Sitting in the front row of a rock concert exposes us to a sound pressure (or sound level) of $1 \times 10^{-1}$ W/m$^2$ (or 110 decibels), and a normal conversation is typically around $1 \times 10^{-6}$ W/m$^2$ (or 60 decibels). How many decibels are you exposed to if a friend is talking in your ear at a rock concert? *Note:* 160 decibels causes perforation of the eardrums. *Hint:* Add the sound pressures and convert to decibels.

**60. Sound.** A whisper corresponds to $1 \times 10^{-10}$ W/m$^2$ (or 20 decibels) and a normal conversation is typically around $1 \times 10^{-6}$ W/m$^2$ (or 60 decibels). How many decibels are you exposed to if one friend is whispering in your ear, while the other one is talking at a normal level? *Hint:* Add the sound pressures and convert to decibels.

**For Exercises 61 and 62, refer to the following:**

There are two types of waves associated with an earthquake: *compression* and *shear*. The compression, or longitudinal, waves displace material behind the earthquake's path. Longitudinal waves travel at great speeds and are often called "primary waves" or simply "P" waves. Shear, or transverse, waves displace material at right angles to the earthquake's path. Transverse waves do not travel as rapidly through the Earth's crust and mantle as do longitudinal waves, and they are called "secondary" or "S" waves.

**61. Earthquakes.** If a seismologist records the energy of P waves as $4.5 \times 10^{12}$ joules and the energy of S waves as $7.8 \times 10^8$ joules, what is the total energy (sum the two energies)? What would the combined effect be on the Richter scale?

**62. Earthquakes.** Repeat Exercise 61, assuming the energy associated with the P waves is $5.2 \times 10^{11}$ joules and the energy associated with the S waves is $4.1 \times 10^9$ joules.

**63. Photography.** In photographic quality assurance, logarithms are used to determine, for instance, the density. Density is the common logarithm of the opacity, which is the quotient of the amount of incident light and the amount of transmitted light. What is the density of a photographic material that only transmits 90% of the incident light?

**64. pH Scale.** The pH scale measures how acidic or basic a substance is. pH is defined as the negative logarithm of the hydrogen ion activity in an aqueous solution, $a_H$. Thus, if $a_H = 0.01$, then $pH = -\log 0.01 = 2$. Determine the pH of a liquid with $a_H = 0.00407$. Round your answer to the nearest hundredth.

**65. pH Scale.** How many times more acidic is a substance with $pH = 3.2$ than a substance with $pH = 4.4$? Round your answer to the nearest integer.

**66. Information Theory.** In information theory, logarithms in base 2 are often used. The capacity $C$ of a noisy channel with bandwidth $W$ and signal and noise powers $S$ and $N$ is $C = W \log_2\left(1 + \dfrac{S}{N}\right)$. The signal noise ratio $R$ is given by $R = 10 \log\left(\dfrac{S}{N}\right)$. Assuming a channel with a bandwidth of 3 megahertz and a signal noise ratio $R = 2$ dB, calculate the channel capacity.

## ■ CATCH THE MISTAKE

**In Exercises 67–70, simplify if possible and explain the mistake that is made.**

**67.** $3 \log 5 - \log 25$

**Solution:**

| | |
|---|---|
| Apply the quotient property (6). | $\dfrac{3 \log 5}{\log 25}$ |
| Write $25 = 5^2$. | $\dfrac{3 \log 5}{\log 5^2}$ |
| Apply the power property (7). | $\dfrac{3 \log 5}{2 \log 5}$ |
| Simplify. | $\dfrac{3}{2}$ |

This is incorrect. The correct answer is log 5. What mistake was made?

**68.** $\ln 3 + 2 \ln 4 - 3 \ln 2$

**Solution:**

| | |
|---|---|
| Apply the power property (7). | $\ln 3 + \ln 4^2 - \ln 2^3$ |
| Simplify. | $\ln 3 + \ln 16 - \ln 8$ |
| Apply property (5). | $\ln (3 + 16 - 8)$ |
| Simplify. | $\ln 11$ |

This is incorrect. The correct answer is ln 6. What mistake was made?

**69.** $\log_2 x + \log_3 y - \log_4 z$

**Solution:**

| | |
|---|---|
| Apply the product property (5). | $\log_6 xy - \log_4 z$ |
| Apply the quotient property (6). | $\log_{24} xyz$ |

This is incorrect. What mistake was made?

**70.** $2(\log 3 - \log 5)$

**Solution:**

| | |
|---|---|
| Apply the quotient property (6). | $2\left(\log \dfrac{3}{5}\right)$ |
| Apply the power property (7). | $\left(\log \dfrac{3}{5}\right)^2$ |
| Apply a calculator to approximate. | $\approx 0.0492$ |

This is incorrect. What mistake was made?

## ▪ CONCEPTUAL

**In Exercises 71–74, determine whether each statement is true or false.**

**71.** $\log e = \dfrac{1}{\ln 10}$

**72.** $\ln e = \dfrac{1}{\log 10}$

**73.** $\ln(xy)^3 = (\ln x + \ln y)^3$

**74.** $\dfrac{\ln a}{\ln b} = \dfrac{\log a}{\log b}$

**75.** $\log 12x^3 = 36 \log x$

**76.** $e^{\ln x^2} = x^2$

## ▪ CHALLENGE

**77.** Prove the quotient rule: $\log_b\left(\dfrac{M}{N}\right) = \log_b M - \log_b N$.

   *Hint:* Let $u = \log_b M$ and $v = \log_b N$. Write both in exponential form and find the quotient $\log_b\left(\dfrac{M}{N}\right)$.

**78.** Prove the power rule: $\log_b M^p = p \log_b M$. *Hint:* Let $u = \log_b M$. Write this log in exponential form and find $\log_b M^p$.

**79.** Write in terms of simpler logarithmic forms.

$$\log_b\left(\sqrt{\dfrac{x^2}{y^3 z^{-5}}}\right)^6$$

**80.** Show that $\log_b\left(\dfrac{1}{x}\right) = -\log_b x$.

**81.** Show that $\log_b\left(\dfrac{a^2}{b^3}\right)^{-3} = 9 - \dfrac{6}{\log_a b}$.

**82.** Given that $\log_b 2 = 0.4307$ and $\log_b 3 = 0.6826$, find $\log_b \sqrt{48}$. Do not use a calculator.

## ▪ TECHNOLOGY

**83.** Use a graphing calculator to plot $y = \ln(2x)$ and $y = \ln 2 + \ln x$. Are they the same graph?

**84.** Use a graphing calculator to plot $y = \ln(2 + x)$ and $y = \ln 2 + \ln x$. Are they the same graph?

**85.** Use a graphing calculator to plot $y = \dfrac{\log x}{\log 2}$ and $y = \log x - \log 2$. Are they the same graph?

**86.** Use a graphing calculator to plot $y = \log\left(\dfrac{x}{2}\right)$ and $y = \log x - \log 2$. Are they the same graph?

**87.** Use a graphing calculator to plot $y = \ln(x^2)$ and $y = 2 \ln x$. Are they the same graph?

**88.** Use a graphing calculator to plot $y = (\ln x)^2$ and $y = 2 \ln x$. Are they the same graph?

**89.** Use a graphing calculator to plot $y = \ln x$ and $y = \dfrac{\log x}{\log e}$. Are they the same graph?

**90.** Use a graphing calculator to plot $y = \log x$ and $y = \dfrac{\ln x}{\ln 10}$. Are they the same graph?

## ▪ PREVIEW TO CALCULUS

In calculus we prove that the derivative of $f + g$ is $f' + g'$ and that the derivative of $f - g$ is $f' - g'$. It is also shown in calculus that if $f(x) = \ln x$ then $f'(x) = \dfrac{1}{x}$.

**91.** Use these properties to find the derivative of $f(x) = \ln x^2$.

**92.** Use these properties to find the derivative of $f(x) = \ln \dfrac{1}{x}$.

**93.** Find the derivative of $f(x) = \ln \dfrac{1}{x^2}$.

**94.** Find the derivative of $f(x) = \ln x^2 + \ln x^3$.

# EXPONENTIAL AND LOGARITHMIC EQUATIONS

## SKILLS OBJECTIVES

- Solve exponential equations.
- Solve logarithmic equations.
- Solve application problems involving exponential and logarithmic equations.

## CONCEPTUAL OBJECTIVE

- Understand how exponential and logarithmic equations are solved using properties of one-to-one functions and inverses.

## Solving Exponential Equations

To solve algebraic equations such as $x^2 - 9 = 0$, the goal is to solve for the variable, $x$, by finding the values of $x$ that make the statement true. Exponential and logarithmic equations have the variable $(x)$ buried within an exponent or a logarithm, but the goal is the same. Find the value(s) of $x$ that makes the statement true.

$$\text{Exponential equation:} \quad e^{2x+1} = 5$$

$$\text{Logarithmic equation:} \quad \log(3x - 1) = 7$$

There are two methods for solving exponential and logarithmic equations that are based on the properties of one-to-one functions and inverses. To solve simple exponential and logarithmic equations, we will use one-to-one properties. To solve more complicated exponential and logarithmic equations, we will use properties of inverses. The following box summarizes the one-to-one and inverse properties that hold true when $b > 0$ and $b \neq 1$.

### ONE-TO-ONE PROPERTIES

| | | |
|---|---|---|
| $b^x = b^y$ | if and only if | $x = y$ |
| $\log_b x = \log_b y$ | if and only if | $x = y$ |

### INVERSE PROPERTIES

$$b^{\log_b x} = x \quad x > 0$$
$$\log_b b^x = x$$

The following strategies are outlined for solving simple and complicated exponential equations using the one-to-one and inverse properties.

## STRATEGIES FOR SOLVING EXPONENTIAL EQUATIONS

| TYPE OF EQUATION | STRATEGY | EXAMPLE |
|---|---|---|
| Simple | 1. Rewrite both sides of the equation in terms of the same base. | $2^{x-3} = 32$ <br> $2^{x-3} = 2^5$ |
| | 2. Use the one-to-one property to equate the exponents. | $x - 3 = 5$ |
| | 3. Solve for the variable. | $\boxed{x = 8}$ |
| Complicated | 1. Isolate the exponential expression. | $3e^{2x} - 2 = 7$ <br> $3e^{2x} = 9$ <br> $e^{2x} = 3$ |
| | 2. Take the same logarithm* of both sides. | $\ln e^{2x} = \ln 3$ |
| | 3. Simplify using the inverse properties. | $2x = \ln 3$ |
| | 4. Solve for the variable. | $\boxed{x = \frac{1}{2} \ln 3}$ |

*Take the logarithm with base that is equal to the base of the exponent and use the property $\log_b b^x = x$ or take the natural logarithm and use the property in $M^p = p \ln M$.

## EXAMPLE 1  Solving a Simple Exponential Equation

Solve the exponential equations using the one-to-one property.

**a.** $3^x = 81$     **b.** $5^{7-x} = 125$     **c.** $\left(\frac{1}{2}\right)^{4y} = 16$

**Solution (a):**

Substitute $81 = 3^4$.                     $3^x = 3^4$

Use the one-to-one property to identify $x$.     $\boxed{x = 4}$

**Solution (b):**

Substitute $125 = 5^3$.                     $5^{7-x} = 5^3$

Use the one-to-one property.             $7 - x = 3$

Solve for $x$.                           $\boxed{x = 4}$

**Solution (c):**

Substitute $\left(\frac{1}{2}\right)^{4y} = \left(\frac{1}{2^{4y}}\right) = 2^{-4y}$.     $2^{-4y} = 16$

Substitute $16 = 2^4$.                     $2^{-4y} = 2^4$

Use the one-to-one property to identify $y$.     $\boxed{y = -1}$

■ **Answer: a.** $x = 4$    **b.** $y = -3$

■ **YOUR TURN** Solve the following equations:

        **a.** $2^{x-1} = 8$     **b.** $\left(\frac{1}{3}\right)^y = 27$

In Example 1, we were able to rewrite the equation in a form with the same bases so that we could use the one-to-one property. In Example 2, we will not be able to write both sides in a form with the same bases. Instead, we will use properties of inverses.

### EXAMPLE 2  Solving a More Complicated Exponential Equation with a Base Other Than 10 or *e*

Solve the exponential equations exactly and then approximate the answers to four decimal places.

**a.** $5^{3x} = 16$    **b.** $4^{3x+2} = 71$

**Solution (a):**

| | |
|---|---|
| Take the natural logarithm of both sides of the equation. | $\ln 5^{3x} = \ln 16$ |
| Use the power property on the left side of the equation. | $3x \ln 5 = \ln 16$ |
| Divide both sides of the equation by 3 ln 5. | $\boxed{x = \dfrac{\ln 16}{3 \ln 5}}$ |
| Use a calculator to approximate $x$ to four decimal places. | $\boxed{x \approx 0.5742}$ |

**Solution (b):**

| | |
|---|---|
| Rewrite in logarithmic form. | $3x + 2 = \log_4 71$ |
| Subtract 2 from both sides. | $3x = \log_4 71 - 2$ |
| Divide both sides by 3. | $x = \dfrac{\log_4 71 - 2}{3}$ |
| Use the change-of-base formula, $\log_4 71 = \dfrac{\ln 71}{\ln 4}$. | $\boxed{x = \dfrac{\dfrac{\ln 71}{\ln 4} - 2}{3}}$ |
| Use a calculator to approximate $x$ to four decimal places. | $x \approx \dfrac{3.07487356 - 2}{3} \approx \boxed{0.3583}$ |

*Technology Tip*

```
((ln(71)/ln(4)-2
)/3
        .3582911866
```

We could have proceeded in an alternative way by taking either the natural log or the common log of both sides and using the power property (instead of using the change-of-base formula) to evaluate the logarithm with base 4.

| | |
|---|---|
| Take the natural logarithm of both sides. | $\ln\left(4^{3x+2}\right) = \ln 71$ |
| Use the power property (7). | $(3x + 2)\ln 4 = \ln 71$ |
| Divide by ln 4. | $3x + 2 = \dfrac{\ln 71}{\ln 4}$ |
| Subtract 2 and divide by 3. | $\boxed{x = \dfrac{\dfrac{\ln 71}{\ln 4} - 2}{3}}$ |
| Use a calculator to approximate $x$. | $x \approx \dfrac{3.07487356 - 2}{3} \approx \boxed{0.3583}$ |

■ **YOUR TURN**  Solve the equation $5^{y^2} = 27$ exactly and then approximate the answer to four decimal places.

■ **Answer:**
$y = \pm\sqrt{\log_5 27} \approx \pm 1.4310$

**EXAMPLE 3** **Solving a More Complicated Exponential Equation with Base 10 or $e$**

Solve the exponential equation $4e^{x^2} = 64$ exactly and then approximate the answer to four decimal places.

**Solution:**

Divide both sides by 4. $\quad\quad\quad e^{x^2} = 16$

Take the natural logarithm (ln) of both sides. $\quad\quad \ln\left(e^{x^2}\right) = \ln 16$

Simplify the left side with the property of inverses. $\quad\quad x^2 = \ln 16$

Solve for $x$ using the square-root method. $\quad\quad \boxed{x = \pm\sqrt{\ln 16}}$

Use a calculator to approximate $x$ to four decimal places. $\quad\quad \boxed{x \approx \pm 1.6651}$

**■ Answer:** $x = \dfrac{\log_{10} 7 + 3}{2} \approx 1.9225$

**■ YOUR TURN** Solve the equation $10^{2x-3} = 7$ exactly and then approximate the answer to four decimal places.

---

The graph of the function $e^{2x} - 4e^x + 3$ is shown. The $x$-intercepts are $x \approx 1.10$ and $x = 0$.

| X | Y1 |
|---|---|
| -1 | 1.664 |
| 0 | 0 |
| 1.099 | .0023 |
| 1.5 | 5.159 |
| 2 | 28.04 |

Y1☐e^(2X)-4e^(X⌐

**■ Answer:** $x = \log 2 \approx 0.3010$

 **EXAMPLE 4** **Solving an Exponential Equation Quadratic in Form**

Solve the equation $e^{2x} - 4e^x + 3 = 0$ exactly and then approximate the answer to four decimal places.

**Solution:**

Let $u = e^x$. (*Note:* $u^2 = e^x \cdot e^x = e^{2x}$.) $\quad\quad u^2 - 4u + 3 = 0$

Factor. $\quad\quad (u - 3)(u - 1) = 0$

Solve for $u$. $\quad\quad u = 3 \quad$ or $\quad u = 1$

Substitute $u = e^x$. $\quad\quad e^x = 3 \quad$ or $\quad e^x = 1$

Take the natural logarithm (ln) of both sides. $\quad \ln(e^x) = \ln 3 \quad$ or $\quad \ln(e^x) = \ln 1$

Simplify with the properties of logarithms. $\quad \boxed{x = \ln 3} \quad$ or $\quad \boxed{x = \ln 1}$

Approximate or evaluate exactly the right sides. $\quad \boxed{x \approx 1.0986} \quad$ or $\quad \boxed{x = 0}$

**■ YOUR TURN** Solve the equation $100^x - 10^x - 2 = 0$ exactly and then approximate the answer to four decimal places.

## Solving Logarithmic Equations

We can solve simple logarithmic equations using the property of one-to-one functions. For more complicated logarithmic equations, we can employ properties of logarithms and properties of inverses. **Solutions must be checked to eliminate extraneous solutions**.

## STRATEGIES FOR SOLVING LOGARITHMIC EQUATIONS

| TYPE OF EQUATION | STRATEGY | EXAMPLE |
|---|---|---|
| Simple | 1. Combine logarithms on each side of the equation using properties. | $\log(x - 3) + \log x = \log 4$ <br> $\log x(x - 3) = \log 4$ |
| | 2. Use the one-to-one property to equate the arguments. | $x(x - 3) = 4$ |
| | 3. Solve for the variable. | $x^2 - 3x - 4 = 0$ <br> $(x - 4)(x + 1) = 0$ <br> $x = -1, 4$ |
| | 4. Check the results and eliminate any extraneous solutions. | Eliminate $x = -1$ because $\log(-1)$ is undefined. $\boxed{x = 4}$ |
| Complicated | 1. Combine and isolate the logarithmic expressions. | $\log_5(x + 2) - \log_5 x = 2$ <br> $\log_5\left(\dfrac{x + 2}{x}\right) = 2$ |
| | 2. Rewrite the equation in exponential form. | $\dfrac{x + 2}{x} = 5^2$ |
| | 3. Solve for the variable. | $x + 2 = 25x$ <br> $24x = 2$ <br> $\boxed{x = \dfrac{1}{12}}$ |
| | 4. Check the results and eliminate any extraneous solutions. | $\log_5\left(\dfrac{1}{12} + 2\right) - \log_5\left(\dfrac{1}{12}\right)$ <br> $= \log_5\left(\dfrac{25}{12}\right) - \log_5\left(\dfrac{1}{12}\right)$ <br> $= \log_5\left[\dfrac{25/12}{1/12}\right] = \log_5[25] = 2 \checkmark$ |

 **EXAMPLE 5   Solving a Simple Logarithmic Equation**

Solve the equation $\log_4(2x - 3) = \log_4(x) + \log_4(x - 2)$.

**Solution:**

Apply the product property (5) on the right side.     $\log_4(2x - 3) = \log_4[x(x - 2)]$

Apply the property of one-to-one functions.     $2x - 3 = x(x - 2)$

Distribute and simplify.     $x^2 - 4x + 3 = 0$

Factor.     $(x - 3)(x - 1) = 0$

Solve for $x$.     $x = 3 \quad \text{or} \quad x = 1$

The possible solution $x = 1$ must be eliminated because it is not in the domain of two of the logarithmic functions.

$$x = 1: \overbrace{\log_4(-1)}^{\text{undefined}} \overset{?}{=} \log_4(1) + \overbrace{\log_4(-1)}^{\text{undefined}}$$

$\boxed{x = 3}$

> **Study Tip**
>
> Solutions should be checked in the original equation to eliminate extraneous solutions.

■ **YOUR TURN** Solve the equation $\ln(x + 8) = \ln(x) + \ln(x + 3)$.

■ **Answer:** $x = 2$

**EXAMPLE 6** **Solving a More Complicated Logarithmic Equation**

Solve the equation $\log_3(9x) - \log_3(x - 8) = 4$.

**Solution:**

Employ the quotient property (6) on the left side.

$$\log_3\left(\frac{9x}{x-8}\right) = 4$$

Write in exponential form. $\quad \log_b x = y \Rightarrow x = b^y$

$$\frac{9x}{x-8} = 3^4$$

Simplify the right side.

$$\frac{9x}{x-8} = 81$$

Multiply the equation by the LCD, $x - 8$.

$$9x = 81(x - 8)$$

Eliminate parentheses.

$$9x = 81x - 648$$

Solve for $x$.

$$-72x = -648$$

$$\boxed{x = 9}$$

*Check:* $\log_3[9 \cdot 9] - \log_3[9 - 8] = \log_3[81] - \log_3 1 = 4 - 0 = 4$

■ **Answer:** $x = 2$

■ **YOUR TURN** Solve the equation $\log_2(4x) - \log_2(2) = 2$.

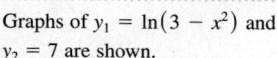
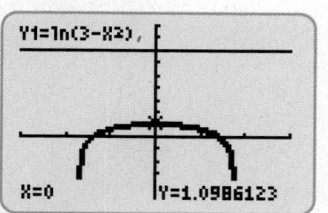
**EXAMPLE 7** **Solving a Logarithmic Equation with No Solution**

Solve the equation $\ln(3 - x^2) = 7$.

**Solution:**

Write in exponential form.

$$3 - x^2 = e^7$$

Simplify.

$$x^2 = 3 - e^7$$

$3 - e^7$ is negative.

$$x^2 = \text{negative real number}$$

There are no real numbers that when squared yield a negative real number. Therefore, there is no real solution .

## Applications

Archaeologists determine the age of a fossil by how much carbon 14 is present at the time of discovery. The number of grams of carbon 14 based on the radioactive decay of the isotope is given by

$$A = A_0 e^{-0.000124t}$$

where $A$ is the number of grams of carbon 14 at the present time, $A_0$ is the number of grams of carbon 14 while alive, and $t$ is the number of years since death. Using the inverse properties, we can isolate $t$.

| WORDS | MATH |
|---|---|
| Divide by $A_0$. | $\dfrac{A}{A_0} = e^{-0.000124t}$ |
| Take the natural logarithm of both sides. | $\ln\left(\dfrac{A}{A_0}\right) = \ln\left(e^{-0.000124t}\right)$ |
| Simplify the right side utilizing properties of inverses. | $\ln\left(\dfrac{A}{A_0}\right) = -0.000124t$ |
| Solve for $t$. | $t = -\dfrac{1}{0.000124}\ln\left(\dfrac{A}{A_0}\right)$ |

Let's assume that animals have approximately 1000 mg of carbon 14 in their bodies when they are alive. If a fossil has 200 mg of carbon 14, approximately how old is the fossil? Substituting $A = 200$ and $A_0 = 1000$ into our equation for $t$, we find

$$t = -\frac{1}{0.000124} \ln\left(\frac{1}{5}\right) \approx 12{,}979.338$$

The fossil is approximately 13,000 years old.

**EXAMPLE 8**   **Calculating How Many Years It Will Take for Money to Double**

You save $1000 from a summer job and put it in a CD earning 5% compounding continuously. How many years will it take for your money to double? Round to the nearest year.

**Solution:**

| | |
|---|---|
| Recall the compound continuous interest formula. | $A = Pe^{rt}$ |
| Substitute $P = 1000$, $A = 2000$, and $r = 0.05$. | $2000 = 1000e^{0.05t}$ |
| Divide by 1000. | $2 = e^{0.05t}$ |
| Take the natural logarithm of both sides. | $\ln 2 = \ln\left(e^{0.05t}\right)$ |
| Simplify with the property $\ln e^x = x$. | $\ln 2 = 0.05t$ |
| Solve for $t$. | $t = \dfrac{\ln 2}{0.05} \approx 13.8629$ |

It will take almost ☐14 years☐ for your money to double.

**Answer:** approximately 11 years

■ **YOUR TURN**   How long will it take $1000 to triple (become $3000) in a savings account earning 10% a year compounding continuously? Round your answer to the nearest year.

When an investment is compounded continuously, how long will it take for that investment to double?

| WORDS | MATH |
|---|---|
| Write the interest formula for compounding continuously. | $A = Pe^{rt}$ |
| Let $A = 2P$ (investment doubles). | $2P = Pe^{rt}$ |
| Divide both sides of the equation by $P$. | $2 = e^{rt}$ |
| Take the natural log of both sides of the equation. | $\ln 2 = \ln e^{rt}$ |
| Simplify the right side by applying the property $\ln e^x = x$. | $\ln 2 = rt$ |
| Divide both sides by $r$ to get the exact value for $t$. | $t = \dfrac{\ln 2}{r}$ |
| Now, approximate $\ln 2 \approx 0.7$. | $t \approx \dfrac{0.7}{r}$ |
| Multiply the numerator and denominator by 100. | $t \approx \dfrac{70}{100r}$ |

This is the "rule of 70."

If we divide 70 by the interest rate (compounding continuously), we get the approximate time for an investment to double. In Example 8, the interest rate (compounding continuously) is 5%. Dividing 70 by 5 yields 14 years.

**SECTION**
**3.4 SUMMARY**

### Strategy for Solving Exponential Equations

| TYPE OF EQUATION | STRATEGY |
|---|---|
| Simple | 1. Rewrite both sides of the equation in terms of the same base. |
| | 2. Use the one-to-one property to equate the exponents. |
| | 3. Solve for the variable. |
| Complicated | 1. Isolate the exponential expression. |
| | 2. Take the same logarithm* of both sides. |
| | 3. Simplify using the inverse properties. |
| | 4. Solve for the variable. |

*Take the logarithm with the base that is equal to the base of the exponent and use the property $\log_b b^x = x$ or take the natural logarithm and use the property in $M^p = p \ln M$.

### Strategy for Solving Logarithmic Equations

| TYPE OF EQUATION | STRATEGY |
|---|---|
| Simple | 1. Combine logarithms on each side of the equation using properties. |
| | 2. Use the one-to-one property to equate the arguments. |
| | 3. Solve for the variable. |
| | 4. Check the results and eliminate any extraneous solutions. |
| Complicated | 1. Combine and isolate the logarithmic expressions. |
| | 2. Rewrite the equation in exponential form. |
| | 3. Solve for the variable. |
| | 4. Check the results and eliminate any extraneous solutions. |

**SECTION**
**3.4 EXERCISES**

■ **SKILLS**

**In Exercises 1–14, solve the exponential equations exactly for $x$.**

**1.** $2^{x^2} = 16$      **2.** $169^x = 13$      **3.** $\left(\frac{2}{3}\right)^{x+1} = \frac{27}{8}$      **4.** $\left(\frac{3}{5}\right)^{x+1} = \frac{25}{9}$      **5.** $e^{2x+3} = 1$

**6.** $10^{x^2-1} = 1$      **7.** $7^{2x-5} = 7^{3x-4}$      **8.** $125^x = 5^{2x-3}$      **9.** $2^{x^2+12} = 2^{7x}$      **10.** $5^{x^2-3} = 5^{2x}$

**11.** $9^x = 3^{x^2-4x}$      **12.** $16^{x-1} = 2^{x^2}$      **13.** $e^{5x-1} = e^{x^2+3}$      **14.** $10^{x^2-8} = 100^x$

**In Exercises 15–40, solve the exponential equations exactly and then approximate your answers to three decimal places.**

**15.** $27 = 2^{3x-1}$      **16.** $15 = 7^{3-2x}$      **17.** $3e^x - 8 = 7$      **18.** $5e^x + 12 = 27$

**19.** $9 - 2e^{0.1x} = 1$      **20.** $21 - 4e^{0.1x} = 5$      **21.** $2(3^x) - 11 = 9$      **22.** $3(2^x) + 8 = 35$

**23.** $e^{3x+4} = 22$      **24.** $e^{x^2} = 73$      **25.** $3e^{2x} = 18$      **26.** $4(10^{3x}) = 20$

**27.** $4e^{2x+1} = 17$      **28.** $5(10^{x^2+2x+1}) = 13$      **29.** $3(4^{x^2-4}) = 16$      **30.** $7 \cdot \left(\frac{1}{4}\right)^{6-5x} = 3$

**31.** $e^{2x} + 7e^x - 3 = 0$      **32.** $e^{2x} - 4e^x - 5 = 0$      **33.** $(3^x - 3^{-x})^2 = 0$      **34.** $(3^x - 3^{-x})(3^x + 3^{-x}) = 0$

**35.** $\dfrac{2}{e^x - 5} = 1$      **36.** $\dfrac{17}{e^x + 4} = 2$      **37.** $\dfrac{20}{6 - e^{2x}} = 4$      **38.** $\dfrac{4}{3 - e^{3x}} = 8$

**39.** $\dfrac{4}{10^{2x} - 7} = 2$      **40.** $\dfrac{28}{10^x + 3} = 4$

**In Exercises 41–58, solve the logarithmic equations exactly.**

**41.** $\log_3(2x + 1) = 4$

**42.** $\log_2(3x - 1) = 3$

**43.** $\log_2(4x - 1) = -3$

**44.** $\log_4(5 - 2x) = -2$

**45.** $\ln x^2 - \ln 9 = 0$

**46.** $\log x^2 + \log x = 3$

**47.** $\log_5(x - 4) + \log_5 x = 1$

**48.** $\log_2(x - 1) + \log_2(x - 3) = 3$

**49.** $\log(x - 3) + \log(x + 2) = \log(4x)$

**50.** $\log_2(x + 1) + \log_2(4 - x) = \log_2(6x)$

**51.** $\log(4 - x) + \log(x + 2) = \log(3 - 2x)$

**52.** $\log(3 - x) + \log(x + 3) = \log(1 - 2x)$

**53.** $\log_4(4x) - \log_4\left(\dfrac{x}{4}\right) = 3$

**54.** $\log_3(7 - 2x) - \log_3(x + 2) = 2$

**55.** $\log(2x - 5) - \log(x - 3) = 1$

**56.** $\log_3(10 - x) - \log_3(x + 2) = 1$

**57.** $\log_4(x^2 + 5x + 4) - 2\log_4(x + 1) = 2$

**58.** $\log_2(x + 1) + \log_2(x + 5) - \log_2(2x + 5) = 2$

**In Exercises 59–72, solve the logarithmic equations exactly and then approximate your answers, if possible, to three decimal places.**

**59.** $\log(2x + 5) = 2$

**60.** $\ln(4x - 7) = 3$

**61.** $\ln(x^2 + 1) = 4$

**62.** $\log(x^2 + 4) = 2$

**63.** $\ln(2x + 3) = -2$

**64.** $\log(3x - 5) = -1$

**65.** $\log(2 - 3x) + \log(3 - 2x) = 1.5$

**66.** $\log_2(3 - x) + \log_2(1 - 2x) = 5$

**67.** $\ln(x) + \ln(x - 2) = 4$

**68.** $\ln(4x) + \ln(2 + x) = 2$

**69.** $\log_7(1 - x) - \log_7(x + 2) = \log_7 x$

**70.** $\log_5(x + 1) - \log_5(x - 1) = \log_5 x$

**71.** $\ln\sqrt{x + 4} - \ln\sqrt{x - 2} = \ln\sqrt{x + 1}$

**72.** $\log(\sqrt{1 - x}) - \log(\sqrt{x + 2}) = \log x$

## ▪ APPLICATIONS

**73. Health.** After strenuous exercise, Sandy's heart rate $R$ (beats per minute) can be modeled by

$$R(t) = 151e^{-0.055t}, \quad 0 \le t \le 15$$

where $t$ is the number of minutes that have elapsed after she stops exercising.

**a.** Find Sandy's heart rate at the end of exercising (when she stops at time $t = 0$).

**b.** Determine how many minutes it takes after Sandy stops exercising for her heart rate to drop to 100 beats per minute. Round to the nearest minute.

**c.** Find Sandy's heart rate 15 minutes after she had stopped exercising.

**74. Business.** A local business purchased a new company van for $45,000. After 2 years the book value of the van is $30,000.

**a.** Find an exponential model for the value of the van using $V(t) = V_0 e^{kt}$ where $V$ is the value of the van in dollars and $t$ is time in years.

**b.** Approximately how many years will it take for the book value of the van to drop to $20,000?

**75. Money.** If money is invested in a savings account earning 3.5% interest compounded yearly, how many years will pass until the money triples?

**76. Money.** If money is invested in a savings account earning 3.5% interest compounded monthly, how many years will pass until the money triples?

**77. Money.** If $7500 is invested in a savings account earning 5% interest compounded quarterly, how many years will pass until there is $20,000?

**78. Money.** If $9000 is invested in a savings account earning 6% interest compounded continuously, how many years will pass until there is $15,000?

**For Exercises 79, 80, and 87, refer to the following:**

$$\text{Richter scale: } M = \frac{2}{3}\log\left(\frac{E}{E_0}\right) \qquad E_0 = 10^{4.4} \text{ joules}$$

**79. Earthquakes.** On September 25, 2003, an earthquake that measured 7.4 on the Richter scale shook Hokkaido, Japan. How much energy (joules) did the earthquake emit?

**80. Earthquakes.** Again, on that same day (September 25, 2003), a second earthquake that measured 8.3 on the Richter scale shook Hokkaido, Japan. How much energy (joules) did the earthquake emit?

**For Exercises 81, 82, and 88, refer to the following:**

Decibel: $D = 10 \log\left(\dfrac{I}{I_T}\right)$   $I_T = 1 \times 10^{-12}$ W/m$^2$

**81. Sound.** Matt likes to drive around campus in his classic Mustang with the stereo blaring. If his boom stereo has a sound intensity of 120 decibels, how many watts per square meter does the stereo emit?

**82. Sound.** The New York Philharmonic has a sound intensity of 100 decibels. How many watts per square meter does the orchestra emit?

**83. Anesthesia.** When a person has a cavity filled, the dentist typically administers a local anesthetic. After leaving the dentist's office, one's mouth often remains numb for several more hours. If a shot of anesthesia is injected into the bloodstream at the time of the procedure ($t = 0$), and the amount of anesthesia still in the bloodstream $t$ hours after the initial injection is given by $A = A_0 e^{-0.5t}$, in how many hours will only 10% of the original anesthetic still be in the bloodstream?

**84. Investments.** Money invested in an account that compounds interest continuously at a rate of 3% a year is modeled by $A = A_0 e^{0.03t}$, where $A$ is the amount in the investment after $t$ years and $A_0$ is the initial investment. How long will it take the initial investment to double?

**85. Biology.** The U.S. Fish and Wildlife Service is releasing a population of the endangered Mexican gray wolf in a protected area along the New Mexico and Arizona border. They estimate the population of the Mexican gray wolf to be approximated by

$$P(t) = \frac{200}{1 + 24e^{-0.2t}}$$

How many years will it take for the population to reach 100 wolves?

**86. Introducing a New Car Model.** If the number of new model Honda Accord hybrids purchased in North America is given by $N = \dfrac{100{,}000}{1 + 10e^{-2t}}$, where $t$ is the number of weeks after Honda releases the new model, how many weeks will it take after the release until there are 50,000 Honda hybrids from that batch on the road?

**87. Earthquakes.** A P wave measures 6.2 on the Richter scale, and an S wave measures 3.3 on the Richter scale. What is their combined measure on the Richter scale?

**88. Sound.** You and a friend get front row seats to a rock concert. The music level is 100 decibels, and your normal conversation is 60 decibels. If your friend is telling you something during the concert, how many decibels are you subjecting yourself to?

■ **CATCH THE MISTAKE**

**In Exercises 89–92, explain the mistake that is made.**

**89.** Solve the equation: $4e^x = 9$.

**Solution:**

Take the natural log of both sides.   $\ln(4e^x) = \ln 9$

Apply the property of inverses.   $4x = \ln 9$

Solve for $x$.   $x = \dfrac{\ln 9}{4} \approx 0.55$

This is incorrect. What mistake was made?

**90.** Solve the equation: $\log(x) + \log(3) = 1$.

**Solution:**

Apply the product property (5).   $\log(3x) = 1$

Exponentiate (base 10).   $10^{\log(3x)} = 1$

Apply the properties of inverses.   $3x = 1$

Solve for $x$.   $x = \dfrac{1}{3}$

This is incorrect. What mistake was made?

**91.** Solve the equation: $\log(x) + \log(x + 3) = 1$ for $x$.

**Solution:**

Apply the product property (5).   $\log(x^2 + 3x) = 1$

Exponentiate both sides (base 10).   $10^{\log(x^2 + 3x)} = 10^1$

Apply the property of inverses.   $x^2 + 3x = 10$

Factor.   $(x + 5)(x - 2) = 0$

Solve for $x$.   $x = -5$ and $x = 2$

This is incorrect. What mistake was made?

**92.** Solve the equation: $\log x + \log 2 = \log 5$.

**Solution:**

Combine the logarithms on the left.   $\log(x + 2) = \log 5$

Apply the property of one-to-one functions.   $x + 2 = 5$

Solve for $x$.   $x = 3$

This is incorrect. What mistake was made?

## ▪ CONCEPTUAL

**In Exercises 93–98, determine whether each statement is true or false.**

**93.** The sum of logarithms with the same base is equal to the logarithm of the product.

**94.** A logarithm squared is equal to two times the logarithm.

**95.** $e^{\log x} = x$

**96.** $e^x = -2$ has no solution.

**97.** $\log_3(x^2 + x - 6) = 1$ has two solutions.

**98.** The division of two logarithms with the same base is equal to the logarithm of the subtraction.

## ▪ CHALLENGE

**99.** Solve for $x$ in terms of $b$:

$$\frac{1}{3}\log_b(x^3) + \frac{1}{2}\log_b(x^2 - 2x + 1) = 2$$

**100.** Solve exactly:

$$2\log_b(x) + 2\log_b(1 - x) = 4$$

**101.** Solve $y = \dfrac{3000}{1 + 2e^{-0.2t}}$ for $t$ in terms of $y$.

**102.** State the range of values of $x$ that the following identity holds: $e^{\ln(x^2 - a)} = x^2 - a$.

**103.** A function called the hyperbolic cosine is defined as the average of exponential growth and exponential decay by $f(x) = \dfrac{e^x + e^{-x}}{2}$. If we restrict the domain of $f$ to $[0, \infty)$, find its inverse.

**104.** A function called the hyperbolic sine is defined by $f(x) = \dfrac{e^x - e^{-x}}{2}$. Find its inverse.

## ▪ TECHNOLOGY

**105.** Solve the equation $\ln 3x = \ln(x^2 + 1)$. Using a graphing calculator, plot the graphs $y = \ln(3x)$ and $y = \ln(x^2 + 1)$ in the same viewing rectangle. Zoom in on the point where the graphs intersect. Does this agree with your solution?

**106.** Solve the equation $10^{x^2} = 0.001^x$. Using a graphing calculator, plot the graphs $y = 10^{x^2}$ and $y = 0.001^x$ in the same viewing rectangle. Does this confirm your solution?

**107.** Use a graphing utility to help solve $3^x = 5x + 2$.

**108.** Use a graphing utility to help solve $\log x^2 = \ln(x - 3) + 2$.

**109.** Use a graphing utility to graph $y = \dfrac{e^x + e^{-x}}{2}$. State the domain. Determine whether there are any symmetry and asymptote.

**110.** Use a graphing utility to graph $y = \dfrac{e^x + e^{-x}}{e^x - e^{-x}}$. State the domain. Determine whether there are any symmetry and asymptote.

## ▪ PREVIEW TO CALCULUS

**111.** The hyperbolic sine function is defined by $\sinh x = \dfrac{e^x - e^{-x}}{2}$. Find its inverse function $\sinh^{-1} x$.

**112.** The hyperbolic tangent is defined by $\tanh x = \dfrac{e^x - e^{-x}}{e^x + e^{-x}}$. Find its inverse function $\tanh^{-1} x$.

**In Exercises 113–114, refer to the following:**

In calculus, to find the derivative of a function of the form $y = k^x$, where $k$ is a constant, we apply logarithmic differentiation. The first step in this process consists of writing $y = k^x$ in an equivalent form using the natural logarithm. Use the properties of this section to write an equivalent form of the following implicitly defined functions.

**113.** $y = 2^x$

**114.** $y = 4^x \cdot 3^{x+1}$

**SKILLS OBJECTIVES**

- Apply exponential growth and exponential decay models to biological, demographic, and economic phenomena.
- Represent distributions by means of a Gaussian model.
- Use logistic growth models to represent phenomena involving limits to growth.
- Solve problems such as species populations, credit card payoff, and wearoff of anesthesia through logarithmic models.

**CONCEPTUAL OBJECTIVE**

- Recognize exponential growth, exponential decay, Gaussian distributions, logistic growth, and logarithmic models.

The following table summarizes the five primary models that involve exponential and logarithmic functions:

| NAME | MODEL | GRAPH | APPLICATIONS |
|---|---|---|---|
| Exponential growth | $f(t) = ce^{kt} \quad k > 0$ | | World populations, bacteria growth, appreciation, global spread of the HIV virus |
| Exponential decay | $f(t) = ce^{-kt} \quad k > 0$ | | Radioactive decay, carbon dating, depreciation |
| Gaussian (normal) distribution | $f(x) = ce^{-(x-a)^2/k}$ | | Bell curve (grade distribution), life expectancy, height/weight charts, intensity of a laser beam, IQ tests |
| Logistic growth | $f(t) = \dfrac{a}{1 + ce^{-kt}}$ | | Conservation biology, learning curve, spread of virus on an island, carrying capacity |
| Logarithmic | $f(t) = a + c \log t$ <br> $f(t) = a + c \ln t$ | | Population of species, anesthesia wearing off, time to pay off credit cards |

# Exponential Growth Models

Quite often one will hear that something "grows exponentially," meaning that it grows very fast and at increasing speed. In mathematics, the precise meaning of **exponential growth** is a *growth rate of a function that is proportional to its current size*. Let's assume you get a 5% raise every year in a government job. If your annual starting salary out of college is $40,000, then your first raise will be $2000. Fifteen years later your annual salary will be approximately $83,000 and your next 5% raise will be around $4150. The raise is always 5% of the current salary, so the larger the current salary, the larger the raise.

In Section 3.1, we saw that interest that is compounded continuously is modeled by $A = Pe^{rt}$. Here $A$ stands for amount and $P$ stands for principal. There are similar models for populations; these take the form $N(t) = N_0e^{rt}$, where $N_0$ represents the number of people at time $t = 0$, $r$ is the annual growth rate, $t$ is time in years, and $N$ represents the number of people at time $t$. In general, any model of the form $f(x) = ce^{kx}$, $k > 0$, models exponential growth.

 **EXAMPLE 1   World Population Projections**

The world population is the total number of humans on Earth at a given time. In 2000 the world population was 6.1 billion and in 2005 the world population was 6.5 billion. Find the annual growth rate and determine what year the population will reach 9 billion.

**Solution:**

Assume an exponential growth model.                              $N(t) = N_0e^{rt}$

Let $t = 0$ correspond to 2000.                                  $N(0) = N_0 = 6.1$

In 2005, $t = 5$, the population was 6.5 billion.                $6.5 = 6.1e^{5r}$

Solve for $r$.                                                   $$\dfrac{6.5}{6.1} = e^{5r}$$

$$\ln\left(\dfrac{6.5}{6.1}\right) = \ln\left(e^{5r}\right)$$

$$\ln\left(\dfrac{6.5}{6.1}\right) = 5r$$

$$r \approx 0.012702681$$

The annual growth rate is approximately $\boxed{1.3\%}$ per year.

Assuming the growth rate stays the same, write a population model.           $N(t) = 6.1e^{0.013t}$

Let $N(t) = 9$.                                                              $9 = 6.1e^{0.013t}$

Solve for $t$.                                                              $$e^{0.013t} = \dfrac{9}{6.1}$$

$$\ln\left(e^{0.013t}\right) = \ln\left(\dfrac{9}{6.1}\right)$$

$$0.013t = \ln\left(\dfrac{9}{6.1}\right)$$

$$t \approx 29.91813894$$

In $\boxed{2030}$ the world population will reach 9 billion if the same growth rate is maintained.

■ **Answer:** 1% per year; 2115

■ **YOUR TURN**  The population of North America (United States and Canada) was 300 million in 1995, and in 2005 the North American population was 332 million. Find the annual growth rate (round to the nearest percent) and use that rounded growth rate to determine what year the population will reach 1 billion.

## Exponential Decay Models

We mentioned radioactive decay briefly in Section 3.1. Radioactive decay is the process in which a radioactive isotope of an element (atoms) loses energy by emitting radiation in the form of particles. This results in loss of mass of the isotope, which we measure as a reduction in the rate of radioactive emission. This process is random, but given a large number of atoms, the decay rate is directly proportional to the mass of the radioactive substance. Since the mass is decreasing, we say this represents *exponential decay*, $m = m_0 e^{-rt}$, where $m_0$ represents the initial mass at time $t = 0$, $r$ is the decay rate, $t$ is time, and $m$ represents the mass at time $t$. In general, any model of the form $f(x) = ce^{-kx}$, $k > 0$, models **exponential decay**.

Typically, the decay rate $r$ is expressed in terms of the half-life $h$. Recall (Section 3.1) that half-life is the time it takes for a quantity to decrease by half.

| WORDS | MATH |
|---|---|
| Write the radioactive decay model. | $m = m_0 e^{-rt}$ |
| Divide both sides by $m_0$. | $\dfrac{m}{m_0} = e^{-rt}$ |
| The remaining mass of the radioactive isotope is half of the initial mass when $t = h$. | $\dfrac{1}{2} = e^{-rh}$ |
| Solve for $r$. | |
| Take the natural logarithm of both sides. | $\ln\left(\dfrac{1}{2}\right) = \ln\left(e^{-rh}\right)$ |
| Simplify. | $\underbrace{\ln 1}_{0} - \ln 2 = -rh$ |
| | $rh = \ln 2$ |
| | $\boxed{r = \dfrac{\ln 2}{h}}$ |

### Technology Tip

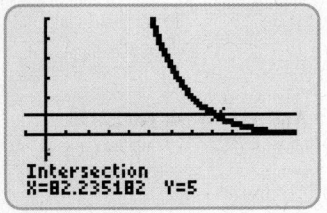

Graphs of $Y_1 = 500e^{-0.56x}$ with $x = t$ and $Y_2 = 5$ are shown.

```
Plot1 Plot2 Plot3
\Y1■500e^(-.056X
)
\Y2■5
```

```
Intersection
X=82.235182  Y=5
```

### EXAMPLE 2    Radioactive Decay

The radioactive isotope of potassium $^{42}$K, which is vital in the diagnosis of brain tumors, has a half-life of 12.36 hours.

**a.** Determine the exponential decay model that represents the mass of $^{42}$K.

**b.** If 500 milligrams of potassium-42 are taken, how many milligrams of this isotope will remain after 48 hours?

**c.** How long will it take for the original 500-milligram sample to decay to a mass of 5 milligrams?

**Solution (a):**

Write the relationship between rate of decay and half-life.     $r = \dfrac{\ln 2}{h}$

Let $h = 12.36$.     $r \approx 0.056$

Write the exponential decay model for the mass of $^{42}$K.     $\boxed{m = m_0 e^{-0.056t}}$

**Solution (b):**

Let $m_0 = 500$ and $t = 48$.                    $m = 500e^{-(0.056)(48)} \approx 34.00841855$

There are approximately ⬚ 34 milligrams ⬚ of $^{42}$K still in the body after 48 hours.

*Note:* Had we used the full value of $r = 0.056079868$, the resulting mass would have been $m = 33.8782897$, which is approximately 34 milligrams.

**Solution (c):**

Write the exponential decay model
for the mass of $^{42}$K.                          $m = m_0 e^{-0.056t}$

Let $m = 5$ and $m_0 = 500$.                        $5 = 500e^{-0.056t}$

Solve for $t$.

Divide by 500.                                      $e^{-0.056t} = \dfrac{5}{500} = \dfrac{1}{100}$

Take the natural logarithm
of both sides.                                      $\ln(e^{-0.056t}) = \ln\left(\dfrac{1}{100}\right)$

Simplify.                                           $-0.056t = \ln\left(\dfrac{1}{100}\right)$

Divide by $-0.056$ and approximate
with a calculator.                                  $t \approx 82.2352$

It will take approximately ⬚ 82 hours ⬚ for the original 500-milligram substance to decay to a mass of 5 milligrams.

- - - - - - - - - - - - - - - - - - - - - - - - - - - - - - - - - - - - - - - - -

■ **YOUR TURN**   The radioactive element radon-222 has a half-life of 3.8 days.

    **a.** Determine the exponential decay model that represents the mass of radon-222.

    **b.** How much of a 64-gram sample of radon-222 will remain after 7 days? Round to the nearest gram.

    **c.** How long will it take for the original 64-gram sample to decay to a mass of 4 grams? Round to the nearest day.

■ **Answer: a.** $m = m_0 e^{-0.1824t}$
        **b.** 18 g
        **c.** 15 days

## Gaussian (Normal) Distribution Models

If your instructor plots the grades from the last test, typically you will see a **Gaussian (normal) distribution** of scores, otherwise known as the *bell-shaped curve*. Other examples of phenomena that tend to follow a Gaussian distribution are SAT scores, height distributions of adults, and standardized tests like IQ assessments.

The graph to the right represents a Gaussian distribution of IQ scores. The average score, which for IQ is 100, is the $x$-value at which the maximum occurs. The typical probability distribution is

$$F(x) = \frac{1}{\sigma\sqrt{2\pi}}\, e^{-(x-\mu)^2/2\sigma^2}$$

where $\mu$ is the average or mean value and the variance is $\sigma^2$.

Any model of the form $f(x) = ce^{-(x-a)^2/k}$ is classified as a **Gaussian model**.

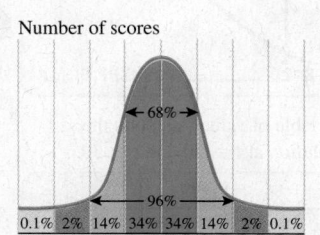

Number of scores

0.1% | 2% | 14% | 34% | 34% | 14% | 2% | 0.1%
55  70  85  100 115 130 145
Intelligence quotient
(Score on Wechsler Adult Intelligence Scale)

### EXAMPLE 3 Weight Distributions

Suppose each member of a Little League football team is weighed and the weight distribution follows the Gaussian model $f(x) = 10e^{-(x-100)^2/25}$.

**a.** Graph the weight distribution.
**b.** What is the average weight of a member of this team?
**c.** Approximately how many boys weigh 95 pounds?

**Solution:**

**a.**

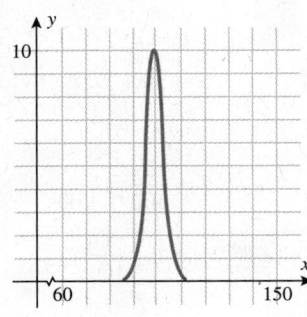

**b.** 100 pounds

**c.** $f(95) = 10e^{-(95-100)^2/25}$

$$= 10e^{-25/25}$$

$$= 10e^{-1}$$

$$\approx 3.6788$$

Approximately 4 boys weigh 95 pounds.

## Logistic Growth Models

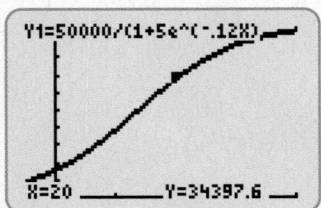

Earlier in this section, we discussed exponential growth models for populations that experience uninhibited growth. Now we will turn our attention to *logistic growth*, which models population growth when there are factors that impact the ability to grow, such as food and space. For example, if 10 rabbits are dropped off on an uninhabited island, they will reproduce and the population of rabbits on that island will experience rapid growth. The population will continue to increase rapidly until the rabbits start running out of space or food on the island. In other words, under favorable conditions the growth is not restricted, while under less favorable conditions the growth becomes restricted. This type of growth is represented by **logistic growth models**, $f(x) = \dfrac{a}{1 + ce^{-kx}}$. Ultimately, the population of rabbits reaches the island's *carrying capacity*, $a$.

### EXAMPLE 4 Number of Students on a College Campus

In 2008 the University of Central Florida was the sixth largest university in the country. The number of students can be modeled by the function

$$f(t) = \frac{50,000}{1 + 5e^{-0.12t}},$$ where $t$ is time in years and

$t = 0$ corresponds to 1970.

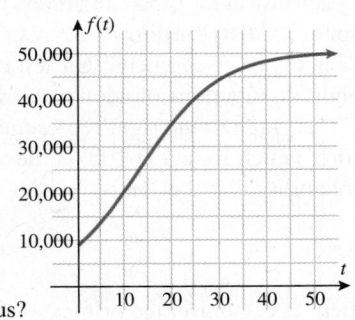

**a.** How many students attended UCF in 1990?
Round to the nearest thousand.
**b.** How many students attended UCF in 2000?
**c.** What is the carrying capacity of the UCF main campus?

Round all answers to the nearest thousand.

**Solution (a):** Let $t = 20$.     $f(20) = \dfrac{50{,}000}{1 + 5e^{-0.12(20)}} \approx \boxed{34{,}000}$

**Solution (b):** Let $t = 30$.     $f(30) = \dfrac{50{,}000}{1 + 5e^{-0.12(30)}} \approx \boxed{44{,}000}$

**Solution (c):** As $t$ increases, the UCF student population approaches $\boxed{50{,}000}$.

# Logarithmic Models

Homeowners typically ask the question, "If I increase my payment, how long will it take to pay off my current mortgage?" In general, a loan over $t$ years with an annual interest rate $r$ with $n$ periods per year corresponds to an interest rate per period of $i = \dfrac{r}{n}$. Typically, loans are paid in equal payments consisting of the principal $P$ plus total interest divided by the total number of periods over the life of the loan $nt$. The periodic payment $R$ is given by

$$R = P\,\dfrac{i}{1 - (1 + i)^{-nt}}$$

We can find the time (in years) it will take to pay off the loan as a function of periodic payment by solving for $t$.

| WORDS | MATH |
|---|---|
| Multiply both sides by $1 - (1 + i)^{-nt}$. | $R[1 - (1 + i)^{-nt}] = Pi$ |
| Eliminate the brackets. | $R - R(1 + i)^{-nt} = Pi$ |
| Subtract $R$. | $-R(1 + i)^{-nt} = Pi - R$ |
| Divide by $-R$. | $(1 + i)^{-nt} = 1 - \dfrac{Pi}{R}$ |
| Take the natural log of both sides. | $\ln(1 + i)^{-nt} = \ln\left(1 - \dfrac{Pi}{R}\right)$ |
| Use the power property for logarithms. | $-nt\ln(1 + i) = \ln\left(1 - \dfrac{Pi}{R}\right)$ |
| Isolate $t$. | $t = -\dfrac{\ln\left(1 - \dfrac{Pi}{R}\right)}{n\ln(1 + i)}$ |
| Let $i = \dfrac{r}{n}$. | $\boxed{t = -\dfrac{\ln\left(1 - \dfrac{Pr}{nR}\right)}{n\ln\left(1 + \dfrac{r}{n}\right)}}$ |

*Technology Tip*

Use the keystrokes [2nd] [Calc] [5:Intersect] to find the points of intersection.

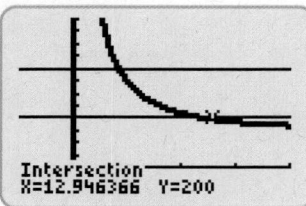

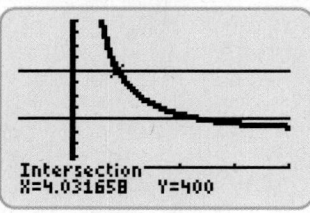

**EXAMPLE 5   Paying Off Credit Cards**

James owes $15,000 on his credit card. The annual interest rate is 13% compounded monthly.

**a.** Find the time it will take to pay off his credit card if he makes payments of $200 per month.

**b.** Find the time it will take to pay off his credit card if he makes payments of $400 per month.

Let $P = 15,000$, $r = 0.13$, and $n = 12$.

$$t = -\frac{\ln\left(1 - \dfrac{15,000(0.13)}{12R}\right)}{12\ln\left(1 + \dfrac{0.13}{12}\right)}$$

**Solution (a):** Let $R = 200$.

$$t = -\frac{\ln\left(1 - \dfrac{15,000(0.13)}{12(200)}\right)}{12\ln\left(1 + \dfrac{0.13}{12}\right)} \approx 13$$

$200 monthly payments will allow James to pay off his credit card in about $\boxed{13 \text{ years}}$.

**Solution (b):** Let $R = 400$.

$$t = -\frac{\ln\left(1 - \dfrac{15,000(0.13)}{12(400)}\right)}{12\ln\left(1 + \dfrac{0.13}{12}\right)} \approx 4$$

$400 monthly payments will allow James to pay off the balance in approximately $\boxed{4 \text{ years}}$. It is important to note that doubling the payment reduced the time to pay off the balance by less than a third.

---

**SECTION**
**3.5   SUMMARY**

In this section, we discussed five main types of models that involve exponential and logarithmic functions.

| NAME | MODEL | APPLICATIONS |
|---|---|---|
| Exponential growth | $f(t) = ce^{kt}, k > 0$ | Uninhibited growth (populations/inflation) |
| Exponential decay | $f(t) = ce^{-kt}, k > 0$ | Carbon dating, depreciation |
| Gaussian (normal) distributions | $f(x) = ce^{-(x-a)^2/k}$ | Bell curves (standardized tests, height/weight charts, distribution of power flux of laser beams) |
| Logistic growth | $f(t) = \dfrac{a}{1 + ce^{-kt}}$ | Conservation biology (growth limited by factors like food and space), learning curve |
| Logarithmic | $f(t) = a + c\log t$ <br> $f(t) = a + c\ln t$ <br> or quotients of logarithmic functions | Time to pay off credit cards, annuity planning |

■ **SKILLS**

In Exercises 1–6, match the function with the graph (a to f) and the model name (i to v).

**1.** $f(t) = 5e^{2t}$

**2.** $N(t) = 28e^{-t/2}$

**3.** $T(x) = 4e^{-(x-80)^2/10}$

**4.** $P(t) = \dfrac{200}{1 + 5e^{-0.4t}}$

**5.** $D(x) = 4 + \log(x - 1)$

**6.** $h(t) = 2 + \ln(t + 3)$

**Model Name**

**i.** Logarithmic      **ii.** Logistic      **iii.** Gaussian      **iv.** Exponential growth      **v.** Exponential decay

**Graphs**

**a.**

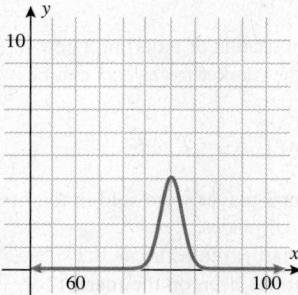

**b.**

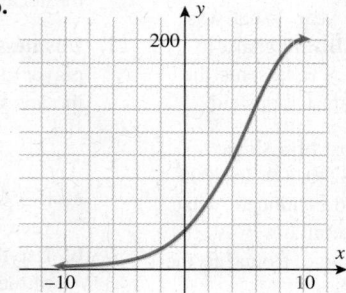

**c.**

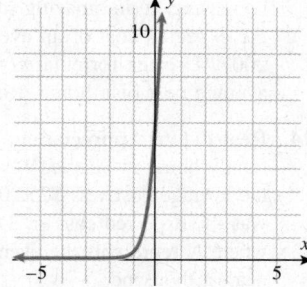

**d.**

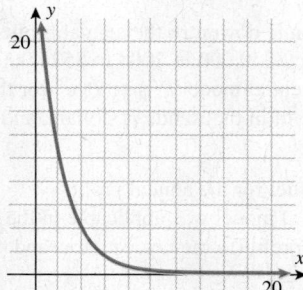

**e.**

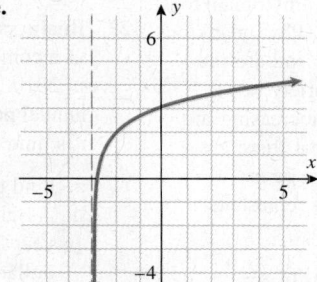

**f.**

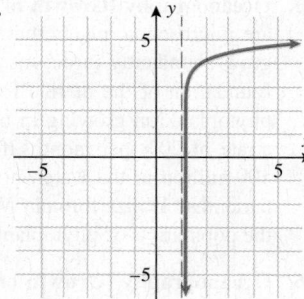

■ **APPLICATIONS**

**7. Population Growth.** The population of the Philippines in 2003 was 80 million. It increases 2.36% per year. What was the expected population of the Philippines in 2010? Apply the formula $N = N_0 e^{rt}$, where $N$ represents the number of people.

**8. Population Growth.** China's urban population is growing at 2.5% a year, compounding continuously. If there were 13.7 million people in Shanghai in 1996, approximately how many people will there be in 2016? Apply the formula $N = N_0 e^{rt}$, where $N$ represents the number of people.

**9. Population Growth.** Port St. Lucie, Florida, had the United States' fastest growth rate among cities with a population of 100,000 or more between 2003 and 2004. In 2003 the population was 103,800 and increasing at a rate of 12% per year. In what year should the population reach 200,000? (Let $t = 0$ correspond to 2003.) Apply the formula $N = N_0 e^{rt}$, where $N$ represents the number of people.

**10. Population Growth.** San Francisco's population has been declining since the "dot com" bubble burst. In 2002 the population was 776,000. If the population is declining at a rate of 1.5% per year, in what year will the population be 700,000? (Let $t = 0$ correspond to 2002.) Apply the formula $N = N_0 e^{-rt}$, where $N$ represents the number of people.

11. **Cellular Phone Plans.** The number of cell phones in China is exploding. In 2007 there were 487.4 million cell phone subscribers, and the number is increasing at a rate of 16.5% per year. How many cell phone subscribers were there in 2010 according to this model? Use the formula $N = N_0 e^{rt}$, where $N$ represents the number of cell phone subscribers. Let $t = 0$ correspond to 2007.

12. **Bacteria Growth.** A colony of bacteria is growing exponentially. Initially, 500 bacteria were in the colony. The growth rate is 20% per hour. (a) How many bacteria should be in the colony in 12 hours? (b) How many in 1 day? Use the formula $N = N_0 e^{rt}$, where $N$ represents the number of bacteria.

13. **Real Estate Appreciation.** In 2004 the average house in Birmingham, AL cost $185,000, and real estate prices were increasing at an amazing rate of 30% per year. What was the expected cost of an average house in Birmingham in 2007? Use the formula $N = N_0 e^{rt}$, where $N$ represents the average cost of a home. Round to the nearest thousand.

14. **Real Estate Appreciation.** The average cost of a single family home in Seattle, WA in 2004 was $230,000. In 2005 the average cost was $252,000. If this trend continued, what was the expected cost in 2007? Use the formula $N = N_0 e^{rt}$, where $N$ represents the average cost of a home. Round to the nearest thousand.

15. **Oceanography (Growth of Phytoplankton).** Phytoplankton are microscopic plants that live in the ocean. Phytoplankton grow abundantly in oceans around the world and are the foundation of the marine food chain. One variety of phytoplankton growing in tropical waters is increasing at a rate of 20% per month. If it is estimated that there are 100 million in the water, how many will there be in 6 months? Utilize formula $N = N_0 e^{rt}$, where $N$ represents the population of phytoplankton.

16. **Oceanography (Growth of Phytoplankton).** In Arctic waters there are an estimated 50,000,000 phytoplankton. The growth rate is 12% per month. How many phytoplankton will there be in 3 months? Utilize formula $N = N_0 e^{rt}$, where $N$ represents the population of phytoplankton.

17. **HIV/AIDS.** In 2003 an estimated 1 million people had been infected with HIV in the United States. If the infection rate increases at an annual rate of 2.5% a year compounding continuously, how many Americans will be infected with the HIV virus by 2015?

18. **HIV/AIDS.** In 2003 there were an estimated 25 million people who have been infected with HIV in sub-Saharan Africa. If the infection rate increases at an annual rate of 9% a year compounding continuously, how many Africans will be infected with the HIV virus by 2015?

19. **Anesthesia.** When a person has a cavity filled, the dentist typically gives a local anesthetic. After leaving the dentist's office, one's mouth often is numb for several more hours. If 100 milliliters of anesthesia is injected into the local tissue at the time of the procedure ($t = 0$), and the amount of anesthesia still in the local tissue $t$ hours after the initial injection is given by $A = 100e^{-0.5t}$, how much remains in the local tissue 4 hours later?

20. **Anesthesia.** When a person has a cavity filled, the dentist typically gives a local anesthetic. After leaving the dentist's office, one's mouth often is numb for several more hours. If 100 milliliters of anesthesia is injected into the local tissue at the time of the procedure ($t = 0$), and the amount of anesthesia still in the local tissue $t$ hours after the initial injection is given by $A = 100e^{-0.5t}$, how much remains in the local tissue 12 hours later?

21. **Business.** The sales $S$ (in thousands of units) of a new mp3 player after it has been on the market for $t$ years can be modeled by

$$S(t) = 750(1 - e^{-kt})$$

a. If 350,000 units of the mp3 player were sold in the first year, find $k$ to four decimal places.
b. Use the model found in part (a) to estimate the sales of the mp3 player after it has been on the market for 3 years.

22. **Business.** During an economic downturn the annual profits of a company dropped from $850,000 in 2008 to $525,000 in 2010. Assume the exponential model $P(t) = P_0 e^{kt}$ for the annual profit where $P$ is profit in thousands of dollars, and $t$ is time in years.

a. Find the exponential model for the annual profit.
b. Assuming the exponential model was applicable in the year 2012, estimate the profit (to the nearest thousand dollars) for the year 2012.

23. **Radioactive Decay.** Carbon-14 has a half-life of 5730 years. How long will it take 5 grams of carbon-14 to be reduced to 2 grams?

24. **Radioactive Decay.** Radium-226 has a half-life of 1600 years. How long will it take 5 grams of radium-226 to be reduced to 2 grams?

25. **Radioactive Decay.** The half-life of uranium-238 is 4.5 billion years. If 98% of uranium-238 remains in a fossil, how old is the fossil?

26. **Decay Levels in the Body.** A drug has a half-life of 12 hours. If the initial dosage is 5 milligrams, how many milligrams will be in the patient's body in 16 hours?

**In Excercises 27–30, use the following formula for Newton's Law of Cooling:**

If you take a hot dinner out of the oven and place it on the kitchen countertop, the dinner cools until it reaches the temperature of the kitchen. Likewise, a glass of ice set on a table in a room eventually melts into a glass of water at that room temperature. The rate at which the hot dinner cools or the ice in the glass melts at any given time is proportional to the difference between its temperature and the temperature of its surroundings (in this case, the room). This is called **Newton's law of cooling** (or warming) and is modeled by

$$T = T_S + (T_0 - T_S)e^{-kt}$$

where $T$ is the temperature of an object at time $t$, $T_s$ is the temperature of the surrounding medium, $T_0$ is the temperature of the object at time $t = 0$, $t$ is the time, and $k$ is a constant.

27. **Newton's Law of Cooling.** An apple pie is taken out of the oven with an internal temperature of 325°F. It is placed on a rack in a room with a temperature of 72°F. After 10 minutes, the temperature of the pie is 200°F. What will the temperature of the pie be 30 minutes after coming out of the oven?

28. **Newton's Law of Cooling.** A cold drink is taken out of an ice chest with a temperature of 38°F and placed on a picnic table with a surrounding temperature of 75°F. After 5 minutes, the temperature of the drink is 45°F. What will the temperature of the drink be 20 minutes after it is taken out of the chest?

29. **Forensic Science (Time of Death).** A body is discovered in a hotel room. At 7:00 A.M. a police detective found the body's temperature to be 85°F. At 8:30 A.M. a medical examiner measures the body's temperature to be 82°F. Assuming the room in which the body was found had a constant temperature of 74°F, how long has the victim been dead? (Normal body temperature is 98.6°F.)

30. **Forensic Science (Time of Death).** At 4 A.M. a body is found in a park. The police measure the body's temperature to be 90°F. At 5 A.M. the medical examiner arrives and determines the temperature to be 86°F. Assuming the temperature of the park was constant at 60°F, how long has the victim been dead?

31. **Depreciation of Automobile.** A new Lexus IS250 has a book value of $38,000, and after 1 year has a book value of $32,000. What is the car's value in 4 years? Apply the formula $N = N_0 e^{-rt}$, where $N$ represents the value of the car. Round to the nearest hundred.

32. **Depreciation of Automobile.** A new Hyundai Triburon has a book value of $22,000, and after 2 years a book value of $14,000. What is the car's value in 4 years? Apply the formula $N = N_0 e^{-rt}$, where $N$ represents the value of the car. Round to the nearest hundred.

33. **Automotive.** A new model BMW convertible coupe is designed and produced in time to appear in North America in the fall. BMW Corporation has a limited number of new models available. The number of new model BMW convertible coupes purchased in North America is given by $N = \dfrac{100,000}{1 + 10e^{-2t}}$, where $t$ is the number of weeks after the BMW is released.

   a. How many new model BMW convertible coupes will have been purchased 2 weeks after the new model becomes available?
   b. How many after 30 weeks?
   c. What is the maximum number of new model BMW convertible coupes that will be sold in North America?

34. **iPhone.** The number of iPhones purchased is given by $N = \dfrac{2,000,000}{1 + 2e^{-4t}}$, where $t$ is the time in weeks after they are made available for purchase.

   a. How many iPhones are purchased within the first 2 weeks?
   b. How many iPhones are purchased within the first month?

35. **Spread of a Disease.** The number of MRSA (methicillin-resistant *Staphylococcus aureus*) cases has been rising sharply in England and Wales since 1997. In 1997, 2422 cases were reported. The number of cases reported in 2003 was 7684. How many cases might be expected in 2010? (Let $t = 0$ correspond to 1997.) Use the formula $N = N_0 e^{-rt}$, where $N$ represents the number of cases reported.

36. **Spread of a Virus.** Dengue fever, an illness carried by mosquitoes, is occurring in one of the worst outbreaks in decades across Latin America and the Caribbean. In 2004, 300,000 cases were reported, and 630,000 cases in 2007. How many cases in 2010? (Let $t = 0$ be 2004.) Use the formula $N = N_0 e^{-rt}$, where $N$ represents the number of cases.

37. **Carrying Capacity.** The Virginia Department of Fish and Game stock a mountain lake with 500 trout. Officials believe the lake can support no more than 10,000 trout. The number of trout is given by $N = \dfrac{10,000}{1 + 19e^{-1.56t}}$, where $t$ is time in years. How many years will it take for the trout population to reach 5000?

38. **Carrying Capacity.** The World Wildlife Fund has placed 1000 rare pygmy elephants in a conservation area in Borneo. They believe 1600 pygmy elephants can be supported in this environment. The number of elephants is given by $N = \dfrac{1600}{1 + 0.6e^{-0.14t}}$, where $t$ is time in years. How many years will it take the herd to reach 1200 elephants?

**39. Lasers.** The intensity of a laser beam is given by the ratio of power to area. A particular laser beam has an intensity function given by $I = e^{-r^2}$ mW/cm$^2$, where $r$ is the radius off the center axis given in centimeters. Where is the beam brightest (largest intensity)?

**40. Lasers.** The intensity of a laser beam is given by the ratio of power to area. A particular laser beam has an intensity function given by $I = e^{-r^2}$ mW/cm$^2$, where $r$ is the radius off the center axis given in centimeters. What percentage of the on-axis intensity ($r = 0$) corresponds to $r = 2$ cm?

**41. Grade Distribution.** Suppose the first test in this class has a normal, or bell-shaped, grade distribution of test scores, with an average score of 75. An approximate function that models your class's grades on test 1 is $N(x) = 10e^{-(x-75)^2/25^2}$, where $N$ represents the number of students who received the score $x$.

   **a.** Graph this function.
   **b.** What is the average grade?
   **c.** Approximately how many students scored a 50?
   **d.** Approximately how many students scored 100?

**42. Grade Distribution.** Suppose the final exam in this class has a normal, or bell-shaped, grade distribution of exam scores, with an average score of 80. An approximate function that models your class's grades on the exam is $N(x) = 10e^{-(x-80)^2/16^2}$, where $N$ represents the number of students who received the score $x$.

   **a.** Graph this function.
   **b.** What is the average grade?
   **c.** Approximately how many students scored a 60?
   **d.** Approximately how many students scored 100?

**43. Time to Pay Off Debt.** Diana just graduated from medical school owing $80,000 in student loans. The annual interest rate is 9%.

   **a.** Approximately how many years will it take to pay off her student loan if she makes a monthly payment of $750?
   **b.** Approximately how many years will it take to pay off her loan if she makes a monthly payment of $1000?

**44. Time to Pay Off Debt.** Victor owes $20,000 on his credit card. The annual interest rate is 17%.

   **a.** Approximately how many years will it take him to pay off this credit card if he makes a monthly payment of $300?
   **b.** Approximately how many years will it take him to pay off this credit card if he makes a monthly payment of $400?

**For Exercises 45 and 46, refer to the following:**

A local business borrows $200,000 to purchase property. The loan has an annual interest rate of 8% compounded monthly and a minimum monthly payment of $1467.

**45. Time to Pay Off Debt/Business.**

   **a.** Approximately how many years will it take the business to pay off the loans if only the minimum payment is made?
   **b.** How much interest will the business pay over the life of the loan if only the minimum payment is made?

**46. Time to Pay Off Debt/Business.**

   **a.** Approximately how many years will it take the business to pay off the loan if the minimum payment is doubled?
   **b.** How much interest will the business pay over the life of the loan if the minimum payment is doubled?
   **c.** How much in interest will the business save by doubling the minimum payment (see Exercise 45, part b)?

## ▪ CATCH THE MISTAKE

**In Exercises 47 and 48, explain the mistake that is made.**

**47.** The city of Orlando, Florida, has a population that is growing at 7% a year, compounding continuously. If there were 1.1 million people in greater Orlando in 2006, approximately how many people will there be in 2016? Apply the formula $N = N_0 e^{rt}$, where $N$ represents the number of people.

**Solution:**

Use the population growth model. $\qquad N = N_0 e^{rt}$

Let $N_0 = 1.1$, $r = 7$, and $t = 10$. $\qquad N = 1.1e^{(7)(10)}$

Approximate with a calculator. $\qquad 2.8 \times 10^{30}$

This is incorrect. What mistake was made?

**48.** The city of San Antonio, Texas, has a population that is growing at 5% a year, compounding continuously. If there were 1.3 million people in the greater San Antonio area in 2006, approximately how many people will there be in 2016? Apply the formula $N = N_0 e^{rt}$, where $N$ represents the number of people.

**Solution:**

Use the population growth model. $\qquad N = N_0 e^{rt}$

Let $N_0 = 1.3$, $r = 5$, and $t = 10$. $\qquad N = 1.3e^{(5)(10)}$

Approximate with a calculator. $\qquad 6.7 \times 10^{21}$

This is incorrect. What mistake was made?

■ **CONCEPTUAL**

**In Exercises 49–52, determine whether each statement is true or false.**

49. When a species gets placed on an endangered species list, the species begins to grow rapidly, and then reaches a carrying capacity. This can be modeled by logistic growth.

50. A professor has 400 students one semester. The number of names (of her students) she is able to memorize can be modeled by a logarithmic function.

51. The spread of lice at an elementary school can be modeled by exponential growth.

52. If you purchase a laptop computer this year ($t = 0$), then the value of the computer can be modeled with exponential decay.

■ **CHALLENGE**

**In Exercises 53 and 54, refer to the logistic model $f(t) = \dfrac{a}{1 + ce^{-kt}}$, where $a$ is the carrying capacity.**

53. As $c$ increases, does the model reach the carrying capacity in less time or more time?

54. As $k$ increases, does the model reach the carrying capacity in less time or more time?

55. A culture of 100 bacteria grows at a rate of 20% every day. Two days later, 60 of the same type of bacteria are placed in a culture that allows a 30% daily growth rate. After how many days do both cultures have the same population?

56. Consider the quotient $Q = \dfrac{P_1 e^{r_1 t}}{P_2 e^{r_2 t}}$ of two models of exponential growth.

   **a.** If $r_1 > r_2$, what can you say about $Q$?

   **b.** If $r_1 < r_2$, what can you say about $Q$?

57. Consider the models of exponential decay $f(t) = (2 + c)e^{-k_1 t}$ and $g(t) = ce^{-k_2 t}$. Suppose that $f(1) = g(1)$, what is the relationship between $k_1$ and $k_2$?

58. Suppose that both logistic growth models $f(t) = \dfrac{a_1}{1 + c_1 e^{-k_1 t}}$ and $g(t) = \dfrac{a_2}{1 + c_2 e^{-k_2 t}}$ have horizontal asymptote $y = 100$.

   What can you say about the corresponding carrying capacities?

■ **TECHNOLOGY**

59. Wing Shan just graduated from dental school owing $80,000 in student loans. The annual interest is 6%. Her time $t$ to pay off the loan is given by

$$t = -\frac{\ln\left[1 - \dfrac{80,000(0.06)}{nR}\right]}{n \ln\left(1 + \dfrac{0.06}{n}\right)}$$

where $n$ is the number of payment periods per year and $R$ is the periodic payment.

**a.** Use a graphing utility to graph

$$t_1 = -\frac{\ln\left[1 - \dfrac{80,000(0.06)}{12x}\right]}{12 \ln\left(1 + \dfrac{0.06}{12}\right)} \text{ as } Y_1 \text{ and}$$

$$t_2 = -\frac{\ln\left[1 - \dfrac{80,000(0.06)}{26x}\right]}{26 \ln\left(1 + \dfrac{0.06}{26}\right)} \text{ as } Y_2.$$

Explain the difference in the two graphs.

**b.** Use the ⟨TRACE⟩ key to estimate the number of years that it will take Wing Shan to pay off her student loan if she can afford a monthly payment of $800.

**c.** If she can make a biweekly payment of $400, estimate the number of years that it will take her to pay off the loan.

**d.** If she adds $200 more to her monthly or $100 more to her biweekly payment, estimate the number of years that it will take her to pay off the loan.

**60.** Amy has a credit card debt in the amount of $12,000. The annual interest is 18%. Her time $t$ to pay off the loan is given by

$$t = -\frac{\ln\left[1 - \dfrac{12,000(0.18)}{nR}\right]}{n\ln\left(1 + \dfrac{0.18}{n}\right)}$$

where $n$ is the number of payment periods per year and $R$ is the periodic payment.

**a.** Use a graphing utility to graph

$$t_1 = -\frac{\ln\left[1 - \dfrac{12,000(0.18)}{12x}\right]}{12\ln\left(1 + \dfrac{0.18}{12}\right)} \text{ as } Y_1 \text{ and}$$

$$t_2 = -\frac{\ln\left[1 - \dfrac{12,000(0.18)}{26x}\right]}{26\ln\left(1 + \dfrac{0.18}{26}\right)} \text{ as } Y_2.$$

Explain the difference in the two graphs.

**b.** Use the TRACE key to estimate the number of years that it will take Amy to pay off her credit card if she can afford a monthly payment of $300.

**c.** If she can make a biweekly payment of $150, estimate the number of years that it will take her to pay off the credit card.

**d.** If Amy adds $100 more to her monthly or $50 more to her biweekly payment, estimate the number of years that it will take her to pay off the credit card.

**PREVIEW TO CALCULUS**

**In Exercises 61–64, refer to the following:**

In calculus, we find the derivative, $f'(x)$, of a function $f(x)$ by allowing $h$ to approach 0 in the difference quotient $\dfrac{f(x+h)-f(x)}{h}$ of functions involving exponential functions.

**61.** Find the difference quotient of the exponential growth model $f(x) = Pe^{kx}$, where $P$ and $k$ are positive constants.

**62.** Find the difference quotient of the exponential decay model $f(x) = Pe^{-kx}$, where $P$ and $k$ are positive constants.

**63.** Use the fact that $\dfrac{e^h - 1}{h} = 1$ when $h$ is close to zero to find the derivative of $f(x) = e^x + x$.

**64.** Find the difference quotient of $f(x) = \cosh x$ and use it to prove that $(\cosh x)' = \sinh x$.

# CHAPTER 3 INQUIRY-BASED LEARNING PROJECT

Among other ideas, in Chapters 1 and 2 you studied functions and their inverses. For instance, you worked with this familiar quadratic function: $y = x^2$. In words, this means "squaring $x$ equals $y$." The equation of its inverse function can be written $x = y^2$; "squaring $y$ equals $x$." Of course, we call $y$ the "square root of $x$." In order to write this relationship with $y$ in terms of $x$, mathematicians devised the symbol for square root, and so we write $y = \sqrt{x}$.

Keep these ideas in mind as you look now at an exponential function and the need to define a new function and new symbol for its inverse.

**1.** Lef $f$ be the base 10 exponential function, $f(x) = 10^x$.

**a.** Graph the exponential function $y = 10^x$ by plotting points.

| x | y |
|---|---|
| −3 | |
| −2 | |
| −1 | |
| 0 | |
| 1 | |
| 2 | |
| 3 | |

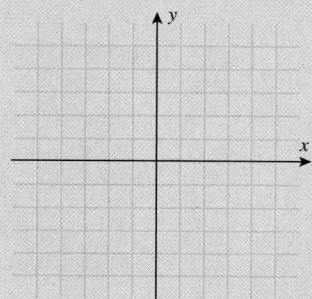

**b.** Discuss whether or not $f(x) = 10^x$ has an inverse function. How did you determine this?

**c.** Using the definition of inverse function, complete the table below for the function $y = f^{-1}(x)$. Then plot the points to make a graph.

| x | y |
|---|---|
| | |
| | |
| | |
| | |
| | |
| | |

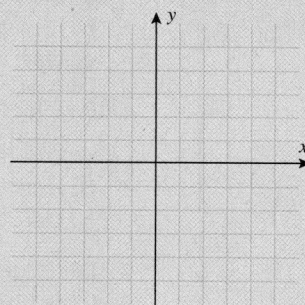

**d.** In part (a) $y = 10^x$, so we could say, "10 to the power of x equals $y$." Write a similar statement about the inverse relationship between x and y in part (d). How would you write this as an equation?

**2.** If you wanted to obtain the graph of $y = f^{-1}(x)$ using your graphing calculator, you would need to solve for $y$ in the equation you wrote in part (d) above. To this end, we need a new symbol to represent the relationship $x = 10^y$. We will call $y$ the "base 10 logarithm of $x$" and write $y = \log_{10}(x)$.

**a.** The base 10 logarithm is also called the common logarithm. Use the "log" key on your graphing calculator to graph $y = \log_{10}(x)$. How does this graph differ from the one you sketched in part 1(c)?

**b.** What are the domain and range of $y = \log_{10}(x)$?

# MODELING OUR WORLD

The following table summarizes the average yearly temperature in degrees Fahrenheit (°F) and carbon dioxide emissions in parts per million (ppm) for **Mauna Loa, Hawaii**.

| YEAR | 1960 | 1965 | 1970 | 1975 | 1980 | 1985 | 1990 | 1995 | 2000 | 2005 |
|---|---|---|---|---|---|---|---|---|---|---|
| TEMPERATURE | 44.45 | 43.29 | 43.61 | 43.35 | 46.66 | 45.71 | 45.53 | 47.53 | 45.86 | 46.23 |
| $CO_2$ EMISSIONS (PPM) | 316.9 | 320.0 | 325.7 | 331.1 | 338.7 | 345.9 | 354.2 | 360.6 | 369.4 | 379.7 |

In the Modeling Our World in Chapters 1 and 2, the temperature and carbon emissions were modeled with *linear functions* and *polynomial functions*, respectively. Now, let us model these same data using *exponential* and *logarithmic functions*.

1. Plot the temperature data, with time on the horizontal axis and temperature on the vertical axis. Let $t = 1$ correspond to 1960.

2. Find a *logarithmic function* with base $e$, $f(t) = A \ln (Bt)$, that models the temperature in Mauna Loa.

   a. Apply data from 1965 and 2005.
   b. Apply data from 2000 and 2005.
   c. Apply regression and all data given.

3. Predict what the temperature will be in Mauna Loa in 2020.

   a. Use the line found in Exercise 2(a).
   b. Use the line found in Exercise 2(b).
   c. Use the line found in Exercise 2(c).

4. Predict what the temperature will be in Mauna Loa in 2100.

   a. Use the line found in Exercise 2(a).
   b. Use the line found in Exercise 2(b).
   c. Use the line found in Exercise 2(c).

5. Do your models support the claim of "global warming"? Explain. Do these logarithmic models give similar predictions to the linear models found in Chapter 1 and the polynomial models found in Chapter 2?

6. Plot the carbon dioxide emissions data, with time on the horizontal axis and carbon dioxide emissions on the vertical axis. Let $t = 0$ correspond to 1960.

7. Find an *exponential function* with base $e$, $f(t) = Ae^{bt}$, that models the $CO_2$ emissions (ppm) in Mauna Loa.

   a. Apply data from 1960 and 2005.
   b. Apply data from 1960 and 2000.
   c. Apply regression and all data given.

**8.** Predict the expected $CO_2$ levels in Mauna Loa in 2020.

  **a.** Use the line found in Exercise 7(a).
  **b.** Use the line found in Exercise 7(b).
  **c.** Use the line found in Exercise 7(c).

**9.** Predict the expected $CO_2$ levels in Mauna Loa in 2100.

  **a.** Use the line found in Exercise 7(a).
  **b.** Use the line found in Exercise 7(b).
  **c.** Use the line found in Exercise 7(c).

**10.** Do your models support the claim of "global warming"? Explain. Do these exponential models give similar predictions to the linear models found in Chapter 1 or the polynomial models found in Chapter 2?

**11.** Comparing the models developed in Chapters 1 and 2, do you believe that global temperatures are best modeled with a linear, polynomial, or logarithmic function?

**12.** Comparing the models developed in Chapters 1 and 2, do you believe that $CO_2$ emissions are best modeled by linear, polynomial, or exponential functions?

# CHAPTER 3 REVIEW

| SECTION | CONCEPT | KEY IDEAS/FORMULAS |
|---|---|---|
| 3.1 | **Exponential functions and their graphs** | |
| | Evaluating exponential functions | $f(x) = b^x \qquad b > 0, b \neq 1$ |
| | Graphs of exponential functions | $y$-intercept $(0, 1)$ $\qquad$ Horizontal asymptote: $y = 0$; the points $(1, b)$ and $(-1, 1/b)$ |
| | The natural base $e$ | $f(x) = e^x$ |
| | Applications of exponential functions | Doubling time: $P = P_0 2^{t/d}$ <br><br> Compound interest: $A = P\left(1 + \dfrac{r}{n}\right)^{nt}$ <br><br> Compounded continuously: $A = Pe^{rt}$ |
| 3.2 | **Logarithmic functions and their graphs** | $y = \log_b x \qquad x > 0$ <br> $b > 0, b \neq 1$ |
| | Evaluating logarithms | $y = \log_b x$ and $x = b^y$ |
| | Common and natural logarithms | $y = \log x \qquad$ Common (base 10) <br> $y = \ln x \qquad$ Natural (base $e$) |
| | Graphs of logarithmic functions | $x$-intercept $(1, 0)$ $\qquad$ Vertical asymptote: $x = 0$; the points $(b, 1)$ and $(1/b, -1)$ |
| | Applications of logarithms | Decibel scale: <br><br> $D = 10 \log\left(\dfrac{I}{I_T}\right) \qquad I_T = 1 \times 10^{-12}\ \text{W/m}^2$ <br><br> Richter scale: <br><br> $M = \dfrac{2}{3} \log\left(\dfrac{E}{E_0}\right) \qquad E_0 = 10^{4.4}$ joules |
| 3.3 | **Properties of logarithms** | |
| | Properties of logarithms | 1. $\log_b 1 = 0$ <br> 2. $\log_b b = 1$ <br> 3. $\log_b b^x = x$ <br> 4. $b^{\log_b x} = x \qquad x > 0$ <br> Product property: <br> 5. $\log_b MN = \log_b M + \log_b N$ <br> Quotient property: <br> 6. $\log_b\left(\dfrac{M}{N}\right) = \log_b M - \log_b N$ <br> Power property: <br> 7. $\log_b M^p = p \log_b M$ |
| | Change-of-base formula | $\log_b M = \dfrac{\log M}{\log b} \quad$ or $\quad \log_b M = \dfrac{\ln M}{\ln b}$ |

| SECTION | CONCEPT | KEY IDEAS/FORMULAS |
|---------|---------|--------------------|
| 3.4 | **Exponential and logarithmic equations** | |
| | Solving exponential equations | *Simple exponential equations* |
| | | 1. Rewrite both sides of the equation in terms of the same base. |
| | | 2. Use the one-to-one property to equate the exponents. |
| | | 3. Solve for the variable. |
| | | *Complicated exponential equations* |
| | | 1. Isolate the exponential expression. |
| | | 2. Take the same logarithm of both sides. |
| | | 3. Simplify using the inverse properties. |
| | | 4. Solve for the variable. |
| | Solving logarithmic equations | *Simple logarithmic equations* |
| | | 1. Combine logarithms on each side of the equation using properties. |
| | | 2. Use the one-to-one property to equate the exponents. |
| | | 3. Solve for the variable. |
| | | 4. Check the results and eliminate any extraneous solutions. |
| | | *Complicated logarithmic equations* |
| | | 1. Combine and isolate the logarithmic expressions. |
| | | 2. Rewrite the equation in exponential form. |
| | | 3. Solve for the variable. |
| | | 4. Check the results and eliminate any extraneous solutions. |
| 3.5 | **Exponential and logarithmic models** | |
| | Exponential growth models | $f(x) = ce^{kx} \quad k > 0$ |
| | Exponential decay models | $f(x) = ce^{-kx} \quad k > 0$ |
| | Gaussian (normal) distribution models | $f(x) = ce^{-(x-a)^2/k}$ |
| | Logistic growth models | $f(x) = \dfrac{a}{1 + ce^{-kx}}$ |
| | Logarithmic models | $f(x) = a + c \log x$ $f(x) = a + c \ln x$ |

## 3.1 Exponential Functions and Their Graphs

**Approximate each number using a calculator and round your answer to two decimal places.**

**1.** $8^{4.7}$    **2.** $\pi^{2/5}$    **3.** $4 \cdot 5^{0.2}$    **4.** $1.2^{1.2}$

**Approximate each number using a calculator and round your answer to two decimal places.**

**5.** $e^{3.2}$    **6.** $e^{\pi}$    **7.** $e^{\sqrt{\pi}}$    **8.** $e^{-2.5\sqrt{3}}$

**Evaluate each exponential function for the given values.**

**9.** $f(x) = 2^{4-x}$        $f(-2.2)$

**10.** $f(x) = -2^{x+4}$        $f(1.3)$

**11.** $f(x) = \left(\frac{2}{5}\right)^{1-6x}$        $f\left(\frac{1}{2}\right)$

**12.** $f(x) = \left(\frac{4}{7}\right)^{5x+1}$        $f\left(\frac{1}{5}\right)$

**Match the graph with the function.**

**13.** $y = 2^{x-2}$      **14.** $y = -2^{2-x}$

**15.** $y = 2 + 3^{x+2}$      **16.** $y = -2 - 3^{2-x}$

**a.**

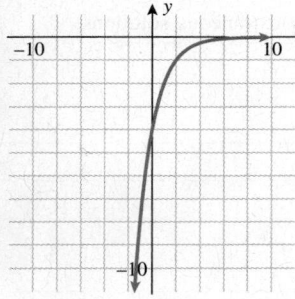

**b.**

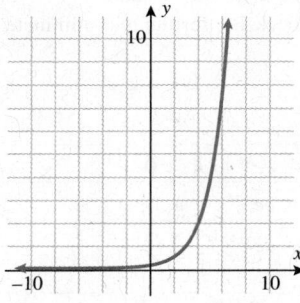

**c.**

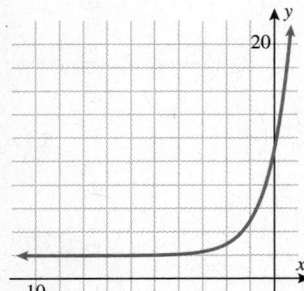

**d.**

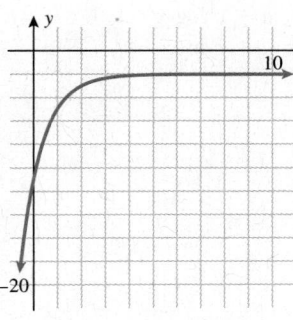

**State the y-intercept and the horizontal asymptote, and graph the exponential function.**

**17.** $y = -6^{-x}$      **18.** $y = 4 - 3^x$

**19.** $y = 1 + 10^{-2x}$      **20.** $y = 4^x - 4$

**State the y-intercept and horizontal asymptote, and graph the exponential function.**

**21.** $y = e^{-2x}$      **22.** $y = e^{x-1}$

**23.** $y = 3.2e^{x/3}$      **24.** $y = 2 - e^{1-x}$

## Applications

**25. Compound Interest.** If $4500 is deposited into an account paying 4.5% compounding semiannually, how much will you have in the account in 7 years?

**26. Compound Interest.** How much money should be put in a savings account now that earns 4.0% a year compounded quarterly if you want $25,000 in 8 years?

**27. Compound Interest.** If $13,450 is put in a money market account that pays 3.6% a year compounded continuously, how much will be in the account in 15 years?

**28. Compound Interest.** How much money should be invested today in a money market account that pays 2.5% a year compounded continuously if you desire $15,000 in 10 years?

## 3.2 Logarithmic Functions and Their Graphs

**Write each logarithmic equation in its equivalent exponential form.**

**29.** $\log_4 64 = 3$      **30.** $\log_4 2 = \frac{1}{2}$

**31.** $\log\left(\frac{1}{100}\right) = -2$      **32.** $\log_{16} 4 = \frac{1}{2}$

**Write each exponential equation in its equivalent logarithmic form.**

**33.** $6^3 = 216$      **34.** $10^{-4} = 0.0001$

**35.** $\frac{4}{169} = \left(\frac{2}{13}\right)^2$      **36.** $\sqrt[3]{512} = 8$

**Evaluate the logarithms exactly.**

**37.** $\log_7 1$      **38.** $\log_4 256$

**39.** $\log_{1/6} 1296$      **40.** $\log 10^{12}$

**Approximate the common and natural logarithms utilizing a calculator. Round to two decimal places.**

**41.** $\log 32$          **42.** $\ln 32$

**43.** $\ln 0.125$       **44.** $\log 0.125$

**State the domain of the logarithmic function in interval notation.**

**45.** $f(x) = \log_3(x + 2)$    **46.** $f(x) = \log_2(2 - x)$

**47.** $f(x) = \log(x^2 + 3)$    **48.** $f(x) = \log(3 - x^2)$

**Match the graph with the function.**

**49.** $y = \log_7 x$         **50.** $y = -\log_7(-x)$

**51.** $y = \log_7(x + 1) - 3$    **52.** $y = -\log_7(1 - x) + 3$

**a.**

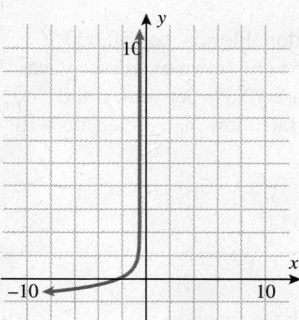

**b.**

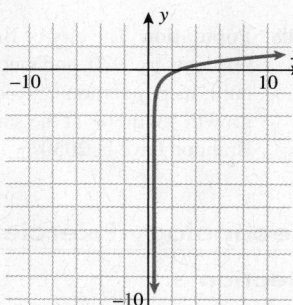

**c.**

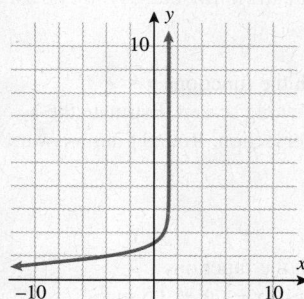

**d.**

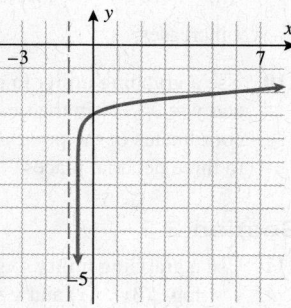

**Graph the logarithmic function with transformation techniques.**

**53.** $f(x) = \log_4(x - 4) + 2$    **54.** $f(x) = \log_4(x + 4) - 3$

**55.** $f(x) = -\log_4(x) - 6$    **56.** $f(x) = -2\log_4(-x) + 4$

## Applications

**57. Chemistry.** Calculate the pH value of milk, assuming it has a concentration of hydrogen ions given by $H^+ = 3.16 \times 10^{-7}$.

**58. Chemistry.** Calculate the pH value of Coca-Cola, assuming it has a concentration of hydrogen ions given by $H^+ = 2.0 \times 10^{-3}$.

**59. Sound.** Calculate the decibels associated with a teacher speaking to a medium-sized class if the sound intensity is $1 \times 10^{-7}$ W/m².

**60. Sound.** Calculate the decibels associated with an alarm clock if the sound intensity is $1 \times 10^{-4}$ W/m².

## 3.3 Properties of Logarithms

**Use the properties of logarithms to simplify each expression.**

**61.** $\log_{2.5} 2.5$    **62.** $\log_2 \sqrt{16}$    **63.** $2.5^{\log_{2.5} 6}$    **64.** $e^{-3\ln 6}$

**Write each expression as a sum or difference of logarithms.**

**65.** $\log_c x^a y^b$         **66.** $\log_3 x^2 y^{-3}$

**67.** $\log_j \left( \dfrac{rs}{t^3} \right)$       **68.** $\log x^c \sqrt{x + 5}$

**69.** $\log \left[ \dfrac{a^{1/2}}{b^{3/2} c^{2/5}} \right]$    **70.** $\log_7 \left[ \dfrac{c^3 d^{1/3}}{e^6} \right]^{1/3}$

**Evaluate the logarithms using the change-of-base formula.**

**71.** $\log_8 3$    **72.** $\log_5 \frac{1}{2}$    **73.** $\log_\pi 1.4$    **74.** $\log_{\sqrt{3}} 2.5$

## 3.4 Exponential and Logarithmic Equations

**Solve the exponential equations exactly for $x$.**

**75.** $4^x = \frac{1}{256}$        **76.** $3^{x^2} = 81$

**77.** $e^{3x-4} = 1$        **78.** $e^{\sqrt{x}} = e^{4.8}$

**79.** $\left(\frac{1}{3}\right)^{x+2} = 81$    **80.** $100^{x^2-3} = 10$

**Solve the exponential equation. Round your answer to three decimal places.**

**81.** $e^{2x+3} - 3 = 10$      **82.** $2^{2x-1} + 3 = 17$

**83.** $e^{2x} + 6e^x + 5 = 0$    **84.** $4e^{0.1x} = 64$

**85.** $(2^x - 2^{-x})(2^x + 2^{-x}) = 0$    **86.** $5(2^x) = 25$

**Solve the logarithmic equations exactly.**

**87.** $\log(3x) = 2$

**88.** $\log_3(x + 2) = 4$

**89.** $\log_4 x + \log_4 2x = 8$

**90.** $\log_6 x + \log_6(2x - 1) = \log_6 3$

**Solve the logarithmic equations. Round your answers to three decimal places.**

**91.** $\ln x^2 = 2.2$

**92.** $\ln(3x - 4) = 7$

**93.** $\log_3(2 - x) - \log_3(x + 3) = \log_3 x$

**94.** $4\log(x + 1) - 2\log(x + 1) = 1$

## 3.5 Exponential and Logarithmic Models

**95. Compound Interest.** If Tania needs $30,000 a year from now for a down payment on a new house, how much should she put in a 1-year CD earning 5% a year compounding continuously so that she will have exactly $30,000 a year from now?

**96. Stock Prices.** Jeremy is tracking the stock value of Best Buy (BBY on the NYSE). In 2003 he purchased 100 shares at $28 a share. The stock did not pay dividends because the company reinvested all earnings. In 2005 Jeremy cashed out and sold the stock for $4000. What was the annual rate of return on BBY?

**97. Compound Interest.** Money is invested in a savings account earning 4.2% interest compounded quarterly. How many years will pass until the money doubles?

**98. Compound Interest.** If $9000 is invested in an investment earning 8% interest compounded continuously, how many years will pass until there is $22,500?

**99. Population.** Nevada has the fastest-growing population according to the U.S. Census Bureau. In 2004 the population of Nevada was 2.62 million and increasing at an annual rate of 3.5%. What is the expected population in 2014? (Let $t = 0$ be 2004.) Apply the formula $N = N_0 e^{rt}$, where $N$ is the population.

**100. Population.** The Hispanic population in the United States is the fastest growing of any ethnic group. In 1996 there were an estimated 28.3 million Hispanics in the United States, and in 2000 there were an estimated 32.5 million. What is the expected population of Hispanics in the United States in 2014? (Let $t = 0$ be 1996.) Apply the formula $N = N_0 e^{rt}$, where $N$ is the population.

**101. Bacteria Growth.** Bacteria are growing exponentially. Initially, there were 1000 bacteria; after 3 hours there were 2500. How many bacteria should be expected in 6 hours? Apply the formula $N = N_0 e^{rt}$, where $N$ is the number of bacteria.

**102. Population.** In 2003 the population of Phoenix, Arizona, was 1,388,215. In 2004 the population was 1,418,041. What is the expected population in 2014? (Let $t = 0$ be 2003.) Apply the formula $N = N_0 e^{rt}$, where $N$ is the population.

**103. Radioactive Decay.** Strontium-90 has a half-life of 28 years. How long will it take for 20 grams of this to decay to 5 grams? Apply the formula $N = N_0 e^{-rt}$, where $N$ is the number of grams.

**104. Radioactive Decay.** Plutonium-239 has a half-life of 25,000 years. How long will it take for 100 grams to decay to 20 grams? Apply the formula $N = N_0 e^{-rt}$, where $N$ is the number of grams.

**105. Wild Life Population.** The *Boston Globe* reports that the fish population of the Essex River in Massachusetts is declining. In 2003 it was estimated there were 5600 fish in the river, and in 2004 there were only 2420 fish. How many fish should there have been in 2010 if this trend continued? Apply the formula $N = N_0 e^{-rt}$, where $N$ is the number of fish.

**106. Car Depreciation.** A new Acura TSX costs $28,200. In 2 years the value will be $24,500. What is the expected value in 6 years? Apply the formula $N = N_0 e^{-rt}$, where $N$ is the value of the car.

**107. Carrying Capacity.** The carrying capacity of a species of beach mice in St. Croix is given by $M = 1000(1 - e^{-0.035t})$, where $M$ is the number of mice and $t$ is time in years ($t = 0$ corresponds to 1998). How many mice should there have been in 2010?

**108. Population.** The city of Brandon, Florida, had 50,000 residents in 1970, and since the crosstown expressway was built, its population has increased 2.3% per year. If the growth continues at the same rate, how many residents will Brandon have in 2030?

## Technology Exercises

### Section 3.1

**109.** Use a graphing utility to graph the function $f(x) = \left(1 + \dfrac{\sqrt{2}}{x}\right)^x$. Determine the horizontal asymptote as $x$ increases.

**110.** Use a graphing utility to graph the functions $y = e^{-x+2}$ and $y = 3^x + 1$ in the same viewing screen. Estimate the coordinates of the point of intersection. Round your answers to three decimal places.

### Section 3.2

**111.** Use a graphing utility to graph the functions $y = \log_{2.4}(3x - 1)$ and $y = \log_{0.8}(x - 1) + 3.5$ in the same viewing screen. Estimate the coordinates of the point of intersection. Round your answers to three decimal places.

**112.** Use a graphing utility to graph the functions $y = \log_{2.5}(x - 1) + 2$ and $y = 3.5^{x-2}$ in the same viewing screen. Estimate the coordinates of the point(s) of intersection. Round your answers to three decimal places.

## Section 3.3

**113.** Use a graphing utility to graph $f(x) = \log_2\left(\dfrac{x^3}{x^2 - 1}\right)$ and

$g(x) = 3\log_2 x - \log_2(x + 1) - \log_2(x - 1)$ in the same viewing screen. Determine the domain where the two functions give the same graph.

**114.** Use a graphing utility to graph $f(x) = \ln\left(\dfrac{9 - x^2}{x^2 - 1}\right)$

and $g(x) = \ln(3 - x) + \ln(3 + x) - \ln(x + 1) - \ln(x - 1)$ in the same viewing screen. Determine the domain where the two functions give the same graph.

## Section 3.4

**115.** Use a graphing utility to graph $y = \dfrac{e^x - e^{-x}}{e^x + e^{-x}}$. State the

domain. Determine if there are any symmetry and asymptote.

**116.** Use a graphing utility to graph $y = \dfrac{1}{e^x - e^{-x}}$. State the

domain. Determine if there are any symmetry and asymptote.

## Section 3.5

**117.** A drug with initial dosage of 4 milligrams has a half-life of 18 hours. Let (0, 4) and (18, 2) be two points.

**a.** Determine the equation of the dosage.
**b.** Use [STAT] [CALC] [ExpReg] to model the equation of the dosage.
**c.** Are the equations in (a) and (b) the same?

**118.** In Exercise 105, let $t = 0$ be 2003 and (0, 5600) and (1, 2420) be the two points.

**a.** Use [STAT] [CALC] [ExpReg] to model the equation for the fish population.
**b.** Using the equation found in (a), how many fish should be expected in 2010?
**c.** Does the answer in (b) agree with the answer in Exercise 105?

1. Simplify $\log 10^{x^3}$.

2. Use a calculator to evaluate $\log_5 326$ (round to two decimal places).

3. Find the exact value of $\log_{1/3} 81$.

4. Rewrite the expression $\ln\left[\dfrac{e^{5x}}{x(x^4 + 1)}\right]$ in a form with no logarithms of products, quotients, or powers.

**In Exercises 5–20, solve for $x$, exactly if possible. If an approximation is required, round your answer to three decimal places.**

5. $e^{x^2-1} = 42$

6. $e^{2x} - 5e^x + 6 = 0$

7. $27e^{0.2x+1} = 300$

8. $3^{2x-1} = 15$

9. $3\ln(x - 4) = 6$

10. $\log(6x + 5) - \log 3 = \log 2 - \log x$

11. $\ln(\ln x) = 1$

12. $\log_2(3x - 1) - \log_2(x - 1) = \log_2(x + 1)$

13. $\log_6 x + \log_6(x - 5) = 2$

14. $\ln(x + 2) - \ln(x - 3) = 2$

15. $\ln x + \ln(x + 3) = 1$

16. $\log_2\left(\dfrac{2x + 3}{x - 1}\right) = 3$

17. $\dfrac{12}{1 + 2e^x} = 6$

18. $\ln x + \ln(x - 3) = 2$

19. State the domain of the function $f(x) = \log\left(\dfrac{x}{x^2 - 1}\right)$.

20. State the range of $x$ values for which the following is true: $10^{\log(4x-a)} = 4x - a$.

**In Exercises 21–24, find all intercepts and asymptotes, and graph.**

21. $f(x) = 3^{-x} + 1$

22. $f(x) = \left(\frac{1}{2}\right)^x - 3$

23. $f(x) = \ln(2x - 3) + 1$

24. $f(x) = \log(1 - x) + 2$

25. **Interest.** If $5000 is invested at a rate of 6% a year, compounded quarterly, what is the amount in the account after 8 years?

26. **Interest.** If $10,000 is invested at a rate of 5%, compounded continuously, what is the amount in the account after 10 years?

27. **Sound.** A lawn mower's sound intensity is approximately $1 \times 10^{-3}$ W/m$^2$. Assuming your threshold of hearing is $1 \times 10^{-12}$ W/m$^2$, calculate the decibels associated with the lawn mower.

28. **Population.** The population in Seattle, Washington, has been increasing at a rate of 5% a year. If the population continues to grow at that rate, and in 2004 there are 800,000 residents, how many residents will there be in 2014? *Hint: $N = N_0 e^{rt}$.*

29. **Earthquake.** An earthquake is considered moderate if it is between 5 and 6 on the Richter scale. What is the energy range in joules for a moderate earthquake?

30. **Radioactive Decay.** The mass $m(t)$ remaining after $t$ hours from a 50-gram sample of a radioactive substance is given by the equation $m(t) = 50e^{-0.0578t}$. After how long will only 30 grams of the substance remain? Round your answer to the nearest hour.

31. **Bacteria Growth.** The number of bacteria in a culture is increasing exponentially. Initially, there were 200 in the culture. After 2 hours there are 500. How many should be expected in 8 hours? Round your answer to the nearest hundred.

32. **Carbon Decay.** Carbon-14 has a half-life of 5730 years. How long will it take for 100 grams to decay to 40 grams?

33. **Spread of a Virus.** The number of people infected by a virus is given by $N = \dfrac{2000}{1 + 3e^{-0.4t}}$, where $t$ is time in days. In how many days will 1000 people be infected?

34. **Oil Consumtion.** The world consumption of oil was 76 million barrels per day in 2002. In 2004 the consumption was 83 million barrels per day. How many barrels are expected to be consumed in 2014?

35. Use a graphing utility to graph $y = \dfrac{e^x - e^{-x}}{2}$. State the domain. Determine if there are any symmetry and asymptote.

36. Use a graphing utility to help solve the equation $4^{3-x} = 2x - 1$. Round your answer to two decimal places.

1. Find the domain and range of the function $f(x) = \dfrac{3}{\sqrt{x^2 - 9}}$.

2. If $f(x) = 1 + 3x$ and $g(x) = x^2 - 1$, find

   **a.** $f + g$    **b.** $f - g$    **c.** $f \cdot g$    **d.** $\dfrac{f}{g}$

   and state the domain of each.

3. Write the function below as a composite of two functions $f$ and $g$. (More than one answer is correct.)

   $$f(g(x)) = \frac{1 - e^{2x}}{1 + e^{2x}}$$

4. Determine whether $f(x) = \sqrt[5]{x^3 + 1}$ is one-to-one. If $f$ is one-to-one, find its inverse $f^{-1}$.

5. Find the quadratic function whose vertex is $(-2, 3)$ and goes through the point $(1, -1)$.

6. Write the polynomial $f(x) = 3x^3 + 6x^2 - 15x - 18$ as a product of linear factors.

7. Solve the equation $e^x + \sqrt{e^x} - 12 = 0$. Round your answer to three decimal places.

8. Using the function $f(x) = 4x - x^2$, evaluate the difference quotient $\dfrac{f(x + h) - f(x)}{h}$.

9. Given the piecewise-defined function

   $$f(x) = \begin{cases} 5 & -2 < x \le 0 \\ 2 - \sqrt{x} & 0 < x < 4 \\ x - 3 & x \ge 4 \end{cases}$$

   find

   **a.** $f(4)$    **b.** $f(0)$    **c.** $f(1)$    **d.** $f(-4)$

   **e.** State the domain and range in interval notation.

   **f.** Determine the intervals where the function is increasing, decreasing, or constant.

10. Sketch the graph of the function $y = \sqrt{1 - x}$ and identify all transformations.

11. Determine whether the function $f(x) = \sqrt{x - 4}$ is one-to-one.

12. The volume of a cylinder with circular base is 400 cubic inches. Its height is 10 inches. Find its radius. Round your answer to three decimal places.

13. Find the vertex of the parabola associated with the quadratic function $f(x) = -4x^2 + 8x - 5$.

14. Find a polynomial of minimum degree (there are many) that has the zeros $x = -5$ (multiplicity 2) and $x = 9$ (multiplicity 4).

15. Use synthetic division to find the quotient $Q(x)$ and remainder $r(x)$ of $(3x^2 - 4x^3 - x^4 + 7x - 20) \div (x + 4)$.

16. Given the zero $x = 2 + i$ of the polynomial $P(x) = x^4 - 7x^3 + 13x^2 + x - 20$, determine all the other zeros and write the polynomial as the product of linear factors.

17. Find the vertical and slant asymptotes of $f(x) = \dfrac{x^2 + 7}{x - 3}$.

18. Graph the rational function $f(x) = \dfrac{3x}{x + 1}$. Give all asymptotes.

19. Graph the function $f(x) = 5x^2 (7 - x)^2 (x + 3)$.

20. If $5400 is invested at 2.75% compounded monthly, how much is in the account after 4 years?

21. Give the exact value of $\log_3 243$.

22. Write the expression $\frac{1}{2} \ln(x + 5) - 2 \ln(x + 1) - \ln(3x)$ as a single logarithm.

23. Solve the logarithmic equation exactly: $10^{2 \log(4x+9)} = 121$.

24. Give an exact solution to the exponential equation $5^{x^2} = 625$.

25. If $8500 is invested at 4% compounded continuously, how many years will pass until there is $12,000?

26. Use a graphing utility to help solve the equation $e^{3-2x} = 2^{x-1}$. Round your answer to two decimal places.

27. Strontium-90 with an initial amount of 6 grams has a half-life of 28 years.

    **a.** Use [STAT] [CALC] [ExpReg] to model the equation of the amount remaining.

    **b.** How many grams will remain after 32 years? Round your answer to two decimal places.

# 4

# Trigonometric Functions of Angles

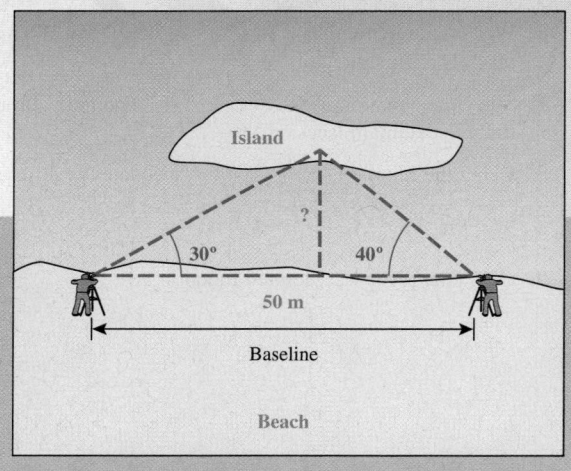

**S**urveyors use trigonometry to indirectly measure distances. Since angles are easier to measure than distances, surveyors set up a baseline between two stations and measure the distance between the two stations and the angles made by the baseline and some third station.

   If there are two stations along the shoreline and the distance along the beach between the two stations is 50 meters and the angles between the baseline (beach) and the line of sight to the island are 30° and 40°, then the Law of Sines can be used to find the shortest distance from the beach to the island.*

---

*See Section 4.4, Exercises 47 and 48.

**IN THIS CHAPTER** angle measure will be defined in terms of both degrees and radians. Then the six trigonometric functions will be defined for acute angles in terms of right triangle ratios. Next the trigonometric functions will be defined for nonacute angles. Lastly, the Law of Sines and the Law of Cosines will be used to solve oblique triangles.

# TRIGONOMETRIC FUNCTIONS OF ANGLES

| 4.1 Angle Measure | 4.2 Right Triangle Trigonometry | 4.3 Trigonometric Functions of Angles | 4.4 The Law of Sines | 4.5 The Law of Cosines |
|---|---|---|---|---|
| • Angles and Their Measure<br>• Coterminal Angles<br>• Arc Length<br>• Area of a Circular Sector<br>• Linear and Angular Speeds | • Right Triangle Ratios<br>• Evaluating Trigonometric Functions Exactly for Special Angle Measures<br>• Solving Right Triangles | • Trigonometric Functions: The Cartesian Plane<br>• Ranges of the Trigonometric Functions<br>• Reference Angles and Reference Right Triangles<br>• Evaluating Trigonometric Functions for Nonacute Angles | • Solving Oblique Triangles | • Solving Oblique Triangles Using the Law of Cosines<br>• The Area of a Triangle |

## LEARNING OBJECTIVES

- Understand angle measures in both degrees and radians, and convert between the two.
- Find trigonometric function values for acute angles.
- Find trigonometric function values for any (acute or nonacute) angle.
- Use the Law of Sines to solve oblique triangles.
- Use the Law of Cosines to solve oblique triangles.

**SKILLS OBJECTIVES**

- Convert angle measure between degrees and radians.
- Find the complement or supplement of an angle.
- Identify coterminal angles.
- Calculate the length of an arc along a circle.
- Calculate the area of a circular sector.

**CONCEPTUAL OBJECTIVES**

- Understand that degrees and radians are both angle measures.
- Realize that radians are unitless (dimensionless).
- Understand the relationship between linear speed and angular speed.

## Angles and Their Measure

An **angle** is formed when a ray is rotated around its endpoint. The common endpoint is called the **vertex**.

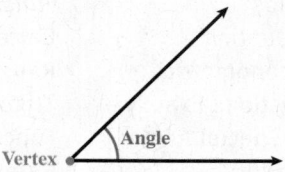

The ray in its original position is called the **initial ray** or the **initial side** of an angle. In the Cartesian plane, we assume the initial side of an angle is the positive *x*-axis. The ray after it is rotated is called the **terminal ray** or the **terminal side** of an angle. Rotation in a counterclockwise direction corresponds to a **positive angle**, whereas rotation in a clockwise direction corresponds to a **negative angle**.

*Study Tip*

Positive angle: counterclockwise
Negative angle: clockwise

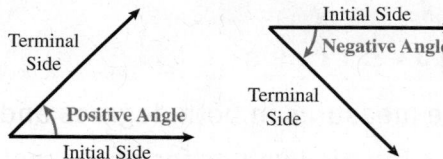

Lengths, or distances, can be measured in different units: feet, miles, and meters are three common units. In order to compare angles of different sizes, we need a standard unit of measure. One way to measure the size of an angle is with **degree measure**.

**DEFINITION**    **Degree Measure of Angles**

An angle formed by one complete counterclockwise rotation has **measure 360 degrees**, denoted 360°.

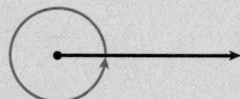

One complete counterclockwise revolution = 360°

| WORDS | MATH |
|---|---|
| 360° represents 1 complete counterclockwise rotation. | $\dfrac{360°}{360°} = 1$ |
| 180° represents a $\frac{1}{2}$ counterclockwise rotation. | $\dfrac{180°}{360°} = \dfrac{1}{2}$ |
| 90° represents a $\frac{1}{4}$ counterclockwise rotation. | $\dfrac{90°}{360°} = \dfrac{1}{4}$ |
| 1° represents a $\frac{1}{360}$ counterclockwise rotation. | $\dfrac{1°}{360°} = \dfrac{1}{360}$ |

The Greek letter $\theta$ (theta) is the most common name for an angle in mathematics. Other common names of angles are $\alpha$ (alpha), $\beta$ (beta), and $\gamma$ (gamma).

**WORDS**

An angle measuring exactly 90° is called a **right angle**.

A right angle is often represented by the adjacent sides of a rectangle, indicating that the two rays are *perpendicular*.

**MATH**

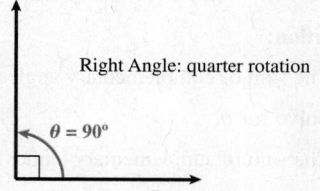

Right Angle: quarter rotation

$\theta = 90°$

An angle measuring exactly 180° is called a **straight angle**.

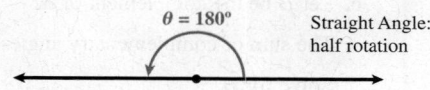

$\theta = 180°$     Straight Angle: half rotation

An angle measuring greater than 0°, but less than 90°, is called an **acute angle**.

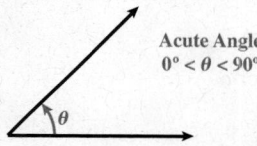

Acute Angle
$0° < \theta < 90°$

$\theta$

An angle measuring greater than 90°, but less than 180°, is called an **obtuse angle**.

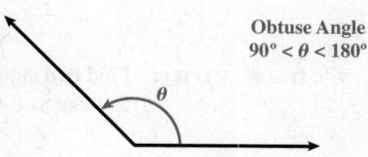

Obtuse Angle
$90° < \theta < 180°$

$\theta$

If the sum of the measures of two positive angles is 90°, the angles are called **complementary**. We say that $\alpha$ is the **complement** of $\beta$ (and vice versa).

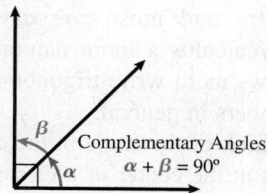

$\beta$

Complementary Angles
$\alpha + \beta = 90°$

$\alpha$

If the sum of the measures of two positive angles is 180°, the angles are called **supplementary**. We say that $\alpha$ is the **supplement** of $\beta$ (and vice versa).

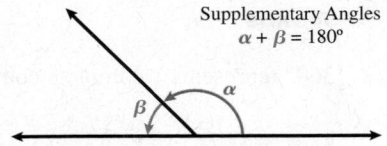

Supplementary Angles
$\alpha + \beta = 180°$

**EXAMPLE 1**  **Finding Measures of Complementary and Supplementary Angles**

Find the measure of each angle.

**a.** Find the complement of 50°.

**b.** Find the supplement of 110°.

**c.** Represent the complement of $\alpha$ in terms of $\alpha$.

**d.** Find two supplementary angles such that the first angle is twice as large as the second angle.

**Solution:**

**a.** The sum of complementary angles is 90°.   $\theta + 50° = 90°$

Solve for $\theta$.   $\theta = \boxed{40°}$

**b.** The sum of supplementary angles is 180°.   $\theta + 110° = 180°$

Solve for $\theta$.   $\theta = \boxed{70°}$

**c.** Let $\beta$ be the complement of $\alpha$.

The sum of complementary angles is 90°.   $\alpha + \beta = 90°$

Solve for $\beta$.   $\beta = \boxed{90° - \alpha}$

**d.** The sum of supplementary angles is 180°.   $\alpha + \beta = 180°$

Let $\beta = 2\alpha$.   $\alpha + 2\alpha = 180°$

Solve for $\alpha$.   $3\alpha = 180°$

$\alpha = 60°$

Substitute $\alpha = 60°$ into $\beta = 2\alpha$.   $\beta = 120°$

The angles have measures $\boxed{60°}$ and $\boxed{120°}$.

■ **Answer:** The angles have measures 45° and 135°.

■ **YOUR TURN**  Find two supplementary angles such that the first angle is 3 times as large as the second angle.

It is important not to confuse an angle with its measure. In Example 1(d), angle $\alpha$ is a rotation and the measure of that rotation is 60°.

In geometry and most everyday applications, angles are measured in degrees. However, in calculus a more natural angle measure is *radian measure*. Using radian measure allows us to write trigonometric functions as functions of not only angles but also real numbers in general.

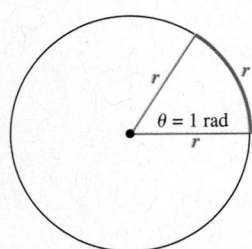

$\theta = 1$ rad

Now we think of the angle in the context of a circle. A **central angle** is an angle that has its vertex at the center of a circle. When the intercepted arc's length is equal to the radius, the measure of the central angle is 1 **radian**.

**DEFINITION**    **Radian Measure**

If a central angle $\theta$ in a circle with radius $r$ intercepts
an arc on the circle of length $s$ (**arc length**), then the
measure of $\theta$, in **radians**, is given by

$$\theta (\text{in radians}) = \frac{s}{r}$$

*Note:* The formula is valid only if $s$ (arc length) and $r$
(radius) are expressed in the same units.

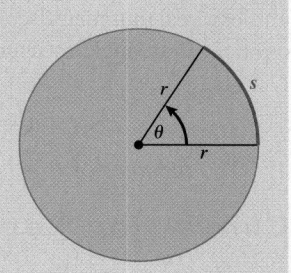

▼ CAUTION

To correctly calculate radians from
the formula $\theta = \frac{s}{r}$, the radius and
arc length must be expressed in the
same units.

Note that both $s$ and $r$ are measured in units of length. When both are given in the same
units, the units cancel, giving the number of radians as a *dimensionless* (unitless) real
number. One full rotation corresponds to an arc length equal to the circumference $2\pi r$ of
the circle with radius $r$. We see then that one full rotation is equal to $2\pi$ radians.

$$\theta_{\text{full rotation}} = \frac{2\pi r}{r} = 2\pi$$

 **EXAMPLE 2**    **Finding the Radian Measure of an Angle**

What is the measure (in radians) of a central angle $\theta$ that intercepts an arc of length
6 centimeters on a circle with radius 2 meters?

**COMMON MISTAKE**

A common mistake is to forget to first put the radius and arc length in the same units.

⭐ **CORRECT**

Write the formula relating radian
measure to arc length and radius.

$$\theta (\text{in radians}) = \frac{s}{r}$$

Substitute $s = 6$ cm and $r = 2$ m
into the radian expression.

$$\theta = \frac{6 \text{ cm}}{2 \text{ m}}$$

Convert the radius (2) meters to
centimeters: 2 m = 200 cm.

$$\theta = \frac{6 \text{ cm}}{200 \text{ cm}}$$

The units, cm, cancel and the
result is a unitless real number.

$$\theta = 0.03 \text{ rad}$$

❌ **INCORRECT**

Substitute $s = 6$ cm and $r = 2$ m into
the radian expression.

$$\theta = \frac{6 \text{ cm}}{2 \text{ m}}$$

Simplify.    $\theta = 3$ rad

**ERROR**

▼ CAUTION

Units for arc length and radius must
be the same to use $\theta = \frac{s}{r}$.

■ **YOUR TURN**    What is the measure (in radians) of a central angle $\theta$ that intercepts
an arc of length 12 millimeters on a circle with radius 4 centimeters?

■ **Answer:** 0.3 rad

In the above example, the units, cm, canceled, therefore correctly giving *radians* as a unitless real number. Because radians are unitless, the word radians (or rad) is often omitted. If an angle measure is given simply as a real number, then radians are implied.

| WORDS | MATH |
|---|---|
| The measure of $\theta$ is 4 degrees. | $\theta = 4°$ |
| The measure of $\theta$ is 4 radians. | $\theta = 4$ |

## Converting Between Degrees and Radians

An angle corresponding to one full rotation is said to have measure 360° or $2\pi$ radians. Therefore, $180° = \pi$ rad.

■ To convert degrees to radians, multiply the degree measure by $\dfrac{\pi}{180°}$.

■ To convert radians to degrees, multiply the radian measure by $\dfrac{180°}{\pi}$.

**EXAMPLE 3** **Converting Between Degrees and Radians**

Convert:

**a.** 45° to radians    **b.** 472° to radians    **c.** $\dfrac{2\pi}{3}$ to degrees

**Solution (a):**

Multiply 45° by $\dfrac{\pi}{180°}$.  $\qquad\qquad\qquad (45°)\left(\dfrac{\pi}{180°}\right) = \dfrac{45°\pi}{180°}$

Simplify.  $\qquad\qquad\qquad\qquad\qquad\qquad = \dfrac{\pi}{4}$ radians

*Note*: $\dfrac{\pi}{4}$ is the exact value. A calculator can be used to approximate this expression.

Scientific and graphing calculators have a $\pi$ button (on most scientific calculators, it requires using a shift or second command). The decimal approximation rounded to three decimal places is 0.785.

Exact value:  $\qquad\qquad\qquad\qquad\qquad$ $\boxed{\dfrac{\pi}{4}}$

Approximate value:  $\qquad\qquad\qquad\qquad$ $\boxed{0.785}$

**Solution (b):**

Multiply 472° by $\dfrac{\pi}{180°}$.  $\qquad\qquad\qquad$ $472°\left(\dfrac{\pi}{180°}\right)$

Simplify (factor out the common 4).  $\qquad = \boxed{\dfrac{118}{45}\pi}$

Approximate with a calculator.  $\qquad\qquad \boxed{\approx 8.238}$

**Solution (c):**

Multiply $\dfrac{2\pi}{3}$ by $\dfrac{180°}{\pi}$.  $\qquad\qquad\qquad$ $\dfrac{2\pi}{3} \cdot \dfrac{180°}{\pi}$

Simplify.  $\qquad\qquad\qquad\qquad\qquad\qquad = \boxed{120°}$

■ **Answer:**
   **a.** $\dfrac{\pi}{3}$ or approximately 1.047

   **b.** $\dfrac{23}{9}\pi$ or approximately 8.029

   **c.** 270°

■ **YOUR TURN** Convert:

**a.** 60° to radians    **b.** 460° to radians    **c.** $\dfrac{3\pi}{2}$ to degrees

# Coterminal Angles

## Angles in Standard Position

If the *initial side* of an angle is aligned along the *positive x-axis* and the *vertex* of the angle is positioned at the *origin*, then the angle is said to be in *standard position*.

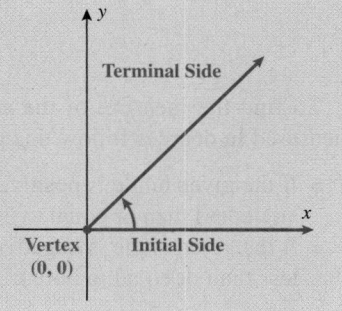

**DEFINITION**   **Standard Position**

An angle is said to be in **standard position** if its initial side is along the positive x-axis and its vertex is at the origin.

We say that an angle lies in the quadrant in which its terminal side lies. Angles in standard position with terminal sides along the x-axis or y-axis (90°, 180°, 270°, 360°, etc.) are called **quadrantal angles**.

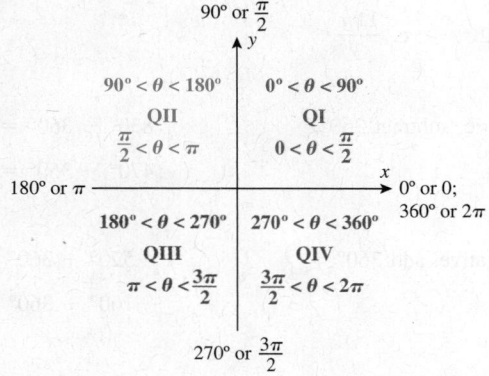

## Coterminal Angles

**DEFINITION**   **Coterminal Angles**

Two angles in standard position with the same terminal side are called **coterminal angles**.

For example, $-40°$ and $320°$ are measures of coterminal angles; their terminal rays are identical even though they are formed by rotations in opposite directions. The angles $60°$ and $420°$ are also coterminal; angles larger than 360° or less than $-360°$ are generated by continuing the rotation beyond one full circle. Thus, all coterminal angles have the same initial side (positive x-axis) and the same terminal side, just different amounts and/or direction of rotation.

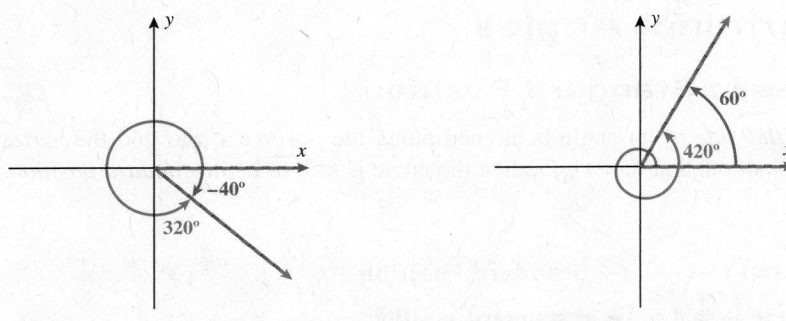

To find the measure of the smallest nonnegative coterminal angle of a given angle measured in degrees follow this procedure:

- If the given angle is positive, subtract 360° (repeatedly until the result is a positive angle less than or equal to 360°).
- If the given angle is negative, add 360° (repeatedly until the result is a positive angle less than or equal to 360°).

Similarly, if the angle is measured in radians, subtract or add equivalently $2\pi$ until your result is a positive angle less than or equal to $2\pi$.

 **EXAMPLE 4** **Finding Measures of Coterminal Angles**

Determine the angle with the smallest possible positive measure that is coterminal with each of the following angles:

**a.** 830°    **b.** −520°    **c.** $\dfrac{11\pi}{3}$

**Solution (a):**

Since 830° is positive, subtract 360°.        $830° - 360° = 470°$

Subtract 360° again.        $470° - 360° = \boxed{110°}$

**Solution (b):**

Since −520° is negative, add 360°.        $-520° + 360° = -160°$

Add 360° again.        $-160° + 360° = \boxed{200°}$

**Solution (c):**

Since $\dfrac{11\pi}{3}$ is positive, subtract $2\pi$.        $\dfrac{11\pi}{3} - 2\pi = \boxed{\dfrac{5\pi}{3}}$

■ **Answer: a.** 180°
   **b.** 290°
   **c.** $\dfrac{11\pi}{6}$

■ **YOUR TURN** Determine the angle with the smallest possible positive measure that is coterminal with each of the following angles:

**a.** 900°    **b.** −430°    **c.** $-\dfrac{13\pi}{6}$

## Applications of Radian Measure

We now look at applications of radian measure that involve calculating *arc lengths*, *areas of circular sectors*, and *angular and linear speeds*. All of these applications are related to the definition of radian measure.

# Arc Length

**Study Tip**

To use the relationship
$$s = r\theta$$
the angle $\theta$ must be in radians.

**DEFINITION**   **Arc Length**

If a central angle $\theta$ in a circle with radius $r$ intercepts an arc on the circle of length $s$, then the **arc length** $s$ is given by

$$s = r\theta \qquad \theta \text{ is given in radians}$$

**EXAMPLE 5**   **Finding Arc Length When the Angle Has Degree Measure**

The International Space Station (ISS) is in an approximately circular orbit 400 kilometers above the surface of the Earth. If the ground station tracks the space station when it is within a 45° central angle of this circular orbit above the tracking antenna, how many kilometers does the ISS cover while it is being tracked by the ground station? Assume that the radius of the Earth is 6400 kilometers. Round to the nearest kilometer.

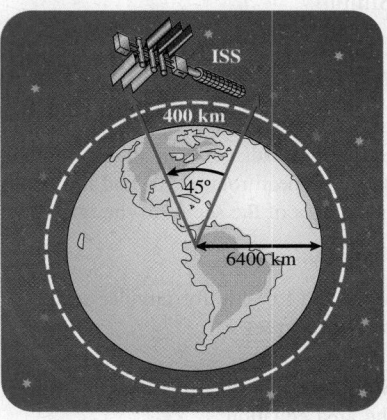

**Technology Tip**

Use the TI to evaluate the expression for $s$.

$$s = (6800 \text{ km})(45°)\left(\frac{\pi}{180°}\right)$$

Press [2nd] [∧] for $\pi$. Type [6800] [x] [45] [x] [2nd] [∧] [÷] [180] [ENTER].

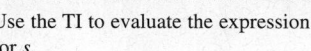

```
6800*45*π/180
        5340.707511
```

**Solution:**

Write the formula for arc length when the angle has degree measure.

$$s = r\theta_d\left(\frac{\pi}{180°}\right)$$

Substitute $r = 6400 + 400 = 6800$ km and $\theta_d = 45°$.

$$s = (6800 \text{ km})(45°)\left(\frac{\pi}{180°}\right)$$

Evaluate with a calculator.

$$s \approx 5340.708 \text{ km}$$

Round to the nearest kilometer.

$$s \approx \boxed{5341 \text{ km}}$$

**Study Tip**

When the angle is given in degrees, the arc length formula becomes
$$s = r \cdot \theta_d\left(\frac{\pi}{180°}\right)$$

The ISS travels approximately 5341 kilometers during the ground station tracking.

▪ **YOUR TURN**   If the ground station in Example 5 could track the ISS within a 60° central angle, how far would the ISS travel during the tracking?

■ **Answer:** 7121 km

# Area of a Circular Sector

**Study Tip**

To use the relationship
$$A = \frac{1}{2}r^2\theta$$
the angle $\theta$ must be in radians.

**DEFINITION**   **Area of a Circular Sector**

The **area of a sector of a circle** with radius $r$ and central angle $\theta$ is given by

$$A = \frac{1}{2}r^2\theta \qquad \theta \text{ is given in radians}$$

| WORDS | MATH |
|---|---|
| Write the ratio of the area of the sector to the area of the entire circle. | $\dfrac{A}{\pi r^2}$ |
| Write the ratio of the central angle $\theta$ to the measure of one full rotation. | $\dfrac{\theta}{2\pi}$ |
| The ratios must be equal (proportionality of sector to circle). | $\dfrac{A}{\pi r^2} = \dfrac{\theta}{2\pi}$ |
| Multiply both sides of the equation by $\pi r^2$. | $\pi r^2 \cdot \dfrac{A}{\pi r^2} = \dfrac{\theta}{2\pi} \cdot \pi r^2$ |
| Simplify. | $A = \dfrac{1}{2} r^2 \theta$ |

### EXAMPLE 6  Finding the Area of a Sector When the Angle Has Degree Measure

Sprinkler heads come in all different sizes depending on the angle of rotation desired. If a sprinkler head rotates 90° and has enough pressure to keep a constant 25-foot spray, what is the area of the sector of the lawn that gets watered? Round to the nearest square foot.

**Solution:**

| | |
|---|---|
| Write the formula for circular sector area in degrees. | $A = \dfrac{1}{2} r^2 \theta_d \left( \dfrac{\pi}{180°} \right)$ |
| Substitute $r = 25$ ft and $\theta_d = 90°$ into the area equation. | $A = \dfrac{1}{2}(25 \text{ ft})^2 (90°) \left( \dfrac{\pi}{180°} \right)$ |
| Simplify. | $A = \left( \dfrac{625\pi}{4} \right) \text{ft}^2 \approx 490.87 \text{ ft}^2$ |
| Round to the nearest square foot. | $A \approx \boxed{491 \text{ ft}^2}$ |

**■ YOUR TURN** If a sprinkler head rotates 180° and has enough pressure to keep a constant 30-foot spray, what is the area of the sector of the lawn it can water? Round to the nearest square foot.

## Linear and Angular Speeds

Recall the relationship between distance, rate (assumed to be constant), and time: $d = rt$. Rate is speed, and in words this formula can be rewritten as

$$\text{distance} = \text{speed} \cdot \text{time} \quad \text{or} \quad \text{speed} = \frac{\text{distance}}{\text{time}}$$

It is important to note that we assume speed is constant. If we think of a car driving around a circular track, the distance it travels is the arc length $s$; and if we let $v$ represent speed and $t$ represent time, we have the formula for speed along a circular path (*linear speed*):

$$v = \frac{s}{t}$$

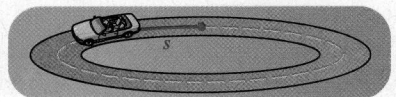

**DEFINITION**    **Linear Speed**

If a point $P$ moves along the circumference of a circle at a constant speed, then the **linear speed** $v$ is given by

$$v = \frac{s}{t}$$

where $s$ is the arc length and $t$ is the time.

**EXAMPLE 7**    **Linear Speed**

A car travels at a constant speed around a circular track with circumference equal to 2 miles. If the car records a time of 15 minutes for 9 laps, what is the linear speed of the car in miles per hour?

**Solution:**

Calculate the distance traveled around the circular track.

$$s = (9 \text{ laps})\left(\frac{2 \text{ mi}}{\text{lap}}\right) = 18 \text{ mi}$$

Substitute $t = 15$ min and $s = 18$ mi into $v = \frac{s}{t}$.

$$v = \frac{18 \text{ mi}}{15 \text{ min}}$$

Convert the linear speed from miles per minute to miles per hour.

$$v = \left(\frac{18 \text{ mi}}{15 \text{ min}}\right)\left(\frac{60 \text{ min}}{1 \text{ hr}}\right)$$

Simplify.

$$v = \boxed{72 \text{ mph}}$$

■ **YOUR TURN**    A car travels at a constant speed around a circular track with circumference equal to 3 miles. If the car records a time of 12 minutes for 7 laps, what is the linear speed of the car in miles per hour?

■ **Answer:** 105 mph

To calculate linear speed, we find how fast a position along the circumference of a circle is changing. To calculate *angular speed*, we find how fast the central angle is changing.

**DEFINITION**    **Angular Speed**

If a point $P$ moves along the circumference of a circle at a constant speed, then the central angle $\theta$ that is formed with the terminal side passing through point $P$ also changes over some time $t$ at a constant speed. The **angular speed** $\omega$ (omega) is given by

$$\omega = \frac{\theta}{t} \qquad \text{where } \theta \text{ is given in radians}$$

▶ **EXAMPLE 8    Angular Speed**

A lighthouse in the middle of a channel rotates its light in a circular motion with constant speed. If the beacon of light completes 1 rotation every 10 seconds, what is the angular speed of the beacon in radians per minute?

**Solution:**

Calculate the angle measure in radians associated with 1 rotation.                $\theta = 2\pi$

Substitute $\theta = 2\pi$ and $t = 10$ sec into $\omega = \dfrac{\theta}{t}$.

$$\omega = \frac{2\pi \text{ (rad)}}{10 \text{ sec}}$$

Convert the angular speed from radians per second to radians per minute.

$$\omega = \frac{2\pi \text{ (rad)}}{10 \text{ sec}} \cdot \frac{60 \text{ sec}}{1 \text{ min}}$$

Simplify.                $\omega = \boxed{12\pi \text{ rad/min}}$

■ **Answer:** $\omega = 3\pi$ rad/min

■ **YOUR TURN**   If the lighthouse in Example 8 is adjusted so that the beacon rotates 1 time every 40 seconds, what is the angular speed of the beacon in radians per minute?

## Relationship Between Linear and Angular Speeds

*Angular speed* and *linear speed* are related through the *radius*.

| WORDS | MATH |
|---|---|
| Write the definition of radian measure. | $\theta = \dfrac{s}{r}$ |
| Write the definition of arc length ($\theta$ in radians). | $s = r\theta$ |
| Divide both sides by $t$. | $\dfrac{s}{t} = \dfrac{r\theta}{t}$ |
| Rewrite the right side of the equation. | $\dfrac{s}{t} = r\dfrac{\theta}{t}$ |
| Recall the definitions of **linear** and **angular** speeds. | $v = \dfrac{s}{t}$ and $\omega = \dfrac{\theta}{t}$ |
| Substitute $v = \dfrac{s}{t}$ and $\omega = \dfrac{\theta}{t}$ into $\dfrac{s}{t} = r\dfrac{\theta}{t}$. | $v = r\omega$ |

**Study Tip**

This relationship between linear and angular speed assumes the angle is given in radians.

### RELATING LINEAR AND ANGULAR SPEEDS

If a point $P$ moves at a constant speed along the circumference of a circle with radius $r$, then the **linear speed** $v$ and the **angular speed** $\omega$ are related by

$$v = r\omega \qquad \text{or} \qquad \omega = \frac{v}{r}$$

*Note:* This relationship is true only when $\theta$ is given in radians.

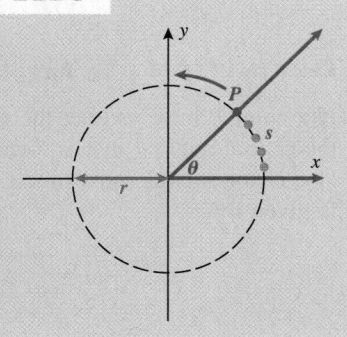

Notice that tires of two different radii with the same angular speed have different linear speeds. The larger tire has the faster linear speed.

## EXAMPLE 9    Relating Linear and Angular Speeds

A Ford F-150 truck comes standard with tires that have a diameter of 25.7 inches (17″ rims). If the owner decides to upgrade to tires with a diameter of 28.2 inches (19″ rims) without having the onboard computer updated, how fast will the truck *actually* be traveling when the speedometer reads 75 miles per hour?

### Solution:

The computer onboard the F-150 "thinks" the tires are 25.7 inches in diameter and knows the angular speed. Use the programmed tire diameter and speedometer reading to calculate the angular speed. Then use that angular speed and the upgraded tire diameter to get the actual speed (linear speed).

**STEP 1**  *Calculate the angular speed of the tires.*

Write the formula for the angular speed.    $\omega = \dfrac{v}{r}$

Substitute $v = 75$ mph and

$r = \dfrac{25.7}{2} = 12.85$ in. into the formula.    $\omega = \dfrac{75 \text{ mi/hr}}{12.85 \text{ in.}}$

$1 \text{ mi} = 5280 \text{ ft} = 63{,}360 \text{ in.}$    $\omega = \dfrac{75(63{,}360) \text{ in./hr}}{12.85 \text{ in.}}$

Simplify.    $\omega \approx 369{,}805 \text{ rad/hr}$

**STEP 2**  *Calculate the actual linear speed of the truck.*

Write the linear speed formula.    $v = r\omega$

Substitute $r = \dfrac{28.2}{2} = 14.1$ in.

and $\omega \approx 369{,}805$ rad/hr.    $v = (14.1 \text{ in.})(369{,}805 \text{ rad/hr})$

Simplify.    $v \approx 5{,}214{,}251 \text{ in./hr}$

$1 \text{ mi} = 5280 \text{ ft} = 63{,}360 \text{ in.}$    $v \approx \dfrac{5{,}214{,}251 \text{ in./hr}}{63{,}360 \text{ in./mi}}$

$v \approx \boxed{82.296 \text{ mph}}$

Although the speedometer indicates a speed of 75 miles per hour, the actual speed is approximately $\boxed{82 \text{ miles per hour}}$.

*Study Tip*

We could have solved Example 9 the following way:

$$\frac{75 \text{ mph}}{25.7} = \frac{x}{28.2}$$

$$x = \left(\frac{28.2}{25.7}\right)(75)$$

$$\approx 82.296 \text{ mph}$$

■ **YOUR TURN**    Suppose the owner of the Ford F-150 truck in Example 9 decides to downsize the tires from their original 25.7-inch diameter to a 24.4-inch diameter. If the speedometer indicates a speed of 65 miles per hour, what is the actual speed of the truck?

■ **Answer:** approximately 62 mph

**SECTION**
**4.1** SUMMARY

Angle measures can be converted between degrees and radians in the following way:

- To convert degrees to radians, multiply the degree measure by $\dfrac{\pi}{180°}$.

- To convert radians to degrees, multiply the radian measure by $\dfrac{180°}{\pi}$.

(Remember that $\pi = 180°$.)

Coterminal angles in standard position have terminal sides that coincide.

The length of a circular arc is given by $s = r\theta$, where $\theta$ is the central angle given in radians and $r$ is the radius of the circle.

The area of a circular sector is given by $A = \dfrac{1}{2}r^2\theta$, where $\theta$ is the central angle given in radians and $r$ is the radius of the circle.

Linear speed, $v = \dfrac{s}{t}$, and angular speed, $\omega = \dfrac{\theta}{t}$, are related through the radius: $v = r\omega$.

**SECTION**
**4.1** EXERCISES

■ **SKILLS**

**In Exercises 1–6, find (a) the complement and (b) the supplement of the given angles.**

**1.** 18°    **2.** 39°    **3.** 42°    **4.** 57°    **5.** 89°    **6.** 75°

**In Exercises 7–12, find the measure (in radians) of a central angle $\theta$ that intercepts an arc of length $s$ on a circle with radius $r$.**

**7.** $r = 22$ in., $s = 4$ in.    **8.** $r = 6$ in., $s = 1$ in.    **9.** $r = 100$ cm, $s = 20$ mm

**10.** $r = 1$ m, $s = 2$ cm    **11.** $r = \frac{1}{4}$ in., $s = \frac{1}{32}$ in.    **12.** $r = \frac{3}{4}$ cm, $s = \frac{3}{14}$ cm

**In Exercises 13–28, convert from degrees to radians. Leave the answers in terms of $\pi$.**

**13.** 30°    **14.** 60°    **15.** 45°    **16.** 90°    **17.** 315°    **18.** 270°

**19.** 75°    **20.** 100°    **21.** 170°    **22.** 340°    **23.** 780°    **24.** 540°

**25.** −210°    **26.** −320°    **27.** −3600°    **28.** 1800°

**In Exercises 29–42, convert from radians to degrees.**

**29.** $\dfrac{\pi}{6}$    **30.** $\dfrac{\pi}{4}$    **31.** $\dfrac{3\pi}{4}$    **32.** $\dfrac{7\pi}{6}$    **33.** $\dfrac{3\pi}{8}$    **34.** $\dfrac{11\pi}{9}$    **35.** $\dfrac{5\pi}{12}$

**36.** $\dfrac{7\pi}{3}$    **37.** $9\pi$    **38.** $-6\pi$    **39.** $\dfrac{19\pi}{20}$    **40.** $\dfrac{13\pi}{36}$    **41.** $-\dfrac{7\pi}{15}$    **42.** $-\dfrac{8\pi}{9}$

**In Exercises 43–50, convert from radians to degrees. Round your answers to the nearest hundredth of a degree.**

**43.** 4    **44.** 3    **45.** 0.85    **46.** 3.27

**47.** −2.7989    **48.** −5.9841    **49.** $2\sqrt{3}$    **50.** $5\sqrt{7}$

**In Exercises 51–56, convert from degrees to radians. Round your answers to three significant digits.**

**51.** 47°    **52.** 65°    **53.** 112°    **54.** 172°    **55.** 56.5°    **56.** 298.7°

**In Exercises 57–68, state in which quadrant or on which axis each angle with the given measure in standard position would lie.**

**57.** 145°    **58.** 175°    **59.** 270°    **60.** 180°    **61.** −540°    **62.** −450°

**63.** $\dfrac{2\pi}{5}$    **64.** $\dfrac{4\pi}{7}$    **65.** $\dfrac{13\pi}{4}$    **66.** $\dfrac{18\pi}{11}$    **67.** 2.5    **68.** 11.4

**In Exercises 69–80, determine the angle of the smallest possible positive measure that is coterminal with each of the angles whose measure is given. Use degree or radian measures accordingly.**

**69.** $412°$          **70.** $379°$          **71.** $-92°$          **72.** $-187°$          **73.** $-390°$          **74.** $945°$

**75.** $\dfrac{29\pi}{3}$          **76.** $\dfrac{47\pi}{7}$          **77.** $-\dfrac{313\pi}{9}$          **78.** $-\dfrac{217\pi}{4}$          **79.** $-30$          **80.** $42$

**In Exercises 81–88, find the exact length of the arc made by the indicated central angle and radius of each circle.**

**81.** $\theta = \dfrac{\pi}{12},\ r = 8\ \text{ft}$          **82.** $\theta = \dfrac{\pi}{8},\ r = 6\ \text{yd}$          **83.** $\theta = \tfrac{1}{2},\ r = 5\ \text{in.}$          **84.** $\theta = \tfrac{3}{4},\ r = 20\ \text{m}$

**85.** $\theta = 22°,\ r = 18\ \mu\text{m}$          **86.** $\theta = 14°,\ r = 15\ \mu\text{m}$          **87.** $\theta = 8°,\ r = 1500\ \text{km}$          **88.** $\theta = 3°,\ r = 1800\ \text{km}$

**In Exercises 89–94, find the area of the circular sector given the indicated radius and central angle. Round your answers to three significant digits.**

**89.** $\theta = \dfrac{3\pi}{8},\ r = 2.2\ \text{km}$          **90.** $\theta = \dfrac{5\pi}{6},\ r = 13\ \text{mi}$          **91.** $\theta = 56°,\ r = 4.2\ \text{cm}$

**92.** $\theta = 27°,\ r = 2.5\ \text{mm}$          **93.** $\theta = 1.2°,\ r = 1.5\ \text{ft}$          **94.** $\theta = 14°,\ r = 3.0\ \text{ft}$

**In Exercises 95–98, find the linear speed of a point that moves with constant speed in a circular motion if the point travels along the circle of arc length s in time t.**

**95.** $s = 2\ \text{m},\ t = 5\ \text{sec}$          **96.** $s = 12\ \text{ft},\ t = 3\ \text{min}$          **97.** $s = 68{,}000\ \text{km},\ t = 250\ \text{hr}$          **98.** $s = 7524\ \text{mi},\ t = 12\ \text{days}$

**In Exercises 99–102, find the distance traveled (arc length) of a point that moves with constant speed v along a circle in time t.**

**99.** $v = 2.8\ \text{m/sec},\ t = 3.5\ \text{sec}$          **100.** $v = 6.2\ \text{km/hr},\ t = 4.5\ \text{hr}$

**101.** $v = 4.5\ \text{mi/hr},\ t = 20\ \text{min}$          **102.** $v = 5.6\ \text{ft/sec},\ t = 2\ \text{min}$

**In Exercises 103–106, find the angular speed (radians/second) associated with rotating a central angle $\theta$ in time t.**

**103.** $\theta = 25\pi,\ t = 10\ \text{sec}$          **104.** $\theta = \dfrac{3\pi}{4},\ t = \dfrac{1}{6}\ \text{sec}$          **105.** $\theta = 200°,\ t = 5\ \text{sec}$          **106.** $\theta = 60°,\ t = 0.2\ \text{sec}$

**In Exercises 107–110, find the linear speed of a point traveling at a constant speed along the circumference of a circle with radius r and angular speed $\omega$.**

**107.** $\omega = \dfrac{2\pi\ \text{rad}}{3\ \text{sec}},\ r = 9\ \text{in.}$          **108.** $\omega = \dfrac{3\pi\ \text{rad}}{4\ \text{sec}},\ r = 8\ \text{cm}$          **109.** $\omega = \dfrac{\pi\ \text{rad}}{20\ \text{sec}},\ r = 5\ \text{mm}$          **110.** $\omega = \dfrac{5\pi\ \text{rad}}{16\ \text{sec}},\ r = 24\ \text{ft}$

**In Exercises 111–114, find the distance a point travels along a circle over a time t, given the angular speed $\omega$ and radius r of the circle. Round your answers to three significant digits.**

**111.** $r = 5\ \text{cm},\ \omega = \dfrac{\pi\ \text{rad}}{6\ \text{sec}},\ t = 10\ \text{sec}$          **112.** $r = 2\ \text{mm},\ \omega = 6\pi\,\dfrac{\text{rad}}{\text{sec}},\ t = 11\ \text{sec}$

**113.** $r = 5.2\ \text{in.},\ \omega = \dfrac{\pi\ \text{rad}}{15\ \text{sec}},\ t = 10\ \text{min}$          **114.** $r = 3.2\ \text{ft},\ \omega = \dfrac{\pi\ \text{rad}}{4\ \text{sec}},\ t = 3\ \text{min}$

**■ APPLICATIONS**

**For Exercises 115 and 116, refer to the following:**

A common school locker combination lock is shown. The lock has a dial with 40 calibration marks numbered 0 to 39. A combination consists of three of these numbers (e.g., 5-35-20). To open the lock, the following steps are taken:

Tacojim/iStockphoto

- Turn the dial clockwise two full turns.
- Continue turning clockwise until the first number of the combination.
- Turn the dial counterclockwise one full turn.
- Continue turning counterclockwise until the second number is reached.
- Turn the dial clockwise again until the third number is reached.
- Pull the shank and the lock will open.

**115. Combination Lock.** Given that the initial position of the dial is at zero (shown in the illustration), how many degrees is the dial rotated in total (sum of clockwise and counterclockwise rotations) in opening the lock if the combination is 35-5-20?

**116. Combination Lock.** Given that the initial position of the dial is at zero (shown in the illustration), how many degrees is the dial rotated in total (sum of clockwise and counterclockwise rotations) in opening the lock if the combination is 20-15-5?

**117. Tires.** A car owner decides to upgrade from tires with a diameter of 24.3 inches to tires with a diameter of 26.1 inches. If she doesn't update the onboard computer, how fast will she actually be traveling when the speedometer reads 65 miles per hour? Round to the nearest miles per hour.

**118. Tires.** A car owner decides to upgrade from tires with a diameter of 24.8 inches to tires with a diameter of 27.0 inches. If she doesn't update the onboard computer, how fast will she actually be traveling when the speedometer reads 70 miles per hour? Round to the nearest miles per hour.

**For Exercises 119 and 120, refer to the following:**

NASA explores artificial gravity as a way to counter the physiologic effects of extended weightlessness for future space exploration. NASA's centrifuge has a 58-foot-diameter arm.

Courtesy NASA

**119. NASA.** If two humans are on opposite (red and blue) ends of the centrifuge and their linear speed is 200 miles per hour, how fast is the arm rotating? Express the answer in radians per second to two significant digits.

**120. NASA.** If two humans are on opposite (red and blue) ends of the centrifuge and they rotate one full rotation every second, what is their linear speed in feet per second?

**For Exercises 121–124, refer to the following:**

A collimator is a device used in radiation treatment that narrows beams or waves, causing the waves to be more aligned in a specific direction. The use of a collimator facilitates the focusing of radiation to treat an affected region of tissue beneath the skin. In the figure, $d_s$ is the distance from the radiation source to the skin and $d_t$ is the distance from the outer layer of skin to the targeted tissue. The field size on the skin (diameter of the circular treated skin) is $2f_s$, and $2f_d$ is the targeted field size at depth $d_t$ (the diameter of the targeted tissue at the specified depth beneath the skin surface).

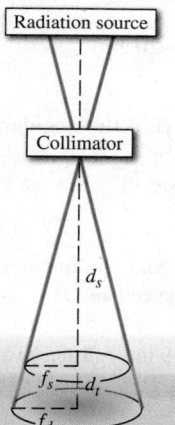

**121. Health/Medicine.** Radiation treatment is applied to a field size of 8 centimeters at a depth 2.5 centimeters below the skin surface. If the treatment head is positioned 80 centimeters from the skin, find the targeted field size to the nearest millimeter.

**122. Health/Medicine.** Radiation treatment is applied to a field size of 4 centimeters lying at a depth of 3.5 centimeters below the skin surface. If the field size on the skin is required to be 3.8 centimeters, find the distance from the skin that the radiation source must be located to the nearest millimeter.

**123. Health/Medicine.** Radiation treatment is applied to a field size on the skin of 3.75 centimeters to reach an affected region of tissue with field size of 4 centimeters at some depth below the skin. If the treatment head is positioned 60 centimeters from the skin surface, find the desired depth below the skin to the target area to the nearest millimeter.

**124. Health/Medicine.** Radiation treatment is applied to a field size on the skin of 4.15 centimeters to reach an affected area lying 4.5 centimeters below the skin surface. If the treatment head is positioned 60 centimeters from the skin surface, find the field size of the targeted area to the nearest millimeter.

**For Exercises 125 and 126, refer to the following:**

Sniffers outside a chemical munitions disposal site monitor the atmosphere surrounding the site to detect any toxic gases. In the event that there is an accidental release of toxic fumes, the data provided by the sniffers make it possible to determine both the distance $d$ that the fumes reach as well as the angle of spread $\theta$ that sweep out a circular sector.

**125. Environment.** If the maximum angle of spread is 105° and the maximum distance at which the toxic fumes were detected was 9 miles from the site, find the area of the circular sector affected by the accidental release.

**126. Environment.** To protect the public from the fumes, officials must secure the perimeter of this area. Find the perimeter of the circular sector in Exercise 125.

**For Exercises 127 and 128, refer to the following:**

The structure of human DNA is a *linear* double helix formed of nucleotide base pairs (two nucleotides) that are stacked with spacing of 3.4 angstroms ($3.4 \times 10^{-12}$ m), and each base pair is rotated 36° with respect to an adjacent pair and has 10 base pairs per helical turn. The DNA of a virus or a bacterium, however, is a *circular* double helix (see the figure below) with the structure varying among species.

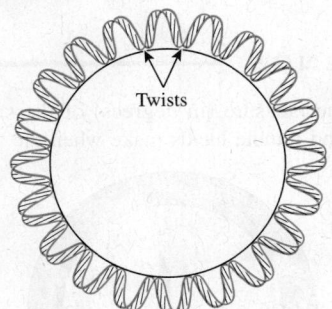

(*Source*: http://www.biophysics.org/Portals/1/
PDFs/Education/Vologodskii.pdf.)

**127. Biology.** If the circular DNA of a virus has 10 twists (or turns) per circle and an inner diameter of 4.5 nanometers, find the arc length between consecutive twists of the DNA.

**128. Biology.** If the circular DNA of a virus has 40 twists (or turns) per circle and an inner diameter of 2.0 nanometers, find the arc length between consecutive twists of the DNA.

## ■ CATCH THE MISTAKE

**In Exercises 129 and 130, explain the mistake that is made.**

**129.** If the radius of a set of tires on a car is 15 inches and the tires rotate 180° per second, how fast is the car traveling (linear speed) in miles per hour?

**Solution:**

Write the formula for
linear speed.                     $v = r\omega$

Let $r = 15$ in. and           $v = (15 \text{ in.})\left(\dfrac{180°}{\text{sec}}\right)$
$\omega = 180°$ per sec.

Simplify.                         $v = 2700\ \dfrac{\text{in.}}{\text{sec}}$

Let 1 mi = 5280 ft
= 63,360 in. and              $v = \left(\dfrac{2700 \cdot 3600}{63,360}\right)$ mph
1 hr = 3600 sec.

Simplify.                         $v \approx 153.4$ mph

This is incorrect. The correct answer is approximately 2.7 miles per hour. What mistake was made?

**130.** If a bicycle has tires with radius 10 inches and the tires rotate 90° per $\frac{1}{2}$ second, how fast is the bicycle traveling (linear speed) in miles per hour?

**Solution:**

Write the formula for
linear speed.                     $v = r\omega$

Let $r = 10$ in. and           $v = (10 \text{ in.})\left(\dfrac{180°}{\text{sec}}\right)$
$\omega = 180°$ per sec.

Simplify.                         $v = \dfrac{1800 \text{ in.}}{\text{sec}}$

Let 1 mi = 5280 ft
= 63,360 in. and              $v = \left(\dfrac{1800 \cdot 3600}{63,360}\right)$ mph
1 hr = 3600 sec.

Simplify.                         $v \approx 102.3$ mph

This is incorrect. The correct answer is approximately 1.8 miles per hour. What mistake was made?

■ **CONCEPTUAL**

**In Exercises 131–134, determine whether each statement is true or false.**

**131.** If the radius of a circle doubles, then the arc length (associated with a fixed central angle) doubles.

**132.** If the radius of a circle doubles, then the area of the sector (associated with a fixed central angle) doubles.

**133.** If the angular speed doubles, then the number of revolutions doubles.

**134.** If the central angle of a sector doubles, then the area corresponding to the sector is double the area of the original sector.

■ **CHALLENGE**

**135.** What is the measure (in degrees) of the smaller angle the hour and minute hands make when the time is 12:20?

**136.** What is the measure (in degrees) of the smaller angle the hour and minute hands make when the time is 9:10?

**137.** Find the area of the shaded region below:

**138.** Find the perimeter of the shaded region in Exercise 137.

■ **TECHNOLOGY**

**In Exercises 139 and 140, find the measure in degrees of a central angle θ that intercepts an arc on a circle with indicated radius r and arc length s.**

**139.** $r = 78.6$ cm, $s = 94.4$ cm

**140.** $r = 14.2$ in., $s = 23.8$ in.

■ **PREVIEW TO CALCULUS**

**In calculus we work with real numbers; thus, the measure of an angle must be in radians.**

**141.** What is the measure (in radians) of a central angle θ that intercepts an arc of length $2\pi$ centimeters on a circle of radius 10 centimeters?

**142.** Determine the angle of the smallest possible positive measure (in radians) that is coterminal with the angle 750°.

**143.** The area of a sector of a circle with radius 3 inches and central angle θ is $\frac{3\pi}{2}$ in.². What is the radian measure of θ?

**144.** An object is rotating at 600° per second, find the central angle θ, in radians, when $t = 3$ sec.

**SKILLS OBJECTIVES**

- Learn the trigonometric functions as ratios of sides of a right triangle.
- Evaluate trigonometric functions exactly for special angles.
- Evaluate trigonometric functions using a calculator.

**CONCEPTUAL OBJECTIVES**

- Understand that right triangle ratios are based on the properties of similar triangles.
- Understand the difference between evaluating trigonometric functions exactly and using a calculator.

The word **trigonometry** stems from the Greek words *trigonon*, which means triangle, and *metrein*, which means to measure. Trigonometry began as a branch of geometry and was utilized extensively by early Greek mathematicians to determine unknown distances. The major *trigonometric functions*, including *sine*, *cosine*, and *tangent*, were first defined as ratios of sides in a right triangle. This is the way we will define them in this section. Since the two angles, besides the right angle, in a right triangle have to be acute, a second kind of definition was needed to extend the domain of trigonometric functions to nonacute angles in the Cartesian plane (Section 4.3). Starting in the eighteenth century, broader definitions of the trigonometric functions came into use, under which the functions are associated with points along the unit circle (Section 5.1).

## Right Triangle Ratios

### Similar Triangles

The word *similar* in mathematics means identical in shape, although not necessarily the same size. It is important to note that two triangles can have the exact same shape (same angles) but have different sizes.

**DEFINITION**   **Similar Triangles**

**Similar triangles** are triangles with equal corresponding angle measures (equal angles).

**Study Tip**

Although an angle and its measure are fundamentally different, out of convenience when "equal angles" is stated, this implies "equal angle measures."

## Right Triangles

A **right triangle** is a triangle in which one of the angles is a right angle 90°. Since one angle is 90°, the other two angles must be complementary (sum to 90°), so that the sum of all three angles is 180°. The longest side of a right triangle, called the **hypotenuse**, is opposite the right angle. The other two sides are called the **legs** of the right triangle.

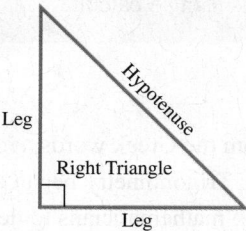

The *Pythagorean theorem* relates the sides of a right triangle. It says that the sum of the squares of the lengths of the two legs is equal to the square of the length of the hypotenuse. It is important to note that length (a synonym of distance) is always positive.

### PYTHAGOREAN THEOREM

In any right triangle, the square of the length of the longest side (hypotenuse) is equal to the sum of the squares of the lengths of the other two sides (legs).

$$a^2 + b^2 = c^2$$

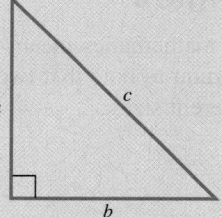

**Study Tip**

The Pythagorean theorem applies only to *right* triangles.

It is important to note that the Pythagorean theorem applies *only* to right triangles. It is also important to note that it does not matter which side is called *a* or *b*, as long as the square of the longest side is equal to the sum of the squares of the shorter sides.

*Right-triangle trigonometry* relies on the properties of similar triangles. Since similar triangles have the same shape (equal corresponding angles), the sides opposite the corresponding angles must be proportional.

# Right Triangle Ratios

The concept of similar triangles, one of the basic insights in trigonometry, allows us to determine the length of a side of one triangle if we know the length of certain sides of a similar triangle. Consider the following similar triangles:

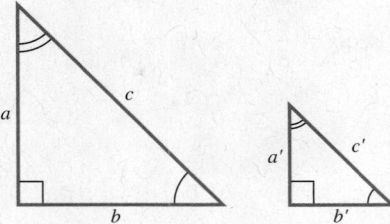

In similar triangles, the sides opposite corresponding angles must be proportional so the following ratios hold true:

$$\frac{a}{a'} = \frac{b}{b'} = \frac{c}{c'}$$

Separate the common ratios into three equations:

$$\frac{a}{a'} = \frac{b}{b'} \qquad \frac{b}{b'} = \frac{c}{c'} \qquad \frac{a}{a'} = \frac{c}{c'}$$

For any right triangle, there are six possible ratios of sides that can be calculated for each acute angle $\theta$:

$$\frac{b}{c} \qquad \frac{a}{c} \qquad \frac{b}{a} \qquad \frac{c}{b} \qquad \frac{c}{a} \qquad \frac{a}{b}$$

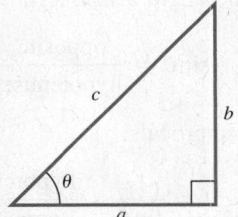

These ratios are referred to as **trigonometric ratios** or **trigonometric functions**, since they depend on the angle $\theta$, and each is given a name:

| FUNCTION NAME | ABBREVIATION | | WORDS | MATH |
|---|---|---|---|---|
| Sine | sin | | The sine of $\theta$ | $\sin \theta$ |
| Cosine | cos | | The cosine of $\theta$ | $\cos \theta$ |
| Tangent | tan | | The tangent of $\theta$ | $\tan \theta$ |
| Cosecant | csc | | The cosecant of $\theta$ | $\csc \theta$ |
| Secant | sec | | The secant of $\theta$ | $\sec \theta$ |
| Cotangent | cot | | The cotangent of $\theta$ | $\cot \theta$ |

Sine, cosine, tangent, cotangent, secant, and cosecant are names given to specific ratios of lengths of sides of right triangles.

*Study Tip*

Notice that

$$\csc\theta = \frac{1}{\sin\theta}$$

$$\sec\theta = \frac{1}{\cos\theta}$$

$$\cot\theta = \frac{1}{\tan\theta}$$

**DEFINITION**     **Trigonometric Functions**

Let $\theta$ be an acute angle in a right triangle, then

$$\sin\theta = \frac{b}{c} \qquad \cos\theta = \frac{a}{c} \qquad \tan\theta = \frac{b}{a}$$

$$\csc\theta = \frac{c}{b} \qquad \sec\theta = \frac{c}{a} \qquad \cot\theta = \frac{a}{b}$$

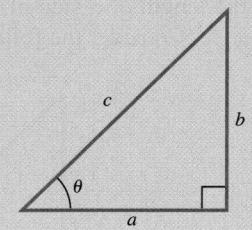

The following terminology will be used throughout this text (refer to the right triangle above):

- The **hypotenuse** is always opposite the right angle.
- One leg ($b$) is **opposite** the angle $\theta$.
- One leg ($a$) is **adjacent** to the angle $\theta$.

Also notice that since $\sin\theta = \frac{b}{c}$ and $\cos\theta = \frac{a}{c}$, then $\tan\theta = \frac{\sin\theta}{\cos\theta} = \frac{\frac{b}{c}}{\frac{a}{c}} = \frac{b}{a}$.

Using this terminology, we arrive at an alternative definition that is easier to remember.

*Study Tip*

Trigonometric functions are functions of a specified angle. Always specify the angle. "Sin" alone means nothing. Sin $\theta$ specifies the angle dependency. The same is true for the other five trigonometric functions.

**DEFINITION**     **Trigonometric Functions (Alternate Form)**

For an acute angle $\theta$ in a right triangle:

$$\sin\theta = \frac{\text{opposite}}{\text{hypotenuse}} \qquad \cos\theta = \frac{\text{adjacent}}{\text{hypotenuse}} \qquad \tan\theta = \frac{\text{opposite}}{\text{adjacent}}$$

and their reciprocals:

$$\csc\theta = \frac{1}{\sin\theta} = \frac{\text{hypotenuse}}{\text{opposite}}$$

$$\sec\theta = \frac{1}{\cos\theta} = \frac{\text{hypotenuse}}{\text{adjacent}}$$

$$\cot\theta = \frac{1}{\tan\theta} = \frac{\text{adjacent}}{\text{opposite}}$$

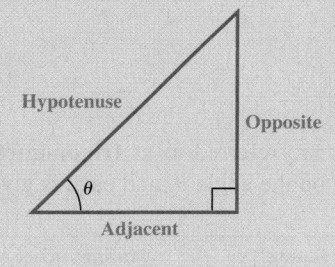

*Study Tip*

SOHCAHTOA

SOH: $\text{Sin}\,\theta = \dfrac{\text{Opposite}}{\text{Hypotenuse}}$

CAH: $\text{Cos}\,\theta = \dfrac{\text{Adjacent}}{\text{Hypotenuse}}$

TOA: $\text{Tan}\,\theta = \dfrac{\text{Opposite}}{\text{Adjacent}}$

## Reciprocal Identities

The three main trigonometric functions should be learned in terms of the following ratios:

$$\sin\theta = \frac{\text{opposite}}{\text{hypotenuse}} \qquad \cos\theta = \frac{\text{adjacent}}{\text{hypotenuse}} \qquad \tan\theta = \frac{\text{opposite}}{\text{adjacent}}$$

*Study Tip*

You need to learn only the three main trigonometric ratios: $\sin\theta$, $\cos\theta$, and $\tan\theta$. The other three can always be calculated as reciprocals of these main three for an acute angle $\theta$.

The remaining three trigonometric functions can be derived from $\sin\theta$, $\cos\theta$, and $\tan\theta$ using the *reciprocal identities*. Recall that the **reciprocal** of $x$ is $\dfrac{1}{x}$ for $x \neq 0$.

## RECIPROCAL IDENTITIES

$$\csc\theta = \frac{1}{\sin\theta} \qquad \sec\theta = \frac{1}{\cos\theta} \qquad \cot\theta = \frac{1}{\tan\theta}$$

# Evaluating Trigonometric Functions Exactly for Special Angle Measures

There are three special acute angles that are very important in trigonometry: $30°, 45°,$ and $60°.$ We can combine the relationships governing their side lengths

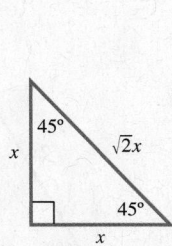 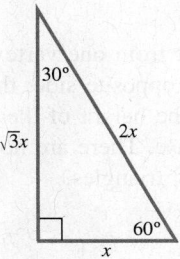

with the trigonometric ratios developed in this section to evaluate the trigonometric functions for the special angle measures of $30°, 45°,$ and $60°.$

Consider a $45°\text{-}45°\text{-}90°$ triangle.

| WORDS | MATH |
|---|---|
| A $45°\text{-}45°\text{-}90°$ triangle is an isosceles (two legs are equal) right triangle. | 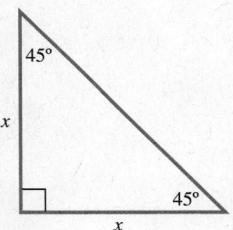 |

Apply the Pythagorean theorem.

$$x^2 + x^2 = \text{hypotenuse}^2$$

Simplify the left side of the equation.

$$2x^2 = \text{hypotenuse}^2$$

Solve for the hypotenuse.

$$\text{hypotenuse} = \pm\sqrt{2x^2} = \pm\sqrt{2}\,|x|$$

$x$ and the hypotenuse are lengths and must be positive.

$$\text{hypotenuse} = \sqrt{2}\,x$$

The hypotenuse of a $45°\text{-}45°\text{-}90°$ triangle is $\sqrt{2}$ times the length of either leg.

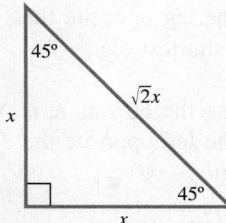

Let us now determine the relationship of the sides of a 30°-60°-90° triangle. We start with an equilateral triangle (equal sides and equal angles of measure 60°).

**WORDS**                                                 **MATH**

Draw an equilateral triangle with sides $2x$.

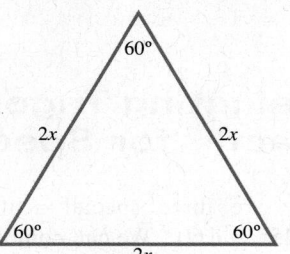

Draw a line segment from one vertex that is perpendicular to the opposite side; this line segment represents the height of the triangle, $h$, and bisects the base. There are now two identical 30°-60°-90° triangles.

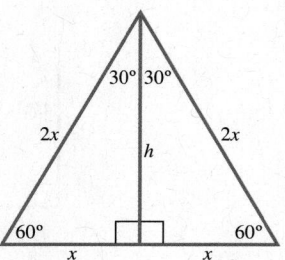

Notice that in each triangle the hypotenuse is twice the shortest leg, which is opposite the 30° angle.

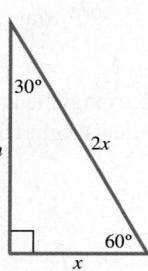

To find the length $h$, use the Pythagorean theorem.

$$h^2 + x^2 = (2x)^2$$
$$h^2 + x^2 = 4x^2$$

Solve for $h$.

$$h^2 = 3x^2$$
$$h = \pm\sqrt{3x^2} = \pm\sqrt{3}\,|x|$$

$h$ and $x$ are lengths and must be positive.

$$h = \sqrt{3}x$$

The hypotenuse of a 30°-60°-90° is twice the length of the leg opposite the 30° angle, the shortest leg.

The leg opposite the 60° angle is $\sqrt{3}$ times the length of the leg opposite the 30° angle, the shortest leg.

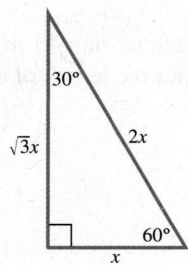

**EXAMPLE 1   Evaluating the Trigonometric Functions Exactly for 30°**

Evaluate the six trigonometric functions for an angle that measures 30°.

**Solution:**

Label the sides (opposite, adjacent, and hypotenuse) of the 30°-60°-90° triangle with respect to the **30°** angle.

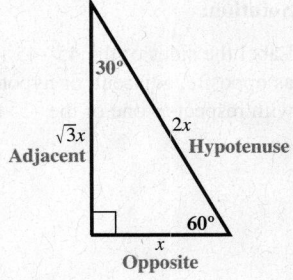

Use the right triangle ratio definitions of sine, cosine, and tangent.

$$\sin 30° = \frac{\text{opposite}}{\text{hypotenuse}} = \frac{x}{2x} = \frac{1}{2}$$

$$\cos 30° = \frac{\text{adjacent}}{\text{hypotenuse}} = \frac{\sqrt{3}x}{2x} = \frac{\sqrt{3}}{2}$$

$$\tan 30° = \frac{\text{opposite}}{\text{adjacent}} = \frac{x}{\sqrt{3}x} = \frac{1}{\sqrt{3}} = \frac{1}{\sqrt{3}} \cdot \frac{\sqrt{3}}{\sqrt{3}} = \frac{\sqrt{3}}{3}$$

Use the reciprocal identities to obtain the value of the cosecant, secant, and cotangent functions.

$$\csc 30° = \frac{1}{\sin 30°} = \frac{1}{\frac{1}{2}} = 2$$

$$\sec 30° = \frac{1}{\cos 30°} = \frac{1}{\frac{\sqrt{3}}{2}} = \frac{2}{\sqrt{3}} = \frac{2}{\sqrt{3}} \cdot \frac{\sqrt{3}}{\sqrt{3}} = \frac{2\sqrt{3}}{3}$$

$$\cot 30° = \frac{1}{\tan 30°} = \frac{1}{\frac{\sqrt{3}}{3}} = \frac{3}{\sqrt{3}} = \frac{3}{\sqrt{3}} \cdot \frac{\sqrt{3}}{\sqrt{3}} = \sqrt{3}$$

The six trigonometric functions evaluated for an angle measuring 30° are

$$\boxed{\sin 30° = \frac{1}{2}} \qquad \boxed{\cos 30° = \frac{\sqrt{3}}{2}} \qquad \boxed{\tan 30° = \frac{\sqrt{3}}{3}}$$

$$\boxed{\csc 30° = 2} \qquad \boxed{\sec 30° = \frac{2\sqrt{3}}{3}} \qquad \boxed{\cot 30° = \sqrt{3}}$$

■ **YOUR TURN**  Evaluate the six trigonometric functions for an angle that measures 60°.

In comparing our answers in Example 1 and Your Turn, we see that the following cofunction relationships are true. We call these *cofunction* relationships.

$$\sin 30° = \cos 60° \qquad \sec 30° = \csc 60° \qquad \tan 30° = \cot 60°$$

$$\sin 60° = \cos 30° \qquad \sec 60° = \csc 30° \qquad \tan 60° = \cot 30°$$

Notice that 30° and 60° are complementary angles.

■ **Answer:**

$$\sin 60° = \frac{\sqrt{3}}{2} \qquad \cos 60° = \frac{1}{2}$$

$$\tan 60° = \sqrt{3} \qquad \csc 60° = \frac{2\sqrt{3}}{3}$$

$$\sec 60° = 2 \qquad \cot 60° = \frac{\sqrt{3}}{3}$$

**EXAMPLE 2** **Evaluating the Trigonometric Functions Exactly for 45°**

Evaluate the six trigonometric functions for an angle that measures 45°.

**Solution:**

Label the sides of the 45°-45°-90° triangle
as opposite, adjacent, or hypotenuse
with respect to one of the 45° angles.

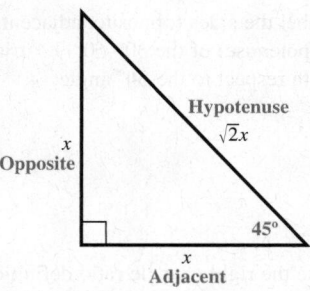

Use the right triangle ratio definitions of sine, cosine, and tangent.

$$\sin 45° = \frac{\text{opposite}}{\text{hypotenuse}} = \frac{x}{\sqrt{2}x} = \frac{1}{\sqrt{2}} = \frac{1}{\sqrt{2}} \cdot \frac{\sqrt{2}}{\sqrt{2}} = \frac{\sqrt{2}}{2}$$

$$\cos 45° = \frac{\text{adjacent}}{\text{hypotenuse}} = \frac{x}{\sqrt{2}x} = \frac{1}{\sqrt{2}} = \frac{1}{\sqrt{2}} \cdot \frac{\sqrt{2}}{\sqrt{2}} = \frac{\sqrt{2}}{2}$$

$$\tan 45° = \frac{\text{opposite}}{\text{adjacent}} = \frac{x}{x} = 1$$

Use the reciprocal identities to obtain the values of the cosecant, secant, and cotangent
functions.

$$\csc 45° = \frac{1}{\sin 45°} = \frac{1}{\frac{\sqrt{2}}{2}} = \frac{2}{\sqrt{2}} = \frac{2}{\sqrt{2}} \cdot \frac{\sqrt{2}}{\sqrt{2}} = \sqrt{2}$$

$$\sec 45° = \frac{1}{\cos 45°} = \frac{1}{\frac{\sqrt{2}}{2}} = \frac{2}{\sqrt{2}} = \frac{2}{\sqrt{2}} \cdot \frac{\sqrt{2}}{\sqrt{2}} = \sqrt{2}$$

$$\cot 45° = \frac{1}{\tan 45°} = \frac{1}{1} = 1$$

### Study Tip

$\sin 45° = \dfrac{\sqrt{2}}{2}$ is exact, whereas if
we evaluate with a calculator, we get
an approximation:

$$\sin 45° \approx 0.7071$$

The six trigonometric functions evaluated for an angle measuring 45° are

| | | |
|---|---|---|
| $\sin 45° = \dfrac{\sqrt{2}}{2}$ | $\cos 45° = \dfrac{\sqrt{2}}{2}$ | $\tan 45° = 1$ |
| $\csc 45° = \sqrt{2}$ | $\sec 45° = \sqrt{2}$ | $\cot 45° = 1$ |

We see that the following *cofunction* relationships are true

$$\sin 45° = \cos 45° \qquad \sec 45° = \csc 45° \qquad \tan 45° = \cot 45°$$

since 45° and 45° are complementary angles.

The trigonometric function values for the three special angle measures, 30°, 45°, and 60°,
are summarized in the following table.

## Trigonometric Function Values for Special Angles

| θ | | | | | | | |
| DEGREES | RADIANS | $\sin\theta$ | $\cos\theta$ | $\tan\theta$ | $\cot\theta$ | $\sec\theta$ | $\csc\theta$ |
|---|---|---|---|---|---|---|---|
| 30° | $\dfrac{\pi}{6}$ | $\dfrac{1}{2}$ | $\dfrac{\sqrt{3}}{2}$ | $\dfrac{\sqrt{3}}{3}$ | $\sqrt{3}$ | $\dfrac{2\sqrt{3}}{3}$ | $2$ |
| 45° | $\dfrac{\pi}{4}$ | $\dfrac{\sqrt{2}}{2}$ | $\dfrac{\sqrt{2}}{2}$ | $1$ | $1$ | $\sqrt{2}$ | $\sqrt{2}$ |
| 60° | $\dfrac{\pi}{3}$ | $\dfrac{\sqrt{3}}{2}$ | $\dfrac{1}{2}$ | $\sqrt{3}$ | $\dfrac{\sqrt{3}}{3}$ | $2$ | $\dfrac{2\sqrt{3}}{3}$ |

It is important to **learn** the special values in **red** for sine and cosine. All other values in the table can be found through reciprocals or quotients of these two functions. Remember that the tangent function is the ratio of the sine to cosine functions.

$$\sin\theta = \frac{\text{opposite}}{\text{hypotenuse}} \qquad \cos\theta = \frac{\text{adjacent}}{\text{hypotenuse}} \qquad \tan\theta = \frac{\sin\theta}{\cos\theta} = \frac{\dfrac{\text{opposite}}{\text{hypotenuse}}}{\dfrac{\text{adjacent}}{\text{hypotenuse}}} = \frac{\text{opposite}}{\text{adjacent}}$$

**Study Tip**

If you memorize the values for sine and cosine for the angles given in the table, then the other trigonometric function values in the table can be found using the quotient and reciprocal identities.

## Using Calculators to Evaluate (Approximate) Trigonometric Functions

We now turn our attention to using calculators to evaluate trigonometric functions, which often results in an approximation. Scientific and graphing calculators have buttons for sine (sin), cosine (cos), and tangent (tan) functions.

**EXAMPLE 3    Evaluating Trigonometric Functions with a Calculator**

Use a calculator to find the values of

**a.** $\sin 75°$    **b.** $\tan 67°$    **c.** $\sec 52°$    **d.** $\cos\left(\dfrac{\pi}{6}\right)$    **e.** $\tan\left(\dfrac{\pi}{8}\right)$

Round your answers to four decimal places.

**Solution:**

**a.** 0.965925826    $\approx 0.9659$

**b.** 2.355852366    $\approx 2.3559$

**c.** $\cos 52° \approx 0.615661475$    $1/x$ (or $x^{-1}$)    1.624269245    $\approx 1.6243$

**d.** 0.866025403    $\approx 0.8660$

**e.** 0.414213562    $\approx 0.4142$

*Note:* We know $\cos\left(\dfrac{\pi}{6}\right) = \dfrac{\sqrt{3}}{2} \approx 0.8660$.

**Study Tip**

In calculating secant, cosecant, and cotangent function values with a calculator, it is important not to round the number until after using the reciprocal function key $1/x$.

■ **YOUR TURN** Use a calculator to find the values of

**a.** $\cos 22°$    **b.** $\tan 81°$    **c.** $\csc 37°$    **d.** $\sin\left(\dfrac{\pi}{4}\right)$    **e.** $\cot\left(\dfrac{\pi}{12}\right)$

Round your answers to four decimal places.

■ **Answer: a.** 0.9272    **b.** 6.3138
**c.** 1.6616    **d.** 0.7071
**e.** 3.7321

When calculating secant, cosecant, and cotangent function values with a calculator, it is important not to round the number until after using the reciprocal function key $1/x$ or $x^{-1}$ in order to be as accurate as possible.

## Solving Right Triangles

A triangle has three angles and three sides. To *solve a triangle* means to find the length of all three sides and the measures of all three angles.

**EXAMPLE 4   Solving a Right Triangle Given an Angle and a Side**

Solve the right triangle—find $a$, $b$, and $\alpha$.

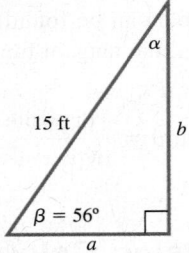

**Solution:**

**STEP 1 Solve for $\alpha$.**

The two acute angles in a right triangle are complementary.

$$\alpha + 56° = 90°$$

Solve for $\alpha$.

$$\boxed{\alpha = 34°}$$

**STEP 2 Solve for $a$.**

Cosine of an angle is equal to the adjacent side over the hypotenuse.

$$\cos 56° = \frac{a}{15}$$

Solve for $a$.

$$a = 15\cos 56°$$

Evaluate the right side of the expression using a calculator.

$$a \approx 8.38789$$

Round $a$ to two significant digits.

$$\boxed{a \approx 8.4 \text{ ft}}$$

**STEP 3 Solve for $b$.**

Notice that there are two ways to solve for $b$: trigonometric functions or the Pythagorean theorem. Although it is tempting to use the Pythagorean theorem, it is better to use the given information with trigonometric functions than to use a value that has already been rounded, which could make results less accurate.

Sine of an angle is equal to the opposite side over the hypotenuse.

$$\sin 56° = \frac{b}{15}$$

Solve for $b$.

$$b = 15\sin 56°$$

Evaluate the right side of the expression using a calculator.

$$b \approx 12.43556$$

Round $b$ to two significant digits.

$$\boxed{b \approx 12 \text{ ft}}$$

STEP 4 **Check.**

Check the trigonometric values of the specific angles by calculating the trigonometric ratios.

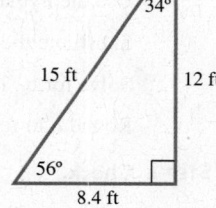

$$\sin 34° \stackrel{?}{=} \frac{8.4}{15} \qquad \cos 34° \stackrel{?}{=} \frac{12}{15} \qquad \tan 34° \stackrel{?}{=} \frac{8.4}{12}$$

$$0.5592 \approx 0.56 \qquad 0.8290 \approx 0.80 \qquad 0.6745 \approx 0.70$$

■ **YOUR TURN** Solve the right triangle— find $a$, $b$, and $\theta$.

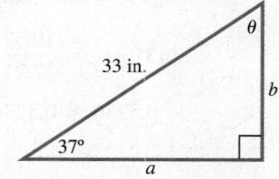

■ **Answer:** $\theta = 53°$, $a \approx 26$ in., $b \approx 20$ in.

Sometimes in solving a right triangle, the side lengths are given and we need to find the angles. To do this, we can work backwards from the table of known values. For example, if $\cos \theta = \frac{1}{2}$, what is $\theta$? We see from the table of exact values that $\theta = 60°$ or $\frac{\pi}{3}$. To find an angle that is not listed in the table, we use the inverse cosine function, $\cos^{-1}$, key on a calculator. In a later section, we will discuss inverse trigonometric functions, but for now we will simply use the inverse trigonometric function keys on a calculator to determine the unknown angle.

### EXAMPLE 5    Solving a Right Triangle Given Two Sides

Solve the right triangle—find $a$, $\alpha$, and $\beta$.

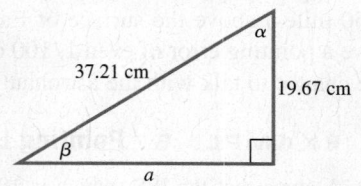

**Solution:**

STEP 1 **Solve for $\alpha$.**

Cosine of an angle is equal to the adjacent side over hypotenuse.

$$\cos \alpha = \frac{19.67 \text{ cm}}{37.21 \text{ cm}}$$

Evaluate the right side using a calculator.

$$\cos \alpha \approx 0.528621338$$

Write the angle $\alpha$ in terms of the inverse cosine function.

$$\alpha \approx \cos^{-1} 0.528621338$$

Use a calculator to evaluate the inverse cosine function.

$$\alpha \approx 58.08764854°$$

Round $\alpha$ to the nearest hundredth of a degree.

$$\boxed{\alpha \approx 58.09°}$$

STEP 2 **Solve for $\beta$.**

The two acute angles in a right triangle are complementary.

$$\alpha + \beta = 90°$$

Substitute $\alpha \approx 58.09°$.

$$58.09 + \beta \approx 90°$$

Solve for $\beta$.

$$\boxed{\beta \approx 31.91°}$$

The answer is already rounded to the nearest hundredth of a degree.

*Technology Tip*

To find $\cos^{-1}\left(\dfrac{19.67}{37.21}\right)$, first press

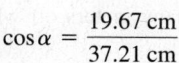 ENTER .

Next, press 2nd COS for $\cos^{-1}$ and 2nd (−) for the answer, ANS

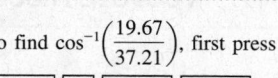

Or enter the entire expression as $\cos^{-1}\left(\dfrac{19.67}{37.21}\right)$. Press 2nd COS

19.67 ÷ 37.21 ) ENTER .

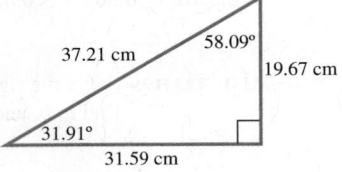

```
19.67/37.21
        .5286213383
cos⁻¹(Ans)
        58.08764854
cos⁻¹(19.67/37.21
)
        58.08764854
```

Using a scientific calculator, press

$\boxed{\cos^{-1}}$ $\boxed{(}$ $\boxed{19.67}$ $\boxed{\div}$ $\boxed{37.21}$

$\boxed{)}$ $\boxed{\text{ENTER}}$ .

■ **Answer:** $a \approx 16.0\,\text{mi}$, $\alpha \approx 43.0°$,
$\beta \approx 47.0°$

### Study Tip

To find a length in a right triangle,
use the sine, cosine, or tangent
function. To find an angle measure
in a right triangle, given the proper
ratio of side lengths, use the inverse
sine, inverse cosine, or inverse
tangent function.

### Technology Tip

To calculate $400 \tan 0.01°$, press

```
400tan(0.01)
        .0698131708
```

STEP 3 **Solve for a.**

Use the Pythagorean theorem. $\qquad a^2 + b^2 = c^2$

Substitute the given values for $b$ and $c$. $\quad a^2 + 19.67^2 = 37.21^2$

Solve for $a$. $\qquad\qquad\qquad\qquad a \approx 31.5859969$

Round $a$ to four significant digits. $\qquad \boxed{a \approx 31.59\,\text{cm}}$

STEP 4 **Check.**

Check the trigonometric values of the specific
angles by calculating the trigonometric ratio.

$$\sin 31.91° \overset{?}{=} \frac{19.67}{37.21} \qquad \sin 58.09° \overset{?}{=} \frac{31.59}{37.21}$$

$$0.5286 \approx 0.5286 \qquad\qquad 0.8489 \approx 0.8490$$

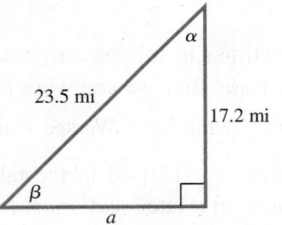

■ **YOUR TURN** Solve the right triangle—
find $a$, $\alpha$, and $\beta$.

## Applications

Suppose NASA wants to talk with the International Space Station (ISS), which is
traveling at a speed of 17,700 miles per hour (7900 meters per second), 400 kilometers
(250 miles) above the surface of Earth. If the antennas at the ground station in Houston
have a pointing error of even 1/100 of a degree, that is, 0.01°, the ground station will miss
the chance to talk with the astronauts.

### EXAMPLE 6   Pointing Error

Assume that the ISS (which is 108 meters long and 73 meters wide) is in a
400-kilometer low Earth orbit. If the communications antennas have a 0.01° pointing
error, how many meters off will the communications link be?

**Solution:**

Draw a right triangle that depicts this scenario.

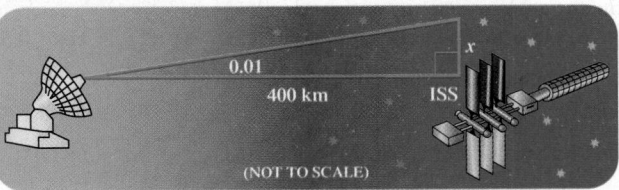

(NOT TO SCALE)

Identify the tangent ratio. $\qquad\qquad\qquad \tan 0.01° = \dfrac{x}{400}$

Solve for $x$. $\qquad\qquad\qquad\qquad\qquad x = (400\,\text{km})\tan 0.01°$

Evaluate the expression on the right. $\qquad\qquad x \approx 0.06981317\,\text{km}$

400 kilometers is accurate to three significant digits, so we express the answer to three
significant digits.

The pointing error causes the signal to be off by $\boxed{69.8\,\text{meters}}$ . Since the ISS is only
108 meters long, it is possible that the signal will be missed by the astronaut crew.

In navigation, the word **bearing** means the direction in which a vessel is pointed. **Heading** is the direction in which the vessel is actually traveling. Heading and bearing are only synonyms when there is no wind. Direction is often given as a bearing, which is the measure of an acute angle with respect to the north–south vertical line. "The plane has a bearing of N 20° E" means that the plane is pointed 20° to the east of due north.

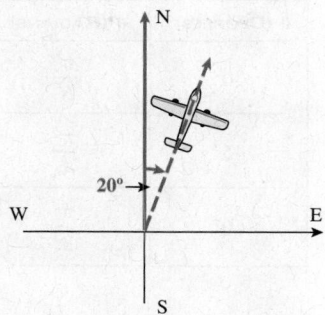

## EXAMPLE 7    Bearing (Navigation)

A jet takes off bearing N 28° E and flies 5 miles, and then makes a left (90°) turn and flies 12 miles farther. If the control tower operator wants to locate the plane, what bearing should she use?

**Solution:**

Draw a picture that represents this scenario.

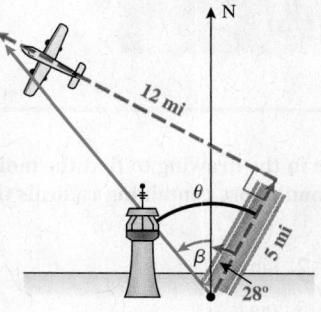

Identify the tangent ratio.

$$\tan\theta = \frac{12}{5}$$

Use the inverse tangent function to solve for $\theta$.

$$\theta = \tan^{-1}\left(\frac{12}{5}\right) \approx 67.4°$$

Subtract 28° from $\theta$ to find the bearing, $\beta$.

$$\beta \approx 67.4° - 28° \approx 39.4°$$

Round to the nearest degree.

$$\boxed{\beta \approx \text{N } 39° \text{ W}}$$

The trigonometric functions defined in terms of ratios of side lengths of right triangles are given by

$$\sin \theta = \frac{\text{opposite}}{\text{hypotenuse}}$$

$$\cos \theta = \frac{\text{adjacent}}{\text{hypotenuse}}$$

$$\tan \theta = \frac{\text{opposite}}{\text{adjacent}}$$

And the remaining three trigonometric functions can be found using the reciprocal identities:

$$\csc \theta = \frac{1}{\sin \theta} \quad \sin \theta \neq 0$$

$$\sec \theta = \frac{1}{\cos \theta} \quad \cos \theta \neq 0$$

$$\cot \theta = \frac{1}{\tan \theta} \quad \tan \theta \neq 0$$

The following table lists the values of the sine and cosine functions for special acute angles:

| $\theta$ (DEGREES) | $\theta$ (RADIANS) | $\sin \theta$ | $\cos \theta$ | $\tan \theta$ |
|---|---|---|---|---|
| 30° | $\dfrac{\pi}{6}$ | $\dfrac{1}{2}$ | $\dfrac{\sqrt{3}}{2}$ | $\dfrac{\sqrt{3}}{3}$ |
| 45° | $\dfrac{\pi}{4}$ | $\dfrac{\sqrt{2}}{2}$ | $\dfrac{\sqrt{2}}{2}$ | 1 |
| 60° | $\dfrac{\pi}{3}$ | $\dfrac{\sqrt{3}}{2}$ | $\dfrac{1}{2}$ | $\sqrt{3}$ |

**▪ SKILLS**

In Exercises 1–6, refer to the triangle in the drawing to find the indicated trigonometric function values. Rationalize any denominators containing radicals that you encounter in the answers.

**1.** $\cos \theta$        **2.** $\sin \theta$        **3.** $\sec \theta$

**4.** $\csc \theta$        **5.** $\tan \theta$        **6.** $\cot \theta$

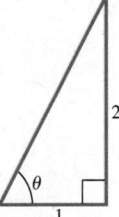

For Exercises 7–12, refer to the triangle in the drawing to find the indicated trigonometric function values. Rationalize any denominators containing radicals that you encounter in the answers.

**7.** $\sin \theta$        **8.** $\cos \theta$        **9.** $\sec \theta$

**10.** $\csc \theta$        **11.** $\cot \theta$        **12.** $\tan \theta$

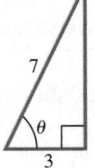

In Exercises 13–18, match the trigonometric function values.

     **a.** $\dfrac{1}{2}$    **b.** $\dfrac{\sqrt{3}}{2}$    **c.** $\dfrac{\sqrt{2}}{2}$

**13.** $\sin 30°$     **14.** $\sin 60°$     **15.** $\cos\left(\dfrac{\pi}{6}\right)$     **16.** $\cos\left(\dfrac{\pi}{3}\right)$     **17.** $\sin 45°$     **18.** $\cos\left(\dfrac{\pi}{4}\right)$

In Exercises 19–21, use the results in Exercises 13–18 and the trigonometric quotient identity $\tan \theta = \dfrac{\sin \theta}{\cos \theta}$ to calculate the following values:

**19.** $\tan 30°$  **20.** $\tan\left(\dfrac{\pi}{4}\right)$  **21.** $\tan 60°$

In Exercises 22–30, use the results in Exercises 13–21 and the reciprocal identities $\csc \theta = \dfrac{1}{\sin \theta}$, $\sec \theta = \dfrac{1}{\cos \theta}$, and $\cot \theta = \dfrac{1}{\tan \theta}$ to calculate the following values:

**22.** $\csc 30°$  **23.** $\sec 30°$  **24.** $\cot\left(\dfrac{\pi}{6}\right)$  **25.** $\csc\left(\dfrac{\pi}{3}\right)$  **26.** $\sec 60°$  **27.** $\cot 60°$

**28.** $\csc 45°$  **29.** $\sec\left(\dfrac{\pi}{4}\right)$  **30.** $\cot\left(\dfrac{\pi}{4}\right)$

In Exercises 31–46, use a calculator to evaluate the trigonometric functions for the indicated angle values. Round your answers to four decimal places.

**31.** $\sin 37°$  **32.** $\sin 17.8°$  **33.** $\cos 82°$  **34.** $\cos 21.9°$  **35.** $\sin\left(\dfrac{\pi}{12}\right)$  **36.** $\sin\left(\dfrac{5\pi}{9}\right)$

**37.** $\cos\left(\dfrac{6\pi}{5}\right)$  **38.** $\cos\left(\dfrac{13\pi}{7}\right)$  **39.** $\tan 54°$  **40.** $\tan 43.2°$  **41.** $\tan\left(\dfrac{\pi}{8}\right)$  **42.** $\cot\left(\dfrac{3\pi}{5}\right)$

**43.** $\csc\left(\dfrac{10\pi}{19}\right)$  **44.** $\sec\left(\dfrac{4\pi}{9}\right)$  **45.** $\cot 55°$  **46.** $\cot 29°$

In Exercises 47–54, refer to the right triangle diagram and the given information to find the indicated measure. Write your answers for angle measures in decimal degrees.

**47.** $\alpha = 55°$, $c = 22$ ft; find $a$.

**48.** $\alpha = 55°$, $c = 22$ ft; find $b$.

**49.** $\alpha = 20.5°$, $b = 14.7$ mi; find $a$.

**50.** $\beta = 69.3°$, $a = 0.752$ mi; find $b$.

**51.** $\beta = 25°$, $a = 11$ km; find $c$.

**52.** $\beta = 75°$, $b = 26$ km; find $c$.

**53.** $b = 2.3$ m, $c = 4.9$ m; find $\alpha$.

**54.** $b = 7.8$ m, $c = 13$ m; find $\beta$.

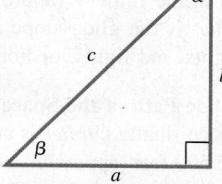

In Exercises 55–66, refer to the right triangle diagram and the given information to solve the right triangle. Write your answers for angle measures in decimal degrees.

**55.** $\alpha = 32°$ and $c = 12$ ft

**56.** $\alpha = 65°$ and $c = 37$ ft

**57.** $\beta = 72°$ and $c = 9.7$ mm

**58.** $\beta = 45°$ and $c = 7.8$ mm

**59.** $\alpha = 54.2°$ and $a = 111$ mi

**60.** $\beta = 47.2°$ and $a = 9.75$ mi

**61.** $a = 42.5$ ft and $b = 28.7$ ft

**62.** $a = 19.8$ ft and $c = 48.7$ ft

**63.** $a = 35,236$ km and $c = 42,766$ km

**64.** $b = 0.1245$ mm and $c = 0.8763$ mm

**65.** $\beta = 25.4°$ and $b = 11.6$ in.

**66.** $\beta = 39.21°$ and $b = 6.3$ m

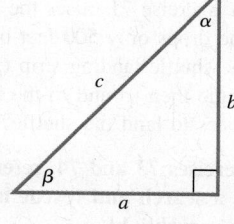

■ **APPLICATIONS**

Exercises 67 and 68 illustrate a mid-air refueling scenario that military aircraft often enact. Assume the elevation angle that the hose makes with the plane being fueled is $\theta = 30°$.

**67. Mid-Air Refueling.** If the hose is 150 feet long, what should be the altitude difference $a$ between the two planes? Round to the nearest foot.

**68. Mid-Air Refueling.** If the smallest acceptable altitude difference $a$ between the two planes is 100 feet, how long should the hose be? Round to the nearest foot.

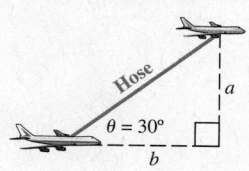

**Exercises 69–72 are based on the idea of a glide slope (the angle the flight path makes with the ground).**

Precision Approach Path Indicator (PAPI) lights are used as a visual approach slope aid for pilots landing aircraft. A typical glide path for commercial jet airliners is 3°. The space shuttle has an outer glide approach of 18°–20°. PAPI lights are typically configured as a row of four lights. All four lights are on, but in different combinations of red or white. If all four lights are white, then the angle of descent is too high; if all four lights are red, then the angle of descent is too low; and if there are two white and two red, then the approach is perfect.

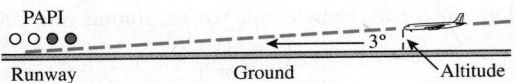

**69. Glide Path of a Commercial Jet Airliner.** If a commercial jetliner is 5000 feet (about 1 mile) ground distance from the runway, what should the altitude of the plane be to achieve two red and two white PAPI lights? (Assume this corresponds to a 3° glide path.)

**70. Glide Path of a Commercial Jet Airliner.** If a commercial jetliner is at an altitude of 450 feet when it is 5200 feet from the runway (approximately 1 mile ground distance), what is the glide slope angle? Will the pilot see white lights, red lights, or both?

**71. Glide Path of the Space Shuttle _Orbiter_.** If the pilot of the space shuttle _Orbiter_ is at an altitude of 3000 feet when she is 15,500 feet (approximately 3 miles) from the shuttle landing facility (ground distance), what is her glide slope angle (round to the nearest degree)? Is she too high or too low?

**72. Glide Path of the Space Shuttle _Orbiter_.** If the same pilot in Exercise 71 raises the nose of the gliding shuttle so that she drops only 500 feet by the time she is 7800 feet from the shuttle landing strip (ground distance), what is her glide angle then (round to the nearest degree)? Is she within the specs to land the shuttle?

**In Exercises 73 and 74, refer to the illustration below, which shows a search and rescue helicopter with a 30° field of view with a searchlight.**

**73. Search and Rescue.** If the search and rescue helicopter is flying at an altitude of 150 feet above sea level, what is the diameter of the circle illuminated on the surface of the water?

**74. Search and Rescue.** If the search and rescue helicopter is flying at an altitude of 500 feet above sea level, what is the diameter of the circle illuminated on the surface of the water?

**For Exercises 75–78, refer to the following:**

Geostationary orbits are useful because they cause a satellite to appear stationary with respect to a fixed point on the rotating Earth. As a result, an antenna (dish TV) can point in a fixed direction and maintain a link with the satellite. The satellite orbits in the direction of Earth's rotation at an altitude of approximately 35,000 kilometers.

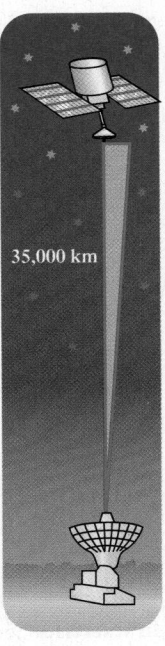

**75. Dish TV.** If your dish TV antenna has a pointing error of 0.000278°, how long would the satellite have to be in order to maintain a link? Round your answer to the nearest meter.

**76. Dish TV.** If your dish TV antenna has a pointing error of 0.000139°, how long would the satellite have to be in order to maintain a link? Round your answer to the nearest meter.

**77. Dish TV.** If the satellite in a geostationary orbit (at 35,000 kilometers) was only 10 meters long, about how accurate would the pointing of the dish have to be? Give the answer in degrees to two significant digits.

**78. Dish TV.** If the satellite in a geostationary orbit (at 35,000 kilometers) was only 30 meters long, about how accurate would the pointing of the dish have to be? Give the answer in degrees to two significant digits.

**79. Angle of Inclination (Skiing).** The angle of inclination of a mountain with triple black diamond ski trails is 65°. If a skier at the top of the mountain is at an elevation of 4000 feet, how long is the ski run from the top to the base of the mountain? Round to the nearest foot.

**80. Bearing (Navigation).** If a plane takes off bearing N 33° W and flies 6 miles and then makes a right (90°) turn and flies 10 miles further, what bearing will the traffic controller use to locate the plane?

**For Exercises 81 and 82, refer to the following:**

The structure of molecules is critical to the study of materials science and organic chemistry, and has countless applications to a variety of interesting phenomena. Trigonometry plays a critical role in determining the bonding angles of molecules. For instance, the structure of the $(FeCl_4Br_2)^{-3}$ ion (dibromatetetrachlorideferrate III) is shown in the figure below.

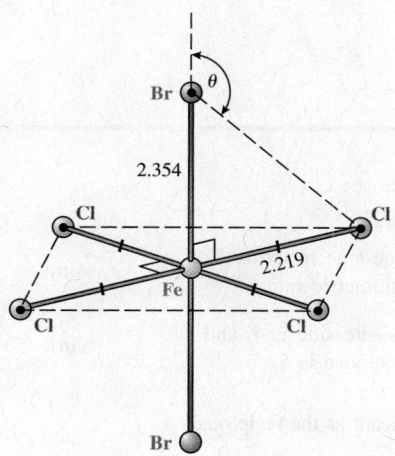

81. **Chemistry.** Determine the angle $\theta$ [i.e., the angle between the axis containing the apical bromide atom (Br) and the segment connecting Br to Cl].

82. **Chemistry.** Now, suppose one of the chlorides (Cl) is removed. The resulting structure is triagonal in nature, resulting in the following structure. Does the angle $\theta$ change? If so, what is its new value?

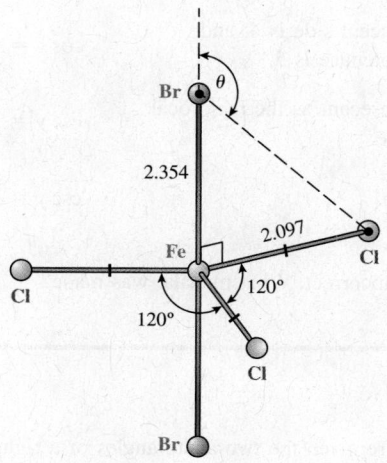

83. **Construction.** Two neighborhood kids are planning to build a treehouse in Tree I, and connect it with a zipline to Tree II that is 40 yards away. The base of the treehouse will be 20 feet above the ground, and a platform will be nailed into Tree II, 3 feet above the ground. The plan is to connect the base of the treehouse on Tree I to an anchor 2 feet above the platform on Tree II.

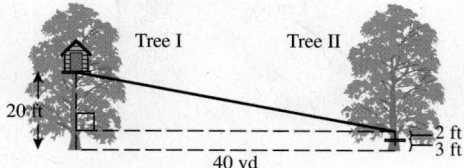

How much zipline (in feet) will they need? Round your answer to the nearest foot.

84. **Construction.** In Exercise 83, what is the angle of depression $\beta$ that the zipline makes with Tree I? Express your answer in two significant digits.

85. **Construction.** A pool that measures 5 feet above the ground is to be placed between the trees directly in the path of the zipline in Exercise 83. Assuming that a rider of the zipline dangles at most 3 feet below the wire anywhere in route, what is the closest the edge of the pool can be placed to tree 2 so that the pool will not impede a rider's trip down the zipline?

86. **Construction.** If the treehouse is to be built so that its base is now 22 feet above the base of tree 1, where should the anchor on tree 2 (to which the zipline is connected) be placed in order to ensure the same angle of depression found in Exercise 84?

**For Exercises 87 and 88, refer to the following:**

A canal constructed by a water-users association can be approximated by an isosceles triangle (see the figure below). When the canal was originally constructed, the depth of the canal was 5.0 feet and the angle defining the shape of the canal was 60°.

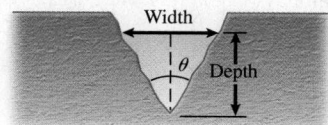

87. **Environmental Science.** If the width of the water surface today is 4.0 feet, find the depth of the water running through the canal.

88. **Environmental Science.** One year later a survey is performed to measure the effects of erosion on the canal. It is determined that when the water depth is 4.0 feet, the width of the water surface is 5.0 feet. Find the angle $\theta$ defining the shape of the canal to the nearest degree. Has erosion affected the shape of the canal? Explain.

**For Exercises 89 and 90, refer to the following:**

After breaking a femur, a patient is placed in traction. The end of a femur of length *l* is lifted to an elevation forming an angle θ with the horizontal (angle of elevation).

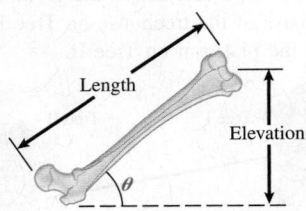

Length

Elevation

θ

**89. Health/Medicine.** A femur 18 inches long is placed into traction, forming an angle of 15° with the horizontal. Find the height of elevation at the end of the femur.

**90. Health/Medicine.** A femur 18 inches long is placed in traction with an elevation of 6.2 inches. What is the angle of elevation of the femur?

## ▪ CATCH THE MISTAKE

**For Exercises 91–94, explain the mistake that is made.**

For the triangle in the drawing, calculate the indicated trigonometric function values.

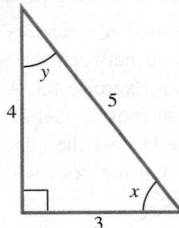

y

4

5

x

3

**91. Calculate sin *y*.**

**Solution:**

Formulate sine in terms of trigonometric ratios.

$$\sin y = \frac{\text{opposite}}{\text{hypotenuse}}$$

The opposite side is 4, and the hypotenuse is 5.

$$\sin y = \frac{4}{5}$$

This is incorrect. What mistake was made?

**92. Calculate tan *x*.**

**Solution:**

Formulate tangent in terms of trigonometric ratios.

$$\tan x = \frac{\text{adjacent}}{\text{opposite}}$$

The adjacent side is 3, and the opposite side is 4.

$$\tan x = \frac{3}{4}$$

This is incorrect. What mistake was made?

**93. Calculate sec *x*.**

**Solution:**

Formulate sine in terms of trigonometric ratios.

$$\sin x = \frac{\text{opposite}}{\text{hypotenuse}}$$

The opposite side is 4, and the hypotenuse is 5.

$$\sin x = \frac{4}{5}$$

Write secant as the reciprocal of sine.

$$\sec x = \frac{1}{\sin x}$$

Simplify.

$$\sec x = \frac{1}{\frac{4}{5}} = \frac{5}{4}$$

This is incorrect. What mistake was made?

**94. Calculate csc *y*.**

**Solution:**

Formulate cosine in terms of trigonometric ratios.

$$\cos y = \frac{\text{adjacent}}{\text{hypotenuse}}$$

The adjacent side is 4, and the hypotenuse is 5.

$$\cos y = \frac{4}{5}$$

Write cosecant as the reciprocal of cosine.

$$\csc y = \frac{1}{\cos y}$$

Simplify.

$$\csc y = \frac{1}{\frac{4}{5}} = \frac{5}{4}$$

This is incorrect. What mistake was made?

## ▪ CONCEPTUAL

**In Exercises 95–98, determine whether each statement is true or false.**

**95.** If you are given the measures of two sides of a right triangle, you can solve the right triangle.

**96.** If you are given the measures of one side and one acute angle of a right triangle, you can solve the right triangle.

**97.** If you are given the two acute angles of a right triangle, you can solve the right triangle.

**98.** If you are given the hypotenuse of a right triangle and the angle opposite the hypotenuse, you can solve the right triangle.

**In Exercises 99–102, use trignometric ratios and the assumption that $a$ is much larger than $b$.**

Thus far, in this text we have discussed trigonometric values only for acute angles, or for $0° < \theta < 90°$. How do we determine these values when $\theta$ is approximately $0°$ or $90°$? We will formally consider these cases in the next section, but for now, draw and label a right triangle that has one angle very close to $0°$, so that the opposite side is very small compared to the adjacent side. Then the hypotenuse and the adjacent side will be very close to the same length.

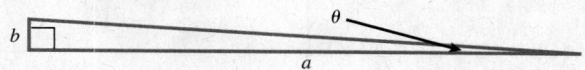

**99.** Approximate $\sin 0°$ without using a calculator.

**100.** Approximate $\cos 0°$ without using a calculator.

**101.** Approximate $\cos 90°$ without using a calculator.

**102.** Approximate $\sin 90°$ without using a calculator.

## ▪ CHALLENGE

**For Exercises 103 and 104, consider the following diagram:**

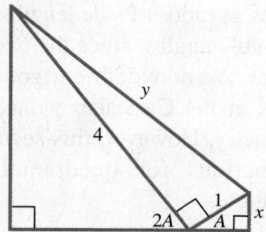

**103.** Determine $x$.

**104.** Determine $y$.

## ▪ TECHNOLOGY

**105.** Calculate $\sec 70°$ in the following two ways:

  **a.** Find $\cos 70°$ to three decimal places and then divide 1 by that number. Write that number to five decimal places.

  **b.** With a calculator in degree mode, enter 70, cos, 1/x, and round the result to five decimal places.

**106.** Calculate $\csc 40°$ in the following two ways:

  **a.** Find $\sin 40°$ to three decimal places and then divide 1 by that number. Write this last result to five decimal places.

  **b.** With a calculator in degree mode, enter 40, sin, 1/x, and round the result to five decimal places.

**107.** Calculate $\cot 54.9°$ in the following two ways:

  **a.** Find $\tan 54.9°$ to three decimal places and then divide 1 by that number. Write that number to five decimal places.

  **b.** With a calculator in degree mode, enter 54.9, tan, 1/x, and round the result to five decimal places.

**108.** Calculate $\sec 18.6°$ in the following two ways:

  **a.** Find $\cos 18.6°$ to three decimal places and then divide 1 by that number. Write that number to five decimal places.

  **b.** With a calculator in degree mode, enter 18.6, cos, 1/x, and round the result to five decimal places.

## ▪ PREVIEW TO CALCULUS

In calculus, the value of $F(b) - F(a)$ of a function $F(x)$ at $x = a$ and $x = b$ plays an important role in the calculation of definite integrals. In Exercises 109–112, find the exact value of $F(b) - F(a)$.

**109.** $F(x) = \sec x, a = \dfrac{\pi}{6}, b = \dfrac{\pi}{3}$

**110.** $F(x) = \sin^3 x, a = 0, b = \dfrac{\pi}{4}$

**111.** $F(x) = \tan x + 2\cos x, a = 0, b = \dfrac{\pi}{3}$

**112.** $F(x) = \dfrac{\cot x - 4\sin x}{\cos x}, a = \dfrac{\pi}{4}, b = \dfrac{\pi}{3}$

**SKILLS OBJECTIVES**

- Calculate trigonometric function values for nonacute angles.
- Determine the reference angle of a nonacute angle.
- Calculate the trigonometric function values for quadrantal angles.

**CONCEPTUAL OBJECTIVES**

- Understand that right triangle ratio definitions of trigonometric functions for acute angles are consistent with definitions of trigonometric functions for all angles in the Cartesian plane.
- Understand why some trigonometric functions are undefined for quadrantal angles.
- Understand that the ranges of the sine and cosine functions are bounded, whereas the ranges for the other four trigonometric functions are unbounded.

In Section 4.2, we defined trigonometric functions as ratios of side lengths of right triangles. This definition holds only for acute ($0° < \theta < 90°$) angles, since the two angles in a right triangle other than the right angle must be acute. We now define trigonometric functions as ratios of $x$- and $y$-coordinates and distances in the Cartesian plane, which for acute angles is consistent with right triangle trigonometry. However, this second approach also enables us to formulate trigonometric functions for quadrantal angles (whose terminal side lies along an axis) and nonacute angles.

## Trigonometric Functions: The Cartesian Plane

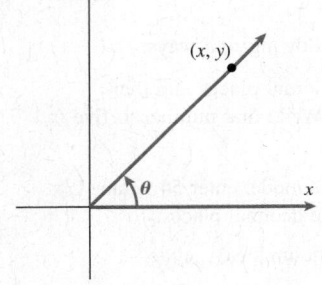

To define the trigonometric functions in the Cartesian plane, let us start with an acute angle $\theta$ in standard position. Choose any point $(x, y)$ on the terminal side of the angle as long as it is not the vertex (the origin).

A right triangle can be drawn so that the right angle is made when a perpendicular segment connects the point $(x, y)$ to the $x$-axis. Notice that the side opposite $\theta$ has length $y$ and the other leg of the right triangle has length $x$.

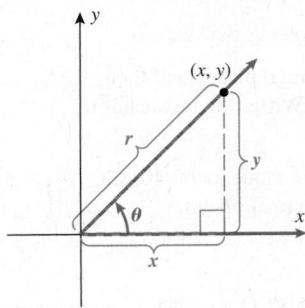

The distance $r$ from the origin $(0, 0)$ to the point $(x, y)$ can be found using the distance formula.

$$r = \sqrt{(x - 0)^2 + (y - 0)^2}$$
$$r = \sqrt{x^2 + y^2}$$
$$r > 0$$

Since $r$ is a distance and $x$ and $y$ are not both zero, $r$ is always positive.

Using our first definition of trigonometric functions in terms of right triangle ratios (Section 4.2), we know that $\sin\theta = \dfrac{\text{opposite}}{\text{hypotenuse}}$. From this picture, we see that sine can also be defined by the relation $\sin\theta = \dfrac{y}{r}$. Similar reasoning holds for all six trigonometric functions and leads us to the second definition of the trigonometric functions, in terms of ratios of coordinates of a point and distances in the Cartesian plane.

---

**DEFINITION**    **Trigonometric Functions**

Let $(x, y)$ be a point, other than the origin, on the terminal side of an angle $\theta$ in standard position. Let $r$ be the distance from the point $(x, y)$ to the origin. Then the six trigonometric functions are defined as

$$\sin\theta = \frac{y}{r} \qquad \cos\theta = \frac{x}{r} \qquad \tan\theta = \frac{y}{x} \quad (x \neq 0)$$

$$\csc\theta = \frac{r}{y} \quad (y \neq 0) \qquad \sec\theta = \frac{r}{x} \quad (x \neq 0) \qquad \cot\theta = \frac{x}{y} \quad (y \neq 0)$$

where $r = \sqrt{x^2 + y^2}$, or $x^2 + y^2 = r^2$. The distance $r$ is positive: $r > 0$.

---

**EXAMPLE 1    Calculating Trigonometric Function Values for Acute Angles**

The terminal side of an angle $\theta$ in standard position passes through the point $(2, 5)$. Calculate the values of the six trigonometric functions for angle $\theta$.

**Solution:**

**STEP 1  Draw the angle and label the point (2, 5).**

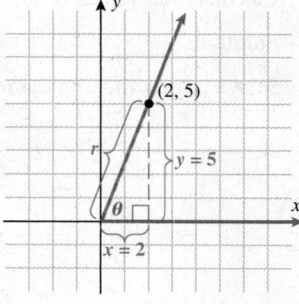

**STEP 2  Calculate the distance r.**    $r = \sqrt{2^2 + 5^2} = \sqrt{29}$

**STEP 3  Formulate the trigonometric functions in terms of x, y, and r.**

Let $x = 2, y = 5, r = \sqrt{29}$.

$$\sin\theta = \frac{y}{r} = \frac{5}{\sqrt{29}} \qquad\qquad \cos\theta = \frac{x}{r} = \frac{2}{\sqrt{29}} \qquad\qquad \tan\theta = \frac{y}{x} = \frac{5}{2}$$

$$\csc\theta = \frac{r}{y} = \frac{\sqrt{29}}{5} \qquad\qquad \sec\theta = \frac{r}{x} = \frac{\sqrt{29}}{2} \qquad\qquad \cot\theta = \frac{x}{y} = \frac{2}{5}$$

**STEP 4** **Rationalize any denominators containing a radical.**

$$\sin\theta = \frac{5}{\sqrt{29}} \cdot \frac{\sqrt{29}}{\sqrt{29}} = \frac{5\sqrt{29}}{29} \qquad \cos\theta = \frac{2}{\sqrt{29}} \cdot \frac{\sqrt{29}}{\sqrt{29}} = \frac{2\sqrt{29}}{29}$$

**STEP 5** **Write the values of the six trigonometric functions for $\theta$.**

$$\sin\theta = \frac{5\sqrt{29}}{29} \qquad \cos\theta = \frac{2\sqrt{29}}{29} \qquad \tan\theta = \frac{5}{2}$$

$$\csc\theta = \frac{\sqrt{29}}{5} \qquad \sec\theta = \frac{\sqrt{29}}{2} \qquad \cot\theta = \frac{2}{5}$$

*Note:* In Example 1, we could have used the values of the sine, cosine, and tangent functions along with the reciprocal identities to calculate the cosecant, secant, and cotangent function values.

■ **YOUR TURN** The terminal side of an angle $\theta$ in standard position passes through the point $(3, 7)$. Calculate the values of the six trigonometric functions for angle $\theta$.

**Study Tip**

There is no need to memorize definitions for secant, cosecant, and cotangent functions, since their values can be derived from the reciprocals of the sine, cosine, and tangent function values.

■ **Answer:**

$$\sin\theta = \frac{7\sqrt{58}}{58} \qquad \cos\theta = \frac{3\sqrt{58}}{58}$$

$$\tan\theta = \frac{7}{3} \qquad \csc\theta = \frac{\sqrt{58}}{7}$$

$$\sec\theta = \frac{\sqrt{58}}{3} \qquad \cot\theta = \frac{3}{7}$$

We can now find values for nonacute angles (angles with measure greater than or equal to $90°$) as well as negative angles.

**EXAMPLE 2** **Calculating Trigonometric Function Values for Nonacute Angles**

The terminal side of an angle $\theta$ in standard position passes through the point $(-4, -7)$. Calculate the values of the six trigonometric functions for angle $\theta$.

**Solution:**

**STEP 1** **Draw the angle and label the point $(-4, -7)$.**

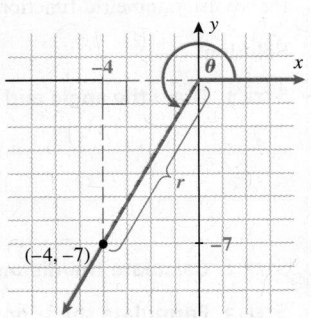

**STEP 2** **Calculate the distance $r$.** $\qquad r = \sqrt{(-4)^2 + (-7)^2} = \sqrt{65}$

**STEP 3** **Formulate the trigonometric functions in terms of $x$, $y$, and $r$.**

Let $x = -4$, $y = -7$, and $r = \sqrt{65}$.

$$\sin\theta = \frac{y}{r} = \frac{-7}{\sqrt{65}} \qquad \cos\theta = \frac{x}{r} = \frac{-4}{\sqrt{65}} \qquad \tan\theta = \frac{y}{x} = \frac{-7}{-4} = \frac{7}{4}$$

$$\csc\theta = \frac{r}{y} = \frac{\sqrt{65}}{-7} \qquad \sec\theta = \frac{r}{x} = \frac{\sqrt{65}}{-4} \qquad \cot\theta = \frac{x}{y} = \frac{-4}{-7} = \frac{4}{7}$$

STEP 4   **Rationalize the radical denominators in the sine and cosine functions.**

$$\sin\theta = \frac{y}{r} = \frac{-7}{\sqrt{65}} \cdot \frac{\sqrt{65}}{\sqrt{65}} = -\frac{7\sqrt{65}}{65}$$

$$\cos\theta = \frac{x}{r} = \frac{-4}{\sqrt{65}} \cdot \frac{\sqrt{65}}{\sqrt{65}} = -\frac{4\sqrt{65}}{65}$$

STEP 5   **Write the values of the six trigonometric functions for $\theta$.**

$$\sin\theta = -\frac{7\sqrt{65}}{65} \qquad \cos\theta = -\frac{4\sqrt{65}}{65} \qquad \tan\theta = \frac{7}{4}$$

$$\csc\theta = -\frac{\sqrt{65}}{7} \qquad \sec\theta = -\frac{\sqrt{65}}{4} \qquad \cot\theta = \frac{4}{7}$$

■ **YOUR TURN**   The terminal side of an angle $\theta$ in standard position passes through the point $(-3, -5)$. Calculate the values of the six trigonometric functions for angle $\theta$.

■ **Answer:**

$$\sin\theta = -\frac{5\sqrt{34}}{34} \qquad \cos\theta = -\frac{3\sqrt{34}}{34}$$

$$\tan\theta = \frac{5}{3} \qquad \csc\theta = -\frac{\sqrt{34}}{5}$$

$$\sec\theta = -\frac{\sqrt{34}}{3} \qquad \cot\theta = \frac{3}{5}$$

## Algebraic Signs of Trigonometric Functions

We have defined trigonometric functions as ratios of $x$, $y$, and $r$. Since $r$ is the distance from the origin to the point $(x, y)$ and distance is never negative, $r$ is always taken as the positive solution to $r^2 = x^2 + y^2$, so $r = \sqrt{x^2 + y^2}$.

The $x$-coordinate is positive in quadrants **I** and **IV** and negative in quadrants **II** and **III**.
The $y$-coordinate is positive in quadrants **I** and **II** and negative in quadrants **III** and **IV**.
Recall the definition of the six trigonometric functions in the Cartesian plane:

$$\sin\theta = \frac{y}{r} \qquad\qquad \cos\theta = \frac{x}{r} \qquad\qquad \tan\theta = \frac{y}{x} \quad (x \neq 0)$$

$$\csc\theta = \frac{r}{y} \;\; (y \neq 0) \qquad \sec\theta = \frac{r}{x} \;\; (x \neq 0) \qquad \cot\theta = \frac{x}{y} \;\; (y \neq 0)$$

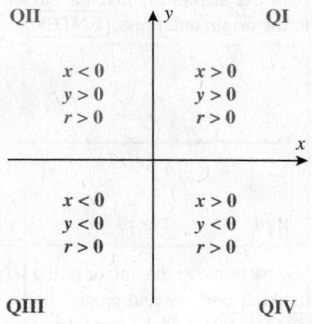

Therefore, the algebraic sign, $+$ or $-$, of each trigonometric function will depend on which quadrant contains the terminal side of angle $\theta$. Let us look at the three main trigonometric functions: sine, cosine, and tangent. In quadrant I, all three functions are positive since $x$, $y$, and $r$ are all positive. However, in quadrant II, only sine is positive since $y$ and $r$ are both positive. In quadrant III, only tangent is positive, and in quadrant IV, only cosine is positive. The expression "**A**ll **S**tudents **T**ake **C**alculus" helps us remember which of the three main trigonometric functions are positive in each quadrant.

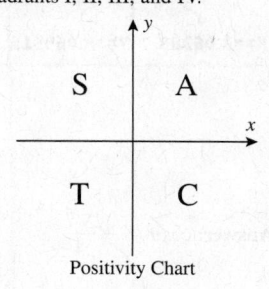
| PHRASE | QUADRANT | POSITIVE TRIGONOMETRIC FUNCTION |
|---|---|---|
| All | I | All three: sine, cosine, and tangent |
| Students | II | Sine |
| Take | III | Tangent |
| Calculus | IV | Cosine |

The following table indicates the algebraic sign of all six trigonometric functions according to the quadrant in which the terminal side of an angle $\theta$ lies. Notice that the reciprocal functions have the same sign.

| TERMINAL SIDE OF $\theta$ IN QUADRANT | $\sin\theta$ | $\cos\theta$ | $\tan\theta$ | $\cot\theta$ | $\sec\theta$ | $\csc\theta$ |
|:---:|:---:|:---:|:---:|:---:|:---:|:---:|
| I | + | + | + | + | + | + |
| II | + | − | − | − | − | + |
| III | − | − | + | + | − | − |
| IV | − | + | − | − | + | − |

**Technology Tip**

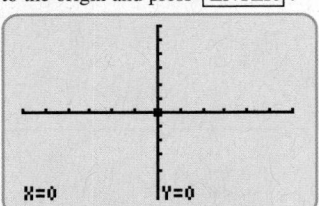

To draw the terminal side of the angle $\theta$ in quadrant III through the point $(-3, -4)$, press GRAPH 2nd: DRAW ▼ 2:Line( ENTER .

Now use arrows to move the cursor to the origin and press ENTER .

Use ◄ to move the cursor to the left to about $x = -3$ and press ENTER . Use ▼ to move the cursor down to about $y = -4$ and press ENTER .

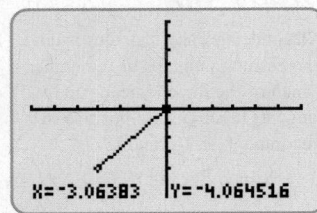

■ **Answer:** $\cos\theta = -\dfrac{\sqrt{7}}{4}$

**EXAMPLE 3   Evaluating a Trigonometric Function When One Trigonometric Function Value and the Quadrant of the Terminal Side Is Known**

If $\cos\theta = -\dfrac{3}{5}$ and the terminal side of angle $\theta$ lies in quadrant III, find $\sin\theta$.

**Solution:**

STEP 1 **Draw some angle $\theta$ in quadrant III.**

STEP 2 **Identify known quantities from the information given.**

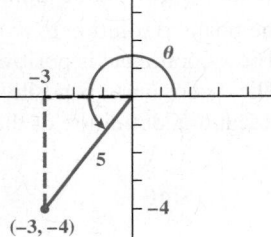

Recall that $\cos\theta = \dfrac{x}{r}$ and $r > 0$.     $\cos\theta = -\dfrac{3}{5} = \dfrac{-3}{5} = \dfrac{x}{r}$

Identify $x$ and $r$.     $x = -3$ and $r = 5$

STEP 3 **Since $x$ and $r$ are known, find $y$.**

Substitute $x = -3$ and $r = 5$ into $x^2 + y^2 = r^2$.     $(-3)^2 + y^2 = 5^2$

Solve for $y$.     $9 + y^2 = 25$

$$y^2 = 16$$
$$y = \pm 4$$

STEP 4 **Select the sign of $y$ based on quadrant information.**

Since the terminal side of angle $\theta$ lies in quadrant III, $y < 0$.     $y = -4$

STEP 5 **Find $\sin\theta$.**     $\sin\theta = \dfrac{y}{r} = \dfrac{-4}{5}$

$$\boxed{\sin\theta = -\dfrac{4}{5}}$$

■ **YOUR TURN**  If $\sin\theta = -\dfrac{3}{4}$ and the terminal side of angle $\theta$ lies in quadrant III, find $\cos\theta$.

We can also make a table showing the values of the trigonometric functions when the terminal side of angle $\theta$ lies along each axis (i.e., when $\theta$ is any of the quadrantal angles).

When the terminal side lies along the $x$-axis, then $y = 0$. When $y = 0$, notice that $r = \sqrt{x^2 + y^2} = \sqrt{x^2} = |x|$. When the terminal side lies along the positive $x$-axis, $x > 0$; and when the terminal side lies along the negative $x$-axis, $x < 0$. Therefore, when the terminal side of the angle lies on the positive $x$-axis, then $y = 0$, $x > 0$, and $r = x$; and when the terminal side lies along the negative $x$-axis, then $y = 0$, $x < 0$, and $r = |x|$. A similar argument can be made when the terminal side lies along the $y$-axis, which results in $r = |y|$.

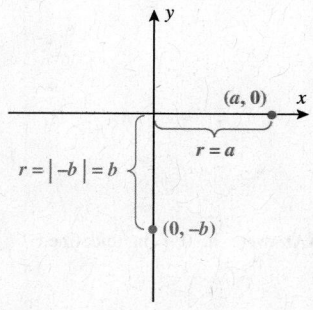

| TERMINAL SIDE OF $\theta$ LIES ALONG THE | $\sin\theta$ | $\cos\theta$ | $\tan\theta$ | $\cot\theta$ | $\sec\theta$ | $\csc\theta$ |
|---|---|---|---|---|---|---|
| Positive $x$-axis (e.g., $0°$ or $360°$ or $0$ or $2\pi$) | 0 | 1 | 0 | undefined | 1 | undefined |
| Positive $y$-axis $\left(\text{e.g., } 90° \text{ or } \dfrac{\pi}{2}\right)$ | 1 | 0 | undefined | 0 | undefined | 1 |
| Negative $x$-axis (e.g., $180°$ or $\pi$) | 0 | $-1$ | 0 | undefined | $-1$ | undefined |
| Negative $y$-axis $\left(\text{e.g., } 270° \text{ or } \dfrac{3\pi}{2}\right)$ | $-1$ | 0 | undefined | 0 | undefined | $-1$ |

## EXAMPLE 4  Working with Values of the Trigonometric Functions for Quadrantal Angles

Evaluate each of the following expressions, if possible:

**a.** $\cos 540° + \sin 270°$  **b.** $\cot\left(\dfrac{\pi}{2}\right) + \tan\left(-\dfrac{\pi}{2}\right)$

**Solution (a):**

The terminal side of an angle with measure $540°$ lies along the negative $x$-axis.

$$540° - 360° = 180°$$

Evaluate cosine of an angle whose terminal side lies along the negative $x$-axis.

$$\cos 540° = -1$$

Evaluate sine of an angle whose terminal side lies along the negative $y$-axis.

$$\sin 270° = -1$$

Sum the sine and cosine values.

$$\cos 540° + \sin 270° = -1 + (-1)$$

$$\cos 540° + \sin 270° = \boxed{-2}$$

*Check:* Evaluate this expression with a calculator.

**Solution (b):**

Evaluate cotangent of an angle whose terminal side lies along the positive $y$-axis.

$$\cot\left(\dfrac{\pi}{2}\right) = 0$$

The terminal side of an angle with measure $-\dfrac{\pi}{2}$ lies along the negative $y$-axis.

$$\tan\left(-\dfrac{\pi}{2}\right) = \tan\left(\dfrac{3\pi}{2}\right)$$

The tangent function is undefined for an angle whose terminal side lies along the negative $y$-axis.

$\tan\left(-\dfrac{\pi}{2}\right)$ is $\boxed{\text{undefined}}$

Even though $\cot\left(\dfrac{\pi}{2}\right)$ is defined, since $\tan\left(-\dfrac{\pi}{2}\right)$ is undefined, the sum of the two expressions is also undefined.

■ **Answer: a.** $0$   **b.** undefined

■ **YOUR TURN**  Evaluate each of the following expressions, if possible:

  **a.** $\csc\left(\dfrac{\pi}{2}\right) + \sec\pi$   **b.** $\csc(-630°) + \sec(-630°)$

# Ranges of the Trigonometric Functions

Thus far, we have discussed what the algebraic sign of a trigonometric function value for an angle in a particular quadrant, but we haven't discussed how to find actual values of the trigonometric functions for nonacute angles. We will need to define *reference angles* and reference right triangles. However, before we proceed, let's get a feel for the ranges (set of values of the functions) we will expect.

Let us start with an angle $\theta$ in quadrant I and the sine function defined as the ratio $\sin\theta = \dfrac{y}{r}$.

$$\sin\theta = \frac{y}{r}$$

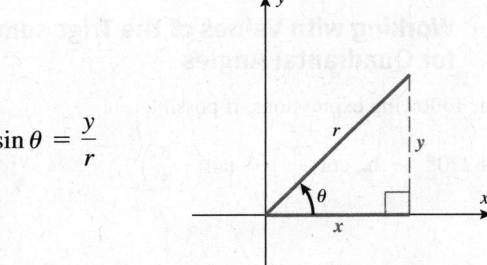

If we keep the value of $r$ constant, then as the measure of $\theta$ increases toward 90° or $\dfrac{\pi}{2}$, $y$ increases. Notice that the value of $y$ approaches the value of $r$ until they are equal when $\theta = 90°\left(\text{or } \dfrac{\pi}{2}\right)$, and $y$ can never be larger than $r$.

$$y \leq r$$

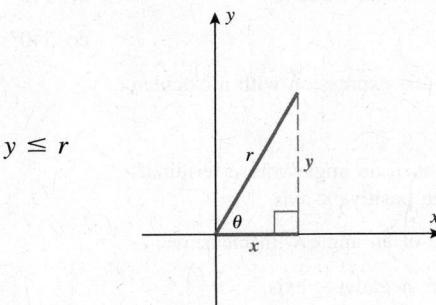

A similar analysis can be conducted in quadrant IV as $\theta$ approaches $-90°$ from $0°$ (note that $y$ is negative in quadrant IV). A result that is valid in all four quadrants is $|y| \leq r$.

| WORDS | MATH |
|---|---|
| Write the absolute value inequality as a double inequality. | $-r \leq y \leq r$ |
| Divide both sides by $r$. | $-1 \leq \dfrac{y}{r} \leq 1$ |
| Let $\sin\theta = \dfrac{y}{r}$. | $-1 \leq \sin\theta \leq 1$ |

Similarly, by allowing $\theta$ to approach $0°$ and $180°$, we can show that $|x| \leq r$, which leads to the range of the cosine function: $-1 \leq \cos\theta \leq 1$. Sine and cosine values range between $-1$ and $1$ and since secant and cosecant are reciprocals of the cosine and sine functions, respectively, their ranges are stated as

$$\sec\theta \leq -1 \text{ or } \sec\theta \geq 1 \qquad \csc\theta \leq -1 \text{ or } \csc\theta \geq 1$$

Since $\tan\theta = \dfrac{y}{x}$ and $\cot\theta = \dfrac{x}{y}$ and since $x < y, x = y$, and $x > y$ are all possible, the values of the tangent and cotangent functions can be any real numbers (positive, negative, or zero). The following box summarizes the ranges of the trigonometric functions.

### RANGES OF THE TRIGONOMETRIC FUNCTIONS

For any angle $\theta$ for which the trigonometric functions are defined, the six trigonometric functions have the following ranges:

- $-1 \leq \sin\theta \leq 1$
- $-1 \leq \cos\theta \leq 1$
- $\sec\theta \leq -1$ or $\sec\theta \geq 1$
- $\csc\theta \leq -1$ or $\csc\theta \geq 1$
- $\tan\theta$ and $\cot\theta$ can equal any real number.

▶ **EXAMPLE 5    Determining Whether a Value Is Within the Range of a Trigonometric Function**

Determine whether each statement is possible or not.

**a.** $\cos\theta = 1.001$

**b.** $\cot\theta = 0$

**c.** $\sec\theta = \dfrac{\sqrt{3}}{2}$

**Solution (a):**  Not possible, because $1.001 > 1$.

**Solution (b):**  Possible, because $\cot 90° = 0$.

**Solution (c):**  Not possible, because $\dfrac{\sqrt{3}}{2} \approx 0.866 < 1$.

▪ **YOUR TURN**  Determine whether each statement is possible or not.

        **a.** $\sin\theta = -1.1$    **b.** $\tan\theta = 2$    **c.** $\csc\theta = \sqrt{3}$

▪ **Answer:  a.** not possible
           **b.** possible
           **c.** possible

# Reference Angles and Reference Right Triangles

Now that we know the trigonometric function ranges and their algebraic signs in each of the four quadrants, we can evaluate the trigonometric functions of nonacute angles. Before we do that, however, we first must discuss *reference angles* and *reference right triangles*.

Every nonquadrantal angle in standard position has a corresponding *reference angle* and *reference right triangle*. We have already calculated the trigonometric function values for quadrantal angles.

**Study Tip**

The reference angle is the acute angle that the terminal side makes with the *x*-axis, not the *y*-axis.

**DEFINITION** **Reference Angle**

For angle $\theta$, $0° < \theta < 360°$ or $0 < \theta < 2\pi$, in standard position whose terminal side lies in one of the four quadrants, there exists a **reference angle** $\alpha$, which is the acute angle formed by the terminal side of angle $\theta$ and the *x*-axis.

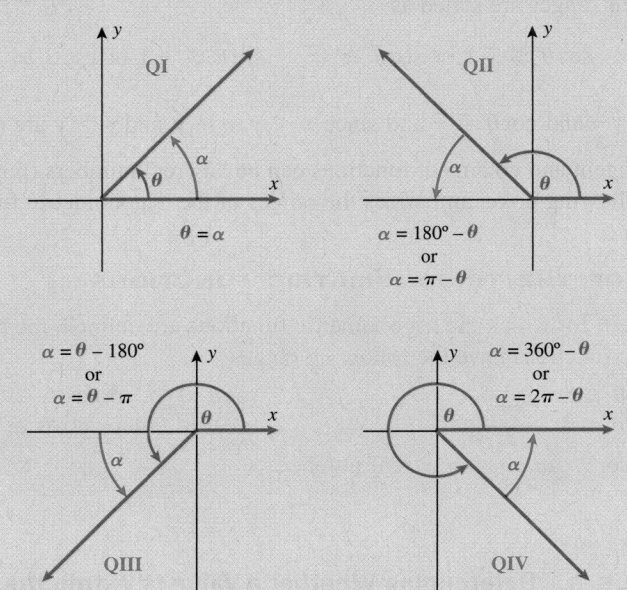

The reference angle is the positive, acute angle that the terminal side makes with the *x*-axis.

## EXAMPLE 6 Finding Reference Angles

Find the reference angle for each angle given.

**a.** 210°    **b.** $\dfrac{3\pi}{4}$    **c.** 422°

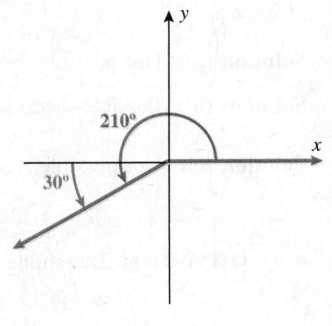

**Solution (a):**

The terminal side of angle $\theta$ lies in quadrant III.

The reference angle is formed by the terminal side and the negative *x*-axis.

$210° - 180° = \boxed{30°}$

**Solution (b):**

The terminal side of angle $\theta$ lies in quadrant II.

The reference angle is formed by the terminal side and the negative $x$-axis.

$$\pi - \frac{3\pi}{4} = \boxed{\frac{\pi}{4}}$$

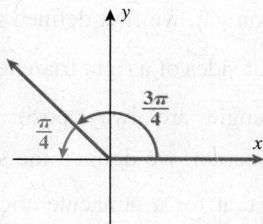

**Solution (c):**

The terminal side of angle $\theta$ lies in quadrant I.

The reference angle is formed by the terminal side and the positive $x$-axis.

$$422° - 360° = \boxed{62°}$$

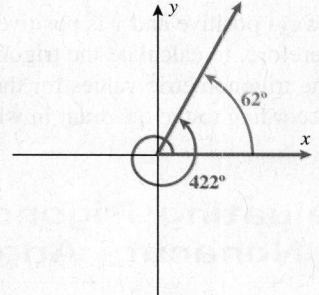

..............................................................

■ **YOUR TURN** Find the reference angle for each angle given.

a. $160°$   b. $\dfrac{7\pi}{4}$   c. $600°$

■ **Answer:**

a. $20°$   b. $\dfrac{\pi}{4}$   c. $60°$

---

**DEFINITION** | **Reference Right Triangle**

To form a **reference right triangle** for angle $\theta$, where $0° < \theta < 360°$ or $0 < \theta < 2\pi$, drop a perpendicular line from the terminal side of the angle to the $x$-axis. The right triangle now has reference angle $\alpha$ as one of its acute angles.

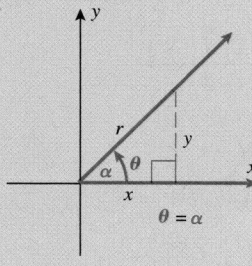

$\theta = \alpha$

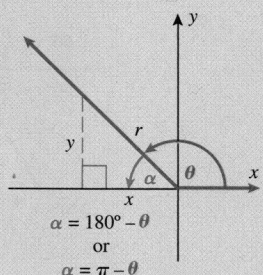

$\alpha = 180° - \theta$
or
$\alpha = \pi - \theta$

$\alpha = \theta - 180°$
or
$\alpha = \theta - \pi$

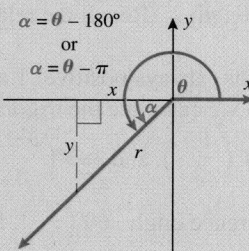

$\alpha = 360° - \theta$
or
$\alpha = 2\pi - \theta$

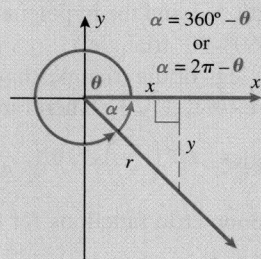

In Section 4.2, we first defined the trigonometric functions of an acute angle as ratios of lengths of sides of a right triangle. For example, $\sin \theta = \dfrac{\text{opposite}}{\text{hypotenuse}}$. The lengths of the sides of triangles are always positive.

In this section, we defined the sine function of any angle as $\sin \theta = \dfrac{y}{r}$. Notice in the above box that for a nonacute angle $\theta$, $\sin \theta = \dfrac{y}{r}$; and for the acute reference angle $\alpha$,

**Study Tip**

To find the trigonometric function values of nonacute angles, first find the trigonometric values of the reference angle and then use the quadrant information to determine the algebraic sign.

$\sin \alpha = \dfrac{|y|}{r}$. The only difference between these two expressions is the algebraic sign, since $r$ is always positive and $y$ is positive or negative depending on the quadrant.

Therefore, to calculate the trigonometric function values for a nonacute angle, simply find the trigonometric values for the reference angle and determine the correct algebraic sign according to the quadrant in which the terminal side lies.

## Evaluating Trigonometric Functions for Nonacute Angles

Let's look at a specific example before we generalize a procedure for evaluating trigonometric function values for nonacute angles.

Suppose we have the angles in standard position with measure **60°, 120°, 240°,** and **300°** or $\dfrac{\pi}{3}, \dfrac{2\pi}{3}, \dfrac{4\pi}{3}$, or $\dfrac{5\pi}{3}$, respectively. Notice that the reference angle for all of these angles is **60°** or $\dfrac{\pi}{3}$.

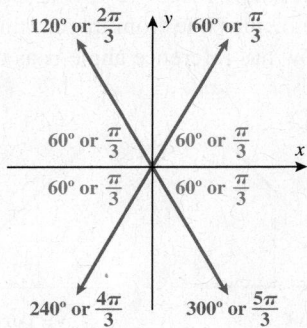

If we draw reference triangles and let the shortest leg have length 1, we find that the other leg has length $\sqrt{3}$ and the hypotenuse has length 2. (Recall the relationships for side lengths of a 30°–60°–90° triangle.)

Notice that the legs of the triangles have lengths (always positive) 1 and $\sqrt{3}$; however, the coordinates are $(\pm 1, \pm \sqrt{3})$. Therefore, when we calculate the trigonometric functions for any of the angles, $60°\left(\dfrac{\pi}{3}\right)$, $120°\left(\dfrac{2\pi}{3}\right)$, $240°\left(\dfrac{4\pi}{3}\right)$, and $300°\left(\dfrac{5\pi}{3}\right)$, we can simply calculate the trigonometric functions for the reference angle, $60°\left(\dfrac{\pi}{3}\right)$, and determine the algebraic sign (+ or −) for the particular trigonometric function and quadrant.

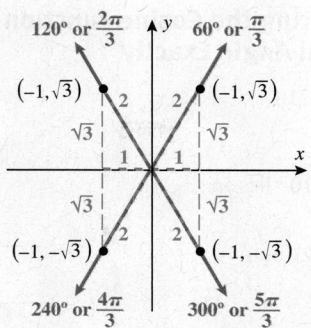

**Study Tip**

The value of a trigonometric function of an angle is the same as the trigonometric value of its reference angle, except there may be an algebraic sign (+ or −) difference between the two values.

To find the value of $\cos 120°$, we first recognize that the terminal side of an angle with $120°$ measure lies in quadrant II. We also know that cosine is negative in quadrant II. We then calculate the cosine of the reference angle, $60°$.

$$\cos 60° = \frac{\text{adjacent}}{\text{hypotenuse}} = \frac{1}{2}$$

Since we know $\cos 120°$ is negative because it lies in quadrant II, we know that

$$\cos 120° = -\frac{1}{2}$$

Similarly, we know that $\cos 240° = -\frac{1}{2}$ and $\cos 300° = \frac{1}{2}$.

For any angle whose terminal side lies along one of the axes, we consult the table in this section for the values of the trigonometric functions for quadrantal angles. If the terminal side lies in one of the four quadrants, then the angle is said to be nonquadrantal and the following procedure can be used.

**PROCEDURE FOR EVALUATING FUNCTION VALUES FOR ANY NONQUADRANTAL ANGLE $\theta$**

**Step 1:**
- If $0° < \theta < 360°$ or $0 < \theta < 2\pi$, proceed to Step 2.
- If $\theta < 0°$, add $360°$ as many times as needed to get a coterminal angle with measure between $0°$ and $360°$. Similarly, if $\theta < 0$, add $2\pi$ as many times as needed to get a coterminal angle with measure between $0$ and $2\pi$.
- If $\theta > 360°$, subtract $360°$ as many times as needed to get a coterminal angle with measure between $0°$ and $360°$. Similarly, if $\theta > 2\pi$, subtract $2\pi$ as many times as needed to get a coterminal angle with measure between $0$ and $2\pi$.

**Step 2:** Find the quadrant in which the terminal side of the angle in Step 1 lies.

**Step 3:** Find the reference angle $\alpha$ of the angle found in Step 1.

**Step 4:** Find the trigonometric function values for the reference angle $\alpha$.

**Step 5:** Determine the correct algebraic signs (+ or −) for the trigonometric function values based on the quadrant identified in Step 2.

**Step 6:** Combine the trigonometric values found in Step 4 with the algebraic signs in Step 5 to give the trigonometric function values of $\theta$.

We follow the above procedure for all angles except when we get to Step 4. In Step 4, we evaluate exactly if possible the special angles $\left( 30°, 45°, 60° \text{ or } \dfrac{\pi}{6}, \dfrac{\pi}{4}, \dfrac{\pi}{3} \right)$; otherwise, we use a calculator to approximate.

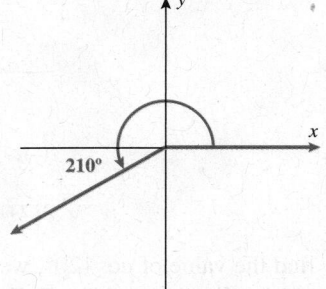
### EXAMPLE 7 Evaluating the Cosine Function of a Special Angle Exactly

Find the exact value of $\cos 210°$.

**Solution:**

The terminal side of $\theta = 210°$ lies in quadrant III.

Find the reference angle for $\theta = 210°$.      $210° - 180° = 30°$

Find the value of the cosine of the reference angle.      $\cos 30° = \dfrac{\sqrt{3}}{2}$

Determine the algebraic sign for the cosine in quadrant III.      Negative $(-)$

Combine the algebraic sign of the cosine in quadrant III with the value of the cosine of the reference angle.      $\cos 210° = \boxed{-\dfrac{\sqrt{3}}{2}}$

■ **Answer:** $-\dfrac{1}{2}$

■ **YOUR TURN** Find the exact value of $\sin 330°$.

### EXAMPLE 8 Evaluating the Cosecant Function of a Special Angle Exactly

Find the exact value of $\csc\left(-\dfrac{7\pi}{6}\right)$.

**Solution:**

Add $2\pi$ to get a coterminal angle between 0 and $2\pi$.      $-\dfrac{7\pi}{6} + 2\pi = \dfrac{5\pi}{6}$

The terminal side of the angle lies in quadrant II.

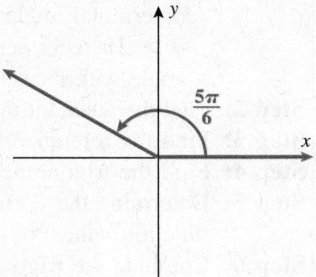

Find the reference angle for the angle with measure $\dfrac{5\pi}{6}$.      $\pi - \dfrac{5\pi}{6} = \dfrac{\pi}{6}$

Find the value of the cosecant of the reference angle.      $\csc\left(\dfrac{\pi}{6}\right) = \dfrac{1}{\sin\left(\dfrac{\pi}{6}\right)} = \dfrac{1}{\dfrac{1}{2}} = 2$

Determine the algebraic sign for the
cosecant in quadrant II.                                              Positive (+)

Combine the algebraic sign of the
cosecant in quadrant II with the value                    $\csc\left(-\dfrac{7\pi}{6}\right) = \boxed{2}$
of the cosecant of the reference angle.

■ **YOUR TURN** Find the exact value of $\sec\left(-\dfrac{11\pi}{6}\right)$.

■ **Answer:** $\dfrac{2\sqrt{3}}{3}$

## EXAMPLE 9    Finding Exact Angle Measures Given Trigonometric Function Values

Find all values of $\theta$ where $0° \le \theta \le 360°$, when $\sin\theta = -\dfrac{\sqrt{3}}{2}$.

**Solution:**

Determine in which quadrants sine is negative.                    QIII and QIV

Since the absolute value of $\sin\theta$ is $\dfrac{\sqrt{3}}{2}$, the
                                                                               $\sin 60° = \dfrac{\sqrt{3}}{2}$
reference angle has measure 60°.

Determine the angles between 180° and 360°
in quadrants III and IV with reference angle 60°.

    Quadrant III:                                            $180° + 60° = 240°$

    Quadrant IV:                                             $360° - 60° = 300°$

The two angles are $\boxed{240°}$ and $\boxed{300°}$.

■ **YOUR TURN** Find all values of $\theta$ where $0° \le \theta \le 360°$, when $\cos\theta = -\dfrac{\sqrt{3}}{2}$.

■ **Answer:** 150° and 210°

## EXAMPLE 10    Finding Approximate Angle Measures Given Trigonometric Function Values

Find the measure of an angle $\theta$ (rounded to the nearest degree) if $\sin\theta = -0.6293$ and
the terminal side of $\theta$ (in standard position) lies in quadrant III, where $0° \le \theta \le 360°$.

**Solution:**

The sine of the reference angle is 0.6293.                    $\sin\alpha = 0.6293$

Find the reference angle.                                            $\alpha = \sin^{-1}(0.6293) \approx 38.998°$

Round the reference angle to the
nearest degree.                                                         $\alpha \approx 39°$

Find $\theta$, which lies in quadrant III.                          $\theta \approx 180° + 39° \approx 219°$

                                                                               $\boxed{\theta \approx 219°}$

Check with a calculator.                                            $\sin 219° \approx -0.6293$

### Technology Tip

When $\sin\theta = -0.6293$, use the
$\boxed{\sin^{-1}}$ key and the absolute value to
find the reference angle.

```
sin⁻¹(0.6293)
        38.99849667
```

■ **YOUR TURN** Find the measure of $\theta$, the smallest positive angle (rounded to the
nearest degree), if $\cos\theta = -0.5299$ and the terminal side of $\theta$
(in standard position) lies in quadrant II.

■ **Answer:** 122°

The trigonometric functions are defined in the Cartesian plane for any angle as follows:

Let $(x, y)$ be a point, other than the origin, on the terminal side of an angle $\theta$ in standard position. Let $r$ be the distance from the point $(x, y)$ to the origin. Then the sine, cosine, and tangent functions are defined as

$$\sin \theta = \frac{y}{r} \qquad \cos \theta = \frac{x}{r} \qquad \tan \theta = \frac{y}{x} \quad (x \neq 0)$$

The range of the sine and cosine functions is $[-1, 1]$, whereas the range of the secant and cosecant functions is $(-\infty, -1] \cup [1, \infty)$.

Reference angles and reference right triangles can be used to evaluate trigonometric functions for nonacute angles.

**SKILLS**

In Exercises 1–14, the terminal side of an angle $\theta$ in standard position passes through the indicated point. Calculate the values of the six trigonometric functions for angle $\theta$.

**1.** $(3, 6)$
**2.** $(8, 4)$
**3.** $\left(\frac{1}{2}, \frac{2}{5}\right)$
**4.** $\left(\frac{4}{7}, \frac{2}{3}\right)$
**5.** $(-2, 4)$

**6.** $(-1, 3)$
**7.** $(-4, -7)$
**8.** $(-9, -5)$
**9.** $\left(-\sqrt{2}, \sqrt{3}\right)$
**10.** $\left(-\sqrt{3}, \sqrt{2}\right)$

**11.** $\left(-\sqrt{5}, -\sqrt{3}\right)$
**12.** $\left(-\sqrt{6}, -\sqrt{5}\right)$
**13.** $\left(-\frac{10}{3}, -\frac{4}{3}\right)$
**14.** $\left(-\frac{2}{9}, -\frac{1}{3}\right)$

In Exercises 15–24, indicate the quadrant in which the terminal side of $\theta$ must lie in order for the information to be true.

**15.** $\cos\theta$ is positive and $\sin\theta$ is negative.

**16.** $\cos\theta$ is negative and $\sin\theta$ is positive.

**17.** $\tan\theta$ is negative and $\sin\theta$ is positive.

**18.** $\tan\theta$ is positive and $\cos\theta$ is negative.

**19.** $\sec\theta$ and $\csc\theta$ are both positive.

**20.** $\sec\theta$ and $\csc\theta$ are both negative.

**21.** $\cot\theta$ and $\cos\theta$ are both positive.

**22.** $\cot\theta$ and $\sin\theta$ are both negative.

**23.** $\tan\theta$ is positive and $\sec\theta$ is negative.

**24.** $\cot\theta$ is negative and $\csc\theta$ is positive.

In Exercises 25–36, find the indicated trigonometric function values.

**25.** If $\cos\theta = -\dfrac{3}{5}$, and the terminal side of $\theta$ lies in quadrant III, find $\sin\theta$.

**26.** If $\tan\theta = -\dfrac{5}{12}$, and the terminal side of $\theta$ lies in quadrant II, find $\cos\theta$.

**27.** If $\sin\theta = \dfrac{60}{61}$, and the terminal side of $\theta$ lies in quadrant II, find $\tan\theta$.

**28.** If $\cos\theta = \dfrac{40}{41}$, and the terminal side of $\theta$ lies in quadrant IV, find $\tan\theta$.

**29.** If $\tan\theta = \dfrac{84}{13}$, and the terminal side of $\theta$ lies in quadrant III, find $\sin\theta$.

**30.** If $\sin\theta = -\dfrac{7}{25}$, and the terminal side of $\theta$ lies in quadrant IV, find $\cos\theta$.

**31.** If $\sec\theta = -2$, and the terminal side of $\theta$ lies in quadrant III, find $\tan\theta$.

**32.** If $\cot\theta = 1$, and the terminal side of $\theta$ lies in quadrant I, find $\sin\theta$.

**33.** If $\csc \theta = \dfrac{2}{\sqrt{3}}$ and the terminal side of $\theta$ lies in quadrant II, find $\cot \theta$.

**34.** If $\sec \theta = -\dfrac{13}{5}$ and the terminal side of $\theta$ lies in quadrant II, find $\csc \theta$.

**35.** If $\cot \theta = -\sqrt{3}$ and the terminal side of $\theta$ lies in quadrant IV, find $\sec \theta$.

**36.** If $\cot \theta = -\dfrac{13}{84}$ and the terminal side of $\theta$ lies in quadrant II, find $\csc \theta$.

**In Exercises 37–46, evaluate each expression, if possible.**

**37.** $\cos(-270°) + \sin 450°$     **38.** $\sin(-270°) + \cos 450°$     **39.** $\sin 630° + \tan(-540°)$     **40.** $\cos(-720°) + \tan 720°$

**41.** $\cos(3\pi) - \sec(-3\pi)$     **42.** $\sin\left(-\dfrac{5\pi}{2}\right) + \csc\left(\dfrac{3\pi}{2}\right)$     **43.** $\csc\left(-\dfrac{7\pi}{2}\right) - \cot\left(\dfrac{7\pi}{2}\right)$     **44.** $\sec(-3\pi) + \tan(3\pi)$

**45.** $\tan 720° + \sec 720°$     **46.** $\cot 450° - \cos(-450°)$

**In Exercises 47–56, determine whether each statement is possible or not.**

**47.** $\sin \theta = -0.999$     **48.** $\cos \theta = 1.0001$     **49.** $\cos \theta = \dfrac{2\sqrt{6}}{3}$     **50.** $\sin \theta = \dfrac{\sqrt{2}}{10}$     **51.** $\tan \theta = 4\sqrt{5}$

**52.** $\cot \theta = -\dfrac{\sqrt{6}}{7}$     **53.** $\sec \theta = -\dfrac{4}{\sqrt{7}}$     **54.** $\csc \theta = \dfrac{\pi}{2}$     **55.** $\cot \theta = 500$     **56.** $\sec \theta = 0.9996$

**In Exercises 57–68, evaluate the following expressions *exactly*:**

**57.** $\cos 240°$     **58.** $\cos 120°$     **59.** $\sin\left(\dfrac{5\pi}{3}\right)$     **60.** $\sin\left(\dfrac{7\pi}{4}\right)$

**61.** $\tan 210°$     **62.** $\sec 135°$     **63.** $\tan(-315°)$     **64.** $\sec(-330°)$

**65.** $\csc\left(\dfrac{11\pi}{6}\right)$     **66.** $\csc\left(-\dfrac{4\pi}{3}\right)$     **67.** $\cot(-315°)$     **68.** $\cot 150°$

**In Exercises 69–76, find all possible values of $\theta$, where $0° \le \theta \le 360°$.**

**69.** $\cos \theta = \dfrac{\sqrt{3}}{2}$     **70.** $\sin \theta = \dfrac{\sqrt{3}}{2}$     **71.** $\sin \theta = -\dfrac{1}{2}$     **72.** $\cos \theta = -\dfrac{1}{2}$

**73.** $\cos \theta = 0$     **74.** $\sin \theta = 0$     **75.** $\sin \theta = -1$     **76.** $\cos \theta = -1$

**In Exercises 77–90, find the smallest positive measure of $\theta$ (rounded to the nearest degree) if the indicated information is true.**

**77.** $\sin \theta = 0.9397$ and the terminal side of $\theta$ lies in quadrant II.

**78.** $\cos \theta = 0.7071$ and the terminal side of $\theta$ lies in quadrant IV.

**79.** $\cos \theta = -0.7986$ and the terminal side of $\theta$ lies in quadrant II.

**80.** $\sin \theta = -0.1746$ and the terminal side of $\theta$ lies in quadrant III.

**81.** $\tan \theta = -0.7813$ and the terminal side of $\theta$ lies in quadrant IV.

**82.** $\cos \theta = -0.3420$ and the terminal side of $\theta$ lies in quadrant III.

**83.** $\tan \theta = -0.8391$ and the terminal side of $\theta$ lies in quadrant II.

**84.** $\tan \theta = 11.4301$ and the terminal side of $\theta$ lies in quadrant III.

**85.** $\sin \theta = -0.3420$ and the terminal side of $\theta$ lies in quadrant IV.

**86.** $\sin \theta = -0.4226$ and the terminal side of $\theta$ lies in quadrant III.

**87.** $\sec \theta = 1.0001$ and the terminal side of $\theta$ lies in quadrant I.

**88.** $\sec \theta = -3.1421$ and the terminal side of $\theta$ lies in quadrant II.

**89.** $\csc \theta = -2.3604$ and the terminal side of $\theta$ lies in quadrant IV.

**90.** $\csc \theta = -1.0001$ and the terminal side of $\theta$ lies in quadrant III.

■ **APPLICATIONS**

**In Exercises 91–94, refer to the following:**

When light passes from one substance to another, such as from air to water, its path bends. This is called refraction and is what is seen in eyeglass lenses, camera lenses, and gems. The rule governing the change in the path is called *Snell's law*, named after a Dutch astronomer: $n_1 \sin \theta_1 = n_2 \sin \theta_2$, where $n_1$ and $n_2$ are the indices of refraction of the different substances and $\theta_1$ and $\theta_2$ are the respective angles that light makes with a line perpendicular to the surface at the boundary between substances. The figure shows the path of light rays going from air to water. Assume that the index of refraction in air is 1.

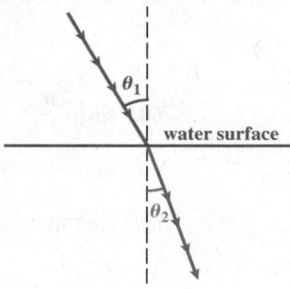

**91.** If light rays hit the water's surface at an angle of 30° from the perpendicular and are refracted to an angle of 22° from the perpendicular, then what is the refraction index for water? Round the answer to two significant digits.

**92.** If light rays hit a glass surface at an angle of 30° from the perpendicular and are refracted to an angle of 18° from the perpendicular, then what is the refraction index for that glass? Round the answer to two significant digits.

**93.** If the refraction index for a diamond is 2.4, then to what angle is light refracted if it enters the diamond at an angle of 30°? Round the answer to two significant digits.

**94.** If the refraction index for a rhinestone is 1.9, then to what angle is light refracted if it enters the rhinestone at an angle of 30°? Round the answer to two significant digits.

**For Exercises 95 and 96, refer to the following:**

An orthotic knee brace can be used to treat knee injuries by locking the knee at an angle $\theta$ chosen to facilitate healing. The angle $\theta$ is measured from the metal bar on the side of the brace on the thigh to the metal bar on the side of the brace on the calf (see the figure on the left). To make working with the brace more convenient, rotate the image such that the thigh

aligns with the positive $x$-axis (see the figure on the right below).

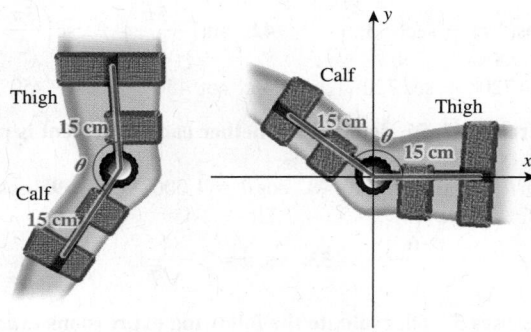

**95. Health/Medicine.** If $\theta = 165°$, find the measure of the reference angle. What is the physical meaning of the reference angle?

**96. Health/Medicine.** If $\theta = 160°$, find the measure of the reference angle. What would an angle greater than 180° represent?

**For Exercises 97 and 98, refer to the following:**

Water covers two-thirds of the Earth's surface and every living thing is dependent on it. For example, the human body is made up of over 70% water. The water molecule is composed of one oxygen atom and two hydrogen atoms and exhibits a bent shape with the oxygen molecule at the center. The angle $\theta$ between the O-H bonds is 104.5°.

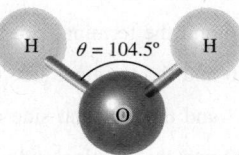

(*Source:* http://www.wiley.com/college/boyer/0470003790/ reviews/pH/ph_water.htm.)

**97. Chemistry.** Sketch the water molecule in the $xy$-coordinate system in a convenient manner for illustrating angles. Find the reference angle. Illustrate both the angle $\theta$ and the reference angle on the sketch.

**98. Chemistry.** Find $\cos(104.5°)$ using the reference angle found in Exercise 97.

## ■ CATCH THE MISTAKE

**In Exercises 99 and 100, explain the mistake that is made.**

**99.** Evaluate the expression $\sec 120°$ exactly.

**Solution:**

$120°$ lies in quadrant II.
The reference angle is $30°$.

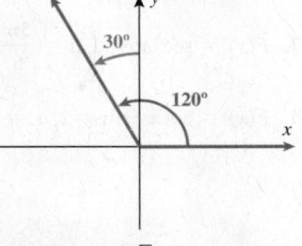

Find the cosine of the reference angle.

$$\cos 30° = \frac{\sqrt{3}}{2}$$

Cosine is negative in quadrant II.

$$\cos 120° = -\frac{\sqrt{3}}{2}$$

Secant is the reciprocal of cosine.

$$\sec 120° = -\frac{2}{\sqrt{3}} = -\frac{2\sqrt{3}}{3}$$

This is incorrect. What mistake was made?

**100.** Find the measure of the smallest positive angle $\theta$ (rounded to the nearest degree) if $\cos\theta = -0.2388$ and the terminal side of $\theta$ (in standard position) lies in quadrant III.

**Solution:**

Evaluate with a calculator.

$$\theta = \cos^{-1}(-0.2388) = 103.8157°$$

Approximate to the nearest degree.

$$\theta \approx 104°$$

This is incorrect. What mistake was made?

## ■ CONCEPTUAL

**In Exercises 101–108, determine whether each statement is true or false.**

**101.** It is possible for all six trigonometric functions of the same angle to have positive values.

**102.** It is possible for all six trigonometric functions of the same angle to have negative values.

**103.** The trigonometric function value for any angle with negative measure must be negative.

**104.** The trigonometric function value for any angle with positive measure must be positive.

**105.** $\sec^2\theta - 1$ can be negative for some value of $\theta$.

**106.** $(\sec\theta)(\csc\theta)$ is negative only when the terminal side of $\theta$ lies in quadrant II or IV.

**107.** $\cos\theta = \cos(\theta + 360°n)$, where $n$ is an integer.

**108.** $\sin\theta = \sin(\theta + 2\pi n)$, where $n$ is an integer.

## ■ CHALLENGE

**109.** If the terminal side of angle $\theta$ passes through the point $(-3a, 4a)$, find $\cos\theta$. Assume $a > 0$.

**110.** If the terminal side of angle $\theta$ passes through the point $(-3a, 4a)$, find $\sin\theta$. Assume $a > 0$.

**111.** Find the equation of the line with negative slope that passes through the point $(a, 0)$ and makes an acute angle $\theta$ with the $x$-axis. The equation of the line will be in terms of $x$, $a$, and a trigonometric function of $\theta$. Assume $a > 0$.

**112.** Find the equation of the line with positive slope that passes through the point $(a, 0)$ and makes an acute angle $\theta$ with the $x$-axis. The equation of the line will be in terms of $x$, $a$, and a trigonometric function of $\theta$. Assume $a > 0$.

**113.** If $\tan\theta = \dfrac{a}{b}$, where $a$ and $b$ are positive, and if $\theta$ lies in quadrant III, find $\sin\theta$.

**114.** If $\tan\theta = -\dfrac{a}{b}$, where $a$ and $b$ are positive, and if $\theta$ lies in quadrant II, find $\cos\theta$.

**115.** If $\csc\theta = -\dfrac{a}{b}$, where $a$ and $b$ are positive, and if $\theta$ lies in quadrant IV, find $\cot\theta$.

**116.** If $\sec\theta = -\dfrac{a}{b}$, where $a$ and $b$ are positive, and if $\theta$ lies in quadrant III, find $\tan\theta$.

## ■ TECHNOLOGY

**In Exercises 117–124, use a calculator to evaluate the following expressions. If you get an error, explain why.**

**117.** $\cos 270°$

**118.** $\tan 270°$

**119.** $\cot 270°$

**120.** $\sin(-270°)$

**121.** $\cos(-270°)$

**122.** $\csc(-270°)$

**123.** $\sec(-270°)$

**124.** $\sec 270°$

■PREVIEW TO CALCULUS

In calculus, the value $F(b) - F(a)$ of a function $F(x)$ at $x = a$ and $x = b$ plays an important role in the calculation of definite integrals.

In Exercises 125–128, find the exact value of $F(b) - F(a)$.

**125.** $F(x) = 2\tan x + \cos x, a = -\dfrac{\pi}{6}, b = \dfrac{\pi}{4}$

**127.** $F(x) = \sec^2 x + 1, a = \dfrac{5\pi}{6}, b = \dfrac{4\pi}{3}$

**126.** $F(x) = \sin^2 x + \cos^2 x, a = \dfrac{3\pi}{4}, b = \dfrac{7\pi}{6}$

**128.** $F(x) = \cot x - \csc^2 x, a = \dfrac{7\pi}{6}, b = \dfrac{7\pi}{4}$

## SECTION
## 4.4 THE LAW OF SINES

### SKILLS OBJECTIVES

■ Solve AAS or ASA triangle cases.
■ Solve ambiguous SSA triangle cases.

### CONCEPTUAL OBJECTIVES

■ Understand the derivation of the Law of Sines.
■ Understand that the ambiguous case can yield no triangle, one triangle, or two triangles.
■ Understand why an AAA case cannot be solved.

## Solving Oblique Triangles

Thus far we have discussed only *right* triangles. There are, however, two types of triangles, right and *oblique*. An **oblique triangle** is any triangle that does not have a right angle. An oblique triangle is either an **acute triangle**, having three acute angles, or an **obtuse triangle**, having one obtuse (between 90° and 180°) angle.

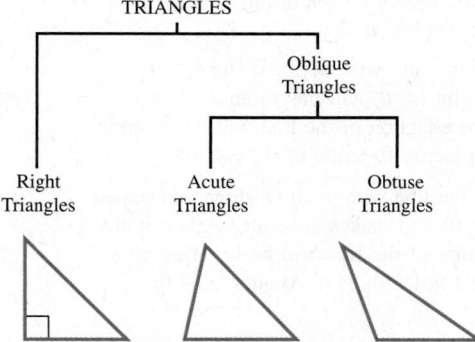

It is customary to label oblique triangles in the following way:

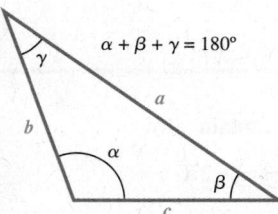

$\alpha + \beta + \gamma = 180°$

■ angle $\alpha$ (alpha) opposite side $a$
■ angle $\beta$ (beta) opposite side $b$
■ angle $\gamma$ (gamma) opposite side $c$

Remember that the sum of the three angles of any triangle must equal 180°. In Section 4.3, we solved right triangles. In this section, we solve oblique triangles, which means we find the lengths of all three sides and the measures of all three angles.

## Four Cases

To solve an oblique triangle, *we need to know the length of one side* and one of the following three:

- two angles
- one angle and another side
- the other two sides

This requirement leads to the following four possible cases to consider:

### REQUIRED INFORMATION TO SOLVE OBLIQUE TRIANGLES

| CASE | WHAT'S GIVEN | EXAMPLES/NAMES |
|------|--------------|----------------|
| **Case 1** | Measures of one side and two angles | **AAS: Angle-Angle-Side** 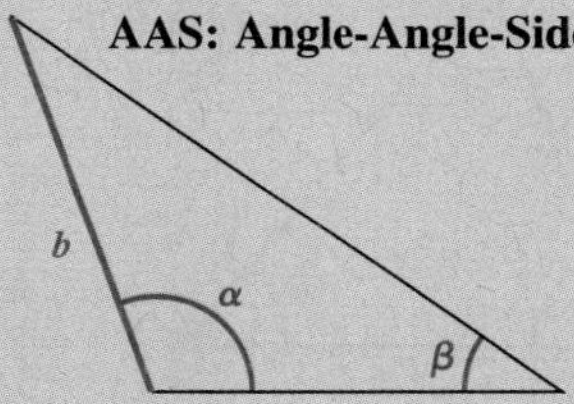  **ASA: Angle-Side-Angle** 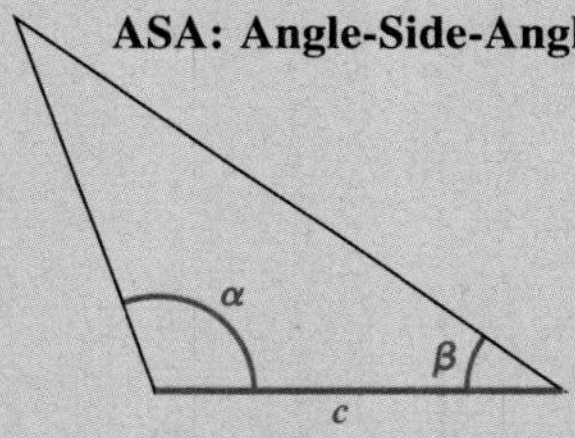  |
| **Case 2** | Measures of two sides and the angle opposite one of them | 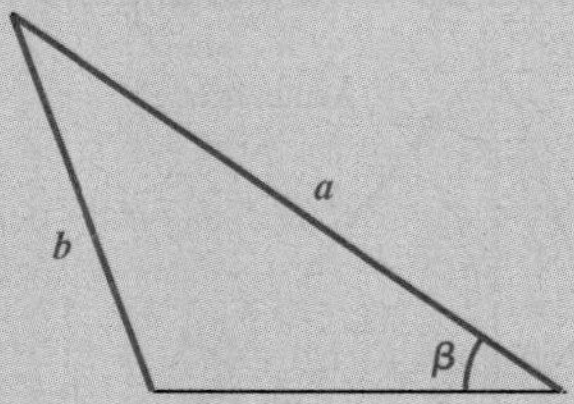 **SSA: Side-Side-Angle** |
| **Case 3** | Measures of two sides and the angle between them | 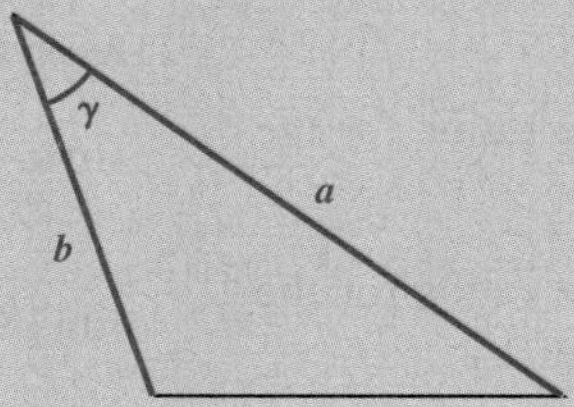 **SAS: Side-Angle-Side** |
| **Case 4** | Measures of three sides | 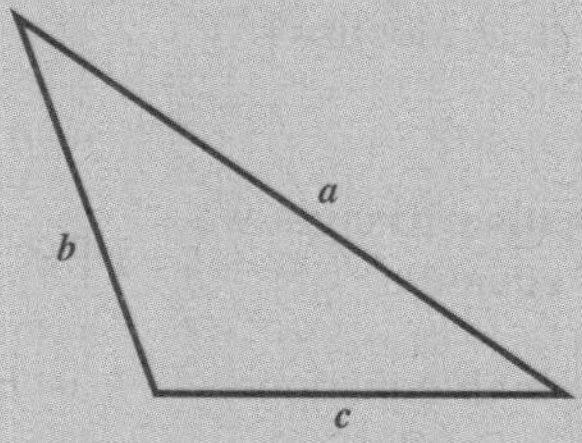 **SSS: Side-Side-Side** |

Notice that there is **no AAA case**, because two similar triangles can have the same angle measures but different side lengths.

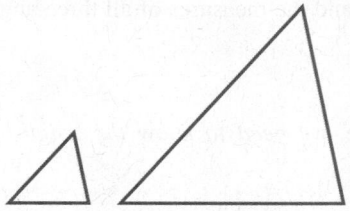

That is why at least the length of one side must be known.

In this section, we will derive the Law of Sines, which will enable us to solve Case 1 and Case 2 problems. In the next section, we will derive the Law of Cosines, which will enable us to solve Case 3 and Case 4 problems.

## The Law of Sines

Let us start with two oblique triangles, an acute triangle and an obtuse triangle.

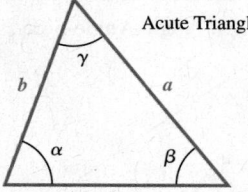
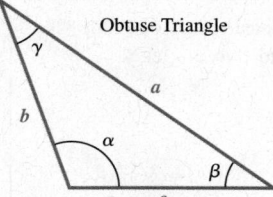

The following discussion applies to both triangles. First, construct an altitude (perpendicular) $h$ from the vertex at angle $\gamma$ to the side (or its extension) opposite $\gamma$.

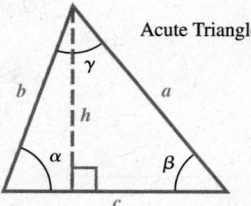
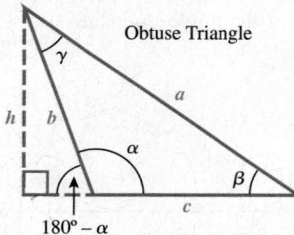

| WORDS | MATH |
|---|---|
| Formulate sine ratios for the acute triangle. | $\sin\alpha = \dfrac{h}{b}$ and $\sin\beta = \dfrac{h}{a}$ |
| Formulate sine ratios for the obtuse triangle. | $\sin(180° - \alpha) = \dfrac{h}{b}$ and $\sin\beta = \dfrac{h}{a}$ |
| For the obtuse triangle, apply the sine difference identity.* | $\sin(180° - \alpha) = \sin 180° \cos\alpha - \cos 180° \sin\alpha$<br>$= 0 \cdot \cos\alpha - (-1)\sin\alpha$<br>$= \sin\alpha$ |
| Therefore, in either triangle we find the same equation. | $\sin\alpha = \dfrac{h}{b}$ and $\sin\beta = \dfrac{h}{a}$ |
| Solve for $h$ in both equations. | $h = b\sin\alpha$ and $h = a\sin\beta$ |
| Since $h$ is equal to itself, equate the expressions for $h$. | $b\sin\alpha = a\sin\beta$ |

*The sine difference identify, $\sin(x - y) = \sin x \cdot \cos y - \cos x \cdot \sin y$ is derived in Section 6.2.

Divide both sides by $ab$.
$$\frac{b \sin \alpha}{ab} = \frac{a \sin \beta}{ab}$$

Divide out common factors.
$$\frac{\sin \alpha}{a} = \frac{\sin \beta}{b}$$

In a similar manner, we can extend an altitude (perpendicular) from angle $\alpha$, and we will find that $\dfrac{\sin \gamma}{c} = \dfrac{\sin \beta}{b}$. Equating these two expressions leads us to the third ratio of the *Law of Sines*: $\dfrac{\sin \alpha}{a} = \dfrac{\sin \gamma}{c}$.

### THE LAW OF SINES

For a triangle with sides of lengths $a$, $b$, and $c$, and opposite angles of measures $\alpha$, $\beta$, and $\gamma$, the following is true:

$$\frac{\sin \alpha}{a} = \frac{\sin \beta}{b} = \frac{\sin \gamma}{c}$$

In other words, the ratio of the sine of an angle in a triangle to its opposite side is equal to the ratios of the sines of the other two angles to their opposite sides.

Notice that in both cases 1 and 2 where an angle and the side opposite that angle are known, the Law of Sines can be used as long as one other piece of information is known (i.e., side length or angle measure).

Some things to note before we begin solving oblique triangles are:

- The angles and sides share the same progression of magnitude:
  - The longest side of a triangle is opposite the largest angle.
  - The shortest side of a triangle is opposite the smallest angle.
- Draw the triangle and label the angles and sides.
- If two angle measures are known, start by determining the third angle.
- Whenever possible, in successive steps always return to given values rather than refer to calculated (approximate) values.

Keeping these pointers in mind will help you determine whether your answers are reasonable.

*Study Tip*

When an angle and the side opposite that angle are known, the Law of Sines can be used provided one other piece of information (side length/angle measure) is known.

*Study Tip*

Remember that the longest side is opposite the largest angle; the shortest side is opposite the smallest angle.

*Study Tip*

Always use given values rather than calculated (approximated) values for better accuracy.

## Case 1: Two Angles and One Side (AAS or ASA)

### EXAMPLE 1   Using the Law of Sines to Solve a Triangle (AAS)

Solve the triangle.

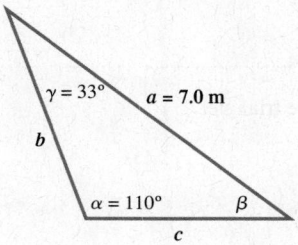

$\gamma = 33°$   $a = 7.0$ m
$b$
$\alpha = 110°$   $\beta$
$c$

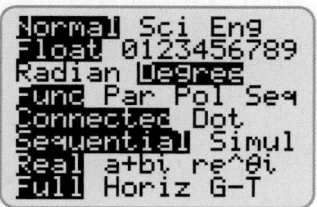
**Answer:** $\gamma = 32°$, $a \approx 42$ ft, $c \approx 23$ ft

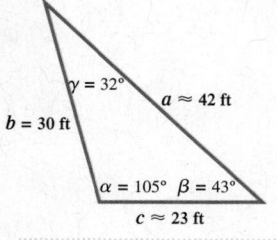

**Solution:**

This is an AAS (angle-angle-side) case because two angles and a side are given and the side is opposite one of the angles.

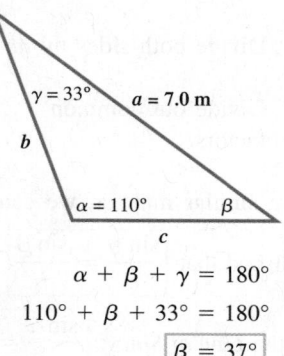

**STEP 1** Find $\beta$.

The sum of the measures of
the angles in a triangle is 180°.

Let $\alpha = 110°$ and $\gamma = 33°$.

Solve for $\beta$.

$$\alpha + \beta + \gamma = 180°$$
$$110° + \beta + 33° = 180°$$
$$\boxed{\beta = 37°}$$

**STEP 2** Find $b$.

Use the Law of Sines with the known side $a$.

$$\frac{\sin \alpha}{a} = \frac{\sin \beta}{b}$$

Isolate $b$.

$$b = \frac{a \sin \beta}{\sin \alpha}$$

Let $\alpha = 110°$, $\beta = 37°$, and $a = 7$ m.

$$b = \frac{7 \sin 37°}{\sin 110°}$$

Use a calculator to approximate $b$.

$$b \approx 4.483067 \text{ m}$$

Round $b$ to two significant digits.

$$\boxed{b \approx 4.5 \text{ m}}$$

**STEP 3** Find $c$.

Use the Law of Sines with the known side $a$.

$$\frac{\sin \alpha}{a} = \frac{\sin \gamma}{c}$$

Isolate $c$.

$$c = \frac{a \sin \gamma}{\sin \alpha}$$

Let $\alpha = 110°$, $\gamma = 33°$, and $a = 7$ m.

$$c = \frac{(7 \text{ m}) \sin 33°}{\sin 110°}$$

Use a calculator to approximate $c$.

$$c \approx 4.057149 \text{ m}$$

Round $c$ to two significant digits.

$$\boxed{c \approx 4.1 \text{ m}}$$

**STEP 4** Draw and label the triangle.

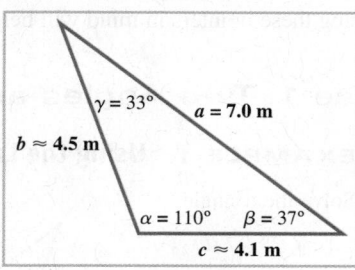

**YOUR TURN** Solve the triangle.

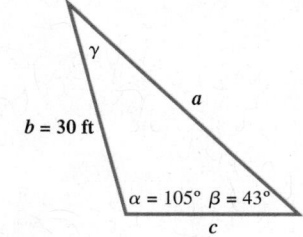

**EXAMPLE 2    Using the Law of Sines to Solve a Triangle (ASA)**

Solve the triangle.

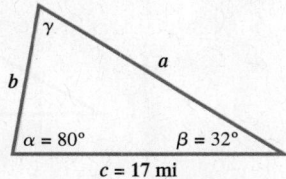

**Solution:**

This is an ASA (angle-side-angle) case because two angles and a side are given and the side is not opposite one of the angles.

**STEP 1** Find $\gamma$.

| | |
|---|---|
| The sum of the measures of the angles in a triangle is 180°. | $\alpha + \beta + \gamma = 180°$ |
| Let $\alpha = 80°$ and $\beta = 32°$. | $80° + 32° + \gamma = 180°$ |
| Solve for $\gamma$. | $\boxed{\gamma = 68°}$ |

**STEP 2** Find $b$.

| | |
|---|---|
| Write the Law of Sines to include the known side $c$. | $\dfrac{\sin \beta}{b} = \dfrac{\sin \gamma}{c}$ |
| Isolate $b$. | $b = \dfrac{c \sin \beta}{\sin \gamma}$ |
| Let $\beta = 32°$, $\gamma = 68°$, and $c = 17$ mi. | $b = \dfrac{(17 \text{ mi}) \sin 32°}{\sin 68°}$ |
| Use a calculator to approximate $b$. | $b \approx 9.7161177$ mi |
| Round $b$ to two significant digits. | $\boxed{b \approx 9.7 \text{ mi}}$ |

**STEP 3** Find $a$.

| | |
|---|---|
| Write the Law of Sines again incorporating the known side $c$. | $\dfrac{\sin \alpha}{a} = \dfrac{\sin \gamma}{c}$ |
| Isolate $a$. | $a = \dfrac{c \sin \alpha}{\sin \gamma}$ |
| Let $\alpha = 80°$, $\gamma = 68°$, and $c = 17$ mi. | $a = \dfrac{(17 \text{ mi}) \sin 80°}{\sin 68°}$ |
| Use a calculator to approximate $a$. | $a \approx 18.056539$ mi |
| Round $a$ to two significant digits. | $\boxed{a \approx 18 \text{ mi}}$ |

**STEP 4** Draw and label the triangle.

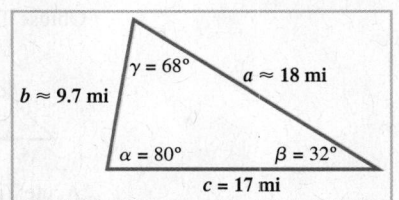

**Technology Tip**

**Step 2:** Use the calculator to find $b = \dfrac{17 \sin 32°}{\sin 68°}$.

```
17sin(32)/sin(68
)
        9.716117734
```

**Step 3:** Use the calculator to find $a = \dfrac{17 \sin 80°}{\sin 68°}$.

```
17sin(80)/sin(68
)
        18.0565394
■
```

■ **Answer:** $\alpha = 35°$, $b \approx 21$ in., $c \approx 18$ in.

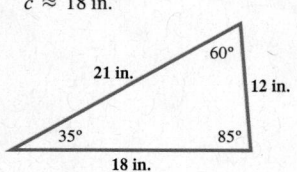

■ **YOUR TURN** Solve the triangle.

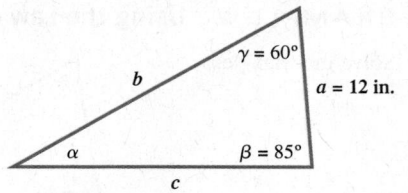

## Case 2 (Ambiguous Case): Two Sides and One Angle (SSA)

If we are given the measures of two sides and an angle opposite one of the sides, then we call that Case 2, SSA (side-side-angle). This case is called the ambiguous case, because the given information by itself can represent one triangle, two triangles, or no triangle at all. If the angle given is acute, then the possibilities are zero, one, or two triangles. If the angle given is obtuse, then the possibilities are zero or one triangle. The possibilities come from the fact that $\sin \alpha = k$, where $0 < k < 1$, has two solutions for $\alpha$: one in quadrant I (acute angle) and one in quadrant II (obtuse angle).

In the figure on the left, note that

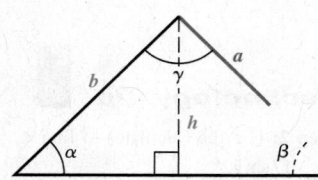

■ $h = b \sin \alpha$ by the definition of the sine ratio,
■ $a$ may turn out to be smaller than, equal to, or larger than $h$.

Since $0 < \sin \alpha < 1$, then $h < b$.

### Given Angle ($\alpha$) Is Acute

| CONDITION | PICTURE | NUMBER OF TRIANGLES |
|---|---|---|
| $0 < a < h$, in this case, $\sin \beta > 1$ (impossible) | No Triangle | 0 |
| $a = h$, in this case, $\sin \beta = 1$ | Right Triangle | 1 |
| $h < a < b$, in this case, $0 < \sin \beta < 1$ | Acute Triangle / Obtuse Triangle | 2 |
| $a \geq b$, in this case, $0 < \sin \beta < 1$ | Acute Triangle | 1 |

## Given Angle (α) Is Obtuse

| CONDITION | PICTURE | NUMBER OF TRIANGLES |
|---|---|---|
| $a \le b$, in this case, $\sin\beta \ge 1$ (impossible) | No Triangle | 0 |
| $a > b$, in this case, $0 < \sin\beta < 1$ | One Triangle | 1 |

### EXAMPLE 3   Solving the Ambiguous Case (SSA)—One Triangle

Solve the triangle $a = 23$ ft, $b = 11$ ft, and $\alpha = 122°$.

**Solution:**

This is the ambiguous case because the measures of two sides and an angle opposite one of those sides are given. Since the given angle $\alpha$ is obtuse and $a > b$, we expect one triangle.

**STEP 1** Find $\beta$.

Use the Law of Sines.

$$\frac{\sin\alpha}{a} = \frac{\sin\beta}{b}$$

Isolate $\sin\beta$.

$$\sin\beta = \frac{b\sin\alpha}{a}$$

Let $a = 23$ ft, $b = 11$ ft, and $\alpha = 122°$.

$$\sin\beta = \frac{(11\text{ ft})\sin122°}{23\text{ ft}}$$

Use a calculator to evaluate the right side. $\sin\beta \approx 0.40558822$

Use a calculator to approximate $\beta$. $\beta \approx \sin^{-1}(0.40558822) \approx \boxed{24°}$

**STEP 2** Find $\gamma$.

The measures of angles in a triangle sum to 180°.

$$\alpha + \beta + \gamma = 180°$$

Substitute $\alpha = 122°$ and $\beta \approx 24°$.

$$122° + 24° + \gamma \approx 180°$$

Solve for $\gamma$. $\boxed{\gamma \approx 34°}$

**STEP 3** Find $c$.

Use the Law of Sines.

$$\frac{\sin\alpha}{a} = \frac{\sin\gamma}{c}$$

Isolate $c$.

$$c = \frac{a\sin\gamma}{\sin\alpha}$$

Substitute $a = 23$ ft, $\alpha = 122°$, and $\gamma \approx 34°$.

$$c \approx \frac{(23\text{ ft})\sin34°}{\sin122°}$$

Use a calculator to evaluate $c$. $\boxed{c \approx 15\text{ ft}}$

STEP 4 Draw and label the triangle.

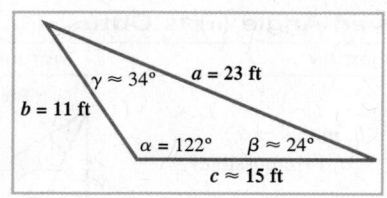

■ **Answer:** $\beta \approx 32°, \gamma \approx 15°,$
$b \approx 35$ mm

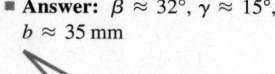

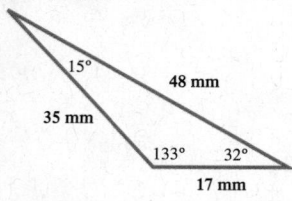

■ **YOUR TURN** Solve the triangle $\alpha = 133°, a = 48$ mm, and $c = 17$ mm.

## EXAMPLE 4 Solving the Ambiguous Case (SSA)— Two Triangles

Solve the triangle $a = 8.1$ m, $b = 8.3$ m, and $\alpha = 72°$.

**Solution:**

This is the ambiguous case because the measures of two sides and an angle opposite one of those sides are given. Since the given angle $\alpha$ is acute and $a < b$, we expect two triangles.

STEP 1 Find $\beta$.

| | |
|---|---|
| Write the Law of Sines for the given information. | $\dfrac{\sin \alpha}{a} = \dfrac{\sin \beta}{b}$ |
| Isolate $\sin \beta$. | $\sin \beta = \dfrac{b \sin \alpha}{a}$ |
| Let $a = 8.1$ m, $b = 8.3$ m, and $\alpha = 72°$. | $\sin \beta = \dfrac{(8.3 \text{ m}) \sin 72°}{8.1 \text{ m}}$ |
| Use a calculator to evaluate the right side. | $\sin \beta \approx 0.974539393$ |
| Use a calculator to approximate $\beta$. Note that $\beta$ can be acute or obtuse. | $\beta \approx \sin^{-1}(0.974539393) \approx 77°$ |
| This is the quadrant I solution ($\beta$ is acute). | $\boxed{\beta_1 \approx 77°}$ |
| The quadrant II solution ($\beta$ is obtuse) is $\beta_2 = 180 - \beta_1$. | $\boxed{\beta_2 \approx 103°}$ |

STEP 2 Find $\gamma$.

| | |
|---|---|
| The measures of the angles in a triangle sum to 180°. | $\alpha + \beta + \gamma = 180°$ |
| Substitute $\alpha = 72°$ and $\beta_1 \approx 77°$. | $72° + 77° + \gamma_1 \approx 180°$ |
| Solve for $\gamma_1$. | $\boxed{\gamma_1 \approx 31°}$ |
| Substitute $\alpha = 72°$ and $\beta_2 \approx 103°$. | $72° + 103° + \gamma_2 \approx 180°$ |
| Solve for $\gamma_2$. | $\boxed{\gamma_2 \approx 5°}$ |

STEP 3 Find $c$.

Use the Law of Sines.

$$\frac{\sin \alpha}{a} = \frac{\sin \gamma}{c}$$

Isolate $c$.

$$c = \frac{a \sin \gamma}{\sin \alpha}$$

Substitute $a = 8.1$ m, $\alpha = 72°$, and $\gamma_1 \approx 31°$.

$$c_1 \approx \frac{(8.1 \text{ m}) \sin 31°}{\sin 72°}$$

Use a calculator to evaluate $c_1$.

$$\boxed{c_1 \approx 4.4 \text{ m}}$$

Substitute $a = 8.1$ m, $\alpha = 72°$, and $\gamma_2 \approx 5°$.

$$c_2 \approx \frac{(8.1 \text{ m}) \sin 5°}{\sin 72°}$$

Use a calculator to evaluate $c_2$.

$$\boxed{c_2 \approx 0.74 \text{ m}}$$

STEP 4 Draw and label the two triangles.

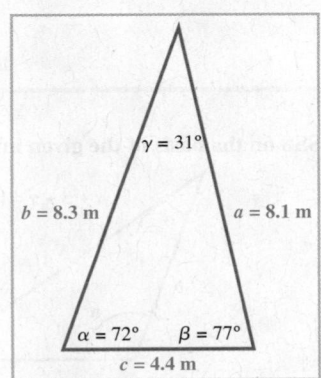

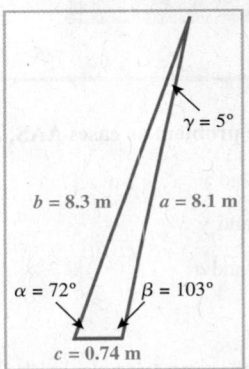

**Study Tip**

Notice that when there are two solutions in the SSA case, one triangle will be obtuse.

## EXAMPLE 5   Solving the Ambiguous Case (SSA)—No Triangle

Solve the triangle $\alpha = 107°$, $a = 6$, and $b = 8$.

**Solution:**

This is the ambiguous case because the measures of two sides and an angle opposite one of those sides are given. Since the given angle $\alpha$ is obtuse and $a < b$, we expect no triangle since the longer side is not opposite the largest angle.

Write the Law of Sines.

$$\frac{\sin \alpha}{a} = \frac{\sin \beta}{b}$$

Isolate $\sin \beta$.

$$\sin \beta = \frac{b \sin \alpha}{a}$$

Let $\alpha = 107°$, $a = 6$, and $b = 8$.

$$\sin \beta = \frac{8 \sin 107°}{6}$$

Use a calculator to evaluate the right side.

$$\sin \beta \approx 1.28 > 1$$

Since the range of the sine function is $[-1, 1]$, there is no angle $\beta$ such that $\sin \beta \approx 1.28$. Therefore, there is $\boxed{\text{no triangle}}$ with the given measurements.

*Note:* Had the geometric contradiction not been noticed, your work analytically will show a contradiction of $\sin \beta > 1$.

In this section, we solved oblique triangles. When given the measures of three parts of a triangle, we classify the triangle according to the given data (sides and angles). Four cases arise:

- one side and two angles (AAS or ASA)
- two sides and the angle opposite one of the sides (SSA)
- two sides and the angle between sides (SAS)
- three sides (SSS)

The Law of Sines

$$\frac{\sin \alpha}{a} = \frac{\sin \beta}{b} = \frac{\sin \gamma}{c}$$

can be used to solve the first two cases (AAS or ASA, and SSA). It is important to note that the SSA case is called the ambiguous case because any one of three results is possible: no triangle, one triangle, or two triangles.

**SECTION**
**4.4 EXERCISES**

**▪ SKILLS**

In Exercises 1–6, classify each triangle problem as cases AAS, ASA, SAS, SSA, or SSS on the basis of the given information.

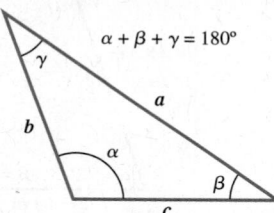

$\alpha + \beta + \gamma = 180°$

**1.** $c, a$, and $\alpha$       **2.** $c, a$, and $\gamma$

**3.** $a, b$, and $c$       **4.** $a, b$, and $\gamma$

**5.** $\alpha, \beta$, and $c$       **6.** $\beta, \gamma$, and $a$

In Exercises 7–16, solve each of the following triangles with the given measures.

**7.** $\alpha = 45°, \beta = 60°, a = 10$ m       **8.** $\beta = 75°, \gamma = 60°, b = 25$ in.

**9.** $\alpha = 46°, \gamma = 72°, b = 200$ cm       **10.** $\gamma = 100°, \beta = 40°, a = 16$ ft

**11.** $\alpha = 16.3°, \gamma = 47.6°, c = 211$ yd       **12.** $\beta = 104.2°, \gamma = 33.6°, a = 26$ in.

**13.** $\alpha = 30°, \beta = 30°, c = 12$ m       **14.** $\alpha = 45°, \gamma = 75°, c = 9$ in.

**15.** $\beta = 26°, \gamma = 57°, c = 100$ yd       **16.** $\alpha = 80°, \gamma = 30°, b = 3$ ft

In Exercises 17–34, the measures of two sides and an angle are given. Determine whether a triangle (or two) exist, and if so, solve the triangle(s).

**17.** $a = 4, b = 5, \alpha = 16°$     **18.** $b = 30, c = 20, \beta = 70°$     **19.** $a = 12, c = 12, \gamma = 40°$

**20.** $b = 111, a = 80, \alpha = 25°$     **21.** $a = 21, b = 14, \beta = 100°$     **22.** $a = 13, b = 26, \alpha = 120°$

**23.** $\alpha = 30°, b = 18, a = 9$     **24.** $\alpha = 45°, b = \sqrt{2}, a = 1$     **25.** $\alpha = 34°, b = 7, a = 10$

**26.** $\alpha = 71°, b = 5.2, a = 5.2$     **27.** $\alpha = 21.3°, b = 6.18, a = 6.03$     **28.** $\alpha = 47.3°, b = 7.3, a = 5.32$

**29.** $\alpha = 116°, b = 4\sqrt{3}, a = 5\sqrt{2}$     **30.** $\alpha = 51°, b = 4\sqrt{3}, a = 4\sqrt{5}$     **31.** $b = 500, c = 330, \gamma = 40°$

**32.** $b = 16, a = 9, \beta = 137°$     **33.** $a = \sqrt{2}, b = \sqrt{7}, \beta = 106°$     **34.** $b = 15.3, c = 27.2, \gamma = 11.6°$

**■ APPLICATIONS**

**For Exercises 35 and 36, refer to the following:**

**NASA Kennedy Space Center**

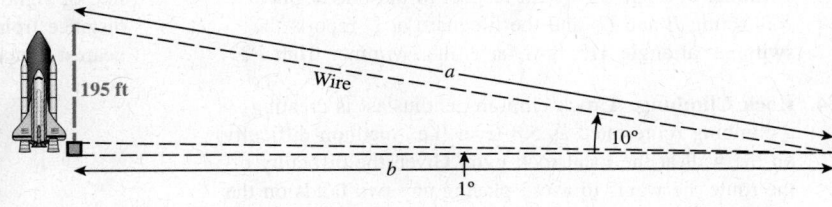

On the launch pad at Kennedy Space Center, there is an escape basket that can hold four astronauts. The basket slides down a wire that is attached 195 feet high, above the base of the launch pad. The angle of inclination measured from where the basket would touch the ground to the base of the launch pad is 1°, and the angle of inclination from that same point to where the wire is attached is 10°.

**35. NASA.** How long is the wire $a$?

**36. NASA.** How far from the launch pad does the basket touch the ground? That is, find $b$.

**37. Hot-Air Balloon.** A hot-air balloon is sighted at the same time by two friends who are 1.0 mile apart on the same side of the balloon. The angles of elevation from the two friends are 20.5° and 25.5°. How high is the balloon?

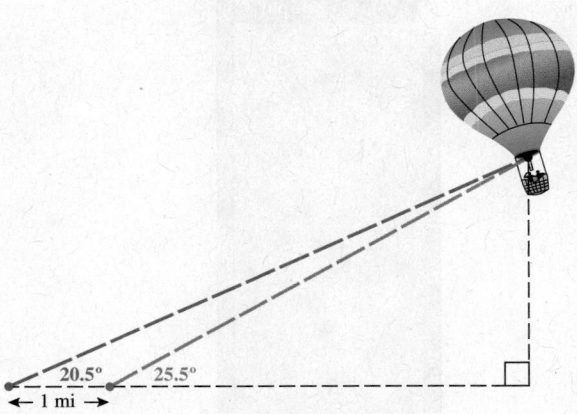

**38. Hot-Air Balloon.** A hot-air balloon is sighted at the same time by two friends who are 2 miles apart on the same side of the balloon. The angles of elevation from the two friends are 10° and 15°. How high is the balloon?

**39. Rocket Tracking.** A tracking station has two telescopes that are 1.0 mile apart. The telescopes can lock onto a rocket after it is launched and record the angles of elevation to the rocket. If the angles of elevation from telescopes A and B are 30° and 80°, respectively, then how far is the rocket from telescope A?

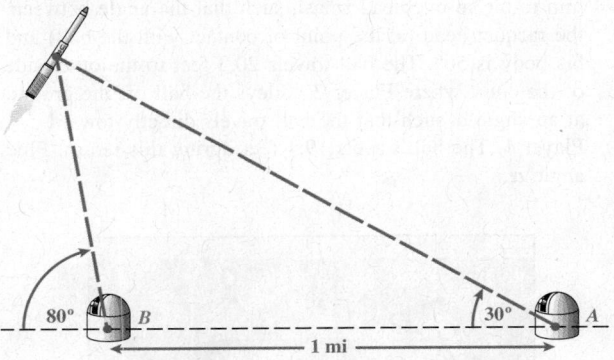

**40. Rocket Tracking.** Given the data in Exercise 39, how far is the rocket from telescope B?

**41. Distance Across River.** An engineer wants to construct a bridge across a fast-moving river. Using a straight-line segment between two points that are 100 feet apart along his side of the river, he measures the angles formed when sighting the point on the other side where he wants to have the bridge end. If the angles formed at points A and B are 65° and 15°, respectively, how far is it from point A to the point on the other side of the river? Round to the nearest foot.

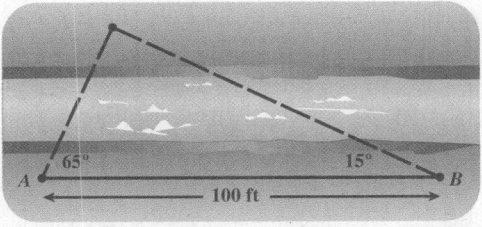

**42. Distance Across River.** Given the data in Exercise 41, how far is it from point B to the point on the other side of the river? Round to the nearest foot.

**43. Lifeguard Posts.** Two lifeguard chairs, labeled $P$ and $Q$, are located 400 feet apart. A troubled swimmer is spotted by both lifeguards. If the lifeguard at $P$ reports the swimmer at angle 35° (with respect to the line segment connecting $P$ and $Q$) and the lifeguard at $Q$ reports the swimmer at angle 41°, how far is the swimmer from $P$?

**44. Rock Climbing.** A rock climbing enthusiast is creating a climbing route rated as 5.8 level (i.e., medium difficulty) on the wall at the local rock gym. Given the difficulty of the route, he wants to avoid placing any two holds on the same vertical or horizontal line on the wall. If he places holds at $P$, $Q$, and $R$ such that $\angle QPR = 40°$, $QR = 6$ feet, and $QP = 4.5$ feet, how far is the hold at $P$ from the hold at $R$?

**45. Tennis.** After a long rally between two friends playing tennis, Player 2 lobs the ball into Player 1's court, enabling him to hit an overhead smash such that the angle between the racquet head (at the point of contact with the ball) and his body is 56°. The ball travels 20.3 feet to the other side of the court where Player 2 volleys the ball off the ground at an angle $\alpha$ such that the ball travels directly toward Player 1. The ball travels 19.4 feet during this return. Find angle $\alpha$.

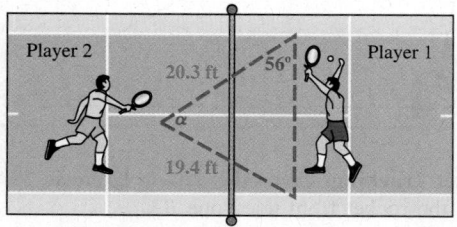

**46. Tennis.** Shocked by the move Player 1 made in Exercise 45, Player 2 is forced to quickly deflect the ball straight back to Player 1. Player 1 reaches behind himself and is able to contact the ball at the same height above the ground with which Player 1 initially hit it. If the angle between Player 1's racquet position at the end of the previous shot and its current position at the point of contact of this shot is 130°, and the angle with which it contacts the ball is 25°, how far has the ball traveled horizontally as a result of Player 2's hit?

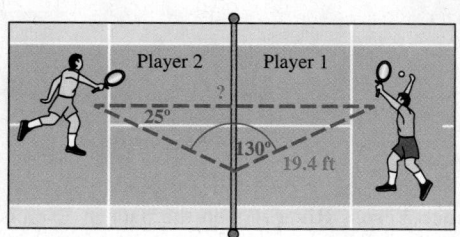

**47. Surveying.** There are two stations along the shoreline and the distance along the beach between the two stations is 50 meters. The angles between the baseline (beach) and the line of sight to the island are 30° and 40°. Find the shortest distance from the beach to the island. Round to the nearest meter.

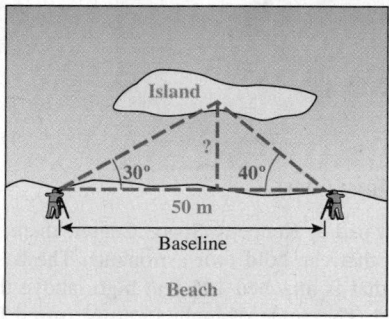

**48. Surveying.** There are two stations along a shoreline and the distance along the beach between the two stations is 200 feet. The angles between the baseline (beach) and the line of sight to the island are 30° and 50°. Find the shortest distance from the beach to the island. Round to the nearest foot.

**49. Bowling.** The 6-8 split is common in bowling. To make this split, a bowler stands dead center and throws the ball hard and straight directly toward the right of the 6 pin. The distance from the ball at the point of release to the 8 pin is 63.2 feet. See the diagram. How far does the ball travel from the bowler to the 6 pin?

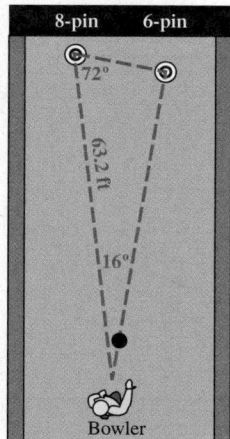

**50. Bowling.** A bowler is said to get a strike on the "Brooklyn side" of the head pin if he hits the head pin on the side opposite the pocket. (For a right-handed bowler, the pocket is to the right of the head pin.) There is a small range for the angle at which the ball must contact the head pin in order to convert all of the pins. If the measurements are as shown, how far does the ball travel (assuming it is thrown straight with no hook) before it contacts the head pin?

**For Exercises 51 and 52, refer to the following:**

To quantify the torque (rotational force) of the elbow joint of a human arm (see the figure to the right), it is necessary to identify angles $A$, $B$, and $C$ as well as lengths $a$, $b$, and $c$. Measurements performed on an arm determine that the measure of angle $C$ is $95°$, the measure of angle $A$ is $82°$, and the length of the muscle $a$ is 23 centimeters.

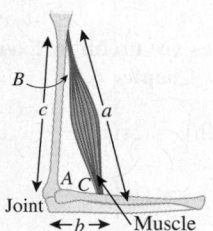

**51. Health/Medicine.** Find the length of the forearm from the elbow joint to the muscle attachment $b$.

**52. Health/Medicine.** Find the length of the upper arm from the muscle attachment to the elbow joint $c$.

■ **CATCH THE MISTAKE**

**In Exercises 53 and 54, explain the mistake that is made.**

**53.** Solve the triangle $\alpha = 120°$, $a = 7$, and $b = 9$.

**Solution:**

| | |
|---|---|
| Use the Law of Sines to find $\beta$. | $\dfrac{\sin \alpha}{a} = \dfrac{\sin \beta}{b}$ |
| Let $\alpha = 120°$, $a = 7$, and $b = 9$. | $\dfrac{\sin 120°}{7} = \dfrac{\sin \beta}{9}$ |
| Solve for $\sin \beta$. | $\sin \beta = 1.113$ |
| Solve for $\beta$. | $\beta = 42°$ |
| Sum the angle measures to $180°$. | $120° + 42° + \gamma = 180°$ |
| Solve for $\gamma$. | $\gamma = 18°$ |
| Use the Law of Sines to find $c$. | $\dfrac{\sin \alpha}{a} = \dfrac{\sin \gamma}{c}$ |
| Let $\alpha = 120°$, $a = 7$, and $\gamma = 18°$. | $\dfrac{\sin 120°}{7} = \dfrac{\sin 18°}{c}$ |
| Solve for $c$. | $c = 2.5$ |

$\alpha = 120°$, $\beta = 42°$, $\gamma = 18°$, $a = 7$, $b = 9$, and $c = 2.5$.

This is incorrect. The longest side is not opposite the longest angle. There is no triangle that makes the original measurements work. What mistake was made?

**54.** Solve the triangle $\alpha = 40°$, $a = 7$, and $b = 9$.

**Solution:**

| | |
|---|---|
| Use the Law of Sines to find $\beta$. | $\dfrac{\sin \alpha}{a} = \dfrac{\sin \beta}{b}$ |
| Let $\alpha = 40°$, $a = 7$, and $b = 9$. | $\dfrac{\sin 40°}{7} = \dfrac{\sin \beta}{9}$ |
| Solve for $\sin \beta$. | $\sin \beta = 0.826441212$ |
| Solve for $\beta$. | $\beta = 56°$ |
| Find $\gamma$. | $40° + 56° + \gamma = 180°$ |
| | $\gamma = 84°$ |
| Use the Law of Sines to find $c$. | $\dfrac{\sin \alpha}{a} = \dfrac{\sin \gamma}{c}$ |
| Let $\alpha = 40°$, $a = 7$, and $\gamma = 84°$. | $\dfrac{\sin 40°}{7} = \dfrac{\sin 84°}{c}$ |
| Solve for $c$. | $c = 11$ |

$\alpha = 40°$, $\beta = 56°$, $\gamma = 84°$, $a = 7$, $b = 9$ and $c = 11$.

This is incorrect. What mistake was made?

■ **CONCEPTUAL**

**In Exercises 55–60, determine whether each statment is true or false.**

**55.** The Law of Sines applies only to right triangles.

**57.** An acute triangle is an oblique triangle.

**59.** If you are given two sides that have the same length in a triangle, then there can be at most one triangle.

**56.** If you are given the measures of two sides and any angle, there is a unique solution for the triangle.

**58.** An obtuse triangle is an oblique triangle.

**60.** If $\alpha$ is obtuse and $\beta = \dfrac{\alpha}{2}$, then the situation is unambiguous.

# ▪ CHALLENGE

The following identities are useful in Exercises 61 and 62, and will be derived in Chapter 6.

$$\sin x + \sin y = 2\sin\left(\frac{x+y}{2}\right)\cos\left(\frac{x-y}{2}\right)$$

$$\sin(2x) = 2\sin x \cos x$$

$$\sin(x \pm y) = \sin x \cos y \pm \cos x \sin y$$

$$\cos(x \pm y) = \cos x \cos y \pm \sin x \sin y$$

**61. Mollweide's Identity.** For any triangle, the following identity is true. It is often used to check the solution of a triangle since all six pieces of information (three sides and three angles) are involved. Derive the identity using the Law of Sines.

$$(a+b)\sin\left(\tfrac{1}{2}\gamma\right) = c\cos\left[\tfrac{1}{2}(\alpha - \beta)\right]$$

**62. The Law of Tangents.** Use the Law of Sines and trigonometric identities to show that for any triangle, the following is true:

$$\frac{a-b}{a+b} = \frac{\tan\left[\tfrac{1}{2}(\alpha - \beta)\right]}{\tan\left[\tfrac{1}{2}(\alpha + \beta)\right]}$$

**63.** Use the Law of Sines to prove that all angles in an equilateral triangle must have the same measure.

**64.** Suppose that you have a triangle with side lengths $a$, $b$, and $c$, and angles $\alpha$, $\beta$, and $\gamma$, respectively, directly across from them. If it is known that $a = \dfrac{1}{\sqrt{2}}b, c = 2$, $\alpha$ is an acute angle, and $\beta = 2\alpha$, solve the triangle.

# ▪ TECHNOLOGY

For Exercises 65–70, let $A$, $B$, and $C$ be the lengths of the three sides with $X$, $Y$, and $Z$ as the opposite corresponding angles. Write a program to solve the given triangle with a calculator.

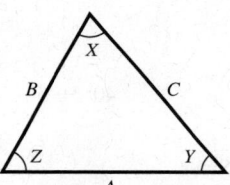

**65.** $A = 10, Y = 40°$, and $Z = 72°$

**66.** $B = 42.8, X = 31.6°$, and $Y = 82.2°$

**67.** $A = 22, B = 17$, and $X = 105°$

**68.** $B = 16.5, C = 9.8$, and $Z = 79.2°$

**69.** $A = 25.7, C = 12.2$, and $X = 65°$

**70.** $A = 54.6, B = 12.9$, and $Y = 23°$

# ▪ PREVIEW TO CALCULUS

In calculus, some applications of the derivative require the solution of triangles. In Exercises 71–74, solve each triangle using the Law of Sines.

**71.** In an oblique triangle $ABC$, $\beta = 45°$, $\gamma = 60°$, and $b = 20$ in. Find the length of $a$. Round your answer to the nearest unit.

**72.** In an oblique triangle $ABC$, $\beta = \dfrac{2\pi}{9}, \gamma = \dfrac{5\pi}{9}$, and $a = 200$ ft. Find the length of $c$. Round your answer to the nearest unit.

**73.** In an oblique triangle $ABC$, $b = 14$ m, $c = 14$ m, and $\alpha = \dfrac{4\pi}{7}$. Find the length of $a$. Round your answer to the nearest unit.

**74.** In an oblique triangle $ABC$, $b = 30$ cm, $c = 45$ cm, and $\gamma = 35°$. Find the length of $a$. Round your answer to the nearest unit.

**SKILLS OBJECTIVES**

- Solve SAS triangles.
- Solve SSS triangles.
- Find the area of triangles in the SAS case.
- Find the area of triangles in the SSS case.

**CONCEPTUAL OBJECTIVES**

- Understand the derivation of the Law of Cosines.
- Develop a strategy for which angles (larger or smaller) and which method (the Law of Sines or the Law of Cosines) to select to solve oblique triangles.

## Solving Oblique Triangles Using the Law of Cosines

In Section 4.4, we learned that to solve oblique triangles means to find all three side lengths and angle measures, and that at least one side length must be known. We need two additional pieces of information to solve an oblique triangle (combinations of side lengths and/or angles). We found that there are four cases:

- Case 1: AAS or ASA (measures of two angles and a side are given)
- Case 2: SSA (measures of two sides and an angle opposite one of the sides are given)
- Case 3: SAS (measures of two sides and the angle between them are given)
- Case 4: SSS (measures of three sides are given)

We used the Law of Sines to solve Case 1 and Case 2 triangles. Now, we need the *Law of Cosines* to solve Case 3 and Case 4 triangles.

| WORDS | MATH |
|---|---|
| Start with an oblique (acute) triangle. | |

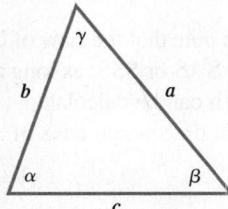

Drop a perpendicular line segment from $\gamma$ to side $c$ with height $h$.

The result is two right triangles within the larger triangle.

Use the Pythagorean theorem to write the relationship between the side lengths in both right triangles.

Triangle 1:
$$x^2 + h^2 = b^2$$

Triangle 2:
$$(c - x)^2 + h^2 = a^2$$

Solve for $h^2$ in both equations.

Triangle 1: $\qquad\qquad\qquad\qquad\qquad\qquad h^2 = b^2 - x^2$

Triangle 2: $\qquad\qquad\qquad\qquad\qquad\qquad h^2 = a^2 - (c - x)^2$

Since the segment of length $h$ is shared,
set $h^2 = h^2$, for the two triangles. $\qquad\quad b^2 - x^2 = a^2 - (c - x)^2$

Multiply out the squared binomial on the right. $\quad b^2 - x^2 = a^2 - (c^2 - 2cx + x^2)$

Eliminate the parentheses. $\qquad\qquad\qquad b^2 - x^2 = a^2 - c^2 + 2cx - x^2$

Add $x^2$ to both sides. $\qquad\qquad\qquad\qquad b^2 = a^2 - c^2 + 2cx$

Isolate $a^2$. $\qquad\qquad\qquad\qquad\qquad a^2 = b^2 + c^2 - 2cx$

Notice that $\cos\alpha = \dfrac{x}{b}$. Let $x = b\cos\alpha$. $\qquad \boxed{a^2 = b^2 + c^2 - 2bc\cos\alpha}$

*Note:* If we instead drop the perpendicular line segment with length $h$ from the angle $\alpha$ or the angle $\beta$, we can derive the other two parts of the Law of Cosines:

$$\boxed{b^2 = a^2 + c^2 - 2ac\cos\beta} \quad \text{and} \quad \boxed{c^2 = a^2 + b^2 - 2ab\cos\gamma}$$

### THE LAW OF COSINES

For a triangle with sides of length $a$, $b$, and $c$, and opposite angle measures $\alpha$, $\beta$, and $\gamma$, the following equations are true:

$$a^2 = b^2 + c^2 - 2bc\cos\alpha$$
$$b^2 = a^2 + c^2 - 2ac\cos\beta$$
$$c^2 = a^2 + b^2 - 2ab\cos\gamma$$

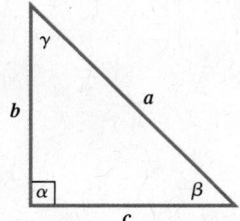

It is important to note that the Law of Cosines can be used to find side lengths or angles in any triangle in cases SAS or SSS, as long as three of the four variables in any of the equations are known, the fourth can be calculated.

Notice that in the special case of a right triangle (say, $\alpha = 90°$),

$$a^2 = b^2 + c^2 - 2bc\underbrace{\cos 90°}_{0}$$

one of the equations of the Law of Cosines reduces to the Pythagorean theorem:

$$\underbrace{a^2}_{\text{hyp}} = \underbrace{b^2}_{\text{leg}} + \underbrace{c^2}_{\text{leg}}$$

The Pythagorean theorem can thus be regarded as a special case of the Law of Cosines.

## Case 3: Solving Oblique Triangles (SAS)

We now solve SAS triangle problems where the measures of two sides and the angle between them are given. We start by using the Law of Cosines to solve for the length of the side opposite the given angle. We then can apply either the Law of Sines or the Law of Cosines to find the second angle measure.

## EXAMPLE 1    Using the Law of Cosines to Solve a Triangle (SAS)

Solve the triangle $a = 13$, $c = 6.0$, and $\beta = 20°$.

**Solution:**

The measures of two sides and the angle
between them are given (SAS).

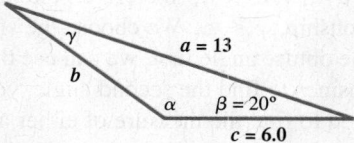

Notice that the Law of Sines can't be used, because it requires the measures of at
least one angle and the side opposite that angle.

STEP 1 Find $b$.

| | |
|---|---|
| Apply the Law of Cosines that involves $\beta$. | $b^2 = a^2 + c^2 - 2ac \cos \beta$ |
| Let $a = 13, c = 6.0$, and $\beta = 20°$. | $b^2 = 13^2 + 6^2 - 2(13)(6) \cos 20°$ |
| Evaluate the right side with a calculator. | $b^2 \approx 58.40795$ |
| Solve for $b$. | $b \approx \pm 7.6425$ |
| Round to two significant digits; $b$ can only be positive. | $\boxed{b \approx 7.6}$ |

STEP 2 Find $\gamma$.

| | |
|---|---|
| Use the Law of Sines to find the smaller angle measure, $\gamma$. | $\dfrac{\sin \gamma}{c} = \dfrac{\sin \beta}{b}$ |
| Isolate $\sin \gamma$. | $\sin \gamma = \dfrac{c \sin \beta}{b}$ |
| Let $b \approx 7.6, c = 6.0$, and $\beta = 20°$. | $\sin \gamma \approx \dfrac{6 \sin 20°}{7.6}$ |
| Apply the inverse sine function. | $\gamma \approx \sin^{-1}\left(\dfrac{6 \sin 20°}{7.6}\right)$ |
| Evaluate the right side with a calculator. | $\gamma \approx 15.66521°$ |
| Round to the nearest degree. | $\boxed{\gamma \approx 16°}$ |

STEP 3 Find $\alpha$.

| | |
|---|---|
| The angle measures must sum to 180°. | $\alpha + 20° + 16° \approx 180°$ |
| Solve for $\alpha$. | $\boxed{\alpha \approx 144°}$ |

▪ **YOUR TURN** Solve the triangle $b = 4.2$, $c = 1.8$, and $\alpha = 35°$.

Notice the steps we took in solving an SAS triangle:

1. Find the length of the side opposite the given angle using the Law of Cosines.
2. Solve for the smaller angle using the Law of Sines.
3. Solve for the larger angle using the fact that angles of a triangle sum to 180°.

You may be thinking, "Would it matter if we had solved for $\alpha$ before solving for $\gamma$?"
Yes, it does matter—in this problem you cannot solve for $\alpha$ by the Law of Sines before

finding $\gamma$. The Law of Sines can be used only on the smaller angle (opposite the shortest side). If we had tried to use the Law of Sines with the obtuse angle $\alpha$, the inverse sine would have resulted in $\alpha = 36°$. Since the sine function is positive in QI and QII, we would not know whether that angle was $\alpha = 36°$ or its supplementary angle $\alpha = 144°$. Notice that $c < a$; therefore, the angles opposite those sides must have the same relationship, $\gamma < \alpha$. We choose the smaller angle first. Alternatively, if we want to solve for the obtuse angle first, we can use the Law of Cosines to solve for $\alpha$. If you use the Law of Cosines to find the second angle, you can choose either angle. The Law of Cosines can be used to find the measure of either acute or obtuse angles.

## Case 4: Solving Oblique Triangles (SSS)

We now solve oblique triangles when all three side lengths are given (the SSS case). In this case, start by finding the largest angle (opposite the largest side) using the Law of Cosines. Then apply the Law of Sines to find either of the remaining two angles. Lastly, find the third angle with the triangle angle sum identity.

**EXAMPLE 2    Using the Law of Cosines to Solve a Triangle (SSS)**

Solve the triangle $a = 8, b = 6$, and $c = 7$.

**Solution:**

**STEP 1** Identify the largest angle, which is $\alpha$.

Write the equation of the Law of Cosines that involves $\alpha$.

$$a^2 = b^2 + c^2 - 2bc\cos\alpha$$

Let $a = 8, b = 6$, and $c = 7$.

$$8^2 = 6^2 + 7^2 - 2(6)(7)\cos\alpha$$

Simplify and isolate $\cos\alpha$.

$$\cos\alpha = \frac{6^2 + 7^2 - 8^2}{2(6)(7)} = 0.25$$

Approximate with a calculator.

$$\alpha = \cos^{-1}(0.25) \approx \boxed{75.5°}$$

**STEP 2** Find either of the remaining angles. We will solve for $\beta$.

Write the Law of Sines.

$$\frac{\sin\alpha}{a} = \frac{\sin\beta}{b}$$

Isolate $\sin\beta$.

$$\sin\beta = \frac{b\sin\alpha}{a}$$

Let $a = 8, b = 6$, and $\alpha = 75.5°$.

$$\sin\beta \approx \frac{6\sin 75.5°}{8}$$

Approximate with a calculator.

$$\beta \approx \sin^{-1}\left(\frac{6\sin 75.5°}{8}\right) \approx \boxed{46.6°}$$

**STEP 3** Find the third angle, $\gamma$.

The sum of the angle measures is 180°.

$$75.5° + 46.6° + \gamma \approx 180°$$

Solve for $\gamma$.

$$\boxed{\gamma \approx 57.9°}$$

### Technology Tip

**Step 1:** Use the calculator to find the value of $\alpha$.

```
(6²+7²-8²)/(2*6*
7)
            .25
cos⁻¹(Ans)
      75.52248781
```

```
cos⁻¹((6²+7²-8²)/
(2*6*7))
      75.52248781
```

**Step 2:** Use the calculator to find $\beta$.

```
6sin(75.5)/8
      .7261107303
sin⁻¹(Ans)
      46.56132609
sin⁻¹((6sin(75.5)
/8)
      46.56132609
▪
```

▪ **Answer:** $\alpha \approx 38.2°, \beta \approx 60.0°, \gamma \approx 81.8°$

▪ **YOUR TURN** Solve the triangle $a = 5, b = 7$, and $c = 8$.

# The Area of a Triangle

The general formula for the area of a triangle and the sine function together can be used to develop a formula for the area of a triangle when the measures of two sides and the angle between them are given.

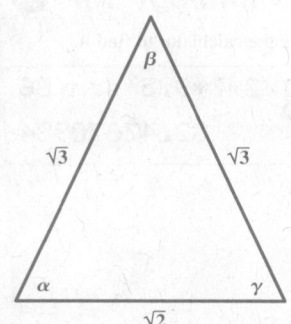

| **WORDS** | **MATH** |
|---|---|
| Start with an acute triangle, given $b$, $c$, and $\alpha$. | 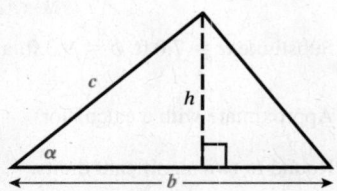 |
| Write the sine ratio in the right triangle for the acute angle $\alpha$. | $\sin \alpha = \dfrac{h}{c}$ |
| Solve for $h$. | $h = c \sin \alpha$ |
| Write the formula for area of a triangle. | $A_{\text{triangle}} = \dfrac{1}{2} bh$ |
| Substitute $h = c \sin \alpha$. | $\boxed{A_{\text{SAS}} = \dfrac{1}{2} bc \sin \alpha}$ |

Now we can calculate the area of this triangle with the given information (the measures of two sides and the angle between them: $b$, $c$, and $\alpha$). Similarly, it can be shown that the other formulas for SAS triangles are

$$\boxed{A_{\text{SAS}} = \frac{1}{2} ab \sin \gamma} \quad \text{and} \quad \boxed{A_{\text{SAS}} = \frac{1}{2} ac \sin \beta}$$

## AREA OF A TRIANGLE (SAS)

For any triangle where the measures of two sides and the angle between them are known, the area for that triangle is given by one of the following formulas (depending on which angle and side measures are given):

$$A_{\text{SAS}} = \frac{1}{2} bc \sin \alpha \qquad \text{when } b, c, \text{ and } \alpha \text{ are known}$$

$$A_{\text{SAS}} = \frac{1}{2} ab \sin \gamma \qquad \text{when } a, b, \text{ and } \gamma \text{ are known}$$

$$A_{\text{SAS}} = \frac{1}{2} ac \sin \beta \qquad \text{when } a, c, \text{ and } \beta \text{ are known}$$

In other words, the area of a triangle equals one-half the product of two of its sides and the sine of the angle between them.

**EXAMPLE 3   Finding the Area of a Triangle (SAS Case)**

Find the area of the triangle $a = 7.0$ ft, $b = 9.3$ ft, and $\gamma = 86°$.

**Solution:**

| | |
|---|---|
| Apply the area formula where *a*, *b*, and *γ* are given. | $A = \dfrac{1}{2}ab\sin\gamma$ |
| Substitute $a = 7.0$ ft, $b = 9.3$ ft, and $\gamma = 86°$. | $A = \dfrac{1}{2}(7.0\text{ ft})(9.3\text{ ft})\sin 86°$ |
| Approximate with a calculator. | $A \approx 32.47071 \text{ ft}^2$ |
| Round to two significant digits. | $\boxed{A \approx 32 \text{ ft}^2}$ |

■ **Answer:** 6.2 m²

■ **YOUR TURN** Find the area of the triangle $a = 3.2$ m, $c = 5.1$ m, and $\beta = 49°$.

The Law of Cosines can be used to develop a formula for the area of an SSS triangle, called **Heron's formula**.

| WORDS | MATH |
|---|---|
| Start with any of the formulas for SAS triangles. | $A = \dfrac{1}{2}ab\sin\gamma$ |
| Square both sides. | $A^2 = \dfrac{1}{4}a^2b^2\sin^2\gamma$ |
| Isolate $\sin^2\gamma$. | $\dfrac{4A^2}{a^2b^2} = \sin^2\gamma$ |
| Apply the Pythagorean identity. | $\dfrac{4A^2}{a^2b^2} = 1 - \cos^2\gamma$ |
| Factor the difference of the two squares on the right. | $\dfrac{4A^2}{a^2b^2} = (1 - \cos\gamma)(1 + \cos\gamma)$ |
| Solve the Law of Cosines, $c^2 = a^2 + b^2 - 2ab\cos\gamma$, for $\cos\gamma$. | $\cos\gamma = \dfrac{a^2 + b^2 - c^2}{2ab}$ |
| Substitute $\cos\gamma = \dfrac{a^2 + b^2 - c^2}{2ab}$ into $\dfrac{4A^2}{a^2b^2} = (1 - \cos\gamma)(1 + \cos\gamma)$. | $\dfrac{4A^2}{a^2b^2} = \left[1 - \dfrac{a^2 + b^2 - c^2}{2ab}\right]\left[1 + \dfrac{a^2 + b^2 - c^2}{2ab}\right]$ |
| Combine the expressions in brackets. | $\dfrac{4A^2}{a^2b^2} = \left[\dfrac{2ab - a^2 - b^2 + c^2}{2ab}\right]\left[\dfrac{2ab + a^2 + b^2 - c^2}{2ab}\right]$ |

| Group the terms in the numerators on the right. | $$\frac{4A^2}{a^2b^2} = \left[\frac{-\left(a^2 - 2ab + b^2\right) + c^2}{2ab}\right]\left[\frac{\left(a^2 + 2ab + b^2\right) - c^2}{2ab}\right]$$ |
|---|---|
| Write the numerators on the right as the difference of two squares. | $$\frac{4A^2}{a^2b^2} = \left[\frac{c^2 - (a - b)^2}{2ab}\right]\left[\frac{(a + b)^2 - c^2}{2ab}\right]$$ |
| Factor the numerators on the right. Recall: $x^2 - y^2 = (x - y)(x + y)$. | $$\frac{4A^2}{a^2b^2} = \left[\frac{(c - [a - b])(c + [a - b])}{2ab}\right]\left[\frac{([a + b] - c)([a + b] + c)}{2ab}\right]$$ |
| Simplify. | $$\frac{4A^2}{a^2b^2} = \left[\frac{(c - a + b)(c + a - b)}{2ab}\right]\left[\frac{(a + b - c)(a + b + c)}{2ab}\right]$$ |
| | $$\frac{4A^2}{a^2b^2} = \frac{(c - a + b)(c + a - b)(a + b - c)(a + b + c)}{4a^2b^2}$$ |
| Solve for $A^2$ by multiplying both sides by $\dfrac{a^2b^2}{4}$. | $$A^2 = \frac{1}{16}(c - a + b)(c + a - b)(a + b - c)(a + b + c)$$ |
| The semiperimeter $s$ is half the perimeter of the triangle. | $$s = \frac{a + b + c}{2}$$ |
| Manipulate each of the four factors: | $$c - a + b = a + b + c - 2a = 2s - 2a = 2(s - a)$$ $$c + a - b = a + b + c - 2b = 2s - 2b = 2(s - b)$$ $$a + b - c = a + b + c - 2c = 2s - 2c = 2(s - c)$$ $$a + b + c = 2s$$ |
| Substitute in these values for the four factors. | $$A^2 = \frac{1}{16}\cdot 2(s - a)\cdot 2(s - b)\cdot 2(s - c)\cdot 2s$$ |
| Simplify. | $$A^2 = s(s - a)(s - b)(s - c)$$ |
| Solve for $A$ (area is always positive). | $$A = \boxed{\sqrt{s(s - a)(s - b)(s - c)}}$$ |

## AREA OF A TRIANGLE (SSS CASE—HERON'S FORMULA)

For any triangle where the lengths of the three sides are known, the area for that triangle is given by the following formula:

$$A_{SSS} = \sqrt{s(s - a)(s - b)(s - c)}$$

where $a$, $b$, and $c$ are the lengths of the sides of the triangle and $s$ is half the perimeter of the triangle, called the semiperimeter.

$$s = \frac{a + b + c}{2}$$

**Technology Tip**

Use the calculator to find $A$.

```
√(10(10-5)(10-6)
(10-9))
      14.14213562
```

**Answer:** $2\sqrt{14} \approx 7.5$ sq units

**EXAMPLE 4    Finding the Area of a Triangle (SSS Case)**

Find the area of the triangle $a = 5$, $b = 6$, and $c = 9$.

**Solution:**

| | |
|---|---|
| Find the semiperimeter $s$. | $s = \dfrac{a + b + c}{2}$ |
| Substitute $a = 5$, $b = 6$, and $c = 9$. | $s = \dfrac{5 + 6 + 9}{2}$ |
| Simplify. | $s = 10$ |
| Write the formula for the area of a triangle in the SSS case (Heron's formula). | $A = \sqrt{s(s - a)(s - b)(s - c)}$ |
| Substitute $a = 5$, $b = 6$, $c = 9$, and $s = 10$. | $A = \sqrt{10(10 - 5)(10 - 6)(10 - 9)}$ |
| Simplify the radicand. | $A = \sqrt{10 \cdot 5 \cdot 4 \cdot 1}$ |
| Evaluate the radical. | $\boxed{A = 10\sqrt{2} \approx 14 \text{ sq units}}$ |

**YOUR TURN** Find the area of the triangle $a = 3$, $b = 5$, and $c = 6$.

# SECTION 4.5 SUMMARY

We can solve any triangle given three measures, as long as one of the measures is a side length. Depending on the information given, we either apply the **Law of Sines**

$$\frac{\sin\alpha}{a} = \frac{\sin\beta}{b} = \frac{\sin\gamma}{c}$$

and the angle sum identity, or we apply a combination of the **Law of Cosines**,

$$a^2 = b^2 + c^2 - 2bc\cos\alpha \qquad b^2 = a^2 + c^2 - 2ac\cos\beta \qquad c^2 = a^2 + b^2 - 2ab\cos\gamma$$

the Law of Sines, and the angle sum identity. The table below summarizes the strategies for solving oblique triangles covered in Sections 4.4 and 4.5.

| OBLIQUE TRIANGLE | WHAT'S KNOWN | PROCEDURE FOR SOLVING |
|---|---|---|
| AAS or ASA | Two angles and a side | Step 1: Find the remaining angle with $\alpha + \beta + \gamma = 180°$. <br> Step 2: Find the remaining sides with the Law of Sines. |
| SSA | Two sides and an angle opposite one of the sides | This is the ambiguous case, so there is either no triangle, one triangle, or two triangles. If the given angle is obtuse, then there is either one or no triangle. If the given angle is acute, then there is no triangle, one triangle, or two triangles. <br> Step 1: Apply the Law of Sines to find one of the angles. <br> Step 2: Find the remaining angle with $\alpha + \beta + \gamma = 180°$. <br> Step 3: Find the remaining side with the Law of Sines. <br> If two triangles exist, then the angle found in Step 1 can be either acute or obtuse, and Step 2 and Step 3 must be performed for each triangle. |
| SAS | Two sides and an angle between the sides | Step 1: Find the third side with the Law of Cosines. <br> Step 2: Find the smaller angle with the Law of Sines. <br> Step 3: Find the remaining angle with $\alpha + \beta + \gamma = 180°$. |
| SSS | Three sides | Step 1: Find the largest angle with the Law of Cosines. <br> Step 2: Find either remaining angle with the Law of Sines. <br> Step 3: Find the last remaining angle with $\alpha + \beta + \gamma = 180°$. |

Formulas for calculating the areas of triangles (SAS and SSS cases) were derived. The three area formulas for the SAS case depend on which angles and sides are given.

$$A_{SAS} = \frac{1}{2}bc\sin\alpha \qquad A_{SAS} = \frac{1}{2}ab\sin\gamma \qquad A_{SAS} = \frac{1}{2}ac\sin\beta$$

The Law of Cosines was instrumental in developing a formula for the area of a triangle (SSS case) when all three sides are given.

$$(Heron's\ formula) \quad A_{SSS} = \sqrt{s(s-a)(s-b)(s-c)} \quad \text{where} \quad s = \frac{a+b+c}{2}$$

## SECTION
## 4.5 EXERCISES

### ▪ SKILLS

In Exercises 1–28, solve each triangle.

**1.** $a = 4$, $c = 3$, $\beta = 100°$

**2.** $a = 6$, $b = 10$, $\gamma = 80°$

**3.** $b = 7$, $c = 2$, $\alpha = 16°$

**4.** $b = 5$, $a = 6$, $\gamma = 170°$

**5.** $b = 5$, $c = 5$, $\alpha = 20°$

**6.** $a = 4.2$, $b = 7.3$, $\gamma = 25°$

**7.** $a = 9$, $c = 12$, $\beta = 23°$

**8.** $b = 6$, $c = 13$, $\alpha = 16°$

**9.** $a = 4$, $c = 8$, $\beta = 60°$

**10.** $b = 3$, $c = \sqrt{18}$, $\alpha = 45°$

**11.** $a = 8$, $b = 5$, $c = 6$

**12.** $a = 6$, $b = 9$, $c = 12$

**13.** $a = 4$, $b = 4$, $c = 5$

**14.** $a = 17$, $b = 20$, $c = 33$

**15.** $a = 8.2$, $b = 7.1$, $c = 6.3$

**16.** $a = 1492$, $b = 2001$, $c = 1776$

**17.** $a = 4$, $b = 5$, $c = 10$

**18.** $a = 1.3$, $b = 2.7$, $c = 4.2$

**19.** $a = 12$, $b = 5$, $c = 13$

**20.** $a = 4$, $b = 5$, $c = \sqrt{41}$

**21.** $\alpha = 40°$, $\beta = 35°$, $a = 6$

**22.** $b = 11.2$, $a = 19.0$, $\gamma = 13.3°$

**23.** $\alpha = 31°$, $b = 5$, $a = 12$

**24.** $a = 11$, $c = 12$, $\gamma = 60°$

**25.** $a = \sqrt{7}$, $b = \sqrt{8}$, $c = \sqrt{3}$

**26.** $\beta = 106°$, $\gamma = 43°$, $a = 1$

**27.** $b = 11$, $c = 2$, $\beta = 10°$

**28.** $\alpha = 25°$, $a = 6$, $c = 9$

In Exercises 29–50, find the area of each triangle with measures given.

**29.** $a = 8$, $c = 16$, $\beta = 60°$

**30.** $b = 6$, $c = 4\sqrt{3}$, $\alpha = 30°$

**31.** $a = 1$, $b = \sqrt{2}$, $\alpha = 45°$

**32.** $b = 2\sqrt{2}$, $c = 4$, $\beta = 45°$

**33.** $a = 6$, $b = 8$, $\gamma = 80°$

**34.** $b = 9$, $c = 10$, $\alpha = 100°$

**35.** $a = 4$, $c = 7$, $\beta = 27°$

**36.** $a = 6.3$, $b = 4.8$, $\gamma = 17°$

**37.** $b = 100$, $c = 150$, $\alpha = 36°$

**38.** $c = 0.3$, $a = 0.7$, $\beta = 145°$

**39.** $a = 15$, $b = 15$, $c = 15$

**40.** $a = 1$, $b = 1$, $c = 1$

**41.** $a = 7$, $b = \sqrt{51}$, $c = 10$

**42.** $a = 9$, $b = 40$, $c = 41$

**43.** $a = 6$, $b = 10$, $c = 9$

**44.** $a = 40$, $b = 50$, $c = 60$

**45.** $a = 14.3$, $b = 15.7$, $c = 20.1$

**46.** $a = 146.5$, $b = 146.5$, $c = 100$

**47.** $a = 14{,}000$, $b = 16{,}500$, $c = 18{,}700$

**48.** $a = \sqrt{2}$, $b = \sqrt{3}$, $c = \sqrt{5}$

**49.** $a = 80$, $b = 75$, $c = 160$

**50.** $a = 19$, $b = 23$, $c = 3$

■ **APPLICATIONS**

**51. Aviation.** A plane flew due north at 500 miles per hour for 3 hours. A second plane, starting at the same point and at the same time, flew southeast at an angle 150° clockwise from due north at 435 miles per hour for 3 hours. At the end of the 3 hours, how far apart were the two planes? Round to the nearest mile.

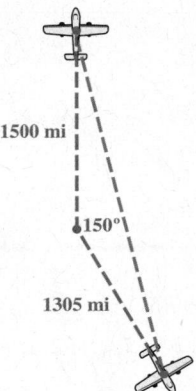

1500 mi

150°

1305 mi

**52. Aviation.** A plane flew due north at 400 miles per hour for 4 hours. A second plane, starting at the same point and at the same time, flew southeast at an angle 120° clockwise from due north at 300 miles per hour for 4 hours. At the end of the 4 hours, how far apart were the two planes? Round to the nearest mile.

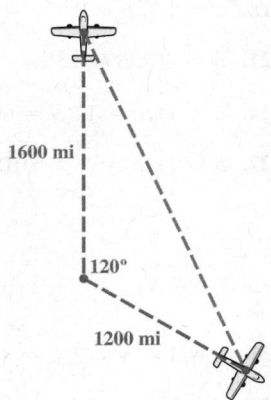

1600 mi

120°

1200 mi

**53. Aviation.** A plane flew N 30° W at 350 miles per hour for 2.5 hours. A second plane, starting at the same point and at the same time, flew 35° at an angle clockwise from due north at 550 miles per hour for 2.5 hours. At the end of 2.5 hours, how far apart were the two planes? Round to the nearest mile.

**54. Aviation.** A plane flew N 30° W at 350 miles per hour for 3 hours. A second plane starts at the same point and takes off at the same time. It is known that after 3 hours, the two planes are 2100 miles apart. Find the original bearing of the second plane, to the nearest hundredth of a degree.

**55. Sliding Board.** A 40-foot slide leaning against the bottom of a building's window makes a 55° angle with the building. The angle formed with the building by the line of sight from the top of the window to the point on the ground where the slide ends is 40°. How tall is the window?

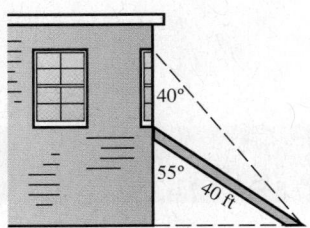

40°

55°
40 ft

**56. Airplane Slide.** An airplane door is 6 feet high. If a slide attached to the bottom of the open door is at an angle of 40° with the ground, and the angle formed by the line of sight from where the slide touches the ground to the top of the door is 45°, how long is the slide?

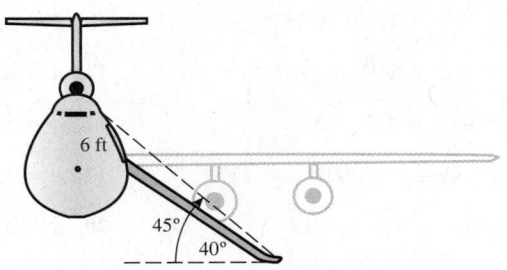

6 ft

45°
40°

**For Exercises 57 and 58, refer to the following:**

To quantify the torque (rotational force) of the elbow joint of a human arm (see the figure to the right), it is necessary to identify angles A, B, and C as well as lengths a, b, and c. Measurements performed on an arm determine that the measure of angle C is 105°, the length of the muscle a is 25.5 centimeters, and the length of the forearm from the elbow joint to the muscle attachment b is 1.76 centimeters.

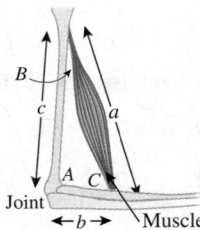

B

c

a

A C

Joint

←b→  Muscle

**57. Health/Medicine.** Find the length of the upper arm from the muscle attachment to the elbow joint c.

**58. Health/Medicine.** Find the measure of angle B.

**59. Law Enforcement.** Two members of a SWAT team and the thief they are to apprehend are positioned as follows:

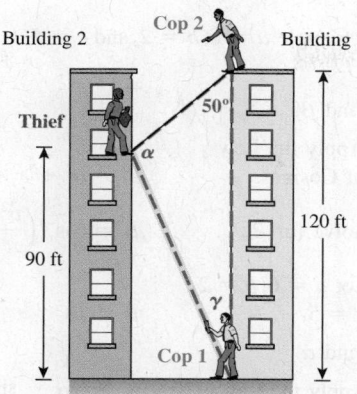

When the signal is given, Cop 2 shoots a zipline across to the window where the thief is spotted (at a 50° angle to Building 1) and Cop 1 shines a very bright light directly at the thief. Find the angle $\gamma$ at which Cop 1 holds the light to shine it directly at the thief. Round to the nearest hundredth degree.

**60. Law Enforcement.** In reference to Exercise 59, what angle does the zipline make with respect to Building 2?

**61. Surveying.** A glaciologist needs to determine the length across a certain crevice on Mendenhall glacier in order to circumvent it with his team. He has the following measurements:

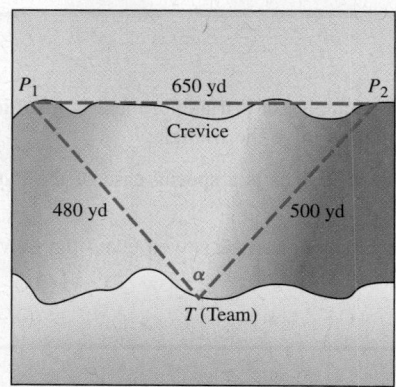

Find $\alpha$.

**62. Surveying.** A glaciologist needs to determine the length across a certain crevice on Mendenhall glacier in order to circumvent it with her team. She has the following measurements:

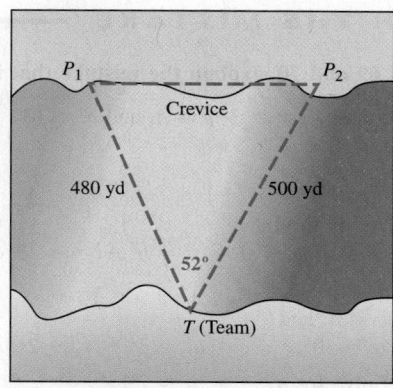

Find the approximate length across the crevice.

**63. Parking Lot.** A parking lot is to have the shape of a parallelogram that has adjacent sides measuring 200 feet and 260 feet. The acute angle between two adjacent sides is 65°. What is the area of the parking lot?

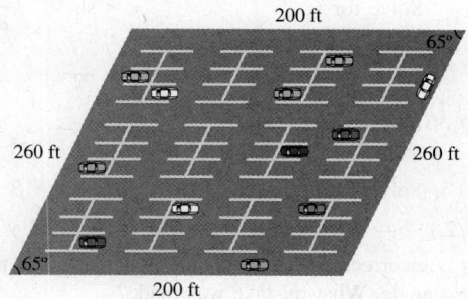

**64. Parking Lot.** A parking lot is to have the shape of a parallelogram that has adjacent sides measuring 250 feet and 300 feet. The acute angle between two adjacent sides is 55°. What is the area of the parking lot?

**65. Regular Hexagon.** A regular hexagon has sides measuring 3 feet. What is its area? Recall that the measure of an angle of a regular $n$-gon is given by the formula

$$\text{angle} = \frac{180°(n - 2)}{n}.$$

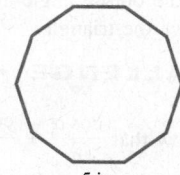

3 ft                 5 in.

**66. Regular Decagon.** A regular decagon has sides measuring 5 inches. What is its area?

**67. Geometry.** A quadrilateral $ABCD$ has sides of lengths $AB = 2$, $BC = 3$, $CD = 4$, and $DA = 5$. The angle between $AB$ and $BC$ is 135°. Find the area of $ABCD$.

**68. Geometry.** A quadrilateral $ABCD$ has sides of lengths $AB = 5$, $BC = 6$, $CD = 7$, and $DA = 8$. The angle between $AB$ and $BC$ is 135°. Find the area of $ABCD$.

■ **CATCH THE MISTAKE**

**In Exercises 69 and 70, explain the mistake that is made.**

**69.** Solve the triangle $b = 3$, $c = 4$, and $\alpha = 30°$.

**Solution:**

**Step 1:** Find $a$.

Apply the Law
of Cosines. $\qquad a^2 = b^2 + c^2 - 2bc\cos\alpha$

Let $b = 3$,
$c = 4$, and
$\alpha = 30°$. $\qquad a^2 = 3^2 + 4^2 - 2(3)(4)\cos 30°$

Solve for $a$. $\qquad a \approx 2.1$

**Step 2:** Find $\gamma$.

Apply the Law
of Sines. $\qquad \dfrac{\sin\alpha}{a} = \dfrac{\sin\gamma}{c}$

Solve for $\sin\gamma$. $\qquad \sin\gamma = \dfrac{c\sin\alpha}{a}$

Solve for $\gamma$. $\qquad \gamma = \sin^{-1}\left(\dfrac{c\sin\alpha}{a}\right)$

Let $a = 2.1$, $c = 4$,
and $\alpha = 30°$. $\qquad \gamma \approx 72°$

**Step 3:** Find $\beta$.

$\alpha + \beta + \gamma = 180° \qquad 30° + \beta + 72° = 180°$

Solve for $\beta$. $\qquad\qquad\qquad\qquad \beta \approx 78°$

$a \approx 2.1$, $b = 3$, $c = 4$, $\alpha = 30°$, $\beta \approx 78°$, and $\gamma \approx 72°$

This is incorrect. The longest side is not opposite the largest angle. What mistake was made?

**70.** Solve the triangle $a = 6$, $b = 2$, and $c = 5$.

**Solution:**

**Step 1:** Find $\beta$.

Apply the Law
of Cosines. $\qquad b^2 = a^2 + c^2 - 2ac\cos\beta$

Solve for $\beta$. $\qquad \beta = \cos^{-1}\left(\dfrac{a^2 + c^2 - b^2}{2ac}\right)$

Let $a = 6$, $b = 2$,
$c = 5$. $\qquad \beta \approx 18°$

**Step 2:** Find $\alpha$.

Apply the Law
of Sines. $\qquad \dfrac{\sin\alpha}{a} = \dfrac{\sin\beta}{b}$

Solve for $\alpha$. $\qquad \alpha = \sin^{-1}\left(\dfrac{a\sin\beta}{b}\right)$

Let $a = 6$, $b = 2$,
and $\beta = 18°$. $\qquad \alpha \approx 68°$

**Step 3:** Find $\gamma$. $\qquad \alpha + \beta + \gamma = 180°$

$68° + 18° + \gamma = 180°$

$\gamma \approx 94°$

$a = 6$, $b = 2$, $c = 5$, $\alpha \approx 68°$, $\beta \approx 18°$, and $\gamma \approx 94°$

This is incorrect. The longest side is not opposite the largest angle. What mistake was made?

■ **CONCEPTUAL**

**In Exercises 71–76, determine whether each statement is true or false.**

**71.** Given the lengths of all three sides of a triangle, there is insufficient information to solve the triangle.

**72.** Given three angles of a triangle, there is insufficient information to solve the triangle.

**73.** The Pythagorean theorem is a special case of the Law of Cosines.

**74.** The Law of Cosines is a special case of the Pythagorean theorem.

**75.** If an obtuse triangle is isosceles, then knowing the measure of the obtuse angle and a side adjacent to it is sufficient to solve the triangle.

**76.** All acute triangles can be solved using the Law of Cosines.

■ **CHALLENGE**

**77.** Show that $\dfrac{\cos\alpha}{a} + \dfrac{\cos\beta}{b} + \dfrac{\cos\gamma}{c} = \dfrac{a^2 + b^2 + c^2}{2abc}$.
*Hint:* Use the Law of Cosines.

**78.** Show that $a = c\cos\beta + b\cos\gamma$. *Hint:* Use the Law of Cosines.

**The following half-angle identities are useful in Exercises 79 and 80, and will be derived in Chapter 6.**

$$\cos\left(\frac{x}{2}\right) = \sqrt{\frac{1 + \cos x}{2}} \qquad \tan\left(\frac{x}{2}\right) = \sqrt{\frac{1 - \cos x}{1 + \cos x}}$$

**79.** Consider the following diagram and express $\cos\left(\dfrac{X}{2}\right)$ in terms of $a$.

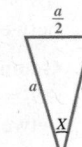

**80.** Using the diagram in Exercise 77, express $\tan\left(\dfrac{X}{2}\right)$ in terms of $a$.

**81.** Show that the area for an SAA triangle is given by

$$A = \frac{a^2 \sin \beta \sin \gamma}{2 \sin \alpha}$$

Assume that $\alpha$, $\beta$, and $a$ are given.

**82.** Show that the area of an isosceles triangle with equal sides of length $s$ is given by

$$A_{\text{isosceles}} = \frac{1}{2} s^2 \sin \theta$$

where $\theta$ is the angle between the two equal sides.

**83.** Find the area of the shaded region.

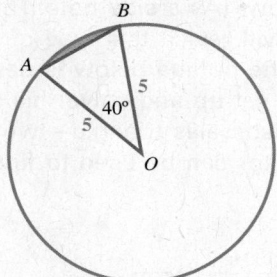

**84.** Find the area of the shaded region.

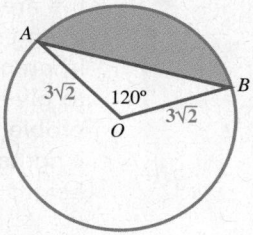

**■ TECHNOLOGY**

For Exercises 85–90, let $A$, $B$, and $C$ be the lengths of the three sides with $X$, $Y$, and $Z$ as the corresponding angle measures in a triangle. Write a program using a TI calculator to solve each triangle with the given measures.

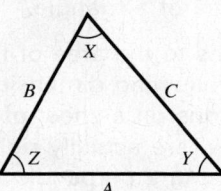

**85.** $B = 45$, $C = 57$, and $X = 43°$

**86.** $B = 24.5$, $C = 31.6$, and $X = 81.5°$

**87.** $A = 29.8$, $B = 37.6$, and $C = 53.2$

**88.** $A = 100$, $B = 170$, and $C = 250$

**89.** $A = \sqrt{12}$, $B = \sqrt{21}$, and $Z = 62.8°$

**90.** $A = 1235$, $B = 987$, and $C = 1456$

**■ PREVIEW TO CALCULUS**

In calculus, some applications of the derivative require the solution of triangles. In Exercises 91–94, solve each triangle using the Law of Cosines.

**91.** Two ships start moving from the same port at the same time. One moves north at 40 miles per hour, while the other moves southeast at 50 miles per hour. Find the distance between the ships 4 hours later. Round your answer to the nearest mile.

**92.** An airport radar detects two planes approaching. The distance between the planes is 80 miles; the closest plane is 60 miles from the airport and the other plane is 70 miles from the airport. What is the angle (in degrees) formed by the planes and the airport?

**93.** An athlete runs along a circular track, of radius 100 meters, runs from $A$ to $B$ and then decides to take a shortcut to go to $C$. If the measure of angle $BAC$ is $\frac{2\pi}{9}$, find the distance covered by the athlete if the distance from $A$ to $B$ is 153 meters. Round your answer to the nearest integer.

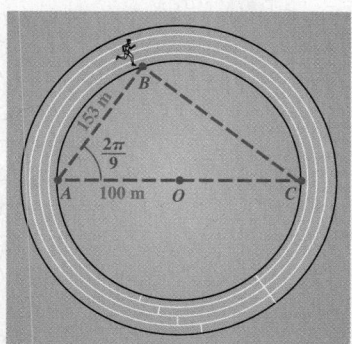

**94.** A regular pentagon is inscribed in a circle of radius 10 feet. Find its perimeter. Round your answer to the nearest tenth.

Dr. Parkinson has acquired two 30-foot sections of fence from her neighbor Mr. Wilson. She has decided to build a triangular corral for her animals. She plans to use a barn wall as the third side. (The barn wall is 100 feet long—see the diagram below.) As her contractor, you are expected to maximize the corral area. You have decided to approach this from a trigonometric viewpoint. Hence, you want to find the angle $\theta$ that maximizes the area. To do this, follow the steps below. (As a side note: This problem is an example of **optimization** and you will revisit this type of problem in precalculus and/or calculus courses. The outline below is designed to give you an understanding of how to set up and solve this type of problem. Realize that this triangle is an isosceles triangle—two equal side lengths—and that its perpendicular bisector can be used to find the height of the triangle.)

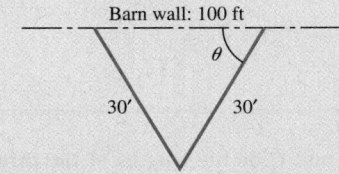

1. Write out the general formula for the area of a triangle.

2. To get an understanding of what happens to the area of the triangle as the angle $\theta$ changes, you will calculate the following dimensions using right triangle trigonometry. Do these calculations on a sheet of scratch paper. Since none of the triangles formed below are actually right triangles, you will need to construct a right triangle (using a perpendicular bisector) along with using the sine and cosine relationships to help you identify the base and height. (Use two decimals.)

| $\theta$ | 20° | 40° | 60° | 80° |
|---|---|---|---|---|
| $b(\theta) =$ base | | | | |
| $h(\theta) =$ height | | | | |
| $A(\theta) =$ area | | | | |

You don't need to do every example in the chart by hand. However, do as many as you need to see what patterns emerge for calculating each base, height, and area. When you see the pattern, you will hopefully then be able to write a function for each piece of information. You can then use the table in your graphing calculator to list all the answers. However, you are encouraged to do at least two by hand before jumping to the function writing. Also be sure to check that the results you get on your table agree with the numbers you get by hand.

3. Write the base $b(\theta)$ of the triangle as a function of $\theta$. (Show how you arrived at this answer.) Describe what happens to the base values as the $\theta$ values increase.

**4.** Write the height $h(\theta)$ of the triangle as a function of $\theta$. (Show how you arrived at this answer.) Describe what happens to the height values as the $\theta$ values increase.

**5.** Write the area $A(\theta)$ as a function of $\theta$ using your results from 3 and 4. Describe what happens to your area values as $\theta$ increases.

**6.** Specify the **domain** for the area within the context of this problem. (**Vocabulary reminder**: The domain for this problem is the set of values of $\theta$ that makes sense from a physical standpoint; that is, you wouldn't build a corral using $\theta = -20°$.)

**7.** Use a graphing utility to graph your area function on its domain.

**8.** Estimate the maximum area and the $\theta$ that this corresponds to.

**9.** What can you conclude about the shape of the triangle that yields the maximum area in this example?

When solving triangles using the Law of Sines, it is important to keep in mind the domain and range of the inverse sine function, because it can play a role in determining your answers. Make sure to check your answers for reasonableness, especially when solving an obtuse triangle, as you will see next.

For a triangle $ABC$, two side lengths and the measure of the angle between them are given below.

$$b = 24 \qquad c = 8 \qquad A = 15°$$

1. How many triangles are possible with these measurements? Explain.

2. Make a careful sketch of a triangle and label the given information. Also label the unknown side $a$, and the unknown angles opposite sides $b$ and $c$, as $B$ and $C$, respectively. What can you say about angle $B$?

3. Explain why the Law of Cosines is needed for this problem.

4. Find the length of side $a$. Round to three significant digits.

5. Suppose a fellow student now wants to find the measure of angle $B$, and decides to use the Law of Sines. Shown below are the steps he wrote out to illustrate his process for computing the measure of $B$ and $C$. Look at the chart he filled in below.

$$B = \sin^{-1}\left[\frac{24}{16.4}\sin(15)\right] \approx 22.3°$$

$$C = 180° - (15° + 22.3°) = 142.7°$$

| SIDES | | ANGLES | |
|---|---|---|---|
| $a$ | 16.4 | $A$ | 15° |
| $b$ | 24 | $B$ | 22.3° |
| $c$ | 8 | $C$ | 142.7° |

What is wrong with the answers given by this student?

6. Because your calculator gives positive values of $\sin^{-1}x$ only between 0 and 90°, the answer this student got for the measure of angle $B$ does not make sense. Show what he needs to do to correct his error.

The Intergovernmental Panel on Climate Change (IPCC) claims that carbon dioxide ($CO_2$) production from increased industrial activity (such as fossil fuel burning and other human activities) has increased the $CO_2$ concentrations in the atmosphere. Because it is a greenhouse gas, elevated $CO_2$ levels will increase global mean (average) temperature. In this section, we will examine the increasing rate of carbon emissions on Earth.

In 1955 there were (globally) 2 billion tons of carbon emitted per year. In 2005 the carbon emission had more than tripled, reaching approximately 7 billion tons of carbon emitted per year. Currently, we are on the path to doubling our current carbon emissions in the next 50 years.

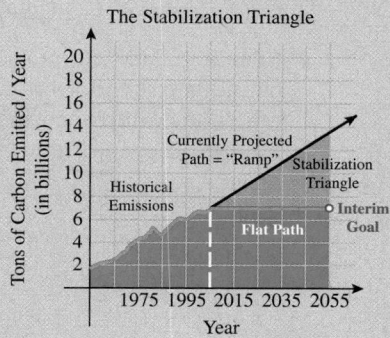

Two Princeton professors* (Stephen Pacala and Rob Socolow) introduced the Climate Carbon Wedge concept. A "wedge" is a strategy to reduce carbon emissions that grow in a 50-year time period from 0 to 1.0 GtC/yr (gigatons of carbon per year).

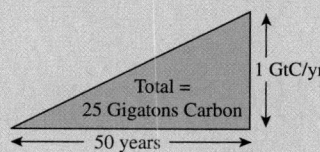

1. Consider eight scenarios (staying on path of one of the seven wedges). A check is done at the 10-year mark. What total GtC per year would we have to measure to correspond to the following projected paths?

   **a.** Flat path (no increase) over 50 years (2005 to 2055)

   **b.** Increase of 1 GtC over 50 years (2005 to 2055)

   **c.** Increase of 2 GtC over 50 years (2005 to 2055)

   **d.** Increase of 3 GtC over 50 years (2005 to 2055)

   **e.** Increase of 4 GtC over 50 years (2005 to 2055)

   **f.** Increase of 5 GtC over 50 years (2005 to 2055)

   **g.** Increase of 6 GtC over 50 years (2005 to 2055)

   **h.** Increase of 7 GtC over 50 years (2005 to 2055) (projected path)

---

*S. Pacala and R. Socolow, "Stabilization Wedges: Solving the Climate Problem for the Next 50 Years with Current Technologies," *Science*, Vol. 305 (2004).

**2.** Consider the angle $\theta$ in each wedge. For each of the seven wedges (and the flat path), find the GtC/yr rate in terms of $\tan\theta$.

**a.** Flat path

**b.** Increase of 1 GtC/50 years

**c.** Increase of 2 GtC/50 years

**d.** Increase of 3 GtC/50 years

**e.** Increase of 4 GtC/50 years

**f.** Increase of 5 GtC/50 years

**g.** Increase of 6 GtC/50 years

**h.** Increase of 7 GtC/50 years (projected path)

**3.** Research the "climate carbon wedge" concept and discuss the types of changes (transportation efficiency, transportation conservation, building efficiency, efficiency in electricity production, alternate energies, etc.) the world would have to make that would correspond to each of the seven wedges.

**a.** Flat path

**b.** Wedge 1

**c.** Wedge 2

**d.** Wedge 3

**e.** Wedge 4

**f.** Wedge 5

**g.** Wedge 6

**h.** Wedge 7

| SECTION | CONCEPT | KEY IDEAS/FORMULAS |
|---|---|---|
| 4.1 | **Angle measure** | |
| | Angles and their measure | *Degrees and Radians* |

One complete counterclockwise rotation

Right Angle

Converting between degrees and radians (Remember that $\pi = 180°$.)

- Degrees to radians: Multiply by $\dfrac{\pi}{180°}$

- Radians to degrees: Multiply by $\dfrac{180°}{\pi}$

| | Coterminal angles | Two angles in standard position with the same terminal side |
|---|---|---|
| | Arc length | $s = r\theta$           $\theta$ is in radians. |
| | Area of a circular sector | $A = \dfrac{1}{2}r^2\theta$       $\theta$ is in radians. |
| | Linear and angular speeds | **Linear speed** $v$ is given by |

$$v = \frac{s}{t}$$

where $s$ is the arc length (or distance along the arc) and $t$ is time.

**Angular speed** $\omega$ is given by

$$\omega = \frac{\theta}{t}$$

where $\theta$ is given in radians.

Linear and angular speeds are related through the radius of the circle:

$$v = r\omega \quad \text{or} \quad \omega = \frac{v}{r}$$

| 4.2 | **Right triangle trigonometry** | |
|---|---|---|
| | Right triangle ratios | $\sin\theta = \dfrac{\text{opposite}}{\text{hypotenuse}}$    (SOH) |

$\cos\theta = \dfrac{\text{adjacent}}{\text{hypotenuse}}$    (CAH)

$\tan\theta = \dfrac{\text{opposite}}{\text{adjacent}}$    (TOA)

**Reciprocal identities**

$$\cot \theta = \frac{1}{\tan \theta} \qquad \csc \theta = \frac{1}{\sin \theta} \qquad \sec \theta = \frac{1}{\cos \theta}$$

Evaluating trigonometric functions exactly for special angle measures

| $\theta$ | $\sin \theta$ | $\cos \theta$ |
| --- | --- | --- |
| 30° | $\dfrac{1}{2}$ | $\dfrac{\sqrt{3}}{2}$ |
| 45° | $\dfrac{\sqrt{2}}{2}$ | $\dfrac{\sqrt{2}}{2}$ |
| 60° | $\dfrac{\sqrt{3}}{2}$ | $\dfrac{1}{2}$ |

The other trigonometric functions can be found for these values using $\tan \theta = \dfrac{\sin \theta}{\cos \theta}$ and the reciprocal identities.

Solving right triangles

**4.3** **Trigonometric functions of angles**

Trigonometric functions: The Cartesian plane

$$\sin \theta = \frac{y}{r} \qquad \cos \theta = \frac{x}{r} \qquad \tan \theta = \frac{y}{x}$$

$$\csc \theta = \frac{r}{y} \qquad \sec \theta = \frac{r}{x} \qquad \cot \theta = \frac{x}{y}$$

where $x^2 + y^2 = r^2 \Rightarrow r = \sqrt{x^2 + y^2}$

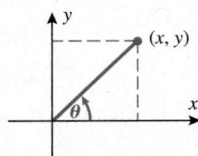

The distance $r$ is positive: $r > 0$.

**Algebraic signs of trigonometric functions**

| $\theta$ | QI | QII | QIII | QIV |
| --- | --- | --- | --- | --- |
| $\sin \theta$ | + | + | − | − |
| $\cos \theta$ | + | − | − | + |
| $\tan \theta$ | + | − | + | − |

**Trigonometric function values for quadrantal angles.**

| $\theta$ | 0° | 90° | 180° | 270° |
| --- | --- | --- | --- | --- |
| $\sin \theta$ | 0 | 1 | 0 | −1 |
| $\cos \theta$ | 1 | 0 | −1 | 0 |
| $\tan \theta$ | 0 | undefined | 0 | undefined |
| $\cot \theta$ | undefined | 0 | undefined | 0 |
| $\sec \theta$ | 1 | undefined | −1 | undefined |
| $\csc \theta$ | undefined | 1 | undefined | −1 |

| SECTION | CONCEPT | KEY IDEAS/FORMULAS |
|---|---|---|
| | Ranges of the trigonometric functions | $\sin\theta$ and $\cos\theta$: $[-1, 1]$ <br> $\tan\theta$ and $\cot\theta$: $(-\infty, \infty)$ <br> $\sec\theta$ and $\csc\theta$: $(-\infty, -1] \cup [1, \infty)$ |
| | Reference angles and reference right triangles | The reference angle $\alpha$ for angle $\theta$ (between $0°$ and $360°$) is given by <br><br> ■ QI: $\alpha = \theta$ <br> ■ QII: $\alpha = 180° - \theta$ or $\pi - \theta$ <br> ■ QIII: $\alpha = \theta - 180°$ or $\theta - \pi$ <br> ■ QIV: $\alpha = 360° - \theta$ or $2\pi - \theta$ |
| | Evaluating trigonometric functions for nonacute angles | |
| 4.4 | **The Law of Sines** | |
| | Solving oblique triangles | Oblique (Nonright) Triangles <br> 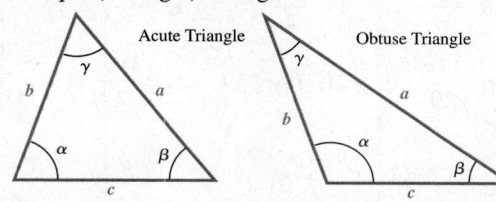 <br> **The Law of Sines** <br> $$\frac{\sin\alpha}{a} = \frac{\sin\beta}{b} = \frac{\sin\gamma}{c}$$ <br> Use for: <br> ■ AAS (or ASA) triangles <br> ■ SSA triangles (ambiguous case) |
| 4.5 | **The Law of Cosines** | |
| | Solving oblique triangles using the Law of Cosines | $a^2 = b^2 + c^2 - 2bc\cos\alpha$ <br> $b^2 = a^2 + c^2 - 2ac\cos\beta$ <br> $c^2 = a^2 + b^2 - 2ab\cos\gamma$ <br><br> Use for: <br> ■ SAS triangles <br> ■ SSS triangles |
| | The area of a triangle | **The area of a triangle (SAS case)** <br> $A_{SAS} = \frac{1}{2}bc\sin\alpha$ when $b$, $c$, and $\alpha$ are known. <br><br> $A_{SAS} = \frac{1}{2}ab\sin\gamma$ when $a$, $b$, and $\gamma$ are known. <br><br> $A_{SAS} = \frac{1}{2}ac\sin\beta$ when $a$, $c$, and $\beta$ are known. <br><br> **The area of a triangle (SSS case)** <br> Use Heron's formula for the SSS case: <br> $$A_{SSS} = \sqrt{s(s-a)(s-b)(s-c)}$$ <br> where $a$, $b$, and $c$ are the lengths of the sides of the triangle and $s$ is half the perimeter of the triangle, called the semiperimeter. <br> $$s = \frac{a+b+c}{2}$$ |

## 4.1 Angle Measure

Find (a) the complement and (b) the supplement of the given angles.

1. 28°  2. 17°  3. 35°

4. 78°  5. 89.01°  6. 0.013°

Convert from degrees to radians. Leave your answers in terms of $\pi$.

7. 135°  8. 240°  9. 330°  10. 180°

11. 216°  12. 108°  13. 1620°  14. 900°

Convert from radians to degrees.

15. $\dfrac{\pi}{3}$  16. $\dfrac{11\pi}{6}$  17. $\dfrac{5\pi}{4}$  18. $\dfrac{2\pi}{3}$

19. $\dfrac{5\pi}{9}$  20. $\dfrac{17\pi}{10}$  21. $10\pi$  22. $\dfrac{31\pi}{2}$

### Applications

23. **Clock.** What is the measure (in degrees) of the angle that the minute hand sweeps in exactly 25 minutes?

24. **Clock.** What is the measure (in degrees) of the angle that the second hand sweeps in exactly 15 seconds?

25. A ladybug is clinging to the outer edge of a child's spinning disk. The disk is 4 inches in diameter and is spinning at 60 revolutions per minute. How fast is the ladybug traveling in inches/minute?

26. How fast is a motorcyclist traveling in miles per hour if his tires are 30 inches in diameter and the angular speed of the tire is $10\pi$ radians per second?

## 4.2 Right Triangle Trigonometry

Use the following triangle to find the indicated trigonometric functions. Rationalize any denominators that you encounter in the answers.

27. $\cos\theta$

28. $\sin\theta$

29. $\sec\theta$

30. $\csc\theta$

31. $\tan\theta$

32. $\cot\theta$

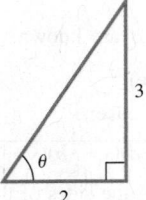

Label each trigonometric function value with the corresponding value (a–c).

a. $\dfrac{\sqrt{3}}{2}$   b. $\dfrac{1}{2}$   c. $\dfrac{\sqrt{2}}{2}$

33. $\sin 30°$  34. $\cos 30°$  35. $\cos 60°$

36. $\sin 60°$  37. $\sin 45°$  38. $\cos 45°$

Use a calculator to approximate the following trigonometric function values. Round the answers to four decimal places.

39. $\sin 42°$  40. $\cos 57°$  41. $\cos 17.3°$  42. $\tan 25.2°$

43. $\cot 33°$  44. $\sec 16.8°$  45. $\csc 40.25°$  46. $\cot 19.76°$

The following exercises illustrate a mid-air refueling scenario that U.S. military aircraft often use. Assume the elevation angle that the hose makes with the plane being fueled is $\theta = 30°$.

47. **Mid-Air Refueling.** If the hose is 150 feet long, what should the altitude difference $a$ be between the two planes?

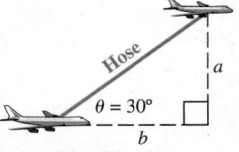

48. **Mid-Air Refueling.** If the smallest acceptable altitude difference, $a$, between the two planes is 100 feet, how long should the hose be?

## 4.3 Trigonometric Functions of Angles

In the following exercises, the terminal side of an angle $\theta$ in standard position passes through the indicated point. Calculate the values of the six trigonometric functions for angle $\theta$.

49. $(6, -8)$  50. $(-24, -7)$  51. $(-6, 2)$  52. $(-40, 9)$

53. $(\sqrt{3}, 1)$  54. $(-9, -9)$  55. $\left(\frac{1}{2}, -\frac{1}{4}\right)$  56. $\left(-\frac{3}{4}, \frac{5}{6}\right)$

57. $(-1.2, -2.4)$  58. $(0.8, -2.4)$

Evaluate the following expressions exactly:

59. $\sin 330°$  60. $\cos(-300°)$  61. $\tan 150°$

62. $\cot 315°$  63. $\sec(-150°)$  64. $\csc 210°$

65. $\sin\left(\dfrac{7\pi}{4}\right)$  66. $\cos\left(\dfrac{7\pi}{6}\right)$  67. $\tan\left(-\dfrac{2\pi}{3}\right)$

68. $\cot\left(\dfrac{4\pi}{3}\right)$  69. $\sec\left(\dfrac{5\pi}{4}\right)$  70. $\csc\left(-\dfrac{8\pi}{3}\right)$

71. $\sec\left(\dfrac{5\pi}{6}\right)$  72. $\cos\left(-\dfrac{11\pi}{6}\right)$

## 4.4  The Law of Sines

Solve the given triangles.

73. $\alpha = 10°, \beta = 20°, a = 4$

74. $\beta = 40°, \gamma = 60°, b = 10$

75. $\alpha = 5°, \beta = 45°, c = 10$

76. $\beta = 60°, \gamma = 70°, a = 20$

77. $\gamma = 11°, \alpha = 11°, c = 11$

78. $\beta = 20°, \gamma = 50°, b = 8$

79. $\alpha = 45°, \gamma = 45°, b = 2$

80. $\alpha = 60°, \beta = 20°, c = 17$

81. $\alpha = 12°, \gamma = 22°, a = 99$

82. $\beta = 102°, \gamma = 27°, a = 24$

**Two sides and an angle are given. Determine whether a triangle (or two) exist and, if so, solve the triangle.**

83. $a = 7, b = 9, \alpha = 20°$

84. $b = 24, c = 30, \beta = 16°$

85. $a = 10, c = 12, \alpha = 24°$

86. $b = 100, c = 116, \beta = 12°$

87. $a = 40, b = 30, \beta = 150°$

88. $b = 2, c = 3, \gamma = 165°$

89. $a = 4, b = 6, \alpha = 10°$

90. $c = 25, a = 37, \gamma = 4°$

## 4.5  The Law of Cosines

Solve each triangle.

91. $a = 40, b = 60, \gamma = 50°$

92. $b = 15, c = 12, \alpha = 140°$

93. $a = 24, b = 25, c = 30$

94. $a = 6, b = 6, c = 8$

95. $a = \sqrt{11}, b = \sqrt{14}, c = 5$

96. $a = 22, b = 120, c = 122$

97. $b = 7, c = 10, \alpha = 14°$

98. $a = 6, b = 12, \gamma = 80°$

99. $b = 10, c = 4, \alpha = 90°$

100. $a = 4, b = 5, \gamma = 75°$

101. $a = 10, b = 11, c = 12$

102. $a = 22, b = 24, c = 25$

103. $b = 16, c = 18, \alpha = 100°$

104. $a = 25, c = 25, \beta = 9°$

105. $b = 12, c = 40, \alpha = 10°$

106. $a = 26, b = 20, c = 10$

107. $a = 26, b = 40, c = 13$

108. $a = 1, b = 2, c = 3$

109. $a = 6.3, b = 4.2, \alpha = 15°$

110. $b = 5, c = 6, \beta = 35°$

**Find the area of each triangle described.**

111. $b = 16, c = 18, \alpha = 100°$

112. $a = 25, c = 25, \beta = 9°$

113. $a = 10, b = 11, c = 12$

114. $a = 22, b = 24, c = 25$

115. $a = 26, b = 20, c = 10$

116. $a = 24, b = 32, c = 40$

117. $b = 12, c = 40, \alpha = 10°$

118. $a = 21, c = 75, \beta = 60°$

## Applications

119. **Area of Inscribed Triangle.** The area of a triangle inscribed in a circle can be found if you know the lengths of the sides of the triangle and the radius of the circle: $A = \dfrac{abc}{4r}$. Find the radius of the circle that circumscribes the triangle if all the sides of the triangle measure 9.0 inches and the area of the triangle is 35 square inches.

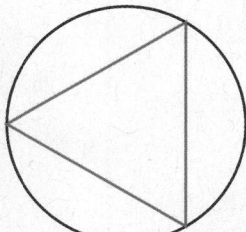

120. **Area of Inscribed Triangle.** The area of a triangle inscribed in a circle can be found if you know the lengths of the sides of the triangle and the radius of the circle: $A = \dfrac{abc}{4r}$. Find the radius of the circle that circumscribes the triangle if the sides of the triangle measure 9, 12, and 15 inches and the area of the triangle is 54 square inches.

1. A 5-foot girl is standing *in* the Grand Canyon, and she wants to estimate the depth of the canyon. The sun casts her shadow 6 inches along the ground. To measure the shadow cast by the top of the canyon, she walks the length of the shadow. She takes 200 steps and estimates that each step is roughly 3 feet. Approximately how tall is the Grand Canyon?

2. Fill in the values in the table.

| $\theta$ | $\sin\theta$ | $\cos\theta$ | $\tan\theta$ | $\cot\theta$ | $\sec\theta$ | $\csc\theta$ |
|---|---|---|---|---|---|---|
| 30° | | | | | | |
| 45° | | | | | | |
| 60° | | | | | | |

3. What is the difference between $\cos\theta = \frac{2}{3}$ and $\cos\theta \approx 0.6\overline{6}$?

4. Fill in the table with exact values for the quadrantal angles and the algebraic signs for the quadrants.

| | 0° | QI | 90° | QII | 180° | QIII | 270° | QIV | 360° |
|---|---|---|---|---|---|---|---|---|---|
| $\sin\theta$ | | | | | | | | | |
| $\cos\theta$ | | | | | | | | | |

5. If $\cot\theta < 0$ and $\sec\theta > 0$, in which quadrant does the terminal side of $\theta$ lie?

6. Evaluate $\sin 210°$ exactly.

7. Convert $\dfrac{13\pi}{4}$ to degree measure.

8. Convert 260° to radian measure. Leave the answer in terms of $\pi$.

9. What is the area of the sector swept by the second hand of a clock in 25 seconds? Assume the radius of the sector is 3 inches.

10. What is the measure in radians of the smaller angle between the hour and minute hands at 10:10?

**Solve the triangles if possible.**

11. $\alpha = 30°, \beta = 40°, b = 10$

12. $\alpha = 47°, \beta = 98°, \gamma = 35°$

13. $a = 7, b = 9, c = 12$

14. $\alpha = 45°, a = 8, b = 10$

15. $a = 1, b = 1, c = 2$

16. $a = \dfrac{23}{7}, c = \dfrac{5}{7}, \beta = 61.2°$

17. $\alpha = 110°, \beta = 20°, a = 5$

18. $b = \dfrac{\sqrt{5}}{2}, c = 3\sqrt{5}, \alpha = 45°$

**In Exercises 19 and 20, find the areas of the given triangles.**

19. $\gamma = 72°, a = 10, b = 12$

20. $a = 7, b = 10, c = 13$

1. Find the average rate of change for $f(x) = \dfrac{5}{x}$ from $x = 2$ to $x = 4$.

2. Use interval notation to express the domain of the function $f(x) = \sqrt{x^2 - 25}$.

3. Using the function $f(x) = 5 - x^2$, evaluate the difference quotient $\dfrac{f(x + h) - f(x)}{h}$.

4. Given the piecewise-defined function
$$f(x) = \begin{cases} x^2 & x < 0 \\ 2x - 1 & 0 \le x < 5 \\ 5 - x & x \ge 5 \end{cases}$$
   find:
   **a.** $f(0)$   **b.** $f(4)$   **c.** $f(5)$   **d.** $f(-4)$
   **e.** State the domain and range in interval notation.
   **f.** Determine the intervals where the function is increasing, decreasing, or constant.

5. Evaluate $g(f(-1))$ for $f(x) = \sqrt[3]{x - 7}$ and $g(x) = \dfrac{5}{3 - x}$.

6. Find the inverse of the function $f(x) = \dfrac{5x + 2}{x - 3}$.

7. Find the quadratic function that has the vertex $(0, 7)$ and goes through the point $(2, -1)$.

8. Find all of the real zeros and state the multiplicity of each for the function $f(x) = \frac{1}{7}x^5 + \frac{2}{9}x^3$.

9. Graph the rational function $f(x) = \dfrac{x^2 + 3}{x - 2}$. Give all asymptotes.

10. Factor the polynomial $P(x) = 4x^4 - 4x^3 + 13x^2 + 18x + 5$ as a product of linear factors.

11. How much money should be put in a savings account now that earns 5.5% a year compounded continuously, if you want to have $85,000 in 15 years?

12. Evaluate $\log_{4.7} 8.9$ using the change-of-base formula. Round the answer to three decimal places.

13. Solve the equation $5(10^{2x}) = 37$ for $x$. Round the answer to three decimal places.

14. Solve for $x$: $\ln\sqrt{6 - 3x} - \frac{1}{2}\ln(x + 2) = \ln(x)$.

15. In a 45°-45°-90° triangle, if the two legs have a length of 15 feet, how long is the hypotenuse?

16. **Height of a tree.** The shadow of a tree measures $15\frac{1}{3}$ feet. At the same time of day the shadow of a 6-foot pole measures 2.3 feet. How tall is the tree?

17. Convert 432° to radians.

18. Convert $\dfrac{5\pi}{9}$ to degrees.

19. Find the exact value of $\tan\left(\dfrac{4\pi}{3}\right)$.

20. Find the exact value of $\sec\left(-\dfrac{7\pi}{6}\right)$.

21. Use a calculator to find the value of $\csc 37°$. Round your answer to four decimal places.

22. In the right triangle below, find $a$, $b$, and $\theta$. Round each to the nearest tenth.

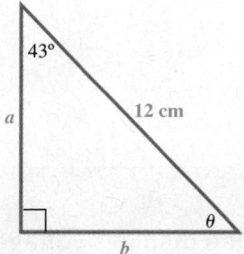

23. Solve the triangle below. Round the side lengths to the nearest centimeter.

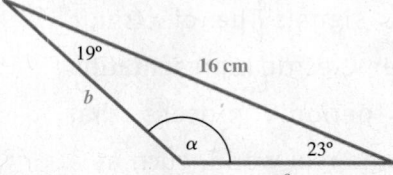

24. Solve the triangle $a = 2$, $b = 4$, and $c = 5$. Round your answer to the nearest degree.

# 5

# Trigonometric Functions of Real Numbers

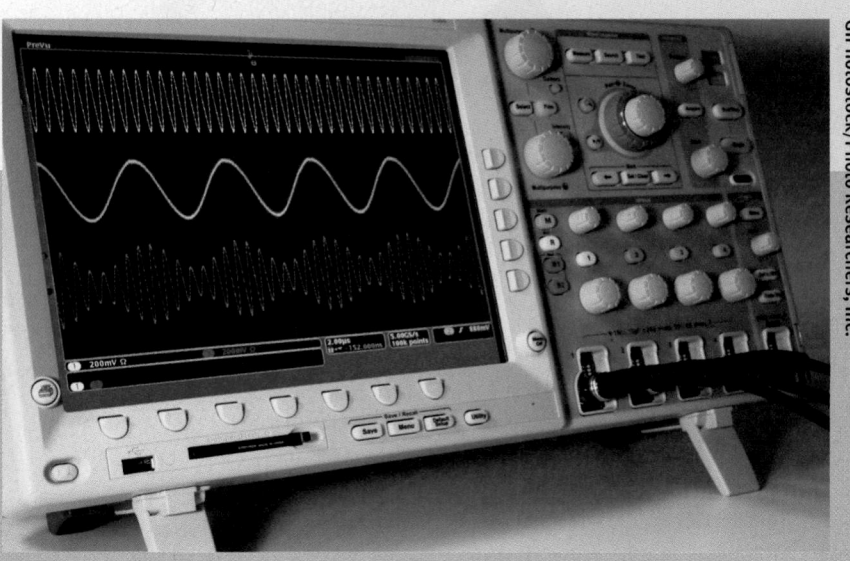

**A**n oscilloscope displays voltage (vertical axis) as a function of time (horizontal axis) of an electronic signal. The electronic signal is an electric representation of some periodic process that occurs in the real world, such as a human pulse or a sound wave.

Oscilloscopes are used in medicine, the sciences, and engineering, and allow the shape of a signal to be displayed, which allows the amplitude and frequency of the repetitive signal to then be determined. The oscilloscope above displays a *sine* wave.

we will use the unit circle approach to define trigonometric functions. We will graph the sine and cosine functions and find periods, amplitudes, and phase shifts. Applications such as harmonic motion will be discussed. Combinations of sinusoidal functions will be discussed through a technique called the addition of ordinates. Lastly, we will discuss the graphs of the other trigonometric functions (tangent, cotangent, secant, and cosecant).

# TRIGONOMETRIC FUNCTIONS OF REAL NUMBERS

## 5.1
Trigonometric Functions:
The Unit Circle Approach

- Trigonometric Functions and the Unit Circle
- Properties of Trigonometric (Circular) Functions

## 5.2
Graphs of Sine and Cosine Functions

- The Graphs of Sinusoidal Functions
- Graphing a Shifted Sinusoidal Function:
  $y = A \sin(Bx + C) + D$
  and
  $y = A \cos(Bx + C) + D$
- Harmonic Motion
- Graphing Sums of Functions: Addition of Ordinates

## 5.3
Graphs of Other Trigonometric Functions

- Graphing the Tangent, Cotangent, Secant, and Cosecant Functions
- Translations of Trigonometric Functions

## LEARNING OBJECTIVES

- Define trigonometric functions using the unit circle approach.
- Graph a sinusoidal function and determine its amplitude, period, and phase shift.
- Graph tangent, cotangent, secant, and cosecant functions.

## SKILLS OBJECTIVES

- Draw the unit circle showing the special angles, and label cosine and sine values.
- Determine the domain and range of trigonometric (circular) functions.
- Classify trigonometric functions as even or odd.

## CONCEPTUAL OBJECTIVES

- Understand that the definition of trigonometric functions using the unit circle approach is consistent with both of the previous definitions (right triangle trigonometry and trigonometric functions of nonacute angles in the Cartesian plane).
- Relate $x$-coordinates and $y$-coordinates of points on the unit circle to the values of cosine and sine functions.
- Visualize the periodic properties of trigonometric (circular) functions.

Recall that the first definition of trigonometric functions we developed was in terms of ratios of sides of right triangles (Section 4.2). Then in Section 4.3 we superimposed right triangles on the Cartesian plane, which led to a second definition of trigonometric functions (for any angle) in terms of ratios of $x$- and $y$-coordinates of a point and the distance from the origin to that point. In this section, we inscribe the right triangles into the unit circle in the Cartesian plane, which will yield a third definition of trigonometric functions. It is important to note that all three definitions are consistent with one another.

## Trigonometric Functions and the Unit Circle

Note: In radians, $\theta = \dfrac{s}{r}$, and since $r = 1$, we know that $\theta = s$.

Recall that the equation for the **unit circle** centered at the origin is given by $x^2 + y^2 = 1$. The term *circular function* is often used as a synonym for trigonometric function, but it is important to note that a circle is not a function (it does not pass the vertical line test).

If we form a central angle $\theta$ in the unit circle such that the terminal side lies in quadrant I, we can use the previous two definitions of the sine and cosine functions when $r = 1$ (i.e., in the unit circle).

| TRIGONOMETRIC FUNCTION | RIGHT TRIANGLE TRIGONOMETRY | CARTESIAN PLANE |
|---|---|---|
| $\sin\theta$ | $\dfrac{\text{opposite}}{\text{hypotenuse}} = \dfrac{y}{1} = y$ | $\dfrac{y}{r} = \dfrac{y}{1} = y$ |
| $\cos\theta$ | $\dfrac{\text{adjacent}}{\text{hypotenuse}} = \dfrac{x}{1} = x$ | $\dfrac{x}{r} = \dfrac{x}{1} = x$ |

Notice that the point $(x, y)$ on the unit circle can be written as $(\cos\theta, \sin\theta)$. We can now summarize the exact values for **sine** and **cosine** in the illustration on the following page.

The following observations are consistent with properties of trigonometric functions we've studied already:

- $\sin\theta > 0$ in QI and QII.
- $\cos\theta > 0$ in QI and QIV.
- The unit circle equation $x^2 + y^2 = 1$ leads to the Pythagorean identity $\cos^2\theta + \sin^2\theta = 1$.

### Study Tip

$(\cos\theta, \sin\theta)$ represents a unique point $(x, y)$ on the unit circle.

$(x, y) = (\cos\theta, \sin\theta)$, where $\theta$ is the central angle whose terminal side intersects the unit circle at $(x, y)$.

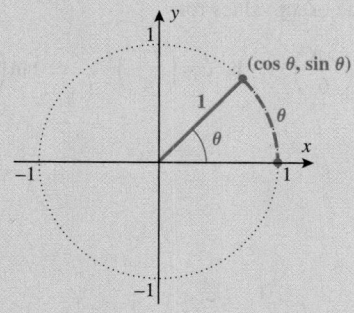

## Trigonometric (Circular) Functions

Using the unit circle relationship, $(x, y) = (\cos\theta, \sin\theta)$, where $\theta$ is the central angle whose terminal side intersects the unit circle at the point $(x, y)$, we can now define the remaining trigonometric functions using this unit circle approach and the quotient and reciprocal identities. Because the trigonometric functions are defined in terms of the unit *circle*, the trigonometric functions are often called **circular functions**.

---

**DEFINITION**     **Trigonometric Functions**

**Unit Circle Approach**

Let $(x, y)$ be any point on the unit circle. If $\theta$ is a real number that represents the distance from the point $(1, 0)$ along the circumference to the point $(x, y)$, then

$$\sin\theta = y \qquad\qquad \cos\theta = x \qquad\qquad \tan\theta = \frac{y}{x} \quad x \neq 0$$

$$\csc\theta = \frac{1}{y} \quad y \neq 0 \qquad \sec\theta = \frac{1}{x} \quad x \neq 0 \qquad \cot\theta = \frac{x}{y} \quad y \neq 0$$

## Technology Tip

Use a TI/scientific calculator to check the values for $\sin\left(\dfrac{7\pi}{4}\right)$, $\cos\left(\dfrac{5\pi}{6}\right)$, and $\tan\left(\dfrac{3\pi}{2}\right)$. Be sure to set the TI in radian mode.

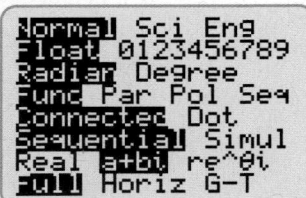

```
sin(7π/4)
          -.7071067812
-√(2)/2
          -.7071067812
```

```
cos(5π/6)
          -.8660254038
-√(3)/2
          -.8660254038
■
```

Since $\tan\left(\dfrac{3\pi}{2}\right)$ is undefined, TI will display an error message.

```
tan(3π/2)
■
```

```
ERR:DOMAIN
1⬛Quit
2:Goto
```

**EXAMPLE 1** **Finding Exact Trigonometric (Circular) Function Values**

Find the exact values for

**a.** $\sin\left(\dfrac{7\pi}{4}\right)$    **b.** $\cos\left(\dfrac{5\pi}{6}\right)$    **c.** $\tan\left(\dfrac{3\pi}{2}\right)$

**Solution (a):**

The angle $\dfrac{7\pi}{4}$ corresponds to the coordinates $\left(\dfrac{\sqrt{2}}{2}, -\dfrac{\sqrt{2}}{2}\right)$ on the unit circle.

The value of the sine function is the $y$-coordinate.    $\boxed{\sin\left(\dfrac{7\pi}{4}\right) = -\dfrac{\sqrt{2}}{2}}$

**Solution (b):**

The angle $\dfrac{5\pi}{6}$ corresponds to the coordinate $\left(-\dfrac{\sqrt{3}}{2}, \dfrac{1}{2}\right)$ on the unit circle.

The value of the cosine function is the $x$-coordinate.    $\boxed{\cos\left(\dfrac{5\pi}{6}\right) = -\dfrac{\sqrt{3}}{2}}$

**Solution (c):**

The angle $\dfrac{3\pi}{2}$ corresponds to the coordinate $(0, -1)$ on the unit circle.

The value of the cosine function is the $x$-coordinate.    $\cos\left(\dfrac{3\pi}{2}\right) = 0$

The value of the sine function is the $y$-coordinate.    $\sin\left(\dfrac{3\pi}{2}\right) = -1$

Tangent is the ratio of sine to cosine.    $\tan\left(\dfrac{3\pi}{2}\right) = \dfrac{\sin\left(\dfrac{3\pi}{2}\right)}{\cos\left(\dfrac{3\pi}{2}\right)}$

Let $\cos\left(\dfrac{3\pi}{2}\right) = 0$ and $\sin\left(\dfrac{3\pi}{2}\right) = -1$.    $\tan\left(\dfrac{3\pi}{2}\right) = \dfrac{-1}{0}$

$\boxed{\tan\left(\dfrac{3\pi}{2}\right) \text{ is undefined.}}$

■**Answer: a.** $\dfrac{1}{2}$    **b.** $\dfrac{\sqrt{2}}{2}$    **c.** $-\sqrt{3}$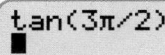

■ **YOUR TURN** Find the exact values for

**a.** $\sin\left(\dfrac{5\pi}{6}\right)$    **b.** $\cos\left(\dfrac{7\pi}{4}\right)$    **c.** $\tan\left(\dfrac{2\pi}{3}\right)$

**EXAMPLE 2  Solving Equations Involving Trigonometric (Circular) Functions**

Use the unit circle to find all values of $\theta$, $0 \le \theta \le 2\pi$, for which $\sin\theta = -\frac{1}{2}$.

**Solution:**

The value of sine is the $y$-coordinate.

Since the value of sine is negative, $\theta$ must lie in quadrant III or quadrant IV.

There are two values for $\theta$ that are greater than or equal to zero and less than or equal to $2\pi$ that correspond to $\sin\theta = -\frac{1}{2}$.

$$\boxed{\theta = \frac{7\pi}{6}, \frac{11\pi}{6}}$$

■ **YOUR TURN** Find all values of $\theta$, $0 \le \theta \le 2\pi$, for which $\cos\theta = -\frac{1}{2}$.

■ **Answer:** $\theta = \dfrac{2\pi}{3}, \dfrac{4\pi}{3}$

# Properties of Trigonometric (Circular) Functions

| WORDS | MATH |
|---|---|
| For a point $(x, y)$ that lies on the unit circle, $x^2 + y^2 = 1$. | $-1 \le x \le 1$ and $-1 \le y \le 1$ |
| Since $(x, y) = (\cos\theta, \sin\theta)$, the following holds. | $-1 \le \cos\theta \le 1$ and $-1 \le \sin\theta \le 1$ |
| State the **domain and range of the cosine and sine functions**. | Domain: $(-\infty, \infty)$   Range: $[-1, 1]$ |
| Since $\cot\theta = \dfrac{\cos\theta}{\sin\theta}$ and $\csc\theta = \dfrac{1}{\sin\theta}$, the values for $\theta$ that make $\sin\theta = 0$ must be eliminated from the **domain of the cotangent and cosecant functions**. (The integer multiples of $\pi$, i.e., $\pm\pi, \pm 2\pi, \pm 3\pi, \ldots$ can be written as $n\pi$.) | Domain: $\theta \ne n\pi$, $n$ an integer |
| Since $\tan\theta = \dfrac{\sin\theta}{\cos\theta}$ and $\sec\theta = \dfrac{1}{\cos\theta}$, the values for $\theta$ that make $\cos\theta = 0$ must be eliminated from the **domain of the tangent and secant functions**. | Domain: $\theta \ne \dfrac{(2n + 1)\pi}{2}$, $n$ an integer |

The following box summarizes the domains and ranges of the trigonometric functions.

### DOMAINS AND RANGES OF THE TRIGONOMETRIC (CIRCULAR) FUNCTIONS

For any real number $\theta$ and integer $n$:

| FUNCTION | DOMAIN | RANGE |
|---|---|---|
| $\sin \theta$ | $(-\infty, \infty)$ | $[-1, 1]$ |
| $\cos \theta$ | $(-\infty, \infty)$ | $[-1, 1]$ |
| $\tan \theta$ | all real numbers such that $\theta \neq \dfrac{(2n+1)\pi}{2}$ | $(-\infty, \infty)$ |
| $\cot \theta$ | all real numbers such that $\theta \neq n\pi$ | $(-\infty, \infty)$ |
| $\sec \theta$ | all real numbers such that $\theta \neq \dfrac{(2n+1)\pi}{2}$ | $(-\infty, -1] \cup [1, \infty)$ |
| $\csc \theta$ | all real numbers such that $\theta \neq n\pi$ | $(-\infty, -1] \cup [1, \infty)$ |

Recall from algebra that **even functions** are functions for which $f(-x) = f(x)$ and **odd functions** are functions for which $f(-x) = -f(x)$.

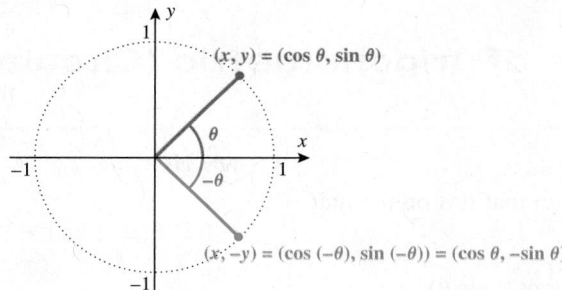

The **cosine function is an even function**.   $\boxed{\cos \theta = \cos(-\theta)}$

The **sine function is an odd function**.   $\boxed{\sin(-\theta) = -\sin \theta}$

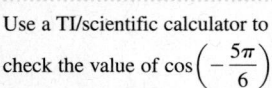
### EXAMPLE 3   Using Properties of Trigonometric (Circular) Functions

Evaluate $\cos\left(-\dfrac{5\pi}{6}\right)$.

**Solution:**

The cosine function is an even function. $\qquad \cos\left(-\dfrac{5\pi}{6}\right) = \cos\left(\dfrac{5\pi}{6}\right)$

Use the unit circle to evaluate cosine. $\qquad \cos\left(\dfrac{5\pi}{6}\right) = -\dfrac{\sqrt{3}}{2}$

$$\cos\left(-\dfrac{5\pi}{6}\right) = \boxed{-\dfrac{\sqrt{3}}{2}}$$

■ **YOUR TURN** Evaluate $\sin\left(-\dfrac{5\pi}{6}\right)$.

It is important to note that although trigonometric functions can be evaluated exactly for some special angles, a calculator can be used to approximate trigonometric functions for any angle. It is important to set the calculator to radian mode first, since $\theta$ is a real number.

 **EXAMPLE 4  Evaluating Trigonometric (Circular) Functions with a Calculator**

Use a calculator to evaluate $\sin\left(\dfrac{7\pi}{12}\right)$. Round the answer to four decimal places.

⭐ **CORRECT**

Evaluate with a calculator.

0.965925826

Round to four decimal places.

$$\sin\left(\dfrac{7\pi}{12}\right) \approx \boxed{0.9659}$$

❌ **INCORRECT**

Evaluate with a calculator.

0.031979376   **ERROR**
(Calculator in degree mode)

Many calculators automatically reset to degree mode after every calculation, so make sure to always check what mode the calculator indicates.

▪ **YOUR TURN**  Use a calculator to evaluate $\tan\left(\dfrac{9\pi}{5}\right)$. Round the answer to four decimal places.

**EXAMPLE 5  Even and Odd Trigonometric (Circular) Functions**

Show that the secant function is an even function.

**Solution:**

Show that $\sec(-\theta) = \sec\theta$.

Secant is the reciprocal of cosine.
$$\sec(-\theta) = \dfrac{1}{\cos(-\theta)}$$

Cosine is an even function, $\cos(-\theta) = \cos\theta$.
$$\sec(-\theta) = \dfrac{1}{\cos\theta}$$

Secant is the reciprocal of cosine, $\sec\theta = \dfrac{1}{\cos\theta}$.
$$\sec(-\theta) = \dfrac{1}{\cos\theta} = \sec\theta$$

Since $\sec(-\theta) = \sec\theta$, $\boxed{\text{the secant function is an even function}}$.

*Study Tip*

Set the calculator in radian mode before evaluating trigonometric functions in radians. Alternatively, convert the radian measure to degrees before evaluating the trigonometric function value.

*Technology Tip*

Use the TI/scientific calculator to evaluate $\sin\left(\dfrac{7\pi}{12}\right)$. Press 2nd ∧ for $\pi$.

```
sin(7π/12)
         .9659258263
```

▪ **Answer:** $-0.7265$

## SECTION 5.1 SUMMARY

In this section, we have defined trigonometric functions as circular functions. Any point $(x, y)$ that lies on the unit circle satisfies the equation $x^2 + y^2 = 1$. The Pythagorean identity $\cos^2\theta + \sin^2\theta = 1$ can also be represented on the unit circle where $(x, y) = (\cos\theta, \sin\theta)$, and where $\theta$ is the central angle whose terminal side intersects the unit circle at the point $(x, y)$. The cosine function is an even function, $\cos(-\theta) = \cos\theta$; the sine function is an odd function, $\sin(-\theta) = -\sin\theta$.

■ SKILLS

In Exercises 1–14, find the *exact* values of the indicated trigonometric functions using the unit circle.

**1.** $\sin\left(\dfrac{5\pi}{3}\right)$    **2.** $\cos\left(\dfrac{5\pi}{3}\right)$    **3.** $\cos\left(\dfrac{7\pi}{6}\right)$    **4.** $\sin\left(\dfrac{7\pi}{6}\right)$

**5.** $\sin\left(\dfrac{3\pi}{4}\right)$    **6.** $\cos\left(\dfrac{3\pi}{4}\right)$    **7.** $\tan\left(\dfrac{7\pi}{4}\right)$    **8.** $\cot\left(\dfrac{7\pi}{4}\right)$

**9.** $\sec\left(\dfrac{5\pi}{4}\right)$    **10.** $\csc\left(\dfrac{5\pi}{3}\right)$    **11.** $\tan\left(\dfrac{4\pi}{3}\right)$    **12.** $\cot\left(\dfrac{11\pi}{6}\right)$

**13.** $\csc\left(\dfrac{5\pi}{6}\right)$    **14.** $\cot\left(\dfrac{2\pi}{3}\right)$

In Exercises 15–34, use the unit circle and the fact that sine is an odd function and cosine is an even function to find the *exact* values of the indicated functions.

**15.** $\sin\left(-\dfrac{2\pi}{3}\right)$    **16.** $\sin\left(-\dfrac{5\pi}{4}\right)$    **17.** $\sin\left(-\dfrac{\pi}{3}\right)$    **18.** $\sin\left(-\dfrac{7\pi}{6}\right)$    **19.** $\cos\left(-\dfrac{3\pi}{4}\right)$

**20.** $\cos\left(-\dfrac{5\pi}{3}\right)$    **21.** $\cos\left(-\dfrac{5\pi}{6}\right)$    **22.** $\cos\left(-\dfrac{7\pi}{4}\right)$    **23.** $\sin\left(-\dfrac{5\pi}{4}\right)$    **24.** $\sin\left(-\pi\right)$

**25.** $\sin\left(-\dfrac{3\pi}{2}\right)$    **26.** $\sin\left(-\dfrac{\pi}{3}\right)$    **27.** $\cos\left(-\dfrac{\pi}{4}\right)$    **28.** $\cos\left(-\dfrac{3\pi}{4}\right)$    **29.** $\cos\left(-\dfrac{\pi}{2}\right)$

**30.** $\cos\left(-\dfrac{7\pi}{6}\right)$    **31.** $\csc\left(-\dfrac{5\pi}{6}\right)$    **32.** $\sec\left(-\dfrac{7\pi}{4}\right)$    **33.** $\tan\left(-\dfrac{11\pi}{6}\right)$    **34.** $\cot\left(-\dfrac{11\pi}{6}\right)$

In Exercises 35–54, use the unit circle to find all of the exact values of $\theta$ that make the equation true in the indicated interval.

**35.** $\cos\theta = \dfrac{\sqrt{3}}{2}, 0 \le \theta \le 2\pi$      **36.** $\cos\theta = -\dfrac{\sqrt{3}}{2}, 0 \le \theta \le 2\pi$      **37.** $\sin\theta = -\dfrac{\sqrt{3}}{2}, 0 \le \theta \le 2\pi$

**38.** $\sin\theta = \dfrac{\sqrt{3}}{2}, 0 \le \theta \le 2\pi$      **39.** $\sin\theta = 0, 0 \le \theta \le 4\pi$      **40.** $\sin\theta = -1, 0 \le \theta \le 4\pi$

**41.** $\cos\theta = -1, 0 \le \theta \le 4\pi$      **42.** $\cos\theta = 0, 0 \le \theta \le 4\pi$      **43.** $\tan\theta = -1, 0 \le \theta \le 2\pi$

**44.** $\cot\theta = 1, 0 \le \theta \le 2\pi$      **45.** $\sec\theta = -\sqrt{2}, 0 \le \theta \le 2\pi$      **46.** $\csc\theta = \sqrt{2}, 0 \le \theta \le 2\pi$

**47.** $\csc\theta$ is undefined, $0 \le \theta \le 2\pi$      **48.** $\sec\theta$ is undefined, $0 \le \theta \le 2\pi$      **49.** $\tan\theta$ is undefined, $0 \le \theta \le 2\pi$

**50.** $\cot\theta$ is undefined, $0 \le \theta \le 2\pi$      **51.** $\csc\theta = -2, 0 \le \theta \le 2\pi$      **52.** $\cot\theta = -\sqrt{3}, 0 \le \theta \le 2\pi$

**53.** $\sec\theta = \dfrac{2\sqrt{3}}{3}, 0 \le \theta \le 2\pi$      **54.** $\tan\theta = \dfrac{\sqrt{3}}{3}, 0 \le \theta \le 2\pi$

■ APPLICATIONS

For Exercises 55 and 56, refer to the following:

The average daily temperature in Peoria, Illinois, can be predicted by the formula $T = 50 - 28\cos\left[\dfrac{2\pi(x-31)}{365}\right]$, where $x$ is the number of the day in the year (January 1 = 1, February 1 = 32, etc.) and $T$ is in degrees Fahrenheit.

**55. Atmospheric Temperature.** What is the expected temperature on February 15?

**56. Atmospheric Temperature.** What is the expected temperature on August 15? (Assume it is not a leap year.)

**For Exercises 57 and 58, refer to the following:**

The human body temperature normally fluctuates during the day. A person's body temperature can be predicted by the formula $T \approx 99.1 - 0.5 \sin\left(x + \dfrac{\pi}{12}\right)$, where $x$ is the number of hours since midnight and $T$ is in degrees Fahrenheit.

**57. Body Temperature.** What is the person's temperature at 6:00 A.M.?

**58. Body Temperature.** What is the person's temperature at 9:00 P.M.?

**For Exercises 59 and 60, refer to the following:**

The height of the water in a harbor changes with the tides. The height of the water at a particular hour during the day can be determined by the formula $h(x) = 5 + 4.8 \sin\left[\dfrac{\pi}{6}(x + 4)\right]$, where $x$ is the number of hours since midnight and $h$ is the height of the tide in feet.

Bill Brooks/Alamy

Bill Brooks/Alamy

**59. Tides.** What is the height of the tide at 3:00 P.M.?

**60. Tides.** What is the height of the tide at 5:00 A.M.?

**61. Yo-Yo Dieting.** A woman has been yo-yo dieting for years. Her weight changes throughout the year as she gains and loses weight. Her weight in a particular month can be determined by the formula $w(x) = 145 + 10 \cos\left(\dfrac{\pi}{6}x\right)$, where $x$ is the month and $w$ is in pounds. If $x = 1$ corresponds to January, how much does she weigh in June?

**62. Yo-Yo Dieting.** How much does the woman in Exercise 61 weigh in December?

**63. Seasonal Sales.** The average number of guests visiting the Magic Kingdom at Walt Disney World per day is given by $n(x) = 30,000 + 20,000 \sin\left[\dfrac{\pi}{2}(x + 1)\right]$, where $n$ is the number of guests and $x$ is the month. If January corresponds to $x = 1$, how many people on average are visiting the Magic Kingdom per day in February?

**64. Seasonal Sales.** How many guests are visiting the Magic Kingdom in Exercise 63 in December?

**For Exercises 65 and 66, refer to the following:**

During the course of treatment of an illness, the concentration of a drug in the bloodstream in micrograms per microliter fluctuates during the dosing period of 8 hours according to the model

$$C(t) = 15.4 - 4.7 \sin\left(\dfrac{\pi}{4}t + \dfrac{\pi}{2}\right), \quad 0 \le t \le 8$$

*Note*: This model does not apply to the first dose of the medication.

**65. Health/Medicine.** Find the concentration of the drug in the bloodstream at the beginning of a dosing period.

**66. Health/Medicine.** Find the concentration of the drug in the bloodstream 6 hours after taking a dose of the drug.

**In Exercises 67 and 68, refer to the following:**

By analyzing available empirical data, it has been determined that the body temperature of a particular species fluctuates during a 24-hour day according to the model

$$T(t) = 36.3 - 1.4 \cos\left[\dfrac{\pi}{12}(t - 2)\right], \quad 0 \le t \le 24$$

where $T$ represents temperature in degrees Celsius and $t$ represents time in hours measured from 12:00 A.M. (midnight).

**67. Biology.** Find the approximate body temperature at midnight. Round your answer to the nearest degree.

**68. Biology.** Find the approximate body temperature at 2:45 P.M. Round your answer to the nearest degree.

**■ CATCH THE MISTAKE**

**In Exercises 69 and 70, explain the mistake that is made.**

**69.** Use the unit circle to evaluate $\tan\left(\dfrac{5\pi}{6}\right)$ exactly.

**Solution:**

Tangent is the ratio of sine to cosine.

$$\tan\left(\frac{5\pi}{6}\right) = \frac{\sin\left(\dfrac{5\pi}{6}\right)}{\cos\left(\dfrac{5\pi}{6}\right)}$$

Use the unit circle to identify sine and cosine.

$$\sin\left(\frac{5\pi}{6}\right) = -\frac{\sqrt{3}}{2} \quad \text{and} \quad \cos\left(\frac{5\pi}{6}\right) = \frac{1}{2}$$

Substitute values for sine and cosine.

$$\tan\left(\frac{5\pi}{6}\right) = \frac{-(\sqrt{3}/2)}{1/2}$$

Simplify.

$$\tan\left(\frac{5\pi}{6}\right) = -\sqrt{3}$$

This is incorrect. What mistake was made?

**70.** Use the unit circle to evaluate $\sec\left(\dfrac{11\pi}{6}\right)$ exactly.

**Solution:**

Secant is the reciprocal of cosine.

$$\sec\left(\frac{11\pi}{6}\right) = \frac{1}{\cos\left(\dfrac{11\pi}{6}\right)}$$

Use the unit circle to evaluate cosine.

$$\cos\left(\frac{11\pi}{6}\right) = -\frac{1}{2}$$

Substitute the value for cosine.

$$\sec\left(\frac{11\pi}{6}\right) = \frac{1}{-\dfrac{1}{2}}$$

Simplify.

$$\sec\left(\frac{11\pi}{6}\right) = -2$$

This is incorrect. What mistake was made?

**■ CONCEPTUAL**

**In Exercises 71–76, determine whether each statement is true or false.**

**71.** $\sin(2n\pi + \theta) = \sin\theta$, $n$ an integer.

**72.** $\cos(2n\pi + \theta) = \cos\theta$, $n$ an integer.

**73.** $\sin\theta = 1$ when $\theta = \dfrac{(2n+1)\pi}{2}$, $n$ an integer.

**74.** $\cos\theta = 1$ when $\theta = n\pi$, $n$ an integer.

**75.** $\tan(\theta + 2n\pi) = \tan\theta$, $n$ an integer.

**76.** $\tan\theta = 0$ if and only if $\theta = \dfrac{(2n+1)\pi}{2}$, $n$ an integer.

**77.** Is cosecant an even or an odd function? Justify your answer.

**78.** Is tangent an even or an odd function? Justify your answer.

**■ CHALLENGE**

**79.** Find all the values of $\theta$, $0 \le \theta \le 2\pi$, for which the equation $\sin\theta = \cos\theta$ is true.

**80.** Find all the values of $\theta$ ($\theta$ is any real number) for which the equation $\sin\theta = \cos\theta$ is true.

**81.** Find all the values of $\theta$, $0 \le \theta \le 2\pi$, for which the equation $2\sin\theta = \csc\theta$ is true.

**82.** Find all the values of $\theta$, $0 \le \theta \le 2\pi$, for which the equation $\cos\theta = \frac{1}{4}\sec\theta$ is true.

**83.** Find all the values of $\theta$ ($\theta$ is any real number) for which the equation $3\csc\theta = 4\sin\theta$ is true.

**84.** Find all the values of $\theta$ ($\theta$ is any real number) for which the equation $4\cos\theta = 3\sec\theta$ is true.

**85.** Does there exist an angle $0 \le \theta < 2\pi$ such that $\tan\theta = \cot\theta$?

**86.** Does there exist an angle $0 \le \theta < 2\pi$ such that $\sec\theta = \csc(-\theta)$?

■ **TECHNOLOGY**

87. Use a calculator to approximate $\sin 423°$. What do you expect $\sin(-423°)$ to be? Verify your answer with a calculator.

88. Use a calculator to approximate $\cos 227°$. What do you expect $\cos(-227°)$ to be? Verify your answer with a calculator.

89. Use a calculator to approximate $\tan 81°$. What do you expect $\tan(-81°)$ to be? Verify your answer with a calculator.

90. Use a calculator to approximate $\csc 211°$. What do you expect $\csc(-211°)$ to be? Verify your answer with a calculator.

**For Exercises 91–94, refer to the following:**

Set the calculator in parametric and radian modes and let

$$X_1 = \cos T$$
$$Y_1 = \sin T$$

Set the window so that $0 \leq T \leq 2\pi$, step $= \dfrac{\pi}{15}$, $-2 \leq X \leq 2$, and $-2 \leq Y \leq 2$. To approximate the sine or cosine of a T value, use the $\boxed{\text{TRACE}}$ key, type in the T value, and read the corresponding coordinates from the screen.

91. Approximate $\cos\left(\dfrac{\pi}{3}\right)$, take 5 steps of $\dfrac{\pi}{15}$ each, and read the $x$-coordinate.

92. Approximate $\sin\left(\dfrac{\pi}{3}\right)$, take 5 steps of $\dfrac{\pi}{15}$ each, and read the $y$-coordinate.

93. Approximate $\sin\left(\dfrac{2\pi}{3}\right)$ to four decimal places.

94. Approximate $\cos\left(\dfrac{5\pi}{4}\right)$ to four decimal places.

■ **PREVIEW TO CALCULUS**

The Fundamental Theorem of Calculus establishes that the definite integral $\int_a^b f(x)\,dx$ equals $F(b) - F(a)$, where $F$ is any antiderivative of a continuous function $f$.

In Exercises 95–98, use the information below to find the exact value of each definite integral.

| FUNCTION | $\sin x$ | $\cos x$ | $\sec^2 x$ | $\csc x \cot x$ |
|---|---|---|---|---|
| ANTIDERIVATIVE | $-\cos x$ | $\sin x$ | $\tan x$ | $-\csc x$ |

95. $\displaystyle\int_0^{\pi} \sin x\,dx$

96. $\displaystyle\int_{\pi/4}^{5\pi/6} \cos x\,dx$

97. $\displaystyle\int_{7\pi/6}^{5\pi/4} \sec^2 x\,dx$

98. $\displaystyle\int_{5\pi/3}^{11\pi/6} \csc x \cot x\,dx$

## SKILLS OBJECTIVES

- Graph the sine and cosine functions.
- Determine the domain and range of the sine and cosine functions.
- Determine the amplitude and period of sinusoidal functions.
- Determine the phase shift of a sinusoidal function.
- Solve harmonic motion problems.
- Graph sums of functions.

## CONCEPTUAL OBJECTIVES

- Understand why the graphs of the sine and cosine functions are called sinusoidal graphs.
- Understand the cyclic nature of periodic functions.
- Visualize harmonic motion as a sinusoidal function.

# The Graphs of Sinusoidal Functions

The following are examples of things that repeat in a predictable way (are roughly periodic):

- heartbeat
- tide levels
- time of sunrise
- average outdoor temperature for the time of year

The trigonometric functions are *strictly* periodic. In the unit circle, the value of any of the trigonometric functions is the same for any coterminal angle (same initial and terminal sides no matter how many full rotations the angle makes). For example, if we add (or subtract) multiples of $2\pi$ to (from) the angle $\theta$, the values for sine and cosine are unchanged.

$$\sin(\theta + 2n\pi) = \sin\theta \qquad \text{or} \qquad \cos(\theta + 2n\pi) = \cos\theta \quad (n \text{ is any integer})$$

**DEFINITION**  **Periodic Function**

A function $f$ is called a **periodic function** if there is a positive number $p$ such that

$$f(x + p) = f(x) \qquad \text{for all } x \text{ in the domain of } f$$

If $p$ is the smallest such number for which this equation holds, then $p$ is called the **fundamental period**.

You will see in this chapter that sine, cosine, secant, and cosecant have fundamental period $2\pi$, but that tangent and cotangent have fundamental period $\pi$.

## The Graph of $f(x) = \sin x$

Let us start by point-plotting the sine function. We select special values for the sine function that we already know.

| x | f(x) = sin x | (x, y) |
|---|---|---|
| 0 | $\sin 0 = 0$ | $(0, 0)$ |
| $\dfrac{\pi}{4}$ | $\sin\left(\dfrac{\pi}{4}\right) = \dfrac{\sqrt{2}}{2}$ | $\left(\dfrac{\pi}{4}, \dfrac{\sqrt{2}}{2}\right)$ |
| $\dfrac{\pi}{2}$ | $\sin\left(\dfrac{\pi}{2}\right) = 1$ | $\left(\dfrac{\pi}{2}, 1\right)$ |
| $\dfrac{3\pi}{4}$ | $\sin\left(\dfrac{3\pi}{4}\right) = \dfrac{\sqrt{2}}{2}$ | $\left(\dfrac{3\pi}{4}, \dfrac{\sqrt{2}}{2}\right)$ |
| $\pi$ | $\sin \pi = 0$ | $(\pi, 0)$ |
| $\dfrac{5\pi}{4}$ | $\sin\left(\dfrac{5\pi}{4}\right) = -\dfrac{\sqrt{2}}{2}$ | $\left(\dfrac{5\pi}{4}, -\dfrac{\sqrt{2}}{2}\right)$ |
| $\dfrac{3\pi}{2}$ | $\sin\left(\dfrac{3\pi}{2}\right) = -1$ | $\left(\dfrac{3\pi}{2}, -1\right)$ |
| $\dfrac{7\pi}{4}$ | $\sin\left(\dfrac{7\pi}{4}\right) = -\dfrac{\sqrt{2}}{2}$ | $\left(\dfrac{7\pi}{4}, -\dfrac{\sqrt{2}}{2}\right)$ |
| $2\pi$ | $\sin(2\pi) = 0$ | $(2\pi, 0)$ |

**Study Tip**

Note that either notation, $y = \sin x$ or $f(x) = \sin x$, can be used.

By plotting the above coordinates $(x, y)$, we can obtain the graph of one **period**, or **cycle**, of the graph of $y = \sin x$. Note that $\dfrac{\sqrt{2}}{2} \approx 0.7$.

**Study Tip**

Looking at the graph of $f(x) = \sin x$, we are reminded that $\sin x > 0$ when $0 < x < \pi$ and $\sin x < 0$ when $\pi < x < 2\pi$. We also see that when $x = \dfrac{3\pi}{4}, \dfrac{5\pi}{4},$ or $\dfrac{7\pi}{4}$, the reference angle is $\dfrac{\pi}{4}$.

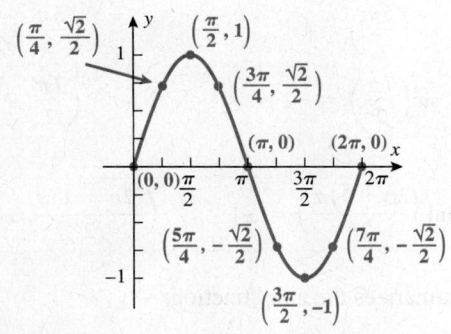

We can extend the graph horizontally in both directions (left and right) since the domain of the sine function is the set of all real numbers.

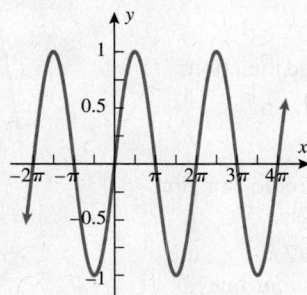

From here on, we are no longer showing angles on the unit circle but are now showing angles as *real numbers* in radians on the *x*-axis of the *Cartesian* graph. Therefore, we no longer illustrate a "terminal side" to an angle—the physical arcs and angles no longer exist; only their measures exist, as values of the *x*-coordinate.

## Technology Tip

Set a TI/scientific calculator to radian mode by typing $\boxed{\text{MODE}}$.

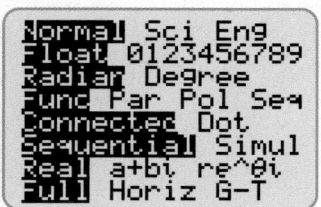

Set the window at Xmin at $-2\pi$,

Xmax at $4\pi$, Xsc1 at $\dfrac{\pi}{2}$, Ymin at

$-1$, Ymax at 1, and Ysc1 at 1.

Setting Xsc1 at $\dfrac{\pi}{2}$ will mark the

labels on the $x$-axis in terms of

multiples of $\dfrac{\pi}{2}$.

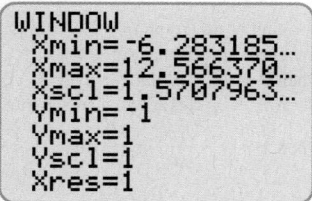

Use $\boxed{\text{Y}=}$ to enter the function

sin(X).

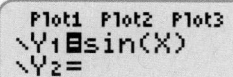

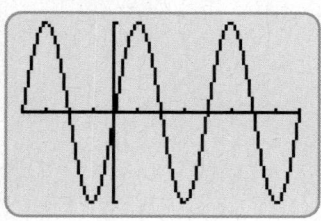

If we graph the function $f(x) = \sin x$, the $x$-intercepts correspond to values of $x$ at which the sine function is equal to zero.

| $x$ | $f(x) = \sin x$ | $(x, y)$ |
|---|---|---|
| 0 | $\sin 0 = 0$ | $(0, 0)$ |
| $\pi$ | $\sin \pi = 0$ | $(\pi, 0)$ |
| $2\pi$ | $\sin(2\pi) = 0$ | $(2\pi, 0)$ |
| $3\pi$ | $\sin(3\pi) = 0$ | $(3\pi, 0)$ |
| $4\pi$ | $\sin(4\pi) = 0$ | $(4\pi, 0)$ |
| ... | | |
| $n\pi$ | $\sin(n\pi) = 0$ | $(n\pi, 0)$, $n$ is an integer. |

Notice that the point $(0, 0)$ is both a $y$-intercept and an $x$-intercept but all $x$-intercepts have the form $(n\pi, 0)$. The maximum value of the sine function is 1, and the minimum value of the sine function is $-1$, which occurs at odd multiples of $\dfrac{\pi}{2}$.

| $x$ | $f(x) = \sin x$ | $(x, y)$ |
|---|---|---|
| $\dfrac{\pi}{2}$ | $\sin\left(\dfrac{\pi}{2}\right) = 1$ | $\left(\dfrac{\pi}{2}, 1\right)$ |
| $\dfrac{3\pi}{2}$ | $\sin\left(\dfrac{3\pi}{2}\right) = -1$ | $\left(\dfrac{3\pi}{2}, -1\right)$ |
| $\dfrac{5\pi}{2}$ | $\sin\left(\dfrac{5\pi}{2}\right) = 1$ | $\left(\dfrac{5\pi}{2}, 1\right)$ |
| $\dfrac{7\pi}{2}$ | $\sin\left(\dfrac{7\pi}{2}\right) = -1$ | $\left(\dfrac{7\pi}{2}, -1\right)$ |
| ... | ... | ... |
| $\dfrac{(2n + 1)\pi}{2}$ | $\sin\left(\dfrac{(2n + 1)\pi}{2}\right) = \pm 1$ | $\left(\dfrac{(2n + 1)\pi}{2}, \pm 1\right)$, $n$ is an integer. |

The following box summarizes the sine function:

### SINE FUNCTION $f(x) = \sin x$

- Domain: $(-\infty, \infty)$ or $-\infty < x < \infty$
- Range: $[-1, 1]$ or $-1 \leq y \leq 1$
- The sine function is an odd function:
  - symmetric about the origin
  - $\sin(-x) = -\sin x$
- The sine function is a periodic function with fundamental period $2\pi$.
- The $x$-intercepts, $0, \pm\pi, \pm 2\pi, \ldots$, are of the form $n\pi$, where $n$ is an integer.
- The maximum (1) and minimum ($-1$) values of the sine function correspond to $x$-values of the form $\dfrac{(2n + 1)\pi}{2}$, such as $\pm\dfrac{\pi}{2}, \pm\dfrac{3\pi}{2}, \pm\dfrac{5\pi}{2}, \ldots$.

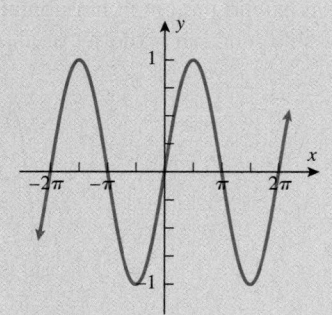

# The Graph of $f(x) = \cos x$

Let us start by point-plotting the cosine function.

| $x$ | $f(x) = \cos x$ | $(x, y)$ |
|---|---|---|
| 0 | $\cos 0 = 1$ | $(0, 1)$ |
| $\dfrac{\pi}{4}$ | $\cos\left(\dfrac{\pi}{4}\right) = \dfrac{\sqrt{2}}{2}$ | $\left(\dfrac{\pi}{4}, \dfrac{\sqrt{2}}{2}\right)$ |
| $\dfrac{\pi}{2}$ | $\cos\left(\dfrac{\pi}{2}\right) = 0$ | $\left(\dfrac{\pi}{2}, 0\right)$ |
| $\dfrac{3\pi}{4}$ | $\cos\left(\dfrac{3\pi}{4}\right) = -\dfrac{\sqrt{2}}{2}$ | $\left(\dfrac{3\pi}{4}, -\dfrac{\sqrt{2}}{2}\right)$ |
| $\pi$ | $\cos \pi = -1$ | $(\pi, -1)$ |
| $\dfrac{5\pi}{4}$ | $\cos\left(\dfrac{5\pi}{4}\right) = -\dfrac{\sqrt{2}}{2}$ | $\left(\dfrac{5\pi}{4}, -\dfrac{\sqrt{2}}{2}\right)$ |
| $\dfrac{3\pi}{2}$ | $\cos\left(\dfrac{3\pi}{2}\right) = 0$ | $\left(\dfrac{3\pi}{2}, 0\right)$ |
| $\dfrac{7\pi}{4}$ | $\cos\left(\dfrac{7\pi}{4}\right) = \dfrac{\sqrt{2}}{2}$ | $\left(\dfrac{7\pi}{4}, \dfrac{\sqrt{2}}{2}\right)$ |
| $2\pi$ | $\cos(2\pi) = 1$ | $(2\pi, 1)$ |

By plotting the above coordinates $(x, y)$, we can obtain the graph of one period, or cycle, of the graph of $y = \cos x$. Note that $\dfrac{\sqrt{2}}{2} \approx 0.7$.

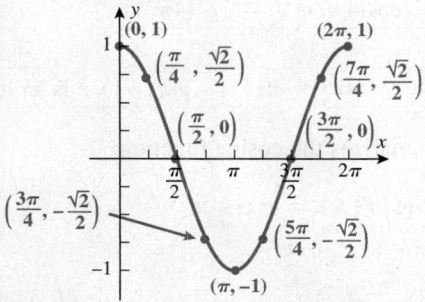

We can extend the graph horizontally in both directions (left and right) since the domain of the cosine function is all real numbers.

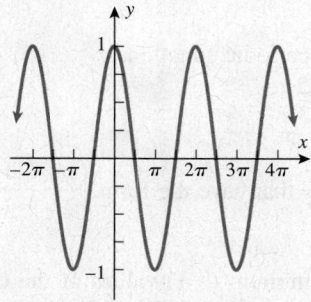

If we graph the function $f(x) = \cos x$, the $x$-intercepts correspond to values of $x$ at which the cosine function is equal to zero.

**Technology Tip**

Set the window at Xmin at

$-2\pi$, Xmax at $4\pi$, Xscl at $\dfrac{\pi}{2}$,

Ymin at $-1$, Ymax at 1, and

Yscl at 1. Setting Xscl at $\dfrac{\pi}{2}$ will

mark the labels on the $x$-axis in

terms of multiples of $\dfrac{\pi}{2}$.

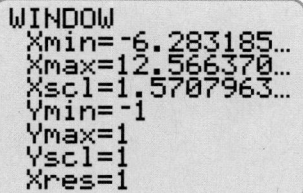

Use $\boxed{Y=}$ to enter the function
cos(X).

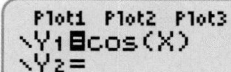

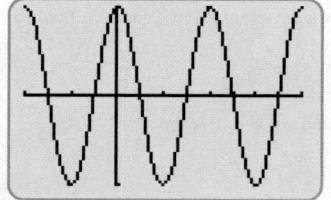

| $x$ | $f(x) = \cos x$ | $(x, y)$ |
|---|---|---|
| $\dfrac{\pi}{2}$ | $\cos\left(\dfrac{\pi}{2}\right) = 0$ | $\left(\dfrac{\pi}{2}, 0\right)$ |
| $\dfrac{3\pi}{2}$ | $\cos\left(\dfrac{3\pi}{2}\right) = 0$ | $\left(\dfrac{3\pi}{2}, 0\right)$ |
| $\dfrac{5\pi}{2}$ | $\cos\left(\dfrac{5\pi}{2}\right) = 0$ | $\left(\dfrac{5\pi}{2}, 0\right)$ |
| $\dfrac{7\pi}{2}$ | $\cos\left(\dfrac{7\pi}{2}\right) = 0$ | $\left(\dfrac{7\pi}{2}, 0\right)$ |
| $\ldots$ | $\ldots$ | $\ldots$ |
| $\dfrac{(2n + 1)\pi}{2}$ | $\cos\left(\dfrac{(2n + 1)\pi}{2}\right) = 0$ | $\left(\dfrac{(2n + 1)\pi}{2}, 0\right)$, $n$ is an integer. |

The point $(0, 1)$ is the $y$-intercept, and there are several $x$-intercepts of the form $\left(\dfrac{(2n + 1)\pi}{2}, 0\right)$. The maximum value of the cosine function is 1 and the minimum value of the cosine function is $-1$; these values occur at integer multiples of $\pi$, i.e., $n\pi$.

| $x$ | $f(x) = \cos x$ | $(x, y)$ |
|---|---|---|
| 0 | $\cos 0 = 1$ | $(0, 1)$ |
| $\pi$ | $\cos \pi = -1$ | $(\pi, -1)$ |
| $2\pi$ | $\cos(2\pi) = 1$ | $(2\pi, 1)$ |
| $3\pi$ | $\cos(3\pi) = -1$ | $(3\pi, -1)$ |
| $4\pi$ | $\cos(4\pi) = 1$ | $(4\pi, 1)$ |
| $\ldots$ | $\ldots$ | $\ldots$ |
| $n\pi$ | $\cos(n\pi) = \pm 1$ | $(n\pi, \pm 1)$, $n$ is an integer. |

The following box summarizes the cosine function:

**COSINE FUNCTION** $f(x) = \cos x$

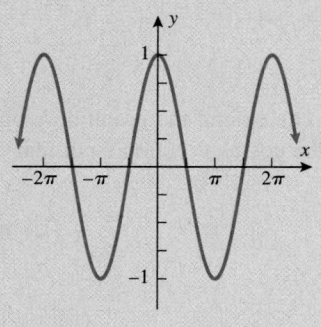

- Domain: $(-\infty, \infty)$ or $-\infty < x < \infty$
- Range: $[-1, 1]$ or $-1 \le y \le 1$
- The cosine function is an even function:
  - symmetric about the $y$-axis
  - $\cos(-x) = \cos x$
- The cosine function is a periodic function with fundamental period $2\pi$.
- The $x$-intercepts, $\pm\dfrac{\pi}{2}, \pm\dfrac{3\pi}{2}, \pm\dfrac{5\pi}{2}, \ldots$, are odd integer multiples of $\dfrac{\pi}{2}$ that have the form $\dfrac{(2n + 1)\pi}{2}$, where $n$ is an integer.

- The maximum (1) and minimum $(-1)$ values of the cosine function correspond to $x$-values of the form $n\pi$, such as $0, \pm\pi, \pm 2\pi, \ldots$.

## The Amplitude and Period of Sinusoidal Graphs

In mathematics, the word **sinusoidal** means "resembling the sine function." Let us start by graphing $f(x) = \sin x$ and $f(x) = \cos x$ on the same graph. Notice that they have similar characteristics (domain, range, period, and shape).

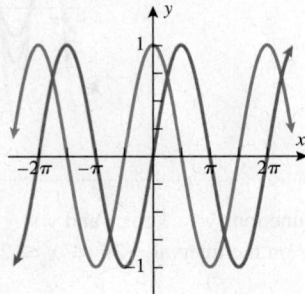

In fact, if we were to shift the cosine graph to the right $\dfrac{\pi}{2}$ units, the two graphs would be identical. For that reason we refer to any graphs of the form $y = \cos x$ or $y = \sin x$ as **sinusoidal functions**.

We now turn our attention to graphs of the form $y = A\sin(Bx)$ and $y = A\cos(Bx)$, which are graphs like $y = \sin x$ and $y = \cos x$ that have been stretched or compressed vertically and horizontally.

### EXAMPLE 1    Vertical Stretching and Compressing

Plot the functions $y = 2\sin x$ and $y = \frac{1}{2}\sin x$ on the same graph with $y = \sin x$ on the interval $-4\pi \leq x \leq 4\pi$.

**Solution:**

STEP 1  Make a table with the coordinate values of the graphs.

| $x$ | 0 | $\dfrac{\pi}{2}$ | $\pi$ | $\dfrac{3\pi}{2}$ | $2\pi$ |
|---|---|---|---|---|---|
| $\sin x$ | 0 | 1 | 0 | $-1$ | 0 |
| $2\sin x$ | 0 | 2 | 0 | $-2$ | 0 |
| $\frac{1}{2}\sin x$ | 0 | $\frac{1}{2}$ | 0 | $-\frac{1}{2}$ | 0 |

STEP 2  Label the points on the graph and connect with a smooth curve over one period, $0 \leq x \leq 2\pi$.

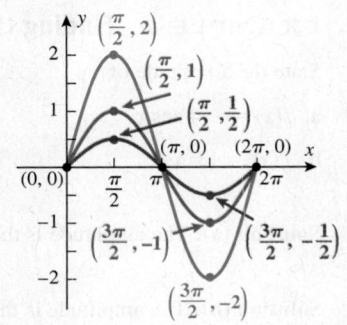

STEP 3  Extend the graph in both directions (repeat every $2\pi$).

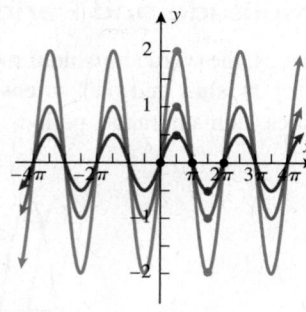

■ **Answer:**

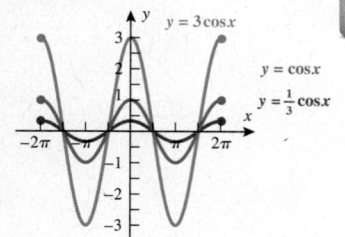

■ **YOUR TURN**  Plot the functions $y = 3\cos x$ and $y = \frac{1}{3}\cos x$ on the same graph with $y = \cos x$ on the interval $-2\pi \leq x \leq 2\pi$.

Notice in Example 1 and the corresponding Your Turn that:

■ $y = 2\sin x$ has the shape and period of $y = \sin x$ but is stretched vertically.
■ $y = \frac{1}{2}\sin x$ has the shape and period of $y = \sin x$ but is compressed vertically.
■ $y = 3\cos x$ has the shape and period of $y = \cos x$ but is stretched vertically.
■ $y = \frac{1}{3}\cos x$ has the shape and period of $y = \cos x$ but is compressed vertically.

In general, functions of the form $y = A\sin x$ and $y = A\cos x$ are stretched vertically when $|A| > 1$ and compressed vertically when $|A| < 1$.

The **amplitude** of a periodic function is half the difference between the maximum value of the function and the minimum value of the function. For the functions $y = \sin x$ and $y = \cos x$, the maximum value is 1 and the minimum value is $-1$. Therefore, the amplitude of each of these two functions is $|A| = \frac{1}{2}|1 - (-1)| = 1$.

## AMPLITUDE OF SINUSOIDAL FUNCTIONS

For sinusoidal functions of the form $y = A\sin(Bx)$ and $y = A\cos(Bx)$, the **amplitude** is $|A|$. When $|A| < 1$, the graph is compressed vertically, and when $|A| > 1$, the graph is stretched vertically.

### EXAMPLE 2   Finding the Amplitude of Sinusoidal Functions

State the amplitude of

**a.** $f(x) = -4\cos x$

**b.** $g(x) = \frac{1}{5}\sin x$

**Solution (a):** The amplitude is the magnitude of $-4$.          $A = |-4| = \boxed{4}$

**Solution (b):** The amplitude is the magnitude of $\frac{1}{5}$.          $A = \left|\frac{1}{5}\right| = \boxed{\frac{1}{5}}$

# EXAMPLE 3    Horizontal Stretching and Compressing

Plot the functions $y = \cos(2x)$ and $y = \cos\left(\frac{1}{2}x\right)$ on the same graph with $y = \cos x$ on the interval $-2\pi \le x \le 2\pi$.

**Solution:**

STEP 1  Make a table with the coordinate values of the graphs. It is necessary only to select the points that correspond to x-intercepts, $(y = 0)$, and maximum and minimum points, $(y = \pm 1)$. Usually, the period is divided into four subintervals (which you will see in Examples 5 to 7).

**Technology Tip**

Set the window at Xmin at $-2\pi$, Xmax at $2\pi$, Xsc1 at $\frac{\pi}{2}$, Ymin at $-1$, Ymax at $1$, and Ysc1 at $1$. Setting Xsc1 at $\frac{\pi}{2}$ will mark the labels on the x-axis in terms of multiples of $\frac{\pi}{2}$.

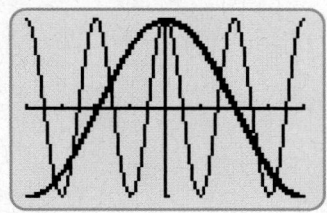

| $x$ | 0 | $\frac{\pi}{4}$ | $\frac{\pi}{2}$ | $\frac{3\pi}{4}$ | $\pi$ | $\frac{5\pi}{4}$ | $\frac{3\pi}{2}$ | $\frac{7\pi}{4}$ | $2\pi$ |
|---|---|---|---|---|---|---|---|---|---|
| $\cos x$ | 1 | | 0 | | $-1$ | | 0 | | 1 |
| $\cos(2x)$ | 1 | 0 | $-1$ | 0 | 1 | 0 | $-1$ | 0 | 1 |
| $\cos\left(\frac{1}{2}x\right)$ | 1 | | | | 0 | | | | $-1$ |

STEP 2  Label the points on the graph and connect with a smooth curve.

$y = \cos x$

$y = \cos(2x)$

$y = \cos\left(\dfrac{1}{2}x\right)$

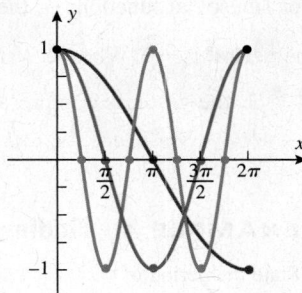

STEP 3  Extend the graph to cover the entire interval: $-2\pi \le x \le 2\pi$.

$y = \cos x$

$y = \cos(2x)$

$y = \cos\left(\dfrac{1}{2}x\right)$

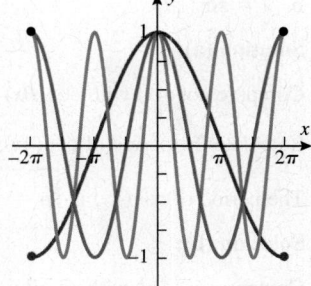

■ **Answer:**

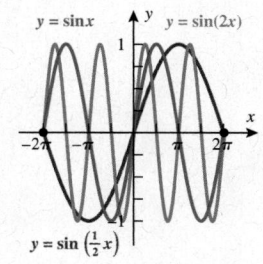

■ **YOUR TURN**  Plot the functions $y = \sin(2x)$ and $y = \sin\left(\frac{1}{2}x\right)$ on the same graph with $y = \sin x$ on the interval $-2\pi \le x \le 2\pi$.

Notice in Example 3 and the corresponding Your Turn that:

- $y = \cos(2x)$ has the shape and amplitude of $y = \cos x$ but is compressed horizontally.
- $y = \cos\left(\frac{1}{2}x\right)$ has the shape and amplitude of $y = \cos x$ but is stretched horizontally.
- $y = \sin(2x)$ has the shape and amplitude of $y = \sin x$ but is compressed horizontally.
- $y = \sin\left(\frac{1}{2}x\right)$ has the shape and amplitude of $y = \sin x$ but is stretched horizontally.

In general, functions of the form $y = \sin(Bx)$ and $y = \cos(Bx)$, with $B > 0$, are compressed horizontally when $B > 1$ and stretched horizontally when $0 < B < 1$. Negative arguments ($B < 0$) are included in the context of *reflections*.

The period of the functions $y = \sin x$ and $y = \cos x$ is $2\pi$. To find the period of a function of the form $y = A\sin(Bx)$ or $y = A\cos(Bx)$, set $Bx$ equal to $2\pi$ and solve for $x$.

$$Bx = 2\pi$$
$$x = \frac{2\pi}{B}$$

**PERIOD OF SINUSOIDAL FUNCTIONS**

For sinusoidal functions of the form $y = A\sin(Bx)$ and $y = A\cos(Bx)$, with $B > 0$, the **period** is $\frac{2\pi}{B}$. When $0 < B < 1$, the graph is stretched horizontally, and when $B > 1$, the graph is compressed horizontally since the period is smaller than $2\pi$.

**Study Tip**

When $B$ is negative, the period is $\frac{2\pi}{|B|}$.

**EXAMPLE 4    Finding the Period of a Sinusoidal Function**

State the period of

**a.** $y = \cos(4x)$

**b.** $y = \sin\left(\frac{1}{3}x\right)$

**Solution (a):**

Compare $\cos(4x)$ with $\cos(Bx)$ to identify $B$.　　　　　$B = 4$

Calculate the period of $\cos(4x)$, using $p = \frac{2\pi}{B}$.　　$p = \frac{2\pi}{4} = \frac{\pi}{2}$

The period of $\cos(4x)$ is $\boxed{p = \frac{\pi}{2}}$.

**Solution (b):**

Compare $\sin\left(\frac{1}{3}x\right)$ with $\sin(Bx)$ to identify $B$.　$B = \frac{1}{3}$

Calculate the period of $\sin\left(\frac{1}{3}x\right)$, using $p = \frac{2\pi}{B}$.　$p = \frac{2\pi}{\frac{1}{3}} = 6\pi$

The period of $\sin\left(\frac{1}{3}x\right)$ is $\boxed{p = 6\pi}$.

**Answer:**
**a.** $p = \frac{2\pi}{3}$　**b.** $p = 4\pi$

**YOUR TURN** State the period of

**a.** $y = \sin(3x)$　　**b.** $y = \cos\left(\frac{1}{2}x\right)$

Now that you know the basic graphs of $y = \sin x$ and $y = \cos x$, you can sketch one cycle (period) of these graphs with the following $x$-values: $0, \dfrac{\pi}{2}, \pi, \dfrac{3\pi}{2}, 2\pi$. For a period of $2\pi$, we used steps of $\dfrac{\pi}{2}$. Therefore, for functions of the form $y = A\sin(Bx)$ or $y = A\cos(Bx)$, when we start at the origin and as long as we include these four basic values during one period, we are able to sketch the graphs.

**Study Tip**

Divide the period by 4 to get the key values along the $x$-axis for graphing.

**STRATEGY FOR SKETCHING GRAPHS OF SINUSOIDAL FUNCTIONS**

To graph $y = A\sin(Bx)$ or $y = A\cos(Bx)$ with $B > 0$:

**Step 1:** Find the amplitude $|A|$ and period $\dfrac{2\pi}{B}$.

**Step 2:** Divide the period into four subintervals of equal lengths.

**Step 3:** Make a table and evaluate the function for $x$-values from Step 2 starting at $x = 0$.

**Step 4:** Draw the $xy$-plane (label the $y$-axis from $-|A|$ to $|A|$) and plot the points found in Step 3.

**Step 5:** Connect the points with a sinusoidal curve (with amplitude $|A|$).

**Step 6:** Extend the graph over one or two additional periods in both directions (left and right).

**Technology Tip**

Use a TI calculator to check the graph of $y = 3\sin(2x)$.

**EXAMPLE 5    Graphing Sinusoidal Functions of the Form $y = A\sin(Bx)$**

Use the strategy for graphing a sinusoidal function to graph $y = 3\sin(2x)$.

**Solution:**

**STEP 1** Find the amplitude and period for $A = 3$ and $B = 2$.

$$|A| = |3| = 3 \quad \text{and} \quad p = \frac{2\pi}{B} = \frac{2\pi}{2} = \pi$$

**STEP 2** Divide the period $\pi$ into four equal steps.    $\dfrac{\pi}{4}$

**STEP 3** Make a table starting at $x = 0$ to the period $x = \pi$ in steps of $\dfrac{\pi}{4}$.

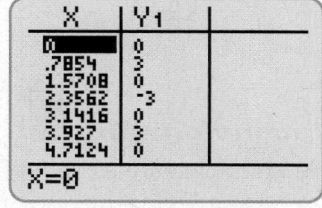

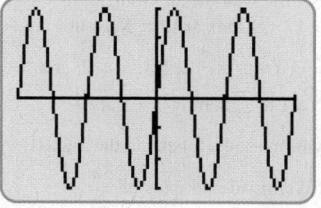

| $x$ | $y = 3\sin(2x)$ | $(x, y)$ |
|---|---|---|
| $0$ | $3[\sin 0] = 3[0] = 0$ | $(0, 0)$ |
| $\dfrac{\pi}{4}$ | $3\left[\sin\left(\dfrac{\pi}{2}\right)\right] = 3[1] = 3$ | $\left(\dfrac{\pi}{4}, 3\right)$ |
| $\dfrac{\pi}{2}$ | $3[\sin \pi] = 3[0] = 0$ | $\left(\dfrac{\pi}{2}, 0\right)$ |
| $\dfrac{3\pi}{4}$ | $3\left[\sin\left(\dfrac{3\pi}{2}\right)\right] = 3[-1] = -3$ | $\left(\dfrac{3\pi}{4}, -3\right)$ |
| $\pi$ | $3[\sin(2\pi)] = 3[0] = 0$ | $(\pi, 0)$ |

STEP 4 Draw the *xy*-plane and label the points in the table.

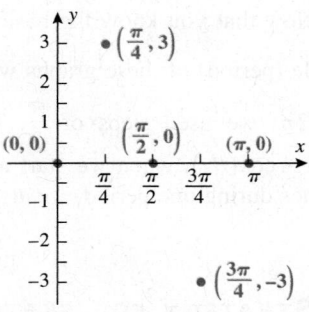

STEP 5 Connect the points with a sinusoidal curve.

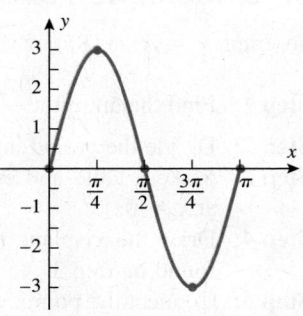

STEP 6 Repeat over several periods (to the left and right).

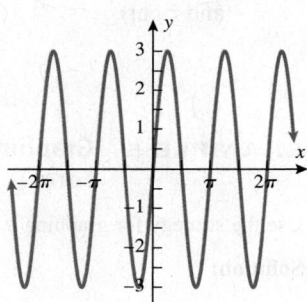

■ **Answer:**

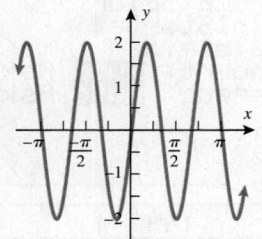

**Technology Tip**

Use a TI calculator to check the graph of $y = -2\cos(\frac{1}{3}x)$.
Set the window at Xmin at $-12\pi$, Xmax at $12\pi$, Xsc1 at $\frac{3\pi}{2}$, Ymin at $-2$, Ymax at $2$, and Ysc1 at 1. Setting Xsc1 at $\frac{3\pi}{2}$ will mark the labels on the *x*-axis in terms of multiples of $\frac{3\pi}{2}$.

■ **YOUR TURN** Use the strategy for graphing sinusoidal functions to graph $y = 2\sin(3x)$.

**EXAMPLE 6** **Graphing Sinusoidal Functions of the Form $y = A\cos(Bx)$**

Use the strategy for graphing a sinusoidal function to graph $y = -2\cos(\frac{1}{3}x)$.

**Solution:**

STEP 1 Find the amplitude for $A = -2$.

$$|A| = |-2| = 2$$

Find the period for $B = \frac{1}{3}$.

$$p = \frac{2\pi}{B} = \frac{2\pi}{\frac{1}{3}} = 6\pi$$

STEP 2 Divide the period $6\pi$ into four equal steps.

$$\frac{6\pi}{4} = \frac{3\pi}{2}$$

**STEP 3**  Make a table starting at $x = 0$ and completing one period of $6\pi$ in steps of $\dfrac{3\pi}{2}$.

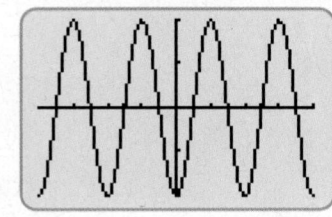

| x | $y = -2\cos\left(\tfrac{1}{3}x\right)$ | $(x, y)$ |
|---|---|---|
| 0 | $-2[\cos 0] = -2[1] = -2$ | $(0, -2)$ |
| $\dfrac{3\pi}{2}$ | $-2\left[\cos\left(\dfrac{\pi}{2}\right)\right] = -2[0] = 0$ | $\left(\dfrac{3\pi}{2}, 0\right)$ |
| $3\pi$ | $-2[\cos\pi] = -2[-1] = 2$ | $(3\pi, 2)$ |
| $\dfrac{9\pi}{2}$ | $-2\left[\cos\left(\dfrac{3\pi}{2}\right)\right] = -2[0] = 0$ | $\left(\dfrac{9\pi}{2}, 0\right)$ |
| $6\pi$ | $-2[\cos(2\pi)] = -2[1] = -2$ | $(6\pi, -2)$ |

**STEP 4**  Draw the *xy*-plane and label the points in the table.

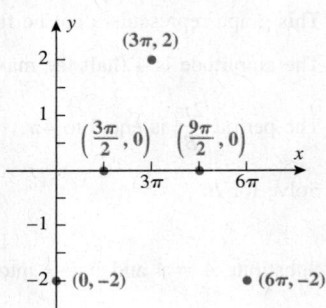

**STEP 5**  Connect the points with a sinusoidal curve.

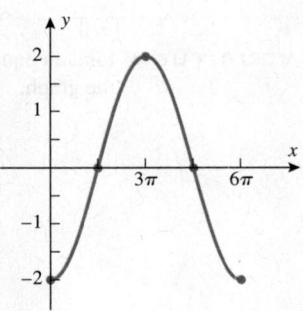

**STEP 6**  Repeat over several periods (to the left and right).

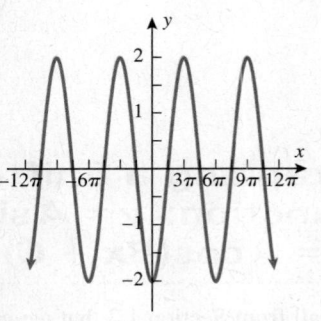

■ **Answer:**

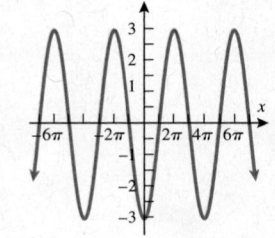

■ **YOUR TURN**  Use the strategy for graphing a sinusoidal function to graph
$$y = -3\cos\left(\tfrac{1}{2}x\right).$$

Notice in Example 6 and the corresponding Your Turn that when *A* is negative, the result is a reflection of the original function (sine or cosine) about the *x*-axis.

**EXAMPLE 7** **Finding an Equation for a Sinusoidal Graph**

Find an equation for the graph.

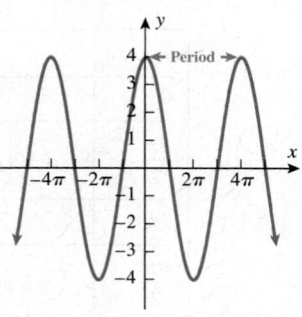

**Solution:**

This graph represents a cosine function. $y = A\cos(Bx)$

The amplitude is 4 (half the maximum spread). $|A| = 4$

The period $\dfrac{2\pi}{B}$ is equal to $4\pi$. $\dfrac{2\pi}{B} = 4\pi$

Solve for $B$. $B = \dfrac{1}{2}$

Substitute $A = 4$ and $B = \frac{1}{2}$ into $y = A\cos(Bx)$. $\boxed{y = 4\cos\left(\dfrac{1}{2}x\right)}$

■ **Answer:** $y = 6\sin(2x)$

■ **YOUR TURN** Find an equation for the graph.

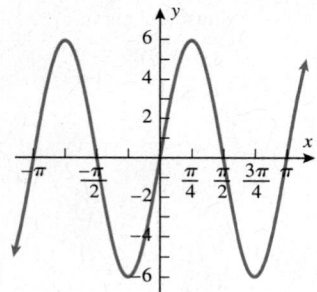

# Graphing a Shifted Sinusoidal Function: $y = A\sin(Bx + C) + D$ and $y = A\cos(Bx + C) + D$

Recall from Section 1.3 that we graph functions using horizontal and vertical translations (shifts) in the following way ($c > 0$):

- To graph $f(x + c)$, shift $f(x)$ to the **left** $c$ units.
- To graph $f(x - c)$, shift $f(x)$ to the **right** $c$ units.
- To graph $f(x) + c$, shift $f(x)$ **up** $c$ units.
- To graph $f(x) - c$, shift $f(x)$ **down** $c$ units.

To graph functions of the form $y = A \sin(Bx + C) + D$ and $y = A \cos(Bx + C) + D$, utilize the strategy below.

### STRATEGY FOR GRAPHING $y = A\sin(Bx + C) + D$ AND $y = A\cos(Bx + C) + D$

A strategy for graphing $y = A \sin(Bx + C) + D$ is outlined below. The same strategy can be used to graph $y = A \cos(Bx + C) + D$.

**Step 1:** Find the amplitude $|A|$.

**Step 2:** Find the period $\dfrac{2\pi}{B}$ and **phase shift** $-\dfrac{C}{B}$.

**Step 3:** Graph $y = A \sin(Bx + C)$ over one period $\left(\text{from } -\dfrac{C}{B} \text{ to } -\dfrac{C}{B} + \dfrac{2\pi}{B}\right)$.

**Step 4:** Extend the graph over several periods.

**Step 5:** Shift the graph of $y = A \sin(Bx + C)$ vertically $D$ units.

*Note:* If we rewrite the function in **standard form**, we get

$$y = A \sin\left[B\left(x + \frac{C}{B}\right)\right] + D$$

which makes it easier to identify the **phase shift**.

    If $B < 0$, we can use properties of even and odd functions

$$\sin(-x) = -\sin x \qquad \cos(-x) = \cos x$$

to rewrite the function with $B > 0$.

**Study Tip**

Rewriting in standard form

$$y = A \sin\left[B\left(x + \frac{C}{B}\right)\right]$$

makes identifying the phase shift easier.

### EXAMPLE 8   Graphing Functions of the Form $y = A\cos(Bx \pm C)$

Graph $y = 5\cos(4x + \pi)$ over one period.

**Solution:**

STEP 1  Find the amplitude.         $|A| = |5| = 5$

STEP 2  Calculate the period and phase shift.

The interval for one period is from $0$ to $2\pi$.     $4x + \pi = 0$    to   $4x + \pi = 2\pi$

Solve for $x$.                  $x = -\dfrac{\pi}{4}$   to   $x = -\dfrac{\pi}{4} + \dfrac{\pi}{2}$

Identify the phase shift.        $-\dfrac{C}{B} = -\dfrac{\pi}{4}$

Identify the period $\dfrac{2\pi}{B}$      $\dfrac{2\pi}{B} = \dfrac{2\pi}{4} = \dfrac{\pi}{2}$

STEP 3  Graph.

Draw a cosine function starting at $x = -\dfrac{\pi}{4}$ with period $\dfrac{\pi}{2}$ and amplitude 5.

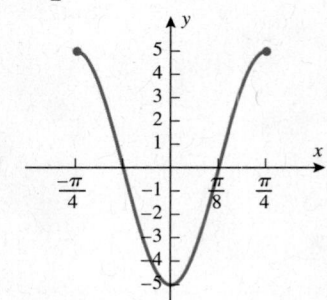

**Study Tip**

An alternative method for finding the period and phase shift is to first write the function in standard form.

$$y = 5\cos\left[4\left(x + \frac{\pi}{4}\right)\right]$$

$$B = 4$$

$$\text{Period} = \frac{2\pi}{B} = \frac{2\pi}{4} = \frac{\pi}{2}.$$

Phase shift $= \dfrac{\pi}{4}$ units to the left.

■ **Answer:**

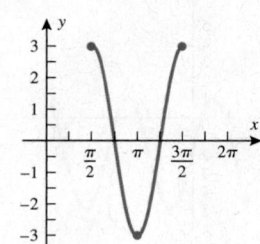

■ **YOUR TURN** Graph $y = 3\cos(2x - \pi)$ over one period.

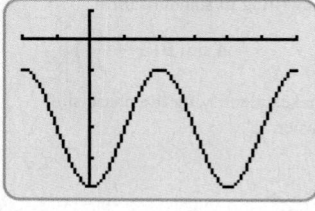

**EXAMPLE 9    Graphing Sinusoidal Functions**

Graph $y = -3 + 2\cos(2x - \pi)$.

**Solution:**

**STEP 1**  Find the amplitude.               $|A| = |2| = 2$

**STEP 2**  Find the phase shift and period.

Set $2x - \pi$ equal to 0 and $2\pi$.     $2x - \pi = 0$    to    $2x - \pi = 2\pi$

Solve for $x$.                 $x = \dfrac{\pi}{2}$    to        $x = \dfrac{\pi}{2} + \pi$

Identify phase shift and period.     $-\dfrac{C}{B} = \dfrac{\pi}{2}$

$\dfrac{2\pi}{B} = \pi$

**STEP 3**  Graph $y = 2\cos(2x - \pi)$ starting at $x = \dfrac{\pi}{2}$ over one period, $\pi$.

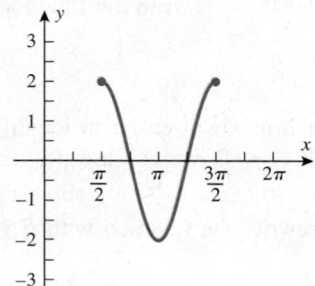

**STEP 4**  Extend the graph of $y = 2\cos(2x - \pi)$ over several periods.

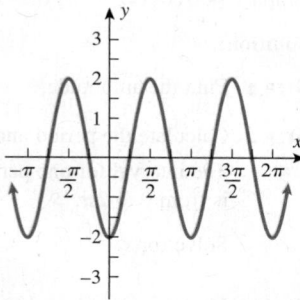

**STEP 5**  Shift the graph of $y = 2\cos(2x - \pi)$ down three units to arrive at the graph of $y = -3 + 2\cos(2x - \pi)$.

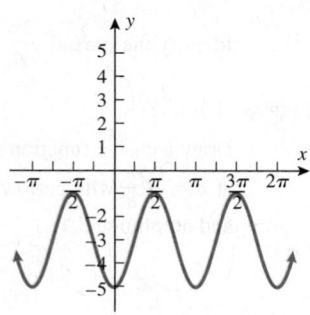

■ **Answer:**

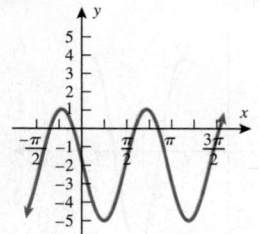

■ **YOUR TURN**  Graph $y = -2 + 3\sin(2x + \pi)$.

# Harmonic Motion

One of the most important applications of sinusoidal functions is in describing *harmonic motion*, which we define as the symmetric periodic movement of an object or quantity about a center (equilibrium) position or value. The oscillation of a pendulum is a form of harmonic motion. Other examples are the recoil of a spring balance scale when a weight is placed on the tray and the variation of current or voltage within an AC circuit.

There are three types of harmonic motion: **simple harmonic motion**, **damped harmonic motion**, and **resonance**.

## Simple Harmonic Motion

Simple harmonic motion is the kind of *unvarying* periodic motion that would occur in an ideal situation in which no resistive forces, such as friction, cause the amplitude of oscillation to decrease over time: the amplitude stays in exactly the same range in each period as time—the variable on the horizontal axis—increases. It will also occur if energy is being supplied at the correct rate to overcome resistive forces. Simple harmonic motion occurs, for example, in an AC electric circuit when a power source is consistently supplying energy. When you are swinging on a swing and "pumping" energy into the swing to keep it in motion at a constant period and amplitude, you are sustaining simple harmonic motion.

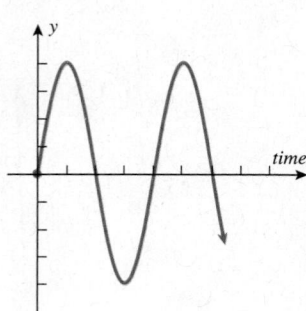

## Damped Harmonic Motion

In damped harmonic motion, the amplitude of the periodic motion decreases as time increases. If you are on a moving swing and stop "pumping" new energy into the swing, the swing will continue moving with a constant period, but the amplitude—the height to which the swing will rise—will diminish with each cycle as the swing is slowed down by friction with the air or between its own moving parts.

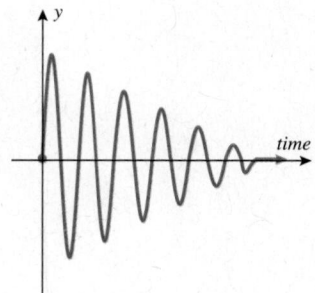

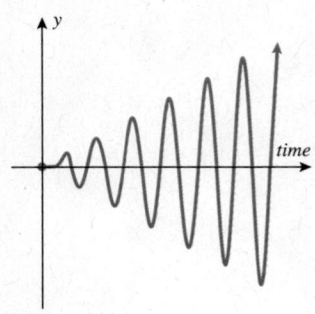

## Resonance

Resonance occurs when the amplitude of periodic motion increases as time increases. It is caused when the energy applied to an oscillating object or system is more than what is needed to oppose friction or other forces and sustain simple harmonic motion. Instead, the applied energy *increases* the amplitude of harmonic motion with each cycle. With resonance, eventually, the amplitude becomes unbounded and the result is disastrous. Bridges have collapsed because of resonance. On the previous page are pictures of the Tacoma Narrows Bridge (near Seattle, Washington) that collapsed due to high winds resulting in resonance. Military soldiers know that when they march across a bridge, they must break cadence to prevent resonance.

## Examples of Harmonic Motion

If we hang a weight from a spring, then while the resulting "system" is at rest we say it is in the equilibrium position.

If we then pull down on the weight and release it, the elasticity in the spring pulls the weight up and causes it to start oscillating up and down.

If we neglect friction and air resistance, we can imagine that the combination of the weight and the spring will oscillate indefinitely; the height of the weight with respect to the equilibrium position can be modeled by a simple sinusoidal function. This is an example of **simple harmonic motion**.

### SIMPLE HARMONIC MOTION

The position of a point oscillating around an equilibrium position at time $t$ is modeled by the sinusoidal function

$$y = A \sin(\omega t) \qquad \text{or} \qquad y = A \cos(\omega t)$$

Here $|A|$ is the amplitude and the period is $\dfrac{2\pi}{\omega}$, where $\omega > 0$.

*Note:* The symbol $\omega$ (Greek lowercase omega) represents the angular frequency.

**EXAMPLE 10    Simple Harmonic Motion**

Let the height of the seat of a swing be equal to zero when the swing is at rest. Assume that a child starts swinging until she reaches the highest she can swing and keeps her effort constant. Suppose the height $h(t)$ of the seat can be given by

$$h(t) = 8 \sin\left(\frac{\pi}{2}t\right)$$

where $t$ is time in seconds and $h$ is the height in feet. Note that positive $h$ indicates height reached swinging forward and negative $h$ indicates height reached swinging backward. Assume that $t = 0$ is when the child passes through the equilibrium position swinging forward.

**a.** Graph the height function $h(t)$ for $0 \le t \le 4$.

**b.** What is the maximum height above the resting level reached by the seat of the swing?

**c.** What is the period of the swinging child?

**Solution (a):**

Make a table with integer values of $t$.    $0 \le t \le 4$

| $t$ (SECONDS) | $y = h(t) = 8 \sin\left(\frac{\pi}{2}t\right)$ (FEET) | $(t,\ y)$ |
|:---:|:---:|:---:|
| 0 | $8 \sin 0 = 0$ | $(0, 0)$ |
| 1 | $8 \sin\left(\dfrac{\pi}{2}\right) = 8$ | $(1, 8)$ |
| 2 | $8 \sin \pi = 0$ | $(2, 0)$ |
| 3 | $8 \sin\left(\dfrac{3\pi}{2}\right) = -8$ | $(3, -8)$ |
| 4 | $8 \sin(2\pi) = 0$ | $(4, 0)$ |

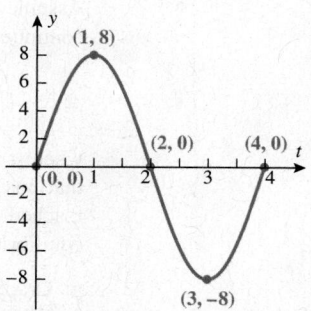

Labeling the time and height on the original diagram, we see that the maximum height is 8 feet and the period is 4 seconds.

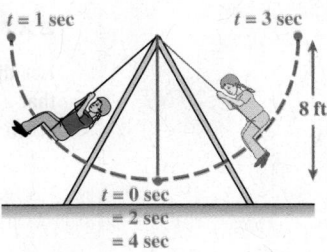

**Solutions (b) and (c):**

$$h(t) = 8 \sin\left(\frac{\pi}{2}t\right)$$

The maximum height above the equilibrium is the amplitude.

$$\boxed{A = 8 \text{ ft}}$$

The period is $\dfrac{2\pi}{\omega}$.

$$\boxed{p = \frac{2\pi}{\dfrac{\pi}{2}} = 4 \text{ sec}}$$

**Damped harmonic motion** can be modeled by a sinusoidal function whose amplitude decreases as time increases. If we again hang a weight from a spring so that it is suspended at rest and then pull down on the weight and release, the weight will oscillate about the equilibrium point. This time we will not neglect friction and air resistance: The weight will oscillate closer and closer to the equilibrium point over time until the weight eventually comes to rest at the equilibrium point. This is an example of damped harmonic motion.

The product of any decreasing function and the original periodic function will describe damped oscillatory motion. Here are two examples of functions that describe damped harmonic motion:

$$y = \frac{1}{t}\sin(\omega t) \qquad y = e^{-t}\cos(\omega t)$$

where $e^{-t}$ is a decreasing exponential function (exponential decay).

### EXAMPLE 11  Damped Harmonic Motion

Assume that the child in Example 10 decides to stop pumping and allows the swing to continue until she eventually comes to rest. Assume that

$$h(t) = \frac{8}{t}\cos\left(\frac{\pi}{2}t\right)$$

where $t$ is time in seconds and $h$ is the height in feet above the resting position. Note that positive $h$ indicates height reached swinging forward and negative $h$ indicates height reached swinging backward, assuming that $t = 1$ is when the child passes through the equilibrium position swinging backward and stops "pumping."

**a.** Graph the height function $h(t)$ for $1 \leq t \leq 8$.
**b.** What is the height above the resting level at 4 seconds? At 8 seconds? After 1 minute?

**Solution (a):**

Make a table with integer values of $t$.  $\qquad 1 \le t \le 8$

| $t$ (SECONDS) | $y = h(t) = \dfrac{8}{t}\cos\left(\dfrac{\pi}{2}t\right)$ (FEET) | $(t, y)$ |
|:---:|:---:|:---:|
| 1 | $\dfrac{8}{1}\cos\left(\dfrac{\pi}{2}\right) = 0$ | $(1, 0)$ |
| 2 | $\dfrac{8}{2}\cos\pi = -4$ | $(2, -4)$ |
| 3 | $\dfrac{8}{3}\cos\left(\dfrac{3\pi}{2}\right) = 0$ | $(3, 0)$ |
| 4 | $\dfrac{8}{4}\cos(2\pi) = 2$ | $(4, 2)$ |
| 5 | $\dfrac{8}{5}\cos\left(\dfrac{5\pi}{2}\right) = 0$ | $(5, 0)$ |
| 6 | $\dfrac{8}{6}\cos(3\pi) = -\dfrac{4}{3}$ | $\left(6, -\dfrac{4}{3}\right)$ |
| 7 | $\dfrac{8}{7}\cos\left(\dfrac{7\pi}{2}\right) = 0$ | $(7, 0)$ |
| 8 | $\dfrac{8}{8}\cos(4\pi) = 1$ | $(8, 1)$ |

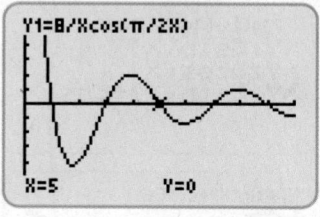
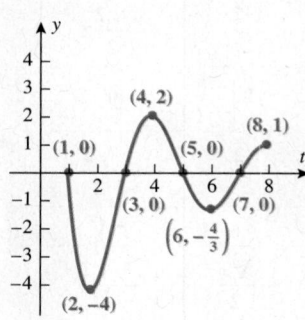

**Solution (b):**

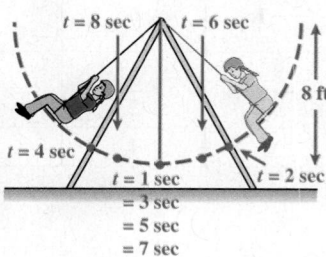

The height is 2 feet when $t$ is 4 seconds.  $\qquad \dfrac{8}{4}\cos(2\pi) = 2$

The height is 1 foot when $t$ is 8 seconds.  $\qquad \dfrac{8}{8}\cos(4\pi) = 1$

The height is 0.13 feet when $t$ is 1 minute (60 seconds).  $\qquad \dfrac{8}{60}\cos(30\pi) = 0.1333$

**Resonance** can be represented by the product of any increasing function and the original sinusoidal function. Here are two examples of functions that result in resonance as time increases:

$$y = t \cos(\omega t) \qquad y = e^t \sin(\omega t)$$

## Graphing Sums of Functions: Addition of Ordinates

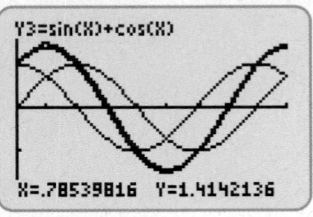
Since you have the ability to graph sinusoidal functions, let us now consider graphing sums of functions such as

$$y = x - \sin\left(\frac{\pi x}{2}\right) \qquad y = \sin x + \cos x \qquad y = 3 \sin x + \cos(2x)$$

The method for graphing these sums is called the **addition of ordinates**, because we add the corresponding $y$-values (ordinates). The following table illustrates the ordinates ($y$-values) of the two sinusoidal functions $\sin x$ and $\cos x$; adding the corresponding ordinates leads to the $y$-values of $y = \sin x + \cos x$.

| $x$ | $\sin x$ | $\cos x$ | $y = \sin x + \cos x$ |
|---|---|---|---|
| $0$ | $0$ | $1$ | $1$ |
| $\dfrac{\pi}{4}$ | $\dfrac{\sqrt{2}}{2}$ | $\dfrac{\sqrt{2}}{2}$ | $\sqrt{2}$ |
| $\dfrac{\pi}{2}$ | $1$ | $0$ | $1$ |
| $\dfrac{3\pi}{4}$ | $\dfrac{\sqrt{2}}{2}$ | $-\dfrac{\sqrt{2}}{2}$ | $0$ |
| $\pi$ | $0$ | $-1$ | $-1$ |
| $\dfrac{5\pi}{4}$ | $-\dfrac{\sqrt{2}}{2}$ | $-\dfrac{\sqrt{2}}{2}$ | $-\sqrt{2}$ |
| $\dfrac{3\pi}{2}$ | $-1$ | $0$ | $-1$ |
| $\dfrac{7\pi}{4}$ | $-\dfrac{\sqrt{2}}{2}$ | $\dfrac{\sqrt{2}}{2}$ | $0$ |
| $2\pi$ | $0$ | $1$ | $1$ |

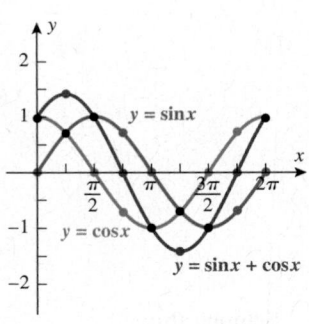

Using a graphing utility, we can graph $Y_1 = \sin X$, $Y_2 = \cos X$, and $Y_3 = Y_1 + Y_2$.

**EXAMPLE 12** **Graphing Sums of Functions**

Graph $y = x - \sin\left(\dfrac{\pi x}{2}\right)$ on the interval $0 \le x \le 4$.

**Solution:**

Let $y_1 = x$ and $y_2 = -\sin\left(\dfrac{\pi x}{2}\right)$.

State the amplitude and period
of the graph of $y_2$.

$$|A| = |-1| = 1,\, p = 4$$

Make a table of $x$- and
$y$-values of $y_1$, $y_2$, and
$y = y_1 + y_2$.

| $x$ | $y_1 = x$ | $y_2 = -\sin\left(\dfrac{\pi x}{2}\right)$ | $y = x + \left[-\sin\left(\dfrac{\pi x}{2}\right)\right]$ |
|---|---|---|---|
| 0 | 0 | 0 | 0 |
| 1 | 1 | −1 | 0 |
| 2 | 2 | 0 | 2 |
| 3 | 3 | 1 | 4 |
| 4 | 4 | 0 | 4 |

Graph $y_1 = x$, $y_2 = -\sin\left(\dfrac{\pi x}{2}\right)$,

and $y = x - \sin\left(\dfrac{\pi x}{2}\right)$.

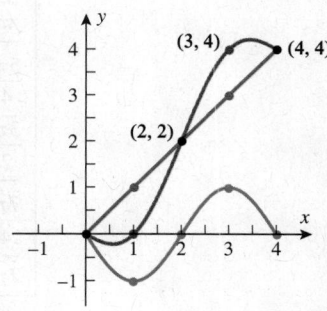

*Technology Tip*

To display the graphs of $x$,
$-\sin\left(\dfrac{\pi x}{2}\right)$, and $x - \sin\left(\dfrac{\pi x}{2}\right)$ in the
same $[0, 4]$ by $[-1, 5]$ viewing
window, enter $Y_1 = x$,
$Y_2 = -\sin\left(\dfrac{\pi x}{2}\right)$, and
$Y_3 = x - \sin\left(\dfrac{\pi x}{2}\right)$.

To graph $Y_3$ using a thicker line, use
the ◄ key to go to the left of $Y_3$,
press ENTER , and select the
thicker line.

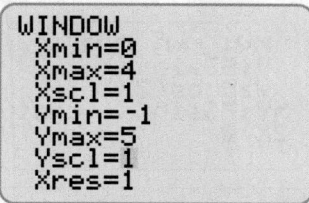

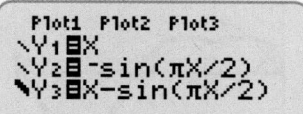

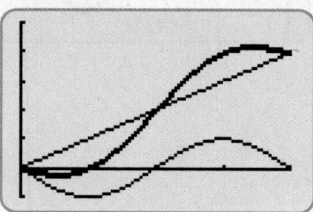

*Technology Tip*

To display the graphs of $3\sin x$, $\cos(2x)$, and $3\sin x + \cos(2x)$ in the same $[0, 2\pi]$ by $[-5, 5]$ viewing window, enter $Y_1 = 3\sin x$, $Y_2 = \cos(2x)$, and $Y_3 = 3\sin x + \cos(2x)$.

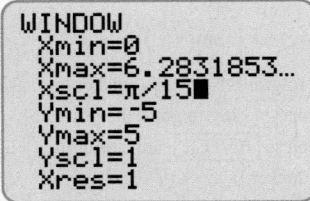

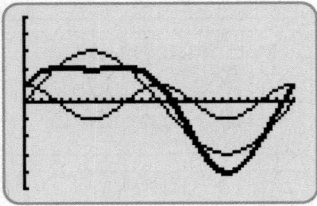

**EXAMPLE 13** **Graphing Sums of Sine and Cosine Functions**

Graph $y = 3\sin x + \cos(2x)$ on the interval $0 \le x \le 2\pi$.

**Solution:**

Let $y_1 = 3\sin x$, and state the amplitude and period of its graph.

$$|A| = 3, p = 2\pi$$

Let $y_2 = \cos(2x)$, and state the amplitude and period of its graph.

$$|A| = 1, p = \pi$$

Make a table of $x$- and $y$-values of $y_1$, $y_2$, and $y = y_1 + y_2$.

| $x$ | $y_1 = 3\sin x$ | $y_2 = \cos(2x)$ | $y = 3\sin x + \cos(2x)$ |
|---|---|---|---|
| $0$ | $0$ | $1$ | $1$ |
| $\dfrac{\pi}{4}$ | $\dfrac{3\sqrt{2}}{2}$ | $0$ | $\dfrac{3\sqrt{2}}{2}$ |
| $\dfrac{\pi}{2}$ | $3$ | $-1$ | $2$ |
| $\dfrac{3\pi}{4}$ | $\dfrac{3\sqrt{2}}{2}$ | $0$ | $\dfrac{3\sqrt{2}}{2}$ |
| $\pi$ | $0$ | $1$ | $1$ |
| $\dfrac{5\pi}{4}$ | $-\dfrac{3\sqrt{2}}{2}$ | $0$ | $-\dfrac{3\sqrt{2}}{2}$ |
| $\dfrac{3\pi}{2}$ | $-3$ | $-1$ | $-4$ |
| $\dfrac{7\pi}{4}$ | $-\dfrac{3\sqrt{2}}{2}$ | $0$ | $-\dfrac{3\sqrt{2}}{2}$ |
| $2\pi$ | $0$ | $1$ | $1$ |

Graph $y_1 = 3\sin x$, $y_2 = \cos(2x)$, and $y = 3\sin x + \cos(2x)$.

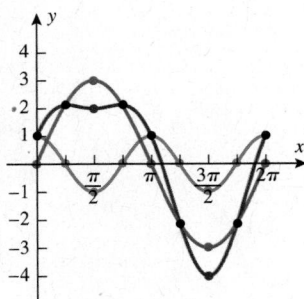

**EXAMPLE 14**   **Graphing Sums of Cosine Functions**

Graph $y = \cos\left(\dfrac{x}{2}\right) - \cos x$ on the interval $0 \leq x \leq 4\pi$.

**Solution:**

Let $y_1 = \cos\left(\dfrac{x}{2}\right)$ and
state the amplitude
and period of its graph.

$$|A| = 1, p = 4\pi$$

Let $y_2 = -\cos x$ and
state the amplitude
and period of its graph.

$$|A| = |-1| = 1, p = 2\pi$$

Make a table of $x$- and
$y$-values of $y_1$, $y_2$, and
$y = y_1 + y_2$.

| $x$ | $y_1 = \cos\left(\dfrac{x}{2}\right)$ | $y_2 = -\cos x$ | $y = \cos\left(\dfrac{x}{2}\right) + (-\cos x)$ |
|---|---|---|---|
| $0$ | $1$ | $-1$ | $0$ |
| $\dfrac{\pi}{2}$ | $\dfrac{\sqrt{2}}{2}$ | $0$ | $\dfrac{\sqrt{2}}{2}$ |
| $\pi$ | $0$ | $1$ | $1$ |
| $\dfrac{3\pi}{2}$ | $-\dfrac{\sqrt{2}}{2}$ | $0$ | $-\dfrac{\sqrt{2}}{2}$ |
| $2\pi$ | $-1$ | $-1$ | $-2$ |
| $\dfrac{5\pi}{2}$ | $-\dfrac{\sqrt{2}}{2}$ | $0$ | $-\dfrac{\sqrt{2}}{2}$ |
| $3\pi$ | $0$ | $1$ | $1$ |
| $\dfrac{7\pi}{2}$ | $\dfrac{\sqrt{2}}{2}$ | $0$ | $\dfrac{\sqrt{2}}{2}$ |
| $4\pi$ | $1$ | $-1$ | $0$ |

Graph $y_1 = \cos\left(\dfrac{x}{2}\right)$, $y_2 = -\cos x$,

and $y = \cos\left(\dfrac{x}{2}\right) - \cos x$.

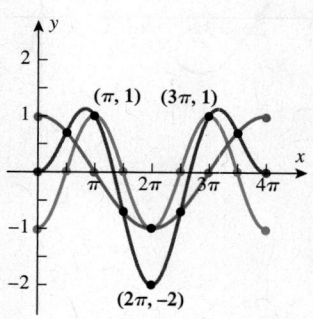

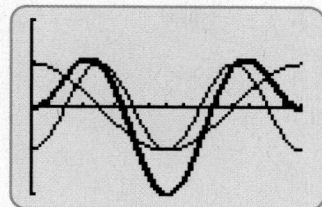

**SECTION**

**5.2** SUMMARY

The sine function is an odd function, and its graph is symmetric about the origin. The cosine function is an even function, and its graph is symmetric about the $y$-axis. Graphs of the form $y = A\sin(Bx)$ and $y = A\cos(Bx)$ have amplitude $|A|$ and period $\dfrac{2\pi}{B}$.

To graph sinusoidal functions, point-plotting can be used. A more efficient way is to first determine the amplitude and period. Divide the period into four equal parts and choose the values of the division points starting at 0 for $x$. Make a table of those four points and graph them (this is the graph of one period) by labeling the four coordinates and drawing a smooth sinusoidal curve. Extend the graph to the left and right.

To find an equation of a sinusoidal function given its graph, start by first finding the amplitude (half the distance between the maximum and minimum values) so you can find $A$. Then determine the period so you can find $B$. Graphs of the form $y = A\sin(Bx + C) + D$ and $y = A\cos(Bx + C) + D$ can be graphed using graph-shifting techniques.

Harmonic motion is one of the primary applications of sinusoidal functions. To graph combinations of trigonometric functions, add the corresponding $y$-values of the individual functions.

**SECTION**

**5.2** EXERCISES

■ SKILLS

**In Exercises 1–10, match the function with its graph (a–j).**

**1.** $y = -\sin x$     **2.** $y = \sin x$     **3.** $y = \cos x$     **4.** $y = -\cos x$     **5.** $y = 2\sin x$

**6.** $y = 2\cos x$     **7.** $y = \sin\left(\frac{1}{2}x\right)$     **8.** $y = \cos\left(\frac{1}{2}x\right)$     **9.** $y = -2\cos\left(\frac{1}{2}x\right)$     **10.** $y = -2\sin\left(\frac{1}{2}x\right)$

**a.**

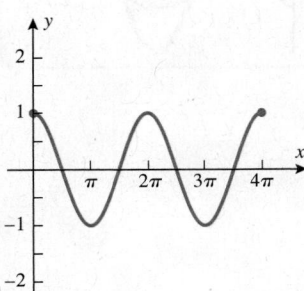

**b.**

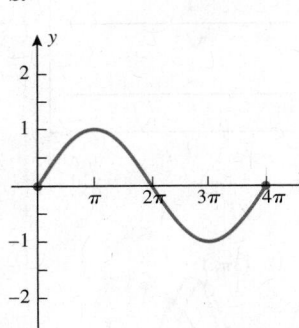

**c.**

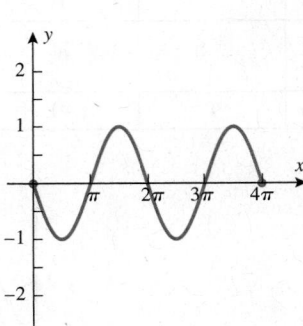

**d.**

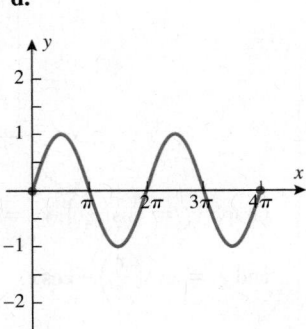

**e.**

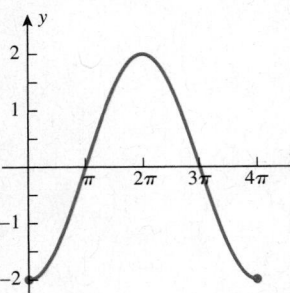

**f.**

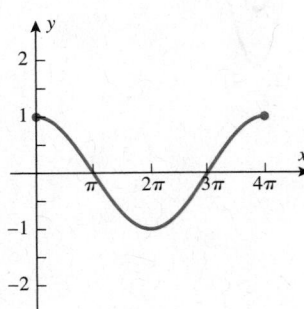

**g.**

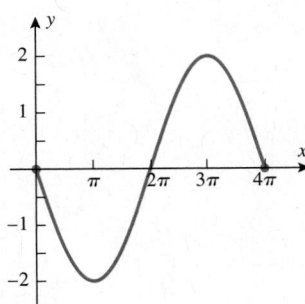

**h.**

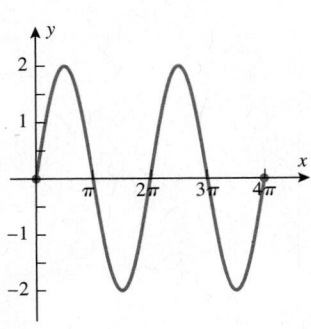

**i.**

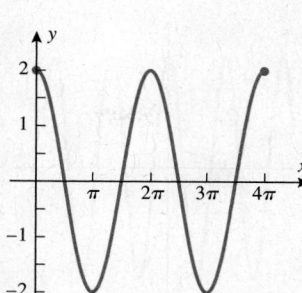

**j.**

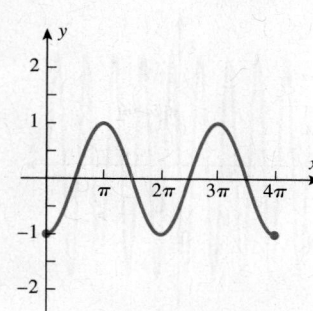

**In Exercises 11–20, state the amplitude and period of each function.**

**11.** $y = \dfrac{3}{2}\cos(3x)$     **12.** $y = \dfrac{2}{3}\sin(4x)$     **13.** $y = -\sin(5x)$     **14.** $y = -\cos(7x)$     **15.** $y = \dfrac{2}{3}\cos\left(\dfrac{3}{2}x\right)$

**16.** $y = \dfrac{3}{2}\sin\left(\dfrac{2}{3}x\right)$     **17.** $y = -3\cos(\pi x)$     **18.** $y = -2\sin(\pi x)$     **19.** $y = 5\sin\left(\dfrac{\pi}{3}x\right)$     **20.** $y = 4\cos\left(\dfrac{\pi}{4}x\right)$

**In Exercises 21–32, graph the given function over one period.**

**21.** $y = 8\cos x$     **22.** $y = 7\sin x$     **23.** $y = \sin(4x)$     **24.** $y = \cos(3x)$

**25.** $y = -3\cos\left(\dfrac{1}{2}x\right)$     **26.** $y = -2\sin\left(\dfrac{1}{4}x\right)$     **27.** $y = -3\sin(\pi x)$     **28.** $y = -2\cos(\pi x)$

**29.** $y = 5\cos(2\pi x)$     **30.** $y = 4\sin(2\pi x)$     **31.** $y = -3\sin\left(\dfrac{\pi}{4}x\right)$     **32.** $y = -4\sin\left(\dfrac{\pi}{2}x\right)$

**In Exercises 33–40, graph the given function over the interval $[-2p, 2p]$, where $p$ is the period of the function.**

**33.** $y = -4\cos\left(\dfrac{1}{2}x\right)$     **34.** $y = -5\sin\left(\dfrac{1}{2}x\right)$     **35.** $y = -\sin(6x)$     **36.** $y = -\cos(4x)$

**37.** $y = 3\cos\left(\dfrac{\pi}{4}x\right)$     **38.** $y = 4\sin\left(\dfrac{\pi}{4}x\right)$     **39.** $y = \sin(4\pi x)$     **40.** $y = \cos(6\pi x)$

**In Exercises 41–48, find the equation for each graph.**

**41.**

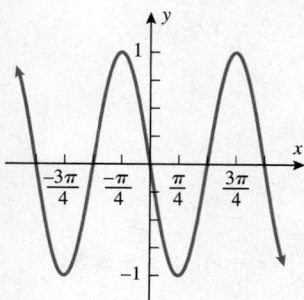

**42.**

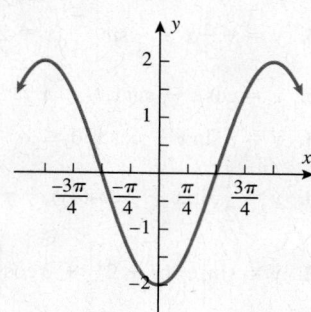

**43.**

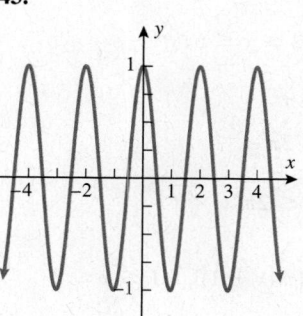

**44.**

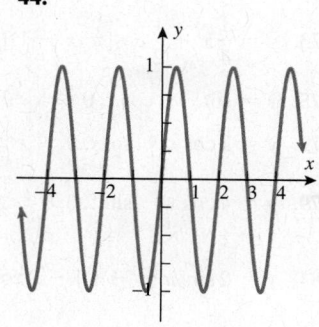

**45.** 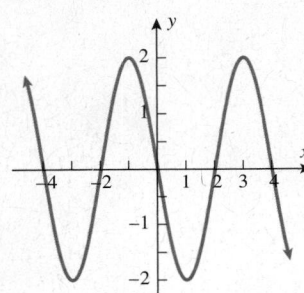  **46.** 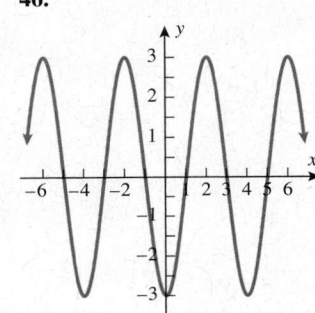  **47.** 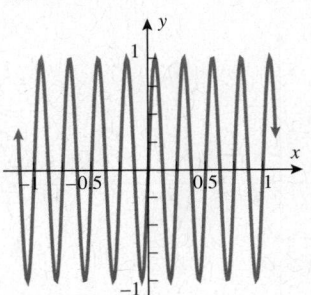  **48.**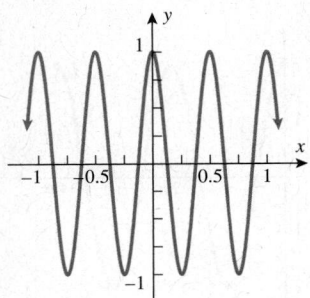

**In Exercises 49–60, state the amplitude, period, and phase shift (including direction) of the given function and graph.**

**49.** $y = 2\sin(\pi x - 1)$

**50.** $y = 4\cos(x + \pi)$

**51.** $y = -5\cos(3x + 2)$

**52.** $y = -7\sin(4x - 3)$

**53.** $y = 6\sin[-\pi(x + 2)]$

**54.** $y = 3\sin\left[-\dfrac{\pi}{2}(x - 1)\right]$

**55.** $y = 3\sin(2x + \pi)$

**56.** $y = -4\cos(2x - \pi)$

**57.** $y = -\dfrac{1}{4}\cos\left(\dfrac{1}{4}x - \dfrac{\pi}{2}\right)$

**58.** $y = \dfrac{1}{2}\sin\left(\dfrac{1}{3}x + \pi\right)$

**59.** $y = 2\cos\left[\dfrac{\pi}{2}(x - 4)\right]$

**60.** $y = -5\sin[-\pi(x + 1)]$

**In Exercises 61–66, sketch the graph of the function over the indicated interval.**

**61.** $y = \dfrac{1}{2} + \dfrac{3}{2}\cos(2x + \pi),\ \left[-\dfrac{3\pi}{2}, \dfrac{3\pi}{2}\right]$

**62.** $y = \dfrac{1}{3} + \dfrac{2}{3}\sin(2x - \pi),\ \left[-\dfrac{3\pi}{2}, \dfrac{3\pi}{2}\right]$

**63.** $y = \dfrac{1}{2} - \dfrac{1}{2}\sin\left(\dfrac{1}{2}x - \dfrac{\pi}{4}\right),\ \left[-\dfrac{7\pi}{2}, \dfrac{9\pi}{2}\right]$

**64.** $y = -\dfrac{1}{2} + \dfrac{1}{2}\cos\left(\dfrac{1}{2}x + \dfrac{\pi}{4}\right),\ \left[-\dfrac{9\pi}{2}, \dfrac{7\pi}{2}\right]$

**65.** $y = -3 + 4\sin[\pi(x - 2)],\ [0, 4]$

**66.** $y = 4 - 3\cos[\pi(x + 1)],\ [-1, 3]$

**In Exercises 67–94, add the ordinates of the individual functions to graph each summed function on the indicated interval.**

**67.** $y = 2x - \cos(\pi x),\ 0 \le x \le 4$

**68.** $y = 3x - 2\cos(\pi x),\ 0 \le x \le 4$

**69.** $y = \dfrac{1}{3}x + 2\cos(2x),\ 0 \le x \le 2\pi$

**70.** $y = \dfrac{1}{4}x + 3\cos\left(\dfrac{x}{2}\right),\ 0 \le x \le 4\pi$

**71.** $y = x - \cos\left(\dfrac{3\pi}{2}x\right),\ 0 \le x \le 6$

**72.** $y = -2x + 2\sin\left(\dfrac{\pi}{2}x\right),\ -2 \le x \le 2$

**73.** $y = \dfrac{1}{4}x - \dfrac{1}{2}\cos[\pi(x - 1)],\ 2 \le x \le 6$

**74.** $y = -\dfrac{1}{3}x + \dfrac{1}{3}\sin\left[\dfrac{\pi}{6}(x + 2)\right],\ -2 \le x \le 10$

**75.** $y = \sin x - \cos x,\ 0 \le x \le 2\pi$

**76.** $y = \cos x - \sin x,\ 0 \le x \le 2\pi$

**77.** $y = 3\cos x + \sin x,\ 0 \le x \le 2\pi$

**78.** $y = 3\sin x - \cos x,\ 0 \le x \le 2\pi$

**79.** $y = 4\cos x - \sin(2x),\ 0 \le x \le 2\pi$

**80.** $y = \dfrac{1}{2}\sin x + 2\cos(4x),\ -\pi \le x \le \pi$

**81.** $y = 2\sin[\pi(x - 1)] - 2\cos[\pi(x + 1)],\ -1 \le x \le 2$

**82.** $y = \sin\left[\dfrac{\pi}{4}(x + 2)\right] + 3\cos\left[\dfrac{3\pi}{3}(x - 1)\right],\ 1 \le x \le 5$

**83.** $y = \cos\left(\dfrac{x}{2}\right) + \cos(2x),\ 0 \le x \le 4\pi$

**84.** $y = \sin(2x) + \sin(3x),\ -\pi \le x \le \pi$

**85.** $y = \sin\left(\dfrac{x}{2}\right) + \sin(2x), 0 \le x \le 4\pi$

**86.** $y = -\sin\left(\dfrac{\pi}{4}x\right) - 3\sin\left(\dfrac{5\pi}{4}x\right), 0 \le x \le 4$

**87.** $y = -\dfrac{1}{3}\sin\left(\dfrac{\pi}{6}x\right) + \dfrac{2}{3}\sin\left(\dfrac{5\pi}{6}x\right), 0 \le x \le 3$

**88.** $y = 8\cos x - 6\cos\left(\dfrac{1}{2}x\right), -2\pi \le x \le 2\pi$

**89.** $y = -\dfrac{1}{4}\cos\left(\dfrac{\pi}{6}x\right) - \dfrac{1}{2}\cos\left(\dfrac{\pi}{3}x\right), 0 \le x \le 12$

**90.** $y = 2\cos\left(\dfrac{3}{2}x\right) - \cos\left(\dfrac{1}{2}x\right), -2\pi \le x \le 2\pi$

**91.** $y = 2\sin\left(\dfrac{x}{2}\right) - \cos(2x), 0 \le x \le 4\pi$

**92.** $y = 2\cos\left(\dfrac{x}{2}\right) + \sin(2x), 0 \le x \le 4\pi$

**93.** $y = 2\sin[\pi(x-1)] + 3\sin\left[2\pi\left(x + \dfrac{1}{2}\right)\right], -2 \le x \le 2$

**94.** $y = -\dfrac{1}{2}\cos\left(x + \dfrac{\pi}{3}\right) - 2\cos\left(x - \dfrac{\pi}{6}\right), -\pi \le x \le \pi$

## ■ APPLICATIONS

**For Exercises 95 and 96, refer to the following:**

An analysis of demand $d$ for widgets manufactured by WidgetsRUs (measured in thousands of units per week) indicates that demand can be modeled by the graph below, where $t$ is time in months since January 2010 (note that $t = 0$ corresponds to January 2010).

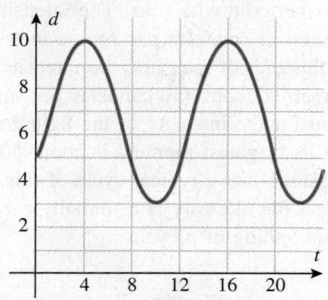

**95. Business.** Find the amplitude of the graph.

**96. Business.** Find the period of the graph.

**For Exercises 97 and 98, refer to the following:**

Researchers have been monitoring oxygen levels (milligrams per liter) in the water of a lake and have found that the oxygen levels fluctuate with an eight-week period. The following tables illustrate data from eight weeks.

**97. Environment.** Find the amplitude of the oxygen level fluctuations.

| Week: $t$ | 0 (initial measurement) | 1 | 2 | 3 | 4 | 5 | 6 | 7 | 8 |
|---|---|---|---|---|---|---|---|---|---|
| Oxygen levels: mg/L | 7 | | 7.7 | 8 | 7.7 | 7 | 6.3 | 6 | 6.3 | 7 |

**98. Environment.** Find the amplitude of the oxygen level fluctuations.

| Week: $t$ | 0 (initial measurement) | 1 | 2 | 3 | 4 | 5 | 6 | 7 | 8 |
|---|---|---|---|---|---|---|---|---|---|
| Oxygen levels: mg/L | 7 | | 8.4 | 9 | 8.4 | 7 | 5.6 | 5 | 5.6 | 7 |

**For Exercises 99–102, refer to the following:**

A weight hanging on a spring will oscillate up and down about its equilibrium position after it is pulled down and released.

This is an example of simple harmonic motion. This motion would continue forever if there were not any friction or air resistance. Simple harmonic motion can be described with the function $y = A\cos\left(t\sqrt{\dfrac{k}{m}}\right)$, where $|A|$ is the amplitude, $t$ is the time in seconds, $m$ is the mass of the weight, and $k$ is a constant particular to the spring.

**99. Simple Harmonic Motion.** If the height of the spring is measured in centimeters and the mass in grams, then what are the amplitude and mass if $y = 4\cos\left(\dfrac{t\sqrt{k}}{2}\right)$?

**100. Simple Harmonic Motion.** If a spring is measured in centimeters and the mass in grams, then what are the amplitude and mass if $y = 3\cos\left(3t\sqrt{k}\right)$?

**101. Frequency of Oscillations.** The frequency of the oscillations in cycles per second is determined by $f = \dfrac{1}{p}$, where $p$ is the period. What is the frequency for the oscillation modeled by $y = 3\cos\left(\dfrac{t}{2}\right)$?

**102. Frequency of Oscillations.** The frequency of the oscillations $f$ is given by $f = \dfrac{1}{p}$, where $p$ is the period. What is the frequency of oscillation modeled by $y = 3.5\cos(3t)$?

**103. Sound Waves.** A pure tone created by a vibrating tuning fork shows up as a sine wave on an oscilloscope's screen. A tuning fork vibrating at 256 hertz (Hz) gives the tone middle C and can have the equation $y = 0.005\sin[(2\pi)(256t)]$, where the amplitude is in centimeters (cm) and the time $t$ in seconds. What are the amplitude and frequency of the wave where the frequency is $\dfrac{1}{p}$ in cycles per second?

*Note:* 1 hertz = 1 cycle per second.

**104. Sound Waves.** A pure tone created by a vibrating tuning fork shows up as a sine wave on an oscilloscope's screen. A tuning fork vibrating at 288 hertz gives the tone D and can have the equation $y = 0.005\sin[(2\pi)(288t)]$, where the amplitude is in centimeters (cm) and the time $t$ in seconds. What are the amplitude and frequency of the wave where the frequency is $\dfrac{1}{p}$ in cycles per second?

**105. Sound Waves.** If a sound wave is represented by $y = 0.008\sin(750\pi t)$ cm, what are its amplitude and frequency? See Exercise 103.

**106. Sound Waves.** If a sound wave is represented by $y = 0.006\cos(1000\pi t)$ cm, what are its amplitude and frequency? See Exercise 103.

**For Exercises 107–110, refer to the following:**

When an airplane flies faster than the speed of sound, the sound waves that are formed take on a cone shape, and where the cone hits the ground, a sonic boom is heard. If $\theta$ is the angle of the vertex of the cone, then $\sin\left(\dfrac{\theta}{2}\right) = \dfrac{330\,\text{m/sec}}{V} = \dfrac{1}{M}$, where $V$ is the speed of the plane and $M$ is the Mach number.

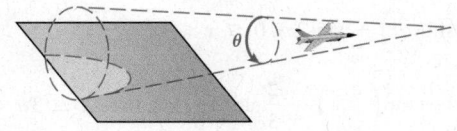

**107. Sonic Booms.** What is the speed of the plane if the plane is flying at Mach 2?

**108. Sonic Booms.** What is the Mach number if the plane is flying at 990 meters per second?

**109. Sonic Booms.** What is the speed of the plane if the cone angle is 60°?

**110. Sonic Booms.** What is the speed of the plane if the cone angle is 30°?

**For Exercises 111 and 112, refer to the following:**

With the advent of summer come fireflies. They are intriguing because they emit a flashing luminescence that beckons their mate to them. It is known that the speed and intensity of the flashing are related to the temperature—the higher the temperature, the quicker and more intense the flashing becomes. If you ever watch a single firefly, you will see that the intensity of the flashing is periodic with time. The intensity of light emitted is measured in *candelas per square meter* (of firefly). To give an idea of this unit of measure, the intensity of a picture on a typical TV screen is about 450 candelas per square meter. The measurement for the intensity of the light emitted by a typical firefly at its brightest moment is about 50 candelas per square meter. Assume that a typical cycle of this flashing is 4 seconds and that the intensity is essentially zero candelas at the beginning and ending of a cycle.

**111. Bioluminescence in Fireflies.** Find an equation that describes this flashing. What is the intensity of the flashing at 4 minutes?

**112. Bioluminescence in Fireflies.** Graph the equation from Exercise 111 for a period of 30 seconds.

# ■ CATCH THE MISTAKE

**In Exercises 113 and 114, explain the mistake that is made.**

**113.** Graph the function $y = -2\cos x$.

**Solution:**

Find the amplitude. $\qquad\qquad |A| = |-2| = 2$

The graph of
$y = -2\cos x$ is
similar to the graph
of $y = \cos x$ with
amplitude 2.

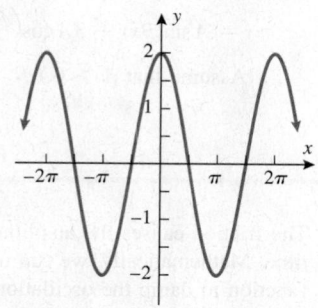

This is incorrect. What mistake was made?

**114.** Graph the function $y = -\sin(2x)$.

**Solution:**

Make a table with values.

| $x$ | $y = -\sin(2x)$ | $(x, y)$ |
|---|---|---|
| 0 | $y = -\sin 0 = 0$ | $(0, 0)$ |
| $\dfrac{\pi}{2}$ | $y = -\sin \pi = 0$ | $(0, 0)$ |
| $\pi$ | $y = -\sin(2\pi) = 0$ | $(0, 0)$ |
| $\dfrac{3\pi}{2}$ | $y = -\sin(3\pi) = 0$ | $(0, 0)$ |
| $2\pi$ | $y = -\sin(4\pi) = 0$ | $(0, 0)$ |

Graph the function
by plotting these
points and connecting
them with a
sinusoidal curve.

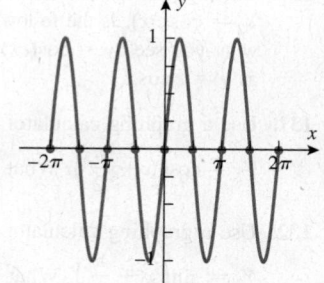

This is incorrect. What mistake was made?

# ■ CONCEPTUAL

**In Exercises 115–118, determine whether each statement is true or false. (*A* and *B* are positive real numbers.)**

**115.** The graph of $y = -A\cos(Bx)$ is the graph of
$y = A\cos(Bx)$ reflected about the $x$-axis.

**116.** The graph of $y = A\sin(-Bx)$ is the graph of
$y = A\sin(Bx)$ reflected about the $x$-axis.

**117.** The graph of $y = -A\cos(-Bx)$ is the graph of
$y = A\cos(Bx)$.

**118.** The graph of $y = -A\sin(-Bx)$ is the graph of
$y = A\sin(Bx)$.

**In Exercises 119–122, *A* and *B* are positive real numbers.**

**119.** Find the $y$-intercept of the function $y = A\cos(Bx)$.

**120.** Find the $y$-intercept of the function $y = A\sin(Bx)$.

**121.** Find the $x$-intercepts of the function $y = A\sin(Bx)$.

**122.** Find the $x$-intercepts of the function $y = A\cos(Bx)$.

■ **CHALLENGE**

**123.** Find the $y$-intercept of $y = -A \sin\left(Bx + \dfrac{\pi}{6}\right)$.

**124.** Find the $y$-intercept of $y = A \cos(Bx - \pi) + C$.

**125.** Find the $x$-intercept(s) of $y = A \sin(Bx) + A$.

**126.** Find an expression involving $C$ and $A$ that describes the values of $C$ for which the graph of $y = A \cos(Bx) + C$ does not cross the $x$-axis. (Assume that $A > 0$.)

**127.** What is the range of $y = 2A \sin(Bx + C) - \dfrac{A}{2}$?

**128.** Can the $y$-coordinate of a point on the graph of
$$y = A \sin(Bx) + 3A \cos\left(\dfrac{B}{2}x\right) \text{ exceed } 4A? \text{ Explain.}$$
(Assume that $A > 0$.)

■ **TECHNOLOGY**

**129.** Use a graphing calculator to graph $Y_1 = 5 \sin x$ and $Y_2 = \sin(5x)$. Is the following statement true based on what you see? $y = \sin(cx)$ has the same graph as $y = c \sin x$.

**130.** Use a graphing calculator to graph $Y_1 = 3 \cos x$ and $Y_2 = \cos(3x)$. Is the following statement true based on what you see? $y = \cos(cx)$ has the same graph as $y = c \cos x$.

**131.** Use a graphing calculator to graph $Y_1 = \sin x$ and $Y_2 = \cos\left(x - \dfrac{\pi}{2}\right)$. What do you notice?

**132.** Use a graphing calculator to graph $Y_1 = \cos x$ and $Y_2 = \sin\left(x + \dfrac{\pi}{2}\right)$. What do you notice?

**133.** Use a graphing calculator to graph $Y_1 = \cos x$ and $Y_2 = \cos(x + c)$, where

    **a.** $c = \dfrac{\pi}{3}$, and explain the relationship between $Y_2$ and $Y_1$.

    **b.** $c = -\dfrac{\pi}{3}$, and explain the relationship between $Y_2$ and $Y_1$.

**134.** Use a graphing calculator to graph $Y_1 = \sin x$ and $Y_2 = \sin(x + c)$, where

    **a.** $c = \dfrac{\pi}{3}$, and explain the relationship between $Y_2$ and $Y_1$.

    **b.** $c = -\dfrac{\pi}{3}$, and explain the relationship between $Y_2$ and $Y_1$.

**For Exercises 135 and 136, refer to the following:**

*Damped oscillatory motion*, or *damped oscillation*, occurs when things in oscillatory motion experience friction or resistance.

The friction causes the amplitude to decrease as a function of time. Mathematically, we can use a negative exponential function to damp the oscillations in the form of

$$f(t) = e^{-t} \sin t$$

**135. Damped Oscillation.** Graph the functions $Y_1 = e^{-t}$, $Y_2 = \sin t$, and $Y_3 = e^{-t} \sin t$ in the same viewing window (let $t$ range from 0 to $2\pi$). What happens as $t$ increases?

**136. Damped Oscillation.** Graph $Y_1 = e^{-t} \sin t$, $Y_2 = e^{-2t} \sin t$, and $Y_3 = e^{-4t} \sin t$ in the same viewing window. What happens to $Y = e^{-kt} \sin t$ as $k$ increases?

**137.** Use a graphing calculator to graph $Y_1 = \sin x$ and $Y_2 = \sin x + c$, where

    **a.** $c = 1$, and explain the relationship between $Y_2$ and $Y_1$.

    **b.** $c = -1$, and explain the relationship between $Y_2$ and $Y_1$.

**138.** Use a graphing calculator to graph $Y_1 = \cos x$ and $Y_2 = \cos x + c$, where

    **a.** $c = \dfrac{1}{2}$, and explain the relationship between $Y_2$ and $Y_1$.

    **b.** $c = -\dfrac{1}{2}$, and explain the relationship between $Y_2$ and $Y_1$.

**139.** What is the amplitude of the function $y = 3 \cos x + 4 \sin x$? Use a graphing calculator to graph $Y_1 = 3 \cos x$, $Y_2 = 4 \sin x$, and $Y_3 = 3 \cos x + 4 \sin x$ in the same viewing window.

**140.** What is the amplitude of the function $y = \sqrt{3} \cos x - \sin x$? Use a graphing calculator to graph $Y_1 = \sqrt{3} \cos x$, $Y_2 = \sin x$, and $Y_3 = \sqrt{3} \cos x - \sin x$ in the same viewing window.

## ▪ PREVIEW TO CALCULUS

In calculus, the definite integral $\int_a^b f(x)\,dx$ is used to find the area below the graph of $f$, above the x-axis, between $x = a$ and $x = b$. For example, $\int_0^2 x\,dx = 2$, as you can see in the following figure:

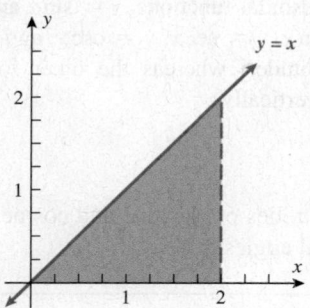

The Fundamental Theorem of Calculus establishes that the definite integral $\int_a^b f(x)\,dx$ equals $F(b) - F(a)$, where $F$ is any antiderivative of a continuous function $f$.

In Exercises 141–144, first shade the area corresponding to the definite integral and then use the information below to find the exact value of the area.

| FUNCTION | $\sin x$ | $\cos x$ |
|---|---|---|
| ANTIDERIVATIVE | $-\cos x$ | $\sin x$ |

**141.** $\displaystyle\int_0^\pi \sin x\,dx$

**142.** $\displaystyle\int_{-\pi/2}^{\pi/2} \cos x\,dx$

**143.** $\displaystyle\int_0^{\pi/2} \cos x\,dx$

**144.** $\displaystyle\int_0^{\pi/2} \sin x\,dx$

---

## SECTION 5.3 GRAPHS OF OTHER TRIGONOMETRIC FUNCTIONS

### SKILLS OBJECTIVES

- Determine the domain and range of the tangent, cotangent, secant, and cosecant functions.
- Graph basic tangent, cotangent, secant, and cosecant functions.
- Determine the period of tangent, cotangent, secant, and cosecant functions.
- Graph translated tangent, cotangent, secant, and cosecant functions.

### CONCEPTUAL OBJECTIVES

- Relate domain restrictions to vertical asymptotes.
- Understand the pattern that vertical asymptotes follow.
- Understand the relationships between the graphs of the cosine and secant functions and the sine and cosecant functions.

## Graphing the Tangent, Cotangent, Secant, and Cosecant Functions

Section 5.2 focused on graphing sinusoidal functions (sine and cosine). We now turn our attention to graphing the other trigonometric functions: tangent, cotangent, secant, and cosecant. We know the graphs of the sine and cosine functions, and we can get the graphs of the other trigonometric functions from the sinusoidal functions. Recall the reciprocal and quotient identities:

$$\tan x = \frac{\sin x}{\cos x} \qquad \cot x = \frac{\cos x}{\sin x} \qquad \sec x = \frac{1}{\cos x} \qquad \csc x = \frac{1}{\sin x}$$

Recall that in graphing rational functions, a *vertical asymptote* is found by setting the denominator of the rational function equal to zero (as long as the numerator and denominator have no common factors). As you will see in this section, tangent and secant functions have graphs with vertical asymptotes at the $x$-values where cosine is equal to zero, and cotangent and cosecant functions have graphs with vertical asymptotes at the $x$-values where sine is equal to zero.

One important difference between the sinusoidal functions, $y = \sin x$ and $y = \cos x$, and the other four trigonometric functions ($y = \tan x$, $y = \sec x$, $y = \csc x$, and $y = \cot x$) is that the sinusoidal functions have defined amplitudes, whereas the other four trigonometric functions do not (since they are unbounded vertically).

## The Tangent Function

Since the tangent function is a quotient that relies on the sine and cosine functions, let us start with a table of values for the quadrantal angles.

| $x$ | $\sin x$ | $\cos x$ | $\tan x = \dfrac{\sin x}{\cos x}$ | $(x, y)$ OR ASYMPTOTE |
|---|---|---|---|---|
| $0$ | $0$ | $1$ | $0$ | $(0, 0)$ |
| $\dfrac{\pi}{2}$ | $1$ | $0$ | undefined | vertical asymptote: $x = \dfrac{\pi}{2}$ |
| $\pi$ | $0$ | $-1$ | $0$ | $(\pi, 0)$ |
| $\dfrac{3\pi}{2}$ | $-1$ | $0$ | undefined | vertical asymptote: $x = \dfrac{3\pi}{2}$ |
| $2\pi$ | $0$ | $1$ | $0$ | $(2\pi, 0)$ |

Notice that the $x$-intercepts correspond to integer multiples of $\pi$ and vertical asymptotes correspond to odd integer multiples of $\dfrac{\pi}{2}$.

We know that the graph of the tangent function is undefined at the odd integer multiples of $\dfrac{\pi}{2}$, so its graph cannot cross the vertical asymptotes. The question is, what happens between the asymptotes? We know the $x$-intercepts, so let us now make a table for special values of $x$.

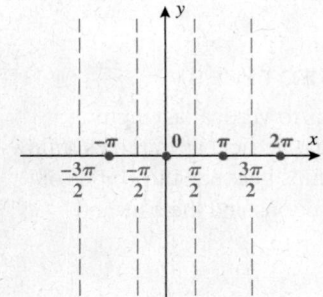

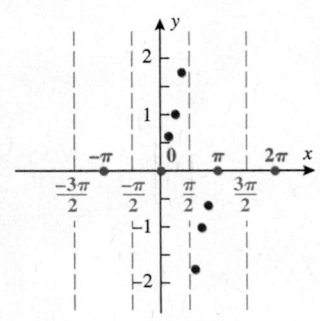

| $x$ | $\sin x$ | $\cos x$ | $\tan x = \dfrac{\sin x}{\cos x}$ | $(x, y)$ |
|---|---|---|---|---|
| $\dfrac{\pi}{6}$ | $\dfrac{1}{2}$ | $\dfrac{\sqrt{3}}{2}$ | $\dfrac{1}{\sqrt{3}} = \dfrac{\sqrt{3}}{3} \approx 0.577$ | $\left(\dfrac{\pi}{6}, 0.577\right)$ |
| $\dfrac{\pi}{4}$ | $\dfrac{\sqrt{2}}{2}$ | $\dfrac{\sqrt{2}}{2}$ | $1$ | $\left(\dfrac{\pi}{4}, 1\right)$ |
| $\dfrac{\pi}{3}$ | $\dfrac{\sqrt{3}}{2}$ | $\dfrac{1}{2}$ | $\sqrt{3} \approx 1.732$ | $\left(\dfrac{\pi}{3}, 1.732\right)$ |
| $\dfrac{2\pi}{3}$ | $\dfrac{\sqrt{3}}{2}$ | $-\dfrac{1}{2}$ | $-\sqrt{3} \approx -1.732$ | $\left(\dfrac{2\pi}{3}, -1.732\right)$ |
| $\dfrac{3\pi}{4}$ | $\dfrac{\sqrt{2}}{2}$ | $-\dfrac{\sqrt{2}}{2}$ | $-1$ | $\left(\dfrac{3\pi}{4}, -1\right)$ |
| $\dfrac{5\pi}{6}$ | $\dfrac{1}{2}$ | $-\dfrac{\sqrt{3}}{2}$ | $\dfrac{1}{-\sqrt{3}} = -\dfrac{\sqrt{3}}{3} \approx -0.577$ | $\left(\dfrac{5\pi}{6}, -0.577\right)$ |

What happens to $\tan x$ as $x$ approaches $\dfrac{\pi}{2}$? We know $\tan x$ is undefined at $x = \dfrac{\pi}{2}$ but we must consider $x$-values both larger and smaller than $\dfrac{\pi}{2} \approx 1.571$.

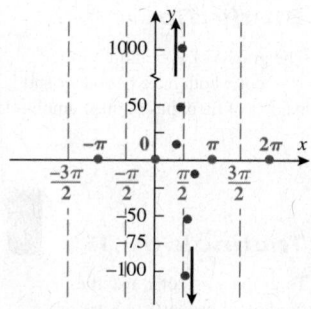

| | approaching from the left → | | | $\dfrac{\pi}{2}$ | ← approaching from the right | | |
|---|---|---|---|---|---|---|---|
| $x$ | 1.5 | 1.55 | 1.57 | 1.571 | 1.58 | 1.59 | 1.65 |
| $\tan x$ | 14.1 | 48.1 | 1255.8 | undefined | $-108.6$ | $-52.1$ | $-12.6$ |

$\underbrace{\qquad\qquad\qquad}_{\tan x \text{ gets larger}}$ $\underbrace{\qquad\qquad\qquad}_{\tan x \text{ gets more negative}}$

The arrows on the graph on the right indicate increasing without bound (in the positive and negative directions).

## GRAPH OF $y = \tan x$

1. The $x$-intercepts occur at multiples of $\pi$.  $(n\pi, 0)$

2. Vertical asymptotes occur at odd integer multiples of $\dfrac{\pi}{2}$.  $x = \dfrac{(2n + 1)\pi}{2}$

3. The domain is the set of all real numbers except odd integer multiples of $\dfrac{\pi}{2}$.  $x \neq \dfrac{(2n + 1)\pi}{2}$

4. The range is the set of all real numbers.  $(-\infty, \infty)$

5. $y = \tan x$ has period $\pi$.

6. $y = \tan x$ is an odd function (symmetric about the origin).  $\tan(-x) = -\tan x$

7. The graph has no defined amplitude, since the funtion is unbounded.

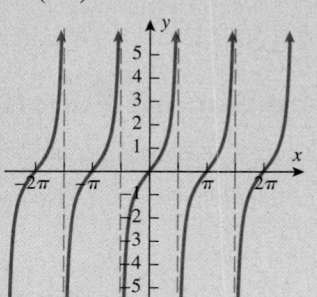

*Note: n* is an integer.

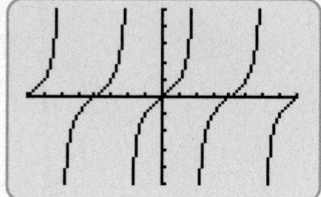
## The Cotangent Function

The cotangent function is similar to the tangent function in that it is a quotient involving the sine and cosine functions. The difference is that cotangent has cosine in the numerator and sine in the denominator: $\cot x = \dfrac{\cos x}{\sin x}$. The graph of $y = \tan x$ has $x$-intercepts corresponding to integer multiples of $\pi$ and vertical asymptotes corresponding to odd integer multiples of $\dfrac{\pi}{2}$.

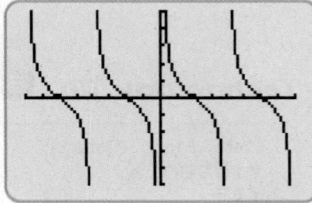
The graph of the cotangent function is the reverse in that it has $x$-intercepts corresponding to odd integer multiples of $\dfrac{\pi}{2}$ and vertical asymptotes corresponding to integer multiples of $\pi$. This is because the $x$-intercepts occur when the numerator, $\cos x$, is equal to 0 and the vertical asymptotes occur when the denominator, $\sin x$, is equal to 0.

### GRAPH OF $y = \cot x$

1. The $x$-intercepts occur at odd integer multiples of $\dfrac{\pi}{2}$.  $\left(\dfrac{(2n + 1)\pi}{2}, 0\right)$

2. Vertical asymptotes occur at integer multiples of $\pi$.  $x = n\pi$

3. The domain is the set of all real numbers except integer multiples of $\pi$.  $x \neq n\pi$

4. The range is the set of all real numbers.  $(-\infty, \infty)$

5. $y = \cot x$ has period $\pi$.

6. $y = \cot x$ is an odd function (symmetric about the origin).  $\cot(-x) = -\cot x$

7. The graph has no defined amplitude, since the funtion is unbounded.

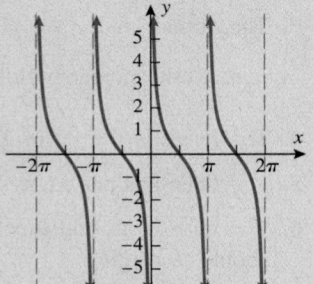

*Note: n* is an integer.

## The Secant Function

Since $y = \cos x$ has period $2\pi$, the secant function, which is the reciprocal of the cosine function, $\sec x = \dfrac{1}{\cos x}$, also has period $2\pi$. We now illustrate values of the secant function with a table.

| $x$ | $\cos x$ | $\sec x = \dfrac{1}{\cos x}$ | $(x, y)$ OR ASYMPTOTE |
|---|---|---|---|
| 0 | 1 | 1 | $(0, 1)$ |
| $\dfrac{\pi}{2}$ | 0 | undefined | vertical asymptote: $x = \dfrac{\pi}{2}$ |
| $\pi$ | $-1$ | $-1$ | $(\pi, -1)$ |
| $\dfrac{3\pi}{2}$ | 0 | undefined | vertical asymptote: $x = \dfrac{3\pi}{2}$ |
| $2\pi$ | 1 | 1 | $(2\pi, 1)$ |

Again, we ask the same question: What happens as $x$ approaches the vertical asymptotes? The secant function grows without bound in either the positive or negative direction.

If we graph $y = \cos x$ (the "guide" function) and $y = \sec x$ on the same graph, we notice the following:

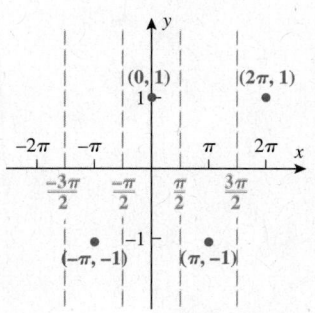

- The $x$-intercepts of $y = \cos x$ correspond to the vertical asymptotes of $y = \sec x$.
- The range of cosine is $[-1, 1]$ and the range of secant is $(-\infty, -1] \cup [1, \infty)$.
- When cosine is positive, secant is positive, and when one is negative, the other is negative.

The cosine function is used as the guide function to graph the secant function.

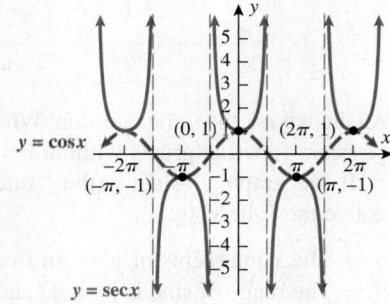

## GRAPH OF $y = \sec x$

1. There are no $x$-intercepts.

$$\dfrac{1}{\cos x} \neq 0$$

2. Vertical asymptotes occur at odd integer multiples of $\dfrac{\pi}{2}$.

$$x = \dfrac{(2n+1)\pi}{2}$$

3. The domain is the set of all real numbers except odd integer multiples of $\dfrac{\pi}{2}$.

$$x \neq \dfrac{(2n+1)\pi}{2}$$

4. The range is $(-\infty, -1] \cup [1, \infty)$.

5. $y = \sec x$ has period $2\pi$.

6. $y = \sec x$ is an even function (symmetric about the $y$-axis).

$$\sec(-x) = \sec x$$

7. The graph has no defined amplitude, since the function is unbounded.

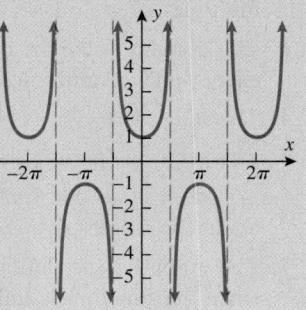

*Note: $n$ is an integer.*

### Technology Tip

To graph $y = \sec x$, enter as $1/\cos x$.

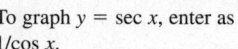

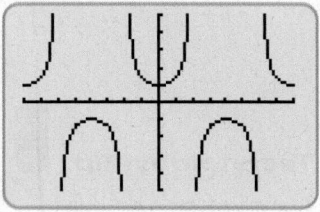

## The Cosecant Function

Since $y = \sin x$ has period $2\pi$, the cosecant function, which is the reciprocal of the sine function, $\csc x = \dfrac{1}{\sin x}$, also has period $2\pi$. We now illustrate values of cosecant with a table.

| $x$ | $\sin x$ | $\csc x = \dfrac{1}{\sin x}$ | $(x, y)$ OR ASYMPTOTE |
|---|---|---|---|
| 0 | 0 | undefined | vertical asymptote: $x = 0$ |
| $\dfrac{\pi}{2}$ | 1 | 1 | $\left(\dfrac{\pi}{2}, 1\right)$ |
| $\pi$ | 0 | undefined | vertical asymptote: $x = \pi$ |
| $\dfrac{3\pi}{2}$ | $-1$ | $-1$ | $\left(\dfrac{3\pi}{2}, -1\right)$ |
| $2\pi$ | 0 | undefined | vertical asymptote: $x = 2\pi$ |

Again, we ask the same question: What happens as $x$ approaches the vertical asymptotes? The cosecant function grows without bound in either the positive or negative direction.

If we graph $y = \sin x$ (the "guide" function) and $y = \csc x$ on the same graph, we notice the following:

- The $x$-intercepts of $y = \sin x$ correspond to the vertical asymptotes of $y = \csc x$.
- The range of sine is $[-1, 1]$ and the range of cosecant is $(-\infty, -1] \cup [1, \infty)$.
- When sine is positive, cosecant is positive, and when one is negative, the other is negative.

The sine function is used as the guide function to graph the cosecant function.

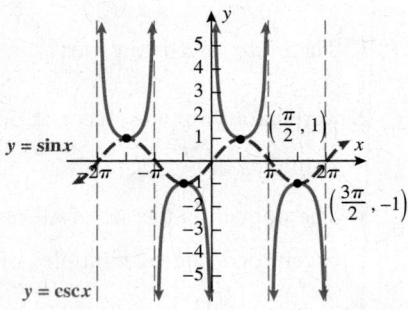

### GRAPH OF $y = \csc x$

1. There are no $x$-intercepts.      $\dfrac{1}{\sin x} \neq 0$

2. Vertical asymptotes occur at integer multiples of $\pi$.      $x = n\pi$

3. The domain is the set of all real numbers except integer multiples of $\pi$.      $x \neq n\pi$

4. The range is $(-\infty, -1] \cup [1, \infty)$.

5. $y = \csc x$ has period $2\pi$.

6. $y = \csc x$ is an odd function (symmetric about the origin).      $\csc(-x) = -\csc x$

7. The graph has no defined amplitude, since the function is unbounded.

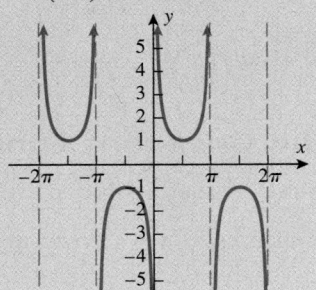

*Note: $n$ is an integer.*

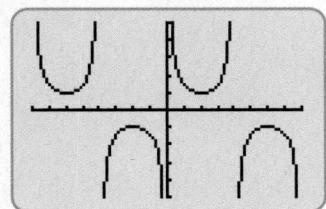
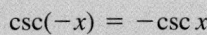

# Graphing More General Tangent, Cotangent, Secant, and Cosecant Functions

| FUNCTION | $y = \sin x$ | $y = \cos x$ | $y = \tan x$ | $y = \cot x$ | $y = \sec x$ | $y = \csc x$ |
|---|---|---|---|---|---|---|
| Graph of One Period | | | | | | |
| Domain | $(-\infty, \infty)$ | $(-\infty, \infty)$ | $x \neq \dfrac{(2n + 1)\pi}{2}$ | $x \neq n\pi$ | $x \neq \dfrac{(2n + 1)\pi}{2}$ | $x \neq n\pi$ |
| Range | $[-1, 1]$ | $[-1, 1]$ | $(-\infty, \infty)$ | $(-\infty, \infty)$ | $(-\infty, -1] \cup [1, \infty)$ | $(-\infty, -1] \cup [1, \infty)$ |
| Amplitude | 1 | 1 | none | none | none | none |
| Period | $2\pi$ | $2\pi$ | $\pi$ | $\pi$ | $2\pi$ | $2\pi$ |
| $x$-intercepts | $(n\pi, 0)$ | $\left( \dfrac{(2n + 1)\pi}{2}, 0 \right)$ | $(n\pi, 0)$ | $\left( \dfrac{(2n + 1)\pi}{2}, 0 \right)$ | none | none |
| Vertical Asymptotes | none | none | $x = \dfrac{(2n + 1)\pi}{2}$ | $x = n\pi$ | $x = \dfrac{(2n + 1)\pi}{2}$ | $x = n\pi$ |

*Note: n* is an integer.

We use these basic functions as the starting point for graphing general tangent, cotangent, secant, and cosecant functions.

## GRAPHING TANGENT AND COTANGENT FUNCTIONS

Graphs of $y = A \tan (Bx)$ and $y = A \cot (Bx)$ can be obtained using the following steps (assume $B > 0$):

**Step 1:** Calculate the period $\dfrac{\pi}{B}$.

**Step 2:** Find two neighboring vertical asymptotes.

For $y = A \tan (Bx)$:  $Bx = -\dfrac{\pi}{2}$  and  $Bx = \dfrac{\pi}{2}$

For $y = A \cot (Bx)$:  $Bx = 0$  and  $Bx = \pi$

**Step 3:** Find the $x$-intercept between the two asymptotes.

For $y = A \tan (Bx)$:  Solve for $x$: $Bx = 0 \Rightarrow x = 0$

For $y = A \cot (Bx)$:  Solve for $x$: $Bx = \dfrac{\pi}{2} \Rightarrow x = \dfrac{\pi}{2B}$

**Step 4:** Draw the vertical asymptotes and label the $x$-intercept.

**Step 5:** Divide the interval between the asymptotes into four equal parts. Set up a table with coordinates corresponding to the points in the interval.

**Step 6:** Connect the points with a smooth curve. Use arrows to indicate the behavior toward the asymptotes.

- If $A > 0$
  - $y = A \tan (Bx)$ increases from left to right.
  - $y = A \cot (Bx)$ decreases from left to right.
- If $A < 0$
  - $y = A \tan (Bx)$ decreases from left to right.
  - $y = A \cot (Bx)$ increases from left to right.

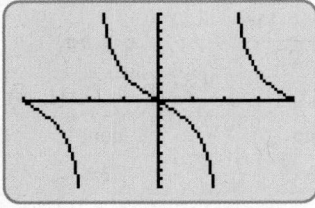

**EXAMPLE 1  Graphing $y = A\tan(Bx)$**

Graph $y = -3\tan(2x)$ on the interval $-\dfrac{\pi}{2} \le x \le \dfrac{\pi}{2}$.

**Solution:** $A = -3$, $B = 2$

**STEP 1** Calculate the period.

$$\dfrac{\pi}{B} = \dfrac{\pi}{2}$$

**STEP 2** Find two vertical asymptotes.

$$Bx = -\dfrac{\pi}{2} \quad \text{and} \quad Bx = \dfrac{\pi}{2}$$

Substitute $B = 2$ and solve for $x$.

$$x = -\dfrac{\pi}{4} \quad \text{and} \quad x = \dfrac{\pi}{4}$$

**STEP 3** Find the $x$-intercept between the asymptotes.

$$Bx = 0$$
$$x = 0$$

**STEP 4** Draw the vertical asymptotes $x = -\dfrac{\pi}{4}$ and $x = \dfrac{\pi}{4}$ and label the $x$-intercept $(0, 0)$.

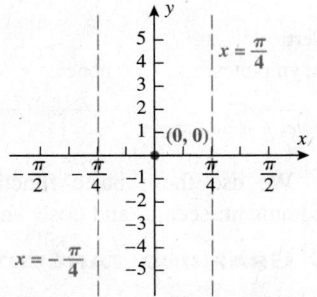

**STEP 5** Divide the period $\dfrac{\pi}{2}$ into four equal parts, in steps of $\dfrac{\pi}{8}$. Set up a table with coordinates corresponding to values of $y = -3\tan(2x)$.

| $x$ | $y = -3\tan(2x)$ | $(x, y)$ |
|:---:|:---:|:---:|
| $-\dfrac{\pi}{4}$ | undefined | vertical asymptote, $x = -\dfrac{\pi}{4}$ |
| $-\dfrac{\pi}{8}$ | 3 | $\left(-\dfrac{\pi}{8}, 3\right)$ |
| $0$ | $0$ | $(0, 0)$ |
| $\dfrac{\pi}{8}$ | $-3$ | $\left(\dfrac{\pi}{8}, -3\right)$ |
| $\dfrac{\pi}{4}$ | undefined | vertical asymptote, $x = \dfrac{\pi}{4}$ |

**STEP 6** Graph the points from the table and connect with a smooth curve. Repeat to the right and left until you reach the interval endpoints. Notice the distance between the vertical asymptotes is the period length $\frac{\pi}{2}$.

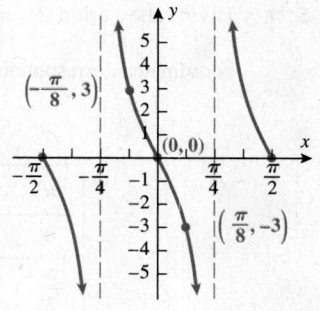

■ **Answer:**

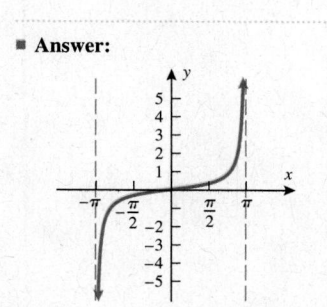

■ **YOUR TURN** Graph $y = \frac{1}{3} \tan\left(\frac{1}{2}x\right)$ on the interval $-\pi \leq x \leq \pi$.

---

**EXAMPLE 2   Graphing $y = A\cot(Bx)$**

Graph $y = 4\cot\left(\frac{1}{2}x\right)$ on the interval $-2\pi \leq x \leq 2\pi$.

**Solution:** $A = 4$, $B = \frac{1}{2}$

**STEP 1** Calculate the period.

$$\frac{\pi}{B} = 2\pi$$

**STEP 2** Find two vertical asymptotes.

Substitute $B = \frac{1}{2}$ and solve for $x$.

$$Bx = 0 \quad \text{and} \quad Bx = \pi$$
$$x = 0 \quad \text{and} \quad x = 2\pi$$

**STEP 3** Find the $x$-intercept between the asymptotes.

$$Bx = \frac{\pi}{2}$$
$$x = \pi$$

**STEP 4** Draw the vertical asymptotes $x = 0$ and $x = 2\pi$ and label the $x$-intercept $(\pi, 0)$.

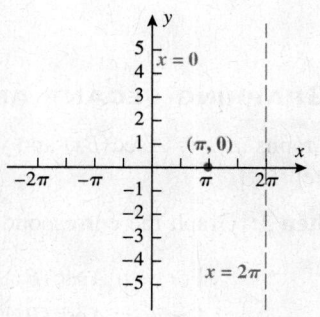

**Technology Tip**

To graph $y = 4\cot\left(\frac{1}{2}x\right)$ on the interval $-2\pi \leq x \leq 2\pi$, enter $y = 4\left[\tan\left(\frac{1}{2}x\right)\right]^{-1}$.

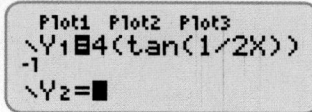

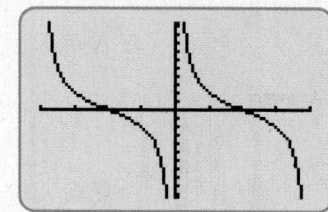

STEP 5 Divide the period $2\pi$ into four equal parts, in steps of $\frac{\pi}{2}$. Set up a table with coordinates corresponding to values of $y = 4\cot\left(\frac{1}{2}x\right)$.

| $x$ | $y = 4\cot\left(\frac{1}{2}x\right)$ | $(x, y)$ |
|---|---|---|
| $0$ | undefined | vertical asymptote, $x = 0$ |
| $\frac{\pi}{2}$ | $4$ | $\left(\frac{\pi}{2}, 4\right)$ |
| $\pi$ | $0$ | $(\pi, 0)$ |
| $\frac{3\pi}{2}$ | $-4$ | $\left(\frac{3\pi}{2}, -4\right)$ |
| $2\pi$ | undefined | vertical asymptote, $x = 2\pi$ |

STEP 6 Graph the points from the table and connect with a smooth curve. Repeat to the right and left until you reach the interval endpoints.

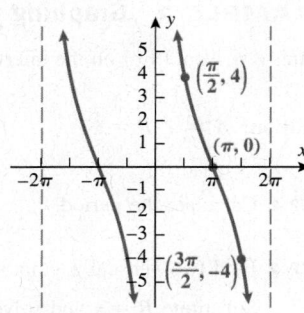

■ **Answer:**

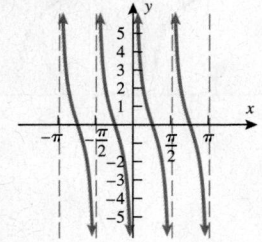

■ **YOUR TURN** Graph $y = 2\cot(2x)$ on the interval $-\pi \le x \le \pi$.

## GRAPHING SECANT AND COSECANT FUNCTIONS

Graphs of $y = A\sec(Bx)$ and $y = A\csc(Bx)$ can be obtained using the following steps:

**Step 1:** Graph the corresponding guide function with a dashed curve.

For $y = A\sec(Bx)$, use $y = A\cos(Bx)$ as a guide.

For $y = A\csc(Bx)$, use $y = A\sin(Bx)$ as a guide.

**Step 2:** Draw the asymptotes, which correspond to the $x$-intercepts of the guide function.

**Step 3:** Draw the U shape between the asymptotes. If the guide function has a positive value between the asymptotes, the U opens upward; and if the guide function has a negative value, the U opens downward.

**EXAMPLE 3    Graphing $y = A\sec(Bx)$**

Graph $y = 2\sec(\pi x)$ on the interval $-2 \le x \le 2$.

**Solution:**

STEP 1 Graph the corresponding guide
function with a dashed curve.

For $y = 2\sec(\pi x)$, use
$y = 2\cos(\pi x)$ as a guide.

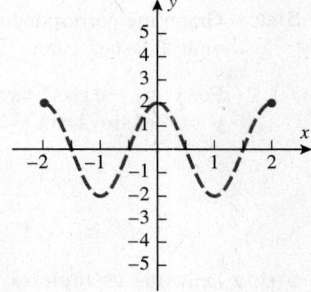

STEP 2 Draw the **asymptotes**, which correspond
to the $x$-intercepts of the guide function.

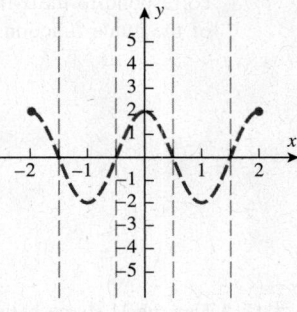

STEP 3 Use the U shape between the asymptotes.
If the guide function is positive, the U opens
upward, and if the guide function is negative,
the U opens downward.

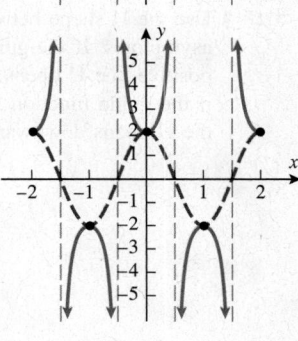

**Technology Tip**

To graph $y = 2\sec(\pi x)$ on the
interval $-2 \le x \le 2$, enter
$y = [2\cos(\pi x)]^{-1}$.

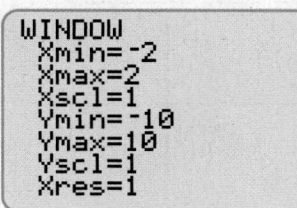

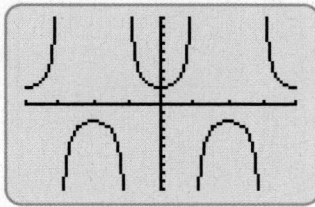

■ **YOUR TURN**   Graph $y = -\sec(2\pi x)$ on the interval $-1 \le x \le 1$.

■ **Answer:**

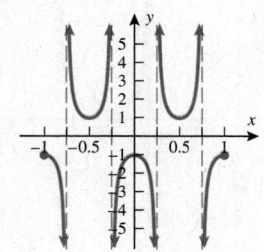

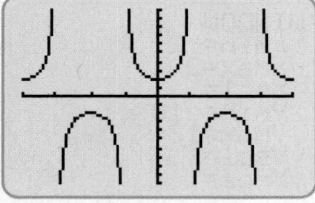
### EXAMPLE 4 Graphing $y = A\csc(Bx)$

Graph $y = -3\csc(2\pi x)$ on the interval $-1 \le x \le 1$.

**Solution:**

**STEP 1** Graph the corresponding guide function with a dashed curve.

For $y = -3\csc(2\pi x)$, use $y = -3\sin(2\pi x)$ as a guide.

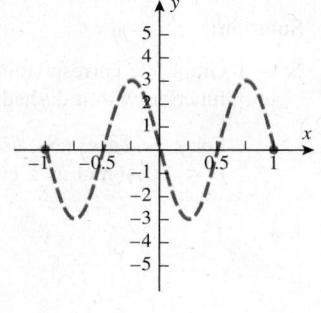

**STEP 2** Draw the **asymptotes**, which correspond to the $x$-intercepts of the guide function.

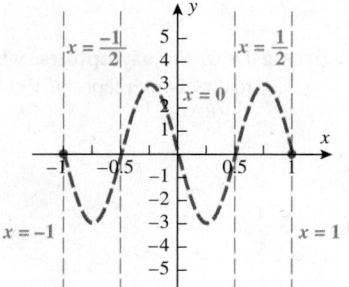

**STEP 3** Use the U shape between the asymptotes. If the guide function is positive, the U opens upward, and if the guide function is negative, the U opens downward.

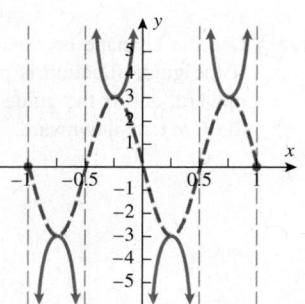

■ **Answer:**

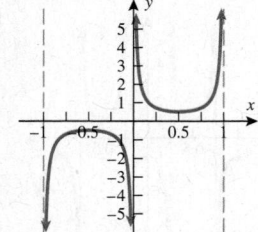

■ **YOUR TURN** Graph $y = \frac{1}{2}\csc(\pi x)$ on the interval $-1 \le x \le 1$.

## Translations of Trigonometric Functions

Vertical translations and horizontal translations (phase shifts) of the tangent, cotangent, secant, and cosecant functions are graphed the same way as vertical and horizontal translations of sinusoidal graphs. For tangent and cotangent functions, we follow the same procedure as we did with sinusoidal functions. For secant and cosecant functions, we graph the guide function first and then translate up or down depending on the sign of the vertical shift.

**EXAMPLE 5   Graphing $y = A \tan(Bx + C) + D$**

Graph $y = 1 - \tan\left(x - \dfrac{\pi}{2}\right)$ on $-\pi \le x \le \pi$. State the domain and range on the interval.

There are two ways to approach graphing this function. Both will be illustrated.

**Solution (1):**

Plot $y = \tan x$, and then do the following:

■ Shift the curve to the right $\dfrac{\pi}{2}$ units.

$\qquad\qquad y = \tan\left(x - \dfrac{\pi}{2}\right)$

■ Reflect the curve about the $x$-axis (because of the negative sign).

$\qquad\qquad y = -\tan\left(x - \dfrac{\pi}{2}\right)$

■ Shift the entire graph up one unit.

$\qquad\qquad y = 1 - \tan\left(x - \dfrac{\pi}{2}\right)$

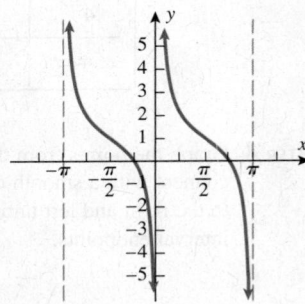

**Solution (2):** Graph $y = -\tan\left(x - \dfrac{\pi}{2}\right)$, and then shift the entire graph up one unit, because $D = 1$.

**STEP 1**  Calculate the period.

$\qquad\qquad \dfrac{\pi}{B} = \pi$

**STEP 2**  Find two vertical asymptotes.

Solve for $x$.

$\qquad\qquad x - \dfrac{\pi}{2} = -\dfrac{\pi}{2}$  and  $x - \dfrac{\pi}{2} = \dfrac{\pi}{2}$

$\qquad\qquad x = 0$  and  $x = \pi$

**STEP 3**  Find the $x$-intercept between the asymptotes.

$\qquad\qquad x - \dfrac{\pi}{2} = 0$

$\qquad\qquad x = \dfrac{\pi}{2}$

**STEP 4**  Draw the vertical asymptotes $x = 0$ and $x = \pi$ and label the $x$-intercept $\left(\dfrac{\pi}{2}, 0\right)$.

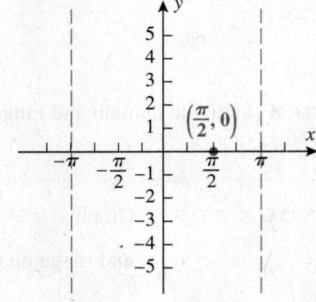

### Technology Tip

To obtain the graph of

$$y = 1 - \tan\left(x - \frac{\pi}{2}\right) \text{ on the}$$

interval $-\pi \leq x \leq \pi$, enter

$$y = 1 - \tan\left(x - \frac{\pi}{2}\right).$$

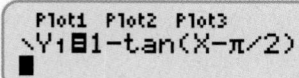

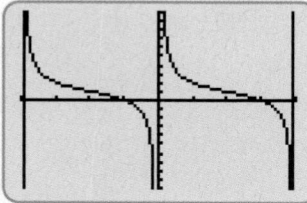

**STEP 5** Divide the period $\pi$ into four equal parts, in steps of $\frac{\pi}{4}$. Set up a table with coordinates corresponding to values of $y = -\tan\left(x - \frac{\pi}{2}\right)$ between the two asymptotes.

| $x$ | $y = -\tan\left(x - \frac{\pi}{2}\right)$ | $(x, y)$ |
|---|---|---|
| $x = 0$ | undefined | vertical asymptote, $x = 0$ |
| $\dfrac{\pi}{4}$ | 1 | $\left(\dfrac{\pi}{4}, 1\right)$ |
| $\dfrac{\pi}{2}$ | 0 | $\left(\dfrac{\pi}{2}, 0\right)$ ($x$-intercept) |
| $\dfrac{3\pi}{4}$ | $-1$ | $\left(\dfrac{3\pi}{4}, -1\right)$ |
| $x = \pi$ | undefined | vertical asymptote, $x = \pi$ |

**STEP 6** Graph the points from the table and connect with a smooth curve. Repeat to the right and left until reaching the interval endpoints.

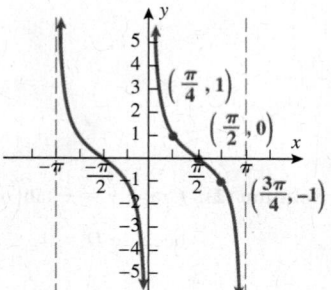

**STEP 7** Shift the entire graph up one unit to arrive at the graph of

$$y = 1 - \tan\left(x - \frac{\pi}{2}\right).$$

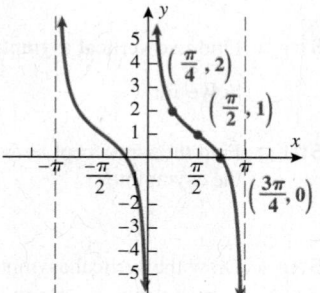

■ **Answer:**

Domain:

$$\left[-\pi, -\frac{\pi}{2}\right) \cup \left(-\frac{\pi}{2}, \frac{\pi}{2}\right) \cup \left(\frac{\pi}{2}, \pi\right]$$

Range: $(-\infty, \infty)$

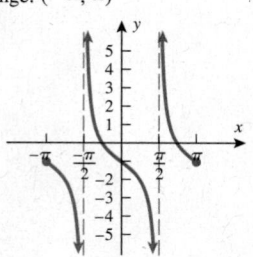

**STEP 8** State the domain and range on the interval.   Domain: $(-\pi, 0) \cup (0, \pi)$
Range: $(-\infty, \infty)$

■ **YOUR TURN** Graph $y = -1 + \cot\left(x + \frac{\pi}{2}\right)$ on $-\pi \leq x \leq \pi$. State the domain and range on the interval.

**EXAMPLE 6   Graphing $y = A\csc(Bx + C) + D$**

Graph $y = 1 - \csc(2x - \pi)$ on $-\pi \leq x \leq \pi$. State the domain and range on the interval.

**Solution:**

Graph $y = -\csc(2x - \pi)$, and shift the entire graph up one unit to arrive at the graph of $y = 1 - \csc(2x - \pi)$.

STEP 1   Draw the guide function,
$y = -\sin(2x - \pi)$.

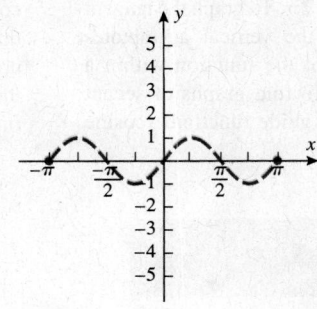

STEP 2   Draw the **vertical asymptotes** of
$y = -\csc(2x - \pi)$ that correspond
to the *x*-intercepts of
$y = -\sin(2x - \pi)$.

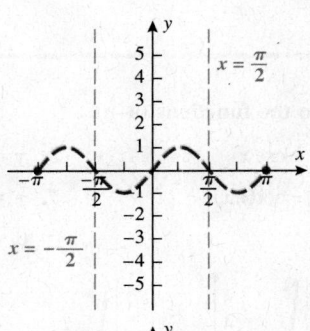

STEP 3   Use the U shape between the
asymptotes. If the guide function is
positive, the U opens upward, and if
the guide function is negative, the U
opens downward.

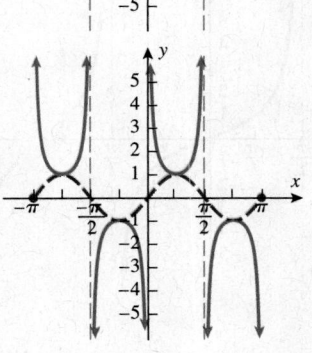

STEP 4   Shift the entire graph up one unit
to arrive at the graph of
$y = 1 - \csc(2x - \pi)$.

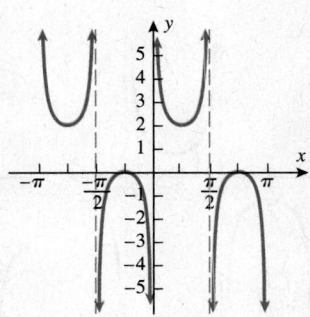

**■ Answer:**
Domain:

$$\left[-1, -\tfrac{1}{2}\right) \cup \left(-\tfrac{1}{2}, \tfrac{1}{2}\right) \cup \left(\tfrac{1}{2}, 1\right]$$

Range: $(-\infty, -3] \cup [-1, \infty)$

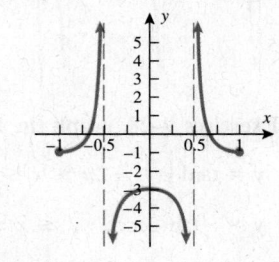

STEP 5   State the domain and
range on the interval.

Domain: $\left(-\pi, -\dfrac{\pi}{2}\right) \cup \left(-\dfrac{\pi}{2}, 0\right) \cup \left(0, \dfrac{\pi}{2}\right) \cup \left(\dfrac{\pi}{2}, \pi\right)$

Range: $(-\infty, 0] \cup [2, \infty)$

**■ YOUR TURN**   Graph $y = -2 + \sec(\pi x - \pi)$ on $-1 \leq x \leq 1$. State the domain and range on the interval.

SECTION
5.3 SUMMARY

The tangent and cotangent functions have period $\pi$, whereas the secant and cosecant functions have period $2\pi$. To graph the tangent and cotangent functions, first identify the vertical asymptotes and x-intercepts, and then find values of the function within a period (i.e., between the asymptotes). To find graphs of secant and cosecant functions, first graph their guide functions (cosine and sine, respectively), and then label vertical asymptotes that correspond to x-intercepts of the guide function. The graphs of the secant and cosecant functions resemble the letter U opening up or down. The secant and cosecant functions are positive when their guide function is positive and negative when their guide function is negative.

SECTION
5.3 EXERCISES

■ SKILLS

**In Exercises 1–8, match the graphs to the functions (a–h).**

**1.** $y = -\tan x$      **2.** $y = -\csc x$      **3.** $y = \sec(2x)$      **4.** $y = \csc(2x)$

**5.** $y = \cot(\pi x)$      **6.** $y = -\cot(\pi x)$      **7.** $y = 3\sec x$      **8.** $y = 3\csc x$

a.
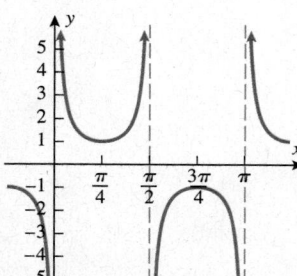

b.
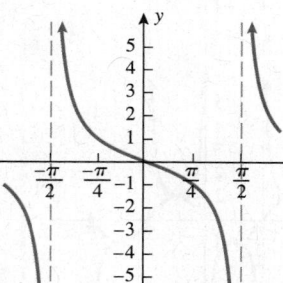

c.
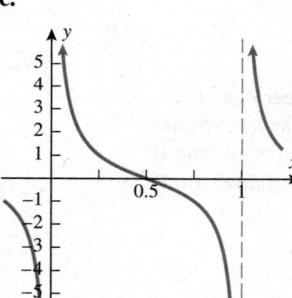

d.
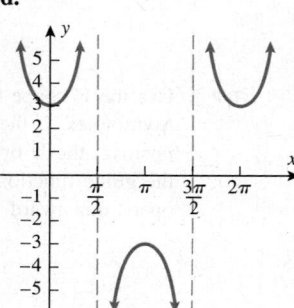

e.
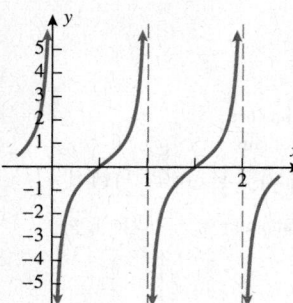

f.
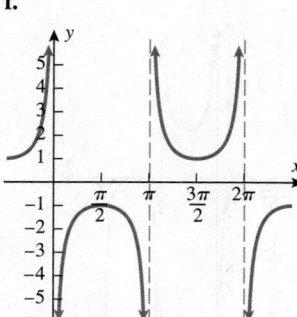

g.
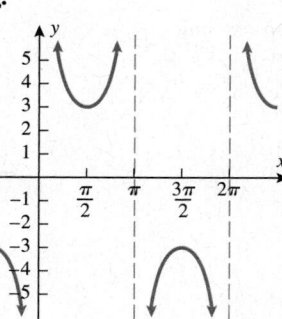

h.
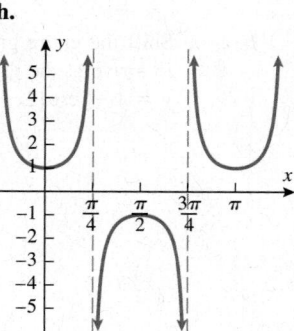

**In Exercises 9–28, graph the functions over the indicated intervals.**

**9.** $y = \tan\left(\frac{1}{2}x\right), \ -2\pi \le x \le 2\pi$      **10.** $y = \cot\left(\frac{1}{2}x\right), \ -2\pi \le x \le 2\pi$      **11.** $y = -\cot(2\pi x), \ -1 \le x \le 1$

**12.** $y = -\tan(2\pi x), \ -1 \le x \le 1$      **13.** $y = 2\tan(3x), \ -\pi \le x \le \pi$      **14.** $y = 2\tan\left(\frac{1}{3}x\right), \ -3\pi \le x \le 3\pi$

**15.** $y = -\dfrac{1}{4}\cot\left(\dfrac{x}{2}\right),\ -2\pi \le x \le 2\pi$

**16.** $y = -\dfrac{1}{2}\tan\left(\dfrac{x}{4}\right),\ -4\pi \le x \le 4\pi$

**17.** $y = -\tan\left(x - \dfrac{\pi}{2}\right),\ -\pi \le x \le \pi$

**18.** $y = \tan\left(x + \dfrac{\pi}{4}\right),\ -\pi \le x \le \pi$

**19.** $y = 2\tan\left(x + \dfrac{\pi}{6}\right),\ -\pi \le x \le \pi$

**20.** $y = -\dfrac{1}{2}\tan(x + \pi),\ -\pi \le x \le \pi$

**21.** $y = \cot\left(x - \dfrac{\pi}{4}\right),\ -\pi \le x \le \pi$

**22.** $y = -\cot\left(x + \dfrac{\pi}{2}\right),\ -\pi \le x \le \pi$

**23.** $y = -\dfrac{1}{2}\cot\left(x + \dfrac{\pi}{3}\right),\ -\pi \le x \le \pi$

**24.** $y = 3\cot\left(x - \dfrac{\pi}{6}\right),\ -\pi \le x \le \pi$

**25.** $y = \tan(2x - \pi),\ -2\pi \le x \le 2\pi$

**26.** $y = \cot(2x - \pi),\ -2\pi \le x \le 2\pi$

**27.** $y = \cot\left(\dfrac{x}{2} + \dfrac{\pi}{4}\right),\ -\pi \le x \le \pi$

**28.** $y = \tan\left(\dfrac{x}{3} - \dfrac{\pi}{3}\right),\ -\pi \le x \le \pi$

**In Exercises 29–46, graph the functions over the indicated intervals.**

**29.** $y = \sec(\tfrac{1}{2}x),\ -2\pi \le x \le 2\pi$

**30.** $y = \csc(\tfrac{1}{2}x),\ -2\pi \le x \le 2\pi$

**31.** $y = -\csc(2\pi x),\ -1 \le x \le 1$

**32.** $y = -\sec(2\pi x),\ -1 \le x \le 1$

**33.** $y = \dfrac{1}{3}\sec\left(\dfrac{\pi}{2}x\right),\ -4 \le x \le 4$

**34.** $y = \dfrac{1}{2}\csc\left(\dfrac{\pi}{3}x\right),\ -6 \le x \le 6$

**35.** $y = -3\csc\left(\dfrac{x}{3}\right),\ -6\pi \le x \le 0$

**36.** $y = -4\sec\left(\dfrac{x}{2}\right),\ -4\pi \le x \le 4\pi$

**37.** $y = 2\sec(3x),\ 0 \le x \le 2\pi$

**38.** $y = 2\csc\left(\dfrac{1}{3}x\right),\ -3\pi \le x \le 3\pi$

**39.** $y = -3\csc\left(x - \dfrac{\pi}{2}\right)$, over at least one period

**40.** $y = 5\sec\left(x + \dfrac{\pi}{4}\right)$, over at least one period

**41.** $y = \tfrac{1}{2}\sec(x - \pi)$, over at least one period

**42.** $y = -4\csc(x + \pi)$, over at least one period

**43.** $y = 2\sec(2x - \pi),\ -2\pi \le x \le 2\pi$

**44.** $y = 2\csc(2x + \pi),\ -2\pi \le x \le 2\pi$

**45.** $y = -\tfrac{1}{4}\sec(3x + \pi)$

**46.** $y = -\dfrac{2}{3}\csc\left(4x - \dfrac{\pi}{2}\right),\ -\pi \le x \le \pi$

**In Exercises 47–56, graph the functions over at least one period.**

**47.** $y = 3 - 2\sec\left(x - \dfrac{\pi}{2}\right)$

**48.** $y = -3 + 2\csc\left(x + \dfrac{\pi}{2}\right)$

**49.** $y = \dfrac{1}{2} + \dfrac{1}{2}\tan\left(x - \dfrac{\pi}{2}\right)$

**50.** $y = \dfrac{3}{4} - \dfrac{1}{4}\cot\left(x + \dfrac{\pi}{2}\right)$

**51.** $y = -2 + 3\csc(2x - \pi)$

**52.** $y = -1 + 4\sec(2x + \pi)$

**53.** $y = -1 - \sec\left(\dfrac{1}{2}x - \dfrac{\pi}{4}\right)$

**54.** $y = -2 + \csc\left(\dfrac{1}{2}x + \dfrac{\pi}{4}\right)$

**55.** $y = -2 - 3\cot\left(2x - \dfrac{\pi}{4}\right),\ -\pi \le x \le \pi$

**56.** $y = -\dfrac{1}{4} + \dfrac{1}{2}\sec\left(\pi x + \dfrac{\pi}{4}\right),\ -2 \le x \le 2$

**In Exercises 57–66, state the domain and range of the functions.**

**57.** $y = \tan\left(\pi x - \dfrac{\pi}{2}\right)$

**58.** $y = \cot\left(x - \dfrac{\pi}{2}\right)$

**59.** $y = 2\sec(5x)$

**60.** $y = -4\sec(3x)$

**61.** $y = 2 - \csc(\tfrac{1}{2}x - \pi)$

**62.** $y = 1 - 2\sec(\tfrac{1}{2}x + \pi)$

**63.** $y = -3\tan\left(\dfrac{\pi}{4}x - \pi\right) + 1$

**64.** $y = \dfrac{1}{4}\cot\left(2\pi x + \dfrac{\pi}{3}\right) - 3$

**65.** $y = -2 + \dfrac{1}{2}\sec\left(\pi x + \dfrac{\pi}{2}\right)$

**66.** $y = \dfrac{1}{2} - \dfrac{1}{3}\csc\left(3x - \dfrac{\pi}{2}\right)$

■ **APPLICATIONS**

**67. Tower of Pisa.** The angle between the ground and the Tower of Pisa is about 85°. Its inclination measured at the base is 4.2 meters. What is the vertical distance from the top of the tower to the ground?

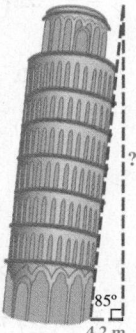

85°
4.2 m

**68. Architecture.** The angle of elevation from the top of a building 40 feet tall to the top of another building 75 feet tall is $\dfrac{\pi}{6}$. What is the distance between the buildings?

**69. Lighthouse.** A lighthouse is located on a small island 3 miles offshore. The distance $x$ is given by $x = 3\tan(\pi t)$, where $t$ is the time measured in seconds. Suppose that at midnight the light beam forms a straight angle with the shoreline. Find $x$ at

**a.** $t = \frac{2}{3}$ s  **b.** $t = \frac{3}{4}$ s  **c.** 1 s

**d.** $t = \frac{5}{4}$ s  **e.** $t = \frac{4}{3}$ s

Round to the nearest length.

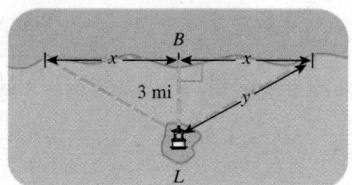

**70. Lighthouse.** If the length of the light beam is determined by $y = 3\left|\sec(\pi t)\right|$, find $y$ at

**a.** $t = \frac{2}{3}$ s  **b.** $t = \frac{3}{4}$ s  **c.** 1 s

**d.** $t = \frac{5}{4}$ s  **e.** $t = \frac{4}{3}$ s

Round to the nearest length.

■ **CATCH THE MISTAKE**

**In Exercises 71 and 72, explain the mistake that is made.**

**71.** Graph $y = 3\csc(2x)$.

**Solution:**

Graph the guide function, $y = \sin(2x)$.

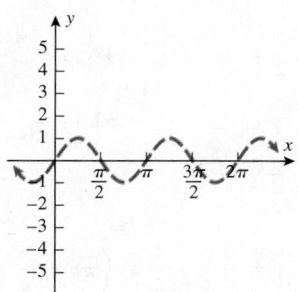

Draw vertical asymptotes at $x$-values that correspond to $x$-intercepts of the guide function.

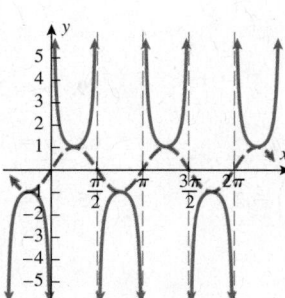

Draw the cosecant function.

This is incorrect. What mistake was made?

**72.** Graph $y = \tan(4x)$.

**Solution:**

**Step 1:** Calculate the period.   $\dfrac{\pi}{B} = \dfrac{\pi}{4}$

**Step 2:** Find two vertical asymptotes.   $4x = 0$ and $4x = \pi$

Solve for $x$.   $x = 0$ and $x = \dfrac{\pi}{4}$

**Step 3:** Find the $x$-intercept between the asymptotes.   $4x = \dfrac{\pi}{2}$

$x = \dfrac{\pi}{8}$

**Step 4:** Draw the vertical asymptotes $x = 0$ and $x = \dfrac{\pi}{4}$ and label the $x$-intercept $\left(\dfrac{\pi}{8}, 0\right)$.

**Step 5:** Graph.

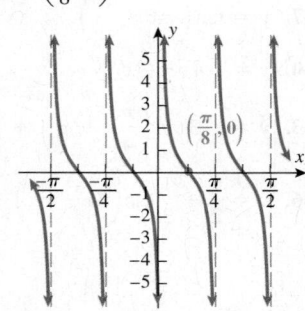

This is incorrect. What mistake was made?

**■ CONCEPTUAL**

In Exercises 73 and 74, determine whether each statement is true or false.

73. $\sec\left(x - \dfrac{\pi}{2}\right) = \csc x$

74. $\csc\left(x - \dfrac{\pi}{2}\right) = \sec x$

75. For what values of $n$ do $y = \tan x$ and $y = \tan(x - n\pi)$ have the same graph?

76. For what values of $n$ do $y = \csc x$ and $y = \csc(x - n\pi)$ have the same graph?

77. Solve the equation $\tan(2x - \pi) = 0$ for $x$ in the interval $[-\pi, \pi]$ by graphing.

78. Solve the equation $\csc(2x + \pi) = 0$ for $x$ in the interval $[-\pi, \pi]$ by graphing.

79. Find the $x$-intercepts of $y = A\tan(Bx + C)$.

80. For what $x$-values does the graph of $y = -A\sec\left(\dfrac{\pi}{2}x\right)$ lie above the $x$-axis? (Assume $A > 0$.)

81. How many solutions are there to the equation $\tan x = x$? Explain.

82. For what values of $A$ do the graphs of $y = A\sin(Bx + C)$ and $y = -2\csc\left(\dfrac{\pi}{6}x - \pi\right)$ never intersect?

**■ TECHNOLOGY**

83. What is the amplitude of the function $y = \cos x + \sin x$? Use a graphing calculator to graph $Y_1 = \cos x$, $Y_2 = \sin x$, and $Y_3 = \cos x + \sin x$ in the same viewing window.

84. Graph $Y_1 = \cos x + \sin x$ and $Y_2 = \sec x + \csc x$ in the same viewing window. Based on what you see, is $Y_1 = \cos x + \sin x$ the guide function for $Y_2 = \sec x + \csc x$?

85. What is the period of the function $y = \tan x + \cot x$? Use a graphing calculator to graph $Y_1 = \tan x + \cot x$ and $Y_3 = 2\csc(2x)$ in the same viewing window.

86. What is the period of the function $y = \tan\left(2x + \dfrac{\pi}{2}\right)$? Use a graphing calculator to graph $Y_1 = \tan\left(2x + \dfrac{\pi}{2}\right)$, $Y_2 = \tan\left(2x - \dfrac{\pi}{2}\right)$, and $Y_3 = \tan\left(-2x + \dfrac{\pi}{2}\right)$ in the same viewing window. Describe the relationships of $Y_1$ and $Y_2$ and $Y_2$ and $Y_3$.

**■ PREVIEW TO CALCULUS**

In calculus, the definite integral $\int_a^b f(x)\,dx$ is used to find the area below the graph of a continuous function $f$, above the $x$-axis, and between $x = a$ and $x = b$. The Fundamental Theorem of Calculus establishes that the definite integral $\int_a^b f(x)\,dx$ equals $F(b) - F(a)$, where $F$ is any antiderivative of a continuous function $f$.

In Exercises 87–90, first shade the area corresponding to the definite integral and then use the information below to find the exact value of the area.

| FUNCTION | $\tan x$ | $\cot x$ | $\sec x$ | $\csc x$ |
|---|---|---|---|---|
| ANTIDERIVATIVE | $-\ln\lvert\cos x\rvert$ | $\ln\lvert\sin x\rvert$ | $\ln\lvert\sec x + \tan x\rvert$ | $-\ln\lvert\csc x + \cot x\rvert$ |

87. $\displaystyle\int_0^{\pi/4} \tan x\,dx$

88. $\displaystyle\int_{\pi/4}^{\pi/2} \cot x\,dx$

89. $\displaystyle\int_0^{\pi/4} \sec x\,dx$

90. $\displaystyle\int_{\pi/4}^{\pi/2} \csc x\,dx$

Perhaps in previous chapters you have solved problems involving how fast a car travels if the tires rotate at 300 rpm's or how to calculate the angular velocity if you know the linear velocity. The following problem uses the rolling wheel idea but in a different way. You will be asked to trace the path of a speck on the outer edge of a wheel as it rolls down the road. The connection to this chapter is that you will need to find the $(x, y)$ coordinates of the speck using functions involving $\sin(\theta)$ and $\cos(\theta)$. Historically, this problem has two significant results. It is connected to the solution of how to build a perfect clock (a major breakthrough) and the fastest path from a point $A$ to a point $B$, where $B$ is below $A$ but not directly below $A$.

In order to trace the path of a point $(x, y)$ on the outer edge of a tire, we will assume the tire has a radius of 15 inches and rolls toward the right. To get started, $(x, y)$ will be the point touching the $x$-axis and $\theta$ will be 0 (see the diagram below). $\theta$ stands for how many degrees the tire has rotated. You will do this for one full revolution in 30° increments.

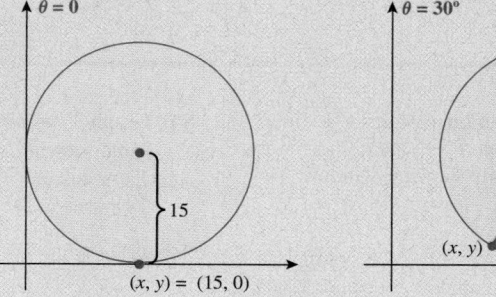

**1.** Fill in the chart. See the diagrams above for help. (Use one decimal.)

| $\theta$ | 0° | 30° | 60° | 90° | 120° | 150° | 180° | 210° | 240° | 270° | 300° | 330° | 360° |
|---|---|---|---|---|---|---|---|---|---|---|---|---|---|
| $x$ | | | | | | | | | | | | | |
| $y$ | | | | | | | | | | | | | |

Getting started:

- The height $y$ can be found using right triangle trigonometry with the side $b$ and the fact that the radius of the tires is 15 inches.

- The $x$-coordinate is $a$ units behind (or ahead of) the center of the circle (tire). Identify where the center is located and then subtract (or add) $a$ from this result. Notice that $a$ is also calculated using right triangle trigonometry.

**2.** On a sheet of graph paper, plot the points $(x, y)$ in your chart. You should see a smooth curve; otherwise, something is off.

**3.** Find the lateral position of the speck $x$ in terms of $\theta$: $x(\theta) =$

**4.** Find the vertical position of the speck $y$ in terms of $\theta$: $y(\theta) =$

# MODELING OUR WORLD

Some would argue that temperatures are oscillatory in nature: that we are not experiencing global warming at all, but instead a natural cycle in Earth's temperature. In the Modeling Our World features in Chapters 1—3, you modeled mean temperatures with linear, polynomial, and logarithmic models—all of which modeled increasing temperatures. Looking at the data another way, we can demonstrate—over a short period of time—how it might appear to be oscillatory, which we can model with a sinusoidal curve. Be warned, however, that even the stock market, which increases gradually over time, looks sinusoidal over a short period.

The following table summarizes average yearly temperature in degree Fahrenheit (°F) and carbon dioxide emissions in parts per million (ppm) for the Mauna Loa Observatory in Hawaii.

| Year | 1960 | 1965 | 1970 | 1975 | 1980 | 1985 | 1990 | 1995 | 2000 | 2005 |
|---|---|---|---|---|---|---|---|---|---|---|
| Temperature | 44.45 | 43.29 | 43.61 | 43.35 | 46.66 | 45.71 | 45.53 | 47.53 | 45.86 | 46.23 |
| $CO_2$ Emissions (ppm) | 316.9 | 320.0 | 325.7 | 331.1 | 338.7 | 345.9 | 354.2 | 360.6 | 369.4 | 379.7 |

**1.** Find a *sinusoidal function* of the form $f(t) = k + A\sin(Bt)$ that models the temperature in Mauna Loa. Assume that the peak amplitude occurs in 1980 and again in 2010 (at 46.66°). Let $t = 0$ correspond to 1960.

**2.** Do your models support the claim of global warming? Explain.

**3.** You have modeled these same data with different types of models—oscillatory and nonoscillatory. Over the short 30-year period from 1980 to 2010, you have a sinusoidal model that can fit the data, but does it prove anything in the long term?

**4.** Would a resonance-type sinusoidal function of the form $f(t) = k + A\sin(Bt)$ perhaps be a better fit for 1960 to 2005? Develop a function of this form that models the data.

| SECTION | CONCEPT | KEY IDEAS/FORMULAS |
|---------|---------|--------------------|
| 5.1 | **Trigonometric functions: The unit circle approach** | |
| | Trigonometric functions and the unit circle | |

| | Properties of trigonometric (circular) functions | Cosine is an even function. $$\cos(-\theta) = \cos\theta$$ Sine is an odd function. $$\sin(-\theta) = -\sin\theta$$ |

## 5.2    Graphs of sine and cosine functions

The graphs of sinusoidal functions

$f(x) = \sin x$

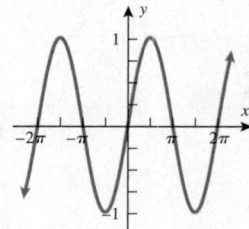

Odd Function

$\sin(-x) = -\sin x$

$f(x) = \cos x$

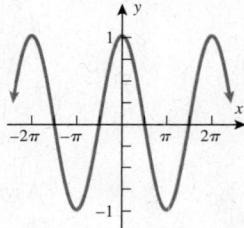

Even Function

$\cos(-x) = \cos(x)$

### The amplitude and period of sinusoidal graphs

$y = A\sin(Bx)$    or    $y = A\cos(Bx)$, $B > 0$

Amplitude $= |A|$

- $|A| > 1$ stretch vertically.
- $|A| < 1$ compress vertically.

Period $= \dfrac{2\pi}{B}$

- $B > 1$ compress horizontally.
- $B < 1$ stretch horizontally.

Graphing a shifted sinusoidal function:

$y = A\sin(Bx + C) + D$

and

$y = A\cos(Bx + C) + D$

- $y = A\sin(Bx \pm C) = A\sin\left[B\left(x \pm \dfrac{C}{B}\right)\right]$ has period $\dfrac{2\pi}{B}$ and a

  phase shift of $\dfrac{C}{B}$ units to the left $(+)$ or the right $(-)$.

- $y = A\cos(Bx \pm C) = A\cos\left[B\left(x \pm \dfrac{C}{B}\right)\right]$ has period $\dfrac{2\pi}{B}$ and a

  phase shift of $\dfrac{C}{B}$ units to the left $(+)$ or the right $(-)$.

- To graph $y = A\sin(Bx + C) + D$ or $y = A\cos(Bx + C) + D$, start with the graph of $y = A\sin(Bx + C)$ or $y = A\cos(Bx + C)$ and shift up or down $D$ units.

| SECTION | CONCEPT | KEY IDEAS/FORMULAS |
|---------|---------|--------------------|
| | Harmonic motion | ■ Simple<br>■ Damped<br>■ Resonance |
| | Graphing sums of functions:<br>Addition of ordinates | |
| 5.3 | **Graphs of other<br>trigonometric functions** | |
| | Graphing the tangent,<br>cotangent, secant, and<br>cosecant functions | **The tangent function**<br>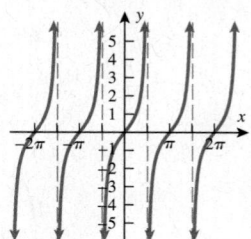<br>$x$-intercepts: $(n\pi, 0)$<br><br>Asymptotes: $x = \dfrac{(2n + 1)\pi}{2}$<br><br>Period: $\pi$<br>Amplitude: none<br><br>**The cotangent function**<br>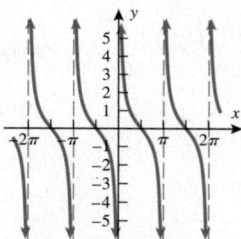<br>Asymptotes: $x = n\pi$<br><br>$x$-intercepts: $\left(\dfrac{(2n + 1)\pi}{2}, 0\right)$<br><br>Period: $\pi$<br>Amplitude: none |

**The secant function**

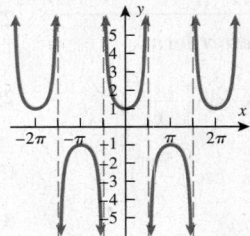

Asymptotes: $x = \dfrac{(2n + 1)\pi}{2}$

Period: $2\pi$
Amplitude: none
$x$-intercepts: none

**The cosecant function**

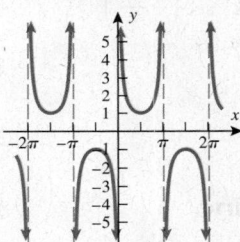

Asymptotes: $x = n\pi$
Period: $2\pi$
Amplitude: none
$x$-intercepts: none

**Graphing more general tangent, cotangent, secant, and cosecant functions**

$y = A\tan(Bx),\ y = A\cot(Bx),\ y = A\sec(Bx),\ y = A\csc(Bx)$

| | | |
|---|---|---|
| Translations of trigonometric functions | | $y = A\tan(Bx + C)$  or  $y = A\cot(Bx + C)$ |

To find asymptotes, set $Bx + C$ equal to

■ $-\dfrac{\pi}{2}$ and $\dfrac{\pi}{2}$ for tangent.

■ $0$ and $\pi$ for cotangent.

To find $x$-intercepts, set $Bx + C$ equal to

■ $0$ for tangent.

■ $\dfrac{\pi}{2}$ for cotangent.

$y = A\sec(Bx + C)$  or  $y = A\csc(Bx + C)$

To graph $y = A\sec(Bx + C)$, use $y = A\cos(Bx + C)$ as the guide.

To graph $y = A\csc(Bx + C)$, use $y = A\sin(Bx + C)$ as the guide.

Intercepts on the guide function correspond to vertical asymptotes of secant or cosecant functions.

## 5.1 Trigonometric Functions: The Unit Circle Approach

**Find each trigonometric function value in *exact* form.**

1. $\tan\left(\dfrac{5\pi}{6}\right)$
2. $\cos\left(\dfrac{5\pi}{6}\right)$
3. $\sin\left(\dfrac{11\pi}{6}\right)$

4. $\sec\left(\dfrac{11\pi}{6}\right)$
5. $\cot\left(\dfrac{5\pi}{4}\right)$
6. $\csc\left(\dfrac{5\pi}{4}\right)$

7. $\sin\left(\dfrac{3\pi}{2}\right)$
8. $\cos\left(\dfrac{3\pi}{2}\right)$
9. $\cos\pi$

10. $\tan\left(\dfrac{7\pi}{4}\right)$
11. $\cos\left(\dfrac{\pi}{3}\right)$
12. $\sin\left(\dfrac{11\pi}{6}\right)$

13. $\sin\left(-\dfrac{7\pi}{4}\right)$
14. $\tan\left(-\dfrac{2\pi}{3}\right)$
15. $\csc\left(-\dfrac{3\pi}{2}\right)$

16. $\cot\left(-\dfrac{5\pi}{6}\right)$
17. $\cos\left(-\dfrac{7\pi}{6}\right)$
18. $\sec\left(-\dfrac{3\pi}{4}\right)$

19. $\tan\left(-\dfrac{13\pi}{6}\right)$
20. $\cos\left(-\dfrac{14\pi}{3}\right)$

## 5.2 Graphs of Sine and Cosine Functions

**Refer to the graph of the sinusoidal function to answer the questions.**

21. Determine the period of the function.

22. Determine the amplitude of the function.

23. Write an equation for the sinusoidal function.

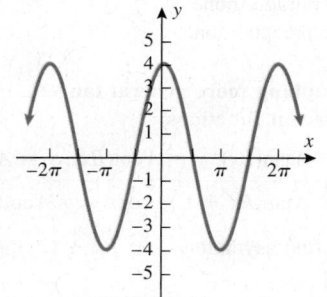

**Refer to the graph of the sinusoidal function to answer the questions.**

24. Determine the period of the function.

25. Determine the amplitude of the function.

26. Write an equation for the sinusoidal function.

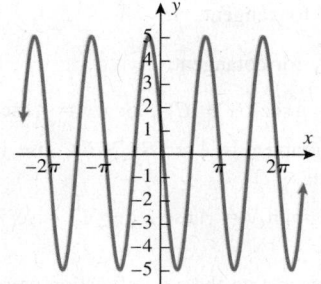

**Determine the amplitude and period of each function.**

27. $y = -2\cos(2\pi x)$
28. $y = \dfrac{1}{3}\sin\left(\dfrac{\pi}{2}x\right)$

29. $y = \dfrac{1}{5}\sin(3x)$
30. $y = -\dfrac{7}{6}\cos(6x)$

**Graph each function from $-2\pi$ to $2\pi$.**

31. $y = -2\sin\left(\dfrac{x}{2}\right)$
32. $y = 3\sin(3x)$

33. $y = \dfrac{1}{2}\cos(2x)$
34. $y = -\dfrac{1}{4}\cos\left(\dfrac{x}{2}\right)$

**State the amplitude, period, phase shift, and vertical shift of each function.**

35. $y = 2 + 3\sin\left(x - \dfrac{\pi}{2}\right)$

36. $y = 3 - \dfrac{1}{2}\sin\left(x + \dfrac{\pi}{4}\right)$

37. $y = -2 - 4\cos\left[3\left(x + \dfrac{\pi}{4}\right)\right]$

38. $y = -1 + 2\cos\left[2\left(x - \dfrac{\pi}{3}\right)\right]$

39. $y = -\dfrac{1}{2} + \dfrac{1}{3}\cos\left(\pi x - \dfrac{1}{2}\right)$

40. $y = \dfrac{3}{4} - \dfrac{1}{6}\sin\left(\dfrac{\pi}{6}x + \dfrac{\pi}{3}\right)$

**Graph each function from $-\pi$ to $\pi$.**

41. $y = 3x - \cos(2x)$

42. $y = -\dfrac{1}{2}\cos(4x) + \dfrac{1}{2}\cos(2x)$

43. $y = 2\sin\left(\dfrac{1}{3}x\right) - 3\sin(3x)$

44. $y = 5\cos x + 3\sin\left(\dfrac{x}{2}\right)$

## 5.3 Graphs of Other Trigonometric Functions

**State the domain and range of each function.**

45. $y = 4\tan\left(x + \dfrac{\pi}{2}\right)$

46. $y = \cot 2\left(x - \dfrac{\pi}{2}\right)$

**47.** $y = 3 \sec(2x)$

**48.** $y = 1 + 2 \csc x$

**49.** $y = -\dfrac{1}{2} + \dfrac{1}{4} \sec\left(\pi x - \dfrac{2\pi}{3}\right)$

**50.** $y = 3 - \dfrac{1}{2} \csc(2x - \pi)$

**Graph each function on the interval** $[-2\pi, 2\pi]$.

**51.** $y = -\tan\left(x - \dfrac{\pi}{4}\right)$

**52.** $y = 1 + \cot(2x)$

**53.** $y = 2 + \sec(x - \pi)$

**54.** $y = -\csc\left(x + \dfrac{\pi}{4}\right)$

**55.** $y = \dfrac{1}{2} + 2 \csc\left(2x - \dfrac{\pi}{2}\right)$

**56.** $y = -1 - \dfrac{1}{2} \sec\left(\pi x - \dfrac{3\pi}{4}\right)$

## Technology Exercises

### Section 5.1

**In Exercises 57 and 58, refer to the following:**

A graphing calculator can be used to graph the unit circle with parametric equations (these will be covered in more detail in Section 9.9). For now, set the calculator in parametric and radian modes and let

$$X_1 = \cos T$$
$$Y_1 = \sin T$$

Set the window so that $0 \le T \le 2\pi$, step $= \dfrac{\pi}{15}$, $-2 \le X \le 2$, and $-2 \le Y \le 2$. To approximate the sine or cosines of a T value, use the $\boxed{\text{TRACE}}$ key, enter the T value, and read the corresponding coordinates from the screen.

**57.** Use the above steps to approximate $\cos\left(\dfrac{13\pi}{12}\right)$ to four decimal places.

**58.** Use the above steps to approximate $\sin\left(\dfrac{5\pi}{6}\right)$ to four decimal places.

### Section 5.2

**59.** Use a graphing calculator to graph $Y_1 = \cos x$ and $Y_2 = \cos(x + c)$, where

    **a.** $c = \dfrac{\pi}{6}$, and explain the relationship between $Y_2$ and $Y_1$.

    **b.** $c = -\dfrac{\pi}{6}$, and explain the relationship between $Y_2$ and $Y_1$.

**60.** Use a graphing calculator to graph $Y_1 = \sin x$ and $Y_2 = \sin x + c$, where

    **a.** $c = \dfrac{1}{2}$, and explain the relationship between $Y_2$ and $Y_1$.

    **b.** $c = -\dfrac{1}{2}$, and explain the relationship between $Y_2$ and $Y_1$.

### Section 5.3

**61.** What is the amplitude of the function $y = 4\cos x - 3\sin x$? Use a graphing calculator to graph $Y_1 = 4\cos x$, $Y_2 = 3\sin x$, and $Y_3 = 4\cos x - 3\sin x$ in the same viewing window.

**62.** What is the amplitude of the function $y = \sqrt{3}\sin x + \cos x$? Use a graphing calculator to graph $Y_1 = \sqrt{3}\sin x$, $Y_2 = \cos x$, and $Y_3 = \sqrt{3}\sin x + \cos x$ in the same viewing window.

1. State the amplitude and period of $y = -5\sin(3x)$.

2. Graph $y = -2\cos\left(\frac{1}{2}x\right)$ on the interval $-4\pi \leq x \leq 4\pi$.

3. Graph $y = 1 + 3\sin(x + \pi)$ on the interval $-3\pi \leq x \leq 3\pi$.

4. Graph $y = 4 - \sin\left(x - \frac{\pi}{2}\right)$ on the interval $-6\pi \leq x \leq 6\pi$.

5. Graph $y = -2 - \cos\left(x + \frac{\pi}{2}\right)$ on the interval $-4\pi \leq x \leq 4\pi$.

6. Graph $y = 3 + 2\cos\left(x + \frac{3\pi}{2}\right)$ on the interval $-5\pi \leq x \leq 5\pi$.

7. Graph $y = \tan\left(\pi x - \frac{\pi}{2}\right)$ over two periods.

8. The vertical asymptotes of $y = 2\csc(3x - \pi)$ correspond to the _____ of $y = 2\sin(3x - \pi)$.

9. State the $x$-intercepts of $y = \tan(2x)$ for all $x$.

10. State the phase shift and vertical shift for $y = -\cot\left(\frac{\pi}{3}x - \pi\right)$.

11. State the range of $y = -3\sec\left(2x + \frac{\pi}{3}\right) - 1$.

12. State the domain of $y = \tan\left(2x - \frac{\pi}{6}\right) + 3$.

13. Graph $y = -2\csc\left(x + \frac{\pi}{2}\right)$ over two periods.

14. Find the $x$-intercept(s) of $y = \frac{6}{\sqrt{3}} - 3\sec\left(6x - \frac{5\pi}{6}\right)$.

15. True or false: The equation $2\sin\theta = 2.0001$ has no solution.

16. On what $x$-intervals does the graph of $y = \cos(2x)$ lie below the $x$-axis?

17. Write the equation of a sine function that has amplitude 4, vertical shift $\frac{1}{2}$ down, phase shift $\frac{3}{2}$ to the left, and period $\pi$.

18. Write the equation of a cotangent function that has period $\pi$, vertical shift 0.01 up, and no phase shift.

19. Graph $y = \cos(3x) - \frac{1}{2}\sin(3x)$ for $0 \leq x \leq \pi$.

20. $y = -\frac{1}{5}\cos\left(\frac{x}{3}\right)$

    a. Graph the function over one period.
    b. Determine the amplitude, period, and phase shift.

21. $y = 4\sin(2\pi x)$

    a. Graph the function over one period.
    b. Determine the amplitude, period, and phase shift.

22. $y = -2\sin(3x + 4\pi) + 1$

    a. Write the sinusoidal function in standard form.
    b. Determine its amplitude, period, and phase shift.
    c. Graph the function over one period.

23. $y = 6 + 5\cos(2x - \pi)$

    a. Write the sinusoidal function in standard form.
    b. Determine its amplitude, period, and phase shift.
    c. Graph the function over one period.

24. Graph the function $y = 2\cos x - \sin x$ on the interval $[-\pi, \pi]$ by adding the ordinates of each individual function.

1. Find the domain of $f(x) = \dfrac{4}{\sqrt{15 + 3x}}$. Express the domain in interval notation.

2. On February 24, the gasoline price (per gallon) was $1.94; on May 24, its price per gallon was $2.39. Find the average rate of change per month in the gasoline price from February 24 to May 24.

3. Write the function whose graph is the graph of $y = |x|$, but stretched by a factor of 2, shifted up four units, and shifted to the left six units. Graph the function on the interval $[-10, 10]$.

4. Given $f(x) = 2x - 5$ and $g(x) = x^2 + 7$, find

   a. $f + g$

   b. $f - g$

   c. $f \cdot g$

   d. $f/g$

   e. $f \circ g$

5. Find the inverse function of the one-to-one function $f(x) = \dfrac{x - 2}{3x + 5}$. Find the domain and range of both $f$ and $f^{-1}$.

6. For $f(x) = -x^2(2x - 6)^3(x + 5)^4$

   a. list each zero and its multiplicity.

   b. sketch the graph.

7. Divide $(6x^4 - 5x^3 + 6x^2 + 7x - 4)$ by $(2x^2 - 1)$ using long division. Express the answer in the form $Q(x) = ?$ and $r(x) = ?$.

8. For the polynomial function $f(x) = x^4 + x^3 - 7x^2 - x + 6$

   a. factor as a product of linear and/or irreducible quadratic factors.

   b. graph the function.

9. Factor the polynomial $P(x) = x^4 - 4x^2 - 5$ as a product of linear factors.

10. Given $f(x) = \dfrac{x^2 - 5x - 14}{2x^2 + 14x + 20}$,

   a. determine the vertical, horizontal, or slant asymptotes (if they exist).

   b. graph the function.

11. If $3000 is deposited into an account paying 1.2% compounded quarterly, how much will you have in the account in 10 years?

12. Approximate $\log_2 19$ utilizing a calculator. Round to two decimal places.

13. Write $\ln\left(\dfrac{a^3}{b^2c^5}\right)$ as a sum or difference of constant multiples of logarithms.

14. Solve the exponential equation $4^{3x-2} + 5 = 23$. Round your answer to three decimal places.

15. Solve the exponential equation $\log(x + 2) + \log(x + 3) = \log(2x + 10)$. Round your answer to three decimal places.

16. Find the area of a circular sector with radius $r = 6.5$ cm and central angle $\theta = \dfrac{4\pi}{5}$. Round your answer to the nearest integer.

17. Solve the right triangle $\beta = 27°$, $c = 14$ in. Round your answer to the nearest hundredth.

18. The terminal side of an angle $\theta$ in standard position passes through the point $(3, -2)$. Calculate the exact value of the six trigonometric functions for angle $\theta$.

19. Solve the triangle $\alpha = 68°$, $a = 24$ m, and $b = 24.5$ m.

20. Solve the triangle $a = 5$, $b = 6$, and $c = 7$.

21. Given that $\sin\theta = \dfrac{1}{2}$ and $\dfrac{\pi}{2} < \theta < \pi$, find the exact value of all the other trigonometric functions.

22. Graph the function $y = 4\cos(2x + \pi)$ over one period.

23. The frequency of the oscillations $f$ is given by $f = \dfrac{1}{p}$, where $p$ is the period. What is the frequency of the oscillations modeled by $y = 1.14\sin(4t)$?

24. Graph the function $y = -2 + 5\csc\left(4x - \dfrac{\pi}{2}\right)$ over two periods. State the range of the function.

# 6

# Analytic Trigonometry

© Jason Brindel Commercial/Alamy

When you press a touch-tone button to dial a phone number, how does the phone system know which key you have pressed? Dual Tone Multi-Frequency (DTMF), also known as Touch-Tone dialing, was developed by Bell Labs in the 1960s. The Touch-Tone system also introduced a standardized *keypad* layout.

The keypad is laid out in a 4 × 3 matrix, with each row representing a low frequency and each column representing a high frequency.

| FREQUENCY | 1209 Hz | 1336 Hz | 1477 Hz |
|---|---|---|---|
| 697 Hz | 1 | 2 | 3 |
| 770 Hz | 4 | 5 | 6 |
| 852 Hz | 7 | 8 | 9 |
| 941 Hz | * | 0 | # |

When you press the number 8, the phone sends a sinusoidal tone that combines a low-frequency tone of 852 hertz and a high-frequency tone of 1336 hertz. The result can be found using sum-to-product *trigonometric identities*.

# ANALYTIC TRIGONOMETRY

| 6.1 Verifying Trigonometric Identities | 6.2 Sum and Difference Identities | 6.3 Double-Angle and Half-Angle Identities | 6.4 Product-to-Sum and Sum-to-Product Identities | 6.5 Inverse Trigonometric Functions | 6.6 Trigonometric Equations |
|---|---|---|---|---|---|
| • Fundamental Identities<br>• Simplifying Trigonometric Expressions Using Identities<br>• Verifying Identities | • Sum and Difference Identities for the Cosine Function<br>• Sum and Difference Identities for the Sine Function<br>• Sum and Difference Identities for the Tangent Function | • Double-Angle Identities<br>• Half-Angle Identities | • Product-to-Sum Identities<br>• Sum-to-Product Identities | • Inverse Sine Function<br>• Inverse Cosine Function<br>• Inverse Tangent Function<br>• Remaining Inverse Trigonometric Functions<br>• Finding Exact Values for Expressions Involving Inverse Trigonometric Functions | • Solving Trigonometric Equations by Inspection<br>• Solving Trigonometric Equations Using Algebraic Techniques<br>• Solving Trigonometric Equations That Require the Use of Inverse Functions<br>• Using Trigonometric Identities to Solve Trigonometric Equations |

## LEARNING OBJECTIVES

- Verify trigonometric identities.
- Use the sum and difference identities to simplify trigonometric expressions.
- Use the double-angle and half-angle identities to simplify trigonometric expressions.
- Use the product-to-sum and sum-to-product identities to simplify trigonometric expressions.
- Evaluate the inverse trigonometric functions for specific values.
- Solve trigonometric equations.

589

## SKILLS OBJECTIVES

- Apply fundamental identities.
- Simplify trigonometric expressions using identities.
- Verify trigonometric identities.

## CONCEPTUAL OBJECTIVES

- Understand that there is more than one way to verify an identity.
- Understand that identities must hold for all values in the domain of the functions that are related by the identities.

## Fundamental Identities

In mathematics, an **identity** is an equation that is true for *all* values of the variable for which the expressions in the equation are defined. If an equation is true for only *some* values of the variable, it is a **conditional equation**.

The following boxes summarize trigonometric identities that have been discussed in Chapters 4 and 5.

### RECIPROCAL IDENTITIES

| RECIPROCAL IDENTITIES | EQUIVALENT FORMS | DOMAIN RESTRICTIONS |
|---|---|---|
| $\csc x = \dfrac{1}{\sin x}$ | $\sin x = \dfrac{1}{\csc x}$ | $x \neq n\pi \quad n = $ integer |
| $\sec x = \dfrac{1}{\cos x}$ | $\cos x = \dfrac{1}{\sec x}$ | $x \neq \dfrac{n\pi}{2} \quad n = $ odd integer |
| $\cot x = \dfrac{1}{\tan x}$ | $\tan x = \dfrac{1}{\cot x}$ | $x \neq \dfrac{n\pi}{2} \quad n = $ integer |

### QUOTIENT IDENTITIES

| QUOTIENT IDENTITIES | DOMAIN RESTRICTIONS |
|---|---|
| $\tan x = \dfrac{\sin x}{\cos x}$ | $\cos x \neq 0 \quad x \neq \dfrac{n\pi}{2} \quad n = $ odd integer |
| $\cot x = \dfrac{\cos x}{\sin x}$ | $\sin x \neq 0 \quad x \neq n\pi \quad n = $ integer |

### PYTHAGOREAN IDENTITIES

$$\sin^2 x + \cos^2 x = 1 \qquad \tan^2 x + 1 = \sec^2 x \qquad 1 + \cot^2 x = \csc^2 x$$

In Chapter 5, we discussed even and odd trigonometric functions, which like even and odd functions in general have these respective properties:

| TYPE OF FUNCTION | ALGEBRAIC IDENTITY | GRAPH |
|---|---|---|
| Even | $f(-x) = f(x)$ | Symmetry about the $y$-axis |
| Odd | $f(-x) = -f(x)$ | Symmetry about the origin |

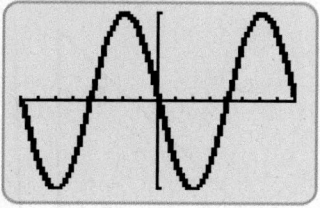

We already learned in Chapter 5 that the sine function is an odd function and the cosine function is an even function. Combining this knowledge with the reciprocal and quotient identities, we arrive at the *even-odd identities*, which we can add to our list of basic identities.

**EVEN-ODD IDENTITIES**

$$\text{Odd} \begin{cases} \sin(-x) = -\sin x \\ \csc(-x) = -\csc x \\ \tan(-x) = -\tan x \\ \cot(-x) = -\cot x \end{cases} \qquad \text{Even} \begin{cases} \cos(-x) = \cos x \\ \sec(-x) = \sec x \end{cases}$$

## Cofunctions

Recall complementary angles (Section 4.1). Notice the *co* in *co*sine, *co*secant, and *co*tangent functions. These *cofunctions* are based on the relationship of *co*mplementary angles. Let us look at a right triangle with labled sides and angles.

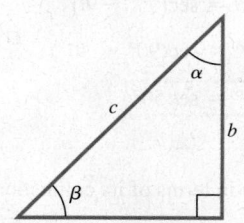

$$\left. \begin{aligned} \sin\beta &= \frac{\text{opposite of } \beta}{\text{hypotenuse}} = \frac{b}{c} \\ \cos\alpha &= \frac{\text{adjacent to } \alpha}{\text{hypotenuse}} = \frac{b}{c} \end{aligned} \right\} \sin\beta = \cos\alpha$$

Recall that the sum of the measures of the three angles in a triangle is 180°. In a right triangle, one angle is 90°; therefore, the two acute angles are complementary angles (the measures sum to 90°). You can see in the triangle above that $\beta$ and $\alpha$ are *co*mplementary angles. In other words, the sine of an angle is the same as the *co*sine of the *co*mplement of that angle. This is true for all *trigonometric cofunction* pairs.

**COFUNCTION THEOREM**

A trigonometric function of an angle is always equal to the cofunction of the complement of the angle. If $\alpha + \beta = 90° \left( \text{or } \alpha + \beta = \dfrac{\pi}{2} \right)$, then

$$\sin\beta = \cos\alpha$$
$$\sec\beta = \csc\alpha$$
$$\tan\beta = \cot\alpha$$

Alternate form of cofunction identities:

$$\sin\theta = \cos\left(\frac{\pi}{2} - \theta\right)$$

$$\cos\theta = \sin\left(\frac{\pi}{2} - \theta\right)$$

$$\tan\theta = \cot\left(\frac{\pi}{2} - \theta\right)$$

$$\cot\theta = \tan\left(\frac{\pi}{2} - \theta\right)$$

$$\sec\theta = \csc\left(\frac{\pi}{2} - \theta\right)$$

$$\csc\theta = \sec\left(\frac{\pi}{2} - \theta\right)$$

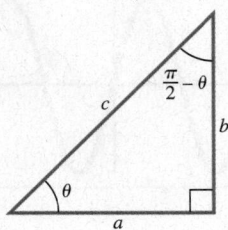

**COFUNCTION IDENTITIES**

| | |
|---|---|
| $\sin\theta = \cos(90° - \theta)$ | $\cos\theta = \sin(90° - \theta)$ |
| $\tan\theta = \cot(90° - \theta)$ | $\cot\theta = \tan(90° - \theta)$ |
| $\sec\theta = \csc(90° - \theta)$ | $\csc\theta = \sec(90° - \theta)$ |

**EXAMPLE 1    Writing Trigonometric Function Values in Terms of Their Cofunctions**

Write each function or function value in terms of its cofunction.

**a.** $\sin 30°$        **b.** $\tan x$        **c.** $\csc 40°$

**Solution (a):**

Cosine is the cofunction of sine.                        $\sin\theta = \cos(90° - \theta)$

Substitute $\theta = 30°$.                                 $\sin 30° = \cos(90° - 30°)$

Simplify.                                                     $\boxed{\sin 30° = \cos 60°}$

**Solution (b):**

Cotangent is the cofunction of tangent.              $\tan\theta = \cot(90° - \theta)$

Substitute $\theta = x$.                                   $\boxed{\tan x = \cot(90° - x)}$

**Solution (c):**

Cosecant is the cofunction of secant.                 $\csc\theta = \sec(90° - \theta)$

Substitute $\theta = 40°$.                                 $\csc 40° = \sec(90° - 40°)$

Simplify.                                                     $\boxed{\csc 40° = \sec 50°}$

■ **Answer: a.** $\sin 45°$ **b.** $\sec(90° - y)$

■ **YOUR TURN** Write each function or function value in terms of its cofunction.

**a.** $\cos 45°$        **b.** $\csc y$

# Simplifying Trigonometric Expressions Using Identities

We can use the fundamental identities and algebraic manipulation to simplify more complicated trigonometric expressions. In simplifying trigonometric expressions, one approach is to first convert all expressions into sines and cosines and then simplify.

 **EXAMPLE 2    Simplifying Trigonometric Expressions**

Simplify $\tan x \sin x + \cos x$.

**Solution:**

Write the tangent function in terms of the sine and cosine functions: $\tan x = \dfrac{\sin x}{\cos x}$.

$$\tan x \cdot \sin x + \cos x$$
$$= \frac{\sin x}{\cos x} \sin x + \cos x$$

Simplify.

$$= \frac{\sin^2 x}{\cos x} + \cos x$$

Write as a fraction with a single quotient by finding a common denominator, $\cos x$.

$$= \frac{\sin^2 x + \cos^2 x}{\cos x}$$

Use the Pythagorean identity:
$\sin^2 x + \cos^2 x = 1$.

$$= \frac{1}{\cos x}$$

Use the reciprocal identity $\sec x = \dfrac{1}{\cos x}$.

$$= \boxed{\sec x}$$

▪ **YOUR TURN**  Simplify $\cot x \cos x + \sin x$.

▪ **Answer:** $\csc x$

In Example 2, $\tan x$ and $\sec x$ are not defined for odd integer multiples of $\dfrac{\pi}{2}$. In the Your Turn, $\cot x$ and $\csc x$ are not defined for integer multiples of $\pi$. Both the original expression and the simplified form are governed by the same restrictions. There are times when the original expression is subject to more domain restrictions than the simplified form and thus special attention must be given to domain restrictions.

For example, the algebraic expression $\dfrac{x^2 - 1}{x + 1}$ is under the domain restriction $x \neq -1$ because that value for $x$ makes the value of the denominator equal to zero. If we forget to state the domain restrictions, we might simplify the algebraic expression as $\dfrac{x^2 - 1}{x + 1} = \dfrac{(x - 1)(x + 1)}{(x + 1)} = x - 1$ and assume this is true for all values of $x$. The correct simplification is $\dfrac{x^2 - 1}{x + 1} = x - 1$ for $x \neq -1$. In fact, if we were to graph both the original expression $y = \dfrac{x^2 - 1}{x + 1}$ and the line $y = x - 1$, they would coincide, except that the graph of the original expression would have a "hole" or discontinuity at $x = -1$. In this chapter, it is assumed that the domain of the simplified expression is the same as the domain of the original expression.

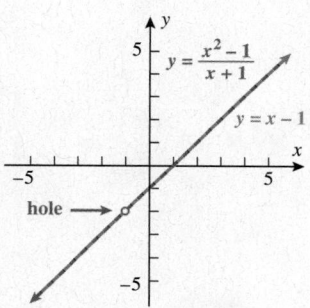

### EXAMPLE 3  Simplifying Trigonometric Expressions

Simplify $\dfrac{1}{\csc^2 x} + \dfrac{1}{\sec^2 x}$.

**Solution:**

Rewrite the expression in terms of quotients squared.

$$\frac{1}{\csc^2 x} + \frac{1}{\sec^2 x} = \left(\frac{1}{\csc x}\right)^2 + \left(\frac{1}{\sec x}\right)^2$$

Use the reciprocal identities to write the cosecant and secant functions in terms of sines and cosines:
$\sin x = \dfrac{1}{\csc x}$ and $\cos x = \dfrac{1}{\sec x}$.

$$= \sin^2 x + \cos^2 x$$

Use the Pythagorean identity:
$\sin^2 x + \cos^2 x = 1$.

$$= \boxed{1}$$

▪ **YOUR TURN**  Simplify $\dfrac{1}{\cos^2 x} - 1$.

▪ **Answer:** $\tan^2 x$

## Verifying Identities

We will now use the trigonometric identities to verify, or establish, other trigonometric identities. For example, verify that

$$(\sin x - \cos x)^2 - 1 = -2\sin x \cos x$$

The good news is that we will know we are done when we get there, since we know the desired identity. But how do we get there? How do we verify that the identity is true? Remember that it must be true for *all* $x$, not just some $x$. Therefore, it is not enough to simply select values for $x$ and show it is true for those specific values.

| WORDS | MATH |
|---|---|
| Start with one side of the equation (the more complicated side). | $(\sin x - \cos x)^2 - 1$ |
| Remember that $(a - b)^2 = a^2 - 2ab + b^2$ and expand $(\sin x - \cos x)^2$. | $= \sin^2 x - 2\sin x \cos x + \cos^2 x - 1$ |
| Group the $\sin^2 x$ and $\cos^2 x$ terms and use the Pythagorean identity. | $= -2\sin x \cos x + \underbrace{(\sin^2 x + \cos^2 x)}_{1} - 1$ |
| Simplify. | $= -2\sin x \cos x$ |

When we arrive at the right side of the equation, then we have succeeded in verifying the identity. In verifying trigonometric identities, there is no one procedure that works for all identities. You must manipulate one side of the equation until it looks like the other side.

The following suggestions help guide the way in verifying trigonometric identities.

### GUIDELINES FOR VERIFYING TRIGONOMETRIC IDENTITIES

- Start with the more complicated side of the equation.
- Combine all sums and differences of fractions (quotients) into a single fraction (quotient).
- Use fundamental trigonometric identities.
- Use algebraic techniques to manipulate one side of the equation until the other side of the equation is achieved.
- Sometimes it is helpful to convert all trigonometric functions into sines and cosines.

It is important to note that trigonometric identities must be valid for all values of the independent variable (usually, $x$ or $\theta$) for which the expressions in the equation are defined (domain of the equation).

## EXAMPLE 4    Verifying Trigonometric Identities

Verify the identity $\dfrac{\tan x - \cot x}{\tan x + \cot x} = \sin^2 x - \cos^2 x.$

**Solution:**

Start with the more complicated side of the equation.

$$\frac{\tan x - \cot x}{\tan x + \cot x}$$

Use the quotient identity to write the tangent and cotangent functions in terms of the sine and cosine functions.

$$= \frac{\dfrac{\sin x}{\cos x} - \dfrac{\cos x}{\sin x}}{\dfrac{\sin x}{\cos x} + \dfrac{\cos x}{\sin x}}$$

Multiply by $\dfrac{\sin x \cos x}{\sin x \cos x}.$

$$= \left( \frac{\dfrac{\sin x}{\cos x} - \dfrac{\cos x}{\sin x}}{\dfrac{\sin x}{\cos x} + \dfrac{\cos x}{\sin x}} \right) \left( \frac{\sin x \cos x}{\sin x \cos x} \right)$$

Simplify.

$$= \frac{\sin^2 x - \cos^2 x}{\sin^2 x + \cos^2 x}$$

Use the Pythagorean identity: $\sin^2 x + \cos^2 x = 1.$

$$= \boxed{\sin^2 x - \cos^2 x}$$

### Technology Tip

Graphs of $y_1 = \dfrac{\tan x - \cot x}{\tan x + \cot x}$ and $y_2 = \sin^2 x - \cos^2 x.$

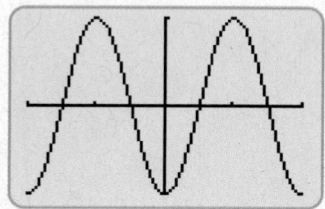

## EXAMPLE 5    Determining Whether a Trigonometric Equation Is an Identity

Determine whether $\left(1 - \cos^2 x\right)\left(1 + \cot^2 x\right) = 0$, is an identity, a conditional equation, or a contradiction.

**Solution:**

Use the quotient identity to write the cotangent function in terms of the sine and cosine functions.

$$(1 - \cos^2 x)(1 + \cot^2 x)$$
$$= \left(1 - \cos^2 x\right)\left(1 + \frac{\cos^2 x}{\sin^2 x}\right)$$

Combine the expression in the second parentheses so that it is a single quotient.

$$= \left(1 - \cos^2 x\right)\left(\frac{\sin^2 x + \cos^2 x}{\sin^2 x}\right)$$

Use the Pythagorean identity.

$$= \underbrace{\left(1 - \cos^2 x\right)}_{\sin^2 x}\left(\frac{\overbrace{\sin^2 x + \cos^2 x}^{1}}{\sin^2 x}\right)$$

Eliminate the parentheses.

$$= \frac{\sin^2 x}{\sin^2 x}$$

Simplify.

$$= 1$$

Since $1 \neq 0$, this is not an identity, but rather a $\boxed{\text{contradiction}}$.

**EXAMPLE 6  Determine Whether a Trigonometric Equation Is an Identity**

Determine whether $\sin^4 x - \cos^4 x = 0$ is an identity, a conditional equation, or a contradiction.

**Solution:**

Factor the left side of the equation.

$$\sin^4 x - \cos^4 x$$
$$= \left(\sin^2 x + \cos^2 x\right)\left(\sin^2 x - \cos^2 x\right) = 0$$

Apply the Pythagorean identity,
$\sin^2 x + \cos^2 x = 1$.

$$= \left(\sin^2 x - \cos^2 x\right) = 0$$

Factor the left side of the equation again.

$$= (\sin x - \cos x)(\sin x + \cos x) = 0$$

Solve.

$$\sin x = \cos x \quad \text{or} \quad \sin x = -\cos x$$

Notice that when $x = \dfrac{\pi}{4}$ and $x = \dfrac{5\pi}{4}$ the equation is satisfied, but for $x = \dfrac{3\pi}{4}$ and $x = \dfrac{7\pi}{4}$ the equation is not satisfied. Since this equation is true for some (but not all values) of $x$, it is a $\boxed{\text{conditional equation}}$.

**▶ EXAMPLE 7  Verifying Trigonometric Identities**

Verify that $\dfrac{\sin(-x)}{\cos(-x)\tan(-x)} = 1$.

**Solution:**

Start with the left side of the equation.

$$\frac{\sin(-x)}{\cos(-x)\tan(-x)}$$

Use the even-odd identities.

$$= \frac{-\sin x}{-\cos x \tan x}$$

Simplify.

$$= \frac{\sin x}{\cos x \tan x}$$

Use the quotient identity to write the tangent function in terms of the sine and cosine functions.

$$= \frac{\sin x}{\cos x \left(\dfrac{\sin x}{\cos x}\right)}$$

Divide out the cosine term in the denominator.

$$= \frac{\sin x}{\sin x}$$

Simplify.

$$= 1$$

We have verified that $\dfrac{\sin(-x)}{\cos(-x)\tan(-x)} = 1$.

**Study Tip**

Start with the more complicated expression (side) and manipulate until reaching the simpler expression (on the other side).

So far we have discussed working with only one side of the identity until arriving at the other side. Another method for verifying identities is to work with (simplify) each side separately and use identities and algebraic techniques to arrive at the same result on both sides.

**EXAMPLE 8** **Verifying an Identity by Simplifying Both Sides Separately**

Verify that $\dfrac{\sin x + 1}{\sin x} = -\dfrac{\cot^2 x}{1 - \csc x}$.

**Solution:**

Left-hand side: $\dfrac{\sin x + 1}{\sin x} = \dfrac{\sin x}{\sin x} + \dfrac{1}{\sin x} = 1 + \csc x$

Right-hand side: $\dfrac{-\cot^2 x}{1 - \csc x} = \dfrac{1 - \csc^2 x}{1 - \csc x} = \dfrac{(1 - \csc x)(1 + \csc x)}{(1 - \csc x)} = 1 + \csc x$

Since the left-hand side equals the right-hand side, the equation is an identity.

---

## SECTION 6.1 SUMMARY

We combined the fundamental trigonometric identities—reciprocal, quotient, Pythagorean, even-odd, and cofunction—with algebraic techniques to simplify trigonometric expressions and verify more complex trigonometric identities. Two steps that we often use in both simplifying trigonometric expressions and verifying trigonometric identities are: (1) writing all trigonometric functions in terms of the sine and cosine functions, and (2) combining sums or differences of quotients into a single quotient.

When verifying trigonometric identities, we typically work with the more complicated side (keeping the other side in mind as our goal). Another approach to verifying trigonometric identities is to work on each side separately and arrive at the same result.

---

## SECTION 6.1 EXERCISES

### ▪ SKILLS

**In Exercises 1–6, use the cofunction identities to fill in the blanks.**

**1.** $\sin 60° = \cos$_____

**2.** $\sin 45° = \cos$_____

**3.** $\cos x = \sin$_____

**4.** $\cot A = \tan$_____

**5.** $\csc 30° = \sec$_____

**6.** $\sec B = \csc$_____

**In Exercises 7–14, write the trigonometric function values in terms of its cofunction.**

**7.** $\sin(x + y)$

**8.** $\sin(60° - x)$

**9.** $\cos(20° + A)$

**10.** $\cos(A + B)$

**11.** $\cot(45° - x)$

**12.** $\sec(30° - \theta)$

**13.** $\csc(60° - \theta)$

**14.** $\tan(40° + \theta)$

**In Exercises 15–38, simplify each of the trigonometric expressions.**

**15.** $\sin x \csc x$

**16.** $\tan x \cot x$

**17.** $\sec(-x)\cot x$

**18.** $\tan(-x)\cos(-x)$

**19.** $\csc(-x)\sin x$

**20.** $\cot(-x)\tan x$

**21.** $\sec x \cos(-x) + \tan^2 x$

**22.** $\sec(-x)\tan(-x)\cos(-x)$

**23.** $(\sin^2 x)(\cot^2 x + 1)$

**24.** $(\cos^2 x)(\tan^2 x + 1)$

**25.** $(\sin x - \cos x)(\sin x + \cos x)$

**26.** $(\sin x + \cos x)^2$

**27.** $\dfrac{\csc x}{\cot x}$

**28.** $\dfrac{\sec x}{\tan x}$

**29.** $\dfrac{1 - \cot(-x)}{1 + \cot x}$

**30.** $\sec^2 x - \tan^2(-x)$

**31.** $\dfrac{1 - \cos^4 x}{1 + \cos^2 x}$

**32.** $\dfrac{1 - \sin^4 x}{1 + \sin^2 x}$

**33.** $\dfrac{1 - \cot^4 x}{1 - \cot^2 x}$

**34.** $\dfrac{1 - \tan^4(-x)}{1 - \tan^2 x}$

**35.** $1 - \dfrac{\sin^2 x}{1 - \cos x}$

**36.** $1 - \dfrac{\cos^2 x}{1 + \sin x}$

**37.** $\dfrac{\tan x - \cot x}{\tan x + \cot x} + 2\cos^2 x$

**38.** $\dfrac{\tan x - \cot x}{\tan x + \cot x} + \cos^2 x$

**In Exercises 39–64, verify each of the trigonometric identities.**

**39.** $(\sin x + \cos x)^2 + (\sin x - \cos x)^2 = 2$

**40.** $(1 - \sin x)(1 + \sin x) = \cos^2 x$

**41.** $(\csc x + 1)(\csc x - 1) = \cot^2 x$

**42.** $(\sec x + 1)(\sec x - 1) = \tan^2 x$

**43.** $\tan x + \cot x = \csc x \sec x$

**44.** $\csc x - \sin x = \cot x \cos x$

**45.** $\dfrac{2 - \sin^2 x}{\cos x} = \sec x + \cos x$

**46.** $\dfrac{2 - \cos^2 x}{\sin x} = \csc x + \sin x$

**47.** $[\cos(-x) - 1][1 + \cos x] = -\sin^2 x$

**48.** $\tan(-x)\cot x = -1$

**49.** $\dfrac{\sec(-x)\cot x}{\csc(-x)} = -1$

**50.** $\csc(-x) - 1 = \dfrac{\cot^2 x}{\csc(-x) + 1}$

**51.** $\dfrac{1}{\csc^2 x} + \dfrac{1}{\sec^2 x} = 1$

**52.** $\dfrac{1}{\cot^2 x} - \dfrac{1}{\tan^2 x} = \sec^2 x - \csc^2 x$

**53.** $\dfrac{1}{1 - \sin x} + \dfrac{1}{1 + \sin x} = 2\sec^2 x$

**54.** $\dfrac{1}{1 - \cos x} + \dfrac{1}{1 + \cos x} = 2\csc^2 x$

**55.** $\dfrac{\sin^2 x}{1 - \cos x} = 1 + \cos x$

**56.** $\dfrac{\cos^2 x}{1 - \sin x} = 1 + \sin x$

**57.** $\sec x + \tan x = \dfrac{1}{\sec x - \tan x}$

**58.** $\csc x + \cot x = \dfrac{1}{\csc x - \cot x}$

**59.** $\dfrac{\csc x - \tan x}{\sec x + \cot x} = \dfrac{\cos x - \sin^2 x}{\sin x + \cos^2 x}$

**60.** $\dfrac{\sec x + \tan x}{\csc x + 1} = \tan x$

**61.** $\dfrac{\cos^2 x + 1 + \sin x}{\cos^2 x + 3} = \dfrac{1 + \sin x}{2 + \sin x}$

**62.** $\dfrac{\sin x + 1 - \cos^2 x}{\cos^2 x} = \dfrac{\sin x}{1 - \sin x}$

**63.** $\sec x(\tan x + \cot x) = \dfrac{\csc x}{\cos^2 x}$

**64.** $\tan x(\csc x - \sin x) = \cos x$

**In Exercises 65–78, determine whether each equation is a conditional equation or an identity.**

**65.** $\cos^2 x(\tan x - \sec x)(\tan x + \sec x) = 1$

**66.** $\cos^2 x(\tan x - \sec x)(\tan x + \sec x) = \sin^2 x - 1$

**67.** $\dfrac{\csc x \cot x}{\sec x \tan x} = \cot^3 x$

**68.** $\sin x \cos x = 0$

**69.** $\sin x + \cos x = \sqrt{2}$

**70.** $\sin^2 x + \cos^2 x = 1$

**71.** $\tan^2 x - \sec^2 x = 1$

**72.** $\sec^2 x - \tan^2 x = 1$

**73.** $\sin x = \sqrt{1 - \cos^2 x}$

**74.** $\csc x = \sqrt{1 + \cot^2 x}$

**75.** $\sqrt{\sin^2 x + \cos^2 x} = 1$

**76.** $\sqrt{\sin^2 x + \cos^2 x} = \sin x + \cos x$

**77.** $(\sin x - \cos x)^2 = \sin^2 x - \cos^2 x$

**78.** $[\sin(-x) - 1][\sin(-x) + 1] = \cos^2 x$

## ■ APPLICATIONS

**79. Area of a Circle.** Show that the area of a circle with radius $r = \sec x$ is equal to $\pi + \pi(\tan x)^2$.

**80. Area of a Triangle.** Show that the area of a triangle with base $b = \cos x$ and height $h = \sec x$ is equal to $\frac{1}{2}$.

**81. Pythagorean Theorem.** Find the length of the hypotenuse of a right triangle whose legs have lengths 1 and $\tan\theta$.

**82. Pythagorean Theorem.** Find the length of the hypotenuse of a right triangle whose legs have lengths 1 and $\cot\theta$.

## ▪CATCH THE MISTAKE

**In Exercises 83–86, explain the mistake that is made.**

**83.** Verify the identity $\dfrac{\cos x}{1 - \tan x} + \dfrac{\sin x}{1 - \cot x} = \sin x + \cos x$.

**Solution:**

Start with the left side of the equation. $\dfrac{\cos x}{1 - \tan x} + \dfrac{\sin x}{1 - \cot x}$

Write the tangent and cotangent functions in terms of sines and cosines.

$= \dfrac{\cos x}{1 - \dfrac{\sin x}{\cos x}} + \dfrac{\sin x}{1 - \dfrac{\cos x}{\sin x}}$

Cancel the common cosine in the first term and sine in the second term.

$= \dfrac{1}{1 - \sin x} + \dfrac{1}{1 - \cos x}$

This is incorrect. What mistake was made?

**84.** Verify the identity $\dfrac{\cos^3 x \sec x}{1 - \sin x} = 1 + \sin x$.

**Solution:**

Start with the equation on the left. $\dfrac{\cos^3 x \sec x}{1 - \sin x}$

Rewrite secant in terms of sine. $= \dfrac{\cos^3 x \dfrac{1}{\sin x}}{1 - \sin x}$

Simplify. $= \dfrac{\cos^3 x}{1 - \sin^2 x}$

Use the Pythagorean identity. $= \dfrac{\cos^3 x}{\cos^2 x}$

Simplify. $= \cos x$

This is incorrect. What mistakes were made?

**85.** Determine whether the equation is a conditional equation or an identity: $\dfrac{\tan x}{\cot x} = 1$.

**Solution:**

Start with the left side. $\dfrac{\tan x}{\cot x}$

Rewrite the tangent and cotangent functions in terms of sines and cosines. $= \dfrac{\dfrac{\sin x}{\cos x}}{\dfrac{\cos x}{\sin x}}$

Simplify. $= \dfrac{\sin^2 x}{\cos^2 x} = \tan^2 x$

Let $x = \dfrac{\pi}{4}$. *Note:* $\tan\left(\dfrac{\pi}{4}\right) = 1$. $= 1$

Since $\dfrac{\tan x}{\cot x} = 1$, this equation is an identity.

This is incorrect. What mistake was made?

**86.** Determine whether the equation is a conditional equation or an identity: $|\sin x| - \cos x = 1$.

**Solution:**

Start with the left side of the equation. $|\sin x| - \cos x$

Let $x = \dfrac{n\pi}{2}$, where $n$ is an odd integer. $\left|\sin\left(\dfrac{n\pi}{2}\right)\right| - \cos\left(\dfrac{n\pi}{2}\right)$

Simplify. $|\pm 1| - 0 = 1$

Since $|\sin x| - \cos x = 1$, this is an identity.

This is incorrect. What mistake was made?

## ▪CONCEPTUAL

**In Exercises 87 and 88, determine whether each statement is true or false.**

**87.** If an equation is true for some values (but not all values), then it is still an identity.

**88.** If an equation has an infinite number of solutions, then it is an identity.

**89.** In which quadrants is the equation $\cos\theta = \sqrt{1 - \sin^2\theta}$ true?

**90.** In which quadrants is the equation $-\cos\theta = \sqrt{1 - \sin^2\theta}$ true?

**91.** In which quadrants is the equation $\csc\theta = -\sqrt{1 + \cot^2\theta}$ true?

**92.** In which quadrants is the equation $\sec\theta = \sqrt{1 + \tan^2\theta}$ true?

**93.** Do you think that $\sin(A + B) = \sin A + \sin B$? Why?

**94.** Do you think that $\cos\left(\tfrac{1}{2}A\right) = \tfrac{1}{2}\cos A$? Why?

**95.** Do you think $\tan(2A) = 2\tan A$? Why?

**96.** Do you think $\cot(A^2) = (\cot A)^2$? Why?

## ▪CHALLENGE

**97.** Simplify $(a\sin x + b\cos x)^2 + (b\sin x - a\cos x)^2$.

**98.** Simplify $\dfrac{1 + \cot^3 x}{1 + \cot x} + \cot x$.

**99.** Show that $\csc\left(\dfrac{\pi}{2} + \theta + 2n\pi\right) = \sec\theta$, $n$ an integer.

**100.** Show that $\sec\left(\dfrac{\pi}{2} - \theta - 2n\pi\right) = \csc\theta$, $n$ an integer.

**101.** Simplify $\csc\left(2\pi - \dfrac{\pi}{2} - \theta\right) \cdot \sec\left(\theta - \dfrac{\pi}{2}\right) \cdot \sin(-\theta)$.

**102.** Simplify $\tan\theta \cdot \cot(2\pi - \theta)$.

■ **TECHNOLOGY**

**In the next section, you will learn the sum and difference identities. In Exercises 103–106, we illustrate these identities with graphing calculators.**

**103.** Determine the correct sign ($+$ or $-$) for
$\cos(A + B) = \cos A \cos B \pm \sin A \sin B$ by graphing
$Y_1 = \cos(A + B)$, $Y_2 = \overset{?}{\cos} A \cos B + \sin A \sin B$, and
$Y_2 = \cos A \cos B - \sin A \sin B$ in the same viewing rectangle for several values of $A$ and $B$.

**104.** Determine the correct sign ($+$ or $-$) for
$\cos(A - B) = \cos A \cos B \pm \sin A \sin B$ by graphing
$Y_1 = \cos(A - B)$, $Y_2 = \overset{?}{\cos} A \cos B + \sin A \sin B$, and
$Y_2 = \cos A \cos B - \sin A \sin B$ in the same viewing rectangle for several values of $A$ and $B$.

**105.** Determine the correct sign ($+$ or $-$) for
$\sin(A + B) = \sin A \cos B \pm \cos A \sin B$ by graphing
$Y_1 = \sin(A + B)$, $Y_2 = \overset{?}{\sin} A \cos B + \cos A \sin B$, and
$Y_2 = \sin A \cos B - \cos A \sin B$ in the same viewing rectangle for several values of $A$ and $B$.

**106.** Determine the correct sign ($+$ or $-$) for
$\sin(A - B) = \sin A \cos B \pm \cos A \sin B$ by graphing
$Y_1 = \sin(A - B)$, $Y_2 = \overset{?}{\sin} A \cos B + \cos A \sin B$, and
$Y_2 = \sin A \cos B - \cos A \sin B$ in the same viewing rectangle for several values of $A$ and $B$.

■ **PREVIEW TO CALCULUS**

**For Exercises 107–110, refer to the following:**

In calculus, when integrating expressions such as $\sqrt{a^2 - x^2}$, $\sqrt{a^2 + x^2}$, and $\sqrt{x^2 - a^2}$, trigonometric functions are used as "dummy" functions to eliminate the radical. Once the integration is performed, the trigonometric function is "unsubstituted." These trigonometric substitutions (and corresponding trigonometric identities) are used to simplify these types of expressions.

When simplifying, it is important to remember that

$$|x| = \begin{cases} x & \text{if } x \geq 0 \\ -x & \text{if } x < 0 \end{cases}$$

| EXPRESSIONS | SUBSTITUTION | | TRIGONOMETRIC IDENTITY |
|---|---|---|---|
| $\sqrt{a^2 - x^2}$ | $x = a \sin\theta$ | $-\dfrac{\pi}{2} \leq \theta \leq \dfrac{\pi}{2}$ | $1 - \sin^2\theta = \cos^2\theta$ |
| $\sqrt{a^2 + x^2}$ | $x = a \tan\theta$ | $-\dfrac{\pi}{2} \leq \theta \leq \dfrac{\pi}{2}$ | $1 + \tan^2\theta = \sec^2\theta$ |
| $\sqrt{x^2 - a^2}$ | $x = a \sec\theta$ | $0 \leq \theta < \dfrac{\pi}{2}$ or $\pi \leq \theta < \dfrac{3\pi}{2}$ | $\sec^2\theta - 1 = \tan^2\theta$ |

**107.** Start with the expression $\sqrt{a^2 - x^2}$ and let $x = a\sin\theta$, assuming $-\dfrac{\pi}{2} \leq \theta \leq \dfrac{\pi}{2}$. Simplify the original expression so that it contains no radicals.

**108.** Start with the expression $\sqrt{a^2 + x^2}$ and let $x = a\tan\theta$, assuming $-\dfrac{\pi}{2} < \theta < \dfrac{\pi}{2}$. Simplify the original expression so that it contains no radicals.

**109.** Start with the expression $\sqrt{x^2 - a^2}$ and let $x = a\sec\theta$, assuming $0 \leq \theta < \dfrac{\pi}{2}$. Simplify the original expression so that it contains no radicals.

**110.** Use a trigonometric substitution to simplify the expression $\sqrt{9 - x^2}$ so that it contains no radicals.

**SKILLS OBJECTIVES**

- Find exact values of trigonometric functions of certain rational multiples of $\pi$ by using the sum and difference identities.
- Develop new identities from the sum and difference identities.

**CONCEPTUAL OBJECTIVE**

- Understand that a trigonometric function of a sum is not the sum of the trigonometric functions.

In this section, we will consider trigonometric functions with arguments that are sums and differences. In general, $f(A + B) \neq f(A) + f(B)$. First, it is important to note that function notation is not distributive:

$$\cos(A + B) \neq \cos A + \cos B$$

This principle is easy to prove. Let $A = \pi$ and $B = 0$; then

$$\cos(A + B) = \cos(\pi + 0) = \cos(\pi) = -1$$
$$\cos A + \cos B = \cos \pi + \cos 0 = -1 + 1 = 0$$

In this section, we will derive some new and important identities.

- Sum and difference identities for the cosine, sine, and tangent functions
- Cofunction identities

We begin with the familiar distance formula, from which we can derive the sum and difference identities for the cosine function. From there we can derive the sum and difference formulas for the sine and tangent functions.

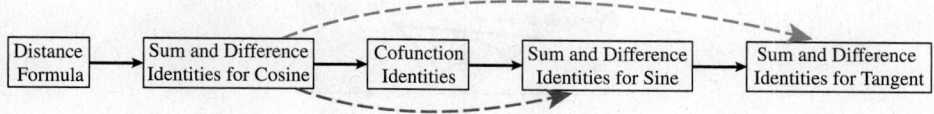

Before we start deriving and working with trigonometric sum and difference identities, let us first discuss why these are important. Sum and difference (and later product-to-sum and sum-to-product) identities are important because they allow calculation in functional (analytic) form and often lead to evaluating expressions *exactly* (as opposed to approximating them with calculators). The identities developed in this chapter are useful in such applications as musical sound, where they allow the determination of the "beat" frequency. In calculus, these identities will simplify the integration and differentiation processes.

## Sum and Difference Identities for the Cosine Function

Recall from Section 5.1 that the unit circle approach gave the relationship between the coordinates along the unit circle and the sine and cosine functions. Specifically, the $x$-coordinate corresponded to the value of the cosine function and the $y$-coordinate corresponded to the value of the sine function.

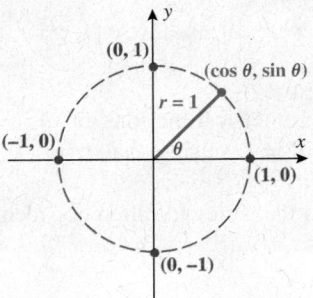

Let us now draw the unit circle with two angles $\alpha$ and $\beta$, realizing that the two terminal sides of these angles form a third angle, $\alpha - \beta$.

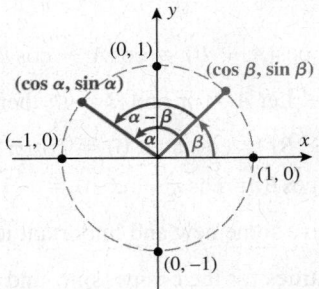

If we label the points $P_1 = (\cos\alpha, \sin\alpha)$ and $P_2 = (\cos\beta, \sin\beta)$, we can then draw a **segment** connecting points $P_1$ and $P_2$.

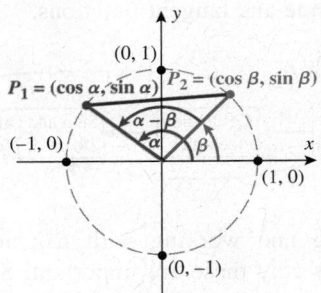

If we rotate the angle clockwise so the central angle $\alpha - \beta$ is in standard position, then the two points where the initial and terminal sides intersect the unit circle are $P_4 = (1, 0)$ and $P_3 = (\cos(\alpha - \beta), \sin(\alpha - \beta))$, respectively.

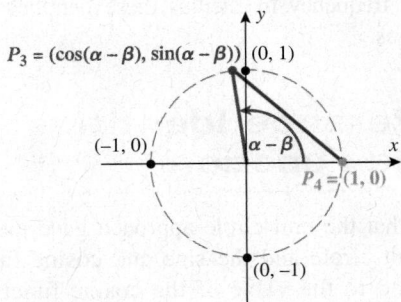

The distance from $P_1$ to $P_2$ is equal to the length of the **segment** joining the points. Similarly, the distance from $P_3$ to $P_4$ is equal to the length of the **segment** joining the points. Since the lengths of the **segments** are equal, we say that the distances are equal: $d(P_1, P_2) = d(P_3, P_4)$.

**Study Tip**

The distance from point $P_1 = (x_1, y_1)$ to $P_2 = (x_2, y_2)$ is given by the distance formula
$$d(P_1, P_2) = \sqrt{(x_2 - x_1)^2 + (y_2 - y_1)^2}.$$

| WORDS | MATH |
|---|---|
| Set the distances (segment lengths) equal. | $d(P_1, P_2) = d(P_3, P_4)$ |
| Apply the distance formula | $\sqrt{(x_2 - x_1)^2 + (y_2 - y_1)^2} = \sqrt{(x_4 - x_3)^2 + (y_4 - y_3)^2}$ |

Substitute $P_1 = (x_1, y_1) = (\cos\alpha, \sin\alpha)$ and $P_2 = (x_2, y_2) = (\cos\beta, \sin\beta)$ into the left side of the equation and $P_3 = (x_3, y_3) = (\cos(\alpha - \beta), \sin(\alpha - \beta))$ and $P_4 = (x_4, y_4) = (1, 0)$ into the right side of the equation.

$$\sqrt{[\cos\beta - \cos\alpha]^2 + [\sin\beta - \sin\alpha]^2} = \sqrt{[1 - \cos(\alpha - \beta)]^2 + [0 - \sin(\alpha - \beta)]^2}$$

| WORDS | MATH |
|---|---|
| Square both sides of the equation. | $[\cos\beta - \cos\alpha]^2 + [\sin\beta - \sin\alpha]^2 = [1 - \cos(\alpha - \beta)]^2 + [0 - \sin(\alpha - \beta)]^2$ |
| Eliminate the brackets. | $\cos^2\beta - 2\cos\beta\cos\alpha + \cos^2\alpha + \sin^2\beta - 2\sin\beta\sin\alpha + \sin^2\alpha$ $= 1 - 2\cos(\alpha - \beta) + \cos^2(\alpha - \beta) + \sin^2(\alpha - \beta)$ |
| Regroup terms on each side and use the Pythagorean identity. | $\underbrace{\cos^2\alpha + \sin^2\alpha}_{1} - 2\cos\alpha\cos\beta - 2\sin\alpha\sin\beta + \underbrace{\cos^2\beta + \sin^2\beta}_{1}$ $= 1 - 2\cos(\alpha - \beta) + \underbrace{\cos^2(\alpha - \beta) + \sin^2(\alpha - \beta)}_{1}$ |
| Simplify. | $2 - 2\cos\alpha\cos\beta - 2\sin\alpha\sin\beta = 2 - 2\cos(\alpha - \beta)$ |
| Subtract 2 from both sides. | $-2\cos\alpha\cos\beta - 2\sin\alpha\sin\beta = -2\cos(\alpha - \beta)$ |
| Divide by $-2$. | $\cos\alpha\cos\beta + \sin\alpha\sin\beta = \cos(\alpha - \beta)$ |
| Write the **difference identity for the cosine function**. | $\boxed{\cos(\alpha - \beta) = \cos\alpha\cos\beta + \sin\alpha\sin\beta}$ |

We can now derive the sum identity for the cosine function from the difference identity for the cosine function and the properties of even and odd functions.

| WORDS | MATH |
|---|---|
| Apply the difference identity. | $\cos(\alpha + \beta) = \cos[\alpha - (-\beta)]$ $\cos(\alpha + \beta) = \cos\alpha\cos(-\beta) + \sin\alpha\sin(-\beta)$ |
| Simplify the left side and use properties of even and odd functions on the right side. | $\cos(\alpha + \beta) = \cos\alpha(\cos\beta) + \sin\alpha(-\sin\beta)$ |
| Write the **sum identity for the cosine function**. | $\boxed{\cos(\alpha + \beta) = \cos\alpha\cos\beta - \sin\alpha\sin\beta}$ |

**SUM AND DIFFERENCE IDENTITIES FOR THE COSINE FUNCTION**

| Sum | $\cos(A + B) = \cos A\cos B - \sin A\sin B$ |
|---|---|
| Difference | $\cos(A - B) = \cos A\cos B + \sin A\sin B$ |

## EXAMPLE 1 Finding Exact Values for the Cosine Function

Evaluate each of the following cosine expressions exactly:

**a.** $\cos\left(\dfrac{7\pi}{12}\right)$

**b.** $\cos 15°$

### Technology Tip

**a.** Use a calculator to check the values for $\cos\left(\dfrac{7\pi}{12}\right)$ and $\dfrac{\sqrt{2} - \sqrt{6}}{4}$.

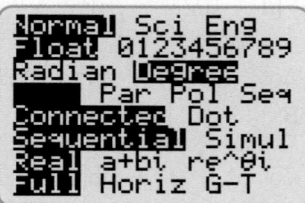

```
cos(7π/12)
       -.2588190451
(√(2)-√(6))/4
       -.2588190451
```

**b.** Use a calculator to check the values of $\cos 15°$ and $\dfrac{\sqrt{2} + \sqrt{6}}{4}$. Be sure the calculator is set in degree mode.

```
Normal Sci Eng
Float 0123456789
Radian Degree
      Par Pol Seq
Connected Dot
Sequential Simul
Real a+bi re^θi
Full Horiz G-T
```

```
cos(15)
       .9659258263
(√(2)+√(6))/4
       .9659258263
■
```

**Solution (a):**

Write $\dfrac{7\pi}{12}$ as a sum of known "special" angles.

$$\cos\left(\frac{7\pi}{12}\right) = \cos\left(\frac{4\pi}{12} + \frac{3\pi}{12}\right)$$

Simplify.

$$\cos\left(\frac{7\pi}{12}\right) = \cos\left(\frac{\pi}{3} + \frac{\pi}{4}\right)$$

Write the sum identity for the cosine function.

$$\cos(A + B) = \cos A \cos B - \sin A \sin B$$

Substitute $A = \dfrac{\pi}{3}$ and $B = \dfrac{\pi}{4}$.

$$\cos\left(\frac{7\pi}{12}\right) = \cos\left(\frac{\pi}{3}\right)\cos\left(\frac{\pi}{4}\right) - \sin\left(\frac{\pi}{3}\right)\sin\left(\frac{\pi}{4}\right)$$

Evaluate the expressions on the right exactly.

$$\cos\left(\frac{7\pi}{12}\right) = \frac{1}{2}\frac{\sqrt{2}}{2} - \frac{\sqrt{3}}{2}\frac{\sqrt{2}}{2}$$

Simplify.

$$\boxed{\cos\left(\frac{7\pi}{12}\right) = \frac{\sqrt{2} - \sqrt{6}}{4}}$$

**Solution (b):**

Write $15°$ as a difference of known "special" angles.

$$\cos 15° = \cos(45° - 30°)$$

Write the difference identity for the cosine function.

$$\cos(A - B) = \cos A \cos B + \sin A \sin B$$

Substitute $A = 45°$ and $B = 30°$.

$$\cos 15° = \cos 45° \cos 30° + \sin 45° \sin 30°$$

Evaluate the expressions on the right exactly.

$$\cos 15° = \frac{\sqrt{2}}{2}\frac{\sqrt{3}}{2} + \frac{\sqrt{2}}{2}\frac{1}{2}$$

Simplify.

$$\boxed{\cos 15° = \frac{\sqrt{6} + \sqrt{2}}{4}}$$

■ **YOUR TURN** Use the sum or difference identities for the cosine function to evaluate each cosine expression exactly.

**a.** $\cos\left(\dfrac{5\pi}{12}\right)$  **b.** $\cos 75°$

■ **Answer: a.** $\dfrac{\sqrt{6} - \sqrt{2}}{4}$

**b.** $\dfrac{\sqrt{6} - \sqrt{2}}{4}$

Example 1 illustrates an important characteristic of the sum and difference identities: that we can now find the exact trigonometric function value of angles that are multiples of $15°$ $\left(\text{or, equivalently, } \dfrac{\pi}{12}\right)$, since each of these can be written as a sum or difference of angles for which we know the trigonometric function values exactly.

## EXAMPLE 2   Writing a Sum or Difference as a Single Cosine Expression

Use the sum or the difference identity for the cosine function to write each of the following expressions as a single cosine expression:

**a.** $\sin(5x)\sin(2x) + \cos(5x)\cos(2x)$

**b.** $\cos x\cos(3x) - \sin x\sin(3x)$

**Solution (a):**

Because of the positive sign, this will be a cosine of a difference.

Reverse the expression and write the formula.

$$\cos A\cos B + \sin A\sin B = \cos(A - B)$$

Identify $A$ and $B$.

$$A = 5x \quad \text{and} \quad B = 2x$$

Substitute $A = 5x$ and $B = 2x$ into the difference identity.

$$\cos(5x)\cos(2x) + \sin(5x)\sin(2x) = \cos(5x - 2x)$$

Simplify.

$$\cos(5x)\cos(2x) + \sin(5x)\sin(2x) = \boxed{\cos(3x)}$$

Notice that if we had selected $A = 2x$ and $B = 5x$ instead, the result would have been $\cos(-3x)$, but since the cosine function is an even function, this would have simplified to $\cos(3x)$.

**Solution (b):**

Because of the negative sign, this will be a cosine of a sum.

Reverse the expression and write the formula.

$$\cos A\cos B - \sin A\sin B = \cos(A + B)$$

Identify $A$ and $B$.

$$A = x \quad \text{and} \quad B = 3x$$

Substitute $A = x$ and $B = 3x$ into the sum identity.

$$\cos x\cos(3x) - \sin x\sin(3x) = \cos(x + 3x)$$

Simplify.

$$\cos x\cos(3x) - \sin x\sin(3x) = \boxed{\cos(4x)}$$

■ **YOUR TURN**  Write as a single cosine expression.

$$\cos(4x)\cos(7x) + \sin(4x)\sin(7x)$$

### *Technology Tip*

a.

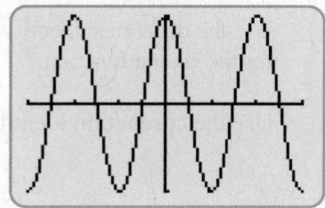

b.

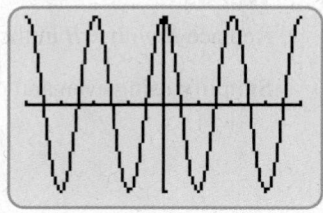

■ **Answer:** $\cos(3x)$

# Sum and Difference Identities for the Sine Function

We can now use the cofunction identities (Section 6.1) together with the sum and difference identities for the cosine function to develop the sum and difference identities for the sine function.

| WORDS | MATH |
|---|---|
| Start with the cofunction identity. | $\sin\theta = \cos\left(\dfrac{\pi}{2} - \theta\right)$ |
| Let $\theta = A + B$. | $\sin(A + B) = \cos\left[\dfrac{\pi}{2} - (A + B)\right]$ |
| Regroup the terms in the cosine expression. | $\sin(A + B) = \cos\left[\left(\dfrac{\pi}{2} - A\right) - B\right]$ |
| Use the difference identity for the cosine function. | $\sin(A + B) = \cos\left(\dfrac{\pi}{2} - A\right)\cos B + \sin\left(\dfrac{\pi}{2} - A\right)\sin B$ |
| Use the cofunction identities. | $\sin(A + B) = \underbrace{\cos\left(\dfrac{\pi}{2} - A\right)}_{\sin A}\cos B + \underbrace{\sin\left(\dfrac{\pi}{2} - A\right)}_{\cos A}\sin B$ |
| Simplify. | $\boxed{\sin(A + B) = \sin A \cos B + \cos A \sin B}$ |

Now we can derive the difference identity for the sine function using the sum identity for the sine function and the properties of even and odd functions.

| WORDS | MATH |
|---|---|
| Replace $B$ with $-B$ in the sum identity. | $\sin(A + (-B)) = \sin A \cos(-B) + \cos A \sin(-B)$ |
| Simplify using even and odd identities. | $\boxed{\sin(A - B) = \sin A \cos B - \cos A \sin B}$ |

**SUM AND DIFFERENCE IDENTITIES FOR THE SINE FUNCTION**

| | |
|---|---|
| Sum | $\sin(A + B) = \sin A \cos B + \cos A \sin B$ |
| Difference | $\sin(A - B) = \sin A \cos B - \cos A \sin B$ |

**EXAMPLE 3  Finding Exact Values for the Sine Function**

Use the sum or the difference identity for the sine function to evaluate each sine expression exactly.

**a.** $\sin\left(\dfrac{5\pi}{12}\right)$    **b.** $\sin 75°$

**Solution (a):**

Write $\dfrac{5\pi}{12}$ as a sum of known "special" angles.

$$\sin\left(\frac{5\pi}{12}\right) = \sin\left(\frac{2\pi}{12} + \frac{3\pi}{12}\right)$$

Simplify.

$$\sin\left(\frac{5\pi}{12}\right) = \sin\left(\frac{\pi}{6} + \frac{\pi}{4}\right)$$

Write the sum identity for the sine function.

$$\sin(A + B) = \sin A \cos B + \cos A \sin B$$

Substitute $A = \dfrac{\pi}{6}$ and $B = \dfrac{\pi}{4}$.

$$\sin\left(\frac{5\pi}{12}\right) = \sin\left(\frac{\pi}{6}\right)\cos\left(\frac{\pi}{4}\right) + \cos\left(\frac{\pi}{6}\right)\sin\left(\frac{\pi}{4}\right)$$

Evaluate the expressions on the right exactly.

$$\sin\left(\frac{5\pi}{12}\right) = \left(\frac{1}{2}\right)\left(\frac{\sqrt{2}}{2}\right) + \left(\frac{\sqrt{3}}{2}\right)\left(\frac{\sqrt{2}}{2}\right)$$

Simplify.

$$\sin\left(\frac{5\pi}{12}\right) = \frac{\sqrt{2} + \sqrt{6}}{4}$$

**Solution (b):**

Write 75° as a sum of known "special" angles.

$$\sin 75° = \sin(45° + 30°)$$

Write the sum identity for the sine function.

$$\sin(A + B) = \sin A \cos B + \cos A \sin B$$

Substitute $A = 45°$ and $B = 30°$.

$$\sin 75° = \sin 45° \cos 30° + \cos 45° \sin 30°$$

Evaluate the expressions on the right exactly.

$$\sin 75° = \left(\frac{\sqrt{2}}{2}\right)\left(\frac{\sqrt{3}}{2}\right) + \left(\frac{\sqrt{2}}{2}\right)\left(\frac{1}{2}\right)$$

Simplify.

$$\sin 75° = \frac{\sqrt{6} + \sqrt{2}}{4}$$

<br />

■ **YOUR TURN** Use the sum or the difference identity for the sine function to evaluate each sine expression exactly.

    **a.** $\sin\left(\dfrac{7\pi}{12}\right)$      **b.** $\sin 15°$

**Technology Tip**

Use a calculator to check the values of $\sin\left(\dfrac{5\pi}{12}\right)$ and $\dfrac{\sqrt{2} + \sqrt{6}}{4}$.

Be sure the calculator is in radian mode.

■ **Answer: a.** $\dfrac{\sqrt{6} + \sqrt{2}}{4}$

    **b.** $\dfrac{\sqrt{6} - \sqrt{2}}{4}$

We see in Example 3 that the sum and difference identities allow us to calculate exact values for trigonometric functions of angles that are multiples of 15° $\left(\text{or, equivalently, } \dfrac{\pi}{12}\right)$, as we saw with the cosine function.

### EXAMPLE 4   Writing a Sum or Difference as a Single Sine Expression

Graph $y = 3\sin x \cos(3x) + 3\cos x \sin(3x)$.

**Solution:**

Use the sum identity for the sine function to write the expression as a single sine expression.

Factor out the common 3.

$$y = 3[\sin x \cos(3x) + \cos x \sin(3x)]$$

Write the sum identity for the sine function.

$$\sin A \cos B + \cos A \sin B = \sin(A + B)$$

Identify $A$ and $B$.

$$A = x \quad \text{and} \quad B = 3x$$

Substitute $A = x$ and $B = 3x$ into the sum identity.

$$\sin x \cos(3x) + \cos x \sin(3x) = \sin(x + 3x) = \sin(4x)$$

Simplify.

$$y = 3[\underbrace{\sin x \cos(3x) + \cos x \sin(3x)}_{\sin(4x)}]$$

Graph $y = 3\sin(4x)$.

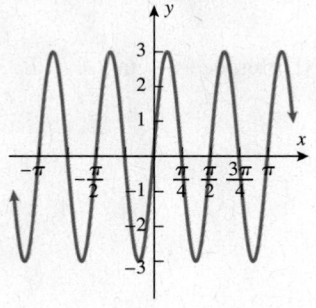

**Technology Tip**

Graphs of
$y_1 = 3\sin x \cos(3x) + 3\cos x \sin(3x)$
and $y_2 = 3\sin(4x)$.

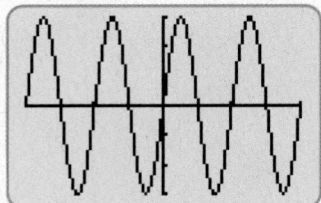

# Sum and Difference Identities for the Tangent Function

We now develop the sum and difference identities for the tangent function.

| WORDS | MATH |
|---|---|

Start with the quotient identity.

$$\tan x = \frac{\sin x}{\cos x}$$

Let $x = A + B$.

$$\tan(A + B) = \frac{\sin(A + B)}{\cos(A + B)}$$

Use the sum identities for the sine and cosine functions.

$$\tan(A + B) = \frac{\sin A \cos B + \cos A \sin B}{\cos A \cos B - \sin A \sin B}$$

Multiply the numerator and denominator by $\dfrac{1}{\cos A \cos B}$.

$$\tan(A + B) = \frac{\dfrac{\sin A \cos B + \cos A \sin B}{\cos A \cos B}}{\dfrac{\cos A \cos B - \sin A \sin B}{\cos A \cos B}} = \frac{\dfrac{\sin A \,\overline{\cos B}}{\cos A \,\overline{\cos B}} + \dfrac{\overline{\cos A}\,\sin B}{\overline{\cos A}\,\cos B}}{\dfrac{\overline{\cos A}\,\overline{\cos B}}{\overline{\cos A}\,\overline{\cos B}} - \dfrac{\sin A \sin B}{\cos A \cos B}}$$

Simplify.

$$\tan(A + B) = \frac{\left(\dfrac{\sin A}{\cos A}\right) + \left(\dfrac{\sin B}{\cos B}\right)}{1 - \left(\dfrac{\sin A}{\cos A}\right)\left(\dfrac{\sin B}{\cos B}\right)}$$

Write the expressions inside the parentheses in terms of the tangent function.

$$\boxed{\tan(A + B) = \frac{\tan A + \tan B}{1 - \tan A \tan B}}$$

Replace $B$ with $-B$.

$$\tan(A - B) = \frac{\tan A + \tan(-B)}{1 - \tan A \tan(-B)}$$

Since the tangent function is an odd function, $\tan(-B) = -\tan B$.

$$\boxed{\tan(A - B) = \frac{\tan A - \tan B}{1 + \tan A \tan B}}$$

---

**SUM AND DIFFERENCE IDENTITIES FOR THE TANGENT FUNCTION**

Sum $\qquad \tan(A + B) = \dfrac{\tan A + \tan B}{1 - \tan A \tan B}$

Difference $\qquad \tan(A - B) = \dfrac{\tan A - \tan B}{1 + \tan A \tan B}$

### EXAMPLE 5  Finding Exact Values for the Tangent Function

Find the exact value of $\tan(\alpha + \beta)$ if $\sin \alpha = -\frac{1}{3}$ and $\cos \beta = -\frac{1}{4}$ and the terminal side of $\alpha$ lies in quadrant III and the terminal side of $\beta$ lies in quadrant II.

**Solution:**

STEP 1  Write the sum identity for the tangent function.

$$\tan(\alpha + \beta) = \frac{\tan \alpha + \tan \beta}{1 - \tan \alpha \tan \beta}$$

STEP 2  Find $\tan \alpha$.

The terminal side of $\alpha$ lies in quadrant III.

$$\sin \alpha = \frac{y}{r} = -\frac{1}{3}.$$

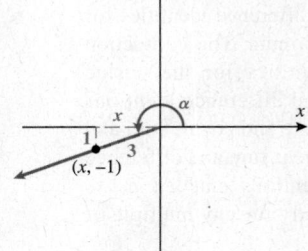

Solve for $x$. $\left(\text{Recall } x^2 + y^2 = r^2.\right)$

$$x^2 + (-1)^2 = 3^2$$
$$x = \pm\sqrt{8}$$

Take the negative sign since $x$ is negative in quadrant III.

$$x = -2\sqrt{2}$$

Find $\tan \alpha$.

$$\tan \alpha = \frac{y}{x} = \frac{-1}{-2\sqrt{2}} = \frac{1}{2\sqrt{2}} \cdot \frac{\sqrt{2}}{\sqrt{2}} = \frac{\sqrt{2}}{4}$$

STEP 3  Find $\tan \beta$.

The terminal side of $\beta$ lies in quadrant II.

$$\cos \beta = -\frac{1}{4} = \frac{x}{r}.$$

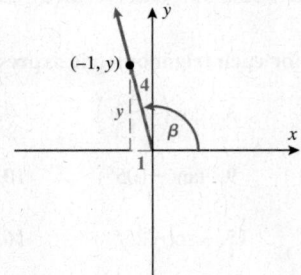

Solve for $y$. $\left(\text{Recall } x^2 + y^2 = r^2.\right)$

$$(-1)^2 + y^2 = 4^2$$
$$y = \pm\sqrt{15}$$

Take the positive sign since $y$ is positive in quadrant II.

$$y = \sqrt{15}$$

Find $\tan \beta$.

$$\tan \beta = \frac{y}{x} = \frac{\sqrt{15}}{-1} = -\sqrt{15}$$

STEP 4  Substitute $\tan \alpha = \frac{\sqrt{2}}{4}$ and $\tan \beta = -\sqrt{15}$ into the sum identity for the tangent function.

$$\tan(\alpha + \beta) = \frac{\frac{\sqrt{2}}{4} - \sqrt{15}}{1 - \left(\frac{\sqrt{2}}{4}\right)(-\sqrt{15})}$$

Multiply the numerator and the denominator by 4.

$$\tan(\alpha + \beta) = \frac{4\left(\frac{\sqrt{2}}{4} - \sqrt{15}\right)}{4\left(1 + \frac{\sqrt{30}}{4}\right)}$$

$$= \frac{\sqrt{2} - 4\sqrt{15}}{4 + \sqrt{30}}$$

The expression $\boxed{\tan(\alpha + \beta) = \dfrac{\sqrt{2} - 4\sqrt{15}}{4 + \sqrt{30}}}$ can be simplified further if we rationalize the denominator.

**Technology Tip**

If $\sin \alpha = -\frac{1}{3}$ and $\alpha$ is in QIII, then $\alpha = \pi + \sin^{-1}\left(\frac{1}{3}\right)$. If $\cos \beta = -\frac{1}{4}$ and $\beta$ is in QII, then $\beta = \pi - \cos^{-1}\left(\frac{1}{4}\right)$. Now use the graphing calculator to find $\tan(\alpha + \beta)$ by entering

```
tan(π+sin-1(1/3)+
π-cos-1(1/4))
        -1.485426269
```

In Step 4, use the graphing calculator to evaluate both expressions

$$\frac{\frac{\sqrt{2}}{4} - \sqrt{15}}{1 - \left(\frac{\sqrt{2}}{4}\right)(-\sqrt{15})} \text{ and }$$

$$\frac{\sqrt{2} - 4\sqrt{15}}{4 + \sqrt{30}} \text{ by entering}$$

```
(√(2)/4-√(15))/(
1-√(2)/4*-√(15))
        -1.485426269
(√(2)-4√(15))/(4
+√(30))
        -1.485426269
■
```

It is important to note in Example 5 that right triangles have been superimposed in the Cartesian plane. The coordinate pair $(x, y)$ can have positive or negative values, but the radius $r$ is always positive. When right triangles are superimposed, with one vertex at the point $(x, y)$ and another vertex at the origin, it is important to understand that triangles have positive side lengths.

## SECTION
## 6.2 SUMMARY

In this section, we derived the sum and difference identities for the cosine function using the distance formula. The cofunction identities and sum and difference identities for the cosine function were used to derive the sum and difference identities for the sine function. We combined the sine and cosine sum and difference identities to determine the tangent sum and difference identities. The sum and difference identities enabled us to evaluate a trigonometric expression exactly for any multiple of $15° \left( \text{i.e., } \dfrac{\pi}{12} \right).$

$$\cos(A + B) = \cos A \cos B - \sin A \sin B$$
$$\cos(A - B) = \cos A \cos B + \sin A \sin B$$
$$\sin(A + B) = \sin A \cos B + \cos A \sin B$$
$$\sin(A - B) = \sin A \cos B - \cos A \sin B$$
$$\tan(A + B) = \frac{\tan A + \tan B}{1 - \tan A \tan B}$$
$$\tan(A - B) = \frac{\tan A - \tan B}{1 + \tan A \tan B}$$

## SECTION
## 6.2 EXERCISES

### ▪ SKILLS

In Exercises 1–16, find the exact value for each trigonometric expression.

**1.** $\sin\left(\dfrac{\pi}{12}\right)$ **2.** $\cos\left(\dfrac{\pi}{12}\right)$ **3.** $\cos\left(-\dfrac{5\pi}{12}\right)$ **4.** $\sin\left(-\dfrac{5\pi}{12}\right)$ **5.** $\tan\left(-\dfrac{\pi}{12}\right)$ **6.** $\tan\left(\dfrac{13\pi}{12}\right)$

**7.** $\sin 105°$ **8.** $\cos 195°$ **9.** $\tan(-105°)$ **10.** $\tan 165°$ **11.** $\cot\left(\dfrac{\pi}{12}\right)$ **12.** $\cot\left(-\dfrac{5\pi}{12}\right)$

**13.** $\sec\left(-\dfrac{11\pi}{12}\right)$ **14.** $\sec\left(-\dfrac{13\pi}{12}\right)$ **15.** $\csc(-255°)$ **16.** $\csc(-15°)$

In Exercises 17–28, write each expression as a single trigonometric function.

**17.** $\sin(2x)\sin(3x) + \cos(2x)\cos(3x)$

**18.** $\sin x \sin(2x) - \cos x \cos(2x)$

**19.** $\sin x \cos(2x) - \cos x \sin(2x)$

**20.** $\sin(2x)\cos(3x) + \cos(2x)\sin(3x)$

**21.** $\cos(\pi - x)\sin x + \sin(\pi - x)\cos x$

**22.** $\sin\left(\dfrac{\pi}{3}x\right)\cos\left(-\dfrac{\pi}{2}x\right) - \cos\left(\dfrac{\pi}{3}x\right)\sin\left(-\dfrac{\pi}{2}x\right)$

**23.** $(\sin A - \sin B)^2 + (\cos A - \cos B)^2 - 2$

**24.** $(\sin A + \sin B)^2 + (\cos A + \cos B)^2 - 2$

**25.** $2 - (\sin A + \cos B)^2 - (\cos A + \sin B)^2$

**26.** $2 - (\sin A - \cos B)^2 - (\cos A + \sin B)^2$

**27.** $\dfrac{\tan 49° - \tan 23°}{1 + \tan 49° \tan 23°}$

**28.** $\dfrac{\tan 49° + \tan 23°}{1 - \tan 49° \tan 23°}$

In Exercises 29–34, find the exact value of the indicated expression using the given information and identities.

**29.** Find the exact value of $\cos(\alpha + \beta)$ if $\cos \alpha = -\dfrac{1}{3}$ and $\cos \beta = -\dfrac{1}{4}$ and the terminal side of $\alpha$ lies in quadrant III and the terminal side of $\beta$ lies in quadrant II.

**30.** Find the exact value of $\cos(\alpha - \beta)$ if $\cos \alpha = \dfrac{1}{3}$ and $\cos \beta = -\dfrac{1}{4}$ and the terminal side of $\alpha$ lies in quadrant IV and the terminal side of $\beta$ lies in quadrant II.

31. Find the exact value of $\sin(\alpha - \beta)$ if $\sin \alpha = -\frac{3}{5}$ and $\sin \beta = \frac{1}{5}$ and the terminal side of $\alpha$ lies in quadrant III and the terminal side of $\beta$ lies in quadrant I.

32. Find the exact value of $\sin(\alpha + \beta)$ if $\sin \alpha = -\frac{3}{5}$ and $\sin \beta = \frac{1}{5}$ and the terminal side of $\alpha$ lies in quadrant III and the terminal side of $\beta$ lies in quadrant II.

33. Find the exact value of $\tan(\alpha + \beta)$ if $\sin \alpha = -\frac{3}{5}$ and $\cos \beta = -\frac{1}{4}$ and the terminal side of $\alpha$ lies in quadrant III and the terminal side of $\beta$ lies in quadrant II.

34. Find the exact value of $\tan(\alpha - \beta)$ if $\sin \alpha = -\frac{3}{5}$ and $\cos \beta = -\frac{1}{4}$ and the terminal side of $\alpha$ lies in quadrant III and the terminal side of $\beta$ lies in quadrant II.

**In Exercises 35–52, determine whether each equation is a conditional equation or an identity.**

35. $\sin(A + B) + \sin(A - B) = 2 \sin A \cos B$

36. $\cos(A + B) + \cos(A - B) = 2 \cos A \cos B$

37. $\sin\left(x - \dfrac{\pi}{2}\right) = \cos\left(x + \dfrac{\pi}{2}\right)$

38. $\sin\left(x + \dfrac{\pi}{2}\right) = \cos\left(x + \dfrac{\pi}{2}\right)$

39. $\dfrac{\sqrt{2}}{2}(\sin x + \cos x) = \sin\left(x + \dfrac{\pi}{4}\right)$

40. $\sqrt{3}\cos x + \sin x = 2\cos\left(x + \dfrac{\pi}{3}\right)$

41. $\sin^2 x = \dfrac{1 - \cos(2x)}{2}$

42. $\cos^2 x = \dfrac{1 + \cos(2x)}{2}$

43. $\sin(2x) = 2 \sin x \cos x$

44. $\cos(2x) = \cos^2 x - \sin^2 x$

45. $\sin(A + B) = \sin A + \sin B$

46. $\cos(A + B) = \cos A + \cos B$

47. $\tan(\pi + B) = \tan B$

48. $\tan(A - \pi) = \tan A$

49. $\cot(3\pi + x) = \dfrac{1}{\tan x}$

50. $\csc(2x) = 2 \sec x \csc x$

51. $\dfrac{1 + \tan x}{1 - \tan x} = \tan\left(x - \dfrac{\pi}{4}\right)$

52. $\cot\left(x + \dfrac{\pi}{4}\right) = \dfrac{1 - \tan x}{1 + \tan x}$

**In Exercises 53–62, graph each of the functions by first rewriting it as a sine, cosine, or tangent of a difference or sum.**

53. $y = \cos\left(\dfrac{\pi}{3}\right)\sin x + \cos x \sin\left(\dfrac{\pi}{3}\right)$

54. $y = \cos\left(\dfrac{\pi}{3}\right)\sin x - \cos x \sin\left(\dfrac{\pi}{3}\right)$

55. $y = \sin x \sin\left(\dfrac{\pi}{4}\right) + \cos x \cos\left(\dfrac{\pi}{4}\right)$

56. $y = \sin x \sin\left(\dfrac{\pi}{4}\right) - \cos x \cos\left(\dfrac{\pi}{4}\right)$

57. $y = -\sin x \cos(3x) - \cos x \sin(3x)$

58. $y = \sin x \sin(3x) + \cos x \cos(3x)$

59. $y = \dfrac{1 + \tan x}{1 - \tan x}$

60. $y = \dfrac{\sqrt{3} - \tan x}{1 + \sqrt{3}\tan x}$

61. $y = \dfrac{1 + \sqrt{3}\tan x}{\sqrt{3} - \tan x}$

62. $y = \dfrac{1 - \tan x}{1 + \tan x}$

## ■ APPLICATIONS

**In Exercises 63 and 64, refer to the following:**

Sum and difference identities can be used to simplify more complicated expressions. For instance, the sine and cosine function can be represented by infinite polynomials called power series.

$$\cos x = 1 - \dfrac{x^2}{2!} + \dfrac{x^4}{4!} - \dfrac{x^6}{6!} + \dfrac{x^8}{8!} - \cdots$$

$$\sin x = x - \dfrac{x^3}{3!} + \dfrac{x^5}{5!} - \dfrac{x^7}{7!} + \dfrac{x^9}{9!} - \cdots$$

63. **Power Series.** Find the power series that represents $\cos\left(x - \dfrac{\pi}{4}\right)$.

64. **Power Series.** Find the power series that represents $\sin\left(x + \dfrac{3\pi}{2}\right)$.

**For Exercises 65 and 66, use the following:**

A nonvertical line makes an angle with the $x$-axis. In the figure, we see that the line $L_1$ makes an acute angle $\theta_1$ with the $x$-axis. Similarly, the line $L_2$ makes an acute angle $\theta_2$ with the $x$-axis.

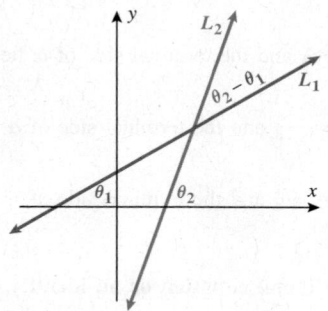

$\tan\theta_1 = $ slope of $L_1 = m_1$

$\tan\theta_2 = $ slope of $L_2 = m_2$

**65. Angle Between Two Lines.** Show that

$$\tan(\theta_2 - \theta_1) = \frac{m_2 - m_1}{1 + m_1 m_2}$$

**66. Relating Tangent and Slope.** Show that

$$\tan(\theta_1 - \theta_2) = \frac{m_1 - m_2}{1 + m_1 m_2}$$

**For Exercises 67 and 68, refer to the following:**

An electric field $E$ of a wave with constant amplitude $A$, propagating a distance $z$, is given by

$$E = A\cos(kz - ct)$$

where $k$ is the propagation wave number, which is related to the wavelength $\lambda$ by $k = \dfrac{2\pi}{\lambda}$, and where $c = 3.0 \times 10^8$ m/s is the speed of light in a vacuum, and $t$ is time in seconds.

**67. Electromagnetic Wave Propagation.** Use the cosine difference identity to express the electric field in terms of both sine and cosine functions. When the quotient of the propagation distance $z$ and the wavelength $\lambda$ are equal to an integer, what do you notice?

**68. Electromagnetic Wave Propagation.** Use the cosine difference identity to express the electric field in terms of both sine and cosine functions. When $t = 0$, what do you notice?

**69. Biology.** By analyzing available empirical data, it has been determined that the body temperature of a species fluctuates according to the model

$$T(t) = 38 - 2.5\cos\left[\frac{\pi}{6}(t - 3)\right], \quad 0 \le t \le 24$$

where $T$ represents temperature in degrees Celsius and $t$ represents time (in hours) measured from 12:00 P.M. (noon). Use an identity to express $T(t)$ in terms of the sine function.

**70. Health/Medicine.** During the course of treatment of an illness, the concentration of a drug (in micrograms per milliliter) in the bloodstream fluctuates during the dosing period of 8 hours according to the model

$$C(t) = 15.4 - 4.7\sin\left(\frac{\pi}{4}t + \frac{\pi}{2}\right), \quad 0 \le t \le 8$$

Use an identity to express the concentration $C(t)$ in terms of the cosine function.

*Note:* This model does not apply to the first dose of the medication as there will be no medication in the bloodstream.

## ▪ CATCH THE MISTAKE

**In Exercises 71 and 72, explain the mistake that is made.**

**71.** Find the exact value of $\tan\left(\dfrac{5\pi}{12}\right)$.

**Solution:**

Write $\dfrac{5\pi}{12}$ as a sum.          $\tan\left(\dfrac{\pi}{4} + \dfrac{\pi}{6}\right)$

Distribute.          $\tan\left(\dfrac{\pi}{4}\right) + \tan\left(\dfrac{\pi}{6}\right)$

Evaluate the tangent function for $\dfrac{\pi}{4}$ and $\dfrac{\pi}{6}$.          $1 + \dfrac{\sqrt{3}}{3}$

This is incorrect. What mistake was made?

**72.** Find the exact value of $\tan\left(-\dfrac{7\pi}{6}\right)$.

**Solution:**

The tangent function is an even function.          $\tan\left(\dfrac{7\pi}{6}\right)$

Write $\dfrac{7\pi}{6}$ as a sum.          $\tan\left(\pi + \dfrac{\pi}{6}\right)$

Use the tangent sum identity, $\tan(A + B) = \dfrac{\tan A + \tan B}{1 - \tan A \tan B}$.          $\dfrac{\tan\pi + \tan\left(\dfrac{\pi}{6}\right)}{1 - \tan\pi\tan\left(\dfrac{\pi}{6}\right)}$

Evaluate the tangent functions on the right.          $\dfrac{0 + \dfrac{1}{\sqrt{3}}}{1 - 0}$

Simplify.          $\dfrac{\sqrt{3}}{3}$

This is incorrect. What mistake was made?

### ▪ CONCEPTUAL

**In Exercises 73–76, determine whether each statement is true or false.**

**73.** $\cos 15° = \cos 45° - \cos 30°$

**74.** $\sin\left(\dfrac{\pi}{2}\right) = \sin\left(\dfrac{\pi}{3}\right) + \sin\left(\dfrac{\pi}{6}\right)$

**75.** $\tan\left(x + \dfrac{\pi}{4}\right) = 1 + \tan x$

**76.** $\cot\left(\dfrac{\pi}{4} - x\right) = \dfrac{1 + \tan x}{1 - \tan x}$

### ▪ CHALLENGE

**77.** Verify that $\sin(A + B + C) = \sin A \cos B \cos C +$ $\cos A \sin B \cos C + \cos A \cos B \sin C - \sin A \sin B \sin C$.

**78.** Verify that $\cos(A + B + C) = \cos A \cos B \cos C -$ $\sin A \sin B \cos C - \sin A \cos B \sin C - \cos A \sin B \sin C$.

**79.** Although in general the statement $\sin(A - B) = \sin A - \sin B$ is not true, it is true for some values. Determine some values of $A$ and $B$ that make this statement true.

**80.** Although in general the statement $\sin(A + B) = \sin A + \sin B$ is not true, it is true for some values. Determine some values of $A$ and $B$ that make this statement true.

### ▪ TECHNOLOGY

**81.** In Exercise 63, you showed that the difference quotient for $f(x) = \sin x$ is $\cos x\left(\dfrac{\sin h}{h}\right) - \sin x\left(\dfrac{1 - \cos h}{h}\right)$.

Plot $Y_1 = \cos x\left(\dfrac{\sin h}{h}\right) - \sin x\left(\dfrac{1 - \cos h}{h}\right)$ for

**a.** $h = 1$ **b.** $h = 0.1$ **c.** $h = 0.01$

What function does the difference quotient for $f(x) = \sin x$ resemble when $h$ approaches zero?

**82.** Show that the difference quotient for $f(x) = \cos x$ is $-\sin x\left(\dfrac{\sin h}{h}\right) - \cos x\left(\dfrac{1 - \cos h}{h}\right)$.

Plot $Y_1 = -\sin x\left(\dfrac{\sin h}{h}\right) - \cos x\left(\dfrac{1 - \cos h}{h}\right)$ for

**a.** $h = 1$ **b.** $h = 0.1$ **c.** $h = 0.01$

What function does the difference quotient for $f(x) = \cos x$ resemble when $h$ approaches zero?

**83.** Show that the difference quotient for $f(x) = \sin(2x)$ is $\cos(2x)\left[\dfrac{\sin(2h)}{h}\right] - \sin(2x)\left[\dfrac{1 - \cos(2h)}{h}\right]$.

Plot $Y_1 = \cos(2x)\left[\dfrac{\sin(2h)}{h}\right] - \sin(2x)\left[\dfrac{1 - \cos(2h)}{h}\right]$ for

**a.** $h = 1$ **b.** $h = 0.1$ **c.** $h = 0.01$

What function does the difference quotient for $f(x) = \sin(2x)$ resemble when $h$ approaches zero?

**84.** Show that the difference quotient for $f(x) = \cos(2x)$ is $-\sin(2x)\left[\dfrac{\sin(2h)}{h}\right] - \cos(2x)\left[\dfrac{1 - \cos(2h)}{h}\right]$.

Plot $Y_1 = -\sin(2x)\left[\dfrac{\sin(2h)}{h}\right] - \cos(2x)\left[\dfrac{1 - \cos(2h)}{h}\right]$ for

**a.** $h = 1$ **b.** $h = 0.1$ **c.** $h = 0.01$

What function does the difference quotient for $f(x) = \cos(2x)$ resemble when $h$ approaches zero?

### ▪ PREVIEW TO CALCULUS

In calculus, one technique used to solve differential equations consists of the separation of variables. For example, consider the equation $x^2 + 3y\dfrac{f(y)}{g(x)} = 0$, which is equivalent to $3yf(y) = -x^2g(x)$. Here each side of the equation contains only one type of variable, either $x$ or $y$.

In Exercises 85–88, use the sum and difference identities to separate the variables in each equation.

**85.** $\sin(x + y) = 0$

**86.** $\cos(x - y) = 0$

**87.** $\tan(x + y) = 2$

**88.** $\cos(x + y) = \sin y$

## Double-Angle Identities

In previous chapters, we could only evaluate trigonometric functions exactly for reference angles of $30°$, $45°$, and $60°$ or $\dfrac{\pi}{6}$, $\dfrac{\pi}{4}$, and $\dfrac{\pi}{3}$; note that as of the previous section, we now can include multiples of $\dfrac{\pi}{12}$ among these "special" angles. Now, we can use *double-angle identities* to also evaluate the trigonometric function values for other angles that are even integer multiples of the special angles or to verify other trigonometric identities. One important distinction now is that we will be able to find exact values of many functions using the double-angle identities without needing to know the value of the angle.

### Derivation of Double-Angle Identities

To derive the double-angle identities, we let $A = B$ in the sum identities.

| WORDS | MATH |
|---|---|
| Write the identity for the sine of a sum. | $\sin(A + B) = \sin A \cos B + \cos A \sin B$ |
| Let $B = A$. | $\sin(A + A) = \sin A \cos A + \cos A \sin A$ |
| Simplify. | $\boxed{\sin(2A) = 2\sin A \cos A}$ |
| Write the identity for the cosine of a sum. | $\cos(A + B) = \cos A \cos B - \sin A \sin B$ |
| Let $B = A$. | $\cos(A + A) = \cos A \cos A - \sin A \sin A$ |
| Simplify. | $\boxed{\cos(2A) = \cos^2 A - \sin^2 A}$ |

We can write the double-angle identity for the cosine function two other ways if we use the Pythagorean identity:

**1.** Write the identity for the cosine function of a double angle.

$$\cos(2A) = \cos^2 A - \sin^2 A$$

Use the Pythagorean identity for the cosine function.

$$\cos(2A) = \underbrace{\cos^2 A}_{1-\sin^2 A} - \sin^2 A$$

Simplify.

$$\boxed{\cos(2A) = 1 - 2\sin^2 A}$$

**2.** Write the identity for the cosine
function of a double angle.

$$\cos(2A) = \cos^2 A - \sin^2 A$$

Use the Pythagorean identity
for the sine function.

$$\cos(2A) = \cos^2 A - \underbrace{\sin^2 A}_{1-\cos^2 A}$$

Simplify.

$$\boxed{\cos(2A) = 2\cos^2 A - 1}$$

The tangent function can always be written as a quotient, $\tan(2A) = \dfrac{\sin(2A)}{\cos(2A)}$, if
$\sin(2A)$ and $\cos(2A)$ are known. Here we write the double-angle identity for the tangent
function in terms of only the tangent function.

Write the tangent of a sum identity.

$$\tan(A + B) = \frac{\tan A + \tan B}{1 - \tan A \tan B}$$

Let $B = A$.

$$\tan(A + A) = \frac{\tan A + \tan A}{1 - \tan A \tan A}$$

Simplify.

$$\boxed{\tan(2A) = \frac{2\tan A}{1 - \tan^2 A}}$$

## DOUBLE-ANGLE IDENTITIES

| SINE | COSINE | TANGENT |
|---|---|---|
| $\sin(2A) = 2\sin A\cos A$ | $\cos(2A) = \cos^2 A - \sin^2 A$ | $\tan(2A) = \dfrac{2\tan A}{1 - \tan^2 A}$ |
| | $\cos(2A) = 1 - 2\sin^2 A$ | |
| | $\cos(2A) = 2\cos^2 A - 1$ | |

## Applying Double-Angle Identities

### EXAMPLE 1    Finding Exact Values Using Double-Angle Identities

If $\cos x = \frac{2}{3}$, find $\sin(2x)$ given $\sin x < 0$.

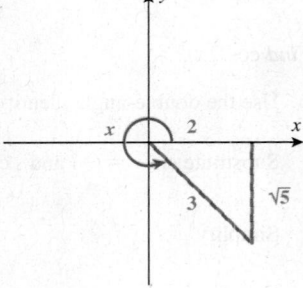

**Solution:**

*Find $\sin x$.*

Use the Pythagorean identity.

$$\sin^2 x + \cos^2 x = 1$$

Substitute $\cos x = \frac{2}{3}$.

$$\sin^2 x + \left(\frac{2}{3}\right)^2 = 1$$

Solve for $\sin x$, which is negative.

$$\sin x = -\sqrt{1 - \frac{4}{9}}$$

Simplify.

$$\sin x = -\frac{\sqrt{5}}{3}$$

*Find* $\sin(2x)$.

Use the double-angle formula for the sine function.          $\sin(2x) = 2\sin x \cos x$

Substitute $\sin x = -\dfrac{\sqrt{5}}{3}$ and $\cos x = \dfrac{2}{3}$.          $\sin(2x) = 2\left(-\dfrac{\sqrt{5}}{3}\right)\left(\dfrac{2}{3}\right)$

Simplify.          $\boxed{\sin(2x) = -\dfrac{4\sqrt{5}}{9}}$

■ **Answer:** $\sin(2x) = \dfrac{4\sqrt{2}}{9}$

■ **YOUR TURN**  If $\cos x = -\frac{1}{3}$, find $\sin(2x)$ given $\sin x < 0$.

---

### EXAMPLE 2  Finding Exact Values Using Double-Angle Identities

If $\sin x = -\frac{4}{5}$ and $\cos x < 0$, find $\sin(2x)$, $\cos(2x)$, and $\tan(2x)$.

**Solution:**

*Solve for* $\cos x$.

Use the Pythagorean identity.          $\sin^2 x + \cos^2 x = 1$

Substitute $\sin x = -\frac{4}{5}$.          $\left(-\dfrac{4}{5}\right)^2 + \cos^2 x = 1$

Simplify.          $\cos^2 x = \dfrac{9}{25}$

Solve for $\cos x$, which is negative.          $\cos x = -\sqrt{\dfrac{9}{25}} = -\dfrac{3}{5}$

*Find* $\sin(2x)$.

Use the double-angle identity for the sine function.          $\sin(2x) = 2\sin x \cos x$

Substitute $\sin x = -\frac{4}{5}$ and $\cos x = -\frac{3}{5}$.          $\sin(2x) = 2\left(-\dfrac{4}{5}\right)\left(-\dfrac{3}{5}\right)$

Simplify.          $\boxed{\sin(2x) = \dfrac{24}{25}}$

*Find* $\cos(2x)$.

Use the double-angle identity for the cosine function.          $\cos(2x) = \cos^2 x - \sin^2 x$

Substitute $\sin x = -\frac{4}{5}$ and $\cos x = -\frac{3}{5}$.          $\cos(2x) = \left(-\dfrac{3}{5}\right)^2 - \left(-\dfrac{4}{5}\right)^2$

Simplify.          $\boxed{\cos(2x) = -\dfrac{7}{25}}$

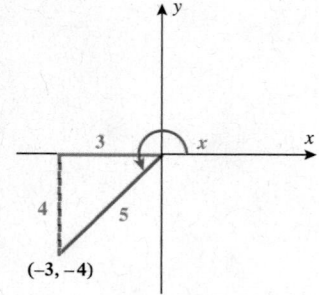

**Technology Tip**

If $\sin x = -\frac{4}{5}$ and $\cos x < 0$, then $x$ is in QIII and a value for $x$ is $x = \pi + \sin^{-1}\left(\frac{4}{5}\right)$. Now use the graphing calculator to find $\sin(2x)$, $\cos(2x)$, and $\tan(2x)$.

```
sin(2(π+sin⁻¹(4/5
)))
               .96
Ans▶Frac
            24/25
```

```
cos(2(π+sin⁻¹(4/5
)))
              -.28
Ans▶Frac
            -7/25
```

```
tan(2(π+sin⁻¹(4/5
)))
       -3.428571429
Ans▶Frac
            -24/7
```

*Find* $\tan(2x)$.

| | |
|---|---|
| Use the quotient identity. | $\tan\theta = \dfrac{\sin\theta}{\cos\theta}$ |
| Let $\theta = 2x$. | $\tan(2x) = \dfrac{\sin(2x)}{\cos(2x)}$ |
| Substitute $\sin(2x) = \frac{24}{25}$ and $\cos(2x) = -\frac{7}{25}$. | $\tan(2x) = \dfrac{\dfrac{24}{25}}{-\dfrac{7}{25}}$ |
| Simplify. | $\boxed{\tan(2x) = -\dfrac{24}{7}}$ |

*Note:* We could also have found $\tan(2x)$ first by finding $\tan x = \dfrac{\sin x}{\cos x}$ and then using the value for $\tan x$ in the double-angle identity, $\tan(2A) = \dfrac{2\tan A}{1 - \tan^2 A}$.

■ **YOUR TURN**  If $\cos x = \frac{3}{5}$ and $\sin x < 0$, find $\sin(2x)$, $\cos(2x)$, and $\tan(2x)$.

■ **Answer:** $\sin(2x) = -\frac{24}{25}$, $\cos(2x) = -\frac{7}{25}$, $\tan(2x) = \frac{24}{7}$

## EXAMPLE 3   Verifying Trigonometric Identities Using Double-Angle Identities

Verify the identity $(\sin x - \cos x)^2 = 1 - \sin(2x)$.

**Solution:**

| | |
|---|---|
| Start with the left side of the equation. | $\boxed{(\sin x - \cos x)^2}$ |
| Expand by squaring. | $= \sin^2 x - 2\sin x \cos x + \cos^2 x$ |
| Group the $\sin^2 x$ and $\cos^2 x$ terms. | $= \sin^2 x + \cos^2 x - 2\sin x \cos x$ |
| Apply the Pythagorean identity. | $= \underbrace{\sin^2 x + \cos^2 x}_{1} - 2\sin x \cos x$ |
| Apply the sine double-angle identity. | $= 1 - \underbrace{2\sin x \cos x}_{\sin(2x)}$ |
| Simplify. | $= \boxed{1 - \sin(2x)}$ |

## ▶ EXAMPLE 4   Verifying Multiple-Angle Identities

Verify the identity $\cos(3x) = \left(1 - 4\sin^2 x\right)\cos x$.

**Solution:**

| | |
|---|---|
| Write the cosine of a sum identity. | $\cos(A + B) = \cos A \cos B - \sin A \sin B$ |
| Let $A = 2x$ and $B = x$. | $\cos(2x + x) = \cos(2x)\cos x - \sin(2x)\sin x$ |
| Apply the double-angle identities. | $\cos(3x) = \underbrace{\cos(2x)}_{1 - 2\sin^2 x}\cos x - \underbrace{\sin(2x)}_{2\sin x \cos x}\sin x$ |
| Simplify. | $\cos(3x) = \cos x - 2\sin^2 x \cos x - 2\sin^2 x \cos x$ |
| | $\cos(3x) = \cos x - 4\sin^2 x \cos x$ |
| Factor out the common cosine term. | $\boxed{\cos(3x) = \left(1 - 4\sin^2 x\right)\cos x}$ |

Graphs of $y = \dfrac{\cot x - \tan x}{\cot x + \tan x}$ and $y = \cos(2x)$.

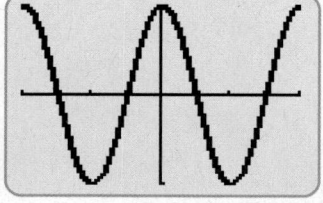

**EXAMPLE 5** **Simplifying Trigonometric Expressions Using Double-Angle Identities**

Graph $y = \dfrac{\cot x - \tan x}{\cot x + \tan x}$.

**Solution:**

Simplify $y = \dfrac{\cot x - \tan x}{\cot x + \tan x}$ first.

Write the cotangent and tangent functions in terms of the sine and cosine functions.

$$y = \dfrac{\dfrac{\cos x}{\sin x} - \dfrac{\sin x}{\cos x}}{\dfrac{\cos x}{\sin x} + \dfrac{\sin x}{\cos x}}$$

Multiply the numerator and the denominator by $\sin x \cos x$.

$$y = \left(\dfrac{\dfrac{\cos x}{\sin x} - \dfrac{\sin x}{\cos x}}{\dfrac{\cos x}{\sin x} + \dfrac{\sin x}{\cos x}}\right)\left(\dfrac{\sin x \cos x}{\sin x \cos x}\right)$$

Simplify.

$$y = \dfrac{\cos^2 x - \sin^2 x}{\cos^2 x + \sin^2 x}$$

Use the double-angle and Pythagorean identities.

$$y = \dfrac{\overbrace{\cos^2 x - \sin^2 x}^{\cos(2x)}}{\underbrace{\cos^2 x + \sin^2 x}_{1}}$$

$$\boxed{y = \cos(2x)}$$

Graph $y = \cos(2x)$.

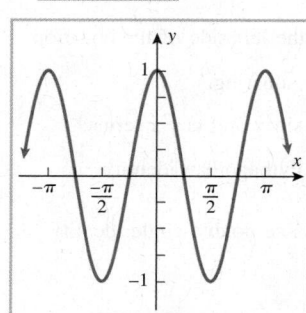

# Half-Angle Identities

We now use the *double-angle identities* to develop the *half-angle identities*. Like the double-angle identities, the half-angle identities will allow us to find certain exact values of trigonometric functions and to verify other trigonometric identities. The *half-angle identities* come directly from the double-angle identities. We start by rewriting the second and third forms of the cosine double-angle identity to obtain identities for the square of the sine and cosine functions, $\sin^2$ and $\cos^2$.

| WORDS | MATH |
|---|---|
| Write the second form of the cosine double-angle identity. | $\cos(2A) = 1 - 2\sin^2 A$ |
| *Find $\sin^2 A$.* | |
| Isolate the $2\sin^2 A$ term on one side of the equation. | $2\sin^2 A = 1 - \cos(2A)$ |
| Divide both sides by 2. | $\boxed{\sin^2 A = \dfrac{1 - \cos(2A)}{2}}$ |

*Find $\cos^2 A$.*

Write the third form of the
cosine double-angle identity.

$$\cos(2A) = 2\cos^2 A - 1$$

Isolate the $2\cos^2 A$ term on
one side of the equation.

$$2\cos^2 A = 1 + \cos^2 A$$

Divide both sides by 2.

$$\boxed{\cos^2 A = \frac{1 + \cos(2A)}{2}}$$

*Find $\tan^2 A$.*

Taking the quotient of these
leads us to another identity.

$$\tan^2 A = \frac{\sin^2 A}{\cos^2 A} = \frac{\dfrac{1 - \cos(2A)}{2}}{\dfrac{1 + \cos(2A)}{2}}$$

Simplify.

$$\boxed{\tan^2 A = \frac{1 - \cos(2A)}{1 + \cos(2A)}}$$

These three identities for the squared functions—really, alternative forms of the double-angle identities—are used in calculus as power reduction formulas (identities that allow us to reduce the power of the trigonometric function from 2 to 1):

$$\boxed{\sin^2 A = \frac{1 - \cos(2A)}{2}} \qquad \boxed{\cos^2 A = \frac{1 + \cos(2A)}{2}} \qquad \boxed{\tan^2 A = \frac{1 - \cos(2A)}{1 + \cos(2A)}}$$

We can now use these forms of the double-angle identities to derive the *half-angle identities*.

| WORDS | MATH |
|---|---|

For the *sine half-angle identity*,
start with the double-angle formula
involving both the sine and cosine
functions, $\cos(2x) = 1 - 2\sin^2 x$,
and solve for $\sin^2 x$.

$$\sin^2 x = \frac{1 - \cos(2x)}{2}$$

Solve for $\sin x$.

$$\sin x = \pm\sqrt{\frac{1 - \cos(2x)}{2}}$$

Let $x = \dfrac{A}{2}$.

$$\sin\left(\frac{A}{2}\right) = \pm\sqrt{\frac{1 - \cos\left(2 \cdot \dfrac{A}{2}\right)}{2}}$$

Simplify.

$$\boxed{\sin\left(\frac{A}{2}\right) = \pm\sqrt{\frac{1 - \cos A}{2}}}$$

For the *cosine half-angle identity*, start with the double-angle formula involving only the cosine function, $\cos(2x) = 2\cos^2 x - 1$, and solve for $\cos^2 x$.

$$\cos^2 x = \frac{1 + \cos(2x)}{2}$$

Solve for $\cos x$.

$$\cos x = \pm\sqrt{\frac{1 + \cos(2x)}{2}}$$

Let $x = \dfrac{A}{2}$.

$$\cos\left(\frac{A}{2}\right) = \pm\sqrt{\frac{1 + \cos\left(2 \cdot \frac{A}{2}\right)}{2}}$$

Simplify.

$$\boxed{\cos\left(\frac{A}{2}\right) = \pm\sqrt{\frac{1 + \cos A}{2}}}$$

For the *tangent half-angle identity*, start with the quotient identity.

$$\tan\left(\frac{A}{2}\right) = \frac{\sin\left(\frac{A}{2}\right)}{\cos\left(\frac{A}{2}\right)}$$

Substitute half-angle identities for the sine and cosine functions.

$$\tan\left(\frac{A}{2}\right) = \frac{\pm\sqrt{\frac{1 - \cos A}{2}}}{\pm\sqrt{\frac{1 + \cos A}{2}}}$$

Simplify.

$$\boxed{\tan\left(\frac{A}{2}\right) = \pm\sqrt{\frac{1 - \cos A}{1 + \cos A}}}$$

*Note:* We can also find $\tan\left(\dfrac{A}{2}\right)$ by starting with the identity $\tan^2 x = \dfrac{1 - \cos(2x)}{1 + \cos(2x)}$, solving for $\tan x$, and letting $x = \dfrac{A}{2}$. The tangent function also has two other similar forms for $\tan\left(\dfrac{A}{2}\right)$ (see Exercises 131 and 132).

### HALF-ANGLE IDENTITIES

| SINE | COSINE | TANGENT |
|---|---|---|
| $\sin\left(\dfrac{A}{2}\right) = \pm\sqrt{\dfrac{1 - \cos A}{2}}$ | $\cos\left(\dfrac{A}{2}\right) = \pm\sqrt{\dfrac{1 + \cos A}{2}}$ | $\tan\left(\dfrac{A}{2}\right) = \pm\sqrt{\dfrac{1 - \cos A}{1 + \cos A}}$ |
| | | $\tan\left(\dfrac{A}{2}\right) = \dfrac{\sin A}{1 + \cos A}$ |
| | | $\tan\left(\dfrac{A}{2}\right) = \dfrac{1 - \cos A}{\sin A}$ |

It is important to note that these identities hold for any real number $A$ or any angle with either degree measure or radian measure $A$ as long as both sides of the equation are defined. The sign ($+$ or $-$) is determined by the sign of the trigonometric function in the quadrant that contains $\dfrac{A}{2}$.

### EXAMPLE 6   Finding Exact Values Using Half-Angle Identities

Use a half-angle identity to find $\cos 15°$.

**Solution:**

Write $\cos 15°$ in terms of a half angle.

$$\cos 15° = \cos\left(\frac{30°}{2}\right)$$

Write the half-angle identity for the cosine function.

$$\cos\left(\frac{A}{2}\right) = \pm\sqrt{\frac{1 + \cos A}{2}}$$

Substitute $A = 30°$.

$$\cos\left(\frac{30°}{2}\right) = \pm\sqrt{\frac{1 + \cos 30°}{2}}$$

Simplify.

$$\cos 15° = \pm\sqrt{\frac{1 + \frac{\sqrt{3}}{2}}{2}}$$

15° is in quadrant I, where the cosine function is positive.

$$\cos 15° = \sqrt{\frac{2 + \sqrt{3}}{4}} = \boxed{\frac{\sqrt{2 + \sqrt{3}}}{2}}$$

**Technology Tip**

Use a TI calculator to check the values of $\cos 15°$ and $\sqrt{\frac{2 + \sqrt{3}}{4}}$. Be sure the calculator is in degree mode.

```
cos(15)
           .9659258263
√((2+√(3))/4)
           .9659258263
```

■ **YOUR TURN**  Use a half-angle identity to find $\sin 22.5°$.

■ **Answer:** $\sin 22.5° = \frac{\sqrt{2 - \sqrt{2}}}{2}$

### EXAMPLE 7   Finding Exact Values Using Half-Angle Identities

Use a half-angle identity to find $\tan\left(\frac{11\pi}{12}\right)$.

**Solution:**

Write $\tan\left(\frac{11\pi}{12}\right)$ in terms of a half angle.

$$\tan\left(\frac{11\pi}{12}\right) = \tan\left(\frac{\frac{11\pi}{6}}{2}\right)$$

Write the half-angle identity for the tangent function.*

$$\tan\left(\frac{A}{2}\right) = \frac{1 - \cos A}{\sin A}$$

Substitute $A = \frac{11\pi}{6}$.

$$\tan\left(\frac{\frac{11\pi}{6}}{2}\right) = \frac{1 - \cos\left(\frac{11\pi}{6}\right)}{\sin\left(\frac{11\pi}{6}\right)}$$

Simplify.

$$\tan\left(\frac{11\pi}{12}\right) = \frac{1 - \frac{\sqrt{3}}{2}}{-\frac{1}{2}}$$

$$\tan\left(\frac{11\pi}{12}\right) = \boxed{\sqrt{3} - 2}$$

**Technology Tip**

Use a TI calculator to check the values of $\tan\left(\frac{11\pi}{12}\right)$ and $\sqrt{3} - 2$. Be sure the calculator is in radian mode.

```
tan(11π/12)
          -.2679491924
√(3)-2
          -.2679491924
▪
```

$\frac{11\pi}{12}$ is in quadrant II, where tangent is negative. Notice that if we approximate $\tan\left(\frac{11\pi}{12}\right)$ with a calculator, we find that $\tan\left(\frac{11\pi}{12}\right) \approx -0.2679$ and $\sqrt{3} - 2 \approx -0.2679$.

*This form of the tangent half-angle identity was selected because of mathematical simplicity. If we had selected either of the other forms, we would have obtained an expression that had a square root within a square root or a radical in the denominator (requiring rationalization).

■ **YOUR TURN**  Use a half-angle identity to find $\tan\left(\frac{\pi}{8}\right)$.

■ **Answer:** $\frac{\sqrt{2}}{2 + \sqrt{2}}$ or $\sqrt{2} - 1$

## EXAMPLE 8 Finding Exact Values Using Half-Angle Identities

If $\cos x = \dfrac{3}{5}$ and $\dfrac{3\pi}{2} < x < 2\pi$, find $\sin\left(\dfrac{x}{2}\right)$, $\cos\left(\dfrac{x}{2}\right)$, and $\tan\left(\dfrac{x}{2}\right)$.

**Solution:**

Determine in which quadrant $\dfrac{x}{2}$ lies.

Since $\dfrac{3\pi}{2} < x < 2\pi$, we divide by 2. $\qquad \dfrac{3\pi}{4} < \dfrac{x}{2} < \pi$

$\dfrac{x}{2}$ lies in quadrant II; therefore, the sine function is positive and both the cosine and tangent functions are negative.

Write the half-angle identity for the sine function. $\quad \sin\left(\dfrac{x}{2}\right) = \pm\sqrt{\dfrac{1-\cos x}{2}}$

Substitute $\cos x = \dfrac{3}{5}$. $\quad \sin\left(\dfrac{x}{2}\right) = \pm\sqrt{\dfrac{1-\dfrac{3}{5}}{2}}$

Simplify. $\quad \sin\left(\dfrac{x}{2}\right) = \pm\sqrt{\dfrac{1}{5}} = \pm\dfrac{\sqrt{5}}{5}$

Since $\dfrac{x}{2}$ lies in quadrant II, choose the positive value for the sine function. $\quad \boxed{\sin\left(\dfrac{x}{2}\right) = \dfrac{\sqrt{5}}{5}}$

Write the half-angle identity for the cosine function. $\quad \cos\left(\dfrac{x}{2}\right) = \pm\sqrt{\dfrac{1+\cos x}{2}}$

Substitute $\cos x = \dfrac{3}{5}$. $\quad \cos\left(\dfrac{x}{2}\right) = \pm\sqrt{\dfrac{1+\dfrac{3}{5}}{2}}$

Simplify. $\quad \cos\left(\dfrac{x}{2}\right) = \pm\sqrt{\dfrac{4}{5}} = \pm\dfrac{2\sqrt{5}}{5}$

Since $\dfrac{x}{2}$ lies in quadrant II, choose the negative value for the cosine function. $\quad \boxed{\cos\left(\dfrac{x}{2}\right) = -\dfrac{2\sqrt{5}}{5}}$

Use the quotient identity for tangent. $\quad \tan\left(\dfrac{x}{2}\right) = \dfrac{\sin\left(\dfrac{x}{2}\right)}{\cos\left(\dfrac{x}{2}\right)}$

Substitute $\sin\left(\dfrac{x}{2}\right) = \dfrac{\sqrt{5}}{5}$ and $\cos\left(\dfrac{x}{2}\right) = -\dfrac{2\sqrt{5}}{5}$. $\quad \tan\left(\dfrac{x}{2}\right) = \dfrac{\dfrac{\sqrt{5}}{5}}{-\dfrac{2\sqrt{5}}{5}}$

Simplify. $\quad \boxed{\tan\left(\dfrac{x}{2}\right) = -\dfrac{1}{2}}$

■ **YOUR TURN** If $\cos x = -\dfrac{3}{5}$ and $\pi < x < \dfrac{3\pi}{2}$, find $\sin\left(\dfrac{x}{2}\right)$, $\cos\left(\dfrac{x}{2}\right)$, and $\tan\left(\dfrac{x}{2}\right)$.

**Technology Tip**

If $\cos x = \dfrac{3}{5}$ and $\dfrac{3\pi}{2} < x < 2\pi$,

then $x$ is in QIV, $\dfrac{x}{2}$ is in QII, and $x = 2\pi - \cos^{-1}\left(\dfrac{3}{5}\right)$. Now use the graphing calculator to find $\sin\left(\dfrac{x}{2}\right)$, $\cos\left(\dfrac{x}{2}\right)$, and $\tan\left(\dfrac{x}{2}\right)$.

```
sin((2π-cos⁻¹(3/5
))/2)
          .4472135955
√(5)/5
          .4472135955
```

```
cos((2π-cos⁻¹(3/5
))/2)
         -.894427191
-2√(5)/5
         -.894427191
■
```

```
tan((2π-cos⁻¹(3/5
))/2)
              -.5
Ans►Frac
             -1/2
```

■**Answer:** $\sin\left(\dfrac{x}{2}\right) = \dfrac{2\sqrt{5}}{5}$, $\cos\left(\dfrac{x}{2}\right) = -\dfrac{\sqrt{5}}{5}$, $\tan\left(\dfrac{x}{2}\right) = -2$

**EXAMPLE 9**  **Using Half-Angle Identities to Verify Other Identities**

Verify the identity $\cos^2\left(\dfrac{x}{2}\right) = \dfrac{\tan x + \sin x}{2\tan x}$.

**Solution:**

Write the cosine half-angle identity.

$$\cos\left(\frac{x}{2}\right) = \pm\sqrt{\frac{1+\cos x}{2}}$$

Square both sides of the equation.

$$\cos^2\left(\frac{x}{2}\right) = \frac{1+\cos x}{2}$$

Multiply the numerator and denominator on the right side by $\tan x$.

$$\cos^2\left(\frac{x}{2}\right) = \left(\frac{1+\cos x}{2}\right)\left(\frac{\tan x}{\tan x}\right)$$

Simplify.

$$\cos^2\left(\frac{x}{2}\right) = \frac{\tan x + \cos x\tan x}{2\tan x}$$

Note that $\cos x\tan x = \sin x$.

$$\boxed{\cos^2\left(\frac{x}{2}\right) = \frac{\tan x + \sin x}{2\tan x}}$$

*Technology Tip*

Graphs of $y_1 = \cos^2\left(\dfrac{x}{2}\right)$ and

$y_2 = \dfrac{\tan x + \sin x}{2\tan x}$.

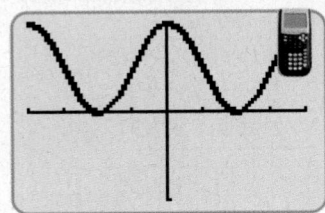

An alternative solution is to start with the right-hand side.

**Solution (alternative):**

Start with the right-hand side.

$$\frac{\tan x + \sin x}{2\tan x}$$

Write this expression as the sum of two expressions.

$$= \frac{\tan x}{2\tan x} + \frac{\sin x}{2\tan x}$$

Simplify.

$$= \frac{1}{2} + \frac{1}{2}\frac{\sin x}{\tan x}$$

Write $\tan x = \dfrac{\sin x}{\cos x}$.

$$= \frac{1}{2} + \frac{1}{2}\frac{\sin x}{\dfrac{\sin x}{\cos x}}$$

$$= \frac{1}{2}(1 + \cos x)$$

$$= \cos^2\left(\frac{x}{2}\right)$$

**EXAMPLE 10**  **Using Half-Angle Identities to Verify Other Trigonometric Identities**

Verify the identity $\tan x = \csc(2x) - \cot(2x)$.

**Solution:**

Write the third half-angle formula for the tangent function.

$$\tan\left(\frac{A}{2}\right) = \frac{1-\cos A}{\sin A}$$

Write the right side as a difference of two expressions having the same denominator.

$$\tan\left(\frac{A}{2}\right) = \frac{1}{\sin A} - \frac{\cos A}{\sin A}$$

Substitute the reciprocal and quotient identities, respectively, on the right.

$$\tan\left(\frac{A}{2}\right) = \csc A - \cot A$$

Let $A = 2x$.

$$\boxed{\tan x = \csc(2x) - \cot(2x).}$$

Notice in Example 10 that we started with the third half-angle identity for the tangent function. In Example 11 we will start with the second half-angle identity for the tangent function. In general, you select the form that appears to lead to the desired expression.

### Technology Tip

Graphs of $y_1 = \dfrac{\sin(2\pi x)}{1 + \cos(2\pi x)}$ and $y_2 = \tan(\pi x)$.

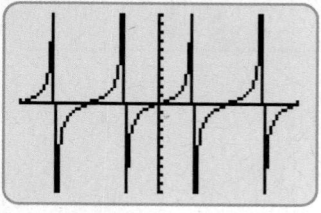

■ **Answer:**

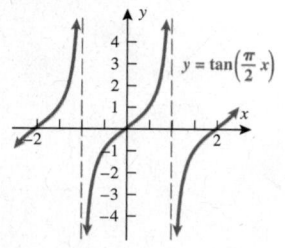

### EXAMPLE 11 Using Half-Angle Identities to Simplify Trigonometric Expressions

Graph $y = \dfrac{\sin(2\pi x)}{1 + \cos(2\pi x)}$.

**Solution:**

Simplify the trigonometric expression using a half-angle identity for the tangent function.

Write the second half-angle identity for the tangent function.

$$\tan\left(\frac{A}{2}\right) = \frac{\sin A}{1 + \cos A}$$

Let $A = 2\pi x$.

$$\tan(\pi x) = \frac{\sin(2\pi x)}{1 + \cos(2\pi x)}$$

Graph $y = \tan(\pi x)$.

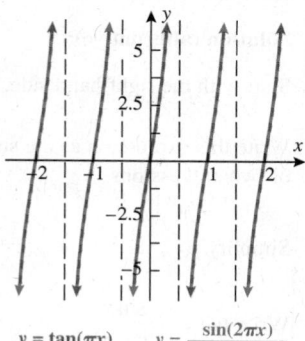

$$y = \tan(\pi x) \qquad y = \frac{\sin(2\pi x)}{1 + \cos(2\pi x)}$$

■ **YOUR TURN** Graph $y = \dfrac{1 - \cos(\pi x)}{\sin(\pi x)}$.

## SECTION 6.3 SUMMARY

In this section, we derived the double-angle identities from the sum identities. We then used the double-angle identities to find exact values of trigonometric functions, to verify other trigonometric identities, and to simplify trigonometric expressions.

$$\sin(2A) = 2\sin A \cos A$$
$$\cos(2A) = \cos^2 A - \sin^2 A$$
$$= 1 - 2\sin^2 A$$
$$= 2\cos^2 A - 1$$
$$\tan(2A) = \frac{2\tan A}{1 - \tan^2 A}$$

The double-angle identities were used to derive the half-angle identities. We then used the half-angle identities to find certain

exact values of trigonometric functions, verify other trigonometric identities, and simplify trigonometric expressions.

$$\sin\left(\frac{A}{2}\right) = \pm\sqrt{\frac{1 - \cos A}{2}} \qquad \cos\left(\frac{A}{2}\right) = \pm\sqrt{\frac{1 + \cos A}{2}}$$

$$\tan\left(\frac{A}{2}\right) = \pm\sqrt{\frac{1 - \cos A}{1 + \cos A}}$$

We determine the sign, $+$ or $-$, by first deciding which quadrant contains $\dfrac{A}{2}$ and then finding the sign of the indicated trigonometric function in that quadrant.

Recall that there are three forms of the tangent half-angle identity. There is no need to memorize the other forms of the tangent half-angle identity, since they can be derived by first using the Pythagorean identity and algebraic manipulation.

## SECTION
### 6.3 EXERCISES

■ SKILLS

In Exercises 1–12, use the double-angle identities to answer the following questions:

1. If $\sin x = \dfrac{1}{\sqrt{5}}$ and $\cos x < 0$, find $\sin(2x)$.

2. If $\sin x = \dfrac{1}{\sqrt{5}}$ and $\cos x < 0$, find $\cos(2x)$.

3. If $\cos x = \dfrac{5}{13}$ and $\sin x < 0$, find $\tan(2x)$.

4. If $\cos x = -\dfrac{5}{13}$ and $\sin x < 0$, find $\tan(2x)$.

5. If $\tan x = \dfrac{12}{5}$ and $\pi < x < \dfrac{3\pi}{2}$, find $\sin(2x)$.

6. If $\tan x = \dfrac{12}{5}$ and $\pi < x < \dfrac{3\pi}{2}$, find $\cos(2x)$.

7. If $\sec x = \sqrt{5}$ and $\sin x > 0$, find $\tan(2x)$.

8. If $\sec x = \sqrt{3}$ and $\sin x < 0$, find $\tan(2x)$.

9. If $\csc x = -2\sqrt{5}$ and $\cos x < 0$, find $\sin(2x)$.

10. If $\csc x = -\sqrt{13}$ and $\cos x > 0$, find $\sin(2x)$.

11. If $\cos x = -\dfrac{12}{13}$ and $\csc x < 0$, find $\cot(2x)$.

12. If $\sin x = \dfrac{12}{13}$ and $\cot x < 0$, find $\csc(2x)$.

In Exercises 13–24, simplify each expression. Evaluate the resulting expression exactly, if possible.

13. $\dfrac{2\tan 15°}{1 - \tan^2 15°}$

14. $\dfrac{2\tan\left(\dfrac{\pi}{8}\right)}{1 - \tan^2\left(\dfrac{\pi}{8}\right)}$

15. $\sin\left(\dfrac{\pi}{8}\right)\cos\left(\dfrac{\pi}{8}\right)$

16. $\sin 15° \cos 15°$

17. $\cos^2(2x) - \sin^2(2x)$

18. $\cos^2(x + 2) - \sin^2(x + 2)$

19. $\dfrac{2\tan\left(\dfrac{5\pi}{12}\right)}{1 - \tan^2\left(\dfrac{5\pi}{12}\right)}$

20. $\dfrac{2\tan\left(\dfrac{x}{2}\right)}{1 - \tan^2\left(\dfrac{x}{2}\right)}$

21. $1 - 2\sin^2\left(\dfrac{7\pi}{12}\right)$

22. $2\sin^2\left(-\dfrac{5\pi}{8}\right) - 1$

23. $2\cos^2\left(-\dfrac{7\pi}{12}\right) - 1$

24. $1 - 2\cos^2\left(-\dfrac{\pi}{8}\right)$

In Exercises 25–40, use the double-angle identities to verify each identity.

25. $\csc(2A) = \frac{1}{2}\csc A \sec A$

26. $\cot(2A) = \frac{1}{2}(\cot A - \tan A)$

27. $(\sin x - \cos x)(\cos x + \sin x) = -\cos(2x)$

28. $(\sin x + \cos x)^2 = 1 + \sin(2x)$

29. $\cos^2 x = \dfrac{1 + \cos(2x)}{2}$

30. $\sin^2 x = \dfrac{1 - \cos(2x)}{2}$

31. $\cos^4 x - \sin^4 x = \cos(2x)$

32. $\cos^4 x + \sin^4 x = 1 - \frac{1}{2}\sin^2(2x)$

33. $8\sin^2 x\cos^2 x = 1 - \cos(4x)$

34. $[\cos(2x) - \sin(2x)][\sin(2x) + \cos(2x)] = \cos(4x)$

35. $-\frac{1}{2}\sec^2 x = -2\sin^2 x\csc^2(2x)$

36. $4\csc(4x) = \dfrac{\sec x \csc x}{\cos(2x)}$

37. $\sin(3x) = \sin x(4\cos^2 x - 1)$

38. $\tan(3x) = \dfrac{\tan x(3 - \tan^2 x)}{(1 - 3\tan^2 x)}$

39. $\frac{1}{2}\sin(4x) = 2\sin x\cos x - 4\sin^3 x\cos x$

40. $\cos(4x) = [\cos(2x) - \sin(2x)][(\cos(2x) + \sin(2x)]$

**In Exercises 41–50, graph the functions.**

**41.** $y = \dfrac{\sin(2x)}{1 - \cos(2x)}$

**42.** $y = \dfrac{2\tan x}{2 - \sec^2 x}$

**43.** $y = \dfrac{\cot x + \tan x}{\cot x - \tan x}$

**44.** $y = \frac{1}{2}\tan x \cot x \sec x \csc x$

**45.** $y = \sin(2x)\cos(2x)$

**46.** $y = 3\sin(3x)\cos(-3x)$

**47.** $y = 1 - \dfrac{\tan x \cot x}{\sec x \csc x}$

**48.** $y = 3 - 2\dfrac{\sec(2x)}{\csc(2x)}$

**49.** $y = \dfrac{\sin(2x)}{\cos x} - 3\cos(2x)$

**50.** $y = 2 + \dfrac{\sin(2x)}{\cos x} - 3\cos(2x)$

**In Exercises 51–66, use the half-angle identities to find the exact values of the trigonometric expressions.**

**51.** $\sin 15°$

**52.** $\cos 22.5°$

**53.** $\cos\left(\dfrac{11\pi}{12}\right)$

**54.** $\sin\left(\dfrac{\pi}{8}\right)$

**55.** $\cos 75°$

**56.** $\sin 75°$

**57.** $\tan 67.5°$

**58.** $\tan 202.5°$

**59.** $\sec\left(-\dfrac{9\pi}{8}\right)$

**60.** $\csc\left(\dfrac{9\pi}{8}\right)$

**61.** $\cot\left(\dfrac{13\pi}{8}\right)$

**62.** $\cot\left(\dfrac{7\pi}{8}\right)$

**63.** $\sec\left(\dfrac{5\pi}{8}\right)$

**64.** $\csc\left(-\dfrac{5\pi}{8}\right)$

**65.** $\cot(-135°)$

**66.** $\cot 105°$

**In Exercises 67–82, use the half-angle identities to find the desired function values. Assume that $x \geq 0$.**

**67.** If $\cos x = \dfrac{5}{13}$ and $\sin x < 0$, find $\sin\left(\dfrac{x}{2}\right)$.

**68.** If $\cos x = -\dfrac{5}{13}$ and $\sin x < 0$, find $\cos\left(\dfrac{x}{2}\right)$.

**69.** If $\tan x = \dfrac{12}{5}$ and $\pi < x < \dfrac{3\pi}{2}$, find $\sin\left(\dfrac{x}{2}\right)$.

**70.** If $\tan x = \dfrac{12}{5}$ and $\pi < x < \dfrac{3\pi}{2}$, find $\cos\left(\dfrac{x}{2}\right)$.

**71.** If $\sec x = \sqrt{5}$ and $\sin x > 0$, find $\tan\left(\dfrac{x}{2}\right)$.

**72.** If $\sec x = \sqrt{3}$ and $\sin x < 0$, find $\tan\left(\dfrac{x}{2}\right)$.

**73.** If $\csc x = 3$ and $\cos x < 0$, find $\sin\left(\dfrac{x}{2}\right)$.

**74.** If $\csc x = -3$ and $\cos x > 0$, find $\cos\left(\dfrac{x}{2}\right)$.

**75.** If $\cos x = -\dfrac{1}{4}$ and $\csc x < 0$, find $\cot\left(\dfrac{x}{2}\right)$.

**76.** If $\cos x = \dfrac{1}{4}$ and $\cot x < 0$, find $\csc\left(\dfrac{x}{2}\right)$.

**77.** If $\cot x = -\dfrac{24}{5}$ and $\dfrac{\pi}{2} < x < \pi$, find $\cos\left(\dfrac{x}{2}\right)$.

**78.** If $\cot x = -\dfrac{24}{5}$ and $\dfrac{\pi}{2} < x < \pi$, find $\sin\left(\dfrac{x}{2}\right)$.

**79.** If $\sin x = -0.3$ and $\sec x > 0$, find $\tan\left(\dfrac{x}{2}\right)$.

**80.** If $\sin x = -0.3$ and $\sec x < 0$, find $\cot\left(\dfrac{x}{2}\right)$.

**81.** If $\sec x = 2.5$ and $\tan x > 0$, find $\cot\left(\dfrac{x}{2}\right)$.

**82.** If $\sec x = -3$ and $\cot x < 0$, find $\tan\left(\dfrac{x}{2}\right)$.

**In Exercises 83–88, simplify each expression using half-angle identities. Do not evaluate.**

**83.** $\sqrt{\dfrac{1 + \cos\left(\dfrac{5\pi}{6}\right)}{2}}$

**84.** $\sqrt{\dfrac{1 - \cos\left(\dfrac{\pi}{4}\right)}{2}}$

**85.** $\dfrac{\sin 150°}{1 + \cos 150°}$

**86.** $\dfrac{1 - \cos 150°}{\sin 150°}$

**87.** $\sqrt{\dfrac{1 - \cos\left(\dfrac{5\pi}{4}\right)}{1 + \cos\left(\dfrac{5\pi}{4}\right)}}$

**88.** $\sqrt{\dfrac{1 - \cos 15°}{1 + \cos 15°}}$

**In Exercises 89–100, use the half-angle identities to verify the identities.**

**89.** $\sin^2\left(\dfrac{x}{2}\right) + \cos^2\left(\dfrac{x}{2}\right) = 1$

**90.** $\cos^2\left(\dfrac{x}{2}\right) - \sin^2\left(\dfrac{x}{2}\right) = \cos x$

**91.** $\sin(-x) = -2\sin\left(\dfrac{x}{2}\right)\cos\left(\dfrac{x}{2}\right)$

**92.** $2\cos^2\left(\dfrac{x}{4}\right) = 1 + \cos\left(\dfrac{x}{2}\right)$

**93.** $\tan^2\left(\dfrac{x}{2}\right) = \dfrac{1 - \cos x}{1 + \cos x}$

**94.** $\tan^2\left(\dfrac{x}{2}\right) = (\csc x - \cot x)^2$

**95.** $\tan\left(\dfrac{A}{2}\right) + \cot\left(\dfrac{A}{2}\right) = 2\csc A$

**96.** $\cot\left(\dfrac{A}{2}\right) - \tan\left(\dfrac{A}{2}\right) = 2\cot A$

**97.** $\csc^2\left(\dfrac{A}{2}\right) = \dfrac{2(1 + \cos A)}{\sin^2 A}$

**98.** $\sec^2\left(\dfrac{A}{2}\right) = \dfrac{2(1 - \cos A)}{\sin^2 A}$

**99.** $\csc\left(\dfrac{A}{2}\right) = \pm\,|\csc A|\,\sqrt{2 + 2\cos A}$

**100.** $\sec\left(\dfrac{A}{2}\right) = \pm\,|\csc A|\,\sqrt{2 - 2\cos A}$

**In Exercises 101–108, graph the functions.**

**101.** $y = 4\cos^2\left(\dfrac{x}{2}\right)$

**102.** $y = -6\sin^2\left(\dfrac{x}{2}\right)$

**103.** $y = \dfrac{1 - \tan^2\left(\dfrac{x}{2}\right)}{1 + \tan^2\left(\dfrac{x}{2}\right)}$

**104.** $y = 1 - \left[\sin\left(\dfrac{x}{2}\right) + \cos\left(\dfrac{x}{2}\right)\right]^2$

**105.** $y = 4\sin^2\left(\dfrac{x}{2}\right) - 1$

**106.** $y = -\dfrac{1}{6}\cos^2\left(\dfrac{x}{2}\right) + 2$

**107.** $y = \sqrt{\dfrac{1 - \cos(2x)}{1 + \cos(2x)}}\quad 0 \le x < \pi$

**108.** $y = \sqrt{\dfrac{1 + \cos(3x)}{2}} + 3\quad 0 \le x \le \dfrac{\pi}{3}$

■ **APPLICATIONS**

**109. Business/Economics.** Annual cash flow of a stock fund (measured as a percentage of total assets) has fluctuated in cycles. The highs were roughly +12% of total assets and lows were roughly −8% of total assets. This cash flow can be modeled by the function

$$C(t) = 12 - 20\sin^2 t$$

Use a double-angle identity to express $C(t)$ in terms of the cosine function.

**110. Business.** Computer sales are generally subject to seasonal fluctuations. An analysis of the sales of a computer manufacturer during 2008–2010 is approximated by the function

$$s(t) = 0.098\cos^2 t + 0.387 \quad 1 \le t \le 12$$

where $t$ represents time in quarters ($t = 1$ represents the end of the first quarter of 2008), and $s(t)$ represents computer sales (quarterly revenue) in millions of dollars. Use a double-angle identity to express $s(t)$ in terms of the cosine function.

**For Exercises 111 and 112, refer to the following:**

An ore-crusher wheel consists of a heavy disk spinning on its axle. The normal (crushing) force $F$, in pounds, between the

wheel and the inclined track is determined by

$$F = W\sin\theta + \frac{1}{2}\psi^2\left[\frac{C}{R}(1 - \cos 2\theta) + \frac{A}{l}\sin 2\theta\right]$$

where $W$ is the weight of the wheel in pounds, $\theta$ is the angle of the axis, $C$ and $A$ are moments of inertia, $R$ is the radius of the wheel, $l$ is the distance from the wheel to the pin where the axle is attached, and $\psi$ is the speed in rpm that the wheel is spinning. The optimum crushing force occurs when the angle $\theta$ is between 45° and 90°.

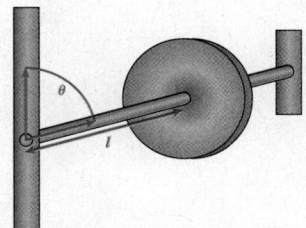

**111. Ore-Crusher Wheel.** Find $F$ if the angle is 60°, $W$ is 500 lb, $\psi$ is 200 rpm, $\dfrac{C}{R} = 750$, and $\dfrac{A}{l} = 3.75$.

**112. Ore-Crusher Wheel.** Find $F$ if the angle is 75°, $W$ is 500 lb, $\psi$ is 200 rpm, $\dfrac{C}{R} = 750$, and $\dfrac{A}{l} = 3.75$.

**113. Area of an Isosceles Triangle.** Consider the triangle below, where the vertex angle measures $\theta$, the equal sides measure $a$, the height is $h$, and half the base is $b$. (In an isosceles triangle, the perpendicular dropped from the vertex angle divides the triangle into two congruent triangles.) The two triangles formed are right triangles.

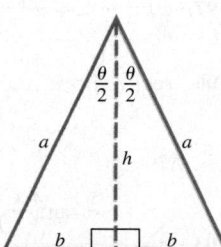

In the right triangles, $\sin\left(\dfrac{\theta}{2}\right) = \dfrac{b}{a}$ and $\cos\left(\dfrac{\theta}{2}\right) = \dfrac{h}{a}$. Multiply each side of each equation by $a$ to get $b = a\sin\left(\dfrac{\theta}{2}\right), h = a\cos\left(\dfrac{\theta}{2}\right)$.

The area of the entire isosceles triangle is $A = \frac{1}{2}(2b)h = bh$. Substitute the values for $b$ and $h$ into the area formula. Show that the area is equivalent to $\left(\dfrac{a^2}{2}\right)\sin\theta$.

**114. Area of an Isosceles Triangle.** Use the results from Exercise 113 to find the area of an isosceles triangle whose equal sides measure 7 inches and whose base angles each measure 75°.

**115.** With the information given in the diagram below, compute $y$.

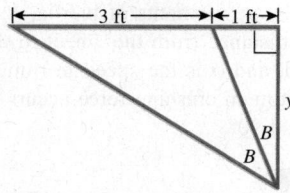

**116.** With the information given in the diagram below, compute $x$.

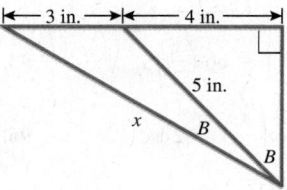

**For Exercises 117 and 118, refer to the following:**

Monthly profits can be expressed as a function of sales, that is, $p(s)$. A financial analysis of a company has determined that the sales $s$ in thousands of dollars are also related to monthly profits $p$ in thousands of dollars by the relationship:

$$\tan\theta = \frac{p}{s} \quad \text{for } 0 \le s \le 50, 0 \le p < 40$$

Based on sales and profits, it can be determined that the domain for angle $\theta$ is $0 \le \theta \le 38°$.

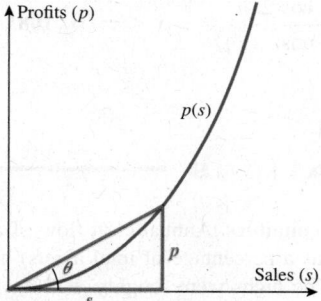

**117. Business.** If monthly profits are \$3000 and monthly sales are \$4000, find $\tan\left(\dfrac{\theta}{2}\right)$.

**118. Business.** If monthly profits are $p$ and monthly sales are $s$ (where $p < s$), find $\tan\left(\dfrac{\theta}{2}\right)$.

# ■ CATCH THE MISTAKE

**In Exercises 119–122, explain the mistake that is made.**

**119.** If $\cos x = \frac{1}{3}$, find $\sin(2x)$ given $\sin x < 0$.

**Solution:**

Write the double-angle identity for the sine function.
$$\sin(2x) = 2\sin x \cos x$$

Solve for $\sin x$ using the Pythagorean identity.
$$\sin^2 x + \left(\frac{1}{3}\right)^2 = 1$$
$$\sin x = \frac{2\sqrt{2}}{3}$$

Substitute $\cos x = \frac{1}{3}$ and $\sin x = \frac{2\sqrt{2}}{3}$.
$$\sin(2x) = 2\left(\frac{2\sqrt{2}}{3}\right)\left(\frac{1}{3}\right)$$

Simplify.
$$\sin(2x) = \frac{4\sqrt{2}}{9}$$

This is incorrect. What mistake was made?

**121.** If $\cos x = -\frac{1}{3}$, find $\sin\left(\frac{x}{2}\right)$ given $\pi < x < \frac{3\pi}{2}$.

**Solution:**

Write the half-angle identity for the sine function.
$$\sin\left(\frac{x}{2}\right) = \pm\sqrt{\frac{1 - \cos x}{2}}$$

Substitute $\cos x = -\frac{1}{3}$.
$$\sin\left(\frac{x}{2}\right) = \pm\sqrt{\frac{1 + \frac{1}{3}}{2}}$$

Simplify.
$$\sin\left(\frac{x}{2}\right) = \pm\sqrt{\frac{2}{3}} = \pm\frac{\sqrt{2}}{\sqrt{3}}$$

The sine function is negative.
$$\sin\left(\frac{x}{2}\right) = -\frac{\sqrt{2}}{\sqrt{3}}$$

This is incorrect. What mistake was made?

**120.** If $\sin x = \frac{1}{3}$, find $\tan(2x)$ given $\cos x < 0$.

**Solution:**

Use the quotient identity.
$$\tan(2x) = \frac{\sin(2x)}{\cos x}$$

Use the double-angle formula for the sine function.
$$\tan(2x) = \frac{2\sin x \cos x}{\cos x}$$

Cancel the common cosine factors.
$$\tan(2x) = 2\sin x$$

Substitute $\sin x = \frac{1}{3}$.
$$\tan(2x) = \frac{2}{3}$$

This is incorrect. What mistake was made?

**122.** If $\cos x = \frac{1}{3}$, find $\tan^2\left(\frac{x}{2}\right)$.

**Solution:**

Use the quotient identity.
$$\tan^2\left(\frac{x}{2}\right) = \frac{\sin^2\left(\frac{x}{2}\right)}{\cos^2 x}$$

Use the half-angle identity for the sine function.
$$\tan^2\left(\frac{x}{2}\right) = \frac{\frac{1 - \cos x}{2}}{\cos^2 x}$$

Simplify.
$$\tan^2\left(\frac{x}{2}\right) = \frac{1}{2}\left(\frac{1}{\cos^2 x} - \frac{\cos x}{\cos^2 x}\right)$$
$$\tan^2\left(\frac{x}{2}\right) = \frac{1}{2}\left(\frac{1}{\cos^2 x} - \frac{1}{\cos x}\right)$$

Substitute $\cos x = \frac{1}{3}$.
$$\tan^2\left(\frac{x}{2}\right) = \frac{1}{2}\left(\frac{1}{\frac{1}{9}} - \frac{1}{\frac{1}{3}}\right)$$
$$\tan^2\left(\frac{x}{2}\right) = 3$$

This is incorrect. What mistake was made?

# ■ CONCEPTUAL

**For Exercises 123–130, determine whether each statement is true or false.**

**123.** $\sin(2A) + \sin(2A) = \sin(4A)$

**124.** $\cos(4A) - \cos(2A) = \cos(2A)$

**125.** If $\tan x > 0$, then $\tan(2x) > 0$.

**126.** If $\sin x > 0$, then $\sin(2x) > 0$.

**127.** $\sin\left(\frac{A}{2}\right) + \sin\left(\frac{A}{2}\right) = \sin A$

**128.** $\cos\left(\frac{A}{2}\right) + \cos\left(\frac{A}{2}\right) = \cos A$

**129.** If $\tan x > 0$, then $\tan\left(\frac{x}{2}\right) > 0$.

**130.** If $\sin x > 0$, then $\sin\left(\frac{x}{2}\right) > 0$.

**131.** Given $\tan\left(\frac{A}{2}\right) = \pm\sqrt{\frac{1 - \cos A}{1 + \cos A}}$, verify $\tan\left(\frac{A}{2}\right) = \frac{\sin A}{1 + \cos A}$. Substitute $A = \pi$ into the identity and explain your results.

**132.** Given $\tan\left(\frac{A}{2}\right) = \pm\sqrt{\frac{1 - \cos A}{1 + \cos A}}$, verify $\tan\left(\frac{A}{2}\right) = \frac{1 - \cos A}{\sin A}$. Substitute $A = \pi$ into the identity and explain your results.

▪CHALLENGE

**133.** Is the identity $\tan(2x) = \dfrac{2\tan x}{1 - \tan^2 x}$ true for $x = \dfrac{\pi}{4}$? Explain.

**134.** Is the identity $2\csc(2x) = \dfrac{1 + \tan^2 x}{\tan x}$ true for $x = \dfrac{\pi}{2}$? Explain.

**135.** Prove that $\cot\left(\dfrac{A}{4}\right) = \pm\sqrt{\dfrac{1 + \cos\left(\dfrac{A}{2}\right)}{1 - \cos\left(\dfrac{A}{2}\right)}}$.

**136.** Prove that $\cot\left(-\dfrac{A}{2}\right)\sec\left(\dfrac{A}{2}\right)\csc\left(-\dfrac{A}{2}\right)\tan\left(\dfrac{A}{2}\right) = 2\csc A$.

**137.** Find the values of $x$ in the interval $[0, 2\pi]$ for which $\tan\left(\dfrac{x}{2}\right) > 0$.

**138.** Find the values of $x$ in the interval $[0, 2\pi]$ for which $\cot\left(\dfrac{x}{2}\right) \le 0$.

▪TECHNOLOGY

One cannot *prove* that an equation is an identity using technology, but rather one uses it as a first step to see whether or not the equation *seems* to be an identity.

**139.** With a graphing calculator, plot $Y_1 = 1 - \dfrac{(2x)^2}{2!} + \dfrac{(2x)^4}{4!}$ and $Y_2 = \cos(2x)$ for $x$ range $[-1, 1]$. Is $Y_1$ a good approximation to $Y_2$?

**140.** With a graphing calculator, plot $Y_1 = (2x) - \dfrac{(2x)^3}{3!} + \dfrac{(2x)^5}{5!}$ and $Y_2 = \sin(2x)$ for $x$ range $[-1, 1]$. Is $Y_1$ a good approximation to $Y_2$?

**141.** With a graphing calculator, plot $Y_1 = \left(\dfrac{x}{2}\right) - \dfrac{\left(\dfrac{x}{2}\right)^3}{3!} + \dfrac{\left(\dfrac{x}{2}\right)^5}{5!}$ and $Y_2 = \sin\left(\dfrac{x}{2}\right)$ for $x$ range $[-1, 1]$. Is $Y_1$ a good approximation to $Y_2$?

**142.** Using a graphing calculator, plot $Y_1 = 1 - \dfrac{\left(\dfrac{x}{2}\right)^2}{2!} + \dfrac{\left(\dfrac{x}{2}\right)^4}{4!}$ and $Y_2 = \cos\left(\dfrac{x}{2}\right)$ for $x$ range $[-1, 1]$. Is $Y_1$ a good approximation to $Y_2$?

▪PREVIEW TO CALCULUS

In calculus, we work with the derivative of expressions containing trigonometric functions. Usually, it is better to work with a simplified version of these expressions.

   In Exercises 143–146, simplify each expression using the double-angle and half-angle identities.

**143.** $\dfrac{\dfrac{2\sin x}{\cos x}}{\dfrac{\cos^2 x - \sin^2 x}{\cos^2 x}}$

**144.** $\cos^4 x - 6\sin^2 x\cos^2 x + \sin^4 x$

**145.** $3\sin x\cos^2 x - \sin^3 x$

**146.** $\sqrt{\dfrac{1 - \sqrt{\dfrac{1 + \cos x}{2}}}{1 + \sqrt{\dfrac{1 + \cos x}{2}}}}$

# PRODUCT-TO-SUM AND SUM-TO-PRODUCT IDENTITIES

## SKILLS OBJECTIVES

- Express products of trigonometric functions as sums of trigonometric functions.
- Express sums of trigonometric functions as products of trigonometric functions.

## CONCEPTUAL OBJECTIVES

- Understand that the sum and difference identities are used to derive product-to-sum identities.
- Understand that the product-to-sum identities are used to derive the sum-to-product identities.

In calculus, often it is helpful to write products of trigonometric functions as sums of other trigonometric functions, and vice versa. In this section, we discuss the *product-to-sum identities*, which convert products to sums, and *sum-to-product identities*, which convert sums to products.

## Product-to-Sum Identities

The *product-to-sum identities* are derived from the sum and difference identities.

| WORDS | MATH |
|---|---|
| Write the identity for the cosine of a sum. | $\cos A \cos B - \sin A \sin B = \cos(A + B)$ |
| Write the identity for the cosine of a difference. | $\cos A \cos B + \sin A \sin B = \cos(A - B)$ |
| Add the two identities. | $2\cos A \cos B = \cos(A + B) + \cos(A - B)$ |
| Divide both sides by 2. | $\boxed{\cos A \cos B = \dfrac{1}{2}[\cos(A + B) + \cos(A - B)]}$ |
| | $\cos A \cos B + \sin A \sin B = \cos(A - B)$ |
| Subtract the sum identity from the difference identity. | $-\cos A \cos B + \sin A \sin B = -\cos(A + B)$ |
| | $2\sin A \sin B = \cos(A - B) - \cos(A + B)$ |
| Divide both sides by 2. | $\boxed{\sin A \sin B = \dfrac{1}{2}[\cos(A - B) - \cos(A + B)]}$ |
| Write the identity for the sine of a sum. | $\sin A \cos B + \cos A \sin B = \sin(A + B)$ |
| Write the identity for the sine of a difference. | $\sin A \cos B - \cos A \sin B = \sin(A - B)$ |
| Add the two identities. | $2\sin A \cos B = \sin(A + B) + \sin(A - B)$ |
| Divide both sides by 2. | $\boxed{\sin A \cos B = \dfrac{1}{2}[\sin(A + B) + \sin(A - B)]}$ |

**PRODUCT-TO-SUM IDENTITIES**

**1.** $\cos A \cos B = \frac{1}{2}[\cos(A + B) + \cos(A - B)]$

**2.** $\sin A \sin B = \frac{1}{2}[\cos(A - B) - \cos(A + B)]$

**3.** $\sin A \cos B = \frac{1}{2}[\sin(A + B) + \sin(A - B)]$

---

### EXAMPLE 1 Illustrating a Product-to-Sum Identity for Specific Values

Show that product-to-sum identity (3) is true when $A = 30°$ and $B = 90°$.

**Solution:**

Write product-to-sum identity (3). $\qquad \sin A \cos B = \dfrac{1}{2}[\sin(A + B) + \sin(A - B)]$

Let $A = 30°$ and $B = 90°$. $\qquad \sin 30° \cos 90° = \dfrac{1}{2}[\sin(30° + 90°) + \sin(30° - 90°)]$

Simplify. $\qquad \sin 30° \cos 90° = \dfrac{1}{2}[\sin 120° + \sin(-60°)]$

Evaluate the trigonometric functions. $\qquad \dfrac{1}{2} \cdot 0 = \dfrac{1}{2}\left[\dfrac{\sqrt{3}}{2} - \dfrac{\sqrt{3}}{2}\right]$

Simplify. $\qquad\qquad 0 = 0$

---

**Technology Tip**

Graphs of $y_1 = \cos(4x)\cos(3x)$ and $y_2 = \frac{1}{2}[\cos(7x) + \cos x]$.

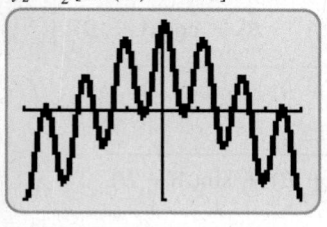

■ **Answer:** $\frac{1}{2}[\cos(7x) + \cos(3x)]$

### EXAMPLE 2 Convert a Product to a Sum

Convert the product $\cos(4x)\cos(3x)$ to a sum.

**Solution:**

Write product-to-sum identity (1). $\qquad \cos A \cos B = \dfrac{1}{2}[\cos(A + B) + \cos(A - B)]$

Let $A = 4x$ and $B = 3x$. $\qquad \cos(4x)\cos(3x) = \dfrac{1}{2}[\cos(4x + 3x) + \cos(4x - 3x)]$

Simplify. $\qquad \boxed{\cos(4x)\cos(3x) = \dfrac{1}{2}[\cos(7x) + \cos x]}$

■ **YOUR TURN** Convert the product $\cos(2x)\cos(5x)$ to a sum.

### EXAMPLE 3   Converting Products to Sums

Express $\sin(2x)\sin(3x)$ in terms of cosines.

#### COMMON MISTAKE

A common mistake that is often made is calling the product of two sines the square of a sine.

| ⭐ **CORRECT** | ❌ **INCORRECT** |
|---|---|
| Write product-to-sum identity (2). | Multiply the two sine functions. |
| $\sin A \sin B$ | $\sin(2x)\sin(3x) = \sin^2(6x^2)$   **ERROR** |
| $= \dfrac{1}{2}[\cos(A - B) - \cos(A + B)]$ | |
| Let $A = 2x$ and $B = 3x$. | |
| $\sin(2x)\sin(3x)$ | |
| $= \dfrac{1}{2}[\cos(2x - 3x) - \cos(2x + 3x)]$ | |
| Simplify. | |
| $\sin(2x)\sin(3x)$ | |
| $= \dfrac{1}{2}[\cos(-x) - \cos(5x)]$ | |
| The cosine function is an even function; thus, | |
| $\sin(2x)\sin(3x) = \dfrac{1}{2}[\cos x - \cos(5x)]$. | |

▼ **CAUTION**

1. $\sin A \sin B \neq \sin^2(AB)$.

2. The argument must be the same in order to use the identity:
$\sin A \sin A = (\sin A)^2 = \sin^2 A$.

■ **YOUR TURN**   Express $\sin x \sin(2x)$ in terms of cosines.

■ **Answer:** $\frac{1}{2}[\cos x - \cos(3x)]$

## Sum-to-Product Identities

The *sum-to-product identities* can be obtained from the product-to-sum identities.

| **WORDS** | **MATH** |
|---|---|
| Write the identity for the product of the sine and cosine functions. | $\dfrac{1}{2}[\sin(x + y) + \sin(x - y)] = \sin x \cos y$ |
| Let $x + y = A$ and $x - y = B$, then $x = \dfrac{A + B}{2}$ and $y = \dfrac{A - B}{2}$. | |
| Substitute these values into the identity. | $\dfrac{1}{2}[\sin A + \sin B] = \sin\left(\dfrac{A + B}{2}\right)\cos\left(\dfrac{A - B}{2}\right)$ |
| Multiply by 2. | $\sin A + \sin B = 2\sin\left(\dfrac{A + B}{2}\right)\cos\left(\dfrac{A - B}{2}\right)$ |

The other three *sum-to-product* identities can be found similarly. All are summarized in the box below.

**SUM-TO-PRODUCT IDENTITIES**

**4.** $\sin A + \sin B = 2\sin\left(\dfrac{A+B}{2}\right)\cos\left(\dfrac{A-B}{2}\right)$

**5.** $\sin A - \sin B = 2\sin\left(\dfrac{A-B}{2}\right)\cos\left(\dfrac{A+B}{2}\right)$

**6.** $\cos A + \cos B = 2\cos\left(\dfrac{A+B}{2}\right)\cos\left(\dfrac{A-B}{2}\right)$

**7.** $\cos A - \cos B = -2\sin\left(\dfrac{A+B}{2}\right)\sin\left(\dfrac{A-B}{2}\right)$

**EXAMPLE 4   Illustrating a Sum-to-Product Identity for Specific Values**

Show that sum-to-product identity (7) is true when $A = 30°$ and $B = 90°$.

**Solution:**

Write the sum-to-product identity (7).

$$\cos A - \cos B = -2\sin\left(\frac{A+B}{2}\right)\sin\left(\frac{A-B}{2}\right)$$

Let $A = 30°$ and $B = 90°$.

$$\cos 30° - \cos 90° = -2\sin\left(\frac{30° + 90°}{2}\right)\sin\left(\frac{30° - 90°}{2}\right)$$

Simplify.

$$\cos 30° - \cos 90° = -2\sin 60° \sin(-30°)$$

The sine function is an odd function.

$$\cos 30° - \cos 90° = 2\sin 60° \sin 30°$$

Evaluate the trigonometric functions.

$$\frac{\sqrt{3}}{2} - 0 = 2\left(\frac{\sqrt{3}}{2}\right)\left(\frac{1}{2}\right)$$

Simplify.

$$\frac{\sqrt{3}}{2} = \frac{\sqrt{3}}{2}$$

**EXAMPLE 5   Convert a Sum to a Product**

Convert $-9[\sin(2x) - \sin(10x)]$, a trigonometric expression containing a sum, to a product.

**Solution:**

The expression inside the brackets is in the form of identity (5).

$$\sin A - \sin B = 2\sin\left(\frac{A-B}{2}\right)\cos\left(\frac{A+B}{2}\right)$$

Let $A = 2x$ and $B = 10x$.

$$\sin(2x) - \sin(10x) = 2\sin\left(\frac{2x - 10x}{2}\right)\cos\left(\frac{2x + 10x}{2}\right)$$

Simplify.

$$\sin(2x) - \sin(10x) = 2\sin(-4x)\cos(6x)$$

The sine function is an odd function.

$$\sin(2x) - \sin(10x) = -2\sin(4x)\cos(6x)$$

Multiply both sides by $-9$.

$$\boxed{-9[\sin(2x) - \sin(10x)] = 18\sin(4x)\cos(6x)}$$

### EXAMPLE 6    Simplifying a Trigonometric Expression

Simplify the expression $\sin\left(\dfrac{x+y}{2}\right)\cos\left(\dfrac{x-y}{2}\right) + \sin\left(\dfrac{x-y}{2}\right)\cos\left(\dfrac{x+y}{2}\right)$.

**Solution:**

Use identities (4) and (5).

$$\underbrace{\sin\left(\frac{x+y}{2}\right)\cos\left(\frac{x-y}{2}\right)}_{\frac{1}{2}[\sin x + \sin y]} + \underbrace{\sin\left(\frac{x-y}{2}\right)\cos\left(\frac{x+y}{2}\right)}_{\frac{1}{2}[\sin x - \sin y]}$$

$$= \frac{1}{2}\sin x + \frac{1}{2}\sin y + \frac{1}{2}\sin x - \frac{1}{2}\sin y$$

Simplify.

$$= \boxed{\sin x}$$

**Technology Tip**

Graphs of
$y_1 = -9[\sin(2x) - \sin(10x)]$ and
$y_2 = 18\sin(4x)\cos(6x)$.

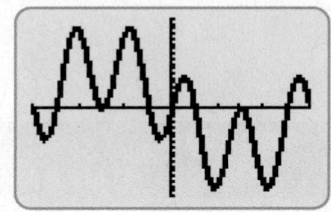

## Applications

In music, a note is a fixed pitch (frequency) that is given a name. If two notes are sounded simultaneously, then they combine to produce another note often called a "beat." The beat frequency is the difference of the two frequencies. The more rapid the beat, the further apart the two frequencies of the notes are. When musicians "tune" their instruments, they use a tuning fork to sound a note and then tune the instrument until the beat is eliminated; hence, the fork and instrument are in tune with each other. Mathematically, a note or tone is represented as $A\cos(2\pi ft)$, where $A$ is the amplitude (loudness), $f$ is the frequency in hertz, and $t$ is time in seconds. The following figure summarizes common notes and frequencies:

| C | D | E | F | G | A | B |
|---|---|---|---|---|---|---|
| 262 Hz | 294 Hz | 330 Hz | 349 Hz | 392 Hz | 440 Hz | 494 Hz |

### EXAMPLE 7    Music

Express the musical tone when a C and G are simultaneously struck (assume with the same loudness).
Find the beat frequency $f_2 - f_1$. Assume uniform loudness, $A = 1$.

**Solution:**

Write the mathematical description of a C note.                 $\cos(2\pi f_1 t)$, $f_1 = 262\,\text{Hz}$

Write the mathematical description of a G note.                 $\cos(2\pi f_2 t)$, $f_2 = 392\,\text{Hz}$

Add the two notes.                                              $\cos(524\pi t) + \cos(784\pi t)$

Use a sum-to-product identity:
$\cos(524\pi t) + \cos(784\pi t)$.      $= 2\cos\left(\dfrac{524\pi t + 784\pi t}{2}\right)\cos\left(\dfrac{524\pi t - 784\pi t}{2}\right)$

Simplify.                                                       $= 2\cos(654\pi t)\cos(-130\pi t)$

Cosine is an even function:
$\cos(-x) = \cos x$.                                            $= 2\cos(654\pi t)\cos(130\pi t)$

Identify average frequency                                      $= 2\underbrace{\cos(327\,\pi t)}_{\substack{\text{average}\\\text{frequency}}}\underbrace{\cos(130\,\pi t)}_{\substack{\text{beats per}\\\text{second}}}$
and beat of the tone.

The beat frequency can also be found by subtracting $f_1$ from $f_2$.

Therefore, the tone of average frequency, 327 hertz, has a beat of 130 hertz (beats/per second).

$$f_2 - f_1 = 392 - 262 = 130\,\text{Hz}$$

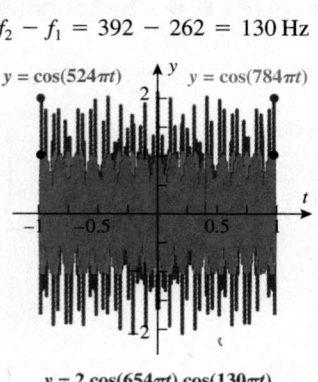

$y = \cos(524\pi t)$   $y = \cos(784\pi t)$

$y = 2\cos(654\pi t)\cos(130\pi t)$

In this section, we used the sum and difference identities to derive the product-to-sum identities. The product-to-sum identities allowed us to express products as sums.

$$\cos A \cos B = \frac{1}{2}[\cos(A + B) + \cos(A - B)]$$

$$\sin A \sin B = \frac{1}{2}[\cos(A - B) - \cos(A + B)]$$

$$\sin A \cos B = \frac{1}{2}[\sin(A + B) + \sin(A - B)]$$

We then used the product-to-sum identities to derive the sum-to-product identities. The sum-to-product identities allow us to express sums as products.

$$\sin A + \sin B = 2 \sin\left(\frac{A + B}{2}\right)\cos\left(\frac{A - B}{2}\right)$$

$$\sin A - \sin B = 2 \sin\left(\frac{A - B}{2}\right)\cos\left(\frac{A + B}{2}\right)$$

$$\cos A + \cos B = 2 \cos\left(\frac{A + B}{2}\right)\cos\left(\frac{A - B}{2}\right)$$

$$\cos A - \cos B = -2 \sin\left(\frac{A + B}{2}\right)\sin\left(\frac{A - B}{2}\right)$$

▪ **SKILLS**

**In Exercises 1–14, write each product as a sum or difference of sines and/or cosines.**

**1.** $\sin(2x)\cos x$

**2.** $\cos(10x)\sin(5x)$

**3.** $5\sin(4x)\sin(6x)$

**4.** $-3\sin(2x)\sin(4x)$

**5.** $4\cos(-x)\cos(2x)$

**6.** $-8\cos(3x)\cos(5x)$

**7.** $\sin\left(\frac{3x}{2}\right)\sin\left(\frac{5x}{2}\right)$

**8.** $\sin\left(\frac{\pi x}{2}\right)\sin\left(\frac{5\pi x}{2}\right)$

**9.** $\cos\left(\frac{2x}{3}\right)\cos\left(\frac{4x}{3}\right)$

**10.** $\sin\left(-\frac{\pi}{4}x\right)\cos\left(-\frac{\pi}{2}x\right)$

**11.** $-3\cos(0.4x)\cos(1.5x)$

**12.** $2\sin(2.1x)\sin(3.4x)$

**13.** $4\sin\left(-\sqrt{3}x\right)\cos\left(3\sqrt{3}x\right)$

**14.** $-5\cos\left(-\frac{\sqrt{2}}{3}x\right)\sin\left(\frac{5\sqrt{2}}{3}x\right)$

**In Exercises 15–28, write each expression as a product of sines and/or cosines.**

**15.** $\cos(5x) + \cos(3x)$

**16.** $\cos(2x) - \cos(4x)$

**17.** $\sin(3x) - \sin x$

**18.** $\sin(10x) + \sin(5x)$

**19.** $\sin\left(\dfrac{x}{2}\right) - \sin\left(\dfrac{5x}{2}\right)$

**20.** $\cos\left(\dfrac{x}{2}\right) - \cos\left(\dfrac{5x}{2}\right)$

**21.** $\cos\left(\dfrac{2}{3}x\right) + \cos\left(\dfrac{7}{3}x\right)$

**22.** $\sin\left(\dfrac{2}{3}x\right) + \sin\left(\dfrac{7}{3}x\right)$

**23.** $\sin(0.4x) + \sin(0.6x)$

**24.** $\cos(0.3x) - \cos(0.5x)$

**25.** $\sin(\sqrt{5}x) - \sin(3\sqrt{5}x)$

**26.** $\cos(-3\sqrt{7}x) - \cos(2\sqrt{7}x)$

**27.** $\cos\left(-\dfrac{\pi}{4}x\right) + \cos\left(\dfrac{\pi}{6}x\right)$

**28.** $\sin\left(\dfrac{3\pi}{4}x\right) + \sin\left(\dfrac{5\pi}{4}x\right)$

**In Exercises 29–34, simplify the trigonometric expressions.**

**29.** $\dfrac{\cos(3x) - \cos x}{\sin(3x) + \sin x}$

**30.** $\dfrac{\sin(4x) + \sin(2x)}{\cos(4x) - \cos(2x)}$

**31.** $\dfrac{\cos x - \cos(3x)}{\sin(3x) - \sin x}$

**32.** $\dfrac{\sin(4x) + \sin(2x)}{\cos(4x) + \cos(2x)}$

**33.** $\dfrac{\cos(5x) + \cos(2x)}{\sin(5x) - \sin(2x)}$

**34.** $\dfrac{\sin(7x) - \sin(2x)}{\cos(7x) - \cos(2x)}$

**In Exercises 35–42, verify the identities.**

**35.** $\dfrac{\sin A + \sin B}{\cos A + \cos B} = \tan\left(\dfrac{A + B}{2}\right)$

**36.** $\dfrac{\sin A - \sin B}{\cos A + \cos B} = \tan\left(\dfrac{A - B}{2}\right)$

**37.** $\dfrac{\cos A - \cos B}{\sin A + \sin B} = -\tan\left(\dfrac{A - B}{2}\right)$

**38.** $\dfrac{\cos A - \cos B}{\sin A - \sin B} = -\tan\left(\dfrac{A + B}{2}\right)$

**39.** $\dfrac{\sin A + \sin B}{\sin A - \sin B} = \tan\left(\dfrac{A + B}{2}\right)\cot\left(\dfrac{A - B}{2}\right)$

**40.** $\dfrac{\cos A - \cos B}{\cos A + \cos B} = -\tan\left(\dfrac{A + B}{2}\right)\tan\left(\dfrac{A - B}{2}\right)$

**41.** $\dfrac{\cos(A + B) + \cos(A - B)}{\sin(A + B) + \sin(A - B)} = \cot A$

**42.** $\dfrac{\cos(A - B) - \cos(A + B)}{\sin(A + B) + \sin(A - B)} = \tan B$

■ **APPLICATIONS**

**43. Business.** An analysis of the monthly costs and monthly revenues of a toy store indicates that monthly costs fluctuate (increase and decrease) according to the function

$$C(t) = \sin\left(\dfrac{\pi}{6}t + \pi\right)$$

and monthly revenues fluctuate (increase and decrease) according to the function

$$R(t) = \sin\left(\dfrac{\pi}{6}t + \dfrac{5\pi}{3}\right)$$

Find the function that describes how the monthly profits fluctuate: $P(t) = R(t) - C(t)$. Using identities in this section, express $P(t)$ in terms of a cosine function.

**44. Business.** An analysis of the monthly costs and monthly revenues of an electronics manufacturer indicates that monthly costs fluctuate (increase and decrease) according to the function

$$C(t) = \cos\left(\dfrac{\pi}{3}t + \dfrac{\pi}{3}\right)$$

and monthly revenues fluctuate (increase and decrease) according to the function

$$R(t) = \cos\left(\dfrac{\pi}{3}t\right)$$

Find the function that describes how the monthly profits fluctuate: $P(t) = R(t) - C(t)$. Using identities in this section, express $P(t)$ in terms of a sine function.

**45. Music.** Write a mathematical description of a tone that results from simultaneously playing a G and a B. What is the beat frequency? What is the average frequency?

**46. Music.** Write a mathematical description of a tone that results from simultaneously playing an F and an A. What is the beat frequency? What is the average frequency?

**47. Optics.** Two optical signals with uniform ($A = 1$) intensities and wavelengths of $1.55\ \mu m$ and $0.63\ \mu m$ are "beat" together. What is the resulting sum if their individual signals are given by $\sin\left(\dfrac{2\pi tc}{1.55\ \mu m}\right)$ and $\sin\left(\dfrac{2\pi tc}{0.63\ \mu m}\right)$, where $c = 3.0 \times 10^8$ m/s?

*Note:* $1\ \mu m = 10^{-6}$ m.

**48. Optics.** The two optical signals in Exercise 47 are beat together. What are the average frequency and the beat frequency?

**For Exercises 49 and 50, refer to the following:**

Touch-tone keypads have the following simultaneous low and high frequencies.

| FREQUENCY | 1209 Hz | 1336 Hz | 1477 Hz |
|-----------|---------|---------|---------|
| 697 Hz    | 1       | 2       | 3       |
| 770 Hz    | 4       | 5       | 6       |
| 852 Hz    | 7       | 8       | 9       |
| 941 Hz    | *       | 0       | #       |

The signal given when a key is pressed is $\sin(2\pi f_1 t) + \sin(2\pi f_2 t)$, where $f_1$ is the low frequency and $f_2$ is the high frequency.

**49. Touch-Tone Dialing.** What is the mathematical function that models the sound of dialing 4?

**50. Touch-Tone Dialing.** What is the mathematical function that models the sound of dialing 3?

**51. Area of a Triangle.** A formula for finding the area of a triangle when given the measures of the angles and one side is Area $= \dfrac{a^2 \sin B \sin C}{2 \sin A}$, where $a$ is the side opposite angle $A$. If the measures of angles $B$ and $C$ are $52.5°$ and $7.5°$, respectively, and if $a = 10$ ft, use the appropriate product-to-sum identity to change the formula so that you can solve for the area of the triangle exactly.

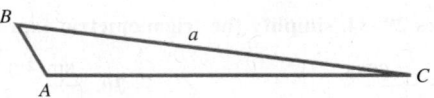

**52. Area of a Triangle.** If the measures of angles $B$ and $C$ in Exercise 51 are $75°$ and $45°$, respectively, and if $a = 12$ in., use the appropriate product-to-sum identity to change the formula so that you can solve for the area of the triangle exactly.

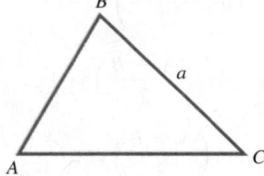

■ **CATCH THE MISTAKE**

**In Exercises 53 and 54, explain the mistake that is made.**

**53.** Simplify the expression $(\cos A - \cos B)^2 + (\sin A - \sin B)^2$.

**Solution:**

Expand by squaring.

$\cos^2 A - 2\cos A \cos B + \cos^2 B + \sin^2 A - 2\sin A \sin B + \sin^2 B$

Group terms.

$\cos^2 A + \sin^2 A - 2\cos A \cos B - 2\sin A \sin B + \cos^2 B + \sin^2 B$

Simplify using the Pythagorean identity.

$\underbrace{\cos^2 A + \sin^2 A}_{1} - 2\cos A \cos B - 2\sin A \sin B + \underbrace{\cos^2 B + \sin^2 B}_{1}$

Factor the common 2.    $2(1 - \cos A \cos B - \sin A \sin B)$

Simplify.                $2(1 - \cos AB - \sin AB)$

This is incorrect. What mistakes were made?

**54.** Simplify the expression $(\sin A - \sin B)(\cos A + \cos B)$.

**Solution:**

Multiply the expressions using the distributive property.

$\sin A \cos A + \sin A \cos B - \sin B \cos A - \sin B \cos B$

Cancel the second and third terms.

$\sin A \cos A - \sin B \cos B$

Use the product-to-sum identity.

$\underset{\frac{1}{2}[\sin(A + A) + \sin(A - A)]}{\sin A \cos A} - \underset{\frac{1}{2}[\sin(B + B) + \sin(B - B)]}{\sin B \cos B}$

Simplify.    $= \dfrac{1}{2}\sin(2A) - \dfrac{1}{2}\sin(2B)$

This is incorrect. What mistake was made?

## ■CONCEPTUAL

**In Exercises 55–58, determine whether each statement is true or false.**

**55.** $\cos A \cos B = \cos AB$

**56.** $\sin A \sin B = \sin AB$

**57.** The product of two cosine functions is a sum of two other cosine functions.

**58.** The product of two sine functions is a difference of two cosine functions.

**59.** Write $\sin A \sin B \sin C$ as a sum or difference of sines and cosines.

**60.** Write $\cos A \cos B \cos C$ as a sum or difference of sines and cosines.

## ■CHALLENGE

**61.** Prove the addition formula
$\cos(A + B) = \cos A \cos B - \sin A \sin B$
using the identities of this section.

**62.** Prove the difference formula
$\sin(A - B) = \sin A \cos B - \sin B \cos A$
using the identities of this section.

**63.** Graph $y = 1 - 3\sin(\pi x)\sin\left(-\dfrac{\pi}{6}x\right)$.

**64.** Graph $y = 4\sin(2x - 1)\cos(2 - x)$.

**65.** Graph $y = -\cos\left(\dfrac{2\pi}{3}x\right)\cos\left(\dfrac{5\pi}{6}x\right)$.

**66.** Graph $y = x - \cos(2x)\sin(3x)$.

## ■TECHNOLOGY

**67.** Suggest an identity $4\sin x \cos x \cos(2x) =$ _____ by graphing $Y_1 = 4\sin x \cos x \cos(2x)$ and determining the function based on the graph.

**68.** Suggest an identity $1 + \tan x \tan(2x) =$ _____ by graphing $Y_1 = 1 + \tan x \tan(2x)$ and determining the function based on the graph.

**69.** With a graphing calculator, plot $Y_1 = \sin(4x)\sin(2x)$, $Y_2 = \sin(6x)$, and $Y_3 = \frac{1}{2}[\cos(2x) - \cos(6x)]$ in the same viewing rectangle $[0, 2\pi]$ by $[-1, 1]$. Which graphs are the same?

**70.** With a graphing calculator, plot $Y_1 = \cos(4x)\cos(2x)$, $Y_2 = \cos(6x)$, and $Y_3 = \frac{1}{2}[\cos(6x) + \cos(2x)]$ in the same viewing rectangle $[0, 2\pi]$ by $[-1, 1]$. Which graphs are the same?

## ■PREVIEW TO CALCULUS

**In calculus, the method of separation of variables is used to solve certain differential equations. Given an equation with two variables, the method consists of writing the equation in such a way that each side of the equation contains only one type of variable.**

**In Exercises 71–74, use the product-to-sum and sum-to-product identities to separate the variables $x$ and $y$ in each equation.**

**71.** $\sin\left(\dfrac{x + y}{2}\right)\sin\left(\dfrac{x - y}{2}\right) = \dfrac{1}{5}$

**72.** $\dfrac{1}{2} = \sin\left(\dfrac{x + y}{2}\right)\cos\left(\dfrac{x - y}{2}\right)$

**73.** $\sin(x + y) = 1 + \sin(x - y)$

**74.** $2 + \cos(x + y) = \cos(x - y)$

**SKILLS OBJECTIVES**

- Develop inverse trigonometric functions.
- Find values of inverse trigonometric functions.
- Graph inverse trigonometric functions.

**CONCEPTUAL OBJECTIVES**

- Understand the different notations for inverse trigonometric functions.
- Understand why domain restrictions on trigonometric functions are needed for inverse trigonometric functions to exist.
- Extend properties of inverse functions to develop inverse trigonometric identities.

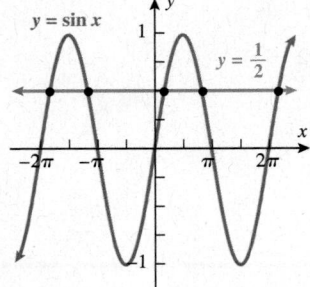

In Section 1.5, we discussed one-to-one functions and inverse functions. Here we present a summary of that section. A function is one-to-one if it passes the horizontal line test: No two $x$-values map to the same $y$-value.

Notice that the sine function does not pass the horizontal line test. However, if we restrict the domain to $-\dfrac{\pi}{2} \le x \le \dfrac{\pi}{2}$, then the restricted function is one-to-one.

Recall that if $y = f(x)$, then $x = f^{-1}(y)$.

The following are the properties of inverse functions:

1. If $f$ is a one-to-one function, then the inverse function $f^{-1}$ exists.
2. The domain of $f^{-1}$ = the range of $f$.
   The range of $f^{-1}$ = the domain of $f$.
3. $f^{-1}(f(x)) = x$ for all $x$ in the domain of $f$.
   $f(f^{-1}(x)) = x$ for all $x$ in the domain of $f^{-1}$.
4. The graph of $f^{-1}$ is the reflection of the graph of $f$ about the line $y = x$. If the point $(a, b)$ lies on the graph of a function, then the point $(b, a)$ lies on the graph of its inverse.

## Inverse Sine Function

Let us start with the sine function with the restricted domain $\left[-\dfrac{\pi}{2}, \dfrac{\pi}{2}\right]$.

$$y = \sin x \qquad \text{Domain: } \left[-\dfrac{\pi}{2}, \dfrac{\pi}{2}\right] \qquad \text{Range: } [-1, 1]$$

| $x$ | $y$ |
|---|---|
| $-\dfrac{\pi}{2}$ | $-1$ |
| $-\dfrac{\pi}{4}$ | $-\dfrac{\sqrt{2}}{2}$ |
| $0$ | $0$ |
| $\dfrac{\pi}{4}$ | $\dfrac{\sqrt{2}}{2}$ |
| $\dfrac{\pi}{2}$ | $1$ |

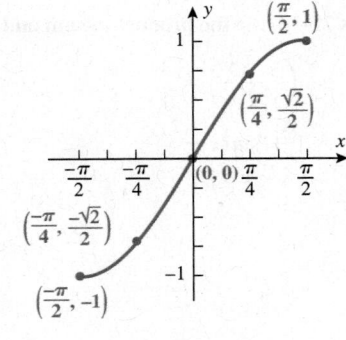

By the properties of inverse functions, the inverse sine function will have a domain of $[-1, 1]$ and a range of $\left[-\frac{\pi}{2}, \frac{\pi}{2}\right]$. To find the inverse sine function, we interchange the $x$- and $y$-values of $y = \sin x$.

$$y = \sin^{-1} x \qquad \text{Domain: } [-1, 1] \qquad \text{Range: } \left[-\frac{\pi}{2}, \frac{\pi}{2}\right]$$

| $x$ | $y$ |
|---|---|
| $-1$ | $-\dfrac{\pi}{2}$ |
| $-\dfrac{\sqrt{2}}{2}$ | $-\dfrac{\pi}{4}$ |
| $0$ | $0$ |
| $\dfrac{\sqrt{2}}{2}$ | $\dfrac{\pi}{4}$ |
| $1$ | $\dfrac{\pi}{2}$ |

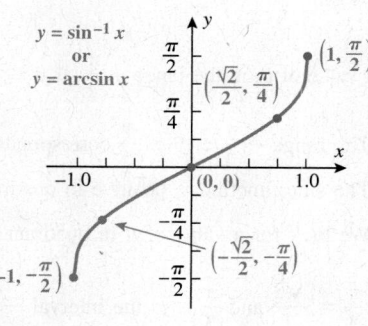

**Study Tip**

The inverse sine function gives an angle on the right half of the unit circle (QI and QIV).

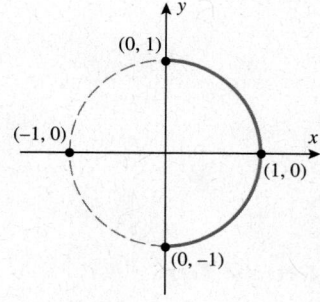

Notice that the inverse sine function, like the sine function, is an odd function (symmetric about the origin).

If the sine of an angle is known, and the angle is between $-\frac{\pi}{2}$ and $\frac{\pi}{2}$, what is the measure of that angle? The inverse sine function determines that angle measure. Another notation for the inverse sine function is $\arcsin x$.

**Technology Tip**

To graph $y = \sin^{-1} x$, use $[-1, 1]$ as the domain and $\left[-\frac{\pi}{2}, \frac{\pi}{2}\right]$ as the range.

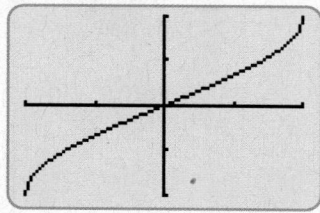

### INVERSE SINE FUNCTION

$$\underbrace{y = \sin^{-1} x \text{ or } y = \arcsin x}_{\text{"y is the inverse sine of x"}} \qquad \text{means} \qquad \underbrace{x = \sin y}_{\substack{\text{"y is the angle measure} \\ \text{whose sine equals x"}}}$$

$$\text{where } -1 \leq x \leq 1 \text{ and } -\frac{\pi}{2} \leq y \leq \frac{\pi}{2}$$

**Study Tip**

Trigonometric functions take angle measures and return real numbers. Inverse trigonometric functions take real numbers and return angle measures.

It is important to note that the $-1$ as the superscript indicates an inverse function. Therefore, the inverse sine function should not be interpreted as a reciprocal:

$$\sin^{-1} x \neq \frac{1}{\sin x}$$

**EXAMPLE 1** **Finding Exact Values of an Inverse Sine Function**

Find the exact value of each of the following expressions:

**a.** $\sin^{-1}\left(\dfrac{\sqrt{3}}{2}\right)$ **b.** $\arcsin\left(-\dfrac{1}{2}\right)$

**Solution (a):**

Let $\theta = \sin^{-1}\left(\dfrac{\sqrt{3}}{2}\right)$.     $\sin\theta = \dfrac{\sqrt{3}}{2}$ for $-\dfrac{\pi}{2} \le \theta \le \dfrac{\pi}{2}$

Which value of $\theta$, in the range $-\dfrac{\pi}{2} \le \theta \le \dfrac{\pi}{2}$, corresponds to a sine value of $\dfrac{\sqrt{3}}{2}$?

- The range $-\dfrac{\pi}{2} \le \theta \le \dfrac{\pi}{2}$ corresponds to quadrants I and IV.
- The sine function is positive in quadrant I.
- We look for a value of $\theta$ in quadrant I that has a sine value of $\dfrac{\sqrt{3}}{2}$.     $\theta = \dfrac{\pi}{3}$

$\sin\dfrac{\pi}{3} = \dfrac{\sqrt{3}}{2}$ and $\dfrac{\pi}{3}$ is in the interval $\left[-\dfrac{\pi}{2}, \dfrac{\pi}{2}\right]$.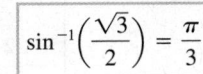

*Calculator Confirmation:* Since $\dfrac{\pi}{3} = 60°$, if our calculator is set in degree mode, we should find that $\sin^{-1}\left(\dfrac{\sqrt{3}}{2}\right)$ is equal to 60°.

**Solution (b):**

Let $\theta = \arcsin\left(-\dfrac{1}{2}\right)$.     $\sin\theta = -\dfrac{1}{2}$ for $-\dfrac{\pi}{2} \le \theta \le \dfrac{\pi}{2}$

Which value of $\theta$, in the range $-\dfrac{\pi}{2} \le \theta \le \dfrac{\pi}{2}$, corresponds to a sine value of $-\dfrac{1}{2}$?

- The range $-\dfrac{\pi}{2} \le \theta \le \dfrac{\pi}{2}$ corresponds to quadrants I and IV.
- The sine function is negative in quadrant IV.
- We look for a value of $\theta$ in quadrant IV that has a sine value of $-\frac{1}{2}$.     $\theta = -\dfrac{\pi}{6}$

$\sin\left(-\dfrac{\pi}{6}\right) = -\dfrac{1}{2}$ and $-\dfrac{\pi}{6}$ is in the interval $\left[-\dfrac{\pi}{2}, \dfrac{\pi}{2}\right]$.     $\boxed{\arcsin\left(-\dfrac{1}{2}\right) = -\dfrac{\pi}{6}}$

*Calculator Confirmation:* Since $-\dfrac{\pi}{6} = -30°$, if our calculator is set in degree mode, we should find that $\sin^{-1}\left(-\frac{1}{2}\right)$ is equal to $-30°$.

**■ YOUR TURN** Find the exact value of each of the following expressions:

**a.** $\sin^{-1}\left(-\dfrac{\sqrt{3}}{2}\right)$ **b.** $\arcsin\left(\dfrac{1}{2}\right)$

**Study Tip**

In Example 1, note that the graphs help identify the desired angles.

**a.**

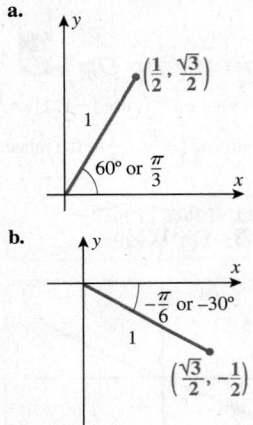

**■ Answer: a.** $-\dfrac{\pi}{3}$ **b.** $\dfrac{\pi}{6}$

In Example 1, it is important to note that in part (a), both $60°$ and $120°$ correspond to the sine function equal to $\dfrac{\sqrt{3}}{2}$ and only one of them is valid, which is why the domain restrictions are necessary for inverse functions except for quadrantal angles. There are always two angles (values) from 0 to $360°$ or 0 to $2\pi$ (except that only $90°$, or $\dfrac{\pi}{2}$, and $270°$, or $\dfrac{3\pi}{2}$, correspond to 1 and $-1$, respectively) that correspond to the sine function equal to a particular value.

It is important to note that the inverse sine function has a domain $[-1, 1]$. For example, $\sin^{-1} 3$ does not exist because 3 is not in the domain of the inverse sine function. Notice that calculator evaluation of $\sin^{-1} 3$ says *error*. Calculators can be used to evaluate inverse sine functions when an exact evaluation is not feasible, just as they are for the basic trigonometric functions. For example, $\sin^{-1} 0.3 \approx 17.46°$, or 0.305 radians.

We now state the properties relating the sine function and the inverse sine function that follow directly from properties of inverse functions.

**Technology Tip**

Use a TI calculator to find $\sin^{-1} 3$ and $\sin^{-1} 0.3$. Be sure to set the calculator in radian mode.

```
sin-1(3)
█
```

```
ERR:DOMAIN
1▊Quit
2:Goto
```

```
sin-1(3)
sin-1(0.3)
         .304692654
█
```

### SINE-INVERSE SINE IDENTITIES

$$\sin^{-1}(\sin x) = x \qquad \text{for} \qquad -\dfrac{\pi}{2} \le x \le \dfrac{\pi}{2}$$

$$\sin(\sin^{-1} x) = x \qquad \text{for} \qquad -1 \le x \le 1$$

For example, $\sin^{-1}\left[\sin\left(\dfrac{\pi}{12}\right)\right] = \dfrac{\pi}{12}$, since $\dfrac{\pi}{12}$ is in the interval $\left[-\dfrac{\pi}{2}, \dfrac{\pi}{2}\right]$. However, you must be careful not to overlook the domain restriction for which these identities hold, as illustrated in the next example.

▶ **EXAMPLE 2  Using Inverse Identities to Evaluate Expressions Involving Inverse Sine Functions**

Find the exact value of each of the following trigonometric expressions:

**a.** $\sin\left[\sin^{-1}\left(\dfrac{\sqrt{2}}{2}\right)\right]$    **b.** $\sin^{-1}\left[\sin\left(\dfrac{3\pi}{4}\right)\right]$

**Solution (a):**

Write the appropriate identity.                $\sin(\sin^{-1} x) = x$ for $-1 \le x \le 1$

Let $x = \dfrac{\sqrt{2}}{2}$, which is in the interval $[-1, 1]$.

Since the domain restriction is met,          $\boxed{\sin\left[\sin^{-1}\left(\dfrac{\sqrt{2}}{2}\right)\right] = \dfrac{\sqrt{2}}{2}}$
the identity can be used.

**a.** Check the answer of $\sin\left[\sin^{-1}\left(\dfrac{\sqrt{2}}{2}\right)\right]$ with a calculator.

```
sin(sin-1(√(2)/2)
)
           .7071067812
√(2)/2
           .7071067812
■
```

**b.** Check the answer of $\sin^{-1}\left[\sin\left(\dfrac{3\pi}{4}\right)\right]$ with a calculator in radian mode.

```
sin-1(sin(3π/4))
           .7853981634
π/4
           .7853981634
■
```

■ **Answer: a.** $-\dfrac{1}{2}$   **b.** $\dfrac{\pi}{6}$

---

**Solution (b):**

### COMMON MISTAKE

Ignoring the domain restrictions on inverse identities.

**⊕ CORRECT**

Write the appropriate identity.

$$\sin^{-1}(\sin x) = x \text{ for } -\frac{\pi}{2} \le x \le \frac{\pi}{2}$$

Let $x = \dfrac{3\pi}{4}$, which is *not* in the interval $\left[-\dfrac{\pi}{2}, \dfrac{\pi}{2}\right]$.

Since the domain restriction is not met, the identity cannot be used. Instead, we look for a value in the domain that corresponds to the same value of sine.

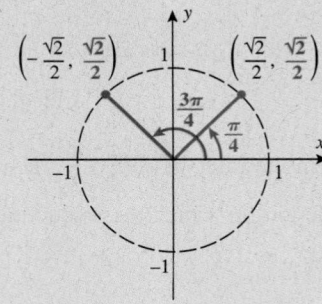

Substitute $\sin\dfrac{3\pi}{4} = \sin\dfrac{\pi}{4}$ into the expression.

$$\sin^{-1}\left[\sin\left(\frac{3\pi}{4}\right)\right] = \sin^{-1}\left[\sin\left(\frac{\pi}{4}\right)\right]$$

Since $\dfrac{\pi}{4}$ is in the interval $\left[-\dfrac{\pi}{2}, \dfrac{\pi}{2}\right]$, we can use the identity.

$$\sin^{-1}\left[\sin\left(\frac{3\pi}{4}\right)\right] = \sin^{-1}\left[\sin\left(\frac{\pi}{4}\right)\right] = \boxed{\dfrac{\pi}{4}}$$

**⊗ INCORRECT**

$\sin^{-1}(\sin x) = x$     **ERROR**

Let $x = \dfrac{3\pi}{4}$.

(Forgot the domain restriction.)

$$\sin^{-1}\left[\sin\left(\frac{3\pi}{4}\right)\right] = \frac{3\pi}{4}$$
          **INCORRECT**

---

■ **YOUR TURN** Find the exact value of each of the following trigonometric expressions:

**a.** $\sin\left[\sin^{-1}\left(-\dfrac{1}{2}\right)\right]$     **b.** $\sin^{-1}\left[\sin\left(\dfrac{5\pi}{6}\right)\right]$

# Inverse Cosine Function

The cosine function is also not a one-to-one function, so we must restrict the domain in order to develop the inverse cosine function.

$$y = \cos x \qquad \text{Domain: } [0, \pi] \qquad \text{Range: } [-1, 1]$$

| $x$ | $y$ |
|---|---|
| $0$ | $1$ |
| $\dfrac{\pi}{4}$ | $\dfrac{\sqrt{2}}{2}$ |
| $\dfrac{\pi}{2}$ | $0$ |
| $\dfrac{3\pi}{4}$ | $-\dfrac{\sqrt{2}}{2}$ |
| $\pi$ | $-1$ |

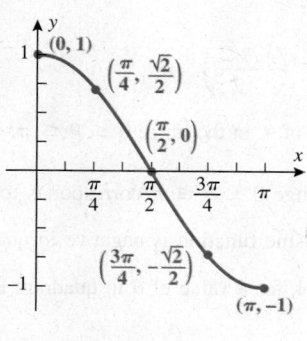

**Technology Tip**

To graph $y = \cos^{-1} x$, use $[-1, 1]$ as the domain and $[0, \pi]$ as the range.

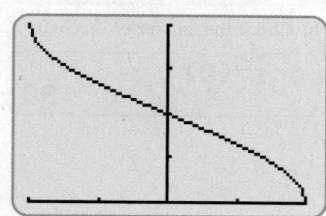

By the properties of inverses, the inverse cosine function will have a domain of $[-1, 1]$ and a range of $[0, \pi]$. To find the inverse cosine function, we interchange the $x$- and $y$-values of $y = \cos x$.

$$y = \cos^{-1} x \qquad \text{Domain: } [-1, 1] \qquad \text{Range: } [0, \pi]$$

| $x$ | $y$ |
|---|---|
| $-1$ | $\pi$ |
| $-\dfrac{\sqrt{2}}{2}$ | $\dfrac{3\pi}{4}$ |
| $0$ | $\dfrac{\pi}{2}$ |
| $\dfrac{\sqrt{2}}{2}$ | $\dfrac{\pi}{4}$ |
| $1$ | $0$ |

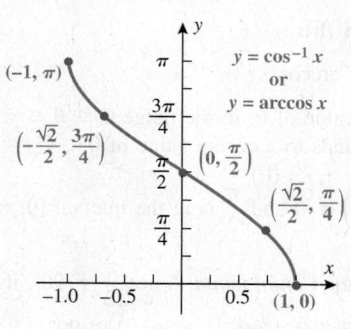

Notice that the inverse cosine function, unlike the cosine function, is not symmetric about the $y$-axis or the origin. Although the inverse sine and inverse cosine functions have the same domain, they behave differently. The inverse sine function increases on its domain (from left to right), whereas the inverse cosine function decreases on its domain (from left to right).

If the cosine of an angle is known and the angle is between 0 and $\pi$, what is the measure of that angle? The inverse cosine function determines that angle measure. Another notation for the inverse cosine function is arccos $x$.

**Study Tip**

The inverse cosine function gives an angle on the top half of the unit circle (QI and QII).

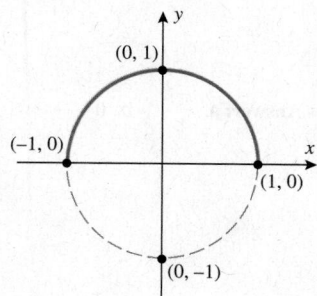

## INVERSE COSINE FUNCTION

$$\underbrace{y = \cos^{-1} x \text{ or } y = \arccos x}_{\text{"}y\text{ is the inverse cosine of }x\text{"}} \quad \text{means} \quad \underbrace{x = \cos y}_{\substack{\text{"}y\text{ is the angle measure} \\ \text{whose cosine equals }x\text{"}}}$$

$$\text{where } -1 \le x \le 1 \text{ and } 0 \le y \le \pi$$

**Study Tip**

$$\cos^{-1} x \ne \frac{1}{\cos x}$$

**EXAMPLE 3    Finding Exact Values of an Inverse Cosine Function**

Find the exact value of each of the following expressions:

**a.** $\cos^{-1}\left(-\dfrac{\sqrt{2}}{2}\right)$     **b.** $\arccos 0$

**Solution (a):**

Let $\theta = \cos^{-1}\left(-\dfrac{\sqrt{2}}{2}\right)$.          $\cos\theta = -\dfrac{\sqrt{2}}{2}$ when $0 \le \theta \le \pi$

Which value of $\theta$, in the range $0 \le \theta \le \pi$, corresponds to a cosine value of $-\dfrac{\sqrt{2}}{2}$?

- The range $0 \le \theta \le \pi$ corresponds to quadrants I and II.
- The cosine function is negative in quadrant II.
- We look for a value of $\theta$ in quadrant II that has a cosine value of $-\dfrac{\sqrt{2}}{2}$.    $\theta = \dfrac{3\pi}{4}$

$\cos\left(\dfrac{3\pi}{4}\right) = -\dfrac{\sqrt{2}}{2}$ and $\dfrac{3\pi}{4}$ is in the interval $[0, \pi]$.     $\boxed{\cos^{-1}\left(-\dfrac{\sqrt{2}}{2}\right) = \dfrac{3\pi}{4}}$

*Calculator Confirmation:* Since $\dfrac{3\pi}{4} = 135°$, if our calculator is set in degree mode, we should find that $\cos^{-1}\left(-\dfrac{\sqrt{2}}{2}\right)$ is equal to $135°$.

**Solution (b):**

Let $\theta = \arccos 0$.          $\cos\theta = 0$ when $0 \le \theta \le \pi$

Which value of $\theta$, in the range $0 \le \theta \le \pi$, corresponds to a cosine value of 0?     $\theta = \dfrac{\pi}{2}$

$\cos\left(\dfrac{\pi}{2}\right) = 0$ and $\dfrac{\pi}{2}$ is in the interval $[0, \pi]$.     $\boxed{\arccos 0 = \dfrac{\pi}{2}}$

*Calculator Confirmation:* Since $\dfrac{\pi}{2} = 90°$, if our calculator is set in degree mode, we should find that $\cos^{-1} 0$ is equal to $90°$.

- **Answer: a.** $\dfrac{\pi}{4}$    **b.** 0

■ **YOUR TURN** Find the exact value of each of the following expressions:

**a.** $\cos^{-1}\left(\dfrac{\sqrt{2}}{2}\right)$     **b.** $\arccos 1$

We now state the properties relating the cosine function and the inverse cosine function that follow directly from the properties of inverses.

**COSINE-INVERSE COSINE IDENTITIES**

$$\cos^{-1}(\cos x) = x \quad \text{for} \quad 0 \le x \le \pi$$

$$\cos(\cos^{-1} x) = x \quad \text{for} \quad -1 \le x \le 1$$

As was the case with inverse identities for the sine function, you must be careful not to overlook the domain restrictions governing when each of these identities hold.

### EXAMPLE 4  Using Inverse Identities to Evaluate Expressions Involving Inverse Cosine Functions

Find the exact value of each of the following trigonometric expressions:

**a.** $\cos\left[\cos^{-1}\left(-\dfrac{1}{2}\right)\right]$     **b.** $\cos^{-1}\left[\cos\left(\dfrac{7\pi}{4}\right)\right]$

**Technology Tip**

**a.** Check the answer of $\cos\left[\cos^{-1}\left(-\tfrac{1}{2}\right)\right]$ with a calculator.

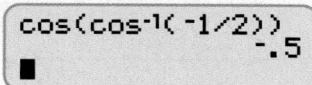

**b.** Check the answer of $\cos^{-1}\left[\cos\left(\dfrac{7\pi}{4}\right)\right]$. Be sure to set the calculator to radian mode.

```
cos-1(cos(7π/4))
          .7853981634
π/4
          .7853981634
■
```

**Solution (a):**

Write the appropriate identity.                 $\cos(\cos^{-1}x) = x$ for $-1 \le x \le 1$

Let $x = -\dfrac{1}{2}$, which is in the interval $[-1, 1]$.

Since the domain restriction is met,

the identity can be used.       $\cos\left[\cos^{-1}\left(-\dfrac{1}{2}\right)\right] = \boxed{-\dfrac{1}{2}}$

**Solution (b):**

Write the appropriate identity.                 $\cos^{-1}(\cos x) = x$ for $0 \le x \le \pi$

Let $x = \dfrac{7\pi}{4}$, which is *not* in the interval $[0, \pi]$.

Since the domain restriction is not met, the identity cannot be used.

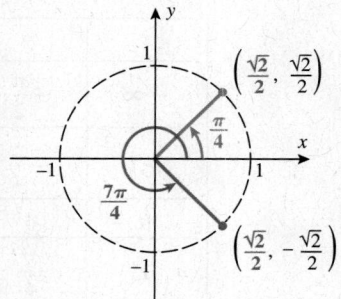

Instead, we find another angle in the interval that has the same cosine value.       $\cos\left(\dfrac{7\pi}{4}\right) = \cos\left(\dfrac{\pi}{4}\right)$

Substitute $\cos\left(\dfrac{7\pi}{4}\right) = \cos\left(\dfrac{\pi}{4}\right)$ into the expression.       $\cos^{-1}\left[\cos\left(\dfrac{7\pi}{4}\right)\right] = \cos^{-1}\left[\cos\left(\dfrac{\pi}{4}\right)\right]$

Since $\dfrac{\pi}{4}$ is in the interval $[0, \pi]$, we can use the identity.       $= \boxed{\dfrac{\pi}{4}}$

■ **YOUR TURN** Find the exact value of each of the following trigonometric expressions:

**a.** $\cos\left[\cos^{-1}\left(\dfrac{1}{2}\right)\right]$     **b.** $\cos^{-1}\left[\cos\left(-\dfrac{\pi}{6}\right)\right]$

■ **Answer: a.** $\dfrac{1}{2}$   **b.** $\dfrac{\pi}{6}$

**Study Tip**

The inverse tangent function gives an angle on the right half of the unit circle (QI and QIV).

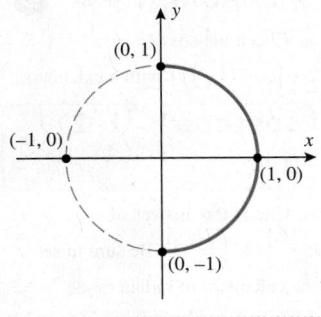

# Inverse Tangent Function

The tangent function, too, is not a one-to-one function (it fails the horizontal line test). Let us start with the tangent function with a restricted domain:

$$y = \tan x \quad \text{Domain: } \left(-\frac{\pi}{2}, \frac{\pi}{2}\right) \quad \text{Range: } (-\infty, \infty)$$

| $x$ | $y$ |
|---|---|
| $-\dfrac{\pi}{2}$ | $-\infty$ |
| $-\dfrac{\pi}{4}$ | $-1$ |
| $0$ | $0$ |
| $\dfrac{\pi}{4}$ | $1$ |
| $\dfrac{\pi}{2}$ | $\infty$ |

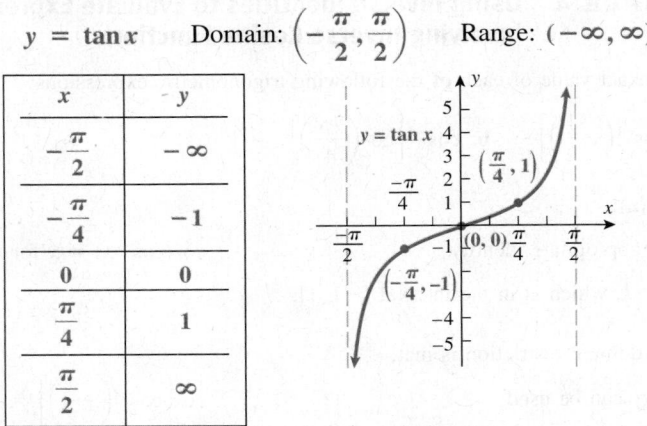

By the properties of inverse functions, the inverse tangent function will have a domain of $(-\infty, \infty)$ and a range of $\left(-\frac{\pi}{2}, \frac{\pi}{2}\right)$. To find the inverse tangent function, interchange $x$ and $y$ values.

**Technology Tip**

To graph $y = \tan^{-1} x$, use $(-\infty, \infty)$ as the domain and $\left(-\frac{\pi}{2}, \frac{\pi}{2}\right)$ as the range.

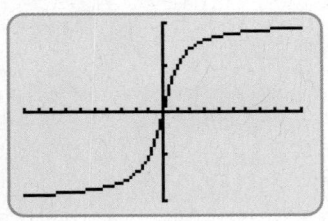

$$y = \tan^{-1} x \quad \text{Domain: } (-\infty, \infty) \quad \text{Range: } \left(-\frac{\pi}{2}, \frac{\pi}{2}\right)$$

| $x$ | $y$ |
|---|---|
| $-\infty$ | $-\dfrac{\pi}{2}$ |
| $-1$ | $-\dfrac{\pi}{4}$ |
| $0$ | $0$ |
| $1$ | $\dfrac{\pi}{4}$ |
| $\infty$ | $\dfrac{\pi}{2}$ |

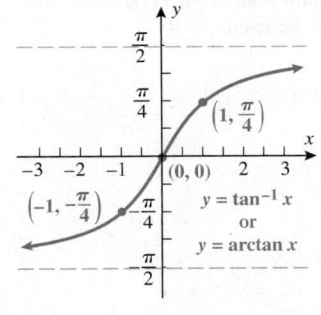

Notice that the inverse tangent function, like the tangent function, is an odd function (it is symmetric about the origin).

The inverse tangent function allows us to answer the question: If the tangent of an angle is known, what is the measure of that angle? Another notation for the inverse tangent function is arctan $x$.

**INVERSE TANGENT FUNCTION**

$$\underbrace{y = \tan^{-1} x \text{ or } y = \arctan x}_{\text{"}y \text{ is the inverse tangent of } x\text{"}} \quad \text{means} \quad \underbrace{x = \tan y}_{\substack{\text{"}y \text{ is the angle measure} \\ \text{whose tangent equals } x\text{"}}}$$

$$\text{where } -\frac{\pi}{2} < y < \frac{\pi}{2}$$

# EXAMPLE 5  Finding Exact Values of an Inverse Tangent Function

Find the exact value of each of the following expressions:

**a.** $\tan^{-1}(\sqrt{3})$    **b.** $\arctan 0$

**Solution (a):**

Let $\theta = \tan^{-1}(\sqrt{3})$.

$\tan \theta = \sqrt{3}$ when

$$-\frac{\pi}{2} < \theta < \frac{\pi}{2}$$

Which value of $\theta$, in the range $-\frac{\pi}{2} < \theta < \frac{\pi}{2}$,

corresponds to a tangent value of $\sqrt{3}$?

$$\theta = \frac{\pi}{3}$$

$\tan\left(\frac{\pi}{3}\right) = \sqrt{3}$ and $\frac{\pi}{3}$ is in the interval $\left(-\frac{\pi}{2}, \frac{\pi}{2}\right)$.    $\boxed{\tan^{-1}(\sqrt{3}) = \frac{\pi}{3}}$

*Calculator Confirmation:* Since $\frac{\pi}{3} = 60°$, if our calculator is set in degree mode, we should find that $\tan^{-1}(\sqrt{3})$ is equal to 60°.

**Solution (b):**

Let $\theta = \arctan 0$.

$\tan \theta = 0$ when $-\frac{\pi}{2} < \theta < \frac{\pi}{2}$

Which value of $\theta$, in the range $-\frac{\pi}{2} < \theta < \frac{\pi}{2}$,

corresponds to a tangent value of 0?

$$\theta = 0$$

$\tan 0 = 0$, and 0 is in the interval $\left(-\frac{\pi}{2}, \frac{\pi}{2}\right)$.    $\boxed{\arctan 0 = 0}$

*Calculator Confirmation:* $\tan^{-1} 0$ is equal to 0.

## Technology Tip

**a.** Use a calculator to check the answer for $\tan^{-1}(\sqrt{3})$.

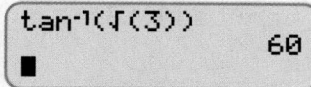

Radian mode:

**b.** Use a calculator to check the answer for $\arctan 0$.

tan⁻¹(0)
■                    0

We now state the properties relating the tangent function and the inverse tangent function that follow directly from the properties of inverses.

## TANGENT-INVERSE TANGENT IDENTITIES

$$\tan^{-1}(\tan x) = x \qquad \text{for} \qquad -\frac{\pi}{2} < x < \frac{\pi}{2}$$

$$\tan(\tan^{-1} x) = x \qquad \text{for} \qquad -\infty < x < \infty$$

**EXAMPLE 6** Using Inverse Identities to Evaluate Expressions Involving Inverse Tangent Functions

Find the exact value of each of the following trigonometric expressions:

**a.** $\tan(\tan^{-1} 17)$   **b.** $\tan^{-1}\left[\tan\left(\dfrac{2\pi}{3}\right)\right]$

**Solution (a):**

Write the appropriate identity. $\qquad\qquad \tan(\tan^{-1} x) = x$ for $-\infty < x < \infty$

Let $x = 17$, which is in the interval $(-\infty, \infty)$.

Since the domain restriction is met, the identity can be used.   $\boxed{\tan(\tan^{-1} 17) = 17}$

**Solution (b):**

Write the appropriate identity. $\qquad\qquad \tan^{-1}(\tan x) = x$ for $-\dfrac{\pi}{2} < x < \dfrac{\pi}{2}$

Let $x = \dfrac{2\pi}{3}$, which is *not* in the interval $\left(-\dfrac{\pi}{2}, \dfrac{\pi}{2}\right)$.

Since the domain restriction is not met, the identity cannot be used.

Instead, we find another angle in the interval that has the same tangent value. $\qquad\qquad \tan\left(\dfrac{2\pi}{3}\right) = \tan\left(-\dfrac{\pi}{3}\right)$

Substitute $\tan\left(\dfrac{2\pi}{3}\right) = \tan\left(-\dfrac{\pi}{3}\right)$ into the expression. $\qquad \tan^{-1}\left[\tan\left(\dfrac{2\pi}{3}\right)\right] = \tan^{-1}\left[\tan\left(-\dfrac{\pi}{3}\right)\right]$

Since $-\dfrac{\pi}{3}$ is in the interval $\left(-\dfrac{\pi}{2}, \dfrac{\pi}{2}\right)$, we can use the identity. $\qquad \tan^{-1}\left[\tan\left(\dfrac{2\pi}{3}\right)\right] = \boxed{-\dfrac{\pi}{3}}$

■ **YOUR TURN** Find the exact value of $\tan^{-1}\left[\tan\left(\dfrac{7\pi}{6}\right)\right]$.

# Remaining Inverse Trigonometric Functions

The remaining three inverse trigonometric functions are defined similarly to the previous ones.

- Inverse cotangent function: $\cot^{-1} x$ or $\text{arccot}\, x$
- Inverse secant function: $\sec^{-1} x$ or $\text{arcsec}\, x$
- Inverse cosecant function: $\csc^{-1} x$ or $\text{arccsc}\, x$

A table summarizing all six of the inverse trigonometric functions is given below:

| INVERSE FUNCTION | $y = \sin^{-1}x$ | $y = \cos^{-1}x$ | $y = \tan^{-1}x$ | $y = \cot^{-1}x$ | $y = \sec^{-1}x$ | $y = \csc^{-1}x$ |
|---|---|---|---|---|---|---|
| DOMAIN | $[-1, 1]$ | $[-1, 1]$ | $(-\infty, \infty)$ | $(-\infty, \infty)$ | $(-\infty, -1] \cup [1, \infty)$ | $(-\infty, -1] \cup [1, \infty)$ |
| RANGE | $\left[-\dfrac{\pi}{2}, \dfrac{\pi}{2}\right]$ | $[0, \pi]$ | $\left(-\dfrac{\pi}{2}, \dfrac{\pi}{2}\right)$ | $(0, \pi)$ | $\left[0, \dfrac{\pi}{2}\right) \cup \left(\dfrac{\pi}{2}, \pi\right]$ | $\left[-\dfrac{\pi}{2}, 0\right) \cup \left(0, \dfrac{\pi}{2}\right]$ |
| GRAPH | | | | | | |

## EXAMPLE 7 Finding the Exact Value of Inverse Trigonometric Functions

Find the exact value of the following expressions:

**a.** $\cot^{-1}\left(\sqrt{3}\right)$   **b.** $\csc^{-1}\left(\sqrt{2}\right)$   **c.** $\sec^{-1}\left(-\sqrt{2}\right)$

**Solution (a):**

Let $\theta = \cot^{-1}\left(\sqrt{3}\right)$.                          $\cot\theta = \sqrt{3}$ when $0 < \theta < \pi$

Which value of $\theta$, in the range $0 < \theta < \pi$,          $\theta = \dfrac{\pi}{6}$
corresponds to a cotangent value of $\sqrt{3}$?

$\cot\left(\dfrac{\pi}{6}\right) = \sqrt{3}$ and $\dfrac{\pi}{6}$ is in the interval $(0, \pi)$.          $\boxed{\cot^{-1}\left(\sqrt{3}\right) = \dfrac{\pi}{6}}$

**Solution (b):**

Let $\theta = \csc^{-1}\left(\sqrt{2}\right)$.                          $\csc\theta = \sqrt{2}$

Which value of $\theta$, in the range

$\left[-\dfrac{\pi}{2}, 0\right) \cup \left(0, \dfrac{\pi}{2}\right]$, corresponds          $\theta = \dfrac{\pi}{4}$

to a cosecant value of $\sqrt{2}$?

$\csc\left(\dfrac{\pi}{4}\right) = \sqrt{2}$ and $\dfrac{\pi}{4}$ is in the

interval $\left[-\dfrac{\pi}{2}, 0\right) \cup \left(0, \dfrac{\pi}{2}\right]$.          $\boxed{\csc^{-1}\left(\sqrt{2}\right) = \dfrac{\pi}{4}}$

**Solution (c):**

Let $\theta = \sec^{-1}\left(-\sqrt{2}\right)$.                          $\sec\theta = -\sqrt{2}$

Which value of $\theta$, in the range

$\left[0, \dfrac{\pi}{2}\right) \cup \left(\dfrac{\pi}{2}, \pi\right]$, corresponds          $\theta = \dfrac{3\pi}{4}$

to a secant value of $-\sqrt{2}$?

$\sec\left(\dfrac{3\pi}{4}\right) = -\sqrt{2}$ and $\dfrac{3\pi}{4}$ is in the

interval $\left[0, \dfrac{\pi}{2}\right) \cup \left(\dfrac{\pi}{2}, \pi\right]$.          $\boxed{\sec^{-1}\left(-\sqrt{2}\right) = \dfrac{3\pi}{4}}$

*Technology Tip*

$\cot^{-1}\left(\sqrt{3}\right) = \tan^{-1}\left(\dfrac{1}{\sqrt{3}}\right)$,

$\csc^{-1}\left(\sqrt{2}\right) = \sin^{-1}\left(\dfrac{1}{\sqrt{2}}\right)$, and

$\sec^{-1}\left(-\sqrt{2}\right) = \cos^{-1}\left(-\dfrac{1}{\sqrt{2}}\right)$.

```
tan-1(1/√(3))
            .5235987756
π/6
            .5235987756
```

```
sin-1(1/√(2))
            .7853981634
π/4
            .7853981634
```

```
cos-1(-1/√(2))
            2.35619449
3π/4
            2.35619449
■
```

How do we approximate the inverse secant, inverse cosecant, and inverse cotangent functions with a calculator? Scientific calculators have keys ($\sin^{-1}$, $\cos^{-1}$, and $\tan^{-1}$) for three of the inverse trigonometric functions but not for the other three. Recall that we find the cosecant, secant, and cotangent function values by taking sine, cosine, or tangent, and finding the reciprocal.

**Study Tip**

$\sec^{-1}x \neq \dfrac{1}{\cos^{-1}x}$

$\csc^{-1}x \neq \dfrac{1}{\sin^{-1}x}$

$\cot^{-1}x \neq \dfrac{1}{\tan^{-1}x}$

$$\csc x = \frac{1}{\sin x} \qquad \sec x = \frac{1}{\cos x} \qquad \cot x = \frac{1}{\tan x}$$

However, *the reciprocal approach cannot be used for inverse functions*. The three inverse trigonometric functions $\csc^{-1}x$, $\sec^{-1}x$, and $\cot^{-1}x$ cannot be found by finding the reciprocal of $\sin^{-1}x$, $\cos^{-1}x$, or $\tan^{-1}x$.

$$\csc^{-1}x \neq \frac{1}{\sin^{-1}x} \qquad \sec^{-1}x \neq \frac{1}{\cos^{-1}x} \qquad \cot^{-1}x \neq \frac{1}{\tan^{-1}x}$$

Instead, we seek the equivalent $\sin^{-1}x$, $\cos^{-1}x$, or $\tan^{-1}x$ values by algebraic means, always remembering to look within the correct domain and range.

| WORDS | MATH | | |
|---|---|---|---|
| Start with the inverse secant function. | $y = \sec^{-1}x$ | for $x \leq -1$ | or $x \geq 1$ |
| Write the equivalent secant expression. | $\sec y = x$ | for $0 \leq y < \dfrac{\pi}{2}$ | or $\dfrac{\pi}{2} < y \leq \pi$ |
| Apply the reciprocal identity. | $\dfrac{1}{\cos y} = x$ | | |
| Simplify using algebraic techniques. | $\cos y = \dfrac{1}{x}$ | | |
| Write the result in terms of the inverse cosine function. | $y = \cos^{-1}\left(\dfrac{1}{x}\right)$ | | |
| Therefore, we have the relationship: | $\sec^{-1}x = \cos^{-1}\left(\dfrac{1}{x}\right)$ | for $x \leq -1$ | or $x \geq 1$ |

The other relationships will be found in the exercises and are summarized below:

**INVERSE SECANT, INVERSE COSECANT, AND INVERSE COTANGENT IDENTITIES**

$$\sec^{-1}x = \cos^{-1}\left(\frac{1}{x}\right) \qquad \text{for} \qquad x \leq -1 \text{ or } x \geq 1$$

$$\csc^{-1}x = \sin^{-1}\left(\frac{1}{x}\right) \qquad \text{for} \qquad x \leq -1 \text{ or } x \geq 1$$

$$\cot^{-1}x = \begin{cases} \tan^{-1}\left(\dfrac{1}{x}\right) & \text{for} \quad x > 0 \\ \pi + \tan^{-1}\left(\dfrac{1}{x}\right) & \text{for} \quad x < 0 \end{cases}$$

### EXAMPLE 8 Using Inverse Identities

**a.** Find the exact value of $\sec^{-1} 2$.
**b.** Use a calculator to find the value of $\cot^{-1} 7$.

**Solution (a):**

Let $\theta = \sec^{-1} 2$.                        $\sec\theta = 2$ on $\left[0, \dfrac{\pi}{2}\right) \cup \left(\dfrac{\pi}{2}, \pi\right]$

Substitute the reciprocal identity.           $\dfrac{1}{\cos\theta} = 2$

Solve for $\cos\theta$.                            $\cos\theta = \dfrac{1}{2}$

The restricted interval $\left[0, \dfrac{\pi}{2}\right) \cup \left(\dfrac{\pi}{2}, \pi\right]$ corresponds to quadrants I and II.

The cosine function is positive in quadrant I.      $\theta = \dfrac{\pi}{3}$

$$\boxed{\sec^{-1} 2 = \cos^{-1}\left(\dfrac{1}{2}\right) = \dfrac{\pi}{3}}$$

**Solution (b):**

Since we do not know an exact value that would correspond to the cotangent function equal to 7, we proceed using identities and a calculator.

Select the correct identity, given that $x = 7 > 0$.      $\cot^{-1} x = \tan^{-1}\left(\dfrac{1}{x}\right)$

Let $x = 7$.                                       $\cot^{-1} 7 = \tan^{-1}\left(\dfrac{1}{7}\right)$

Evaluate the right side with a calculator.      $\boxed{\cot^{-1} 7 \approx 8.13°}$

**Technology Tip**

Use the inverse trigonometry function identities to find

**a.** $\sec^{-1} 2 = \cos^{-1}\left(\frac{1}{2}\right)$

**b.** $\cot^{-1} 7 = \tan^{-1}\left(\frac{1}{7}\right)$

```
cos⁻¹(1/2)
          1.047197551
π/3
          1.047197551
```

```
tan⁻¹(1/7)
          .1418970546
Ans*180/π
          8.130102354
```

# Finding Exact Values for Expressions Involving Inverse Trigonometric Functions

We will now find exact values of trigonometric expressions that involve inverse trigonometric functions.

**EXAMPLE 9    Finding Exact Values of Trigonometric Expressions Involving Inverse Trigonometric Functions**

Find the exact value of $\cos\left[\sin^{-1}\left(\frac{2}{3}\right)\right]$.

**Solution:**

**STEP 1** Let $\theta = \sin^{-1}\left(\frac{2}{3}\right)$.     $\sin\theta = \frac{2}{3}$ when $-\frac{\pi}{2} \le \theta \le \frac{\pi}{2}$

The range $-\frac{\pi}{2} \le \theta \le \frac{\pi}{2}$ corresponds to quadrants I and IV.

The sine function is positive in quadrant I.

**STEP 2** Draw angle $\theta$ in quadrant I.

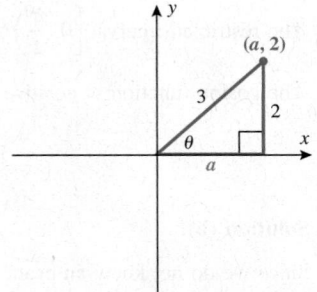

Label the sides known
from the sine value.         $\sin\theta = \frac{2}{3} = \dfrac{\text{opposite}}{\text{hypotenuse}}$

**STEP 3** Find the unknown side length $a$.     $a^2 + 2^2 = 3^2$

Solve for $a$.     $a = \pm\sqrt{5}$

Since $\theta$ is in quadrant I, $a$ is positive.     $a = \sqrt{5}$

**STEP 4** Find $\cos\left[\sin^{-1}\left(\frac{2}{3}\right)\right]$.

Substitute $\theta = \sin^{-1}\left(\frac{2}{3}\right)$.     $\cos\left[\sin^{-1}\left(\frac{2}{3}\right)\right] = \cos\theta$

Find $\cos\theta$.

$\cos\theta = \dfrac{\text{adjacent}}{\text{hypotenuse}} = \dfrac{\sqrt{5}}{3}$

$$\boxed{\cos\left[\sin^{-1}\left(\frac{2}{3}\right)\right] = \frac{\sqrt{5}}{3}}$$

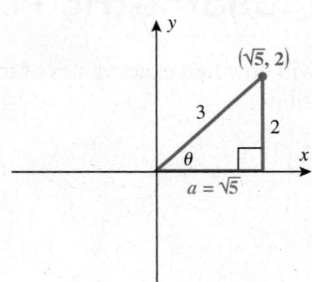

■ **Answer:** $\dfrac{2\sqrt{2}}{3}$

■ **YOUR TURN** Find the exact value of $\sin\left[\cos^{-1}\left(\frac{1}{3}\right)\right]$.

**EXAMPLE 10**  **Finding Exact Values of Trigonometric Expressions Involving Inverse Trigonometric Functions**

Find the exact value of $\tan\left[\cos^{-1}\left(-\frac{7}{12}\right)\right]$.

**Solution:**

**STEP 1**  Let $\theta = \cos^{-1}\left(-\frac{7}{12}\right)$.       $\cos\theta = -\dfrac{7}{12}$ when $0 \le \theta \le \pi$

The range $0 \le \theta \le \pi$ corresponds to quadrants I and II.

The cosine function is negative in quadrant II.

**STEP 2**  Draw angle $\theta$ in quadrant II.

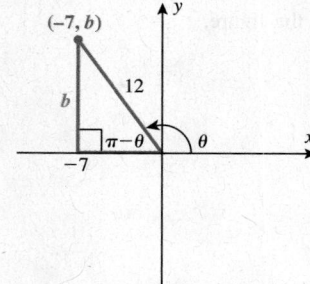

Label the sides known from the cosine value.       $\cos\theta = -\dfrac{7}{12} = \dfrac{\text{adjacent}}{\text{hypotenuse}}$

**STEP 3**  Find the length of the unknown side $b$.       $b^2 + (-7)^2 = 12^2$

Solve for $b$.       $b = \pm\sqrt{95}$

Since $\theta$ is in quadrant II, $b$ is positive.       $b = \sqrt{95}$

**STEP 4**  Find $\tan\left[\cos^{-1}\left(-\frac{7}{12}\right)\right]$.

Substitute $\theta = \cos^{-1}\left(-\frac{7}{12}\right)$.       $\tan\left[\cos^{-1}\left(-\dfrac{7}{12}\right)\right] = \tan\theta$

Find $\tan\theta$.

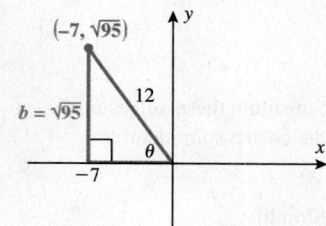

$\tan\theta = \dfrac{\text{opposite}}{\text{adjacent}} = \dfrac{\sqrt{95}}{-7}$

$\boxed{\tan\left[\cos^{-1}\left(-\dfrac{7}{12}\right)\right] = -\dfrac{\sqrt{95}}{7}}$

**■ YOUR TURN**  Find the exact value of $\tan\left[\sin^{-1}\left(-\frac{3}{7}\right)\right]$.

**■ Answer:** $-\dfrac{3\sqrt{10}}{20}$

**EXAMPLE 11** **Using Identities to Find Exact Values of Trigonometric Expressions Involving Inverse Trigonometric Functions**

Find the exact value of $\cos\left[\sin^{-1}\left(\frac{3}{5}\right) + \tan^{-1}1\right]$.

**Solution:**

Recall the cosine sum identity: $\qquad\qquad\qquad\qquad \cos(A + B) = \cos A \cos B - \sin A \sin B$

Let $A = \sin^{-1}\left(\frac{3}{5}\right)$ and $B = \tan^{-1}1$.

$$\cos\left[\sin^{-1}\left(\frac{3}{5}\right) + \tan^{-1}1\right] = \cos\left[\sin^{-1}\left(\frac{3}{5}\right)\right]\cos(\tan^{-1}1) - \sin\left[\sin^{-1}\left(\frac{3}{5}\right)\right]\sin(\tan^{-1}1)$$

From the figure,

$$A = \sin^{-1}\left(\frac{3}{5}\right) \Rightarrow \sin A = \frac{3}{5}$$

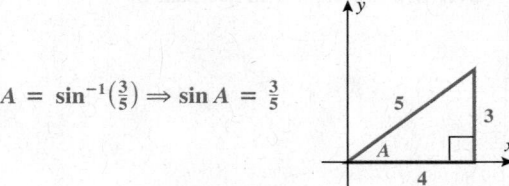

we see that

$$\cos\left[\sin^{-1}\left(\frac{3}{5}\right)\right] = \cos A = \frac{4}{5}$$

$$\sin\left[\sin^{-1}\left(\frac{3}{5}\right)\right] = \sin A = \frac{3}{5}$$

From the figure,

$$B = \tan^{-1}(1) \Rightarrow \tan B = 1$$

we see that

$$\cos(\tan^{-1}1) = \cos B = \frac{\sqrt{2}}{2}$$

$$\sin(\tan^{-1}1) = \sin B = \frac{\sqrt{2}}{2}$$

Substitute these values into the cosine sum identity:

$$\cos\left[\sin^{-1}\left(\frac{3}{5}\right) + \tan^{-1}1\right] = \left(\frac{4}{5}\right)\left(\frac{\sqrt{2}}{2}\right) - \left(\frac{3}{5}\right)\left(\frac{\sqrt{2}}{2}\right)$$

Simplify.

$$= \boxed{\frac{\sqrt{2}}{10}}$$

▪**Answer:** $\dfrac{7\sqrt{2}}{10}$

▪ **YOUR TURN** Find the exact value of $\sin\left[\cos^{-1}\left(\frac{3}{5}\right) + \tan^{-1}1\right]$.

**EXAMPLE 12**   **Writing Trigonometric Expressions Involving Inverse Trigonometric Functions in Terms of a Single Variable**

Write the expression $\cos(\tan^{-1}u)$ as an equivalent expression in terms of only the variable $u$.

**Solution:** Let $\theta = \tan^{-1}u$; therefore, $\tan\theta = u = \dfrac{u}{1}$.

Realize that $u$ can be positive or negative. Since the range of the inverse tangent function is $\left(-\dfrac{\pi}{2}, \dfrac{\pi}{2}\right)$, sketch the angle $\theta$ in both quadrants I and IV and draw the corresponding two right triangles. Recalling that the tangent ratio is opposite over adjacent, we label those corresponding sides with $u$ and 1, respectively. Then solving for the hypotenuse using the Pythagorean theorem gives $\sqrt{u^2 + 1}$.

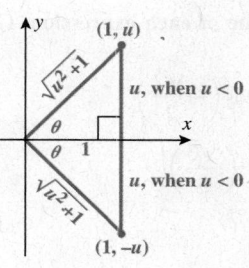

Substitute $\theta = \tan^{-1}u$ into $\cos(\tan^{-1}u)$.

$$\cos(\tan^{-1}u) = \cos\theta$$

Use the right triangle ratio for cosine: adjacent over hypotenuse.

$$= \frac{1}{\sqrt{u^2 + 1}}$$

Rationalize the denominator.

$$\cos(\tan^{-1}u) = \frac{1}{\sqrt{u^2 + 1}} \cdot \frac{\sqrt{u^2 + 1}}{\sqrt{u^2 + 1}}$$

$$= \boxed{\frac{\sqrt{u^2 + 1}}{u^2 + 1}}$$

■ **YOUR TURN** Write the expression $\sin(\tan^{-1}u)$ as an equivalent expression in terms of only the variable $u$.

■ **Answer:** $\dfrac{u\sqrt{u^2 + 1}}{u^2 + 1}$

---

**SECTION**
**6.5 SUMMARY**

If a trigonometric function value of an angle or of a real number is known, what is that number, as defined by the domain restriction? Inverse trigonometric functions determine the angle measure (or the value of the argument). To define the inverse trigonometric relations as functions, we first restrict the trigonometric functions to domains in which they are one-to-one functions. Exact values

for inverse trigonometric functions can be found when the function values are those of the special angles. Inverse trigonometric functions also provide a means for evaluating one trigonometric function when we are given the value of another. It is important to note that the $-1$ as a superscript indicates an inverse function, not a reciprocal.

| INVERSE FUNCTION | $y = \sin^{-1}x$ | $y = \cos^{-1}x$ | $y = \tan^{-1}x$ | $y = \cot^{-1}x$ | $y = \sec^{-1}x$ | $y = \csc^{-1}x$ |
|---|---|---|---|---|---|---|
| DOMAIN | $[-1, 1]$ | $[-1, 1]$ | $(-\infty, \infty)$ | $(-\infty, \infty)$ | $(-\infty, -1] \cup [1, \infty)$ | $(-\infty, -1] \cup [1, \infty)$ |
| RANGE | $\left[-\dfrac{\pi}{2}, \dfrac{\pi}{2}\right]$ | $[0, \pi]$ | $\left(-\dfrac{\pi}{2}, \dfrac{\pi}{2}\right)$ | $(0, \pi)$ | $\left[0, \dfrac{\pi}{2}\right) \cup \left(\dfrac{\pi}{2}, \pi\right]$ | $\left[-\dfrac{\pi}{2}, 0\right) \cup \left(0, \dfrac{\pi}{2}\right]$ |
| GRAPH |  |  |  |  |  |  |

## SECTION 6.5 EXERCISES

■ SKILLS

**In Exercises 1–16, find the exact value of each expression. Give the answer in radians.**

1. $\arccos\left(\dfrac{\sqrt{2}}{2}\right)$
2. $\arccos\left(-\dfrac{\sqrt{2}}{2}\right)$
3. $\arcsin\left(-\dfrac{\sqrt{3}}{2}\right)$
4. $\arcsin\left(\dfrac{1}{2}\right)$

5. $\cot^{-1}(-1)$
6. $\tan^{-1}\left(\dfrac{\sqrt{3}}{3}\right)$
7. $\operatorname{arcsec}\left(\dfrac{2\sqrt{3}}{3}\right)$
8. $\operatorname{arccsc}(-1)$

9. $\csc^{-1}2$
10. $\sec^{-1}(-2)$
11. $\arctan(-\sqrt{3})$
12. $\operatorname{arccot}(\sqrt{3})$

13. $\sin^{-1}0$
14. $\tan^{-1}1$
15. $\sec^{-1}(-1)$
16. $\cot^{-1}0$

**In Exercises 17–32, find the exact value of each expression. Give the answer in degrees.**

17. $\cos^{-1}\left(\dfrac{1}{2}\right)$
18. $\cos^{-1}\left(-\dfrac{\sqrt{3}}{2}\right)$
19. $\sin^{-1}\left(\dfrac{\sqrt{2}}{2}\right)$
20. $\sin^{-1}0$

21. $\cot^{-1}\left(-\dfrac{\sqrt{3}}{3}\right)$
22. $\tan^{-1}(-\sqrt{3})$
23. $\arctan\left(\dfrac{\sqrt{3}}{3}\right)$
24. $\operatorname{arccot}1$

25. $\operatorname{arccsc}(-2)$
26. $\csc^{-1}\left(-\dfrac{2\sqrt{3}}{3}\right)$
27. $\operatorname{arcsec}(-\sqrt{2})$
28. $\operatorname{arccsc}(-\sqrt{2})$

29. $\sin^{-1}(-1)$
30. $\arctan(-1)$
31. $\operatorname{arccot}0$
32. $\operatorname{arcsec}(-1)$

**In Exercises 33–42, use a calculator to evaluate each expression. Give the answer in degrees and round it to two decimal places.**

33. $\cos^{-1}(0.5432)$
34. $\sin^{-1}(0.7821)$
35. $\tan^{-1}(1.895)$
36. $\tan^{-1}(3.2678)$

37. $\sec^{-1}(1.4973)$
38. $\sec^{-1}(2.7864)$
39. $\csc^{-1}(-3.7893)$
40. $\csc^{-1}(-6.1324)$

41. $\cot^{-1}(-4.2319)$
42. $\cot^{-1}(-0.8977)$

**In Exercises 43–52, use a calculator to evaluate each expression. Give the answer in radians and round it to two decimal places.**

43. $\sin^{-1}(-0.5878)$
44. $\sin^{-1}(0.8660)$
45. $\cos^{-1}(0.1423)$
46. $\tan^{-1}(-0.9279)$

47. $\tan^{-1}(1.3242)$
48. $\cot^{-1}(2.4142)$
49. $\cot^{-1}(-0.5774)$
50. $\sec^{-1}(-1.0422)$

51. $\csc^{-1}(3.2361)$
52. $\csc^{-1}(-2.9238)$

**In Exercises 53–76, evaluate each expression exactly, if possible. If not possible, state why.**

53. $\sin^{-1}\left[\sin\left(\dfrac{5\pi}{12}\right)\right]$
54. $\sin^{-1}\left[\sin\left(-\dfrac{5\pi}{12}\right)\right]$
55. $\sin[\sin^{-1}(1.03)]$
56. $\sin[\sin^{-1}(1.1)]$

57. $\sin^{-1}\left[\sin\left(-\dfrac{7\pi}{6}\right)\right]$
58. $\sin^{-1}\left[\sin\left(\dfrac{7\pi}{6}\right)\right]$
59. $\cos^{-1}\left[\cos\left(\dfrac{4\pi}{3}\right)\right]$
60. $\cos^{-1}\left[\cos\left(-\dfrac{5\pi}{3}\right)\right]$

61. $\cot\left[\cot^{-1}(\sqrt{3})\right]$
62. $\cot^{-1}\left[\cot\left(\dfrac{5\pi}{4}\right)\right]$
63. $\sec^{-1}\left[\sec\left(-\dfrac{\pi}{3}\right)\right]$
64. $\sec\left[\sec^{-1}\left(\dfrac{1}{2}\right)\right]$

65. $\csc\left[\csc^{-1}\left(\dfrac{1}{2}\right)\right]$
66. $\csc\left[\csc^{-1}\left(\dfrac{7\pi}{6}\right)\right]$
67. $\cot(\cot^{-1}0)$
68. $\cot^{-1}\left[\cot\left(-\dfrac{\pi}{4}\right)\right]$

69. $\tan^{-1}\left[\tan\left(-\dfrac{\pi}{4}\right)\right]$
70. $\tan^{-1}\left[\tan\left(\dfrac{\pi}{4}\right)\right]$
71. $\sec(\sec^{-1}0)$
72. $\csc^{-1}(\csc\pi)$

73. $\cot^{-1}\left[\cot\left(\dfrac{8\pi}{3}\right)\right]$
74. $\tan^{-1}[\tan(8\pi)]$
75. $\csc^{-1}\left[\csc\left(\dfrac{15\pi}{4}\right)\right]$
76. $\sec^{-1}\left[\sec\left(\dfrac{17\pi}{2}\right)\right]$

**In Exercises 77–88, evaluate each expression exactly.**

77. $\cos\left[\sin^{-1}\left(\dfrac{3}{4}\right)\right]$

78. $\sin\left[\cos^{-1}\left(\dfrac{2}{3}\right)\right]$

79. $\sin\left[\tan^{-1}\left(\dfrac{12}{5}\right)\right]$

80. $\cos\left[\tan^{-1}\left(\dfrac{7}{24}\right)\right]$

81. $\tan\left[\sin^{-1}\left(\dfrac{3}{5}\right)\right]$

82. $\tan\left[\cos^{-1}\left(\dfrac{2}{5}\right)\right]$

83. $\sec\left[\sin^{-1}\left(\dfrac{\sqrt{2}}{5}\right)\right]$

84. $\sec\left[\cos^{-1}\left(\dfrac{\sqrt{7}}{4}\right)\right]$

85. $\csc\left[\cos^{-1}\left(\dfrac{1}{4}\right)\right]$

86. $\csc\left[\sin^{-1}\left(\dfrac{1}{4}\right)\right]$

87. $\cot\left[\sin^{-1}\left(\dfrac{60}{61}\right)\right]$

88. $\cot\left[\sec^{-1}\left(\dfrac{41}{9}\right)\right]$

89. $\cos\left[\tan^{-1}\left(\dfrac{3}{4}\right) - \sin^{-1}\left(\dfrac{4}{5}\right)\right]$

90. $\cos\left[\tan^{-1}\left(\dfrac{12}{5}\right) + \sin^{-1}\left(\dfrac{3}{5}\right)\right]$

91. $\sin\left[\cos^{-1}\left(\dfrac{5}{13}\right) + \tan^{-1}\left(\dfrac{4}{3}\right)\right]$

92. $\sin\left[\cos^{-1}\left(\dfrac{3}{5}\right) - \tan^{-1}\left(\dfrac{5}{12}\right)\right]$

93. $\sin\left[2\cos^{-1}\left(\dfrac{3}{5}\right)\right]$

94. $\cos\left[2\sin^{-1}\left(\dfrac{3}{5}\right)\right]$

95. $\tan\left[2\sin^{-1}\left(\dfrac{5}{13}\right)\right]$

96. $\tan\left[2\cos^{-1}\left(\dfrac{5}{13}\right)\right]$

**For each of the following expressions, write an equivalent expression in terms of only the variable $u$.**

97. $\cos(\sin^{-1}u)$

98. $\sin(\cos^{-1}u)$

99. $\tan(\cos^{-1}u)$

100. $\tan(\sin^{-1}u)$

■ **APPLICATIONS**

**For Exercises 101 and 102, refer to the following:**

Annual sales of a product are generally subject to seasonal fluctuations and are approximated by the function

$$s(t) = 4.3\cos\left(\dfrac{\pi}{6}t\right) + 56.2 \quad 0 \le t \le 11$$

where $t$ represents time in months ($t = 0$ represents January) and $s(t)$ represents monthly sales of the product in thousands of dollars.

101. **Business.** Find the month(s) in which monthly sales are $56,200.

102. **Business.** Find the month(s) in which monthly sales are $51,900.

**For Exercises 103 and 104, refer to the following:**

Allergy sufferers' symptoms fluctuate with pollen levels. Pollen levels are often reported to the public on a scale of 0–12, which is meant to reflect the levels of pollen in the air. For example, a pollen level between 4.9 and 7.2 indicates that pollen levels will likely cause symptoms for many individuals allergic to the predominant pollen of the season (*Source*: http://www.pollen.com). The pollen levels at a single location were measured and averaged for each month. Over a period of 6 months, the levels fluctuated according to the model

$$p(t) = 5.5 + 1.5\sin\left(\dfrac{\pi}{6}t\right) \quad 0 \le t \le 6$$

where $t$ is measured in months and $p(t)$ is the pollen level.

103. **Biology/Health.** In which month(s) was the monthly average pollen level 7.0?

104. **Biology/Health.** In which month(s) was the monthly average pollen level 6.25?

105. **Alternating Current.** Alternating electrical current in amperes (A) is modeled by the equation $i = I\sin(2\pi ft)$, where $i$ is the current, $I$ is the maximum current, $t$ is time in seconds, and $f$ is the frequency in hertz is the number of cycles per second. If the frequency is 5 hertz and maximum current is 115 angstrom, what time $t$ corresponds to a current of 85 angstrom? Find the smallest positive value of $t$.

106. **Alternating Current.** If the frequency is 100 hertz and maximum current is 240 angstrom, what time $t$ corresponds to a current of 100 angstrom? Find the smallest positive value of $t$.

107. **Hours of Daylight.** The number of hours of daylight in San Diego, California, can be modeled with $H(t) = 12 + 2.4\sin(0.017t - 1.377)$, where $t$ is the day of the year (January 1, $t = 1$, etc.). For what value of $t$ is the number of hours of daylight equal to 14.4? If May 31 is the 151st day of the year, what month and day correspond to that value of $t$?

108. **Hours of Daylight.** Repeat Exercise 107. For what value of $t$ is the number of hours of daylight equal to 9.6? What month and day correspond to the value of $t$? (You may have to count backwards.)

109. **Money.** A young couple get married and immediately start saving money. They renovate a house and are left with less and less saved money. They have children after 10 years and are in debt until their children are in college. They then save until retirement. A formula that represents the percentage of their annual income that they either save (positive) or are in debt (negative) is given by $P(t) = 12.5\cos(0.157t) + 2.5$, where $t = 0$ corresponds

to the year they were married. How many years into their marriage do they first accrue debt?

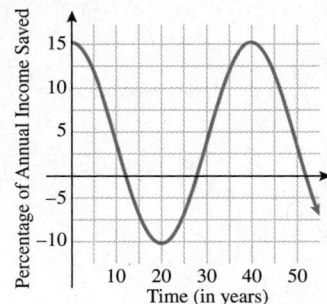

Percentage of Annual Income Saved vs. Time (in years)

110. **Money.** For the couple in Exercise 109, how many years into their marriage are they back to saving 15% of their annual income?

111. **Viewing Angle of Painting.** A museum patron whose eye level is 5 feet above the floor is studying a painting that is 8 feet in height and mounted on the wall 4 feet above the floor. If the patron is $x$ feet from the wall, use $\tan(\alpha + \beta)$ to express $\tan\theta$, where $\theta$ is the angle that the patron's eye sweeps from the top to the bottom of the painting.

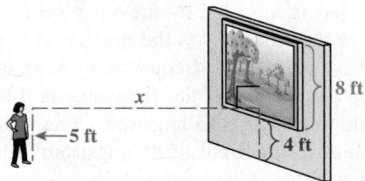

112. **Viewing Angle of Painting.** Using the equation for $\tan\theta$ in Exercise 111, solve for $\theta$ using the inverse tangent. Then find the measure of the angles $\theta$ for $x = 10$ and $x = 20$ (to the nearest degree).

113. **Earthquake Movement.** The horizontal movement of a point that is $k$ kilometers away from an earthquake's fault line can be estimated with

$$M = \frac{f}{2}\left[ 1 - \frac{2\tan^{-1}\left(\frac{k}{d}\right)}{\pi} \right]$$

where $M$ is the movement of the point in meters, $f$ is the total horizontal displacement occurring along the fault line, $k$ is the distance of the point from the fault line, and $d$ is the depth in kilometers of the focal point of the earthquake. If an earthquake produces a displacement $f$ of 2 meters and the depth of the focal point is 4 kilometers, then what is the movement $M$ of a point that is 2 kilometers from the fault line? of a point 10 kilometers from the fault line?

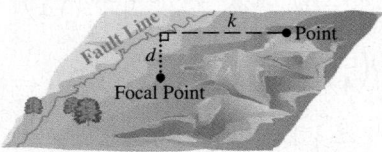

114. **Earthquake Movement.** Repeat Exercise 113. If an earthquake produces a displacement $f$ of 3 meters and the depth of the focal point is 2.5 kilometers, then what is the movement $M$ of a point that is 5 kilometers from the fault line? of a point 10 kilometers from the fault line?

115. **Laser Communication.** A laser communication system depends on a narrow beam, and a direct line of sight is necessary for communication links. If a transmitter/receiver for a laser system is placed between two buildings (see the figure) and the other end of the system is located on a low-earth-orbit satellite, then the link is operational only when the satellite and the ground system have a line of sight (when the buildings are not in the way). Find the angle $\theta$ that corresponds to the system being operational (i.e., find the maximum value of $\theta$ that permits the system to be operational). Express $\theta$ in terms of inverse tangent functions and the distance from the shorter building.

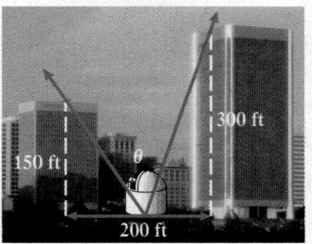

116. **Laser Communication.** Repeat Exercise 115, assuming that the ground system is on top of a 20-foot tower.

■ **CATCH THE MISTAKE**

In Exercises 117–120, explain the mistake that is made.

117. Evaluate the expression exactly: $\sin^{-1}\left[\sin\left(\frac{3\pi}{5}\right)\right]$.

**Solution:**

Use the identity $\sin^{-1}(\sin x) = x$ on $0 \le x \le \pi$.

Since $\frac{3\pi}{5}$ is in the interval

$[0, \pi]$, the identity can be used.
$$\sin^{-1}\left[\sin\left(\frac{3\pi}{5}\right)\right] = \frac{3\pi}{5}$$

This is incorrect. What mistake was made?

118. Evaluate the expression exactly: $\cos^{-1}\left[\cos\left(-\frac{\pi}{5}\right)\right]$.

**Solution:**

Use the identity $\cos^{-1}(\cos x) = x$ on $-\frac{\pi}{2} \le x \le \frac{\pi}{2}$.

Since $-\frac{\pi}{5}$ is in the interval

$\left[-\frac{\pi}{2}, \frac{\pi}{2}\right]$, the identity can be used.
$$\cos^{-1}\left[\cos\left(-\frac{\pi}{5}\right)\right] = -\frac{\pi}{5}$$

This is incorrect. What mistake was made?

**119.** Evaluate the expression exactly: $\cot^{-1}(2.5)$.

**Solution:**

Use the reciprocal identity.     $\cot^{-1}(2.5) = \dfrac{1}{\tan^{-1}(2.5)}$

Evaluate $\tan^{-1}(2.5) = 1.19$.     $\cot^{-1}(2.5) = \dfrac{1}{1.19}$

Simplify.     $\cot^{-1}(2.5) = 0.8403$

This is incorrect. What mistake was made?

**120.** Evaluate the expression exactly: $\csc^{-1}\left(\dfrac{1}{4}\right)$.

**Solution:**

Use the reciprocal identity.     $\csc^{-1}\left(\dfrac{1}{4}\right) = \dfrac{1}{\sin^{-1}\left(\dfrac{1}{4}\right)}$

Evaluate $\sin^{-1}\left(\dfrac{1}{4}\right) = 14.478$.     $\csc^{-1}\left(\dfrac{1}{4}\right) = \dfrac{1}{14.478}$

Simplify.     $\csc^{-1}\left(\dfrac{1}{4}\right) = 0.0691$

This is incorrect. What mistake was made?

## ▪ CONCEPTUAL

**In Exercises 121–124, determine whether each statement is true or false.**

**121.** The inverse secant function is an even function.

**122.** The inverse cosecant function is an odd function.

**123.** $\csc^{-1}(\csc\theta) = \theta$, for all $\theta$ in the domain of cosecant.

**124.** $\sin^{-1}(2x) \cdot \csc^{-1}(2x) = 1$, for all $x$ for which both functions are defined.

**125.** Explain why $\sec^{-1}\left(\dfrac{1}{2}\right)$ does not exist.

**126.** Explain why $\csc^{-1}\left(\dfrac{1}{2}\right)$ does not exist.

## ▪ CHALLENGE

**127.** Evaluate exactly: $\sin\left[\cos^{-1}\left(\dfrac{\sqrt{2}}{2}\right) + \sin^{-1}\left(-\dfrac{1}{2}\right)\right]$.

**128.** Determine the $x$-values for which

$$\sin^{-1}\left[2\sin\left(\dfrac{3x}{2}\right)\cos\left(\dfrac{3x}{2}\right)\right] = 3x$$

**129.** Evaluate exactly: $\sin(2\sin^{-1}1)$.

**130.** Let $f(x) = 2 - 4\sin\left(x - \dfrac{\pi}{2}\right)$.

   **a.** State an accepted domain of $f(x)$ so that $f(x)$ is a one-to-one function.

   **b.** Find $f^{-1}(x)$ and state its domain.

**131.** Let $f(x) = 3 + \cos\left(x - \dfrac{\pi}{4}\right)$.

   **a.** State an accepted domain of $f(x)$ so that $f(x)$ is a one-to-one function.

   **b.** Find $f^{-1}(x)$ and state its domain.

**132.** Let $f(x) = 1 - \tan\left(x + \dfrac{\pi}{3}\right)$.

   **a.** State an accepted domain of $f(x)$ so that $f(x)$ is a one-to-one function.

   **b.** Find $f^{-1}(x)$ and state its domain.

**133.** Let $f(x) = 2 + \dfrac{1}{4}\cot\left(2x - \dfrac{\pi}{6}\right)$.

   **a.** State an accepted domain of $f(x)$ so that $f(x)$ is a one-to-one function.

   **b.** Find $f^{-1}(x)$ and state its domain.

**134.** Let $f(x) = -\csc\left(\dfrac{\pi}{4}x - 1\right)$.

   **a.** State an accepted domain of $f(x)$ so that $f(x)$ is a one-to-one function.

   **b.** Find $f^{-1}(x)$ and state its domain.

## ▪ TECHNOLOGY

**135.** Use a graphing calculator to plot $Y_1 = \sin(\sin^{-1}x)$ and $Y_2 = x$ for the domain $-1 \leq x \leq 1$. If you then increase the domain to $-3 \leq x \leq 3$, you get a different result. Explain the result.

**136.** Use a graphing calculator to plot $Y_1 = \cos(\cos^{-1}x)$ and $Y_2 = x$ for the domain $-1 \leq x \leq 1$. If you then increase the domain to $-3 \leq x \leq 3$, you get a different result. Explain the result.

**137.** Use a graphing calculator to plot $Y_1 = \csc^{-1}(\csc x)$ and $Y_2 = x$. Determine the domain for which the following statement is true: $\csc^{-1}(\csc x) = x$. Give the domain in terms of $\pi$.

**138.** Use a graphing calculator to plot $Y_1 = \sec^{-1}(\sec x)$ and $Y_2 = x$. Determine the domain for which the following statement is true: $\sec^{-1}(\sec x) = x$. Give the domain in terms of $\pi$.

**139.** Given $\tan x = \dfrac{40}{9}$ and $\pi < x < \dfrac{3\pi}{2}$:

   **a.** Find $\sin(2x)$ using the double-angle identity.

**b.** Use the inverse of tangent to find $x$ in quadrant III and use a calculator to find $\sin(2x)$. Round to five decimal places.

**c.** Are the results in (a) and (b) the same?

**140.** Given $\sin x = -\dfrac{1}{\sqrt{10}}$ and $\dfrac{3\pi}{2} < x < 2\pi$:

   **a.** Find $\tan(2x)$ using the double-angle identity.

   **b.** Use the inverse of sine to find $x$ in quadrant IV and find $\tan(2x)$.

   **c.** Are the results in (a) and (b) the same?

## ■ PREVIEW TO CALCULUS

In calculus, we study the derivatives of inverse trigonometric functions. In order to obtain these formulas, we use the definitions of the functions and a right triangle. Thus, if $y = \sin^{-1}x$, then $\sin y = x$; the right triangle associated with this equation is given below, where we can see that $\cos y = \sqrt{1 - x^2}$.

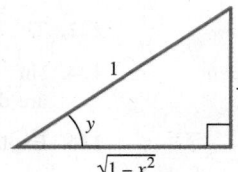

In Exercises 141–144, use this idea to find the indicated expression.

**141.** If $y = \tan^{-1}x$, find $\sec^2 y$.

**142.** If $y = \cos^{-1}x$, find $\sin y$.

**143.** If $y = \sec^{-1}x$, find $\sec y \tan y$.

**144.** If $y = \cot^{-1}x$, find $\csc^2 y$.

## SECTION
## 6.6 TRIGONOMETRIC EQUATIONS

### SKILLS OBJECTIVES

- Solve trigonometric equations by inspection.
- Solve trigonometric equations using algebraic techniques.
- Solve trigonometric equations using inverse functions.
- Solve trigonometric equations (involving more than one trigonometric function) using trigonometric identities.

### CONCEPTUAL OBJECTIVES

- Understand that solving trigonometric equations is similar to solving algebraic equations.
- Realize that the goal in solving trigonometric equations is to find the value(s) for the independent variable that make(s) the equation a true statement.

## Solving Trigonometric Equations by Inspection

The goal in solving equations in one variable is to find the values for that variable which make the equation true. For example, $9x = 72$ can be solved by inspection by asking the question, "9 times what is 72?" The answer is $x = 8$. We approach simple trigonometric equations the same way we approach algebraic equations: We inspect the equation and determine the solution.

## EXAMPLE 1   Solving a Trigonometric Equation by Inspection

Solve each of the following equations on the interval $[0, 2\pi]$:

**a.** $\sin x = \frac{1}{2}$     **b.** $\cos(2x) = \frac{1}{2}$

**Solution (a):**

Ask the question, "sine of what angles is $\frac{1}{2}$?"

$$x = \frac{\pi}{6} \quad \text{or} \quad x = \frac{5\pi}{6}$$

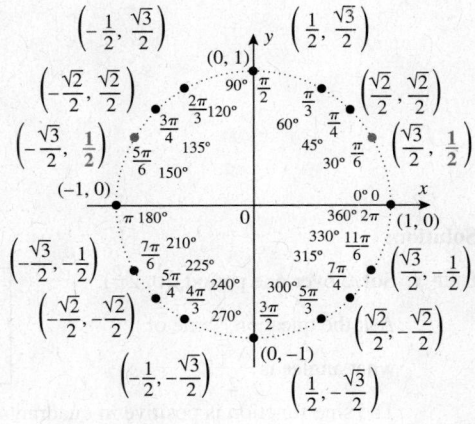

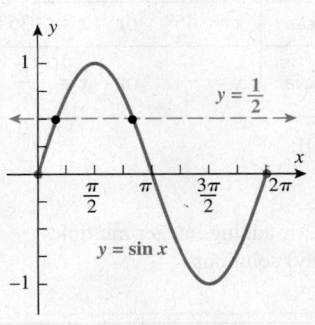

**Solution (b):**

Ask the question, "cosine of what angles is $\frac{1}{2}$?"

In this case, the angle is equal to $2x$.

$$2x = \frac{\pi}{3} \quad \text{or} \quad 2x = \frac{5\pi}{3}$$

Solve for $x$:   $x = \dfrac{\pi}{6} \quad \text{or} \quad x = \dfrac{5\pi}{6}$.

If the solution set for $x$ is over $[0, 2\pi)$, then the solution set for $2x$ is over $[0, 4\pi)$.

Notice that $x = \dfrac{7\pi}{6} \quad \text{or} \quad x = \dfrac{11\pi}{6}$ also satisfy the equation.

$\cos(2x) = \frac{1}{2}$.

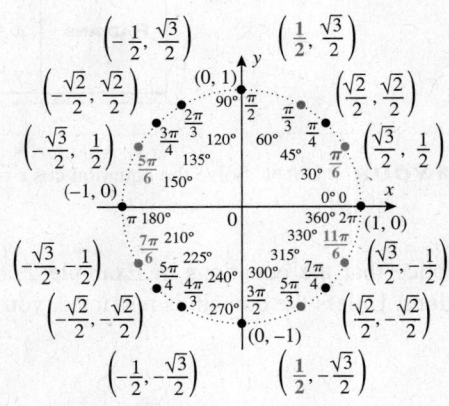

**Study Tip**

Recall the special triangle.

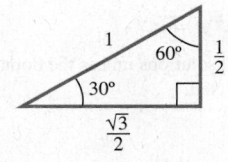

$\sin 30° = \frac{1}{2}$

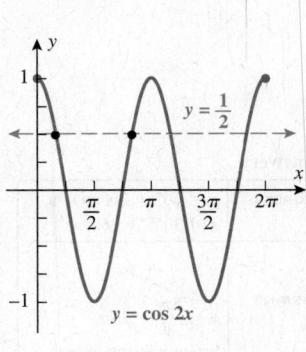

· · · · · · · · · · · · · · · · · · · · · · · · · · · · · · · · · · · · · · · · · · · · · · · · · · · · · · · · · · · · · · · · · · · · · · · · · · ·

■ **YOUR TURN** Solve each of the following equations on the interval $[0, 2\pi)$:

**a.** $\cos x = \frac{1}{2}$     **b.** $\sin(2x) = \frac{1}{2}$

■ **Answer: a.** $x = \dfrac{\pi}{3}, \dfrac{5\pi}{3}$

**b.** $x = \dfrac{\pi}{12}, \dfrac{5\pi}{12}, \dfrac{13\pi}{12}, \dfrac{17\pi}{12}$

**Technology Tip**

Use the fact that a solution to the equation $\sin x = \dfrac{\sqrt{2}}{2}$ is the same as a point of intersection of $y = \sin x$ and $y = \dfrac{\sqrt{2}}{2}$ over one period, $[0, 2\pi)$ or $[0, 360°)$.

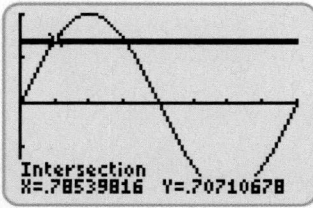

**Study Tip**

Find *all* solutions unless the domain is restricted.

**EXAMPLE 2** **Solving a Trigonometric Equation by Inspection**

Solve the equation $\sin x = \dfrac{\sqrt{2}}{2}$.

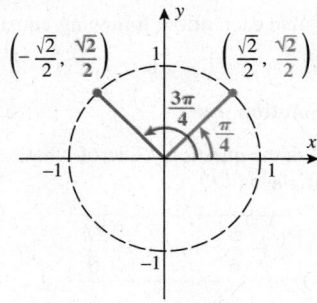

**Solution:**

**STEP 1** Solve over one period, $[0, 2\pi)$.

Ask the question, "sine of what angles is $\dfrac{\sqrt{2}}{2}$?"

The sine function is positive in quadrants I and II.

| DEGREES | $x = 45°$ or $x = 135°$ |
|---------|--------------------------|
| RADIANS | $x = \dfrac{\pi}{4}$ or $x = \dfrac{3\pi}{4}$ |

**STEP 2** Solve over all real numbers.

Since the sine function has a period of 360° or $2\pi$, adding integer multiples of 360° or $2\pi$ will give the other (infinitely many) solutions.

| DEGREES | $x = 45° + 360°n$ or $x = 135° + 360°n$ |
|---------|------------------------------------------|
| RADIANS | $x = \dfrac{\pi}{4} + 2n\pi$ or $x = \dfrac{3\pi}{4} + 2n\pi$, where $n$ is any integer |

**▪ YOUR TURN** Solve the equation $\cos x = \dfrac{1}{2}$.

**▪ Answer:**

| DEGREES | $x = 60° + 360°n$ or $x = 300° + 360°n$ |
|---------|------------------------------------------|
| RADIANS | $x = \dfrac{\pi}{3} + 2n\pi$ or $x = \dfrac{5\pi}{3} + 2n\pi$, where $n$ is any integer |

Notice that the equations in Example 2 and Your Turn have an infinite number of solutions. Unless the domain is restricted, you must find *all* solutions.

## EXAMPLE 3 Solving a Trigonometric Equation by Inspection

Solve the equation $\tan(2x) = -\sqrt{3}$.

**Solution:**

<table>
<tr><td rowspan="2">STEP 1</td><td rowspan="2">Solve over one period, $[0, \pi)$.<br><br>Ask the question, "tangent of what angles is $-\sqrt{3}$?" Note that the angle in this case is $2x$.</td><td>DEGREES</td><td>$2x = 120°$</td></tr>
<tr><td>RADIANS</td><td>$2x = \dfrac{2\pi}{3}$</td></tr>
</table>

The tangent function is negative in quadrants II and IV. Since $[0, \pi)$ includes quadrants I and II, we find only the angle in quadrant II. (The solution corresponding to quadrant IV will be found when we extend the solution over all real numbers.)

STEP 2    Solve over all $x$.

| | | |
|---|---|---|
| Since the tangent function has a period of $180°$, or $\pi$, adding integer multiples of $180°$ or $\pi$ will give all of the other solutions. | **DEGREES** | $2x = 120° + 180°n$ |
| | **RADIANS** | $2x = \dfrac{2\pi}{3} + n\pi,$<br>where $n$ is any integer |

| | | |
|---|---|---|
| Solve for $x$ by dividing by 2. | **DEGREES** | $x = 60° + 90°n$ |
| | **RADIANS** | $x = \dfrac{\pi}{3} + \dfrac{n}{2}\pi,$<br>where $n$ is any integer |

*Note:*

- There are infinitely many solutions. If we graph $y = \tan(2x)$ and $y = -\sqrt{3}$, we see that there are infinitely many points of intersection.

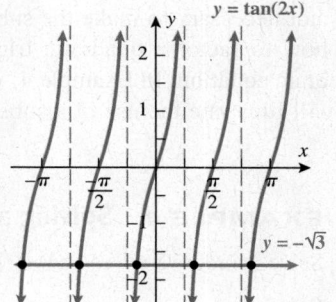

$y = \tan(2x)$

$y = -\sqrt{3}$

- Had we restricted the domain to $0 \le x < 2\pi$, the solutions (in radians) would be the values given to the right in the table.

| $n$ | $x = \dfrac{\pi}{3} + \dfrac{n}{2}\pi$ |
|---|---|
| 0 | $x = \dfrac{\pi}{3}$ |
| 1 | $x = \dfrac{5\pi}{6}$ |
| 2 | $x = \dfrac{4\pi}{3}$ |
| 3 | $x = \dfrac{11\pi}{6}$ |

Notice that only $n = 0, 1, 2, 3$ yield $x$-values in the domain $0 \le x < 2\pi$.

---

### Technology Tip

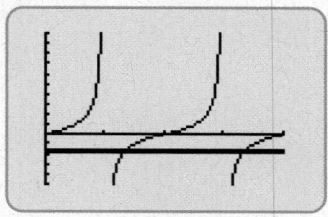

To find the point of intersection, use `2nd` `TRACE` for `CALC`; move the down arrow to `5: Intersect`; type `ENTER` for the first curve, `ENTER` for the second curve, `0.8` for guess, and `ENTER`.

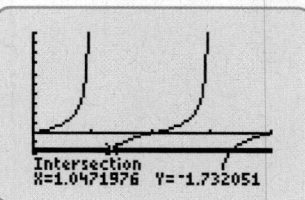

For the second answer, you need a number close to the answer for the guess. Type `2.5` for guess, and `ENTER`.

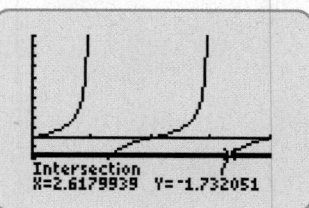

Notice that in Step 2 of Example 2, $2n\pi$ was added to get all of the solutions, whereas in Step 2 of Example 3, we added $n\pi$ to the argument of the tangent function. The reason that we added $2n\pi$ in Example 2 and $n\pi$ in Example 3 is because the sine function has period $2\pi$, whereas the tangent function has period $\pi$.

# Solving Trigonometric Equations Using Algebraic Techniques

We now will use algebraic techniques to solve trigonometric equations. Let us first start with linear and quadratic equations. For linear equations, we solve for the variable by isolating it. For quadratic equations, we often employ factoring or the quadratic formula. If we can let $x$ represent the trigonometric function and the resulting equation is either linear or quadratic, then we use techniques learned in solving algebraic equations.

| TYPE | EQUATION | SUBSTITUTION | ALGEBRAIC EQUATION |
|---|---|---|---|
| Linear trigonometric equation | $4\sin\theta - 2 = -4$ | $u = \sin\theta$ | $4u - 2 = -4$ |
| Quadratic trigonometric equation | $2\cos^2\theta + \cos\theta - 1 = 0$ | $u = \cos\theta$ | $2u^2 + u - 1 = 0$ |

It is not necessary to make the substitution, though it is convenient. Frequently, one can see how to factor a quadratic trigonometric equation without first converting it to an algebraic equation. In Example 4, we will not use a substitution. However, in Example 5, we will illustrate the use of a substitution.

**EXAMPLE 4  Solving a Linear Trigonometric Equation**

Solve $4\sin\theta - 2 = -4$ on $0 \le \theta < 2\pi$.

**Solution:**

STEP 1  Solve for $\sin\theta$.                                     $4\sin\theta - 2 = -4$

Add 2.                                                             $4\sin\theta = -2$

Divide by 4.                                                       $\sin\theta = -\dfrac{1}{2}$

STEP 2  Find the values of $\theta$ on $0 \le \theta < 2\pi$ that satisfy the equation $\sin\theta = -\frac{1}{2}$.

The sine function is negative in quadrants III and IV.

$\sin\left(\dfrac{7\pi}{6}\right) = -\dfrac{1}{2}$ and $\sin\left(\dfrac{11\pi}{6}\right) = -\dfrac{1}{2}$.         $\boxed{\theta = \dfrac{7\pi}{6}}$ or $\boxed{\theta = \dfrac{11\pi}{6}}$

■ **Answer:** $\theta = \dfrac{\pi}{3}$ or $\dfrac{5\pi}{3}$

■ **YOUR TURN** Solve $2\cos\theta + 1 = 2$ on $0 \le \theta < 2\pi$.

**EXAMPLE 5** **Solving a Quadratic Trigonometric Equation**

Solve $2\cos^2\theta + \cos\theta - 1 = 0$ on $0 \le \theta < 2\pi$.

**Solution:**

**Technology Tip**

Plot1  Plot2  Plot3
\Y1■2(cos(X))²+c
os(X)-1

STEP 1  Solve for $\cos\theta$.

$$2\cos^2\theta + \cos\theta - 1 = 0$$

Let $u = \cos\theta$.

$$2u^2 + u - 1 = 0$$

Factor the quadratic equation.

$$(2u - 1)(u + 1) = 0$$

Set each factor equal to 0.

$$2u - 1 = 0 \quad\text{or}\quad u + 1 = 0$$

Solve each for $u$.

$$u = \frac{1}{2} \quad\text{or}\quad u = -1$$

Substitute $u = \cos\theta$.

$$\cos\theta = \frac{1}{2} \quad\text{or}\quad \cos\theta = -1$$

STEP 2  Find the values of $\theta$ on $0 \le \theta < 2\pi$ which satisfy the equation $\cos\theta = \frac{1}{2}$.

The cosine function is positive in quadrants I and IV.

$$\cos\left(\frac{\pi}{3}\right) = \frac{1}{2} \quad\text{and}\quad \cos\left(\frac{5\pi}{3}\right) = \frac{1}{2}.$$

$$\boxed{\theta = \frac{\pi}{3}} \quad\text{or}\quad \boxed{\theta = \frac{5\pi}{3}}$$

STEP 3  Find the values of $\theta$ on $0 \le \theta < 2\pi$ that satisfy the equation $\cos\theta = -1$.

$$\cos\pi = -1.$$

$$\boxed{\theta = \pi}$$

The solutions to $2\cos^2\theta + \cos\theta - 1 = 0$ on $0 \le \theta < 2\pi$ are $\theta = \frac{\pi}{3}, \theta = \frac{5\pi}{3}$, and $\theta = \pi$.

■ **YOUR TURN** Solve $2\sin^2\theta - \sin\theta - 1 = 0$ on $0 \le \theta < 2\pi$.

■ **Answer:** $\theta = \frac{\pi}{2}, \frac{7\pi}{6}$, or $\frac{11\pi}{6}$

# Solving Trigonometric Equations That Require the Use of Inverse Functions

Thus far, we have been able to solve the trigonometric equations exactly. Now we turn our attention to situations that require using a calculator and inverse functions to approximate a solution to a trigonometric equation.

**Study Tip**

If Example 5 asked for the solution to the trigonometric equation over all real numbers, then the solutions would be $\theta = \frac{\pi}{3} \pm 2n\pi, \frac{5\pi}{3} \pm 2n\pi$, and $\pi \pm 2n\pi$.

*Technology Tip*

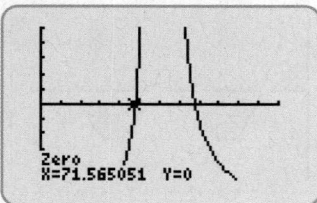

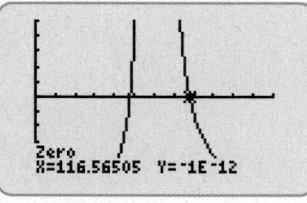

**EXAMPLE 6  Solving a Trigonometric Equation That Requires the Use of Inverse Functions**

Solve $\tan^2\theta - \tan\theta = 6$ on $0° \le \theta < 180°$.

**Solution:**

STEP 1  Solve for $\tan\theta$.

Subtract 6.                                    $\tan^2\theta - \tan\theta - 6 = 0$

Factor the quadratic trigonometric
expression on the left.                    $(\tan\theta - 3)(\tan\theta + 2) = 0$

Set the factors equal to 0.       $\tan\theta - 3 = 0$   or   $\tan\theta + 2 = 0$

Solve for $\tan\theta$.                    $\tan\theta = 3$   or       $\tan\theta = -2$

STEP 2  Solve $\tan\theta = 3$ on $0° \le \theta < 180°$.

The tangent function is positive on $0° \le \theta < 180°$ only in quadrant I.

Write the equivalent inverse notation to $\tan\theta = 3$.        $\theta = \tan^{-1}3$

Use a calculator to evaluate (approximate) $\theta$.        $\boxed{\theta \approx 71.6°}$

STEP 3  Solve $\tan\theta = -2$ on $0° \le \theta < 180°$.

The tangent function is negative on $0° \le \theta < 180°$ only in quadrant II.

A calculator gives values of the inverse tangent in quadrants I and IV.

We will call the reference angle in quadrant IV "$\alpha$."

Write the equivalent inverse notation
to $\tan\alpha = -2$.                                            $\alpha = \tan^{-1}(-2)$

Use a calculator to evaluate (approximate) $\alpha$.            $\alpha \approx -63.4°$

To find the value of $\theta$ in quadrant II, add 180°.            $\theta = \alpha + 180°$

$\boxed{\theta \approx 116.6°}$

The solutions to $\tan^2\theta - \tan\theta = 6$ on $0° \le \theta < 180°$ are $\theta = 71.6°$ and $\theta = 116.6°$.

■ **Answer:** $\theta \approx 63.4°$ or $108.4°$

■ **YOUR TURN**  Solve $\tan^2\theta + \tan\theta = 6$ on $0° \le \theta < 180°$.

Recall that in solving algebraic quadratic equations, one method (when factoring is not obvious or possible) is to use the Quadratic Formula.

$$ax^2 + bx + c = 0 \text{ has solutions } x = \frac{-b \pm \sqrt{b^2 - 4ac}}{2a}$$

EXAMPLE 7   **Solving a Quadratic Trigonometric Equation That Requires the Use of the Quadratic Formula and Inverse Functions**

**Technology Tip**

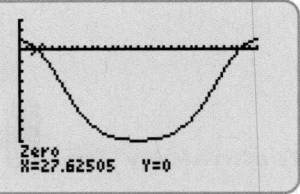

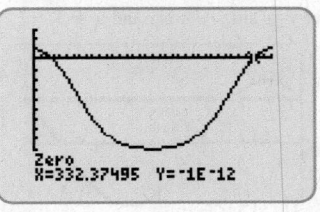

Solve $2\cos^2\theta + 5\cos\theta - 6 = 0$ on $0° \leq \theta < 360°$.

**Solution:**

STEP 1   Solve for $\cos\theta$.                    $2\cos^2\theta + 5\cos\theta - 6 = 0$

Let $u = \cos\theta$.                    $2u^2 + 5u - 6 = 0$

Use the Quadratic Formula,       $u = \dfrac{-5 \pm \sqrt{5^2 - 4(2)(-6)}}{2(2)}$
$a = 2, b = 5, c = -6$.

Simplify.                     $u = \dfrac{-5 \pm \sqrt{73}}{4}$

Use a calculator to approximate
the solution.               $u \approx -3.3860$   or   $u \approx 0.8860$

Let $u = \cos\theta$.        $\cos\theta \approx -3.3860$   or   $\cos\theta \approx 0.8860$

STEP 2   Solve $\cos\theta = -3.3860$ on $0° \leq \theta < 360°$.

Recall that the range of the cosine function is $[-1, 1]$; therefore, the cosine function can never equal a number outside that range.

Since $-3.3860 < -1$, the equation $\cos\theta = -3.3860$ has *no solution*.

STEP 3   Solve $\cos\theta = 0.8860$ on $0° \leq \theta < 360°$.

The cosine function is positive in quadrants I and IV. Since a calculator gives inverse cosine values only in quadrants I and II, we will have to use a reference angle to get the quadrant IV solution.

Write the equivalent inverse
notation for $\cos\theta = 0.8860$.        $\theta = \cos^{-1}(0.8860)$

Use a calculator to evaluate
(approximate) the solution.        $\boxed{\theta \approx 27.6°}$

To find the second solution
(in quadrant IV), subtract the        $\theta = 360° - 27.6°$
reference angle from 360°.        $\boxed{\theta \approx 332.4°}$

The solutions to $2\cos^2\theta + 5\cos\theta - 6 = 0$ on $0° \leq \theta < 360°$ are $\theta \approx 27.6°$ and $\theta \approx 332.4°$.

■ **YOUR TURN**   Solve $2\sin^2\theta - 5\sin\theta - 6 = 0$ on $0° \leq \theta < 360°$.

■ **Answer:**  $\theta \approx 242.4°$ or $297.6°$

# Using Trigonometric Identities to Solve Trigonometric Equations

We now consider trigonometric equations that involve more than one trigonometric function. Trigonometric identities are an important part of solving these types of equations.

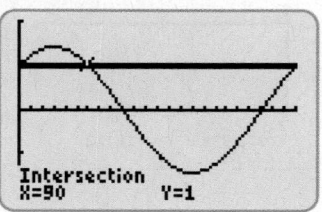

## Technology Tip

Find the points of intersection of $y = \sin x + \cos x$ and $y = 1$.

Intersection
X=90          Y=1

In radians, the $x$-coordinates will be in decimal form as opposed to multiples of $\pi$. In this screen shot degrees is used, which allows for more familiar known exact values to be illustrated.

**EXAMPLE 8**    **Using Trigonometric Identities to Solve Trigonometric Equations**

Solve $\sin x + \cos x = 1$ on $0 \le x < 2\pi$.

**Solution:**

Square both sides.                          $\sin^2 x + 2\sin x \cos x + \cos^2 x = 1$

Label the Pythagorean identity.            $\underbrace{\sin^2 x + \cos^2 x}_{1} + 2\sin x \cos x = 1$

Subtract 1 from both sides.                 $2\sin x \cos x = 0$

Use the Zero Product Property.              $\sin x = 0 \quad \text{or} \quad \cos x = 0$

Solve for $x$ on $0 \le x < 2\pi$.          $x = 0 \quad \text{or} \quad x = \pi \quad \text{or} \quad x = \dfrac{\pi}{2} \quad \text{or} \quad x = \dfrac{3\pi}{2}$

Because we squared the equation, we have to check for extraneous solutions.

Check $x = 0$.                              $\sin 0 + \cos 0 = 0 + 1 = 1 \quad \checkmark$

Check $x = \pi$.                            $\sin \pi + \cos \pi = 0 - 1 = -1 \quad \times$

Check $x = \dfrac{\pi}{2}$.                 $\sin\left(\dfrac{\pi}{2}\right) + \cos\left(\dfrac{\pi}{2}\right) = 1 + 0 = 1 \quad \checkmark$

Check $x = \dfrac{3\pi}{2}$.                $\sin\left(\dfrac{3\pi}{2}\right) + \cos\left(\dfrac{3\pi}{2}\right) = -1 + 0 = -1 \quad \times$

The solutions to $\sin x + \cos x = 1$ on $0 \le x < 2\pi$ are $\boxed{x = 0}$ and $\boxed{x = \dfrac{\pi}{2}}$.

■ **Answer:** $x = \dfrac{\pi}{2}$ or $x = \pi$

■ **YOUR TURN** Solve $\sin x - \cos x = 1$ on $0 \le x < 2\pi$.

**EXAMPLE 9  Using Trigonometric Identities to Solve Trigonometric Equations**

Solve $\sin(2x) = \sin x$ on $0 \le x < 2\pi$.

## COMMON MISTAKE

Dividing by a trigonometric function (which could be equal to zero).

⭐ **CORRECT**

Use the double-angle formula for sine.

$$\underbrace{\sin(2x)}_{2\sin x\cos x} = \sin x$$

Subtract $\sin x$.

$$2\sin x \cos x - \sin x = 0$$

Factor out the common $\sin x$.

$$(\sin x)(2\cos x - 1) = 0$$

Set each factor equal to 0.

$$\sin x = 0 \quad \text{or} \quad 2\cos x - 1 = 0$$

$$\sin x = 0 \quad \text{or} \quad \cos x = \frac{1}{2}$$

Solve $\sin x = 0$ for $x$ on $0 \le x < 2\pi$.

$$\boxed{x = 0} \quad \text{or} \quad \boxed{x = \pi}$$

Solve $\cos x = \frac{1}{2}$ for $x$ on $0 \le x < 2\pi$.

$$\boxed{x = \frac{\pi}{3}} \quad \text{or} \quad \boxed{x = \frac{5\pi}{3}}$$

❌ **INCORRECT**

$$2\sin x \cos x = \sin x$$

Divide by $\sin x$.  **ERROR**

$$2\cos x = 1$$

Solve for $\cos x$.

$$\cos x = \frac{1}{2}$$

Missing solutions from $\sin x = 0$.

The solutions to $\sin(2x) = \sin x$ are $x = 0, \dfrac{\pi}{3}, \pi$, and $\dfrac{5\pi}{3}$.

▼ **CAUTION**

Do not divide equations by trigonometric functions, as they can sometimes equal zero.

∙ **YOUR TURN** Solve $\sin(2x) = \cos x$ on $0 \le x < 2\pi$.

∎ **Answer:** $x = \dfrac{\pi}{2}, \dfrac{3\pi}{2}, \dfrac{\pi}{6},$ or $\dfrac{5\pi}{6}$

**EXAMPLE 10** **Using Trigonometric Identities to Solve Trigonometric Equations**

Solve $\sin x + \csc x = -2$.

**Solution:**

Use the reciprocal identity.

$$\sin x + \underbrace{\csc x}_{\frac{1}{\sin x}} = -2$$

Add 2.

$$\sin x + 2 + \frac{1}{\sin x} = 0$$

Multiply by $\sin x$. *Note:* $\sin x \neq 0$.

$$\sin^2 x + 2\sin x + 1 = 0$$

Factor as a perfect square.

$$(\sin x + 1)^2 = 0$$

Solve for $\sin x$.

$$\sin x = -1$$

Solve for $x$ on one period of the sine function, $[0, 2\pi)$.

$$x = \frac{3\pi}{2}$$

Add integer multiples of $2\pi$ to obtain all solutions.

$$\boxed{x = \frac{3\pi}{2} + 2n\pi}$$

**EXAMPLE 11** **Using Trigonometric Identities and Inverse Functions to Solve Trigonometric Equations**

Solve $3\cos^2\theta + \sin\theta = 3$ on $0° \le \theta < 360°$.

**Solution:**

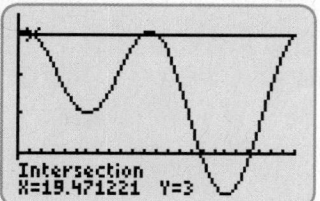
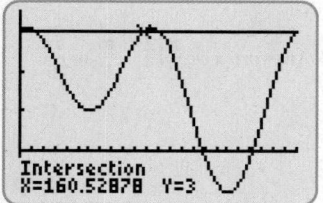
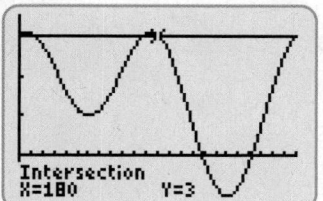
Use the Pythagorean identity.

$$3\underbrace{\cos^2\theta}_{1 - \sin^2\theta} + \sin\theta = 3$$

Subtract 3.

$$3(1 - \sin^2\theta) + \sin\theta - 3 = 0$$

Eliminate the parentheses.

$$3 - 3\sin^2\theta + \sin\theta - 3 = 0$$

Simplify.

$$-3\sin^2\theta + \sin\theta = 0$$

Factor the common $\sin\theta$.

$$\sin\theta(1 - 3\sin\theta) = 0$$

Set each factor equal to 0.

$$\sin\theta = 0 \quad \text{or} \quad 1 - 3\sin\theta = 0$$

Solve for $\sin\theta$.

$$\sin\theta = 0 \quad \text{or} \quad \sin\theta = \frac{1}{3}$$

Solve $\sin\theta = 0$ for $x$ on $0° \le \theta < 360°$.

$$\boxed{\theta = 0°} \quad \text{or} \quad \boxed{\theta = 180°}$$

Solve $\sin\theta = \frac{1}{3}$ for $x$ on $0° \le \theta < 360°$.

The sine function is positive in quadrants I and II.

A calculator gives inverse values only in quadrant I.

Write the equivalent inverse notation for $\sin\theta = \frac{1}{3}$.

$$\theta = \sin^{-1}\left(\frac{1}{3}\right)$$

Use a calculator to approximate the quadrant I solution.

$$\boxed{\theta \approx 19.5°}$$

To find the quadrant II solution, subtract the reference angle from 180°.

$$\theta \approx 180° - 19.5°$$
$$\boxed{\theta \approx 160.5°}$$

# Applications

 **EXAMPLE 12** **Applications Involving Trigonometric Equations**

Light bends (refracts) according to Snell's law, which states

$$n_i \sin(\theta_i) = n_r \sin(\theta_r)$$

where

- $n_i$ is the refractive index of the medium the light is leaving.
- $\theta_i$ is the incident angle between the light ray and the normal (perpendicular) to the interface between mediums.
- $n_r$ is the refractive index of the medium the light is entering.
- $\theta_r$ is the refractive angle between the light ray and the normal (perpendicular) to the interface between mediums.

Janis Christie/Getty Images, Inc.

Assume that light is going from air into a diamond. Calculate the refractive angle $\theta_r$ if the incidence angle is $\theta_i = 32°$ and the index of refraction values for air and diamond are $n_i = 1.00$ and $n_r = 2.417$, respectively.

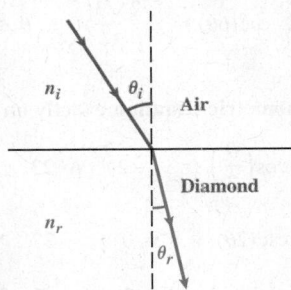

**Solution:**

Write Snell's law. $\qquad\qquad\qquad\qquad n_i \sin(\theta_i) = n_r \sin(\theta_r)$

Substitute $\theta_i = 32°$, $n_i = 1.00$, and $n_r = 2.417$. $\qquad \sin 32° = 2.417 \sin \theta_r$

Isolate $\sin \theta_r$ and simplify. $\qquad\qquad\qquad \sin \theta_r = \dfrac{\sin 32°}{2.417} \approx 0.21925$

Solve for $\theta_r$ using the inverse sine function. $\qquad \theta_r \approx \sin^{-1}(0.21925) \approx 12.665°$

Round to the nearest degree. $\qquad\qquad\qquad \boxed{\theta_r \approx 13°}$

---

**SECTION**
**6.6** SUMMARY

In this section, we began by solving basic trigonometric equations that contained only one trigonometric function. Some such equations can be solved exactly by inspection, and others can be solved exactly using algebraic techniques similar to those of linear and quadratic equations. Calculators and inverse functions are needed when exact values are not known. It is important to note that calculators give the inverse function in only one of the two relevant quadrants. The other quadrant solutions must be found using reference angles. Trigonometric identities are useful for solving equations that involve more than one trigonometric function. With trigonometric identities we can transform such equations into equations involving only one trigonometric function, and then we can apply algebraic techniques.

**SECTION**
# 6.6 EXERCISES

■ SKILLS

In Exercises 1–20, solve the given trigonometric equation exactly over the indicated interval.

**1.** $\cos\theta = -\dfrac{\sqrt{2}}{2}, 0 \le \theta < 2\pi$

**2.** $\sin\theta = -\dfrac{\sqrt{2}}{2}, 0 \le \theta < 2\pi$

**3.** $\csc\theta = -2, 0 \le \theta < 4\pi$

**4.** $\sec\theta = -2, 0 \le \theta < 4\pi$

**5.** $\tan\theta = 0$, all real numbers

**6.** $\cot\theta = 0$, all real numbers

**7.** $\sin(2\theta) = -\dfrac{1}{2}, 0 \le \theta < 2\pi$

**8.** $\cos(2\theta) = \dfrac{\sqrt{3}}{2}, 0 \le \theta < 2\pi$

**9.** $\sin\left(\dfrac{\theta}{2}\right) = -\dfrac{1}{2}$, all real numbers

**10.** $\cos\left(\dfrac{\theta}{2}\right) = -1$, all real numbers

**11.** $\tan(2\theta) = \sqrt{3}, -2\pi \le \theta < 2\pi$

**12.** $\tan(2\theta) = -\sqrt{3}$, all real numbers

**13.** $\sec\theta = -2, -2\pi \le \theta < 0$

**14.** $\csc\theta = \dfrac{2\sqrt{3}}{3}, -\pi \le \theta < \pi$

**15.** $\cot(4\theta) = -\dfrac{\sqrt{3}}{3}$, all real numbers

**16.** $\tan(5\theta) = 1$, all real numbers

**17.** $\sec(3\theta) = -1, -2\pi \le \theta \le 0$

**18.** $\sec(4\theta) = \sqrt{2}, 0 \le \theta \le \pi$

**19.** $\csc(3\theta) = 1, -2\pi \le \theta \le 0$

**20.** $\csc(6\theta) = -\dfrac{2\sqrt{3}}{3}, 0 \le \theta \le \pi$

In Exercises 21–40, solve the given trigonometric equation exactly on $0 \le \theta < 2\pi$.

**21.** $2\sin(2\theta) = \sqrt{3}$

**22.** $2\cos\left(\dfrac{\theta}{2}\right) = -\sqrt{2}$

**23.** $3\tan(2\theta) - \sqrt{3} = 0$

**24.** $4\tan\left(\dfrac{\theta}{2}\right) - 4 = 0$

**25.** $2\cos(2\theta) + 1 = 0$

**26.** $4\csc(2\theta) + 8 = 0$

**27.** $\sqrt{3}\cot\left(\dfrac{\theta}{2}\right) - 3 = 0$

**28.** $\sqrt{3}\sec(2\theta) + 2 = 0$

**29.** $\tan^2\theta - 1 = 0$

**30.** $\sin^2\theta + 2\sin\theta + 1 = 0$

**31.** $2\cos^2\theta - \cos\theta = 0$

**32.** $\tan^2\theta - \sqrt{3}\tan\theta = 0$

**33.** $\csc^2\theta + 3\csc\theta + 2 = 0$

**34.** $\cot^2\theta = 1$

**35.** $\sin^2\theta + 2\sin\theta - 3 = 0$

**36.** $2\sec^2\theta + \sec\theta - 1 = 0$

**37.** $\sec^2\theta - 1 = 0$

**38.** $\csc^2\theta - 1 = 0$

**39.** $\sec^2(2\theta) - \dfrac{4}{3} = 0$

**40.** $\csc^2(2\theta) - 4 = 0$

In Exercises 41–60, solve the given trigonometric equation on $0° \le \theta < 360°$ and express the answer in degrees rounded to two decimal places.

**41.** $\sin(2\theta) = -0.7843$

**42.** $\cos(2\theta) = 0.5136$

**43.** $\tan\left(\dfrac{\theta}{2}\right) = -0.2343$

**44.** $\sec\left(\dfrac{\theta}{2}\right) = 1.4275$

**45.** $5\cot\theta - 9 = 0$

**46.** $5\sec\theta + 6 = 0$

**47.** $4\sin\theta + \sqrt{2} = 0$

**48.** $3\cos\theta - \sqrt{5} = 0$

**49.** $4\cos^2\theta + 5\cos\theta - 6 = 0$

**50.** $6\sin^2\theta - 13\sin\theta - 5 = 0$

**51.** $6\tan^2\theta - \tan\theta - 12 = 0$

**52.** $6\sec^2\theta - 7\sec\theta - 20 = 0$

**53.** $15\sin^2(2\theta) + \sin(2\theta) - 2 = 0$

**54.** $12\cos^2\left(\dfrac{\theta}{2}\right) - 13\cos\left(\dfrac{\theta}{2}\right) + 3 = 0$

**55.** $\cos^2\theta - 6\cos\theta + 1 = 0$

**56.** $\sin^2\theta + 3\sin\theta - 3 = 0$

**57.** $2\tan^2\theta - \tan\theta - 7 = 0$

**58.** $3\cot^2\theta + 2\cot\theta - 4 = 0$

**59.** $\csc^2(3\theta) - 2 = 0$

**60.** $\sec^2\left(\dfrac{\theta}{2}\right) - 2 = 0$

In Exercises 61–88, solve the trigonometric equations exactly on the indicated interval, $0 \le x < 2\pi$.

**61.** $\sin x = \cos x$

**62.** $\sin x = -\cos x$

**63.** $\sec x + \cos x = -2$

**64.** $\sin x + \csc x = 2$

**65.** $\sec x - \tan x = \dfrac{\sqrt{3}}{3}$

**66.** $\sec x + \tan x = 1$

**67.** $\csc x + \cot x = \sqrt{3}$

**68.** $\csc x - \cot x = \dfrac{\sqrt{3}}{3}$

**69.** $2\sin x - \csc x = 0$

**70.** $2\sin x + \csc x = 3$

**71.** $\sin(2x) = 4\cos x$

**72.** $\sin(2x) = \sqrt{3}\sin x$

**73.** $\sqrt{2}\sin x = \tan x$

**74.** $\cos(2x) = \sin x$

**75.** $\tan(2x) = \cot x$

**76.** $3\cot(2x) = \cot x$

**77.** $\sqrt{3}\sec x = 4\sin x$

**78.** $\sqrt{3}\tan x = 2\sin x$

**79.** $\sin^2 x - \cos(2x) = -\tfrac{1}{4}$

**80.** $\sin^2 x - 2\sin x = 0$

**81.** $\cos^2 x + 2\sin x + 2 = 0$

**82.** $2\cos^2 x = \sin x + 1$

**83.** $2\sin^2 x + 3\cos x = 0$

**84.** $4\cos^2 x - 4\sin x = 5$

**85.** $\cos(2x) + \cos x = 0$

**86.** $2\cot x = \csc x$

**87.** $\tfrac{1}{4}\sec(2x) = \sin(2x)$

**88.** $-\tfrac{1}{4}\csc\left(\tfrac{1}{2}x\right) = \cos\left(\tfrac{1}{2}x\right)$

In Exercises 89–98, solve each trigonometric equation on $0° \le \theta < 360°$. Express solutions in degrees and round to two decimal places.

**89.** $\cos(2x) + \tfrac{1}{2}\sin x = 0$

**90.** $\sec^2 x = \tan x + 1$

**91.** $6\cos^2 x + \sin x = 5$

**92.** $\sec^2 x = 2\tan x + 4$

**93.** $\cot^2 x - 3\csc x - 3 = 0$

**94.** $\csc^2 x + \cot x = 7$

**95.** $2\sin^2 x + 2\cos x - 1 = 0$  **96.** $\sec^2 x + \tan x - 2 = 0$

**97.** $\dfrac{1}{16}\csc^2\left(\dfrac{x}{4}\right) - \cos^2\left(\dfrac{x}{4}\right) = 0$  **98.** $-\dfrac{1}{4}\sec^2\left(\dfrac{x}{8}\right) + \sin^2\left(\dfrac{x}{8}\right) = 0$

## ▪ APPLICATIONS

**For Exercises 99 and 100, refer to the following:**

Computer sales are generally subject to seasonal fluctuations. The sales of QualComp computers during 2008–2010 is approximated by the function

$$s(t) = 0.120\sin(0.790t - 2.380) + 0.387 \quad 1 \le t \le 12$$

where $t$ represents time in quarters ($t = 1$ represents the end of the first quarter of 2008), and $s(t)$ represents computer sales (quarterly revenue) in millions of dollars.

**99. Business.** Find the quarter(s) in which the quarterly sales are $472,000.

**100. Business.** Find the quarter(s) in which the quarterly sales are $507,000.

**For Exercises 101 and 102, refer to the following:**

Allergy sufferers' symptoms fluctuate with the concentration of pollen in the air. At one location the pollen concentration, measured in grains per cubic meter, of grasses fluctuates throughout the day according to the function:

$$p(t) = 35 - 26\cos\left(\dfrac{\pi}{12}t - \dfrac{7\pi}{6}\right), \quad 0 \le t \le 24$$

where $t$ is measured in hours and $t = 0$ is 12:00 A.M.

**101. Biology/Health.** Find the time(s) of day when the grass pollen level is 41 grains per cubic meter. Round to the nearest hour.

**102. Biology/Health.** Find the time(s) of day when the grass pollen level is 17 grains per cubic meter. Round to the nearest hour.

**103. Sales.** Monthly sales of soccer balls are approximated by

$$S = 400\sin\left(\dfrac{\pi}{6}x\right) + 2000, \text{ where } x \text{ is the number of the}$$

month (January is $x = 1$, etc.). During which month do sales reach 2400?

**104. Sales.** Monthly sales of soccer balls are approximated by

$$S = 400\sin\left(\dfrac{\pi}{6}x\right) + 2000, \text{ where } x \text{ is the number of the}$$

month (January is $x = 1$, etc.). During which two months do sales reach 1800?

**105. Home Improvement.** A rain gutter is constructed from a single strip of sheet metal by bending as shown below and on the right, so that the base and sides are the same length. Express the area of the cross section of the rain gutter as a function of the angle $\theta$ (note that the expression will also involve $x$).

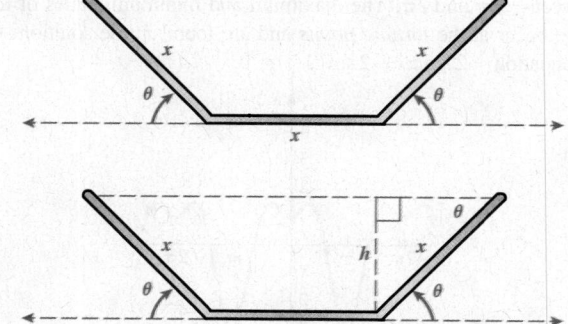

**106. Home Improvement.** A rain gutter is constructed from a single strip of sheet metal by bending as shown above, so that the base and sides are the same length. When the area of the cross section of the rain gutter is expressed as a function of the angle $\theta$, you can then determine the value of $\theta$ that produces the cross section with the greatest possible area. The angle is found by solving the equation $\cos^2\theta - \sin^2\theta + \cos\theta = 0$. Which angle gives the maximum area?

**107. Deer Population.** The number of deer on an island is given by $D = 200 + 100 \sin\left(\dfrac{\pi}{2}x\right)$, where $x$ is the number of years since 2000. Which is the first year after 2000 that the number of deer reaches 300?

**108. Deer Population.** The number of deer on an island is given by $D = 200 + 100 \sin\left(\dfrac{\pi}{6}x\right)$, where $x$ is the number of years since 2000. Which is the first year after 2000 that the number of deer reaches 150?

**109. Optics.** Assume that light is going from air into a diamond. Calculate the refractive angle $\theta_r$ if the incidence angle is $\theta_i = 75°$ and the index of refraction values for air and diamond are $n_i = 1.00$ and $n_r = 2.417$, respectively. Round to the nearest degree. (See Example 12 for Snell's law.)

**110. Optics.** Assume that light is going from a diamond into air. Calculate the refractive angle $\theta_r$ if the incidence angle is $\theta_i = 15°$ and the index of refraction values for diamond and air are $n_i = 2.417$ and $n_r = 1.00$, respectively. Round to the nearest degree. (See Example 12 for Snell's law.)

**111. Air in Lungs.** If a person breathes in and out every 3 seconds, the volume of air in the lungs can be modeled by $A = 2\sin\left(\dfrac{\pi}{3}x\right)\cos\left(\dfrac{\pi}{3}x\right) + 3$, where $A$ is in liters of air and $x$ is in seconds. How many seconds into the cycle is the volume of air equal to 4 liters?

**112. Air in Lungs.** For the function given in Exercise 111, how many seconds into the cycle is the volume of air equal to 2 liters?

**For Exercises 113 and 114, refer to the following:**

The figure below shows the graph of $y = 2\cos x - \cos(2x)$ between $-2\pi$ and $2\pi$. The maximum and minimum values of the curve occur at the *turning points* and are found in the solutions of the equation $-2\sin x + 2\sin(2x) = 0$.

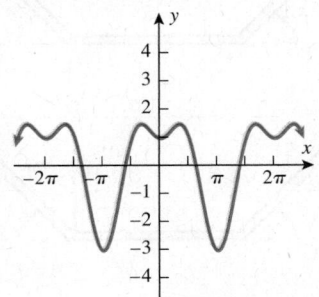

**113. Finding Turning Points.** Solve for the coordinates of the turning points of the curve between 0 and $2\pi$.

**114. Finding Turning Points.** Solve for the coordinates of the turning points of the curve between $-2\pi$ and 0.

**115. Business.** An analysis of a company's costs and revenue shows that annual costs of producing their product as well as annual revenues from the sale of a product are generally subject to seasonal fluctuations and are approximated by the function

$$C(t) = 2.3 + 0.25\sin\left(\dfrac{\pi}{6}t\right) \qquad 0 \le t \le 11$$

$$R(t) = 2.3 + 0.5\cos\left(\dfrac{\pi}{6}t\right) \qquad 0 \le t \le 11$$

where $t$ represents time in months ($t = 0$ represents January), $C(t)$ represents the monthly costs of producing the product in millions of dollars, and $R(t)$ represents monthly revenue from sales of the product in millions of dollars. Find the month(s) in which the company breaks even. *Hint:* A company breaks even when its profit is zero.

**116. Business.** An analysis of a company's costs and revenue shows that the annual costs of producing its product as well as annual revenues from the sale of a product are generally subject to seasonal fluctuations and are approximated by the function

$$C(t) = 25.7 + 0.2\sin\left(\dfrac{\pi}{6}t\right) \qquad 0 \le t \le 11$$

$$R(t) = 25.7 + 9.6\cos\left(\dfrac{\pi}{6}t\right) \qquad 0 \le t \le 11$$

where $t$ represents time in months ($t = 0$ represents January), $C(t)$ represents the monthly costs of producing the product in millions of dollars, and $R(t)$ represents monthly revenue from sales of the product in millions of dollars. Find the month(s) in which the company breaks even. *Hint:* A company breaks even when its profit is zero.

**For Exercises 117 and 118, refer to the following:**

By analyzing available empirical data, it has been determined that the body temperature of a species fluctuates according to the model

$$T(t) = 37.10 + 1.40\sin\left(\dfrac{\pi}{24}t\right)\cos\left(\dfrac{\pi}{24}t\right) \qquad 0 \le t \le 24$$

where $T$ represents temperature in degrees Celsius and $t$ represents time (in hours) measured from 12:00 A.M. (midnight).

**117. Biology/Health.** Find the time(s) of day the body temperature is 37.28°C. Round to the nearest hour.

**118. Biology/Health.** Find the time(s) of day the body temperature is 36.75°C. Round to the nearest hour.

■ **CATCH THE MISTAKE**

**In Exercises 119–122, explain the mistake that is made.**

**119.** Solve $\sqrt{2 + \sin\theta} = \sin\theta$ on $0 \leq \theta \leq 2\pi$.

**Solution:**

| | |
|---|---|
| Square both sides. | $2 + \sin\theta = \sin^2\theta$ |
| Gather all terms to one side. | $\sin^2\theta - \sin\theta - 2 = 0$ |
| Factor. | $(\sin\theta - 2)(\sin\theta + 1) = 0$ |
| Set each factor equal to zero. | $\sin\theta - 2 = 0$ or $\sin\theta + 1 = 0$ |
| Solve for $\sin\theta$. | $\sin\theta = 2$ or $\sin\theta = -1$ |
| Solve $\sin\theta = 2$ for $\theta$. | no solution |
| Solve $\sin\theta = -1$ for $\theta$. | $\theta = \dfrac{3\pi}{2}$ |

This is incorrect. What mistake was made?

**120.** Solve $\sqrt{3\sin\theta - 2} = -\sin\theta$ on $0 \leq \theta \leq 2\pi$.

**Solution:**

| | |
|---|---|
| Square both sides. | $3\sin\theta - 2 = \sin^2\theta$ |
| Gather all terms to one side. | $\sin^2\theta - 3\sin\theta + 2 = 0$ |
| Factor. | $(\sin\theta - 2)(\sin\theta - 1) = 0$ |
| Set each factor equal to zero. | $\sin\theta - 2 = 0$ or $\sin\theta - 1 = 0$ |
| Solve for $\sin\theta$. | $\sin\theta = 2$ or $\sin\theta = 1$ |
| Solve $\sin\theta = 2$ for $\theta$. | no solution |
| Solve $\sin\theta = 1$ for $\theta$. | $\theta = \dfrac{\pi}{2}$ |

This is incorrect. What mistake was made?

**121.** Solve $3\sin(2x) = 2\cos x$ on $0° \leq \theta \leq 180°$.

**Solution:**

| | |
|---|---|
| Use the double-angle identity for the sine function. | $3\underbrace{\sin(2x)}_{2\sin x\cos x} = 2\cos x$ |
| Simplify. | $6\sin x\cos x = 2\cos x$ |
| Divide by $2\cos x$. | $3\sin x = 1$ |
| Divide by 3. | $\sin x = \dfrac{1}{3}$ |
| Write the equivalent inverse notation. | $x = \sin^{-1}\left(\dfrac{1}{3}\right)$ |
| Use a calculator to approximate the solution. | $x \approx 19.47°$, QI solution |
| The QII solution is: | $x \approx 180° - 19.47° \approx 160.53°$ |

This is incorrect. What mistake was made?

**122.** Solve $\sqrt{1 + \sin x} = \cos x$ on $0 \leq x \leq 2\pi$.

**Solution:**

| | |
|---|---|
| Square both sides. | $1 + \sin x = \cos^2 x$ |
| Use the Pythagorean identity. | $1 + \sin x = \underbrace{\cos^2 x}_{1 - \sin^2 x}$ |
| Simplify. | $\sin^2 x + \sin x = 0$ |
| Factor. | $\sin x(\sin x + 1) = 0$ |
| Set each factor equal to zero. | $\sin x = 0$ or $\sin x + 1 = 0$ |
| Solve for $\sin x$. | $\sin x = 0$ or $\sin x = -1$ |
| Solve for $x$. | $x = 0, \pi, \dfrac{3\pi}{2}, 2\pi$ |

This is incorrect. What mistake was made?

■ **CONCEPTUAL**

**In Exercises 123–126, determine whether each statement is true or false.**

**123.** Linear trigonometric equations always have one solution on $[0, 2\pi]$.

**124.** Quadratic trigonometric equations always have two solutions on $[0, 2\pi]$.

**125.** If a trigonometric equation has all real numbers as its solution, then it is an identity.

**126.** If a trigonometric equation has an infinite number of solutions, then it is an identity.

## ■ CHALLENGE

**127.** Solve $16\sin^4\theta - 8\sin^2\theta = -1$ over $0 \le \theta \le 2\pi$.

**128.** Solve $\left|\cos\left(\theta + \dfrac{\pi}{4}\right)\right| = \dfrac{\sqrt{3}}{2}$ over all real numbers.

**129.** Solve for the smallest positive $x$ that makes this statement true:

$$\sin\left(x + \frac{\pi}{4}\right) + \sin\left(x - \frac{\pi}{4}\right) = \frac{\sqrt{2}}{2}$$

**130.** Solve for the smallest positive $x$ that makes this statement true:

$$\cos x \cos 15° + \sin x \sin 15° = 0.7$$

**131.** Find all real numbers $x$ such that $\dfrac{1 - \cos\left(\dfrac{x}{3}\right)}{1 + \cos\left(\dfrac{x}{3}\right)} + 1 = 0$.

**132.** Find all real numbers $\theta$ such that $\sec^4\left(\dfrac{1}{3}\theta\right) - 1 = 0$.

**133.** Find all real numbers $\theta$ such that $\csc^4\left(\dfrac{\pi}{4}\theta - \pi\right) - 4 = 0$.

**134.** Find all real numbers $x$ such that $2\tan(3x) = \sqrt{3} - \sqrt{3}\tan^2(3x)$.

## ■ TECHNOLOGY

Graphing calculators can be used to find approximate solutions to trigonometric equations. For the equation $f(x) = g(x)$, let $Y_1 = f(x)$ and $Y_2 = g(x)$. The $x$-values that correspond to points of intersections represent solutions.

**135.** With a graphing utility, solve the equation $\sin\theta = \cos(2\theta)$ on $0 \le \theta \le \pi$.

**136.** With a graphing utility, solve the equation $\csc\theta = \sec\theta$ on $0 \le \theta \le \dfrac{\pi}{2}$.

**137.** With a graphing utility, solve the equation $\sin\theta = \sec\theta$ on $0 \le \theta \le \pi$.

**138.** With a graphing utility, solve the equation $\cos\theta = \csc\theta$ on $0 \le \theta \le \pi$.

**139.** With a graphing utility, find all of the solutions to the equation $\sin\theta = e^\theta$ for $\theta \ge 0$.

**140.** With a graphing utility, find all of the solutions to the equation $\cos\theta = e^\theta$ for $\theta \ge 0$.

Find the smallest positive values of $x$ that make the statement true. Give the answer in degrees and round to two decimal places.

**141.** $\sec(3x) + \csc(2x) = 5$

**142.** $\cot(5x) + \tan(2x) = -3$

**143.** $e^x - \tan x = 0$      **144.** $e^x + 2\sin x = 1$

**145.** $\ln x - \sin x = 0$      **146.** $\ln x - \cos x = 0$

## ■ PREVIEW TO CALCULUS

In calculus, the definite integral is used to find the area between two intersecting curves (functions). When the curves correspond to trigonometric functions, we need to solve trigonometric equations.

In Exercises 147–150, solve each trigonometric equation within the indicated interval.

**147.** $\cos x = 2 - \cos x$, $0 \le x \le 2\pi$

**148.** $\cos(2x) = \sin x$, $-\dfrac{\pi}{2} \le x \le \dfrac{\pi}{6}$

**149.** $2\sin x = \tan x$, $-\dfrac{\pi}{3} \le x \le \dfrac{\pi}{3}$

**150.** $\sin(2x) - \cos(2x) = 0$, $0 < x \le \pi$

# CHAPTER 6 INQUIRY-BASED LEARNING PROJECT

*When it comes to identities, don't always let your intuition be your guide.*

1. Suppose a fellow student claims that the equation $\sin(a + b) = \sin a + \sin b$ is an identity. He's wondering if you can help because he's not sure how to verify his claim, but says, "It just seems intuitively so." Can you help this student?

   **a.** First, let's understand the student's claim. What does it *mean* to say that $\sin(a + b) = \sin a + \sin b$ "is an identity"?

   **b.** If you decided to try and verify the student's claim, you'd start with one side of his equation and try to manipulate that side until it looks like the other side. But, that may turn out to be a lot of unnecessary work *if*, in fact, the student's claim is false. So, instead, try something else.
   Consider a right triangle with angles $a$ and $b$. Calculate the values in the chart below, using various values of $a$ and $b$.

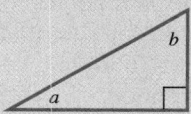

| a | b | a + b | sin(a + b) | sin a | sin b | sin a + sin b |
|---|---|---|---|---|---|---|
|   |   |   |   |   |   |   |
|   |   |   |   |   |   |   |

   **c.** What does your data tell you about the student's claim? Explain.

   **d.** In this example, you discovered that function notation is not distributive. Now, show the student how to write the *sum identity for the sine function*; that is,

$$\sin(a + b) = \underline{\hspace{4cm}}$$

   (This identity is derived in this chapter.)

2. Word has gotten out that you are really good at helping others understand trigonometric identities. Another of your fellow students asks whether $\sin(2a) = 2\sin a$ is an identity.

   **a.** How many values of $a$ would you need to check to determine whether the student's equation is an identity? Explain.

   **b.** Show how to convince the student that his equation is *not* an identity.

   **c.** Try to discover the *double-angle identity* $\sin(2a) = \underline{\hspace{3cm}}$: For the right triangle below, fill out the chart (exact values) and look for a pattern.

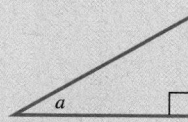

| a | sin(2a) | sin a | cos a |
|---|---|---|---|
| 30° |   |   |   |
| 45° |   |   |   |
| 60° |   |   |   |
| 90° |   |   |   |

# MODELING OUR WORLD

In the Modeling Our World feature in Chapter 5, you modeled mean *temperatures* with sinusoidal models. Now we consider *carbon emissions*, which are greenhouse gases that have been shown to negatively affect the ozone layer. Over the last 50 years, we have increased our global carbon emissions at an alarming rate. Recall that the graph of the inverse tangent function increases rapidly and then levels off at the horizontal asymptote, $y = \dfrac{\pi}{2} \approx 1.57$. To achieve a similar plateau with carbon emissions, drastic environmental regulations will need to be enacted.

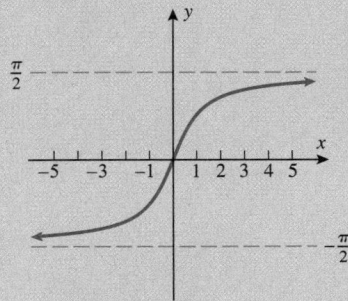

The carbon emissions data over the last 50 years suggest an almost linear climb (similar to the inverse tangent graph from $x = 0$ to $x = 1$). If the world started reducing carbon emissions, they might possibly reach a plateau level.

The following table summarizes average yearly temperature in degrees Fahrenheit (°F) and carbon dioxide emissions in parts per million (ppm) for Mauna Loa, Hawaii.

| YEAR | 1960 | 1965 | 1970 | 1975 | 1980 | 1985 | 1990 | 1995 | 2000 | 2005 |
|---|---|---|---|---|---|---|---|---|---|---|
| TEMPERATURE | 44.45 | 43.29 | 43.61 | 43.35 | 46.66 | 45.71 | 45.53 | 47.53 | 45.86 | 46.23 |
| $CO_2$ EMISSIONS (PPM) | 316.9 | 320.0 | 325.7 | 331.1 | 338.7 | 345.9 | 354.2 | 360.6 | 369.4 | 379.7 |

1. Plot the carbon emissions data with time on the horizontal axis and $CO_2$ emissions (in ppm) on the vertical axis. Let $t = 0$ correspond to 1960.

2. Find an *inverse tangent function* of the form $f(x) = A\tan^{-1}(Bx) + k$ that models the carbon emissions in Mauna Loa.

   a. Use the data from 1960, 1985, and 2005.

   b. Use the data from 1960, 1965, and 1995.

3. According to your model, what are the expected carbon emissions in 2050?

4. Describe the ways by which the world might be able to reach a plateau level of carbon emissions instead of the predicted increased rates.

| SECTION | CONCEPT | KEY IDEAS/FORMULAS |
|---------|---------|--------------------|

**6.1** — **Verifying trigonometric identities**

Identities must hold for *all* values of $x$ (not just some values of $x$) for which both sides of the equation are defined.

Fundamental identities

*Reciprocal identities*

$$\csc\theta = \frac{1}{\sin\theta} \qquad \sec\theta = \frac{1}{\cos\theta} \qquad \cot\theta = \frac{1}{\tan\theta}$$

*Quotient identities*

$$\tan\theta = \frac{\sin\theta}{\cos\theta} \qquad \cot\theta = \frac{\cos\theta}{\sin\theta}$$

*Pythagorean identities*

$$\sin^2\theta + \cos^2\theta = 1$$
$$\tan^2\theta + 1 = \sec^2\theta$$
$$1 + \cot^2\theta = \csc^2\theta$$

*Cofunction identities*

$$\sin\theta = \cos\left(\frac{\pi}{2} - \theta\right) \qquad \csc\theta = \sec\left(\frac{\pi}{2} - \theta\right)$$

$$\cos\theta = \sin\left(\frac{\pi}{2} - \theta\right) \qquad \sec\theta = \csc\left(\frac{\pi}{2} - \theta\right)$$

$$\tan\theta = \cot\left(\frac{\pi}{2} - \theta\right) \qquad \cot\theta = \tan\left(\frac{\pi}{2} - \theta\right)$$

Simplifying trigonometric expressions using identities

Use the reciprocal, quotient, or Pythagorean identities to simplify trigonometric expressions.

Verifying identities

- Convert all trigonometric expressions to sines and cosines.
- Write all sums or differences of fractions as a single fraction.

**6.2** — **Sum and difference identities**

$$f(A \pm B) \neq f(A) \pm f(B)$$
For trigonometric functions, we have the sum and difference identities.

Sum and difference identities for the cosine function

$$\cos(A + B) = \cos A \cos B - \sin A \sin B$$
$$\cos(A - B) = \cos A \cos B + \sin A \sin B$$

Sum and difference identities for the sine function

$$\sin(A + B) = \sin A \cos B + \cos A \sin B$$
$$\sin(A - B) = \sin A \cos B - \cos A \sin B$$

Sum and difference identities for the tangent function

$$\tan(A + B) = \frac{\tan A + \tan B}{1 - \tan A \tan B}$$

$$\tan(A - B) = \frac{\tan A - \tan B}{1 + \tan A \tan B}$$

**6.3** — **Double-angle and half-angle identities**

Double-angle identities

$$\sin(2A) = 2\sin A \cos A$$
$$\cos(2A) = \cos^2 A - \sin^2 A$$
$$= 1 - 2\sin^2 A = 2\cos^2 A - 1$$
$$\tan(2A) = \frac{2\tan A}{1 - \tan^2 A}$$

| SECTION | CONCEPT | KEY IDEAS/FORMULAS |
|---|---|---|
| | Half-angle identities | $\sin\left(\dfrac{A}{2}\right) = \pm\sqrt{\dfrac{1 - \cos A}{2}}$ |
| | | $\cos\left(\dfrac{A}{2}\right) = \pm\sqrt{\dfrac{1 + \cos A}{2}}$ |
| | | $\tan\left(\dfrac{A}{2}\right) = \pm\sqrt{\dfrac{1 - \cos A}{1 + \cos A}} = \dfrac{\sin A}{1 + \cos A} = \dfrac{1 - \cos A}{\sin A}$ |

**6.4**    **Product-to-sum and sum-to-product identities**

Product-to-sum identities

$$\cos A \cos B = \tfrac{1}{2}[\cos(A + B) + \cos(A - B)]$$

$$\sin A \sin B = \tfrac{1}{2}[\cos(A - B) - \cos(A + B)]$$

$$\sin A \cos B = \tfrac{1}{2}[\sin(A + B) + \sin(A - B)]$$

Sum-to-product identities

$$\sin A + \sin B = 2\sin\left(\dfrac{A + B}{2}\right)\cos\left(\dfrac{A - B}{2}\right)$$

$$\sin A - \sin B = 2\sin\left(\dfrac{A - B}{2}\right)\cos\left(\dfrac{A + B}{2}\right)$$

$$\cos A + \cos B = 2\cos\left(\dfrac{A + B}{2}\right)\cos\left(\dfrac{A - B}{2}\right)$$

$$\cos A - \cos B = -2\sin\left(\dfrac{A + B}{2}\right)\sin\left(\dfrac{A - B}{2}\right)$$

**6.5**    **Inverse trigonometric functions**

| $\sin^{-1}x$ or $\arcsin x$ | $\cos^{-1}x$ or $\arccos x$ |
|---|---|
| $\tan^{-1}x$ or $\arctan x$ | $\cot^{-1}x$ or $\operatorname{arccot} x$ |
| $\sec^{-1}x$ or $\operatorname{arcsec} x$ | $\csc^{-1}x$ or $\operatorname{arccsc} x$ |

Inverse sine function

**Definition**

$y = \sin^{-1}x$   means   $x = \sin y$

$-1 \le x \le 1$   and   $-\dfrac{\pi}{2} \le y \le \dfrac{\pi}{2}$

**Identities**

$\sin^{-1}(\sin x) = x$   for   $-\dfrac{\pi}{2} \le x \le \dfrac{\pi}{2}$

$\sin(\sin^{-1}x) = x$   for   $-1 \le x \le 1$

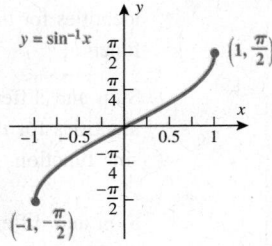

Inverse cosine function

**Definition**

$y = \cos^{-1}x$   means   $x = \cos y$

$-1 \le x \le 1$   and   $0 \le y \le \pi$

**Identities**

$\cos^{-1}(\cos x) = x$   for   $0 \le x \le \pi$

$\cos(\cos^{-1}x) = x$   for   $-1 \le x \le 1$

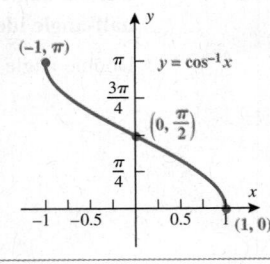

| SECTION | CONCEPT | KEY IDEAS/FORMULAS |
|---|---|---|

Inverse tangent function

**Definition**

$$y = \tan^{-1}x \quad \text{means} \quad x = \tan y$$

$$-\infty < x < \infty \quad \text{and} \quad -\frac{\pi}{2} < y < \frac{\pi}{2}$$

**Identities**

$$\tan^{-1}(\tan x) = x \quad \text{for} \quad -\frac{\pi}{2} < x < \frac{\pi}{2}$$

$$\tan(\tan^{-1}x) = x \quad \text{for} \quad -\infty < x < \infty$$

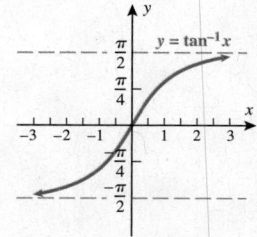

Remaining inverse trigonometric functions

**Inverse cotangent function**
**Definition**

$$y = \cot^{-1}x \quad \text{means} \quad x = \cot y$$

$$-\infty < x < \infty \quad \text{and} \quad 0 < y < \pi$$

**Identity**

$$\cot^{-1}x = \begin{cases} \tan^{-1}\left(\dfrac{1}{x}\right), x > 0 \\ \pi + \tan^{-1}\left(\dfrac{1}{x}\right), x < 0 \end{cases}$$

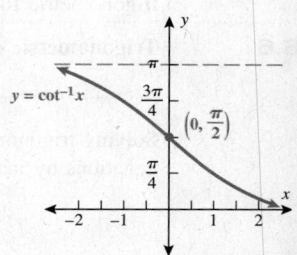

**Inverse secant function**
**Definition**

$$y = \sec^{-1}x \quad \text{means} \quad x = \sec y$$

$$x \le -1 \quad \text{or} \quad x \ge 1 \quad \text{and}$$

$$0 \le y < \frac{\pi}{2} \quad \text{or} \quad \frac{\pi}{2} < y \le \pi$$

**Identity**

$$\sec^{-1}x = \cos^{-1}\left(\frac{1}{x}\right) \quad \text{for} \quad x \le -1 \quad \text{or} \quad x \ge 1$$

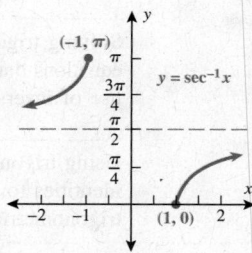

**Inverse cosecant function**

**Definition**

$y = \csc^{-1}x$   means   $x = \csc y$

$x \leq -1$   or   $x \geq 1$   and

$-\dfrac{\pi}{2} \leq y < 0$   or   $0 < y \leq \dfrac{\pi}{2}$

**Identity**

$\csc^{-1}x = \sin^{-1}\left(\dfrac{1}{x}\right)$

for   $x \leq -1$   or   $x \geq 1$

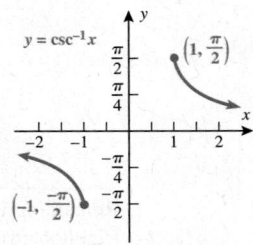

| | | |
| --- | --- | --- |
| | Finding exact values for expressions involving inverse trigonometric functions | |
| 6.6 | **Trigonometric equations** | Goal: Find the values of the variable that make the equation true. |
| | Solving trigonometric equations by inspection | Solve: $\sin\theta = \dfrac{\sqrt{2}}{2}$ on $0 \leq \theta \leq 2\pi$.<br><br>Answer: $\theta = \dfrac{\pi}{4}$   or   $\theta = \dfrac{3\pi}{4}$.<br><br>Solve: $\sin\theta = \dfrac{\sqrt{2}}{2}$ on all real numbers.<br><br>Answer: $\theta = \begin{cases} \dfrac{\pi}{4} + 2n\pi \\ \dfrac{3\pi}{4} + 2n\pi \end{cases}$   where $n$ is an integer. |
| | Solving trigonometric equations using algebraic techniques | Transform trigonometric equations into linear or quadratic algebraic equations by making a substitution such as $x = \sin\theta$. Then use algebraic methods for solving linear and quadratic equations. If an expression is squared, always check for extraneous solutions. |
| | Solving trigonometric equations that require the use of inverse functions | Follow the same procedures outlined by inspection or algebraic methods. Finding the solution requires the use of inverse functions and a calculator. Be careful: Calculators only give one solution (the one in the range of the inverse function). |
| | Using trigonometric identities to solve trigonometric equations | Use trigonometric identities to transform an equation with multiple trigonometric functions into an equation with only one trigonometric function. Then use the methods outlined above. |

## 6.1 Verifying Trigonometric Identities

**Use the cofunction identities to fill in the blanks.**

1. $\sin 30° = \cos$ _____

2. $\cos A = \sin$ _____

3. $\tan 45° = \cot$ _____

4. $\csc 60° = \sec$ _____

5. $\sec 30° = \csc$ _____

6. $\cot 60° = \tan$ _____

**Simplify the following trigonometric expressions:**

7. $\tan x(\cot x + \tan x)$

8. $(\sec x + 1)(\sec x - 1)$

9. $\dfrac{\tan^4 x - 1}{\tan^2 x - 1}$

10. $\sec^2 x(\cot^2 x - \cos^2 x)$

11. $\cos x[\cos(-x) - \tan(-x)] - \sin x$

12. $\dfrac{\tan^2 x + 1}{2\sec^2 x}$

13. $\dfrac{\csc^3(-x) + 8}{\csc x - 2}$

14. $\dfrac{\csc^2 x - 1}{\cot x}$

**Verify the trigonometric identities.**

15. $(\tan x + \cot x)^2 - 2 = \tan^2 x + \cot^2 x$

16. $\csc^2 x - \cot^2 x = 1$

17. $\dfrac{1}{\sin^2 x} - \dfrac{1}{\tan^2 x} = 1$

18. $\dfrac{1}{\csc x + 1} + \dfrac{1}{\csc x - 1} = \dfrac{2\tan x}{\cos x}$

19. $\dfrac{\tan^2 x - 1}{\sec^2 x + 3\tan x + 1} = \dfrac{\tan x - 1}{\tan x + 2}$

20. $\cot x(\sec x - \cos x) = \sin x$

**Determine whether each of the following equations is a conditional equation or an identity:**

21. $2\tan^2 x + 1 = \dfrac{1 + \sin^2 x}{\cos^2 x}$

22. $\sin x - \cos x = 0$

23. $\cot^2 x - 1 = \tan^2 x$

24. $\cos^2 x(1 + \cot^2 x) = \cot^2 x$

25. $\left(\cot x - \dfrac{1}{\tan x}\right)^2 = 0$

26. $\csc x + \sec x = \dfrac{1}{\sin x + \cos x}$

## 6.2 Sum and Difference Identities

**Find the exact value for each trigonometric expression.**

27. $\cos\left(\dfrac{7\pi}{12}\right)$

28. $\sin\left(\dfrac{\pi}{12}\right)$

29. $\tan(-15°)$

30. $\cot 105°$

**Write each expression as a single trigonometric function.**

31. $\sin(4x)\cos(3x) - \cos(4x)\sin(3x)$

32. $\sin(-x)\sin(-2x) + \cos(-x)\cos(-2x)$

33. $\dfrac{\tan(5x) - \tan(4x)}{1 + \tan(5x)\tan(4x)}$

34. $\dfrac{\tan\left(\dfrac{\pi}{4}\right) + \tan\left(\dfrac{\pi}{3}\right)}{1 - \tan\left(\dfrac{\pi}{4}\right)\tan\left(\dfrac{\pi}{3}\right)}$

**Find the exact value of the indicated expression using the given information and identities.**

35. Find the exact value of $\tan(\alpha - \beta)$ if $\sin\alpha = -\dfrac{3}{5}$, $\sin\beta = -\dfrac{24}{25}$, the terminal side of $\alpha$ lies in quadrant IV, and the terminal side of $\beta$ lies in quadrant III.

36. Find the exact value of $\cos(\alpha + \beta)$ if $\cos\alpha = -\dfrac{5}{13}$, $\sin\beta = \dfrac{7}{25}$, the terminal side of $\alpha$ lies in quadrant II, and the terminal side of $\beta$ also lies in quadrant II.

37. Find the exact value of $\cos(\alpha - \beta)$ if $\cos\alpha = \dfrac{9}{41}$, $\cos\beta = \dfrac{7}{25}$, the terminal side of $\alpha$ lies in quadrant IV, and the terminal side of $\beta$ lies in quadrant I.

38. Find the exact value of $\sin(\alpha - \beta)$ if $\sin\alpha = -\dfrac{5}{13}$, $\cos\beta = -\dfrac{4}{5}$, the terminal side of $\alpha$ lies in quadrant III, and the terminal side of $\beta$ lies in quadrant II.

**Determine whether each of the following equations is a conditional equation or an identity:**

39. $2\cos A\cos B = \cos(A + B) + \cos(A - B)$

40. $2\sin A\sin B = \cos(A - B) - \cos(A + B)$

**Graph the following functions:**

**41.** $y = \cos\left(\dfrac{\pi}{2}\right)\cos x - \sin\left(\dfrac{\pi}{2}\right)\sin x$

**42.** $y = \sin\left(\dfrac{2\pi}{3}\right)\cos x + \cos\left(\dfrac{2\pi}{3}\right)\sin x$

**43.** $y = \dfrac{2\tan\left(\dfrac{x}{3}\right)}{1 - \tan^2\left(\dfrac{x}{3}\right)}$

**44.** $y = \dfrac{\tan(\pi x) - \tan x}{1 + \tan(\pi x)\tan x}$

## 6.3 Double-Angle and Half-Angle Identities

**Use double-angle identities to answer the following questions:**

**45.** If $\sin x = \dfrac{3}{5}$ and $\dfrac{\pi}{2} < x < \pi$, find $\cos(2x)$.

**46.** If $\cos x = \dfrac{7}{25}$ and $\dfrac{3\pi}{2} < x < 2\pi$, find $\sin(2x)$.

**47.** If $\cot x = -\dfrac{11}{61}$ and $\dfrac{3\pi}{2} < x < 2\pi$, find $\tan(2x)$.

**48.** If $\tan x = -\dfrac{12}{5}$ and $\dfrac{\pi}{2} < x < \pi$, find $\cos(2x)$.

**49.** If $\sec x = \dfrac{25}{24}$ and $0 < x < \dfrac{\pi}{2}$, find $\sin(2x)$.

**50.** If $\csc x = \dfrac{5}{4}$ and $\dfrac{\pi}{2} < x < \pi$, find $\tan(2x)$.

**Simplify each of the following expressions. Evaluate exactly, if possible.**

**51.** $\cos^2 15° - \sin^2 15°$

**52.** $\dfrac{2\tan\left(-\dfrac{\pi}{12}\right)}{1 - \tan^2\left(-\dfrac{\pi}{12}\right)}$

**53.** $6\sin\left(\dfrac{\pi}{12}\right)\cos\left(\dfrac{\pi}{12}\right)$

**54.** $1 - 2\sin^2\left(\dfrac{\pi}{8}\right)$

**Verify the following identities:**

**55.** $\sin^3 A - \cos^3 A = (\sin A - \cos A)\left[1 + \tfrac{1}{2}\sin(2A)\right]$

**56.** $2\sin A\cos^3 A - 2\sin^3 A\cos A = \cos(2A)\sin(2A)$

**57.** $\tan A = \dfrac{\sin(2A)}{1 + \cos(2A)}$

**58.** $\tan A = \dfrac{1 - \cos(2A)}{\sin(2A)}$

**59. Launching a Missile.** When launching a missile for a given range, the minimum velocity needed is related to the angle $\theta$ of the launch, and the velocity is determined by $V = \dfrac{2\cos(2\theta)}{1 + \cos(2\theta)}$. Show that $V$ is equivalent to $1 - \tan^2\theta$.

**60. Launching a Missile.** When launching a missile for a given range, the minimum velocity needed is related to the angle $\theta$ of the launch, and the velocity is determined by $V = \dfrac{2\cos(2\theta)}{1 + \cos(2\theta)}$. Find the value of $V$ when $\theta = \dfrac{\pi}{6}$.

**Use half-angle identities to find the exact value of each of the following trigonometric expressions:**

**61.** $\sin(-22.5°)$

**62.** $\cos 67.5°$

**63.** $\cot\left(\dfrac{3\pi}{8}\right)$

**64.** $\csc\left(-\dfrac{7\pi}{8}\right)$

**65.** $\sec(-165°)$

**66.** $\tan(-75°)$

**Use half-angle identities to find each of the following values:**

**67.** If $\sin x = -\dfrac{7}{25}$ and $\pi < x < \dfrac{3\pi}{2}$, find $\sin\left(\dfrac{x}{2}\right)$.

**68.** If $\cos x = -\dfrac{4}{5}$ and $\dfrac{\pi}{2} < x < \pi$, find $\cos\left(\dfrac{x}{2}\right)$.

**69.** If $\tan x = \dfrac{40}{9}$ and $\pi < x < \dfrac{3\pi}{2}$, find $\tan\left(\dfrac{x}{2}\right)$.

**70.** If $\sec x = \dfrac{17}{15}$ and $\dfrac{3\pi}{2} < x < 2\pi$, find $\sin\left(\dfrac{x}{2}\right)$.

**Simplify each expression using half-angle identities. Do not evaluate.**

**71.** $\sqrt{\dfrac{1 - \cos\left(\dfrac{\pi}{6}\right)}{2}}$

**72.** $\sqrt{\dfrac{1 - \cos\left(\dfrac{11\pi}{6}\right)}{1 + \cos\left(\dfrac{11\pi}{6}\right)}}$

**Verify each of the following identities:**

**73.** $\left[\sin\left(\dfrac{A}{2}\right) + \cos\left(\dfrac{A}{2}\right)\right]^2 = 1 + \sin A$

**74.** $\sec^2\left(\dfrac{A}{2}\right) + \tan^2\left(\dfrac{A}{2}\right) = \dfrac{3 - \cos A}{1 + \cos A}$

**75.** $\csc^2\left(\dfrac{A}{2}\right) + \cot^2\left(\dfrac{A}{2}\right) = \dfrac{3 + \cos A}{1 - \cos A}$

**76.** $\tan^2\left(\dfrac{A}{2}\right) + 1 = \sec^2\left(\dfrac{A}{2}\right)$

Graph each of the following functions.
*Hint:* Use trigonometric identities first.

**77.** $y = \sqrt{\dfrac{1 - \cos\left(\dfrac{\pi}{12}x\right)}{2}}$

**78.** $y = \cos^2\left(\dfrac{x}{2}\right) - \sin^2\left(\dfrac{x}{2}\right)$

**79.** $y = -\sqrt{\dfrac{1 - \cos x}{1 + \cos x}}$

**80.** $y = \sqrt{\dfrac{1 + \cos(3x - 1)}{2}}$

## 6.4 Product-to-Sum and Sum-to-Product Identities

Write each product as a sum or difference of sines and/or cosines.

**81.** $6\sin(5x)\cos(2x)$      **82.** $3\sin(4x)\sin(2x)$

Write each expression as a product of sines and/or cosines.

**83.** $\cos(5x) - \cos(3x)$      **84.** $\sin\left(\dfrac{5x}{2}\right) + \sin\left(\dfrac{3x}{2}\right)$

**85.** $\sin\left(\dfrac{4x}{3}\right) - \sin\left(\dfrac{2x}{3}\right)$      **86.** $\cos(7x) + \cos x$

Simplify each trigonometric expression.

**87.** $\dfrac{\cos(8x) + \cos(2x)}{\sin(8x) - \sin(2x)}$

**88.** $\dfrac{\sin(5x) + \sin(3x)}{\cos(5x) + \cos(3x)}$

Verify the identities.

**89.** $\dfrac{\sin A + \sin B}{\cos A - \cos B} = -\cot\left(\dfrac{A - B}{2}\right)$

**90.** $\dfrac{\sin A - \sin B}{\cos A - \cos B} = -\cot\left(\dfrac{A + B}{2}\right)$

**91.** $\csc\left(\dfrac{A - B}{2}\right) = \dfrac{2\sin\left(\dfrac{A + B}{2}\right)}{\cos B - \cos A}$

**92.** $\sec\left(\dfrac{A + B}{2}\right) = \dfrac{2\sin\left(\dfrac{A - B}{2}\right)}{\sin A - \sin B}$

## 6.5 Inverse Trigonometric Functions

Find the exact value of each expression. Give the answer in radians.

**93.** $\arctan 1$      **94.** $\operatorname{arccsc}(-2)$

**95.** $\cos^{-1}0$      **96.** $\sin^{-1}(-1)$

**97.** $\sec^{-1}\left(\dfrac{2}{\sqrt{3}}\right)$      **98.** $\cot^{-1}\left(-\sqrt{3}\right)$

Find the exact value of each expression. Give the answer in degrees.

**99.** $\csc^{-1}(-1)$      **100.** $\arctan(-1)$

**101.** $\operatorname{arccot}\left(\dfrac{\sqrt{3}}{3}\right)$      **102.** $\cos^{-1}\left(\dfrac{\sqrt{2}}{2}\right)$

**103.** $\sin^{-1}\left(-\dfrac{\sqrt{3}}{2}\right)$      **104.** $\sec^{-1}1$

Use a calculator to evaluate each expression. Give the answer in degrees and round to two decimal places.

**105.** $\sin^{-1}(-0.6088)$      **106.** $\tan^{-1}(1.1918)$

**107.** $\sec^{-1}(1.0824)$      **108.** $\cot^{-1}(-3.7321)$

Use a calculator to evaluate each expression. Give the answer in radians and round to two decimal places.

**109.** $\cos^{-1}(-0.1736)$      **110.** $\tan^{-1}(0.1584)$

**111.** $\csc^{-1}(-10.0167)$      **112.** $\sec^{-1}(-1.1223)$

Evaluate each expression exactly, if possible. If not possible, state why.

**113.** $\sin^{-1}\left[\sin\left(-\dfrac{\pi}{4}\right)\right]$      **114.** $\cos\left[\cos^{-1}\left(-\dfrac{\sqrt{2}}{2}\right)\right]$

**115.** $\tan\left[\tan^{-1}\left(-\sqrt{3}\right)\right]$      **116.** $\cot^{-1}\left[\cot\left(\dfrac{11\pi}{6}\right)\right]$

**117.** $\csc^{-1}\left[\csc\left(\dfrac{2\pi}{3}\right)\right]$      **118.** $\sec\left[\sec^{-1}\left(-\dfrac{2\sqrt{3}}{3}\right)\right]$

Evaluate each expression exactly.

**119.** $\sin\left[\cos^{-1}\left(\dfrac{11}{61}\right)\right]$      **120.** $\cos\left[\tan^{-1}\left(\dfrac{40}{9}\right)\right]$

**121.** $\tan\left[\cot^{-1}\left(\dfrac{6}{7}\right)\right]$      **122.** $\cot\left[\sec^{-1}\left(\dfrac{25}{7}\right)\right]$

**123.** $\sec\left[\sin^{-1}\left(\dfrac{1}{6}\right)\right]$      **124.** $\csc\left[\cot^{-1}\left(\dfrac{5}{12}\right)\right]$

## 6.6 Trigonometric Equations

Solve the given trigonometric equation on the indicated interval.

**125.** $\sin(2\theta) = -\dfrac{\sqrt{3}}{2}, 0 \le \theta \le 2\pi$

**126.** $\sec\left(\dfrac{\theta}{2}\right) = 2, -2\pi \le \theta \le 2\pi$

**127.** $\sin\left(\dfrac{\theta}{2}\right) = -\dfrac{\sqrt{2}}{2}, -2\pi \le \theta \le 2\pi$

**128.** $\csc(2\theta) = 2, 0 \le \theta \le 2\pi$

**129.** $\tan\left(\dfrac{1}{3}\theta\right) = -1, 0 \le \theta \le 6\pi$

**130.** $\cot(4\theta) = -\sqrt{3}, -\pi \le \theta \le \pi$

Solve each trigonometric equation exactly on $0 \le \theta \le 2\pi$.

**131.** $4\cos(2\theta) + 2 = 0$

**132.** $\sqrt{3}\tan\left(\dfrac{\theta}{2}\right) - 1 = 0$

**133.** $2\tan(2\theta) + 2 = 0$

**134.** $2\sin^2\theta + \sin\theta - 1 = 0$

**135.** $\tan^2\theta + \tan\theta = 0$

**136.** $\sec^2\theta - 3\sec\theta + 2 = 0$

Solve the given trigonometric equations on $0° \le \theta \le 360°$ and express the answer in degrees to two decimal places.

**137.** $\tan(2\theta) = -0.3459$     **138.** $6\sin\theta - 5 = 0$

**139.** $4\cos^2\theta + 3\cos\theta = 0$     **140.** $12\cos^2\theta - 7\cos\theta + 1 = 0$

**141.** $\csc^2\theta - 3\csc\theta - 1 = 0$   **142.** $2\cot^2\theta + 5\cot\theta - 4 = 0$

Solve each trigonometric equation exactly on the interval $0 \le \theta \le 2\pi$.

**143.** $\sec x = 2\sin x$     **144.** $3\tan x + \cot x = 2\sqrt{3}$

**145.** $\sqrt{3}\tan x - \sec x = 1$     **146.** $2\sin(2x) = \cot x$

**147.** $\sqrt{3}\tan x = 2\sin x$     **148.** $2\sin x = 3\cot x$

**149.** $\cos^2 x + \sin x + 1 = 0$     **150.** $2\cos^2 x - \sqrt{3}\cos x = 0$

**151.** $\cos(2x) + 4\cos x + 3 = 0$  **152.** $\sin(2x) + \sin x = 0$

**153.** $\tan^2\left(\frac{1}{2}x\right) - 1 = 0$     **154.** $\cot^2\left(\frac{1}{3}x\right) - 1 = 0$

Solve each trigonometric equation on $0° \le \theta \le 360°$. Give the answers in degrees and round to two decimal places.

**155.** $\csc^2 x + \cot x = 1$     **156.** $8\cos^2 x + 6\sin x = 9$

**157.** $\sin^2 x + 2 = 2\cos x$     **158.** $\cos(2x) = 3\sin x - 1$

**159.** $\cos x - 1 = \cos(2x)$     **160.** $12\cos^2 x + 4\sin x = 11$

## Technology Exercises

### Section 6.1

**161.** Is $\cos 73° = \sqrt{1 - \sin^2 73°}$? Use a calculator to find each of the following:

  **a.** $\cos 73°$

  **b.** $1 - \sin 73°$

  **c.** $\sqrt{1 - \sin^2 73°}$

  Which results are the same?

**162.** Is $\csc 28° = \sqrt{1 + \cot^2 28°}$? Use a calculator to find each of the following:

  **a.** $\cot 28°$

  **b.** $1 + \cot 28°$

  **c.** $\sqrt{1 + \cot^2 28°}$

  Which results are the same?

### Section 6.2

Recall that the difference quotient for a function $f$ is given by
$$\dfrac{f(x + h) + f(x)}{h}.$$

**163.** Show that the difference quotient for $f(x) = \sin(3x)$ is
$$[\cos(3x)]\left[\dfrac{\sin(3h)}{h}\right] - [\sin(3x)]\left[\dfrac{1 - \cos(3h)}{h}\right].$$

Plot $Y_1 = [\cos(3x)]\left[\dfrac{\sin(3h)}{h}\right] - [\sin(3x)]\left[\dfrac{1 - \cos(3h)}{h}\right]$

for

  **a.** $h = 1$

  **b.** $h = 0.1$

  **c.** $h = 0.01$

What function does the difference quotient for $f(x) = \sin(3x)$ resemble when $h$ approaches zero?

**164.** Show that the difference quotient for $f(x) = \cos(3x)$ is
$$[-\sin(3x)]\left[\dfrac{\sin(3h)}{h}\right] - [\cos(3x)]\left[\dfrac{1 - \cos(3h)}{h}\right].$$

Plot $Y_1 = [-\sin(3x)]\left[\dfrac{\sin(3h)}{h}\right] - [\cos(3x)]\left[\dfrac{1 - \cos(3h)}{h}\right]$

for

  **a.** $h = 1$

  **b.** $h = 0.1$

  **c.** $h = 0.01$

What function does the difference quotient for $f(x) = \cos(3x)$ resemble when $h$ approaches zero?

## Section 6.3

**165.** With a graphing calculator, plot $Y_1 = \tan(2x)$, $Y_2 = 2\tan x$, and $Y_3 = \dfrac{2\tan x}{1 - \tan^2 x}$ in the same viewing rectangle $[-2\pi, 2\pi]$ by $[-10, 10]$. Which graphs are the same?

**166.** With a graphing calculator, plot $Y_1 = \cos(2x)$, $Y_2 = 2\cos x$, and $Y_3 = 1 - 2\sin^2 x$ in the same viewing rectangle $[-2\pi, 2\pi]$ by $[-2, 2]$. Which graphs are the same?

**167.** With a graphing calculator, plot $Y_1 = \cos\left(\dfrac{x}{2}\right)$, $Y_2 = \dfrac{1}{2}\cos x$, and $Y_3 = -\sqrt{\dfrac{1 + \cos x}{2}}$ in the same viewing rectangle $[\pi, 2\pi]$ by $[-1, 1]$. Which graphs are the same?

**168.** With a graphing calculator, plot $Y_1 = \sin\left(\dfrac{x}{2}\right)$, $Y_2 = \dfrac{1}{2}\sin x$, and $Y_3 = -\sqrt{\dfrac{1 - \cos x}{2}}$ in the same viewing rectangle $[2\pi, 4\pi]$ by $[-1, 1]$. Which graphs are the same?

## Section 6.4

**169.** With a graphing calculator, plot $Y_1 = \sin(5x)\cos(3x)$, $Y_2 = \sin(4x)$, and $Y_3 = \frac{1}{2}[\sin(8x) + \sin(2x)]$ in the same viewing rectangle $[0, 2\pi]$ by $[-1, 1]$. Which graphs are the same?

**170.** With a graphing calculator, plot $Y_1 = \sin(3x)\cos(5x)$, $Y_2 = \cos(4x)$, and $Y_3 = \frac{1}{2}[\sin(8x) - \sin(2x)]$ in the same viewing rectangle $[0, 2\pi]$ by $[-1, 1]$. Which graphs are the same?

## Section 6.5

**171.** Given $\cos x = -\dfrac{1}{\sqrt{5}}$ and $\dfrac{\pi}{2} < x < \pi$:

   **a.** Find $\cos(2x)$ using the double-angle identity.
   **b.** Use the inverse of cosine to find $x$ in quadrant II and to find $\cos(2x)$.
   **c.** Are the results in (a) and (b) the same?

**172.** Given $\cos x = \dfrac{5}{12}$ and $\dfrac{3\pi}{2} < x < 2\pi$:

   **a.** Find $\cos\left(\frac{1}{2}x\right)$ using the half-angle identity.
   **b.** Use the inverse of cosine to find $x$ in quadrant IV and to find $\cos\left(\frac{1}{2}x\right)$. Round to five decimal places.
   **c.** Are the results in (a) and (b) the same?

## Section 6.6

**Find the smallest positive value of $x$ that makes each statement true. Give the answer in radians and round to four decimal places.**

**173.** $\ln x + \sin x = 0$

**174.** $\ln x + \cos x = 0$

1. For what values of $x$ does the quotient identity

   $\tan x = \dfrac{\sin x}{\cos x}$ not hold?

2. Is the equation $\sqrt{\sin^2 x + \cos^2 x} = \sin x + \cos x$ a conditional equation or an identity?

3. Evaluate $\sin\left(-\dfrac{\pi}{8}\right)$ exactly.

4. Evaluate $\tan\left(\dfrac{7\pi}{12}\right)$ exactly.

5. If $\cos x = \dfrac{2}{5}$ and $\dfrac{3\pi}{2} < x < 2\pi$, find $\sin\left(\dfrac{x}{2}\right)$.

6. If $\sin x = -\dfrac{1}{5}$ and $\pi < x < \dfrac{3\pi}{2}$, find $\cos(2x)$.

7. Write $\cos(7x)\cos(3x) - \sin(3x)\sin(7x)$ as a cosine or sine of a sum or difference.

8. Write $-\dfrac{2\tan x}{1 - \tan^2 x}$ as a single tangent function.

9. Write $\sqrt{\dfrac{1 + \cos(a + b)}{2}}$ as a single cosine function if $a + b$ is an angle in quadrant II. $\left(\text{Assume } \dfrac{\pi}{2} < a + b < \pi.\right)$

10. Write $2\sin\left(\dfrac{x + 3}{2}\right)\cos\left(\dfrac{x - 3}{2}\right)$ as a sum of two sine functions.

11. Write $10\cos(3 - x) + 10\cos(x + 3)$ as a product of two cosine functions.

12. In the expression $\sqrt{9 - u^2}$, let $u = 3\sin x$. What is the resulting expression?

**Solve the trigonometric equations exactly, if possible. Otherwise, use a calculator to approximate solution(s).**

13. $2\sin\theta = -\sqrt{3}$ on all real numbers.

14. $2\cos^2\theta + \cos\theta - 1 = 0$ on $0 \le \theta \le 2\pi$

15. $\sin 2\theta = \dfrac{1}{2}\cos\theta$ over $0 \le \theta \le 360°$

16. $\sqrt{\sin x + \cos x} = -1$ over $0 \le \theta \le 2\pi$

17. Determine whether $(1 + \cot x)^2 = \csc^2 x$ is a conditional or an identity.

18. Evaluate $\csc\left(-\dfrac{\pi}{12}\right)$ exactly.

19. If $\sin x = -\dfrac{5}{13}$ and $\pi < x < \dfrac{3\pi}{2}$, find $\cos\left(\dfrac{x}{2}\right)$.

20. If $\cos x = -0.26$ and $\dfrac{\pi}{2} < x < \pi$, find $\sin(2x)$.

21. Express $y = \sqrt{\dfrac{1 + \dfrac{\sqrt{2}}{2}\left[\cos\left(\dfrac{\pi}{3}x\right) + \sin\left(\dfrac{\pi}{3}x\right)\right]}{1 - \dfrac{\sqrt{2}}{2}\left[\cos\left(\dfrac{\pi}{3}x\right) + \sin\left(\dfrac{\pi}{3}x\right)\right]}}$

   as a cotangent function.

22. Calculate $\csc\left(\csc^{-1}\sqrt{2}\right)$.

23. Determine an interval on which $f(x) = a + b\csc(\pi x + c)$ is one-to-one, and determine the inverse of $f(x)$ on this interval. Assume that $a$, $b$, and $c$ are all positive.

24. Find the range of $y = -\dfrac{\pi}{4} + \arctan(2x - 3)$.

25. Solve $\cos\left(\dfrac{\pi}{4}\theta\right) = -\dfrac{1}{2}$, for all real numbers.

26. Solve $\sqrt{\dfrac{1 - \cos(2\pi x)}{1 + \cos(2\pi x)}} = -\dfrac{1}{\sqrt{3}}$, for all real numbers.

27. Solve $\dfrac{\sqrt{3}}{\csc\left(\dfrac{x}{3}\right)} = \cos\left(\dfrac{x}{3}\right)$, for all real numbers.

28. Show that the difference quotient for $f(x) = \cos\left(\frac{1}{2}x\right)$ is

    $$-\sin\left(\frac{1}{2}x\right)\left[\frac{\sin\left(\frac{1}{2}h\right)}{h}\right] - \cos\left(\frac{1}{2}x\right)\left[\frac{1 - \cos\left(\frac{1}{2}h\right)}{h}\right].$$

    Plot $Y_1 = -\sin\left(\frac{1}{2}x\right)\left[\dfrac{\sin\left(\frac{1}{2}h\right)}{h}\right] - \cos(2x)\left[\dfrac{1 - \cos\left(\frac{1}{2}h\right)}{h}\right]$

    for

    a. $h = 1$

    b. $h = 0.1$

    c. $h = 0.01$

    What function does the difference quotient for $f(x) = \cos\left(\frac{1}{2}x\right)$ resemble when $h$ approaches zero?

29. Given $\tan x = \dfrac{3}{4}$ and $\pi < x < \dfrac{3\pi}{2}$:

    a. Find $\sin\left(\frac{1}{2}x\right)$ using the half-angle identity.

    b. Use the inverse of tangent to find $x$ in quadrant III and to find $\sin\left(\frac{1}{2}x\right)$. Round to five decimal places.

    c. Are the results in (a) and (b) the same?

1. Find the exact value of the following trigonometric functions:

   a. $\sin\left(\dfrac{7\pi}{3}\right)$

   b. $\tan\left(-\dfrac{5\pi}{3}\right)$

   c. $\csc\left(\dfrac{11\pi}{6}\right)$

2. Find the exact value of the following trigonometric functions:

   a. $\sec\left(\dfrac{5\pi}{6}\right)$

   b. $\cos\left(-\dfrac{3\pi}{4}\right)$

   c. $\cot\left(\dfrac{7\pi}{6}\right)$

3. Find the exact value of the following inverse trigonometric functions:

   a. $\cos^{-1}\left(-\dfrac{1}{2}\right)$

   b. $\csc^{-1}(-2)$

   c. $\cot\left(-\sqrt{3}\right)$

4. For the relation $x^2 - y^2 = 25$, determine whether $y$ is a function of $x$.

5. Determine whether the function $g(x) = \sqrt{2 - x^2}$ is odd or even.

6. For the function $y = 5(x - 4)^2$, identify all of the transformations of $y = x^2$.

7. Find the composite function, $f \circ g$, and state the domain for $f(x) = x^3 - 1$ and $g(x) = \dfrac{1}{x}$.

8. Find the inverse of the function $f(x) = \sqrt[3]{x} - 1$.

9. Find the vertex of the parabola associated with the quadratic function $f(x) = \frac{1}{4}x^2 + \frac{3}{5}x - \frac{6}{25}$.

10. Find a polynomial of minimum degree that has the zeros $x = -\sqrt{7}$ (multiplicity 2), $x = 0$ (multiplicity 3), $x = \sqrt{7}$ (multiplicity 2).

11. Use long division to find the quotient $Q(x)$ and the remainder $r(x)$ of $(5x^3 - 4x^2 + 3) \div (x^2 + 1)$.

12. Given the zero $x = 4i$ of the polynomial $P(x) = x^4 + 2x^3 + x^2 + 32x - 240$, determine all the other zeros and write the polynomial in terms of a product of linear factors.

13. Find the vertical and horizontal asymptotes of the function $f(x) = \dfrac{0.7x^2 - 5x + 11}{x^2 - x - 6}$.

14. If $5400 is invested at 2.25% compounded continuously, how much is in the account after 4 years?

15. Use interval notation to express the domain of the function $f(x) = \log_4(x + 3)$.

16. Use properties of logarithms to simplify the expression $\log_\pi 1$.

17. Give an exact solution to the logarithmic equation $\log_5(x + 2) + \log_5(6 - x) = \log_5(3x)$.

18. If money is invested in a savings account earning 4% compounded continuously, how many years will it take for the money to triple?

19. Use a calculator to evaluate $\cos 62°$. Round the answer to four decimal places.

20. **Angle of Inclination (Skiing).** The angle of inclination of a mountain with triple black diamond ski trails is 63°. If a skier at the top of the mountain is at an elevation of 4200 feet, how long is the ski run from the top to the base of the mountain?

21. Convert $-105°$ to radians. Leave the answer in terms of $\pi$.

22. Find all of the exact values of $\theta$, when $\tan\theta = 1$ and $0 \le \theta \le 2\pi$.

23. Determine whether the equation $\cos^2 x - \sin^2 x = 1$ is a conditional equation or an identity.

24. Simplify $\dfrac{2\tan\left(-\dfrac{\pi}{8}\right)}{1 - \tan^2\left(-\dfrac{\pi}{8}\right)}$ and evaluate exactly.

25. Evaluate exactly the expression $\tan\left[\sin^{-1}\left(\dfrac{5}{13}\right)\right]$.

26. With a graphing calculator, plot $Y_1 = \sin x \cos(3x)$, $Y_2 = \cos(4x)$, and $Y_3 = \frac{1}{2}[\sin(4x) - \sin(2x)]$ in the same viewing rectangle $[0, 2\pi]$ by $[-1, 1]$. Which graphs are the same?

27. Find the smallest positive value of $x$ that makes the statement true. Give the answer in radians and round to four decimal places.

$$\ln x - \sin(2x) = 0$$

# 7

# Vectors, the Complex Plane, and Polar Coordinates

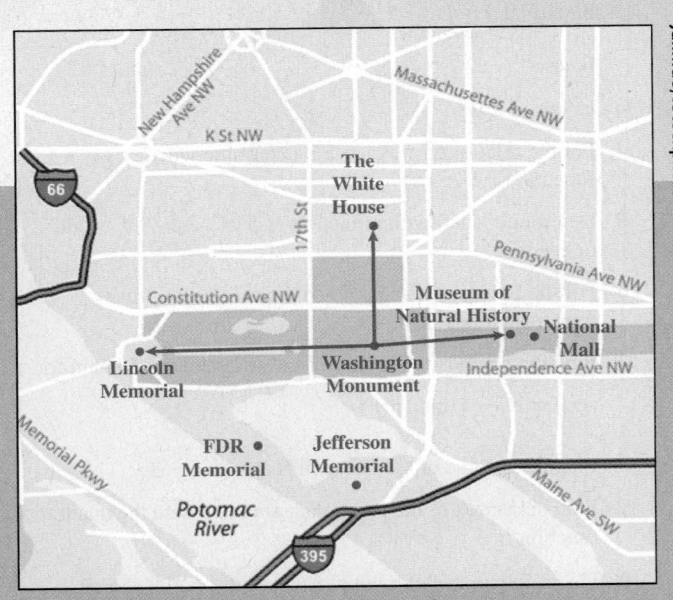

A coordinate system is used to locate a point in a plane. In the Cartesian plane, rectangular coordinates $(x, y)$ are used to describe the location of a point. For example, we can say that the Museum of Natural History in Washington, D.C., is at the corner of Constitution Avenue and 12th Street. But we can also describe the location of the Museum of Natural History as being $\frac{1}{4}$ mile east-northeast of the Washington Monument. Instead of using a grid of streets running east-west and north-south, it is sometimes more convenient to give a location with respect to a distance and direction from a fixed point. In the *polar coordinate system*, the location of a point is given in *polar coordinates* as $(r, \theta)$, where $r$ is the distance and $\theta$ is the direction angle of the point from a fixed reference point (origin).

IN THIS CHAPTER vectors will be defined and combined with the Law of Sines and the Law of Cosines to find resulting velocity and force vectors. The dot product (product of two vectors) is defined and used in physical problems like calculating work. Trigonometric functions are then used to define complex numbers in polar form. Lastly, we define polar coordinates and examine polar equations and their corresponding graphs.

# VECTORS, THE COMPLEX PLANE, AND POLAR COORDINATES

## 7.1 Vectors

## 7.2 The Dot Product

## 7.3 Polar (Trigonometric) Form of Complex Numbers

## 7.4 Products, Quotients, Powers, and Roots of Complex Numbers

## 7.5 Polar Coordinates and Graphs of Polar Equations

- Magnitude and Direction of Vectors
- Vector Operations
- Horizontal and Vertical Components of a Vector
- Unit Vectors
- Resultant Vectors

- The Dot Product
- Angle Between Two Vectors
- Work

- Complex Numbers in Rectangular Form
- Complex Numbers in Polar Form

- Products of Complex Numbers
- Quotients of Complex Numbers
- Powers of Complex Numbers
- Roots of Complex Numbers

- Polar Coordinates
- Converting Between Polar and Rectangular Coordinates
- Graphs of Polar Equations

## LEARNING OBJECTIVES

- Find the direction and magnitude of a vector.
- Find the dot product of two vectors.
- Express complex numbers in polar form.
- Use De Moivre's theorem to find a complex number raised to a power.
- Convert between rectangular and polar coordinates.

## Magnitude and Direction of Vectors

What is the difference between velocity and speed? Speed (55 miles per hour) has only *magnitude*, whereas velocity (55 miles per hour west) has both *magnitude* and *direction*. We use **scalars**, which are real numbers, to denote magnitudes such as speed and mass. We use **vectors**, which have magnitude *and* direction, to denote quantities such as velocity (speed in a certain direction) and force (weight in a certain direction).

A vector quantity is geometrically denoted by a **directed line segment**, which is a line segment with an arrow representing direction. There are many ways to denote a vector. For example, the vector shown in the margin can be denoted as $\mathbf{u}$, $\vec{u}$, or $\overrightarrow{AB}$, where $A$ is the **initial point** and $B$ is the **terminal point**.

It is customary in books to use the bold letter to represent a vector and when handwritten (as in your class notes and homework) to use the arrow on top to denote a vector.

In this section, we will limit our discussion to vectors in a plane (two-dimensional). It is important to note that geometric representation can be extended to three dimensions and algebraic representation can be extended to any higher dimension, as you will see in the exercises.

### Geometric Interpretation of Vectors

The *magnitude* of a vector can be denoted one of two ways: $|\mathbf{u}|$ or $\|\mathbf{u}\|$. We will use the former notation.

**Study Tip**

The magnitude of a vector is the distance between the initial and terminal points of the vector.

> **MAGNITUDE: |U|**
>
> The **magnitude** of a vector $\mathbf{u}$, denoted $|\mathbf{u}|$, is the length of the directed line segment, that is the distance between the initial and terminal points of the vector.

Two vectors have the **same direction** if they are parallel and point in the same direction. Two vectors have **opposite direction** if they are parallel and point in opposite directions.

> **EQUAL VECTORS: U = V**
>
> Two vectors $\mathbf{u}$ and $\mathbf{v}$ are **equal** ($\mathbf{u} = \mathbf{v}$) if and only if they have the same magnitude ($|\mathbf{u}| = |\mathbf{v}|$) and the same direction.

| Equal Vectors $\mathbf{u} = \mathbf{v}$ | Same Magnitude but Opposite Direction $\mathbf{u} = -\mathbf{v}$ | Same Magnitude $|\mathbf{u}| = |\mathbf{v}|$ | Different Magnitude | Same Direction Different Magnitude |
|---|---|---|---|---|

It is important to note that vectors do not have to coincide to be equal.

**VECTOR ADDITION: U + V**

Two vectors, **u** and **v**, can be added together using either of the following approaches:

- The **tail-to-tip** (or head-to-tail) method: Sketch the initial point of one vector at the terminal point of the other vector. The **sum, u + v,** is the **resultant** vector from the tail end of **u** to the tip end of **v**.

  [or]

- The parallelogram method: Sketch the initial points of the vectors at the same point. The sum **u + v** is the diagonal of the parallelogram formed by **u** and **v**.

The difference, **u − v,** is the

- Resultant vector from the tip of **v** to the tip of **u,** when the tails of **v** and **u** coincide.

  [or]

- The other diagonal formed by the parallelogram method.

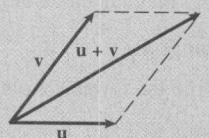

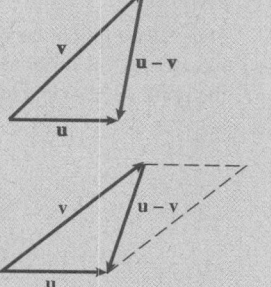

> **Study Tip**
>
> Equal vectors can be translated (shifted) so that they coincide.

## Algebraic Interpretation of Vectors

Since vectors that have the same direction and magnitude are equal, any vector can be translated to an equal vector with its initial point located at the origin in the Cartesian plane. Therefore, we will now consider vectors in a rectangular coordinate system.

A vector with its initial point at the origin is called a **position vector**, or a vector in **standard position**. A position vector **u** with its terminal point at the point $(a, b)$ is denoted:

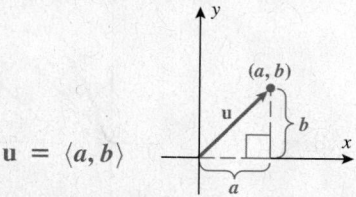

$$\mathbf{u} = \langle a, b \rangle$$

where the real numbers $a$ and $b$ are called the **components** of vector **u**.

Notice the subtle difference between coordinate notation and vector notation. The point is denoted with parentheses, $(a, b)$, whereas the vector is denoted with angled brackets, $\langle a, b \rangle$. The notation $\langle a, b \rangle$ denotes a vector whose initial point is $(0, 0)$ and terminal point is $(a, b)$.

The vector with initial point $(3, 4)$ and terminal point $(8, 10)$ is equal to the vector $\langle 5, 6 \rangle$, which has initial point $(0, 0)$ and terminal point $(5, 6)$.

Recall that the geometric definition of the *magnitude* of a vector is the *length* of the vector.

## MAGNITUDE: |u|

The **magnitude** (or norm) of a vector, $\mathbf{u} = \langle a, b \rangle$, is

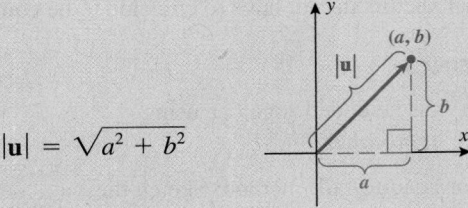

$$|\mathbf{u}| = \sqrt{a^2 + b^2}$$

### EXAMPLE 1   Finding the Magnitude of a Vector

Find the magnitude of the vector $\mathbf{u} = \langle 3, -4 \rangle$.

**Solution:**

Write the formula for magnitude of a vector.    $|\mathbf{u}| = \sqrt{a^2 + b^2}$

Let $a = 3$ and $b = -4$.    $|\mathbf{u}| = \sqrt{3^2 + (-4)^2}$

Simplify.    $|\mathbf{u}| = \boxed{\sqrt{25} = 5}$

*Note:* If we graph the vector $\mathbf{u} = \langle 3, -4 \rangle$, we see that the distance from the origin to the point $(3, -4)$ is five units.

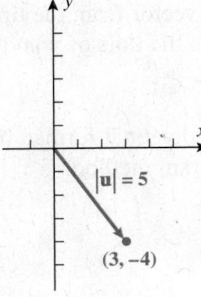

■ **Answer:** $\sqrt{26}$

■ **YOUR TURN** Find the magnitude of the vector $\mathbf{v} = \langle -1, 5 \rangle$.

## DIRECTION ANGLE OF A VECTOR

The positive angle between the $x$-axis and a position vector is called the **direction angle**, denoted $\theta$.

$$\tan \theta = \frac{b}{a}, \text{ where } a \neq 0$$

## EXAMPLE 2  Finding the Direction Angle of a Vector

Find the direction angle of the vector $\mathbf{v} = \langle -1, 5 \rangle$.

**Solution:**

Start with $\tan\theta = \dfrac{b}{a}$ and let $a = -1$ and $b = 5$.

$\tan\theta = \dfrac{5}{-1}$

With a calculator, approximate $\tan^{-1}(-5)$.

$\tan^{-1}(-5) \approx -78.7°$

The calculator gives a **quadrant IV** angle.

The point $(-1, 5)$ lies in quadrant II.

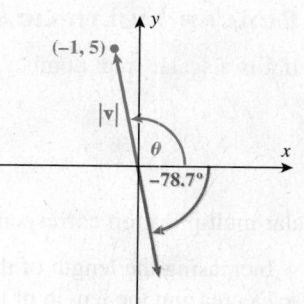

Add 180°.

$\theta = -78.7° + 180° = 101.3°$

$\boxed{\theta = 101.3°}$

**Technology Tip**

Use the calculator to find $\theta$.

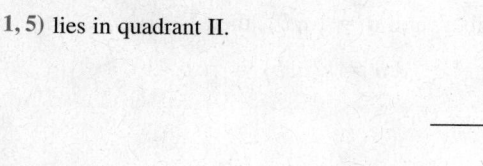

tan⁻¹( -5)
      -78.69006753

■ **YOUR TURN**  Find the direction angle of the vector $\mathbf{u} = \langle 3, -4 \rangle$.

■ **Answer:** 306.9°

Recall that two vectors are equal if they have the same magnitude and direction. Algebraically, this corresponds to their corresponding vector components ($a$ and $b$) being equal.

### EQUAL VECTORS: U = V

The vectors $\mathbf{u} = \langle a, b \rangle$ and $\mathbf{v} = \langle c, d \rangle$ are **equal** (that is, $\mathbf{u} = \mathbf{v}$) if and only if $a = c$ and $b = d$.

# Vector Operations

Vector addition is done geometrically with the tail-to-tip rule. Algebraically, vector addition is performed component by component.

### VECTOR ADDITION: U + V

If $\mathbf{u} = \langle a, b \rangle$ and $\mathbf{v} = \langle c, d \rangle$, then $\mathbf{u} + \mathbf{v} = \langle a + c, b + d \rangle$.

## EXAMPLE 3  Adding Vectors

Let $\mathbf{u} = \langle 2, -7 \rangle$ and $\mathbf{v} = \langle -3, 4 \rangle$. Find $\mathbf{u} + \mathbf{v}$.

**Solution:**

Let $\mathbf{u} = \langle 2, -7 \rangle$ and $\mathbf{v} = \langle -3, 4 \rangle$
in the addition formula.

$\mathbf{u} + \mathbf{v} = \langle 2 + (-3), -7 + 4 \rangle$

Simplify.

$\mathbf{u} + \mathbf{v} = \boxed{\langle -1, -3 \rangle}$

■ **YOUR TURN**  Let $\mathbf{u} = \langle 1, 2 \rangle$ and $\mathbf{v} = \langle -5, -4 \rangle$. Find $\mathbf{u} + \mathbf{v}$.

■ **Answer:** $\mathbf{u} + \mathbf{v} = \langle -4, -2 \rangle$

We now summarize vector operations. As we have seen, addition and subtraction are performed algebraically component by component. Multiplication, however, is not as straightforward. To perform **scalar multiplication** of a vector (to multiply a vector by a real number), we multiply each component by the scalar. In Section 7.2, we will study a form of multiplication for two vectors that is defined as long as the vectors have the same number of components; it gives a result known as the *dot product*, and is useful in solving common problems in physics.

### SCALAR MULTIPLICATION: $k\mathbf{u}$

If $k$ is a scalar (real number) and $\mathbf{u} = \langle a, b \rangle$, then

$$k\mathbf{u} = k\langle a, b \rangle = \langle ka, kb \rangle$$

Scalar multiplication corresponds to

- Increasing the length of the vector: $|k| > 1$
- Decreasing the length of the vector: $|k| < 1$
- Changing the direction of the vector: $k < 0$

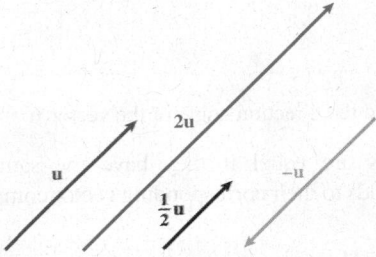

The following box is a summary of vector operations:

### VECTOR OPERATIONS

If $\mathbf{u} = \langle a, b \rangle$, $\mathbf{v} = \langle c, d \rangle$, and $k$ is a scalar, then

$$\mathbf{u} + \mathbf{v} = \langle a + c, b + d \rangle$$

$$\mathbf{u} - \mathbf{v} = \langle a - c, b - d \rangle$$

$$k\mathbf{u} = k\langle a, b \rangle = \langle ka, kb \rangle$$

The zero vector, $\mathbf{0} = \langle 0, 0 \rangle$, is a vector in any direction with a magnitude equal to zero. We now can state the algebraic properties (associative, commutative, and distributive) of vectors.

### ALGEBRAIC PROPERTIES OF VECTORS

$$\mathbf{u} + \mathbf{v} = \mathbf{v} + \mathbf{u}$$

$$(\mathbf{u} + \mathbf{v}) + \mathbf{w} = \mathbf{u} + (\mathbf{v} + \mathbf{w})$$

$$(k_1 k_2)\mathbf{u} = k_1(k_2\mathbf{u})$$

$$k(\mathbf{u} + \mathbf{v}) = k\mathbf{u} + k\mathbf{v}$$

$$(k_1 + k_2)\mathbf{u} = k_1\mathbf{u} + k_2\mathbf{u}$$

$$0\mathbf{u} = \mathbf{0} \qquad 1\mathbf{u} = \mathbf{u} \qquad -1\mathbf{u} = -\mathbf{u}$$

$$\mathbf{u} + (-\mathbf{u}) = \mathbf{0}$$

# Horizontal and Vertical Components of a Vector

The **horizontal component** $a$ and **vertical component** $b$ of a vector **u** are related to the magnitude of the vector, $|\mathbf{u}|$, through the sine and cosine of the direction angle.

$$\cos\theta = \frac{a}{|\mathbf{u}|} \qquad \sin\theta = \frac{b}{|\mathbf{u}|}$$

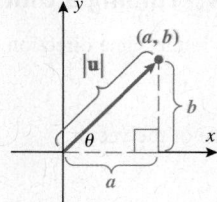

### HORIZONTAL AND VERTICAL COMPONENTS OF A VECTOR

The horizontal and vertical components of vector **u**, with magnitude $|\mathbf{u}|$ and direction angle $\theta$, are given by

horizontal component: $a = |\mathbf{u}|\cos\theta$

vertical component: $b = |\mathbf{u}|\sin\theta$

The vector **u** can then be written as $\mathbf{u} = \langle a, b \rangle = \langle |\mathbf{u}|\cos\theta, |\mathbf{u}|\sin\theta \rangle$.

---

**EXAMPLE 4** **Finding the Horizontal and Vertical Components of a Vector**

Find the vector that has a magnitude of 6 and a direction angle of 15°.

**Solution:**

| | |
|---|---|
| Write the horizontal and vertical components of a vector **u**. | $a = |\mathbf{u}|\cos\theta$ and $b = |\mathbf{u}|\sin\theta$ |
| Let $|\mathbf{u}| = 6$ and $\theta = 15°$. | $a = 6\cos 15°$ and $b = 6\sin 15°$ |
| Use a calculator to approximate the sine and cosine functions of 15°. | $a \approx 5.8$ and $b \approx 1.6$ |
| Let $\mathbf{u} = \langle a, b \rangle$. | $\mathbf{u} = \boxed{\langle 5.8, 1.6 \rangle}$ |

---

■ **YOUR TURN** Find the vector that has a magnitude of 3 and direction angle of 75°.

■ **Answer:** $\mathbf{u} = \langle 0.78, 2.9 \rangle$

# Unit Vectors

A **unit vector** is any vector with magnitude equal to 1 or $|\mathbf{u}| = 1$. It is often useful to be able to find a unit vector in the same direction of some vector **v**. A unit vector can be formed from any nonzero vector as follows:

### FINDING A UNIT VECTOR

If **v** is a nonzero vector, then

$$\mathbf{u} = \frac{\mathbf{v}}{|\mathbf{v}|} = \frac{1}{|\mathbf{v}|} \cdot \mathbf{v}$$

is a **unit vector** in the same direction as **v**. In other words, multiplying any nonzero vector by the reciprocal of its magnitude results in a unit vector.

*Study Tip*

Multiplying a nonzero vector by the reciprocal of its magnitude results in a unit vector.

It is important to notice that since the magnitude is always a scalar, then the reciprocal of the magnitude is always a scalar. A scalar times a vector is a vector.

 **EXAMPLE 5** **Finding a Unit Vector**

Find a unit vector in the same direction as $\mathbf{v} = \langle -3, -4 \rangle$.

**Solution:**

Find the magnitude of the vector
$\mathbf{v} = \langle -3, -4 \rangle$.

$$|\mathbf{v}| = \sqrt{(-3)^2 + (-4)^2}$$

Simplify.

$$|\mathbf{v}| = 5$$

Multiply $\mathbf{v}$ by the reciprocal of its magnitude.

$$\frac{1}{|\mathbf{v}|} \cdot \mathbf{v}$$

Let $|\mathbf{v}| = 5$ and $\mathbf{v} = \langle -3, -4 \rangle$.

$$\frac{1}{5} \langle -3, -4 \rangle$$

Simplify.

$$\boxed{\left\langle -\frac{3}{5}, -\frac{4}{5} \right\rangle}$$

*Check:* The unit vector, $\left\langle -\frac{3}{5}, -\frac{4}{5} \right\rangle$, should have a magnitude of 1.

$$\sqrt{\left(-\frac{3}{5}\right)^2 + \left(-\frac{4}{5}\right)^2} = \sqrt{\frac{25}{25}} = 1$$

■ **Answer:** $\left\langle \frac{5}{13}, -\frac{12}{13} \right\rangle$

■ **YOUR TURN** Find a unit vector in the same direction as $\mathbf{v} = \langle 5, -12 \rangle$.

Two important unit vectors are the horizontal and vertical unit vectors $\mathbf{i}$ and $\mathbf{j}$. The unit vector $\mathbf{i}$ has an initial point at the origin and terminal point at $(1, 0)$. The unit vector $\mathbf{j}$ has an initial point at the origin and terminal point at $(0, 1)$. We can use these unit vectors to represent vectors algebraically. For example, the vector $\langle 3, -4 \rangle = 3\mathbf{i} - 4\mathbf{j}$.

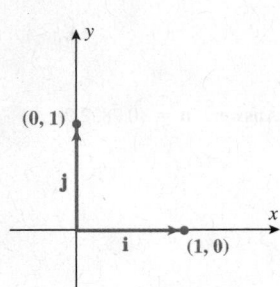

## Resultant Vectors

Vectors arise in many applications. **Velocity vectors** and **force vectors** are two that we will discuss. For example, suppose that you are at the beach and "think" that you are swimming straight out at a certain speed (magnitude and direction). This is your **apparent velocity** with respect to the water. After a few minutes you turn around to look at the shore, and you are farther out than you thought and appear to have drifted down the beach. This is because of the current of the water. When the **current velocity** and the apparent velocity are added together, the result is the **actual** or **resultant velocity**.

EXAMPLE 6 Resultant Velocities

A boat's speedometer reads 25 miles per hour (which is relative to the water) and sets a course due east (90° from due north). If the river is moving 10 miles per hour due north, what is the resultant (actual) velocity of the boat?

Solution:

Draw a picture.

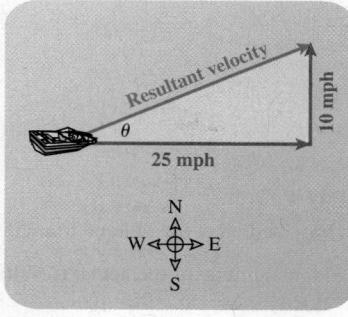

Label the horizontal and vertical components of the resultant vector.

$\langle 25, 10 \rangle$

Determine the magnitude of the resultant vector.

$$\sqrt{25^2 + 10^2} = 5\sqrt{29} \approx 27 \text{ mph}$$

Determine the direction angle.

$$\tan \theta = \frac{10}{25}$$

Solve for $\theta$.

$$\theta = \tan^{-1}\left(\frac{2}{5}\right) \approx 22°$$

The actual velocity of the boat has magnitude 27 miles per hour and the boat is headed 22° north of east or 68° east of north .

In Example 6, the three vectors formed a right triangle. In Example 7, the three vectors form an oblique triangle.

EXAMPLE 7 Resultant Velocities

A speedboat traveling 30 miles per hour has a compass heading of 100° east of north. The current velocity has a magnitude of 15 miles per hour and its heading is 22° east of north. Find the resultant (actual) velocity of the boat.

Solution:

Draw a picture.

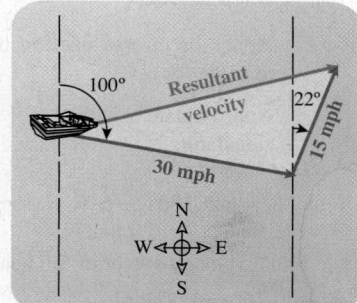

Label the **supplementary angles** to 100°.

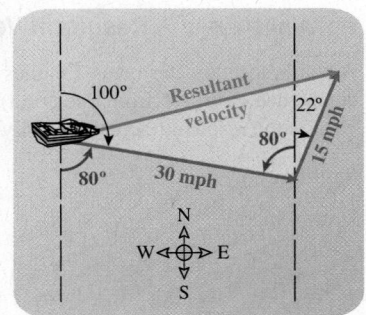

Draw and label the oblique triangle.

The magnitude of the actual (resultant) velocity is *b*.

The heading of the actual (resultant) velocity is 100° − α.

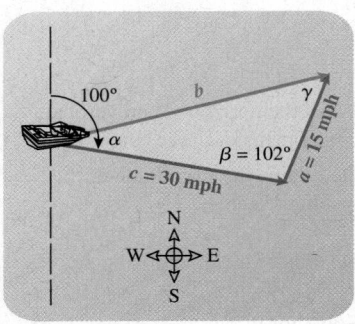

Use the Law of Sines and the Law of Cosines to solve for α and *b*.

**Find *b*:** Apply the Law of Cosines.    $b^2 = a^2 + c^2 - 2ac \cos \beta$

Let $a = 15$, $c = 30$, and
$\beta = 102°$.    $b^2 = 15^2 + 30^2 - 2(15)(30) \cos 102°$

Solve for *b*.    $\boxed{b \approx 36 \text{ mph}}$

**Find α:** Apply the Law of Sines.    $\dfrac{\sin \alpha}{a} = \dfrac{\sin \beta}{b}$

Isolate $\sin \alpha$.    $\sin \alpha = \dfrac{a}{b} \sin \beta$

Let $a = 15$, $b = 36$,
and $\beta = 102°$.    $\sin \alpha = \dfrac{15}{36} \sin 102°$

Apply the inverse sine function
to solve for α.    $\alpha = \sin^{-1}\left(\dfrac{15}{36} \sin 102°\right)$

Approximate α with a
calculator.    $\alpha \approx 24°$

Actual heading: $100° - \alpha = 100° - 24° = \boxed{76°}$

The actual velocity vector of the boat has magnitude $\boxed{36 \text{ miles per hour}}$ and the boat is headed $\boxed{76° \text{ east of north}}$.

Two vectors combine to yield a resultant vector. The opposite vector to the resultant vector is called the **equilibrant**.

### EXAMPLE 8  Finding an Equilibrant

A skier is being pulled up a slope by a handle lift. Let $F_1$ represent the vertical force due to gravity and $F_2$ represent the force of the skier pushing against the side of the mountain, at an angle of $35°$ to the horizontal. If the weight of the skier is 145 pounds, that is, $|F_1| = 145$, find the magnitude of the equilibrant force $F_3$ required to hold the skier in place (i.e., to keep the skier from sliding down the mountain). Assume that the side of the mountain is a frictionless surface.

**Technology Tip**

Use a TI calculator to find
$|F_3| = 145 \sin 35°$.

```
145sin(35)
        83.16858327
```

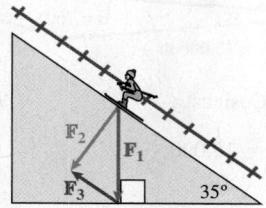

**Solution:**

The angle between vectors $F_1$ and $F_2$ is $35°$.

The magnitude of vector $F_3$ is the force required to hold the skier in place.

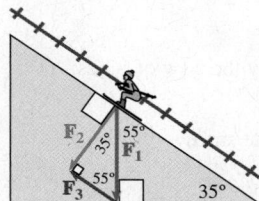

Relate the magnitudes (side lengths) to the given angle using the sine ratio.

$$\sin 35° = \frac{|F_3|}{|F_1|}$$

Solve for $|F_3|$.

$$|F_3| = |F_1| \sin 35°$$

Let $|F_1| = 145$.

$$|F_3| = 145 \sin 35°$$

$$|F_3| = 83.16858$$

A force of approximately $\boxed{83 \text{ pounds}}$ is required to keep the skier from sliding down the hill.

### EXAMPLE 9  Resultant Forces

A barge runs aground outside the channel. A single tugboat cannot generate enough force to pull the barge off the sandbar. A second tugboat comes to assist. The following diagram illustrates the force vectors, $F_1$ and $F_2$, from the tugboats. What is the resultant force vector of the two tugboats?

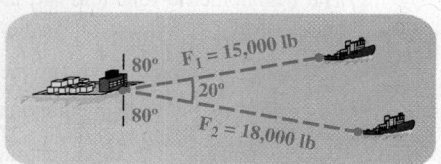

Use the calculator to find $b$.

```
15000²+18000²-2*
15000*18000cos(1
60)
        1056434015
√(Ans)
        32502.83088
```

Use the calculator to find $\alpha$.

```
15000/32503sin(1
60)
        .1578408808
sin⁻¹(Ans)
        9.08159538
```

*Study Tip*

In Example 9, $\beta = 160°$ because the angle between the paths of the tugboats is 20°.

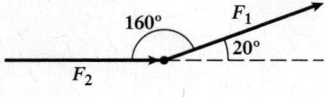

**Solution:**

Using the tail-to-tip rule, we can add these two vectors and form a triangle:

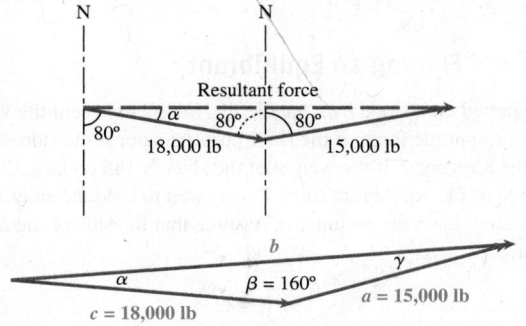

**Find $b$:** Apply the Law of Cosines.

$$b^2 = a^2 + c^2 - 2ac\cos\beta$$

Let $a = 15{,}000$, $c = 18{,}000$, and $\beta = 160°$.

$$b^2 = 15{,}000^2 + 18{,}000^2$$
$$- 2(15{,}000)(18{,}000)\cos 160°$$

Solve for $b$.

$$\boxed{b = 32{,}503 \text{ lb}}$$

**Find $\alpha$:** Apply the Law of Sines.

$$\frac{\sin\alpha}{a} = \frac{\sin\beta}{b}$$

Isolate $\sin\alpha$.

$$\sin\alpha = \frac{a}{b}\sin\beta$$

Let $a = 15{,}000$, $b = 32{,}503$, and $\beta = 160°$.

$$\sin\alpha = \frac{15{,}000}{32{,}503}\sin 160°$$

Apply the inverse sine function to solve for $\alpha$.

$$\alpha = \sin^{-1}\left(\frac{15{,}000}{32{,}503}\sin 160°\right)$$

Approximate $\alpha$ with a calculator.

$$\boxed{\alpha \approx 9.08°}$$

The resulting force is $\boxed{32{,}503 \text{ pounds}}$ at an angle of $\boxed{9° \text{ from the tug pulling with a force of 18,000 pounds}}$.

In this section, we discussed scalars (real numbers) and vectors. Scalars have only magnitude, whereas vectors have both magnitude and direction.

$$\text{Vector:} \quad \mathbf{u} = \langle a, b \rangle$$

$$\text{Magnitude:} \quad |\mathbf{u}| = \sqrt{a^2 + b^2}$$

$$\text{Direction } (\theta)\text{:} \quad \tan\theta = \frac{b}{a}$$

We defined vectors both algebraically and geometrically and gave interpretations of magnitude and vector addition in both methods.

Vector addition is performed algebraically component by component.

$$\langle a, b \rangle + \langle c, d \rangle = \langle a + c, b + d \rangle.$$

The trigonometric functions are used to express the horizontal and vertical components of a vector.

$$\text{Horizontal component:} \quad a = |\mathbf{u}|\cos\theta$$

$$\text{Vertical component:} \quad b = |\mathbf{u}|\sin\theta$$

Velocity and force vectors illustrate applications of the Law of Sines and the Law of Cosines.

**SKILLS**

**In Exercises 1–6, find the magnitude of the vector $\overrightarrow{AB}$.**

**1.** $A = (2, 7)$ and $B = (5, 9)$     **2.** $A = (-2, 3)$ and $B = (3, -4)$     **3.** $A = (4, 1)$ and $B = (-3, 0)$

**4.** $A = (-1, -1)$ and $B = (2, -5)$     **5.** $A = (0, 7)$ and $B = (-24, 0)$     **6.** $A = (-2, 1)$ and $B = (4, 9)$

**In Exercises 7–16, find the magnitude and direction angle of the given vector.**

**7.** $\mathbf{u} = \langle 3, 8 \rangle$     **8.** $\mathbf{u} = \langle 4, 7 \rangle$     **9.** $\mathbf{u} = \langle 5, -1 \rangle$     **10.** $\mathbf{u} = \langle -6, -2 \rangle$     **11.** $\mathbf{u} = \langle -4, 1 \rangle$

**12.** $\mathbf{u} = \langle -6, 3 \rangle$     **13.** $\mathbf{u} = \langle -8, 0 \rangle$     **14.** $\mathbf{u} = \langle 0, 7 \rangle$     **15.** $\mathbf{u} = \langle \sqrt{3}, 3 \rangle$     **16.** $\mathbf{u} = \langle -5, -5 \rangle$

**In Exercises 17–24, perform the indicated vector operation, given $\mathbf{u} = \langle -4, 3 \rangle$ and $\mathbf{v} = \langle 2, -5 \rangle$.**

**17.** $\mathbf{u} + \mathbf{v}$     **18.** $\mathbf{u} - \mathbf{v}$     **19.** $3\mathbf{u}$     **20.** $-2\mathbf{u}$

**21.** $2\mathbf{u} + 4\mathbf{v}$     **22.** $5(\mathbf{u} + \mathbf{v})$     **23.** $6(\mathbf{u} - \mathbf{v})$     **24.** $2\mathbf{u} - 3\mathbf{v} + 4\mathbf{u}$

**In Exercises 25–34, find the vector, given its magnitude and direction angle.**

**25.** $|\mathbf{u}| = 7, \theta = 25°$     **26.** $|\mathbf{u}| = 5, \theta = 75°$     **27.** $|\mathbf{u}| = 16, \theta = 100°$     **28.** $|\mathbf{u}| = 8, \theta = 200°$     **29.** $|\mathbf{u}| = 4, \theta = 310°$

**30.** $|\mathbf{u}| = 8, \theta = 225°$     **31.** $|\mathbf{u}| = 9, \theta = 335°$     **32.** $|\mathbf{u}| = 3, \theta = 315°$     **33.** $|\mathbf{u}| = 2, \theta = 120°$     **34.** $|\mathbf{u}| = 6, \theta = 330°$

**In Exercises 35–44, find a unit vector in the direction of the given vector.**

**35.** $\mathbf{v} = \langle -5, -12 \rangle$     **36.** $\mathbf{v} = \langle 3, 4 \rangle$     **37.** $\mathbf{v} = \langle 60, 11 \rangle$     **38.** $\mathbf{v} = \langle -7, 24 \rangle$     **39.** $\mathbf{v} = \langle 24, -7 \rangle$

**40.** $\mathbf{v} = \langle -10, 24 \rangle$     **41.** $\mathbf{v} = \langle -9, -12 \rangle$     **42.** $\mathbf{v} = \langle 40, -9 \rangle$     **43.** $\mathbf{v} = \langle \sqrt{2}, 3\sqrt{2} \rangle$     **44.** $\mathbf{v} = \langle -4\sqrt{3}, -2\sqrt{3} \rangle$

**In Exercises 45–50, express the vector in terms of unit vectors i and j.**

**45.** $\langle 7, 3 \rangle$     **46.** $\langle -2, 4 \rangle$     **47.** $\langle 5, -3 \rangle$     **48.** $\langle -6, -2 \rangle$     **49.** $\langle -1, 0 \rangle$     **50.** $\langle 0, 2 \rangle$

**In Exercises 51–56, perform the indicated vector operation.**

**51.** $(5\mathbf{i} - 2\mathbf{j}) + (-3\mathbf{i} + 2\mathbf{j})$     **52.** $(4\mathbf{i} - 2\mathbf{j}) + (3\mathbf{i} - 5\mathbf{j})$     **53.** $(-3\mathbf{i} + 3\mathbf{j}) - (2\mathbf{i} - 2\mathbf{j})$

**54.** $(\mathbf{i} - 3\mathbf{j}) - (-2\mathbf{i} + \mathbf{j})$     **55.** $(5\mathbf{i} + 3\mathbf{j}) + (2\mathbf{i} - 3\mathbf{j})$     **56.** $(-2\mathbf{i} + \mathbf{j}) + (2\mathbf{i} - 4\mathbf{j})$

**APPLICATIONS**

**57. Bullet Speed.** A bullet is fired from ground level at a speed of 2200 feet per second at an angle of 30° from the horizontal. Find the magnitude of the horizontal and vertical components of the velocity vector.

**58. Weightlifting.** A 50-pound weight lies on an inclined bench that makes an angle of 40° with the horizontal. Find the component of the weight directed perpendicular to the bench and also the component of the weight parallel to the inclined bench.

**59. Weight of a Boat.** A force of 630 pounds is needed to pull a speedboat and its trailer up a ramp that has an incline of 13°. What is the combined weight of the boat and its trailer?

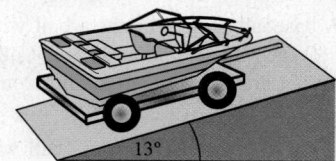

**60. Weight of a Boat.** A force of 500 pounds is needed to pull a speedboat and its trailer up a ramp that has an incline of 16°. What is the weight of the boat and its trailer?

**61. Speed and Direction of a Ship.** A ship's captain sets a course due north at 10 miles per hour. The water is moving at 6 miles per hour due west. What is the actual velocity of the ship, and in what direction is it traveling?

**62. Speed and Direction of a Ship.** A ship's captain sets a course due west at 12 miles per hour. The water is moving at 3 miles per hour due north. What is the actual velocity of the ship, and in what direction is it traveling?

**63. Heading and Airspeed.** A plane has a compass heading of 60° east of due north and an airspeed of 300 miles per hour. The wind is blowing at 40 miles per hour with a heading of 30° west of due north. What are the plane's actual heading and airspeed?

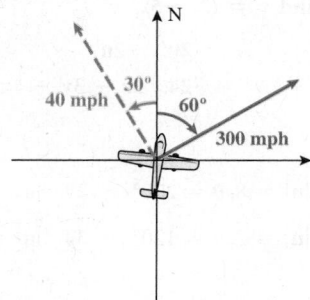

**64. Heading and Airspeed.** A plane has a compass heading of 30° east of due north and an airspeed of 400 miles per hour. The wind is blowing at 30 miles per hour with a heading of 60° west of due north. What are the plane's actual heading and airspeed?

**65. Sliding Box.** A box weighing 500 pounds is held in place on an inclined plane that has an angle of 30°. What force is required to hold it in place?

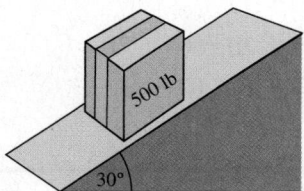

**66. Sliding Box.** A box weighing 500 pounds is held in place on an inclined plane that has an angle of 10°. What force is required to hold it in place?

**67. Baseball.** A baseball player throws a ball with an initial velocity of 80 feet per second at an angle of 40° with the horizontal. What are the vertical and horizontal components of the velocity?

**68. Baseball.** A baseball pitcher throws a ball with an initial velocity of 100 feet per second at an angle of 5° with the horizontal. What are the vertical and horizontal components of the velocity?

**For Exercises 69 and 70, refer to the following:**

In a post pattern in football, the receiver in motion runs past the quarterback parallel to the line of scrimmage (*A*), runs perpendicular to the line of scrimmage (*B*), and then cuts toward the goal post (*C*).

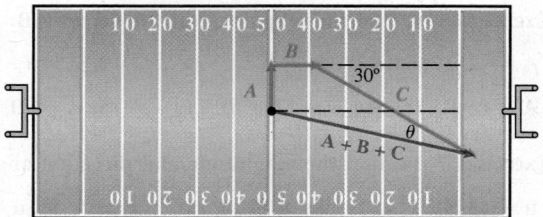

**69. Football.** A receiver runs the post pattern. If the magnitudes of the vectors are $|A| = 4$ yd, $|B| = 12$ yd, and $|C| = 20$ yd, find the magnitude of the resultant vector **A + B + C**.

**70. Football.** A receiver runs the post pattern. If the magnitudes of the vectors are $|A| = 4$ yd, $|B| = 12$ yd, and $|C| = 20$ yd, find the direction angle $\theta$.

**71. Resultant Force.** A force with a magnitude of 100 pounds and another with a magnitude of 400 pounds are acting on an object. The two forces have an angle of 60° between them. What is the direction of the resultant force with respect to the force of 400 pounds?

**72. Resultant Force.** A force with a magnitude of 100 pounds and another with a magnitude of 400 pounds are acting on an object. The two forces have an angle of 60° between them. What is the magnitude of the resultant force?

**73. Resultant Force.** A force of 1000 pounds is acting on an object at an angle of 45° from the horizontal. Another force of 500 pounds is acting at an angle of −40° from the horizontal. What is the magnitude of the resultant force?

**74. Resultant Force.** A force of 1000 pounds is acting on an object at an angle of 45° from the horizontal. Another force of 500 pounds is acting at an angle of −40° from the horizontal. What is the angle of the resultant force?

**75. Resultant Force.** Forces with magnitudes of 200 N and 180 N act on a hook. The angle between these two forces is 45°. Find the direction and magnitude of the resultant of these forces.

**76. Resultant Force.** Forces with magnitudes of 100 N and 50 N act on a hook. The angle between these two forces is 30°. Find the direction and magnitude of the resultant of these forces.

**77. Exercise Equipment.** A tether ball weighing 5 pounds is pulled outward from a pole by a horizontal force **u** until the rope makes a 45° angle with the pole. Determine the resulting tension (in pounds) on the rope and magnitude of **u**.

**78. Exercise Equipment.** A tether ball weighing 8 pounds is pulled outward from a pole by a horizontal force **u** until the rope makes a 60° angle with the pole. Determine the resulting tension (in pounds) on the rope and magnitude of **u**.

**79. Recreation.** A freshman wishes to sign up for four different clubs during orientation. Each club is positioned at a different table in the gym and the clubs of interest to him are positioned at A, B, C, and D, as pictured below. He starts at the entrance way O and walks directly toward A, followed by B and C, then to D, and then back to O.

**a.** Find the resultant vector of all his movement.

**b.** How far did he walk during this sign-up adventure?

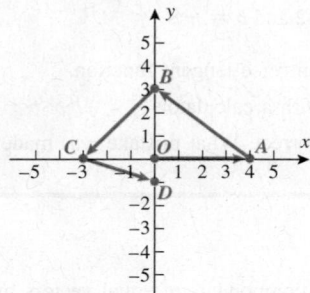

**80. Recreation.** A freshman wishes to sign up for three different clubs during orientation. Each club is positioned at a different table in the gym and the clubs of interest to him are positioned at A, B, and C, as pictured below. He starts at the entrance way O at the far end of the gym, walks directly toward A, followed by B and C, and then exits the gym through the exit P at the opposite end.

**a.** Find the resultant vector of all his movement.

**b.** How far did he walk during this sign-up adventure?

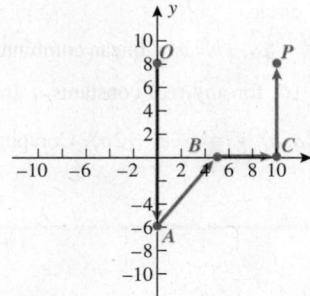

**81. Torque.** *Torque* is the tendency for an arm to rotate about a pivot point. If a force **F** is applied at an angle $\theta$ to turn an arm of length L, as pictured below, then the magnitude of the torque $= L|\mathbf{F}|\sin\theta$.

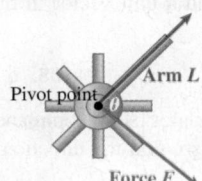

Assume that a force of 45 N is applied to a bar 0.2 meter wide on a sewer shut-off valve at an angle 85°. What is the magnitude of the torque in N-m?

**82. Torque.** You walk through a swinging mall door to enter a department store. You exert a force of 40 N applied perpendicular to the door. The door is 0.85 meter wide. Assuming that you pushed the door at its edge and the hinge is the pivot point, find the magnitude of the torque.

**83. Torque.** You walk through a swinging mall door to enter a department store. You exert a force of 40 N applied at an angle 110° to the door. The door is 0.85 meter wide. Assuming that you pushed the door at its edge and the hinge is the pivot point, find the magnitude of the torque.

**84. Torque.** Suppose that within the context of Exercises 82 and 83, the magnitude of the torque turned out to be 0 N-m. When can this occur?

**85. Resultant Force.** A person is walking two dogs fastened to separate leashes that meet in a connective hub, leading to a single leash that she is holding. Dog 1 applies a force N 60° W with a magnitude of 8, and Dog 2 applies a force of N 45° E with a magnitude of 6. Find the magnitude and direction of the force **w** that the walker applies to the leash in order to counterbalance the total force exerted by the dogs.

**86. Resultant Force.** A person is walking three dogs fastened to separate leashes that meet in a connective hub, leading to a single leash that she is holding. Dog 1 applies a force N 60° W with a magnitude of 8, Dog 2 applies a force of N 45° E with a magnitude of 6, and Dog 3 moves directly N with a magnitude of 12. Find the magnitude and direction of the force **w** that the walker applies to the leash in order to counterbalance the total force exerted by the dogs.

**For Exercises 87 and 88, refer to the following:**

Muscle A and muscle B are attached to a bone as indicated in the figure below. Muscle A exerts a force on the bone at angle $\alpha$, while muscle B exerts a force on the bone at angle $\beta$.

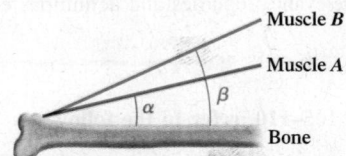

**87. Health/Medicine.** Assume muscle A exerts a force of 900 N on the bone at angle $\alpha = 8°$, while muscle B exerts a force of 750 N on the bone at angle $\beta = 33°$. Find the resultant force and the angle of the force due to muscle A and muscle B on the bone.

**88. Health/Medicine.** Assume muscle A exerts a force of 1000 N on the bone at angle $\alpha = 9°$, while muscle B exerts a force of 820 N on the bone at angle $\beta = 38°$. Find the resultant force and the angle of the force due to muscle A and muscle B on the bone.

■ **CATCH THE MISTAKE**

**In Exercises 89 and 90, explain the mistake that is made.**

**89.** Find the magnitude of the vector $\langle -2, -8 \rangle$.

**Solution:**

Factor the $-1$.                  $-\langle 2, 8 \rangle$

Find the magnitude       $|\langle 2, 8 \rangle| = \sqrt{2^2 + 8^2}$
of $\langle 2,8 \rangle$.                     $= \sqrt{68} = 2\sqrt{17}$

Write the magnitude
of $\langle -2, -8 \rangle$.        $|\langle -2, -8 \rangle| = -2\sqrt{17}$

This is incorrect. What mistake was made?

**90.** Find the direction angle of the vector $\langle -2, -8 \rangle$.

**Solution:**

Write the formula for the direction
angle of $\langle a, b \rangle$.                $\tan \theta = \dfrac{b}{a}$

Let $a = -2$ and $b = -8$.      $\tan \theta = \dfrac{-8}{-2}$

Apply the inverse tangent function.    $\theta = \tan^{-1} 4$

Evaluate with a calculator.         $\theta = 76°$

This is incorrect. What mistake was made?

■ **CONCEPTUAL**

**In Exercises 91–94, determine whether each statment is true or false.**

**91.** The magnitude of the vector $\mathbf{i}$ is the imaginary number $i$.

**92.** The arrow components of equal vectors must coincide.

**93.** The magnitude of a vector is always greater than or equal to the magnitude of its horizontal component.

**94.** The magnitude of a vector is always greater than or equal to the magnitude of its vertical component.

**95.** Would a scalar or a vector represent the following? *The car is driving 72 miles per hour due east (90° with respect to north).*

**96.** Would a scalar or vector represent the following? *The granite has a mass of 131 kilograms.*

**97.** Find the magnitude of the vector $\langle -a, b \rangle$ if $a > 0$ and $b > 0$.

**98.** Find the direction angle of the vector $\langle -a, b \rangle$ if $a > 0$ and $b > 0$.

■ **CHALLENGE**

**99.** Show that if $\mathbf{u}$ is a unit vector in the direction of $\mathbf{v}$, then $\mathbf{v} = |\mathbf{u}|\, \mathbf{u}$.

**100.** Show that if $\mathbf{u} = a\mathbf{i} + b\mathbf{j}$ is a unit vector, then $(a, b)$ lies on the unit circle.

**101.** A vector $\mathbf{u}$ is a *linear combination* of $\mathbf{p}$ and $\mathbf{q}$ if there exist constants $c_1$ and $c_2$ such that $\mathbf{u} = c_1\mathbf{p} + c_2\mathbf{q}$. Show that $\langle -6, 4 \rangle$ is a linear combination of $\langle -8, 4 \rangle$ and $\langle 1, -1 \rangle$.

**102.** Show that $\left\langle -\frac{2}{9}a, \frac{8}{9}b \right\rangle$ is a linear combination of $\langle a, 3b \rangle$ and $\langle -a, -b \rangle$, for any real constants $a$ and $b$.

**103.** Prove that $\mathbf{u} + 3(2\mathbf{v} - \mathbf{u}) = 6\mathbf{v} - 2\mathbf{u}$, showing carefully how all relevant properties and definitions enter the proof.

**104.** Let $\mathbf{u} = \langle 2a, a \rangle$, $\mathbf{v} = \langle -a, -2a \rangle$. Compute $\left| \dfrac{2\mathbf{u}}{|\mathbf{v}|} - \dfrac{3\mathbf{v}}{|\mathbf{u}|} \right|$.

■ **TECHNOLOGY**

**For Exercises 105–110, refer to the following:**

Vectors can be represented as column matrices. For example, the vector $\mathbf{u} = \langle 3, -4 \rangle$ can be represented as a $2 \times 1$ column matrix $\begin{bmatrix} 3 \\ -4 \end{bmatrix}$. With a TI-83 calculator, vectors can be entered as matrices in two ways, directly or via $\boxed{\text{MATRIX}}$.

Directly:

```
[[3][-4]]
        [[3 ]
         [-4]]
■
```

Matrix:

```
[A]
        [[3 ]
         [-4]]
```

Use a calculator to perform the vector operation given $\mathbf{u} = \langle 8, -5 \rangle$ and $\mathbf{v} = \langle -7, 11 \rangle$.

**105.** $\mathbf{u} + 3\mathbf{v}$                 **106.** $-9(\mathbf{u} - 2\mathbf{v})$

Use a calculator to find a unit vector in the direction of the given vector.

**107.** $\mathbf{u} = \langle 10, -24 \rangle$          **108.** $\mathbf{u} = \langle -9, -40 \rangle$

Use the graphing calculator $\boxed{\text{SUM}}$ command to find the magnitude of the given vector. Also, find the direction angle to the nearest degree.

**109.** $\langle -33, 180 \rangle$            **110.** $\langle -20, -30\sqrt{5} \rangle$

■ **PREVIEW TO CALCULUS**

There is a branch of calculus devoted to the study of vector-valued functions; these are functions that map real numbers onto vectors. For example, $\mathbf{v}(t) = \langle t, 2t \rangle$.

**111.** Find the magnitude of the vector-valued function $\mathbf{v}(t) = \langle \cos t, \sin t \rangle$.

**112.** Find the direction of the vector-valued function $\mathbf{v}(t) = \langle -3t, -4t \rangle$.

The difference quotient for the vector-valued function $\mathbf{v}(t)$ is defined as $\dfrac{\mathbf{v}(t + h) - \mathbf{v}(t)}{h}$. In Exercises 113 and 114, find the difference quotient of the vector-valued function.

**113.** $\mathbf{v}(t) = \langle t, t^2 \rangle$

**114.** $\mathbf{v}(t) = \langle t^2 + 1, t^3 \rangle$

**SECTION**
**7.2** THE DOT PRODUCT

**SKILLS OBJECTIVES**

- Find the dot product of two vectors.
- Use the dot product to find the angle between two vectors.
- Determine whether two vectors are parallel or perpendicular.
- Use the dot product to calculate the amount of work associated with a physical problem.

**CONCEPTUAL OBJECTIVE**

- Understand the difference between scalar vector multiplication and the dot product of two vectors.

## The Dot Product

With two-dimensional vectors, there are two types of multiplication defined for vectors: scalar multiplication and the dot product. Scalar multiplication (which we already demonstrated in Section 7.1) is multiplication of a scalar by a vector; the result is a vector. Now we discuss the *dot product* of two vectors. In this case, there are two important things to note: (1) The dot product of two vectors is defined only if the vectors have the same number of components and (2) if the dot product does exist, then the result is a scalar.

**DOT PRODUCT**

The **dot product** of two vectors $\mathbf{u} = \langle a, b \rangle$ and $\mathbf{v} = \langle c, d \rangle$ is given by

$$\mathbf{u} \cdot \mathbf{v} = ac + bd$$

$\mathbf{u} \cdot \mathbf{v}$ is pronounced "u dot v."

### EXAMPLE 1  Finding the Dot Product of Two Vectors

Find the dot product $\langle -7, 3 \rangle \cdot \langle 2, 5 \rangle$.

**Solution:**

Sum the products of the first
components and the products
of the second components.

$$\langle -7, 3 \rangle \cdot \langle 2, 5 \rangle = (-7)(2) + (3)(5)$$

Simplify.

$$= -14 + 15$$

$$= \boxed{1}$$

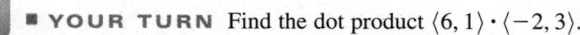

> ■ **YOUR TURN** Find the dot product $\langle 6, 1 \rangle \cdot \langle -2, 3 \rangle$.

The following box summarizes the properties of the dot product:

### PROPERTIES OF THE DOT PRODUCT

1. $\mathbf{u} \cdot \mathbf{v} = \mathbf{v} \cdot \mathbf{u}$
2. $\mathbf{u} \cdot \mathbf{u} = |\mathbf{u}|^2$
3. $\mathbf{0} \cdot \mathbf{u} = 0$
4. $k(\mathbf{u} \cdot \mathbf{v}) = (k\mathbf{u}) \cdot \mathbf{v} = \mathbf{u} \cdot (k\mathbf{v})$
5. $(\mathbf{u} + \mathbf{v}) \cdot \mathbf{w} = \mathbf{u} \cdot \mathbf{w} + \mathbf{v} \cdot \mathbf{w}$
6. $\mathbf{u} \cdot (\mathbf{v} + \mathbf{w}) = \mathbf{u} \cdot \mathbf{v} + \mathbf{u} \cdot \mathbf{w}$

These properties are verified in the exercises.

## Angle Between Two Vectors

We can use the properties of the dot product to develop an equation that relates the angle between two vectors and the dot product of the vectors.

| WORDS | MATH |
|---|---|
| Let $\mathbf{u}$ and $\mathbf{v}$ be two vectors with the same initial point, and let $\theta$ be the angle between them. | |
| The vector $\mathbf{u} - \mathbf{v}$ is opposite angle $\theta$. | |
| A triangle is formed with side lengths equal to the magnitudes of the three vectors. | |

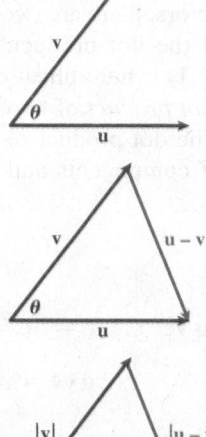

*Study Tip*

The dot product of two vectors
is a scalar.

■ **Answer:** $-9$

Apply the Law of Cosines.

$$|\mathbf{u} - \mathbf{v}|^2 = |\mathbf{u}|^2 + |\mathbf{v}|^2 - 2|\mathbf{u}||\mathbf{v}|\cos\theta$$

Use properties of the dot product
to rewrite the left side of equation.

Property (2):

$$|\mathbf{u} - \mathbf{v}|^2 = (\mathbf{u} - \mathbf{v}) \cdot (\mathbf{u} - \mathbf{v})$$

Property (6):

$$= \mathbf{u} \cdot (\mathbf{u} - \mathbf{v}) - \mathbf{v} \cdot (\mathbf{u} - \mathbf{v})$$

Property (6):

$$= \mathbf{u} \cdot \mathbf{u} - \mathbf{u} \cdot \mathbf{v} - \mathbf{v} \cdot \mathbf{u} + \mathbf{v} \cdot \mathbf{v}$$

Property (2):

$$= |\mathbf{u}|^2 - \mathbf{u} \cdot \mathbf{v} - \mathbf{v} \cdot \mathbf{u} + |\mathbf{v}|^2$$

Property (1):

$$\boxed{= |\mathbf{u}|^2 - 2(\mathbf{u} \cdot \mathbf{v}) + |\mathbf{v}|^2}$$

Substitute this last expression
for the left side of the original
Law of Cosines equation.

$$|\mathbf{u}|^2 - 2(\mathbf{u} \cdot \mathbf{v}) + |\mathbf{v}|^2 = |\mathbf{u}|^2 + |\mathbf{v}|^2 - 2|\mathbf{u}||\mathbf{v}|\cos\theta$$

Simplify.

$$-2(\mathbf{u} \cdot \mathbf{v}) = -2|\mathbf{u}||\mathbf{v}|\cos\theta$$

Isolate $\cos\theta$.

$$\boxed{\cos\theta = \frac{\mathbf{u} \cdot \mathbf{v}}{|\mathbf{u}||\mathbf{v}|}}$$

Notice that $\mathbf{u}$ and $\mathbf{v}$ have to be nonzero vectors, since we divided by them in the last step.

## ANGLE BETWEEN TWO VECTORS

If $\theta$ is the angle between two nonzero vectors $\mathbf{u}$ and $\mathbf{v}$, where $0° \leq \theta \leq 180°$, then

$$\cos\theta = \frac{\mathbf{u} \cdot \mathbf{v}}{|\mathbf{u}||\mathbf{v}|}$$

In the Cartesian plane, there are two angles between two vectors, $\theta$ and $360° - \theta$. **We assume that $\theta$ is the "smaller" angle.**

### EXAMPLE 2  Finding the Angle Between Two Vectors

Find the angle between $\langle 2, -3 \rangle$ and $\langle -4, 3 \rangle$.

**Solution:**

Let $\mathbf{u} = \langle 2, -3 \rangle$ and $\mathbf{v} = \langle -4, 3 \rangle$.

STEP 1  Find $\mathbf{u} \cdot \mathbf{v}$.

$$\mathbf{u} \cdot \mathbf{v} = \langle 2, -3 \rangle \cdot \langle -4, 3 \rangle$$
$$= (2)(-4) + (-3)(3) = -17$$

STEP 2  Find $|\mathbf{u}|$.

$$|\mathbf{u}| = \sqrt{\mathbf{u} \cdot \mathbf{u}} = \sqrt{2^2 + (-3)^2} = \sqrt{13}$$

STEP 3  Find $|\mathbf{v}|$.

$$|\mathbf{v}| = \sqrt{\mathbf{v} \cdot \mathbf{v}} = \sqrt{(-4)^2 + 3^2} = \sqrt{25} = 5$$

STEP 4  Find $\theta$.

$$\cos\theta = \frac{\mathbf{u} \cdot \mathbf{v}}{|\mathbf{u}||\mathbf{v}|} = \frac{-17}{5\sqrt{13}}$$

Approximate $\theta$ with
a calculator.

$$\theta = \cos^{-1}\left(-\frac{17}{5\sqrt{13}}\right) \approx 160.559965°$$

$$\boxed{\theta \approx 161°}$$

STEP 5  Draw a picture to confirm the answer.

Draw the vectors $\langle 2, -3 \rangle$ and $\langle -4, 3 \rangle$.

161° appears to be correct.

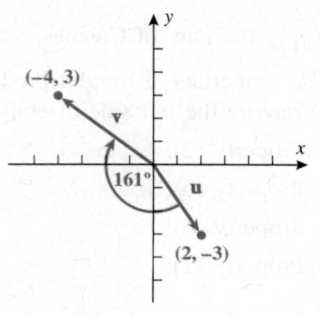

■ **Answer:** 38°

■ **YOUR TURN**  Find the angle between $\langle 1, 5 \rangle$ and $\langle -2, 4 \rangle$.

When two vectors are **parallel**, the angle between them is 0° or 180°.

$\theta = 0°$  $\xrightarrow[\mathbf{v}]{\mathbf{u}}$          $\theta = 180°$  $\xleftarrow[\mathbf{v}]{}\;\xrightarrow[\mathbf{u}]{}$

When two vectors are **perpendicular (orthogonal)**, the angle between them is 90°.

$\theta = 90°$

*Note:* We did not include 270° because the angle $0° \leq \theta \leq 180°$ between two vectors is taken to be the smaller angle.

| **WORDS** | **MATH** |
|---|---|
| When two vectors **u** and **v** are perpendicular, $\theta = 90°$. | $\cos 90° = \dfrac{\mathbf{u} \cdot \mathbf{v}}{|\mathbf{u}||\mathbf{v}|}$ |
| Substitute $\cos 90° = 0$. | $0 = \dfrac{\mathbf{u} \cdot \mathbf{v}}{|\mathbf{u}||\mathbf{v}|}$ |
| Therefore, the dot product of **u** and **v** must be zero. | $\mathbf{u} \cdot \mathbf{v} = 0$ |

### ORTHOGONAL VECTORS

Two vectors **u** and **v** are **orthogonal** (perpendicular) if and only if their dot product is zero.

$$\mathbf{u} \cdot \mathbf{v} = 0$$

**EXAMPLE 3**   **Determining Whether Vectors Are Orthogonal**

Determine whether each pair of vectors is orthogonal.

**a.** $\mathbf{u} = \langle 2, -3 \rangle$ and $\mathbf{v} = \langle 3, 2 \rangle$      **b.** $\mathbf{u} = \langle -7, -3 \rangle$ and $\mathbf{v} = \langle 7, 3 \rangle$

**Solution (a):**

Find the dot product $\mathbf{u} \cdot \mathbf{v}$.

$$\mathbf{u} \cdot \mathbf{v} = (2)(3) + (-3)(2)$$

Simplify.

$$\mathbf{u} \cdot \mathbf{v} = 0$$

Vectors $\mathbf{u}$ and $\mathbf{v}$ are orthogonal, since $\mathbf{u} \cdot \mathbf{v} = 0$.

**Solution (b):**

Find the dot product $\mathbf{u} \cdot \mathbf{v}$.

$$\mathbf{u} \cdot \mathbf{v} = (-7)(7) + (-3)(3)$$

Simplify.

$$\mathbf{u} \cdot \mathbf{v} = -58$$

Vectors $\mathbf{u}$ and $\mathbf{v}$ are not orthogonal, since $\mathbf{u} \cdot \mathbf{v} \neq 0$.

# Work

If you had to carry barbells with weights or pillows for 1 mile, which would you choose? You would probably pick the pillows over the barbell with weights, because the pillows are lighter. It requires less work to carry the pillows than it does to carry the weights. If asked to carry either of them 1 mile or 10 miles, you would probably pick 1 mile, because it's a shorter distance and requires less work. **Work** is done when a *force causes an object to move a certain distance.*

The simplest case is when the force is in the same direction as the displacement—for example, a stagecoach (the horses pull with a force in the same direction). In this case the work is defined as the magnitude of the force times the magnitude of the displacement, distance *d.*

$$W = |\mathbf{F}| d$$

Notice that the magnitude of the force is a scalar, the distance *d* is a scalar, and hence the product is a scalar.

If the horses pull with a force of 1000 pounds and they move the stagecoach 100 feet, the work done by the force is

$$W = (1000 \, \text{lb})(100 \, \text{ft}) = 100{,}000 \, \text{ft-lb}$$

In many physical applications, however, the force is not in the same direction as the displacement, and hence vectors (not just their magnitudes) are required.

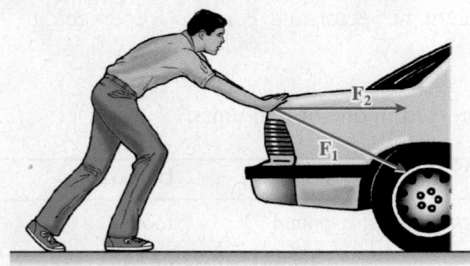

We often want to know how much of a force is applied in a certain direction. For example, when your car runs out of gasoline and you try to push it, some of the force vector $\mathbf{F}_1$ you generate from pushing translates into the horizontal component $\mathbf{F}_2$; hence, the car moves horizontally.

If we let $\theta$ be the angle between the vectors $\mathbf{F}_1$ and $\mathbf{F}_2$, then the horizontal component of $\mathbf{F}_1$ is $\mathbf{F}_2$ where $|F_2| = |F_1| \cos \theta$.

If the man in the picture pushes at an angle of 25° with a force of 150 pounds, then the horizontal component of the force vector $\mathbf{F}_1$ is

$$(150\,\text{lb})(\cos 25°) \approx \boxed{136\,\text{lb}}$$

| WORDS | MATH |
|---|---|
| To develop a generalized formula when the force exerted and the displacement are not in the same direction, we start with the formula for the angle between two vectors. | $\cos \theta = \dfrac{\mathbf{u} \cdot \mathbf{v}}{|\mathbf{u}||\mathbf{v}|}$ |
| We then isolate the dot product $\mathbf{u} \cdot \mathbf{v}$. | $\mathbf{u} \cdot \mathbf{v} = |\mathbf{u}||\mathbf{v}| \cos \theta$ |
| Let $\mathbf{u} = \mathbf{F}$ and $\mathbf{v} = \mathbf{d}$. | $W = \mathbf{F} \cdot \mathbf{d} = |\mathbf{F}||\mathbf{d}| \cos \theta = \underbrace{|\mathbf{F}| \cos \theta}_{\substack{\text{magnitude of force} \\ \text{in direction of displacement}}} \cdot \underbrace{|\mathbf{d}|}_{\text{distance}}$ |

### WORK

If an object is moved from point $A$ to point $B$ by a constant force, then the work associated with this displacement is

$$W = \mathbf{F} \cdot \mathbf{d}$$

where $\mathbf{d}$ is the displacement vector and $\mathbf{F}$ is the force vector.

Work is typically expressed in one of two units:

| SYSTEM | FORCE | DISTANCE | WORK |
|---|---|---|---|
| U.S. customary | pound | foot | ft-lb |
| SI | newton | meter | N-m |

**EXAMPLE 4** **Calculating Work**

How much work is done when a force (in pounds) $\mathbf{F} = \langle 2, 4 \rangle$ moves an object from $(0, 0)$ to $(5, 9)$ (the distance is in feet)?

**Solution:**

| | |
|---|---|
| Find the displacement vector $\mathbf{d}$. | $\mathbf{d} = \langle 5, 9 \rangle$ |
| Apply the work formula, $W = \mathbf{F} \cdot \mathbf{d}$. | $W = \langle 2, 4 \rangle \cdot \langle 5, 9 \rangle$ |
| Calculate the dot product. | $W = (2)(5) + (4)(9)$ |
| Simplify. | $\boxed{W = 46 \text{ ft-lb}}$ |

■ **YOUR TURN** How much work is done when a force (in newtons) $\mathbf{F} = \langle 1, 3 \rangle$ moves an object from $(0, 0)$ to $(4, 7)$ (the distance is in meters)?

■ **Answer:** 25 N-m

---

# SECTION
## 7.2 SUMMARY

In this section, we defined the dot product as a form of multiplication of two vectors. A scalar times a vector results in a vector, whereas the dot product of two vectors is a scalar.

$$\langle a, b \rangle \cdot \langle c, d \rangle = ac + bd$$

We developed a formula that determines the angle $\theta$ between two vectors $\mathbf{u}$ and $\mathbf{v}$.

$$\cos \theta = \frac{\mathbf{u} \cdot \mathbf{v}}{|\mathbf{u}||\mathbf{v}|}$$

Orthogonal (perpendicular) vectors have an angle of 90° between them, and consequently, the dot product of two orthogonal vectors is equal to zero. Work is the result of a force displacing an object. When the force and displacement are in the same direction, the work is equal to the product of the magnitude of the force and the distance (magnitude of the displacement). When the force and displacement are not in the same direction, work is the dot product of the force vector and displacement vector, $\mathbf{W} = \mathbf{F} \cdot \mathbf{d}$.

---

# SECTION
## 7.2 EXERCISES

■ **SKILLS**

In Exercises 1–12, find the indicated dot product.

**1.** $\langle 4, -2 \rangle \cdot \langle 3, 5 \rangle$

**2.** $\langle 7, 8 \rangle \cdot \langle 2, -1 \rangle$

**3.** $\langle -5, 6 \rangle \cdot \langle 3, 2 \rangle$

**4.** $\langle 6, -3 \rangle \cdot \langle 2, 1 \rangle$

**5.** $\langle -7, -4 \rangle \cdot \langle -2, -7 \rangle$

**6.** $\langle 5, -2 \rangle \cdot \langle -1, -1 \rangle$

**7.** $\langle \sqrt{3}, -2 \rangle \cdot \langle 3\sqrt{3}, -1 \rangle$

**8.** $\langle 4\sqrt{2}, \sqrt{7} \rangle \cdot \langle -\sqrt{2}, -\sqrt{7} \rangle$

**9.** $\langle 5, a \rangle \cdot \langle -3a, 2 \rangle$

**10.** $\langle 4x, 3y \rangle \cdot \langle 2y, -5x \rangle$

**11.** $\langle 0.8, -0.5 \rangle \cdot \langle 2, 6 \rangle$

**12.** $\langle -18, 3 \rangle \cdot \langle 10, -300 \rangle$

**In Exercises 13–24, find the angle (round to the nearest degree) between each pair of vectors.**

**13.** $\langle -4, 3 \rangle$ and $\langle -5, -9 \rangle$

**14.** $\langle 2, -4 \rangle$ and $\langle 4, -1 \rangle$

**15.** $\langle -2, -3 \rangle$ and $\langle -3, 4 \rangle$

**16.** $\langle 6, 5 \rangle$ and $\langle 3, -2 \rangle$

**17.** $\langle -4, 6 \rangle$ and $\langle -6, 8 \rangle$

**18.** $\langle 1, 5 \rangle$ and $\langle -3, -2 \rangle$

**19.** $\langle -2, 2\sqrt{3} \rangle$ and $\langle -\sqrt{3}, 1 \rangle$

**20.** $\langle -3\sqrt{3}, -3 \rangle$ and $\langle -2\sqrt{3}, 2 \rangle$

**21.** $\langle -5\sqrt{3}, -5 \rangle$ and $\langle \sqrt{2}, -\sqrt{2} \rangle$

**22.** $\langle -5, -5\sqrt{3} \rangle$ and $\langle 2, -\sqrt{2} \rangle$

**23.** $\langle 4, 6 \rangle$ and $\langle -6, -9 \rangle$

**24.** $\langle 2, 8 \rangle$ and $\langle -12, 3 \rangle$

**In Exercises 25–36, determine whether each pair of vectors is orthogonal.**

**25.** $\langle -6, 8 \rangle$ and $\langle -8, 6 \rangle$

**26.** $\langle 5, -2 \rangle$ and $\langle -5, 2 \rangle$

**27.** $\langle 6, -4 \rangle$ and $\langle -6, -9 \rangle$

**28.** $\langle 8, 3 \rangle$ and $\langle -6, 16 \rangle$

**29.** $\langle 0.8, 4 \rangle$ and $\langle 3, -6 \rangle$

**30.** $\langle -7, 3 \rangle$ and $\langle \frac{1}{7}, -\frac{1}{3} \rangle$

**31.** $\langle 5, -0.4 \rangle$ and $\langle 1.6, 20 \rangle$

**32.** $\langle 12, 9 \rangle$ and $\langle 3, -4 \rangle$

**33.** $\langle \sqrt{3}, \sqrt{6} \rangle$ and $\langle -\sqrt{2}, 1 \rangle$

**34.** $\langle \sqrt{7}, -\sqrt{3} \rangle$ and $\langle 3, 7 \rangle$

**35.** $\langle \frac{4}{3}, \frac{8}{15} \rangle$ and $\langle -\frac{1}{12}, \frac{5}{24} \rangle$

**36.** $\langle \frac{5}{6}, \frac{6}{7} \rangle$ and $\langle \frac{36}{25}, -\frac{49}{36} \rangle$

# ▪ APPLICATIONS

**37. Lifting Weights.** How much work does it take to lift 100 pounds vertically 4 feet?

**38. Lifting Weights.** How much work does it take to lift 150 pounds vertically 3.5 feet?

**39. Raising Wrecks.** How much work is done by a crane to lift a 2-ton car to a level of 20 feet?

**40. Raising Wrecks.** How much work is done by a crane to lift a 2.5-ton car to a level of 25 feet?

**41. Work.** To slide a crate across the floor, a force of 50 pounds at a 30° angle is needed. How much work is done if the crate is dragged 30 feet?

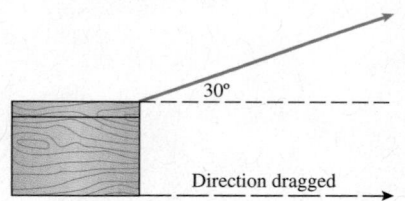

30°

Direction dragged

**42. Work.** To slide a crate across the floor, a force of 800 pounds at a 20° angle is needed. How much work is done if the crate is dragged 50 feet?

**43. Close a Door.** A sliding door is closed by pulling a cord with a constant force of 35 pounds at a constant angle of 45°. The door is moved 6 feet to close it. How much work is done?

**44. Close a Door.** A sliding door is closed by pulling a cord with a constant force of 45 pounds at a constant angle of 55°. The door is moved 6 feet to close it. How much work is done?

**45. Braking Power.** A car that weighs 2500 pounds is parked on a hill in San Francisco with a slant of 40° from the horizontal. How much force will keep it from rolling down the hill?

**46. Towing Power.** A car that weighs 2500 pounds is parked on a hill in San Francisco with a slant of 40° from the horizontal. A tow truck has to remove the car from its parking spot and move it 120 feet up the hill. How much work is required?

**47. Towing Power.** A semitrailer truck that weighs 40,000 pounds is parked on a hill in San Francisco with a slant of 10° from the horizontal. A tow truck has to remove the truck from its parking spot and move it 100 feet up the hill. How much work is required?

**48. Braking Power.** A truck that weighs 40,000 pounds is parked on a hill in San Francisco with a slant of 10° from the horizontal. How much force will keep it from rolling down the hill?

**49. Business.** Suppose that $\mathbf{u} = \langle 2000, 5000 \rangle$ represents the number of units of battery $A$ and $B$, respectively, produced by a company and $\mathbf{v} = \langle 8.40, 6.50 \rangle$ represents the price (in dollars) of a 10-pack of battery $A$ and $B$, respectively. Compute and interpret $\mathbf{u} \cdot \mathbf{v}$.

**50. Demographics.** Suppose that $\mathbf{u} = \langle 120, 80 \rangle$ represents the number of males and females in a high school class, and $\mathbf{v} = \langle 7.2, 5.3 \rangle$ represents the average number of minutes it takes a male and female, respectively, to register. Compute and interpret $\mathbf{u} \cdot \mathbf{v}$.

**51. Geometry.** Use vector methods to show that the diagonals of a rhombus are perpendicular to each other.

**52. Geometry.** Let **u** be a unit vector, and consider the following diagram:

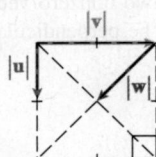

Compute **u** · **v** and **u** · **w**.

**53. Geometry.** Consider the following diagram:

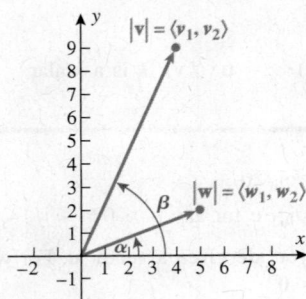

**a.** Compute $\cos\beta$, $\sin\beta$, $\cos\alpha$, and $\sin\alpha$.

**b.** Use (a) to show that $\cos(\alpha - \beta) = \dfrac{\mathbf{v} \cdot \mathbf{w}}{\sqrt{\mathbf{v} \cdot \mathbf{v}} \sqrt{\mathbf{w} \cdot \mathbf{w}}}$.

**54. Geometry.** Consider the diagram in Exercise 53.

**a.** Compute $\cos\beta$, $\sin\beta$, $\cos\alpha$, and $\sin\alpha$.

**b.** Use (a) to show that $\cos(\alpha + \beta) = \dfrac{\mathbf{v} \cdot \langle w_1, -w_2 \rangle}{\sqrt{\mathbf{v} \cdot \mathbf{v}} \sqrt{\mathbf{w} \cdot \mathbf{w}}}$.

**55. Tennis.** A player hits an overhead smash at full arm extension at the top of his racquet, which is 7 feet from the ground. The ball travels 16.3 feet (ignore the effects of gravity). Consult the following diagram:

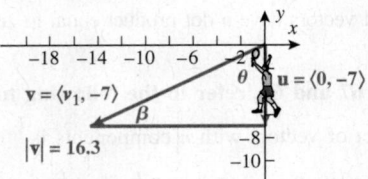

**a.** Determine $v_1$.

**b.** Find the angle $\theta$ with which the player hits this smash.

**56. Tennis.** In Exercise 55, use the dot product to determine the angle $\beta$ with which the ball hits the ground.

**57. Optimization.** Let $\mathbf{u} = \langle a, b \rangle$ be a given vector and suppose that the head of $\mathbf{n} = \langle n_1, n_2 \rangle$ lies on the circle $x^2 + y^2 = r^2$. Find the vector **n** such that $\mathbf{u} \cdot \mathbf{n}$ is as big as possible. Find the actual value of $\mathbf{u} \cdot \mathbf{n}$ in this case.

**58. Optimization.** Let $\mathbf{u} = \langle a, b \rangle$ be a given vector and suppose that the head of $\mathbf{n} = \langle n_1, n_2 \rangle$ lies on the circle $x^2 + y^2 = r^2$. Find the vector **n** such that $\mathbf{u} \cdot \mathbf{n}$ is as small as possible. Find the actual value of $\mathbf{u} \cdot \mathbf{n}$ in this case.

**59. Pursuit Theory.** Assume that the head of **u** is restricted so that its tail is at the origin and its head is on the unit circle in quadrant II or quadrant III. A vector **v** has its tail at the origin and its head must lie on the line $y = 2 - x$ in quadrant I. Find the least value of $\mathbf{u} \cdot \mathbf{v}$.

**60. Pursuit Theory.** Assume that the head of **u** is restricted so that its tail is at the origin and its head is on the unit circle in quadrant I or quadrant IV. A vector **v** has its tail at the origin and its head must lie on the line $y = 2 - x$ in quadrant I. Find the largest value of $\mathbf{u} \cdot \mathbf{v}$.

**■ CATCH THE MISTAKE**

**In Exercises 61 and 62, explain the mistake that is made.**

**61.** Find the dot product $\langle -3, 2 \rangle \cdot \langle 2, 5 \rangle$.

**Solution:**

Multiply component by component. $\quad \langle -3, 2 \rangle \cdot \langle 2, 5 \rangle = \langle (-3)(2), (2)(5) \rangle$

Simplify. $\quad \langle -3, 2 \rangle \cdot \langle 2, 5 \rangle = \langle -6, 10 \rangle$

This is incorrect. What mistake was made?

**62.** Find the dot product $\langle 11, 12 \rangle \cdot \langle -2, 3 \rangle$.

**Solution:**

Multiply the outer and inner components.

$$\langle 11, 12 \rangle \cdot \langle -2, 3 \rangle = (11)(3) + (12)(-2)$$

Simplify. $\quad \langle 11, 12 \rangle \cdot \langle -2, 3 \rangle = 9$

This is incorrect. What mistake was made?

## ▪ CONCEPTUAL

**In Exercises 63–66, determine whether each statement is true or false.**

**63.** A dot product of two vectors is a vector.

**64.** A dot product of two vectors is a scalar.

**65.** Orthogonal vectors have a dot product equal to zero.

**66.** If the dot product of two nonzero vectors is equal to zero, then the vectors must be perpendicular.

**For Exercises 67 and 68, refer to the following to find the dot product:**

The dot product of vectors with $n$ components is

$$\langle a_1, a_2, \ldots, a_n \rangle \cdot \langle b_1, b_2, \ldots, b_n \rangle = a_1 b_1 + a_2 b_2 + \cdots + a_n b_n.$$

**67.** $\langle 3, 7, -5 \rangle \cdot \langle -2, 4, 1 \rangle$

**68.** $\langle 1, 0, -2, 3 \rangle \cdot \langle 5, 2, 3, 1 \rangle$

**In Exercises 69–72, given $u = \langle a, b \rangle$ and $v = \langle c, d \rangle$, show that the following properties are true:**

**69.** $\mathbf{u} \cdot \mathbf{v} = \mathbf{v} \cdot \mathbf{u}$

**70.** $\mathbf{u} \cdot \mathbf{u} = |\mathbf{u}|^2$

**71.** $\mathbf{0} \cdot \mathbf{u} = 0$

**72.** $k(\mathbf{u} \cdot \mathbf{v}) = (k\mathbf{u}) \cdot \mathbf{v} = \mathbf{u} \cdot (k\mathbf{v})$, $k$ is a scalar

## ▪ CHALLENGE

**73.** Show that $\mathbf{u} \cdot (\mathbf{v} + \mathbf{w}) = \mathbf{u} \cdot \mathbf{v} + \mathbf{u} \cdot \mathbf{w}$.

**74.** Show that $|\mathbf{u} - \mathbf{v}|^2 = |\mathbf{u}|^2 + |\mathbf{v}|^2 - 2(\mathbf{u} \cdot \mathbf{v})$.

**75.** The *projection of* $\mathbf{v}$ *onto* $\mathbf{u}$ is defined by $\text{proj}_{\mathbf{u}} \mathbf{v} = \left( \dfrac{\mathbf{u} \cdot \mathbf{v}}{|\mathbf{u}|^2} \right) \mathbf{u}$.

This vector is depicted below. Heuristically, this is the "shadow" of $\mathbf{v}$ on $\mathbf{u}$.

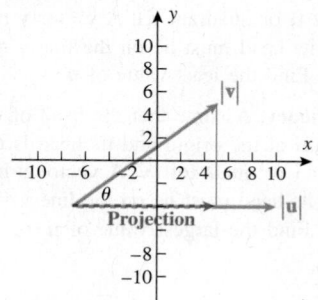

**a.** Compute $\text{proj}_{\mathbf{u}} 2\mathbf{u}$.

**b.** What is $\text{proj}_{\mathbf{u}} c\mathbf{u}$ for any $c > 0$?

**76. a.** Compute $\text{proj}_{\mathbf{u}} 2\mathbf{u}$.

    **b.** What is $\text{proj}_{\mathbf{u}} c\mathbf{u}$ for any $c > 0$?

**77.** Suppose that you are given a vector $\mathbf{u}$. For what vectors $\mathbf{v}$ does $\text{proj}_{\mathbf{u}} \mathbf{v} = \mathbf{0}$?

**78.** True or false: $\text{proj}_{\mathbf{u}}(\mathbf{v} + \mathbf{w}) = \text{proj}_{\mathbf{u}} \mathbf{v} + \text{proj}_{\mathbf{u}} \mathbf{w}$.

**79.** If $\mathbf{u}$ and $\mathbf{v}$ are unit vectors, determine the maximum and minimum value of $(-2\mathbf{u}) \cdot (3\mathbf{v})$.

**80.** Assume that the angle between $\mathbf{u}$ and $\mathbf{v}$ is $\theta = \dfrac{\pi}{3}$. Show that

$$\frac{(\mathbf{u} \cdot \mathbf{v})\mathbf{u}}{|\mathbf{v}|} - \frac{(\mathbf{v} \cdot \mathbf{u})\mathbf{v}}{|\mathbf{u}|} = \frac{|\mathbf{u}|\mathbf{u} - |\mathbf{v}|\mathbf{v}}{2}.$$

## ▪ TECHNOLOGY

**For Exercises 81 and 82, find the indicated dot product with a calculator.**

**81.** $\langle -11, 34 \rangle \cdot \langle 15, -27 \rangle$

**82.** $\langle 23, -350 \rangle \cdot \langle 45, 202 \rangle$

**83.** A rectangle has sides with lengths 18 units and 11 units. Find the angle to one decimal place between the diagonal and the side with length of 18 units. *Hint:* Set up a rectangular coordinate system, and use vectors $\langle 18, 0 \rangle$ to represent the side of length 18 units and $\langle 18, 11 \rangle$ to represent the diagonal.

**84.** The definition of a dot product and the formula to find the angle between two vectors can be extended and applied to vectors with more than two components. A rectangular box has sides with lengths 12 feet, 7 feet, and 9 feet. Find the angle, to the nearest degree, between the diagonal and the side with length 7 feet.

**Use the graphing calculator** $\boxed{\text{SUM}}$ **command to find the angle (round to the nearest degree) between each pair of vectors.**

**85.** $\langle -25, 42 \rangle, \langle 10, 35 \rangle$

**86.** $\langle -12, 9 \rangle, \langle -21, -13 \rangle$

## ▪ PREVIEW TO CALCULUS

There is a branch of calculus devoted to the study of vector-valued functions; these are functions that map real numbers onto vectors. For example, $\mathbf{v}(t) = \langle t, 2t \rangle$.

**87.** Calculate the dot product of the vector-valued functions $\mathbf{u}(t) = \langle 2t, t^2 \rangle$ and $\mathbf{v}(t) = \langle t, -3t \rangle$.

**88.** Calculate the dot product of the vector-valued functions $\mathbf{u}(t) = \langle \cos t, \sin t \rangle$ and $\mathbf{v}(t) = \langle \cos t, -\sin t \rangle$.

**89.** Find the angle between the vector-valued functions $\mathbf{u}(t) = \langle \sin t, \cos t \rangle$ and $\mathbf{v}(t) = \langle \csc t, -\cos t \rangle$ when $t = \dfrac{\pi}{6}$.

**90.** Find the values of $t$ that make the vector-valued functions $\mathbf{u}(t) = \langle \sin t, \sin t \rangle$ and $\mathbf{v}(t) = \langle \cos t, -\sin t \rangle$ orthogonal.

# SECTION 7.3 POLAR (TRIGONOMETRIC) FORM OF COMPLEX NUMBERS

**SKILLS OBJECTIVES**

- Graph a point in the complex plane.
- Convert complex numbers from rectangular form to polar form.
- Convert complex numbers from polar form to rectangular form.

**CONCEPTUAL OBJECTIVES**

- Understand that a complex number can be represented either in rectangular or polar form.
- Relate the horizontal axis in the complex plane to the real component of a complex number.
- Relate the vertical axis in the complex plane to the imaginary component of a complex number.

## Complex Numbers in Rectangular Form

We are already familiar with the **rectangular coordinate system**, where the horizontal axis is called the $x$-axis and the vertical axis is called the $y$-axis. In our study of complex numbers, we refer to the **standard (rectangular) form** as $a + bi$, where $a$ represents the real part and $b$ represents the imaginary part. If we let the horizontal axis be the **real axis** and the vertical axis be the **imaginary axis**, the result is the **complex plane**. The point $a + bi$ is located in the complex plane by finding the coordinates $(a, b)$.

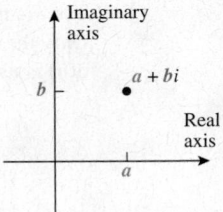

When $b = 0$, the result is a real number, and therefore any numbers along the horizontal axis are real numbers. When $a = 0$, the result is an imaginary number, so any numbers along the vertical axis are imaginary numbers.

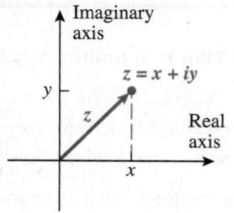

Imaginary axis

$z = x + iy$

$y$

$z$

Real axis

$x$

The variable $z$ is often used to represent a complex number: $z = x + iy$. Complex numbers are analogous to vectors. Suppose we define a vector $\mathbf{z} = \langle x, y \rangle$, whose initial point is the origin and whose terminal point is $(x, y)$; then the magnitude of that vector is $|\mathbf{z}| = \sqrt{x^2 + y^2}$. Similarly, the magnitude, or *modulus*, of a complex number is defined like the magnitude of a position vector in the $xy$-plane, as the distance from the origin $(0, 0)$ to the point $(x, y)$ in the complex plane.

## *Technology Tip*

To use a TI calculator to find the modulus of a complex number, press MATH ▶ CPX ▼

5: ABS ( and enter the complex number.

### DEFINITION Modulus of a Complex Number

The **modulus**, or magnitude, of a complex number $z = x + iy$ is the distance from the origin to the point $(x, y)$ in the complex plane given by

$$|z| = \sqrt{x^2 + y^2}$$

Recall that a complex number $z = x + iy$ has a complex conjugate $\bar{z} = x - iy$. The bar above a complex number denotes its conjugate. Notice that

$$z\bar{z} = (x + iy)(x - iy) = x^2 - i^2 y^2 = x^2 + y^2$$

and therefore the modulus can also be written as

$$|z| = \sqrt{z\bar{z}}$$

## *Technology Tip*

Find the modulus of $z = -3 + 2i$.

MATH ▶ CPX ▼ 5: ABS (

ENTER (−) 3 + 2 2nd

· ) ENTER

```
abs(-3+2i)
        3.605551275
√(13)
        3.605551275
■
```

### EXAMPLE 1 Finding the Modulus of a Complex Number

Find the modulus of $z = -3 + 2i$.

### COMMON MISTAKE

Including the $i$ in the imaginary part.

**★ CORRECT**

Let $x = -3$ and $y = 2$ in $|z| = \sqrt{x^2 + y^2}$.

$$|-3 + 2i| = \sqrt{(-3)^2 + 2^2}$$

Eliminate the parentheses.

$$|-3 + 2i| = \sqrt{9 + 4}$$

Simplify.

$$|z| = |-3 + 2i| = \sqrt{13}$$

**✖ INCORRECT**

Let $x = -3$ and $y = 2i$   **ERROR**

$$|-3 + 2i| = \sqrt{(-3)^2 + (2i)^2}$$

The $i$ is not included in the formula. Only the imaginary part (the coefficient of $i$) is used.

■ **Answer:** $|z| = |2 - 5i| = \sqrt{29}$

■ **YOUR TURN** Find the modulus of $z = 2 - 5i$.

# Complex Numbers in Polar Form

We say that a complex number $z = x + iy$ is in *rectangular* form because it is located at the point $(x, y)$, which is expressed in rectangular coordinates, in the complex plane. Another convenient way of expressing complex numbers is in *polar* form. Recall from our study of vectors (Section 7.1) that vectors have both magnitude and a direction angle. The same is true of numbers in the complex plane. Let $r$ represent the magnitude, or distance from the origin to the point $(x, y)$, and $\theta$ represent the direction angle; then we have the following relationships:

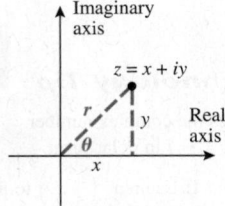

$$r = \sqrt{x^2 + y^2}$$

$$\sin\theta = \frac{y}{r} \qquad \cos\theta = \frac{x}{r} \qquad \text{and} \qquad \tan\theta = \frac{y}{x} \quad (x \neq 0)$$

Isolating $x$ and $y$ in the sinusoidal functions, we find

$$x = r\cos\theta \qquad y = r\sin\theta$$

When we use these expressions for $x$ and $y$, a complex number can be written in *polar* form.

$$z = x + yi = (r\cos\theta) + (r\sin\theta)i = r(\cos\theta + i\sin\theta)$$

### POLAR (TRIGONOMETRIC) FORM OF COMPLEX NUMBERS

The following expression is the **polar form** of a complex number:

$$z = r(\cos\theta + i\sin\theta)$$

where $r$ represents the **modulus** (magnitude) of the complex number and $\theta$ represents the **argument** of $z$.

The following is standard notation for modulus and argument:

$$r = \text{mod}\,z = |z| \qquad \text{and} \qquad \theta = \text{Arg}\,z, \qquad 0 \leq \theta < 2\pi \qquad \text{or} \qquad 0° \leq \theta < 360°$$

## Converting Complex Numbers Between Rectangular and Polar Forms

We can convert back and forth between rectangular and polar (trigonometric) forms of complex numbers using the modulus and trigonometric ratios.

$$r = \sqrt{x^2 + y^2} \qquad \sin\theta = \frac{y}{r} \qquad \cos\theta = \frac{x}{r} \qquad \text{and} \qquad \tan\theta = \frac{y}{x} \quad (x \neq 0)$$

### CONVERTING COMPLEX NUMBERS FROM RECTANGULAR FORM TO POLAR FORM

**Step 1:** Plot the point $z = x + iy$ in the complex plane (note the quadrant).

**Step 2:** Find $r$. Use $r = \sqrt{x^2 + y^2}$.

**Step 3:** Find $\theta$. Apply $\tan\theta = \frac{y}{x}$, $x \neq 0$, where $\theta$ is in the quadrant found in Step 1.

**Step 4:** Write the complex number in polar form: $z = r(\cos\theta + i\sin\theta)$.

Notice that imaginary numbers, $z = bi$, lie on the imaginary axis. Therefore, $\theta = 90°$ if $b > 0$ and $\theta = 270°$ if $b < 0$.

## EXAMPLE 2 Converting from Rectangular to Polar Form

Express the complex number $z = \sqrt{3} - i$ in polar form.

**Solution:**

**STEP 1** Plot the point.

The point lies in **quadrant IV**.

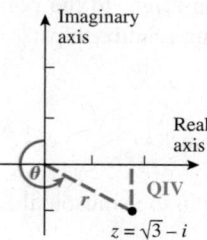

**STEP 2** Find $r$.

Let $x = \sqrt{3}$ and $y = -1$
in $r = \sqrt{x^2 + y^2}$.

$$r = \sqrt{(\sqrt{3})^2 + (-1)^2}$$

Eliminate the parentheses.

$$r = \sqrt{3 + 1}$$

Simplify.

$$\boxed{r = 2}$$

**STEP 3** Find $\theta$.

Let $x = \sqrt{3}$ and $y = -1$
in $\tan\theta = \dfrac{y}{x}$.

$$\tan\theta = -\frac{1}{\sqrt{3}}$$

Solve for $\theta$.

$$\theta = \tan^{-1}\left(-\frac{1}{\sqrt{3}}\right) = -\frac{\pi}{6}$$

Find the reference angle.

$$\text{reference angle} = \frac{\pi}{6}$$

The complex number lies in quadrant IV.

$$\boxed{\theta = \frac{11\pi}{6}}$$

**STEP 4** Write the complex number in polar form.
$z = r(\cos\theta + i\sin\theta)$

$$\boxed{z = 2\left[\cos\left(\frac{11\pi}{6}\right) + i\sin\left(\frac{11\pi}{6}\right)\right]}$$

*Note:* An alternative form is in degrees: $z = 2(\cos 330° + i\sin 330°)$.

■ **YOUR TURN** Express the complex number $z = 1 - i\sqrt{3}$ in polar form.

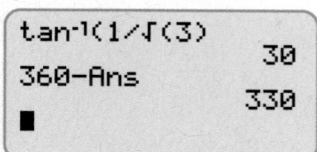
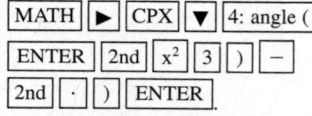
You must be very careful in converting from rectangular to polar form. Remember that the inverse tangent function is a one-to-one function and will yield values in quadrants I and IV. If the point lies in quadrant II or III, add 180° to the angle found through the inverse tangent function.

**EXAMPLE 3  Converting from Rectangular to Polar Form**

Forgetting to confirm the quadrant, which results in using the reference angle instead of the actual angle.

Express the complex number $z = -2 + i$ in polar form.

★ **CORRECT**

**Step 1:** Plot the point.

The point lies in **quadrant II**.

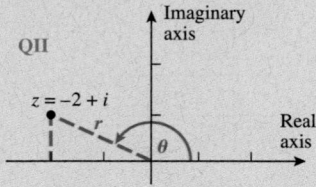

**Step 2:** Find $r$.

Let $x = -2$ and $y = 1$ in.
$r = \sqrt{x^2 + y^2}$.

$$r = \sqrt{(-2)^2 + 1^2}$$

Simplify.

$$\boxed{r = \sqrt{5}}$$

**Step 3:** Find $\theta$.

Let $x = -2$ and $y = 1$ in.
$\tan\theta = \dfrac{y}{x}$.

$$\tan\theta = -\frac{1}{2}$$

$$\theta = \tan^{-1}\left(-\frac{1}{2}\right)$$

$$= -26.565°$$

The complex number lies in quadrant II.

$$\boxed{\theta = -26.6° + 180° = 153.4°}$$

**Step 4:** Write the complex number in
polar form $z = r(\cos\theta + i\sin\theta)$.

$$\boxed{z = \sqrt{5}(\cos 153.4° + i\sin 153.4°)}$$

✖ **INCORRECT**

Evaluate the inverse function with a calculator.

$$\theta = \tan^{-1}\left(-\frac{1}{2}\right) = -26.565°$$

Write the complex number in polar form.

$$z = r(\cos\theta + i\sin\theta)$$
$$z = \sqrt{5}[\cos(-26.6°) + i\sin(-26.6°)]$$

*Note:* $\theta = -26.565°$ lies in quadrant IV, whereas the original point lies in quadrant II. Therefore, we should have added 180° to $\theta$ in order to arrive at a point in quadrant II.

*Technology Tip*

Express the complex number
$z = -2 + i$ in polar form.

```
abs(-2+i)
          2.236067977
√(5)
          2.236067977
angle(-2+i)
          153.4349488
```

---

■ **YOUR TURN** Express the complex number $z = -1 + 2i$ in polar form.

■ **Answer:**
$z = \sqrt{5}(\cos 116.6° + i\sin 116.6°)$

To convert from polar to rectangular form, simply evaluate the trigonometric functions.

### EXAMPLE 4   Converting from Polar to Rectangular Form

Express $z = 4(\cos 120° + i \sin 120°)$ in rectangular form.

**Solution:**

Evaluate the trigonometric functions exactly.

$$z = 4\left(\underbrace{\cos 120°}_{-\frac{1}{2}} + \underbrace{i \sin 120°}_{\frac{\sqrt{3}}{2}}\right)$$

Distribute the 4.

$$z = 4\left(-\frac{1}{2}\right) + 4\left(\frac{\sqrt{3}}{2}\right)i$$

Simplify.

$$\boxed{z = -2 + 2\sqrt{3}i}$$

■ **YOUR TURN** Express $z = 2(\cos 210° + i \sin 210°)$ in rectangular form.

### EXAMPLE 5   Using a Calculator to Convert from Polar to Rectangular Form

Express $z = 3(\cos 109° + i \sin 109°)$ in rectangular form. Round to four decimal places.

**Solution:**

Use a calculator to evaluate the trigonometric functions.

$$z = 3\left(\underbrace{\cos 109°}_{-0.325568} + \underbrace{i \sin 109°}_{0.945519}\right)$$

Simplify.

$$\boxed{z = -0.9767 + 2.8366i}$$

■ **YOUR TURN** Express $z = 7(\cos 217° + i \sin 217°)$ in rectangular form. Round to four decimal places.

## SECTION 7.3 SUMMARY

In the complex plane, the horizontal axis is the real axis and the vertical axis is the imaginary axis. We can express complex numbers in either rectangular or polar form:

**rectangular form:** $z = x + iy$

or

**polar form:** $z = r(\cos\theta + i\sin\theta)$

The modulus of a complex number, $z = x + iy$, is given by

$$|z| = \sqrt{x^2 + y^2}$$

To convert from rectangular to polar form, we use the relationships

$$r = \sqrt{x^2 + y^2} \qquad \text{and} \qquad \tan\theta = \frac{y}{x}, x \neq 0 \text{ and } 0 \leq \theta < 2\pi$$

It is important to note in which quadrant the point lies. To convert from polar to rectangular form, simply evaluate the trigonometric functions.

$$x = r\cos\theta \qquad \text{and} \qquad y = r\sin\theta$$

## SECTION
## 7.3 EXERCISES

**■ SKILLS**

**In Exercises 1–8, graph each complex number in the complex plane.**

**1.** $7 + 8i$          **2.** $3 + 5i$          **3.** $-2 - 4i$          **4.** $-3 - 2i$

**5.** $2$          **6.** $7$          **7.** $-3i$          **8.** $-5i$

**In Exercises 9–24, express each complex number in polar form.**

**9.** $1 - i$          **10.** $2 + 2i$          **11.** $1 + \sqrt{3}i$          **12.** $-3 - \sqrt{3}i$

**13.** $-4 + 4i$          **14.** $\sqrt{5} - \sqrt{5}i$          **15.** $\sqrt{3} - 3i$          **16.** $-\sqrt{3} + i$

**17.** $3 + 0i$          **18.** $-2 + 0i$          **19.** $-\frac{1}{2} - \frac{1}{2}i$          **20.** $\frac{1}{6} - \frac{1}{6}i$

**21.** $-\sqrt{6} - \sqrt{6}i$          **22.** $\frac{1}{3} - \frac{1}{3}i$          **23.** $-5 + 5i$          **24.** $3 + 3i$

**In Exercises 25–40, use a calculator to express each complex number in polar form.**

**25.** $3 - 7i$          **26.** $2 + 3i$          **27.** $-6 + 5i$          **28.** $-4 - 3i$

**29.** $-5 + 12i$          **30.** $24 + 7i$          **31.** $8 - 6i$          **32.** $-3 + 4i$

**33.** $-\dfrac{1}{2} + \dfrac{3}{4}i$          **34.** $-\dfrac{5}{8} - \dfrac{11}{4}i$          **35.** $5.1 + 2.3i$          **36.** $1.8 - 0.9i$

**37.** $-2\sqrt{3} - \sqrt{5}i$          **38.** $-\dfrac{4\sqrt{5}}{3} + \dfrac{\sqrt{5}}{2}i$          **39.** $4.02 - 2.11i$          **40.** $1.78 - 0.12i$

**In Exercises 41–52, express each complex number in rectangular form.**

**41.** $5(\cos 180° + i\sin 180°)$          **42.** $2(\cos 135° + i\sin 135°)$          **43.** $2(\cos 315° + i\sin 315°)$

**44.** $3(\cos 270° + i\sin 270°)$          **45.** $-4(\cos 60° + i\sin 60°)$          **46.** $-4(\cos 210° + i\sin 210°)$

**47.** $\sqrt{3}(\cos 150° + i\sin 150°)$          **48.** $\sqrt{3}(\cos 330° + i\sin 330°)$          **49.** $\sqrt{2}\left[\cos\left(\dfrac{\pi}{4}\right) + i\sin\left(\dfrac{\pi}{4}\right)\right]$

**50.** $2\left[\cos\left(\dfrac{5\pi}{6}\right) + i\sin\left(\dfrac{5\pi}{6}\right)\right]$          **51.** $6\left[\cos\left(\dfrac{3\pi}{4}\right) + i\sin\left(\dfrac{3\pi}{4}\right)\right]$          **52.** $4\left[\cos\left(\dfrac{11\pi}{6}\right) + i\sin\left(\dfrac{11\pi}{6}\right)\right]$

**In Exercises 53–64, use a calculator to express each complex number in rectangular form.**

**53.** $5(\cos 295° + i\sin 295°)$          **54.** $4(\cos 35° + i\sin 35°)$          **55.** $3(\cos 100° + i\sin 100°)$

**56.** $6(\cos 250° + i\sin 250°)$          **57.** $-7(\cos 140° + i\sin 140°)$          **58.** $-5(\cos 320° + i\sin 320°)$

**59.** $3\left[\cos\left(\dfrac{11\pi}{12}\right) + i\sin\left(\dfrac{11\pi}{12}\right)\right]$          **60.** $2\left[\cos\left(\dfrac{4\pi}{7}\right) + i\sin\left(\dfrac{4\pi}{7}\right)\right]$          **61.** $-2\left[\cos\left(\dfrac{3\pi}{5}\right) + i\sin\left(\dfrac{3\pi}{5}\right)\right]$

**62.** $-4\left[\cos\left(\dfrac{15\pi}{11}\right) + i\sin\left(\dfrac{15\pi}{11}\right)\right]$          **63.** $-5\left[\cos\left(\dfrac{4\pi}{9}\right) + i\sin\left(\dfrac{4\pi}{9}\right)\right]$          **64.** $6\left[\cos\left(\dfrac{13\pi}{8}\right) + i\sin\left(\dfrac{13\pi}{8}\right)\right]$

■ **APPLICATIONS**

**65. Road Construction.** Engineers are planning the construction of a bypass in a north–south highway to connect cities $B$ and $C$.

**a.** What is the distance from $A$ to $C$?

**b.** Write the vector $AC$ as a complex number in polar form. (Use degrees for the angle.)

**c.** What is the angle $BAC$?

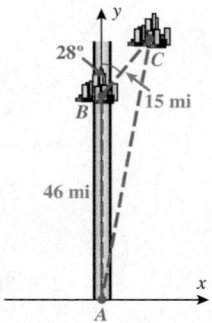

**66. Road Construction.** Engineers are planning the construction of a bypass in a north–south highway to connect cities $B$ and $C$.

**a.** What is the distance from $A$ to $C$?

**b.** Write the vector $AC$ as a complex number in polar form. (Use degrees for the angle.)

**c.** What is the angle $BAC$?

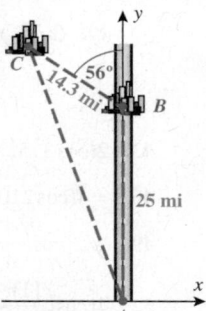

**67. City Map Barcelona.** The city of Barcelona is crossed by the Diagonal Avenue as shown in the map.

**a.** Which complex numbers, in rectangular form, represent the street segment $A$-$B$, $B$-$C$, and $C$-$D$?

**b.** Which complex number, in polar form, represents $A$-$D$?

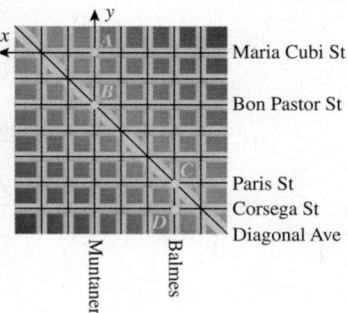

**68. City Map Washington, D.C.** A simplified map of Washington, D.C., is shown below.

**a.** Which complex numbers, in rectangular form, represent the street segment $A$-$B$, $B$-$C$, and $C$-$D$?

**b.** Which complex number, in polar form, represents $A$-$D$?

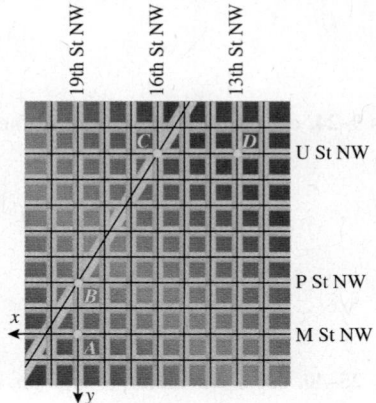

**For Exercises 69 and 70, refer to the following:**

In the design of AC circuits, the voltage across a resistance is regarded as a real number. When the voltage goes across an inductor or a capacitor, it is considered an imaginary number: positive ($I > 0$) in the inductor case and negative ($I < 0$) in the capacitor case. The impedance results from the combination of the voltages in the circuit and is given by the formula

$$z = |z|(\cos\theta + i\sin\theta), \text{ where } |z| = \sqrt{R^2 + I^2}$$
$$\text{and } \theta = \tan^{-1}\left(\frac{I}{R}\right)$$

where $z$ is impedance, $R$ is resistance, and $I$ is inductance.

**69. AC Circuits.** Find the impedance of a circuit with resistance 4 ohms and inductor of 6 ohms. Write your answer in polar form.

**70. AC Circuits.** Find the impedance of a circuit with resistance 7 ohms and capacitor of 5 ohms. Write your answer in polar form.

## ▪CATCH THE MISTAKE

**In Exercises 71 and 72, explain the mistake that is made.**

**71.** Express $z = -3 - 8i$ in polar form.

**Solution:**

Find $r$.     $r = \sqrt{x^2 + y^2} = \sqrt{9 + 64} = \sqrt{73}$

Find $\theta$.     $\tan\theta = \dfrac{8}{3}$

$$\theta = \tan^{-1}\left(\dfrac{8}{3}\right) = 69.44°$$

Write the complex number in polar form.

$$z = \sqrt{73}\,(\cos 69.44° + i\sin 69.44°)$$

This is incorrect. What mistake was made?

**72.** Express $z = -3 + 8i$ in polar form.

**Solution:**

Find $r$.     $r = \sqrt{x^2 + y^2} = \sqrt{9 + 64} = \sqrt{73}$

Find $\theta$.     $\tan\theta = -\dfrac{8}{3}$

$$\theta = \tan^{-1}\left(-\dfrac{8}{3}\right) = -69.44°$$

Write the complex number in polar form.

$$z = \sqrt{73}\,[\cos(-69.44°) + i\sin(-69.44°)]$$

This is incorrect. What mistake was made?

## ▪CONCEPTUAL

**In Exercises 73–76, determine whether each statement is true or false.**

**73.** In the complex plane, any point that lies along the horizontal axis is a real number.

**74.** In the complex plane, any point that lies along the vertical axis is an imaginary number.

**75.** The modulus of $z$ and the modulus of $\bar{z}$ are equal.

**76.** The argument of $z$ and the argument of $\bar{z}$ are equal.

**77.** Find the argument of $z = a$, where $a$ is a positive real number.

**78.** Find the argument of $z = bi$, where $b$ is a positive real number.

**79.** Find the modulus of $z = bi$, where $b$ is a negative real number.

**80.** Find the modulus of $z = a$, where $a$ is a negative real number.

**In Exercises 81 and 82, use a calculator to express the complex number in polar form.**

**81.** $a - 2ai$, where $a > 0$

**82.** $-3a - 4ai$, where $a > 0$

## ▪CHALLENGE

**83.** Suppose that a complex number $z$ lies on the circle $x^2 + y^2 = \pi^2$. If $\cos\left(\dfrac{\theta}{2}\right) = \dfrac{1}{2}$ and $\sin\theta < 0$, find the rectangular form of $z$.

**84.** Suppose that a complex number $z$ lies on the circle $x^2 + y^2 = 8$. If $\sin\left(\dfrac{\theta}{2}\right) = -\dfrac{\sqrt{3}}{2}$ and $\cos\theta < 0$, find the rectangular form of $z$.

**85.** Consider the following diagram:

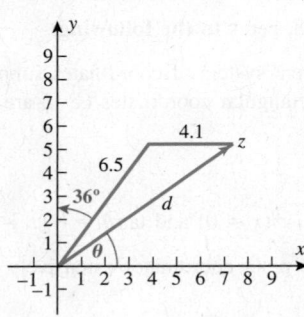

Find $z$ in trigonometric form.
*Hint:* Use the Law of Cosines.

**86.** Consider the following diagram:

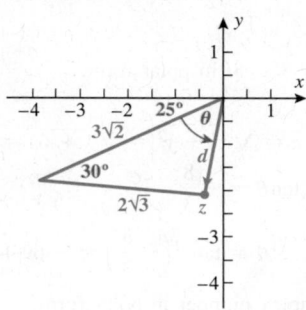

Find $z$ in trigonometric form.
*Hint:* Use the Law of Cosines.

**87.** Consider the complex number in polar form
$z = r(\cos\theta + i\sin\theta)$. What is the polar form of $-z$?

**88.** Consider the complex number in polar form
$z = r(\cos\theta + i\sin\theta)$. What is the polar form of $\bar{z}$?

■ **TECHNOLOGY**

Graphing calculators are able to convert complex numbers from rectangular to polar form using the $\boxed{\text{ABS}}$ command to find the modulus and the angle command to find the argument.

**89.** Find abs$(1 + i)$. Find angle$(1 + i)$. Write $1 + i$ in polar form.

**90.** Find abs$(1 - i)$. Find angle$(1 - i)$. Write $1 - i$ in polar form.

A second way of using a graphing calculator to convert between rectangular and polar coordinates is with the $\boxed{\text{Pol}}$ and $\boxed{\text{Rec}}$ commands.

**91.** Find Pol(2, 1). Write $2 + i$ in polar form.

**92.** Find Rec(345°). Write $3(\cos 45° + i\sin 45°)$ in rectangular form.

Another way of using a graphing calculator to represent complex numbers in rectangular form is to enter the real and imaginary parts as a list of two numbers and use the $\boxed{\text{SUM}}$ command to find the modulus.

**93.** Write $28 - 21i$ in polar form using the $\boxed{\text{SUM}}$ command to find its modulus, and round the angle to the nearest degree.

**94.** Write $-\sqrt{21} + 10i$ in polar form using the $\boxed{\text{SUM}}$ command to find its modulus, and round the angle to the nearest degree.

■ **PREVIEW TO CALCULUS**

**In Exercises 95–98, refer to the following:**

The use of a different system of coordinates simplifies many mathematical expressions and some calculations are performed in an easier way. The rectangular coordinates $(x, y)$ are transformed into polar coordinates by the equations

$$x = r\cos\theta \text{ and } y = r\sin\theta$$

where $r = \sqrt{x^2 + y^2}\ (r \neq 0)$ and $\tan\theta = \dfrac{y}{x}\ (x \neq 0)$. In polar coordinates, the equation of the unit circle $x^2 + y^2 = 1$ is just $r = 1$.

In calculus, we use polar coordinates extensively. Transform the rectangular equation to polar form.

**95.** $x^2 + y^2 = 25$

**96.** $x^2 + y^2 = 4x$

**97.** $y^2 - 2y = -x^2$

**98.** $(x^2 + y^2)^2 - 16(x^2 - y^2) = 0$

# PRODUCTS, QUOTIENTS, POWERS, AND ROOTS OF COMPLEX NUMBERS

## SKILLS OBJECTIVES

- Find the product of two complex numbers.
- Find the quotient of two complex numbers.
- Raise a complex number to an integer power.
- Find the $n$th roots of a complex number.
- Solve a polynomial equation by finding complex roots.

## CONCEPTUAL OBJECTIVES

- Derive the identities for products and quotients of complex numbers.
- Relate De Moivre's theorem (the power rule) for complex numbers to the product rule for complex numbers.

In this section, we will multiply complex numbers, divide complex numbers, raise complex numbers to powers, and find roots of complex numbers.

## Products of Complex Numbers

First, we will derive a formula for the product of two complex numbers.

| WORDS | MATH |
|---|---|
| Start with two complex numbers $z_1$ and $z_2$. | $z_1 = r_1(\cos\theta_1 + i\sin\theta_1)$ and $z_2 = r_2(\cos\theta_2 + i\sin\theta_2)$ |
| Multiply $z_1$ and $z_2$. | $z_1 z_2 = r_1 r_2(\cos\theta_1 + i\sin\theta_1)(\cos\theta_2 + i\sin\theta_2)$ |
| Use the FOIL method to multiply the expressions in parentheses. | $z_1 z_2 = r_1 r_2(\cos\theta_1 \cos\theta_2 + i\cos\theta_1 \sin\theta_2 + i\sin\theta_1 \cos\theta_2 + \underset{-1}{i^2} \sin\theta_1 \sin\theta_2)$ |
| Group the real parts and the imaginary parts. | $z_1 z_2 = r_1 r_2[(\cos\theta_1 \cos\theta_2 - \sin\theta_1 \sin\theta_2) + i(\cos\theta_1 \sin\theta_2 + \sin\theta_1 \cos\theta_2)]$ |
| Apply the cosine and sine sum identities. | $z_1 z_2 = r_1 r_2\left[ \underbrace{(\cos\theta_1 \cos\theta_2 - \sin\theta_1 \sin\theta_2)}_{\cos(\theta_1 + \theta_2)} + i\underbrace{(\cos\theta_1 \sin\theta_2 + \sin\theta_1 \cos\theta_2)}_{\sin(\theta_1 + \theta_2)} \right]$ |
| Simplify. | $z_1 z_2 = r_1 r_2[\cos(\theta_1 + \theta_2) + i\sin(\theta_1 + \theta_2)]$ |

### PRODUCT OF TWO COMPLEX NUMBERS

Let $z_1 = r_1(\cos\theta_1 + i\sin\theta_1)$ and $z_2 = r_2(\cos\theta_2 + i\sin\theta_2)$ be two complex numbers. The complex product $z_1 z_2$ is given by

$$z_1 z_2 = r_1 r_2[\cos(\theta_1 + \theta_2) + i\sin(\theta_1 + \theta_2)]$$

In other words, *when multiplying two complex numbers, multiply the magnitudes and add the arguments.*

### Study Tip

When two complex numbers are multiplied, the magnitudes are multiplied and the arguments are added.

### EXAMPLE 1   Multiplying Complex Numbers

Find the product of $z_1 = 3(\cos 35° + i\sin 35°)$ and $z_2 = 2(\cos 10° + i\sin 10°)$.

**Solution:**

| Set up the product. | $z_1 z_2 = 3(\cos 35° + i\sin 35°) \cdot 2(\cos 10° + i\sin 10°)$ |
|---|---|
| Multiply the magnitudes and add the arguments. | $z_1 z_2 = 3 \cdot 2[\cos(35° + 10°) + i\sin(35° + 10°)]$ |

Simplify. $\qquad z_1z_2 = 6(\cos 45° + i\sin 45°)$

The product is in polar form.
To express the product in
rectangular form, evaluate $\qquad z_1z_2 = 6\left(\dfrac{\sqrt{2}}{2} + i\dfrac{\sqrt{2}}{2}\right) = 3\sqrt{2} + 3i\sqrt{2}$
the trigonometric functions.

Product in polar form: $\qquad \boxed{z_1z_2 = 6(\cos 45° + i\sin 45°)} = 6\left[\cos\left(\dfrac{\pi}{4}\right) + i\sin\left(\dfrac{\pi}{4}\right)\right]$

Product in rectangular form: $\qquad \boxed{z_1z_2 = 3\sqrt{2} + 3i\sqrt{2}}$

■ **Answer:**
$z_1z_2 = 10(\cos 120° + i\sin 120°)$ or
$z_1z_2 = -5 + 5i\sqrt{3}$

■ **YOUR TURN** Find the product of $z_1 = 2(\cos 55° + i\sin 55°)$ and
$z_2 = 5(\cos 65° + i\sin 65°)$. Express the answer in both polar and
rectangular form.

## Quotients of Complex Numbers

We now derive a formula for the quotient of two complex numbers.

| WORDS | MATH |
|---|---|
| Start with two complex numbers $z_1$ and $z_2$. | $z_1 = r_1(\cos\theta_1 + i\sin\theta_1)$ and $z_2 = r_2(\cos\theta_2 + i\sin\theta_2)$ |
| Divide $z_1$ by $z_2$. | $\dfrac{z_1}{z_2} = \dfrac{r_1(\cos\theta_1 + i\sin\theta_1)}{r_2(\cos\theta_2 + i\sin\theta_2)} = \left(\dfrac{r_1}{r_2}\right)\left(\dfrac{\cos\theta_1 + i\sin\theta_1}{\cos\theta_2 + i\sin\theta_2}\right)$ |
| Multiply the numerator and the denominator of the second expression in parentheses by the conjugate of the denominator, $\cos\theta_2 - i\sin\theta_2$. | $\dfrac{z_1}{z_2} = \left(\dfrac{r_1}{r_2}\right)\left(\dfrac{\cos\theta_1 + i\sin\theta_1}{\cos\theta_2 + i\sin\theta_2}\right)\left(\dfrac{\cos\theta_2 - i\sin\theta_2}{\cos\theta_2 - i\sin\theta_2}\right)$ |
| Use the FOIL method to multiply the expressions in parentheses in the last two expressions. | $\dfrac{z_1}{z_2} = \left(\dfrac{r_1}{r_2}\right)\left(\dfrac{\cos\theta_1\cos\theta_2 - i^2\sin\theta_1\sin\theta_2 + i\sin\theta_1\cos\theta_2 - i\sin\theta_2\cos\theta_1}{\cos^2\theta_2 - i^2\sin^2\theta_2}\right)$ |
| Substitute $i^2 = -1$ and group the real parts and the imaginary parts. | $\dfrac{z_1}{z_2} = \left(\dfrac{r_1}{r_2}\right)\left[\dfrac{(\cos\theta_1\cos\theta_2 + \sin\theta_1\sin\theta_2) + i(\sin\theta_1\cos\theta_2 - \sin\theta_2\cos\theta_1)}{\underbrace{\cos^2\theta_2 + \sin^2\theta_2}_{1}}\right]$ |
| Simplify. | $\dfrac{z_1}{z_2} = \left(\dfrac{r_1}{r_2}\right)[(\cos\theta_1\cos\theta_2 + \sin\theta_1\sin\theta_2) + i(\sin\theta_1\cos\theta_2 - \sin\theta_2\cos\theta_1)]$ |
| Use the cosine and sine difference identities. | $\dfrac{z_1}{z_2} = \left(\dfrac{r_1}{r_2}\right)\underbrace{(\cos\theta_1\cos\theta_2 + \sin\theta_1\sin\theta_2)}_{\cos(\theta_1 - \theta_2)} + i\underbrace{(\sin\theta_1\cos\theta_2 - \sin\theta_2\cos\theta_1)}_{\sin(\theta_1 - \theta_2)}$ |
| Simplify. | $\dfrac{z_1}{z_2} = \dfrac{r_1}{r_2}[\cos(\theta_1 - \theta_2) + i\sin(\theta_1 - \theta_2)]$ |

It is important to notice that the argument difference is the argument of the numerator minus the argument of the denominator.

### QUOTIENT OF TWO COMPLEX NUMBERS

Let $z_1 = r_1(\cos\theta_1 + i\sin\theta_1)$ and $z_2 = r_2(\cos\theta_2 + i\sin\theta_2)$ be two complex numbers. The complex quotient $\dfrac{z_1}{z_2}$ is given by

$$\frac{z_1}{z_2} = \frac{r_1}{r_2}[\cos(\theta_1 - \theta_2) + i\sin(\theta_1 - \theta_2)]$$

In other words, *when dividing two complex numbers, divide the magnitudes and subtract the arguments. It is important to note that the argument difference is the argument of the complex number in the numerator minus the argument of the complex number in the denominator.*

### EXAMPLE 2   Dividing Complex Numbers

Let $z_1 = 6(\cos 125° + i\sin 125°)$ and $z_2 = 3(\cos 65° + i\sin 65°)$. Find $\dfrac{z_1}{z_2}$.

**Solution:**

Set up the quotient.

$$\frac{z_1}{z_2} = \frac{6(\cos 125° + i\sin 125°)}{3(\cos 65° + i\sin 65°)}$$

Divide the magnitudes and subtract the arguments.

$$\frac{z_1}{z_2} = \frac{6}{3}[\cos(125° - 65°) + i\sin(125° - 65°)]$$

Simplify.

$$\frac{z_1}{z_2} = 2(\cos 60° + i\sin 60°)$$

The quotient is in polar form. To express the quotient in rectangular form, evaluate the trigonometric functions.

$$\frac{z_1}{z_2} = 2\left(\frac{1}{2} + i\frac{\sqrt{3}}{2}\right) = 1 + i\sqrt{3}$$

Polar form:

$$\boxed{\frac{z_1}{z_2} = 2(\cos 60° + i\sin 60°)}$$

Rectangular form:

$$\boxed{\frac{z_1}{z_2} = 1 + i\sqrt{3}}$$

■ **YOUR TURN** Let $z_1 = 10(\cos 275° + i\sin 275°)$ and $z_2 = 5(\cos 65° + i\sin 65°)$. Find $\dfrac{z_1}{z_2}$. Express the answers in both polar and rectangular form.

*Technology Tip*

Let $z_1 = 6(\cos 125° + i\sin 125°)$ and $z_2 = 3(\cos 65° + i\sin 65°)$.

Find $\dfrac{z_1}{z_2}$. Be sure to include parentheses for $z_1$ and $z_2$.

```
(6(cos(125)+isin
(125)))/(3(cos(6
5)+isin(65)))
   1.0000+1.7321i
√(3)
            1.7321
```

■ **Answer:**

$\dfrac{z_1}{z_2} = 2(\cos 210° + i\sin 210°)$ or

$\dfrac{z_1}{z_2} = -\sqrt{3} - i$

When multiplying or dividing complex numbers, we have considered only those values of $\theta$ such that $0° \le \theta < 360°$. When the value of $\theta$ is negative or greater than or equal to $360°$, find the coterminal angle in the interval $[0°, 360°)$.

# Powers of Complex Numbers

Raising a number to a positive integer power is the same as multiplying that number by itself repeated times.

$$x^3 = x \cdot x \cdot x \qquad (a + b)^2 = (a + b)(a + b)$$

Therefore, raising a complex number to a power that is a positive integer is the same as multiplying the complex number by itself multiple times. Let us illustrate this with the complex number $z = r(\cos\theta + i\sin\theta)$, which we will raise to positive integer powers ($n$).

| WORDS | MATH |
|---|---|
| Take the case $n = 2$. | $z^2 = [r(\cos\theta + i\sin\theta)][r(\cos\theta + i\sin\theta)]$ |
| Apply the product rule (multiply the magnitudes and add the arguments). | $z^2 = r^2[\cos(2\theta) + i\sin(2\theta)]$ |
| Take the case $n = 3$. | $z^3 = z^2 z = \{r^2[\cos(2\theta) + i\sin(2\theta)]\}[r(\cos\theta + i\sin\theta)]$ |
| Apply the product rule (multiply the magnitudes and add the arguments). | $z^3 = r^3[\cos(3\theta) + i\sin(3\theta)]$ |
| Take the case $n = 4$. | $z^4 = z^3 z = \{r^3[\cos(3\theta) + i\sin(3\theta)]\}[r(\cos\theta + i\sin\theta)]$ |
| Apply the product rule (multiply the magnitudes and add the arguments). | $z^4 = r^4[\cos(4\theta) + i\sin(4\theta)]$ |
| The pattern observed for any $n$ is | $z^n = r^n[\cos(n\theta) + i\sin(n\theta)]$ |

Although we will not prove this generalized representation of a complex number raised to a power, it was proved by Abraham De Moivre, and hence its name.

## DE MOIVRE'S THEOREM

If $z = r(\cos\theta + i\sin\theta)$ is a complex number, then

$$z^n = r^n[\cos(n\theta) + i\sin(n\theta)]$$

when $n$ is a positive integer ($n \geq 1$).

In other words, when raising a complex number to a power $n$, raise the magnitude to the same power $n$ and multiply the argument by $n$.

Although De Moivre's theorem was proved for all real numbers $n$, we will only use it for positive integer values of $n$ and their reciprocals ($n$th roots). This is a very powerful theorem. For example, if asked to find $(\sqrt{3} + i)^{10}$, you have two choices: (1) Multiply out the expression algebraically, which we will call the long way or (2) convert to polar coordinates and use De Moivre's theorem, which we will call the short way. We will use De Moivre's theorem.

## EXAMPLE 3   Finding a Power of a Complex Number

Find $(\sqrt{3} + i)^{10}$ and express the answer in rectangular form.

**Technology Tip**

Find $(\sqrt{3} + i)^{10}$ and express the answer in rectangular form.

```
(√(3)+i)^10
512-886.8100135i
(2(cos(30)+isin(
30)))^10
512-886.8100135i
```

**Solution:**

**STEP 1**   Convert to polar form.           $(\sqrt{3} + i)^{10} = [2(\cos 30° + i\sin 30°)]^{10}$

**STEP 2**   Apply De Moivre's theorem       $(\sqrt{3} + i)^{10} = [2(\cos 30° + i\sin 30°)]^{10}$
with $n = 10$.                                     $= 2^{10}[\cos(10 \cdot 30°) + i\sin(10 \cdot 30°)]$

**STEP 3**   Simplify.                        $(\sqrt{3} + i)^{10} = 2^{10}(\cos 300° + i\sin 300°)$

Evaluate $2^{10}$ and the sine
and cosine functions.                          $= 1024\left(\dfrac{1}{2} - i\dfrac{\sqrt{3}}{2}\right)$

Simplify.                                        $\boxed{= 512 - 512i\sqrt{3}}$

■ **YOUR TURN**   Find $(1 + i\sqrt{3})^{10}$ and express the answer in rectangular form.

■ **Answer:** $-512 - 512i\sqrt{3}$

# Roots of Complex Numbers

De Moivre's theorem is the basis for the *nth root theorem*. Before we proceed, let us motivate it with a problem: Solve $x^3 - 1 = 0$. Recall that a polynomial of degree $n$ has $n$ solutions (roots in the complex number system). So the polynomial $P(x) = x^3 - 1$ is of degree 3 and has three solutions (roots). We can solve it algebraically.

| **WORDS** | **MATH** |
|---|---|

List the potential rational roots of the
polynomial $P(x) = x^3 - 1$.

$$x = \pm 1$$

Use synthetic division to test $x = 1$.

$$
\begin{array}{c|cccc}
1 & 1 & 0 & 0 & -1 \\
  &   & 1 & 1 & 1 \\
\hline
  & 1 & 1 & 1 & \boxed{0} \\
  & \multicolumn{3}{c}{\underbrace{\phantom{1\ 1\ 1}}_{x^2 + x + 1}} &
\end{array}
$$

Since $x = 1$ is a zero, then the polynomial
can be written as a product of the linear
factor $(x - 1)$ and a quadratic factor.

$$P(x) = (x - 1)(x^2 + x + 1)$$

Use the quadratic formula on $x^2 + x + 1 = 0$
to solve for $x$.

$$x = \frac{-1 \pm \sqrt{1 - 4}}{2} = \frac{-1 \pm \sqrt{-3}}{2} = -\frac{1}{2} \pm \frac{i\sqrt{3}}{2}$$

So the three solutions to the equation $x^3 - 1 = 0$ are $\boxed{x = 1,\ x = -\dfrac{1}{2} + \dfrac{i\sqrt{3}}{2},\ \text{and}\ x = -\dfrac{1}{2} - \dfrac{i\sqrt{3}}{2}}$.

An alternative approach to solving $x^3 - 1 = 0$ is to use the *nth root theorem* to find the additional complex cube roots of 1.

# Derivation of the *n*th Root Theorem

| WORDS | MATH |
|---|---|
| Let $z$ and $w$ be complex numbers such that $w$ is the $n$th root of $z$. | $w = z^{1/n}$ or $w = \sqrt[n]{z}$, where $n$ is a positive integer |
| Raise both sides of the equation to the $n$th power. | $w^n = z$ |
| Let $z = r(\cos\theta + i\sin\theta)$ and $w = s(\cos\alpha + i\sin\alpha)$. | $[s(\cos\alpha + i\sin\alpha)]^n = r(\cos\theta + i\sin\theta)$ |
| Apply De Moivre's theorem to the left side of the equation. | $s^n[\cos(n\alpha) + i\sin(n\alpha)] = r(\cos\theta + i\sin\theta)$ |
| For these two expressions to be equal, their magnitudes must be equal and their angles must be coterminal. | $s^n = r$ and $n\alpha = \theta + 2k\pi$, where $k$ is any integer |
| Solve for $s$ and $\alpha$. | $s = r^{1/n}$ and $\alpha = \dfrac{\theta + 2k\pi}{n}$ |
| Substitute $s = r^{1/n}$ and $\alpha = \dfrac{\theta + 2k\pi}{n}$ into $w = z^{1/n}$. | $z^{1/n} = r^{1/n}\left[\cos\left(\dfrac{\theta + 2k\pi}{n}\right) + i\sin\left(\dfrac{\theta + 2k\pi}{n}\right)\right]$ |

Notice that when $k = n$, the arguments $\dfrac{\theta}{n} + 2\pi$ and $\dfrac{\theta}{n}$ are coterminal. Therefore, to get distinct roots, let $k = 0, 1, \ldots, n - 1$. If we let $z$ be a given complex number and $w$ be any complex number that satisfies the relationship $z^{1/n} = w$ or $z = w^n$, where $n \geq 2$, then we say that $w$ is a **complex *n*th root** of $z$.

---

**nTH ROOT THEOREM**

The ***n*th roots** of the complex number $z = r(\cos\theta + i\sin\theta)$ are given by

$$w_k = r^{1/n}\left[\cos\left(\frac{\theta}{n} + \frac{2k\pi}{n}\right) + i\sin\left(\frac{\theta}{n} + \frac{2k\pi}{n}\right)\right] \qquad \theta \text{ in radians}$$

or

$$w_k = r^{1/n}\left[\cos\left(\frac{\theta}{n} + \frac{k \cdot 360°}{n}\right) + i\sin\left(\frac{\theta}{n} + \frac{k \cdot 360°}{n}\right)\right] \qquad \theta \text{ in degrees}$$

where $k = 0, 1, 2, \ldots, n - 1$.

---

### EXAMPLE 4   Finding Roots of Complex Numbers

Find the three distinct cube roots of $-4 - 4i\sqrt{3}$, and plot the roots in the complex plane.

**Solution:**

**STEP 1** Write $-4 - 4i\sqrt{3}$ in polar form. $\qquad\qquad\qquad 8(\cos 240° + i\sin 240°)$

**STEP 2** Find the three cube roots.

$$w_k = r^{1/n}\left[\cos\left(\frac{\theta}{n} + \frac{k \cdot 360°}{n}\right) + i\sin\left(\frac{\theta}{n} + \frac{k \cdot 360°}{n}\right)\right]$$

$$\theta = 240°, \; r = 8, \; n = 3, \; k = 0, 1, 2$$

$k = 0$: $\qquad\qquad w_0 = 8^{1/3}\left[\cos\left(\dfrac{240°}{3} + \dfrac{0 \cdot 360°}{3}\right) + i\sin\left(\dfrac{240°}{3} + \dfrac{0 \cdot 360°}{3}\right)\right]$

Simplify. $\qquad\qquad \boxed{w_0 = 2(\cos 80° + i\sin 80°)}$

$k = 1$:

$$w_1 = 8^{1/3}\left[\cos\left(\frac{240°}{3} + \frac{1 \cdot 360°}{3}\right) + i\sin\left(\frac{240°}{3} + \frac{1 \cdot 360°}{3}\right)\right]$$

Simplify.

$$w_1 = 2(\cos 200° + i\sin 200°)$$

$k = 2$:

$$w_2 = 8^{1/3}\left[\cos\left(\frac{240°}{3} + \frac{2 \cdot 360°}{3}\right) + i\sin\left(\frac{240°}{3} + \frac{2 \cdot 360°}{3}\right)\right]$$

Simplify.

$$w_2 = 2(\cos 320° + i\sin 320°)$$

**STEP 3**  Plot the three cube roots in the complex plane.

Notice the following:

- The roots all have a magnitude of 2.
- The roots lie on a circle of radius 2.
- The roots are equally spaced around the circle (120° apart).

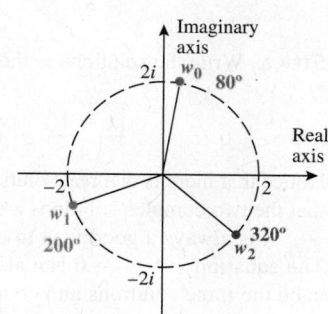

■ **YOUR TURN**  Find the three distinct cube roots of $4 - 4i\sqrt{3}$, and plot the roots in the complex plane.

## Solving Equations Using Roots of Complex Numbers

Let us return to solving the equation $x^3 - 1 = 0$. As stated, $x = 1$ is the real solution to this cubic equation. However, there are two additional (complex) solutions. Since we are finding the zeros of a third-degree polynomial, we expect three solutions. Furthermore, when complex solutions arise in finding the roots of polynomials with real coefficients, they come in conjugate pairs.

▶  **EXAMPLE 5**   **Solving Equations Using Complex Roots**

Find all complex solutions to $x^3 - 1 = 0$.

**Solution:** $x^3 = 1$

**STEP 1**  Write 1 in polar form.            $1 = 1 + 0i = \cos 0° + i\sin 0°$

**STEP 2**  Find the three cube roots of 1.

$$w_k = r^{1/n}\left[\cos\left(\frac{\theta}{n} + \frac{k \cdot 360°}{n}\right) + i\sin\left(\frac{\theta}{n} + \frac{k \cdot 360°}{n}\right)\right]$$

$$r = 1, \theta = 0°, n = 3, k = 0, 1, 2$$

$k = 0$:

$$w_0 = 1^{1/3}\left[\cos\left(\frac{0°}{3} + \frac{0 \cdot 360°}{3}\right) + i\sin\left(\frac{0°}{3} + \frac{0 \cdot 360°}{3}\right)\right]$$

Simplify.

$$w_0 = \cos 0° + i\sin 0°$$

$k = 1$:

$$w_1 = 1^{1/3}\left[\cos\left(\frac{0°}{3} + \frac{1 \cdot 360°}{3}\right) + i\sin\left(\frac{0°}{3} + \frac{1 \cdot 360°}{3}\right)\right]$$

Simplify.

$$w_1 = \cos 120° + i\sin 120°$$

$k = 2$:

$$w_2 = 1^{1/3}\left[\cos\left(\frac{0°}{3} + \frac{2 \cdot 360°}{3}\right) + i\sin\left(\frac{0°}{3} + \frac{2 \cdot 360°}{3}\right)\right]$$

Simplify.

$$w_2 = \cos 240° + i\sin 240°$$

**Technology Tip**

Find the three distinct roots of $-4 - 4i\sqrt{3}$.

*Caution:* If you use a TI calculator to find $(-4 - 4i\sqrt{3})^{1/3}$, the calculator will return only one root.

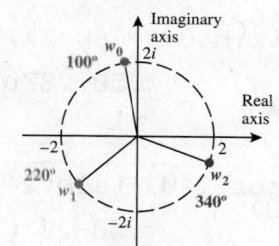

To find all three distinct roots, you need to change to polar form and apply the *n*th root theorem.

■ **Answer:**
$$w_0 = 2(\cos 100° + i\sin 100°)$$
$$w_1 = 2(\cos 220° + i\sin 220°)$$
$$w_2 = 2(\cos 340° + i\sin 340°)$$

**STEP 3** Write the roots in rectangular form.

$w_0$: $\qquad w_0 = \underbrace{\cos 0°}_{1} + i\underbrace{\sin 0°}_{0} = 1$

$w_1$: $\qquad w_1 = \underbrace{\cos 120°}_{-\frac{1}{2}} + i\underbrace{\sin 120°}_{\frac{\sqrt{3}}{2}} = -\frac{1}{2} + i\frac{\sqrt{3}}{2}$

$w_2$: $\qquad w_2 = \underbrace{\cos 240°}_{-\frac{1}{2}} + i\underbrace{\sin 240°}_{-\frac{\sqrt{3}}{2}} = -\frac{1}{2} - i\frac{\sqrt{3}}{2}$

**STEP 4** Write the solutions to the equation $x^3 - 1 = 0$.

$$\boxed{x = 1} \qquad \boxed{x = -\frac{1}{2} + i\frac{\sqrt{3}}{2}} \qquad \boxed{x = -\frac{1}{2} - i\frac{\sqrt{3}}{2}}$$

Notice that there is one real solution and there are two (nonreal) complex solutions and that the two complex solutions are complex conjugates.

It is always a good idea to check that the solutions indeed satisfy the equation. The equation $x^3 - 1 = 0$ can also be written as $x^3 = 1$, so the check in this case is to cube the three solutions and confirm that the result is 1.

$x = 1$: $\qquad\qquad\qquad\qquad 1^3 = 1$

$x = -\frac{1}{2} + \frac{i\sqrt{3}}{2}$: $\qquad \left(-\frac{1}{2} + i\frac{\sqrt{3}}{2}\right)^3 = \left(-\frac{1}{2} + i\frac{\sqrt{3}}{2}\right)^2\left(-\frac{1}{2} + i\frac{\sqrt{3}}{2}\right)$

$$= \left(-\frac{1}{2} - i\frac{\sqrt{3}}{2}\right)\left(-\frac{1}{2} + i\frac{\sqrt{3}}{2}\right)$$

$$= \frac{1}{4} + \frac{3}{4}$$

$$= 1$$

$x = -\frac{1}{2} - \frac{i\sqrt{3}}{2}$: $\qquad \left(-\frac{1}{2} - i\frac{\sqrt{3}}{2}\right)^3 = \left(-\frac{1}{2} - i\frac{\sqrt{3}}{2}\right)^2\left(-\frac{1}{2} - i\frac{\sqrt{3}}{2}\right)$

$$= \left(-\frac{1}{2} + i\frac{\sqrt{3}}{2}\right)\left(-\frac{1}{2} - i\frac{\sqrt{3}}{2}\right)$$

$$= \frac{1}{4} + \frac{3}{4}$$

$$= 1$$

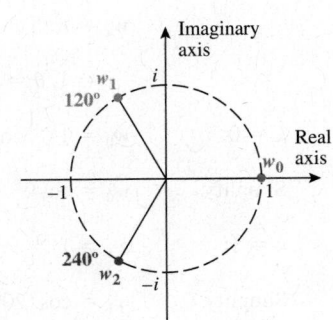

In this section, we multiplied and divided complex numbers and, using De Moivre's theorem, raised complex numbers to integer powers and found the $n$th roots of complex numbers, as follows:

Let $z_1 = r_1(\cos\theta_1 + i\sin\theta_1)$ and
$z_2 = r_2(\cos\theta_2 + i\sin\theta_2)$ be two complex numbers.

The **product** $z_1 z_2$ is given by

$$z_1 z_2 = r_1 r_2 [\cos(\theta_1 + \theta_2) + i\sin(\theta_1 + \theta_2)]$$

The **quotient** $\dfrac{z_1}{z_2}$ is given by

$$\frac{z_1}{z_2} = \frac{r_1}{r_2}[\cos(\theta_1 - \theta_2) + i\sin(\theta_1 - \theta_2)]$$

Let $z = r(\cos\theta + i\sin\theta)$ be a complex number. Then for a positive integer $n$,

$z$ raised to a **power** $n$ is given by

$$z^n = r^n[\cos(n\theta) + i\sin(n\theta)]$$

The **$n$th roots** of $z$ are given by

$$w_k = r^{1/n}\left[\cos\left(\frac{\theta}{n} + \frac{k \cdot 360°}{n}\right) + i\sin\left(\frac{\theta}{n} + \frac{k \cdot 360°}{n}\right)\right]$$

where $\theta$ is in degrees

or

$$w_k = r^{1/n}\left[\cos\left(\frac{\theta}{n} + \frac{k \cdot 2\pi}{n}\right) + i\sin\left(\frac{\theta}{n} + \frac{k \cdot 2\pi}{n}\right)\right]$$

where $\theta$ is in radians and $k = 0, 1, 2, \ldots, n - 1$.

■ SKILLS

**In Exercises 1–10, find the product $z_1 z_2$ and express it in rectangular form.**

1. $z_1 = 4(\cos 40° + i\sin 40°)$ and $z_2 = 3(\cos 80° + i\sin 80°)$

2. $z_1 = 2(\cos 100° + i\sin 100°)$ and $z_2 = 5(\cos 50° + i\sin 50°)$

3. $z_1 = 4(\cos 80° + i\sin 80°)$ and $z_2 = 2(\cos 145° + i\sin 145°)$

4. $z_1 = 3(\cos 130° + i\sin 130°)$ and $z_2 = 4(\cos 170° + i\sin 170°)$

5. $z_1 = 2(\cos 10° + i\sin 10°)$ and $z_2 = 4(\cos 80° + i\sin 80°)$

6. $z_1 = 3(\cos 190° + i\sin 190°)$ and $z_2 = 5(\cos 80° + i\sin 80°)$

7. $z_1 = \sqrt{3}\left[\cos\left(\dfrac{\pi}{12}\right) + i\sin\left(\dfrac{\pi}{12}\right)\right]$ and $z_2 = \sqrt{27}\left[\cos\left(\dfrac{\pi}{6}\right) + i\sin\left(\dfrac{\pi}{6}\right)\right]$

8. $z_1 = \sqrt{5}\left[\cos\left(\dfrac{\pi}{15}\right) + i\sin\left(\dfrac{\pi}{15}\right)\right]$ and $z_2 = \sqrt{5}\left[\cos\left(\dfrac{4\pi}{15}\right) + i\sin\left(\dfrac{4\pi}{15}\right)\right]$

9. $z_1 = 4\left[\cos\left(\dfrac{3\pi}{8}\right) + i\sin\left(\dfrac{3\pi}{8}\right)\right]$ and $z_2 = 3\left[\cos\left(\dfrac{\pi}{8}\right) + i\sin\left(\dfrac{\pi}{8}\right)\right]$

10. $z_1 = 6\left[\cos\left(\dfrac{2\pi}{9}\right) + i\sin\left(\dfrac{2\pi}{9}\right)\right]$ and $z_2 = 5\left[\cos\left(\dfrac{\pi}{9}\right) + i\sin\left(\dfrac{\pi}{9}\right)\right]$

**In Exercises 11–20, find the quotient $\dfrac{z_1}{z_2}$ and express it in rectangular form.**

**11.** $z_1 = 6(\cos 100° + i \sin 100°)$ and $z_2 = 2(\cos 40° + i \sin 40°)$

**12.** $z_1 = 8(\cos 80° + i \sin 80°)$ and $z_2 = 2(\cos 35° + i \sin 35°)$

**13.** $z_1 = 10(\cos 200° + i \sin 200°)$ and $z_2 = 5(\cos 65° + i \sin 65°)$

**14.** $z_1 = 4(\cos 280° + i \sin 280°)$ and $z_2 = 4(\cos 55° + i \sin 55°)$

**15.** $z_1 = \sqrt{12}(\cos 350° + i \sin 350°)$ and $z_2 = \sqrt{3}(\cos 80° + i \sin 80°)$

**16.** $z_1 = \sqrt{40}(\cos 110° + i \sin 110°)$ and $z_2 = \sqrt{10}(\cos 20° + i \sin 20°)$

**17.** $z_1 = 9\left[\cos\left(\dfrac{5\pi}{12}\right) + i \sin\left(\dfrac{5\pi}{12}\right)\right]$ and $z_2 = 3\left[\cos\left(\dfrac{\pi}{12}\right) + i \sin\left(\dfrac{\pi}{12}\right)\right]$

**18.** $z_1 = 8\left[\cos\left(\dfrac{5\pi}{8}\right) + i \sin\left(\dfrac{5\pi}{8}\right)\right]$ and $z_2 = 4\left[\cos\left(\dfrac{3\pi}{8}\right) + i \sin\left(\dfrac{3\pi}{8}\right)\right]$

**19.** $z_1 = 45\left[\cos\left(\dfrac{22\pi}{15}\right) + i \sin\left(\dfrac{22\pi}{15}\right)\right]$ and $z_2 = 9\left[\cos\left(\dfrac{2\pi}{15}\right) + i \sin\left(\dfrac{2\pi}{15}\right)\right]$

**20.** $z_1 = 22\left[\cos\left(\dfrac{11\pi}{18}\right) + i \sin\left(\dfrac{11\pi}{18}\right)\right]$ and $z_2 = 11\left[\cos\left(\dfrac{5\pi}{18}\right) + i \sin\left(\dfrac{5\pi}{18}\right)\right]$

**In Exercises 21–30, find the result of each expression using De Moivre's theorem. Write the answer in rectangular form.**

**21.** $(-1 + i)^5$    **22.** $(1 - i)^4$    **23.** $(-\sqrt{3} + i)^6$    **24.** $(\sqrt{3} - i)^8$    **25.** $(1 - \sqrt{3}i)^4$

**26.** $(-1 + \sqrt{3}i)^5$    **27.** $(4 - 4i)^8$    **28.** $(-3 + 3i)^{10}$    **29.** $(4\sqrt{3} + 4i)^7$    **30.** $(-5 + 5\sqrt{3}i)^7$

**In Exercises 31–40, find all $n$th roots of $z$. Write the answers in polar form, and plot the roots in the complex plane.**

**31.** $2 - 2i\sqrt{3}, n = 2$    **32.** $2 + 2\sqrt{3}i, n = 2$    **33.** $\sqrt{18} - \sqrt{18}i, n = 2$    **34.** $-\sqrt{2} + \sqrt{2}i, n = 2$

**35.** $4 + 4\sqrt{3}i, n = 3$    **36.** $-\dfrac{27}{2} + \dfrac{27\sqrt{3}}{2}i, n = 3$    **37.** $\sqrt{3} - i, n = 3$    **38.** $4\sqrt{2} + 4\sqrt{2}i, n = 3$

**39.** $8\sqrt{2} - 8\sqrt{2}i, n = 4$    **40.** $-\sqrt{128} + \sqrt{128}i, n = 4$

**In Exercises 41–56, find all complex solutions to the given equations.**

**41.** $x^4 - 16 = 0$    **42.** $x^3 - 8 = 0$    **43.** $x^3 + 8 = 0$    **44.** $x^3 + 1 = 0$

**45.** $x^4 + 16 = 0$    **46.** $x^6 + 1 = 0$    **47.** $x^6 - 1 = 0$    **48.** $4x^2 + 1 = 0$

**49.** $x^2 + i = 0$    **50.** $x^2 - i = 0$    **51.** $x^4 - 2i = 0$    **52.** $x^4 + 2i = 0$

**53.** $x^5 + 32 = 0$    **54.** $x^5 - 32 = 0$    **55.** $x^7 - \pi^{14}i = 0$    **56.** $x^7 + \pi^{14} = 0$

■ **APPLICATIONS**

**57. Complex Pentagon.** When you graph the five fifth roots of $-\dfrac{\sqrt{2}}{2} - \dfrac{\sqrt{2}}{2}i$ and connect the points, you form a pentagon. Find the roots and draw the pentagon.

**58. Complex Square.** When you graph the four fourth roots of $16i$ and connect the points, you form a square. Find the roots and draw the square.

**59. Hexagon.** Compute the six sixth roots of $\dfrac{1}{2} - \dfrac{\sqrt{3}}{2}i$, and form a hexagon by connecting successive roots.

**60. Octagon.** Compute the eight eighth roots of $2i$, and form an octagon by connecting successive roots.

# ■ CATCH THE MISTAKE

**In Exercises 61–64, explain the mistake that is made.**

**61.** Let $z_1 = 6(\cos 65° + i \sin 65°)$ and

$z_2 = 3(\cos 125° + i \sin 125°)$. Find $\dfrac{z_1}{z_2}$.

**Solution:**

Use the quotient formula.

$$\frac{z_1}{z_2} = \frac{r_1}{r_2}[\cos(\theta_1 - \theta_2) + i \sin(\theta_1 - \theta_2)]$$

Substitute values.

$$\frac{z_1}{z_2} = \frac{6}{3}[\cos(125° - 65°) + i \sin(125° - 65°)]$$

Simplify. $\dfrac{z_1}{z_2} = 2(\cos 60° + i \sin 60°)$

Evaluate the trigonometric functions.

$$\frac{z_1}{z_2} = 2\left(\frac{1}{2} + i\frac{\sqrt{3}}{2}\right) = 1 + i\sqrt{3}$$

This is incorrect. What mistake was made?

**62.** Let $z_1 = 6(\cos 65° + i \sin 65°)$ and
$z_2 = 3(\cos 125° + i \sin 125°)$. Find $z_1 z_2$.

**Solution:**

Write the product.

$z_1 z_2 = 6(\cos 65° + i \sin 65°) \cdot 3(\cos 125° + i \sin 125°)$

Multiply the magnitudes.

$z_1 z_2 = 18(\cos 65° + i \sin 65°)(\cos 125° + i \sin 125°)$

Multiply the cosine terms and sine terms (add the arguments).

$$z_1 z_2 = 18[\cos(65° + 125°) + i^2 \sin(65° + 125°)]$$

Simplify ($i^2 = -1$).

$$z_1 z_2 = 18(\cos 190° - \sin 190°)$$

This is incorrect. What mistake was made?

**63.** Find $(\sqrt{2} + i\sqrt{2})^6$.

**Solution:**

Raise each term to the sixth power. $(\sqrt{2})^6 + i^6(\sqrt{2})^6$

Simplify. $8 + 8i^6$

Let $i^6 = i^4 \cdot i^2 = -1$. $8 - 8 = 0$

This is incorrect. What mistake was made?

**64.** Find all complex solutions to $x^5 - 1 = 0$.

**Solution:**

Add 1 to both sides. $x^5 = 1$

Raise both sides to the fifth power. $x = 1^{1/5}$

Simplify. $x = 1$

This is incorrect. What mistake was made?

# ■ CONCEPTUAL

**In Exercises 65–70, determine whether the statement is true or false.**

**65.** The product of two complex numbers is a complex number.

**66.** The quotient of two complex numbers is a complex number.

**67.** There are always $n$ distinct real solutions of the equation $x^n - a = 0$, where $a$ is not zero.

**68.** There are always $n$ distinct complex solutions of the equation $x^n - a = 0$, where $a$ is not zero.

**69.** There are $n$ distinct complex zeros of $\dfrac{1}{a + bi}$, where $a$ and $b$ are positive real numbers.

**70.** There exists a complex number for which there is no complex square root.

**71.** The distance between any consecutive pair of the $n$ complex roots of a number is a constant.

**72.** If $2\left[\cos\left(\dfrac{\pi}{2}\right) + i \sin\left(\dfrac{\pi}{2}\right)\right]$ is one of the $n$ complex roots of a number, then $n$ is even.

■ **CHALLENGE**

**In Exercises 73–76, use the following identity:**

In calculus you will see an identity called Euler's formula or identity, $e^{i\theta} = \cos\theta + i\sin\theta$. Notice that when $\theta = \pi$, the identity reduces to $e^{i\pi} + 1 = 0$, which is a beautiful identity in that it relates the five fundamental numbers ($e$, $\pi$, $1$, $i$, and $0$) and the fundamental operations (multiplication, addition, exponents, and equality) in mathematics.

**73.** Let $z_1 = r_1(\cos\theta_1 + i\sin\theta_1) = r_1 e^{i\theta_1}$ and $z_2 = r_2(\cos\theta_2 + i\sin\theta_2) = r_2 e^{i\theta_2}$ be two complex numbers. Use the properties of exponentials to show that $z_1 z_2 = r_1 r_2[\cos(\theta_1 + \theta_2) + i\sin(\theta_1 + \theta_2)]$.

**74.** Let $z_1 = r_1(\cos\theta_1 + i\sin\theta_1) = r_1 e^{i\theta_1}$ and $z_2 = r_2(\cos\theta_2 + i\sin\theta_2) = r_2 e^{i\theta_2}$ be two complex numbers. Use the properties of exponentials to show that $\dfrac{z_1}{z_2} = \dfrac{r_1}{r_2}[\cos(\theta_1 - \theta_2) + i\sin(\theta_1 - \theta_2)]$.

**75.** Let $z = r(\cos\theta + i\sin\theta) = re^{i\theta}$. Use the properties of exponents to show that $z^n = r^n[\cos(n\theta) + i\sin(n\theta)]$.

**76.** Let $z = r(\cos\theta + i\sin\theta) = re^{i\theta}$. Use the properties of exponents to show that
$$w_k = r^{1/n}\left[\cos\left(\frac{\theta}{n} + \frac{2k\pi}{n}\right) + i\sin\left(\frac{\theta}{n} + \frac{2k\pi}{n}\right)\right].$$

**77.** Use De Moivre's theorem to prove the identity $\cos 2\theta = \cos^2\theta - \sin^2\theta$.

**78.** Use De Moivre's theorem to derive an expression for $\sin(3\theta)$.

**79.** Use De Moivre's theorem to derive an expression for $\cos(3\theta)$.

**80.** Calculate $\dfrac{\left(\dfrac{1}{2} + \dfrac{\sqrt{3}}{2}i\right)^{14}}{\left(\dfrac{1}{2} - \dfrac{\sqrt{3}}{2}i\right)^{20}}$.

**81.** Calculate $(1 - i)^n \cdot (1 + i)^m$, where $n$ and $m$ are positive integers.

**82.** Calculate $\dfrac{(1 + i)^n}{(1 - i)^m}$, where $n$ and $m$ are positive integers.

■ **TECHNOLOGY**

**For Exercises 83–88, refer to the following:**

According to the $n$th root theorem, the first of the $n$th roots of the complex number $z = r(\cos\theta + i\sin\theta)$ is given by

$$w_1 = r^{1/n}\left[\cos\left(\frac{\theta}{n} + \frac{2\pi}{n}\right) + i\sin\left(\frac{\theta}{n} + \frac{2\pi}{n}\right)\right], \text{ with } \theta \text{ in radians}$$

or $w_1 = r^{1/n}\left[\cos\left(\dfrac{\theta}{n} + \dfrac{360°}{n}\right) + i\sin\left(\dfrac{\theta}{n} + \dfrac{360°}{n}\right)\right]$,

with $\theta$ in degrees.

Using the graphing calculator to plot the $n$ roots of a complex number $z$, enter $r_1 = r$, $\theta \min = \dfrac{\theta}{n}$, $\theta \max = 2\pi + \dfrac{\theta}{n}$ or

$360° + \dfrac{\theta}{n}$, $\theta \text{ step} = \dfrac{2\pi}{n}$ or $\dfrac{360°}{n}$, $x\min = -r$, $x\max = r$,

$y\min = -r$, $y\max = r$, and $\boxed{\text{MODE}}$ in radians or degrees.

**83.** Find the fifth roots of $\dfrac{\sqrt{3}}{2} - \dfrac{1}{2}i$, and plot the roots with a calculator.

**84.** Find the fourth roots of $-\dfrac{\sqrt{2}}{2} + \dfrac{\sqrt{2}}{2}i$, and plot the roots with a calculator.

**85.** Find the sixth roots of $-\dfrac{1}{2} - \dfrac{\sqrt{3}}{2}i$, and draw the complex hexagon with a calculator.

**86.** Find the fifth roots of $-4 + 4i$, and draw the complex pentagon with a calculator.

**87.** Find the cube roots of $\dfrac{27\sqrt{2}}{2} + \dfrac{27\sqrt{2}}{2}i$, and draw the complex triangle with a calculator.

**88.** Find the fifth roots of $8\sqrt{2}\left(\sqrt{3} - 1\right) + 8\sqrt{2}\left(\sqrt{3} - 1\right)i$, and draw the complex triangle with a calculator.

■ **PREVIEW TO CALCULUS**

**In advanced calculus, complex numbers in polar form are used extensively. Use De Moivre's formula to show that**

**89.** $\cos(2\theta) = \cos^2\theta - \sin^2\theta$

**90.** $\sin(2\theta) = 2\sin\theta\cos\theta$

**91.** $\cos(3\theta) = 4\cos^3\theta - 3\cos\theta$

**92.** $\sin(3\theta) = 3\sin\theta - 4\sin^3\theta$

We have discussed the rectangular and the trigonometric (polar) form of complex numbers in the complex plane. We now turn our attention back to the familiar Cartesian plane, where the horizontal axis represents the $x$-variable, the vertical axis represents the $y$-variable, and points in this plane represent pairs of real numbers. It is often convenient to instead represent real-number plots in the *polar coordinate system*.

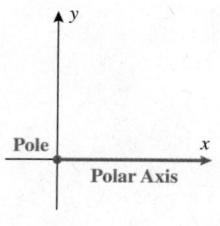

## Polar Coordinates

The **polar coordinate system** is anchored by a point, called the **pole** (taken to be the **origin**), and a ray with a vertex at the pole, called the **polar axis**. The polar axis is normally shown where we expect to find the positive $x$-axis in Cartesian coordinates.

If you align the pole with the origin on the rectangular graph and the polar axis with the positive $x$-axis, you can label a point either with rectangular coordinates $(x, y)$ or with an ordered pair $(r, \theta)$ in **polar coordinates**.

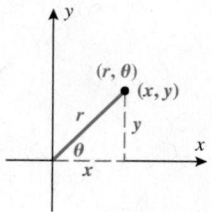

Typically, polar graph paper is used that gives the angles and radii. The graph below gives the angles in radians (the angle also can be given in degrees) and shows the radii from 0 through 5.

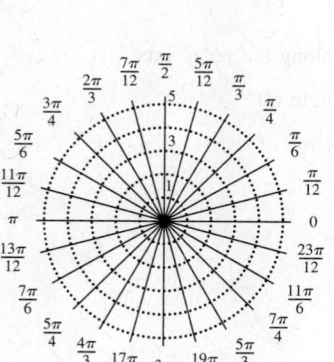

When plotting points in the polar coordinate system, $|r|$ represents the distance from the origin to the point. The following procedure guides us in plotting points in the polar coordinate system.

**POINT-PLOTTING POLAR COORDINATES**

To plot a point $(r, \theta)$:

1. Start on the polar axis and rotate the terminal side of an angle to the value $\theta$.
2. If $r > 0$, the point is $r$ units from the origin in the *same direction* of the terminal side of $\theta$.
3. If $r < 0$, the point is $|r|$ units from the origin in the *opposite direction* of the terminal side of $\theta$.

### EXAMPLE 1   Plotting Points in the Polar Coordinate System

Plot the points in a polar coordinate system.

**a.** $\left(3, \dfrac{3\pi}{4}\right)$     **b.** $(-2, 60°)$

**Solution (a):**

Start by placing a pencil along the polar axis.

Rotate the pencil to the angle $\dfrac{3\pi}{4}$.

Go out (in the direction of the pencil) three units.

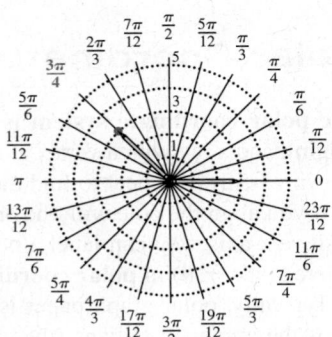

**Solution (b):**

Start by placing a pencil along the polar axis.

Rotate the pencil to the angle 60°.

Go out (opposite the direction of the pencil) two units.

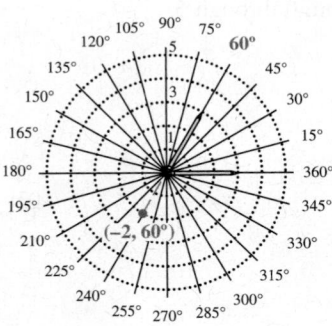

■ **Answer:**

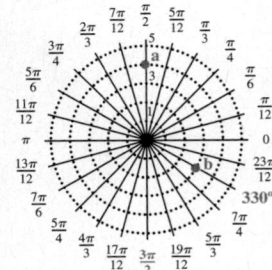

■ **YOUR TURN**  Plot the points in the polar coordinate system.

**a.** $\left(-4, \dfrac{3\pi}{2}\right)$     **b.** $(3, 330°)$

In polar form it is important to note that $(r, \theta)$, the name of the point, is not unique, whereas in rectangular form $(x, y)$ it is unique. For example, $(2, 30°) = (-2, 210°)$.

# Converting Between Polar and Rectangular Coordinates

The relationships between polar and rectangular coordinates are the familiar ones:

$$\sin\theta = \frac{y}{r}$$

$$\cos\theta = \frac{x}{r} \qquad r^2 = x^2 + y^2$$

$$\tan\theta = \frac{y}{x} \quad (x \neq 0)$$

## CONVERTING BETWEEN POLAR AND RECTANGULAR COORDINATES

| FROM | TO | IDENTITIES |
|------|------|------------|
| Polar $(r, \theta)$ | Rectangular $(x, y)$ | $x = r\cos\theta \qquad y = r\sin\theta$ |
| Rectangular $(x, y)$ | Polar $(r, \theta)$ | $r = \sqrt{x^2 + y^2} \qquad \tan\theta = \dfrac{y}{x} \quad (x \neq 0)$ <br> Make sure that $\theta$ is in the correct quadrant. |

### EXAMPLE 2   Converting Between Polar and Rectangular Coordinates

**a.** Convert $(-1, \sqrt{3})$ to polar coordinates.

**b.** Convert $(6\sqrt{2}, 135°)$ to rectangular coordinates.

**Solution (a):** $(-1, \sqrt{3})$ lies in quadrant II.

Identify $x$ and $y$.                $x = -1, \qquad y = \sqrt{3}$

Find $r$.                $r = \sqrt{x^2 + y^2} = \sqrt{(-1)^2 + (\sqrt{3})^2} = \sqrt{4} = 2$

Find $\theta$.                $\tan\theta = \dfrac{\sqrt{3}}{-1} \qquad$ ($\theta$ lies in quadrant II)

Identify $\theta$ from the
unit circle.                $\theta = \dfrac{2\pi}{3}$

Write the point in
polar coordinates.        $\boxed{\left(2, \dfrac{2\pi}{3}\right)}$

*Note:* Other polar coordinates like $\left(2, -\dfrac{4\pi}{3}\right)$ and $\left(-2, \dfrac{5\pi}{3}\right)$ also correspond to the point $(-1, \sqrt{3})$.

**Solution (b):** $(6\sqrt{2}, 135°)$ lies in quadrant II.

Identify $r$ and $\theta$.                $r = 6\sqrt{2} \qquad \theta = 135°$

Find $x$.                $x = r\cos\theta = 6\sqrt{2}\cos 135° = 6\sqrt{2}\left(-\dfrac{\sqrt{2}}{2}\right) = -6$

Find $y$.                $y = r\sin\theta = 6\sqrt{2}\sin 135° = 6\sqrt{2}\left(\dfrac{\sqrt{2}}{2}\right) = 6$

Write the point in
rectangular coordinates.        $\boxed{(-6, 6)}$

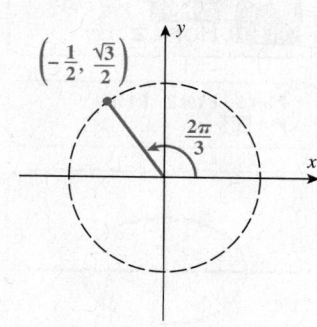

### Technology Tip

```
abs(-1+√(3)i)
              2.00
angle(-1+√(3)i)
            120.00
Ans/180▶Frac
             2/3
■
```

The solution is $\left(2, \frac{2}{3}\pi\right)$.

# Graphs of Polar Equations

We are familiar with equations in rectangular form such as

$$y = 3x + 5 \qquad y = x^2 + 2 \qquad x^2 + y^2 = 9$$
$$\text{(line)} \qquad\quad \text{(parabola)} \qquad\quad \text{(circle)}$$

We now discuss equations in polar form (known as **polar equations**) such as

$$r = 5\theta \qquad r = 2\cos\theta \qquad r = \sin(5\theta)$$

which you will learn to recognize in this section as typical equations whose plots are some general shapes.

Our first example deals with two of the simplest forms of polar equations: when $r$ or $\theta$ is constant. The results are a circle centered at the origin and a line that passes through the origin, respectively.

### EXAMPLE 3 Graphing a Polar Equation of the Form $r$ = Constant or $\theta$ = Constant

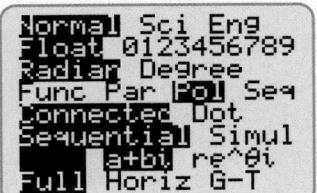
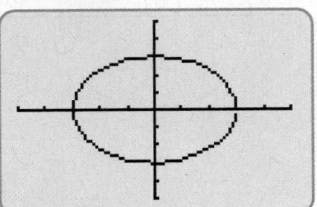
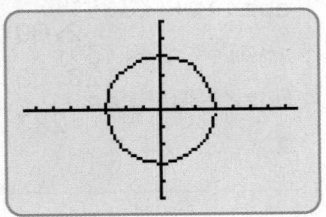
Graph the polar equations.

**a.** $r = 3$    **b.** $\theta = \dfrac{\pi}{4}$

**Solution (a):** Constant value of $r$

Approach 1 (polar coordinates):      $r = 3$ ($\theta$ can take on any value)

     Plot points for arbitrary $\theta$ and $r = 3$.

     Connect the points; a circle with radius 3.

Approach 2 (rectangular coordinates):      $r = 3$

     Square both sides.      $r^2 = 9$

     Remember that in rectangular coordinates $r^2 = x^2 + y^2$.      $x^2 + y^2 = 3^2$

     This is a circle, centered at the origin, with radius 3.

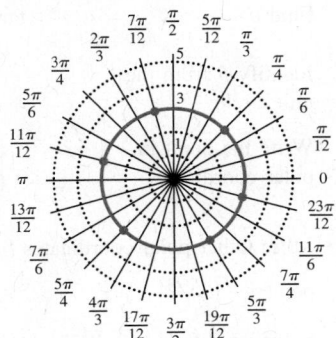

**Solution (b):** Constant value of $\theta$

Approach 1: $\theta = \dfrac{\pi}{4}$ ($r$ can take on any value, positive or negative.)

     Plot points for $\theta = \dfrac{\pi}{4}$ at several arbitrary values of $r$.

     Connect the points. The result is a line passing through the origin with

     slope $= 1 \left[ m = \tan\left(\dfrac{\pi}{4}\right) \right]$.

Approach 2:   $\theta = \dfrac{\pi}{4}$

Take the tangent of both sides.         $\tan\theta = \underbrace{\tan\left(\dfrac{\pi}{4}\right)}_{1}$

Use the identity $\tan\theta = \dfrac{y}{x}$.         $\dfrac{y}{x} = 1$

Multiply by $x$.         $y = x$

The result is a line passing through the origin with slope = 1.

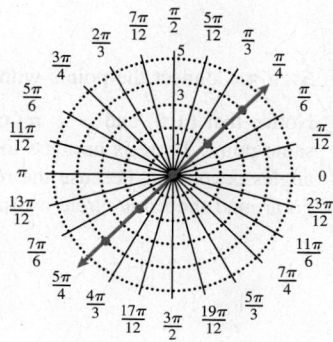

Rectangular equations that depend on varying (not constant) values of $x$ or $y$ can be graphed by point-plotting (making a table and plotting the points). We will use this same procedure for graphing polar equations that depend on varying (not constant) values of $r$ or $\theta$.

▶ **EXAMPLE 4**   **Graphing a Polar Equation of the Form $r = c \cdot \cos\theta$ or $r = c \cdot \sin\theta$**

Graph $r = 4\cos\theta$.

**Solution:**

**STEP 1**  Make a table and find several key values.

| $\theta$ | $r = 4\cos\theta$ | $(r, \theta)$ |
|---|---|---|
| $0$ | $4(1) = 4$ | $(4, 0)$ |
| $\dfrac{\pi}{4}$ | $4\left(\dfrac{\sqrt{2}}{2}\right) \approx 2.8$ | $\left(2.8, \dfrac{\pi}{4}\right)$ |
| $\dfrac{\pi}{2}$ | $4(0) = 0$ | $\left(0, \dfrac{\pi}{2}\right)$ |
| $\dfrac{3\pi}{4}$ | $4\left(-\dfrac{\sqrt{2}}{2}\right) \approx -2.8$ | $\left(-2.8, \dfrac{3\pi}{4}\right)$ |
| $\pi$ | $4(-1) = -4$ | $(-4, \pi)$ |
| $\dfrac{5\pi}{4}$ | $4\left(-\dfrac{\sqrt{2}}{2}\right) \approx -2.8$ | $\left(-2.8, \dfrac{5\pi}{4}\right)$ |
| $\dfrac{3\pi}{2}$ | $4(0) = 0$ | $\left(0, \dfrac{3\pi}{2}\right)$ |
| $\dfrac{7\pi}{4}$ | $4\left(\dfrac{\sqrt{2}}{2}\right) \approx 2.8$ | $\left(2.8, \dfrac{7\pi}{4}\right)$ |
| $2\pi$ | $4(1) = 4$ | $(4, 2\pi)$ |

**Technology Tip**

Graph $r = 4\cos\theta$.

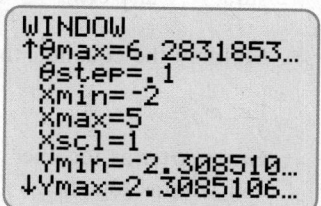

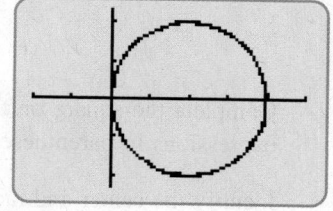

STEP 2 Plot the points in polar coordinates.

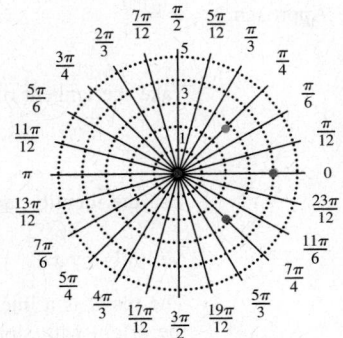

STEP 3 Connect the points with a smooth curve.

Notice that $(4, 0)$ and $(-4, \pi)$ correspond to the same point. There is no need to continue with angles beyond $\pi$, because the result would be to go around the same circle again.

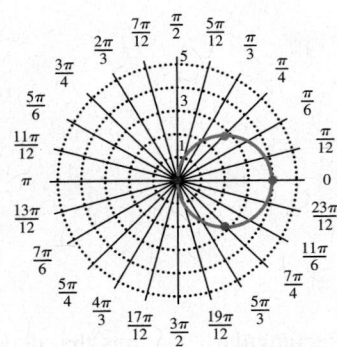

■ **Answer:**

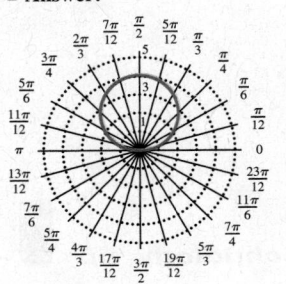

■ **YOUR TURN** Graph $r = 4\sin\theta$.

**Study Tip**

Graphs of $r = a\sin\theta$ and $r = a\cos\theta$ are circles.

Compare the result of Example 4, the graph of $r = 4\cos\theta$, with the result of the Your Turn, the graph of $r = 4\sin\theta$. Notice that they are 90° out of phase (we simply rotate one graph 90° about the pole to get the other graph).

In general, graphs of polar equations of the form $r = a\sin\theta$ and $r = a\cos\theta$ are circles.

| WORDS | MATH | |
|---|---|---|
| Start with the polar form. | $r = a\sin\theta$ | $r = a\cos\theta$ |
| Apply trigonometric ratios: $\sin\theta = \dfrac{y}{r}$ and $\cos\theta = \dfrac{x}{r}$. | $r = a\dfrac{y}{r}$ | $r = a\dfrac{x}{r}$ |
| Multiply the equations by $r$. | $r^2 = ay$ | $r^2 = ax$ |
| Let $r^2 = x^2 + y^2$. | $x^2 + y^2 = ay$ | $x^2 + y^2 = ax$ |
| Group $x$ terms together and $y$ terms together. | $x^2 + (y^2 - ay) = 0$ | $(x^2 - ax) + y^2 = 0$ |
| | $x^2 + \left[y^2 - ay + \left(\dfrac{a}{2}\right)^2\right] = \left(\dfrac{a}{2}\right)^2$ | $\left[x^2 - ax + \left(\dfrac{a}{2}\right)^2\right] + y^2 = \left(\dfrac{a}{2}\right)^2$ |
| Complete the square on the expressions in parentheses. | $x^2 + \left(y - \dfrac{a}{2}\right)^2 = \left(\dfrac{a}{2}\right)^2$ | $\left(x - \dfrac{a}{2}\right)^2 + y^2 = \left(\dfrac{a}{2}\right)^2$ |
| Identify the center and radius. | Center: $\left(0, \dfrac{a}{2}\right)$    Radius: $\dfrac{a}{2}$ | Center: $\left(\dfrac{a}{2}, 0\right)$    Radius: $\dfrac{a}{2}$ |

**EXAMPLE 5** **Graphing a Polar Equation of the Form $r = c \cdot \sin(2\theta)$ or $r = c \cdot \cos(2\theta)$**

Graph $r = 5\sin(2\theta)$.

**Solution:**

STEP 1 Make a table and find key values. Since the argument of the sine function is doubled, the period is halved. Therefore, instead of steps of $\frac{\pi}{4}$, take steps of $\frac{\pi}{8}$.

| $\theta$ | $r = 5\sin(2\theta)$ | $(r, \theta)$ |
|---|---|---|
| $0$ | $5(0) = 0$ | $(0, 0)$ |
| $\frac{\pi}{8}$ | $5\left(\frac{\sqrt{2}}{2}\right) \approx 3.5$ | $\left(3.5, \frac{\pi}{8}\right)$ |
| $\frac{\pi}{4}$ | $5(1) = 5$ | $\left(5, \frac{\pi}{4}\right)$ |
| $\frac{3\pi}{8}$ | $5\left(\frac{\sqrt{2}}{2}\right) \approx 3.5$ | $\left(3.5, \frac{3\pi}{8}\right)$ |
| $\frac{\pi}{2}$ | $5(0) = 0$ | $\left(0, \frac{\pi}{2}\right)$ |

STEP 2 Label the polar coordinates.

The values in the table represent what happens in quadrant I. The same pattern repeats in the other three quadrants. The result is a **four-leaved rose**.

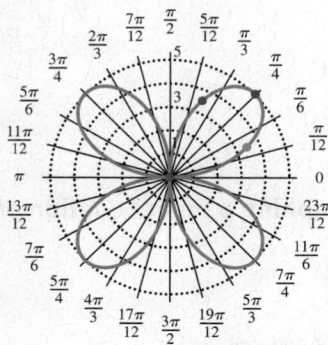

STEP 3 Connect the points with smooth curves.

■ **YOUR TURN** Graph $r = 5\cos(2\theta)$.

Compare the result of Example 5, the graph of $r = 5\sin(2\theta)$, with the result of the Your Turn, the graph of $r = 5\cos(2\theta)$. Notice that they are 45° out of phase (we rotate one graph 45° about the pole to get the other graph).

In general, for $r = a\sin(n\theta)$ or $r = a\cos(n\theta)$, the graph has $n$ leaves (petals) if $n$ is odd and $2n$ leaves (petals) if $n$ is even. As $a$ increases, the leaves (petals) get longer.

The next class of graphs are called **limaçons**, which have equations of the form $r = a \pm b\cos\theta$ or $r = a \pm b\sin\theta$. When $a = b$, the result is a **cardioid** (heart shape).

*Technology Tip*

Graph $r = 5\sin(2\theta)$.

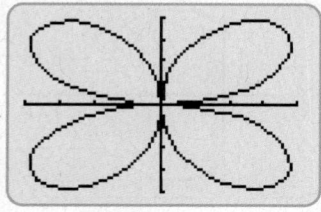

■ **Answer:**

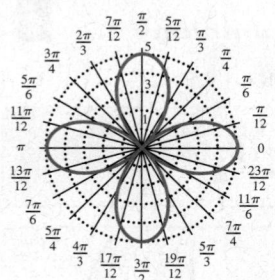

*Study Tip*

Graphs of $r = a\sin(n\theta)$ and $r = a\cos(n\theta)$ are roses with $n$ leaves if $n$ is odd and $2n$ leaves if $n$ is even.

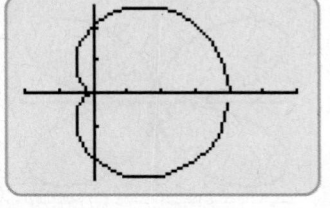
### EXAMPLE 6   The Cardioid as a Polar Equation

Graph $r = 2 + 2\cos\theta$.

**Solution:**

**STEP 1** Make a table and find key values.

This behavior repeats in quadrant III and quadrant IV, because the cosine function has corresponding values in quadrant I and quadrant IV and in quadrant II and quadrant III.

| $\theta$ | $r = 2 + 2\cos\theta$ | $(r, \theta)$ |
|---|---|---|
| 0 | $2 + 2(1) = 4$ | $(4, 0)$ |
| $\dfrac{\pi}{4}$ | $2 + 2\left(\dfrac{\sqrt{2}}{2}\right) = 3.4$ | $\left(3.4, \dfrac{\pi}{4}\right)$ |
| $\dfrac{\pi}{2}$ | $2 + 2(0) = 2$ | $\left(2, \dfrac{\pi}{2}\right)$ |
| $\dfrac{3\pi}{4}$ | $2 + 2\left(-\dfrac{\sqrt{2}}{2}\right) \approx 0.6$ | $\left(0.6, \dfrac{3\pi}{4}\right)$ |
| $\pi$ | $2 + 2(-1) = 0$ | $(0, \pi)$ |

**STEP 2** Plot the points in polar coordinates.

**STEP 3** Connect the points with a smooth curve. The curve is a *cardioid*, a term formed from Greek roots meaning "heart-shaped."

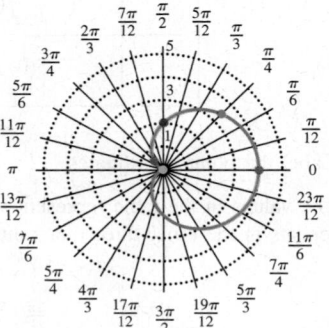

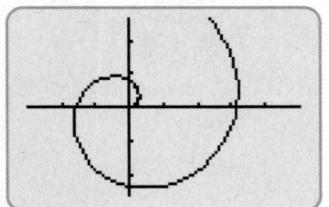
### EXAMPLE 7   Graphing a Polar Equation of the Form $r = c \cdot \theta$

Graph $r = 0.5\theta$.

**Solution:**

**STEP 1** Make a table and find key values.

| $\theta$ | $r = 0.5\theta$ | $(r, \theta)$ |
|---|---|---|
| 0 | $0.5(0) = 0$ | $(0, 0)$ |
| $\dfrac{\pi}{2}$ | $0.5\left(\dfrac{\pi}{2}\right) = 0.8$ | $\left(0.8, \dfrac{\pi}{2}\right)$ |
| $\pi$ | $0.5(\pi) = 1.6$ | $(1.6, \pi)$ |
| $\dfrac{3\pi}{2}$ | $0.5\left(\dfrac{3\pi}{2}\right) = 2.4$ | $\left(2.4, \dfrac{3\pi}{2}\right)$ |
| $2\pi$ | $0.5(2\pi) = 3.1$ | $(3.1, 2\pi)$ |

STEP 2 Plot the points in polar coordinates.

STEP 3 Connect the points with a smooth curve.
The curve is a *spiral*.

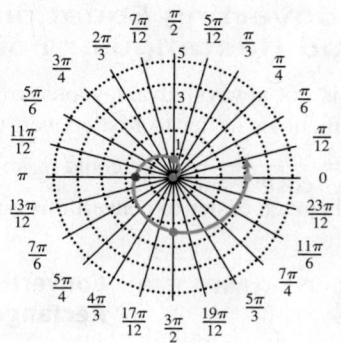

## EXAMPLE 8    Graphing a Polar Equation of the Form $r^2 = c \cdot \sin(2\theta)$ or $r^2 = c \cdot \cos(2\theta)$

Graph $r^2 = 4\cos(2\theta)$.

**Solution:**

STEP 1 Make a table and find key values.

Solving for $r$ yields $r = \pm 2\sqrt{\cos(2\theta)}$. All coordinates $(-r, \theta)$ can be expressed as $(r, \theta + \pi)$. The following table does not have values for $\frac{\pi}{4} < \theta < \frac{3\pi}{4}$, because the corresponding values of $\cos(2\theta)$ are negative and hence $r$ is an imaginary number. The table also does not have values for $\theta > \pi$, because $2\theta > 2\pi$ and the corresponding points are repeated.

| $\theta$ | $\cos(2\theta)$ | $r = \pm 2\sqrt{\cos(2\theta)}$ | $(r, \theta)$ |
|---|---|---|---|
| $0$ | $1$ | $r = \pm 2$ | $(2, 0)$    and    $(-2, 0) = (2, \pi)$ |
| $\dfrac{\pi}{6}$ | $0.5$ | $r = \pm 1.4$ | $\left(1.4, \dfrac{\pi}{6}\right)$ and $\left(-1.4, \dfrac{\pi}{6}\right) = \left(1.4, \dfrac{7\pi}{6}\right)$ |
| $\dfrac{\pi}{4}$ | $0$ | $r = 0$ | $\left(0, \dfrac{\pi}{4}\right)$ |
| $\dfrac{3\pi}{4}$ | $0$ | $r = 0$ | $\left(0, \dfrac{3\pi}{4}\right)$ |
| $\dfrac{5\pi}{6}$ | $0.5$ | $r = \pm 1.4$ | $\left(1.4, \dfrac{5\pi}{6}\right)$ and $\left(-1.4, \dfrac{5\pi}{6}\right) = \left(1.4, \dfrac{11\pi}{6}\right)$ |
| $\pi$ | $1$ | $r = \pm 2$ | $(2, \pi)$    and    $(-2, \pi) = (2, 2\pi)$ |

STEP 2 Plot the points in polar coordinates.

STEP 3 Connect the points with a smooth curve.
The resulting curve is known as a
*lemniscate*.

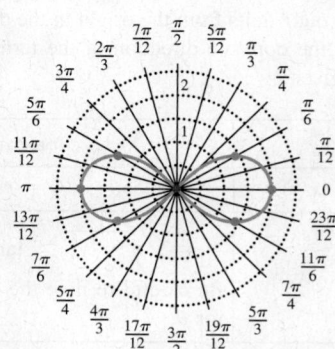

## Converting Equations Between Polar and Rectangular Form

It is not always advantageous to plot an equation in the form in which it is given. It is sometimes easier to first convert to rectangular form and then plot. For example, to plot $r = \dfrac{2}{\cos\theta + \sin\theta}$, we could make a table of values. However, as you will see in Example 9, it is much easier to convert this equation to rectangular coordinates.

*Technology Tip*

Graph $r = \dfrac{2}{\cos\theta + \sin\theta}$.

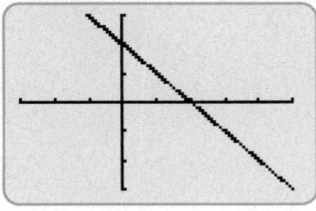

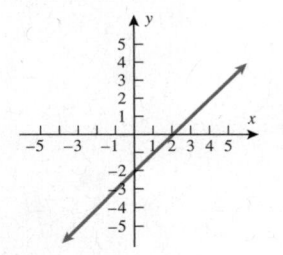

■ **Answer:** $y = x - 2$

### EXAMPLE 9 Converting an Equation from Polar Form to Rectangular Form

Graph $r = \dfrac{2}{\cos\theta + \sin\theta}$.

**Solution:**

Multiply the equation by $\cos\theta + \sin\theta$.

$$r(\cos\theta + \sin\theta) = 2$$

Eliminate parentheses.

$$r\cos\theta + r\sin\theta = 2$$

Convert the result to rectangular form.

$$\underset{x}{\underbrace{r\cos\theta}} + \underset{y}{\underbrace{r\sin\theta}} = 2$$

Simplify. The result is a straight line.

$$\boxed{y = -x + 2}$$

Graph the line.

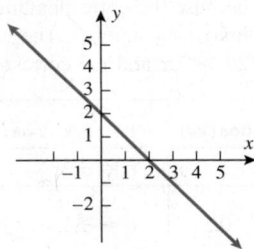

■ **YOUR TURN** Graph $r = \dfrac{2}{\cos\theta - \sin\theta}$.

Graph polar coordinates $(r, \theta)$ in the polar coordinate system first by rotating a ray to get the terminal side of the angle. Then if $r$ is positive, go out $r$ units from the origin in the direction of the terminal side. If $r$ is negative, go out $|r|$ units in the opposite direction of the terminal side. Conversions between polar and rectangular forms are given by

| FROM | TO | IDENTITIES |
|---|---|---|
| Polar $(r, \theta)$ | Rectangular $(x, y)$ | $x = r\cos\theta \qquad y = r\sin\theta$ |
| Rectangular $(x, y)$ | Polar $(r, \theta)$ | $r = \sqrt{x^2 + y^2} \qquad \tan\theta = \dfrac{y}{x}, x \neq 0$<br>Be careful to note the proper quadrant for $\theta$. |

We can graph polar equations by point-plotting. Common shapes that arise are given in the following table. Sine and cosine curves have the same shapes (just rotated). If more than one equation is given, then the top equation corresponds to the actual graph. In this table, $a$ and $b$ are assumed to be positive.

| CLASSIFICATION | DESCRIPTION | POLAR EQUATIONS | GRAPH |
|---|---|---|---|
| Line | Radial line | $\theta = a$ | |
| Circle | Circle centered at the origin | $r = a$ | |
| Circle | Circle that touches the pole and whose center is on the polar axis | $r = a\cos\theta$ | |
| Circle | Circle that touches the pole and whose center is on the line $\theta = \dfrac{\pi}{2}$ | $r = a\sin\theta$ | |
| Limaçon | Cardioid **a = b** | $r = a + b\cos\theta$ <br> $r = a + b\sin\theta$ | |
| Limaçon | Without inner loop $a > b$ | $r = -a - b\cos\theta$ <br> $r = a + b\sin\theta$ | |
| Limaçon | With inner loop $a < b$ | $r = a + b\sin\theta$ <br> $r = a + b\cos\theta$ | |
| Lemniscate | | $r^2 = a^2\cos(2\theta)$ <br> $r^2 = a^2\sin(2\theta)$ | |
| Rose | Three* rose petals | $r = a\sin(3\theta)$ <br> $r = a\cos(3\theta)$ | |

| CLASSIFICATION | DESCRIPTION | POLAR EQUATIONS | GRAPH |
|---|---|---|---|
| Rose | Four*/rose petals | $r = a\sin(2\theta)$ <br> $r = a\cos(2\theta)$ | |
| Spiral | | $r = a\theta$ | |

*In the argument $n\theta$, if $n$ is odd, there are $n$ petals (leaves), and if $n$ is even, there are $2n$ petals (leaves).

**SECTION**
**7.5 EXERCISES**

**▪ SKILLS**

**In Exercises 1–10, plot each indicated point in a polar coordinate system.**

**1.** $\left(3, \dfrac{5\pi}{6}\right)$  **2.** $\left(2, \dfrac{5\pi}{4}\right)$  **3.** $\left(4, \dfrac{11\pi}{6}\right)$  **4.** $\left(1, \dfrac{2\pi}{3}\right)$  **5.** $\left(-2, \dfrac{\pi}{6}\right)$

**6.** $\left(-4, \dfrac{7\pi}{4}\right)$  **7.** $(-4, 270°)$  **8.** $(3, 135°)$  **9.** $(4, 225°)$  **10.** $(-2, 60°)$

**In Exercises 11–20, convert each point to exact polar coordinates. Assume that $0 \le \theta < 2\pi$.**

**11.** $(2, 2\sqrt{3})$  **12.** $(3, -3)$  **13.** $(-1, -\sqrt{3})$  **14.** $(6, 6\sqrt{3})$  **15.** $(-4, 4)$

**16.** $(0, \sqrt{2})$  **17.** $(3, 0)$  **18.** $(-7, -7)$  **19.** $(-\sqrt{3}, -1)$  **20.** $(2\sqrt{3}, -2)$

**In Exercises 21–30, convert each point to exact rectangular coordinates.**

**21.** $\left(4, \dfrac{5\pi}{3}\right)$  **22.** $\left(2, \dfrac{3\pi}{4}\right)$  **23.** $\left(-1, \dfrac{5\pi}{6}\right)$  **24.** $\left(-2, \dfrac{7\pi}{4}\right)$  **25.** $\left(0, \dfrac{11\pi}{6}\right)$

**26.** $(6, 0)$  **27.** $(2, 240°)$  **28.** $(-3, 150°)$  **29.** $(-1, 135°)$  **30.** $(5, 315°)$

**In Exercises 31–34, match the polar graphs with their corresponding equations.**

**31.** $r = 4\cos\theta$  **32.** $r = 2\theta$  **33.** $r = 3 + 3\sin\theta$  **34.** $r = 3\sin(2\theta)$

**a.**

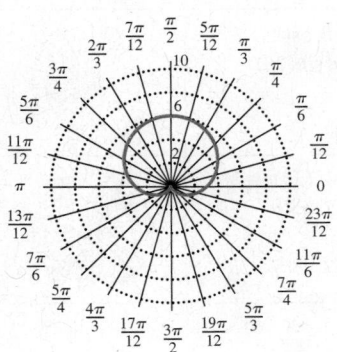

**b.**

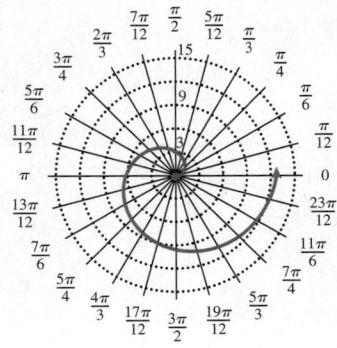

**c.**

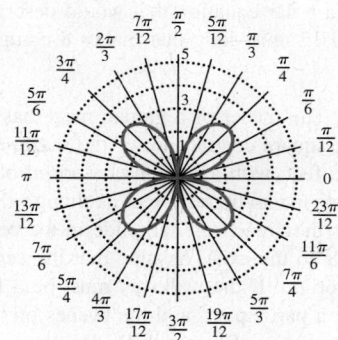

**d.**

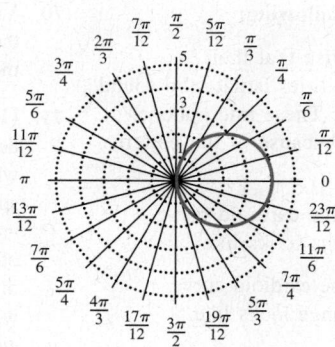

**In Exercises 35–50, graph each equation.**

**35.** $r = 5$

**36.** $\theta = -\dfrac{\pi}{3}$

**37.** $r = 2\cos\theta$

**38.** $r = 3\sin\theta$

**39.** $r = 4\sin(2\theta)$

**40.** $r = 5\cos(2\theta)$

**41.** $r = 3\sin(3\theta)$

**42.** $r = 4\cos(3\theta)$

**43.** $r^2 = 9\cos(2\theta)$

**44.** $r^2 = 16\sin(2\theta)$

**45.** $r = -2\cos\theta$

**46.** $r = -3\sin(3\theta)$

**47.** $r = 4\theta$

**48.** $r = -2\theta$

**49.** $r = -3 + 2\cos\theta$

**50.** $r = 2 + 3\sin\theta$

**In Exercises 51–54, convert the equation from polar to rectangular form. Identify the resulting equation as a line, parabola, or circle.**

**51.** $r(\sin\theta + 2\cos\theta) = 1$

**52.** $r(\sin\theta - 3\cos\theta) = 2$

**53.** $r^2\cos^2\theta - 2r\cos\theta + r^2\sin^2\theta = 8$

**54.** $r^2\cos^2\theta - r\sin\theta = -2$

**In Exercises 55–60, graph the polar equation.**

**55.** $r = -\frac{1}{3}\theta$

**56.** $r = \frac{1}{4}\theta$

**57.** $r = 4\sin(5\theta)$

**58.** $r = -3\cos(4\theta)$

**59.** $r = -2 - 3\cos\theta$

**60.** $r = 4 - 3\sin\theta$

## ▪ APPLICATIONS

**61. Halley's Comet.** Halley's comet travels an elliptical path that can be modeled with the polar equation
$$r = \frac{0.587(1 + 0.967)}{1 - 0.967\cos\theta}.$$ Sketch the graph of the path of Halley's comet.

**62. Dwarf Planet Pluto.** The planet Pluto travels in an elliptical orbit that can be modeled with the polar equation
$$r = \frac{29.62(1 + 0.249)}{1 - 0.249\cos\theta}.$$ Sketch the graph of Pluto's orbit.

**For Exercises 63 and 64, refer to the following:**

Spirals are seen in nature, as in the swirl of a pine cone; they are also used in machinery to convert motions. An Archimedes spiral has the general equation $r = a\theta$. A more general form for the equation of a spiral is $r = a\theta^{1/n}$, where $n$ is a constant that determines how tightly the spiral is wrapped.

**63. Archimedes Spiral.** Compare the Archimedes spiral $r = \theta$ with the spiral $r = \theta^{1/2}$ by graphing both on the same polar graph.

**64. Archimedes Spiral.** Compare the Archimedes spiral $r = \theta$ with the spiral $r = \theta^{4/3}$ by graphing both on the same polar graph.

**For Exercises 65 and 66, refer to the following:**

The *lemniscate motion* occurs naturally in the flapping of birds' wings. The bird's vertical lift and wing sweep create the distinctive figure-eight pattern. The patterns vary with the different wing profiles.

**65. Flapping Wings of Birds.** Compare the following two possible lemniscate patterns by graphing them on the same polar graph: $r^2 = 4\cos(2\theta)$ and $r^2 = \frac{1}{4}\cos(2\theta)$.

**66. Flapping Wings of Birds.** Compare the following two possible lemniscate patterns by graphing them on the same polar graph: $r^2 = 4\cos(2\theta)$ and $r^2 = 4\cos(2\theta + 2)$.

**For Exercises 67 and 68, refer to the following:**

Many microphone manufacturers advertise that their microphones' exceptional pickup capabilities isolate the sound source and minimize background noise. These microphones are described as cardioid microphones because of the pattern formed by the range of the pickup.

67. **Cardioid Pickup Pattern.** Graph the cardioid curve $r = 2 + 2\sin\theta$ to see what the range looks like.

68. **Cardioid Pickup Pattern.** Graph the cardioid curve $r = -4 - 4\sin\theta$ to see what the range looks like.

**For Exercises 69 and 70, refer to the following:**

The sword artistry of the Samurai is legendary in Japanese folklore and myth. The elegance with which a samurai could wield a sword rivals the grace exhibited by modern figure skaters. In more modern times, such legends have been rendered digitally in many different video games (e.g., *Onimusha*). In order to make the characters realistically move across the screen, and in particular, wield various sword motions true to the legends, trigonometric functions are extensively used in constructing the underlying graphics module. One famous movement is a figure eight, swept out with two hands on the sword. The actual path of the tip of the blade as the movement progresses in this figure-eight motion depends essentially on the length $L$ of the sword and the speed with which it is swept out. Such a path is modeled using a polar equation of the form

$$r^2\theta = L\cos(A\theta) \text{ or } r^2\theta = L\sin(A\theta), \ \theta_1 \leq \theta \leq \theta_2$$

whose graphs are called *lemniscates*.

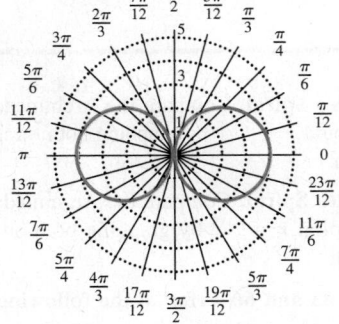

69. **Video Games.** Graph the following equations:

 a. $r^2\theta = 5\cos\theta, 0 \leq \theta \leq 2\pi$

 b. $r^2\theta = 5\cos(2\theta), 0 \leq \theta \leq \pi$

 c. $r^2\theta = 5\cos(4\theta), 0 \leq \theta \leq \dfrac{\pi}{2}$

What do you notice about all of these graphs? Suppose that the movement of the tip of the sword in a game is governed by these graphs. Describe what happens if you change the domain in (b) and (c) to $0 \leq \theta \leq 2\pi$.

70. **Video Games.** Write a polar equation that would describe the motion of a sword 12 units long that makes 8 complete motions in $[0, 2\pi]$.

71. **Home Improvement.** The owner of a garden maze has decided to replace the square central plot of the maze, which is 60 feet × 60 feet, with a section comprised of a spiral to make the participants literally feel as though they are going in circles as they reach the tall slide in the center of the maze (that leads to the exit). Assume that the center of the maze is at the origin. If the walkway must be 3 feet wide to accommodate a participant, and the bushes on either side of the walkway are 1.5 feet thick, how many times can the spiral wrap around before the center is reached? Graph the resulting spiral.

72. **Home Improvement.** Consider the garden maze in Exercise 71, but now suppose that the owner wants the spiral to wrap around exactly 3 times. How wide can the walkway then be throughout the spiral? Graph it.

73. **Magnetic Pendulum.** A magnetic bob is affixed to an arm of length $L$, which is fastened to a pivot point. Three magnets of equal strength are positioned on a plane 8 inches from the center; one is placed on the $x$-axis, one at 120° with respect to the positive $x$-axis, and the other at 240° with respect to the positive $x$-axis. The path swept out is a three-petal rose, as shown below:

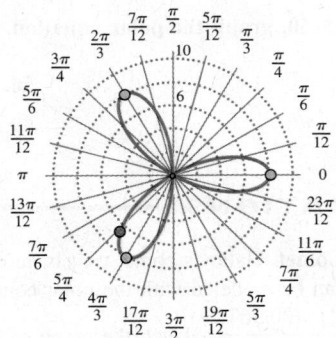

 a. Find the equation of this path.

 b. How many times does the path retrace itself on the interval $[0, 100\pi]$?

74. **Magnetic Pendulum.** In reference to the context of Exercise 73, now position 8 magnets, each 8 units from the origin and at the vertices of a regular octagon, one being on the $x$-axis. Assume that the path of the pendulum is an eight-petal rose.

 a. Find the equation of this path.

 b. Graph this equation.

# CATCH THE MISTAKE

**In Exercises 75 and 76, explain the mistake that is made.**

**75.** Convert $(-2, -2)$ to polar coordinates.

**Solution:**

Label $x$ and $y$.  $x = -2, y = -2$

Find $r$.  $r = \sqrt{x^2 + y^2} = \sqrt{4 + 4} = \sqrt{8} = 2\sqrt{2}$

Find $\theta$.  $\tan \theta = \dfrac{-2}{-2} = 1$

$$\theta = \tan^{-1}(1) = \frac{\pi}{4}$$

Write the point in polar coordinates.  $\left(2\sqrt{2}, \dfrac{\pi}{4}\right)$

This is incorrect. What mistake was made?

**76.** Convert $\left(-\sqrt{3}, 1\right)$ to polar coordinates.

**Solution:**

Label $x$ and $y$.  $x = -\sqrt{3}, y = 1$

Find $r$.  $r = \sqrt{x^2 + y^2} = \sqrt{3 + 1} = \sqrt{4} = 2$

Find $\theta$.  $\tan \theta = \dfrac{1}{-\sqrt{3}} = -\dfrac{1}{\sqrt{3}}$

$$\theta = \tan^{-1}\left(-\frac{1}{\sqrt{3}}\right) = -\frac{\pi}{4}$$

Write the point in polar coordinates.  $\left(2, -\dfrac{\pi}{4}\right)$

This is incorrect. What mistake was made?

# CONCEPTUAL

**In Exercises 77 and 78, determine whether each statement is true or false.**

**77.** All cardioids are limaçons, but not all limaçons are cardioids.

**78.** All limaçons are cardioids, but not all cardioids are limaçons.

**79.** Find the polar equation that is equivalent to a vertical line, $x = a$.

**80.** Find the polar equation that is equivalent to a horizontal line, $y = b$.

**81.** Give another pair of polar coordinates for the point $(a, \theta)$.

**82.** Convert $(-a, b)$ to polar coordinates. Assume that $a > 0, b > 0$.

# CHALLENGE

**83.** Determine the values of $\theta$ at which $r = 4\cos\theta$ and $r\cos\theta = 1$ intersect. Graph both equations.

**84.** Find the Cartesian equation for $r = a\sin\theta + b\cos\theta$, where $a$ and $b$ are positive. Identify the type of graph.

**85.** Find the Cartesian equation for $r = \dfrac{a\sin(2\theta)}{\cos^3\theta - \sin^3\theta}$.

**86.** Identify an equation for the following graph:

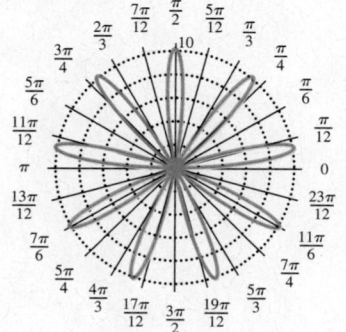

**87.** Consider the equation $r = 2a\cos(\theta - b)$. Sketch the graph for various values of $a$ and $b$, and then give a general description of the graph.

**88.** Consider the equation $r = a\sin(b\theta)$, where $a, b > 0$. Determine the smallest number $M$ for which the graph starts to repeat.

■ TECHNOLOGY

89. Given $r = \cos\left(\dfrac{\theta}{2}\right)$, find the $\theta$-intervals for the inner loop above the $x$-axis.

90. Given $r = 2\cos\left(\dfrac{3\theta}{2}\right)$, find the $\theta$-intervals for the petal in the first quadrant.

91. Given $r = 1 + 3\cos\theta$, find the $\theta$-intervals for the inner loop.

92. Given $r = 1 + \sin(2\theta)$ and $r = 1 - \cos(2\theta)$, find all points of intersection.

93. Given $r = 2 + \sin(4\theta)$ and $r = 1$, find the angles of all points of intersection.

94. Given $r = 2 - \cos(3\theta)$ and $r = 1.5$, find the angles of all points of intersection.

■ PREVIEW TO CALCULUS

**In calculus, when we need to find the area enclosed by two polar curves, the first step consists of finding the points where the curves coincide.**

**In Exercises 95–98, find the points of intersection of the given curves.**

95. $r = 4\sin\theta$ and $r = 4\cos\theta$

96. $r = \cos\theta$ and $r = 2 + 3\cos\theta$

97. $r = 1 - \sin\theta$ and $r = 1 + \cos\theta$

98. $r = 1 + \sin\theta$ and $r = 1 + \cos\theta$

When it comes to raising complex numbers to integer powers, you can do it the Brut force way (i.e., "the long way") or you can take advantage of De Moivre's theorem (i.e., "the short way").

Let us start with the complex number $z = 1 + i$ (rectangular coordinates) or in polar (trigonometric) form can be written as $z = \sqrt{2}\,(\cos 45° + i \sin 45°) =$

$$\sqrt{2}\left[\cos\left(\frac{\pi}{4}\right) + i \sin\left(\frac{\pi}{4}\right)\right]$$

*Brut Force*

$n = 1$: $(1 + i)^1 = $ _____

$n = 2$: $(1 + i)^2 = $ _____

$n = 3$: $(1 + i)^3 = $ _____

$n = 4$: $(1 + i)^4 = $ _____

*De Moivre's Theorem:* $z^n = r^n[\cos(n\theta) + i \sin(n\theta)]$

$n = 1$: $z^1 = r[\cos(\theta) + i\sin(\theta)] = \sqrt{2}\left[\cos\left(\frac{\pi}{4}\right) + i\sin\left(\frac{\pi}{4}\right)\right] = $ _____

$n = 2$: $z^2 = r^2[\cos(2\theta) + i\sin(2\theta)] = (\sqrt{2})^2\left[\cos\left(2\cdot\frac{\pi}{4}\right) + i\sin\left(\frac{\pi}{4}\right)\right] = $ _____

$n = 3$: $z^3 = r^3[\cos(3\theta) + i\sin(3\theta)] = (\sqrt{2})^3\left[\cos\left(3\cdot\frac{\pi}{4}\right) + i\sin\left(\frac{3\pi}{4}\right)\right] = $ _____

$n = 4$: $z^4 = r^4[\cos(4\theta) + i\sin(4\theta)] = (\sqrt{2})^4\left[\cos\left(4\cdot\frac{\pi}{4}\right) + i\sin\left(4\cdot\frac{\pi}{4}\right)\right] = $ _____

At what $n$ would you use De Moivre's theorem?

# MODELING **OUR WORLD**

In the summer of 2008, the average price of unleaded gasoline in the United States topped $4 per gallon. This meant that considering hybrid alternative automobiles was no longer just a "green" pursuit for the environmentally conscious, but an attractive financial option. When hybrids were first introduced, gasoline was roughly $3 per gallon and hybrid owners had to drive three to five years (depending on how many miles per year they drove) before their savings at the pump equaled the initial additional cost of the purchase. With gasoline approaching the $4 per gallon price, the rising price of gasoline allows a consumer to make up the initial additional cost of a hybrid automobile in as little as one to three years, depending on driving habits.

The following table illustrates the approximate gross vehicle weight of both a large SUV and a small hybrid and the approximate fuel economy rates in miles per gallon:

| AUTOMOBILE | WEIGHT | MPG |
|---|---|---|
| Ford Expedition | 7100 lb | 18 |
| Toyota Prius | 2800 lb | 45 |

Recall that the amount of work to push an object that weighs $F$ pounds a distance of $d$ feet along a horizontal is $W = \mathbf{F} \cdot \mathbf{d}$.

1. Calculate how much work it would take to move a Ford Expedition 100 feet.

2. Calculate how much work it would take to move a Toyota Prius 100 feet.

3. Compare the values you calculated in Questions 1 and 2. What is the ratio of work to move the Expedition to work required to move the Prius?

4. Compare the result in Question 3 with the ratio of fuel economy (mpg) for these two vehicles. What can you conclude about the relationship between weight of an automobile and fuel economy?

5. Calculate the work required to move both the Ford Expedition and Toyota Prius 100 feet along an incline that makes a 45° angle with the ground (horizontal).

6. Based on your results in Question 5, do you expect the fuel economy ratios to be the same in this inclined scenario compared with the horizontal? In other words, should consumers in Florida (flat) be guided by the same "numbers" as consumers in the Appalachian Mountains (North Carolina)?

| SECTION | CONCEPT | KEY IDEAS/FORMULAS |
|---|---|---|
| 7.1 | **Vectors** | Vector $\mathbf{u}$ or $\overrightarrow{AB}$ |

| | | |
|---|---|---|
| | Magnitude and direction of vectors | $\|\mathbf{u}\| = \sqrt{a^2 + b^2}$ |

$\tan\theta = \dfrac{b}{a}$    Magnitude (length of a vector): $\mathbf{u} = \langle a, b \rangle$

Geometric: tail-to-tip

$\mathbf{u} = \langle a, b \rangle$  and  $\mathbf{v} = \langle c, d \rangle$

$\mathbf{u} + \mathbf{v} = \langle a + c, b + d \rangle$

| | | |
|---|---|---|
| | Vector operations | Scalar multiplication: $k\langle a, b \rangle = \langle ka, kb \rangle$ |
| | Horizontal and vertical components of a vector | Horizontal component: $a = \|\mathbf{u}\| \cos\theta$<br>Vertical component: $b = \|\mathbf{u}\| \sin\theta$ |
| | Unit vectors | $\mathbf{u} = \dfrac{\mathbf{v}}{\|\mathbf{v}\|}$ |
| | Resultant vectors | ▪ Resultant velocities<br>▪ Resultant forces |
| 7.2 | **The dot product** | ▪ The product of a scalar and a vector is a vector.<br>▪ The dot product of two vectors is a scalar. |
| | The dot product | $\mathbf{u} = \langle a, b \rangle$  and  $\mathbf{v} = \langle c, d \rangle$<br>$\mathbf{u} \cdot \mathbf{v} = ac + bd$ |
| | Angle between two vectors | If $\theta$ is the angle between two nonzero vectors $\mathbf{u}$ and $\mathbf{v}$, where $0° \leq \theta \leq 180°$, then |

$$\cos\theta = \frac{\mathbf{u} \cdot \mathbf{v}}{\|\mathbf{u}\|\|\mathbf{v}\|}$$

Orthogonal (perpendicular) vectors: $\mathbf{u} \cdot \mathbf{v} = 0$

| | | |
|---|---|---|
| | Work | When force and displacement are in the same direction: $W = \|\mathbf{F}\|\|\mathbf{d}\|$. |

When force and displacement are not in the same direction: $W = \mathbf{F} \cdot \mathbf{d}$.

| SECTION | CONCEPT | KEY IDEAS/FORMULAS |
|---------|---------|---------------------|
| 7.3 | **Polar (trigonometric) form of complex numbers** | |
| | Complex numbers in rectangular form | The **modulus**, or magnitude, of a complex number $z = x + iy$ is the distance from the origin to the point $(x, y)$ in the complex plane given by $$\lvert z \rvert = \sqrt{x^2 + y^2}$$ |
| | Complex numbers in polar form | The **polar form** of a complex number is $$z = r(\cos\theta + i\sin\theta)$$ where $r$ represents the **modulus** (magnitude) of the complex number and $\theta$ represents the **argument** of $z$. **Converting complex numbers between rectangular and polar forms** Step 1: Plot the point $z = x + yi$ in the complex plane (note the quadrant). Step 2: Find $r$. Use $r = \sqrt{x^2 + y^2}$. Step 3: Find $\theta$. Use $\tan\theta = \dfrac{y}{x}$, $x \neq 0$, where $\theta$ is in the quadrant found in Step 1. |
| 7.4 | **Products, quotients, powers, and roots of complex numbers** | |
| | Products of complex numbers | Let $z_1 = r_1(\cos\theta_1 + i\sin\theta_1)$ and $z_2 = r_2(\cos\theta_2 + i\sin\theta_2)$ be two complex numbers. The product $z_1 z_2$ is given by $$z_1 z_2 = r_1 r_2[\cos(\theta_1 + \theta_2) + i\sin(\theta_1 + \theta_2)]$$ Multiply the magnitudes and add the arguments. |
| | Quotients of complex numbers | Let $z_1 = r_1(\cos\theta_1 + i\sin\theta_1)$ and $z_2 = r_2(\cos\theta_2 + i\sin\theta_2)$ be two complex numbers. The quotient $\dfrac{z_1}{z_2}$ is given by $$\frac{z_1}{z_2} = \frac{r_1}{r_2}[\cos(\theta_1 - \theta_2) + i\sin(\theta_1 - \theta_2)]$$ Divide the magnitudes and subtract the arguments. |
| | Powers of complex numbers | **De Moivre's theorem** If $z = r(\cos\theta + i\sin\theta)$ is a complex number, then $z^n = r^n[\cos(n\theta) + i\sin(n\theta)]$, $n \geq 1$, where $n$ is an integer. |
| | Roots of complex numbers | The **nth roots** of the complex number $z = r(\cos\theta + i\sin\theta)$ are given by $$w_k = r^{1/n}\left[\cos\left(\frac{\theta}{n} + \frac{k \cdot 360°}{n}\right) + i\sin\left(\frac{\theta}{n} + \frac{k \cdot 360°}{n}\right)\right]$$ $\theta$ in degrees, where $k = 0, 1, 2, \ldots, n - 1$. |

| SECTION | CONCEPT | KEY IDEAS/FORMULAS |
|---|---|---|

**7.5** **Polar coordinates and graphs of polar equations**

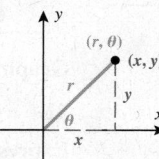

Polar coordinates

To plot a point $(r, \theta)$:

- Start on the polar axis and rotate a ray to form the terminal side of an angle $\theta$.
- If $r > 0$, the point is $r$ units from the origin in the *same direction* as the terminal side of $\theta$.
- If $r < 0$, the point is $|r|$ units from the origin in the *opposite direction* of the terminal side of $\theta$.

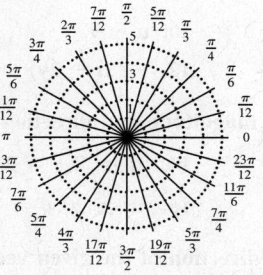

Converting between polar and rectangular coordinates

From polar $(r, \theta)$ to rectangular $(x, y)$:

$$x = r\cos\theta \qquad y = r\sin\theta$$

From rectangular $(x, y)$ to polar $(r, \theta)$:

$$r = \sqrt{x^2 + y^2} \qquad \tan\theta = \frac{y}{x} \quad x \neq 0$$

Graphs of polar equations

Radial line, circle, spiral, rose petals, lemniscate, and limaçon

## 7.1 Vectors

**Find the magnitude of vector $\overrightarrow{AB}$.**

1. $A = (4, -3)$ and $B = (-8, 2)$
2. $A = (-2, 11)$ and $B = (2, 8)$
3. $A = (0, -3)$ and $B = (5, 9)$
4. $A = (3, -11)$ and $B = (9, -3)$

**Find the magnitude and direction angle of the given vector.**

5. $\mathbf{u} = \langle -10, 24 \rangle$
6. $\mathbf{u} = \langle -5, -12 \rangle$
7. $\mathbf{u} = \langle 16, -12 \rangle$
8. $\mathbf{u} = \langle 0, 3 \rangle$

**Perform the vector operation, given that $\mathbf{u} = \langle 7, -2 \rangle$ and $\mathbf{v} = \langle -4, 5 \rangle$.**

9. $2\mathbf{u} + 3\mathbf{v}$
10. $\mathbf{u} - \mathbf{v}$
11. $6\mathbf{u} + \mathbf{v}$
12. $-3(\mathbf{u} + 2\mathbf{v})$

**Find the vector, given its magnitude and direction angle.**

13. $|\mathbf{u}| = 10, \theta = 75°$
14. $|\mathbf{u}| = 8, \theta = 225°$
15. $|\mathbf{u}| = 12, \theta = 105°$
16. $|\mathbf{u}| = 20, \theta = 15°$

**Find a unit vector in the direction of the given vector.**

17. $\mathbf{v} = \langle \sqrt{6}, -\sqrt{6} \rangle$
18. $\mathbf{v} = \langle -11, 60 \rangle$

**Perform the indicated vector operation.**

19. $(3\mathbf{i} - 4\mathbf{j}) + (2\mathbf{i} + 5\mathbf{j})$
20. $(-6\mathbf{i} + \mathbf{j}) - (9\mathbf{i} - \mathbf{j})$

## 7.2 The Dot Product

**Find the indicated dot product.**

21. $\langle 6, -3 \rangle \cdot \langle 1, 4 \rangle$
22. $\langle -6, 5 \rangle \cdot \langle -4, 2 \rangle$
23. $\langle 3, 3 \rangle \cdot \langle 3, -6 \rangle$
24. $\langle -2, -8 \rangle \cdot \langle -1, 1 \rangle$
25. $\langle 0, 8 \rangle \cdot \langle 1, 2 \rangle$
26. $\langle 4, -3 \rangle \cdot \langle -1, 0 \rangle$

**Find the angle (round to the nearest degree) between each pair of vectors.**

27. $\langle 3, 4 \rangle$ and $\langle -5, 12 \rangle$
28. $\langle -4, 5 \rangle$ and $\langle 5, -4 \rangle$
29. $\langle 1, \sqrt{2} \rangle$ and $\langle -1, 3\sqrt{2} \rangle$
30. $\langle 7, -24 \rangle$ and $\langle -6, 8 \rangle$
31. $\langle 3, 5 \rangle$ and $\langle -4, -4 \rangle$
32. $\langle -1, 6 \rangle$ and $\langle 2, -2 \rangle$

**Determine whether each pair of vectors is orthogonal.**

33. $\langle 8, 3 \rangle$ and $\langle -3, 12 \rangle$
34. $\langle -6, 2 \rangle$ and $\langle 4, 12 \rangle$
35. $\langle 5, -6 \rangle$ and $\langle -12, -10 \rangle$
36. $\langle 1, 1 \rangle$ and $\langle -4, 4 \rangle$
37. $\langle 0, 4 \rangle$ and $\langle 0, -4 \rangle$
38. $\langle -7, 2 \rangle$ and $\langle \frac{1}{7}, -\frac{1}{2} \rangle$
39. $\langle 6z, a - b \rangle$ and $\langle a + b, -6z \rangle$
40. $\langle a - b, -1 \rangle$ and $\langle a + b, a^2 - b^2 \rangle$

## 7.3 Polar (Trigonometric) Form of Complex Numbers

**Graph each complex number in the complex plane.**

41. $-6 + 2i$
42. $5i$

**Express each complex number in polar form.**

43. $\sqrt{2} - \sqrt{2}i$
44. $\sqrt{3} + i$
45. $-8i$
46. $-8 - 8i$

**With a calculator, express each complex number in polar form.**

47. $-60 + 11i$
48. $9 - 40i$
49. $15 + 8i$
50. $-10 - 24i$

**Express each complex number in rectangular form.**

51. $6(\cos 300° + i\sin 300°)$
52. $4(\cos 210° + i\sin 210°)$
53. $\sqrt{2}(\cos 135° + i\sin 135°)$
54. $4(\cos 150° + i\sin 150°)$

**With a calculator, express each complex number in rectangular form.**

55. $4(\cos 200° + i\sin 200°)$
56. $3(\cos 350° + i\sin 350°)$

## 7.4 Products, Quotients, Powers, and Roots of Complex Numbers

**Find the product $z_1 z_2$.**

57. $z_1 = 3(\cos 200° + i\sin 200°)$ and $z_2 = 4(\cos 70° + i\sin 70°)$
58. $z_1 = 3(\cos 20° + i\sin 20°)$ and $z_2 = 4(\cos 220° + i\sin 220°)$
59. $z_1 = 7(\cos 100° + i\sin 100°)$ and $z_2 = 3(\cos 140° + i\sin 140°)$
60. $z_1 = (\cos 290° + i\sin 290°)$ and $z_2 = 4(\cos 40° + i\sin 40°)$

**Find the quotient $\frac{z_1}{z_2}$.**

61. $z_1 = \sqrt{6}(\cos 200° + i\sin 200°)$ and $z_2 = \sqrt{6}(\cos 50° + i\sin 50°)$
62. $z_1 = 18(\cos 190° + i\sin 190°)$ and $z_2 = 2(\cos 100° + i\sin 100°)$
63. $z_1 = 24(\cos 290° + i\sin 290°)$ and $z_2 = 4(\cos 110° + i\sin 110°)$
64. $z_1 = \sqrt{200}(\cos 93° + i\sin 93°)$ and $z_2 = \sqrt{2}(\cos 48° + i\sin 48°)$

**Find the result of each expression using De Moivre's theorem. Write the answer in rectangular form.**

65. $(3 + 3i)^4$
66. $(3 + \sqrt{3}i)^4$
67. $(1 + \sqrt{3}i)^5$
68. $(-2 - 2i)^7$

**Find all *n*th roots of *z*. Write the answers in polar form, and plot the roots in the complex plane.**

**69.** $2 + 2\sqrt{3}i, n = 2$    **70.** $-8 + 8\sqrt{3}i, n = 4$

**71.** $-256, n = 4$    **72.** $-18i, n = 2$

**Find all complex solutions to the given equations.**

**73.** $x^3 + 216 = 0$    **74.** $x^4 - 1 = 0$

**75.** $x^4 + 1 = 0$    **76.** $x^3 - 125 = 0$

## 7.5  Polar Coordinates and Graphs of Polar Equations

**Convert each point to exact polar coordinates (assuming that $0 \le \theta < 2\pi$), and then graph the point in the polar coordinate system.**

**77.** $(-2, 2)$    **78.** $(4, -4\sqrt{3})$

**79.** $(-5\sqrt{3}, -5)$    **80.** $(\sqrt{3}, \sqrt{3})$

**81.** $(0, -2)$    **82.** $(11, 0)$

**Convert each polar point to exact rectangular coordinates.**

**83.** $\left(-3, \dfrac{5\pi}{3}\right)$    **84.** $\left(4, \dfrac{5\pi}{4}\right)$

**85.** $\left(2, \dfrac{\pi}{3}\right)$    **86.** $\left(6, \dfrac{7\pi}{6}\right)$

**87.** $\left(1, \dfrac{4\pi}{3}\right)$    **88.** $\left(-3, \dfrac{7\pi}{4}\right)$

**Graph each equation.**

**89.** $r = 4\cos(2\theta)$    **90.** $r = \sin(3\theta)$

**91.** $r = -\theta$    **92.** $r = 4 - 3\sin\theta$

## Technology Exercises

### Section 7.1

**With the graphing calculator [SUM] command, find the magnitude of the given vector. Also, find the direction angle to the nearest degree.**

**93.** $\langle 25, -60\rangle$    **94.** $\langle -70, 10\sqrt{15}\rangle$

### Section 7.2

**With the graphing calculator [SUM] command, find the angle (round to the nearest degree) between each pair of vectors.**

**95.** $\langle 14, 37\rangle, \langle 9, -26\rangle$

**96.** $\langle -23, -8\rangle, \langle 18, -32\rangle$

### Section 7.3

**Another way of using a graphing calculator to represent complex numbers in rectangular form is to enter the real and imaginary parts as a list of two numbers and use the [SUM] command to find the modulus.**

**97.** Write $-\sqrt{23} - 11i$ in polar form using the [SUM] command to find its modulus, and round the angle to the nearest degree.

**98.** Write $11 + \sqrt{23}i$ in polar form using the [SUM] command to find its modulus, and round the angle to the nearest degree.

### Section 7.4

**99.** Find the fourth roots of $-8 + 8\sqrt{3}i$, and draw the complex rectangle with the calculator.

**100.** Find the fourth roots of $8\sqrt{3} + 8i$, and draw the complex rectangle with the calculator.

### Section 7.5

**101.** Given $r = 1 - 2\sin(3\theta)$, find the angles of all points of intersection (where $r = 0$).

**102.** Given $r = 1 + 2\cos(3\theta)$, find the angles of all points of intersection (where $r = 0$).

**1.** Find the magnitude and direction angle of the vector $\mathbf{u} = \langle -5, 12 \rangle$.

**2.** Find a unit vector pointing in the same direction as $\mathbf{v} = \langle -3, -4 \rangle$.

**3.** Perform the indicated operations:

    **a.** $2\langle -1, 4 \rangle - 3\langle 4, 1 \rangle$

    **b.** $\langle -7, -1 \rangle \cdot \langle 2, 2 \rangle$

**4.** In a post pattern in football, the receiver in motion runs past the quarterback parallel to the line of scrimmage ($A$), runs 12 yards perpendicular to the line of scrimmage ($B$), and then cuts toward the goal post ($C$).

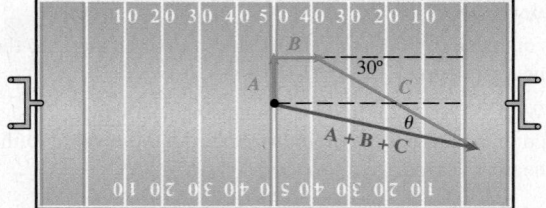

A receiver runs the post pattern. If the magnitudes of the vectors are $|A| = 3$ yd, $|B| = 12$ yd, and $|C| = 18$ yd, find the magnitude of the resultant vector $\mathbf{A} + \mathbf{B} + \mathbf{C}$ and the direction angle $\theta$.

**5.** Find the dot product $\langle 4, -51 \rangle \cdot \langle -2, -\frac{1}{3} \rangle$.

**6.** If the dot product $\langle a, -2a \rangle \cdot \langle 4, 5 \rangle = 18$, find the value of $a$.

**For Exercises 7 and 8, use the complex number**
$z = 16(\cos 120° + i \sin 120°)$.

**7.** Find $z^4$.

**8.** Find the four distinct fourth roots of $z$.

**9.** Convert the point $(3, 210°)$ to rectangular coordinates.

**10.** Convert the polar point $\left( 4, \frac{5\pi}{4} \right)$ to rectangular coordinates.

**11.** Convert the point $(30, -15)$ to polar coordinates.

**12.** Graph $r = 6\sin(2\theta)$.

**13.** Graph $r^2 = 9\cos(2\theta)$.

**14.** Find $x$ such that $\langle x, 1 \rangle$ is perpendicular to $3\mathbf{i} - 4\mathbf{j}$.

**15.** Prove that $\mathbf{u} \cdot (\mathbf{v} - \mathbf{w}) = \mathbf{u} \cdot \mathbf{v} - \mathbf{u} \cdot \mathbf{w}$.

**16.** Construct a unit vector in the opposite direction of $\langle 3, 5 \rangle$.

**17.** Compute $\mathbf{u} \cdot \mathbf{v}$ if $|\mathbf{u}| = 4$, $|\mathbf{v}| = 10$, and $\theta = \dfrac{2\pi}{3}$.

**18.** Determine whether $\mathbf{u}$ and $\mathbf{v}$ are parallel, perpendicular, or neither: $\mathbf{u} = \langle \sin\theta, \cos\theta \rangle$, and $\mathbf{v} = \langle -\cos\theta, \sin\theta \rangle$.

**19.** Find the magnitude of $-\mathbf{i} - \mathbf{j}$.

**20.** Determine $\theta$, when a streetlight is formed as follows:

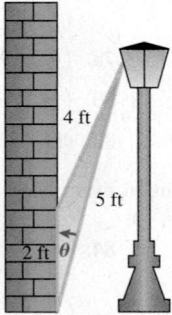

**21.** Two tugboats pull a cruiser off the port of Miami. The first one pulls with a force of 25,000 pounds and the second one pulls with a force of 27,000 pounds. If the angle between the lines connecting the cruiser with the tugboats is 25°, what is the resultant force vector of the two tugboats?

**22.** True or false: If $\mathbf{u} + \mathbf{v}$ is perpendicular to $\mathbf{u} - \mathbf{v}$, then $|\mathbf{u}| = |\mathbf{v}|$.

**23.** Solve $z^4 + 256i = 0$.

**24.** Convert to a Cartesian equation: $r^2 = \tan\theta$.

**25.** With the graphing calculator $\boxed{\text{SUM}}$ command, find the angle (round to the nearest degree) between each pair of vectors: $\langle -8, -11 \rangle$ and $\langle -16, 26 \rangle$.

**26.** Find the fourth roots of $-8\sqrt{3} - 8i$, and draw the complex rectangle with the calculator.

1. Given $f(x) = x^2 - 4$ and $g(x) = \dfrac{1}{\sqrt{3x + 5}}$, find $(f \circ g)(x)$ and the domain of $f$, $g$, and $f \circ g$.

2. Determine whether the function $f(x) = |x^3|$ is even, odd, or neither.

3. Find the quadratic function whose graph has a vertex at $(-1, 2)$ and that passes through the point $(2, -1)$. Express the quadratic function in both standard and general forms.

4. For the polynomial function
   $f(x) = x^5 - 4x^4 + x^3 + 10x^2 - 4x - 8$
   a. List each real zero and its multiplicity.
   b. Determine whether the graph touches or crosses at each $x$-intercept.

5. Find all vertical and horizontal or slant asymptotes (if any) in the following:
   $$f(x) = \frac{x^3 - 3x^2 + 2x - 1}{x^2 - 2x + 1}$$

6. How much money should be invested today in a money market account that pays 1.4% a year compounded continuously if you desire $5000 in 8 years?

7. Write the exponential equation $\sqrt[4]{625} = 5$ in its equivalent logarithmic form.

8. What is the radian measure of an angle of 305°? Express your answer in terms of $\pi$.

9. Find all trigonometric functions of the angle $\theta$. Rationalize any denominators containing radicals that you encounter in your answers.

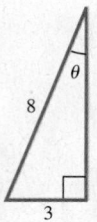

10. Solve the triangle $\alpha = 30°$, $\beta = 30°$, and $c = 4$ in.

11. Solve the triangle $a = 14.2$ m, $b = 16.5$ m, and $\gamma = 50°$.

12. Find the exact value of each trigonometric function:
   a. $\sin\left(\dfrac{3\pi}{2}\right)$
   b. $\cos 0$
   c. $\tan\left(\dfrac{5\pi}{4}\right)$
   d. $\cot\left(\dfrac{11\pi}{6}\right)$
   e. $\sec\left(\dfrac{2\pi}{3}\right)$
   f. $\csc\left(\dfrac{5\pi}{6}\right)$

13. State the amplitude, period, phase shift, and vertical shift of the function $y = 4 - \frac{1}{3}\sin(4x - \pi)$.

14. If $\sin x = \dfrac{1}{\sqrt{3}}$ and $\cos x < 0$, find $\cos(2x)$.

15. Find the exact value of $\tan\left[\cos^{-1}\left(-\frac{3}{5}\right) + \sin^{-1}\left(\frac{1}{2}\right)\right]$.

16. Find $\left(1 + \sqrt{3}i\right)^8$. Express the answer in rectangular form.

# 8

# Systems of Linear Equations and Inequalities

Cryptography is the practice and study of encryption and decryption—encoding data so that it can be decoded only by specific individuals. In other words, it turns a message into gibberish so that only the person who has the deciphering tools can turn that gibberish back into the original message. ATM cards, online shopping sites, and secure military communications all depend on coding and decoding of information. Matrices are used extensively in cryptography. A *matrix* is used as the "key" to encode the data, and then its *inverse matrix* is used as the key to decode the data.*

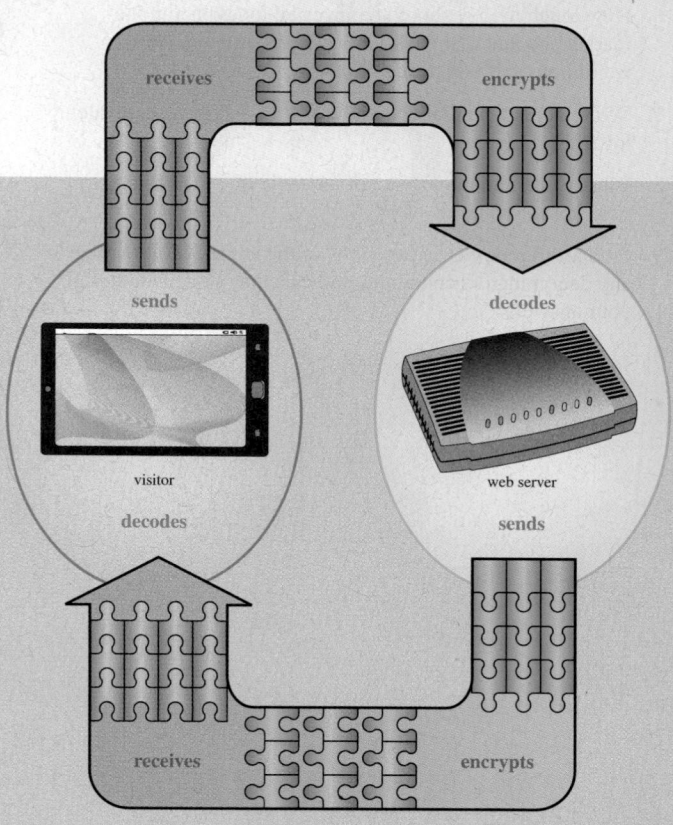

receives        encrypts

sends           decodes

visitor         web server

decodes         sends

receives        encrypts

*Section 8.4, Exercises 87–92.

▶ **IN THIS CHAPTER** we will solve systems of linear equations using the elimination and substitution methods. We will then solve systems of linear equations using matrices three different ways: using augmented matrices (Gauss–Jordan elimination), matrix algebra (inverse matrices), and determinants (Cramer's rule). We will then discuss an application of systems of linear equations that is useful in calculus called partial–fraction decomposition. Finally, we will solve systems of linear inequalities.

# SYSTEMS OF LINEAR EQUATIONS AND INEQUALITIES

| 8.1 Systems of Linear Equations in Two Variables | 8.2 Systems of Linear Equations in Three Variables | 8.3 Systems of Linear Equations and Matrices | 8.4 Matrix Algebra | 8.5 The Determinant of a Square Matrix and Cramer's Rule | 8.6 Partial Fractions | 8.7 Systems of Linear Inequalities in Two Variables |
|---|---|---|---|---|---|---|
| • Solving Systems of Linear Equations in Two Variables <br> • Three Methods and Three Types of Solutions | • Solving Systems of Linear Equations in Three Variables <br> • Types of Solutions | • Matrices <br> • Augmented Matrices <br> • Row Operations on a Matrix <br> • Row–Echelon Form of a Matrix <br> • Gaussian Elimination with Back-Substitution <br> • Gauss–Jordan Elimination <br> • Inconsistent and Dependent Systems | • Equality of Matrices <br> • Matrix Addition and Subtraction <br> • Scalar and Matrix Multiplication <br> • Matrix Equations <br> • Finding the Inverse of a Square Matrix <br> • Solving Systems of Linear Equations Using Matrix Algebra and Inverses of Square Matrices | • Determinant of a $2 \times 2$ Matrix <br> • Determinant of an $n \times n$ Matrix <br> • Cramer's Rule: Systems of Linear Equations in Two Variables <br> • Cramer's Rule: Systems of Linear Equations in Three Variables | • Performing Partial Fraction Decomposition | • Linear Inequalities in Two Variables <br> • Systems of Linear Inequalities in Two Variables <br> • The Linear Programming Model |

## LEARNING OBJECTIVES

- Solve systems of linear equations in two variables using elimination and substitution methods.
- Solve systems of linear equations in three variables using elimination and substitution methods.
- Use Gauss–Jordan elimination (augmented matrices) to solve systems of linear equations in more than two variables.
- Use matrix algebra and inverse matrices to solve systems of linear equations.
- Use Cramer's rule to solve systems of linear equations.
- Perform partial–fraction decomposition on rational expressions.
- Solve systems of linear inequalities in two variables.

**SKILLS OBJECTIVES**

- Solve systems of linear equations in two variables using the substitution method.
- Solve systems of linear equations in two variables using the elimination method.
- Solve systems of linear equations in two variables by graphing.
- Solve applications involving systems of linear equations.

**CONCEPTUAL OBJECTIVES**

- Understand that a system of linear equations has either one solution, no solution, or infinitely many solutions.
- Visualize two lines that intersect at one point, no points (parallel lines), or infinitely many points (same line).

## Solving Systems of Linear Equations in Two Variables

### Overview

A linear equation in two variables is given in standard form by

$$Ax + By = C$$

and the graph of this linear equation is a line, provided that $A$ and $B$ are not both equal to zero. In this section, we discuss **systems of linear equations**, which can be thought of as simultaneous equations. To **solve** a system of linear equations in two variables means to find the solution that satisfies *both* equations. Suppose we are given the following system of equations:

$$x + 2y = 6$$
$$3x - y = 11$$

We can interpret the solution to this system of equations both algebraically and graphically.

| | ALGEBRAIC | GRAPHICAL |
|---|---|---|
| **Solution** | $x = 4$ and $y = 1$ | $(4, 1)$ |
| **Check** | **Equation 1**  **Equation 2**<br>$x + 2y = 6$   $3x - y = 11$<br>$(4) + 2(1) = 6$ ✓  $3(4) - 1 = 11$ ✓ | |
| **Interpretation** | $x = 4$ and $y = 1$ satisfy both equations. | The point $(4, 1)$ lies on both lines. |

This particular example had *one solution*. There are systems of equations that have *no solution* or *infinitely many solutions*. We give these systems special names: **independent**, **inconsistent**, and **dependent**, respectively.

| INDEPENDENT SYSTEM | INCONSISTENT SYSTEM | DEPENDENT SYSTEM |
|---|---|---|
| One solution | No solution | Infinitely many solutions |
| | | |
| Lines have different slopes. | Lines are parallel (same slope and different $y$-intercepts). | Lines coincide (same slope and same $y$-intercept). |

In this section, we discuss three methods for solving systems of two linear equations in two variables: *substitution*, *elimination*, and *graphing*. We use the algebraic methods—substitution and elimination—to find solutions exactly; we then look at a graphical interpretation of the solution (two lines that intersect at one point, parallel lines, or coinciding lines).

We will illustrate each method with the same example given earlier:

$$x + 2y = 6 \qquad \text{Equation (1)}$$
$$3x - y = 11 \qquad \text{Equation (2)}$$

## Substitution Method

The following box summarizes the substitution method for solving systems of two linear equations in two variables:

---

**SUBSTITUTION METHOD**

**Step 1: Solve** one of the equations for one variable
in terms of the other variable.

Equation (2): $y = 3x - 11$

**Step 2: Substitute** the expression found in Step 1
into the *other* equation. The result is an
equation in one variable.

Equation (1): $x + 2(3x - 11) = 6$

**Step 3: Solve** the equation obtained in Step 2.

$x + 6x - 22 = 6$
$7x = 28$
$\boxed{x = 4}$

**Step 4: Back-substitute** the value found in Step 3
into the expression found in Step 1.

$y = 3(4) - 11$
$\boxed{y = 1}$

**Step 5: Check** that the solution satisfies *both* equations.
Substitute (4, 1) into both equations.

Equation (1): $x + 2y = 6$
$(4) + 2(1) = 6$ ✓

Equation (2): $3x - y = 11$
$3(4) - 1 = 11$ ✓

### EXAMPLE 1 Determining by Substitution That a System Has One Solution

Use the substitution method to solve the following system of linear equations:

$$x + y = 8 \qquad \text{Equation (1)}$$
$$3x - y = 4 \qquad \text{Equation (2)}$$

**Solution:**

**STEP 1** Solve Equation (2) for $y$ in terms of $x$.  $\qquad y = 3x - 4$

**STEP 2** Substitute $y = 3x - 4$ into Equation (1).  $\qquad x + (3x - 4) = 8$

**STEP 3** Solve for $x$.  $\qquad x + 3x - 4 = 8$
$$4x = 12$$
$$\boxed{x = 3}$$

**STEP 4** Back-substitute $x = 3$ into Equation (1).  $\qquad 3 + y = 8$
$$\boxed{y = 5}$$

**STEP 5** Check that $(3, 5)$ satisfies *both* equations.

$$\text{Equation (1):} \qquad x + y = 8$$
$$3 + 5 = 8$$

$$\text{Equation (2):} \qquad 3x - y = 4$$
$$3(3) - 5 = 4$$

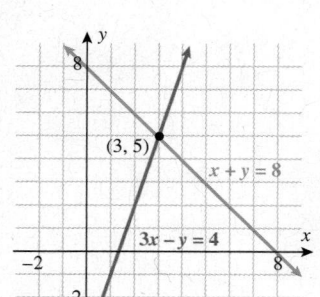

*Note:* The graphs of the two equations are two lines that intersect at the point $(3, 5)$.

### EXAMPLE 2 Determining by Substitution That a System Has No Solution

Use the substitution method to solve the following system of linear equations:

$$x - y = 2 \qquad \text{Equation (1)}$$
$$2x - 2y = 10 \qquad \text{Equation (2)}$$

**Solution:**

**STEP 1** Solve Equation (1) for $y$ in terms of $x$.  $\qquad y = x - 2$

**STEP 2** Substitute $y = x - 2$ into Equation (2).  $\qquad 2x - 2(x - 2) = 10$

**STEP 3** Solve for $x$.  $\qquad 2x - 2x + 4 = 10$
$$4 = 10$$

$4 = 10$ is never true, so this is called an inconsistent system. There is $\boxed{\text{no solution}}$ to this system of linear equations.

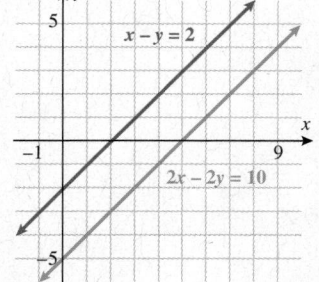

*Note:* The graphs of the two equations are parallel lines.

**EXAMPLE 3**   **Determining by Substitution That a System Has Infinitely Many Solutions**

Use the substitution method to solve the following system of linear equations:

$$x - y = \ \ \ 2 \qquad \text{Equation (1)}$$

$$-x + y = -2 \qquad \text{Equation (2)}$$

**Solution:**

**STEP 1** Solve Equation (1) for $y$ in terms of $x$. $\qquad\qquad y = x - 2$

**STEP 2** Substitute $y = x - 2$ into Equation (2). $\qquad\quad -x + (x - 2) = -2$

**STEP 3** Solve for $x$. $\qquad\qquad\qquad\qquad\qquad\qquad\quad -x + x - 2 = -2$

$$-2 = -2$$

$-2 = -2$ is always true, so this is called a dependent system. Notice, for instance, that the points $(2, 0)$, $(4, 2)$, and $(7, 5)$ all satisfy both equations. In fact, there are $\boxed{\text{infinitely many solutions}}$ to this system of linear equations. All solutions are in the form $(x, y)$, where $\boxed{y = x - 2}$. (The graphs of these two equations are the same line.) If we let $x = a$, then $y = a - 2$. In other words, all of the points $(a, a - 2)$ where $a$ is any real number are solutions to this system of linear equations.

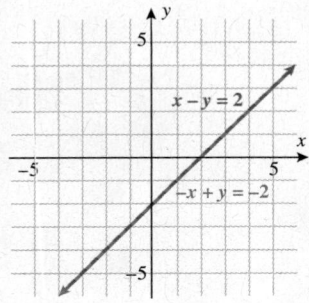

▪ **YOUR TURN** Use the substitution method to solve each system of linear equations.

    **a.** $2x + \ \ y = 3$     **b.** $x - \ \ y = \ \ 2$     **c.** $x + 2y = 1$
         $4x + 2y = 4$          $4x - 3y = 10$        $2x + 4y = 2$

▪ **Answer: a.** no solution
     **b.** $(4, 2)$
     **c.** infinitely many solutions where $y = -\frac{1}{2}x + \frac{1}{2}$ or $\left(a, \dfrac{1 - a}{2}\right)$.

## Elimination Method

We now turn our attention to another method, *elimination*, which is often preferred over substitution and will later be used in higher order systems. In a system of two linear equations in two variables, the equations can be combined, resulting in a third equation in one variable, thus *eliminating* one of the variables. The following is an example of when elimination would be preferred because the $y$ terms sum to zero when the two equations are added together:

$$\begin{array}{r} 2x - y = \ \ 5 \\ -x + y = -2 \\ \hline x \qquad\ = \ \ 3 \end{array}$$

When you cannot eliminate a variable simply by *adding* the two equations, multiply one equation by a constant that will cause the coefficients of some variable in the two equations to match and be opposite in sign.

The following box summarizes the *elimination method*, also called the *addition method*, for solving systems of two linear equations in two variables using the same example given earlier:

$$x + 2y = \ \ 6 \qquad \text{Equation (1)}$$

$$3x - \ \ y = 11 \qquad \text{Equation (2)}$$

## ELIMINATION METHOD

**Step 1*:** **Multiply** the coefficients of one (or both) of the equations so that one of the variables will be eliminated when the two equations are added.

Multiply Equation (2) by 2:
$$6x - 2y = 22$$

**Step 2:** **Eliminate** one of the variables by adding the equation found in Step 1 to the *other* original equation. The result is an equation in one variable.

$$\begin{aligned} x + 2y &= 6 \\ 6x - 2y &= 22 \\ \hline 7x &= 28 \end{aligned}$$

**Step 3:** **Solve** the equation obtained in Step 2.

$$7x = 28$$
$$\boxed{x = 4}$$

**Step 4:** **Back-substitute** the value found in Step 3 into either of the two original equations.

$$(4) + 2y = 6$$
$$2y = 2$$
$$\boxed{y = 1}$$

**Step 5:** **Check** that the solution satisfies *both* equations. Substitute $(4, 1)$ into both equations.

Equation (1):
$$x + 2y = 6$$
$$(4) + 2(1) = 6 \checkmark$$

Equation (2):
$$3x - y = 11$$
$$3(4) - 1 = 11 \checkmark$$

*Step 1 is not necessary in cases where a pair of corresponding terms already sum to zero.

---

### EXAMPLE 4   Applying the Elimination Method When One Variable Is Eliminated by Adding the Two Original Equations

Use the elimination method to solve the following system of linear equations:

$$2x - y = -5 \qquad \text{Equation (1)}$$
$$4x + y = 11 \qquad \text{Equation (2)}$$

**Solution:**

**STEP 1** Not necessary.

**STEP 2** Eliminate $y$ by adding Equation (1) to Equation (2).

$$\begin{aligned} 2x - y &= -5 \\ 4x + y &= 11 \\ \hline 6x &= 6 \end{aligned}$$

**STEP 3** Solve for $x$.

$$\boxed{x = 1}$$

**STEP 4** Back-substitute $x = 1$ into Equation (2). Solve for $y$.

$$4(1) + y = 11$$
$$\boxed{y = 7}$$

**STEP 5** Check that $(1, 7)$ satisfies both equations.

Equation (1): $\qquad 2x - y = -5$
$$2(1) - (7) = -5 \checkmark$$

Equation (2): $\qquad 4x + y = 11$
$$4(1) + (7) = 11 \checkmark$$

*Note:* The graphs of the two given equations correspond to two lines that intersect at the point $(1, 7)$.

### Study Tip

You can eliminate one variable from the system by addition when (1) the coefficients are equal and (2) the signs are opposite.

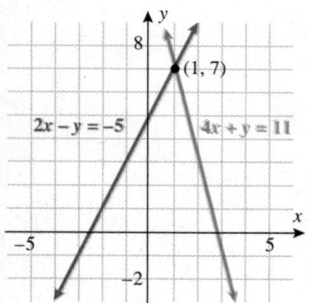

In Example 4, we eliminated the variable $y$ simply by adding the two equations. Sometimes it is necessary to multiply one (Example 5) or both (Example 6) equations by constants prior to adding.

**EXAMPLE 5**   **Applying the Elimination Method When Multiplying One Equation by a Constant Is Necessary**

Use the elimination method to solve the following system of linear equations:

$$-4x + 3y = 23 \qquad \text{Equation (1)}$$
$$12x + 5y = 1 \qquad \text{Equation (2)}$$

**Solution:**

STEP 1 Multiply Equation (1) by 3.

$$-12x + 9y = 69$$

STEP 2 Eliminate $x$ by adding the modified Equation (1) to Equation (2).

$$\begin{array}{r} -12x + 9y = 69 \\ \underline{12x + 5y = 1} \\ 14y = 70 \end{array}$$

STEP 3 Solve for $y$.

$$\boxed{y = 5}$$

STEP 4 Back-substitute $y = 5$ into Equation (2).

$$12x + 5(5) = 1$$

Solve for $x$.

$$12x + 25 = 1$$
$$12x = -24$$
$$\boxed{x = -2}$$

STEP 5 Check that $(-2, 5)$ satisfies both equations.

Equation (1):   $-4(-2) + 3(5) = 23$
                      $8 + 15 = 23$ ✓

Equation (2):   $12(-2) + 5(5) = 1$
                      $-24 + 25 = 1$ ✓

**Study Tip**

Be sure to multiply the **entire** equation by the constant.

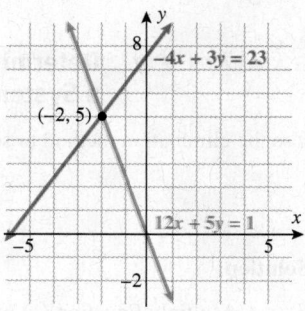

*Note:* The graphs of the two given equations correspond to two lines that intersect at the point $(-2, 5)$.

In Example 5, we eliminated $x$ simply by multiplying the first equation by a constant and adding the result to the second equation. In order to eliminate either of the variables in Example 6, we will have to multiply *both* equations by constants prior to adding.

**EXAMPLE 6    Applying the Elimination Method When Multiplying Both Equations by Constants Is Necessary**

Use the elimination method to solve the following system of linear equations:

$$3x + 2y = 1 \qquad \text{Equation (1)}$$
$$5x + 7y = 9 \qquad \text{Equation (2)}$$

**Solution:**

STEP 1  Multiply Equation (1) by 5 and Equation (2) by $-3$.

$$15x + 10y = \phantom{-}5$$
$$-15x - 21y = -27$$

STEP 2  Eliminate $x$ by adding the modified Equation (1) to the modified Equation (2).

$$\begin{aligned} 15x + 10y &= \phantom{-}5 \\ -15x - 21y &= -27 \\ \hline -11y &= -22 \end{aligned}$$

STEP 3  Solve for $y$.

$$\boxed{y = 2}$$

STEP 4  Back-substitute $y = 2$ into Equation (1). Solve for $x$.

$$3x + 2(2) = 1$$
$$3x = -3$$
$$\boxed{x = -1}$$

STEP 5  Check that $(-1, 2)$ satisfies both equations.

Equation (1):
$$3x + 2y = 1$$
$$3(-1) + 2(2) = 1 \checkmark$$

Equation (2):
$$5x + 7y = 9$$
$$5(-1) + 7(2) = 9 \checkmark$$

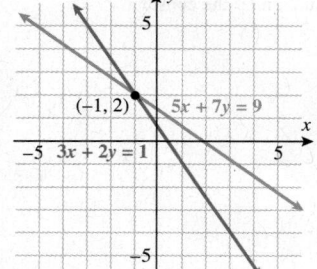

*Note:* The graphs of the two given equations correspond to two lines that intersect at the point $(-1, 2)$.

Notice in Example 6 that we could have also eliminated $y$ by multiplying the first equation by 7 and the second equation by $-2$. Typically, the choice is dictated by which approach will keep the coefficients as simple as possible. In the event that the original coefficients contain fractions or decimals, first rewrite the equations in standard form with integer coefficients and then make the decision.

**EXAMPLE 7    Determining by the Elimination Method That a System Has No Solution**

Use the elimination method to solve the following system of linear equations:

$$-x + \phantom{2}y = 7 \qquad \text{Equation (1)}$$
$$2x - 2y = 4 \qquad \text{Equation (2)}$$

**Solution:**

STEP 1  Multiply Equation (1) by 2.

$$-2x + 2y = 14$$

STEP 2  Eliminate $y$ by adding the modified Equation (1) found in Step 1 to Equation (2).

$$\begin{aligned} -2x + 2y &= 14 \\ 2x - 2y &= \phantom{1}4 \\ \hline 0 &= 18 \end{aligned}$$

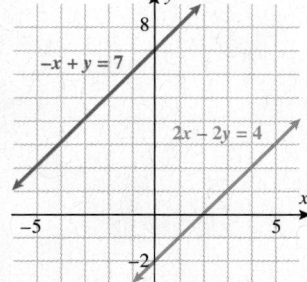

This system is inconsistent since $0 = 18$ is never true. Therefore, there are no values of $x$ and $y$ that satisfy both equations. We say that there is $\boxed{\text{no solution}}$ to this system of linear equations.

*Note:* The graphs of the two equations are two parallel lines.

EXAMPLE 8    **Determining by the Elimination Method That a System Has Infinitely Many Solutions**

Use the elimination method to solve the following system of linear equations:

$$7x + y = 2 \qquad \text{Equation (1)}$$
$$-14x - 2y = -4 \qquad \text{Equation (2)}$$

**Solution:**

STEP 1  Multiply Equation (1) by 2.

$$14x + 2y = 4$$

STEP 2  Add the modified Equation (1) found in Step 1 to Equation (2).

$$\begin{array}{r} 14x + 2y = 4 \\ -14x - 2y = -4 \\ \hline 0 = 0 \end{array}$$

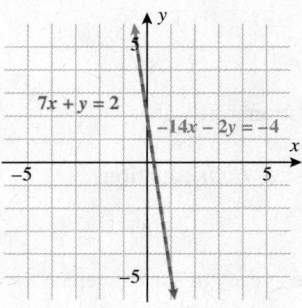

This system is dependent since $0 = 0$ is always true. We say that there are ⎡infinitely many solutions⎤ to this system of linear equations of the form ⎡$y = -7x + 2$⎤ and these can be represented by the points $(a, 2 - 7a)$.

*Note:* The graphs of the two equations are the same line.

■ YOUR TURN  Apply the elimination method to solve each system of linear equations.

**a.** $2x + 3y = 1$
$4x - 3y = -7$

**b.** $x - 5y = 2$
$-10x + 50y = -20$

**c.** $x - y = 14$
$-x + y = 9$

■ **Answer:**
**a.** $(-1, 1)$
**b.** infinitely many solutions of the form $y = \frac{1}{5}x - \frac{2}{5}$ or $\left(a, \dfrac{a-2}{5}\right).$
**c.** no solution

## Graphing Method

A third way to solve a system of linear equations in two variables is to graph the two lines. If the two lines intersect, then the point of intersection is the solution. Graphing is the most labor-intensive method for solving systems of linear equations in two variables. The graphing method is typically not used to solve systems of linear equations when an exact solution is desired. Instead, it is used to interpret or confirm the solution(s) found by the other two methods (substitution and elimination). If you are using a graphing calculator, however, you will get as accurate an answer using the graphing method as you will when applying the other methods.

The following box summarizes the graphing method for solving systems of linear equations in two variables using the same example given earlier:

$$x + 2y = 6 \qquad \text{Equation (1)}$$
$$3x - y = 11 \qquad \text{Equation (2)}$$

**GRAPHING METHOD**

**Step 1\*:** **Write** the equations in slope–intercept form.

Equation (1):      Equation (2):

$$y = -\frac{1}{2}x + 3 \qquad y = 3x - 11$$

**Step 2:** **Graph** the two lines.

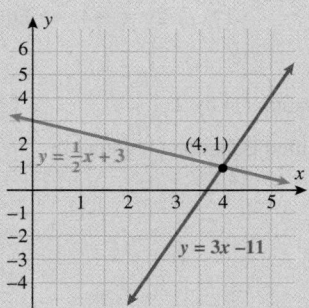

**Step 3:** **Identify** the point of intersection.

$(4, 1)$

**Step 4:** **Check** that the solution satisfies *both* equations.

Equation (1):      Equation (2):

$$x + 2y = 6 \qquad\quad 3x - y = 11$$
$$(4) + 2(1) = 6 \checkmark \qquad 3(4) - 1 = 11 \checkmark$$

\*Step 1 is not necessary when the lines are already in slope–intercept form.

**EXAMPLE 9**   **Determining by Graphing That a System Has One Solution**

Use graphing to solve the following system of linear equations:

$$x + y = 2 \qquad \text{Equation (1)}$$
$$3x - y = 2 \qquad \text{Equation (2)}$$

**Solution:**

**STEP 1** Write each equation in slope–intercept form.

$$y = -x + 2 \qquad \text{Equation (1)}$$
$$y = 3x - 2 \qquad \text{Equation (2)}$$

**STEP 2** Plot both lines on the same graph.

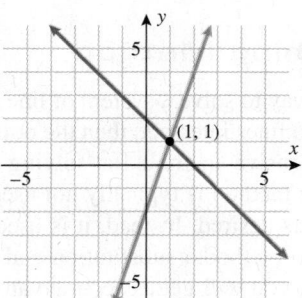

**STEP 3** Identify the point of intersection.

$(1, 1)$

**STEP 4** Check that the point $(1, 1)$ satisfies both equations.

$$x + y = 2$$
$$1 + 1 = 2 \checkmark \qquad \text{Equation (1)}$$

$$3x - y = 2$$
$$3(1) - (1) = 2 \checkmark \qquad \text{Equation (2)}$$

*Note:* There is one solution, because the two lines intersect at one point.

**EXAMPLE 10    Determining by Graphing That a System Has No Solution**

Use graphing to solve the following system of linear equations:

$$2x - 3y = 9 \qquad \text{Equation (1)}$$
$$-4x + 6y = 12 \qquad \text{Equation (2)}$$

**Solution:**

STEP 1 Write each equation in slope–intercept form.

$$y = \frac{2}{3}x - 3 \qquad \text{Equation (1)}$$

$$y = \frac{2}{3}x + 2 \qquad \text{Equation (2)}$$

STEP 2 Plot both lines on the same graph.

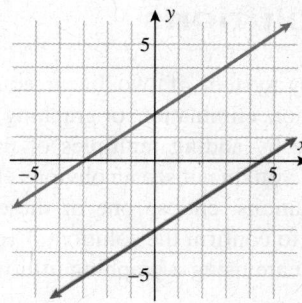

STEP 3 Identify the point of intersection.          None

The two lines are parallel because they have the same slope, but different $y$-intercepts. For this reason there is  no solution —two parallel lines do not intersect.

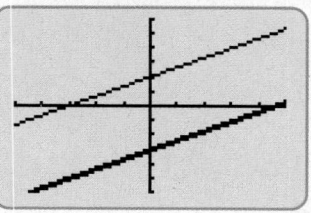
**EXAMPLE 11    Determining by Graphing That a System Has Infinitely Many Solutions**

Use graphing to solve the following system of linear equations:

$$3x + 4y = 12 \qquad \text{Equation (1)}$$
$$\frac{3}{4}x + y = 3 \qquad \text{Equation (2)}$$

**Solution:**

STEP 1 Write each equation in slope–intercept form.

$$y = -\frac{3}{4}x + 3 \quad y = -\frac{3}{4}x + 3$$

STEP 2 Plot both lines on the same graph.

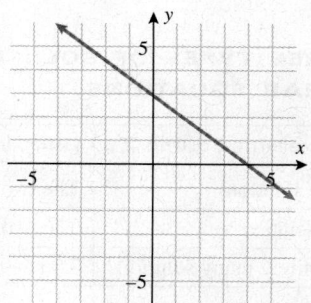

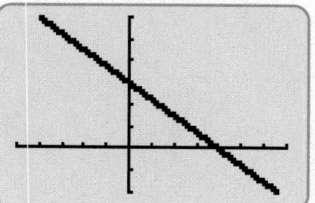

STEP 3 Identify the point of intersection.              Infinitely many points

There are $\boxed{\text{infinitely many solutions, } y = -\frac{3}{4}x + 3}$, since the two lines are identical and coincide. The points that lie along the line are $\left(a, -\frac{3}{4}a + 3\right)$.

■ **YOUR TURN** Utilize graphing to solve each system of linear equations.

a.   $x - 2y = 1$       b.   $x - 2y = 1$       c.   $2x + y = 3$
     $2x - 4y = 2$           $2x + y = 7$           $2x + y = 7$

■ **Answer:**
a. infinitely many solutions of the form $y = \frac{1}{2}x - \frac{1}{2}$
b. $(3, 1)$
c. no solution

# Three Methods and Three Types of Solutions

Given any system of two linear equations in two variables, any of the three methods (substitution, elimination, or graphing) can be utilized. If you find that it is easy to eliminate a variable by adding multiples of the two equations, then elimination is the preferred choice. If you do not see an obvious elimination, then solve the system by substitution. For exact solutions, choose one of these two algebraic methods. You should typically use graphing to confirm the solution(s) you have found by applying the other two methods or when you are using a graphing utility.

**EXAMPLE 12   Identifying Which Method to Use**

State which of the two algebraic methods (elimination or substitution) would be the preferred method to solve each system of linear equations.

a.   $x - 2y = 1$       b. $x = 2y - 1$       c. $7x - 20y = 1$
     $-x + y = 2$           $2x - y = 4$           $5x + 3y = 18$

**Solution:**

a. **Elimination:** Because the $x$ variable is eliminated when the two equations are added.

b. **Substitution:** Because the first equation is easily substituted into the second equation (for $x$).

c. **Either:** There is no preferred method, as both elimination and substitution require substantial work.

Regardless of which method is used to solve systems of two linear equations in two variables, in general, we can summarize the three types of solutions both algebraically and graphically.

**THREE TYPES OF SOLUTIONS TO SYSTEMS OF LINEAR EQUATIONS**

| NUMBER OF SOLUTIONS | GRAPHICAL INTERPRETATION |
| --- | --- |
| One solution | The two lines intersect at one point. |
| No solution | The two lines are parallel. (*Same* slope/*different* y-intercepts.) |
| Infinitely many solutions | The two lines coincide. (*Same* slope/*same* y-intercept.) |

## Applications

Suppose you have two job offers that require sales. One pays a higher base, while the other pays a higher commission. Which job do you take?

### EXAMPLE 13  Deciding Which Job to Take

Suppose that upon graduation you are offered a job selling biomolecular devices to laboratories studying DNA. The Beckman-Coulter Company offers you a job selling its DNA sequencer with an annual base salary of $20,000 plus 5% commission on total sales. The MJ Research Corporation offers you a job selling its PCR Machine that makes copies of DNA with an annual base salary of $30,000 plus 3% commission on sales. Determine what the total sales would have to be to make the Beckman-Coulter job the better offer.

**Solution:**

STEP 1  **Identify the question.**

When would these two jobs have equal compensations?

STEP 2  **Make notes.**

| | |
|---|---|
| Beckman-Coulter salary | 20,000 + 5% of sales |
| MJ Research salary | 30,000 + 3% of sales |

STEP 3  **Set up the equations.**

Let $x$ = total sales and $y$ = compensation.

Equation (1)   Beckman-Coulter:  $y = 20{,}000 + 0.05x$

Equation (2)   MJ Research:  $y = 30{,}000 + 0.03x$

STEP 4  **Solve the system of equations.**
*Substitution method\**

Substitute Equation (1)
into Equation (2).   $20{,}000 + 0.05x = 30{,}000 + 0.03x$

Solve for $x$.   $0.02x = 10{,}000$
$x = 500{,}000$

If you make $500,000 worth of sales per year, the jobs will yield equal compensations. If you sell less than $500,000, the MJ Research job is the better offer, and more than $500,000 , the Beckman-Coulter job is the better offer.

\*The elimination method could also have been used.

STEP 5  **Check the solution.**

Equation (1)   Beckman-Coulter:  $y = 20{,}000 + 0.05(500{,}000) = \$45{,}000$

Equation (2)   MJ Research:  $y = 30{,}000 + 0.03(500{,}000) = \$45{,}000$

*Technology Tip*

The graphs of $Y_1 = 20{,}000 + 0.05x$ and $Y_2 = 30{,}000 + 0.03x$ are shown.

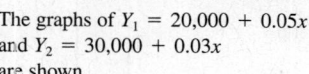

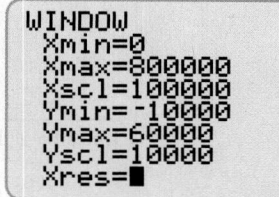

The graphs and table support the solution to the system.

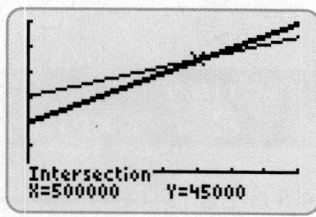

In this section, we discussed two algebraic techniques for solving systems of two linear equations in two variables:

- Substitution method
- Elimination method

The algebraic methods are preferred for exact solutions, and the graphing method is typically used to give a visual interpretation and confirmation of the solution. There are three types of solutions to systems of two linear equations in two variables: one solution, no solution, or infinitely many solutions.

| INDEPENDENT SYSTEM | INCONSISTENT SYSTEM | DEPENDENT SYSTEM |
|---|---|---|
| One solution | No solution | Infinitely many solutions |
| | | |
| Lines have different slopes. | Lines are parallel (same slope and different $y$-intercepts). | Lines coincide (same slope and same $y$-intercept). |

■ SKILLS

**In Exercises 1–20, solve each system of linear equations by substitution.**

**1.** $x + y = 7$
$x - y = 9$

**2.** $x - y = -10$
$x + y = 4$

**3.** $2x - y = 3$
$x - 3y = 4$

**4.** $4x + 3y = 3$
$2x + y = 1$

**5.** $3x + y = 5$
$2x - 5y = -8$

**6.** $6x - y = -15$
$2x - 4y = -16$

**7.** $2u + 5v = 7$
$3u - v = 5$

**8.** $m - 2n = 4$
$3m + 2n = 1$

**9.** $2x + y = 7$
$-2x - y = 5$

**10.** $3x - y = 2$
$3x - y = 4$

**11.** $4r - s = 1$
$8r - 2s = 2$

**12.** $-3p + q = -4$
$6p - 2q = 8$

**13.** $5r - 3s = 15$
$-10r + 6s = -30$

**14.** $-5p - 3q = -1$
$10p + 6q = 2$

**15.** $2x - 3y = -7$
$3x + 7y = 24$

**16.** $4x - 5y = -7$
$3x + 8y = 30$

**17.** $\frac{1}{3}x - \frac{1}{4}y = 0$
$-\frac{2}{3}x + \frac{3}{4}y = 2$

**18.** $\frac{1}{5}x + \frac{2}{3}y = 10$
$-\frac{1}{2}x - \frac{1}{6}y = -7$

**19.** $-3.9x + 4.2y = 15.3$
$-5.4x + 7.9y = 16.7$

**20.** $6.3x - 7.4y = 18.6$
$2.4x + 3.5y = 10.2$

**In Exercises 21–40, solve each system of linear equations by elimination.**

**21.** $x - y = -3$
$x + y = 7$

**22.** $x - y = -10$
$x + y = 8$

**23.** $5x + 3y = -3$
$3x - 3y = -21$

**24.** $-2x + 3y = 1$
$2x - y = 7$

**25.** $2x - 7y = 4$
$5x + 7y = 3$

**26.** $3x + 2y = 6$
$-3x + 6y = 18$

**27.** $2x + 5y = 7$
$3x - 10y = 5$

**28.** $6x - 2y = 3$
$-3x + 2y = -2$

**29.** $2x + 5y = 5$
$-4x - 10y = -10$

**30.** $11x + 3y = 3$
$22x + 6y = 6$

**31.** $3x - 2y = 12$
$4x + 3y = 16$

**32.** $5x - 2y = 7$
$3x + 5y = 29$

**33.** $6x - 3y = -15$
$7x + 2y = -12$

**34.** $7x - 4y = -1$
$3x - 5y = 16$

**35.** $4x - 5y = 22$
$3x + 4y = 1$

**36.** $6x - 5y = 32$
$2x - 6y = 2$

**37.** $\frac{1}{3}x + \frac{1}{2}y = 1$
$\frac{1}{5}x + \frac{7}{2}y = 2$

**38.** $\frac{1}{2}x - \frac{1}{3}y = 0$
$\frac{3}{2}x + \frac{1}{2}y = \frac{3}{4}$

**39.** $3.4x + 1.7y = 8.33$
$-2.7x - 7.8y = 15.96$

**40.** $-0.04x + 1.12y = 9.815$
$2.79x + 1.19y = -0.165$

**In Exercises 41–44, match the systems of equations with the graphs.**

**41.** $3x - y = 1$
$3x + y = 5$
**a.**

**42.** $-x + 2y = -1$
$2x + y = 7$
**b.**

**43.** $2x + y = 3$
$2x + y = 7$
**c.**

**44.** $x - 2y = 1$
$2x - 4y = 2$
**d.**

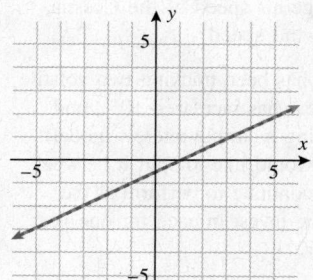 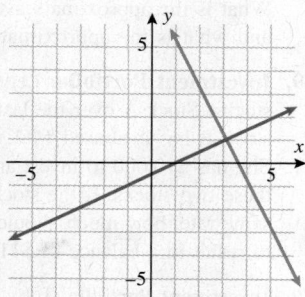 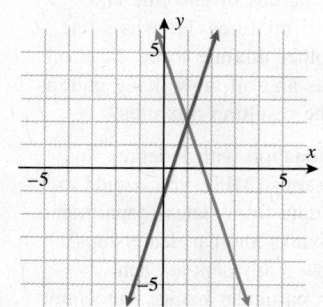 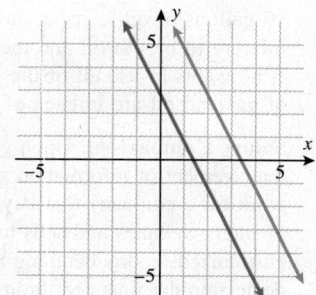

**In Exercises 45–52, solve each system of linear equations by graphing.**

**45.** $y = -x$
$y = x$

**46.** $x - 3y = 0$
$x + 3y = 0$

**47.** $2x + y = -3$
$x + y = -2$

**48.** $x - 2y = -1$
$-x - y = -5$

**49.** $\frac{1}{2}x - \frac{2}{3}y = 4$
$\frac{1}{4}x - y = 6$

**50.** $\frac{1}{5}x - \frac{5}{2}y = 10$
$\frac{1}{15}x - \frac{5}{6}y = \frac{10}{3}$

**51.** $1.6x - y = 4.8$
$-0.8x + 0.5y = 1.5$

**52.** $1.1x - 2.2y = 3.3$
$-3.3x + 6.6y = -6.6$

**In Exercises 53–58, use any method to solve each system of linear equations.**

**53.** $x - y = 2$
$x + y = 4$

**54.** $-0.5x + 0.3y = 0.8$
$-1.5x + 0.9y = 2.4$

**55.** $x - y = 1$
$x + y = 1$

**56.** $x + y = 2$
$x - y = -2$

**57.** $0.02x + 0.05y = 1.25$
$-0.06x - 0.15y = -3.75$

**58.** $x - y = 2$
$x + y = -2$

■ **APPLICATIONS**

**59. Environment.** Approximately 2 million dry erase markers are disposed of by teachers each year. Traditional dry erase markers are toxic and nonbiodegradable. EcoSmart World sells AusPens, which are dry erase markers that are recyclable, refillable, and nontoxic. The markers are available in a kit containing $x$ AusPens and $x$ refill ink bottles, each a different color. One refill ink bottle can refill up to 40 AusPens, and one kit is equivalent to $y$ dry erase markers. If one kit is equivalent to 246 traditional dry erase markers, find the number of AusPens that are in each kit.

**60. Pharmacy.** A pharmacy technician receives an order for 454 grams of a 3% zinc oxide cream. If the pharmacy has 1% and 10% zinc oxide creams in stock, how much of each should be mixed to fill the order?

**61. Mixture.** In chemistry lab, Stephanie has to make a 37 milliliter solution that is 12% HCl. All that is in the lab is 8% and 15% HCl. How many milliliters of each solution should she use to obtain the desired mix?

**62. Mixture.** A mechanic has 340 gallons of gasoline and 10 gallons of oil to make gas/oil mixtures. He wants one mixture to be 4% oil and the other mixture to be 2.5% oil. If he wants to use all of the gas and oil, how many gallons of gas and oil are in each of the resulting mixtures?

**63. Salary Comparison.** Upon graduation with a degree in management of information systems (MIS), you decide to work for a company that buys data from states' departments of motor vehicles and sells to banks and car dealerships customized reports detailing how many cars at each dealership are financed through particular banks. Autocount Corporation offers you a $15,000 base salary and 10% commission on your total annual sales. Polk Corporation offers you a base salary of $30,000 plus a 5% commission on your total annual sales. How many total sales would you have to make per year to earn more money at Autocount?

**64. Salary Comparison.** Two types of residential real estate agents are those who sell existing houses (resale) and those who sell new homes for developers. Resale of existing homes typically earns 6% commission on every sale, and representing developers in selling new homes typically earns a base salary of $15,000 per year plus an additional 1.5% commission, because agents are required to work 5 days a week on site in a new development. Find the total value (dollars) an agent would have to sell per year to make more money in resale than in new homes?

**65. Gas Mileage.** A Honda Accord gets approximately 26 mpg on the highway and 19 mpg in the city. You drove 349.5 miles on a full tank (16 gallons) of gasoline. Approximately how many miles did you drive in the city and how many on the highway?

**66. Wireless Plans.** AT&T is offering a 600-minute peak plan with free mobile-to-mobile and weekend minutes at $59 per month plus $0.13 per minute for every minute over 600. The next plan up is the 800-minute plan that costs $79 per month. You think you may go over 600 minutes, but are not sure you need 800 minutes. How many minutes would you have to talk for the 800-minute plan to be the better deal?

**67. Distance/Rate/Time.** A direct flight on Delta Air Lines from Atlanta to Paris is 4000 miles and takes approximately 8 hours going east (Atlanta to Paris) and 10 hours going west (Paris to Atlanta). Although the plane averages the same airspeed, there is a headwind while traveling west and a tailwind while traveling east, resulting in different air speeds. What is the average air speed of the plane, and what is the average wind speed?

**68. Distance/Rate/Time.** A private pilot flies a Cessna 172 on a trip that is 500 miles each way. It takes her approximately 3 hours to get there and 4 hours to return. What is the approximate average air speed of the Cessna, and what is the approximate wind speed?

**69. Investment Portfolio.** Leticia has been tracking two volatile stocks. Stock A over the last year has increased 10%, and stock B has increased 14% (using a simple interest model). She has $10,000 to invest and would like to split it between these two stocks. If the stocks continue to perform at the same rate, how much should she invest in each for one year to result in a balance of $11,260?

**70. Investment Portfolio.** Toby split his savings into two different investments, one earning 5% and the other earning 7%. He put twice as much in the investment earning the higher rate. In one year, he earned $665 in interest. How much money did he invest in each account?

**71. Break-Even Analysis.** A company produces CD players for a unit cost of $15 per CD player. The company has fixed costs of $120. If each CD player can be sold for $30, how many CD players must be sold to break even? Determine the cost equation first. Next, determine the revenue equation. Use the two equations you have found to determine the break-even point.

**72. Managing a Lemonade Stand.** An elementary-school-age child wants to have a lemonade stand. She would sell each glass of lemonade for $0.25. She has determined that each glass of lemonade costs about $0.10 to make (for lemons and sugar). It costs her $15.00 for materials to make the lemonade stand. How many glasses of lemonade must she sell to break even?

**73. Meal Cost.** An airline is deciding which meals to buy from its provider. If the airline orders the same number of meals of types I and II totaling 150 meals, the cost is $1275; if they order 60% of type I and 40% of type II, the cost is $1260. What is the cost of each type of meal?

**74. Meal Cost.** In a school district, the board of education has decided on two menus to serve in the school cafeterias. The annual budget for the meal plan is $1.2 million and one of the menus is 5% more expensive than the other. What is the annual cost of each menu? Round your answer to the nearest integer.

**75. Population.** The U.S. Census Bureau reports that Florida's population in the year 2008 was 18,328,340 habitants. The number of females exceeded the number of males by 329,910. What is the number of habitants, by gender, in Florida in 2008?

**76. Population.** According to the U.S. Census Bureau, in 2000, the U.S. population was 281,420,906 habitants. Some projections indicate that by 2020 there will be 341,250,007 habitants. The number of senior citizens will increase 30%, while the number of citizens under the age of 65 will increase 20%. Find the number of senior citizens and nonsenior citizens in the year 2000. Round your answer to the nearest integer.

■ **CATCH THE MISTAKE**

**In Exercises 77–80, explain the mistake that is made.**

**77.** Solve the system of equations by elimination.

$$2x + y = -3$$
$$3x + y = 8$$

**Solution:**

Multiply Equation (1) by $-1$.          $2x - y = -3$

Add the result to Equation (2).
$$\underline{3x + y = \phantom{-}8}$$
$$5x \phantom{+ y} = \phantom{-}5$$

Solve for $x$.          $x = 1$

Substitute $x = 1$ into Equation (2).     $3(1) + y = 8$
$$y = 5$$

The answer $(1, 5)$ is incorrect. What mistake was made?

**78.** Solve the system of equations by elimination.

$$4x - y = 12$$
$$4x - y = 24$$

**Solution:**

Multiply Equation (1) by $-1$.          $-4x + y = -12$

Add the result to Equation (2).
$$-4x + y = -12$$
$$\underline{4x - y = \phantom{-}24}$$
$$0 = \phantom{-}12$$

Answer: Infinitely many solutions.

This is incorrect. What mistake was made?

**79.** Solve the system of equations by substitution.

$$x + 3y = -4$$
$$-x + 2y = -6$$

**Solution:**

Solve Equation (1) for $x$.          $x = -3y - 4$

Substitute $x = -3y - 4$
into Equation (2).          $-(-3y - 4) + 2y = -6$

Solve for $y$.          $3y - 4 + 2y = -6$
$$5y = -2$$
$$y = -\frac{2}{5}$$

Substitute $y = -\frac{2}{5}$ into Equation (1).     $x + 3\left(-\frac{2}{5}\right) = -4$

Solve for $x$.          $x = -\frac{14}{5}$

The answer $\left(-\frac{2}{5}, -\frac{14}{5}\right)$ is incorrect. What mistake was made?

**80.** Solve the system of equations by graphing.

$$2x + 3y = \phantom{1}5$$
$$4x + 6y = 10$$

**Solution:**

Write both equations in slope–intercept form.
$$y = -\frac{2}{3}x + \frac{5}{3}$$
$$y = -\frac{2}{3}x + \frac{5}{3}$$

Since these lines have the same slope, they are parallel lines.

Parallel lines do not intersect, so there is no solution.

This is incorrect. What mistake was made?

## ▪ CONCEPTUAL

**In Exercises 81–84, determine whether each statement is true or false on the *xy*-plane.**

**81.** A system of equations represented by a graph of two lines with the same slope always has no solution.

**82.** A system of equations represented by a graph of two lines with slopes that are negative reciprocals always has one solution.

**83.** If two lines do not have exactly one point of intersection, then they must be parallel.

**84.** The system of equations, $Ax - By = 1$ and $-Ax + By = -1$, has no solution.

**85.** The point $(2, -3)$ is a solution to the system of equations

$$Ax + By = -29$$
$$Ax - By = 13$$

Find $A$ and $B$.

**86.** If you graph the lines

$$x - 50y = 100$$
$$x - 48y = -98$$

they appear to be parallel lines. However, there is a unique solution. Explain how this might be possible.

## ▪ CHALLENGE

**87. Energy Drinks.** A nutritionist wishes to market a new vitamin-enriched fruit drink and is preparing two versions of it to distribute at a local health club. She has 100 cups of pineapple juice and 4 cups of super vitamin-enriched pomegranate concentrate. One version of the drink is to contain 2% pomegranate and the other version 4% pomegranate. How much of each drink can she create if drinks are 1 cup and she uses all of the ingredients?

**88. Easter Eggs.** A family is coloring Easter eggs and wants to make 2 shades of purple, "light purple" and "deep purple." They have 30 tablespoons of deep red solution and 2 tablespoons of blue solution. If "light purple" consists of 2% blue solution and "deep purple" consists of 10% blue solution, how much of each version of purple solution can be created?

**89.** The line $y = mx + b$ connects the points $(-2, 4)$ and $(4, -2)$. Find the values of $m$ and $b$.

**90.** Find $b$ and $c$ such that the parabola $y = x^2 + bx + c$ goes through the points $(2, 7)$ and $(-6, 7)$.

**91.** Find $b$ and $c$ such that the parabola $y = bx^2 + bx + c$ goes through the points $(4, 46)$ and $(-2, 10)$.

**92.** The system of equations

$$x^2 + y^2 = 4$$
$$x^2 - y^2 = 2$$

can be solved by a change of variables. Taking $u = x^2$ and $v = y^2$, we can transform the system into

$$u + v = 4$$
$$u - v = 2$$

Find the solutions of the original system.

**93.** The system of equations

$$x^2 + 2y^2 = 11$$
$$4x^2 + y^2 = 16$$

can be solved by a change of variables. Taking $u = x^2$ and $v = y^2$, we can transform the system into

$$u + 2v = 11$$
$$4u + v = 16$$

Find the solutions of the original system.

**94.** The parabola $y = bx^2 - 2x - a$ goes through the points $(-2, a)$ and $(-1, b - 2)$. Find $a$ and $b$.

## ▪ TECHNOLOGY

**95.** Apply a graphing utility to graph the two equations $y = -1.25x + 17.5$ and $y = 2.3x - 14.1$. Approximate the solution to this system of linear equations.

**96.** Apply a graphing utility to graph the two equations $y = 14.76x + 19.43$ and $y = 2.76x + 5.22$. Approximate the solution to this system of linear equations.

**97.** Apply a graphing utility to graph the two equations $23x + 15y = 7$ and $46x + 30y = 14$. Approximate the solution to this system of linear equations.

**98.** Apply a graphing utility to graph the two equations $-3x + 7y = 2$ and $6x - 14y = 3$. Approximate the solution to this system of linear equations.

**99.** Apply a graphing utility to graph the two equations $\frac{1}{3}x - \frac{5}{12}y = \frac{5}{6}$ and $\frac{3}{7}x + \frac{1}{14}y = \frac{29}{28}$. Approximate the solution to this system of linear equations.

**100.** Apply a graphing utility to graph the two equations $\frac{5}{9}x + \frac{11}{13}y = 2$ and $\frac{3}{4}x + \frac{5}{7}y = \frac{13}{14}$. Approximate the solution to this system of linear equations.

## ▪ PREVIEW TO CALCULUS

**For Exercises 101–104, refer to the following:**

In calculus, when integrating rational functions, we decompose the function into partial fractions. This technique involves the solution of systems of equations. For example, suppose

$$\frac{1}{x^2 + x - 2} = \frac{1}{(x - 1)(x + 2)}$$

$$= \frac{A}{x - 1} + \frac{B}{x + 2}$$

$$= \frac{A(x + 2) + B(x - 1)}{(x - 1)(x + 2)}$$

and we want to find $A$ and $B$ such that $1 = A(x + 2) + B(x - 1)$, which is equivalent to $1 = (A + B)x + (2A - B)$. From this equation, we obtain the system of equations

$$A + B = 0$$
$$2A - B = 1$$

which solution is $\left(\frac{1}{3}, -\frac{1}{3}\right)$.

Find the values of $A$ and $B$ that make each equation true.

**101.** $x + 5 = A(x + 2) + B(x - 4)$

**102.** $6x = A(x + 1) + B(x - 2)$

**103.** $x + 1 = A(x + 2) + B(x - 3)$

**104.** $5 = A(x - 2) + B(2x + 1)$

---

**SECTION 8.2** SYSTEMS OF LINEAR EQUATIONS IN THREE VARIABLES

### SKILLS OBJECTIVES

- Solve systems of linear equations in three variables using a combination of both the elimination method and the substitution method.
- Solve application problems using systems of linear equations in three variables.

### CONCEPTUAL OBJECTIVES

- Understand that a graph of a linear equation in three variables corresponds to a plane.
- Identify three types of solutions: one solution (point), no solution, or infinitely many solutions (a single line in three-dimensional space or a plane).

## Solving Systems of Linear Equations in Three Variables

In Section 8.1, we solved systems of two linear equations in two variables. Graphs of linear equations in two variables correspond to lines. Now we turn our attention to linear equations in *three* variables. A **linear equation in three variables**, $x$, $y$, and $z$, is given by

$$Ax + By + Cz = D$$

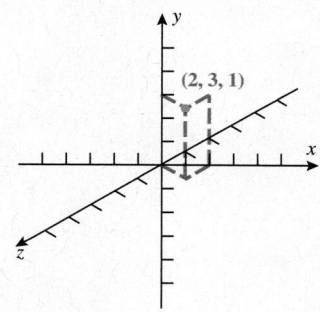

where $A$, $B$, $C$, and $D$ are real numbers that are not all equal to zero. All three variables have degree equal to one, which is why this is called a linear equation in three variables. The graph of any equation in three variables requires a three-dimensional coordinate system.

The $x$-axis, $y$-axis, and $z$-axis are each perpendicular to the other two. For the three-dimensional coordinate system on the right, a point $(x, y, z) = (2, 3, 1)$ is found by starting at the origin, moving two units to the right, three units up, and one unit out toward you.

**Study Tip**

If all three planes are coplaner (the same plane) there are infinitely many solutions.

In two variables, the graph of a linear equation is a line. In three variables, however, the graph of a linear equation is a **plane**. A plane can be thought of as an infinite sheet of paper. When solving systems of linear equations in three variables, we find one of three possibilities: one solution, no solution, or infinitely many solutions.

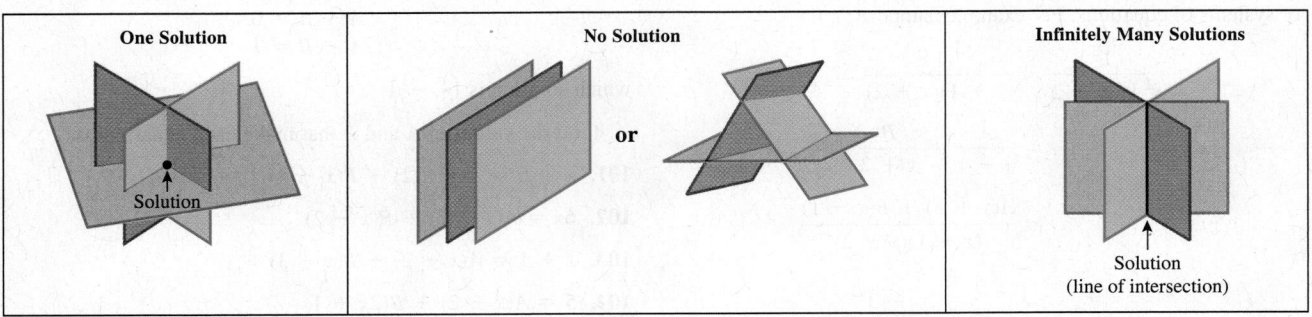

There are many ways to solve systems of linear equations in more than two variables. One method is to combine the elimination and substitution methods, which will be discussed in this section. Other methods involve matrices, which will be discussed in Sections 8.3–8.5. We now outline a procedure for solving systems of linear equations in three variables, which can be extended to solve systems of more than three variables. Solutions are sometimes given as ordered triples of the form $(x, y, z)$.

**SOLVING SYSTEMS OF LINEAR EQUATIONS IN THREE VARIABLES USING ELIMINATION AND SUBSTITUTION**

**Step 1:** Reduce the system of three equations in three variables to two equations in two (of the same) variables by applying elimination.

**Step 2:** Solve the resulting system of two linear equations in two variables by applying elimination or substitution.

**Step 3:** Substitute the solutions in Step 2 into *any* one of the original equations and solve for the third variable.

**Step 4:** Check that the solution satisfies *all* three original equations.

**EXAMPLE 1**   **Solving a System of Linear Equations in Three Variables**

Solve the system:

$$2x + \phantom{2}y + 8z = -1 \quad \text{Equation (1)}$$
$$\phantom{2}x - \phantom{2}y + \phantom{8}z = -2 \quad \text{Equation (2)}$$
$$3x - 2y - 2z = \phantom{-}2 \quad \text{Equation (3)}$$

**Solution:**

Inspecting the three equations, we see that $y$ is easily eliminated when Equations (1) and (2) are added, because the coefficients of $y$, $+1$ and $-1$, are equal in magnitude and opposite in sign. We can also eliminate $y$ from Equation (3) by adding Equation (3) to *either* 2 times Equation (1) *or* $-2$ times Equation (2). Therefore, our plan of attack is to eliminate $y$ from the system of equations, so the result will be two equations in two variables $x$ and $z$.

**STEP 1** Eliminate $y$ in Equation (1) and Equation (2).

Equation (1):
Equation (2):
Add.

$$2x + y + 8z = -1$$
$$x - y + z = -2$$
$$3x \qquad + 9z = -3$$

*Study Tip*

First eliminate the *same* variable from two different pairs of equations.

Eliminate $y$ in Equation (2) and Equation (3).

Multiply Equation (2) by $-2$.
Equation (3):
Add.

$$-2x + 2y - 2z = 4$$
$$3x - 2y - 2z = 2$$
$$x \qquad - 4z = 6$$

**STEP 2** Solve the system of two linear equations in two variables.

$$3x + 9z = -3$$
$$x - 4z = 6$$

Substitution* method: $x = 4z + 6$

$$3(4z + 6) + 9z = -3$$

Distribute.

$$12z + 18 + 9z = -3$$

Combine like terms.

$$21z = -21$$

Solve for $z$.

$$\boxed{z = -1}$$

Substitute $z = -1$ into $x = 4z + 6$.

$$x = 4(-1) + 6 = 2$$

$\boxed{x = 2}$ and $\boxed{z = -1}$ are the solutions to the system of two equations.

**STEP 3** Substitute $x = 2$ and $z = -1$ into any one of the three original equations and solve for $y$.

Substitute $x = 2$ and $z = -1$ into Equation (2).

$$2 - y - 1 = -2$$

Solve for $y$.

$$\boxed{y = 3}$$

**STEP 4** Check that $x = 2$, $y = 3$, and $z = -1$ satisfy all three equations.

Equation (1): $2(2) + 3 + 8(-1) = 4 + 3 - 8 = -1$

Equation (2): $2 - 3 - 1 = -2$

Equation (3): $3(2) - 2(3) - 2(-1) = 6 - 6 + 2 = 2$

The solution is $\boxed{x = 2, y = 3, z = -1, \text{ or } (2, 3, -1)}$.

*Elimination method could also be used.

▪ **YOUR TURN** Solve the system:

$$2x - y + 3z = -1$$
$$x + y - z = 0$$
$$3x + 3y - 2z = 1$$

In Example 1 and the Your Turn, the variable $y$ was eliminated by adding the first and second equations. In practice, any of the three variables can be eliminated, but typically we select the most convenient variable to eliminate. If a variable is missing from one of the equations (has a coefficient of 0), then we eliminate that variable from the other two equations.

**EXAMPLE 2** **Solving a System of Linear Equations in Three Variables When One Variable Is Missing**

Solve the system:
$$x \phantom{+ y} + z = 1 \quad \text{Equation (1)}$$
$$2x + y - z = -3 \quad \text{Equation (2)}$$
$$x + 2y - z = -1 \quad \text{Equation (3)}$$

**Solution:**

Since $y$ is missing from Equation (1), $y$ is the variable to be eliminated in Equation (2) and Equation (3).

**STEP 1** Eliminate $y$.

Multiply Equation (2) by $-2$.
Equation (3):

$$-4x - 2y + 2z = 6$$
$$\underline{x + 2y - z = -1}$$

Add.

$$-3x \phantom{+ 2y} + z = 5$$
$$x + z = 1$$

**STEP 2** Solve the system of two equations.

Equation (1) and the resulting equation in Step 1.

$$-3x + z = 5$$

Multiply the second equation by $(-1)$ and add it to the first equation.

$$x + z = 1$$
$$\underline{3x - z = -5}$$
$$4x \phantom{- z} = -4$$

Solve for $x$.

$$x = -1$$

Substitute $x = -1$ into Equation (1).

$$-1 + z = 1$$

Solve for $z$.

$$z = 2$$

**STEP 3** Substitute $x = -1$ and $z = 2$ into one of the original equations [Equation (2) or Equation (3)] and solve for $y$.

Substitute $x = -1$ and $z = 2$ into $x + 2y - z = -1$.

$$(-1) + 2y - 2 = -1$$

Gather like terms.

$$2y = 2$$

Solve for $y$.

$$y = 1$$

**STEP 4** Check that $x = -1$, $y = 1$, and $z = 2$ satisfy all three equations.

Equation (1): $(-1) + 2 = 1$

Equation (2): $2(-1) + (1) - (2) = -3$

Equation (3): $(-1) + 2(1) - (2) = -1$

The solution is $\boxed{x = -1, y = 1, z = 2}$.

■ **YOUR TURN** Solve the system:
$$x + y + z = 0$$
$$2x \phantom{+ y} + z = -1$$
$$x - y - z = 2$$

# Types of Solutions

Systems of linear equations in three variables have three possible solutions: one solution, infinitely many solutions, or no solution. Examples 1 and 2 each had one solution. Examples 3 and 4 illustrate systems with infinitely many solutions and no solution, respectively.

 **EXAMPLE 3**   **A Dependent System of Linear Equations in Three Variables (Infinitely Many Solutions)**

Solve the system:

$$2x + y - z = 4 \qquad \text{Equation (1)}$$
$$x + y \quad\;\; = 2 \qquad \text{Equation (2)}$$
$$3x + 2y - z = 6 \qquad \text{Equation (3)}$$

**Solution:**

Since $z$ is missing from Equation (2), $z$ is the variable to be eliminated from Equation (1) and Equation (3).

**STEP 1** Eliminate $z$.

Multiply Equation (1) by $(-1)$.

Equation (3):

Add.

$$-2x - y + z = -4$$
$$\underline{3x + 2y - z = \;\; 6}$$
$$x + y \quad\;\; = \;\; 2$$

**STEP 2** Solve the system of two equations: Equation (2) and the resulting equation in Step 1.

$$x + y = \;\; 2$$
$$x + y = \;\; 2$$

Multiply the first equation by $(-1)$ and add it to the second equation.

$$-x - y = -2$$
$$\underline{x + y = \;\; 2}$$
$$0 = \;\; 0$$

This statement is always true; therefore, there are $\boxed{\text{infinitely many solutions}}$. The original system has been reduced to a system of two identical linear equations. Therefore, the equations are dependent (share infinitely many solutions). Typically, to define those infinitely many solutions, we let $z = a$, where $a$ stands for any real number, and then find $x$ and $y$ in terms of $a$. The resulting ordered triple showing the three variables in terms of $a$ is called a **parametric representation** of a line in three dimensions.

**STEP 3** Let $\boxed{z = a}$ and find $x$ and $y$ in terms of $a$.

Solve Equation (2) for $y$.

$$y = 2 - x$$

Let $y = 2 - x$ and $z = a$ in Equation (1).

$$2x + (2 - x) - a = 4$$

Solve for $x$.

$$2x + 2 - x - a = 4$$
$$x - a = 2$$
$$\boxed{x = a + 2}$$

Let $\boxed{x = a + 2}$ in Equation (2).

$$(a + 2) + y = 2$$

Solve for $y$.

$$\boxed{y = -a}$$

The infinitely many solutions are written as $\boxed{(a + 2, -a, a)}$.

STEP 4 Check that $x = a + 2$, $y = -a$, and $z = a$ satisfy all three equations.

Equation (1): $2(a + 2) + (-a) - a = 2a + 4 - a - a = 4$ ✓

Equation (2): $(a + 2) + (-a) = a + 2 - a = 2$ ✓

Equation (3): $3(a + 2) + 2(-a) - a = 3a + 6 - 2a - a = 6$ ✓

■ **Answer:** $(a - 1, a + 1, a)$

■ **YOUR TURN** Solve the system:

$$
\begin{aligned}
x + \phantom{2}y - 2z &= \phantom{-}0 \\
x \phantom{{}+ 2y} - \phantom{2}z &= -1 \\
x - 2y + \phantom{2}z &= -3
\end{aligned}
$$

> **EXAMPLE 4** **An Inconsistent System of Linear Equations in Three Variables (No Solution)**

Solve the system:

$$
\begin{aligned}
x + 2y - \phantom{2}z &= \phantom{-}3 \qquad \text{Equation (1)} \\
2x + \phantom{2}y + 2z &= -1 \qquad \text{Equation (2)} \\
-2x - 4y + 2z &= \phantom{-}5 \qquad \text{Equation (3)}
\end{aligned}
$$

**Solution:**

STEP 1 Eliminate $x$.

Multiply Equation (1) by $-2$.

Equation (2):

Add.

$$
\begin{array}{r}
-2x - 4y + 2z = -6 \\
2x + \phantom{2}y + 2z = -1 \\
\hline
-3y + 4z = -7
\end{array}
$$

Equation (2):

Equation (3):

Add.

$$
\begin{array}{r}
2x + \phantom{2}y + 2z = -1 \\
-2x - 4y + 2z = \phantom{-}5 \\
\hline
-3y + 4z = \phantom{-}4
\end{array}
$$

STEP 2 Solve the system of two equations:

$$
\begin{aligned}
-3y + 4z &= -7 \\
-3y + 4z &= \phantom{-}4
\end{aligned}
$$

Multiply the top equation by $(-1)$ and add it to the second equation.

$$
\begin{array}{r}
3y - 4z = \phantom{1}7 \\
-3y + 4z = \phantom{1}4 \\
\hline
0 = 11
\end{array}
$$

This is a contradiction, or inconsistent statement, and therefore, there is $\boxed{\text{no solution}}$.

So far in this section, we have discussed only systems of *three* linear equations in *three* variables. What happens if we have a system of *two* linear equations in *three* variables? The two linear equations in three variables will always correspond to two planes in three dimensions. The possibilities are no solution (the two planes are parallel) or infinitely many solutions (the two planes intersect in a line or two planes are coplanar).

| NO SOLUTION | INFINITELY MANY SOLUTIONS (LINE) |
|---|---|
| 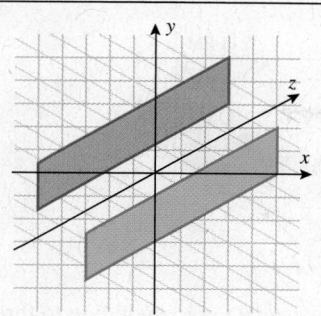 | 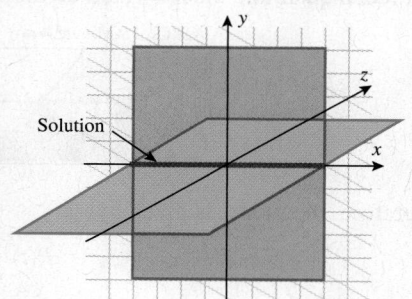 |

### EXAMPLE 5   Solving a System of Two Linear Equations in Three Variables

Solve the system of linear equations:   $x - y + z = 7$     Equation (1)

$\qquad\qquad\qquad\qquad\qquad\quad x + y + 2z = 2$     Equation (2)

**Solution:**

Eliminate $y$ by adding the two equations.

$$\begin{array}{r} x - y + z = 7 \\ x + y + 2z = 2 \\ \hline 2x \quad\; + 3z = 9 \end{array}$$

Therefore, Equation (1) and Equation (2) are both true if $2x + 3z = 9$. Since we know there is a solution, it must be a line. To define the line of intersection, we again turn to parametric representation.

Let $\boxed{z = a}$ , where $a$ is any real number.       $2x + 3a = 9$

Solve for $x$.

$$\boxed{x = \frac{9}{2} - \frac{3}{2}a}$$

Substitute $z = a$ and $x = \frac{9}{2} - \frac{3}{2}a$ into Equation (1).     $\left(\frac{9}{2} - \frac{3}{2}a\right) - y + a = 7$

Solve for $y$.

$$\boxed{y = -\frac{1}{2}a - \frac{5}{2}}$$

The solution is the line in three dimensions given by $\boxed{\left(\frac{9}{2} - \frac{3}{2}a, -\frac{1}{2}a - \frac{5}{2}, a\right)}$ , where $a$ is any real number.

*Note:* Every real number $a$ corresponds to a point on the line of intersection.

| $a$ | $\left(\frac{9}{2} - \frac{3}{2}a, -\frac{1}{2}a - \frac{5}{2}, a\right)$ |
|---|---|
| $-1$ | $(6, -2, -1)$ |
| $0$ | $\left(\frac{9}{2}, -\frac{5}{2}, 0\right)$ |
| $1$ | $(3, -3, 1)$ |

## Modeling with a System of Three Linear Equations

Many times in the real world we see a relationship that looks like a particular function such as a quadratic function and we know particular data points, but we do not know the function. We start with the general function, fit the curve to particular data points, and solve a system of linear equations to determine the specific function parameters.

Suppose you want to model a stock price as a function of time and based on the data you feel a quadratic model would be the best fit.

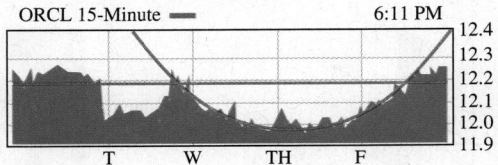

ORCL 15-Minute ▬▬          6:11 PM

Therefore, the model is given by

$$P(t) = at^2 + bt + c$$

where $P(t)$ is the price of the stock at time $t$. If we have data corresponding to three distinct points $[t, P(t)]$, the result is a system of three linear equations in three variables $a$, $b$, and $c$. We can solve the resulting system of linear equations, which determines the coefficients $a$, $b$, and $c$ of the quadratic model for stock price.

### EXAMPLE 6  Stock Value

The Oracle Corporation's stock (ORCL) over 3 days (Wednesday, October 13, to Friday, October 15, 2004) can be approximately modeled by a quadratic function: $f(t) = at^2 + bt + c$. If Wednesday corresponds to $t = 1$, where $t$ is in days, then the following data points approximately correspond to the stock value:

| $t$ | $f(t)$ | Days |
|---|---|---|
| 1 | $12.20 | Wednesday |
| 2 | $12.00 | Thursday |
| 3 | $12.20 | Friday |

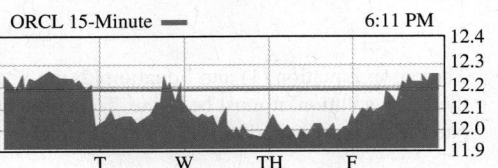

ORCL 15-Minute ▬▬          6:11 PM

Determine the function that models this behavior.

**Solution:**

Substitute the points (1, 12.20), (2, 12.00), and (3, 12.20) into $f(t) = at^2 + bt + c$.

$$a(1)^2 + b(1) + c = 12.20$$

$$a(2)^2 + b(2) + c = 12.00$$

$$a(3)^2 + b(3) + c = 12.20$$

Simplify to a system of three equations in three variables ($a$, $b$, and $c$).

$$a + b + c = 12.20 \qquad \text{Equation (1)}$$
$$4a + 2b + c = 12.00 \qquad \text{Equation (2)}$$
$$9a + 3b + c = 12.20 \qquad \text{Equation (3)}$$

Solve for $a$, $b$, and $c$ by applying the technique of this section.

STEP 1  Eliminate $c$.

| | |
|---|---|
| Multiply Equation (1) by $(-1)$. | $-a - b - c = -12.20$ |
| Equation (2): | $4a + 2b + c = \phantom{-}12.20$ |
| Add. | $3a + b \phantom{+ 2b} = -0.20$ |
| Multiply Equation (1) by $-1$. | $-a - b - c = -12.20$ |
| Equation (3): | $9a + 3b + c = \phantom{-}12.20$ |
| Add. | $8a + 2b \phantom{+ c} = \phantom{-}0$ |

**STEP 2** Solve the system of two equations.

$$3a + b = -0.20$$
$$8a + 2b = 0$$

Multiply the first equation by $-2$ and add to the second equation.

$$-6a - 2b = 0.40$$
$$\underline{8a + 2b = 0}$$

Add.                                                           $$2a = 0.4$$

Solve for $a$.                                                 $$a = 0.2$$

Substitute $a = 0.2$ into $8a + 2b = 0$.                       $$8(0.2) + 2b = 0$$

Simplify.                                                      $$2b = -1.6$$

Solve for $b$.                                                 $$b = -0.8$$

**STEP 3** Substitute $a = 0.2$ and $b = -0.8$ into one of the original three equations.

Substitute $a = 0.2$ and $b = -0.8$
into $a + b + c = 12.20$.                                      $$0.2 - 0.8 + c = 12.20$$

Gather like terms.                                            $$-0.6 + c = 12.20$$

Solve for $c$.                                                $$c = 12.80$$

**STEP 4** Check that $a = 0.2$, $b = -0.8$, and $c = 12.80$ satisfy all three equations.

Equation (1):    $a + b + c = 0.2 - 0.8 + 12.8 = 12.20$

Equation (2):    $4a + 2b + c = 4(0.2) + 2(-0.8) + 12.80$
$$= 0.8 - 1.6 + 12.8 = 12.00$$

Equation (3):    $9a + 3b + c = 9(0.2) + 3(-0.8) + 12.80$
$$= 1.8 - 2.4 + 12.8 = 12.20$$

The model is given by   $\boxed{f(t) = 0.2t^2 - 0.8t + 12.80}$.

# SECTION
## 8.2  SUMMARY

Graphs of linear equations in *two* variables are *lines*, whereas graphs of linear equations in *three* variables are *planes*. Systems of linear equations in three variables have one of three solutions:

- One solution (the intersection point of the three planes)
- No solution (no intersection of all three planes)
- Infinitely many solutions (planes intersect along a line)

When the solution to a system of three linear equations is a line in three dimensions, we use parametric representation to express the solution.

# SECTION
## 8.2  EXERCISES

### ▪ SKILLS

**In Exercises 1–32, solve each system of linear equations.**

**1.**   $x - y + z = 6$
$-x + y + z = 3$
$-x - y - z = 0$

**2.**   $-x - y + z = -1$
$-x + y - z = 3$
$x - y - z = 5$

**3.**   $x + y - z = 2$
$-x - y - z = -3$
$-x + y - z = 6$

**4.**   $x + y + z = -1$
$-x + y - z = 3$
$-x - y + z = 8$

**5.**   $-x + y - z = -1$
$x - y - z = 3$
$x + y - z = 9$

**6.**   $x - y - z = 2$
$-x - y + z = 4$
$-x + y - z = 6$

**7.**   $2x - 3y + 4z = -3$
$-x + y + 2z = 1$
$5x - 2y - 3z = 7$

**8.**   $x - 2y + z = 0$
$-2x + y - z = -5$
$13x + 7y + 5z = 6$

**9.** 
$$3y - 4x + 5z = 2$$
$$2x - 3y - 2z = -3$$
$$3z + 4y - 2x = 1$$

**10.** 
$$2y + z - x = 5$$
$$2x + 3z - 2y = 0$$
$$-2z + y - 4x = 3$$

**11.** 
$$x - y + z = -1$$
$$y - z = -1$$
$$-x + y + z = 1$$

**12.** 
$$-y + z = 1$$
$$x - y + z = -1$$
$$x - y - z = -1$$

**13.** 
$$3x - 2y - 3z = -1$$
$$x - y + z = -4$$
$$2x + 3y + 5z = 14$$

**14.** 
$$3x - y + z = 2$$
$$x - 2y + 3z = 1$$
$$2x + y - 3z = -1$$

**15.** 
$$-3x - y - z = 2$$
$$x + 2y - 3z = 4$$
$$2x - y + 4z = 6$$

**16.** 
$$2x - 3y + z = 1$$
$$x + 4y - 2z = 2$$
$$3x - y + 4z = -3$$

**17.** 
$$3x + 2y + z = 4$$
$$-4x - 3y - z = -15$$
$$x - 2y + 3z = 12$$

**18.** 
$$3x - y + 4z = 13$$
$$-4x - 3y - z = -15$$
$$x - 2y + 3z = 12$$

**19.** 
$$-x + 2y + z = -2$$
$$3x - 2y + z = 4$$
$$2x - 4y - 2z = 4$$

**20.** 
$$2x - y = 1$$
$$-x + z = -2$$
$$-2x + y = -1$$

**21.** 
$$x - z - y = 10$$
$$2x - 3y + z = -11$$
$$y - x + z = -10$$

**22.** 
$$2x + z + y = -3$$
$$2y - z + x = 0$$
$$x + y + 2z = 5$$

**23.** 
$$3x_1 + x_2 - x_3 = 1$$
$$x_1 - x_2 + x_3 = -3$$
$$2x_1 + x_2 + x_3 = 0$$

**24.** 
$$2x_1 + x_2 + x_3 = -1$$
$$x_1 + x_2 - x_3 = 5$$
$$3x_1 - x_2 - x_3 = 1$$

**25.** 
$$2x + 5y = 9$$
$$x + 2y - z = 3$$
$$-3x - 4y + 7z = 1$$

**26.** 
$$x - 2y + 3z = 1$$
$$-2x + 7y - 9z = 4$$
$$x + z = 9$$

**27.** 
$$2x_1 - x_2 + x_3 = 3$$
$$x_1 - x_2 + x_3 = 2$$
$$-2x_1 + 2x_2 - 2x_3 = -4$$

**28.** 
$$x_1 - x_2 - 2x_3 = 0$$
$$-2x_1 + 5x_2 + 10x_3 = -3$$
$$3x_1 + x_2 = 0$$

**29.** 
$$2x + y - z = 2$$
$$x - y - z = 6$$

**30.** 
$$3x + y - z = 0$$
$$x + y + 7z = 4$$

**31.** 
$$4x + 3y - 3z = 5$$
$$6x + 2z = 10$$

**32.** 
$$x + 2y + 4z = 12$$
$$-3x - 4y + 7z = 21$$

## ▪ APPLICATIONS

**33. Business.** A small company has an assembly line that produces three types of widgets. The basic widget is sold for $10 per unit, the midprice widget for $12 per unit, and the top-of-the-line widget for $15 per unit. The assembly line has a daily capacity of producing 300 widgets that may be sold for a total of $3700. Find the quantity of each type of widget produced on a day when the number of basic widgets and top-of-the-line widgets is the same.

**34. Business.** A small company has an assembly line that produces three types of widgets. The basic widget is sold for $10 per unit, the midprice widget for $12 per unit, and the top-of-the-line widget for $15 per unit. The assembly line has a daily capacity of producing 325 widgets that may be sold for a total of $3825. Find the quantity of each type of widget produced on a day when twice as many basic widgets as top-of-the-line widgets are produced.

**Exercises 35 and 36 rely on a selection of Subway sandwiches whose nutrition information is given in the table.**

Suppose you are going to eat only Subway sandwiches for a week (seven days) for lunch and dinner (total of 14 meals).

| SANDWICH | CALORIES | FAT (GRAMS) |
|---|---|---|
| Mediterranean chicken | 350 | 18 |
| Six-inch tuna | 430 | 19 |
| Six-inch roast beef | 290 | 5 |

www.subway.com

**35. Diet.** Your goal is a total of 4840 calories and 190 grams of fat. How many of each sandwich would you eat that week to obtain this goal?

**36. Diet.** Your goal is a total of 4380 calories and 123 grams of fat. How many of each sandwich would you eat that week to obtain this goal?

**Exercises 37 and 38 involve vertical motion and the effect of gravity on an object.**

Because of gravity, an object that is projected upward will eventually reach a maximum height and then fall to the ground. The equation that determines the height $h$ of a projectile $t$ seconds after it is shot upward is given by

$$h = \frac{1}{2}at^2 + v_0 t + h_0$$

where $a$ is the acceleration due to gravity, $h_0$ is the initial height of the object at time $t = 0$, and $v_0$ is the initial velocity of the object at time $t = 0$. Note that a projectile follows the path of a parabola opening down, so $a < 0$.

**37. Vertical Motion.** An object is thrown upward and the following table depicts the height of the ball $t$ seconds after the projectile is released. Find the initial height, initial velocity, and acceleration due to gravity.

| t SECONDS | HEIGHT (FEET) |
|---|---|
| 1 | 36 |
| 2 | 40 |
| 3 | 12 |

**38. Vertical Motion.** An object is thrown upward and the following table depicts the height of the ball $t$ seconds after the projectile is released. Find the initial height, initial velocity, and acceleration due to gravity.

| $t$ SECONDS | HEIGHT (FEET) |
|---|---|
| 1 | 84 |
| 2 | 136 |
| 3 | 156 |

**39. Data Curve-Fitting.** The number of minutes that an average person of age $x$ spends driving a car can be modeled by a quadratic function $y = ax^2 + bx + c$, where $a < 0$ and $18 \le x \le 65$. The following table gives the average number of minutes per day that a person spends driving a car. Determine the quadratic function that models this quantity.

| AGE | AVERAGE DAILY MINUTES DRIVING |
|---|---|
| 20 | 30 |
| 40 | 60 |
| 60 | 40 |

**40. Data Curve-Fitting.** The average age when a woman gets married began increasing during the last century. In 1930 the average age was 18.6, in 1950 the average age was 20.2, and in 2002 the average age was 25.3. Find a quadratic function $y = ax^2 + bx + c$, where $a > 0$ and $18 < y < 35$, that models the average age $y$ when a woman gets married as a function of the year $x$ ($x = 0$ corresponds to 1930). What will the average age be in 2010?

**41. Money.** Tara and Lamar decide to place $20,000 of their savings into investments. They put some in a money market account earning 3% interest, some in a mutual fund that has been averaging 7% a year, and some in a stock that rose 10% last year. If they put $6000 more in the money market than in the mutual fund and the mutual fund and stocks experience the same growth the next year as they did the previous year, they will earn $1180 in a year. How much money did Tara and Lamar put in each of the three investments?

**42. Money.** Tara talks Lamar into putting less money in the money market and more money in the stock (see Exercise 41). They place $20,000 of their savings into investments. They put some in a money market account earning 3% interest, some in a mutual fund that has been averaging 7% a year, and some in a stock that rose 10% last year. If they put $6000 more in the stock than in the mutual fund and the mutual fund and stock experience the same growth the next year as they did the previous year, they will earn $1680 in a year. How much money did Tara and Lamar put in each of the three investments?

**43. Ski Production.** A company produces three types of skis: regular model, trick ski, and slalom ski. They need to fill a customer order of 110 pairs of skis. There are two major production divisions within the company: labor and finishing. Each regular model of skis requires 2 hours of labor and 1 hour of finishing. Each trick ski model requires 3 hours of labor and 2 hours of finishing. Finally, each slalom ski model requires 3 hours of labor and 5 hours of finishing. Suppose the company has only 297 labor hours and 202 finishing hours. How many of each type ski can be made under these restrictions?

**44. Automobile Production.** An automobile manufacturing company produces three types of automobiles: compact car, intermediate, and luxury model. The company has the capability of producing 500 automobiles. Suppose that each compact-model car requires 200 units of steel and 30 units of rubber, each intermediate model requires 300 units of steel and 20 units of rubber, and each luxury model requires 250 units of steel and 45 units of rubber. The number of units of steel available is 128,750, and the number of units of rubber available is 15,625. How many of each type of automobile can be produced with these restraints?

**45. Computer versus Man.** *The Seattle Times* reported a story on November 18, 2006, about a game of Scrabble played between a human and a computer. The best Scrabble player in the United States was pitted against a computer program designed to play the game. Remarkably, the human beat the computer in the best of two out of three games competition. The total points scored by both computer and the man for all three games was 2591. The difference between the first game's total and second game's total was 62 points. The difference between the first game's total and the third game's total was only 2 points. Determine the total number of points scored by both computer and the man for each of the three contests.

**46. Brain versus Computer.** Can the human brain perform more calculations per second than a supercomputer? The calculating speed of the three top supercomputers, IBM's Blue Gene/L, IBM's BGW, and IBM's ASC Purple, has been determined. The speed of IBM's Blue Gene/L is 245 teraflops more than that of IBM's BGW. The computing speed of IBM's BGW is 22 teraflops more than that of IBM's ASC Purple. The combined speed of all three top supercomputers is 568 teraflops. Determine the computing speed (in teraflops) of each supercomputer. A **teraflop** is a measure of a computer's speed and can be expressed as 1 trillion floating-point operations per second. By comparison, it is estimated that the human brain can perform 10 quadrillion calculations per second.

**47. Production.** A factory manufactures three types of golf balls: Eagle, Birdie, and Bogey. The daily production is 10,000 balls. The number of Eagle and Birdie balls combined equals the number of Bogey balls produced. If the factory makes three times more Birdie than Eagle balls, find the daily production of each type of ball.

**48. Pizza.** Three-cheese pizzas are made with a mixture of three types of cheese. The cost of a pizza containing 2 parts of each cheese is $2.40. A pizza made with 2 parts of cheese A, 1 part of cheese B, and 2 parts of cheese C costs $2.20, while a pizza made with 2 parts of cheese A, 2 parts of cheese B, and 3 parts of cheese C costs $2.70. Determine the cost, per part, of each cheese.

**49. TV Commercials.** A TV station sells intervals of time for commercials of 10 seconds for $100, 20 seconds for $180, and 40 seconds for $320. It has 2 minutes for publicity during a game with a total revenue of $1060 for six commercials shown. Find the number of commercials of each length sold by the TV station if there are twice as many 10 second commercials as 40 second commercials.

**50. Airline.** A commercial plane has 270 seats divided into three classes: first class, business, and coach. The first-class seats are a third of the business-class seats. There are 250 more coach seats than first-class seats. Find the number of seats of each class in the airplane.

■ **CATCH THE MISTAKE**

**In Exercises 51 and 52, explain the mistake that is made.**

**51.** Solve the system of equations.

| | |
|---|---|
| Equation (1): | $2x - y + z = 2$ |
| Equation (2): | $x - y = 1$ |
| Equation (3): | $x + z = 1$ |

**Solution:**

| | |
|---|---|
| Equation (2): | $x - y = 1$ |
| Equation (3): | $x + z = 1$ |
| Add Equation (2) and Equation (3). | $-y + z = 2$ |
| Multiply Equation (1) by $(-1)$. | $-2x + y - z = -2$ |
| Add. | $-2x = 0$ |
| Solve for $x$. | $x = 0$ |
| Substitute $x = 0$ into Equation (2). | $0 - y = 1$ |
| Solve for $y$. | $y = -1$ |
| Substitute $x = 0$ into Equation (3). | $0 + z = 1$ |
| Solve for $z$. | $z = 1$ |

The answer is $x = 0$, $y = -1$, and $z = 1$.

This is incorrect. Although $x = 0$, $y = -1$, and $z = 1$ does satisfy the three original equations, it is only one of infinitely many solutions. What mistake was made?

**52.** Solve the system of equations.

| | |
|---|---|
| Equation (1): | $x + 3y + 2z = 4$ |
| Equation (2): | $3x + 10y + 9z = 17$ |
| Equation (3): | $2x + 7y + 7z = 17$ |

**Solution:**

| | |
|---|---|
| Multiply Equation (1) by $-3$. | $-3x - 9y - 6z = -12$ |
| Equation (2): | $3x + 10y + 9z = 17$ |
| Add. | $y + 3z = 5$ |
| Multiply Equation (1) by $-2$. | $-2x - 6y - 4z = -8$ |
| Equation (3): | $2x + 7y + 7z = 17$ |
| Add. | $y + 3z = 9$ |
| Solve the system of two equations. | $y + 3z = 5$ |
| | $y + 3z = 9$ |

Infinitely many solutions.

Let $z = a$, then $y = 5 - 3a$.

| | |
|---|---|
| Substitute $z = a$ and $y = 5 - 3a$ into Equation (1). | $x + 3y + 2z = 4$ |
| | $x + 3(5 - 3a) + 2a = 4$ |
| Eliminate parentheses. | $x + 15 - 9a + 2a = 4$ |
| Solve for $x$. | $x = 7a - 11$ |

The answer is $x = 7a - 11$, $y = 5 - 3a$, and $z = a$.

This is incorrect. There is no solution. What mistake was made?

## ▪CONCEPTUAL

**In Exercises 53–56, determine whether each statement is true or false.**

**53.** A system of linear equations that has more variables than equations cannot have a unique solution.

**54.** A system of linear equations that has the same number of equations as variables always has a unique solution.

**55.** The linear equation $Ax + By = C$ always represents a straight line.

**56.** If the system of linear equations

$$x + 2y + 3z = a$$
$$2x + 3y + z = b$$
$$3x + y + 2z = c$$

has a unique solution $\left(\frac{1}{6}, \frac{1}{6}, \frac{1}{6}\right)$, then the system of equations

$$x + 2y + 3z = 2a$$
$$2x + 3y + z = 2b$$
$$3x + y + 2z = 2c$$

has a unique solution $\left(\frac{1}{3}, \frac{1}{3}, \frac{1}{3}\right)$.

**57.** The circle given by the equation $x^2 + y^2 + ax + by + c = 0$ passes through the points $(-2, 4)$, $(1, 1)$, and $(-2, -2)$. Find $a$, $b$, and $c$.

**58.** The circle given by the equation $x^2 + y^2 + ax + by + c = 0$ passes through the points $(0, 7)$, $(6, 1)$, and $(5, 4)$. Find $a$, $b$, and $c$.

## ▪CHALLENGE

**59.** A fourth-degree polynomial,
$f(x) = ax^4 + bx^3 + cx^2 + dx + e$, with $a < 0$, can be used to represent the following data on the number of deaths per year due to lightning strikes. Assume 1999 corresponds to $x = -2$ and 2003 corresponds to $x = 2$. Use the data to determine $a$, $b$, $c$, $d$, and $e$.

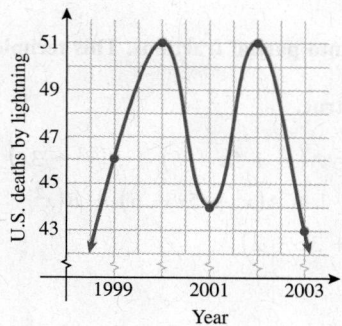

**60.** A copy machine accepts nickels, dimes, and quarters. After 1 hour, there are 30 coins total and their value is $4.60. If there are four more quarters than nickels, how many nickels, quarters, and dimes are in the machine?

**In Exercises 61–64, solve the system of linear equations.**

**61.**
$$2y + z = 3$$
$$4x - z = -3$$
$$7x - 3y - 3z = 2$$
$$x - y - z = -2$$

**62.**
$$-2x - y + 2z = 3$$
$$3x - 4z = 2$$
$$2x + y = -1$$
$$-x + y - z = -8$$

**63.**
$$3x_1 - 2x_2 + x_3 + 2x_4 = -2$$
$$-x_1 + 3x_2 + 4x_3 + 3x_4 = 4$$
$$x_1 + x_2 + x_3 + x_4 = 0$$
$$5x_1 + 3x_2 + x_3 + 2x_4 = -1$$

**64.**
$$5x_1 + 3x_2 + 8x_3 + x_4 = 1$$
$$x_1 + 2x_2 + 5x_3 + 2x_4 = 3$$
$$4x_1 + x_3 - 2x_4 = -3$$
$$x_2 + x_3 + x_4 = 0$$

**65.** Find the values of $A$, $B$, $C$, and $D$ such that the following equation is true:

$$x^3 + x^2 + 2x + 3 = (Ax + B)(x^2 + 3) + (Cx + D)(x^2 + 2)$$

**66.** Find the values of $A$, $B$, $C$, $D$, and $E$ such that the following equation is true:

$$Ax^3(x + 1) + Bx^2(x + 1) + Cx(x + 1) + D(x + 1) + Ex^4$$
$$= 4x^4 + x + 1$$

## ▪ TECHNOLOGY

In Exercises 67 and 68, employ a graphing calculator to solve the system of linear equations (most graphing calculators have the capability of solving linear systems with the user entering the coefficients).

The $\boxed{\text{rref}}$ under the $\boxed{\text{MATRIX}}$ menu will be used to solve the system of equations by entering the coefficients of $x$, $y$, $z$, and the constant.

$\boxed{2^{nd}}$ $\boxed{\text{MATRIX}}$ $\boxed{\blacktriangleright}$ $\boxed{\text{MATH}}$ $\boxed{\blacktriangledown}$ $\boxed{\text{B:rref(}}$ $\boxed{\text{ENTER}}$ $\boxed{2^{nd}}$ $\boxed{[}$ $\boxed{2^{nd}}$ $\boxed{[}$
$\boxed{2}$ $\boxed{,}$ $\boxed{1}$ $\boxed{,}$ $\boxed{8}$ $\boxed{,}$ $\boxed{(-)}$ $\boxed{1}$ $\boxed{2^{nd}}$ $\boxed{]}$ $\boxed{2^{nd}}$ $\boxed{[}$ $\boxed{1}$ $\boxed{,}$ $\boxed{(-)}$ $\boxed{1}$ $\boxed{,}$ $\boxed{1}$ $\boxed{,}$ $\boxed{(-)}$
$\boxed{2}$ $\boxed{2^{nd}}$ $\boxed{]}$ $\boxed{2^{nd}}$ $\boxed{[}$ $\boxed{3}$ $\boxed{,}$ $\boxed{(-)}$ $\boxed{2}$ $\boxed{,}$ $\boxed{(-)}$ $\boxed{2}$ $\boxed{,}$ $\boxed{2}$ $\boxed{2^{nd}}$ $\boxed{]}$ $\boxed{2^{nd}}$ $\boxed{]}$ $\boxed{)}$
$\boxed{\text{ENTER}}$

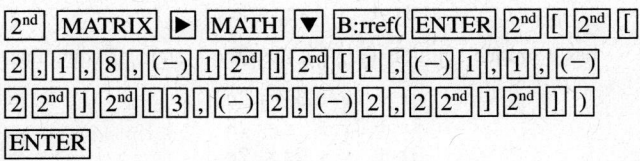

First row gives $x = 2$, second row gives $y = 3$, and third row gives $z = -1$.

*Note:* The TI function $\boxed{\text{rref}}$ stands for reduced row echelon form.

**67.** $\begin{aligned} x - z - y &= 10 \\ 2x - 3y + z &= -11 \\ y - x + z &= -10 \end{aligned}$

**68.** $\begin{aligned} 2x + z + y &= -3 \\ 2y - z + x &= 0 \\ x + y + 2z &= 5 \end{aligned}$

**69.** Some graphing calculators and graphing utilities have the ability to graph in three dimensions (3D) as opposed to the traditional two dimensions (2D). The line must be given in the form $z = ax + by + c$. Rewrite the system of equations in Exercise 67 in this form and graph the three lines in 3D. What is the point of intersection? Compare that with your answer in Exercise 67.

**70.** Some graphing calculators and graphing utilities have the ability to graph in three dimensions (3D) as opposed to the traditional two dimensions (2D). The line must be given in the form $z = ax + by + c$. Rewrite the system of equations in Exercise 68 in this form and graph the three lines in 3D. What is the point of intersection? Compare that with your answer in Exercise 68.

In Exercises 71 and 72, employ a graphing calculator to solve the system of equations.

**71.** $\begin{aligned} 0.2x - 0.7y + 0.8z &= 11.2 \\ -1.2x + 0.3y - 1.5z &= 0 \\ 0.8x - 0.1y + 2.1z &= 6.4 \end{aligned}$

**72.** $\begin{aligned} 1.8x - 0.5y + 2.4z &= 1.6 \\ 0.3x \qquad\quad - 0.6z &= 0.2 \end{aligned}$

## ▪ PREVIEW TO CALCULUS

In calculus, when integrating rational functions, we decompose the function into partial fractions. This technique involves the solution of systems of equations.

In Exercises 73–76, find the values of $A$, $B$, and $C$ that make each equation true.

**73.** $5x^2 + 6x + 2 = A(x^2 + 2x + 5) + (Bx + C)(x + 2)$

**74.** $2x^2 - 3x + 2 = A(x^2 + 1) + (Bx + C)x$

**75.** $3x + 8 = A(x^2 + 5x + 6) + B(x^2 + 3x) + C(x^2 + 2x)$

**76.** $x^2 + x + 1 = A(x^2 + 5x + 6) + B(x^2 + 4x + 3)$
$\qquad\quad + C(x^2 + 3x + 2)$

## SKILLS OBJECTIVES

- Write a system of linear equations as an augmented matrix.
- Perform row operations on an augmented matrix.
- Write a matrix in row–echelon form.
- Solve systems of linear equations using Gaussian elimination with back-substitution.
- Write a matrix in reduced row–echelon form.
- Solve systems of linear equations using Gauss–Jordan elimination.

## CONCEPTUAL OBJECTIVES

- Visualize an augmented matrix as a system of linear equations.
- Understand that solving systems with augmented matrices is equivalent to solving by the method of elimination.
- Recognize matrices that correspond to inconsistent and dependent systems.

# Matrices

Some information is best displayed in a table. For example, the number of calories burned per half hour of exercise depends on the person's weight, as illustrated in the following table. Note that the rows correspond to activities and the columns correspond to weight.

| ACTIVITY | 127–137 LB | 160–170 LB | 180–200 LB |
|---|---|---|---|
| Walking/4 mph | 156 | 183 | 204 |
| Volleyball | 267 | 315 | 348 |
| Jogging/5 mph | 276 | 345 | 381 |

Another example is the driving distance in miles from cities in Arizona (columns) to cities outside the state (rows).

| CITY | FLAGSTAFF | PHOENIX | TUCSON | YUMA |
|---|---|---|---|---|
| Albuquerque, NM | 325 | 465 | 440 | 650 |
| Las Vegas, NV | 250 | 300 | 415 | 295 |
| Los Angeles, CA | 470 | 375 | 490 | 285 |

If we selected only the numbers in each of the preceding tables and placed brackets around them, the result would be a *matrix*.

$$\text{Calories: } \begin{bmatrix} 156 & 183 & 204 \\ 267 & 315 & 348 \\ 276 & 345 & 381 \end{bmatrix} \qquad \text{Miles: } \begin{bmatrix} 325 & 465 & 440 & 650 \\ 250 & 300 & 415 & 295 \\ 470 & 375 & 490 & 285 \end{bmatrix}$$

---

A *matrix* is a rectangular array of numbers written within brackets.

$$\begin{bmatrix} a_{11} & a_{12} & \cdots & a_{1j} & \cdots & a_{1n} \\ a_{21} & a_{22} & \cdots & a_{2j} & \cdots & a_{2n} \\ \vdots & \vdots & \cdots & \vdots & \cdots & \vdots \\ a_{i1} & a_{i2} & \cdots & a_{ij} & \cdots & a_{in} \\ \vdots & \vdots & \cdots & \vdots & \cdots & \vdots \\ a_{m1} & a_{m2} & \cdots & a_{mj} & \cdots & a_{mn} \end{bmatrix}$$

Each number $a_{ij}$ in the matrix is called an **entry** (or **element**) of the matrix. The first subscript $i$ is the **row index**, and the second subscript $j$ is the **column index**. This matrix contains $m$ rows and $n$ columns, and is said to be of **order** $m \times n$.

**Study Tip**

The order of a matrix is always given as the number of rows by the number of columns.

When the number of rows equals the number of columns (i.e., when $m = n$), the matrix is a **square matrix** of order $n$. In a square matrix, the entries $a_{11}, a_{22}, a_{33}, \ldots, a_{nn}$ are the **main diagonal** entries.

The matrix

$$A_{4\times3} = \begin{bmatrix} * & * & * \\ * & * & * \\ * & a_{32} & * \\ * & * & * \end{bmatrix}$$

has order (dimensions) $4 \times 3$, since there are four rows and three columns. The entry $a_{32}$ is in the third row and second column.

### EXAMPLE 1 Finding the Order of a Matrix

Determine the order of each matrix given.

**a.** $\begin{bmatrix} 2 & 1 \\ 3 & 0 \end{bmatrix}$
**b.** $\begin{bmatrix} 1 & -2 & 5 \\ -1 & 3 & 4 \end{bmatrix}$
**c.** $\begin{bmatrix} -2 & 5 & 4 \\ 1 & -\frac{1}{3} & 0 \\ 3 & 8 & 1 \end{bmatrix}$

**d.** $\begin{bmatrix} 4 & 9 & -\frac{1}{2} & 3 \end{bmatrix}$
**e.** $\begin{bmatrix} 3 & -2 \\ 5 & 1 \\ 0 & -\frac{2}{3} \\ 7 & 6 \end{bmatrix}$

**Solution:**

**a.** This matrix has **2** rows and **2** columns, so the order of the matrix is $\boxed{2 \times 2}$.

**b.** This matrix has **2** rows and **3** columns, so the order of the matrix is $\boxed{2 \times 3}$.

**c.** This matrix has **3** rows and **3** columns, so the order of the matrix is $\boxed{3 \times 3}$ or 3 since it is a square matrix.

**d.** This matrix has **1** row and **4** columns, so the order of the matrix is $\boxed{1 \times 4}$.

**e.** This matrix has **4** rows and **2** columns, so the order of the matrix is $\boxed{4 \times 2}$.

A matrix with only one column is called a **column matrix**, and a matrix that has only one row is called a **row matrix**. Notice that in Example 1 the matrices given in parts (a) and (c) are square matrices and the matrix given in part (d) is a row matrix.

You can use matrices as a shorthand way of writing systems of linear equations. There are two ways we can represent systems of linear equations with matrices: as *augmented matrices* or with *matrix equations*. In this section, we will discuss *augmented matrices* and solve systems of linear equations using two methods: *Gaussian elimination with back-substitution* and *Gauss–Jordan elimination*.

## Augmented Matrices

A **coefficient matrix** is a matrix whose elements are the coefficients of a system of linear equations. A particular type of matrix that is used in representing a system of linear equations is an **augmented matrix**. It resembles a coefficient matrix with an additional vertical line and column of numbers, hence the name *augmented*. The following table illustrates examples of augmented matrices that represent systems of linear equations:

| SYSTEM OF LINEAR EQUATIONS | AUGMENTED MATRIX |
|---|---|
| $3x + 4y = 1$ <br> $x - 2y = 7$ | $\begin{bmatrix} 3 & 4 & 1 \\ 1 & -2 & 7 \end{bmatrix}$ |
| $x - y + z = 2$ <br> $2x + 2y - 3z = -3$ <br> $x + y + z = 6$ | $\begin{bmatrix} 1 & -1 & 1 & 2 \\ 2 & 2 & -3 & -3 \\ 1 & 1 & 1 & 6 \end{bmatrix}$ |
| $x + y + z = 0$ <br> $3x + 2y - z = 2$ | $\begin{bmatrix} 1 & 1 & 1 & 0 \\ 3 & 2 & -1 & 2 \end{bmatrix}$ |

Note the following:

- Each row represents an equation.
- The vertical line represents the equal sign.
- The first column represents the coefficients of the variable $x$.
- The second column represents the coefficients of the variable $y$.
- The third column (in the second and third systems) represents the coefficients of the variable $z$.
- The coefficients of the variables are on the left of the equal sign (vertical line) and the constants are on the right.
- Any variable that does not appear in an equation has an implied coefficient of 0.

**EXAMPLE 2   Writing a System of Linear Equations as an Augmented Matrix**

Write each system of linear equations as an augmented matrix.

**a.** $2x - y = 5$
$-x + 2y = 3$

**b.** $3x - 2y + 4z = 5$
$y - 3z = -2$
$7x \quad - z = 1$

**c.** $x_1 - x_2 + 2x_3 - 3 = 0$
$x_1 + x_2 - 3x_3 + 5 = 0$
$x_1 - x_2 + x_3 - 2 = 0$

**Solution:**

**a.**

$$\begin{bmatrix} 2 & -1 & | & 5 \\ -1 & 2 & | & 3 \end{bmatrix}$$

**b.** Note that all missing terms have a 0 coefficient.

$3x - 2y + 4z = 5$
$0x + y - 3z = -2$
$7x + 0y - z = 1$

$$\begin{bmatrix} 3 & -2 & 4 & | & 5 \\ 0 & 1 & -3 & | & -2 \\ 7 & 0 & -1 & | & 1 \end{bmatrix}$$

**c.** Write the constants on the right side of the vertical line in the matrix.

$x_1 - x_2 + 2x_3 = 3$
$x_1 + x_2 - 3x_3 = -5$
$x_1 - x_2 + x_3 = 2$

$$\begin{bmatrix} 1 & -1 & 2 & | & 3 \\ 1 & 1 & -3 & | & -5 \\ 1 & -1 & 1 & | & 2 \end{bmatrix}$$

■ **Answer:**

**a.** $\begin{bmatrix} 2 & 1 & | & 3 \\ 1 & -1 & | & 5 \end{bmatrix}$

**b.** $\begin{bmatrix} -1 & 1 & 1 & | & 7 \\ 1 & -1 & -1 & | & 2 \\ 0 & -1 & 1 & | & -1 \end{bmatrix}$

■ **YOUR TURN** Write each system of linear equations as an augmented matrix.

**a.** $2x + y - 3 = 0$
$x - y = 5$

**b.** $y - x + z = 7$
$x - y - z = 2$
$z - y = -1$

## Row Operations on a Matrix

*Row operations* on a matrix are used to solve a system of linear equations when the system is written as an augmented matrix. Recall from the elimination method in Sections 8.1 and 8.2 that we could interchange equations, multiply an entire equation by a nonzero constant, and add a multiple of one equation to another equation to produce equivalent systems. Because each row in a matrix represents an equation, the operations that produced equivalent systems of equations that were used in the elimination method will also produce equivalent augmented matrices.

**Study Tip**

Each missing term in an equation of the system of linear equations is represented with a zero in the augmented matrix.

### ROW OPERATIONS

The following operations on an augmented matrix will yield an equivalent matrix:

1. Interchange any two rows.
2. Multiply a row by a nonzero constant.
3. Add a multiple of one row to another row.

The following symbols describe these row operations:

1. $R_i \leftrightarrow R_j$ — Interchange row $i$ with row $j$.
2. $cR_i \rightarrow R_i$ — Multiply row $i$ by the constant $c$.
3. $cR_i + R_j \rightarrow R_j$ — Multiply row $i$ by the constant $c$ and add to row $j$, writing the results in row $j$.

**EXAMPLE 3    Applying a Row Operation to an Augmented Matrix**

For each matrix, perform the given operation.

**a.** $\begin{bmatrix} 2 & -1 & | & 3 \\ 0 & 2 & | & 1 \end{bmatrix}$  $R_1 \leftrightarrow R_2$

**b.** $\begin{bmatrix} -1 & 0 & 1 & | & -2 \\ 3 & -1 & 2 & | & 3 \\ 0 & 1 & 3 & | & 1 \end{bmatrix}$  $2R_3 \rightarrow R_3$

**c.** $\begin{bmatrix} 1 & 2 & 0 & 2 & | & 2 \\ 0 & 1 & 2 & 3 & | & 5 \end{bmatrix}$  $R_1 - 2R_2 \rightarrow R_1$

**Solution:**

**a.** Interchange the first row with the second row.

$\begin{bmatrix} 2 & -1 & | & 3 \\ 0 & 2 & | & 1 \end{bmatrix}$  $R_1 \leftrightarrow R_2$  $\boxed{\begin{bmatrix} 0 & 2 & | & 1 \\ 2 & -1 & | & 3 \end{bmatrix}}$

**b.** Multiply the third row by 2.

$\begin{bmatrix} -1 & 0 & 1 & | & -2 \\ 3 & -1 & 2 & | & 3 \\ 0 & 1 & 3 & | & 1 \end{bmatrix}$  $2R_3 \rightarrow R_3$  $\begin{bmatrix} -1 & 0 & 1 & | & -2 \\ 3 & -1 & 2 & | & 3 \\ 0 & 2 & 6 & | & 2 \end{bmatrix}$

**c.** From row 1 subtract 2 times row 2, and write the answer in row 1. Note that finding row 1 minus 2 times row 2 is the same as adding row 1 to the product of $-2$ with row 2.

$R_1 - 2R_2 \rightarrow R_1$  $\begin{bmatrix} 1-2(0) & 2-2(1) & 0-2(2) & 2-2(3) & | & 2-2(5) \\ 0 & 1 & 2 & 3 & | & 5 \end{bmatrix}$

$\boxed{\begin{bmatrix} 1 & 0 & -4 & -4 & | & -8 \\ 0 & 1 & 2 & 3 & | & 5 \end{bmatrix}}$

■ **YOUR TURN**  Perform the operation $R_1 + 2R_3 \rightarrow R_1$ on the matrix.

$\begin{bmatrix} 1 & 0 & -2 & | & -3 \\ 0 & 1 & 2 & | & 3 \\ 0 & 0 & 1 & | & 2 \end{bmatrix}$

■ **Answer:**

$\begin{bmatrix} 1 & 0 & 0 & | & 1 \\ 0 & 1 & 2 & | & 3 \\ 0 & 0 & 1 & | & 2 \end{bmatrix}$

# Row-Echelon Form of a Matrix

We can solve systems of linear equations using augmented matrices with two procedures: *Gaussian elimination with back-substitution*, which uses row operations to transform a matrix into *row–echelon form*, and *Gauss–Jordan elimination*, which uses row operations to transform a matrix into *reduced row–echelon form*.

**Row–Echelon Form**

A matrix is in **row–echelon** form if it has all three of the following properties:

1. Any rows consisting entirely of 0s are at the bottom of the matrix.
2. For each row that does not consist entirely of 0s, the first (leftmost) nonzero entry is 1 (called the leading 1).
3. For two successive nonzero rows, the leading 1 in the higher row is farther to the left than the leading 1 in the lower row.

**Reduced Row–Echelon Form**

If a matrix in row–echelon form has the following additional property, then the matrix is in **reduced row–echelon form**:

4. Every column containing a leading 1 has zeros in every position above and below the leading 1.

**EXAMPLE 4** **Determining Whether a Matrix Is in Row–Echelon Form**

Determine whether each matrix is in row–echelon form. If it is in row–echelon form, determine whether it is in reduced row–echelon form.

a. $\left[\begin{array}{ccc|c} 1 & 3 & 2 & 3 \\ 0 & 1 & 4 & 2 \\ 0 & 0 & 1 & -1 \end{array}\right]$
b. $\left[\begin{array}{ccc|c} 1 & 3 & 2 & 3 \\ 0 & 1 & 1 & 3 \\ 0 & 0 & 0 & 0 \end{array}\right]$
c. $\left[\begin{array}{ccc|c} 1 & 0 & 3 & 2 \\ 0 & 1 & -1 & 5 \end{array}\right]$

d. $\left[\begin{array}{cc|c} 1 & 0 & 1 \\ 0 & 3 & 1 \end{array}\right]$
e. $\left[\begin{array}{ccc|c} 1 & 0 & 0 & 3 \\ 0 & 1 & 0 & 5 \\ 0 & 0 & 1 & 7 \end{array}\right]$
f. $\left[\begin{array}{ccc|c} 1 & 3 & 2 & 3 \\ 0 & 0 & 1 & 2 \\ 0 & 1 & 0 & -3 \end{array}\right]$

**Solution:**

The matrices in (a), (b), (c), and (e) are in row–echelon form. The matrix in (d) is not in row–echelon form, by condition 2; the leading nonzero entry is not a 1 in each row. If the "3" were a "1," the matrix would be in reduced row–echelon form. The matrix in (f) is not in row–echelon form, because of condition 3; the leading 1 in row 2 is not to the left of the leading 1 in row 3. The matrices in (c) and (e) are in reduced row–echelon form, because in the columns containing the leading 1s there are zeros in every position above and below the leading 1.

# Gaussian Elimination with Back-Substitution

Gaussian elimination with back-substitution is a method that uses row operations to transform an augmented matrix into row–echelon form and then uses back-substitution to find the solution to the system of linear equations.

### GAUSSIAN ELIMINATION WITH BACK-SUBSTITUTION

**Step 1:** Write the system of linear equations as an augmented matrix.

**Step 2:** Use row operations to rewrite the augmented matrix in row–echelon form.

**Step 3:** Write the system of linear equations that corresponds to the matrix in row–echelon form found in Step 2.

**Step 4:** Use the system of linear equations found in Step 3 together with back-substitution to find the solution of the system.

The order in which we perform row operations is important. You should move from left to right. Here is an example of Step 2 in the procedure:

$$\left[\begin{array}{ccc|c} 1 & * & * & * \\ * & * & * & * \\ * & * & * & * \end{array}\right] \rightarrow \left[\begin{array}{ccc|c} 1 & * & * & * \\ 0 & * & * & * \\ 0 & * & * & * \end{array}\right] \rightarrow \left[\begin{array}{ccc|c} 1 & * & * & * \\ 0 & 1 & * & * \\ 0 & * & * & * \end{array}\right] \rightarrow \left[\begin{array}{ccc|c} 1 & * & * & * \\ 0 & 1 & * & * \\ 0 & 0 & * & * \end{array}\right] \rightarrow \left[\begin{array}{ccc|c} 1 & * & * & * \\ 0 & 1 & * & * \\ 0 & 0 & 1 & * \end{array}\right]$$

Matrices are not typically used for systems of linear equations in two variables because the methods from Section 8.1 (substitution and elimination) are more efficient. Example 5 illustrates this procedure with a simple system of linear equations in two variables.

**EXAMPLE 5**   **Using Gaussian Elimination with Back-Substitution to Solve a System of Two Linear Equations in Two Variables**

Apply Gaussian elimination with back-substitution to solve the system of linear equations.

$$2x + y = -8$$
$$x + 3y = 6$$

**Solution:**

**STEP 1** Write the system of linear equations as an augmented matrix.   $\begin{bmatrix} 2 & 1 & -8 \\ 1 & 3 & 6 \end{bmatrix}$

**STEP 2** Use row operations to rewrite the matrix in row–echelon form.

Get a 1 in the top left. Interchange rows 1 and 2.

$$\begin{bmatrix} 2 & 1 & -8 \\ 1 & 3 & 6 \end{bmatrix} \quad R_1 \leftrightarrow R_2 \quad \begin{bmatrix} 1 & 3 & 6 \\ 2 & 1 & -8 \end{bmatrix}$$

Get a 0 below the leading 1 in row 1.

$$\begin{bmatrix} 1 & 3 & 6 \\ 2 & 1 & -8 \end{bmatrix} \quad R_2 - 2R_1 \rightarrow R_2 \quad \begin{bmatrix} 1 & 3 & 6 \\ 0 & -5 & -20 \end{bmatrix}$$

Get a leading 1 in row 2. Make the "$-5$" a "1" by dividing by $-5$. Dividing by $-5$ is the same as multiplying by its reciprocal $-\frac{1}{5}$.

$$\begin{bmatrix} 1 & 3 & 6 \\ 0 & -5 & -20 \end{bmatrix} \quad -\frac{1}{5}R_2 \rightarrow R_2 \quad \begin{bmatrix} 1 & 3 & 6 \\ 0 & 1 & 4 \end{bmatrix}$$

The resulting matrix is in row–echelon form.

**STEP 3** Write the system of linear equations corresponding to the row–echelon form of the matrix resulting in Step 2.

$$\begin{bmatrix} 1 & 3 & 6 \\ 0 & 1 & 4 \end{bmatrix} \rightarrow \begin{array}{r} x + 3y = 6 \\ y = 4 \end{array}$$

**STEP 4** Use back-substitution to find the solution to the system.

Let $y = 4$ in the first equation $x + 3y = 6$.          $x + 3(4) = 6$

Solve for $x$.          $x = -6$

The solution to the system of linear equations is $\boxed{x = -6, y = 4}$.

**EXAMPLE 6**   **Using Gaussian Elimination with Back-Substitution to Solve a System of Three Linear Equations in Three Variables**

Use Gaussian elimination with back-substitution to solve the system of linear equations.

$$2x + y + 8z = -1$$
$$x - y + z = -2$$
$$3x - 2y - 2z = 2$$

**Solution:**

**STEP 1** Write the system of linear equations as an augmented matrix.   $\begin{bmatrix} 2 & 1 & 8 & -1 \\ 1 & -1 & 1 & -2 \\ 3 & -2 & -2 & 2 \end{bmatrix}$

STEP 2 Use row operations to rewrite the matrix in row–echelon form.

Get a 1 in the top left.
Interchange rows 1 and 2.

$$R_1 \leftrightarrow R_2 \quad \begin{bmatrix} 1 & -1 & 1 & | & -2 \\ 2 & 1 & 8 & | & -1 \\ 3 & -2 & -2 & | & 2 \end{bmatrix}$$

Get 0s below the leading 1
in row 1.

$$R_2 - 2R_1 \rightarrow R_2 \quad \begin{bmatrix} 1 & -1 & 1 & | & -2 \\ 0 & 3 & 6 & | & 3 \\ 3 & -2 & -2 & | & 2 \end{bmatrix}$$

$$R_3 - 3R_1 \rightarrow R_3 \quad \begin{bmatrix} 1 & -1 & 1 & | & -2 \\ 0 & 3 & 6 & | & 3 \\ 0 & 1 & -5 & | & 8 \end{bmatrix}$$

Get a leading 1 in row 2. Make the
"3" a "1" by dividing by 3.

$$\tfrac{1}{3}R_2 \rightarrow R_2 \quad \begin{bmatrix} 1 & -1 & 1 & | & -2 \\ 0 & 1 & 2 & | & 1 \\ 0 & 1 & -5 & | & 8 \end{bmatrix}$$

Get a zero below the leading
1 in row 2.

$$R_3 - R_2 \rightarrow R_3 \quad \begin{bmatrix} 1 & -1 & 1 & | & -2 \\ 0 & 1 & 2 & | & 1 \\ 0 & 0 & -7 & | & 7 \end{bmatrix}$$

Get a leading 1 in row 3. Make the
"−7" a "1" by dividing by −7.

$$-\tfrac{1}{7}R_3 \rightarrow R_3 \quad \begin{bmatrix} 1 & -1 & 1 & | & -2 \\ 0 & 1 & 2 & | & 1 \\ 0 & 0 & 1 & | & -1 \end{bmatrix}$$

STEP 3 Write the system of linear equations corresponding
to the row–echelon form of the matrix resulting in Step 2.

$$\begin{aligned} x - y + z &= -2 \\ y + 2z &= 1 \\ z &= -1 \end{aligned}$$

STEP 4 Use back-substitution to find the solution to the system.

Let $\boxed{z = -1}$ in the second equation $y + 2z = 1$. $\qquad y + 2(-1) = 1$

Solve for $y$. $\qquad \boxed{y = 3}$

Let $y = 3$ and $z = -1$ in the first equation
$x - y + z = -2$. $\qquad x - (3) + (-1) = -2$

Solve for $x$. $\qquad \boxed{x = 2}$

The solution to the system of linear equations is $\boxed{x = 2, y = 3, \text{ and } z = -1}$.

■ **Answer:** $x = -1, y = 2, z = 1$

■ **YOUR TURN** Use Gaussian elimination with back-substitution to solve the system
of linear equations.

$$\begin{aligned} x + y - z &= 0 \\ 2x + y + z &= 1 \\ 2x - y + 3z &= -1 \end{aligned}$$

# Gauss–Jordan Elimination

In Gaussian elimination with back-substitution, we used row operations to rewrite the matrix in an equivalent row–echelon form. If we continue using row operations until the matrix is in *reduced* row–echelon form, this eliminates the need for back-substitution, and we call this process *Gauss–Jordan elimination*.

> ## GAUSS–JORDAN ELIMINATION
>
> **Step 1:** Write the system of linear equations as an augmented matrix.
> **Step 2:** Use row operations to rewrite the augmented matrix in *reduced* row–echelon form.
> **Step 3:** Write the system of linear equations that corresponds to the matrix in reduced row–echelon form found in Step 2. The result is the solution to the system.

The order in which we perform row operations is important. You should move from left to right. Think of this process as climbing *down* a set of stairs first and then back up the stairs second. On the way *down* the stairs always use operations with rows *above* where you currently are, and on the way back *up* the stairs always use rows *below* where you currently are.

**Study Tip**

For reduced row–echelon form, get 1s along the main diagonal and 0s above and below these 1s.

Down the stairs:

$$
\begin{bmatrix} 1 & * & * & | & * \\ * & * & * & | & * \\ * & * & * & | & * \end{bmatrix} \rightarrow
\begin{bmatrix} 1 & * & * & | & * \\ 0 & * & * & | & * \\ 0 & * & * & | & * \end{bmatrix} \rightarrow
\begin{bmatrix} 1 & * & * & | & * \\ 0 & 1 & * & | & * \\ 0 & * & * & | & * \end{bmatrix} \rightarrow
\begin{bmatrix} 1 & * & * & | & * \\ 0 & 1 & * & | & * \\ 0 & 0 & * & | & * \end{bmatrix} \rightarrow
\begin{bmatrix} 1 & * & * & | & * \\ 0 & 1 & * & | & * \\ 0 & 0 & 1 & | & * \end{bmatrix}
$$

Up the stairs:

$$
\begin{bmatrix} 1 & * & * & | & * \\ 0 & 1 & * & | & * \\ 0 & 0 & 1 & | & * \end{bmatrix} \rightarrow
\begin{bmatrix} 1 & * & * & | & * \\ 0 & 1 & 0 & | & * \\ 0 & 0 & 1 & | & * \end{bmatrix} \rightarrow
\begin{bmatrix} 1 & * & 0 & | & * \\ 0 & 1 & 0 & | & * \\ 0 & 0 & 1 & | & * \end{bmatrix} \rightarrow
\begin{bmatrix} 1 & 0 & 0 & | & * \\ 0 & 1 & 0 & | & * \\ 0 & 0 & 1 & | & * \end{bmatrix}
$$

**EXAMPLE 7**   **Using Gauss–Jordan Elimination to Solve a System of Linear Equations in Three Variables**

Apply Gauss–Jordan elimination to solve the system of linear equations.

$$x - y + 2z = -1$$
$$3x + 2y - 6z = 1$$
$$2x + 3y + 4z = 8$$

**Solution:**

STEP 1 Write the system as an augmented matrix.

$$\begin{bmatrix} 1 & -1 & 2 & | & -1 \\ 3 & 2 & -6 & | & 1 \\ 2 & 3 & 4 & | & 8 \end{bmatrix}$$

STEP 2 Utilize row operations to rewrite the matrix in reduced row–echelon form.

There is already a 1 in the first row/first column.

Get 0s below the leading 1 in row 1.

$$\begin{matrix} R_2 - 3R_1 \rightarrow R_2 \\ R_3 - 2R_1 \rightarrow R_3 \end{matrix} \quad \begin{bmatrix} 1 & -1 & 2 & | & -1 \\ 0 & 5 & -12 & | & 4 \\ 0 & 5 & 0 & | & 10 \end{bmatrix}$$

Get a 1 in row 2/column 2.

$$R_2 \leftrightarrow R_3 \quad \begin{bmatrix} 1 & -1 & 2 & | & -1 \\ 0 & 5 & 0 & | & 10 \\ 0 & 5 & -12 & | & 4 \end{bmatrix}$$

$$\tfrac{1}{5}R_2 \rightarrow R_2 \quad \begin{bmatrix} 1 & -1 & 2 & | & -1 \\ 0 & 1 & 0 & | & 2 \\ 0 & 5 & -12 & | & 4 \end{bmatrix}$$

Get a 0 in row 3/column 2.

$$R_3 - 5R_2 \rightarrow R_3 \quad \begin{bmatrix} 1 & -1 & 2 & | & -1 \\ 0 & 1 & 0 & | & 2 \\ 0 & 0 & -12 & | & -6 \end{bmatrix}$$

Get a 1 in row 3/column 3.

$$-\tfrac{1}{12}R_3 \rightarrow R_3 \quad \begin{bmatrix} 1 & -1 & 2 & | & -1 \\ 0 & 1 & 0 & | & 2 \\ 0 & 0 & 1 & | & \tfrac{1}{2} \end{bmatrix}$$

*Now, go back up the stairs.*

Get 0s above the 1 in row 3/column 3.

$$R_1 - 2R_3 \rightarrow R_1 \quad \begin{bmatrix} 1 & -1 & 0 & | & -2 \\ 0 & 1 & 0 & | & 2 \\ 0 & 0 & 1 & | & \tfrac{1}{2} \end{bmatrix}$$

Get a 0 in row 1/column 2.

$$R_1 + R_2 \rightarrow R_1 \quad \begin{bmatrix} 1 & 0 & 0 & | & 0 \\ 0 & 1 & 0 & | & 2 \\ 0 & 0 & 1 & | & \tfrac{1}{2} \end{bmatrix}$$

STEP 3 Identify the solution.

$$\boxed{x = 0, \ y = 2, \ z = \tfrac{1}{2}}$$

■ **Answer:** $x = -1, y = 2, z = 3$

■ **YOUR TURN** Use an augmented matrix and Gauss–Jordan elimination to solve the system of equations.

$$x + y - z = -2$$
$$3x + y - z = -4$$
$$2x - 2y + 3z = 3$$

**EXAMPLE 8   Solving a System of Four Linear Equations in Four Variables**

Solve the system of equations with Gauss–Jordan elimination.

$$x_1 + x_2 - x_3 + 3x_4 = 3$$
$$3x_2 \quad\quad - 2x_4 = 4$$
$$2x_1 \quad - 3x_3 \quad\quad = -1$$
$$2x_1 \quad\quad\quad + 4x_4 = -6$$

<br>**Study Tip**<br>Careful attention should be paid to order of terms, and zeros should be used for missing terms.

**Solution:**

**STEP 1** Write the system as an augmented matrix.

$$\begin{bmatrix} 1 & 1 & -1 & 3 & | & 3 \\ 0 & 3 & 0 & -2 & | & 4 \\ 2 & 0 & -3 & 0 & | & -1 \\ 2 & 0 & 0 & 4 & | & -6 \end{bmatrix}$$

**STEP 2** Use row operations to rewrite the matrix in reduced row–echelon form.

There is already a 1 in the first row/first column.

Get 0s below the 1 in row 1/column 1.

$R_3 - 2R_1 \to R_3$
$R_4 - 2R_1 \to R_4$

$$\begin{bmatrix} 1 & 1 & -1 & 3 & | & 3 \\ 0 & 3 & 0 & -2 & | & 4 \\ 0 & -2 & -1 & -6 & | & -7 \\ 0 & -2 & 2 & -2 & | & -12 \end{bmatrix}$$

Get a 1 in row 2/column 2.

$R_2 \leftrightarrow R_4$

$$\begin{bmatrix} 1 & 1 & -1 & 3 & | & 3 \\ 0 & -2 & 2 & -2 & | & -12 \\ 0 & -2 & -1 & -6 & | & -7 \\ 0 & 3 & 0 & -2 & | & 4 \end{bmatrix}$$

$-\frac{1}{2}R_2 \leftrightarrow R_2$

$$\begin{bmatrix} 1 & 1 & -1 & 3 & | & 3 \\ 0 & 1 & -1 & 1 & | & 6 \\ 0 & -2 & -1 & -6 & | & -7 \\ 0 & 3 & 0 & -2 & | & 4 \end{bmatrix}$$

Get 0s below the 1 in row 2/column 2.

$R_3 + 2R_2 \to R_3$
$R_4 - 3R_2 \to R_4$

$$\begin{bmatrix} 1 & 1 & -1 & 3 & | & 3 \\ 0 & 1 & -1 & 1 & | & 6 \\ 0 & 0 & -3 & -4 & | & 5 \\ 0 & 0 & 3 & -5 & | & -14 \end{bmatrix}$$

Get a 1 in row 3/column 3.

$-\frac{1}{3}R_3 \to R_3$

$$\begin{bmatrix} 1 & 1 & -1 & 3 & | & 3 \\ 0 & 1 & -1 & 1 & | & 6 \\ 0 & 0 & 1 & \frac{4}{3} & | & -\frac{5}{3} \\ 0 & 0 & 3 & -5 & | & -14 \end{bmatrix}$$

Get a 0 in row 4/column 3.

$R_4 - 3R_3 \to R_4$

$$\begin{bmatrix} 1 & 1 & -1 & 3 & | & 3 \\ 0 & 1 & -1 & 1 & | & 6 \\ 0 & 0 & 1 & \frac{4}{3} & | & -\frac{5}{3} \\ 0 & 0 & 0 & -9 & | & -9 \end{bmatrix}$$

Get a 1 in row 4/column 4.

$$-\frac{1}{9}R_4 \rightarrow R_4 \quad \begin{bmatrix} 1 & 1 & -1 & 3 & | & 3 \\ 0 & 1 & -1 & 1 & | & 6 \\ 0 & 0 & 1 & \frac{4}{3} & | & -\frac{5}{3} \\ 0 & 0 & 0 & 1 & | & 1 \end{bmatrix}$$

*Now go back up the stairs.*

Get 0s above the 1 in row 4/column 4.

$$\begin{array}{l} R_3 - \frac{4}{3}R_4 \rightarrow R_3 \\ R_2 - R_4 \rightarrow R_2 \\ R_1 - 3R_4 \rightarrow R_1 \end{array} \quad \begin{bmatrix} 1 & 1 & -1 & 0 & | & 0 \\ 0 & 1 & -1 & 0 & | & 5 \\ 0 & 0 & 1 & 0 & | & -3 \\ 0 & 0 & 0 & 1 & | & 1 \end{bmatrix}$$

Get 0s above the 1 in row 3/column 3.

$$\begin{array}{l} R_2 + R_3 \rightarrow R_2 \\ R_1 + R_3 \rightarrow R_1 \end{array} \quad \begin{bmatrix} 1 & 1 & 0 & 0 & | & -3 \\ 0 & 1 & 0 & 0 & | & 2 \\ 0 & 0 & 1 & 0 & | & -3 \\ 0 & 0 & 0 & 1 & | & 1 \end{bmatrix}$$

Get a 0 in row 1/column 2.

$$R_1 - R_2 \rightarrow R_1 \quad \begin{bmatrix} 1 & 0 & 0 & 0 & | & -5 \\ 0 & 1 & 0 & 0 & | & 2 \\ 0 & 0 & 1 & 0 & | & -3 \\ 0 & 0 & 0 & 1 & | & 1 \end{bmatrix}$$

**STEP 3** Identify the solution.

$$\boxed{x_1 = -5, x_2 = 2, x_3 = -3, x_4 = 1}$$

# Inconsistent and Dependent Systems

Recall from Section 8.1 that systems of linear equations can be independent, inconsistent, or dependent systems and therefore have *one solution*, *no solution*, or *infinitely many solutions*. All of the systems we have solved so far in this section have been independent systems (unique solution). When solving a system of linear equations using Gaussian elimination or Gauss–Jordan elimination, the following will indicate the three possible types of solutions.

| SYSTEM | TYPE OF SOLUTION | MATRIX DURING GAUSS-JORDAN ELIMINATION | EXAMPLE | |
|---|---|---|---|---|
| Independent | One (unique) solution | Diagonal entries are all 1s, and the 0s occupy all other coefficient positions. | $\begin{bmatrix} 1 & 0 & 0 & \mid & 1 \\ 0 & 1 & 0 & \mid & -3 \\ 0 & 0 & 1 & \mid & 2 \end{bmatrix}$ or | $\begin{array}{l} x = 1 \\ y = -3 \\ z = 2 \end{array}$ |
| Inconsistent | No solution | One row will have only zero entries for coefficients and a nonzero entry for the constant. | $\begin{bmatrix} 1 & 0 & 0 & \mid & 1 \\ 0 & 1 & 0 & \mid & -3 \\ 0 & 0 & 0 & \mid & 2 \end{bmatrix}$ or | $\begin{array}{l} x = 1 \\ y = -3 \\ 0 = 2 \end{array}$ |
| Dependent | Infinitely many solutions | One row will be entirely 0s when the number of equations equals the number of variables. | $\begin{bmatrix} 1 & 0 & -2 & \mid & 1 \\ 0 & 1 & 1 & \mid & -3 \\ 0 & 0 & 0 & \mid & 0 \end{bmatrix}$ or | $\begin{array}{l} x - 2z = 1 \\ y + z = -3 \\ 0 = 0 \end{array}$ |

EXAMPLE 9   **Determining That a System Is Inconsistent: No Solution**

Solve the system of equations.

$$
\begin{aligned}
x + 2y - z &= 3 \\
2x + y + 2z &= -1 \\
-2x - 4y + 2z &= 5
\end{aligned}
$$

**Solution:**

STEP 1  Write the system of equations as an augmented matrix.

$$
\left[\begin{array}{ccc|c}
1 & 2 & -1 & 3 \\
2 & 1 & 2 & -1 \\
-2 & -4 & 2 & 5
\end{array}\right]
$$

STEP 2  Apply row operations to rewrite the matrix in row–echelon form.

Get 0s below the 1 in column 1.

$$
\begin{array}{c}
R_2 - 2R_1 \rightarrow R_2 \\
R_3 + 2R_1 \rightarrow R_3
\end{array}
\left[\begin{array}{ccc|c}
1 & 2 & -1 & 3 \\
0 & -3 & 4 & -7 \\
0 & 0 & 0 & 11
\end{array}\right]
$$

There is no need to continue because row 3 is a contradiction.   $0x + 0y + 0z = 11$ or $0 = 11$

Since this is inconsistent, there is *no solution* to this system of equations.

EXAMPLE 10   **Determining That a System Is Dependent: Infinitely Many Solutions**

Solve the system of equations.

$$
\begin{aligned}
x + z &= 3 \\
2x + y + 4z &= 8 \\
3x + y + 5z &= 11
\end{aligned}
$$

**Solution:**

STEP 1  Write the system of equations as an augmented matrix.

$$
\left[\begin{array}{ccc|c}
1 & 0 & 1 & 3 \\
2 & 1 & 4 & 8 \\
3 & 1 & 5 & 11
\end{array}\right]
$$

STEP 2  Use row operations to rewrite the matrix in reduced row–echelon form.

Get the 0s below the 1 in column 1.

$$
\begin{array}{c}
R_2 - 2R_1 \rightarrow R_2 \\
R_3 - 3R_1 \rightarrow R_3
\end{array}
\left[\begin{array}{ccc|c}
1 & 0 & 1 & 3 \\
0 & 1 & 2 & 2 \\
0 & 1 & 2 & 2
\end{array}\right]
$$

Get a 0 in row 3/column 2.

$$
R_3 - R_2 \rightarrow R_3
\left[\begin{array}{ccc|c}
1 & 0 & 1 & 3 \\
0 & 1 & 2 & 2 \\
0 & 0 & 0 & 0
\end{array}\right]
$$

This matrix is in reduced row–echelon form. This matrix corresponds to a dependent system of linear equations and has infinitely many solutions.

STEP 3  Write the augmented matrix as a system of linear equations.

$$
\begin{aligned}
x + z &= 3 \\
y + 2z &= 2
\end{aligned}
$$

Let $z = a$, where $a$ is any real number, and substitute this into the two equations.

We find that $x = 3 - a$ and $y = 2 - 2a$. The general solution is

$\boxed{x = 3 - a, y = 2 - 2a, z = a}$ for $a$ any real number. Note that $(2, 0, 1)$ and $(3, 2, 0)$ are particular solutions when $a = 1$ and $a = 0$, respectively.

**Study Tip**

In a system with three variables, say, $x$, $y$, and $z$, we typically let $z = a$ (where $a$ is called a parameter) and then solve for $x$ and $y$ in terms of $a$.

A common mistake that is made is to identify a unique solution as no solution when one of the variables is equal to zero. For example, what is the difference between the following two matrices?

$$\begin{bmatrix} 1 & 0 & 2 & | & 1 \\ 0 & 1 & 3 & | & 2 \\ 0 & 0 & 3 & | & 0 \end{bmatrix} \quad \text{and} \quad \begin{bmatrix} 1 & 0 & 2 & | & 1 \\ 0 & 1 & 3 & | & 2 \\ 0 & 0 & 0 & | & 3 \end{bmatrix}$$

The first matrix has a *unique solution*, whereas the second matrix has *no solution*. The third row of the first matrix corresponds to the equation $3z = 0$, which implies that $z = 0$. The third row of the second matrix corresponds to the equation $0x + 0y + 0z = 3$ or $0 = 3$, which is inconsistent, and therefore the system has no solution.

**EXAMPLE 11    Determining That a System Is Dependent: Infinitely Many Solutions**

Solve the system of linear equations.

$$\begin{aligned} 2x + y + z &= 8 \\ x + y - z &= -3 \end{aligned}$$

**Solution:**

**STEP 1** Write the system of equations as an augmented matrix. $\begin{bmatrix} 2 & 1 & 1 & | & 8 \\ 1 & 1 & -1 & | & -3 \end{bmatrix}$

**STEP 2** Use row operations to rewrite the matrix in reduced row–echelon form.

Get a 1 in row 1/column 1. $\qquad R_1 \leftrightarrow R_2 \quad \begin{bmatrix} 1 & 1 & -1 & | & -3 \\ 2 & 1 & 1 & | & 8 \end{bmatrix}$

Get a 0 in row 2/column 1. $\qquad R_2 - 2R_1 \rightarrow R_2 \quad \begin{bmatrix} 1 & 1 & -1 & | & -3 \\ 0 & -1 & 3 & | & 14 \end{bmatrix}$

Get a 1 in row 2/column 2. $\qquad -R_2 \rightarrow R_2 \quad \begin{bmatrix} 1 & 1 & -1 & | & -3 \\ 0 & 1 & -3 & | & -14 \end{bmatrix}$

Get a 0 in row 1/column 2. $\qquad R_1 - R_2 \rightarrow R_1 \quad \begin{bmatrix} 1 & 0 & 2 & | & 11 \\ 0 & 1 & -3 & | & -14 \end{bmatrix}$

This matrix is in reduced row–echelon form.

**STEP 3** Identify the solution.

$$\begin{aligned} x + 2z &= 11 \\ y - 3z &= -14 \end{aligned}$$

Let $z = a$, where $a$ is any real number. Substituting $z = a$ into these two equations gives the infinitely many solutions $\boxed{x = 11 - 2a,\ y = 3a - 14,\ z = a}$.

■ **Answer:** $x = 3a + 2$, $y = -4a - 2$, $z = a$, where $a$ is any real number.

■ **YOUR TURN** Solve the system of equations using an augmented matrix.

$$\begin{aligned} x + y + z &= 0 \\ 3x + 2y - z &= 2 \end{aligned}$$

In Example 10 there were three equations and three unknowns ($x$, $y$, and $z$). In Example 11 there were two equations and three unknowns. Whenever there are more unknowns than equations, the system is dependent, that is, infinitely many solutions.

# Applications

Remember Jared who lost all that weight eating at Subway and is still keeping it off 10 years later? He ate Subway sandwiches for lunch and dinner for one year and lost 235 pounds! The following table gives nutritional information for Subway's 6-inch sandwiches advertised with 6 grams of fat or less.

| SANDWICH | CALORIES | FAT (g) | CARBOHYDRATES (g) | PROTEIN (g) |
|---|---|---|---|---|
| Veggie Delight | 350 | 18 | 17 | 36 |
| Oven-roasted chicken breast | 430 | 19 | 46 | 20 |
| Ham (Black Forest without cheese) | 290 | 5 | 45 | 19 |

## EXAMPLE 12  Subway Diet

Suppose you are going to eat only Subway 6-inch sandwiches for a week (seven days) for both lunch and dinner (total of 14 meals). If your goal is to eat 388 grams of protein and 4900 calories in those 14 sandwiches, how many of each sandwich should you eat that week?

**Solution:**

**STEP 1**  Determine the system of linear equations.

Let three variables represent the number of each type of sandwich you eat in a week.

$$x = \text{number of Veggie Delight sandwiches}$$
$$y = \text{number of chicken breast sandwiches}$$
$$z = \text{number of ham sandwiches}$$

The total number of sandwiches eaten is 14.  $\qquad x + y + z = 14$

The total number of calories consumed is 4900.  $\quad 350x + 430y + 290z = 4900$

The total number of grams of protein
consumed is 388.  $\qquad\qquad 36x + 20y + 19z = 388$

Write an augmented matrix representing this system of linear equations.

$$\begin{bmatrix} 1 & 1 & 1 & | & 14 \\ 350 & 430 & 290 & | & 4900 \\ 36 & 20 & 19 & | & 388 \end{bmatrix}$$

**STEP 2**  Utilize row operations to rewrite the matrix in reduced row–echelon form.

$$\begin{matrix} R_2 - 350R_1 \rightarrow R_2 \\ R_3 - 36R_1 \rightarrow R_3 \end{matrix} \quad \begin{bmatrix} 1 & 1 & 1 & | & 14 \\ 0 & 80 & -60 & | & 0 \\ 0 & -16 & -17 & | & -116 \end{bmatrix}$$

$$\tfrac{1}{80}R_2 \rightarrow R_2 \quad \begin{bmatrix} 1 & 1 & 1 & | & 14 \\ 0 & 1 & -\tfrac{3}{4} & | & 0 \\ 0 & -16 & -17 & | & -116 \end{bmatrix}$$

$$R_3 + 16R_2 \rightarrow R_3 \quad \begin{bmatrix} 1 & 1 & 1 & | & 14 \\ 0 & 1 & -\tfrac{3}{4} & | & 0 \\ 0 & 0 & -29 & | & -116 \end{bmatrix}$$

$$-\tfrac{1}{29}R_3 \rightarrow R_3 \quad \begin{bmatrix} 1 & 1 & 1 & | & 14 \\ 0 & 1 & -\tfrac{3}{4} & | & 0 \\ 0 & 0 & 1 & | & 4 \end{bmatrix}$$

$$\begin{matrix} R_2 + \tfrac{3}{4}R_3 \rightarrow R_2 \\ R_1 - R_3 \rightarrow R_1 \end{matrix} \quad \begin{bmatrix} 1 & 1 & 0 & | & 10 \\ 0 & 1 & 0 & | & 3 \\ 0 & 0 & 1 & | & 4 \end{bmatrix}$$

$$R_1 - R_2 \rightarrow R_1 \quad \begin{bmatrix} 1 & 0 & 0 & | & 7 \\ 0 & 1 & 0 & | & 3 \\ 0 & 0 & 1 & | & 4 \end{bmatrix}$$

**STEP 3** Identify the solution.  $\boxed{x = 7, y = 3, z = 4}$

You should eat $\boxed{\text{7 Veggie Delights, 3 oven-roasted chicken breast, and 4 ham sandwiches}}$.

## Technology Tip

Enter the matrix into the TI or graphing calculator. Press 2nd MATRIX. Use ► EDIT ENTER ENTER.

Now enter the size by typing the number of rows first and the number of columns second. Enter the elements of the matrix one row at a time by pressing the number and ENTER each time.

When done, press 2nd QUIT. To show the matrix $A$, press 2nd MATRIX ENTER ENTER.

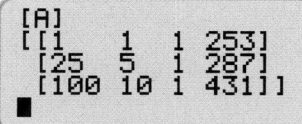

To find the reduced row–echelon form of the original matrix directly use rref (matrix) command. Press 2nd MATRIX ► MATH ▼ B:rref ENTER 2nd MATRIX ENTER ) ► MATH 1:Frac ENTER.

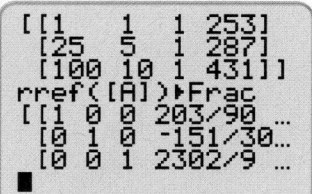

The solution to the system is $a = \tfrac{203}{90}, b = -\tfrac{151}{30}, c = \tfrac{2302}{9}$.

## EXAMPLE 13 Fitting a Curve to Data

The amount of money awarded in medical malpractice suits is rising. This can be modeled with a quadratic function $y = at^2 + bt + c$, where $t > 0$ and $a > 0$. Determine a quadratic function that passes through the three points shown on the graph. Based on this trend, how much money will be spent on malpractice in 2011?

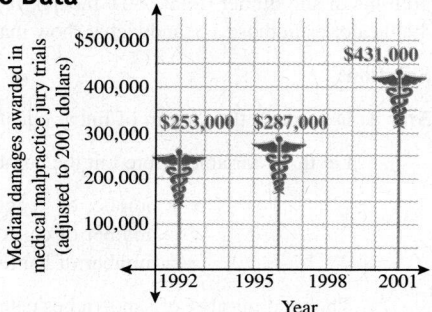

**Solution:**

Let 1991 correspond to $t = 0$ and $y$ represent the number of dollars awarded for malpractice suits. The following data are reflected in the illustration above:

| YEAR | $t$ | $y$ (THOUSANDS OF DOLLARS) | $(t, y)$ |
|------|-----|----------------------------|----------|
| 1992 | 1 | 253 | (1, 253) |
| 1996 | 5 | 287 | (5, 287) |
| 2001 | 10 | 431 | (10, 431) |

Substitute the three points (1, 253), (5, 287), and (10, 431) into the general quadratic equation: $y = at^2 + bt + c$.

| POINT | $y = at^2 + bt + c$ | SYSTEM OF EQUATIONS |
|-------|---------------------|---------------------|
| (1, 253) | $253 = a(1)^2 + b(1) + c$ | $a + b + c = 253$ |
| (5, 287) | $287 = a(5)^2 + b(5) + c$ | $25a + 5b + c = 287$ |
| (10, 431) | $431 = a(10)^2 + b(10) + c$ | $100a + 10b + c = 431$ |

**STEP 1** Write this system of linear equations
as an augmented matrix.

$$\begin{bmatrix} 1 & 1 & 1 & | & 253 \\ 25 & 5 & 1 & | & 287 \\ 100 & 10 & 1 & | & 431 \end{bmatrix}$$

**STEP 2** Apply row operations to rewrite the matrix in reduced row–echelon form.

$$R_2 - 25R_1 \rightarrow R_2 \quad \begin{bmatrix} 1 & 1 & 1 & | & 253 \\ 0 & -20 & -24 & | & -6038 \\ 100 & 10 & 1 & | & 431 \end{bmatrix}$$

$$R_3 - 100R_1 \rightarrow R_3 \quad \begin{bmatrix} 1 & 1 & 1 & | & 253 \\ 0 & -20 & -24 & | & -6038 \\ 0 & -90 & -99 & | & -24{,}869 \end{bmatrix}$$

$$-\tfrac{1}{20}R_2 \rightarrow R_2 \quad \begin{bmatrix} 1 & 1 & 1 & | & 253 \\ 0 & 1 & \frac{6}{5} & | & \frac{3019}{10} \\ 0 & -90 & -99 & | & -24{,}869 \end{bmatrix}$$

$$R_3 + 90R_2 \rightarrow R_3 \quad \begin{bmatrix} 1 & 1 & 1 & | & 253 \\ 0 & 1 & \frac{6}{5} & | & \frac{3019}{10} \\ 0 & 0 & 9 & | & 2302 \end{bmatrix}$$

$$\tfrac{1}{9}R_3 \rightarrow R_3 \quad \begin{bmatrix} 1 & 1 & 1 & | & 253 \\ 0 & 1 & \frac{6}{5} & | & \frac{3019}{10} \\ 0 & 0 & 1 & | & \frac{2302}{9} \end{bmatrix}$$

$$R_2 - \tfrac{6}{5}R_3 \rightarrow R_2 \quad \begin{bmatrix} 1 & 1 & 1 & | & 253 \\ 0 & 1 & 0 & | & -\frac{151}{30} \\ 0 & 0 & 1 & | & \frac{2302}{9} \end{bmatrix}$$

$$R_1 - R_3 \rightarrow R_1 \quad \begin{bmatrix} 1 & 1 & 0 & | & -\frac{25}{9} \\ 0 & 1 & 0 & | & -\frac{151}{30} \\ 0 & 0 & 1 & | & \frac{2302}{9} \end{bmatrix}$$

$$R_1 - R_2 \rightarrow R_1 \quad \begin{bmatrix} 1 & 0 & 0 & | & \frac{203}{90} \\ 0 & 1 & 0 & | & -\frac{151}{30} \\ 0 & 0 & 1 & | & \frac{2302}{9} \end{bmatrix}$$

**STEP 3** Identify the solution.

$$a = \frac{203}{90}, \quad b = -\frac{151}{30}, \quad c = \frac{2302}{9}$$

Substituting $a = \frac{203}{90}$, $b = -\frac{151}{30}$, $c = \frac{2302}{9}$ into $y = at^2 + bt + c$, we find that the thousands of dollars spent on malpractice suits as a function of year is given by

$$\boxed{y = \frac{203}{90}t^2 - \frac{151}{30}t + \frac{2302}{9}} \qquad \text{1991 is } t = 0$$

Notice that all three points lie on this curve.

For 2011, we let $t = 20$, which results in approximately $\boxed{\$1.06\text{ M}}$ in malpractice.

## SECTION 8.3 SUMMARY

In this section, we used augmented matrices to represent a system of linear equations.

$$\begin{array}{l} a_1x + b_1y + c_1z = d_1 \\ a_2x + b_2y + c_2z = d_2 \\ a_3x + b_3y + c_3z = d_3 \end{array} \Leftrightarrow \left[ \begin{array}{ccc|c} a_1 & b_1 & c_1 & d_1 \\ a_2 & b_2 & c_2 & d_2 \\ a_3 & b_3 & c_3 & d_3 \end{array} \right]$$

Any missing terms correspond to a 0 in the matrix. A matrix is in **row–echelon** form if it has all three of the following properties:

1. Any rows consisting entirely of 0s are at the bottom of the matrix.
2. For each row that does not consist entirely of 0s, the first (leftmost) nonzero entry is 1 (called the leading 1).

3. For two successive nonzero rows, the leading 1 in the higher row is farther to the left than the leading 1 in the lower row.

If a matrix in row–echelon form has the following additional property, then the matrix is in **reduced row–echelon form**:

4. Every column containing a leading 1 has zeros in every position above and below the leading 1.

The two methods used for solving systems of linear equations represented as augmented matrices are Gaussian elimination with back-substitution and Gauss–Jordan elimination. In both cases, we represent the system of linear equations as an augmented matrix and then use row operations to rewrite in row–echelon form. With Gaussian elimination we then stop and perform back-substitution to solve the system, and with Gauss–Jordan elimination we continue with row operations until the matrix is in reduced row–echelon form and then identify the solution to the system.

## SECTION 8.3 EXERCISES

### ■ SKILLS

In Exercises 1–6, determine the order of each matrix.

1. $\left[ \begin{array}{ccc} -1 & 3 & 4 \\ 2 & 7 & 9 \end{array} \right]$
2. $\left[ \begin{array}{cc} 0 & 1 \\ 3 & 9 \\ 7 & 8 \end{array} \right]$
3. $\left[ \begin{array}{cccc} 1 & 2 & 3 & 4 \end{array} \right]$
4. $\left[ \begin{array}{c} 3 \\ 7 \\ -1 \\ 10 \end{array} \right]$
5. $[0]$
6. $\left[ \begin{array}{cccc} -1 & 3 & 6 & 8 \\ 2 & 9 & 7 & 3 \\ 5 & 4 & -2 & -10 \\ 6 & 3 & 1 & 5 \end{array} \right]$

In Exercises 7–14, write the augmented matrix for each system of linear equations.

7. $\begin{array}{l} 3x - 2y = 7 \\ -4x + 6y = -3 \end{array}$

8. $\begin{array}{l} -x + y = 2 \\ x - y = -4 \end{array}$

9. $\begin{array}{l} 2x - 3y + 4z = -3 \\ -x + y + 2z = 1 \\ 5x - 2y - 3z = 7 \end{array}$

10. $\begin{array}{l} x - 2y + z = 0 \\ -2x + y - z = -5 \\ 13x + 7y + 5z = 6 \end{array}$

11. $\begin{array}{l} x + y = 3 \\ x - z = 2 \\ y + z = 5 \end{array}$

12. $\begin{array}{l} x - y = -4 \\ y + z = 3 \end{array}$

13. $\begin{array}{l} 3y - 4x + 5z - 2 = 0 \\ 2x - 3y - 2z = -3 \\ 3z + 4y - 2x - 1 = 0 \end{array}$

14. $\begin{array}{l} 2y + z - x - 3 = 2 \\ 2x + 3z - 2y = 0 \\ -2z + y - 4x - 3 = 0 \end{array}$

In Exercises 15–20, write the system of linear equations represented by the augmented matrix. Utilize the variables $x$, $y$, and $z$.

15. $\left[ \begin{array}{cc|c} -3 & 7 & 2 \\ 1 & 5 & 8 \end{array} \right]$

16. $\left[ \begin{array}{ccc|c} -1 & 2 & 4 & 4 \\ 7 & 9 & 3 & -3 \\ 4 & 6 & -5 & 8 \end{array} \right]$

17. $\left[ \begin{array}{ccc|c} -1 & 0 & 0 & 4 \\ 7 & 9 & 3 & -3 \\ 4 & 6 & -5 & 8 \end{array} \right]$

18. $\left[ \begin{array}{ccc|c} 2 & 3 & -4 & 6 \\ 7 & -1 & 5 & 9 \end{array} \right]$

19. $\left[ \begin{array}{cc|c} 1 & 0 & a \\ 0 & 1 & b \end{array} \right]$

20. $\left[ \begin{array}{ccc|c} 3 & 0 & 5 & 1 \\ 0 & -4 & 7 & -3 \\ 2 & -1 & 0 & 8 \end{array} \right]$

**In Exercises 21–30, indicate whether each matrix is in row–echelon form. If it is, determine whether it is in reduced row–echelon form.**

**21.** $\begin{bmatrix} 1 & 0 & | & 3 \\ 1 & 1 & | & 2 \end{bmatrix}$

**22.** $\begin{bmatrix} 0 & 1 & | & 3 \\ 1 & 0 & | & 2 \end{bmatrix}$

**23.** $\begin{bmatrix} 1 & 0 & -1 & | & -3 \\ 0 & 1 & 3 & | & 14 \end{bmatrix}$

**24.** $\begin{bmatrix} 1 & 0 & 0 & | & -3 \\ 0 & 1 & 3 & | & 14 \end{bmatrix}$

**25.** $\begin{bmatrix} 1 & 0 & 1 & | & 3 \\ 0 & 0 & 0 & | & 0 \\ 0 & 1 & 2 & | & 2 \end{bmatrix}$

**26.** $\begin{bmatrix} 1 & 0 & 1 & | & 3 \\ 0 & 1 & 2 & | & 2 \\ 0 & 0 & 0 & | & 0 \end{bmatrix}$

**27.** $\begin{bmatrix} 1 & 0 & 0 & | & 3 \\ 0 & 1 & 0 & | & 2 \\ 0 & 0 & 1 & | & 5 \end{bmatrix}$

**28.** $\begin{bmatrix} -1 & 0 & 0 & | & 3 \\ 0 & -1 & 0 & | & 2 \\ 0 & 0 & -1 & | & 5 \end{bmatrix}$

**29.** $\begin{bmatrix} 1 & 0 & 0 & 1 & | & 3 \\ 0 & 1 & 0 & 3 & | & 2 \\ 0 & 0 & 1 & 0 & | & 5 \\ 0 & 0 & 0 & 1 & | & 0 \end{bmatrix}$

**30.** $\begin{bmatrix} 1 & 0 & 0 & 1 & | & 3 \\ 0 & 1 & 0 & 3 & | & 2 \\ 0 & 0 & 1 & 0 & | & 5 \\ 0 & 0 & 0 & 0 & | & 0 \end{bmatrix}$

**In Exercises 31–40, perform the indicated row operations on each augmented matrix.**

**31.** $\begin{bmatrix} 1 & -2 & | & -3 \\ 2 & 3 & | & -1 \end{bmatrix}$ $R_2 - 2R_1 \rightarrow R_2$

**32.** $\begin{bmatrix} 2 & -3 & | & -4 \\ 1 & 2 & | & 5 \end{bmatrix}$ $R_1 \leftrightarrow R_2$

**33.** $\begin{bmatrix} 1 & -2 & -1 & | & 3 \\ 2 & 1 & -3 & | & 6 \\ 3 & -2 & 5 & | & -8 \end{bmatrix}$ $R_2 - 2R_1 \rightarrow R_2$

**34.** $\begin{bmatrix} 1 & -2 & 1 & | & 3 \\ 0 & 1 & -2 & | & 6 \\ -3 & 0 & -1 & | & -5 \end{bmatrix}$ $R_3 + 3R_1 \rightarrow R_3$

**35.** $\begin{bmatrix} 1 & -2 & 5 & -1 & | & 2 \\ 0 & 3 & 0 & -1 & | & -2 \\ 0 & -2 & 1 & -2 & | & 5 \\ 0 & 0 & 1 & -1 & | & -6 \end{bmatrix}$ $R_3 + R_2 \rightarrow R_2$

**36.** $\begin{bmatrix} 1 & 0 & 5 & -10 & | & 15 \\ 0 & 1 & 2 & -3 & | & 4 \\ 0 & 2 & -3 & 0 & | & -1 \\ 0 & 0 & 1 & -1 & | & -3 \end{bmatrix}$ $R_2 - \frac{1}{2}R_3 \rightarrow R_3$

**37.** $\begin{bmatrix} 1 & 0 & 5 & -10 & | & -5 \\ 0 & 1 & 2 & -3 & | & -2 \\ 0 & 2 & -3 & 0 & | & -1 \\ 0 & -3 & 2 & -1 & | & -3 \end{bmatrix}$ $\begin{aligned} R_3 - 2R_2 \rightarrow R_3 \\ R_4 + 3R_2 \rightarrow R_4 \end{aligned}$

**38.** $\begin{bmatrix} 1 & 0 & 4 & 0 & | & 1 \\ 0 & 1 & 2 & 0 & | & -2 \\ 0 & 0 & 1 & 0 & | & 0 \\ 0 & 0 & 0 & 1 & | & -3 \end{bmatrix}$ $\begin{aligned} R_2 - 2R_3 \rightarrow R_2 \\ R_1 - 4R_3 \rightarrow R_1 \end{aligned}$

**39.** $\begin{bmatrix} 1 & 0 & 4 & 8 & | & 3 \\ 0 & 1 & 2 & -3 & | & -2 \\ 0 & 0 & 1 & 6 & | & 3 \\ 0 & 0 & 0 & 1 & | & -3 \end{bmatrix}$ $\begin{aligned} R_3 - 6R_4 \rightarrow R_3 \\ R_2 + 3R_4 \rightarrow R_2 \\ R_1 - 8R_4 \rightarrow R_1 \end{aligned}$

**40.** $\begin{bmatrix} 1 & 0 & -1 & 5 & | & 2 \\ 0 & 1 & 2 & 3 & | & -5 \\ 0 & 0 & 1 & -2 & | & 2 \\ 0 & 0 & 0 & 1 & | & 1 \end{bmatrix}$ $\begin{aligned} R_3 + 2R_4 \rightarrow R_3 \\ R_2 - 3R_4 \rightarrow R_2 \\ R_1 - 5R_4 \rightarrow R_1 \end{aligned}$

**In Exercises 41–50, use row operations to transform each matrix to reduced row–echelon form.**

**41.** $\begin{bmatrix} 1 & 2 & | & 4 \\ 2 & 3 & | & 2 \end{bmatrix}$

**42.** $\begin{bmatrix} 1 & -1 & | & 3 \\ -3 & 2 & | & 2 \end{bmatrix}$

**43.** $\begin{bmatrix} 1 & -1 & 1 & | & -1 \\ 0 & 1 & -1 & | & -1 \\ -1 & 1 & 1 & | & 1 \end{bmatrix}$

**44.** $\begin{bmatrix} 0 & -1 & 1 & | & 1 \\ 1 & -1 & 1 & | & -1 \\ 1 & -1 & -1 & | & -1 \end{bmatrix}$

**45.** $\begin{bmatrix} 3 & -2 & -3 & | & -1 \\ 1 & -1 & 1 & | & -4 \\ 2 & 3 & 5 & | & 14 \end{bmatrix}$

**46.** $\begin{bmatrix} 3 & -1 & 1 & | & 2 \\ 1 & -2 & 3 & | & 1 \\ 2 & 1 & -3 & | & -1 \end{bmatrix}$

**47.** $\begin{bmatrix} 2 & 1 & -6 & | & 4 \\ 1 & -2 & 2 & | & -3 \end{bmatrix}$

**48.** $\begin{bmatrix} -3 & -1 & 2 & | & -1 \\ -1 & -2 & 1 & | & -3 \end{bmatrix}$

**49.** $\begin{bmatrix} -1 & 2 & 1 & | & -2 \\ 3 & -2 & 1 & | & 4 \\ 2 & -4 & -2 & | & 4 \end{bmatrix}$

**50.** $\begin{bmatrix} 2 & -1 & 0 & | & 1 \\ -1 & 0 & 1 & | & -2 \\ -2 & 1 & 0 & | & -1 \end{bmatrix}$

**In Exercises 51–70, solve the system of linear equations using Gaussian elimination with back-substitution.**

**51.** $\begin{aligned} 2x + 3y &= 1 \\ x + y &= -2 \end{aligned}$

**52.** $\begin{aligned} 3x + 2y &= 11 \\ x - y &= 12 \end{aligned}$

**53.** $\begin{aligned} -x + 2y &= 3 \\ 2x - 4y &= -6 \end{aligned}$

**54.** $\begin{aligned} 3x - y &= -1 \\ 2y + 6x &= 2 \end{aligned}$

**55.** $\begin{aligned} \frac{2}{3}x + \frac{1}{3}y &= \frac{8}{9} \\ \frac{1}{2}x + \frac{1}{4}y &= \frac{3}{4} \end{aligned}$

**56.** $\begin{aligned} 0.4x - 0.5y &= 2.08 \\ -0.3x + 0.7y &= 1.88 \end{aligned}$

**57.** $\begin{aligned} x - z - y &= 10 \\ 2x - 3y + z &= -11 \\ y - x + z &= -10 \end{aligned}$

**58.** $\begin{aligned} 2x + z + y &= -3 \\ 2y - z + x &= 0 \\ x + y + 2z &= 5 \end{aligned}$

**59.** $\begin{aligned} 3x_1 + x_2 - x_3 &= 1 \\ x_1 - x_2 + x_3 &= -3 \\ 2x_1 + x_2 + x_3 &= 0 \end{aligned}$

**60.** $\begin{aligned} 2x_1 + x_2 + x_3 &= -1 \\ x_1 + x_2 - x_3 &= 5 \\ 3x_1 - x_2 - x_3 &= 1 \end{aligned}$

**61.** $\begin{aligned} 2x + 5y &= 9 \\ x + 2y - z &= 3 \\ -3x - 4y + 7z &= 1 \end{aligned}$

**62.** $\begin{aligned} x - 2y + 3z &= 1 \\ -2x + 7y - 9z &= 4 \\ x + z &= 9 \end{aligned}$

**63.** $\begin{aligned} 2x_1 - x_2 + x_3 &= 3 \\ x_1 - x_2 + x_3 &= 2 \\ -2x_1 + 2x_2 - 2x_3 &= -4 \end{aligned}$

**64.** $\begin{aligned} x_1 - x_2 - 2x_3 &= 0 \\ -2x_1 + 5x_2 + 10x_3 &= -3 \\ 3x_1 + x_2 &= 0 \end{aligned}$

**65.** $\begin{aligned} 2x + y - z &= 2 \\ x - y - z &= 6 \end{aligned}$

**66.** $\begin{aligned} 3x + y - z &= 0 \\ x + y + 7z &= 4 \end{aligned}$

**67.** $\begin{aligned} 2y + z &= 3 \\ 4x - z &= -3 \\ 7x - 3y - 3z &= 2 \\ x - y - z &= -2 \end{aligned}$

**68.** $\begin{aligned} -2x - y + 2z &= 3 \\ 3x - 4z &= 2 \\ 2x + y &= -1 \\ -x + y - z &= -8 \end{aligned}$

**69.** $\begin{aligned} 3x_1 - 2x_2 + x_3 + 2x_4 &= -2 \\ -x_1 + 3x_2 + 4x_3 + 3x_4 &= 4 \\ x_1 + x_2 + x_3 + x_4 &= 0 \\ 5x_1 + 3x_2 + x_3 + 2x_4 &= -1 \end{aligned}$

**70.** $\begin{aligned} 5x_1 + 3x_2 + 8x_3 + x_4 &= 1 \\ x_1 + 2x_2 + 5x_3 + 2x_4 &= 3 \\ 4x_1 + x_3 - 2x_4 &= -3 \\ x_2 + x_3 + x_4 &= 0 \end{aligned}$

**In Exercises 71–86, solve the system of linear equations using Gauss–Jordan elimination.**

**71.** $\begin{aligned} x + 3y &= -5 \\ -2x - y &= 0 \end{aligned}$

**72.** $\begin{aligned} 5x - 4y &= 31 \\ 3x + 7y &= -19 \end{aligned}$

**73.** $\begin{aligned} x + y &= 4 \\ -3x - 3y &= 10 \end{aligned}$

**74.** $\begin{aligned} 3x - 4y &= 12 \\ -6x + 8y &= -24 \end{aligned}$

**75.** $\begin{aligned} x - 2y + 3z &= 5 \\ 3x + 6y - 4z &= -12 \\ -x - 4y + 6z &= 16 \end{aligned}$

**76.** $\begin{aligned} x + 2y - z &= 6 \\ 2x - y + 3z &= -13 \\ 3x - 2y + 3z &= -16 \end{aligned}$

**77.** $\begin{aligned} x + y + z &= 3 \\ x - z &= 1 \\ y - z &= -4 \end{aligned}$

**78.** $\begin{aligned} x - 2y + 4z &= 2 \\ 2x - 3y - 2z &= -3 \\ \frac{1}{2}x + \frac{1}{4}y + z &= -2 \end{aligned}$

**79.** $\begin{aligned} x + 2y + z &= 3 \\ 2x - y + 3z &= 7 \\ 3x + y + 4z &= 5 \end{aligned}$

**80.** $\begin{aligned} x + 2y + z &= 3 \\ 2x - y + 3z &= 7 \\ 3x + y + 4z &= 10 \end{aligned}$

**81.** $\begin{aligned} 3x - y + z &= 8 \\ x + y - 2z &= 4 \end{aligned}$

**82.** $\begin{aligned} x - 2y + 3z &= 10 \\ -3x + z &= 9 \end{aligned}$

**83.** $\begin{aligned} 4x - 2y + 5z &= 20 \\ x + 3y - 2z &= 6 \end{aligned}$

**84.** $\begin{aligned} y + z &= 4 \\ x + y &= 8 \end{aligned}$

**85.** $\begin{aligned} x - y - z - w &= 1 \\ 2x + y + z + 2w &= 3 \\ x - 2y - 2z - 3w &= 0 \\ 3x - 4y + z + 5w &= -3 \end{aligned}$

**86.** $\begin{aligned} x - 3y + 3z - 2w &= 4 \\ x + 2y - z &= -3 \\ x + 3z + 2w &= 3 \\ y + z + 5w &= 6 \end{aligned}$

## ■ APPLICATIONS

**87. Astronomy.** Astronomers have determined the number of stars in a small region of the universe to be 2,880,968 classified as red dwarfs, yellow, and blue stars. For every blue star there are 120 red dwarfs; for every red dwarf there are 3000 yellow stars. Determine the number of stars by type in that region of the universe.

**88. Orange Juice.** Orange juice producers use three varieties of oranges: Hamlin, Valencia, and navel. They want to make a juice mixture to sell at $3.00 per gallon. The price per gallon of each variety of juice is $2.50, $3.40, and $2.80, respectively. To maintain their quality standards, they use the same amount of Valencia and navel oranges. Determine the quantity of each juice used to produce 1 gallon of mixture.

**Exercises 89 and 90 rely on a selection of Subway sandwiches whose nutrition information is given in the table below. Suppose you are going to eat only Subway sandwiches for a week (seven days) for lunch and dinner (a total of 14 meals).**

| SANDWICH | CALORIES | FAT (g) | CARBOHYDRATES (g) | PROTEIN (g) |
|---|---|---|---|---|
| Mediterranean chicken | 350 | 18 | 17 | 36 |
| 6-inch tuna | 430 | 19 | 46 | 20 |
| 6-inch roast beef | 290 | 5 | 45 | 19 |
| Turkey–bacon wrap | 430 | 27 | 20 | 34 |

www.subway.com

**89. Diet.** Your goal is a low-fat diet consisting of 526 grams of carbohydrates, 168 grams of fat, and 332 grams of protein. How many of each sandwich would you eat that week to obtain this goal?

**90. Diet.** Your goal is a low-carb diet consisting of 5180 calories, 335 grams of carbohydrates, and 263 grams of fat. How many of each sandwich would you eat that week to obtain this goal?

**Exercises 91 and 92 involve vertical motion and the effect of gravity on an object.**

Because of gravity, an object that is projected upward will eventually reach a maximum height and then fall to the ground. The equation that relates the height $h$ of a projectile $t$ seconds after it is projected upward is given by

$$h = \frac{1}{2}at^2 + v_0t + h_0$$

where $a$ is the acceleration due to gravity, $h_0$ is the initial height of the object at time $t = 0$, and $v_0$ is the initial velocity of the object at time $t = 0$. Note that a projectile follows the path of a parabola opening down, so $a < 0$.

**91. Vertical Motion.** An object is thrown upward, and the table below depicts the height of the ball $t$ seconds after the projectile is released. Find the initial height, initial velocity, and acceleration due to gravity.

| t (SECONDS) | HEIGHT (FEET) |
|---|---|
| 1 | 34 |
| 2 | 36 |
| 3 | 6 |

**92. Vertical Motion.** An object is thrown upward, and the table below depicts the height of the ball $t$ seconds after the projectile is released. Find the initial height, initial velocity, and acceleration due to gravity.

| t (SECONDS) | HEIGHT (FEET) |
|---|---|
| 1 | 54 |
| 2 | 66 |
| 3 | 46 |

**93. Data Curve-Fitting.** The average number of minutes that a person spends driving a car can be modeled by a quadratic function $y = ax^2 + bx + c$, where $a < 0$ and $15 < x < 65$. The table below gives the average number of minutes a day that a person spends driving a car. Determine a quadratic function that models this quantity.

| AGE | AVERAGE DAILY MINUTES DRIVING |
|---|---|
| 16 | 25 |
| 40 | 64 |
| 65 | 40 |

**94. Data Curve-Fitting.** The average age when a woman gets married has been increasing during the last century. In 1920 the average age was 18.4, in 1960 the average age was 20.3, and in 2002 the average age was 25.30. Find a quadratic function $y = ax^2 + bx + c$, where $a > 0$ and $18 < x < 35$, that models the average age $y$ when a woman gets married as a function of the year $x$ ($x = 0$ corresponds to 1920). What will the average age be in 2010?

**95. Chemistry/Pharmacy.** A pharmacy receives an order for 100 milliliters of 5% hydrogen peroxide solution. The pharmacy has a 1.5% and a 30% solution on hand. A technician will mix the 1.5% and 30% solutions to make the 5% solution. How much of the 1.5% and 30% solutions, respectively, will be needed to fill this order? Round to the nearest milliliter.

**96. Chemistry/Pharmacy.** A pharmacy receives an order for 60 grams of a 0.7% hydrocortisone cream. The pharmacy has 1% and 0.5% hydrocortisone creams as well as a Eucerin cream for use as a base (0% hydrocortisone). The technician must use twice as much 0.5% hydrocortisone cream than the Eucerin base. How much of the 1% and 0.5% hydrocortisone creams and Eucerin cream are needed to fill this order?

**97. Business.** A small company has an assembly line that produces three types of widgets. The basic widget is sold for $12 per unit, the midprice widget for $15 per unit, and the top-of-the-line widget for $18 per unit. The assembly line has a daily capacity of producing 375 widgets that may be sold for a total of $5250. Find the quantity of each type of widget produced on a day when twice as many basic widgets as midprice widgets are produced.

**98. Business.** A small company has an assembly line that produces three types of widgets. The basic widget is sold for $10 per unit, the midprice widget for $12 per unit, and the top-of-the-line widget for $15 per unit. The assembly line has a daily capacity of producing 350 widgets that may be sold for a total of $4600. Find the quantity of each type of widget produced on a day when twice as many top-of-the-line widgets as basic widgets are produced.

**99. Money.** Gary and Ginger decide to place $10,000 of their savings into investments. They put some in a money market account earning 3% interest, some in a mutual fund that has been averaging 7% a year, and some in a stock that rose 10% last year. If they put $3000 more in the money market than in the mutual fund and the mutual fund and stocks have the same growth in the next year as they did in the previous year, they will earn $540 in a year. How much money did they put in each of the three investments?

**100. Money.** Ginger talks Gary into putting less money in the money market and more money in the stock (see Exercise 99). They place $10,000 of their savings into investments. They put some in a money market account earning 3% interest, some in a mutual fund that has been averaging 7% a year, and some in a stock that rose 10% last year. If they put $3000 more in the stock than in the mutual fund and the mutual fund and stock have the same growth in the next year as they did in the previous year, they will earn $840 in a year. How much money did they put in each of the three investments?

**101. Manufacturing.** A company produces three products $x$, $y$, and $z$. Each item of product $x$ requires 20 units of steel, 2 units of plastic, and 1 unit of glass. Each item of product $y$ requires 25 units of steel, 5 units of plastic, and no units of glass. Each item of product $z$ requires 150 units of steel, 10 units of plastic, and 0.5 units of glass. The available amounts of steel, plastic, and glass are 2400, 310, and 28, respectively. How many items of each type can the company produce and utilize all the available raw materials?

**102. Geometry.** Find the values of $a$, $b$, and $c$ such that the graph of the quadratic function $y = ax^2 + bx + c$ passes through the points $(1, 5)$, $(-2, -10)$, and $(0, 4)$.

**103. Ticket Sales.** One hundred students decide to buy tickets to a football game. There are three types of tickets: general admission, reserved, and end zone. Each general admission ticket costs $20, each reserved ticket costs $40, and each end zone ticket costs $15. The students spend a total of $2375 for all the tickets. There are five more reserved tickets than general admission tickets, and 20 more end zone tickets than general admission tickets. How many of each type of ticket were purchased by the students?

**104. Exercise and Nutrition.** Ann would like to exercise one hour per day to burn calories and lose weight. She would like to engage in three activities: walking, step-up exercise, and weight training. She knows she can burn 85 calories walking at a certain pace in 15 minutes, 45 calories doing the step-up exercise in 10 minutes, and 137 calories by weight training for 20 minutes.

   **a.** Determine the number of calories per minute she can burn doing each activity.
   **b.** Suppose she has time to exercise for only one hour (60 minutes). She sets a goal of burning 358 calories in one hour and would like to weight train twice as long as walking. How many minutes must she engage in each exercise to burn the required number of calories in one hour?

**105. Geometry.** The circle given by the equation $x^2 + y^2 + ax + by + c = 0$ passes through the points $(4, 4)$, $(-3, -1)$, and $(1, -3)$. Find $a$, $b$, and $c$.

**106. Geometry.** The circle given by the equation $x^2 + y^2 + ax + by + c = 0$ passes through the points $(0, 7)$, $(6, 1)$, and $(5, 4)$. Find $a$, $b$, and $c$.

# ■CATCH THE MISTAKE

**In Exercises 107–110, explain the mistake that is made.**

**107.** Solve the system of equations using an augmented matrix.

$$y - x + z = 2$$
$$x - 2z + y = -3$$
$$x + y + z = 6$$

**Solution:**

**Step 1:** Write as an augmented matrix.
$$\begin{bmatrix} 1 & -1 & 1 & | & 2 \\ 1 & -2 & 1 & | & -3 \\ 1 & 1 & 1 & | & 6 \end{bmatrix}$$

**Step 2:** Reduce the matrix using Gaussian elimination.
$$\begin{bmatrix} 1 & -1 & 1 & | & 2 \\ 0 & 1 & 0 & | & 5 \\ 0 & 0 & 0 & | & -6 \end{bmatrix}$$

**Step 3:** Identify the solution. Row 3 is inconsistent, so there is no solution.

This is incorrect. The correct answer is $x = 1$, $y = 2$, $z = 3$. What mistake was made?

**108.** Perform the indicated row operations on the matrix.

$$\begin{bmatrix} 1 & -1 & 1 & | & 2 \\ 2 & -3 & 1 & | & 4 \\ 3 & 1 & 2 & | & -6 \end{bmatrix}$$

**a.** $R_2 - 2R_1 \rightarrow R_2$
**b.** $R_3 - 3R_1 \rightarrow R_3$

**Solution:**

**a.**
$$\begin{bmatrix} 1 & -1 & 1 & | & 2 \\ 0 & -3 & 1 & | & 4 \\ 3 & 1 & 2 & | & -6 \end{bmatrix}$$

**b.**
$$\begin{bmatrix} 1 & -1 & 1 & | & 2 \\ 2 & -3 & 1 & | & 4 \\ 0 & 1 & 2 & | & -6 \end{bmatrix}$$

This is incorrect. What mistake was made?

**109.** Solve the system of equations using an augmented matrix.

$$3x - 2y + z = -1$$
$$x + y - z = 3$$
$$2x - y + 3z = 0$$

**Solution:**

**Step 1:** Write the system as an augmented matrix.
$$\begin{bmatrix} 3 & -2 & 1 & | & -1 \\ 1 & 1 & -1 & | & 3 \\ 2 & -1 & 3 & | & 0 \end{bmatrix}$$

**Step 2:** Reduce the matrix using Gaussian elimination.
$$\begin{bmatrix} 1 & 0 & 0 & | & 1 \\ 0 & 1 & 0 & | & 2 \\ 0 & 0 & 1 & | & 0 \end{bmatrix}$$

**Step 3:** Identify the answer: Row 3 is inconsistent $1 = 0$, therefore there is no solution.

This is incorrect. What mistake was made?

**110.** Solve the system of equations using an augmented matrix.

$$x + 3y + 2z = 4$$
$$3x + 10y + 9z = 17$$
$$2x + 7y + 7z = 17$$

**Solution:**

**Step 1:** Write the system as an augmented matrix.
$$\begin{bmatrix} 1 & 3 & 2 & | & 4 \\ 3 & 10 & 9 & | & 17 \\ 2 & 7 & 7 & | & 17 \end{bmatrix}$$

**Step 2:** Reduce the matrix using Gaussian elimination.
$$\begin{bmatrix} 1 & 0 & -7 & | & -11 \\ 0 & 1 & 3 & | & 5 \\ 0 & 0 & 0 & | & 4 \end{bmatrix}$$

**Step 3:** Identify the answer: Infinitely many solutions.
$$x = 7t - 11$$
$$y = -3t + 5$$
$$z = t$$

This is incorrect. What mistake was made?

# ■CONCEPTUAL

**In Exercises 111–118, determine whether each of the following statements is true or false:**

**111.** A system of equations represented by a nonsquare coefficient matrix cannot have a unique solution.

**112.** The procedure for Gaussian elimination can be used only for a system of linear equations represented by a square matrix.

**113.** A system of linear equations represented by a square coefficient matrix that has a unique solution has a reduced matrix with 1s along the main diagonal and 0s above and below the 1s.

**114.** A system of linear equations represented by a square coefficient matrix with an all-zero row has infinitely many solutions.

**115.** When a system of linear equations is represented by a square augmented matrix, the system of equations always has a unique solution.

**116.** Gauss–Jordan elimination produces a matrix in reduced row–echelon form.

**117.** An inconsistent system of linear equations has infinitely many solutions.

**118.** Every system of linear equations with a unique solution is represented by an augmented matrix of order $n \times (n + 1)$. (Assume no two rows are identical.)

**CHALLENGE**

**119.** A fourth-degree polynomial $f(x) = ax^4 + bx^3 + cx^2 + dx + k$, with $a < 0$, can be used to represent the data on the number of deaths per year due to lightning strikes (assume 1999 corresponds to $x = 0$).

Use the data below to determine $a$, $b$, $c$, $d$, and $k$.

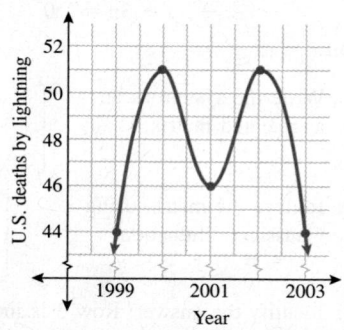

**120.** A copy machine accepts nickels, dimes, and quarters. After one hour, it holds 30 coins total, and their value is $4.60. How many nickels, quarters, and dimes are in the machine?

**121.** A ferry goes down a river from city $A$ to city $B$ in 5 hours. The return trip takes 7 hours. How long will a canoe take to make the trip from $A$ to $B$ if it moves at the river speed?

**122.** Solve the system of equations.

$$\frac{3}{x} - \frac{4}{y} + \frac{6}{z} = 1$$

$$\frac{9}{x} + \frac{8}{y} - \frac{12}{z} = 3$$

$$\frac{9}{x} - \frac{4}{y} + \frac{12}{z} = 4$$

**123.** The sides of a triangle are formed by the lines $x - y = -3$, $3x + 4y = 5$, and $6x + y = 17$. Find the vertices of the triangle.

**124.** A winery has three barrels, $A$, $B$, and $C$, containing mixtures of three different wines, $w_1$, $w_2$, and $w_3$. In barrel $A$, the wines are in the ratio 1:2:3. In barrel $B$, the wines are in the ratio 3:5:7. In barrel $C$, the wines are in the ratio 3:7:9. How much wine must be taken from each barrel to get a mixture containing 17 liters of $w_1$, 35 liters of $w_2$, and 47 liters of $w_3$?

**TECHNOLOGY**

**125.** In Exercise 57, you were asked to solve this system of equations using an augmented matrix.

$$\begin{aligned} x - z - y &= 10 \\ 2x - 3y + z &= -11 \\ y - x + z &= -10 \end{aligned}$$

A graphing calculator or graphing utility can be used to solve systems of linear equations by entering the coefficients of the matrix. Solve this system and confirm your answer with the calculator's answer.

**126.** In Exercise 58, you were asked to solve this system of equations using an augmented matrix.

$$\begin{aligned} 2x + z + y &= -3 \\ 2y - z + x &= 0 \\ x + y + 2z &= 5 \end{aligned}$$

A graphing calculator or graphing utility can be use to solve systems of linear equations by entering the coefficients of the matrix. Solve this system and confirm your answer with the calculator's answer.

**In Exercises 127 and 128, you are asked to model a set of three points with a quadratic function $y = ax^2 + bx + c$ and determine the quadratic function.**

**a.** Set up a system of equations, use a graphing utility or graphing calculator to solve the system by entering the coefficients of the augmented matrix.

**b.** Use the graphing calculator commands $\boxed{\text{STAT}}$ $\boxed{\text{QuadReg}}$ to model the data using a quadratic function. Round your answers to two decimal places.

**127.** $(-6, -8)$, $(2, 7)$, $(7, 1)$

**128.** $(-9, 20)$, $(2, -18)$, $(11, 16)$

# ▪PREVIEW TO CALCULUS

In calculus, when solving systems of linear differential equations with initial conditions, the solution of a system of linear equations is required. In Exercises 129–132, solve each system of equations.

**129.** $\begin{aligned} c_1 + c_2 &= 0 \\ c_1 + 5c_2 &= -3 \end{aligned}$

**130.** $\begin{aligned} 3c_1 + 3c_2 &= 0 \\ 2c_1 + 3c_2 &= 0 \end{aligned}$

**131.** $\begin{aligned} 2c_1 + 2c_2 + 2c_3 &= 0 \\ 2c_1 \quad\quad - 2c_3 &= 2 \\ c_1 - c_2 + c_3 &= 6 \end{aligned}$

**132.** $\begin{aligned} c_1 \quad\quad + c_4 &= 1 \\ c_3 &= 1 \\ c_2 + 3c_4 &= 1 \\ c_1 - 2c_3 &= 1 \end{aligned}$

---

## SECTION
## 8.4 MATRIX ALGEBRA

### SKILLS OBJECTIVES

- Use equality of matrices.
- Add and subtract matrices.
- Perform scalar multiplication.
- Multiply two matrices.
- Write a system of linear equations as a matrix equation.
- Find the inverse of a square matrix.
- Solve systems of linear equations using inverse matrices.

### CONCEPTUAL OBJECTIVES

- Understand what is meant by equal matrices.
- Understand why multiplication of some matrices is undefined.
- Realize that matrix multiplication is *not* commutative.
- Visualize a system of linear equations as a matrix equation.
- Understand that only a square matrix can have an inverse.
- Realize that not every square matrix has an inverse.

## Equality of Matrices

In Section 8.3, we defined a matrix with $m$ rows and $n$ columns to have order $m \times n$.

$$A = \begin{bmatrix} a_{11} & a_{12} & \cdots & a_{1n} \\ a_{21} & a_{22} & \cdots & a_{2n} \\ \vdots & \vdots & \cdots & \vdots \\ a_{m1} & a_{m2} & \cdots & a_{mn} \end{bmatrix}$$

Capital letters are used to represent (or name) a matrix, and lowercase letters are used to represent the entries (elements) of the matrix. The subscripts are used to denote the location (row/column) of each entry. The order of a matrix is often written as a subscript of the matrix name: $A_{m \times n}$. Other words like "size" and "dimension" are used as synonyms of "order." Matrices are a convenient way to represent data.

There is an entire field of study called **matrix algebra** that treats matrices similarly to functions and variables in traditional algebra. This section serves as an introduction to matrix algebra. It is important to pay special attention to the *order* of a matrix, because it determines whether certain operations are defined.

Two matrices are equal if and only if they have the same order, $m \times n$, and all of their corresponding entries are equal.

---

**DEFINITION**   **Equality of Matrices**

Two matrices, $A$ and $B$, are **equal**, written as $A = B$, if and only if *both* of the following are true:

- $A$ and $B$ have the same order $m \times n$.
- Every pair of corresponding entries is equal: $a_{ij} = b_{ij}$ for all $i = 1, 2, \ldots, m$ and $j = 1, 2, \ldots, n$.

---

**EXAMPLE 1**   **Equality of Matrices**

Referring to the definition of equality of matrices, find the indicated entries.

$$\begin{bmatrix} a_{11} & a_{12} & a_{13} \\ a_{21} & a_{22} & a_{23} \\ a_{31} & a_{32} & a_{33} \end{bmatrix} = \begin{bmatrix} 2 & -7 & 1 \\ 0 & 5 & -3 \\ -1 & 8 & 9 \end{bmatrix}$$

Find the main diagonal entries: $a_{11}$, $a_{22}$, and $a_{33}$.

**Solution:**

Since the matrices are equal, their corresponding entries are equal.

$\boxed{a_{11} = 2}$   $\boxed{a_{22} = 5}$   $\boxed{a_{33} = 9}$

## Matrix Addition and Subtraction

Two matrices, $A$ and $B$, can be added or subtracted only if they have the *same order*. Suppose $A$ and $B$ are both of order $m \times n$; then the *sum $A + B$* is found by adding corresponding entries, or taking $a_{ij} + b_{ij}$. The *difference $A - B$* is found by subtracting the entries in $B$ from the corresponding entries in $A$, or finding $a_{ij} - b_{ij}$.

---

**DEFINITION**   **Matrix Addition and Matrix Subtraction**

If $A$ is an $m \times n$ matrix and $B$ is an $m \times n$ matrix, then their **sum** $A + B$ is an $m \times n$ matrix whose entries are given by

$$a_{ij} + b_{ij}$$

and their **difference** $A - B$ is an $m \times n$ matrix whose entries are given by

$$a_{ij} - b_{ij}$$

## EXAMPLE 2   Adding and Subtracting Matrices

Given that $A = \begin{bmatrix} -1 & 3 & 4 \\ -5 & 2 & 0 \end{bmatrix}$ and $B = \begin{bmatrix} 2 & 1 & -3 \\ 0 & -5 & 4 \end{bmatrix}$, find:

**a.** $A + B$     **b.** $A - B$

**Solution:**

Since $A_{2\times 3}$ and $B_{2\times 3}$ have the same order, they can be added or subtracted.

**a.** Write the sum.

$$A + B = \begin{bmatrix} -1 & 3 & 4 \\ -5 & 2 & 0 \end{bmatrix} + \begin{bmatrix} 2 & 1 & -3 \\ 0 & -5 & 4 \end{bmatrix}$$

Add the corresponding entries.

$$= \begin{bmatrix} -1+2 & 3+1 & 4+(-3) \\ -5+0 & 2+(-5) & 0+4 \end{bmatrix}$$

Simplify.

$$= \begin{bmatrix} 1 & 4 & 1 \\ -5 & -3 & 4 \end{bmatrix}$$

**b.** Write the difference.

$$A - B = \begin{bmatrix} -1 & 3 & 4 \\ -5 & 2 & 0 \end{bmatrix} - \begin{bmatrix} 2 & 1 & -3 \\ 0 & -5 & 4 \end{bmatrix}$$

Subtract the corresponding entries.

$$= \begin{bmatrix} -1-2 & 3-1 & 4-(-3) \\ -5-0 & 2-(-5) & 0-4 \end{bmatrix}$$

Simplify.

$$= \begin{bmatrix} -3 & 2 & 7 \\ -5 & 7 & -4 \end{bmatrix}$$

■ **YOUR TURN** Perform the indicated matrix operations, if possible.

$$A = \begin{bmatrix} -4 & 0 \\ 1 & 2 \end{bmatrix} \quad B = \begin{bmatrix} 2 & 3 \\ -4 & 0 \end{bmatrix} \quad C = [2 \quad 9 \quad 5 \quad -1] \quad D = \begin{bmatrix} 0 \\ -3 \\ 4 \\ 2 \end{bmatrix}$$

    **a.** $B - A$     **b.** $C + D$     **c.** $A + B$     **d.** $A + D$

It is important to note that only matrices of the same order can be added or subtracted. For example, if $A = \begin{bmatrix} -1 & 3 & 4 \\ -5 & 2 & 0 \end{bmatrix}$ and $B = \begin{bmatrix} 5 & -3 \\ 12 & 1 \end{bmatrix}$, the sum and difference of these matrices are undefined because $A_{2\times 3}$ and $B_{2\times 2}$ do not have the same order.

A matrix whose entries are all equal to 0 is called a **zero matrix**, denoted **0**. The following are examples of zero matrices:

$2 \times 2$ square zero matrix     $\begin{bmatrix} 0 & 0 \\ 0 & 0 \end{bmatrix}$

$3 \times 2$ zero matrix     $\begin{bmatrix} 0 & 0 \\ 0 & 0 \\ 0 & 0 \end{bmatrix}$

$1 \times 4$ zero matrix     $[0 \quad 0 \quad 0 \quad 0]$

If $A$, an $m \times n$ matrix, is added to the $m \times n$ zero matrix, the result is $A$.

$$A + 0 = A$$

**Technology Tip**

Enter the matrices as $A$ and $B$.

[A]
    [[-1 3 4]
     [-5 2 0]]

[B]
    [[2 1 -3]
     [0 -5 4]]

Now enter $[A] + [B]$ and $[A] - [B]$.

[A]+[B]
    [[1 4 1]
     [-5 -3 4]]
[A]-[B]
    [[-3 2 7]
     [-5 7 -4]]

■ **Answer:**

**a.** $\begin{bmatrix} 6 & 3 \\ -5 & -2 \end{bmatrix}$     **b.** not defined

**c.** $\begin{bmatrix} -2 & 3 \\ -3 & 2 \end{bmatrix}$     **d.** not defined

**Study Tip**

Only matrices of the same order can be added or subtracted.

For example,

$$\begin{bmatrix} 1 & -3 \\ 2 & 5 \end{bmatrix} + \begin{bmatrix} 0 & 0 \\ 0 & 0 \end{bmatrix} = \begin{bmatrix} 1 & -3 \\ 2 & 5 \end{bmatrix}$$

Because of this result, an $m \times n$ zero matrix is called the **additive identity** for $m \times n$ matrices. Similarly, for any matrix $A$, there exists an **additive inverse**, $-A$, such that each entry of $-A$ is the negative of the corresponding entry of $A$.

For example, $A = \begin{bmatrix} 1 & -3 \\ 2 & 5 \end{bmatrix}$ and $-A = \begin{bmatrix} -1 & 3 \\ -2 & -5 \end{bmatrix}$, and adding these two matrices results in a zero matrix: $A + (-A) = \mathbf{0}$.

The same properties that hold for adding real numbers also hold for adding matrices, provided that addition of matrices is defined.

### PROPERTIES OF MATRIX ADDITION

If $A$, $B$, and $C$ are all $m \times n$ matrices and $\mathbf{0}$ is the $m \times n$ zero matrix, then the following are true:

**Commutative property:** $\qquad A + B = B + A$

**Associative property:** $\qquad (A + B) + C = A + (B + C)$

**Additive identity property:** $\qquad A + \mathbf{0} = A$

**Additive inverse property:** $\qquad A + (-A) = \mathbf{0}$

## Scalar and Matrix Multiplication

There are two types of multiplication involving matrices: *scalar multiplication* and *matrix multiplication*. A **scalar** is any real number. *Scalar multiplication* is the multiplication of a matrix by a scalar, or real number, and is defined for all matrices. *Matrix multiplication* is the multiplication of two matrices and is defined only for certain pairs of matrices, depending on the order of each matrix.

## Scalar Multiplication

To multiply a matrix $A$ by a scalar $k$, multiply every entry in $A$ by $k$.

$$3\begin{bmatrix} -1 & 0 & 4 \\ 7 & 5 & -2 \end{bmatrix} = \begin{bmatrix} 3(-1) & 3(0) & 3(4) \\ 3(7) & 3(5) & 3(-2) \end{bmatrix} = \begin{bmatrix} -3 & 0 & 12 \\ 21 & 15 & -6 \end{bmatrix}$$

Here, the scalar is $k = 3$.

### DEFINITION    Scalar Multiplication

If $A$ is an $m \times n$ matrix and $k$ is any real number, then their product $kA$ is an $m \times n$ matrix whose entries are given by

$$ka_{ij}$$

In other words, every entry $a_{ij}$ of $A$ is multiplied by $k$.

In general, uppercase letters are used to denote a matrix and lowercase letters are used to denote scalars. Notice that the elements of each matrix are also represented with lowercase letters, since they are real numbers.

### EXAMPLE 3    Multiplying a Matrix by a Scalar

Given that $A = \begin{bmatrix} -1 & 2 \\ -3 & 4 \end{bmatrix}$ and $B = \begin{bmatrix} 0 & 1 \\ -2 & 3 \end{bmatrix}$, perform:

**a.** $2A$       **b.** $-3B$       **c.** $2A - 3B$

**Solution (a):**

Write the scalar multiplication.

$$2A = 2\begin{bmatrix} -1 & 2 \\ -3 & 4 \end{bmatrix}$$

Multiply all entries of $A$ by 2.

$$2A = \begin{bmatrix} 2(-1) & 2(2) \\ 2(-3) & 2(4) \end{bmatrix}$$

Simplify.

$$2A = \begin{bmatrix} -2 & 4 \\ -6 & 8 \end{bmatrix}$$

**Solution (b):**

Write the scalar multiplication.

$$-3B = -3\begin{bmatrix} 0 & 1 \\ -2 & 3 \end{bmatrix}$$

Multiply all entries of $B$ by $-3$.

$$-3B = \begin{bmatrix} -3(0) & -3(1) \\ -3(-2) & -3(3) \end{bmatrix}$$

Simplify.

$$-3B = \begin{bmatrix} 0 & -3 \\ 6 & -9 \end{bmatrix}$$

**Solution (c):**

Add the results of parts (a) and (b).

$$2A - 3B = 2A + (-3B)$$

$$2A - 3B = \begin{bmatrix} -2 & 4 \\ -6 & 8 \end{bmatrix} + \begin{bmatrix} 0 & -3 \\ 6 & -9 \end{bmatrix}$$

Add the corresponding entries.

$$2A - 3B = \begin{bmatrix} -2+0 & 4+(-3) \\ -6+6 & 8+(-9) \end{bmatrix}$$

Simplify.

$$2A - 3B = \begin{bmatrix} -2 & 1 \\ 0 & -1 \end{bmatrix}$$

■ **YOUR TURN**  For the matrices $A$ and $B$ given in Example 3, find $-5A + 2B$.

***Technology Tip***

Enter matrices as $A$ and $B$.

```
[A]
          [[-1 2]
           [-3 4]]
[B]
          [[0 1]
           [-2 3]]
```

Now enter $2A$, $-3B$, $2A - 3B$.

```
2[A]
          [[-2 4]
           [-6 8]]
-3[B]
          [[0 -3]
           [6 -9]]
■
```

```
2[A]-3[B]
          [[-2 1 ]
           [0 -1]]
■
```

■ **Answer:**
$$-5A + 2B = \begin{bmatrix} 5 & -8 \\ 11 & -14 \end{bmatrix}$$

## Matrix Multiplication

Scalar multiplication is straightforward in that it is defined for all matrices and is performed by multiplying every entry in the matrix by the scalar. Addition of matrices is also an entry-by-entry operation. *Matrix multiplication*, on the other hand, is not as straightforward in that we *do not multiply the corresponding entries* and it is not defined for all matrices. Matrices are multiplied using a row-by-column method.

***Study Tip***

When we multiply matrices, we *do not* multiply corresponding entries.

Before we even try to find the product $AB$ of two matrices $A$ and $B$, we first have to determine whether the product is defined. For the product $AB$ to exist, **the number of columns in the first matrix $A$ must equal the number of rows in the second matrix $B$**. In other words, if the matrix $A_{m \times n}$ has $m$ rows and $n$ columns and the matrix $B_{n \times p}$ has $n$ rows and $p$ columns, then the product $(AB)_{m \times p}$ is defined and has $m$ rows and $p$ columns.

$$
\begin{array}{cccc}
\text{Matrix:} & A & B & AB \\
\text{Order:} & m \times n & n \times p & m \times p
\end{array}
$$

Equal

Order of $AB$

### EXAMPLE 4 Determining Whether the Product of Two Matrices Is Defined

Given the matrices

$$
A = \begin{bmatrix} 1 & -2 & 0 \\ 5 & -1 & 3 \end{bmatrix} \quad B = \begin{bmatrix} 2 & 3 \\ 0 & 7 \\ 4 & 9 \end{bmatrix} \quad C = \begin{bmatrix} 6 & -1 \\ 5 & 2 \end{bmatrix} \quad D = \begin{bmatrix} -3 & -2 \end{bmatrix}
$$

state whether each of the following products exists. If the product exists, state the order of the product matrix.

**a.** $AB$    **b.** $AC$    **c.** $BC$    **d.** $CD$    **e.** $DC$

**Solution:**

Label the order of each matrix: $A_{2 \times 3}$, $B_{3 \times 2}$, $C_{2 \times 2}$, and $D_{1 \times 2}$.

**a.** $AB$ is defined, because $A$ has 3 columns and $B$ has 3 rows.      $A_{2 \times 3} B_{3 \times 2}$
     $AB$ is order $\boxed{2 \times 2}$ .                                        $(AB)_{2 \times 2}$

**b.** $AC$ is $\boxed{\text{not defined}}$ , because $A$ has 3 columns and $C$ has 2 rows.

**c.** $BC$ is defined, because $B$ has 2 columns and $C$ has 2 rows.      $B_{3 \times 2} C_{2 \times 2}$
     $BC$ is order $\boxed{3 \times 2}$ .                                        $(BC)_{3 \times 2}$

**d.** $CD$ is $\boxed{\text{not defined}}$ , because $C$ has 2 columns and $D$ has 1 row.

**e.** $DC$ is defined, because $D$ has 2 columns and $C$ has 2 rows.      $D_{1 \times 2} C_{2 \times 2}$
     $DC$ is order $\boxed{1 \times 2}$ .                                        $(DC)_{1 \times 2}$

Notice that in part (d) we found that $CD$ is not defined, but in part (e) we found that $DC$ is defined. **Matrix multiplication is not commutative**. Therefore, the order in which matrices are multiplied is important in determining whether the product is defined or undefined. For the product of two matrices to exist, the number of *columns* in the *first* matrix $A$ must equal the number of *rows* in the *second* matrix $B$.

■ **YOUR TURN** For the matrices given in Example 4, state whether the following products exist. If the product exists, state the order of the product matrix.

     **a.** $DA$    **b.** $CB$    **c.** $BA$

Now that we can determine whether a product of two matrices is defined and, if so, what the order of the resulting product is, let us turn our attention to how to multiply two matrices.

## DEFINITION  Matrix Multiplication

If $A$ is an $m \times n$ matrix and $B$ is an $n \times p$ matrix, then their product $AB$ is an $m \times p$ matrix whose entries are given by

$$(ab)_{ij} = a_{i1}b_{1j} + a_{i2}b_{2j} + \cdots + a_{in}b_{nj}$$

In other words, the entry $(ab)_{ij}$, which is in the $i$th row and $j$th column of $AB$, is the sum of the products of the corresponding entries in the $i$th row of $A$ and the $j$th column of $B$. Multiply *across* the row and *down* the column.

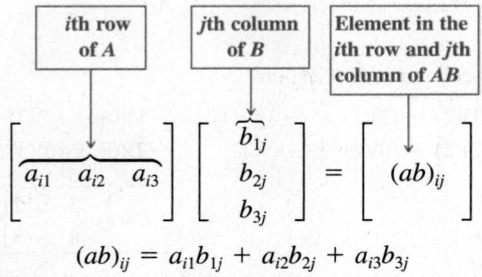

$$(ab)_{ij} = a_{i1}b_{1j} + a_{i2}b_{2j} + a_{i3}b_{3j}$$

## EXAMPLE 5  Multiplication of Two 2 × 2 Matrices

Given $A = \begin{bmatrix} 1 & 2 \\ 3 & 4 \end{bmatrix}$ and $B = \begin{bmatrix} 5 & 6 \\ 7 & 8 \end{bmatrix}$, find $AB$.

### COMMON MISTAKE

Do not multiply entry by entry.

**✪ CORRECT**

Write the product of the two matrices $A$ and $B$.

$$AB = \begin{bmatrix} 1 & 2 \\ 3 & 4 \end{bmatrix}\begin{bmatrix} 5 & 6 \\ 7 & 8 \end{bmatrix}$$

Perform the row-by-column multiplication.

$$AB = \begin{bmatrix} (1)(5) + (2)(7) & (1)(6) + (2)(8) \\ (3)(5) + (4)(7) & (3)(6) + (4)(8) \end{bmatrix}$$

Simplify.

$$AB = \begin{bmatrix} 19 & 22 \\ 43 & 50 \end{bmatrix}$$

**✖ INCORRECT**

Multiply the corresponding entries.

**ERROR**

$$AB \neq \begin{bmatrix} (1)(5) & (2)(6) \\ (3)(7) & (4)(8) \end{bmatrix}$$

*Technology Tip*

Enter the matrices as $A$ and $B$ and calculate $AB$.

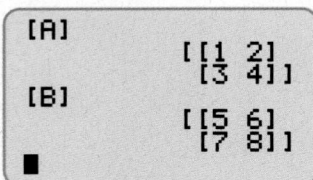

■ **YOUR TURN**  For matrices $A$ and $B$ given in Example 5, find $BA$.

Compare the products obtained in Example 5 and the preceding Your Turn. Note that $AB \neq BA$. Therefore, there is **no commutative property for matrix multiplication**.

■ **Answer:**

$$BA = \begin{bmatrix} 5 & 6 \\ 7 & 8 \end{bmatrix}\begin{bmatrix} 1 & 2 \\ 3 & 4 \end{bmatrix}$$

$$= \begin{bmatrix} 23 & 34 \\ 31 & 46 \end{bmatrix}$$

▪ **Answer:** $AB = \begin{bmatrix} 0 & -5 \\ -1 & -7 \end{bmatrix}$

▶ **EXAMPLE 6   Multiplying Matrices**

For $A = \begin{bmatrix} -1 & 2 & -3 \\ -2 & 0 & 4 \end{bmatrix}$ and $B = \begin{bmatrix} 2 & 0 \\ 1 & 3 \\ -1 & -2 \end{bmatrix}$, find *AB*.

**Solution:**

Since *A* is order $2 \times 3$ and *B* is order $3 \times 2$, the product *AB* is defined and has order $2 \times 2$.
$$A_{2\times3}B_{3\times2} = (AB)_{2\times2}$$

Write the product of the two matrices.
$$AB = \begin{bmatrix} -1 & 2 & -3 \\ -2 & 0 & 4 \end{bmatrix}\begin{bmatrix} 2 & 0 \\ 1 & 3 \\ -1 & -2 \end{bmatrix}$$

Perform the row-by-column multiplication.
$$AB = \begin{bmatrix} (-1)(2) + (2)(1) + (-3)(-1) & (-1)(0) + (2)(3) + (-3)(-2) \\ (-2)(2) + (0)(1) + (4)(-1) & (-2)(0) + (0)(3) + (4)(-2) \end{bmatrix}$$

Simplify.
$$AB = \begin{bmatrix} 3 & 12 \\ -8 & -8 \end{bmatrix}$$

▪ **YOUR TURN** For $A = \begin{bmatrix} 1 & 0 & 2 \\ -3 & -1 & 4 \end{bmatrix}$ and $B = \begin{bmatrix} 0 & -1 \\ 1 & 2 \\ 0 & -2 \end{bmatrix}$, find *AB*.

▶ **EXAMPLE 7   Multiplying Matrices**

For $A = \begin{bmatrix} 1 & 0 & 3 \\ -2 & 5 & -1 \end{bmatrix}$ and $B = \begin{bmatrix} -2 & 0 & 1 \\ -3 & -1 & 4 \\ 0 & 2 & 5 \end{bmatrix}$, find *AB*.

**Solution:**

Since *A* is order $2 \times 3$ and *B* is order $3 \times 3$, the product *AB* is defined and has order $2 \times 3$.
$$A_{2\times3}B_{3\times3} = (AB)_{2\times3}$$

Write the product of the two matrices.
$$AB = \begin{bmatrix} 1 & 0 & 3 \\ -2 & 5 & -1 \end{bmatrix}\begin{bmatrix} -2 & 0 & 1 \\ -3 & -1 & 4 \\ 0 & 2 & 5 \end{bmatrix}$$

Perform the row-by-column multiplication.
$$AB = \begin{bmatrix} (1)(-2) + (0)(-3) + (3)(0) & (1)(0) + (0)(-1) + (3)(2) & (1)(1) + (0)(4) + (3)(5) \\ (-2)(-2) + (5)(-3) + (-1)(0) & (-2)(0) + (5)(-1) + (-1)(2) & (-2)(1) + (5)(4) + (-1)(5) \end{bmatrix}$$

Simplify.
$$AB = \begin{bmatrix} -2 & 6 & 16 \\ -11 & -7 & 13 \end{bmatrix}$$

▪ **Answer: a.** $AB = \begin{bmatrix} 4 & 5 \\ 8 & 10 \\ 12 & 15 \end{bmatrix}$

**b.** does not exist

▪ **YOUR TURN** Given $A = \begin{bmatrix} 1 \\ 2 \\ 3 \end{bmatrix}$ and $B = \begin{bmatrix} 4 & 5 \end{bmatrix}$, find:

**a.** *AB*, if it exists     **b.** *BA*, if it exists

Although we have shown repeatedly that there is no commutative property of multiplication for matrices, matrices do have an associative property of multiplication, as well as a distributive property of multiplication similar to real numbers.

## PROPERTIES OF MATRIX MULTIPLICATION

If $A$, $B$, and $C$ are all matrices for which $AB$, $AC$, $BC$, $A + B$, and $B + C$ are all defined, then the following properties are true:

**Associative property:**   $A(BC) = (AB)C$

**Distributive property:**   $A(B + C) = AB + AC$ or $(A + B)C = AC + BC$

### EXAMPLE 8   Application of Matrix Multiplication

The following table gives fuel and electric requirements per mile associated with gasoline and electric automobiles:

|  | NUMBER OF GALLONS/MILE | NUMBER OF kW-hr/MILE |
|---|---|---|
| Gas car | 0.05 | 0 |
| Hybrid car | 0.02 | 0.1 |
| Electric car | 0 | 0.25 |

The following table gives an average cost for gasoline and electricity:

| Cost per gallon of gasoline | $3.00 |
|---|---|
| Cost per kW-hr of electricity | $0.05 |

a. Let matrix $A$ represent the gasoline and electricity consumption and matrix $B$ represent the costs of gasoline and electricity.
b. Find $AB$ and describe what the entries of the product matrix represent.
c. Assume you drive 12,000 miles per year. What are the yearly costs associated with driving the three types of cars?

**Solution (a):**

$A$ has order $3 \times 2$.

$$A = \begin{bmatrix} 0.05 & 0 \\ 0.02 & 0.1 \\ 0 & 0.25 \end{bmatrix}$$

$B$ has order $2 \times 1$.

$$B = \begin{bmatrix} \$3.00 \\ \$0.05 \end{bmatrix}$$

**Solution (b):**

Find the order of the product matrix $AB$.

$$A_{3\times2}B_{2\times1} = (AB)_{3\times1}$$

$$AB = \begin{bmatrix} 0.05 & 0 \\ 0.02 & 0.1 \\ 0 & 0.25 \end{bmatrix} \begin{bmatrix} \$3.00 \\ \$0.05 \end{bmatrix}$$

Calculate $AB$.

$$= \begin{bmatrix} (0.05)(\$3.00) + (0)(\$0.05) \\ (0.02)(\$3.00) + (0.1)(\$0.05) \\ (0)(\$3.00) + (0.25)(\$0.05) \end{bmatrix}$$

$$AB = \begin{bmatrix} \$0.15 \\ \$0.065 \\ \$0.0125 \end{bmatrix}$$

*Technology Tip*

Enter the matrices as $A$ and $B$ and calculate $AB$.

```
[A]
      [[.05 0  ]
       [.02 .1 ]
       [0   .25]]
[B]
      [[3  ]
       [.05]]
```

```
[A][B]
      [[.15  ]
       [.065 ]
       [.0125]]
```

Interpret the product matrix.

$$AB = \begin{bmatrix} \text{Cost per mile to drive the gas car} \\ \text{Cost per mile to drive the hybrid car} \\ \text{Cost per mile to drive the electric car} \end{bmatrix}$$

**Solution (c):**

Find 12,000AB.

$$12{,}000 \begin{bmatrix} \$0.15 \\ \$0.065 \\ \$0.0125 \end{bmatrix} = \begin{bmatrix} \$1800 \\ \$780 \\ \$150 \end{bmatrix}$$

| GAS/ELECTRIC COSTS PER YEAR ($) | |
|---|---|
| Gas car | 1800 |
| Hybrid car | 780 |
| Electric car | 150 |

# Matrix Equations

**Matrix equations** are another way of writing systems of linear equations.

| WORDS | MATH |
|---|---|
| Start with a matrix equation. | $\begin{bmatrix} 2 & -3 \\ 1 & 5 \end{bmatrix}\begin{bmatrix} x \\ y \end{bmatrix} = \begin{bmatrix} -7 \\ 9 \end{bmatrix}$ |
| Multiply the two matrices on the left. | $\begin{bmatrix} 2x - 3y \\ x + 5y \end{bmatrix} = \begin{bmatrix} -7 \\ 9 \end{bmatrix}$ |
| Apply equality of two matrices. | $2x - 3y = -7$ <br> $x + 5y = \;\;\;9$ |

Let $A$ be a matrix with $m$ rows and $n$ columns, which represents the coefficients in the system. Also, let $X$ be a column matrix of order $n \times 1$ that represents the variables in the system and let $B$ be a column matrix of order $m \times 1$ that represents the constants in the system. Then, a system of linear equations can be written as $AX = B$.

| SYSTEM OF LINEAR EQUATIONS | A | X | B | MATRIX EQUATION: AX = B |
|---|---|---|---|---|
| $3x + 4y = 1$ <br> $x - 2y = 7$ | $\begin{bmatrix} 3 & 4 \\ 1 & -2 \end{bmatrix}$ | $\begin{bmatrix} x \\ y \end{bmatrix}$ | $\begin{bmatrix} 1 \\ 7 \end{bmatrix}$ | $\begin{bmatrix} 3 & 4 \\ 1 & -2 \end{bmatrix}\begin{bmatrix} x \\ y \end{bmatrix} = \begin{bmatrix} 1 \\ 7 \end{bmatrix}$ |
| $x - y + z = 2$ <br> $2x + 2y - 3z = -3$ <br> $x + y + z = 6$ | $\begin{bmatrix} 1 & -1 & 1 \\ 2 & 2 & -3 \\ 1 & 1 & 1 \end{bmatrix}$ | $\begin{bmatrix} x \\ y \\ z \end{bmatrix}$ | $\begin{bmatrix} 2 \\ -3 \\ 6 \end{bmatrix}$ | $\begin{bmatrix} 1 & -1 & 1 \\ 2 & 2 & -3 \\ 1 & 1 & 1 \end{bmatrix}\begin{bmatrix} x \\ y \\ z \end{bmatrix} = \begin{bmatrix} 2 \\ -3 \\ 6 \end{bmatrix}$ |
| $x + y + z = 0$ <br> $3x + 2y - z = 2$ | $\begin{bmatrix} 1 & 1 & 1 \\ 3 & 2 & -1 \end{bmatrix}$ | $\begin{bmatrix} x \\ y \\ z \end{bmatrix}$ | $\begin{bmatrix} 0 \\ 2 \end{bmatrix}$ | $\begin{bmatrix} 1 & 1 & 1 \\ 3 & 2 & -1 \end{bmatrix}\begin{bmatrix} x \\ y \\ z \end{bmatrix} = \begin{bmatrix} 0 \\ 2 \end{bmatrix}$ |

**EXAMPLE 9    Writing a System of Linear Equations as a Matrix Equation**

Write each system of linear equations as a matrix equation.

**a.** $2x - y = 5$
  $-x + 2y = 3$

**b.** $3x - 2y + 4z = 5$
  $y - 3z = -2$
  $7x \quad - z = 1$

**c.** $x_1 - x_2 + 2x_3 - 3 = 0$
  $x_1 + x_2 - 3x_3 + 5 = 0$
  $x_1 - x_2 + x_3 - 2 = 0$

**Solution:**

**a.**
$$\begin{bmatrix} 2 & -1 \\ -1 & 2 \end{bmatrix}\begin{bmatrix} x \\ y \end{bmatrix} = \begin{bmatrix} 5 \\ 3 \end{bmatrix}$$

**b.** Note that all missing terms have 0 coefficients.

$3x - 2y + 4z = 5$
$0x + y - 3z = -2$
$7x + 0y - z = 1$

$$\begin{bmatrix} 3 & -2 & 4 \\ 0 & 1 & -3 \\ 7 & 0 & -1 \end{bmatrix}\begin{bmatrix} x \\ y \\ z \end{bmatrix} = \begin{bmatrix} 5 \\ -2 \\ 1 \end{bmatrix}$$

**c.** Write the constants on the right side of the equal sign.

$x_1 - x_2 + 2x_3 = 3$
$x_1 + x_2 - 3x_3 = -5$
$x_1 - x_2 + x_3 = 2$

$$\begin{bmatrix} 1 & -1 & 2 \\ 1 & 1 & -3 \\ 1 & -1 & 1 \end{bmatrix}\begin{bmatrix} x_1 \\ x_2 \\ x_3 \end{bmatrix} = \begin{bmatrix} 3 \\ -5 \\ 2 \end{bmatrix}$$

■ **YOUR TURN** Write each system of linear equations as a matrix equation.

**a.** $2x + y - 3 = 0$
  $x - y = 5$

**b.** $y - x + z = 7$
  $x - y - z = 2$
  $z - y = -1$

■ **Answer:**
**a.** $\begin{bmatrix} 2 & 1 \\ 1 & -1 \end{bmatrix}\begin{bmatrix} x \\ y \end{bmatrix} = \begin{bmatrix} 3 \\ 5 \end{bmatrix}$

**b.** $\begin{bmatrix} -1 & 1 & 1 \\ 1 & -1 & -1 \\ 0 & -1 & 1 \end{bmatrix}\begin{bmatrix} x \\ y \\ z \end{bmatrix} = \begin{bmatrix} 7 \\ 2 \\ -1 \end{bmatrix}$

# Finding the Inverse of a Square Matrix

Before we discuss solving systems of linear equations in the form $AX = B$, let us first recall how we solve $ax = b$, where $a$ and $b$ are real numbers (not matrices).

| WORDS | MATH |
|---|---|
| Write the linear equation in one variable. | $ax = b$ |
| Multiply both sides by $a^{-1}$ (same as dividing by $a$), provided $a \neq 0$. | $a^{-1}ax = a^{-1}b$ |
| Simplify. | $\underset{1}{\underline{a^{-1}a}}x = a^{-1}b$ |
| | $x = a^{-1}b$ |

Recall that $a^{-1}$, or $\frac{1}{a}$, is the *multiplicative inverse* of $a$ because $a^{-1}a = 1$. And we call 1 the *multiplicative identity*, because any number multiplied by 1 is itself. Before we solve matrix equations, we need to define the *multiplicative identity matrix* and the *multiplicative inverse matrix*.

A square matrix of order $n \times n$ with 1s along the **main diagonal** $(a_{ii})$ and 0s for all other elements is called the **multiplicative identity matrix** $I_n$.

$$I_2 = \begin{bmatrix} 1 & 0 \\ 0 & 1 \end{bmatrix} \qquad I_3 = \begin{bmatrix} 1 & 0 & 0 \\ 0 & 1 & 0 \\ 0 & 0 & 1 \end{bmatrix} \qquad I_4 = \begin{bmatrix} 1 & 0 & 0 & 0 \\ 0 & 1 & 0 & 0 \\ 0 & 0 & 1 & 0 \\ 0 & 0 & 0 & 1 \end{bmatrix}$$

Since a real number multiplied by 1 is itself $(a \cdot 1 = a)$, we expect that a matrix multiplied by the appropriate identity matrix should result in itself. Remember, the order in which matrices are multiplied makes a difference. Notice the appropriate identity matrix may differ, depending on the order of multiplication, but the identity matrix will always be square.

$$A_{m \times n} I_n = A_{m \times n} \quad \text{and} \quad I_m A_{m \times n} = A_{m \times n}$$

### EXAMPLE 10 Multiplying a Matrix by the Multiplicative Identity Matrix $I_n$

For $A = \begin{bmatrix} -2 & 4 & 1 \\ 3 & 7 & -1 \end{bmatrix}$, find $I_2 A$.

**Solution:**

Write the two matrices. $A = \begin{bmatrix} -2 & 4 & 1 \\ 3 & 7 & -1 \end{bmatrix}$ $I_2 = \begin{bmatrix} 1 & 0 \\ 0 & 1 \end{bmatrix}$

Find the product $I_2 A$. $I_2 A = \begin{bmatrix} 1 & 0 \\ 0 & 1 \end{bmatrix} \begin{bmatrix} -2 & 4 & 1 \\ 3 & 7 & -1 \end{bmatrix}$

$$I_2 A = \begin{bmatrix} (1)(-2) + (0)(3) & (1)(4) + (0)(7) & (1)(1) + (0)(-1) \\ (0)(-2) + (1)(3) & (0)(4) + (1)(7) & (0)(1) + (1)(-1) \end{bmatrix}$$

$$I_2 A = \boxed{\begin{bmatrix} -2 & 4 & 1 \\ 3 & 7 & -1 \end{bmatrix}} = A$$

■ **YOUR TURN** For $A$ in Example 10, find $AI_3$.

■ **Answer:**
$AI_3 = \begin{bmatrix} -2 & 4 & 1 \\ 3 & 7 & -1 \end{bmatrix} = A$

The identity matrix $I_n$ will assist us in developing the concept of an *inverse of a square matrix*.

### Study Tip

- Only a *square* matrix can have an inverse.
- Not all square matrices have inverses.

### DEFINITION  Inverse of a Square Matrix

Let $A$ be a square $n \times n$ matrix. If there exists a square $n \times n$ matrix $A^{-1}$ such that

$$AA^{-1} = I_n \quad \text{and} \quad A^{-1}A = I_n$$

then $A^{-1}$, stated as "$A$ inverse," is the **inverse** of $A$.

It is important to note that only a square matrix can have an inverse. Even then, not all square matrices have inverses.

## EXAMPLE 11    Multiplying a Matrix by Its Inverse

Verify that the inverse of $A = \begin{bmatrix} 1 & 3 \\ 2 & 5 \end{bmatrix}$ is $A^{-1} = \begin{bmatrix} -5 & 3 \\ 2 & -1 \end{bmatrix}$.

**Solution:**

Show that $AA^{-1} = I_2$ and $A^{-1}A = I_2$.

Find the product $AA^{-1}$.

$$AA^{-1} = \begin{bmatrix} 1 & 3 \\ 2 & 5 \end{bmatrix}\begin{bmatrix} -5 & 3 \\ 2 & -1 \end{bmatrix}$$

$$= \begin{bmatrix} (1)(-5) + (3)(2) & (1)(3) + (3)(-1) \\ (2)(-5) + (5)(2) & (2)(3) + (5)(-1) \end{bmatrix}$$

$$= \begin{bmatrix} 1 & 0 \\ 0 & 1 \end{bmatrix} = I_2$$

Find the product $A^{-1}A$.

$$A^{-1}A = \begin{bmatrix} -5 & 3 \\ 2 & -1 \end{bmatrix}\begin{bmatrix} 1 & 3 \\ 2 & 5 \end{bmatrix}$$

$$= \begin{bmatrix} (-5)(1) + (3)(2) & (-5)(3) + (3)(5) \\ (2)(1) + (-1)(2) & (2)(3) + (-1)(5) \end{bmatrix}$$

$$= \begin{bmatrix} 1 & 0 \\ 0 & 1 \end{bmatrix} = I_2$$

■ **YOUR TURN** Verify that the inverse of $A = \begin{bmatrix} 1 & 4 \\ 2 & 9 \end{bmatrix}$ is $A^{-1} = \begin{bmatrix} 9 & -4 \\ -2 & 1 \end{bmatrix}$.

**Technology Tip**

Enter the matrices as $A$, and $A^{-1}$ as $B$.

```
[A]
          [[1 3]
           [2 5]]
[B]
          [[-5 3 ]
           [2 -1]]
■
```

Enter $AA^{-1}$ as $AB$, and $A^{-1}$ as $BA$.

```
[A][B]
          [[1 0]
           [0 1]]
[B][A]
          [[1 0]
           [0 1]]
```

■ **Answer:** $AA^{-1} = A^{-1}A = I_2$

Now that we can show that two matrices are inverses of one another, let us describe the process for finding an inverse, if it exists. If an inverse $A^{-1}$ exists, then the matrix $A$ is said to be **nonsingular**. If the inverse does not exist, then the matrix $A$ is said to be **singular**.

Let $A = \begin{bmatrix} 1 & -1 \\ 2 & -3 \end{bmatrix}$ and the inverse be $A^{-1} = \begin{bmatrix} w & x \\ y & z \end{bmatrix}$, where $w$, $x$, $y$, and $z$ are variables to be determined. A matrix and its inverse must satisfy the identity $AA^{-1} = I_2$.

| WORDS | MATH |
|---|---|
| The product of a matrix and its inverse is the identity matrix. | $\begin{bmatrix} 1 & -1 \\ 2 & -3 \end{bmatrix}\begin{bmatrix} w & x \\ y & z \end{bmatrix} = \begin{bmatrix} 1 & 0 \\ 0 & 1 \end{bmatrix}$ |
| Multiply the two matrices on the left. | $\begin{bmatrix} w - y & x - z \\ 2w - 3y & 2x - 3z \end{bmatrix} = \begin{bmatrix} 1 & 0 \\ 0 & 1 \end{bmatrix}$ |
| Equate corresponding matrix elements. | $\begin{array}{cc} w - y = 1 & \quad x - z = 0 \\ 2w - 3y = 0 & \quad 2x - 3z = 1 \end{array}$ and |

Notice that there are two systems of equations, both of which can be solved by several methods (elimination, substitution, or augmented matrices). We will find that $w = 3$, $x = -1$, $y = 2$, and $z = -1$. Therefore, we know the inverse is $A^{-1} = \begin{bmatrix} 3 & -1 \\ 2 & -1 \end{bmatrix}$. But, instead, let us use augmented matrices in order to develop the general procedure.

Write the two systems of equations as two augmented matrices:

$$\begin{array}{cc} \begin{matrix} w & y \end{matrix} & \begin{matrix} x & z \end{matrix} \\ \left[\begin{array}{cc|c} 1 & -1 & 1 \\ 2 & -3 & 0 \end{array}\right] & \left[\begin{array}{cc|c} 1 & -1 & 0 \\ 2 & -3 & 1 \end{array}\right] \end{array}$$

Since the left side is the same for each augmented matrix, we can combine these two matrices into one matrix, thereby simultaneously solving both systems of equations.

$$\begin{bmatrix} 1 & -1 & | & 1 & 0 \\ 2 & -3 & | & 0 & 1 \end{bmatrix}$$

Notice that the right side of the vertical line is the identity matrix $I_2$.

Using Gauss–Jordan elimination, transform the matrix on the left to the identity matrix.

$$\begin{bmatrix} 1 & -1 & | & 1 & 0 \\ 2 & -3 & | & 0 & 1 \end{bmatrix}$$

$R_2 - 2R_1 \rightarrow R_2 \quad \begin{bmatrix} 1 & -1 & | & 1 & 0 \\ 0 & -1 & | & -2 & 1 \end{bmatrix}$

$-R_2 \rightarrow R_2 \quad \begin{bmatrix} 1 & -1 & | & 1 & 0 \\ 0 & 1 & | & 2 & -1 \end{bmatrix}$

$R_1 + R_2 \rightarrow R_1 \quad \begin{bmatrix} 1 & 0 & | & 3 & -1 \\ 0 & 1 & | & 2 & -1 \end{bmatrix}$

The matrix on the right of the vertical line is the inverse $A^{-1} = \begin{bmatrix} 3 & -1 \\ 2 & -1 \end{bmatrix}$.

### FINDING THE INVERSE OF A SQUARE MATRIX

To find the inverse of an $n \times n$ matrix $A$:

**Step 1:** Form the matrix $[A \mid I_n]$.

**Step 2:** Use row operations to transform this entire augmented matrix to $[I_n \mid A^{-1}]$. This is done by applying Gauss–Jordan elimination to reduce $A$ to the identity matrix $I_n$. If this is not possible, then $A$ is a singular matrix and no inverse exists.

**Step 3:** Verify the result by showing that $AA^{-1} = I_n$ and $A^{-1}A = I_n$.

*Technology Tip*

A graphing calculator can be used to find the inverse of $A$. Enter the matrix $A$.

```
[A]
            [[1 2]
             [3 5]]
■
```

To find $A^{-1}$, press [2nd] [MATRIX] [1:[A]] [ENTER] [$x^{-1}$] [ENTER].

```
[A]
            [[1 2]
             [3 5]]
[A]⁻¹
            [[-5 2 ]
             [3  -1]]
```

### ▶ EXAMPLE 12 Finding the Inverse of a 2 × 2 Matrix

Find the inverse of $A = \begin{bmatrix} 1 & 2 \\ 3 & 5 \end{bmatrix}$.

**Solution:**

**STEP 1** Form the matrix $[A \mid I_2]$. $\qquad \begin{bmatrix} 1 & 2 & | & 1 & 0 \\ 3 & 5 & | & 0 & 1 \end{bmatrix}$

**STEP 2** Use row operations to transform $A$ into $I_2$.

$R_2 - 3R_1 \rightarrow R_2 \quad \begin{bmatrix} 1 & 2 & | & 1 & 0 \\ 0 & -1 & | & -3 & 1 \end{bmatrix}$

$-R_2 \rightarrow R_2 \quad \begin{bmatrix} 1 & 2 & | & 1 & 0 \\ 0 & 1 & | & 3 & -1 \end{bmatrix}$

$R_1 - 2R_2 \rightarrow R_1 \quad \begin{bmatrix} 1 & 0 & | & -5 & 2 \\ 0 & 1 & | & 3 & -1 \end{bmatrix}$

Identify the inverse. $\qquad A^{-1} = \begin{bmatrix} -5 & 2 \\ 3 & -1 \end{bmatrix}$

**STEP 3** Check.

$$AA^{-1} = \begin{bmatrix} 1 & 2 \\ 3 & 5 \end{bmatrix}\begin{bmatrix} -5 & 2 \\ 3 & -1 \end{bmatrix} = \begin{bmatrix} 1 & 0 \\ 0 & 1 \end{bmatrix} = I_2$$

$$A^{-1}A = \begin{bmatrix} -5 & 2 \\ 3 & -1 \end{bmatrix}\begin{bmatrix} 1 & 2 \\ 3 & 5 \end{bmatrix} = \begin{bmatrix} 1 & 0 \\ 0 & 1 \end{bmatrix} = I_2$$

■ **YOUR TURN** Find the inverse of $A = \begin{bmatrix} 2 & 3 \\ 5 & 8 \end{bmatrix}$.

■ **Answer:** $A^{-1} = \begin{bmatrix} 8 & -3 \\ -5 & 2 \end{bmatrix}$

This procedure for finding an inverse of a square matrix is used for all square matrices of order $n \times n$. For the special case of a $2 \times 2$ matrix, there is a formula (that will be derived in Exercises 107 and 108) for finding the inverse.

Let $A = \begin{bmatrix} a & b \\ c & d \end{bmatrix}$ represent any $2 \times 2$ matrix; then the inverse matrix is given by

$$A^{-1} = \frac{1}{ad - bc}\begin{bmatrix} d & -b \\ -c & a \end{bmatrix} \quad ad - bc \neq 0$$

The denominator $ad - bc$ is called the *determinant* of the matrix $A$ and will be discussed in Section 8.5.

We found the inverse of $A = \begin{bmatrix} 1 & 2 \\ 3 & 5 \end{bmatrix}$ in Example 12. Let us now find the inverse using this formula.

**WORDS**

Write the formula for $A^{-1}$.

Substitute $a = 1, b = 2, c = 3$, and $d = 5$ into the formula.

Simplify.

**MATH**

$$A^{-1} = \frac{1}{ad - bc}\begin{bmatrix} d & -b \\ -c & a \end{bmatrix}$$

$$A^{-1} = \frac{1}{(1)(5) - (2)(3)}\begin{bmatrix} 5 & -2 \\ -3 & 1 \end{bmatrix}$$

$$A^{-1} = (-1)\begin{bmatrix} 5 & -2 \\ -3 & 1 \end{bmatrix}$$

$$A^{-1} = \begin{bmatrix} -5 & 2 \\ 3 & -1 \end{bmatrix}$$

The result is the same as that we found in Example 12.

**EXAMPLE 13    Finding That No Inverse Exists: Singular Matrix**

Find the inverse of $A = \begin{bmatrix} 1 & -5 \\ -1 & 5 \end{bmatrix}$.

**Solution:**

**STEP 1** Form the matrix $[A \mid I_2]$.

$$\begin{bmatrix} 1 & -5 & | & 1 & 0 \\ -1 & 5 & | & 0 & 1 \end{bmatrix}$$

**STEP 2** Apply row operations to transform $A$ into $I_2$.

$$R_2 + R_1 \rightarrow R_2 \quad \begin{bmatrix} 1 & -5 & | & 1 & 0 \\ 0 & 0 & | & 1 & 1 \end{bmatrix}$$

We cannot convert the left-hand side of the augmented matrix to $I_2$ because of the all-zero row on the left-hand side. Therefore, $\boxed{A \text{ is not invertible}}$; that is, $A$ has no inverse, or $A^{-1}$ does not exist. We say that $A$ is **singular**.

*Study Tip*

If the determinant of a $2 \times 2$ matrix is equal to 0, then its inverse does not exist.

## EXAMPLE 14  Finding the Inverse of a 3 × 3 Matrix

Find the inverse of $A = \begin{bmatrix} 1 & 2 & -1 \\ 0 & 1 & -1 \\ -1 & 0 & -2 \end{bmatrix}$.

**Solution:**

**STEP 1**  Form the matrix $[A \mid I_3]$.

$$\left[\begin{array}{ccc|ccc} 1 & 2 & -1 & 1 & 0 & 0 \\ 0 & 1 & -1 & 0 & 1 & 0 \\ -1 & 0 & -2 & 0 & 0 & 1 \end{array}\right]$$

**STEP 2**  Apply row operations to transform $A$ into $I_3$.

$$R_3 + R_1 \rightarrow R_3 \quad \left[\begin{array}{ccc|ccc} 1 & 2 & -1 & 1 & 0 & 0 \\ 0 & 1 & -1 & 0 & 1 & 0 \\ 0 & 2 & -3 & 1 & 0 & 1 \end{array}\right]$$

$$R_3 - 2R_2 \rightarrow R_3 \quad \left[\begin{array}{ccc|ccc} 1 & 2 & -1 & 1 & 0 & 0 \\ 0 & 1 & -1 & 0 & 1 & 0 \\ 0 & 0 & -1 & 1 & -2 & 1 \end{array}\right]$$

$$-R_3 \rightarrow R_3 \quad \left[\begin{array}{ccc|ccc} 1 & 2 & -1 & 1 & 0 & 0 \\ 0 & 1 & -1 & 0 & 1 & 0 \\ 0 & 0 & 1 & -1 & 2 & -1 \end{array}\right]$$

$$\begin{array}{c} R_2 + R_3 \rightarrow R_2 \\ R_1 + R_3 \rightarrow R_1 \end{array} \quad \left[\begin{array}{ccc|ccc} 1 & 2 & 0 & 0 & 2 & -1 \\ 0 & 1 & 0 & -1 & 3 & -1 \\ 0 & 0 & 1 & -1 & 2 & -1 \end{array}\right]$$

$$R_1 - 2R_2 \rightarrow R_1 \quad \left[\begin{array}{ccc|ccc} 1 & 0 & 0 & 2 & -4 & 1 \\ 0 & 1 & 0 & -1 & 3 & -1 \\ 0 & 0 & 1 & -1 & 2 & -1 \end{array}\right]$$

Identify the inverse.

$$A^{-1} = \begin{bmatrix} 2 & -4 & 1 \\ -1 & 3 & -1 \\ -1 & 2 & -1 \end{bmatrix}$$

**STEP 3**  Check.  $AA^{-1} = \begin{bmatrix} 1 & 2 & -1 \\ 0 & 1 & -1 \\ -1 & 0 & -2 \end{bmatrix}\begin{bmatrix} 2 & -4 & 1 \\ -1 & 3 & -1 \\ -1 & 2 & -1 \end{bmatrix} = \begin{bmatrix} 1 & 0 & 0 \\ 0 & 1 & 0 \\ 0 & 0 & 1 \end{bmatrix} = I_3$

$$A^{-1}A = \begin{bmatrix} 2 & -4 & 1 \\ -1 & 3 & -1 \\ -1 & 2 & -1 \end{bmatrix}\begin{bmatrix} 1 & 2 & -1 \\ 0 & 1 & -1 \\ -1 & 0 & -2 \end{bmatrix} = \begin{bmatrix} 1 & 0 & 0 \\ 0 & 1 & 0 \\ 0 & 0 & 1 \end{bmatrix} = I_3$$

■ **Answer:** $A^{-1} = \begin{bmatrix} 0 & 1 & 1 \\ 1 & -1 & -1 \\ 0 & 2 & 1 \end{bmatrix}$

■ **YOUR TURN**  Find the inverse of $A = \begin{bmatrix} 1 & 1 & 0 \\ -1 & 0 & 1 \\ 2 & 0 & -1 \end{bmatrix}$.

# Solving Systems of Linear Equations Using Matrix Algebra and Inverses of Square Matrices

We can solve systems of linear equations using matrix algebra. We will use a system of three equations and three variables to demonstrate the procedure. However, it can be extended to any square system.

**Linear System of Equations**

$$a_1 x + b_1 y + c_1 z = d_1$$
$$a_2 x + b_2 y + c_2 z = d_2$$
$$a_3 x + b_3 y + c_3 z = d_3$$

**Matrix Form of the System**

$$\underbrace{\begin{bmatrix} a_1 & b_1 & c_1 \\ a_2 & b_2 & c_2 \\ a_3 & b_3 & c_3 \end{bmatrix}}_{A} \underbrace{\begin{bmatrix} x \\ y \\ z \end{bmatrix}}_{X} = \underbrace{\begin{bmatrix} d_1 \\ d_2 \\ d_3 \end{bmatrix}}_{B}$$

Recall that a system of linear equations has a unique solution, no solution, or infinitely many solutions. If a system of $n$ equations in $n$ variables has a unique solution, it can be found using the following procedure:

| WORDS | MATH |
|---|---|
| Write the system of linear equations as a matrix equation. | $A_{n \times n} X_{n \times 1} = B_{n \times 1}$ |
| Multiply both sides of the equation by $A^{-1}$. | $A^{-1}AX = A^{-1}B$ |
| A matrix times its inverse is the identity matrix. | $I_n X = A^{-1}B$ |
| A matrix times the identity matrix is equal to itself. | $X = A^{-1}B$ |

Notice the order in which the right side is multiplied, $X_{n \times 1} = A^{-1}_{n \times n} B_{n \times 1}$, and remember that matrix multiplication is not commutative. Therefore, you multiply both sides of the matrix equation in the same order.

## SOLVING A SYSTEM OF LINEAR EQUATIONS USING MATRIX ALGEBRA: UNIQUE SOLUTION

If a system of linear equations is represented by the matrix equation $AX = B$, where $A$ is a nonsingular square matrix, then the system has a unique solution given by

$$X = A^{-1}B$$

Enter the matrix $A$.

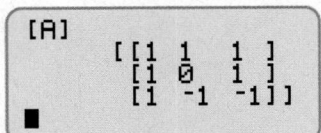

Now use the graphing calculator to find the inverse of $A$, $A^{-1}$.
2nd MATRIX 1:[A] ENTER
$x^{-1}$ ENTER.

```
[[1 1  1 ]
 [1 0  1 ]
 [1 -1 -1]]
[A]⁻¹
 [[.5  0  .5 ]
  [1  -1  0 ]
  [-.5 1  -.5]]
```

To show elements using fractions, press 2nd MATRIX 1:[A] ENTER
$x^{-1}$ MATH 1: *Frac* ENTER
ENTER.

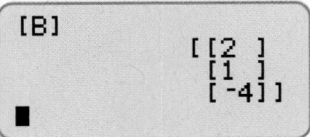

Now enter the matrix $B$:

```
[B]
   [[2 ]
    [1 ]
    [-4]]
■
```

To find $X$ enter $A^{-1}B$, press 2nd
ANS 2nd MATRIX 2:B
ENTER ENTER.

```
Ans[B]
    [[-1]
     [1 ]
     [2 ]]
■
```

The solution to the system is
$x = -1$, $y = 1$, and $z = 2$.

---

▶ **EXAMPLE 15  Solving a System of Linear Equations Using Matrix Algebra**

Solve the system of equations using matrix algebra.

$$\begin{aligned} x + y + z &= 2 \\ x \quad\;\; + z &= 1 \\ x - y - z &= -4 \end{aligned}$$

**Solution:**

Write the system in matrix form.

$$AX = B$$

$$A = \begin{bmatrix} 1 & 1 & 1 \\ 1 & 0 & 1 \\ 1 & -1 & -1 \end{bmatrix} \quad X = \begin{bmatrix} x \\ y \\ z \end{bmatrix} \quad B = \begin{bmatrix} 2 \\ 1 \\ -4 \end{bmatrix}$$

*Find the inverse of A.*

Form the matrix $[A \mid I_3]$.

$$\left[\begin{array}{ccc|ccc} 1 & 1 & 1 & 1 & 0 & 0 \\ 1 & 0 & 1 & 0 & 1 & 0 \\ 1 & -1 & -1 & 0 & 0 & 1 \end{array}\right]$$

$$\begin{array}{c} R_2 - R_1 \to R_2 \\ R_3 - R_1 \to R_3 \end{array} \left[\begin{array}{ccc|ccc} 1 & 1 & 1 & 1 & 0 & 0 \\ 0 & -1 & 0 & -1 & 1 & 0 \\ 0 & -2 & -2 & -1 & 0 & 1 \end{array}\right]$$

$$-R_2 \to R_2 \left[\begin{array}{ccc|ccc} 1 & 1 & 1 & 1 & 0 & 0 \\ 0 & 1 & 0 & 1 & -1 & 0 \\ 0 & -2 & -2 & -1 & 0 & 1 \end{array}\right]$$

$$R_3 + 2R_2 \to R_3 \left[\begin{array}{ccc|ccc} 1 & 1 & 1 & 1 & 0 & 0 \\ 0 & 1 & 0 & 1 & -1 & 0 \\ 0 & 0 & -2 & 1 & -2 & 1 \end{array}\right]$$

$$-\tfrac{1}{2}R_3 \to R_3 \left[\begin{array}{ccc|ccc} 1 & 1 & 1 & 1 & 0 & 0 \\ 0 & 1 & 0 & 1 & -1 & 0 \\ 0 & 0 & 1 & -\frac{1}{2} & 1 & -\frac{1}{2} \end{array}\right]$$

$$R_1 - R_3 \to R_1 \left[\begin{array}{ccc|ccc} 1 & 1 & 0 & \frac{3}{2} & -1 & \frac{1}{2} \\ 0 & 1 & 0 & 1 & -1 & 0 \\ 0 & 0 & 1 & -\frac{1}{2} & 1 & -\frac{1}{2} \end{array}\right]$$

$$R_1 - R_2 \to R_1 \left[\begin{array}{ccc|ccc} 1 & 0 & 0 & \frac{1}{2} & 0 & \frac{1}{2} \\ 0 & 1 & 0 & 1 & -1 & 0 \\ 0 & 0 & 0 & -\frac{1}{2} & 1 & -\frac{1}{2} \end{array}\right]$$

Identify the inverse.

$$A^{-1} = \begin{bmatrix} \frac{1}{2} & 0 & \frac{1}{2} \\ 1 & -1 & 0 \\ -\frac{1}{2} & 1 & -\frac{1}{2} \end{bmatrix}$$

The solution to the system is $X = A^{-1}B$.

$$X = A^{-1}B = \begin{bmatrix} \frac{1}{2} & 0 & \frac{1}{2} \\ 1 & -1 & 0 \\ -\frac{1}{2} & 1 & -\frac{1}{2} \end{bmatrix} \begin{bmatrix} 2 \\ 1 \\ -4 \end{bmatrix}$$

Simplify.

$$X = \begin{bmatrix} x \\ y \\ z \end{bmatrix} = \begin{bmatrix} -1 \\ 1 \\ 2 \end{bmatrix}$$

$$\boxed{x = -1, \, y = 1, \, z = 2}$$

■ **YOUR TURN** Solve the system of equations using matrix algebra.

$$\begin{aligned} x + \; y - z &= 3 \\ y + z &= 1 \\ 2x + 3y + z &= 5 \end{aligned}$$

■ **Answer:** $x = 0, \, y = 2, \, z = -1$

## Cryptography Applications

Cryptography is the practice of hiding information, or secret communication. Let's assume you want to send your ATM PIN code over the Internet, but you don't want hackers to be able to retrieve it. You can represent the PIN code in a matrix and then multiply that PIN matrix by a "key" matrix so that it is encrypted. If the person you send it to has the "inverse key" matrix, he can multiply the encrypted matrix he receives by the inverse key matrix and the result will be the original PIN matrix. Although PIN numbers are typically four digits, we will assume two digits to illustrate the process.

| **WORDS** | **MATH** |
|---|---|
| Suppose the two-digit ATM PIN is 13. | $P = [1 \quad 3]$ |
| Apply any $2 \times 2$ nonsingular matrix as the "key" (encryption) matrix. | $K = \begin{bmatrix} 2 & 3 \\ 5 & 8 \end{bmatrix}$ |
| Multiply the PIN and encryption matrices. | $PK = [1 \quad 3]\begin{bmatrix} 2 & 3 \\ 5 & 8 \end{bmatrix}$ |
| | $= [1(2) + 3(5) \quad 1(3) + 3(8)]$ |
| | $= [17 \quad 27]$ |
| The receiver of the encrypted matrix sees only $[17 \quad 27]$. | |
| The decoding "key" is the inverse matrix $K^{-1}$. | $K^{-1} = \begin{bmatrix} 8 & -3 \\ -5 & 2 \end{bmatrix}$ |

*Study Tip*

$$K = \begin{bmatrix} 2 & 3 \\ 5 & 8 \end{bmatrix}$$

$$K^{-1} = \frac{1}{(2)(8) - (3)(5)}\begin{bmatrix} 8 & -3 \\ -5 & 2 \end{bmatrix}$$

$$= \begin{bmatrix} 8 & -3 \\ -5 & 2 \end{bmatrix}$$

Any receiver who has the decoding key can multiply the received encrypted matrix by the decoding "key" matrix. The result is the original transmitted PIN number.

$$[17 \quad 27]\begin{bmatrix} 8 & -3 \\ -5 & 2 \end{bmatrix} = [17(8) + 27(-5) \quad 17(-3) + 27(2)] = [1 \quad 3]$$

Matrices can be used to represent data. Operations such as equality, addition, subtraction, and scalar multiplication are performed entry by entry. Two matrices can be added or subtracted only if they have the same order. Matrix multiplication, however, requires that the number of columns in the first matrix is equal to the number of rows in the second matrix and is performed using a row-by-column procedure.

### Matrix Multiplication Is Not Commutative: $AB \neq BA$

| OPERATION | ORDER REQUIREMENT |
|---|---|
| Equality | Same: $A_{m \times n} = B_{m \times n}$ |
| Addition | Same: $A_{m \times n} + B_{m \times n}$ |
| Subtraction | Same: $A_{m \times n} - B_{m \times n}$ |
| Scalar multiplication | None: $kA_{m \times n}$ |
| Matrix multiplication | $A_{m \times n} B_{n \times p} = (AB)_{m \times p}$ |

Systems of linear equations can be solved using matrix equations.

| SYSTEM OF LINEAR EQUATIONS | A | X | B | MATRIX EQUATION: $AX = B$ |
|---|---|---|---|---|
| $\begin{aligned} x - y + z &= 2 \\ 2x + 2y - 3z &= -3 \\ x + y + z &= 6 \end{aligned}$ | $\begin{bmatrix} 1 & -1 & 1 \\ 2 & 2 & -3 \\ 1 & 1 & 1 \end{bmatrix}$ | $\begin{bmatrix} x \\ y \\ z \end{bmatrix}$ | $\begin{bmatrix} 2 \\ -3 \\ 6 \end{bmatrix}$ | $\begin{bmatrix} 1 & -1 & 1 \\ 2 & 2 & -3 \\ 1 & 1 & 1 \end{bmatrix} \begin{bmatrix} x \\ y \\ z \end{bmatrix} = \begin{bmatrix} 2 \\ -3 \\ 6 \end{bmatrix}$ |

If this system of linear equations has a unique solution, then the solution is represented by

$$X = A^{-1}B$$

$A^{-1}$ is the inverse of $A$, that is, $AA^{-1} = A^{-1}A = I$, and is found by

$$\left[ A_{n \times n} | I_n \right] \rightarrow \left[ I_n | A_{n \times n}^{-1} \right]$$

■ SKILLS

**In Exercises 1–8, state the order of each matrix.**

**1.** $\begin{bmatrix} -1 & 2 & 4 \\ 7 & -3 & 9 \end{bmatrix}$

**2.** $\begin{bmatrix} 3 & 5 \\ 2 & 6 \\ -1 & -4 \end{bmatrix}$

**3.** $\begin{bmatrix} -4 & 5 \\ 0 & 1 \end{bmatrix}$

**4.** $[-4 \quad 5 \quad 3 \quad 7]$

**5.** $\begin{bmatrix} -3 & 4 & 1 \\ 10 & 8 & 0 \\ -2 & 5 & 7 \end{bmatrix}$

**6.** $\begin{bmatrix} 1 \\ 2 \\ 3 \\ 4 \end{bmatrix}$

**7.** $\begin{bmatrix} -3 & 6 & 0 & 5 \\ 4 & -9 & 2 & 7 \\ 1 & 8 & 3 & 6 \\ 5 & 0 & -4 & 11 \end{bmatrix}$

**8.** $\begin{bmatrix} -1 & 3 & 6 & 9 \\ 2 & 5 & -7 & 8 \end{bmatrix}$

**In Exercises 9–14, solve for the indicated variables.**

9. $\begin{bmatrix} 2 & x \\ y & 3 \end{bmatrix} = \begin{bmatrix} 2 & -5 \\ 1 & 3 \end{bmatrix}$

10. $\begin{bmatrix} -3 & 17 \\ x & y \end{bmatrix} = \begin{bmatrix} -3 & 17 \\ 10 & 12 \end{bmatrix}$

11. $\begin{bmatrix} x+y & 3 \\ x-y & 9 \end{bmatrix} = \begin{bmatrix} -5 & z \\ -1 & 9 \end{bmatrix}$

12. $\begin{bmatrix} x & -4 \\ y & 7 \end{bmatrix} = \begin{bmatrix} 2+y & -4 \\ 5 & 7 \end{bmatrix}$

13. $\begin{bmatrix} 3 & 4 \\ 0 & 12 \end{bmatrix} = \begin{bmatrix} x-y & 4 \\ 0 & 2y+x \end{bmatrix}$

14. $\begin{bmatrix} 9 & 2b+1 \\ -5 & 16 \end{bmatrix} = \begin{bmatrix} a^2 & 9 \\ 2a+1 & b^2 \end{bmatrix}$

**In Exercises 15–24, perform the indicated operations for each expression, if possible.**

$$A = \begin{bmatrix} -1 & 3 & 0 \\ 2 & 4 & 1 \end{bmatrix} \quad B = \begin{bmatrix} 0 & 2 & 1 \\ 3 & -2 & 4 \end{bmatrix} \quad C = \begin{bmatrix} 0 & 1 \\ 2 & -1 \\ 3 & 1 \end{bmatrix} \quad D = \begin{bmatrix} 2 & -3 \\ 0 & 1 \\ 4 & -2 \end{bmatrix}$$

15. $A + B$  16. $C + D$  17. $C - D$  18. $A - B$  19. $B + C$

20. $A + D$  21. $D - B$  22. $C - A$  23. $2A + 3B$  24. $2B - 3A$

**In Exercises 25–44, perform the indicated operations for each expression, if possible.**

$$A = \begin{bmatrix} 1 & 2 & -1 \\ 0 & 3 & 1 \\ 5 & 0 & -2 \end{bmatrix} \quad B = [2 \quad 0 \quad -3] \quad C = \begin{bmatrix} -1 & 7 & 2 \\ 3 & 0 & 1 \end{bmatrix} \quad D = \begin{bmatrix} 3 & 0 \\ 1 & -1 \\ 2 & 5 \end{bmatrix}$$

$$E = \begin{bmatrix} -1 & 0 & 1 \\ 2 & 1 & 4 \\ -3 & 1 & 5 \end{bmatrix} \quad F = \begin{bmatrix} 1 \\ 0 \\ -1 \end{bmatrix} \quad G = \begin{bmatrix} 1 & 2 \\ 3 & 4 \end{bmatrix}$$

25. $CD$  26. $BF$  27. $DC$  28. $(A+E)D$

29. $DG$  30. $2A + 3E$  31. $GD$  32. $ED + C$

33. $-4BD$  34. $-3ED$  35. $B(A+E)$  36. $GC + 5C$

37. $FB + 5A$  38. $A^2$  39. $G^2 + 5G$  40. $C \cdot (2E)$

41. $(2E) \cdot F$  42. $CA + 5C$  43. $DF$  44. $AE$

**In Exercises 45–50, determine whether $B$ is the multiplicative inverse of $A$ using $AA^{-1} = I$.**

45. $A = \begin{bmatrix} 8 & -11 \\ -5 & 7 \end{bmatrix}$  $B = \begin{bmatrix} 7 & 11 \\ 5 & 8 \end{bmatrix}$

46. $A = \begin{bmatrix} 7 & -9 \\ -3 & 4 \end{bmatrix}$  $B = \begin{bmatrix} 4 & 9 \\ 3 & 7 \end{bmatrix}$

47. $A = \begin{bmatrix} 3 & 1 \\ 1 & -2 \end{bmatrix}$  $B = \begin{bmatrix} \frac{2}{7} & \frac{1}{7} \\ \frac{1}{7} & -\frac{3}{7} \end{bmatrix}$

48. $A = \begin{bmatrix} 2 & 3 \\ 1 & -1 \end{bmatrix}$  $B = \begin{bmatrix} \frac{1}{5} & \frac{3}{5} \\ \frac{1}{5} & -\frac{2}{5} \end{bmatrix}$

49. $A = \begin{bmatrix} 1 & -1 & 1 \\ 1 & 0 & -1 \\ 0 & 1 & -1 \end{bmatrix}$  $B = \begin{bmatrix} 1 & 0 & 1 \\ 1 & -1 & 2 \\ 1 & -1 & 1 \end{bmatrix}$

50. $A = \begin{bmatrix} -1 & 0 & -1 \\ -1 & 1 & -2 \\ -1 & 1 & -1 \end{bmatrix}$  $B = \begin{bmatrix} -1 & 1 & -1 \\ -1 & 0 & 1 \\ 0 & -1 & 1 \end{bmatrix}$

**In Exercises 51–62, find $A^{-1}$, if possible.**

51. $A = \begin{bmatrix} 2 & 1 \\ -1 & 0 \end{bmatrix}$

52. $A = \begin{bmatrix} 3 & 1 \\ 2 & 1 \end{bmatrix}$

53. $A = \begin{bmatrix} \frac{1}{3} & 2 \\ 5 & \frac{3}{4} \end{bmatrix}$

54. $A = \begin{bmatrix} \frac{1}{4} & 2 \\ \frac{1}{3} & \frac{2}{3} \end{bmatrix}$

55. $A = \begin{bmatrix} 1 & 1 & 1 \\ 1 & -1 & -1 \\ -1 & 1 & -1 \end{bmatrix}$

56. $A = \begin{bmatrix} 1 & -1 & 1 \\ 1 & 1 & 1 \\ -1 & 2 & -3 \end{bmatrix}$

**57.** $A = \begin{bmatrix} 1 & 0 & 1 \\ 0 & 1 & 1 \\ 1 & -1 & 0 \end{bmatrix}$

**58.** $A = \begin{bmatrix} 1 & 2 & -3 \\ 1 & -1 & -1 \\ 1 & 0 & -4 \end{bmatrix}$

**59.** $A = \begin{bmatrix} 2 & 4 & 1 \\ 1 & 1 & -1 \\ 1 & 1 & 0 \end{bmatrix}$

**60.** $A = \begin{bmatrix} 1 & 0 & 1 \\ 1 & 1 & -1 \\ 2 & 1 & -1 \end{bmatrix}$

**61.** $A = \begin{bmatrix} 1 & 1 & -1 \\ 1 & -1 & 1 \\ 2 & -1 & -1 \end{bmatrix}$

**62.** $A = \begin{bmatrix} 1 & -1 & -1 \\ 1 & 1 & -3 \\ 3 & -5 & 1 \end{bmatrix}$

**In Exercises 63–74, apply matrix algebra to solve the system of linear equations.**

**63.** $\begin{aligned} 2x - y &= 5 \\ x + y &= 1 \end{aligned}$

**64.** $\begin{aligned} 2x - 3y &= 12 \\ x + y &= 1 \end{aligned}$

**65.** $\begin{aligned} 4x - 9y &= -1 \\ 7x - 3y &= \tfrac{5}{2} \end{aligned}$

**66.** $\begin{aligned} 7x - 3y &= 1 \\ 4x - 5y &= -\tfrac{7}{5} \end{aligned}$

**67.** $\begin{aligned} x + y + z &= 1 \\ x - y - z &= -1 \\ -x + y - z &= -1 \end{aligned}$

**68.** $\begin{aligned} x - y + z &= 0 \\ x + y + z &= 2 \\ -x + 2y - 3z &= 1 \end{aligned}$

**69.** $\begin{aligned} x \quad\;\; + z &= 3 \\ y + z &= 1 \\ x - y \quad\;\; &= 2 \end{aligned}$

**70.** $\begin{aligned} x + 2y - 3z &= 1 \\ x - y - z &= 3 \\ x \quad\;\; - 4z &= 0 \end{aligned}$

**71.** $\begin{aligned} 2x + 4y + z &= -5 \\ x + y - z &= 7 \\ x + y \quad\;\; &= 0 \end{aligned}$

**72.** $\begin{aligned} x \quad\;\; + z &= 3 \\ x + y - z &= -3 \\ 2x + y - z &= -5 \end{aligned}$

**73.** $\begin{aligned} x + y - z &= 4 \\ x - y + z &= 2 \\ 2x - y - z &= -3 \end{aligned}$

**74.** $\begin{aligned} x - y - z &= 0 \\ x + y - 3z &= 2 \\ 3x - 5y + z &= 4 \end{aligned}$

## ▪ APPLICATIONS

**75. Smoking.** On January 6 and 10, 2000, the Harris Poll conducted a survey of adult smokers in the United States. When asked, "Have you ever tried to quit smoking?", 70% said yes and 30% said no. Write a 2 × 1 matrix—call it $A$—that represents those smokers. When asked what consequences smoking would have on their lives, 89% believed it would increase their chance of getting lung cancer and 84% believed smoking would shorten their lives. Write a 2 × 1 matrix—call it $B$—that represents those smokers. If there are 46 million adult smokers in the United States

  **a.** What does $46A$ tell us?
  **b.** What does $46B$ tell us?

**76. Women in Science.** According to the study of science and engineering indicators by the National Science Foundation (www.nsf.gov), the number of female graduate students in science and engineering disciplines has increased over the last 30 years. In 1981, 24% of mathematics graduate students were female and 23% of graduate students in computer science were female. In 1991, 32% of mathematics graduate students and 21% of computer science graduate students were female. In 2001, 38% of mathematics graduate students and 30% of computer science graduate students were female. Write three 2 × 1 matrices representing the percentage of female graduate students.

$$A = \begin{bmatrix} \% \text{ female}-\text{math}-1981 \\ \% \text{ female}-\text{C.S.}-1981 \end{bmatrix}$$

$$B = \begin{bmatrix} \% \text{ female}-\text{math}-1991 \\ \% \text{ female}-\text{C.S.}-1991 \end{bmatrix}$$

$$C = \begin{bmatrix} \% \text{ female}-\text{math}-2001 \\ \% \text{ female}-\text{C.S.}-2001 \end{bmatrix}$$

What does $C - B$ tell us? What does $B - A$ tell us? What can you conclude about the number of women pursuing mathematics and computer science graduate degrees?

*Note:* C.S. = computer science.

**77. Registered Voters.** According to the U.S. Census Bureau (www.census.gov), in the 2000 national election, 58.9% of men over the age of 18 were registered voters, but only 41.4% voted; and 62.8% of women over 18 were registered voters, but only 43% actually voted. Write a 2 × 2 matrix with the following data:

$$A = \begin{bmatrix} \text{Percentage of registered} & \text{Percentage of registered} \\ \text{male voters} & \text{female voters} \\ \text{Percent of males} & \text{Percent of females} \\ \text{who voted} & \text{who voted} \end{bmatrix}$$

If we let $B$ be a 2 × 1 matrix representing the total population of males and females over the age of 18 in the United States, or $B = \begin{bmatrix} 100 \text{ M} \\ 110 \text{ M} \end{bmatrix}$, what does $AB$ tell us?

**78. Job Application.** A company has two rubrics for scoring job applicants based on weighting education, experience, and the interview differently.

Matrix $A$

|  | Rubric 1 | Rubric 2 |
|---|---|---|
| Education | 0.5 | 0.6 |
| Experience | 0.3 | 0.1 |
| Interview | 0.2 | 0.3 |

Applicants receive a score from 1 to 10 in each category (education, experience, and interview). Two applicants are shown in matrix $B$.

Matrix $B$

|  | Education | Experience | Interview |
|---|---|---|---|
| Applicant 1 | 8 | 7 | 5 |
| Applicant 2 | 6 | 8 | 8 |

What is the order of $BA$? What does each entry in $BA$ tell us?

**79. Taxes.** The IRS allows an individual to deduct business expenses in the following way: $0.45 per mile driven, 50% of entertainment costs, and 100% of actual expenses. Represent these deductions in the given order as a row matrix $A$. In 2006, Jamie had the following business expenses: $2700 in entertainment, $15,200 actual expenses, and he drove 7523 miles. Represent Jamie's expenses in the given order as a column matrix $B$. Multiply these two matrices to find the total amount of business expenses Jamie can claim on his 2006 federal tax form: $AB$.

**80. Tips on Service.** Marilyn decides to go to the Safety Harbor Spa for a day of pampering. She is treated to a hot stone massage ($85), a manicure and pedicure ($75), and a haircut ($100). Represent the costs of the individual services as a row matrix $A$ (in the given order). She decides to tip her masseur 25%, her nail tech 20%, and her hair stylist 15%. Represent the tipping percentages as a column matrix $B$ (in the given order). Multiply these matrices to find the total amount in tips $AB$ she needs to add to her final bill.

**Use the following tables for Exercises 81 and 82:**

The following table gives fuel and electric requirements per mile associated with gasoline and electric automobiles:

|  | NUMBER OF GALLONS/MILE | NUMBER OF kW-hr/MILE |
|---|---|---|
| SUV full size | 0.06 | 0 |
| Hybrid car | 0.02 | 0.1 |
| Electric car | 0 | 0.3 |

The following table gives an average cost for gasoline and electricity:

| Cost per gallon of gasoline | $3.80 |
|---|---|
| Cost per kW-hr of electricity | $0.05 |

**81. Environment.** Let matrix $A$ represent the gasoline and electricity consumption and matrix $B$ represent the costs of gasoline and electricity. Find $AB$ and describe what the elements of the product matrix represent. *Hint:* $A$ has order $3 \times 2$ and $B$ has order $2 \times 1$.

**82. Environment.** Assume you drive 12,000 miles per year. What are the yearly costs associated with driving the three types of cars in Exercise 81?

**For Exercises 83 and 84, refer to the following:**

The results of a nutritional analysis of one serving of three foods $A$, $B$, and $C$ were

$$X = \begin{bmatrix} \text{Carbohydrates (g)} & \text{Protein (g)} & \text{Fat (g)} \\ 5 & 0 & 2 \\ 5 & 6 & 5 \\ 8 & 4 & 4 \end{bmatrix} \begin{matrix} A \\ B \\ C \end{matrix}$$

It is possible to find the nutritional content of a meal consisting of a combination of the foods $A$, $B$, and $C$ by multiplying the matrix $X$ by a second matrix $N = \begin{bmatrix} r \\ s \\ t \end{bmatrix}$, that is, $XN$, where $r$ is the number of servings of food $A$, $s$ is the number of servings of food $B$, and $t$ is the number of servings of food $C$.

**83. Health/Nutrition.** Find the matrix $N$ that represents a meal consisting of two servings of food $A$ and one serving of food $B$. Find the nutritional content of that meal.

**84. Health/Nutrition.** Find the matrix $N$ that represents a meal consisting of one serving of food $A$ and two servings of food $C$. Find the nutritional content of that meal.

**For Exercises 85 and 86, refer to the following:**

Cell phone companies charge users based on the number of minutes talked, the number of text messages sent, and the number of megabytes of data used. The costs for three cell phone providers are given in the following table:

|  | MINUTES | TEXT MESSAGES | MEGABYTE OF DATA |
|---|---|---|---|
| $C_1$ | $0.04 | $0.05 | $0.15 |
| $C_2$ | $0.06 | $0.05 | $0.18 |
| $C_3$ | $0.07 | $0.07 | $0.13 |

It is possible to find the cost to a cell phone user for each of the three providers by creating a matrix $X$ whose rows are the rows of data in the table and multiplying the matrix $X$ by a second matrix

$N = \begin{bmatrix} m \\ t \\ d \end{bmatrix}$, that is, $XN$, where $m$ is the number of minutes talked,

$t$ is the number of text messages sent, and $d$ is the megabytes of data used.

**85. Telecommunications/Business.** A local business is looking at providing an employee a cell phone for business use. Find the matrix $N$ that represents expected normal cell phone usage of 200 minutes, 25 text messages, and no data usage. Find and interpret $XN$. Which is the better cell phone provider for this employee?

**86. Telecommunications/Business.** A local business is looking at providing an employee a cell phone for business use. Find the matrix $N$ that represents expected normal cell phone usage of 125 minutes, 125 text messages, and 320 megabytes of data usage. Find and interpret $XN$. Which is the better cell phone provider for this employee?

**For Exercises 87–92, apply the following decoding scheme:**

| 1 | A | 10 | J | 19 | S |
|---|---|----|---|----|---|
| 2 | B | 11 | K | 20 | T |
| 3 | C | 12 | L | 21 | U |
| 4 | D | 13 | M | 22 | V |
| 5 | E | 14 | N | 23 | W |
| 6 | F | 15 | O | 24 | X |
| 7 | G | 16 | P | 25 | Y |
| 8 | H | 17 | Q | 26 | Z |
| 9 | I | 18 | R |    |   |

The encoding matrix is $\begin{bmatrix} 1 & 1 & 0 \\ -1 & 0 & 1 \\ 2 & 0 & -1 \end{bmatrix}$. The encrypted matrices are given below. For each of the following, determine the 3-letter word that is originally transmitted. *Hint:* All six words are parts of the body.

**87. Cryptography.** [55  10  −22]

**88. Cryptography.** [31  8  −7]

**89. Cryptography.** [21  12  −2]

**90. Cryptography.** [9  1  5]

**91. Cryptography.** [−10  5  20]

**92. Cryptography.** [40  5  −17]

**For Exercises 93 and 94, refer to the following:**

The results of a nutritional analysis of one serving of three foods $A$, $B$, and $C$ were:

$$Y = \begin{bmatrix} 8 & 4 & 6 \\ 6 & 10 & 5 \\ 10 & 4 & 8 \end{bmatrix} \begin{matrix} A \\ B \\ C \end{matrix}$$

with columns labeled Carbohydrates (g), Protein (g), Fat (g).

The nutritional content of a meal consisting of a combination of the foods $A$, $B$, and $C$ is the product of the matrix $Y$ and a second matrix $N = \begin{bmatrix} r \\ s \\ t \end{bmatrix}$, that is, $YN$, where $r$ is the number of servings of food $A$, $s$ is the number of servings of food $B$, and $t$ is the number of servings of food $C$.

**93. Health/Nutrition.** Use the inverse matrix technique to find the number of servings of foods $A$, $B$, and $C$ necessary to create a meal of 18 grams of carbohydrates, 21 grams of protein, and 22 grams of fat.

**94. Health/Nutrition.** Use the inverse matrix technique to find the number of servings of foods $A$, $B$, and $C$ necessary to create a meal of 14 grams of carbohydrates, 25 grams of protein, and 16 grams of fat.

**For Exercises 95 and 96, refer to the following:**

Cell phone companies charge users based on the number of minutes talked, the number of text messages sent, and the number of megabytes of data used. The costs for three cell phone providers are given in the table:

|       | MINUTES | TEXT MESSAGES | MEGABYTES OF DATA |
|-------|---------|---------------|-------------------|
| $C_1$ | $0.03   | $0.06         | $0.15             |
| $C_2$ | $0.04   | $0.05         | $0.18             |
| $C_3$ | $0.05   | $0.07         | $0.13             |

The cost to a cell phone user for each of the three providers is the product of the matrix $X$ whose rows are the rows of data in the table and the matrix $N = \begin{bmatrix} m \\ t \\ d \end{bmatrix}$ where $m$ is the number of minutes talked, $t$ is the number of text messages sent, and $d$ is the megabytes of data used.

**95. Telecommunications/Business.** A local business is looking at providing an employee a cell phone for business use. The business solicits estimates for their normal monthly usage from three cell phone providers. Company 1 estimates the cost to be $49.50, Company 2 estimates the cost to be $52.00, and Company 3 estimates the cost to be $58.50. Use the inverse matrix technique to find the normal monthly usage for the employee.

**96. Telecommunications/Business.** A local business is looking at providing an employee a cell phone for business use. The business solicits estimates for their normal monthly usage from three cell phone providers. Company 1 estimates the cost to be $82.50, Company 2 estimates the cost to be $85.00, and Company 3 estimates the cost to be $92.50. Use the inverse matrix technique to find the normal monthly usage for the employee.

# ■ CATCH THE MISTAKE

**In Exercises 97–100, explain the mistake that is made.**

**97.** Multiply $\begin{bmatrix} 3 & 2 \\ 1 & 4 \end{bmatrix} \begin{bmatrix} -1 & 3 \\ -2 & 5 \end{bmatrix}$.

**Solution:**

Multiply corresponding elements.

$$\begin{bmatrix} 3 & 2 \\ 1 & 4 \end{bmatrix} \begin{bmatrix} -1 & 3 \\ -2 & 5 \end{bmatrix} = \begin{bmatrix} (3)(-1) & (2)(3) \\ (1)(-2) & (4)(5) \end{bmatrix}$$

Simplify. $\begin{bmatrix} 3 & 2 \\ 1 & 4 \end{bmatrix} \begin{bmatrix} -1 & 3 \\ -2 & 5 \end{bmatrix} = \begin{bmatrix} -3 & 6 \\ -2 & 20 \end{bmatrix}$

This is incorrect. What mistake was made?

**98.** Multiply $\begin{bmatrix} 3 & 2 \\ 1 & 4 \end{bmatrix} \begin{bmatrix} -1 & 3 \\ -2 & 5 \end{bmatrix}$.

**Solution:**

Multiply using column-by-row method.

$$\begin{bmatrix} 3 & 2 \\ 1 & 4 \end{bmatrix} \begin{bmatrix} -1 & 3 \\ -2 & 5 \end{bmatrix} = \begin{bmatrix} (3)(-1) + (1)(3) & (2)(-1) + (4)(3) \\ (3)(-2) + (1)(5) & (2)(-2) + (4)(5) \end{bmatrix}$$

Simplify. $\begin{bmatrix} 3 & 2 \\ 1 & 4 \end{bmatrix} \begin{bmatrix} -1 & 3 \\ -2 & 5 \end{bmatrix} = \begin{bmatrix} 0 & 10 \\ -1 & 16 \end{bmatrix}$

This is incorrect. What mistake was made?

**99.** Find the inverse of $A = \begin{bmatrix} 1 & 0 & 1 \\ -1 & 0 & -1 \\ 1 & 2 & 0 \end{bmatrix}$.

**Solution:**

Write the matrix $[A \mid I_3]$. $\left[\begin{array}{ccc|ccc} 1 & 0 & 1 & 1 & 0 & 0 \\ -1 & 0 & -1 & 0 & 1 & 0 \\ 1 & 2 & 0 & 0 & 0 & 1 \end{array}\right]$

Use Gaussian elimination to reduce $A$.

$\begin{array}{l} R_2 + R_1 \to R_2 \\ R_3 - R_1 \to R_3 \end{array}$ $\left[\begin{array}{ccc|ccc} 1 & 0 & 1 & 1 & 0 & 0 \\ 0 & 0 & 0 & 1 & 1 & 0 \\ 0 & 2 & -1 & -1 & 0 & 1 \end{array}\right]$

$R_2 \leftrightarrow R_3$ $\left[\begin{array}{ccc|ccc} 1 & 0 & 1 & 1 & 0 & 0 \\ 0 & 2 & -1 & -1 & 0 & 1 \\ 0 & 0 & 0 & 1 & 1 & 0 \end{array}\right]$

$\frac{1}{2}R_2 \to R_2$ $\left[\begin{array}{ccc|ccc} 1 & 0 & 1 & 1 & 0 & 0 \\ 0 & 1 & -\frac{1}{2} & -\frac{1}{2} & 0 & \frac{1}{2} \\ 0 & 0 & 0 & 1 & 1 & 0 \end{array}\right]$

$A^{-1} = \begin{bmatrix} 1 & 0 & 0 \\ -\frac{1}{2} & 0 & \frac{1}{2} \\ 1 & 1 & 0 \end{bmatrix}$ is incorrect because $AA^{-1} \neq I_3$.

What mistake was made?

**100.** Find the inverse of $A$ given that $A = \begin{bmatrix} 2 & 5 \\ 3 & 10 \end{bmatrix}$.

**Solution:** $A^{-1} = \dfrac{1}{A}$ $\quad A^{-1} = \dfrac{1}{\begin{bmatrix} 2 & 5 \\ 3 & 10 \end{bmatrix}}$

Simplify. $A^{-1} = \begin{bmatrix} \frac{1}{2} & \frac{1}{5} \\ \frac{1}{3} & \frac{1}{10} \end{bmatrix}$

This is incorrect. What mistake was made?

# ■ CONCEPTUAL

**In Exercises 101–106, determine whether the statements are true or false.**

**101.** If $A = \begin{bmatrix} a_{11} & a_{12} \\ a_{21} & a_{22} \end{bmatrix}$ and $B = \begin{bmatrix} b_{11} & b_{12} \\ b_{21} & b_{22} \end{bmatrix}$, then

$AB = \begin{bmatrix} a_{11}b_{11} & a_{12}b_{12} \\ a_{21}b_{21} & a_{22}b_{22} \end{bmatrix}$.

**102.** If $AB$ is defined, then $AB = BA$.

**103.** $AB$ is defined only if the number of columns in $A$ equals the number of rows in $B$.

**104.** $A + B$ is defined only if $A$ and $B$ have the same order.

**105.** If $A = \begin{bmatrix} a_{11} & a_{12} \\ a_{21} & a_{22} \end{bmatrix}$, then $A^{-1} = \begin{bmatrix} \frac{1}{a_{11}} & \frac{1}{a_{12}} \\ \frac{1}{a_{21}} & \frac{1}{a_{22}} \end{bmatrix}$.

**106.** All square matrices have inverses.

**107.** For $A = \begin{bmatrix} a_{11} & a_{12} \\ a_{21} & a_{22} \end{bmatrix}$, find $A^2$.

**108.** In order for $A^2_{m \times n}$ to be defined, what condition (with respect to $m$ and $n$) must be met?

**109.** For what values of $x$ does the inverse of $A$ not exist, given $A = \begin{bmatrix} x & 6 \\ 3 & 2 \end{bmatrix}$?

**110.** Let $A = \begin{bmatrix} a & 0 & 0 \\ 0 & b & 0 \\ 0 & 0 & c \end{bmatrix}$. Find $A^{-1}$. Assume $abc \neq 0$.

■ **CHALLENGE**

**111.** For $A = \begin{bmatrix} 1 & 1 \\ 1 & 1 \end{bmatrix}$ find $A$, $A^2$, $A^3$, .... What is $A^n$?

**112.** For $A = \begin{bmatrix} 1 & 0 \\ 0 & 1 \end{bmatrix}$ find $A$, $A^2$, $A^3$, .... What is $A^n$?

**113.** If $A_{m \times n} B_{n \times p}$ is defined, explain why $(A_{m \times n} B_{n \times p})^2$ is not defined for $m \neq p$.

**114.** Given $C_{n \times m}$ and $A_{m \times n} = B_{m \times n}$, explain why $AC \neq CB$, if $m \neq n$.

**115.** Verify that $A^{-1} = \dfrac{1}{ad - bc} \begin{bmatrix} d & -b \\ -c & a \end{bmatrix}$ is the inverse of $A = \begin{bmatrix} a & b \\ c & d \end{bmatrix}$, provided $ad - bc \neq 0$.

**116.** Let $A = \begin{bmatrix} a & b \\ c & d \end{bmatrix}$ and form the matrix $[A \mid I_2]$. Apply row operations to transform into $[I_2 \mid A^{-1}]$. Show $A^{-1} = \dfrac{1}{ad - bc} \begin{bmatrix} d & -b \\ -c & a \end{bmatrix}$ such that $ad - bc \neq 0$.

**117.** Why does the square matrix $A = \begin{bmatrix} 2 & 3 \\ 4 & 6 \end{bmatrix}$ not have an inverse?

**118.** Why does the square matrix $A = \begin{bmatrix} 1 & 2 & -1 \\ 2 & 4 & -2 \\ 0 & 1 & 3 \end{bmatrix}$ not have an inverse?

■ **TECHNOLOGY**

**In Exercises 119–124, apply a graphing utility to perform the indicated matrix operations, if possible.**

$$A = \begin{bmatrix} 1 & 7 & 9 & 2 \\ -3 & -6 & 15 & 11 \\ 0 & 3 & 2 & 5 \\ 9 & 8 & -4 & 1 \end{bmatrix} \quad B = \begin{bmatrix} 7 & 9 \\ 8 & 6 \\ -4 & -2 \\ 3 & 1 \end{bmatrix}$$

**119.** $AB$     **120.** $BA$     **121.** $BB$     **122.** $AA$

$$A = \begin{bmatrix} 2 & 1 & 1 \\ -3 & 0 & 2 \\ 4 & -6 & 0 \end{bmatrix}$$

**123.** $A^2$     **124.** $A^5$

**In Exercises 125 and 126, apply a graphing utility to perform the indicated matrix operations.**

$$A = \begin{bmatrix} 1 & 7 & 9 & 2 \\ -3 & -6 & 15 & 11 \\ 0 & 3 & 2 & 5 \\ 9 & 8 & -4 & 1 \end{bmatrix}$$

**125.** Find $A^{-1}$.     **126.** Find $AA^{-1}$.

■ **PREVIEW TO CALCULUS**

**In calculus, when finding the inverse of a vector function, it is fundamental that the matrix of partial derivatives is not singular. In Exercises 127–130, find the inverse of each matrix.**

**127.** $\begin{bmatrix} 2x & 2y \\ 2x & -2y \end{bmatrix}$

**128.** $\begin{bmatrix} 1 & 1 \\ uy & ux \end{bmatrix}$

**129.** $\begin{bmatrix} \cos\theta & \sin\theta \\ -\sin\theta & \cos\theta \end{bmatrix}$

**130.** $\begin{bmatrix} \cos\theta & -r\sin\theta & 0 \\ \sin\theta & r\cos\theta & 0 \\ 0 & 0 & 1 \end{bmatrix}$

# THE DETERMINANT OF A SQUARE MATRIX AND CRAMER'S RULE

SKILLS OBJECTIVES

- Find the determinant of a 2 × 2 matrix.
- Find the determinant of an $n \times n$ matrix.
- Use Cramer's rule to solve a square system of linear equations.

CONCEPTUAL OBJECTIVES

- Derive Cramer's rule.
- Understand that if a determinant of a matrix is equal to zero, then that matrix does not have an inverse.
- Understand that Cramer's rule can be used to find only a unique solution.

In Section 8.3, we discussed Gauss–Jordan elimination as a way to solve systems of linear equations using augmented matrices. Then in Section 8.4, we employed matrix algebra and inverses to solve systems of linear equations that are square (same number of equations as variables). In this section, we will describe another method, called Cramer's rule, for solving systems of linear equations. Cramer's rule is applicable only to square systems. *Determinants* of square matrices play a vital role in Cramer's rule and indicate whether a matrix has an inverse.

## Determinant of a 2 × 2 Matrix

Every square matrix $A$ has a number associated with it called its *determinant*, denoted $\det(A)$ or $|A|$.

---

**DEFINITION**     **Determinant of a 2 × 2 Matrix**

The **determinant** of the 2 × 2 matrix $A = \begin{bmatrix} a & b \\ c & d \end{bmatrix}$ is given by

$$\det(A) = |A| = \begin{vmatrix} a & b \\ c & d \end{vmatrix} = ad - bc$$

---

Although the symbol for determinant, $|\ |$, looks like absolute value bars, the determinant can be any real number (positive, negative, or zero). The determinant of a 2 × 2 matrix is found by finding the product of the main diagonal entries (top left to bottom right) and subtracting the product of the entries along the other diagonal (bottom left to top right).

$$\begin{vmatrix} a & b \\ c & d \end{vmatrix} = ad - bc$$

*Study Tip*

The determinant of a 2 × 2 matrix is found by finding the product of the main diagonal entries and subtracting the product of the other diagonal entries.

## EXAMPLE 1  Finding the Determinant of a 2 × 2 Matrix

Find the determinant of each matrix.

**a.** $\begin{bmatrix} 2 & -5 \\ -1 & 3 \end{bmatrix}$   **b.** $\begin{bmatrix} 0.5 & 0.2 \\ -3.0 & -4.2 \end{bmatrix}$   **c.** $\begin{bmatrix} \frac{2}{3} & 1 \\ 2 & 3 \end{bmatrix}$

**Solution:**

**a.** $\begin{vmatrix} 2 & -5 \\ -1 & 3 \end{vmatrix} = (2)(3) - (-1)(-5) = 6 - 5 = \boxed{1}$

**b.** $\begin{vmatrix} 0.5 & 0.2 \\ -3 & -4.2 \end{vmatrix} = (0.5)(-4.2) - (-3)(0.2) = -2.1 + 0.6 = \boxed{-1.5}$

**c.** $\begin{vmatrix} \frac{2}{3} & 1 \\ 2 & 3 \end{vmatrix} = \left(\frac{2}{3}\right)(3) - (2)(1) = 2 - 2 = \boxed{0}$

In Example 1, we see that determinants are real numbers that can be positive, negative, or zero. Although evaluating determinants of 2 × 2 matrices is a simple process, one **common mistake** is reversing the difference: $\begin{vmatrix} a & b \\ c & d \end{vmatrix} \neq bc - ad$.

■ **YOUR TURN**  Evaluate the determinant $\begin{vmatrix} -2 & 1 \\ -3 & 2 \end{vmatrix}$.

# Determinant of an *n* × *n* Matrix

In order to define the *determinant* of a 3 × 3 or a general *n* × *n* (where *n* ≥ 3) matrix, we first define *minors* and *cofactors* of a square matrix.

### DEFINITION  Minor and Cofactor

Let $A$ be a square matrix of order $n \times n$. Then:

■ The **minor** $M_{ij}$ of the entry $a_{ij}$ is the determinant of the $(n - 1) \times (n - 1)$ matrix obtained when the *i*th row and *j*th column of $A$ are deleted.

■ The **cofactor** $C_{ij}$ of the entry $a_{ij}$ is given by $C_{ij} = (-1)^{i+j} M_{ij}$.

The following table illustrates entries, minors, and cofactors of the matrix:

$$A = \begin{bmatrix} 1 & -3 & 2 \\ 4 & -1 & 0 \\ 5 & -2 & 3 \end{bmatrix}$$

| ENTRY $a_{ij}$ | MINOR $M_{ij}$ | COFACTOR $C_{ij}$ |
|---|---|---|
| $a_{11} = 1$ | For $M_{11}$, delete the first row and first column: $$\begin{bmatrix} 1 & -3 & 2 \\ 4 & -1 & 0 \\ 5 & -2 & 3 \end{bmatrix}$$ $$M_{11} = \begin{vmatrix} -1 & 0 \\ -2 & 3 \end{vmatrix} = -3 - 0 = -3$$ | $C_{11} = (-1)^{1+1}M_{11}$ $= (1)(-3)$ $= -3$ |
| $a_{32} = -2$ | For $M_{32}$, delete the third row and second column: $$\begin{bmatrix} 1 & -3 & 2 \\ 4 & -1 & 0 \\ 5 & -2 & 3 \end{bmatrix}$$ $$M_{32} = \begin{vmatrix} 1 & 2 \\ 4 & 0 \end{vmatrix} = 0 - 8 = -8$$ | $C_{32} = (-1)^{3+2}M_{32}$ $= (-1)(-8)$ $= 8$ |

Notice that the cofactor is simply the minor multiplied by either 1 or $-1$, depending on whether $i + j$ is even or odd. Therefore, we can make the following sign pattern for $3 \times 3$ and $4 \times 4$ matrices and obtain the cofactor by multiplying the minor with the appropriate sign ($+1$ or $-1$):

$$\begin{bmatrix} + & - & + \\ - & + & - \\ + & - & + \end{bmatrix} \qquad \begin{bmatrix} + & - & + & - \\ - & + & - & + \\ + & - & + & - \\ - & + & - & + \end{bmatrix}$$

## DEFINITION   Determinant of an $n \times n$ Matrix

Let $A$ be an $n \times n$ matrix. Then the **determinant** of $A$ is found by summing the entries in *any* row of $A$ (or column of $A$) multiplied by each entries' respective cofactor.

If $A$ is a $3 \times 3$ matrix, the determinant can be given by

$$\det(A) = a_{11}C_{11} + a_{12}C_{12} + a_{13}C_{13}$$

this is called **expanding the determinant by the first row**. It is important to note that any row or column can be used. Typically, the row or column with the most zeros is selected because it makes the arithmetic simpler.

Combining the definitions of minors, cofactors, and determinants, we now give a general definition for the determinant of a $3 \times 3$ matrix.

*Row 1 expansion:* $$\begin{vmatrix} a_1 & b_1 & c_1 \\ a_2 & b_2 & c_2 \\ a_3 & b_3 & c_3 \end{vmatrix} = a_1\begin{vmatrix} b_2 & c_2 \\ b_3 & c_3 \end{vmatrix} - b_1\begin{vmatrix} a_2 & c_2 \\ a_3 & c_3 \end{vmatrix} + c_1\begin{vmatrix} a_2 & b_2 \\ a_3 & b_3 \end{vmatrix}$$

*Column 1 expansion:* $$\begin{vmatrix} a_1 & b_1 & c_1 \\ a_2 & b_2 & c_2 \\ a_3 & b_3 & c_3 \end{vmatrix} = a_1\begin{vmatrix} b_2 & c_2 \\ b_3 & c_3 \end{vmatrix} - a_2\begin{vmatrix} b_1 & c_1 \\ b_3 & c_3 \end{vmatrix} + a_3\begin{vmatrix} b_1 & c_1 \\ b_2 & c_2 \end{vmatrix}$$

Whichever row or column is expanded, an alternating sign scheme is used (see sign arrays above). Notice that in either of the expansions above, each $2 \times 2$ determinant obtained is found by crossing out the row and column containing the entry that is multiplying the determinant.

**EXAMPLE 2    Finding the Determinant of a 3 × 3 Matrix**

For the given matrix, expand the determinant by the *first row*.

$$\begin{bmatrix} 2 & 1 & 3 \\ -1 & 5 & -2 \\ -3 & 7 & 4 \end{bmatrix}$$

**Solution:**

Expand the determinant by the **first** row. Remember the alternating **sign**.

$$\begin{vmatrix} 2 & 1 & 3 \\ -1 & 5 & -2 \\ -3 & 7 & 4 \end{vmatrix} = + 2\begin{vmatrix} 5 & -2 \\ 7 & 4 \end{vmatrix} - 1\begin{vmatrix} -1 & -2 \\ -3 & 4 \end{vmatrix} + 3\begin{vmatrix} -1 & 5 \\ -3 & 7 \end{vmatrix}$$

Evaluate the resulting 2 × 2 determinants.

$$= 2[(5)(4) - (7)(-2)] - 1[(-1)(4) - (-3)(-2)] + 3[(-1)(7) - (-3)(5)]$$

$$= 2[20 + 14] - [-4 - 6] + 3[-7 + 15]$$

Simplify.

$$= 2(34) - (-10) + 3(8)$$

$$= 68 + 10 + 24$$

$$= \boxed{102}$$

■ **Answer:** 156

■ **YOUR TURN**  For the given matrix, expand the determinant by the first row.

$$\begin{bmatrix} 1 & 3 & -2 \\ 2 & 5 & 4 \\ 7 & -1 & 6 \end{bmatrix}$$

Determinants can be expanded by any row *or* column. Typically, the row or column with the most zeros is selected to simplify the arithmetic.

**EXAMPLE 3    Finding the Determinant of a 3 × 3 Matrix**

Find the determinant of the matrix $\begin{vmatrix} -1 & 2 & 0 \\ 4 & 7 & 1 \\ 5 & 3 & 0 \end{vmatrix}$.

**Solution:**

Since there are two 0s in the third column, expand the determinant by the third column. Recall the sign array.

$$\begin{bmatrix} + & - & + \\ - & + & - \\ + & - & + \end{bmatrix}$$

$$\begin{vmatrix} -1 & 2 & 0 \\ 4 & 7 & 1 \\ 5 & 3 & 0 \end{vmatrix} = + 0\begin{vmatrix} 4 & 7 \\ 5 & 3 \end{vmatrix} - 1\begin{vmatrix} -1 & 2 \\ 5 & 3 \end{vmatrix} + 0\begin{vmatrix} -1 & 2 \\ 4 & 7 \end{vmatrix}$$

There is no need to calculate the two determinants that are multiplied by 0s, since 0 times any real number is zero.

$$\begin{vmatrix} -1 & 2 & 0 \\ 4 & 7 & 1 \\ 5 & 3 & 0 \end{vmatrix} = 0 - 1\underbrace{\begin{vmatrix} -1 & 2 \\ 5 & 3 \end{vmatrix}}_{-3-10} + 0$$

Simplify.

$$= -1(-13) = \boxed{13}$$

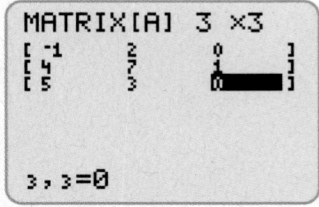

■ **Answer:** 20

■ **YOUR TURN**  Evaluate the determinant $\begin{vmatrix} 1 & -2 & 1 \\ -1 & 0 & 3 \\ -4 & 0 & 2 \end{vmatrix}$.

**EXAMPLE 4**  **Finding the Determinant of a 4 × 4 Matrix**

Find the determinant of the matrix $\begin{vmatrix} 1 & -2 & 3 & 4 \\ -4 & 0 & -1 & 0 \\ -3 & 9 & 6 & 5 \\ -5 & 7 & 2 & 1 \end{vmatrix}$.

**Solution:**

Since there are two 0s in the second row, expand the determinant by the second row.
Recall the sign array for a 4 × 4 matrix.

$$\begin{bmatrix} + & - & + & - \\ - & + & - & + \\ + & - & + & - \\ - & + & - & + \end{bmatrix}$$

$$\begin{bmatrix} 1 & -2 & 3 & 4 \\ -4 & 0 & -1 & 0 \\ -3 & 9 & 6 & 5 \\ -5 & 7 & 2 & 1 \end{bmatrix} = -(-4)\begin{vmatrix} -2 & 3 & 4 \\ 9 & 6 & 5 \\ 7 & 2 & 1 \end{vmatrix} + 0 - (-1)\begin{vmatrix} 1 & -2 & 4 \\ -3 & 9 & 5 \\ -5 & 7 & 1 \end{vmatrix} + 0$$

Evaluate the two 3 × 3 determinants.

$$\begin{vmatrix} -2 & 3 & 4 \\ 9 & 6 & 5 \\ 7 & 2 & 1 \end{vmatrix} = -2\begin{vmatrix} 6 & 5 \\ 2 & 1 \end{vmatrix} - 3\begin{vmatrix} 9 & 5 \\ 7 & 1 \end{vmatrix} + 4\begin{vmatrix} 9 & 6 \\ 7 & 2 \end{vmatrix}$$

$$= -2(6 - 10) - 3(9 - 35) + 4(18 - 42)$$
$$= -2(-4) - 3(-26) + 4(-24)$$
$$= 8 + 78 - 96$$
$$= -10$$

$$\begin{vmatrix} 1 & -2 & 4 \\ -3 & 9 & 5 \\ -5 & 7 & 1 \end{vmatrix} = 1\begin{vmatrix} 9 & 5 \\ 7 & 1 \end{vmatrix} - (-2)\begin{vmatrix} -3 & 5 \\ -5 & 1 \end{vmatrix} + 4\begin{vmatrix} -3 & 9 \\ -5 & 7 \end{vmatrix}$$

$$= 1(9 - 35) + 2(-3 + 25) + 4(-21 + 45)$$
$$= -26 + 2(22) + 4(24)$$
$$= -26 + 44 + 96$$
$$= 114$$

$$\begin{bmatrix} 1 & -2 & 3 & 4 \\ -4 & 0 & -1 & 0 \\ -3 & 9 & 6 & 5 \\ -5 & 7 & 2 & 1 \end{bmatrix} = 4\underbrace{\begin{vmatrix} -2 & 3 & 4 \\ 9 & 6 & 5 \\ 7 & 2 & 1 \end{vmatrix}}_{-10} + \underbrace{\begin{vmatrix} 1 & -2 & 4 \\ -3 & 9 & 5 \\ -5 & 7 & 1 \end{vmatrix}}_{114} = 4(-10) + 114 = \boxed{74}$$

# Cramer's Rule: Systems of Linear Equations in Two Variables

Let's now apply determinants of $2 \times 2$ matrices to solve systems of linear equations in two variables. We begin by solving the general system of two linear equations in two variables:

$$(1) \quad a_1 x + b_1 y = c_1$$
$$(2) \quad a_2 x + b_2 y = c_2$$

**Solve for $x$ using elimination (eliminate $y$).**

Multiply (1) by $b_2$.

$$b_2 a_1 x + b_2 b_1 y = b_2 c_1$$

Multiply (2) by $-b_1$.

$$-b_1 a_2 x - b_1 b_2 y = -b_1 c_2$$

Add the two new equations to eliminate $y$.

$$(a_1 b_2 - a_2 b_1) x = (b_2 c_1 - b_1 c_2)$$

Divide both sides by $(a_1 b_2 - a_2 b_1)$.

$$x = \frac{(b_2 c_1 - b_1 c_2)}{(a_1 b_2 - a_2 b_1)}$$

Write both the numerator and the denominator as determinants.

$$x = \frac{\begin{vmatrix} c_1 & b_1 \\ c_2 & b_2 \end{vmatrix}}{\begin{vmatrix} a_1 & b_1 \\ a_2 & b_2 \end{vmatrix}}$$

**Solve for $y$ using elimination (eliminate $x$).**

Multiply (1) by $-a_2$.

$$-a_2 a_1 x - a_2 b_1 y = -a_2 c_1$$

Multiply (2) by $a_1$.

$$a_1 a_2 x + a_1 b_2 y = a_1 c_2$$

Add the two new equations to eliminate $x$.

$$(a_1 b_2 - a_2 b_1) y = (a_1 c_2 - a_2 c_1)$$

Divide both sides by $(a_1 b_2 - a_2 b_1)$.

$$y = \frac{(a_1 c_2 - a_2 c_1)}{(a_1 b_2 - a_2 b_1)}$$

Write both the numerator and the denominator as determinants.

$$y = \frac{\begin{vmatrix} a_1 & c_1 \\ a_2 & c_2 \end{vmatrix}}{\begin{vmatrix} a_1 & b_1 \\ a_2 & b_2 \end{vmatrix}}$$

Notice that the solutions for $x$ and $y$ involve three determinants. If we let

$$D = \begin{vmatrix} a_1 & b_1 \\ a_2 & b_2 \end{vmatrix} \qquad D_x = \begin{vmatrix} c_1 & b_1 \\ c_2 & b_2 \end{vmatrix} \qquad D_y = \begin{vmatrix} a_1 & c_1 \\ a_2 & c_2 \end{vmatrix},$$

$$\text{then} \quad x = \frac{D_x}{D} \quad \text{and} \quad y = \frac{D_y}{D}.$$

Notice that the real number $D$ is the determinant of the coefficient matrix of the system and cannot equal zero ($D \neq 0$) or there will be no unique solution. These formulas for solving a system of two linear equations in two variables are known as *Cramer's rule*.

CRAMER'S RULE FOR SOLVING SYSTEMS OF
TWO LINEAR EQUATIONS IN TWO VARIABLES

For the system of linear equations

$$a_1x + b_1y = c_1$$
$$a_2x + b_2y = c_2$$

let

$$D = \begin{vmatrix} a_1 & b_1 \\ a_2 & b_2 \end{vmatrix} \qquad D_x = \begin{vmatrix} c_1 & b_1 \\ c_2 & b_2 \end{vmatrix} \qquad D_y = \begin{vmatrix} a_1 & c_1 \\ a_2 & c_2 \end{vmatrix}$$

If $D \neq 0$, then the solution to the system of linear equations is

$$x = \frac{D_x}{D} \qquad y = \frac{D_y}{D}$$

If $D = 0$, then the system of linear equations has either no solution or infinitely many solutions.

Notice that the determinants $D_x$ and $D_y$ are similar to the determinant $D$. A three-step procedure is outlined for setting up the three determinants for a system of two linear equations in two variables:

$$a_1x + b_1y = c_1$$
$$a_2x + b_2y = c_2$$

**Step 1:** Set up $D$.

Apply the coefficients of $x$ and $y$. $\qquad D = \begin{vmatrix} a_1 & b_1 \\ a_2 & b_2 \end{vmatrix}$

**Step 2:** Set up $D_x$.

Start with $D$ and replace the coefficients of $x$
(column 1) with the constants on the right side $\qquad D_x = \begin{vmatrix} c_1 & b_1 \\ c_2 & b_2 \end{vmatrix}$
of the equal sign.

**Step 3:** Set up $D_y$.

Start with $D$ and replace the coefficients of $y$
(column 2) with the constants on the right side $\qquad D_y = \begin{vmatrix} a_1 & c_1 \\ a_2 & c_2 \end{vmatrix}$
of the equal sign.

**Study Tip**

Cramer's rule is only applicable to square systems of linear equations.

**EXAMPLE 5** **Using Cramer's Rule to Solve a System of Two Linear Equations**

Apply Cramer's rule to solve the system.

$$x + 3y = 1$$
$$2x + y = -3$$

**Technology Tip**

A graphing calculator can be used to solve the system using Cramer's rule. Enter the matrix $A$ for the determinant $D_x$, $B$ for $D_y$, $C$ for $D$.

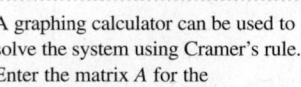

**[A]**
$$\begin{bmatrix} 1 & 3 \\ -3 & 1 \end{bmatrix}$$

**[B]**
$$\begin{bmatrix} 1 & 1 \\ 2 & -3 \end{bmatrix}$$

**[C]**
$$\begin{bmatrix} 1 & 3 \\ 2 & 1 \end{bmatrix}$$

To solve for $x$ and $y$, enter $D_x/D$ as $A/C$ for $x$ and $D_y/D$ as $B/C$ for $y$.

```
det([A])/det([C]
)
                 -2
det([B])/det([C]
)
                  1
```

■ **Answer:** $x = 5, y = -6$

**Solution:**

Set up the three determinants.

$$D = \begin{vmatrix} 1 & 3 \\ 2 & 1 \end{vmatrix}$$

$$D_x = \begin{vmatrix} 1 & 3 \\ -3 & 1 \end{vmatrix}$$

$$D_y = \begin{vmatrix} 1 & 1 \\ 2 & -3 \end{vmatrix}$$

Evaluate the determinants.

$$D = 1 - 6 = -5$$
$$D_x = 1 - (-9) = 10$$
$$D_y = -3 - 2 = -5$$

Solve for $x$ and $y$.

$$x = \frac{D_x}{D} = \frac{10}{-5} = -2$$

$$y = \frac{D_y}{D} = \frac{-5}{-5} = 1$$

$$\boxed{x = -2, y = 1}$$

■ **YOUR TURN** Apply Cramer's rule to solve the system.

$$5x + 4y = 1$$
$$-3x - 2y = -3$$

Recall from Section 8.1 that systems of two linear equations in two variables led to one of three possible outcomes: a unique solution, no solution, and infinitely many solutions. When $D = 0$, Cramer's rule does not apply and the system is either inconsistent (has no solution) or contains dependent equations (has infinitely many solutions).

## Cramer's Rule: Systems of Linear Equations in Three Variables

Cramer's rule can also be used to solve higher order systems of linear equations. The following box summarizes Cramer's rule for solving a system of three equations in three variables:

### CRAMER'S RULE: SOLUTION FOR SYSTEMS OF THREE EQUATIONS IN THREE VARIABLES

The system of linear equations

$$a_1x + b_1y + c_1z = d_1$$
$$a_2x + b_2y + c_2z = d_2$$
$$a_3x + b_3y + c_3z = d_3$$

has the solution

$$x = \frac{D_x}{D} \qquad y = \frac{D_y}{D} \qquad z = \frac{D_z}{D} \qquad D \neq 0$$

where the determinants are given as follows:

Display the coefficients of $x$, $y$, and $z$.

$$D = \begin{vmatrix} a_1 & b_1 & c_1 \\ a_2 & b_2 & c_2 \\ a_3 & b_3 & c_3 \end{vmatrix}$$

Replace the coefficients of $x$ (column 1) in $D$ with the constants on the right side of the equal sign.

$$D_x = \begin{vmatrix} d_1 & b_1 & c_1 \\ d_2 & b_2 & c_2 \\ d_3 & b_3 & c_3 \end{vmatrix}$$

Replace the coefficients of $y$ (column 2) in $D$ with the constants on the right side of the equal sign.

$$D_y = \begin{vmatrix} a_1 & d_1 & c_1 \\ a_2 & d_2 & c_2 \\ a_3 & d_3 & c_3 \end{vmatrix}$$

Replace the coefficients of $z$ (column 3) in $D$ with the constants on the right side of the equal sign.

$$D_z = \begin{vmatrix} a_1 & b_1 & d_1 \\ a_2 & b_2 & d_2 \\ a_3 & b_3 & d_3 \end{vmatrix}$$

**EXAMPLE 6   Using Cramer's Rule to Solve a System of Three Linear Equations**

Use Cramer's rule to solve the system.

$$\begin{aligned} 3x - 2y + 3z &= -3 \\ 5x + 3y + 8z &= -2 \\ x + y + 3z &= 1 \end{aligned}$$

**Solution:**

*Set up the four determinants.*

$D$ contains the coefficients of $x$, $y$, and $z$.

$$D = \begin{vmatrix} 3 & -2 & 3 \\ 5 & 3 & 8 \\ 1 & 1 & 3 \end{vmatrix}$$

*Replace a column with constants on the right side of the equation.*

$$D_x = \begin{vmatrix} 3 & -2 & 3 \\ -2 & 3 & 8 \\ 1 & 1 & 3 \end{vmatrix} \quad D_y = \begin{vmatrix} 3 & -3 & 3 \\ 5 & -2 & 8 \\ 1 & 1 & 3 \end{vmatrix} \quad D_z = \begin{vmatrix} 3 & -2 & -3 \\ 5 & 3 & -2 \\ 1 & 1 & 1 \end{vmatrix}$$

*Evaluate the determinants.*

$$D = 3(9 - 8) - (-2)(15 - 8) + 3(5 - 3) = 23$$

$$D_x = -3(9 - 8) - (-2)(-6 - 8) + 3(-2 - 3) = -46$$

$$D_y = 3(-6 - 8) - (-3)(15 - 8) + 3(5 + 2) = 0$$

$$D_z = 3(3 + 2) - (-2)(5 + 2) - 3(5 - 3) = 23$$

*Solve for $x$, $y$, and $z$.*

$$x = \frac{D_x}{D} = \frac{-46}{23} = -2 \quad y = \frac{D_y}{D} = \frac{0}{23} = 0 \quad z = \frac{D_z}{D} = \frac{23}{23} = 1$$

$$\boxed{x = -2, y = 0, z = 1}$$

■ **YOUR TURN**  Use Cramer's rule to solve the system.

$$\begin{aligned} 2x + 3y + z &= -1 \\ x - y - z &= 0 \\ -3x - 2y + 3z &= 10 \end{aligned}$$

■ **Answer:** $x = 1$, $y = -2$, $z = 3$

As was the case in two equations, when $D = 0$, Cramer's rule does not apply and the system of three equations is either inconsistent (no solution) or contains dependent equations (infinitely many solutions).

## SECTION 8.5 SUMMARY

In this section, **determinants** were discussed for square matrices.

| ORDER | DETERMINANT | ARRAY |
|---|---|---|
| $2 \times 2$ | $\det(A) = |A| = \begin{vmatrix} a & b \\ c & d \end{vmatrix} = ad - bc$ | |
| $3 \times 3$ | $\begin{vmatrix} a_1 & b_1 & c_1 \\ a_2 & b_2 & c_2 \\ a_3 & b_3 & c_3 \end{vmatrix} = a_1 \begin{vmatrix} b_2 & c_2 \\ b_3 & c_3 \end{vmatrix} - b_1 \begin{vmatrix} a_2 & c_2 \\ a_3 & c_3 \end{vmatrix} + c_1 \begin{vmatrix} a_2 & b_2 \\ a_3 & b_3 \end{vmatrix}$ <br> Expansion by first row (any row or column can be used) | $\begin{bmatrix} + & - & + \\ - & + & - \\ + & - & + \end{bmatrix}$ |

**Cramer's rule** was developed for $2 \times 2$ and $3 \times 3$ matrices, but it can be extended to general $n \times n$ matrices. When the coefficient determinant is equal to zero ($D = 0$), then the system is either inconsistent (and has no solution) or represents dependent equations (and has infinitely many solutions), and Cramer's rule does not apply.

| SYSTEM | ORDER | SOLUTION | DETERMINANTS |
|---|---|---|---|
| $a_1x + b_1y = c_1$ <br> $a_2x + b_2y = c_2$ | $2 \times 2$ | $x = \dfrac{D_x}{D}$ $\quad$ $y = \dfrac{D_y}{D}$ | $D = \begin{vmatrix} a_1 & b_1 \\ a_2 & b_2 \end{vmatrix} \neq 0$ <br> $D_x = \begin{vmatrix} c_1 & b_1 \\ c_2 & b_2 \end{vmatrix}$ <br> $D_y = \begin{vmatrix} a_1 & c_1 \\ a_2 & c_2 \end{vmatrix}$ |
| $a_1x + b_1y + c_1z = d_1$ <br> $a_2x + b_2y + c_2z = d_2$ <br> $a_3x + b_3y + c_3z = d_3$ | $3 \times 3$ | $x = \dfrac{D_x}{D}$ $\quad$ $y = \dfrac{D_y}{D}$ $\quad$ $z = \dfrac{D_z}{D}$ | $D = \begin{vmatrix} a_1 & b_1 & c_1 \\ a_2 & b_2 & c_2 \\ a_3 & b_3 & c_3 \end{vmatrix} \neq 0$ <br> $D_x = \begin{vmatrix} d_1 & b_1 & c_1 \\ d_2 & b_2 & c_2 \\ d_3 & b_3 & c_3 \end{vmatrix}$ <br> $D_y = \begin{vmatrix} a_1 & d_1 & c_1 \\ a_2 & d_2 & c_2 \\ a_3 & d_3 & c_3 \end{vmatrix}$ <br> $D_z = \begin{vmatrix} a_1 & b_1 & d_1 \\ a_2 & b_2 & d_2 \\ a_3 & b_3 & d_3 \end{vmatrix}$ |

## SECTION
## 8.5 EXERCISES

### ▪ SKILLS

**In Exercises 1–10, evaluate each 2 × 2 determinant.**

**1.** $\begin{vmatrix} 1 & 2 \\ 3 & 4 \end{vmatrix}$
**2.** $\begin{vmatrix} 1 & -2 \\ -3 & -4 \end{vmatrix}$
**3.** $\begin{vmatrix} 7 & 9 \\ -5 & -2 \end{vmatrix}$
**4.** $\begin{vmatrix} -3 & -11 \\ 7 & 15 \end{vmatrix}$
**5.** $\begin{vmatrix} 0 & 7 \\ 4 & -1 \end{vmatrix}$

**6.** $\begin{vmatrix} 0 & 0 \\ 1 & 0 \end{vmatrix}$
**7.** $\begin{vmatrix} -1.2 & 2.4 \\ -0.5 & 1.5 \end{vmatrix}$
**8.** $\begin{vmatrix} -1.0 & 1.4 \\ 1.5 & -2.8 \end{vmatrix}$
**9.** $\begin{vmatrix} \frac{3}{4} & \frac{1}{3} \\ 2 & \frac{8}{9} \end{vmatrix}$
**10.** $\begin{vmatrix} -\frac{1}{2} & \frac{1}{4} \\ \frac{2}{3} & -\frac{8}{9} \end{vmatrix}$

**In Exercises 11–30, use Cramer's rule to solve each system of equations, if possible.**

**11.** $x + y = -1$
$x - y = 11$

**12.** $x + y = -1$
$x - y = -9$

**13.** $3x + 2y = -4$
$-2x + y = 5$

**14.** $5x + 3y = 1$
$4x - 7y = -18$

**15.** $3x - 2y = -1$
$5x + 4y = -31$

**16.** $x - 4y = -7$
$3x + 8y = 19$

**17.** $7x - 3y = -29$
$5x + 2y = 0$

**18.** $6x - 2y = 24$
$4x + 7y = 41$

**19.** $3x + 5y = 16$
$y - x = 0$

**20.** $-2x - 3y = 15$
$7y + 4x = -33$

**21.** $3x - 5y = 7$
$-6x + 10y = -21$

**22.** $3x - 5y = 7$
$6x - 10y = 14$

**23.** $2x - 3y = 4$
$-10x + 15y = -20$

**24.** $2x - 3y = 2$
$10x - 15y = 20$

**25.** $3x + \frac{1}{2}y = 1$
$4x + \frac{1}{3}y = \frac{5}{3}$

**26.** $\frac{3}{2}x + \frac{9}{4}y = \frac{9}{8}$
$\frac{1}{3}x + \frac{1}{4}y = \frac{1}{12}$

**27.** $0.3x - 0.5y = -0.6$
$0.2x + y = 2.4$

**28.** $0.5x - 0.4y = -3.6$
$10x + 3.6y = -14$

**29.** $y = 17x + 7$
$y = -15x + 7$

**30.** $9x = -45 - 2y$
$4x = -3y - 20$

**In Exercises 31–42, evaluate each 3 × 3 determinant.**

**31.** $\begin{vmatrix} 3 & 1 & 0 \\ 2 & 0 & -1 \\ -4 & 1 & 0 \end{vmatrix}$
**32.** $\begin{vmatrix} 1 & 1 & 0 \\ 0 & 2 & -1 \\ 0 & -3 & 5 \end{vmatrix}$
**33.** $\begin{vmatrix} 2 & 1 & -5 \\ 3 & 0 & -1 \\ 4 & 0 & 7 \end{vmatrix}$
**34.** $\begin{vmatrix} 2 & 1 & -5 \\ 3 & -7 & 0 \\ 4 & -6 & 0 \end{vmatrix}$

**35.** $\begin{vmatrix} 1 & 1 & -5 \\ 3 & -7 & -4 \\ 4 & -6 & 9 \end{vmatrix}$
**36.** $\begin{vmatrix} -3 & 2 & -5 \\ 1 & 8 & 2 \\ 4 & -6 & 9 \end{vmatrix}$
**37.** $\begin{vmatrix} 1 & 3 & 4 \\ 2 & -1 & 1 \\ 3 & -2 & 1 \end{vmatrix}$
**38.** $\begin{vmatrix} -7 & 2 & 5 \\ \frac{7}{8} & 3 & 4 \\ -1 & 4 & 6 \end{vmatrix}$

**39.** $\begin{vmatrix} -3 & 1 & 5 \\ 2 & 0 & 6 \\ 4 & 7 & -9 \end{vmatrix}$
**40.** $\begin{vmatrix} 1 & -1 & 5 \\ 3 & -3 & 6 \\ 4 & 9 & 0 \end{vmatrix}$
**41.** $\begin{vmatrix} -2 & 1 & -7 \\ 4 & -2 & 14 \\ 0 & 1 & 8 \end{vmatrix}$
**42.** $\begin{vmatrix} 5 & -2 & -1 \\ 4 & -9 & -3 \\ 2 & 8 & -6 \end{vmatrix}$

**In Exercises 43–58, apply Cramer's rule to solve each system of equations, if possible.**

**43.** $x + y - z = 0$
$x - y + z = 4$
$x + y + z = 10$

**44.** $-x + y + z = -4$
$x + y - z = 0$
$x + y + z = 2$

**45.** $3x + 8y + 2z = 28$
$-2x + 5y + 3z = 34$
$4x + 9y + 2z = 29$

**46.** $7x + 2y - z = -1$
$6x + 5y + z = 16$
$-5x - 4y + 3z = -5$

**47.** $3x + 5z = 11$
$4y + 3z = -9$
$2x - y = 7$

**48.** $3x - 2z = 7$
$4x + z = 24$
$6x - 2y = 10$

**49.** $x + y - z = 5$
$x - y + z = -1$
$-2x - 2y + 2z = -10$

**50.** $x + y - z = 3$
$x - y + z = -2$
$-2x - 2y + 2z = -6$

**51.** $\quad x + y + z = 9$
$\quad\quad x - y + z = 3$
$\quad\quad -x + y - z = 5$

**52.** $\quad x + y + z = 6$
$\quad\quad x - y - z = 0$
$\quad\quad -x + y + z = 7$

**53.** $\quad x + 2y + 3z = 11$
$\quad\quad -2x + 3y + 5z = 29$
$\quad\quad 4x - y + 8z = 19$

**54.** $8x - 2y + 5z = 36$
$\quad\ 3x + y - z = 17$
$\quad\ 2x - 6y + 4z = -2$

**55.** $\quad x - 4y + 7z = 49$
$\quad\quad -3x + 2y - z = -17$
$\quad\quad 5x + 8y - 2z = -24$

**56.** $\quad \frac{1}{2}x - 2y + 7z = 25$
$\quad\quad x + \frac{1}{4}y - 4z = -2$
$\quad\quad -4x + 5y = -56$

**57.** $\quad 2x + 7y - 4z = -5.5$
$\quad\quad -x - 4y - 5z = -19$
$\quad\quad 4x - 2y - 9z = -38$

**58.** $\quad 4x - 2y + z = -15$
$\quad\quad 3x + y - 2z = -20$
$\quad\quad -6x + y + 5z = 51$

## ▪ APPLICATIONS

**In Exercises 59 and 60, three points, $(x_1, y_1)$, $(x_2, y_2)$, and $(x_3, y_3)$, are collinear if and only if**

$$\begin{vmatrix} x_1 & y_1 & 1 \\ x_2 & y_2 & 1 \\ x_3 & y_3 & 1 \end{vmatrix} = 0$$

**59. Geometry.** Apply determinants to determine whether the points, $(-2, -1)$, $(1, 5)$, and $(3, 9)$, are collinear.

**60. Geometry.** Apply determinants to determine whether the points, $(2, -6)$, $(-7, 30)$, and $(5, -18)$, are collinear.

**For Exercises 61–64, the area of a triangle with vertices, $(x_1, y_1)$, $(x_2, y_2)$, and $(x_3, y_3)$, is given by**

$$\text{Area} = \pm\frac{1}{2}\begin{vmatrix} x_1 & y_1 & 1 \\ x_2 & y_2 & 1 \\ x_3 & y_3 & 1 \end{vmatrix}$$

**where the sign is chosen so that the area is positive.**

**61. Geometry.** Apply determinants to find the area of a triangle with vertices, $(3, 2)$, $(5, 2)$, and $(3, -4)$. Check your answer by plotting these vertices in a Cartesian plane and using the formula for area of a right triangle.

**62. Geometry.** Apply determinants to find the area of a triangle with vertices, $(2, 3)$, $(7, 3)$, and $(7, 7)$. Check your answer by plotting these vertices in a Cartesian plane and using the formula for area of a right triangle.

**63. Geometry.** Apply determinants to find the area of a triangle with vertices, $(1, 2)$, $(3, 4)$, and $(-2, 5)$.

**64. Geometry.** Apply determinants to find the area of a triangle with vertices, $(-1, -2)$, $(3, 4)$, and $(2, 1)$.

**65. Geometry.** An equation of a line that passes through two points $(x_1, y_1)$ and $(x_2, y_2)$ can be expressed as a determinant equation as follows:

$$\begin{vmatrix} x & y & 1 \\ x_1 & y_1 & 1 \\ x_2 & y_2 & 1 \end{vmatrix} = 0$$

Apply the determinant to write an equation of the line passing through the points $(1, 2)$ and $(2, 4)$. Expand the determinant and express the equation of the line in slope–intercept form.

**66. Geometry.** If three points $(x_1, y_1)$, $(x_2, y_2)$, and $(x_3, y_3)$ are collinear (lie on the same line), then the following determinant equation must be satisfied:

$$\begin{vmatrix} x_1 & y_1 & 1 \\ x_2 & y_2 & 1 \\ x_3 & y_3 & 1 \end{vmatrix} = 0$$

Determine whether $(0, 5)$, $(2, 0)$, and $(1, 2)$ are collinear.

**67. Electricity: Circuit Theory.** The following equations come from circuit theory. Find the currents $I_1$, $I_2$, and $I_3$.

$I_1 = I_2 + I_3$

$16 = 4I_1 + 2I_3$

$24 = 4I_1 + 4I_2$

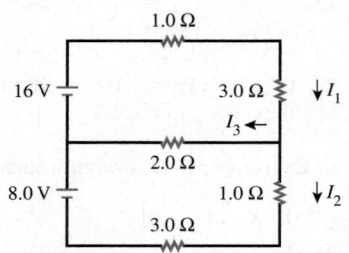

**68. Electricity: Circuit Theory.** The following equations come from circuit theory. Find the currents $I_1$, $I_2$, and $I_3$.

$I_1 = I_2 + I_3$

$24 = 6I_1 + 3I_3$

$36 = 6I_1 + 6I_2$

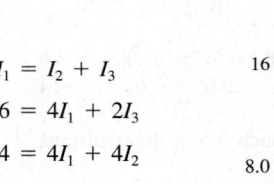

■ **CATCH THE MISTAKE**

**In Exercises 69–72, explain the mistake that is made.**

**69.** Evaluate the determinant $\begin{vmatrix} 2 & 1 & 3 \\ -3 & 0 & 2 \\ 1 & 4 & -1 \end{vmatrix}$.

**Solution:**

Expand the $3 \times 3$ determinant in terms of the $2 \times 2$ determinants.

$$\begin{vmatrix} 2 & 1 & 3 \\ -3 & 0 & 2 \\ 1 & 4 & -1 \end{vmatrix} = 2\begin{vmatrix} 0 & 2 \\ 4 & -1 \end{vmatrix} + 1\begin{vmatrix} -3 & 2 \\ 1 & -1 \end{vmatrix} + 3\begin{vmatrix} -3 & 0 \\ 1 & 4 \end{vmatrix}$$

Expand the $2 \times 2$ determinants.   $= 2(0 - 8) + 1(3 - 2) + 3(-12 - 0)$

Simplify.   $= -16 + 1 - 36 = -51$

This is incorrect. What mistake was made?

**70.** Evaluate the determinant $\begin{vmatrix} 2 & 1 & 3 \\ -3 & 0 & 2 \\ 1 & 4 & -1 \end{vmatrix}$.

**Solution:**

Expand the $3 \times 3$ determinant in terms of the $2 \times 2$ determinants.

$$\begin{vmatrix} 2 & 1 & 3 \\ -3 & 0 & 2 \\ 1 & 4 & -1 \end{vmatrix} = 2\begin{vmatrix} 0 & 2 \\ 4 & -1 \end{vmatrix} - 1\begin{vmatrix} -3 & 2 \\ 1 & -1 \end{vmatrix} + 3\begin{vmatrix} -3 & 2 \\ 1 & -1 \end{vmatrix}$$

Expand the $2 \times 2$ determinants.   $= 2(0 - 8) - 1(3 - 2) + 3(3 - 2)$

Simplify.   $= -16 - 1 + 3 = -14$

This is incorrect. What mistake was made?

**71.** Solve the system of linear equations.

$$2x + 3y = 6$$
$$-x - y = -3$$

**Solution:**

Set up the determinants.

$$D = \begin{vmatrix} 2 & 3 \\ -1 & -1 \end{vmatrix}, D_x = \begin{vmatrix} 2 & 6 \\ -1 & -3 \end{vmatrix}, \text{ and } D_y = \begin{vmatrix} 6 & 3 \\ -3 & -1 \end{vmatrix}$$

Evaluate the determinants.   $D = 1, D_x = 0, \text{ and } D_y = 3$

Solve for $x$ and $y$.   $x = \dfrac{D_x}{D} = \dfrac{0}{1} = 0$ and $y = \dfrac{D_y}{D} = \dfrac{3}{1} = 3$

$x = 0, y = 3$ is incorrect. What mistake was made?

**72.** Solve the system of linear equations.

$$4x - 6y = 0$$
$$4x + 6y = 4$$

**Solution:**

Set up the determinants.

$$D = \begin{vmatrix} 4 & -6 \\ 4 & 6 \end{vmatrix}, D_x = \begin{vmatrix} 0 & -6 \\ 4 & 6 \end{vmatrix}, \text{ and } D_y = \begin{vmatrix} 4 & 0 \\ 4 & 4 \end{vmatrix}$$

Evaluate the determinants.   $D = 48, D_x = 24, \text{ and } D_y = 16$

Solve for $x$ and $y$.   $x = \dfrac{D}{D_x} = \dfrac{48}{24} = 2$ and $y = \dfrac{D_y}{D} = \dfrac{48}{16} = 3$

$x = 2, y = 3$ is incorrect. What mistake was made?

■ **CONCEPTUAL**

**In Exercises 73–76, determine whether each statement is true or false.**

**73.** The value of a determinant changes sign if any two rows are interchanged.

**74.** If all the entries in any column are equal to zero, the value of the determinant is 0.

**75.** $\begin{vmatrix} 2 & 6 & 4 \\ 0 & 2 & 8 \\ 4 & 0 & 10 \end{vmatrix} = 2\begin{vmatrix} 1 & 3 & 2 \\ 0 & 1 & 4 \\ 2 & 0 & 5 \end{vmatrix}$

**76.** $\begin{vmatrix} 3 & 1 & 2 \\ 0 & 2 & 8 \\ 3 & 1 & 2 \end{vmatrix} = 0$

**77.** Calculate the determinant $\begin{vmatrix} a & 0 & 0 \\ 0 & b & 0 \\ 0 & 0 & c \end{vmatrix}$.

**78.** Calculate the determinant $\begin{vmatrix} a_1 & b_1 & c_1 \\ 0 & b_2 & c_2 \\ 0 & 0 & c_3 \end{vmatrix}$.

■ **CHALLENGE**

**79.** Evaluate the determinant:

$$\begin{vmatrix} 1 & -2 & -1 & 3 \\ 4 & 0 & 1 & 2 \\ 0 & 3 & 2 & 4 \\ 1 & -3 & 5 & -4 \end{vmatrix}$$

**80.** For the system of equations

$$3x + 2y = 5$$
$$ax - 4y = 1$$

find $a$ that guarantees no unique solution.

**81.** Show that

$$\begin{vmatrix} a_1 & b_1 & c_1 \\ a_2 & b_2 & c_2 \\ a_3 & b_3 & c_3 \end{vmatrix} = \begin{matrix} a_1b_2c_3 + b_1c_2a_3 + c_1a_2b_3 \\ -a_3b_2c_1 - b_3c_2a_1 - b_1a_2c_3 \end{matrix}$$

by expanding down the second column.

**82.** Show that

$$\begin{vmatrix} a_1 & b_1 & c_1 \\ a_2 & b_2 & c_2 \\ a_3 & b_3 & c_3 \end{vmatrix} = \begin{matrix} a_1b_2c_3 + b_1c_2a_3 + c_1a_2b_3 \\ -a_3b_2c_1 - b_3c_2a_1 - c_3b_1a_2 \end{matrix}$$

by expanding across the third row.

**83.** Show that

$$\begin{vmatrix} a^2 & a & 1 \\ b^2 & b & 1 \\ c^2 & c & 1 \end{vmatrix} = (a - b)(a - c)(b - c)$$

**84.** For the system of equations

$$x + 3y + 2z = 0$$
$$x + ay + 4z = 0$$
$$2y + az = 0$$

find the value(s) of $a$ that guarantees no unique solution.

■ **TECHNOLOGY**

**In Exercises 85–88, apply a graphing utility to evaluate the determinants.**

**85.** $\begin{vmatrix} 1 & 1 & -5 \\ 3 & -7 & -4 \\ 4 & -6 & 9 \end{vmatrix}$  Compare with your answer to Exercise 35.

**86.** $\begin{vmatrix} -3 & 2 & -5 \\ 1 & 8 & 2 \\ 4 & -6 & 9 \end{vmatrix}$  Compare with your answer to Exercise 36.

**87.** $\begin{vmatrix} -3 & 2 & -1 & 3 \\ 4 & 1 & 5 & 2 \\ 17 & 2 & 2 & 8 \\ 13 & -4 & 10 & -11 \end{vmatrix}$

**88.** $\begin{vmatrix} -3 & 21 & 19 & 3 \\ 4 & 1 & 16 & 2 \\ 17 & 31 & 2 & 5 \\ 13 & -4 & 10 & 2 \end{vmatrix}$

**In Exercises 89 and 90, apply Cramer's rule to solve each system of equations and a graphing utility to evaluate the determinants.**

**89.**
$$3.1x + 1.6y - 4.8z = -33.76$$
$$5.2x - 3.4y + 0.5z = -36.68$$
$$0.5x - 6.4y + 11.4z = 25.96$$

**90.**
$$-9.2x + 2.7y + 5.1z = -89.20$$
$$4.3x - 6.9y - 7.6z = 38.89$$
$$2.8x - 3.9y - 3.5z = 34.08$$

■ **PREVIEW TO CALCULUS**

**In calculus, determinants are used when evaluating double and triple integrals through a change of variables. In these cases, the elements of the determinant are functions.**

**In Exercises 91–94, find each determinant.**

**91.** $\begin{vmatrix} \cos\theta & -r\sin\theta \\ \sin\theta & r\cos\theta \end{vmatrix}$

**92.** $\begin{vmatrix} 2x & 2y \\ 2x & 2y - 2 \end{vmatrix}$

**93.** $\begin{vmatrix} \sin\phi\cos\theta & -\rho\sin\phi\sin\theta & \rho\cos\phi\cos\theta \\ \sin\phi\sin\theta & \rho\sin\phi\cos\theta & \rho\cos\phi\sin\theta \\ \cos\phi & 0 & -\rho\sin\phi \end{vmatrix}$

**94.** $\begin{vmatrix} \cos\theta & -r\sin\theta & 0 \\ \sin\theta & r\cos\theta & 0 \\ 0 & 0 & 1 \end{vmatrix}$

**SKILLS OBJECTIVES**

- Decompose rational expressions into sums of partial fractions when the denominators contain:
  - Distinct linear factors
  - Repeated linear factors
  - Distinct irreducible quadratic factors
  - Repeated irreducible quadratic factors

**CONCEPTUAL OBJECTIVE**

- Understand the connection between partial-fraction decomposition and systems of linear equations.

## Performing Partial Fraction Decomposition

In Chapter 2, we studied polynomial functions, and in Section 2.6, we discussed ratios of polynomial functions, called rational functions. Rational expressions are of the form

$$\frac{n(x)}{d(x)} \qquad d(x) \neq 0$$

where the numerator $n(x)$ and the denominator $d(x)$ are polynomials. Examples of rational expressions are

$$\frac{4x - 1}{2x + 3} \qquad \frac{2x + 5}{x^2 - 1} \qquad \frac{3x^4 - 2x + 5}{x^2 + 2x + 4}$$

Suppose we are asked to add two rational expressions: $\dfrac{2}{x + 1} + \dfrac{5}{x - 3}$.

We already possess the skills to accomplish this. We first identify the least common denominator $(x + 1)(x - 3)$ and combine the fractions into a single expression.

$$\frac{2}{x + 1} + \frac{5}{x - 3} = \frac{2(x - 3) + 5(x + 1)}{(x + 1)(x - 3)} = \frac{2x - 6 + 5x + 5}{(x + 1)(x - 3)} = \frac{7x - 1}{x^2 - 2x - 3}$$

How do we do this in reverse? For example, how do we start with $\dfrac{7x - 1}{x^2 - 2x - 3}$ and write this expression as a sum of two simpler expressions?

Partial-Fraction Decomposition

$$\frac{7x - 1}{x^2 - 2x - 3} = \overbrace{\underbrace{\frac{2}{x + 1}}_{\text{Partial Fraction}} + \underbrace{\frac{5}{x - 3}}_{\text{Partial Fraction}}}$$

Each of the two expressions on the right is called a **partial fraction**. The sum of these fractions is called the **partial-fraction decomposition** of $\dfrac{7x - 1}{x^2 - 2x - 3}$.

Partial-fraction decomposition is an important tool in calculus. Calculus operations such as differentiation and integration are often made simpler if you apply partial fractions. The reason partial fractions were not discussed until now is because partial-fraction decomposition *requires the ability to solve systems of linear equations*. Since partial-fraction decomposition is made possible by the techniques of solving systems of linear equations, we consider partial fractions an important application of systems of linear equations.

As mentioned earlier, a rational expression is the ratio of two polynomial expressions $n(x)/d(x)$ and we assume that $n(x)$ and $d(x)$ are polynomials with no common factors other than 1. If the degree of $n(x)$ is less than the degree of $d(x)$, then the rational expression

$n(x)/d(x)$ is said to be **proper**. If the degree of $n(x)$ is greater than or equal to the degree of $d(x)$, the rational expression is said to be **improper**. If the rational expression is improper, it should first be divided using long division.

$$\frac{n(x)}{d(x)} = Q(x) + \frac{r(x)}{d(x)}$$

The result is the sum of a quotient $Q(x)$ and a rational expression, which is the ratio of the remainder $r(x)$ and the divisor $d(x)$. The rational expression $r(x)/d(x)$ is proper, and the techniques outlined in this section can be applied to its partial-fraction decomposition.

Partial-fraction decomposition of proper rational expressions always begins with factoring the denominator $d(x)$. The goal is to write $d(x)$ as a product of distinct linear factors, but that may not always be possible. Sometimes $d(x)$ can be factored into a product of linear factors, where one or more are repeated. And, sometimes the factored form of $d(x)$ contains irreducible quadratic factors, such as $x^2 + 1$. There are times when the irreducible quadratic factors are repeated, such as $(x^2 + 1)^2$. A procedure is now outlined for partial-fraction decomposition.

## PARTIAL-FRACTION DECOMPOSITION

To write a rational expression $\dfrac{n(x)}{d(x)}$ as a sum of partial fractions:

**Step 1:** Determine whether the rational expression is proper or improper.

- Proper:        degree of $n(x) <$ degree of $d(x)$
- Improper:     degree of $n(x) \geq$ degree of $d(x)$

**Step 2:** If proper, proceed to Step 3.

If improper, divide $\dfrac{n(x)}{d(x)}$ using polynomial (long) division and write

the result as $\dfrac{n(x)}{d(x)} = Q(x) + \dfrac{r(x)}{d(x)}$ and proceed to Step 3 with $\dfrac{r(x)}{d(x)}$.

**Step 3:** Factor $d(x)$. One of four possible cases will arise:

*Case 1* Distinct (nonrepeated) *linear* factors: $(ax + b)$

Example: $d(x) = (3x - 1)(x + 2)$

*Case 2* One or more repeated linear factors: $(ax + b)^m$     $m \geq 2$

Example: $d(x) = (x + 5)^2(x - 3)$

*Case 3* One or more distinct irreducible $(ax^2 + bx + c = 0$ has no real roots$)$ quadratic factors: $(ax^2 + bx + c)$

Example: $d(x) = (x^2 + 4)(x + 1)(x - 2)$

*Case 4* One or more repeated irreducible quadratic factors: $(ax^2 + bx + c)^m$

Example: $d(x) = (x^2 + x + 1)^2(x + 1)(x - 2)$

**Step 4:** Decompose the rational expression into a sum of partial fractions according to the procedure outlined in each case in this section.

Step 4 depends on which cases, or types of factors, arise. It is important to note that these four cases are not exclusive and combinations of different types of factors will appear.

## Distinct Linear Factors

### CASE 1: $d(x)$ HAS ONLY DISTINCT (NONREPEATED) LINEAR FACTORS

If $d(x)$ is a polynomial of degree $p$, and it can be factored into $p$ linear factors

$$d(x) = \underbrace{(ax + b)(cx + d)\ldots}_{p \text{ linear factors}}$$

where no two factors are the same, then the partial-fraction decomposition of $\dfrac{n(x)}{d(x)}$ can be written as

$$\frac{n(x)}{d(x)} = \frac{A}{(ax + b)} + \frac{B}{(cx + d)} + \cdots$$

where the numerators, $A$, $B$, and so on are constants to be determined.

The goal is to write a proper rational expression as the sum of proper rational expressions. Therefore, if the denominator is a linear factor (degree 1), then the numerator is a constant (degree 0).

**EXAMPLE 1   Partial-Fraction Decomposition with Distinct Linear Factors**

Find the partial-fraction decomposition of $\dfrac{5x + 13}{x^2 + 4x - 5}$.

**Solution:**

| | |
|---|---|
| Factor the denominator. | $\dfrac{5x + 13}{(x - 1)(x + 5)}$ |
| Express as a sum of two partial fractions. | $\dfrac{5x + 13}{(x - 1)(x + 5)} = \dfrac{A}{(x - 1)} + \dfrac{B}{(x + 5)}$ |
| Multiply the two sides of the equation by the LCD $(x - 1)(x + 5)$. | $5x + 13 = A(x + 5) + B(x - 1)$ |
| Eliminate the parentheses. | $5x + 13 = Ax + 5A + Bx - B$ |
| Group the $x$'s and constants on the right. | $5x + 13 = (A + B)x + (5A - B)$ |
| Identify like terms. | $5x + 13 = (A + B)x + (5A - B)$ |
| Equate the **coefficients of** $x$. | $5 = A + B$ |
| Equate the **constant** terms. | $13 = 5A - B$ |
| Solve the system of two linear equations using any method to solve for $A$ and $B$. | $A = 3, B = 2$ |
| Substitute $A = 3$, $B = 2$ into the partial-fraction decomposition. | $\boxed{\dfrac{5x + 13}{(x - 1)(x + 5)} = \dfrac{3}{(x - 1)} + \dfrac{2}{(x + 5)}}$ |

Check by adding the partial fractions.

$$\frac{3}{(x - 1)} + \frac{2}{(x + 5)} = \frac{3(x + 5) + 2(x - 1)}{(x - 1)(x + 5)} = \frac{5x + 13}{x^2 + 4x - 5}$$

■ **YOUR TURN** Find the partial-fraction decomposition of $\dfrac{4x - 13}{x^2 - 3x - 10}$.

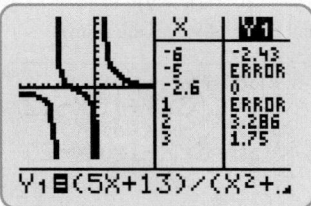
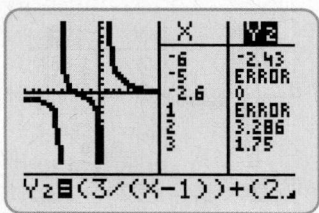
■ **Answer:**

$$\frac{4x - 13}{x^2 - 3x - 10} = \frac{3}{x + 2} + \frac{1}{x - 5}$$

In Example 1, we started with a rational expression that had a numerator of degree 1 and a denominator of degree 2. Partial-fraction decomposition enabled us to write that rational expression as a sum of two rational expressions with degree 0 numerators and degree 1 denominators.

## Repeated Linear Factors

### CASE 2: $d(x)$ HAS AT LEAST ONE REPEATED LINEAR FACTOR

If $d(x)$ can be factored into a product of linear factors, then the partial-fraction decomposition will proceed as in Case 1, with the exception of a repeated factor $(ax + b)^m$, $m \geq 2$. Any linear factor repeated $m$ times will result in the sum of $m$ partial fractions

$$\frac{A}{(ax + b)} + \frac{B}{(ax + b)^2} + \frac{C}{(ax + b)^3} + \cdots + \frac{M}{(ax + b)^m}$$

where the numerators, $A, B, C, \ldots, M$ are constants to be determined.

Note that if $d(x)$ is of degree $p$, the general form of the decomposition will have $p$ partial fractions. If some numerator constants turn out to be zero, then the final decomposition may have fewer than $p$ partial fractions.

### Technology Tip

Use a TI to check the graph of $Y_1 = \dfrac{-3x^2 + 13x - 12}{x^3 - 4x^2 + 4x}$ and its partial-fraction decomposition $Y_2 = \dfrac{-3}{x} + \dfrac{1}{(x - 2)^2}$. The graphs and tables of values are shown.

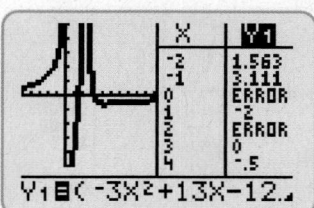

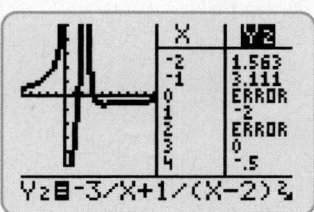

**EXAMPLE 2   Partial-Fraction Decomposition with a Repeated Linear Factor**

Find the partial-fraction decomposition of $\dfrac{-3x^2 + 13x - 12}{x^3 - 4x^2 + 4x}$.

**Solution:**

Factor the denominator. $\dfrac{-3x^2 + 13x - 12}{x(x - 2)^2}$

Express as a sum of three partial fractions. $\dfrac{-3x^2 + 13x - 12}{x(x - 2)^2} = \dfrac{A}{x} + \dfrac{B}{(x - 2)} + \dfrac{C}{(x - 2)^2}$

Multiply both sides by the LCD $x(x - 2)^2$. $-3x^2 + 13x - 12 = A(x - 2)^2 + Bx(x - 2) + Cx$

Eliminate the parentheses. $-3x^2 + 13x - 12 = Ax^2 - 4Ax + 4A + Bx^2 - 2Bx + Cx$

Group like terms on the right. $-3x^2 + 13x - 12 = (A + B)x^2 + (-4A - 2B + C)x + 4A$

Identify like terms on both sides. $-3x^2 + 13x - 12 = (A + B)x^2 + (-4A - 2B + C)x + 4A$

Equate the **coefficients of $x^2$**. $-3 = A + B$ (1)

Equate the **coefficients of $x$**. $13 = -4A - 2B + C$ (2)

Equate the **constant** terms. $-12 = 4A$ (3)

Solve the system of three equations for $A$, $B$, and $C$.

| | |
|---|---|
| Solve (3) for $A$. | $A = -3$ |
| Substitute $A = -3$ into (1). | $B = 0$ |
| Substitute $A = -3$ and $B = 0$ into (2). | $C = 1$ |

Substitute $A = -3$, $B = 0$, $C = 1$ into the partial-fraction decomposition.

$$\frac{-3x^2 + 13x - 12}{x(x-2)^2} = \frac{-3}{x} + \frac{0}{(x-2)} + \frac{1}{(x-2)^2}$$

$$\boxed{\frac{-3x^2 + 13x - 12}{x^3 - 4x^2 + 4x} = \frac{-3}{x} + \frac{1}{(x-2)^2}}$$

Check by adding the partial fractions.

$$\frac{-3}{x} + \frac{1}{(x-2)^2} = \frac{-3(x-2)^2 + 1(x)}{x(x-2)^2} = \frac{-3x^2 + 13x - 12}{x^3 - 4x^2 + 4x}$$

■ **YOUR TURN** Find the partial-fraction decomposition of $\dfrac{x^2 + 1}{x^3 + 2x^2 + x}$.

■ **Answer:**
$$\frac{x^2 + 1}{x^3 + 2x^2 + x} = \frac{1}{x} - \frac{2}{(x+1)^2}$$

## EXAMPLE 3   Partial-Fraction Decomposition with Multiple Repeated Linear Factors

Find the partial-fraction decomposition of $\dfrac{2x^3 + 6x^2 + 6x + 9}{x^4 + 6x^3 + 9x^2}$.

**Solution:**

Factor the denominator.

$$\frac{2x^3 + 6x^2 + 6x + 9}{x^2(x+3)^2}$$

Express as a sum of four partial fractions.

$$\frac{2x^3 + 6x^2 + 6x + 9}{x^2(x+3)^2} = \frac{A}{x} + \frac{B}{x^2} + \frac{C}{(x+3)} + \frac{D}{(x+3)^2}$$

Multiply both sides by the LCD $x^2(x+3)^2$.

$$2x^3 + 6x^2 + 6x + 9 = Ax(x+3)^2 + B(x+3)^2 + Cx^2(x+3) + Dx^2$$

Eliminate the parentheses.

$$2x^3 + 6x^2 + 6x + 9 = Ax^3 + 6Ax^2 + 9Ax + Bx^2 + 6Bx + 9B + Cx^3 + 3Cx^2 + Dx^2$$

Group like terms on the right.

$$2x^3 + 6x^2 + 6x + 9 = (A+C)x^3 + (6A+B+3C+D)x^2 + (9A+6B)x + 9B$$

Identify like terms on both sides.

$$2x^3 + 6x^2 + 6x + 9 = (A+C)x^3 + (6A+B+3C+D)x^2 + (9A+6B)x + 9B$$

| | | |
|---|---|---|
| Equate the **coefficients of $x^3$**. | $2 = A + C$ | (1) |
| Equate the **coefficients of $x^2$**. | $6 = 6A + B + 3C + D$ | (2) |
| Equate the **coefficients of $x$**. | $6 = 9A + 6B$ | (3) |
| Equate the **constant terms**. | $9 = 9B$ | (4) |

Solve the system of four equations for $A$, $B$, $C$, and $D$.

| | |
|---|---|
| Solve Equation (4) for $B$. | $B = 1$ |
| Substitute $B = 1$ into Equation (3) and solve for $A$. | $A = 0$ |
| Substitute $A = 0$ into Equation (1) and solve for $C$. | $C = 2$ |
| Substitute $A = 0$, $B = 1$, and $C = 2$ into Equation (2) and solve for $D$. | $D = -1$ |

Substitute $A = 0$, $B = 1$, $C = 2$, $D = -1$ into the partial-fraction decomposition.

$$\frac{2x^3 + 6x^2 + 6x + 9}{x^2(x + 3)^2} = \frac{0}{x} + \frac{1}{x^2} + \frac{2}{(x + 3)} + \frac{-1}{(x + 3)^2}$$

$$\boxed{\frac{2x^3 + 6x^2 + 6x + 9}{x^2(x + 3)^2} = \frac{1}{x^2} + \frac{2}{(x + 3)} - \frac{1}{(x + 3)^2}}$$

Check by adding the partial fractions.

$$\frac{1}{x^2} + \frac{2}{(x + 3)} - \frac{1}{(x + 3)^2} = \frac{(x + 3)^2 + 2x^2(x + 3) - 1(x^2)}{x^2(x + 3)^2}$$

$$= \frac{2x^3 + 6x^2 + 6x + 9}{x^4 + 6x^3 + 9x^2}$$

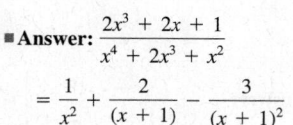

■**Answer:** $\dfrac{2x^3 + 2x + 1}{x^4 + 2x^3 + x^2}$

$= \dfrac{1}{x^2} + \dfrac{2}{(x + 1)} - \dfrac{3}{(x + 1)^2}$

■ **YOUR TURN** Find the partial-fraction decomposition of $\dfrac{2x^3 + 2x + 1}{x^4 + 2x^3 + x^2}$.

## Distinct Irreducible Quadratic Factors

There will be times when a polynomial cannot be factored into a product of linear factors with real coefficients. For example, $x^2 + 4$, $x^2 + x + 1$, and $9x^2 + 3x + 2$ are all examples of *irreducible quadratic* expressions. The general form of an **irreducible quadratic factor** is given by

$$ax^2 + bx + c \quad \text{where } ax^2 + bx + c = 0 \text{ has no real roots}$$

### CASE 3: $d(x)$ HAS A DISTINCT IRREDUCIBLE QUADRATIC FACTOR

If the factored form of $d(x)$ contains an irreducible quadratic factor $ax^2 + bx + c$, then the partial-fraction decomposition will contain a term of the form

$$\frac{Ax + B}{ax^2 + bx + c}$$

where $A$ and $B$ are constants to be determined.

**Study Tip**

In a partial-fraction decomposition, the degree of the numerator is always 1 less than the degree of the denominator.

Recall that for a proper rational expression, the degree of the numerator is less than the degree of the denominator. For irreducible quadratic (degree 2) denominators we assume a linear (degree 1) numerator. For example,

$$\frac{7x^2 + 2}{(2x + 1)(x^2 + 1)} = \underbrace{\frac{A}{(2x + 1)}}_{\substack{\text{Constant numerator} \\ \text{Linear factor}}} + \underbrace{\frac{Bx + C}{(x^2 + 1)}}_{\substack{\text{Linear numerator} \\ \text{Quadratic factor}}}$$

A constant is used in the numerator when the denominator consists of a linear expression and a linear expression is used in the numerator when the denominator consists of a quadratic expression.

**EXAMPLE 4   Partial-Fraction Decomposition with an Irreducible Quadratic Factor**

Find the partial-fraction decomposition of $\dfrac{7x^2 + 2}{(2x + 1)(x^2 + 1)}$.

**Solution:**

The denominator is already in factored form.

$$\frac{7x^2 + 2}{(2x + 1)(x^2 + 1)}$$

Express as a sum of two partial fractions.

$$\frac{7x^2 + 2}{(2x + 1)(x^2 + 1)} = \frac{A}{(2x + 1)} + \frac{Bx + C}{(x^2 + 1)}$$

Multiply both sides by the LCD $(2x + 1)(x^2 + 1)$.

$$7x^2 + 2 = A(x^2 + 1) + (Bx + C)(2x + 1)$$

Eliminate the parentheses.

$$7x^2 + 2 = Ax^2 + A + 2Bx^2 + Bx + 2Cx + C$$

Group like terms on the right.

$$7x^2 + 2 = (A + 2B)x^2 + (B + 2C)x + (A + C)$$

Identify like terms on both sides.

$$7x^2 + 0x + 2 = (A + 2B)x^2 + (B + 2C)x + (A + C)$$

Equate the **coefficients** of $x^2$.

$$7 = A + 2B$$

Equate the **coefficients** of $x$.

$$0 = B + 2C$$

Equate the **constant** terms.

$$2 = A + C$$

Solve the system of three equations for $A$, $B$, and $C$.

$$A = 3,\ B = 2,\ C = -1$$

Substitute $A = 3$, $B = 2$, $C = -1$ into the partial-fraction decomposition.

$$\boxed{\frac{7x^2 + 2}{(2x + 1)(x^2 + 1)} = \frac{3}{(2x + 1)} + \frac{2x - 1}{(x^2 + 1)}}$$

Check by adding the partial fractions.

$$\frac{3}{(2x + 1)} + \frac{2x - 1}{(x^2 + 1)} = \frac{3(x^2 + 1) + (2x - 1)(2x + 1)}{(2x + 1)(x^2 + 1)} = \frac{7x^2 + 2}{(2x + 1)(x^2 + 1)}$$

■ **YOUR TURN** Find the partial-fraction decomposition of $\dfrac{-2x^2 + x + 6}{(x - 1)(x^2 + 4)}$.

**Technology Tip**

Use a TI to check the graph of

$$Y_1 = \frac{7x^2 + 2}{(2x + 1)(x^2 + 1)}$$ and its

partial-fraction decomposition

$$Y_2 = \frac{3}{2x + 1} + \frac{2x - 1}{x^2 + 1}.$$ The graphs

and tables of values are shown.

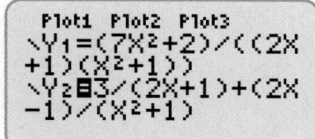

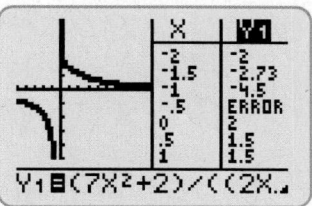

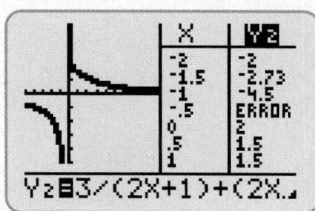

■**Answer:** $\dfrac{-2x^2 + x + 6}{(x - 1)(x^2 + 4)}$

$$= \frac{1}{x - 1} - \frac{3x + 2}{x^2 + 4}$$

## Repeated Irreducible Quadratic Factors

### CASE 4: $d(x)$ HAS A REPEATED IRREDUCIBLE QUADRATIC FACTOR

If the factored form of $d(x)$ contains an irreducible quadratic factor $\left(ax^2 + bx + c\right)^m$, where $b^2 - 4ac < 0$, then the partial-fraction decomposition will contain a series of terms of the form

$$\frac{A_1x + B_1}{ax^2 + bx + c} + \frac{A_2x + B_2}{\left(ax^2 + bx + c\right)^2} + \frac{A_3x + B_3}{\left(ax^2 + bx + c\right)^3} + \cdots + \frac{A_mx + B_m}{\left(ax^2 + bx + c\right)^m}$$

where $A_i$ and $B_i$ with $i = 1, 2, \ldots, m$, are constants to be determined.

**EXAMPLE 5  Partial-Fraction Decomposition with a Repeated Irreducible Quadratic Factor**

Find the partial-fraction decomposition of $\dfrac{x^3 - x^2 + 3x + 2}{\left(x^2 + 1\right)^2}$.

**Solution:**

The denominator is already in factored form.

$$\dfrac{x^3 - x^2 + 3x + 2}{\left(x^2 + 1\right)^2}$$

Express as a sum of two partial fractions.

$$\dfrac{x^3 - x^2 + 3x + 2}{\left(x^2 + 1\right)^2} = \dfrac{Ax + B}{x^2 + 1} + \dfrac{Cx + D}{\left(x^2 + 1\right)^2}$$

Multiply both sides by the LCD $\left(x^2 + 1\right)^2$.

$$x^3 - x^2 + 3x + 2 = (Ax + B)\left(x^2 + 1\right) + Cx + D$$

Eliminate the parentheses.

$$x^3 - x^2 + 3x + 2 = Ax^3 + Bx^2 + Ax + B + Cx + D$$

Group like terms on the right.

$$x^3 - x^2 + 3x + 2 = Ax^3 + Bx^2 + (A + C)x + (B + D)$$

Identify like terms on both sides.

$$x^3 - x^2 + 3x + 2 = Ax^3 + Bx^2 + (A + C)x + (B + D)$$

Equate the **coefficients of $x^3$**.  $\qquad 1 = A \qquad (1)$

Equate the **coefficients of $x^2$**.  $\qquad -1 = B \qquad (2)$

Equate the **coefficients of $x$**.  $\qquad 3 = A + C \qquad (3)$

Equate the **constant terms**.  $\qquad 2 = B + D \qquad (4)$

Substitute $A = 1$ into Equation (3) and solve for $C$.  $\qquad C = 2$

Substitute $B = -1$ into Equation (4) and solve for $D$.  $\qquad D = 3$

Substitute $A = 1, B = -1, C = 2, D = 3$ into the partial-fraction decomposition.

$$\dfrac{x^3 - x^2 + 3x + 2}{\left(x^2 + 1\right)^2} = \dfrac{x - 1}{x^2 + 1} + \dfrac{2x + 3}{\left(x^2 + 1\right)^2}$$

Check by adding the partial fractions.

$$\dfrac{x - 1}{x^2 + 1} + \dfrac{2x + 3}{\left(x^2 + 1\right)^2} = \dfrac{(x - 1)\left(x^2 + 1\right) + (2x + 3)}{\left(x^2 + 1\right)^2} = \dfrac{x^3 - x^2 + 3x + 2}{\left(x^2 + 1\right)^2}$$

■ **Answer:** $\dfrac{3x^3 + x^2 + 4x - 1}{\left(x^2 + 4\right)^2}$

$= \dfrac{3x + 1}{x^2 + 4} - \dfrac{8x + 5}{\left(x^2 + 4\right)^2}$

■ **YOUR TURN** Find the partial-fraction decomposition of $\dfrac{3x^3 + x^2 + 4x - 1}{\left(x^2 + 4\right)^2}$.

## Combinations of All Four Cases

As you probably can imagine, there are rational expressions that have combinations of all four cases, which can lead to a system of several equations when solving for the unknown constants in the numerators of the partial fractions.

**EXAMPLE 6  Partial-Fraction Decomposition**

Find the partial-fraction decomposition of $\dfrac{x^5 + x^4 + 4x^3 - 3x^2 + 4x - 8}{x^2(x^2 + 2)^2}$.

**Solution:**

The denominator is already in factored form.

$$\frac{x^5 + x^4 + 4x^3 - 3x^2 + 4x - 8}{x^2(x^2 + 2)^2}$$

Express as a sum of partial fractions.

There are repeated linear and irreducible quadratic factors.

$$\frac{x^5 + x^4 + 4x^3 - 3x^2 + 4x - 8}{x^2(x^2 + 2)^2} = \frac{A}{x} + \frac{B}{x^2} + \frac{Cx + D}{(x^2 + 2)} + \frac{Ex + F}{(x^2 + 2)^2}$$

Multiply both sides by the LCD $x^2(x^2 + 2)^2$.

$$x^5 + x^4 + 4x^3 - 3x^2 + 4x - 8$$
$$= Ax(x^2 + 2)^2 + B(x^2 + 2)^2 + (Cx + D)x^2(x^2 + 2) + (Ex + F)x^2$$

Eliminate the parentheses.

$$x^5 + x^4 + 4x^3 - 3x^2 + 4x - 8$$
$$= Ax^5 + 4Ax^3 + 4Ax + Bx^4 + 4Bx^2 + 4B + Cx^5 + 2Cx^3 + Dx^4 + 2Dx^2 + Ex^3 + Fx^2$$

Group like terms on the right.

$$x^5 + x^4 + 4x^3 - 3x^2 + 4x - 8$$
$$= (A + C)x^5 + (B + D)x^4 + (4A + 2C + E)x^3 + (4B + 2D + F)x^2 + 4Ax + 4B$$

Equating the coefficients of like terms leads to six equations.

$$A + C = 1$$
$$B + D = 1$$
$$4A + 2C + E = 4$$
$$4B + 2D + F = -3$$
$$4A = 4$$
$$4B = -8$$

Solve this system of equations.

$$A = 1, \quad B = -2, \quad C = 0, \quad D = 3, \quad E = 0, \quad F = -1$$

Substitute $A = 1$, $B = -2$, $C = 0$, $D = 3$, $E = 0$, $F = -1$ into the partial-fraction decomposition.

$$\frac{x^5 + x^4 + 4x^3 - 3x^2 + 4x - 8}{x^2(x^2 + 2)^2} = \frac{1}{x} + \frac{-2}{x^2} + \frac{0x + 3}{(x^2 + 2)} + \frac{0x + -1}{(x^2 + 2)^2}$$

$$\boxed{\frac{x^5 + x^4 + 4x^3 - 3x^2 + 4x - 8}{x^2(x^2 + 2)^2} = \frac{1}{x} - \frac{2}{x^2} + \frac{3}{(x^2 + 2)} - \frac{1}{(x^2 + 2)^2}}$$

Check by adding the partial fractions.

**SECTION**
**8.6 SUMMARY**

A rational expression $\dfrac{n(x)}{d(x)}$ is

- **Proper:** If the degree of the numerator is less than the degree of the denominator.
- **Improper:** If the degree of the numerator is equal to or greater than the degree of the denominator.

**Partial-Fraction Decomposition of Proper Rational Expressions**

1. Distinct (nonrepeated) linear factors

    Example: $\dfrac{3x - 10}{(x - 5)(x + 4)} = \dfrac{A}{x - 5} + \dfrac{B}{x + 4}$

2. Repeated linear factors

    Example: $\dfrac{2x + 5}{(x - 3)^2(x + 1)} = \dfrac{A}{x - 3} + \dfrac{B}{(x - 3)^2} + \dfrac{C}{x + 1}$

3. Distinct irreducible quadratic factors

    Example: $\dfrac{1 - x}{(x^2 + 1)(x^2 + 8)} = \dfrac{Ax + B}{x^2 + 1} + \dfrac{Cx + D}{x^2 + 8}$

4. Repeated irreducible quadratic factors

    Example: $\dfrac{4x^2 - 3x + 2}{(x^2 + 1)^2} = \dfrac{Ax + B}{x^2 + 1} + \dfrac{Cx + D}{(x^2 + 1)^2}$

**SECTION**
**8.6 EXERCISES**

**SKILLS**

**In Exercises 1–6, match the rational expression (1–6) with the form of the partial-fraction decomposition (a–f).**

1. $\dfrac{3x + 2}{x(x^2 - 25)}$
2. $\dfrac{3x + 2}{x(x^2 + 25)}$
3. $\dfrac{3x + 2}{x^2(x^2 + 25)}$
4. $\dfrac{3x + 2}{x^2(x^2 - 25)}$
5. $\dfrac{3x + 2}{x(x^2 + 25)^2}$
6. $\dfrac{3x + 2}{x^2(x^2 + 25)^2}$

a. $\dfrac{A}{x} + \dfrac{B}{x^2} + \dfrac{Cx + D}{x^2 + 25}$

b. $\dfrac{A}{x} + \dfrac{Bx + C}{x^2 + 25} + \dfrac{Dx + E}{(x^2 + 25)^2}$

c. $\dfrac{A}{x} + \dfrac{Bx + C}{x^2 + 25}$

d. $\dfrac{A}{x} + \dfrac{B}{x + 5} + \dfrac{C}{x - 5}$

e. $\dfrac{A}{x} + \dfrac{B}{x^2} + \dfrac{Cx + D}{x^2 + 25} + \dfrac{Ex + F}{(x^2 + 25)^2}$

f. $\dfrac{A}{x} + \dfrac{B}{x^2} + \dfrac{C}{x + 5} + \dfrac{D}{x - 5}$

**In Exercises 7–14, write the form of the partial-fraction decomposition. Do not solve for the constants.**

7. $\dfrac{9}{x^2 - x - 20}$
8. $\dfrac{8}{x^2 - 3x - 10}$
9. $\dfrac{2x + 5}{x^3 - 4x^2}$
10. $\dfrac{x^2 + 2x - 1}{x^4 - 9x^2}$

11. $\dfrac{2x^3 - 4x^2 + 7x + 3}{(x^2 + x + 5)}$
12. $\dfrac{2x^3 + 5x^2 + 6}{(x^2 - 3x + 7)}$
13. $\dfrac{3x^3 - x + 9}{(x^2 + 10)^2}$
14. $\dfrac{5x^3 + 2x^2 + 4}{(x^2 + 13)^2}$

**In Exercises 15–40, find the partial-fraction decomposition for each rational function.**

15. $\dfrac{1}{x(x + 1)}$
16. $\dfrac{1}{x(x - 1)}$
17. $\dfrac{x}{x(x - 1)}$
18. $\dfrac{x}{x(x + 1)}$

19. $\dfrac{9x - 11}{(x - 3)(x + 5)}$
20. $\dfrac{8x - 13}{(x - 2)(x + 1)}$
21. $\dfrac{3x + 1}{(x - 1)^2}$
22. $\dfrac{9y - 2}{(y - 1)^2}$

23. $\dfrac{4x - 3}{x^2 + 6x + 9}$
24. $\dfrac{3x + 1}{x^2 + 4x + 4}$
25. $\dfrac{4x^2 - 32x + 72}{(x + 1)(x - 5)^2}$
26. $\dfrac{4x^2 - 7x - 3}{(x + 2)(x - 1)^2}$

27. $\dfrac{5x^2 + 28x - 6}{(x + 4)(x^2 + 3)}$

28. $\dfrac{x^2 + 5x + 4}{(x - 2)(x^2 + 2)}$

29. $\dfrac{-2x^2 - 17x + 11}{(x - 7)(3x^2 - 7x + 5)}$

30. $\dfrac{14x^2 + 8x + 40}{(x + 5)(2x^2 - 3x + 5)}$

31. $\dfrac{x^3}{(x^2 + 9)^2}$

32. $\dfrac{x^2}{(x^2 + 9)^2}$

33. $\dfrac{2x^3 - 3x^2 + 7x - 2}{(x^2 + 1)^2}$

34. $\dfrac{-x^3 + 2x^2 - 3x + 15}{(x^2 + 8)^2}$

35. $\dfrac{3x + 1}{x^4 - 1}$

36. $\dfrac{2 - x}{x^4 - 81}$

37. $\dfrac{5x^2 + 9x - 8}{(x - 1)(x^2 + 2x - 1)}$

38. $\dfrac{10x^2 - 5x + 29}{(x - 3)(x^2 + 4x + 5)}$

39. $\dfrac{3x}{x^3 - 1}$

40. $\dfrac{5x + 2}{x^3 - 8}$

# ■ APPLICATIONS

**41. Optics.** The relationship between the distance of an object to a lens $d_o$, the distance to the image $d_i$, and the focal length $f$ of the lens is given by

$$\frac{f(d_i + d_o)}{d_i d_o} = 1$$

Use partial-fraction decomposition to write the lens law in terms of sums of fractions. What does each term represent?

**42. Sums.** Find the partial-fraction decomposition of $\dfrac{1}{n(n + 1)}$, and apply it to find the sum of

$$\frac{1}{1 \cdot 2} + \frac{1}{2 \cdot 3} + \frac{1}{3 \cdot 4} + \cdots + \frac{1}{999 \cdot 1000}$$

**In Exercises 43 and 44, refer to the following:**

Laplace transforms are used to solve differential equations. The Laplace transform of $f(t)$ is denoted by $L\{f(t)\}$; thus, $L\{e^{3t}\}$ is the Laplace transform of $f(t) = e^{3t}$. It is known that

$$L\{e^{kt}\} = \frac{1}{s - k} \text{ and } L\{e^{-kt}\} = \frac{1}{s + k}.$$ Then the inverse Laplace

transform of $g(s) = \dfrac{1}{s - k}$ is $L^{-1}\left\{\dfrac{1}{s - k}\right\} = e^{kt}$. Inverse Laplace transforms are linear:

$$L^{-1}\{f(t) + g(t)\} = L^{-1}\{f(t)\} + L^{-1}\{g(t)\}$$

**43. Laplace Transform.** Use partial fractions to find the inverse Laplace transform of $\dfrac{9 + s}{4 - s^2}$.

**44. Laplace Transform.** Use partial fractions to find the inverse Laplace transform of $\dfrac{2s^2 + 3s - 2}{s(s + 1)(s - 2)}$.

# ■ CATCH THE MISTAKE

**In Exercises 45 and 46, explain the mistake that is made.**

**45.** Find the partial-fraction decomposition of $\dfrac{3x^2 + 3x + 1}{x(x^2 + 1)}$.

**Solution:**

Write the partial-fraction decomposition form. $\dfrac{3x^2 + 3x + 1}{x(x^2 + 1)} = \dfrac{A}{x} + \dfrac{B}{x^2 + 1}$

Multiply both sides by the LCD $x(x^2 + 1)$. $3x^2 + 3x + 1 = A(x^2 + 1) + Bx$

Eliminate the parentheses. $3x^2 + 3x + 1 = Ax^2 + Bx + A$

Matching like terms leads to three equations. $A = 3$, $B = 3$, and $A = 1$

This is incorrect. What mistake was made?

**46.** Find the partial-fraction decomposition of $\dfrac{3x^4 - x - 1}{x(x - 1)}$.

**Solution:**

Write the partial-fraction decomposition form. $\dfrac{3x^4 - x - 1}{x(x - 1)} = \dfrac{A}{x} + \dfrac{B}{x - 1}$

Multiply both sides by the LCD $x(x - 1)$. $3x^4 - x - 1 = A(x - 1) + Bx$

Eliminate the parentheses and group like terms. $3x^4 - x - 1 = (A + B)x - A$

Compare like coefficients. $A = 1$, $B = -2$

This is incorrect. What mistake was made?

■ **CONCEPTUAL**

**In Exercises 47–52, determine whether each statement is true or false.**

**47.** Partial-fraction decomposition can be employed only when the degree of the numerator is greater than the degree of the denominator.

**48.** The degree of the denominator of a proper rational expression is equal to the number of partial fractions in its decomposition.

**49.** Partial-fraction decomposition depends on the factors of the denominator.

**50.** A rational function can always be decomposed into partial fractions with linear or irreducible quadratic factors in each denominator.

**51.** The partial-fraction decomposition of a rational function $\dfrac{f(x)}{(x-a)^n}$ has the form $\dfrac{A_1}{(x-a)} + \dfrac{A_2}{(x-a)^2} + \cdots + \dfrac{A_n}{(x-a)^n}$, where all the numbers $A_i$ are nonzero.

**52.** The rational function $\dfrac{1}{x^3+1}$ cannot be decomposed into partial fractions.

■ **CHALLENGE**

**For Exercises 53–58, find the partial-fraction decomposition.**

**53.** $\dfrac{x^2 + 4x - 8}{x^3 - x^2 - 4x + 4}$

**54.** $\dfrac{ax + b}{x^2 - c^2}$    $a, b, c$ are real numbers.

**55.** $\dfrac{2x^3 + x^2 - x - 1}{x^4 + x^3}$

**56.** $\dfrac{-x^3 + 2x - 2}{x^5 - x^4}$

**57.** $\dfrac{x^5 + 2}{\left(x^2 + 1\right)^3}$

**58.** $\dfrac{x^2 - 4}{\left(x^2 + 1\right)^3}$

■ **TECHNOLOGY**

**59.** Apply a graphing utility to graph $y_1 = \dfrac{5x + 4}{x^2 + x - 2}$ and $y_2 = \dfrac{3}{x - 1} + \dfrac{2}{x + 2}$ in the same viewing rectangle. Is $y_2$ the partial-fraction decomposition of $y_1$?

**60.** Apply a graphing utility to graph $y_1 = \dfrac{2x^2 + 2x - 5}{x^3 + 5x}$ and $y_2 = \dfrac{3x + 2}{x^2 + 5} - \dfrac{1}{x}$ in the same viewing rectangle. Is $y_2$ the partial-fraction decomposition of $y_1$?

**61.** Apply a graphing utility to graph $y_1 = \dfrac{x^9 + 8x - 1}{x^5\left(x^2 + 1\right)^3}$ and $y_2 = \dfrac{4}{x} - \dfrac{1}{x^5} + \dfrac{2}{x^2 + 1} - \dfrac{3x + 2}{\left(x^2 + 1\right)^2}$ in the same viewing rectangle. Is $y_2$ the partial-fraction decomposition of $y_1$?

**62.** Apply a graphing utility to graph $y_1 = \dfrac{x^3 + 2x + 6}{(x + 3)\left(x^2 - 4\right)^3}$ and $y_2 = \dfrac{2}{x + 3} + \dfrac{x + 3}{\left(x^2 - 4\right)^3}$ in the same viewing rectangle. Is $y_2$ the partial-fraction decomposition of $y_1$?

**63.** Apply a graphing utility to graph $y_1 = \dfrac{2x^3 - 8x + 16}{(x - 2)^2\left(x^2 + 4\right)}$ and $y_2 = \dfrac{1}{x - 2} + \dfrac{2}{(x - 2)^2} + \dfrac{x + 4}{x^2 + 4}$ in the same viewing rectangle. Is $y_2$ the partial-fraction decomposition of $y_1$?

**64.** Apply a graphing utility to graph $y_1 = \dfrac{3x^3 + 14x^2 + 6x + 51}{\left(x^2 + 3x - 4\right)\left(x^2 + 2x + 5\right)}$ and $y_2 = \dfrac{2}{x - 1} - \dfrac{1}{x + 4} + \dfrac{2x - 3}{x^2 + 2x + 5}$ in the same viewing rectangle. Is $y_2$ the partial-fraction decomposition of $y_1$?

■ **PREVIEW TO CALCULUS**

**In calculus, partial fractions are used to calculate the sums of infinite series. In Exercises 65–68, find the partial-fraction decomposition of the summand.**

**65.** $\displaystyle\sum_{k=1}^{\infty} \dfrac{9}{k(k + 3)}$

**66.** $\displaystyle\sum_{k=1}^{\infty} \dfrac{1}{k(k + 1)}$

**67.** $\displaystyle\sum_{k=1}^{\infty} \dfrac{2k + 1}{k^2(k + 1)^2}$

**68.** $\displaystyle\sum_{k=1}^{\infty} \dfrac{4}{k(k + 1)(k + 2)}$

**SKILLS OBJECTIVES**

- Graph a linear inequality in two variables.
- Graph a system of linear inequalities in two variables.
- Solve an optimization problem using linear programming.

**CONCEPTUAL OBJECTIVES**

- Interpret the difference between solid and dashed lines.
- Interpret an overlapped shaded region as a solution.

## Linear Inequalities in Two Variables

Recall in Section 0.6 that $y = 2x + 1$ is an *equation in two variables* whose graph is a line in the $xy$-plane. We now turn our attention to **linear inequalities in two variables**. For example, if we change the $=$ in $y = 2x + 1$ to $<$, we get $y < 2x + 1$. The solution to this inequality in two variables is the set of all points $(x, y)$ that make this inequality true. Some solutions to this inequality are $(-2, -5)$, $(0, 0)$, $(3, 4)$, $(5, -1)$, . . . .

In fact, the entire region *below* the line $y = 2x + 1$ satisfies the inequality $y < 2x + 1$. If we reverse the sign of the inequality to get $y > 2x + 1$, then the entire region *above* the line $y = 2x + 1$ represents the solution to the inequality.

Any line divides the $xy$-plane into two **half-planes**. For example, the line $y = 2x + 1$ divides the $xy$-plane into two half-planes represented as $y > 2x + 1$ and $y < 2x + 1$. Recall that with inequalities in one variable we used the notation of parentheses and brackets to denote the type of inequality (strict or nonstrict). We use a similar notation with linear inequalities in two variables. If the inequality is a strict inequality, $<$ or $>$, then the line is *dashed*, and, if the inequality includes the equal sign, $\le$ or $\ge$, then a *solid* line is used. The following box summarizes the procedure for graphing a linear inequality in two variables.

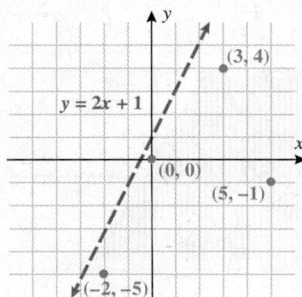

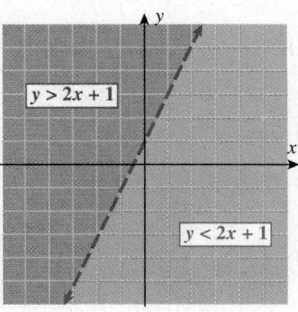

**GRAPHING A LINEAR INEQUALITY IN TWO VARIABLES**

**Step 1:** **Change** the inequality sign, $<$, $\le$, $\ge$, or $>$, to an equal sign, $=$.

**Step 2:** **Draw** the line that corresponds to the resulting equation in Step 1.
- If the inequality is strict, $<$ or $>$, use a **dashed** line.
- If the inequality is not strict, $\le$ or $\ge$, use a **solid** line.

**Step 3:** **Test** a point.
- Select a point in one half-plane and test to see whether it satisfies the inequality. If it does, then so do all the points in that region (half-plane). If not, then none of the points in that half-plane satisfy the inequality.
- Repeat this step for the other half-plane.

**Step 4:** **Shade** the half-plane that satisfies the inequality.

### Study Tip

A dashed line means that the points that lie on the line are not included in the solution of the linear inequality.

The graphing calculator can be used to help in shading the linear inequality $3x + y < 2$. However, it will not show whether the line is solid or dashed. First solve for $y$, $y < -3x + 2$. Then, enter $y_1 = -3x + 2$. Since $y_1 < -3x + 2$, the region below the dashed line is shaded.

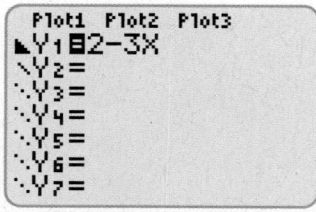

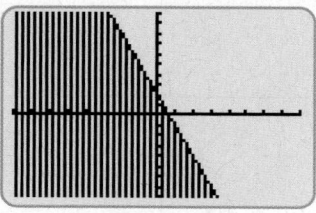

■ **Answer:**

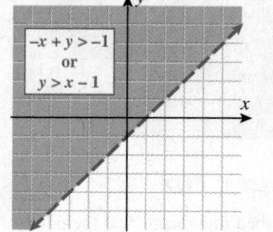

## EXAMPLE 1 Graphing a Strict Linear Inequality in Two Variables

Graph the inequality $3x + y < 2$.

**Solution:**

**STEP 1** Change the inequality sign to an equal sign. $\qquad 3x + y = 2$

**STEP 2** Draw the line.

Convert from standard form to slope–intercept form. $\qquad y = -3x + 2$

Since the inequality $<$ is a strict inequality, use a **dashed** line.

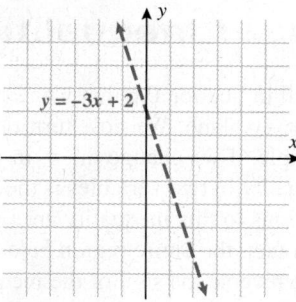

**STEP 3** Test points in each half-plane.

Substitute $(3, 0)$ into $3x + y < 2$. $\qquad 3(3) + 0 < 2$

The point $(3, 0)$ does not satisfy the inequality. $\qquad 9 < 2$

Substitute $(-2, 0)$ into $3x + y < 2$. $\qquad 3(-2) + 0 < 2$

The point $(-2, 0)$ does satisfy the inequality. $\qquad -6 < 2$

**STEP 4** Shade the region containing the point $(-2, 0)$.

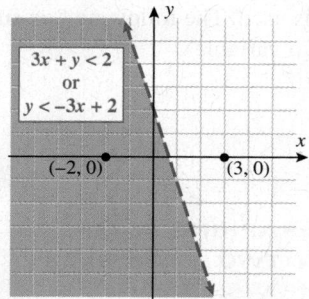

■ **YOUR TURN** Graph the inequality $-x + y > -1$.

**EXAMPLE 2  Graphing a Nonstrict Linear Inequality in Two Variables**

Graph the inequality $2x - 3y \geq 6$.

**Solution:**

STEP 1  Change the inequality sign to an equal sign.     $2x - 3y = 6$

STEP 2  Draw the line.

Convert from standard form to slope–intercept form.     $y = \dfrac{2}{3}x - 2$

Since the inequality $\geq$ is not a strict inequality, use a **solid** line.

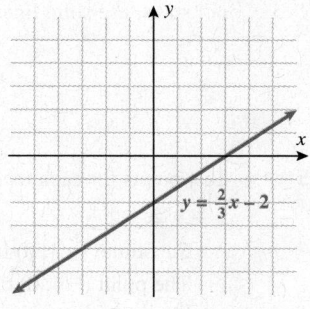

STEP 3  Test points in each half-plane.

Substitute $(5, 0)$ into $2x - 3y \geq 6$.      $2(5) - 3(0) \geq 6$

The point $(5, 0)$ satisfies the inequality.              $10 \geq 6$

Substitute $(0, 0)$ into $2x - 3y \geq 6$.      $2(0) - 3(0) \geq 6$

                                                          $0 \geq 6$

The point $(0, 0)$ does not satisfy the inequality.

STEP 4  Shade the region containing the point $(5, 0)$.

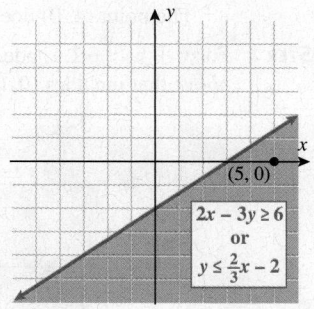

***Technology Tip***

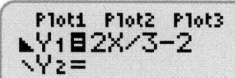

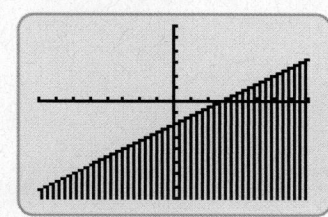

■ **YOUR TURN**  Graph the inequality $x - 2y \leq 6$.

■ **Answer:**

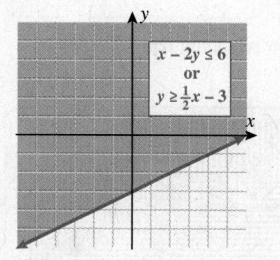

# Systems of Linear Inequalities in Two Variables

**Systems of linear inequalities** are similar to *systems of linear equations*. In systems of linear equations we sought the points that satisfied *all* of the equations. The **solution set of a system of inequalities** contains the points that satisfy *all* of the inequalities. The graph of a system of inequalities can be obtained by simultaneously graphing each individual inequality and finding where the shaded regions intersect (or overlap), if at all.

**EXAMPLE 3  Solving a System of Two Linear Inequalities**

Graph the system of inequalities:     $x + y \geq -2$
$x + y \leq \phantom{-}2$

**Solution:**

STEP 1  Change the inequality signs to equal signs.     $x + y = -2$
$x + y = \phantom{-}2$

STEP 2  Draw the two lines.

Because the inequality signs are
not strict, use solid lines.

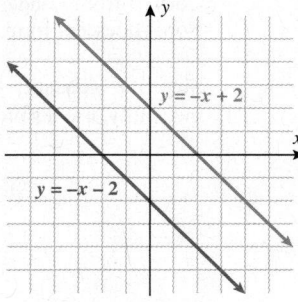

STEP 3  Test points for each inequality.

$x + y \geq -2$

Substitute $(-4, 0)$ into $x + y \geq -2$.     $-4 \geq -2$
The point $(-4, 0)$ does not satisfy
the inequality.
Substitute $(0, 0)$ into $x + y \geq -2$.     $0 \geq -2$
The point $(0, 0)$ does satisfy the inequality.

$x + y \leq 2$

Substitute $(0, 0)$ into $x + y \leq 2$.     $0 \leq 2$
The point $(0, 0)$ does satisfy the inequality.
Substitute $(4, 0)$ into $x + y \leq 2$.     $4 \leq 2$
The point $(4, 0)$ does not satisfy the inequality.

STEP 4  For $x + y \geq -2$, shade the region     For $x + y \leq 2$, shade the region
*above* that includes $(0, 0)$.     *below* that includes $(0, 0)$.

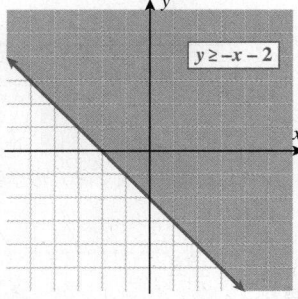     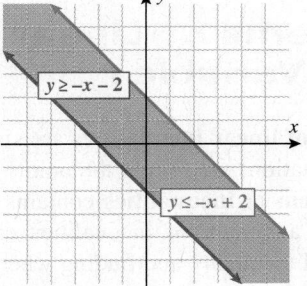

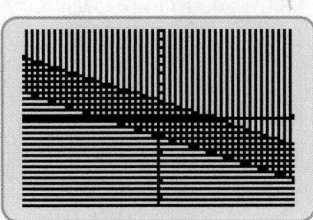
STEP 5  All of the points in the overlapping
region and on the lines constitute
the solution.

Notice that three sample points $(0, 0)$,
$(-1, 1)$, and $(1, -1)$ all lie in the
shaded region and all three satisfy
both inequalities.

**EXAMPLE 4    Solving a System of Two Linear Inequalities with No Solution**

Graph the system of inequalities:

$$x + y \leq -2$$
$$x + y \geq \phantom{-}2$$

**Solution:**

**STEP 1**   Change the inequality signs to equal signs.

$$x + y = -2$$
$$x + y = \phantom{-}2$$

**STEP 2**   Draw the two lines.

Because the inequality signs are not strict, use solid lines.

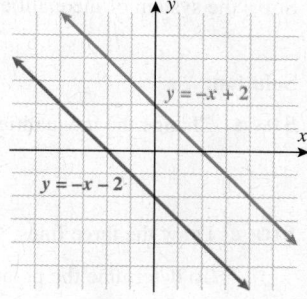

**STEP 3**   Test points for each inequality.

$x + y \leq -2$

Substitute $(-4, 0)$ into $x + y \leq -2$.          $-4 \leq -2$

The point $(-4, 0)$ does satisfy the inequality.

Substitute $(0, 0)$ into $x + y \leq -2$.          $0 \leq -2$

The point $(0, 0)$ does not satisfy the inequality.

$x + y \geq 2$

Substitute $(0, 0)$ into $x + y \geq 2$.          $0 \geq 2$

The point $(0, 0)$ does not satisfy the inequality.

Substitute $(4, 0)$ into $x + y \geq 2$.          $4 \geq 2$

The point $(4, 0)$ does satisfy the inequality.

**STEP 4**   For $x + y \leq -2$, shade the region *below* that includes $(-4, 0)$.

For $x + y \leq 2$, shade the region *above* that includes $(4, 0)$.

**STEP 5**   There is no overlapping region. Therefore, no points satisfy both inequalities. We say there is no solution .

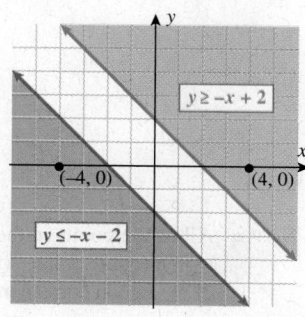

■ **YOUR TURN**   Graph the solution to the system of inequalities.

   **a.** $y > x + 1$         **b.** $y < x + 1$
         $y < x - 1$                $y > x - 1$

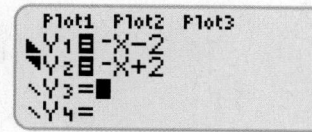
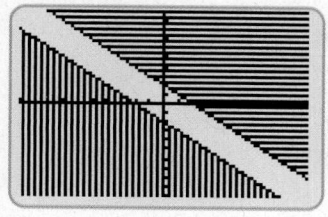

■ **Answer:**

**a.** no solution

**b.**

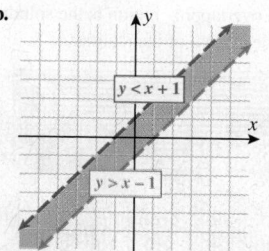

Thus far we have addressed only systems of two linear inequalities. Systems with more than two inequalities are treated in a similar manner. The solution is the set of all points that satisfy *all* of the inequalities. When there are more than two linear inequalities, the solution may be a **bounded** region. We can algebraically determine where the lines intersect by setting the $y$-values equal to each other.

 **EXAMPLE 5** **Solving a System of Multiple Linear Inequalities**

Solve the system of inequalities:
$$y \leq x$$
$$y \geq -x$$
$$y < 3$$

**Solution:**

**STEP 1** Change the inequalities to equal signs.

$$y = x$$
$$y = -x$$
$$y = 3$$

**STEP 2** Draw the three lines.

To determine the points of intersection, set the $y$-values equal.

Point where $y = x$ and $y = -x$ intersect:
$$x = -x$$
$$x = 0$$

Substitute $x = 0$ into $y = x$.
$$(0, 0)$$

Point where $y = -x$ and $y = 3$ intersect:
$$-x = 3$$
$$x = -3$$
$$(-3, 3)$$

Point where $y = 3$ and $y = x$ intersect:
$$x = 3$$
$$(3, 3)$$

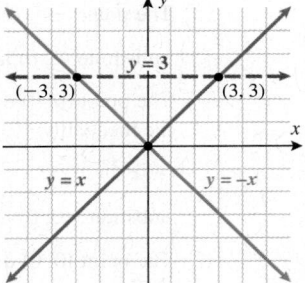

**STEP 3** Test points to determine the shaded half-planes corresponding to $y \leq x$, $y \geq -x$, and $y < 3$.

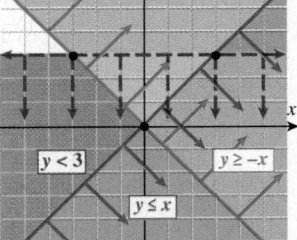

**STEP 4** All of the points in the overlapping region (orange) and along the boundaries of the region corresponding to the lines $y = -x$ and $y = x$ constitute the solution.

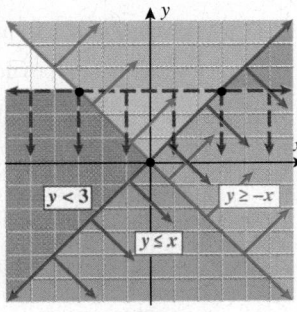

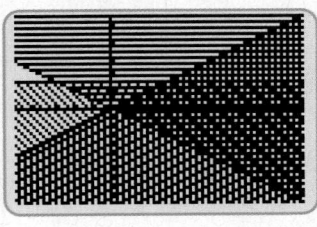

## Applications

In economics, the point where the supply and demand curves intersect is called the **equilibrium point**. **Consumer surplus** is a measure of the amount that consumers benefit by being able to purchase a product for a price less than the maximum they would be willing to pay. **Producer surplus** is a measure of the amount that producers benefit by selling at a market price that is higher than the least they would be willing to sell for.

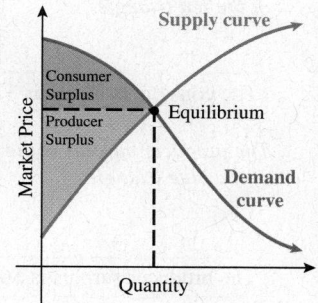

---

**EXAMPLE 6** **Consumer Surplus and Producer Surplus**

The Tesla Motors Roadster is the first electric car that is able to travel 245 miles on a single charge. The price of a 2013 model is approximately $90,000 (including tax and incentives).

Courtesy Tesla Motors

Suppose the supply and demand equations for this electric car are given by

$$P = 90,000 - 0.1x \quad \text{(Demand)}$$
$$P = 10,000 + 0.3x \quad \text{(Supply)}$$

where $P$ is the price in dollars and $x$ is the number of cars produced. Calculate the consumer surplus and the producer surplus for these two equations.

**Solution:**

*Find the equilibrium point.*

$$90,000 - 0.1x = 10,000 + 0.3x$$
$$0.4x = 80,000$$
$$x = 200,000$$

Let $x = 200,000$ in either the supply or demand equation.

$$P = 90,000 - 0.1(200,000) = 70,000$$
$$P = 10,000 + 0.3(200,000) = 70,000$$

According to these models, if the price of a Tesla Motors Roadster is $70,000, then 200,000 cars will be sold and there will be no surplus.

*Write the systems of linear inequalities that correspond to consumer surplus and producer surplus.*

| CONSUMER SURPLUS | PRODUCER SURPLUS |
|---|---|
| $P \leq 90,000 - 0.1x$ | $P \geq 10,000 + 0.3x$ |
| $P \geq 70,000$ | $P \leq 70,000$ |
| $x \geq 0$ | $x \geq 0$ |

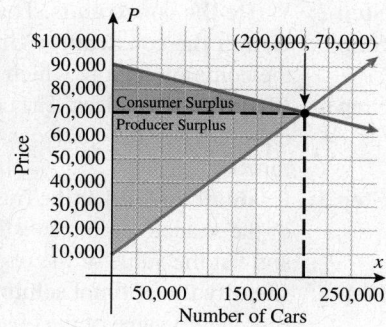

| | |
|---|---|
| *The consumer surplus is the area of the red triangle.* | $A = \frac{1}{2}bh$ |
| | $= \frac{1}{2}(200{,}000)(20{,}000)$ |
| The consumer surplus is \$2B. | $= 2{,}000{,}000{,}000$ |
| *The producer surplus is the area of the blue triangle.* | $A = \frac{1}{2}bh$ |
| | $= \frac{1}{2}(200{,}000)(60{,}000)$ |
| The producer surplus is \$6B. | $= 6{,}000{,}000{,}000$ |

The graph of the systems of linear inequalities in Example 6 are said to be **bounded**, whereas the graphs of the systems of linear inequalities in Examples 3–5 are said to be **unbounded**. Any points that correspond to boundary lines intersecting are called **corner points** or **vertices**. In Example 6, the vertices corresponding to the consumer surplus are the points (0, 90,000), (0, 70,000), and (200,000, 70,000), and the vertices corresponding to the producer surplus are the points (0, 70,000), (0, 10,000), and (200,000, 70,000).

## The Linear Programming Model

Often we seek to maximize or minimize a function subject to constraints. This process is called **optimization**. When the function we seek to minimize or maximize is linear and the constraints are given in terms of linear inequalities, a graphing approach to such problems is called **linear programming**. In linear programming, we start with a linear equation, called the **objective function**, that represents the quantity that is to be maximized or minimized.

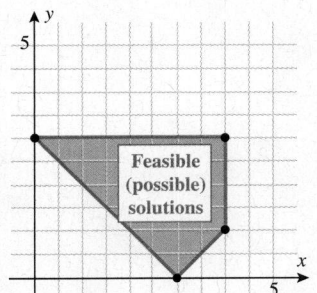

The goal is to minimize or maximize the objective function $z = Ax + By$ subject to *constraints*. In other words, find the points $(x, y)$ that make the value of $z$ the largest (or smallest). The **constraints** are a system of linear inequalities, and the common shaded region represents the **feasible (possible) solutions**.

If the constraints form a bounded region, the maximum or minimum value of the objective function will occur using the coordinates of one of the vertices. If the region is not bounded, then if an optimal solution exists, it will occur at a vertex. A procedure for solving linear programming problems is outlined below:

### SOLVING AN OPTIMIZATION PROBLEM USING LINEAR PROGRAMMING

**Step 1:  Write the objective function.** This expression represents the quantity that is to be minimized or maximized.

**Step 2:  Write the constraints.** This is a system of linear inequalities.

**Step 3:  Graph the constraints.** Graph the system of linear inequalities and shade the common region, which contains the feasible solutions.

**Step 4:  Identify the vertices.** The corner points (vertices) of the shaded region represent possible solutions for maximizing or minimizing the objective function.

**Step 5:  Evaluate the objective function for each vertex.** For each corner point of the shaded region, substitute the coordinates into the objective function and list the value of the objective function.

**Step 6:  Identify the optimal solution.** The largest (maximum) or smallest (minimum) value of the objective function in Step 5 is the optimal solution.

**EXAMPLE 7   Maximizing an Objective Function**

Find the maximum value of $z = 2x + y$ subject to the constraints:

$$x \geq 1 \qquad x \leq 4 \qquad x + y \leq 5 \qquad y \geq 0$$

**Solution:**

STEP 1  Write the objective function.          $z = 2x + y$

STEP 2  Write the constraints.

$$x \geq 1$$
$$x \leq 4$$
$$y \leq -x + 5$$
$$y \geq 0$$

STEP 3  Graph the constraints.

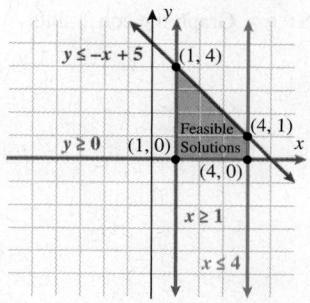

STEP 4  Identify the vertices.          (1, 4), (4, 1), (1, 0), (4, 0)

STEP 5  Evaluate the objective function for each vertex.

| VERTEX | x | y | OBJECTIVE FUNCTION: $z = 2x + y$ |
|--------|---|---|----------------------------------|
| (1, 4) | 1 | 4 | $2(1) + 4 = 6$ |
| (4, 1) | 4 | 1 | $2(4) + 1 = 9$ |
| (1, 0) | 1 | 0 | $2(1) + 0 = 2$ |
| (4, 0) | 4 | 0 | $2(4) + 0 = 8$ |

STEP 6  The maximum value of $z$ is **9**, subject to the given constraints when $x = 4$ and $y = 1$.

■ **YOUR TURN**  Find the maximum value of $z = x + 3y$ subject to the constraints:

$$x \geq 1 \qquad x \leq 3 \qquad y \leq -x + 3 \qquad y \geq 0$$

**Study Tip**

The bounded region is the region that satisfies *all* of the constraints. Only vertices of the bounded region correspond to possible solutions. Even though $y = -x + 5$ and $y = 0$ intersect at $x = 5$, that point of intersection is outside the shaded region and therefore is *not* one of the vertices.

■ **Answer:** The maximum value of $z$ is **7**, which occurs when $x = 1$ and $y = 2$.

**EXAMPLE 8 Minimizing an Objective Function**

Find the minimum value of $z = 4x + 5y$ subject to the constraints:

$$x \geq 0 \qquad 2x + y \leq 6 \qquad x + y \leq 5 \qquad y \geq 0$$

**Solution:**

**STEP 1** Write the objective function.

$z = 4x + 5y$

**STEP 2** Write the constraints.

$x \geq 0$
$y \leq -2x + 6$
$y \leq \ -x + 5$
$y \geq 0$

**STEP 3** Graph the constraints.

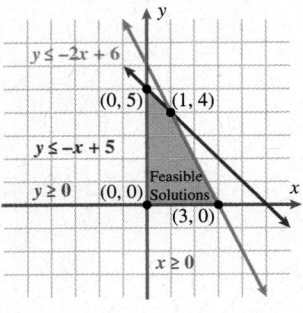

**STEP 4** Identify the vertices.

$(0, 0), (0, 5), (1, 4), (3, 0)$

**STEP 5** Evaluate the objective function for each vertex.

| VERTEX | x | y | OBJECTIVE FUNCTION: $z = 4x + 5y$ |
|--------|---|---|-----------------------------------|
| $(0, 0)$ | 0 | 0 | $4(0) + 5(0) = \mathbf{0}$ |
| $(0, 5)$ | 0 | 5 | $4(0) + 5(5) = \mathbf{25}$ |
| $(1, 4)$ | 1 | 4 | $4(1) + 5(4) = \mathbf{24}$ |
| $(3, 0)$ | 3 | 0 | $4(3) + 5(0) = \mathbf{12}$ |

**STEP 6** | The minimum value of $z$ is **0**, which occurs when $x = 0$ and $y = 0$. |

■ **YOUR TURN** Find the minimum value of $z = 2x + 3y$ subject to the constraints:

$$x \geq 1 \qquad 2x + y \leq 8 \qquad x + y \geq 4$$

*Study Tip*

Maxima or minima of objective functions only occur at the vertices of the shaded region corresponding to the constraints.

■ **Answer:** The minimum value of $z$ is **8**, which occurs when $x = 4$ and $y = 0$.

**EXAMPLE 9    Solving an Optimization Problem Using Linear Programming: Unbounded Region**

Find the maximum value and minimum value of $z = 7x + 3y$ subject to the constraints:

$$y \geq 0 \qquad -2x + y \leq 0 \qquad -x + y \geq -4$$

**Solution:**

STEP 1  Write the objective function.

$z = 7x + 3y$

STEP 2  Write the constraints.

$y \geq 0$
$y \leq 2x$
$y \geq x - 4$

STEP 3  Graph the constraints.

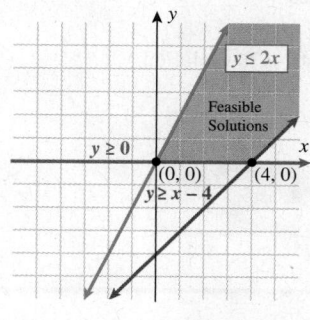

STEP 4  Identify the vertices.

$(0, 0), (4, 0)$

STEP 5  Evaluate the objective function for each vertex.

| VERTEX | x | y | OBJECTIVE FUNCTION: z = 7x + 3y |
|--------|---|---|---------------------------------|
| $(0, 0)$ | 0 | 0 | $7(0) + 3(0) = \mathbf{0}$ |
| $(4, 0)$ | 4 | 0 | $7(4) + 3(0) = \mathbf{28}$ |

STEP 6  The minimum value of $z$ is **0**, which occurs when $x = 0$ and $y = 0$.

There is no maximum value, because if we select a point in the shaded region, say, $(3, 3)$, the objective function at $(3, 3)$ is equal to 30, which is greater than 28.

When the feasible solutions are contained in a bounded region, then a maximum and a minimum exist and are each located at one of the vertices. If the feasible solutions are contained in an unbounded region, then if a maximum or minimum exists, it is located at one of the vertices.

## SECTION 8.7 SUMMARY

**Graphing a Linear Inequality**

1. Change the inequality sign to an equal sign.
2. Draw the line $y = mx + b$. (Dashed for strict inequalities and solid for nonstrict inequalities.)
3. Test a point. (Select a point in one-half plane and test the inequality. Repeat this step for the other half-plane.)
4. Shade the half-plane of the overlapping region that satisfies the linear inequality.

**Graphing a System of Linear Inequalities**

- Draw the individual linear inequalities.
- The overlapped shaded region, if it exists, is the solution.

**Linear Programming Model**

1. Write the objective function.
2. Write the constraints.
3. Graph the constraints.
4. Identify the vertices.
5. Evaluate the objective function for each vertex.
6. Identify the optimal solution.

## SECTION 8.7 EXERCISES

### ▪ SKILLS

**In Exercises 1–4, match the linear inequality with the correct graph.**

**1.** $y > x$      **2.** $y \geq x$      **3.** $y < x$      **4.** $y \leq x$

**a.** 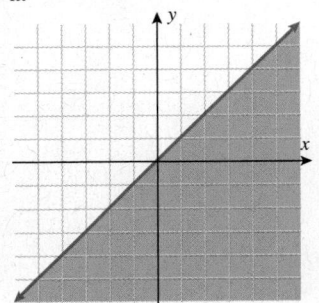    **b.** 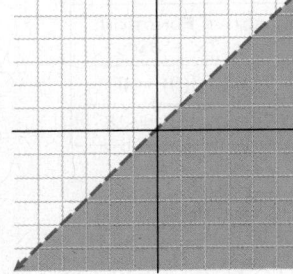    **c.** 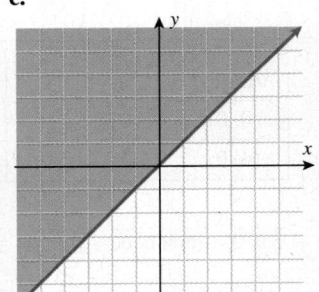    **d.**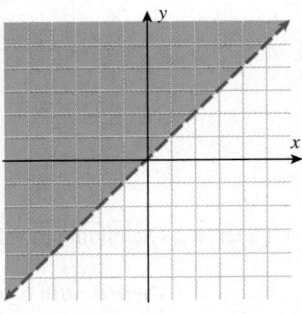

**In Exercises 5–20, graph each linear inequality.**

| | | | |
|---|---|---|---|
| **5.** $y > x - 1$ | **6.** $y \geq -x + 1$ | **7.** $y \leq -x$ | **8.** $y > -x$ |
| **9.** $y \leq -3x + 2$ | **10.** $y < 2x + 3$ | **11.** $y \leq -2x + 1$ | **12.** $y > 3x - 2$ |
| **13.** $3x + 4y < 2$ | **14.** $2x + 3y > -6$ | **15.** $5x + 3y < 15$ | **16.** $4x - 5y \leq 20$ |
| **17.** $4x - 2y \geq 6$ | **18.** $6x - 3y \geq 9$ | **19.** $6x + 4y \leq 12$ | **20.** $5x - 2y \geq 10$ |

**In Exercises 21–50, graph each system of inequalities or indicate that the system has no solution.**

| | | | | |
|---|---|---|---|---|
| **21.** $y \geq x - 1$ <br> $\quad y \leq x + 1$ | **22.** $y > x + 1$ <br> $\quad y < x - 1$ | **23.** $y > 2x + 1$ <br> $\quad y < 2x - 1$ | **24.** $y \leq 2x - 1$ <br> $\quad y \geq 2x + 1$ | **25.** $y \geq 2x$ <br> $\quad y \leq 2x$ |
| **26.** $y > 2x$ <br> $\quad y < 2x$ | **27.** $x > -2$ <br> $\quad x < 4$ | **28.** $y < 3$ <br> $\quad y > 0$ | **29.** $x \geq 2$ <br> $\quad y \leq x$ | **30.** $y \leq 3$ <br> $\quad y \geq x$ |

**31.** $y > x$
$x < 0$
$y < 4$

**32.** $y \le x$
$x \ge 0$
$y \le 1$

**33.** $x + y > 2$
$y < 1$
$x > 0$

**34.** $x + y < 4$
$x > 0$
$y \ge 1$

**35.** $-x + y > 1$
$y < 3$
$x > 0$

**36.** $x - y > 2$
$y < 4$
$x \ge 0$

**37.** $x + 3y > 6$
$y < 1$
$x \ge 1$

**38.** $x + 2y > 4$
$y < 1$
$x \ge 0$

**39.** $y \ge x - 1$
$y \le -x + 3$
$y < x + 2$

**40.** $y < 4 - x$
$y > x - 4$
$y > -x - 4$

**41.** $x + y > -4$
$-x + y < 2$
$y \ge -1$
$y \le 1$

**42.** $y < x + 2$
$y > x - 2$
$y < -x + 2$
$y > -x - 2$

**43.** $y < x + 3$
$x + y \ge 1$
$y \ge 1$
$y \le 3$

**44.** $y \le -x + 2$
$y - x \ge -3$
$y \ge -2$
$y \le 1$

**45.** $y + x < 2$
$y + x \ge 4$
$y \ge -2$
$y \le 1$

**46.** $y - x < 3$
$y + x > 3$
$y \le -2$
$y \ge -4$

**47.** $2x - y < 2$
$2x + y > 2$
$y < 2$

**48.** $3x - y > 3$
$3x + y < 3$
$y < -2$

**49.** $x + 4y > 5$
$x - 4y < 5$
$x > 6$

**50.** $2x - 3y < 6$
$2x + 3y > 6$
$x < 4$

In Exercises 51–54, find the value of the objective function at each of the vertices. What is the maximum value of the objective function? What is the minimum value of the objective function?

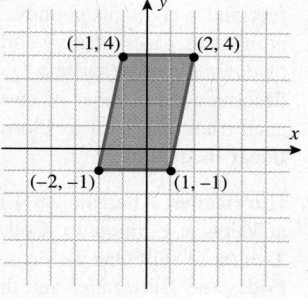

**51.** Objective function: $z = 2x + 3y$

**52.** Objective function: $z = 3x + 2y$

**53.** Objective function: $z = 1.5x + 4.5y$

**54.** Objective function: $z = \frac{2}{3}x + \frac{3}{5}y$

In Exercises 55–62, minimize or maximize each objective function subject to the constraints.

**55.** Minimize $z = 7x + 4y$ subject to
$x \ge 0 \qquad y \ge 0 \qquad -x + y \le 4$

**56.** Maximize $z = 3x + 5y$ subject to
$x \ge 0 \qquad y \ge 0 \qquad -x + y \ge 4$

**57.** Maximize $z = 4x + 3y$ subject to
$x \ge 0 \qquad y \le -x + 4 \qquad y \ge -x$

**58.** Minimize $z = 4x + 3y$ subject to
$x \ge 0 \qquad y \ge 0$
$x + y \le 10 \qquad x + y \ge 0$

**59.** Minimize $z = 2.5x + 3.1y$ subject to
$x \ge 0 \qquad y \ge 0 \qquad x \le 4$
$-x + y \le 2 \qquad x + y \le 6$

**60.** Maximize $z = 2.5x - 3.1y$ subject to
$x \ge 1 \qquad y \le 7 \qquad x \le 3$
$-x + y \ge 2 \qquad x + y \ge 6$

**61.** Maximize $z = \frac{1}{4}x + \frac{2}{5}y$ subject to
$x + y \ge 5 \qquad x + y \le 7$
$-x + y \le 5 \qquad -x + y \ge 3$

**62.** Minimize $z = \frac{1}{3}x - \frac{2}{5}y$ subject to
$x + y \ge 6 \qquad x + y \le 8$
$-x + y \le 6 \qquad -x + y \ge 4$

■ **APPLICATIONS**

For Exercises 63–66, employ the following supply and demand equations:

$$\text{Demand:} \quad P = 80 - 0.01x$$
$$\text{Supply:} \quad P = 20 + 0.02x$$

where $P$ is the price in dollars when $x$ units are produced.

**63. Consumer Surplus.** Write a system of linear inequalities corresponding to the consumer surplus.

**64. Producer Surplus.** Write a system of linear inequalities corresponding to the producer surplus.

**65. Consumer Surplus.** Calculate the consumer surplus given the supply and demand equations.

**66. Producer Surplus.** Calculate the producer surplus given the supply and demand equations.

**67. Hurricanes.** After back-to-back-to-back-to-back hurricanes (Charley, Frances, Ivan, and Jeanne) in Florida in the summer of 2004, FEMA sent disaster relief trucks to Florida. Floridians mainly needed drinking water and generators. Each truck could carry no more than 6000 pounds of cargo or 2400 cubic feet of cargo. Each case of bottled water takes up 1 cubic foot of space and weighs 25 pounds. Each generator takes up 20 cubic feet and weighs 150 pounds. Let $x$ represent the number of cases of water and $y$ represent the number of generators, and write a system of linear inequalities that describes the number of generators and cases of water each truck can haul to Florida.

**68. Hurricanes.** Repeat Exercise 67 with a smaller truck and different supplies. Suppose the smaller trucks that can haul 2000 pounds and 1500 cubic feet of cargo are used to haul plywood and tarps. A case of plywood is 60 cubic feet and weighs 500 pounds. A case of tarps is 10 cubic feet and weighs 50 pounds. Letting $x$ represent the number of cases of plywood and $y$ represent the number of cases of tarps, write a system of linear inequalities that describes the number of cases of tarps and plywood each truck can haul to Florida. Graph the system of linear inequalities.

**69. Hurricanes.** After the 2004 hurricanes in Florida, a student at Valencia Community College decided to create two T-shirts to sell. One T-shirt said, "I survived Charley on Friday the Thirteenth," and the second said, "I survived Charley, Frances, Ivan, and Jeanne." The Charley T-shirt costs him $7 to make and he sold it for $13. The other T-shirt cost him $5 to make and he sold it for $10. He did not want to invest more than $1000. He estimated that the total demand would not exceed 180 T-shirts. Find the number of each type of T-shirt he needed to make to yield maximum profit.

**70. Hurricanes.** After Hurricane Charley devastated central Florida unexpectedly, Orlando residents prepared for Hurricane Frances by boarding up windows and filling up their cars with gas. It took 5 hours of standing in line to get plywood, and lines for gas were just as time-consuming. A student at Seminole Community College decided to do a spoof of the "Got Milk" ads and created two T-shirts: "Got Plywood" showing a line of people in a home improvement store, and "Got Gas" showing a street lined with cars waiting to pump gasoline. The "Got Plywood" shirts cost $8 to make, and she sold them for $13. The "Got Gas" shirts cost $6 to make, and she sold them for $10. She decided to limit her costs to $1400. She estimated that demand for these T-shirts would not exceed 200 T-shirts. Find the number of each type of T-shirt she should have made to yield maximum profit.

**71. Health.** A diet must be designed to provide at least 275 units of calcium, 125 units of iron, and 200 units of Vitamin B. Each ounce of food $A$ contains 10 units of calcium, 15 units of iron, and 20 units of vitamin B. Each ounce of food $B$ contains 20 units of calcium, 10 units of iron, and 15 units of vitamin B.
   **a.** Find a system of inequalities to describe the different quantities of food that may be used (let $x$ = the number of ounces of food $A$ and $y$ = the number of ounces of food $B$).
   **b.** Graph the system of inequalities.
   **c.** Using the graph found in part (b), find two possible solutions (there are infinitely many).

**72. Health.** A diet must be designed to provide at least 350 units of calcium, 175 units of iron, and 225 units of Vitamin B. Each ounce of food $A$ contains 15 units of calcium, 25 units of iron, and 20 units of vitamin B. Each ounce of food $B$ contains 25 units of calcium, 10 units of iron, and 10 units of vitamin B.
   **a.** Find a system of inequalities to describe the different quantities of food that may be used (let $x$ = the number of ounces of food $A$ and $y$ = the number of ounces of food $B$).
   **b.** Graph the system of inequalities.
   **c.** Using the graph found in part (b), find two possible solutions (there are infinitely many).

**73. Business.** A manufacturer produces two types of computer mouse: USB wireless mouse and a Bluetooth mouse. Past sales indicate that it is necessary to produce at least twice as many USB wireless mice than Bluetooth mice. To meet demand, the manufacturer must produce at least 1000 computer mice per hour.
   **a.** Find a system of inequalities describing the production levels of computer mice. Let $x$ be the production level for USB wireless mouse and $y$ be the production level for Bluetooth mouse.
   **b.** Graph the system of inequalities describing the production levels of computer mice.
   **c.** Use your graph in part (b) to find two possible solutions.

**74. Business.** A manufacturer produces two types of mechanical pencil lead: 0.5 millimeter and 0.7 millimeter. Past sales indicate that it is necessary to produce at least 50% more 0.5 millimeter lead than 0.7 millimeter lead. To meet demand, the manufacturer must produce at least 10,000 pieces of pencil lead per hour.
   **a.** Find a system of inequalities describing the production levels of pencil lead. Let $x$ be the production level for 0.5 millimeter pencil lead and $y$ be the production level for 0.7 millimeter pencil lead.
   **b.** Graph the system of inequalities describing the production levels of pencil lead.
   **c.** Use your graph in part (b) to find two possible solutions.

**75. Computer Business.** A computer science major and a business major decide to start a small business that builds and sells desktop computers and laptop computers. They buy the parts, assemble them, load the operating system, and sell the computers to other students. The costs for parts, time to assemble each computer, and profit are summarized in the following table:

|  | DESKTOP | LAPTOP |
|---|---|---|
| Cost of parts | $700 | $400 |
| Time to assemble (hours) | 5 | 3 |
| Profit | $500 | $300 |

They were able to get a small business loan in the amount of $10,000 to cover costs. They plan on making these computers over the summer and selling them the first day of class. They can dedicate at most only 90 hours to assembling these computers. They estimate that the demand for laptops will be at least three times as great as the demand for desktops. How many of each type of computer should they make to maximize profit?

**76. Computer Business.** Repeat Exercise 75 if the two students are able to get a loan for $30,000 to cover costs and they can dedicate at most 120 hours to assembling the computers.

**77. Passenger Ratio.** The Eurostar is a high-speed train that travels between London, Brussels, and Paris. There are 30 cars on each departure. Each train car is designated first-class or second-class. Based on demand for each type of fare, there should always be at least two but no more

than four first-class train cars. The management wants to claim that the ratio of first-class to second-class cars never exceeds 1:8. If the profit on each first-class train car is twice as much as the profit on each second-class train car, find the number of each class of train car that will generate a maximum profit.

**78. Passenger Ratio.** Repeat Exercise 77. This time, assume that there has to be at least one first-class train car and that the profit from each first-class train car is 1.2 times as much as the profit from each second-class train car. The ratio of first-class to second-class cannot exceed 1:10.

**79. Production.** A manufacturer of skis produces two models: a regular ski and a slalom ski. A set of regular skis produces a $25 profit and a set of slalom skis produces a profit of $50. The manufacturer expects a customer demand of at least 200 pairs of regular skis and at least 80 pair of slalom skis. The maximum number of pairs of skis that can be produced by this company is 400. How many of each model of skis should be produced to maximize profits?

**80. Donut Inventory.** A well-known donut store makes two popular types of donuts: crème-filled and jelly-filled. The manager knows from past statistics that the number of dozens of donuts sold is at least 10, but no more than 30. To prepare the donuts for frying, the baker needs (on the average) 3 minutes for a dozen crème-filled and 2 minutes for jelly-filled. The baker has at most two hours available per day to prepare the donuts. How many dozens of each type should be prepared to maximize the daily profit if there is a $1.20 profit for each dozen crème-filled and $1.80 profit for each dozen jelly-filled donuts?

■**CATCH THE MISTAKE**

**In Exercises 81 and 82, explain the mistake that is made.**

**81.** Graph the inequality $y \geq 2x + 1$.

**Solution:**

Graph the line $y = 2x + 1$ with a solid line.

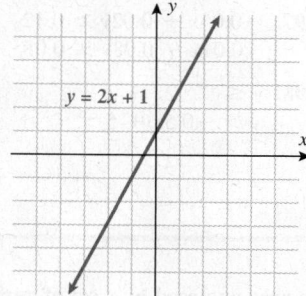

Since the inequality is $\geq$, shade to the *right*.

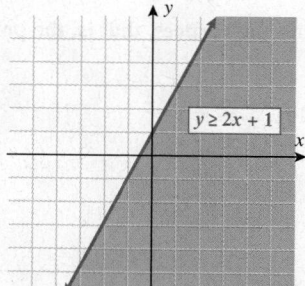

This is incorrect. What mistake was made?

**82.** Graph the inequality $y < 2x + 1$.

**Solution:**

Graph the line $y = 2x + 1$ with a solid line.

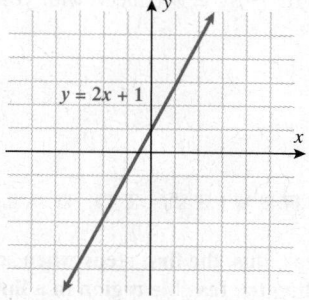

Since the inequality is $<$, shade *below*.

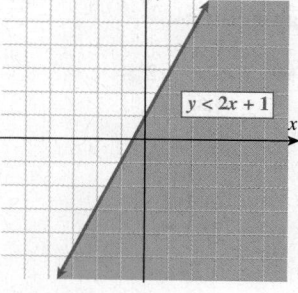

This is incorrect. What mistake was made?

■ CONCEPTUAL

**In Exercises 83–88, determine whether each statement is true or false.**

83. A linear inequality always has a solution that is a half-plane.

84. A dashed curve is used for strict inequalities.

85. A solid curve is used for strict inequalities.

86. A system of linear inequalities always has a solution.

87. An objective function always has a maximum or minimum.

88. An objective function subject to constraints that correspond to a bounded region always has a maximum and a minimum.

■ CHALLENGE

**In Exercises 89 and 90, for the system of linear inequalities, assume $a$, $b$, $c$, and $d$ are real numbers.**

$$x \geq a$$
$$x < b$$
$$y > c$$
$$y \leq d$$

89. Describe the solution when $a < b$ and $c < d$.

90. What will the solution be if $a > b$ and $c > d$?

**For Exercises 91 and 92, use the following system of linear inequalities:**

$$y \leq \quad ax + b$$
$$y \geq -ax + b$$

91. If $a$ and $b$ are positive real numbers, graph the solution.

92. If $a$ and $b$ are negative real numbers, graph the solution.

93. Maximize the objective function $z = 2x + y$ subject to the conditions, where $a > 2$.

$$ax + y \geq -a$$
$$-ax + y \leq \quad a$$
$$ax + y \leq \quad a$$
$$-ax + y \geq -a$$

94. Maximize the objective function $z = x + 2y$ subject to the conditions, where $a > b > 0$.

$$x + y \geq a$$
$$-x + y \leq a$$
$$x + y \leq a + b$$
$$-x + y \geq a - b$$

■ TECHNOLOGY

**In Exercises 95 and 96, apply a graphing utility to graph the following inequalities.**

95. $4x - 2y \geq 6$ (Check with your answer to Exercise 17.)

96. $6x - 3y \geq 9$ (Check with your answer to Exercise 18.)

**In Exercises 97 and 98, use a graphing utility to graph each system of inequalities or indicate that the system has no solution.**

97. $-0.05x + 0.02y \geq 0.12$
    $\quad 0.01x + 0.08y \leq 0.08$

98. $y \leq \quad 2x + 3$
    $y > -0.5x + 5$

■ PREVIEW TO CALCULUS

In calculus, the first steps when solving the problem of finding the area enclosed by a set of curves are similar to those for finding the feasible region in a linear programming problem.

In Exercises 99–102, graph the system of inequalities and identify the vertices, that is, the points of intersection of the given curves.

99. $y \leq x + 2$
    $y \geq x^2$

100. $x \leq 25$
     $x \geq y^2$

101. $y \leq x^2$
     $y \geq x^3$
     $x \geq 0$

102. $y \geq \quad x^3$
     $y \leq -x$
     $y \geq \quad x + 6$

In Section 8.1, you learned how to solve systems of two linear equations in two variables. That is, you determined the set of all points that satisfy both given equations in a system. In Chapter 0 you solved linear inequalities in one variable. Next, you will put these ideas together as you consider systems of linear inequalities in two variables, and their solutions.

**1.** The following graph shows the line $y = 2x + 1$. Notice that the line divides the Cartesian plane into two half-planes—one below and one above the line.

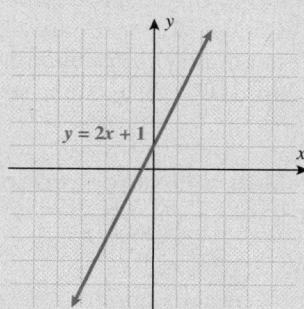

The set of all the points in the half-plane below the line are in the shaded region.

**a.** The set of points *on* the line, together with the points in the shaded region, make up the solution set of the inequality: $y \leq 2x + 1$. To get an idea of what this means, choose several points—a few on the line, a few in the shaded region, and a few in the unshaded region—and evaluate the inequality for each. What do you notice?

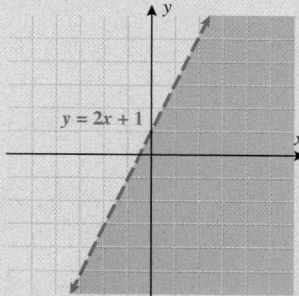

**b.** Write an inequality that has as its solution set the points on the line $y = 2x + 1$ together with all the points above the line.

**c.** Suppose you wanted to graph the solutions to the strict inequality $y < 2x + 1$. How do you think you could alter the graph shown above to do this? Explain.

**2.** To graph a linear inequality, first graph the associated line (either solid or dashed), then choose the appropriate half-plane to shade. Remember, ALL of the points in one of the half-planes are in the solution set of the given inequality, and NONE of the points in the other half-plane are in the solution set. To determine which half-plane to shade, one need only check one test point.

**a.** Graph the linear inequality $3x + 6y < 18$.

**b.** Graph the linear inequality $3x - 6y \leq 18$.

**c.** Now consider the system of two linear inequalities:

$$3x + 6y > 18$$
$$3x - 6y \leq 18$$

Graph the two associated lines together at the right.

Shade the region(s) that contain(s) the points in the solution set of the system of inequalities. Use some test points, if needed.

**d.** How is the region you shaded in part (c) related to the regions you shaded in parts (a) and (b)?

In 2005 hybrid vehicles were introduced in the U.S. market. The demand for hybrids, which are typically powered by a combination of gasoline and electric batteries, was based on popular recognition of petroleum as an increasingly scarce nonrenewable resource, as well as consumers' need to combat rising prices at the gas pumps. In addition to achieving greater fuel economy than conventional internal combustion engine vehicles (ICEVs), their use also results in reduced emissions.

An online "Gas Mileage Impact Calculator," created by the American Council for an Energy-Efficient Economy (www.aceee.org), was used to generate the following tables comparing a conventional sedan (four-door) and an SUV versus their respective hybrid counterparts.

## Gas Mileage Impact Calculator

|  | TOYOTA CAMRY 2.4L 4, AUTO $3.75/GALLON 15,000 MI/YEAR | TOYOTA CAMRY HYBRID 2.4L 4, AUTO $3.75/GALLON 15,000 MI/YEAR |
|---|---|---|
| **Gas consumption** | 611 gallons | 449 gallons |
| **Gas cost** | $2289.75 | $1681.99 |
| **Fuel economy** | 25 mpg | 33 mpg |
| EMISSIONS | | |
| **Carbon dioxide** (greenhouse gas) | 11,601 pounds | 8522 pounds |
| **Carbon monoxide** (poisonous gas) | 235 pounds | 169 pounds |
| **Nitrogen oxides** (lung irritant and smog) | 10 pounds | 7 pounds |
| **Particulate matter** (soot) | 255 grams | 255 grams |
| **Hydrocarbons** (smog) | 6 pounds | 8 pounds |

|  | TOYOTA HIGHLANDER 3.5L 6, AUTO STK $3.75/GALLON 15,000 MI/YEAR | TOYOTA HIGHLANDER HYBRID 3.3L 6, AUTO AWD $3.75/GALLON 15,000 MI/YEAR |
|---|---|---|
| **Gas consumption** | 740 gallons | 576 gallons |
| **Gas cost** | $2773.44 | $2158.33 |
| **Fuel economy** | 20 mpg | 26 mpg |
| EMISSIONS | | |
| **Carbon dioxide** (greenhouse gas) | 14,052 pounds | 10,936 pounds |
| **Carbon monoxide** (poisonous gas) | 229 pounds | 187 pounds |
| **Nitrogen oxides** (lung irritant and smog) | 11 pounds | 8 pounds |
| **Particulate matter** (soot) | 320 grams | 399 grams |
| **Hydrocarbons** (smog) | 7 pounds | 16 pounds |

The MSRP and mileage comparisons for the 2008 models are given below:

|  | CAMRY | CAMRY HYBRID | HIGHLANDER | HIGHLANDER HYBRID |
|---|---|---|---|---|
| **MSRP** | $19,435 | $26,065 | $28,035 | $34,435 |
| **Miles per gallon in city** | 21 | 33 | 18 | 27 |
| **Miles per gallon on highway** | 31 | 34 | 24 | 25 |

For the following questions, assume that you drive 15,000 miles per year (all in the city) and the price of gasoline is $3.75 per gallon.

**1.** Write a linear equation that models the total cost of owning and operating each vehicle $y$ as a function of the number of years of ownership $x$.

   **a.** Camry                   **b.** Camry Hybrid

   **c.** Highlander          **d.** Highlander Hybrid

**2.** Write a linear equation that models the total number of pounds of carbon dioxide each vehicle emits $y$ as a function of the number of years of ownership $x$.

   **a.** Camry                   **b.** Camry Hybrid

   **c.** Highlander          **d.** Highlander Hybrid

**3.** How many years would you have to own and drive the vehicle for the hybrid to be the better deal?

   **a.** Camry Hybrid versus Camry   **b.** Highlander Hybrid versus Highlander

**4.** How many years would you have to own and drive the vehicle for the hybrid to emit 50% less carbon dioxide than its conventional counterpart?

   **a.** Camry Hybrid versus Camry   **b.** Highlander Hybrid versus Highlander

# CHAPTER 8 REVIEW

| SECTION | CONCEPT | KEY IDEAS/FORMULAS |
|---|---|---|
| 8.1 | Systems of linear equations in two variables | $A_1x + B_1y = C_1$<br>$A_2x + B_2y = C_2$ |
| | Solving systems of linear equations in two variables | **Substitution method**<br>Solve for one variable in terms of the other and substitute that expression into the other equation.<br>**Elimination method**<br>Eliminate a variable by adding multiples of the equations.<br>**Graphing method**<br>Graph the two lines. The solution is the point of intersection. Parallel lines have no solution and identical lines have infinitely many solutions. |
| | Three methods and three types of solutions | One solution, no solution, infinitely many solutions |
| 8.2 | Systems of linear equations in three variables | Planes in a three-dimensional coordinate system |
| | Solving systems of linear equations in three variables | Step 1: Reduce the system to two equations and two unknowns.<br>Step 2: Solve the resulting system from Step 1.<br>Step 3: Substitute solutions found in Step 2 into any of the equations to find the third variable.<br>Step 4: Check. |
| | Types of solutions | One solution (point), no solution, or infinitely many solutions (line or the same plane) |
| 8.3 | Systems of linear equations and matrices | |
| | Matrices | $A_{m\times n} = \begin{bmatrix} a_{11} & a_{12} & \cdots & a_{1n} \\ a_{21} & a_{22} & \cdots & a_{2n} \\ \vdots & & & \vdots \\ a_{m1} & a_{m2} & \cdots & a_{mn} \end{bmatrix}$ |
| | Augmented matrices | $\begin{aligned} a_1x + b_1y + c_1z &= d_1 \\ a_2x + b_2y + c_2z &= d_2 \\ a_3x + b_3y + c_3z &= d_3 \end{aligned} \Rightarrow \begin{bmatrix} a_1 & b_1 & c_1 & \vert & d_1 \\ a_2 & b_2 & c_2 & \vert & d_2 \\ a_3 & b_3 & c_3 & \vert & d_3 \end{bmatrix}$ |
| | Row operations on a matrix | 1. $R_i \leftrightarrow R_j$ — Interchange row $i$ with row $j$.<br>2. $cR_i \rightarrow R_i$ — Multiply row $i$ by the constant $c$.<br>3. $cR_i + R_j \rightarrow R_j$ — Multiply row $i$ by the constant $c$ and add to row $j$, writing the results in row $j$. |
| | Row–echelon form of a matrix | A matrix is in **row–echelon form** if it has all three of the following properties:<br>1. Any rows consisting entirely of 0s are at the bottom of the matrix.<br>2. For each row that does not consist entirely of 0s, the first (leftmost) nonzero entry is 1 (called the leading 1).<br>3. For two successive nonzero rows, the leading 1 in the higher row is farther to the left than the leading 1 in the lower row.<br>If a matrix in row–echelon form has the following additional property, then the matrix is in **reduced row–echelon form**:<br>4. Every column containing a leading 1 has zeros in every position above and below the leading 1. |

| SECTION | CONCEPT | KEY IDEAS/FORMULAS |
|---|---|---|
| | Gaussian elimination with back-substitution | Step 1: Write the system of equations as an augmented matrix. Step 2: Apply row operations to transform the matrix into row–echelon form. Step 3: Apply back-substitution to identify the solution. |
| | Gauss–Jordan elimination | Step 1: Write the system of equations as an augmented matrix. Step 2: Apply row operations to transform the matrix into *reduced* row–echelon form. Step 3: Identify the solution. |
| | Inconsistent and dependent systems | No solution or infinitely many solutions |
| 8.4 | **Matrix algebra** | $$\begin{array}{c} \begin{array}{ccccc} \text{Column 1} & \text{Column 2} & \cdots & \text{Column } j & \cdots & \text{Column } n \end{array} \\ \begin{array}{c} \text{Row 1} \\ \text{Row 2} \\ \vdots \\ \text{Row } i \\ \vdots \\ \text{Row } m \end{array} \begin{bmatrix} a_{11} & a_{12} & \cdots & a_{1j} & \cdots & a_{1n} \\ a_{21} & a_{22} & \cdots & a_{2j} & \cdots & a_{2n} \\ \vdots & \vdots & \cdots & \vdots & \cdots & \vdots \\ a_{i1} & a_{i2} & \cdots & a_{ij} & \cdots & a_{in} \\ \vdots & \vdots & \cdots & \vdots & \cdots & \vdots \\ a_{m1} & a_{m2} & \cdots & a_{mj} & \cdots & a_{mn} \end{bmatrix} \end{array}$$ |
| | Equality of matrices | The orders must be the same: $A_{m \times n}$ and $B_{m \times n}$ and corresponding entries are equal. |
| | Matrix addition and subtraction | The orders must be the same: $A_{m \times n}$ and $B_{m \times n}$. Perform operation entry by entry. |
| | Scalar and matrix multiplication | The scalar is multiplied by *all* of the entries. For matrix multiplication <br> ■ The orders must satisfy the relationship: $A_{m \times n}$ and $B_{n \times p}$, resulting in $(AB)_{m \times p}$. <br> ■ Perform multiplication row by column. <br> ■ Matrix multiplication is not commutative: $AB \neq BA$. |
| | Matrix equations | Linear system: $AX = B$. *Front* multiply both sides of the equation by $A^{-1}$ (provided $A^{-1}$ exists), which results in $X = A^{-1}B$. |
| | Finding the inverse of a square matrix | Only square matrices, $n \times n$, have inverses, $A^{-1}A = I_n$. Step 1: Form the matrix $[A \mid I_n]$. Step 2: Use row operations to transform this matrix to $\left[ I_n \mid A^{-1} \right]$. |
| | Solving systems of linear equations using matrix algebra and inverses of square matrices | $AX = B$ Step 1: Find $A^{-1}$. Step 2: $X = A^{-1}B$. |

| | | |
|---------|---------|--------------------|
| 8.5 | **The determinant of a square matrix and Cramer's rule** | Cramer's rule can only be used to solve a system of linear equations with a unique solution. |
| | Determinant of a $2 \times 2$ matrix | $\begin{vmatrix} a & b \\ c & d \end{vmatrix} = ad - bc$ |

Determinant of an $n \times n$ matrix

Let $A$ be a square matrix of order $n \times n$. Then:

- The **minor** $M_{ij}$ of the element $a_{ij}$ is the determinant of the $(n-1) \times (n-1)$ matrix obtained when the $i$th row and $j$th column of $A$ are deleted.
- The **cofactor** $C_{ij}$ of the element $a_{ij}$ is given by $C_{ij} = (-1)^{i+j} M_{ij}$.

$$\begin{bmatrix} 1 & -3 & 2 \\ 4 & -1 & 0 \\ 5 & -2 & 3 \end{bmatrix}$$

$$M_{11} = \begin{vmatrix} -1 & 0 \\ -2 & 3 \end{vmatrix} = -3 - 0 = -3$$

$$C_{11} = (-1)^{1+1} M_{11} = (1)(-3) = -3$$

Sign pattern of cofactors for the determinant of a $3 \times 3$ matrix:

$$\begin{bmatrix} + & - & + \\ - & + & - \\ + & - & + \end{bmatrix}$$

If $A$ is a $3 \times 3$ matrix, the determinant can be given by $\det(A) = a_{11}C_{11} + a_{12}C_{12} + a_{13}C_{13}$. This is called **expanding the determinant by the first row**. (Note that any row or column can be used.)

$$\begin{vmatrix} a_1 & b_1 & c_1 \\ a_2 & b_2 & c_2 \\ a_3 & b_3 & c_3 \end{vmatrix} = a_1 \begin{vmatrix} b_2 & c_2 \\ b_3 & c_3 \end{vmatrix} - b_1 \begin{vmatrix} a_2 & c_2 \\ a_3 & c_3 \end{vmatrix} + c_1 \begin{vmatrix} a_2 & b_2 \\ a_3 & b_3 \end{vmatrix}$$

Cramer's rule: Systems of linear equations in two variables

The system

$$a_1 x + b_1 y = c_1$$
$$a_2 x + b_2 y = c_2$$

has the solution

$$x = \frac{D_x}{D} \qquad y = \frac{D_y}{D} \qquad \text{if } D \neq 0$$

where

$$D = \begin{vmatrix} a_1 & b_1 \\ a_2 & b_2 \end{vmatrix} \qquad D_x = \begin{vmatrix} c_1 & b_1 \\ c_2 & b_2 \end{vmatrix} \qquad D_y = \begin{vmatrix} a_1 & c_1 \\ a_2 & c_2 \end{vmatrix}$$

| SECTION | CONCEPT | KEY IDEAS/FORMULAS |
|---|---|---|

| | Cramer's rule: Systems of linear equations in three variables | The system $$\begin{aligned} a_1x + b_1y + c_1z &= d_1 \\ a_2x + b_2y + c_2z &= d_2 \\ a_3x + b_3y + c_3z &= d_3 \end{aligned}$$ has the solution $$x = \frac{D_x}{D} \qquad y = \frac{D_y}{D} \qquad z = \frac{D_z}{D} \quad \text{if } D \neq 0$$ where $$D = \begin{vmatrix} a_1 & b_1 & c_1 \\ a_2 & b_2 & c_2 \\ a_3 & b_3 & c_3 \end{vmatrix} \qquad D_x = \begin{vmatrix} d_1 & b_1 & c_1 \\ d_2 & b_2 & c_2 \\ d_3 & b_3 & c_3 \end{vmatrix}$$ $$D_y = \begin{vmatrix} a_1 & d_1 & c_1 \\ a_2 & d_2 & c_2 \\ a_3 & d_3 & c_3 \end{vmatrix} \qquad D_z = \begin{vmatrix} a_1 & b_1 & d_1 \\ a_2 & b_2 & d_2 \\ a_3 & b_3 & d_3 \end{vmatrix}$$ |
| 8.6 | **Partial fractions** | $\dfrac{n(x)}{d(x)}$    Factor $d(x)$ |
| | Performing partial fraction decomposition | Write $\dfrac{n(x)}{d(x)}$ as a sum of partial fractions: <br> *Case 1:* Distinct (nonrepeated) **linear** factors <br> *Case 2:* Repeated **linear** factors <br> *Case 3:* Distinct **irreducible quadratic** factors <br> *Case 4:* Repeated **irreducible quadratic** factors. <br><br> **Distinct linear factors** $$\frac{n(x)}{d(x)} = \frac{A}{(ax+b)} + \frac{B}{(cx+d)} + \cdots$$ **Repeated linear factors** $$\frac{n(x)}{d(x)} = \frac{A}{(ax+b)} + \frac{B}{(ax+b)^2} + \cdots + \frac{M}{(ax+b)^m}$$ **Distinct irreducible quadratic factors** $$\frac{n(x)}{d(x)} = \frac{Ax+B}{ax^2+bx+c}$$ **Repeated irreducible quadratic factors** $$\frac{n(x)}{d(x)} = \frac{A_1 x + B_1}{ax^2+bx+c} + \frac{A_2 x + B_2}{\left(ax^2+bx+c\right)^2} +$$ $$\frac{A_3 x + B_3}{\left(ax^2+bx+c\right)^3} + \cdots + \frac{A_m x + B_m}{\left(ax^2+bx+c\right)^m}$$ |
| 8.7 | **Systems of linear inequalities in two variables** | |
| | Linear inequalities in two variables | ■ $\leq$ or $\geq$ use solid lines. <br> ■ $<$ or $>$ use dashed lines. |
| | Systems of linear inequalities in two variables | Solutions are determined graphically by finding the common shaded regions. |
| | The linear programming model | Finding optimal solutions <br> Minimizing or maximizing a function <br> subject to constraints (linear inequalities) |

## 8.1 Systems of Linear Equations in Two Variables

**Solve each system of linear equations.**

**1.** $r - s = 3$
$r + s = 3$

**2.** $3x + 4y = 2$
$x - y = 6$

**3.** $-4x + 2y = 3$
$4x - y = 5$

**4.** $0.25x - 0.5y = 0.6$
$0.5x + 0.25y = 0.8$

**5.** $x + y = 3$
$x - y = 1$

**6.** $3x + y = 4$
$2x + y = 1$

**7.** $4c - 4d = 3$
$c + d = 4$

**8.** $5r + 2s = 1$
$r - s = -3$

**9.** $y = -\frac{1}{2}x$
$y = \frac{1}{2}x + 2$

**10.** $2x + 4y = -2$
$4x - 2y = 3$

**11.** $1.3x - 2.4y = 1.6$
$0.7x - 1.2y = 1.4$

**12.** $\frac{1}{4}x - \frac{3}{4}y = 12$
$\frac{1}{2}y + \frac{1}{4}x = \frac{1}{2}$

**13.** $5x - 3y = 21$
$-2x + 7y = -20$

**14.** $6x - 2y = -2$
$4x + 3y = 16$

**15.** $10x - 7y = -24$
$7x + 4y = 1$

**16.** $\frac{1}{3}x - \frac{2}{9}y = \frac{2}{9}$
$\frac{4}{5}x + \frac{3}{4}y = -\frac{3}{4}$

**Match each system of equations with its graph.**

**17.** $2x - 3y = 4$
$x + 4y = 3$

**18.** $5x - y = 2$
$5x - y = -2$

**19.** $x + 2y = -6$
$2x + 4y = -12$

**20.** $5x + 2y = 3$
$4x - 2y = 6$

**a.**

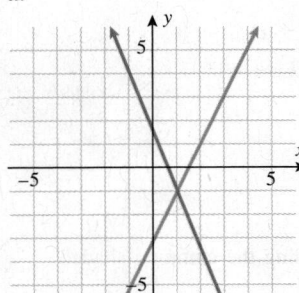

**b.**

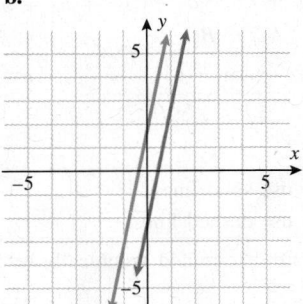

**c.**

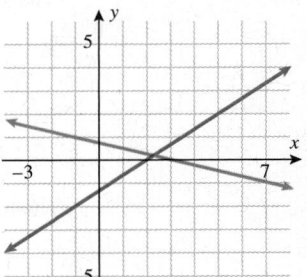

**d.**

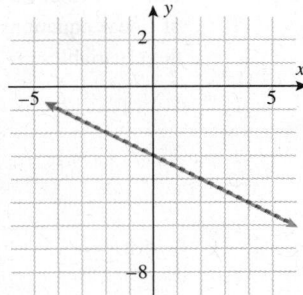

## Applications

**21. Chemistry.** In chemistry lab, Alexandra needs to make a 42-milliliter solution that is 15% NaCl. All that is in the lab is 6% and 18% NaCl. How many milliliters of each solution should she use to obtain the desired mix?

**22. Gas Mileage.** A Nissan Sentra gets approximately 32 mpg on the highway and 18 mpg in the city. Suppose 265 miles were driven on a full tank (12 gallons) of gasoline. Approximately how many miles were driven in the city and how many on the highway?

## 8.2 Systems of Linear Equations in Three Variables

**Solve each system of linear equations.**

**23.** $x + y + z = 1$
$x - y - z = -3$
$-x + y + z = 3$

**24.** $x - 2y + z = 3$
$2x - y + z = -4$
$3x - 3y - 5z = 2$

**25.** $x + y + z = 7$
$x - y - z = 17$
$y + z = 5$

**26.** $x + z = 3$
$-x + y - z = -1$
$x + y + z = 5$

## Applications

**27. Fitting a Curve to Data.** The average number of flights on a commercial plane that a person takes per year can be modeled by a quadratic function $y = ax^2 + bx + c$, where $a < 0$, and $x$ represents age: $16 \leq x \leq 65$. The following table gives the average number of flights per year that a person takes on a commercial airline. Determine a quadratic function that models this quantity. *Note:* Coefficients will be approximate.

| AGE | NUMBER OF FLIGHTS PER YEAR |
|---|---|
| 16 | 2 |
| 40 | 6 |
| 65 | 4 |

**28. Investment Portfolio.** Danny and Paula decide to invest $20,000 of their savings. They put some in an IRA account earning 4.5% interest, some in a mutual fund that has been averaging 8% a year, and some in a stock that earned 12% last year. If they put $4000 more in the IRA than in the mutual fund, and the mutual fund and stock have the same growth in the next year as they did in the previous year, they will earn $1525 in a year. How much money did they put in each of the three investments?

## 8.3 Systems of Linear Equations and Matrices

**Write the augmented matrix for each system of linear equations.**

**29.** $5x + 7y = 2$
$3x - 4y = -2$

**30.** $2.3x - 4.5y = 6.8$
$-0.4x + 2.1y = -9.1$

**31.** $2x - z = 3$
$y - 3z = -2$
$x + 4z = -3$

**32.** $2y - x + 3z = 1$
$4z - 2y + 3x = -2$
$x - y - 4z = 0$

**Indicate whether each matrix is in row–echelon form. If it is, state whether it is in *reduced* row–echelon form.**

**33.** $\begin{bmatrix} 1 & 1 & | & 0 \\ 0 & 1 & | & 2 \end{bmatrix}$

**34.** $\begin{bmatrix} 1 & 2 & | & 0 \\ 0 & 0 & | & 1 \end{bmatrix}$

**35.** $\begin{bmatrix} 2 & 0 & 1 & | & 1 \\ 0 & -2 & 0 & | & 2 \\ 0 & 0 & 2 & | & 3 \end{bmatrix}$

**36.** $\begin{bmatrix} 1 & 0 & 1 & 0 & | & 2 \\ 0 & 0 & 1 & 1 & | & -3 \\ 0 & 1 & 0 & 0 & | & 2 \\ 0 & 0 & 0 & 1 & | & 1 \end{bmatrix}$

**Perform the indicated row operations on each matrix.**

**37.** $\begin{bmatrix} 1 & -2 & | & 1 \\ 0 & -2 & | & 2 \end{bmatrix}$ $\quad -\frac{1}{2}R_2 \rightarrow R_2$

**38.** $\begin{bmatrix} 1 & 4 & | & 1 \\ 2 & -2 & | & 3 \end{bmatrix}$ $\quad R_2 - 2R_1 \rightarrow R_2$

**39.** $\begin{bmatrix} 1 & -2 & 0 & | & 1 \\ 0 & -2 & 3 & | & -2 \\ 0 & 1 & -4 & | & 8 \end{bmatrix}$ $\quad R_2 + R_1 \rightarrow R_1$

**40.** $\begin{bmatrix} 1 & 1 & 1 & 6 & | & 0 \\ 0 & 2 & -2 & 3 & | & -2 \\ 0 & 0 & 1 & -2 & | & 4 \\ 0 & -1 & 3 & -3 & | & 3 \end{bmatrix}$ $\quad \begin{array}{l} -2R_1 + R_2 \rightarrow R_1 \\ R_4 + R_3 \rightarrow R_4 \end{array}$

**Apply row operations to transform each matrix to reduced row–echelon form.**

**41.** $\begin{bmatrix} 1 & 3 & | & 0 \\ 3 & 4 & | & 1 \end{bmatrix}$

**42.** $\begin{bmatrix} 1 & 2 & -1 & | & 0 \\ 0 & 1 & -1 & | & -1 \\ -2 & 0 & 1 & | & -2 \end{bmatrix}$

**43.** $\begin{bmatrix} 4 & 1 & -2 & | & 0 \\ 1 & 0 & -1 & | & 0 \\ -2 & 1 & 1 & | & 12 \end{bmatrix}$

**44.** $\begin{bmatrix} 2 & 3 & 2 & | & 1 \\ 0 & -1 & 1 & | & -2 \\ 1 & 1 & -1 & | & 6 \end{bmatrix}$

**Solve the system of linear equations using augmented matrices.**

**45.** $3x - 2y = 2$
$-2x + 4y = 1$

**46.** $2x - 7y = 22$
$x + 5y = -23$

**47.** $5x - y = 9$
$x + 4y = 6$

**48.** $8x + 7y = 10$
$-3x + 5y = 42$

**49.** $x - 2y + z = 3$
$2x - y + z = -4$
$3x - 3y - 5z = 2$

**50.** $3x - y + 4z = 18$
$5x + 2y - z = -20$
$x + 7y - 6z = -38$

**51.** $x - 4y + 10z = -61$
$3x - 5y + 8z = -52$
$-5x + y - 2z = 8$

**52.** $4x - 2y + 5z = 17$
$x + 6y - 3z = -\frac{17}{2}$
$-2x + 5y + z = 2$

**53.** $3x + y + z = -4$
$x - 2y + z = -6$

**54.** $2x - y + 3z = 6$
$3x + 2y - z = 12$

## Applications

**55. Fitting a Curve to Data.** The average number of flights on a commercial plane that a person takes a year can be modeled by a quadratic function $y = ax^2 + bx + c$, where $a < 0$ and $x$ represents age: $16 < x < 65$. The table below gives the average number of flights per year that a person takes on a commercial airline. Determine a quadratic function that models this quantity by solving for $a$, $b$, and $c$ using matrices and compare with Exercise 27. *Note:* Coefficients will be approximate.

| AGE | NUMBER OF FLIGHTS PER YEAR |
|---|---|
| 16 | 2 |
| 40 | 6 |
| 65 | 4 |

**56. Investment Portfolio.** Danny and Paula decide to invest $20,000 of their savings in investments. They put some in an IRA account earning 4.5% interest, some in a mutual fund that has been averaging 8% a year, and some in a stock that earned 12% last year. If they put $3000 more in the mutual fund than in the IRA, and the mutual fund and stock have the same growth in the next year as they did in the previous year, they will earn $1877.50 in a year. How much money did they put in each of the three investments?

## 8.4 Matrix Algebra

**Calculate the given expression, if possible.**

$$A = \begin{bmatrix} 2 & -3 \\ 0 & 1 \end{bmatrix} \quad B = \begin{bmatrix} 1 & 5 & -1 \\ 3 & 7 & 2 \end{bmatrix} \quad C = \begin{bmatrix} 5 & 0 & 1 \\ 2 & -1 & 4 \\ 0 & 3 & 6 \end{bmatrix}$$

$$D = \begin{bmatrix} 5 & 2 \\ 9 & 7 \end{bmatrix} \quad E = \begin{bmatrix} 2 & 0 & 3 \\ 4 & 1 & -1 \end{bmatrix}$$

**57.** $A + C$

**58.** $B + A$

**59.** $B + E$

**60.** $A + D$

**61.** $2A + D$

**62.** $3E + B$

**63.** $2D - 3A$

**64.** $3B - 4E$

**65.** $5A - 2D$

**66.** $5B - 4E$

**67.** $AB$

**68.** $BC$

**69.** $DA$

**70.** $AD$

**71.** $BC + E$

**72.** $DB$

**73.** $EC$

**74.** $CE$

**Determine whether $B$ is the multiplicative inverse of $A$ using $AA^{-1} = I$.**

**75.** $A = \begin{bmatrix} 6 & 4 \\ 4 & 2 \end{bmatrix} \quad B = \begin{bmatrix} -0.5 & 1 \\ 1 & -1.5 \end{bmatrix}$

**76.** $A = \begin{bmatrix} 1 & -2 \\ 2 & -4 \end{bmatrix} \quad B = \begin{bmatrix} 1 & 2 \\ 2 & -2 \end{bmatrix}$

**77.** $A = \begin{bmatrix} 1 & -2 & 6 \\ 2 & 3 & -2 \\ 0 & -1 & 1 \end{bmatrix} \quad B = \begin{bmatrix} -\frac{1}{7} & \frac{4}{7} & 2 \\ \frac{2}{7} & -\frac{1}{7} & -2 \\ \frac{2}{7} & -\frac{1}{7} & -1 \end{bmatrix}$

**78.** $A = \begin{bmatrix} 0 & 7 & 6 \\ 1 & 0 & -4 \\ -2 & 1 & 0 \end{bmatrix} \quad B = \begin{bmatrix} 1 & 1 & 1 \\ -2 & -2 & -2 \\ 2 & 0 & 6 \end{bmatrix}$

**Find $A^{-1}$, if it exists.**

**79.** $A = \begin{bmatrix} 1 & 2 \\ -3 & 4 \end{bmatrix}$

**80.** $A = \begin{bmatrix} -2 & 7 \\ -4 & 6 \end{bmatrix}$

**81.** $A = \begin{bmatrix} 0 & 1 \\ -2 & 0 \end{bmatrix}$

**82.** $A = \begin{bmatrix} 3 & -1 \\ -2 & 2 \end{bmatrix}$

**83.** $A = \begin{bmatrix} 1 & 3 & -2 \\ 2 & 1 & -1 \\ 0 & 1 & -3 \end{bmatrix}$

**84.** $A = \begin{bmatrix} 0 & 1 & 0 \\ 4 & 1 & 2 \\ -3 & -2 & 1 \end{bmatrix}$

**85.** $A = \begin{bmatrix} -1 & 1 & 0 \\ -2 & 1 & 2 \\ 1 & 2 & 4 \end{bmatrix}$

**86.** $A = \begin{bmatrix} -4 & 4 & 3 \\ 1 & 2 & 2 \\ 3 & -1 & 6 \end{bmatrix}$

**Solve the system of linear equations using matrix algebra.**

**87.** $3x - y = 11$
  $5x + 2y = 33$

**88.** $6x + 4y = 15$
  $-3x - 2y = -1$

**89.** $\frac{5}{8}x - \frac{2}{3}y = -3$
  $\frac{3}{4}x + \frac{5}{6}y = 16$

**90.** $x + y - z = 0$
  $2x - y + 3z = 18$
  $3x - 2y + z = 17$

**91.** $3x - 2y + 4z = 11$
  $6x + 3y - 2z = 6$
  $x - y + 7z = 20$

**92.** $2x + 6y - 4z = 11$
  $-x - 3y + 2z = -\frac{11}{2}$
  $4x + 5y + 6z = 20$

## 8.5 The Determinant of a Square Matrix and Cramer's Rule

**Evaluate each $2 \times 2$ determinant.**

**93.** $\begin{vmatrix} 2 & 4 \\ 3 & 2 \end{vmatrix}$

**94.** $\begin{vmatrix} -2 & -4 \\ -3 & 2 \end{vmatrix}$

**95.** $\begin{vmatrix} 2.4 & -2.3 \\ 3.6 & -1.2 \end{vmatrix}$

**96.** $\begin{vmatrix} -\frac{1}{4} & 4 \\ \frac{3}{4} & -4 \end{vmatrix}$

**Employ Cramer's rule to solve each system of equations, if possible.**

**97.** $x - y = 2$
  $x + y = 4$

**98.** $3x - y = -17$
  $-x + 5y = 43$

**99.** $2x + 4y = 12$
  $x - 2y = 6$

**100.** $-x + y = 4$
  $2x - 6y = -5$

**101.** $-3x = 40 - 2y$
  $2x = 25 + y$

**102.** $3x = 20 + 4y$
  $y - x = -6$

**Evaluate each $3 \times 3$ determinant.**

**103.** $\begin{vmatrix} 1 & 2 & 2 \\ 0 & 1 & 3 \\ 2 & -1 & 0 \end{vmatrix}$

**104.** $\begin{vmatrix} 0 & -2 & 1 \\ 0 & -3 & 7 \\ 1 & -10 & -3 \end{vmatrix}$

**105.** $\begin{vmatrix} a & 0 & -b \\ -a & b & c \\ 0 & 0 & -d \end{vmatrix}$

**106.** $\begin{vmatrix} -2 & -4 & 6 \\ 2 & 0 & 3 \\ -1 & 2 & \frac{3}{4} \end{vmatrix}$

**Employ Cramer's rule to solve each system of equations, if possible.**

**107.** $x + y - 2z = -2$
  $2x - y + z = 3$
  $x + y + z = 4$

**108.** $-x - y + z = 3$
  $x + 2y - 2z = 8$
  $2x + y + 4z = -4$

**109.** $3x + 4z = -1$
  $x + y + 2z = -3$
  $y - 4z = -9$

**110.** $x + y + z = 0$
  $-x - 3y + 5z = -2$
  $2x + y - 3z = -4$

## 8.6 Partial Fractions

Write the form of each partial-fraction decomposition. Do not solve for the constants.

**111.** $\dfrac{4}{(x-1)^2(x+3)(x-5)}$  **112.** $\dfrac{7}{(x-9)(3x+5)^2(x+4)}$

**113.** $\dfrac{12}{x(4x+5)(2x+1)^2}$  **114.** $\dfrac{2}{(x+1)(x-5)(x-9)^2}$

**115.** $\dfrac{3}{x^2+x-12}$  **116.** $\dfrac{x^2+3x-2}{x^3+6x^2}$

**117.** $\dfrac{3x^3+4x^2+56x+62}{(x^2+17)^2}$  **118.** $\dfrac{x^3+7x^2+10}{(x^2+13)^2}$

Find the partial-fraction decomposition for each rational function.

**119.** $\dfrac{9x+23}{(x-1)(x+7)}$  **120.** $\dfrac{12x+1}{(3x+2)(2x-1)}$

**121.** $\dfrac{13x^2+90x-25}{2x^3-50x}$  **122.** $\dfrac{5x^2+x+24}{x^3+8x}$

**123.** $\dfrac{2}{x^2+x}$  **124.** $\dfrac{x}{x(x+3)}$

**125.** $\dfrac{5x-17}{x^2+4x+4}$  **126.** $\dfrac{x^3}{(x^2+64)^2}$

## 8.7 Systems of Linear Inequalities in Two Variables

Graph each linear inequality.

**127.** $y \ge -2x+3$  **128.** $y < x-4$

**129.** $2x+4y > 5$  **130.** $5x+2y \le 4$

**131.** $y \ge -3x+2$  **132.** $y < x-2$

**133.** $3x+8y \le 16$  **134.** $4x-9y \le 18$

Graph each system of inequalities or indicate that the system has no solution.

**135.** $y \ge x+2$
$\quad\;\; y \le x-2$

**136.** $y \ge 3x$
$\quad\;\; y \le 3x$

**137.** $x \le -2$
$\quad\;\; y > \;\; x$

**138.** $\;\; x+3y \ge 6$
$\quad 2x-\;\; y \le 8$

**139.** $3x-4y \le 16$
$\quad 5x+3y > \;9$

**140.** $x+y > -4$
$\quad\; x-y < \;\; 3$
$\quad\quad\quad\; y \ge -2$
$\quad\; x \quad\;\; \le \;\; 8$

Minimize or maximize the objective function subject to the constraints.

**141.** Minimize $z = 2x+y$ subject to

$$x \ge 0 \qquad y \ge 0 \qquad x+y \le 3$$

**142.** Maximize $z = 2x+3y$ subject to

$$x \ge 0 \qquad y \ge 0$$
$$-x+y \le 0 \qquad x \le 3$$

**143.** Minimize $z = 3x-5y$ subject to

$$2x+y > 6 \qquad 2x-y < 6 \qquad x > 0$$

**144.** Maximize $z = -2x+7y$ subject to

$$3x+y < 7 \qquad x-2y > 1 \qquad x \ge 0$$

### Applications

For Exercises 145 and 146, refer to the following:

An art student decides to hand-paint coasters and sell sets at a flea market. She decides to make two types of coaster sets: an ocean watercolor and black-and-white geometric shapes. The cost, profit, and time it takes her to paint each set are summarized in the table below.

|  | OCEAN WATERCOLOR | GEOMETRIC SHAPES |
|---|---|---|
| Cost | $4 | $2 |
| Profit | $15 | $8 |
| Hours | 3 | 2 |

**145. Profit.** If the student's costs cannot exceed $100 and she can spend only 90 hours total painting the coasters, determine the number of each type she should make to maximize her profit.

**146. Profit.** If the student's costs cannot exceed $300 and she can spend only 90 hours painting, determine the number of each type she should make to maximize her profit.

### Technology Exercises

#### Section 8.1

**147.** Apply a graphing utility to graph the two equations $0.4x+0.3y = -0.1$ and $0.5x-0.2y = 1.6$. Find the solution to this system of linear equations.

**148.** Apply a graphing utility to graph the two equations $\frac{1}{2}x + \frac{3}{10}y = \frac{1}{5}$ and $-\frac{5}{3}x + \frac{1}{2}y = \frac{4}{3}$. Find the solution to this system of linear equations.

REVIEW EXERCISES

## Section 8.2

**Employ a graphing calculator to solve the system of equations.**

**149.**
$$5x - 3y + 15z = 21$$
$$-2x + 0.8y - 4z = -8$$
$$2.5x - y + 7.5z = 12$$

**150.**
$$2x - 1.5y + 3z = 9.5$$
$$0.5x - 0.375y + 0.75z = 1.5$$

## Section 8.3

**In Exercises 151 and 152, refer to the following:**

You are asked to model a set of three points with a quadratic function $y = ax^2 + bx + c$ and determine the quadratic function.

**a.** Set up a system of equations; use a graphing utility or graphing calculator to solve the system by entering the coefficients of the augmented matrix.

**b.** Use the graphing calculator commands $\boxed{\text{STAT}}$ $\boxed{\text{QuadReg}}$ to model the data using a quadratic function. Round your answers to two decimal places.

**151.** $(-10, 12.5), (3, -2.8), (9, 8.5)$

**152.** $(-4, 10), (2.5, -9.5), (13.5, 12.6)$

## Section 8.4

**Apply a graphing utility to perform the indicated matrix operations, if possible.**

$$A = \begin{bmatrix} -6 & 0 & 4 \\ 1 & 3 & 5 \\ 2 & -1 & 0 \end{bmatrix} \quad B = \begin{bmatrix} 5 & 1 \\ 0 & 2 \\ -8 & 4 \end{bmatrix} \quad C = \begin{bmatrix} 4 & -3 & 0 \\ 1 & 2 & 5 \end{bmatrix}$$

**153.** ABC

**154.** CAB

**Apply a graphing utility and matrix algebra to solve the system of linear equations.**

**155.**
$$6.1x - 14.2y = 75.495$$
$$-2.3x + 7.2y = -36.495$$

**156.**
$$7.2x + 3.2y - 1.7z = 5.53$$
$$-1.3x + 4.1y + 2.8z = -23.949$$

## Section 8.5

**Apply Cramer's rule to solve each system of equations and a graphing utility to evaluate the determinants.**

**157.**
$$4.5x - 8.7y = -72.33$$
$$-1.4x + 5.3y = 31.32$$

**158.**
$$1.4x + 3.6y + 7.5z = 42.08$$
$$2.1x - 5.7y - 4.2z = 5.37$$
$$1.8x - 2.8y - 6.2z = -9.86$$

## Section 8.6

**159.** Apply a graphing utility to graph $y_1 = \dfrac{x^2 + 4}{x^4 - x^2}$ and
$y_2 = -\dfrac{4}{x^2} + \dfrac{5/2}{x - 1} - \dfrac{5/2}{x + 1}$ in the same viewing rectangle. Is $y_2$ the partial-fraction decomposition of $y_1$?

**160.** Apply a graphing utility to graph
$$y_1 = \frac{x^3 + 6x^2 + 27x + 38}{(x^2 + 8x + 17)(x^2 + 6x + 13)}$$ and
$$y_2 = \frac{2x + 1}{x^2 + 8x + 17} - \frac{x - 3}{x^2 + 6x + 13}$$ in the same viewing rectangle. Is $y_2$ the partial-fraction decomposition of $y_1$?

## Section 8.7

**In Exercises 161 and 162, use a graphing utility to graph each system of inequalities or indicate that the system has no solution.**

**161.** $2x + 5y \geq -15$
$y \leq -\frac{2}{3}x - 1$

**162.** $y \leq 0.5x$
$y > -1.5x + 6$

**163.** Maximize $z = 6.2x + 1.5y$ subject to
$$4x - 3y \leq 5.4$$
$$2x + 4.5y \leq 6.3$$
$$3x - y \geq -10.7$$

**164.** Minimize $z = 1.6x - 2.8y$ subject to
$$y \geq 3.2x - 4.8 \qquad x \geq -2$$
$$y \leq 3.2x + 4.8 \qquad x \leq 4$$

**Solve each system of linear equations using elimination and/or substitution methods.**

**1.** $x - 2y = 1$
$-x + 3y = 2$

**2.** $3x + 5y = -2$
$7x + 11y = -6$

**3.** $x - y = 2$
$-2x + 2y = -4$

**4.** $3x - 2y = 5$
$6x - 4y = 0$

**5.** $x + y + z = -1$
$2x + y + z = 0$
$-x + y + 2z = 0$

**6.** $6x + 9y + z = 5$
$2x - 3y + z = 3$
$10x + 12y + 2z = 9$

**In Exercises 7 and 8, write the system of linear equations as an augmented matrix.**

**7.** $6x + 9y + z = 5$
$2x - 3y + z = 3$
$10x + 12y + 2z = 9$

**8.** $3x + 2y - 10z = 2$
$x + y - z = 5$

**9.** Perform the following row operations.

$$\begin{bmatrix} 1 & 3 & 5 \\ 2 & 7 & -1 \\ -3 & -2 & 0 \end{bmatrix} \begin{matrix} R_2 - 2R_1 \rightarrow R_2 \\ R_3 + 3R_1 \rightarrow R_3 \end{matrix}$$

**10.** Rewrite the following matrix in reduced row–echelon form.

$$\begin{bmatrix} 2 & -1 & 1 & | & 3 \\ 1 & 1 & -1 & | & 0 \\ 3 & 2 & -2 & | & 1 \end{bmatrix}$$

**In Exercises 11 and 12, solve the systems of linear equations using augmented matrices.**

**11.** $6x + 9y + z = 5$
$2x - 3y + z = 3$
$10x + 12y + 2z = 9$

**12.** $3x + 2y - 10z = 2$
$x + y - z = 5$

**13.** Multiply the matrices, if possible.

$$\begin{bmatrix} 1 & -2 & 5 \\ 0 & -1 & 3 \end{bmatrix} \begin{bmatrix} 0 & 4 \\ 3 & -5 \\ -1 & 1 \end{bmatrix}$$

**14.** Add the matrices, if possible.

$$\begin{bmatrix} 1 & -2 & 5 \\ 0 & -1 & 3 \end{bmatrix} + \begin{bmatrix} 0 & 4 \\ 3 & -5 \\ -1 & 1 \end{bmatrix}$$

**15.** Find the inverse of $\begin{bmatrix} 4 & 3 \\ 5 & -1 \end{bmatrix}$, if it exists.

**16.** Find the inverse of $\begin{bmatrix} 1 & -3 & 2 \\ 4 & 2 & 0 \\ -1 & 2 & 5 \end{bmatrix}$, if it exists.

**17.** Solve the system of linear equations with matrix algebra (inverses).

$$3x - y + 4z = 18$$
$$x + 2y + 3z = 20$$
$$-4x + 6y - z = 11$$

**Calculate the determinant.**

**18.** $\begin{vmatrix} 7 & -5 \\ 2 & -1 \end{vmatrix}$

**19.** $\begin{vmatrix} 1 & -2 & -1 \\ 3 & -5 & 2 \\ 4 & -1 & 0 \end{vmatrix}$

**In Exercises 20 and 21, solve the system of linear equations using Cramer's rule.**

**20.** $x - 2y = 1$
$-x + 3y = 2$

**21.** $3x + 5y - 2z = -6$
$7x + 11y + 3z = 2$
$x - y + z = 4$

**22.** A company has two rubrics for scoring job applicants based on weighting education, experience, and the interview differently.

| | Rubric 1 | Rubric 2 |
|---|---|---|
| Education | 0.4 | 0.6 |
| Experience | 0.5 | 0.1 |
| Interview | 0.1 | 0.3 |

**Matrix A:** (Education, Experience, Interview rows)

Applicants receive a score from 1 to 10 in each category (education, experience, and interview). Two applicants are shown in the matrix $B$.

| | Education | Experience | Interview |
|---|---|---|---|
| Applicant 1 | 4 | 7 | 3 |
| Applicant 2 | 6 | 5 | 4 |

**Matrix B:**

What is the order of $BA$? What does each entry in $BA$ tell us?

**Write each rational expression as a sum of partial fractions.**

**23.** $\dfrac{2x + 5}{x^2 + x}$

**24.** $\dfrac{3x - 13}{(x - 5)^2}$

**25.** $\dfrac{5x - 3}{x(x^2 - 9)}$

**26.** $\dfrac{1}{2x^2 + 5x - 3}$

**Graph the inequalities.**

**27.** $-2x + y < 6$

**28.** $4x - y \geq 8$

**In Exercises 29 and 30, graph the system of inequalities.**

**29.** $x + y \leq 4$
$-x + y \geq -2$

**30.** $x + 3y \leq 6$
$2x - y \leq 4$

**31.** Minimize the function $z = 5x + 7y$ subject to the constraints
$x \geq 0 \qquad y \geq 0 \qquad x + y \leq 3 \qquad -x + y \geq 1$

32. Find the maximum value of the objective function $z = 3x + 6y$ given the constraints

$$x \geq 0 \qquad y \geq 0$$
$$x + y \leq 6 \qquad -x + 2y \leq 4$$

33. Apply a graphing utility and matrix algebra to solve the system of linear equations.

$$5.6x - 2.7y = \phantom{-}87.28$$
$$-4.2x + 8.4y = -106.26$$

34. You are asked to model a set of three points with a quadratic function $y = ax^2 + bx + c$.

   a. Set up a system of equations; use a graphing utility or graphing calculator to solve the system by entering the coefficients of the augmented matrix.

   b. Use the graphing calculator commands $\boxed{\text{STAT}}$ $\boxed{\text{QuadReg}}$ to model the data using a quadratic function.

$$(-3, 6), (1, 12), (5, 7)$$

1. Evaluate $g[f(-1)]$, with $f(x) = \sqrt{2x + 11}$ and $g(x) = x^3$.

2. Use interval notation to express the domain of the function $G(x) = \dfrac{9}{\sqrt{1 - 5x}}$.

3. Using the function $f(x) = x^2 - 3x + 2$, evaluate the difference quotient $\dfrac{f(x + h) - f(x)}{h}$.

4. Find all the real zeros (and state the multiplicity) of $f(x) = -4x(x - 7)^2(x + 13)^3$.

5. Find the vertex of the parabola $f(x) = -0.04x^2 + 1.2x - 3$.

6. Factor the polynomial $P(x) = x^4 + 8x^2 - 9$ as a product of linear factors.

7. Find the vertical and horizontal asymptotes of the function $f(x) = \dfrac{5x - 7}{3 - x}$.

8. Approximate $e^\pi$ using a calculator. Round your answer to two decimal places.

9. Evaluate $\log_5 0.2$ exactly.

10. Solve $5^{2x-1} = 11$ for $x$. Round the answer to three decimal places.

11. Evaluate $\log_2 6$ using the change-of-base formula. Round your answer to three decimal places.

12. Solve $\ln(5x - 6) = 2$. Round your answer to three decimal places.

13. Give the exact value of $\cos 30°$.

14. How much money should be put in a savings account now that earns 4.7% a year compounded weekly, if you want to have $65,000 in 17 years?

15. The terminal side of angle $\theta$ in standard position passes through the point $(-5, 2)$. Calculate the exact values of the six trigonometric function for angle $\theta$.

16. Find all values of $\theta$, where $0° \le \theta \le 360°$, when $\cos\theta = -\dfrac{\sqrt{3}}{2}$.

17. Graph the function $y = \tan\left(\frac{1}{4}x\right)$ over the interval $-2\pi \le x \le 2\pi$.

18. Verify the identity $\cos(3x) = \cos x\,(1 - 4\sin^2 x)$.

19. State the domain and range of the function $y = 5\tan\left(x - \dfrac{\pi}{2}\right)$.

20. Simplify the trigonometric expression $\dfrac{\sec^4 x - 1}{\sec^2 x + 1}$.

21. Use the half-angle identities to find the exact value of $\tan\left(-\dfrac{3\pi}{8}\right)$.

22. Write the product $7\sin(-2x)\sin(5x)$ as a sum or difference of sines and/or cosines.

23. Solve the triangle $\beta = 106.3°$, $\gamma = 37.4°$, $a = 76.1$ m.

24. Find the angle (rounded to the nearest degree) between the vectors $\langle 2, 3\rangle$ and $\langle -4, -5\rangle$.

25. Find all complex solutions to $x^3 - 27 = 0$.

26. Graph $\theta = -\dfrac{\pi}{4}$.

27. Given

$$A = \begin{bmatrix} 3 & 4 & -7 \\ 0 & 1 & 5 \end{bmatrix} \quad B = \begin{bmatrix} 8 & -2 & 6 \\ 9 & 0 & -1 \end{bmatrix} \quad C = \begin{bmatrix} 9 & 0 \\ 1 & 2 \end{bmatrix}$$

find $CB$.

28. Solve the system using Gauss–Jordan elimination.

$$\begin{aligned} x - 2y + 3z &= 11 \\ 4x + 5y - z &= -8 \\ 3x + y - 2z &= 1 \end{aligned}$$

29. Use Cramer's rule to solve the system of equations.

$$\begin{aligned} 7x + 5y &= 1 \\ -x + 4y &= -1 \end{aligned}$$

30. Write the matrix equation, find the inverse of the coefficient matrix, and solve the system using matrix algebra.

$$\begin{aligned} 2x + 5y &= -1 \\ -x + 4y &= 7 \end{aligned}$$

31. Graph the system of linear inequalities.

$$\begin{aligned} y &> -x \\ y &\ge -3 \\ x &\le 3 \end{aligned}$$

# 9

# Conics, Systems of Nonlinear Equations and Inequalities, and Parametric Equations

We will now study three types of conic sections or conics: the parabola, the ellipse, and the hyperbola. The trajectory of a basketball is a *parabola*, the Earth's orbit around the Sun is an *ellipse*, and the shape of a cooling tower is a *hyperbola*.

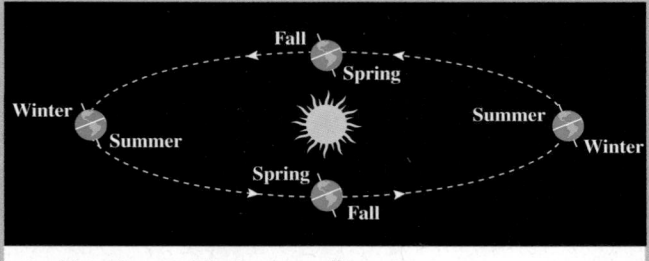

Earth's orbit around the Sun is an *ellipse*.

**IN THIS CHAPTER** we define the three conic sections: the parabola, the ellipse, and the hyperbola. Algebraic equations and the graphs of these conics are discussed. We solve systems of nonlinear equations and inequalities involving parabolas, ellipses, and hyperbolas. We then will determine how rotating the axes changes the equation of a conic, and with our results we will be able to identify the graph of a general second-degree equation as one of the three conics. We will discuss the equations of the conics first in rectangular coordinates and then in polar coordinates. Finally, we will look at parametric equations, which give orientation along a plane curve.

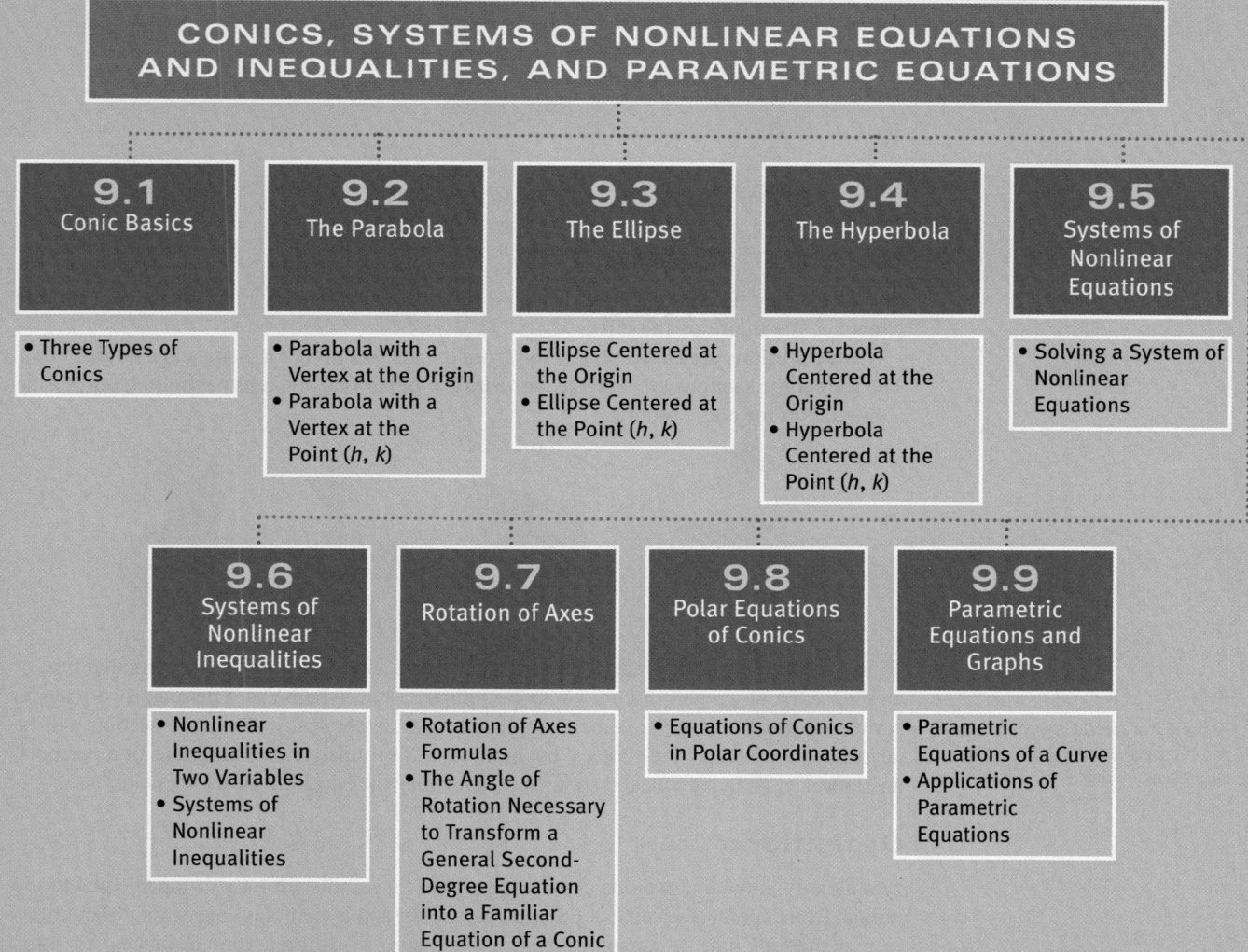

# CONICS, SYSTEMS OF NONLINEAR EQUATIONS AND INEQUALITIES, AND PARAMETRIC EQUATIONS

**9.1**
Conic Basics

- Three Types of Conics

**9.2**
The Parabola

- Parabola with a Vertex at the Origin
- Parabola with a Vertex at the Point $(h, k)$

**9.3**
The Ellipse

- Ellipse Centered at the Origin
- Ellipse Centered at the Point $(h, k)$

**9.4**
The Hyperbola

- Hyperbola Centered at the Origin
- Hyperbola Centered at the Point $(h, k)$

**9.5**
Systems of Nonlinear Equations

- Solving a System of Nonlinear Equations

**9.6**
Systems of Nonlinear Inequalities

- Nonlinear Inequalities in Two Variables
- Systems of Nonlinear Inequalities

**9.7**
Rotation of Axes

- Rotation of Axes Formulas
- The Angle of Rotation Necessary to Transform a General Second-Degree Equation into a Familiar Equation of a Conic

**9.8**
Polar Equations of Conics

- Equations of Conics in Polar Coordinates

**9.9**
Parametric Equations and Graphs

- Parametric Equations of a Curve
- Applications of Parametric Equations

## LEARNING OBJECTIVES

- Identify if a second-degree equation in two variables corresponds to a parabola, an ellipse, or a hyperbola.
- Graph parabolas whose vertex is at the point $(h, k)$.
- Graph an ellipse whose center is at the point $(h, k)$.
- Graph a hyperbola whose center is at the point $(h, k)$.
- Solve systems of nonlinear equations.
- Graph systems of nonlinear inequalities.
- Transform general second-degree equations into recognizable equations of conics by analyzing the rotation of axes.
- Express equations of conics in polar coordinates.
- Express projectile motion using parametric equations.

**SKILLS OBJECTIVES**

- Learn the name of each conic section.
- Define conics.
- Recognize the algebraic equation associated with each conic.

**CONCEPTUAL OBJECTIVES**

- Understand each conic as an intersection of a plane and a cone.
- Understand how the three equations of the conic sections are related to the general form of a second-degree equation in two variables.

## Three Types of Conics

### Names of Conics

The word *conic* is derived from the word *cone*. Let's start with a (right circular) **double cone** (see the figure on the left).

   **Conic sections** are curves that result from the intersection of a plane and a double cone. The four conic sections are a **circle**, an **ellipse**, a **parabola**, and a **hyperbola**. **Conics** is an abbreviation for conic sections.

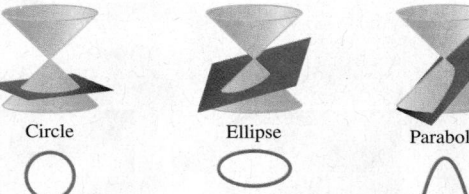

| Circle | Ellipse | Parabola | Hyperbola |

**Study Tip**

A circle is a special type of ellipse. All circles are ellipses, but not all ellipses are circles.

   In Section 0.5, circles were discussed, and we will show that a circle is a particular type of an ellipse. Now we will discuss parabolas, ellipses, and hyperbolas. There are two ways in which we usually describe conics: graphically and algebraically. An entire section will be devoted to each of the three conics, but here we will summarize the definitions of a parabola, an ellipse, and a hyperbola and show how to identify the equations of these conics.

### Definitions

You already know that a circle consists of all points equidistant (at a distance equal to the radius) from a point (the center). Ellipses, parabolas, and hyperbolas have similar definitions in that they all have a constant distance (or a sum or difference of distances) to some reference point(s).

   A **parabola** is the set of all points that are **equidistant from both a line and a point**. An **ellipse** is the set of all points, the **sum of whose distances to two fixed points is constant**. A **hyperbola** is the set of all points, the **difference of whose distances to two fixed points is a constant**.

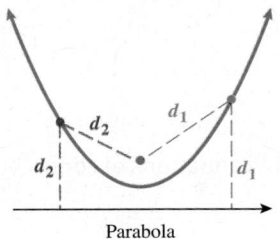

Parabola

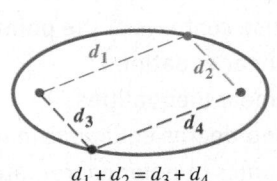

$$d_1 + d_2 = d_3 + d_4$$

Ellipse

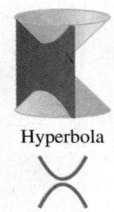

$$|d_2 - d_1| = |d_4 - d_3|$$

Hyperbola

The **general form of a second-degree equation in two variables**, $x$ and $y$, is given by

$$Ax^2 + Bxy + Cy^2 + Dx + Ey + F = 0$$

If we let $A = 1, B = 0, C = 1, D = 0, E = 0$, and $F = -r^2$, this general equation reduces to the equation of a circle centered at the origin: $x^2 + y^2 = r^2$. In fact, all three conics (parabolas, ellipses, and hyperbolas) are special cases of the general second-degree equation.

Recall from Section 0.2 (Quadratic Equations) that the discriminant, $b^2 - 4ac$, determines what types of solutions result from solving a second-degree equation in one variable. If the discriminant is positive, the solutions are two distinct real roots. If the discriminant is zero, the solution is a real repeated root. If the discriminant is negative, the solutions are two complex conjugate roots.

The concept of discriminant is also applicable to second-degree equations in two variables. The discriminant $B^2 - 4AC$ determines the *shape* of the conic section.

| Conic | Discriminant |
|-------|--------------|
| Ellipse | $B^2 - 4AC < 0$ |
| Parabola | $B^2 - 4AC = 0$ |
| Hyperbola | $B^2 - 4AC > 0$ |

**Study Tip**

All circles are ellipses since $B^2 - 4AC < 0$.

Using the discriminant to identify the shape of the conic will not work for degenerate cases (when the polynomial factors). For example,

$$2x^2 - xy - y^2 = 0$$

At first glance, one may think this is a hyperbola because $B^2 - 4AC > 0$, but this is a degenerate case.

$$(2x + y)(x - y) = 0$$

$$2x + y = 0 \qquad \text{or} \qquad x - y = 0$$

$$y = -2x \qquad \text{or} \qquad y = x$$

The graph is two intersecting lines.

We now identify conics from the general form of a second-degree equation in two variables.

**EXAMPLE 1  Determining the Type of Conic**

Determine what type of conic corresponds to each of the following equations:

**a.** $\dfrac{x^2}{a^2} + \dfrac{y^2}{b^2} = 1$  **b.** $y = x^2$  **c.** $\dfrac{x^2}{a^2} - \dfrac{y^2}{b^2} = 1$

**Solution:**

Write the general form of the second-degree equation:

$$Ax^2 + Bxy + Cy^2 + Dx + Ey + F = 0$$

**a.** Identify $A, B, C, D, E$, and $F$.  $A = \dfrac{1}{a^2}, B = 0, C = \dfrac{1}{b^2}, D = 0, E = 0, F = -1$

Calculate the discriminant.  $B^2 - 4AC = -\dfrac{4}{a^2 b^2} < 0$

Since the discriminant is negative, the equation $\dfrac{x^2}{a^2} + \dfrac{y^2}{b^2} = 1$ is that of an **ellipse**.

Notice that if $a = b = r$, then this equation of an ellipse reduces to the general equation of a circle, $x^2 + y^2 = r^2$, centered at the origin, with radius $r$.

**b.** Identify $A$, $B$, $C$, $D$, $E$, and $F$.  $\quad A = 1, B = 0, C = 0, D = 0, E = -1, F = 0$

Calculate the discriminant.  $\quad B^2 - 4AC = 0$

Since the discriminant is zero, the equation $y = x^2$ is a **parabola**.

**c.** Identify $A$, $B$, $C$, $D$, $E$, and $F$.  $\quad A = \dfrac{1}{a^2}, B = 0, C = -\dfrac{1}{b^2}, D = 0, E = 0, F = -1$

Calculate the discriminant.  $\quad B^2 - 4AC = \dfrac{4}{a^2 b^2} > 0$

Since the discriminant is positive, the equation $\dfrac{x^2}{a^2} - \dfrac{y^2}{b^2} = 1$ is a **hyperbola**.

■ **Answer: a.** ellipse
      **b.** hyperbola
      **c.** parabola

■ **YOUR TURN**  Determine what type of conic corresponds to each of the following equations:

    **a.** $2x^2 + y^2 = 4$      **b.** $2x^2 = y^2 + 4$      **c.** $2y^2 = x$

In the next three sections, we will discuss the standard forms of equations and the graphs of parabolas, ellipses, and hyperbolas.

## SECTION 9.1 SUMMARY

In this section, we defined the three conic sections and determined their general equations with respect to the general form of a second-degree equation in two variables:

$$Ax^2 + Bxy + Cy^2 + Dx + Ey + F = 0$$

The following table summarizes the three conics: ellipse, parabola, and hyperbola.

| CONIC | GEOMETRIC DEFINITION: THE SET OF ALL POINTS | DISCRIMINANT |
|---|---|---|
| Ellipse | the sum of whose distances to two fixed points is constant | Negative: $B^2 - 4AC < 0$ |
| Parabola | equidistant to both a line and a point | Zero: $B^2 - 4AC = 0$ |
| Hyperbola | the difference of whose distances to two fixed points is a constant | Positive: $B^2 - 4AC > 0$ |

It is important to note that a circle is a special type of ellipse.

## SECTION 9.1 EXERCISES

■ **SKILLS**

**In Exercises 1–12, identify the conic section as a parabola, ellipse, circle, or hyperbola.**

**1.** $x^2 + xy - y^2 + 2x = -3$      **2.** $x^2 + xy + y^2 + 2x = -3$      **3.** $2x^2 + 2y^2 = 10$      **4.** $x^2 - 4x + y^2 + 2y = 4$

**5.** $2x^2 - y^2 = 4$      **6.** $2y^2 - x^2 = 16$      **7.** $5x^2 + 20y^2 = 25$      **8.** $4x^2 + 8y^2 = 30$

**9.** $x^2 - y = 1$      **10.** $y^2 - x = 2$      **11.** $x^2 + y^2 = 10$      **12.** $x^2 + y^2 = 100$

**SKILLS OBJECTIVES**

- Graph a parabola given the focus, directrix, and vertex.
- Find the equation of a parabola whose vertex is at the origin.
- Find the equation of a parabola whose vertex is at the point $(h, k)$.
- Solve applied problems that involve parabolas.

**CONCEPTUAL OBJECTIVES**

- Derive the general equation of a parabola.
- Identify, draw, and use the focus, directrix, and axis of symmetry.

## Parabola with a Vertex at the Origin

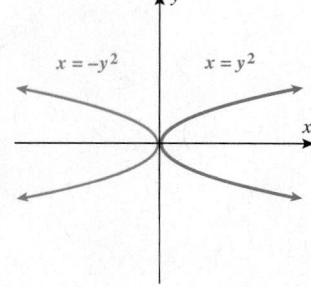

Recall from Section 2.1 that the graphs of quadratic functions such as

$$f(x) = a(x - h)^2 + k \quad \text{or} \quad y = ax^2 + bx + c$$

were *parabolas* that opened either upward or downward. We now expand our discussion to *parabolas* that open to the **right** or **left**. We did not discuss these types of parabolas before because they are not functions (they fail the vertical line test).

---

**DEFINITION** | **Parabola**

A **parabola** is the set of all points in a plane that are equidistant from a fixed line, the **directrix**, and a fixed point not on the line, the **focus**. The line through the focus and perpendicular to the directrix is the **axis of symmetry**. The **vertex** of the parabola is located at the midpoint between the directrix and the focus along the axis of symmetry.

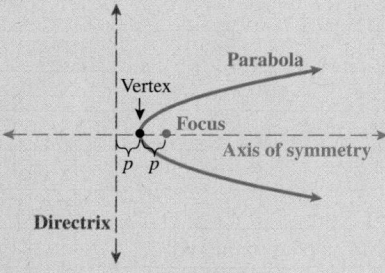

Here $p$ is the distance along the axis of symmetry from the directrix to the vertex and from the vertex to the focus.

---

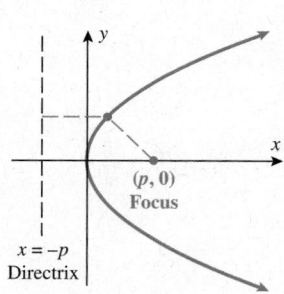

Let's consider a parabola with the vertex at the origin and the focus on the positive $x$-axis. Let the distance from the vertex to the focus be $p$. Therefore, the focus is located at the point $(p, 0)$. Since the distance from the vertex to the focus is $p$, the distance from the vertex to the directrix must also be $p$. Since the axis of symmetry is the $x$-axis, the directrix must be perpendicular to the $x$-axis. Therefore, the directrix is given by $x = -p$. Any point, $(x, y)$, must have the same distance to the focus, $(p, 0)$, as it does to the point $(-p, y)$ of the directrix.

# Derivation of the Equation of a Parabola

| WORDS | MATH |
|---|---|
| Calculate the distance from $(x, y)$ to $(p, 0)$ with the distance formula. | $\sqrt{(x - p)^2 + y^2}$ |
| Calculate the distance from $(x, y)$ to $(-p, y)$ with the distance formula. | $\sqrt{(x - (-p))^2 + 0^2}$ |
| Set the two distances equal to one another. | $\sqrt{(x - p)^2 + y^2} = \sqrt{(x + p)^2}$ |
| Recall that $\sqrt{x^2} = |x|$. | $\sqrt{(x - p)^2 + y^2} = |x + p|$ |
| Square both sides of the equation. | $(x - p)^2 + y^2 = (x + p)^2$ |
| Square the binomials inside the parentheses. | $x^2 - 2px + p^2 + y^2 = x^2 + 2px + p^2$ |
| Simplify. | $\boxed{y^2 = 4px}$ |

The equation $y^2 = 4px$ represents a parabola opening right ($p > 0$) with the vertex at the origin. The following box summarizes parabolas that have a vertex at the origin and a focus along either the $x$-axis or the $y$-axis:

## EQUATION OF A PARABOLA WITH VERTEX AT THE ORIGIN

The standard (conic) form of the equation of a **parabola** with vertex at the origin is given by

| EQUATION | $y^2 = 4px$ | $x^2 = 4py$ |
|---|---|---|
| VERTEX | $(0, 0)$ | $(0, 0)$ |
| FOCUS | $(p, 0)$ | $(0, p)$ |
| DIRECTRIX | $x = -p$ | $y = -p$ |
| AXIS OF SYMMETRY | $x$-axis | $y$-axis |
| $p > 0$ | opens to the right | opens upward |
| $p < 0$ | opens to the left | opens downward |
| GRAPH ($p > 0$) | | |

**EXAMPLE 1    Finding the Focus and Directrix of a Parabola Whose Vertex Is Located at the Origin**

Find the focus and directrix of a parabola whose equation is $y^2 = 8x$.

**Solution:**

Compare this parabola with the general equation of a parabola.

$$y^2 = 4px$$
$$y^2 = 8x$$

Let $y^2 = 8x$.                                                        $4px = 8x$

Solve for $p$ (assume $x \neq 0$).                                    $4p = 8$
$$p = 2$$

The focus of a parabola of the form $y^2 = 4px$ is $(p, 0)$.    $\boxed{\text{Focus } (2, 0)}$

The directrix of a parabola of the form $y^2 = 4px$ is $x = -p$.    $\boxed{\text{Directrix } x = -2}$ .

■ **YOUR TURN**  Find the focus and directrix of a parabola whose equation is $y^2 = 16x$.

■**Answer:** The focus is $(4, 0)$ and the directrix is $x = -4$.

## Graphing a Parabola with a Vertex at the Origin

When a seamstress starts with a pattern for a custom-made suit, the pattern is used as a guide. The pattern is not sewn into the suit, but rather removed once it is used to determine the exact shape and size of the fabric to be sewn together. The focus and directrix of a parabola are similar to the pattern used by a seamstress. Although the focus and directrix define a parabola, they do not appear on the graph of a parabola.

We can draw an approximate sketch of a parabola whose vertex is at the origin with three pieces of information. We know that the vertex is located at $(0, 0)$. Additional information that we seek is the direction in which the parabola opens and approximately how wide or narrow to draw the parabolic curve. The direction toward which the parabola opens is found from the equation. An equation of the form $y^2 = 4px$ opens either left or right. It opens right if $p > 0$ and opens left if $p < 0$. An equation of the form $x^2 = 4py$ opens either up or down. It opens up if $p > 0$ and opens down if $p < 0$. How narrow or wide should we draw the parabolic curve? If we select a few points that satisfy the equation, we can use those as graphing aids.

In Example 1, we found that the focus of that parabola is located at $(2, 0)$. If we select the $x$-coordinate of the focus $x = 2$, and substitute that value into the equation of the parabola $y^2 = 8x$, we find the corresponding $y$ values to be $y = -4$ and $y = 4$. If we plot the three points $(0, 0)$, $(2, -4)$, and $(2, 4)$ and then connect the points with a parabolic curve, we get the graph on the right.

The line segment that passes through the focus $(2, 0)$ is parallel to the directrix $x = -2$, and whose endpoints are on the parabola is called the **latus rectum**. The latus rectum in this case has length 8. The latus rectum is a graphing aid that assists us in determining how wide or how narrow to draw the parabola.

In general, the points on a parabola of the form $y^2 = 4px$ that lie above and below the focus $(p, 0)$ satisfy the equation $y^2 = 4p^2$ and are located at $(p, -2p)$ and $(p, 2p)$. The latus rectum will have length $4|p|$. Similarly, a parabola of the form $x^2 = 4py$ will have a horizontal latus rectum of length $4|p|$.

### Study Tip

The focus and directrix define a parabola, but do not appear on its graph.

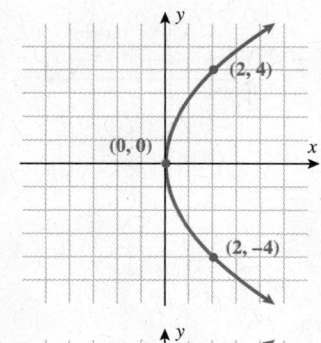

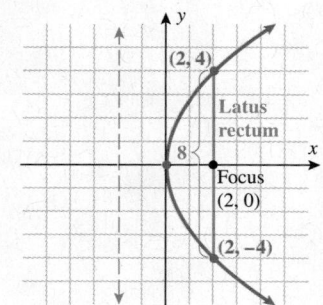

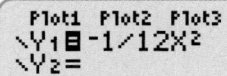
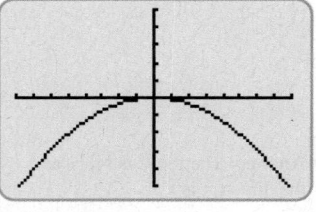
### EXAMPLE 2 Graphing a Parabola Whose Vertex Is at the Origin, Using the Focus, Directrix, and Latus Rectum as Graphing Aids

Determine the focus, directrix, and length of the latus rectum of the parabola $x^2 = -12y$. Employ these to assist in graphing the parabola.

**Solution:**

Compare this parabola with the general equation of a parabola.     $x^2 = 4py$     $x^2 = -12y$

Solve for $p$.                                                           $4p = -12$

$$p = -3$$

A parabola of the form $x^2 = 4py$ has focus $(0, p)$, directrix $y = -p$, and a latus rectum of length $4|p|$. For this parabola, $p = -3$; therefore, the focus is $\boxed{(0, -3)}$, the directrix is $\boxed{y = 3}$, and the length of the latus rectum is $\boxed{12}$.

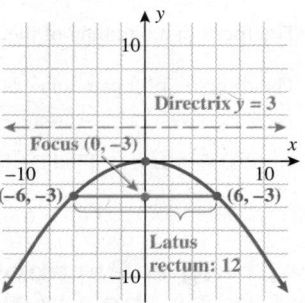

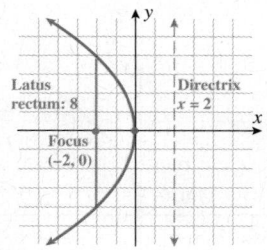
■ **YOUR TURN** Find the focus, directrix, and length of the latus rectum of the parabola $y^2 = -8x$, and use these to graph the parabola.

## Finding the Equation of a Parabola with a Vertex at the Origin

Thus far we have started with the equation of a parabola and then determined its focus and directrix. Let's now reverse the process. For example, if we know the focus and directrix of a parabola, how do we find the equation of the parabola? If we are given the focus and directrix, then we can find the vertex, which is the midpoint between the focus and the directrix. If the vertex is at the origin, then we know the general equation of the parabola that corresponds to the focus.

### EXAMPLE 3 Finding the Equation of a Parabola Given the Focus and Directrix When the Vertex Is at the Origin

Find the standard form of the equation of a parabola whose focus is at the point $\left(0, \frac{1}{2}\right)$ and whose directrix is $y = -\frac{1}{2}$. Graph the equation.

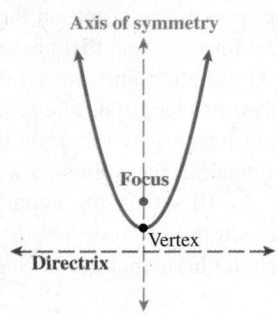

**Solution:**

The midpoint of the segment joining the focus and the directrix along the axis of symmetry is the vertex.

Calculate the midpoint between $\left(0, \frac{1}{2}\right)$ and $\left(0, -\frac{1}{2}\right)$.

$$\text{Vertex} = \left(\frac{0 + 0}{2}, \frac{\frac{1}{2} - \frac{1}{2}}{0}\right) = (0, 0).$$

A parabola with vertex at $(0, 0)$, focus at $(0, p)$, and directrix $y = -p$ corresponds to the equation $x^2 = 4py$.

Identify $p$ given that the focus is $(0, p) = \left(0, \frac{1}{2}\right)$.    $p = \dfrac{1}{2}$

Substitute $p = \frac{1}{2}$ into the standard equation of a parabola with vertex at the origin $x^2 = 4py$.    $x^2 = 2y$

Now that the equation is known, a few points can be selected, and the parabola can be point-plotted. Alternatively, the length of the latus rectum can be calculated to sketch the approximate width of the parabola.

To graph $x^2 = 2y$, first calculate the latus rectum.    $4|p| = 4\left(\dfrac{1}{2}\right) = 2$

Label the focus, directrix, and latus rectum, and draw a parabolic curve whose vertex is at the origin that intersects with the latus rectum's endpoints.

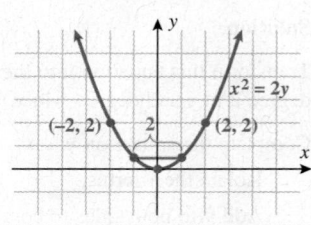

- - - - - - - - - - - - - - - - - - - - - - - - - - - - - - - - - - - - - - - - - - - - - - -

■ **YOUR TURN**  Find the equation of a parabola whose focus is at the point $(-5, 0)$ and whose directrix is $x = 5$.

■**Answer:** $y^2 = -20x$

Before we proceed to parabolas with general vertices, let's first make a few observations: The larger the latus rectum, the more rapidly the parabola widens. An alternative approach for graphing the parabola is to plot a few points that satisfy the equation of the parabola, which is the approach in most textbooks.

## Parabola with a Vertex at the Point (*h*, *k*)

Recall (Section 0.5) that the graph of $x^2 + y^2 = r^2$ is a circle with radius $r$ centered at the origin, whereas the graph of $(x - h)^2 + (y - k)^2 = r^2$ is a circle with radius $r$ centered at the point $(h, k)$. In other words, the center is shifted from the origin to the point $(h, k)$. This same translation (shift) can be used to describe parabolas whose vertex is at the point $(h, k)$.

**Study Tip**

When $(h, k) = (0, 0)$, the vertex of the parabola is located at the origin.

**EQUATION OF A PARABOLA WITH VERTEX AT THE POINT (*h*, *k*)**

The standard (conic) form of the equation of a parabola with vertex at the point $(h, k)$ is given by

| EQUATION | $(y - k)^2 = 4p(x - h)$ | $(x - h)^2 = 4p(y - k)$ |
|---|---|---|
| VERTEX | $(h, k)$ | $(h, k)$ |
| FOCUS | $(p + h, k)$ | $(h, p + k)$ |
| DIRECTRIX | $x = -p + h$ | $y = -p + k$ |
| AXIS OF SYMMETRY | $y = k$ | $x = h$ |
| $p > 0$ | opens to the right | opens upward |
| $p < 0$ | opens to the left | opens downward |

In order to find the vertex of a parabola given a general second-degree equation, first complete the square (Section 0.2) in order to identify $(h, k)$. Then determine whether the parabola opens up, down, left, or right. Identify points that lie on the graph of the parabola. Intercepts are often the easiest points to find, since they are the points where one of the variables is set equal to zero.

### Technology Tip

Use a TI to check the graph of $y^2 - 6y - 2x + 8 = 0$. Use $(y - 3)^2 = 2x + 1$ to solve for $y$ first. That is, $y_1 = 3 + \sqrt{2x + 1}$ or $y_2 = 3 - \sqrt{2x + 1}$.

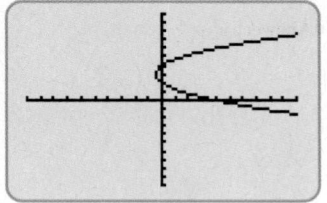

### EXAMPLE 4  Graphing a Parabola with Vertex ($h$, $k$)

Graph the parabola given by the equation $y^2 - 6y - 2x + 8 = 0$.

**Solution:**

Transform this equation into the form $(y - k)^2 = 4p(x - h)$, since this equation is of degree 2 in $y$ and degree 1 in $x$. We know this parabola opens either to the left or right.

Complete the square on $y$: $\qquad\qquad\qquad\qquad\qquad y^2 - 6y - 2x + 8 = 0$

Isolate the $y$ terms. $\qquad\qquad\qquad\qquad\qquad\quad y^2 - 6y = 2x - 8$

Add 9 to both sides to complete the square. $\qquad y^2 - 6y + 9 = 2x - 8 + 9$

Write the left side as a perfect square. $\qquad\qquad (y - 3)^2 = 2x + 1$

Factor out a 2 on the right side. $\qquad\qquad\qquad (y - 3)^2 = 2\left(x + \dfrac{1}{2}\right)$

Compare with $(y - k)^2 = 4p(x - h)$ and identify $(h, k)$ and $p$.

$$(h, k) = \left(-\dfrac{1}{2}, 3\right)$$

$$4p = 2 \Rightarrow p = \dfrac{1}{2}$$

### Study Tip

It is often easier to find the intercepts by converting to the general form of the equation.

The vertex is at the point $\left(-\dfrac{1}{2}, 3\right)$, and since $p = \dfrac{1}{2}$ is positive, the parabola opens to the right. Since the parabola's vertex lies in quadrant II and it opens to the right, we know there are two $y$-intercepts and one $x$-intercept. Apply the general equation $y^2 - 6y - 2x + 8 = 0$ to find the intercepts.

Find the $y$-intercepts (set $x = 0$). $\qquad\qquad\qquad y^2 - 6y + 8 = 0$

Factor. $\qquad\qquad\qquad\qquad\qquad\qquad (y - 2)(y - 4) = 0$

Solve for $y$. $\qquad\qquad\qquad\qquad\qquad\quad y = 2 \quad \text{or} \quad y = 4$

Find the $x$-intercept (set $y = 0$). $\qquad\qquad\qquad -2x + 8 = 0$

Solve for $x$. $\qquad\qquad\qquad\qquad\qquad\qquad\qquad x = 4$

■ **Answer:**
Vertex: $\left(-\dfrac{9}{5}, -2\right)$
$x$-intercept: $x = -1$
$y$-intercepts: $y = -5$ and $y = 1$

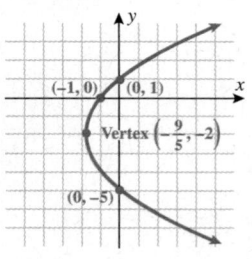

Label the following points and connect them with a smooth curve:

| | |
|---|---|
| Vertex: | $\left(-\dfrac{1}{2}, 3\right)$ |
| $y$-intercepts: | $(0, 2)$ and $(0, 4)$ |
| $x$-intercept: | $(4, 0)$ |

......................................................................................................................

■ **YOUR TURN** For the equation $y^2 + 4y - 5x - 5 = 0$, identify the vertex and the intercepts, and graph.

### EXAMPLE 5    Graphing a Parabola with Vertex (*h*, *k*)

Graph the parabola given by the equation $x^2 - 2x - 8y - 7 = 0$.

**Solution:**

Transform this equation into the form $(x - h)^2 = 4p(y - k)$, since this equation is degree 2 in $x$ and degree 1 in $y$. We know this parabola opens either upward or downward.

Complete the square on $x$:

$$x^2 - 2x - 8y - 7 = 0$$

Isolate the $x$ terms.

$$x^2 - 2x = 8y + 7$$

Add 1 to both sides to complete the square.

$$x^2 - 2x + 1 = 8y + 7 + 1$$

Write the left side as a perfect square.

$$(x - 1)^2 = 8y + 8$$

Factor out the 8 on the right side.

$$(x - 1)^2 = 8(y + 1)$$

Compare with $(x - h)^2 = 4p(y - k)$ and identify $(h, k)$ and $p$.

$$(h, k) = (1, -1)$$

$$4p = 8 \Rightarrow p = 2$$

The vertex is at the point $(1, -1)$, and since $p = 2$ is positive, the parabola opens upward. Since the parabola's vertex lies in quadrant IV and it opens upward, we know there are two $x$-intercepts and one $y$-intercept. Use the general equation $x^2 - 2x - 8y - 7 = 0$ to find the intercepts.

Find the $y$-intercept (set $x = 0$).

$$-8y - 7 = 0$$

Solve for $y$.

$$y = -\frac{7}{8}$$

Find the $x$-intercepts (set $y = 0$).

$$x^2 - 2x - 7 = 0$$

Solve for $x$.

$$x = \frac{2 \pm \sqrt{4 + 28}}{2} = \frac{2 \pm \sqrt{32}}{2} = \frac{2 \pm 4\sqrt{2}}{2} = 1 \pm 2\sqrt{2}$$

Label the following points and connect with a smooth curve:

Vertex:        $(1, -1)$

$y$-intercept:    $\left(0, -\frac{7}{8}\right)$

$x$-intercepts:   $\left(1 - 2\sqrt{2}, 0\right)$ and $\left(1 + 2\sqrt{2}, 0\right)$

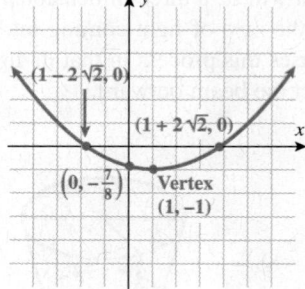

■ **YOUR TURN**   For the equation $x^2 + 2x + 8y - 7 = 0$, identify the vertex and the intercepts, and graph.

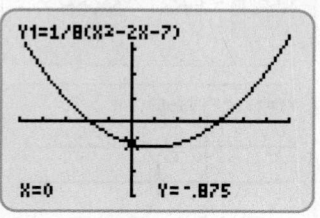
■**Answer:**
Vertex: $(-1, 1)$
$x$-intercepts: $x = -1 \pm 2\sqrt{2}$
$y$-intercept: $y = \frac{7}{8}$

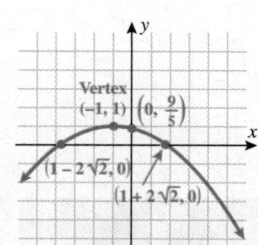

Use a graphing calculator to check the graph of $y^2 + 6y - 12x + 33 = 0$. Use $y^2 + 6y - (12x - 33) = 0$ to solve for $y$ first. That is,
$y_1 = -3 + 2\sqrt{3x - 6}$ or
$y_2 = -3 - 2\sqrt{3x - 6}$.

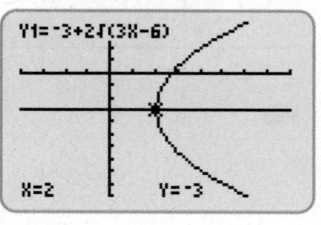

■**Answer:** $y^2 + 6y + 8x - 7 = 0$

## EXAMPLE 6   Finding the Equation of a Parabola with Vertex (*h*, *k*)

Find the general form of the equation of a parabola whose vertex is located at the point $(2, -3)$ and whose focus is located at the point $(5, -3)$.

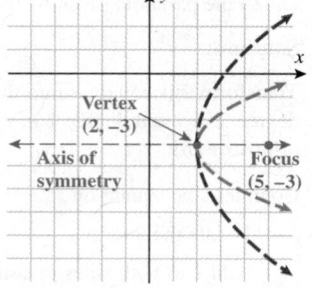

**Solution:**

Draw a Cartesian plane and label the vertex and focus. The vertex and focus share the same axis of symmetry $y = -3$, and indicate a parabola opening to the right.

Write the standard (conic) equation of a parabola opening to the right.

$$(y - k)^2 = 4p(x - h) \qquad p > 0$$

Substitute the vertex $(h, k) = (2, -3)$, into the standard equation.

$$[y - (-3)]^2 = 4p(x - 2)$$

Find $p$.

　　The general form of the vertex is $(h, k)$ and the focus is $(h + p, k)$.

　　For this parabola, the vertex is $(2, -3)$ and the focus is $(5, -3)$.

　　Find $p$ by taking the difference of the $x$-coordinates. $\qquad p = 3$

Substitute $p = 3$ into $[y - (-3)]^2 = 4p(x - 2)$. $\qquad (y + 3)^2 = 4(3)(x - 2)$

Eliminate the parentheses. $\qquad y^2 + 6y + 9 = 12x - 24$

Simplify. $\qquad \boxed{y^2 + 6y - 12x + 33 = 0}$

■ **YOUR TURN** Find the equation of the parabola whose vertex is located at $(2, -3)$ and whose focus is located at $(0, -3)$.

## Applications

If we start with a parabola in the $xy$-plane and rotate it around its axis of symmetry, the result will be a three-dimensional paraboloid. Solar cookers illustrate the physical property that the rays of light coming into a parabola should be reflected to the focus. A flashlight reverses this process in that its light source at the focus illuminates a parabolic reflector to direct the beam outward.

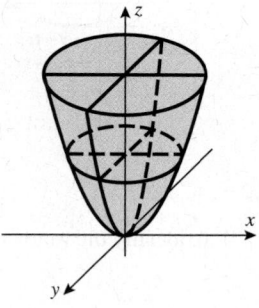

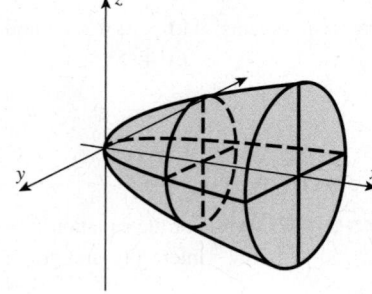

**Satellite dish**

A satellite dish is in the shape of a paraboloid. Functioning as an antenna, the parabolic dish collects all of the incoming signals and reflects them to a single point, the focal point, which is where the receiver is located. In Examples 7 and 8, and in the Applications Exercises, the intention is not to find the three-dimensional equation of the paraboloid, but rather the equation of the plane parabola that's rotated to generate the paraboloid.

### EXAMPLE 7  Finding the Location of the Receiver in a Satellite Dish

A satellite dish is 24 feet in diameter at its opening and 4 feet deep in its center. Where should the receiver be placed?

**Solution:**

Draw a parabola with a vertex at the origin representing the center cross section of the satellite dish.

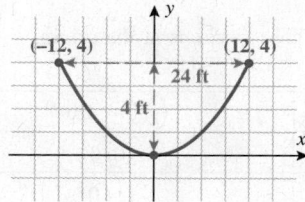

Write the standard equation of a parabola opening upward with vertex at (0, 0).

$$x^2 = 4py$$

The point (12, 4) lies on the parabola, so substitute (12, 4) into $x^2 = 4py$.

$$(12)^2 = 4p(4)$$

Simplify.

$$144 = 16p$$

Solve for $p$.

$$p = 9$$

Substitute $p = 9$ into the focus $(0, p)$.

$$\text{focus: } (0, 9)$$

> The receiver should be placed 9 feet from the vertex of the dish.

Parabolic antennas work for sound in addition to light. Have you ever wondered how the sound of the quarterback calling audible plays is heard by the sideline crew? The crew holds a parabolic system with a microphone at the focus. All of the sound in the direction of the parabolic system is reflected toward the focus, where the microphone amplifies and records the sound.

### EXAMPLE 8  Finding the Equation of a Parabolic Sound Dish

If the parabolic sound dish the sideline crew is holding has a 2-foot diameter at the opening and the microphone is located 6 inches from the vertex, find the equation that governs the center cross section of the parabolic sound dish.

**Solution:**

Write the standard equation of a parabola opening to the right with the vertex at the origin (0, 0).

$$x = 4py^2$$

The focus is located 6 inches ($\frac{1}{2}$ foot) from the vertex.

$$(p, 0) = \left(\frac{1}{2}, 0\right)$$

Solve for $p$.

$$p = \frac{1}{2}$$

Let $p = \frac{1}{2}$ in $x = 4py^2$.

$$x = 4\left(\frac{1}{2}\right)y^2$$

Simplify.

$$\boxed{x = 2y^2}$$

## SECTION
## 9.2 SUMMARY

In this section, we discussed parabolas whose vertex is at the origin.

| EQUATION | $y^2 = 4px$ | $x^2 = 4py$ |
|---|---|---|
| VERTEX | $(0, 0)$ | $(0, 0)$ |
| FOCUS | $(p, 0)$ | $(0, p)$ |
| DIRECTRIX | $x = -p$ | $y = -p$ |
| AXIS OF SYMMETRY | $x$-axis | $y$-axis |
| $p > 0$ | opens to the right | opens upward |
| $p < 0$ | opens to the left | opens downward |
| GRAPH | | |

For parabolas whose vertex is at the point, $(h, k)$:

| EQUATION | $(y - k)^2 = 4p(x - h)$ | $(x - h)^2 = 4p(y - k)$ |
|---|---|---|
| VERTEX | $(h, k)$ | $(h, k)$ |
| FOCUS | $(p + h, k)$ | $(h, p + k)$ |
| DIRECTRIX | $x = -p + h$ | $y = -p + k$ |
| AXIS OF SYMMETRY | $y = k$ | $x = h$ |
| $p > 0$ | opens to the right | opens upward |
| $p < 0$ | opens to the left | opens downward |

**SECTION**
# 9.2 EXERCISES

■ SKILLS

**In Exercises 1–4, match the parabola to the equation.**

**1.** $y^2 = 4x$
**a.**

**2.** $y^2 = -4x$
**b.**

**3.** $x^2 = -4y$
**c.**

**4.** $x^2 = 4y$
**d.**

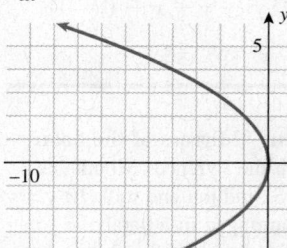
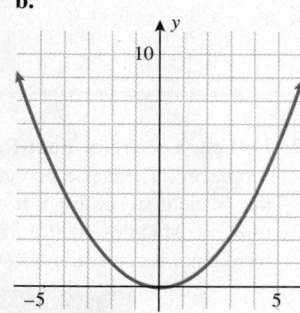
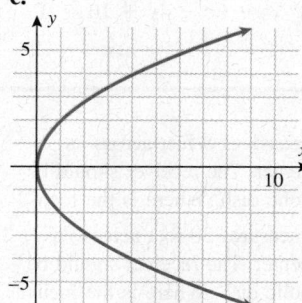
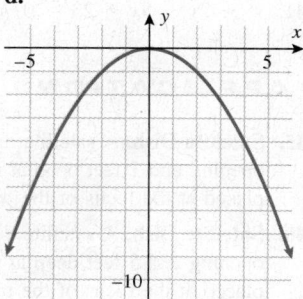

**In Exercises 5–8, match the parabola to the equation.**

**5.** $(y - 1)^2 = 4(x - 1)$
**a.**

**6.** $(y + 1)^2 = -4(x - 1)$
**b.**

**7.** $(x + 1)^2 = -4(y + 1)$
**c.**

**8.** $(x - 1)^2 = 4(y - 1)$
**d.**

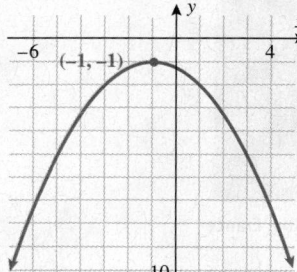
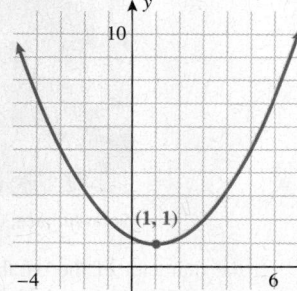
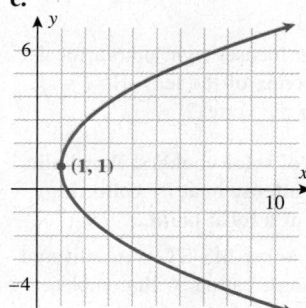
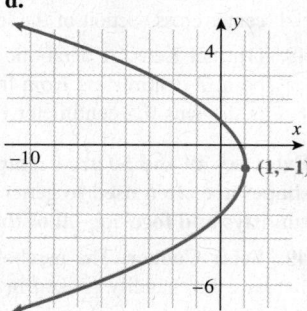

**In Exercises 9–20, find an equation for the parabola described.**

**9.** Vertex at $(0, 0)$; focus at $(0, 3)$

**10.** Vertex at $(0, 0)$; focus at $(2, 0)$

**11.** Vertex at $(0, 0)$; focus at $(-5, 0)$

**12.** Vertex at $(0, 0)$; focus at $(0, -4)$

**13.** Vertex at $(3, 5)$; focus at $(3, 7)$

**14.** Vertex at $(3, 5)$; focus at $(7, 5)$

**15.** Vertex at $(2, 4)$; focus at $(0, 4)$

**16.** Vertex at $(2, 4)$; focus at $(2, -1)$

**17.** Focus at $(2, 4)$; directrix at $y = -2$

**18.** Focus at $(2, -2)$; directrix at $y = 4$

**19.** Focus at $(3, -1)$; directrix at $x = 1$

**20.** Focus at $(-1, 5)$; directrix at $x = 5$

**In Exercises 21–24, write an equation for each parabola.**

**21.**

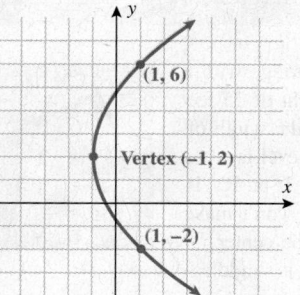

**22.**

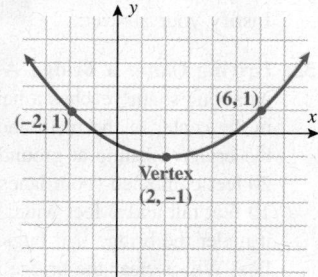

**23.**

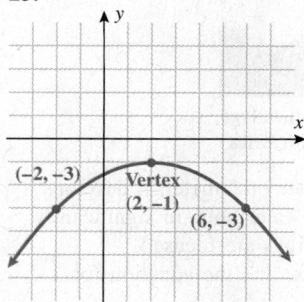

**24.**

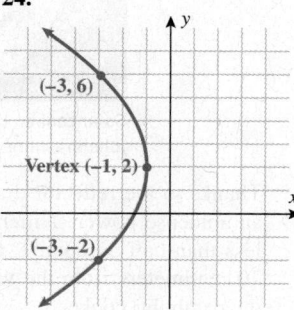

**In Exercises 25–32, find the focus, vertex, directrix, and length of latus rectum and graph the parabola.**

**25.** $x^2 = 8y$       **26.** $x^2 = -12y$       **27.** $y^2 = -2x$       **28.** $y^2 = 6x$

**29.** $x^2 = 16y$       **30.** $x^2 = -8y$       **31.** $y^2 = 4x$       **32.** $y^2 = -16x$

**In Exercises 33–44, find the vertex and graph the parabola.**

**33.** $(y - 2)^2 = 4(x + 3)$       **34.** $(y + 2)^2 = -4(x - 1)$       **35.** $(x - 3)^2 = -8(y + 1)$       **36.** $(x + 3)^2 = -8(y - 2)$

**37.** $(x + 5)^2 = -2y$       **38.** $y^2 = -16(x + 1)$       **39.** $y^2 - 4y - 2x + 4 = 0$       **40.** $x^2 - 6x + 2y + 9 = 0$

**41.** $y^2 + 2y - 8x - 23 = 0$       **42.** $x^2 - 6x - 4y + 10 = 0$       **43.** $x^2 - x + y - 1 = 0$       **44.** $y^2 + y - x + 1 = 0$

## ▪ APPLICATIONS

**45. Satellite Dish.** A satellite dish measures 8 feet across its opening and 2 feet deep at its center. The receiver should be placed at the focus of the parabolic dish. Where is the focus?

**46. Satellite Dish.** A satellite dish measures 30 feet across its opening and 5 feet deep at its center. The receiver should be placed at the focus of the parabolic dish. Where is the focus?

**47. Eyeglass Lens.** Eyeglass lenses can be thought of as very wide parabolic curves. If the focus occurs 2 centimeters from the center of the lens and the lens at its opening is 5 centimeters, find an equation that governs the shape of the center cross section of the lens.

**48. Optical Lens.** A parabolic lens focuses light onto a focal point 3 centimeters from the vertex of the lens. How wide is the lens 0.5 centimeter from the vertex?

**Exercises 49 and 50 are examples of solar cookers. Parabolic shapes are often used to generate intense heat by collecting sun rays and focusing all of them at a focal point.**

**49. Solar Cooker.** The parabolic cooker MS-ST10 is delivered as a kit, handily packed in a single carton, with complete assembly instructions and even the necessary tools.

© AP/Wide World Photos

Solar cooker, Ubuntu Village,
Johannesburg, South Africa

Thanks to the reflector diameter of 1 meter, it develops an immense power: 1 liter of water boils in significantly less than half an hour. If the rays are focused 40 centimeters from the vertex, find the equation for the parabolic cooker.

**50. Le Four Solaire at Font-Romeur "Mirrors of the Solar Furnace."** There is a reflector in the Pyrenees Mountains that is eight stories high. It cost $2 million and took 10 years to build. Made of 9000 mirrors arranged in a parabolic formation, it can reach 6000°F just from the Sun hitting it!

Mark Antman/The Image Works

Solar furnace, Odellio, France

If the diameter of the parabolic mirror is 100 meters and the sunlight is focused 25 meters from the vertex, find the equation for the parabolic dish.

**51. Sailing Under a Bridge.** A bridge with a parabolic shape has an opening 80 feet wide at the base (where the bridge meets the water), and the height in the center of the bridge is 20 feet. A sailboat whose mast reaches 17 feet above the water is traveling under the bridge 10 feet from the center of the bridge. Will it clear the bridge without scraping its mast? Justify your answer.

**52. Driving Under a Bridge.** A bridge with a parabolic shape reaches a height of 25 feet in the center of the road, and the width of the bridge opening at ground level is 20 feet combined (both lanes). If an RV is 10 feet tall and 8 feet wide, it won't make it under the bridge if it hugs the center line. Will it clear the bridge if it straddles the center line? Justify your answer.

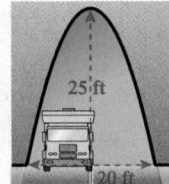

**53. Parabolic Telescope.** The Arecibo radio telescope in Puerto Rico has an enormous reflecting surface, or radio mirror. The huge "dish" is 1000 feet in diameter and 167 feet deep and covers an area of about 20 acres. Using these dimensions, determine the focal length of the telescope. Find the equation for the dish portion of the telescope.

**54. Suspension Bridge.** If one parabolic segment of a suspension bridge is 300 feet and if the cables at the vertex are suspended 10 feet above the bridge, whereas the height of the cables 150 feet from the vertex reaches 60 feet, find the equation of the parabolic path of the suspension cables.

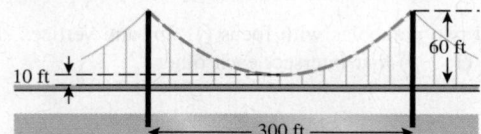

**55. Health.** In a meditation state, the pulse rate (pulses per minute) can be modeled by $p(t) = 0.18t^2 - 5.4t + 95.5$, where $t$ is in minutes. What is the minimum pulse rate according to this model?

**56. Health.** In a distress situation, the pulse rate (pulses per minutes) can be modeled by $p(t) = -1.1t^2 + 22t + 80$, where $t$ is the time in seconds. What is the maximum pulse rate according to this model?

**57. Business.** The profit, in thousands of dollars, for a product is $P(x) = -x^2 + 60x - 500$ where $x$ is the production level in hundreds of units. Find the production level that maximizes the profit. Find the maximum profit.

**58. Business.** The profit, in thousands of dollars, for a product is $P(x) = -x^2 + 80x - 1200$ where $x$ is the production level in hundreds of units. Find the production level that maximizes the profit. Find the maximum profit.

## ▪ CATCH THE MISTAKE

**In Exercises 59 and 60, explain the mistake that is made.**

**59.** Find an equation for a parabola whose vertex is at the origin and whose focus is at the point (3, 0).

**Solution:**

Write the general equation for a parabola whose vertex is at the origin.    $x^2 = 4py$

The focus of this parabola is $(p, 0) = (3, 0)$.    $p = 3$

Substitute $p = 3$ into $x^2 = 4py$.    $x^2 = 12y$

This is incorrect. What mistake was made?

**60.** Find an equation for a parabola whose vertex is at the point (3, 2) and whose focus is located at (5, 2).

**Solution:**

Write the equation associated with a parabola whose vertex is (3, 2).    $(x - h)^2 = 4p(y - k)$

Substitute (3, 2) into $(x - h)^2 = 4p(y - k)$.    $(x - 3)^2 = 4p(y - 2)$

The focus is located at (5, 2); therefore, $p = 5$.

Substitute $p = 5$ into $(x - 3)^2 = 4p(y - 2)$.    $(x - 3)^2 = 20(y - 2)$

This is incorrect. What mistake(s) was made?

## ▪ CONCEPTUAL

**In Exercises 61–64, determine whether each statement is true or false.**

**61.** The vertex lies on the graph of a parabola.

**62.** The focus lies on the graph of a parabola.

**63.** The directrix lies on the graph of a parabola.

**64.** The endpoints of the latus rectum lie on the graph of a parabola.

**In Exercises 65 and 66, use the following equation:**

$$\frac{(y - k)^2}{(x - h)} = 4$$

**65.** Find the directrix of the parabola.

**66.** Determine whether the parabola opens to the right or to the left.

**In Exercises 67 and 68, use the following information about the graph of the parabola:**

Axis of symmetry: $x = 6$
Directrix: $y = 4$
Focus: (6, 9)

**67.** Find the vertex of the parabola.

**68.** Find the equation of the parabola.

### ▪ CHALLENGE

**69.** Derive the standard equation of a parabola with its vertex at the origin, opening upward $x^2 = 4py$. [Calculate the distance $d_1$ from any point on the parabola $(x, y)$ to the focus $(0, p)$. Calculate the distance $d_2$ from any point on the parabola $(x, y)$ to the directrix $(-p, y)$. Set $d_1 = d_2$.]

**70.** Derive the standard equation of a parabola opening right, $y^2 = 4px$. [Calculate the distance $d_1$ from any point on the parabola $(x, y)$ to the focus $(p, 0)$. Calculate the distance $d_2$ from any point on the parabola $(x, y)$ to the directrix $(x, -p)$. Set $d_1 = d_2$.]

**71.** Two parabolas with the same axis of symmetry, $y = 6$, intersect at the point $(4, 2)$. If the directrix of one of these parabolas is the $y$-axis and the directrix of the other parabola is $x = 8$, find the equations of the parabolas.

**72.** Two parabolas with the same axis of symmetry, $x = 9$, intersect at the point $(6, -5)$. If the directrix of one of these parabolas is $y = -11$ and the directrix of the other parabola is $y = 1$, find the equations of the parabolas.

**73.** Find the points of intersection of the parabolas with foci $\left(0, \frac{3}{2}\right)$ and $\left(0, -\frac{3}{4}\right)$, and directresses $y = \frac{1}{2}$ and $y = -\frac{5}{4}$, respectively.

**74.** Find two parabolas with focus $(1, 2p)$ and vertices $(1, p)$ and $(1, -p)$ that intersect each other.

### ▪ TECHNOLOGY

**75.** With a graphing utility, plot the parabola $x^2 - x + y - 1 = 0$. Compare with the sketch you drew for Exercise 43.

**76.** With a graphing utility, plot the parabola $y^2 + y - x + 1 = 0$. Compare with the sketch you drew for Exercise 44.

**77.** In your mind, picture the parabola given by $(y + 3.5)^2 = 10(x - 2.5)$. Where is the vertex? Which way does this parabola open? Now plot the parabola with a graphing utility.

**78.** In your mind, picture the parabola given by $(x + 1.4)^2 = -5(y + 1.7)$. Where is the vertex? Which way does this parabola open? Now plot the parabola with a graphing utility.

**79.** In your mind, picture the parabola given by $(y - 1.5)^2 = -8(x - 1.8)$. Where is the vertex? Which way does this parabola open? Now plot the parabola with a graphing utility.

**80.** In your mind, picture the parabola given by $(x + 2.4)^2 = 6(y - 3.2)$. Where is the vertex? Which way does this parabola open? Now plot the parabola with a graphing utility.

### ▪ PREVIEW TO CALCULUS

**In calculus, to find the area between two curves, first we need to find the point of intersection of the two curves. In Exercises 81–84, find the points of intersection of the two parabolas.**

**81.** Parabola I: vertex: $(0, -1)$; directrix: $y = -\frac{5}{4}$
Parabola II: vertex: $(0, 7)$; directrix: $y = \frac{29}{4}$

**82.** Parabola I: vertex: $(0, 0)$; focus: $(0, 1)$
Parabola II: vertex: $(1, 0)$; focus: $(1, 1)$

**83.** Parabola I: vertex: $\left(5, \frac{5}{3}\right)$; focus: $\left(5, \frac{29}{12}\right)$
Parabola II: vertex: $\left(\frac{13}{2}, \frac{289}{24}\right)$; focus: $\left(\frac{13}{2}, \frac{253}{24}\right)$

**84.** Parabola I: focus: $\left(-2, -\frac{35}{4}\right)$; directrix: $y = -\frac{37}{4}$
Parabola II: focus: $\left(2, -\frac{101}{4}\right)$; directrix: $y = -\frac{99}{4}$

## SKILLS OBJECTIVES

- Graph an ellipse given the center, major axis, and minor axis.
- Find the equation of an ellipse centered at the origin.
- Find the equation of an ellipse centered at the point $(h, k)$.
- Solve applied problems that involve ellipses.

## CONCEPTUAL OBJECTIVES

- Derive the general equation of an ellipse.
- Understand the meaning of major and minor axes and foci.
- Understand the properties of an ellipse that result in a circle.
- Interpret eccentricity in terms of the shape of the ellipse.

# Ellipse Centered at the Origin

## Definition of an Ellipse

If we were to take a piece of string, tie loops at both ends, and tack the ends down so that the string had lots of slack, we would have the picture on the right. If we then took a pencil and pulled the string taut and traced our way around for one full rotation, the result would be an ellipse. See the second figure on the right.

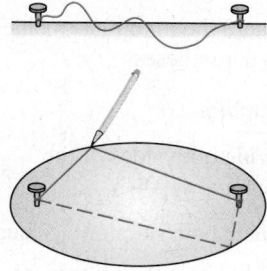

| DEFINITION | Ellipse |
|---|---|

An **ellipse** is the set of all points in a plane the sum of whose distances from two fixed points is constant. These two fixed points are called **foci** (plural of focus). A line segment through the foci called the **major axis** intersects the ellipse at the **vertices**. The midpoint of the line segment joining the vertices is called the **center**. The line segment that intersects the center and joins two points on the ellipse and is perpendicular to the major axis is called the **minor axis**.

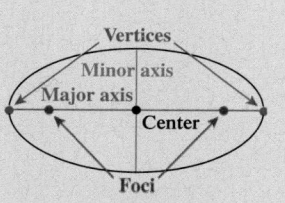

Let's start with an ellipse whose center is located at the origin. Using graph-shifting techniques, we can later extend the characteristics of an ellipse centered at a point other than the origin. Ellipses can vary from the shape of circles to something quite elongated, either horizontally or vertically, that resembles the shape of a racetrack. We say that the ellipse has either greater (elongated) or lesser (circular) *eccentricity*; as we will see, there is a simple mathematical definition of *eccentricity*. It can be shown that the standard equation of an ellipse with its center at the origin is given by one of two forms, depending on whether the orientation of the major axis of the ellipse is horizontal or vertical. For $a > b > 0$, if the major axis is horizontal, then the equation is given by $\dfrac{x^2}{a^2} + \dfrac{y^2}{b^2} = 1$, and if the major axis is vertical, then the equation is given by $\dfrac{x^2}{b^2} + \dfrac{y^2}{a^2} = 1$.

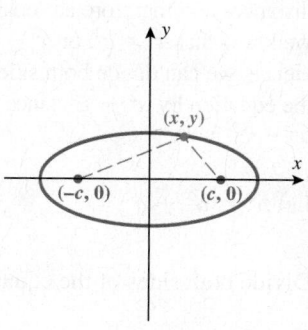

Let's consider an ellipse with its center at the origin and the foci on the $x$-axis. Let the distance from the center to the focus be $c$. Therefore, the foci are located at the points $(-c, 0)$ and $(c, 0)$. The line segment containing the foci is called the major axis, and it lies along the $x$-axis. The sum of the two distances from the foci to any point $(x, y)$ must be constant.

**925**

## Derivation of the Equation of an Ellipse

| WORDS | MATH |
|---|---|
| Calculate the distance from $(x, y)$ to $(-c, 0)$ by applying the distance formula. | $\sqrt{[x - (-c)]^2 + y^2}$ |
| Calculate the distance from $(x, y)$ to $(c, 0)$ by applying the distance formula. | $\sqrt{(x - c)^2 + y^2}$ |
| The sum of these two distances is equal to a constant ($2a$ for convenience). | $\sqrt{[x - (-c)]^2 + y^2} + \sqrt{(x - c)^2 + y^2} = 2a$ |
| Isolate one radical. | $\sqrt{[x - (-c)]^2 + y^2} = 2a - \sqrt{(x - c)^2 + y^2}$ |
| Square both sides of the equation. | $(x + c)^2 + y^2 = 4a^2 - 4a\sqrt{(x - c)^2 + y^2} + (x - c)^2 + y^2$ |
| Square the binomials inside the parentheses. | $x^2 + 2cx + c^2 + y^2 = 4a^2 - 4a\sqrt{(x - c)^2 + y^2}$ $\qquad + x^2 - 2cx + c^2 + y^2$ |
| Simplify. | $4cx - 4a^2 = -4a\sqrt{(x - c)^2 + y^2}$ |
| Divide both sides of the equation by $-4$. | $a^2 - cx = a\sqrt{(x - c)^2 + y^2}$ |
| Square both sides of the equation. | $(a^2 - cx)^2 = a^2\left[(x - c)^2 + y^2\right]$ |
| Square the binomials inside the parentheses. | $a^4 - 2a^2cx + c^2x^2 = a^2(x^2 - 2cx + c^2 + y^2)$ |
| Distribute the $a^2$ term. | $a^4 - 2a^2cx + c^2x^2 = a^2x^2 - 2a^2cx + a^2c^2 + a^2y^2$ |
| Group the $x$ and $y$ terms together, respectively, on one side and constants on the other side. | $c^2x^2 - a^2x^2 - a^2y^2 = a^2c^2 - a^4$ |
| Factor out the common factors. | $(c^2 - a^2)x^2 - a^2y^2 = a^2(c^2 - a^2)$ |
| Multiply both sides of the equation by $-1$. | $(a^2 - c^2)x^2 + a^2y^2 = a^2(a^2 - c^2)$ |
| We can make the argument that $a > c$ in order for a point to be on the ellipse (and not on the $x$-axis). Thus, since $a$ and $c$ represent distances and therefore are positive, we know that $a^2 > c^2$, or $a^2 - c^2 > 0$. Hence, we can divide both sides of the equation by $a^2 - c^2$, since $a^2 - c^2 \neq 0$. | $x^2 + \dfrac{a^2y^2}{(a^2 - c^2)} = a^2$ |
| Let $b^2 = a^2 - c^2$. | $x^2 + \dfrac{a^2y^2}{b^2} = a^2$ |
| Divide both sides of the equation by $a^2$. | $\boxed{\dfrac{x^2}{a^2} + \dfrac{y^2}{b^2} = 1}$ |

The equation $\dfrac{x^2}{a^2} + \dfrac{y^2}{b^2} = 1$ represents an ellipse with its center at the origin with the foci along the $x$-axis, since $a > b$. The following box summarizes ellipses that have their center at the origin and foci along either the $x$-axis or $y$-axis:

### EQUATION OF AN ELLIPSE WITH CENTER AT THE ORIGIN

The **standard form of the equation of an ellipse** with its center at the origin is given by

| ORIENTATION OF MAJOR AXIS | Horizontal (along the $x$-axis) | Vertical (along the $y$-axis) |
|---|---|---|
| EQUATION | $\dfrac{x^2}{a^2} + \dfrac{y^2}{b^2} = 1 \quad a > b > 0$ | $\dfrac{x^2}{b^2} + \dfrac{y^2}{a^2} = 1 \quad a > b > 0$ |
| FOCI | $(-c, 0)$ and $(c, 0)$ where $c^2 = a^2 - b^2$ | $(0, -c)$ and $(0, c)$ where $c^2 = a^2 - b^2$ |
| VERTICES | $(-a, 0)$ and $(a, 0)$ | $(0, -a)$ and $(0, a)$ |
| OTHER INTERCEPTS | $(0, b)$ and $(0, -b)$ | $(b, 0)$ and $(-b, 0)$ |
| GRAPH | (graph of horizontal ellipse with points $(0,b)$, $(-c,0)$, $(c,0)$, $(-a,0)$, $(a,0)$, $(0,0)$, $(0,-b)$) | (graph of vertical ellipse with points $(0,a)$, $(0,c)$, $(-b,0)$, $(0,0)$, $(b,0)$, $(0,-c)$, $(0,-a)$) |

In both cases, the value of $c$, the distance along the major axis from the center to the focus, is given by $c^2 = a^2 - b^2$. The length of the major axis is $2a$ and the length of the minor axis is $2b$.

Notice that when $a = b$, the equation $\dfrac{x^2}{a^2} + \dfrac{y^2}{b^2} = 1$ simplifies to $\dfrac{x^2}{a^2} + \dfrac{y^2}{a^2} = 1$ or $x^2 + y^2 = a^2$, which corresponds to a circle. The vertices correspond to intercepts when an ellipse is centered at the origin. One of the first things we notice about an ellipse is its *eccentricity*. The **eccentricity**, denoted $e$, is given by $e = \dfrac{c}{a}$, where $0 < e < 1$. The circle is a limiting form of an ellipse, $c = 0$. In other words, if the eccentricity is close to 0, then the ellipse resembles a circle, whereas if the eccentricity is close to 1, then the ellipse is quite elongated, or eccentric.

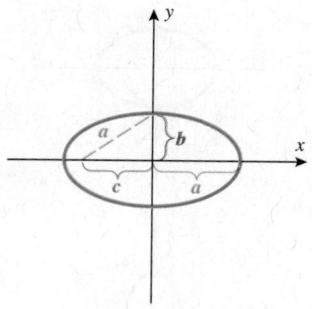

## Graphing an Ellipse with Center at the Origin

The equation of an ellipse in standard form can be used to graph an ellipse. Although an ellipse is defined in terms of the foci, the foci are not part of the graph. It is important to note that if the divisor of the term with $x^2$ is larger than the divisor of the term with $y^2$, then the ellipse is elongated horizontally.

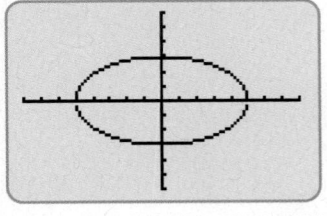
## EXAMPLE 1    Graphing an Ellipse with a Horizontal Major Axis

Graph the ellipse given by $\frac{x^2}{25} + \frac{y^2}{9} = 1$.

**Solution:**

| | |
|---|---|
| Since $25 > 9$, the major axis is horizontal. | $a^2 = 25$ and $b^2 = 9$ |
| Solve for $a$ and $b$. | $a = 5$ and $b = 3$ |
| Identify the vertices: $(-a, 0)$ and $(a, 0)$. | $(-5, 0)$ and $(5, 0)$ |
| Identify the endpoints ($y$-intercepts) on the minor axis: $(0, -b)$ and $(0, b)$. | $(0, -3)$ and $(0, 3)$ |

Graph by labeling the points $(-5, 0)$, $(5, 0)$, $(0, -3)$, and $(0, 3)$ and connecting them with a smooth curve.

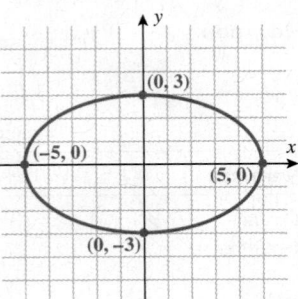

If the divisor of $x^2$ is larger than the divisor of $y^2$, then the major axis is horizontal along the $x$-axis, as in Example 1. If the divisor of $y^2$ is larger than the divisor of $x^2$, then the major axis is vertical along the $y$-axis, as you will see in Example 2.

■ **Answer:**

**a.**

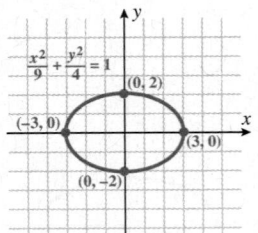

**b.**

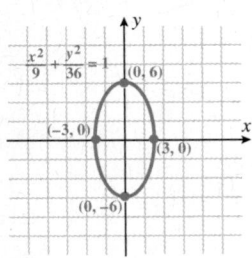

## EXAMPLE 2    Graphing an Ellipse with a Vertical Major Axis

Graph the ellipse given by $16x^2 + y^2 = 16$.

**Solution:**

| | |
|---|---|
| Write the equation in standard form by dividing by 16. | $\frac{x^2}{1} + \frac{y^2}{16} = 1$ |
| Since $16 > 1$, this ellipse is elongated vertically. | $a^2 = 16$ and $b^2 = 1$ |
| Solve for $a$ and $b$. | $a = 4$ and $b = 1$ |
| Identify the vertices: $(0, -a)$ and $(0, a)$. | $(0, -4)$ and $(0, 4)$ |
| Identify the $x$-intercepts on the minor axis: $(-b, 0)$ and $(b, 0)$. | $(-1, 0)$ and $(1, 0)$ |

Graph by labeling the points $(0, -4)$, $(0, 4)$, $(-1, 0)$, and $(1, 0)$ and connecting them with a smooth curve.

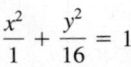
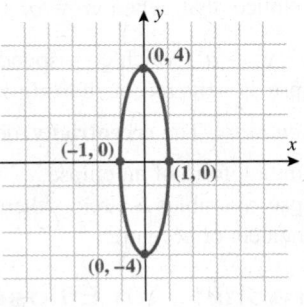

■ **YOUR TURN**  Graph the ellipses:

$$\textbf{a. } \frac{x^2}{9} + \frac{y^2}{4} = 1 \qquad \textbf{b. } \frac{x^2}{9} + \frac{y^2}{36} = 1$$

# Finding the Equation of an Ellipse with Center at the Origin

What if we know the vertices and the foci of an ellipse and want to find the equation to which it corresponds? The axis on which the foci and vertices are located is the major axis. Therefore, we will have the standard equation of an ellipse, and $a$ will be known (from the vertices). Since $c$ is known from the foci, we can use the relation $c^2 = a^2 - b^2$ to determine the unknown $b$.

### EXAMPLE 3  Finding the Equation of an Ellipse Centered at the Origin

Find the standard form of the equation of an ellipse with foci at $(-3, 0)$ and $(3, 0)$ and vertices $(-4, 0)$ and $(4, 0)$.

**Solution:**

The major axis lies along the $x$-axis, since it contains the foci and vertices.

Write the corresponding general equation of an ellipse.  $\dfrac{x^2}{a^2} + \dfrac{y^2}{b^2} = 1$

Identify $a$ from the vertices:

  Match vertices $(-4, 0) = (-a, 0)$ and $(4, 0) = (a, 0)$.  $a = 4$

Identify $c$ from the foci:

  Match foci $(-3, 0) = (-c, 0)$ and $(3, 0) = (c, 0)$.  $c = 3$

Substitute $a = 4$ and $c = 3$ into $b^2 = a^2 - c^2$.  $b^2 = 4^2 - 3^2$

Simplify.  $b^2 = 7$

Substitute $a^2 = 16$ and $b^2 = 7$ into $\dfrac{x^2}{a^2} + \dfrac{y^2}{b^2} = 1$.  $\dfrac{x^2}{16} + \dfrac{y^2}{7} = 1$

The equation of the ellipse is  $\boxed{\dfrac{x^2}{16} + \dfrac{y^2}{7} = 1}$.

■ **YOUR TURN**  Find the standard form of the equation of an ellipse with vertices at $(0, -6)$ and $(0, 6)$ and foci $(0, -5)$ and $(0, 5)$.

■ **Answer:** $\dfrac{x^2}{11} + \dfrac{y^2}{36} = 1$

# Ellipse Centered at the Point (*h, k*)

We can use graph-shifting techniques to graph ellipses that are centered at a point other than the origin. For example, to graph $\dfrac{(x - h)^2}{a^2} + \dfrac{(y - k)^2}{b^2} = 1$ (assuming $h$ and $k$ are positive constants), start with the graph of $\dfrac{x^2}{a^2} + \dfrac{y^2}{b^2} = 1$ and shift to the right $h$ units and up $k$ units. The center, the vertices, the foci, and the major and minor axes all shift. In other words, the two ellipses are identical in shape and size, except that the ellipse $\dfrac{(x - h)^2}{a^2} + \dfrac{(y - k)^2}{b^2} = 1$ is centered at the point $(h, k)$.

The following table summarizes the characteristics of ellipses centered at a point other than the origin:

**EQUATION OF AN ELLIPSE WITH CENTER AT THE POINT $(h, k)$**

The **standard form of the equation of an ellipse** with its center at the point $(h, k)$ is given by

| ORIENTATION OF MAJOR AXIS | Horizontal (parallel to the $x$-axis) | Vertical (parallel to the $y$-axis) |
|---|---|---|
| EQUATION | $\dfrac{(x - h)^2}{a^2} + \dfrac{(y - k)^2}{b^2} = 1$ | $\dfrac{(x - h)^2}{b^2} + \dfrac{(y - k)^2}{a^2} = 1$ |
| GRAPH | | |
| FOCI | $(h - c, k)$ and $(h + c, k)$ | $(h, k - c)$ and $(h, k + c)$ |
| VERTICES | $(h - a, k)$ and $(h + a, k)$ | $(h, k - a)$ and $(h, k + a)$ |

In both cases, $a > b > 0$, $c^2 = a^2 - b^2$, the length of the major axis is $2a$, and the length of the minor axis is $2b$.

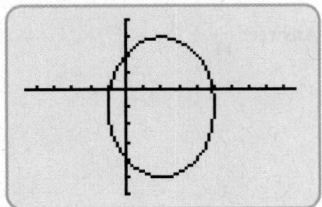
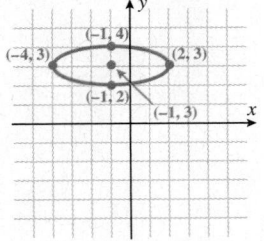

**EXAMPLE 4** **Graphing an Ellipse with Center $(h, k)$ Given the Equation in Standard Form**

Graph the ellipse given by $\dfrac{(x - 2)^2}{9} + \dfrac{(y + 1)^2}{16} = 1$.

**Solution:**

Write the equation in the form

$$\dfrac{(x - h)^2}{b^2} + \dfrac{(y - k)^2}{a^2} = 1. \qquad \dfrac{(x - 2)^2}{3^2} + \dfrac{[y - (-1)]^2}{4^2} = 1$$

Identify $a$, $b$, and the center $(h, k)$.　　$a = 4$, $b = 3$, and $(h, k) = (2, -1)$

Draw a graph and label the center: $(2, -1)$.

Since $a = 4$, the vertices are up 4 and down four units from the center: $(2, -5)$ and $(2, 3)$.

Since $b = 3$, the endpoints of the minor axis are to the left and right three units: $(-1, -1)$ and $(5, -1)$.

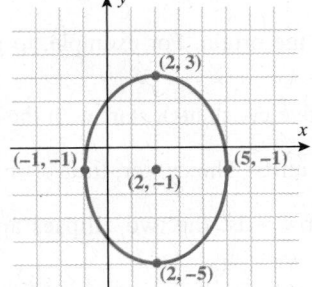

■ **YOUR TURN** Graph the ellipse given by $\dfrac{(x + 1)^2}{9} + \dfrac{(y - 3)^2}{1} = 1$.

All active members of the Lambda Chi fraternity are college students, but not all college students are members of the Lambda Chi fraternity. Similarly, all circles are ellipses, but not all ellipses are circles. When $a = b$, the standard equation of an ellipse simplifies to a standard equation of a circle. Recall that when we are given the equation of a circle in general form, we first complete the square in order to express the equation in standard form, which allows the center and radius to be identified. We use that same approach when the equation of an ellipse is given in a general form.

**EXAMPLE 5    Graphing an Ellipse with Center ($h$, $k$) Given an Equation in General Form**

Graph the ellipse given by $4x^2 + 24x + 25y^2 - 50y - 39 = 0$.

**Solution:**

Transform the general equation into standard form.

Group $x$ terms together and $y$ terms together and add 39 to both sides.

$$(4x^2 + 24x) + (25y^2 - 50y) = 39$$

Factor out the 4 common to the $x$ terms and the 25 common to the $y$ terms.

$$4(x^2 + 6x) + 25(y^2 - 2y) = 39$$

Complete the square on $x$ and $y$.

$$4(x^2 + 6x + 9) + 25(y^2 - 2y + 1) = 39 + 4(9) + 25(1)$$

Simplify.

$$4(x + 3)^2 + 25(y - 1)^2 = 100$$

Divide by 100.

$$\frac{(x + 3)^2}{25} + \frac{(y - 1)^2}{4} = 1$$

Since $25 > 4$, this is an ellipse with a horizontal major axis.

Now that the equation of the ellipse is in standard form, compare to $\frac{(x - h)^2}{a^2} + \frac{(y - k)^2}{b^2} = 1$ and identify $a$, $b$, $h$, $k$.

$$a = 5, \ b = 2, \text{ and } (h, k) = (-3, 1)$$

Since $a = 5$, the vertices are five units to left and right of the center.

$$(-8, 1) \text{ and } (2, 1)$$

Since $b = 2$, the endpoints of the minor axis are up and down two units from the center.

$$(-3, -1) \text{ and } (-3, 3)$$

Graph.

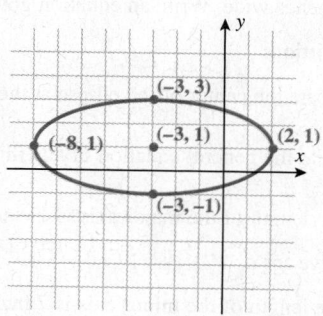

**Technology Tip**

Use a graphing calculator to check the graph of $4x^2 + 24x + 25y^2 - 50y - 39 = 0$.

Use $\frac{(x + 3)^2}{25} + \frac{(y - 1)^2}{4} = 1$ to solve for $y$ first. That is,

$$y_1 = 1 + 2\sqrt{1 - \frac{(x + 3)^2}{25}} \text{ or}$$

$$y_2 = 1 - 2\sqrt{1 - \frac{(x + 3)^2}{25}}.$$

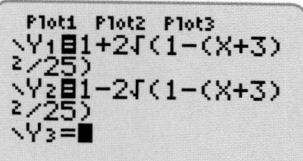

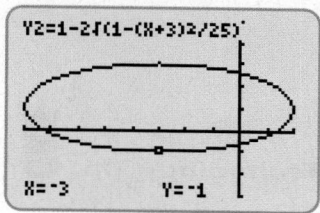

■**Answer:**

$$\frac{(x + 4)^2}{1} + \frac{(y - 1)^2}{4} = 1$$

Center: $(-4, 1)$

Vertices: $(-4, -1)$ and $(-4, 3)$

Endpoints of minor axis: $(-5, 1)$ and $(-3, 1)$

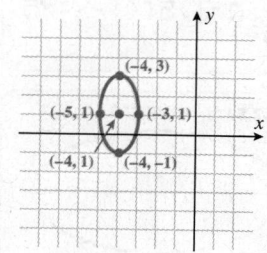

■ **YOUR TURN**    Write the equation $4x^2 + 32x + y^2 - 2y + 61 = 0$ in standard form. Identify the center, vertices, and endpoints of the minor axis, and graph.

## Applications

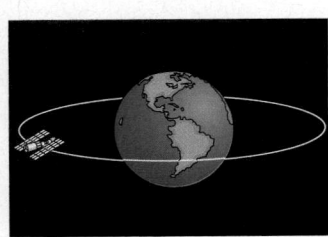

There are many examples of ellipses all around us. On Earth we have racetracks, and in our solar system, the planets travel in elliptical orbits with the Sun as a focus. Satellites are in elliptical orbits around Earth. Most communications satellites are in a *geosynchronous* (GEO) orbit—they orbit Earth once each day. In order to stay over the same spot on Earth, a *geostationary* satellite has to be directly above the equator; it circles Earth in exactly the time it takes Earth to turn once on its axis, and its orbit has to follow the path of the equator as Earth rotates. Otherwise, from Earth the satellite would appear to move in a north–south line every day.

If we start with an ellipse in the *xy*-plane and rotate it around its major axis, the result is a three-dimensional ellipsoid.

 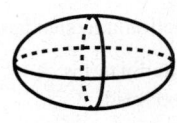

A football and a blimp are two examples of ellipsoids. The ellipsoidal shape allows for a more aerodynamic path.

PhotoDisc, Inc.

Peter Phipp/Age Fotostock America, Inc.

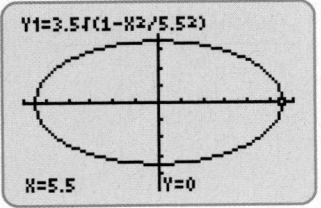
### EXAMPLE 6   An Official NFL Football

A longitudinal section (that includes the two vertices and the center) of an official Wilson NFL football is an ellipse. The longitudinal section is approximately 11 inches long and 7 inches wide. Write an equation governing the elliptical longitudinal section.

**Solution:**

Locate the center of the ellipse at the origin and orient the football horizontally.

Write the general equation of an ellipse centered at the origin. $\qquad \dfrac{x^2}{a^2} + \dfrac{y^2}{b^2} = 1$

The length of the major axis is 11 inches. $\qquad\qquad 2a = 11$

Solve for *a*. $\qquad\qquad a = 5.5$

The length of the minor axis is 7 inches. $\qquad\qquad 2b = 7$

Solve for *b*. $\qquad\qquad b = 3.5$

Substitute $a = 5.5$ and $b = 3.5$ into $\dfrac{x^2}{a^2} + \dfrac{y^2}{b^2} = 1$. $\qquad \boxed{\dfrac{x^2}{5.5^2} + \dfrac{y^2}{3.5^2} = 1}$

## SECTION
## 9.3  SUMMARY

In this section, we first analyzed ellipses that are centered at the origin.

| ORIENTATION OF MAJOR AXIS | Horizontal along the $x$-axis | Vertical along the $y$-axis |
|---|---|---|
| EQUATION | $\dfrac{x^2}{a^2} + \dfrac{y^2}{b^2} = 1 \quad a > b > 0$ | $\dfrac{x^2}{b^2} + \dfrac{y^2}{a^2} = 1 \quad a > b > 0$ |
| FOCI* | $(-c, 0)$ and $(c, 0)$ | $(0, -c)$ and $(0, c)$ |
| VERTICES | $(-a, 0)$ and $(a, 0)$ | $(0, -a)$ and $(0, a)$ |
| OTHER INTERCEPTS | $(0, -b)$ and $(0, b)$ | $(-b, 0)$ and $(b, 0)$ |
| GRAPH | | |

$*c^2 = a^2 - b^2$

For ellipses centered at the origin, we can graph an ellipse by finding all four intercepts.

For ellipses **centered at the point $(h, k)$,** the major and minor axes and endpoints of the ellipse all shift accordingly. When $a = b$, the ellipse is a circle.

| ORIENTATION OF MAJOR AXIS | Horizontal (parallel to the $x$-axis) | Vertical (parallel to the $y$-axis) |
|---|---|---|
| EQUATION | $\dfrac{(x-h)^2}{a^2} + \dfrac{(y-k)^2}{b^2} = 1$ | $\dfrac{(x-h)^2}{b^2} + \dfrac{(y-k)^2}{a^2} = 1$ |
| GRAPH | | |
| FOCI | $(h - c, k)$ and $(h + c, k)$ | $(h, k - c)$ and $(h, k + c)$ |
| VERTICES | $(h - a, k)$ and $(h + a, k)$ | $(h, k - a)$ and $(h, k + a)$ |

■ SKILLS

**In Exercises 1–4, match the equation to the ellipse.**

**1.** $\dfrac{x^2}{36} + \dfrac{y^2}{16} = 1$

**2.** $\dfrac{x^2}{16} + \dfrac{y^2}{36} = 1$

**3.** $\dfrac{x^2}{8} + \dfrac{y^2}{72} = 1$

**4.** $4x^2 + y^2 = 1$

**a.**

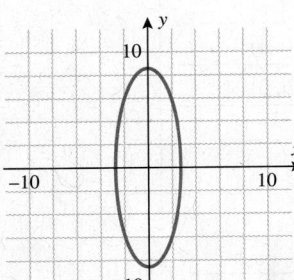

**b.**

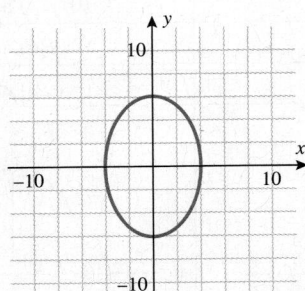

**c.**

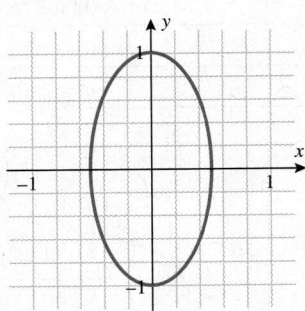

**d.**

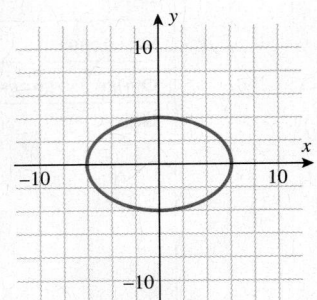

**In Exercises 5–16, graph each ellipse. Label the center and vertices.**

**5.** $\dfrac{x^2}{25} + \dfrac{y^2}{16} = 1$

**6.** $\dfrac{x^2}{49} + \dfrac{y^2}{9} = 1$

**7.** $\dfrac{x^2}{16} + \dfrac{y^2}{64} = 1$

**8.** $\dfrac{x^2}{25} + \dfrac{y^2}{144} = 1$

**9.** $\dfrac{x^2}{100} + y^2 = 1$

**10.** $9x^2 + 4y^2 = 36$

**11.** $\dfrac{4}{9}x^2 + 81y^2 = 1$

**12.** $\dfrac{4}{25}x^2 + \dfrac{100}{9}y^2 = 1$

**13.** $4x^2 + y^2 = 16$

**14.** $x^2 + y^2 = 81$

**15.** $8x^2 + 16y^2 = 32$

**16.** $10x^2 + 25y^2 = 50$

**In Exercises 17–24, find the standard form of the equation of an ellipse with the given characteristics.**

**17.** Foci: $(-4, 0)$ and $(4, 0)$    Vertices: $(-6, 0)$ and $(6, 0)$

**18.** Foci: $(-1, 0)$ and $(1, 0)$    Vertices: $(-3, 0)$ and $(3, 0)$

**19.** Foci: $(0, -3)$ and $(0, 3)$    Vertices: $(0, -4)$ and $(0, 4)$

**20.** Foci: $(0, -1)$ and $(0, 1)$    Vertices: $(0, -2)$ and $(0, 2)$

**21.** Major axis vertical with length of 8, minor axis length of 4, and centered at $(0, 0)$

**22.** Major axis horizontal with length of 10, minor axis length of 2, and centered at $(0, 0)$

**23.** Vertices $(0, -7)$ and $(0, 7)$ and endpoints of minor axis $(-3, 0)$ and $(3, 0)$

**24.** Vertices $(-9, 0)$ and $(9, 0)$ and endpoints of minor axis $(0, -4)$ and $(0, 4)$

**In Exercises 25–28, match each equation with the ellipse.**

**25.** $\dfrac{(x-3)^2}{4} + \dfrac{(y+2)^2}{25} = 1$

**26.** $\dfrac{(x+3)^2}{4} + \dfrac{(y-2)^2}{25} = 1$

**27.** $\dfrac{(x-3)^2}{25} + \dfrac{(y+2)^2}{4} = 1$

**28.** $\dfrac{(x+3)^2}{25} + \dfrac{(y-2)^2}{4} = 1$

**a.**

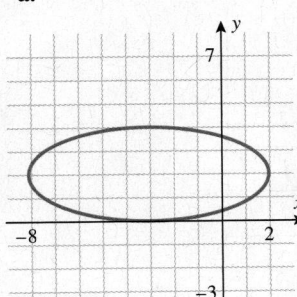

**b.**

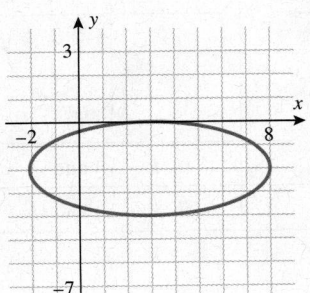

**c.**

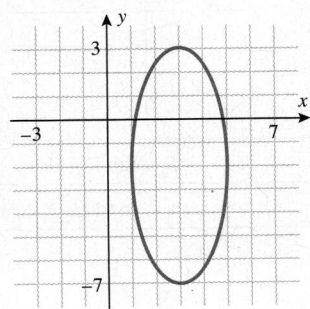

**d.**

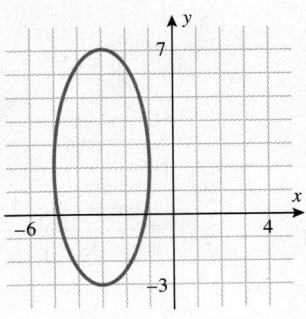

**In Exercises 29–38, graph each ellipse. Label the center and vertices.**

**29.** $\dfrac{(x-1)^2}{16} + \dfrac{(y-2)^2}{4} = 1$

**30.** $\dfrac{(x+1)^2}{36} + \dfrac{(y+2)^2}{9} = 1$

**31.** $10(x+3)^2 + (y-4)^2 = 80$

**32.** $3(x+3)^2 + 12(y-4)^2 = 36$

**33.** $x^2 + 4y^2 - 24y + 32 = 0$

**34.** $25x^2 + 2y^2 - 4y - 48 = 0$

**35.** $x^2 - 2x + 2y^2 - 4y - 5 = 0$

**36.** $9x^2 - 18x + 4y^2 - 27 = 0$

**37.** $5x^2 + 20x + y^2 + 6y - 21 = 0$

**38.** $9x^2 + 36x + y^2 + 2y + 36 = 0$

**In Exercises 39–46, find the standard form of the equation of an ellipse with the given characteristics.**

**39.** Foci: $(-2, 5)$ and $(6, 5)$   Vertices: $(-3, 5)$ and $(7, 5)$

**40.** Foci: $(2, -2)$ and $(4, -2)$   Vertices: $(0, -2)$ and $(6, -2)$

**41.** Foci: $(4, -7)$ and $(4, -1)$   Vertices: $(4, -8)$ and $(4, 0)$

**42.** Foci: $(2, -6)$ and $(2, -4)$   Vertices: $(2, -7)$ and $(2, -3)$

**43.** Major axis vertical with length of 8, minor axis length of 4, and centered at $(3, 2)$

**44.** Major axis horizontal with length of 10, minor axis length of 2, and centered at $(-4, 3)$

**45.** Vertices $(-1, -9)$ and $(-1, 1)$ and endpoints of minor axis $(-4, -4)$ and $(2, -4)$

**46.** Vertices $(-2, 3)$ and $(6, 3)$ and endpoints of minor axis $(2, 1)$ and $(2, 5)$

# ■ APPLICATIONS

**47. Carnival Ride.** The Zipper, a favorite carnival ride, maintains an elliptical shape with a major axis of 150 feet and a minor axis of 30 feet. Assuming it is centered at the origin, find an equation for the ellipse.

Courtesy Chance Morgan, Inc.

**Zipper**

**48. Carnival Ride.** A Ferris wheel traces an elliptical path with both a major and minor axis of 180 feet. Assuming it is centered at the origin, find an equation for the ellipse (circle).

Tina Buckman/Index Stock

Ferris wheel, Barcelona, Spain

**For Exercises 49 and 50, refer to the following information:**

A high school wants to build a football field surrounded by an elliptical track. A regulation football field must be 120 yards long and 30 yards wide.

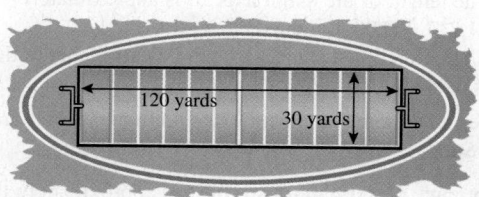

120 yards

30 yards

**49. Sports Field.** Suppose the elliptical track is centered at the origin and has a horizontal major axis of length 150 yards and a minor axis length of 40 yards.

   **a.** Write an equation for the ellipse.
   **b.** Find the width of the track at the end of the field. Will the track completely enclose the football field?

**50. Sports Field.** Suppose the elliptical track is centered at the origin and has a horizontal major axis of length 150 yards. How long should the minor axis be in order to enclose the field?

**For Exercises 51 and 52, refer to orbits in our solar system:**

The planets have elliptical orbits with the Sun as one of the foci. Pluto (orange), the planet furthest from the Sun, has a very elongated, or flattened, elliptical orbit, whereas Earth (royal blue) has an almost circular orbit. Because of Pluto's flattened path, it is not always the planet furthest from the Sun.

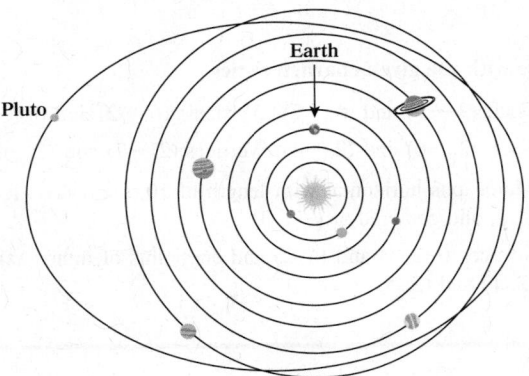

**51. Planetary Orbits.** The orbit of the dwarf planet Pluto has approximately the following characteristics (assume the Sun is the focus):

■ The length of the major axis $2a$ is approximately 11,827,000,000 kilometers.
■ The perihelion distance from the dwarf planet to the Sun is 4,447,000,000 kilometers.

Determine the equation for Pluto's elliptical orbit around the Sun.

**52. Planetary Orbits.** Earth's orbit has approximately the following characteristics (assume the Sun is the focus):

■ The length of the major axis $2a$ is approximately 299,700,000 kilometers.
■ The perihelion distance from Earth to the Sun is 147,100,000 kilometers.

Determine the equation for Earth's elliptical orbit around the Sun.

**For Exercises 53 and 54, refer to the following information:**

Asteroids orbit the Sun in elliptical patterns and often cross paths with Earth's orbit, making life a little tense now and again. A few asteroids have orbits that cross Earth's orbit—called "Apollo asteroids" or "Earth-crossing asteroids." In recent years, asteroids have passed within 100,000 kilometers of Earth!

**53. Asteroids.** Asteroid 433, or Eros, is the second largest near-Earth asteroid. The semimajor axis is 150 million kilometers and the eccentricity is 0.223, where eccentricity is defined as $e = \sqrt{1 - \dfrac{b^2}{a^2}}$, where $a$ is the semimajor axis or $2a$ is the major axis, and $b$ is the semiminor axis or $2b$ is the minor axis. Find the equation of Eros's orbit. Round $a$ and $b$ to the nearest million kilometers.

**54. Asteroids.** The asteroid Toutatis is the largest near-Earth asteroid. The semimajor axis is 350 million kilometers and the eccentricity is 0.634, where eccentricity is defined as $e = \sqrt{1 - \dfrac{b^2}{a^2}}$, where $a$ is the semimajor axis or $2a$ is the major axis, and $b$ is the semimajor axis or $2b$ is the minor axis. On September 29, 2004, it missed Earth by 961,000 miles. Find the equation of Toutatis's orbit.

**55. Halley's Comet.** The eccentricity of Halley's Comet is approximately 0.967. If a comet had $e$ almost equal to 1, what would its orbit appear to be from Earth?

**56. Halley's Comet.** The length of the semimajor axis is 17.8 AU (astronomical units) and the eccentricity is approximately 0.967. Find the equation of Halley's Comet. (Assume 1 AU = 150 million km.)

**57. Medicine.** The second time that a drug is given to a patient, the relationship between the drug concentration $c$ (in milligrams per $cm^3$) and the time $t$ (in hours) is given by

$$t^2 + 9c^2 - 6t - 18c + 9 = 0$$

Determine the highest concentration of drug in the patient's bloodstream.

**58. Fuel Transportation.** Tanks built to transport fuel and other hazardous materials have an elliptical cross section, which makes them more stable for the transportation of these materials. If the lengths of the major and minor axes of the elliptical cross section are 8 feet and 6 feet, respectively, and the tank is 30 feet long, find the volume of the tank. Round your answer to the nearest integer. *Hint:* The area of an ellipse is $\pi \cdot a \cdot b$.

**For Exercises 59 and 60, refer to the following:**

An elliptical trainer is an exercise machine that can be used to simulate stair climbing, walking, or running. The stride length is the length of a step on the trainer (forward foot to rear foot). The minimum step-up height is the height of a pedal at its lowest point, while the maximum step-up height is the height of a pedal at its highest point.

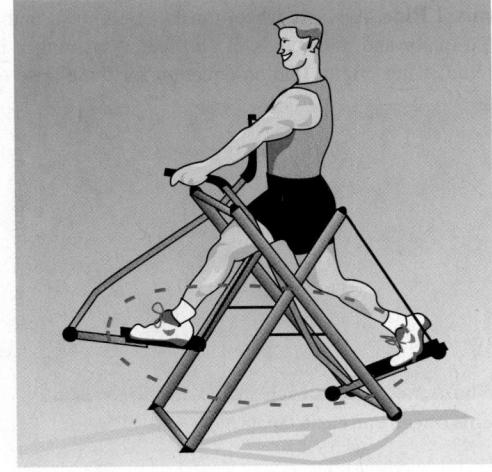

**59. Health/Exercise.** An elliptical trainer has a stride length of 16 inches. The maximum step-up height is 12.5 inches, while the minimum step-up height is 2.5 inches.

a. Find the equation of the ellipse traced by the pedals assuming the origin lies at the pedal axle (center of the ellipse is at the origin).

b. Use the approximation to the perimeter of an ellipse $p = \pi\sqrt{2(a^2 + b^2)}$ to find the distance, to the nearest inch, traveled in one complete step (revolution of a pedal).

c. How many steps, to the nearest step, are necessary to travel a distance of one mile?

**60. Health/Exercise.** An elliptical trainer has a stride length of 18 inches. The maximum step-up height is 13.5 inches, while the minimum step-up height is 3.5 inches. Find the equation of the ellipse traced by the pedals assuming the origin lies at the pedal axle.

a. Find the equation of the ellipse traced by the pedals assuming the origin lies at the pedal axle (center of the ellipse is at the origin).

b. Use the approximation to the perimeter of an ellipse $p = \pi\sqrt{2(a^2 + b^2)}$ to find the distance, to the nearest inch, traveled in one complete step (revolution of a pedal).

c. How many steps, to the nearest step, are necessary to travel a distance of one mile?

■ CATCH THE MISTAKE ────────────────

**In Exercises 61 and 62, explain the mistake that is made.**

**61.** Graph the ellipse given by $\dfrac{x^2}{6} + \dfrac{y^2}{4} = 1$.

**Solution:**

Write the standard form of the equation of an ellipse.

$$\frac{x^2}{a^2} + \frac{y^2}{b^2} = 1$$

Identify $a$ and $b$.

$a = 6, b = 4$

Label the vertices and the endpoints of the minor axis, $(-6, 0), (6, 0), (0, -4),$ $(0, 4)$, and connect with an elliptical curve.

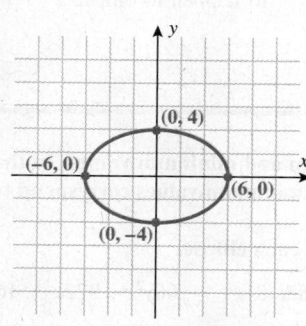

This is incorrect. What mistake was made?

**62.** Determine the foci of the ellipse $\dfrac{x^2}{16} + \dfrac{y^2}{9} = 1$.

**Solution:**

Write the general equation of a horizontal ellipse.

$$\frac{x^2}{a^2} + \frac{y^2}{b^2} = 1$$

Identify $a$ and $b$.

$a = 4, b = 3$

Substitute $a = 4, b = 3$ into $c^2 = a^2 + b^2$.

$c^2 = 4^2 + 3^2$

Solve for $c$.

$c = 5$

Foci are located at $(-5, 0)$ and $(5, 0)$.

The points $(-5, 0)$ and $(5, 0)$ are located outside of the ellipse.

This is incorrect. What mistake was made?

■ CONCEPTUAL ────────────────

**In Exercises 63–66, determine whether each statement is true or false.**

**63.** If you know the vertices of an ellipse, you can determine the equation for the ellipse.

**64.** If you know the foci and the endpoints of the minor axis, you can determine the equation for the ellipse.

**65.** Ellipses centered at the origin have symmetry with respect to the $x$-axis, $y$-axis, and the origin.

**66.** All ellipses are circles, but not all circles are ellipses.

**67.** How many ellipses, with major and minor axes parallel to the coordinate axes, have focus $(-2, 0)$ and pass through the point $(-2, 2)$?

**68.** How many ellipses have vertices $(-3, 0)$ and $(3, 0)$?

**69.** If two ellipses intersect each other, what is the minimum number of intersection points?

**70.** If two ellipses intersect each other, what is the maximum number of intersection points?

■ **CHALLENGE**

**71.** The eccentricity of an ellipse is defined as $e = \dfrac{c}{a}$. Compare the eccentricity of the orbit of Pluto to that of Earth (refer to Exercises 51 and 52).

**72.** The eccentricity of an ellipse is defined as $e = \dfrac{c}{a}$. Since $a > c > 0$, then $0 < e < 1$. Describe the shape of an ellipse when

   **a.** $e$ is close to zero
   **b.** $e$ is close to one
   **c.** $e = 0.5$

**73.** Find the equation of an ellipse centered at the origin containing the points $(1, 3)$ and $(4, 2)$.

**74.** Find the equation of an ellipse centered at the origin containing the points $\left(1, \dfrac{6\sqrt{5}}{5}\right)$ and $\left(-\dfrac{5}{3}, 2\right)$.

**75.** Find the equation of an ellipse centered at $(2, -3)$ that passes through the points $\left(1, -\dfrac{1}{3}\right)$ and $(5, -3)$.

**76.** Find the equation of an ellipse centered at $(1, -2)$ that passes through the points $(1, -4)$ and $(2, -2)$.

■ **TECHNOLOGY**

**77.** Graph the following three ellipses: $x^2 + y^2 = 1$, $x^2 + 5y^2 = 1$, and $x^2 + 10y^2 = 1$. What can be said to happen to the ellipse $x^2 + cy^2 = 1$ as $c$ increases?

**78.** Graph the following three ellipses: $x^2 + y^2 = 1$, $5x^2 + y^2 = 1$, and $10x^2 + y^2 = 1$. What can be said to happen to the ellipse $cx^2 + y^2 = 1$ as $c$ increases?

**79.** Graph the following three ellipses: $x^2 + y^2 = 1$, $5x^2 + 5y^2 = 1$, and $10x^2 + 10y^2 = 1$. What can be said to happen to the ellipse $cx^2 + cy^2 = 1$ as $c$ increases?

**80.** Graph the equation $\dfrac{x^2}{9} - \dfrac{y^2}{16} = 1$. Notice what a difference the sign makes. Is this an ellipse?

**81.** Graph the following three ellipses: $x^2 + y^2 = 1$, $0.5x^2 + y^2 = 1$, and $0.05x^2 + y^2 = 1$. What can be said to happen to ellipse $cx^2 + y^2 = 1$ as $c$ decreases?

**82.** Graph the following three ellipses: $x^2 + y^2 = 1$, $x^2 + 0.5y^2 = 1$, and $x^2 + 0.05y^2 = 1$. What can be said to happen to ellipse $x^2 + cy^2 = 1$ as $c$ decreases?

■ **PREVIEW TO CALCULUS**

In calculus, the derivative of a function is used to find its maximum and minimum values. In the case of an ellipse, with major and minor axes parallel to the coordinate axes, the maximum and minimum values correspond to the $y$-coordinate of the vertices that lie on its vertical axis of symmetry.

   In Exercises 83–86, find the maximum and minimum values of each ellipse.

**83.** $4x^2 + y^2 - 24x + 10y + 57 = 0$

**84.** $9x^2 + 4y^2 + 72x + 16y + 124 = 0$

**85.** $81x^2 + 100y^2 - 972x + 1600y + 1216 = 0$

**86.** $25x^2 + 16y^2 + 200x + 256y - 176 = 0$

SKILLS OBJECTIVES

- Find a hyperbola's foci and vertices.
- Find the equation of a hyperbola centered at the origin.
- Graph a hyperbola using asymptotes as graphing aids.
- Find the equation of a hyperbola centered at the point $(h, k)$.
- Solve applied problems that involve hyperbolas.

CONCEPTUAL OBJECTIVES

- Derive the general equation of a hyperbola.
- Identify, apply, and graph the transverse axis, vertices, and foci.
- Use asymptotes to determine the shape of a hyperbola.

## Hyperbola Centered at the Origin

The definition of a hyperbola is similar to the definition of an ellipse. An ellipse is the set of all points, the *sum* of whose distances from two points (the foci) is constant. A *hyperbola* is the set of all points, the *difference* of whose distances from two points (the foci) is constant. What distinguishes their equations is a minus sign.

**Ellipse** centered at the origin: $\quad \dfrac{x^2}{a^2} + \dfrac{y^2}{b^2} = 1$

**Hyperbola** centered at the origin: $\quad \dfrac{x^2}{a^2} - \dfrac{y^2}{b^2} = 1$

**DEFINITION**    **Hyperbola**

A **hyperbola** is the set of all points in a plane the difference of whose distances from two fixed points is a positive constant. These two fixed points are called **foci**. The hyperbola has two separate curves called **branches**. The two points where the hyperbola intersects the line joining the foci are called **vertices**. The line segment joining the vertices is called the **transverse axis of the hyperbola**. The midpoint of the transverse axis is called the **center**.

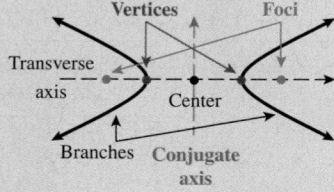

Let's consider a hyperbola with the center at the origin and the foci on the $x$-axis. Let the distance from the center to the focus be $c$. Therefore, the foci are located at the points $(-c, 0)$ and $(c, 0)$. The difference of the two distances from the foci to any point $(x, y)$ must be constant. We then can follow a similar analysis as done with an ellipse.

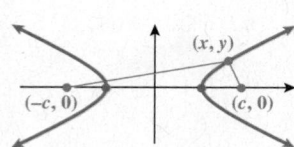

## Derivation of the Equation of a Hyperbola

| WORDS | MATH |
|---|---|
| The difference of these two distances is equal to a constant ($2a$ for convenience). | $$\sqrt{[x - (-c)]^2 + y^2} - \sqrt{(x - c)^2 + y^2} = \pm 2a$$ |
| Following the same procedure that we did with an ellipse leads to: | $$(c^2 - a^2)x^2 - a^2y^2 = a^2(c^2 - a^2)$$ |
| We can make the argument that $c > a$ in order for a point to be on the hyperbola (and not on the $x$-axis). Therefore, since $a$ and $c$ represent distances and therefore are positive, we know that $c^2 > a^2$, or $c^2 - a^2 > 0$. Hence, we can divide both sides of the equation by $c^2 - a^2$, since $c^2 - a^2 \neq 0$. | $$x^2 - \frac{a^2y^2}{(c^2 - a^2)} = a^2$$ |
| Let $b^2 = c^2 - a^2$. | $$x^2 - \frac{a^2y^2}{b^2} = a^2$$ |
| Divide both sides of the equation by $a^2$. | $$\frac{x^2}{a^2} - \frac{y^2}{b^2} = 1$$ |

The equation $\dfrac{x^2}{a^2} - \dfrac{y^2}{b^2} = 1$ represents a hyperbola with its center at the origin, with the foci along the $x$-axis. The following box summarizes hyperbolas that have their center at the origin and foci along either the $x$-axis or $y$-axis:

### EQUATION OF A HYPERBOLA WITH CENTER AT THE ORIGIN

The **standard form of the equation of a hyperbola** with its center at the origin is given by

| ORIENTATION OF TRANSVERSE AXIS | Horizontal (along the $x$-axis) | Vertical (along the $y$-axis) |
|---|---|---|
| EQUATION | $\dfrac{x^2}{a^2} - \dfrac{y^2}{b^2} = 1$ | $\dfrac{y^2}{a^2} - \dfrac{x^2}{b^2} = 1$ |
| FOCI | $(-c, 0)$ and $(c, 0)$ where $c^2 = a^2 + b^2$ | $(0, -c)$ and $(0, c)$ where $c^2 = a^2 + b^2$ |
| ASYMPTOTES | $y = \dfrac{b}{a}x$ and $y = -\dfrac{b}{a}x$ | $y = \dfrac{a}{b}x$ and $y = -\dfrac{a}{b}x$ |
| VERTICES | $(-a, 0)$ and $(a, 0)$ | $(0, -a)$ and $(0, a)$ |
| TRANSVERSE AXIS | Horizontal length $2a$ | Vertical length $2a$ |
| GRAPH | | |

Note that for $\dfrac{x^2}{a^2} - \dfrac{y^2}{b^2} = 1$, if $x = 0$, then $-\dfrac{y^2}{b^2} = 1$, which yields an imaginary number for $y$.

However, when $y = 0$, $\dfrac{x^2}{a^2} = 1$, and therefore $x = \pm a$. The vertices for this hyperbola are $(-a, 0)$ and $(a, 0)$.

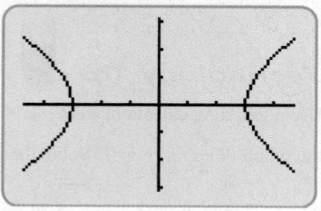
### EXAMPLE 1 Finding the Foci and Vertices of a Hyperbola Given the Equation

Find the foci and vertices of the hyperbola given by $\dfrac{x^2}{9} - \dfrac{y^2}{4} = 1$.

**Solution:**

Compare to the standard equation of a hyperbola, $\dfrac{x^2}{a^2} - \dfrac{y^2}{b^2} = 1$.    $a^2 = 9, b^2 = 4$

Solve for $a$ and $b$.    $a = 3, b = 2$

Substitute $a = 3$ into the vertices, $(-a, 0)$ and $(a, 0)$.    $(-3, 0)$ and $(3, 0)$

Substitute $a = 3, b = 2$ into $c^2 = a^2 + b^2$.    $c^2 = 3^2 + 2^2$

Solve for $c$.    $c^2 = 13$

$c = \sqrt{13}$

Substitute $c = \sqrt{13}$ into the foci, $(-c, 0)$ and $(c, 0)$.    $\left(-\sqrt{13}, 0\right)$ and $\left(\sqrt{13}, 0\right)$

The vertices are $\boxed{(-3, 0)}$ and $\boxed{(3, 0)}$, and the foci are $\boxed{\left(-\sqrt{13}, 0\right)}$ and $\boxed{\left(\sqrt{13}, 0\right)}$.

■ **YOUR TURN** Find the vertices and foci of the hyperbola $\dfrac{y^2}{16} - \dfrac{x^2}{20} = 1$.

### EXAMPLE 2 Finding the Equation of a Hyperbola Given Foci and Vertices

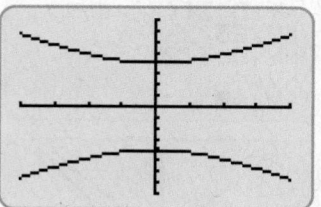
Find the standard form of the equation of a hyperbola whose vertices are located at $(0, -4)$ and $(0, 4)$ and whose foci are located at $(0, -5)$ and $(0, 5)$.

**Solution:**

The center is located at the midpoint of the segment joining the vertices.    $\left(\dfrac{0 + 0}{2}, \dfrac{-4 + 4}{2}\right) = (0, 0)$

Since the foci and vertices are located on the $y$-axis, the standard equation is given by:    $\dfrac{y^2}{a^2} - \dfrac{x^2}{b^2} = 1$

The vertices $(0, \pm a)$ and the foci $(0, \pm c)$ can be used to identify $a$ and $c$.    $a = 4, c = 5$

Substitute $a = 4, c = 5$ into $b^2 = c^2 - a^2$.    $b^2 = 5^2 - 4^2$

Solve for $b$.    $b^2 = 25 - 16 = 9$

$b = 3$

Substitute $a = 4$ and $b = 3$ into $\dfrac{y^2}{a^2} - \dfrac{x^2}{b^2} = 1$.    $\boxed{\dfrac{y^2}{16} - \dfrac{x^2}{9} = 1}$

■ **YOUR TURN** Find the equation of a hyperbola whose vertices are located at $(-2, 0)$ and $(2, 0)$ and whose foci are located at $(-4, 0)$ and $(4, 0)$.

## Graphing a Hyperbola Centered at the Origin

To graph a hyperbola, we use the vertices and asymptotes. The asymptotes are found by the equations $y = \pm\dfrac{b}{a}x$ or $y = \pm\dfrac{a}{b}x$, depending on whether the transverse axis is horizontal or vertical. An easy way to draw these graphing aids is to first draw the rectangular box that passes through the vertices and the points $(0, \pm b)$ or $(\pm b, 0)$. The **conjugate axis** is perpendicular to the transverse axis and has length $2b$. The asymptotes pass through the center of the hyperbola and the corners of the rectangular box.

$$\frac{x^2}{a^2} - \frac{y^2}{b^2} = 1 \qquad\qquad\qquad \frac{y^2}{a^2} - \frac{x^2}{b^2} = 1$$

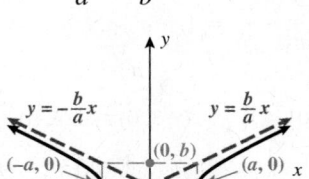

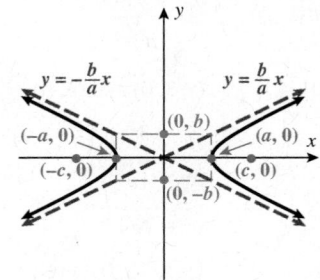

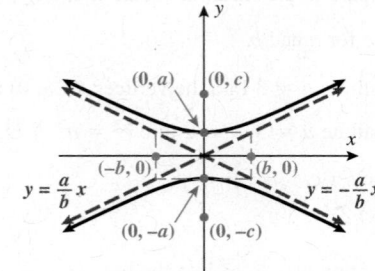

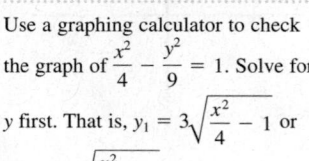

### Technology Tip

Use a graphing calculator to check the graph of $\dfrac{x^2}{4} - \dfrac{y^2}{9} = 1$. Solve for $y$ first. That is, $y_1 = 3\sqrt{\dfrac{x^2}{4} - 1}$ or $y_2 = -3\sqrt{\dfrac{x^2}{4} - 1}$.

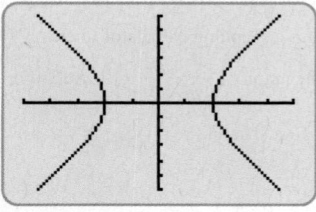

To add the two asymptotes, enter $y_3 = \frac{3}{2}x$ or $y_4 = -\frac{3}{2}x$.

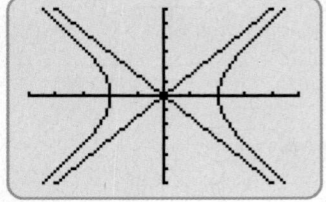

### EXAMPLE 3 Graphing a Hyperbola Centered at the Origin with a Horizontal Transverse Axis

Graph the hyperbola given by $\dfrac{x^2}{4} - \dfrac{y^2}{9} = 1$.

**Solution:**

Compare $\dfrac{x^2}{2^2} - \dfrac{y^2}{3^2} = 1$ to the general equation $\dfrac{x^2}{a^2} - \dfrac{y^2}{b^2} = 1$.

Identify $a$ and $b$. $\qquad\qquad\qquad\qquad\qquad\qquad a = 2$ and $b = 3$

The transverse axis of this hyperbola lies on the $x$-axis.

Label the vertices $(-a, 0) = (-2, 0)$ and $(a, 0) = (2, 0)$ and the points $(0, -b) = (0, -3)$ and $(0, b) = (0, 3)$. Draw the rectangular box that passes through those points. Draw the **asymptotes** that pass through the center and the corners of the rectangle.

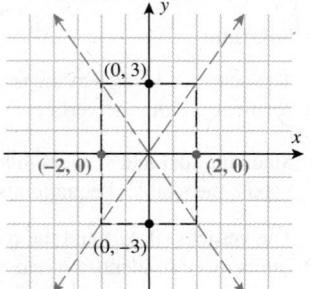

Draw the two **branches** of the hyperbola, each passing through a vertex and guided by the asymptotes.

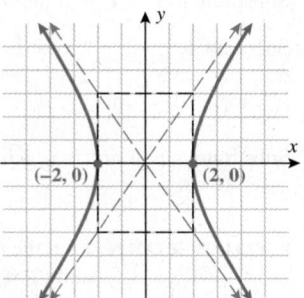

In Example 3, if we let $y = 0$, then $\frac{x^2}{4} = 1$ or $x = \pm 2$. Thus the vertices are $(-2, 0)$ and $(2, 0)$, and the transverse axis lies along the $x$-axis. Note that if $x = 0$, $y = \pm 3i$.

**EXAMPLE 4** **Graphing a Hyperbola Centered at the Origin with a Vertical Transverse Axis**

Graph the hyperbola given by $\frac{y^2}{16} - \frac{x^2}{4} = 1$.

**Solution:**

Compare $\frac{y^2}{4^2} - \frac{x^2}{2^2} = 1$ to the general equation $\frac{y^2}{a^2} - \frac{x^2}{b^2} = 1$.

Identify $a$ and $b$.            $a = 4$ and $b = 2$

The transverse axis of this hyperbola lies along the $y$-axis.

Label the vertices $(0, -a) = \mathbf{(0, -4)}$ and $(0, a) = \mathbf{(0, 4)}$, and the points $(-b, 0) = (-2, 0)$ and $(b, 0) = (2, 0)$. Draw the rectangular box that passes through those points. Draw the **asymptotes** that pass through the center and the corners of the rectangle.

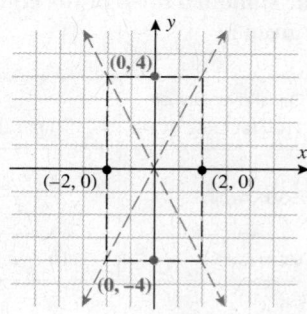

Draw the two **branches** of the hyperbola, each passing through a vertex and guided by the asymptotes.

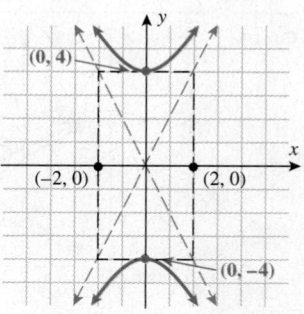

■ **YOUR TURN** Graph the hyperbolas:

     **a.** $\frac{y^2}{1} - \frac{x^2}{4} = 1$      **b.** $\frac{x^2}{4} - \frac{y^2}{1} = 1$

***Technology Tip***

Use a graphing calculator to check the graph of $\frac{y^2}{16} - \frac{x^2}{4} = 1$. Solve for $y$ first. That is, $y_1 = 4\sqrt{1 + \frac{x^2}{4}}$ or $y_2 = -4\sqrt{1 + \frac{x^2}{4}}$. To add the two asymptotes, enter $y_3 = 2x$ or $y_4 = -2x$.

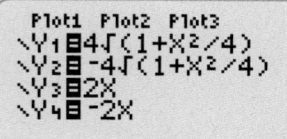

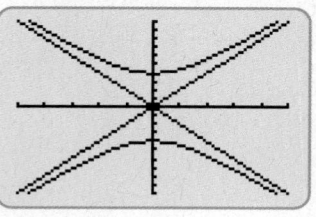

■ **Answer:**
    **a.**

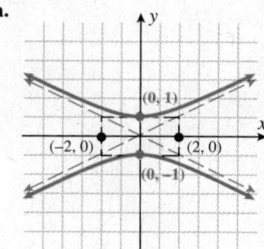

    **b.**

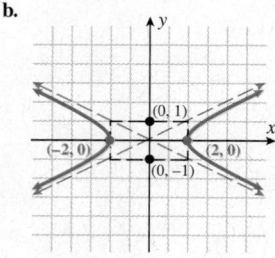

# Hyperbola Centered at the Point (h, k)

We can use graph-shifting techniques to graph hyperbolas that are centered at a point other than the origin—say, $(h, k)$. For example, to graph $\dfrac{(x-h)^2}{a^2} - \dfrac{(y-k)^2}{b^2} = 1$, start with the graph of $\dfrac{x^2}{a^2} - \dfrac{y^2}{b^2} = 1$ and shift to the right $h$ units and up $k$ units. The center, the vertices, the foci, the transverse and conjugate axes, and the asymptotes all shift. The following table summarizes the characteristics of hyperbolas centered at a point other than the origin:

## EQUATION OF A HYPERBOLA WITH CENTER AT THE POINT (*h, k*)

The **standard form of the equation of a hyperbola** with its center at the point $(h, k)$ is given by

| ORIENTATION OF TRANSVERSE AXIS | Horizontal (parallel to the *x*-axis) | Vertical (parallel to the *y*-axis) |
|---|---|---|
| EQUATION | $\dfrac{(x-h)^2}{a^2} - \dfrac{(y-k)^2}{b^2} = 1$ | $\dfrac{(y-k)^2}{a^2} - \dfrac{(x-h)^2}{b^2} = 1$ |
| VERTICES | $(h-a, k)$ and $(h+a, k)$ | $(h, k-a)$ and $(h, k+a)$ |
| FOCI | $(h-c, k)$ and $(h+c, k)$ where $c^2 = a^2 + b^2$ | $(h, k-c)$ and $(h, k+c)$ where $c^2 = a^2 + b^2$ |
| GRAPH | | |

**EXAMPLE 5**   **Graphing a Hyperbola with Center Not at the Origin**

Graph the hyperbola $\dfrac{(y-2)^2}{16} - \dfrac{(x-1)^2}{9} = 1$.

**Solution:**

Compare $\dfrac{(y-2)^2}{4^2} - \dfrac{(x-1)^2}{3^2} = 1$ to the general equation $\dfrac{(y-k)^2}{a^2} - \dfrac{(x-h)^2}{b^2} = 1$.

Identify $a$, $b$, and $(h, k)$.                        $a = 4$, $b = 3$, and $(h, k) = (1, 2)$

The transverse axis of this hyperbola lies along $x = 2$, which is parallel to the $y$-axis.

Label the vertices $(h, k - a) = (1, -2)$ and
$(h, k + a) = (1, 6)$ and the points $(h - b, k) = (-2, 2)$
and $(h + b, k) = (4, 2)$. Draw the rectangular box that
passes through those points. Draw the **asymptotes** that
pass through the center $(h, k) = (1, 2)$ and the corners
of the rectangle. Draw the two **branches** of the hyperbola,
each passing through a vertex and guided by the
asymptotes.

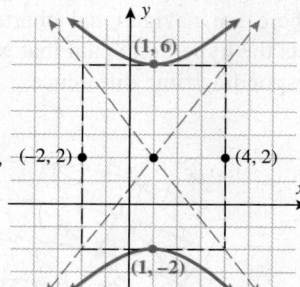

**Technology Tip**

Use a graphing calculator to check the
graph of $\dfrac{(y-2)^2}{16} - \dfrac{(x-1)^2}{9} = 1$.

Solve for $y$ first. That is,

$y_1 = 2 + 4\sqrt{1 + \dfrac{(x-1)^2}{9}}$  or

$y_2 = 2 - 4\sqrt{1 + \dfrac{(x-1)^2}{9}}$.

To add the two asymptotes, enter

$y_3 = \dfrac{4}{3}(x-1) + 2$  or

$y_4 = -\dfrac{4}{3}(x-1) + 2$.

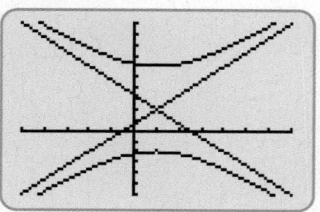

**EXAMPLE 6**   **Transforming an Equation of a Hyperbola to Standard Form**

Graph the hyperbola $9x^2 - 16y^2 - 18x + 32y - 151 = 0$.

**Solution:**

Complete the square on the $x$
terms and $y$ terms, respectively.

$$9(x^2 - 2x) - 16(y^2 - 2y) = 151$$

$$9(x^2 - 2x + 1) - 16(y^2 - 2y + 1) = 151 + 9 - 16$$

$$9(x-1)^2 - 16(y-1)^2 = 144$$

$$\frac{(x-1)^2}{16} - \frac{(y-1)^2}{9} = 1$$

Compare $\dfrac{(x-1)^2}{16} - \dfrac{(y-1)^2}{9} = 1$ to the general form $\dfrac{(x-h)^2}{a^2} - \dfrac{(y-k)^2}{b^2} = 1$.

Identify $a$, $b$, and $(h, k)$.                        $a = 4$, $b = 3$, and $(h, k) = (1, 1)$

The transverse axis of this hyperbola lies along $y = 1$.

Label the vertices $(h - a, k) = (-3, 1)$ and
$(h + a, k) = (5, 1)$ and the points
$(h, k - b) = (1, -2)$ and $(h, k + b) = (1, 4)$.
Draw the rectangular box that passes through these
points. Draw the **asymptotes** that pass through the
center $(1, 1)$ and the corners of the box. Draw the
two **branches** of the hyperbola, each passing through
a vertex and guided by the asymptotes.

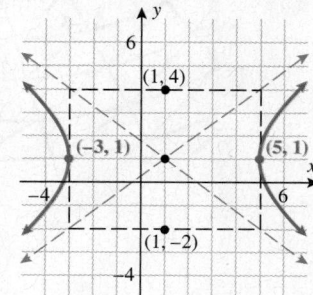

## Applications

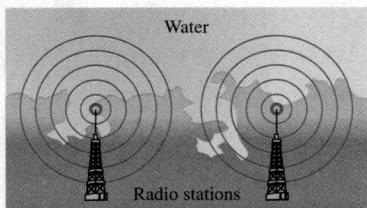

Nautical navigation is assisted by hyperbolas. For example, suppose that two radio stations on a coast are emitting simultaneous signals. If a boat is at sea, it will be slightly closer to one station than the other station, which results in a small time difference between the received signals from the two stations. Recall that a hyperbola is the set of all points whose differences of the distances from two points (the foci—or the radio stations) are constant. Therefore, if the boat follows the path associated with a constant time difference, that path will be hyperbolic.

The synchronized signals would intersect one another in associated hyperbolas. Each time difference corresponds to a different path. The radio stations are the foci of the hyperbolas. This principle forms the basis of a hyperbolic radio navigation system known as *LORAN* (**LO**ng-**RA**nge **N**avigation).

There are navigational charts that correspond to different time differences. A ship selects the hyperbolic path that will take it to the desired port, and the loran chart lists the corresponding time difference.

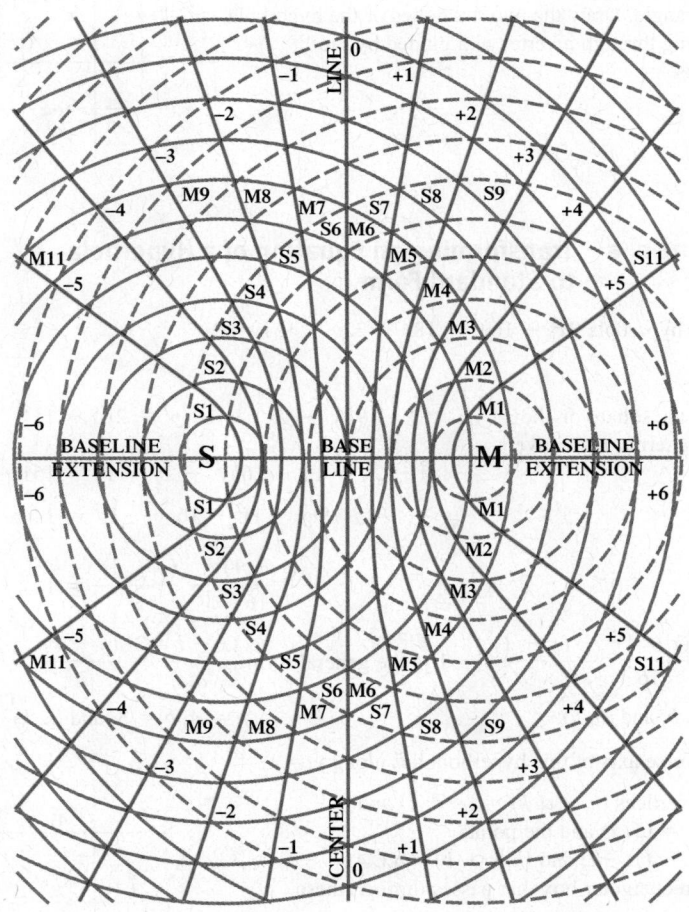

## EXAMPLE 7 Nautical Navigation Using Loran

Two LORAN stations are located 200 miles apart along a coast. If a ship records a time difference of 0.00043 second and continues on the hyperbolic path corresponding to that difference, where does it reach shore? Assume that the speed of the radio signal is 186,000 miles per second.

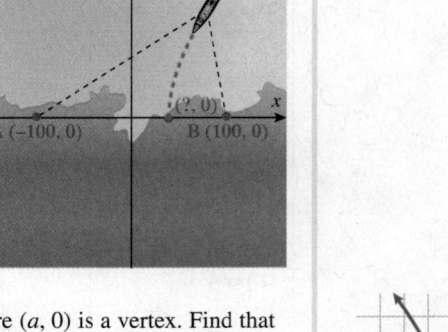

**Solution:**

Draw the $xy$-plane and the two stations corresponding to the foci at $(-100, 0)$ and $(100, 0)$. Draw the ship somewhere in quadrant I.

The hyperbola corresponds to a path where the difference of the distances between the ship and the respective stations remains constant. The constant is $2a$, where $(a, 0)$ is a vertex. Find that difference by using $d = rt$.

Substitute $r = 186{,}000$ miles/second and $t = 0.00043$ second into $d = rt$.

$$d = (186{,}000 \text{ miles/second})(0.00043 \text{ second}) \approx 80 \text{ miles}$$

Set the constant equal to $2a$.          $2a = 80$

Find a vertex $(a, 0)$.          $(40, 0)$

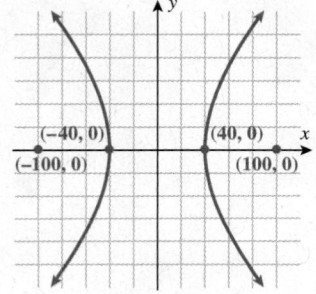

The ship reaches shore between the two stations, 60 miles from station B and 140 miles from station A.

## SECTION 9.4 SUMMARY

In this section, we discussed hyperbolas centered at the origin.

| | | |
|---|---|---|
| **EQUATION** | $\dfrac{x^2}{a^2} - \dfrac{y^2}{b^2} = 1$ | $\dfrac{y^2}{a^2} - \dfrac{x^2}{b^2} = 1$ |
| **TRANSVERSE AXIS** | Horizontal ($x$-axis), length $2a$ | Vertical ($y$-axis), length $2a$ |
| **CONJUGATE AXIS** | Vertical ($y$-axis), length $2b$ | Horizontal ($x$-axis), length $2b$ |
| **VERTICES** | $(-a, 0)$ and $(a, 0)$ | $(0, -a)$ and $(0, a)$ |
| **FOCI** | $(-c, 0)$ and $(c, 0)$ where $c^2 = a^2 + b^2$ | $(0, -c)$ and $(0, c)$ where $c^2 = a^2 + b^2$ |
| **ASYMPTOTE** | $y = \dfrac{b}{a}x$ and $y = -\dfrac{b}{a}x$ | $y = \dfrac{a}{b}x$ and $y = -\dfrac{a}{b}x$ |
| **GRAPH** | | |

For a hyperbola centered at $(h, k)$, the vertices, foci, and asymptotes all shift accordingly.

| ORIENTATION OF TRANSVERSE AXIS | Horizontal (parallel to the $x$-axis) | Vertical (parallel to the $y$-axis) |
|---|---|---|
| EQUATION | $\dfrac{(x-h)^2}{a^2} - \dfrac{(y-k)^2}{b^2} = 1$ | $\dfrac{(y-k)^2}{a^2} - \dfrac{(x-h)^2}{b^2} = 1$ |
| VERTICES | $(h-a, k)$ and $(h+a, k)$ | $(h, k-a)$ and $(h, k+a)$ |
| FOCI | $(h-c, k)$ and $(h+c, k)$ where $c^2 = a^2 + b^2$ | $(h, k-c)$ and $(h, k+c)$ where $c^2 = a^2 + b^2$ |
| GRAPH | $y = \dfrac{b}{a}(x-h)+k$   $y = -\dfrac{b}{a}(x-h)+k$   $(h, k+b)$   $(h-a, k)$   $(h, k)$   $(h+a, k)$   $(h, k-b)$ | $y = \dfrac{a}{b}(x-h)+k$   $(h, k+a)$   $(h-b, k)$   $(h, k)$   $(h+b, k)$   $(h, k-a)$   $y = -\dfrac{a}{b}(x-h)+k$ |

■ **SKILLS**

In Exercises 1–4, match each equation with the corresponding hyperbola.

**1.** $\dfrac{x^2}{36} - \dfrac{y^2}{16} = 1$     **2.** $\dfrac{y^2}{36} - \dfrac{x^2}{16} = 1$     **3.** $\dfrac{x^2}{8} - \dfrac{y^2}{72} = 1$     **4.** $4y^2 - x^2 = 1$

**a.**     **b.**     **c.**     **d.**

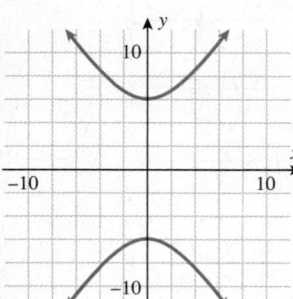 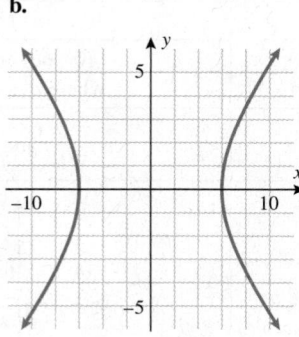 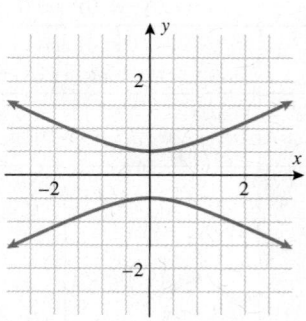 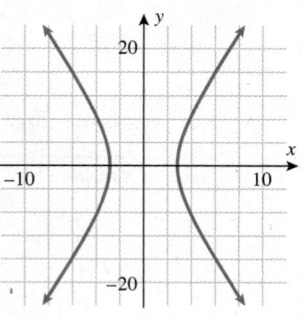

In Exercises 5–16, graph each hyperbola.

**5.** $\dfrac{x^2}{25} - \dfrac{y^2}{16} = 1$     **6.** $\dfrac{x^2}{49} - \dfrac{y^2}{9} = 1$     **7.** $\dfrac{y^2}{16} - \dfrac{x^2}{64} = 1$     **8.** $\dfrac{y^2}{144} - \dfrac{x^2}{25} = 1$

**9.** $\dfrac{x^2}{100} - y^2 = 1$     **10.** $9y^2 - 4x^2 = 36$     **11.** $\dfrac{4y^2}{9} - 81x^2 = 1$     **12.** $\dfrac{4}{25}x^2 - \dfrac{100}{9}y^2 = 1$

**13.** $4x^2 - y^2 = 16$     **14.** $y^2 - x^2 = 81$     **15.** $8y^2 - 16x^2 = 32$     **16.** $10x^2 - 25y^2 = 50$

**In Exercises 17–24, find the standard form of an equation of the hyperbola with the given characteristics.**

17. Vertices: $(-4, 0)$ and $(4, 0)$   Foci: $(-6, 0)$ and $(6, 0)$

18. Vertices: $(-1, 0)$ and $(1, 0)$   Foci: $(-3, 0)$ and $(3, 0)$

19. Vertices: $(0, -3)$ and $(0, 3)$   Foci: $(0, -4)$ and $(0, 4)$

20. Vertices: $(0, -1)$ and $(0, 1)$   Foci: $(0, -2)$ and $(0, 2)$

21. Center: $(0, 0)$; transverse: $x$-axis; asymptotes: $y = x$ and $y = -x$

22. Center: $(0, 0)$; transverse: $y$-axis; asymptotes: $y = x$ and $y = -x$

23. Center: $(0, 0)$; transverse axis: $y$-axis; asymptotes: $y = 2x$ and $y = -2x$

24. Center: $(0, 0)$; transverse axis: $x$-axis; asymptotes: $y = 2x$ and $y = -2x$

**In Exercises 25–28, match each equation with the hyperbola.**

25. $\dfrac{(x - 3)^2}{4} - \dfrac{(y + 2)^2}{25} = 1$

26. $\dfrac{(x + 3)^2}{4} - \dfrac{(y - 2)^2}{25} = 1$

27. $\dfrac{(y - 3)^2}{25} - \dfrac{(x + 2)^2}{4} = 1$

28. $\dfrac{(y + 3)^2}{25} - \dfrac{(x - 2)^2}{4} = 1$

a.

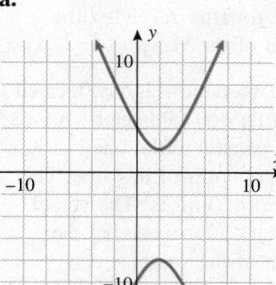

b.

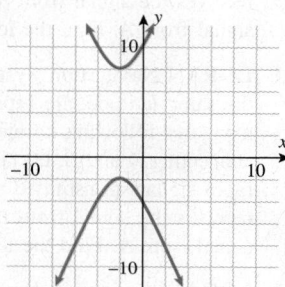

c.

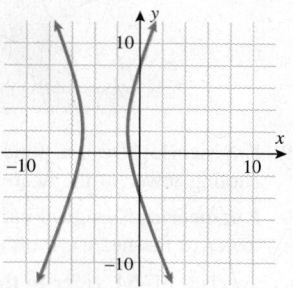

d.

**In Exercises 29–38, graph each hyperbola.**

29. $\dfrac{(x - 1)^2}{16} - \dfrac{(y - 2)^2}{4} = 1$

30. $\dfrac{(y + 1)^2}{36} - \dfrac{(x + 2)^2}{9} = 1$

31. $10(y + 3)^2 - (x - 4)^2 = 80$

32. $3(x + 3)^2 - 12(y - 4)^2 = 36$

33. $x^2 - 4x - 4y^2 = 0$

34. $-9x^2 + y^2 + 2y - 8 = 0$

35. $-9x^2 - 18x + 4y^2 - 8y - 41 = 0$

36. $25x^2 - 50x - 4y^2 - 8y - 79 = 0$

37. $x^2 - 6x - 4y^2 - 16y - 8 = 0$

38. $-4x^2 - 16x + y^2 - 2y - 19 = 0$

**In Exercises 39–42, find the standard form of the equation of a hyperbola with the given characteristics.**

39. Vertices: $(-2, 5)$ and $(6, 5)$    Foci: $(-3, 5)$ and $(7, 5)$

40. Vertices: $(1, -2)$ and $(3, -2)$    Foci: $(0, -2)$ and $(4, -2)$

41. Vertices: $(4, -7)$ and $(4, -1)$    Foci: $(4, -8)$ and $(4, 0)$

42. Vertices: $(2, -6)$ and $(2, -4)$    Foci: $(2, -7)$ and $(2, -3)$

## ■ APPLICATIONS

43. **Ship Navigation.** Two loran stations are located 150 miles apart along a coast. If a ship records a time difference of 0.0005 second and continues on the hyperbolic path corresponding to that difference, where will it reach shore?

44. **Ship Navigation.** Two loran stations are located 300 miles apart along a coast. If a ship records a time difference of 0.0007 second and continues on the hyperbolic path corresponding to that difference, where will it reach shore? Round to the nearest mile.

45. **Ship Navigation.** If the captain of the ship in Exercise 43 wants to reach shore between the stations and 30 miles from one of them, what time difference should he look for?

46. **Ship Navigation.** If the captain of the ship in Exercise 44 wants to reach shore between the stations and 50 miles from one of them, what time difference should he look for?

47. **Light.** If the light from a lamp casts a hyperbolic pattern on the wall due to its lampshade, calculate the equation of the hyperbola if the distance between the vertices is 2 feet and the foci are half a foot from the vertices.

48. **Special Ops.** A military special ops team is calibrating its recording devices used for passive ascertaining of enemy location. They place two recording stations, alpha and bravo, 3000 feet apart (alpha is due east of bravo). The team detonates small explosives 300 feet west of alpha and records the time it takes each station to register an explosion. The team also sets up a second set of explosives directly north of the alpha station. How many feet north of alpha should the team set off the explosives if it wants to record the same difference in times as on the first explosion?

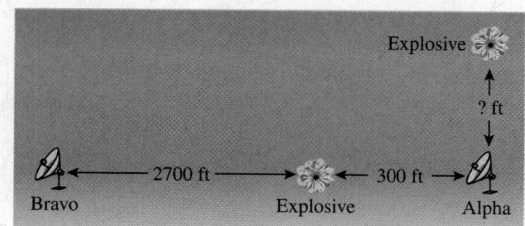

**For Exercises 49 and 50, refer to the following:**

Nuclear cooling towers are typically built in the shape of a hyperboloid. The cross section of a cooling tower forms a hyperbola. The cooling tower pictured is 450 feet tall and modeled by the equation $\dfrac{x^2}{8100} - \dfrac{y^2}{16,900} = 1$

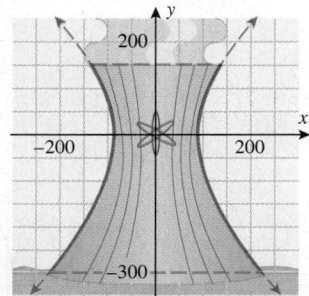

**49. Engineering/Design.** Find the diameter of the top of the cooling tower to the nearest foot.

**50. Engineering/Design.** Find the diameter of the base of the tower to the nearest foot.

**In Exercises 51–54, refer to the following:**

The navigation system loran (long-range navigation) uses the reflection properties of a hyperbola. Two synchronized radio signals are transmitted at a constant speed by two distant radio stations (foci of the hyperbola). Based on the order of arrival and the interval between the signals, the location of the craft along a branch of a hyperbola can be determined. The distance between the radio stations and the craft remains constant. With the help of a third station, the location of the craft can be determined exactly as the intersection of the branches of two hyperbolas.

**51. LORAN Navigation System.** Two radio stations, located at the same latitude, are separated by 200 kilometers. A vessel navigates following a trajectory parallel to the line connecting $A$ and $B$, 50 kilometers north of this line. The radio signal transmitted travels at 320 m/μs. The vessel receives the signal from $B$, 400 μs after receiving the signal from $A$. Find the location of the vessel.

**52. LORAN Navigation System.** Two radio stations, located at the same latitude, are separated by 300 kilometers. A vessel navigates following a trajectory parallel to the line connecting $A$ and $B$, 80 kilometers north of this line. The radio signals transmitted travel at 350 m/μs. The vessel receives the signal from $B$, 380 μs after receiving the signal from $A$. Find the location of the vessel.

**53. LORAN Navigation System.** Two radio stations, located at the same latitude, are separated by 460 kilometers. A vessel navigates following a trajectory parallel to the line connecting $A$ and $B$, 60 kilometers north of this line. The radio signals transmitted travel at 420 m/μs. The vessel receives the signal from $B$, 500 μs after receiving the signal from $A$. Find the location of the vessel.

**54. LORAN Navigation System.** Two radio stations, located at the same latitude, are separated by 520 kilometers. A vessel navigates following a trajectory parallel to the line connecting $A$ and $B$, 40 kilometers north of this line. The radio signals transmitted travel at 500 m/μs. The vessel receives the signal from $B$, 450 μs after receiving the signal from $A$. Find the location of the vessel.

## ■ CATCH THE MISTAKE

**In Exercises 55 and 56, explain the mistake that is made.**

**55.** Graph the hyperbola $\dfrac{y^2}{4} - \dfrac{x^2}{9} = 1$.

**Solution:**

Compare the equation to the standard form and solve for $a$ and $b$.     $a = 2, b = 3$

Label the vertices $(-a, 0)$ and $(a, 0)$.     $(-2, 0)$ and $(2, 0)$

Label the points $(0, -b)$ and $(0, b)$.     $(0, -3)$ and $(0, 3)$

Draw the rectangle connecting these four points, and align the asymptotes so that they pass through the center and the corner of the boxes. Then draw the hyperbola using the vertices and asymptotes.

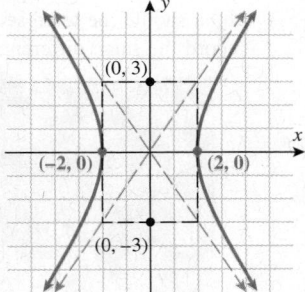

This is incorrect. What mistake was made?

**56.** Graph the hyperbola $\dfrac{x^2}{1} - \dfrac{y^2}{4} = 1$.

**Solution:**

Compare the equation to the general form and solve for $a$ and $b$.     $a = 2, b = 1$

Label the vertices $(-a, 0)$ and $(a, 0)$.     $(-2, 0)$ and $(2, 0)$

Label the points $(0, -b)$ and $(0, b)$.     $(0, -1)$ and $(0, 1)$

Draw the rectangle connecting these four points, and align the asymptotes so that they pass through the center and the corner of the boxes. Then draw the hyperbola using the vertices and asymptotes.

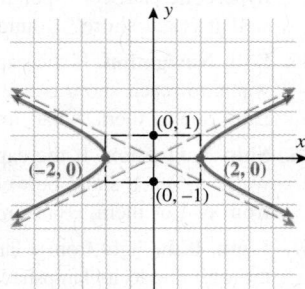

This is incorrect. What mistake was made?

## ■CONCEPTUAL

**In Exercises 57–60, determine whether each statement is true or false.**

**57.** If you know the vertices of a hyperbola, you can determine the equation for the hyperbola.

**58.** If you know the foci and vertices, you can determine the equation for the hyperbola.

**59.** Hyperbolas centered at the origin have symmetry with respect to the $x$-axis, $y$-axis, and the origin.

**60.** The center and foci are part of the graph of a hyperbola.

**61.** If the point $(p, q)$ lies on the hyperbola $\dfrac{x^2}{a^2} - \dfrac{y^2}{b^2} = 1$, find three other points that lie on the hyperbola.

**62.** Given the hyperbola $\dfrac{x^2}{4} - \dfrac{y^2}{b^2} = 1$, find $b$ such that the asymptotes are perpendicular to each other.

**63.** A vertical line intersects the hyperbola $\dfrac{x^2}{9} - \dfrac{y^2}{4} = 1$, at the point $(p, q)$, and intersects the hyperbola $\dfrac{x^2}{9} - \dfrac{y^2}{16} = 1$ at the point $(p, r)$. Determine the relationship between $q$ and $r$. Assume $p$, $r$, and $q$ are positive real numbers.

**64.** Does the line $y = \dfrac{2b}{a}x$ intersect the hyperbola $\dfrac{x^2}{a^2} - \dfrac{y^2}{b^2} = 1$?

## ■CHALLENGE

**65.** Find the general equation of a hyperbola whose asymptotes are perpendicular.

**66.** Find the general equation of a hyperbola whose vertices are $(3, -2)$ and $(-1, -2)$ and whose asymptotes are the lines $y = 2x - 4$ and $y = -2x$.

**67.** Find the asymptotes of the graph of the hyperbola given by $9y^2 - 16x^2 - 36y - 32x - 124 = 0$.

**68.** Find the asymptotes of the graph of the hyperbola given by $5x^2 - 4y^2 + 20x + 8y - 4 = 0$.

**69.** If the line $3x + 5y - 7 = 0$ is perpendicular to one of the asymptotes of the graph of the hyperbola given by $\dfrac{x^2}{a^2} - \dfrac{y^2}{b^2} = 1$ with vertices at $(\pm 3, 0)$, find the foci.

**70.** If the line $2x - y + 9 = 0$ is perpendicular to one of the asymptotes of the graph of the hyperbola given by $\dfrac{y^2}{a^2} - \dfrac{x^2}{b^2} = 1$ with vertices at $(0, \pm 1)$, find the foci.

## ■TECHNOLOGY

**71.** Graph the following three hyperbolas: $x^2 - y^2 = 1$, $x^2 - 5y^2 = 1$, and $x^2 - 10y^2 = 1$. What can be said to happen to the hyperbola $x^2 - cy^2 = 1$ as $c$ increases?

**72.** Graph the following three hyperbolas: $x^2 - y^2 = 1$, $5x^2 - y^2 = 1$, and $10x^2 - y^2 = 1$. What can be said to happen to the hyperbola $cx^2 - y^2 = 1$ as $c$ increases?

**73.** Graph the following three hyperbolas: $x^2 - y^2 = 1$, $0.5x^2 - y^2 = 1$, and $0.05x^2 - y^2 = 1$. What can be said to happen to the hyperbola $cx^2 - y^2 = 1$ as $c$ decreases?

**74.** Graph the following three hyperbolas: $x^2 - y^2 = 1$, $x^2 - 0.5y^2 = 1$, and $x^2 - 0.05y^2 = 1$. What can be said to happen to the hyperbola $x^2 - cy^2 = 1$ as $c$ decreases?

## ■PREVIEW TO CALCULUS

**In Exercises 75 and 76, refer to the following:**

In calculus, we study hyperbolic functions. The hyperbolic sine is defined by $\sinh u = \dfrac{e^u - e^{-u}}{2}$; the hyperbolic cosine is defined by $\cosh u = \dfrac{e^u + e^{-u}}{2}$.

**75.** If $x = \cosh u$ and $y = \sinh u$, show that $x^2 - y^2 = 1$.

**76.** If $x = \dfrac{e^u + e^{-u}}{e^u - e^{-u}}$ and $y = \dfrac{2}{e^u - e^{-u}}$, show that $x^2 - y^2 = 1$.

**In Exercises 77 and 78, refer to the following:**

In calculus, we use the difference quotient $\dfrac{f(x + h) - f(x)}{h}$ to find the derivative of the function $f$.

**77.** Find the derivative of $y = f(x)$, where $y^2 - x^2 = 1$ and $y < 0$.

**78.** Find the difference quotient of $y = f(x)$, where $4x^2 + y^2 = 1$ and $y > 0$.

### SKILLS OBJECTIVES

- Solve a system of nonlinear equations with elimination.
- Solve a system of nonlinear equations with substitution.
- Eliminate extraneous solutions.

### CONCEPTUAL OBJECTIVES

- Interpret the algebraic solution graphically.
- Understand the types of solutions: distinct number of solutions, no solution, and infinitely many solutions.
- Understand that equations of conic sections are nonlinear equations.

## Solving a System of Nonlinear Equations

In Chapter 8, we discussed solving systems of *linear* equations. We applied elimination and substitution to solve systems of linear equations in two variables, and we employed matrices to solve systems of linear equations in three or more variables. Recall that a system of linear equations in two variables has one of three types of solutions:

| | | |
|---|---|---|
| **One solution** | Two lines that intersect at one point | 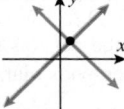 |
| **No solution** | Two parallel lines (never intersect) | 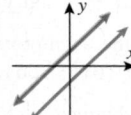 |
| **Infinitely many solutions** | Two lines that coincide (same line) | 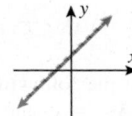 |

Notice that systems of *linear* equations in two variables always corresponded to *lines*. Now we turn our attention to systems of *nonlinear* equations in two variables. If any of the equations in a system of equations is nonlinear, then the system is a nonlinear system. The following are systems of nonlinear equations:

$$\begin{cases} y = x^2 + 1 \text{ (Parabola)} \\ y = 2x + 2 \text{ (Line)} \end{cases} \quad \begin{cases} x^2 + y^2 = 25 \text{ (Circle)} \\ y = x \text{ (Line)} \end{cases} \quad \begin{cases} \dfrac{x^2}{9} + \dfrac{y^2}{4} = 1 \text{ (Ellipse)} \\ \dfrac{y^2}{16} - \dfrac{x^2}{25} = 1 \text{ (Hyperbola)} \end{cases}$$

To find the solution to these systems, we ask the question, "At what point(s)—if any—do the graphs of these equations intersect?" Since some nonlinear equations represent conics, this is a convenient time to discuss systems of nonlinear equations.

How many points of intersection do a line and a parabola have? The answer depends on which line and which parabola. As we see in the following graphs, the answer can be one, two, or none.

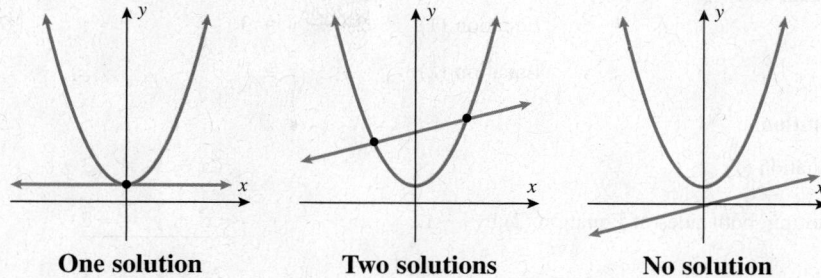

How many points of intersection do a parabola and an ellipse have? One, two, three, four, or no points of intersection correspond to one solution, two solutions, three solutions, four solutions, or no solution, respectively.

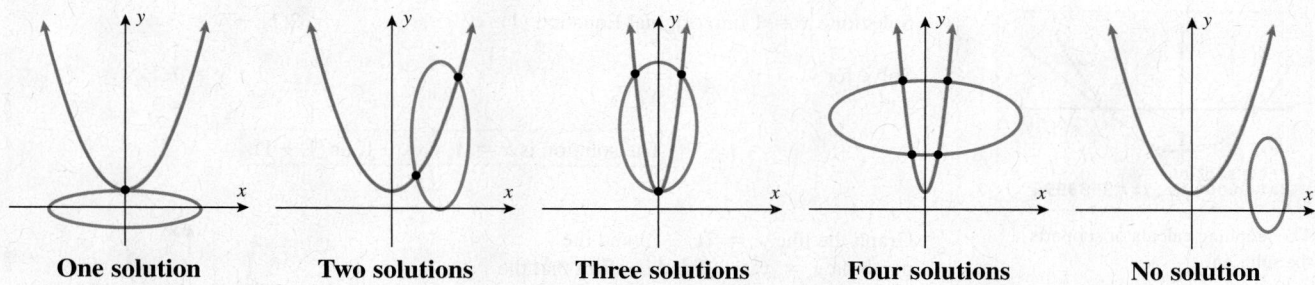

How many points of intersection do a parabola and a hyperbola have? The answer depends on which parabola and which hyperbola. As we see in the following graphs, the answer can be one, two, three, four, or none.

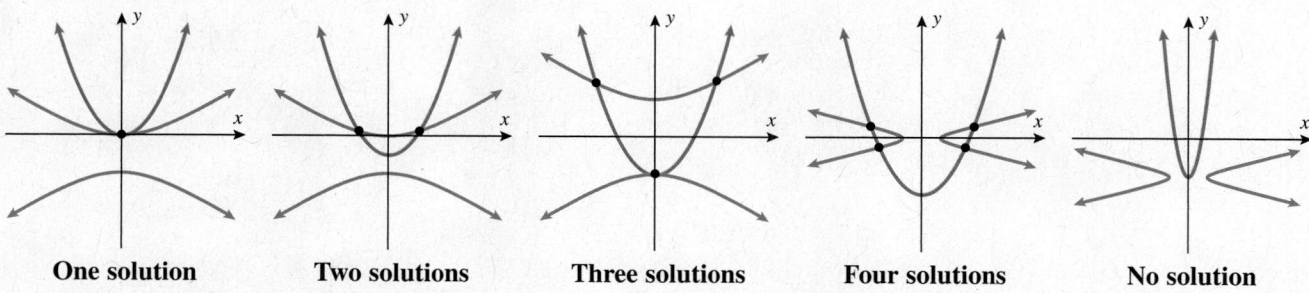

## Using Elimination to Solve Systems of Nonlinear Equations

The first three examples in this section use elimination to solve systems of two nonlinear equations. In linear systems, we can eliminate either variable. In nonlinear systems, the variable to eliminate is the one that is raised to the same power in both equations.

## Technology Tip

Use a graphing calculator to solve the system of equations. Solve for $y$ in each equation first; that is, $y_1 = 2x - 3$ and $y_2 = x^2 - 2$.

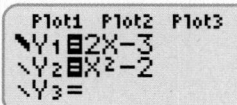

Use the keystrokes:

2nd CALC ▼ 5:Intersect
ENTER .

When prompted by the question "First curve?" type ENTER .

When prompted by the question "Second curve?" type ENTER .
When prompted by the question "Guess?" type ENTER .

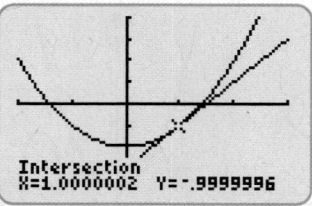

The graphing calculator supports the solution.

**EXAMPLE 1** **Solving a System of Two Nonlinear Equations by Elimination: One Solution**

Solve the system of equations, and graph the corresponding line and parabola to verify the answer.

$$\text{Equation (1):} \qquad 2x - y = 3$$
$$\text{Equation (2):} \qquad x^2 - y = 2$$

**Solution:**

| | |
|---|---|
| Equation (1): | $2x - y = \ \ 3$ |
| Multiply both sides of Equation (2) by $-1$. | $-x^2 + y = -2$ |
| Add. | $2x - x^2 = \ \ 1$ |
| Gather all terms to one side. | $x^2 - 2x + 1 = 0$ |
| Factor. | $(x - 1)^2 = 0$ |
| Solve for $x$. | $x = 1$ |
| Substitute $x = 1$ into original Equation (1). | $2(1) - y = 3$ |
| Solve for $y$. | $y = -1$ |

> The solution is $x = 1$, $y = -1$, or $(1, -1)$.

Graph the line $y = 2x - 3$ and the parabola $y = x^2 - 2$ and confirm that the point of intersection is $(1, -1)$.

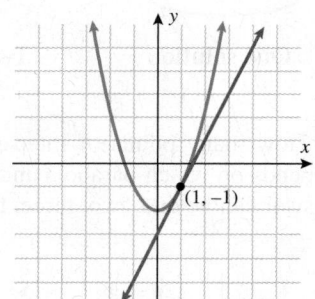

**EXAMPLE 2  Solving a System of Two Nonlinear Equations with Elimination: More Than One Solution**

Solve the system of equations, and graph the corresponding parabola and circle to verify the answer.

$$\text{Equation (1):} \quad -x^2 + y = -7$$

$$\text{Equation (2):} \quad x^2 + y^2 = 9$$

**Solution:**

| | |
|---|---|
| Equation (1): | $-x^2 + y = -7$ |
| Equation (2): | $x^2 + y^2 = \phantom{-}9$ |
| Add. | $y^2 + y = \phantom{-}2$ |
| Gather all terms to one side. | $y^2 + y - 2 = 0$ |
| Factor. | $(y + 2)(y - 1) = 0$ |
| Solve for $y$. | $y = -2 \quad \text{or} \quad y = 1$ |
| Substitute $y = -2$ into Equation (2). | $x^2 + (-2)^2 = 9$ |
| Solve for $x$. | $x = \pm\sqrt{5}$ |
| Substitute $y = 1$ into Equation (2). | $x^2 + (1)^2 = 9$ |
| Solve for $x$. | $x = \pm\sqrt{8} = \pm 2\sqrt{2}$ |

There are four solutions: $\boxed{\left(-\sqrt{5}, -2\right), \left(\sqrt{5}, -2\right), \left(-2\sqrt{2}, 1\right), \text{ and } \left(2\sqrt{2}, 1\right)}$

Graph the parabola $y = x^2 - 7$ and the circle $x^2 + y^2 = 9$ and confirm the four points of intersection.

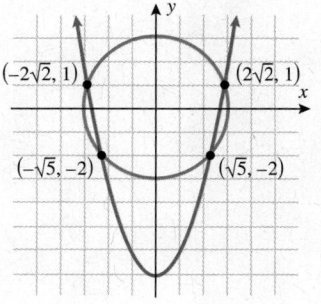

***Technology Tip***

Use a graphing calculator to solve the system of equations. Solve for $y$ in each equation first; that is, $y_1 = x^2 - 7$, $y_2 = \sqrt{9 - x^2}$, and $y_3 = -\sqrt{9 - x^2}$.

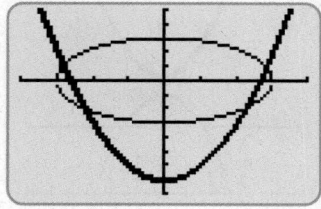

*Note:* The circle appears elliptical because the $x$- and $y$-axes are not of equal scale. The zoom square feature can give the appearance of a circle.

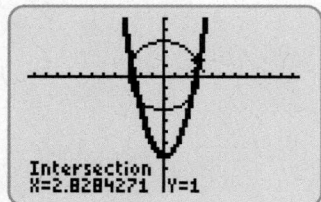

## Technology Tip

Use a graphing calculator to solve the system of equations. Solve for $y$ in each equation first; that is, $y_1 = -x^2 + 3$ and $y_2 = x^2 + 5$.

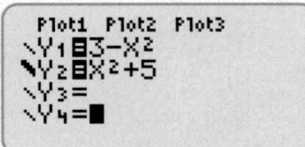

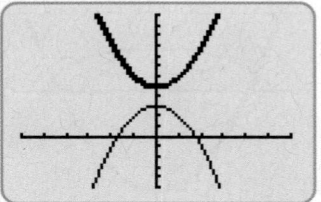

*Note:* The graphs do not intersect each other. There is no solution to the system.

**EXAMPLE 3   Solving a System of Two Nonlinear Equations with Elimination: No Solution**

Solve the system of equations, and graph the corresponding parabolas to verify the answer.

$$\text{Equation (1):} \qquad x^2 + y = 3$$

$$\text{Equation (2):} \qquad -x^2 + y = 5$$

**Solution:**

| | |
|---|---|
| Equation (1): | $x^2 + y = 3$ |
| Equation (2): | $-x^2 + y = 5$ |
| Add. | $2y = 8$ |
| Solve for $y$. | $y = 4$ |
| Substitute $y = 4$ into Equation (1). | $x^2 + 4 = 3$ |
| Simplify. | $x^2 = -1$ |

$x^2 = -1$ has no real solution.

There is   no solution   to this system of nonlinear equations.

Graph the parabola $x^2 + y = 3$ and the parabola $y = x^2 + 5$ and confirm there are no points of intersection.

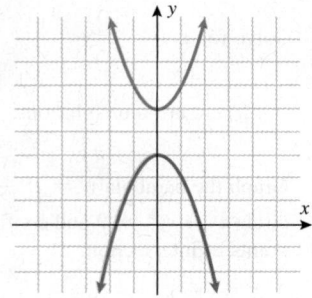

**EXAMPLE 4**   **Solving a System of Nonlinear Equations with Elimination**

Solve the system of nonlinear equations with elimination.

$$\text{Equation (1):} \quad \frac{x^2}{4} + y^2 = 1$$

$$\text{Equation (2):} \quad x^2 - y^2 = 1$$

**Solution:**

Add Equations (1) and (2) to eliminate $y^2$.

$$\frac{x^2}{4} + y^2 = 1$$
$$\underline{x^2 - y^2 = 1}$$
$$\frac{5}{4}x^2 = 2$$

Solve for $x$.

$$x^2 = \frac{8}{5}$$

$$x = \pm\sqrt{\frac{8}{5}}$$

Let $x = \pm\sqrt{\frac{8}{5}}$ in Equation (2).

$$\left(\pm\sqrt{\frac{8}{5}}\right)^2 - y^2 = 1$$

Solve for $y$.

$$y^2 = \frac{8}{5} - 1 = \frac{3}{5}$$

$$y = \pm\sqrt{\frac{3}{5}}$$

There are four solutions:

$$\left(-\sqrt{\frac{8}{5}}, -\sqrt{\frac{3}{5}}\right), \left(-\sqrt{\frac{8}{5}}, \sqrt{\frac{3}{5}}\right), \left(\sqrt{\frac{8}{5}}, -\sqrt{\frac{3}{5}}\right), \text{ and } \left(\sqrt{\frac{8}{5}}, \sqrt{\frac{3}{5}}\right)$$

A calculator can be used to approximate these solutions:

$$\sqrt{\frac{8}{5}} \approx 1.26$$

$$\sqrt{\frac{3}{5}} \approx 0.77$$

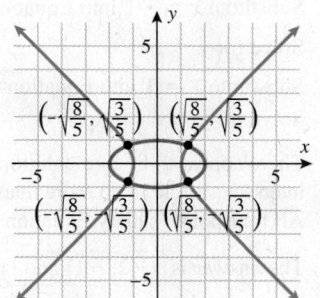

**■ Answer:**
**a.** $(-1, 2)$ and $(2, 5)$

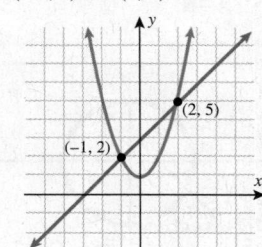

**b.** no solution

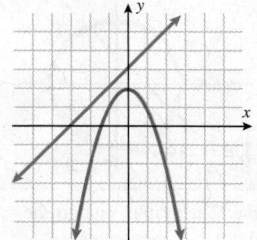

**c.** no solution

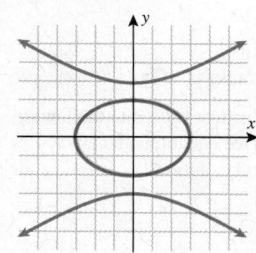

............................................................................................................

**■ YOUR TURN**  Solve the following systems of nonlinear equations:

**a.**  $-x + y = 3$
    $x^2 - y = -1$

**b.**  $x^2 + y = 2$
    $-x + y = 3$

**c.**  $\dfrac{x^2}{9} + \dfrac{y^2}{4} = 1$

    $\dfrac{y^2}{9} - \dfrac{x^2}{16} = 1$

## Using Substitution to Solve Systems of Nonlinear Equations

Elimination is based on the idea of eliminating one of the variables and solving the remaining equation in one variable. This is not always possible with nonlinear systems. For example, a system consisting of a circle and a line

$$x^2 + y^2 = 5$$
$$-x + y = 1$$

cannot be solved with elimination, because both variables are raised to different powers in each equation. We now turn to the substitution method. It is important to always check solutions, because extraneous solutions are possible.

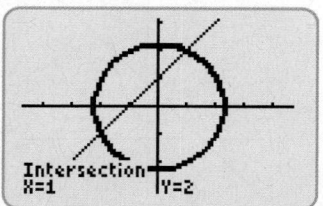
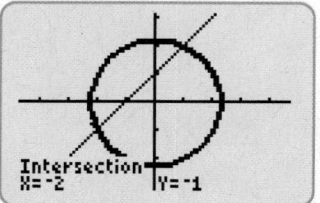
**■ Answer:** (2, 3) and (3, 2)

### EXAMPLE 5  Solving a System of Nonlinear Equations with Substitution

Solve the system of equations, and graph the corresponding circle and line to verify the answer.

Equation (1):    $x^2 + y^2 = 5$

Equation (2):    $-x + y = 1$

**Solution:**

Rewrite Equation (2) with $y$ isolated.

Equation (1): $\qquad\qquad\qquad\qquad\qquad\qquad x^2 + y^2 = 5$

Equation (2): $\qquad\qquad\qquad\qquad\qquad\qquad y = x + 1$

Substitute Equation (2), $y = x + 1$, into Equation (1). $\quad x^2 + (x + 1)^2 = 5$

Eliminate the parentheses. $\qquad\qquad\qquad\qquad x^2 + x^2 + 2x + 1 = 5$

Gather like terms. $\qquad\qquad\qquad\qquad\qquad\qquad 2x^2 + 2x - 4 = 0$

Divide by 2. $\qquad\qquad\qquad\qquad\qquad\qquad\qquad x^2 + x - 2 = 0$

Factor. $\qquad\qquad\qquad\qquad\qquad\qquad\qquad (x + 2)(x - 1) = 0$

Solve for $x$. $\qquad\qquad\qquad\qquad\qquad\qquad x = -2 \quad \text{or} \quad x = 1$

Substitute $x = -2$ into Equation (1). $\qquad\qquad (-2)^2 + y^2 = 5$

Solve for $y$. $\qquad\qquad\qquad\qquad\qquad\qquad y = -1 \quad \text{or} \quad y = 1$

Substitute $x = 1$ into Equation (1). $\qquad\qquad (1)^2 + y^2 = 5$

Solve for $y$. $\qquad\qquad\qquad\qquad\qquad\qquad y = -2 \quad \text{or} \quad y = 2$

There appear to be four solutions: $(-2, -1)$, $(-2, 1)$, $(1, -2)$, and $(1, 2)$, but a line can intersect a circle in no more than two points. Therefore, at least two solutions are *extraneous*. All four points satisfy Equation (1), but only $(-2, -1)$ and $(1, 2)$ also satisfy Equation (2).

The answer is $\boxed{(-2, -1) \text{ and } (1, 2)}$.

Graph the circle $x^2 + y^2 = 5$ and the line $y = x + 1$ and confirm the two points of intersection.

*Note:* After solving for $x$, had we substituted back into the linear Equation (2) instead of Equation (1), extraneous solutions would not have appeared. In general, **substitute back into the lowest-degree equation, and always check solutions.**

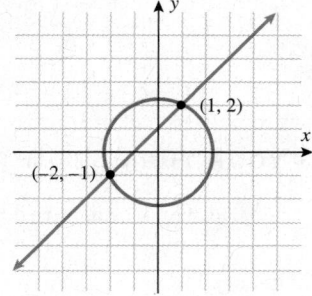

**■ YOUR TURN** Solve the system of equations $x^2 + y^2 = 13$ and $x + y = 5$.

In Example 6, the equation $xy = 2$ can also be shown to be a rotated hyperbola (Section 9.7). For now, we can express this equation in terms of a reciprocal function $y = \dfrac{2}{x}$, a topic we discussed in Section 1.2.

---

**EXAMPLE 6**   **Solving a System of Nonlinear Equations with Substitution**

Solve the system of equations.

$$\text{Equation (1):}\qquad x^2 + y^2 = 5$$

$$\text{Equation (2):}\qquad xy = 2$$

**Solution:**

Since Equation (2) tells us that $xy = 2$, we know that neither $x$ nor $y$ can be zero.

Solve Equation (2) for $y$.
$$y = \frac{2}{x}$$

Substitute $y = \dfrac{2}{x}$ into Equation (1).
$$x^2 + \left(\frac{2}{x}\right)^2 = 5$$

Eliminate the parentheses.
$$x^2 + \frac{4}{x^2} = 5$$

Multiply by $x^2$.
$$x^4 + 4 = 5x^2$$

Collect the terms to one side.
$$x^4 - 5x^2 + 4 = 0$$

Factor.
$$\left(x^2 - 4\right)\left(x^2 - 1\right) = 0$$

Solve for $x$.
$$x = \pm 2 \quad \text{or} \quad x = \pm 1$$

Substitute $x = -2$ into Equation (2), $xy = 2$, and solve for $y$.
$$y = -1$$

Substitute $x = 2$ into Equation (2), $xy = 2$, and solve for $y$.
$$y = 1$$

Substitute $x = -1$ into Equation (2), $xy = 2$, and solve for $y$.
$$y = -2$$

Substitute $x = 1$ into Equation (2), $xy = 2$, and solve for $y$.
$$y = 2$$

Check to see that there are four solutions: $\boxed{(-2, -1), (-1, -2), (2, 1), \text{ and } (1, 2)}$.

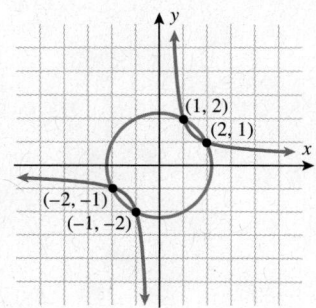

*Note:* It is important to check the solutions either algebraically or graphically (see the graph on the left).

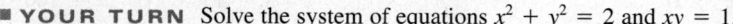

■ **YOUR TURN**   Solve the system of equations $x^2 + y^2 = 2$ and $xy = 1$.

■ **Answer:** $(-1, -1)$ and $(1, 1)$

## Applications

Use a graphing calculator to solve the system of equations. Solve for $y$ in each equation first; that is, $y_1 = \dfrac{400{,}000}{x}$ and $y_2 = 40 + \dfrac{237{,}600}{x-40}$.

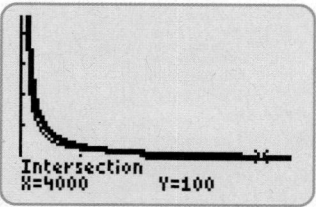

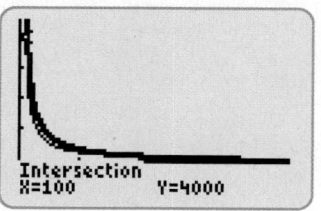

*Note:* The graphs support the solutions to the system.

### EXAMPLE 7   Calculating How Much Fence to Buy

A couple buy a rectangular piece of property advertised as 10 acres (approximately 400,000 square feet). They want two fences to divide the land into an internal grazing area and a surrounding riding path. If they want the riding path to be 20 feet wide, one fence will enclose the property and one internal fence will sit 20 feet inside the outer fence. If the internal grazing field is 237,600 square feet, how many linear feet of fencing should they buy?

**Solution:**

Use the five-step procedure for solving word problems from Section 0.1, and use two variables.

STEP 1  **Identify the question.**

How many linear feet of fence should they buy? Or, what is the sum of the perimeters of the two fences?

STEP 2  **Make notes or draw a sketch.**

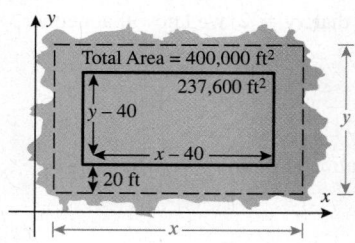

STEP 3  **Set up the equations.**

$x =$ length of property          $x - 40 =$ length of internal field
$y =$ width of property          $y - 40 =$ width of internal field

Equation (1):                  $xy = 400{,}000$

Equation (2):      $(x - 40)(y - 40) = 237{,}600$

STEP 4  **Solve the system of equations.**

*Substitution Method*

Since Equation (1) tells us that $xy = 400{,}000$, we know that neither $x$ nor $y$ can be zero.

Solve Equation (1) for $y$.                          $y = \dfrac{400{,}000}{x}$

Substitute $y = \dfrac{400{,}000}{x}$ into Equation (2).      $(x - 40)\left(\dfrac{400{,}000}{x} - 40\right) = 237{,}600$

Eliminate the parentheses.      $400{,}000 - 40x - \dfrac{16{,}000{,}000}{x} + 1600 = 237{,}600$

Multiply by the LCD, $x$.        $400{,}000x - 40x^2 - 16{,}000{,}000 + 1600x = 237{,}600x$

Collect like terms on one side.        $40x^2 - 164{,}000x + 16{,}000{,}000 = 0$

Divide by 40.                $x^2 - 4100x + 400{,}000 = 0$

Factor.                  $(x - 4000)(x - 100) = 0$

Solve for $x$.                $x = 4000$   or   $x = 100$

| | |
|---|---|
| Substitute $x = 4000$ into the original Equation (1). | $4000y = 400,000$ |
| Solve for $y$. | $y = 100$ |
| Substitute $x = 100$ into the original Equation (1). | $100y = 400,000$ |
| Solve for $y$. | $y = 4000$ |

The two solutions yield the same dimensions: $4000 \times 100$. The inner field has the dimensions $3960 \times 60$. Therefore, the sum of the perimeters of the two fences is

$$2(4000) + 2(100) + 2(3960) + 2(60) = 8000 + 200 + 7920 + 120 = 16,240$$

> The couple should buy 16,240 linear feet of fencing.

**STEP 5  Check the solution.**

The point $(4000, 100)$ satisfies both Equation (1) and Equation (2).

It is important to note that some nonlinear equations are not conic sections (they could be exponential, logarithmic, or higher-degree polynomial equations). These systems of linear equations are typically solved by the substitution method (see the exercises).

## SECTION 9.5 SUMMARY

In this section, systems of two equations were discussed when at least one of the equations is nonlinear (e.g., conics). The substitution method and elimination method can *sometimes* be applied to nonlinear systems. When graphing the two equations, the points of intersection are the solutions of the system. Systems of nonlinear equations can have more than one solution. Also, extraneous solutions can appear, so it is important to always check solutions.

## SECTION 9.5 EXERCISES

■ SKILLS

**In Exercises 1–12, solve the system of equations by applying the elimination method.**

**1.** $x^2 - y = -2$
   $-x + y = 4$

**2.** $x^2 + y = 2$
   $2x + y = -1$

**3.** $x^2 + y = 1$
   $2x + y = 2$

**4.** $x^2 - y = 2$
   $-2x + y = -3$

**5.** $x^2 + y = -5$
   $-x + y = 3$

**6.** $x^2 - y = -7$
   $x + y = -2$

**7.** $x^2 + y^2 = 1$
   $x^2 - y = -1$

**8.** $x^2 + y^2 = 1$
   $x^2 + y = -1$

**9.** $x^2 + y^2 = 3$
   $4x^2 + y = 0$

**10.** $x^2 + y^2 = 6$
   $-7x^2 + y = 0$

**11.** $x^2 + y^2 = -6$
   $-2x^2 + y = 7$

**12.** $x^2 + y^2 = 5$
   $3x^2 + y = 9$

**In Exercises 13–24, solve the system of equations by applying the substitution method.**

**13.** $x + y = 2$
$x^2 + y^2 = 2$

**14.** $x - y = -2$
$x^2 + y^2 = 2$

**15.** $xy = 4$
$x^2 + y^2 = 10$

**16.** $xy = -3$
$x^2 + y^2 = 12$

**17.** $y = x^2 - 3$
$y = -4x + 9$

**18.** $y = -x^2 + 5$
$y = 3x - 4$

**19.** $x^2 + xy - y^2 = 5$
$x - y = -1$

**20.** $x^2 + xy + y^2 = 13$
$x + y = -1$

**21.** $2x - y = 3$
$x^2 + y^2 - 2x + 6y = -9$

**22.** $x^2 + y^2 - 2x - 4y = 0$
$-2x + y = -3$

**23.** $4x^2 + 12xy + 9y^2 = 25$
$-2x + y = 1$

**24.** $-4xy + 4y^2 = 8$
$3x + y = 2$

**In Exercises 25–40, solve the system of equations by applying any method.**

**25.** $x^3 - y^3 = 63$
$x - y = 3$

**26.** $x^3 + y^3 = -26$
$x + y = -2$

**27.** $4x^2 - 3xy = -5$
$-x^2 + 3xy = 8$

**28.** $2x^2 + 5xy = 2$
$x^2 - xy = 1$

**29.** $2x^2 - xy = 28$
$4x^2 - 9xy = 28$

**30.** $-7xy + 2y^2 = -3$
$-3xy + y^2 = 0$

**31.** $4x^2 + 10y^2 = 26$
$-2x^2 + 2y^2 = -6$

**32.** $x^3 + y^3 = 19$
$x^3 - y^3 = -35$

**33.** $\log_x(2y) = 3$
$\log_x(y) = 2$

**34.** $\log_x(y) = 1$
$\log_x(2y) = \frac{1}{2}$

**35.** $\dfrac{1}{x^3} + \dfrac{1}{y^2} = 17$
$\dfrac{1}{x^3} - \dfrac{1}{y^2} = -1$

**36.** $\dfrac{2}{x^2} + \dfrac{3}{y^2} = \dfrac{5}{6}$
$\dfrac{4}{x^2} - \dfrac{9}{y^2} = 0$

**37.** $2x^2 + 4y^4 = -2$
$6x^2 + 3y^4 = -1$

**38.** $x^2 + y^2 = -2$
$x^2 + y^2 = -1$

**39.** $2x^2 - 5y^2 + 8 = 0$
$x^2 - 7y^2 + 4 = 0$

**40.** $x^2 + y^2 = 4x + 6y - 12$
$9x^2 + 4y^2 = 36x + 24y - 36$

**In Exercises 41 and 44, graph each equation and find the point(s) of intersection.**

**41.** The parabola $y = x^2 - 6x + 11$ and the line $y = -x + 7$

**42.** The circle $x^2 + y^2 - 4x - 2y + 5 = 0$ and the line $-x + 3y = 6$

**43.** The ellipse $9x^2 - 18x + 4y^2 + 8y - 23 = 0$ and the line $-3x + 2y = 1$.

**44.** The parabola $y = -x^2 + 2x$ and the circle $x^2 + 6x + y^2 - 4y + 12 = 0$.

**▪ APPLICATIONS**

**45. Numbers.** The sum of two numbers is 10, and the difference of their squares is 40. Find the numbers.

**46. Numbers.** The difference of two numbers is 3, and the difference of their squares is 51. Find the numbers.

**47. Numbers.** The product of two numbers is equal to the reciprocal of the difference of their reciprocals. The product of the two numbers is 72. Find the numbers.

**48. Numbers.** The ratio of the sum of two numbers to the difference of the two numbers is 9. The product of the two numbers is 80. Find the numbers.

**49. Geometry.** A rectangle has a perimeter of 36 centimeters and an area of 80 square centimeters. Find the dimensions of the rectangle.

**50. Geometry.** Two concentric circles have perimeters that add up to $16\pi$ and areas that add up to $34\pi$. Find the radii of the two circles.

**51. Horse Paddock.** An equestrian buys a 5-acre rectangular parcel (approximately 200,000 square feet) and is going to fence in the entire property and then divide the parcel into two halves with a fence. If 2200 linear feet of fencing is required, what are the dimensions of the parcel?

52. **Dog Run.** A family moves into a new home and decides to fence in the yard to give its dog room to roam. If the area that will be fenced in is rectangular and has an area of 11,250 square feet, and the length is twice as much as the width, how many linear feet of fence should the family buy?

53. **Footrace.** Your college algebra professor and Jeremy Wariner (2004 Olympic Gold Medalist in the men's 400 meter) decided to race. The race was 400 meters and Jeremy gave your professor a 1-minute head start, and still crossed the finish line 1 minute 40 seconds before your professor. If Jeremy ran five times faster than your professor, what was each person's average speed?

54. **Footrace.** You decided to race Jeremy Wariner for 800 meters. At that distance, Jeremy runs approximately twice as fast as you. He gave you a 1-minute head start and crossed the finish line 20 seconds before you. What were each of your average speeds?

55. **Velocity.** Two cars start moving simultaneously in the same direction. The first car moves at 50 miles per hour; the speed of the second car is 40 miles per hour. A half-hour later, another car starts moving in the same direction. The third car reaches the first one 1.5 hours after it reached the second car. Find the speed of the third car.

56. **Design.** Two boxes are constructed to contain the same volume. In the first box, the width is 16 centimeters larger than the depth and the length is five times the depth. In the second box, both the length and width are 4 centimeters shorter and the depth is 25% larger than in the first box. Find the dimensions of the second box.

57. **Numbers.** Find a number consisting of four digits such that

- the sum of the squares of the thousands and the units is 13.
- the sum of the squares of the hundreds and tens is 85.
- the hundreds is one more than the tens.
- the thousands is one more than the units.
- when 1089 is subtracted from the number, the result has the same digits but in inverse order.

58. **Numbers.** Find a number consisting of three digits such that

- the sum of the cubes of the hundreds and units is 9.
- the tens is one more than twice the hundreds.
- the hundreds is one more than the units.

■ **CATCH THE MISTAKE** ─────────────────────

**In Exercises 59 and 60, explain the mistake that is made.**

59. Solve the system of equations: $x^2 + y^2 = 4$
$x + y = 2$

**Solution:**

Multiply the second equation by $(-1)$ and add to the first equation. $\qquad x^2 - x = 2$

Subtract 2. $\qquad x^2 - x - 2 = 0$

Factor. $\qquad (x + 1)(x - 2) = 0$

Solve for $x$. $\qquad x = -1 \quad \text{and} \quad x = 2$

Substitute $x = -1$ and $x = 2$ into $x + y = 2$. $\qquad -1 + y = 2 \quad \text{and} \quad 2 + y = 2$

Solve for $y$. $\qquad y = 3 \quad \text{and} \quad y = 0$

The answer is $(-1, 3)$ and $(2, 0)$.

This is incorrect. What mistake was made?

60. Solve the system of equations: $x^2 + y^2 = 5$
$2x - y = 0$

**Solution:**

Solve the second equation for $y$. $\qquad y = 2x$

Substitute $y = 2x$ into the first equation. $\qquad x^2 + (2x)^2 = 5$

Eliminate the parentheses. $\qquad x^2 + 4x^2 = 5$

Gather like terms. $\qquad 5x^2 = 5$

Solve for $x$. $\qquad x = -1 \quad \text{and} \quad x = 1$

Substitute $x = -1$ into the first equation. $\qquad (-1)^2 + y^2 = 5$

Solve for $y$. $\qquad y = -2 \quad \text{and} \quad y = 2$

Substitute $x = 1$ into the first equation. $\qquad (1)^2 + y^2 = 5$

Solve for $y$. $\qquad y = -2 \quad \text{and} \quad y = 2$

The answers are $(-1, -2)$, $(-1, 2)$, $(1, -2)$, and $(1, 2)$.

This is incorrect. What mistake was made?

## ▪CONCEPTUAL

**In Exercises 61–64, determine whether each statement is true or false.**

**61.** A system of equations representing a line and a parabola can intersect in at most three points.

**62.** A system of equations representing a line and a cubic function can intersect in at most three places.

**63.** The elimination method can always be used to solve systems of two nonlinear equations.

**64.** The substitution method always works for solving systems of nonlinear equations.

**65.** A circle and a line have at most two points of intersection. A circle and a parabola have at most four points of intersection. What is the greatest number of points of intersection that a circle and an $n$th-degree polynomial can have?

**66.** A line and a parabola have at most two points of intersection. A line and a cubic function have at most three points of intersection. What is the greatest number of points of intersection that a line and an $n$th-degree polynomial can have?

## ▪CHALLENGE

**67.** Find a system of equations representing a line and a parabola that has only one real solution.

**68.** Find a system of equations representing a circle and a parabola that has only one real solution.

**In Exercises 69–72, solve each system of equations.**

**69.**
$$x^4 + 2x^2y^2 + y^4 = 25$$
$$x^4 - 2x^2y^2 + y^4 = 9$$

**70.**
$$x^4 + 2x^2y^2 + y^4 = 169$$
$$x^4 - 2x^2y^2 + y^4 = 25$$

**71.**
$$x^4 + 2x^2y^2 + y^4 = -25$$
$$x^4 - 2x^2y^2 + y^4 = -9$$

**72.**
$$x^4 + 2x^2y^2 + y^4 = -169$$
$$x^4 - 2x^2y^2 + y^4 = -25$$

## ▪TECHNOLOGY

**In Exercises 73–78, use a graphing utility to solve the systems of equations.**

**73.**
$$y = e^x$$
$$y = \ln x$$

**74.**
$$y = 10^x$$
$$y = \log x$$

**75.**
$$2x^3 + 4y^2 = 3$$
$$xy^3 = 7$$

**76.**
$$3x^4 - 2xy + 5y^2 = 19$$
$$x^4y = 5$$

**77.**
$$5x^3 + 2y^2 = 40$$
$$x^3y = 5$$

**78.**
$$4x^4 + 2xy + 3y^2 = 60$$
$$x^4y = 8 - 3x^4$$

## ▪PREVIEW TO CALCULUS

**In calculus, when finding the derivative of equations in two variables, we typically use implicit differentiation. A more direct approach is used when an equation can be solved for one variable in terms of the other variable.**

**In Exercises 79–82, solve each equation for $y$ in terms of $x$.**

**79.** $x^2 + 4y^2 = 8, y < 0$

**80.** $y^2 + 2xy + 4 = 0, y > 0$

**81.** $x^3y^3 = 9y, y > 0$

**82.** $3xy = -x^3y^2, y < 0$

## SKILLS OBJECTIVES

- Graph a nonlinear inequality in two variables.
- Graph a system of nonlinear inequalities in two variables.

## CONCEPTUAL OBJECTIVES

- Understand that a nonlinear inequality in two variables may be represented by either a bounded or an unbounded region.
- Interpret an overlapping shaded region as a solution.

## Nonlinear Inequalities in Two Variables

Linear inequalities are expressed in the form $Ax + By \leq C$. Specific expressions can involve either of the strict or either of the nonstrict inequalities. Examples of **nonlinear inequalities in two variables** are

$$9x^2 + 16y^2 \geq 1 \qquad x^2 + y^2 > 1 \qquad y \leq -x^2 + 3 \qquad \text{and} \qquad \frac{x^2}{20} - \frac{y^2}{81} < 1$$

We follow the same procedure as we did with linear inequalities. We change the inequality to an equal sign, graph the resulting nonlinear equation, test points from the two regions, and shade the region that makes the inequality true. For strict inequalities, $<$ or $>$, we use dashed curves, and for nonstrict inequalities, $\leq$ or $\geq$, we use solid curves.

 **EXAMPLE 1** **Graphing a Strict Nonlinear Inequality in Two Variables**

Graph the inequality $x^2 + y^2 > 1$.

**Solution:**

STEP 1 Change the inequality sign to an equal sign. $\qquad x^2 + y^2 = 1$

The equation is the equation of a circle.

STEP 2 Draw the graph of the circle.

The center is $(0, 0)$ and the radius is 1.

Since the inequality $>$ is a strict inequality, draw the circle as a **dashed** curve.

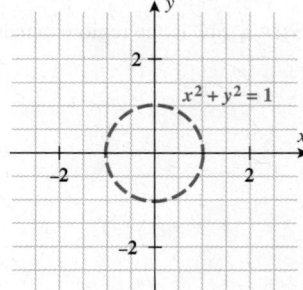

STEP 3 Test points in each region (outside the circle and inside the circle).

Substitute $(2, 0)$ into $x^2 + y^2 > 1$. $\qquad\qquad\qquad 4 \geq 1$

The point $(2, 0)$ satisfies the inequality.

Substitute $(0, 0)$ into $x^2 + y^2 > 1$. $\qquad\qquad\qquad 0 \geq 1$

The point $(0, 0)$ does not satisfy the inequality.

STEP 4 Shade the region containing the point $(2, 0)$.

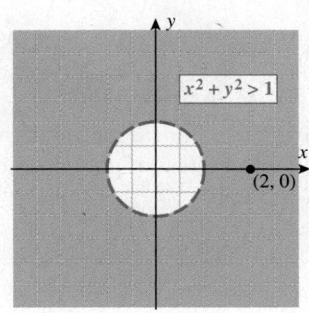

### Technology Tip

Use a graphing calculator to graph the inequality $y \leq -x^2 + 3$. Enter $y_1 = -x^2 + 3$. For $\leq$, use the arrow key to move the cursor to the left of $Y_1$ and type $\boxed{\text{ENTER}}$ until you see ◥.

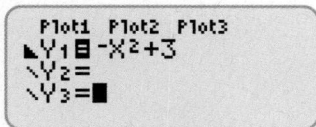

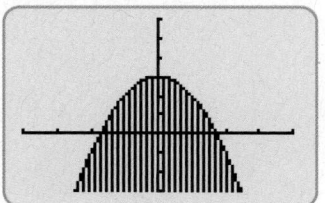

*Note:* The parabola should be drawn solid.

■ **Answer:**

**a.**

**b.**

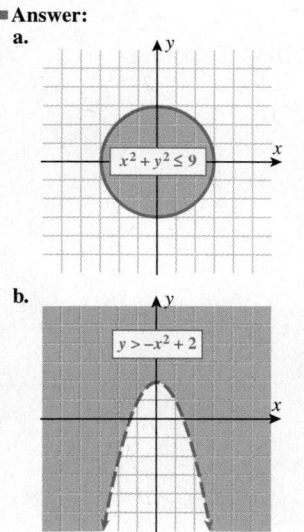

### EXAMPLE 2 Graphing a Nonstrict Nonlinear Inequality in Two Variables

Graph the inequality $y \leq -x^2 + 3$.

**Solution:**

STEP 1 Change the inequality sign to an equal sign. $\qquad y = -x^2 + 3$

The equation is that of a parabola.

STEP 2 Graph the parabola.

Reflect the base function, $f(x) = x^2$, about the $x$-axis and shift up three units. Since the inequality $\leq$ is a nonstrict inequality, draw the parabola as a **solid** curve.

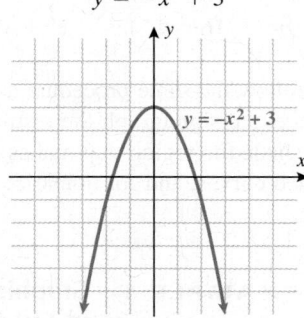

STEP 3 Test points in each region (inside the parabola and outside the parabola).

Substitute $(3, 0)$ into $y \leq -x^2 + 3$. $\qquad 0 \leq -6$

The point $(3, 0)$ does not satisfy the inequality.

Substitute $(0, 0)$ into $y \leq -x^2 + 3$. $\qquad 0 \leq 3$

The point $(0, 0)$ does satisfy the inequality.

STEP 4 Shade the region containing the point $(0, 0)$.

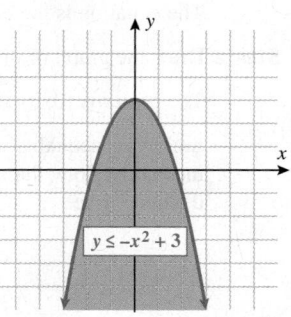

■ **YOUR TURN** Graph the following inequalities:

$\qquad$ **a.** $x^2 + y^2 \leq 9 \qquad$ **b.** $y > -x^2 + 2$

## Systems of Nonlinear Inequalities

To solve a system of inequalities, first graph the inequalities and shade the region containing the points that satisfy each inequality. The overlap of all the shaded regions is the solution.

**EXAMPLE 3** **Graphing a System of Inequalities**

Graph the solution to the system of inequalities: $y \geq x^2 - 1$
$\qquad\qquad\qquad\qquad\qquad\qquad y < x + 1$

**Solution:**

STEP 1 Change the inequality signs to equal signs.

$y = x^2 - 1$
$y = x + 1$

STEP 2 The resulting equations represent a parabola (to be drawn solid) and a line (to be drawn dashed). Graph the two equations.

To determine the points of intersection, set the $y$-values equal to each other.

$x^2 - 1 = x + 1$

Write the quadratic equation in standard form.

$x^2 - x - 2 = 0$

Factor.

$(x - 2)(x + 1) = 0$

Solve for $x$.

$x = 2 \quad \text{or} \quad x = -1$

Substitute $x = 2$ into $y = x + 1$.

$(2, 3)$

Substitute $x = -1$ into $y = x + 1$.

$(-1, 0)$

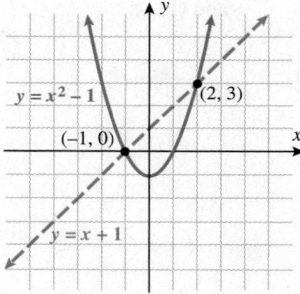

STEP 3 Test points and shade the regions.

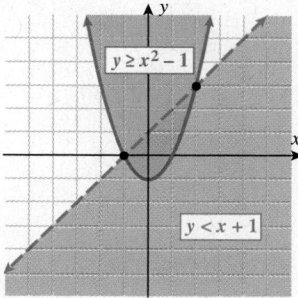

STEP 4 Shade the common region.

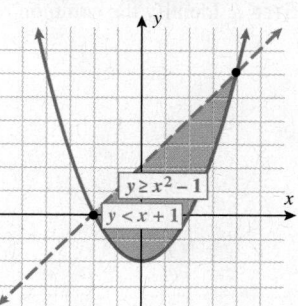

■ **YOUR TURN** Graph the solution to the system of inequalities: $x^2 + y^2 < 9$
$\qquad\qquad\qquad\qquad\qquad\qquad\qquad\qquad\qquad\qquad\qquad y > 0$

*Technology Tip*

Use a graphing calculator to graph the solution to the system of inequalities $y \geq x^2 - 1$ and $y < x + 1$.

First enter $y_2 = x^2 - 1$. For $\geq$, use the arrow key to move the cursor to the left of $Y_1$ and type ENTER until you see ◥. Next enter $y_2 = x + 1$. For $<$, use the arrow key to move the cursor to the left of $Y_1$ and type ENTER until you see ◣.

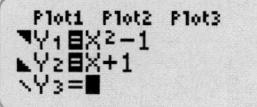

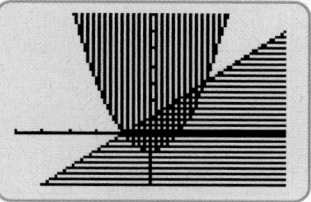

*Note:* The parabola should be drawn solid, and the line should be drawn dashed.

*Study Tip*

The points of intersection correspond to the vertices of the bounded region.

■ **Answer:**

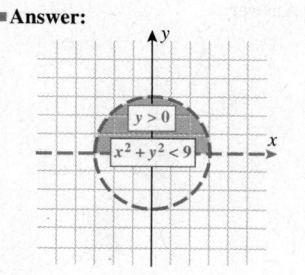

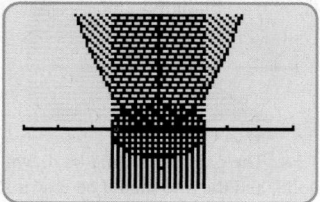
### EXAMPLE 4  Solving a System of Nonlinear Inequalities

Solve the system of inequalities:  $\begin{aligned} x^2 + y^2 &< 2 \\ y &\geq x^2 \end{aligned}$

**Solution:**

**STEP 1** Change the inequality signs to equal signs.
$$\begin{aligned} x^2 + y^2 &= 2 \\ y &= x^2 \end{aligned}$$

**STEP 2** The resulting equations correspond to a circle (to be drawn dashed) and a parabola (to be drawn solid). Graph the two inequalities.

To determine the points of intersection, solve the system of equations by substitution.
$$x^2 + \underbrace{\left(x^2\right)^2}_{y} = 2$$

$$x^4 + x^2 - 2 = 0$$

Factor.  $$\left(x^2 + 2\right)\left(x^2 - 1\right) = 0$$

Solve for $x$.  $$\underbrace{x^2 = -2}_{\text{no solution}} \quad \text{or} \quad \underbrace{x^2 = 1}_{x = \pm 1}$$

The points of intersection are $(-1, 1)$ and $(1, 1)$.

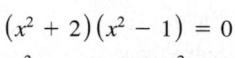

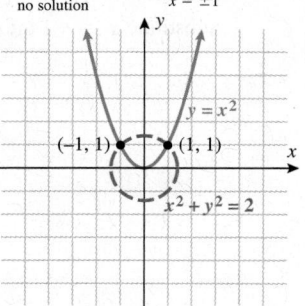

**STEP 3** Test points and shade the region.

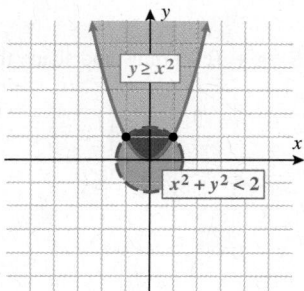

**STEP 4** Identify the common region as the solution.

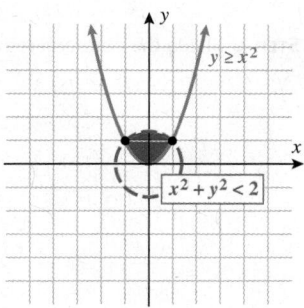

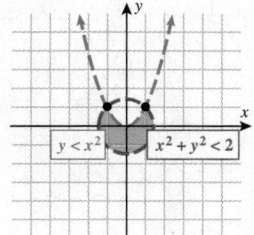
■ **YOUR TURN** Solve the system of inequalities:  $\begin{aligned} x^2 + y^2 &< 2 \\ y &< x^2 \end{aligned}$

It is important to note that any inequality based on an equation whose graph is not a line is considered a nonlinear inequality.

### EXAMPLE 5   Solving a System of Nonlinear Inequalities

Solve the system of inequalities:   $(x - 1)^2 + \dfrac{y^2}{4} < 1$

$$y \geq \sqrt{x}$$

**Solution:**

STEP 1  Change the inequality signs to equal signs.

$$(x - 1)^2 + \frac{y^2}{4} = 1$$
$$y = \sqrt{x}$$

STEP 2  The resulting equations correspond to an ellipse (to be drawn dashed) and the square-root function (to be drawn solid). Graph the two inequalities.

To determine the points of intersection, solve the system of equations by substitution.

$$(x - 1)^2 + \frac{(\sqrt{x})^2}{4} = 1$$

Multiply by 4.

$$4(x - 1)^2 + x = 4$$

Expand the binomial squared.

$$4(x^2 - 2x + 1) + x = 4$$

Distribute.

$$4x^2 - 8x + 4 + x = 4$$

Combine like terms and gather terms to one side.

$$4x^2 - 7x = 0$$

Factor.

$$x(4x - 7) = 0$$

Solve for $x$.

$$x = 0 \quad \text{and} \quad x = \frac{7}{4}$$

The points of intersection are $(0, 0)$ and $\left(\dfrac{7}{4}, \sqrt{\dfrac{7}{4}}\right)$.

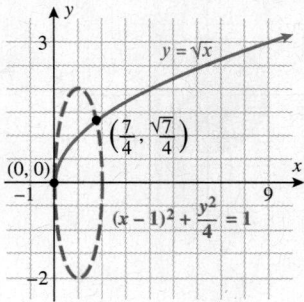

STEP 3  Shade the solution.

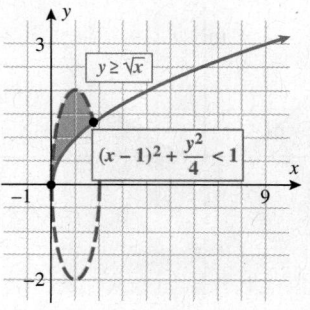

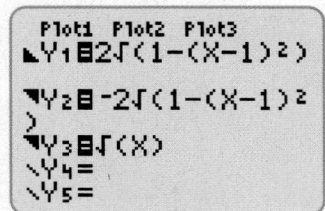
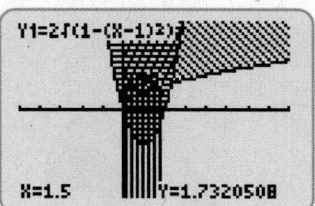

## SECTION
## 9.6 SUMMARY

In this section, we discussed nonlinear inequalities in two variables. Sometimes these result in bounded regions (e.g., $x^2 + y^2 \leq 1$), and sometimes these result in unbounded regions (e.g., $x^2 + y^2 > 1$).

When solving systems of inequalities, we first graph each of the inequalities separately and then look for the intersection (overlap) of all shaded regions.

## SECTION
## 9.6 EXERCISES

■ SKILLS

**In Exercises 1–12, match the nonlinear inequality with the correct graph.**

**1.** $x^2 + y^2 < 25$

**2.** $x^2 + y^2 \leq 9$

**3.** $\dfrac{x^2}{9} + \dfrac{y^2}{16} \geq 1$

**4.** $\dfrac{x^2}{4} + \dfrac{y^2}{9} > 1$

**5.** $y \geq x^2 - 3$

**6.** $x^2 \geq 16y$

**7.** $x \geq y^2 - 4$

**8.** $\dfrac{x^2}{9} + \dfrac{y^2}{25} \geq 1$

**9.** $9x^2 + 9y^2 < 36$

**10.** $(x - 2)^2 + (y + 3)^2 \leq 9$

**11.** $\dfrac{x^2}{4} - \dfrac{y^2}{9} \geq 1$

**12.** $\dfrac{y^2}{16} - \dfrac{x^2}{9} < 1$

**a.**

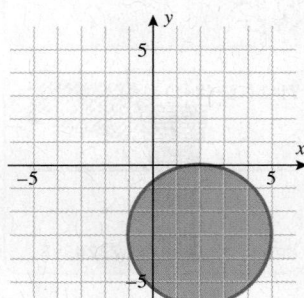

**b.**

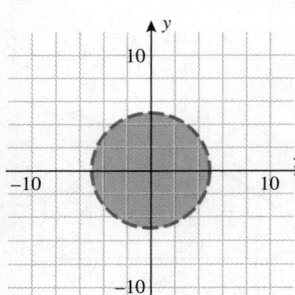

**c.**

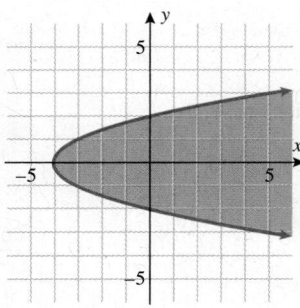

**d.**

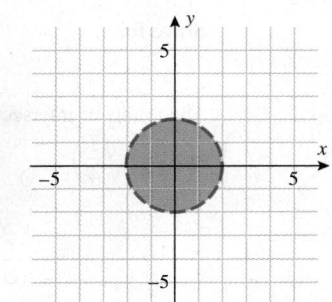

**e.**

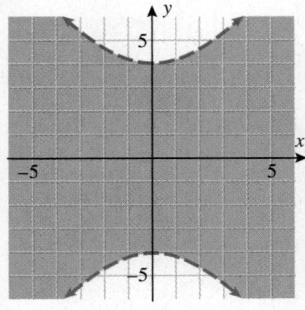

**f.**

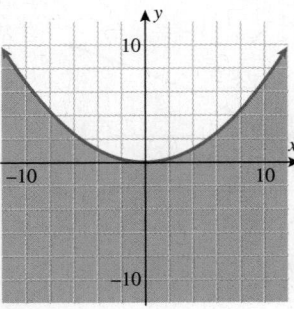

**g.**

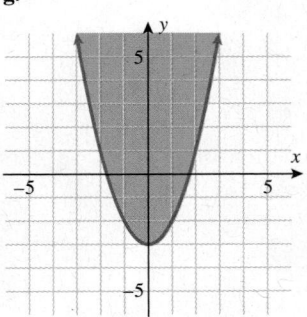

**h.**

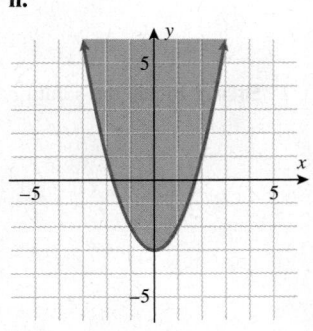

**i.**

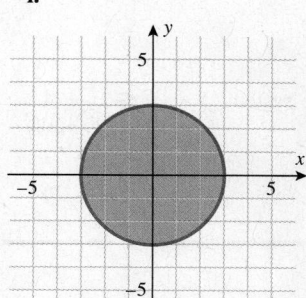

**j.**

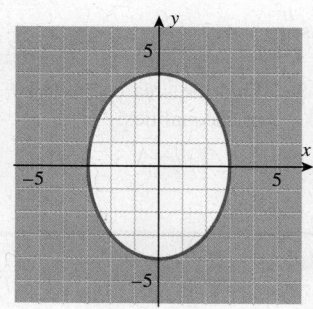

**k.**

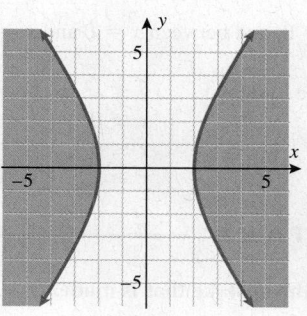

**l.**

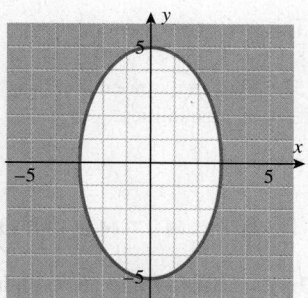

**In Exercises 13–30, graph the nonlinear inequality.**

**13.** $y \le x^2 - 2$

**14.** $y \ge -x^2 + 3$

**15.** $x^2 + y^2 > 4$

**16.** $x^2 + y^2 < 16$

**17.** $x^2 + y^2 - 2x + 4y + 4 \ge 0$

**18.** $x^2 + y^2 + 2x - 2y - 2 \le 0$

**19.** $3x^2 + 4y^2 \le 12$

**20.** $\dfrac{(x-2)^2}{9} + \dfrac{(y+1)^2}{25} > 1$

**21.** $9x^2 + 16y^2 - 18x + 96y + 9 > 0$

**22.** $\dfrac{(x-2)^2}{4} - \dfrac{(y+3)^2}{1} \ge 1$

**23.** $9x^2 - 4y^2 \ge 26$

**24.** $\dfrac{(y+1)^2}{9} - \dfrac{(x+2)^2}{16} < 1$

**25.** $36x^2 - 9y^2 \ge 324$

**26.** $25x^2 - 36y^2 + 200x + 144y - 644 \ge 0$

**27.** $y \ge e^x$

**28.** $y \le \ln x$

**29.** $y < -x^3$

**30.** $y > -x^4$

**In Exercises 31–50, graph each system of inequalities or indicate that the system has no solution.**

**31.** $y < x + 1$
  $y \le x^2$

**32.** $y < x^2 + 4x$
  $y \le 3 - x$

**33.** $y \ge 2 + x$
  $y \le 4 - x^2$

**34.** $y \ge (x - 2)^2$
  $y \le 4 - x$

**35.** $y \le -(x + 2)^2$
  $y > -5 + x$

**36.** $y \ge (x - 1)^2 + 2$
  $y \le 10 - x$

**37.** $-x^2 + y > -1$
  $x^2 + y < 1$

**38.** $x < -y^2 + 1$
  $x > y^2 - 1$

**39.** $y \ge x^2$
  $x \ge y^2$

**40.** $y < x^2$
  $x > y^2$

**41.** $x^2 + y^2 < 36$
  $2x + y > 3$

**42.** $x^2 + y^2 < 36$
  $y > 6$

**43.** $x^2 + y^2 < 25$
  $y \ge 6 + x$

**44.** $(x - 1)^2 + (y + 2)^2 \le 36$
  $y \ge x - 3$

**45.** $x^2 + y^2 \le 9$
  $y \ge 1 + x^2$

**46.** $x^2 + y^2 \ge 16$
  $x^2 + (y - 3)^2 \le 9$

**47.** $x^2 - y^2 < 4$
  $y > 1 - x^2$

**48.** $\dfrac{x^2}{4} - \dfrac{y^2}{9} \le 1$
  $y \ge x - 5$

**49.** $y < e^x$
  $y > \ln x \qquad x > 0$

**50.** $y < 10^x$
  $y > \log x \qquad x > 0$

## ▪ APPLICATIONS

**51.** Find the area enclosed by the system of inequalities.
  $x^2 + y^2 < 9$
  $x > 0$

**52.** Find the area enclosed by the system of inequalities.
  $x^2 + y^2 \le 5$
  $x \le 0$
  $y \ge 0$

**In Exercises 53 and 54, refer to the following:**

The area enclosed by the ellipse $\dfrac{x^2}{a^2} + \dfrac{y^2}{b^2} = 1$ is given by $ab\pi$.

**53.** Find the area enclosed by the system of inequalities.
  $4x^2 + y^2 \le 16$
  $x \le 0$
  $y \ge 0$

**54.** Find the area enclosed by the system of inequalities.
  $9x^2 + 4y^2 \ge 36$
  $x^2 + y^2 \le 9$

**In Exercises 55 and 56, refer to the following:**

The area below $y = x^2$, above $y = 0$, and between $x = 0$ and $x = a$ is $\dfrac{a^3}{3}$.

**55.** Find the area enclosed by the system of inequalities.

$$y \le x^2$$
$$x \ge 0$$
$$x \le 6$$
$$y \ge x - 6$$

**56.** Find the area enclosed by the system of inequalities.

$$y \le x^2 + 4$$
$$y \ge x$$
$$x \ge -3$$
$$x \le 3$$

## ■ CATCH THE MISTAKE

**In Exercises 57 and 58, explain the mistake that is made.**

**57.** Graph the system of inequalities: $\quad x^2 + y^2 < 1$
$$x^2 + y^2 > 4$$

**Solution:**

Draw the circles
$x^2 + y^2 = 1$ and
$x^2 + y^2 = 4$.

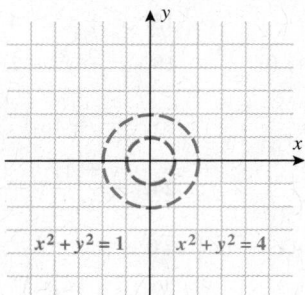

Shade outside $x^2 + y^2 = 1$
and inside $x^2 + y^2 = 4$.

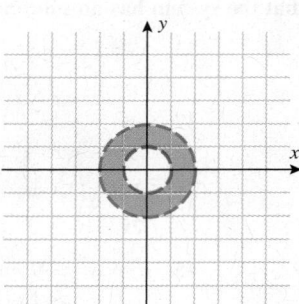

This is incorrect. What mistake was made?

**58.** Graph the system of inequalities: $\quad x > -y^2 + 1$
$$x < y^2 - 1$$

**Solution:**

Draw the parabolas
$x = -y^2 + 1$ and
$x = y^2 - 1$.

Shade the region
between the curves.

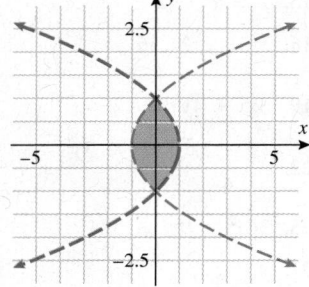

This is incorrect. What mistake was made?

## ■ CONCEPTUAL

**In Exercises 59–66, determine whether each statement is true or false.**

**59.** A nonlinear inequality always represents a bounded region.

**60.** A system of inequalities always has a solution.

**61.** The solution to the following system of equations is symmetric with respect to the y-axis:

$$\frac{x^2}{a^2} - \frac{y^2}{b^2} \le 1$$
$$y \ge x^2 - 2a$$

**62.** The solution to the following system of equations is symmetric with respect to the origin:

$$\frac{x^2}{a^2} - \frac{y^2}{b^2} \le 1$$
$$y \ge \sqrt[3]{x}$$

**63.** The solution to the following system of equations is symmetric with respect to the origin:

$$\frac{x^2}{a^2} - \frac{y^2}{b^2} \ge 1$$
$$\frac{x^2}{4a^2} + \frac{y^2}{a^2} \le 1$$

**64.** The solution to the following system of equations is bounded:

$$\frac{x^2}{a^2} - \frac{y^2}{b^2} \le 1$$
$$x \ge -2a$$
$$x \le 2a$$

**65.** The following systems of inequalities have the same solution:

$$16x^2 - 25y^2 \geq 400$$
$$x \geq -6$$
$$x \leq 6$$

$$\frac{y^2}{25} - \frac{x^2}{16} \geq 1$$
$$y \geq -6$$
$$y \leq 6$$

**66.** The solution to the following system of inequalities is unbounded:

$$\frac{x^2}{a^2} - \frac{y^2}{b^2} \leq 1$$
$$\frac{y^2}{a^2} - \frac{x^2}{b^2} \leq 1$$

■ CHALLENGE

**67.** For the system of nonlinear inequalities $\begin{aligned}x^2 + y^2 \geq a^2 \\ x^2 + y^2 \leq b^2\end{aligned}$, what restriction must be placed on the values of $a$ and $b$ for this system to have a solution? Assume that $a$ and $b$ are real numbers.

**68.** Can $x^2 + y^2 < -1$ ever have a real solution? What types of numbers would $x$ and/or $y$ have to be to satisfy this inequality?

**69.** Find a positive real number $a$ such that the area enclosed by the curves is the same.

$$x^2 + y^2 = 144 \quad \text{and} \quad \frac{x^2}{a^2} + \frac{y^2}{4^2} = 1$$

**70.** If the area of the regions enclosed by $x^2 + y^2 = 1$ and $\frac{x^2}{a^2} + \frac{y^2}{b^2} = 1$ are equal, what can you say about $a$ and $b$?

**71.** If the solution to

$$4x^2 + 9y^2 \leq 36$$
$$(x - h)^2 \leq 4y$$

is symmetric with respect to the $y$-axis, what can you say about $h$?

**72.** The solution to

$$\frac{x^2}{a^2} + \frac{y^2}{b^2} \leq 1$$
$$y \geq x$$

is located in quadrants I, II, and III. If the sections in quadrants I and III have the same area, what can you say about $a$ and $b$?

■ TECHNOLOGY

**In Exercises 73–80, use a graphing utility to graph the inequalities.**

**73.** $x^2 + y^2 - 2x + 4y + 4 \geq 0$

**74.** $x^2 + y^2 + 2x - 2y - 2 \leq 0$

**75.** $y \geq e^x$

**76.** $y \leq \ln x$

**77.** $y < e^x$
$y > \ln x \quad x > 0$

**78.** $y < 10^x$
$y > \log x \quad x > 0$

**79.** $x^2 - 4y^2 + 5x - 6y + 18 \geq 0$

**80.** $x^2 - 2xy + 4y^2 + 10x - 25 \leq 0$

■ PREVIEW TO CALCULUS

**In calculus, the problem of finding the area enclosed by a set of curves can be seen as the problem of finding the area enclosed by a system of inequalities.**

**In Exercises 81–84, graph the system of inequalities.**

**81.** $y \leq x^3 - x$
$y \geq x^2 - 1$

**82.** $y \leq x^3$
$y \geq 2x - x^2$

**83.** $y \geq x^3 - 2x^2$
$y \leq x^2$
$y \leq 5$

**84.** $y \leq \sqrt{1 - x^2}$
$y \geq x^2$
$y \leq 2x$

SKILLS OBJECTIVES

- Transform general second-degree equations into recognizable equations of conics by analyzing rotation of axes.
- Determine the angle of rotation that will transform a general second-degree equation into a familiar equation of a conic section.
- Graph a rotated conic.

CONCEPTUAL OBJECTIVE

- Understand how the equation of a conic section is altered by rotation of axes.

## Rotation of Axes Formulas

In Sections 9.1 through 9.4, we learned to recognize equations of parabolas, ellipses, and hyperbolas that were centered at any point in the Cartesian plane and whose vertices and foci were aligned either along or parallel to either the $x$-axis or the $y$-axis. We learned, for example, that the equation of an ellipse centered at the origin takes the form

$$\frac{x^2}{a^2} + \frac{y^2}{b^2} = 1$$

where the major and minor axes are, respectively, either the $x$- or the $y$-axis depending on whether $a$ is greater than or less than $b$. Now let us look at an equation of a conic section whose graph is *not* aligned with the $x$- or $y$-axis: the equation $5x^2 - 8xy + 5y^2 - 9 = 0$.

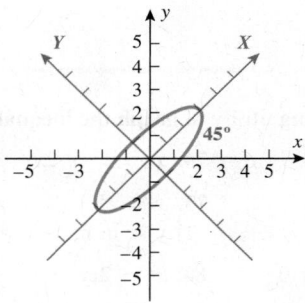

This graph can be thought of as an ellipse that started with the major axis along the $x$-axis and the minor axis along the $y$-axis and then was rotated counterclockwise $45°$. A new $XY$-coordinate system can be introduced that has the same origin but is rotated by a certain amount from the standard $xy$-coordinate system. In this example, the major axis of the ellipse lies along the new $X$-axis and the minor axis lies along the new $Y$-axis. We will see that we can write the equation of this ellipse as

$$\frac{X^2}{9} + \frac{Y^2}{1} = 1$$

We will now develop the *rotation of axes formulas*, which allow us to transform the generalized second-degree equation in $xy$, that is, $Ax^2 + Bxy + Cy^2 + Dx + Ey + F = 0$, into an equation in $XY$ of a conic that is familiar to us.

**WORDS**

Let the new $XY$-coordinate system be displaced from the $xy$-coordinate system by rotation through an angle $\theta$. Let $P$ represent some point a distance $r$ from the origin.

**MATH**

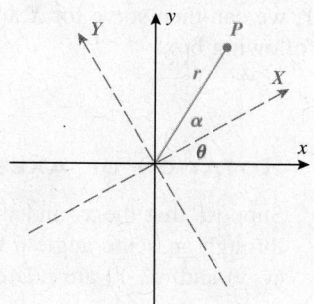

We can represent the point $P$ as either the point $(x, y)$ or the point $(X, Y)$.

We define the angle $\alpha$ as the angle $r$ makes with the $X$-axis and $\alpha + \theta$ as the angle $r$ makes with the $x$-axis.

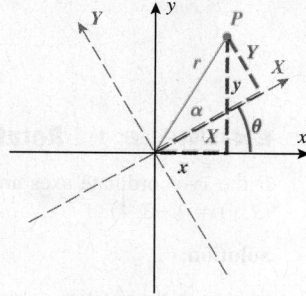

We can represent the point $P$ in polar coordinates using the following relationships:

$$x = r\cos(\alpha + \theta)$$
$$y = r\sin(\alpha + \theta)$$
$$X = r\cos\alpha$$
$$Y = r\sin\alpha$$

Let us now derive the relationships between the two coordinate systems.

**WORDS**

Start with the $x$-term and write the cosine identity for a sum.

Eliminate the parentheses and group $r$ with the $\alpha$-terms.

Substitute according to the relationships $X = r\cos\alpha$ and $Y = r\sin\alpha$.

Start with the $y$-term and write the sine identity for a sum.

Eliminate the parentheses and group $r$ with the $\alpha$-terms.

Substitute according to the relationships $X = r\cos\alpha$ and $Y = r\sin\alpha$.

**MATH**

$$x = r\cos(\alpha + \theta)$$
$$= r(\cos\alpha\cos\theta - \sin\alpha\sin\theta)$$

$$x = (r\cos\alpha)\cos\theta - (r\sin\alpha)\sin\theta$$

$$\boxed{x = X\cos\theta - Y\sin\theta}$$

$$y = r\sin(\alpha + \theta)$$
$$= r(\sin\alpha\cos\theta + \cos\alpha\sin\theta)$$

$$y = (r\sin\alpha)\cos\theta + (r\cos\alpha)\sin\theta$$

$$\boxed{y = Y\cos\theta + X\sin\theta}$$

By treating the highlighted equations for $x$ and $y$ as a system of linear equations in $X$ and $Y$, we can then solve for $X$ and $Y$ in terms of $x$ and $y$. The results are summarized in the following box:

---

### ROTATION OF AXES FORMULAS

Suppose that the $x$- and $y$-axes in the rectangular coordinate plane are rotated through an acute angle $\theta$ to produce the $X$- and $Y$-axes. Then, the coordinates $(x, y)$ and $(X, Y)$ are related according to the following equations:

$$x = X\cos\theta - Y\sin\theta \qquad\qquad X = x\cos\theta + y\sin\theta$$
$$y = X\sin\theta + Y\cos\theta \qquad\text{or}\qquad Y = -x\sin\theta + y\cos\theta$$

---

### EXAMPLE 1  Rotating the Axes

If the $xy$-coordinate axes are rotated 60°, find the $XY$-coordinates of the point $(x, y) = (-3, 4)$.

**Solution:**

Start with the rotation formulas.

$$X = x\cos\theta + y\sin\theta$$
$$Y = -x\sin\theta + y\cos\theta$$

Let $x = -3$, $y = 4$, and $\theta = 60°$.

$$X = -3\cos 60° + 4\sin 60°$$
$$Y = -(-3)\sin 60° + 4\cos 60°$$

Simplify.

$$X = -3\underbrace{\cos 60°}_{\frac{1}{2}} + 4\underbrace{\sin 60°}_{\frac{\sqrt{3}}{2}}$$

$$Y = 3\underbrace{\sin 60°}_{\frac{\sqrt{3}}{2}} + 4\underbrace{\cos 60°}_{\frac{1}{2}}$$

$$X = -\frac{3}{2} + 2\sqrt{3}$$

$$Y = \frac{3\sqrt{3}}{2} + 2$$

The $XY$-coordinates are $\boxed{\left(-\dfrac{3}{2} + 2\sqrt{3},\ \dfrac{3\sqrt{3}}{2} + 2\right)}$.

---

■ **YOUR TURN** If the $xy$-coordinate axes are rotated 30°, find the $XY$-coordinates of the point $(x, y) = (3, -4)$.

■ **Answer:**
$$\left(\frac{3\sqrt{3}}{2} - 2,\ -\frac{3}{2} - 2\sqrt{3}\right)$$

## EXAMPLE 2   Rotating an Ellipse

Show that the graph of the equation $5x^2 - 8xy + 5y^2 - 9 = 0$ is an ellipse aligning with coordinate axes that are rotated by 45°.

**Solution:**

Start with the rotation formulas.

$$x = X\cos\theta - Y\sin\theta$$

$$y = X\sin\theta + Y\cos\theta$$

Let $\theta = 45°$.

$$x = X\cos 45° - Y\sin 45°$$
$$\qquad \frac{\sqrt{2}}{2} \qquad\quad \frac{\sqrt{2}}{2}$$

$$y = X\sin 45° + Y\cos 45°$$
$$\qquad \frac{\sqrt{2}}{2} \qquad\quad \frac{\sqrt{2}}{2}$$

Simplify.

$$x = \frac{\sqrt{2}}{2}(X - Y)$$

$$y = \frac{\sqrt{2}}{2}(X + Y)$$

Substitute $x = \frac{\sqrt{2}}{2}(X - Y)$ and $y = \frac{\sqrt{2}}{2}(X + Y)$ into $5x^2 - 8xy + 5y^2 - 9 = 0$.

$$5\left[\frac{\sqrt{2}}{2}(X - Y)\right]^2 - 8\left[\frac{\sqrt{2}}{2}(X - Y)\right]\left[\frac{\sqrt{2}}{2}(X + Y)\right] + 5\left[\frac{\sqrt{2}}{2}(X + Y)\right]^2 - 9 = 0$$

Simplify.

$$\frac{5}{2}\left(X^2 - 2XY + Y^2\right) - 4\left(X^2 - Y^2\right) + \frac{5}{2}\left(X^2 + 2XY + Y^2\right) - 9 = 0$$

$$\frac{5}{2}X^2 - 5XY + \frac{5}{2}Y^2 - 4X^2 + 4Y^2 + \frac{5}{2}X^2 + 5XY + \frac{5}{2}Y^2 = 9$$

Combine like terms.

$$X^2 + 9Y^2 = 9$$

Divide by 9.

$$\boxed{\frac{X^2}{9} + \frac{Y^2}{1} = 1}$$

This (as discussed earlier) is an ellipse whose major axis is along the $X$-axis.

The vertices are at the points $(X, Y) = (\pm 3, 0)$.

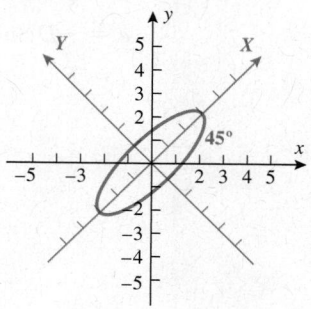

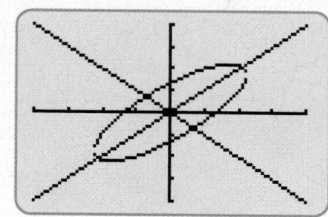

# The Angle of Rotation Necessary to Transform a General Second-Degree Equation into a Familiar Equation of a Conic

In Section 9.1, we stated that the general second-degree equation

$$Ax^2 + Bxy + Cy^2 + Dx + Ey + F = 0$$

corresponds to a graph of a conic. Which type of conic it is depends on the value of the discriminant, $B^2 - 4AC$. In Sections 9.2–9.4, we discussed graphs of parabolas, ellipses, and hyperbolas with vertices along either the axes or lines parallel (or perpendicular) to the axes. In all cases the value of $B$ was taken to be zero. When the value of $B$ is nonzero, the result is a conic with vertices along the new $XY$-axes (or, respectively, parallel and perpendicular to them), which are the original $xy$-axes rotated through an angle $\theta$. If given $\theta$, we can determine the rotation equations as illustrated in Example 2, but how do we find the angle $\theta$ that represents the *angle of rotation*?

To find the angle of rotation, let us start with a general second-degree polynomial equation:

$$Ax^2 + Bxy + Cy^2 + Dx + Ey + F = 0$$

We want to transform this equation into an equation in $X$ and $Y$ that does not contain an $XY$-term. Suppose we rotate our coordinates by an angle $\theta$ and use the rotation equations

$$x = X\cos\theta - Y\sin\theta \qquad y = X\sin\theta + Y\cos\theta$$

in the general second-degree polynomial equation; then the result is

$$A(X\cos\theta - Y\sin\theta)^2 + B(X\cos\theta - Y\sin\theta)(X\sin\theta + Y\cos\theta)$$
$$+ C(X\cos\theta + Y\sin\theta)^2 + D(X\cos\theta - Y\sin\theta) + E(X\sin\theta + Y\cos\theta) + F = 0$$

If we expand these expressions and collect like terms, the result is an equation of the form

$$aX^2 + bXY + cY^2 + dX + eY + f = 0$$

where

$$a = A\cos^2\theta + B\sin\theta\cos\theta + C\sin^2\theta$$
$$b = B(\cos^2\theta - \sin^2\theta) + 2(C - A)\sin\theta\cos\theta$$
$$c = A\sin^2\theta - B\sin\theta\cos\theta + C\cos^2\theta$$
$$d = D\cos\theta + E\sin\theta$$
$$e = -D\sin\theta + E\cos\theta$$
$$f = F$$

| WORDS | MATH |
|---|---|
| We do not want this new equation to have an $XY$-term, so we set $b = 0$. | $B(\cos^2\theta - \sin^2\theta) + 2(C - A)\sin\theta\cos\theta = 0$ |
| We can use the double-angle formulas to simplify. | $\underbrace{B(\cos^2\theta - \sin^2\theta)}_{\cos(2\theta)} + (C - A)\underbrace{2\sin\theta\cos\theta}_{\sin(2\theta)} = 0$ |
| Subtract the $\sin(2\theta)$ term from both sides of the equation. | $B\cos(2\theta) = (A - C)\sin(2\theta)$ |
| Divide by $B\sin(2\theta)$. | $\dfrac{B\cos(2\theta)}{B\sin(2\theta)} = \dfrac{(A - C)\sin(2\theta)}{B\sin(2\theta)}$ |
| Simplify. | $\boxed{\cot(2\theta) = \dfrac{A - C}{B}}$ |

## ANGLE OF ROTATION FORMULA

To transform the equation of a conic

$$Ax^2 + Bxy + Cy^2 + Dx + Ey + F = 0$$

into an equation in $X$ and $Y$ without an $XY$-term, rotate the $xy$-axes by an acute angle $\theta$ that satisfies the equation

$$\cot(2\theta) = \frac{A - C}{B} \quad \text{or} \quad \tan(2\theta) = \frac{B}{A - C}$$

Notice that the trigonometric equation $\cot(2\theta) = \dfrac{A - C}{B}$ or $\tan(2\theta) = \dfrac{B}{A - C}$ can be solved exactly for some values of $\theta$ (Example 3) and will have to be approximated with a calculator for other values of $\theta$ (Example 4).

## EXAMPLE 3   Determining the Angle of Rotation I: The Value of the Cotangent Function Is That of a Known (Special) Angle

Determine the angle of rotation necessary to transform the following equation into an equation in $X$ and $Y$ with no $XY$-term:

$$3x^2 + 2\sqrt{3}xy + y^2 + 2x - 2\sqrt{3}y = 0$$

**Solution:**

| | |
|---|---|
| Identify the $A$, $B$, and $C$ parameters in the equation. | $\underset{A}{3x^2} + \underset{B}{2\sqrt{3}\,xy} + \underset{C}{1y^2} + 2x - 2\sqrt{3}y = 0$ |
| Write the rotation formula. | $\cot(2\theta) = \dfrac{A - C}{B}$ |
| Let $A = 3, B = 2\sqrt{3}$, and $C = 1$. | $\cot(2\theta) = \dfrac{3 - 1}{2\sqrt{3}}$ |
| Simplify. | $\cot(2\theta) = \dfrac{1}{\sqrt{3}}$ |
| Apply the reciprocal identity. | $\tan(2\theta) = \sqrt{3}$ |

From our knowledge of trigonometric exact values, we know that $2\theta = 60°$ or $\boxed{\theta = 30°}$.

**Technology Tip**

To find the angle of rotation, use

$\theta = \dfrac{1}{2}\tan^{-1}\left(\dfrac{B}{A - C}\right)$ and set a

graphing calculator to degree mode. Substitute $A = 3$, $B = 2\sqrt{3}$, $C = 1$.

```
1/2tan-1(2√(3)/(3
-1))
                 30
```

**Technology Tip**

To find the angle of rotation, use

$\theta = \dfrac{1}{2} \tan^{-1}\left(\dfrac{B}{A-C}\right)$ and set

a graphing calculator to degree mode. Substitute $A = 4$, $B = 2$, and $C = -6$.

```
1/2tan⁻¹(2/(4-(⁻6
)))
        5.654966237
■
```

**EXAMPLE 4** **Determining the Angle of Rotation II: The Argument of the Cotangent Function Needs to Be Approximated with a Calculator**

Determine the angle of rotation necessary to transform the following equation into an equation in $X$ and $Y$ with no $XY$-term. Round to the nearest tenth of a degree.

$$4x^2 + 2xy - 6y^2 - 5x + y - 2 = 0$$

**Solution:**

Identify the $A$, $B$, and $C$ parameters in the equation.

$$\underset{A}{4x^2} + \underset{B}{2xy} - \underset{C}{6y^2} - 5x + y - 2 = 0$$

Write the rotation formula.

$$\cot(2\theta) = \frac{A-C}{B}$$

Let $A = 4$, $B = 2$, and $C = -6$.

$$\cot(2\theta) = \frac{4 - (-6)}{2}$$

Simplify.

$$\cot(2\theta) = 5$$

Apply the reciprocal identity.

$$\tan(2\theta) = \frac{1}{5} = 0.2$$

Write the result as an inverse tangent function.

$$2\theta = \tan^{-1}(0.2)$$

With a calculator evaluate the right side of the equation.

$$2\theta \approx 11.31°$$

Solve for $\theta$ and round to the nearest tenth of a degree.

$$\boxed{\theta = 5.7°}$$

Special attention must be given when evaluating the inverse tangent function on a calculator, as the result is always in quadrant I or IV. If $2\theta$ turns out to be negative, then 180° must be added so that $2\theta$ is in quadrant II (as opposed to quadrant IV). Then $\theta$ will be an acute angle lying in quadrant I.

Recall that we stated (without proof) in Section 9.1 that we can identify a general equation

$$Ax^2 + Bxy + Cy^2 + Dx + Ey + F = 0$$

as that of a particular conic depending on the discriminant.

| Parabola | $B^2 - 4AC = 0$ |
|---|---|
| Ellipse | $B^2 - 4AC < 0$ |
| Hyperbola | $B^2 - 4AC > 0$ |

## EXAMPLE 5    Graphing a Rotated Conic

For the equation $x^2 + 2xy + y^2 - \sqrt{2}x - 3\sqrt{2}y + 6 = 0$:

**a.** Determine which conic the equation represents.

**b.** Find the rotation angle required to eliminate the $XY$-term in the new coordinate system.

**c.** Transform the equation in $x$ and $y$ into an equation in $X$ and $Y$.

**d.** Graph the resulting conic.

**Solution (a):**

Identify $A$, $B$, and $C$.

$$\underset{A}{1x^2} + \underset{B}{2xy} + \underset{C}{1y^2} - \sqrt{2}x - 3\sqrt{2}y + 6 = 0$$

$$A = 1, B = 2, C = 1$$

Compute the discriminant.

$$B^2 - 4AC = 2^2 - 4(1)(1) = 0$$

Since the discriminant equals zero, the equation represents a **parabola**.

**Solution (b):**

Write the rotation formula.

$$\cot(2\theta) = \frac{A - C}{B}$$

Let $A = 1, B = 2,$ and $C = 1$.

$$\cot(2\theta) = \frac{1 - 1}{2}$$

Simplify.

$$\cot(2\theta) = 0$$

Write the cotangent function in terms of the sine and cosine functions.

$$\frac{\cos(2\theta)}{\sin(2\theta)} = 0$$

The numerator must equal zero.

$$\cos(2\theta) = 0$$

From our knowledge of trigonometric exact values, we know that $2\theta = 90°$ or $\boxed{\theta = 45°}$.

Now enter

$$y_1 = \frac{-2x + 3\sqrt{2} + \sqrt{-8\sqrt{2}x - 6}}{2}$$

and

$$y_2 = \frac{-2x + 3\sqrt{2} - \sqrt{-8\sqrt{2}x - 6}}{2}.$$

To graph the $X$- and $Y$-axes, enter
$y_3 = \tan(45)x$ and

$$y_4 = -\frac{1}{\tan(45)}x.$$

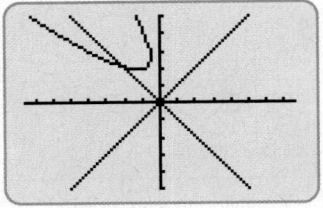

**Solution (c):**

Start with the equation
$x^2 + 2xy + y^2 - \sqrt{2}x - 3\sqrt{2}y + 6 = 0$,
and use the rotation formulas
with $\theta = 45°$.

Find $x^2$, $xy$, and $y^2$.

$$x = X\cos 45° - Y\sin 45° = \frac{\sqrt{2}}{2}(X - Y)$$

$$y = X\sin 45° + Y\cos 45° = \frac{\sqrt{2}}{2}(X + Y)$$

$$x^2 = \left[\frac{\sqrt{2}}{2}(X - Y)\right]^2 = \frac{1}{2}\left(X^2 - 2XY + Y^2\right)$$

$$xy = \left[\frac{\sqrt{2}}{2}(X - Y)\right]\left[\frac{\sqrt{2}}{2}(X + Y)\right] = \frac{1}{2}\left(X^2 - Y^2\right)$$

$$y^2 = \left[\frac{\sqrt{2}}{2}(X + Y)\right]^2 = \frac{1}{2}\left(X^2 + 2XY + Y^2\right)$$

Substitute the values
for $x$, $y$, $x^2$, $xy$,
and $y^2$ into the
original equation.

$$x^2 + 2xy + y^2 - \sqrt{2}x - 3\sqrt{2}y + 6 = 0$$

$$\frac{1}{2}\left(X^2 - 2XY + Y^2\right) + 2\frac{1}{2}\left(X^2 - Y^2\right)$$

$$+ \frac{1}{2}\left(X^2 + 2XY + Y^2\right) - \sqrt{2}\left[\frac{\sqrt{2}}{2}(X - Y)\right]$$

$$- 3\sqrt{2}\left[\frac{\sqrt{2}}{2}(X + Y)\right] + 6 = 0$$

Eliminate the parentheses
and combine like terms.

$$2X^2 - 4X - 2Y + 6 = 0$$

Divide by 2.

$$X^2 - 2X - Y + 3 = 0$$

Add $Y$.

$$Y = \left(X^2 - 2X\right) + 3$$

Complete the square on $X$.

$$Y = (X - 1)^2 + 2$$

**Solution (d):**

This is a parabola opening
upward in the $XY$-coordinate
system shifted to the right
one unit and up two units.

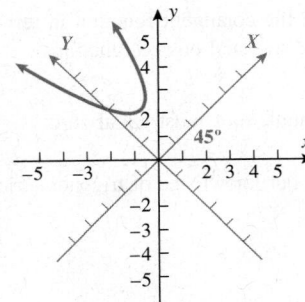

In this section, we found that the graph of the general second-degree equation

$$Ax^2 + Bxy + Cy^2 + Dx + Ey + F = 0$$

can represent conics in a system of rotated axes.

The following are the rotation formulas relating the $xy$-coordinate system to a rotated coordinate system with axes $X$ and $Y$

$$x = X\cos\theta - Y\sin\theta$$
$$y = X\sin\theta + Y\cos\theta$$

where the rotation angle $\theta$ is found from the equation

$$\cot(2\theta) = \frac{A - C}{B} \quad \text{or} \quad \tan(2\theta) = \frac{B}{A - C}$$

**SECTION**
**9.7 EXERCISES**

■ SKILLS

In Exercises 1–8, the coordinates of a point in the $xy$-coordinate system are given. Assuming that the $XY$-axes are found by rotating the $xy$-axes by the given angle $\theta$, find the corresponding coordinates for the point in the $XY$-system.

1. $(2, 4)$, $\theta = 45°$
2. $(5, 1)$, $\theta = 60°$
3. $(-3, 2)$, $\theta = 30°$
4. $(-4, 6)$, $\theta = 45°$
5. $(-1, -3)$, $\theta = 60°$
6. $(4, -4)$, $\theta = 45°$
7. $(0, 3)$, $\theta = 60°$
8. $(-2, 0)$, $\theta = 30°$

In Exercises 9–24, (a) identify the type of conic from the discriminant, (b) transform the equation in $x$ and $y$ into an equation in $X$ and $Y$ (without an $XY$-term) by rotating the $x$- and $y$-axes by the indicated angle $\theta$ to arrive at the new $X$- and $Y$-axes, and (c) graph the resulting equation (showing both sets of axes).

9. $xy - 1 = 0$, $\theta = 45°$
10. $xy - 4 = 0$, $\theta = 45°$
11. $x^2 + 2xy + y^2 + \sqrt{2}x - \sqrt{2}y - 1 = 0$, $\theta = 45°$
12. $2x^2 - 4xy + 2y^2 - \sqrt{2}x + 1 = 0$, $\theta = 45°$
13. $y^2 - \sqrt{3}xy + 3 = 0$, $\theta = 30°$
14. $x^2 - \sqrt{3}xy - 3 = 0$, $\theta = 60°$
15. $7x^2 - 2\sqrt{3}xy + 5y^2 - 8 = 0$, $\theta = 60°$
16. $4x^2 + \sqrt{3}xy + 3y^2 - 45 = 0$, $\theta = 30°$
17. $3x^2 + 2\sqrt{3}xy + y^2 + 2x - 2\sqrt{3}y - 2 = 0$, $\theta = 30°$
18. $x^2 + 2\sqrt{3}xy + 3y^2 - 2\sqrt{3}x + 2y - 4 = 0$, $\theta = 60°$
19. $7x^2 + 4\sqrt{3}xy + 3y^2 - 9 = 0$, $\theta = \dfrac{\pi}{6}$
20. $37x^2 + 42\sqrt{3}xy + 79y^2 - 400 = 0$, $\theta = \dfrac{\pi}{3}$
21. $7x^2 - 10\sqrt{3}xy - 3y^2 + 24 = 0$, $\theta = \dfrac{\pi}{3}$
22. $9x^2 + 14\sqrt{3}xy - 5y^2 + 48 = 0$, $\theta = \dfrac{\pi}{6}$
23. $x^2 - 2xy + y^2 - \sqrt{2}x - \sqrt{2}y - 8 = 0$, $\theta = \dfrac{\pi}{4}$
24. $x^2 + 2xy + y^2 + 3\sqrt{2}x + \sqrt{2}y = 0$, $\theta = \dfrac{\pi}{4}$

In Exercises 25–38, determine the angle of rotation necessary to transform the equation in $x$ and $y$ into an equation in $X$ and $Y$ with no $XY$-term.

25. $x^2 + 4xy + y^2 - 4 = 0$
26. $3x^2 + 5xy + 3y^2 - 2 = 0$
27. $2x^2 + \sqrt{3}xy + 3y^2 - 1 = 0$
28. $4x^2 + \sqrt{3}xy + 3y^2 - 1 = 0$
29. $2x^2 + \sqrt{3}xy + y^2 - 5 = 0$
30. $2\sqrt{3}x^2 + xy + 3\sqrt{3}y^2 + 1 = 0$
31. $\sqrt{2}x^2 + xy + \sqrt{2}y^2 - 1 = 0$
32. $x^2 + 10xy + y^2 + 2 = 0$
33. $12\sqrt{3}x^2 + 4xy + 8\sqrt{3}y^2 - 1 = 0$
34. $4x^2 + 2xy + 2y^2 - 7 = 0$
35. $5x^2 + 6xy + 4y^2 - 1 = 0$
36. $x^2 + 2xy + 12y^2 + 3 = 0$
37. $3x^2 + 10xy + 5y^2 - 1 = 0$
38. $10x^2 + 3xy + 2y^2 + 3 = 0$

In Exercises 39–48, graph the second-degree equation. (*Hint:* Transform the equation into an equation that contains no $xy$-term.)

39. $21x^2 + 10\sqrt{3}xy + 31y^2 - 144 = 0$
40. $5x^2 + 6xy + 5y^2 - 8 = 0$
41. $8x^2 - 20xy + 8y^2 + 18 = 0$
42. $3y^2 - 26\sqrt{3}xy - 23x^2 - 144 = 0$
43. $3x^2 + 2\sqrt{3}xy + y^2 + 2x - 2\sqrt{3}y - 12 = 0$
44. $3x^2 - 2\sqrt{3}xy + y^2 - 2x - 2\sqrt{3}y - 4 = 0$
45. $37x^2 - 42\sqrt{3}xy + 79y^2 - 400 = 0$
46. $71x^2 - 58\sqrt{3}xy + 13y^2 + 400 = 0$
47. $x^2 + 2xy + y^2 + 5\sqrt{2}x + 3\sqrt{2}y = 0$
48. $7x^2 - 4\sqrt{3}xy + 3y^2 - 9 = 0$

■ CONCEPTUAL

In Exercises 49–52, determine whether each statement is true or false.

49. The graph of the equation $x^2 + kxy + 9y^2 = 5$, where $k$ is any positive constant less than 6, is an ellipse.

50. The graph of the equation $x^2 + kxy + 9y^2 = 5$, where $k$ is any constant greater than 6, is a parabola.

51. The reciprocal function is a rotated hyperbola.

52. The equation $\sqrt{x} + \sqrt{y} = 3$ can be transformed into the equation $X^2 + Y^2 = 9$.

## ▪ CHALLENGE

**53.** Determine the equation in $X$ and $Y$ that corresponds to $\dfrac{x^2}{a^2} + \dfrac{y^2}{b^2} = 1$ when the axes are rotated through

    **a.** 90°    **b.** 180°

**54.** Determine the equation in $X$ and $Y$ that corresponds to $\dfrac{x^2}{a^2} - \dfrac{y^2}{b^2} = 1$ when the axes are rotated through

    **a.** 90°    **b.** 180°

**55.** Identify the conic section with equation $y^2 + ax^2 = x$ for $a < 0, a > 0, a = 0$, and $a = 1$.

**56.** Identify the conic section with equation $x^2 - ay^2 = y$ for $a < 0, a > 0, a = 0$, and $a = 1$.

## ▪ TECHNOLOGY

**For Exercises 57–62, refer to the following:**

To use a function-driven software or graphing utility to graph a general second-degree equation, you need to solve for $y$. Let us consider a general second-degree equation $Ax^2 + Bxy + Cy^2 + Dx + Ey + F = 0$.

Group $y^2$ terms together, $y$ terms together, and the remaining terms together.

$$Ax^2 + \underline{Bxy} + \underline{Cy^2} + Dx + \underline{Ey} + F = 0$$

$$Cy^2 + (Bxy + Ey) + \left(Ax^2 + Dx + F\right) = 0$$

Factor out the common $y$ in the first set of parentheses.

$$Cy^2 + y(Bx + E) + \left(Ax^2 + Dx + F\right) = 0$$

Now this is a quadratic equation in $y$: $ay^2 + by + c = 0$.

Use the quadratic formula to solve for $y$.

$$Cy^2 + y(Bx + E) + \left(Ax^2 + Dx + F\right) = 0$$

$$a = C, b = Bx + E, c = Ax^2 + Dx + F$$

$$y = \frac{-b \pm \sqrt{b^2 - 4ac}}{2a} \qquad y = \frac{-(Bx + E) \pm \sqrt{(Bx + E)^2 - 4(C)\left(Ax^2 + Dx + F\right)}}{2(C)}$$

$$y = \frac{-(Bx + E) \pm \sqrt{B^2x^2 + 2BEx + E^2 - 4ACx^2 - 4CDx - 4CF}}{2C}$$

$$y = \frac{-(Bx + E) \pm \sqrt{\left(B^2 - 4AC\right)x^2 + (2BE - 4CD)x + \left(E^2 - 4CF\right)}}{2C}$$

**Case I:** $B^2 - 4AC = 0 \rightarrow$ The second-degree equation $Ax^2 + Bxy + Cy^2 + Dx + Ey + F = 0$ is a parabola.

$$y = \frac{-(Bx + E) \pm \sqrt{(2BE - 4CD)x + \left(E^2 - 4CF\right)}}{2C}$$

**Case II:** $B^2 - 4AC < 0 \rightarrow$ The second-degree equation $Ax^2 + Bxy + Cy^2 + Dx + Ey + F = 0$ is an ellipse.

$$y = \frac{-(Bx + E) \pm \sqrt{\left(B^2 - 4AC\right)x^2 + (2BE - 4CD)x + \left(E^2 - 4CF\right)}}{2C}$$

**Case III:** $B^2 - 4AC > 0 \rightarrow$ The second-degree equation $Ax^2 + Bxy + Cy^2 + Dx + Ey + F = 0$ is a hyperbola.

$$y = \frac{-(Bx + E) \pm \sqrt{\left(B^2 - 4AC\right)x^2 + (2BE - 4CD)x + \left(E^2 - 4CF\right)}}{2C}$$

**57.** Use a graphing utility to explore the second-degree equation $3x^2 + 2\sqrt{3}xy + y^2 + Dx + Ey + F = 0$ for the following values of $D, E$, and $F$:

    **a.** $D = 1, E = 3, F = 2$

    **b.** $D = -1, E = -3, F = 2$

Show the angle of rotation to the nearest degree. Explain the differences.

58. Use a graphing utility to explore the second-degree equation $x^2 + 3xy + 3y^2 + Dx + Ey + F = 0$ for the following values of $D$, $E$, and $F$:

    **a.** $D = 2, E = 6, F = -1$

    **b.** $D = 6, E = 2, F = -1$

    Show the angle of rotation to the nearest degree. Explain the differences.

59. Use a graphing utility to explore the second-degree equation $2x^2 + 3xy + y^2 + Dx + Ey + F = 0$ for the following values of $D$, $E$, and $F$:

    **a.** $D = 2, E = 1, F = -2$

    **b.** $D = 2, E = 1, F = 2$

    Show the angle of rotation to the nearest degree. Explain the differences.

60. Use a graphing utility to explore the second-degree equation $2\sqrt{3}x^2 + xy + \sqrt{3}y^2 + Dx + Ey + F = 0$ for the following values of $D$, $E$, and $F$:

    **a.** $D = 2, E = 1, F = -1$

    **b.** $D = 2, E = 6, F = -1$

    Show the angle of rotation to the nearest degree. Explain the differences.

61. Use a graphing utility to explore the second-degree equation $Ax^2 + Bxy + Cy^2 + 2x + y - 1 = 0$ for the following values of $A$, $B$, and $C$:

    **a.** $A = 4, B = -4, C = 1$

    **b.** $A = 4, B = 4, C = -1$

    **c.** $A = 1, B = -4, C = 4$

    Show the angle of rotation to the nearest degree. Explain the differences.

62. Use a graphing utility to explore the second-degree equation $Ax^2 + Bxy + Cy^2 + 3x + 5y - 2 = 0$ for the following values of $A$, $B$, and $C$:

    **a.** $A = 1, B = -4, C = 4$

    **b.** $A = 1, B = 4, D = -4$

    Show the angle of rotation to the nearest degree. Explain the differences.

■ **PREVIEW TO CALCULUS**

In calculus, when finding the area between two curves, we need to find the points of intersection of the curves. In Exercises 63–66, find the points of intersection of the rotated conic sections.

63. $x^2 + 2xy = 10$
$3x^2 - xy = 2$

64. $x^2 - 3xy + 2y^2 = 0$
$x^2 + xy = 6$

65. $2x^2 - 7xy + 2y^2 = -1$
$x^2 - 3xy + y^2 = 1$

66. $4x^2 + xy + 4y^2 = 22$
$-3x^2 + 2xy - 3y^2 = -11$

**SECTION**
## 9.8 POLAR EQUATIONS OF CONICS

**SKILLS OBJECTIVES**

■ Define conics in terms of eccentricity.
■ Express equations of conics in polar form.
■ Graph the polar equations of conics.

**CONCEPTUAL OBJECTIVE**

■ Define all conics in terms of a focus and a directrix.

## Equations of Conics in Polar Coordinates

In Section 9.1, we discussed parabolas, ellipses, and hyperbolas in terms of geometric definitions. Then in Sections 9.2–9.4, we examined the rectangular equations of these conics. The equations for ellipses and hyperbolas when their centers are at the origin were simpler than when they were not (when the conics were shifted). In Section 7.5, we discussed polar coordinates and graphing of polar equations. In this section, we develop a more unified definition of the three conics in terms of a single focus and a directrix. You will see in this section that if the *focus* is located at the origin, then equations of conics are simpler when written in polar coordinates.

## Alternative Definition of Conics

Recall that when we work with rectangular coordinates, we define a parabola (Sections 9.1 and 9.2) in terms of a fixed point (focus) and a line (directrix), whereas we define an ellipse and hyperbola (Sections 9.1, 9.3, and 9.4) in terms of two fixed points (the foci). However, it is possible to define all three conics in terms of a single focus and a directrix.

The following alternative representation of conics depends on a parameter called *eccentricity*.

### ALTERNATIVE DESCRIPTION OF CONICS

Let $D$ be a fixed line (the **directrix**), $F$ be a fixed point (a **focus**) not on $D$, and $e$ be a fixed positive number (**eccentricity**). The set of all points $P$ such that the ratio of the distance from $P$ to $F$ to the distance from $P$ to $D$ equals the constant $e$ defines a conic section.

$$\frac{d(P, F)}{d(P, D)} = e$$

- If $e = 1$, the conic is a **parabola**.
- If $e < 1$, the conic is an **ellipse**.
- If $e > 1$, the conic is a **hyperbola**.

When $e = 1$, the result is a parabola, described by the same definition we used previously in Section 9.1. When $e \neq 1$, the result is either an ellipse or a hyperbola. The major axis of an ellipse passes through the focus and is perpendicular to the directrix. The transverse axis of a hyperbola also passes through the focus and is perpendicular to the directrix. If we let $c$ represent the distance from the focus to the center and $a$ represent the distance from the vertex to the center, then eccentricity is given by

$$e = \frac{c}{a}$$

In polar coordinates, if we locate the focus of a conic at the pole and the directrix is either perpendicular or parallel to the polar axis, then we have four possible scenarios:

- The directrix is *perpendicular* to the polar axis and $p$ units to the *right* of the pole.
- The directrix is *perpendicular* to the polar axis and $p$ units to the *left* of the pole.
- The directrix is *parallel* to the polar axis and $p$ units *above* the pole.
- The directrix is *parallel* to the polar axis and $p$ units *below* the pole.

Let us take the case in which the directrix is perpendicular to the polar axis and $p$ units to the right of the pole.

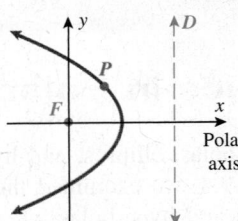

In polar coordinates $(r, \theta)$, we see that the distance from the focus to a point $P$ is equal to $r$, that is, $d(P, F) = r$, and the distance from $P$ to the closest point on the directrix is $d(P, D) = p - r\cos\theta$.

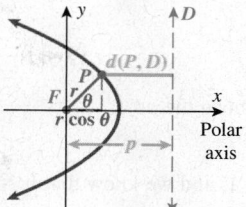

| WORDS | MATH |
|---|---|
| Substitute $d(P, F) = r$ and $d(P, D) = p - r\cos\theta$ | |
| into the formula for eccentricity, $\dfrac{d(P, F)}{d(P, D)} = e$. | $\dfrac{r}{p - r\cos\theta} = e$ |
| Multiply the result by $p - r\cos\theta$. | $r = e(p - r\cos\theta)$ |
| Eliminate the parentheses. | $r = ep - er\cos\theta$ |
| Add $er\cos\theta$ to both sides of the equation. | $r + er\cos\theta = ep$ |
| Factor out the common $r$. | $r + (1 + e\cos\theta) = ep$ |
| Divide both sides by $1 + e\cos\theta$. | $r = \dfrac{ep}{1 + e\cos\theta}$ |

We need not derive the other three cases here, but note that if the directrix is perpendicular to the polar axis and $p$ units to the *left* of the pole, the resulting polar equation is

$$r = \frac{ep}{1 - e\cos\theta}$$

If the directrix is parallel to the polar axis, the directrix is either above $(y = p)$ or below $(y = -p)$ the polar axis and we get the sine function instead of the cosine function, as summarized in the following box:

## POLAR EQUATIONS OF CONICS

The following polar equations represent conics with one focus at the origin and with eccentricity $e$. It is assumed that the positive $x$-axis represents the polar axis.

| EQUATION | DESCRIPTION |
|---|---|
| $r = \dfrac{ep}{1 + e\cos\theta}$ | The directrix is *vertical* and $p$ units to the *right* of the pole. |
| $r = \dfrac{ep}{1 - e\cos\theta}$ | The directrix is *vertical* and $p$ units to the *left* of the pole. |
| $r = \dfrac{ep}{1 + e\sin\theta}$ | The directrix is *horizontal* and $p$ units *above* the pole. |
| $r = \dfrac{ep}{1 - e\sin\theta}$ | The directrix is *horizontal* and $p$ units *below* the pole. |

| ECCENTRICITY | THE CONIC IS A ___ | THE ___ IS PERPENDICULAR TO THE DIRECTRIX |
|---|---|---|
| $e = 1$ | Parabola | Axis of symmetry |
| $e < 1$ | Ellipse | Major axis |
| $e > 1$ | Hyperbola | Transverse axis |

*Technology Tip*

Be sure to set the calculator to radian and polar modes.

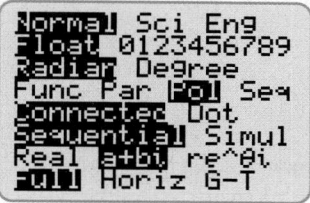

Use $\boxed{\text{Y}=}$ to enter the polar equation $r = \dfrac{3}{1 + \sin\theta}$.

$\boxed{\text{r1}=}$ $\boxed{3}$ $\boxed{\div}$ $\boxed{(}$ $\boxed{(}$ $\boxed{1}$ $\boxed{+}$ $\boxed{\sin}$
$\boxed{\text{X, T, }\theta\text{, n}}$ $\boxed{)}$ $\boxed{)}$

To enter the equation of the directrix $y = 3$, use its polar form.

$$y = 3 \quad r\sin\theta = 3 \quad r = \frac{3}{\sin\theta}$$

Now enter $\boxed{\text{r2}=}$ $\boxed{3}$ $\boxed{\div}$ $\boxed{\sin}$
$\boxed{\text{X, T, }\theta\text{, n}}$ $\boxed{)}$ .

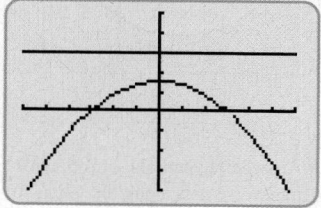

### EXAMPLE 1   Finding the Polar Equation of a Conic

Find a polar equation for a parabola that has its focus at the origin and whose directrix is the line $y = 3$.

**Solution:**

The directrix is horizontal and above the pole.

$$r = \frac{ep}{1 + e\sin\theta}$$

A parabola has eccentricity $e = 1$, and we know that $p = 3$.

$$\boxed{r = \frac{3}{1 + \sin\theta}}$$

■ **Answer:** $r = \dfrac{3}{1 - \cos\theta}$

▮ **YOUR TURN** Find a polar equation for a parabola that has its focus at the origin and whose directrix is the line $x = -3$.

**Technology Tip**

Use $\boxed{Y=}$ to enter the polar

equation $r = \dfrac{10}{3 + 2\cos\theta}$.

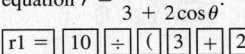

$\boxed{r1 =}$ $\boxed{10}$ $\boxed{\div}$ $\boxed{(}$ $\boxed{3}$ $\boxed{+}$ $\boxed{2}$

$\boxed{\cos}$ $\boxed{X, T, \theta, n}$ $\boxed{)}$ $\boxed{)}$

To enter the equation of the directrix $x = 5$, use its polar form.

$$x = 5 \quad r\cos\theta = 5 \quad r = \frac{5}{\cos\theta}$$

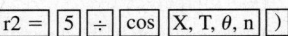

$\boxed{r2 =}$ $\boxed{5}$ $\boxed{\div}$ $\boxed{\cos}$ $\boxed{X, T, \theta, n}$ $\boxed{)}$

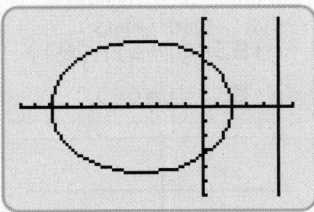

■ **Answer:** hyperbola, $e = 5$, with transverse axis along the $y$-axis

### EXAMPLE 2   Identifying a Conic from Its Equation

Identify the type of conic represented by the equation $r = \dfrac{10}{3 + 2\cos\theta}$.

**Solution:**

To identify the type of conic, we need to rewrite the equation in the form:

$$r = \frac{ep}{1 \pm e\cos\theta}$$

Divide the numerator and denominator by 3.

$$r = \frac{\dfrac{10}{3}}{\left(1 + \dfrac{2}{3}\cos\theta\right)}$$

Identify $e$ in the denominator.

$$= \frac{\dfrac{10}{3}}{\left(1 + \dfrac{\overset{2}{\overbrace{\tfrac{2}{3}}}}{e}\cos\theta\right)}$$

The numerator is equal to $ep$.

$$= \frac{\overset{p}{5} \cdot \overset{e}{\tfrac{2}{3}}}{\left(1 + \dfrac{\tfrac{2}{3}}{e}\cos\theta\right)}$$

Since $e = \frac{2}{3} < 1$, the conic is an $\boxed{\text{ellipse}}$. The directrix is $x = 5$, so the major axis is along the $x$-axis (perpendicular to the directrix).

▮ **YOUR TURN** Identify the type of conic represented by the equation

$$r = \frac{10}{2 - 10\sin\theta}$$

In Example 2 we found that the polar equation $r = \dfrac{10}{3 + 2\cos\theta}$ is an ellipse with its major axis along the $x$-axis. We will graph this ellipse in Example 3.

## EXAMPLE 3   Graphing a Conic from Its Equation

The graph of the polar equation $r = \dfrac{10}{3 + 2\cos\theta}$ is an ellipse.

a. Find the vertices.
b. Find the center of the ellipse.
c. Find the lengths of the major and minor axes.
d. Graph the ellipse.

**Solution (a):**

From Example 2 we see that $e = \frac{2}{3}$, which corresponds to an ellipse, and $x = 5$ is the directrix.
   The major axis is perpendicular to the directrix. Therefore, the major axis lies along the polar axis. To find the vertices (which lie along the major axis), let $\theta = 0$ and $\theta = \pi$.

$\theta = 0$:
$$r = \frac{10}{3 + 2\cos\theta} = \frac{10}{5} = 2$$

$\theta = \pi$:
$$r = \frac{10}{3 + 2\cos\pi} = \frac{10}{1} = 10$$

The vertices are the points $\boxed{V_1 = (2,0)}$ and $\boxed{V_2 = (10,\pi)}$.

**Solution (b):**

The vertices in rectangular coordinates are $V_1 = (2,0)$ and $V_2 = (-10,0)$.

The midpoint (in rectangular coordinates) between the two vertices is the point $(-4,0)$, which corresponds to the point $\boxed{(4,\pi)}$ in polar coordinates.

**Solution (c):**

The length of the major axis, $2a$, is the distance between the vertices.   $\boxed{2a = 12}$

The length $a = 6$ corresponds to the distance from the center to a vertex.

Apply the formula $e = \dfrac{c}{a}$ with $a = 6$ and $e = \frac{2}{3}$ to find $c$.
$$c = ae = 6\left(\frac{2}{3}\right) = 4$$

Let $a = 6$ and $c = 4$ in $b^2 = a^2 - c^2$.
$$b^2 = 6^2 - 4^2 = 20$$

Solve for $b$.
$$b = 2\sqrt{5}$$

The length of the minor axis is $\boxed{2b = 4\sqrt{5}}$.

**Solution (d):**

Graph the ellipse.

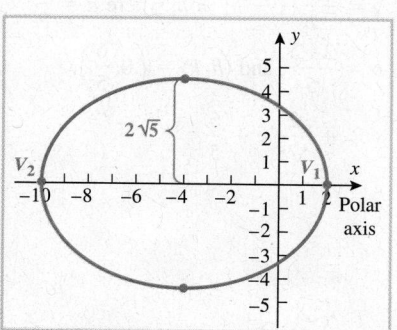

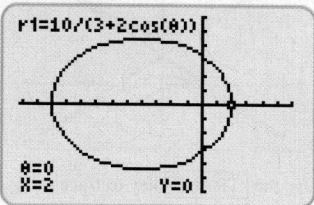
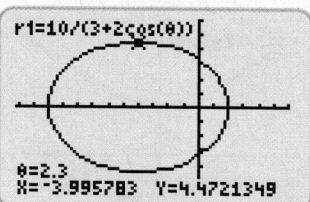
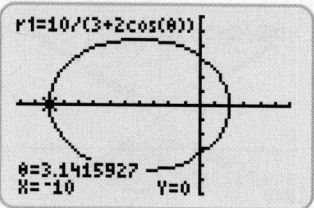
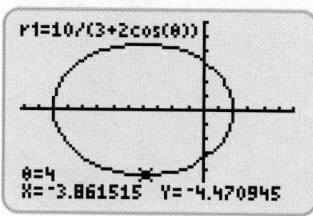

**Technology Tip**

Use $\boxed{Y=}$ to enter the polar

equation $r = \dfrac{2}{2 + 3\sin\theta}$.

$\boxed{\text{r1}} = \boxed{2}\,\boxed{\div}\,\boxed{(}\,\boxed{2}\,\boxed{+}\,\boxed{3}$
$\boxed{\sin}\,\boxed{\text{X, T, }\theta\text{, n}}\,\boxed{)}\,\boxed{)}$

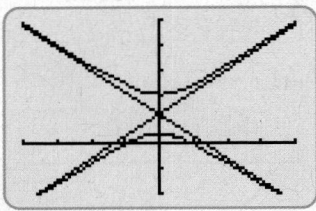

Use the $\boxed{\text{TRACE}}$ key to trace the
vertices of the hyperbola.

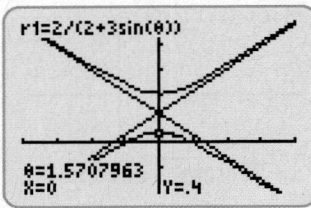

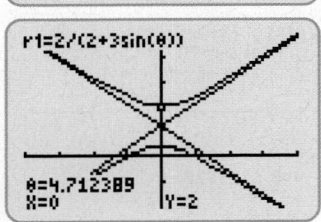

**EXAMPLE 4   Identifying and Graphing a Conic from Its Equation**

Identify and graph the conic defined by the equation $r = \dfrac{2}{2 + 3\sin\theta}$.

**Solution:**

Rewrite the equation in
the form $r = \dfrac{ep}{1 + e\sin\theta}$.

$$r = \frac{2}{2 + 3\sin\theta} = \frac{\overset{\overset{p}{\left(\frac{2}{3}\right)}}{}\,\overset{\overset{e}{\left(\frac{3}{2}\right)}}{}}{1 + \underset{e}{\left(\frac{3}{2}\right)}\sin\theta}$$

The conic is a *hyperbola* since $e = \frac{3}{2} > 1$.

The directrix is horizontal and $\frac{2}{3}$ unit above the pole (origin).

To find the vertices, let $\theta = \dfrac{\pi}{2}$ and $\theta = \dfrac{3\pi}{2}$.

$\theta = \dfrac{\pi}{2}$:

$$r = \frac{2}{2 + 3\sin\left(\dfrac{\pi}{2}\right)} = \frac{2}{5}$$

$\theta = \dfrac{3\pi}{2}$:

$$r = \frac{2}{2 + 3\sin\left(\dfrac{3\pi}{2}\right)} = \frac{2}{-1} = -2$$

The vertices in polar coordinates are $\left(\dfrac{2}{5}, \dfrac{\pi}{2}\right)$ and $\left(-2, \dfrac{3\pi}{2}\right)$.

The vertices in rectangular coordinates are $V_1 = \left(0, \frac{2}{5}\right)$ and $V_2 = (0, 2)$.

The center is the midpoint between the vertices: $\left(0, \frac{6}{5}\right)$.

The distance from the center to a focus is $c = \frac{6}{5}$.

Apply the formula $e = \dfrac{c}{a}$ with $c = \dfrac{6}{5}$ and
$e = \dfrac{3}{2}$ to find $a$.

$$a = \frac{c}{e} = \frac{\dfrac{6}{5}}{\dfrac{3}{2}} = \frac{4}{5}$$

Let $a = \frac{4}{5}$ and $c = \frac{6}{5}$ in $b^2 = c^2 - a^2$.

$$b^2 = \left(\frac{6}{5}\right)^2 - \left(\frac{4}{5}\right)^2 = \frac{20}{25}$$

Solve for $b$.

$$b = \frac{2\sqrt{5}}{5}$$

The asymptotes are given by
$y = \pm\dfrac{a}{b}(x - h) + k$, where $a = \dfrac{4}{5}$,

$b = \dfrac{2\sqrt{5}}{5}$, and $(h, k) = \left(0, \dfrac{6}{5}\right)$.

$$y = \pm\frac{2}{\sqrt{5}}x + \frac{6}{5}$$

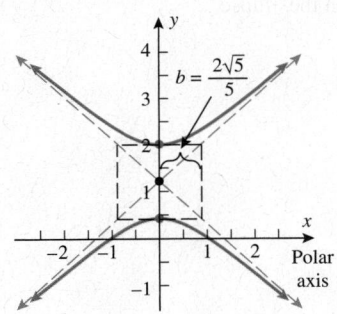

It is important to note that although we relate specific points (vertices, foci, etc.) to rectangular coordinates, another approach to finding a rough sketch is to simply point-plot the equation in polar coordinates.

### EXAMPLE 5   Graphing a Conic by Point-Plotting in Polar Coordinates

Sketch a graph of the conic $r = \dfrac{4}{1 - \sin\theta}$.

**Solution:**

**STEP 1** The conic is a parabola because the equation is in the form

$$r = \frac{(4)(1)}{1 - (1)\sin\theta}.$$

Make a table with key values for $\theta$ and $r$.

| $\theta$ | $r = \dfrac{4}{1 - \sin\theta}$ | $(r, \theta)$ |
|---|---|---|
| $0$ | $r = \dfrac{4}{1 - \sin 0} = \dfrac{4}{1} = 4$ | $(4, 0)$ |
| $\dfrac{\pi}{2}$ | $r = \dfrac{4}{1 - \sin\dfrac{\pi}{2}} = \dfrac{4}{1 - 1} = \dfrac{4}{0}$ | undefined |
| $\pi$ | $r = \dfrac{4}{1 - \sin\pi} = \dfrac{4}{1} = 4$ | $(4, \pi)$ |
| $\dfrac{3\pi}{2}$ | $r = \dfrac{4}{1 - \sin\dfrac{3\pi}{2}} = \dfrac{4}{1 - (-1)} = \dfrac{4}{2} = 2$ | $\left(2, \dfrac{3\pi}{2}\right)$ |
| $2\pi$ | $r = \dfrac{4}{1 - \sin(2\pi)} = \dfrac{4}{1} = 4$ | $(4, 2\pi)$ |

**STEP 2** Plot the points on a polar graph and connect them with a smooth parabolic curve.

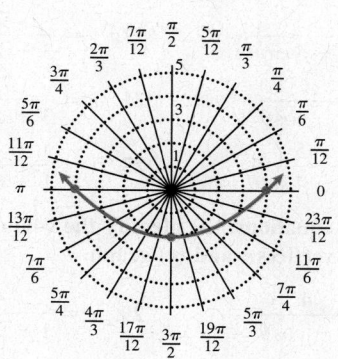

**Technology Tip**

Use $\boxed{Y=}$ to enter the polar equation $r = \dfrac{4}{1 - \sin\theta}$.

$\boxed{r1} = \boxed{4} \boxed{\div} \boxed{(} \boxed{(} \boxed{1} \boxed{-} \boxed{\sin}$
$\boxed{X, T, \theta, n} \boxed{)} \boxed{)}$

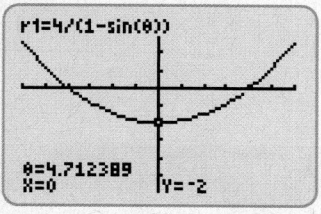

In this section, we found that we could graph polar equations of conics by identifying a single focus and the directrix. There are four possible equations in terms of eccentricity $e$:

| EQUATION | DESCRIPTION |
|---|---|
| $r = \dfrac{ep}{1 + e\cos\theta}$ | The directrix is *vertical* and $p$ units to the *right* of the pole. |
| $r = \dfrac{ep}{1 - e\cos\theta}$ | The directrix is *vertical* and $p$ units to the *left* of the pole. |
| $r = \dfrac{ep}{1 + e\sin\theta}$ | The directrix is *horizontal* and $p$ units *above* the pole. |
| $r = \dfrac{ep}{1 - e\sin\theta}$ | The directrix is *horizontal* and $p$ units *below* the pole. |

■ SKILLS

In Exercises 1–14, find the polar equation that represents the conic described (assume that a focus is at the origin).

| Conic | Eccentricity | Directrix | | Conic | Eccentricity | Directrix |
|---|---|---|---|---|---|---|
| **1.** Ellipse | $e = \frac{1}{2}$ | $y = -5$ | | **2.** Ellipse | $e = \frac{1}{3}$ | $y = 3$ |
| **3.** Hyperbola | $e = 2$ | $y = 4$ | | **4.** Hyperbola | $e = 3$ | $y = -2$ |
| **5.** Parabola | $e = 1$ | $x = 1$ | | **6.** Parabola | $e = 1$ | $x = -1$ |
| **7.** Ellipse | $e = \frac{3}{4}$ | $x = 2$ | | **8.** Ellipse | $e = \frac{2}{3}$ | $x = -4$ |
| **9.** Hyperbola | $e = \frac{4}{3}$ | $x = -3$ | | **10.** Hyperbola | $e = \frac{3}{2}$ | $x = 5$ |
| **11.** Parabola | $e = 1$ | $y = -3$ | | **12.** Parabola | $e = 1$ | $y = 4$ |
| **13.** Ellipse | $e = \frac{3}{5}$ | $y = 6$ | | **14.** Hyperbola | $e = \frac{8}{5}$ | $y = 5$ |

In Exercises 15–26, identify the conic (parabola, ellipse, or hyperbola) that each polar equation represents.

**15.** $r = \dfrac{4}{1 + \cos\theta}$

**16.** $r = \dfrac{3}{2 - 3\sin\theta}$

**17.** $r = \dfrac{2}{3 + 2\sin\theta}$

**18.** $r = \dfrac{3}{2 - 2\cos\theta}$

**19.** $r = \dfrac{2}{4 + 8\cos\theta}$

**20.** $r = \dfrac{1}{4 - \cos\theta}$

**21.** $r = \dfrac{7}{3 + \cos\theta}$

**22.** $r = \dfrac{4}{5 + 6\sin\theta}$

**23.** $r = \dfrac{40}{5 + 5\sin\theta}$

**24.** $r = \dfrac{5}{5 - 4\sin\theta}$

**25.** $r = \dfrac{1}{1 - 6\cos\theta}$

**26.** $r = \dfrac{5}{3 - 3\sin\theta}$

In Exercises 27–42, for the given polar equations: (a) identify the conic as either a parabola, an ellipse, or a hyperbola; (b) find the eccentricity and vertex (or vertices); and (c) graph.

**27.** $r = \dfrac{2}{1 + \sin\theta}$

**28.** $r = \dfrac{4}{1 - \cos\theta}$

**29.** $r = \dfrac{4}{1 - 2\sin\theta}$

**30.** $r = \dfrac{3}{3 + 8\cos\theta}$

**31.** $r = \dfrac{2}{2 + \sin\theta}$

**32.** $r = \dfrac{1}{3 - \sin\theta}$

**33.** $r = \dfrac{1}{2 - 2\sin\theta}$

**34.** $r = \dfrac{1}{1 - 2\sin\theta}$

**35.** $r = \dfrac{4}{3 + \cos\theta}$    **36.** $r = \dfrac{2}{5 + 4\sin\theta}$    **37.** $r = \dfrac{6}{2 + 3\sin\theta}$    **38.** $r = \dfrac{6}{1 + \cos\theta}$

**39.** $r = \dfrac{2}{5 + 5\cos\theta}$    **40.** $r = \dfrac{10}{6 - 3\cos\theta}$    **41.** $r = \dfrac{6}{3\cos\theta + 1}$    **42.** $r = \dfrac{15}{3\sin\theta + 5}$

## ▪ APPLICATIONS

**For Exercises 43 and 44, refer to the following:**

Planets travel in elliptical orbits around a single focus, the Sun. Pluto (orange), the dwarf planet furthest from the Sun, has a pronounced elliptical orbit, whereas Earth (royal blue) has an almost circular orbit. The polar equation of a planet's orbit can be expressed as

$$r = \frac{a\left(1 - e^2\right)}{\left(1 - e\cos\theta\right)}$$

where $e$ is the eccentricity and $2a$ is the length of the major axis. It can also be shown that the perihelion distance (minimum distance from the Sun to a planet) and the aphelion distance (maximum distance from the Sun to the planet) can be represented by $r = a(1 - e)$ and $r = a(1 + e)$, respectively.

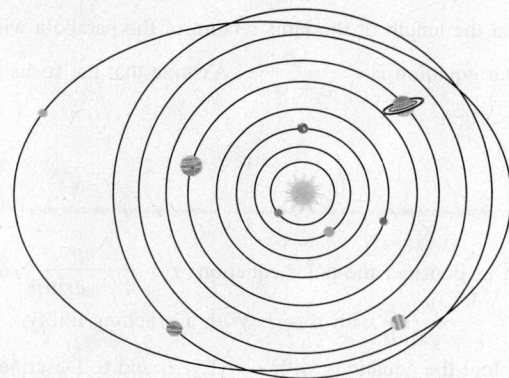

**43. Planetary Orbits.** Pluto's orbit is summarized in the picture below. Find the eccentricity of Pluto's orbit. Find the polar equation that governs Pluto's orbit.

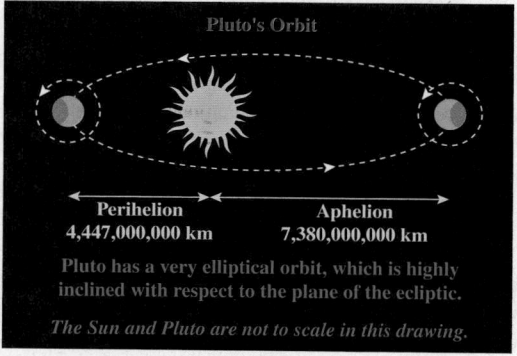

Pluto's Orbit

Perihelion
4,447,000,000 km

Aphelion
7,380,000,000 km

Pluto has a very elliptical orbit, which is highly inclined with respect to the plane of the ecliptic.

*The Sun and Pluto are not to scale in this drawing.*

**44. Planetary Orbits.** Earth's orbit is summarized in the picture below. Find the eccentricity of Earth's orbit. Find the polar equation that governs Earth's orbit.

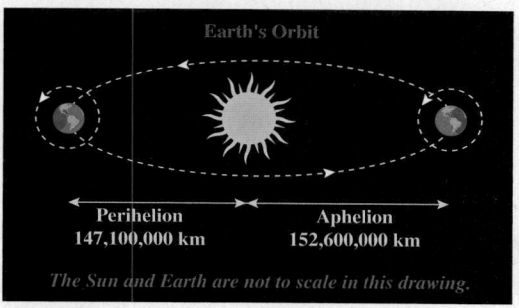

Earth's Orbit

Perihelion
147,100,000 km

Aphelion
152,600,000 km

*The Sun and Earth are not to scale in this drawing.*

**For Exercises 45 and 46, refer to the following:**

Asteroids, meteors, and comets all orbit the Sun in elliptical patterns and often cross paths with Earth's orbit, making life a little tense now and again. Asteroids are large rocks (bodies under 1000 kilometers across), meteors range from sand particles to rocks, and comets are masses of debris. A few asteroids have orbits that cross Earth's orbits—called Apollos or Earth-crossing asteroids. In recent years, asteroids have passed within 100,000 kilometers of Earth!

**45. Asteroids.** The asteroid 433 or Eros is the second largest near-Earth asteroid. The semimajor axis of its orbit is 150 million kilometers and the eccentricity is 0.223. Find the polar equation of Eros's orbit.

**46. Asteroids.** The asteroid Toutatis is the largest near-Earth asteroid. The semimajor axis of its orbit is 350 million kilometers and the eccentricity is 0.634. On September 29, 2004, it missed Earth by 961,000 miles. Find the polar equation of Toutatis's orbit.

**47. Earth's Orbit.** A simplified model of Earth's orbit around the Sun is given by $r = \dfrac{1}{1 + 0.0167\cos\theta}$. Find the center of the orbit in

  **a.** rectangular coordinates
  **b.** polar coordinates

**48. Uranus's Orbit.** A simplified model of Uranus's orbit around the Sun is given by $r = \dfrac{1}{1 + 0.0461\cos\theta}$. Find the center of the orbit in

  **a.** rectangular coordinates
  **b.** polar coordinates

**49. Orbit of Halley's Comet.** A simplified model of the orbit of Halley's Comet around the Sun is given by $r = \dfrac{1}{1 + 0.967\sin\theta}$. Find the center of the orbit in rectangular coordinates.

**50. Orbit of the Hale–Bopp Comet.** A simplified model of the orbit of the Hale–Bopp Comet around the Sun is given by $r = \dfrac{1}{1 + 0.995\sin\theta}$. Find the center of the orbit in rectangular coordinates.

## ▪ CONCEPTUAL

**51.** When $0 < e < 1$, the conic is an ellipse. Does the conic become more elongated or elliptical as $e$ approaches 1 or as $e$ approaches 0?

**52.** Show that $r = \dfrac{ep}{1 - e\sin\theta}$ is the polar equation of a conic with a horizontal directrix that is $p$ units *below* the pole.

**53.** Convert from rectangular to polar coordinates to show that the equation of a hyperbola, $\dfrac{x^2}{a^2} - \dfrac{y^2}{b^2} = 1$, in polar form is $r^2 = -\dfrac{b^2}{1 - e^2\cos^2\theta}$.

**54.** Convert from rectangular to polar coordinates to show that the equation of an ellipse, $\dfrac{x^2}{a^2} + \dfrac{y^2}{b^2} = 1$, in polar form is $r^2 = \dfrac{b^2}{1 - e^2\cos^2\theta}$.

## ▪ CHALLENGE

**55.** Find the major diameter of the ellipse with polar equation $r = \dfrac{ep}{1 + e\cos\theta}$ in terms of $e$ and $p$.

**56.** Find the minor diameter of the ellipse with polar equation $r = \dfrac{ep}{1 + e\cos\theta}$ in terms of $e$ and $p$.

**57.** Find the center of the ellipse with polar equation $r = \dfrac{ep}{1 + e\cos\theta}$ in terms of $e$ and $p$.

**58.** Find the length of the latus rectum of the parabola with polar equation $r = \dfrac{p}{1 + \cos\theta}$. Assume that the focus is at the origin.

## ▪ TECHNOLOGY

**59.** Let us consider the polar equations $r = \dfrac{ep}{1 + e\cos\theta}$ and $r = \dfrac{ep}{1 - e\cos\theta}$ with eccentricity $e = 1$. With a graphing utility, explore the equations with $p = 1, 2,$ and 6. Describe the behavior of the graphs as $p \to \infty$ and also the difference between the two equations.

**60.** Let us consider the polar equations $r = \dfrac{ep}{1 + e\sin\theta}$ and $r = \dfrac{ep}{1 - e\sin\theta}$ with eccentricity $e = 1$. With a graphing utility, explore the equations with $p = 1, 2,$ and 6. Describe the behavior of the graphs as $p \to \infty$ and also the difference between the two equations.

**61.** Let us consider the polar equations $r = \dfrac{ep}{1 + e\cos\theta}$ and $r = \dfrac{ep}{1 - e\cos\theta}$ with $p = 1$. With a graphing utility, explore the equations with $e = 1.5, 3,$ and 6. Describe the behavior of the graphs as $e \to \infty$ and also the difference between the two equations.

**62.** Let us consider the polar equations $r = \dfrac{ep}{1 + e\sin\theta}$ and $r = \dfrac{ep}{1 - e\sin\theta}$ with $p = 1$. With a graphing utility, explore the equations with $e = 1.5, 3,$ and 6. Describe the behavior of the graphs as $e \to \infty$ and also the difference between the two equations.

**63.** Let us consider the polar equations $r = \dfrac{ep}{1 + e\cos\theta}$ and $r = \dfrac{ep}{1 - e\cos\theta}$ with $p = 1$. With a graphing utility, explore the equations with $e = 0.001, 0.5, 0.9,$ and 0.99. Describe the behavior of the graphs as $e \to 1$ and also the difference between the two equations. Be sure to set the window parameters properly.

**64.** Let us consider the polar equations $r = \dfrac{ep}{1 + e\sin\theta}$ and $r = \dfrac{ep}{1 - e\sin\theta}$ with $p = 1$. With a graphing utility, explore the equations with $e = 0.001, 0.5, 0.9,$ and 0.99. Describe the behavior of the graphs as $e \to 1$ and also the difference between the two equations. Be sure to set the window parameters properly.

**65.** Let us consider the polar equation $r = \dfrac{5}{5 + 2\sin\theta}$.

Explain why the graphing utility gives the following graphs with the specified window parameters:

**a.** $[-2, 2]$ by $[-2, 2]$ with $\theta$ step $= \dfrac{\pi}{2}$

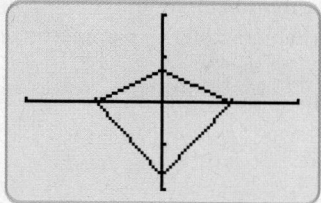

**b.** $[-2, 2]$ by $[-2, 2]$ with $\theta$ step $= \dfrac{\pi}{3}$

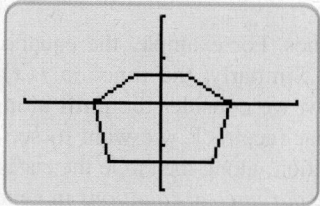

**66.** Let us consider the polar equation $r = \dfrac{2}{1 + \cos\theta}$. Explain why a graphing utility gives the following graphs with the specified window parameters:

**a.** $[-2, 2]$ by $[-4, 4]$ with $\theta$ step $= \dfrac{\pi}{2}$

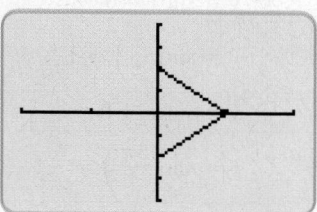

**b.** $[-2, 2]$ by $[-4, 4]$ with $\theta$ step $= \dfrac{\pi}{3}$

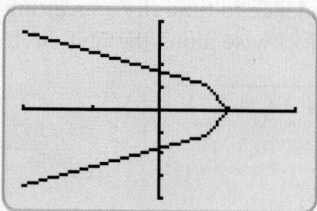

**67.** Let us consider the polar equation $r = \dfrac{6}{1 + 3\sin\theta}$.

Explain why a graphing utility gives the following graphs with the specified window parameters:

**a.** $[-8, 8]$ by $[-2, 4]$ with $\theta$ step $= \dfrac{\pi}{2}$

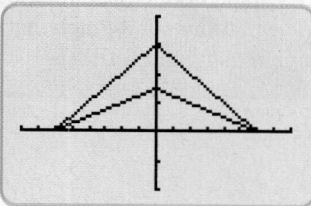

**b.** $[-4, 8]$ by $[-2, 6]$ with $\theta$ step $= 0.4\pi$

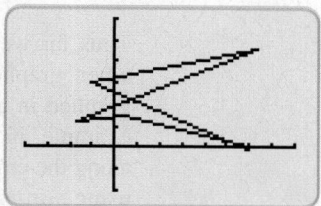

**68.** Let us consider the polar equation $r = \dfrac{2}{1 - \sin\theta}$. Explain why a graphing utility gives the following graphs with the specified window parameters:

**a.** $[-4, 4]$ by $[-2, 4]$ with $\theta$ step $= \dfrac{\pi}{3}$

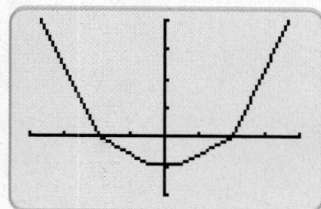

**b.** $[-4, 4]$ by $[-2, 6]$ with $\theta$ step $= 0.8\pi$

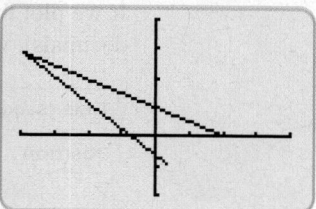

■ **PREVIEW TO CALCULUS**

**In calculus, when finding the area between two polar curves, we need to find the points of intersection of the two curves. In Exercises 69–72, find the values of $\theta$ where the two conic sections intersect on $[0, 2\pi]$.**

**69.** $r = \dfrac{2}{2 + \sin\theta}$, $r = \dfrac{2}{2 + \cos\theta}$

**70.** $r = \dfrac{1}{3 + 2\sin\theta}$, $r = \dfrac{1}{3 - 2\sin\theta}$

**71.** $r = \dfrac{1}{4 - 3\sin\theta}$, $r = \dfrac{1}{-1 + 7\sin\theta}$

**72.** $r = \dfrac{1}{5 + 2\cos\theta}$, $r = \dfrac{1}{10 - 8\cos\theta}$

**SKILLS OBJECTIVES**

- Graph parametric equations.
- Find an equation (in rectangular form) that corresponds to a graph defined parametrically.
- Find parametric equations for a graph that is defined by an equation in rectangular form.

**CONCEPTUAL OBJECTIVES**

- Understand that the results of increasing the value of the parameter reveal the orientation of a curve or the direction of motion along it.
- Use time as a parameter in parametric equations.

## Parametric Equations of a Curve

Thus far we have talked about graphs in planes. For example, the equation $x^2 + y^2 = 1$ when graphed in a plane is the unit circle. Similarly, the function $f(x) = \sin x$ when graphed in a plane is a sinusoidal curve. Now, we consider the **path along a curve**. For example, if a car is being driven on a circular racetrack, we want to see the movement along the circle. We can determine where (position) along the circle the car is at some time $t$ using *parametric equations*. Before we define *parametric equations* in general, let us start with a simple example.

Let $x = \cos t$ and $y = \sin t$ and $t \geq 0$. We then can make a table of some corresponding values.

| $t$ SECONDS | $x = \cos t$ | $y = \sin t$ | $(x, y)$ |
|---|---|---|---|
| $0$ | $x = \cos 0 = 1$ | $y = \sin 0 = 0$ | $(1, 0)$ |
| $\dfrac{\pi}{2}$ | $x = \cos\left(\dfrac{\pi}{2}\right) = 0$ | $y = \sin\left(\dfrac{\pi}{2}\right) = 1$ | $(0, 1)$ |
| $\pi$ | $x = \cos \pi = -1$ | $y = \sin \pi = 0$ | $(-1, 0)$ |
| $\dfrac{3\pi}{2}$ | $x = \cos\left(\dfrac{3\pi}{2}\right) = 0$ | $y = \sin\left(\dfrac{3\pi}{2}\right) = -1$ | $(0, -1)$ |
| $2\pi$ | $x = \cos(2\pi) = 1$ | $y = \sin(2\pi) = 0$ | $(1, 0)$ |

If we plot these points and note the correspondence to time (by converting all numbers to decimals), we will be tracing a *path* counterclockwise along the unit circle.

| TIME (SECONDS) | $t = 0$ | $t = 1.57$ | $t = 3.14$ | $t = 4.71$ |
|---|---|---|---|---|
| POSITION | $(1, 0)$ | $(0, 1)$ | $(-1, 0)$ | $(0, -1)$ |

Notice that at time $t = 6.28$ seconds we are back to the point $(1, 0)$.

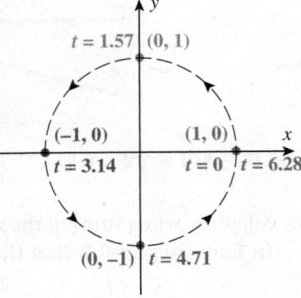

We can see that the path represents the unit circle, since $x^2 + y^2 = \cos^2 t + \sin^2 t = 1$.

**Parametric Equations**

Let $x = f(t)$ and $y = g(t)$ be functions defined for $t$ on some interval. The set of points $(x, y) = [f(t), g(t)]$ represents a **plane curve**. The equations

$$x = f(t) \quad \text{and} \quad y = g(t)$$

are called **parametric equations** of the curve. The variable $t$ is called the **parameter**.

Parametric equations are useful for showing movement along a curve. We insert arrows in the graph to show **direction**, or **orientation**, along the curve as $t$ increases.

**EXAMPLE 1** **Graphing a Curve Defined by Parametric Equations**

Graph the curve defined by the parametric equations

$$x = t^2 \quad y = (t - 1) \quad t \text{ in } [-2, 2]$$

Indicate the orientation with arrows.

**Solution:**

STEP 1 Make a table and find values for $t$, $x$, and $y$.

| $t$ | $x = t^2$ | $y = (t - 1)$ | $(x, y)$ |
|---|---|---|---|
| $t = -2$ | $x = (-2)^2 = 4$ | $y = (-2 - 1) = -3$ | $(4, -3)$ |
| $t = -1$ | $x = (-1)^2 = 1$ | $y = (-1 - 1) = -2$ | $(1, -2)$ |
| $t = 0$ | $x = 0^2 = 0$ | $y = (0 - 1) = -1$ | $(0, -1)$ |
| $t = 1$ | $x = 1^2 = 1$ | $y = (1 - 1) = 0$ | $(1, 0)$ |
| $t = 2$ | $x = 2^2 = 4$ | $y = (2 - 1) = 1$ | $(4, 1)$ |

STEP 2 Plot the points in the $xy$-plane.

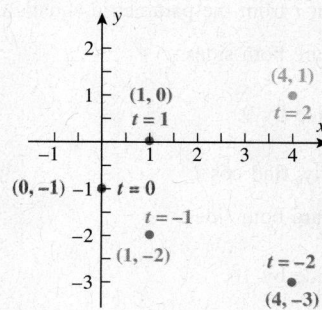

STEP 3 Connect the points with a smooth curve and use arrows to indicate direction.

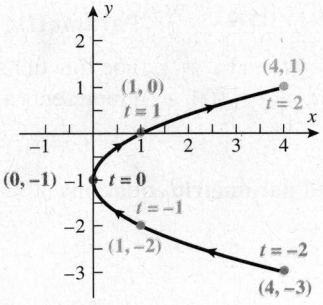

The shape of the graph appears to be a parabola. The parametric equations are $x = t^2$ and $y = (t - 1)$. If we solve the second equation for $t$, getting $t = y + 1$, and substitute this expression into $x = t^2$, the result is $x = (y + 1)^2$. The graph of $x = (y + 1)^2$ is a parabola with vertex at the point $(0, -1)$ and opening to the right.

■ **Answer:**

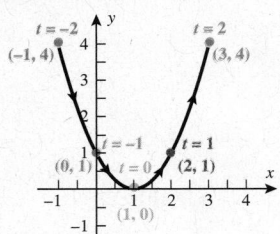

■ **YOUR TURN** Graph the curve defined by the parametric equations

$$x = t + 1 \qquad y = t^2 \qquad t \text{ in } [-2, 2]$$

Indicate the orientation with arrows.

Sometimes it is easier to show the rectangular equivalent of the curve and eliminate the parameter.

 **EXAMPLE 2**  **Graphing a Curve Defined by Parametric Equations by First Finding an Equivalent Rectangular Equation**

Graph the curve defined by the parametric equations

$$x = 4\cos t \qquad y = 3\sin t \qquad t \text{ is any real number}$$

Indicate the orientation with arrows.

**Solution:**

One approach is to point-plot as in Example 1. A second approach is to find the equivalent rectangular equation that represents the curve.

We apply the Pythagorean identity. $\qquad\qquad \sin^2 t + \cos^2 t = 1$

Find $\sin^2 t$ from the parametric equation for $y$. $\qquad y = 3\sin t$

    Square both sides. $\qquad\qquad\qquad\qquad y^2 = 9\sin^2 t$

    Divide by 9. $\qquad\qquad\qquad\qquad\qquad \sin^2 t = \dfrac{y^2}{9}$

Similarly, find $\cos^2 t$. $\qquad\qquad\qquad\qquad x = 4\cos t$

    Square both sides. $\qquad\qquad\qquad\qquad x^2 = 16\cos^2 t$

    Divide by 16. $\qquad\qquad\qquad\qquad\qquad \cos^2 t = \dfrac{x^2}{16}$

Substitute $\sin^2 t = \dfrac{y^2}{9}$ and $\cos^2 t = \dfrac{x^2}{16}$ into $\sin^2 t + \cos^2 t = 1$. $\qquad\qquad \dfrac{y^2}{9} + \dfrac{x^2}{16} = 1$

The curve is an ellipse centered at the origin and elongated horizontally.

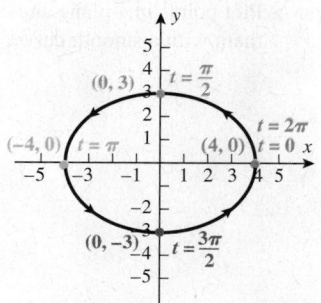

The orientation is counterclockwise. For example, when $t = 0$, the position is $(4, 0)$; when $t = \dfrac{\pi}{2}$, the position is $(0, 3)$; and when $t = \pi$, the position is $(-4, 0)$.

# Applications of Parametric Equations

Parametric equations can be used to describe motion in many applications. Two that we will discuss are the *cycloid* and a *projectile*. Suppose that you paint a red **X** on a bicycle tire. As the bicycle moves in a straight line, if you watch the motion of the red **X**, you will see that it follows the path of a **cycloid**.

The parametric equations that define a cycloid are

$$x = a(t - \sin t) \qquad \text{and} \qquad y = a(1 - \cos t)$$

where $t$ is any real number.

## EXAMPLE 3 Graphing a Cycloid

Graph the cycloid given by $x = 2(t - \sin t)$ and $y = 2(1 - \cos t)$ for $t$ in $[0, 4\pi]$.

**Solution:**

STEP 1 Make a table and find key values for $t$, $x$, and $y$.

| $t$ | $x = 2(t - \sin t)$ | $y = 2(1 - \cos t)$ | $(x, y)$ |
|---|---|---|---|
| $t = 0$ | $x = 2(0 - 0) = 0$ | $y = 2(1 - 1) = 0$ | $(0, 0)$ |
| $t = \pi$ | $x = 2(\pi - 0) = 2\pi$ | $y = 2[1 - (-1)] = 4$ | $(2\pi, 4)$ |
| $t = 2\pi$ | $x = 2(2\pi - 0) = 4\pi$ | $y = 2(1 - 1) = 0$ | $(4\pi, 0)$ |
| $t = 3\pi$ | $x = 2(3\pi - 0) = 6\pi$ | $y = 2[1 - (-1)] = 4$ | $(6\pi, 4)$ |
| $t = 4\pi$ | $x = 2(4\pi - 0) = 8\pi$ | $y = 2(1 - 1) = 0$ | $(8\pi, 0)$ |

STEP 2 Plot points in a plane and connect them with a smooth curve.

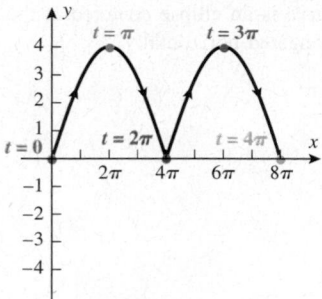

Another example of parametric equations describing real-world phenomena is *projectile motion*. The accompanying photo of a golfer hitting a golf ball presents an example of a projectile.

Joshua Dalsimer/© Corbis; iStockphoto (golf ball)

Let $v_0$ be the initial velocity of an object, $\theta$ be the initial angle of inclination with the horizontal, and $h$ be the initial height above the ground. Then the parametric equations describing the **projectile motion** (which will be developed in calculus) are

$$x = (v_0 \cos \theta)t \qquad \text{and} \qquad y = -\tfrac{1}{2}gt^2 + (v_0 \sin \theta)t + h$$

where $t$ is the time and $g$ is the constant acceleration due to gravity (9.8 meters per square second or 32 feet per square second).

### EXAMPLE 4 Graphing Projectile Motion

Suppose a golfer hits his golf ball with an initial velocity of 160 feet per second at an angle of 30° with the ground. How far is his drive, assuming the length of the drive is from the tee to where the ball first hits the ground? Graph the curve representing the path of the golf ball. Assume that he hits the ball straight off the tee and down the fairway.

**Solution:**

STEP 1 Find the parametric equations that describe the golf ball that the golfer drove.

First, write the parametric equations for projectile motion.

$$x = (v_0 \cos \theta)t \quad \text{and} \quad y = -\tfrac{1}{2}gt^2 + (v_0 \sin \theta)t + h$$

Let $g = 32$ ft/sec$^2$, $v_0 = 160$ ft/sec, $h = 0$, and $\theta = 30°$.

$$x = (160 \cdot \cos 30°)t \quad \text{and} \quad y = -16t^2 + (160 \cdot \sin 30°)t$$

Evaluate the sine and cosine functions and simplify.

$$x = 80\sqrt{3}\,t \quad \text{and} \quad y = -16t^2 + 80t$$

STEP 2   Graph the projectile motion.

| $t$ | $x = 80\sqrt{3}\,t$ | $y = -16t^2 + 80t$ | $(x, y)$ |
|---|---|---|---|
| $t = 0$ | $x = 80\sqrt{3}(0) = 0$ | $y = -16(0)^2 + 80(0) = 0$ | $(0, 0)$ |
| $t = 1$ | $x = 80\sqrt{3}(1) \approx 139$ | $y = -16(1)^2 + 80(1) = 64$ | $(139, 64)$ |
| $t = 2$ | $x = 80\sqrt{3}(2) \approx 277$ | $y = -16(2)^2 + 80(2) = 96$ | $(277, 96)$ |
| $t = 3$ | $x = 80\sqrt{3}(3) \approx 416$ | $y = -16(3)^2 + 80(3) = 96$ | $(416, 96)$ |
| $t = 4$ | $x = 80\sqrt{3}(4) \approx 554$ | $y = -16(4)^2 + 80(4) = 64$ | $(554, 64)$ |
| $t = 5$ | $x = 80\sqrt{3}(5) \approx 693$ | $y = -16(5)^2 + 80(5) = 0$ | $(693, 0)$ |

*Technology Tip*

Graph $x = 80\sqrt{3}\,t$ and $y = -16t^2 + 80t$.

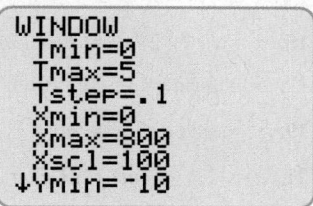

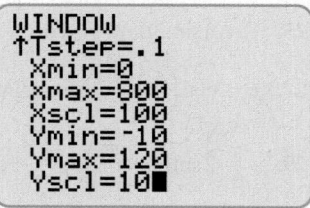

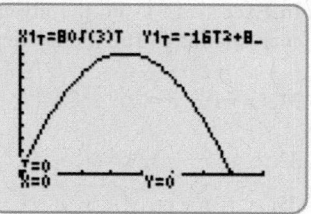

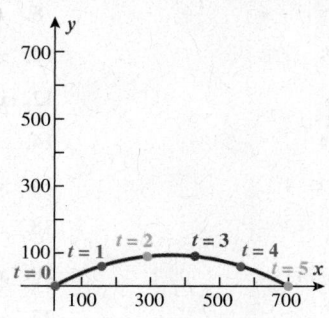

We can see that we selected our time increments well (the last point, $(693, 0)$, corresponds to the ball hitting the ground 693 feet from the tee).

STEP 3   Identify the horizontal distance from the tee to where the ball first hits the ground.

Algebraically, we can determine the distance of the tee shot by setting the height $y$ equal to zero.

$$y = -16t^2 + 80t = 0$$

Factor (divide) the common, $-16t$.

$$-16t(t - 5) = 0$$

Solve for $t$.

$$t = 0 \text{ or } t = 5$$

The ball hits the ground after 5 seconds.

Let $t = 5$ in the horizontal distance, $x = 80\sqrt{3}\,t$.

$$x = 80\sqrt{3}(5) \approx 693$$

> The ball hits the ground 693 feet from the tee.

With parametric equations, we can also determine when the ball lands (5 seconds).

## SECTION
## 9.9   SUMMARY

Parametric equations are a way of describing as a function of $t$, the parameter, the path an object takes along a curve in the $xy$-plane. Parametric equations have equivalent rectangular equations. Typically, the method of graphing a set of parametric equations is to eliminate $t$ and graph the corresponding rectangular equation. Once the curve is found, orientation along the curve can be determined by finding points corresponding to different $t$-values. Two important applications are cycloids and projectiles, whose paths we can trace using parametric equations.

**SECTION**
**9.9** EXERCISES

■ SKILLS

In Exercises 1–30, graph the curve defined by the parametric equations.

**1.** $x = t + 1$, $y = \sqrt{t}$, $t \geq 0$

**2.** $x = 3t$, $y = t^2 - 1$, $t$ in $[0, 4]$

**3.** $x = -3t$, $y = t^2 + 1$, $t$ in $[0, 4]$

**4.** $x = t^2 - 1$, $y = t^2 + 1$, $t$ in $[-3, 3]$

**5.** $x = t^2$, $y = t^3$, $t$ in $[-2, 2]$

**6.** $x = t^3 + 1$, $y = t^3 - 1$, $t$ in $[-2, 2]$

**7.** $x = \sqrt{t}$, $y = t$, $t$ in $[0, 10]$

**8.** $x = t$, $y = \sqrt{t^2 + 1}$, $t$ in $[0, 10]$

**9.** $x = (t + 1)^2$, $y = (t + 2)^3$, $t$ in $[0, 1]$

**10.** $x = (t - 1)^3$, $y = (t - 2)^2$, $t$ in $[0, 4]$

**11.** $x = e^t$, $y = e^{-t}$, $-\ln 3 \leq t \leq \ln 3$

**12.** $x = e^{-2t}$, $y = e^{2t} + 4$, $-\ln 2 \leq t \leq \ln 3$

**13.** $x = 2t^4 - 1$, $y = t^8 + 1$, $0 \leq t \leq 4$

**14.** $x = 3t^6 - 1$, $y = 2t^3$, $-1 \leq t \leq 1$

**15.** $x = t(t - 2)^3$, $y = t(t - 2)^3$, $0 \leq t \leq 4$

**16.** $x = -t\sqrt[3]{t}$, $y = -5t^8 - 2$, $-3 \leq t \leq 3$

**17.** $x = 3 \sin t$, $y = 2 \cos t$, $t$ in $[0, 2\pi]$

**18.** $x = \cos(2t)$, $y = \sin t$, $t$ in $[0, 2\pi]$

**19.** $x = \sin t + 1$, $y = \cos t - 2$, $t$ in $[0, 2\pi]$

**20.** $x = \tan t$, $y = 1$, $t$ in $\left[-\dfrac{\pi}{4}, \dfrac{\pi}{4}\right]$

**21.** $x = 1$, $y = \sin t$, $t$ in $[-2\pi, 2\pi]$

**22.** $x = \sin t$, $y = 2$, $t$ in $[0, 2\pi]$

**23.** $x = \sin^2 t$, $y = \cos^2 t$, $t$ in $[0, 2\pi]$

**24.** $x = 2 \sin^2 t$, $y = 2 \cos^2 t$, $t$ in $[0, 2\pi]$

**25.** $x = 2 \sin(3t)$, $y = 3 \cos(2t)$, $t$ in $[0, 2\pi]$

**26.** $x = 4 \cos(2t)$, $y = t$, $t$ in $[0, 2\pi]$

**27.** $x = \cos\left(\dfrac{t}{2}\right) - 1$, $y = \sin\left(\dfrac{t}{2}\right) + 1$, $-2\pi \leq t \leq 2\pi$

**28.** $x = \sin\left(\dfrac{t}{3}\right) + 3$, $y = \cos\left(\dfrac{t}{3}\right) - 1$, $0 \leq t \leq 6\pi$

**29.** $x = 2 \sin\left(t + \dfrac{\pi}{4}\right)$, $y = -2 \cos\left(t + \dfrac{\pi}{4}\right)$, $-\dfrac{\pi}{4} \leq t \leq \dfrac{7\pi}{4}$

**30.** $x = -3 \cos^2(3t)$, $y = 2 \cos(3t)$, $-\dfrac{\pi}{3} \leq t \leq \dfrac{\pi}{3}$

In Exercises 31–40, the given parametric equations define a plane curve. Find an equation in rectangular form that also corresponds to the plane curve.

**31.** $x = \dfrac{1}{t}$, $y = t^2$

**32.** $x = t^2 - 1$, $y = t^2 + 1$

**33.** $x = t^3 + 1$, $y = t^3 - 1$

**34.** $x = 3t$, $y = t^2 - 1$

**35.** $x = t$, $y = \sqrt{t^2 + 1}$

**36.** $x = \sin^2 t$, $y = \cos^2 t$

**37.** $x = 2 \sin^2 t$, $y = 2 \cos^2 t$

**38.** $x = \sec^2 t$, $y = \tan^2 t$

**39.** $x = 4(t^2 + 1)$, $y = 1 - t^2$

**40.** $x = \sqrt{t - 1}$, $y = \sqrt{t}$

■ APPLICATIONS

For Exercises 41–50, recall that the flight of a projectile can be modeled with the parametric equations

$$x = (v_0 \cos \theta)t \qquad y = -16t^2 + (v_0 \sin \theta)t + h$$

where $t$ is in seconds, $v_0$ is the initial velocity, $\theta$ is the angle with the horizontal, and $x$ and $y$ are in feet.

**41. Flight of a Projectile.** A projectile is launched from the ground at a speed of 400 feet per second at an angle of 45° with the horizontal. After how many seconds does the projectile hit the ground?

**42. Flight of a Projectile.** A projectile is launched from the ground at a speed of 400 feet per second at an angle of 45° with the horizontal. How far does the projectile travel (what is the horizontal distance), and what is its maximum altitude?

**43. Flight of a Baseball.** A baseball is hit at an initial speed of 105 miles per hour and an angle of 20° at a height of 3 feet above the ground. If home plate is 420 feet from the back fence, which is 15 feet tall, will the baseball clear the back fence for a home run?

**44. Flight of a Baseball.** A baseball is hit at an initial speed of 105 miles per hour and an angle of 20° at a height of 3 feet above the ground. If there is no back fence or other obstruction, how far does the baseball travel (horizontal distance), and what is its maximum height?

**45. Bullet Fired.** A gun is fired from the ground at an angle of 60°, and the bullet has an initial speed of 700 feet per second. How high does the bullet go? What is the horizontal (ground) distance between the point where the gun is fired and the point where the bullet hits the ground?

**46. Bullet Fired.** A gun is fired from the ground at an angle of 60°, and the bullet has an initial speed of 2000 feet per second. How high does the bullet go? What is the horizontal (ground) distance between the point where the gun is fired and the point where the bullet hits the ground?

**47. Missile Fired.** A missile is fired from a ship at an angle of 30°, an initial height of 20 feet above the water's surface, and a speed of 4000 feet per second. How long will it be before the missile hits the water?

**48. Missile Fired.** A missile is fired from a ship at an angle of 40°, an initial height of 20 feet above the water's surface, and a speed of 5000 feet per second. Will the missile be able to hit a target that is 2 miles away?

**49. Path of a Projectile.** A projectile is launched at a speed of 100 feet per second at an angle of 35° with the horizontal. Plot the path of the projectile on a graph. Assume that $h = 0$.

**50. Path of a Projectile.** A projectile is launched at a speed of 150 feet per second at an angle of 55° with the horizontal. Plot the path of the projectile on a graph. Assume that $h = 0$.

**For Exercises 51 and 52, refer to the following:**

Modern amusement park rides are often designed to push the envelope in terms of speed, angle, and ultimately $g$'s, and usually take the form of gargantuan roller coasters or skyscraping towers. However, even just a couple of decades ago, such creations were depicted only in fantasy-type drawings, with their creators never truly believing their construction would become a reality. Nevertheless, thrill rides still capable of nauseating any would-be rider were still able to be constructed; one example is the *Calypso*. This ride is a not-too-distant cousin of the more well-known *Scrambler*. It consists of four rotating arms (instead of three like the Scrambler), and on each of these arms, four cars (equally spaced around the circumference of a circular frame) are attached. Once in motion, the main piston to which the four arms are connected rotates clockwise, while each of the four arms themselves rotates counterclockwise. The combined motion appears as a blur to any onlooker from the crowd, but the motion of a single rider is much less chaotic. In fact, a single rider's path can be modeled by the following graph:

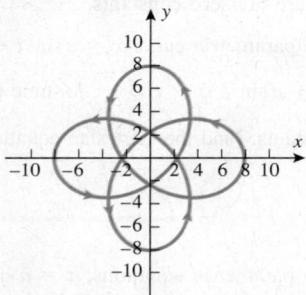

The equation of this graph is defined parametrically by

$$x(t) = A\cos t + B\cos(-3t)$$
$$y(t) = A\sin t + B\sin(-3t) \quad 0 \le t \le 2\pi$$

**51. Amusement Rides.** What is the location of the rider at $t = 0$, $t = \dfrac{\pi}{2}$, $t = \pi$, $t = \dfrac{3\pi}{2}$, and $t = 2\pi$?

**52. Amusement Rides.** Suppose that the ride conductor was rather sinister and speeded up the ride to twice the speed. How would you modify the parametric equations to model such a change? Now vary the values of $A$ and $B$. What do you think these parameters are modeling in this problem?

■**CATCH THE MISTAKE**

**In Exercises 53 and 54, explain the mistake that is made.**

**53.** Find the rectangular equation that corresponds to the plane curve defined by the parametric equations $x = t + 1$ and $y = \sqrt{t}$. Describe the plane curve.

**Solution:**

Square $y = \sqrt{t}$.                $y^2 = t$

Substitute $t = y^2$ into $x = t + 1$.    $x = y^2 + 1$

The graph of $x = y^2 + 1$ is a parabola opening to the right with its vertex at $(1, 0)$.

This is incorrect. What mistake was made?

**54.** Find the rectangular equation that corresponds to the plane curve defined by the parametric equations $x = \sqrt{t}$ and $y = t - 1$. Describe the plane curve.

**Solution:**

Square $x = \sqrt{t}$.                $x^2 = t$

Substitute $t = x^2$ into $y = t - 1$.    $y = x^2 - 1$

The graph of $y = x^2 - 1$ is a parabola opening up with its vertex at $(0, -1)$.

This is incorrect. What mistake was made?

■ **CONCEPTUAL**

**In Exercises 55 and 56, determine whether each statement is true or false.**

**55.** Curves given by equations in rectangular form have orientation.

**56.** Curves given by parametric equations have orientation.

**57.** Determine what type of curve the parametric equations $x = \sqrt{t}$ and $y = \sqrt{1-t}$ define.

**58.** Determine what type of curve the parametric equations $x = \ln t$ and $y = t$ define.

■ **CHALLENGE**

**59.** Prove that $x = a\tan t$, $y = b\sec t$, $0 \le t \le 2\pi$, $t \ne \dfrac{\pi}{2}, \dfrac{3\pi}{2}$ are parametric equations for a hyperbola. Assume that $a$ and $b$ are nonzero constants.

**60.** Prove that $x = a\csc\left(\dfrac{t}{2}\right)$, $y = b\cot\left(\dfrac{t}{2}\right)$, $0 \le t \le 4\pi$, $t \ne \pi, 3\pi$ are parametric equations for a hyperbola. Assume that $a$ and $b$ are nonzero constants.

**61.** Consider the parametric curve $x = a\sin^2 t - b\cos^2 t$, $y = b\cos^2 t + a\sin^2 t$, $0 \le t \le \dfrac{\pi}{2}$. Assume that $a$ and $b$ are nonzero constants. Find the Cartesian equation for this curve.

**62.** Consider the parametric curve $x = a\sin t + a\cos t$, $y = a\cos t - a\sin t$, $0 \le t \le 2\pi$. Assume that $a$ is not zero. Find the Cartesian equation for this curve.

**63.** Consider the parametric curve $x = e^{at}$, $y = be^t$, $t > 0$. Assume that $a$ is a positive integer and $b$ is a positive real number. Determine the Cartesian equation.

**64.** Consider the parametric curve $x = a\ln t$, $y = \ln(bt)$, $t > 0$. Assume that $b$ is a positive integer and $a$ is a positive real number. Determine the Cartesian equation.

■ **TECHNOLOGY**

**65.** Consider the parametric equations: $x = a\sin t - \sin(at)$ and $y = a\cos t + \cos(at)$. With a graphing utility, explore the graphs for $a = 2, 3$, and $4$.

**66.** Consider the parametric equations: $x = a\cos t - b\cos(at)$ and $y = a\sin t + \sin(at)$. With a graphing utility, explore the graphs for $a = 3$ and $b = 1$, $a = 4$ and $b = 2$, and $a = 6$ and $b = 2$. Find the $t$-interval that gives one cycle of the curve.

**67.** Consider the parametric equations: $x = \cos(at)$ and $y = \sin(bt)$. With a graphing utility, explore the graphs for $a = 2$ and $b = 4$, $a = 4$ and $b = 2$, $a = 1$ and $b = 3$, and $a = 3$ and $b = 1$. Find the $t$-interval that gives one cycle of the curve.

**68.** Consider the parametric equations: $x = a\sin(at) - \sin t$ and $y = a\cos(at) - \cos t$. With a graphing utility, explore the graphs for $a = 2$ and $3$. Describe the $t$-interval for each case.

**69.** Consider the parametric equations $x = a\cos(at) - \sin t$ and $y = a\sin(at) - \cos t$. With a graphing utility, explore the graphs for $a = 2$ and $3$. Describe the $t$-interval for each case.

**70.** Consider the parametric equations $x = a\sin(at) - \cos t$ and $y = a\cos(at) - \sin t$. With a graphing utility, explore the graphs for $a = 2$ and $3$. Describe the $t$-interval for each case.

■ **PREVIEW TO CALCULUS**

**In calculus, some operations can be simplified by using parametric equations. Finding the points of intersection (if they exist) of two curves given by parametric equations is a standard procedure.**

**In Exercises 71–74, find the points of intersection of the given curves given $s$ and $t$ are any real numbers.**

**71.** Curve I: $x = t$, $y = t^2 - 1$
Curve II: $x = s + 1$, $y = 4 - s$

**72.** Curve I: $x = t^2 + 3$, $y = t$
Curve II: $x = s + 2$, $y = 1 - s$

**73.** Curve I: $x = 100t$, $y = 80t - 16t^2$
Curve II: $x = 100 - 200t$, $y = -16t^2 + 144t - 224$

**74.** Curve I: $x = t^2$, $y = t + 1$
Curve II: $x = 2 + s$, $y = 1 - s$

# CHAPTER 9 INQUIRY-BASED LEARNING PROJECT

### "And the Rockets Red Glare . . ."

Scientists at Vandenberg Air Force Base are interested in tracing the path of some newly designed rockets. They will launch two rockets at 100 feet per second. One will depart at 45°, the other at 60°. From vector analysis and gravity, you determine the following coordinates $(x, y)$ as a function of time $t$ where $y$ stands for height in feet above the ground and $x$ stands for lateral distance traveled.

| 45° | 60° |
|---|---|
| $x = 100 \cos(45°)t$ | $x = 100 \cos(60°)t$ |
| $y = -16t^2 + 100 \sin(45°)t$ | $y = -16t^2 + 100 \sin(60°)t$ |

**1.** For each angle (45°, 60°), fill in the chart (round to one decimal place). You can do this by hand (very slowly) or use the table capabilities of a calculator or similar device.

| $t$ | 0 | 0.5 | 1.0 | 1.5 | 2.0 | 2.5 | 3.0 | 3.5 | 4.0 | 4.5 | 5.0 |
|---|---|---|---|---|---|---|---|---|---|---|---|
| $X_{45}$ | | | | | | | | | | | |
| $Y_{45}$ | | | | | | | | | | | |
| $X_{60}$ | | | | | | | | | | | |
| $Y_{60}$ | | | | | | | | | | | |

**2.** What are a few things worth noting when looking at your table values? Think about the big picture and the fact that you are dealing with projectiles.

Show your work for the following:

**3.** Which rocket traveled higher and by how much? Recall that the $y$ variable is the height. (List the heights of each rocket.)

**4.** When each rocket first hits the ground, which one has traveled farther laterally and by how much? (List distances of each.)

**5.** Which rocket was in the air longer and by how much? (List the times of each.)

**6.** For each rocket, write $t$ in terms of $x$. Then substitute this value into the $y$ equation. This is called "eliminating the parameter" and puts $y$ as a function of $x$. Simplify completely. Use exact values. Reduce the fractions to their lowest terms.

# MODELING OUR WORLD

In the Modeling Our World (MOW) features in Chapters 1–3, you used the average yearly temperature in degrees Fahrenheit (°F) and carbon dioxide emissions in parts per million (ppm) collected by NOAA in Mauna Loa, Hawaii, to develop linear (Chapter 1) and nonlinear (Chapters 2 and 3) models. In the following exercises, you will determine when these different models actually predict the same temperatures and carbon emissions. It is important to realize that not only can different models be used to predict trends, but also the choice of data those models are fitted to also affects the models and hence the predicted values.

| Year | 1960 | 1965 | 1970 | 1975 | 1980 | 1985 | 1990 | 1995 | 2000 | 2005 |
|---|---|---|---|---|---|---|---|---|---|---|
| Temperature | 44.45 | 43.29 | 43.61 | 43.35 | 46.66 | 45.71 | 45.53 | 47.53 | 45.86 | 46.23 |
| $CO_2$ emissions (ppm) | 316.9 | 320.0 | 325.7 | 331.1 | 338.7 | 345.9 | 354.2 | 360.6 | 369.4 | 379.7 |

1. Solve the system of nonlinear equations governing mean temperature that was found by using two data points:

   Equation (1): Use the linear model developed in MOW Chapter 1, Exercise 2(a).

   Equation (2): Use the quadratic model found in MOW Chapter 2, Exercise 2(a).

2. For what year do the models used in Exercise 1 agree? Compare the value given by the models that year to the actual data for the year.

3. Solve the system of nonlinear equations governing mean temperature that was found by applying regression (all data points):

   Equation (1): Use the linear model developed in MOW Chapter 1, Exercise 2(c).

   Equation (2): Use the quadratic model found in MOW Chapter 2, Exercise 2(c).

4. For what year do the models used in Exercise 3 agree? Compare the value given by the models that year to the actual data for the year.

5. Solve the system of nonlinear equations governing carbon dioxide emissions that was found by using two data points:

   Equation (1): Use the linear model developed in MOW Chapter 1, Exercise 7(a).

   Equation (2): Use the quadratic model found in MOW Chapter 2, Exercise 7(a).

6. For what year do the models used in Exercise 5 agree? Compare the value given by the models that year to the actual data for the year.

7. Solve the system of nonlinear equations governing carbon emissions that was found by applying regression (all data points):

   Equation (1): Use the linear model developed in MOW Chapter 1, Exercise 7(c).

   Equation (2): Use the quadratic model found in MOW Chapter 2, Exercise 7(c).

8. For what year do the models used in Exercise 7 agree? Compare the value given by the models that year to the actual data for the year.

| SECTION | CONCEPT | KEY IDEAS/FORMULAS |
|---|---|---|
| 9.1 | **Conic basics** | |
| | Three types of conics | **Parabola, ellipse, and hyperbola:** **Parabola:** Distances from a point to a reference point (focus) and a reference line (directrix) are equal. **Ellipse:** Sum of the distances between the point and two reference points (foci) is constant. **Hyperbola:** Difference of the distances between the point and two reference points (foci) is constant. |
| 9.2 | **The parabola** | |
| | Parabola with a vertex at the origin | 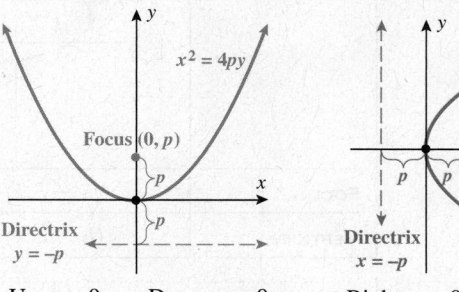 Up: $p > 0$    Down: $p < 0$    Right: $p > 0$    Left: $p < 0$ |

| | Parabola with a vertex at the point $(h, k)$ | |
|---|---|---|

| EQUATION | $(y - k)^2 = 4p(x - h)$ | $(x - h)^2 = 4p(y - k)$ |
|---|---|---|
| VERTEX | $(h, k)$ | $(h, k)$ |
| FOCUS | $(p + h, k)$ | $(h, p + k)$ |
| DIRECTRIX | $x = -p + h$ | $y = -p + k$ |
| AXIS OF SYMMETRY | $y = k$ | $x = h$ |
| $p > 0$ | opens to the right | opens upward |
| $p < 0$ | opens to the left | opens downward |

| 9.3 | **The ellipse** | |
|---|---|---|
| | Ellipse centered at the origin | 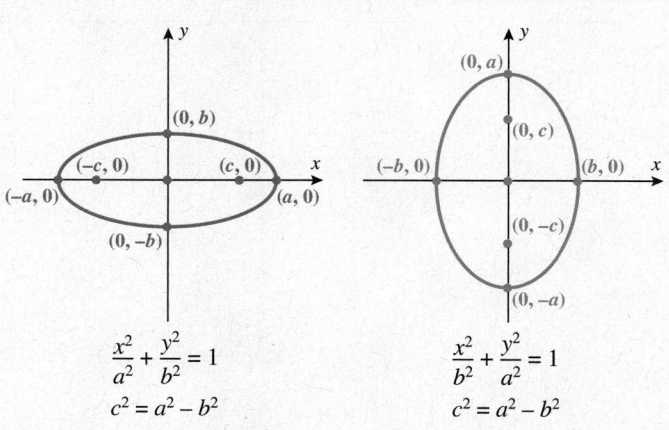 |

$$\frac{x^2}{a^2} + \frac{y^2}{b^2} = 1$$
$$c^2 = a^2 - b^2$$

$$\frac{x^2}{b^2} + \frac{y^2}{a^2} = 1$$
$$c^2 = a^2 - b^2$$

Ellipse centered
at the point $(h, k)$

| ORIENTATION OF MAJOR AXIS | Horizontal (parallel to the $x$-axis) | Vertical (parallel to the $y$-axis) |
|---|---|---|
| EQUATION | $\dfrac{(x-h)^2}{a^2} + \dfrac{(y-k)^2}{b^2} = 1$ | $\dfrac{(x-h)^2}{b^2} + \dfrac{(y-k)^2}{a^2} = 1$ |
| GRAPH | | |
| FOCI | $(h-c, k)$ and $(h+c, k)$ | $(h, k-c)$ and $(h, k+c)$ |
| VERTICES | $(h-a, k)$ and $(h+a, k)$ | $(h, k-a)$ and $(h, k+a)$ |

Graph (Horizontal): points labeled $(h, k+b)$, $(h-a, k)$, $(h, k)$, $(h+a, k)$, $(h-c, k)$, $(h+c, k)$, $(h, k-b)$.

Graph (Vertical): points labeled $(h, k+a)$, $(h, k+c)$, $(h-b, k)$, $(h+b, k)$, $(h, k)$, $(h, k-c)$, $(h, k-a)$.

## 9.4  The hyperbola

Hyperbola centered
at the origin

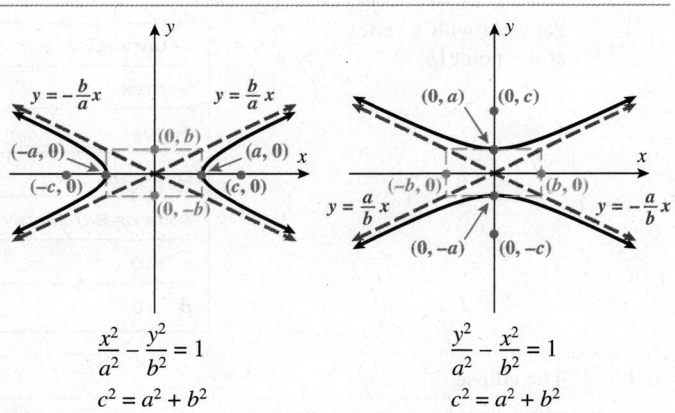

$\dfrac{x^2}{a^2} - \dfrac{y^2}{b^2} = 1$

$c^2 = a^2 + b^2$

$\dfrac{y^2}{a^2} - \dfrac{x^2}{b^2} = 1$

$c^2 = a^2 + b^2$

| Section | Concept | Key Ideas/Formulas |
|---|---|---|

| Hyperbola centered at the point $(h, k)$ | | |
|---|---|---|

| Orientation of Transverse Axis | Horizontal (parallel to the $x$-axis) | Vertical (parallel to the $y$-axis) |
|---|---|---|
| Equation | $\dfrac{(x-h)^2}{a^2} - \dfrac{(y-k)^2}{b^2} = 1$ | $\dfrac{(y-k)^2}{a^2} - \dfrac{(x-h)^2}{b^2} = 1$ |
| Vertices | $(h-a, k)$ and $(h+a, k)$ | $(h, k-a)$ and $(h, k+a)$ |
| Foci | $(h-c, k)$ and $(h+c, k)$ where $c^2 = a^2 + b^2$ | $(h, k-c)$ and $(h, k+c)$ where $c^2 = a^2 + b^2$ |
| Graph | | |

| | | |
|---|---|---|
| **9.5** | **Systems of nonlinear equations** | There is no procedure guaranteed to solve nonlinear equations. |
| | Solving a system of nonlinear equations | **Elimination** <br> Eliminate a variable by either adding one equation to or subtracting one equation from the other. <br><br> **Substitution** <br> Solve for one variable in terms of the other and substitute into the second equation. |
| **9.6** | **Systems of nonlinear inequalities** | Solutions are determined graphically by finding the common shaded regions. <br> ■ $\leq$ or $\geq$ use solid curves. <br> ■ $<$ or $>$ use dashed curves. |
| | Nonlinear inequalities in two variables | Step 1: Rewrite the inequality as an equation. <br> Step 2: Graph the equation. <br> Step 3: Test points. <br> Step 4: Shade. |
| | Systems of nonlinear inequalities | Graph the individual inequalities and the solution in the common (overlapping) shaded region. |
| **9.7** | **Rotation of axes** | |
| | Rotation of axes formulas | $x = X \cos\theta - Y \sin\theta$ <br> $y = X \sin\theta + Y \cos\theta$ |
| | The angle of rotation necessary to transform a general second-degree equation into a familiar equation of a conic | $\cot(2\theta) = \dfrac{A - C}{B}$ or $\tan(2\theta) = \dfrac{B}{A - C}$ |

| SECTION | CONCEPT | KEY IDEAS/FORMULAS |
|---|---|---|
| 9.8 | **Polar equations of conics** | All three conics (parabolas, ellipses, and hyperbolas) are defined in terms of a single focus and a directrix. |
|  | Equations of conics in polar coordinates | The directrix is *vertical* and *p* units to the *right* of the pole. $$r = \frac{ep}{1 + e\cos\theta}$$ The directrix is *vertical* and *p* units to the *left* of the pole. $$r = \frac{ep}{1 - e\cos\theta}$$ The directrix is *horizontal* and *p* units *above* the pole. $$r = \frac{ep}{1 + e\sin\theta}$$ The directrix is *horizontal* and *p* units *below* the pole. $$r = \frac{ep}{1 - e\sin\theta}$$ |
| 9.9 | **Parametric equations and graphs** |  |
|  | Parametric equations of a curve | Parametric equations: $x = f(t)$ and $y = g(t)$ <br> Plane curve: $(x, y) = (f(t), g(t))$ |
|  | Applications of parametric equations | Cycloids and projectiles |

## 9.1 Conic Basics

**Determine whether each statement is true or false.**

1. The focus is a point on the graph of the parabola.

2. The graph of $y^2 = 8x$ is a parabola that opens upward.

3. $\dfrac{x^2}{9} - \dfrac{y^2}{1} = 1$ is the graph of a hyperbola that has a horizontal transverse axis.

4. $\dfrac{(x+1)^2}{9} + \dfrac{(y-3)^2}{16} = 1$ is a graph of an ellipse whose center is $(1, 3)$.

## 9.2 The Parabola

**Find an equation for the parabola described.**

5. Vertex at $(0, 0)$; Focus at $(3, 0)$

6. Vertex at $(0, 0)$; Focus at $(0, 2)$

7. Vertex at $(0, 0)$; Directrix at $x = 5$

8. Vertex at $(0, 0)$; Directrix at $y = 4$

9. Vertex at $(2, 3)$; Focus at $(2, 5)$

10. Vertex at $(-1, -2)$; Focus at $(1, -2)$

11. Focus at $(1, 5)$; Directrix at $y = 7$

12. Focus at $(2, 2)$; Directrix at $x = 0$

**Find the focus, vertex, directrix, and length of the latus rectum, and graph the parabola.**

13. $x^2 = -12y$

14. $x^2 = 8y$

15. $y^2 = x$

16. $y^2 = -6x$

17. $(y + 2)^2 = 4(x - 2)$

18. $(y - 2)^2 = -4(x + 1)$

19. $(x + 3)^2 = -8(y - 1)$

20. $(x - 3)^2 = -8(y + 2)$

21. $x^2 + 5x + 2y + 25 = 0$

22. $y^2 + 2y - 16x + 1 = 0$

## Applications

23. **Satellite Dish.** A satellite dish measures 10 feet across its opening and 2 feet deep at its center. The receiver should be placed at the focus of the parabolic dish. Where should the receiver be placed?

24. **Clearance Under a Bridge.** A bridge with a parabolic shape reaches a height of 40 feet in the center of the road, and the width of the bridge opening at ground level is 30 feet combined (both lanes). If an RV is 14 feet tall and 8 feet wide, will it make it through the tunnel?

## 9.3 The Ellipse

**Graph each ellipse.**

25. $\dfrac{x^2}{9} + \dfrac{y^2}{64} = 1$

26. $\dfrac{x^2}{81} + \dfrac{y^2}{49} = 1$

27. $25x^2 + y^2 = 25$

28. $4x^2 + 8y^2 = 64$

**Find the standard form of an equation of the ellipse with the given characteristics.**

29. Foci: $(-3, 0)$ and $(3, 0)$   Vertices: $(-5, 0)$ and $(5, 0)$

30. Foci: $(0, -2)$ and $(0, 2)$   Vertices: $(0, -3)$ and $(0, 3)$

31. Major axis vertical with length of 16, minor axis length of 6, and centered at $(0, 0)$

32. Major axis horizontal with length of 30, minor axis length of 20, and centered at $(0, 0)$

**Graph each ellipse.**

33. $\dfrac{(x-7)^2}{100} + \dfrac{(y+5)^2}{36} = 1$

34. $20(x + 3)^2 + (y - 4)^2 = 120$

35. $4x^2 - 16x + 12y^2 + 72y + 123 = 0$

36. $4x^2 - 8x + 9y^2 - 72y + 147 = 0$

**Find the standard form of an equation of the ellipse with the given characteristics.**

37. Foci: $(-1, 3)$ and $(7, 3)$   Vertices: $(-2, 3)$ and $(8, 3)$

38. Foci: $(1, -3)$ and $(1, -1)$   Vertices: $(1, -4)$ and $(1, 0)$

## Applications

39. **Planetary Orbits.** Jupiter's orbit is summarized in the picture. Utilize the fact that the Sun is a focus to determine an equation for Jupiter's elliptical orbit around the Sun. Round to the nearest hundred thousand kilometers.

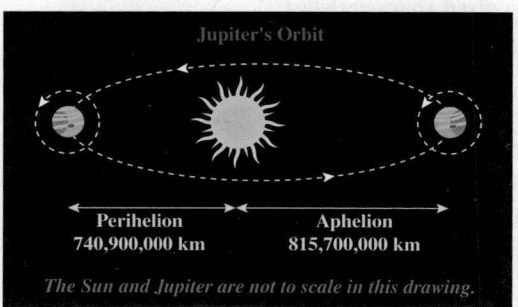

Jupiter's Orbit

Perihelion
740,900,000 km

Aphelion
815,700,000 km

*The Sun and Jupiter are not to scale in this drawing.*

**40. Planetary Orbits.** Mars's orbit is summarized in the picture that follows. Utilize the fact that the Sun is a focus to determine an equation for Mars's elliptical orbit around the Sun. Round to the nearest million kilometers.

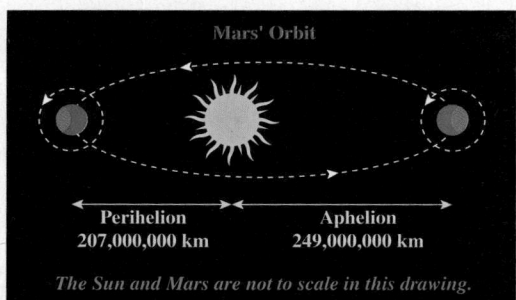

Mars' Orbit

Perihelion
207,000,000 km

Aphelion
249,000,000 km

*The Sun and Mars are not to scale in this drawing.*

## 9.4 The Hyperbola

**Graph each hyperbola.**

**41.** $\dfrac{x^2}{9} - \dfrac{y^2}{64} = 1$

**42.** $\dfrac{x^2}{81} - \dfrac{y^2}{49} = 1$

**43.** $x^2 - 25y^2 = 25$

**44.** $8y^2 - 4x^2 = 64$

**Find the standard form of an equation of the hyperbola with the given characteristics.**

**45.** Vertices: $(-3, 0)$ and $(3, 0)$     Foci: $(-5, 0)$ and $(5, 0)$

**46.** Vertices: $(0, -1)$ and $(0, 1)$     Foci: $(0, -3)$ and $(0, 3)$

**47.** Center: $(0, 0)$; Transverse: $y$-axis; Asymptotes: $y = 3x$ and $y = -3x$

**48.** Center: $(0, 0)$; Transverse axis: $y$-axis; Asymptotes: $y = \frac{1}{2}x$ and $y = -\frac{1}{2}x$

**Graph each hyperbola.**

**49.** $\dfrac{(y - 1)^2}{36} - \dfrac{(x - 2)^2}{9} = 1$

**50.** $3(x + 3)^2 - 12(y - 4)^2 = 72$

**51.** $8x^2 - 32x - 10y^2 - 60y - 138 = 0$

**52.** $2x^2 + 12x - 8y^2 + 16y + 6 = 0$

**Find the standard form of an equation of the hyperbola with the given characteristics.**

**53.** Vertices: $(0, 3)$ and $(8, 3)$     Foci: $(-1, 3)$ and $(9, 3)$

**54.** Vertices: $(4, -2)$ and $(4, 0)$     Foci: $(4, -3)$ and $(4, 1)$

### Applications

**55. Ship Navigation.** Two loran stations are located 220 miles apart along a coast. If a ship records a time difference of 0.00048 second and continues on the hyperbolic path corresponding to that difference, where would it reach shore? Assume that the speed of radio signals is 186,000 miles per second.

**56. Ship Navigation.** Two loran stations are located 400 miles apart along a coast. If a ship records a time difference of 0.0008 second and continues on the hyperbolic path corresponding to that difference, where would it reach shore?

## 9.5 Systems of Nonlinear Equations

**Solve the system of equations with the elimination method.**

**57.** $\begin{aligned} x^2 + y &= -3 \\ x - y &= 5 \end{aligned}$

**58.** $\begin{aligned} x^2 + y^2 &= 4 \\ x^2 + y &= 2 \end{aligned}$

**59.** $\begin{aligned} x^2 + y^2 &= 5 \\ 2x^2 - y &= 0 \end{aligned}$

**60.** $\begin{aligned} x^2 + y^2 &= 16 \\ 6x^2 + y^2 &= 16 \end{aligned}$

**Solve the system of equations with the substitution method.**

**61.** $\begin{aligned} x + y &= 3 \\ x^2 + y^2 &= 4 \end{aligned}$

**62.** $\begin{aligned} xy &= 4 \\ x^2 + y^2 &= 16 \end{aligned}$

**63.** $\begin{aligned} x^2 + xy + y^2 &= -12 \\ x - y &= 2 \end{aligned}$

**64.** $\begin{aligned} 3x + y &= 3 \\ x - y^2 &= -9 \end{aligned}$

**Solve the system of equations by applying any method.**

**65.** $\begin{aligned} x^3 - y^3 &= -19 \\ x - y &= -1 \end{aligned}$

**66.** $\begin{aligned} 2x^2 + 4xy &= 9 \\ x^2 - 2xy &= 0 \end{aligned}$

**67.** $\begin{aligned} \dfrac{2}{x^2} + \dfrac{1}{y^2} &= 15 \\ \dfrac{1}{x^2} - \dfrac{1}{y^2} &= -3 \end{aligned}$

**68.** $\begin{aligned} x^2 + y^2 &= 2 \\ x^2 + y^2 &= 4 \end{aligned}$

## 9.6 Systems of Nonlinear Inequalities

**Graph the nonlinear inequality.**

**69.** $y \geq x^2 + 3$

**70.** $x^2 + y^2 > 16$

**71.** $y \leq e^x$

**72.** $y < -x^3 + 2$

**73.** $y \geq \ln(x - 1)$

**74.** $9x^2 + 4y^2 \leq 36$

**Solve each system of inequalities and shade the region on a graph, or indicate that the system has no solution.**

**75.** $\begin{aligned} y &\geq x^2 - 2 \\ y &\leq -x^2 + 2 \end{aligned}$

**76.** $\begin{aligned} x^2 + y^2 &\leq 4 \\ y &\leq x \end{aligned}$

**77.** $\begin{aligned} y &\geq (x + 1)^2 - 2 \\ y &\leq 10 - x \end{aligned}$

**78.** $\begin{aligned} 3x^2 + 3y^2 &\leq 27 \\ y &\geq x - 1 \end{aligned}$

**79.** $\begin{aligned} 4y^2 - 9x^2 &\leq 36 \\ y &\geq x + 1 \end{aligned}$

**80.** $\begin{aligned} 9x^2 + 16y^2 &\leq 144 \\ y &\geq 1 - x^2 \end{aligned}$

## 9.7 Rotation of Axes

**The coordinates of a point in the $xy$-coordinate system are given. Assuming the $X$- and $Y$-axes are found by rotating the $x$- and $y$-axes by the indicated angle $\theta$, find the corresponding coordinates for the point in the $XY$-system.**

**81.** $(-3, 2)$,  $\theta = 60°$

**82.** $(4, -3)$,  $\theta = 45°$

**Transform the equation of the conic into an equation in $X$ and $Y$ (without an $XY$-term) by rotating the $x$- and $y$-axes through the indicated angle $\theta$. Then graph the resulting equation.**

**83.** $2x^2 + 4\sqrt{3}xy - 2y^2 - 16 = 0$,  $\theta = 30°$

**84.** $25x^2 + 14xy + 25y^2 - 288 = 0$,  $\theta = \dfrac{\pi}{4}$

Determine the angle of rotation necessary to transform the equation in $x$ and $y$ into an equation in $X$ and $Y$ with no $XY$-term.

**85.** $4x^2 + 2\sqrt{3}xy + 6y^2 - 9 = 0$

**86.** $4x^2 + 5xy + 4y^2 - 11 = 0$

Graph the second-degree equation.

**87.** $x^2 + 2xy + y^2 + \sqrt{2}x - \sqrt{2}y + 8 = 0$

**88.** $76x^2 + 48\sqrt{3}xy + 28y^2 - 100 = 0$

## 9.8 Polar Equations of Conics

Find the polar equation that represents the conic described.

**89.** An ellipse with eccentricity $e = \frac{3}{7}$ and directrix $y = -7$

**90.** A parabola with directrix $x = 2$

Identify the conic (parabola, ellipse, or hyperbola) that each polar equation represents.

**91.** $r = \dfrac{6}{4 - 5\cos\theta}$

**92.** $r = \dfrac{2}{5 + 3\sin\theta}$

For the given polar equations, find the eccentricity and vertex (or vertices), and graph the curve.

**93.** $r = \dfrac{4}{2 + \cos\theta}$

**94.** $r = \dfrac{6}{1 - \sin\theta}$

## 9.9 Parametric Equations and Graphs

Graph the curve defined by the parametric equations.

**95.** $x = \sin t, y = 4\cos t$ for $t$ in $[-\pi, \pi]$

**96.** $x = 5\sin^2 t, y = 2\cos^2 t$ for $t$ in $[-\pi, \pi]$

**97.** $x = 4 - t^2, y = t^2$ for $t$ in $[-3, 3]$

**98.** $x = t + 3, y = 4$ for $t$ in $[-4, 4]$

The given parametric equations define a plane curve. Find an equation in rectangular form that also corresponds to the plane curve.

**99.** $x = 4 - t^2, y = t$

**100.** $x = 5\sin^2 t, y = 2\cos^2 t$

**101.** $x = 2\tan^2 t, y = 4\sec^2 t$

**102.** $x = 3t^2 + 4, y = 3t^2 - 5$

## Technology Exercises

### Section 9.2

**103.** In your mind, picture the parabola given by $(x - 0.6)^2 = -4(y + 1.2)$. Where is the vertex? Which way does this parabola open? Now plot the parabola with a graphing utility.

**104.** In your mind, picture the parabola given by $(y - 0.2)^2 = 3(x - 2.8)$. Where is the vertex? Which way does this parabola open? Now plot the parabola with a graphing utility.

**105.** Given is the parabola $y^2 + 2.8y + 3x - 6.85 = 0$.
  **a.** Solve the equation for $y$, and use a graphing utility to plot the parabola.
  **b.** Transform the equation into the form $(y - k)^2 = 4p(x - h)$. Find the vertex. Which way does the parabola open?
  **c.** Do (a) and (b) agree with each other?

**106.** Given is the parabola $x^2 - 10.2x - y + 24.8 = 0$.
  **a.** Solve the equation for $y$, and use a graphing utility to plot the parabola.
  **b.** Transform the equation into the form $(x - h)^2 = 4p(y - k)$. Find the vertex. Which way does the parabola open?
  **c.** Do (a) and (b) agree with each other?

### Section 9.3

**107.** Graph the following three ellipses: $4x^2 + y^2 = 1$, $4(2x)^2 + y^2 = 1$, and $4(3x)^2 + y^2 = 1$. What can be said to happen to ellipse $4(cx)^2 + y^2 = 1$ as $c$ increases?

**108.** Graph the following three ellipses: $x^2 + 4y^2 = 1$, $x^2 + 4(2y)^2 = 1$, and $x^2 + 4(3y)^2 = 1$. What can be said to happen to ellipse $x^2 + 4(cy)^2 = 1$ as $c$ increases?

### Section 9.4

**109.** Graph the following three hyperbolas: $4x^2 - y^2 = 1$, $4(2x)^2 - y^2 = 1$, and $4(3x)^2 - y^2 = 1$. What can be said to happen to hyperbola $4(cx)^2 - y^2 = 1$ as $c$ increases?

**110.** Graph the following three hyperbolas: $x^2 - 4y^2 = 1$, $x^2 - 4(2y)^2 = 1$, and $x^2 - 4(3y)^2 = 1$. What can be said to happen to hyperbola $x^2 - 4(cy)^2 = 1$ as $c$ increases?

### Section 9.5

With a graphing utility, solve the following systems of equations:

**111.** $7.5x^2 + 1.5y^2 = 12.25$
$x^2y = 1$

**112.** $4x^2 + 2xy + 3y^2 = 12$
$x^3y = 3 - 3x^3$

### Section 9.6

With a graphing utility, graph the following systems of nonlinear inequalities:

**113.** $y \geq 10^x - 1$
$y \leq 1 - x^2$

**114.** $x^2 + 4y^2 \leq 36$
$y \geq e^x$

## Section 9.7

**115.** With a graphing utility, explore the second-degree equation $Ax^2 + Bxy + Cy^2 + 10x - 8y - 5 = 0$ for the following values of $A$, $B$, and $C$:

**a.** $A = 2, B = -3, C = 5$
**b.** $A = 2, B = 3, C = -5$

Show the angle of rotation to one decimal place. Explain the differences.

**116.** With a graphing utility, explore the second-degree equation $Ax^2 + Bxy + Cy^2 + 2x - y = 0$ for the following values of $A$, $B$, and $C$:

**a.** $A = 1, B = -2, C = -1$
**b.** $A = 1, B = 2, D = 1$

Show the angle of rotation to the nearest degree. Explain the differences.

## Section 9.8

**117.** Let us consider the polar equation $r = \dfrac{8}{4 + 5\sin\theta}$. Explain why a graphing utility gives the following graph with the specified window parameters:

$$[-6, 6] \text{ by } [-3, 9] \text{ with } \theta \text{ step} = \frac{\pi}{4}$$

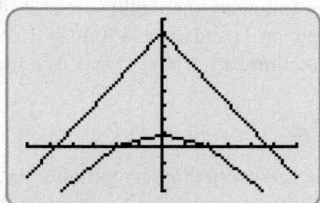

**118.** Let us consider the polar equation $r = \dfrac{9}{3 - 2\sin\theta}$. Explain why a graphing utility gives the following graph with the specified window parameters:

$$[-6, 6] \text{ by } [-3, 9] \text{ with } \theta \text{ step} = \frac{\pi}{2}$$

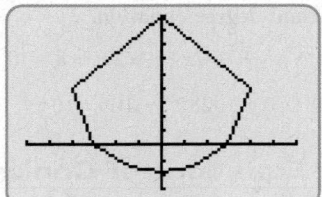

## Section 9.9

**119.** Consider the parametric equations $x = a\cos(at) + b\sin(bt)$ and $y = a\sin(at) + b\cos(bt)$. Use a graphing utility to explore the graphs for $(a, b) = (2, 3)$ and $(a, b) = (3, 2)$. Describe the $t$-interval for each case.

**120.** Consider the parametric equations $x = a\sin(at) - b\cos(bt)$ and $y = a\cos(at) - b\sin(bt)$. Use a graphing utility to explore the graphs for $(a, b) = (1, 2)$ and $(a, b) = (2, 1)$. Describe the $t$-interval for each case.

**Match the equation to the graph.**

**1.** $x = 16y^2$

**2.** $y = 16x^2$

**3.** $x^2 + 16y^2 = 1$

**4.** $x^2 - 16y^2 = 1$

**5.** $16x^2 + y^2 = 1$

**6.** $16y^2 - x^2 = 1$

**a.**

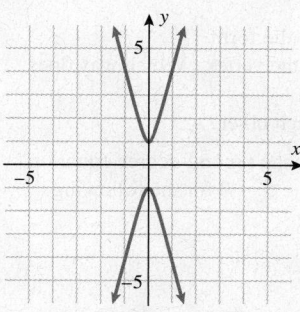

**b.**

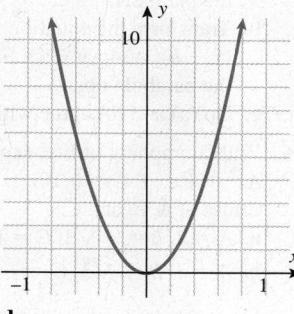

**c.**

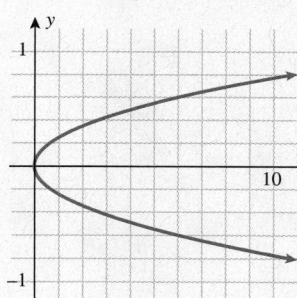

**d.**

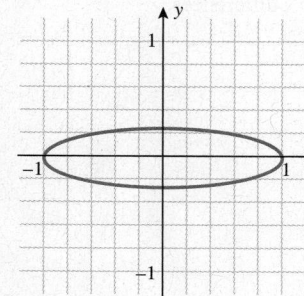

**e.**

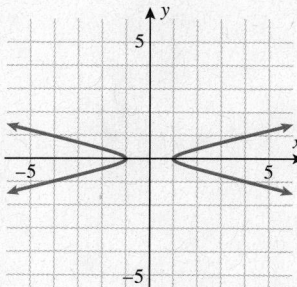

**f.**

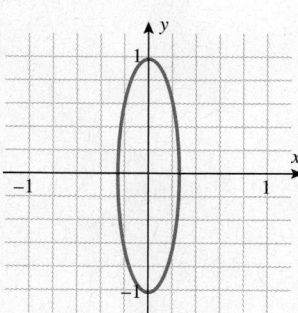

**Find the equation of the conic with the given characteristics.**

**7.** Parabola    vertex: $(0, 0)$    focus: $(-4, 0)$

**8.** Parabola    vertex: $(0, 0)$    directrix: $y = 2$

**9.** Parabola    vertex: $(-1, 5)$    focus: $(-1, 2)$

**10.** Parabola    vertex: $(2, -3)$    directrix: $x = 0$

**11.** Ellipse    center: $(0, 0)$
vertices: $(0, -4), (0, 4)$
foci: $(0, -3), (0, 3)$

**12.** Ellipse    center: $(0, 0)$
vertices: $(-3, 0), (3, 0)$
foci: $(-1, 0), (1, 0)$

**13.** Ellipse    vertices: $(2, -6), (2, 6)$
foci: $(2, -4), (2, 4)$

**14.** Ellipse    vertices: $(-7, -3), (-4, -3)$
foci: $(-6, -3), (-5, -3)$

**15.** Hyperbola    vertices: $(-1, 0)$ and $(1, 0)$
asymptotes: $y = -2x$ and $y = 2x$

**16.** Hyperbola    vertices: $(0, -1)$ and $(0, 1)$
asymptotes: $y = -\frac{1}{3}x$ and $y = \frac{1}{3}x$

**17.** Hyperbola    foci: $(2, -6), (2, 6)$
vertices: $(2, -4), (2, 4)$

**18.** Hyperbola    foci: $(-7, -3), (-4, -3)$
vertices: $(-6, -3), (-5, -3)$

**Graph the following equations:**

**19.** $9x^2 + 18x - 4y^2 + 16y - 43 = 0$

**20.** $4x^2 - 8x + y^2 + 10y + 28 = 0$

**21.** $y^2 + 4y - 16x + 20 = 0$

**22.** $x^2 - 4x + y + 1 = 0$

**23. Eyeglass Lens.** Eyeglass lenses can be thought of as very wide parabolic curves. If the focus occurs 1.5 centimeters from the center of the lens, and the lens at its opening is 4 centimeters across, find an equation that governs the shape of the lens.

**24. Planetary Orbits.** The planet Uranus's orbit is described in the following picture with the Sun as a focus of the elliptical orbit. Write an equation for the orbit.

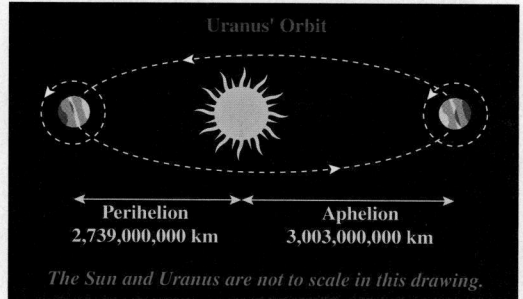

**Graph the following nonlinear inequalities:**

**25.** $y < x^3 + 1$

**26.** $y^2 \geq 16x$

**Graph the following systems of nonlinear inequalities:**

**27.**
$$y \le 4 - x^2$$
$$16x^2 + 25y^2 \le 400$$

**28.** $y \le e^{-x}$
$$y \ge x^2 - 4$$

**29.** Identify the conic represented by the equation
$$r = \frac{12}{3 + 2\sin\theta}.$$ State the eccentricity.

**30.** Use rotation of axes to transform the equation in $x$ and $y$ into an equation in $X$ and $Y$ that has no $XY$-term:
$6\sqrt{3}x^2 + 6xy + 4\sqrt{3}y^2 = 21\sqrt{3}$. State the rotation angle.

**31.** A golf ball is hit with an initial speed of 120 feet per second at an angle of 45° with the ground. How long will the ball stay in the air? How far will the ball travel (horizontal distance) before it hits the ground?

**32.** Describe (classify) the plane curve defined by the parametric equations $x = \sqrt{1 - t}$ and $y = \sqrt{t}$ for $t$ in $[0, 1]$.

**33.** Use a graphing utility to graph the following nonlinear inequality:
$$x^2 + 4xy - 9y^2 - 6x + 8y + 28 \le 0$$

**34.** Use a graphing utility to solve the following systems of equations:
$$0.1225x^2 + 0.0289y^2 = 1$$
$$y^3 = 11x$$
Round your answers to three decimal places.

**35.** Given is the parabola $x^2 + 4.2x - y + 5.61 = 0$.
   **a.** Solve the equation for $y$ and use a graphing utility to plot the parabola.
   **b.** Transform the equation into the form $(x - h)^2 = 4p(y - k)$. Find the vertex. Which way does the parabola open?
   **c.** Do (a) and (b) agree with each other?

**36.** With a graphing utility, explore the second-degree equation $Ax^2 + Bxy + Cy^2 + 10x - 8y - 5 = 0$ for the following values of $A$, $B$, and $C$:
   **a.** $A = 2, B = -\sqrt{3}, C = 1$
   **b.** $A = 2, B = \sqrt{3}, C = -1$

Show the angle of rotation to one decimal place. Explain the differences.

1. Solve for $x$: $(x + 2)^2 - (x + 2) - 20 = 0$.

2. Find an equation of a circle centered at $(5, 1)$ and passing through the point $(6, -2)$.

3. Evaluate the difference quotient $\dfrac{f(x + h) - f(x)}{h}$ for the function $f(x) = 8 - 7x$.

4. Write an equation that describes the following variation: $I$ is directly proportional to both $P$ and $t$, and $I = 90$ when $P = 1500$ and $t = 2$.

5. Find the quadratic function that has vertex $(7, 7)$ and goes through the point $(10, 10)$.

6. **Compound Interest.** How much money should you put in a savings account now that earns 4.7% interest a year compounded weekly if you want to have $65,000 in 17 years?

7. Solve the logarithmic equation exactly: $\log x^2 - \log 16 = 0$.

8. In a 30°-60°-90° triangle, if the shortest leg has length 8 inches, what are the lengths of the other leg and the hypotenuse?

9. Use a calculator to evaluate $\cot(-27°)$. Round your answer to four decimal places.

10. **Sound Waves.** If a sound wave is represented by $y = 0.007 \sin(850\pi t)$ cm, what are its amplitude and frequency?

11. For the trigonometric expression $\tan\theta (\csc\theta + \cos\theta)$, perform the operations and simplify. Write the answer in terms of $\sin\theta$ and $\cos\theta$.

12. Find the exact value of $\cos\left(-\dfrac{11\pi}{12}\right)$.

13. Solve the trigonometric equation $4\cos^2 x + 4\cos 2x + 1 = 0$ exactly over the interval $0 \le \theta \le 2\pi$.

14. **Airplane Speed.** A plane flew due north at 450 miles per hour for 2 hours. A second plane, starting at the same point and at the same time, flew southeast at an angle of 135° clockwise from due north at 375 miles per hour for 2 hours. At the end of 2 hours, how far apart were the two planes? Round to the nearest mile.

15. Find the vector with magnitude $|\mathbf{u}| = 15$ and direction angle $\theta = 110°$.

16. Given $z_1 = 5(\cos 15° + i\sin 15°)$ and $z_2 = 2(\cos 75° + i\sin 75°)$, find the product $z_1 z_2$ and express it in rectangular form.

17. At a food court, 3 medium sodas and 2 soft pretzels cost $6.77. A second order of 5 medium sodas and 4 soft pretzels costs $12.25. Find the cost of a soda and the cost of a soft pretzel.

18. Find the partial-fraction decomposition for the rational expression $\dfrac{3x + 5}{(x - 3)\left(x^2 + 5\right)}$.

19. Graph the system of inequalities or indicate that the system has no solution.
$$y \ge 3x - 2$$
$$y \le 3x + 2$$

20. Solve the system using Gauss–Jordan elimination.
$$\begin{aligned} x - 2y + z &= 7 \\ -3x + y + 2z &= -11 \end{aligned}$$

21. Given $A = \begin{bmatrix} 3 & 4 & -7 \\ 0 & 1 & 5 \end{bmatrix}$, $B = \begin{bmatrix} 8 & -2 & 6 \\ 9 & 0 & -1 \end{bmatrix}$, and $C = \begin{bmatrix} 9 & 0 \\ 1 & 2 \end{bmatrix}$, find $2B - 3A$.

22. Use Cramer's rule to solve the system of equations.
$$\begin{aligned} 25x + 40y &= -12 \\ 75x - 105y &= 69 \end{aligned}$$

23. Find the standard form of the equation of an ellipse with foci $(6, 2)$ and $(6, -6)$ and vertices $(6, 3)$ and $(6, -7)$.

24. Find the standard form of the equation of a hyperbola with vertices $(5, -2)$ and $(5, 0)$ and foci $(5, -3)$ and $(5, 1)$.

25. Solve the system of equations.
$$\begin{aligned} x + y &= 6 \\ x^2 + y^2 &= 20 \end{aligned}$$

26. Use a graphing utility to graph the following equation:
$$x^2 - 3xy + 10y^2 - 1 = 0$$

27. Use a graphing utility to graph the following system of nonlinear inequalities:
$$\begin{aligned} y &\ge e^{-0.3x} - 3.5 \\ y &\le 4 - x^2 \end{aligned}$$

# 10

# Sequences and Series

Gaillardia Flower (55), Kenneth M. Highfil/Photo Researchers, Inc.; Michaelmas Daisy (89), Maxine Adcock/Photo Researchers, Inc.; Yellow Iris (3), Edward Kinsman/Photo Researchers, Inc.; Blue Columbine (5), Jeffrey Lepore/Photo Researchers, Inc.; Gerbera Daisy (34), Bonnie Sue Rauch/Photo Researchers, Inc.; Erect Dayflower (2), Michael Lustbader/Photo Researchers, Inc.; Calla Lilies (1), Adam Jones/Photo Researchers, Inc.; Cosmos Flower (8), Maria Mosolova/Photo Researchers, Inc.; Lemon Symphony (21), Bonnie Sue Rauch/Photo Researchers, Inc.; Black-Eyed Susan (13), Rod Planck/Photo Researchers, Inc.

A famous sequence that appears throughout nature is the *Fibonacci sequence*, where each term in the sequence is the sum of the previous two numbers:

$$1, 1, 2, 3, 5, 8, 13, 21, 34, 55, 89, \ldots$$

The number of petals in certain flowers are numbers in the Fibonacci sequence.

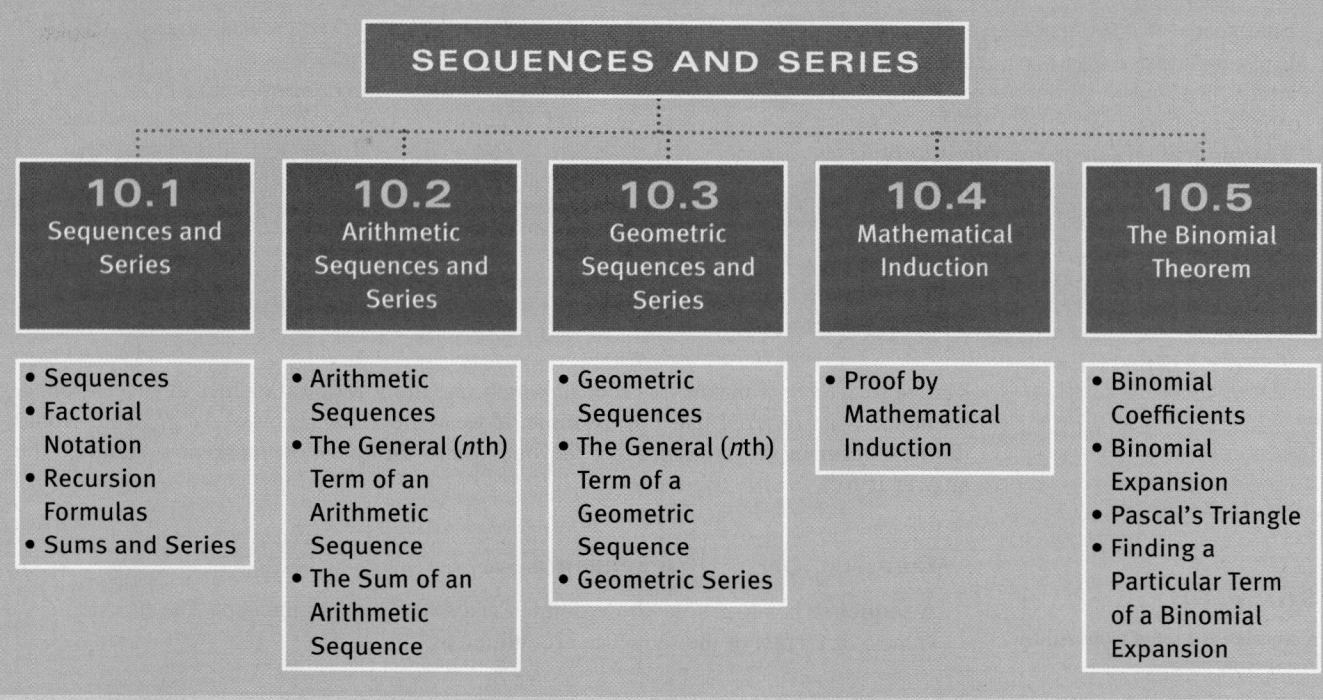

**IN THIS CHAPTER** we will first define a sequence and a series and then discuss two particular kinds of sequences and series called arithmetic and geometric. We will then discuss mathematical proof by induction. Lastly, we will discuss the Binomial theorem, which allows us an efficient way to perform binomial expansions.

## SEQUENCES AND SERIES

### 10.1 Sequences and Series
- Sequences
- Factorial Notation
- Recursion Formulas
- Sums and Series

### 10.2 Arithmetic Sequences and Series
- Arithmetic Sequences
- The General (*n*th) Term of an Arithmetic Sequence
- The Sum of an Arithmetic Sequence

### 10.3 Geometric Sequences and Series
- Geometric Sequences
- The General (*n*th) Term of a Geometric Sequence
- Geometric Series

### 10.4 Mathematical Induction
- Proof by Mathematical Induction

### 10.5 The Binomial Theorem
- Binomial Coefficients
- Binomial Expansion
- Pascal's Triangle
- Finding a Particular Term of a Binomial Expansion

## LEARNING OBJECTIVES

- Use sigma notation to represent a series.
- Find the sum of an arithmetic sequence.
- Determine whether an infinite geometric series converges.
- Prove mathematical statements using mathematical induction.
- Perform binomial expansions.

### SKILLS OBJECTIVES

- Find terms of a sequence given the general term.
- Look for a pattern in a sequence and find the general term.
- Apply factorial notation.
- Apply recursion formulas.
- Use summation (sigma) notation to represent a series.
- Evaluate a series.

### CONCEPTUAL OBJECTIVES

- Understand the difference between a sequence and a series.
- Understand the difference between a finite series and an infinite series.

## Sequences

The word *sequence* means an order in which one thing follows another in succession. A sequence is an ordered list. For example, if we write $x, 2x^2, 3x^3, 4x^4, 5x^5, ?$, what would the next term in the *sequence* be, the one where the question mark now stands? The answer is $6x^6$.

### Study Tip

A sequence is a set of terms written in a specific order

$$a_1, a_2, a_3, \ldots a_n, \ldots$$

where $a_1$ is called the first term, $a_2$ is called the second term, and $a_n$ is called the $n$th term.

> **DEFINITION**    **A Sequence**
>
> A **sequence** is a function whose domain is a set of positive integers. The function values, or **terms**, of the sequence are written as
>
> $$a_1, a_2, a_3, \ldots, a_n, \ldots$$
>
> Rather than using function notation, sequences are usually written with subscript (or index) notation, $a_{\text{subscript}}$.

A **finite sequence** has the domain $\{1, 2, 3, \ldots, n\}$ for some positive integer $n$. An **infinite sequence** has the domain of all positive integers $\{1, 2, 3, \ldots\}$. There are times when it is convenient to start the indexing at 0 instead of 1:

$$a_0, a_1, a_2, a_3, \ldots, a_n, \ldots$$

Sometimes a pattern in the sequence can be obtained and the sequence can be written using a *general term*. In the previous example, $x, 2x^2, 3x^3, 4x^4, 5x^5, 6x^6, \ldots$, each term has the same exponent and coefficient. We can write this sequence as $a_n = nx^n$, $n = 1, 2, 3, 4, 5, 6, \ldots$, where $a_n$ is called the **general** or **$n$th term**.

> **EXAMPLE 1**    **Finding Several Terms of a Sequence, Given the General Term**
>
> Find the first four ($n = 1, 2, 3, 4$) terms of each of the following sequences, given the general term.
>
> **a.** $a_n = 2n - 1$
>
> **b.** $b_n = \dfrac{(-1)^n}{n + 1}$

**Solution (a):**                                                    $a_n = 2n - 1$

Find the first term, $n = 1$.                                        $a_1 = 2(1) - 1 = 1$
Find the second term, $n = 2$.                                       $a_2 = 2(2) - 1 = 3$
Find the third term, $n = 3$.                                        $a_3 = 2(3) - 1 = 5$
Find the fourth term, $n = 4$.                                       $a_4 = 2(4) - 1 = 7$

The first four terms of the sequence are $\boxed{1, 3, 5, 7}$.

**Solution (b):**                                                    $b_n = \dfrac{(-1)^n}{n + 1}$

Find the first term, $n = 1$.                                        $b_1 = \dfrac{(-1)^1}{1 + 1} = -\dfrac{1}{2}$

Find the second term, $n = 2$.                                       $b_2 = \dfrac{(-1)^2}{2 + 1} = \dfrac{1}{3}$

Find the third term, $n = 3$.                                        $b_3 = \dfrac{(-1)^3}{3 + 1} = -\dfrac{1}{4}$

Find the fourth term, $n = 4$.                                       $b_4 = \dfrac{(-1)^4}{4 + 1} = \dfrac{1}{5}$

The first four terms of the sequence are $\boxed{-\frac{1}{2}, \frac{1}{3}, -\frac{1}{4}, \frac{1}{5}}$.

■ **YOUR TURN**  Find the first four terms of the sequence $a_n = \dfrac{(-1)^n}{n^2}$.

■ **Answer:** $-1, \frac{1}{4}, -\frac{1}{9}, \frac{1}{16}$

### EXAMPLE 2    Finding the General Term, Given Several Terms of the Sequence

Find the general term of the sequence, given the first five terms.

**a.** $1, \frac{1}{4}, \frac{1}{9}, \frac{1}{16}, \frac{1}{25}, \ldots$          **b.** $-1, 4, -9, 16, -25, \ldots$

**Solution (a):**

Write 1 as $\frac{1}{1}$.                                            $\dfrac{1}{1}, \dfrac{1}{4}, \dfrac{1}{9}, \dfrac{1}{16}, \dfrac{1}{25}, \ldots$

Notice that each denominator is an integer squared.                  $\dfrac{1}{1^2}, \dfrac{1}{2^2}, \dfrac{1}{3^2}, \dfrac{1}{4^2}, \dfrac{1}{5^2}, \ldots$

Identify the general term.                                           $\boxed{a_n = \dfrac{1}{n^2} \qquad n = 1, 2, 3, 4, 5, \ldots}$

**Solution (b):**

Notice that each term includes an integer squared.                   $-1^2, 2^2, -3^2, 4^2, -5^2, \ldots$

Identify the general term.                                           $\boxed{b_n = (-1)^n n^2 \qquad n = 1, 2, 3, 4, 5, \ldots}$

■ **YOUR TURN**  Find the general term of the sequence, given the first five terms.

**a.** $-\frac{1}{2}, \frac{1}{4}, -\frac{1}{6}, \frac{1}{8}, -\frac{1}{10}, \ldots$          **b.** $\frac{1}{2}, \frac{1}{4}, \frac{1}{8}, \frac{1}{16}, \frac{1}{32}, \ldots$

**Study Tip**

$(-1)^n$ or $(-1)^{n+1}$ is a way to represent an alternating sequence.

■ **Answer:**
**a.** $a_n = \dfrac{(-1)^n}{2n}$  **b.** $a_n = \dfrac{1}{2^n}$

Parts (b) in both Example 1 and Example 2 are called **alternating** sequences, because the terms alternate signs (positive and negative). If the odd-indexed terms, $a_1, a_3, a_5, \ldots,$ are negative and the even-indexed terms, $a_2, a_4, a_6, \ldots,$ are positive, we include $(-1)^n$ in the general term. If the opposite is true, and the odd-indexed terms are positive and the even-indexed terms are negative, we include $(-1)^{n+1}$ in the general term.

# Factorial Notation

**Technology Tip**

Find 0!, 1!, 2!, 3!, 4!, and 5!.

Scientific calculators:

| Press | Display |
|-------|---------|
| 0 ! = | 1 |
| 1 ! = | 1 |
| 2 ! = | 2 |
| 3 ! = | 6 |
| 4 ! = | 24 |
| 5 ! = | 120 |

Graphing calculators:

| Press | Display |
|-------|---------|
| 0 MATH PRB 4:! ENTER | 1 |
| 1 MATH PRB 4:! ENTER | 1 |
| 2 MATH PRB 4:! ENTER | 2 |
| 3 MATH PRB 4:! ENTER | 6 |
| 4 MATH PRB 4:! ENTER | 24 |
| 5 MATH PRB 4:! ENTER | 120 |

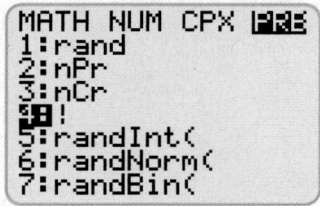

Many important sequences that arise in mathematics involve terms that are defined with products of consecutive positive integers. The products are expressed in *factorial notation*.

---

**DEFINITION**　　**Factorial**

If $n$ is a positive integer, then $n!$ (stated as "$n$ factorial") is the product of all positive integers from $n$ down to 1.

$$n! = n(n-1)(n-2)\cdots 3 \cdot 2 \cdot 1 \qquad n \geq 2$$

and $0! = 1$ and $1! = 1$.

---

The values of $n!$ for the first six nonnegative integers are

$$0! = 1$$
$$1! = 1$$
$$2! = 2 \cdot 1 = 2$$
$$3! = 3 \cdot 2 \cdot 1 = 6$$
$$4! = 4 \cdot 3 \cdot 2 \cdot 1 = 24$$
$$5! = 5 \cdot 4 \cdot 3 \cdot 2 \cdot 1 = 120$$

Notice that $4! = 4 \cdot 3 \cdot 2 \cdot 1 = 4 \cdot 3!$. In general, we can apply the formula $n! = n[(n-1)!]$. Often the brackets are not used, and the notation $n! = n(n-1)!$ implies calculating the factorial $(n-1)!$ and then multiplying that quantity by $n$. For example, to find 6!, we employ the relationship $n! = n(n-1)!$ and set $n = 6$:

$$6! = 6 \cdot 5! = 6 \cdot 120 = 720$$

## EXAMPLE 3　Finding the Terms of a Sequence Involving Factorials

Find the first four terms of the sequence, given the general term $a_n = \dfrac{x^n}{n!}$.

**Solution:**

Find the first term, $n = 1$. 　　　　　$a_1 = \dfrac{x^1}{1!} = x$

Find the second term, $n = 2$. 　　　　$a_2 = \dfrac{x^2}{2!} = \dfrac{x^2}{2 \cdot 1} = \dfrac{x^2}{2}$

Find the third term, $n = 3$. 　　　　　$a_3 = \dfrac{x^3}{3!} = \dfrac{x^3}{3 \cdot 2 \cdot 1} = \dfrac{x^3}{6}$

Find the fourth term, $n = 4$. 　　　　$a_4 = \dfrac{x^4}{4!} = \dfrac{x^4}{4 \cdot 3 \cdot 2 \cdot 1} = \dfrac{x^4}{24}$

The first four terms of the sequence are $\boxed{x, \dfrac{x^2}{2}, \dfrac{x^3}{6}, \dfrac{x^4}{24}}$.

**EXAMPLE 4   Evaluating Expressions with Factorials**

Evaluate each factorial expression.

**a.** $\dfrac{6!}{2! \cdot 3!}$     **b.** $\dfrac{(n+1)!}{(n-1)!}$

**Solution (a):**

Expand each factorial in the numerator and denominator.

$$\frac{6!}{2! \cdot 3!} = \frac{6 \cdot 5 \cdot 4 \cdot 3 \cdot 2 \cdot 1}{2 \cdot 1 \cdot 3 \cdot 2 \cdot 1}$$

Cancel the $3 \cdot 2 \cdot 1$ in both the numerator and denominator.

$$= \frac{6 \cdot 5 \cdot 4}{2 \cdot 1}$$

Simplify.

$$= \frac{6 \cdot 5 \cdot 2}{1} = 60$$

$$\boxed{\frac{6!}{2! \cdot 3!} = 60}$$

**Solution (b):**

Expand each factorial in the numerator and denominator.

$$\frac{(n+1)!}{(n-1)!} = \frac{(n+1)(n)(n-1)(n-2)\cdots 3 \cdot 2 \cdot 1}{(n-1)(n-2)\cdots 3 \cdot 2 \cdot 1}$$

Cancel the $(n-1)(n-2)\cdots 3 \cdot 2 \cdot 1$ in both the numerator and denominator.

$$\frac{(n+1)!}{(n-1)!} = (n+1)(n)$$

Alternatively,

$$\frac{(n+1)!}{(n-1)!} = \frac{(n+1)(n)(n-1)!}{(n-1)!}$$

$$\boxed{\frac{(n+1)!}{(n-1)!} = n^2 + n}$$

### COMMON MISTAKE

In Example 4 we found $\dfrac{6!}{2! \cdot 3!} = 60$. It is important to note that $2! \cdot 3! \neq 6!$.

▪ **YOUR TURN**  Evaluate each factorial expression.

**a.** $\dfrac{3! \cdot 4!}{2! \cdot 6!}$     **b.** $\dfrac{(n+2)!}{n!}$

**Technology Tip**

Evaluate $\dfrac{6!}{2!3!}$.

Scientific calculators:

| Press | Display |
|---|---|
| 6 [!] [÷] [(] [2] [!] [x] | 60 |
| 3 [!] [)] [=] | |

Graphing calculators:

6 [MATH] [▶] [PRB] [▼] [4: !]
[ENTER] [÷] [(] [2] [MATH] [▶]
[PRB] [▼] [4: !] [ENTER] [x] [3]
[MATH] [▶] [PRB] [▼] [4: !]
[ENTER] [)] [ENTER].

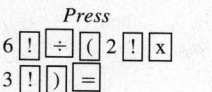

**Study Tip**

In general, $m!n! \neq (mn)!$.

▪ **Answer:**

**a.** $\frac{1}{10}$     **b.** $(n+2)(n+1)$

## Recursion Formulas

Another way to define a sequence is **recursively**, or using a **recursion formula**. The first few terms are listed, and the recursion formula determines the remaining terms based on previous terms. For example, the famous Fibonacci sequence is 1, 1, 2, 3, 5, 8, 13, 21, 34, 55, 89, . . . . Each term in the Fibonacci sequence is found by adding the previous two terms.

$$1 + 1 = 2 \qquad 1 + 2 = 3 \qquad 2 + 3 = 5$$
$$3 + 5 = 8 \qquad 5 + 8 = 13 \qquad 8 + 13 = 21$$
$$13 + 21 = 34 \qquad 21 + 34 = 55 \qquad 34 + 55 = 89$$

We can define the Fibonacci sequence using a general term:

$$a_1 = 1, \ a_2 = 1, \quad \text{and} \quad a_n = a_{n-2} + a_{n-1} \qquad n \geq 3$$

The Fibonacci sequence is found in places we least expect it (e.g., pineapples, broccoli, and flowers). The number of petals in certain flowers is a Fibonacci number. For example, a wild rose has 5 petals, lilies and irises have 3 petals, and daisies have 34, 55, or even 89 petals. The number of spirals in an Italian broccoli is a Fibonacci number (13).

**EXAMPLE 5  Using a Recursion Formula to Find a Sequence**

Find the first four terms of the sequence $a_n$ if $a_1 = 2$ and $a_n = 2a_{n-1} - 1, n \geq 2$.

**Solution:**

Write the first term, $n = 1$.                  $a_1 = 2$

Find the second term, $n = 2$.            $a_2 = 2a_1 - 1 = 2(2) - 1 = 3$

Find the third term, $n = 3$.               $a_3 = 2a_2 - 1 = 2(3) - 1 = 5$

Find the fourth term, $n = 4$.             $a_4 = 2a_3 - 1 = 2(5) - 1 = 9$

The first four terms of the sequence are $\boxed{2, 3, 5, 9}$.

■ **Answer:** $1, \frac{1}{2}, \frac{1}{12}, \frac{1}{288}$

■ **YOUR TURN** Find the first four terms of the sequence

$$a_1 = 1 \qquad \text{and} \qquad a_n = \frac{a_{n-1}}{n!} \qquad n \geq 2$$

## Sums and Series

When we add the terms in a sequence, the result is a *series*.

**DEFINITION**  **Series**

Given the infinite sequence $a_1, a_2, a_3, \ldots, a_n, \ldots$, the sum of all of the terms in the infinite sequence is called an **infinite series** and is denoted by

$$a_1 + a_2 + a_3 + \cdots + a_n + \cdots$$

and the sum of only the first $n$ terms is called a **finite series**, or **$n$th partial sum**, and is denoted by

$$S_n = a_1 + a_2 + a_3 + \cdots + a_n$$

The capital Greek letter $\Sigma$ (sigma) corresponds to the capital S in our alphabet. Therefore, we use $\Sigma$ as a shorthand way to represent a sum (series). For example, the sum of the first five terms of the sequence $1, 4, 9, 16, 25, \ldots, n^2, \ldots$ can be represented using **sigma (or summation) notation**:

$$\sum_{n=1}^{5} n^2 = (1)^2 + (2)^2 + (3)^2 + (4)^2 + (5)^2$$

$$= 1 + 4 + 9 + 16 + 25$$

This is read "the sum as $n$ goes from 1 to 5 of $n^2$." The letter $n$ is called the **index of summation**, and often other letters are used instead of $n$. It is important to note that the sum can start at other integers besides 1.

If we wanted the sum of all of the terms in the sequence, we would represent that infinite series using summation notation as

$$\sum_{n=1}^{\infty} n^2 = 1 + 4 + 9 + 16 + 25 + \cdots$$

**EXAMPLE 6 Writing a Series Using Sigma Notation**

Represent each of the following series using sigma notation:

**a.** $1 + 1 + \frac{1}{2} + \frac{1}{6} + \frac{1}{24} + \frac{1}{120}$    **b.** $8 + 27 + 64 + 125 + \cdots$

**Solution (a):**

Write 1 as $\frac{1}{1}$.

$$\frac{1}{1} + \frac{1}{1} + \frac{1}{2} + \frac{1}{6} + \frac{1}{24} + \frac{1}{120}$$

Notice that we can write the denominators using factorials.

$$= \frac{1}{1} + \frac{1}{1} + \frac{1}{2!} + \frac{1}{3!} + \frac{1}{4!} + \frac{1}{5!}$$

Recall that $0! = 1$ and $1! = 1$.

$$= \frac{1}{0!} + \frac{1}{1!} + \frac{1}{2!} + \frac{1}{3!} + \frac{1}{4!} + \frac{1}{5!}$$

Identify the general term.

$$a_n = \frac{1}{n!} \qquad n = 0, 1, 2, 3, 4, 5$$

Write the finite series using sigma notation.

$$\boxed{\sum_{n=0}^{5} \frac{1}{n!}}$$

**Solution (b):**

Write the infinite series as a sum of terms cubed.

$$8 + 27 + 64 + 125 + \cdots$$
$$= 2^3 + 3^3 + 4^3 + 5^3 + \cdots$$

Identify the general term of the series.

$$a_n = n^3 \qquad n \geq 2$$

Write the infinite series using sigma notation.

$$\boxed{\sum_{n=2}^{\infty} n^3}$$

■ **YOUR TURN** Represent each of the following series using sigma notation:

**a.** $1 - \frac{1}{2} + \frac{1}{6} - \frac{1}{24} + \frac{1}{120} - \cdots$

**b.** $4 + 8 + 16 + 32 + 64 + \cdots$

■ **Answer:**

**a.** $\displaystyle\sum_{n=1}^{\infty} \frac{(-1)^{n+1}}{n!}$    **b.** $\displaystyle\sum_{n=2}^{\infty} 2^n$

Now that we are comfortable with sigma (summation) notation, let's turn our attention to evaluating a series (calculating the sum). You can always evaluate a finite series. However, you cannot always evaluate an infinite series.

**EXAMPLE 7 Evaluating a Finite Series**

Evaluate the series $\sum_{i=0}^{4} (2i + 1)$.

**Solution:**

Write out the partial sum.

$$\sum_{i=0}^{4} (2i + 1) = 1 + 3 + 5 + 7 + 9$$

$$\begin{array}{ccccc} & (i=1) & & (i=3) & \\ & \downarrow & & \downarrow & \\ 1 & +3 & +5 & +7 & +9 \\ \uparrow & & \uparrow & & \uparrow \\ (i=0) & & (i=2) & & (i=4) \end{array}$$

Simplify.

$$= 25$$

$$\boxed{\sum_{i=0}^{4} (2i + 1) = 25}$$

**Technology Tip**

2nd $\boxed{LIST}$ $\boxed{\blacktriangleright}$ $\boxed{MATH}$ $\boxed{\blacktriangledown}$
$\boxed{5:sum(}$ $\boxed{ENTER}$ 2nd $\boxed{LIST}$ $\boxed{\blacktriangleright}$
$\boxed{OPS}$ $\boxed{\blacktriangledown}$ $\boxed{5:seq(}$ $\boxed{ENTER}$ 2
$\boxed{ALPHA}$ $\boxed{I}$ $\boxed{+}$ $\boxed{1}$ $\boxed{,}$ $\boxed{ALPHA}$ $\boxed{I}$
$\boxed{,}$ $\boxed{0}$ $\boxed{,}$ $\boxed{4}$ $\boxed{,}$ $\boxed{1}$ $\boxed{)}$ $\boxed{)}$ $\boxed{ENTER}$.

```
sum(seq(2I+1,I,0
,4,1))
                25
```

■ **YOUR TURN** Evaluate the series $\sum_{n=1}^{5} (-1)^n n$.

■ **Answer:** $-3$

*Study Tip*

The sum of a finite series always exists. The sum of an infinite series may or may not exist.

Infinite series may or may not have a finite sum. For example, if we keep adding $1 + 1 + 1 + 1 + \cdots$, then there is no single real number that the series sums to because the sum continues to grow without bound. However, if we add $0.9 + 0.09 + 0.009 + 0.0009 + \cdots$, this sum is $0.9999\ldots = 0.\overline{9}$, which is a rational number, and it can be proven that $0.\overline{9} = 1$.

*Technology Tip*

**a.** [2nd] [LIST] [▶] [MATH] [▼]
[5:sum(] [ENTER] [2nd] [LIST] [▶]
[OPS] [▼] [5:seq(] [ENTER] [3] [÷]
[10] [^] [ALPHA] [N] [,] [ALPHA]
[N] [,] [1] [,] [10] [,] [1] [)] [)] [ENTER].

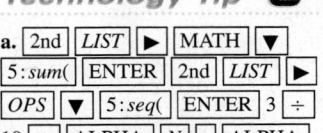

```
sum(seq(3/10^N,N
,1,10,1))
         .3333333333
```

**b.** [2nd] [LIST] [▶] [MATH] [▼]
[5:sum(] [ENTER] [2nd] [LIST] [▶]
[OPS] [▼] [5:seq(] [ALPHA] [N]
[$x^2$] [,] [^] [ALPHA] [N] [,] [1] [,]
[100] [,] [1] [)] [)] [ENTER].

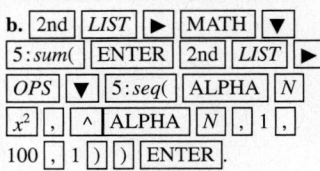

```
sum(seq(N²,N,1,1
00,1))
          338350
```

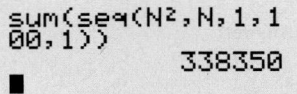

■ **Answer: a.** Series diverges.
 **b.** Series converges to $\frac{2}{3}$.

**EXAMPLE 8** **Evaluating an Infinite Series, If Possible**

Evaluate the following infinite series, if possible.

**a.** $\displaystyle\sum_{n=1}^{\infty} \frac{3}{10^n}$   **b.** $\displaystyle\sum_{n=1}^{\infty} n^2$

**Solution (a):**

Expand the series.
$$\sum_{n=1}^{\infty} \frac{3}{10^n} = \frac{3}{10} + \frac{3}{100} + \frac{3}{1000} + \frac{3}{10,000} + \cdots$$

Write in decimal form.
$$\sum_{n=1}^{\infty} \frac{3}{10^n} = 0.3 + 0.03 + 0.003 + 0.0003 + \cdots$$

Calculate the sum.
$$\sum_{n=1}^{\infty} \frac{3}{10^n} = 0.333333\overline{3} = \frac{1}{3}$$

$$\boxed{\sum_{n=1}^{\infty} \frac{3}{10^n} = \frac{1}{3}}$$

**Solution (b):**

Expand the series.
$$\sum_{n=1}^{\infty} n^2 = 1 + 4 + 9 + 16 + 25 + 36 + \cdots$$

This sum is infinite since it continues to grow without any bound.

In part (a) we say that the series **converges** to $\frac{1}{3}$ and in part (b) we say that the series **diverges**.

■ **YOUR TURN** Evaluate the following infinite series, if possible.

**a.** $\displaystyle\sum_{n=1}^{\infty} 2n$   **b.** $\displaystyle\sum_{n=1}^{\infty} 6\left(\frac{1}{10}\right)^n$

## Applications

The average stock price for Home Depot Inc (HD) was \$37 in 2007, \$28 in 2008, and \$23 in 2009. If $a_n$ is the yearly average stock price, where $n = 0$ corresponds to 2007, then $\frac{1}{3}\sum_{n=0}^{2} a_n$ tells us the average yearly stock price over the three-year period 2007 to 2009.

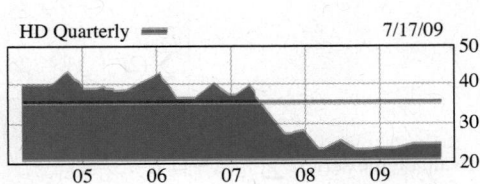

**SECTION**
**10.1** SUMMARY

In this section, we discussed finite and infinite sequences and series. When the terms of a sequence are added together, the result is a series.

**Finite sequence:** $a_1, a_2, a_3, \ldots, a_n$
**Infinite sequence:** $a_1, a_2, a_3, \ldots, a_n, \ldots$

**Finite series:** $a_1 + a_2 + a_3 + \cdots + a_n$
**Infinite series:** $a_1 + a_2 + a_3 + \cdots + a_n + \cdots$

**Factorial** notation was also introduced:

$$n! = n(n-1)\cdots 3 \cdot 2 \cdot 1 \quad n \geq 2$$

and $0! = 1$ and $1! = 1$.

The sum of a finite series is always finite.

The sum of an infinite series is either convergent or divergent.

Sigma notation is used to express a series.

■ **Finite series:** $\displaystyle\sum_{i=1}^{n} a_i = a_1 + a_2 + \cdots + a_n$

■ **Infinite series:** $\displaystyle\sum_{n=1}^{\infty} a_n = a_1 + a_2 + a_3 + \cdots$

**SECTION**
**10.1** EXERCISES

■ SKILLS

**In Exercises 1–12, write the first four terms of each sequence. Assume $n$ starts at 1.**

**1.** $a_n = n$

**2.** $a_n = n^2$

**3.** $a_n = 2n - 1$

**4.** $a_n = x^n$

**5.** $a_n = \dfrac{n}{(n+1)}$

**6.** $a_n = \dfrac{(n+1)}{n}$

**7.** $a_n = \dfrac{2^n}{n!}$

**8.** $a_n = \dfrac{n!}{(n+1)!}$

**9.** $a_n = (-1)^n x^{n+1}$

**10.** $a_n = (-1)^{n+1} n^2$

**11.** $a_n = \dfrac{(-1)^n}{(n+1)(n+2)}$

**12.** $a_n = \dfrac{(n-1)^2}{(n+1)^2}$

**In Exercises 13–20, find the indicated term of each sequence given.**

**13.** $a_n = \left(\dfrac{1}{2}\right)^n \quad a_9 = ?$

**14.** $a_n = \dfrac{n}{(n+1)^2} \quad a_{15} = ?$

**15.** $a_n = \dfrac{(-1)^n n!}{(n+2)!} \quad a_{19} = ?$

**16.** $a_n = \dfrac{(-1)^{n+1}(n-1)(n+2)}{n} \quad a_{13} = ?$

**17.** $a_n = \left(1 + \dfrac{1}{n}\right)^2 \quad a_{100} = ?$

**18.** $a_n = 1 - \dfrac{1}{n^2} \quad a_{10} = ?$

**19.** $a_n = \log 10^n \quad a_{23} = ?$

**20.** $a_n = e^{\ln n} \quad a_{49} = ?$

**In Exercises 21–28, write an expression for the $n$th term of the given sequence. Assume $n$ starts at 1.**

**21.** $2, 4, 6, 8, 10, \ldots$

**22.** $3, 6, 9, 12, 15, \ldots$

**23.** $\dfrac{1}{2 \cdot 1}, \dfrac{1}{3 \cdot 2}, \dfrac{1}{4 \cdot 3}, \dfrac{1}{5 \cdot 4}, \dfrac{1}{6 \cdot 5}, \cdots$

**24.** $\dfrac{1}{2}, \dfrac{1}{4}, \dfrac{1}{8}, \dfrac{1}{16}, \dfrac{1}{32}, \cdots$

**25.** $-\dfrac{2}{3}, \dfrac{4}{9}, -\dfrac{8}{27}, \dfrac{16}{81}, \cdots$

**26.** $\dfrac{1}{2}, \dfrac{3}{4}, \dfrac{9}{8}, \dfrac{27}{16}, \dfrac{81}{32}, \cdots$

**27.** $1, -1, 1, -1, 1, \ldots$

**28.** $\dfrac{1}{3}, -\dfrac{2}{4}, \dfrac{3}{5}, -\dfrac{4}{6}, \dfrac{5}{7}, \cdots$

**In Exercises 29–40, simplify each ratio of factorials.**

**29.** $\dfrac{9!}{7!}$

**30.** $\dfrac{4!}{6!}$

**31.** $\dfrac{29!}{27!}$

**32.** $\dfrac{32!}{30!}$

**33.** $\dfrac{75!}{77!}$

**34.** $\dfrac{100!}{103!}$

**35.** $\dfrac{97!}{93!}$

**36.** $\dfrac{101!}{98!}$

**37.** $\dfrac{(n-1)!}{(n+1)!}$

**38.** $\dfrac{(n+2)!}{n!}$

**39.** $\dfrac{(2n+3)!}{(2n+1)!}$

**40.** $\dfrac{(2n+2)!}{(2n-1)!}$

**In Exercises 41–50, write the first four terms of the sequence defined by each recursion formula. Assume the sequence begins at $n = 1$.**

**41.** $a_1 = 7$    $a_n = a_{n-1} + 3$

**42.** $a_1 = 2$    $a_n = a_{n-1} + 1$

**43.** $a_1 = 1$    $a_n = n \cdot a_{n-1}$

**44.** $a_1 = 2$    $a_n = (n + 1) \cdot a_{n-1}$

**45.** $a_1 = 100$    $a_n = \dfrac{a_{n-1}}{n!}$

**46.** $a_1 = 20$    $a_n = \dfrac{a_{n-1}}{n^2}$

**47.** $a_1 = 1, a_2 = 2$    $a_n = a_{n-1} \cdot a_{n-2}$

**48.** $a_1 = 1, a_2 = 2$    $a_n = \dfrac{a_{n-2}}{a_{n-1}}$

**49.** $a_1 = 1, a_2 = -1$    $a_n = (-1)^n [a_{n-1}^2 + a_{n-2}^2]$

**50.** $a_1 = 1, a_2 = -1$    $a_n = (n - 1) a_{n-1} + (n - 2)a_{n-2}$

**In Exercises 51–64, evaluate each finite series.**

**51.** $\displaystyle\sum_{n=1}^{5} 2$

**52.** $\displaystyle\sum_{n=1}^{5} 7$

**53.** $\displaystyle\sum_{n=0}^{4} n^2$

**54.** $\displaystyle\sum_{n=1}^{4} \frac{1}{n}$

**55.** $\displaystyle\sum_{n=1}^{6} (2n - 1)$

**56.** $\displaystyle\sum_{n=1}^{6} (n + 1)$

**57.** $\displaystyle\sum_{n=0}^{4} 1^n$

**58.** $\displaystyle\sum_{n=0}^{4} 2^n$

**59.** $\displaystyle\sum_{n=0}^{3} (-x)^n$

**60.** $\displaystyle\sum_{n=0}^{3} (-x)^{n+1}$

**61.** $\displaystyle\sum_{k=0}^{5} \frac{2^k}{k!}$

**62.** $\displaystyle\sum_{k=0}^{5} \frac{(-1)^k}{k!}$

**63.** $\displaystyle\sum_{k=0}^{5} \frac{x^k}{k!}$

**64.** $\displaystyle\sum_{k=0}^{4} \frac{(-1)^k x^k}{k!}$

**In Exercises 65–68, evaluate each infinite series, if possible.**

**65.** $\displaystyle\sum_{j=0}^{\infty} 2 \cdot (0.1)^j$

**66.** $\displaystyle\sum_{j=0}^{\infty} 5 \cdot \left(\tfrac{1}{10}\right)^j$

**67.** $\displaystyle\sum_{j=0}^{\infty} n^j$    $n \geq 1$

**68.** $\displaystyle\sum_{j=0}^{\infty} 1^j$

**In Exercises 69–76, use sigma notation to represent each sum.**

**69.** $1 - \dfrac{1}{2} + \dfrac{1}{4} - \dfrac{1}{8} + \cdots + \dfrac{1}{64}$

**70.** $1 + \dfrac{1}{2} + \dfrac{1}{4} + \dfrac{1}{8} + \cdots + \dfrac{1}{64} + \cdots$

**71.** $1 - 2 + 3 - 4 + 5 - 6 + \cdots$

**72.** $1 + 2 + 3 + 4 + 5 + \cdots + 21 + 22 + 23$

**73.** $\dfrac{2 \cdot 1}{1} + \dfrac{3 \cdot 2 \cdot 1}{1} + \dfrac{4 \cdot 3 \cdot 2 \cdot 1}{2 \cdot 1} + \dfrac{5 \cdot 4 \cdot 3 \cdot 2 \cdot 1}{3 \cdot 2 \cdot 1} + \dfrac{6 \cdot 5 \cdot 4 \cdot 3 \cdot 2 \cdot 1}{4 \cdot 3 \cdot 2 \cdot 1}$

**74.** $1 + \dfrac{2}{1} + \dfrac{2^2}{2 \cdot 1} + \dfrac{2^3}{3 \cdot 2 \cdot 1} + \dfrac{2^4}{4 \cdot 3 \cdot 2 \cdot 1} + \cdots$

**75.** $1 - x + \dfrac{x^2}{2} - \dfrac{x^3}{6} + \dfrac{x^4}{24} - \dfrac{x^5}{120} + \cdots$

**76.** $x + x^2 + \dfrac{x^3}{2} + \dfrac{x^4}{6} + \dfrac{x^5}{24} + \dfrac{x^6}{120}$

## ▪ APPLICATIONS

**77. Money.** Upon graduation Jessica receives a commission from the U.S. Navy to become an officer and a $20,000 signing bonus for selecting aviation. She puts the entire bonus in an account that earns 6% interest compounded monthly. The balance in the account after $n$ months is

$$A_n = 20{,}000 \left(1 + \frac{0.06}{12}\right)^n \quad n = 1, 2, 3, \ldots$$

Her commitment to the Navy is 6 years. Calculate $A_{72}$. What does $A_{72}$ represent?

**78. Money.** Dylan sells his car during his freshman year and puts $7000 in an account that earns 5% interest compounded quarterly. The balance in the account after $n$ quarters is

$$A_n = 7000 \left(1 + \frac{0.05}{4}\right)^n \quad n = 1, 2, 3, \ldots$$

Calculate $A_{12}$. What does $A_{12}$ represent?

**79. Salary.** An attorney is trying to calculate the costs associated with going into private practice. If she hires a paralegal to assist her, she will have to pay the paralegal $20 per hour. To be competitive with most firms, she will have to give her paralegal a $2 per hour raise each year. Find a general term of a sequence $a_n$ that would represent the hourly salary of a paralegal with $n$ years of experience. What will be the paralegal's salary with 20 years of experience?

**80. NFL Salaries.** A player in the NFL typically has a career that lasts 3 years. The practice squad makes the league minimum of $275,000 (2004) in the first year, with a $75,000 raise per year. Write the general term of a sequence $a_n$ that represents the salary of an NFL player making the league minimum during his entire career. Assuming $n = 1$ corresponds to the first year, what does $\sum_{n=1}^{3} a_n$ represent?

**81. Salary.** Upon graduation Sheldon decides to go to work for a local police department. His starting salary is $30,000 per year, and he expects to get a 3% raise per year. Write the recursion formula for a sequence that represents his annual salary after $n$ years on the job. Assume $n = 0$ represents his first year making $30,000.

**82. *Escherichia coli*.** A single cell of bacteria reproduces through a process called binary fission. *Escherichia coli* cells divide into two every 20 minutes. Suppose the same rate of division is maintained for 12 hours after the original cell enters the body. How many *E. coli* bacteria cells would be in the body 12 hours later? Suppose there is an infinite nutrient source so that the *E. coli* bacteria cells maintain the same rate of division for 48 hours after the original cell enters the body. How many *E. coli* bacteria cells would be in the body 48 hours later?

**83. AIDS/HIV.** A typical person has 500 to 1500 T cells per drop of blood in the body. HIV destroys the T cell count at a rate of 50–100 cells per drop of blood per year, depending on how aggressive it is in the body. Generally, the onset of AIDS occurs once the body's T cell count drops below 200. Write a sequence that represents the total number of T cells in a person infected with HIV. Assume that before infection the person has a 1000 T cell count ($a_0 = 1000$) and the rate at which the infection spreads corresponds to a loss of 75 T cells per drop of blood per year. How much time will elapse until this person has full-blown AIDS?

**84. Company Sales.** Lowe's reported total sales from 2003 through 2004 in the billions. The sequence $a_n = 3.8 + 1.6n$ represents the total sales in billions of dollars. Assuming $n = 3$ corresponds to 2003, what were the reported sales in 2003 and 2004? What does $\frac{1}{2} \cdot \sum_{n=3}^{4} a_n$ represent?

**85. Cost of Eating Out.** A college student tries to save money by bringing a bag lunch instead of eating out. He will be able to save $100 per month. He puts the money into his savings account, which draws 1.2% interest and is compounded monthly. The balance in his account after $n$ months of bagging his lunch is
$$A_n = 100,000[(1.001)^n - 1] \qquad n = 1, 2, \ldots$$
Calculate the first four terms of this sequence. Calculate the amount after 3 years (36 months).

**86. Cost of Acrylic Nails.** A college student tries to save money by growing her own nails out and not spending $50 per month on acrylic fills. She will be able to save $50 per month. She puts the money into her savings account, which draws 1.2% interest and is compounded monthly. The balance in her account after $n$ months of natural nails is
$$A_n = 50,000[(1.001)^n - 1] \qquad n = 1, 2, \ldots$$
Calculate the first four terms of this sequence. Calculate the amount after 4 years (48 months).

**87. Math and Engineering.** The formula $\sum_{n=0}^{\infty} \dfrac{x^n}{n!}$ can be used to approximate the function $y = e^x$. Estimate $e^2$ by using the sum of the first five terms and compare this result with the calculator value of $e^2$.

**88. Home Prices.** If the inflation rate is 3.5% per year and the average price of a home is $195,000, the average price of a home after $n$ years is given by $A_n = 195,000(1.035)^n$. Find the average price of the home after 6 years.

**89. Approximating Functions.** Polynomials can be used to approximate transcendental functions such as $\ln(x)$ and $e^x$, which are found in advanced mathematics and engineering. For example, $\sum_{n=0}^{\infty}(-1)^n \dfrac{(x - 1)^{n+1}}{n + 1}$ can be used to approximate $\ln(x)$, when $x$ is close to 1. Use the first five terms of the series to approximate $\ln(1.1)$ and compare with the value indicated by your calculator for $\ln(1.1)$.

**90. Future Value of an Annuity.** The future value of an ordinary annuity is given by the formula $FV = PMT[((1 + i)^n - 1)/i]$, where $PMT =$ amount paid into the account at the end of each period, $i =$ interest rate per period, and $n =$ number of compounding periods. If you invest $5000 at the end of each year for 5 years, you will have an accumulated value of $FV$ as given in the above formula at the end of the $n$th year. Determine how much is in the account at the end of each year for the next 5 years if $i = 0.06$.

■ **CATCH THE MISTAKE**

**In Exercises 91–94, explain the mistake that is made.**

**91.** Simplify the ratio of factorials $\dfrac{(3!)(5!)}{6!}$.

**Solution:**

Express 6! in factored form. $\dfrac{(3!)(5!)}{(3!)(2!)}$

Cancel the 3! in the numerator and denominator. $\dfrac{(5!)}{(2!)}$

Write out the factorials. $\dfrac{5 \cdot 4 \cdot 3 \cdot 2 \cdot 1}{2 \cdot 1}$

Simplify. $5 \cdot 4 \cdot 3 = 60$

$\dfrac{(3!)(5!)}{(3!)(2!)} \neq 60$. What mistake was made?

**92.** Simplify the factorial expression $\dfrac{2n(2n - 2)!}{(2n + 2)!}$.

**Solution:**

Express factorials in factored form.

$$\dfrac{2n(2n - 2)(2n - 4)(2n - 6) \cdots}{(2n + 2)(2n)(2n - 2)(2n - 4)(2n - 6) \cdots}$$

Cancel common terms. $\dfrac{1}{2n + 2}$

This is incorrect. What mistake was made?

**93.** Find the first four terms of the sequence defined by $a_n = (-1)^{n+1}n^2$.

**Solution:**

Find the $n = 1$ term. $a_1 = -1$

Find the $n = 2$ term. $a_2 = 4$

Find the $n = 3$ term. $a_3 = -9$

Find the $n = 4$ term. $a_4 = 16$

The sequence $-1, 4, -9, 16, \ldots$ is incorrect. What mistake was made?

**94.** Evaluate the series $\sum_{k=0}^{3}(-1)^{k+1}k^2$.

**Solution:**

Write out the sum. $\sum_{k=0}^{3}(-1)^{k+1}k^2 = -1 + 4 - 9$

Simplify the sum. $\sum_{k=0}^{3}(-1)^{k+1}k^2 = -6$

This is incorrect. What mistake was made?

■ **CONCEPTUAL**

**In Exercises 95–100, determine whether each statement is true or false.**

**95.** $\sum_{k=0}^{n} cx^k = c\sum_{k=0}^{n} x^k$

**96.** $\sum_{i=1}^{n}(a_i + b_i) = \sum_{i=1}^{n} a_i + \sum_{i=1}^{n} b_i$

**97.** $\sum_{k=1}^{n} a_k b_k = \sum_{k=1}^{n} a_k \cdot \sum_{k=1}^{n} b_k$

**98.** $(a!)(b!) = (ab)!$

**99.** $\sum_{k=1}^{\infty} a_k = \infty$

**100.** If $m! < n!$, then $m < n$.

■ **CHALLENGE**

**101.** Write the first four terms of the sequence defined by the recursion formula

$$a_1 = C \qquad a_n = a_{n-1} + D \qquad D \neq 0$$

**102.** Write the first four terms of the sequence defined by the recursion formula

$$a_1 = C \qquad a_n = Da_{n-1} \qquad D \neq 0$$

**103. Fibonacci Sequence.** An explicit formula for the $n$th term of the Fibonacci sequence is

$$F_n = \dfrac{(1 + \sqrt{5})^n - (1 - \sqrt{5})^n}{2^n\sqrt{5}}$$

Apply algebra (not your calculator) to find the first two terms of this sequence and verify that these are indeed the first two terms of the Fibonacci sequence.

**104.** Let $a_n = \sqrt{a_{n-1}}$ for $n \geq 2$ and $a_1 = 7$. Find the first five terms of this sequence and make a generalization for the $n$th term.

**■TECHNOLOGY**

**105.** The sequence defined by $a_n = \left(1 + \dfrac{1}{n}\right)^n$ approaches the number $e$ as $n$ gets large. Use a graphing calculator to find $a_{100}$, $a_{1000}$, $a_{10,000}$, and keep increasing $n$ until the terms in the sequence approach 2.7183.

**106.** The Fibonacci sequence is defined by $a_1 = 1$, $a_2 = 1$, and $a_n = a_{n-2} + a_{n-1}$ for $n \geq 3$. The ratio $\dfrac{a_{n+1}}{a_n}$ is an approximation of the golden ratio. The ratio approaches a constant $\phi$ (phi) as $n$ gets large. Find the golden ratio using a graphing utility.

**107.** Use a graphing calculator "SUM" to sum $\sum_{k=0}^{5} \dfrac{2^k}{k!}$. Compare it with your answer to Exercise 61.

**108.** Use a graphing calculator "SUM" to sum $\sum_{k=0}^{5} \dfrac{(-1)^k}{k!}$. Compare it with your answer to Exercise 62.

**■PREVIEW TO CALCULUS**

In calculus, we study the convergence of sequences. A sequence is *convergent* when its terms approach a limiting value. For example, $a_n = \dfrac{1}{n}$ is convergent because its terms approach zero. If the terms of a sequence satisfy $a_1 \leq a_2 \leq a_3 \leq \ldots \leq a_n \leq \ldots$, the sequence is *monotonic nondecreasing*. If $a_1 \geq a_2 \geq a_3 \geq \ldots \geq a_n \geq \ldots$, the sequence is *monotonic nonincreasing*.

In Exercises 109–112, classify each sequence as monotonic or not monotonic. If the sequence is monotonic, determine whether it is nondecreasing or nonincreasing.

**109.** $a_n = \dfrac{4n}{n+5}$

**110.** $a_n = \sin\left(\dfrac{n\pi}{4}\right)$

**111.** $a_n = \dfrac{2 + (-1)^n}{n+4}$

**112.** $a_n = \dfrac{3n^2}{5n^2 + 1}$

**SECTION 10.2 — ARITHMETIC SEQUENCES AND SERIES**

**SKILLS OBJECTIVES**

- Recognize an arithmetic sequence.
- Find the general, or *n*th, term of an arithmetic sequence.
- Evaluate a finite arithmetic series.
- Use arithmetic sequences and series to model real-world problems.

**CONCEPTUAL OBJECTIVE**

- Understand the difference between an arithmetic sequence and an arithmetic series.

## Arithmetic Sequences

The word *arithmetic* (with emphasis on the third syllable) often implies adding or subtracting of numbers. *Arithmetic sequences* are sequences whose terms are found by adding a constant to each previous term. The sequence 1, 3, 5, 7, 9, . . . is arithmetic because each successive term is found by adding 2 to the previous term.

**DEFINITION** **Arithmetic Sequences**

A sequence is **arithmetic** if the difference of any two consecutive terms is constant: $a_{n+1} - a_n = d$, where the number $d$ is called the **common difference**. Each term in the sequence is found by adding the same real number $d$ to the previous term, so that $a_{n+1} = a_n + d$.

**EXAMPLE 1    Identifying the Common Difference in Arithmetic Sequences**

Determine whether each sequence is arithmetic. If so, find the common difference for each of the arithmetic sequences.

**a.** $5, 9, 13, 17, \ldots$    **b.** $18, 9, 0, -9, \ldots$    **c.** $\frac{1}{2}, \frac{5}{4}, 2, \frac{11}{4}, \ldots$

**Solution (a):**

| | |
|---|---|
| Label the terms. | $a_1 = 5, a_2 = 9, a_3 = 13, a_4 = 17, \ldots$ |
| Find the difference $d = a_{n+1} - a_n$. | $d = a_2 - a_1 = 9 - 5 = \boxed{4}$ |
| Check that the difference of the next two successive pairs of terms is also 4. | $d = a_3 - a_2 = 13 - 9 = 4$ |
| | $d = a_4 - a_3 = 17 - 13 = 4$ |

There is a common difference of $\boxed{4}$. Therefore, this sequence is arithmetic and each successive term is found by adding 4 to the previous term.

**Study Tip**

We check several terms to confirm that a series is arithmetic.

**Solution (b):**

| | |
|---|---|
| Label the terms. | $a_1 = 18, a_2 = 9, a_3 = 0, a_4 = -9, \ldots$ |
| Find the difference $d = a_{n+1} - a_n$. | $d = a_2 - a_1 = 9 - 18 = \boxed{-9}$ |
| Check that the difference of the next two successive pairs of terms is also $-9$. | $d = a_3 - a_2 = 0 - 9 = -9$ |
| | $d = a_4 - a_3 = -9 - 0 = -9$ |

There is a common difference of $\boxed{-9}$. Therefore, this sequence is arithmetic and each successive term is found by subtracting 9 from (i.e., adding $-9$ to) the previous term.

**Solution (c):**

| | |
|---|---|
| Label the terms. | $a_1 = \dfrac{1}{2}, a_2 = \dfrac{5}{4}, a_3 = 2, a_4 = \dfrac{11}{4}, \ldots$ |
| Find the difference $d = a_{n+1} - a_n$. | $d = a_2 - a_1 = \dfrac{5}{4} - \dfrac{1}{2} = \boxed{\dfrac{3}{4}}$ |
| Check that the difference of the next two successive pairs of terms is also $\frac{3}{4}$. | $d = a_3 - a_2 = 2 - \dfrac{5}{4} = \dfrac{3}{4}$ |
| | $d = a_4 - a_3 = \dfrac{11}{4} - 2 = \dfrac{3}{4}$ |

There is a common difference of $\boxed{\dfrac{3}{4}}$. Therefore, this sequence is arithmetic and each successive term is found by adding $\frac{3}{4}$ to the previous term.

■ **Answer:** **a.** $-5$    **b.** $\frac{2}{3}$

■ **YOUR TURN** Find the common difference for each of the arithmetic sequences.

**a.** $7, 2, -3, -8, \ldots$    **b.** $1, \frac{5}{3}, \frac{7}{3}, 3, \ldots$

# The General (*n*th) Term of an Arithmetic Sequence

To find a formula for the general, or *n*th, term of an arithmetic sequence, write out the first several terms and look for a pattern.

First term, $n = 1$.      $a_1$

Second term, $n = 2$.      $a_2 = a_1 + d$

Third term, $n = 3$.      $a_3 = a_2 + d = (a_1 + d) + d = a_1 + 2d$

Fourth term, $n = 4$.      $a_4 = a_3 + d = (a_1 + 2d) + d = a_1 + 3d$

In general, the *n*th term is given by $a_n = a_1 + (n - 1)d$.

### THE *n*TH TERM OF AN ARITHMETIC SEQUENCE

The ***n*th term** of an arithmetic sequence with common difference $d$ is given by

$$a_n = a_1 + (n - 1)d \qquad \text{for } n \geq 1$$

## EXAMPLE 2   Finding the *n*th Term of an Arithmetic Sequence

Find the 13th term of the arithmetic sequence 2, 5, 8, 11, . . . .

**Solution:**

Identify the common difference.            $d = 5 - 2 = 3$

Identify the first ($n = 1$) term.            $a_1 = 2$

Substitute $a_1 = 2$ and $d = 3$ into $a_n = a_1 + (n - 1)d$.    $a_n = 2 + 3(n - 1)$

Substitute $n = 13$ into $a_n = 2 + 3(n - 1)$.      $a_{13} = 2 + 3(13 - 1) = \boxed{38}$

■ **YOUR TURN** Find the 10th term of the arithmetic sequence 3, 10, 17, 24, . . . .

▶ ## EXAMPLE 3   Finding the Arithmetic Sequence

The 4th term of an arithmetic sequence is 16, and the 21st term is 67. Find $a_1$ and $d$ and construct the sequence.

**Solution:**

Write the 4th and 21st terms.           $a_4 = 16$ and $a_{21} = 67$

Adding $d$ 17 times to $a_4$ results in $a_{21}$.      $a_{21} = a_4 + 17d$

Substitute $a_4 = 16$ and $a_{21} = 67$.      $67 = 16 + 17d$

Solve for $d$.                   $\boxed{d = 3}$

Substitute $d = 3$ into $a_n = a_1 + (n - 1)d$.    $a_n = a_1 + 3(n - 1)$

Let $a_4 = 16$.               $16 = a_1 + 3(4 - 1)$

Solve for $a_1$.               $\boxed{a_1 = 7}$

The arithmetic sequence that starts at 7 and has a common difference of 3 is $\boxed{7, 10, 13, 16, \dots}$.

■ **YOUR TURN** Construct the arithmetic sequence whose 7th term is 26 and whose 13th term is 50.

**Technology Tip**

2nd | LIST | ▶ | OPS | ▼ | 5:seq(
ENTER | 2 | + | 3 | ( | ALPHA
N | − | 1 | ) | , | ALPHA | N | ,
13 | , | 1 | ) | ENTER .

seq(2+3(N−1),N,1
3,13,1)
         {38}

■ **Answer:** 66

■ **Answer:** 2, 6, 10, 14, . . .

# The Sum of an Arithmetic Sequence

What is the sum of the first 100 counting numbers

$$1 + 2 + 3 + 4 + \cdots + 99 + 100 = ?$$

If we write this sum twice (one in ascending order and one in descending order) and add, we get 100 pairs of 101.

$$
\begin{array}{c}
\phantom{00}1 + \phantom{0}2 + \phantom{0}3 + \phantom{0}4 + \cdots + 99 + 100 \\
100 + 99 + 98 + 97 + \cdots + \phantom{0}2 + \phantom{00}1 \\
\hline
101 + 101 + 101 + 101 + \cdots + 101 + 101 = 100\,(101)
\end{array}
$$

Since we added twice the sum, we divide by 2.

$$1 + 2 + 3 + 4 + \cdots + 99 + 100 = \frac{(101)(100)}{2} = 5050$$

Now, let us develop the sum of a general arithmetic series.

The sum of the first $n$ terms of an arithmetic sequence is called the **$n$th partial sum**, or **finite arithmetic series**, and is denoted by $S_n$. An arithmetic sequence can be found by starting at the first term and adding the common difference to each successive term, and so the $n$th partial sum, or finite series, can be found the same way, but terminating the sum at the $n$th term:

$$S_n = a_1 + a_2 + a_3 + a_4 + \cdots$$
$$S_n = a_1 + (a_1 + d) + (a_1 + 2d) + (a_1 + 3d) + \cdots + (a_n)$$

Similarly, we can start with the $n$th term and find terms going backward by subtracting the common difference until we arrive at the first term:

$$S_n = a_n + a_{n-1} + a_{n-2} + a_{n-3} + \cdots$$
$$S_n = a_n + (a_n - d) + (a_n - 2d) + (a_n - 3d) + \cdots + (a_1)$$

Add these two representations of the $n$th partial sum. Notice that the $d$ terms are eliminated:

$$S_n = a_1 + (a_1 + d) + (a_1 + 2d) + (a_1 + 3d) + \cdots + (a_n)$$
$$S_n = a_n + (a_n - d) + (a_n - 2d) + (a_n - 3d) + \cdots + (a_1)$$
$$\overline{2S_n = \underbrace{(a_1 + a_n) + (a_1 + a_n) + (a_1 + a_n) + \cdots + (a_1 + a_n)}_{n(a_1 + a_n)}}$$

$$2S_n = n(a_1 + a_n) \quad \text{or} \quad S_n = \frac{n}{2}(a_1 + a_n)$$

**DEFINITION**  **Evaluating a Finite Arithmetic Series**

The sum of the first $n$ terms of an arithmetic sequence ($n$th *partial sum*), called a **finite arithmetic series**, is given by the formula

$$S_n = \frac{n}{2}(a_1 + a_n) \quad n \geq 2$$

For an arithmetic sequence, let $a_n = a_1 + (n-1)d$.

$$S_n = \frac{n}{2}[a_1 + a_1 + (n-1)d]$$
$$= \frac{n}{2}[2a_1 + (n-1)d] = na_1 + \frac{n(n-1)d}{2}$$

## EXAMPLE 4  Evaluating a Finite Arithmetic Series

Evaluate the finite arithmetic series $\sum_{k=1}^{100} k$.

**Solution:**

Expand the arithmetic series.

$$\sum_{k=1}^{100} k = 1 + 2 + 3 + \cdots + 99 + 100$$

This is the sum of an arithmetic sequence of numbers with a common difference of 1.

Identify the parameters of the arithmetic sequence.

$$a_1 = 1, a_n = 100, \text{ and } n = 100$$

Substitute these values into $S_n = \dfrac{n}{2}(a_1 + a_n)$.

$$S_{100} = \frac{100}{2}(1 + 100)$$

Simplify.

$$\boxed{S_{100} = 5050}$$

The sum of the first 100 natural numbers is 5050.

■ **YOUR TURN** Evaluate the following finite arithmetic series:

**a.** $\sum_{k=1}^{30} k$  **b.** $\sum_{k=1}^{20}(2k + 1)$

**Technology Tip**

To find the sum of the series $\sum_{k=1}^{100} k$, press

2nd | LIST | ▶ | MATH | ▼ |
5:*sum(* | ENTER | 2nd | LIST |
▶ | OPS | ▼ | 5:*seq(* | ENTER |
ALPHA | K | , | ALPHA | K | , |
1 | , | 100 | , | 1 | ) | ) | ENTER |.

```
sum(seq(K,K,1,10
0,1))
              5050
```

■ **Answer: a.** 465   **b.** 440

## ▶ EXAMPLE 5  Finding the *n*th Partial Sum of an Arithmetic Sequence

Find the sum of the first 20 terms of the arithmetic sequence 3, 8, 13, 18, 23, . . . .

**Solution:**

Recall the partial sum formula.

$$S_n = \frac{n}{2}(a_1 + a_n)$$

Find the 20th partial sum of this arithmetic sequence.

$$S_{20} = \frac{20}{2}(a_1 + a_{20})$$

Recall that the general *n*th term of an arithmetic sequence is given by

$$a_n = a_1 + (n - 1)d$$

Note that the first term of the arithmetic sequence is 3.

$$a_1 = 3$$

This is an arithmetic sequence with a common difference of 5.

$$d = 5$$

Substitute $a_1 = 3$ and $d = 5$ into $a_n = a_1 + (n - 1)d$.

$$a_n = 3 + (n - 1)5$$

Substitute $n = 20$ to find the 20th term.

$$a_{20} = 3 + (20 - 1)5 = 98$$

Substitute $a_1 = 3$ and $a_{20} = 98$ into the partial sum.

$$\boxed{S_{20} = 10(3 + 98) = 1010}$$

The sum of the first 20 terms of this arithmetic sequence is 1010.

**Technology Tip**

To find the sum of the series $\sum_{n=1}^{20} 3 + (n - 1)5$, press

2nd | LIST | ▶ | MATH | ▼ |
5:*sum(* | ENTER | 2nd | LIST |
▶ | OPS | ▼ | 5:*seq(* | ENTER |
3 | + | ( | ALPHA | N | − | 1 | ) |
5 | , | ALPHA | N | , | 1 | , | 20 | , | 1 |
) | ) | ENTER |.

```
sum(seq(3+(N-1)5
,N,1,20,1))
              1010
■
```

■ **YOUR TURN** Find the sum of the first 25 terms of the arithmetic sequence 2, 6, 10, 14, 18, . . . .

■ **Answer:** 1250

## Applications

### EXAMPLE 6   Marching Band Formation

Suppose a band has 18 members in the first row, 22 members in the second row, and 26 members in the third row and continues with that pattern for a total of nine rows. How many marchers are there all together?

The Ohio State University marching band

**Solution:**

The number of members in each row forms an arithmetic sequence with a common difference of 4, and the first row has 18 members.

$$a_1 = 18 \quad d = 4$$

Calculate the $n$th term of the sequence $a_n = a_1 + (n - 1)d$.

$$a_n = 18 + (n - 1)4$$

Find the 9th term, $n = 9$.

$$a_9 = 18 + (9 - 1)4 = 50$$

Calculate the sum $S_n = \dfrac{n}{2}(a_1 + a_n)$ of the nine rows.

$$S_9 = \dfrac{9}{2}(a_1 + a_9)$$

$$= \dfrac{9}{2}(18 + 50)$$

$$= \dfrac{9}{2}(68)$$

$$= \boxed{306}$$

There are 306 members in the marching band.

■ **Answer:** 328

■ **YOUR TURN**   Suppose a bed of tulips is arranged in a garden so that there are 20 tulips in the first row, 26 tulips in the second row, and 32 tulips in the third row and the rows continue with that pattern for a total of 8 rows. How many tulips are there all together?

## SECTION
# 10.2 SUMMARY

In this section, arithmetic sequences were defined as sequences of which each successive term is found by adding the same constant $d$ to the previous term. Formulas were developed for the general, or $n$th, term of an arithmetic sequence, and for the $n$th partial sum of an arithmetic sequence, also called a finite arithmetic series.

$$a_n = a_1 + (n - 1)d \qquad n \geq 1$$

$$S_n = \frac{n}{2}(a_1 + a_n) = na_1 + \frac{n(n-1)}{2}d$$

## SECTION
# 10.2 EXERCISES

### ▪ SKILLS

**In Exercises 1–10, determine whether each sequence is arithmetic. If it is, find the common difference.**

**1.** $2, 5, 8, 11, 14, \ldots$

**2.** $9, 6, 3, 0, -3, -6, \ldots$

**3.** $1^2 + 2^2 + 3^2 + \cdots$

**4.** $1! + 2! + 3! + \cdots$

**5.** $3.33, 3.30, 3.27, 3.24, \ldots$

**6.** $0.7, 1.2, 1.7, 2.2, \ldots$

**7.** $4, \frac{14}{3}, \frac{16}{3}, 6, \ldots$

**8.** $2, \frac{7}{3}, \frac{8}{3}, 3, \ldots$

**9.** $10^1, 10^2, 10^3, 10^4, \ldots$

**10.** $120, 60, 30, 15, \ldots$

**In Exercises 11–20, find the first four terms of each sequence described. Determine whether the sequence is arithmetic, and if so, find the common difference.**

**11.** $a_n = -2n + 5$

**12.** $a_n = 3n - 10$

**13.** $a_n = n^2$

**14.** $a_n = \frac{n^2}{n!}$

**15.** $a_n = 5n - 3$

**16.** $a_n = -4n + 5$

**17.** $a_n = 10(n - 1)$

**18.** $a_n = 8n - 4$

**19.** $a_n = (-1)^n n$

**20.** $a_n = (-1)^{n+1} 2n$

**In Exercises 21–28, find the general, or $n$th, term of each arithmetic sequence given the first term and the common difference.**

**21.** $a_1 = 11 \qquad d = 5$

**22.** $a_1 = 5 \qquad d = 11$

**23.** $a_1 = -4 \qquad d = 2$

**24.** $a_1 = 2 \qquad d = -4$

**25.** $a_1 = 0 \qquad d = \frac{2}{3}$

**26.** $a_1 = -1 \qquad d = -\frac{3}{4}$

**27.** $a_1 = 0 \qquad d = e$

**28.** $a_1 = 1.1 \qquad d = -0.3$

**In Exercises 29–32, find the specified term for each arithmetic sequence given.**

**29.** The 10th term of the sequence $7, 20, 33, 46, \ldots$

**30.** The 19th term of the sequence $7, 1, -5, -11, \ldots$

**31.** The 100th term of the sequence $9, 2, -5, -12, \ldots$

**32.** The 90th term of the sequence $13, 19, 25, 31, \ldots$

**33.** The 21st term of the sequence $\frac{1}{3}, \frac{7}{12}, \frac{5}{6}, \frac{13}{12}, \ldots$

**34.** The 33rd term of the sequence $\frac{1}{5}, \frac{8}{15}, \frac{13}{15}, \frac{6}{5}, \ldots$

**In Exercises 35–40, for each arithmetic sequence described, find $a_1$ and $d$ and construct the sequence by stating the general, or $n$th, term.**

**35.** The 5th term is 44 and the 17th term is 152.

**36.** The 9th term is $-19$ and the 21st term is $-55$.

**37.** The 7th term is $-1$ and the 17th term is $-41$.

**38.** The 8th term is 47 and the 21st term is 112.

**39.** The 4th term is 3 and the 22nd term is 15.

**40.** The 11th term is $-3$ and the 31st term is $-13$.

**In Exercises 41–52, find each sum given.**

**41.** $\displaystyle\sum_{k=1}^{23} 2k$
**42.** $\displaystyle\sum_{k=0}^{20} 5k$
**43.** $\displaystyle\sum_{n=1}^{30} (-2n + 5)$
**44.** $\displaystyle\sum_{n=0}^{17} (3n - 10)$
**45.** $\displaystyle\sum_{j=3}^{14} 0.5j$
**46.** $\displaystyle\sum_{j=1}^{33} \frac{j}{4}$

**47.** $2 + 7 + 12 + 17 + \cdots + 62$
**48.** $1 - 3 - 7 - \cdots - 75$
**49.** $4 + 7 + 10 + \cdots + 151$

**50.** $2 + 0 - 2 - \cdots - 56$
**51.** $\frac{1}{6} - \frac{1}{6} - \frac{1}{2} - \cdots - \frac{13}{2}$
**52.** $\frac{11}{12} + \frac{7}{6} + \frac{17}{12} + \cdots + \frac{14}{3}$

**In Exercises 53–58, find the indicated partial sum of each arithmetic series.**

**53.** The first 18 terms of $1 + 5 + 9 + 13 + \cdots$

**54.** The first 21 terms of $2 + 5 + 8 + 11 + \cdots$

**55.** The first 43 terms of $1 + \frac{1}{2} + 0 - \frac{1}{2} - \cdots$

**56.** The first 37 terms of $3 + \frac{3}{2} + 0 - \frac{3}{2} - \cdots$

**57.** The first 18 terms of $-9 + 1 + 11 + 21 + 31 + \cdots$

**58.** The first 21 terms of $-2 + 8 + 18 + 28 + \cdots$

### ▪ APPLICATIONS

**59. Comparing Salaries.** Colin and Camden are twin brothers graduating with B.S. degrees in biology. Colin takes a job at the San Diego Zoo making $28,000 for his first year with a $1500 raise per year every year after that. Camden accepts a job at Florida Fish and Wildlife making $25,000 with a guaranteed $2000 raise per year. How much will each of the brothers have made in a total of 10 years?

**60. Comparing Salaries.** On graduating with a Ph.D. in optical sciences, Jasmine and Megan choose different career paths. Jasmine accepts a faculty position at the University of Arizona making $80,000 with a guaranteed $2000 raise every year. Megan takes a job with the Boeing Corporation making $90,000 with a guaranteed $5000 raise each year. Calculate how much each woman will have made after 15 years.

**61. Theater Seating.** You walk into the premiere of Brad Pitt's new movie, and the theater is packed, with almost every seat filled. You want to estimate the number of people in the theater. You quickly count to find that there are 22 seats in the front row, and there are 25 rows in the theater. Each row appears to have one more seat than the row in front of it. How many seats are in that theater?

**62. Field of Tulips.** Every spring the Skagit County Tulip Festival plants more than 100,000 bulbs. In honor of the Tri-Delta sorority that has sent 120 sisters from the University of Washington to volunteer for the festival, Skagit County has planted tulips in the shape of $\triangle\triangle\triangle$. In each of the triangles there are 20 rows of tulips, each row having one less than the row before. How many tulips are planted in each delta if there is one tulip in the first row?

**63. World's Largest Champagne Fountain.** From December 28 to 30, 1999, Luuk Broos, director of Maison Luuk-Chalet Fontain, constructed a 56-story champagne fountain at the Steigenberger Kurhaus Hotel, Scheveningen, Netherlands. The fountain consisted of 30,856 champagne glasses. Assuming there was one glass at the top and the number of glasses in each row forms an arithmetic sequence, how many were on the bottom row (story)? How many glasses less did each successive row (story) have? Assume each story is one row.

**64. Stacking of Logs.** If 25 logs are laid side by side on the ground, and 24 logs are placed on top of those, and 23 logs are placed on the 3rd row, and the pattern continues until there is a single log on the 25th row, how many logs are in the stack?

**65. Falling Object.** When a skydiver jumps out of an airplane, she falls approximately 16 feet in the 1st second, 48 feet during the 2nd second, 80 feet during the 3rd second, 112 feet during the 4th second, and 144 feet during the 5th second, and this pattern continues. If she deploys her parachute after 10 seconds have elapsed, how far will she have fallen during those 10 seconds?

**66. Falling Object.** If a penny is dropped out of a plane, it falls approximately 4.9 meters during the 1st second, 14.7 meters during the 2nd second, 24.5 meters during the 3rd second, and 34.3 meters during the 4th second. Assuming this pattern continues, how many meters will the penny have fallen after 10 seconds?

**67. Grocery Store.** A grocer has a triangular display of oranges in a window. There are 20 oranges in the bottom row and the number of oranges decreases by one in each row above this row. How many oranges are in the display?

**68. Salary.** Suppose your salary is $45,000 and you receive a $1500 raise for each year you work for 35 years.
a. How much will you earn during the 35th year?
b. What is the total amount you earned over your 35-year career?

**69. Theater Seating.** At a theater, seats are arranged in a triangular pattern of rows with each succeeding row having one more seat than the previous row. You count the number of seats in the fourth row and determine that there are 26 seats.
a. How many seats are in the first row?
b. Now, suppose there are 30 rows of seats. How many total seats are there in the theater?

**70. Mathematics.** Find the exact sum of

$$\frac{1}{e} + \frac{3}{e} + \frac{5}{e} + \cdots + \frac{23}{e}$$

# ▪ CATCH THE MISTAKE

**In Exercises 71–74, explain the mistake that is made.**

**71.** Find the general, or $n$th, term of the arithmetic sequence 3, 4, 5, 6, 7, . . . .

**Solution:**

The common difference of this sequence is 1.  $d = 1$

The first term is 3.  $a_1 = 3$

The general term is $a_n = a_1 + nd$.  $a_n = 3 + n$

This is incorrect. What mistake was made?

**72.** Find the general, or $n$th, term of the arithmetic sequence 10, 8, 6, . . . .

**Solution:**

The common difference of this sequence is 2.  $d = 2$

The first term is 10.  $a_1 = 10$

The general term is $a_n = a_1 + (n-1)d$.  $a_n = 10 + 2(n-1)$

This is incorrect. What mistake was made?

**73.** Find the sum $\sum_{k=0}^{10}(2n + 1)$.

**Solution:**

The sum is given by $S_n = \dfrac{n}{2}(a_1 + a_n)$, where $n = 10$.

Identify the 1st and 10th terms.  $a_1 = 1, a_{10} = 21$

Substitute $a_1 = 1$, $a_{10} = 21$, and $n = 10$ into $S_n = \dfrac{n}{2}(a_1 + a_n)$.  $S_{10} = \dfrac{10}{2}(1 + 21) = 110$

This is incorrect. What mistake was made?

**74.** Find the sum $3 + 9 + 15 + 21 + 27 + 33 + \cdots + 87$.

**Solution:**

This is an arithmetic sequence with common difference of 6.  $d = 6$

The general term is given by $a_n = a_1 + (n-1)d$.  $a_n = 3 + (n-1)6$

87 is the 15th term of the series.  $a_{15} = 3 + (15-1)6 = 87$

The sum of the series is $S_n = \dfrac{n}{2}(a_n - a_1)$.  $S_{15} = \dfrac{15}{2}(87 - 3) = 630$

This is incorrect. What mistake was made?

# ▪ CONCEPTUAL

**In Exercises 75–78, determine whether each statement is true or false.**

**75.** An arithmetic sequence and a finite arithmetic series are the same.

**76.** The sum of all infinite and finite arithmetic series can always be found.

**77.** An alternating sequence cannot be an arithmetic sequence.

**78.** The common difference of an arithmetic sequence is always positive.

# ▪ CHALLENGE

**79.** Find the sum $a + (a + b) + (a + 2b) + \cdots + (a + nb)$.

**80.** Find the sum $\sum_{k=-29}^{30} \ln e^k$.

**81.** The wave number $\lambda$ (reciprocal of wave length) of certain light waves in the spectrum of light emitted by hydrogen is given by $\lambda = R\left(\dfrac{1}{k^2} - \dfrac{1}{n^2}\right)$, $n > k$, where $R = 109{,}678$. A

series of lines is given by holding $k$ constant and varying the value of $n$. Suppose $k = 2$ and $n = 3, 4, 5, \ldots$. Find what value the wave number of the series approaches as $n$ increases.

**82.** In a certain arithmetic sequence $a_1 = -4$ and $d = 6$. If $S_n = 570$, find the value of $n$.

# ▪ TECHNOLOGY

**83.** Use a graphing calculator "SUM" to sum the natural numbers from 1 to 100.

**84.** Use a graphing calculator to sum the even natural numbers from 1 to 100.

**85.** Use a graphing calculator to sum the odd natural numbers from 1 to 100.

**86.** Use a graphing calculator to find $\sum_{n=1}^{30}(-2n + 5)$. Compare it with your answer to Exercise 43.

**87.** Use a graphing calculator to find $\sum_{n=1}^{100}[-59 + 5(n - 1)]$.

**88.** Use a graphing calculator to find $\sum_{n=1}^{200}\left[-18 + \tfrac{4}{5}(n - 1)\right]$.

■ **PREVIEW TO CALCULUS**

In calculus, when estimating certain integrals, we use sums of the form $\sum_{i=1}^{n} f(x_i)\Delta x$, where $f$ is a function and $\Delta x$ is a constant.

In Exercises 89–92, find the indicated sum.

**89.** $\sum_{i=1}^{100} f(x_i)\Delta x$, where $f(x_i) = 2i$ and $\Delta x = 0.1$

**90.** $\sum_{i=1}^{50} f(x_i)\Delta x$, where $f(x_i) = 4i - 2$ and $\Delta x = 0.01$

**91.** $\sum_{i=1}^{43} f(x_i)\Delta x$, where $f(x_i) = 6 + i$ and $\Delta x = 0.001$

**92.** $\sum_{i=1}^{85} f(x_i)\Delta x$, where $f(x_i) = 6 - 7i$ and $\Delta x = 0.2$

## SECTION 10.3 GEOMETRIC SEQUENCES AND SERIES

### SKILLS OBJECTIVES

- Recognize a geometric sequence.
- Find the general, or $n$th, term of a geometric sequence.
- Evaluate a finite geometric series.
- Evaluate an infinite geometric series, if it exists.
- Use geometric sequences and series to model real-world problems.

### CONCEPTUAL OBJECTIVES

- Understand the difference between a geometric sequence and a geometric series.
- Distinguish between an arithmetic sequence and a geometric sequence.
- Understand why it is not possible to evaluate all infinite geometric series.

## Geometric Sequences

In Section 10.2, we discussed *arithmetic* sequences, where successive terms had a *common difference*. In other words, each term was found by adding the same constant to the previous term. In this section, we discuss *geometric* sequences, where successive terms have a *common ratio*. In other words, each term is found by multiplying the previous term by the same constant. The sequence $4, 12, 36, 108, \ldots$ is geometric because each successive term is found by multiplying the previous term by 3.

**DEFINITION**   **Geometric Sequences**

A sequence is **geometric** if each term in the sequence is found by multiplying the previous term by a number $r$, so that $a_{n+1} = r \cdot a_n$. Because $\dfrac{a_{n+1}}{a_n} = r$, the number $r$ is called the **common ratio**.

**EXAMPLE 1** **Identifying the Common Ratio in Geometric Sequences**

Find the common ratio for each of the geometric sequences.

**a.** $5, 20, 80, 320, \ldots$    **b.** $1, -\frac{1}{2}, \frac{1}{4}, -\frac{1}{8}, \ldots$    **c.** $\$5000, \$5500, \$6050, \$6655, \ldots$

**Solution (a):**

Label the terms.

Find the ratio $r = \dfrac{a_{n+1}}{a_n}$.

$a_1 = 5, a_2 = 20, a_3 = 80, a_4 = 320, \ldots$

$r = \dfrac{a_2}{a_1} = \dfrac{20}{5} = 4$

$r = \dfrac{a_3}{a_2} = \dfrac{80}{20} = 4$

$r = \dfrac{a_4}{a_3} = \dfrac{320}{80} = 4$

The common ratio is 4.

**Solution (b):**

Label the terms.

Find the ratio $r = \dfrac{a_{n+1}}{a_n}$.

$a_1 = 1, a_2 = -\dfrac{1}{2}, a_3 = \dfrac{1}{4}, a_4 = -\dfrac{1}{8}, \ldots$

$r = \dfrac{a_2}{a_1} = \dfrac{-1/2}{1} = -\dfrac{1}{2}$

$r = \dfrac{a_3}{a_2} = \dfrac{1/4}{-1/2} = -\dfrac{1}{2}$

$r = \dfrac{a_4}{a_3} = \dfrac{-1/8}{1/4} = -\dfrac{1}{2}$

The common ratio is $-\frac{1}{2}$.

**Solution (c):**

Label the terms.

Find the ratio $r = \dfrac{a_{n+1}}{a_n}$.

$a_1 = \$5000, a_2 = \$5500, a_3 = \$6050, a_4 = \$6655, \ldots$

$r = \dfrac{a_2}{a_1} = \dfrac{\$5500}{\$5000} = 1.1$

$r = \dfrac{a_3}{a_2} = \dfrac{\$6050}{\$5500} = 1.1$

$r = \dfrac{a_4}{a_3} = \dfrac{\$6655}{\$6050} = 1.1$

The common ratio is 1.1.

■ **YOUR TURN** Find the common ratio of each geometric series.

**a.** $1, -3, 9, -27, \ldots$    **b.** $320, 80, 20, 5, \ldots$

■ **Answer: a.** $-3$    **b.** $\frac{1}{4}$ or 0.25

# The General (*n*th) Term of a Geometric Sequence

To find a formula for the general, or *n*th, term of a geometric sequence, write out the first several terms and look for a pattern.

| WORDS | MATH |
|---|---|
| First term, $n = 1$. | $a_1$ |
| Second term, $n = 2$. | $a_2 = a_1 \cdot r$ |
| Third term, $n = 3$. | $a_3 = a_2 \cdot r = (a_1 \cdot r) \cdot r = a_1 \cdot r^2$ |
| Fourth term, $n = 4$. | $a_4 = a_3 \cdot r = (a_1 \cdot r^2) \cdot r = a_1 \cdot r^3$ |

In general, the $n$th term is given by $a_n = a_1 \cdot r^{n-1}$.

### THE $n$TH TERM OF A GEOMETRIC SEQUENCE

The **$n$th term** of a geometric sequence with common ratio $r$ is given by

$$a_n = a_1 \cdot r^{n-1} \qquad \text{for } n \geq 1$$

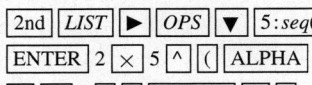

### *Technology Tip*

Use $\boxed{seq}$ to find the $n$th term of the sequence by setting the initial index value equal to the final index value. To find the 7th term of the geometric sequence $a_n = 2 \cdot 5^{n-1}$, press

$\boxed{\text{2nd}}\ \boxed{\text{LIST}}\ \boxed{\blacktriangleright}\ \boxed{\text{OPS}}\ \boxed{\blacktriangledown}\ \boxed{5:seq(}$
$\boxed{\text{ENTER}}\ \boxed{2}\ \boxed{\times}\ \boxed{5}\ \boxed{\wedge}\ \boxed{()}\ \boxed{\text{ALPHA}}$
$\boxed{N}\ \boxed{-}\ \boxed{1}\ \boxed{)}\ \boxed{,}\ \boxed{\text{ALPHA}}\ \boxed{N}\ \boxed{,}$
$\boxed{7}\ \boxed{,}\ \boxed{7}\ \boxed{,}\ \boxed{1}\ \boxed{)}\ \boxed{\text{ENTER}}$.

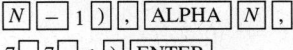

```
seq(2*5^(N-1),N,
7,7,1)
            {31250}
■
```

■ **Answer:** 49,152

### EXAMPLE 2   Finding the $n$th Term of a Geometric Sequence

Find the 7th term of the sequence 2, 10, 50, 250, . . . .

**Solution:**

Identify the common ratio.

$$r = \frac{10}{2} = \frac{50}{10} = \frac{250}{50} = 5$$

Identify the first ($n = 1$) term. $\qquad a_1 = 2$

Substitute $a_1 = 2$ and $r = 5$ into $a_n = a_1 \cdot r^{n-1}$. $\qquad a_n = 2 \cdot 5^{n-1}$

Substitute $n = 7$ into $a_n = 2 \cdot 5^{n-1}$. $\qquad a_7 = 2 \cdot 5^{7-1} = 2 \cdot 5^6 = 31{,}250$

> The 7th term of the geometric sequence is 31,250.

■ **YOUR TURN** Find the 8th term of the sequence 3, 12, 48, 192, . . . .

### EXAMPLE 3   Finding the Geometric Sequence

Find the geometric sequence whose 5th term is 0.01 and whose common ratio is 0.1.

**Solution:**

Label the common ratio and 5th term. $\qquad a_5 = 0.01$ and $r = 0.1$

Substitute $a_5 = 0.01$, $n = 5$, and $r = 0.1$
into $a_n = a_1 \cdot r^{n-1}$. $\qquad 0.01 = a_1 \cdot (0.1)^{5-1}$

Solve for $a_1$. $\qquad a_1 = \dfrac{0.01}{(0.1)^4} = \dfrac{0.01}{0.0001} = 100$

> The geometric sequence that starts at 100 and has a common ratio of 0.1 is
> 100, 10, 1, 0.1, 0.01, . . . .

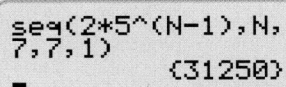

■ **Answer:** 81, 27, 9, 3, 1, . . .

■ **YOUR TURN** Find the geometric sequence whose 4th term is 3 and whose common ratio is $\frac{1}{3}$.

# Geometric Series

The sum of the terms of a geometric sequence is called a **geometric series**.

$$a_1 + a_1 \cdot r + a_1 \cdot r^2 + a_1 \cdot r^3 + \cdots$$

If we only sum the first $n$ terms of a geometric sequence, the result is a **finite geometric series** given by

$$S_n = a_1 + a_1 \cdot r + a_1 \cdot r^2 + a_1 \cdot r^3 + \cdots + a_1 \cdot r^{n-1}$$

To develop a formula for this $n$th partial sum, we multiply the above equation by $r$:

$$r \cdot S_n = a_1 \cdot r + a_1 \cdot r^2 + a_1 \cdot r^3 + \cdots + a_1 \cdot r^{n-1} + a_1 \cdot r^n$$

   Subtracting the **second** equation from the **first** equation, we find that all of the terms on the right side drop out except the *first* term in the **first** equation and the *last* term in the **second** equation:

$$S_n = a_1 + a_1 \cdot r + a_1 \cdot r^2 + \cdots + a_1 r^{n-1}$$
$$-rS_n = \qquad - a_1 \cdot r - a_1 \cdot r^2 - \cdots - a_1 r^{n-1} - a_1 r^n$$
$$\overline{S_n - rS_n = a_1 \qquad\qquad\qquad\qquad\qquad\qquad -a_1 r^n}$$

Factor the $S_n$ out of the left side and the $a_1$ out of the right side:

$$S_n(1 - r) = a_1(1 - r^n)$$

Divide both sides by $(1 - r)$, assuming $r \neq 1$. The result is a general formula for the sum of a finite geometric series:

$$S_n = a_1 \frac{(1 - r^n)}{(1 - r)} \qquad r \neq 1$$

## EVALUATING A FINITE GEOMETRIC SERIES

The sum of the first $n$ terms of a geometric sequence, called a **finite geometric series**, is given by the formula

$$S_n = a_1 \frac{(1 - r^n)}{(1 - r)} \qquad r \neq 1$$

It is important to note that a finite geometric series can also be written in sigma (summation) notation:

$$S_n = \sum_{k=1}^{n} a_1 \cdot r^{k-1} = a_1 + a_1 \cdot r + a_1 \cdot r^2 + a_1 \cdot r^3 + \cdots + a_1 \cdot r^{n-1}$$

**Study Tip**

The underscript $k = 1$ applies only when the summation starts at the $a_1$ term. It is important to note which term is the starting term.

## EXAMPLE 4   Evaluating a Finite Geometric Series

Evaluate each finite geometric series.

**a.** $\displaystyle\sum_{k=1}^{13} 3 \cdot (0.4)^{k-1}$

**b.** The first nine terms of the series $1 + 2 + 4 + 8 + 16 + 32 + 64 + \cdots$

**Solution (a):**

Identify $a_1$, $n$, and $r$.
$$a_1 = 3,\ n = 13,\ \text{and } r = 0.4$$

Substitute $a_1 = 3$, $n = 13$, and $r = 0.4$ into $S_n = a_1 \dfrac{(1 - r^n)}{(1 - r)}$.
$$S_{13} = 3\,\frac{\left(1 - 0.4^{13}\right)}{(1 - 0.4)}$$

Simplify.
$$\boxed{S_{13} \approx 4.99997}$$

**Solution (b):**

Identify the first term and common ratio.
$$a_1 = 1 \text{ and } r = 2$$

Substitute $a_1 = 1$ and $r = 2$ into $S_n = a_1 \dfrac{(1 - r^n)}{(1 - r)}$.
$$S_n = \frac{(1 - 2^n)}{(1 - 2)}$$

To sum the first nine terms, let $n = 9$.
$$S_9 = \frac{(1 - 2^9)}{(1 - 2)}$$

Simplify.
$$\boxed{S_9 = 511}$$

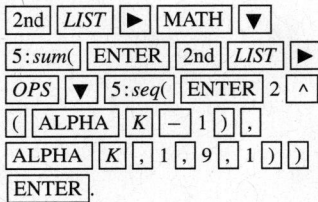
The sum of an infinite geometric sequence is called an **infinite geometric series**. Some infinite geometric series *converge* (yield a finite sum) and some *diverge* (do not have a finite sum). For example,

$$\frac{1}{2} + \frac{1}{4} + \frac{1}{8} + \frac{1}{16} + \frac{1}{32} + \cdots + \frac{1}{2^n} + \cdots = 1 \quad \text{(converges)}$$

$$2 + 4 + 8 + 16 + 32 + \cdots + 2^n + \cdots \quad \text{(diverges)}$$

For infinite geometric series that converge, the partial sum $S_n$ approaches a single number as $n$ gets large. The formula used to evaluate a finite geometric series

$$S_n = a_1 \frac{(1 - r^n)}{(1 - r)}$$

can be extended to an infinite geometric series for certain values of $r$. If $|r| < 1$, then when $r$ is raised to a power, it continues to get smaller, approaching 0. For those values of $r$, the infinite geometric series converges to a finite sum.

$$\text{Let } n \to \infty; \text{ then } a_1 \frac{(1 - r^n)}{(1 - r)} \to a_1 \frac{(1 - 0)}{(1 - r)} = \frac{a_1}{1 - r}, \text{ if } |r| < 1.$$

## EVALUATING AN INFINITE GEOMETRIC SERIES

The **sum of an infinite geometric series** is given by the formula

$$\sum_{n=1}^{\infty} a_1 r^{n-1} = \sum_{n=0}^{\infty} a_1 \cdot r^n = a_1 \frac{1}{(1-r)} \qquad |r| < 1$$

### EXAMPLE 5    Determining Whether the Sum of an Infinite Series Exists

Determine whether the sum exists for each of the geometric series.

**a.** $3 + 15 + 75 + 375 + \cdots$    **b.** $8 + 4 + 2 + 1 + \frac{1}{2} + \frac{1}{4} + \frac{1}{8} + \cdots$

**Solution (a):**

Identify the common ratio.    $r = 5$

Since 5 is greater than 1, the  sum does not exist .    $|r| = 5 > 1$

**Solution (b):**

Identify the common ratio.    $r = \dfrac{1}{2}$

Since $\frac{1}{2}$ is less than 1, the  sum exists .    $|r| = \dfrac{1}{2} < 1$

■ **YOUR TURN** Determine whether the sum exists for each of the geometric series.

**a.** $81 + 9 + 1 + \frac{1}{9} + \cdots$    **b.** $1 + 5 + 25 + 125 + \cdots$

Do you expect $\frac{1}{4} + \frac{1}{12} + \frac{1}{36} + \frac{1}{64} + \cdots$ and $\frac{1}{4} - \frac{1}{12} + \frac{1}{36} - \frac{1}{64} + \cdots$ to sum to the same number? The answer is no, because the second series is an alternating series and terms are both added and subtracted. Hence, we would expect the second series to sum to a smaller number than the first series sums to.

### EXAMPLE 6    Evaluating an Infinite Geometric Series

Evaluate each infinite geometric series.

**a.** $1 + \frac{1}{3} + \frac{1}{9} + \frac{1}{27} + \cdots$    **b.** $1 - \frac{1}{3} + \frac{1}{9} - \frac{1}{27} + \cdots$

**Solution (a):**

Identify the first term and the common ratio.    $a_1 = 1 \qquad r = \dfrac{1}{3}$

Since $|r| = \frac{1}{3} < 1$, the sum of the series exists.

Substitute $a_1 = 1$ and $r = \frac{1}{3}$ into

$$\sum_{n=0}^{\infty} a_1 \cdot r^n = \frac{a_1}{(1-r)}.$$

$$\frac{1}{1 - \dfrac{1}{3}}$$

Simplify.

$$= \frac{1}{\dfrac{2}{3}} = \frac{3}{2}$$

$$\boxed{1 + \frac{1}{3} + \frac{1}{9} + \frac{1}{27} + \cdots = \frac{3}{2}}$$

**Solution (b):**

Identify the first term and the common ratio. $\qquad a_1 = 1 \qquad r = -\dfrac{1}{3}$

Since $|r| = \left|-\dfrac{1}{3}\right| = \dfrac{1}{3} < 1$, the sum of the series exists.

Substitute $a_1 = 1$ and $r = -\dfrac{1}{3}$ into $\displaystyle\sum_{n=0}^{\infty} a_1 \cdot r^n = \dfrac{a_1}{(1-r)}$.

Simplify. $\qquad = \dfrac{1}{1-(-1/3)} = \dfrac{1}{1+(1/3)} = \dfrac{1}{4/3} = \dfrac{3}{4}$

$$1 - \frac{1}{3} + \frac{1}{9} - \frac{1}{27} + \cdots = \frac{3}{4}$$

Notice that the alternating series summed to $\dfrac{3}{4}$, whereas the positive series summed to $\dfrac{3}{2}$.

■ **Answer: a.** $\dfrac{3}{8}$ **b.** $\dfrac{3}{16}$

■ **YOUR TURN** Find the sum of each infinite geometric series.

a. $\dfrac{1}{4} + \dfrac{1}{12} + \dfrac{1}{36} + \dfrac{1}{108} + \cdots$ b. $\dfrac{1}{4} - \dfrac{1}{12} + \dfrac{1}{36} - \dfrac{1}{108} + \cdots$

It is important to note the restriction on the common ratio $r$. The absolute value of the common ratio has to be strictly less than 1 for an infinite geometric series to converge. Otherwise, the infinite geometric series diverges.

**EXAMPLE 7  Evaluating an Infinite Geometric Series**

Evaluate the infinite geometric series, if possible.

a. $\displaystyle\sum_{n=0}^{\infty} 2\left(-\dfrac{1}{4}\right)^n$ b. $\displaystyle\sum_{n=1}^{\infty} 3 \cdot 2^{n-1}$

**Solution (a):**

Identify $a_1$ and $r$. $\qquad \displaystyle\sum_{n=0}^{\infty} 2\left(-\dfrac{1}{4}\right)^n = \underset{a_1}{2} - \dfrac{1}{2} + \dfrac{1}{8} - \dfrac{1}{32} + \dfrac{1}{128} - \cdots$

Since $|r| = \left|-\dfrac{1}{4}\right| = \dfrac{1}{4} < 1$, the infinite geometric series converges. $\qquad \displaystyle\sum_{n=0}^{\infty} a_1 \cdot r^n = \dfrac{a_1}{(1-r)}$

Let $a_1 = 2$ and $r = -\dfrac{1}{4}$. $\qquad = \dfrac{2}{[1-(-1/4)]}$

Simplify. $\qquad = \dfrac{2}{1+(1/4)} = \dfrac{2}{5/4} = \dfrac{8}{5}$

This infinite geometric series converges. $\qquad \displaystyle\sum_{n=0}^{\infty} 2\left(-\dfrac{1}{4}\right)^n = \dfrac{8}{5}$

**Solution (b):**

Identify $a_1$ and $r$. $\qquad \displaystyle\sum_{n=1}^{\infty} 3 \cdot (2)^{n-1} = \underset{a_1}{3} + 6 + 12 + 24 + 48 + \cdots$

Since $r = 2 > 1$, this infinite geometric series diverges.

## Applications

Suppose you are given a job offer with a guaranteed percentage raise per year. What will your annual salary be 10 years from now? That answer can be obtained using a geometric sequence. Suppose you want to make voluntary contributions to a retirement account directly debited from your paycheck every month. Suppose the account earns a fixed percentage rate: How much will you have in 30 years if you deposit $50 a month? What is the difference in the total you will have in 30 years if you deposit $100 a month instead? These important questions about your personal finances can be answered using geometric sequences and series.

---

**EXAMPLE 8    Future Salary: Geometric Sequence**

Suppose you are offered a job as an event planner for the PGA Tour. The starting salary is $45,000, and employees are given a 5% raise per year. What will your annual salary be during the 10th year with the PGA Tour?

**Solution:**

Every year the salary is 5% more than the previous year.

Label the year 1 salary. $\qquad\qquad\qquad a_1 = 45,000$

Calculate the year 2 salary. $\qquad\qquad a_2 = 1.05 \cdot a_1$

Calculate the year 3 salary. $\qquad\qquad a_3 = 1.05 \cdot a_2$

$\qquad\qquad\qquad\qquad\qquad\qquad\quad = 1.05(1.05 \cdot a_1) = (1.05)^2 a_1$

Calculate the year 4 salary. $\qquad\qquad a_4 = 1.05 \cdot a_3$

$\qquad\qquad\qquad\qquad\qquad\qquad\quad = 1.05(1.05)^2 a_1 = (1.05)^3 a_1$

Identify the year $n$ salary. $\qquad\qquad a_n = 1.05^{n-1} a_1$

Substitute $n = 10$ and $a_1 = 45,000$. $\qquad a_{10} = (1.05)^9 \cdot 45,000$

Simplify. $\qquad\qquad\qquad\qquad\qquad a_{10} \approx 69,809.77$

During your 10th year with the company, your salary will be $69,809.77.

........................................................................

■ **YOUR TURN** Suppose you are offered a job with AT&T at $37,000 per year with a guaranteed raise of 4% every year. What will your annual salary be after 15 years with the company?

■ **Answer:** $64,072.03

---

**EXAMPLE 9    Savings Growth: Geometric Series**

Karen has maintained acrylic nails by paying for them with money earned from a part-time job. After hearing a lecture from her economics professor on the importance of investing early in life, she decides to remove the acrylic nails, which cost $50 per month, and do her own manicures. She has that $50 automatically debited from her checking account on the first of every month and put into a money market account that earns 3% interest compounded monthly. What will the balance be in the money market account exactly 2 years from the day of her initial $50 deposit?

Use a calculator to find
$$S_{24} = 50(1.0025) \frac{(1 - 1.0025^{24})}{(1 - 1.0025)}.$$

Scientific calculators:

| Press | Display |
|-------|---------|
| 50 $\boxed{\times}$ 1.0025 $\boxed{\times}$ | 1238.23 |
| $\boxed{(}$ 1 $\boxed{-}$ 1.0025 | |
| $\boxed{x^y}$ 24 $\boxed{)}$ $\boxed{\div}$ $\boxed{(}$ | |
| 1 $\boxed{-}$ 1.0025 $\boxed{)}$ $\boxed{=}$ | |

Graphing calculators:

50 $\boxed{\times}$ 1.0025 $\boxed{\times}$ $\boxed{(}$ 1 $\boxed{-}$ 1.0025

$\boxed{\wedge}$ 24 $\boxed{)}$ $\boxed{\div}$ $\boxed{(}$ 1 $\boxed{-}$ 1.0025 $\boxed{)}$

$\boxed{\text{ENTER}}$

```
50*1.0025*(1-1.0
025^24)/(1-1.002
5)
        1238.228737
■
```

■ **Answer:** $5105.85

**Solution:**

Recall the compound interest formula. $\qquad A = P\left(1 + \frac{r}{n}\right)^{nt}$

Substitute $r = 0.03$ and $n = 12$ into
the compound interest formula. $\qquad A = P\left(1 + \frac{0.03}{12}\right)^{12t}$

$$= P(1.0025)^{12t}$$

Let $t = \frac{n}{12}$, where $n$ is the number of months
of the investment. $\qquad A_n = P(1.0025)^n$

The first deposit of $50 will gain interest for 24 months. $\quad A_{24} = 50(1.0025)^{24}$

The second deposit of $50 will gain interest for 23 months. $\quad A_{23} = 50(1.0025)^{23}$

The third deposit of $50 will gain interest for 22 months. $\quad A_{22} = 50(1.0025)^{22}$

The last deposit of $50 will gain interest for 1 month. $\quad A_1 = 50(1.0025)^1$

Sum the amounts accrued from the 24 deposits.

$$A_1 + A_2 + \cdots + A_{24} = 50(1.0025) + 50(1.0025)^2 + 50(1.0025)^3 + \cdots + 50(1.0025)^{24}$$

Identify the first term and common ratio. $\qquad a_1 = 50(1.0025)$ and $r = 1.0025$

Sum the first $n$ terms of a geometric series. $\qquad S_n = a_1 \frac{(1 - r^n)}{(1 - r)}$

Substitute $n = 24$, $a_1 = 50(1.0025)$,
and $r = 1.0025$. $\qquad S_{24} = 50(1.0025) \frac{(1 - 1.0025^{24})}{(1 - 1.0025)}$

Simplify. $\qquad S_{24} \approx 1238.23$

> Karen will have $1238.23 saved in her money market account in 2 years.

■ **YOUR TURN** Repeat Example 9 with Karen putting $100 (instead of $50) in the
same money market account. Assume she does this for 4 years
(instead of 2 years).

In this section, we discussed geometric sequences, in which each
successive term is found by multiplying the previous term by a
constant, so that $a_{n+1} = r \cdot a_n$. That constant, $r$, is called the
common ratio. The $n$th term of a geometric sequence is given by
$a_n = a_1 r^{n-1}$, $n \geq 1$ or $a_{n+1} = a_1 r^n$, $n \geq 0$. The sum of the terms
of a geometric sequence is called a geometric series. Finite
geometric series converge to a number. Infinite geometric series
converge to a number if the absolute value of the common ratio is
less than 1. If the absolute value of the common ratio is greater

than or equal to 1, the infinite geometric series diverges and
the sum does not exist. Many real-world applications involve
geometric sequences and series, such as growth of salaries and
annuities through percentage increases.

**Finite Geometric Series:** $\quad \sum_{k=1}^{n} a_1 r^{k-1} = a_1 \frac{(1 - r^n)}{(1 - r)} \quad r \neq 1$

**Infinite Geometric Series:** $\quad \sum_{k=1}^{\infty} a_1 r^{k-1} = a_1 \frac{1}{(1 - r)} \quad |r| < 1$

**SECTION**
**10.3** EXERCISES

■ SKILLS

In Exercises 1–8, determine whether each sequence is geometric. If it is, find the common ratio.

**1.** $1, 3, 9, 27, \ldots$ **2.** $2, 4, 8, 16, \ldots$ **3.** $1, 4, 9, 16, 25, \ldots$ **4.** $1, \frac{1}{4}, \frac{1}{9}, \frac{1}{16}, \ldots$

**5.** $8, 4, 2, 1, \ldots$ **6.** $8, -4, 2, -1, \ldots$ **7.** $800, 1360, 2312, 3930.4, \ldots$ **8.** $7, 15.4, 33.88, 74.536, \ldots$

In Exercises 9–16, write the first five terms of each geometric series.

**9.** $a_1 = 6 \quad r = 3$ **10.** $a_1 = 17 \quad r = 2$ **11.** $a_1 = 1 \quad r = -4$ **12.** $a_1 = -3 \quad r = -2$

**13.** $a_1 = 10{,}000 \quad r = 1.06$ **14.** $a_1 = 10{,}000 \quad r = 0.8$ **15.** $a_1 = \frac{2}{3} \quad r = \frac{1}{2}$ **16.** $a_1 = \frac{1}{10} \quad r = -\frac{1}{5}$

In Exercises 17–24, write the formula for the $n$th term of each geometric series.

**17.** $a_1 = 5 \quad r = 2$ **18.** $a_1 = 12 \quad r = 3$ **19.** $a_1 = 1 \quad r = -3$ **20.** $a_1 = -4 \quad r = -2$

**21.** $a_1 = 1000 \quad r = 1.07$ **22.** $a_1 = 1000 \quad r = 0.5$ **23.** $a_1 = \frac{16}{3} \quad r = -\frac{1}{4}$ **24.** $a_1 = \frac{1}{200} \quad r = 5$

In Exercises 25–30, find the indicated term of each geometric sequence.

**25.** 7th term of the sequence $-2, 4, -8, 16, \ldots$ **26.** 10th term of the sequence $1, -5, 25, -225, \ldots$

**27.** 13th term of the sequence $\frac{1}{3}, \frac{2}{3}, \frac{4}{3}, \frac{8}{3}, \ldots$ **28.** 9th term of the sequence $100, 20, 4, 0.8, \ldots$

**29.** 15th term of the sequence $1000, 50, 2.5, 0.125, \ldots$ **30.** 8th term of the sequence $1000, -800, 640, -512, \ldots$

In Exercises 31–40, find the sum of each finite geometric series.

**31.** $\dfrac{1}{3} + \dfrac{2}{3} + \dfrac{2^2}{3} + \cdots + \dfrac{2^{12}}{3}$ **32.** $1 + \dfrac{1}{3} + \dfrac{1}{3^2} + \dfrac{1}{3^3} + \cdots + \dfrac{1}{3^{10}}$

**33.** $2 + 6 + 18 + 54 + \cdots + 2(3^9)$ **34.** $1 + 4 + 16 + 64 + \cdots + 4^9$

**35.** $\displaystyle\sum_{n=0}^{10} 2(0.1)^n$ **36.** $\displaystyle\sum_{n=0}^{11} 3(0.2)^n$ **37.** $\displaystyle\sum_{n=1}^{8} 2(3)^{n-1}$ **38.** $\displaystyle\sum_{n=1}^{9} \frac{2}{3}(5)^{n-1}$ **39.** $\displaystyle\sum_{k=0}^{13} 2^k$ **40.** $\displaystyle\sum_{k=0}^{13} \left(\frac{1}{2}\right)^k$

In Exercises 41–54, find the sum of each infinite geometric series, if possible.

**41.** $\displaystyle\sum_{n=0}^{\infty} \left(\frac{1}{2}\right)^n$ **42.** $\displaystyle\sum_{n=1}^{\infty} \left(\frac{1}{3}\right)^n$ **43.** $\displaystyle\sum_{n=1}^{\infty} \left(-\frac{1}{3}\right)^n$ **44.** $\displaystyle\sum_{n=0}^{\infty} \left(-\frac{1}{2}\right)^n$ **45.** $\displaystyle\sum_{n=0}^{\infty} 1^n$

**46.** $\displaystyle\sum_{n=0}^{\infty} 1.01^n$ **47.** $\displaystyle\sum_{n=0}^{\infty} -9\left(\frac{1}{3}\right)^n$ **48.** $\displaystyle\sum_{n=0}^{\infty} -8\left(-\frac{1}{2}\right)^n$ **49.** $\displaystyle\sum_{n=0}^{\infty} 10{,}000(0.05)^n$ **50.** $\displaystyle\sum_{n=0}^{\infty} 200(0.04)^n$

**51.** $\displaystyle\sum_{n=1}^{\infty} 0.4^n$ **52.** $0.3 + 0.03 + 0.003 + 0.0003 + \cdots$ **53.** $\displaystyle\sum_{n=0}^{\infty} 0.99^n$ **54.** $\displaystyle\sum_{n=0}^{\infty} \left(\frac{5}{4}\right)^n$

■ APPLICATIONS

**55. Salary.** Jeremy is offered a government job with the Department of Commerce. He is hired on the "GS" scale at a base rate of $34,000 with a 2.5% increase in his salary per year. Calculate what his salary will be after he has been with the Department of Commerce for 12 years.

**56. Salary.** Alison is offered a job with a small start-up company that wants to promote loyalty to the company with incentives for employees to stay with the company. The company offers her a starting salary of $22,000 with a guaranteed 15% raise per year. What will her salary be after she has been with the company for 10 years?

**57. Depreciation.** Brittany, a graduating senior in high school, receives a laptop computer as a graduation gift from her Aunt Jeanine so that she can use it when she gets to the University of Alabama. If the laptop costs $2000 new and depreciates 50% per year, write a formula for the value of the laptop $n$ years after it was purchased. How much will the laptop be worth when Brittany graduates from college (assuming she will graduate in 4 years)? How much will it be worth when she finishes graduate school? Assume graduate school is another 3 years.

**58. Depreciation.** Derek is deciding between a new Honda Accord and the BMW 325 series. The BMW costs $35,000 and the Honda costs $25,000. If the BMW depreciates at 20% per year and the Honda depreciates at 10% per year, find formulas for the value of each car $n$ years after it is purchased. Which car is worth more in 10 years?

**59. Bungee Jumping.** A bungee jumper rebounds 70% of the height jumped. Assuming the bungee jump is made with a cord that stretches to 100 feet, how far will the bungee jumper travel upward on the fifth rebound?

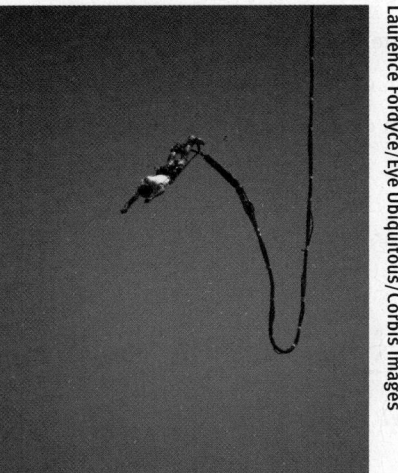

Laurence Fordyce/Eye Ubiquitous/Corbis Images

**60. Bungee Jumping.** A bungee jumper rebounds 65% of the height jumped. Assuming the bungee cord stretches 200 feet, how far will the bungee jumper travel upward on the eighth rebound?

**61. Population Growth.** One of the fastest-growing universities in the country is the University of Central Florida. The student populations each year starting in 2000 were 36,000, 37,800, 39,690, 41,675, . . . . Assuming this rate has continued, how many students are enrolled at UCF in 2010?

**62. Web Site Hits.** The Web site for Matchbox 20 (www. matchboxtwenty.com) has noticed that every week the number of hits to its Web site increases 5%. If there were 20,000 hits this week, how many will there be exactly 52 weeks from now if this rate continues?

**63. Rich Man's Promise.** A rich man promises that he will give you $1000 on January 1, and every day after that, he will pay you 90% of what he paid you the day before. How many days will it take before you are making less than $1? How much will the rich man pay out for the entire month of January? Round to the nearest dollar.

**64. Poor Man's Clever Deal.** A poor man promises to work for you for $0.01 the first day, $0.02 on the second day, $0.04 on the third day; his salary will continue to double each day. If he started on January 1 how much would he be paid to work on January 31? How much in total would he make during the month? Round to the nearest dollar.

**65. Investing Lunch.** A newlywed couple decides to stop going out to lunch every day and instead bring their lunch to work. They estimate it will save them $100 per month. They invest that $100 on the first of every month in an account that is compounded monthly and pays 5% interest. How much will be in the account at the end of 3 years?

**66. Pizza as an Investment.** A college freshman decides to stop ordering late-night pizzas (for both health and cost reasons). He realizes that he has been spending $50 a week on pizzas. Instead, he deposits $50 into an account that compounds weekly and pays 4% interest. (Assume 52 weeks annually.) How much money will be in the account after 52 weeks?

**67. Tax-Deferred Annuity.** Dr. Schober contributes $500 from her paycheck (weekly) to a tax-deferred investment account. Assuming the investment earns 6% and is compounded weekly, how much will be in the account after 26 weeks? 52 weeks?

**68. Saving for a House.** If a new graduate decides she wants to save for a house and she is able to put $300 every month into an account that earns 5% compounded monthly, how much will she have in the account after 5 years?

**69. House Values.** In 2008 you buy a house for $195,000. The value of the house appreciates 6.5% per year, on the average. How much is the house worth after 15 years?

**70. The Bouncing Ball Problem.** A ball is dropped from a height of 9 feet. Assume that on each bounce, the ball rebounds to one-third of its previous height. Find the total distance that the ball travels.

**71. Probability.** A fair coin is tossed repeatedly. The probability that the first head occurs on the $n$th toss is given by the function $p(n) = \left(\frac{1}{2}\right)^n$, where $n \geq 1$. Show that

$$\sum_{n=1}^{\infty} \left(\frac{1}{2}\right)^n = 1.0$$

**72. Salary.** Suppose you work for a supervisor who gives you two different options to choose from for your monthly pay. Option 1: The company pays you 1 cent for the first day of work, 2 cents the second day, 4 cents for the third day, 8 cents for the fourth day, and so on for 30 days. Option 2: You can receive a check right now for $10,000,000. Which pay option is better? How much better is it?

## ▪ CATCH THE MISTAKE

**In Exercises 73–76, explain the mistake that is made.**

**73.** Find the $n$th term of the geometric sequence

$$-1, \tfrac{1}{3}, -\tfrac{1}{9}, \tfrac{1}{27}, \dots .$$

**Solution:**

Identify the first term and common ratio.
$$a_1 = -1 \text{ and } r = \frac{1}{3}$$

Substitute $a_1 = -1$ and $r = \tfrac{1}{3}$ into $a_n = a_1 \cdot r^{n-1}$.
$$a_n = (-1) \cdot \left(\frac{1}{3}\right)^{n-1}$$

Simplify.
$$a_n = \frac{-1}{3^{n-1}}$$

This is incorrect. What mistake was made?

**74.** Find the sum of the first $n$ terms of the finite geometric series

$$2, 4, 8, 16, \dots .$$

**Solution:**

Write the sum in sigma notation.
$$\sum_{k=1}^{n} (2)^k$$

Identify the first term and common ratio.
$$a_1 = 1 \text{ and } r = 2$$

Substitute $a_1 = 1$ and $r = 2$ into $S_n = a_1 \dfrac{(1 - r^n)}{(1 - r)}$.
$$S_n = 1\frac{(1 - 2^n)}{(1 - 2)}$$

Simplify.
$$S_n = 2^n - 1$$

This is incorrect. What mistake was made?

**75.** Find the sum of the finite geometric series $\displaystyle\sum_{n=1}^{8} 4(-3)^n$.

**Solution:**

Identify the first term and common ratio.
$$a_1 = 4 \text{ and } r = -3$$

Substitute $a_1 = 4$ and $r = -3$ into $S_n = a_1 \dfrac{(1 - r^n)}{(1 - r)}$.
$$S_n = 4\frac{[1 - (-3)^n]}{[1 - (-3)]}$$
$$= 4\frac{[1 - (-3)^n]}{4}$$

Simplify.
$$S_n = [1 - (-3)^n]$$

Substitute $n = 8$.
$$S_8 = [1 - (-3)^8] = -6560$$

This is incorrect. What mistake was made?

**76.** Find the sum of the infinite geometric series $\displaystyle\sum_{n=1}^{\infty} 2 \cdot 3^{n-1}$.

**Solution:**

Identify the first term and common ratio.
$$a_1 = 2 \text{ and } r = 3$$

Substitute $a_1 = 2$ and $r = 3$ into $S_\infty = a_1 \dfrac{1}{(1 - r)}$.
$$S_\infty = 2\frac{1}{(1 - 3)}$$

Simplify.
$$S_\infty = -1$$

This is incorrect. The series does not sum to $-1$. What mistake was made?

## ▪ CONCEPTUAL

**In Exercises 77–80, determine whether each statement is true or false.**

**77.** An alternating sequence cannot be a geometric sequence.

**78.** All finite and infinite geometric series can always be evaluated.

**79.** The common ratio of a geometric sequence can be positive or negative.

**80.** An infinite geometric series can be evaluated if the common ratio is less than or equal to 1.

## ▪ CHALLENGE

**81.** State the conditions for the sum

$$a + a \cdot b + a \cdot b^2 + \cdots + a \cdot b^n + \cdots$$

to exist. Assuming those conditions are met, find the sum.

**82.** Find the sum of $\displaystyle\sum_{k=0}^{20} \log 10^{2^k}$.

**83.** Represent the repeating decimal $0.474747\dots$ as a fraction (ratio of two integers).

**84.** Suppose the sum of an infinite geometric series is

$$S = \frac{2}{1 - x}, \text{ where } x \text{ is a variable.}$$

**a.** Write out the first five terms of the series.

**b.** For what values of $x$ will the series converge?

■**TECHNOLOGY**

**85.** Sum the series $\sum_{k=1}^{50}(-2)^{k-1}$. Apply a graphing utility to confirm your answer.

**86.** Does the sum of the infinite series $\sum_{n=0}^{\infty}\left(\frac{1}{3}\right)^n$ exist? Use a graphing calculator to find it.

**87.** Apply a graphing utility to plot $y_1 = 1 + x + x^2 + x^3 + x^4$ and $y_2 = \dfrac{1}{1-x}$. Based on what you see, what do you expect the geometric series $\sum_{n=0}^{\infty} x^n$ to sum to?

**88.** Apply a graphing utility to plot $y_1 = 1 - x + x^2 - x^3 + x^4$ and $y_2 = \dfrac{1}{1+x}$. Based on what you see, what do you expect the geometric series $\sum_{n=0}^{\infty}(-1)^n x^n$ to sum to?

■**PREVIEW TO CALCULUS**

In calculus, we study the convergence of geometric series. A geometric series with ratio $r$ diverges if $|r| \geq 1$. If $|r| < 1$, then the geometric series converges to the sum

$$\sum_{n=0}^{\infty} ar^n = \frac{a}{1-r}$$

In Exercises 89–92, determine the convergence or divergence of the series. If the series is convergent, find its sum.

**89.** $1 + \dfrac{2}{3} + \dfrac{4}{9} + \dfrac{8}{27} + \cdots$

**90.** $1 + \dfrac{5}{4} + \dfrac{25}{16} + \dfrac{125}{64} + \cdots$

**91.** $\dfrac{3}{8} + \dfrac{3}{32} + \dfrac{3}{128} + \dfrac{3}{512} + \cdots$

**92.** $\sum_{n=0}^{\infty} \dfrac{\pi}{3}\left(-\dfrac{8}{9}\right)^n$

**SECTION**

# 10.4 MATHEMATICAL INDUCTION

**SKILLS OBJECTIVES**

■ Know the steps required to prove a statement by mathematical induction.
■ Prove mathematical statements using mathematical induction.

**CONCEPTUAL OBJECTIVES**

■ Understand that just because there appears to be a pattern, the pattern is not necessarily true for all values.
■ Understand that when mathematical ideas are accepted, it is because they can be proved.

## Proof by Mathematical Induction

| $n$ | $n^2 - n + 41$ | PRIME? |
|---|---|---|
| 1 | 41 | Yes |
| 2 | 43 | Yes |
| 3 | 47 | Yes |
| 4 | 53 | Yes |
| 5 | 61 | Yes |

Is the expression $n^2 - n + 41$ *always* a prime number if $n$ is a natural number? Your instinct may lead you to try a few values for $n$.

It appears that the statement might be true for all natural numbers. However, what about when $n = 41$?

$$n^2 - n + 41 = (41)^2 - 41 + 41 = 41^2$$

We find that when $n = 41$, $n^2 - n + 41$ is not prime. The moral of the story is that just because a pattern seems to exist for *some* values, the pattern is not necessarily true for *all* values. We must look for a way to show whether a statement is true for all values. In this section, we talk about *mathematical induction*, which is a way to show a statement is true for all values.

Mathematics is based on logic and proof (not assumptions or belief). One of the most famous mathematical statements was Fermat's Last Theorem. Pierre de Fermat (1601–1665) conjectured that there are no positive integer values for $x$, $y$, and $z$ such that $x^n + y^n = z^n$, if $n \geq 3$. Although mathematicians *believed* that this theorem was true, no one was able to

*prove* it until 350 years after the assumption was made. Professor Andrew Wiles at Princeton University received a $50,000 prize for successfully proving Fermat's Last Theorem in 1994.

*Mathematical induction* is a technique used in precalculus and even in very advanced mathematics to prove many kinds of mathematical statements. In this section, you will use it to prove statements like "If $x > 1$, then $x^n > 1$ for all natural numbers $n$."

The principle of mathematical induction can be illustrated by a row of standing dominos, as in the image here. We make two assumptions:

1. The first domino is knocked down.
2. If a domino is knocked down, then the domino immediately following it will also be knocked down.

If both of these assumptions are true, then it is also true that all of the dominos will fall.

## PRINCIPLE OF MATHEMATICAL INDUCTION

Let $S_n$ be a statement involving the positive integer $n$. To prove that $S_n$ is true for all positive integers, the following steps are required:

**Step 1:** Show that $S_1$ is true.
**Step 2:** Assume $S_k$ is true and show that $S_{k+1}$ is true ($k = 1, 2, 3, \ldots$).

Combining Steps 1 and 2 proves the statement is true for all positive integers (natural numbers).

### EXAMPLE 1   Using Mathematical Induction

Apply the principle of mathematical induction to prove this statement:

If $x > 1$, then $x^n > 1$ for all natural numbers $n$.

**Solution:**

**STEP 1** Show the statement is true for $n = 1$.          $x^1 > 1$ because $x > 1$

**STEP 2** Assume the statement is true for $n = k$.          $x^k > 1$

Show the statement is true for $k + 1$.

Multiply both sides by $x$.          $x^k \cdot x > 1 \cdot x$

(Since $x > 1$, this step does not reverse the inequality sign.)

Simplify.          $x^{k+1} > x$

Recall that $x > 1$.          $x^{k+1} > x > 1$

Therefore, we have shown that $x^{k+1} > 1$.

This completes the induction proof. Thus, the following statement is true:

"If $x > 1$, then $x^n > 1$ for **all** natural numbers $n$."

### EXAMPLE 2   Using Mathematical Induction

Use mathematical induction to prove that $n^2 + n$ is divisible by 2 for all natural numbers (positive integers) $n$.

**Solution:**

**STEP 1** Show the statement we are testing is true for $n = 1$.          $1^2 + 1 = 2$

2 is divisible by 2.          $\dfrac{2}{2} = 1$

STEP 2 Assume the statement is true for $n = k$.

$$\frac{k^2 + k}{2} = \text{an integer}$$

Show it is true for $k + 1$ where $k \geq 1$.

$$\frac{(k + 1)^2 + (k + 1)}{2} \stackrel{?}{=} \text{an integer}$$

$$\frac{k^2 + 2k + 1 + k + 1}{2} \stackrel{?}{=} \text{an integer}$$

Regroup terms.

$$\frac{(k^2 + k) + 2(k + 1)}{2} \stackrel{?}{=} \text{an integer}$$

$$\frac{(k^2 + k)}{2} + \frac{2(k + 1)}{2} \stackrel{?}{=} \text{an integer}$$

**Study Tip**

Mathematical induction is not always the best approach. Example 3 can be shown via arithmetic series.

We assumed $\dfrac{k^2 + k}{2} = \text{an integer}$.  $\qquad$ an integer $+ (k + 1) \stackrel{?}{=} \text{an integer}$

Since $k$ is a natural number (integer). $\qquad$ an integer $+$ an integer $= \text{an integer}$

This completes the induction proof. The following statement is true:

$$\text{“}n^2 + n \text{ is divisible by 2 for all natural numbers } n.\text{”}$$

Mathematical induction is often used to prove formulas for partial sums.

**Technology Tip**

To visualize what needs to be proved in the partial–sum formula, use the [sum] command to find the sum of the series $\sum_{k=1}^{n} k$ on the left side for an arbitrary $n$ value, say, $n = 100$. Press

| 2nd | | LIST | | ▶ | | MATH | | ▼ |

| 5:sum( | | ENTER | | 2nd | | LIST | | ▶ |

| OPS | | ▼ | | 5:seq( | | ENTER |

| ALPHA | | N | | , | | ALPHA | | N | | , |

| 1 | | , | | 100 | | , | | 1 | | ) | | ) | | ENTER |.

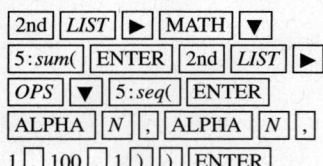

Now calculate the sum by substituting $n = 100$ into $n(n + 1)/2$ on the right side.

```
sum(seq(N,N,1,10
0,1))
             5050
100(100+1)/2
             5050
```

*Note:* The Solutions to the left and right side of the formula agree with each other.

**EXAMPLE 3  Proving a Partial–Sum Formula with Mathematical Induction**

Apply mathematical induction to prove the following partial–sum formula:

$$1 + 2 + 3 + \cdots + n = \frac{n(n + 1)}{2} \text{ for all positive integers } n$$

**Solution:**

STEP 1 Show the formula is true for $n = 1$. $\qquad 1 = \dfrac{1(1 + 1)}{2} = \dfrac{2}{2} = 1$

STEP 2 Assume the formula is true for $n = k$. $\qquad 1 + 2 + 3 + \cdots + k = \dfrac{k(k + 1)}{2}$

Show it is true for $n = k + 1$.

$$1 + 2 + 3 + \cdots + k + (k + 1) \stackrel{?}{=} \frac{(k + 1)(k + 2)}{2}$$

$$\underbrace{1 + 2 + 3 + \cdots + k}_{\frac{k(k + 1)}{2}} + (k + 1) \stackrel{?}{=} \frac{(k + 1)(k + 2)}{2}$$

$$\frac{k(k + 1)}{2} + (k + 1) \stackrel{?}{=} \frac{(k + 1)(k + 2)}{2}$$

$$\frac{k(k + 1) + 2(k + 1)}{2} \stackrel{?}{=} \frac{(k + 1)(k + 2)}{2}$$

$$\frac{k^2 + 3k + 2}{2} \stackrel{?}{=} \frac{(k + 1)(k + 2)}{2}$$

$$\frac{(k + 1)(k + 2)}{2} = \frac{(k + 1)(k + 2)}{2}$$

This completes the induction proof. The following statement is true:

$$\text{“}1 + 2 + 3 + \cdots + n = \frac{n(n + 1)}{2} \text{ for all positive integers } n.\text{”}$$

## SECTION
## 10.4 SUMMARY

Just because we believe something is true does not mean that it is. In mathematics we rely on proof. In this section, we discussed *mathematical induction*, a process of proving some kinds of mathematical statements. The two-step procedure for mathematical induction is to (1) show the statement is true for $n = 1$, then (2) assume the statement is true for $n = k$ (any positive integer) and show the statement must be true for $n = k + 1$. The combination of Steps 1 and 2 proves the statement.

## SECTION
## 10.4 EXERCISES

### ▪ SKILLS

**In Exercises 1–24, prove each statement using mathematical induction for all positive integers $n$.**

**1.** $n^2 \leq n^3$

**2.** If $0 < x < 1$, then $0 < x^n < 1$.

**3.** $2n \leq 2^n$

**4.** $5^n < 5^{n+1}$

**5.** $n! > 2^n \quad n \geq 4$    (Show it is true for $n = 4$, instead of $n = 1$.)

**6.** $(1 + c)^n \geq nc \quad c > 1$

**7.** $n(n + 1)(n - 1)$ is divisible by 3.

**8.** $n^3 - n$ is divisible by 3.

**9.** $n^2 + 3n$ is divisible by 2.

**10.** $n(n + 1)(n + 2)$ is divisible by 6.

**11.** $2 + 4 + 6 + 8 + \cdots + 2n = n(n + 1)$

**12.** $1 + 3 + 5 + 7 + \cdots + (2n - 1) = n^2$

**13.** $1 + 3 + 3^2 + 3^3 + \cdots + 3^n = \dfrac{3^{n+1} - 1}{2}$

**14.** $2 + 4 + 8 + \cdots + 2^n = 2^{n+1} - 2$

**15.** $1^2 + 2^2 + 3^2 + \cdots + n^2 = \dfrac{n(n + 1)(2n + 1)}{6}$

**16.** $1^3 + 2^3 + 3^3 + \cdots + n^3 = \dfrac{n^2(n + 1)^2}{4}$

**17.** $\dfrac{1}{1 \cdot 2} + \dfrac{1}{2 \cdot 3} + \dfrac{1}{3 \cdot 4} + \cdots + \dfrac{1}{n(n + 1)} = \dfrac{n}{n + 1}$

**18.** $\dfrac{1}{2 \cdot 3} + \dfrac{1}{3 \cdot 4} + \cdots + \dfrac{1}{(n + 1)(n + 2)} = \dfrac{n}{2(n + 2)}$

**19.** $(1 \cdot 2) + (2 \cdot 3) + (3 \cdot 4) + \cdots + n(n + 1) = \dfrac{n(n + 1)(n + 2)}{3}$

**20.** $(1 \cdot 3) + (2 \cdot 4) + (3 \cdot 5) + \cdots + n(n + 2) = \dfrac{n(n + 1)(2n + 7)}{6}$

**21.** $1 + x + x^2 + x^3 + \cdots + x^{n-1} = \dfrac{1 - x^n}{1 - x} \quad x \neq 1$

**22.** $\dfrac{1}{2} + \dfrac{1}{4} + \dfrac{1}{8} + \cdots + \dfrac{1}{2^n} = 1 - \dfrac{1}{2^n}$

**23.** The sum of an arithmetic sequence: $a_1 + (a_1 + d) + (a_1 + 2d) + \cdots + [a_1 + (n - 1)d] = \dfrac{n}{2}[2a_1 + (n - 1)d]$.

**24.** The sum of a geometric sequence: $a_1 + a_1 r + a_1 r^2 + \cdots + a_1 r^{n-1} = a_1\left(\dfrac{1 - r^n}{1 - r}\right), r \neq 1$.

■ **APPLICATIONS**

**The Tower of Hanoi.** This is a game with three pegs and $n$ disks (largest on the bottom and smallest on the top). The goal is to move this entire tower of disks to another peg (in the same order). The challenge is that you may move only one disk at a time, and at no time can a larger disk be resting on a smaller disk. You may want to first go online to www.mazeworks.com/hanoi/index/htm and play the game.

Andy Washnik

**Tower of Hanoi**

25. What is the smallest number of moves needed if there are three disks?

26. What is the smallest number of moves needed if there are four disks?

27. What is the smallest number of moves needed if there are five disks?

28. What is the smallest number of moves needed if there are $n$ disks? Prove it by mathematical induction.

29. **Telephone Infrastructure.** Suppose there are $n$ cities that are to be connected with telephone wires. Apply mathematical induction to prove that the number of telephone wires required to connect the $n$ cities is given by $\dfrac{n(n-1)}{2}$. Assume each city has to connect directly with any other city.

30. **Geometry.** Prove, with mathematical induction, that the sum of the measures of the interior angles in degrees of a regular polygon of $n$ sides is given by the formula $(n-2)(180°)$ for $n \geq 3$. *Hint:* Divide a polygon into triangles. For example, a four-sided polygon can be divided into two triangles. A five-sided polygon can be divided into three triangles. A six-sided polygon can be divided into four triangles, and so on.

■ **CONCEPTUAL**

**In Exercises 31 and 32, determine whether each statement is true or false.**

31. Assume $S_k$ is true. If it can be shown that $S_{k+1}$ is true, then $S_n$ is true for all $n$, where $n$ is any positive integer.

32. Assume $S_1$ is true. If it can be shown that $S_2$ and $S_3$ are true, then $S_n$ is true for all $n$, where $n$ is any positive integer.

■ **CHALLENGE**

33. Apply mathematical induction to prove
$$\sum_{k=1}^{n} k^4 = \frac{n(n+1)(2n+1)(3n^2+3n-1)}{30}$$

34. Apply mathematical induction to prove
$$\sum_{k=1}^{n} k^5 = \frac{n^2(n+1)^2(2n^2+2n-1)}{12}$$

35. Apply mathematical induction to prove
$$\left(1+\frac{1}{1}\right)\left(1+\frac{1}{2}\right)\left(1+\frac{1}{3}\right)\cdots\left(1+\frac{1}{n}\right) = n+1$$

36. Apply mathematical induction to prove that $x+y$ is a factor of $x^{2n}-y^{2n}$.

37. Apply mathematical induction to prove that $x-y$ is a factor of $x^{2n}-y^{2n}$.

38. Apply mathematical induction to prove
$$\ln(c_1 \cdot c_2 \cdot c_3 \cdots c_n) = \ln c_1 + \ln c_2 + \cdots + \ln c_n$$

39. Use a graphing calculator to sum the series $\dfrac{1}{2} + \dfrac{1}{4} + \dfrac{1}{8} + \cdots + \dfrac{1}{2^n}$ and evaluate the expression $1 - \dfrac{1}{2^n}$ for $n=8$. Do they agree with each other? Do your answers confirm the proof for Exercise 22?

■TECHNOLOGY

**40.** Use a graphing calculator to sum the series
$(1 \cdot 2) + (2 \cdot 3) + (3 \cdot 4) + \cdots + n(n + 1)$ and evaluate
the expression $\dfrac{n(n + 1)(n + 2)}{3}$ for $n = 200$. Do they
agree with each other? Do your answers confirm the proof
for Exercise 19?

■PREVIEW TO CALCULUS

Several of the results studied in calculus must be proved by mathematical induction. In Exercises 41–44, apply mathematical
induction to prove each formula.

**41.** $(\pi + 1) + (\pi + 2) + (\pi + 3) + \cdots + (\pi + n)$
$= \dfrac{n(2\pi + n + 1)}{2}$

**42.** $(1 + 1) + (2 + 4) + (3 + 9) + \cdots + (n + n^2)$
$= \dfrac{n(n + 1)(n + 2)}{3}$

**43.** $(1 + 1) + (2 + 8) + (3 + 27) + \cdots + (n + n^3)$
$= \dfrac{n(n + 1)(n^2 + n + 2)}{4}$

**44.** $(1 + 1) + (4 + 8) + (9 + 27) + \cdots + (n^2 + n^3)$
$= \dfrac{n(n + 1)(n + 2)(3n + 1)}{12}$

**SECTION**
## 10.5 THE BINOMIAL THEOREM

**SKILLS OBJECTIVES**

■ Evaluate a binomial coefficient with the
Binomial theorem.
■ Evaluate a binomial coefficient with Pascal's triangle.
■ Expand a binomial raised to a positive integer power.
■ Find a particular term of a binomial expansion.

**CONCEPTUAL OBJECTIVE**

■ Recognize patterns in binomial expansions.

## Binomial Coefficients

A **binomial** is a polynomial that has two terms. The following are all examples of binomials:

$$x^2 + 2y \qquad a + 3b \qquad 4x^2 + 9$$

In this section, we will develop a formula for the expression for raising a binomial to a
power $n$, where $n$ is a positive integer.

$$(x^2 + 2y)^6 \qquad (a + 3b)^4 \qquad (4x^2 + 9)^5$$

To begin, let's start by writing out the expansions of $(a + b)^n$ for several values of $n$.

$$(a + b)^1 = a + b$$
$$(a + b)^2 = a^2 + 2ab + b^2$$
$$(a + b)^3 = a^3 + 3a^2b + 3ab^2 + b^3$$
$$(a + b)^4 = a^4 + 4a^3b + 6a^2b^2 + 4ab^3 + b^4$$
$$(a + b)^5 = a^5 + 5a^4b + 10a^3b^2 + 10a^2b^3 + 5ab^4 + b^5$$

There are several *patterns* that all of the **binomial expansions** have:

1. The number of terms in each resulting polynomial is always *one more* than the power of the binomial $n$. Thus, there are $n + 1$ terms in each expansion.

$$n = 3: \quad (a + b)^3 = \underbrace{a^3 + 3a^2b + 3ab^2 + b^3}_{\text{four terms}}$$

2. Each expansion has symmetry. For example, $a$ and $b$ can be interchanged and you will arrive at the same expansion. Furthermore, the powers of *a* **decrease** by 1 in each successive term, and the powers of *b* **increase** by 1 in each successive term.

$$(a + b)^3 = a^3b^0 + 3a^2b^1 + 3a^1b^2 + a^0b^3$$

3. The sum of the powers of each term in the expansion is $n$.

$$n = 3: \quad (a + b)^3 = a^3b^0 \overset{3+0=3}{\quad} + 3a^2b^1 \overset{2+1=3}{\quad} + 3a^1b^2 \overset{1+2=3}{\quad} + a^0b^3 \overset{0+3=3}{\quad}$$

4. The coefficients **increase** and **decrease** in a symmetric manner.

$$(a + b)^5 = 1a^5 + 5a^4b + 10a^3b^2 + 10a^2b^3 + 5ab^4 + 1b^5$$

Using these patterns, we can develop a generalized formula for $(a + b)^n$.

$$(a + b)^n = \Box a^n + \Box a^{n-1}b + \Box a^{n-2}b^2 + \cdots + \Box a^2b^{n-2} + \Box ab^{n-1} + \Box b^n$$

We know that there are $n + 1$ terms in the expansion. We also know that the sum of the powers of each term must equal $n$. The powers increase and decrease by 1 in each successive term, and if we interchanged $a$ and $b$, the result would be the same expansion. The question that remains is, what coefficients go in the blanks?

We know that the coefficients must increase and then decrease in a symmetric order (similar to walking up and then down a hill). It turns out that the *binomial coefficients* are represented by a symbol that we will now define.

---

**DEFINITION**    **Binomial Coefficients**

For nonnegative integers $n$ and $k$, where $n \geq k$, the symbol $\binom{n}{k}$ is called the **binomial coefficient** and is defined by

$$\binom{n}{k} = \frac{n!}{(n - k)!k!} \qquad \binom{n}{k} \text{ is read "} n \text{ choose } k\text{."}$$

---

You will see in the following sections that "$n$ choose $k$" comes from counting combinations of $n$ things taken $k$ at a time.

### Technology Tip

| Press | Display |
|---|---|
| 6 [nCr] 4 [=] | 15 |
| 5 [nCr] 5 [=] | 1 |
| 4 [nCr] 0 [=] | 1 |
| 10 [nCr] 9 [=] | 10 |

```
6 nCr 4
                    15
5 nCr 5
                     1
4 nCr 0
                     1
```

```
10 nCr 9
                    10
■
```

**EXAMPLE 1    Evaluating a Binomial Coefficient**

Evaluate the following binomial coefficients:

a. $\binom{6}{4}$    b. $\binom{5}{5}$    c. $\binom{4}{0}$    d. $\binom{10}{9}$

**Solution:**

Select the top number as $n$ and the bottom number as $k$ and substitute into the binomial coefficient formula $\binom{n}{k} = \frac{n!}{(n - k)!k!}$.

**a.** $\dbinom{6}{4} = \dfrac{6!}{(6-4)!4!} = \dfrac{6!}{2!4!} = \dfrac{6 \cdot 5 \cdot 4 \cdot 3 \cdot 2 \cdot 1}{(2 \cdot 1)(4 \cdot 3 \cdot 2 \cdot 1)} = \dfrac{6 \cdot 5}{2} = \boxed{15}$

**b.** $\dbinom{5}{5} = \dfrac{5!}{(5-5)!5!} = \dfrac{5!}{0!5!} = \dfrac{1}{0!} = \dfrac{1}{1} = \boxed{1}$

**c.** $\dbinom{4}{0} = \dfrac{4!}{(4-0)!0!} = \dfrac{4!}{4!0!} = \dfrac{1}{0!} = \boxed{1}$

**d.** $\dbinom{10}{9} = \dfrac{10!}{(10-9)!9!} = \dfrac{10!}{1!9!} = \dfrac{10 \cdot 9!}{9!} = \boxed{10}$

■ **YOUR TURN** Evaluate the following binomial coefficients:

$$\textbf{a. } \dbinom{9}{6} \qquad \textbf{b. } \dbinom{8}{6}$$

■ **Answer: a.** 84 **b.** 28

Parts (b) and (c) of Example 1 lead to the general formulas

$$\dbinom{n}{n} = 1 \quad \text{and} \quad \dbinom{n}{0} = 1$$

# Binomial Expansion

Let's return to the question of the binomial expansion and how to determine the coefficients:

$$(a+b)^n = \square a^n + \square a^{n-1}b + \square a^{n-2}b^2 + \cdots + \square a^2 b^{n-2} + \square ab^{n-1} + \square b^n$$

The symbol $\dbinom{n}{k}$ is called a binomial coefficient because the coefficients in the blanks in the binomial expansion are equivalent to this symbol.

**THE BINOMIAL THEOREM**

Let $a$ and $b$ be real numbers; then for any positive integer $n$,

$$(a+b)^n = \dbinom{n}{0}a^n + \dbinom{n}{1}a^{n-1}b + \dbinom{n}{2}a^{n-2}b^2 + \cdots + \dbinom{n}{n-2}a^2 b^{n-2} + \dbinom{n}{n-1}ab^{n-1} + \dbinom{n}{n}b^n$$

or in sigma (summation) notation as

$$(a+b)^n = \sum_{k=0}^{n} \dbinom{n}{k}a^{n-k}b^k$$

## EXAMPLE 2    Applying the Binomial Theorem

Expand $(x+2)^3$ with the Binomial theorem.

**Solution:**

Substitute $a = x$, $b = 2$, and $n = 3$ into the equation of the Binomial theorem.

$$(x+2)^3 = \sum_{k=0}^{3} \dbinom{3}{k}x^{3-k}2^k$$

Expand the summation.

$$= \dbinom{3}{0}x^3 + \dbinom{3}{1}x^2 \cdot 2 + \dbinom{3}{2}x \cdot 2^2 + \dbinom{3}{3}2^3$$

Find the binomial coefficients.

$$= x^3 + 3x^2 \cdot 2 + 3x \cdot 2^2 + 2^3$$

Simplify.

$$= \boxed{x^3 + 6x^2 + 12x + 8}$$

■ **YOUR TURN** Expand $(x+5)^4$ with the Binomial theorem.

■ **Answer:**
$x^4 + 20x^3 + 150x^2 + 500x + 625$

## EXAMPLE 3   Applying the Binomial Theorem

Expand $(2x - 3)^4$ with the Binomial theorem.

**Solution:**

Substitute $a = 2x$, $b = -3$, and $n = 4$ into the equation of the Binomial theorem.

$$(2x - 3)^4 = \sum_{k=0}^{4} \binom{4}{k}(2x)^{4-k}(-3)^k$$

Expand the summation.

$$= \binom{4}{0}(2x)^4 + \binom{4}{1}(2x)^3(-3) + \binom{4}{2}(2x)^2(-3)^2 + \binom{4}{3}(2x)(-3)^3 + \binom{4}{4}(-3)^4$$

Find the binomial coefficients.

$$= (2x)^4 + 4(2x)^3(-3) + 6(2x)^2(-3)^2 + 4(2x)(-3)^3 + (-3)^4$$

Simplify.

$$\boxed{= 16x^4 - 96x^3 + 216x^2 - 216x + 81}$$

■ **YOUR TURN** Expand $(3x - 2)^4$ with the Binomial theorem.

# Pascal's Triangle

Instead of writing out the Binomial theorem and calculating the binomial coefficients using factorials every time you want to do a binomial expansion, we now present an alternative, more convenient way of remembering the binomial coefficients, called **Pascal's triangle**.

Notice that the first and last number in every row is 1. Each of the other numbers is found by adding the two numbers directly above it. For example,

$$3 = 2 + 1 \qquad 4 = 1 + 3 \qquad 10 = 6 + 4$$

Let's arrange values of $\binom{n}{k}$ in a triangular pattern. Notice that the *value* of the binomial coefficients below are given in the margin.

Pascal's triangle

```
            1
          1   1
        1   2   1
      1   3   3   1
    1   4   6   4   1
  1   5  10  10   5   1
```

$$\binom{0}{0}$$

$$\binom{1}{0} \quad \binom{1}{1}$$

$$\binom{2}{0} \quad \binom{2}{1} \quad \binom{2}{2}$$

$$\binom{3}{0} \quad \binom{3}{1} \quad \binom{3}{2} \quad \binom{3}{3}$$

$$\binom{4}{0} \quad \binom{4}{1} \quad \binom{4}{2} \quad \binom{4}{3} \quad \binom{4}{4}$$

$$\binom{5}{0} \quad \binom{5}{1} \quad \binom{5}{2} \quad \binom{5}{3} \quad \binom{5}{4} \quad \binom{5}{5}$$

It turns out that the numbers in Pascal's triangle are exactly the coefficients in a binomial expansion.

$$1$$
$$1a + 1b$$
$$1a^2 + 2ab + 1b^2$$
$$1a^3 + 3a^2b + 3ab^2 + 1b^3$$
$$1a^4 + 4a^3b + 6a^2b^2 + 4ab^3 + 1b^4$$
$$1a^5 + 5a^4b + 10a^3b^2 + 10a^2b^3 + 5ab^4 + 1b^5$$

The top row is called the *zero row* because it corresponds to the binomial raised to the zero power, $n = 0$. Since each row in Pascal's triangle starts and ends with a 1 and all other values are found by adding the two numbers directly above it, we can now easily calculate the sixth row.

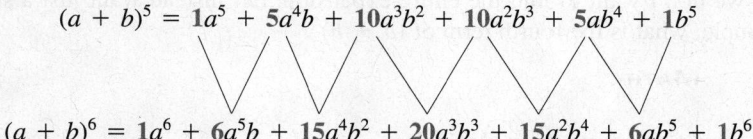

$$(a + b)^5 = 1a^5 + 5a^4b + 10a^3b^2 + 10a^2b^3 + 5ab^4 + 1b^5$$

$$(a + b)^6 = 1a^6 + 6a^5b + 15a^4b^2 + 20a^3b^3 + 15a^2b^4 + 6ab^5 + 1b^6$$

### EXAMPLE 4  Applying Pascal's Triangle in a Binomial Expansion

Use Pascal's triangle to determine the binomial expansion of $(x + 2)^5$.

**Solution:**

Write the binomial expansion with blanks for coefficients.

$$(x + 2)^5 = \Box x^5 + \Box x^4 \cdot 2 + \Box x^3 \cdot 2^2 + \Box x^2 \cdot 2^3 + \Box x \cdot 2^4 + \Box 2^5$$

Write the binomial coefficients in the *fifth* row of Pascal's triangle.

$$1, 5, 10, 10, 5, 1$$

Substitute these coefficients into the blanks of the binomial expansion.

$$(x + 2)^5 = 1x^5 + 5x^4 \cdot 2 + 10x^3 \cdot 2^2 + 10x^2 \cdot 2^3 + 5x \cdot 2^4 + 1 \cdot 2^5$$

Simplify.   $\boxed{(x + 2)^5 = x^5 + 10x^4 + 40x^3 + 80x^2 + 80x + 32}$

■ **YOUR TURN**  Apply Pascal's triangle to determine the binomial expansion of $(x + 3)^4$.

■ **Answer:**
$x^4 + 12x^3 + 54x^2 + 108x + 81$

### EXAMPLE 5  Applying Pascal's Triangle in a Binomial Expansion

Use Pascal's triangle to determine the binomial expansion of $(2x + 5)^4$.

**Solution:**

Write the binomial expansion with blanks for coefficients.

$$(2x + 5)^4 = \Box (2x)^4 + \Box (2x)^3 \cdot 5 + \Box (2x)^2 \cdot 5^2 + \Box (2x) \cdot 5^3 + \Box 5^4$$

Write the binomial coefficients in the *fourth* row of Pascal's triangle.

$$1, 4, 6, 4, 1$$

Substitute these coefficients into the blanks of the binomial expansion.

$$(2x + 5)^4 = 1(2x)^4 + 4(2x)^3 \cdot 5 + 6(2x)^2 \cdot 5^2 + 4(2x) \cdot 5^3 + 1 \cdot 5^4$$

Simplify.   $\boxed{(2x + 5)^4 = 16x^4 + 160x^3 + 600x^2 + 1000x + 625}$

■ **Answer:**
**a.** $27x^3 + 54x^2 + 36x + 8$
**b.** $243x^5 - 810x^4 + 1080x^3 - 720x^2$
       $+ 240x - 32$

■ **YOUR TURN** Use Pascal's triangle to determine the binomial expansion of
   **a.** $(3x + 2)^3$     **b.** $(3x - 2)^5$

# Finding a Particular Term of a Binomial Expansion

What if we don't want to find the entire expansion, but instead want just a single term? For example, what is the fourth term of $(a + b)^5$?

| **WORDS** | **MATH** |
|---|---|
| Recall the sigma notation. | $(a + b)^n = \sum_{k=0}^{n} \binom{n}{k} a^{n-k} b^k$ |
| Let $n = 5$. | $(a + b)^5 = \sum_{k=0}^{5} \binom{5}{k} a^{5-k} b^k$ |
| Expand. | $(a + b)^5 = \binom{5}{0}a^5 + \binom{5}{1}a^4b + \binom{5}{2}a^3b^2 + \underbrace{\binom{5}{3}a^2b^3}_{\text{fourth term}} + \binom{5}{4}ab^4 + \binom{5}{5}b^5$ |
| Simplify the fourth term. | $10a^2b^3$ |

> **FINDING A PARTICULAR TERM OF A BINOMIAL EXPANSION**
>
> The $(r + 1)$ term of the expansion $(a + b)^n$ is $\binom{n}{r} a^{n-r} b^r$.

**Technology Tip**

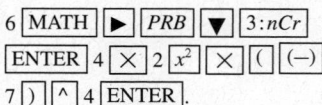

6 MATH ▶ PRB ▼ 3:nCr
ENTER 4 × 2 $x^2$ × ( (−)
7 ) ^ 4 ENTER.

```
6 nCr 4*2²*(-7)^
4
            144060
```

■ **Answer:** $1080x^3$

### EXAMPLE 6   Finding a Particular Term of a Binomial Expansion

Find the fifth term of the binomial expansion of $(2x - 7)^6$.

**Solution:**

Recall that the $r + 1$ term of $(a + b)^n$ is $\binom{n}{r} a^{n-r} b^r$.

For the fifth term, let $r = 4$.   $\binom{n}{4} a^{n-4} b^4$

For this expansion, let $a = 2x$, $b = -7$, and $n = 6$.   $\binom{6}{4}(2x)^{6-4}(-7)^4$

Note that $\binom{6}{4} = 15$.   $15(2x)^2(-7)^4$

Simplify.   $\boxed{144{,}060x^2}$

★ **YOUR TURN** What is the third term of the binomial expansion of $(3x - 2)^5$?

## SECTION 10.5 SUMMARY

In this section, we developed a formula for expanding a binomial raised to a non-negative integer power, $n$. The patterns that surfaced were

- that the expansion displays symmetry between the two terms
- every expansion has $n + 1$ terms
- the powers sum to $n$
- the coefficients, called binomial coefficients, are ratios of factorials

$$(a + b)^n = \sum_{k=0}^{n} \binom{n}{k} a^{n-k} b^k$$

$$\binom{n}{k} = \frac{n!}{(n - k)!k!}$$

Also, Pascal's triangle, a shortcut method for evaluating the binomial coefficients, was discussed. The patterns in the triangle are that every row begins and ends with 1 and all other numbers are found by adding the two numbers in the row above the entry.

```
          1
        1   1
      1   2   1
    1   3   3   1
  1   4   6   4   1
1   5   10   10   5   1
```

Lastly, a formula was given for finding a particular term of a binomial expansion; the $(r + 1)$ term of $(a + b)^n$ is $\binom{n}{r} a^{n-r} b^r$.

## SECTION 10.5 EXERCISES

### ▪ SKILLS

**In Exercises 1–10, evaluate each binomial coefficient.**

1. $\binom{7}{3}$

2. $\binom{8}{2}$

3. $\binom{10}{8}$

4. $\binom{23}{21}$

5. $\binom{17}{0}$

6. $\binom{100}{0}$

7. $\binom{99}{99}$

8. $\binom{52}{52}$

9. $\binom{48}{45}$

10. $\binom{29}{26}$

**In Exercises 11–32, expand each expression using the Binomial theorem.**

11. $(x + 2)^4$

12. $(x + 3)^5$

13. $(y - 3)^5$

14. $(y - 4)^4$

15. $(x + y)^5$

16. $(x - y)^6$

17. $(x + 3y)^3$

18. $(2x - y)^3$

19. $(5x - 2)^3$

20. $(a - 7b)^3$

21. $\left(\frac{1}{x} + 5y\right)^4$

22. $\left(2x + \frac{3}{y}\right)^4$

23. $(x^2 + y^2)^4$

24. $(r^3 - s^3)^3$

25. $(ax + by)^5$

26. $(ax - by)^5$

27. $(\sqrt{x} + 2)^6$

28. $(3 + \sqrt{y})^4$

29. $(a^{3/4} + b^{1/4})^4$

30. $(x^{2/3} + y^{1/3})^3$

31. $(x^{1/4} + 2\sqrt{y})^4$

32. $(\sqrt{x} - 3y^{1/4})^8$

**In Exercises 33–36, expand each expression using Pascal's triangle.**

33. $(r - s)^4$

34. $(x^2 + y^2)^7$

35. $(ax + by)^6$

36. $(x + 3y)^4$

**In Exercises 37–44, find the coefficient $C$ of the given term in each binomial expansion.**

| Binomial | Term | Binomial | Term | Binomial | Term |
|---|---|---|---|---|---|
| 37. $(x + 2)^{10}$ | $Cx^6$ | 38. $(3 + y)^9$ | $Cy^5$ | 39. $(y - 3)^8$ | $Cy^4$ |
| 40. $(x - 1)^{12}$ | $Cx^5$ | 41. $(2x + 3y)^7$ | $Cx^3y^4$ | 42. $(3x - 5y)^9$ | $Cx^2y^7$ |
| 43. $(x^2 + y)^8$ | $Cx^8y^4$ | 44. $(r - s^2)^{10}$ | $Cr^6s^8$ | | |

## ▪ APPLICATIONS

**45. Lottery.** In a state lottery in which 6 numbers are drawn from a possible 40 numbers, the number of possible 6-number combinations is equal to $\binom{40}{6}$. How many possible combinations are there?

**46. Lottery.** In a state lottery in which 6 numbers are drawn from a possible 60 numbers, the number of possible 6-number combinations is equal to $\binom{60}{6}$. How many possible combinations are there?

**47. Poker.** With a deck of 52 cards, 5 cards are dealt in a game of poker. There are a total of $\binom{52}{5}$ different 5-card poker hands that can be dealt. How many possible hands are there?

**48. Canasta.** In the card game Canasta, two decks of cards including the jokers are used and 11 cards are dealt to each person. There are a total of $\binom{108}{11}$ different 11-card Canasta hands that can be dealt. How many possible hands are there?

## ▪ CATCH THE MISTAKE

**In Exercises 49 and 50, explain the mistake that is made.**

**49.** Evaluate the expression $\binom{7}{5}$.

**Solution:**

Write out the binomial coefficient in terms of factorials.

$$\binom{7}{5} = \frac{7!}{5!}$$

Write out the factorials.

$$\binom{7}{5} = \frac{7!}{5!} = \frac{7 \cdot 6 \cdot 5 \cdot 4 \cdot 3 \cdot 2 \cdot 1}{5 \cdot 4 \cdot 3 \cdot 2 \cdot 1}$$

Simplify.

$$\binom{7}{5} = \frac{7!}{5!} = \frac{7 \cdot 6}{1} = 42$$

This is incorrect. What mistake was made?

**50.** Expand $(x + 2y)^4$.

**Solution:**

Write out the expansion with blanks.

$$(x + 2y)^4 = \square x^4 + \square x^3 y + \square x^2 y^2 + \square xy^3 + \square y^4$$

Write out the terms from the fifth row of Pascal's triangle.

$$1, 4, 6, 4, 1$$

Substitute these coefficients into the expansion.

$$(x + 2y)^4 = x^4 + 4x^3 y + 6x^2 y^2 + 4xy^3 + y^4$$

This is incorrect. What mistake was made?

## ▪ CONCEPTUAL

**In Exercises 51–56, determine whether each statement is true or false.**

**51.** The binomial expansion of $(x + y)^{10}$ has 10 terms.

**52.** The binomial expansion of $(x^2 + y^2)^{15}$ has 16 terms.

**53.** $\binom{n}{n} = 1$

**54.** $\binom{n}{-n} = -1$

**55.** The coefficient of $x^8$ in the expansion of $(2x - 1)^{12}$ is 126,720.

**56.** The sixth term of the binomial expansion of $(x^2 + y)^{10}$ is $252x^5 y^5$.

## ▪ CHALLENGE

**57.** Show that $\binom{n}{k} = \binom{n}{n-k}$, if $0 \leq k \leq n$.

**58.** Show that if $n$ is a positive integer, then

$$\binom{n}{0} + \binom{n}{1} + \binom{n}{2} + \cdots + \binom{n}{n} = 2^n$$

*Hint:* Let $2^n = (1 + 1)^n$ and use the Binomial theorem to expand.

**59.** Show that $\binom{n}{k} = \binom{n-1}{k-1} + \binom{n-1}{k}$ for $k < n$ and $n \geq 2$.

**60.** Show that $(n - 2k)\binom{n}{k} = n\left[\binom{n-1}{k} - \binom{n-1}{k-1}\right]$ for $n > k$ and $n \geq 2$.

■ TECHNOLOGY

**61.** With a graphing utility, plot $y_1 = 1 - 3x + 3x^2 - x^3$, $y_2 = -1 + 3x - 3x^2 + x^3$, and $y_3 = (1 - x)^3$ in the same viewing screen. Which is the binomial expansion of $(1 - x)^3$, $y_1$ or $y_2$?

**62.** With a graphing utility, plot $y_1 = (x + 3)^4$, $y_2 = x^4 + 4x^3 + 6x^2 + 4x + 1$, and $y_3 = x^4 + 12x^3 + 54x^2 + 108x + 81$. Which is the binomial expansion of $(x + 3)^4$, $y_2$ or $y_3$?

**63.** With a graphing utility, plot $y_1 = 1 - 3x$, $y_2 = 1 - 3x + 3x^2$, $y_3 = 1 - 3x + 3x^2 - x^3$, and $y_4 = (1 - x)^3$ for $-1 < x < 1$. What do you notice happening each time an additional term is added to the series? Now, let $1 < x < 2$. Does the same thing happen?

**64.** With a graphing utility, plot $y_1 = 1 - \dfrac{3}{x}$, $y_2 = 1 - \dfrac{3}{x} + \dfrac{3}{x^2}$, $y_3 = 1 - \dfrac{3}{x} + \dfrac{3}{x^2} - \dfrac{1}{x^3}$, and $y_4 = \left(1 - \dfrac{1}{x}\right)^3$ for $1 < x < 2$.

What do you notice happening each time an additional term is added to the series? Now, let $0 < x < 1$. Does the same thing happen?

**65.** With a graphing utility, plot $y_1 = 1 + \dfrac{3}{x}$, $y_2 = 1 + \dfrac{3}{x} + \dfrac{3}{x^2}$, $y_3 = 1 + \dfrac{3}{x} + \dfrac{3}{x^2} - \dfrac{1}{x^3}$, and $y_4 = \left(1 + \dfrac{1}{x}\right)^3$ for $1 < x < 2$. What do you notice happening each time an additional term is added to the series? Now, let $0 < x < 1$. Does the same thing happen?

**66.** With a graphing utility, plot $y_1 = 1 + \dfrac{x}{1!}$, $y_2 = 1 + \dfrac{x}{1!} + \dfrac{x^2}{2!}$, $y_3 = 1 + \dfrac{x}{1!} + \dfrac{x^2}{2!} - \dfrac{x^3}{3!}$, and $y_4 = e^x$ for $-1 < x < 1$. What do you notice happening each time an additional term is added to the series? Now, let $1 < x < 2$. Does the same thing happen?

■ PREVIEW TO CALCULUS

In calculus, the difference quotient $\dfrac{f(x + h) - f(x)}{h}$ of a function $f$ is used to find the derivative of the function $f$.

In Exercises 67 and 68, use the Binomial theorem to find the difference quotient of each function.

**67.** $f(x) = x^n$

**68.** $f(x) = (2x)^n$

**69.** In calculus, we learn that the derivative of $f(x) = (x + 1)^n$ is $f'(x) = n(x + 1)^{n-1}$. Using the Binomial theorem, find an expression for $f'$ using sigma notation.

**70.** In calculus, we learn that the antiderivative of $f(x) = (x + 1)^n$ is $F(x) = \dfrac{(x + 1)^{n+1}}{n + 1}$ for $n \neq -1$. Using the Binomial theorem, find an expression for $F(x)$ using sigma notation.

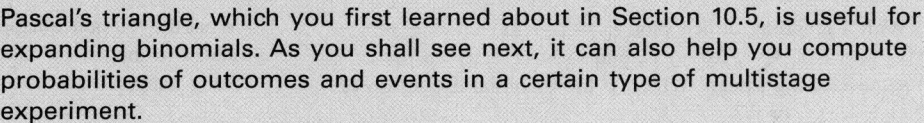

# CHAPTER 10 INQUIRY-BASED LEARNING PROJECT

Pascal's triangle, which you first learned about in Section 10.5, is useful for expanding binomials. As you shall see next, it can also help you compute probabilities of outcomes and events in a certain type of multistage experiment.

1. Suppose a math teacher gives her students a pop quiz, including 2 true/false questions. Since Cameron didn't study, he decides to randomly guess for the true/false portion of the quiz. Each of his answers will either be right (R) or wrong (W). There are four possible outcomes for his answers: RR, RW, WR, and WW. These outcomes may be organized according to the number of correct answers given in each possible outcome, as shown below.

| RANDOMLY GUESSING ON 2 TRUE/FALSE QUIZ QUESTIONS | | | |
|---|---|---|---|
| Number of correct answers given | 2 | 1 | 0 |
| Outcomes | RR | RW, WR | WW |
| Number of ways | 1 | 2 | 1 |

a. Cameron's math teacher will give several more pop quizzes this term, with various numbers of true/false questions on each quiz. Complete the following tables for randomly guessing on true/false quizzes with 1 question, 3 questions, and 4 questions.

| RANDOMLY GUESSING ON 1 TRUE/FALSE QUIZ QUESTION | | |
|---|---|---|
| Number of correct answers given | 1 | 0 |
| Outcomes | | |
| Number of ways | | |

| RANDOMLY GUESSING ON 3 TRUE/FALSE QUIZ QUESTIONS | |
|---|---|
| Number of correct answers given | |
| Outcomes | |
| Number of ways | |

| RANDOMLY GUESSING ON 4 TRUE/FALSE QUIZ QUESTIONS | |
|---|---|
| Number of correct answers given | |
| Outcomes | |
| Number of ways | |

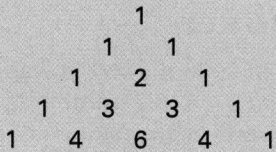

```
          1
        1   1
      1   2   1
    1   3   3   1
  1   4   6   4   1
```

**b.** Notice that the "Number of ways" row of each table in part (a) are the rows of Pascal's triangle, shown above. Notice that the first and last entry of each row is a 1. Describe how to find the other entries.

**c.** Extend Pascal's triangle for four more rows, to the row that begins 1   8 .... How can you interpret each of the entries in the 1   8 ... row, in the context of randomly guessing on a true/false quiz?

**d.** What is the sum of the entries in each of the rows of Pascal's triangle? Try to find a formula for the sum of the entries in the $n$th row. What do these numbers represent, in terms of randomly guessing on a true/false quiz?

**2.** Use Pascal's triangle to find the probability of each event $E$ given in parts (a) and (b) below.

**a.** $E$ is the event of guessing 4 answers correctly on a 6-question true/false quiz.

**b.** $E$ is the event of guessing *at least* 5 answers correctly on an 8-question true/false quiz.

**3.** Randomly guessing on a true/false quiz is an example of a multistage experiment in which there are *two equally likely outcomes* at each stage. Pascal's triangle may also be used to solve similar probability problems, as with flipping a coin or births of boys and girls.

Show how to use Pascal's triangle to find the probability of each of the following events.

**a.** No boys in a family with 4 children.

**b.** At least one boy in a family with 6 children.

**c.** All 10 heads when flipping a coin 10 times.

# MODELING OUR WORLD

In 2005 the world was producing 7 billion tons of carbon emissions per year. In 2055 this number is projected to double with the worldwide production of carbon emissions equaling 14 billion tons per year.

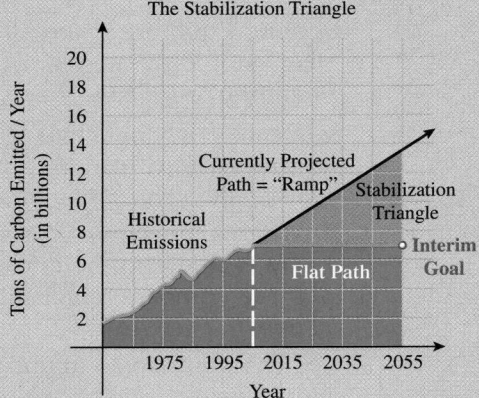

1. Determine the equation of the line for the projected path: an increase of 7 gigatons of carbon (GtC) over 50 years (2005–2055). Calculate the slope of the line.

2. What is the increase (per year) in the rate of carbon emissions per year based on the projected path model?

3. Develop a model in terms of a finite series that yields the total additional billions of tons of carbon emitted over the 50-year period (2005–2055) for the projected path over the flat path.

4. Calculate the total additional billions of tons of carbon of the projected path over the flat path [i.e., sum the series in (3)].

5. Discuss possible ways to provide the reduction between the projected path and the flat path based on the proposals given by Pacala and Socolow (professors at Princeton).*

*S. Pacala and R. Socolow, "Stabilization Wedges: Solving the Climate Problem for the Next 50 Years with Current Technologies," *Science*, Vol. 305 (2004).

# CHAPTER 10 REVIEW

| SECTION | CONCEPT | KEY IDEAS/FORMULAS |
|---|---|---|
| 10.1 | **Sequences and series** | |
| | Sequences | $a_1, a_2, a_3, \ldots, a_n, \ldots$    $a_n$ is the general term. |
| | Factorial notation | $n! = n(n-1)(n-2) \cdots 3 \cdot 2 \cdot 1$    $n \geq 2$ <br> $0! = 1$  and  $1! = 1$ |
| | Recursion formulas | When $a_n$ is defined by previous terms $a_{n-i}$ ($i = 1, 2, \ldots$). |
| | Sums and series | Infinite series: <br> $$\sum_{n=1}^{\infty} a_n = a_1 + a_2 + a_3 + \cdots + a_n + \cdots$$ <br> Finite series, or $n$th partial sum, $S_n$: <br> $$S_n = a_1 + a_2 + a_3 + \cdots + a_n$$ |
| 10.2 | **Arithmetic sequences and series** | |
| | Arithmetic sequences | $a_{n+1} = a_n + d$  or  $a_{n+1} - a_n = d$ <br> $d$ is called the **common difference**. |
| | The general ($n$th) term of an arithmetic sequence | $a_n = a_1 + (n-1)d$  for  $n \geq 1$ |
| | The sum of an arithmetic sequence | $S_n = \dfrac{n}{2}(a_1 + a_n)$ |
| 10.3 | **Geometric sequences and series** | |
| | Geometric sequences | $a_{n+1} = r \cdot a_n$  or  $\dfrac{a_{n+1}}{a_n} = r$ <br> $r$ is called the **common ratio**. |
| | The general ($n$th) term of a geometric sequence | $a_n = a_1 \cdot r^{n-1}$  for  $n \geq 1$ |
| | Geometric series | Finite series: $S_n = a_1 \dfrac{(1 - r^n)}{(1 - r)}$    $r \neq 1$ <br><br> Infinite series: $\displaystyle\sum_{n=0}^{\infty} a_1 r^n = a_1 \dfrac{1}{(1 - r)}$    $|r| < 1$ |
| 10.4 | **Mathematical induction** | |
| | Proof by mathematical induction | Prove that $S_n$ is true for all positive integers: <br> Step 1: Show that $S_1$ is true. <br> Step 2: Assume $S_n$ is true for $S_k$ and show it is true for $S_{k+1}$ <br> ($k$ = positive integer). |

| SECTION | CONCEPT | KEY IDEAS/FORMULAS |
|---------|---------|---------------------|
| 10.5 | **The Binomial theorem** | |
| | Binomial coefficients | $\binom{n}{k} = \dfrac{n!}{(n-k)!k!}$ $\binom{n}{n} = 1 \quad \text{and} \quad \binom{n}{0} = 1$ |
| | Binomial expansion | $(a+b)^n = \displaystyle\sum_{k=0}^{n} \binom{n}{k} a^{n-k} b^k$ |
| | Pascal's triangle | Shortcut way of remembering binomial coefficients. Each term is found by adding the two numbers in the row directly above it. |
| | Finding a particular term of a binomial expansion | The $(r+1)$ term of the expansion $(a+b)^n$ is $\binom{n}{r} a^{n-r} b^r$. |

## 10.1 Sequences and Series

**Write the first four terms of each sequence. Assume $n$ starts at 1.**

1. $a_n = n^3$

2. $a_n = \dfrac{n!}{n}$

3. $a_n = 3n + 2$

4. $a_n = (-1)^n x^{n+2}$

**Find the indicated term of each sequence.**

5. $a_n = \left(\dfrac{2}{3}\right)^n \qquad a_5 = ?$

6. $a_n = \dfrac{n^2}{3^n} \qquad a_8 = ?$

7. $a_n = \dfrac{(-1)^n(n-1)!}{n(n+1)!} \qquad a_{15} = ?$

8. $a_n = 1 + \dfrac{1}{n} \qquad a_{10} = ?$

**Write an expression for the $n$th term of each given sequence.**

9. $3, -6, 9, -12, \ldots$

10. $1, \frac{1}{2}, 3, \frac{1}{4}, 5, \frac{1}{6}, 7, \frac{1}{8}, \ldots$

11. $-1, 1, -1, 1, \ldots$

12. $1, 10, 10^2, 10^3, \ldots$

**Simplify each ratio of factorials.**

13. $\dfrac{8!}{6!}$

14. $\dfrac{20!}{23!}$

15. $\dfrac{n(n-1)!}{(n+1)!}$

16. $\dfrac{(n-2)!}{n!}$

**Write the first four terms of each sequence defined by the recursion formula.**

17. $a_1 = 5 \qquad a_n = a_{n-1} - 2$

18. $a_1 = 1 \qquad a_n = n^2 \cdot a_{n-1}$

19. $a_1 = 1, a_2 = 2 \qquad a_n = (a_{n-1})^2 \cdot (a_{n-2})$

20. $a_1 = 1, a_2 = 2 \qquad a_n = \dfrac{a_{n-2}}{(a_{n-1})^2}$

**Evaluate each finite series.**

21. $\displaystyle\sum_{n=1}^{5} 3$

22. $\displaystyle\sum_{n=1}^{4} \dfrac{1}{n^2}$

23. $\displaystyle\sum_{n=1}^{6} (3n+1)$

24. $\displaystyle\sum_{k=0}^{5} \dfrac{2^{k+1}}{k!}$

**Use sigma (summation) notation to represent each sum.**

25. $-1 + \frac{1}{2} - \frac{1}{4} + \frac{1}{8} + \cdots - \frac{1}{64}$

26. $2 + 4 + 6 + 8 + 10 + \cdots + 20$

27. $1 + x + \dfrac{x^2}{2} + \dfrac{x^3}{6} + \dfrac{x^4}{24} + \cdots$

28. $x - x^2 + \dfrac{x^3}{2} - \dfrac{x^4}{6} + \dfrac{x^5}{24} - \dfrac{x^6}{120} + \cdots$

## Applications

29. **A Marine's Investment.** With the prospect of continued fighting in Iraq, in December 2004, the Marine Corps offered bonuses of as much as $30,000—in some cases, tax-free—to persuade enlisted personnel with combat experience and training to reenlist. Suppose a Marine put his entire $30,000 reenlistment bonus in an account that earned 4% interest compounded monthly. The balance in the account after $n$ months would be

$$A_n = 30{,}000\left(1 + \dfrac{0.04}{12}\right)^n \qquad n = 1, 2, 3, \ldots$$

His commitment to the Marines is 5 years. Calculate $A_{60}$. What does $A_{60}$ represent?

30. **Sports.** The NFL minimum salary for a rookie is $180,000. Suppose a rookie enters the league making the minimum and gets a $30,000 raise each year. Write the general term $a_n$ of a sequence that represents the salary of an NFL player making the league minimum during his entire career. Assuming $n = 1$ corresponds to the first year, what does $\sum_{n=1}^{4} a_n$ represent?

## 10.2 Arithmetic Sequences and Series

**Determine whether each sequence is arithmetic. If it is, find the common difference.**

31. $7, 5, 3, 1, -1, \ldots$

32. $1^3 + 2^3 + 3^3 + \cdots$

33. $1, \frac{3}{2}, 2, \frac{5}{2}, \ldots$

34. $a_n = -n + 3$

35. $a_n = \dfrac{(n+1)!}{n!}$

36. $a_n = 5(n-1)$

**Find the general, or $n$th, term of each arithmetic sequence given the first term and the common difference.**

37. $a_1 = -4 \qquad d = 5$

38. $a_1 = 5 \qquad d = 6$

39. $a_1 = 1 \qquad d = -\frac{2}{3}$

40. $a_1 = 0.001 \qquad d = 0.01$

**For each arithmetic sequence described below, find $a_1$ and $d$ and construct the sequence by stating the general, or $n$th, term.**

41. The 5th term is 13 and the 17th term is 37.

42. The 7th term is $-14$ and the 10th term is $-23$.

43. The 8th term is 52 and the 21st term is 130.

44. The 11th term is $-30$ and the 21st term is $-80$.

**Find each sum.**

45. $\displaystyle\sum_{k=1}^{20} 3k$

46. $\displaystyle\sum_{n=1}^{15} (n+5)$

47. $2 + 8 + 14 + 20 + \cdots + 68$

48. $\frac{1}{4} - \frac{1}{4} - \frac{3}{4} - \cdots - \frac{31}{4}$

**Applications**

**49. Salary.** Upon graduating with MBAs, Bob and Tania opt for different career paths. Bob accepts a job with the U.S. Department of Transportation making $45,000 with a guaranteed $2000 raise every year. Tania takes a job with Templeton Corporation making $38,000 with a guaranteed $4000 raise every year. Calculate how many total dollars both Bob and Tania will have each made after 15 years.

**50. Gravity.** When a skydiver jumps out of an airplane, she falls approximately 16 feet in the 1st second, 48 feet during the 2nd second, 80 feet during the 3rd second, 112 feet during the 4th second, and 144 feet during the 5th second, and this pattern continues. If she deploys her parachute after 5 seconds have elapsed, how far will she have fallen during those 5 seconds?

## 10.3 Geometric Sequences and Series

**Determine whether each sequence is geometric. If it is, find the common ratio.**

**51.** $2, -4, 8, -16, \ldots$     **52.** $1, \dfrac{1}{2^2}, \dfrac{1}{3^2}, \dfrac{1}{4^2}, \ldots$

**53.** $20, 10, 5, \dfrac{5}{2}, \ldots$     **54.** $\dfrac{1}{100}, \dfrac{1}{10}, 1, 10, \ldots$

**Write the first five terms of each geometric series.**

**55.** $a_1 = 3 \quad r = 2$     **56.** $a_1 = 10 \quad r = \dfrac{1}{4}$

**57.** $a_1 = 100 \quad r = -4$     **58.** $a_1 = -60 \quad r = -\dfrac{1}{2}$

**Write the formula for the $n$th term of each geometric series.**

**59.** $a_1 = 7 \quad r = 2$     **60.** $a_1 = 12 \quad r = \dfrac{1}{3}$

**61.** $a_1 = 1 \quad r = -2$     **62.** $a_1 = \dfrac{32}{5} \quad r = -\dfrac{1}{4}$

**Find the indicated term of each geometric sequence.**

**63.** 25th term of the sequence $2, 4, 8, 16, \ldots$

**64.** 10th term of the sequence $\dfrac{1}{2}, 1, 2, 4, \ldots$

**65.** 12th term of the sequence $100, -20, 4, -0.8, \ldots$

**66.** 11th term of the sequence $1000, -500, 250, -125, \ldots$

**Evaluate each geometric series, if possible.**

**67.** $\dfrac{1}{2} + \dfrac{3}{2} + \dfrac{3^2}{2} + \cdots + \dfrac{3^8}{2}$

**68.** $1 + \dfrac{1}{2} + \dfrac{1}{2^2} + \dfrac{1}{2^3} + \cdots + \dfrac{1}{2^{10}}$

**69.** $\displaystyle\sum_{n=1}^{8} 5(3)^{n-1}$     **70.** $\displaystyle\sum_{n=1}^{7} \dfrac{2}{3}(5)^n$

**71.** $\displaystyle\sum_{n=0}^{\infty} \left(\dfrac{2}{3}\right)^n$     **72.** $\displaystyle\sum_{n=1}^{\infty} \left(-\dfrac{1}{5}\right)^{n+1}$

**Applications**

**73. Salary.** Murad is fluent in four languages and is offered a job with the U.S. government as a translator. He is hired on the "GS" scale at a base rate of $48,000 with a 2% increase in his salary per year. Calculate what his salary will be *after* he has been with the U.S. government for 12 years.

**74. Boat Depreciation.** Upon graduating from Auburn University, Philip and Steve get jobs at Disney Ride and Show Engineering and decide to buy a ski boat together. If the boat costs $15,000 new, and depreciates 20% per year, write a formula for the value of the boat $n$ years after it was purchased. How much will the boat be worth when Philip and Steve have been working at Disney for 3 years?

## 10.4 Mathematical Induction

**Prove each statement using mathematical induction for all positive integers $n$.**

**75.** $3n \le 3^n$     **76.** $4^n < 4^{n+1}$

**77.** $2 + 7 + 12 + 17 + \cdots + (5n - 3) = \dfrac{n}{2}(5n - 1)$

**78.** $2n^2 > (n + 1)^2 \quad n \ge 3$

## 10.5 The Binomial Theorem

**Evaluate each binomial coefficient.**

**79.** $\dbinom{11}{8}$     **80.** $\dbinom{10}{0}$     **81.** $\dbinom{22}{22}$     **82.** $\dbinom{47}{45}$

**Expand each expression using the Binomial theorem.**

**83.** $(x - 5)^4$     **84.** $(x + y)^5$     **85.** $(2x - 5)^3$

**86.** $(x^2 + y^3)^4$     **87.** $(\sqrt{x} + 1)^5$     **88.** $(x^{2/3} + y^{1/3})^6$

**Expand each expression using Pascal's triangle.**

**89.** $(r - s)^5$     **90.** $(ax + by)^4$

**Find the coefficient $C$ of the term in each binomial expansion.**

| Binomial | Term |
|---|---|
| **91.** $(x - 2)^8$ | $Cx^6$ |
| **92.** $(3 + y)^7$ | $Cy^4$ |
| **93.** $(2x + 5y)^6$ | $Cx^2y^4$ |
| **94.** $(r^2 - s)^8$ | $Cr^8s^4$ |

**Applications**

**95. Lottery.** In a state lottery in which 6 numbers are drawn from a possible 53 numbers, the number of possible 6-number combinations is equal to $\dbinom{53}{6}$. How many possible combinations are there?

**96. Canasta.** In the card game Canasta, two decks of cards including the jokers are used, and 13 cards are dealt to each person. A total of $\binom{108}{13}$ different 13-card Canasta hands can be dealt. How many possible hands are there?

## Technology Exercises

### Section 10.1

**97.** Use a graphing calculator "SUM" to find the sum of the series $\sum_{n=1}^{6} \frac{1}{n^2}$.

**98.** Use a graphing calculator "SUM" to find the sum of the infinite series $\sum_{n=1}^{\infty} \frac{1}{n}$, if possible.

### Section 10.2

**99.** Use a graphing calculator to sum $\sum_{n=1}^{75} \left[ \frac{3}{2} + \frac{6}{7}(n-1) \right]$.

**100.** Use a graphing calculator to sum $\sum_{n=1}^{264} \left[ -19 + \frac{1}{3}(n-1) \right]$.

### Section 10.3

**101.** Apply a graphing utility to plot
$y_1 = 1 - 2x + 4x^2 - 8x^3 + 16x^4$ and $y_2 = \dfrac{1}{1+2x}$, and let $x$ range from $[-0.3, 0.3]$. Based on what you see, what do you expect the geometric series $\sum_{n=0}^{\infty} (-1)^n (2x)^n$ to sum to in this range of $x$-values?

**102.** Does the sum of the infinite series $\sum_{n=0}^{\infty} \left( \dfrac{e}{\pi} \right)^n$ exist? Use a graphing calculator to find it and round to four decimal places.

### Section 10.4

**103.** Use a graphing calculator to sum the series $2 + 7 + 12 + 17 + \cdots + (5n - 3)$ and evaluate the expression $\dfrac{n}{2}(5n - 1)$ for $n = 200$. Do they agree with each other? Do your answers confirm the proof for Exercise 77?

**104.** Use a graphing calculator to plot the graphs of $y_1 = 2x^2$ and $y_2 = (x + 1)^2$ in the $[100, 1000]$ by $[10{,}000, 2{,}500{,}000]$ viewing rectangle. Do your results confirm the proof for Exercise 78?

### Section 10.5

**105.** With a graphing utility, plot $y_1 = 1 + 8x$, $y_2 = 1 + 8x + 24x^2$, $y_3 = 1 + 8x + 24x^2 + 32x^3$, $y_4 = 1 + 8x + 24x^2 + 32x^3 + 16x^4$, and $y_5 = (1 + 2x)^4$ for $-0.1 < x < 0.1$. What do you notice happening each time an additional term is added to the series? Now, let $0.1 < x < 1$. Does the same thing happen?

**106.** With a graphing utility, plot $y_1 = 1 - 8x$, $y_2 = 1 - 8x + 24x^2$, $y_3 = 1 - 8x + 24x^2 - 32x^3$, $y_4 = 1 - 8x + 24x^2 - 32x^3 + 16x^4$, and $y_5 = (1 - 2x)^4$ for $-0.1 < x < 0.1$. What do you notice happening each time an additional term is added to the series? Now, let $0.1 < x < 1$. Does the same thing happen?

**For Exercises 1–5, use the sequence** $1, x, x^2, x^3, \ldots$

1. Write the $n$th term of the sequence.

2. Classify this sequence as arithmetic, geometric, or neither.

3. Find the $n$th partial sum of the series $S_n$.

4. Assuming this sequence is infinite, write its series using sigma notation.

5. Assuming this sequence is infinite, what condition would have to be satisfied in order for the sum to exist?

6. Find the following sum: $\frac{1}{3} + \frac{1}{9} + \frac{1}{27} + \frac{1}{81} + \cdots$.

7. Find the following sum: $\sum_{n=1}^{10} 3 \cdot \left(\frac{1}{4}\right)^n$.

8. Find the following sum: $\sum_{k=1}^{50} (2k + 1)$.

9. Write the following series using sigma notation, then find its sum: $2 + 7 + 12 + 17 + \cdots + 497$.

10. Use mathematical induction to prove that $2 + 4 + 6 + \cdots + 2n = n^2 + n$.

11. Evaluate $\frac{7!}{2!}$.

12. Find the third term of $(2x + y)^5$.

**In Exercises 13 and 14, evaluate each expression.**

13. $\binom{15}{12}$    14. $\binom{k}{k}$

15. Simplify the expression $\frac{42!}{7! \cdot 37!}$.

16. Simplify the expression $\frac{(n + 2)!}{(n - 2)!}$ for $n \geq 2$.

17. Expand the expression $\left(x^2 + \frac{1}{x}\right)^5$.

18. Use the Binomial theorem to expand the binomial $(3x - 2)^4$.

**Prove each statement using mathematical induction for all positive integers** $n$.

19. $3 + 7 + 11 + \cdots + 4n - 1 = 2n^2 + n$

20. $2^1 + 1^3 + 2^2 + 2^3 + 2^3 + 3^3 + 2^4 + 4^3 + \cdots + 2^n + n^3$
$$= 2^{n+1} - 2 + \frac{n^2(n + 1)^2}{4}$$

**Find the sum of each infinite geometric series, if possible.**

21. $\sum_{n=0}^{\infty} \left(\frac{2}{5}\right)^n$

22. $1 + \frac{3}{4} + \frac{9}{16} + \frac{27}{64} + \cdots$

**Apply sigma notation to represent each series.**

23. $\frac{5}{8} + \frac{5}{10} + \frac{5}{12} + \frac{5}{14} + \cdots$

24. $\frac{1}{4} + \frac{5}{8} + \frac{7}{16} + \frac{17}{32} + \frac{31}{64} + \frac{65}{128} + \cdots$

**In Exercises 25 and 26, expand the expression using the Binomial theorem.**

25. $(2 - 3x)^7$    26. $(x^2 + y^3)^6$

27. Find the constant term in the expression $\left(x^3 + \frac{1}{x^3}\right)^{20}$.

28. Use a graphing calculator to sum $\sum_{n=1}^{125} \left[-\frac{11}{4} + \frac{5}{6}(n - 1)\right]$.

1. Find the difference quotient $\dfrac{f(x + h) - f(x)}{h}$ of the function $f(x) = \dfrac{x^2}{x + 1}$.

2. Given $f(x) = x^2 + x$ and $g(x) = \dfrac{1}{x + 3}$, find $(f \circ g)(x)$.

3. Write the polynomial function $f(x) = x^4 - 4x^3 - 4x^2 - 4x - 5$ as a product of linear factors.

4. Find the inverse of the function $f(x) = 5x - 4$.

5. Use long division to divide the polynomials: $(-6x^5 + 3x^3 + 2x^2 - 7) \div (x^2 + 3)$.

6. Write the logarithmic equation $\log 0.001 = -3$ in its equivalent exponential form.

7. Solve for $x$: $\ln(5x - 6) = 2$. Round to three decimal places.

8. **Sprinkler Coverage.** A sprinkler has a 21-foot spray and it rotates through an angle of 50°. What is the area that the sprinkler covers?

9. Find the exact value of $\sin\left(-\dfrac{7\pi}{4}\right)$.

10. If $\tan x = \dfrac{7}{24}$ and $\pi < x < \dfrac{3\pi}{2}$, find $\cos(2x)$.

11. Solve the trigonometric equation exactly $2\cos^2\theta - \cos\theta - 1 = 0$ over $0 \le \theta \le 2\pi$.

12. Given $\gamma = 53°$, $a = 18$, and $c = 17$, determine if a triangle (or two) exist and if so solve the triangles.

13. Express the complex number $\sqrt{2} - \sqrt{2}i$ in polar form.

14. Solve the system of linear equations.
$$8x - 5y = 15$$
$$y = \frac{8}{5}x + 10$$

15. Solve the system of linear equations.
$$2x - y + z = 1$$
$$x - y + 4z = 3$$

16. Maximize the objective function $z = 4x + 5y$, subject to the constraints $x + y \le 5$, $x \ge 1$, $y \ge 2$.

17. Solve the system using Gauss–Jordan elimination.
$$x + 5y - 2z = 3$$
$$3x + y + 2z = -3$$
$$2x - 4y + 4z = 10$$

18. Given
$$A = \begin{bmatrix} 3 & 4 & -7 \\ 0 & 1 & 5 \end{bmatrix} \quad B = \begin{bmatrix} 8 & -2 & 6 \\ 9 & 0 & -1 \end{bmatrix} \quad C = \begin{bmatrix} 9 & 0 \\ 1 & 2 \end{bmatrix}$$
find $C(A + B)$.

19. Calculate the determinant.
$$\begin{vmatrix} 2 & 5 & -1 \\ 1 & 4 & 0 \\ -2 & 1 & 3 \end{vmatrix}$$

20. Find the equation of a parabola with vertex $(3, 5)$ and directrix $x = 7$.

21. Graph $x^2 + y^2 < 4$.

22. The parametric equations $x = 2\sin t$, $y = 3\cos t$ define a plane curve. Find an equation in rectangular form that also corresponds to the plane curve.

23. Find the sum of the finite series $\sum_{n=1}^{4} \dfrac{2^{n-1}}{n!}$.

24. Classify the sequence as arithmetic, geometric, or neither.
$$5, 15, 45, 135, \ldots$$

25. The number of subsets with $k$ elements of a set with $n$ elements is given by $\dfrac{n!}{k!(n - k)!}$. Find the number of subsets with 3 elements of a set with 7 elements.

26. Find the binomial expansion of $(x - x^2)^5$.

# Answers To Odd Numbered Exercises*

## CHAPTER 0

### Section 0.1

**1.** $m = 2$

**3.** $t = \frac{7}{5}$

**5.** $x = -10$

**7.** $n = 2$

**9.** $x = 12$

**11.** $t = -\frac{15}{2}$

**13.** $x = -1$

**15.** $p = -\frac{9}{2}$

**17.** $x = \frac{1}{4}$

**19.** $x = -\frac{3}{2}$

**21.** $a = -8$

**23.** $x = -15$

**25.** $c = -\frac{35}{13}$

**27.** $m = \frac{60}{11}$

**29.** $x = 36$

**31.** $p = 8$

**33.** $y = -2$

**35.** $p = 2$

**37.** no solution

**39.** 12 mi

**41.** 270 units

**43.** $r_1 = 3$ ft, $r_2 = 6$ ft

**45.** 5.25 ft

**47.** $20,000 at 4%, $100,000 at 7%

**49.** $3000 at 10%, $5500 at 2%, $5500 at 40%

**51.** 70 ml of 5% HCl, 30 ml of 15% HCl

**53.** 9 min

**55.** $3.07 per gallon

**57.** 233 ml

**59.** 2.3 mph

**61.** walker: 4 mph, jogger: 6 mph

**63.** bicyclist: 6 min, walker: 18 min

**65.** 22.5 hr

**67.** 2.4 hr

**69.** 2 field goals, 6 touchdowns

**71.** 3.5 ft from the center

**73.** Fulcrum is 0.4 unit from Maria and 0.6 unit from Max.

**75.** Should have subtracted $4x$ and added 7 to both sides; $x = 5$

**77.** $x = \dfrac{c - b}{a}$

**79.** $\dfrac{P - 2l}{2} = w$

**81.** $\dfrac{2A}{b} = h$

**83.** $\dfrac{A}{l} = w$

**85.** $\dfrac{V}{lw} = h$

**87.** Janine's average speed is 58 mph, Tricia's average speed is 70 mph.

**89.** $x = 2$

**91.** all real numbers

**93.** $191,983.35

**95.** Option B: better for 5 or few plays/mo
Option A: better for 6 or more plays/mo

### Section 0.2

**1.** $x = 3$ or $x = 2$

**3.** $p = 5$ or $p = 3$

**5.** $x = -4$ or $x = 3$

**7.** $x = -\frac{1}{4}$

**9.** $y = \frac{1}{3}$

**11.** $y = 0$ or $y = 2$

**13.** $p = \frac{2}{3}$

**15.** $x = -3$ or $x = 3$

**17.** $x = -6$ or $x = 2$

**19.** $p = -5$ or $p = 5$

**21.** $x = -2$ or $x = 2$

**23.** $p = \pm2\sqrt{2}$

**25.** $x = \pm 3i$

**27.** $x = -3, 9$

**29.** $x = \dfrac{-3 \pm 2i}{2}$

**31.** $x = \dfrac{2 \pm 3\sqrt{3}}{5}$

**33.** $x = -2, 4$

**35.** $x = -3, 1$

**37.** $t = 1, 5$

**39.** $y = 1, 3$

**41.** $p = \dfrac{-4 \pm \sqrt{10}}{2}$

**43.** $x = \frac{1}{2}, 3$

**45.** $x = \dfrac{4 \pm 3\sqrt{2}}{2}$

**47.** $t = \dfrac{-3 \pm \sqrt{13}}{2}$

**49.** $s = \dfrac{-1 \pm i\sqrt{3}}{2}$

**51.** $x = \dfrac{3 \pm \sqrt{57}}{6}$

**53.** $x = 1 \pm 4i$

**55.** $x = \dfrac{-7 \pm \sqrt{109}}{10}$

**57.** $x = \dfrac{-4 \pm \sqrt{34}}{3}$

**59.** $v = -2, 10$

**61.** $t = -6, 1$

**63.** $x = -7, 1$

**65.** $p = 4 \pm 2\sqrt{3}$

**67.** $w = \dfrac{-1 \pm i\sqrt{167}}{8}$

**69.** $p = \dfrac{9 \pm \sqrt{69}}{6}$

**71.** $t = \dfrac{10 \pm \sqrt{130}}{10}$

**73.** $x = -0.3, 0.4$

**75.** $t = 8$ (Aug. 2003) and $t = 12$ (Dec. 2003)

**77.** 31,000 units

**79.** $1 per bottle

**81.** 3 days

**83.** **a.** 55.25 sq in.
**b.** $4x^2 + 30x + 55.25$
**c.** $4x^2 + 30x$ represents the increase in usable area of the paper.
**d.** $x \approx 0.3$ in.

**85.** 20 in.

**87.** 17, 18

**89.** Length: 15 ft, width: 9 ft

**91.** Base: 6, height: 20

**93.** Impact with ground in 2.5 sec

**95.** 21.2 ft

**97.** 5 ft $\times$ 5 ft

**99.** 2.3 ft

**101.** 10 days

**103.** The problem is factored incorrectly. The correction would be $t = -1, 6$.

**105.** When taking the square root of both sides, the $i$ is missing from the right side. The correction would be $a = \pm\frac{3}{4}i$.

**107.** false

**109.** true

---

*Answers that require a proof, graph, or otherwise lengthy solution are not included.

**111.** $x^2 - 2ax + a^2 = 0$

**113.** $x^2 - 7x + 10 = 0$

**115.** $t = \pm\sqrt{\dfrac{2s}{g}}$

**117.** $c = \pm\sqrt{a^2 + b^2}$

**119.** $x = 0, \pm 2$

**121.** $x = -1, \pm 2$

**123.** $\dfrac{-b}{2a} + \dfrac{\sqrt{b^2 - 4ac}}{2a} - \dfrac{b}{2a} - \dfrac{\sqrt{b^2 - 4ac}}{2a} = \dfrac{-2b}{2a} = \dfrac{-b}{a}$

**125.** $x^2 - 6x + 4 = 0$

**127.** 250 mph

**129.** $ax^2 - bx + c = 0$

**131.** Small jet: 300 mph, 757: 400 mph

**133.** $x = -1, 2$

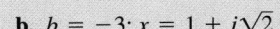

**135. a.** $x = -2, 4$

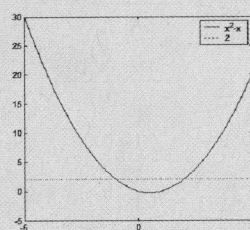

$b = -1: x = 1$

**b.** $b = -3: x = 1 \pm i\sqrt{2}$

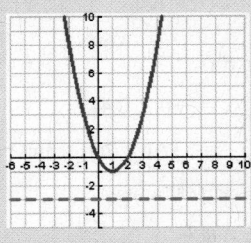

$b = 0: x = 0, 2$

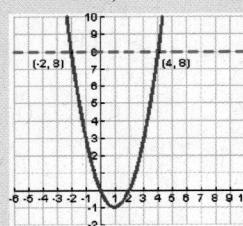

$b = 5: x = 1 \pm \sqrt{6}$

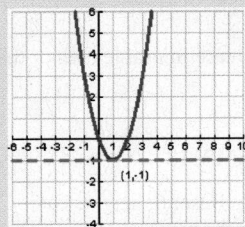

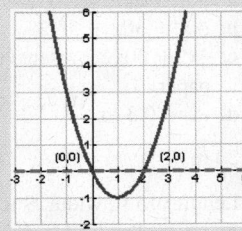

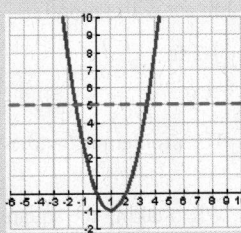

**13.** $x \neq -\frac{1}{5}, \frac{1}{2}, x = -3$

**15.** $t \neq 1$, no solution

**17.** $x = 3$ or $x = 4$

**19.** $x = -\frac{3}{4}$ or $x = 2$

**21.** no solution

**23.** $x = 5$

**25.** $y = -\frac{1}{2}$

**27.** $x = 5$

**29.** $x = -9$ or $x = 7$

**31.** $x = 4$

**33.** $y = 0, 25$

**35.** $s = 3, 6$

**37.** $x = -3, -1$

**39.** $x = 0$

**41.** $x = 1$ and $x = 5$

**43.** $x = 7$

**45.** $x = -3$ and $x = -\frac{15}{4}$

**47.** $x = \frac{5}{2}$

**49.** no solution

**51.** $x = 1$

**53.** $x = 4$ and $x = -8$

**55.** $x = 1, 5$

**57.** $x = 7$

**59.** $x = 4$

**61.** $x = 0, x = -8$

**63.** $x = \pm 1, x = \pm\sqrt{2}$

**65.** $x = \dfrac{\pm i\sqrt{6}}{2}, x = \pm i\sqrt{2}$

**67.** $t = \frac{5}{4}, t = 3$

**69.** $x = \pm 1, \pm i, x = \pm\frac{1}{2}, \pm\frac{1}{2}i$

**71.** $y = -\frac{3}{4}, y = 1$

**73.** $z = 1$

**75.** $t = -27, t = 8$

**77.** $x = -\frac{4}{3}, x = 0$

**79.** $u = \pm 8, u = \pm 1$

**81.** $x = 0, -3, 4$

**83.** $p = 0, \pm\frac{3}{2}$

**85.** $u = 0, \pm 2, \pm 2i$

**87.** $x = \pm 3, 5$

**89.** $y = -2, 5, 7$

**91.** $x = 0, 3, -1$

**93.** $t = \pm 5$

**95.** $y = 2, 3$

**97.** $p = 10$ or $p = 4$

**99.** $y = 5$ or $y = 3$

**101.** $t = 4$ or $t = 2$

**103.** $x = 8$ or $x = -1$

**105.** $y = 0$ or $y = \frac{2}{3}$

**107.** $x = -\frac{23}{14}$ or $x = \frac{47}{14}$

**109.** $x = 13$ or $x = -3$

**111.** $p = 7$ or $p = -13$

**113.** $y = 9$ or $y = -5$

**115.** $x = \pm\sqrt{5}$ or $x = \pm\sqrt{3}$

**117.** $x = \pm 2$

**119.** January and September

**121.** 162 cm

**123.** 7.5 cm in front of lens

**125.** Object distance = 6 cm
image distance = 3 cm

**127.** 132 ft

**129.** 25 cm

**131.** 80% of the speed of light

**133.** no solution

**135.** Cannot cross multiply—must multiply by LCD first; $p = \frac{6}{5}$

**137.** false

**139.** $x = \dfrac{a - b}{c}$

**141.** $x = -2$

**143.** $x = \dfrac{by}{a - y - cy}, x \neq 0, -\dfrac{b}{c + 1}$

## Section 0.3

**1.** $x \neq 2$, no solution

**3.** $p \neq 1$, no solution

**5.** $x \neq -2, x = -10$

**7.** $n \neq -1, 0$, no solution

**9.** $a \neq 0, -3$, no solution

**11.** $n \neq 1, n = \frac{53}{11}$

**145.** $x = \frac{313}{64} \cong 4.89$

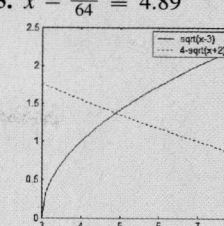

**147.** $x = 81$

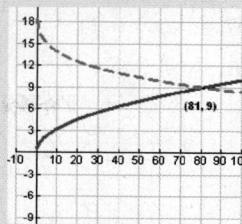

## Section 0.4

**1.** $[-2, 3)$ 
... $-3 -2 -1\ 0\ 1\ 2\ 3\ 4$ ...

**3.** $(-3, 5]$ 
... $-3 -2 -1\ 0\ 1\ 2\ 3\ 4\ 5$ ...

**5.** $[4, 6]$ 
... $3\ 4\ 5\ 6\ 7$ ...

**7.** $[-8, -6]$ 
... $-9 -8 -7 -6 -5$ ...

**9.** $\varnothing$ 
... $-3 -2 -1\ 0\ 1\ 2\ 3$ ...

**11.** $[1, 4)$ 
... $0\ 1\ 2\ 3\ 4$ ...

**13.** $[-1, 2)$ 
... $-2 -1\ 0\ 1\ 2\ 3$ ...

**15.** $(-\infty, 4) \cup (4, \infty)$ 
... $2\ 3\ 4\ 5\ 6\ 7$ ...

**17.** $(-\infty, -3] \cup [3, \infty)$ 
... $-3 -2 -1\ 0\ 1\ 2\ 3$ ...

**19.** $(-3, 2]$ 
... $-4 -3 -2 -1\ 0\ 1\ 2\ 3\ 4$ ...

**21.** $(-3, \infty)$          **23.** $(-\infty, 6)$

**25.** $(-\infty, 1)$         **27.** $(-\infty, -0.5)$

**29.** $[-8, 4)$             **31.** $(-6, 6)$

**33.** $\left[\frac{1}{2}, \frac{5}{4}\right]$          **35.** $[-4.5, 0.5]$

**37.** $\left[-1, \frac{3}{2}\right]$          **39.** $\left(\frac{1}{3}, \frac{1}{2}\right)$

**41.** $\left(-\infty, -\frac{1}{2}\right] \cup [3, \infty)$

**43.** $\left(-\infty, -1 - \sqrt{5}\right] \cup \left[-1 + \sqrt{5}, \infty\right)$

**45.** $\left(2 - \sqrt{10}, 2 + \sqrt{10}\right)$          **47.** $(-\infty, 0] \cup [3, \infty)$

**49.** $(-\infty, -3) \cup (3, \infty)$          **51.** $(-\infty, -2] \cup [0, 1]$

**53.** $(0, 1) \cup (1, \infty)$          **55.** $(-\infty, -2) \cup [-1, 2)$

**57.** $(-\infty, -5] \cup (-2, 0]$          **59.** $(-2, 2)$

**61.** $\mathbb{R}$ (consistent)          **63.** $[-3, 3) \cup (3, \infty)$

**65.** $(-3, -1] \cup (3, \infty)$          **67.** $(-\infty, -4) \cup (2, 5]$

**69.** $(-\infty, -2) \cup (2, \infty)$          **71.** $(-\infty, 2) \cup (6, \infty)$

**73.** $[3, 5]$          **75.** $\mathbb{R}$

**77.** $(-\infty, 2] \cup [5, \infty)$          **79.** $\mathbb{R}$

**81.** $\left(-\infty, -\frac{3}{2}\right] \cup \left[\frac{3}{2}, \infty\right)$          **83.** $(-\infty, -3) \cup (3, \infty)$

**85.** $[-3, 3]$          **87.** $0.9\, r_T \le r_R \le 1.1\, r_T$

**89.** $4{,}386.25 \le T \le 15{,}698.75$

**91.** 285,700 units

**93.** Between 33% and 71% intensities

**95.** Between 30 and 100 orders

**97.** For years 3–5, the car is worth more than you owe. In the first 3 years you owe more than the car is worth.

**99.** 75 sec

**101.** A price increase less than \$1 per bottle or greater than \$20 per bottle

**103.** Win: $d < 4$, tie: $d = 4$

**105.** When the number of units sold was between 25 and 75 units.

**107.** Forgot to flip the sign when dividing by $-3$. Answer should be $[2, \infty)$.

**109.** Cannot divide by $x$ $(-\infty, 0) \cup (3, \infty)$

**111.** true          **113.** false

**115.** $\mathbb{R}$          **117.** no solution

**119. a.** $(-2, 5)$

**b.**

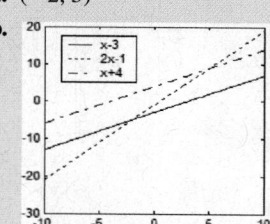

**c.** agree

**121.** $\left(-\frac{1}{2}, \infty\right)$

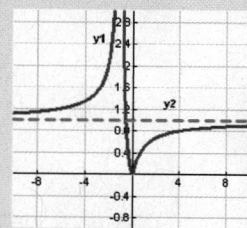

## Section 0.5

**1.** $d = 4$, $(3, 3)$          **3.** $d = 4\sqrt{2}$, $(1, 2)$

**5.** $d = 3\sqrt{10}$, $\left(-\frac{17}{2}, \frac{7}{2}\right)$          **7.** $d = 5$, $\left(-5, \frac{1}{2}\right)$

**9.** $d = 4\sqrt{2}, (-4, -6)$  **11.** $d = 5, \left(\frac{3}{2}, \frac{11}{6}\right)$

**13.**

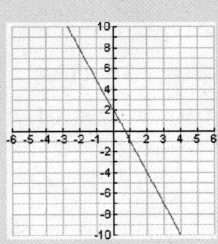

**15.**

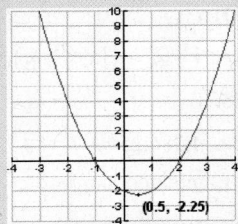

(0.5, -2.25)

**17.**

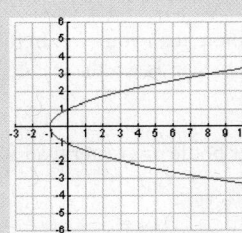

**19.** $(3, 0), (0, -6)$  **21.** $(4, 0)$, no $y$-intercept

**23.** $(\pm 2, 0), (0, \pm 4)$  **25.** $x$-axis

**27.** $x$-axis  **29.** $y$-axis

**31.**

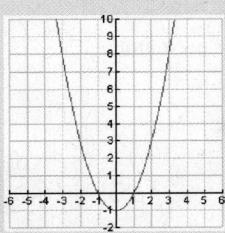

**33.**

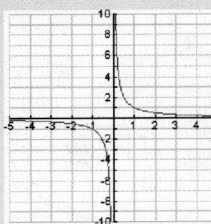

**35.**

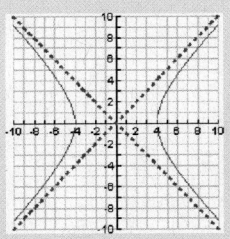

**37.** $(x - 5)^2 + (y - 7)^2 = 81$

**39.** $(x + 11)^2 + (y - 12)^2 = 169$

**41.** $(x - 5)^2 + (y + 3)^2 = 12$

**43.** $\left(x - \frac{2}{3}\right)^2 + \left(y + \frac{3}{5}\right)^2 = \frac{1}{16}$

**45.** $(2, -5), r = 7$  **47.** $(4, 9), r = 2\sqrt{5}$

**49.** $\left(\frac{2}{5}, \frac{1}{7}\right), r = \frac{2}{3}$  **51.** $(5, 7), r = 9$

**53.** $(1, 3), r = 3$  **55.** $(5, -3), r = 2\sqrt{3}$

**57.** $(3, 2), r = 2\sqrt{3}$  **59.** $\left(\frac{1}{2}, -\frac{1}{2}\right), r = \frac{1}{2}$

**61.**

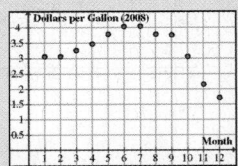

**63.** 268 mi  **65.** $330 million

**67.** $x^2 + y^2 = 2,250,000$  **69.** $x^2 + y^2 = 40,000$

**71.** $x \geq 1$ or $[1, \infty)$; the demand model is defined when at least 1000 units per day are demanded.

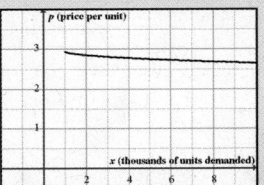

**73.** The equation is not linear—you need more than two points to plot the graph.

**75.** The center should be $(4, -3)$.

**77.** false  **79.** true

**81.** single point $(-5, 3)$  **83.** origin

**85.** $(x - 3)^2 + (y + 2)^2 = 20$  **87.** $4c = a^2 + b^2$

**89.** $y$-axis

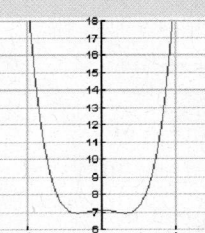

**91. a.** $(5.5, -1.5), r = 6.3$

**b.** $y = -1.5 \pm \sqrt{39.69 - (x - 5.5)^2}$

**c.**

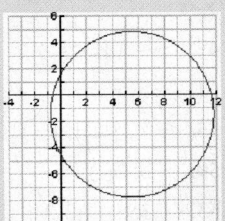

## Section 0.6

**1.** 3

**3.** $-2$

**5.** $-\frac{19}{10}$

**7.** 2.379

**9.** $-3$

**11.** $(0.5, 0), (0, -1), m = 2$, increasing

**13.** $(1, 0), (0, 1), m = -1$, decreasing

**15.** none, $(0, 1), m = 0$, horizontal

**17.** $\left(\frac{3}{2}, 0\right), (0, -3)$

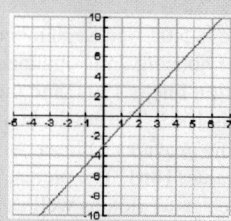

**19.** $(4, 0), (0, 2)$

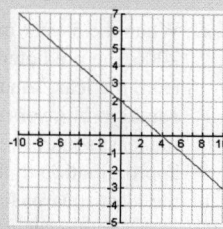

**21.** $(2, 0), \left(0, -\frac{4}{3}\right)$

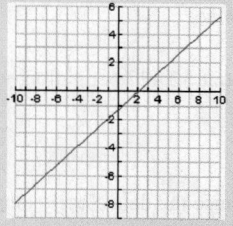

**23.** $(-2, 0), (0, -2)$

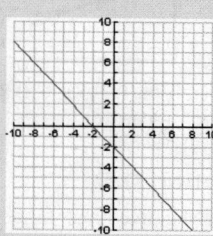

**25.** $(-1, 0)$, none

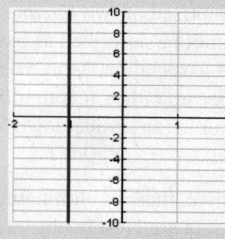

**27.** none, $(0, 1.5)$

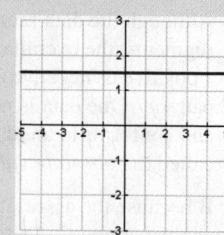

**29.** $\left(-\frac{7}{2}, 0\right)$, none

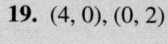

**31.** $y = \frac{2}{5}x - 2$   $m = \frac{2}{5}$   $y$-intercept: $(0, -2)$

**33.** $y = -\frac{1}{3}x + 2$   $m = -\frac{1}{3}$   $y$-intercept: $(0, 2)$

**35.** $y = 4x - 3$   $m = 4$   $y$-intercept: $(0, -3)$

**37.** $y = -2x + 4$   $m = -2$   $y$-intercept: $(0, 4)$

**39.** $y = \frac{2}{3}x - 2$   $m = \frac{2}{3}$   $y$-intercept: $(0, -2)$

**41.** $y = -\frac{3}{4}x + 6$   $m = -\frac{3}{4}$   $y$-intercept: $(0, 6)$

**43.** $y = 2x + 3$

**45.** $y = -\frac{1}{3}x$

**47.** $y = 2$

**49.** $x = \frac{3}{2}$

**51.** $y = 5x + 2$

**53.** $y = -3x - 4$

**55.** $y = \frac{3}{4}x - \frac{7}{4}$

**57.** $y = 4$

**59.** $x = -1$

**61.** $y = \frac{3}{5}x + \frac{1}{5}$

**63.** $y = -5x - 16$

**65.** $y = \frac{1}{6}x - \frac{121}{3}$

**67.** $y = -3x + 1$

**69.** $y = \frac{3}{2}x$

**71.** $x = 3$

**73.** $y = 7$

**75.** $y = \frac{6}{5}x + 6$

**77.** $x = -6$

**79.** $x = \frac{2}{5}$

**81.** $y = x - 1$

**83.** $y = -2x + 3$

**85.** $y = -\frac{1}{2}x + 1$

**87.** $y = 2x + 7$

**89.** $y = \frac{3}{2}x$

**91.** $y = 5$

**93.** $y = 2$

**95.** $y = \frac{3}{2}x - 4$

**97.** $y = \frac{5}{4}x + \frac{3}{2}$

**99.** $y = \frac{3}{7}x + \frac{5}{2}$

**101.** $C(h) = 1200 + 25h$; $2000

**103.** $375

**105.** 347 units

**107.** $F = \frac{9}{5}C + 32$, $-40°C = -40°F$

**109.** $\frac{1}{50}$ in./yr

**111.** 0.06 oz/yr, 6 lb 12.4 oz

**113.** $y$-intercept is the flat monthly fee of $35.

**115.** $-0.35$ in./yr, 2.75 in.

**117.** 2.4 plastic bags per year (in billions), 404 billion

**119. a.** $(1, 31.93)$ $(2, 51.18)$ $(5, 111.83)$

    **b.** $m = 25.59$. This means that when you buy one bottle of Hoisin it costs $31.93 per bottle.

    **c.** $m = 31.93$. This means that when you buy two bottles of Hoisin it costs $25.59 per bottle.

    **d.** $m = 22.366$. This means that when you buy five bottles of Hoisin it costs $22.37 per bottle.

**121.** The computations used to calculate the $x$- and $y$-intercepts should be reversed. So, the $x$-intercept is $(3, 0)$ and the $y$-intercept is $(0, -2)$.

**123.** The denominator and numerator in the slope computation should be switched, resulting in the slope being undefined.

**125.** true

**127.** false

**129.** Any vertical line is perpendicular to a line with slope 0.

**131.** $y = -\dfrac{A}{B}x + 1$

**133.** $y = \dfrac{B}{A}x + (2B - 1)$

**135.** $b_1 = b_2$

**137.** perpendicular

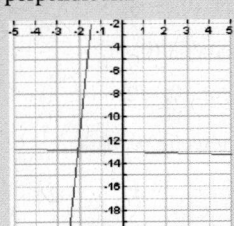

**139.** perpendicular

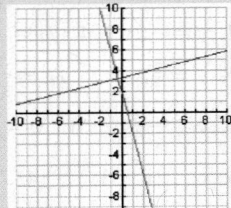

**141.** neither

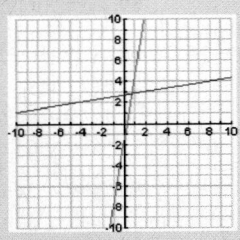

## Section 0.7

**1.** $y = kx$

**3.** $V = kx^3$

**5.** $z = km$

**7.** $f = \dfrac{k}{\lambda}$

**9.** $F = \dfrac{kw}{L}$

**11.** $v = kgt$

**13.** $R = \dfrac{k}{PT}$

**15.** $y = k\sqrt{x}$

**17.** $d = rt$

**19.** $V = lwh$

**21.** $A = \pi r^2$

**23.** $V = \dfrac{\pi}{16}hr^2$

**25.** $V = \dfrac{400,000}{P}$

**27.** $F = \dfrac{2\pi}{\lambda L}$

**29.** $t = \dfrac{19.2}{s}$

**31.** $R = \dfrac{4.9}{I^2}$

**33.** $R = \dfrac{0.01L}{A}$

**35.** $F = \dfrac{0.025m_1 m_2}{d^2}$

**37.** $W = 7.5H$

**39.** 1292 mph

**41.** $F = 1.618H$

**43.** 24 cm

**45.** \$37.50

**47.** 20,000

**49.** 600 $w/m^2$

**51.** Bank of America: 1.5%; Navy Federal Credit Union: 3%

**53.** $\frac{11}{12}$ or 0.92 atm

**55.** Should be $y$ is <u>inversely</u> proportional to $x$

**57.** true

**59.** b

**61.** $\sigma_{p_1}^2 = 1.23 C_n^2 k^{7/6} L^{11/6}$

**63. a.** $y = 2.93x + 201.72$

**b.** $120.07$, $y = 120.074x^{0.259}$

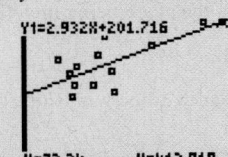

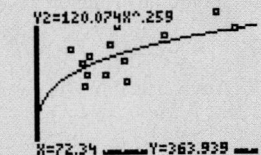

**c.** When the oil price is \$72.70 per barrel in September 2006, the predicted stock index obtained from the least squares regression line is 415, and from the equation of direct variation it is 364. The least squares regression line provides a closer approximation to the actual value, 417.

**65. a.** $y = -141.73x + 2,419.35$

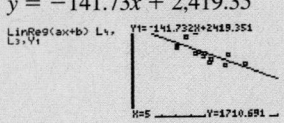

**b.** $3,217.69$, $y = \dfrac{3217.69}{x^{0.41}}$

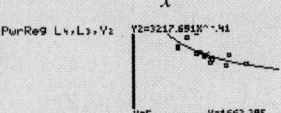

**c.** When the 5-year maturity rate is 5.02% in September 2006, the predicted number of housing units obtained from the least squares regression line is 1708, and the equation of inverse variation is 1661. The equation of the least squares regression line provides a closer approximation to the actual value, 1861. The picture of the least squares line, with the scatterplot, as well as the computations using the TI-8* is as follows:

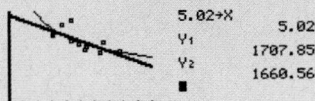

**67. a.** $y = 0.218x + 0.898$   **b.** about \$2.427 per gallon, yes

**c.** \$3.083

## Section 0.8

**1.** Negative linear association because the data closely cluster around what is reasonably described as a linear with negative slope.

**3.** Although the data seem to be comprised of two *linear* segments, the overall data set cannot be described as having a positive or negative direction of association. Moreover, the pattern of the data is not linear, per se; rather, it is nonlinear and conforms to an identifiable curve (an upside down V called the *absolute value* function).

**5.** **B** because the association is positive, thereby eliminating choices A and C. And, since the data are closely clustered around a linear curve, the bigger of the two correlation coefficients, 0.80 and 0.20, is more appropriate.

**7.** **C** because the association is negative, thereby eliminating choices B and D. And, the data are more loosely clustered around a linear curve than are those pictured in #6. So, the correlation coefficient is the negative choice closer to 0.

**9. a.**

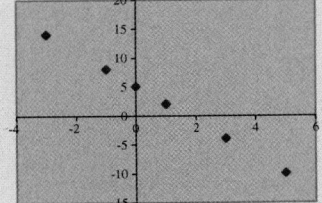

**b.** The data seem to be nearly perfectly aligned to a line with negative slope. So, it is reasonable to guess that the correlation coefficient is very close to −1.

**c.** The equation of the best fit line is $y = -3x + 5$ with a correlation coefficient of $r = -1$.

**d.** There is a perfect negative linear association between $x$ and $y$.

**11. a.**

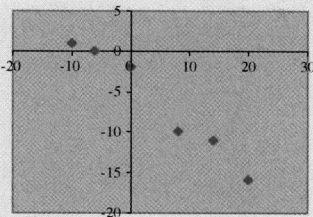

**b.** The data tends to fall from left to right, so that the correlation coefficient should be negative. Also, the data do not seem to stray too far from a linear curve, so the $r$ value should be reasonably close to −1, but not equal to it. A reasonable guess would be around −0.90.

**c.** The equation of the best fit line is approximately $y = -0.5844x - 3.801$ with a correlation coefficient of about $r = 0.9833$.

**d.** There is a strong (but not perfect) negative linear relationship between $x$ and $y$.

**13. a.**

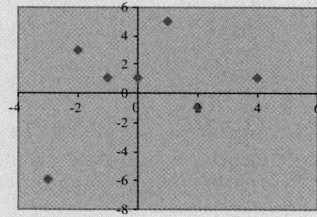

**b.** The data seems to rise from left to right, but it is difficult to be certain about this relationship since the data stray considerably away from an identifiable line. As such, it is reasonable to guess that $r$ is a rather small value close to 0, say around 0.30.

**c.** The equation of the best fit line is approximately $y = 0.5x + 0.5$ with a correlation coefficient of about 0.349.

**d.** There is a very loose (bordering on unidentifiable) positive linear relationship between $x$ and $y$.

**15. a.**

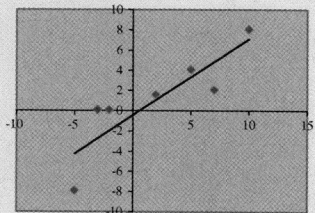

The equation of the best fit line is about $y = 0.7553x - 0.4392$ with a correlation coefficient of about $r = 0.868$.

**b.** The values $x = 0$ and $x = -6$ are within the range of the data set, so that using the best fit line for predictive purposes is reasonable. This is not the case for the values $x = 12$ and $x = -15$. The predicted value of $y$ when $x = 0$ is approximately −0.4392, and the predicted value of $y$ when $x = -6$ is −4.971.

**c.** Solve the equation $2 = 0.7553x - 0.4392$ for $x$ to obtain: $2.4392 = 0.7553x$ so that $x = 3.229$. So, using the best fit line, you would expect to get a $y$-value of 2 when $x$ is approximately 3.229.

**17. a.**

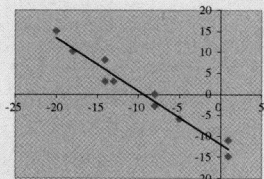

The equation of the best fit line is about $y = -1.2631x - 11.979$ with a correlation coefficient of about $r = -0.980$.

**b.** The values $x = -15$, −6, and 0 are within the range of the data set, so that using the best fit line for predictive purposes is reasonable. This is not the case for the value $x = 12$. The predicted value of $y$ when $x = -15$ is approximately 6.9675, the predicted value of $y$ when $x = -6$ is about −4.4004, and the predicted value of $y$ when $x = 0$ is −11.979.

**c.** Solve the equation $2 = -1.2631x - 11.979$ for $x$ to obtain: $13.979 = -1.2631x$ so that $x = -11.067$. So, using the best fit line, you would expect to get a $y$-value of 2 when $x$ is approximately −11.067.

**19. a.** The scatterplot for the entire data set is:

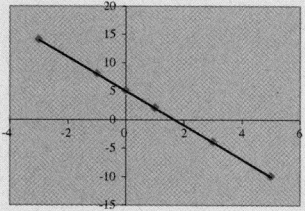

The equation of the best fit line is $y = -3x + 5$ with a correlation coefficient of $r = -1$.

**b.** The scatterplot for the data set obtained by removing the starred data point $(5, -10)$ is:

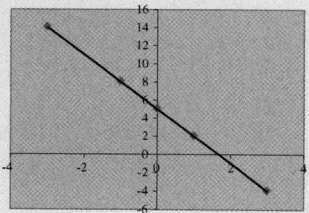

The equation of the best fit line of this modified data set is $y = -3x + 5$ with a correlation coefficient of $r = -1$.

c. Removing the data point did not result in the slightest change in either the equation of the best fit line or the correlation coefficient. This is reasonable since the relationship between $x$ and $y$ in the original data set is perfectly linear, so that all of the points lie ON the same line. As such, removing one of them has no effect on the line itself.

**21. a.** The scatterplot for the entire data set is:

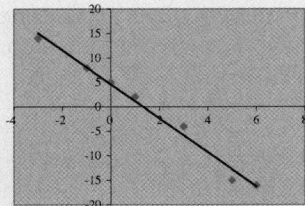

The equation of the best fit line is $y = -3.4776x + 4.6076$ with a correlation coefficient of about $r = -0.993$.

**b.** The scatterplot for the data set obtained by removing the starred data points $(3, -4)$ and $(6, -16)$ is:

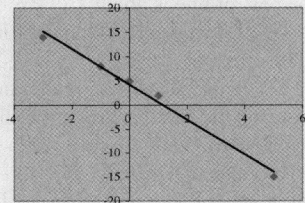

The equation of the best fit line of this modified data set is $y = -3.6534x + 4.2614$ with a correlation coefficient of $r = -0.995$.

**c.** Removing the data point did change both the best fit line and the correlation coefficient, but only very slightly.

**23. a.**

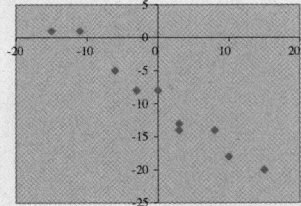

**b.** The correlation coefficient is approximately $r = -0.980$. This is identical to the $r$-value from Problem 17. This makes sense because simply interchanging the $x$ and $y$-values does not change how the points cluster together in the $xy$-plane.

**c.** The equation of the best fit line for the paired data $(y, x)$ is $x = -0.7607y - 9.4957$.

**d.** It is not reasonable to use the best fit line in (c) to find the predicted value of $x$ when $y = 23$ because this value falls outside the range of the given data. However, it is okay

to use the best fit line to find the predicted values of $x$ when $y = 2$ or $y = -16$. Indeed, the predicted value of $x$ when $y = 2$ is about $-11.0171$, and the predicted value of $x$ when $y = -16$ is about $2.6755$.

**25.** First, note that the scatterplot is given by

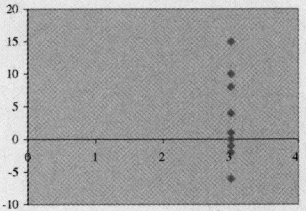

The paired data all lie identically on the vertical line $x = 3$. As such, you might think that the square of the correlation coefficient would be 1 and the best fit line is, in fact, $x = 3$. However, since there is absolutely no *variation* in the $x$-values for this data set, it turns out that in the formula for the correlation coefficient

$$r = \frac{n \sum xy - \left(\sum x\right)\left(\sum y\right)}{\sqrt{n \sum x^2 - \left(\sum x\right)^2} \cdot \sqrt{n \sum y^2 - \left(\sum y\right)^2}}$$

the quantity $\sqrt{n \sum x^2 - \left(\sum x\right)^2}$ turns out to be zero. (Check this on Excel for this data set!) As such, there is no meaningful $r$-value for this data set.

Also, the best fit line is definitely the vertical line $x = 3$, but the technology cannot provide it because its slope is undefined.

**27.** The $y$-intercept $1.257$ is mistakenly interpreted as the slope. The correct interpretation is that for every unit increase in $x$, the $y$-value increases by about $5.175$.

**29. a.** Here is a table listing all of the correlation coefficients between each of the events and the total points:

| Event | $r$ |
|---|---|
| 100 m | $-0.714$ |
| Long Jump | $0.768$ |
| Shot Put | $0.621$ |
| High Jump | $0.627$ |
| 400 m | $-0.704$ |
| 1500 m | $-0.289$ |
| 110 m hurdle | $-0.653$ |
| Discus | $0.505$ |
| Pole Vault | $0.283$ |
| Javeline | $0.421$ |

Long jump has the strongest relationship to the total points.

**b.** The correlation coefficient between *long jump* and *total events* is $r = 0.768$.

**c.** The equation of the best fit line between the two events in (b) is $y = 838.70x + 1957.77$.

**d.** Evaluate the equation in (c) at $x = 40$ to get the total points are about 35,506.

**31. a.** The following is a scatterplot illustrating the relationship between *left thumb length* and *total both scores*.

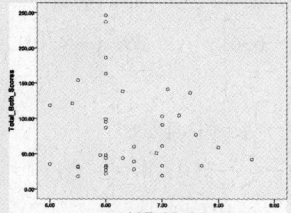

**b.** $r = -0.105$

**c.** The correlation coefficient ($r = -0.105$) indicates a weak relationship between left thumb length and total both scores.

**d.** The equation of the best fit line for these two events is $y = -7.62x + 127.73$.

**e.** No, given the weak correlation coefficient between total both scores and left thumb length, one could not use the best fit line to produce accurate predictions.

**33. a.** A scatterplot illustrating the relationship between *% residents immunized* and *% residents with influenza* is shown below.

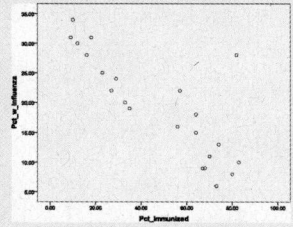

**b.** The correlation coefficient between *% residents immunized* and *% residents with influenza* is $r = -0.812$

**c.** Based on the correlation coefficient ($r = -0.812$), we would believe that there is a strong relationship between % residents immunized and % residents with influenza.

**d.** The equation of the best fit line that describes the relationship between *% residents immunized* and *% residents with influenza* is $y = -0.27x + 32.20$.

**e.** Since $r = -0.812$ indicates a strong relationship between % residents immunized and % residents with influenza, we can make a reasonably accurate prediction. However it will not be completely accurate.

**35. a.** A scatterplot illustrating the relationship between *average wait times* and *average rating of enjoyment* is shown below.

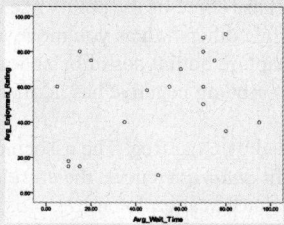

**b.** The correlation coefficient between *average wait times* and *average rating of enjoyment* is $r = 0.348$.

**c.** The correlation coefficient ($r = 0.348$) indicates a somewhat weak relationship between average wait times and average rating of enjoyment.

**d.** The equation of the best fit line that describes the relationship between *average wait times* and *average rating of enjoyment* is $y = 0.31x + 37.83$.

**e.** No, given the somewhat weak correlation coefficient between average wait times and average rating of enjoyment, one could not use the best fit line to produce accurate predictions.

**37. a.** A scatterplot illustrating the relationship between *average wait times* and *average rating of enjoyment* for *Park 2* is shown below.

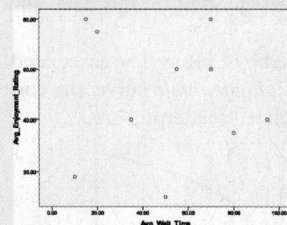

**b.** The correlation coefficient between *average wait times* and *average rating of enjoyment* is $r = -0.064$.

**c.** The correlation coefficient ($r = -0.064$) indicates a weak relationship between average wait times and average rating of enjoyment for Park 2.

**d.** The equation of the best fit line that describes the relationship between *average wait times* and *average rating of enjoyment* is $y = -0.05x + 52.53$.

**e.** No, given the weak correlation coefficient between average wait times and average rating of enjoyment for Park 2, one could not use the best fit line to produce accurate predictions.

**39. a.** The scatterplot for this data set is given by

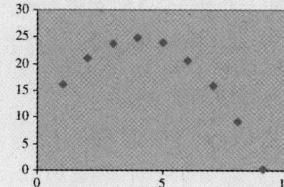

**b.** The equation of the best fit *line* is
$y = -1.9867x + 27.211$ with a correlation coefficient of
$r = -0.671$. This line does not seem to accurately
describe the data because some of the points rise as you
move left to right, while others fall as you move left to
right; a line cannot capture both types of behavior
simultaneously. Also, $r$ being negative has no meaning
here.

**c.** The best fit is provided by QuadReg. The associated
equation of the best fit *quadratic* curve, the correlation
coefficient, and associated scatterplot are:

 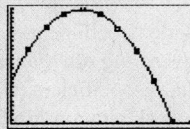

**41. a.** The scatterplot for this data set is given by

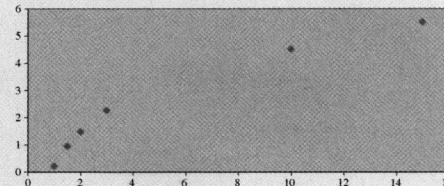

**b.** The equation of the best fit *line* is $y = 0.3537x + 0.5593$
with a correlation coefficient of $r = 0.971$. This line
seems to provide a very good fit for this data, although
not perfect.

**c.** The best fit is provided by LnReg. The associated
equation of the best fit *logarithmic* curve, the correlation
coefficient, and associated scatterplot are:

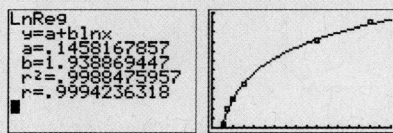

## Chapter 0 Review

**1.** $x = \frac{16}{7}$     **3.** $p = -\frac{8}{25}$     **5.** $x = 27$

**7.** $y = -\frac{17}{5}$     **9.** $b = \frac{6}{7}$     **11.** $x = -\frac{6}{17}$

**13.** \$5000@20%; \$20,000@8%

**15.** 60 ml of 5%; 90 ml of 10%

**17.** $b = -3, 7$    **19.** $x = 0, 8$    **21.** $q = \pm13$

**23.** $x = 2 \pm 4i$    **25.** $x = -2, 6$    **27.** $x = \frac{1 \pm \sqrt{33}}{2}$

**29.** $t = -1, \frac{7}{3}$    **31.** $f = \frac{1 \pm \sqrt{337}}{48}$    **33.** $q = \frac{3 \pm \sqrt{69}}{10}$

**35.** $x = -1, \frac{5}{2}$    **37.** $x = -3, \frac{2}{7}$    **39.** $h = 1$ ft, $b = 4$ ft

**41.** $x = \frac{6 \pm \sqrt{39}}{3}$    **43.** $t = -\frac{34}{5}, t \neq -4, 0$

**45.** $x = -\frac{1}{2}, x \neq 0$    **47.** $x = 6$    **49.** $x = 125$

**51.** no solution    **53.** $x \cong -0.6$    **55.** $y = \frac{1}{4}, 1$

**57.** $x = -\frac{125}{8}, 1$    **59.** $x = -\frac{1}{8}, -1$    **61.** $x = \pm2, \pm3i$

**63.** $x = 0, -8, 4$    **65.** $p = \pm2, 3$    **67.** $p = -\frac{1}{2}, \frac{5}{2}, 3$

**69.** $y = \pm9$    **71.** no solution    **73.** $x = 0.9667, 1.7$

**75.** $(4, \infty)$        **77.** $[8, 12]$

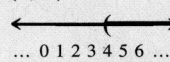

... 0 1 2 3 4 5 6 ...       ... 7 8 9 10 11 12 ...

**79.** $\left(-\infty, \frac{5}{3}\right)$    **81.** $\left(-\frac{3}{2}, \infty\right)$    **83.** $(4, 9]$

**85.** $\left[3, \frac{7}{2}\right]$    **87.** $[-6, 6]$    **89.** $(-\infty, 0] \cup [4, \infty)$

**91.** $\left(-\infty, -\frac{3}{4}\right) \cup (4, \infty)$

**93.** $(0, 3)$    **95.** $(-\infty, -6] \cup [9, \infty)$

**97.** $(-\infty, 2) \cup (4, 5]$    **99.** $(-\infty, -11) \cup (3, \infty)$

**101.** $(-\infty, -3) \cup (3, \infty)$    **103.** $\mathbb{R}$

**105.** $3\sqrt{5}$        **107.** $\sqrt{205}$

**109.** $\left(\frac{5}{2}, 6\right)$        **111.** $(3.85, 5.3)$

**113.** $(\pm2, 0), (0, \pm1)$    **115.** $(\pm3, 0)$, no $y$-intercepts

**117.** $y$-axis        **119.** origin

**121.**                  **123.**

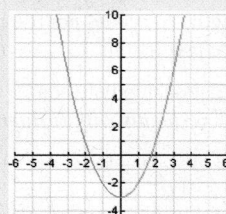   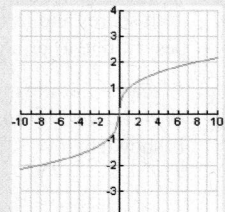

**125.**

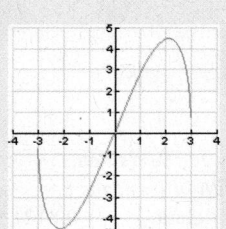

**127.** $(-2, -3), r = 9$      **129.** not a circle

**131.** $y = -2x - 2$      **133.** $y = 6$

**135.** $y = \frac{5}{6}x + \frac{4}{3}$      **137.** $y = -2x - 1$

**139.** $y = \frac{2}{3}x + \frac{1}{3}$      **141.** $C = 2\pi r$

**143.** $A = \pi r^2$

## Chapter 0 Practice Test

**1.** $p = -3$  **3.** $t = -4, 7$  **5.** $x = -\frac{1}{2}, \frac{8}{3}$

**7.** $y = -8$  **9.** $x = 4$  **11.** $y = 1$

**13.** $x = 0, 2, 6$  **15.** $(-\infty, 17]$  **17.** $\left(-\frac{32}{5}, -6\right]$

**19.** $(-\infty, -1] \cup \left[\frac{4}{3}, \infty\right)$  **21.** $\left(-\frac{1}{2}, 3\right]$

**23.** $\sqrt{82}$

**25.**

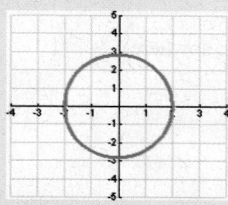

**27.** $(6, 0), (0, -2)$

**29.** $y = \frac{8}{3}x - 8$

**31.** $y = x + 5$

**33.** $y = -2x + 3$

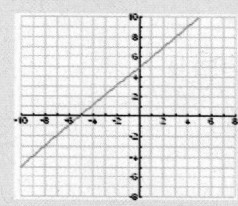

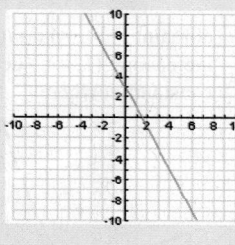

**35.** $F = \dfrac{30m}{P}$

# CHAPTER 1

## Section 1.1

**1.** not a function
**3.** not a function
**5.** function
**7.** not a function
**9.** not a function
**11.** function
**13.** not a function
**15.** function
**17.** not a function

**19. a.** 5  **b.** 1  **c.** $-3$
**21. a.** 3  **b.** 2  **c.** 5
**23. a.** $-5$  **b.** $-5$  **c.** $-5$
**25. a.** 2  **b.** $-8$  **c.** $-5$
**27.** 1
**29.** $-3$ and 1
**31.** $[-4, 4]$
**33.** 6
**35.** $-7$
**37.** 6
**39.** $-1$
**41.** $-33$
**43.** $-\frac{7}{6}$
**45.** $\frac{2}{3}$
**47.** 4
**49.** $8 - x - a$
**51.** $(-\infty, \infty)$
**53.** $(-\infty, \infty)$
**55.** $(-\infty, 5) \cup (5, \infty)$
**57.** $(-\infty, -2) \cup (-2, 2) \cup (2, \infty)$
**59.** $(-\infty, \infty)$
**61.** $(-\infty, 7]$
**63.** $\left[-\frac{5}{2}, \infty\right)$
**65.** $(-\infty, -2] \cup [2, \infty)$
**67.** $(3, \infty)$
**69.** $(-\infty, \infty)$
**71.** $(-\infty, -4) \cup (-4, \infty)$

**73.** $\left(-\infty, \frac{3}{2}\right)$  **75.** $(-\infty, -2) \cup (3, \infty)$

**77.** $(-\infty, -4] \cup [4, \infty)$  **79.** $\left(-\infty, \frac{3}{2}\right)$

**81.** $(-\infty, \infty)$  **83.** $x = -2, 4$  **85.** $x = -1, 5, 6$

**87.** $T(6) = 64.8°F, T(12) = 90°F$  **89.** 27 ft, $[0, 2.8]$

**91.** $V(x) = x(10 - 2x)^2, (0, 5)$

**93.** $E(4) \approx 84$ yen  **95.** 229 people
   $E(7) \approx 84$ yen
   $E(8) \approx 83$ yen

**97. a.** $A(x) = x(x - 3.375)$
   **b.** $A(4.5) \approx 5$. The area in the window is approximately 5 sq in.
   **c.** $A(8.5) \approx 44$. This is not possible because the window would be larger than the entire envelope (32 sq in.).

**99.** Yes, for every input (year), there corresponds a unique output (federal funds rate).

**101.** $(1989, 4000), (1993, 6000), (1997, 6000), (2001, 8000),$ $(2005, 11000)$

**103. a.** $F(50) = 0$  **b.** $g(50) = 1000$  **c.** $H(50) = 2000$

**105.** Should apply the <u>vertical</u> line test to determine if the relationship describes a function, which it is a function.

**107.** $f(x + 1) \neq f(x) + f(1)$, in general.

**109.** $G(-1 + h) \neq G(-1) + G(h)$, in general.

**111.** false  **113.** true  **115.** $A = 2$

**117.** $C = -5, D = -2$

**119.** $(-\infty, -a) \cup (-a, a) \cup (a, \infty)$

**121.** Warmest: noon, 90°F. The values of $T$ outside the interval $[6, 18]$ are too small to be considered temperatures in Florida.

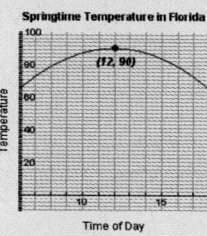

**123.** Shift graph of $f(x)$ two units to the right.

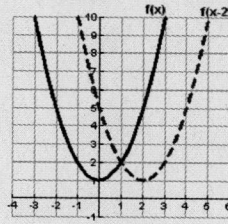

**125.** $f'(x) = 3x^2 + 1$

**127.** $f'(x) = \dfrac{8}{(x + 3)^2}$

## Section 1.2

**1.** neither　　　**3.** odd　　　**5.** even

**7.** even　　　**9.** neither　　　**11.** neither

**13.** neither　　　**15.** neither

**17. a.** $(-\infty, \infty)$　**b.** $[-1, \infty)$　**c.** increasing: $(-1, \infty)$,
decreasing: $(-3, -2)$, constant: $(-\infty, -3) \cup (-2, -1)$
**d.** 0　**e.** $-1$　**f.** 2

**19. a.** $[-7, 2]$　**b.** $[-5, 4]$　**c.** increasing: $(-4, 0)$,
decreasing: $(-7, -4) \cup (0, 2)$, constant: nowhere　**d.** 4
**e.** 1　**f.** $-5$

**21. a.** $(-\infty, \infty)$　**b.** $(-\infty, \infty)$　**c.** increasing:
$(-\infty, -3) \cup (4, \infty)$, decreasing: nowhere,
constant: $(-3, 4)$　**d.** 2　**e.** 2　**f.** 2

**23. a.** $(-\infty, \infty)$　**b.** $[-4, \infty)$　**c.** increasing: $(0, \infty)$,
decreasing: $(-\infty, 0)$, constant: nowhere　**d.** $-4$　**e.** 0　**f.** 0

**25. a.** $(-\infty, 0) \cup (0, \infty)$　**b.** $(-\infty, 0) \cup (0, \infty)$
**c.** increasing: $(-\infty, 0) \cup (0, \infty)$, decreasing: nowhere,
constant: nowhere　**d.** undefined　**e.** 3　**f.** $-3$

**27. a.** $(-\infty, 0) \cup (0, \infty)$　**b.** $(-\infty, 5) \cup [7]$
**c.** increasing: $(-\infty, 0)$, decreasing: $(5, \infty)$,
constant: $(0, 5)$　**d.** undefined　**e.** 3　**f.** 7

**29.** $2x + h - 1$　　　**31.** $2x + h + 3$

**33.** $2x + h - 3$　　　**35.** $-6x - 3h + 5$

**37.** $3x^2 + 3xh + h^2 + 2x + h$

**39.** $\dfrac{-2}{(x + h - 2)(x - 2)}$

**41.** $\dfrac{-2}{\sqrt{1 - 2(x + h)} + \sqrt{1 - 2x}}$

**43.** $\dfrac{-4}{\sqrt{x(x + h)}\left(\sqrt{x} + \sqrt{x + h}\right)}$

**45.** 13　　　**47.** 1　　　**49.** $-2$　　　**51.** $-1$

**53.** domain: $(-\infty, \infty)$　range: $(-\infty, 2]$
increasing: $(-\infty, 2)$　decreasing: nowhere
constant: $(2, \infty)$

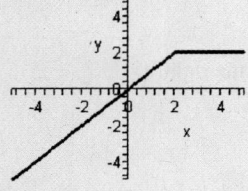

**55.** domain: $(-\infty, \infty)$　range: $[0, \infty)$
increasing: $(0, \infty)$　decreasing: $(-1, 0)$
constant: $(-\infty, -1)$

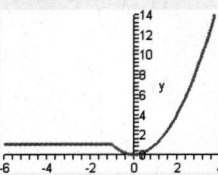

**57.** domain: $(-\infty, \infty)$　range: $(-\infty, \infty)$
increasing: $(-\infty, \infty)$　decreasing: nowhere
constant: nowhere

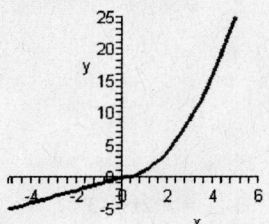

**59.** domain: $(-\infty, \infty)$　range: $[1, \infty)$
increasing: $(1, \infty)$　decreasing: $(-\infty, 1)$
constant: nowhere

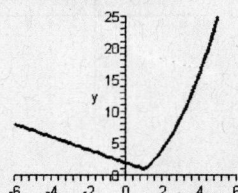

**61.**

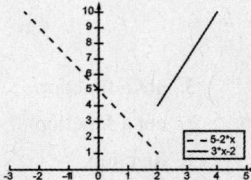

domain: $(-\infty, 2) \cup (2, \infty)$
range: $(1, \infty)$
increasing: $(2, \infty)$
decreasing: $(-\infty, 2)$

**63.** domain: $(-\infty, \infty)$　range: $[-1, 3]$
increasing: $(-1, 3)$　decreasing: nowhere
constant: $(-\infty, -1) \cup (3, \infty)$

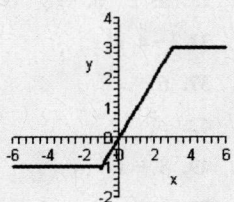

**65.** domain: $(-\infty, \infty)$   range: $[1, 4]$
increasing: $(1, 2)$   decreasing: nowhere
constant: $(-\infty, 1) \cup (2, \infty)$

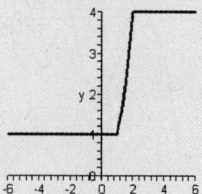

**67.** domain: $(-\infty, -2) \cup (-2, \infty)$
range: $(-\infty, \infty)$   increasing: $(-2, 1)$
decreasing: $(-\infty, -2) \cup (1, \infty)$
constant: nowhere

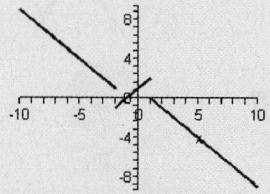

open holes $(-2, 1), (-2, -1), (1, 2)$, closed hole $(1, 0)$

**69.** domain: $(-\infty, \infty)$   range: $[0, \infty)$
increasing: $(0, \infty)$   decreasing: nowhere
constant: $(-\infty, 0)$

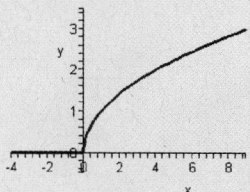

**71.** domain: $(-\infty, \infty)$   range: $(-\infty, \infty)$
increasing: nowhere
decreasing: $(-\infty, 0) \cup (0, \infty)$
constant: nowhere

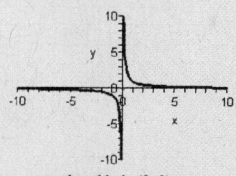

closed hole $(0, 0)$

**73.** domain: $(-\infty, 1) \cup (1, \infty)$
range: $(-\infty, -1) \cup (-1, \infty)$ increasing: $(-1, 1)$
decreasing: $(-\infty, -1) \cup (1, \infty)$
constant: nowhere

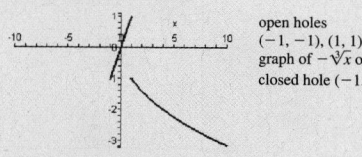

open holes
$(-1, -1), (1, 1), (1, -1)$
graph of $-\sqrt[3]{x}$ on $(-\infty, -1)$
closed hole $(-1, 1)$

**75.** domain: $(-\infty, \infty)$   range: $(-\infty, 2) \cup [4, \infty)$
increasing: $(-\infty, -2) \cup (0, 2) \cup (2, \infty)$
decreasing: $(-2, 0)$   constant: nowhere

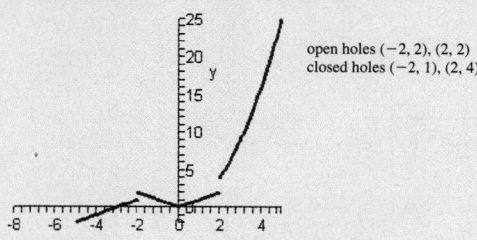

open holes $(-2, 2), (2, 2)$
closed holes $(-2, 1), (2, 4)$

**77.** domain: $(-\infty, 1) \cup (1, \infty)$
range: $(-\infty, 1) \cup (1, \infty)$
increasing: $(-\infty, 1) \cup (1, \infty)$
decreasing: nowhere   constant: nowhere

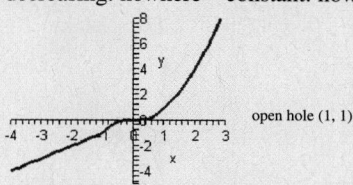

open hole $(1, 1)$

**79.** Profit is increasing from October through December and decreasing from January through October.

**81.** $C(x) = \begin{cases} 10x, & 0 \leq x \leq 50 \\ 9x, & 50 < x \leq 100 \\ 8x, & x > 100 \end{cases}$

**83.** $C(x) = \begin{cases} 250x, & 0 \leq x \leq 10 \\ 175x + 750, & x > 10 \end{cases}$

**85.** $C(x) = \begin{cases} 1000 + 35x, & 0 \leq x \leq 100 \\ 2000 + 25x, & x > 100 \end{cases}$

**87.** $R(x) = \begin{cases} 50{,}000 + 3x, & 0 \leq x \leq 100{,}000 \\ -50{,}000 + 4x, & x > 100{,}000 \end{cases}$

**89.** $P(x) = 65x - 800$

**91.** $f(x) = 0.80 + 0.17[\![x]\!], x \geq 0$

**93.** $f(t) = 3(-1)^{[\![t]\!]}, t \geq 0$

**95. a.** 20 per yr         **b.** 110 per yr

**97.** 0 ft/sec

**99.** Demand for the product is increasing at an approximate rate of 236 units over the first quarter.

**101.** Should exclude the origin since $x = 0$ is not in the domain. The range should be $(0, \infty)$.

**103.** The portion of $C(x)$ for $x > 30$ should be:
$15 + \underbrace{x - 30}_{\substack{\text{Number miles} \\ \text{beyond first 30}}}$

**105.** false                         **107.** yes, if $a = 2b$

**109.** yes, if $a = -4, b = -5$  **111.** odd  **113.** odd

**115.** domain: $\mathbb{R}$
range: set of integers

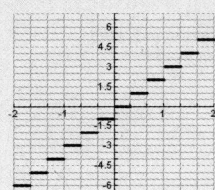

**117.** $f'(x) = 0$      **119.** $f'(x) = 2ax + b$

## Section 1.3

**1.** $y = |x| + 3$   **3.** $y = |-x| = |x|$    **5.** $y = 3|x|$

**7.** $y = x^3 - 4$   **9.** $y = (x + 1)^3 + 3$   **11.** $y = -x^3$

**13.**

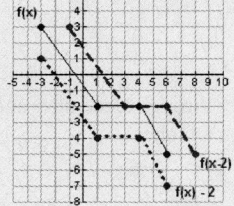

**15.**

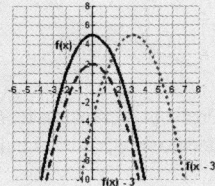

**17.**

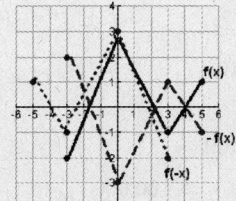

**19.**

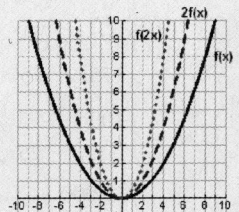

**21.**

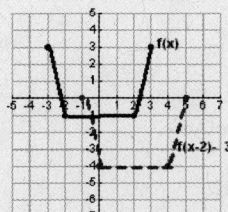

**23.**

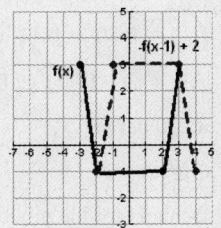

**25.**

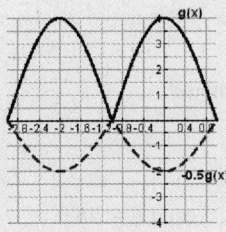

**27.**

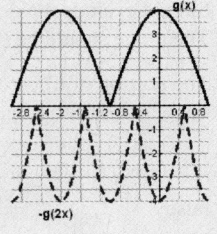

**29.**

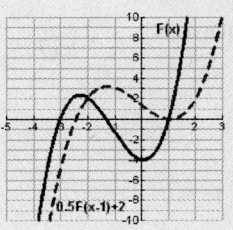

**31.**

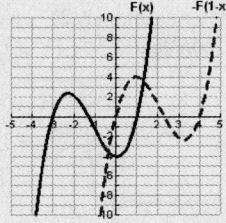

**33.**

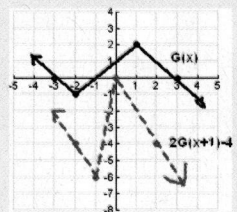

**35.**

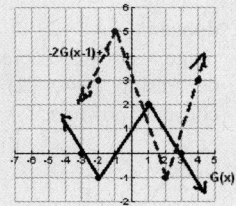

**37.**

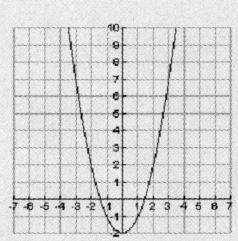

**39.**

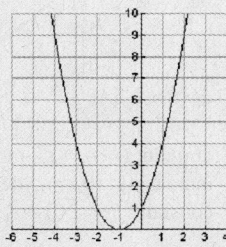

**41.**

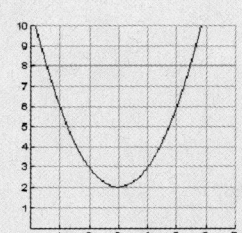

**43.**

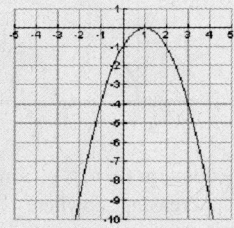

**45.**

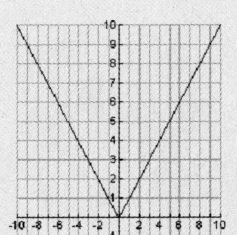

**47.**

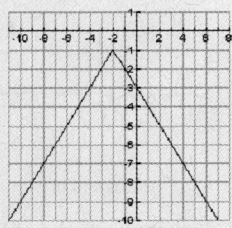

**49.**

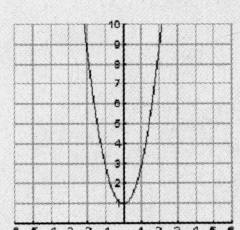

**51.**

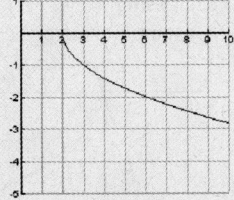

**53.**

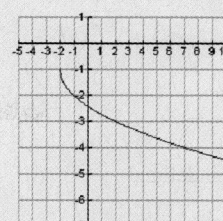

**55.**

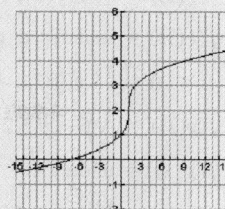

**57.**

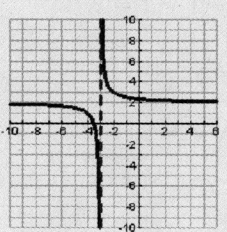

**59.**

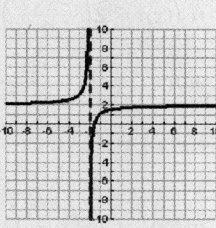

**61.**

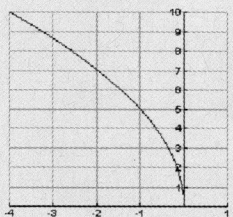

**63.** $f(x) = (x - 3)^2 + 2$

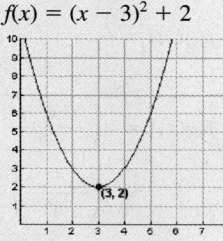

**65.** $f(x) = -(x + 1)^2 + 1$

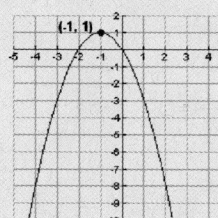

**67.** $f(x) = 2(x - 2)^2 - 5$

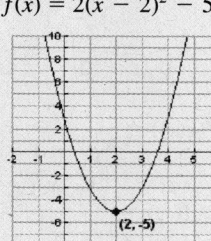

**69.** $S(x) = 10x$ and $S(x) = 10x + 50$

**71.** $T(x) = 0.33(x - 6500)$

**73.** $f(x) = 7.00 + 0.30x$, $f(x + 2) = 7.60 + 0.30x$

**75.** $Q(t) = P(t + 50)$

**77. a.** $\text{BSA}(w) = \sqrt{\dfrac{9w}{200}}$

**b.** $\text{BSA}(w - 3) = \sqrt{\dfrac{9(w - 3)}{200}}$

**79.** (b) is wrong − shift right three units.

**81.** (b) should be deleted since $|3 - x| = |x - 3|$.
The correct sequence of steps would be:
$(a) \rightarrow (c)^* \rightarrow (d)$, where
(c)*: Shift to the right three units.

**83.** true          **85.** true          **87.** true

**89.** $(a + 3, b + 2)$          **91.** $(a - 1, 2b - 1)$

**93.** Any part of the graph of $y = f(x)$ that is below the $x$-axis is reflected above it for the graph of $y = |f(x)|$.

**a.**

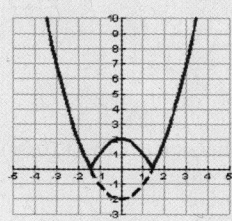

**b.**

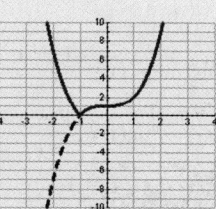

**95.** If $a > 1$, then the graph is a horizontal compression. If $0 < a < 1$, then the graph is a horizontal expansion.

**a.**

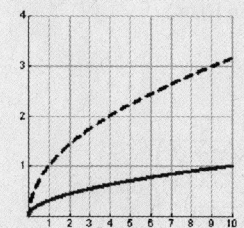

**b.**

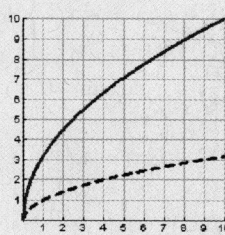

**97.** Each horizontal line in the graph of $y = [\![x]\!]$ is stretched by a factor of 2. Any portion of the graph that is below the $x$-axis is reflected above it. Also, there is a vertical shift up of one unit.

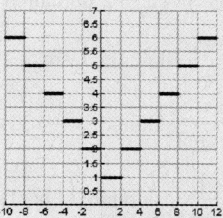

**99.** $f'(x) = 3x^2 + 1$, $g'(x) = 2(x - 1)$, $g'$ is obtained by shifting $f'$ left five units.

**101.** $f'(x) = 2$, $g'(x) = 2$, $f'$ and $g'$ are the same.

## Section 1.4

**1.**

$$\left.\begin{array}{l} f(x) + g(x) = x + 2 \\ f(x) - g(x) = 3x \\ f(x) \cdot g(x) = -2x^2 + x + 1 \end{array}\right\} \text{domain: } (-\infty, \infty)$$

$$\frac{f(x)}{g(x)} = \frac{2x + 1}{1 - x} \text{ domain: } (-\infty, 1) \cup (1, \infty)$$

**3.** 
$$\left.\begin{array}{l} f(x) + g(x) = 3x^2 - x - 4 \\ f(x) - g(x) = x^2 - x + 4 \\ f(x) \cdot g(x) = 2x^4 - x^3 - 8x^2 + 4x \end{array}\right\} \text{domain: } (-\infty, \infty)$$

$$\frac{f(x)}{g(x)} = \frac{2x^2 - x}{x^2 - 4} \quad \text{domain: } (-\infty, -2) \cup (-2, 2) \cup (2, \infty)$$

**5.**
$$\left.\begin{array}{l} f(x) + g(x) = \dfrac{1 + x^2}{x} \\[4pt] f(x) - g(x) = \dfrac{1 - x^2}{x} \\[4pt] f(x) \cdot g(x) = 1 \\[4pt] \dfrac{f(x)}{g(x)} = \dfrac{1}{x^2} \end{array}\right\} \text{domain: } (-\infty, 0) \cup (0, \infty)$$

**7.**
$$\left.\begin{array}{l} f(x) + g(x) = 3\sqrt{x} \\ f(x) - g(x) = -\sqrt{x} \\ f(x) \cdot g(x) = 2x \end{array}\right\} \text{domain } [0, \infty)$$

$$\frac{f(x)}{g(x)} = \frac{1}{2} \text{ domain: } (0, \infty)$$

**9.**
$$\left.\begin{array}{l} f(x) + g(x) = \sqrt{4 - x} + \sqrt{x + 3} \\ f(x) - g(x) = \sqrt{4 - x} - \sqrt{x + 3} \\ f(x) \cdot g(x) = \sqrt{4 - x} \cdot \sqrt{x + 3} \end{array}\right\} \text{domain: } [-3, 4]$$

$$\frac{f(x)}{g(x)} = \frac{\sqrt{4 - x}\sqrt{x + 3}}{x + 3} \text{ domain: } (-3, 4]$$

**11.** $(f \circ g)(x) = 2x^2 - 5$ domain: $(-\infty, \infty)$
$(g \circ f)(x) = 4x^2 + 4x - 2$ domain: $(-\infty, \infty)$

**13.** $(f \circ g)(x) = \dfrac{1}{x + 1}$ domain: $(-\infty, -1) \cup (-1, \infty)$

$(g \circ f)(x) = \dfrac{2x - 1}{x - 1}$ domain: $(-\infty, 1) \cup (1, \infty)$

**15.** $(f \circ g)(x) = \dfrac{1}{|x - 1|}$ domain: $(-\infty, 1) \cup (1, \infty)$

$(g \circ f)(x) = \dfrac{1}{|x| - 1}$ domain: $(-\infty, -1) \cup (-1, 1) \cup (1, \infty)$

**17.** $(f \circ g)(x) = \sqrt{x + 4}$ domain: $[-4, \infty)$
$(g \circ f)(x) = \sqrt{x - 1} + 5$ domain: $[1, \infty)$

**19.** $(f \circ g)(x) = x$ domain: $(-\infty, \infty)$
$(g \circ f)(x) = x$ domain: $(-\infty, \infty)$

**21.** 15     **23.** 13     **25.** $26\sqrt{3}$

**27.** $\frac{110}{3}$     **29.** 11     **31.** $3\sqrt{2}$

**33.** undefined     **35.** undefined     **37.** 13

**39.** $f(g(1)) = \frac{1}{3}$   $g(f(2)) = 2$

**41.** $f(g(1)) = $ undefined   $g(f(2)) = $ undefined

**43.** $f(g(1)) = \frac{1}{3}$   $g(f(2)) = 4$

**45.** $f(g(1)) = \sqrt{5}$   $g(f(2)) = 6$

**47.** $f(g(1)) = $ undefined   $g(f(2)) = $ undefined

**49.** $f(g(1)) = \sqrt[3]{3}$   $g(f(2)) = 4$

**51.** $f(g(x)) = 2\left(\dfrac{x - 1}{2}\right) + 1 = x - 1 + 1 = x$

$g(f(x)) = \dfrac{(2x + 1) - 1}{2} = \dfrac{2x}{2} = x$

**53.** $f(g(x)) = \sqrt{(x^2 + 1) - 1} = \sqrt{x^2} = \underbrace{|x|}_{\text{Since } x \geq 1} = x$

$g(f(x)) = \left(\sqrt{x - 1}\right)^2 + 1 = (x - 1) + 1 = x$

**55.** $f(g(x)) = \dfrac{1}{\frac{1}{x}} = x$   $g(f(x)) = \dfrac{1}{\frac{1}{x}} = x$

**57.** $f(g(x)) = 4\left(\dfrac{\sqrt{x + 9}}{2}\right)^2 - 9$

$= 4\left(\dfrac{x + 9}{4}\right) - 9 = x$

$g(f(x)) = \dfrac{\sqrt{(4x^2 - 9) + 9}}{2}$

$= \dfrac{\sqrt{4x^2}}{2} = \dfrac{2x}{2} = x$

**59.** $f(g(x)) = \dfrac{1}{\frac{x+1}{x} - 1} = \dfrac{1}{\frac{x+1-x}{x}} = \dfrac{1}{\frac{1}{x}} = x$

$g(f(x)) = \dfrac{\frac{1}{x-1} + 1}{\frac{1}{x-1}} = \dfrac{\frac{1+x-1}{x-1}}{\frac{1}{x-1}} = \dfrac{\frac{x}{x-1}}{\frac{1}{x-1}} = x$

**61.** $f(x) = 2x^2 + 5x$   $g(x) = 3x - 1$

**63.** $f(x) = \dfrac{2}{|x|}$   $g(x) = x - 3$

**65.** $f(x) = \dfrac{3}{\sqrt{x} - 2}$   $g(x) = x + 1$

**67.** $F(C(K)) = \frac{9}{5}(K - 273.15) + 32$

**69. a.** $A(x) = \left(\dfrac{x}{4}\right)^2$   **b.** $A(100) = 625 \text{ ft}^2$

   **c.** $A(200) = 2500 \text{ ft}^2$

**71. a.** $C(p) = 62,000 - 20p$
   **b.** $R(p) = 600,000 - 200p$
   **c.** $P(p) = 538,000 - 180p$

**73. a.** $C(n(t)) = -10t^2 + 500t + 1375$

**b.** $C(n(16)) = 6815$

The cost of production on a day when the assembly line was running for 16 hours is $6,815,000.

**75. a.** $A(r(t)) = \pi\left(10t - 0.2t^2\right)^2$

**b.** 11,385 sq mi

**77.** $A(t) = \pi\left[150\sqrt{t}\right]^2 = 22,500\pi t$ ft²

**79.** $d(h) = \sqrt{h^2 + 4}$

**81.** Must exclude $-2$ from the domain

**83.** $(f \circ g)(x) = f(g(x))$, not $f(x) \cdot g(x)$

**85.** Function notation, not multiplication

**87.** false       **89.** true

**91.** $(g \circ f)(x) = \dfrac{1}{x}$ domain: $x \neq 0, a$

**93.** $(g \circ f)(x) = x$ domain: $[-a, \infty)$

**95.**

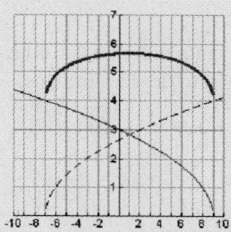

domain: $[-7, 9]$

**97.**

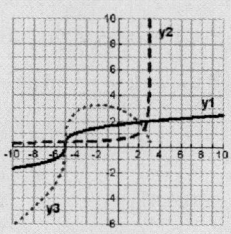

domain: $(-\infty, 3) \cup (-3, -1] \cup [4, 6) \cup (6, \infty)$

**99.** $H'(x) = F'(x) + G'(x)$

**101.** $H'(x) \neq F'(x)G'(x)$

## Section 1.5

**1.** not a function

**3.** function, not one-to-one

**5.** function, not one-to-one

**7.** function, one-to-one

**9.** function, not one-to-one

**11.** not one-to-one function

**13.** one-to-one function

**15.** not one-to-one function

**17.** one-to-one function

**19.**

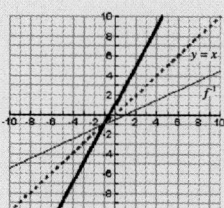

**21.**

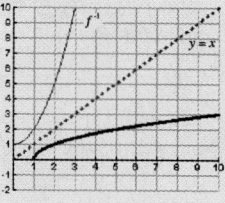

**23.**

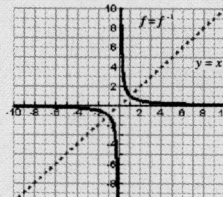

**25.**

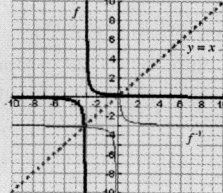

**27.**

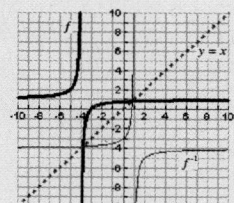

**29.**

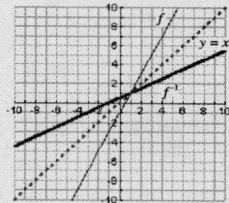

**31.**

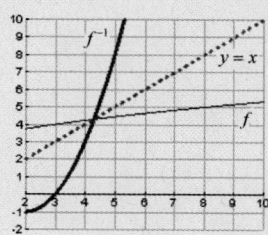

**33.**

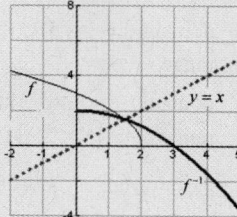

**35.**

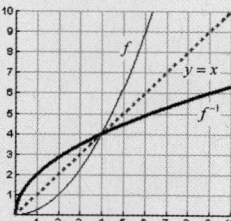

**37.** $f^{-1}(x) = -\frac{1}{3}x + \frac{2}{3}$

domain $f$: $(-\infty, \infty)$ domain $f^{-1}$: $(-\infty, \infty)$

range $f$: $(-\infty, \infty)$   range $f^{-1}$: $(-\infty, \infty)$

**39.** $f^{-1}(x) = \sqrt[3]{x-1}$

domain $f$: $(-\infty, \infty)$  domain $f^{-1}$: $(-\infty, \infty)$
range $f$: $(-\infty, \infty)$  range $f^{-1}$: $(-\infty, \infty)$

**41.** $f^{-1}(x) = x^2 + 3$

domain $f$: $[3, \infty)$  domain $f^{-1}$: $[0, \infty)$
range $f$: $[0, \infty)$  range $f^{-1}$: $[3, \infty)$

**43.** $f^{-1}(x) = \sqrt{x+1}$

domain $f$: $[0, \infty)$  domain $f^{-1}$: $[-1, \infty)$
range $f$: $[-1, \infty)$  range $f^{-1}$: $[0, \infty)$

**45.** $f^{-1}(x) = -2 + \sqrt{x+3}$

domain $f$: $[-2, \infty)$  domain $f^{-1}$: $[-3, \infty)$
range $f$: $[-3, \infty)$  range $f^{-1}$: $[-2, \infty)$

**47.** $f^{-1}(x) = \dfrac{2}{x}$

domain $f$: $(-\infty, 0) \cup (0, \infty)$
range $f$: $(-\infty, 0) \cup (0, \infty)$
domain $f^{-1}$: $(-\infty, 0) \cup (0, \infty)$
range $f^{-1}$: $(-\infty, 0) \cup (0, \infty)$

**49.** $f^{-1}(x) = \dfrac{3x-2}{x} = 3 - \dfrac{2}{x}$

domain $f$: $(-\infty, 3) \cup (3, \infty)$
range $f$: $(-\infty, 0) \cup (0, \infty)$
domain $f^{-1}$: $(-\infty, 0) \cup (0, \infty)$
range $f^{-1}$: $(-\infty, 3) \cup (3, \infty)$

**51.** $f^{-1}(x) = \dfrac{5x-1}{x+7}$

domain $f$: $(-\infty, 5) \cup (5, \infty)$
range $f$: $(-\infty, -7) \cup (-7, \infty)$
domain $f^{-1}$: $(-\infty, -7) \cup (-7, \infty)$
range $f^{-1}$: $(-\infty, 5) \cup (5, \infty)$

**53.** $f^{-1}(x) = \dfrac{1}{x^2}$

domain $f$ = range $f^{-1}$: $(0, \infty)$
range $f$ = domain $f^{-1}$: $(0, \infty)$

**55.** $f^{-1}(x) = \dfrac{2x^2+1}{x^2-1}$

domain $f$ = range $f^{-1}$: $(-\infty, -1] \cup (2, \infty)$
range $f$ = domain $f^{-1}$: $(-\infty, -1) \cup (-1, 1) \cup (1, \infty)$

**57.** not one-to-one.

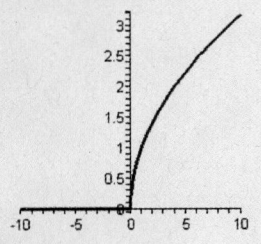

**59.** one-to-one

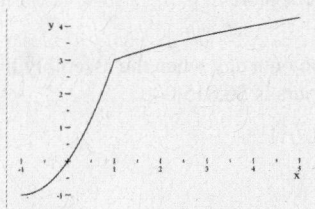

$$f^{-1}(x) = \begin{cases} x^3, & x \le -1, \\ -1 + \sqrt{x+1}, & -1 < x \le 1, \\ (x-2)^2, & x > 1 \end{cases}$$

**61.** one-to-one

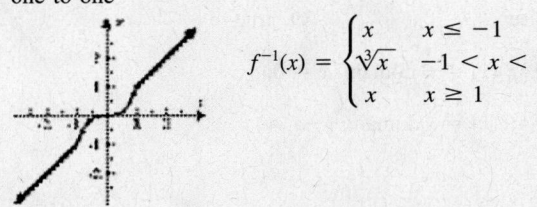

$$f^{-1}(x) = \begin{cases} x & x \le -1 \\ \sqrt[3]{x} & -1 < x < 1 \\ x & x \ge 1 \end{cases}$$

**63.** $f^{-1}(x) = \frac{5}{9}(x-32)$  The inverse function represents the conversion from degrees Fahrenheit to degrees Celsius.

**65.** $C(x) = \begin{cases} 250x, & 0 \le x \le 10 \\ 2500 + 175(x-10), & x > 10 \end{cases}$

$C^{-1}(x) = \begin{cases} \dfrac{x}{250}, & 0 \le x \le 2500 \\ \dfrac{x-750}{175}, & x > 2500 \end{cases}$

**67.** $E(x) = 5.25x$, $E^{-1}(x) = \dfrac{x}{5.25}$, $x \ge 0$ The inverse function tells you how many hours you need to work to attain a certain take home pay.

**69.** Domain: $[0, 24]$ Range: $[97.5528, 101.70]$

**71.** Domain: $[97.5528, 101.70]$ Range: $[0, 24]$

**73.** $M(x) = \begin{cases} 0.60x, & 0 \le x \le 15 \\ 0.60(15) + 0.90(x-15), & x > 15 \end{cases}$

$M^{-1}(x) = \begin{cases} \dfrac{5x}{3}, & 0 \le x \le 9 \\ \dfrac{10x}{9} + 5, & x > 9 \end{cases}$

**75.** $V(x) = \begin{cases} 20{,}000 - 600x, & 0 \le x \le 5, \\ 21{,}500 - 900x, & x > 5 \end{cases}$

$V^{-1}(x) = \begin{cases} \dfrac{21{,}500-x}{900}, & 0 \le x \le 17{,}000 \\ \dfrac{20{,}000-x}{600}, & 17{,}000 < x \le 20{,}000 \end{cases}$

**77.** Not a function since the graph does not pass the vertical line test

**79.** Must restrict the domain to a portion on which $f$ is one-to-one, say $x \geq 0$. Then, the calculation will be valid.

**81.** false      **83.** false      **85.** $(b, 0)$

**87.** $f(x) = \sqrt{1 - x^2}, \quad 0 \leq x \leq 1,$

$f^{-1}(x) = \sqrt{1 - x^2}, \quad 0 \leq x \leq 1$
Domain and range of both are $[0, 1]$.

**89.** $m \neq 0$

**91.** $a = 4, f^{-1}(x) = \dfrac{1 - 2x}{x}, (-\infty, 0) \cup (0, \infty)$

**93.** not one-to-one      **95.** not one-to-one

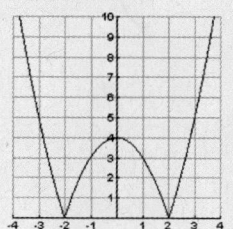 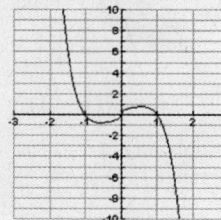

**97.** no      **99.**

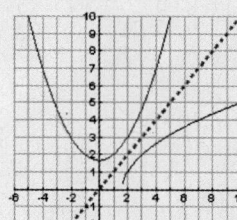 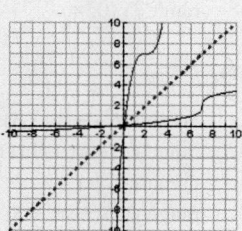

To be inverses, restrict the domain of the parabola to $[0, \infty)$.

**101. a.** $f^{-1}(x) = \dfrac{x - 1}{2}$    **b.** $f'(x) = 2$    **c.** $(f^{-1})'(x) = \frac{1}{2}$

**103. a.** $f^{-1}(x) = x^2 - 2, x \geq 0$    **b.** $f'(x) = \dfrac{1}{2\sqrt{x + 2}}$

     **c.** $(f^{-1})'(x) = 2x$

## Review Exercises

**1.** yes      **3.** no      **5.** yes      **7.** no

**9. a.** 2   **b.** 4   **c.** $x = -3, 4$

**11. a.** 0   **b.** $-2$   **c.** $x \approx -5, 2$

**13.** 5      **15.** $-665$      **17.** $-2$      **19.** 4

**21.** $(-\infty, \infty)$      **23.** $(-\infty, -4) \cup (-4, \infty)$      **25.** $[4, \infty)$

**27.** $D = 18$      **29.** odd      **31.** odd

**33. a.** $[-5, \infty)$   **b.** $[-3, \infty)$   **c.** increasing:
     $(-5, -3) \cup (3, \infty)$, decreasing: $(-1, 1)$,
     constant: $(-3, 1) \cup (1, 3)$   **d.** 2   **e.** 3   **f.** 1

**35. a.** $[-6, 6]$   **b.** $[0, 3] \cup \{-3, -2, -1\}$
     **c.** increasing: $(0, 3)$, decreasing: $(0, 3)$,
     contant: $(-6, -4) \cup (-4, -2) \cup (-2, 0)$
     **d.** $-1$   **e.** $-2$   **f.** 3

**37.** $3x^2 + 3xh + h^2$      **39.** $1 - \dfrac{1}{x(x + h)}$

**41.** $-2$

**43.** domain: $(-\infty, \infty)$
     range: $(0, \infty)$

**45.** domain: $(-\infty, \infty)$
     range: $[-1, \infty)$

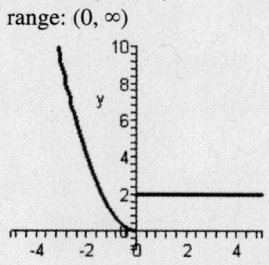 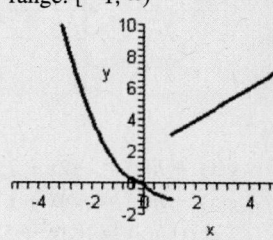

open hole $(0, 0)$, closed hole $(0, 2)$      open hole $(1, 3)$, closed hole $(1, -1)$

**47.** \$29,000 per year

**49.**              **51.**

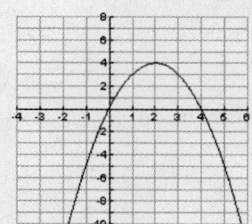 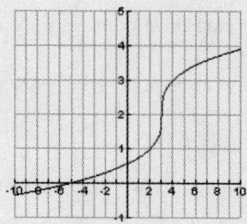

**53.**              **55.**

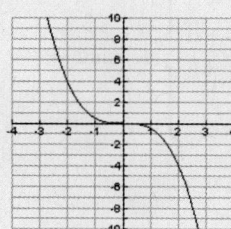 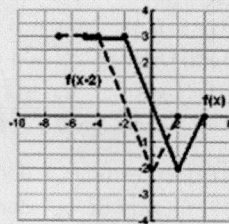

**57.**

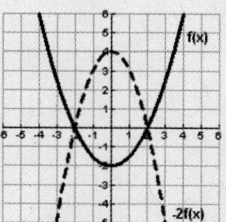

**59.** $y = \sqrt{x + 3}$   domain: $[-3, \infty)$

**61.** $y = \sqrt{x - 2} + 3$   domain: $[2, \infty)$

**63.** $y = 5\sqrt{x} - 6$   domain: $[0, \infty)$

**65.** $y = (x+2)^2 - 12$

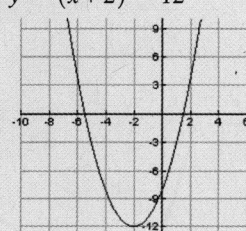

**67.**

$g(x) + h(x) = -2x - 7$
$g(x) - h(x) = -4x - 1$  } domain: $(-\infty, \infty)$
$g(x) \cdot h(x) = -3x^2 + 5x + 12$

$\dfrac{g(x)}{h(x)} = \dfrac{-3x - 4}{x - 3}$   domain: $(-\infty, 3) \cup (3, \infty)$

**69.**

$g(x) + h(x) = \dfrac{1}{x^2} + \sqrt{x}$

$g(x) - h(x) = \dfrac{1}{x^2} - \sqrt{x}$   } domain: $(0, \infty)$

$g(x) \cdot h(x) = \dfrac{1}{x^{3/2}}$

$\dfrac{g(x)}{h(x)} = \dfrac{1}{x^{5/2}}$

**71.**

$g(x) + h(x) = \sqrt{x - 4} + \sqrt{2x + 1}$
$g(x) - h(x) = \sqrt{x - 4} - \sqrt{2x + 1}$   } domain: $[4, \infty)$
$g(x) \cdot h(x) = \sqrt{x - 4} \cdot \sqrt{2x + 1}$
$\dfrac{g(x)}{h(x)} = \dfrac{\sqrt{x - 4}}{\sqrt{2x + 1}}$

**73.** $(f \circ g)(x) = 6x - 1$ domain: $(-\infty, \infty)$
$(g \circ f)(x) = 6x - 7$ domain: $(-\infty, \infty)$

**75.** $(f \circ g)(x) = \dfrac{8 - 2x}{13 - 3x}$
domain: $(-\infty, 4) \cup \left(4, \frac{13}{3}\right) \cup \left(\frac{13}{3}, \infty\right)$
$(g \circ f)(x) = \dfrac{x + 3}{4x + 10}$
domain: $(-\infty, -3) \cup \left(-3, -\frac{5}{2}\right) \cup \left(-\frac{5}{2}, \infty\right)$

**77.** $(f \circ g)(x) = \sqrt{(x - 3)(x + 3)}$
domain: $(-\infty, -3] \cup [3, \infty)$
$(g \circ f)(x) = x - 9$ domain: $[5, \infty)$

**79.** $f(g(3)) = 857, g(f(-1)) = 51$

**81.** $f(g(3)) = \frac{17}{31}, g(f(-1)) = 1$

**83.** $f(g(3)) = 12, g(f(-1)) = 2$

**85.** $f(x) = 3x^2 + 4x + 7, g(x) = x - 2$

**87.** $f(x) = \dfrac{1}{\sqrt{x}}, \ g(x) = x^2 + 7$

**89.** $A(t) = 625\pi(t + 2)$ in$^2$

**91.** yes     **93.** yes     **95.** yes

**97.** not one-to-one   **99.** one-to-one

**101.**                     **103.**

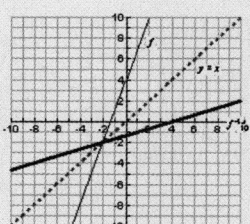     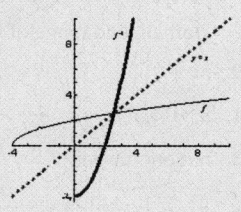

**105.** $f^{-1}(x) = \frac{1}{2}(x - 1) = \dfrac{x - 1}{2}$
domain $f$: $(-\infty, \infty)$   domain $f^{-1}$: $(-\infty, \infty)$
range $f$: $(-\infty, \infty)$   range $f^{-1}$: $(-\infty, \infty)$

**107.** $f^{-1}(x) = x^2 - 4$
domain $f$: $[-4, \infty)$   domain $f^{-1}$: $[0, \infty)$
range $f$: $[0, \infty)$   range $f^{-1}$: $[-4, \infty)$

**109.** $f^{-1}(x) = \dfrac{6 - 3x}{x - 1}$
domain $f$: $(-\infty, -3) \cup (-3, \infty)$
range $f$: $(-\infty, 1) \cup (1, \infty)$
domain $f^{-1}$: $(-\infty, 1) \cup (1, \infty)$
range $f^{-1}$: $(-\infty, -3) \cup (-3, \infty)$

**111.** $S(x) = 22{,}000 + 0.08x, S^{-1}(x) = \dfrac{x - 22{,}000}{0.08}$,
sales required to earn a desired income

**113.** domain: $(-\infty, -1) \cup (3, \infty)$

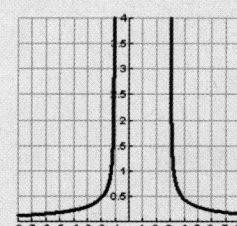

**115. a.** $(-\infty, 2) \cup (2, \infty)$   **b.** $\{-1, 0, 1\} \cup (2, \infty)$
**c.** increasing: $(2, \infty)$, decreasing: $(-\infty, -1)$, constant: $(-1, 2)$

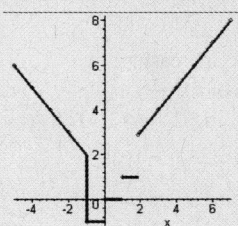

**117.** The graph of $f$ can be obtained by shifting the graph of $g$ two units to the left. That is, $f(x) = g(x + 2)$.

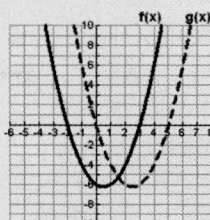

**119.** domain: $[-1.5, 4)$          **121.** yes

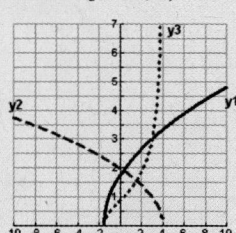 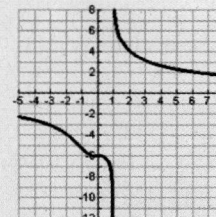

## Practice Test

**1.** b          **3.** c          **5.** $\dfrac{\sqrt{x-2}}{x^2+11}$ domain: $[2, \infty)$

**7.** $x + 9$ domain: $(2, \infty)$     **9.** 4     **11.** neither

**13.** domain: $[3, \infty)$   range: $(-\infty, 2]$

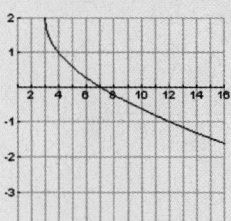

**15.** domain: $(-\infty, -1) \cup (-1, \infty)$   range: $[1, \infty)$

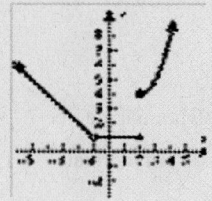

**17. a.** $-2$     **b.** 4     **c.** $-3$     **d.** $x = -3, 2$

**19.** $6x + 3h - 4$          **21.** $-32$

**23.** $f^{-1}(x) = x^2 + 5$
domain $f$: $[5, \infty)$   domain $f^{-1}$: $[0, \infty)$
range $f$: $[0, \infty)$   range $f^{-1}$: $[5, \infty)$

**25.** $f^{-1}(x) = \dfrac{5x - 1}{x + 2}$
domain $f$: $(-\infty, 5) \cup (5, \infty)$
range $f$: $(-\infty, -2) \cup (-2, \infty)$
domain $f^{-1}$: $(-\infty, -2) \cup (-2, \infty)$
range $f^{-1}$: $(-\infty, 5) \cup (5, \infty)$

**27.** $[0, \infty)$          **29.** $P(t) = \frac{9}{10}t + 10$

**31.** quadrant III, "quarter of unit circle"

**33.** $C(x) = \begin{cases} 15, & 0 \le x \le 30 \\ x-15, & x > 30 \end{cases}$

# CHAPTER 2

## Section 2.1

**1.** b          **3.** a          **5.** b          **7.** c

**9.**                              **11.**

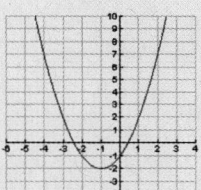 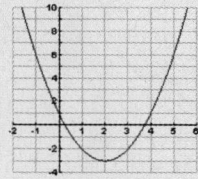

**13.**                             **15.**

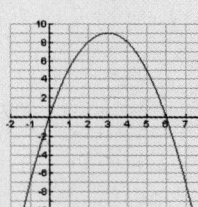 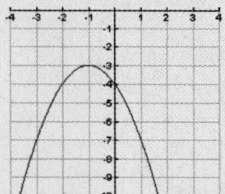

**17.**                             **19.**

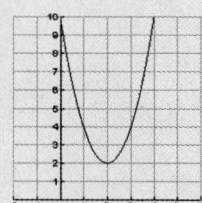 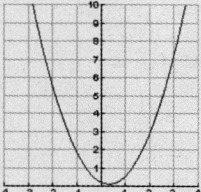

**21.**

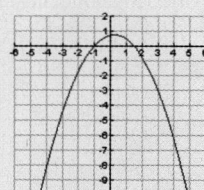

**23.** $f(x) = (x + 3)^2 - 12$

**25.** $f(x) = -(x + 5)^2 + 28$

**27.** $f(x) = 2(x + 2)^2 - 10$

**29.** $f(x) = -4(x - 2)^2 + 9$

**31.** $f(x) = (x + 5)^2 - 25$

**33.** $f(x) = \frac{1}{2}(x - 4)^2 - 5$

**35.**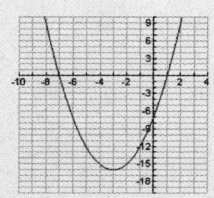

**37.**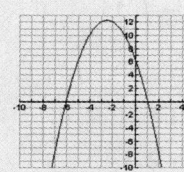

**39.**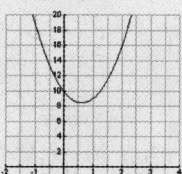

**41.**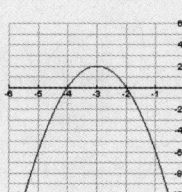

**43.**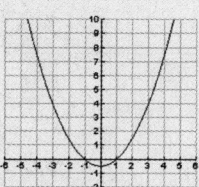

**45.** $\left(\frac{1}{33}, \frac{494}{33}\right)$

**47.** $\left(7, -\frac{39}{2}\right)$

**49.** $\left(\frac{15}{28}, \frac{829}{392}\right)$

**51.** $(-75, 12.95)$

**53.** $(21.67, -24.65)$

**55.** $y = -2(x + 1)^2 + 4$

**57.** $y = -5(x - 2)^2 + 5$

**59.** $y = \frac{5}{9}(x + 1)^2 - 3$

**61.** $y = 10(x + 2)^2 - 4$

**63.** $y = 12\left(x - \frac{1}{2}\right)^2 - \frac{3}{4}$

**65.** $y = \frac{5}{4}(x - 2.5)^2 - 3.5$

**67. a.** 350,000 units    **b.** $12,262,500

**69.** He is gaining weight during January of 2010 and losing weight from February 2010 to June 2011.

**71. a.** 120 ft    **b.** 50 yd    **73.** 2,083,333 sq ft

**75. a.** 1 sec, 116 ft    **b.** 3.69 sec

**77. a.** 26,000 ft    **b.** 8944 ft

**79. a.** 100 boards    **b.** $24,000

**81.** 15 to 16 or 64 to 65 units to break even.

**83. a.** $f(t) = \frac{28}{27}t^2 + 16$    **b.** 219 million

**85. a.** $y = -0.01(t - 225)^2 + 400$    **b.** 425 min

**87.** Step 2 is wrong: Vertex is $(-3, -1)$. Step 4 is wrong: The $x$-intercepts are $(-2, 0), (-4, 0)$. Should graph $y = (x + 3)^2 - 1$.

**89.** Step 2 is wrong: $(-x^2 + 2x) = -(x^2 - 2x)$

**91.** true                    **93.** false

**95.** $f(x) = a\left(x + \dfrac{b}{2a}\right)^2 + \dfrac{4ac - b^2}{4a}$

**97. a.** 62,500 sq ft    **b.** 79,577 sq ft

**99.** $x = 5$

**101. a.** $(1425, 4038.25)$    **b.** $(0, -23)$
 **c.** $(4.04, 0), (2845.96, 0)$
 **d.** $x = 1425$

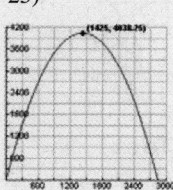

**103. a.** $y = -2x^2 + 12.8x + 4.32$
 **b.** $y = -2(x - 3.2)^2 + 24.8, (3.2, 24.8)$
 **c.** yes

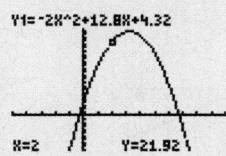

**105.** Plot

**107.** $\dfrac{(x - 0)^2}{9} + \dfrac{(y - 2)^2}{4} = 1$    ellipse

**109.** $(x + 3)^2 = 20\left(y + \frac{1}{5}\right)$    parabola

## Section 2.2

**1.** polynomial; degree 5        **3.** polynomial, degree 7

**5.** not a polynomial            **7.** not a polynomial

**9.** not a polynomial            **11.** h

**13.** b                **15.** e                **17.** c

**19.**                    **21.**

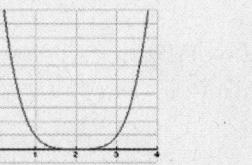

**23.**

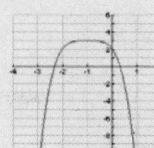

**25.** 3 (multiplicity 1), −4 (multiplicity 3)

**27.** 0 (multiplicity 2), 7 (multiplicity 2), −4 (multiplicity 1)

**29.** 0 (multiplicity 2), 1 (multiplicity 2)

**31.** 0 (multiplicity 1), $\frac{3}{2}$ (multiplicity 1), $-\frac{9}{4}$ (multiplicity 1)

**33.** 0 (multiplicity 2), −3 (multiplicity 1)

**35.** 0 (multiplicity 4)

**37.** $P(x) = x(x + 3)(x - 1)(x - 2)$

**39.** $P(x) = x(x + 5)(x + 3)(x - 2)(x - 6)$

**41.** $P(x) = (2x + 1)(3x - 2)(4x - 3)$

**43.** $P(x) = x^2 - 2x - 1$

**45.** $P(x) = x^2(x + 2)^3$

**47.** $P(x) = (x + 3)^2(x - 7)^5$

**49.** $P(x) = x^2(x + 1)(x + \sqrt{3})^2(x - \sqrt{3})^2$

**51.** $f(x) = (x - 2)^3$  **a.** 2 (multiplicity 3)
**b.** crosses at 2  **c.** (0, −8)  **d.** falls left, rises right
**e.**

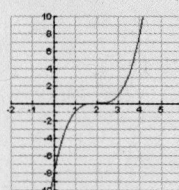

**53.** $f(x) = x(x - 3)(x + 3)$  **a.** 0, 3, −3 (multiplicity 1)
**b.** crosses at each zero  **c.** (0, 0)  **d.** falls left, rises right
**e.**

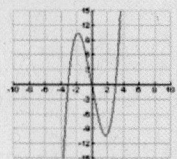

**55.** $f(x) = -x(x - 2)(x + 1)$  **a.** 0, 2, −1 (multiplicity 1)
**b.** crosses at each zero  **c.** (0, 0)  **d.** falls right, rises left
**e.**

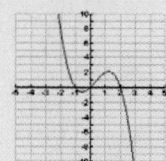

**57.** $f(x) = -x^3(x + 3)$  **a.** 0 (multiplicity 3), −3 (multiplicity 1)
**b.** crosses at both 0 and −3  **c.** (0, 0)  **d.** falls left and
right, without bound
**e.**

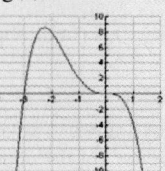

**59.** $f(x) = 12x^4(x - 4)(x + 1)$  **a.** 0 (multiplicity 4),
4 (multiplicity 1), −1 (multiplicity 1)
**b.** touches at 0 and crosses at 4 and −1
**c.** (0, 0)  **d.** rises left and right, without bound
**e.**

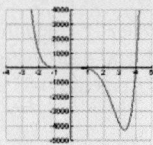

**61.** $f(x) = 2x^3(x - 4)(x + 1)$  **a.** 0 (multiplicity 3),
4 (multiplicity 1), −1 (multiplicity 1)
**b.** crosses at each zero  **c.** (0, 0)  **d.** falls left, rises right
**e.**

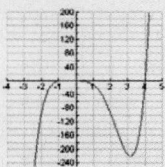

**63.** $f(x) = (x - 2)(x + 2)(x - 1)$  **a.** 1, 2, −2 (multiplicity 1)
**b.** crosses at each zero  **c.** (0, 4)  **d.** falls left, rises right
**e.**

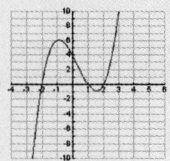

**65.** $f(x) = -(x + 2)^2(x - 1)^2$  **a.** −2 (multiplicity 2),
1 (multiplicity 2)  **b.** touches at both −2 and 1  **c.** (0, −4)
**d.** falls left and right, without bound
**e.**

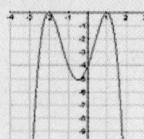

**67.** $f(x) = x^2(x - 2)^3(x + 3)^2$  **a.** 0 (multiplicity 2),
2 (multiplicity 3), −3 (multiplicity 2)
**b.** touches at both 0 and −3, and crosses at 2
**c.** (0, 0)  **d.** falls left, and rises right
**e.**

**69. a.** $-3$ (multiplicity 1), $-1$ (multiplicity 2), 2 (multiplicity 1)
**b.** even **c.** negative **d.** (0, 6)
**e.** $f(x) = -(x + 1)^2(x - 2)(x + 3)$

**71. a.** 0 (multiplicity 2), $-2$ (multiplicity 2), $\frac{3}{2}$ (multiplicity 1)
**b.** odd **c.** positive **d.** (0, 0)
**e.** $f(x) = x^2(2x - 3)(x + 2)^2$

**73. a.** Revenue for the company is increasing when advertising costs are less than \$400,000. Revenue for the company is decreasing when advertising costs are between \$400,000 and \$600,000.
**b.** The zeros of the revenue function occur when \$0 and \$600,000 are spent on advertising. When either \$0 or \$600,000 is spent on advertising, the company's revenue is \$0.

**75.** The velocity of air in the trachea is increasing when the radius of the trachea is between 0 and 0.45 cm and decreasing when the radius of the trachea is between 0.45 cm and 0.65 cm.

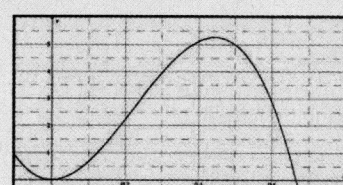

**77.** 6th degree polynomial   **79.** down

**81.** 4th degree   **83.** 4

**85.** between 35 and 39 degrees

**87.** If $h$ is a zero of a polynomial, then $(x - h)$ is a factor of it. So, in this case the function would be:
$P(x) = (x + 2)(x + 1)(x - 3)(x - 4)$

**89.** The zeros are correct. But it is a fifth degree polynomial. The graph should touch at 1 (since even multiplicity) and cross at $-2$. The graph should look like:

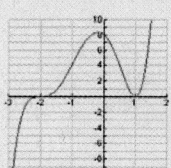

**91.** false   **93.** true   **95.** $n$

**97.** $f(x) = (x + 1)^2(x - 3)^5$, $g(x) = (x + 1)^4(x - 3)^3$

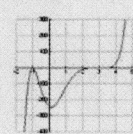
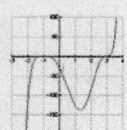

$h(x) = (x + 1)^6(x - 3)$

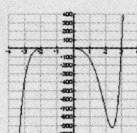

**99.** $0, a, -b$

**101.** no $x$-intercepts

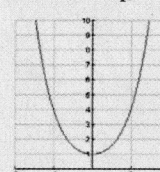

**103.** $y = -2x^5$, yes

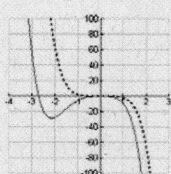

**105.** $x$-intercepts: $(-2.25, 0), (6.2, 0), (14.2, 0)$ zeros: $-2.25$ (multiplicity 2), 6.2 (multiplicity 1), 14.2, (multiplicity 1)

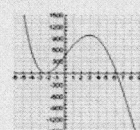

**107.**

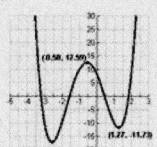

$(-2.56, -17.12)$
$(-0.58, 12.59)$
$(1.27, -11.73)$ ·

**109.** $x = 1.154$   **111.** $x = -0.865, x = 1.363$

## Section 2.3

**1.** $Q(x) = 3x - 3, \quad r(x) = -11$

**3.** $Q(x) = 3x - 28, \quad r(x) = 130$

**5.** $Q(x) = x - 4, \quad r(x) = 12$

**7.** $Q(x) = 3x + 5, \quad r(x) = 0$

**9.** $Q(x) = 2x - 3, \quad r(x) = 0$

**11.** $Q(x) = 4x^2 + 4x + 1, \quad r(x) = 0$

**13.** $Q(x) = 2x^2 - x - \frac{1}{2}, \quad r(x) = \frac{15}{2}$

**15.** $Q(x) = 4x^2 - 10x - 6, \quad r(x) = 0$

**17.** $Q(x) = -2x^2 - 3x - 9,$
$r(x) = -27x^2 + 3x + 9$

**19.** $Q(x) = x^2 + 1, \quad r(x) = 0$

**21.** $Q(x) = x^2 + x + \frac{1}{6}, \quad r(x) = -\frac{121}{6}x + \frac{121}{3}$

**23.** $Q(x) = -3x^3 + 5.2x^2 + 3.12x - 0.128,$
$r(x) = 0.9232$

**25.** $Q(x) = x^2 - 0.6x + 0.09, \quad r(x) = 0$

**27.** $Q(x) = 3x + 1, \quad r(x) = 0$

**29.** $Q(x) = 7x - 10, \quad r(x) = 15$

**31.** $Q(x) = -x^3 + 3x - 2, \quad r(x) = 0$

**33.** $Q(x) = x^3 - x^2 + x - 1, \quad r(x) = 2$

**35.** $Q(x) = x^3 - 2x^2 + 4x - 8$, $r(x) = 0$

**37.** $Q(x) = 2x^2 - 6x + 2$, $r(x) = 0$

**39.** $Q(x) = 2x^3 - \frac{5}{3}x^2 + \frac{53}{9}x + \frac{106}{27}$, $r(x) = -\frac{112}{81}$

**41.** $Q(x) = 2x^3 + 6x^2 - 18x - 54$, $r(x) = 0$

**43.** $Q(x) = x^6 + x^5 + x^4 - 7x^3 - 7x^2 - 4x - 4$, $r(x) = -3$

**45.** $Q(x) = x^5 + \sqrt{5}x^4 - 44x^3 - 44\sqrt{5}x^2 - 245x - 245\sqrt{5}$, $r(x) = 0$

**47.** $Q(x) = 2x - 7$, $r(x) = 0$

**49.** $Q(x) = x^2 - 9$, $r(x) = 0$

**51.** $Q(x) = x + 6$, $r(x) = -x + 1$

**53.** $Q(x) = x^4 - 2x^3 - 4x + 7$, $r(x) = 0$

**55.** $Q(x) = x^4 + 2x^3 + 8x^2 + 18x + 36$, $r(x) = 71$

**57.** $Q(x) = x^2 + 1$, $r(x) = -24$

**59.** $Q(x) = x^6 + x^5 + x^4 + x^3 + x^2 + x + 1$, $r(x) = 0$

**61.** $3x^2 + 2x + 1$ ft          **63.** $x^2 + 1$ hr

**65.** Should have subtracted each term in the long division rather than adding them.

**67.** Forgot the "0" placeholder.

**69.** true          **71.** false

**73.** false          **75.** yes

**77.** $Q(x) = x^{2n} + 2x^n + 1$, $r(x) = 0$

**79.** $2x - 1$          **81.** $x^3 - 1$

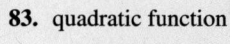

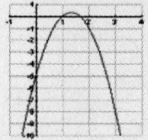

**83.** quadratic function

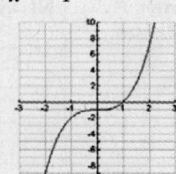

**85.** $(2x - 5) + \dfrac{10}{x + 2}$

**87.** $(2x^2 - 2x + 3) - \dfrac{x - 3}{x^2 + x + 1}$

## Section 2.4

**1.** $-4, 1, 3$; $P(x) = (x - 1)(x + 4)(x - 3)$

**3.** $-3, \frac{1}{2}, 2$; $P(x) = (2x - 1)(x + 3)(x - 2)$

**5.** $-3, 5$; $P(x) = (x^2 + 4)(x - 5)(x + 3)$

**7.** $-3, 1$; $P(x) = (x - 1)(x + 3)(x^2 - 2x + 2)$

**9.** $-2, -1$ (both multiplicity 2);
     $P(x) = (x + 2)^2(x + 1)^2$

**11.** $\pm 1, \pm 2, \pm 4$

**13.** $\pm 1, \pm 2, \pm 3, \pm 4, \pm 6, \pm 12$

**15.** $\pm\frac{1}{2}, \pm 1, \pm 2, \pm 4, \pm 8$

**17.** $\pm 1, \pm 2, \pm 4, \pm 5, \pm 10, \pm 20, \pm\frac{1}{5}, \pm\frac{2}{5}, \pm\frac{4}{5}$

**19.** $\pm 1, \pm 2, \pm 4, \pm 8$; rational zeros: $-4, -1, 2, 1$

**21.** $\pm 1, \pm 3, \pm\frac{1}{2}, \pm\frac{3}{2}$; rational zeros: $\frac{1}{2}, 1, 3$

**23.**

| POSITIVE REAL ZEROS | NEGATIVE REAL ZEROS |
|---|---|
| 1 | 1 |

**25.**

| POSITIVE REAL ZEROS | NEGATIVE REAL ZEROS |
|---|---|
| 1 | 0 |

**27.**

| POSITIVE REAL ZEROS | NEGATIVE REAL ZEROS |
|---|---|
| 2 | 1 |
| 0 | 1 |

**29.**

| POSITIVE REAL ZEROS | NEGATIVE REAL ZEROS |
|---|---|
| 1 | 1 |

**31.**

| POSITIVE REAL ZEROS | NEGATIVE REAL ZEROS |
|---|---|
| 2 | 2 |
| 0 | 2 |
| 2 | 0 |
| 0 | 0 |

**33.**

| POSITIVE REAL ZEROS | NEGATIVE REAL ZEROS |
|---|---|
| 4 | 0 |
| 2 | 0 |
| 0 | 0 |

**35. a.** Number of sign variations for $P(x)$: 0

Number of sign variations for $P(-x)$: 3

| POSITIVE REAL ZEROS | NEGATIVE REAL ZEROS |
|---|---|
| 0 | 3 |
| 0 | 1 |

   **b.** possible rational zeros: $\pm1, \pm2, \pm3, \pm6$

   **c.** rational zeros: $-1, -2, -3$

   **d.** $P(x) = (x + 1)(x + 2)(x + 3)$

**37. a.** Number of sign variations for $P(x)$: 2

Number of sign variations for $P(-x)$: 1

| POSITIVE REAL ZEROS | NEGATIVE REAL ZEROS |
|---|---|
| 2 | 1 |
| 0 | 1 |

   **b.** possible rational zeros: $\pm1, \pm7$

   **c.** rational zeros: $-1, 1, 7$

   **d.** $P(x) = (x + 1)(x - 1)(x - 7)$

**39. a.** Number of sign variations for $P(x)$: 1

Number of sign variations for $P(-x)$: 2

| POSITIVE REAL ZEROS | NEGATIVE REAL ZEROS |
|---|---|
| 1 | 2 |
| 1 | 0 |

   **b.** possible rational zeros: $\pm1, \pm2, \pm5, \pm10$

   **c.** rational zeros: $0, 1, -2, -5$

   **d.** $P(x) = x(x - 1)(x + 2)(x + 5)$

**41. a.** Number of sign variations for $P(x)$: 4

Number of sign variations for $P(-x)$: 0

| POSITIVE REAL ZEROS | NEGATIVE REAL ZEROS |
|---|---|
| 4 | 0 |
| 2 | 0 |
| 0 | 0 |

   **b.** possible rational zeros: $\pm1, \pm2, \pm13, \pm26$

   **c.** rational zeros: $1, 2$

   **d.** $P(x) = (x - 1)(x - 2)(x^2 - 4x + 13)$

**43. a.** Number of sign variations for $P(x)$: 2

Number of sign variations for $P(-x)$: 1

| POSITIVE REAL ZEROS | NEGATIVE REAL ZEROS |
|---|---|
| 2 | 1 |
| 0 | 1 |

   **b.** possible rational zeros: $\pm1, \pm\frac{1}{2}, \pm\frac{1}{5}, \pm\frac{1}{10}$

   **c.** rational zeros: $-1, -\frac{1}{2}, \frac{1}{5}$

   **d.** $P(x) = (x - 1)(2x + 1)(5x - 1)$

**45. a.** Number of sign variations for $P(x)$: 1

Number of sign variations for $P(-x)$: 2

| POSITIVE REAL ZEROS | NEGATIVE REAL ZEROS |
|---|---|
| 1 | 2 |
| 1 | 0 |

   **b.** possible rational zeros: $\pm1, \pm2, \pm5, \pm10, \pm\frac{1}{2}, \pm\frac{1}{3}, \pm\frac{1}{6}, \pm\frac{2}{3}$, $\pm\frac{5}{2}, \pm\frac{5}{3}, \pm\frac{5}{6}, \pm\frac{10}{3}$

   **c.** rational zeros: $-1, -\frac{5}{2}, \frac{2}{3}$

   **d.** $P(x) = 6(x + 1)\left(x + \frac{5}{2}\right)\left(x - \frac{2}{3}\right)$

**47. a.** Number of sign variations for $P(x)$: 4

Number of sign variations for $P(-x)$: 0

| POSITIVE REAL ZEROS | NEGATIVE REAL ZEROS |
|---|---|
| 4 | 0 |
| 2 | 0 |
| 0 | 0 |

   **b.** possible rational zeros: $\pm1, \pm2, \pm4$

   **c.** rational zeros: $1$

   **d.** $P(x) = (x - 1)^2(x^2 + 4)$

**49. a.** Number of sign variations for $P(x)$: 1

Number of sign variations for $P(-x)$: 1

| POSITIVE REAL ZEROS | NEGATIVE REAL ZEROS |
|---|---|
| 1 | 1 |

   **b.** possible rational zeros:
$\pm1, \pm2, \pm3, \pm4, \pm6, \pm9, \pm12, \pm18, \pm36$

   **c.** rational zeros: $-1, 1$

   **d.** $P(x) = (x + 1)(x - 1)(x^2 + 9)(x^2 + 4)$

**51. a.** Number of sign variations for $P(x)$: 4

Number of sign variations for $P(-x)$: 0

| POSITIVE REAL ZEROS | NEGATIVE REAL ZEROS |
|---|---|
| 4 | 0 |
| 2 | 0 |
| 0 | 0 |

**b.** possible rational zeros:

$\pm 1, \pm 5, \pm\frac{1}{2}, \pm\frac{1}{4}, \pm\frac{5}{2}, \pm\frac{5}{4}$

**c.** rational zeros: $\frac{1}{2}$

**d.** $P(x) = 4\left(x - \frac{1}{2}\right)^2(x^2 - 4x + 5)$

**53.**

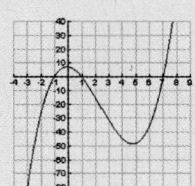

**55.**

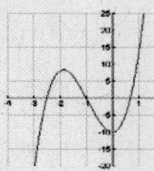

**57.** $x = 1.34$

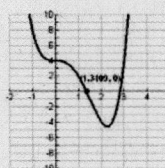

**59.** $x = 0.22$

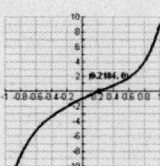

**61.** $x = -0.43$

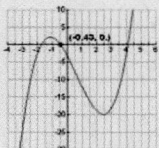

**63.** $x = 2.88$    **65.** 6 in. $\times$ 8 in.    **67.** 30 cows

**69.** $P(x) = -0.0002x^2 + 8x - 1500$; 0 or 2 positive real zeros

**71.** 18 hr

**73.** It is true that one can get 5 negative zeros here, but there may be just 1 or 3.

| POSITIVE REAL ZEROS | NEGATIVE REAL ZEROS |
|---|---|
| 0 | 5 |
| 0 | 3 |
| 0 | 1 |

**75.** true    **77.** false    **79.** false

**81.** $b, c$    **83.** $a, c,$ and $-c$

**85.** possible rational zeros:

$\pm 1, \pm 2, \pm 4, \pm 8, \pm 16, \pm 32$    zeros: 2

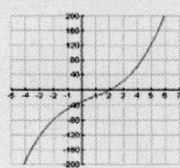

**87. a.** $-\frac{3}{4}, \frac{2}{3}$    **b.** $(3x - 2)(4x + 3)(x^2 + 2x + 5)$

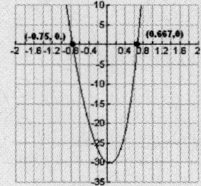

**89.** $1, 5, -2; (-2, -1) \cup (5, \infty)$

**91.** $-\frac{1}{2}, 3, \pm\sqrt{2}; \left(-\sqrt{2}, -\frac{1}{2}\right) \cup \left(\frac{1}{2}, 3\right)$

## Section 2.5

**1.** $x = \pm 2i; P(x) = (x + 2i)(x - 2i)$

**3.** $x = 1 \pm i; P(x) = (x - (1 - i))(x - (1 + i))$

**5.** $x = \pm 2, \pm 2i; P(x) = (x - 2)(x + 2)(x - 2i)(x + 2i)$

**7.** $x = \pm\sqrt{5}, \pm i\sqrt{5};$

$P(x) = (x - \sqrt{5})(x + \sqrt{5})(x - i\sqrt{5})(x + i\sqrt{5})$

**9.** $-i$    **11.** $-2i, 3 + i$

**13.** $1 + 3i, 2 - 5i$    **15.** $i, 1 + i$

**17.** $P(x) = x^3 - 2x^2 + 5x$

**19.** $P(x) = x^3 - 3x^2 + 28x - 26$

**21.** $P(x) = x^4 - 2x^3 + 11x^2 - 18x + 18$

**23.** $\pm 2i, -3, 5; P(x) = (x - 2i)(x + 2i)(x - 5)(x + 3)$

**25.** $\pm i, 1, 3; P(x) = (x - i)(x + i)(x - 3)(x - 1)$

**27.** $\pm 3i, 1$ (multiplicity 2); $P(x) = (x - 3i)(x + 3i)(x - 1)^2$

**29.** $1 \pm i, -1 \pm 2\sqrt{2};$

$P(x) = (x - (1 + i))(x - (1 - i)) \cdot$

$(x - (-1 - 2\sqrt{2}))(x - (-1 + 2\sqrt{2}))$

**31.** $3 \pm i, \pm 2;$

$P(x) = (x - (3 + i))(x - (3 - i))(x - 2)(x + 2)$

**33.** $2 \pm i, 1, 4;$
$P(x) = (x - (2 + i))(x - (2 - i))(x - 1)(x - 4)$

**35.** $P(x) = (x + 3i)(x - 3i)(x - 1)$

**37.** $P(x) = (x + i)(x - i)(x - 5)$

**39.** $P(x) = (x + 2i)(x - 2i)(x + 1)$

**41.** $P(x) = (x - 3)(x - (-1 + i\sqrt{5}))(x - (-1 - i\sqrt{5}))$

**43.** $P(x) = (x + 3)(x - 5)(x + 2i)(x - 2i)$

**45.** $P(x) = (x + 1)(x - 5)(x + 2i)(x - 2i)$

**47.** $P(x) = (x - 1)(x - 2)(x - (2 - 3i))(x - (2 + 3i))$

**49.** $P(x) = -(x + 1)(x - 2)(x - (2 - i))(x - (2 + i))$

**51.** $P(x) = (x - 1)^2(x + 2i)(x - 2i)$

**53.** $P(x) = (x - 1)(x + 1)(x - 2i)(x + 2i)(x - 3i)(x + 3i)$

**55.** $P(x) = (2x - 1)^2(x - (2 - i))(x - (2 + i))$

**57.** $P(x) = (x - 1)(x + 1)(3x - 2)(x - 2i)(x + 2i)$

**59.** Yes. In such case, $P(x)$ is always above the $x$-axis since the leading coefficient is positive, indicating that the end behavior should resemble that of $y = x^{2n}$, for some positive integer $n$. So, profit is always positive and increasing.

**61.** No. In such case, it crosses the $x$-axis and looks like $y = -x^3$. So, profit is decreasing.

**63.** Since the profit function is a third-degree polynomial, we know that the function has three zeros and at most two turning points. Looking at the graph, we can see there is one real zero where $t \le 0$. There are no real zeros when $t > 0$, so the other two zeros must be complex conjugates. Therefore, the company always has a profit greater than approximately 5.1 million dollars and, in fact, the profit will increase toward infinity as $t$ increases.

**65.** Since the concentration function is a third-degree polynomial, we know that the function has three zeros and at most two turning points. Looking at the graph, we can see there is one real zero sometimes $t \ge 8$. The remaining zeros are a complex conjugate pair. Therefore, the concentration of the drug in the bloodstream will decrease to zero as the hours go by. Note that the concentration will not approach negative infinity since concentration is a nonnegative quantity.

**67.** Step 2 is an error. In general, the additive inverse of a real root need not be a root. This is being confused with the fact that complex roots occur in conjugate pairs.

**69.** false          **71.** true

**73.** No. Complex zeros occur in conjugate pairs. So, the collection of complex solutions contributes an even number of zeros, thereby requiring there to be at least one real zero.

**75.** $P(x) = x^6 + 3b^2x^4 + 3b^4x^2 + b^6$

**77.** $P(x) = x^6 + (2a^2 + b^2)x^4 + (a^4 + 2a^2b^2)x^2 + b^2a^4$

**79.** All roots are complex.

| REAL ZEROS | COMPLEX ZEROS | |
|---|---|---|
| 0 | 4 | 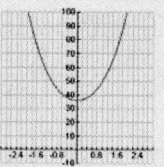 |
| 2 | 2 | |
| 4 | 0 | |

**81.** $\frac{3}{5}, \pm i, \pm 2i;$
$P(x) = -5(x - 0.6)(x - 2i)(x + 2i)(x - i)(x + i)$

**83. a.** $f(x) = (x + 1)(x - i)(x + i)$
**b.** $f(x) = (x + 1)(x^2 + 1)$

**85. a.** $f(x) = (x + 2i)(x - 2i)(x + i)(x - i)$
**b.** $f(x) = (x^2 + 4)(x^2 + 1)$

## Section 2.6

**1.** $(-\infty, -4) \cup (-4, 3) \cup (3, \infty)$

**3.** $(-\infty, -2) \cup (-2, 2) \cup (2, \infty)$

**5.** $(-\infty, \infty)$

**7.** $(-\infty, -2) \cup (-2, 3) \cup (3, \infty)$

**9.** HA: $y = 0$ VA: $x = -2$

**11.** HA: none VA: $x = -5$

**13.** HA: none VA: $x = \frac{1}{2}, x = -\frac{4}{3}$

**15.** HA: $y = \frac{1}{3}$ VA: none

**17.** $y = x + 6$          **19.** $y = 2x + 24$          **21.** $y = 4x + \frac{11}{2}$

**23.** b          **25.** a          **27.** e

**29.** 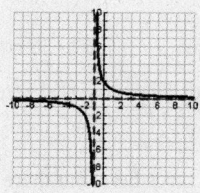          **31.**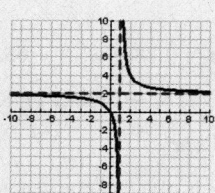

**33.** 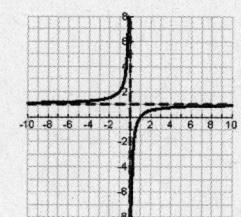          **35.**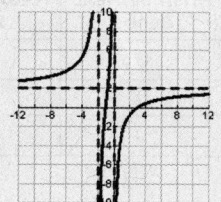

**37.**

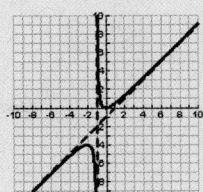

**39.**

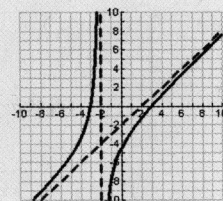

**41.**

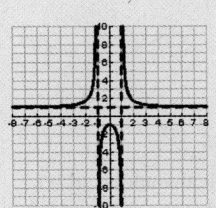

**43.**

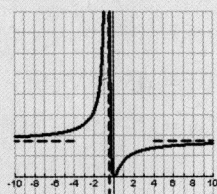

**45.**

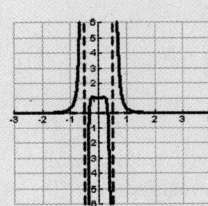

**47.**

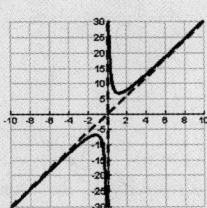

**49.**

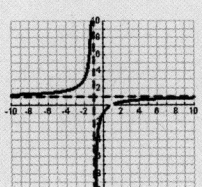

**51.**

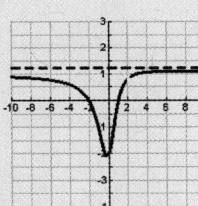

**53.**

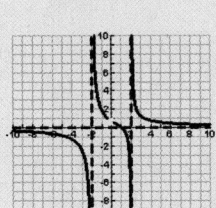

**55.** $y = \frac{1}{2}$

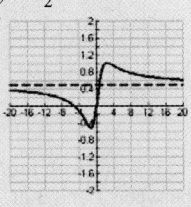

**57. a.** $x$-intercept: (2, 0); $y$-intercept: (0, 0.5)
  **b.** HA: $y = 0$    VA: $x = -1, x = 4$
  **c.** $f(x) = \dfrac{x-2}{(x+1)(x-4)}$

**59. a.** $x$-intercept: (0, 0); $y$-intercept: (0, 0)
  **b.** HA: $y = -3$    VA: $x = -4, x = 4$
  **c.** $f(x) = \dfrac{-3x^2}{(x+4)(x-4)}$

**61. a.** 4500 people  **b.** 6 mo  **c.** stabilizes around 9500

**63. a.** $C(1) \cong 0.0198$  **b.** $C(60) \cong 0.0324$
  **c.** $C(300) \cong 0$
  **d.** $y = 0$; after several days, $C(t) \cong 0$

**65. a.** $N(0) = 52$ wpm  **b.** $N(12) \cong 107$ wpm
  **c.** $N(36) \cong 120$ wpm  **d.** $y = 130$; 130 wpm

**67.** $y = 10$, 10 oz of food  **69.** $\dfrac{2w^2 + 1000}{w}$

**71.** 2000 or 8000 units; average profit of $16 per unit.

**73.** The concentration of the drug in the bloodstream 15 hours after taking the dose is approximately 25.4 μg/mL. There are two times, 1 hour and 15 hours, after taking the medication at which the concentration of the drug in the bloodstream is approximately 25.4 μg/mL. The first time, approximately 1 hour, occurs as the concentration of the drug is increasing to a level high enough that the body will be able to maintain a concentration of approximately 25 μg/mL throughout the day. The second time, approximately 15 hours, occurs many hours later in the day as the concentration of the medication in the bloodstream drops.

**75.** $f(x) = \dfrac{x-1}{x^2-1} = \dfrac{\cancel{x-1}}{\cancel{(x-1)}(x+1)} = \dfrac{1}{x+1}$ with a hole at $x = 1$. So $x = 1$ is not a vertical asymptote.

**77.** In Step 2, the ratio of the leading coefficients should be $\dfrac{-1}{1}$. So the horizontal asymptote is $y = -1$.

**79.** true  **81.** false

**83.** HA: $y = 1$    VA: $x = c, x = -d$

**85.** Two possibilities: $y = \dfrac{4x^2}{(x+3)(x-1)}$ and
  $y = \dfrac{4x^5}{(x+3)^3(x-1)^2}$

**87.** $f(x) = \dfrac{x^3+1}{x^2+1}$

**89.** VA: $x = -2$, yes  **91.** HA: $y = 0$   VA: $x = 0, x = -\frac{1}{3}$
  Intercepts: $\left(-\frac{2}{5}, 0\right)$, yes

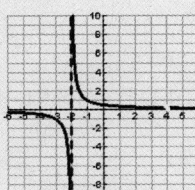
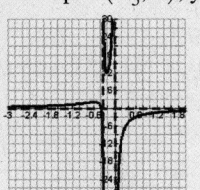

**93. a.** $f$: HA: $y = 0$ VA: $x = 3$
  $g$: HA: $y = 2$ VA: $x = 3$
  $h$: HA: $y = -3$ VA: $x = 3$
  **b.** graphs of $f$ and $g$: as
  $x \to \pm\infty, f(x) \to 0$ and $g(x) \to 2$

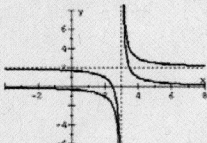

**c.** graphs of *g* and *h* below:

as $x \to \pm\infty$, $g(x) \to 2$ and $h(x) \to -3$

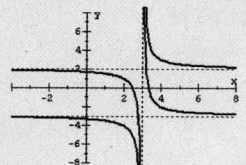

**d.** $g(x) = \dfrac{2x - 5}{x - 3}$, $h(x) = \dfrac{-3x + 10}{x - 3}$ yes

**95.** $x = -2, x = -1, x = 5$

**97.** $x = \frac{2}{3}, x = -\frac{1}{2}$

## Review Exercises

**1.** b

**3.** a

**5.**

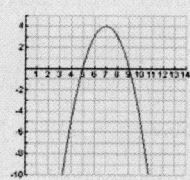

**7.**

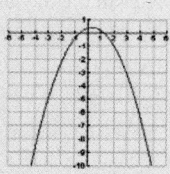

**9.** $f(x) = \left(x - \frac{3}{2}\right)^2 - \frac{49}{4}$

**11.** $f(x) = 4(x + 1)^2 - 11$

**13.**

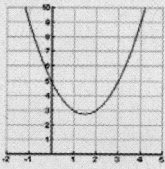

**15.**

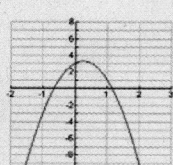

**17.** $\left(\frac{5}{26}, \frac{599}{52}\right)$

**19.** $\left(-\frac{2}{15}, \frac{451}{125}\right)$

**21.** $y = \frac{1}{9}(x + 2)^2 + 3$

**23.** $y = 5.6(x - 2.7)^2 + 3.4$

**25. a.** $P(x) = -2x^2 + \frac{35}{3}x - 14$

**b.** $x \cong 4.1442433, 1.68909$

**c.**

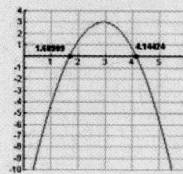

**d.** (1.6891, 4.144) or 1689 to 4144

**27.** $A(x) = -\frac{1}{2}(x - 1)^2 + \frac{9}{2}$, maximum at $x = 1$

base: 3 units, height: 3 units

**29.** yes, 6     **31.** no     **33.** d     **35.** a

**37.**

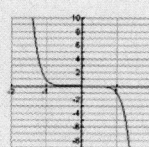

**39.**

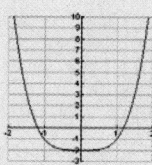

**41.** 6 (multiplicity 5), $-4$ (multiplicity 2)

**43.** $0, -2, 2, 3, -3$, all multiplicity 1

**45.** $f(x) = x(x + 3)(x - 4)$

**47.** $f(x) = x(5x + 2)(4x - 3)$

**49.** $f(x) = x^4 - 2x^3 - 11x^2 + 12x + 36$

**51.** $f(x) = (x - 7)(x + 2)$     **a.** $-2, 7$ (both multiplicity 1)

**b.** crosses at $-2, 7$   **c.** $(0, -14)$   **d.** rises right and left

**e.**

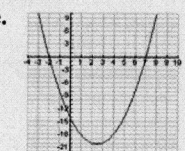

**53.** $f(x) = 6x^7 + 3x^5 - x^2 + x - 4$   **a.** (0.8748, 0) with
multiplicity 1   **b.** crosses at its only real zero   **c.** $(0, -4)$
**d.** falls left and rises right

**e.**

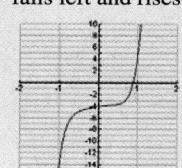

**55. a.**

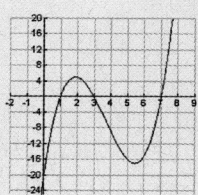

**b.** 1, 3, 7 (all with multiplicity 1)

**c.** between 1 and 3 hr, and more than 7 hr is financially
beneficial

**57.** $Q(x) = x + 4$,   $r(x) = 2$

**59.** $Q(x) = 2x^3 - 4x^2 - 2x - \frac{7}{2}$,   $r(x) = -23$

**61.** $Q(x) = x^3 + 2x^2 + x - 4$,   $r(x) = 0$

**63.** $Q(x) = x^5 - 8x^4 + 64x^3 - 512x^2 + 4096x - 32,768$,
$r(x) = 262,080$

**65.** $Q(x) = x + 3$,   $r(x) = -4x - 8$

**67.** $Q(x) = x^2 - 5x + 7, \quad r(x) = -15$

**69.** $3x^3 + 2x^2 - x + 4$ ft

**71.** $f(-2) = -207$      **73.** $g(1) = 0$

**75.** no      **77.** yes

**79.** $P(x) = x(x + 2)(x - 4)^2$    **81.** $P(x) = x^2(x + 3)(x - 2)^2$

**83.**

| POSITIVE REAL ZEROS | NEGATIVE REAL ZEROS |
|---|---|
| 1 | 1 |

**85.**

| POSITIVE REAL ZEROS | NEGATIVE REAL ZEROS |
|---|---|
| 5 | 2 |
| 5 | 0 |
| 3 | 2 |
| 3 | 0 |
| 1 | 2 |
| 1 | 0 |

**87.** possible rational zeros: $\pm1, \pm2, \pm3, \pm6$

**89.** possible rational zeros: $\pm1, \pm2, \pm4, \pm8, \pm16, \pm32, \pm64, \pm\frac{1}{2}$

**91.** possible rational zeros: $\pm1, \pm\frac{1}{2}$; zeros: $\frac{1}{2}$

**93.** possible rational zeros: $\pm1, \pm2, \pm4, \pm8, \pm16$; zeros: $1, 2, 4, -2$

**95. a.**

| POSITIVE REAL ZEROS | NEGATIVE REAL ZEROS |
|---|---|
| 1 | 0 |

**b.** $\pm1, \pm5$
**c.** $-1$ is a lower bound, 5 is an upper bound.
**d.** none   **e.** not possible
**f.**

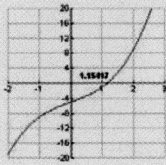

**97. a.**

| POSITIVE REAL ZEROS | NEGATIVE REAL ZEROS |
|---|---|
| 3 | 0 |
| 1 | 0 |

**b.** $\pm1, \pm2, \pm3, \pm4, \pm6, \pm12$
**c.** $-4$ is a lower bound, 12 is an upper bound.

**d.** $1, 2, 6$   **e.** $P(x) = (x - 1)(x - 6)(x - 2)$
**f.**

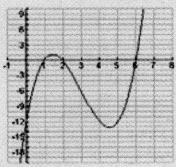

**99. a.**

| POSITIVE REAL ZEROS | NEGATIVE REAL ZEROS |
|---|---|
| 0 | 0 |
| 0 | 2 |
| 2 | 2 |
| 2 | 0 |

**b.** $\pm1, \pm2, \pm3, \pm4, \pm6, \pm8 \pm12, \pm24$
**c.** $-4$ is a lower bound, 8 is an upper bound.
**d.** $-2, -1, 1, 6$
**e.** $P(x) = (x - 2)(x + 1)(x + 2)(x - 6)$
**f.**

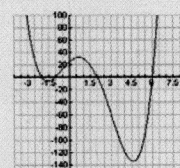

**101.** $P(x) = (x - 5i)(x + 5i)$

**103.** $P(x) = (x - (1 - 2i))(x - (1 + 2i))$

**105.** $2i, 3 - i$      **107.** $-i, 2 + I$

**109.** $-i, 4, -1; P(x) = (x - i)(x + i)(x - 4)(x + 1)$

**111.** $3i, 1 \pm i; P(x) = (x - 3i)(x + 3i)(x - (1 + i))(x - (1 - i))$

**113.** $P(x) = (x - 3)(x + 3)(x - 3i)(x + 3i)$

**115.** $P(x) = (x - 2i)(x + 2i)(x - 1)$

**117.** HA: $y = -1$   VA: $x = -2$

**119.** HA: none   VA: $x = -1$   Slant: $y = 4x - 4$

**121.** HA: $y = 2$   VA: none

**123.**                  **125.**

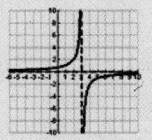 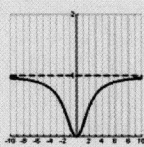

**127.**

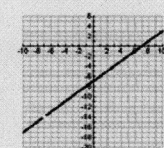

**129. a.** $(480, -1211)$  **b.** $(0, -59)$  **c.** $(-12.14, 0), (972.14, 0)$
**d.** $x = 480$

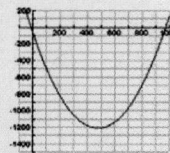

**131.** $x$-intercepts: $(-1, 0), (0.4, 0), (2.8, 0)$; zeros: $-1, 0.4, 2.8$,
each with multiplicity 1

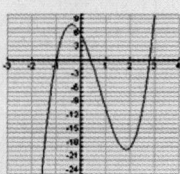

**133.** linear function

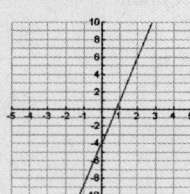

**135. a.** $-2$ (multiplicity 2), 3, 4
**b.** $P(x) = (x + 2)^2(x - 3)(x - 4)$

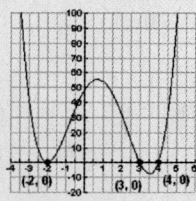

**137.** $\frac{7}{2}, -2 \pm 3i$; $P(x) = (2x - 7)(x + 2 - 3i)(x + 2 + 3i)$

**139. a.** yes, one-to-one  **b.** $f^{-1}(x) = \dfrac{-3 - x}{x - 2}$

**c.**

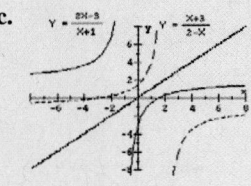

## Practice Test

**1.**

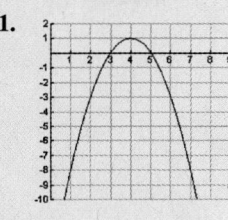

**3.** $\left(3, \frac{1}{2}\right)$                 **5.** $f(x) = x(x - 2)^3(x - 1)^2$

**7.** $Q(x) = -2x^2 - 2x - \frac{11}{2}$,  $r(x) = -\frac{19}{2}x + \frac{7}{2}$

**9.** yes                 **11.** $P(x) = (x - 7)(x + 2)(x - 1)$

**13.** yes, complex zero

**15.** possible rational zeros: $\pm 1, \pm 2, \pm 3, \pm 4, \pm 6, \pm 12, \pm\frac{1}{3}, \pm\frac{2}{3}, \pm\frac{4}{3}$

**17.** $\frac{3}{2}, \pm 2i$                 **19.** degree 3

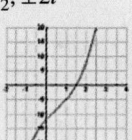     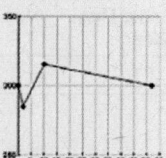

**21.** degree 3

**23. a.** $x$-intercept: $(0, 0)$, $y$-intercept: $(0, 0)$
**b.** $x = \pm 2$  **c.** $y = 0$  **d.** none
**e.**

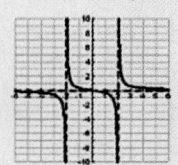

**25. a.** $x$-intercept: $(3, 0)$, $y$-intercept: $\left(0, \frac{3}{8}\right)$
**b.** $x = -2, x = 4$  **c.** $y = 0$
**d.** none  **e.**

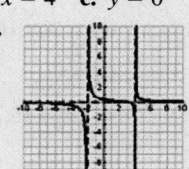

**27. a.** $y = x^2 - 3x - 7.99$
**b.** $y = (x - 1.5)^2 - 10.24$  **c.** $(-1.7, 0)$ and $(4.7, 0)$
**d.** yes

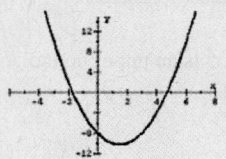

## Cumulative Test

**1.** $f(2) = \frac{15}{2}, f(-1) = -5, f(1 + h) = 4 + 4h - \dfrac{1}{\sqrt{h + 3}}$,

$f(-x) = -4x - \dfrac{1}{\sqrt{2 - x}}$

**3.** $f(-3) = \frac{7}{2}, f(0) = -\frac{5}{2}, f(4) = -\frac{7}{18}$, $f(1)$ is undefined.

**5.** $\dfrac{1}{\sqrt{x + h} + \sqrt{x}} + \dfrac{2x + h}{x^2(x + h)^2}$

**7. a.**

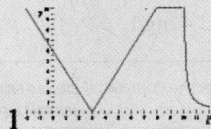

**b.** domain: $(-\infty, 10) \cup (10, \infty)$, range: $[0, \infty)$

**c.** increasing: $(3, 8)$, decreasing: $(-\infty, 3) \cup (10, \infty)$, constant: $(8, 10)$

**9.** $-\frac{1}{28}$            **11.** neither

**13.** right one unit and then up three units

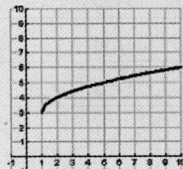

**15.** $g(f(-1)) = 0$      **17.** $f(x) = (x + 2)^2 + 3$

**19.** $Q(x) = 4x^2 + 4x + 1$, $r(x) = -8$

**21.** possible rational zeros:

$\pm 1, \pm 2, \pm 3, \pm 4, \pm 6, \pm\frac{1}{2}, \pm\frac{1}{3}, \pm\frac{1}{4}, \pm\frac{1}{6}, \pm\frac{1}{12}, \pm\frac{2}{3}, \pm\frac{3}{2}, \pm\frac{3}{4}, \pm\frac{1}{4}$

zeros: $-2, -\frac{3}{4}, \frac{1}{3}$

**23.** $P(x) = (x + 1)(x - 2)(x - 4)$

**25.** HA: $y = 0$   VA: $x = \pm 2$

**27.** $f(x) = \dfrac{3(x + 1)}{x(2x - 3)}$    $x$-intercepts: $(-1, 0)$

HA: $y = 0$
VA: $x = 0$, $x = \frac{3}{2}$
yes

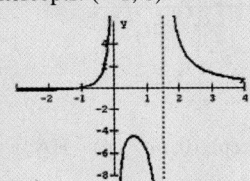

# CHAPTER 3

## Section 3.1

**1.** $\frac{1}{25}$    **3.** 4    **5.** 27    **7.** 9.7385    **9.** 7.3891

**11.** 0.0432    **13.** 27    **15.** 16    **17.** 4

**19.** 19.81    **21.** f    **23.** e    **25.** b

**27.** $y$-intercept: $(0, 1)$   HA: $y = 0$
domain: $(-\infty, \infty)$   range: $(0, \infty)$
other points: $\left(-1, \frac{1}{6}\right)$, $(1, 6)$

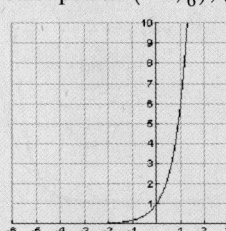

**29.** $y$-intercept: $(0, 1)$   HA: $y = 0$
domain: $(-\infty, \infty)$   range: $(0, \infty)$
other points: $(1, 0.1)$, $(-1, 10)$

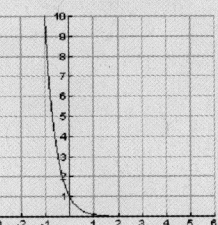

**31.** $y$-intercept: $(0, 1)$   HA: $y = 0$
domain: $(-\infty, \infty)$   range: $(0, \infty)$
other points: $(1, e)$, $(2, e^2)$

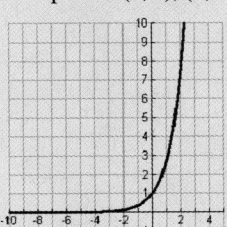

**33.** $y$-intercept: $(0, 1)$   HA: $y = 0$
domain: $(-\infty, \infty)$   range: $(0, \infty)$
other points: $\left(1, \frac{1}{e}\right)$, $(-1, e)$

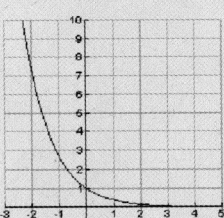

**35.** $y$-intercept: $(0, 0)$    HA: $y = -1$
domain: $(-\infty, \infty)$    range: $(-1, \infty)$
other points: $(2, 3)$, $(1, 1)$

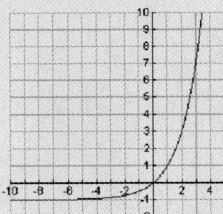

**37.** $y$-intercept: $(0, 1)$    HA: $y = 2$
domain: $(-\infty, \infty)$    range: $(-\infty, 2)$
other points: $(1, 2 - e)$, $\left(-1, 2 - \frac{1}{e}\right)$

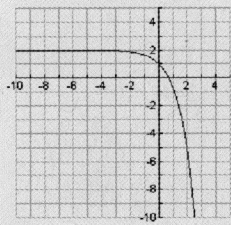

**39.** *y*-intercept: (0, 6)   HA: *y* = 5
domain: $(-\infty, \infty)$   range: $(5, \infty)$
other points: (1, 5.25), (−1, 9)

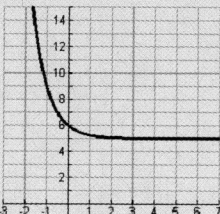

**41.** *y*-intercept: (0, *e* − 4)   HA: *y* = −4
domain: $(-\infty, \infty)$   range: $(-4, \infty)$
other points: (−1, −3), $(1, e^2 - 4)$

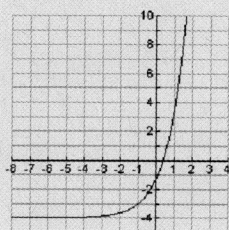

**43.** *y*-intercept: (0, 3)   HA: *y* = 0
domain: $(-\infty, \infty)$   range: $(0, \infty)$
other points: (2, 3*e*), $\left(1, 3\sqrt{e}\right)$

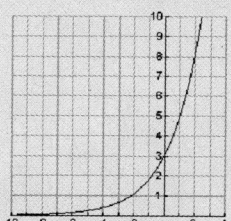

**45.** *y*-intercept: (0, 5)   HA: *y* = 1
domain: $(-\infty, \infty)$   range: $(1, \infty)$
other points: (0, 5), (2, 2)

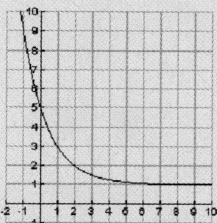

**47.** 10.4 million

**49.** $P(30) = 1500\left(2^{30/5}\right) \cong 96{,}000$

**51.** 168 mg          **53.** 2 mg

**55.** $3031          **57.** $3448.42

**59.** $13,011.03          **61.** $4319.55

**63.** $13,979.42          **65.** 3.4 mg/L

**67.**

| *p* (PRICE PER UNIT) | *D(p)*—APPROXIMATE DEMAND FOR PRODUCT IN UNITS |
|---|---|
| 1.00 | 1,955,000 |
| 5.00 | 1,020,500 |
| 10.00 | 452,810 |
| 20.00 | 89,147 |
| 40.00 | 3455 |
| 60.00 | 134 |
| 80.00 | 5 |
| 90.00 | 1 |

**69.** The mistake is that $4^{-1/2} \neq 4^2$. Rather,
$$4^{-1/2} = \frac{1}{4^{1/2}} = \frac{1}{2}.$$

**71.** *r* = 0.025 rather than 2.5

**73.** false          **75.** true

**77.**

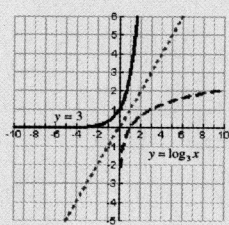

**79.**

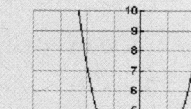

**81.** *y*-intercept: (0, *be* − *a*)   HA: *y* = −*a*

**83.** Domain: $(-\infty, \infty)$

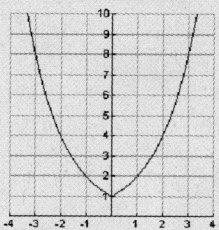

**85.**

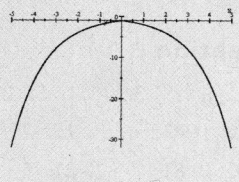

**87.**

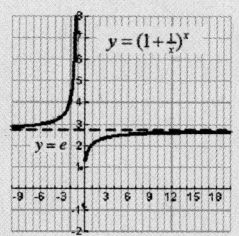

**89.** close on the interval (−3, 3)

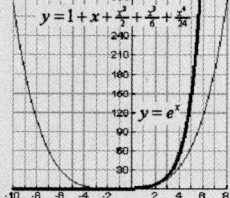

1110

**91.** as $x$ increases,
$f(x) \rightarrow e$, $g(x) \rightarrow e^2$, $h(x) \rightarrow e^4$

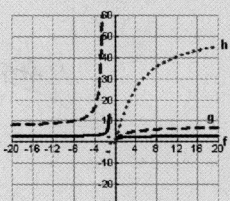

**93. a.**

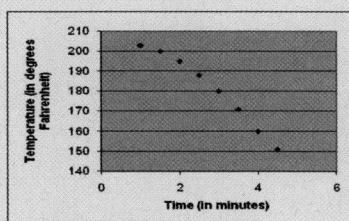

**b.** The best fit exponential curve is $y = 228.34\,(0.9173)^x$ with $r^2 = 0.9628$. This best fit curve is shown below on the scatterplot. The fit is very good, as evidenced by the fact that the square of the correlation coefficient is very close to 1.

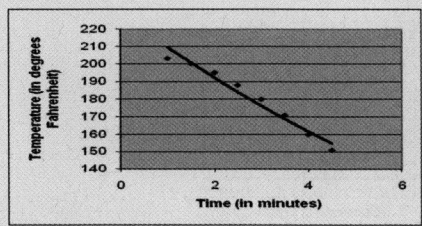

**c. (i)** Compute the $y$-value when $x = 6$ to obtain about 136°F.
  **(ii)** The temperature of the soup the moment it was taken out of the microwave is the $y$-value at $x = 0$, namely, about 228°F.
**d.** The shortcoming of this model for large values of $x$ is that the curve approaches the $x$-axis, not 72°. As such, it is no longer useful for describing the temperature beyond the $x$-value at which the temperature is 72°.

**95.** odd

## Section 3.2

**1.** $81^{1/4} = 3$  **3.** $2^{-5} = \frac{1}{32}$  **5.** $10^{-2} = 0.01$

**7.** $10^4 = 10{,}000$  **9.** $\left(\frac{1}{4}\right)^{-3} = 64$  **11.** $e^{-1} = \frac{1}{e}$

**13.** $e^0 = 1$  **15.** $e^x = 5$  **17.** $x^z = y$

**19.** $y^x = x + y$  **21.** $\log(0.00001) = -5$

**23.** $\log_5 78{,}125 = 5^7$  **25.** $\log_{225}(15) = \frac{1}{2}$

**27.** $\log_{2/5}\left(\frac{8}{125}\right) = 3$  **29.** $\log_{1/27}(3) = -\frac{1}{3}$  **31.** $\ln 6 = x$

**33.** $\log_y x = z$  **35.** 0  **37.** 5

**39.** 7  **41.** $-6$  **43.** undefined

**45.** undefined  **47.** 1.46  **49.** 5.94

**51.** undefined  **53.** $-8.11$  **55.** $(-5, \infty)$

**57.** $\left(-\infty, \frac{5}{2}\right)$  **59.** $\left(-\infty, \frac{7}{2}\right)$  **61.** $(-\infty, 0) \cup (0, \infty)$

**63.** $\mathbb{R}$  **65.** $(-2, 5)$  **67.** b

**69.** c  **71.** d

**73.** domain: $(1, \infty)$  **75.** domain: $(0, \infty)$
  range: $(-\infty, \infty)$    range: $(-\infty, \infty)$

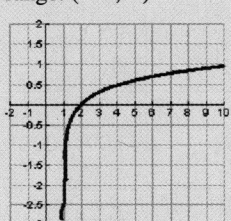  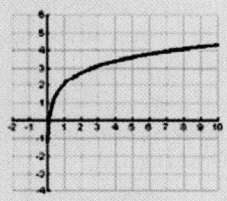

**77.** domain: $(-2, \infty)$  **79.** domain: $(0, \infty)$
  range: $(-\infty, \infty)$    range: $(-\infty, \infty)$

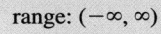

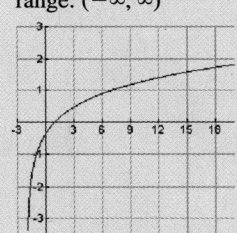  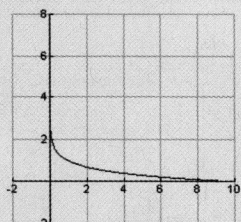

**81.** domain: $(-4, \infty)$  **83.** domain: $(0, \infty)$
  range: $(-\infty, \infty)$    range: $(-\infty, \infty)$

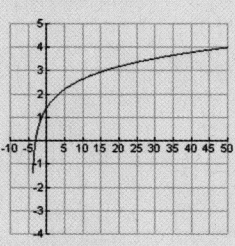  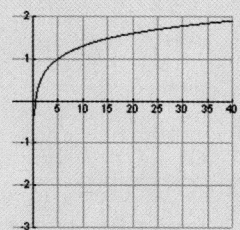

**85.** 60 dB  **87.** 117 dB  **89.** 8.5  **91.** 6.6  **93.** 3.3

**95.** Normal rainwater: 5.6
  Acid rain/tomato juice: 4

**97.** 3.6  **99.** 13,236 yr  **101.** 25 dB loss

**103. a.**

| Usage | Wavelength | Frequency |
|---|---|---|
| Super Low Frequency— Communication with Submarines | 10,000,000 m | 30 Hz |
| Ultra Low Frequency— Communication within Mines | 1,000,000 m | 300 Hz |
| Very Low Frequency— Avalanche Beacons | 100,000 m | 3000 Hz |
| Low Frequency— Navigation, AM Longwave Broadcasting | 10,000 m | 30,000 Hz |
| Medium Frequency— AM Bradcasts, Amatuer Radio | 1,000 m | 300,000 Hz |
| High Frequency— Shortwave broadcasts, Citizens Band Radio | 100 m | 3,000,000 Hz |
| Very High Frequency— FM Radio, Television | 10 m | 30,000,000 Hz |
| Ultra High Frequency— Television, Mobile Phones | 0.050 m | 6,000,000,000 Hz |

**b.**

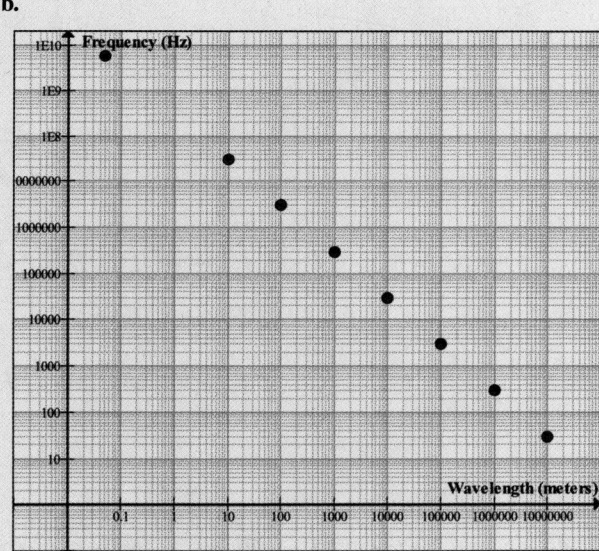

**105.** $\log_2 4 = x$ is equivalent to $2^x = 4$ (not $x = 2^4$).

**107.** The domain is the set of all real numbers such that $x + 5 > 0$, which is written as $(-5, \infty)$.

**109.** false **111.** true

**113.** domain: $(a, \infty)$ range: $(-\infty, \infty)$
$x$-intercept: $(a + e^b, 0)$

**115.**

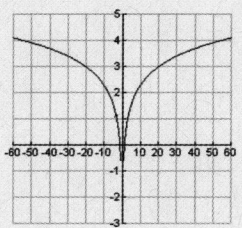

**117.** $y = x$

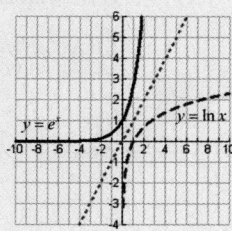

**119.** $x$-intercept: $(1, 0)$
VA: $x = 0$

**121.** $(0, \infty)$

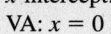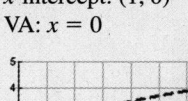

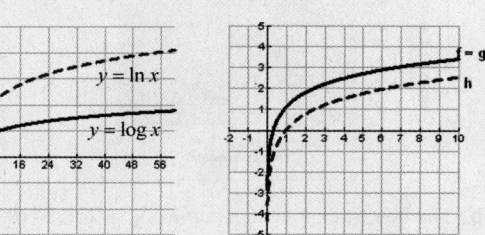

**123. a.**

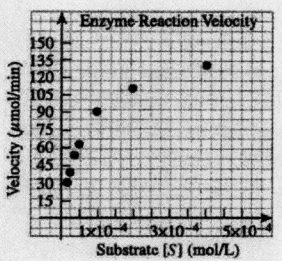

**b.** A reasonable estimate for $V_{\max}$ is about 156 $\mu$mol/min.

**c.** $K_m$ is the value of $[S]$ that results in the velocity being half of its maximum value, which by (b) is about 156. So, we need the value of $[S]$ that corresponds to $v = 78$. From the graph, this is very difficult to ascertain because of the very small units. We can simply say that it occurs between 0.0001 and 0.0002. A more accurate estimate can be obtained if a best fit curve is known.

**d. (i)** $v = 33.70 \ln([S]) + 395.80$ with $r^2 = 0.9984$.
It is shown on the scatterplot below.

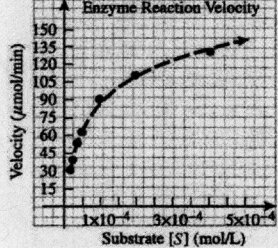

**(ii)** Using the equation, we must solve the following equation for [S]:

$$100 = 33.70 \ln([S]) + 395.80$$
$$-295.80 = 33.70 \ln[S]$$
$$-8.77745 = \ln[S]$$
$$e^{-8.77745} = S$$
$$S = 0.000154171$$

**125.** $f'(x) = e^x$  **127.** $(f^{-1})'(x) = \dfrac{1}{x}$

## Section 3.3

**1.** 0  **3.** 1  **5.** 8

**7.** $-3$  **9.** $\frac{3}{2}$  **11.** 5

**13.** $x + 5$  **15.** 8  **17.** $\frac{1}{9}$

**19.** $\dfrac{7}{x^3}$  **21.** $3 \log_b(x) + 5 \log_b(y)$

**23.** $\frac{1}{2} \log_b(x) + \frac{1}{3} \log_b(y)$  **25.** $\frac{1}{3} \log_b(r) - \frac{1}{2} \log_b(s)$

**27.** $\log_b(x) - \log_b(y) - \log_b(z)$  **29.** $2 \log x + \frac{1}{2} \log(x + 5)$

**31.** $3 \ln(x) + 2 \ln(x - 2) - \frac{1}{2} \ln(x^2 + 5)$

**33.** $2 \log(x - 1) - \log(x - 3) - \log(x + 3)$

**35.** $\frac{1}{2} \ln(x + 5) - \frac{1}{2} \ln(x - 1)$  **37.** $\log_b(x^3 y^5)$

**39.** $\log_b\!\left(\dfrac{u^5}{v^2}\right)$  **41.** $\log_b\!\left(x^{1/2} y^{2/3}\right)$  **43.** $\log\!\left(\dfrac{u^2}{v^3 z^2}\right)$

**45.** $\ln\!\left(\dfrac{x^2 - 1}{(x^2 + 3)^2}\right)$  **47.** $\ln\!\left(\dfrac{(x + 3)^{1/2}}{x(x + 2)^{1/3}}\right)$  **49.** 1.2091

**51.** $-2.3219$  **53.** 1.6599  **55.** 2.0115

**57.** 3.7856  **59.** 110 dB  **61.** 5.5

**63.** 0.0458  **65.** 16 times

**67.** $3 \log 5 - \log 5^2 = 3 \log 5 - 2 \log 5 = \log 5$

**69.** Cannot apply the product and quotient properties to logarithms with different bases. Cannot reduce the given expression further without using the change of base formula.

**71.** true  **73.** false  **75.** false

**79.** $6 \log_b x - 9 \log_b y + 15 \log_b z$

**83.** yes  **85.** no

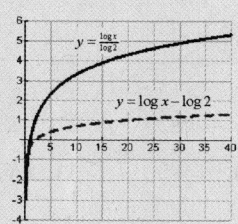

**87.** no  **89.** yes

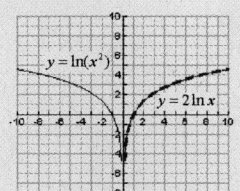  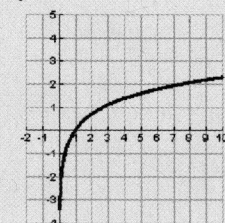

**91.** $f'(x) = \frac{1}{x} + \frac{1}{x} = \frac{2}{x}$  **93.** $f'(x) = -\frac{2}{x}$

## Section 3.4

**1.** $x = \pm 2$  **3.** $x = -4$  **5.** $x = -\frac{3}{2}$

**7.** $x = -1$  **9.** $x = 3, 4$  **11.** $x = 0, 6$

**13.** $x = 1, 4$  **15.** $x = \dfrac{\log_2(27) + 1}{3} \approx 1.918$

**17.** $x = \ln 5 \approx 1.609$  **19.** $x = 10 \ln 4 \approx 13.863$

**21.** $x = \log_3(10) \approx 2.096$  **23.** $x = \dfrac{\ln(22) - 4}{3} \approx -0.303$

**25.** $x = \dfrac{\ln 6}{2} \approx 0.896$  **27.** 0.223  **29.** $\pm 2.282$

**31.** $x = \ln\!\left(\dfrac{-7 + \sqrt{61}}{2}\right) \approx -0.904$  **33.** $x = 0$

**35.** $x = \ln 7 \approx 1.946$  **37.** $x = 0$

**39.** $x = \dfrac{\log_{10}(9)}{2} \approx 0.477$  **41.** $x = 40$

**43.** $x = \frac{9}{32}$  **45.** $x = \pm 3$  **47.** $x = 5$

**49.** $x = 6$  **51.** $x = -1$  **53.** no solution

**55.** $x = \frac{25}{8}$  **57.** $x = -\frac{4}{5}$  **59.** $x = 47.5$

**61.** $x \approx \pm 7.321$  **63.** $x \approx -1.432$  **65.** $x \cong -1.25$

**67.** $x \approx 8.456$  **69.** $x = \dfrac{-3 + \sqrt{13}}{2} \cong 0.303$

**71.** $x \approx 3.646$

**73. a.** 151 beats per min  **b.** 7 min  **c.** 66 beats per min

**75.** 31.9 yr  **77.** 19.74 yr  **79.** $3.16 \times 10^{15}$ J

**81.** 1 W/m²  **83.** 4.61 hr  **85.** 15.89 yr

**87.** 6.2

**89.** $\ln(4e^x) \neq 4x$. Should first divide both sides by 4, then take the natural log:

$$4e^x = 9$$
$$e^x = \frac{9}{4}$$
$$\ln(e^x) = \ln\!\left(\tfrac{9}{4}\right)$$
$$x = \ln\!\left(\tfrac{9}{4}\right)$$

**91.** $x = -5$ is not a solution since $\log(-5)$ is not defined.

**93.** true      **95.** false      **97.** false

**99.** $x = \dfrac{1 + \sqrt{1 + 4b^2}}{2}$      **101.** $t = -5\ln\left(\dfrac{3000 - y}{2y}\right)$

**103.** $f^{-1}(x) = \ln\left(x + \sqrt{x^2 - 1}\right)$

**105.** $x = \dfrac{3 \pm \sqrt{5}}{2}$      **107.**

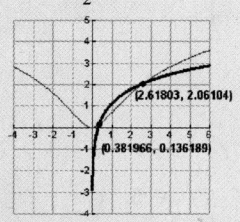

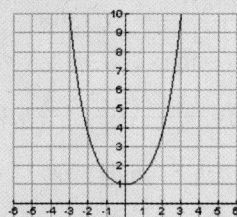

**109.** domain: $(-\infty, \infty)$    $y$-axis symmetry

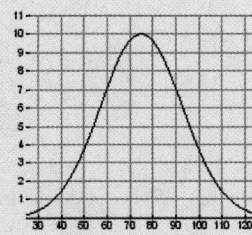

**111.** $f^{-1}(x) = \ln\left(x + \sqrt{x^2 + 1}\right)$      **113.** $\ln y = x\ln 2$

## Section 3.5

**1.** c (iv)      **3.** a (iii)      **5.** f (i)

**7.** 94 million      **9.** 5.5 yr, 2008

**11.** 799.6 subscribers    **13.** $455,000    **15.** 332 million

**17.** 1.45 million      **19.** 13.53 ml

**21. a.** $k = -\ln\left(\dfrac{8}{15}\right) \cong 0.6286$

     **b.** 636,000 mp3 players

**23.** 7575 yr      **25.** 131,158,556 years old

**27.** 105°F      **29.** 3.8 hr before 7 A.M.

**31.** $19,100

**33. a.** 84,520    **b.** 100,000    **c.** 100,000

**35.** 29,551 cases    **37.** 1.89 yr    **39.** $r = 0$

**41. a.**           **b.** 75   **c.** 4   **d.** 4

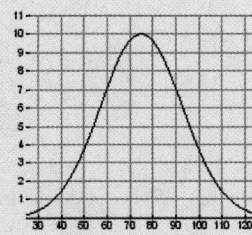

**43. a.** 18 yr   **b.** 10 yr      **45. a.** 30 yr   **b.** $328,120

**47.** $r = 0.07$, not 7    **49.** true      **51.** false

**53.** less time      **55.** about 10.9 days

**57.** $k_1 = k_2 + \ln\left(\dfrac{2 + c}{c}\right)$

**59. a.** For the same periodic payment, it will take Wing Shan fewer years to pay off the loan if she can afford to pay biweekly.

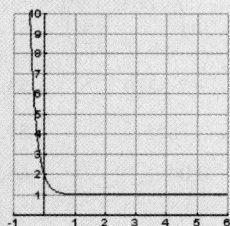

     **b.** 11.58 yr    **c.** 10.33 yr    **d.** 8.54 yr, 7.69 yr, respectively

**61.** $Pe^{kx}\dfrac{(e^{kh} - 1)}{h}$      **63.** $f'(x) = e^x + 1$

## Review Exercises

**1.** 17,559.94    **3.** 5.52    **5.** 24.53    **7.** 5.89

**9.** 73.52    **11.** 6.25    **13.** b    **15.** c

**17.** $y$-intercept: $(0, -1)$     **19.** $y$-intercept: $(0, 2)$
     HA: $y = 0$                HA: $y = 1$

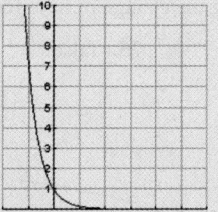 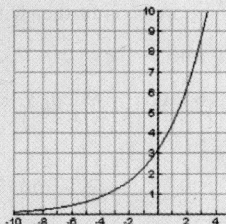

**21.** $y$-intercept: $(0, 1)$     **23.** $y$-intercept: $(0, 3.2)$
     HA: $y = 0$                HA: $y = 0$

**25.** $6144.68      **27.** $23,080.29      **29.** $4^3 = 64$

**31.** $10^{-2} = \dfrac{1}{100}$    **33.** $\log_6 216 = 3$    **35.** $\log_{2/13}\left(\dfrac{4}{169}\right) = 2$

**37.** 0      **39.** $-4$      **41.** 1.51      **43.** $-2.08$

**45.** $(-2, \infty)$    **47.** $(-\infty, \infty)$    **49.** b      **51.** d

**53.**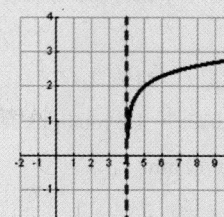

**55.**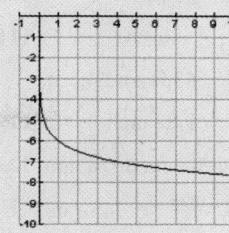

**57.** 6.5  **59.** 50 dB  **61.** 1

**63.** 6  **65.** $a \log_c (x) + b \log_c (y)$

**67.** $\log_j (r) + \log_j (s) - 3 \log_j (t)$

**69.** $\frac{1}{2} \log (a) - \frac{3}{2} \log (b) - \frac{2}{5} \log (c)$

**71.** 0.5283  **73.** 0.2939  **75.** $x = -4$

**77.** $x = \frac{4}{3}$  **79.** $x = -6$  **81.** $x \approx -0.218$

**83.** no solution  **85.** $x = 0$  **87.** $x = \frac{100}{3}$

**89.** $x = 128\sqrt{2}$  **91.** $x \approx \pm 3.004$  **93.** $x \approx 0.449$

**95.** $28,536.88  **97.** 16.6 yr  **99.** 3.72 million

**101.** 6250 bacteria  **103.** 56 yr  **105.** 16 fish

**107.** 343 mice

**109.** HA: $y = e^{\sqrt{2}} \approx 4.11$  **111.** (2.376, 2.071)

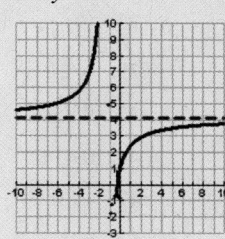  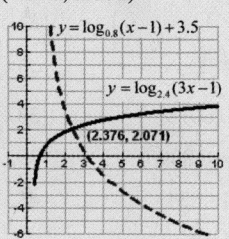

**113.** $(0, \infty)$

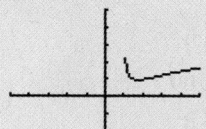

**115.** domain: $(-\infty, \infty)$  symmetric origin
HA: $y = -1$ (as $x \to -\infty$), $y = 1$ (as $x \to \infty$)

**117. a.** $N = 4e^{-0.038508t} \approx 4(0.9622)^t$  **b.** $N = 4(0.9622)^t$
**c.** yes

## Practice Test

**1.** $x^3$  **3.** $-4$

**5.** $x = \pm\sqrt{1 + \ln 42} \approx \pm 2.177$

**7.** $x = \dfrac{-1 + \ln\left(\frac{300}{27}\right)}{0.2} \cong 7.04$

**9.** $x = 4 + e^2 \approx 11.389$

**11.** $x = e^e \approx 15.154$  **13.** $x = 9$

**15.** $x = \dfrac{-3 \pm \sqrt{9 - 4(-e)}}{2} \approx 0.729$

**17.** $x = \ln\left(\frac{1}{2}\right) \approx -0.693$  **19.** $(-1, 0) \cup (1, \infty)$

**21.** $x$-intercept: none
$y$-intercept: (0, 2)
HA: $y = 1$

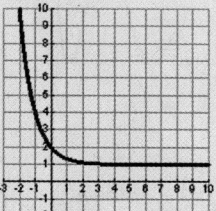

**23.** $x$-intercept: $\left(\dfrac{3 + \frac{1}{e}}{2}, 0\right)$
$y$-intercept: none
VA: $x = \frac{3}{2}$

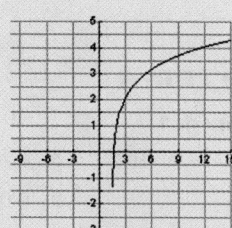

**25.** $8051.62  **27.** 90 dB

**29.** $7.9 \times 10^{11} < E < 2.5 \times 10^{13}$ J

**31.** 7800 bacteria  **33.** 3 days

**35.** domain $(-\infty, \infty)$
symmetric origin

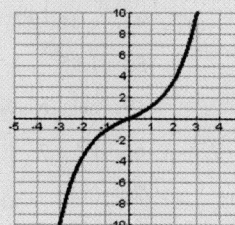

## Cumulative Test

**1.** domain: $(-\infty, -3) \cup (3, \infty)$; range: $(0, \infty)$

**3.** $g(x) = e^{2x}$ and $f(x) = \dfrac{1 - x}{1 + x}$ or

$g(x) = e^x$ and $f(x) = \dfrac{1 - x^2}{1 + x^2}$

**5.** $f(x) = -\frac{4}{9}x^2 - \frac{16}{9}x + \frac{11}{9}$     **7.** 2.197

**9. a.** 1     **b.** 5     **c.** 1     **d.** undefined
   **e.** domain: $(-2, \infty)$   range: $(0, \infty)$
   **f.** Increasing: $(4, \infty)$, decreasing: $(0, 4)$, constant: $(-2, 0)$

**11.** yes     **13.** $(1, -1)$

**15.** $Q(x) = -x^3 + 3x - 5, r(x) = 0$

**17.** HA: none   VA: $x = 3$   Slant: $y = x + 3$

**19.**

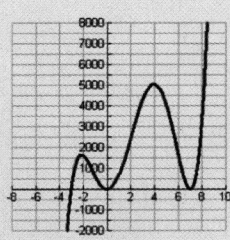

**21.** 5     **23.** $x = 0.5$     **25.** 8.62 yr

**27. a.** $N = 6e^{-0.247553t} \approx 6(0.9755486421)^t$
   **b.** 2.72 g

## CHAPTER 4

### Section 4.1

**1. a.** $72°$   **b.** $162°$   **3. a.** $48°$   **b.** $138°$   **5. a.** $1°$   **b.** $91°$

**7.** 0.18     **9.** 0.02     **11.** 0.125

**13.** $\frac{\pi}{6}$     **15.** $\frac{\pi}{4}$     **17.** $\frac{7\pi}{4}$

**19.** $\frac{5\pi}{12}$     **21.** $\frac{17\pi}{18}$     **23.** $\frac{13\pi}{3}$

**25.** $-\frac{7\pi}{6}$     **27.** $-20\pi$     **29.** $30°$

**31.** $135°$     **33.** $67.5°$     **35.** $75°$

**37.** $1620°$     **39.** $171°$     **41.** $-84°$

**43.** $229.18°$     **45.** $48.70°$     **47.** $-160.37°$

**49.** $198.48°$     **51.** 0.820     **53.** 1.95

**55.** 0.986     **57.** QII     **59.** negative $y$-axis

**61.** negative $x$-axis     **63.** I     **65.** IV

**67.** II     **69.** $52°$     **71.** $268°$

**73.** $330°$     **75.** $\frac{5\pi}{3}$     **77.** $\frac{11\pi}{9}$

**79.** 1.42     **81.** $\frac{2\pi}{3}$ ft     **83.** $\frac{5}{2}$ in.

**85.** $\frac{11\pi}{5}\ \mu$m     **87.** $\frac{200\pi}{3}$ km     **89.** 2.85 km²

**91.** 8.62 cm²     **93.** 0.0236 ft²     **95.** $\frac{2}{5}$ m/sec

**97.** 272 km/hr     **99.** 9.8 m     **101.** 1.5 mi

**103.** $\frac{5\pi}{2}$ rad/sec     **105.** $\frac{2\pi}{9}$ rad/sec     **107.** $6\pi$ in./sec

**109.** $\frac{\pi}{4}$ mm/sec     **111.** 26.2 cm

**113.** 653 in. or 54.5 ft     **115.** $1{,}440°$

**117.** 69.82 mph     **119.** 10.11 rad/sec = 1.6 rotations/sec

**121.** 7.8 cm or 78 mm   **123.** 4.0 cm or 40 mm

**125.** $\frac{189\pi}{8} \cong 74$ sq mi

**127.** $\dfrac{\left(4.5 \times 10^{-9}\right)}{2}\dfrac{\pi}{5} \cong 1.4 \times 10^{-9}$ m or 1.4 nm

**129.** Angular velocity must be expressed in radians (not degrees) per second. Use $\pi\,\frac{\text{rad}}{\text{sec}}$ in place of $\frac{180°}{\text{sec}}$.

**131.** true     **133.** true     **135.** $110°$

**137.** $\frac{15\pi}{2}$ units²     **139.** $68.8°$     **141.** $\theta = \frac{\pi}{5}$

**143.** $\frac{\pi}{3}$

### Section 4.2

**1.** $\frac{\sqrt{5}}{5}$     **3.** $\sqrt{5}$     **5.** 2

**7.** $\frac{2\sqrt{10}}{7}$     **9.** $\frac{7}{3}$     **11.** $\frac{3\sqrt{10}}{20}$

**13.** a     **15.** b     **17.** c

**19.** $\frac{\sqrt{3}}{3}$     **21.** $\sqrt{3}$     **23.** $\frac{2\sqrt{3}}{3}$

**25.** $\frac{2\sqrt{3}}{3}$     **27.** $\frac{\sqrt{3}}{3}$     **29.** $\sqrt{2}$

**31.** 0.6018     **33.** 0.1392     **35.** 0.2588

**37.** $-0.8090$     **39.** 1.3764     **41.** 0.4142

**43.** 1.0034     **45.** 0.7002     **47.** 18 ft

**49.** 5.50 mi     **51.** 12 km     **53.** $62°$

**55.** $\beta = 58°, a \approx 6.4$ ft, $b \approx 10$ ft

**57.** $\alpha = 18°, b \approx 9.2$ mm, $a \approx 3.0$ mm

**59.** $\beta = 35.8°, c \approx 137$ mi, $b \approx 80.1$ mi

**61.** $\alpha \approx 56.0°; \beta \approx 34.0°; c \approx 51.3$ ft

**63.** $\alpha \approx 55.480°; \beta \approx 34.520°; b \approx 24{,}235$ km

**65.** $c \approx 27.0$ in.; $a \approx 24.4$ in.; $\alpha \approx 64.6°$

**67.** 88 ft     **69.** 260 ft     **71.** $11.0°$; too low

**73.** 80 ft     **75.** 170 m     **77.** $0.000016°$

**79.** 4,414 ft     **81.** $136.69°$     **83.** 120.93 ft

**85.** 24 ft     **87.** 3.5 ft     **89.** 4.7 in.

**91.** Opposite side has length 3, not 4.

**93.** $\sec x = \dfrac{1}{\cos x}$, not $\dfrac{1}{\sin x}$.     **95.** true

**97.** false    **99.** 0    **101.** 0

**103.** $\frac{1}{2}$    **105. a.** 0.342; 2.92398   **b.** 2.92380

**107. a.** 1.423; 0.70281   **b.** 0.70281

**109.** $\frac{6-2\sqrt{3}}{3}$    **111.** $\sqrt{3}-1$

## Section 4.3

**1.** $\sin\theta = \frac{2\sqrt{5}}{5}$, $\cos\theta = \frac{\sqrt{5}}{5}$, $\tan\theta = 2$, $\csc\theta = \frac{\sqrt{5}}{2}$, $\sec\theta = \sqrt{5}$, $\cot\theta = \frac{1}{2}$

**3.** $\sin\theta = \frac{4\sqrt{41}}{41}$, $\cos\theta = \frac{5\sqrt{41}}{41}$, $\tan\theta = \frac{4}{5}$, $\csc\theta = \frac{\sqrt{41}}{4}$, $\sec\theta = \frac{\sqrt{41}}{5}$, $\cot\theta = \frac{5}{4}$

**5.** $\sin\theta = \frac{2\sqrt{5}}{5}$, $\cos\theta = -\frac{\sqrt{5}}{5}$, $\tan\theta = -2$, $\csc\theta = \frac{\sqrt{5}}{2}$, $\sec\theta = -\sqrt{5}$, $\cot\theta = -\frac{1}{2}$

**7.** $\sin\theta = -\frac{7\sqrt{65}}{65}$, $\cos\theta = -\frac{4\sqrt{65}}{65}$, $\tan\theta = \frac{7}{4}$, $\csc\theta = -\frac{\sqrt{65}}{7}$, $\sec\theta = -\frac{\sqrt{65}}{4}$, $\cot\theta = \frac{4}{7}$

**9.** $\sin\theta = \frac{\sqrt{15}}{5}$, $\cos\theta = -\frac{\sqrt{10}}{5}$, $\tan\theta = -\frac{\sqrt{6}}{2}$, $\csc\theta = \frac{\sqrt{15}}{3}$, $\sec\theta = -\frac{\sqrt{10}}{2}$, $\cot\theta = -\frac{\sqrt{6}}{3}$

**11.** $\sin\theta = -\frac{\sqrt{6}}{4}$, $\cos\theta = -\frac{\sqrt{10}}{4}$, $\tan\theta = \frac{\sqrt{15}}{5}$, $\csc\theta = -\frac{2\sqrt{6}}{3}$, $\sec\theta = -\frac{2\sqrt{10}}{5}$, $\cot\theta = \frac{\sqrt{15}}{3}$

**13.** $\sin\theta = -\frac{2\sqrt{29}}{29}$, $\cos\theta = -\frac{5\sqrt{29}}{29}$, $\tan\theta = \frac{2}{5}$, $\csc\theta = -\frac{\sqrt{29}}{2}$, $\sec\theta = -\frac{\sqrt{29}}{5}$, $\cot\theta = \frac{5}{2}$

**15.** QIV    **17.** QII    **19.** QI

**21.** QI    **23.** QIII    **25.** $-\frac{4}{5}$

**27.** $-\frac{60}{11}$    **29.** $-\frac{84}{85}$    **31.** $-\sqrt{3}$

**33.** $-\frac{\sqrt{3}}{3}$    **35.** $\frac{2\sqrt{3}}{3}$    **37.** 1

**39.** $-1$    **41.** 0    **43.** 1

**45.** 1    **47.** possible    **49.** not possible

**51.** possible    **53.** possible    **55.** possible

**57.** $-\frac{1}{2}$    **59.** $-\frac{\sqrt{3}}{2}$    **61.** $\frac{\sqrt{3}}{3}$

**63.** 1    **65.** $-2$    **67.** 1

**69.** $\theta = 30°$ or $330°$    **71.** $\theta = 210°$ or $330°$

**73.** $\theta = 90°$ or $270°$    **75.** $\theta = 270°$    **77.** 110°

**79.** 143°    **81.** 322°    **83.** 140°

**85.** 340°    **87.** 1°    **89.** 335°

**91.** 1.3    **93.** 12°

**95.** 15°; The lower leg is bent at the knee in a backward direction at an angle of 15°.

**97.** 75.5°

**99.** Reference angle is measured between the terminal side and the $x$-axis, not the $y$-axis. The reference angle is 60°, $\sec 120° = -2$

**101.** true    **103.** false    **105.** false

**107.** true    **109.** $-\frac{3}{5}$

**111.** $y = (\tan\theta)(a-x)$    **113.** $-\dfrac{a}{\sqrt{a^2 + b^2}}$

**115.** $-\dfrac{\sqrt{a^2 - b^2}}{b}$    **117.** 0    **119.** 0

**121.** 0    **123.** does not exist

**125.** $\dfrac{12 + 3\sqrt{2} + \sqrt{3}}{6}$    **127.** $\frac{8}{3}$

## Section 4.4

**1.** SSA    **3.** SSS    **5.** ASA

**7.** $\gamma = 75°$, $b \approx 12.2$ m, $c \approx 13.66$ m

**9.** $\beta = 62°$, $a \approx 163$ cm, $c \approx 215$ cm

**11.** $\beta = 116.1°$, $a \approx 80.2$ yd, $b \approx 256.6$ yd

**13.** $\gamma = 120°$, $a \approx 7$ m, $b \approx 7$ m

**15.** $\alpha = 97°$, $a \approx 118$ yd, $b \approx 52$ yd

**17.** $\beta_1 \approx 20°$, $\gamma_1 \approx 144°$, $c_1 \approx 9$; $\beta_2 \approx 160°$, $\gamma_2 \approx 4°$, $c_2 \approx 1$

**19.** $\alpha \approx 40°$, $\beta \approx 100°$, $b \approx 18$

**21.** no triangle

**23.** $\beta = 90°$, $\gamma \approx 60°$, $c \approx 16$

**25.** $\beta \approx 23°$, $\gamma \approx 123°$, $c \approx 15$

**27.** $\beta_1 \approx 21.9°$, $\gamma_1 \approx 136.8°$, $c_1 \approx 11.36$; $\beta_2 \approx 158.1°$, $\gamma_2 \approx 0.6°$, $c_2 \approx 0.17$

**29.** $\beta \approx 62°$, $\gamma \approx 2°$, $c \approx 0.275$

**31.** $\beta_1 \approx 77°$, $\alpha_1 \approx 63°$, $a_1 \approx 457$; $\beta_2 \approx 103°$, $\alpha_2 \approx 37°$, $a_2 \approx 309$

**33.** $\alpha \approx 31°$, $\gamma \approx 43°$, $c \approx 2$

**35.** 1,246 ft    **37.** 1.7 mi    **39.** 1.3 mi

**41.** 26 ft    **43.** 270 ft    **45.** 63.83°

**47.** each 76.5 ft    **49.** 60.14 ft    **51.** 1.2 cm

**53.** The value of $\beta$ is incorrect. Should be $\sin\beta = \frac{9\sin 120°}{7}$.

**55.** false    **57.** true    **59.** true

**71.** 27 in.    **73.** 22 m

## Section 4.5

**1.** $b \approx 5, \gamma \approx 33°, \alpha \approx 47°$  **3.** $a \approx 5, \gamma \approx 6°, \beta \approx 158°$

**5.** $a \approx 2, \beta \approx 80°, \gamma \approx 80°$  **7.** $b \approx 5, \alpha \approx 43°, \gamma \approx 114°$

**9.** $b \approx 7, \alpha \approx 30°, \gamma \approx 90°$  **11.** $\alpha \approx 93°, \beta \approx 39°, \gamma \approx 48°$

**13.** $\gamma \approx 77°, \beta \approx 51.32°, \alpha \approx 51°$

**15.** $\alpha \approx 75°, \beta \approx 57°, \gamma \approx 48°$

**17.** no triangle

**19.** $\gamma \approx 90°, \beta \approx 23°, \alpha \approx 67°$

**21.** $\gamma = 105°, b \approx 5, c \approx 9$

**23.** $\beta \approx 12°, \gamma \approx 137°, c \approx 16$

**25.** $\beta \approx 77°, \alpha \approx 66°, \gamma \approx 37°$

**27.** $\gamma \approx 2°, \alpha \approx 168°, a \approx 13$

**29.** 55.4  **31.** 0.5  **33.** 23.6

**35.** 6.4  **37.** 4,408.4  **39.** 97.4

**41.** 25.0  **43.** 26.7  **45.** 111.64

**47.** 111,632,076  **49.** no triangle  **51.** 2710 mi

**53.** 1280 mi  **55.** 16 ft  **57.** 26.0 cm

**59.** 21.67°  **61.** 83.07°  **63.** 47,128 sq ft

**65.** 23.38 sq ft  **67.** 8.73

**69.** Should have used the smaller angle $\beta$ in Step 2

**71.** false  **73.** true  **75.** true

**79.** $\cos\left(\frac{x}{2}\right) = \sqrt{\dfrac{1 - \cos\left(2\cos^{-1}\left(\frac{1}{4}\right)\right)}{2}}$  **83.** 0.69 sq units

**91.** 333 mi  **93.** 28 m

## Review Exercises

**1. a.** 62°  **b.** 152°  **3. a.** 55°  **b.** 145°

**5. a.** 0.99°  **b.** 90.99°  **7.** $\frac{3\pi}{4}$

**9.** $\frac{11\pi}{6}$  **11.** $\frac{6\pi}{5}$

**13.** $9\pi$  **15.** 60°  **17.** 225°

**19.** 100°  **21.** 1800°  **23.** 150°

**25.** 754 in./min  **27.** $\frac{2\sqrt{13}}{13}$  **29.** $\frac{\sqrt{13}}{2}$

**31.** $\frac{3}{2}$  **33.** b  **35.** b

**37.** c  **39.** 0.6691  **41.** 0.9548

**43.** 1.5399  **45.** 1.5477  **47.** 75 ft

**49.** $\sin \theta = -\frac{4}{5}, \cos \theta = \frac{3}{5}, \tan \theta = -\frac{4}{3}$, $\cot \theta = -\frac{3}{4}, \sec \theta = \frac{5}{3}, \csc \theta = -\frac{5}{4}$

**51.** $\sin \theta = \frac{\sqrt{10}}{10}, \cos \theta = -\frac{3\sqrt{10}}{10}, \tan \theta = -\frac{1}{3}$, $\cot \theta = -3, \sec \theta = -\frac{\sqrt{10}}{3}, \csc \theta = \sqrt{10}$

**53.** $\sin \theta = \frac{1}{2}, \cos \theta = \frac{\sqrt{3}}{2}, \tan \theta = \frac{\sqrt{3}}{3}$, $\cot \theta = \sqrt{3}, \sec \theta = \frac{2\sqrt{3}}{3}, \csc \theta = 2$

**55.** $\sin \theta = -\frac{\sqrt{5}}{5}, \cos \theta = \frac{2\sqrt{5}}{5}, \tan \theta = -\frac{1}{2}$, $\cot \theta = -2, \sec \theta = \frac{\sqrt{5}}{2}, \csc \theta = -\sqrt{5}$

**57.** $\sin \theta = -\frac{\sqrt{7.2}}{3}, \cos \theta = -\frac{\sqrt{7.2}}{6}, \tan \theta = 2$, $\cot \theta = \frac{1}{2}, \sec \theta = -\frac{\sqrt{7.2}}{1.2}, \csc \theta = -\frac{\sqrt{7.2}}{2.4}$

**59.** $-\frac{1}{2}$  **61.** $-\frac{\sqrt{3}}{3}$  **63.** $-\frac{2\sqrt{3}}{3}$

**65.** $-\frac{\sqrt{2}}{2}$  **67.** $\sqrt{3}$  **69.** $-\sqrt{2}$

**71.** $-\frac{2\sqrt{3}}{3}$  **73.** $\gamma = 150°, b \approx 8, c \approx 12$

**75.** $\gamma = 130°, a \approx 1, b \approx 9$

**77.** $\beta = 158°, a \approx 11, b \approx 22$

**79.** $\beta = 90°, a \approx \sqrt{2}, c \approx \sqrt{2}$

**81.** $\beta = 146°, b \approx 266, c \approx 178$

**83.** $\beta_1 \approx 26°, \gamma_1 \approx 134°, c_1 \approx 15$; $\beta_2 \approx 154°, \gamma_2 \approx 6°, c_2 \approx 2$

**85.** $\gamma_1 \approx 29°, \alpha_1 \approx 127°, b_1 \approx 20$; $\gamma_2 \approx 151°, \beta_2 \approx 5°, b_2 \approx 2$

**87.** no triangle

**89.** $\beta_1 \approx 15°, \gamma_1 \approx 155°, c_1 \approx 10$; $\beta_2 \approx 165°, \gamma_2 \approx 5°, c_2 \approx 2$

**91.** $c \approx 46, \alpha \approx 42°, \beta \approx 88°$

**93.** $\gamma \approx 75°, \beta \approx 54°, \alpha \approx 51°$

**95.** $\gamma = 90°, \beta \approx 48°, \alpha \approx 42°$

**97.** $a \approx 4, \beta \approx 28°, \gamma \approx 138°$

**99.** $a \approx 11, \beta \approx 68°, \gamma \approx 22°$

**101.** $\gamma \approx 70°, \beta \approx 59°, \alpha \approx 51°$

**103.** $a \approx 26, \beta \approx 37°, \gamma \approx 43°$

**105.** $a \approx 28, \beta \approx 4°, \gamma \approx 166°$

**107.** no triangle  **109.** $\beta \approx 10°, \gamma \approx 155°, c \approx 10.3$

**111.** 141.8  **113.** 51.5  **115.** 89.8

**117.** 41.7  **119.** 5.2 in.

## Practice Test

**1.** 6000 ft

**3.** exact value versus approximate value

**5.** QIV      **7.** 585°      **9.** $\frac{15\pi}{4}$ in$^2$

**11.** $\gamma = 110°$, $a \approx 7.8$, $c \approx 14.6$

**13.** $\gamma \approx 96.4°$, $\beta \approx 48.2°$, $\alpha \approx 35.4°$

**15.** no triangle

**17.** $\gamma = 50°$, $b \approx 1.82$, $c \approx 4.08$      **19.** 57

## Cumulative Test

**1.** $-\frac{5}{8}$      **3.** $-2x - h$      **5.** 1

**7.** $y = -2x^2 + 7$

**9.** VA: $x = 2$, HA: none, SA: $y = x + 2$

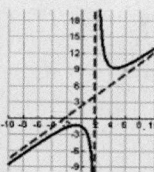

**11.** \$37,250      **13.** $x \approx 0.440$      **15.** $15\sqrt{2}$ ft

**17.** $\frac{12\pi}{5}$      **19.** $\sqrt{3}$      **21.** 1.6616

**23.** $\alpha = 138°$, $c \approx 8$ cm, $c \approx 9$ cm

# CHAPTER 5

## Section 5.1

**1.** $-\frac{\sqrt{3}}{2}$   **3.** $-\frac{\sqrt{3}}{2}$   **5.** $\frac{\sqrt{2}}{2}$   **7.** $-1$

**9.** $-\sqrt{2}$   **11.** $\sqrt{3}$   **13.** 2   **15.** $-\frac{\sqrt{3}}{2}$

**17.** $-\frac{\sqrt{3}}{2}$   **19.** $-\frac{\sqrt{2}}{2}$   **21.** $-\frac{\sqrt{3}}{2}$   **23.** $\frac{\sqrt{2}}{2}$

**25.** 1   **27.** $\frac{\sqrt{2}}{2}$   **29.** 0   **31.** $-2$

**33.** $\frac{\sqrt{3}}{3}$   **35.** $\theta = \frac{\pi}{6}, \frac{11\pi}{6}$   **37.** $\theta = \frac{4\pi}{3}, \frac{5\pi}{3}$

**39.** $\theta = 0, \pi, 2\pi, 3\pi, 4\pi$   **41.** $\theta = \pi, 3\pi$

**43.** $\theta = \frac{3\pi}{4}, \frac{7\pi}{4}$   **45.** $\theta = \frac{3\pi}{4}, \frac{5\pi}{4}$   **47.** $\theta = 0, \pi, 2\pi$

**49.** $\theta = \frac{\pi}{2}, \frac{3\pi}{2}$   **51.** $\theta = \frac{7\pi}{6}, \frac{11\pi}{6}$   **53.** $\theta = \frac{5\pi}{6}, \frac{11\pi}{6}$

**55.** 22.9°F   **57.** 99.1°F   **59.** 2.6 ft

**61.** 135 lb   **63.** 10,000 guests

**65.** 10.7 $\mu$g/$\mu$L   **67.** 35°C

**69.** Should have used $\cos\left(\frac{5\pi}{6}\right) = -\frac{\sqrt{3}}{2}$ and $\sin\left(\frac{5\pi}{6}\right) = \frac{1}{2}$

**71.** true   **73.** false   **75.** true

**77.** odd     **79.** $\theta = \frac{\pi}{4}, \frac{5\pi}{4}$     **81.** $\theta = \frac{\pi}{4}, \frac{3\pi}{4}, \frac{5\pi}{4}, \frac{7\pi}{4}$

**83.** $\theta = \frac{\pi}{3} + n\pi, \frac{2\pi}{3} + n\pi$     **85.** $\theta = \frac{\pi}{4}, \frac{3\pi}{4}, \frac{5\pi}{4}, \frac{7\pi}{4}$

**87.** $0.891; -0.891$     **89.** $6.314; -6.314$

**91.** 0.5     **93.** 0.866     **95.** 2

**97.** $\frac{3 - \sqrt{3}}{3}$

## Section 5.2

**1.** c     **3.** a     **5.** h     **7.** b

**9.** e     **11.** $\frac{3}{2}; p = \frac{2\pi}{3}$   **13.** $1; p = \frac{2\pi}{5}$   **15.** $\frac{2}{3}; p = \frac{4\pi}{3}$

**17.** $3; p = 2$     **19.** $5; p = 6$

**21.** 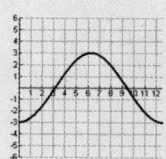     **23.**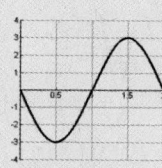

**25.** 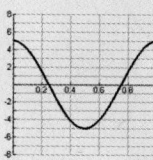     **27.**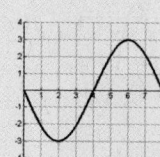

**29.** 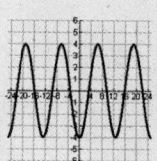     **31.**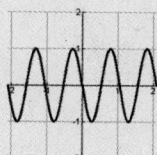

**33.** 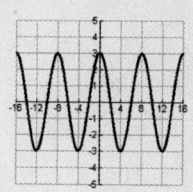     **35.**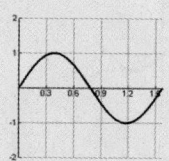

**37.**     **39.**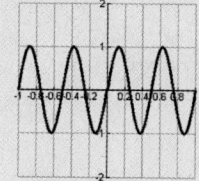

**41.** $y = -\sin(2x)$     **43.** $y = \cos(\pi x)$

**45.** $y = -2\sin\left(\frac{\pi}{2}x\right)$     **47.** $y = \sin(8\pi x)$

**49.** $2; 2; \frac{1}{\pi}$

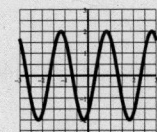

**51.** $5; \frac{\pi}{2}; -\frac{2}{3}$

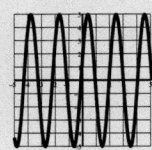

**53.** $6; 2; -2$

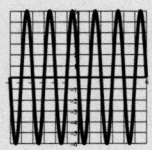

**55.** $3; \pi; \frac{\pi}{2}$ left

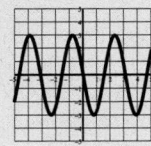

**57.** $\frac{1}{4}; 8\pi; 2\pi$ right

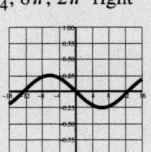

**59.** $2; 4; -4$ right

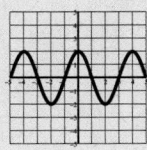

**61.**

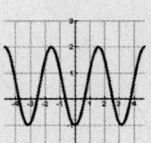

**63.**

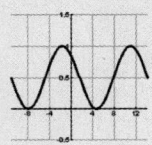

**65.**

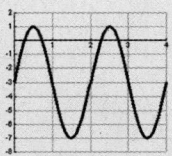

**67.**

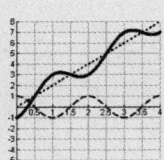

**69.**

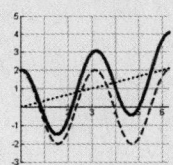

**71.**

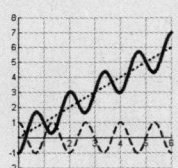

**73.**

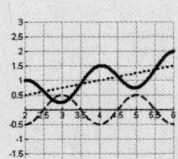

**75.**

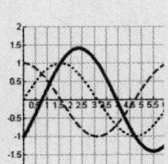

**77.**

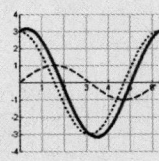

**79.**

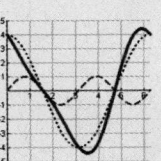

**81.**

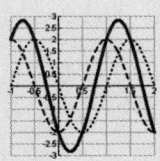

**83.**

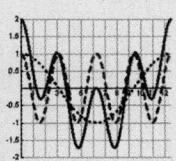

**85.**

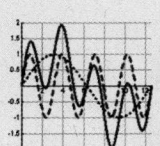

**87.**

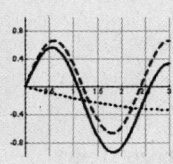

**89.**

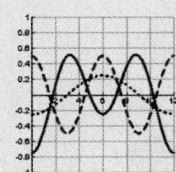

**91.**

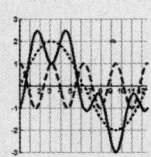

**93.**

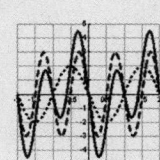

**95.** 3.5 or 3500 widgets

**97.** 1 mg/L

**99.** 4 cm; 4 g

**101.** $\frac{1}{4\pi}$ cycles/sec

**103.** 0.005 cm; 256 Hz

**105.** 0.008 cm; 375 Hz

**107.** 660 m/sec

**109.** 660 m/sec

**111.** $y = 25 - 25\cos\left(\frac{\pi t}{2}\right)$; 0 candelas/m$^2$

**113.** The correct graph is reflected over the $x$-axis.

**115.** true

**117.** false

**119.** $(0, A)$

**121.** $x = \frac{n\pi}{B}$

**123.** $\left(0, -\frac{A}{2}\right)$

**125.** $\left(\frac{3\pi}{2B} + \frac{2n\pi}{B}, 0\right)$

**127.** $\left[-\frac{5A}{2}, \frac{3A}{2}\right]$

**129.** no

**131.** graphs same

**133.** **a.** left $\frac{\pi}{3}$ units   **b.** right $\frac{\pi}{3}$ units

**135.** $y_1 = e^{-t}, y_2 = \sin t, y_3 = e^{-t}\sin t$

As $t$ increases, the graph of $y_1$ approaches the $t$-axis from above, the graph of $y_2$ oscillates, keeping its same form, the graph of $y_3$ oscillates, but dampens so that it approaches the $t$-axis from below and above.

**137.** **a.** $y_1 = \sin x$(solid), $y_2 = \sin x + 1$ (dashed)
The graph of $y_2$ is that of $y_1$ shifted up one unit.

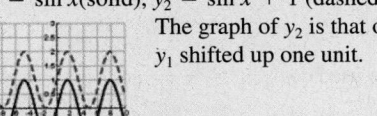

**b.** $y_1 = \sin x$ (solid)
$\quad y_2 = \sin x - 1$ (dashed)

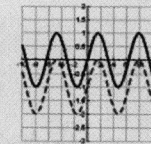

The graph of $y_2$ is that of $y_1$ shifted down 1 unit.

**139.** 5

**141.** 2

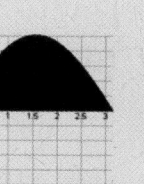

**143.** 1

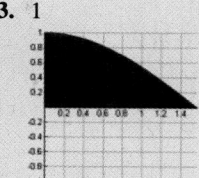

## Section 5.3

**1.** b          **3.** h          **5.** c          **7.** d

**9.**

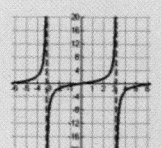

**11.**

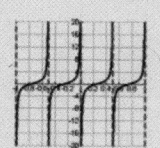

**13.**

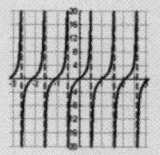

**15.**

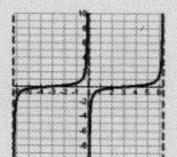

**17.**

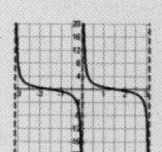

**19.**

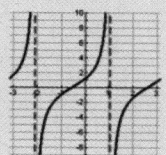

**21.**

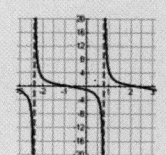

**23.**

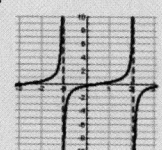

**25.**

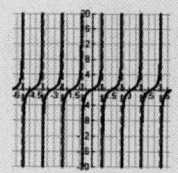

**27.**

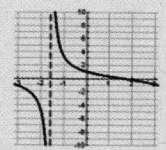

**29.**

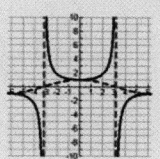

**31.**

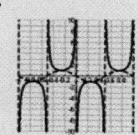

**33.**

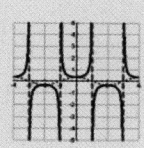

**35.**

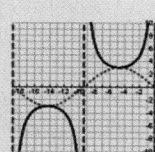

**37.**

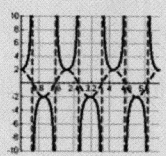

**39.**

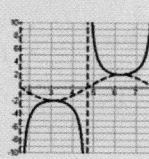

**41.**

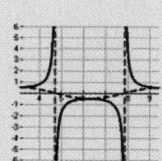

**43.**

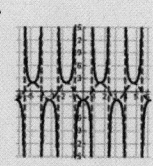

**45.**

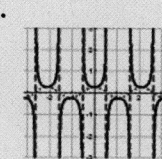

**47.**

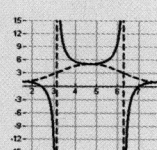

**49.**

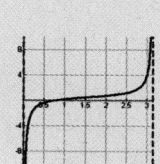

**51.**

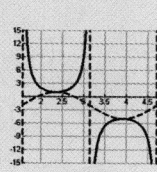

**53.**

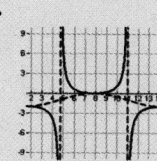

**55.**

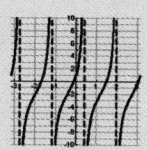

**57.** domain: $x \neq n$, $n$ an integer     range: $\mathbb{R}$

**59.** domain: $x \neq \frac{2n+1}{10}\pi$, $n$ an integer
range: $(-\infty, -2] \cup [2, \infty)$

**61.** domain: $x \neq 2n\pi$, $n$ an integer     range: $(-\infty, 1] \cup [3, \infty)$

**63.** domain: $x \neq 4n + 6$, $n$ an integer    range: $\mathbb{R}$

**65.** domain: $x \neq n$, $n$ an integer    range: $\left(-\infty, -\frac{5}{2}\right] \cup \left[-\frac{3}{2}, \infty\right)$

**67.** 48 m

**69. a.** $-5.2$ mi    **b.** $-3$ mi    **c.** 0    **d.** 3 mi    **e.** 5.2 mi

**71.** Forgot that the amplitude is 3, not 1. Guide function should have been $y = 3\sin(2x)$.

**73.** true    **75.** $n$, $n$ an integer

**77.** $x = 0, \pm\frac{\pi}{2}, \pm\pi$    **79.** $x = \frac{n\pi - C}{B}$, $n$ an integer

**81.** infinitely many solutions

**83.** $\sqrt{2}$
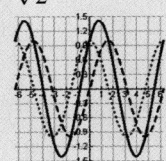

**85.** $\pi$
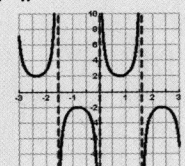

**87.** $-\ln\frac{\sqrt{2}}{2}$
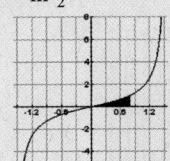

**89.** $\ln\left(\sqrt{2} + 1\right)$
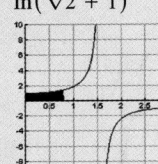

## Review Exercises

**1.** $-\frac{\sqrt{3}}{3}$    **3.** $-\frac{1}{2}$    **5.** 1

**7.** $-1$    **9.** $-1$    **11.** $\frac{1}{2}$

**13.** $\frac{\sqrt{2}}{2}$    **15.** 1    **17.** $-\frac{\sqrt{3}}{2}$

**19.** $\frac{-\sqrt{3}}{3}$    **21.** $2\pi$    **23.** $y = 4\cos x$

**25.** 5    **27.** $2; p = 1$    **29.** $\frac{1}{5}; p = \frac{2\pi}{3}$

**31.**
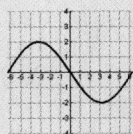

**33.**
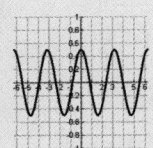

**35.** $3; 2\pi; \frac{\pi}{2}; 2$ (up)    **37.** $4; \frac{2\pi}{3}; -\frac{\pi}{4}; -2$ (down)

**39.** $\frac{1}{3}; 2; \frac{1}{2\pi}; \frac{1}{2}$ (down)

**41.**
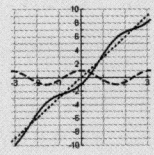

**43.**
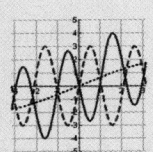

**45.** domain: $x \neq n\pi$, $n$ an integer    range: $\mathbb{R}$

**47.** domain: $x \neq \frac{2n + 1}{4}\pi$, $n$ an integer
range: $(-\infty, -3] \cup [3, \infty)$

**49.** domain: $x \neq \frac{6n+7}{6}$, $n$ an integer
range: $\left(-\infty, -\frac{3}{4}\right] \cup \left[-\frac{1}{4}, \infty\right)$

**51.**
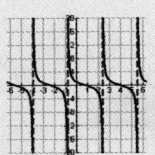

**53.**
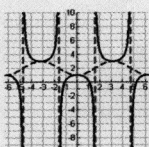

**55.**
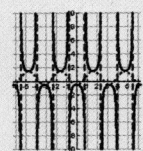

**57.** $-0.9659$

**59. a.** $y_1 = \cos x$ (solid)
$y_2 = \cos\left(x + \frac{\pi}{6}\right)$ (dashed)
The graph of $y_2$ is that of $y_1$ shifted left $\frac{\pi}{6}$ units.
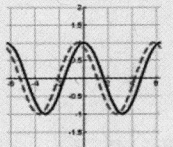

**b.** $y_1 = \cos x$ (solid)
$y_2 = \cos\left(x - \frac{\pi}{6}\right)$ (dashed)
The graph of $y_2$ is that of $y_1$ shifted right $\frac{\pi}{6}$ units.
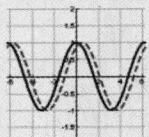

**61.** approximately 5

## Practice Test

**1.** $5, p = \frac{2\pi}{3}$

**3.**
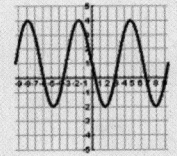

**5.**
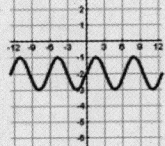

**7.**
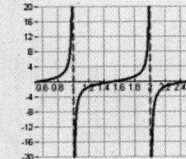

**9.** $x = \frac{n\pi}{2}$, $n$ an integer

**11.** $(-\infty, -4] \cup [2, \infty)$

**13.**

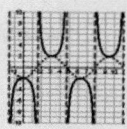

**15.** true

**17.** $y = 4\sin\left[\pi\left(x + \frac{3}{2}\right)\right] - \frac{1}{2}$

**19.**

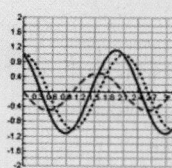

**21. a.**

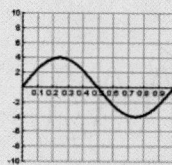

**b.** 4    **c.** 1

**23. a.** $y = 6 + 5\cos\left[2\left(x - \frac{\pi}{2}\right)\right]$
**b.** amplitude: 5, period: $\pi$, phase shift: $\frac{\pi}{2}$
**c.**

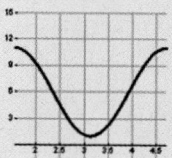

## Cumulative Test

**1.** $(-5, \infty)$

**3.** $y = 2|x + 6| + 4$

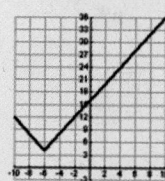

**5.** $f^{-1}(x) = \frac{5x + 2}{1 - 3x}$
domain $f$ = range $f^{-1}$: $\left(-\infty, -\frac{5}{3}\right) \cup \left(-\frac{5}{3}, \infty\right)$
domain $f^{-1}$ = range $f$: $\left(-\infty, \frac{1}{3}\right) \cup \left(\frac{1}{3}, \infty\right)$

**7.** $Q(x) = 3x^2 - \frac{5}{2}x + \frac{9}{2}$,    $r(x) = \frac{9}{2}x + \frac{1}{2}$

**9.** $P(x) = \left(x - \sqrt{5}\right)\left(x + \sqrt{5}\right)(x - i)(x + i)$

**11.** \$3382

**13.** $3\ln a - 2\ln b - 5\ln c$

**15.** $x = 1$

**17.** $\alpha = 63°$, $b \approx 6.36$ in., $a \approx 12.47$ in.

**19.** $\beta \approx 71.17°$, $\gamma \approx 40.83°$, $c \approx 16.92$ m or
$\beta = 108.83°$, $\gamma = 3.17°$, $c \approx 1.43$ m

**21.** $\cos\theta = -\frac{\sqrt{3}}{2}$, $\tan\theta = -\frac{\sqrt{3}}{3}$, $\cot\theta = -\sqrt{3}$,
$\sec\theta = -\frac{2\sqrt{3}}{3}$, $\csc\theta = 2$

**23.** $f = \frac{2}{\pi}$

# CHAPTER 6

## Section 6.1

**1.** $30°$       **3.** $90° - x$       **5.** $60°$

**7.** $\cos(90° - x - y)$   **9.** $\sin(70° - A)$   **11.** $\tan(45° + x)$

**13.** $\sec(30° + \theta)$   **15.** 1       **17.** $\csc x$

**19.** $-1$       **21.** $\sec^2 x$       **23.** 1

**25.** $\sin^2 x - \cos^2 x$   **27.** $\sec x$       **29.** 1

**31.** $\sin^2 x$       **33.** $\csc^2 x$       **35.** $-\cos x$

**37.** 1       **65.** conditional   **67.** identity

**69.** conditional   **71.** conditional   **73.** conditional

**75.** identity   **77.** conditional   **81.** $|\sec\theta|$

**83.** Simplified the two fractions in Step 2 incorrectly

**85.** $\tan^2 x = 1$ is a conditional, which does not hold for all values of $x$.

**87.** false       **89.** QI or QIV   **91.** QI or QII

**93.** no       **95.** no       **97.** $a^2 + b^2$

**101.** $\sec\theta$       **103.** $\cos A \cos B - \sin A \sin B$

**105.** $\sin A \cos B + \cos A \sin B$

**107.** $|a|\cos\theta$       **109.** $|a|\tan\theta$

## Section 6.2

**1.** $\frac{\sqrt{6} - \sqrt{2}}{4}$       **3.** $\frac{\sqrt{6} - \sqrt{2}}{4}$       **5.** $-2 + \sqrt{3}$

**7.** $\frac{\sqrt{2} + \sqrt{6}}{4}$       **9.** $2 + \sqrt{3}$       **11.** $2 + \sqrt{3}$

**13.** $\sqrt{2} - \sqrt{6}$   **15.** $\sqrt{6} - \sqrt{2}$   **17.** $\cos x$

**19.** $-\sin x$       **21.** 0       **23.** $-2\cos(A - B)$

**25.** $-2\sin(A + B)$   **27.** $\tan(26°)$   **29.** $\frac{1 + 2\sqrt{30}}{12}$

**31.** $\dfrac{-6\sqrt{6}+4}{25}$  **33.** $\dfrac{192-25\sqrt{15}}{-119}$  **35.** identity

**37.** conditional  **39.** identity  **41.** identity

**43.** identity  **45.** conditional  **47.** identity

**49.** identity  **51.** conditional

**53.** $y=\sin\left(x+\dfrac{\pi}{3}\right)$  **55.** $y=\cos\left(x-\dfrac{\pi}{4}\right)$

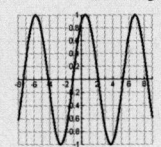  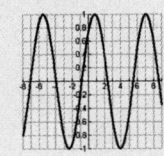

**57.** $y=-\sin 4x$  **59.** $y=\tan\left(x-\dfrac{\pi}{4}\right)$

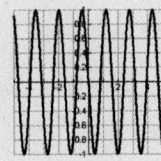  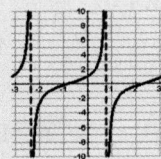

**61.** $y=\tan\left(x+\dfrac{\pi}{6}\right)$

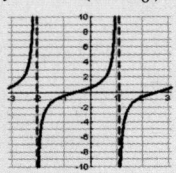

**63.** $\dfrac{\sqrt{2}}{2}\left(1+x-\dfrac{x^2}{2!}-\dfrac{x^3}{3!}+\dfrac{x^4}{4!}+\dfrac{x^5}{5!}--++\cdots\right)$

**67.** $E=A\cos(kz)\cos(ct)$  **69.** $T(t)=38-2.5\sin\left(\dfrac{\pi}{6}t\right)$

**71.** $\tan(A+B)\neq\tan A+\tan B$. Should have used

$$\tan(A+B)=\dfrac{\tan A+\tan B}{1-\tan A\tan B}$$

**73.** false  **75.** false

**79.** $B=2m\pi,\quad A=2n\pi;\ n,m$ integers

**81. a.**  **b.**  **c.**

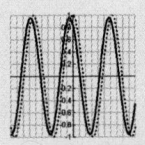  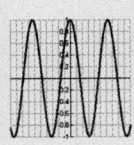  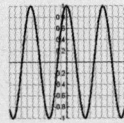

$y=\cos x$ as $h\to 0$

**83. a.**  **b.**  **c.**

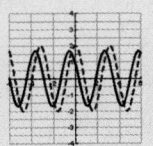  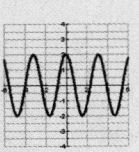  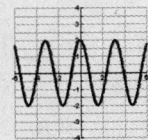

$y=2\cos(2x)$ as $h\to 0$

**85.** $\tan x=-\tan y$  **87.** $\tan x=\dfrac{2-\tan y}{1+2\tan y}$

## Section 6.3

**1.** $-\dfrac{4}{5}$  **3.** $\dfrac{120}{119}$  **5.** $\dfrac{120}{169}$

**7.** $-\dfrac{4}{3}$  **9.** $\dfrac{\sqrt{19}}{10}$  **11.** $\dfrac{119}{120}$

**13.** $\dfrac{\sqrt{3}}{3}$  **15.** $\dfrac{\sqrt{2}}{4}$  **17.** $\cos(4x)$

**19.** $-\dfrac{\sqrt{3}}{3}$  **21.** $-\dfrac{\sqrt{3}}{2}$  **23.** $-\dfrac{\sqrt{3}}{2}$

**41.**  **43.**

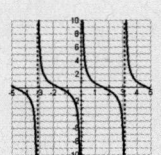  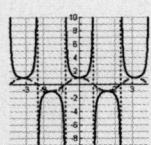

**45.**  **47.**

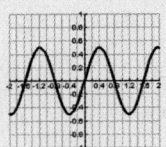  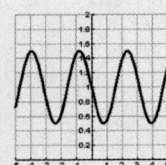

**49.**

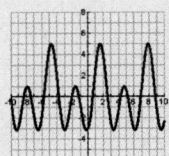

**51.** $\dfrac{\sqrt{2-\sqrt{3}}}{2}$  **53.** $-\dfrac{\sqrt{2+\sqrt{3}}}{2}$  **55.** $\dfrac{\sqrt{2-\sqrt{3}}}{2}$

**57.** $\sqrt{3+2\sqrt{2}}$  **59.** $-\dfrac{2}{\sqrt{2+\sqrt{2}}}$

**61.** $-\dfrac{1}{\sqrt{3+2\sqrt{2}}}$ or $1-\sqrt{2}$

**63.** $-\dfrac{2}{\sqrt{2-\sqrt{2}}}$  **65.** $1$  **67.** $\dfrac{2\sqrt{13}}{13}$  **69.** $\dfrac{3\sqrt{13}}{13}$

**71.** $\dfrac{\sqrt{5}-1}{2}$ or $\sqrt{\dfrac{3-\sqrt{5}}{2}}$  **73.** $\sqrt{\dfrac{3+2\sqrt{2}}{6}}$

**75.** $-\dfrac{\sqrt{15}}{5}$  **77.** $\sqrt{\dfrac{1-\dfrac{24}{\sqrt{601}}}{2}}$

**79.** $-\sqrt{\dfrac{1-\sqrt{0.91}}{1-\sqrt{0.91}}}$  **81.** $\sqrt{\dfrac{7}{3}}$  **83.** $\cos\left(\dfrac{5\pi}{12}\right)$

**85.** $\tan(75°)$  **87.** $-\tan\left(\dfrac{5\pi}{8}\right)$

**101.**  **103.**

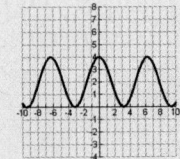

**105.**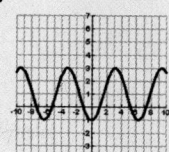

**107.**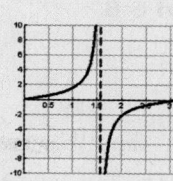

**109.** $C(t) = 2 + 10 \cos(2t)$

**111.** 22,565,385 lb

**115.** $\sqrt{2}$ ft

**117.** $\frac{1}{3}$

**119.** Should use $\sin x = -\frac{2\sqrt{2}}{3}$ since we are assuming that $\sin x < 0$.

**121.** If $\pi < x < \frac{3\pi}{2}$, then $\frac{\pi}{2} < \frac{x}{2} < \frac{3\pi}{4}$, so that $\sin\left(\frac{x}{2}\right)$ is positive, not negative.

**123.** false

**125.** false

**127.** false

**129.** false

**131.** cannot evaluate the identity at $A = \pi$

**133.** no

**137.** $0 < x < \pi$

**139.** 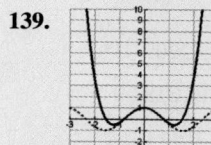 $y_1$ (dotted graph) is a good approximation of $y_2$ on $[-1, 1]$.

**141.** 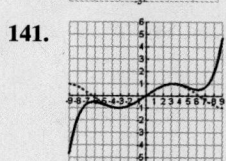 $y_1$ (dotted graph) is a good approximation of $y_2$ on $[-1, 1]$.

**143.** $\tan(2x)$

**145.** $\sin(3x)$

## Section 6.4

**1.** $\frac{1}{2}[\sin(3x) + \sin x]$

**3.** $\frac{5}{2}[\cos(2x) - \cos(10x)]$

**5.** $2[\cos x + \cos(3x)]$

**7.** $\frac{1}{2}[\cos x - \cos(4x)]$

**9.** $\frac{1}{2}[\cos(2\pi x) - \cos(3\pi x)]\left[\cos(2x) + \cos\left(\frac{2x}{3}\right)\right]$

**11.** $-\frac{3}{2}[\cos(1.9x) + \cos(1.1x)]$  **13.** $2\left[\sin\left(2\sqrt{3}x\right) - \sin\left(4\sqrt{3}x\right)\right]$

**15.** $2\cos(4x)\cos x$

**17.** $2\sin x \cos(2x)$

**19.** $-2\sin x \cos\left(\frac{3x}{2}\right)$

**21.** $2\cos\left(\frac{3}{2}x\right)\cos\left(\frac{5}{6}x\right)$

**23.** $2\sin(0.5x)\cos(0.1x)$

**25.** $-2\sin\left(\sqrt{5}x\right)\cos\left(2\sqrt{5}x\right)$

**27.** $2\cos\left(\frac{\pi}{24}x\right)\cos\left(\frac{5\pi}{24}x\right)$

**29.** $-\tan x$

**31.** $\tan(2x)$

**33.** $\cot\left(\frac{3x}{2}\right)$

**43.** $P(t) = \sqrt{3}\cos\left(\frac{\pi}{6}t + \frac{4}{3}\pi\right)$

**45.** $2\cos(886\pi t)\cos(102\pi t)$; 102 Hz; 443 Hz

**47.** $2\sin\left[\frac{2\pi tc}{2}\left(\frac{1}{1.55} + \frac{1}{0.63}\right)10^6\right]$
$\cdot \cos\left[\frac{2\pi tc}{2}\left(\frac{1}{1.55} - \frac{1}{0.63}\right)10^6\right]$

**49.** $2\sin(1979\pi t)\cos(439\pi t)$

**51.** 5.98 ft$^2$

**53.** $\cos A \cos B \neq \cos(AB)$ and $\sin A \sin B \neq \sin(AB)$, should have used the product-to-sum identities.

**55.** false  **57.** true

**59.** $\frac{1}{4}[\sin(A - B + C) + \sin(C - A + B) - \sin(A + B + C) - \sin(A + B - C)]$

**63.** 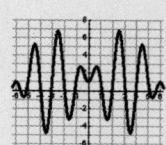  **65.**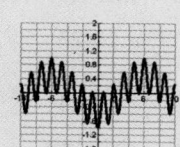

**67.** $\sin(4x)$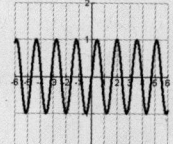

**69.** $y_1 = \sin(4x)\sin(2x)$ (solid), $y_2 = \sin(6x)$ (dashed), $y_3 = \frac{1}{2}[\cos(2x) - \cos(6x)]$

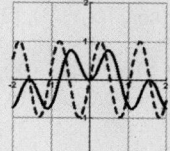 $Y_1$ and $Y_3$ are the same.

**71.** $\cos x = \cos y - \frac{2}{5}$  **73.** $2\sin y = \sec x$

## Section 6.5

**1.** $\frac{\pi}{4}$  **3.** $-\frac{\pi}{3}$  **5.** $\frac{3\pi}{4}$

**7.** $\frac{\pi}{6}$  **9.** $\frac{\pi}{6}$  **11.** $-\frac{\pi}{3}$

**13.** 0  **15.** $\pi$  **17.** 60°

**19.** 45°  **21.** 120°  **23.** 30°

**25.** −30°  **27.** 135°  **29.** −90°

**31.** 90°  **33.** 57.10°  **35.** 62.18°

**37.** 48.10°  **39.** −15.30°  **41.** 166.70°

**43.** −0.63  **45.** 1.43  **47.** 0.92

**49.** 2.09    **51.** 0.31    **53.** $\frac{5\pi}{12}$

**55.** undefined    **57.** $\frac{\pi}{6}$    **59.** $\frac{2\pi}{3}$

**61.** $\sqrt{3}$    **63.** $\frac{\pi}{3}$    **65.** undefined

**67.** 0    **69.** $-\frac{\pi}{4}$    **71.** not possible

**73.** $\frac{2\pi}{3}$    **75.** $-\frac{\pi}{4}$    **77.** $\frac{\sqrt{7}}{4}$    **79.** $\frac{12}{13}$

**81.** $\frac{3}{4}$    **83.** $\frac{5\sqrt{23}}{23}$    **85.** $\frac{4\sqrt{15}}{15}$    **87.** $\frac{11}{60}$

**89.** $\frac{24}{25}$    **91.** $\frac{56}{65}$    **93.** $\frac{24}{25}$    **95.** $\frac{120}{119}$

**97.** $\sqrt{1-u^2}$    **99.** $\frac{\sqrt{1-u^2}}{u}$    **101.** April and October

**103.** 3rd mo    **105.** 0.026476 sec = 26 ms

**107.** 173.4; June 22–23    **109.** 11 yr

**111.** $\tan\theta = \frac{8x}{x^2-7}$    **113.** 0.70 m; 0.24 m

**115.** $\theta = \pi - \tan^{-1}\left(\frac{300}{200-x}\right) - \tan^{-1}\left(\frac{150}{x}\right)$

**117.** The identity $\sin^{-1}(\sin x) = x$ is valid only for $x$ in the interval $\left[-\frac{\pi}{2}, \frac{\pi}{2}\right]$, not $[0, \pi]$.

**119.** In general, $\cot^{-1}x \neq \frac{1}{\tan^{-1}x}$.

**121.** false    **123.** false

**125.** $\frac{1}{2}$ is not in the domain of the inverse secant function.

**127.** $\frac{\sqrt{6}-\sqrt{2}}{4}$    **129.** 0

**131. a.** $\left[\frac{\pi}{4}, \frac{5\pi}{4}\right]$    **b.** $f^{-1}(x) = \frac{\pi}{4} + \cos^{-1}(x-3)$, $[2, 4]$

**133. a.** $\left(-\frac{\pi}{12}, \frac{5\pi}{12}\right)$    **b.** $f^{-1}(x) = \frac{\pi}{12} + \frac{1}{2}\cot^{-1}(4x-8)$, $\mathbb{R}$

**135.** $Y_1 = \sin\left(\sin^{-1}x\right)$, $Y_2 = x$

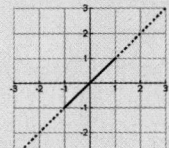

Identity $\sin\left(\sin^{-1}x\right) = x$ only holds for $-1 \leq x \leq 1$.

**137.** $Y_1 = \csc^{-1}(\csc x)$, $Y_2 = x$

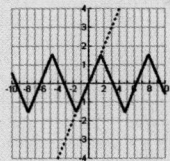

$x \in \left[-\frac{\pi}{2}, 0\right) \cup \left(0, \frac{\pi}{2}\right]$

**139. a.** $\frac{720}{1681}$    **b.** 0.42832    **c.** yes

**141.** $\sec^2 y = 1 + x^2$    **143.** $\sec y \tan y = x\sqrt{x^2 - 1}$

## Section 6.6

**1.** $\frac{3\pi}{4}, \frac{5\pi}{4}$    **3.** $\frac{7\pi}{6}, \frac{11\pi}{6}, \frac{19\pi}{6}, \frac{23\pi}{6}$

**5.** $n\pi$, $n$ an integer    **7.** $\frac{7\pi}{12}, \frac{11\pi}{12}, \frac{19\pi}{12}, \frac{23\pi}{12}$

**9.** $\frac{7\pi}{3} + 4n\pi, \frac{11\pi}{3} + 4n\pi$, $n$ an integer

**11.** $\frac{\pi}{6}, \frac{2\pi}{3}, \frac{7\pi}{6}, \frac{5\pi}{3}, -\frac{\pi}{3}, -\frac{5\pi}{6}, -\frac{4\pi}{3}, -\frac{11\pi}{6}$

**13.** $-\frac{2\pi}{3}, -\frac{4\pi}{3}$    **15.** $\frac{\pi(2+3n)}{12}$, $n$ an integer

**17.** $\frac{(2n+1)\pi}{3}$, $n$ an integer    **19.** $-\frac{\pi}{2}, -\frac{7\pi}{6}, -\frac{11\pi}{6}$

**21.** $\frac{\pi}{6}, \frac{2\pi}{3}, \frac{7\pi}{6}, \frac{4\pi}{3}$    **23.** $\frac{\pi}{12}, \frac{7\pi}{12}, \frac{13\pi}{12}, \frac{19\pi}{12}$

**25.** $\frac{\pi}{3}, \frac{2\pi}{3}, \frac{4\pi}{3}, \frac{5\pi}{3}$    **27.** $\frac{2\pi}{3}$

**29.** $\frac{\pi}{4}, \frac{3\pi}{4}, \frac{5\pi}{4}, \frac{7\pi}{4}$    **31.** $\frac{\pi}{2}, \frac{3\pi}{2}, \frac{\pi}{3}, \frac{5\pi}{3}$

**33.** $\frac{7\pi}{6}, \frac{11\pi}{6}, \frac{3\pi}{2}$    **35.** $\frac{\pi}{2}$

**37.** $0, \pi$

**39.** $\frac{\pi}{12}, \frac{5\pi}{12}, \frac{7\pi}{12}, \frac{11\pi}{12}, \frac{7\pi}{12}, \frac{13\pi}{12}, \frac{17\pi}{12}, \frac{19\pi}{12}, \frac{23\pi}{12}$

**41.** 115.83°, 295.83°, 154.17°, 334.17°

**43.** 333.63°    **45.** 29.05°, 209.05°

**47.** 200.70°, 339.30°    **49.** 41.41°, 318.59°

**51.** 56.31°, 126.87°, 236.31°, 306.87°

**53.** 101.79°, 281.79°, 168.21°, 348.21°, 9.74°, 189.74°, 80.26°, 260.26°

**55.** 80.12°, 279.88°

**57.** 64.93°, 121.41°, 244.93°, 301.41°

**59.** 15°, 45°, 75°, 105°, 135°, 165°, 195°, 225°, 255°, 285°, 315°, 345°

**61.** $\frac{\pi}{4}, \frac{5\pi}{4}$    **63.** $\pi$    **65.** $\frac{\pi}{6}$    **67.** $\frac{\pi}{3}$

**69.** $\frac{\pi}{4}, \frac{3\pi}{4}, \frac{5\pi}{4}, \frac{7\pi}{4}$    **71.** $\frac{\pi}{2}, \frac{3\pi}{2}$

**73.** $0, \pi, 2\pi, \frac{\pi}{4}, \frac{7\pi}{4}$    **75.** $\frac{\pi}{6}, \frac{5\pi}{6}, \frac{3\pi}{2}, \frac{\pi}{2}, \frac{7\pi}{6}, \frac{11\pi}{6}$

**77.** $\frac{\pi}{6}, \frac{\pi}{3}, \frac{7\pi}{6}, \frac{4\pi}{3}$    **79.** $\frac{\pi}{6}, \frac{5\pi}{6}, \frac{7\pi}{6}, \frac{11\pi}{6}$

**81.** $\frac{3\pi}{2}$    **83.** $\frac{2\pi}{3}, \frac{4\pi}{3}$    **85.** $\frac{\pi}{3}, \frac{5\pi}{3}, \pi$

**87.** $\frac{\pi}{24}, \frac{5\pi}{24}, \frac{13\pi}{24}, \frac{17\pi}{24}, \frac{25\pi}{24}, \frac{29\pi}{24}, \frac{37\pi}{24}, \frac{41\pi}{24}$

**89.** 57.47°, 122.53°, 216.38°, 323.62°

**91.** 30°, 150°, 199.47°, 340.53°

**93.** 14.48°, 165.52°, 270°

**95.** 111.47°, 248.53°    **97.** $\frac{\pi}{3}, \frac{5\pi}{3}$

**99.** 4th quarter of 2008, 2nd quarter of 2009, and 4th quarter of 2010

**101.** 9 P.M.        **103.** March

**105.** $A = x^2\left[\sin\theta + \frac{\sin(2\theta)}{2}\right]$

**107.** 2001        **109.** 24°        **111.** $\frac{3}{4}$ sec

**113.** $(0, 1), \left(\frac{\pi}{3}, \frac{3}{2}\right), \left(\frac{5\pi}{3}, \frac{3}{2}\right), (\pi, -3), (2\pi, 1)$

**115.** March and September

**117.** 1 A.M. and 11 A.M.

**119.** The value $\theta = \frac{3\pi}{2}$ does not satisfy the original equation.
$\sqrt{2 + \sin\left(\frac{3\pi}{2}\right)} = \sqrt{2 - 1} = 1$, while $\sin\left(\frac{3\pi}{2}\right) = -1$.
So, this value of $\theta$ is an extraneous solution.

**121.** Cannot divide by $\cos x$ since it could be zero. Factor as
$2\cos x(3\sin x - 1) = 0$.

**123.** false        **125.** true        **127.** $\frac{\pi}{6}, \frac{5\pi}{6}, \frac{7\pi}{6}, \frac{11\pi}{6}$

**129.** $\frac{\pi}{6}$ or 30°        **131.** no solution

**133.** $5 + 2n$, $n$ an integer        **135.** $\frac{\pi}{6}, \frac{5\pi}{6}$

**137.** no solutions

**139.** infinitely many negative solutions

**141.** 7.39°        **143.** 79.07°        **145.** 127.1°

**147.** $x = 0, 2\pi$        **149.** $x = 0, \frac{\pi}{3}, -\frac{\pi}{3}$

## Review Exercises

**1.** 60°        **3.** 45°        **5.** 60°

**7.** $\sec^2 x$        **9.** $\sec^2 x$        **11.** $\cos^2 x$

**13.** $-\left(4 + 2\csc x + \csc^2 x\right)$        **21.** identity

**23.** conditional        **25.** identity        **27.** $\frac{\sqrt{2} - \sqrt{6}}{4}$

**29.** $\sqrt{3} - 2$        **31.** $\sin x$        **33.** $\tan x$

**35.** $\frac{117}{44}$        **37.** $-\frac{897}{1025}$        **39.** identity

**41.**        **43.**

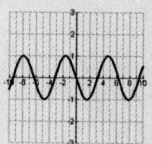        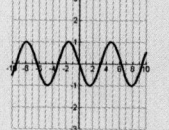

**45.** $\frac{7}{25}$        **47.** $\frac{671}{1800}$        **49.** $\frac{336}{625}$

**51.** $\frac{\sqrt{3}}{2}$        **53.** $\frac{3}{2}$        **61.** $-\frac{\sqrt{2-\sqrt{2}}}{2}$

**63.** $\frac{1}{\sqrt{3+2\sqrt{2}}}$        **65.** $\frac{2}{\sqrt{2+\sqrt{3}}}$        **67.** $\frac{7\sqrt{2}}{10}$

**69.** $-\frac{5}{4}$        **71.** $\sin\left(\frac{\pi}{12}\right)$

**77.**        **79.**

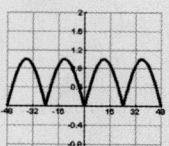        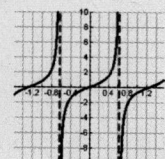

**81.** $3[\sin(7x) + \sin(3x)]$        **83.** $-2\sin(4x)\sin(x)$

**85.** $2\sin\left(\frac{x}{3}\right)\cos x$        **87.** $\cot(3x)$        **93.** $\frac{\pi}{4}$

**95.** $\frac{\pi}{2}$        **97.** $\frac{\pi}{6}$        **99.** $-90°$

**101.** 60°        **103.** $-60°$        **105.** $-37.50°$

**107.** 22.50°        **109.** 1.75        **111.** $-0.10$

**113.** $-\frac{\pi}{4}$        **115.** $\sqrt{3}$        **117.** $\frac{\pi}{3}$

**119.** $\frac{60}{61}$        **121.** $\frac{7}{6}$        **123.** $\frac{6\sqrt{35}}{35}$

**125.** $\frac{2\pi}{3}, \frac{5\pi}{3}, \frac{5\pi}{6}, \frac{11\pi}{6}$        **127.** $-\frac{\pi}{2}, -\frac{3\pi}{2}$        **129.** $\frac{9\pi}{4}, \frac{21\pi}{4}$

**131.** $\frac{\pi}{3}, \frac{2\pi}{3}, \frac{4\pi}{3}, \frac{5\pi}{3}$        **133.** $\frac{3\pi}{8}, \frac{11\pi}{8}, \frac{7\pi}{8}, \frac{15\pi}{8}$

**135.** $0, \pi, 2\pi, \frac{3\pi}{4}, \frac{7\pi}{4}$

**137.** 80.46°, 260.46°, 170.46°, 350.46°

**139.** 90°, 270°, 138.59°, 221.41°

**141.** 17.62°, 162.38°        **143.** $\frac{\pi}{4}, \frac{5\pi}{4}$        **145.** $\pi, \frac{\pi}{3}$

**147.** $0, \pi, 2\pi, \frac{\pi}{6}, \frac{11\pi}{6}$        **149.** $\frac{3\pi}{2}$        **151.** $\pi$

**153.** $\frac{\pi}{2}, \frac{3\pi}{2}$        **155.** 90°, 270°, 135°, 315°

**157.** 0°, 360°        **159.** 90°, 270°, 60°, 300°

**161. a.** 0.2924    **b.** 0.0437    **c.** 0.2924

**163. a.**        **b.**

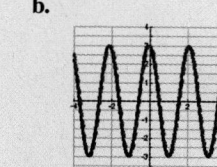

**c.**

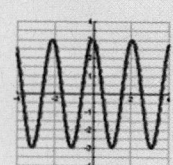

$y = 3\cos(3x)$ as $h \to 0$

**165.** $y_1 = \tan(2x)$ (solid), $y_2 = 2\tan x$ (dashed),

$y_3 = \dfrac{2\tan x}{1 - \tan^2 x}$

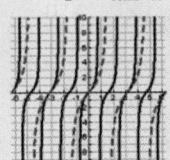

$Y_1$ and $Y_3$ are the same.

**167.** $y_1 = \cos\left(\frac{x}{2}\right)$ (solid), $y_2 = \frac{1}{2}\cos x$ (dashed),

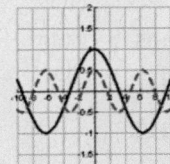

$y_3 = \sqrt{\dfrac{1 + \cos x}{2}}$

$Y_1$ and $Y_3$ are the same.

**169.** $y_1 = \sin(5x)\cos(3x)$ (solid), $y_2 = \sin(4x)$ (dashed),
$y_3 = \frac{1}{2}[\sin(8x) + \sin(2x)]$

$Y_1$ and $Y_3$ are the same.

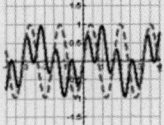

**171. a.** $-\frac{3}{5}$    **b.** $-0.6$    **c.** yes

**173.** 0.579 rad

## Practice Test

**1.** $x = \frac{(2n+1)\pi}{2}$, $n$ an integer    **3.** $-\frac{\sqrt{2-\sqrt{2}}}{2}$

**5.** $\frac{\sqrt{30}}{10}$    **7.** $\cos(10x)$    **9.** $\cos\left(\frac{a+b}{2}\right)$

**11.** $20\cos x\cos 3$

**13.** $\theta = \frac{4\pi}{3} + 2n\pi, \frac{5\pi}{3} + 2n\pi$, $n$ an integer

**15.** $14.48°, 165.52°, 90°, 270°$    **17.** conditional

**19.** $-\frac{\sqrt{26}}{26}$    **21.** $\cot\left(\frac{\pi}{6}x + \frac{\pi}{8}\right)$

**23.** $\left[c - \frac{1}{2}, c\right) \cup \left(c, c + \frac{1}{2}\right]; f^{-1}(x) = \frac{1}{\pi}\csc^{-1}\left(\frac{x-a}{b}\right) - \frac{c}{\pi}$

**25.** $\frac{8}{3} + 8n, \frac{16}{3} + 8n$, $n$ an integer

**27.** $\frac{\pi}{2} + 6n\pi, \frac{7\pi}{2} + 6n\pi$, $n$ an integer

**29. a.** $\sqrt{\frac{9}{10}}$    **b.** 0.3163    **c.** yes

## Cumulative Test

**1. a.** $\frac{\sqrt{3}}{2}$    **b.** $\sqrt{3}$    **c.** $-2$

**3. a.** $\frac{2\pi}{3}$    **b.** $-\frac{\pi}{6}$    **c.** $\frac{5\pi}{6}$

**5.** even    **7.** $\frac{1}{x^3} - 1; (-\infty, 0) \cup (0, \infty)$

**9.** $\left(-\frac{6}{5}, -\frac{3}{5}\right)$    **11.** $Q(x) = 5x - 4, r(x) = -5x + 7$

**13.** HA: $y = 0.7$; VA: $x = -2, x = 3$

**15.** $(-3, \infty)$    **17.** 4    **19.** 0.4695

**21.** $-\frac{7\pi}{12}$    **23.** conditional    **25.** $\frac{5}{12}$

**27.** 1.3994

# CHAPTER 7

## Section 7.1

**1.** $\sqrt{13}$    **3.** $5\sqrt{2}$    **5.** 25

**7.** $\sqrt{73}, 69.4°$    **9.** $\sqrt{26}, 348.7°$    **11.** $\sqrt{17}, 166.0°$

**13.** $8, 180°$    **15.** $2\sqrt{3}, 60°$    **17.** $\langle -2, -2 \rangle$

**19.** $\langle -12, 9 \rangle$    **21.** $\langle 0, -14 \rangle$    **23.** $\langle -36, 48 \rangle$

**25.** $\langle 6.3, 3.0 \rangle$    **27.** $\langle -2.8, 15.8 \rangle$    **29.** $\langle 2.6, -3.1 \rangle$

**31.** $\langle 8.2, -3.8 \rangle$    **33.** $\langle -1, 1.7 \rangle$    **35.** $\langle -\frac{5}{13}, -\frac{12}{13} \rangle$

**37.** $\langle \frac{60}{61}, \frac{11}{61} \rangle$    **39.** $\langle \frac{24}{25}, -\frac{7}{25} \rangle$    **41.** $\langle -\frac{3}{5}, -\frac{4}{5} \rangle$

**43.** $\langle \frac{\sqrt{10}}{10}, \frac{3\sqrt{10}}{10} \rangle$    **45.** $7\vec{i} + 3\vec{j}$    **47.** $5\vec{i} - 3\vec{j}$

**49.** $-\vec{i} + 0\vec{j}$    **51.** $2\vec{i} + 0\vec{j}$    **53.** $-5\vec{i} + 5\vec{j}$

**55.** $7\vec{i} + 0\vec{j}$    **57.** H: 1905 ft/sec; V: 1100 ft/sec

**59.** 2801 lb    **61.** 11.7 mph, $31°$ west of due north

**63.** $52.41°$ east of due north, 303 mph    **65.** 250 lb

**67.** V: 51.4 ft/sec; H: 61.3 ft/sec    **69.** 29.93 yd

**71.** $10.9°$    **73.** 1156 lb

**75.** $23.75°, 351.16$    **77.** $5\sqrt{2}, 5$

**79. a.** $|\overrightarrow{OA}| = 4, |\overrightarrow{OA}| = 5,$
$|\overrightarrow{OA}| = 3\sqrt{2}, |\overrightarrow{OA}| = \sqrt{10}, |\overrightarrow{OA}| = 1$
**b.** $\left(10 + \sqrt{10} + 3\sqrt{2}\right)$ units

**81.** 8.97 Nm    **83.** 31.95 Nm

**85.** $8.67, 18.05°$ counterclockwise of south

**87.** 1611 N; $19°$

**89.** Magnitude cannot be negative. Oserve that
$|\langle -2, -8 \rangle| = \sqrt{(-2)^2 + (-8)^2} = \sqrt{68} = 2\sqrt{17}.$

**91.** false    **93.** true    **95.** vector

**97.** $\sqrt{a^2 + b^2}$    **105.** $[[-13][28]]$    **107.** $[[5/13][-12/13]]$

**109.** $183, -79.61114$    **111.** 1    **113.** $\langle 1, 2t + h \rangle$

## Section 7.2

**1.** 2  **3.** $-3$  **5.** 42

**7.** 11  **9.** $-13a$  **11.** $-1.4$

**13.** 98°  **15.** 109°  **17.** 3°

**19.** 30°  **21.** 105°  **23.** 180°

**25.** not orthogonal  **27.** orthogonal  **29.** not orthogonal

**31.** orthogonal  **33.** orthogonal  **35.** orthogonal

**37.** 400 ft-lb  **39.** 80,000 ft-lb  **41.** 1299 ft-lb

**43.** 148 ft-lb  **45.** 1607 lb  **47.** 694,593 ft-lb

**49.** $49,300; total cost

**53. a.** $\cos \beta = \dfrac{v_1}{\sqrt{v_1^2 + v_2^2}}$, $\sin \beta = \dfrac{v_2}{\sqrt{v_1^2 + v_2^2}}$,

$\cos \alpha = \dfrac{w_1}{\sqrt{w_1^2 + w_2^2}}$, $\sin \alpha = \dfrac{w_2}{\sqrt{w_1^2 + w_2^2}}$

**55. a.** $-14.72$  **b.** 64.57°

**57.** $\vec{n} = \langle r, 0 \rangle$; $\vec{u} \cdot \vec{n} = |\vec{u}|r$  **59.** $-2$

**61.** The dot product of two vectors is a scalar, not a vector.

**63.** false  **65.** true  **67.** 17

**75. a.** $\text{proj}_{-\vec{u}}\, 2\vec{u} = -2\vec{u}$  **b.** $\text{proj}_{\vec{u}}\, c\vec{u} = -c\vec{u}$

**77.** $\vec{u}$ is perpendicular to $\vec{v}$, $\theta = 90°$

**79.** $-6, 6$  **81.** $-1083$  **83.** 31.4°

**85.** 1220  **87.** $2t^2 - 3t^3$  **89.** 1.518 rad

## Section 7.3

**1.** $-8$

**9.** $\sqrt{2}\left[\cos\left(\frac{7\pi}{4}\right) + i\sin\left(\frac{7\pi}{4}\right)\right] = \sqrt{2}\left[\cos(315°) + i\sin(315°)\right]$

**11.** $2\left[\cos\left(\frac{\pi}{3}\right) + i\sin\left(\frac{\pi}{3}\right)\right] = 2[\cos(60°) + i\sin(60°)]$

**13.** $4\sqrt{2}\left[\cos\left(\frac{3\pi}{4}\right) + i\sin\left(\frac{3\pi}{4}\right)\right] = 4\sqrt{2}[\cos(135°) + i\sin(135°)]$

**15.** $2\sqrt{3}\left[\cos\left(\frac{5\pi}{3}\right) + i\sin\left(\frac{5\pi}{3}\right)\right] = 2\sqrt{3}[\cos(300°) + i\sin(300°)]$

**17.** $3[\cos(0) + i\sin(0)] = 3[\cos(0°) + i\sin(0°)]$

**19.** $\frac{\sqrt{2}}{2}\left[\cos\left(\frac{5\pi}{4}\right) + i\sin\left(\frac{5\pi}{4}\right)\right] = \frac{\sqrt{2}}{2}\left[\cos(225°) + i\sin(225°)\right]$

**21.** $2\sqrt{3}\left[\cos\left(\frac{5\pi}{4}\right) + i\sin\left(\frac{5\pi}{4}\right)\right] =$
$2\sqrt{3}[\cos(225°) + i\sin(225°)]$

**23.** $5\sqrt{2}\left[\cos\left(\frac{3\pi}{4}\right) + i\sin\left(\frac{3\pi}{4}\right)\right] =$
$5\sqrt{2}[\cos(135°) + i\sin(135°)]$

**25.** $\sqrt{58}[\cos(293.2°) + i\sin(293.2°)]$

**27.** $\sqrt{61}[\cos(140.2°) + i\sin(140.2°)]$

**29.** $13[\cos(112.6°) + i\sin(112.6°)]$

**31.** $10[\cos(323.1°) + i\sin(323.1°)]$

**33.** $\frac{\sqrt{13}}{4}[\cos(123.7°) + i\sin(123.7°)]$

**35.** $5.59[\cos(24.27°) + i\sin(24.27°)]$

**37.** $\sqrt{17}[\cos(212.84°) + i\sin(212.84°)]$

**39.** $4.54[\cos(332.31°) + i\sin(332.31°)]$

**41.** $-5$  **43.** $\sqrt{2} - \sqrt{2}i$  **45.** $-2 - 2\sqrt{3}i$

**47.** $-\frac{3}{2} + \frac{\sqrt{3}}{2}i$  **49.** $1 + i$  **51.** $-3\sqrt{2} + 3\sqrt{2}i$

**53.** $2.1131 - 4.5315i$  **55.** $-0.5209 + 2.9544i$

**57.** $5.3623 - 4.4995i$  **59.** $-2.8978 + 0.7765i$

**61.** $0.6180 - 1.9021i$  **63.** $-0.87 - 4.92i$

**65. a.** 59.7 mi  **b.** $59.7[\cos(68.8°) + i\sin(68.8°)]$  **c.** 6.8°

**67. a.** $\overrightarrow{AB} = B - A = -2i$, $\overrightarrow{BC} = C - B = 3 - 3i$,
$\overrightarrow{CD} = D - C = -i$
**b.** $3\sqrt{5}[\cos(297°) + i\sin(297°)]$

**69.** $z = 2\sqrt{13}[\cos(56.31°) + i\sin(56.31°)]$

**71.** The point is in QIII not QI. Add 180° to $\tan^{-1}\left(\frac{8}{3}\right)$.

**73.** true  **75.** true  **77.** 0°

**79.** $\sqrt{b^2} = |b|$  **81.** $a\sqrt{5}[\cos(296.6°) + i\sin(296.6°)]$

**83.** $-\frac{\pi}{2} - \frac{\pi\sqrt{3}}{2}i$  **85.** $8.79[\cos(28°) + i\sin(28°)]$

**87.** $-z = r[\cos(\theta + \pi) + i\sin(\theta + \pi)]$

**89.** $1.41421, 45°, 1.4142[\cos(45°) + i\sin(45°)]$

**91.** $\sqrt{5}[\cos(26.57°) + i\sin(26.57°)]$

**93.** $35[\cos(323°) + i\sin(323°)]$

**95.** $r = 5$  **97.** $r = 2\sin\theta$

## Section 7.4

**1.** $-6 + 6\sqrt{3}i$  **3.** $-4\sqrt{2} - 4\sqrt{2}i$  **5.** $0 + 8i$

**7.** $\frac{9\sqrt{2}}{2} + \frac{9\sqrt{2}}{2}i$  **9.** $0 + 12i$  **11.** $\frac{3}{2} + \frac{3\sqrt{3}}{2}i$

**13.** $-\sqrt{2} + \sqrt{2}i$    **15.** $0 - 2i$    **17.** $\frac{3}{2} + \frac{3\sqrt{3}}{2}i$

**19.** $-\frac{5}{2} - \frac{5\sqrt{3}}{2}i$    **21.** $4 - 4i$    **23.** $-64 + 0i$

**25.** $-8 + 8\sqrt{3}i$    **27.** $1{,}048{,}576 + 0i$

**29.** $-1{,}048{,}576\sqrt{3} - 1{,}048{,}576i$

**31.** $2[\cos(150°) + i\sin(150°)]$,
$2[\cos(330°) + i\sin(330°)]$

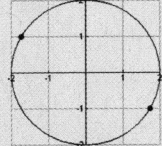

**33.** $\sqrt{6}[\cos(157.5°) + i\sin(157.5°)]$,
$\sqrt{6}[\cos(337.5°) + i\sin(337.5°)]$

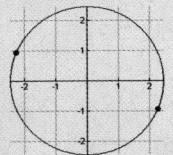

**35.** $2[\cos(20°) + i\sin(20°)]$,
$2[\cos(140°) + i\sin(140°)]$,
$2[\cos(260°) + i\sin(260°)]$

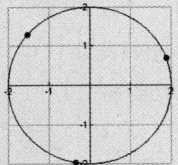

**37.** $\sqrt[3]{2}[\cos(110°) + i\sin(110°)]$, $\sqrt[3]{2}[\cos(230°) + i\sin(230°)]$,
$\sqrt[3]{2}[\cos(350°) + i\sin(350°)]$

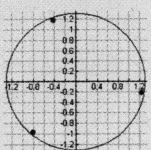

**39.** $2[\cos(78.75°) + i\sin(78.75°)]$,
$2[\cos(168.75°) + i\sin(168.75°)]$,
$2[\cos(258.75°) + i\sin(258.75°)]$,
$2[\cos(348.75°) + i\sin(348.75°)]$

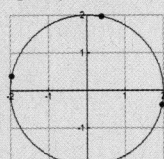

**41.** $\pm 2, \pm 2i$    **43.** $-2, 1-\sqrt{3}i, 1+\sqrt{3}i$

**45.** $\sqrt{2} + \sqrt{2}i, -\sqrt{2} + \sqrt{2}i, -\sqrt{2} - \sqrt{2}i, \sqrt{2} - \sqrt{2}i$

**47.** $1, \frac{1}{2} + \frac{\sqrt{3}}{2}i, -\frac{1}{2} + \frac{\sqrt{3}}{2}i, -1, -\frac{1}{2} - \frac{\sqrt{3}}{2}i, \frac{1}{2} - \frac{\sqrt{3}}{2}i$

**49.** $-\frac{\sqrt{2}}{2} + \frac{\sqrt{2}}{2}i, \frac{\sqrt{2}}{2} - \frac{\sqrt{2}}{2}i$

**51.** $\sqrt[4]{2}\left[\cos\left(\frac{\pi}{8}\right) + i\sin\left(\frac{\pi}{8}\right)\right]$,
$\sqrt[4]{2}\left[\cos\left(\frac{5\pi}{8}\right) + i\sin\left(\frac{5\pi}{8}\right)\right]$,
$\sqrt[4]{2}\left[\cos\left(\frac{9\pi}{8}\right) + i\sin\left(\frac{9\pi}{8}\right)\right]$,
$\sqrt[4]{2}\left[\cos\left(\frac{13\pi}{8}\right) + i\sin\left(\frac{13\pi}{8}\right)\right]$

**53.** $2\left[\cos\left(\frac{\pi}{5}\right) + i\sin\left(\frac{\pi}{5}\right)\right]$,
$2\left[\cos\left(\frac{3\pi}{5}\right) + i\sin\left(\frac{3\pi}{5}\right)\right]$,
$2[\cos(\pi) + i\sin(\pi)]$
$2\left[\cos\left(\frac{7\pi}{5}\right) + i\sin\left(\frac{7\pi}{5}\right)\right]$,
$2\left[\cos\left(\frac{9\pi}{5}\right) + i\sin\left(\frac{9\pi}{5}\right)\right]$

**55.** $\pi^2\left[\cos\left(\frac{\pi}{14}\right) + i\sin\left(\frac{\pi}{14}\right)\right]$,
$\pi^2\left[\cos\left(\frac{5\pi}{14}\right) + i\sin\left(\frac{5\pi}{14}\right)\right]$,
$\pi^2\left[\cos\left(\frac{9\pi}{14}\right) + i\sin\left(\frac{9\pi}{14}\right)\right]$
$\pi^2\left[\cos\left(\frac{13\pi}{14}\right) + i\sin\left(\frac{13\pi}{14}\right)\right]$,
$\pi^2\left[\cos\left(\frac{17\pi}{14}\right) + i\sin\left(\frac{17\pi}{14}\right)\right]$,
$\pi^2\left[\cos\left(\frac{21\pi}{14}\right) + i\sin\left(\frac{21\pi}{14}\right)\right]$
$\pi^2\left[\cos\left(\frac{25\pi}{14}\right) + i\sin\left(\frac{25\pi}{14}\right)\right]$

**57.** $[\cos(45°) + i\sin(45°)]$,
$[\cos(117°) + i\sin(117°)]$,
$[\cos(189°) + i\sin(189°)]$,
$[\cos(261°) + i\sin(261°)]$,
$[\cos(333°) + i\sin(333°)]$

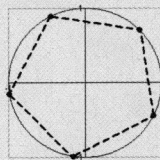

**59.** $[\cos(50° + 60°k) + i\sin(50° + 60°k)]$,
$k = 0, 1, 2, 3, 4, 5$

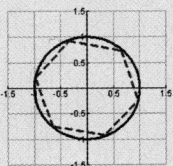

**61.** Reversed order of angles being subtracted.

**63.** Should use DeMoivre's formula. In general,
$(a + b)^6 \neq a^6 + b^6$.

**65.** true    **67.** false    **69.** true

**71.** true    **79.** $\cos(3x) = 4\cos^3 x - 3\cos x$

**81.** $2^{\frac{n+m}{2}} e^{\frac{\pi}{4}(m-n)i}$

**83.** $\left[\cos\left(\frac{11\pi}{6(5)} + \frac{2k\pi}{5}\right) + i\sin\left(\frac{11\pi}{6(5)} + \frac{2k\pi}{5}\right)\right]$,
$k = 0, 1, 2, 3, 4$

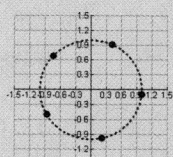

**85.** $\left[\cos\left(\frac{4\pi}{3(6)} + \frac{2k\pi}{6}\right) + i\sin\left(\frac{4\pi}{3(6)} + \frac{2k\pi}{6}\right)\right]$,
$k = 0, 1, 2, 3, 4, 5$

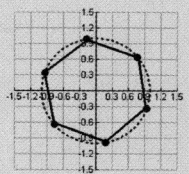

**87.** $(27)^{1/3}\left[\cos\left(\frac{\frac{\pi}{4}}{3} + \frac{2k\pi}{3}\right) + i\sin\left(\frac{\frac{\pi}{4}}{3} + \frac{2k\pi}{3}\right)\right]$,
$k = 0, 1, 2$

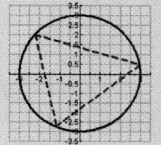

## Section 7.5

**1.** $-10$

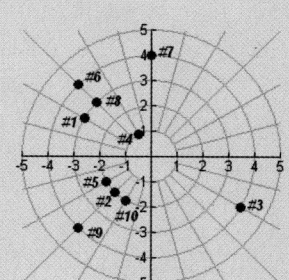

**11.** $\left(4, \frac{\pi}{3}\right)$    **13.** $\left(2, \frac{4\pi}{3}\right)$    **15.** $\left(4\sqrt{2}, \frac{3\pi}{4}\right)$

**17.** $(3, 0)$    **19.** $\left(2, \frac{7\pi}{6}\right)$    **21.** $\left(2, -2\sqrt{3}\right)$

**23.** $\left(\frac{\sqrt{3}}{2}, -\frac{1}{2}\right)$    **25.** $(0, 0)$    **27.** $\left(-1, -\sqrt{3}\right)$

**29.** $\left(\frac{\sqrt{2}}{2}, -\frac{\sqrt{2}}{2}\right)$    **31.** d    **33.** a

**35.**

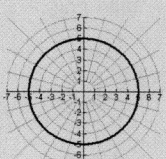

**37.**

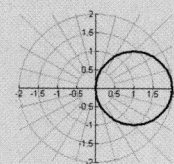

**39.**

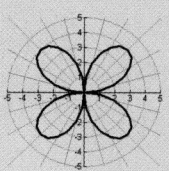

**41.**

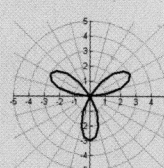

**43.**

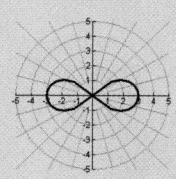

**45.**

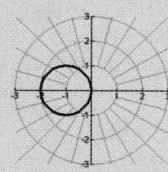

**47.**

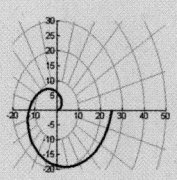

**49.**

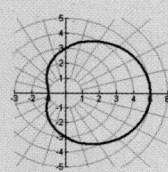

**51.** $y = -2x + 1$, line    **53.** $(x-1)^2 + y^2 = 9$, circle

**55.**

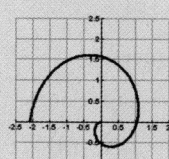

**57.**

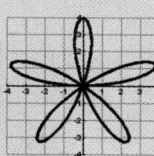

**59.**

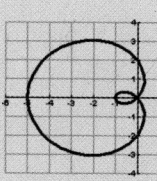

**61.**

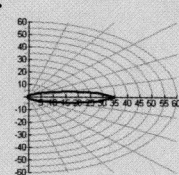

**63.** $r = \sqrt{\theta}$ more tightly wound than graph of $r = \theta$

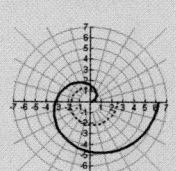

**65.** $r^2 = \frac{1}{4}\cos(2\theta)$ much closer to the origin than graph of $r^2 = 4\cos(2\theta)$

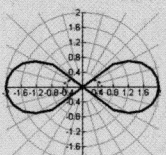

**67.**

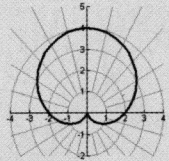

**69. a.–c.** All three graphs are figure eights. Extending the domain in **b** results in twice as fast movement, while doing so in **c** results in movement that is four times as fast.

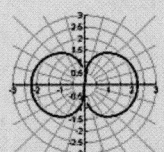

**71.** 6 times, $r = \frac{5}{2\pi}\theta, 0 \le \theta \le 12\pi$

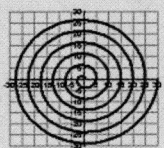

**73. a.** $r = 8\sin(3\theta), 0 \le \theta \le 2\pi$ **b.** 50 times

**75.** The point is in QIII; so needed to add $\pi$ to the angle.

**77.** true **79.** $r = \frac{a}{\cos\theta}$ **81.** $(-a, \theta \pm 180°)$

**83.** $\left(2, \frac{\pi}{3}\right), \left(2, \frac{5\pi}{3}\right)$

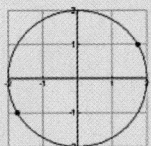

**85.** $x^3 - y^3 - 2axy = 0$

**87.** circle with radius $a$ centered $(a, b)$

**89.** $\theta = \frac{\pi}{2}, \frac{3\pi}{2}$ **91.** $\theta = \frac{\pi}{2}, \theta = \cos^{-1}\left(-\frac{1}{3}\right), \theta = \frac{3\pi}{2}$

**93.** $\theta = \frac{\pi}{8} + \frac{n\pi}{2}, n$ an integer

**95.** $\left(2\sqrt{2}, \frac{\pi}{4}\right), \left(-2\sqrt{2}, \frac{5\pi}{4}\right)$

**97.** $\left(\frac{2 - \sqrt{2}}{2}, \frac{3\pi}{4}\right), \left(\frac{2 + \sqrt{2}}{2}, \frac{7\pi}{4}\right)$

## Review Exercises

**1.** 13 **3.** 13 **5.** 26; 112.6°

**7.** 20; 323.1° **9.** $\langle 2, 11 \rangle$ **11.** $\langle 38, -7 \rangle$ **13.** $\langle 2.6, 9.7 \rangle$

**15.** $\langle -3.1, 11.6 \rangle$ **17.** $\left\langle \frac{\sqrt{2}}{2}, -\frac{\sqrt{2}}{2} \right\rangle$ **19.** $5\vec{i} + 2\vec{j}$

**21.** $-6$ **23.** $-9$ **25.** 16 **27.** 59° **29.** 49°

**31.** 166° **33.** not orthogonal **35.** orthogonal

**37.** not orthogonal **39.** not orthogonal

**41.**

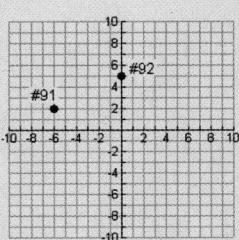

**43.** $2[\cos(315°) + i\sin(315°)]$

**45.** $8[\cos(270°) + i\sin(270°)]$

**47.** $61[\cos(169.6°) + i\sin(169.6°)]$

**49.** $17[\cos(28.1°) + i\sin(28.1°)]$

**51.** $3 - 3\sqrt{3}i$ **53.** $-1 + i$

**55.** $-3.7588 - 1.3681i$

**57.** $-12i$ **59.** $-\frac{21}{2} - \frac{21\sqrt{3}}{2}i$

**61.** $-\frac{\sqrt{3}}{2} + \frac{1}{2}i$ **63.** $-6$

**65.** $-324$ **67.** $16 - 16\sqrt{3}i$

**69.** $2[\cos(30°) + i\sin(30°)],$
$2[\cos(210°) + i\sin(210°)]$

**71.** $4[\cos(45°) + i\sin(45°)],$
$4[\cos(135°) + i\sin(135°)],$
$4[\cos(225°) + i\sin(225°)],$
$4[\cos(315°) + i\sin(315°)]$

**73.** $3 + 3\sqrt{3}i, -6, 3 - 3\sqrt{3}i$

**75.** $\frac{\sqrt{2}}{2} + \frac{\sqrt{2}}{2}i, -\frac{\sqrt{2}}{2} + \frac{\sqrt{2}}{2}i, -\frac{\sqrt{2}}{2} - \frac{\sqrt{2}}{2}i, \frac{\sqrt{2}}{2} - \frac{\sqrt{2}}{2}i$

**77.** $\left(2\sqrt{2}, \frac{3\pi}{4}\right)$  **79.** $\left(10, \frac{7\pi}{6}\right)$

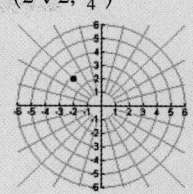  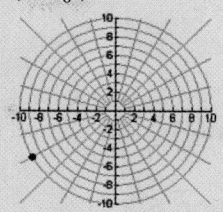

**81.** $\left(2, \frac{3\pi}{2}\right)$

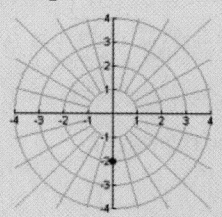

**83.** $\left(-\frac{3}{2}, \frac{3\sqrt{3}}{2}\right)$  **85.** $\left(1, \sqrt{3}\right)$  **87.** $\left(-\frac{1}{2}, -\frac{\sqrt{3}}{2}\right)$

**89.**  **91.**

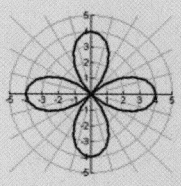  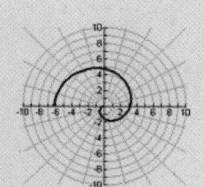

**93.** $65, -67.38014°$  **95.** $40°$

**97.** $12[\cos(246°) + i\sin(246°)]$

**99.** $\sqrt[4]{16}\left[\cos\left(\frac{120°}{4} + \frac{360°k}{4}\right) + i\sin\left(\frac{120°}{4} + \frac{360°k}{4}\right)\right]$,
$k = 0, 1, 2, 3$

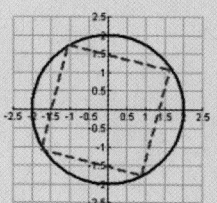

**101.** $\frac{\pi}{18}, \frac{5\pi}{18}, \frac{13\pi}{18}, \frac{17\pi}{18}, \frac{25\pi}{18}, \frac{29\pi}{18}$

## Practice Test

**1.** $13, 112.6°$  **3. a.** $\langle -14, 5 \rangle$  **b.** $-16$

**5.** $9$  **7.** $32{,}768\left[-1 + \sqrt{3}i\right]$

**9.** $\frac{-3\sqrt{3}}{2} - \frac{3}{2}i$  **11.** $\left(15\sqrt{5}, 333.4°\right)$

**13.**

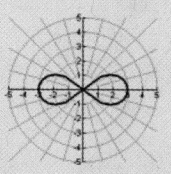

**17.** $-20$  **19.** $\sqrt{2}$  **21.** $50{,}769$ lb, $\alpha \approx 12°$

**23.** $4[\cos(67.5° + 90°k) + i\sin(67.5° + 90°k)]$,
$k = 0, 1, 2, 3$

**25.** $112°$

## Cumulative Test

**1.** $(f \circ g)(x) = \dfrac{-12x - 19}{3x + 5}$,
domains: $f = (-\infty, \infty), g = f \circ g = \left(-\frac{5}{3}, \infty\right)$

**3.** $y = -\frac{1}{3}(x + 1)^2 + 2 = -\frac{1}{3}x^2 - \frac{2}{3}x + \frac{5}{3}$

**5.** no HA, VA: $x = 1$, slant: $y = x - 1$

**7.** $\log_{625} 5 = \frac{1}{4}$

**9.** $\sin\theta = \frac{3}{8}, \cos\theta = \frac{\sqrt{55}}{8}, \tan\theta = \frac{3\sqrt{55}}{55}$
$\cot\theta = \frac{\sqrt{55}}{3}, \sec\theta = \frac{8\sqrt{55}}{55}, \csc\theta = \frac{8}{3}$

**11.** $c \approx 13.1$ m, $\alpha \approx 56.1°, \beta = 73.9°$

**13.** Amplitude $= \frac{1}{3}$, Period $= \frac{\pi}{2}$, Phase Shift $= \frac{\pi}{4}$ (right),
Vertical Shift $= 4$ (up)

**15.** $\frac{25\sqrt{3} - 48}{11}$

# CHAPTER 8

## Section 8.1

**1.** $(8, -1)$  **3.** $(1, -1)$  **5.** $(1, 2)$

**7.** $u = \frac{32}{17}, v = \frac{11}{17}$  **9.** no solution

**11.** infinitely many solutions  **13.** infinitely many solutions

**15.** $(1, 3)$  **17.** $(6, 8)$  **19.** $(-6.24, -2.15)$

**21.** $(2, 5)$  **23.** $(-3, 4)$  **25.** $\left(1, -\frac{2}{7}\right)$

**27.** $\left(\frac{19}{7}, \frac{11}{35}\right)$  **29.** infinitely many solutions

**31.** $(4, 0)$  **33.** $(-2, 1)$  **35.** $(3, -2)$

**37.** $\left(\frac{75}{32}, \frac{7}{16}\right)$  **39.** $(4.2, -3.5)$  **41.** c

**43.** d

**45.** $(0, 0)$

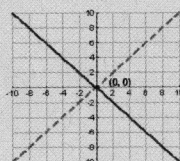

**47.** $(-1, -1)$

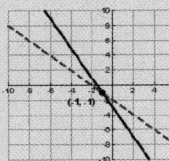

**49.** $(0, -6)$

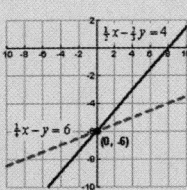

**51.** no solutions

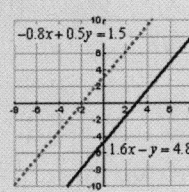

**53.** $(3, 1)$

**55.** $(1, 0)$

**57.** Infinitely many solutions: $\left(a, \frac{1.25 - 0.02a}{0.05}\right)$

**59.** 6 AusPens per kit

**61.** 15.86 ml of 8% HCl, 21.14 ml of 15% HCl

**63.** $300,000 of sales

**65.** 169 highway miles, 180.5 city miles

**67.** plane speed: 450 mph, wind speed: 50 mph

**69.** 10% stock: $3500, 14% stock: $6500

**71.** 8 CD players

**73.** Type I: $8; Type II: $9

**75.** males: 8,999,215; females: 9,329,125

**77.** Every term is the first equation is not multiplied by $-1$ correctly. The equation should be $-2x - y = 3$, and the resulting solution should be $x = 11, y = -25$.

**79.** Did not distribute $-1$ correctly. In Step 3, the calculation should be $-(-3y - 4) = 3y + 4$.

**81.** false        **83.** false        **85.** $A = -4, B = 7$

**87.** 2% drink: 8 cups, 4% drink: 96 cups

**89.** $(-1, 2)$        **91.** $(2, 6)$

**93.** $\left(\sqrt{3}, -2\right), \left(\sqrt{3}, 2\right), \left(-\sqrt{3}, -2\right), \left(-\sqrt{3}, 2\right)$

**95.** $(8.9, 6.4)$        **97.** Infinitely many solutions

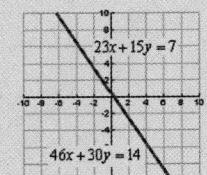

**99.** $(2.426, -0.059)$        **101.** $A = \frac{3}{2}, B = -\frac{1}{2}$

**103.** $A = \frac{4}{5}, B = \frac{1}{5}$

## Section 8.2

**1.** $x = -\frac{3}{2}, y = -3, z = \frac{9}{2}$        **3.** $x = -2, y = \frac{9}{2}, z = \frac{1}{2}$

**5.** $x = 5, y = 3, z = -1$        **7.** $x = \frac{90}{31}, y = \frac{103}{31}, z = \frac{9}{31}$

**9.** $x = -\frac{13}{4}, y = \frac{1}{2}, z = -\frac{5}{2}$        **11.** $x = -2, y = -1, z = 0$

**13.** $x = 2, y = 5, z = -1$        **15.** no solution

**17.** no solution

**19.** $x = 1 - a, y = -\left(a + \frac{1}{2}\right), z = a$

**21.** $x = 41 + 4a, y = 31 + 3a, z = a$

**23.** $x_1 = -\frac{1}{2}, x_2 = \frac{7}{4}, x_3 = -\frac{3}{4}$

**25.** no solution

**27.** $x_1 = 1, x_2 = -1 + a, x_3 = a$

**29.** $x = \frac{2}{3}a + \frac{8}{3}, y = -\frac{1}{3}a - \frac{10}{3}, z = a$

**31.** $x = a, y = \frac{20}{3} - \frac{13}{3}a, z = 5 - 3a$

**33.** 100 basic widgets, 100 midprice widgets, and 100 top-of-the-line widgets produced

**35.** 6 Mediterranean chicken sandwiches
3 six-in. tuna sandwiches
5 six-in. roast beef sandwiches

**37.** $h_0 = 0, v_0 = 52, a = -32$

**39.** $y = -0.0625x^2 + 5.25x - 50$

**41.** money market: $10,000,
mutual fund: $4000, stock: $6000

**43.** 33 regular model skis, 72 trick skis,
5 slalom skis

**45.** game 1: 885 points, game 2: 823 points,
game 3: 883 points

**47.** eagle balls: 1250, birdie balls: 3750,
bogey balls: 5000

**49.** 10 sec: 2, 20 sec: 3, 40 sec: 1

**51.** Equation (2) and Equation (3) must be added correctly – should be $2x - y + z = 2$. Also, should begin by eliminating one variable from Equation (1).

**53.** true

**55.** $a = 4, b = -2, c = -4$

**57.** $x^2 + y^2 + 4x - 2y - 4 = 0$

**59.** $a = -\frac{55}{24}, b = -\frac{1}{4}, c = \frac{223}{24}, d = \frac{1}{4}, e = 44$

**61.** no solution

**63.** $x_1 = -2, x_2 = 1, x_3 = -4, x_4 = 5$

**65.** $A = 0, B = 1, C = 1, D = 0$

**67.** $x = 41 + 4a, y = 31 + 3a, z = a$

**69.** same as answer in Example 57

**71.** $\left(-\frac{80}{7}, -\frac{80}{7}, \frac{48}{7}\right)$

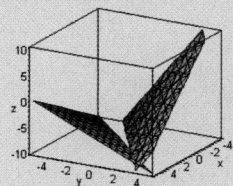

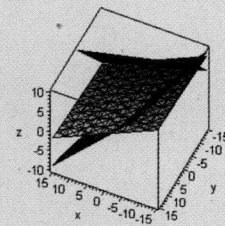

**73.** $A = 2, B = 3, C = -4$

**75.** $A = \frac{4}{3}, B = -1, C = -\frac{1}{3}$

## Section 8.3

**1.** $2 \times 3$

**3.** $1 \times 4$

**5.** $1 \times 1$

**7.** $\begin{bmatrix} 3 & -2 & | & 7 \\ -4 & 6 & | & -3 \end{bmatrix}$

**9.** $\begin{bmatrix} 2 & -3 & 4 & | & -3 \\ -1 & 1 & 2 & | & 1 \\ 5 & -2 & -3 & | & 7 \end{bmatrix}$

**11.** $\begin{bmatrix} 1 & 1 & 0 & | & 3 \\ 1 & 0 & -1 & | & 2 \\ 0 & 1 & 1 & | & 5 \end{bmatrix}$

**13.** $\begin{bmatrix} -4 & 3 & 5 & | & 2 \\ 2 & -3 & -2 & | & -3 \\ -2 & 4 & 3 & | & 1 \end{bmatrix}$

**15.** $\begin{cases} -3x + 7y = 2 \\ x + 5y = 8 \end{cases}$

**17.** $\begin{cases} -x = 4 \\ 7x + 9y + 3z = -3 \\ 4x + 6y - 5z = 8 \end{cases}$

**19.** $\begin{cases} x = a \\ y = b \end{cases}$

**21.** not reduced form

**23.** reduced form

**25.** not reduced form

**27.** reduced form

**29.** reduced form

**31.** $\begin{bmatrix} 1 & -2 & | & -3 \\ 0 & 7 & | & 5 \end{bmatrix}$

**33.** $\begin{bmatrix} 1 & -2 & -1 & | & 3 \\ 0 & 5 & -1 & | & 0 \\ 3 & -2 & 5 & | & 8 \end{bmatrix}$

**35.** $\begin{bmatrix} 1 & -2 & 5 & -1 & | & 2 \\ 0 & 1 & 1 & -3 & | & 3 \\ 0 & -2 & 1 & -2 & | & 5 \\ 0 & 0 & 1 & -1 & | & -6 \end{bmatrix}$

**37.** $\begin{bmatrix} 1 & 0 & 5 & -10 & | & -5 \\ 0 & 1 & 2 & -3 & | & -2 \\ 0 & 0 & -7 & 6 & | & 3 \\ 0 & 0 & 8 & -10 & | & -9 \end{bmatrix}$

**39.** $\begin{bmatrix} 1 & 0 & 4 & 0 & | & 27 \\ 0 & 1 & 2 & 0 & | & -11 \\ 0 & 0 & 1 & 0 & | & 21 \\ 0 & 0 & 0 & 1 & | & -3 \end{bmatrix}$

**41.** $\begin{bmatrix} 1 & 0 & | & -8 \\ 0 & 1 & | & 6 \end{bmatrix}$

**43.** $\begin{bmatrix} 1 & 0 & 0 & | & -2 \\ 0 & 1 & 0 & | & -1 \\ 0 & 0 & 1 & | & 0 \end{bmatrix}$

**45.** $\begin{bmatrix} 1 & 0 & 0 & | & 2 \\ 0 & 1 & 0 & | & 5 \\ 0 & 0 & 1 & | & -1 \end{bmatrix}$

**47.** $\begin{bmatrix} 1 & 0 & -2 & | & 1 \\ 0 & 1 & -2 & | & 2 \end{bmatrix}$

**49.** $\begin{bmatrix} 1 & 0 & 1 & | & 1 \\ 0 & 1 & 1 & | & -\frac{1}{2} \\ 0 & 0 & 0 & | & 0 \end{bmatrix}$

**51.** $x = -7, y = 5$

**53.** $x - 2y = -3$ or $x = 2a - 3, y = a$

**55.** no solution

**57.** $x = 4a + 41, y = 31 + 3a, z = a$

**59.** $x_1 = -\frac{1}{2}, x_2 = \frac{7}{4}, x_3 = -\frac{3}{4}$

**61.** no solution

**63.** $x_1 = 1, x_2 = a - 1, x_3 = a$

**65.** $x = \frac{2}{3}(a + 4), y = -\frac{1}{3}(a + 10), z = a$

**67.** no solution

**69.** $x_1 = -2, x_2 = 1, x_3 = -4, x_4 = 5$

**71.** $(1, -2)$

**73.** no solution

**75.** $(-2, 1, 3)$

**77.** $(3, -2, 2)$

**79.** no solution

**81.** $x = \frac{a}{4} + 3, y = \frac{7a}{4} - \frac{53}{3}, z = a$

**83.** $x = \frac{72 - 11a}{14}, y = \frac{13a + 4}{14}, z = a$

**85.** $x = 1, y = 2, z = -3, w = 1$

**87.** 960 red dwarf, 8 blue stars, 2,880,000 yellow stars

**89.** 2 chicken, 2 tuna, 8 roast beef, 2 turkey bacon

**91.** initial height: 0 ft, initial velocity: 50 ft/sec, acceleration: $-32$ ft/sec$^2$

**93.** $y = -0.053x^2 + 4.58x - 34.76$

**95.** about 88 ml of the 1.5% solution and 12 ml of the 30% solution

**97.** 200 basic widgets, 100 midprice widgets, and 75 top-of-the-line widgets produced

**99.** money market: $5500, mutual fund: $2500, stock: $2000

**101.** product $x$: 25 units, product $y$: 40 units, product $z$: 6 units

**103.** general admission: 25, reserved: 30, end zone: 45

**105.** $a = -\frac{22}{17}, b = -\frac{44}{17}, c = -\frac{280}{17}$

**107.** Need to line up a single variable in a given column before forming the augmented matrix. The correct martrix is

$$\begin{bmatrix} -1 & 1 & 1 & | & 2 \\ 1 & 1 & -2 & | & -3 \\ 1 & 1 & 1 & | & 6 \end{bmatrix}, \text{ after reducing, } \begin{bmatrix} 1 & 0 & 0 & | & 2 \\ 0 & 1 & 0 & | & 1 \\ 0 & 0 & 1 & | & 3 \end{bmatrix}.$$

**109.** Row 3 is not inconsistent. It implies $z = 0$.

**111.** false     **113.** true     **115.** false     **117.** false

**119.** $f(x) = -\frac{11}{6}x^4 + \frac{44}{3}x^3 - \frac{223}{6}x^2 + \frac{94}{3}x + 44$

**121.** 35 hr     **123.** $(-1, 2), (2, -1),$ and $(3, -1)$

**125.**
```
rref([A])
  [[1 0 -4 41]
   [0 1 -3 31]
   [0 0 0 0 ]]
```

**127. a.**
```
rref([A])
  [[1 0 0 -.23653...
   [0 1 0 .928846...
   [0 0 1 6.08846...
```
$y = -0.24x^2 + 0.93x + 6.09$

**b.**
```
QuadReg
 y=ax²+bx+c
 a=-.2365384615
 b=.9288461538
 c=6.088461538
```
$y = -0.24x^2 + 0.93x + 6.09$

**129.** $c_1 = \frac{3}{4}, c_2 = -\frac{3}{4}$     **131.** $c_1 = 2, c_2 = -3, c_3 = 1$

## Section 8.4

**1.** $2 \times 3$     **3.** $2 \times 2$     **5.** $3 \times 3$

**7.** $4 \times 4$     **9.** $x = -5, y = 1$

**11.** $x = -3, y = -2, z = 3$     **13.** $x = 6, y = 3$

**15.** $\begin{bmatrix} -1 & 5 & 1 \\ 5 & 2 & 5 \end{bmatrix}$     **17.** $\begin{bmatrix} -2 & 4 \\ 2 & -2 \\ -1 & 3 \end{bmatrix}$

**19.** not defined     **21.** not defined

**23.** $\begin{bmatrix} -2 & 12 & 3 \\ 13 & 2 & 14 \end{bmatrix}$     **25.** $\begin{bmatrix} 8 & 3 \\ 11 & 5 \end{bmatrix}$

**27.** $\begin{bmatrix} -3 & 21 & 6 \\ -4 & 7 & 1 \\ 13 & 14 & 9 \end{bmatrix}$     **29.** $\begin{bmatrix} 3 & 6 \\ -2 & -2 \\ 17 & 24 \end{bmatrix}$

**31.** not defined     **33.** $[0 \quad 60]$

**35.** $[-6 \quad 1 \quad -9]$     **37.** $\begin{bmatrix} 7 & 10 & -8 \\ 0 & 15 & 5 \\ 23 & 0 & -7 \end{bmatrix}$

**39.** $\begin{bmatrix} 12 & 20 \\ 30 & 42 \end{bmatrix}$     **41.** $\begin{bmatrix} -4 \\ -4 \\ -16 \end{bmatrix}$

**43.** not defined     **45.** yes

**47.** yes     **49.** yes

**51.** $\begin{bmatrix} 0 & -1 \\ 1 & 2 \end{bmatrix}$     **53.** $\begin{bmatrix} -\frac{1}{13} & \frac{8}{39} \\ \frac{20}{39} & -\frac{4}{117} \end{bmatrix}$

**55.** $\begin{bmatrix} \frac{1}{2} & \frac{1}{2} & 0 \\ \frac{1}{2} & 0 & \frac{1}{2} \\ 0 & -\frac{1}{2} & -\frac{1}{2} \end{bmatrix}$     **57.** $A^{-1}$ does not exist.

**59.** $\begin{bmatrix} -\frac{1}{2} & -\frac{1}{2} & \frac{5}{2} \\ \frac{1}{2} & \frac{1}{2} & -\frac{3}{2} \\ 0 & -1 & 1 \end{bmatrix}$     **61.** $\begin{bmatrix} \frac{1}{2} & \frac{1}{2} & 0 \\ \frac{3}{4} & \frac{1}{4} & -\frac{1}{2} \\ \frac{1}{4} & \frac{3}{4} & -\frac{1}{2} \end{bmatrix}$

**63.** $x = 2, y = -1$     **65.** $x = \frac{1}{2}, y = \frac{1}{3}$

**67.** $x = 0, y = 0, z = 1$

**69.** $A^{-1}$ does not exist

**71.** $x = -1, y = 1, z = -7$     **73.** $x = 3, y = 5, z = 4$

**75.** $A = \begin{bmatrix} 0.70 \\ 0.30 \end{bmatrix}, B = \begin{bmatrix} 0.89 \\ 0.84 \end{bmatrix}$

**a.** $46A = \begin{bmatrix} 32.2 \\ 13.8 \end{bmatrix}$, out of 46 million people, 32.2 million said that they had tried to quit smoking, while 13.8 million said that they had not.

**b.** $46B = \begin{bmatrix} 40.94 \\ 38.64 \end{bmatrix}$, out of 46 million people, 40.94 million believed that smoking would increase the chance of getting lung cancer, and that 38.64 million believed that smoking would shorten their lives.

**77.** $A = \begin{bmatrix} 0.589 & 0.628 \\ 0.414 & 0.430 \end{bmatrix}, B = \begin{bmatrix} 100M \\ 110M \end{bmatrix}$

$AB = \begin{bmatrix} 127.98M \\ 88.7M \end{bmatrix}$ 127.98 million registered voters, of those 88.7 million actually vote

**79.** $A = [0.45 \quad 0.50 \quad 1.00]$

$B = \begin{bmatrix} 7{,}523 \\ 2{,}700 \\ 15{,}200 \end{bmatrix} \quad AB = [19{,}935.35]$

**81.** $AB = \begin{bmatrix} 0.228 \\ 0.081 \\ 0.015 \end{bmatrix}$, total cost per mile to run each type of automobile

**83.** $N = \begin{bmatrix} 2 \\ 1 \\ 0 \end{bmatrix} \quad XN = \begin{bmatrix} 10 \\ 16 \\ 20 \end{bmatrix}$

The nutritional content of the meal is 10 g of carbohydrates, 16 g of protein, and 20 g of fat.

**85.** $N = \begin{bmatrix} 200 \\ 25 \\ 0 \end{bmatrix} \quad XN = \begin{bmatrix} 9.25 \\ 13.25 \\ 15.75 \end{bmatrix}$

Company 1 would charge \$9.25, Company 2 would charge \$13.25, and Company 3 would charge \$15.75, respectively, for 200 minutes of talking and 25 text message. The better cell phone provider for this employee would be Company 1.

**87.** JAW          **89.** LEG          **91.** EYE

**93.** $X = \begin{bmatrix} 8 & 4 & 6 \\ 6 & 10 & 5 \\ 10 & 4 & 8 \end{bmatrix}^{-1} \begin{bmatrix} 18 \\ 21 \\ 22 \end{bmatrix} = \begin{bmatrix} 1 \\ 1 \\ 1 \end{bmatrix}$

The combination of one serving each of food A, B, and C will create a meal of 18 g carbohydrates, 21 g of protein, and 22 g of fat.

**95.** $X = \begin{bmatrix} 0.03 & 0.06 & 0.15 \\ 0.04 & 0.05 & 0.18 \\ 0.05 & 0.07 & 0.13 \end{bmatrix}^{-1} \begin{bmatrix} 49.50 \\ 52.00 \\ 58.50 \end{bmatrix} = \begin{bmatrix} 350 \\ 450 \\ 100 \end{bmatrix}$

The employee's normal monthly usage is 350 minutes talking, 400 text messages, and 100 MB of data usage.

**97.** Not multiplying correctly. It should be:
$\begin{bmatrix} 3 & 2 \\ 1 & 4 \end{bmatrix} \begin{bmatrix} -1 & 3 \\ -2 & 5 \end{bmatrix} = \begin{bmatrix} -7 & 19 \\ -9 & 23 \end{bmatrix}$

**99.** $A$ is not invertible because the identity matrix was not reached.

**101.** false          **103.** true          **105.** false

**107.** $\begin{bmatrix} a_{11}^2 + a_{12}a_{21} & a_{11}a_{12} + a_{12}a_{22} \\ a_{21}a_{11} + a_{22}a_{21} & a_{22}^2 + a_{21}a_{12} \end{bmatrix}$

**109.** $x = 9$

**111.** $A = \begin{bmatrix} 1 & 1 \\ 1 & 1 \end{bmatrix}$, $A^2 = \begin{bmatrix} 2 & 2 \\ 2 & 2 \end{bmatrix}$, $A^3 = 2^{n-1}A, n \geq 1$

**113.** must have $m = p$

**115.** $A \cdot A^{-1} = \begin{bmatrix} a & b \\ c & d \end{bmatrix} \cdot \left( \dfrac{1}{ad - bc} \begin{bmatrix} d & -b \\ -c & a \end{bmatrix} \right)$

$= \dfrac{1}{ad - bc} \left( \begin{bmatrix} a & b \\ c & d \end{bmatrix} \cdot \begin{bmatrix} d & -b \\ -c & a \end{bmatrix} \right)$

$= \dfrac{1}{ad - bc} \begin{bmatrix} ad - bc & 0 \\ 0 & ad - bc \end{bmatrix}$

$= \begin{bmatrix} \frac{ad - bc}{ad - bc} & 0 \\ 0 & \frac{ad - bc}{ad - bc} \end{bmatrix} = \begin{bmatrix} 1 & 0 \\ 0 & 1 \end{bmatrix} = I$

**117.** $ad - bc = 0$

**119.** $\begin{bmatrix} 33 & 35 \\ -96 & -82 \\ 31 & 19 \\ 146 & 138 \end{bmatrix}$          **121.** not defined

**123.** $\begin{bmatrix} 5 & -4 & 4 \\ 2 & -15 & -3 \\ 26 & 4 & -8 \end{bmatrix}$

**125.** $\begin{bmatrix} -\frac{115}{6008} & \frac{431}{6008} & \frac{-1067}{6008} & \frac{103}{751} \\ \frac{411}{6008} & \frac{-391}{6008} & \frac{731}{6008} & \frac{-22}{751} \\ \frac{57}{751} & \frac{28}{751} & \frac{-85}{751} & \frac{3}{751} \\ \frac{-429}{6008} & \frac{145}{6008} & \frac{1035}{6008} & \frac{12}{751} \end{bmatrix}$

**127.** $\begin{bmatrix} \frac{1}{4x} & \frac{1}{4x} \\ \frac{1}{4y} & -\frac{1}{4y} \end{bmatrix}$          **129** $\begin{bmatrix} \cos\theta & -\sin\theta \\ \sin\theta & \cos\theta \end{bmatrix}$

## Section 8.5

**1.** $-2$          **3.** 31          **5.** $-28$

**7.** $-0.6$          **9.** 0          **11.** $x = 5, y = -6$

**13.** $x = -2, y = 1$          **15.** $x = -3, y = -4$

**17.** $x = -2, y = 5$          **19.** $x = 2, y = 2$

**21.** $D = 0$, inconsistent or dependent system

**23.** $D = 0$, inconsistent or dependent system

**25.** $x = \frac{1}{2}, y = -1$          **27.** $x = 1.5, y = 2.1$

**29.** $x = 0, y = 7$          **31.** 7

**33.** $-25$          **35.** $-180$

**37.** 0          **39.** 238

**41.** 0          **43.** $x = 2, y = 3, z = 5$

**45.** $x = -2, y = 3, z = 5$          **47.** $x = 2, y = -3, z = 1$

**49.** $D = 0$, inconsistent or dependent system

**51.** $D = 0$, inconsistent or dependent system

**53.** $x = -3, y = 1, z = 4$          **55.** $x = 2, y = -3, z = 5$

**57.** $x = -2, y = \frac{3}{2}, z = 3$     **59.** yes

**61.** 6 units$^2$     **63.** 6 units$^2$

**65.** $y = 2x$     **67.** $I_1 = \frac{7}{2}, I_2 = \frac{5}{2}, I_3 = 1$

**69.** The second determinant should be subtracted; that is, it should be $-1\begin{bmatrix} -3 & 2 \\ 1 & -1 \end{bmatrix}$.

**71.** In $D_x$ and $D_y$, the column $\begin{bmatrix} 6 \\ -3 \end{bmatrix}$ should replace the column corresponding to the variable that is being solved for in each case. Precisely, $D_x$ should be $\begin{bmatrix} 6 & 3 \\ -3 & -1 \end{bmatrix}$ and $D_y$ should be $\begin{bmatrix} 2 & 6 \\ -1 & -3 \end{bmatrix}$.

**73.** true     **75.** false

**77.** $abc$     **79.** $-419$

**81.** $-b_1\begin{vmatrix} a_2 & c_2 \\ a_3 & c_3 \end{vmatrix} + b_2\begin{vmatrix} a_1 & c_1 \\ a_3 & c_3 \end{vmatrix} - b_3\begin{vmatrix} a_1 & c_1 \\ a_2 & c_2 \end{vmatrix}$

$= -b_1[(a_2)(c_3) - (a_3)(c_2)] + b_2[(a_1)(c_3) - (a_3)(c_1)]$

$\quad - b_3[(a_1)(c_2) - (a_2)(c_1)]$

$= -a_2b_1c_3 + a_3b_1c_2 + a_1b_2c_3 - a_3b_2c_1 - a_1b_3c_2 + a_2b_3c_1$

**85.** $-180$     **87.** $-1019$

**89.** $x = -6.4, y = 1.5, z = 3.4$     **91.** $r$

**93.** $-\rho^2\sin\varphi$

## Section 8.6

**1.** d     **3.** a     **5.** b

**7.** $\dfrac{A}{x-5} + \dfrac{B}{x+4}$     **9.** $\dfrac{A}{x-4} + \dfrac{B}{x} + \dfrac{C}{x^2}$

**11.** $2x - 6 + \dfrac{3x+33}{x^2+x+5}$     **13.** $\dfrac{Ax+B}{x^2+10} + \dfrac{Cx+D}{(x^2+10)^2}$

**15.** $\dfrac{1}{x} - \dfrac{1}{x+1}$     **17.** $\dfrac{1}{x-1}$

**19.** $\dfrac{2}{x-3} + \dfrac{7}{x+5}$     **21.** $\dfrac{3}{x-1} + \dfrac{4}{(x-1)^2}$

**23.** $\dfrac{4}{x+3} - \dfrac{15}{(x+3)^2}$     **25.** $\dfrac{3}{x+1} + \dfrac{1}{x-5} + \dfrac{2}{(x-5)^2}$

**27.** $\dfrac{-2}{x+4} + \dfrac{7x}{x^2+3}$     **29.** $\dfrac{-2}{x-7} + \dfrac{4x-3}{3x^2-7x+5}$

**31.** $\dfrac{x}{x^2+9} - \dfrac{9x}{(x^2+9)^2}$     **33.** $\dfrac{2x-3}{x^2+1} + \dfrac{5x+1}{(x^2+1)^2}$

**35.** $\dfrac{1}{x-1} + \dfrac{1}{2(x+1)} + \dfrac{-3x-1}{2(x^2+1)}$

**37.** $\dfrac{3}{x-1} + \dfrac{2x+5}{x^2+2x-1}$     **39.** $\dfrac{1}{x-1} + \dfrac{1-x}{x^2+x+1}$

**41.** $\dfrac{1}{d_o} + \dfrac{1}{d_i} = \dfrac{1}{f}$     **43.** $-\frac{11}{4}e^{2t} + \frac{7}{4}e^{-2t}$

**45.** The form of the decomposition is incorrect. It should be $\dfrac{A}{x} + \dfrac{Bx+C}{x^2+1}$. Once this correction is made, the correct decomposition is $\dfrac{1}{x} + \dfrac{2x+3}{x^2+1}$.

**47.** false     **49.** true     **51.** false

**53.** $\dfrac{1}{x-1} - \dfrac{1}{x+2} + \dfrac{1}{x-2}$

**55.** $\dfrac{1}{x} + \dfrac{1}{x+1} - \dfrac{1}{x^3}$

**57.** $\dfrac{x}{x^2+1} - \dfrac{2x}{(x^2+1)^2} + \dfrac{x+2}{(x^2+1)^3}$

**59.** yes     **61.** no

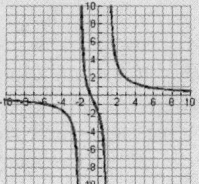   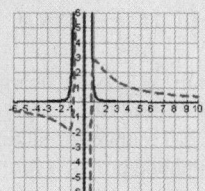

**63.** yes

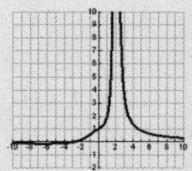

**65.** $\dfrac{3}{k} - \dfrac{3}{k+3}$     **67.** $\dfrac{1}{k^2} - \dfrac{1}{(k+1)^2}$

## Section 8.7

**1.** d     **3.** b

**5.**     **7.**

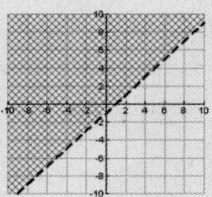   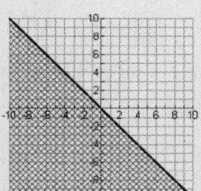

**9.**     **11.**

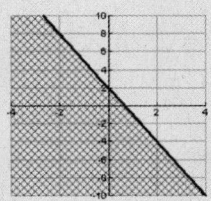    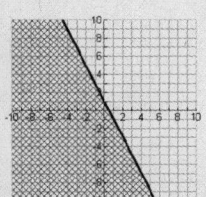

**13.**

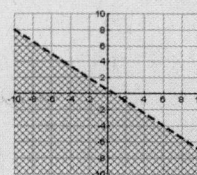

**15.**

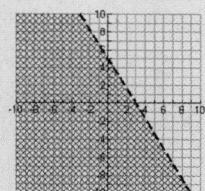

**17.**

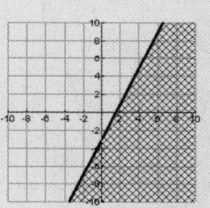

**19.**

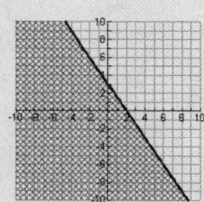

**21.**

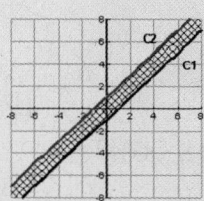

**23.**

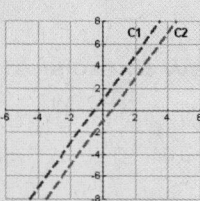

**25.**

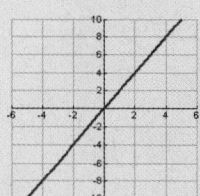

**27.**

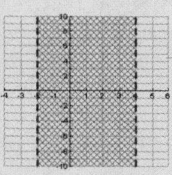

**29.**

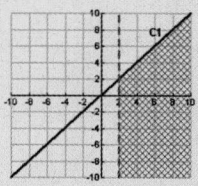

**31.**

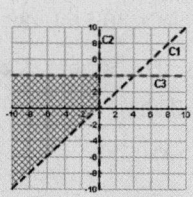

**33.**

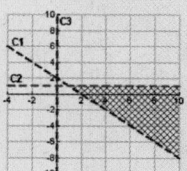

**35.**

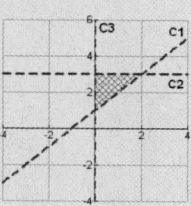

**37.**

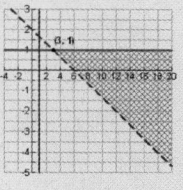

**39.**

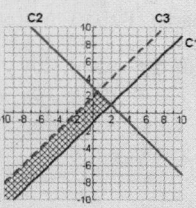

**41.**

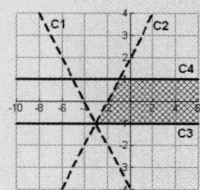

**43.**

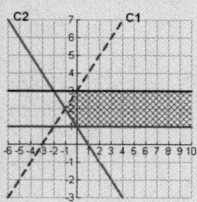

**45.** no solution

**47.**

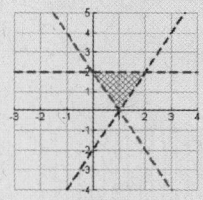

**49.**

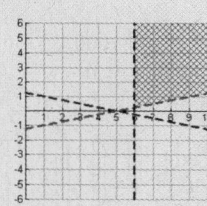

**51.** $f(x, y) = z = 2x + 3y$
$f(-1, 4) = 10$
$f(2, 4) = 16$ (MAX),
$f(-2, -1) = -7$ (MIN),
$f(1, -1) = -1$

**53.** $f(x, y) = z = 1.5x + 4.5y$
$f(-1, 4) = 16.5$
$f(2, 4) = 21$ (MAX)
$f(-2, -1) = -7.5$ (MIN)
$f(1, -1) = -3$

**55.** minimize at $f(0, 0) = 0$

**57.** no maximum

**59.** minimize at $f(0, 0) = 0$

**61.** maximize at $f(1, 6) = \frac{53}{20} = 2.65$

**63.** $\begin{cases} P \le 80 - 0.01x \\ P \ge 60 \\ x \ge 0 \end{cases}$

**65.** 20,000 units$^2$

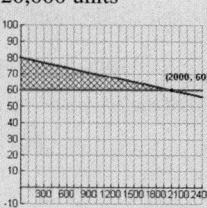

**67.** $\begin{cases} x \ge 0, y \ge 0 \\ x + 20y \le 2400 \\ 25x + 150y \le 6000 \end{cases}$

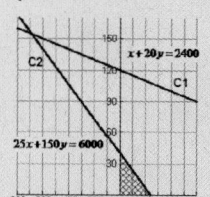

**69.** Frances T-shirts: 130
Charley T-shirts: 50 (profit $950)

**71.** **a.** $275 \leq 10x + 20y$
$125 \leq 15x + 10y$
$200 \leq 20x + 15y$
$x \geq 0, y \geq 0$

**b.**
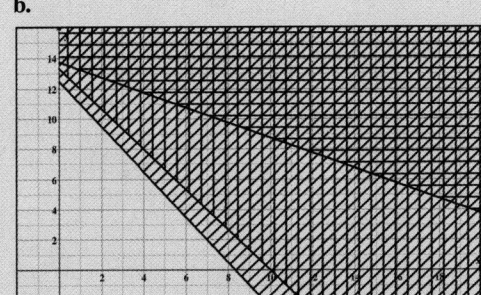

**73.** **a.** $x \geq 2y$
$x + y \geq 1000$
$x \geq 0, y \geq 0$

**b.**
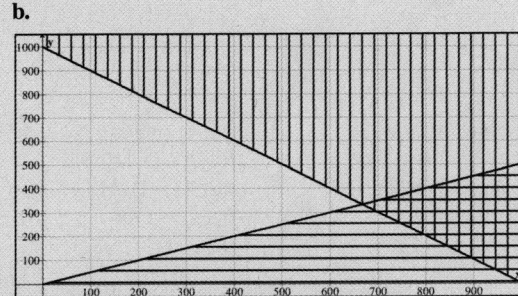

**c.** Two possible solutions would be for the manufacturer to produce 700 USB wireless mice and 300 Bluetooth mice or 800 USB wireless mice and 300 Bluetooth mice.

**75.** laptops: 25, desktops: 0 (profit $7500)

**77.** first-class cars: 3, second-class cars: 27

**79.** 200 of each type of ski

**81.** The shading should be above the line.

**83.** true       **85.** false       **87.** false

**89.** shaded rectangle

**91.**
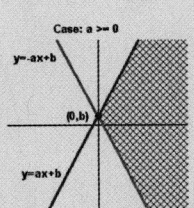

**93.** maximum at $(0, a)$ and is $a$

**95.**                          **97.**
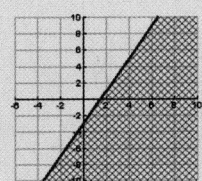          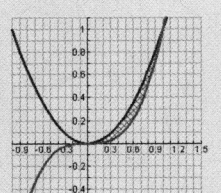

**99.**                          **101.**
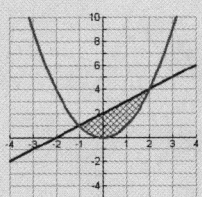          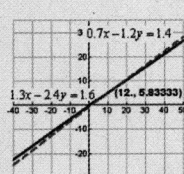

**Review Exercises**

**1.** $(3, 0)$       **3.** $\left(\frac{13}{4}, 8\right)$       **5.** $(2, 1)$       **7.** $\left(\frac{19}{8}, \frac{13}{8}\right)$

**9.** $(-2, 1)$                    **11.** $\left(12, 5.8\overline{3}\right)$

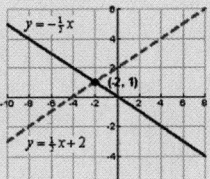

**13.** $(3, -2)$                  **15.** $(-1, 2)$

**17.** c                          **19.** d

**21.** 6% NaCl: 10.5 ml, 18% NaCl: 31.5 ml

**23.** $x = -1, y = -a + 2, z = a$

**25.** no solution

**27.** $y = -0.0050x^2 + 0.4486x - 3.8884$

**29.** $\begin{bmatrix} 5 & 7 & | & 2 \\ 3 & -4 & | & -2 \end{bmatrix}$       **31.** $\begin{bmatrix} 2 & 0 & -1 & | & 3 \\ 0 & 1 & -3 & | & -2 \\ 1 & 0 & 4 & | & -3 \end{bmatrix}$

**33.** no                         **35.** no

**37.** $\begin{bmatrix} 1 & -2 & | & 1 \\ 0 & 1 & | & -1 \end{bmatrix}$       **39.** $\begin{bmatrix} 1 & -4 & 3 & | & -1 \\ 0 & -2 & 3 & | & -2 \\ 0 & 1 & -4 & | & 8 \end{bmatrix}$

**41.** $\begin{bmatrix} 1 & 0 & | & \frac{3}{5} \\ 0 & 1 & | & -\frac{1}{5} \end{bmatrix}$       **43.** $\begin{bmatrix} 1 & 0 & 0 & | & -4 \\ 0 & 1 & 0 & | & 8 \\ 0 & 0 & 1 & | & -4 \end{bmatrix}$

**45.** $x = \frac{5}{4}, y = \frac{7}{8}$      **47.** $x = 2, y = 1$

**49.** $x = -\frac{74}{21}, y = -\frac{73}{21}, z = -\frac{3}{7}$

**51.** $x = 1, y = 3, z = -5$

**53.** $x = -\frac{3}{7}a - 2, y = \frac{2}{7}a + 2, z = a$

**55.** $y = -0.005x^2 + 0.45x - 3.89$      **57.** not defined

**59.** $\begin{bmatrix} 3 & 5 & 2 \\ 7 & 8 & 1 \end{bmatrix}$    **61.** $\begin{bmatrix} 9 & -4 \\ 9 & 9 \end{bmatrix}$

**63.** $\begin{bmatrix} 4 & 13 \\ 18 & 11 \end{bmatrix}$    **65.** $\begin{bmatrix} 0 & -19 \\ -18 & -9 \end{bmatrix}$

**67.** $\begin{bmatrix} -7 & -11 & -8 \\ 3 & 7 & 2 \end{bmatrix}$    **69.** $\begin{bmatrix} 10 & -13 \\ 18 & -20 \end{bmatrix}$

**71.** $\begin{bmatrix} 17 & -8 & 18 \\ 33 & 0 & 42 \end{bmatrix}$    **73.** $\begin{bmatrix} 10 & 9 & 20 \\ 22 & -4 & 2 \end{bmatrix}$

**75.** yes      **77.** yes

**79.** $\begin{bmatrix} \frac{2}{5} & -\frac{1}{5} \\ \frac{3}{10} & \frac{1}{10} \end{bmatrix}$    **81.** $\begin{bmatrix} 0 & -\frac{1}{2} \\ 1 & 0 \end{bmatrix}$

**83.** $\begin{bmatrix} -\frac{1}{6} & \frac{7}{12} & -\frac{1}{12} \\ \frac{1}{2} & -\frac{1}{4} & -\frac{1}{4} \\ \frac{1}{6} & -\frac{1}{12} & -\frac{5}{12} \end{bmatrix}$    **85.** $\begin{bmatrix} 0 & -\frac{2}{5} & \frac{1}{5} \\ 1 & -\frac{2}{5} & \frac{1}{5} \\ -\frac{1}{2} & \frac{3}{10} & \frac{1}{10} \end{bmatrix}$

**87.** $x = 5, y = 4$      **89.** $x = 8, y = 12$

**91.** $x = 1, y = 2, z = 3$      **93.** $-8$

**95.** 5.4      **97.** $x = 3, y = 1$

**99.** $x = 6, y = 0$      **101.** $x = 90, y = 155$

**103.** 11      **105.** $-abd$

**107.** $x = 1, y = 1, z = 2$    **109.** $x = -\frac{15}{7}, y = -\frac{25}{7}, z = \frac{19}{14}$

**111.** $\dfrac{A}{x - 1} + \dfrac{B}{(x - 1)^2} + \dfrac{C}{x + 3} + \dfrac{D}{x - 5}$

**113.** $\dfrac{A}{x} + \dfrac{B}{(2x + 1)^2} + \dfrac{C}{4x + 5} + \dfrac{D}{2x + 1}$

**115.** $\dfrac{A}{x - 3} + \dfrac{B}{x + 4}$    **117.** $\dfrac{Ax + B}{x^2 + 17} + \dfrac{Cx + D}{(x^2 + 17)^2}$

**119.** $\dfrac{4}{x - 1} + \dfrac{5}{x + 7}$    **121.** $\dfrac{1}{2x} + \dfrac{15}{2(x - 5)} - \dfrac{3}{2(x + 5)}$

**123.** $\dfrac{-2}{x + 1} + \dfrac{2}{x}$    **125.** $\dfrac{5}{x + 2} - \dfrac{27}{(x + 2)^2}$

**127.**      **129.**

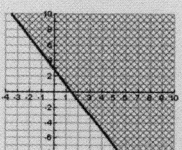     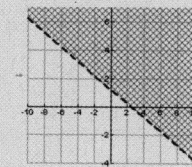

**131.**      **133.**

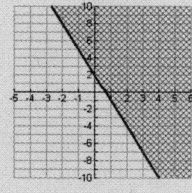     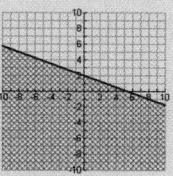

**135.** no solution      **137.**

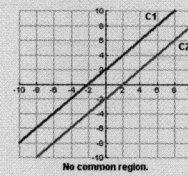     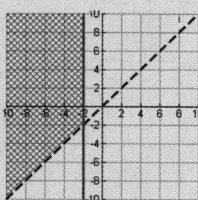

No common region.

**139.**

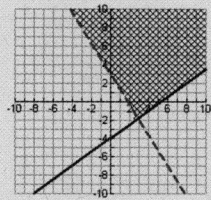

**141.** minimum value of $z$: 0, occurs at $(0, 0)$

**143.** minimum value of $z$: $-30$, occurs at $(0, 6)$

**145.** ocean watercolor: 10
geometric shape: 30 (profit $390)

**147.** $(2, -3)$

**149.** $(3.6, 3, 0.8)$

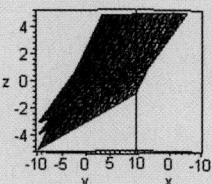

**151. a.**

```
rref([A])
[[1 0 0 .161066…
 [0 1 0 -.04946…
 [0 0 1 -4.1012…
```

$y = 0.16x^2 - 0.05x - 4.10$

**b.**

```
QuadReg
y=ax²+bx+c
a=.1610661269
b=-.0494601889
c=-4.101214575
```

$y = 0.16x^2 - 0.05x - 4.10$

**153.** $\begin{bmatrix} -238 & 206 & 50 \\ -113 & 159 & 135 \\ 40 & -30 & 0 \end{bmatrix}$

**155.** $x = 2.25, y = -4.35$      **157.** $x = -9.5, y = 3.4$

**159.** yes      **161.**

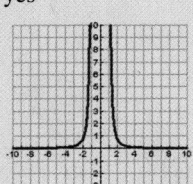 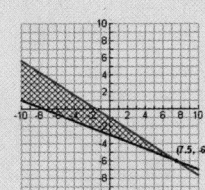

**163.** maximum is 12.06, occurs at (1.8, 0.6)

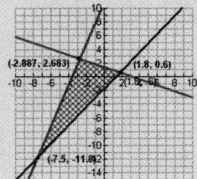

## Practice Test

**1.** $(7, 3)$      **3.** $x = a, y = a - 2$

**5.** $x = 1, y = -5, z = 3$      **7.** $\begin{bmatrix} 6 & 9 & 1 & | & 5 \\ 2 & -3 & 1 & | & 3 \\ 10 & 12 & 2 & | & 9 \end{bmatrix}$

**9.** $\begin{bmatrix} 1 & 3 & 5 \\ 0 & 1 & -11 \\ 0 & 7 & 15 \end{bmatrix}$

**11.** $x = -\frac{1}{3}a + \frac{7}{6}, y = \frac{1}{9}a - \frac{2}{9}, z = a$

**13.** $\begin{bmatrix} -11 & 19 \\ -6 & 8 \end{bmatrix}$      **15.** $\begin{bmatrix} \frac{1}{19} & \frac{3}{19} \\ \frac{5}{19} & -\frac{4}{19} \end{bmatrix}$

**17.** $x = -3, y = 1, z = 7$      **19.** $-31$

**21.** $x = 1, y = -1, z = 2$      **23.** $\dfrac{5}{x} - \dfrac{3}{x + 1}$

**25.** $\dfrac{1}{3x} + \dfrac{2}{3(x - 3)} - \dfrac{1}{x + 3}$

**27.**      **29.**

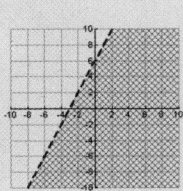 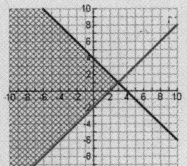

**31.** minimum value of $z$: 7, occurs at (0, 1)

**33.** $(12.5, -6.4)$

## Cumulative Test

**1.** 27      **3.** $2x + h - 3$

**5.** $(15, 6)$      **7.** VA: $x = 3$; HA: $y = -5$

**9.** $-1$      **11.** 2.585      **13.** $\frac{\sqrt{3}}{2}$

**15.** $\sin\theta = \frac{2\sqrt{29}}{29}, \cos\theta = \frac{-5\sqrt{29}}{29}, \tan\theta = \frac{-2}{5}, \cot\theta = -\frac{5}{2},$
$\sec\theta = -\frac{\sqrt{29}}{5}, \csc\theta = \frac{\sqrt{29}}{2}$

**17.**

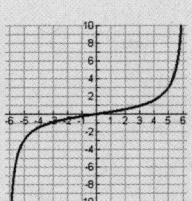

**19.** domain: $x \neq \frac{(2n + 1)\pi}{2} + \frac{\pi}{2} = \frac{(2n + 2)\pi}{2} = (n + 1)\pi$,
$n$ any integer, range: all reals

**21.** 1

**23.** $\alpha = 36.3°, b \approx 123.4$ m, $c \approx 78.1$ m

**25.** $-2, 1 - \sqrt{3}i, 1 + \sqrt{3}i$

**27.** $\begin{bmatrix} 72 & -18 & 54 \\ 26 & -2 & 4 \end{bmatrix}$      **29.** $x = \frac{3}{11}, y = -\frac{2}{11}$

**31.**

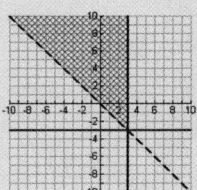

# CHAPTER 9
## Section 9.1

**1.** hyperbola      **3.** circle      **5.** hyperbola

**7.** ellipse      **9.** parabola      **11.** circle

## Section 9.2

**1.** c      **3.** d      **5.** c

**7.** a      **9.** $x^2 = 12y$      **11.** $y^2 = -20x$

**13.** $(x - 3)^2 = 8(y - 5)$      **15.** $(y - 4)^2 = -8(x - 2)$

**17.** $(x - 2)^2 = 4(3)(y - 1) = 12(y - 1)$

**19.** $(y + 1)^2 = 4(1)(x - 2) = 4(x - 2)$

**21.** $(y - 2)^2 = 8(x + 1)$      **23.** $(x - 2)^2 = -8(y + 1)$

**25.** vertex: (0, 0)
focus: (0, 2)
directrix: $y = -2$
length of latus rectum: 8

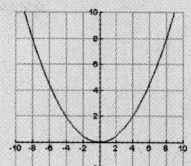

**27.** vertex: (0, 0)
focus: $\left(-\frac{1}{2}, 0\right)$
directrix: $x = \frac{1}{2}$
length of latus rectum: 2

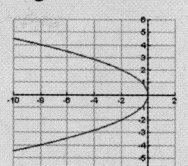

**29.** vertex: (0, 0)
focus: (0, 4)
directrix: $y = -4$
length of latus rectum: 16

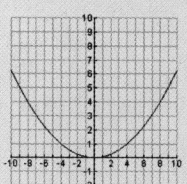

**31.** vertex: (0, 0)
focus: (1, 0)
directrix: $x = -1$
length of latus rectum: 4

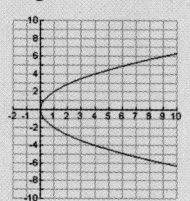

**33.** vertex: $(-3, 2)$

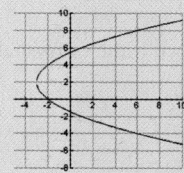

**35.** vertex: $(3, -1)$

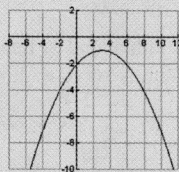

**37.** vertex: $(-5, 0)$

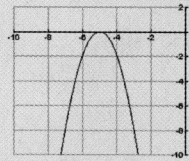

**39.** vertex: (0, 2)

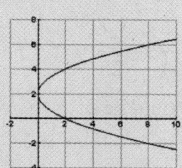

**41.** vertex: $(-3, -1)$

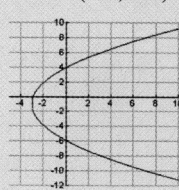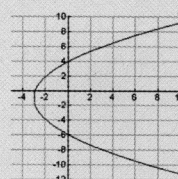

**43.** vertex: $\left(\frac{1}{2}, \frac{5}{4}\right)$

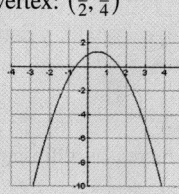

**45.** (0, 2), receiver placed 2 ft from vertex

**47.** opens up: $y = \frac{1}{8}x^2$, for any $x$ in $[-2.5, 2.5]$
opens right: $x = \frac{1}{8}y^2$, for any $y$ in $[-2.5, 2.5]$

**49.** $x^2 = 4(40)y = 160y$

**51.** yes, opening height 18.75 ft, mast 17 ft

**53.** 374.25 ft, $x^2 = 1497y$

**55.** 55 pulses per min

**57.** The maximum profit of $400,000 is achieved when 3000 units are produced.

**59.** If the vertex is at the origin and the focus is at (3, 0), then the parabola must open to the right. So, the general equation is $y^2 = 4px$, for some $p > 0$.

**61.** true

**63.** false

**65.** $x = h - 1$

**67.** $\left(6, \frac{13}{2}\right)$

**69.** Equate $d_1$ and $d_2$ and simplify:
$$\sqrt{(x - 0)^2 + (y - p)^2} = |y + p|$$
$$x^2 = 4py$$

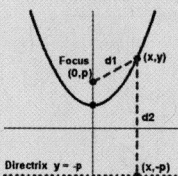

**71.** $(y - 6)^2 = 8(x - 2)$, $(y - 6)^2 = -4(x - 6)$

**73.** (2, 3), $(-2, 3)$

**75.**

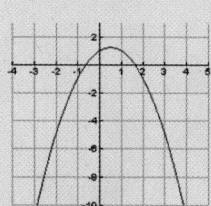

**77.** vertex: $(2.5, -3.5)$
opens right

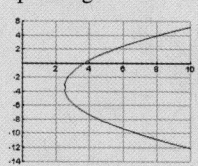

**79.** vertex: (1.8, 1.5)
opens left

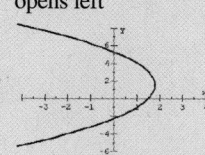

**81.** (2, 3), $(-2, 3)$

**83.** (1, 7), (10, 10)

## Section 9.3

**1.** d

**3.** a

**5.** center: (0, 0)
vertices: $(\pm 5, 0)$, $(0, \pm 4)$

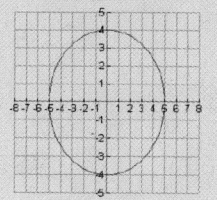

**7.** center: (0, 0)
vertices: $(\pm 4, 0)$, $(0, \pm 8)$

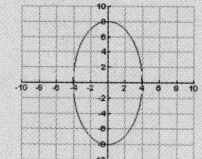

**9.** center: $(0, 0)$
vertices: $(\pm 10, 0)$, $(0, \pm 1)$

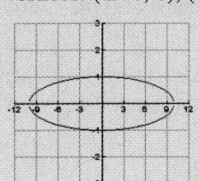

**11.** center: $(0, 0)$
vertices: $\left(\pm \frac{3}{2}, 0\right)$, $\left(0, \pm \frac{1}{9}\right)$

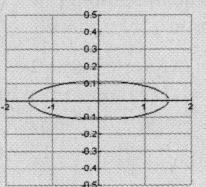

**35.** center: $(1, 1)$
vertices: $\left(1 \pm 2\sqrt{2}, 1\right)$, $(1, 3)$, $(1, -1)$

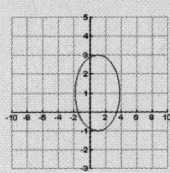

**13.** center: $(0, 0)$
vertices: $(\pm 2, 0)$, $(0, \pm 4)$

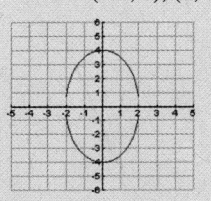

**15.** center: $(0, 0)$
vertices: $(\pm 2, 0)$, $\left(0, \pm \sqrt{2}\right)$

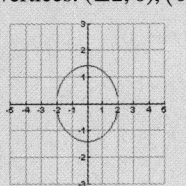

**37.** center: $(-2, -3)$
vertices: $\left(-2 \pm \sqrt{10}, -3\right)$, $\left(-2, -3 \pm 5\sqrt{2}\right)$

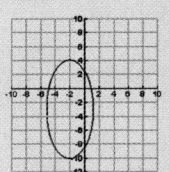

**17.** $\frac{x^2}{36} + \frac{y^2}{20} = 1$

**19.** $\frac{x^2}{7} + \frac{y^2}{16} = 1$

**21.** $\frac{x^2}{4} + \frac{y^2}{16} = 1$

**23.** $\frac{x^2}{9} + \frac{y^2}{49} = 1$

**25.** c

**27.** b

**29.** center: $(1, 2)$
vertices: $(-3, 2)$, $(5, 2)$, $(1, 0)$, $(1, 4)$

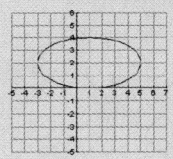

**31.** center: $(-3, 4)$
vertices: $\left(-2\sqrt{2} - 3, 4\right)$, $\left(2\sqrt{2} - 3, 4\right)$,
$\left(-3, 4 + 4\sqrt{5}\right)$, $\left(-3, 4 - 4\sqrt{5}\right)$

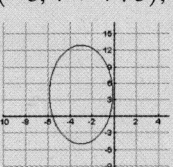

**33.** center: $(0, 3)$
vertices: $(-2, 3)$, $(2, 3)$, $(0, 3)$, $(0, 4)$

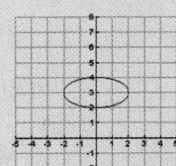

**39.** $\frac{(x - 2)^2}{25} + \frac{(y - 5)^2}{9} = 1$

**41.** $\frac{(x - 4)^2}{7} + \frac{(y + 4)^2}{16} = 1$

**43.** $\frac{(x - 3)^2}{4} + \frac{(y - 2)^2}{16} = 1$

**45.** $\frac{(x + 1)^2}{9} + \frac{(y + 4)^2}{25} = 1$

**47.** $\frac{x^2}{225} + \frac{y^2}{5625} = 1$

**49.** **a.** $\frac{x^2}{5625} + \frac{y^2}{400} = 1$

**b.** width at end of field is 24 yd; no, since width of football field is 30 yd wide

**51.** $\frac{x^2}{5,914,000,000^2} + \frac{y^2}{5,729,000,000^2} = 1$

**53.** $\frac{x^2}{150,000,000^2} + \frac{y^2}{146,000,000^2} = 1$

**55.** straight line       **57.** 2 mg/cm$^3$

**59.** **a.** $\frac{x^2}{64} + \frac{y^2}{25} = 1$   **b.** 42 in.   **c.** 1509 steps

**61.** It should be $a^2 = 6$, $b^2 = 4$, so that
$a = \pm\sqrt{6}$, $b = \pm 2$.

**63.** false       **65.** true       **67.** three ellipses

**69.** one point

**71.** Pluto: $e \cong 0.25$   Earth: $e \cong 0.02$

**73.** $x^2 + 3y^2 = 28$

**75.** $8x^2 + 9y^2 - 32x + 54y + 41 = 0$

**77.** as $c$ increases, ellipse more elongated

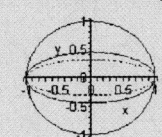

........... $x^2 + 10y^2 = 1$

‒ ‒ ‒ ‒ ‒ $x^2 + 5y^2 = 1$

———— $x^2 + y^2 = 1$

**79.** as $c$ increases, circle gets smaller

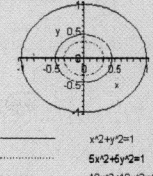

| | |
|---|---|
| —— | x^2+y^2=1 |
| ········· | 5x^2+6y^2=1 |
| ------ | 10x^2+10y^2=1 |

**81.** as $c$ decreases, the major axis becomes longer

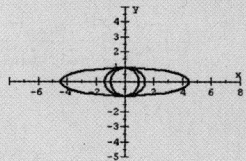

**83.** maximum: $-3$, minimum: $-7$

**85.** maximum: 1, minimum: $-17$

## Section 9.4

**1.** b

**3.** d

**5.**

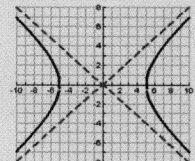

**7.**

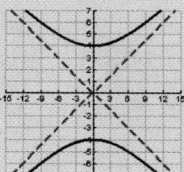

**9.**

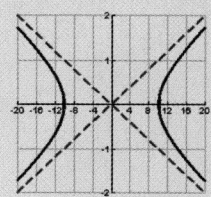

**11.**

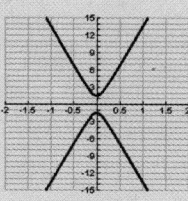

**13.**

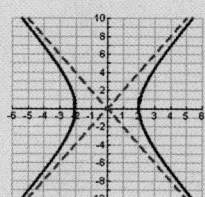

**15.**

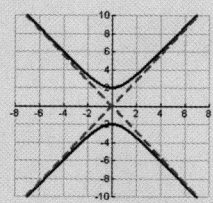

**17.** $\frac{x^2}{16} - \frac{y^2}{20} = 1$

**19.** $\frac{y^2}{9} - \frac{x^2}{7} = 1$

**21.** $x^2 - y^2 = a^2$

**23.** $\frac{y^2}{4} - x^2 = b^2$

**25.** c

**27.** b

**29.**

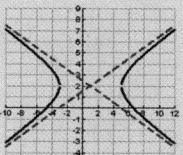

**31.**

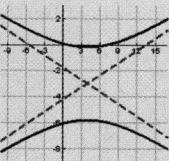

**33.**

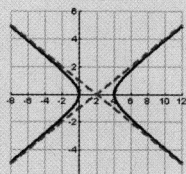

**35.**

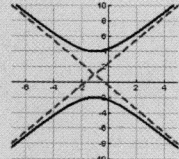

**37.**

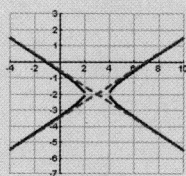

**39.** $\frac{(x-2)^2}{16} - \frac{(y-5)^2}{9} = 1$

**41.** $\frac{(y+4)^2}{9} - \frac{(x-4)^2}{7} = 1$

**43.** Ship will come ashore between the two stations 28.5 mi from one and 121.5 mi from the other.

**45.** 0.000484 sec

**47.** $y^2 - \frac{4}{5}x^2 = 1$

**49.** 275 ft

**51.** (76, 50)

**53.** (109.4, 60)

**55.** The transverse axis should be vertical. The points are (3, 0), $(-3, 0)$ and the vertices are (0, 2), (0, $-2$).

**57.** false

**59.** true

**61.** $(p, -q)$, $(-p, q)$ and $(-p, -q)$

**63.** $r > q$

**65.** $\frac{x^2}{a^2} - \frac{y^2}{a^2} = 1$, which is equivalent to $x^2 - y^2 = a^2$

**67.** $y = -\frac{4}{3}x + \frac{2}{3}$, $y = \frac{4}{3}x + \frac{10}{3}$

**69.** $\left(\pm\sqrt{34}, 0\right)$

**71.** As $c$ increases, the graphs become more squeezed down toward the $x$-axis.

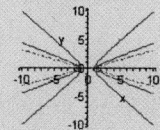

| | |
|---|---|
| ········· | Innermost curve |
| —— | Outermost Curve |
| ------ | Middle Curve |

**73.** As $c$ decreases, the vertices are located at $\left(\pm\frac{1}{c}, 0\right)$ are moving away from the origin.

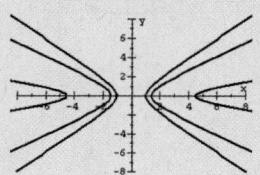

**77.** $\dfrac{-(2x + h)}{\sqrt{1 + (x + h)^2} + \sqrt{1 + x^2}}$

## Section 9.5

**1.** $(2, 6), (-1, 3)$      **3.** $(1, 0)$

**5.** no solution      **7.** $(0, 1)$

**9.** $(0.63, -1.61), (-0.63, -1.61)$

**11.** no solution      **13.** $(1, 1)$

**15.** $\left(2\sqrt{2}, \sqrt{2}\right), \left(-2\sqrt{2}, -\sqrt{2}\right),$
$\left(\sqrt{2}, 2\sqrt{2}\right), \left(-\sqrt{2}, -2\sqrt{2}\right)$

**17.** $(-6, 33), (2, 1)$      **19.** $(3, 4)\ (-2, -1)$

**21.** $(0, -3), \left(\frac{2}{5}, -\frac{11}{5}\right)$      **23.** $(-1, -1), \left(\frac{1}{4}, \frac{3}{2}\right)$

**25.** $(-1, -4), (4, 1)$      **27.** $(1, 3), (-1, -3)$

**29.** $(-4, -1), (4, 1)$

**31.** $(-2, -1), (-2, 1), (2, -1), (2, 1)$

**33.** $(2, 4)$      **35.** $\left(\frac{1}{2}, \frac{1}{3}\right), \left(\frac{1}{2}, -\frac{1}{3}\right)$

**37.** no solution      **39.** no solution

**41.**

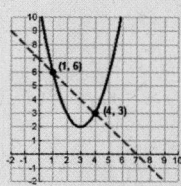

**43.** $8\text{ cm} \times 10\text{ cm}$      **45.** 3 and 7

**47.** 8 and 9, $-8$ and $-9$      **49.** $8\text{ cm} \times 10\text{ cm}$

**51.** $400\text{ ft} \times 500\text{ ft}$ or $\frac{1000}{3}\text{ ft} \times 600\text{ ft}$

**53.** professor: 2 m/sec, Jeremy: 10 m/sec

**55.** 60 mph      **57.** 4763

**59.** In general, $y^2 - y \neq 0$. Must solve this system using substitution.

**61.** false      **63.** false      **65.** $2n$

**67.** Consider $\begin{cases} y = x^2 + 1 \\ y = 1 \end{cases}$. Any system in which the linear equation is the tangent line to the parabola at its vertex will have only one solution.

**69.** $(1, 2), (-1, 2), (1, -2), (-1, -2)$      **71.** no solution

**73.** no solution      **75.** $(-1.57, -1.64)$

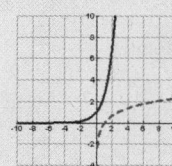 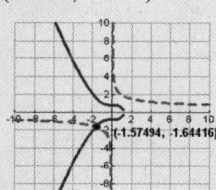

**77.** $(1.067, 4.119), (1.986, 0.638), (-1.017, -4.757)$

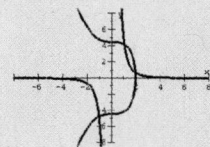

**79.** $y = \sqrt{\dfrac{8 - x^2}{4}}$      **81.** $y = \dfrac{3}{x^{3/2}}$

## Section 9.6

**1.** b    **3.** j    **5.** h    **7.** c    **9.** d    **11.** k

**13.**          **15.**

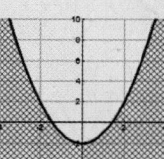 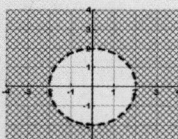

**17.**          **19.**

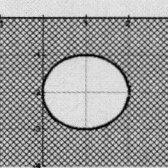 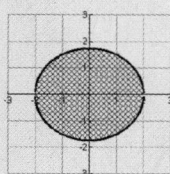

**21.**          **23.**

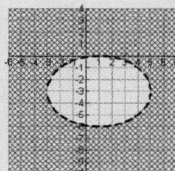 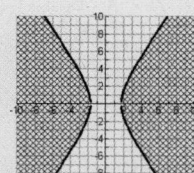

**25.**
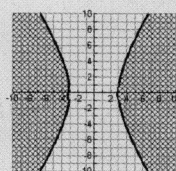

**27.**
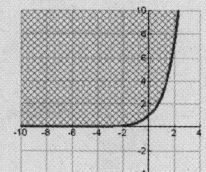

**29.**
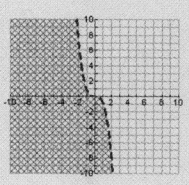

**31.**
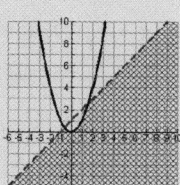

**33.**
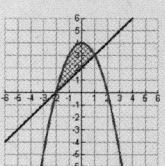

**35.**
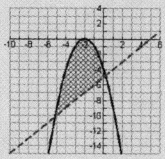

**37.**
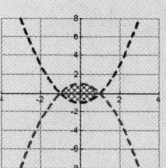

**39.**
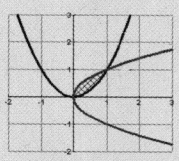

**41.**
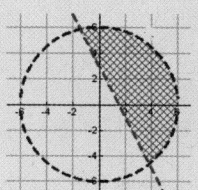

**43.**
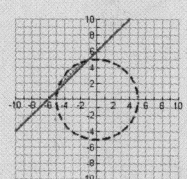

**45.**
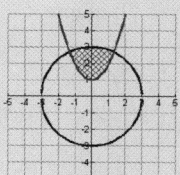

**47.**
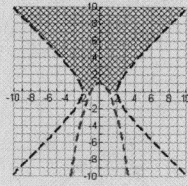

**49.**
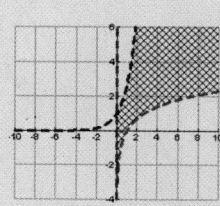

**51.** $\frac{9}{2}\pi$ units$^2$     **53.** $2\pi$ units$^2$     **55.** 90 units$^2$

**57.** There is no common region here—it is empty, as is seen in the graph below:

No common region.

**59.** false            **61.** true

**63.** true             **65.** false

**67.** $0 \le a \le b$      **69.** $a = 36$

**71.** $h = 0$

**73.**
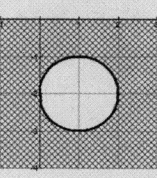

**75.**
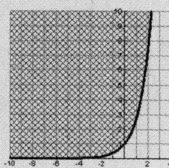

**77.**
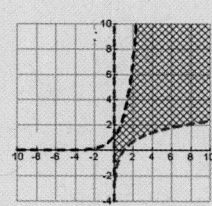

**79.**
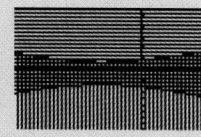

**81.**
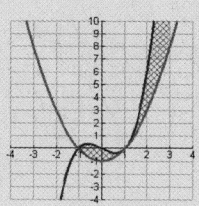

**83.**
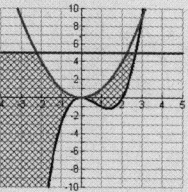

## Section 9.7

**1.** $\left(3\sqrt{2},\, \sqrt{2}\right)$       **3.** $\left(-\frac{3\sqrt{3}}{2} + 1, \frac{3}{2} + \sqrt{3}\right)$

**5.** $\left(-\frac{1 + 3\sqrt{3}}{2},\, \frac{\sqrt{3} - 3}{2}\right)$     **7.** $\left(\frac{3\sqrt{3}}{2}, \frac{3}{2}\right)$

**9. a.** hyperbola   **b.** $\frac{X^2}{2} - \frac{Y^2}{2} = 1$
**c.**
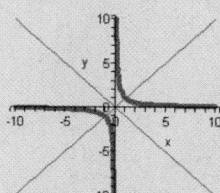

**1147**

**11. a.** parabola **b.** $2X^2 - 2Y - 1 = 0$
**c.**

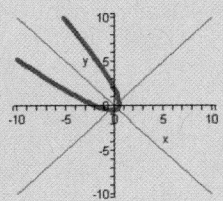

**13. a.** hyperbola **b.** $\frac{X^2}{6} - \frac{Y^2}{2} = 1$
**c.**

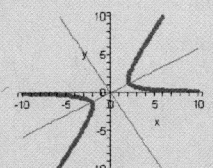

**15. a.** ellipse **b.** $\frac{X^2}{2} + \frac{Y^2}{1} = 1$
**c.**

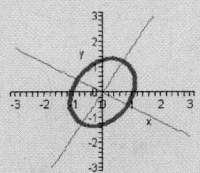

**17. a.** parabola **b.** $2X^2 - 2Y - 1 = 0$
**c.**

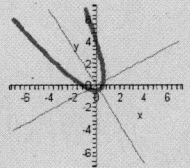

**19. a.** ellipse **b.** $\frac{X^2}{1} + \frac{Y^2}{9} = 1$
**c.**

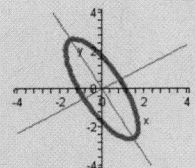

**21. a.** hyperbola **b.** $\frac{X^2}{3} - \frac{Y^2}{2} = 1$
**c.**

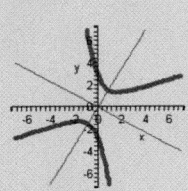

**23. a.** parabola **b.** $Y^2 - X - 4 = 0$
**c.**

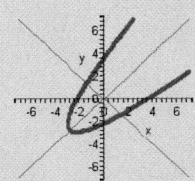

**25.** 45°    **27.** 60°    **29.** 30°    **31.** 45°

**33.** 15°    **35.** 40.3°    **37.** 50.7°

**39.**

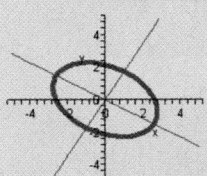

**41.**

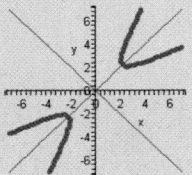

**43.**

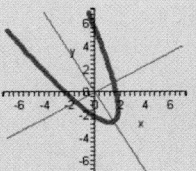

**45.**

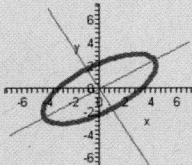

**47.**

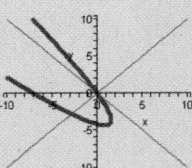

**49.** true    **51.** true

**53. a.** $\dfrac{x^2}{b^2} + \dfrac{y^2}{a^2} = 1$   **b.** The original equation

**55.** $a < 0$: hyperbola; $a = 0$: parabola; $a > 0$: ellipse; $a = 1$: circle

**57.**
  **a.**                       **b.**

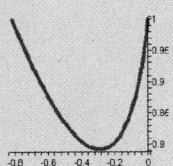

rotation

**59.**

**a.**

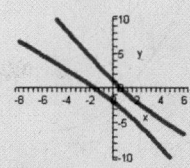

**b.**

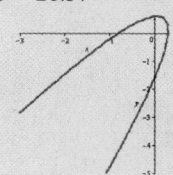

vertices are separating

**61. a.** $-26.57°$     **b.** $19.33°$

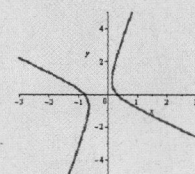

**c.** $26.57°$

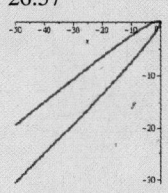

**63.** $(-\sqrt{2}, -2\sqrt{2}), (\sqrt{2}, 2\sqrt{2})$

**65.** $(-1, 0), (1, 0), (3, 1), (-3, -1)$

## Section 9.8

**1.** $r = \dfrac{5}{2 - \sin\theta}$     **3.** $r = \dfrac{8}{1 + 2\sin\theta}$     **5.** $r = \dfrac{1}{1 + \cos\theta}$

**7.** $r = \dfrac{6}{4 + 3\cos\theta}$     **9.** $r = \dfrac{12}{3 - 4\cos\theta}$     **11.** $r = \dfrac{3}{1 - \sin\theta}$

**13.** $r = \dfrac{18}{5 + 3\sin\theta}$     **15.** parabola     **17.** ellipse

**19.** hyperbola     **21.** ellipse     **23.** parabola

**25.** hyperbola

**27. a.** parabola **b.** $e = 1$, $(0, 1)$

**c.**

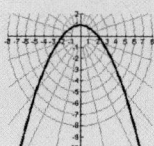

**29. a.** hyperbola **b.** $e = 2$, $(0, -4)$, $\left(0, -\dfrac{4}{3}\right)$

**c.**

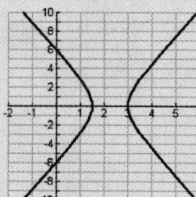

**31. a.** ellipse **b.** $e = \dfrac{1}{2}$, $\left(0, \dfrac{1}{2}\right)$, $(0, -2)$

**c.**

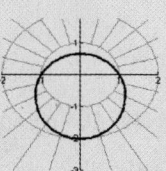

**33. a.** parabola **b.** $e = 1$, $\left(0, -\dfrac{1}{4}\right)$

**c.**

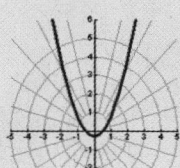

**35. a.** ellipse **b.** $e = \dfrac{1}{3}$, $(1, 0)$, $(-2, 0)$

**c.**

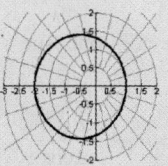

**37. a.** hyperbola **b.** $e = \dfrac{3}{2}$, $\left(0, \dfrac{6}{5}\right)$, $(0, 6)$

**c.**

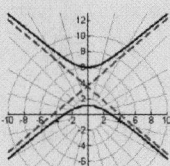

**39. a.** parabola **b.** $e = 1$, $\left(0, \dfrac{1}{5}\right)$

**c.**

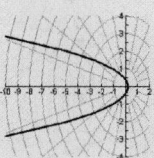

**41. a.** hyperbola **b.** $e = \dfrac{3}{5}$, $\left(\dfrac{15}{8}, \dfrac{\pi}{2}\right)$, $\left(\dfrac{15}{2}, \dfrac{3\pi}{2}\right)$

**c.**

**43.** $0.248$, $r = \dfrac{5{,}913{,}500{,}000\left(1 - 0.248^2\right)}{1 - 0.248\cos\theta}$

**45.** $r = \dfrac{150{,}000{,}000\left(1 - 0.223^2\right)}{1 - 0.223\cos\theta}$

**47. a.** $(-0.0167, 0)$  **b.** $(0.0167, \pi)$   **49.** $(0, -15.406)$

**51.** $e \to 1$: elongated (more elliptical), $e \to 0$: elliptical (circular)

**55.** $\dfrac{2ep}{1 - e^2}$

**57.** $\left(-\dfrac{\frac{ep}{1+e} - \frac{ep}{1-e}}{2}, \pi\right)$

**59.** $r = \dfrac{p}{1 + \cos\theta}$       $r = \dfrac{p}{1 - \cos\theta}$

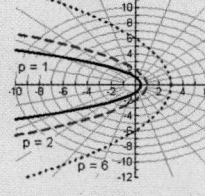    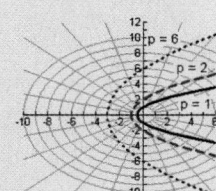

As $p \to \infty$, the graphs get wider, open in opposite directions.

**61.** $r = \dfrac{e}{1 + e\cos\theta}$       $r = \dfrac{e}{1 - e\cos\theta}$

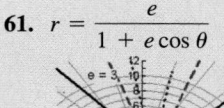    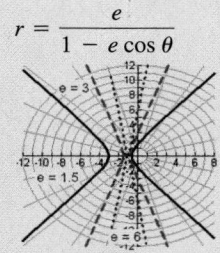

As $e \to \infty$, the graphs get wider, latter family of curves is shifted to the left.

**63.** $r = \dfrac{e}{1 + e\cos\theta}$       $r = \dfrac{e}{1 - e\cos\theta}$

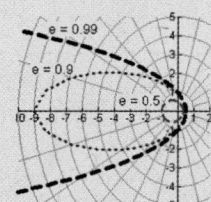

As $e \to 1$, graphs get larger, and centers move accordingly, centers for the latter family of curves move to the right, while the centers for the first family move left.

**69.** $\theta = \dfrac{\pi}{4}, \dfrac{5\pi}{4}$       **71.** $\theta = \dfrac{\pi}{6}, \dfrac{5\pi}{6}$

## Section 9.9

**1.** 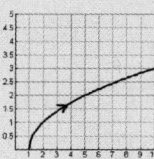   **3.**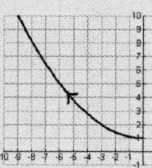

**5.** 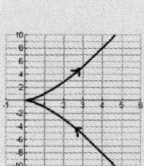   **7.**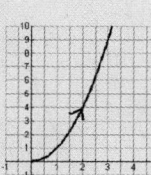

**9.** 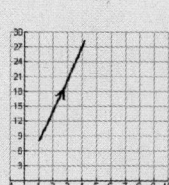   **11.**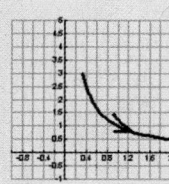

**13.** 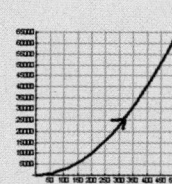   **15.**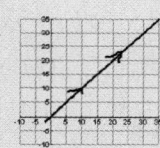

**17.** 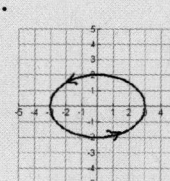   **19.**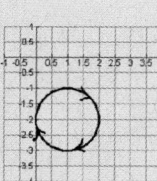

**21.** 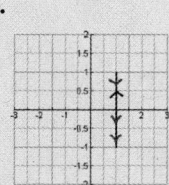   **23.**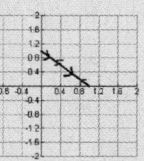

**25.** 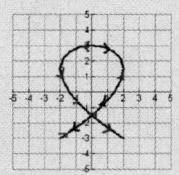   **27.**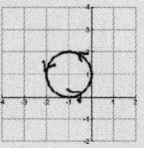

**29.**

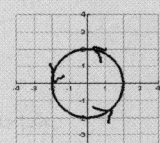

**31.** $y = \frac{1}{x^2}$    **33.** $y = x - 2$    **35.** $y = \sqrt{x^2 + 1}$

**37.** $x + y = 2$    **39.** $x + 4y = 8$    **41.** 17.7 sec

**43.** yes

**45.** distance: 13,261 ft; max height: 5742 ft

**47.** 125 sec

**49.**

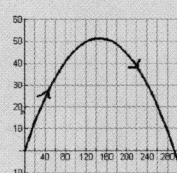

**51.** $t = 0$: $(A + B, 0)$, $t = \frac{\pi}{2}$: $(0, A + B)$, $t = \pi$: $(-A - B, 0)$, $t = \frac{3\pi}{2}$: $(0, -A - B)$, $t = 2\pi$: $(A + B, 0)$

**53.** The original domain must be $t \geq 0$. Only the portion of the parabola where $y \geq 0$ is part of the plane curve.

**55.** false    **57.** quarter circle in QI

**61.** $y = \frac{a-b}{a+b}x + \frac{2ab}{a+b}$    **63.** $y = bx^{1/a}$

**65.** $a = 2$    $a = 3$    $a = 4$

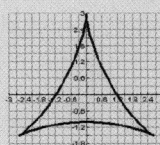 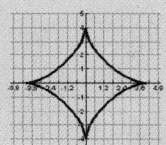 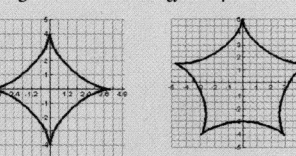

As $a$ increases, distance between vertices and origin gets larger, and number of distinct vertices increases.

**67.** $a = 2, b = 4$    $a = 4, b = 2$

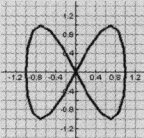 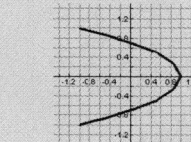

$a = 1, b = 3$    $a = 3, b = 1$

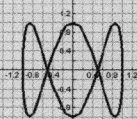

$2\pi$ units of time

**69.** $a = 2$    $a = 3$

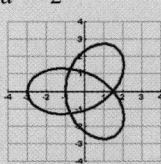 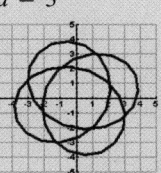

$2\pi$ units of time

**71.** $(-3, 8), (2, 3)$    **73.** $(-100, -96), (1300, -1664)$

## Review Exercises

**1.** false    **3.** true

**5.** $y^2 = 12x$    **7.** $y^2 = -20x$

**9.** $(x - 2)^2 = 8(y - 3)$    **11.** $(x - 1)^2 = -4(y - 6)$

**13.** F: $(0, -3)$ V: $(0, 0)$, D: $y = 3$, LR: 12

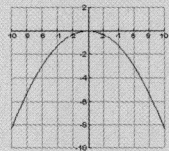

**15.** F: $(\frac{1}{4}, 0)$, V: $(0, 0)$, D: $x = -\frac{1}{4}$, LR: 1

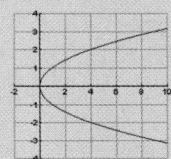

**17.** F: $(3, -2)$, V: $(0, 0)$, D: $x = 1$, LR: 4

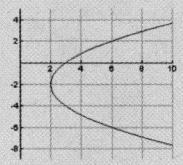

**19.** F: $(-3, -1)$, V: $(-3, 1)$, D: $y = 3$, LR: 8

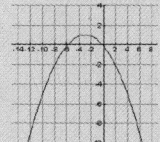

**21.** F: $(-\frac{5}{2}, -\frac{79}{8})$, V: $(-\frac{5}{2}, -\frac{75}{8})$, D: $y = -\frac{71}{8}$, LR: 2

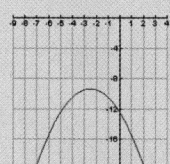

**23.** 3.125 ft from center

**25.**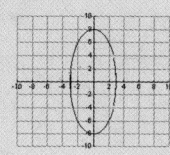

**27.**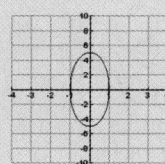

**29.** $\frac{x^2}{25} + \frac{y^2}{16} = 1$

**31.** $\frac{x^2}{9} + \frac{y^2}{64} = 1$

**33.**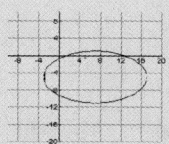

**35.**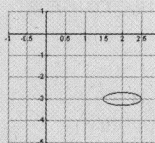

**37.** $\frac{(x-3)^2}{25} + \frac{(y-3)^2}{9} = 1$

**39.** $\frac{(x - (3.74 \times 10^7))^2}{6.058 \times 10^{17}} + \frac{(y-0)^2}{6.044 \times 10^{17}} = 1$

**41.**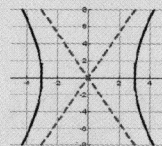

**43.**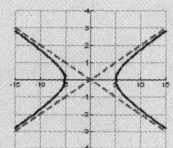

**45.** $\frac{x^2}{9} - \frac{y^2}{16} = 1$

**47.** $\frac{y^2}{9} - x^2 = 1$

**49.**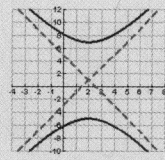

**51.**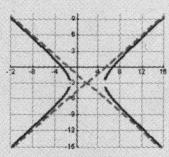

**53.** $\frac{(x-4)^2}{16} - \frac{(y-3)^2}{9} = 1$

**55.** between the stations: 65.36 mi from one, 154.64 mi from the other

**57.** $(-2, -7), (1, -4)$

**59.** $(1, 2), (-1, 2)$

**61.** no solution

**63.** no solution

**65.** $(2, 3), (-3, -2)$

**67.** $\left(\frac{1}{2}, \frac{1}{\sqrt{7}}\right), \left(-\frac{1}{2}, \frac{1}{\sqrt{7}}\right), \left(\frac{1}{2}, -\frac{1}{\sqrt{7}}\right), \left(-\frac{1}{2}, -\frac{1}{\sqrt{7}}\right)$

**69.**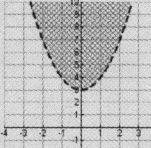

**71.**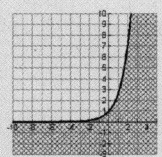

**73.**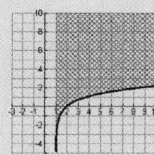

**75.**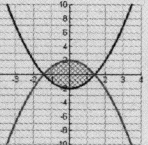

**77.**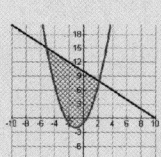

**79.**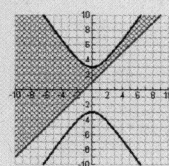

**81.** $\left(-\frac{3}{2} + \sqrt{3}, \frac{3\sqrt{3}}{2} + 1\right)$

**83.** $\frac{x^2}{4} - \frac{y^2}{4} = 1$

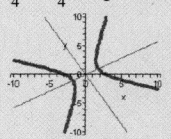

**85.** $60°$

**87.**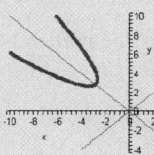

**89.** $r = \dfrac{21}{7 - 3\sin\theta}$

**91.** hyperbola

**93.** $e = \frac{1}{2}, \left(\frac{4}{3}, 0\right), (-4, 0)$

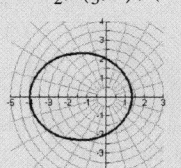

**95.**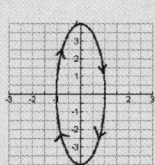

**97.**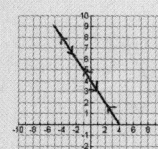

**99.** $x = 4 - y^2$

**101.** $y = 2x + 4$

**103.** $(0.6, -1.2)$, down

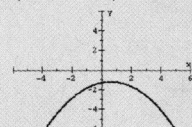

**105. a.** $y = -1.4 \pm \sqrt{-3x + 8.81}$

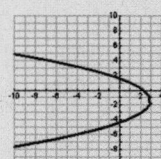

**b.** $(y - (-1.4))^2 = 4\left(-\frac{3}{4}\right)(x - 2.937)$, $(2.937, -1.4)$, left
**c.** yes

**107.** increases minor axis ($x$-axis)

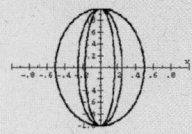

**109.** move toward origin

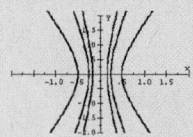

**111.** $(0.635, 2.480)$, $(-0.635, 2.480)$, $(-1.245, 0.645)$, $(1.245, 0.645)$

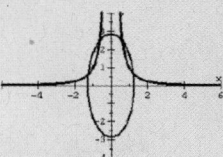

**113.**

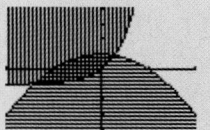

**115. a.** 1.2 rad    **b.** 0.2 rad

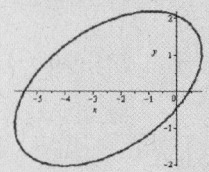

**119.** $a = 2, b = 3$    $a = 3, b = 2$

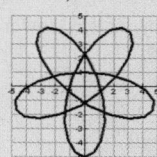

$2\pi$ units of time

## Practice Test

**1.** c          **3.** d          **5.** f

**7.** $y^2 = -16x$

**9.** $(x + 1)^2 = -12(y - 5)$

**11.** $\frac{x^2}{7} + \frac{y^2}{16} = 1$

**13.** $\frac{(x - 2)^2}{20} + \frac{y^2}{36} = 1$

**15.** $x^2 - \frac{y^2}{4} = 1$

**17.** $\frac{y^2}{16} - \frac{(x - 2)^2}{20} = 1$

**19.**                    **21.**

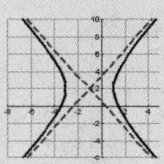      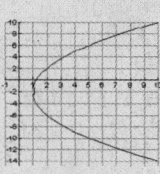

**23.** $x^2 = 6y$

**25.**                    **27.**

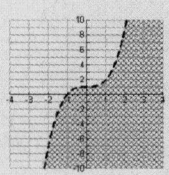      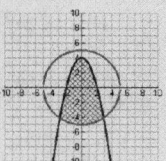

**29.** ellipse, $e = \frac{2}{3}$

**31.** 5.3 sec, 450 ft

**33.**

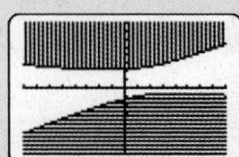

**35. a.** $y = x^2 + 4.2x + 5.61$

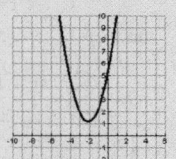

**b.** $(x - (-1.2))^2 = 4\left(\frac{1}{4}\right)(y - 1.2)$, $(-1.2, 1.2)$, up
**c.** yes

## Cumulative Test

**1.** $-6, 3$          **3.** $-7$

**5.** $y = \frac{1}{3}(x - 7)^2 + 7$     **7.** 4

**9.** 1.9626          **11.** $\frac{1}{\cos\theta} + \sin\theta$

**13.** $\frac{\pi}{3}, \frac{2\pi}{3}, \frac{4\pi}{3}, \frac{5\pi}{3}$     **15.** $\langle -5.13, 14.10 \rangle$

**17.** soda: \$1.29; soft pretzel: \$1.45

**19.**

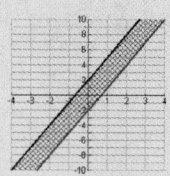

**21.** $\begin{bmatrix} 7 & -16 & 33 \\ 18 & -3 & -17 \end{bmatrix}$   **23.** $\frac{(x-6)^2}{9} + \frac{(y+2)^2}{25} = 1$

**25.** $(2, 4), (4, 2)$

**27.**

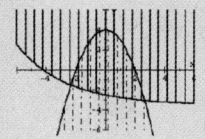

# CHAPTER 10

## Section 10.1

**1.** $1, 2, 3, 4$    **3.** $1, 3, 5, 7$    **5.** $\frac{1}{2}, \frac{2}{3}, \frac{3}{4}, \frac{4}{5}$

**7.** $2, 2, \frac{4}{3}, \frac{2}{3}$    **9.** $-x^2, x^3, -x^4, x^5$

**11.** $-\frac{1}{6}, \frac{1}{12}, -\frac{1}{20}, \frac{1}{30}$   **13.** $\frac{1}{512}$    **15.** $-\frac{1}{420}$

**17.** $\frac{10201}{10000} = 1.0201$    **19.** $23$    **21.** $a_n = 2n$

**23.** $a_n = \frac{1}{(n+1)n}$    **25.** $a_n = \frac{(-1)^n 2^n}{3^n}$   **27.** $a_n = (-1)^{n+1}$

**29.** $72$    **31.** $812$    **33.** $\frac{1}{5852}$

**35.** $83, 156, 160$   **37.** $\frac{1}{(n+1)n}$   **39.** $(2n+3)(2n+2)$

**41.** $7, 10, 13, 16$   **43.** $1, 2, 6, 24$   **45.** $100, 50, \frac{25}{3}, \frac{25}{72}$

**47.** $1, 2, 2, 4$    **49.** $1, -1, -2, 5$   **51.** $10$

**53.** $30$    **55.** $36$    **57.** $5$

**59.** $1 - x + x^2 - x^3$    **61.** $\frac{109}{15}$

**63.** $1 + x + \frac{x^2}{2} + \frac{x^3}{6} + \frac{x^4}{24}$   **65.** $\frac{20}{9}$

**67.** not possible    **69.** $\sum\limits_{n=0}^{6} (-1)^n \frac{1}{2^n}$

**71.** $\sum\limits_{n=1}^{\infty} (-1)^{n-1} n$    **73.** $\sum\limits_{n=1}^{6} \frac{(n+1)!}{(n-1)!} = \sum\limits_{n=1}^{5} n(n+1)$

**75.** $\sum\limits_{n=1}^{\infty} (-1)^{n-1} \frac{x^{n-1}}{(n-1)!} = \sum\limits_{n=0}^{\infty} (-1)^n \frac{x^n}{n!}$

**77.** $\$28,640.89$; total balance in account after 6 yr (or 72 mo)

**79.** $s_n = 20 + 2n$; a paralegal with 20 years experience would make $\$60$ per hour.

**81.** $a_n = 1.03 a_{n-1}$; $a_0 = 30,000$

**83.** $a_{n+1} = 1000 - 75 a_n$; approximately 10.7 yr

**85.** $A_1 = 100, A_2 = 200.10, A_3 = 300.30,$
$A_4 = 400.60, A_{36} = 3663.72$

**87.** $7$; $7.38906$    **89.** $0.0953103$; $0.0953102$

**91.** The mistake is that $6! \neq 3! 2!$, but rather
$6! = 6 \cdot 5 \cdot 4 \cdot 3 \cdot 2 \cdot 1$.

**93.** $(-1)^{n+1} = \begin{cases} 1, & n = 1, 3, 5, \dots \\ -1, & n = 2, 4, 6, \dots \end{cases}$ So, the terms should all be the opposite sign.

**95.** true    **97.** false    **99.** false

**101.** $C, C + D, C + 2D, C + 3D$

**103.** 1 and 1    **105.** $\approx 2.705$; $\approx 2.717$; $\approx 2.718$;

**107.** $\frac{109}{15}$    **109.** monotonic, increasing

**111.** not monotonic

## Section 10.2

**1.** arithmetic, $d = 3$    **3.** not arithmetic

**5.** arithmetic, $d = -0.03$

**7.** arithmetic, $d = \frac{2}{3}$   **9.** not arithmetic

**11.** $3, 1, -1, -3$; arithmetic; $d = -2$

**13.** $1, 4, 9, 16$; not arithmetic

**15.** $2, 7, 12, 17$; arithmetic; $d = 5$

**17.** $0, 10, 20, 30$; arithmetic; $d = 10$

**19.** $-1, 2, -3, 4$; not arithmetic

**21.** $a_n = 11 + (n-1)5 = 5n + 6$

**23.** $a_n = -4 + (n-1)(2) = -6 + 2n$

**25.** $a_n = 0 + (n-1)\frac{2}{3} = \frac{2}{3}n - \frac{2}{3}$

**27.** $a_n = 0 + (n-1)e = en - e$    **29.** $124$

**31.** $-684$    **33.** $\frac{16}{3}$

**35.** $a_5 = 44, a_{17} = 152$; $a_n = 8 + (n-1)9 = 9n - 1$

**37.** $a_7 = -1, a_{17} = -41$; $a_n = 23 + (n-1)(-4) = -4n + 27$

**39.** $a_4 = 3, a_{22} = 15$; $a_n = 1 + (n-1)\frac{2}{3} = \frac{2}{3}n + \frac{1}{3}$

**41.** $552$    **43.** $-780$    **45.** $51$

**47.** $416$    **49.** $3875$

**51.** $\frac{21}{2}\left[\frac{1}{6} - \frac{13}{2}\right] = \frac{21}{2}\left(\frac{1-39}{6}\right) = -\frac{133}{2}$   **53.** $630$

**55.** $S_{43} = \frac{43}{4}(5 - 43) = -\frac{817}{2}$    **57.** $1368$

**59.** Colin: $\$347,500$; Camden: $\$340,000$

**61.** 850 seats

**63.** 1101 glasses on the bottom row, each row had 20 fewer glasses than the one before.

**65.** 1600 ft    **67.** 210 oranges

**69. a.** 23 seats in the first row   **b.** 1125 seats

**71.** $a_n = a_1 + (n-1)d$, not $a_1 + nd$

**73.** There are 11 terms, not 10. So, $n = 11$, and thus,
$$S_{11} = \frac{11}{2}(1 + 21) = 121.$$

**75.** false  **77.** true  **79.** $\dfrac{(n + 1)[2a + bn]}{2}$

**81.** 27,420  **83.** 5050  **85.** 2500

**87.** 18,850  **89.** 1010  **91.** 1.204

**87.** $\displaystyle\sum_{n=0}^{\infty} x^n = \dfrac{1}{1 - x}$

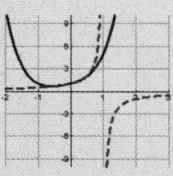

**89.** converges, 3  **91.** converges, $\frac{1}{2}$

## Section 10.3

**1.** yes, $r = 3$  **3.** no

**5.** yes, $r = \frac{1}{2}$  **7.** yes, $r = 1.7$

**9.** 6, 18, 54, 162, 486  **11.** 1, $-4$, 16, $-64$, 256

**13.** 10,000, 10,600, 11,236, 11,910.16, 12,624.77

**15.** $\frac{2}{3}, \frac{1}{3}, \frac{1}{6}, \frac{1}{12}, \frac{1}{24}$  **17.** $a_n = 5(2)^{n-1}$

**19.** $a_n = 1(-3)^{n-1}$  **21.** $a_n = 1000(1.07)^{n-1}$

**23.** $a_n = \frac{16}{3}\left(-\frac{1}{4}\right)^{n-1}$  **25.** $a_7 = -128$

**27.** $a_{13} = \frac{4096}{3}$  **29.** $a_{15} = 6.10 \times 10^{-16}$

**31.** $\frac{8191}{3}$  **33.** 59,048

**35.** $2.\overline{2}$  **37.** 6560

**39.** 16,383  **41.** 2

**43.** $-\frac{1}{4}$  **45.** not possible, diverges

**47.** $-\frac{27}{2}$  **49.** 10,526

**51.** $\frac{2}{3}$  **53.** 100

**55.** $44,610.95

**57.** $a_n = 2000(0.5)^n$; $a_4 = 125$, $a_7 = 16$

**59.** 17 ft  **61.** 58,640 students

**63.** 66 days; $9618  **65.** $3877.64

**67.** 26 weeks: $13,196.88   52 weeks: $26,811.75

**69.** $501,509  **71.** $\dfrac{\frac{1}{2}}{1 - \frac{1}{2}} = 1$

**73.** Should be $r = -\frac{1}{3}$.

**75.** Should use $r = -3$ all the way through the calculation. Also, $a_1 - 12$ (not 4).

**77.** false  **79.** true

**81.** $|b| < 1, \dfrac{a}{1 - b}$  **83.** $\frac{47}{99}$

**85.** $-37,529,996,894,754$

## Section 10.4

**25.** 7 steps  **27.** 31 steps

**31.** false  **39.** $\frac{255}{256}$, yes

## Section 10.5

**1.** 35  **3.** 45  **5.** 1  **7.** 1  **9.** 17,296

**11.** $x^4 + 8x^3 + 24x^2 + 32x + 16$

**13.** $y^5 - 15y^4 + 90y^3 - 270y^2 + 405y - 243$

**15.** $x^5 + 5x^4y + 10x^3y^2 + 10x^2y^3 + 5xy^4 + y^5$

**17.** $x^3 + 9x^2y + 27xy^2 + 27y^3$

**19.** $125x^3 - 150x^2 + 60x - 8$

**21.** $\frac{1}{x^4} + 20\frac{y}{x^3} + 150\frac{y^2}{x^2} + 500\frac{y^3}{x} + 625y^4$

**23.** $x^8 + 4x^6y^2 + 6x^4y^4 + 4x^2y^6 + y^8$

**25.** $a^5x^5 + 5a^4bx^4y + 10a^3b^2x^3y^2 + 10a^2b^2x^2y^3$
$+ 5ab^4xy^4 + b^5y^5$

**27.** $x^3 + 12x^{5/2} + 60x^2 + 160x^{3/2} + 240x + 192x^{1/2} + 64$

**29.** $a^3 + 4a^{9/4}b^{1/4} + 6a^{3/2}b^{1/2} + 4a^{3/4}b^{3/4} + b$

**31.** $x + 8x^{3/4}y^{1/2} + 24x^{1/2}y + 32x^{1/4}y^{3/2} + 16y^2$

**33.** $r^4 - 4r^3s + 6r^2s^2 - 4rs^3 + s^4$

**35.** $a^6x^6 + 6a^5bx^5y + 15a^4b^2x^4y^2 + 20a^3b^3x^3y^3$
$+ 15a^2b^4x^2y^4 + 6ab^5xy^5 + b^6y^6$

**37.** 3360  **39.** 5670  **41.** 22,680

**43.** 70  **45.** 3,838,380  **47.** 2,598,960

**49.** $\dbinom{7}{5} \neq \dfrac{7!}{5!}$, but rather $\dfrac{7!}{5!2!} = \dfrac{7 \cdot 6 \cdot 5!}{5!(2 \cdot 1)} = 21.$

**51.** false  **53.** true  **55.** true

**61.** $1 - 3x + 3x^2 - x^3$

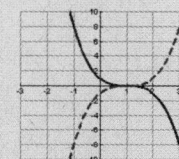

**63.** graphs of the respective functions get closer to the graph of $y_4 = (1 - x)^3$ when $1 < x < 2$, when $x > 1$, no longer true

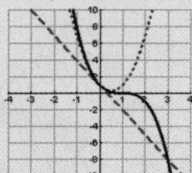

**65.** graph of the curve better approximation to the graph of $y = \left(1 + \frac{1}{x}\right)^3$, for $1 < x < 2$; no, does not get closer to this graph if $0 < x < 1$

**67.** $\sum_{k=1}^{n}\binom{n}{k}x^{n-k}h^{k-1}$  **69.** $\sum_{k=0}^{n-1}\frac{n!}{(n-1-k)!k!}x^{n-1-k}$

## Review Exercises

**1.** $1, 8, 27, 64$    **3.** $5, 8, 11, 14$

**5.** $a_5 = \frac{32}{243} = 0.13$    **7.** $a_{15} = -\frac{1}{3600}$

**9.** $a_n = (-1)^{n+1}3n$    **11.** $a_n = (-1)^n$

**13.** $56$    **15.** $\frac{1}{n+1}$

**17.** $5, 3, 1, -1$    **19.** $1, 2, 4, 32$

**21.** $15$    **23.** $69$    **25.** $\sum_{n=1}^{7}\frac{(-1)^n}{2^{n-1}}$    **27.** $\sum_{n=0}^{\infty}\frac{x^n}{n!}$

**29.** \$36,639.90; amount in the account after 5 yr

**31.** arithmetic, $d = -2$

**33.** arithmetic, $d = \frac{1}{2}$

**35.** arithmetic, $d = 1$

**37.** $a_n = -4 + (n-1)(5) = 5n - 9$

**39.** $a_n = 1 + (n-1)\left(-\frac{2}{3}\right) = -\frac{2}{3}n + \frac{5}{3}$

**41.** $a_1 = 5, d = 2, a_n = 5 + (n-1)(2) = 2n + 3$

**43.** $a_1 = 10, d = 6, a_n = 10 + (n-1)6 = 6n + 4$

**45.** $630$    **47.** $420$

**49.** Bob: \$885,000    Tania: \$990,000

**51.** geometric, $r = -2$    **53.** geometric, $r = \frac{1}{2}$

**55.** $3, 6, 12, 24, 48$    **57.** $100, -400, 1600, -6400, 25,600$

**59.** $a_n = a_1 r^{n-1} = 7 \cdot 2^{n-1}$  **61.** $a_n = 1(-2)^{n-1}$

**63.** $a_{25} = 33,554,432$    **65.** $a_{12} = -2.048 \times 10^{-6}$

**67.** $4920.50$    **69.** $16,400$    **71.** $3$

**73.** \$60,875.61    **79.** $165$    **81.** $1$

**83.** $x^4 - 20x^3 + 150x^2 - 500x + 625$

**85.** $8x^3 - 60x^2 + 150x - 125$

**87.** $x^{5/2} + 5x^2 + 10x^{3/2} + 10x + 5x^{1/2} + 1$

**89.** $r^5 - 5r^4s + 10r^3s^2 - 10r^2s^3 + 5rs^4 - s^5$

**91.** $112$    **93.** $37,500$    **95.** $22,957,480$

**97.** $\frac{5369}{3600}$    **99.** $\frac{34,875}{14}$

**101.** $\frac{1}{1 + 2x}$

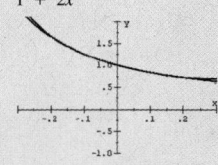

**103.** $99,900$, yes

**105.** graphs become better approximations of the graph of $y = (1 + 2x)^4$ for $-0.1 < x < 0.1$; does not get closer for $0.1 < x < 1$

## Practice Test

**1.** $x^{n-1}$    **3.** $S_n = \frac{1 - x^n}{1 - x}$    **5.** $|x| < 1$

**7.** $1 - \left(\frac{1}{4}\right)^{10} \approx 1$    **9.** $24,950$    **11.** $2520$

**13.** $455$    **15.** $20,254$

**17.** $x^{10} + 5x^7 + 10x^4 + 10x + \frac{5}{x^2} + \frac{1}{x^5}$

**21.** $\frac{5}{3}$    **23.** $\sum_{n=1}^{\infty}\frac{5}{2(n+3)}$

**25.** $128 - 1344x + 6048x^2 - 15120x^3 + 22680x^4 - 20412x^5$
$+ 10206x^6 - 2187x^7$

**27.** $184,756$

## Cumulative Test

**1.** $\dfrac{x^2 + hx + 2x + h}{(x+1)(x+h+1)}$

**3.** $f(x) = (x - 5)(x + 1)(x - i)(x + i)$

**5.** $x = -8$    **7.** $2x + h - 3$    **9.** $(15, 6)$

**11.** VA: $x = 3$    HA: $y = -5$    **13.** $2.585$

**15.** no solution

**17.** $z(1, 4) = 24$

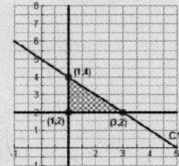

**19.** $\begin{bmatrix} 99 & 18 & -9 \\ 29 & 4 & 7 \end{bmatrix}$    **21.** $-16(x - 3) = (y - 5)^2$

**23.** $3$    **25.** $35$

# Applications Index

## A

Archaeology, carbon dating, 372, 390–391

Architecture
college campus design, 75
Tower of Pisa inclination, 576

Art/Music/Theater/Entertainment
art business, 901
college architecture, 75
concert sound levels, 382, 394
music tones and beats, 638
photography, 383
stained glass profits, 178
suspense novels, 178
theater seating, 1038
viewing angle of paintings, 660
Walt Disney World profit, 335
wedding planning, 178
world's largest champagne
fountain, 1038

Astronomy, *see* Physics and Astronomy

Automotive
average driving times, 795, 819
braking power, 716
car value, 61, 89, 221, 405
depreciation of vehicle, 1050
gas mileage, 782, 898
gasoline and electric vehicles, 845
gasoline/oil mixtures, 782
manufacturing, 795
monthly driving costs, 89
motorcycle angular speeds, 512
new model availability, 393, 394, 405
rental car costs, 89
tire size and speed, 436
trip time, 278
velocity, 963
wrecks, 716

Aviation
air speed, 782
commercial plane seats, 796
distance and air speed, 1017
distances traveled, 500
glide paths of jets, 454
hot-air balloon, 487
Mach numbers, 98
mid-air refueling, 453, 512
military aircraft, 98, 453, 512

navigation, 451, 454, 706
search-and-rescue helicopters, 454
slide length, 500
sonic booms and plane speeds, 556
U.S. Navy commission, 1028
wind speed, 17, 782

## B

Biology/Zoology
alligator length, 16
bacterial growth, 404, 416
bioluminescence in fireflies, 556
bird wing-flapping, 753
body temperature, 525, 612, 676
career salaries, 1038
carrying capacity, 405, 416
deer population, 676
DNA, 437
dogwalking, 707
*E. coli* reproduction rate, 1029
food amounts for cats, 324
human body temperature, 525
human height, 89
human lung volume, 676
pollen levels, 659, 675
snake length, 16
trout population, 405
tulip festival, 1038
virus spread, 323
wild life population, 416
wolf population, 394

Business
agriculture, 221, 296
annual sales, 659
art business profit, 901
assembly lines, 794, 820
author royalties, 178
bakery profit, 296, 889
balancing financials, 31
break-even analysis, 30, 296, 676, 782
budgeting, 16, 178
business expenses, 194, 845
cash flow of stock fund, 627
cell phone costs, 845–846
computer business, 889
computer mice, 888
computer sales, 627, 675
consumer surplus, 887

costs, 89, 90, 178, 205, 334, 637, 783, 795
delivery services, 17
demand function, 296
demand modeling, 555
electronics costs and revenues, 637
grocery display, 1038
GS salary scale, 1049
information management, 782
job applicant scoring, 845
lemonade stand entrepreneur, 782
Levi's jeans sales, 98
manufacturing costs, 205, 246
maximizing profit, 889, 923
mechanical pencils, 888
monthly costs and revenues, 637
monthly sales, 628, 659, 675
NASCAR revenue, 75
newspaper deliveries, 17
NFL salaries, 1071
operating costs, 89
part-time work, 16
Poor Man's Clever Deal, 1050
price changes, 16
price increases for profit, 30
producer surplus, 887
production costs, 250
production levels, 30, 794, 796, 820, 888, 923
product pricing, 716
profit, 30, 61, 178, 250, 338, 628, 889, 901, 923
profit function, 194, 252, 296, 304, 305, 324, 334, 335
projected revenue, 61
ranching, 251
real estate, 205, 782
revenue, 60, 61, 75, 334, 637, 1029
revenue function, 268
revenue maximization, 252
salary/commission, 233, 335
salary comparison, 355, 782, 1038, 1050, 1072
salary raises, 194, 1029, 1038, 1047, 1049, 1071, 1072
sales, 98, 233, 404, 525, 627, 628, 659, 675, 820, 1029
seasonal sales, 525

# Subject Index

## A

AAS (angle-angle-side) method, for solving triangles, 477, 479–480
Abscissa, defined, 63
Absolute value, defined, 41
Absolute value equations
  defined, 41
  solving, 41–43
Absolute value functions
  defined, 164
  properties and graphing of, 175, 182–183
Absolute value inequalities
  properties of, 57
  solving, 57–58
Acute angles
  defined, 423
  trigonometric function values for, 459–460
Acute triangles, 476. *See also* Oblique triangles
Addition
  of functions, 196–198
  of matrices, 824–826
  of vectors, 695, 697, 700–704
Addition method, *see* Elimination method
Addition of ordinates, 548–551
Additive identity property, for matrices, 826
Additive inverse property, for matrices, 826
Adjacent angles, defined, 442
Algebra, fundamental theorem of, 298–299
Algebraic expressions, defined, 4
Algebraic functions, exponential functions vs., 342
Algebraic techniques, solving trigonometric equations with, 666–667
Allometric growth, modeling of, 92
Alternating sequences, sign in, 1021
Ambiguous case, of oblique triangles, 482–486
Amplitude
  defined, 534
  in graphing, 537–542

in harmonic motion, 543–548
of sinusoidal functions, 533–536
Angles. *See also* Double-angle identities; Half-angle identities
  acute, 423, 459–460
  adjacent, 442
  coterminal, 427–428
  defined, 422
  nonacute, 460–461, 466–471
  opposite, 442
  quadrantal, 427, 463–464, 560
  reference, 464–467
  rotation of, 978–982
  special angles, 443–447
  standard position of, 427
  types of, 423–424
  vectors and, 710–713
Angle measure. *See also* Inverse trigonometric functions; Radian measure
  complementary and supplementary, 423–424
  degrees and radians, 422–426
Angle of rotation
  and conics, 978–982
  formula for, 979
Angular speed
  defined, 431
  and linear speed, 431–433
Applications (word problems), 7–8. *See also Applications Index*
  distance–rate–time problems, 12–14
  geometry problems, 9
  interest problems, 9–11
  mixture problems, 11–12
Approximations
  for exponential functions, 343
  for irrational zeros, 291–294
  for logarithmic functions, 360–362
  for trigonometric functions, 447–448, 469, 471, 523, 667–669
Arc length, defined, 429
Area
  of circular sector, 429–430
  of triangles, 495–499, 504–505
Argument, of function, 149
Arithmetic sequences, 1031–1036
  defined, 1031

general (*n*th) term of, 1033–1034
  sum of, 1034–1036
Arithmetic series, evaluating, 1034–1036
ASA (angle-side-angle) method, for solving triangles, 477, 481–482
Associative property, for matrices, 826, 831
Asymptotes. *See also* Sinusoidal functions; Trigonometric functions, graphing
  defined, 309
  of exponential functions, 344–347
  graphing, 314–320
  horizontal, 308–309, 311–320
  in hyperbolas, 941, 943–946
  slant, 308–309, 313–320
  vertical, 308–311, 314–320, 560
Augmented matrix/matrices
  defined, 801
  solving linear equations with, 804–810
  writing linear equations using, 801–802
Average rate of change, of functions, 167–170
Axis/axes
  in complex plane, 719
  of ellipses, 925, 928, 986–991
  of hyperbolas, 939, 986–991
  of parabolas, 911, 986–991
  in polar coordinate system, 741–742
  in rectangular coordinate system, 63, 719
  reflection about, 186–188, 364–365
  rotation of, 974–976
  of symmetry, 239, 911
Axis of symmetry, of parabola, 911

## B

Bases, of logarithms, 361–362
Base 10, defined, 361
Base *b*
  defined, 342
  and logarithmic functions, 359
Bell-shaped curve, 396
Best fit line, 113–120
  finding by linear regression, 114–118
  for prediction, 118–120

Binomials, defined, 1057
Binomial coefficients
   defined, 1058
   evaluating, 1058–1059
   and Pascal's triangle, 1060–1062
Binomial expansion
   finding terms of, 1062
   Pascal's triangle and, 1060–1062
   principles of, 1057–1058
   using binomial theorem, 1059–1060
Binomial theorem
   binomial expansion with, 1059–1060
   defined, 1059
Bisection method, for finding zeros,
   291–294
Bounded graphs, 880–882
Boyle's law, 2
Branches, of hyperbola, 939

**C**
Calculators
   absolute values, 42, 57
   asymptotes, 316–320, 561–570, 572
   best fit line, 114–115
   circles, 71
   complex number mode, 26
   complex numbers, 722–724, 731, 733
   complex roots, 734–736
   complex zeros, 300–303
   composite functions, 200
   conversion of degrees and radians, 426
   correlation coefficients, 109–110
   creating scatterplots, 104
   determinants, 850
   domain restrictions, 154
   double- and half-angle identities,
      615–620
   drawing angles, 462
   exponential equations, 386–388
   exponential functions, 343, 345, 347,
      352–353
   factorial notation, 1022–1023
   finding exact values, 604–607, 609
   finding zeros, 260, 281–283, 287,
      292–293, 300–303
   functions, 151–152. *See also specific
      functions*
   graphing conics, 914, 916–918,
      928–931, 942–944, 946
   graphing inequalities, 966–969
   graphing lines, 82
   interest problems, 352–353
   inverse functions, 216–218
   inverse trigonometric functions,
      641–651, 653

linear equations and systems of, 5–6,
   779–780, 839–841
linear inequalities, 50–51, 876–880
logarithms, 361–362
logarithmic equations, 388–390
logarithmic functions, 364–365
logistic growth modeling, 400
matrix functions, 786, 788–790,
   814–815, 825, 827, 829,
   835–836, 838
midpoint formula, 64
modulus of complex number, 720
natural base (*e*), 348–349, 361–362
nonlinear equations, 955–956, 958
partial-fraction decomposition,
   865–866, 869
periodic functions, 530, 532,
   537–539, 547
piecewise-defined functions,
   171–174, 218
polar and rectangular forms, 722–724
polar equation graphs, 744–750,
   987–991
polynomial functions, 262, 264–265
polynomial inequalities, 52–54
quadratic equations, 20, 26
quadratic functions, 246–247
quadratic in form equations, 39–40
radian measures, 429
radical equations, 36–37
rational equations, 33–34
rational functions, 313
rational inequalities, 55
reciprocal functions, 447–448, 562
rotation of axes, 977, 979–981
sequences and series, 1022–1026,
   1033, 1035, 1042–1044, 1054, 1062
solving triangles, 480–481, 493,
   494, 498
sums and differences, 606, 607, 609
sums of functions, 548–551
symmetry in graphing, 68, 69, 165
transformations, 184–186, 188, 191,
   346–347, 364–365
trigonometric equations, 664–670, 672
trigonometric functions, 445–446,
   448–450, 520–523, 595, 711
using Cramer's rule, 855–856
Calculus
   partial-fraction decomposition in,
      863–864
   products and sums of
      functions, 631
Cardioids, graphing, 747–748
Carrying capacity, 340, 400, 416

Cartesian coordinate system
   converting with polar, 743
   defined, 63
   elements of, 63
   trigonometric functions in, 529–530
Cartesian plane
   trigonometric functions in, 458–464
   unit circle and, 518–519
Center
   of circle, 71–72
   of ellipse, 925
   of hyperbola, 939
Central angles, defined, 425
Change, average rate in functions,
   167–170
Change-of-base formula, for logarithms,
   380–381
Circles
   arc length and, 429
   central angles in, 425
   circular sector, 429–430
   defined, 70
   equations of, 71–72
   graphing, 71–72, 744–746, 751
Circular functions. *See also
   Trigonometric functions*
   defined, 519
   properties of, 521–523
Coefficients
   in augmented matrices, 801–802
   binomial, 1058–1062
   leading, 22–24, 238, 241, 256
Cofactors, of square matrix, 850–851
Cofunctions, trigonometric, identities,
   591–592
Cofunction theorem, 591
Column index, of matrix, 800
Column matrix, defined, 801
Combined variation
   defined, 96
   modeling with, 96
Common difference
   defined, 1031
   and sequence terms, 1031–1033
Common logarithmic function
   defined, 361
   properties of, 361–362, 376
Common ratios
   defined, 1040
   in geometric sequences, 1040–1042
Commutative property, for matrices, 826,
   828–829
Complementary angles
   defined, 423
   measures of, 424

Rectangular coordinate system, elements
of, 63
Rectangular form
complex numbers in, 719–724
converting to polar form, 721–724, 750
Recursion formulas, for sequences,
1023–1024
Reduced row-echelon form
Gauss-Jordan elimination and,
807–810
properties of, 803–804
Reference angles, 464
defined, 466
finding, 466–467
Reference right triangles, defined, 467
Reflection about axes
defined, 187
graphing, 186–188, 364–365
and sinusoidal functions, 536, 539
Relations
defined, 144
functions and, 145–146
Remainders, in polynomial division,
271–276, 280–283
Remainder theorem
defined, 281
in evaluation of polynomials, 281
Repeated roots, 27
defined, 260–261
finding, 260–261
Resonance, characteristics of, 544, 548
Response variables, 102–106, 146
Resultant vectors
defined, 695
solving for, 700–704
Richter scale, logarithmic application,
367
Right angle, defined, 423
Right triangles
characteristics of, 440
defined, 440
ratios of, 441–443
reference, 467
solving, 448–450
Right triangle ratios. *See also*
Trigonometric functions
applications of, 450–451
properties of, 441–443
Rigid transformations, defined, 189
Rising lines, slope and, 80–81
Roots
of complex numbers, 733–736
square, 21–24, 163
Roots (solution)
complex, 26, 27, 298
defined, 4

imaginary, 21
real, 26, 27
repeated, 27, 260–261
Rotation
angle of, 978–982
and radian measure, 424–425
Rotation of axes
derivation of formulas, 974–976
formulas for, 974–976
Row-echelon form, properties of,
803–804
Row index, of matrix, 800
Row matrix, defined, 801
Row operations
Gauss elimination and, 803–806
Gauss-Jordan elimination and,
807–810
Rule of 4 (expression of functions), 148

**S**
SAS (side-angle-side) method
area of SAS triangle, 495–497
for solving triangles, 493–494
Scalars
and matrices, 826–827
vectors vs., 694
Scalar multiplication
of matrices, 826–827
of vectors, 698
Scatterplots
creating, 104–106
defined, 102, 131
relationships between variables,
102–103
Secant function
defined, 441–442, 459
graphing, 562–563, 565, 568–569
inverse, 650–653
for special angles, 443–447
and unit circle, 518–519
Secant line, and average rate of change,
167–170
Second-degree equation, defined, 5.
*See also* Quadratic equations
Sequences. *See also* Series
arithmetic, 1031–1036
defined, 1020
factorial notation and, 1022–1023
finding terms of, 1020–1024
geometric, 1040–1048
modeling, 1068
recursion formulas and, 1023–1024
sums of, *see* Series
Series. *See also* Sequences
applications of, 1026, 1036
arithmetic, 1034–1036

defined, 1024
evaluating, 1025–1026, 1034–1036,
1043–1046
geometric, 1043–1048
modeling, 1068
Sets
elements of, 144
solution, 4
union and intersection of, 49, 53–58
Sides, of angles, 422, 427
Sigma notation, defined, 1024
Sign
in alternating sequences, 1021
Descartes's rule of, 284–287
and inequalities, 47, 49–50
of trigonometric functions, 461–464
variation in, 286–287
Similar triangles, defined, 439
Simple harmonic motion
characteristics of, 543
examples of, 544–546
Simple interest (finance)
defined, 10
joint variation and, 95–96
problems, 9–11
Simplification
of algebraic expressions, 4, 7
of trigonometric expressions, 592–593,
618, 624, 635
Sines, Law of, *see* Law of Sines
Sine function, 439. *See also* Law of
Sines; Sinusoidal functions
defined, 441–442, 459
graphing, 528–530, 548–551
inverse, 640–644
inverse function, 506, 640–644
inverse identities, 643–644
for special angles, 443–447
sum and difference identities, 605–607
and unit circle, 518–519
vectors and, 699
Singular matrices, characteristics of,
835, 837
Sinusoidal functions
amplitude of, 533–536
graphing, 528–532, 537–542, 548–551
harmonic motion and, 543–548
modeling of, 579
period of, 536–537
Slant asymptotes
defined, 314
in graphing, 314–320
locating, 314
Slope
in average rate of change, 167–170
of common functions, 161–164

### Parabola

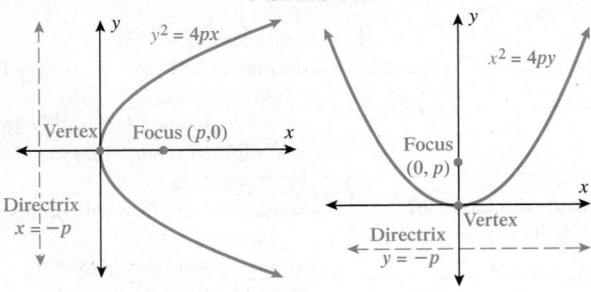

### Ellipse

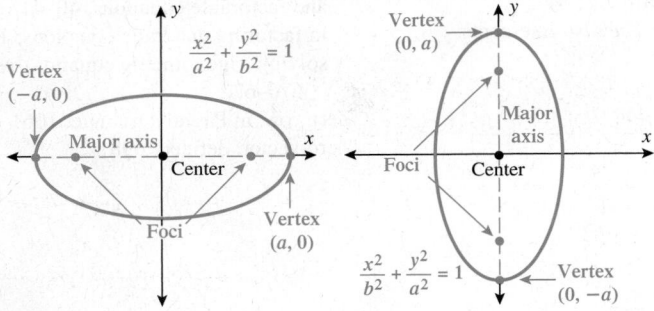

### Hyperbola

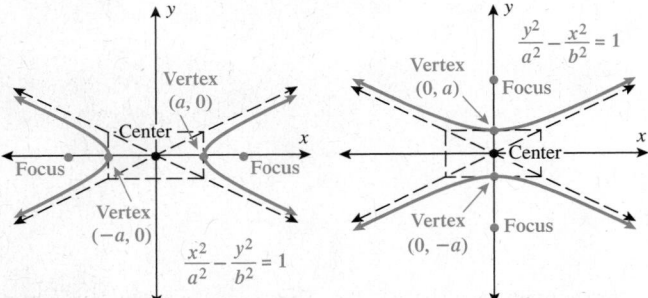

1. Infinite Sequence:

$$\{a_n\} = a_1, a_2, a_3, \ldots, a_n, \ldots$$

2. Summation Notation:

$$\sum_{i=1}^{n} a_i = a_1 + a_2 + a_3 + \cdots + a_n$$

3. $n$th Term of an Arithmetic Sequence:

$$a_n = a_1 + (n-1)d$$

4. Sum of First $n$ Terms of an Arithmetic Sequence:

$$S_n = \frac{n}{2}(a_1 + a_n)$$

5. $n$th Term of a Geometric Sequence:

$$a_n = a_1 r^{n-1}$$

6. Sum of First $n$ Terms of a Geometric Sequence:

$$S_n = \frac{a_1(1-r^n)}{1-r} \quad (r \neq 1)$$

7. Sum of an Infinite Geometric Series with $|r| < 1$:

$$S = \frac{a_1}{1-r}$$

1. $n! = n(n-1)(n-2) \cdots 3 \cdot 2 \cdot 1$; $1! = 1$; $0! = 1$

2. $\displaystyle \binom{n}{r} = \frac{n!}{r!(n-r)!}$

3. Binomial theorem:

$$(a+b)^n = \binom{n}{0}a^n + \binom{n}{1}a^{n-1}b$$
$$+ \binom{n}{2}a^{n-2}b^2 + \cdots + \binom{n}{n}b^n$$

1. $_nP_r$, the number of permutations of $n$ elements taken $r$ at a time, is given by

$$_nP_r = \frac{n!}{(n-r)!}.$$

2. $_nC_r$, the number of combinations of $n$ elements taken $r$ at a time, is given by

$$_nC_r = \frac{n!}{(n-r)!r!}.$$

3. *Probability of an Event:* $P(E) = \dfrac{n(E)}{n(S)}$, where

$n(E) =$ the number of outcomes in event $E$ and
$n(S) =$ the number of outcomes in the sample space.

| $y = \sin^{-1}x$ | $x = \sin y$ | $-\dfrac{\pi}{2} \le y \le \dfrac{\pi}{2}$ | $-1 \le x \le 1$ |
|---|---|---|---|
| $y = \cos^{-1}x$ | $x = \cos y$ | $0 \le y \le \pi$ | $-1 \le x \le 1$ |
| $y = \tan^{-1}x$ | $x = \tan y$ | $-\dfrac{\pi}{2} < y < \dfrac{\pi}{2}$ | $x$ is any real number |
| $y = \cot^{-1}x$ | $x = \cot y$ | $0 < y < \pi$ | $x$ is any real number |
| $y = \sec^{-1}x$ | $x = \sec y$ | $0 \le y \le \pi, y \ne \dfrac{\pi}{2}$ | $x \le -1$ or $x \ge 1$ |
| $y = \csc^{-1}x$ | $x = \csc y$ | $-\dfrac{\pi}{2} \le y \le \dfrac{\pi}{2}, y \ne 0$ | $x \le -1$ or $x \ge 1$ |

## GRAPHS OF THE INVERSE TRIGONOMETRIC FUNCTIONS

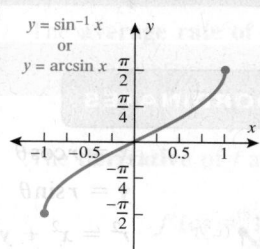

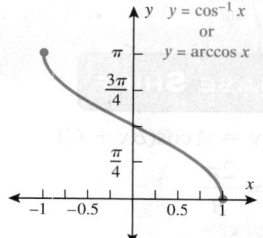

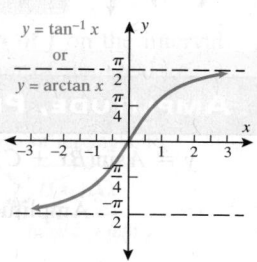

## VECTORS

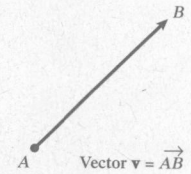

Vector $\mathbf{v} = \vec{AB}$

**Vector Addition**

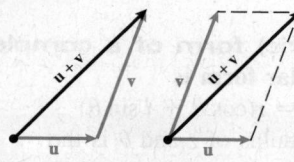

For vectors $\mathbf{u} = \langle a, b \rangle$ and $\mathbf{v} = \langle c, d \rangle$, and real number $k$,

$$\mathbf{u} = a\mathbf{i} + b\mathbf{j}$$
$$|\mathbf{u}| = \sqrt{a^2 + b^2}$$
$$\mathbf{u} + \mathbf{v} = \langle a + c, b + d \rangle$$
$$k\mathbf{u} = \langle ka, kb \rangle$$
$$\mathbf{u} \cdot \mathbf{v} = ac + bd$$
$$\cos\theta = \frac{\mathbf{u} \cdot \mathbf{v}}{|\mathbf{u}||\mathbf{v}|}$$

**Scalar Multiplication**

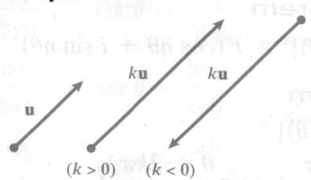

$(k > 0)$   $(k < 0)$

$$\text{Comp}_{\mathbf{v}}\,\mathbf{u} = |\mathbf{u}| \cos\theta = \frac{\mathbf{u} \cdot \mathbf{v}}{|\mathbf{u}|}$$

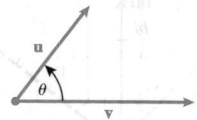

# EXACT VALUES OF TRIGONOMETRIC FUNCTIONS

| $x$ degrees | $x$ radians | $\sin x$ | $\cos x$ | $\tan x$ |
|---|---|---|---|---|
| 0° | 0 | 0 | 1 | 0 |
| 30° | $\dfrac{\pi}{6}$ | $\dfrac{1}{2}$ | $\dfrac{\sqrt{3}}{2}$ | $\dfrac{\sqrt{3}}{3}$ |
| 45° | $\dfrac{\pi}{4}$ | $\dfrac{\sqrt{2}}{2}$ | $\dfrac{\sqrt{2}}{2}$ | 1 |
| 60° | $\dfrac{\pi}{3}$ | $\dfrac{\sqrt{3}}{2}$ | $\dfrac{1}{2}$ | $\sqrt{3}$ |
| 90° | $\dfrac{\pi}{2}$ | 1 | 0 | — |

# ANGLE MEASUREMENT

$\pi$ radians $= 180°$

$s = r\theta \quad A = \frac{1}{2}r^2\theta \quad$ ($\theta$ in radians)

To convert from degrees to radians, multiply by $\dfrac{\pi}{180°}$.

To convert from radians to degrees, multiply by $\dfrac{180°}{\pi}$.

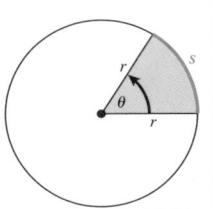

# OBLIQUE TRIANGLES

## Law of Sines

In any triangle,
$$\frac{\sin\alpha}{a} = \frac{\sin\beta}{b} = \frac{\sin\gamma}{c}.$$

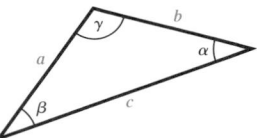

## Law of Cosines

$$a^2 = b^2 + c^2 - 2bc\cos\alpha$$
$$b^2 = a^2 + c^2 - 2ac\cos\beta$$
$$c^2 = a^2 + b^2 - 2ab\cos\gamma$$

# CIRCULAR FUNCTIONS (COSθ, SINθ)

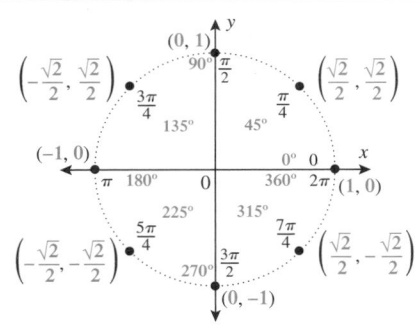

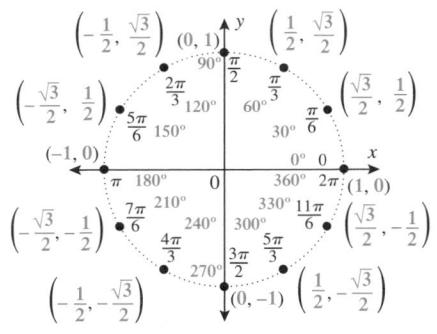

# STUDENT'S SOLUTIONS MANUAL

## VICTOR MAYMESKUL
*Georgia Southern University*

*to accompany*

# FUNDAMENTALS OF DIFFERENTIAL EQUATIONS
### SIXTH EDITION
*and*
# FUNDAMENTALS OF DIFFERENTIAL EQUATIONS AND BOUNDARY VALUE PROBLEMS
### FOURTH EDITION

## R. Kent Nagle

## Edward B. Saff
*Vanderbilt Unviersity*

## A. David Snider
*University of South Florida*

PEARSON

Addison
Wesley

Boston    San Francisco    New York
London    Toronto    Sydney    Tokyo    Singapore    Madrid
Mexico City    Munich    Paris    Cape Town    Hong Kong    Montreal

Reproduced by Pearson Addison-Wesley from electronic files supplied by the author.

Copyright © 2004 Pearson Education, Inc.
Publishing as Pearson Addison-Wesley, 75 Arlington Street, Boston MA 02116

ISBN    0-321-17319-8

5 VH 06

# Contents

# CHAPTER 1: Introduction

**EXERCISES 1.1:  Background, page 5**

1. This equation involves only ordinary derivatives of $x$ with respect to $t$, and the highest derivative has the second order. Thus it is an ordinary differential equation of the second order with independent variable $t$ and dependent variable $x$. It is linear because $x$, $dx/dt$, and $d^2x/dt^2$ appear in additive combination (even with constant coefficients) of their first powers.

3. This equation is an ODE because it contains no partial derivatives. Since the highest order derivative is $dy/dx$, the equation is a first order equation. This same term also shows us that the independent variable is $x$ and the dependent variable is $y$. This equation is nonlinear because of the $y$ in the denominator of the term $[y(2-3x)]/[x(1-3y)]$.

5. This equation is an ODE because it contains only ordinary derivatives. The term $dp/dt$ is the highest order derivative and thus shows us that this is a first order equation. This term also shows us that the independent variable is $t$ and the dependent variable is $p$. This equation is nonlinear since in the term $kp(P-p) = kPp - kp^2$ the dependent variable $p$ is squared (compare with equation (7) on page 5 of the text).

7. This equation is an ordinary first order differential equation with independent variable $x$ and dependent variable $y$. It is nonlinear because it contains the square of $dy/dx$.

9. This equation contains only ordinary derivative of $y$ with respect to $x$. Hence, it is an ordinary differential equation of the second order (the highest order derivative is $d^2y/dx^2$) with independent variable $x$ and dependent variable $y$. This equation is of the form (7) on page 5 of the text and, therefore, is linear.

# Chapter 1

**11.** This equation contains partial derivatives, thus it is a PDE. Because the highest order derivative is a second order partial derivative, the equation is a second order equation. The terms $\partial N/\partial t$ and $\partial N/\partial r$ show that the independent variables are $t$ and $r$ and the dependent variable is $N$.

**13.** Since the rate of change of a quantity means its derivative, denoting the coefficient proportionality between $dp/dt$ and $p(t)$ by $k$ $(k > 0)$, we get

$$\frac{dp}{dt} = kp.$$

**15.** In this problem, $T \geq M$ (coffee is hotter than the air), and $T$ is a decreasing function of $t$, that is $dT/dt \leq 0$. Thus

$$\frac{dT}{dt} = k(M - T),$$

where $k > 0$ is the proportionality constant.

**17.** In classical physics, the instantaneous acceleration, $a$, of an object moving in a straight line is given by the second derivative of distance, $x$, with respect to time, $t$; that is

$$\frac{d^2 x}{dt^2} = a.$$

Integrating both sides with respect to $t$ and using the given fact that $a$ is constant we obtain

$$\frac{dx}{dt} = at + C. \tag{1.1}$$

The instantaneous velocity, $v$, of an object is given by the first derivative of distance, $x$, with respect to time, $t$. At the beginning of the race, $t = 0$, both racers have zero velocity. Therefore we have $C = 0$. Integrating equation (1.1) with respect to $t$ we obtain

$$x = \frac{1}{2} at^2 + C_1.$$

For this problem we will use the starting position for both competitors to be $x = 0$ at $t = 0$. Therefore, we have $C_1 = 0$. This gives us a general equation used for both racers as

$$x = \frac{1}{2} at^2 \qquad \text{or} \qquad t = \sqrt{\frac{2x}{a}},$$

where the acceleration constant $a$ has different values for Kevin and for Alison. Kevin covers the last $\frac{1}{4}$ of the full distance, $L$, in 3 seconds. This means Kevin's acceleration, $a_K$, is determined by:

$$t_K - t_{3/4} = 3 = \sqrt{\frac{2L}{a_K}} - \sqrt{\frac{2(3L/4)}{a_K}},$$

where $t_K$ is the time it takes for Kevin to finish the race. Solving this equation for $a_K$ gives,

$$a_K = \frac{\left(\sqrt{2} - \sqrt{3/2}\right)^2}{9} L.$$

Therefore the time required for Kevin to finish the race is given by:

$$t_K = \sqrt{\frac{2L}{\left(\sqrt{2} - \sqrt{3/2}\right)^2 L/9}} = \frac{3}{\sqrt{2} - \sqrt{3/2}} \sqrt{2} = 12 + 6\sqrt{3} \approx 22.39 \, \text{sec}.$$

Alison covers the last $1/3$ of the distance, $L$, in 4 seconds. This means Alison's acceleration, $a_A$, is found by:

$$t_A - t_{2/3} = 4 = \sqrt{\frac{2L}{a_A}} - \sqrt{\frac{2(2L/3)}{a_A}},$$

where $t_A$ is the time required for Alison to finish the race. Solving this equation for $a_A$ gives

$$a_A = \frac{\left(\sqrt{2} - \sqrt{4/3}\right)^2}{16} L.$$

Therefore the time required for Alison to finish the race is given by:

$$t_A = \sqrt{\frac{2L}{\left(\sqrt{2} - \sqrt{4/3}\right)^2 (L/16)}} = \frac{4}{\sqrt{2} - \sqrt{4/3}} \sqrt{2} = 12 + 4\sqrt{6} \approx 21.80 \, \text{sec}.$$

The time required for Alison to finish the race is less than Kevin; therefore Alison wins the race by $6\sqrt{3} - 4\sqrt{6} \approx 0.594$ seconds.

## EXERCISES 1.2:  Solutions and Initial Value Problems, page 14

1.  (a) Differentiating $\phi(x)$ yields $\phi'(x) = 6x^2$. Substitution $\phi$ and $\phi'$ for $y$ and $y'$ into the given equation, $xy' = 3y$, gives

$$x\left(6x^2\right) = 3\left(2x^3\right),$$

which is an identity on $(-\infty, \infty)$. Thus $\phi(x)$ is an explicit solution on $(-\infty, \infty)$.

**(b)** We compute

$$\frac{d\phi}{dx} = \frac{d}{dx}\left(e^x - x\right) = e^x - 1.$$

Functions $\phi(x)$ and $\phi'(x)$ are defined for all real numbers and

$$\frac{d\phi}{dx} + \phi(x)^2 = (e^x - 1) + (e^x - x)^2 = (e^x - 1) + \left(e^{2x} - 2xe^x + x^2\right) = e^{2x} + (1 - 2x)e^x + x^2 - 1,$$

which is identically equal to the right-hand side of the given equation. Thus $\phi(x)$ is an explicit solution on $(-\infty, \infty)$.

**(c)** Note that the function $\phi(x) = x^2 - x^{-1}$ is not defined at $x = 0$. Differentiating $\phi(x)$ twice yields

$$\frac{d\phi}{dx} = \frac{d}{dx}\left(x^2 - x^{-1}\right) = 2x - (-1)x^{-2} = 2x + x^{-2};$$

$$\frac{d^2\phi}{dx^2} = \frac{d}{dx}\left(\frac{d\phi}{dx}\right) = \frac{d}{dx}\left(2x + x^{-2}\right) = 2 + (-2)x^{-3} = 2\left(1 - x^{-3}\right).$$

Therefore

$$x^2 \frac{d^2\phi}{dx^2} = x^2 \cdot 2\left(1 - x^{-3}\right) = 2\left(x^2 - x^{-1}\right) = 2\phi(x),$$

and $\phi(x)$ is an explicit solution to the differential equation $x^2 y'' = 2y$ on any interval not containing the point $x = 0$, in particular, on $(0, \infty)$.

**3.** Since $y = \sin x + x^2$, we have $y' = \cos x + 2x$ and $y'' = -\sin x + 2$. These functions are defined on $(-\infty, \infty)$. Substituting these expressions into the differential equation $y'' + y = x^2 + 2$ gives

$$y'' + y = -\sin x + 2 + \sin x + x^2 = 2 + x^2 = x^2 + 2 \qquad \text{for all } x \text{ in } (-\infty, \infty).$$

Therefore, $y = \sin x + x^2$ is a solution to the differential equation on the interval $(-\infty, \infty)$.

**5.** Differentiating $x(t) = \cos 2t$, we get

$$\frac{dx}{dt} = \frac{d}{dt}\left(\cos 2t\right) = (-\sin 2t)(2) = -2\sin 2t.$$

So,

$$\frac{dx}{dt} + tx = -2\sin 2t + t\cos 2t \not\equiv \sin 2t$$

on any interval. Therefore, $x(t)$ is not a solution to the given differential equation.

7. We differentiate $y = e^{2x} - 3e^{-x}$ twice:

$$\frac{dy}{dx} = \frac{d}{dx}\left(e^{2x} - 3e^{-x}\right) = e^{2x}(2) - 3e^{-x}(-1) = 2e^{2x} + 3e^{-x};$$
$$\frac{d^2y}{dx^2} = \frac{d}{dx}\left(\frac{dy}{dx}\right) = \frac{d}{dx}\left(2e^{2x} + 3e^{-x}\right) = 2e^{2x}(2) + 3e^{-x}(-1) = 4e^{2x} - 3e^{-x}.$$

Substituting $y$, $y'$, and $y''$ into the differential equation and collecting similar terms, we get

$$\frac{d^2y}{dx^2} - \frac{dy}{dx} - 2y = \left(4e^{2x} - 3e^{-x}\right) - \left(2e^{2x} + 3e^{-x}\right) - 2\left(e^{2x} - 3e^{-x}\right)$$
$$= (4 - 2 - 2)e^{2x} + (-3 - 3 - 2(-3))e^{-x} = 0.$$

Hence $y = e^{2x} - 3e^{-x}$ is an explicit solution to the given differential equation.

9. Differentiating the equation $x^2 + y^2 = 6$ implicitly, we obtain

$$2x + 2yy' = 0 \qquad \Rightarrow \qquad y' = -\frac{x}{y}.$$

Since there can be no function $y = f(x)$ that satisfies the differential equation $y' = x/y$ and the differential equation $y' = -x/y$ on the same interval, we see that $x^2 + y^2 = 6$ does not define an implicit solution to the differential equation.

11. Differentiating the equation $e^{xy} + y = x - 1$ implicitly with respect to $x$ yields

$$\frac{d}{dx}\left(e^{xy} + y\right) = \frac{d}{dx}(x - 1)$$
$$\Rightarrow \qquad e^{xy}\frac{d}{dx}(xy) + \frac{dy}{dx} = 1$$
$$\Rightarrow \qquad e^{xy}\left(y + x\frac{dy}{dx}\right) + \frac{dy}{dx} = 1$$
$$\Rightarrow \qquad ye^{xy} + \frac{dy}{dx}\left(xe^{xy} + 1\right) = 1$$
$$\Rightarrow \qquad \frac{dy}{dx} = \frac{1 - ye^{xy}}{1 + xe^{xy}} = \frac{e^{xy}\left(e^{-xy} - y\right)}{e^{xy}\left(e^{-xy} + x\right)} = \frac{e^{-xy} - y}{e^{-xy} + x}.$$

5

Chapter 1

Therefore, the function $y(x)$ defined by $e^{xy} + y = x - 1$ is an implicit solution to the given differential equation.

**13.** Differentiating the equation $\sin y + xy - x^3 = 2$ implicitly with respect to $x$, we obtain

$$y' \cos y + xy' + y - 3x^2 = 0$$
$$\Rightarrow \quad (\cos y + x)y' = 3x^2 - y \quad \Rightarrow \quad y' = \frac{3x^2 - y}{\cos y + x}.$$

Differentiating the second equation above again, we obtain

$$(-y' \sin y + 1)y' + (\cos y + x)y'' = 6x - y'$$
$$\Rightarrow \quad (\cos y + x)y'' = 6x - y' + (y')^2 \sin y - y' = 6x - 2y' + (y')^2 \sin y$$
$$\Rightarrow \quad y'' = \frac{6x - 2y' + (y')^2 \sin y}{\cos y + x}.$$

Multiplying the right-hand side of this last equation by $y'/y' = 1$ and using the fact that

$$y' = \frac{3x^2 - y}{\cos y + x},$$

we get

$$y'' = \frac{6x - 2y' + (y')^2 \sin y}{\cos y + x} \cdot \frac{y'}{(3x^2 - y)/(\cos y + x)}$$
$$= \frac{6xy' - 2(y')^2 + (y')^3 \sin y}{3x^2 - y}.$$

Thus $y$ is an implicit solution to the differential equation.

**15.** We differentiate $\phi(x)$ and substitute $\phi$ and $\phi'$ into the differential equation for $y$ and $y'$. This yields

$$\phi(x) = Ce^{3x} + 1 \quad \Rightarrow \quad \frac{d\phi(x)}{dx} = (Ce^{3x} + 1)' = 3Ce^{3x};$$
$$\frac{d\phi}{dx} - 3\phi = (3Ce^{3x}) - 3(Ce^{3x} + 1) = (3C - 3C)e^{3x} - 3 = -3,$$

which holds for any constant $C$ and any $x$ on $(-\infty, \infty)$. Therefore, $\phi(x) = Ce^{3x} + 1$ is a one-parameter family of solutions to $y' - 3y = -3$ on $(-\infty, \infty)$. Graphs of these functions for $C = 0, \pm 0.5, \pm 1$, and $\pm 2$ are sketched in Figure 1-A.

6

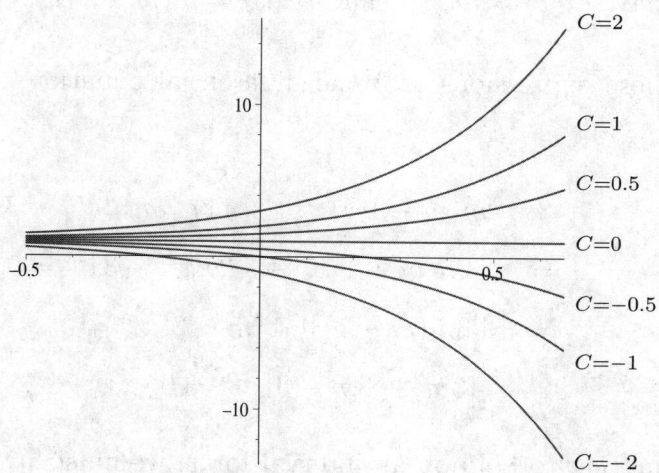

**Figure 1–A**: Graphs of the functions $y = Ce^{3x} + 1$ for $C = 0$, $\pm 0.5$, $\pm 1$, and $\pm 2$.

**17.** Differentiating $\phi(x)$, we find that

$$
\begin{aligned}
\phi'(x) &= \left(\frac{2}{1 - ce^x}\right)' = \left[2\left(1 - ce^x\right)^{-1}\right]' \\
&= 2(-1)\left(1 - ce^x\right)^{-2}\left(1 - ce^x\right)' = 2ce^x\left(1 - ce^x\right)^{-2}.
\end{aligned}
\tag{1.2}
$$

On the other hand, substitution of $\phi(x)$ for $y$ into the right-hand side of the given equation yields

$$
\begin{aligned}
\frac{\phi(x)(\phi(x) - 2)}{2} &= \frac{1}{2}\frac{2}{1 - ce^x}\left(\frac{2}{1 - ce^x} - 2\right) \\
&= \frac{2}{1 - ce^x}\left(\frac{1}{1 - ce^x} - 1\right) = \frac{2}{1 - ce^x}\frac{1 - (1 - ce^x)}{1 - ce^x} = \frac{2ce^x}{(1 - ce^x)^2},
\end{aligned}
$$

which is identical to $\phi'(x)$ found in (1.2).

**19.** Squaring and adding the terms $dy/dx$ and $y$ in the equation $(dy/dx)^2 + y^2 + 3 = 0$ gives a nonnegative number. Therefore when these two terms are added to 3, the left-hand side will always be greater than or equal to three and hence can never equal the right-hand side which is zero.

# Chapter 1

**21.** For $\phi(x) = x^m$, we have $\phi'(x) = mx^{m-1}$ and $\phi''(x) = m(m-1)x^{m-2}$.

    **(a)** Substituting these expressions into the differential equation, $3x^2 y'' + 11xy' - 3y = 0$, gives

$$3x^2 \left[m(m-1)x^{m-2}\right] + 11x\left[mx^{m-1}\right] - 3x^m = 0$$
$$\Rightarrow \quad 3m(m-1)x^m + 11mx^m - 3x^m = 0$$
$$\Rightarrow \quad [3m(m-1) + 11m - 3]\,x^m = 0$$
$$\Rightarrow \quad [3m^2 + 8m - 3]\,x^m = 0.$$

For the last equation to hold on an interval for $x$, we must have

$$3m^2 + 8m - 3 = (3m-1)(m+3) = 0.$$

Thus either $(3m-1) = 0$ or $(m+3) = 0$, which gives $m = \dfrac{1}{3}, -3$.

    **(b)** Substituting the above expressions for $\phi(x)$, $\phi'(x)$, and $\phi''(x)$ into the differential equation, $x^2 y'' - xy' - 5y = 0$, gives

$$x^2 \left[m(m-1)x^{m-2}\right] - x\left[mx^{m-1}\right] - 5x^m = 0 \quad \Rightarrow \quad [m^2 - 2m - 5]\,x^m = 0.$$

For the last equation to hold on an interval for $x$, we must have

$$m^2 - 2m - 5 = 0.$$

To solve for $m$ we use the quadratic formula:

$$m = \frac{2 \pm \sqrt{4 + 20}}{2} = 1 \pm \sqrt{6}.$$

**23.** In this problem, $f(x,y) = x^3 - y^3$ and so

$$\frac{\partial f}{\partial y} = \frac{\partial \left(x^3 - y^3\right)}{\partial y} = -3y^2.$$

Clearly, $f$ and $\partial f/\partial y$ (being polynomials) are continuous on the whole $xy$-plane. Thus the hypotheses of Theorem 1 are satisfied, and the initial value problem has a unique solution for *any* initial data, in particular, for $y(0) = 6$.

**25.** Writing

$$\frac{dx}{dt} = -\frac{4t}{x} = -4tx^{-1},$$

we see that $f(t,x) = -4tx^{-1}$ and $\partial f(t,x)/\partial x = \partial(-4tx^{-1})/\partial x = 4tx^{-2}$. The functions $f(t,x)$ and $\partial f(t,x)/\partial x$ are not continuous only when $x = 0$. Therefore, they are continuous in any rectangle $R$ that contains the point $(2, -\pi)$, but does not intersect the $t$-axis; for instance, $R = \{(t,x) : 1 < t < 3, -2\pi < x < 0\}$. Thus, Theorem 1 applies, and the given initial problem has a unique solution.

**26.** Here $f(x,y) = 3x - \sqrt[3]{y-1}$ and $\partial f(x,y)/\partial y = -\frac{1}{3}(y-1)^{-2/3}$. Unfortunately, $\partial f/\partial y$ is not continuous or defined when $y = 1$. So there is no rectangle containing $(2,1)$ in which both $f$ and $\partial f/\partial y$ are continuous. Therefore, we are not guaranteed a unique solution to this initial value problem.

**27.** Rewriting the differential equation in the form $dy/dx = x/y$, we conclude that $f(x,y) = x/y$. Since $f$ is not continuous when $y = 0$, there is no rectangle containing the point $(1,0)$ in which $f$ is continuous. Therefore, Theorem 1 cannot be applied.

**29. (a)** Clearly, both functions $\phi_1(x) \equiv 0$ and $\phi_2(x) = (x-2)^3$ satisfy the initial condition, $y(2) = 0$. Next, we check that they also satisfy the differential equation $dy/dx = 3y^{2/3}$.

$$\frac{d\phi_1}{dx} = \frac{d}{dx}(0) = 0 = 3\phi_1(x)^{2/3};$$
$$\frac{d\phi_2}{dx} = \frac{d}{dx}\left[(x-2)^3\right] = 3(x-2)^2 = 3\left[(x-2)^3\right]^{2/3} = 3\phi_2(x)^{2/3}.$$

Hence both functions, $\phi_1(x)$ and $\phi_2(x)$, are solutions to the initial value problem of Exapmle 9.

**(b)** In this initial value problem,

$$f(x,y) = 3y^{2/3} \qquad \Rightarrow \qquad \frac{\partial f(x,y)}{\partial y} = 3\frac{2}{3}y^{2/3-1} = \frac{2}{y^{1/3}},$$

$x_0 = 0$ and $y_0 = 10^{-7}$. The function $f(x,y)$ is continuous everywhere; $\partial f(x,y)/\partial y$ is continuous in any region which does not intersect the $x$-axis (where $y = 0$). In particular,

9

# Chapter 1

both functions, $f(x,y)$ and $\partial f(x,y)/\partial y$, are continuous in the rectangle

$$R = \{(x,y) : -1 < x < 1, (1/2)10^{-7} < y < (2)10^{-7}\}$$

containing the initial point $(0, 10^{-7})$. Thus, it follows from Theorem 1 that the given initial value problem has a unique solution in an interval about $x_0$.

**31.** **(a)** To try to apply Theorem 1 we must first write the equation in the form $y' = f(x,y)$. Here $f(x,y) = 4xy^{-1}$ and $\partial f(x,y)/\partial y = -4xy^{-2}$. Neither $f$ nor $\partial f/\partial y$ are continuous or defined when $y = 0$. Therefore there is no rectangle containing $(x_0, 0)$ in which both $f$ and $\partial f/\partial y$ are continuous, so Theorem 1 cannot be applied.

**(b)** Suppose for the moment that there is such a solution $y(x)$ with $y(x_0) = 0$ and $x_0 \neq 0$. Substituting into the differential equation we get

$$y(x_0)y'(x_0) - 4x_0 = 0 \tag{1.3}$$

or

$$0 \cdot y'(x_0) - 4x_0 = 0 \qquad \Rightarrow \qquad 4x_0 = 0.$$

Thus $x_0 = 0$, which is a contradiction.

**(c)** Taking $C = 0$ in the implicit solution $4x^2 - y^2 = C$ given in Example 5 on page 9 gives $4x^2 - y^2 = 0$ or $y = \pm 2x$. Both solutions $y = 2x$ and $y = -2x$ satisfy $y(0) = 0$.

**EXERCISES 1.3:   Direction Fields, page 22**

**1.** **(a)** For $y = \pm 2x$,

$$\frac{dy}{dx} = \frac{d}{dx}(\pm 2x) = \pm 2 \qquad \text{and} \qquad \frac{4x}{y} = \frac{4x}{\pm 2x} = \pm 2, \quad x \neq 0.$$

Thus $y = 2x$ and $y = -2x$ are solutions to the differential equation $dy/dx = 4x/y$ on any interval not containing the point $x = 0$.

**(b)** , **(c)** See Figures B.1 and B.2 in the answers of the text.

10

**(d)** As $x \to \infty$ or $x \to -\infty$, the solution in part (b) increases unboundedly and has the lines $y = 2x$ and $y = -2x$, respectively, as slant asymptotes. The solution in part (c) also increases without bound as $x \to \infty$ and approaches the line $y = 2x$, while it is not even defined for $x < 0$.

**3.** From Figure B.3 in the answers section of the text, we conclude that, regardless of the initial velocity, $v(0)$, the corresponding solution curve $v = v(t)$ has the line $v = 8$ as a horizontal asymptote, that is, $\lim_{t \to \infty} v(t) = 8$. This explains the name "terminal velocity" for the value $v = 8$.

**5. (a)** The graph of the directional field is shown in Figure B.4 in the answers section of the text.

**(b), (c)** The direction field indicates that all solution curves (other than $p(t) \equiv 0$) will approach the horizontal line (asymptote) $p = 1.5$ as $t \to +\infty$. Thus $\lim_{t \to +\infty} p(t) = 1.5$.

**(d)** No. The direction field shows that populations greater than 1500 will steadily decrease, but can never reach 1500 or any smaller value, i.e., the solution curves cannot cross the line $p = 1.5$. Indeed, the constant function $p(t) \equiv 1.5$ is a solution to the given logistic equation, and the uniqueness part of Theorem 1, page 12, prevents intersections of solution curves.

**6. (a)** The slope of a solution to the differential equation $dy/dx = x + \sin y$ is given by $dy/dx$. Therefore the slope at $(1, \pi/2)$ is equal to

$$\frac{dy}{dx} = 1 + \sin \frac{\pi}{2} = 2.$$

**(b)** The solution curve is increasing if the slope of the curve is greater than zero. From part (a) we know the slope to be $x + \sin y$. The function $\sin y$ has values ranging from $-1$ to $1$; therefore if $x$ is greater than 1 then the slope will always have a value greater than zero. This tells us that the solution curve is increasing.

**(c)** The second derivative of every solution can be determined by finding the derivative of

11

the differential equation $dy/dx = x + \sin y$. Thus

$$\frac{d}{dx}\left(\frac{dy}{dx}\right) = \frac{d}{dx}(x + \sin y);$$

$$\Rightarrow \quad \frac{d^2y}{dx^2} = 1 + (\cos y)\frac{dy}{dx} \quad \text{(chain rule)}$$

$$= 1 + (\cos y)(x + \sin y) = 1 + x\cos y + \sin y \cos y;$$

$$\Rightarrow \quad \frac{d^2y}{dx^2} = 1 + x\cos y + \frac{1}{2}\sin 2y.$$

(d) Relative minima occur when the first derivative, $dy/dx$, is equal to zero and the second derivative, $d^2y/dx^2$, is greater than zero. The value of the first derivative at the point $(0,0)$ is given by

$$\frac{dy}{dx} = 0 + \sin 0 = 0.$$

This tells us that the solution has a critical point at the point $(0,0)$. Using the second derivative found in part (c) we have

$$\frac{d^2y}{dx^2} = 1 + 0 \cdot \cos 0 + \frac{1}{2}\sin 0 = 1.$$

This tells us the point $(0,0)$ is a relative minimum.

7. (a) The graph of the directional field is shown in Figure B.5 in the answers section of the text.

(b) The direction field indicates that all solution curves with $p(0) > 1$ will approach the horizontal line (asymptote) $p = 2$ as $t \to +\infty$. Thus $\lim_{t \to +\infty} p(t) = 2$ when $p(0) = 3$.

(c) The direction field shows that a population between 1000 and 2000 (that is $1 < p(0) < 2$) will approach the horizontal line $p = 2$ as $t \to +\infty$.

(d) The direction field shows that an initial population less than 1000 (that is $0 \le p(0) < 1$) will approach zero as $t \to +\infty$.

(e) As noted in part (d), the line $p = 1$ is an asymptote. The direction field indicates that a population of 900 ($p(0) = 0.9$) steadily decreases with time and therefore cannot increase to 1100.

9. **(a)** The function $\phi(x)$, being a solution to the given initial value problem, satisfies

$$\frac{d\phi}{dx} = x - \phi(x), \qquad \phi(0) = 1. \tag{1.4}$$

Thus

$$\frac{d^2\phi}{dx^2} = \frac{d}{dx}\left(\frac{d\phi}{dx}\right) = \frac{d}{dx}(x - \phi(x)) = 1 - \frac{d\phi}{dx} = 1 - x + \phi(x),$$

where we have used (1.4) substituting (twice) $x - \phi(x)$ for $d\phi/dx$.

**(b)** First we note that any solution to the given differential equation on an interval $I$ is continuously diferentiable on $I$. Indeed, if $y(x)$ is a solution on $I$, then $y'(x)$ does exist on $I$, and so $y(x)$ is continuous on $I$ because it is differentiable. This immediately implies that $y'(x)$ is continuous as the difference of two continuous functions, $x$ and $y(x)$.

From (1.4) we conclude that

$$\frac{d\phi}{dx}\bigg|_{x=0} = [x - \phi(x)]\big|_{x=0} = 0 - \phi(0) = -1 < 0$$

and so the continuity of $\phi'(x)$ implies that, for $|x|$ small enough, $\phi'(x) < 0$. By the Monotonicity Test, negative derivative of a function results that the function itself is decreasing.

When $x$ increases from zero, as far as $\phi(x) > x$, one has $\phi'(x) < 0$ and so $\phi(x)$ decreases. On the other hand, the function $y = x$ increases unboundedly, as $x \to \infty$. Thus, by intermediate value theorem, there is a point, say, $x^* > 0$, where the curve $y = \phi(x)$ crosses the line $y = x$. At this point, $\phi(x^*) = x^*$ and hence $\phi'(x^*) = x^* - \phi(x^*) = 0$.

**(c)** From (b) we conclude that $x^*$ is a critical point for $\phi(x)$ (its derivative vanishes at this point). Also, from part (a), we see that

$$\phi''(x^*) = 1 - \phi'(x^*) = 1 > 0.$$

Hence, by Second Derivative Test, $\phi(x)$ has a relative minimum at $x^*$.

**(d)** Remark that the arguments, used in part (c), can be applied to *any* point $\widetilde{x}$, where $\phi'(\widetilde{x}) = 0$, to conclude that $\phi(x)$ has a relative minimum at $\widetilde{x}$. Since a continuously differentiable function on an interval cannot have two relative minima on an interval without having a point of relative maximum, we conclude that $x^*$ is the only point where $\phi'(x) = 0$. Continuity of $\phi'(x)$ implies that it has the same sign for all $x > x^*$ and, therefore, it is positive there since it is positive for $x > x^*$ and close to $x^*$ ($\phi'(x^*) = 0$ and $\phi''(x^*) > 0$). By Monotonicity Test, $\phi(x)$ increases for $x > x^*$.

(e) For $y = x - 1$, $dy/dx = 1$ and $x - y = x - (x - 1) = 1$. Thus the given differential equation is satisfied, and $y = x - 1$ is indeed a solution.

To show that the curve $y = \phi(x)$ always stays above the line $y = x - 1$, we note that the initial value problem

$$\frac{dy}{dx} = x - y, \qquad y(x_0) = y_0 \tag{1.5}$$

has a unique solution for any $x_0$ and $y_0$. Indeed, functions $f(x, y) = x - y$ and $\partial f / \partial y \equiv -1$ are continuous on the whole $xy$-plane, and Theorem 1, Section 1.2, applies. This implies that the curve $y = \phi(x)$ always stays above the line $y = x - 1$:

$$\phi(0) = 1 > -1 = (x - 1)\big|_{x=0},$$

and the existence of a point $\tilde{x}$ with $\phi(\tilde{x}) \leq (\tilde{x} - 1)$ would imply, by intermediate value theorem, the existence of a point $x_0$, $0 < x_0 \leq \tilde{x}$, satisfying $y_0 := \phi(x_0) = x_0 - 1$ and, therefore, there would be two solutions to the initial value problem (1.5).

Since, from part (a), $\phi''(x) = 1 - \phi'(x) = 1 - x + \phi(x) = \phi(x) - (x - 1) > 0$, we also conclude that $\phi'(x)$ is an increasing function and $\phi'(x) < 1$. Thus there exists $\lim_{x \to \infty} \phi'(x) \leq 1$. The strict inequality would imply that the values of the function $y = \phi(x)$, for $x$ large enough, become smaller than those of $y = x - 1$. Therefore,

$$\lim_{x \to \infty} \phi'(x) = 1 \qquad \Leftrightarrow \qquad \lim_{x \to \infty} [x - \phi(x)] = 1,$$

and so the line $y = x - 1$ is a slant asymptote for $\phi(x)$.

(f), (g) The direction field for given differential equation and the curve $y = \phi(x)$ are shown in Figure B.6 in the answers of the text.

**11.** For this equation, the isoclines are given by $2x = c$. These are vertical lines $x = c/2$. Each element of the direction field associated with a point on $x = c/2$ has slope $c$. (See Figure B.7 in the answers of the text.)

**13.** For the equation $\partial y/\partial x = -x/y$, the isoclines are the curves $-x/y = c$. These are lines that pass through the origin and have equations of the form $y = mx$, where $m = -1/c$, $c \neq 0$. If we let $c = 0$ in $-x/y = c$, we see that the $y$-axis ($x = 0$) is also an isocline. Each element of the direction field associated with a point on an isocline has slope $c$ and is, therefore, perpendicular to that isocline. Since circles have the property that at any point on the circle the tangent at that point is perpendicular to a line from that point to the center of the circle, we see that the solution curves will be circles with their centers at the origin. But since we cannot have $y = 0$ (since $-x/y$ would then have a zero in the denominator) the solutions will not be defined on the $x$-axis. (Note however that a related form of this differential equation is $yy' + x = 0$. This equation has implicit solutions given by the equations $y^2 + x^2 = C$. These solutions will be circles.) The graph of $\phi(x)$, the solution to the equation satisfying the initial condition $y(0) = 4$, is the upper semicircle with center at the origin and passing through the point $(0, 4)$ (see Figure B.8 in the answers of the text).

**15.** For the equation $dy/dx = 2x^2 - y$, the isoclines are the curves $2x^2 - y = c$, or $y = 2x^2 - c$. The curve $y = 2x^2 - c$ is a parabola which is open upward and has the vertex at $(0, -c)$. Three of them, for $c = -1$, $0$, and $2$ (dotted curves), as well as the solution curve satisfying the initial condition $y(0) = 0$, are depicted in Figure B.9.

**17.** The isoclines for the equation

$$\frac{dy}{dx} = 3 - y + \frac{1}{x}$$

are given by

$$3 - y + \frac{1}{x} = c \qquad \Leftrightarrow \qquad y = \frac{1}{x} + 3 - c,$$

which are hyperbolas having $x = 0$ as a vertical asymptote and $y = 3 - c$ as a horizontal asymptote. Each element of the direction field associated with a point on such a hyperbola has slope $c$. For $x > 0$ large enough: if an isocline is located *above* the line $y = 3$, then $c \leq 0$,

15

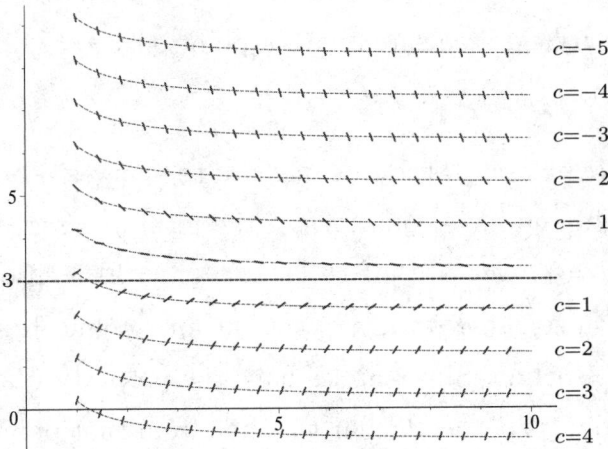

**Figure 1–B**: Isoclines and the direction field for Problem 17.

and so the elements of the direction field have *negative* or *zero slope*; if an isocline is located *below* the line $y = 3$, then $c > 0$, and so the elements of the direction field have *positive slope*. In other words, for $x > 0$ large enough, at any point above the line $y = 3$ a solution curve decreases passing through this point, and any solution curve increases passing through a point below $y = 3$. The direction field for this differential equation is depicted in Figure 1-B. From this picture we conclude that any solution to the differential equation $dy/dx = 3 - y + 1/x$ has the line $y = 3$ as a horizontal asymptote.

**19.** Integrating both sides of the equation $dy/y = -dx/x$ yields

$$\int \frac{1}{y}\, dy = -\int \frac{1}{x}\, dx \quad \Rightarrow \quad \ln|y| = -\ln|x| + C_1 \quad \Rightarrow \quad \ln|y| = \ln \frac{e^{C_1}}{|x|}$$

$$\Rightarrow \quad |y| = \frac{e^{C_1}}{|x|} \quad \Rightarrow \quad |y| = \frac{C_2}{|x|},$$

where $C_1$ is an arbitrary constant and so $C_2 := e^{C_1}$ is an arbitrary *positive* constant. The last equality can be written as

$$y = \pm \frac{C_2}{x} = \frac{C}{x},$$

where $C = \pm C_2$ is *any nonzero* constant. The value $C = 0$ gives $y \equiv 0$ (for $x \neq 0$), which is, clearly, also a solution to the given equation.

## EXERCISES 1.4:   The Approximation Method of Euler, page 28

**1.** In this initial value problem, $f(x, y) = x/y$, $x_0 = 0$, and $y_0 = -1$. Thus, with $h = 0.1$, the recursive formulas (2) and (3) on page 25 of the text become

$$x_{n+1} = x_n + h = x_n + 0.1\,,$$
$$y_{n+1} = y_n + hf(x_n, y_n) = y_n + 0.1 \cdot \left(\frac{x_n}{y_n}\right), \qquad n = 0, 1, \ldots.$$

We set $n = 0$ in these formulas and obtain

$$x_1 = x_0 + 0.1 = 0 + 0.1 = 0.1\,,$$
$$y_1 = y_0 + 0.1 \cdot \left(\frac{x_0}{y_0}\right) = -1 + 0.1 \cdot \left(\frac{0}{-1}\right) = -1.$$

Putting $n = 1$ in the recursive formulas yields

$$x_2 = x_1 + 0.1 = 0.1 + 0.1 = 0.2\,,$$
$$y_2 = y_1 + 0.1 \cdot \left(\frac{x_1}{y_1}\right) = -1 + 0.1 \cdot \left(\frac{0.1}{-1}\right) = -1.01\,.$$

Continuing in the same manner, we find for $n = 2$, 3, and 4:

$$x_3 = 0.2 + 0.1 = 0.3\,, \qquad y_3 = -1.01 + 0.1 \cdot \left(\frac{0.2}{-1.01}\right) = -1.02980\,;$$

$$x_4 = 0.3 + 0.1 = 0.4\,, \qquad y_4 = -1.02980 + 0.1 \cdot \left(\frac{0.3}{-1.02980}\right) = -1.05893\,;$$

$$x_5 = 0.4 + 0.1 = 0.5\,, \qquad y_5 = -1.05893 + 0.1 \cdot \left(\frac{0.4}{-1.05893}\right) = -1.09671\,,$$

where we have rounded off all answers to five decimal places.

**2.** In this problem, $x_0 = 0$, $y_0 = 4$, $h = 0.1$, and $f(x, y) = -x/y$. Thus, the recursive formulas given in equations (2) and (3) on page 25 of the text become

$$x_{n+1} = x_n + h = x_n + 0.1\,,$$

# Chapter 1

$$y_{n+1} = y_n + hf(x_n, y_n) = y_n + 0.1 \cdot \left( -\frac{x_n}{y_n} \right), \qquad n = 0, 1, 2, \ldots .$$

To find an approximation for the solution at the point $x_1 = x_0 + 0.1 = 0.1$, we let $n = 0$ in the last recursive formula to find

$$y_1 = y_0 + 0.1 \cdot \left( -\frac{x_0}{y_0} \right) = 4 + 0.1 \cdot (0) = 4.$$

To approximate the value of the solution at the point $x_2 = x_1 + 0.1 = 0.2$, we let $n = 1$ in the last recursive formula to obtain

$$y_2 = y_1 + 0.1 \cdot \left( -\frac{x_1}{y_1} \right) = 4 + 0.1 \cdot \left( -\frac{0.1}{4} \right) = 4 - \frac{1}{400} = 3.9975 \approx 3.998 \,.$$

Continuing in this way we find

$$x_3 = x_2 + 0.1 = 0.3 \,, \qquad y_3 = y_2 + 0.1 \cdot \left( -\frac{x_2}{y_2} \right) = 3.9975 + 0.1 \cdot \left( -\frac{0.2}{3.9975} \right) \approx 3.992 \,,$$

$$x_4 = 0.4 \,, \qquad\qquad y_4 \approx 3.985 \,,$$

$$x_5 = 0.5 \,, \qquad\qquad y_5 \approx 3.975 \,,$$

where all of the answers have been rounded off to three decimal places.

**3.** Here $f(x, y) = y(2 - y)$, $x_0 = 0$, and $y_0 = 3$. We again use recursive formulas from Euler's method with $h = 0.1$. Setting $n = 0$, 1, 2, 3, and 4 and rounding off results to three decimal places, we get

$$x_1 = x_0 + 0.1 = 0.1 \,, \qquad y_1 = y_0 + 0.1 \cdot [y_0(2 - y_0)] = 3 + 0.1 \cdot [3(2 - 3)] = 2.700;$$

$$x_2 = 0.1 + 0.1 = 0.2 \,, \qquad y_2 = 2.700 + 0.1 \cdot [2.700(2 - 2.700)] = 2.511;$$

$$x_3 = 0.2 + 0.1 = 0.3 \,, \qquad y_3 = 2.511 + 0.1 \cdot [2.511(2 - 2.511)] \approx 2.383;$$

$$x_4 = 0.3 + 0.1 = 0.4 \,, \qquad y_4 = 2.383 + 0.1 \cdot [2.383(2 - 2.383)] \approx 2.292;$$

$$x_5 = 0.4 + 0.1 = 0.5 \,, \qquad y_5 = 2.292 + 0.1 \cdot [2.292(2 - 2.292)] \approx 2.225 \,.$$

**5.** In this problem, $f(x, y) = (y^2 + y)/x$, $x_0 = y_0 = 1$, and $h = 0.2$. The recursive formulas (2) and (3) on page 25 of the text, applied succesively with $n = 1$, 2, 3, and 4, yield

$$x_1 = x_0 + 0.2 = 1.2 \,, \qquad y_1 = y_0 + 0.2 \left( \frac{y_0^2 + y_0}{x_0} \right) = 1 + 0.2 \left( \frac{1^2 + 1}{1} \right) = 1.400;$$

$$x_2 = 1.2 + 0.2 = 1.4, \qquad y_2 = 1.400 + 0.2\left(\frac{1.400^2 + 1.400}{1.2}\right) \approx 1.960;$$

$$x_3 = 1.4 + 0.2 = 1.6, \qquad y_3 = 1.960 + 0.2\left(\frac{1.960^2 + 1.960}{1.4}\right) \approx 2.789;$$

$$x_4 = 1.6 + 0.2 = 1.8, \qquad y_4 = 2.789 + 0.2\left(\frac{2.789^2 + 2.789}{1.6}\right) \approx 4.110.$$

**7.** For this problem notice that the independent variable is $t$ and the dependent variable is $x$. Hence, the recursive formulas given in equations (2) and (3) on page 25 of the text become

$$t_{n+1} = t_n + h \qquad \text{and} \qquad \phi(t_{n+1}) \approx x_{n+1} = x_n + h f(t_n, x_n), \qquad n = 0, 1, 2, \dots.$$

For this problem, $f(t, x) = 1 + t\sin(tx)$, $t_0 = 0$, and $x_0 = 0$. Thus the second recursive formula above becomes

$$x_{n+1} = x_n + h\left[1 + t_n \sin(t_n x_n)\right], \qquad n = 0, 1, 2, \dots.$$

For the case $N = 1$, we have $h = (1 - 0)/1 = 1$ which gives us

$$t_1 = 0 + 1 = 1 \qquad \text{and} \qquad \phi(1) \approx x_1 = 0 + 1 \cdot (1 + 0 \cdot \sin 0) = 1.$$

For the case $N = 2$, we have $h = 1/2 = 0.5$. Thus we have

$$t_1 = 0 + 0.5 = 0.5, \qquad\qquad x_1 = 0 + 0.5 \cdot (1 + 0 \cdot \sin 0) = 0.5,$$

and

$$t_2 = 0.5 + 0.5 = 1, \qquad\qquad \phi(1) \approx x_2 = 0.5 + 0.5 \cdot [1 + 0.5 \cdot \sin(0.25)] \approx 1.06185.$$

For the case $N = 4$, we have $h = 1/4 = 0.25$, and so the recursive formulas become

$$t_{n+1} = t_n + 0.25 \qquad \text{and} \qquad x_{n+1} = x_n + 0.25 \cdot [1 + t_n \sin(t_n x_n)].$$

Therefore, we have

$$t_1 = 0 + 0.25 = 0.25, \qquad\qquad x_1 = 0 + 0.25 \cdot [1 + 0 \cdot \sin(0)] = 0.25.$$

Plugging these values into the recursive equations above yields

$$t_2 = 0.25 + 0.25 = 0.5 \quad \text{and} \quad x_2 = 0.25 + 0.25 \cdot [1 + 0.25 \cdot \sin(0.0625)] = 0.503904\,.$$

Continuing in this way gives

$$t_3 = 0.75 \quad \text{and} \quad x_3 = 0.503904 + 0.25 \cdot [1 + 0.5 \cdot \sin(0.251952)] = 0.785066\,,$$

$$t_4 = 1.00 \quad \text{and} \quad \phi(1) \approx x_4 = 1.13920\,.$$

For $N = 8$, we have $h = 1/8 = 0.125$. Thus, the recursive formulas become

$$t_{n+1} = t_n + 0.125 \quad \text{and} \quad x_{n+1} = x_n + 0.125 \cdot [1 + t_n \sin(t_n x_n)]\,.$$

Using these formulas and starting with $t_0 = 0$ and $x_0 = 0$, we can fill in Table 1-A. From this we see that $\phi(1) \approx x_8 = 1.19157$, which is rounded to five decimal places.

---

**Table 1–A**: Euler's method approximations for the solution of $x' = 1 + t\sin(tx)$, $x(0) = 0$, at $t = 1$ with 8 steps ($h = 1/8$).

| $n$ | $t_n$ | $x_n$ |
|---|---|---|
| 1 | 0.125 | 0.125 |
| 2 | 0.250 | 0.250244 |
| 3 | 0.375 | 0.377198 |
| 4 | 0.500 | 0.508806 |
| 5 | 0.625 | 0.649535 |
| 6 | 0.750 | 0.805387 |
| 7 | 0.875 | 0.983634 |
| 8 | 1.000 | 1.191572 |

---

**9.** To approximate the solution on the whole interval $[1, 2]$ by Euler's method with the step $h = 0.1$, we first approximate the solution at the points $x_n = 1 + 0.1n$, $n = 1, \ldots, 10$. Then, on each subinterval $[x_n, x_{n+1}]$, we approximate the solution by the linear interval, connecting

$(x_n, y_n)$ with $(x_{n+1}, y_{n+1})$, $n = 0, 1, \ldots, 9$. Since $f(x, y) = x^{-2} - yx^{-1} - y^2$, the recursive formulas have the form

$$x_{n+1} = x_n + 0.1 \,,$$
$$y_{n+1} = y_n + 0.1 \left( \frac{1}{x_n^2} - \frac{y_n}{x_n} - y_n^2 \right), \qquad n = 0, 1, \ldots, 9 \,,$$

$x_0 = 1$, $y_0 = -1$. Therefore,

$$x_1 = \; 1 + 0.1 = 1.1 \,, \quad y_1 = -1 + 0.1 \left( \frac{1}{1^2} - \frac{-1}{1} - (-1)^2 \right) = -0.9 \,;$$

$$x_2 = 1.1 + 0.1 = 1.2 \,, \quad y_2 = -0.9 + 0.1 \left( \frac{1}{1.1^2} - \frac{-0.9}{1.1} - (-0.9)^2 \right) \approx -0.81653719 \,;$$

$$x_3 = 1.2 + 0.1 = 1.3 \,, \quad y_3 = -0.81653719 + 0.1 \left( \frac{1}{1.2^2} - \frac{-0.81653719}{1.2} - (-0.81653719)^2 \right)$$
$$\approx -0.74572128 \,;$$

$$x_4 = 1.3 + 0.1 = 1.4 \,, \quad y_4 = -0.74572128 + 0.1 \left( \frac{1}{1.3^2} - \frac{-0.74572128}{1.3} - (-0.74572128)^2 \right)$$
$$\approx -0.68479653 \,;$$

etc.

The results of these computations (rounded to five decimal places) are shown in Table 1-B.

---

**Table 1–B**: Euler's method approximations for the solutions of $y' = x^{-2} - yx^{-1} - y^2$, $y(1) = -1$, on $[1, 2]$ with $h = 0.1$.

| $n$ | $x_n$ | $y_n$ | $n$ | $x_n$ | $y_n$ |
|---|---|---|---|---|---|
| 0 | 1.0 | $-1.00000$ | 6 | 1.6 | $-0.58511$ |
| 1 | 1.1 | $-0.90000$ | 7 | 1.7 | $-0.54371$ |
| 2 | 1.2 | $-0.81654$ | 8 | 1.8 | $-0.50669$ |
| 3 | 1.3 | $-0.74572$ | 9 | 1.9 | $-0.47335$ |
| 4 | 1.4 | $-0.68480$ | 10 | 2.0 | $-0.44314$ |
| 5 | 1.5 | $-0.63176$ | | | |

---

The function $y(x) = -1/x = x^{-1}$, obviously, satisfies the initial condition, $y(1) = -1$. Further

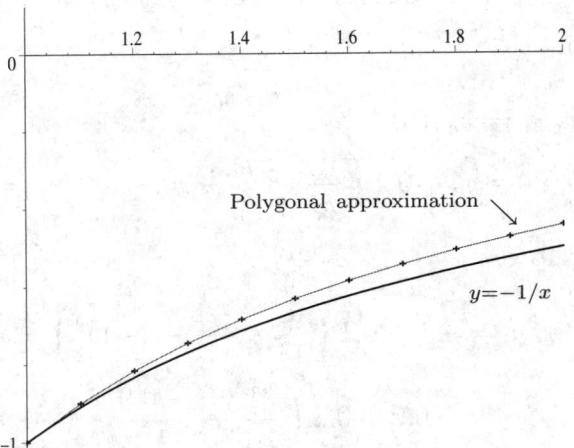

**Figure 1–C**: Polygonal line approximation and the actual solution for Problem 9.

we compute both sides of the given differential equation:

$$y'(x) = \left(-x^{-1}\right)' = x^{-2},$$
$$f(x, y(x)) = x^{-2} - \left(-x^{-1}\right) x^{-1} - \left(-x^{-1}\right)^2 = x^{-2} + x^{-2} - x^{-2} = x^{-2}.$$

Thus, the function $y(x) = -1/x$ is, indeed, the solution to the given initial value problem.

The graphs of the obtained polygonal line approximation and the actual solution are sketched in Figure 1-C.

**11.** In this problem, the independent variable is $t$ and the dependent variable is $x$; $f(t, x) = 1 + x^2$, $t_0 = 0$, and $x_0 = 0$.

The function $\phi(t) = \tan t$ satisfies the initial condition: $\phi(0) = \tan 0 = 0$. The differential equation is also satisfied:

$$\frac{d\phi}{dt} = \sec^2 t = 1 + \tan^2 t = 1 + \phi(t)^2.$$

Therefore, $\phi(t)$ is the solution to the given initial value problem.

For approximation of $\phi(t)$ at the point $t = 1$ with $N = 20$ steps, we take the step size $h = (1 - t_0)/20 = 0.05$. Thus, the recursive formulas for Euler's method are

$$t_{n+1} = t_n + 0.05,$$

$$x_{n+1} = x_n + 0.05\left(1 + x_n^2\right).$$

Applying these formulas with $n = 0, 1, \ldots, 19$, we obtain

$$x_1 = x_0 + 0.05\left(1 + x_0^2\right) = 0.05,$$

$$x_2 = x_1 + 0.05\left(1 + x_1^2\right) = 0.05 + 0.05\left(1 + 0.05^2\right) = 0.100125,$$

$$x_3 = x_2 + 0.05\left(1 + x_2^2\right) = 0.100125 + 0.05\left(1 + 0.100125^2\right) \approx 0.150626,$$

$$\vdots$$

$$x_{19} = x_{18} + 0.05\left(1 + x_{18}^2\right) \approx 1.328148,$$

$$\phi(1) \approx x_{20} = x_{19} + 0.05\left(1 + x_{19}^2\right) = 1.328148 + 0.05\left(1 + 1.328148^2\right) \approx 1.466347,$$

which is a good enough approximation to $\phi(1) = \tan 1 \approx 1.557408$.

13. From Problem 12, $y_n = (1 + 1/n)^n$ and so $\lim_{n\to\infty}\left[(e - y_n)/(1/n)\right]$ is a 0/0 indeterminant. If we let $h = 1/n$ in $y_n$ and use L'Hospital's rule, we get

$$\lim_{n\to\infty}\frac{e - y_n}{1/n} = \lim_{h\to 0}\frac{e - (1+h)^{1/h}}{h} = \lim_{h\to 0}\frac{g(h)}{h} = \lim_{h\to 0}\frac{g'(h)}{1},$$

where $g(h) = e - (1+h)^{1/h}$. Writing $(1+h)^{1/h}$ as $e^{\ln(1+h)/h}$ the function $g(h)$ becomes

$$g(h) = e - e^{\ln(1+h)/h}.$$

The first derivative is given by

$$g'(h) = 0 - \frac{d}{dh}\left[e^{\ln(1+h)/h}\right] = -e^{\ln(1+h)/h}\frac{d}{dh}\left[\frac{1}{h}\ln(1+h)\right].$$

Substituting Maclaurin's series for $\ln(1+h)$ we obtain

$$g'(h) = -(1+h)^{1/h}\frac{d}{dh}\left[\frac{1}{h}\left(h - \frac{1}{2}h^2 + \frac{1}{3}h^3 - \frac{1}{4}h^4 + \cdots\right)\right]$$

23

$$= -(1+h)^{1/h} \frac{d}{dh}\left[1 - \frac{1}{2}h + \frac{1}{3}h^2 - \frac{1}{4}h^3 + \cdots\right]$$

$$= -(1+h)^{1/h}\left[-\frac{1}{2} + \frac{2}{3}h - \frac{3}{4}h^2 + \cdots\right].$$

Hence

$$\lim_{h \to 0} g'(h) = \lim_{h \to 0}\left\{-(1+h)^{1/h}\left[-\frac{1}{2} + \frac{2}{3}h - \frac{3}{4}h^2 + \cdots\right]\right\}$$

$$= \left[-\lim_{h \to 0}(1+h)^{1/h}\right] \cdot \left[\lim_{h \to 0}\left\{-\frac{1}{2} + \frac{2}{3}h - \frac{3}{4}h^2 + \cdots\right\}\right].$$

From calculus we know that $e = \lim\limits_{h \to 0}(1+h)^{1/h}$, which gives

$$\lim_{h \to 0} g'(h) = -e\left(-\frac{1}{2}\right) = \frac{e}{2}.$$

So we have

$$\lim_{n \to \infty} \frac{e - y_n}{1/n} = \frac{e}{2}.$$

**15.** The independent variable in this problem is the time $t$ and the dependent variable is the temperature $T(t)$ of a body. Thus, we will use the recursive formulas (2) and (3) on page 25 with $x$ replaced by $t$ and $y$ replaced by $T$. In the differential equation describing the Newton's Law of Cooling, $f(t, T) = K(M(t) - T)$. With the suggested values of $K = 1\,(\text{min})^{-1}$, $M(t) \equiv 70°$, $h = 0.1$, and the initial condition $T(0) = 100°$, the initial value problem becomes

$$\frac{dT}{dt} = 70 - T, \qquad T(0) = 100,$$

and so the recursive formulas are

$$t_{n+1} = t_n + 0.1\,,$$

$$T_{n+1} = T_n + 0.1(70 - T_n).$$

For $n = 0$,

$$t_1 = t_0 + 0.1 = 0.1\,, \qquad T_1 = T_0 + 0.1(70 - T_0) = 100 + 0.1(70 - 100) = 97\,;$$

for $n = 1$,

$$t_2 = t_1 + 0.1 = 0.2, \qquad T_2 = T_1 + 0.1(70 - T_1) = 97 + 0.1(70 - 97) = 94.3;$$

for $n = 2$,

$$t_3 = t_2 + 0.1 = 0.3, \qquad T_3 = T_2 + 0.1(70 - T_2) = 94.3 + 0.1(70 - 94.3) = 91.87.$$

---

**Table 1–C**: Euler's method approximations for the solutions of $T' = K(M - T)$, $T(0) = 100$, with $K = 1$, $M = 70$, and $h = 0.1$.

| $n$ | $t_n$ | $T_n$ | $n$ | $t_n$ | $T_n$ |
|---|---|---|---|---|---|
| 0 | 0.0 | 100.00 | 11 | 1.1 | 79.414 |
| 1 | 0.1 | 97.000 | 12 | 1.2 | 78.473 |
| 2 | 0.2 | 94.300 | 13 | 1.3 | 77.626 |
| 3 | 0.3 | 91.870 | 14 | 1.4 | 76.863 |
| 4 | 0.4 | 89.683 | 15 | 1.5 | 76.177 |
| 5 | 0.5 | 87.715 | 16 | 1.6 | 75.559 |
| 6 | 0.6 | 85.943 | 17 | 1.7 | 75.003 |
| 7 | 0.7 | 84.349 | 18 | 1.8 | 74.503 |
| 8 | 0.8 | 82.914 | 19 | 1.9 | 74.053 |
| 9 | 0.9 | 81.623 | 20 | 2.0 | 73.647 |
| 10 | 1.0 | 80.460 | | | |

---

By continuing this way and rounding results to three decimal places, we fill in Table 1-C. From this table we conclude that

**(a)** the temperature of a body after 1 minute $T(1) \approx 80.460°$ and

**(b)** its temperature after 2 minutes $T(2) \approx 73.647°$.

**16.** For this problem notice that the independent variable is $t$ and the dependent variable is $T$. Hence, in the recursive formulas for Euler's method, the $t$ will take the place of the $x$ and the

# Chapter 1

$T$ will take the place of the $y$. Also we see that $h = 0.1$ and $f(t, T) = K\left(M^4 - T^4\right)$, where $K = 40^{-4}$ and $M = 70$. The recursive formulas (2) and (3) on page 25 of the text become

$$t_{n+1} = t_n + 0.1\,,$$
$$T_{n+1} = T_n + hf\left(t_n, T_n\right) = T_n + 0.1\left(40^{-4}\right)\left(70^4 - T_n^4\right), \qquad n = 0, 1, 2, \ldots.$$

From the initial condition, $T(0) = 100$, we see that $t_0 = 0$ and $T_0 = 100$. Therefore, for $n = 0$,

$$t_1 = t_0 + 0.1 = 0 + 0.1 = 0.1\,,$$
$$T_1 = T_0 + 0.1\left(40^{-4}\right)\left(70^4 - T_0^4\right) = 100 + 0.1\left(40^{-4}\right)\left(70^4 - 100^4\right) \approx 97.0316,$$

where we have rounded off to four decimal places. For $n = 1$, we have

$$t_2 = t_1 + 0.1 = 0.1 + 0.1 = 0.2\,,$$
$$T_2 = T_1 + 0.1\left(40^{-4}\right)\left(70^4 - T_1^4\right) = 97.0316 + 0.1\left(40^{-4}\right)\left(70^4 - 97.0316^4\right) \approx 94.5068\,.$$

By continuing this way, we fill in Table 1-D.

---

**Table 1–D**: Euler's method approximations for the solution of $T' = K\left(M^4 - T^4\right)$, $T(0) = 100$, with $K = 40^{-4}$, $M = 70$, and $h = 0.1$.

| $n$ | $t_n$ | $T_n$ | $n$ | $t_n$ | $T_n$ | $n$ | $t_n$ | $T_n$ |
|---|---|---|---|---|---|---|---|---|
| 0 | 0 | 100 | 7 | 0.7 | 85.9402 | 14 | 1.4 | 79.5681 |
| 1 | 0.1 | 97.0316 | 8 | 0.8 | 84.7472 | 15 | 1.5 | 78.9403 |
| 2 | 0.2 | 94.5068 | 9 | 0.9 | 83.6702 | 16 | 1.6 | 78.3613 |
| 3 | 0.3 | 92.3286 | 10 | 1.0 | 82.6936 | 17 | 1.7 | 77.8263 |
| 4 | 0.4 | 90.4279 | 11 | 1.1 | 81.8049 | 18 | 1.8 | 77.3311 |
| 5 | 0.5 | 88.7538 | 12 | 1.2 | 80.9934 | 19 | 1.9 | 76.8721 |
| 6 | 0.6 | 87.2678 | 13 | 1.3 | 80.2504 | 20 | 2.0 | 76.4459 |

---

From this table we see that

$$T(1) = T(t_{10}) \approx T_{10} = 82.694 \qquad \text{and} \qquad T(2) = T(t_{20}) \approx T_{20} = 76.446\,.$$

# CHAPTER 2: First Order Differential Equations

**EXERCISES 2.2:**    Separable Equations, page 46

1. This equation is separable because we can separate variables by multiplying both sides by $dx$ and dividing by $2y^3 + y + 4$.

3. This equation is separable because

$$\frac{dy}{dx} = \frac{ye^{x+y}}{x^2+2} = \left(\frac{e^x}{x^2+2}\right) ye^y = g(x)p(y).$$

5. Writing the equation in the form

$$\frac{ds}{dt} = \frac{s+1}{st} - s^2,$$

we see that the right-hand side cannot be represented in the form $g(t)p(s)$. Therefore, the equation is not separable.

7. Multiplying both sides of the equation by $y^2 dx$ and integrating yields

$$y^2 dy = (1 - x^2)dx \quad \Rightarrow \quad \int y^2 dy = \int (1 - x^2)dx$$

$$\Rightarrow \quad \frac{1}{3}y^3 = x - \frac{1}{3}x^3 + C_1 \quad \Rightarrow \quad y^3 = 3x - x^3 + C \quad \Rightarrow \quad y = \sqrt[3]{3x - x^3 + C},$$

where $C := 3C_1$ is an arbitrary constant.

9. To separate variables, we divide the equation by $y$ and multiply by $dx$. This results

$$\frac{dy}{dx} = y(2 + \sin x) \quad \Rightarrow \quad \frac{dy}{y} = (2 + \sin x)dx$$

$$\Rightarrow \quad \int \frac{dy}{y} = \int (2 + \sin x)dx \quad \Rightarrow \quad \ln|y| = 2x - \cos x + C_1$$

$$\Rightarrow \quad |y| = e^{2x - \cos x + C_1} = e^{C_1}e^{2x - \cos x} = C_2 e^{2x - \cos x},$$

# Chapter 2

where $C_1$ is an arbitrary constant and, therefore, $C_2 := e^{C_1}$ is an arbitrary *positive* constant.

We can rewrite the above solution in the form

$$y = \pm C_2 e^{2x - \cos x} = C e^{2x - \cos x}, \qquad (2.1)$$

with $C := C_2$ or $C = -C_2$. Thus $C$ is an arbitrary *nonzero* constant. The value $C = 0$ in (2.1) gives $y(x) \equiv 0$, which is, clearly, is also a solution to the differential equation. Therefore, the answer to the problem is given by (2.1) with an arbitrary constant $C$.

**11.** Separating variables, we obtain

$$\frac{dy}{\sec^2 y} = \frac{dx}{1 + x^2}.$$

Using the trigonometric identities $\sec y = 1/\cos y$ and $\cos^2 y = (1 + \cos 2y)/2$ and integrating, we get

$$\frac{dy}{\sec^2 y} = \frac{dx}{1 + x^2} \qquad \Rightarrow \qquad \frac{(1 + \cos 2y)dy}{2} = \frac{dx}{1 + x^2}$$

$$\Rightarrow \qquad \int \frac{(1 + \cos 2y)dy}{2} = \int \frac{dx}{1 + x^2}$$

$$\Rightarrow \qquad \frac{1}{2}\left(y + \frac{1}{2}\sin 2y\right) = \arctan x + C_1$$

$$\Rightarrow \qquad 2y + \sin 2y = 4\arctan x + 4C_1 \qquad \Rightarrow \qquad 2y + \sin 2y = 4\arctan x + C.$$

The last equation defines implicit solutions to the given differential equation.

**13.** Writing the given equation in the form $dx/dt = x - x^2$, we separate the variables to get

$$\frac{dx}{x - x^2} = dt.$$

Integrate (the left side is integrated by partial fractions, with $1/(x - x^2) = 1/x + 1/(1 - x)$) to obtain:

$$\ln|x| - \ln|1 - x| = t + c \qquad \Rightarrow \qquad \ln\left|\frac{x}{1 - x}\right| = t + c$$

$$\Rightarrow \qquad \frac{x}{1 - x} = \pm e^{t+c} = Ce^t, \qquad \text{where } C = e^c$$

$$\Rightarrow \qquad x = Ce^t - xCe^t \qquad \Rightarrow \qquad x + xCe^t = Ce^t$$

$$\Rightarrow \qquad x\left(1 + Ce^t\right) = Ce^t \qquad \Rightarrow \qquad x = \frac{Ce^t}{1 + Ce^t}.$$

Note: When $C$ is replaced by $-K$, this answer can also be written as $x = Ke^t/(Ke^t - 1)$. Further we observe that since we divide by $x - x^2 = x(1 - x)$, then $x \equiv 0$ and $x \equiv 1$ are also solutions. Allowing $K$ to be zero gives $x \equiv 0$, but no choice for $K$ will give $x \equiv 1$, so we list this as a separate solution.

**15.** To separate variables, we move the term containin $dx$ to the right-hand side of the equation and divide both sides of the result by $y$. This yields

$$y^{-1}dy = -ye^{\cos x} \sin x \, dx \qquad \Rightarrow \qquad y^{-2}dy = -e^{\cos x} \sin x \, dx.$$

Integrating the last equation, we obtain

$$\int y^{-2}dy = \int \left(-e^{\cos x} \sin x\right) dx \qquad \Rightarrow \qquad -y^{-1} + C = \int e^u du \quad (u = \cos x)$$

$$\Rightarrow \qquad -\frac{1}{y} + C = e^u = e^{\cos x} \qquad \Rightarrow \qquad y = \frac{1}{C - e^{\cos x}},$$

where $C$ is an arbitrary constant.

**17.** First we find a general solution to the equation. Separating variables and integrating, we get

$$\frac{dy}{dx} = x^3(1 - y) \qquad \Rightarrow \qquad \frac{dy}{1 - y} = x^3 dx$$

$$\Rightarrow \qquad \int \frac{dy}{1 - y} = \int x^3 dx \qquad \Rightarrow \qquad -\ln|1 - y| + C_1 = \frac{x^4}{4}$$

$$\Rightarrow \qquad |1 - y| = \exp\left(C_1 - \frac{x^4}{4}\right) = Ce^{-x^4/4}.$$

To find $C$, we use the initial condition, $y(0) = 3$. Thus, substitution 3 for $y$ and 0 for $x$ into the last equation yields

$$|1 - 3| = Ce^{-0^4/4} \qquad \Rightarrow \qquad 2 = C.$$

Therefore, $|1 - y| = 2e^{-x^4/4}$. Finally, since $1 - y(0) = 1 - 3 < 0$, on an interval containing $x = 0$ one has $1 - y(x) < 0$ and so $|1 - y(x)| = y(x) - 1$. The solution to the problem is then

$$y - 1 = 2e^{-x^4/4} \qquad \text{or} \qquad y = 2e^{-x^4/4} + 1.$$

# Chapter 2

**19.** For a general solution, separate variables and integrate:

$$\frac{dy}{d\theta} = y\sin\theta \qquad \Rightarrow \qquad \frac{dy}{y} = \sin\theta\,d\theta$$

$$\Rightarrow \qquad \int\frac{dy}{y} = \int\sin\theta\,d\theta \qquad \Rightarrow \qquad \ln|y| = -\cos\theta + C_1$$

$$\Rightarrow \qquad |y| = e^{-\cos\theta + C_1} = Ce^{-\cos\theta} \qquad \Rightarrow \qquad y = -Ce^{-\cos\theta}$$

(because at the initial point, $\theta = \pi$, $y(\pi) < 0$). We substitute now the initial condition, $y(\pi) = -3$, and obtain

$$-3 = y(\pi) = -Ce^{-\cos\pi} = -Ce \qquad \Rightarrow \qquad C = 3e^{-1}.$$

Hence, the answer is given by $y = -3e^{-1}e^{-\cos\theta} = -3e^{-1-\cos\theta}$.

**21.** Separate variables to obtain

$$\frac{1}{2}(y+1)^{-1/2}\,dy = \cos x\,dx.$$

Integrating, we have

$$(y+1)^{1/2} = \sin x + C.$$

Using the fact that $y(\pi) = 0$, we find

$$1 = \sin\pi + C \qquad \Rightarrow \qquad C = 1.$$

Thus

$$(y+1)^{1/2} = \sin x + 1 \qquad \Rightarrow \qquad y = (\sin x + 1)^2 - 1 = \sin^2 x + 2\sin x.$$

**23.** We have

$$\frac{dy}{dx} = 2x\cos^2 y \qquad \Rightarrow \qquad \frac{dy}{\cos^2 y} = 2x\,dx \qquad \Rightarrow \qquad \sec^2 y\,dy = 2x\,dx$$

$$\Rightarrow \qquad \int\sec^2 y\,dy = \int 2x\,dx \qquad \Rightarrow \qquad \tan y = x^2 + C.$$

Since $y = \pi/4$ when $x = 0$, we get $\tan(\pi/4) = 0^2 + C$ and so $C = 1$. The solution, therefore, is

$$\tan y = x^2 + 1 \qquad \Leftrightarrow \qquad y = \arctan\left(x^2 + 1\right).$$

**25.** By separating variables we obtain $(1+y)^{-1}dy = x^2\,dx$. Integrating yields

$$\ln|1+y| = \frac{x^3}{3} + C\,. \tag{2.2}$$

Substituting $y = 3$ and $x = 0$ from the initial condition, we get $\ln 4 = 0 + C$, which implies that $C = \ln 4$. By substituting this value for $C$ into equation (2.2) above, we have

$$\ln|1+y| = \frac{x^3}{3} + \ln 4\,.$$

Hence,

$$e^{\ln|1+y|} = e^{(x^3/3) + \ln 4} = e^{x^3/3}e^{\ln 4} = 4e^{x^3/3}$$

$$\Rightarrow \quad 1+y = 4e^{x^3/3} \quad \Rightarrow \quad y = 4e^{x^3/3} - 1\,.$$

We can drop the absolute signs above because we are assuming from the initial condition that $y$ is close to 3 and therefore $1 + y$ is positive.

**27. (a)** The differential equation $dy/dx = e^{x^2}$ separates if we multiply by $dx$. We integrate the separated equation from $x = 0$ to $x = x_1$ to obtain

$$\int_0^{x_1} e^{x^2}\,dx = \int_{x=0}^{x=x_1} dy = y\,\Big|_{x=0}^{x=x_1} = y(x_1) - y(0).$$

If we let $t$ be the variable of integration and replace $x_1$ by $x$ and $y(0)$ by 0, then we can express the solution to the initial value problem as

$$y(x) = \int_0^x e^{t^2}\,dt.$$

**(b)** The differential equation $dy/dx = e^{x^2}y^{-2}$ separates if we multiply by $y^2$ and $dx$. We integrate the separated equation from $x = 0$ to $x = x_1$ to obtain

$$\int_0^{x_1} e^{x^2}\,dx = \int_0^{x_1} y^2\,dy = \frac{1}{3}y^3\,\Big|_{x=0}^{x=x_1} = \frac{1}{3}\left[y(x_1)^3 - y(0)^3\right].$$

Chapter 2

If we let $t$ be the variable of integration and replace $x_1$ by $x$ and $y(0)$ by 1 in the above equation, then we can express the initial value problem as

$$\int_0^x e^{t^2}\,dt = \frac{1}{3}\left[y(x)^3 - 1\right].$$

Solving for $y(x)$ we arrive at

$$y(x) = \left[1 + 3\int_0^x e^{t^2}\,dt\right]^{1/3}. \tag{2.3}$$

(c) The differential equation $dy/dx = \sqrt{1 + \sin x}\,(1 + y^2)$ separates if we divide by $(1 + y^2)$ and multiply by $dx$. We integrate the separated equation from $x = 0$ to $x = x_1$ and find

$$\int_0^{x_1} \sqrt{1 + \sin x}\,dx = \int_{x=0}^{x=x_1} (1 + y^2)^{-1}\,dy = \tan^{-1} y(x_1) - \tan^{-1} y(0).$$

If we let $t$ be the variable of integration and replace $x_1$ by $x$ and $y(0)$ by 1 then we can express the solution to the initial value problem by

$$y(x) = \tan\left[\int_0^x \sqrt{1 + \sin t}\,dt + \frac{\pi}{4}\right].$$

(d) We will use Simpson's rule (Appendix B) to approximate the definite integral found in part (b). (Simpson's rule is implemented on the website for the text.) Simpson's rule requires an even number of intervals, but we don't know how many are required to obtain the desired three-place accuracy. Rather than make an error analysis, we will compute the approximate value of $y(0.5)$ using 2, 4, 6, ... intervals for Simpson's rule until the approximate values for $y(0.5)$ change by less than five in the fourth place.

For $n = 2$, we divide $[0, 0.5]$ into 4 equal subintervals. Thus each interval will be of length $(0.5 - 0)/4 = 1/8 = 0.125$. Therefore, the integral is approximated by

$$\int_0^{0.5} e^{x^2}\,dx = \frac{1}{24}\left[e^0 + 4e^{(0.125)^2} + 2e^{(0.25)^2} + 4e^{(0.325)^2} + e^{(0.5)^2}\right] \approx 0.544999003.$$

Substituting this value into equation (2.3) from part (b) yields

$$y(0.5) \approx [1 + 3(0.544999003)]^{1/3} \approx 1.38121 \,.$$

Repeating these calculations for $n = 3$, 4, and 5 yields Table 2-A.

**Table 2–A**: Successive approximations for $y(0.5)$ using Simpson's rule.

| Number of Intervals | $y(0.5)$ |
|---|---|
| 6 | 1.38120606 |
| 8 | 1.38120520 |
| 10 | 1.38120497 |

Since these values do not change by more than 5 in the fourth place, we can conclude that the first three places are accurate and that we have obtained an approximate solution $y(0.5) \approx 1.381 \,.$

**29.** **(a)** Separating variables and integrating yields

$$\frac{dy}{y^{1/3}} = dx \quad \Rightarrow \quad \int \frac{dy}{y^{1/3}} = \int dx$$

$$\Rightarrow \quad \frac{1}{2/3} y^{2/3} = x + C_1 \quad \Rightarrow \quad y = \left( \frac{2}{3} x + \frac{2}{3} C_1 \right)^{3/2} = \left( \frac{2x}{3} + C \right)^{3/2} \,.$$

**(b)** Using the initial condition, $y(0) = 0$, we find that

$$0 = y(0) = \left[ \frac{2(0)}{3} + C \right]^{3/2} = C^{3/2} \quad \Rightarrow \quad C = 0 \,,$$

and so $y = (2x/3 + 0)^{3/2} = (2x/3)^{3/2}$, $x \geq 0$, is a solution to the initial value problem.

**(c)** The function $y(x) \equiv 0$, clearly, satisfies both, the differential equation $dy/dx = y^{1/3}$ and the initial condition $y(0) = 0$.

**(d)** In notation of Theorem 1 on page 12, $f(x, y) = y^{1/3}$ and so

$$\frac{\partial f}{\partial y} = \frac{d}{dy} \left( y^{1/3} \right) = \frac{1}{3} y^{-2/3} = \frac{1}{3y^{2/3}} \,.$$

33

**Chapter 2**

Since $\partial f/\partial y$ is not continuous when $y = 0$, there is no rectangle containing the point $(0,0)$ in which both, $f$ and $\partial f/\partial y$, are continuous. Therefore, Theorem 1 does not apply to this initial value problem.

30. **(a)** Dividing the equation by $(y+1)^{2/3}$ and multiplying by $dx$ separate variables. Thus we get

$$\frac{dy}{dx} = (x-3)(y+1)^{2/3} \quad \Rightarrow \quad \frac{dy}{(y+1)^{2/3}} = (x-3)dx$$

$$\Rightarrow \quad \int \frac{dy}{(y+1)^{2/3}} = \int (x-3)dx \quad \Rightarrow \quad 3(y+1)^{1/3} = \frac{x^2}{2} - 3x + C_1$$

$$\Rightarrow \quad y+1 = \left(\frac{x^2}{6} - x + \frac{C_1}{3}\right)^3 \quad \Rightarrow \quad y = -1 + \left(\frac{x^2}{6} - x + C\right)^3. \quad (2.4)$$

**(b)** Substitution $y(x) \equiv -1$ into the differential equation gives

$$\frac{d(-1)}{dx} = (x-3)[(-1)+1]^{2/3} \quad \Rightarrow \quad 0 = (x-3)\cdot 0,$$

which is an identity. Therefore, $y(x) \equiv -1$ is, indeed, a solution.

**(c)** With any choice of constant $C$, $x^2/6 - x + C$ is a quadratic polynomial which is not identically zero. So, in (2.4), $y = -1 + (x^2/6 - x + C)^3 \neq -1$ for all $C$, and the solution $y(x) \equiv -1$ was lost in separation of variables.

31. **(a)** Separating variables and integrating yields

$$\frac{dy}{y^3} = x\,dx \quad \Rightarrow \quad \int \frac{dy}{y^3} = \int x\,dx$$

$$\Rightarrow \quad \frac{1}{-2}y^{-2} = \frac{1}{2}x^2 + C_1 \quad \Rightarrow \quad y^{-2} = -x^2 - 2C_1$$

$$\Rightarrow \quad x^2 + y^{-2} = C, \quad (2.5)$$

where $C := -2C_1$ is an arbitrary constant.

**(b)** To find the solution satisfying the initial condition $y(0) = 1$, we substitute in (2.5) 0 for $x$ and 1 for $y$ and obtain

$$0^2 + 1^{-2} = C \quad \Rightarrow \quad C = 1 \quad \Rightarrow \quad x^2 + y^{-2} = 1.$$

34

Solving for $y$ yields

$$y = \pm \frac{1}{\sqrt{1 - x^2}} .$$ (2.6)

Since, at the initial point, $x = 0$, $y(0) = 1 > 1$, we choose the positive sign in the above expression for $y$. Thus, the solution is

$$y = \frac{1}{\sqrt{1 - x^2}} .$$

Similarly we find solutions for the other two initial conditions:

$$y(0) = \frac{1}{2} \quad \Rightarrow \quad C = 4 \quad \Rightarrow \quad y = \frac{1}{\sqrt{4 - x^2}} ;$$

$$y(0) = 2 \quad \Rightarrow \quad C = \frac{1}{4} \quad \Rightarrow \quad y = \frac{1}{\sqrt{(1/4) - x^2}} .$$

(c) For the solution to the first initial problem in (b), $y(0) = 1$, the domain is the set of all values of $x$ satisfying two conditions

$$\begin{cases} 1 - x^2 \geq 0 & \text{(for existence of the square root)} \\ 1 - x^2 \neq 0 & \text{(for existence of the quotient)} \end{cases} \quad \Rightarrow \quad 1 - x^2 > 0.$$

Solving for $x$, we get

$$x^2 < 1 \quad \Rightarrow \quad |x| < 1 \quad \text{or} \quad -1 < x < 1.$$

In the same manner, we find domains for solutions to the other two initial value problems:

$$y(0) = \frac{1}{2} \quad \Rightarrow \quad -2 < x < 2 ;$$

$$y(0) = 2 \quad \Rightarrow \quad -\frac{1}{2} < x < \frac{1}{2} .$$

(d) First, we find the solution to the initial value problem $y(0) = a$, $a > 0$, and its domain. Following the lines used in (b) and (c) for particular values of $a$, we conclude that

$$y(0) = a \quad \Rightarrow \quad 0^2 + a^{-2} = C \quad \Rightarrow \quad y = \frac{1}{\sqrt{a^{-2} - x^2}} \quad \text{and so its domain is}$$

$$a^{-2} - x^2 > 0 \quad \Rightarrow \quad x^2 < a^{-2} \quad \Rightarrow \quad -\frac{1}{a} < x < \frac{1}{a} .$$

As $a \to +0$, $1/a \to +\infty$, and the domain expands to the whole real line; as $a \to +\infty$, $1/a \to 0$, and the domain shrinks to $x = 0$.

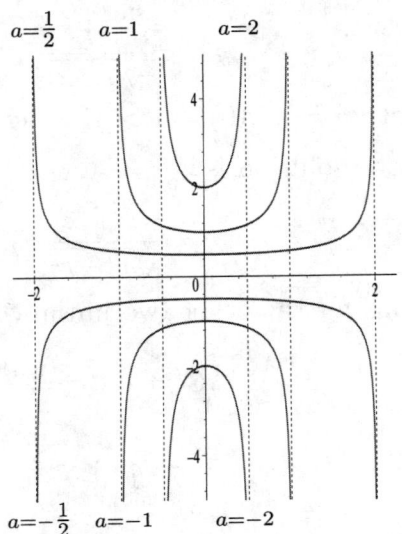

**Figure 2–A**: Solutions to the initial value problem $y' = xy^3$, $y(0) = a$, $a \pm 0.5$, $\pm 1$, and $\pm 2$.

**(e)** For the values $a = 1/2$, 1, and 2 the solutions are found in (b); for $a = -1$, we just have to choose the negative sign in (2.6); similarly, we reverse signs in the other two solutions in (b) to obtain the answers for $a = -1/2$ and $-2$. The graphs of these functions are shown in Figure 2-A.

**33.** Let $A(t)$ be the number of kilograms of salt in the tank at $t$ minutes after the process begins. Then we have

$$\frac{dA(t)}{dt} = \text{rate of salt in } - \text{ rate of salt out.}$$

$$\text{rate of salt in } = 10 \text{ L/min } \times 0.3 \text{ kg/L } = 3 \text{ kg/min.}$$

Since the tank is kept uniformly mixed, $A(t)/400$ is the mass of salt per liter that is flowing out of the tank at time $t$. Thus we have

$$\text{rate of salt out} = 10 \text{ L/min } \times \frac{A(t)}{400} \text{ kg/L} = \frac{A(t)}{40} \text{ kg/min.}$$

Therefore,

$$\frac{dA}{dt} = 3 - \frac{A}{40} = \frac{120 - A}{40}.$$

Separating this differential equation and integrating yield

$$\frac{40}{120 - A} dA = dt \qquad \Rightarrow \qquad -40 \ln|120 - A| = t + C$$

$$\Rightarrow \qquad \ln|120 - A| = -\frac{t}{40} + C, \quad \text{where } -\frac{C}{40} \text{ is replaced by } C$$

$$\Rightarrow \qquad 120 - A = Ce^{-t/40}, \quad \text{where } C \text{ can now be positive or negative}$$

$$\Rightarrow \qquad A = 120 - Ce^{-t/40}.$$

There are 2 kg of salt in the tank initially, thus $A(0) = 2$. Using this initial condition, we find

$$2 = 120 - C \qquad \Rightarrow \qquad C = 118.$$

Substituting this value of $C$ into the solution, we have

$$A = 120 - 118e^{-t/40}.$$

Thus

$$A(10) = 120 - 118e^{-10/40} \approx 28.1 \text{ kg}.$$

Note: There is a detailed discussion of mixture problems in Section 3.2.

**35.** In Problem 34 we saw that the differential equation $dT/dt = k(M - T)$ can be solved by separation of variables to yield

$$T = Ce^{kt} + M.$$

When the oven temperature is $120°$ we have $M = 120$. Also $T(0) = 40$. Thus

$$40 = C + 120 \qquad \Rightarrow \qquad C = -80.$$

Because $T(45) = 90$, we have

$$90 = -80e^{45k} + 120 \qquad \Rightarrow \qquad \frac{3}{8} = e^{45k} \qquad \Rightarrow \qquad 45k = \ln\left(\frac{3}{8}\right).$$

Thus $k = \ln(3/8)/45 \approx -0.02180$. This $k$ is independent of $M$. Therefore, we have the general equation

$$T(t) = Ce^{-0.02180t} + M.$$

(a) We are given that $M = 100$. To find $C$ we must solve the equation $T(0) = 40 = C + 100$. This gives $C = -60$. Thus the equation becomes

$$T(t) = -60e^{-0.02180t} + 100.$$

We want to solve for $t$ when $T(t) = 90$. This gives us

$$90 = -60e^{-0.02180t} + 100 \qquad \Rightarrow \qquad \frac{1}{6} = e^{-0.02180t}$$

$$\Rightarrow \qquad -0.0218t = \ln\left(\frac{1}{6}\right) \qquad \Rightarrow \qquad 0.0218t = \ln 6 \, .$$

Therefore $t = \ln 6 / 0.0218 \approx 82.2$ min.

(b) Here $M = 140$, so we solve

$$T(0) = 40 = C + 140 \qquad \Rightarrow \qquad C = -100.$$

As above, solving for $t$ in the equation

$$T(t) = -100e^{-0.02180t} + 140 = 90 \qquad \Rightarrow \qquad t \approx 31.8 \, .$$

(c) With $M = 80$, we solve

$$40 = C + 80,$$

yielding $C = -40$. Setting

$$T(t) = -40e^{-0.02180t} + 80 = 90 \qquad \Rightarrow \qquad -\frac{1}{4} = e^{-0.02180t} \, .$$

This last equation is impossible because an exponential function is never negative. Hence it never attains desired temperature. The physical nature of this problem would lead us to expect this result. A further discussion of Newton's law of cooling is given in Section 3.3.

**37.** The differential equation

$$\frac{dP}{dt} = \frac{r}{100} P$$

separates if we divide by $P$ and multiply by $dt$.

$$\int \frac{1}{P}\, dP = \frac{r}{100}\int dt \qquad \Rightarrow \qquad \ln P = \frac{r}{100}t + C \qquad \Rightarrow \qquad P(t) = Ke^{rt/100},$$

where $K$ is the initial amount of money in the savings account, $K = \$1000$, and $r\%$ is the interest rate, $r = 5$. This results in

$$P(t) = 1000e^{5t/100}. \tag{2.7}$$

(a) To determine the amount of money in the account after 2 years we substitute $t = 2$ into equation (2.7), which gives

$$P(2) = 1000e^{10/100} = \$1105.17.$$

(b) To determine when the account will reach \$4000 we solve equation (2.7) for $t$ with $P = \$4000$:

$$4000 = 1000e^{5t/100} \qquad \Rightarrow \qquad e^{5t/100} = 4 \qquad \Rightarrow \qquad t = 20\ln 4 \approx 27.73 \text{ years.}$$

(c) To determine the amount of money in the account after $3\frac{1}{2}$ years we need to determine the value of each \$1000 deposit after $3\frac{1}{2}$ years has passed. This means that the initial \$1000 is in the account for the entire $3\frac{1}{2}$ years and grows to the amount which is given by $P_0 = 1000e^{5(3.5)/100}$. For the growth of the \$1000 deposited after 12 months, we take $t = 2.5$ in equation (2.7) because that is how long this \$1000 will be in the account. This gives $P_1 = 1000e^{5(2.5)/100}$. Using the above reasoning for the remaining deposits we arrive at $P_2 = 1000e^{5(1.5)/100}$ and $P_3 = 1000e^{5(0.5)/100}$. The total amount is determined by the sum of the $P_i$'s.

$$P = 1000\left[e^{5(3.5)/100} + e^{5(2.5)/100} + e^{5(1.5)/100} + e^{5(0.5)/100}\right] \approx \$4,427.59.$$

**39.** Let $s(t)$, $t > 0$, denote the distance traveled by driver A from the time $t = 0$ when he ran out of gas to time $t$. Then driver A's velocity $v_A(t) = ds/dt$ is a solution to the initial value problem

$$\frac{dv_A}{dt} = -kv_A^2, \qquad v_A(0) = v_B,$$

where $v_B$ is driver B's constant velocity, and $k > 0$ is a positive constant. Separating variables we get

$$\frac{dv_A}{v_A^2} = -k\,dt \qquad \Rightarrow \qquad \int \frac{dv_A}{v_A^2} = -\int k\,dt \qquad \Rightarrow \qquad \frac{1}{v_A(t)} = kt + C\,.$$

From the initial condition we find

$$\frac{1}{v_B} = \frac{1}{v_A(0)} = k \cdot 0 + C = C \qquad \Rightarrow \qquad C = \frac{1}{v_B}\,.$$

Thus

$$v_A(t) = \frac{1}{kt + 1/v_B} = \frac{v_B}{v_B kt + 1}\,.$$

The function $s(t)$ therefore satisfies

$$\frac{ds}{dt} = \frac{v_B}{v_B kt + 1}\,, \qquad s(0) = 0.$$

Integrating we obtain

$$s(t) = \int \frac{v_B}{v_B kt + 1}\,dt = \frac{1}{k} \ln\left(v_B kt + 1\right) + C_1\,.$$

To find $C_1$ we use the initial condition:

$$0 = s(0) = \frac{1}{k} \ln\left(v_B k \cdot 0 + 1\right) + C_1 = C_1 \qquad \Rightarrow \qquad C_1 = 0.$$

So,

$$s(t) = \frac{1}{k} \ln\left(v_B kt + 1\right).$$

At the moment $t = t_1$ when driver A's speed was halved, i.e., $v_A(t_1) = v_A(0)/2 = v_B/2$, we have

$$\frac{1}{2} v_B = v_A(t_1) = \frac{v_B}{v_B kt_1 + 1} \qquad \text{and} \qquad 1 = s(t_1) = \frac{1}{k} \ln\left(v_B kt_1 + 1\right)$$

$$\Rightarrow \qquad v_B kt_1 + 1 = 2 \qquad \text{and so} \qquad k = \ln\left(v_B kt_1 + 1\right) = \ln 2$$

$$\Rightarrow \qquad s(t) = \frac{1}{\ln 2} \ln\left(v_B t \ln 2 + 1\right).$$

Since driver B was 3 miles behind driver A at time $t = 0$, and his speed remained constant, he finished the race at time $t_B = (3+2)/v_B = 5/v_B$. At this moment, driver A had already gone

$$s(t_B) = \frac{1}{\ln 2} \ln\left(v_B t_B \ln 2 + 1\right) = \frac{1}{\ln 2} \ln\left(\frac{5}{v_B} v_B \ln 2 + 1\right)$$

$$= \frac{1}{\ln 2} \ln\left(5 \ln 2 + 1\right) \approx 2.1589 > 2 \text{ miles},$$

i.e., A won the race.

**EXERCISES 2.3:   Linear Equations, page 54**

**1.** Writing

$$\frac{dy}{dx} - x^{-2} y = -x^{-2} \cos x,$$

we see that this equation has the form (4) on page 50 of the text with $P(x) = -x^{-2}$ and $Q(x) = -x^{-2} \cos x$. Therefore, it is linear.

Isolating $dy/dx$ yields

$$\frac{dy}{dx} = \frac{y - \cos x}{x^2}.$$

Since the right-hand side cannot be represented as a product $g(x)p(y)$, the equation is not separable.

**3.** In this equation, the independent variable is $t$ and the dependent variable is $x$. Dividing by $x$, we obtain

$$\frac{dx}{dt} = \frac{\sin t}{x} - t^2.$$

Therefore, it is neither linear, because of the $\sin t/x$ term, nor separable, because the right-hand side is not a product of functions of single variables $x$ and $t$.

**5.** This is a linear equation with independent variable $t$ and dependent variable $y$. This is also a separable equation because

$$\frac{dy}{dt} = \frac{y(t-1)}{t^2 + 1} = \left(\frac{t-1}{t^2+1}\right) y = g(t)p(y).$$

# Chapter 2

**7.** In this equation, $P(x) \equiv -1$ and $Q(x) = e^{3x}$. Hence the integrating factor

$$\mu(x) = \exp\left(\int P(x)dx\right) = \exp\left(\int (-1)dx\right) = e^{-x}.$$

Multiplying both sides of the equation by $\mu(x)$ and integrating, we obtain

$$e^{-x}\frac{dy}{dx} - e^{-x}y = e^{-x}e^{3x} = e^{2x} \quad \Rightarrow \quad \frac{d\left(e^{-x}y\right)}{dx} = e^{2x}$$

$$\Rightarrow \quad e^{-x}y = \int e^{2x}dx = \frac{1}{2}e^{2x} + C$$

$$\Rightarrow \quad y = \left(\frac{1}{2}e^{2x} + C\right)e^x = \frac{e^{3x}}{2} + Ce^x.$$

**9.** This is a linear equation with dependent variable $r$ and independent variable $\theta$. The method we will use to solve this equation is exactly the same as the method we use to solve an equation in the variables $x$ and $y$ since these variables are just dummy variables. Thus we have $P(\theta) = \tan\theta$ and $Q(\theta) = \sec\theta$ which are continuous on any interval not containing odd multiples of $\pi/2$. We proceed as usual to find the integrating factor $\mu(\theta)$. We have

$$\mu(\theta) = \exp\left(\int \tan\theta\, d\theta\right) = e^{-\ln|\cos\theta| + C} = K \cdot \frac{1}{|\cos\theta|} = K|\sec\theta|, \quad \text{where } K = e^C.$$

Thus we have

$$\mu(\theta) = \sec\theta,$$

where we can drop the absolute value sign by making $K = 1$ if $\theta$ is in an interval where $\sec\theta$ is positive or by making $K = -1$ if $\sec\theta$ is negative. Multiplying the equation by the integrating factor yields

$$\sec\theta\frac{dr}{d\theta} + (\sec\theta\tan\theta)r = \sec^2\theta \quad \Rightarrow \quad D_\theta(r\sec\theta) = \sec^2\theta.$$

Integrating with respect to $\theta$ yields

$$r\sec\theta = \int \sec^2\theta\, d\theta = \tan\theta + C \quad \Rightarrow \quad r = \cos\theta\tan\theta + C\cos\theta \quad \Rightarrow \quad r = \sin\theta + C\cos\theta.$$

Because of the continuity of $P(\theta)$ and $Q(\theta)$ this solution is valid on any open interval that has end points that are consecutive odd multiples of $\pi/2$.

**11.** Choosing $t$ as the independent variable and $y$ as the dependent variable, we put the equation put into standard form:

$$t + y + 1 - \frac{dy}{dt} = 0 \quad \Rightarrow \quad \frac{dy}{dt} - y = t + 1. \tag{2.8}$$

Thus $P(t) \equiv -1$ and so $\mu(t) = \exp\left[\int(-1)dt\right] = e^{-t}$. We multiply both sides of the second equation in (2.8) by $\mu(t)$ and integrate. This yields

$$e^{-t}\frac{dy}{dt} - e^{-t}y = (t+1)e^{-t} \quad \Rightarrow \quad \frac{d}{dt}\left(e^{-t}y\right) = (t+1)e^{-t}$$

$$\Rightarrow \quad e^{-t}y = \int(t+1)e^{-t}dt = -(t+1)e^{-t} + \int e^{-t}dt$$

$$= -(t+1)e^{-t} - e^{-t} + C = -(t+2)e^{-t} + C$$

$$\Rightarrow \quad y = e^t\left(-(t+2)e^{-t} + C\right) = -t - 2 + Ce^t,$$

where we have used integration by parts to find $\int(t+1)e^{-t}dt$.

**13.** In this problem, the independent variable is $y$ and the dependent variable is $x$. So, we divide the equation by $y$ to rewrite it in standard form.

$$y\frac{dx}{dy} + 2x = 5y^2 \quad \Rightarrow \quad \frac{dx}{dy} + \frac{2}{y}x = 5y^2.$$

Therefore, $P(y) = 2/y$ and the integrating factor, $\mu(y)$, is

$$\mu(y) = \exp\left(\int \frac{2}{y}\,dy\right) = \exp\left(2\ln|y|\right) = |y|^2 = y^2.$$

Multiplying the equation (in standard form) by $y^2$ and integrating yield

$$y^2\frac{dx}{dy} + 2y\,x = 5y^4 \quad \Rightarrow \quad \frac{d}{dy}\left(y^2 x\right) = 5y^4$$

$$\Rightarrow \quad y^2 x = \int 5y^4\,dy = y^5 + C \quad \Rightarrow \quad x = y^{-2}\left(y^5 + C\right) = y^3 + Cy^{-2}.$$

**15.** To put this linear equation in standard form, we divide by $(x^2 + 1)$ to obtain

$$\frac{dy}{dx} + \frac{x}{x^2+1}y = \frac{x}{x^2+1}. \tag{2.9}$$

# Chapter 2

Here $P(x) = x/(x^2 + 1)$, so

$$\int P(x)\, dx = \int \frac{x}{x^2 + 1}\, dx = \frac{1}{2}\ln(x^2 + 1).$$

Thus the integrating factor is

$$\mu(x) = e^{(1/2)\ln(x^2+1)} = e^{\ln\left[(x^2+1)^{1/2}\right]} = (x^2 + 1)^{1/2}.$$

Multiplying equation (2.9) by $\mu(x)$ yields

$$(x^2 + 1)^{1/2}\frac{dy}{dx} + \frac{x}{(x^2+1)^{1/2}}\, y = \frac{x}{(x^2+1)^{1/2}},$$

which becomes

$$\frac{d}{dx}\left[(x^2 + 1)^{1/2}y\right] = \frac{x}{(x^2+1)^{1/2}}.$$

Now we integrate both sides and solve for $y$ to find

$$(x^2 + 1)^{1/2}y = (x^2 + 1)^{1/2} + C \qquad \Rightarrow \qquad y = 1 + C(x^2 + 1)^{-1/2}.$$

This solution is valid for all $x$ since $P(x)$ and $Q(x)$ are continuous for all $x$.

**17.** This is a linear equation with $P(x) = -1/x$ and $Q(x) = xe^x$ which is continuous on any interval not containing 0. Therefore, the integrating factor is given by

$$\mu(x) = \exp\left[\int\left(-\frac{1}{x}\right)dx\right] = e^{-\ln x} = \frac{1}{x}, \qquad \text{for } x > 0.$$

Multiplying the equation by this integrating factor yields

$$\frac{1}{x}\frac{dy}{dx} - \frac{y}{x^2} = e^x \qquad \Rightarrow \qquad D_x\left(\frac{y}{x}\right) = e^x.$$

Integrating gives

$$\frac{y}{x} = e^x + C \qquad \Rightarrow \qquad y = xe^x + Cx.$$

Now applying the initial condition, $y(1) = e - 1$, we have

$$e - 1 = e + C \qquad \Rightarrow \qquad C = -1.$$

Thus, the solution is

$$y = xe^x - x, \quad \text{on the interval } (0, \infty).$$

Note: This interval is the largest interval containing the initial value $x = 1$ in which $P(x)$ and $Q(x)$ are continuous.

**19.** In this problem, $t$ is the independent variable and $x$ is the dependent variable. One can notice that the left-hand side is the derivative of $xt^3$ with respect to $t$. Indeed, using product rule for differentiation, we get

$$\frac{d}{dt}\left(xt^3\right) = \frac{dx}{dt}t^3 + x\frac{d\left(t^3\right)}{dt} = t^3\frac{dx}{dt} + 3t^2 x.$$

Thus the equation becomes

$$\frac{d}{dt}\left(xt^3\right) = t \quad \Rightarrow \quad xt^3 = \int t\,dt = \frac{t^2}{2} + C$$

$$\Rightarrow \quad x = t^{-3}\left(\frac{t^2}{2} + C\right) = \frac{1}{2t} + \frac{C}{t^3}.$$

(Of course, one could divide the given equation by $t^3$ to get standard form, conclude that $P(t) = 3/t$, find that $\mu(t) = t^3$, multiply by $t^3$ back, and come up with the original equation.) We now use the initial condition, $x(2) = 0$, to find $C$.

$$0 = x(2) = \frac{1}{2(2)} + \frac{C}{2^3} \quad \Rightarrow \quad \frac{1}{4} + \frac{C}{8} = 0 \quad \Rightarrow \quad C = -2.$$

Hence, the solution is $x = 1/(2t) - 2/(t^3)$.

**21.** Putting the equation in standard form yields

$$\frac{dy}{dx} + \frac{\sin x}{\cos x}y = 2x\cos x \quad \Rightarrow \quad \frac{dy}{dx} + (\tan x)y = 2x\cos x.$$

Therefore, $P(x) = \tan x$ and so

$$\mu(x) = \exp\left(\int \tan x\,dx\right) = \exp\left(-\ln|\cos x|\right) = |\cos x|^{-1}.$$

At the initial point, $x = \pi/4$, $\cos(\pi/4) > 0$ and, therefore, we can take $\mu(x) = (\cos x)^{-1}$. Multiplying the standard form of the given equation by $\mu(x)$ gives

$$\frac{1}{\cos x}\frac{dy}{dx} + \frac{\sin x}{\cos^2 x}y = 2x \qquad \Rightarrow \qquad \frac{d}{dx}\left(\frac{1}{\cos x}y\right) = 2x$$

$$\Rightarrow \qquad \frac{1}{\cos x}y = \int 2x\,dx = x^2 + C \qquad \Rightarrow \qquad y = \cos x\left(x^2 + C\right).$$

From the initial condition, we find $C$:

$$\frac{-15\sqrt{2}\pi^2}{32} = y\left(\frac{\pi}{4}\right) = \cos\frac{\pi}{4}\left[\left(\frac{\pi}{4}\right)^2 + C\right] \qquad \Rightarrow \qquad C = -\pi^2.$$

Hence, the solution is given by $y = \cos x\left(x^2 - \pi^2\right)$.

23. We proceed similarly to Example 2 on page 52 and obtain an analog of the initial value problem (13), that is,

$$\frac{dy}{dt} + 5y = 40e^{-20t}, \qquad y(0) = 10. \tag{2.10}$$

Thus $P(t) \equiv 5$ and $\mu(t) = \exp\left(\int 5dt\right) = e^{5t}$. Multiplying the differential equation in (2.10) by $\mu(t)$ and integrating, we obtain

$$e^{5t}\frac{dy}{dt} + 5e^{5t}y = 40e^{-20t}e^{5t} = 40e^{-15t}$$

$$\Rightarrow \qquad \frac{d\left(e^{5t}y\right)}{dt} = 40e^{-15t} \qquad \Rightarrow \qquad e^{5t}y = \int 40e^{-15t}\,dt = \frac{40}{-15}e^{-15t} + C.$$

Therefore, a general solution to the differential equation in (2.10) is

$$y = e^{-5t}\left(\frac{40}{-15}e^{-15t} + C\right) = Ce^{-5t} - \frac{8}{3}e^{-20t}.$$

Finally, we find $C$ using the initial condition.

$$10 = y(0) = Ce^{-5\cdot 0} - \frac{8}{3}e^{-20\cdot 0} = C - \frac{8}{3} \qquad \Rightarrow \qquad C = 10 + \frac{8}{3} = \frac{38}{3}.$$

Hence, the mass of $RA_2$ for $t \geq 0$ is given by

$$y(t) = \frac{38}{3}e^{-5t} - \frac{8}{3}e^{-20t}.$$

**25. (a)** This is a linear problem and so an integrating factor is

$$\mu(x) = \exp\left(\int 2x\,dx\right) = \exp\left(x^2\right).$$

Multiplying the equation by this integrating factor yields

$$e^{x^2}\frac{dy}{dx} + 2xe^{x^2}y = e^{x^2} \qquad \Rightarrow \qquad D_x\left(ye^{x^2}\right) = e^{x^2}$$

$$\Rightarrow \quad \int_2^x D_t\left(ye^{t^2}\right)dt = \int_2^x e^{t^2}\,dt,$$

where we have changed the dummy variable $x$ to $t$ and integrated with respect to $t$ from 2 (since the initial value for $x$ in the initial condition is 2) to $x$. Thus, since $y(2) = 1$,

$$ye^{x^2} - e^4 = \int_2^x e^{t^2}\,dt \quad \Rightarrow \quad y = e^{-x^2}\left(e^4 + \int_2^x e^{t^2}\,dt\right) = e^{4-x^2} + e^{-x^2}\int_2^x e^{t^2}\,dt.$$

**(b)** We will use Simpson's rule (page A.3 of the Appendix B) to approximate the definite integral found in part (a) with upper limit $x = 3$. Simpson's rule requires an even number of intervals, but we don't know how many are required to obtain the desired 3 place accuracy. Rather than make an error analysis, we will compute the approximate value of $y(3)$ using 4, 6, 8, 10, 12, ... intervals for Simpson's rule until the approximate values for $y(3)$ change by less than 5 in the fourth place. For $n = 2$ we divide $[2,3]$ into 4 equal subintervals. Thus, each subinterval will be of length $(3-2)/4 = 1/4$. Therefore, the integral is approximated by

$$\int_2^3 e^{t^2}\,dt \approx \frac{1}{12}\left[e^{(2)^2} + e^{(2.25)^2} + e^{(2.5)^2} + e^{(2.75)^2} + e^{(3)^2}\right] \approx 1460.354350.$$

Dividing this by $e^{(3)^2}$ and adding $e^{4-3^2} = e^{-5}$, gives

$$y(3) \approx 0.186960.$$

Doing calculations for 6, 8, 10, and 12 intervals yields Table 2-B.

47

**Table 2–B**: Successive approximations for $y(3)$ using Simpson's rule.

| Number of Intervals | $y(3)$ |
|:---:|:---:|
| 6 | 0.183905 |
| 8 | 0.183291 |
| 10 | 0.183110 |
| 12 | 0.183043 |

Since the last 3 approximate values do not change by more than 5 in the fourth place, it appears that their first three places are accurate and the approximate solution is $y(3) \approx 0.183$.

27. **(a)** The given differential equation is in standard form. Thus $P(x) = \sqrt{1 + \sin^2 x}$. Since we cannot express $\int P(x)\,dx$ as an elementary function, we use fundamental theorem of calculus to conclude that, with any fixed constant $a$,

$$\left( \int_{a}^{x} P(t)dt \right)' = P(x),$$

that is, the above definite integral with variable upper bound is an antiderivative of $P(x)$. Since, in the formula for $\mu(x)$, one can choose any antiderivative of $P(x)$, we take the above definite integral with $a = 0$. (Such a choice of $a$ comes from the initial point $x = 0$ and makes it easy to satisfy the initial condition.) Therefore, the integrating factor $\mu(x)$ can be chosen as

$$\mu(x) = \exp\left( \int_{0}^{x} \sqrt{1 + \sin^2 t}\,dt \right).$$

Multiplying the differential equaion by $\mu(x)$ and integrating from $x = 0$ to $x = s$, we obtain

$$\frac{d[\mu(x)y]}{dx} = \mu(x)x \qquad \Rightarrow \qquad d[\mu(x)y] = \mu(x)x\,dx$$

$$\Rightarrow \quad \int_0^s d[\mu(x)y] = \int_0^s \mu(x)x\,dx \qquad \Rightarrow \quad \mu(x)y(x)\,\Big|_{x=0}^{x=s} = \int_0^s \mu(x)x\,dx$$

$$\Rightarrow \quad \mu(s)y(s) - \mu(0)y(0) = \int_0^s \mu(x)x\,dx\,.$$

From the initial condition, $y(0) = 2$. Also, note that

$$\mu(0) = \exp\left(\int_0^0 \sqrt{1+\sin^2 t}\,dt\right) = e^0 = 1.$$

This yields $\mu(0)y(0) = 2$ and so

$$\mu(s)y(s) = \int_0^s \mu(x)x\,dx + 2\,.$$

Dividing by $\mu(s)$ and interchanging $x$ and $s$ give the required.

**(b)** The values of $\mu(x)$, $x = 0.1$, $0.2$, ..., $1.0$, approximated by using Simpson's rule, are given in Table 2-C.

---

**Table 2–C**: Approximations of $\nu(x) = \int_0^x \sqrt{1+\sin^2 t}\,dt$ and $\mu(x) = e^{\nu(x)}$ using Simpson's rule.

| $x$ | $\nu(x)$ | $\mu(x)$ | $x$ | $\nu(x)$ | $\mu(x)$ |
|-----|----------|----------|-----|----------|----------|
| 0.0 | 0.0      | 1.0000   | 0.6 | 0.632016 | 1.881401 |
| 0.1 | 0.100166 | 1.105354 | 0.7 | 0.748903 | 2.114679 |
| 0.2 | 0.201315 | 1.223010 | 0.8 | 0.869917 | 2.386713 |
| 0.3 | 0.304363 | 1.355761 | 0.9 | 0.994980 | 2.704670 |
| 0.4 | 0.410104 | 1.506975 | 1.0 | 1.123865 | 3.076723 |
| 0.5 | 0.519172 | 1.680635 |     |          |          |

---

We now use these values of $\mu(x)$ to approximate $\int_0^1 \mu(s)s\,ds$ by applying Simpson's rule again. With $n = 5$ and

$$h = \frac{1-0}{2n} = 0.1$$

49

Chapter 2

the Simpson's rule becomes

$$\int_0^1 \mu(s)s\,ds \approx \frac{0.1}{3}[\mu(0)(0) + 4\mu(0.1)(0.1) + 2\mu(0.2)(0.2) + 4\mu(0.3)(0.3)$$

$$+2\mu(0.4)(0.4) + 4\mu(0.5)(0.5) + 2\mu(0.6)(0.6) + 4\mu(0.7)(0.7)$$

$$+2\mu(0.8)(0.8) + 4\mu(0.9)(0.9) + \mu(1.0)(1.0)] \approx 1.064539\,.$$

Therefore,

$$y(1) \approx \frac{1}{\mu(1)} \int_0^1 \mu(s)s\,ds + \frac{2}{\mu(1)} = \frac{1}{3.076723} \cdot 1.064539 + \frac{2}{3.076723} = 0.9960\,.$$

(c) We rewrite the differential equation in the form used in Euler's method,

$$\frac{dy}{dx} = x - \sqrt{1 + \sin^2 x}\,y\,, \qquad y(0) = 2,$$

and conclude that $f(x,y) = x - \sqrt{1 + \sin^2 x}\,y$. Thus the recursive formulas (2) and (3) on page 25 of the text become

$$x_{n+1} = x_n + h,$$
$$y_{n+1} = y_n + h\left(x_n - \sqrt{1 + \sin^2 x_n}\,y_n\right), \qquad n = 0, 1, \ldots,$$

$x_0 = 0$, $y_0 = 2$. With $h = 0.1$ we need $(1 - 0)/0.1$ steps to get an approximation at $x = 1$.

$n = 0: \quad x_1 = 0.1\,, \quad y_1 = (2) + 0.1[(0) - \sqrt{1 + \sin^2(0)}\,(2)] = 1.8000;$
$n = 1: \quad x_2 = 0.2\,, \quad y_2 = (1.8) + 0.1[(0.1) - \sqrt{1 + \sin^2(0.1)}\,(1.8)] \approx 1.6291;$
$n = 2: \quad x_3 = 0.3\,, \quad y_3 = (1.6291) + 0.1[(0.2) - \sqrt{1 + \sin^2(0.2)}\,(1.6291)] \approx 1.4830;$
$\vdots$

Results of these computations, rounded off to four decimal places, are given in Table 2-D. Thus Euler's method with step $h = 0.1$ gives $y(1) \approx 0.9486$.

Next we take $h = 0.05$ and fill in the Table 2-E. So, with step $h = 0.05$, we have $y(1) \approx 0.9729$.

50

**Table 2–D**: Euler's method approximations for the solution of $y' + y\sqrt{1 + \sin^2 x} = x$, $y(0) = 2$, at $x = 1$ with $h = 0.1$.

| $k$ | $x_k$ | $y_k$ | $k$ | $x_k$ | $y_k$ | $k$ | $x_k$ | $y_k$ |
|---|---|---|---|---|---|---|---|---|
| 0 | 0.0 | 2.0000 | 4 | 0.4 | 1.3584 | 8 | 0.8 | 1.0304 |
| 1 | 0.1 | 1.8000 | 5 | 0.5 | 1.2526 | 9 | 0.9 | 0.9836 |
| 2 | 0.2 | 1.6291 | 6 | 0.6 | 1.1637 | 10 | 1.0 | 0.9486 |
| 3 | 0.3 | 1.4830 | 7 | 0.7 | 1.0900 | | | |

**Table 2–E**: Euler's method approximations for the solution of $y' + y\sqrt{1 + \sin^2 x} = x$, $y(0) = 2$, at $x = 1$ with $h = 0.05$.

| $n$ | $x_n$ | $y_n$ | $n$ | $x_n$ | $y_n$ | $n$ | $x_n$ | $y_n$ |
|---|---|---|---|---|---|---|---|---|
| 0 | 0.00 | 2.0000 | 7 | 0.35 | 1.4368 | 14 | 0.70 | 1.1144 |
| 1 | 0.05 | 1.9000 | 8 | 0.40 | 1.3784 | 15 | 0.75 | 1.0831 |
| 2 | 0.10 | 1.8074 | 9 | 0.45 | 1.3244 | 16 | 0.80 | 1.0551 |
| 3 | 0.15 | 1.7216 | 10 | 0.50 | 1.2747 | 17 | 0.85 | 1.0301 |
| 4 | 0.20 | 1.6420 | 11 | 0.55 | 1.2290 | 18 | 0.90 | 1.0082 |
| 5 | 0.25 | 1.5683 | 12 | 0.60 | 1.1872 | 19 | 0.95 | 0.9892 |
| 6 | 0.30 | 1.5000 | 13 | 0.65 | 1.1490 | 20 | 1.00 | 0.9729 |

**29.** In the presented form, the equation

$$\frac{dy}{dx} = \frac{1}{e^{4y} + 2x}$$

is, clearly, not linear. But, if we switch the roles of variables and consider $y$ as the independent variable and $x$ as the dependent variable (using the connection between derivatives of inverse functions, that is, the formula $y'(x) = 1/x'(y)$), then the equation transforms to

$$\frac{dx}{dy} = e^{4y} + 2x \qquad \Rightarrow \qquad \frac{dx}{dy} - 2x = e^{4y}.$$

This is a linear equation with $P(y) = -2$. Thus the integrating factor is

$$\mu(y) = \exp\left(\int (-2)dy\right) = e^{-2y}$$

Chapter 2

and so

$$\frac{d}{dy}\left(e^{-2y}x\right) = e^{-2y}e^{4y} = e^{2y} \quad \Rightarrow \quad e^{-2y}x = \int e^{2y}\,dy = \frac{e^{2y}}{2} + C.$$

Solving for $x$ yields

$$x = e^{2y}\left(\frac{e^{2y}}{2} + C\right) = \frac{e^{4y}}{2} + Ce^{2y}.$$

31. **(a)** On the interval $0 \le x \le 2$, we have $P(x) = 1$. Thus we are solving the equation

$$\frac{dy}{dx} + y = x, \qquad y(0) = 1.$$

The integrating factor is given by

$$\mu(x) = \exp\left(\int dx\right) = e^x.$$

Multiplying the equation by the integrating factor, we obtain

$$e^x \frac{dy}{dx} + e^x y = xe^x \quad \Rightarrow \quad D_x\left[e^x y\right] = xe^x \quad \Rightarrow \quad e^x y = \int xe^x\,dx.$$

Calculating this integral by parts and dividing by $e^x$ yields

$$y = e^{-x}\left(xe^x - e^x + C\right) = x - 1 + Ce^{-x}.$$

**(b)** Using the initial condition, $y(0) = 1$, we see that

$$1 = y(0) = 0 - 1 + C = -1 + C \quad \Rightarrow \quad C = 2.$$

Thus the solution becomes

$$y = x - 1 + 2e^{-x}.$$

**(c)** In the interval $x > 2$, we have $P(x) = 3$. Therefore, the integrating factor is given by

$$\mu(x) = \exp\left(\int 3\,dx\right) = e^{3x}.$$

Multiplying the equation by this factor and solving yields

$$e^{3x}\frac{dy}{dx} + 3e^{3x}y = xe^{3x} \quad \Rightarrow \quad D_x\left(e^{3x}y\right) = xe^{3x} \quad \Rightarrow \quad e^{3x}y = \int xe^{3x}\,dx.$$

Integrating by parts and dividing by $e^{3x}$ gives

$$y = e^{-3x}\left[\frac{1}{3}xe^{3x} - \frac{1}{9}e^{3x} + C\right] = \frac{x}{3} - \frac{1}{9} + Ce^{-3x}.$$

**(d)** We want the value of the initial point for the solution in part (c) to be the value of the solution found in part (b) at the point $x = 2$. This value is given by

$$y(2) = 2 - 1 + 2e^{-2} = 1 + 2e^{-2}.$$

Thus the initial point we seek is

$$y(2) = 1 + 2e^{-2}.$$

Using this initial point to find the constant $C$ given in part (c) yields

$$1 + 2e^{-2} = y(2) = \frac{2}{3} - \frac{1}{9} + Ce^{-6} \quad \Rightarrow \quad C = \frac{4}{9}e^6 + 2e^4.$$

Thus, the solution of the equation on the interval $x > 2$ is given by

$$y = \frac{x}{3} - \frac{1}{9} + \left[\frac{4}{9}e^6 + 2e^4\right]e^{-3x}.$$

Patching these two solutions together gives us a continuous solution to the original equation on the interval $x \geq 0$:

$$y = \begin{cases} x - 1 + 2e^{-x}, & 0 \leq x \leq 2; \\ \frac{x}{3} - \frac{1}{9} + \left(\frac{4}{9}e^6 + 2e^4\right)e^{-3x}, & 2 < x. \end{cases}$$

**(e)** The graph of the solution is given in Figure B.18 of the answers in the text.

**33. (a)** Writing the equation in standard form yields

$$\frac{dy}{dx} + \frac{2}{x}y = 3.$$

Therefore, $P(x) = 2/x$ and

$$\mu(x) = \exp\left(\int \frac{2}{x}\,dx\right) = \exp\left(2\ln|x|\right) = |x|^2 = x^2.$$

Hence

$$\frac{d}{dx}\left(x^2 y\right) = 3x^2 \quad \Rightarrow \quad x^2 y = \int 3x^2\,dx = x^3 + C \quad \Rightarrow \quad y = x + \frac{C}{x^2}$$

Chapter 2

is a general solution to the given differential equation. Unless $C = 0$ and so $y = x$, the function $y = x + C/x^2$ is not defined when $x = 0$. Therefore, among all solutions, the only function defined at $x = 0$ is $\phi(x) = x$, and the initial value problem with $y(0) = y_0$ has a solution (and unique) if and only if

$$y_0 = \phi(x)\Big|_{x=0} = 0.$$

(b) Standard form of the equation $xy' - 2y = 3x$ is

$$\frac{dy}{dx} - \frac{2}{x}y = 3.$$

This gives $P(x) = -2/x$, $\mu(x) = \exp\left[\int(-2/x)dx\right] = x^{-2}$, and

$$\frac{d}{dx}\left(x^{-2}y\right) = 3x^{-2} \quad \Rightarrow \quad x^{-2}y = \int 3x^{-2}\,dx = -3x^{-1} + C \quad \Rightarrow \quad y = -3x + Cx^2.$$

Therefore, any solution is a polynomial and so is defined for all real numbers. Moreover, any solution satisfies the initial condition $y(0) = 0$ because

$$-3x + Cx^2\Big|_{x=0} = -3(0) + C(0)^2 = 0$$

and, therefore, is a solution to the initial value problem. (This also implies that the initial value problem with $y(0) = y_0 \neq 0$ has no solution.)

35. (a) This part of the problem is similar to Problem 33 in Section 2.2. So, we proceed in the same way.

Let $A(t)$ denote the mass of salt in the tank at $t$ minutes after the process begins. Then we have

$$\text{rate of input} = 5 \text{ L/min} \times 0.2 \text{ kg/L} = 1 \text{ kg/min},$$
$$\text{rate of exit} = 5 \text{ L/min} \times \frac{A(t)}{500} \text{ kg/L} = \frac{A(t)}{100} \text{ kg/min},$$
$$\frac{dA}{dt} = 1 - \frac{A}{100} = \frac{100 - A}{100}.$$

Separating this differential equation yields $dA/(100 - A) = dt/100$. Integrating, we obtain

$$-\ln|100 - A| = \frac{t}{100} + C_1 \quad \Rightarrow \quad |100 - A| = e^{-t/100 - C_1} = e^{-C_1}e^{-t/100}$$

54

$$\Rightarrow \quad 100 - A = Ce^{-t/100} \quad \left(C = \pm e^{-C_1}\right) \quad \Rightarrow \quad A = 100 - Ce^{-t/100}.$$

The initial condition, $A(0) = 5$ (initially, there were 5 kg of salt in the tank) implies that

$$5 = A(0) = 100 - C \quad \Rightarrow \quad C = 95.$$

Substituting this value of $C$ into the solution, we have

$$A(t) = 100 - 95e^{-t/100}.$$

Thus the mass of salt in the tank after 10 min is

$$A(10) = 100 - 95e^{-10/100} \approx 14.04 \text{ kg},$$

which gives the concentration $14.04 \, \text{kg}/500 \, \text{L} \approx 0.0281 \, \text{kg/L}$.

(b) After the leak develops, the system satisfies a new differential equation. While the rate of input remains the same, 1 kg/min, the rate of exit is now different. Since, every minute, 5 liters of the solution is coming in and $5 + 1 = 6$ liters are going out, the volume of the solution in the tank decreases by $6 - 5 = 1$ liter per minute. Thus, for $t \geq 10$, the volume of the solution in the tank is $500 - 1 \cdot (t - 10) = 510 - t$ liters. This gives the concentration of salt in the tank

$$\frac{A(t)}{510 - t} \text{ kg/L} \tag{2.11}$$

and

$$\text{rate of exit} = 6 \text{ L/min} \times \frac{A(t)}{510 - t} \text{ kg/L} = \frac{6A(t)}{510 - t} \text{ kg/min}.$$

Hence, the differential equation, for $t > 10$, becomes

$$\frac{dA}{dt} = 1 - \frac{6A}{510 - t} \quad \Rightarrow \quad \frac{dA}{dt} + \frac{6A}{510 - t} = 1$$

with the initial condition $A(10) = 14.04$ (the value found in (a)). This equation is a linear equation. We have

$$\mu(t) = \exp\left(\int \frac{6}{510 - t} \, dt\right) = \exp\left(-6 \ln|510 - t|\right) = (510 - t)^{-6}$$

$$\Rightarrow \quad \frac{d}{dt}\left[(510-t)^{-6}A\right] = 1 \cdot (510-t)^{-6} = (510-t)^{-6}$$

$$\Rightarrow \quad (510-t)^{-6}A = \int (510-t)^{-6}dt = \frac{1}{5}(510-t)^{-5} + C$$

$$\Rightarrow \quad A = \frac{1}{5}(510-t) + C(510-t)^6.$$

Using the initial condition, $A(10) = 14.04$, we compute $C$.

$$14.04 = A(10) = \frac{1}{5}(510-10) + C(510-10)^6 \quad \Rightarrow \quad C = -\frac{85.96}{(500)^6}.$$

Therefore,

$$A(t) = \frac{1}{5}(510-t) - \frac{85.96}{(500)^6}(510-t)^6 = \frac{1}{5}(510-t) - 85.96\left(\frac{510-t}{500}\right)^6$$

and, according to (2.11), the concentration of salt is given by

$$\frac{A(t)}{510-t} = \frac{1}{5} - \frac{85.96}{510-t} \cdot \left(\frac{510-t}{500}\right)^6.$$

20 minutes after the leak develops, that is, when $t = 30$, the concentration will be

$$\frac{1}{5} - \frac{85.96}{510-30} \cdot \left(\frac{510-30}{500}\right)^6 \approx 0.0598 \text{ kg/L}.$$

**37.** We are solving the equation

$$\frac{dx}{dt} + 2x = 1 - \cos\left(\frac{\pi t}{12}\right), \qquad x(0) = 10.$$

This is a linear problem with dependent variable $x$ and independent variable $t$ so that $P(t) = 2$. Therefore, to solve this equation we first must find the integrating factor $\mu(t)$.

$$\mu(t) = \exp\left(\int 2\, dt\right) = e^{2t}.$$

Multiplying the equation by this factor yields

$$e^{2t}\frac{dx}{dt} + 2xe^{2t} = e^{2t}\left[1 - \cos\left(\frac{\pi t}{12}\right)\right] = e^{2t} - e^{2t}\cos\left(\frac{\pi t}{12}\right)$$

$$\Rightarrow \quad xe^{2t} = \int e^{2t}\, dt - \int e^{2t}\cos\left(\frac{\pi t}{12}\right)dt = \frac{1}{2}e^{2t} - \int e^{2t}\cos\left(\frac{\pi t}{12}\right)dt.$$

The last integral can be found by integrating by parts twice which leads back to an integral similar to the original. Combining these two similar integrals and simplifying, we obtain

$$\int e^{2t} \cos\left(\frac{\pi t}{12}\right) dt = \frac{e^{2t}\left[2\cos\left(\frac{\pi t}{12}\right) + \frac{\pi}{12}\sin\left(\frac{\pi t}{12}\right)\right]}{4 + \left(\frac{\pi}{12}\right)^2} + C.$$

Thus we see that

$$x(t) = \frac{1}{2} - \frac{2\cos\left(\frac{\pi t}{12}\right) + \frac{\pi}{12}\sin\left(\frac{\pi t}{12}\right)}{4 + \left(\frac{\pi}{12}\right)^2} + Ce^{-2t}.$$

Using the initial condition, $t = 0$ and $x = 10$, to solve for $C$, we obtain

$$C = \frac{19}{2} + \frac{2}{4 + \left(\frac{\pi}{12}\right)^2}.$$

Therefore, the desired solution is

$$x(t) = \frac{1}{2} - \frac{2\cos\left(\frac{\pi t}{12}\right) + \frac{\pi}{12}\sin\left(\frac{\pi t}{12}\right)}{4 + \left(\frac{\pi}{12}\right)^2} + \left[\frac{19}{2} + \frac{2}{4 + \left(\frac{\pi}{12}\right)^2}\right] e^{-2t}.$$

**39.** Let $T_j(t)$, $j = 0, 1, 2, \ldots$, denote the temperature in the classroom for $9 + j \le t < 10 + j$, where $t = 13$ denotes $1 : 00$ P.M., $t = 14$ denotes $2 : 00$ P.M., etc. Then

$$T(9) = 0, \tag{2.12}$$

and the continuity of the temperature implies that

$$\lim_{t \to 10 + j} = T_{j+1}(10 + j), \qquad j = 0, 1, 2, \ldots . \tag{2.13}$$

According to the work of the heating unit, the temperature satisfies the equation

$$\frac{dT_j}{dt} = \begin{cases} 1 - T_j, & \text{if } j = 2k \\ -T_j, & \text{if } j = 2k + 1 \end{cases}, \qquad 9 + j < t < 10 + j \quad k = 0, 1, \ldots .$$

The general solutions of these equations are:

for $j$ even

$$\frac{dT_j}{dt} = 1 - T_j \qquad \Rightarrow \qquad \frac{dT_j}{1 - T_j} = dt$$

$$\Rightarrow \qquad \ln|1 - T_j| = -t + c_j \qquad \Rightarrow \qquad T_j(t) = 1 - C_j e^{-t};$$

for $j$ odd

$$\frac{dT_j}{dt} = -T_j \qquad \Rightarrow \qquad \frac{dT_j}{-T_j} = dt$$

$$\Rightarrow \qquad \ln|T_j| = -t + c_j \qquad \Rightarrow \qquad T_j(t) = C_j e^{-t};$$

where $C_j \neq 0$ are constants. From (2.12) we have:

$$0 = T_0(9) = \left(1 - C_0 e^{-t}\right)\Big|_{t=9} = 1 - C_0 e^{-9} \qquad \Rightarrow \qquad C_0 = e^9.$$

Also from (2.13), for even values of $j$ (say, $j = 2k$) we get

$$\left(1 - C_{2k} e^{-t}\right)\Big|_{t=9+(2k+1)} = C_{2k+1} e^{-t}\Big|_{t=9+(2k+1)}$$

$$\Rightarrow \qquad 1 - C_{2k} e^{-(10+2k)} = C_{2k+1} e^{-(10+2k)}$$

$$\Rightarrow \qquad C_{2k+1} = e^{10+2k} - C_{2k}.$$

Similarly from (2.13) for odd values of $j$ (say, $j = 2k + 1$) we get

$$C_{2k+1} e^{-t}\Big|_{t=9+(2k+2)} = \left(1 - C_{2k+2} e^{-t}\right)\Big|_{t=9+(2k+2)}$$

$$\Rightarrow \qquad C_{2k+1} e^{-(11+2k)} = 1 - C_{2k+2} e^{-(11+2k)}$$

$$\Rightarrow \qquad C_{2k+2} = e^{11+2k} - C_{2k+1}.$$

In general we see that for any integer $j$ (even or odd) the following formula holds:

$$C_j = e^{9+j} - C_{j-1}.$$

Using this recurrence formula we successively compute

$$C_1 = e^{10} - C_0 = e^{10} - e^9 = e^9(e - 1)$$

$$C_2 = e^{11} - C_1 = e^{11} - e^{10} + e^9 = e^9(e^2 - e + 1)$$

$$\vdots$$

$$C_j = e^9 \sum_{k=0}^{j} (-1)^{j-k} e^k.$$

Therefore, the temperature at noon (when $t = 12$ and $j = 3$) is

$$T_3(12) = C_3 e^{-12} = e^{-12} e^9 \sum_{k=0}^{3} (-1)^{3-k} e^k = 1 - e^{-1} + e^{-2} - e^{-3} \approx 0.718 = 71.8^\circ \text{ F}.$$

At 5 P.M.(when $t = 17$ and $j = 8$), we find

$$T_8(17) = 1 - C_8 e^{-17} = 1 - e^{-17} e^9 \sum_{k=0}^{8} (-1)^{8-k} e^k = \sum_{k=1}^{8} (-1)^{k+1} e^{-k}$$

$$= e^{-1} \cdot \frac{1 - (-e^{-1})^8}{1 + e^{-1}} \approx 0.269 = 26.9^\circ \text{ F}.$$

## EXERCISES 2.4:  Exact Equations, page 65

**1.** In this equation, $M(x, y) = x^2 y + x^4 \cos x$ and $N(x, y) = -x^3$. Taking partial derivatives, we obtain

$$\frac{\partial M}{\partial y} = \frac{\partial}{\partial y} \left( x^2 y + x^4 \right) = x^2 \neq -3x^2 = \frac{\partial N}{\partial x} .$$

Therefore, according to Theorem 2 on page 61 of the text, the equation is not exact.

Rewriting the equation in the form

$$\frac{dy}{dx} = \frac{x^2 y + x^4 \cos x}{x^3} = \frac{1}{x} y + x \cos x, \tag{2.14}$$

we conclude that it is not separable because the right-hand side in (2.14) cannot be factored as $p(x)q(y)$. We also see that the equation is linear with $y$ as the dependent variable.

**3.** Here $M(x, y) = y e^{xy} + 2x$, $N(x, y) = x e^{xy} - 2y$. Thus

$$\frac{\partial M}{\partial y} = \frac{\partial}{\partial y} \left( y e^{xy} + 2x \right) = e^{xy} + y \frac{\partial}{\partial y} \left( e^{xy} \right) = e^{xy} + y e^{xy} x = e^{xy}(1 + yx),$$

$$\frac{\partial N}{\partial x} = \frac{\partial}{\partial x} \left( x e^{xy} - 2y \right) = e^{xy} + x \frac{\partial}{\partial x} \left( e^{xy} \right) = e^{xy} + x e^{xy} y = e^{xy}(1 + xy),$$

$\partial M/\partial y = \partial N/\partial x$, and the equation is exact.

We write the equation in the form

$$\frac{dy}{dx} = -\frac{y e^{xy} + 2x}{x e^{xy} - 2y}$$

and conclude that it is not separable because the right-hand side cannot be represented as a product of two functions of single variables $x$ and $y$. Also, the right-hand side is not linear with respect to $y$ which implies that the equation is not linear with $y$ as the dependent variable. Similarly, choosing $x$ as the dependent variable (taking the reciprocals of both sides) we conclude that the equation is not linear either.

**5.** The differential equation is not separable because $(2xy + \cos y)$ cannot be factored. This equation can be put in standard form by defining $x$ as the dependent variable and $y$ as the independent variable. This gives

$$\frac{dx}{dy} + \frac{2}{y}x = \frac{-\cos y}{y^2},$$

so we see that the differential equation is linear.

If we set $M(x,y) = y^2$ and $N(x,y) = 2xy + \cos y$ we are able to see that the differential equation is also exact because $M_y(x,y) = 2y = N_x(x,y)$.

**7.** In this problem, the variables are $r$ and $\theta$, $M(r,\theta) = \theta$, and $N(r,\theta) = 3r - \theta - 1$. Because

$$\frac{\partial M}{\partial \theta} = 1 \neq 3 = \frac{\partial N}{\partial r},$$

the equation is not exact. With $r$ as the dependent variable, the equation takes the form

$$\frac{dr}{d\theta} = -\frac{3r - \theta - 1}{\theta} = -\frac{3}{\theta}r + \frac{\theta + 1}{\theta},$$

and it is linear. Since the right-hand side in the above equation cannot be factored as $p(\theta)q(r)$, the equation is not separable.

**9.** We have that $M(x,y) = 2xy + 3$ and $N(x,y) = x^2 - 1$. Therefore, $M_y(x,y) = 2x = N_x(x,y)$ and so the equation is exact. We will solve this equation by first integrating $M(x,y)$ with respect to $x$, although integration of $N(x,y)$ with respect to $y$ is equally easy. Thus

$$F(x,y) = \int (2xy + 3)\, dx = x^2 y + 3x + g(y).$$

Differentiating $F(x,y)$ with respect to $y$ gives $F_y(x,y) = x^2 + g'(y) = N(x,y) = x^2 - 1$. From this we see that $g' = -1$. (As a partial check we note that $g'(y)$ does not involve $x$.) Integrating gives

$$g(y) = \int (-1)\, dy = -y.$$

Since the constant of integration will be incorporated into the parameter of the solution, it is not written here. Substituting this expression for $g(y)$ into the expression that we found for $F(x,y)$ yields

$$F(x,y) = x^2 y + 3x - y.$$

Therefore, the solution of the differential equation is

$$x^2 y + 3x - y = C \quad \Rightarrow \quad y = \frac{C - 3x}{x^2 - 1}.$$

*The given equation could be solved by the method of grouping.* To see this, express the differential equation in the form

$$(2xy\, dx + x^2\, dy) + (3\, dx - dy) = 0.$$

The first term of the left-hand side we recognize as the total differential of $x^2 y$. The second term is the total differential of $(3x - y)$. Thus we again find that

$$F(x,y) = x^2 y + 3x - y$$

and, again, the solution is $x^2 y + 3x - y = C$.

**11.** Computing partial derivatives of $M(x,y) = \cos x \cos y + 2x$ and $N(x,y) = -(\sin x \sin y + 2y)$, we obtain

$$\frac{\partial M}{\partial y} = \frac{\partial}{\partial y}\left(\cos x \cos y + 2x\right) = -\cos x \sin y,$$
$$\frac{\partial N}{\partial x} = \frac{\partial}{\partial x}\left[-(\sin x \sin y + 2y)\right] = -\cos x \sin y,$$
$$\Rightarrow \quad \frac{\partial M}{\partial y} = \frac{\partial N}{\partial x},$$

and the equation is exact.

Chapter 2

Integrating $M(x,y)$ with respect to $x$ yields

$$F(x,y) = \int M(x,y)dx = \int (\cos x \cos y + 2x)\,dx$$

$$= \cos y \int \cos x\,dx + \int 2x\,dx = \sin x \cos y + x^2 + g(y).$$

To find $g(y)$, we compute the partial derivative of $F(x,y)$ with respect to $y$ and compare the result with $N(x,y)$.

$$\frac{\partial F}{\partial y} = \frac{\partial}{\partial y}\left[\sin x \cos y + x^2 + g(y)\right] = -\sin x \sin y + g'(y) = -(\sin x \sin y + 2y)$$

$$\Rightarrow \quad g'(y) = -2y \quad \Rightarrow \quad g(y) = \int (-2y)dy = -y^2.$$

(We take the integration constant $C = 0$.) Therefore,

$$F(x,y) = \sin x \cos y + x^2 - y^2 = c$$

is a general solution to the given equation.

13. In this equation, the variables are $y$ and $t$, $M(y,t) = t/y$, $N(y,t) = 1 + \ln y$. Since

$$\frac{\partial M}{\partial t} = \frac{\partial}{\partial t}\left(\frac{t}{y}\right) = \frac{1}{y} \quad \text{and} \quad \frac{\partial N}{\partial y} = \frac{\partial}{\partial y}(1 + \ln y) = \frac{1}{y},$$

the equation is exact.

Integrating $M(y,t)$ with respect to $y$, we get

$$F(y,t) = \int \frac{t}{y}\,dy = t \ln|y| + g(t) = t \ln y + g(t).$$

(From $N(y,t) = 1 + \ln y$ we conclude that $y > 0$.) Therefore,

$$\frac{\partial F}{\partial t} = \frac{\partial}{\partial t}[t\ln y + g(t)] = \ln y + g'(t) = 1 + \ln y$$

$$\Rightarrow \quad g'(t) = 1 \quad \Rightarrow \quad g(t) = t$$

$$\Rightarrow \quad F(y,t) = t\ln y + t,$$

and a general solution is given by $t\ln y + t = c$ (or, explicitly, $t = c/(\ln y + 1)$).

**15.** This differential equation is expressed in the variables $r$ and $\theta$. Since the variables $x$ and $y$ are dummy variables, this equation is solved in exactly the same way as an equation in $x$ and $y$. We will look for a solution with independent variable $\theta$ and dependent variable $r$. We see that the differential equation is expressed in the differential form

$$M(r,\theta)\, dr + N(r,\theta)\, d\theta = 0, \quad \text{where} \quad M(r,\theta) = \cos\theta \text{ and } N(r,\theta) = -r\sin\theta + e^{\theta}.$$

This implies that

$$M_{\theta}(r,\theta) = -\sin\theta = N_r(r,\theta),$$

and so the equation is exact. Therefore, to solve the equation we need to find a function $F(r,\theta)$ that has $\cos\theta\, dr + (-r\sin\theta + e^{\theta})\, d\theta$ as its total differential. Integrating $M(r,\theta)$ with respect to $r$ we see that

$$F(r,\theta) = \int \cos\theta\, dr = r\cos\theta + g(\theta)$$

$$\Rightarrow \quad F_{\theta}(r,\theta) = -r\sin\theta + g'(\theta) = N(r,\theta) = -r\sin\theta + e^{\theta}.$$

Thus we have that

$$g'(\theta) = e^{\theta} \quad \Rightarrow \quad g(\theta) = e^{\theta},$$

where the constant of integration will be incorporated into the parameter of the solution. Substituting this expression for $g(\theta)$ into the expression we found for $F(r,\theta)$ yields

$$F(r,\theta) = r\cos\theta + e^{\theta}.$$

From this we see that the solution is given by the one parameter family $r\cos\theta + e^{\theta} = C$, or, solving for $r$,

$$r = \frac{C - e^{\theta}}{\cos\theta} = (C - e^{\theta})\sec\theta.$$

**17.** Partial derivatives of $M(x,y) = 1/y$ and $N(x,y) = -\left(3y - x/y^2\right)$ are

$$\frac{\partial M}{\partial y} = \frac{\partial}{\partial y}\left(\frac{1}{y}\right) = -\frac{1}{y^2} \quad \text{and} \quad \frac{\partial N}{\partial x} = \frac{\partial}{\partial x}\left(-3y + \frac{x}{y^2}\right) = \frac{1}{y^2}.$$

Since $\partial M/\partial y \neq \partial N/\partial x$, the equation is not exact.

Chapter 2

**19.** Taking partial derivatives of $M(x,y) = 2x + y/(1+x^2y^2)$ and $N(x,y) = -2y + x/(1+x^2y^2)$ with respect to $y$ and $x$, respectively, we get

$$\frac{\partial M}{\partial y} = \frac{\partial}{\partial y}\left(2x + \frac{y}{1+x^2y^2}\right) = \frac{(1)(1+x^2y^2) - yx^2(2y)}{(1+x^2y^2)^2} = \frac{1-x^2y^2}{(1+x^2y^2)^2},$$

$$\frac{\partial N}{\partial x} = \frac{\partial}{\partial x}\left(-2y + \frac{x}{1+x^2y^2}\right) = \frac{(1)(1+x^2y^2) - xy^2(2x)}{(1+x^2y^2)^2} = \frac{1-x^2y^2}{(1+x^2y^2)^2}.$$

Therefore, the equation is exact.

$$F(x,y) = \int\left(2x + \frac{y}{1+x^2y^2}\right)dx = x^2 + \int\frac{d(xy)}{1+(xy)^2} = x^2 + \arctan(xy) + g(y)$$

$$\frac{\partial F}{\partial y} = \frac{\partial}{\partial y}\left[x^2 + \arctan(xy) + g(y)\right] = \frac{x}{1+(xy)^2} + g'(y) = -2y + \frac{x}{1+x^2y^2}$$

$$\Rightarrow \quad g'(y) = -2y \quad \Rightarrow \quad g(y) = -y^2$$

$$\Rightarrow \quad F(x,y) = x^2 - y^2 + \arctan(xy)$$

and a general solution then is given implicitly by $x^2 - y^2 + \arctan(xy) = c$.

**21.** We check the equation for exactness. We have $M(x,y) = 1/x + 2y^2x$, $N(x,y) = 2yx^2 - \cos y$,

$$\frac{\partial M}{\partial y} = \frac{\partial}{\partial y}\left(\frac{1}{x} + 2y^2x\right) = 4yx,$$

$$\frac{\partial N}{\partial x} = \frac{\partial}{\partial x}\left(2yx^2 - \cos y\right) = 4yx.$$

Thus $\partial M/\partial y = \partial N/\partial x$. Integrating $M(x,y)$ with respect to $x$ yields

$$F(x,y) = \int\left(\frac{1}{x} + 2y^2x\right)dx = \ln|x| + x^2y^2 + g(y).$$

Therefore,

$$\frac{\partial F}{\partial y} = \frac{\partial}{\partial y}\left[\ln|x| + x^2y^2 + g(y)\right] = 2x^2y + g'(y) = N(x,y) = 2yx^2 - \cos y$$

$$\Rightarrow \quad g'(y) = -\cos y \quad \Rightarrow \quad g(y) = \int(-\cos y)dy = -\sin y$$

$$\Rightarrow \quad F(x,y) = \ln|x| + x^2y^2 - \sin y,$$

and a general solution to the given differential equation is

$$\ln|x| + x^2y^2 - \sin y = c.$$

Substituting the initial condition, $y = \pi$ when $x = 1$, we find $c$.

$$\ln|1| + 1^2\pi^2 - \sin\pi = c \quad \Rightarrow \quad c = \pi^2.$$

Therefore, the answer is given implicitly by $\ln|x| + x^2y^2 - \sin y = \pi^2$. (We also used the fact that at the initial point, $(1, \pi)$, $x > 0$ to skip the absolute value sign in the logarithmic term.)

**23.** Here $M(t, y) = e^t y + te^t y$ and $N(t, y) = te^t + 2$. Thus $M_y(t, y) = e^t + te^t = N_t(t, y)$ and so the equation is exact. To find $F(t, y)$ we first integrate $N(t, y)$ with respect to $y$ to obtain

$$F(t, y) = \int (te^t + 2)\, dy = (te^t + 2)y + h(t),$$

where we have chosen to integrate $N(t, y)$ because this integration is more easily accomplished. Thus

$$F_t(t, y) = e^t y + te^t y + h'(t) = M(t, y) = e^t y + te^t y$$
$$\Rightarrow \quad h'(t) = 0 \quad \Rightarrow \quad h(t) = C.$$

We will incorporate this constant into the parameter of the solution. Combining these results gives $F(t, y) = te^t y + 2y$. Therefore, the solution is given by $te^t y + 2y = C$. Solving for $y$ yields $y = C/(te^t + 2)$. Now we use the initial condition $y(0) = -1$ to find the solution that passes through the point $(0, -1)$. Thus

$$y(0) = \frac{C}{0 + 2} = -1 \quad \Rightarrow \quad \frac{C}{2} = -1 \quad \Rightarrow \quad C = -2.$$

This gives us the solution

$$y = -\frac{2}{te^t + 2}.$$

**25.** One can check that the equation is not exact $(\partial M/\partial y \neq \partial N/\partial x)$, but it is separable because it can be written in the form

$$y^2 \sin x\, dx + \frac{1 - y}{x}\, dy = 0 \quad \Rightarrow \quad y^2 \sin x\, dx = \frac{y - 1}{x}\, dy$$
$$\Rightarrow \quad x \sin x\, dx = \frac{y - 1}{y^2}\, dy.$$

Integrating both sides yields

$$\int x \sin x \, dx = \int \frac{y-1}{y^2} \, dy \qquad \Rightarrow \qquad x(-\cos x) - \int (-\cos x) dx = \int \left( \frac{1}{y} - \frac{1}{y^2} \right) dy$$

$$\Rightarrow \qquad -x \cos x + \sin x = \ln|y| + \frac{1}{y} + C,$$

where we applied integration by parts to find $\int x \sin x \, dx$. Substitution of the initial condition, $y(\pi) = 1$, results

$$-\pi \cos \pi + \sin \pi = \ln|1| + \frac{1}{1} + C \qquad \Rightarrow \qquad C = \pi - 1.$$

So, the solution to the initial value problem is

$$-x \cos x + \sin x = \ln y + 1/y + \pi - 1.$$

(Since $y(\pi) = 1 > 0$, we have removed the absolute value sign in the logarithmic term.)

**27. (a)** We want to find $M(x, y)$ so that for $N(x, y) = \sec^2 y - x/y$ we have

$$M_y(x, y) = N_x(x, y) = -\frac{1}{y}.$$

Therefore, we must integrate this last expression with respect to $y$. That is,

$$M(x, y) = \int \left( -\frac{1}{y} \right) dy = -\ln|y| + f(x),$$

where $f(x)$, the "constant" of integration, is a function only of $x$.

**(b)** We want to find $M(x, y)$ so that for

$$N(x, y) = \sin x \cos y - xy - e^{-y}$$

we have

$$M_y(x, y) = N_x(x, y) = \cos x \cos y - y.$$

Therefore, we must integrate this last expression with respect to $y$. That is

$$M(x, y) = \int (\cos x \cos y - y) \, dy = \cos x \int \cos y \, dy - \int y \, dy$$

$$= \cos x \sin y - \frac{y^2}{2} + f(x),$$

where $f(x)$, a function only of $x$, is the "constant" of integration.

**29. (a)** We have $M(x,y) = y^2 + 2xy$ and $N(x,y) = -x^2$. Therefore $M_y(x,y) = 2y + 2x$ and $N_x(x,y) = -2x$. Thus $M_y(x,y) \neq N_x(x,y)$, so the differential equation is not exact.

**(b)** If we multiply $(y^2 + 2xy)dx - x^2 dy = 0$ by $y^{-2}$, we obtain

$$\left(1 + \frac{2x}{y}\right) dx - \frac{x^2}{y^2} dy = 0.$$

In this equation we have $M(x,y) = 1 + 2xy^{-1}$ and $N(x,y) = -x^2 y^{-2}$. Therefore,

$$\frac{\partial M(x,y)}{\partial y} = -\frac{2x}{y^2} = \frac{\partial N(x,y)}{\partial x}.$$

So the new differential equation is exact.

**(c)** Following the method for solving exact equations we integrate $M(x,y)$ in part (b) with respect to $x$ to obtain

$$F(x,y) = \int \left(1 + 2\frac{x}{y}\right) dx = x + \frac{x^2}{y} + g(y).$$

To determine $g(y)$, take the partial derivative of both sides of the above equation with respect to $y$ to obtain

$$\frac{\partial F}{\partial y} = -\frac{x^2}{y^2} + g'(y).$$

Substituting $N(x,y)$ (given in part (b)) for $\partial F/\partial y$, we can now solve for $g'(y)$ to obtain

$$N(x,y) = -\frac{x^2}{y^2} = -\frac{x^2}{y^2} + g'(y) \quad \Rightarrow \quad g'(y) = 0.$$

The integral of $g'(y)$ will yield a constant and the choice of the constant of integration is not important so we can take $g(y) = 0$. Hence we have $F(x,y) = x + x^2/y$ and the solution to the equation is given implicitly by

$$x + \frac{x^2}{y} = C.$$

Solving the above equation for $y$, we obtain

$$y = \frac{x^2}{C - x}.$$

# Chapter 2

**(d)** By dividing both sides by $y^2$ we lost the solution $y \equiv 0$.

**31.** Following the proof of Theorem 2, we come to the expression (10) on page 63 of the text for $g'(y)$, that is

$$g'(y) = N(x,y) - \frac{\partial}{\partial y} \int_{x_0}^{x} M(s,y)\, ds \qquad (2.15)$$

(where we have replaced the integration variable $t$ by $s$). In other words, $g(y)$ is an antiderivative of the right-hand side in (2.15). Since an antiderivative is defined up to an additive constant and, in Theorem 2, such a constant can be chosen arbitrarily (that is, $g(y)$ can be *any* antiderivative), we choose $g(y)$ that vanishes at $y_0$. According to fundamental theorem of calculus, this function can be written in the form

$$g(y) = \int_{y_0}^{y} g'(t)\, dt = \int_{y_0}^{y} \left[ N(x,t) - \frac{\partial}{\partial t} \int_{x_0}^{x} M(s,t)\, ds \right] dt$$

$$= \int_{y_0}^{y} N(x,t)\, dt - \int_{y_0}^{y} \frac{\partial}{\partial t} \left[ \int_{x_0}^{x} M(s,t)\, ds \right] dt$$

$$= \int_{y_0}^{y} N(x,t)\, dt - \left[ \int_{x_0}^{x} M(s,t)\, ds \right] \Bigg|_{t=y_0}^{t=y}$$

$$= \int_{y_0}^{y} N(x,t)\, dt - \int_{x_0}^{x} M(s,y)\, ds + \int_{x_0}^{x} M(s,y_0)\, ds \,.$$

Substituting this function into the formula (9) on page 63 of the text, we conclude that

$$F(x,y) = \int_{x_0}^{x} M(t,y)\, dt + \left[ \int_{y_0}^{y} N(x,t)\, dt - \int_{x_0}^{x} M(s,y)\, ds + \int_{x_0}^{x} M(s,y_0)\, ds \right]$$

$$= \int_{y_0}^{y} N(x,t)\, dt + \int_{x_0}^{x} M(s,y_0)\, ds \,.$$

**(a)** In the differential form used in Example 1, $M(x,y) = 2xy^2 + 1$ and $N(x,y) = 2x^2 y$.

Thus, $N(x,t) = 2x^2t$ and $M(s, y_0) = 2s \cdot 0^2 + 1 = 1$, and (18) yields

$$F(x,y) = \int_0^y (2x^2t)\, dt + \int_0^x 1 \cdot ds = x^2 \int_0^y 2t\, dt + \int_0^x ds$$

$$= x^2 t^2 \Big|_{t=0}^{t=y} + s \Big|_{s=0}^{s=x} = x^2 y^2 + x.$$

**(b)** Since $M(x,y) = 2xy - \sec^2 x$ and $N(x,y) = x^2 + 2y$, we have

$$N(x,t) = x^2 + 2t \quad \text{and} \quad M(s, y_0) = 2s \cdot 0 - \sec^2 s = -\sec^2 s,$$

$$F(x,y) = \int_0^y (x^2 + 2t)\, dt + \int_0^x (-\sec^2 s)\, ds$$

$$= (x^2 t + t^2) \Big|_{t=0}^{t=y} - \tan s \Big|_{s=0}^{s=x} = x^2 y + y^2 - \tan x.$$

**(c)** Here, $M(x,y) = 1 + e^x y + x e^x y$ and $N(x,y) = x e^x + 2$. Therefore,

$$N(x,t) = x e^x + 2 \quad \text{and} \quad M(s, y_0) = 1 + e^s \cdot 0 + s e^s \cdot 0 = 1,$$

$$F(x,y) = \int_0^y (x e^x + 2)\, dt + \int_0^x 1 \cdot ds$$

$$= (x e^x + 2) t \Big|_{t=0}^{t=y} + s \Big|_{s=0}^{s=x} = (x e^x + 2) y + x,$$

which is identical to $F(x,y)$ obtained in Example 3.

**32. (a)** The slope of the orthogonal curves, say $m_\perp$, must be $-1/m$, where $m$ is the slope of the original curves. Therefore, we have

$$m_\perp = \frac{F_y(x,y)}{F_x(x,y)} \quad \Rightarrow \quad \frac{dy}{dx} = \frac{F_y(x,y)}{F_x(x,y)} \quad \Rightarrow \quad F_y(x,y)\, dx - F_x(x,y)\, dy = 0.$$

**(b)** Let $F(x,y) = x^2 + y^2$. Then we have $F_x(x,y) = 2x$ and $F_y(x,y) = 2y$. Plugging these expressions into the final result of part (a) gives

$$2y\, dx - 2x\, dy = 0 \quad \Rightarrow \quad y\, dx - x\, dy = 0.$$

Chapter 2

To find the orthogonal trajectories, we must solve this differential equation. To this end, note that this equation is separable and thus

$$\int \frac{1}{x}\, dx = \int \frac{1}{y}\, dy \qquad \Rightarrow \qquad \ln|x| = \ln|y| + C$$
$$\Rightarrow \qquad e^{\ln|x|-C} = e^{\ln|y|} \qquad \Rightarrow \qquad y = kx, \quad \text{where } k = \pm e^{-C}.$$

Therefore, the orthogonal trajectories are lines through the origin.

(c) Let $F(x,y) = xy$. Then we have $F_x(x,y) = y$ and $F_y(x,y) = x$. Plugging these expressions into the final result of part (a) gives

$$x\, dx - y\, dy = 0.$$

To find the orthogonal trajectories, we must solve this differential equation. To this end, note that this equation is separable and thus

$$\int x\, dx = \int y\, dy \qquad \Rightarrow \qquad \frac{x^2}{2} = \frac{y^2}{2} + C \qquad \Rightarrow \qquad x^2 - y^2 = k,$$

where $k := 2C$. Therefore, the orthogonal trajectories are hyperbolas.

33. We use notations and results of Problem 32, that is, for a family of curves given by $F(x,y) = k$, the orthogonal trajectories satisfy the differential equation

$$\frac{\partial F(x,y)}{\partial y}\, dx - \frac{\partial F(x,y)}{\partial x}\, dy = 0. \tag{2.16}$$

(a) In this problem, $F(x,y) = 2x^2 + y^2$ and the equation (2.16) becomes

$$\frac{\partial(2x^2 + y^2)}{\partial y}\, dx - \frac{\partial(2x^2 + y^2)}{\partial x}\, dy = 0 \qquad \Rightarrow \qquad 2y\, dx - 4x\, dy = 0. \tag{2.17}$$

Separating variables and integrating yield

$$2y\, dx = 4x\, dy \qquad \Rightarrow \qquad \frac{dx}{x} = \frac{2dy}{y} \qquad \Rightarrow \qquad \int \frac{dx}{x} = \int \frac{2dy}{y}$$
$$\Rightarrow \qquad \ln|x| = 2\ln|y| + c_1 \qquad \Rightarrow \qquad e^{\ln|x|} = e^{2\ln|y|+c_1}$$
$$\Rightarrow \qquad |x| = e^{c_1}|y|^2 = c_2 y^2 \qquad \Rightarrow \qquad x = \pm c_2 y^2 = c y^2,$$

where $c$ as any nonzero constant.

Separating variables, we divided the equation (2.17) by $xy$. As a result, we lost two constant solutions $x \equiv 0$ and $y \equiv 0$ (see the discussion on pages 44–45 of Section 2.2 of the text). Thus the orthogonal trajectories for the family $2x^2 + y^2 = k$ are $x = cy^2$, $c \neq 0$, $x \equiv 0$, and $y \equiv 0$. (Note that $x \equiv 0$ can be obtained from $x = cy^2$ by taking $c = 0$ while $y \equiv 0$ cannot.)

**(b)** First we rewrite the equation defining the family of curves in the form $F(x, y) = k$ by dividing it by $x^4$. This yields $yx^{-4} = k$. We use (2.17) to set up an equation for the orthogonal trajectories:

$$\frac{\partial F}{\partial x} = -4yx^{-5}, \qquad \frac{\partial F}{\partial y} = x^{-4} \qquad \Rightarrow \qquad x^{-4}\,dx - \left(-4yx^{-5}\right) dy = 0.$$

Solving this separable equation yields

$$x^{-4}\,dx = -4yx^{-5}\,dy = 0 \qquad \Rightarrow \qquad x\,dx = -4y\,dy$$

$$\Rightarrow \qquad \int x\,dx = \int (-4y)\,dy \qquad \Rightarrow \qquad \frac{x^2}{2} = -2y^2 + c_1 \qquad \Rightarrow \qquad x^2 + 4y^2 = c.$$

Thus, the family of orthogonal trajectories is $x^2 + 4y^2 = c$.

**(c)** Taking logarithm of both sides of the equation, we obtain

$$\ln y = kx \qquad \Rightarrow \qquad \frac{\ln y}{x} = k,$$

and so $F(x, y) = (\ln y)/x$, $\partial F/\partial x = -(\ln y)/x^2$, $\partial F/\partial y = 1/(xy)$. The equation (2.17) becomes

$$\frac{1}{xy}\,dx - \left(-\frac{\ln y}{x^2}\right) dy = 0 \qquad \Rightarrow \qquad \frac{1}{xy}\,dx = -\frac{\ln y}{x^2}\,dy.$$

Separating variables and integrating, we obtain

$$x\,dx = -y \ln y\,dy \qquad \Rightarrow \qquad \int x\,dx = -\int y \ln y\,dy$$

$$\Rightarrow \qquad \frac{x^2}{2} = -\frac{y^2}{2}\ln y + \int \frac{y^2}{2}\cdot\frac{1}{y}\,dy = -\frac{y^2}{2}\ln y + \frac{y^2}{4} + c_1$$

$$\Rightarrow \qquad \frac{x^2}{2} + \frac{y^2}{2}\ln y - \frac{y^2}{4} = c_1 \qquad \Rightarrow \qquad 2x^2 + 2y^2 \ln y - y^2 = c,$$

where $c := 4c_1$, and we have used integration by parts to find $\int y \ln y\,dy$.

**(d)** We divide the equation, $y^2 = kx$, by $x$ and get $y^2/x = k$. Thus, $F(x,y) = y^2/x$ and

$$\frac{\partial F}{\partial x} = -\frac{y^2}{x^2}, \qquad \frac{\partial F}{\partial y} = \frac{2y}{x}$$

$$\Rightarrow \qquad \frac{2y}{x}\,dx - \left(-\frac{y^2}{x^2}\right)dy = 0 \qquad \Rightarrow \qquad \frac{2y}{x}\,dx = \left(-\frac{y^2}{x^2}\right)dy$$

$$\Rightarrow \qquad 2x\,dx = -y\,dy \qquad \Rightarrow \qquad x^2 = -\frac{y^2}{2} + c_1 \qquad \Rightarrow \qquad 2x^2 + y^2 = c.$$

**35.** Applying Leibniz's theorem, we switch the order of differentiation (with respect to $y$) and integration. This yields

$$g' = N(x,y) - \int\limits_{x_0}^{x} \left(\frac{\partial}{\partial y} M(t,y)\right) dt.$$

Therefore, $g'$ is differentiable (even continuously) with respect to $x$ as a difference of two (continuously) differentiable functions, $N(x,y)$ and an integral with variable upper bound of a continuous function $M_y'(t,y)$. Taking partial derivatives of both sides with respect to $x$ and using fundamental theorem of calculus, we obtain

$$\frac{\partial(g')}{\partial x} = \frac{\partial}{\partial x}\left[N(x,y) - \int\limits_{x_0}^{x}\left(\frac{\partial}{\partial y}M(t,y)\right)dt\right]$$

$$= \frac{\partial}{\partial x}N(x,y) - \frac{\partial}{\partial x}\left[\int\limits_{x_0}^{x}\left(\frac{\partial}{\partial y}M(t,y)\right)dt\right] = \frac{\partial}{\partial x}N(x,y) - \frac{\partial}{\partial y}M(x,y) = 0$$

due to (5). Thus $\partial(g')/\partial x \equiv 0$ which implies that $g'$ does not depend on $x$ (a consequence of mean value theorem).

## EXERCISES 2.5: Special Integrating Factors, page 71

**1.** Here $M(x,y) = 2y^3 + 2y^2$ and $N(x,y) = 3y^2x + 2xy$. Computing

$$\frac{\partial M}{\partial y} = 6y^2 + 4y \qquad \text{and} \qquad \frac{\partial N}{\partial x} = 3y^2 + 2y,$$

we conclude that this equation is not exact. Note that these functions, as well as $M$ itself, depend on $y$ only. Then, clearly, so does the expression $(\partial N/\partial x - \partial M/\partial y)/M$, and the equation has an integrating factor depending on $y$ alone. Also, since

$$\frac{\partial M/\partial y - \partial N/\partial x}{N} = \frac{(6y^2 + 4y) - (3y^2 + 2y)}{3y^2x + 2xy} = \frac{3y^2 + 2y}{x(3y^2 + 2y)} = \frac{1}{x},$$

the equation has an integrating factor depending on $x$.

Writing the equation in the form

$$\frac{dx}{dy} = -\frac{3y^2x + 2xy}{2y^3 + y^2} = -\frac{xy(3y+2)}{2y^2(y+1)} = -\frac{y(3y+2)}{2y^2(y+1)} x$$

we conclude that it is separable and linear with $x$ as the dependent variable.

**3.** This equation is not separable because of the factor $(y^2 + 2xy)$. It is not linear because of the factor $y^2$. To see if it is exact, we compute $M_y(x, y)$ and $N_x(x, y)$, and see that

$$M_y(x, y)2y + 2x \neq -2x = N_x(x, y).$$

Therefore, the equation is not exact. To see if we can find an integrating factor of the form $\mu(x)$, we compute

$$\frac{\dfrac{\partial M}{\partial y} - \dfrac{\partial N}{\partial x}}{N} = \frac{2y + 4x}{-x^2},$$

which is not a function of $x$ alone. To see if we can find an integrating factor of the form $\mu(y)$, we compute

$$\frac{\dfrac{\partial N}{\partial x} - \dfrac{\partial M}{\partial y}}{M} = \frac{-4x - 2y}{y^2 + 2xy} = \frac{-2(2x + y)}{y(y + 2x)} = \frac{-2}{y}.$$

Thus the equation has an integrating factor that is a function of $y$ alone.

**5.** In this problem, $M(x, y) = 2y^2x - y$ and $N(x, y) = x$. Therefore,

$$\frac{\partial M}{\partial y} = 4yx - 1 \quad \text{and} \quad \frac{\partial N}{\partial x} = 1 \quad \Rightarrow \quad \frac{\partial N}{\partial x} - \frac{\partial M}{\partial y} = 2 - 4yx.$$

The equation is not exact, because $\partial M/\partial y \neq \partial N/\partial x$, but it has an integrating factor depending just on $y$ since

$$\frac{\partial N/\partial x - \partial M/\partial y}{M} = \frac{2 - 4yx}{2y^2x - y} = \frac{-2(2yx - 1)}{y(2yx - 1)} = \frac{-2}{y}.$$

Isolating $dy/dx$, we obtain

$$\frac{dy}{dx} = \frac{y - 2y^2 x}{x} = \frac{y}{x} - 2y^2 .$$

The right-hand side cannot be factorized as $p(x)q(y)$, and so the equation is not separable. Also, it is not linear with $y$ as the dependent variable (because of $2y^2$ term). By taking the reciprocals we also conclude that it is not linear with the dependent variable $x$.

**7.** The equation $(3x^2 + y)\,dx + (x^2 y - x)\,dy = 0$ is not separable or linear. To see if it is exact, we compute

$$\frac{\partial M}{\partial y} = 1 \neq 2xy - 1 = \frac{\partial N}{\partial x} .$$

Thus, the equation is not exact. To see if we can find an integrating factor, we compute

$$\frac{\partial M/\partial y - \partial N/\partial x}{N} = \frac{2 - 2xy}{x^2 y - x} = \frac{-2(xy - 1)}{x(xy - 1)} = \frac{-2}{x} .$$

From this we see that the integrating factor will be

$$\mu(x) = \exp\left(\int \frac{-2}{x}\,dx\right) = \exp\left(-2\ln|x|\right) = x^{-2}.$$

To solve the equation, we multiply it by the integrating factor $x^{-2}$ to obtain

$$\left(3 + yx^{-2}\right)dx + \left(y - x^{-1}\right)dy = 0.$$

This is now exact. Thus, we want to find $F(x, y)$. To do this, we integrate $M(x, y) = 3 + yx^{-2}$ with respect to $x$ to get

$$F(x, y) = \int \left(3 + yx^{-2}\right)dx = 3x - yx^{-1} + g(y)$$

$$\Rightarrow \qquad F_y(x, y) = -x^{-1} + g'(y) = N(x, y) = y - x^{-1}$$

$$\Rightarrow \qquad g'(y) = y \qquad \Rightarrow \qquad g(y) = \frac{y^2}{2} .$$

Therefore,

$$F(x, y) = 3x - yx^{-1} + \frac{y^2}{2} .$$

And so we see that an implicit solution is

$$\frac{y^2}{2} - \frac{y}{x} + 3x = C.$$

Since $\mu(x) = x^{-2}$ we must check to see if the solution $x \equiv 0$ was either gained or lost. The function $x \equiv 0$ is a solution to the original equation, but is not given by the above implicit solution for any choice of $C$. Hence,

$$\frac{y^2}{2} - \frac{y}{x} + 3x = C \qquad \text{and} \qquad x \equiv 0$$

are solutions.

**9.** We compute partial derivatives of $M(x, y) = 2y^2 + 2y + 4x^2$ and $N(x, y) = 2xy + x$.

$$\frac{\partial M}{\partial y} = \frac{\partial}{\partial y}\left(2y^2 + 2y + 4x^2\right) = 4y + 2, \qquad \frac{\partial N}{\partial x} = \frac{\partial}{\partial x}\left(2xy + x\right) = 2y + 1.$$

Although the equation is not exact $(\partial M/\partial y \neq \partial N/\partial x)$, the quotient

$$\frac{\partial M/\partial y - \partial N/\partial x}{N} = \frac{(4y + 2) - (2y + 1)}{2xy + x} = \frac{2y + 1}{x(2y + 1)} = \frac{1}{x}$$

depends on $x$ only, and so the equation has an integrating factor, which can be found by applying formula (8) on page 70 of the text. Namely,

$$\mu(x) = \exp\left(\int \frac{1}{x}\,dx\right) = \exp\left(\ln|x|\right) = |x|.$$

Note that if $\mu$ is an integrating factor, then $-\mu$ is an integrating factor as well. This observation allows us to take $\mu(x) = x$. Multiplying given differential equation by $x$ yields an exact equation

$$\left(2y^2 + 2y + 4x^2\right)x\,dx + x^2\left(2y + 1\right)dy = 0.$$

Therefore,

$$F(x, y) = \int x^2(2y + 1)\,dy = x^2\left(y^2 + y\right) + h(x)$$

$$\Rightarrow \quad \frac{\partial F}{\partial x} = 2x\left(y^2 + y\right) + h'(x) = \left(2y^2 + 2y + 4x^2\right)x$$

$$\Rightarrow \quad h'(x) = 4x^3 \quad \Rightarrow \quad h(x) = \int 4x^3\,dx = x^4$$

$$\Rightarrow \quad F(x, y) = x^2\left(y^2 + y\right) + x^4 = x^2y^2 + x^2y + x^4,$$

and $x^2y^2 + x^2y + x^4 = c$ is a general solution.

# Chapter 2

**11.** In this differential equation, $M(x, y) = y^2 + 2xy$, $N(x, y) = -x^2$. Therefore,

$$\frac{\partial M}{\partial y} = 2y + 2x, \qquad \frac{\partial N}{\partial x} = -2x,$$

and so $(\partial N/\partial x - \partial M/\partial y)/M = (-4x - 2y)/(y^2 + 2xy) = -2/y$ is a function of $y$. Then

$$\mu(y) = \exp\left[\int \left(-\frac{2}{y}\right) dy\right] = \exp\left(-2\ln|y|\right) = y^{-2}.$$

Multiplying the differential equation by $\mu(y)$ and solving the obtained exact equation, we get

$$y^{-2}\left(y^2 + 2xy\right) dx - y^{-2}x^2 dy = 0$$

$$\Rightarrow \qquad F(x, y) = \int \left(-y^{-2}x^2\right) dy = y^{-1}x^2 + h(x)$$

$$\Rightarrow \qquad \frac{\partial F}{\partial x} = \frac{\partial}{\partial x}\left[y^{-1}x^2 + h(x)\right] = 2y^{-1}x + h'(x) = y^{-2}\left(y^2 + 2xy\right) = 1 + 2xy^{-1}$$

$$\Rightarrow \qquad h'(x) = 1 \qquad \Rightarrow \qquad h(x) = x \qquad \Rightarrow \qquad F(x, y) = y^{-1}x^2 + x.$$

Since we multiplied given equation by $\mu(y) = y^{-2}$ (in fact, divided by $y^2$) to get an exact equation, we could lose the solution $y \equiv 0$, and this, indeed, happened: $y \equiv 0$ is, clearly, a solution to the original equation. Thus a general solution is

$$y^{-1}x^2 + x = c \qquad \text{and} \qquad y \equiv 0.$$

**13.** We will multiply the equation by the factor $x^n y^m$ and try to make it exact. Thus, we have

$$\left(2x^n y^{m+2} - 6x^{n+1}y^{m+1}\right) dx + \left(3x^{n+1}y^{m+1} - 4x^{n+2}y^m\right) dy = 0.$$

We want $M_y(x, y) = N_x(x, y)$. Since

$$M_y(x, y) = 2(m + 2)x^n y^{m+1} - 6(m + 1)x^{n+1}y^m,$$

$$N_x(x, y) = 3(n + 1)x^n y^{m+1} - 4(n + 2)x^{n+1}y^m,$$

we need

$$2(m + 2) = 3(n + 1) \qquad \text{and} \qquad 6(m + 1) = 4(n + 2).$$

Solving these equations simultaneously, we obtain $n = 1$ and $m = 1$. So,

$$\mu(x, y) = xy.$$

With these choices for $n$ and $m$ we obtain the exact equation

$$(2xy^3 - 6x^2y^2)\, dx + (3x^2y^2 - 4x^3y)\, dy = 0.$$

Solving this equation, we have

$$F(x, y) = \int (2xy^3 - 6x^2y^2)\, dx = x^2y^3 - 2x^3y^2 + g(y)$$
$$\Rightarrow \quad F_y(x, y) = 3x^2y^2 - 4x^3y + g'(y) = N(x, y) = 3x^2y^2 - 4x^3y.$$

Therefore, $g'(y) = 0$. Since the constant of integration can be incorporated into the constant $C$ of the solution, we can pick $g(y) \equiv 0$. Thus, we have

$$F(x, y) = x^2y^3 - 2x^3y^2$$

and the solution becomes

$$x^2y^3 - 2x^3y^2 = C.$$

Since we have multiplied the original equation by $xy$ we could have added the extraneous solutions $y \equiv 0$ or $x \equiv 0$. But, since $y \equiv 0$ implies that $dy/dx \equiv 0$ or $x \equiv 0$ implies that $dx/dy \equiv 0$, $y \equiv 0$ and $x \equiv 0$ are solutions of the original equation as well as the transformed equation.

**15.** Assume that, for a differential equation

$$M(x, y)dx + N(x, y)dy = 0, \tag{2.18}$$

the expression

$$\frac{\partial N/\partial x - \partial M/\partial y}{xM - yN} = H(xy) \tag{2.19}$$

is a function of $xy$ only. Denoting

$$\mu(z) = \exp\left(\int H(z)dz\right)$$

and multiplying (2.18) by $\mu(xy)$, we get a differential equation

$$\mu(xy)M(x,y)dx + \mu(xy)N(x,y)dy = 0. \tag{2.20}$$

Let us check it for exactness. First we note that

$$\mu'(z) = \left[\exp\left(\int H(z)dz\right)\right]' = \exp\left(\int H(z)dz\right)\left[\int H(z)dz\right]' = \mu(z)H(z).$$

Next, using this fact, we compute partial derivatives of the coefficients in (2.20).

$$\frac{\partial}{\partial y}\{\mu(xy)M(x,y)\} = \mu'(xy)\frac{\partial(xy)}{\partial y}M(x,y) + \mu(xy)\frac{\partial M(x,y)}{\partial y}$$

$$= \mu(xy)H(xy)\,xM(x,y) + \mu(xy)\frac{\partial M(x,y)}{\partial y}$$

$$= \mu(xy)\left[H(xy)\,xM(x,y) + \frac{\partial M(x,y)}{\partial y}\right],$$

$$\frac{\partial}{\partial x}\{\mu(xy)N(x,y)\} = \mu'(xy)\frac{\partial(xy)}{\partial x}N(x,y) + \mu(xy)\frac{\partial N(x,y)}{\partial x}$$

$$= \mu(xy)H(xy)\,yN(x,y) + \mu(xy)\frac{\partial N(x,y)}{\partial x}$$

$$= \mu(xy)\left[H(xy)\,yN(x,y) + \frac{\partial N(x,y)}{\partial x}\right].$$

But (2.19) implies that

$$\frac{\partial N}{\partial x} - \frac{\partial M}{\partial y} = (xM - yN)H(xy) \quad \Leftrightarrow \quad yNH(xy) + \frac{\partial N}{\partial x} = xMH(xy) + \frac{\partial M}{\partial y},$$

and, therefore,

$$\frac{\partial[\mu(xy)M(x,y)]}{\partial y} = \frac{\partial[\mu(xy)N(x,y)]}{\partial x}.$$

This means that the equation (2.20) is exact.

17. (a) Expressing the family $y = x - 1 + ke^{-x}$ in the form $(y - x + 1)e^x = k$, we have (with notation of Problem 32) $F(x,y) = (y - x + 1)e^x$. We compute

$$\frac{\partial F}{\partial x} = \frac{\partial}{\partial x}\left[(y - x + 1)e^x\right] = \frac{\partial(y - x + 1)}{\partial x}e^x + (y - x + 1)\frac{d(e^x)}{dx}$$

$$= -e^x + (y - x + 1)e^x = (y - x)e^x,$$

$$\frac{\partial F}{\partial y} = \frac{\partial}{\partial y} \left[ (y - x + 1)e^x \right] = \frac{\partial(y - x + 1)}{\partial y} e^x = e^x.$$

Now we can use the result of Problem 32 to derive an equation for the orthogonal trajectories (i.e., velocity potentials) of the given family of curves:

$$\frac{\partial F}{\partial y} dx - \frac{\partial F}{\partial x} dy = 0 \quad \Rightarrow \quad e^x dx - (y - x)e^x dy = 0 \quad \Rightarrow \quad dx + (x - y)dy = 0.$$

**(b)** In the differential equation $dx + (x - y)dy = 0$, $M = 1$ and $N = x - y$. Therefore,

$$\frac{\partial N/\partial x - \partial M/\partial y}{M} = \frac{\partial(x - y)/\partial x - \partial(1)/\partial y}{(1)} = 1,$$

and an integrating factor $\mu(y)$ is given by $\mu(y) = \exp\left[\int(1)dy\right] = e^y$. Multiplying the equation from part (a) by $\mu(y)$ yields an exact equation, and we look for its solutions of the form $G(x, y) = c$.

$$e^y dx + (x - y)e^y dy = 0$$
$$\Rightarrow \quad G(x, y) = \int e^y dx = xe^y + g(y)$$
$$\Rightarrow \quad \frac{\partial G}{\partial y} = xe^y + g'(y) = (x - y)e^y \quad \Rightarrow \quad g'(y) = -ye^y$$
$$\Rightarrow \quad g(y) = \int(-ye^y)dy = -\left(ye^y - \int e^y dy\right) = -ye^y + e^y.$$

Thus, the velocity potentials are given by

$$G(x, y) = xe^y - ye^y + e^y = c \quad \text{or} \quad x = y - 1 + ce^{-y}.$$

## EXERCISES 2.6:    Substitutions and Transformations, page 78

**1.** We can write the equation in the form

$$\frac{dy}{dx} = (y - 4x - 1)^2 = [(y - 4x) - 1]^2 = G(y - 4x),$$

where $G(t) = (t - 1)^2$. Thus, it is of the form $dy/dx = G(ax + by)$.

**3.** In this equation, the variables are $x$ and $t$. Its coefficients, $t + x + 2$ and $3t - x - 6$, are linear functions of $x$ and $t$. Therefore, given equation is an equation with linear coefficients.

# Chapter 2

**5.** The given differential equation is not homogeneous due to the $e^{-2x}$ terms. The equation $(ye^{-2x} + y^3) \, dx - e^{-2x} dy = 0$ is a Bernoulli equation because it can be written in the form $dy/dx + P(x)y = Q(x)y^n$ as follows:

$$\frac{dy}{dx} - y = e^{2x}y^3.$$

The differential equation does not have linear coefficients nor is it of the form $y' = G(ax + by)$.

**7.** Here, the variables are $y$ and $\theta$. Writing

$$\frac{dy}{d\theta} = -\frac{y^3 - \theta y^2}{2\theta^2 y} = -\frac{(y/\theta)^3 - (y/\theta)^2}{2(y/\theta)},$$

we see that the right-hand side is a function of $y/\theta$ alone. Hence, the equation is homogeneous.

**9.** First, we write the equation in the form

$$\frac{dy}{dx} = \frac{-3x^2 + y^2}{xy - x^3 y^{-1}} = \frac{y^3 - 3x^2 y}{xy^2 - x^3} = \frac{(y/x)^3 - 3(y/x)}{(y/x)^2 - 1}.$$

Therefore, it is homogeneous, and we we make a substitution $y/x = u$ or $y = xu$. Then $y' = u + xu'$, and the equation becomes

$$u + x\frac{du}{dx} = \frac{u^3 - 3u}{u^2 - 1}.$$

Separating variables and integrating yield

$$\frac{du}{dx} = \frac{u^3 - 3u}{u^2 - 1} - u = -\frac{2u}{u^2 - 1} \quad \Rightarrow \quad \frac{u^2 - 1}{u} \, du = -\frac{2}{x} \, dx$$

$$\Rightarrow \quad \int \frac{u^2 - 1}{u} \, du = -\int \frac{2}{x} \, dx \quad \Rightarrow \quad \int \left( u - \frac{1}{u} \right) du = -2 \int \frac{dx}{x}$$

$$\Rightarrow \quad \frac{1}{2} u^2 - \ln|u| = -2\ln|x| + C_1 \quad \Rightarrow \quad u^2 - \ln\left(u^2\right) + \ln(x^4) = C.$$

Substituting back $y/x$ for $u$ and simplifying, we finally get

$$\left(\frac{y}{x}\right)^2 - \ln\left(\frac{y^2}{x^2}\right) + \ln(x^4) = C \quad \Rightarrow \quad \frac{y^2}{x^2} + \ln\left(\frac{x^6}{y^2}\right) = C,$$

which can also be written as

$$\ln\left(\frac{y^2}{x^6}\right) - \frac{y^2}{x^2} = K.$$

**11.** From

$$\frac{dx}{dy} = \frac{xy - y^2}{x^2} = \frac{y}{x} - \left(\frac{y}{x}\right)^2$$

we conclude that given equation is homogeneous. Let $u = y/x$. Then $y = xu$ and $y' = u + xu'$. Substitution yields

$$u + x\frac{du}{dx} = u - u^2 \quad \Rightarrow \quad x\frac{du}{dx} = -u^2 \quad \Rightarrow \quad -\frac{du}{u^2} = \frac{dx}{x}$$

$$\Rightarrow \quad -\int \frac{du}{u^2} = \int \frac{dx}{x} \quad \Rightarrow \quad \frac{1}{u} = \ln|x| + C$$

$$\Rightarrow \quad \frac{x}{y} = \ln|x| + C \quad \Rightarrow \quad y = \frac{x}{\ln|x| + C}.$$

Note that, solving this equation, we have performed two divisions: by $x^2$ and $u^2$. In doing this, we lost two solutions, $x \equiv 0$ and $u \equiv 0$. (The latter gives $y \equiv 0$.) Therefore, a general solution to the given equation is

$$y = \frac{x}{\ln|x| + C}, \qquad x \equiv 0, \qquad \text{and} \qquad y \equiv 0.$$

**13.** Since we can express $f(t, x)$ in the form $G(x/t)$, that is, (dividing numerator and denominator by $t^2$)

$$\frac{x^2 + t\sqrt{t^2 + x^2}}{tx} = \frac{(x/t)^2 + \sqrt{(x/t)^2}}{(x/t)},$$

the equation is homogeneous. Substituting $v = x/t$ and $dx/dt = v + tdv/dt$ into the equation yields

$$v + t\frac{dv}{dt} = v + \frac{\sqrt{1 + v^2}}{v} \quad \Rightarrow \quad t\frac{dv}{dt} = \frac{\sqrt{1 + v^2}}{v}.$$

This transformed equation is separable. Thus we have

$$\frac{v}{\sqrt{1 + v^2}}\, dv = \frac{1}{t}\, dt \quad \Rightarrow \quad \sqrt{1 + v^2} = \ln|t| + C,$$

where we have integrated with the integration on the left hand side being accomplished by the substitution $u = 1 + v^2$. Substituting $x/t$ for $v$ in this equation gives the solution to the original equation which is

$$\sqrt{1 + \frac{x^2}{t^2}} = \ln|t| + C.$$

# Chapter 2

**15.** This equation is homogeneous because

$$\frac{dy}{dx} = \frac{x^2 - y^2}{3xy} = \frac{1 - (y/x)^2}{3(y/x)}.$$

Thus, we substitute $u = y/x$ ($y = xu$ and so $y' = u + xu'$) to get

$$u + x\frac{du}{dx} = \frac{1 - u^2}{3u} \quad \Rightarrow \quad x\frac{du}{dx} = \frac{1 - 4u^2}{3u} \quad \Rightarrow \quad \frac{3u\,du}{1 - 4u^2} = \frac{dx}{x}$$

$$\Rightarrow \quad \int \frac{3u\,du}{1 - 4u^2} = \int \frac{dx}{x} \quad \Rightarrow \quad -\frac{3}{8}\ln\left|1 - 4u^2\right| = \ln|x| + C_1$$

$$\Rightarrow \quad -3\ln\left|1 - 4\left(\frac{y}{x}\right)^2\right| = 8\ln|x| + C_2$$

$$\Rightarrow \quad 3\ln(x^2) - 3\ln\left|x^2 - 4y^2\right| = 8\ln|x| + C_2,$$

which, after some algebra, gives $\left(x^2 - 4y^2\right)^3 x^2 = C$.

**17.** With the substitutions $z = x + y$ and $dz/dx = 1 + dy/dx$ or $dy/dx = dz/dx - 1$ this equation becomes the separable equation

$$\frac{dz}{dx} - 1 = \sqrt{z} - 1 \quad \Rightarrow \quad \frac{dz}{dx} = \sqrt{z}$$

$$\Rightarrow \quad z^{-1/2}\,dz = dx \quad \Rightarrow \quad 2z^{1/2} = x + C.$$

Substituting $x + y$ for $z$ in this solution gives the solution of the original equation

$$2\sqrt{x + y} = x + C$$

which, on solving for $y$, yields

$$y = \left(\frac{x}{2} + \frac{C}{2}\right)^2 - x.$$

Thus, we have

$$y = \frac{(x + C)^2}{4} - x.$$

**19.** The right-hand side of this equation has the form $G(x - y)$ with $G(t) = (t + 5)^2$. Thus we substitute

$$t = x - y \quad \Rightarrow \quad y = x - t \quad \Rightarrow \quad y' = 1 - t',$$

separate variables, and integrate.

$$1 - \frac{dt}{dx} = (t+5)^2$$

$$\Rightarrow \quad \frac{dt}{dx} = 1 - (t+5)^2 = (1 - t - 5)(1 + t + 5) = -(t+4)(t+6)$$

$$\Rightarrow \quad \frac{dt}{(t+4)(t+6)} = -dx \quad \Rightarrow \quad \int \frac{dt}{(t+4)(t+6)} = -\int dx$$

$$\Rightarrow \quad \frac{1}{2} \int \left( \frac{1}{t+4} - \frac{1}{t+6} \right) dt = -\int dx \quad \Rightarrow \quad \ln \left| \frac{t+4}{t+6} \right| = -2x + C_1$$

$$\Rightarrow \quad \ln \left| \frac{x-y+4}{x-y+6} \right| = -2x + C_1 \quad \Rightarrow \quad \frac{x-y+6}{x-y+4} = C_2 e^{2x}$$

$$\Rightarrow \quad 1 + \frac{2}{x-y+4} = C_2 e^{2x} \quad \Rightarrow \quad y = x + 4 + \frac{2}{Ce^{2x}+1}.$$

Also, the solution

$$t + 4 \equiv 0 \quad \Rightarrow \quad y = x + 4$$

has been lost in separation variables.

**21.** This is a Bernoulli equation with $n = 2$. So, we make a substitution $u = y^{1-n} = y^{-1}$. We have $y = u^{-1}$, $y' = -u^{-2}u'$, and the equation becomes

$$-\frac{1}{u^2} \frac{du}{dx} + \frac{1}{ux} = \frac{x^2}{u^2} \quad \Rightarrow \quad \frac{du}{dx} - \frac{1}{x} u = -x^2.$$

The last equation is a linear equation with $P(x) = -1/x$. Following the procedure of solving linear equations, we find an integrating factor $\mu(x) = 1/x$ and multiply the equation by $\mu(x)$ to get

$$\frac{1}{x} \frac{du}{dx} - \frac{1}{x^2} u = -x \quad \Rightarrow \quad \frac{d}{dx} \left( \frac{1}{x} u \right) = -x$$

$$\Rightarrow \quad \frac{1}{x} u = \int (-x) dx = -\frac{1}{2} x^2 + C_1 \quad \Rightarrow \quad u = -\frac{1}{2} x^3 + C_1 x$$

$$\Rightarrow \quad y = \frac{1}{-x^3/2 + C_1 x} = \frac{2}{Cx - x^3}.$$

Also, $y \equiv 0$ is a solution which was lost when we multiplied the equation by $u^2$ (in terms of $y$, divided by $y^2$) to obtain a linear equation.

# Chapter 2

**23.** This is a Bernoulli equation with $n = 2$. Dividing it by $y^2$ and rewriting gives

$$y^{-2}\frac{dy}{dx} - 2x^{-1}y^{-1} = -x^2.$$

Making the substitution $v = y^{-1}$ and hence $dv/dx = -y^{-2}dy/dx$, the above equation becomes

$$\frac{dv}{dx} + 2\frac{v}{x} = x^2.$$

This is a linear equation in $v$ and $x$. The integrating factor $\mu(x)$ is given by

$$\mu(x) = \exp\left(\int \frac{2}{x}\,dx\right) = \exp\left(2\ln|x|\right) = x^2.$$

Multiplying the linear equation by this integrating factor and solving, we have

$$x^2\frac{dv}{dx} + 2vx = x^4 \qquad \Rightarrow \qquad D_x\left(x^2 v\right) = x^4$$

$$\Rightarrow \qquad x^2 v = \int x^4\,dx = \frac{x^5}{5} + C_1 \qquad \Rightarrow \qquad v = \frac{x^3}{5} + \frac{C_1}{x^2}.$$

Substituting $y^{-1}$ for $v$ in this solution gives a solution to the original equation. Therefore, we find

$$y^{-1} = \frac{x^3}{5} + \frac{C_1}{x^2} \qquad \Rightarrow \qquad y = \left(\frac{x^5 + 5C_1}{5x^2}\right)^{-1}.$$

Letting $C = 5C_1$ and simplifying yields

$$y = \frac{5x^2}{x^5 + C}.$$

Note: $y \equiv 0$ is also a solution to the original equation. It was lost in the first step when we divided by $y^2$.

**25.** In this Bernoulli equation, $n = 3$. Dividing the equation by $x^3$, we obtain

$$x^{-3}\frac{dx}{dt} + \frac{1}{t}x^{-2} = -t.$$

Now we make a substitution $u = x^{-2}$ to obtain a linear equation. Since $u' = -2x^{-3}x'$, the equation becomes

$$-\frac{1}{2}\frac{du}{dt} + \frac{1}{t}u = -t \qquad \Rightarrow \qquad \frac{du}{dt} - \frac{2}{t}u = 2t$$

$$\Rightarrow \qquad \mu(t) = \exp\left(-\int \frac{2}{t}\, dt\right) = t^{-2}$$

$$\Rightarrow \qquad \frac{d\left(t^{-2}u\right)}{dt} = \frac{2}{t} \qquad \Rightarrow \qquad t^{-2}u = \int \frac{2}{t}\, dt = 2\ln|t| + C$$

$$\Rightarrow \qquad u = 2t^2 \ln|t| + Ct^2 \qquad \Rightarrow \qquad x^{-2} = 2t^2 \ln|t| + Ct^2\,.$$

$x \equiv 0$ is also a solution, which we lost dividing the equation by $x^3$.

**27.** This equation is a Bernoulli equation with $n = 2$, because it can be written in the form

$$\frac{dr}{d\theta} - \frac{2}{\theta}\, r = r^2\theta^{-2}.$$

Dividing by $r^2$ and making the substitution $u = r^{-1}$, we obtain a linear equation.

$$r^{-2}\frac{dr}{d\theta} - \frac{2}{\theta}\, r^{-1} = \theta^{-2} \qquad \Rightarrow \qquad -\frac{du}{d\theta} - \frac{2}{\theta}\, u = \theta^{-2}$$

$$\Rightarrow \qquad \frac{du}{d\theta} + \frac{2}{\theta}\, u = -\theta^{-2} \qquad \Rightarrow \qquad \mu(\theta) = \exp\left(\int \frac{2}{\theta}\, d\theta\right) = \theta^2$$

$$\Rightarrow \qquad \frac{d\left(\theta^2 u\right)}{d\theta} = -1 \qquad \Rightarrow \qquad \theta^2 u = -\theta + C \qquad \Rightarrow \qquad u = \frac{-\theta + C}{\theta^2}\,.$$

Making back substitution (and adding the lost solution $r \equiv 0$), we obtain a general solution

$$r = \frac{\theta^2}{C - \theta} \qquad \text{and} \qquad r \equiv 0.$$

**29.** Solving for $h$ and $k$ in the linear system

$$\begin{cases} -3h + k - 1 = 0 \\ h + k + 3 = 0 \end{cases}$$

gives $h = -1$ and $k = -2$. Thus, we make the substitutions $x = u - 1$ and $y = v - 2$, so that $dx = du$ and $dy = dv$, to obtain

$$(-3u + v)\, du + (u + v)\, dv = 0.$$

This is the same transformed equation that we encountered in Example 4 on page 77 of the text. There we found that its solution is

$$v^2 + 2uv - 3u^2 = C.$$

# Chapter 2

Substituting $x + 1$ for $u$ and $y + 2$ for $v$ gives the solution to the original equation

$$(y+2)^2 + 2(x+1)(y+2) - 3(x+1)^2 = C.$$

**31.** In this equation with linear coefficients, we make a substitution $x = u + h$, $y = v + k$, where $h$ and $k$ satisfy

$$\begin{cases} 2h - k = 0 \\ 4h + k = 3 \end{cases} \Rightarrow \begin{cases} k = 2h \\ 4h + 2h = 3 \end{cases} \Rightarrow \begin{matrix} k = 1, \\ h = 1/2. \end{matrix}$$

Thus $x = u + 1/2$, $y = v + 1$. As $dx = du$ and $dy = dv$, substitution yields

$$(2u - v)du + (4u + v)dv = 0 \qquad \Rightarrow \qquad \frac{du}{dv} = -\frac{4u + v}{2u - v} = -\frac{4(u/v) + 1}{2(u/v) - 1}$$

$$\Rightarrow \qquad z = \frac{u}{v} \qquad \Rightarrow \qquad u = vz \qquad \Rightarrow \qquad \frac{du}{dv} = z + v\frac{dz}{dv}$$

$$\Rightarrow \qquad z + v\frac{dz}{dv} = -\frac{4z + 1}{2z - 1} \qquad \Rightarrow \qquad v\frac{dz}{dv} = -\frac{4z + 1}{2z - 1} - z = -\frac{(2z + 1)(z + 1)}{2z - 1}$$

$$\Rightarrow \qquad \frac{2z - 1}{(2z + 1)(z + 1)}dz = -\frac{1}{v}dv \qquad \Rightarrow \qquad \int \frac{2z - 1}{(2z + 1)(z + 1)}dz = -\int \frac{1}{v}dv.$$

To find the integral in the left-hand side of the above equation, we use the partial fraction decomposition

$$\frac{2z - 1}{(2z + 1)(z + 1)} = -\frac{4}{2z + 1} + \frac{3}{z + 1}.$$

Therefore, the integration yields

$$-2\ln|2z + 1| + 3\ln|z + 1| = -\ln|v| + C_1 \qquad \Rightarrow \qquad |z + 1|^3|v| = e^{C_1}|2z + 1|^2$$

$$\Rightarrow \qquad \left(\frac{u}{v} + 1\right)^3 v = C_2\left(2\frac{u}{v} + 1\right)^2 \qquad \Rightarrow \qquad (u + v)^3 = C_2(2u + v)^2$$

$$\Rightarrow \qquad (x - 1/2 + y - 1)^3 = C_2(2x - 1 + y - 1)^2 \qquad \Rightarrow \qquad (2x + 2y - 3)^3 = C(2x + y - 2)^2.$$

**33.** In Problem 1, we found that the given equation is of the form $dy/dx = G(y - 4x)$ with $G(u) = (u - 1)^2$. Thus we make a substitution $u = y - 4x$ to get

$$\frac{dy}{dx} = (y - 4x - 1)^2 \qquad \Rightarrow \qquad 4 + \frac{du}{dx} = (u - 1)^2$$

$$\Rightarrow \quad \frac{du}{dx} = (u-1)^2 - 4 = (u-3)(u+1) \quad \Rightarrow \quad \int \frac{du}{(u-3)(u+1)} = \int dx \,.$$

To integrate the left-hand side, we use partial fractions:

$$\frac{1}{(u-3)(u+1)} = \frac{1}{4}\left(\frac{1}{u-3} - \frac{1}{u+1}\right).$$

Thus

$$\frac{1}{4}\left(\ln|u-3| - \ln|u+1|\right) = x + C_1 \quad \Rightarrow \quad \ln\left|\frac{u-3}{u+1}\right| = 4x + C_2$$

$$\Rightarrow \quad \frac{u-3}{u+1} = Ce^{4x} \quad \Rightarrow \quad u = \frac{Ce^{4x}+3}{1-Ce^{4x}}$$

$$\Rightarrow \quad y = 4x + \frac{Ce^{4x}+3}{1-Ce^{4x}}, \tag{2.21}$$

where $C \neq 0$ is an arbitrary constant. Separating variables, we lost the constant solutions $u \equiv 3$ and $u \equiv -1$, that is, $y = 4x+3$ and $y = 4x-1$. While $y = 4x+3$ can be obtained from (2.21) by setting $C = 0$, the solution $y = 4x-1$ is not included in (2.21). Therefore, a general solution to the given equation is

$$y = 4x + \frac{Ce^{4x}+3}{1-Ce^{4x}} \quad \text{and} \quad y = 4x-1.$$

**35.** This equation has linear coefficients. Thus we make a substitution $t = u+h$ and $x = v+k$ with $h$ and $k$ satisfying

$$\begin{cases} h+k+2 = 0 \\ 3h-k-6 = 0 \end{cases} \quad \Rightarrow \quad \begin{aligned} h &= 1, \\ k &= -3. \end{aligned}$$

As $dt = du$ and $dx = dv$, the substitution yields

$$(u+v)dv + (3u-v)du = 0 \quad \Rightarrow \quad \frac{du}{dv} = -\frac{u+v}{3u-v} = -\frac{(u/v)+1}{3(u/v)-1}.$$

With $z = u/v$, we have $u = vz$, $u' = z + vz'$, and the equation becomes

$$z + v\frac{dz}{dv} = -\frac{z+1}{3z-1} \quad \Rightarrow \quad v\frac{dz}{dv} = -\frac{3z^2+1}{3z-1}$$

$$\Rightarrow \quad \frac{3z-1}{3z^2+1}\,dz = -\frac{1}{v}\,dv \quad \Rightarrow \quad \int \frac{3z-1}{3z^2+1}\,dz = -\int \frac{1}{v}\,dv$$

$$\Rightarrow \quad \int \frac{3zdz}{3z^2+1} - \int \frac{dz}{3z^2+1} = -\ln|v| + C_1$$

$$\Rightarrow \quad \frac{1}{2}\ln(3z^2+1) - \frac{1}{\sqrt{3}}\arctan\left(z\sqrt{3}\right) = -\ln|v| + C_1$$

$$\Rightarrow \quad \ln\left[(3z^2+1)v^2\right] - \frac{2}{\sqrt{3}}\arctan\left(z\sqrt{3}\right) = C_2.$$

Making back substitution, after some algebra we get

$$\ln\left[3(t-1)^2 + (x+3)^2\right] + \frac{2}{\sqrt{3}}\arctan\left[\frac{x+3}{\sqrt{3}(t-1)}\right] = C.$$

**37.** In Problem 5, we have written the equation in the form

$$\frac{dy}{dx} - y = e^{2x}y^3 \quad \Rightarrow \quad y^{-3}\frac{dy}{dx} - y^{-2} = e^{2x}.$$

Making a substitution $u = y^{-2}$ (and so $u' = -2y^{-3}y'$) in this Bernoulli equation, we get

$$\frac{du}{dx} + 2u = -2e^{2x} \quad \Rightarrow \quad \mu(x) = \exp\left(\int 2dx\right) = e^{2x}$$

$$\Rightarrow \quad \frac{d(e^{2x}u)}{dx} = -2e^{2x}e^{2x} = -2e^{4x} \quad \Rightarrow \quad e^{2x}u = \int(-2e^{4x})\,dx = -\frac{1}{2}e^{4x} + C$$

$$\Rightarrow \quad u = -\frac{1}{2}e^{2x} + Ce^{-2x} \quad \Rightarrow \quad y^{-2} = -\frac{1}{2}e^{2x} + Ce^{-2x}.$$

The constant function $y \equiv 0$ is also a solution, which we lost dividing the equation by $y^3$.

**39.** Since the equation is homogeneous, we make a substitution $u = y/\theta$. Thus we get

$$\frac{dy}{d\theta} = -\frac{(y/\theta)^3 - (y/\theta)^2}{2(y/\theta)} \quad \Rightarrow \quad u + \theta\frac{du}{d\theta} = -\frac{u^3-u^2}{2u} = -\frac{u^2-u}{2}$$

$$\Rightarrow \quad \theta\frac{du}{d\theta} = -\frac{u^2+u}{2} \quad \Rightarrow \quad \frac{2du}{u(u+1)} = -\frac{d\theta}{\theta}$$

$$\Rightarrow \quad \int\frac{2du}{u(u+1)} = -\int\frac{d\theta}{\theta} \quad \Rightarrow \quad \ln\frac{u^2}{(u+1)^2} = -\ln|\theta| + C_1$$

$$\Rightarrow \quad \frac{u^2}{(u+1)^2} = \frac{C}{\theta}, \quad C \neq 0.$$

Back substitution $u = y/\theta$ yields

$$\frac{y^2}{(y+\theta)^2} = \frac{C}{\theta} \quad \Rightarrow \quad \theta y^2 = C(y+\theta)^2, \quad C \neq 0.$$

When $C = 0$, the above formula gives $\theta \equiv 0$ or $y \equiv 0$, which were lost in separating variables. Also, we lost another solution, $u + 1 \equiv 0$ or $y = -\theta$. Thus, the answer is

$$\theta y^2 = C(y + \theta)^2 \quad \text{and} \quad y = -\theta,$$

where $C$ is an arbitrary constant.

**41.** The right-hand side of (8) from Example 2 of the text can be written as

$$y - x - 1 + (x - y + 2)^{-1} = -(x - y + 2) + 1 + (x - y + 2)^{-1} = G(x - y + 2)$$

with $G(v) = -v + v^{-1} + 1$. With $v = x - y + 2$, we have $y' = 1 - v'$, and the equation becomes

$$1 - \frac{dv}{dx} = -v + v^{-1} + 1 \quad \Rightarrow \quad \frac{dv}{dx} = \frac{v^2 - 1}{v} \quad \Rightarrow \quad \frac{v}{v^2 - 1} dv = dx$$
$$\Rightarrow \quad \ln|v^2 - 1| = 2x + C_1 \quad \Rightarrow \quad v^2 - 1 = Ce^{2x}, \quad C \neq 0.$$

Dividing by $v^2 - 1$, we lost constant solutions $v = \pm 1$, which can be obtained by taking $C = 0$ in the above formula. Therefore, a general solution to the given equation is

$$(x - y + 2)^2 = Ce^{2x} + 1,$$

where $C$ is an arbitrary constant.

**43. (a)** If $f(tx, ty) = f(x, y)$ for any $t$, then, substituting $t = 1/x$, we obtain

$$f(tx, ty) = f\left(\frac{1}{x} \cdot x, \frac{1}{x} \cdot y\right) = f\left(1, \frac{y}{x}\right),$$

which shows that $f(x, y)$ depends, in fact, on $y/x$ alone.

**(b)** Since

$$\frac{dy}{dx} = -\frac{M(x, y)}{N(x, y)} =: f(x, y)$$

and the function $f(x, y)$ satisfies

$$f(tx, ty) = -\frac{M(tx, ty)}{N(tx, ty)} = -\frac{t^n M(x, y)}{t^n N(x, y)} = -\frac{M(x, y)}{N(x, y)} = f(x, y),$$

we apply (a) to conclude that the equation $M(x, y)dx + N(x, y)dy = 0$ is homogeneous.

# Chapter 2

**45.** To obtain (17), we divide given equations:

$$\frac{dy}{dx} = -\frac{4x + y}{2x - y} = \frac{4 + (y/x)}{(y/x) - 2}.$$

Therefore, the equation is homogeneous, and the substitution $u = y/x$ yields

$$u + x\frac{du}{dx} = \frac{4 + u}{u - 2} \qquad \Rightarrow \qquad x\frac{du}{dx} = \frac{4 + u}{u - 2} - u = \frac{-u^2 + 3u + 4}{u - 2}$$

$$\Rightarrow \qquad \frac{u - 2}{u^2 - 3u - 4}\,du = -\frac{1}{x}\,dx \qquad \Rightarrow \qquad \int \frac{u - 2}{u^2 - 3u - 4}\,du = -\int \frac{1}{x}\,dx\,.$$

Using partial fractions, we get

$$\frac{u - 2}{u^2 - 3u - 4} = \frac{2}{5}\frac{1}{u - 4} + \frac{3}{5}\frac{1}{u + 1},$$

and so

$$\frac{2}{5}\ln|u - 4| + \frac{3}{5}\ln|u + 1| = -\ln|x| + C_1$$

$$\Rightarrow \qquad (u - 4)^2(u + 1)^3 x^5 = C$$

$$\Rightarrow \qquad \left(\frac{y}{x} - 4\right)^2\left(\frac{y}{x} + 1\right)^3 x^5 = C \qquad \Rightarrow \qquad (y - 4x)^2(y + x)^3 = C.$$

## REVIEW PROBLEMS:    page 81

**1.** Separation variables yields

$$\frac{y - 1}{e^y}\,dy = e^x\,dx \qquad \Rightarrow \qquad (y - 1)e^{-y}\,dy = e^x\,dx$$

$$\Rightarrow \qquad \int (y - 1)e^{-y}\,dy = \int e^x\,dx$$

$$\Rightarrow \qquad -(y - 1)e^{-y} + \int e^{-y}\,dy = e^x + C \qquad \Rightarrow \qquad -(y - 1)e^{-y} - e^{-y} = e^x + C$$

$$\Rightarrow \qquad e^x + ye^{-y} = -C,$$

and we can replace $-C$ by $K$.

**3.** The differential equation is an exact equation with $M = 2xy - 3x^2$ and $N = x^2 - 2y^{-3}$ because $M_y = 2x = N_x$. To solve this problem we will follow the procedure for solving exact equations given in Section 2.4. First we integrate $M(x, y)$ with respect to $x$ to get

$$F(x, y) = \int \left(2xy - 3x^2\right) dx + g(y)$$
$$\Rightarrow \quad F(x, y) = x^2 y - x^3 + g(y). \tag{2.22}$$

To determine $g(y)$ take the partial derivative with respect to $y$ of both sides and substitute $N(x, y)$ for $\partial F(x, y)/\partial y$ to obtain

$$N = x^2 - 2y^{-3} = x^2 + g'(y).$$

Solving for $g'(y)$ yields

$$g'(y) = -2y^{-3}.$$

Since the choice of the constant of integration is arbitrary we will take $g(y) = y^{-2}$. Hence, from equation (2.22) we have $F(x, y) = x^2 y - x^3 + y^{-2}$ and the solution to the differential equation is given implicitly by $x^2 y - x^3 + y^{-2} = C$.

**5.** In this problem,

$$M(x, y) = \sin(xy) + xy \cos(xy), \qquad N(x, y) = 1 + x^2 \cos(xy).$$

We check the equation for exactness:

$$\frac{\partial M}{\partial y} = [x \cos(xy)] + [x \cos(xy) - xy \sin(xy)x] = 2x \cos(xy) - x^2 y \sin(xy),$$
$$\frac{\partial N}{\partial x} = 0 + [2x \cos(xy) - x^2 \sin(xy)y] = 2x \cos(xy) - x^2 y \sin(xy).$$

Therefore, the equation is exact. So, we use the method discussed in Section 2.4 and obtain

$$F(x, y) = \int N(x, y)dy = \int \left[1 + x^2 \cos(xy)\right] dy = y + x \sin(xy) + h(x)$$
$$\Rightarrow \quad \frac{\partial F}{\partial x} = \sin(xy) + x \cos(xy)y + h'(x) = M(x, y) = \sin(xy) + xy \cos(xy)$$
$$\Rightarrow \quad h'(x) = 0 \quad \Rightarrow \quad h(x) \equiv 0,$$

and a general solution is given implicitly by $y + x \sin(xy) = c$.

**7.** This equation is separable. Separating variables and integrating, we get

$$t^3 y^2\, dt = -t^4 y^{-6}\, dy \qquad \Rightarrow \qquad \frac{dt}{t} = -\frac{dy}{y^8}$$

$$\Rightarrow \qquad \ln|t| + C_1 = \frac{1}{7}\, y^{-7} \qquad \Rightarrow \qquad y = (7\ln|t| + C)^{-1/7}\,.$$

The function $t \equiv 0$ is also a solution. (We lost it when divided the equation by $t^4$.)

**9.** The given differential equation can be written in the form

$$\frac{dy}{dx} + \frac{1}{3x}\, y = -\frac{x}{3}\, y^{-1}\,.$$

This is a Bernoulli equation with $n = -1$, $P(x) = 1/(3x)$, and $Q(x) = -x/3$. To transform this equation into a linear equation, we first multiply by $y$ to obtain

$$y\frac{dy}{dx} + \frac{1}{3x}\, y^2 = -\frac{1}{3}\, x.$$

Next we make the substitution $v = y^2$. Since $v' = 2yy'$, the transformed equation is

$$\frac{1}{2}\, v' + \frac{1}{3x}\, v = -\frac{1}{3}\, x,$$

$$\Rightarrow \qquad v' + \frac{2}{3x}\, v = -\frac{2}{3}\, x. \qquad (2.23)$$

The above equation is linear, so we can solve it for $v$ using the method for solving linear equations discussed in Section 2.3. Following this procedure, the integrating factor $\mu(x)$ is found to be

$$\mu(x) = \exp\left(\int \frac{2}{3x}\, dx\right) = \exp\left(\frac{2}{3}\ln|x|\right) = x^{2/3}.$$

Multiplying equation (2.23) by $x^{2/3}$ gives

$$x^{2/3} v' + \frac{2}{3x^{1/3}}\, v = -\frac{2}{3}\, x^{5/3} \qquad \Rightarrow \qquad \left(x^{2/3} v\right)' = -\frac{2}{3}\, x^{5/3}.$$

We now integrate both sides and solve for $v$ to find

$$x^{2/3} v = \int \frac{-2}{3}\, x^{5/3}\, dx = \frac{-1}{4}\, x^{8/3} + C \qquad \Rightarrow \qquad v = \frac{-1}{4}\, x^2 + Cx^{-2/3}.$$

Substituting $v = y^2$ gives the solution

$$y^2 = -\frac{1}{4}\, x^2 + Cx^{-2/3} \qquad \Rightarrow \qquad (x^2 + 4y^2)x^{2/3} = 4C$$

or, cubing both sides, $(x^2 + 4y^2)^3 x^2 = C_1$, where $C_1 := (4C)^3$ is an arbitrary constant.

**11.** The right-hand side of this equation is of the form $G(t-x)$ with $G(u) = 1 + \cos^2 u$. Thus we make a substitution

$$t - x = u \quad \Rightarrow \quad x = t - u \quad \Rightarrow \quad x' = 1 - u',$$

which yields

$$1 - \frac{du}{dt} = 1 + \cos^2 u \quad \Rightarrow \quad \frac{du}{dt} = -\cos^2 u$$

$$\Rightarrow \quad \sec^2 u \, du = -dt \quad \Rightarrow \quad \int \sec^2 u \, du = -\int dt$$

$$\Rightarrow \quad \tan u = -t + C \quad \Rightarrow \quad \tan(t - x) + t = C.$$

**13.** This is a linear equation with $P(x) = -1/x$. Following the method for solving linear equations given on page 51 of the text, we find that an integrating factor $\mu(x) = 1/x$, and so

$$\frac{d[(1/x)y]}{dx} = \frac{1}{x} x^2 \sin 2x = x \sin 2x$$

$$\Rightarrow \quad \frac{y}{x} = \int x \sin 2x \, dx = -\frac{1}{2} x \cos 2x + \frac{1}{2} \int \cos 2x \, dx = -\frac{1}{2} x \cos 2x + \frac{1}{4} \sin 2x + C$$

$$\Rightarrow \quad y = -\frac{x^2}{2} \cos 2x + \frac{x}{4} \sin 2x + Cx.$$

**15.** The right-hand side of the differential equation $y' = 2 - \sqrt{2x - y + 3}$ is a function of $2x - y$ and so can be solved using the method for equations of the form $y' = G(ax + by)$ on page 74 of the text. By letting $z = 2x - y$ we can transform the equation into a separable one. To solve, we differentiate $z = 2x - y$ with respect to $x$ to obtain

$$\frac{dz}{dx} = 2 - \frac{dy}{dx} \quad \Rightarrow \quad \frac{dy}{dx} = 2 - \frac{dz}{dx}.$$

Substituting $z = 2x - y$ and $y' = 2 - z'$ into the differential equation yields

$$2 - \frac{dz}{dx} = 2 - \sqrt{z + 3} \quad \text{or} \quad \frac{dz}{dx} = \sqrt{z + 3}.$$

To solve this equation we divide by $\sqrt{z + 3}$, multiply by $dx$, and integrate to obtain

$$\int (z + 3)^{-1/2} \, dz = \int dx \quad \Rightarrow \quad 2(z + 3)^{1/2} = x + C.$$

Chapter 2

Thus we get

$$z + 3 = \frac{(x+C)^2}{4} .$$

Finally, replacing $z$ by $2x - y$ yields

$$2x - y + 3 = \frac{(x+C)^2}{4} .$$

Solving for $y$, we obtain

$$y = 2x + 3 - \frac{(x+C)^2}{4} .$$

**17.** This equation is a Bernoulli equation with $n = 2$. So, we divide it by $y^2$ and substitute $u = y^{-1}$ to get

$$-\frac{du}{d\theta} + 2u = 1 \quad \Rightarrow \quad \frac{du}{d\theta} - 2u = -1 \quad \Rightarrow \quad \mu(\theta) = \exp\left[\int (-2)d\theta\right] = e^{-2\theta}$$

$$\Rightarrow \quad \frac{d\left(e^{-2\theta}u\right)}{d\theta} = -e^{-2\theta} \quad \Rightarrow \quad e^{-2\theta}u = \int \left(-e^{-2\theta}\right) d\theta = \frac{e^{-2\theta}}{2} + C_1$$

$$\Rightarrow \quad y^{-1} = \frac{1}{2} + C_1 e^{2\theta} = \frac{1 + Ce^{2\theta}}{2} \quad \Rightarrow \quad y = \frac{2}{1 + Ce^{2\theta}} .$$

This formula, together with $y \equiv 0$, gives a general solution to the given equation.

**19.** In the differential equation $M(x,y) = x^2 - 3y^2$ and $N(x,y) = 2xy$. The differential equation is not exact because

$$\frac{\partial M}{\partial y} = -6y \neq 2x = \frac{\partial N}{\partial x} .$$

However, because $(\partial M/\partial y - \partial N/\partial x)/N = (-8y)/(2xy) = -4/x$ depends only on $x$, we can determine $\mu(x)$ from equation (8) on page 70 of the text. This gives

$$\mu(x) = \exp\left(\int \frac{-4}{x} dx\right) = x^{-4}.$$

When we multiply the differential equation by $\mu(x) = x^{-4}$ we get the exact equation

$$(x^{-2} - 3x^{-4}y^2) dx + 2x^{-3}y dy = 0.$$

To find $F(x,y)$ we integrate $(x^{-2} - 3x^{-4}y^2)$ with respect to $x$:

$$F(x,y) = \int (x^{-2} - 3x^{-4}y^2) dx = -x^{-1} + x^{-3}y^2 + g(y).$$

Next we take the partial derivative of $F$ with respect to $y$ and substitute $2x^{-3}y$ for $\partial F/\partial y$:

$$2x^{-3}y = 2x^{-3}y + g'(y).$$

Thus $g'(y) = 0$ and since the choice of the constant of integration is not important, we will take $g(y) \equiv 0$. Hence, we have $F(x,y) = -x^{-1} + x^{-3}y^2$ and the implicit solution to the differential equation is

$$-x^{-1} + x^{-3}y^2 = C.$$

Solving for $y^2$ yields $y^2 = x^2 + Cx^3$.

Finally we check to see if any solutions were lost in the process. We multiplied by the integrating factor $\mu(x) = x^{-4}$ so we check $x \equiv 0$. This is also a solution to the original equation.

**21.** This equation has linear coefficients. Therefore, we are looking for a substitution $x = u + h$ and $y = v + k$ with $h$ and $k$ satisfying

$$\begin{cases} -2h + k - 1 = 0 \\ h + k - 4 = 0 \end{cases} \Rightarrow \begin{aligned} h &= 1, \\ k &= 3. \end{aligned}$$

So, $x = u + 1$ $(dx = du)$ and $y = v + 3$ $(dy = dv)$, and the equation becomes

$$(-2u + v)du + (u + v)dv = 0 \quad \Rightarrow \quad \frac{dv}{du} = \frac{2u - v}{u + v} = \frac{2 - (v/u)}{1 + (v/u)}.$$

With $z = v/u$, we have $v' = z + uz'$, and so

$$z + u\frac{dz}{du} = \frac{2 - z}{1 + z} \quad \Rightarrow \quad u\frac{dz}{du} = \frac{2 - z}{1 + z} - z = \frac{-z^2 - 2z + 2}{1 + z}$$

$$\Rightarrow \quad \frac{z + 1}{z^2 + 2z - 2}dz = -\frac{du}{u} \quad \Rightarrow \quad \int \frac{1 + z}{z^2 + 2z - 2}dz = -\int \frac{du}{u}$$

$$\Rightarrow \quad \frac{1}{2}\ln\left|z^2 + 2z - 2\right| = -\ln|u| + C_1 \quad \Rightarrow \quad \left(z^2 + 2z - 2\right)u^2 = C_2.$$

Back substitution, $z = v/u = (y - 3)/(x - 1)$, yields

$$v^2 + 2uv - 2u^2 = C_2 \quad \Rightarrow \quad (y - 3)^2 + 2(x - 1)(y - 3) - 2(x - 1)^2 = C_2$$

$$\Rightarrow \quad y^2 - 8y - 2x^2 - 2x + 2xy = C.$$

**23.** Given equation is homogeneous because

$$\frac{dy}{dx} = \frac{x - y}{x + y} = \frac{1 - (y/x)}{1 + (y/x)}.$$

Therefore, substituting $u = y/x$, we obtain a separable equation.

$$u + x\frac{du}{dx} = \frac{1 - u}{1 + u} \qquad \Rightarrow \qquad x\frac{du}{dx} = \frac{-u^2 - 2u + 1}{1 + u}$$

$$\Rightarrow \qquad \frac{u + 1}{u^2 + 2u - 1}\,du = -\frac{dx}{x} \qquad \Rightarrow \qquad \int \frac{1 + u}{u^2 + 2u - 1}\,du = -\int \frac{dx}{x}$$

$$\Rightarrow \qquad \frac{1}{2}\ln|u^2 + 2u - 1| = -\ln|x| + C_1 \qquad \Rightarrow \qquad (u^2 + 2u - 1)\,x^2 = C,$$

and, substituting back $u = y/x$, after some algebra we get a general solution $y^2 + 2xy - x^2 = C$.

**25.** In this differential form, $M(x, y) = y(x - y - 2)$ and $N(x, y) = x(y - x + 4)$. Therefore,

$$\frac{\partial M}{\partial y} = x - 2y - 2, \qquad \frac{\partial N}{\partial x} = y - 2x + 4$$

$$\Rightarrow \qquad \frac{\partial N/\partial x - \partial M/\partial y}{M} = \frac{(y - 2x + 4) - (x - 2y - 2)}{y(x - y - 2)} = \frac{-3(x - y - 2)}{y(x - y - 2)} = \frac{-3}{y},$$

which is a function of $y$ alone. Therefore, the equation has a special integrating factor $\mu(y)$. We use formula (9) on page 70 of the text to find that $\mu(y) = y^{-3}$. Multiplying the equation by $\mu(y)$ yields

$$y^{-2}(x - y - 2)\,dx + xy^{-3}(y - x + 4)\,dy = 0$$

$$\Rightarrow \qquad F(x, y) = \int y^{-2}(x - y - 2)\,dx = \frac{y^{-2}x^2}{2} - \left(y^{-1} + 2y^{-2}\right)x + g(y)$$

$$\Rightarrow \qquad \frac{\partial F}{\partial y} = -y^{-3}x^2 - \left(-y^{-2} - 4y^{-3}\right)x + g'(y) = N(x, y) = xy^{-3}(y - x + 4)$$

$$\Rightarrow \qquad g'(x) = 0 \qquad \Rightarrow \qquad g(y) \equiv 0,$$

and so

$$F(x, y) = \frac{y^{-2}x^2}{2} - x\left(y^{-1} + 2y^{-2}\right) = C_1 \qquad \Rightarrow \qquad x^2 y^{-2} - 2xy^{-1} - 4xy^{-2} = C$$

is a general solution. In addition, $y \equiv 0$ is a solution that we lost when multiplied the equation by $\mu(y) = y^{-3}$ (i.e., divided by $y^3$).

**27.** This equation has linear coefficients. Thus we make a substitution $x = u + h$, $y = v + k$ with $h$ and $k$ satisfying

$$\begin{cases} 3h - k - 5 = 0 \\ h - k + 1 = 0 \end{cases} \Rightarrow \quad \begin{aligned} h &= 3, \\ k &= 4. \end{aligned}$$

With this substitution,

$$(3u - v)du + (u - v)dv = 0 \quad \Rightarrow \quad \frac{dv}{du} = -\frac{3u - v}{u - v} = -\frac{3 - (v/u)}{1 - (v/u)}$$

$$\Rightarrow \quad z = \frac{v}{u}, \quad v = uz, \quad v' = z + uz'$$

$$\Rightarrow \quad z + u\frac{dz}{du} = -\frac{3 - z}{1 - z} \quad \Rightarrow \quad u\frac{dz}{du} = -\frac{3 - z}{1 - z} - z = -\frac{z^2 - 3}{z - 1}$$

$$\Rightarrow \quad \frac{z - 1}{z^2 - 3}dz = -\frac{du}{u} \quad \Rightarrow \quad \int \frac{z - 1}{z^2 - 3}dz = -\int \frac{du}{u}.$$

We use partial fractions to find the integral in the left-hand side. Namely,

$$\frac{z - 1}{z^2 - 3} = \frac{A}{z - \sqrt{3}} + \frac{B}{z + \sqrt{3}}, \quad A = \frac{1}{2} - \frac{1}{2\sqrt{3}}, \quad B = \frac{1}{2} + \frac{1}{2\sqrt{3}}.$$

Therefore, integration yields

$$A\ln\left|z - \sqrt{3}\right| + B\ln\left|z + \sqrt{3}\right| = -\ln|u| + C_1$$

$$\Rightarrow \quad \left(z - \sqrt{3}\right)^{1-1/\sqrt{3}}\left(z + \sqrt{3}\right)^{1+1/\sqrt{3}}u^2 = C$$

$$\Rightarrow \quad \left(v - u\sqrt{3}\right)^{1-1/\sqrt{3}}\left(v + u\sqrt{3}\right)^{1+1/\sqrt{3}} = C$$

$$\Rightarrow \quad (v^2 - 3u^2)\left(\frac{v + u\sqrt{3}}{v - u\sqrt{3}}\right)^{1/\sqrt{3}} = C$$

$$\Rightarrow \quad \left[(y - 4)^2 - 3(x - 3)^2\right]\left[\frac{(y - 4) + (x - 3)\sqrt{3}}{(y - 4) - (x - 3)\sqrt{3}}\right]^{1/\sqrt{3}} = C.$$

**29.** Here $M(x, y) = 4xy^3 - 9y^2 + 4xy^2$ and $N(x, y) = 3x^2y^2 - 6xy + 2x^2y$. We compute

$$\frac{\partial M}{\partial y} = 12xy^2 - 18y + 8xy, \quad \frac{\partial N}{\partial x} = 6xy^2 - 6y + 4xy,$$

$$\frac{\partial M/\partial y - \partial N/\partial x}{N} = \frac{(12xy^2 - 18y + 8xy) - (6xy^2 - 6y + 4xy)}{3x^2y^2 - 6xy + 2x^2y} = \frac{2y(3xy - 6 + 2x)}{xy(3xy - 6 + 2x)} = \frac{2}{x},$$

# Chapter 2

which is a function of $x$ alone. Thus, the equation has a special integrating factor

$$\mu(x) = \exp\left(\int \frac{2}{x}\, dx\right) = x^2.$$

Multiplying the equation by $\mu(x)$, we find that

$$F(x,y) = \int x^2 \left(4xy^3 - 9y^2 + 4xy^2\right) dx = x^4 y^3 - 3x^3 y^2 + x^4 y^2 + g(y)$$

$$\Rightarrow \quad \frac{\partial F}{\partial y} = 3x^4 y^2 - 6x^3 y + 2x^4 y + g'(y) = x^2 N(x,y) = x^2 \left(3x^2 y^2 - 6xy + 2x^2 y\right)$$

$$\Rightarrow \quad g'(y) = 0 \quad \Rightarrow \quad g(y) \equiv 0$$

$$\Rightarrow \quad F(x,y) = x^4 y^3 - 3x^3 y^2 + x^4 y^2 = C$$

is a general solution.

**31.** In this problem,

$$\frac{\partial M}{\partial y} = -1, \qquad \frac{\partial N}{\partial x} = 1, \qquad \text{and so} \qquad \frac{\partial M/\partial y - \partial N/\partial x}{N} = -\frac{2}{x}.$$

Therefore, the equation has a special integrating factor

$$\mu(x) = \exp\left[\int \left(\frac{-2}{x}\right) dx\right] = x^{-2}.$$

We multiply the given equation by $\mu(x)$ to get an exact equation.

$$\left(x - \frac{y}{x^2}\right) dx + \frac{1}{x}\, dy = 0$$

$$\Rightarrow \quad F(x,y) = \int \left(\frac{1}{x}\right) dy = \frac{y}{x} + h(x)$$

$$\Rightarrow \quad \frac{\partial F}{\partial x} = -\frac{y}{x^2} + h'(x) = x - \frac{y}{x^2} \quad \Rightarrow \quad h'(x) = x \quad \Rightarrow \quad h(x) = \frac{x^2}{2},$$

and a general solution is given by

$$F(x,y) = \frac{y}{x} + \frac{x^2}{2} = C \quad \text{and} \quad x \equiv 0.$$

(The latter has been lost in multiplication by $\mu(x)$.) Substitution the initial values, $y = 3$ when $x = 1$, yields

$$\frac{3}{1} + \frac{1^2}{2} = C \quad \Rightarrow \quad C = \frac{7}{2}.$$

Hence, the answer is

$$\frac{y}{x} + \frac{x^2}{2} = \frac{7}{2} \quad \Rightarrow \quad y = -\frac{x^3}{2} + \frac{7x}{2}.$$

**33.** Choosing $x$ as the dependent variable, we transform the equation to

$$\frac{dx}{dt} + x = -(t+3).$$

This equation is linear, $P(t) \equiv 1$. So, $\mu(t) = \exp\left(\int dt\right) = e^t$ and

$$\frac{d\left(e^t x\right)}{dt} = -(t+3)e^t$$

$$\Rightarrow \quad e^t x = -\int (t+3)e^t \, dt = -(t+3)e^t + \int e^t \, dt = -(t+2)e^t + C$$

$$\Rightarrow \quad x = -(t+2) + Ce^{-t}.$$

Using the initial condition, $x(0) = 1$, we find that

$$1 = x(0) = -(0+2) + Ce^{-0} \quad \Rightarrow \quad C = 3,$$

and so $x = -t - 2 + 3e^{-t}$.

**35.** For $M(x,y) = 2y^2 + 4x^2$ and $N(x,y) = -xy$, we compute

$$\frac{\partial M}{\partial y} = 4y, \qquad \frac{\partial N}{\partial x} = -y \quad \Rightarrow \quad \frac{\partial M/\partial y - \partial N/\partial x}{N} = \frac{4y - (-y)}{-xy} = \frac{-5}{x},$$

which is a function of $x$ only. Using (8) on page 70 of the text, we find an integrating factor $\mu(x) = x^{-5}$ and multiply the equation by $\mu(x)$ to get an exact equation,

$$x^{-5}\left(2y^2 + 4x^2\right) dx - x^{-4}y \, dy = 0.$$

Hence,

$$F(x,y) = \int \left(-x^{-4}y\right) dy = -\frac{x^{-4}y^2}{2} + h(x)$$

$$\Rightarrow \quad \frac{\partial F}{\partial x} = \frac{4x^{-5}y^2}{2} + h'(x) = x^{-5}M(x,y) = 2x^{-5}y^2 + 4x^{-3}$$

$$\Rightarrow \quad h'(x) = 4x^{-3} \quad \Rightarrow \quad h(x) = -2x^{-2}$$

$$\Rightarrow \quad F(x,y) = -\frac{x^{-4}y^2}{2} - 2x^{-2} = C.$$

We find $C$ by substituting the initial condition, $y(1) = -2$:

$$-\frac{(1)^{-4}(-2)^2}{2} - 2(1)^{-2} = C \quad \Rightarrow \quad C = -4.$$

So, the solution is

$$-\frac{x^{-4}y^2}{2} - 2x^{-2} = -4$$

$$\Rightarrow \quad y^2 + 4x^2 = 8x^4$$

$$\Rightarrow \quad y^2 = 8x^4 - 4x^2 = 4x^2\left(2x^2 - 1\right)$$

$$\Rightarrow \quad y = -2x\sqrt{2x^2 - 1}\,,$$

where, taking the square root, we have chosen the negative sign because of the initial negative value for $y$.

**37.** In this equation with linear coefficients we make a substitution $x = u + h$, $y = v + k$ with $h$ and $k$ such that

$$\begin{cases} 2h - k = 0 \\ h + k = 3 \end{cases} \quad \Rightarrow \quad \begin{cases} k = 2h \\ h + (2h) = 3 \end{cases} \quad \Rightarrow \quad \begin{matrix} k = 2, \\ h = 1. \end{matrix}$$

Therefore,

$$(2u - v)du + (u + v)dv = 0$$

$$\Rightarrow \quad \frac{dv}{du} = \frac{v - 2u}{v + u} = \frac{(v/u) - 2}{(v/u) + 1}$$

$$\Rightarrow \quad z = v/u, \quad v = uz, \quad v' = z + uz'$$

$$\Rightarrow \quad z + u\frac{dz}{du} = \frac{z - 2}{z + 1} \quad \Rightarrow \quad u\frac{dz}{du} = -\frac{z^2 + 2}{z + 1}$$

$$\Rightarrow \quad \frac{z + 1}{z^2 + 2}dz = -\frac{du}{u}\,.$$

Integration yields

$$\int \frac{z + 1}{z^2 + 2}dz = -\int \frac{du}{u} \quad \Rightarrow \quad \int \frac{z\,dz}{z^2 + 2} + \int \frac{dz}{z^2 + 2} = -\int \frac{du}{u}$$

$$\Rightarrow \quad \frac{1}{2}\ln\left(z^2+2\right)+\frac{1}{\sqrt{2}}\arctan\left(\frac{z}{\sqrt{2}}\right)=-\ln|u|+C_1$$

$$\Rightarrow \quad \ln\left[\left(z^2+2\right)u^2\right]+\sqrt{2}\arctan\left(\frac{z}{\sqrt{2}}\right)=C$$

$$\Rightarrow \quad \ln\left(v^2+2u^2\right)+\sqrt{2}\arctan\left(\frac{v}{u\sqrt{2}}\right)=C$$

$$\Rightarrow \quad \ln\left[(y-2)^2+2(x-1)^2\right]+\sqrt{2}\arctan\left[\frac{y-2}{(x-1)\sqrt{2}}\right]=C.$$

The initial condition, $y(0)=2$, gives $C=\ln 2$, and so the answer is

$$\ln\left[(y-2)^2+2(x-1)^2\right]+\sqrt{2}\arctan\left[\frac{y-2}{(x-1)\sqrt{2}}\right]=\ln 2.$$

**39.** Multiplying the equation by $y$, we get

$$y\frac{dy}{dx}-\frac{2}{x}y^2=\frac{1}{x}.$$

We substitute $u=y^2$ and obtain

$$\frac{1}{2}\frac{du}{dx}-\frac{2}{x}u=\frac{1}{x} \qquad \Rightarrow \qquad \frac{du}{dx}-\frac{4}{x}u=\frac{2}{x},$$

which is linear and has an integrating factor

$$\mu(x)=\exp\left[\int\left(-\frac{4}{x}\right)dx\right]=x^{-4}.$$

Hence,

$$\frac{d\left(x^{-4}u\right)}{dx}=2x^{-5}$$

$$\Rightarrow \quad x^{-4}u=\int\left(2x^{-5}\right)dx=-\frac{x^{-4}}{2}+C$$

$$\Rightarrow \quad x^{-4}y^2=-\frac{x^{-4}}{2}+C$$

$$\Rightarrow \quad y^2=-\frac{1}{2}+Cx^4.$$

Substitution $y(1)=3$ yields

$$3^2=-\frac{1}{2}+C(1)^4 \qquad \text{or} \qquad C=\frac{19}{2}.$$

Therefore, the solution to the given initial value problem is

$$y^2 = -\frac{1}{2} + \frac{19x^4}{2} \qquad \text{or} \qquad y = \sqrt{\frac{19x^4 - 1}{2}} \,.$$

# CHAPTER 3: Mathematical Models and Numerical Methods Involving First Order Equations

**EXERCISES 3.2: Compartmental Analysis, page 98**

1. Let $x(t)$ denote the mass of salt in the tank at time $t$ with $t = 0$ denoting the moment when the process started. Thus we have $x(0) = 0.5$ kg. We use the mathematical model described by equation (1) on page 90 of the text to find $x(t)$. Since the solution is entering the tank with rate 8 L/min and contains 0.05 kg/L of salt,

$$\text{input rate} = 8\,(\text{L/min}) \cdot 0.05\,(\text{kg/L}) = 0.4\,(\text{kg/min}).$$

We can determine the concentration of salt in the tank by dividing $x(t)$ by the volume of the solution, which remains constant, 100 L, because the flow rate in is the same as the flow rate out. Therefore, the concentration of salt at time $t$ is $x(t)/100$ kg/L and

$$\text{output rate} = \frac{x(t)}{100}\,(\text{kg/L}) \cdot 8\,(\text{L/min}) = \frac{2x(t)}{25}\,(\text{kg/min}).$$

Then the equation (1) yields

$$\frac{dx}{dt} = 0.4 - \frac{2x}{25} \qquad \Rightarrow \qquad \frac{dx}{dt} + \frac{2x}{25} = 0.4\,, \qquad x(0) = 0.5\,.$$

This equation is linear, has integrating factor $\mu(t) = \exp\left[\int (2/25)dt\right] = e^{2t/25}$, and so

$$\frac{d\left(e^{2t/25}x\right)}{dt} = 0.4e^{2t/25}$$

$$\Rightarrow \qquad e^{2t/25}x = 0.4\left(\frac{25}{2}\right)e^{2t/25} + C = 5e^{2t/25} + C \qquad \Rightarrow \qquad x = 5 + Ce^{-2t/25}.$$

Using the initial condition, we find $C$.

$$0.5 = x(0) = 5 + C \qquad \Rightarrow \qquad C = -4.5\,,$$

and so the mass of salt in the tank after $t$ minutes is

$$x(t) = 5 - 4.5e^{-2t/25}.$$

If the concentration of salt in the tank is 0.02 kg/L, then the mass of salt is $0.02 \times 100 = 2$ kg, and, to find this moment, we solve

$$5 - 4.5e^{-2t/25} = 2 \quad \Rightarrow \quad e^{-2t/25} = \frac{2}{3} \quad \Rightarrow \quad t = \frac{25\ln(3/2)}{2} \approx 5.07 \text{ (min)}.$$

**3.** Let $x(t)$ be the volume of nitric acid in the tank at time $t$. The tank initially held 200 L of a 0.5% nitric acid solution; therefore, $x(0) = 200 \times 0.005 = 1$. Since 6 L of 20% nitric acid solution are flowing into the tank per minute, the rate at which nitric acid is entering is $6 \times 0.2 = 1.2$ L/min. Because the rate of flow out of the tank is 8 L/min and the rate of flow in is only 6 L/min, there is a net loss in the tank of 2 L of solution every minute. Thus, at any time $t$, the tank will be holding $200 - 2t$ liters of solution. Combining this with the fact that the volume of nitric acid in the tank at time $t$ is $x(t)$, we see that the concentration of nitric acid in the tank at time $t$ is $x(t)/(200 - 2t)$. Here we are assuming that the tank is kept well stirred. The rate at which nitric acid flows out of the tank is, therefore, $8 \times [x(t)/(200 - 2t)]$ L/min. From all of these facts, we see that

$$\text{input rate} = 1.2 \text{ L/min},$$
$$\text{output rate} = \frac{8x(t)}{200 - 2t} \text{ L/min}.$$

We know that

$$\frac{dx}{dt} = \text{input rate} - \text{output rate}.$$

Thus we must solve the differential equation

$$\frac{dx}{dt} = 1.2 - \frac{4x(t)}{100 - t}, \qquad x(0) = 1.$$

This is the linear equation

$$\frac{dx}{dt} + \frac{4}{100 - t}x = 1.2, \qquad x(0) = 1.$$

An integrating factor for this equation has the form

$$\mu(t) = \exp\left(\int \frac{4}{100-t}\,dt\right) = e^{-4\ln(100-t)} = (100-t)^{-4}.$$

Multiplying the linear equation by the integrating factor yields

$$(100-t)^{-4}\frac{dx}{dt} + 4x(100-t)^{-5} = (1.2)(100-t)^{-4}$$
$$\Rightarrow \quad D_t\left[(100-t)^{-4}x\right] = (1.2)(100-t)^{-4}$$
$$\Rightarrow \quad (100-t)^{-4}x = 1.2\int (100-t)^{-4}\,dt = \frac{1.2}{3}(100-t)^{-3} + C$$
$$\Rightarrow \quad x(t) = (0.4)(100-t) + C(100-t)^4.$$

To find the value of $C$, we use the initial condition $x(0) = 1$. Therefore,

$$x(0) = (0.4)(100) + C(100)^4 = 1 \quad \Rightarrow \quad C = \frac{-39}{100^4} = -3.9 \times 10^{-7}.$$

This means that at time $t$ there is

$$x(t) = (0.4)(100-t) - (3.9 \times 10^{-7})(100-t)^4$$

liters of nitric acid in the tank. When the percentage of nitric acid in the tank is 10%, the concentration of nitric acid is 0.1. Thus we want to solve the equation

$$\frac{x(t)}{200-2t} = 0.1.$$

Therefore, we divide the solution $x(t)$ that we found above by $2(100-t)$ and solve for $t$. That is, we solve

$$(0.2) - (1.95 \times 10^{-7})(100-t)^3 = 0.1$$
$$\Rightarrow \quad t = -\left[0.1 \cdot \frac{10^7}{1.95}\right]^{1/3} + 100 \approx 19.96 \text{ (min)}.$$

5. Let $x(t)$ denote the volume of chlorine in the pool at time $t$. Then in the formula

$$\text{rate of change} = \text{input rate} - \text{output rate}$$

105

# Chapter 3

we have

$$\text{input rate} = 5 \,(\text{gal/min}) \cdot \frac{0.001\%}{100\%} = 5 \cdot 10^{-5} \,(\text{gal/min}),$$

$$\text{output rate} = 5 \,(\text{gal/min}) \cdot \frac{x(t)\,(\text{gal})}{10{,}000\,(\text{gal})} = 5 \cdot 10^{-4} x(t) \,(\text{gal/min}),$$

and the equation for $x(t)$ becomes

$$\frac{dx}{dt} = 5 \cdot 10^{-5} - 5 \cdot 10^{-4} x \qquad \Rightarrow \qquad \frac{dx}{dt} + 5 \cdot 10^{-4} x = 5 \cdot 10^{-5}.$$

This is a linear equation. Solving yields

$$x(t) = 0.1 + C e^{5 \cdot 10^{-4} t} = 0.1 + C e^{-0.0005t}.$$

Using the initial condition,

$$x(0) = 10{,}000\,(\text{gal}) \cdot \frac{0.01\%}{100\%} = 1\,(\text{gal}),$$

we find the value of $C$:

$$1 = 0.1 + C e^{-0.0005 \cdot 0} \qquad \Rightarrow \qquad C = 0.9 \,.$$

Therefore, $x(t) = 0.1 + 0.9 e^{-0.0005t}$ and the concentration of chlorine, say, $c(t)$, in the pool at time $t$ is

$$c(t) = \frac{x(t)\,(\text{gal})}{10{,}000\,(\text{gal})} \cdot 100\% = \frac{x(t)}{100}\,\% = 0.001 + 0.009 e^{-0.0005t}\,\%.$$

After 1 hour (i.e., $t = 60$ min),

$$c(60) = 0.001 + 0.009 e^{-0.0005 \cdot 60} = 0.001 + 0.009 e^{-0.03} \approx 0.0097\,\%.$$

To answer the second question, we solve the equation

$$c(t) = 0.001 + 0.009 e^{-0.0005t} = 0.002 \qquad \Rightarrow \qquad t = \frac{\ln(1/9)}{-0.0005} \approx 4394.45\,(\text{min}) \approx 73.24\,(\text{h}).$$

**7.** Let $x(t)$ denote the mass of salt in the first tank at time $t$. Assuming that the initial mass is $x(0) = x_0$, we use the mathematical model described by equation (1) on page 90 of the text to find $x(t)$. We can determine the concentration of salt in the first tank by dividing $x(t)$ by the its volume, i.e., $x(t)/60$ kg/gal. Note that the volume of brine in this tank remains constant because the flow rate in is the same as the flow rate out. Then

$$\text{output rate}_1 = (3 \text{ gal/min}) \cdot \left( \frac{x(t)}{60} \text{ kg/gal} \right) = \frac{x(t)}{20} \text{ kg/min}.$$

Since the incoming liquid is pure water, we conclude that

$$\text{input rate}_1 = 0.$$

Therefore, $x(t)$ satisfies the initial value problem

$$\frac{dx}{dt} = \text{input rate}_1 - \text{output rate}_1 = -\frac{x}{20}, \qquad x(0) = x_0.$$

This equation is linear and separable. Solving and using the initial condition to evaluate the arbitrary constant, we find

$$x(t) = x_0 e^{-t/20}.$$

Now, let $y(t)$ denote the mass of salt in the second tank at time $t$. Since initially this tank contained only pure water, we have $y(0) = 0$. The function $y(t)$ can be described by the same mathematical model. We get

$$\text{input rate}_2 = \text{output rate}_1 = \frac{x(t)}{20} = \frac{x_0}{20} e^{-t/20} \text{ kg/min}.$$

Further since the volume of the second tank also remains constant, we have

$$\text{output rate}_2 = (3 \text{ gal/min}) \cdot \left( \frac{y(t)}{60} \text{ kg/gal} \right) = \frac{y(t)}{20} \text{ kg/min}.$$

Therefore, $y(t)$ satisfies the initial value problem

$$\frac{dy}{dt} = \text{input rate}_2 - \text{output rate}_2 = \frac{x_0}{20} e^{-t/20} - \frac{y(t)}{20}, \qquad y(0) = 0.$$

or

$$\frac{dy}{dt} + \frac{y(t)}{20} = \frac{x_0}{20} e^{-t/20}, \qquad y(0) = 0.$$

# Chapter 3

This is a linear equation in standard form. Using the method given on page 51 of the text we find the general solution to be

$$y(t) = \frac{x_0}{20} te^{-t/20} + Ce^{-t/20}.$$

The constant $C$ can be found from the initial condition:

$$0 = y(0) = \frac{x_0}{20} \cdot 0 \cdot e^{-0/20} + Ce^{-0/20} \qquad \Rightarrow \qquad C = 0.$$

Therefore, $y(t) = (x_0/20) te^{-t/20}$. To investigate $y(t)$ for maximum value we calculate

$$\frac{dy}{dt} = \frac{x_0}{20} e^{-t/20} - \frac{y(t)}{20} = \frac{x_0}{20} e^{-t/20} \left(1 - \frac{t}{20}\right).$$

Thus

$$\frac{dy}{dt} = 0 \qquad \Leftrightarrow \qquad 1 - \frac{t}{20} = 0 \qquad \Leftrightarrow \qquad t = 20,$$

which is the point of global maximum (notice that $dy/dt > 0$ for $t < 20$ and $dy/dt < 0$ for $t > 20$). In other words, at this moment the water in the second tank will taste saltiest, and comparing concentrations, it will be

$$\frac{y(20)/60}{x_0/60} = \frac{y(20)}{x_0} = \frac{1}{20} \cdot 20 \cdot e^{-20/20} = e^{-1}$$

times as salty as the original brine.

9. Let $p(t)$ be the population of splake in the lake at time $t$. We start counting the population in 1980. Thus, we let $t = 0$ correspond to the year 1980. By the Malthusian law stated on page 93 of the text, we have

$$p(t) = p_0 e^{kt}.$$

Since $p_0 = p(0) = 1000$, we see that

$$p(t) = 1000 e^{kt}.$$

To find $k$ we use the fact that the population of splake was 3000 in 1987. Therefore,

$$p(7) = 3000 = 1000 e^{k \cdot 7} \qquad \Rightarrow \qquad 3 = e^{k \cdot 7} \qquad \Rightarrow \qquad k = \frac{\ln 3}{7}.$$

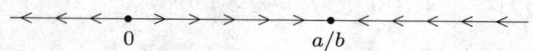

**Figure 3–A**: The phase line for $p' = (a - bp)p$.

Putting this value for $k$ into the equation for $p(t)$ gives

$$p(t) = 1000e^{(t\ln 3)/7} = 1000 \cdot 3^{t/7}.$$

To estimate the population in 2010 we plug $t = 2010 - 1980 = 30$ into this formula to get

$$p(30) = 1000 \cdot 3^{30/7} \approx 110,868 \text{ splakes.}$$

**11.** In this problem, the dependent variable is $p$, the independent variable is $t$, and the function $f(t,p) = (a-bp)p$. Since $f(t,p) = f(p)$, i.e., does not depend on $t$, the equation is autonomous. To find equilibrium solutions, we solve

$$f(p) = 0 \quad \Rightarrow \quad (a - bp)p = 0 \quad \Rightarrow \quad p_1 = 0, \quad p_2 = \frac{a}{b}.$$

Thus, $p_1(t) \equiv 0$ and $p_2(t) \equiv a/b$ are equilibrium solutions. For $p_1 < p < p_2$, $f(p) > 0$, and $f(p) < 0$ when $p > p_2$. (Also, $f(p) < 0$ for $p < p_1$.) Thus the phase line for the given equation is as it is shown in Figure 3-A. From this picture, we conclude that the equilibrium $p = p_1$ is a source while $p = p_2$ is a sink. Thus, regardless of an initial point $p_0 > 0$, the solution to the corresponding initial value problem will approach $p_2 = a/b$ as $t \to \infty$.

**13.** With year 1980 corresponding to $t = 0$, the data given can be written as

$$t_0 = 0, \qquad p_0 = p(t_0) = 1000;$$
$$t_a = 1987 - 1980 = 7, \quad p_a = p(t_a) = 3000;$$
$$t_b = 1994 - 1980 = 14, \quad p_b = p(t_b) = 5000.$$

Since $t_b = 2t_a$, we can use formulas in Problem 12 to compute parameters $p_1$ and $A$ in the logistic model (14) on page 94 of the text. We have:

$$p_1 = \frac{(3000)(5000) - 2(1000)(5000) + (1000)(3000)}{(3000)^2 - (1000)(5000)}(3000) = 6000;$$

$$A = \frac{1}{(6000)7} \ln\left[\frac{5000(3000 - 1000)}{1000(5000 - 3000)}\right] = \frac{\ln 5}{42000}.$$

Thus the formula (15) on page 95 of the text becomes

$$p(t) = \frac{p_0 p_1}{p_0 + (p_1 - p_0)e^{-Ap_1 t}} = \frac{(1000)(6000)}{(1000) + (6000 - 1000)e^{-(\ln 5/42000)6000t}} = \frac{6000}{1 + 5^{1-t/7}}. \quad (3.1)$$

In the year 2010, $t = 2010 - 1980 = 30$, and the estimated population of splake is

$$p(30) = \frac{6000}{1 + 5^{1-30/7}} \approx 5970.$$

Taking the limit in (3.1), as $t \to \infty$, yields

$$\lim_{t\to\infty} p(t) = \lim_{t\to\infty} \frac{6000}{1 + 5^{1-t/7}} = \frac{6000}{1 + \lim_{t\to\infty} 5^{1-t/7}} = 6000.$$

Therefore, the predicted limiting population is 6000.

**15.** Counting time from the year 1970, we have the following data:

$$t_0 = 0, \qquad\qquad p_0 = p(t_0) = 300;$$
$$t_a = 1975 - 1970 = 5, \quad p_a = p(t_a) = 1200;$$
$$t_b = 1980 - 1970 = 10, \quad p_b = p(t_b) = 1500.$$

Since $t_b = 2t_a$, we use the formulas in Problem 12 to find parameters in the logistic model.

$$p_1 = \left[\frac{(1200)(1500) - 2(300)(1500) + (300)(1200)}{(1200)^2 - (300)(1500)}\right](1200) = \frac{16800}{11};$$

$$A = \frac{1}{(16800/11)5} \ln\left[\frac{(1500)(1200 - 300)}{(300)(1500 - 1200)}\right] = \frac{11\ln(15)}{84000}.$$

Therefore,

$$p(t) = \frac{300(16800/11)}{300 + [(16800/11) - 300]e^{-\ln(15)t/5}} = \frac{16800}{11 + 3 \cdot 15^{1-t/5}}.$$

In the year 2010, $t = 2010 - 1970 = 40$, and so the estimated population of alligators is

$$p(40) = \frac{16800}{11 + 3 \cdot 15^{1-40/5}} = \frac{16800}{11 + 3 \cdot 15^{-7}} \approx 1527.$$

Taking the limit of $p(t)$, as $t \to \infty$, we get the predicted limiting population of

$$\lim_{t\to\infty} \frac{16800}{11 + 3 \cdot 15^{1-t/5}} = \frac{16800}{11} \approx 1527.$$

**16.** By definition,

$$p'(t) = \lim_{h \to 0} \frac{p(t+h) - p(t)}{h}.$$

Replacing $h$ by $-h$ in the above equation, we obtain

$$p'(t) = \lim_{h \to 0} \frac{p(t-h) - p(t)}{-h} = \lim_{h \to 0} \frac{p(t) - p(t-h)}{h}.$$

Adding the previous two equations together yields

$$
\begin{aligned}
2p'(t) &= \lim_{h \to 0} \left[ \frac{p(t+h) - p(t)}{h} + \frac{p(t) - p(t-h)}{h} \right] \\
&= \lim_{h \to 0} \left[ \frac{p(t+h) - p(t-h)}{h} \right].
\end{aligned}
$$

Thus

$$p'(t) = \lim_{h \to 0} \left[ \frac{p(t+h) - p(t-h)}{2h} \right].$$

**19.** This problem can be regarded as a compartmental analysis problem for the population of fish. If we let $m(t)$ denote the mass in million tons of a certain species of fish, then the mathematical model for this process is given by

$$\frac{dm}{dt} = \text{increase rate} - \text{decrease rate}.$$

The increase rate of fish is given by $2m$ million tons/yr. The decrease rate of fish is given as 15 million tons/yr. Substituting these rates into the above equation we obtain

$$\frac{dm}{dt} = 2m - 15, \qquad m(0) = 7 \text{ (million tons)}.$$

This equation is linear and separable. Using the initial condition, $m(0) = 7$ to evaluate the arbitrary constant we obtain

$$m(t) = -\frac{1}{2} e^{2t} + \frac{15}{2}.$$

Knowing this equation we can now find when all the fish will be gone. To determine when all the fish will be gone we set $m(t) = 0$ and solve for $t$. This gives

$$0 = -\frac{1}{2} e^{2t} + \frac{15}{2}$$

and, hence,

$$t = \frac{1}{2} \ln(15) \approx 1.354 \text{ (years)}.$$

To determine the fishing rate required to keep the fish mass constant we solve the general problem

$$\frac{dm}{dt} = 2m - r, \qquad m(0) = 7,$$

with $r$ as the fishing rate. Thus we obtain

$$m(t) = Ke^{2t} + \frac{r}{2}.$$

The initial mass was given to be 7 million tons. Substituting this into the above equation we can find the arbitrary constant $K$:

$$m(0) = 7 = K + \frac{r}{2} \qquad \Rightarrow \qquad K = 7 - \frac{r}{2}.$$

Thus $m(t)$ is given by

$$m(t) = \left(7 - \frac{r}{2}\right)e^{2t} + \frac{r}{2}.$$

A fishing rate of $r = 14$ million tons/year will give a constant mass of fish by canceling out the coefficient of the $e^{2t}$ term.

21. Let $D = D(t)$, $S(t)$, and $V(t)$ denote the diameter, surface area, and volume of the snowball at time $t$, respectively. From geometry, we know that $V = \pi D^3/6$ and $S = \pi D^2$. Since we are given that $V'(t)$ is proportional to $S(t)$, the equation describing the melting process is

$$\frac{dV}{dt} = kS \qquad \Rightarrow \qquad \frac{d}{dt}\left(\frac{\pi}{6}D^3\right) = k\left(\pi D^2\right)$$

$$\Rightarrow \qquad \frac{\pi}{2}D^2\frac{dD}{dt} = k\pi D^2 \qquad \Rightarrow \qquad \frac{dD}{dt} = 2k = \text{const.}$$

Solving, we get $D = 2kt + C$. Initially, $D(0) = 4$, and we also know that $D(30) = 3$. These data allow us to find $k$ and $C$.

$$4 = D(0) = 2k \cdot 0 + C \qquad \Rightarrow \qquad C = 4;$$

$$3 = D(30) = 2k \cdot 30 + C = 2k \cdot 30 + 4 \qquad \Rightarrow \qquad 2k = -\frac{1}{30}.$$

Thus

$$D(t) = -\frac{t}{30} + 4.$$

The diameter $D(t)$ of the snowball will be 2 inches when

$$-\frac{t}{30} + 4 = 2 \quad \Rightarrow \quad t = 60\,(\text{min}) = 1\,(\text{h}),$$

and the snowball will disappear when

$$-\frac{t}{30} + 4 = 0 \quad \Rightarrow \quad t = 120\,(\text{min}) = 2\,(\text{h}).$$

**23.** If $m(t)$ (with $t$ measured in "days") denotes the mass of a radioactive substance, the law of decay says that

$$\frac{dm}{dt} = km(t),$$

with the decay constant $k$ depending on the substance. Solving this equation yields

$$m(t) = Ce^{kt}.$$

If the initial mass of the substance is $m(0) = m_0$, then, similarly to the equation (11) on page 93 of the text, we find that

$$m(t) = m_0 e^{kt}. \tag{3.2}$$

In this problem, $m_0 = 50$ g, and we know that $m(3) = 10$ g. These data yield

$$10 = m(3) = 50 \cdot e^{k(3)} \quad \Rightarrow \quad k = -\frac{\ln 5}{3},$$

and so the decay is governed by the equation

$$m(t) = 50e^{-(\ln 5)t/3} = (50)5^{-t/3}.$$

After 4 days, the remaining amount will be $m(4) = (50)5^{-4/3}$ g, which is

$$\frac{(50)5^{-4/3}}{50} \cdot 100\% = 5^{-4/3} \cdot 100\% \approx 11.7\%$$

of the original amount.

## Chapter 3

**25.** Let $M(t)$ denote the mass of carbon-14 present in the burnt wood of the campfire. Then since carbon-14 decays at a rate proportional to its mass, we have

$$\frac{dM}{dt} = -\alpha M,$$

where $\alpha$ is the proportionality constant. This equation is linear and separable. Using the initial condition, $M(0) = M_0$ we obtain

$$M(t) = M_0 e^{-\alpha t}.$$

Given the half-life of carbon-14 to be 5600 years, we solve for $\alpha$ since we have

$$\frac{1}{2} M_0 = M_0 e^{-\alpha(5600)} \quad \Rightarrow \quad \frac{1}{2} = e^{-\alpha(5600)},$$

which yields

$$\alpha = \frac{\ln(0.5)}{-5600} \approx 0.000123776.$$

Thus,

$$M(t) = M_0 e^{-0.000123776t}.$$

Now we are told that after $t$ years 2% of the original amount of carbon-14 remains in the campfire and we are asked to determine $t$. Thus

$$0.02 M_0 = M_0 e^{-0.000123776t} \quad \Rightarrow \quad 0.02 = e^{-0.000123776t}$$

$$\Rightarrow \quad t = \frac{\ln 0.02}{-0.000123776} \approx 31,606 \text{ (years)}.$$

**27.** The element Hh decays according to the general law of a radioactive decay, which is described by (3.2) (this time, with $t$ measured in "years"). Since the initial mass of Hh is $m_0 = 1$ kg and the decay constant $k = k_{Hh} = -2/\text{yr}$, we get

$$Hh(t) = e^{k_{Hh}t} = e^{-2t}. \tag{3.3}$$

For It, the process is more complicated: it has an incoming mass from the decay of Hh and, at the same, looses its mass decaying to Bu. (This process is very similar to "brine solution" problems.) Thus we use the general idea in getting a differential equation describing this process:

$$\text{rate of change} = \text{input rate} - \text{output rate}. \tag{3.4}$$

The "input rate" is the rate of mass coming from Hh's decay, which is opposite to the rate of decay of Hh (Hh looses the mass but It gains it), i.e.,

$$\text{input rate} = -\frac{d\text{Hh}}{dt} = 2e^{-2t}, \tag{3.5}$$

where we have used (3.3). The "output rate" is the rate with which It decays, which (again, according to the general law of a radioactive decay) is proportional to its current mass. Since the decay constant for It is $k = k_{\text{It}} = -1/\text{yr}$,

$$\text{output rate} = k_{\text{It}}\text{It}(t) = -\text{It}(t). \tag{3.6}$$

Therefore, combining (3.4)–(3.6) we get the equation for It, that is,

$$\frac{d\text{It}(t)}{dt} = 2e^{-2t} - \text{It}(t) \qquad \Rightarrow \qquad \frac{d\text{It}(t)}{dt} + \text{It}(t) = 2e^{-2t}.$$

This is a linear equation with $P(t) \equiv 1$ and an integrating factor $\mu(t) = \exp\left[\int (1)dt\right] = e^t$. Multiplying the equation by $\mu(t)$ yields

$$\frac{d\left[e^t\text{It}(t)\right]}{dt} = 2e^{-t} \qquad \Rightarrow \qquad e^t\text{It}(t) = -2e^{-t} + C \qquad \Rightarrow \qquad \text{It}(t) = -2e^{-2t} + Ce^{-t}.$$

Initially, there were no It, which means that $\text{It}(0) = 0$. With this initial condition we find that

$$0 = \text{It}(0) = -2e^{-2(0)} + Ce^{-(0)} = -2 + C \qquad \Rightarrow \qquad C = 2,$$

and the mass of It remaining after $t$ years is

$$\text{It}(t) = -2e^{-2t} + 2e^{-t} = 2\left(e^{-t} - e^{-2t}\right). \tag{3.7}$$

The element Bu only gains its mass from It, and the rate with which it does this is opposite to the rate with which It looses its mass. Hence (3.6) yields

$$\frac{d\text{Bu}(t)}{dt} = \text{It}(t) = 2\left(e^{-t} - e^{-2t}\right).$$

# Chapter 3

Integrating, we obtain

$$Bu(t) = 2 \int \left( e^{-t} - e^{-2t} \right) dt = -2e^{-t} + e^{-2t} + C,$$

and the initial condition $Bu(0) = 0$ gives $C = 1$. Therefore,

$$Bu(t) = -2e^{-t} + e^{-2t} + 1.$$

## EXERCISES 3.3:  Heating and Cooling of Buildings, page 107

1. Let $T(t)$ denote the temperature of coffee at time $t$ (in minutes). According to the Newton's Law (1) on page 102 of the text,

$$\frac{dT}{dt} = K[21 - T(t)],$$

where we have taken $H(t) \equiv U(t) \equiv 0$, $M(t) \equiv 21°\,C$, with the initial condition $T(0) = 95°\,C$. Solving this initial value problem yields

$$\frac{dT}{21 - T} = K\,dt \quad \Rightarrow \quad -\ln|T - 21| = Kt + C_1 \quad \Rightarrow \quad T(t) = 21 + Ce^{-Kt};$$

$$95 = T(0) = 21 + Ce^{-K(0)} \quad \Rightarrow \quad C = 74 \quad \Rightarrow \quad T(t) = 21 + 74e^{-Kt}.$$

To find $K$, we use the fact that after $5\,\text{min}$ the temperature of coffee was $80°\,C$. Thus

$$80 = T(5) = 21 + 74e^{-K(5)} \quad \Rightarrow \quad K = \frac{\ln(74/59)}{5},$$

and so

$$T(t) = 21 + 74e^{-\ln(74/59)t/5} = 21 + 74\left(\frac{74}{59}\right)^{-t/5}.$$

Finally, we solve the equation $T(t) = 50$ to find the time appropriate for drinking coffee:

$$50 = 21 + 74\left(\frac{74}{59}\right)^{-t/5} \quad \Rightarrow \quad \left(\frac{74}{59}\right)^{-t/5} = \frac{29}{74} \quad \Rightarrow \quad t = \frac{5\ln(74/29)}{\ln(74/59)} \approx 20.7\,(\text{min}).$$

3. This problem is similar to one of cooling a building. In this problem we have no additional heating or cooling so we can say that the rate of change of the wine's temperature, $T(t)$ is given by Newton's law of cooling

$$\frac{dT}{dt} = K[M(t) - T(t)],$$

where $M(t) = 32$ is the temperature of ice. This equation is linear and is rewritten in the standard form as

$$\frac{dT}{dt} + KT(t) = 32K.$$

We find that the integrating factor is $e^{Kt}$. Multiplying both sides by $e^{Kt}$ and integrating gives

$$e^{Kt}\frac{dT}{dt} + e^{Kt}KT(t) = 32Ke^{Kt} \quad \Rightarrow \quad e^{Kt}T(t) = \int 32Ke^{Kt}\,dt$$

$$\Rightarrow \quad e^{Kt}T(t) = 32e^{Kt} + C \quad \Rightarrow \quad T(t) = 32 + Ce^{-Kt}.$$

By setting $t = 0$ and using the initial temperature 70°F, we find the constant $C$.

$$70 = 32 + C \quad \Rightarrow \quad C = 38.$$

Knowing that it takes 15 minutes for the wine to chill to 60°F, we can find the constant, $K$:

$$60 = 32 + 38e^{-K(15)}.$$

Solving for $K$ yields

$$K = \frac{-1}{15}\ln\left(\frac{60-32}{38}\right) \approx 0.02035.$$

Therefore,

$$T(t) = 32 + 38e^{-0.02035t}.$$

We can now determine how long it will take for the wine to reach 56°F. Using our equation for temperature $T(t)$, we set

$$56 = 32 + 38e^{-0.02035t}$$

and, solving for $t$, obtain

$$t = \frac{-1}{0.02035}\ln\left(\frac{56-32}{38}\right) \approx 22.6 \text{ min.}$$

5. This problem can be treated as one similar to that of a cooling building. If we assume the air surrounding the body has not changed since the death, we can say that the rate of change of the body's temperature, $T(t)$ is given by Newton's law of cooling:

$$\frac{dT}{dt} = K[M(t) - T(t)],$$

where $M(t)$ represents the surrounding temperature which we've assumed to be a constant 16°C. This differential equation is linear and is solved using an integrating factor of $e^{Kt}$. Rewriting the above equation in standard form, multiplying both sides by $e^{Kt}$ and integrating gives

$$\frac{dT}{dt} + KT(t) = K(16) \qquad \Rightarrow \qquad e^{Kt}\frac{dT}{dt} + e^{Kt}KT(t) = 16Ke^{Kt}$$

$$\Rightarrow \qquad e^{Kt}T(t) = 16e^{Kt} + C \qquad \Rightarrow \qquad T(t) = 16 + Ce^{-Kt}.$$

Let us take $t = 0$ as the time at which the person died. Then $T(0) = 37°C$ (normal body temperature) and we get

$$37 = 16 + C \qquad \Rightarrow \qquad C = 21.$$

Now we know that at sometime, say $X$ hours after death, the body temperature was measured to be 34.5°C and that at $X + 1$ hours after death the body temperature was measured to be 33.7°C. Therefore, we have

$$34.5 = 16 + 21e^{-KX} \qquad \text{and} \qquad 33.7 = 16 + 21e^{-K(X+1)}.$$

Solving the first equation for $KX$ we arrive at

$$KX = -\ln\left(\frac{34.5 - 16}{21}\right) = 0.12675. \tag{3.8}$$

Substituting this value into the second equation we, can solve for $K$ as follows:

$$33.7 = 16 + 21e^{-0.12675-K}$$

$$\Rightarrow \qquad K = -\left[0.12675 + \ln\left(\frac{33.7 - 16}{21}\right)\right] = 0.04421.$$

This results in an equation for the body temperature of

$$T(t) = 16 + 21e^{-0.04421t}.$$

From equation (3.8) we now find the number of hours $X$ before 12 Noon when the person died.

$$X = \frac{0.12675}{K} = \frac{0.12675}{0.04421} \approx 2.867 \text{ (hours)}.$$

Therefore, the time of death is 2.867 hours (2 hours and 52 min) before Noon or $9:08$ A.M.

**7.** The temperature function $T(t)$ changes according to Newton's law of cooling (1) on page 102 of the text. Similarly to Example 1 we conclude that, with $H(t) \equiv U(t) \equiv 0$ and the outside temperature $M(t) \equiv 35°C$, a general solution formula (4) on page 102 becomes

$$T(t) = 35 + Ce^{-Kt}.$$

To find $C$, we use the initial condition,

$$T(0) = T(\text{at noon}) = 24°C,$$

and get

$$24 = T(0) = 35 + Ce^{-K(0)} \quad \Rightarrow \quad C = 24 - 35 = -11 \quad \Rightarrow \quad T(t) = 35 - 11e^{-Kt}.$$

The time constant for the building $1/K = 4\,\text{hr}$; so $K = 1/4$ and $T(t) = 35 - 11e^{-t/4}$.

At $2:00\,\text{P.M.}$ $t = 2$, and $t = 6$ at $6:00\,\text{P.M.}$ Substituting this values into the solution, we obtain that the temperature

$$\text{at } 2:00\,\text{P.M. will be} \quad T(2) = 35 - 11e^{-2/4} \approx 28.3°C;$$
$$\text{at } 6:00\,\text{P.M. will be} \quad T(6) = 35 - 11e^{-6/4} \approx 32.5°C.$$

Finally, we solve the equation

$$T(t) = 35 - 11e^{-t/4} = 27$$

to find the time when the temperature inside the building reaches $27°C$.

$$35 - 11e^{-t/4} = 27 \quad \Rightarrow \quad 11e^{-t/4} = 8 \quad \Rightarrow \quad t = 4\ln\left(\frac{11}{8}\right) \approx 1.27.$$

Thus, the temperature inside the building will be $27°C$ at $1.27\,\text{hr}$ after noon, that is, at $1:16:12\,\text{P.M.}$

**9.** Since we are evaluating the temperature in a warehouse, we can assume that any heat generated by people or equipment in the warehouse will be negligible. Therefore, we have $H(t) = 0$.

119

# Chapter 3

Also, we are assuming that there is no heating or air conditioning in the warehouse. Therefore, we have that $U(t)$. We are also given that the outside temperature has a sinusoidal fluctuation. Thus, as in Example 2, page 103, we see that

$$M(t) = M_0 - B \cos \omega t \,,$$

where $M_0$ is the average outside temperature, $B$ is a positive constant for the magnitude of the temperature shift from this average, and $\omega = \pi/2$ radians per hour. To find $M_0$ and $B$, we are given that at $2:00$ A.M., $M(t)$ reaches a low of $16°C$ and at $2:00$ P.M. it reaches a high of $32°C$. This gives

$$M_0 = \frac{16 + 32}{2} = 24°C.$$

By letting $t = 0$ at $2:00$ A.M. (so that low for the outside temperature corresponds to the low for the negative cosine function), we can calculate the constant $B$. That is

$$16 = 24 - B \cos 0 = 24 - B \qquad \Rightarrow \qquad B = 8.$$

Therefore, we see that

$$M(t) = 24 - 8 \cos \omega t,$$

where $\omega = \pi/12$. As in Example 2, using the fact that $B_0 = M_0 + H_0/K = M_0 + 0/K = M_0$, we see that

$$T(t) = 24 - 8F(t) + Ce^{-Kt} \,,$$

where

$$F(t) = \frac{\cos \omega t + (\omega/K) \sin \omega t}{1 + (\omega/K)^2} = \left[ 1 + \left( \frac{\omega}{K} \right)^2 \right]^{-1/2} \cos(\omega t - \alpha).$$

In the last expression, $\alpha$ is chosen such that $\tan \alpha = \omega/K$. By assuming that the exponential term dies off, we obtain

$$T(t) = 24 - 8 \left[ 1 + \left( \frac{\omega}{K} \right)^2 \right]^{-1/2} \cos(\omega t - \alpha).$$

This function will reach a minimum when $\cos(\omega t - \alpha) = 1$ and it will reach a maximum when $\cos(\omega t - \alpha) = -1$.

For the case when the time constant for the building is 1, we see that $1/K = 1$ which implies that $K = 1$. Therefore, the temperature will reach a maximum of $K$

$$T = 24 + 8\left[1 + \left(\frac{\pi}{12}\right)^2\right]^{-1/2} \approx 31.7°C.$$

It will reach a minimum of

$$T = 24 - 8\left[1 + \left(\frac{\pi}{12}\right)^2\right]^{-1/2} \approx 16.3°C.$$

For the case when the time constant of the building is 5, we have

$$\frac{1}{K} = 5 \qquad \Rightarrow \qquad K = \frac{1}{5}.$$

Then, the temperature will reach a maximum of

$$T = 24 + 8\left[1 + \left(\frac{5\pi}{12}\right)^2\right]^{-1/2} \approx 28.9°C,$$

and a minimum of

$$T = 24 - 8\left[1 + \left(\frac{5\pi}{12}\right)^2\right]^{-1/2} \approx 19.1°C.$$

**11.** As in Example 3, page 105 of the text, this problem involves a thermostat to regulate the temperature in the van. Hence, we have

$$U(t) = K_U \left[T_D - T(t)\right],$$

where $T_D$ is the desired temperature 16°C and $K_U$ is a proportionality constant. We will assume that $H(t) = 0$ and that the outside temperature $M(t)$ is a constant 35°C. The time constant for the van is $1/K = 2$ hr, hence $K = 0.5$. Since the time constant for the van with its air conditioning system is $1/K_1 = 1/3$ hr, then $K_1 = K + K_U = 3$. Therefore, $K_U = 3 - 0.5 = 2.5$. The temperature in the van is governed by the equation

$$\frac{dT}{dt} = (0.5)(35 - T) + (2.5)(16 - T) = 57.5 - 3T.$$

Solving this separable equation yields

$$T(t) = 19.17 + Ce^{-3t}.$$

When $t = 0$ we are given $T(0) = 55$. Using this information to solve for $C$ gives $C = 35.83$. Hence, the van temperature is given by

$$T(t) = 19.17 + 35.83e^{-3t}.$$

To find out when the temperature in the van will reach 27°C, we let $T(t) = 27$ and solve for $t$. Thus, we see that

$$27 = 19.17 + 35.83e^{-3t} \qquad \Rightarrow \qquad e^{-3t} = \frac{7.83}{35.83} \approx 0.2185$$

$$\Rightarrow \qquad t \approx \frac{\ln(0.2185)}{3} \approx 0.5070 \text{ (hr)} \qquad \text{or} \qquad 30.4 \text{ min.}$$

13. Since the time constant is 64, we have $K = 1/64$. The temperature in the tank increases at the rate of 2°F for every 1000 Btu. Furthermore, every hour of sunlight provides an input of 2000 Btu to the tank. Thus,

$$H(t) = 2 \times 2 = 4°\text{F per hr.}$$

We are given that $T(0) = 110$, and that the temperature $M(t)$ outside the tank is a constant 80°F. Hence the temperature in the tank is governed by

$$\frac{dT}{dt} = \frac{1}{64}[80 - T(t)] + 4 = -\frac{1}{64}T(t) + 5.25, \qquad T(0) = 110.$$

Solving this separable equation gives

$$T(t) = 336 + Ce^{-t/64}.$$

To find $C$, we use the initial condition to see that

$$T(0) = 110 = 336 + C \qquad \Rightarrow \qquad C = -226.$$

This yields the equation

$$T(t) = 336 - 226e^{-t/64}.$$

After 12 hours of sunlight, the temperature will be

$$T(12) = 336 - 226e^{-12/64} \approx 148.6°\text{F}.$$

**15.** The equation $dT/dt = k\left(M^4 - T^4\right)$ is separable. Separation variables yields

$$\frac{dT}{T^4 - M^4} = -k\,dt \qquad \Rightarrow \qquad \int \frac{dT}{T^4 - M^4} = -\int k\,dt = -kt + C_1. \qquad (3.9)$$

Since $T^4 - M^4 = \left(T^2 - M^2\right)\left(T^2 + M^2\right)$, we have

$$\frac{1}{T^4 - M^4} = \frac{1}{2M^2}\frac{\left(M^2 + T^2\right) + \left(M^2 - T^2\right)}{\left(T^2 - M^2\right)\left(T^2 + M^2\right)} = \frac{1}{2M^2}\left[\frac{1}{T^2 - M^2} - \frac{1}{T^2 + M^2}\right],$$

and the integral in the left-hand side of (3.9) becomes

$$\int \frac{dT}{T^4 - M^4} = \frac{1}{2M^2}\left[\int \frac{dT}{T^2 - M^2} - \int \frac{dT}{T^2 + M^2}\right] = \frac{1}{4M^3}\left[\ln\frac{T - M}{T + M} - 2\arctan\left(\frac{T}{M}\right)\right].$$

Thus a general solution to Stefan's equation is given implicitly by

$$\frac{1}{4M^3}\left[\ln\frac{T - M}{T + M} - 2\arctan\left(\frac{T}{M}\right)\right] = -kt + C_1$$

or

$$T - M = C(T + M)\exp\left[2\arctan\left(\frac{T}{M}\right) - 4M^3 kt\right].$$

When $T$ is close to $M$,

$$M^4 - T^4 = (M - T)(M + T)\left(M^2 + T^2\right) \approx (M - T)(2M)\left(2M^2\right) \approx 4M^3(M - T),$$

and so

$$\frac{dT}{dt} \approx k \cdot 4M^3(M - T)4M^3 = k_1(M - T)$$

with $k_1 = 4M^3 k$, which constitutes Newton's law.

## EXERCISES 3.4:  Newtonian Mechanics, page 115

**1.** This problem is a particular case of Example 1 on page 110 of the text. Therefore, we can use the general formula (6) on page 111 with $m = 5$, $b = 50$, and $v_0 = v(0) = 0$. But let us follow the general idea of Section 3.4, find an equation of the motion, and solve it.

# Chapter 3

With given data, the force due to gravity is $F_1 = mg = 5g$ and the air resistance force is $F_2 = -50v$. Therefore, the velocity $v(t)$ satisfies

$$m\frac{dv}{dt} = F_1 + F_2 = 5g - 50v \qquad \Rightarrow \qquad \frac{dv}{dt} = g - 10v, \qquad v(0) = 0.$$

Separating variables yields

$$\frac{dv}{10v - g} = -dt \qquad \Rightarrow \qquad \frac{1}{10}\ln|10v - g| = -t + C_1$$

$$\Rightarrow \qquad v(t) = \frac{g}{10} + Ce^{-10t}.$$

Substituting the initial condition, $v(0) = 0$, we get $C = -g/10$, and so

$$v(t) = \frac{g}{10}\left(1 - e^{-10t}\right).$$

Integrating this equation yields

$$x(t) = \int v(t)\,dt = \int \frac{g}{10}\left(1 - e^{-10t}\right)dt = \frac{g}{10}\left(t + \frac{1}{10}e^{-10t}\right) + C,$$

and we find $C$ using the initial condition $x(0) = 0$:

$$0 = \frac{g}{10}\left(0 + \frac{1}{10}e^{-10(0)}\right) + C \qquad \Rightarrow \qquad C = -\frac{g}{100}$$

$$\Rightarrow \qquad x(t) = \frac{g}{10}t + \frac{g}{100}\left(e^{-10t} - 1\right) = (0.981)t + (0.0981)e^{-10t} - 0.0981 \text{ (m)}.$$

When the object hits the ground, $x(t) = 1000\,\text{m}$. Thus we solve

$$(0.981)t + (0.0981)e^{-10t} - 0.0981 = 1000,$$

which gives ($t$ is nonnegative!) $t \approx 1019.468 \approx 1019\,\text{sec}$.

3. For this problem, $m = 500$ kg, $v_0 = 0$, $g = 9.81$ m/sec$^2$, and $b = 50$ kg/sec. We also see that the object has 1000 m to fall before it hits the ground. Plugging these variables into equation (6) on page 111 of the text gives the equation

$$x(t) = \frac{(500)(9.81)}{50}t + \frac{500}{50}\left(0 - \frac{(500)(9.81)}{50}\right)\left(1 - e^{-50t/500}\right)$$

$$\Rightarrow \qquad x(t) = 98.1t + 981e^{-t/10} - 981.$$

To find out when the object will hit the ground, we solve $x(t) = 1000$ for $t$. Therefore, we have

$$1000 = 98.1t + 981e^{-t/10} - 981 \qquad \Rightarrow \qquad 98.1t + 981e^{-t/10} = 1981.$$

In this equation, if we ignore the term $981e^{-t/10}$ we will find that $t \approx 20.2$. But this means that we have ignored the term similar to $981e^{-2} \approx 132.8$ which we see is to large to ignore. Therefore, we must try to approximate $t$. We will use Newton's method on the equation

$$f(t) = 98.1t + 981e^{-t/10} - 1981 = 0.$$

(If we can find a root to this equation, we will have found the $t$ we want.) Newton's method generates a sequence of approximations given by the formula

$$t_{n+1} = t_n - \frac{f(t_n)}{f'(t_n)}.$$

Since $f'(t) = 98.1 - 98.1e^{-t/10} = 98.1\left(1 - e^{-t/10}\right)$, the recursive equation above becomes

$$t_{n+1} = t_n - \frac{t_n + 10e^{-t_n/10} - (1981/98.1)}{1 - e^{-t_n/10}}. \tag{3.10}$$

To start the process, let $t_0 = 1981/98.1 \approx 20.19368$, which was the approximation we obtained when we neglected the exponential term. Then, by equation (3.10) above we have

$$t_1 = 20.19368 - \frac{20.19368 + 10e^{-2.019368} - 20.19368}{1 - e^{-2.019368}}$$

$$\Rightarrow \qquad t_1 \approx 18.663121.$$

To find $t_2$ we plug this value for $t_1$ into equation (3.10). This gives $t_2 \approx 18.643753$. Continuing this process, we find that $t_3 \approx 18.643749$. Since $t_2$ and $t_3$ agree to four decimal places, an approximation for the time it takes the object to strike the ground is $t \approx 18.6437$ sec.

**5.** We proceed similarly to the solution of Problem 1 to get

$$F_1 = 5g, \qquad F_2 = -10g$$

$$\Rightarrow \qquad 5\frac{dv}{dt} = F_1 + F_2 = 5g - 10v$$

$$\Rightarrow \qquad \frac{dv}{dt} = g - 2v, \qquad v(0) = 50.$$

Solving this iniial value problem yields

$$v(t) = \frac{g}{2} + Ce^{-2t};$$

$$50 = v(0) = \frac{g}{2} + Ce^{-2(0)} \qquad \Rightarrow \qquad C = \frac{100 - g}{2}$$

$$\Rightarrow \qquad v(t) = \frac{g}{2} + \frac{100 - g}{2}e^{-2t}.$$

We now integrate $v(t)$ to obtain the equation of the motion of the object:

$$x(t) = \int v(t)\,dt = \int \left( \frac{g}{2} + \frac{100 - g}{2}e^{-2t} \right) dt = \frac{g}{2}t - \frac{100 - g}{4}e^{-2t} + C,$$

where $C$ is such that $x(0) = 0$. Computing

$$0 = x(0) = \frac{g}{2}(0) - \frac{100 - g}{4}e^{-2(0)} + C \qquad \Rightarrow \qquad C = \frac{100 - g}{4},$$

we answer the first question in this problem, that is,

$$x(t) = \frac{g}{2}t - \frac{100 - g}{4}e^{-2t} + \frac{100 - g}{4} \approx 4.905t + 22.5475 - 22.5475\,e^{-2t}.$$

Answering the second question, we solve the equation $x(t) = 500$ to find time $t$ when the object passes $500\,\mathrm{m}$, and so strikes the ground.

$$4.905t + 22.5475 - 22.5475\,e^{-2t} = 500 \qquad \Rightarrow \qquad t \approx 97.34\,(\mathrm{sec}).$$

7. Since the air resistance force has different coefficients of proportionality for closed and for opened chute, we need two differential equations describing the motion. Let $x_1(t)$, $x_1(0) = 0$, denote the distance the parachutist has fallen in $t$ seconds, and let $v_1(t) = dx/dt$ denote her velocity. With $m = 75$, $b = b_1 = 30$ N-sec/m, and $v_0 = 0$ the initial value problem (4) on page 111 of the text becomes

$$75\frac{dv_1}{dt} = 75g - 30v_1 \qquad \Rightarrow \qquad \frac{dv_1}{dt} + \frac{2}{5}v_1 = g, \qquad v_1(0) = 0.$$

This is a linear equation. Solving yields

$$d\left(e^{2t/5}v_1\right) = e^{2t/5}g\,dt \qquad \Rightarrow \qquad v_1(t) = \frac{5g}{2} + C_1 e^{-2t/5};$$

$$0 = v_1(0) = \frac{5g}{2} + C_1 e^0 = \frac{5g}{2} + C_1 \qquad \Rightarrow \qquad C_1 = -\frac{5g}{2}$$

$$\Rightarrow \qquad v_1(t) = \frac{5g}{2}\left(1 - e^{-2t/5}\right)$$

$$\Rightarrow \qquad x_1(t) = \int_0^t v_1(s)ds = \frac{5g}{2}\left(s + \frac{5}{2}e^{-2s/5}\right)\Big|_{s=0}^{s=t} = \frac{5g}{2}\left(t + \frac{5}{2}e^{-2t/5} - \frac{5}{2}\right).$$

To find the time $t_*$ when the chute opens, we solve

$$20 = v_1(t_*) \qquad \Rightarrow \qquad 20 = \frac{5g}{2}\left(1 - e^{-2t_*/5}\right) \qquad \Rightarrow \qquad t_* = -\frac{5}{2}\ln\left(1 - \frac{8}{g}\right) \approx 4.225\,(\text{sec}).$$

By this time the parachutist has fallen

$$x_1(t_*) = \frac{5g}{2}\left(t_* + \frac{5}{2}e^{-2t_*/5} - \frac{5}{2}\right) \approx \frac{5g}{2}\left(4.225 + \frac{5}{2}e^{-2\cdot4.225/5} - \frac{5}{2}\right) \approx 53.62\,(\text{m}),$$

and so she is $2000 - 53.62 = 1946.38$ m above the ground. Setting the second equation, we for convenience reset the time $t$. Denoting by $x_2(t)$ the distance passed by the parachutist from the moment when the chute opens, and by $v_2(t) := x_2'(t)$ – her velocity, we have

$$75\frac{dv_2}{dt} = 75g - 90v_2, \qquad v_2(0) = v_1(t_*) = 20, \quad x_2(0) = 0.$$

Solving, we get

$$v_2(t) = \frac{5g}{6} + C_2 e^{-6t/5};$$

$$20 = v_2(0) = \frac{5g}{6} + C_2 \qquad \Rightarrow \qquad C_2 = 20 - \frac{5g}{6}$$

$$\Rightarrow \qquad v_2(t) = \frac{5g}{6} + \left(20 - \frac{5g}{6}\right)e^{-6t/5}$$

$$\Rightarrow \qquad x_2(t) = \int_0^t v_2(s)ds = \left[\frac{5g}{6}s - \frac{5}{6}\left(20 - \frac{5g}{6}\right)e^{-6s/5}\right]\Big|_{s=0}^{s=t}$$

$$= \frac{5g}{6}t + \frac{5}{6}\left(20 - \frac{5g}{6}\right)\left(1 - e^{-6t/5}\right).$$

With the chute open, the parachutist falls 1946.38 m. It takes $t^*$ seconds, where $t^*$ satisfies $x_2(t^*) = 1946.38$. Solving yields

$$\frac{5g}{6} t^* + \frac{5}{6}\left(20 - \frac{5g}{6}\right)\left(1 - e^{-6t^*/5}\right) = 1946.38 \qquad \Rightarrow \qquad t^* \approx 236.884 \,(\text{sec}).$$

Therefore, the parachutist will hit the ground after $t^* + t_* \approx 241.1$ seconds.

9. This problem is similar to Example 1 on page 110 of the text with the addition of a buoyancy force of magnitude $(1/40)mg$. If we let $x(t)$ be the distance below the water at time $t$ and $v(t)$ the velocity, then the total force acting on the object is

$$F = mg - bv - \frac{1}{40} mg.$$

We are given $m = 100$ kg, $g = 9.81$ m/sec$^2$, and $b = 10$ kg/sec. Applying Newton's Second Law gives

$$100\frac{dv}{dt} = (100)(9.81) - 10v - \frac{10}{4}(9.81) \qquad \Rightarrow \qquad \frac{dv}{dt} = 9.56 - (0.1)v\,.$$

Solving this equation by separation of variables, we have

$$v(t) = 95.65 + Ce^{-t/10}.$$

Since $v(0) = 0$, we find $C = -95.65$ and, hence,

$$v(t) = 95.65 - 95.65e^{-t/10}.$$

Integrating yields

$$x(t) = 95.65t + 956.5e^{-t/10} + C_1\,.$$

Using the fact that $x(0) = 0$, we find $C_1 = -956.5$. Therefore, the equation of motion of the object is

$$x(t) = 95.65t + 956.5e^{-t/10} - 956.5\,.$$

To determine when the object is traveling at the velocity of 70 m/sec, we solve $v(t) = 70$. That is,

$$70 = 95.65 - 95.65e^{-t/10} = 95.65\left(1 - e^{-t/10}\right)$$

$$\Rightarrow \qquad t = -10\ln\left(1 - \frac{70}{95.65}\right) \approx 13.2 \text{ sec}.$$

**11.** Let $v(t) = V[x(t)]$. Then, using the chain rule, we get

$$\frac{dv}{dt} = \frac{dV}{dx}\frac{dx}{dt} = \frac{dV}{dx}V$$

and so, for $V(x)$, the initial value problem (4) on page 111 of the text becomes

$$m\frac{dV}{dx}V = mg - bV, \qquad V(0) = V[x(0)] = v(0) = v_0.$$

This differential equation is separable. Solving yields

$$\frac{V}{g - (b/m)V}dV = dx \qquad \Rightarrow \qquad \frac{m}{b}\left[\frac{g}{g - (b/m)V} - 1\right]dV = dx$$

$$\Rightarrow \qquad \int \frac{m}{b}\left[\frac{g}{g - (b/m)V} - 1\right]dV = \int dx$$

$$\Rightarrow \qquad \frac{m}{b}\left[-\frac{mg}{b}\ln|g - (b/m)V| - V\right] = x + C$$

$$\Rightarrow \qquad mg\ln|mg - bV| + bV = -\frac{b^2 x}{m} + C_1.$$

Substituting the initial condition, $V(0) = v_0$, we find that $C_1 = mg\ln|mg - bv_0| + bv_0$ and hence

$$mg\ln|mg - bV| + bV = -\frac{b^2 x}{m} + mg\ln|mg - bv_0| + bv_0$$

$$\Rightarrow \qquad e^{bV}|mg - bV|^{mg} = e^{bv_0}|mg - bv_0|^{mg}e^{-b^2 x/m}.$$

**13.** There are two forces acting on the shell: a constant force due to the downward pull of gravity and a force due to air resistance that acts in opposition to the motion of the shell. All of the motion occurs along a vertical axis. On this axis, we choose the origin to be the point where the shell was shot from and let $x(t)$ denote the position upward of the shell at time $t$. The forces acting on the object can be expressed in terms of this axis. The force due to gravity is

$$F_1 = -mg,$$

where $g$ is the acceleration due to gravity near Earth. Note we have a minus force because our coordinate system was chosen with up as positive and gravity acts in a downward direction. The force due to air resistance is

$$F_2 = -(0.1)v^2.$$

The negative sign is present because air resistance acts in opposition to the motion of the object. Therefore the net force acting on the shell is

$$F = F_1 + F_2 = -mg - (0.1)v^2.$$

We now apply Newton's second law to obtain

$$m\frac{dv}{dt} = -\left[mg + (0.1)v^2\right].$$

Because the initial velocity of the shell is 500 m/sec, a model for the velocity of the rising shell is expressed as the initial-value problem

$$m\frac{dv}{dt} = -\left[mg + (0.1)v^2\right], \qquad v(t=0) = 500, \qquad\qquad (3.11)$$

where $g = 9.81$. Separating variables, we get

$$\frac{dv}{10mg + v^2} = -\frac{dt}{10m}$$

and so

$$\int \frac{dv}{10mg + v^2} = -\int \frac{dt}{10m} \qquad \Rightarrow \qquad \frac{1}{\sqrt{10mg}}\tan^{-1}\left(\frac{v}{\sqrt{10mg}}\right) = -\frac{t}{10m} + C.$$

Setting $m = 3$, $g = 9.81$ and $v = 500$ when $t = 0$, we find

$$C = \frac{1}{\sqrt{10(3)(9.81)}}\tan^{-1}\left(\frac{500}{\sqrt{10(3)(9.81)}}\right) \approx 0.08956.$$

Thus the equation of velocity $v$ as a function of time $t$ is

$$\frac{1}{\sqrt{10mg}}\tan^{-1}\left(\frac{v}{\sqrt{10mg}}\right) = -\frac{t}{10m} + 0.08956.$$

From physics we know that when the shell reaches its maximum height the shell's velocity will be zero; therefore $t_{\max}$ will be

$$\begin{aligned} t_{\max} &= -10(3)\left[\frac{1}{\sqrt{10(3)(9.81)}}\tan^{-1}\left(\frac{0}{\sqrt{10(3)(9.81)}}\right) - 0.08956\right] \\ &= -(30)(-0.08956) \approx 2.69 \text{ (seconds).} \end{aligned}$$

Using equation (3.11) and noting that $dv/dt = (dv/dx)(dx/dt) = (dv/dx)v$, we can determine the maximum height attained by the shell. With the above substitution, equation (3.11) becomes

$$mv\frac{dv}{dx} = -\left(mg + 0.1v^2\right), \qquad v(0) = 500.$$

Using separation of variables and integration, we get

$$\frac{v\,dv}{10mg + v^2} = -\frac{dx}{10m} \quad \Rightarrow \quad \frac{1}{2}\ln\left(10mg + v^2\right) = -\frac{x}{10m} + C \quad \Rightarrow \quad 10mg + v^2 = Ke^{-x/(5m)}.$$

Setting $v = 500$ when $x = 0$, we find

$$K = e^0\left(10(3)(9.81) + (500)^2\right) = 250294.3.$$

Thus the equation of velocity as a function of distance is

$$v^2 + 10mg = (250294.3)e^{-x/(5m)}.$$

The maximum height will occur when the shell's velocity is zero, therefore $x_{max}$ is

$$x_{max} = -5(3)\ln\left(\frac{0 + 10(3)(9.81)}{250294.3}\right) \approx 101.19 \text{ (meters)}.$$

15. The total torque exerted on the flywheel is the sum of the torque exerted by the motor and the retarding torque due to friction. Thus, by Newton's second law for rotation, we have

$$I\frac{d\omega}{dt} = T - k\omega \qquad \text{with} \qquad \omega(0) = \omega_0,$$

where $I$ is the moment of inertia of the flywheel, $\omega(t)$ is the angular velocity, $d\omega/dt$ is the angular acceleration, $T$ is the constant torque exerted by the motor, and $k$ is a positive constant of proportionality for the torque due to friction. Solving this separable equation gives

$$\omega(t) = \frac{T}{k} + Ce^{-kt/I}.$$

Using the initial condition $\omega(0) = \omega_0$ we find $C = (\omega_0 - T/k)$. Hence,

$$\omega(t) = \frac{T}{k} + \left(\omega_0 - \frac{T}{k}\right)e^{-kt/I}.$$

# Chapter 3

**17.** Since the motor is turned off, its torque is $T = 0$, and the only torque acting on the flywheel is the retarding one, $-5\sqrt{\omega}$. Then Newton's second law for rotational motion becomes

$$I\frac{d\omega}{dt} = -5\sqrt{\omega} \quad \text{with} \quad \omega(0) = \omega_0 = 225 \text{ (rad/sec)} \quad \text{and} \quad I = 50 \text{ (kg/m}^2\text{)} .$$

The general solution to this separable equation is

$$\sqrt{\omega(t)} = -\frac{5}{2I}t + C = -0.05t + C.$$

Using the initial condition, we find

$$\sqrt{\omega(0)} = -0.05 \cdot 0 + C \quad \Rightarrow \quad C = \sqrt{\omega(0)} = \sqrt{225} = 15.$$

Thus

$$t = \frac{1}{0.05}\left[15 - \sqrt{\omega(t)}\right] = 20\left[15 - \sqrt{\omega(t)}\right].$$

At the moment $t = t_{\text{stop}}$ when the flywheel stops rotating we have $\omega(t_{\text{stop}}) = 0$ and so

$$t_{\text{stop}} = 20(15 - \sqrt{0}) = 300 \text{ (sec)}.$$

**19.** There are three forces acting on the object: $F_1$, the force due to gravity, $F_2$, the air resistance force, and $F_3$, the friction force. Using Figure 3.11 (with 30° replaced by 45°), we obtain

$$F_1 = mg\sin 45° = mg\sqrt{2}/2,$$
$$F_2 = -3v,$$
$$F_3 = -\mu N = -\mu mg\cos 45° = -\mu mg\sqrt{2}/2,$$

and so the equation describing the motion is

$$m\frac{dv}{dt} = \frac{mg\sqrt{2}}{2} - \frac{\mu mg\sqrt{2}}{2} - 3v \quad \Rightarrow \quad \frac{dv}{dt} = 0.475g\sqrt{2} - \frac{v}{20}$$

with the initial condition $v(0) = 0$. Solving yields

$$v(t) = 9.5g\sqrt{2} + Ce^{-t/20};$$
$$0 = v(0) = 9.5g\sqrt{2} + C \quad \Rightarrow \quad C = -9.5g\sqrt{2}$$

$$\Rightarrow \qquad v(t) = 9.5g\sqrt{2}\left(1 - e^{-t/20}\right).$$

Since $x(0) = 0$, integrating the above equation, we obtain

$$
\begin{aligned}
x(t) &= \int_0^t v(s)ds = \int_0^t 9.5g\sqrt{2}\left(1 - e^{-s/20}\right)ds = 9.5g\sqrt{2}\left(s + 20e^{-s/20}\right)\Big|_{s=0}^{s=t} \\
&= 9.5g\sqrt{2}\left(t + 20e^{-t/20} - 20\right) \approx 131.8t + 2636e^{-t/20} - 2636.
\end{aligned}
$$

The object reaches the end of the inclined plane when

$$x(t) = 131.8t + 2636e^{-t/20} - 2636 = 10 \qquad \Rightarrow \qquad t \approx 1.768\,(\text{sec}).$$

**21.** In this problem there are two forces acting on a sailboat: A constant horizontal force due to the wind and a force due to the water resistance that acts in opposition to the motion of the sailboat. All of the motion occurs along a horizontal axis. On this axis, we choose the origin to be the point where the hard blowing wind begins and $x(t)$ denotes the distance the sailboat travels in time $t$. The forces on the sailboat can be expressed in terms of this axis. The force due to the wind is

$$F_1 = 600 \text{ N}.$$

The force due to water resistance is

$$F_2 = -100v \text{ N}.$$

Applying Newton's second law we obtain

$$m\frac{dv}{dt} = 600 - 100v.$$

Since the initial velocity of the sailboat is 1 m/sec, a model for the velocity of the moving sailboat is expressed as the initial-value problem

$$m\frac{dv}{dt} = 600 - 100v, \qquad v(0) = 1.$$

Using separation of variables, we get, with $m = 50$ kg,

$$\frac{dv}{6 - v} = 2dt \qquad \Rightarrow \qquad -6\ln(6 - v) = 2t + C.$$

Therefore, the velocity is given by $v(t) = 6 - Ke^{-2t}$. Setting $v = 1$ when $t = 0$, we find that

$$1 = 6 - K \qquad \Rightarrow \qquad K = 5.$$

Thus the equation for velocity $v(t)$ is $v(t) = 6 - 5e^{-2t}$. The limiting velocity of the sailboat under these conditions is found by letting time approach infinity:

$$\lim_{t \to \infty} v(t) = \lim_{t \to \infty} \left(6 - 5e^{-2t}\right) = 6 \text{ (m/sec)}.$$

To determine the equation of motion we will use the equation of velocity obtained previously and substitute $dx/dt$ for $v(t)$ to obtain

$$\frac{dx}{dt} = 6 - 5e^{-2t}, \qquad x(0) = 0.$$

Integrating this equation we obtain

$$x(t) = 6t + \frac{5}{2}e^{-2t} + C_1.$$

Setting $x = 0$ when $t = 0$, we find

$$0 = 0 + \frac{5}{2} + C_1 \qquad \Rightarrow \qquad C_1 = -\frac{5}{2}.$$

Thus the equation of motion for the sailboat is given by

$$x(t) = 6t + \frac{5}{2}e^{-2t} - \frac{5}{2}.$$

23. In this problem, there are two forces acting on a boat: the wind force $F_1$ and the water resistance force $F_2$. Since the proportionality constant in the water resistance force is different for the velocities below and above of a certain limit (5 m/sec for the boat A and 6 m/sec for the boat B), for each boat we have two differential equations. (Compare with Problem 7.) Let $x_1^{(A)}(t)$ denote the distance passed by the boat A for the time $t$, $v_1^{(A)}(t) := dx_1^{(A)}(t)/dt$. Then the equation describing the motion of the boat A before it reaches the velocity 5 m/sec is

$$m \frac{dv_1^{(A)}}{dt} = F_1 + F_2 = 650 - b_1 v_1^{(A)} \qquad \Rightarrow \qquad \frac{dv_1^{(A)}}{dt} = \frac{65}{6} - \frac{4}{3}v_1^{(A)}. \tag{3.12}$$

Solving this linear equation and using the initial condition, $v_1^{(A)}(0) = 2$, we get

$$v_1^{(A)}(t) = \frac{65}{8} - \frac{49}{8} e^{-4t/3},$$

and so

$$x_1^{(A)}(t) = \int\limits_0^t \left( \frac{65}{8} - \frac{49}{8} e^{-4s/3} \right) ds = \frac{65}{8} t - \frac{147}{32} \left( e^{-4t/3} - 1 \right).$$

The boat A will have the velocity 5 m/sec at $t = t_*$ satisfying

$$\frac{65}{8} - \frac{49}{8} e^{-4t_*/3} = 5 \qquad \Rightarrow \qquad t_* = -\frac{3 \ln(25/49)}{4} \approx 0.5 \,(\text{sec}),$$

and it will be

$$x_1^{(A)}(t_*) = \frac{65}{8} t_* - \frac{147}{32} \left( e^{-4t_*/3} - 1 \right) \approx 1.85 \,(\text{m})$$

away from the starting point or, equivalently, $500 - 1.85 = 498.15$ meters away from the finish. Similarly to (3.12), resetting the time, we obtain an equation of the motion of the boat A starting from the moment when its velocity reaches 5 m/sec. Denoting by $x_2^{(A)}(t)$ the distance passed by the boat A and by $v_2^{(A)}(t)$ its velocity, we get $x_2^{(A)}(0) = 0$, $v_2^{(A)}(0) = 5$, and

$$m \frac{dv_2^{(A)}}{dt} = 650 - b_2 v_2^{(A)}$$

$$\Rightarrow \qquad \frac{dv_2^{(A)}}{dt} = \frac{65}{6} - v_2^{(A)} \qquad \Rightarrow \qquad v_2^{(A)}(t) = \frac{65}{6} - \frac{35}{6} e^{-t}$$

$$\Rightarrow \qquad x_2^{(A)}(t) = \int\limits_0^t \left( \frac{65}{6} - \frac{35}{6} e^{-s} \right) ds = \frac{65}{6} t + \frac{35}{6} \left( e^{-t} - 1 \right).$$

Solving the equation $x_2^{(A)}(t) = 498.15$, we find the time (counting from the moment when the boat A's velocity has reached 5 m/sec) $t^* \approx 46.5$ sec, which is necessary to come to the end of the first leg. Therefore, the total time for the boat A is $t_* + t^* \approx 0.5 + 46.5 = 47$ sec.

Similarly, for the boat B, we find that

$$v_1^{(B)}(t) = \frac{65}{8} - \frac{49}{8} e^{-5t/3}, \quad x_1^{(B)}(t) = \frac{65}{8} t + \frac{147}{40} \left( e^{-5t/3} - 1 \right), \quad t_* = -\frac{3 \ln(17/49)}{5} \approx 0.635 \,;$$

$$v_2^{(B)}(t) = \frac{65}{5} - \frac{35}{5} e^{-5t/6}, \quad x_2^{(B)}(t) = \frac{65}{5} t + \frac{42}{5} \left( e^{-5t/6} - 1 \right), \quad t^* \approx 38.895 \,.$$

Thus, $t_* + t^* < 40$ sec, and so the boat B will be leading at the end of the first leg.

# Chapter 3

**25. (a)** From Newton's second law we have

$$m \frac{dv}{dt} = \frac{-GMm}{r^2}.$$

Dividing both sides by $m$, the mass of the rocket, and letting $g = GM/R^2$ we get

$$\frac{dv}{dt} = \frac{-gR^2}{r^2},$$

where $g$ is the gravitational force of Earth, $R$ is the radius of Earth and $r$ is the distance between Earth and the projectile.

**(b)** Using the equation found in part (a), letting $dv/dt = (dv/dr)(dr/dt)$ and knowing that $dr/dt = v$, we get

$$v \frac{dv}{dr} = -\frac{gR^2}{r^2}.$$

**(c)** The differential equation found in part (b) is separable and can be written in the form

$$v\,dv = -\frac{gR^2}{r^2}\,dr.$$

If the projectile leaves Earth with a velocity of $v_0$ we have the initial value problem

$$v\,dv = -\frac{gR^2}{r^2}\,dr, \qquad v\bigg|_{r=R} = v_0.$$

Integrating we get

$$\frac{v^2}{2} = \frac{gR^2}{r} + K,$$

where $K$ is an arbitrary constant. We can find the constant $K$ by using the initial value as follows:

$$K = \frac{v_0^2}{2} - \frac{gR^2}{R} = \frac{v_0^2}{2} - gR.$$

Substituting this formula for $K$ and solving for the velocity we obtain

$$v^2 = \frac{2gR^2}{r} + v_0^2 - 2gR.$$

**(d)** In order for the velocity of the projectile to always remain positive, $(2gR^2/r) + v_0^2$ must be greater than $2gR$ as $r$ approaches infinity. This means

$$\lim_{r \to \infty} \left( \frac{2gR^2}{r} + v_0^2 \right) > 2gR \qquad \Rightarrow \qquad v_0^2 > 2gR.$$

Therefore, $v_0^2 - 2gR > 0$.

(e) Using the equation $v_e = \sqrt{2gR}$ for the escape velocity and converting meters to kilometers we have

$$v_e = \sqrt{2gR} = \sqrt{2 \cdot 9.81 \text{ m/sec}^2 \cdot (1 \text{ km}/1000 \text{ m})(6370 \text{ km})} \approx 11.18 \text{ km/sec}.$$

(f) Similarly to (e), we find

$$v_e = \sqrt{2(g/6)R} = \sqrt{2(9.81/6)(1/1000)(1738)} = 2.38 \text{ (km/sec)}.$$

## EXERCISES 3.5:   Electrical Circuits, page 122

1. In this problem, $R = 5\,\Omega$, $L = 0.05\,\text{H}$, and the voltage function is given by $E(t) = 5\cos 120t$ V. Substituting these data into a general solution (3) to the Kirchhoff's equation (2) yields

$$
\begin{aligned}
I(t) &= e^{-Rt/L}\left(\int e^{Rt/L}\,\frac{E(t)}{L}\,dt + K\right) \\
&= e^{-5t/0.05}\left(\int e^{5t/0.05}\,\frac{5\cos 120t}{0.05}\,dt + K\right) = e^{-100t}\left(100\int e^{100t}\cos 120t\,dt + K\right).
\end{aligned}
$$

Using the integral tables, we evaluate the integral in the right-hand side and obtain

$$I(t) = e^{-100t}\left[100\,\frac{e^{100t}\,(100\cos 120t + 120\sin 120t)}{(100)^2 + (120)^2} + K\right] = \frac{\cos 120t + 1.2\sin 120t}{2.44} + Ke^{-100t}.$$

The initial condition, $I(0) = 1$, implies that

$$1 = I(0) = \frac{\cos(120(0)) + 1.2\sin(120(0))}{2.44} + Ke^{-100(0)} = \frac{1}{2.44} + K \quad\Rightarrow\quad K = 1 - \frac{1}{2.44} = \frac{1.44}{2.44}$$

and so

$$I(t) = \frac{1.44e^{-100t} + \cos 120t + 1.2\sin 120t}{2.44}.$$

The subsequent inductor voltage is then determined by

$$
\begin{aligned}
E_L(t) = L\,\frac{dI}{dt} &= 0.05\,\frac{d}{dt}\left(\frac{1.44e^{-100t} + \cos 120t + 1.2\sin 120t}{2.44}\right) \\
&= \frac{-7.2e^{-100t} - 6\sin 120t + 7.2\cos 120t}{2.44}.
\end{aligned}
$$

**3.** In this $RC$ circuit, $R = 100\,\Omega$, $C = 10^{-12}$ F, the initial charge of the capacitor is $Q = q(0) = 0$ coulombs, and the applied constant voltage is $V = 5$ volts. Thus we can use a general equation for the charge $q(t)$ of the capacitor derived in Example 2. Substitution of given data yields

$$q(t) = CV + [Q - CV]e^{-t/RC} = 10^{-12}(5)\left(1 - e^{-t/(100 \cdot 10^{-12})}\right) = 5 \cdot 10^{-12}\left(1 - e^{-10^{10}t}\right)$$

and so

$$E_C(t) = \frac{q(t)}{C} = 5\left(1 - e^{-10^{10}t}\right).$$

Solving the equation $E_C(t) = 3$, we get

$$5\left(1 - e^{-10^{10}t}\right) = 3 \qquad \Rightarrow \qquad e^{-10^{10}t} = 0.4 \qquad \Rightarrow \qquad t = -\frac{\ln 0.4}{10^{10}} \approx 9.2 \times 10^{-11}\ (\text{sec}).$$

Therefore, it will take about $9.2 \times 10^{-11}$ seconds for the voltage to reach 3 volts at the receiving gate.

**5.** Let $V(t)$ denote the voltage across an element, and let $I(t)$ be the current through this element. Then for the power, say $P = P(t)$, generated or dissipated by the element we have

$$P = I(t)V(t). \tag{3.13}$$

We use formulas given in (a), (b), and (c) on page 119–120 of the text to find $P$ for a resistor, an inductor, and a capacitor.

**(a)** *Resistor.* In this case,

$$V(t) = E_R(t) = RI(t),$$

and substitution into (3.13) yields

$$P_R = I(t)\,[RI(t)] = I(t)^2 R.$$

**(b)** *Inductor.* We have

$$V(t) = E_L(t) = L\frac{dI(t)}{dt}$$

$$\Rightarrow \qquad P_L = I(t)\left[L\frac{dI(t)}{dt}\right] = \frac{L}{2}\left[2I(t)\frac{dI(t)}{dt}\right] = \frac{L}{2}\frac{d\,[I(t)^2]}{dt} = \frac{d\,[LI(t)^2/2]}{dt}.$$

**(c)** *Capacitor.* Here, with $q(t)$ denoting the electrical charge on the capacitor,

$$V(t) = E_C(t) = \frac{1}{C}q(t) \quad \Rightarrow \quad q(t) = CE_C(t) \quad \Rightarrow \quad I(t) = \frac{dq(t)}{dt} = \frac{d[CE_C(t)]}{dt}$$

and so

$$P_C = \frac{d[CE_C(t)]}{dt}E_C(t) = \frac{C}{2}\left[2E_C(t)\frac{dE_C(t)}{dt}\right] = \frac{C}{2}\frac{d[E_C(t)^2]}{dt} = \frac{d[CE_C(t)^2/2]}{dt}.$$

**7.** First, we find a formula for the current $I(t)$. Given that $R = 3\,\Omega$, $L = 10\,\text{H}$, and the voltage function $E(t)$ is a constant, say, $V$, the formula (3) on page 121 (which describes currents in $RL$ circuits) becomes

$$I(t) = e^{-3t/10}\left(\int e^{3t/10}\frac{V}{10}\,dt + K\right) = e^{-3t/10}\left(\frac{V}{3}e^{3t/10} + K\right) = \frac{V}{3} + Ke^{-3t/10}.$$

The initial condition, $I(0) = 0$ (there were no current in the electromagnet before the voltage source was applied), yields

$$0 = \frac{V}{3} + Ke^{-3(0)/10} \quad \Rightarrow \quad K = -\frac{V}{3} \quad \Rightarrow \quad I(t) = \frac{V}{3}\left(1 - e^{-3t/10}\right).$$

Next, we find the limiting value $I_\infty$ of $I(t)$, that is,

$$I_\infty = \lim_{t\to\infty}\left[\frac{V}{3}\left(1 - e^{-3t/10}\right)\right] = \frac{V}{3}(1 - 0) = \frac{V}{3}.$$

Therefore, we are looking for the moment $t$ when $I(t) = (0.9)I_\infty = (0.9)V/3$. Solving yields

$$\frac{0.9V}{3} = \frac{V}{3}\left(1 - e^{-3t/10}\right) \quad \Rightarrow \quad e^{-3t/10} = 0.1 \quad \Rightarrow \quad t = -\frac{10\ln 0.1}{3} \approx 7.68.$$

Thus it takes approximately 7.68 seconds for the electromagnet to reach 90% of its final value.

## EXERCISES 3.6: Improved Euler's Method, page 132

**1.** Given the step size $h$ and considering equally spaced points we have

$$x_{n+1} = x_n + nh, \qquad n = 0, 1, 2, \dots.$$

Euler's method is defined by equation (4) on page 125 of the text to be

$$y_{n+1} = y_n + hf(x_n, y_n), \qquad n = 0, 1, 2, \dots ,$$

where $f(x, y) = 5y$. Starting with the given value of $y_0 = 1$, we compute

$$y_1 = y_0 + h(5y_0) = 1 + 5h.$$

We can then use this value to compute $y_2$ to be

$$y_2 = y_1 + h(5y_1) = (1 + 5h)y_1 = (1 + 5h)^2.$$

Proceeding in this manner, we can generalize to $y_n$:

$$y_n = (1 + 5h)^n.$$

Referring back to our equation for $x_n$ and using the given values of $x_0 = 0$ and $x_1 = 1$ we find

$$1 = nh \qquad \Rightarrow \qquad n = \frac{1}{h}.$$

Substituting this back into the formula for $y_n$ we find the approximation to the initial value problem

$$y' = 5y, \qquad y(0) = 1$$

at $x = 1$ to be $(1 + 5h)^{1/h}$.

**3.** In this initial value problem, $f(x, y) = y$, $x_0 = 0$, and $y_0 = 1$. Formula (8) on page 127 of the text then becomes

$$y_{n+1} = y_n + \frac{h}{2}(y_n + y_{n+1}).$$

Solving this equation for $y_{n+1}$ yields

$$\left(1 - \frac{h}{2}\right) y_{n+1} = \left(1 + \frac{h}{2}\right) y_n \qquad \Rightarrow \qquad y_{n+1} = \left(\frac{1 + h/2}{1 - h/2}\right) y_n, \qquad n = 0, 1, \dots . \quad (3.14)$$

If $n \geq 1$, we can use (3.14) to express $y_n$ in terms of $y_{n-1}$ and substitute this expression into the right-hand side of (3.14). Continuing this process, we get

$$y_{n+1} = \left(\frac{1 + h/2}{1 - h/2}\right) \left[\left(\frac{1 + h/2}{1 - h/2}\right) y_{n-1}\right] = \left(\frac{1 + h/2}{1 - h/2}\right)^2 y_{n-1} = \dots = \left(\frac{1 + h/2}{1 - h/2}\right)^{n+1} y_0 .$$

In order to approximate the solution $\phi(x) = e^x$ at the point $x = 1$ with $N$ steps, we take $h = (x - x_0)/N = 1/N$, and so $N = 1/h$. Then the above formula becomes

$$y_N = \left(\frac{1+h/2}{1-h/2}\right)^N y_0 = \left(\frac{1+h/2}{1-h/2}\right)^N = \left(\frac{1+h/2}{1-h/2}\right)^{1/h}$$

and hence

$$e = \phi(1) \approx y_N = \left(\frac{1+h/2}{1-h/2}\right)^{1/h}.$$

Substituting $h = 10^{-k}$, $k = 0, 1, 2, 3$, and $4$, we fill in Table 3-A.

**Table 3–A:** Approximations $\left(\dfrac{1+h/2}{1+h/2}\right)^{1/h}$ to $e \approx 2.718281828\ldots$.

| $h$ | Approximation | Error |
|---|---|---|
| 1 | 3 | 0.281718172 |
| $10^{-1}$ | 2.720551414 | 0.002269586 |
| $10^{-2}$ | 2.718304481 | 0.000022653 |
| $10^{-3}$ | 2.718282055 | 0.000000227 |
| $10^{-4}$ | 2.718281831 | 0.000000003 |

These approximations are better then those in Tables 3.4 and 3.5 of the text.

**5.** In this problem, we have $f(x, y) = 4y$. Thus, we have

$$f(x_n, y_n) = 4y_n \quad \text{and} \quad f(x_n + h, y_n + hf(x_n, y_n)) = 4[y_n + h(4y_n)] = 4y_n + 16hy_n.$$

By equation (9) on page 128 of the text, we have

$$y_{n+1} = y_n + \frac{h}{2}(4y_n + 4y_n + 16hy_n) = (1 + 4h + 8h^2) y_n. \tag{3.15}$$

Since the initial condition $y(0) = 1/3$ implies that $x_0 = 0$ and $y_0 = 1/3$, equation (3.15) above yields

$$y_1 = (1 + 4h + 8h^2) y_0 = \frac{1}{3}(1 + 4h + 8h^2),$$

$$y_2 = \left(1 + 4h + 8h^2\right) y_1 = \left(1 + 4h + 8h^2\right) \left(\frac{1}{3}\right) \left(1 + 4h + 8h^2\right) = \frac{1}{3}\left(1 + 4h + 8h^2\right)^2,$$

$$y_3 = \left(1 + 4h + 8h^2\right) y_2 = \left(1 + 4h + 8h^2\right) \left(\frac{1}{3}\right) \left(1 + 4h + 8h^2\right)^2 = \frac{1}{3}\left(1 + 4h + 8h^2\right)^3.$$

Continuing this way we see that

$$y_n = \frac{1}{3}\left(1 + 4h + 8h^2\right)^n. \tag{3.16}$$

(This can be proved by induction using equation (3.15) above.) We are looking for an approximation to our solution at the point $x = 1/2$. Therefore, we have

$$h = \frac{1/2 - x_0}{n} = \frac{1/2 - 0}{n} = \frac{1}{2n} \qquad \Rightarrow \qquad n = \frac{1}{2h}.$$

Substituting this value for $n$ into equation (3.16) yields

$$y_n = \frac{1}{3}\left(1 + 4h + 8h^2\right)^{1/(2h)}.$$

7. For this problem, $f(x, y) = x - y^2$. We need to approximate the solution on the interval $[1, 1.5]$ using a step size of $h = 0.1$. Thus the number of steps needed is $N = 5$. The inputs to the subroutine on page 129 are $x_0 = 1$, $y_0 = 0$, $c = 1.5$, and $N = 5$. For Step 3 of the subroutine we have

$$F = f(x, y) = x - y^2,$$
$$G = f(x + h, y + hF) = (x + h) - (y + hF)^2 = (x + h) - \left[y + h(x - y^2)\right]^2.$$

Starting with $x = x_0 = 1$ and $y = y_0 = 0$ we get $h = 0.1$ (as specified) and

$$F = 1 - 0^2 = 1,$$
$$G = (1 + 0.1) - \left[0 + 0.1(1 - 0^2)\right]^2 = 1.1 - (0.1)^2 = 1.09.$$

Hence in Step 4 we compute

$$x = 1 + 0.1 = 1.1,$$
$$y = 0 + 0.05(1 + 1.09) = 0.1045.$$

Thus the approximate value of the solution at 1.1 is 0.1045. Next we repeat Step 3 with $x = 1.1$ and $y = 0.1045$ to obtain

$$F = 1.1 + (0.1045)^2 \approx 1.0891,$$

$$G = (1.1 + 0.1) - \left[0.1045 + 0.1\left(1.1 - (0.1045)^2\right)\right]^2 \approx 1.1545.$$

Hence in Step 4 we compute

$$x = 1.1 + 0.1 = 1.2,$$

$$y = 0.1045 + 0.05(1.0891 + 1.1545) \approx 0.21668.$$

Thus the approximate value of the solution at 1.2 is 0.21668. By continuing in this way, we fill in Table 3-B. (The reader can also use the software provided free with the text.)

---

**Table 3–B**: Improved Euler's method to approximate the solution of $y' = x - y^2$, $y(1) = 0$, with $h = 0.1$.

| $i$ | $x$ | $y$ |
|---|---|---|
| 0 | 1 | 0 |
| 1 | 1.1 | 0.10450 |
| 2 | 1.2 | 0.21668 |
| 3 | 1.3 | 0.33382 |
| 4 | 1.4 | 0.45300 |
| 5 | 1.5 | 0.57135 |

---

**9.** In this initial value problem, $f(x, y) = x + 3\cos(xy)$, $x_0 = 0$, and $y_0 = 0$. To approximate the solution on $[0, 2]$ with a step size $h = 0.2$, we need $N = 10$ steps. The functions $F$ and $G$ in the improved Euler's method subroutine are

$$\begin{aligned} F &= f(x, y) = x + 3\cos(xy); \\ G &= f(x + h, y + hF) = x + h + 3\cos[(x + h)(y + hF)] \\ &= x + 0.2 + 3\cos[(x + 0.2)(y + 0.2\{x + 3\cos(xy)\})]. \end{aligned}$$

Starting with $x = x_0 = 0$ and $y = y_0 = 0$, we compute

$$F = 0 + 3\cos(0 \cdot 0) = 3\,;$$

$$G = 0 + 0.2 + 3\cos[(0 + 0.2)(0 + 0.2\,\{0 + 3\cos(0 \cdot 0)\})] \approx 3.178426\,.$$

Using these values, we find on Step 4 that

$$x = 0 + 0.2 = 0.2\,,$$

$$y = 0 + 0.1(3 + 3.178426) \approx 0.617843\,.$$

With these new values of $x$ and $y$, we repeat the Step 3 and obtain

$$F = 0.2 + 3\cos(0.2 \cdot 0.617843) \approx 3.177125\,;$$

$$G = 0.2 + 0.2 + 3\cos[(0.2 + 0.2)(0.617843 + 0.2\,\{0.2 + 3\cos(0.2 \cdot 0.617843)\})] \approx 3.030865\,.$$

Step 4 then yields an approximation of the solution at $x = 0.4$:

$$x = 0.2 + 0.2 = 0.4\,,$$

$$y = 0.617843 + 0.1(3.177125 + 3.030865) \approx 1.238642\,.$$

By continuing in this way, we obtain Table 3-C.

---

**Table 3–C**: Improved Euler's method approximations to the solution of $y' = x + 3\cos(xy)$, $y(0) = 0$, on $[0, 2]$ with $h = 0.2$.

| $i$ | $x$ | $y \approx$ | $i$ | $x$ | $y \approx$ |
|---|---|---|---|---|---|
| 0 | 0 | 0 | 6 | 1.2 | 1.884609 |
| 1 | 0.2 | 0.617843 | 7 | 1.4 | 1.724472 |
| 2 | 0.4 | 1.238642 | 8 | 1.6 | 1.561836 |
| 3 | 0.6 | 1.736531 | 9 | 1.8 | 1.417318 |
| 4 | 0.8 | 1.981106 | 10 | 2.0 | 1.297794 |
| 5 | 1.0 | 1.997052 | | | |

---

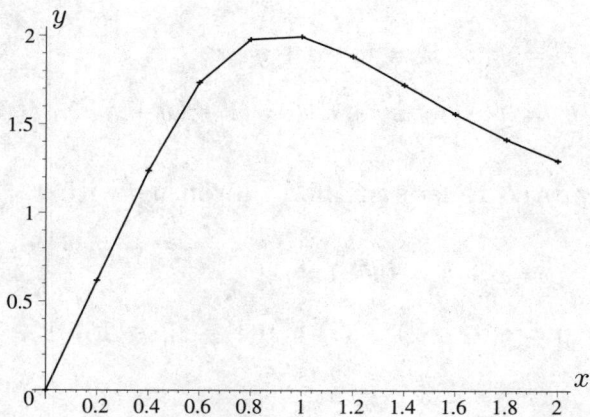

**Figure 3–B**: Polygonal line approximation to the solution of $y' = x + 3\cos(xy)$, $y(0) = 0$.

A polygonal line, approximating the graph of the solution to the given initial value problem, which has vertices at points $(x, y)$ from Table 3-C, is sketched in Figure 3-B.

**13.** We want to approximate the solution $\phi(x)$ to $y' = 1 - y + y^3$, $y(0) = 0$, at $x = 1$. (In other words, we want to find an approximate value for $\phi(1)$.) To do this, we will use the algorithm on page 130 of the text. (We assume that the reader has a programmable calculator or microcomputer available and can transform the step-by-step outline on page 130 into an executable program. Alternatively, the reader can use the software provided free with the text.)

The inputs to the program are $x_0 = 0$, $y_0 = 0$, $c = 1$, $\varepsilon = 0.003$, and, say, $M = 100$. Notice that by Step 6 of the improved Euler's method with tolerance, the computations should terminate when two successive approximations differ by less that 0.003. The initial value for $h$ in Step 1 of the improved Euler's method subroutine is

$$h = (1 - 0)2^{-0} = 1.$$

For the given equation, we have $f(x, y) = 1 - y + y^3$, and so the numbers $F$ and $G$ in Step 3 of the improved Euler's method subroutine are

$$F = f(x, y) = 1 - y + y^3,$$
$$G = f(x + h, y + hF) = 1 - (y + hF) + (y + hF)^3.$$

From Step 4 of the improved Euler's method subroutine with $x = 0$, $y = 0$, and $h = 1$, we get

$$x = x + h = 0 + 1 = 1,$$
$$y = y + \frac{h}{2}(F + G) = 0 + \frac{1}{2}\left[1 + (1 - 1 + 1^3)\right] = 1.$$

Thus,

$$\phi(1) \approx y(1; 1) = 1.$$

The algorithm (Step 1 of the improved Euler's method subroutine) next sets $h = 2^{-1} = 0.5$. The inputs to the subroutine are $x = 0$, $y = 0$, $c = 1$, and $N = 2$. For Step 3 of the subroutine we have

$$F = 1 - 0 + 0 = 1,$$
$$G = 1 - [0 + 0.5(1)] + [0 + 0.5(1)]^3 = 0.625.$$

Hence in Step 4 we compute

$$x = 0 + 0.5 = 0.5,$$
$$y = 0 + 0.25(1 + 0.625) = 0.40625.$$

Thus the approximate value of the solution at 0.5 is 0.40625. Next we repeat Step 3 with $x = 0.5$ and $y = 0.40625$ to obtain

$$F = 1 - 0.40625 + (0.40625)^3 = 0.6607971,$$
$$G = 1 - [0.40625 + 0.5(0.6607971)] + [0.40625 + 0.5(0.6607971)]^3 \approx 0.6630946.$$

In Step 4 we compute

$$x = 0.5 + 0.5 = 1,$$

**Table 3–D**: Improved Euler's method approximations to $\phi(1)$, where $\phi(x)$ is the solution to $y' = 1 - y + y^3$, $y(0) = 0$.

| $h$ | $y(1; h) \approx \phi(1)$ |
|-----|---------------------------|
| 1 | 1.0 |
| $2^{-1}$ | 0.7372229 |
| $2^{-2}$ | 0.7194115 |
| $2^{-3}$ | 0.7169839 |

$$y = 0.40625 + 0.25(0.6607971 + 0.6630946) \approx 0.7372229\,.$$

Thus the approximate value of the solution at $x = 1$ is 0.7372229. Further outputs of the algorithm are given in Table 3-D.

Since

$$\left| y(1; 2^{-3}) - y(1; 2^{-2}) \right| = |0.7169839 - 0.7194115| < 0.003\,,$$

the algorithm stops (see Step 6 of the improved Euler's method with tolerance) and prints out that $\phi(1)$ is approximately 0.71698.

**15.** For this problem, $f(x, y) = (x + y + 2)^2$. We want to approximate the solution, satisfying $y(0) = -2$, on the interval $[0, 1.4]$ to find the point, with two decimal places of accuracy, where it crosses the $x$-axis, that is $y = 0$. Our approach is to use a step size of 0.005 and look for a change in the sign of $y$. This requires 280 steps. For this procedure inputs to the improved Euler's method subroutine are $x_0 = 0$, $y_0 = -2$, $c = 1.4$, and $N = 280$. We will stop the subroutine when we see a sign change in the value of $y$. (The subroutine is implemented on the software package provided free with the text.)

For Step 3 of the subroutine we have

$$F = f(x, y) = (x + y + 2)^2\,,$$
$$G = f(x + h, y + hF) = (x + h + y + hF + 2)^2 = [x + y + 2 + h(1 + F)]^2\,.$$

147

Starting with the inputs $x = x_0 = 0$, $y = y_0 = -2$, and $h = 0.005$ we obtain

$$F = (0 - 2 + 2)^2 = 0,$$
$$G = [0 - 2 + 2 + 0.005(1 + 0)]^2 = 0.000025.$$

Thus, in Step 4 we compute

$$x = 0 + 0.005 = 0.005,$$
$$y = -2 + 0.005(0 + 0.000025)(1/2) \approx -2.$$

Thus the approximate value of the solution at $x = 0.005$ is $-2$. We continue with Steps 3 and 4 of the improved Euler's method subroutine until we arrive at $x = 1.270$ and $y \approx -0.04658269$. The next iteration, with $x = 1.275$, yields $y \approx 0.006295411$. This tells us that $y = 0$ is occurs somewhere between $x = 1.270$ and $x = 1.275$. Therefore, rounding off to two decimal places yields $x = 1.27$.

**17.** In this initial value problem, $f(x, y) = -20y$, $x_0 = 0$, and $y_0 = 1$. By applying formula (4) on page 125 of the text, we can find a general formula for $y_n$ in terms of $h$. Indeed,

$$y_n = y_{n-1} + h(-20y_{n-1}) = (1 - 20h)y_{n-1} = \cdots = (1 - 20h)^n y_0 = (1 - 20h)^n = [c(h)]^n,$$

where $c(h) = 1 - 20h$. For suggested values of $h$, we have

$$
\begin{array}{llll}
h = 0.1 & \Rightarrow & c(0.1) = -1 & \Rightarrow & x_n = 0.1n, & y_n = (-1)^n, & n = 1, \ldots, 10; \\
h = 0.025 & \Rightarrow & c(0.025) = 0.5 & \Rightarrow & x_n = 0.025n, & y_n = (0.5)^n, & n = 1, \ldots, 40; \\
h = 0.2 & \Rightarrow & c(0.2) = -3 & \Rightarrow & x_n = 0.2n, & y_n = (-3)^n, & n = 1, \ldots, 5.
\end{array}
$$

These values are shown in Table 3-E.

Thus, for $h = 0.1$ we have alternating $y_n = \pm 1$; for $h = 0.2$, $y_n$'s have an increasing magnitude and alternating sign; $h = 0.025$ is a good step size. From this example we conclude that, in Euler's method, one should be very careful in choosing a step size. Wrong choice can even lead to a diverging process.

**Table 3–E**: Euler's method approximations to the solution of $y' = -20y$, $y(0) = 1$, on $[0, 1]$ with $h = 0.1$, $0.2$, and $0.025$.

| $x_n$ | $y_n$ ($h = 0.2$) | $y_n$ ($h = 0.1$) | $y_n$ ($h = 0.025$) |
|---|---|---|---|
| 0.1 | | $-1$ | 0.062500 |
| 0.2 | $-3$ | 1 | 0.003906 |
| 0.3 | | $-1$ | 0.000244 |
| 0.4 | 9 | 1 | 0.000015 |
| 0.5 | | $-1$ | 0.000001 |
| 0.6 | $-27$ | 1 | 0.000000 |
| 0.7 | | $-1$ | 0.000000 |
| 0.8 | 81 | 1 | 0.000000 |
| 0.9 | | $-1$ | 0.000000 |
| 1.0 | $-243$ | 1 | 0.000000 |

19. In this problem, the variables are $t$ and $p$. With suggested values of parameters, the initial value problem (13) becomes

$$\frac{dp}{dt} = 3p - p^r, \qquad p(0) = 1.$$

Therefore, $f(t, p) = 3p - p^r$ and, with $h = 0.25$, functions $F$ and $G$ in improved Euler's method subroutine have the form

$$
\begin{aligned}
F &= f(t, p) = 3p - p^r; \\
G &= f(t + 0.25, p + 0.25F) = 3[p + 0.25F] - [p + 0.25F]^r \\
&= 3\left[p + 0.25\left(3p - p^r\right)\right] - \left[p + 0.25\left(3p - p^r\right)\right]^r.
\end{aligned}
$$

The results of computations are shown in Table 3-F.

These results indicate that the limiting populations for $r = 1.5$, $r = 2$, and $r = 3$ are $p_\infty = 9$, $p_\infty = 3$, and $p_\infty = \sqrt{3}$, respectively.

Since the right-hand side of the given logistic equation, $f(t, p) = 3p - p^r$, does not depend on $t$, we conclude that this equation is autonomous. Therefore, its equilibrium solutions (if any)

**Table 3–F**: Improved Euler's method approximations to the solution of $p' = 3p - p^r$, $p(0) = 1$, on $[0, 5]$ with $h = 0.25$ for $r = 1.5$, 2, and 3.

| $x_n$ | $y_n$ $(r = 1.5)$ | $y_n$ $(r = 2)$ | $y_n$ $(r = 3)$ |
|---|---|---|---|
| 0.25 | 1.582860 | 1.531250 | 1.390625 |
| 0.5 | 2.351441 | 2.049597 | 1.553472 |
| 0.75 | 3.267498 | 2.440027 | 1.628847 |
| 1.0 | 4.253156 | 2.686754 | 1.669992 |
| 1.25 | 5.216751 | 2.829199 | 1.694056 |
| 1.5 | 6.083402 | 2.908038 | 1.708578 |
| 1.75 | 6.811626 | 2.950802 | 1.717479 |
| 2.0 | 7.392146 | 2.973767 | 1.722980 |
| 2.25 | 7.837090 | 2.986037 | 1.726396 |
| 2.5 | 8.168507 | 2.992574 | 1.728522 |
| 2.75 | 8.410362 | 2.996053 | 1.729847 |
| 3.0 | 8.584317 | 2.997903 | 1.730674 |
| 3.25 | 8.708165 | 2.998886 | 1.731191 |
| 3.5 | 8.795710 | 2.999408 | 1.731513 |
| 3.75 | 8.857285 | 2.999685 | 1.731715 |
| 4.0 | 8.900443 | 2.999833 | 1.731841 |
| 4.25 | 8.930619 | 2.999911 | 1.731920 |
| 4.5 | 8.951682 | 2.999953 | 1.731969 |
| 4.75 | 8.966366 | 2.999975 | 1.732000 |
| 5.0 | 8.976596 | 2.999987 | 1.732019 |

can be found by solving

$$f(p) = 3p - p^r = 0 \quad \Leftrightarrow \quad p\left(3 - p^{r-1}\right) = 0 \quad \Leftrightarrow \quad p = 0 \quad \text{or} \quad p = 3^{1/(r-1)}.$$

The condition $r > 1$ implies that $f(p) > 0$ on $\left(0, 3^{1/(r-1)}\right)$ and $f(p) < 0$ on $\left(3^{1/(r-1)}, \infty\right)$. Therefore, $p = 3^{1/(r-1)}$ is a sink and, regardless of the initial value $p(0) = p_0 > 0$, there holds

$$\lim_{t \to \infty} p(t) = 3^{1/(r-1)}.$$

**21.** We will use the improved Euler's method with $h = 2/3$ to approximate the solution of the problem

$$\left\{ \left[ 75 - 20 \cos\left(\frac{\pi t}{12}\right) \right] - T(t) \right\} + 0.1 + 1.5[70 - T(t)], \qquad T(0) = 65,$$

with $K = 0.2$. Since $h = 2/3$, it will take 36 steps to go from $t = 0$ to $t = 24$. By simplifying the above expression, we obtain

$$\frac{dT}{dt} = (75K + 105.1) - 20K \cos\left(\frac{\pi t}{12}\right) - (K + 1.5)T(t), \qquad T(0) = 65.$$

(Note that here $t$ takes the place of $x$ and $T$ takes the place of $y$.) Therefore, with $K = 0.2$ the inputs to the subroutine are $t_0 = 0$, $T_0 = 65$, $c = 24$, and $N = 36$. For Step 3 of the subroutine we have

$$\begin{aligned} F &= f(t, T) = (75K + 105.1) - 20K \cos\left(\frac{\pi t}{12}\right) - (K + 1.5)T, & (3.17) \\ G &= f(t + h, T + hF) \\ &= (75K + 105.1) - 20K \cos\left(\frac{\pi(t + h)}{12}\right) - (K + 1.5)\{T + hF\}. & (3.18) \end{aligned}$$

For Step 4 in the subroutine we have

$$t = t + h,$$
$$T = T + \frac{h}{2}(F + G).$$

Now, starting with $t = t_0 = 0$ and $T = T_0 = 65$, and $h = 2/3$ (as specified) we have Step 3 of the subroutine to be

$$F = [75(0.2) + 105.1] - 20(0.2) \cos 0 - [(0.2) + 1.5](65) = 5.6\,,$$
$$G = [75(0.2) + 105.1] - 20(0.2) \cos\left[\frac{\pi(0.6667)}{12}\right] - [(0.2) + 1.5][65 + (0.6667)(5.6)] \approx -0.6862\,.$$

Hence in Step 4 we compute

$$t = 0 + 0.6667 = 0.6667$$
$$T = 65 + 0.3333(5.6 - 0.6862) \approx 66.638\,.$$

**Table 3–G**: Improved Euler's method to approximate the temperature in a building over a 24-hour period (with $K = 0.2$).

| Time | $t_n$ | $T_n$ |
|---|---|---|
| Midnight | 0 | 65 |
| 12:40 A.M. | 0.6667 | 66.63803 |
| 1:20 A.M. | 1.3333 | 67.52906 |
| 2:00 A.M. | 2.0000 | 68.07270 |
| 2:40 A.M. | 2.6667 | 68.46956 |
| 3:20 A.M. | 3.3333 | 68.81808 |
| 4:00 A.M. | 4.0000 | 69.16392 |
| 8:00 A.M. | 8.0000 | 71.48357 |
| Noon | 12.000 | 72.90891 |
| 4:00 P.M. | 16.000 | 72.07140 |
| 8:00 P.M. | 20.000 | 69.80953 |
| Midnight | 24.000 | 68.38519 |

Recalling that $t_0$ is midnight, we see that these results imply that at 0.6667 hours after midnight (or 12 : 40 A.M.) the temperature is approximately 66.638. Continuing with this process for $n = 1, 2, \ldots, 35$ gives us the approximate temperatures in a building with $K = 0.2$ over a 24 hr period. These results are given in Table 3-G. (This is just a partial table.)

The next step is to redo the above work with $K = 0.4$. That is, we substitute $K = 0.4$ and $h = 2/3 \approx 0.6667$ into equations (3.17) and (3.18) above. This yields

$$F = 135.1 - 8\cos\left(\frac{\pi t}{12}\right) - 1.9T,$$

$$G = 135.1 - 8\cos\left[\frac{\pi(t + 0.6667)}{12}\right] - 1.9(T + 0.6667F),$$

and

$$T = T + (0.3333)(F + G).$$

Then, using these equations, we go through the process of first finding $F$, then using this result to find $G$, and finally using both results to find $T$. (This process must be done for

$n = 0, 1, 2, \ldots, 35$.) Lastly, we redo this work with $K = 0.6$ and $h = 2/3$. By so doing, we obtain the results given in the table in the answers of the text. (Note that the values for $T_0$, $T_6$, $T_{12}$, $T_{18}$, $T_{24}$, $T_{30}$, and $T_{36}$ are given in the answers.)

## EXERCISES 3.7: Higher Order Numerical Methods: Taylor and Runge-Kutta, page 142

**1.** In this problem, $f(x, y) = \cos(x + y)$. Applying formula (4) on page 135 of the text we compute

$$\frac{\partial f(x, y)}{\partial x} = \frac{\partial}{\partial x}\left[\cos(x + y)\right] = -\sin(x + y)\frac{\partial}{\partial x}(x + y) = -\sin(x + y);$$

$$\frac{\partial f(x, y)}{\partial y} = \frac{\partial}{\partial y}\left[\cos(x + y)\right] = -\sin(x + y)\frac{\partial}{\partial y}(x + y) = -\sin(x + y);$$

$$f_2(x, y) = \frac{\partial f(x, y)}{\partial x} + \left[\frac{\partial f(x, y)}{\partial y}\right]f(x, y) = -\sin(x + y) + \left[-\sin(x + y)\right]\cos(x + y)$$
$$= -\sin(x + y)[1 + \cos(x + y)],$$

and so, with $p = 2$, (5) and (6) on page 135 yield

$$x_{n+1} = x_n + h,$$

$$y_{n+1} = y_n + h\cos(x_n + y_n) - \frac{h^2}{2}\sin(x_n + y_n)\left[1 + \cos(x_n + y_n)\right].$$

**3.** Here we have $f(x, y) = x - y$ and so

$$f_2(x, y) = \frac{\partial(x - y)}{\partial x} + \frac{\partial(x - y)}{\partial y}(x - y) = 1 + (-1)(x - y) = 1 - x + y.$$

To obtain $f_3(x, y)$ and then $f_4(x, y)$, we differentiate the equation $y'' = f_2(x, y)$ twice. This yields

$$y'''(x) = [f_2(x, y)]' = (1 - x + y)' = -1 + y' = -1 + x - y =: f_3(x, y);$$

$$y^{(4)}(x) = [f_3(x, y)]' = (-1 + x - y)' = 1 - y' = 1 - x + y =: f_4(x, y).$$

153

## Chapter 3

Therefore, the recursive formulas of order 4 for the Taylor method are

$$
\begin{aligned}
x_{n+1} &= x_n + h, \\
y_{n+1} &= y_n + h\left(x_n - y_n\right) + \frac{h^2}{2}\left(1 - x_n + y_n\right) + \frac{h^3}{3!}\left(-1 + x_n - y_n\right) + \frac{h^4}{4!}\left(1 - x_n + y_n\right) \\
&= y_n + h\left(x_n - y_n\right) + \frac{h^2}{2}\left(1 - x_n + y_n\right) - \frac{h^3}{6}\left(1 - x_n + y_n\right) + \frac{h^4}{24}\left(1 - x_n + y_n\right) \\
&= y_n + h + \left(1 - x_n + y_n\right)\left(-h + \frac{h^2}{2} - \frac{h^3}{6} + \frac{h^4}{24}\right) \\
&= y_n + h\left(x_n - y_n\right) + \left(1 - x_n - y_n\right)\left(\frac{h^2}{2} - \frac{h^3}{6} + \frac{h^4}{24}\right).
\end{aligned}
$$

**5.** For the Taylor method of *order* 2, we need to find (see equation (4) on page 135 of the text)

$$
f_2(x, y) = \frac{\partial f(x, y)}{\partial x} + \left[\frac{\partial f(x, y)}{\partial y}\right] f(x, y)
$$

for $f(x, y) = x + 1 - y$. Thus, we have

$$
f_2(x, y) = 1 + (-1)(x + 1 - y) = y - x.
$$

Therefore, by equations (5) and (6) on page 135 of the text, we see that the recursive formulas with $h = 0.25$ become

$$
\begin{aligned}
x_{n+1} &= x_n + 0.25, \\
y_{n+1} &= y_n + 0.25\left(x_n + 1 - y_n\right) + \frac{(0.25)^2}{2}\left(y_n - x_n\right).
\end{aligned}
$$

By starting with $x_0 = 0$ and $y_0 = 1$ (the initial values for the problem), we find

$$
y_1 = 1 + \frac{0.0625}{2} \approx 1.03125.
$$

Plugging this value into the recursive formulas yields

$$
y_2 = 1.03125 + 0.25(0.25 + 1 - 1.03125) + \left(\frac{0.0625}{2}\right)(1.03125 - 0.25) \approx 1.11035.
$$

By continuing in this way, we can fill in the first three columns in Table 3-H.

For the Taylor method of *order* 4, we need to find $f_3$ and $f_4$. Thus, we have

$$f_3(x,y) = \frac{\partial f_2(x,y)}{\partial x} + \left[\frac{\partial f_2(x,y)}{\partial y}\right] f(x,y) = -1 + 1 \cdot (x+1-y) = x - y,$$

$$f_4(x,y) = \frac{\partial f_3(x,y)}{\partial x} + \left[\frac{\partial f_3(x,y)}{\partial y}\right] f(x,y) = 1 + (-1) \cdot (x+1-y) = y - x.$$

Hence, by equation (6) on page 135 of the text, we see that the recursive formula for $y_{n+1}$ for the Taylor method of order 4 with $h = 0.25$ is given by

$$y_{n+1} = y_n + 0.25\,(x_n+1-y_n) + \frac{(0.25)^2}{2}\,(y_n-x_n) + \frac{(0.25)^3}{6}\,(x_n-y_n) + \frac{(0.25)^4}{24}\,(y_n-x_n).$$

By starting with $x_0 = 0$ and $y_0 = 1$, we can fill in the fourth column of Table 3-H.

**Table 3–H**: Taylor approximations of order 2 and 4 for the equation $y' = x + 1 - y$.

| $n$ | $x_n$ | $y_n$ (order 2) | $y_n$ (order 4) |
|---|---|---|---|
| 0 | 0 | 1 | 1 |
| 1 | 0.25 | 1.03125 | 1.02881 |
| 2 | 0.50 | 1.11035 | 1.10654 |
| 3 | 0.75 | 1.22684 | 1.22238 |
| 4 | 1.00 | 1.37253 | 1.36789 |

Thus, the approximation (rounded to 4 decimal places) of the solution by the Taylor method at the point $x = 1$ is given by $\phi_2(1) = 1.3725$ if we use order 2 and by $\phi_4(1) = 1.3679$ if we use order 4. The actual solution is $y = x + e^{-x}$ and so has the value $y(1) = 1 + e^{-1} \approx 1.3678794$ at $x = 1$. Comparing these results, we see that

$$|y(1) - \phi_2(1)| = 0.00462 \quad \text{and} \quad |y(1) - \phi_4(1)| = 0.00002\,.$$

7. We will use the 4th order Runge-Kutta subroutine described on page 138 of the text. Since $x_0 = 0$ and $h = 0.25$, we need $N = 4$ steps to approximate the solution at $x = 1$. With $f(x,y) = 2y - 6$, we set $x = x_0 = 0$, $y = y_0 = 1$ and go to Step 3 to compute $k_j$'s.

$$k_1 = hf(x,y) = 0.25[2(1) - 6] = -1\,;$$

$$k_2 = hf(x + h/2, y + k_1/2) = 0.25[2(1 + (-1)/2) - 6] = -1.25\,;$$

$$k_3 = hf(x + h/2, y + k_2/2) = 0.25[2(1 + (-1.25)/2) - 6] = -1.3125\,;$$

$$k_4 = hf(x + h, y + k_3) = 0.25[2(1 + (-1.3125)) - 6] = -1.65625\,.$$

Step 4 then yields

$$x = 0 + 0.25 = 0.25\,,$$

$$y = 1 + \frac{1}{6}\left(k_1 + 2k_2 + 2k_3 + k_4\right) = 1 + \frac{1}{6}\left(-1 - 2 \cdot 1.25 - 2 \cdot 1.3125 - 1.65625\right) \approx -0.29688\,.$$

Now we go back to Step 3 and recalculate $k_j$'s for new values of $x$ and $y$.

$$k_1 = 0.25[2(-0.29688) - 6] = -1.64844\,;$$

$$k_2 = 0.25[2(-0.29688 + (-1.64844)/2) - 6] = -2.06055\,;$$

$$k_3 = 0.25[2(-0.29688 + (-2.06055)/2) - 6] = -2.16358\,;$$

$$k_4 = 0.25[2(-0.29688 + (-2.16358)) - 6] = -2.73022\,;$$

$$x = 0.25 + 0.25 = 0.5\,,$$

$$y = -0.29688 + \frac{1}{6}\left(-1.64844 - 2 \cdot 2.06055 - 2 \cdot 2.16358 - 2.73022\right) \approx -2.43470\,.$$

We repeat the cycle two more times:

$$k_1 = 0.25[2(-2.43470) - 6] = -2.71735\,;$$

$$k_2 = 0.25[2(-2.43470 + (-2.71735)/2) - 6] = -3.39670\,;$$

$$k_3 = 0.25[2(-2.43470 + (-3.39670)/2) - 6] = -3.56652\,;$$

$$k_4 = 0.25[2(-2.43470 + (-3.56652)) - 6] = -4.50060\,;$$

$$x = 0.5 + 0.25 = 0.75\,,$$

$$y = -2.43470 + \frac{1}{6}\left(-2.71735 - 2 \cdot 3.39670 - 2 \cdot 3.56652 - 4.50060\right) \approx -5.95876$$

and

$$k_1 = 0.25[2(-5.95876) - 6] = -4.47938\,;$$

$$k_2 = 0.25[2(-5.95876 + (-4.47938)/2) - 6] = -5.59922\,;$$

$$k_3 = 0.25[2(-5.95876 + (-5.59922)/2) - 6] = -5.87918 \,;$$

$$k_4 = 0.25[2(-5.95876 + (-5.87918)) - 6] = -7.41895 \,;$$

$$x = 0.75 + 0.25 = 1.00 \,,$$

$$y = -5.95876 + \frac{1}{6}(-4.47938 - 2 \cdot 5.59922 - 2 \cdot 5.87918 - 7.41895) \approx -11.7679 \,.$$

Thus $\phi(1) \approx -11.7679$. The actual solution, $\phi(x) = 3 - 2e^{2x}$, evaluated at $x = 1$, gives

$$\phi(1) = 3 - 2e^{2(1)} = 3 - 2e^2 \approx -11.7781 \,.$$

9. For this problem we will use the 4th order Runge-Kutta subroutine with $f(x, y) = x + 1 - y$. Using the step size of $h = 0.25$, the number of steps needed is $N = 4$ to approximate the solution at $x = 1$. For Step 3 we have

$$k_1 = hf(x, y) = 0.25(x + 1 - y),$$

$$k_2 = hf\left(x + \frac{h}{2}, y + \frac{k_1}{2}\right) = 0.25(0.875x + 1 - 0.875y),$$

$$k_3 = hf\left(x + \frac{h}{2}, y + \frac{k_2}{2}\right) = 0.25(0.890625x + 1 - 0.890625y),$$

$$k_4 = hf(x + h, y + k_3) = 0.25(0.77734375x + 1 - 0.77734375y).$$

Hence, in Step 4 we have

$$x = x + 0.25 \,,$$

$$y = y + \frac{1}{6}(k_1 + 2k_2 + 2k_3 + k_4) \,.$$

Using the initial conditions $x_0 = 0$ and $y_0 = 1$, $c = 1$, and $N = 4$ for Step 3 we obtain

$$k_1 = 0.25(0 + 1 - 1) = 0,$$

$$k_2 = 0.25(0.875(0) + 1 - 0.875(1)) = 0.03125,$$

$$k_3 = 0.25(0.890625(0) + 1 - 0.890625(1)) \approx 0.0273438,$$

$$k_4 = 0.25(0.77734375(0) + 1 - 0.77734375(1)) \approx 0.0556641.$$

Thus, Step 4 gives

$$x = 0 + 0.25 = 0.25 \,,$$

$$y \approx 1 + \frac{1}{6}\left[0 + 2(0.03125) + 2(0.0273438) + 0.0556641\right] \approx 1.02881.$$

Thus the approximate value of the solution at 0.25 is 1.02881. By repeating Steps 3 and 4 of the algorithm we fill in the following Table 3-I.

**Table 3–I**: 4th order Runge-Kutta subroutine approximations for $y' = x + 1 - y$ at $x = 1$ with $h = 0.25$.

| $x$ | 0 | 0.25 | 0.50 | 0.75 | 1.0 |
|---|---|---|---|---|---|
| $y$ | 1 | 1.02881 | 1.10654 | 1.22238 | 1.36789 |

Thus, our approximation at $x = 1$ is approximately 1.36789. Comparing this with Problem 5, we see we have obtained accuracy to four decimal places as we did with the Taylor method of order four, but without having to compute any partial derivatives.

11. In this problem, $f(x, y) = 2x^{-4} - y^2$. To find the root of the solution within two decimal places of accuracy, we choose a step size $h = 0.005$ in 4th order Runge-Kutta subroutine. It will require $(2 - 1)/0.005 = 200$ steps to approximate the solution on $[1, 2]$. With the initial input $x = x_0 = 1$, $y = y_0 = -0.414$, we get

$k_1 = hf(x, y) = 0.005[2(1)^{-4} - (-0.414)^2] = 0.009143;$

$k_2 = hf(x + h/2, y + k_1/2) = 0.005[2(1 + 0.005/2)^{-4} - (-0.414 + 0.009143/2)^2] = 0.009062;$

$k_3 = hf(x + h/2, y + k_2/2) = 0.005[2(1 + 0.005/2)^{-4} - (-0.414 + 0.009062/2)^2] = 0.009062;$

$k_4 = hf(x + h, y + k_3) = 0.005[2(1 + 0.005)^{-4} - (-0.414 + 0.009062)^2] = 0.008983;$

$\Downarrow$

$x = 1 + 0.005 = 1.005,$

$y = -0.414 + \frac{1}{6}(0.009143 + 2 \cdot 0.009062 + 2 \cdot 0.009062 + 0.008983) \approx -0.404937;$

$\vdots$

On the 82nd step we get

$$x = 1.405 + 0.005 = 1.410\,,$$

$$y = -0.004425 + \frac{1}{6}\,(0.002566 + 2 \cdot 0.002548 + 2 \cdot 0.002548 + 0.002530) \approx -0.001876\,,$$

and the next step gives

$$k_1 = 0.005[2(1.410)^{-4} - (-0.001876)^2] = 0.002530\,;$$

$$k_2 = 0.005[2(1.410 + 0.005/2)^{-4} - (-0.001876 + 0.002530/2)^2] = 0.002512\,;$$

$$k_3 = 0.005[2(1.410 + 0.005/2)^{-4} - (-0.001876 + 0.002512/2)^2] = 0.002512\,;$$

$$k_4 = 0.005[2(1.410 + 0.005)^{-4} - (-0.001876 + 0.002512)^2] = 0.002494\,;$$

$$\Downarrow$$

$$x = 1.410 + 0.005 = 1.415\,,$$

$$y = -0.414 + \frac{1}{6}\,(0.002530 + 2 \cdot 0.002512 + 2 \cdot 0.002512 + 0.002494) \approx 0.000636\,.$$

Since $y(1.41) < 0$ and $y(1.415) > 0$ we conclude that the root of the solution is on the interval $(1.41, 1.415)$.

As a check, we apply the 4th order Runge-Kutta subroutine to approximate the solution to the given initial value problem on $[1, 1.5]$ with a step size $h = 0.001$, which requires $N = (1.5 - 1)/0.001 = 500$ steps. This yields $y(1.413) \approx -0.000367$, $y(1.414) \approx 0.000134$, and so, within two decimal places of accuracy, $x \approx 1.41$.

13. For this problem $f(x,y) = y^2 - 2e^x y + e^{2x} + e^x$. We want to find the vertical asymptote located in the interval $[0, 2]$ within two decimal places of accuracy using the Forth Order Runge-Kutta subroutine. One approach is to use a step size of $0.005$ and look for $y$ to approach infinity. This would require 400 steps. We will stop the subroutine when the value of $y$ ("blows up") becomes very large. For Step 3 we have

$$k_1 = hf(x,y) = 0.005\left(y^2 - 2e^x y + e^{2x} + e^x\right),$$

$$k_2 = hf\left(x + \frac{h}{2}, y + \frac{k_1}{2}\right) = 0.005\left[\left(y + \frac{k_1}{2}\right)^2 - 2e^{(x+h/2)}\left(y + \frac{k_1}{2}\right) + e^{2(x+h/2)} + e^{(x+h/2)}\right],$$

$$k_3 = hf\left(x + \frac{h}{2}, y + \frac{k_2}{2}\right) = 0.005\left[\left(y + \frac{k_2}{2}\right)^2 - 2e^{(x+h/2)}\left(y + \frac{k_2}{2}\right) + e^{2(x+h/2)} + e^{(x+h/2)}\right],$$

$$k_4 = hf(x+h, y+k_3) = 0.005\left[(y+k_3)^2 - 2e^{(x+h)}(y+k_3) + e^{2(x+h)} + e^{(x+h)}\right].$$

Hence in Step 4 we have

$$x = x + 0.005\,,$$

$$y = y + \frac{1}{6}\left(k_1 + 2k_2 + 2k_3 + k_4\right).$$

Using the initial conditions $x_0 = 0$, $y_0 = 3$, $c = 2$, and $N = 400$ on Step 3 we obtain

$$k_1 = 0.005\left(3^2 - 2e^0(3) + e^{2(0)} + e^0\right) = 0.025\,,$$

$$k_2 = 0.005\left[(3 + 0.0125)^2 - 2e^{(0+0.0025)}(3 + 0.0125) + e^{2(0+0.0025)} + e^{(0+0.0025)}\right] \approx 0.02522\,,$$

$$k_3 = 0.005\left[(3 + 0.01261)^2 - 2e^{(0+0.0025)}(3 + 0.01261) + e^{2(0+0.0025)} + e^{(0+0.0025)}\right] \approx 0.02522\,,$$

$$k_4 = 0.005\left[(3 + 0.02522)^2 - 2e^{(0+0.0025)}(3 + 0.02522) + e^{2(0+0.0025)} + e^{(0+0.0025)}\right] \approx 0.02543\,.$$

Thus, Step 4 yields

$$x = 0 + 0.005 = 0.005$$

and

$$y \approx 3 + \frac{1}{6}\left(0.025 + 2(0.02522) + 2(0.02522) + 0.02543\right) \approx 3.02522\,.$$

Thus the approximate value at $x = 0.005$ is $3.02522$. By repeating Steps 3 and 4 of the subroutine we find that, at $x = 0.505$, $y = 2.0201 \cdot 10^{13}$. The next iteration gives a floating point overflow. This would lead one to think the asymptote occurs at $x = 0.51$.

As a check lets apply the 4th order Runge-Kutta subroutine with the initial conditions $x_0 = 0$, $y_0 = 3$, $c = 1$, and $N = 400$. This gives a finer step size of $h = 0.0025$. With these inputs, we find $y(0.5025) \approx 4.0402 \cdot 10^{13}$.

Repeating the subroutine one more time with a step size of $0.00125$, we obtain the value $y(0.50125) \approx 8.0804 \cdot 10^{13}$. Therefore we conclude that the vertical asymptote occurs at $x = 0.50$ and not at $0.51$ as was earlier thought.

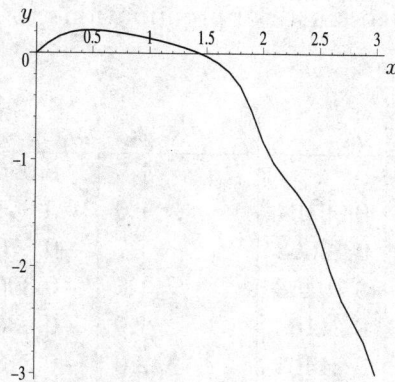

**Figure 3–C**: Polygonal line approximation to the solution of $y' = \cos(5y) - x$, $y(0) = 0$, on $[0, 3]$.

15. Here $f(x, y) = \cos(5y) - x$, $x_0 = 0$, and $y_0 = 0$. With a step size $h = 0.1$ we take $N = 30$ in order to approximate the solution on $[0, 3]$. We set $x = x_0 = 0$, $y = y_0 = 0$ and compute

$$k_1 = hf(x, y) = 0.1[\cos(5 \cdot 0) - 0] = 0.1\,;$$

$$k_2 = hf(x + h/2, y + k_1/2) = 0.1[\cos(5(0 + 0.1/2)) - (0 + 0.1/2)] = 0.091891\,;$$

$$k_3 = hf(x + h/2, y + k_2/2) = 0.1[\cos(5(0 + 0.091891/2)) - (0 + 0.1/2)] = 0.092373\,;$$

$$k_4 = hf(x + h, y + k_3) = 0.1[\cos(5(0 + 0.092373)) - (0 + 0.1)] = 0.079522\,;$$

$$\Downarrow$$

$$x = 0 + 0.1 = 0.1\,,$$

$$y = 0 + \frac{1}{6}(0.1 + 2 \cdot 0.091891 + 2 \cdot 0.092373 + 0.079522) \approx 0.091342\,;$$

$$\vdots$$

The results of computations are shown in Table 3-J.

Using these value, we sketch a polygonal line approximating the graph of the solution on $[0, 3]$. See Figure 3-C.

**Table 3–J**: 4th order Runge-Kutta approximations to the solution of $y' = \cos(5y) - x$, $y(0) = 0$, on $[0, 3]$ with $h = 0.1$.

| $x_n$ | $y_n$ | | $x_n$ | $y_n$ |
|---|---|---|---|---|
| 0 | 0 | | 1.5 | −0.02668 |
| 0.1 | 0.09134 | | 1.6 | −0.85748 |
| 0.2 | 0.15663 | | 1.7 | −0.17029 |
| 0.3 | 0.19458 | | 1.8 | −0.30618 |
| 0.4 | 0.21165 | | 1.9 | −0.53517 |
| 0.5 | 0.21462 | | 2.0 | −0.81879 |
| 0.6 | 0.20844 | | 2.1 | −1.02887 |
| 0.7 | 0.19629 | | 2.2 | −1.17307 |
| 0.8 | 0.18006 | | 2.3 | −1.30020 |
| 0.9 | 0.16079 | | 2.4 | −1.45351 |
| 1.0 | 0.13890 | | 2.5 | −1.69491 |
| 1.1 | 0.11439 | | 2.6 | −2.03696 |
| 1.2 | 0.08686 | | 2.7 | −2.30917 |
| 1.3 | 0.05544 | | 2.8 | −2.50088 |
| 1.4 | 0.01855 | | 2.9 | −2.69767 |
| | | | 3.0 | −2.99510 |

**17.** Taylor method of order 2 has recursive formulas given by equations (5) and (6) on page 135 of the text: that is

$$x_{j+1} = x_j + h \qquad \text{and} \qquad y_{j+1} = y_j + h f(x_j, y_j) + \frac{h^2}{2!} f_2(x_j, y_j).$$

With $f(x, y) = y$, we have

$$f_2(x, y) = y'' = \frac{\partial f(x, y)}{\partial x} + \left[ \frac{\partial f(x, y)}{\partial y} \right] f(x, y) = 0 + 1 \cdot (y) = y.$$

Therefore, since $h = 1/n$, the recursive formula for $y_{j+1}$ is given by the equation

$$y_{j+1} = y_j + \frac{1}{n} y_j + \frac{1}{2n^2} y_j = \left( 1 + \frac{1}{n} + \frac{1}{2n^2} \right) y_j.$$

We are starting the process at $x_0 = 0$ and $y_0 = 1$, and we are taking steps of size $1/n$ until we reach $x = 1$. This means that we will take $n$ steps. Thus, $y_n$ will be an approximation for the solution to the differential equation at $x = 1$. Since the actual solution is $y = e^x$, this means that $y_n \approx e$. To find the equation we are looking for, we see that

$$y_1 = \left(1 + \frac{1}{n} + \frac{1}{2n^2}\right) y_0 = \left(1 + \frac{1}{n} + \frac{1}{2n^2}\right),$$

$$y_2 = \left(1 + \frac{1}{n} + \frac{1}{2n^2}\right) y_1 = \left(1 + \frac{1}{n} + \frac{1}{2n^2}\right)^2,$$

$$y_3 = \left(1 + \frac{1}{n} + \frac{1}{2n^2}\right) y_2 = \left(1 + \frac{1}{n} + \frac{1}{2n^2}\right)^3,$$

$$y_4 = \left(1 + \frac{1}{n} + \frac{1}{2n^2}\right) y_3 = \left(1 + \frac{1}{n} + \frac{1}{2n^2}\right)^4,$$

$$\vdots$$

$$y_n = \left(1 + \frac{1}{n} + \frac{1}{2n^2}\right) y_{n-1} = \left(1 + \frac{1}{n} + \frac{1}{2n^2}\right)^n.$$

(This can be proved rigorously by mathematical induction.) As we observed above, $y_n \approx e$, and so we have

$$e \approx \left(1 + \frac{1}{n} + \frac{1}{2n^2}\right)^n.$$

**19.** In this initial value problem, the independent variable is $u$, the dependent variable is $v$, $u_0 = 2$, $v_0 = 0.1$, and

$$f(u, v) = u\left(\frac{u}{2} + 1\right) v^3 + \left(u + \frac{5}{2}\right) v^2.$$

We will use the classical 4th order Runge-Kutta algorithm with tolerance given on page 139 of the text but, since the stopping criteria should be based on the relative error, we will replace the condition $|z - v| < \varepsilon$ in Step 6 by $|(z - v)/v| < \varepsilon$ (see Step 6' on page 138).

We start with $m = 0$, $N = 2^m = 1$, and a step size $h = (3 - 2)/N = 1$. Setting $u = u_0 = 2$, $v = v_0 = 0.1$, on Step 4 we compute

$$k_1 = hf(u, v) = (1)\left[2\left(\frac{2}{2} + 1\right)(0.1)^3 + \left(2 + \frac{5}{2}\right)(0.1)^2\right] = 0.049;$$

$$k_2 = hf\left(u + h/2, v + k_1/2\right) = (1)\left[(2 + 1/2)\left(\frac{2 + 1/2}{2} + 1\right)(0.1 + 0.049/2)^3\right.$$

$$\left. + \left((2 + 1/2) + \frac{5}{2}\right)(0.1 + 0.049/2)^2\right] = 0.088356;$$

163

$$k_3 = hf(u + h/2, v + k_2/2) = (1) \left[ (2 + 1/2) \left( \frac{2 + 1/2}{2} + 1 \right) (0.1 + 0.088356/2)^3 \right.$$

$$\left. + \left( (2 + 1/2) + \frac{5}{2} \right) (0.1 + 0.088356/2)^2 \right] = 0.120795 \, ;$$

$$k_4 = hf(u + h, v + k_3) = (1) \left[ (2 + 1) \left( \frac{2 + 1}{2} + 1 \right) (0.1 + 0.120795)^3 \right.$$

$$\left. + \left( (2 + 1) + \frac{5}{2} \right) (0.1 + 0.120795)^2 \right] = 0.348857 \, .$$

So,

$$u = u + h = 2 + 1 = 3 \, ,$$

$$v = v + \frac{1}{6} (0.049 + 2 \cdot 0.088356 + 2 \cdot 0.120795 + 0.348857) \approx 0.236027 \, .$$

Because the relative error between two successive approximations, $v(3; 2^0) = 0.236027$ and $v = 0.1$ is $\varepsilon = |(0.236027 - 0.1)/0.236027| \approx 0.576320 > 0.0001$, we go back to Step 2 and set $m = 1$, take $N = 2^m = 2$ on Step 3, compute $h = 1/N = 0.5$, and use the 4th order Runge-Kutta subroutine on page 138 of the text to find $v(3; 0.5)$. This takes two steps and yields

$$k_1 = (0.5) \left[ 2 \left( \frac{2}{2} + 1 \right) (0.1)^3 + \left( 2 + \frac{5}{2} \right) (0.1)^2 \right] = 0.0245;$$

$$k_2 = (0.5) \left[ (2 + 0.5/2) \left( \frac{2 + 0.5/2}{2} + 1 \right) (0.1 + 0.0245/2)^3 \right.$$

$$\left. + \left( (2 + 0.5/2) + \frac{5}{2} \right) (0.1 + 0.0245/2)^2 \right] = 0.033306 \, ;$$

$$k_3 = (0.5) \left[ (2 + 0.5/2) \left( \frac{2 + 0.5/2}{2} + 1 \right) (0.1 + 0.033306/2)^3 \right.$$

$$\left. + \left( (2 + 0.5/2) + \frac{5}{2} \right) (0.1 + 0.033306/2)^2 \right] = 0.036114 \, ;$$

$$k_4 = (0.5) \left[ (2 + 0.5) \left( \frac{2 + 0.5}{2} + 1 \right) (0.1 + 0.036114)^3 \right.$$

$$\left. + \left( (2 + 0.5) + \frac{5}{2} \right) (0.1 + 0.036114)^2 \right] = 0.053410 \, .$$

This gives

$$u = 2 + 0.5 = 2.5\,,$$

$$v = 0.1 + \frac{1}{6}\,(0.0245 + 2 \cdot 0.033306 + 2 \cdot 0.036114 + 0.053410) \approx 0.136125\,.$$

We compute $k_j$'s again and find an approximate value of $v(3)$.

$$k_1 = (0.5)\left[2.5\left(\frac{2.5}{2} + 1\right)(0.136125)^3 + \left(2.5 + \frac{5}{2}\right)(0.136125)^2\right] = 0.053419;$$

$$k_2 = (0.5)\left[(2.5 + 0.5/2)\left(\frac{2.5 + 0.5/2}{2} + 1\right)(0.136125 + 0.053419/2)^3\right.$$

$$\left. + \left((2.5 + 0.5/2) + \frac{5}{2}\right)(0.136125 + 0.053419/2)^2\right] = 0.083702;$$

$$k_3 = (0.5)\left[(2.5 + 0.5/2)\left(\frac{2.5 + 0.5/2}{2} + 1\right)(0.136125 + 0.083702/2)^3\right.$$

$$\left. + \left((2.5 + 0.5/2) + \frac{5}{2}\right)(0.136125 + 0.083702/2)^2\right] = 0.101558;$$

$$k_4 = (0.5)\left[(2.5 + 0.5)\left(\frac{2.5 + 0.5}{2} + 1\right)(0.136125 + 0.101558)^3\right.$$

$$\left. + \left((2.5 + 0.5) + \frac{5}{2}\right)(0.136125 + 0.101558)^2\right] = 0.205709\,.$$

Therefore, at $u = 2.5 + 0.5 = 3.0$,

$$v = 0.136125 + \frac{1}{6}\,(0.053419 + 2 \cdot 0.083702 + 2 \cdot 0.101558 + 0.205709) \approx 0.241066\,.$$

This time the relative error is

$$\varepsilon = \left|\frac{v(3;2^{-1}) - v(3;2^0)}{v(3;2^{-1})}\right| = \frac{0.241066 - 0.236027}{0.241066} \approx 0.020903 > 0.0001\,.$$

Thus we set $m = 2$, $N = 2^m = 4$, $h = 1/N = 0.25$, repeat computations with this new step, and find that $v(3;2^{-2}) \approx 0.241854$ and

$$\varepsilon = \left|\frac{v(3;2^{-2}) - v(3;2^{-1})}{v(3;2^{-1})}\right| = \frac{0.241854 - 0.241066}{0.241854} \approx 0.003258 > 0.0001\,.$$

We continue increasing $m$ and get

$$m = 3, \; h = 0.125, \quad v(3; 2^{-3}) = 0.241924, \; \varepsilon = \left| \frac{0.241924 - 0.241854}{0.241924} \right| \approx 0.00029 > 10^{-4};$$

$$m = 4, \; h = 0.0625, \; v(3; 2^{-4}) = 0.241929, \; \varepsilon = \left| \frac{0.241929 - 0.241924}{0.241929} \right| \approx 0.00002 < 10^{-4}.$$

Therefore, within an accuracy of $0.0001$, $v(3) \approx 0.24193$.

# CHAPTER 4: Linear Second Order Equations

**EXERCISES 4.1:   Introduction: The Mass-Spring Oscillator, page 159**

**1.** With $b = 0$ and $F_{\text{ext}} = 0$, equation (3) on page 155 becomes

$$my'' + ky = 0.$$

Substitution $y = \sin \omega t$, where $\omega = \sqrt{k/m}$, yields

$$
\begin{aligned}
m(\sin \omega t)'' + k(\sin \omega t) &= -m\omega^2 \sin \omega t + k \sin \omega t \\
&= \sin \omega t \left(-m\omega^2 + k\right) = \sin \omega t \left(-m(k/m) + k\right) = 0.
\end{aligned}
$$

Thus $y = \sin \omega t$ is indeed a solution.

**3.** Differentiating $y(t)$, we find

$$
\begin{aligned}
y &= 2 \sin 3t + \cos 3t \\
\Rightarrow \quad y' &= 6 \cos 3t - 3 \sin 3t \\
\Rightarrow \quad y'' &= -18 \sin 3t - 9 \cos 3t.
\end{aligned}
$$

Substituting $y$, $y'$, and $y''$ into the given equation, we get

$$
\begin{aligned}
2y'' + 18y &= 2(-18 \sin 3t - 9 \cos 3t) + 18(2 \sin 3t + \cos 3t) \\
&= [2(-18) + 18(2)] \sin 3t + [2(-9) + 18(1)] \cos 3t = 0.
\end{aligned}
$$

Next, we check that the initial conditions are satisfied.

$$
\begin{aligned}
y(0) &= (2 \sin 3t + \cos 3t) \big|_{t=0} = 2 \sin 0 + \cos 0 = 1, \\
y'(0) &= (6 \cos 3t - 3 \sin 3t) \big|_{t=0} = 6 \cos 0 - 3 \sin 0 = 6.
\end{aligned}
$$

Writing $y(t)$ in the form

$$y(t) = \sqrt{5}\left(\frac{2}{\sqrt{5}}\sin 3t + \frac{1}{\sqrt{5}}\cos 3t\right) = \sqrt{5}\sin(3t + \gamma),$$

where $\gamma = \arctan(1/2)$, we conclude that $|y(t)| = \sqrt{5}|\sin(3t + \gamma)|$, and so $\max|y(t)| = \sqrt{5}$ (since $\max|\sin(3t + \gamma)| = 1$).

**5.** We differentiate $y(t)$ twice and obtain

$$
\begin{aligned}
y(t) &= e^{-2t}\sin(\sqrt{2}t) \\
y'(t) &= e^{-2t}[(-2)\sin(\sqrt{2}t) + \sqrt{2}\cos(\sqrt{2}t)] \\
y''(t) &= e^{-2t}\left[(-2)^2\sin(\sqrt{2}t) + (-2)\sqrt{2}\cos(\sqrt{2}t) + (-2)\sqrt{2}\cos(\sqrt{2}t) - (\sqrt{2})^2\sin(\sqrt{2}t)\right] \\
&= e^{-2t}\left[2\sin(\sqrt{2}t) - 4\sqrt{2}\cos(\sqrt{2}t)\right].
\end{aligned}
$$

Substituting these functions into the differential equation, we get

$$
\begin{aligned}
my'' + by' + ky = y'' + 4y' + 6y &= e^{-2t}\left[2\sin(\sqrt{2}t) - 4\sqrt{2}\cos(\sqrt{2}t)\right] \\
&\quad + 4e^{-2t}[(-2)\sin(\sqrt{2}t) + \sqrt{2}\cos(\sqrt{2}t)] + 6e^{-2t}\sin(\sqrt{2}t) \\
&= e^{-2t}\left[(2 - 8 + 6)\sin(\sqrt{2}t) + (-4\sqrt{2} + 4\sqrt{2})\cos(\sqrt{2}t)\right] = 0.
\end{aligned}
$$

Therefore, $y = e^{-2t}\sin(\sqrt{2}t)$ is a solution. As $t \to +\infty$, $e^{-2t} \to 0$ while $\sin(\sqrt{2}t)$ remains bounded. Therefore, $\lim_{t\to+\infty} y(t) = 0$.

**7.** For $y = A\cos 5t + B\sin 5t$,

$$y' = -5A\sin 5t + 5B\cos 5t, \qquad y'' = -25A\cos 5t - 25B\sin 5t.$$

Inserting $y$, $y'$, and $y''$ into the given equation and matching coefficients yield

$$
\begin{aligned}
& y'' + 2y' + 4y = 3\sin 5t \\
\Rightarrow \quad & (-25A\cos 5t - 25B\sin 5t) + 2(-5A\sin 5t + 5B\cos 5t) + 4(A\cos 5t + B\sin 5t) \\
& \qquad = (-21A + 10B)\cos 5t + (-10A - 21B)\sin 5t = 3\sin 5t \\
\Rightarrow \quad & \begin{aligned} -21A + 10B &= 0, \\ -10A - 21B &= 3 \end{aligned} \qquad \Rightarrow \qquad \begin{aligned} A &= -30/541, \\ B &= -63/541. \end{aligned}
\end{aligned}
$$

Thus, $y = -(30/541)\cos 5t - (63/541)\sin 5t$ is a synchronous solution to $y'' + 2y' + 4y = 3\sin 5t$.

**9.** We differentiate $y = A \cos 2t + B \sin 2t$ twice to get

$$y' = -2A \sin 2t + 2B \cos 2t \quad \text{and} \quad y'' = -4A \cos 2t - 4B \sin 2t,$$

substitute $y$, $y'$, and $y''$ into the given equation, and compare coefficients. This yields

$$y'' + 2y' + 4y = (-4A \cos 2t - 4B \sin 2t) + 2(-2A \sin 2t + 2B \cos 2t) + 4(A \cos 2t + B \sin 2t)$$

$$= 4B \cos 2t - 4A \sin 2t = 3 \cos 2t + 4 \sin 2t$$

$$\Rightarrow \quad \begin{matrix} 4B = 3, \\ -4A = 4 \end{matrix} \quad \Rightarrow \quad \begin{matrix} A = -1, \\ B = 3/4 \end{matrix} \quad \Rightarrow \quad y = -\cos 2t + (3/4) \sin 2t.$$

## EXERCISES 4.2: Homogeneous Linear Equations; The General Solution, page 167

**1.** The auxiliary equation for this problem is $r^2 + 5r + 6 = (r+2)(r+3) = 0$, which has the roots $r = -2$ and $r = -3$. Thus $\{e^{-2t}, e^{-3t}\}$ is a set of two linearly independent solutions for this differential equation. Therefore, a general solution is given by

$$y(t) = c_1 e^{-2t} + c_2 e^{-3t},$$

where $c_1$ and $c_2$ are arbitrary constants.

**3.** The auxiliary equation, $r^2 + 8r + 16 = (r+4)^2 = 0$, has a double root $r = -4$. Therefore, $e^{-4t}$ and $te^{-4t}$ are two linearly independent solutions for this differential equation, and a general solution is given by

$$y(t) = c_1 e^{-4t} + c_2 te^{-4t},$$

where $c_1$ and $c_2$ are arbitrary constants.

**5.** The auxiliary equation for this problem is $r^2 + r - 1 = 0$. By the quadratic formula, we have

$$r = \frac{-1 \pm \sqrt{1+4}}{2} = \frac{-1 \pm \sqrt{5}}{2}.$$

Therefore, a general solution is

$$z(t) = c_1 e^{(-1-\sqrt{5})t/2} + c_2 e^{(-1+\sqrt{5})t/2}.$$

**7.** Solving the auxiliary equation, $2r^2 + 7r - 4 = 0$, yields $r = 1/2, -4$. Thus a general solution is given by

$$u(t) = c_1 e^{t/2} + c_2 e^{-4t},$$

where $c_1$ and $c_2$ are arbitrary constants.

**9.** The auxiliary equation for this problem is $r^2 - r - 11 = 0$, which has roots

$$r = \frac{1 \pm \sqrt{1 + 4 \cdot 11}}{2} = \frac{1 \pm 3\sqrt{5}}{2}.$$

Thus, a general solution to the given equation is

$$y(t) = c_1 e^{(1+3\sqrt{5})t/2} + c_2 e^{(1-3\sqrt{5})t/2}.$$

**11.** Solving the auxiliary equation, $4r^2 + 20r + 25 = (2r + 5)^2 = 0$, we conclude that $r = -5/2$ is its double root. Therefore, a general solution to the given differential equation is

$$w(t) = c_1 e^{-5t/2} + c_2 t e^{-5t/2}.$$

**13.** The auxiliary equation for this problem is $r^2 + 2r - 8 = 0$, which has roots $r = -4, 2$. Thus, a general solution is given by

$$y(t) = c_1 e^{-4t} + c_2 e^{2t},$$

where $c_1$, $c_2$ are arbitrary constants. To satisfy the initial conditions, $y(0) = 3$, $y'(0) = -12$, we find the derivative $y'(t) = -4c_1 e^{-4t} + 2c_2 e^{2t}$ and solve the system

$$
\begin{aligned}
y(0) &= c_1 e^{-4 \cdot 0} + c_2 e^{2 \cdot 0} = c_1 + c_2 = 3, \\
y'(0) &= -4c_1 e^{-4 \cdot 0} + 2c_2 e^{2 \cdot 0} = -4c_1 + 2c_2 = -12
\end{aligned}
\qquad \Rightarrow \qquad
\begin{aligned}
c_1 &= 3, \\
c_2 &= 0.
\end{aligned}
$$

Therefore, the solution to the given initial value problem is

$$y(t) = (3)e^{-4t} + (0)e^{2t} = 3e^{-4t}.$$

**15.** The auxiliary equation for this equation is $r^2 + 2r + 1 = (r + 1)^2 = 0$. We see that $r = -1$ is a repeated root. Thus, two linearly independent solutions are $y_1(t) = e^{-t}$ and $y_2(t) = te^{-t}$. This means that a general solution is given by $y(t) = c_1 e^{-t} + c_2 t e^{-t}$.

To find the constants $c_1$ and $c_2$, we substitute the initial conditions into the general solution and its derivative, $y'(t) = -c_1 e^{-t} + c_2 \left( e^{-t} - te^{-t} \right)$, and obtain

$$y(0) = 1 = c_1 e^0 + c_2 \cdot 0 = c_1,$$
$$y'(0) = -3 = -c_1 e^0 + c_2 \left( e^0 - 0 \right) = -c_1 + c_2.$$

So, $c_1 = 1$ and $c_2 = -2$. Therefore, the solution that satisfies the initial conditions is given by

$$y(t) = e^{-t} - 2te^{-t}.$$

**17.** The auxiliary equation for this problem, $r^2 - 2r - 2 = 0$, has roots $r = 1 \pm \sqrt{3}$. Thus, a general solution is given by $z(t) = c_1 e^{(1+\sqrt{3})t} + c_2 e^{(1-\sqrt{3})t}$. Differentiating, we find that $z'(t) = c_1(1+\sqrt{3})e^{(1+\sqrt{3})t} + c_2(1-\sqrt{3})e^{(1-\sqrt{3})t}$. Substitution of $z(t)$ and $z'(t)$ into the initial conditions yields the system

$$
\begin{aligned}
z(0) &= c_1 + c_2 = 0, \\
z'(0) &= c_1(1+\sqrt{3}) + c_2(1-\sqrt{3}) = \sqrt{3}(c_1 - c_2) = 3
\end{aligned}
\quad \Rightarrow \quad
\begin{aligned}
c_1 &= \sqrt{3}/2, \\
c_2 &= -\sqrt{3}/2.
\end{aligned}
$$

Thus, the solution satisfying the given initial conditions is

$$z(t) = \frac{\sqrt{3}}{2} e^{(1+\sqrt{3})t} - \frac{\sqrt{3}}{2} e^{(1-\sqrt{3})t} = \frac{\sqrt{3}}{2} \left( e^{(1+\sqrt{3})t} - e^{(1-\sqrt{3})t} \right).$$

**19.** Here, the auxiliary equation is $r^2 - 4r - 5 = (r-5)(r+1) = 0$, which has roots $r = 5, -1$. Consequently, a general solution to the differential equation is $y(t) = c_1 e^{5t} + c_2 e^{-t}$, where $c_1$ and $c_2$ are arbitrary constants. To find the solution that satisfies the initial conditions, $y(-1) = 3$ and $y'(-1) = 9$, we first differentiate the solution found above, then plug in $y$ and $y'$ into the initial conditions. This gives

$$y(-1) = 3 = c_1 e^{-5} + c_2 e$$
$$y'(-1) = 9 = 5c_1 e^{-5} - c_2 e.$$

Solving this system yields $c_1 = 2e^5$, $c_2 = e^{-1}$. Thus $y(t) = 2e^{5(t+1)} + e^{-(t+1)}$ is the desired solution.

# Chapter 4

**21. (a)** With $y(t) = e^{rt}$, $y'(t) = re^{rt}$, the equation becomes

$$are^{rt} + be^{rt} = (ar + b)e^{rt} = 0.$$

Since the function $e^{rt}$ is never zero on $(-\infty, \infty)$, to satisfy the above equation we must have

$$ar + b = 0.$$

**(b)** Solving the characteristic equation, $ar + b = 0$, obtained in part (a), we get $r = -b/a$. So $y(t) = e^{rt} = e^{-bt/a}$, and a general solution is given by $y = ce^{-bt/a}$, where $c$ is an arbitrary constant.

**23.** We form the characteristic equation, $5r + 4 = 0$, and find its root $r = -4/5$. Therefore, $y(t) = ce^{-4t/5}$ is a general solution to the given equation.

**25.** The characteristic equation, $6r - 13 = 0$, has the root $r = 13/6$. Therefore, a general solution is given by $w(t) = ce^{13t/6}$.

**27.** Assuming that $y_1(t) = e^{-t}\cos 2t$ and $y_2(t) = e^{-t}\sin 2t$ are linearly dependent on $(0, 1)$, we conclude that, for some constant $c$ and all $t \in (0, 1)$,

$$y_1(t) = cy_2(t) \quad \Rightarrow \quad e^{-t}\cos 2t = ce^{-t}\sin 2t \quad \Rightarrow \quad \cos 2t = c\sin 2t.$$

Choosing, say, $t = \pi/4$, we get $\cos(\pi/2) = c\sin(\pi/2)$ or $c = 0$. This implies that

$$\cos 2t \equiv 0 \cdot \sin 2t \equiv 0, \qquad t \in (0, 1),$$

which is a contradiction. Thus, $y_1(t)$ and $y_2(t)$ are linearly independent on $(0, 1)$ (and so on $(-\infty, \infty)$; see Problem 33(a) below).

**29.** These functions are linearly independent, because the equality $y_1(t) \equiv cy_2(t)$ would imply that, for some constant $c$,

$$te^{2t} \equiv ce^{2t} \quad \Rightarrow \quad t \equiv c$$

on $(0, 1)$.

**31.** Using the trigonometric identity $1 + \tan^2 t \equiv \sec^2 t$, we conclude that

$$y_1(t) = \tan^2 t - \sec^2 t \equiv -1 \qquad \Rightarrow \qquad y_2(t) \equiv 3 \equiv (-3)y_1(t),$$

and so $y_1(t)$ and $y_2(t)$ are linearly dependent on $(0, 1)$ (even on $(-\infty, \infty)$).

**33. (a)** True. Since $y_1(t)$ and $y_2(t)$ are linearly dependent on $[a, b]$, there exists a constant $c$ such that $y_1(t) = cy_2(t)$ (or $y_2(t) = cy_1(t)$) for all $t$ in $[a, b]$. In particular, this equality is satisfied on any smaller interval $[c, d]$, and so $y_1(t)$ and $y_2(t)$ are linearly dependent on $[c, d]$.

**(b)** False. As an example, consider $y_1(t) = t$ and $y_2(t) = |t|$ on $[-1, 1]$. For $t$ in $[0, 1]$, $y_2(t) = t = y_1(t)$, and so $y_2(t) \equiv c_1 y_1(t)$ with constant $c_1 = 1$. For $t$ in $[-1, 0]$, we have $y_2(t) = -t = -y_1(t)$, and so $y_2(t) \equiv c_2 y_1(t)$ with constant $c_2 = -1$. Therefore, these two functions are linearly dependent on $[0, 1]$ and on $[-1, 0]$. Since $c_1 \neq c_2$, there is no such a constant $c$ that $y_1(t) \equiv cy_2(t)$ on $[-1, 1]$. So, $y_1(t)$ and $y_2(t)$ are linearly independent on $[-1, 1]$.

**35. (a)** No, because, for $t \geq 0$, $y_2(t) = |t^3| = t^3 = y_1(t)$.

**(b)** No, because, for $t \leq 0$, $y_2(t) = |t^3| = -t^3 = -y_1(t)$.

**(c)** Yes, because there is no constant $c$ such that $y_2(t) = cy_1(t)$ is satisfied for all $t$ (for positive $t$ we have $c = 1$, and $c = -1$ for negative $t$).

**(d)** While $y_1'(t) = 3t^2$ on $(-\infty, \infty)$, for the derivative of $y_2(t)$ we consider three different cases: $t < 0$, $t = 0$, and $t > 0$. For $t < 0$, $y_2(t) = -t^3$, $y_2'(t) = -3t^2$, and so

$$W[y_1, y_2](t) = \begin{vmatrix} t^3 & -t^3 \\ 3t^2 & -3t^2 \end{vmatrix} = t^3(-3t^2) - 3t^2(-t^3) = 0.$$

Similarly, for $t > 0$, $y_2(t) = t^3$, $y_2'(t) = 3t^2$, and

$$W[y_1, y_2](t) = \begin{vmatrix} t^3 & t^3 \\ 3t^2 & 3t^2 \end{vmatrix} = t^3 \cdot 3t^2 - 3t^2 \cdot t^3 = 0.$$

For $t = 0$, $y_1'(0) = 3 \cdot 0^2 = 0$ and $y_2'(0) = 0$. The latter follows from the fact that one-sided derivatives of $y_2(t)$, $3t^2$ and $-3t^2$, are both zero at $t = 0$. Also, $y_1(0) = y_2(0) = 0$. Hence

$$W[y_1, y_2](0) = \begin{vmatrix} 0 & 0 \\ 0 & 0 \end{vmatrix} = 0,$$

and so $W[y_1, y_2](t) \equiv 0$ on $(-\infty, \infty)$. This result does not contradict part (b) in Problem 34 because these functions are not a pair of solutions to a homogeneous linear equation with constant coefficients.

37. If $y_1(t)$ and $y_2(t)$ are solutions to the equation $ay'' + by' + c = 0$, then, by Abel's formula, $W[y_1, y_2](t) = Ce^{-bt/a}$, where $C$ is a constant depending on $y_1$ and $y_2$. Thus, if $C \neq 0$, then $W[y_1, y_2](t) \neq 0$ for any $t$ in $(-\infty, \infty)$, because the exponential function, $e^{-bt/a}$, is never zero. For $C = 0$, $W[y_1, y_2](t) \equiv 0$ on $(-\infty, \infty)$.

39. **(a)** A linear combination of $y_1(t) = 1$, $y_2(t) = t$, and $y_3(t) = t^2$,

$$C_1 \cdot 1 + C_2 \cdot t + C_3 \cdot t^2 = C_1 + C_2 t + C_3 t^2,$$

is a polynomial of degree at most two and so can have at most two real roots, unless it is a zero polynomial, i.e., has all zero coefficients. Therefore, the above linear combination vanishes on $(-\infty, \infty)$ if and only if $C_1 = C_2 = C_3 = 0$, and $y_1(t)$, $y_2(t)$, and $y_3(t)$ are linearly independent on $(-\infty, \infty)$.

**(b)** Since

$$5y_1(t) + 3y_2(t) + 15y_3(t) = -15 + 15\sin^2 t + 15\cos^2 t = 15(-1 + \sin^2 t + \cos^2 t) \equiv 0$$

on $(-\infty, \infty)$ (the Pythagorean identity), given functions are linearly dependent.

**(c)** These functions are linearly independent. Indeed, since the function $e^t$ does not vanish on $(-\infty, \infty)$,

$$C_1 y_1 + C_2 y_2 + C_3 y_3 = C_1 e^t + C_2 t e^t + C_3 t^2 e^t = \left(C_1 + C_2 t + C_3 t^2\right) e^t = 0$$

if and only if $C_1 + C_2 t + C_3 t^2 = 0$. But functions $1$, $t$, and $t^2$ are linearly independent on $(-\infty, \infty)$ (see (a)) and so their linear combination is identically zero if and only if $C_1 = C_2 = C_3 = 0$.

**(d)** By the definition of $\cosh t$,

$$y_3(t) = \cosh t = \frac{e^t + e^{-t}}{2} = \frac{1}{2} e^t + \frac{1}{2} e^{-t} = \frac{1}{2} y_1(t) + \frac{1}{2} y_2(t),$$

and given functions are linearly dependent on $(-\infty, \infty)$.

**41.** The auxiliary equation for this problem is $r^3 + r^2 - 6r + 4 = 0$. Factoring yields

$$
\begin{aligned}
r^3 + r^2 - 6r + 4 &= \left(r^3 - r^2\right) + \left(2r^2 - 2r\right) + (-4r + 4) \\
&= r^2(r - 1) + 2r(r - 1) - 4(r - 1) = (r - 1)(r^2 + 2r - 4).
\end{aligned}
$$

Thus the roots of the auxiliary equation are

$$r = 1 \quad \text{and} \quad r = \frac{-2 \pm \sqrt{(-2)^2 - 4(1)(-4)}}{2} = -1 \pm \sqrt{5}.$$

Therefore, the functions $e^t$, $e^{(-1-\sqrt{5})t}$, and $e^{(-1+\sqrt{5})t}$ are solutions to the given equation, and they are linearly independent on $(-\infty, \infty)$ (see Problem 40). Hence, a general solution to $y''' + y'' - 6y' + 4y = 0$ is given by

$$y(t) = c_1 e^t + c_2 e^{(-1-\sqrt{5})t} + c_3 e^{(-1+\sqrt{5})t}.$$

**42.** The auxiliary equation associated with this differential equation is $r^3 - 6r^2 - r + 6 = 0$. We see, by inspection, that $r = 1$ is a root. Dividing the cubic polynomial $r^3 - 6r^2 - r + 6$ by $r - 1$, we find that

$$r^3 - 6r^2 - r + 6 = (r - 1)(r^2 - 5r - 6) = (r - 1)(r + 1)(r - 6).$$

Hence $r = -1, 1, 6$ are the roots to the auxiliary equation, and a general solution is

$$y(t) = c_1 e^{-t} + c_2 e^t + c_3 e^{6t}.$$

**43.** Factoring the auxiliary polynomial yields

$$
\begin{aligned}
r^3 + 2r^2 - 4r - 8 &= \left(r^3 + 2r^2\right) - (4r + 8) \\
&= r^2(r + 2) - 4(r + 2) = (r + 2)\left(r^2 - 4\right) = (r + 2)(r + 2)(r - 2).
\end{aligned}
$$

Therefore, the auxiliary equation has a double root $-2$ and a root 2. The functions $e^{-2t}$, $te^{-2t}$, and $e^{2t}$ form a linearly independent solution set. Therefore, a general solution in this problem is

$$z(t) = c_1 e^{-2t} + c_2 t e^{-2t} + c_3 e^{2t}.$$

**45.** By inspection, we see that $r = 2$ is a root of the auxiliary equation, $r^3 + 3r^2 - 4r - 12 = 0$. Dividing the polynomial $r^3 + 3r^2 - 4r - 12$ by $r - 2$ yields

$$r^3 + 3r^2 - 4r - 12 = (r - 2)\left(r^2 + 5r + 6\right) = (r - 2)(r + 2)(r + 3).$$

Hence, two other roots of the auxiliary equation are $r = -2$ and $r = -3$. The functions $e^{-3t}$, $e^{-2t}$, and $e^{2t}$ are three linearly independent solutions to the given equation, and a general solution is given by

$$y(t) = c_1 e^{-3t} + c_2 e^{-2t} + c_3 e^{2t}.$$

**47.** First we find a general solution to the equation $y''' - y' = 0$. Its characteristic equation, $r^3 - r = 0$, has roots $r = 0, -1$, and 1, and so a general solution is given by

$$y(t) = c_1 e^{(0)t} + c_2 e^{(-1)t} + c_3 e^{(1)t} = c_1 + c_2 e^{-t} + c_3 e^{t}.$$

Differentiating $y(t)$ twice yields

$$y'(t) = -c_2 e^{-t} + c_3 e^{t}, \qquad y''(t) = c_2 e^{-t} + c_3 e^{t}.$$

Now we substitute $y$, $y'$, and $y''$ into the initial conditions and find $c_1$, $c_2$, and $c_3$.

$$
\begin{array}{lclcl}
y(0) = c_1 + c_2 + c_3 & = & 2, & & c_1 = 3, \\
y'(0) = -c_2 + c_3 & = & 3, & \Rightarrow & c_2 = -2, \\
y''(0) = c_2 + c_3 & = & -1 & & c_3 = 1.
\end{array}
$$

Therefore, the solution to the given initial value problem is

$$y(t) = 3 - 2e^{-t} + e^{t}.$$

**49. (a)** To find the roots of the auxiliary equation, $p(r) := 3r^3 + 18r^2 + 13r - 19 = 0$, one can use Newton's method or intermediate value theorem. We note that

$$p(-5) = -9 < 0, \qquad p(-4) = 25 > 0,$$
$$p(-2) = 3 > 0, \qquad p(-1) = -17 < 0,$$
$$p(0) = -19 < 0, \qquad p(1) = 15 > 0.$$

Therefore, the roots of $p(r)$ belong to the intervals $[-5, -4]$, $[-2, -1]$, and $[0, 1]$, and we can take $r = -5$, $r = -2$, and $r = 0$ as initial quesses. Approximation yields $r_1 \approx -4.832$, $r_2 \approx -1.869$, and $r_3 \approx 0.701$. So, a general solution is given by

$$y(t) = c_1 e^{r_1 t} + c_2 e^{r_2 t} + c_3 e^{r_3 t} = c_1 e^{-4.832t} + c_2 e^{-1.869t} + c_3 e^{0.701t}.$$

**(b)** The auxiliary equation, $r^4 - 5r^2 + 5 = 0$, is of quadratic type. The substitution $s = r^2$ yields

$$s^2 - 5s + 5 = 0 \quad \Rightarrow \quad s = \frac{5 \pm \sqrt{5}}{2} \quad \Rightarrow \quad r = \pm\sqrt{s} = \pm\sqrt{\frac{5 \pm \sqrt{5}}{2}}.$$

Therefore,

$$r_1 = \sqrt{\frac{5 - \sqrt{5}}{2}} \approx 1.176\,, \qquad r_2 = \sqrt{\frac{5 + \sqrt{5}}{2}} \approx 1.902\,, \qquad r_3 = -r_1\,, \quad \text{and} \quad r_4 = -r_2$$

are the roots of the auxiliary equation, and a general solution to $y^{(\text{iv})} - 5y'' + 5y = 0$ is given by $y(t) = c_1 e^{r_1 t} + c_2 e^{-r_1 t} + c_3 e^{r_2 t} + c_4 e^{-r_2 t}$.

**(c)** We can use numerical tools to find the roots of the auxiliary fifth degree polynomial equation $r^5 - 3r^4 - 5r^3 + 15r^2 + 4r - 12 = 0$. Alternatively, one can involve the rational root theorem and examine the divisors of the free coefficient, $-12$. These divisors are $\pm1$, $\pm2$, $\pm3$, $\pm4$, $\pm6$, and $\pm12$. By inspection, $r = \pm1$, $\pm2$, and $3$ satisfy the equation. Thus, a general solution is $y(t) = c_1 e^{-t} + c_2 e^t + c_3 e^{-2t} + c_4 e^{2t} + c_5 e^{3t}$.

## EXERCISES 4.3: Auxiliary Equations with Complex Roots, page 177

**1.** The auxiliary equation in this problem is $r^2 + 9 = 0$, which has roots $r = \pm 3i$. We see that $\alpha = 0$ and $\beta = 3$. Thus, a general solution to the differential equation is given by

$$y(t) = c_1 e^{(0)t} \cos 3t + c_2 e^{(0)t} \sin 3t = c_1 \cos 3t + c_2 \sin 3t.$$

**3.** The auxiliary equation, $r^2 - 6r + 10 = 0$, has roots $r = \left(6 \pm \sqrt{6^2 - 40}\right)/2 = 3 \pm i$. So $\alpha = 3$, $\beta = 1$, and

$$z(t) = c_1 e^{3t} \cos t + c_2 e^{3t} \sin t$$

is a general solution.

**5.** This differential equation has the auxiliary equation $r^2 + 4r + 6 = 0$. The roots of this auxiliary equation are $r = \left(-4 \pm \sqrt{16 - 24}\right)/2 = -2 \pm \sqrt{2}\,i$. We see that $\alpha = -2$ and $\beta = \sqrt{2}$. Thus, a general solution to the differential equation is given by

$$w(t) = c_1 e^{-2t} \cos \sqrt{2}t + c_2 e^{-2t} \sin \sqrt{2}t.$$

**7.** The auxiliary equation for this problem is given by

$$4r^2 - 4r + 26 = 0 \quad \Rightarrow \quad 2r^2 - 2r + 13 = 0 \quad \Rightarrow \quad r = \frac{2 \pm \sqrt{4 - 104}}{4} = \frac{1}{2} \pm \frac{5}{2}\,i.$$

Therefore, $\alpha = 1/2$ and $\beta = 5/2$. Thus, a general solution is given by

$$y(t) = c_1 e^{t/2} \cos\left(\frac{5t}{2}\right) + c_2 e^{t/2} \sin\left(\frac{5t}{2}\right).$$

**9.** The associated auxiliary equation, $r^2 - 8r + 7 = 0$, has two real roots, $r = 1,\ 7$. Thus the answer is

$$y(t) = c_1 e^t + c_2 e^{7t}.$$

**11.** The auxiliary equation for this problem is $r^2 + 10r + 25 = (r + 5)^2 = 0$. We see that $r = -5$ is a repeated root. Thus two linearly independent solutions are $z_1(t) = e^{-5t}$ and $z_2(t) = te^{-5t}$. This means that a general solution is given by

$$z(t) = c_1 e^{-5t} + c_2 te^{-5t},$$

where $c_1$ and $c_2$ are arbitrary constants.

**13.** Solving the auxiliary equation yields complex roots

$$r^2 + 2r + 5 = 0 \quad \Rightarrow \quad r = \frac{-2 \pm \sqrt{2^2 - 4(1)(5)}}{2} = -1 \pm 2i.$$

So, $\alpha = -1$, $\beta = 2$, and a general solution is given by

$$y(t) = c_1 e^{-t} \cos 2t + c_2 e^{-t} \sin 2t.$$

**15.** First, we find the roots of the auxiliary equation.

$$r^2 + 10r + 41 = 0 \quad \Rightarrow \quad r = \frac{-10 \pm \sqrt{10^2 - 4(1)(41)}}{2} = -5 \pm 4i.$$

These are complex numbers with $\alpha = -5$ and $\beta = 4$. Hence, a general solution to the given differential equation is

$$y(t) = c_1 e^{-5t} \cos 4t + c_2 e^{-5t} \sin 4t.$$

**17.** The auxiliary equation in this problem, $r^2 - r + 7 = 0$, has the roots

$$r = \frac{1 \pm \sqrt{1^2 - 4(1)(7)}}{2} = \frac{1 \pm \sqrt{-27}}{2} = \frac{1}{2} \pm \frac{3\sqrt{3}}{2}\, i.$$

Therefore, a general solution is

$$y(t) = c_1 e^{t/2} \cos\left(\frac{3\sqrt{3}}{2}\, t\right) + c_2 e^{t/2} \sin\left(\frac{3\sqrt{3}}{2}\, t\right).$$

**19.** The auxiliary equation, $r^3 + r^2 + 3r - 5 = 0$, is a cubic equation. Since any cubic equation has a real root, first we examine the divisors of the free coefficient, 5, to find integer real roots (if any). By inspection, $r = 1$ satisfies the equation. Dividing $r^3 + r^2 + 3r - 5$ by $r - 1$ yields

$$r^3 + r^2 + 3r - 5 = (r - 1)(r^2 + 2r + 5).$$

Therefore, the other two roots of the auxiliary equation are the roots of the quadratic equation $r^2 + 2r + 5 = 0$, which are $r = -1 \pm 2i$. A general solution to the given equation is then given by

$$y(t) = c_1 e^t + c_2 e^{-t} \cos 2t + c_3 e^{-t} \sin 2t.$$

**21.** The auxiliary equation for this problem is $r^2 + 2r + 2 = 0$, which has the roots

$$r = \frac{-2 \pm \sqrt{4 - 8}}{2} = -1 \pm i.$$

# Chapter 4

So, a general solution is given by

$$y(t) = c_1 e^{-t} \cos t + c_2 e^{-t} \sin t \,,$$

where $c_1$ and $c_2$ are arbitrary constants. To find the solution that satisfies the initial conditions, $y(0) = 2$ and $y'(0) = 1$, we first differentiate the solution found above, then plug in given initial conditions. This yields $y'(t) = c_1 e^{-t}(-\cos t - \sin t) + c_2 e^{-t}(\cos t - \sin t)$ and

$$y(0) = c_1 = 2,$$
$$y'(0) = -c_1 + c_2 = 1 \,.$$

Thus $c_1 = 2$, $c_2 = 3$, and the solution is given by

$$y(t) = 2e^{-t} \cos t + 3e^{-t} \sin t \,.$$

**23.** The auxiliary equation for this problem is $r^2 - 4r + 2 = 0$. The roots of this equation are

$$r = \frac{4 \pm \sqrt{16 - 8}}{2} = 2 \pm \sqrt{2} \,,$$

which are real numbers. A general solution is given by $w(t) = c_1 e^{(2+\sqrt{2})t} + c_2 e^{(2-\sqrt{2})t}$, where $c_1$ and $c_2$ are arbitrary constants. To find the solution that satisfies the initial conditions, $w(0) = 0$ and $w'(0) = 1$, we first differentiate the solution found above, then plug in our initial conditions. This gives

$$w(0) = c_1 + c_2 = 0,$$
$$w'(0) = \left(2 + \sqrt{2}\right) c_1 + \left(2 - \sqrt{2}\right) c_2 = 1 \,.$$

Solving this system of equations yields $c_1 = 1/(2\sqrt{2})$ and $c_2 = -1/(2\sqrt{2})$. Thus

$$w(t) = \frac{1}{2\sqrt{2}} e^{(2+\sqrt{2})t} - \frac{1}{2\sqrt{2}} e^{(2-\sqrt{2})t} = \frac{\sqrt{2}}{4} \left(e^{(2+\sqrt{2})t} - e^{(2-\sqrt{2})t}\right)$$

is the desired solution.

**25.** The auxiliary equation, $r^2 - 2r + 2 = 0$, has the roots $r = 1 \pm i$. Thus, a general solution is

$$y(t) = c_1 e^t \cos t + c_2 e^t \sin t,$$

where $c_1$ and $c_2$ are arbitrary constants. To find the solution that satisfies the initial conditions, $y(\pi) = e^\pi$ and $y'(\pi) = 0$, we find $y'(t) = c_1 e^t(\cos t - \sin t) + c_2 e^t(\sin t + \cos t)$ and solve the system

$$e^\pi = y(\pi) = -c_1 e^\pi,$$
$$0 = y'(\pi) = -c_1 e^\pi - c_2 e^\pi.$$

This yields $c_1 = -1$, $c_2 = -c_1 = 1$. So, the answer is

$$y(t) = -e^t \cos t + e^t \sin t = e^t(\sin t - \cos t).$$

**27.** To solve the auxiliary equation, $r^3 - 4r^2 + 7r - 6 = 0$, which is of the third order, we find its real root first. Examining the divisors of $-6$, that is, $\pm 1, \pm 2, \pm 3$, and $\pm 6$, we find that $r = 2$ satisfies the equation. Next, we divide $r^3 - 4r^2 + 7r - 6$ by $r - 2$ and obtain

$$r^3 - 4r^2 + 7r - 6 = (r - 2)(r^2 - 2r + 3).$$

Therefore, the other two roots of the auxiliary equation are

$$r = \frac{2 \pm \sqrt{4 - 12}}{2} = 1 \pm \sqrt{2}i,$$

and a general solution to the given differential equation is given by

$$y(t) = c_1 e^{2t} + c_2 e^t \cos \sqrt{2}t + c_3 e^t \sin \sqrt{2}t.$$

Next, we find the derivatives,

$$y'(t) = 2c_1 e^{2t} + c_2 e^t \left(\cos \sqrt{2}t - \sqrt{2}\sin \sqrt{2}t\right) + c_3 e^t \left(\sin \sqrt{2}t + \sqrt{2}\cos \sqrt{2}t\right),$$
$$y''(t) = 4c_1 e^{2t} + c_2 e^t \left(-\cos \sqrt{2}t - 2\sqrt{2}\sin \sqrt{2}t\right) + c_3 e^t \left(-\sin \sqrt{2}t + 2\sqrt{2}\cos \sqrt{2}t\right),$$

and substitute $y$, $y'$, and $y''$ into the initial conditions. This yields

$$
\begin{aligned}
c_1 + c_2 &= 1, & c_1 &= 1, \\
2c_1 + c_2 + \sqrt{2}c_3 &= 0, & \Rightarrow \qquad c_2 &= 0, \\
4c_1 - c_2 + 2\sqrt{2}c_3 &= 0 & c_3 &= -\sqrt{2}.
\end{aligned}
$$

With these values of the constants $c_1$, $c_2$, and $c_3$, the solution becomes

$$ y(t) = e^{2t} - \sqrt{2}e^t \sin\sqrt{2}t. $$

**29. (a)** As it was stated in Section 4.2, third order linear homogeneous differential equations with constant coefficients can be handled in the same way as second order equations. Therefore, we look for the roots of the auxiliary equation $r^3 - r^2 + r + 3 = 0$. By the rational root theorem, the only possible rational roots are $r = \pm 1$ and $\pm 3$. By checking these values, we find that one of the roots of the auxiliary equation is $r = -1$. Factorization yields

$$ r^3 - r^2 + r + 3 = (r+1)(r^2 - 2r + 3). $$

Using the quadratic formula, we find that the other two roots are

$$ r = \frac{2 \pm \sqrt{4-12}}{2} = 1 \pm \sqrt{2}\,i. $$

A general solution is, therefore,

$$ y(t) = c_1 e^{-t} + c_2 e^t \cos\sqrt{2}t + c_3 e^t \sin\sqrt{2}t. $$

**(b)** By inspection, $r = 2$ is a root of the auxiliary equation, $r^3 + 2r^2 + 5r - 26 = 0$. Since

$$ r^3 + 2r^2 + 5r - 26 = (r-2)\left(r^2 + 4r + 13\right), $$

the other two roots are the roots of $r^2 + 4r + 13 = 0$, that is, $r = -2 \pm 3i$. Therefore, a general solution to the given equation is

$$ y(t) = c_1 e^{2t} + c_2 e^{-2t} \cos 3t + c_3 e^{-2t} \sin 3t. $$

**(c)** The fourth order auxiliary equation $r^4 + 13r^2 + 36 = 0$ can be reduced to a quadratic equation by making a substitution $s = r^2$. This yields

$$s^2 + 13r + 36 = 0 \quad \Rightarrow \quad s = \frac{-13 \pm \sqrt{169 - 144}}{2} = \frac{-13 \pm 5}{2}.$$

Thus, $s = (-13+5)/2 = -4$ or $s = (-13-5)/2 = -9$, and the solutions to the auxiliary equation are $r = \pm\sqrt{-4} = \pm 2i$ and $r = \pm\sqrt{-9} = \pm 3i$. A general solution, therefore, has the form

$$y(t) = c_1 \cos 2t + c_2 \sin 2t + c_3 \cos 3t + c_4 \sin 3t.$$

**31. (a)** Comparing the equation $y'' + 16y = 0$ with the mass-spring model (16) in Example 4, we conclude that the damping coefficient $b = 0$ and the stiffness constant $k = 16 > 0$. Thus, solutions should have an oscillatory behavior.

Indeed, the auxiliary equation, $r^2 + 16 = 0$, has roots $r = \pm 4i$, and a general solution is given by

$$y(t) = c_1 \cos 4t + c_2 \sin 4t.$$

Evaluating $y'(t)$ and substituting the initial conditions, we get

$$\begin{aligned} y(0) &= c_1 = 2, \\ y'(0) &= 4c_2 = 0 \end{aligned} \quad \Rightarrow \quad \begin{aligned} c_1 &= 2, \\ c_2 &= 0 \end{aligned} \quad \Rightarrow \quad y(t) = 2\cos 4t.$$

**(b)** Positive damping $b = 100$ and stiffness $k = 1$ imply that the displacement $y(t)$ tends to zero, as $t \to \infty$.

To confirm this prediction, we solve the given initial value problem explicitly. The roots of the associated equation are

$$r = \frac{-100 \pm \sqrt{100^2 - 4}}{2} = -50 \pm \sqrt{2499}.$$

Thus the roots $r_1 = -50 - \sqrt{2499}$ and $r_2 = -50 + \sqrt{2499}$ are both negative. A general solution is given by

$$y(t) = c_1 e^{r_1 t} + c_2 e^{r_2 t} \quad \Rightarrow \quad y'(t) = c_1 r_1 e^{r_1 t} + c_2 r_2 e^{r_2 t}.$$

Solving the initial value problem yields

$$y(0) = 1 = c_1 + c_2, \qquad \Rightarrow \qquad c_1 = r_2/(r_2 - r_1),$$
$$y'(0) = 0 = c_1 r_1 + c_2 r_2 \qquad\qquad c_2 = r_1/(r_1 - r_2),$$

and so the desired solution is

$$y(t) = \frac{-50 + \sqrt{2499}}{2\sqrt{2499}} e^{(-50 - \sqrt{2499})t} + \frac{50 + \sqrt{2499}}{2\sqrt{2499}} e^{(-50 + \sqrt{2499})t}.$$

Since both powers in exponential functions tend to $-\infty$ as $t \to \infty$, $y(t) \to 0$.

(c) The corresponding mass-spring model has negative damping $b = -6$ and positive stiffness $k = 8$. Thus the magnitude $|y(t)|$ of the displacement $y(t)$ will increase without bound, as $t \to \infty$. Moreover, because of the positive initial displacement and initial zero velocity, the mass will move in the negative direction. Thus, our guess is that $y(t) \to -\infty$ as $t \to \infty$.

Now we find the actual solution. Since the roots of the auxiliary equation are $r = 2$ and $r = 4$, a general solution to the given equation is $y(t) = c_1 e^{2t} + c_2 e^{4t}$. Next, we find $c_1$ and $c_2$ satisfying the initial conditions.

$$y(0) = 1 = c_1 + c_2, \qquad \Rightarrow \qquad c_1 = 2,$$
$$y'(0) = 0 = 2c_1 + 4c_2 \qquad\qquad c_2 = -1.$$

Thus, the desired solution is

$$y(t) = 2e^{2t} - e^{4t},$$

and it approaches $-\infty$ as $t \to \infty$.

(d) In this problem, the stiffness $k = -3$ is negative. In the mass-spring model, this means that the spring forces the mass to move in the same direction as the sign of the displacement is. Initially, the displacement $y(0) = -2$ is negative, and the mass has no initial velocity. Thus the mass, when released, will move in the negative direction, and the spring will enforce this movement. So, we expect that $y(t) \to -\infty$ as $t \to \infty$.

To find the actual solution, we solve the auxiliary equation $r^2 + 2r - 3 = 0$ and obtain $r = -3, 1$. Therefore, a general solution is given by $y(t) = c_1 e^{-3t} + c_2 e^t$. We find $c_1$ and

$c_2$ from the initial conditions.

$$y(0) = -2 = c_1 + c_2, \qquad \Rightarrow \qquad c_1 = -1/2,$$
$$y'(0) = 0 = -3c_1 + c_2 \qquad\qquad\qquad c_2 = -3/2.$$

Thus, the solution to the initial value problem is

$$y(t) = -\frac{e^{-3t}}{2} - \frac{3e^t}{2},$$

and, as $t \to \infty$, it approaches $-\infty$.

(e) As in the previous problem, we have negative stiffness $k = -6$. But this time the initial displacement, $y(0) = 1$, as well as the initial velocity, $y'(0) = 1$, is positive. So, the mass will start moving in the positive direction, and will continue doing this (due to the negative stiffness) with increasing velocity. Thus our prediction is that $y(t) \to \infty$ when $t \to \infty$.

Indeed, the roots of the characteristic equation in this problem are $r = -2$ and $3$, and so a general solution has the form $y(t) = c_1 e^{-2t} + c_2 e^{3t}$. To satisfy the initial conditions, we solve the system

$$y(0) = 1 = c_1 + c_2, \qquad \Rightarrow \qquad c_1 = 2/5,$$
$$y'(0) = 1 = -2c_1 + 3c_2 \qquad\qquad\qquad c_2 = 3/5.$$

Thus, the solution to the initial value problem is

$$y(t) = \frac{2e^{-2t}}{5} + \frac{3e^{3t}}{5},$$

and it approaches $\infty$ as $t \to \infty$.

**33.** From Example 3 we see that, in the study of a vibrating spring with damping, we have the initial value problem

$$my''(t) + by'(t) + ky(t) = 0; \qquad y(0) = y_0, \qquad y'(0) = v_0,$$

where $m$ is the mass of the spring system, $b$ is the damping constant, $k$ is the spring constant, $y(0)$ is the initial displacement, $y'(0)$ is the initial velocity, and $y(t)$ is the displacement of the mass from the equilibrium at time $t$.

# Chapter 4

**(a)** We want to determine the equation of motion for a spring system with $m = 10$ kg, $b = 60$ kg/sec, $k = 250$ kg/sec$^2$, $y(0) = 0.3$ m, and $y'(0) = -0.1$ m/sec. That is, we seek the solution to the initial value problem

$$10y''(t) + 60y'(t) + 250y(t) = 0; \qquad y(0) = 0.3, \qquad y'(0) = -0.1.$$

The auxiliary equation for the above differential equation is

$$10r^2 + 60r + 250 = 0 \qquad \Rightarrow \qquad r^2 + 6r + 25 = 0,$$

which has the roots

$$r = \frac{-6 \pm \sqrt{36 - 100}}{2} = \frac{-6 \pm 8i}{2} = -3 \pm 4i.$$

Hence $\alpha = -3$ and $\beta = 4$, and the displacement $y(t)$ has the form

$$y(t) = c_1 e^{-3t} \cos 4t + c_2 e^{-3t} \sin 4t.$$

We find $c_1$ and $c_2$ by using the initial conditions. We first differentiate $y(t)$ to get

$$y'(t) = (-3c_1 + 4c_2)e^{-3t} \cos 4t + (-4c_1 - 3c_2)e^{-3t} \sin 4t.$$

Substituting $y$ and $y'$ into the initial conditions, we obtain the system

$$y(0) = 0.3 = c_1,$$
$$y'(0) = -0.1 = -3c_1 + 4c_2.$$

Solving, we find that $c_1 = 0.3$ and $c_2 = 0.2$. Therefore the equation of motion is given by

$$y(t) = 0.3e^{-3t} \cos 4t + 0.2e^{-3t} \sin 4t \text{ (m)}.$$

**(b)** From Problem 32 we know that the frequency of oscillation is given by $\beta/(2\pi)$. In part (a) we found that $\beta = 4$. Therefore the frequency of oscillation is $4/(2\pi) = 2/\pi$.

**(c)** We see a decrease in the frequency of oscillation. We also have the introduction of the factor $e^{-3t}$, which causes the solution to decay to zero. This is a result of energy loss due to the damping.

**35.** The equation of the motion of a swinging door is similar to that for mass-spring model (with the mass $m$ replaced by the moment of inertia $I$ and the displacement $y(t)$ replaced by the angle $\theta$ that the door is open). So, from the discussion following Example 3 we conclude that the door will not continually swing back and forth (that is, the solution $\theta(t)$ will not oscillate) if $b \geq \sqrt{4Ik} = 2\sqrt{Ik}$.

**37. (a)** The auxiliary equation for this problem is $r^4 + 2r^2 + 1 = (r^2 + 1)^2 = 0$. This equation has the roots $r_1 = r_2 = -i$, $r_3 = r_4 = i$. Thus, $\cos t$ and $\sin t$ are solutions and, since the roots are repeated, we get two more solutions by multiplying $\cos t$ and $\sin t$ by $t$, that is, $t \cos t$ and $t \sin t$ are also solutions. This gives a general solution

$$y(t) = c_1 \cos t + c_2 \sin t + c_3 t \cos t + c_4 t \sin t.$$

**(b)** The auxiliary equation in this problem is

$$r^4 + 4r^3 + 12r^2 + 16r + 16 = (r^2 + 2r + 4)^2 = 0.$$

The roots of the quadratic equation $r^2 + 2r + 4 = 0$ are

$$r = \frac{-2 \pm \sqrt{4 - 16}}{2} = -1 \pm \sqrt{3}i.$$

Hence the roots of the auxiliary equation are $r_1 = r_2 = -1 - \sqrt{3}i$ and $r_3 = r_4 = -1 + \sqrt{3}i$. Thus two linearly independent solutions are $e^{-t}\cos(\sqrt{3}t)$ and $e^{-t}\sin(\sqrt{3}t)$, and we get two more linearly independent by multiplying them by $t$. This gives a general solution of the form

$$y(t) = (c_1 + c_2 t)e^{-t}\cos(\sqrt{3}t) + (c_3 + c_4 t)e^{-t}\sin(\sqrt{3}t).$$

**39. (a)** Comparing given equation with the Cauchy-Euler equation (21) in general form, we conclude that $a = 3$, $b = 11$, and $c = -3$. Thus, the substitution $x = e^t$ leads to the equation (22) in Problem 38 with these values of parameters. That is,

$$a\frac{d^2y}{dt^2} + (b - a)\frac{dy}{dt} + cy = 0 \qquad \Rightarrow \qquad 3\frac{d^2y}{dt^2} + 8\frac{dy}{dt} - 3y = 0.$$

**(b)** The auxiliary equation to the differential equation obtained in (a) is $3r^2 + 8r - 3 = 0$, which has the roots

$$r = \frac{-8 \pm \sqrt{64 - 4(3)(-3)}}{6} = \frac{-8 \pm 10}{6} \qquad \Rightarrow \qquad r = -3, \frac{1}{3}.$$

This yields a general solution $y(t) = c_1 e^{t/3} + c_2 e^{-3t}$.

**(c)** Since $x = e^t$, we can express $y(t)$ as a function of $x$ by writing

$$y = c_1 e^{t/3} + c_2 e^{-3t} = c_1 \left(e^t\right)^{1/3} + c_2 \left(e^t\right)^{-3} = c_1 x^{1/3} + c_2 x^{-3}.$$

**41.** This equation is a Cauchy-Euler equation. The substitution $x = e^t$ leads to the equation (22) with $a = 1$, $b = 2$, and $c = -6$. Thus we have

$$a\frac{d^2y}{dt^2} + (b-a)\frac{dy}{dt} + cy = 0 \qquad \Rightarrow \qquad \frac{d^2y}{dt^2} + \frac{dy}{dt} - 6y = 0.$$

The auxiliary equation, $r^2 + r - 6 = 0$, has the roots $r = -3$ and $r = 2$. Therefore, a general solution can be written as

$$y = c_1 e^{-3t} + c_2 e^{2t} = c_1 \left(e^t\right)^{-3} + c_2 \left(e^t\right)^2 = c_1 x^{-3} + c_2 x^2.$$

**43.** The substitution $x = e^t$ yields the equation

$$\frac{d^2y}{dt^2} + (9-1)\frac{dy}{dt} + 17y = 0 \qquad \Rightarrow \qquad \frac{d^2y}{dt^2} + 8\frac{dy}{dt} + 17y = 0.$$

Solving the characteristic equation, $r^2 + 8r + 17 = 0$, we get

$$r = \frac{-8 \pm \sqrt{64 - 68}}{2} = -4 \pm i.$$

Thus, the roots are complex with $\alpha = -4$, $\beta = 1$, and a general solution, as a function of $t$, is given by $y(t) = c_1 e^{-4t} \cos t + c_2 e^{-4t} \sin t$. Now we make the back substitution. Since $x = e^t$, we have $t = \ln x$ and so

$$y = \left(e^t\right)^{-4} (c_1 \cos t + c_2 \sin t) = x^{-4} \left[c_1 \cos(\ln x) + c_2 \sin(\ln x)\right].$$

**EXERCISES 4.4:**  Nonhomogeneous Equations: The Method of Undetermined Coefficients, page 186

1. We cannot use the method of undetermined coefficients to find a particular solution because of the $t^{-1}$ term, which is not a polynomial.

3. Rewriting the right-hand side in the form $3^t = e^{(\ln 3)t} = e^{rt}$, where $r = \ln 3$, we conclude that the method of undetermined coefficients can be applied.

5. Since $\sec \theta = 1/\cos \theta$, we cannot use the method of undetermined coefficients.

7. Given equation is not an equation with constant coefficients. Thus the method of undetermined coefficients cannot be applied.

9. The roots of the auxiliary equation, $r^2 + 3 = 0$, are $r = \pm \sqrt{3}i$. Since they are different from zero, we look for a particular solution of the form $y_p(t) \equiv A$. Substitution into the original equation yields

$$(A)'' + 3A = -9 \qquad \Rightarrow \qquad 3A = -9 \qquad \Rightarrow \qquad A = -3.$$

Thus, $y_p(t) \equiv -3$ is a particular solution to the given nonhomogeneous equation.

11. The auxiliary equation in this problem, $2r^2 + 1 = 0$, has complex roots. Therefore, $e^{2t}$ is not a solution to the corresponding homogeneous equation, and a particular solution to the original nonhomogeneous equation has the form $z_p(t) = Ae^{2t}$. Substituting this expression into the equation, we find the constant $A$.

$$2\left(Ae^{2t}\right)'' + Ae^{2t} = 2\left(4Ae^{2t}\right) + Ae^{2t} = 9Ae^{2t} = 9e^{2t} \qquad \Rightarrow \qquad A = 1.$$

Hence, $z_p(t) = e^{2t}$.

12. This equation is a linear first order differential equation with constant coefficients. The corresponding homogeneous equation, $2x' + x = 0$, can be solved by the methods of Chapter 2. Alternatively, one can use the result of Problem 21 in Section 4.2. Either approach yields

# Chapter 4

$x_h(t) = Ce^{-t/2}$. So, the homogeneous equation does not have a polynomial solution (other than $x(t) \equiv 0$), and we look for a particular solution to the nonhomogeneous equation of the form $x_p(t) = A_2 t^2 + A_1 t + A_0$. Substitution into the original differential equation yields

$$2x_p'(t) + x_p(t) = 2(2A_2 t + A_1) + A_2 t^2 + A_1 t + A_0 = A_2 t^2 + (4A_2 + A_1)t + (2A_1 + A_0) = 3t^2.$$

By equating coefficients we obtain

$$A_2 = 3,$$
$$4A_2 + A_1 = 0 \quad \Rightarrow \quad A_1 = -12,$$
$$2A_1 + A_0 = 0 \quad \Rightarrow \quad A_0 = 24.$$

Therefore, a particular solution is $x_p(t) = 3t^2 - 12t + 24$.

**13.** The right-hand side of the original nonhomogeneous equation suggest us the form

$$y_p(t) = t^s(A\cos 3t + B\sin 3t)$$

for a particular solution. Since the roots of the auxiliary equation, $r^2 - r + 9 = 0$, are different from $3i$, neither $\cos 3t$ nor $\sin 3t$ is a solution to the corresponding homogeneous equation. Therefore, we can choose $s = 0$, and so

$$y_p(t) = A\cos 3t + B\sin 3t,$$
$$y_p'(t) = -3A\sin 3t + 3B\cos 3t,$$
$$y_p''(t) = -9A\cos 3t - 9B\sin 3t.$$

Substituting these expressions into the original equation and equating the corresponding coefficients, we conclude that

$$(-9A\cos 3t - 9B\sin 3t) - (-3A\sin 3t + 3B\cos 3t) + 9(A\cos 3t + B\sin 3t) = 3\sin 3t$$
$$\Rightarrow \quad -3B\cos 3t + 3A\sin 3t = 3\sin 3t \quad \Rightarrow \quad A = 1, \ B = 0.$$

Hence, the answer is $y_p(t) = \cos 3t$.

**15.** For this problem, the corresponding homogeneous equation is $y'' - 5y' + 6y = 0$, which has the associated auxiliary equation $r^2 - 5r + 6 = 0$. The roots of this equation are $r = 3$ and $r = 2$. Therefore, neither $y = e^x$ nor $y = xe^x$ satisfies the homogeneous equation, and in the expression $y_p(x) = x^s(Ax + B)e^x$ for a particular solution we can take $s = 0$. So

$$y_p(x) = (Ax + B)e^x$$

$$\Rightarrow \quad y_p'(x) = (Ax + B + A)e^x$$

$$\Rightarrow \quad y_p''(x) = (Ax + B + 2A)e^x$$

$$\Rightarrow \quad (Ax + B + 2A)e^x - 5(Ax + B + A)e^x + 6(Ax + B)e^x = xe^x$$

$$\Rightarrow \quad (2Ax - 3A + 2B)e^x = xe^x \quad \Rightarrow \quad \begin{matrix} 2A = 1, \\ -3A + 2B = 0 \end{matrix} \quad \Rightarrow \quad \begin{matrix} A = 1/2, \\ B = 3/4 \,, \end{matrix}$$

and $y_p(x) = (x/2 + 3/4)e^x$.

**16.** The corresponding homogeneous equation has the auxiliary equation $r^2 - 1 = 0$, whose roots are $r = \pm 1$. Thus, in the expression $\theta_p(t) = (A_1 t + A_0)\cos t + (B_1 t + B_0)\sin t$ none of the terms is a solution to the homogeneous equation. We find

$$\theta_p(t) = (A_1 t + A_0)\cos t + (B_1 t + B_0)\sin t$$

$$\Rightarrow \quad \theta_p'(t) = A_1 \cos t - (A_1 t + A_0)\sin t + B_1 \sin t + (B_1 t + B_0)\cos t$$

$$= (B_1 t + A_1 + B_0)\cos t + (-A_1 t - A_0 + B_1)\sin t$$

$$\Rightarrow \quad \theta_p''(t) = B_1 \cos t - (B_1 t + B_0 + A_1)\sin t - A_1 \sin t + (-A_1 t - A_0 + B_1)\cos t$$

$$= (-A_1 t - A_0 + B_1)\cos t + (-B_1 t - B_0 - 2A_1)\sin t.$$

Substituting these expressions into the original differential equation, we get

$$\begin{aligned} \theta_p'' - \theta_p &= (-A_1 t - A_0 + 2B_1)\cos t + (-B_1 t - B_0 - 2A_1)\sin t \\ &\qquad - (A_1 t + A_0)\cos t - (B_1 t + B_0)\sin t \\ &= -2A_1 t \cos t + (-2A_0 + 2B_1)\cos t - 2B_1 t \sin t + (-2A_1 - 2B_0)\sin t \\ &= t\sin t. \end{aligned}$$

Chapter 4

Equating the coefficients, we see that

$$-2A_1 = 0 \qquad \Rightarrow \qquad A_1 = 0,$$
$$-2A_0 + 2B_1 = 0 \qquad \Rightarrow \qquad B_1 = A_0,$$
$$-2B_1 = 1 \qquad \Rightarrow \qquad B_1 = -\frac{1}{2} \quad \text{and so} \quad A_0 = -\frac{1}{2},$$
$$-2A_1 - 2B_0 = 0 \qquad \Rightarrow \qquad B_0 = 0.$$

Therefore, a particular solution of the nonhomogeneous equation $\theta'' - \theta = t\sin t$ is given by

$$\theta_p(t) = -\frac{t\sin t + \cos t}{2}.$$

**17.** The right-hand side of the original equation suggests that a particular solution should be of the form $y_p(t) = At^s e^t$. Since $r = 1$ is a double root of the corresponding auxiliary equation, $r^2 - 2r + 1 = (r-1)^2 = 0$, we take $s = 2$. Hence

$$y_p(t) = At^2 e^t \qquad \Rightarrow \qquad y_p'(t) = A\left(t^2 + 2t\right)e^t \qquad \Rightarrow \qquad y_p''(t) = A\left(t^2 + 4t + 2\right)e^t.$$

Substituting these expressions into the original equation, we find the constant $A$.

$$A\left(t^2 + 4t + 2\right)e^t - 2A\left(t^2 + 2t\right)e^t + At^2 e^t = 8e^t \qquad \Rightarrow \qquad 2Ae^t = 8e^t \qquad \Rightarrow \qquad A = 4.$$

Thus, $y_p(t) = 4t^2 e^t$.

**19.** According to the right-hand side of the given equation, a particular solution has the form $y_p(t) = t^s(A_1 t + A_0)e^{-3t}$. To choose $s$, we solve the auxiliary equation, $4r^2 + 11r - 3 = 0$, and find that $r = -3$ is its simple root. Therefore, we take $s = 1$, and so

$$y_p(t) = t\left(A_1 t + A_0\right)e^{-3t} = \left(A_1 t^2 + A_0 t\right)e^{-3t}.$$

Differentiating yields

$$y_p'(t) = \left[-3A_1 t^2 + (2A_1 - 3A_0)t + A_0\right]e^{-3t},$$
$$y_p''(t) = \left[9A_1 t^2 + (9A_0 - 12A_1)t + 2A_1 - 6A_0\right]e^{-3t}.$$

Substituting $y$, $y'$, and $y''$ into the original equation, after some algebra we get

$$[-26A_1t + (8A_1 - 13A_0)]e^{-3t} = -2te^{-3t} \quad \Rightarrow \quad \begin{array}{l} -26A_1 = -2, \\ 8A_1 - 13A_0 = 0 \end{array} \quad \Rightarrow \quad \begin{array}{l} A_1 = 1/13, \\ A_0 = 8/169. \end{array}$$

Therefore,

$$y_p(t) = \left(\frac{t}{13} + \frac{8}{169}\right) te^{-3t}.$$

**21.** The nonhomogeneous term of the original equation is $te^{2t}$. Therefore, a particular solution has the form $x_p(t) = t^s \left(A_1t + A_0\right) e^{2t}$. The corresponding homogeneous differential equation has the auxiliary equation $r^2 - 4r + 4 = (r-2)^2 = 0$. Since $r = 2$ is its double root, $s$ is chosen to be 2. Thus a particular solution to the nonhomogeneous equation has the form

$$x_p(t) = t^2 \left(A_1t + A_0\right) e^{2t} = \left(A_1t^3 + A_0t^2\right) e^{2t}.$$

We compute

$$x'_p = \left(3A_1t^2 + 2A_0t\right) e^{2t} + 2\left(A_1t^3 + A_0t^2\right) e^{2t},$$
$$x''_p = (6A_1t + 2A_0) e^{2t} + 4\left(3A_1t^2 + 2A_0t\right) e^{2t} + 4\left(A_1t^3 + A_0t^2\right) e^{2t}.$$

Substituting these expressions into the original differential equation yields

$$\begin{aligned} x''_p - 4x'_p + 4x_p &= (6A_1t + 2A_0) e^{2t} + 4\left(3A_1t^2 + 2A_0t\right) e^{2t} + 4\left(A_1t^3 + A_0t^2\right) e^{2t} \\ &\quad -4\left(3A_1t^2 + 2A_0t\right) e^{2t} - 8\left(A_1t^3 + A_0t^2\right) e^{2t} + 4\left(A_1t^3 + A_0t^2\right) e^{2t} \\ &= (6A_1t + 2A_0) e^{2t} = te^{2t}. \end{aligned}$$

Equating coefficients yields $A_0 = 0$ and $A_1 = 1/6$. Therefore $x_p(t) = t^3e^{2t}/6$ is a particular solution to the given nonhomogeneous equation.

**23.** The right-hand side of this equation suggests that $y_p(\theta) = \theta^s(A_2\theta^2 + A_1\theta + A_0)$. We choose $s = 1$ because $r = 0$ is a simple root of the auxiliary equation, $r^2 - 7r = 0$. Therefore,

$$y_p(\theta) = \theta(A_2\theta^2 + A_1\theta + A_0) = A_2\theta^3 + A_1\theta^2 + A_0\theta$$
$$\Rightarrow \quad y'_p(\theta) = 3A_2\theta^2 + 2A_1\theta + A_0 \quad \Rightarrow \quad y''_p(\theta) = 6A_2\theta + 2A_1.$$

So,

$$y_p'' - 7y_p' = (6A_2\theta + 2A_1) - 7\left(3A_2\theta^2 + 2A_1\theta + A_0\right) = -21A_2\theta^2 + (6A_2 - 14A_1)\theta + 2A_1 - 7A_0 = \theta^2.$$

Comparing the corresponding coefficients, we find $A_2$, $A_1$, and $A_0$.

$$
\begin{aligned}
-21A_2 &= 1, & A_2 &= -1/21, \\
6A_2 - 14A_1 &= 0, & \Rightarrow \qquad A_1 &= 3A_2/7 = -1/49, \\
2A_1 - 7A_0 &= 0 & A_0 &= 2A_1/7 = -2/343.
\end{aligned}
$$

Hence

$$y_p(\theta) = -\frac{1}{21}\theta^3 - \frac{1}{49}\theta^2 - \frac{2}{343}\theta.$$

**25.** We look for a particular solution of the form $y_p(t) = t^s(A\cos 3t + B\sin 3t)e^{2t}$. Since $r = 2 + 3i$ is not a root of the auxiliary equation, which is $r^2 + 2r + 4 = 0$, we can take $s = 0$. Thus,

$$
\begin{aligned}
y_p(t) &= (A\cos 3t + B\sin 3t)e^{2t} \\
\Rightarrow \qquad y_p'(t) &= [(2A + 3B)\cos 3t + (-3A + 2B)\sin 3t]e^{2t} \\
\Rightarrow \qquad y_p''(t) &= [(-5A + 12B)\cos 3t + (-12A - 5B)\sin 3t]e^{2t}.
\end{aligned}
$$

Next, we substitute $y_p$, $y_p'$, and $y_p''$ into the original equation and compare the corresponding coefficients.

$$y_p'' + 2y_p' + 4y_p = [(3A + 18B)\cos 3t + (-18A + 3B)\sin 3t]e^{2t} = 111e^{2t}\cos 3t$$

$$
\Rightarrow \qquad
\begin{aligned}
3A + 18B &= 111, \\
-18A + 3B &= 0.
\end{aligned}
$$

This system has the solution $A = 1$, $B = 6$. So,

$$y_p(t) = (\cos 3t + 6\sin 3t)e^{2t}.$$

**27.** The right-hand side of this equation suggests that

$$y_p(t) = t^s\left(A_3t^3 + A_2t^2 + A_1t + A_0\right)\cos 3t + t^s\left(B_3t^3 + B_2t^2 + B_1t + B_0\right)\sin 3t.$$

To choose $s$, we find the roots of the characteristic equation, which is $r^2 + 9 = 0$. Since $r = \pm 3i$ are its simple roots, we take $s = 1$. Thus

$$y_p(t) = t\left(A_3 t^3 + A_2 t^2 + A_1 t + A_0\right)\cos 3t + t\left(B_3 t^3 + B_2 t^2 + B_1 t + B_0\right)\sin 3t.$$

**29.** The characteristic equation $r^2 - 6r + 9 = (r-3)^2 = 0$ has a double root $r = 3$. Therefore, a particular solution is of the form

$$y_p(t) = t^2\left(A_6 t^6 + A_5 t^5 + A_4 t^4 + A_3 t^3 + A_2 t^2 + A_1 t + A_0\right)e^{3t}.$$

**31.** From the form of the right-hand side, we conclude that a particular solution should be of the form

$$y_p(t) = t^s\left[\left(A_3 t^3 + A_2 t^2 + A_1 t + A_0\right)\cos t + \left(B_3 t^3 + B_2 t^2 + B_1 t + B_0\right)\sin t\right]e^{-t}.$$

Since $r = -1 \pm i$ are simple roots of the characteristic equation, $r^2 + 2r + 2 = 0$, we should take $s = 1$. Therefore,

$$y_p(t) = t\left[\left(A_3 t^3 + A_2 t^2 + A_1 t + A_0\right)\cos t + \left(B_3 t^3 + B_2 t^2 + B_1 t + B_0\right)\sin t\right]e^{-t}.$$

**33.** The right-hand side of the equation suggests that $y_p(t) = t^s(A\cos t + B\sin t)$. By inspection, we see that $r = i$ is not a root of the corresponding auxiliary equation, $r^3 - r^2 + 1 = 0$. Thus, with $s = 0$,

$$y_p(t) = A\cos t + B\sin t,$$
$$y_p'(t) = -A\sin t + B\cos t,$$
$$y_p''(t) = -A\cos t - B\sin t,$$
$$y_p'''(t) = A\sin t - B\cos t,$$

and substitution into the original equation yields

$$(A\sin t - B\cos t) - (-A\cos t - B\sin t) + (A\cos t + B\sin t) = \sin t$$
$$\Rightarrow \quad (2A - B)\cos t + (A + 2B)\sin t = \sin t$$
$$\Rightarrow \quad \begin{matrix} 2A - B = 0, \\ A + 2B = 1 \end{matrix} \quad \Rightarrow \quad \begin{matrix} A = 1/5, \\ B = 2/5 \end{matrix} \quad \Rightarrow \quad y_p(t) = \frac{1}{5}\cos t + \frac{2}{5}\sin t.$$

**35.** We look for a particular solution of the form $y_p(t) = t^s(A_1 t + A_0)e^t$, and choose $s = 1$ because the auxiliary equation, $r^3 + r^2 - 2 = (r - 1)(r^2 + 2r + 2) = 0$ has $r = 1$ as a simple root. Hence,

$$y_p(t) = t(A_1 t + A_0)e^t = (A_1 t^2 + A_0 t)e^t$$
$$\Rightarrow \quad y_p'(t) = \left[A_1 t^2 + (2A_1 + A_0)t + A_0\right]e^t$$
$$\Rightarrow \quad y_p''(t) = \left[A_1 t^2 + (4A_1 + A_0)t + (2A_1 + 2A_0)\right]e^t$$
$$\Rightarrow \quad y_p'''(t) = \left[A_1 t^2 + (6A_1 + A_0)t + (6A_1 + 3A_0)\right]e^t$$
$$\Rightarrow \quad y''' + y'' - 2y = \left[10A_1 t + (8A_1 + 5A_0)\right]e^t = te^t.$$

Equating the corresponding coefficients, we find that

$$\begin{aligned} 10A_1 &= 1, \\ 8A_1 + 5A_0 &= 0 \end{aligned} \quad \Rightarrow \quad \begin{aligned} A_1 &= 1/10, \\ A_0 &= -8A_1/5 = -4/25 \end{aligned} \quad \Rightarrow \quad y_p(t) = \left(\frac{1}{10}t^2 - \frac{4}{25}t\right)e^t.$$

## EXERCISES 4.5:   The Superposition Principle and Undetermined Coefficients Revisited, page 192

**1.** Let $g_1(t) := \sin t$ and $g_2(t) := e^{2t}$. Then $y_1(t) = \cos t$ is a solution to

$$y'' - y' + y = g_1(t)$$

and $y_2(t) = e^{2t}/3$ is a solution to

$$y'' - y' + y = g_2(t).$$

**(a)** The right-hand side of the given equation is $5\sin t = 5g_1(t)$. Therefore, the function $y(t) = 5y_1(t) = 5\cos t$ is a solution to $y'' - y' + y = 5\sin t$.

**(b)** We can express $\sin t - 3e^{2t} = g_1(t) - 3g_2(t)$. So, by the superposition principle the desired solution is $y(t) = y_1(t) - 3y_2(t) = \cos t - e^{2t}$.

**(c)** Since $4\sin t + 18e^{2t} = 4g_1(t) + 18g_2(t)$, the function

$$y(t) = 4y_1(t) + 18y_2(t) = 4\cos t + 6e^{2t}$$

is a solution to the given equation.

**3.** The corresponding homogeneous equation, $y'' - y = 0$, has the associated auxiliary equation $r^2 - 1 = (r-1)(r+1) = 0$. This gives $r = \pm 1$ as the roots of this equation, and a general solution to the homogeneous equation is $y_h(t) = c_1 e^t + c_2 e^{-t}$. Combining this solution with the particular solution, $y_p(t) = -t$, we find that a general solution is given by

$$y(t) = y_p(t) + y_h(t) = -t + c_1 e^t + c_2 e^{-t}.$$

**5.** The corresponding auxiliary equation, $r^2 - r - 2 = 0$, has the roots $r = -1, 2$. Hence, a general solution to the corresponding homogeneous equation is $\theta_h(t) = c_1 e^{2t} + c_2 e^{-t}$. By the superposition principle, a general solution to the original nonhomogeneous equation is

$$\theta(t) = \theta_p(t) + \theta_h(t) = t - 1 + c_1 e^{2t} + c_2 e^{-t}.$$

**7.** First, we rewrite the equation in standard form, that is,

$$y'' - 2y' + y = 2e^x.$$

The corresponding homogeneous equation, $y'' - 2y' + y = 0$, has the associated auxiliary equation $r^2 - 2r + 1 = (r-1)^2 = 0$. Thus $r = 1$ is its double root, and a general solution to the homogeneous equation is $y_h(x) = c_1 x e^x + c_2 e^x$. Combining this with the particular solution, $y_p(x) = x^2 e^x$, we find that a general solution is given by

$$y(x) = y_p(x) + y_h(x) = x^2 e^x + c_1 x e^x + c_2 e^x.$$

**9.** We can write the nonhomogeneous term as a difference

$$t^2 + 4t - t^2 e^t \sin t = (t^2 + 4t) - (t^2 e^t \sin t) = g_1(t) - g_2(t).$$

Both, $g_1(t)$ and $g_2(t)$, have a form suitable for the method of undetermined coefficients. Therefore, we can apply this method to find particular solutions $y_{p,1}(t)$ and $y_{p,2}(t)$ to

$$3y'' + 2y' + 8y = g_1(t) \qquad \text{and} \qquad 3y'' + 2y' + 8y = g_2(t),$$

respectively. Then, by the superposition principle, $y_p(t) = y_{p,1}(t) - y_{p,2}(t)$ is a particular solution to the given equation.

# Chapter 4

**11.** The answer is "no", because the method of undetermined coefficients cannot be applied to

$$y'' - 6y' - 4y = \frac{1}{t}.$$

**13.** In the original form, the function $\sin^2 t$ does not fit any of the cases in the method of undetermined coefficients. But it can be written as $\sin^2 t = (1 - \cos 2t)/2$, and so

$$2t + \sin^2 t + 3 = 2t + \frac{1 - \cos 2t}{2} + 3 = \left(2t + \frac{7}{2}\right) - \left(\frac{1}{2}\cos 2t\right).$$

Now, the method of undetermined coefficients can be applied to each term in the above difference to find a particular solution to the corresponding nonhomogeneous equation, and the difference of these particular solutions, by the superposition principle, is a particular solution to the original equation. Thus, the answer is "yes".

**15.** "No", because the given equation is not an equation with constant coefficients.

**17.** The auxiliary equation in this problem is $r^2 - 1 = 0$ with roots $r = \pm 1$. Hence,

$$y_h(t) = c_1 e^t + c_2 e^{-t}$$

is a general solution to the corresponding homogeneous equation. Next, we find a particular solution $y_p(t)$ to the original nonhomogeneous equation. The method of undetermined coefficients yields

$$y_p(t) = At + B \quad \Rightarrow \quad y_p'(t) \equiv A \quad \Rightarrow \quad y_p''(t) \equiv 0;$$
$$y_p'' - y_p = 0 - (At + B) = -At - B = -11t + 1 \quad \Rightarrow \quad A = 11, \ B = -1$$
$$\Rightarrow \quad y_p(t) = 11t - 1.$$

By the superposition principle, a general solution is given by

$$y(t) = y_p(t) + y_h(t) = 11t - 1 + c_1 e^t + c_2 e^{-t}.$$

**19.** Solving the auxiliary equation, $r^2 - 3r + 2 = 0$, we find that $r = 1, 2$. Therefore, a general solution to the homogeneous equation, $y'' - 3y' + 2y = 0$, is

$$y_h(x) = c_1 e^x + c_2 e^{2x}.$$

By the method of undetermined coefficients, a particular solution $y_p(x)$ to the original equation has the form $y_p(x) = x^s(A \cos x + B \sin x)e^x$. We choose $s = 0$ because $r = 1 + i$ is not a root of the auxiliary equation. So,

$$y_p(x) = (A \cos x + B \sin x)e^x$$

$$\Rightarrow \quad y_p'(x) = [(A + B) \cos x + (B - A) \sin x]e^x$$

$$\Rightarrow \quad y_p''(x) = (2B \cos x - 2A \sin x)e^x .$$

Substituting these expressions into the equation, we compare the corresponding coefficients and find $A$ and $B$.

$$\{(2B \cos x - 2A \sin x) - 3[(A + B) \cos x + (B - A) \sin x] + 2(A \cos x + B \sin x)\} e^x = e^x \sin x$$

$$\Rightarrow \quad -(A + B) \cos x + (A - B) \sin x = \sin x \quad \Rightarrow \quad \begin{matrix} A + B = 0, \\ A - B = 1 \end{matrix} \quad \Rightarrow \quad \begin{matrix} A = 1/2, \\ B = -1/2. \end{matrix}$$

Therefore,

$$y_p(x) = \frac{(\cos x - \sin x)e^x}{2}$$

and

$$y(x) = \frac{(\cos x - \sin x)e^x}{2} + c_1 e^x + c_2 e^{2x}$$

is a general solution to the given nonhomogeneous equation.

**21.** Since the roots of the auxiliary equation, which is $r^2 + 2r + 2 = 0$, are $r = -1 \pm i$, we have a general solution to the corresponding homogeneous equation

$$y_h(\theta) = c_1 e^{-\theta} \cos \theta + c_2 e^{-\theta} \sin \theta = (c_1 \cos \theta + c_2 \sin \theta) e^{-\theta} ,$$

and look for a particular solution of the form

$$y_p(\theta) = \theta^s(A \cos \theta + B \sin \theta)e^{-\theta} \qquad \text{with} \qquad s = 1.$$

Differentiating $y_p(\theta)$, we get

$$y_p'(\theta) = (A \cos \theta + B \sin \theta)e^{-\theta} + \theta \left[(A \cos \theta + B \sin \theta)e^{-\theta}\right]' ,$$

199

Chapter 4

$$y_p''(\theta) = 2\left[(A\cos\theta + B\sin\theta)e^{-\theta}\right]' + \theta\left[(A\cos\theta + B\sin\theta)e^{-\theta}\right]''$$
$$= 2\left[(B-A)\cos\theta - (B+A)\sin\theta\right]e^{-\theta} + \theta\left[(A\cos\theta + B\sin\theta)e^{-\theta}\right]''.$$

(Note that we did not evaluate the terms containing the factor $\theta$ because they give zero result when substituted into the original equation.) Therefore,

$$y_p'' + 2y_p' + 2y_p = 2\left[(B-A)\cos\theta - (B+A)\sin\theta\right]e^{-\theta} + 2(A\cos\theta + B\sin\theta)e^{-\theta}$$
$$= 2\left(B\cos\theta - A\sin\theta\right)e^{-\theta} = e^{-\theta}\cos\theta.$$

Hence $A = 0$, $B = 1/2$, $y_p(\theta) = (1/2)\theta e^{-\theta}\sin\theta$, and a general solution is given by

$$y(\theta) = \frac{1}{2}\theta e^{-\theta}\sin\theta + (c_1\cos\theta + c_2\sin\theta)e^{-\theta}.$$

**23.** The corresponding homogeneous equation, $y' - y = 0$, is separable. Solving yields

$$\frac{dy}{dt} = y \quad\Rightarrow\quad \frac{dy}{y} = dt \quad\Rightarrow\quad \ln|y| = t + c \quad\Rightarrow\quad y = \pm e^c e^t = Ce^t,$$

where $C \neq 0$ is an arbitrary constant. By inspection, $y \equiv 0$ is also a solution. Therefore, $y_h(t) = Ce^t$, where $C$ is an arbitrary constant, is a general solution to the homogeneous equation. (Alternatively, one can apply the method of solving first order linear equations in Section 2.3 or the method discussed in Problem 21, Section 4.2.) A particular solution has the form $y_p(t) = A$. Substitution into the original equation yields

$$(A)' - A = 1 \quad\Rightarrow\quad A = -1.$$

Thus $y(t) = Ce^t - 1$ is a general solution. To satisfy the initial condition, $y(0) = 0$, we find

$$0 = y(0) = Ce^0 - 1 = C - 1 \quad\Rightarrow\quad C = 1.$$

So, the answer is $y(t) = e^t - 1$.

**25.** The auxiliary equation, $r^2 + 1 = 0$, has roots $r = \pm i$. Therefore, a general solution to the corresponding homogeneous equation is $z_h(x) = c_1\cos x + c_2\sin x$, and a particular solution

200

to the original equation has the form $z_p(x) = Ae^{-x}$. Substituting this function into the given equation, we find the constant $A$.

$$z'' + z = \left(Ae^{-x}\right)'' + Ae^{-x} = 2Ae^{-x} = 2e^{-x} \quad \Rightarrow \quad A = 1,$$

and a general solution to the given nonhomogeneous equation is

$$z(x) = e^{-x} + c_1 \cos x + c_2 \sin x.$$

Next, since $z'(x) = -e^{-x} - c_1 \sin x + c_2 \cos x$, from the initial conditions we get a system for determining constants $c_1$ and $c_2$.

$$\begin{aligned} 0 &= z(0) = 1 + c_1, \\ 0 &= z'(0) = -1 + c_2 \end{aligned} \quad \Rightarrow \quad \begin{aligned} c_1 &= -1, \\ c_2 &= 1. \end{aligned}$$

Hence, $z = (x) = e^{-x} - \cos x + \sin x$ is the solution to the given initial value problem.

**27.** The roots of the auxiliary equation, $r^2 - r - 2 = 0$, are $r = -1$ and $r = 2$. This gives a general solution to the corresponding homogeneous equation of the form $y_h(x) = c_1 e^{-x} + c_2 e^{2x}$. We use the superposition principle to find a particular solution to the nonhomogeneous equation.

**(i)** For the equation

$$y'' - y' - 2y = \cos x,$$

a particular solution has the form $y_{p,1}(x) = A\cos x + B\sin x$. Substitution into the above equation yields

$$(-A\cos x - B\sin x) - (-A\sin x + B\cos x) - 2(A\cos x + B\sin x)$$
$$= (-3A - B)\cos x + (A - 3B)\sin x = \cos x$$

$$\Rightarrow \quad \begin{aligned} -3A - B &= 1, \\ A - 3B &= 0 \end{aligned} \quad \Rightarrow \quad \begin{aligned} A &= -3/10, \\ B &= -1/10. \end{aligned}$$

So, $y_{p,1}(x) = -(3/10)\cos x - (1/10)\sin x$.

Chapter 4

**(ii)** For the equation

$$y'' - y' - 2y = \sin 2x,$$

a particular solution has the form $y_{p,2}(x) = A\cos 2x + B\sin 2x$. Substitution yields

$$(-4A\cos 2x - 4B\sin 2x) - (-2A\sin 2x + 2B\cos 2x) - 2(A\cos 2x + B\sin 2x)$$

$$= (-6A - 2B)\cos 2x + (2A - 6B)\sin 2x = \sin 2x$$

$$\Rightarrow \quad \begin{array}{l} -6A - 2B = 0, \\ 2A - 6B = 1 \end{array} \quad \Rightarrow \quad \begin{array}{l} A = 1/20, \\ B = -3/20. \end{array}$$

So,

$$y_{p,2}(x) = \frac{1}{20}\cos 2x - \frac{3}{20}\sin 2x.$$

Therefore, a general solution to the original equation is

$$\begin{aligned} y(x) &= y_{p,1}(x) - y_{p,2}(x) + y_h(x) \\ &= -\frac{3}{10}\cos x - \frac{1}{10}\sin x - \frac{1}{20}\cos 2x + \frac{3}{20}\sin 2x + c_1 e^{-x} + c_2 e^{2x}. \end{aligned}$$

Next, we find $c_1$ and $c_2$ such that the initial conditions are satisfied.

$$\begin{array}{l} -7/20 = y(0) = -3/10 - 1/20 + c_1 + c_2, \\ 1/5 = y'(0) = -1/10 + 2(3/20) - c_1 + 2c_2 \end{array} \Rightarrow \begin{array}{l} c_1 + c_2 = 0, \\ -c_1 + 2c_2 = 0 \end{array} \Rightarrow \begin{array}{l} c_1 = 0, \\ c_2 = 0. \end{array}$$

With these constants, the solution becomes

$$y(x) = -\frac{3}{10}\cos x - \frac{1}{10}\sin x - \frac{1}{20}\cos 2x + \frac{3}{20}\sin 2x.$$

**29.** The roots of the auxiliary equation, $r^2 - 1 = 0$, are $r = \pm 1$. Therefore, a general solution to the corresponding homogeneous equation is

$$y_h(\theta) = c_1 e^{\theta} + c_2 e^{-\theta}.$$

**(i)** For the equation

$$y'' - y = \sin\theta,$$

a particular solution has the form $y_{p,1}(x) = A \cos\theta + B \sin\theta$. Substitution into the equation yields

$$(-A\cos\theta - B\sin\theta) - (A\cos\theta + B\sin\theta) = -2A\cos\theta - 2B\sin\theta = \sin\theta$$

$$\Rightarrow \quad \begin{matrix} -2A = 0, \\ -2B = 1 \end{matrix} \quad \Rightarrow \quad \begin{matrix} A = 0, \\ B = -1/2. \end{matrix}$$

So, $y_{p,1}(\theta) = -(1/2)\sin\theta$.

**(ii)** For the equation

$$y'' - y = e^{2\theta},$$

a particular solution has the form $y_{p,2}(\theta) = Ae^{2\theta}$. Substitution yields

$$\left(Ae^{2\theta}\right)'' - \left(Ae^{2\theta}\right) = 3Ae^{2\theta} = e^{2\theta} \quad \Rightarrow \quad A = 1/3,$$

and $y_{p,2}(\theta) = (1/3)e^{2\theta}$.

By the superposition principle, a particular solution to the original nonhomogeneous equation is given by

$$y_p(\theta) = y_{p,1}(\theta) - y_{p,2}(\theta) = -(1/2)\sin\theta - (1/3)e^{2\theta},$$

and a general solution is

$$y(\theta) = y_p(\theta) + y_h(\theta) = -(1/2)\sin\theta - (1/3)e^{2\theta} + c_1 e^\theta + c_2 e^{-\theta}.$$

Next, we satisfy the initial conditions.

$$\begin{matrix} 1 = y(0) = -1/3 + c_1 + c_2, \\ -1 = y'(0) = -1/2 - 2/3 + c_1 - c_2 \end{matrix} \quad \Rightarrow \quad \begin{matrix} c_1 + c_2 = 4/3, \\ c_1 - c_2 = 1/6 \end{matrix} \quad \Rightarrow \quad \begin{matrix} c_1 = 3/4, \\ c_2 = 7/12. \end{matrix}$$

Therefore, the solution to the given initial value problem is

$$y(\theta) = -\frac{1}{2}\sin\theta - \frac{1}{3}e^{2\theta} + \frac{3}{4}e^\theta + \frac{7}{12}e^{-\theta}.$$

# Chapter 4

**31.** For the nonhomogeneous term $\sin t + t \cos t$, a particular solution has the form

$$y_{p,1}(t) = (A_1 t + A_0)t^s \cos t + (B_1 t + B_0)t^s \sin t.$$

For $10^t = e^{t \ln 10}$, a particular solution should be of the form

$$y_{p,2}(t) = Ct^p e^{t \ln 10} = Ct^p 10^t.$$

Since the roots of the auxiliary equation, $r^2 + 1 = 0$, are $r = \pm i$, we choose $s = 1$ and $p = 0$. Thus, by the superposition principle,

$$y_p(t) = y_{p,1}(t) + y_{p,2}(t) = (A_1 t + A_0)t \cos t + (B_1 t + B_0)t \sin t + C \cdot 10^t.$$

**33.** The roots of the auxiliary equation, which is $r^2 - r - 2 = 0$, are $r = -1$, $2$. The right-hand side of the given equation is a sum of two terms, $e^t \cos t$ and $-t^2 + t + 1$. Corresponding particular solutions have the forms

$$y_{p,1}(t) = (A \cos t + B \sin t)t^s e^t \quad \text{and} \quad y_{p,2}(t) = (C_2 t^2 + C_1 t + C_0)t^p,$$

and we can take $s = p = 0$ since neither $r = 1 + i$ nor $r = 0$ is a root of the auxiliary equation. By the superposition principle,

$$y_p(t) = (A \cos t + B \sin t)e^t + C_2 t^2 + C_1 t + C_0.$$

**35.** Since the roots of the auxiliary equation are

$$r = \frac{4 \pm \sqrt{16 - 20}}{2} = 2 \pm i,$$

which are different from $5$ and $3i$, a particular solution has the form

$$y_p(t) = (A_1 t + A_0) \cos 3t + (B_1 t + B_0) \sin 3t + Ce^{5t}.$$

(The last term corresponds to $e^{5t}$ in the right-hand side of the original equation, and the first two come from $t \sin 3t - \cos 3t$.)

**37.** Clearly, $r = 0$ is not a root of the auxiliary equation, $r^3 - 2r^2 - r + 2 = 0$. (One can find the roots, say, using the factorization $r^3 - 2r^2 - r + 2 = (r-2)(r-1)(r+1)$, but they are not needed for the form of a particular solution: the only important thing is that they are different from zero.) Therefore, a particular solution has the form

$$y_p(t) = A_2 t^2 + A_1 t + A_0.$$

Substitution into the original equation yields

$$
\begin{aligned}
y_p''' - 2y_p'' - y_p' + 2y_p &= (0) - 2(2A_2) - (2A_2 t + A_1) + 2(A_2 t^2 + A_1 t + A_0) \\
&= 2A_2 t^2 + (A_1 - 2A_2)t + (A_0 - A_1 - 4A_2) = 2t^2 + 4t - 9.
\end{aligned}
$$

Equating the coefficients, we obtain

$$
\begin{aligned}
2A_2 &= 2, & A_2 &= 1, \\
2A_1 - 2A_2 &= 4, & \Rightarrow \qquad A_1 &= 3, \\
2A_0 - A_1 - 4A_2 &= -9, & A_0 &= -1.
\end{aligned}
$$

Therefore, $y_p(t) = t^2 + 3t - 1$.

**39.** The auxiliary equation in this problem is $r^3 + r^2 - 2 = 0$. By inspection, we see that $r = 0$ is not a root. Next, we find that $r = 1$ is a simple root because

$$\left.\left(r^3 + r^2 - 2\right)\right|_{r=1} = 0 \qquad \text{and} \qquad \left.\left(r^3 + r^2 - 2\right)'\right|_{r=1} = \left.\left(3r^2 + 2r\right)\right|_{r=1} \neq 0.$$

Therefore, by the superposition principle, a particular solution has the form

$$y_p(t) = t(A_1 t + A_0)e^t + B = (A_1 t^2 + A_0 t)e^t + B.$$

Differentiating, we get

$$
\begin{aligned}
y_p'(t) &= \left[A_1 t^2 + (A_0 + 2A_1)t + A_0\right] e^t, \\
y_p''(t) &= \left[A_1 t^2 + (A_0 + 4A_1)t + 2A_0 + 2A_1\right] e^t, \\
y_p'''(t) &= \left[A_1 t^2 + (A_0 + 6A_1)t + 3A_0 + 6A_1\right] e^t.
\end{aligned}
$$

# Chapter 4

We substitute $y_p$ and its derivatives into the original equation and equate the corresponding coefficients. This yields

$$\left\{\left[A_1t^2 + (A_0 + 6A_1)t + 3A_0 + 6A_1\right] + \left[A_1t^2 + (A_0 + 4A_1)t + 2A_0 + 2A_1\right]\right.$$
$$\left. -2\left[A_1t^2 + A_0t\right]\right\}e^t - 2B = te^t + 1$$

$$\Rightarrow \quad [10A_1t + 8A_1 + 5A_0]\,e^t - 2B = te^t + 1$$

$$10A_1 = 1, \qquad\qquad A_1 = 1/10,$$

$$\Rightarrow \quad 8A_1 + 5A_0 = 0, \qquad \Rightarrow \quad A_0 = -4/25,$$

$$-2B = 1 \qquad\qquad B = -1/2.$$

Hence, a particular solution is

$$y_p(t) = \left(\frac{1}{10}t - \frac{4}{25}\right)te^t - \frac{1}{2}.$$

**41.** The characteristic equation in this problem is $r^2 + 2r + 5 = 0$, which has roots $r = -1 \pm 2i$. Therefore, a general solution to the corresponding homogeneous equation is given by

$$y_h(t) = (c_1\cos 2t + c_2\sin 2t)\,e^{-t}. \qquad\qquad (4.1)$$

**(a)** For $0 \le t \le 3\pi/2$, $g(t) \equiv 10$, and so the equation becomes

$$y'' + 2y' + 5y = 10.$$

Hence a particular solution has the form $y_p(t) \equiv A$. Substitution into the equation yields

$$(A)'' + 2(A)' + 5(A) = 10 \quad \Rightarrow \quad 5A = 10 \quad \Rightarrow \quad A = 2,$$

and so, on $[0, 3\pi/2]$, a general solution to the original equation is

$$y_1(t) = (c_1\cos 2t + c_2\sin 2t)\,e^{-t} + 2.$$

We find $c_1$ and $c_2$ by substituting this function into the initial conditions.

$$0 = y_1(0) = c_1 + 2, \qquad\qquad c_1 = -2,$$
$$0 = y_1'(0) = -c_1 + 2c_2 \qquad \Rightarrow \qquad c_2 = -1$$
$$\Rightarrow \quad y_1(t) = -(2\cos 2t + \sin 2t)\,e^{-t} + 2.$$

**(b)** For $t > 3\pi/2$, $g(t) \equiv 0$, and so the given equation becomes homogeneous. Thus, a general solution, $y_2(t)$, is given by (4.1), i.e.,

$$y_2(t) = y_h(t) = (c_1 \cos 2t + c_2 \sin 2t)\, e^{-t}.$$

**(c)** We want to satisfy the conditions

$$
\begin{aligned}
y_1(3\pi/2) &= y_2(3\pi/2), \\
y_1'(3\pi/2) &= y_2'(3\pi/2).
\end{aligned}
$$

Evaluating $y_1$, $y_2$, and their derivatives at $t = 3\pi/2$, we solve the system

$$
\begin{aligned}
2e^{-3\pi/2} + 2 &= -c_1 e^{-3\pi/2}, \\
0 &= (c_1 - 2c_2)e^{3\pi/2}
\end{aligned}
\quad\Rightarrow\quad
\begin{aligned}
c_1 &= -2\left(e^{3\pi/2} + 1\right), \\
c_2 &= -\left(e^{3\pi/2} + 1\right).
\end{aligned}
$$

**43.** Recall that the motion of a mass-spring system is governed by the equation

$$my'' + by' + ky = g(t),$$

where $m$ is the mass, $b$ is the damping coefficient, $k$ is the spring constant, and $g(t)$ is the external force. Thus, we have an initial value problem

$$y'' + 4y' + 3y = 5\sin t, \qquad y(0) = \frac{1}{2}, \quad y'(0) = 0.$$

The roots of the auxiliary equation, $r^2 + 4r + 3 = 0$, are $r = -3, -1$, and a general solution to the corresponding homogeneous equation is

$$y_h(t) = c_1 e^{-3t} + c_2 e^{-t}.$$

We look for a particular solution to the original equation of the form $y_p(t) = A\cos t + B\sin t$. Substituting this function into the equation, we get

$$
\begin{aligned}
y_p'' + 4y_p' + 3y_p &= (-A\cos t - B\sin t) + 4(-A\sin t + B\cos t) + 3(A\cos t + B\sin t) \\
&= (2A + 4B)\cos t + (2B - 4A)\sin t = 5\sin t
\end{aligned}
$$

$$
\begin{aligned}
2A + 4B &= 0, \\
2B - 4A &= 5
\end{aligned}
\quad\Rightarrow\quad
\begin{aligned}
A &= -1, \\
B &= 1/2.
\end{aligned}
$$

207

Thus, a general solution to the equation describing the motion is

$$y(t) = -\cos t + \frac{1}{2}\sin t + c_1 e^{-3t} + c_2 e^{-t}.$$

Differentiating, we find $y'(t) = \sin t + (1/2)\cos t - 3c_1 e^{-3t} - c_2 e^{-t}$. Initial conditions give

$$y(0) = -1 + c_1 + c_2 = 1/2, \qquad \Rightarrow \qquad c_1 = -1/2,$$
$$y'(0) = 1/2 - 3c_1 - c_2 = 0 \qquad\qquad\qquad c_2 = 2.$$

Hence, the equation of motion is

$$y(t) = -\cos t + \frac{1}{2}\sin t - \frac{1}{2}e^{-3t} + 2e^{-t}.$$

**45. (a)** With $m = k = 1$ and $L = \pi$ given initial value problem becomes

$$y(t) = 0, \qquad t \leq -\frac{\pi}{2V},$$

$$y'' + y' = \begin{cases} \cos Vt, & -\pi/(2V) < t < \pi/(2V), \\ 0, & t \geq \pi/(2V). \end{cases}$$

The corresponding homogeneous equation $y'' + y = 0$ is the simple harmonic equation whose general solution is

$$y_h(t) = C_1 \cos t + C_2 \sin t. \tag{4.2}$$

First, we find the solution to the given problem for $-\pi/(2V) < t < \pi/(2V)$. The nonhomogeneous term, $\cos Vt$, suggests a particular solution of the form

$$y_p(t) = A \cos Vt + B \sin Vt.$$

Substituting $y_p(t)$ into the equation yields

$$(A \cos Vt + B \sin Vt)'' + (A \cos Vt + B \sin Vt) = \cos Vt$$

$$\Rightarrow \qquad (-V^2 A \cos Vt - V^2 B \sin Vt) + (A \cos Vt + B \sin Vt) = \cos Vt$$

$$\Rightarrow \qquad (1 - V^2) A \cos Vt + (1 - V^2) B \sin Vt = \cos Vt.$$

Equating coefficients, we get

$$A = \frac{1}{1 - V^2}, \qquad B = 0,$$

Thus a general solution on $(-\pi/(2V), \pi/(2V))$ is

$$y_1(t) = y_h(t) + y_p(t) = C_1 \cos t + C_2 \sin t + \frac{1}{1 - V^2} \cos Vt. \qquad (4.3)$$

Since $y(t) \equiv 0$ for $t \le -\pi/(2V)$, the initial conditions for the above solution are

$$y_1\left(-\frac{\pi}{2V}\right) = y_1'\left(-\frac{\pi}{2V}\right) = 0.$$

From (4.3) we obtain

$$y_1\left(-\frac{\pi}{2V}\right) = C_1 \cos\left(-\frac{\pi}{2V}\right) + C_2 \sin\left(-\frac{\pi}{2V}\right) = 0$$

$$y_1'\left(-\frac{\pi}{2V}\right) = -C_1 \sin\left(-\frac{\pi}{2V}\right) + C_2 \cos\left(-\frac{\pi}{2V}\right) + \frac{V}{1 - V^2} = 0.$$

Solving the system yields

$$C_1 = \frac{V}{V^2 - 1} \sin \frac{\pi}{2V}, \qquad C_2 = \frac{V}{V^2 - 1} \cos \frac{\pi}{2V},$$

and

$$\begin{aligned}
y_1(t) &= \frac{V}{V^2 - 1} \sin \frac{\pi}{2V} \cos t + \frac{V}{V^2 - 1} \cos \frac{\pi}{2V} \sin t + \frac{1}{1 - V^2} \cos Vt \\
&= \frac{V}{V^2 - 1} \sin\left(t + \frac{\pi}{2V}\right) - \frac{1}{V^2 - 1} \cos Vt, \qquad -\frac{\pi}{2V} < t < \frac{\pi}{2V}.
\end{aligned}$$

For $t > \pi/(2V)$ given equation is homogeneous, and its general solution, $y_2(t)$, is given by (4.2). That is,

$$y_2(t) = C_3 \cos t + C_4 \sin t.$$

From the initial conditions

$$y_2\left(\frac{\pi}{2V}\right) = y_1\left(\frac{\pi}{2V}\right),$$

$$y_2'\left(\frac{\pi}{2V}\right) = y_1'\left(\frac{\pi}{2V}\right),$$

we conclude that

$$C_3 \cos \frac{\pi}{2V} + C_4 \sin \frac{\pi}{2V} = \frac{V}{V^2 - 1} \sin \frac{\pi}{V},$$

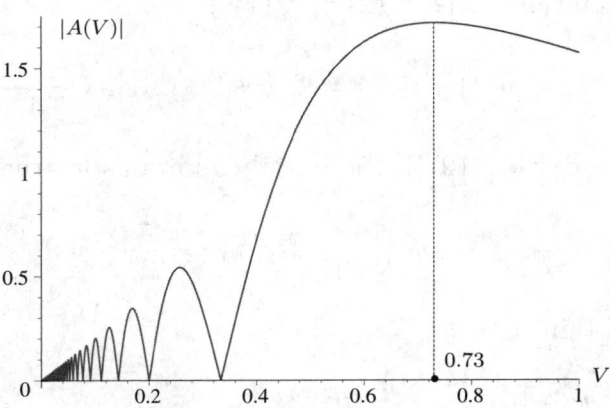

**Figure 4–A**: The graph of the function $|A(V)|$.

$$-C_3 \sin \frac{\pi}{2V} + C_4 \cos \frac{\pi}{2V} = \frac{V}{V^2 - 1} \cos \frac{\pi}{V} + \frac{V}{V^2 - 1} = \frac{2V}{V^2 - 1} \cos^2 \frac{\pi}{2V} \, .$$

The solution of this system is

$$C_3 = 0, \qquad C_4 = \frac{2V}{V^2 - 1} \cos \frac{\pi}{2V} \, .$$

So,

$$y_2(t) = \frac{2V}{V^2 - 1} \cos \frac{\pi}{2V} \sin t.$$

**(b)** The graph of the function

$$|A(V)| = \left| \frac{2V}{V^2 - 1} \cos \frac{\pi}{2V} \right|$$

is given in Figure 4-A. From this graph, we find that the most violent shaking of the vehicle (the maximum of $|A(V)|$) happens when the speed $V \approx 0.73$ .

**47.** The auxiliary equation in this problem is $r^2 + 9 = 0$ with roots $r = \pm 3i$. So, a general solution to the corresponding homogeneous equation is

$$y_h = c_1 \cos 3t + c_2 \sin 3t.$$

The form of a particular solution, corresponding to the right-hand side, is

$$y_p(t) = A \cos 6t + B \sin 6t.$$

Substitution into the original equation yields

$$-27(A\cos 6t + B\sin 6t) = 27\cos 6t \quad\Rightarrow\quad A = -1,\ B = 0 \quad\Rightarrow\quad y_p(t) = -\cos 6t.$$

Therefore, a general solution has the form

$$y(t) = c_1\cos 3t + c_2\sin 3t - \cos 6t.$$

In (a)–(c), we have the same boundary condition at $t = 0$, that is, $y(0) = -1$. This yields

$$-1 = y(0) = c_1 - 1 \quad\Rightarrow\quad c_1 = 0.$$

Hence, all the solutions satisfying this condition are given by

$$y(t) = c_2\sin 3t - \cos 6t. \tag{4.4}$$

(a) The second boundary condition gives $3 = y(\pi/6) = c_2 + 1 \quad\Rightarrow\quad c_2 = 2$, and the answer is $y = 2\sin 3t - \cos 6t$.

(b) This time we have $5 = y(\pi/3) = c_2 \cdot 0 - 1 \quad\Rightarrow\quad 5 = -1$, and so there is no solution of the form (4.4) satisfying this second boundary condition.

(c) Now we have $-1 = y(\pi/3) = c_2 \cdot 0 - 1 \quad\Rightarrow\quad -1 = -1$, which is a true identity. This means that any function in (4.4) satisfies both boundary conditions.

## EXERCISES 4.6:   Variation of Parameters, page 197

1. The auxiliary equation in this problem is $r^2 + 4 = 0$, which has the roots $r = \pm 2i$. Therefore, $y_1(t) = \cos 2t$ and $y_2(t) = \sin 2t$ are two linearly independent solutions, and a general solution to the corresponding homogeneous equation is given by

$$y_h(t) = c_1\cos 2t + c_2\sin 2t.$$

Using the variation of parameters method, we look for a particular solution to the original nonhomogeneous equation of the form

$$y_p(t) = v_1(t)y_1(t) + v_2(t)y_2(t) = v_1(t)\cos 2t + v_2(t)\sin 2t.$$

# Chapter 4

The system (9) on page 195 in the text becomes

$$v_1'(t)\cos 2t + v_2'(t)\sin 2t = 0$$
$$-2v_1'(t)\sin 2t + 2v_2'(t)\cos 2t = \tan 2t. \tag{4.5}$$

Multiplying the first equation in (4.5) by $\sin 2t$, the second equation by $(1/2)\cos 2t$, and adding the resulting equations together, we get

$$v_2'(t) = \frac{1}{2}\sin 2t \qquad \Rightarrow \qquad v_2 = \frac{1}{2}\int \sin 2t\, dt = -\frac{1}{4}\cos 2t + c_3.$$

From the first equation in (4.5) we also obtain

$$v_1'(t) = -v_2'(t)\tan 2t = -\frac{1}{2}\frac{\sin^2 2t}{\cos 2t} = -\frac{1}{2}\frac{1 - \cos^2 2t}{\cos 2t} = \frac{1}{2}(\cos 2t - \sec 2t)$$

$$\Rightarrow \qquad v_1(t) = \frac{1}{2}\int (\cos 2t - \sec 2t)\, dt = \frac{1}{4}(\sin 2t - \ln|\sec 2t + \tan 2t|) + c_4.$$

We take $c_3 = c_4 = 0$ since we need just one particular solution. Thus

$$
\begin{aligned}
y_p(t) &= \frac{1}{4}(\sin 2t - \ln|\sec 2t + \tan 2t|)\cos 2t - \frac{1}{4}\cos 2t \sin 2t \\
&= -\frac{1}{4}\cos 2t \ln|\sec 2t + \tan 2t|
\end{aligned}
$$

and a general solution to the given equation is

$$y(t) = y_h(t) + y_p(t) = c_1\cos 2t + c_2\sin 2t - \frac{1}{4}\cos 2t \ln|\sec 2t + \tan 2t|.$$

**2.** From Example 1 on page 196 in the text, we know that functions $y_1(t) = \cos t$ and $y_2(t) = \sin t$ are two linearly independent solutions to the corresponding homogeneous equation, and so its general solution is given by

$$y_h(t) = c_1\cos t + c_2\sin t.$$

Now we apply the method of variation of parameters to find a particular solution to the original equation. By the formula (3) on page 194 in the text, $y_p(t)$ has the form

$$y_p(t) = v_1(t)y_1(t) + v_2(t)y_2(t).$$

Since

$$y_1'(t) = (\cos t)' = -\sin t, \qquad y_2'(t) = (\sin t)' = \cos t,$$

the system (9) on page 195 becomes

$$\begin{aligned} v_1'(t)\cos t + v_2'(t)\sin t &= 0, \\ -v_1'(t)\sin t + v_2'(t)\cos t &= \sec t. \end{aligned} \tag{4.6}$$

Multiplying the first equation by $\sin t$ and the second equation by $\cos t$ yields

$$v_1'(t)\sin t \cos t + v_2'(t)\sin^2 t = 0,$$
$$-v_1'(t)\sin t \cos t + v_2'(t)\cos^2 t = 1.$$

Adding these equations together, we obtain

$$v_2'(t)\left(\cos^2 t + \sin^2 t\right) = 1 \qquad \text{or} \qquad v_2'(t) = 1.$$

From the first equation in (4.6), we can now find $v_1'(t)$:

$$v_1'(t) = -v_2'(t)\,\frac{\sin t}{\cos t} = -\tan t.$$

So,

$$\begin{array}{ll} v_1'(t) = -\tan t, & v_1(t) = -\int \tan t\,dt = \ln|\cos t| + c_3, \\ v_2'(t) = 1 & v_2(t) = \int dt = t + c_4. \end{array} \quad \Rightarrow$$

Since we are looking for a particular solution, we can take $c_3 = c_4 = 0$ and get

$$y_p(t) = \cos t \ln|\cos t| + t\sin t.$$

Thus a general solution to the given equation is

$$y(t) = y_p(t) + y_h(t) = \cos t \ln|\cos t| + t\sin t + c_1\cos t + c_2\sin t.$$

**3.** First, we can simplify the equation by dividing both sides by 2. This yields

$$x'' - x' - 2x = e^{3t}.$$

This equation has associated homogeneous equation $x'' - x' - 2x = 0$. The roots of the associated auxiliary equation, $r^2 - r - 2 = 0$, are $r = 2$ and $r = -1$. Therefore, a general solution to this equation is

$$x_h(t) = c_1 e^{2t} + c_2 e^{-t}.$$

For the variation of parameters method, we let

$$x_p(t) = v_1(t)x_1(t) + v_2(t)x_2(t), \qquad \text{where} \qquad x_1(t) = e^{2t} \quad \text{and} \quad x_2(t) = e^{-t}.$$

Thus, $x_1'(t) = 2e^{2t}$ and $x_2'(t) = -e^{-t}$. This means that we have to solve the system

$$e^{2t}v_1' + e^{-t}v_2' = 0,$$
$$2e^{2t}v_1' - e^{-t}v_2' = e^{3t}.$$

Adding these two equations yields

$$3e^{2t}v_1' = e^{3t} \qquad \Rightarrow \qquad v_1' = \frac{1}{3}e^t \qquad \Rightarrow \qquad v_1(t) = \frac{1}{3}e^t.$$

Substututing $v_1'$ into the first equation, we get

$$\frac{1}{3}e^{3t} + e^{-t}v_2' = 0 \qquad \Rightarrow \qquad v_2' = -\frac{1}{3}e^{4t} \qquad \Rightarrow \qquad v_2(t) = -\frac{1}{12}e^{4t}.$$

Therefore,

$$x_p(t) = \frac{1}{3}e^t e^{2t} - \frac{1}{12}e^{4t}e^{-t} = \frac{1}{4}e^{3t},$$

and a general solution is

$$x(t) = c_1 e^{2t} + c_2 e^{-t} + \frac{1}{4}e^{3t}.$$

5. This equation has associated homogeneous equation $y'' - 2y' + y = 0$. Its auxiliary equation, $r^2 - 2r + 1 = 0$, has a double root $r = 1$. Thus a general solution to the homogeneous equation is

$$y_h(t) = c_1 e^t + c_2 t e^t.$$

For the variation of parameters method, we let

$$y_p(t) = v_1(t)y_1(t) + v_2(t)y_2(t), \qquad \text{where} \qquad y_1(t) = e^t \quad \text{and} \quad y_2(t) = t e^t.$$

Thus, $y_1'(t) = e^t$ and $y_2'(t) = te^t + e^t$. This means that we want to solve the system (see system (9) on page 195 of text)

$$e^t v_1' + te^t v_2' = 0,$$
$$e^t v_1' + \left(te^t + e^t\right) v_2' = t^{-1}e^t.$$

Subtracting these two equations yields

$$e^t v_2' = t^{-1}e^t \quad \Rightarrow \quad v_2' = t^{-1}.$$

So

$$v_2(t) = \int t^{-1}\, dt = \ln|t| + c_3\,.$$

Also, we have from the first equation of the system

$$e^t v_1' = -te^t v_2' = -te^t t^{-1} = -e^t \quad \Rightarrow \quad v_1' = -1.$$

So,

$$v_1(t) = -t + c_4\,.$$

By letting $c_3$ and $c_4$ equal to zero, and plugging the expressions found above for $v_1(t)$ and $v_2(t)$ into the equation defining $y_p(t)$, we obtain a particular solution

$$y_p(t) = -te^t + te^t \ln|t|.$$

We obtain a general solution of the nonhomogeneous equation by adding this expression for $y_p(t)$ to the expression for $y_h(t)$. Thus, we obtain

$$y(t) = c_1 e^t + c_2 te^t - te^t + te^t \ln|t| = c_1 e^t + (c_2 - 1)te^t + te^t \ln|t|.$$

If we let $C_1 = c_1$ and $C_2 = c_2 - 1$, we can express this general solution in the form

$$y(t) = C_1 e^t + C_2 te^t + te^t \ln|t|.$$

# Chapter 4

**7.** The auxiliary equation in this problem is $r^2 + 16 = 0$, which has the roots $r = \pm 4i$. Therefore, $y_1(\theta) = \cos 4\theta$ and $y_2(\theta) = \sin 4\theta$ are two linearly independent solutions, and a general solution to the corresponding homogeneous equation is given by

$$y_h(\theta) = c_1 \cos 4\theta + c_2 \sin 4\theta.$$

Using the variation of parameters method, we look for a particular solution to the original nonhomogeneous equation of the form

$$y_p(\theta) = v_1(\theta)y_1(\theta) + v_2(\theta)y_2(\theta) = v_1(\theta)\cos 4\theta + v_2(\theta)\sin 4\theta.$$

The system (9) on page 195 in the text becomes

$$
\begin{aligned}
v_1'(\theta)\cos 4\theta + v_2'(\theta)\sin 4\theta &= 0, \\
-4v_1'(\theta)\sin 4\theta + 4v_2'(\theta)\cos 4\theta &= \sec 4\theta.
\end{aligned}
\tag{4.7}
$$

Multiplying the first equation in (4.7) by $\sin 4\theta$ and the second equation by $(1/4)\cos 4\theta$, and adding the resulting equations together, we get

$$v_2'(\theta) = \frac{1}{4} \qquad \Rightarrow \qquad v_2 = \frac{1}{4}\theta + c_3.$$

From the first equation in (4.7) we also obtain

$$v_1'(\theta) = -\frac{1}{4}\tan 4\theta \qquad \Rightarrow \qquad v_1(\theta) = -\frac{1}{4}\int \tan 4\theta \, d\theta = \frac{1}{16}\ln|\cos 4\theta| + c_4.$$

Taking $c_3 = c_4 = 0$, we obtain

$$y_p(\theta) = \frac{\cos 4\theta}{16}\ln|\cos 4\theta| + \frac{1}{4}\theta \sin 4\theta$$

$$\Rightarrow \quad y(\theta) = c_1 \cos 4\theta + c_2 \sin 4\theta + \frac{\theta}{4}\sin 4\theta + \frac{\cos 4\theta}{16}\ln|\cos 4\theta|.$$

**9.** In this problem, the corresponding homogeneous equation is the same as that in Problem 1. Hence $y_1(t) = \cos 2t$ and $y_2(t) = \sin 2t$ are two linearly independent solutions, and a general solution to the homogeneous equation is given by

$$y_h(t) = c_1 \cos 2t + c_2 \sin 2t,$$

and, in the variation of parameters method, a particular solution has the form

$$y_p(t) = v_1(t)\cos 2t + v_2(t)\sin 2t,$$

where $v_1'(t)$, $v_2'(t)$ satisfy the system

$$v_1'(t)\cos 2t + v_2'(t)\sin 2t = 0,$$
$$-2v_1'(t)\sin 2t + 2v_2'(t)\cos 2t = \csc^2 2t.$$

Multiplying the first equation by $\sin 2t$ and the second equation by $(1/2)\cos 2t$, and adding the resulting equations, we get

$$v_2'(t) = \frac{1}{2}\csc^2 2t\cos 2t \qquad \Rightarrow \qquad v_2 = \frac{1}{2}\int \csc^2 2t\cos 2t\,dt = -\frac{1}{4}\csc 2t + c_3\,.$$

From the first equation in the system above we also find

$$v_1'(t) = -v_2'(t)\tan 2t = -\frac{1}{2}\csc^2 2t\cos 2t\tan 2t = -\frac{1}{2}\csc 2t$$
$$\Rightarrow \qquad v_1(t) = -\frac{1}{2}\int \csc 2t\,dt = \frac{1}{4}\ln|\csc 2t + \cot 2t| + c_4\,.$$

With $c_3 = c_4 = 0$,

$$y_p(t) = \frac{1}{4}\cos 2t\ln|\csc 2t + \cot 2t| - \frac{1}{4}\csc 2t\sin 2t = \frac{1}{4}\left(\cos 2t\ln|\csc 2t + \cot 2t| - 1\right)$$
$$\Rightarrow \qquad y(t) = c_1\cos 2t + c_2\sin 2t + \frac{1}{4}\left(\cos 2t\ln|\csc 2t + \cot 2t| - 1\right).$$

**11.** This equation is similar to that in Example 1 on page 196 in the text. Only the nonhomogeneous term is different. Thus we will follow steps in Example 1. Two independent solutions to the corresponding homogeneous equation, $y'' + y = 0$, are $y_1(t) = \cos t$ and $y_2(t) = \sin t$. A particular solution to the original equation is of the form

$$y_p(t) = v_1(t)\cos t + v_2(t)\sin t,$$

where $v_1(t)$ and $v_2(t)$ satisfy

$$v_1'(t)\cos t + v_2'(t)\sin t = 0,$$
$$-v_1'(t)\sin t + v_2'(t)\cos t = \tan^2 t.$$

# Chapter 4

Multiplying the first equation by $\sin t$ and the second equation by $\cos t$, and adding them together yield

$$v_2'(t) = \tan^2 t \cos t = (\sec^2 t - 1)\cos t = \sec t - \cos t.$$

We find $v_1'(t)$ from the first equation in the system.

$$v_1'(t) = -v_2'(t)\tan t = -(\sec t - \cos t)\tan t = \sin t - \frac{\sin t}{\cos^2 t}.$$

Integrating, we get

$$v_1(t) = \int \left(\sin t - \frac{\sin t}{\cos^2 t}\right) dt = -\cos t - \sec t,$$

$$v_2(t) = \int (\sec t - \cos t)\, dt = \ln|\sec t + \tan t| - \sin t,$$

where we have taken zero integration constants. Therefore,

$$y_p(t) = -(\cos t + \sec t)\cos t + (\ln|\sec t + \tan t| - \sin t)\sin t = \sin t \ln|\sec t + \tan t| - 2,$$

and a general solution is given by

$$y(t) = c_1 \cos t + c_2 \sin t + \sin t \ln|\sec t + \tan t| - 2.$$

**13.** The corresponding homogeneous equation in this problem is the same as that in Problem 1 (with $y$ replaced by $v$). Similarly to the solution of Problem 1, we conclude that $v_1(t) = \cos 2t$ and $v_2(t) = \sin 2t$ are two linearly independent solutions of the corresponding homogeneous equation, and a particular solution to the original equation can be found as

$$v_p(t) = u_1(t)\cos 2t + u_2(t)\sin 2t,$$

where $u_1(t)$ and $u_2(t)$ satisfy

$$u_1'(t)\cos 2t + u_2'(t)\sin 2t = 0,$$
$$-2u_1'(t)\sin 2t + 2u_2'(t)\cos 2t = \sec^4 2t.$$

Multiplying the first equation by $\sin 2t$ and the second equation by $(1/2)\cos 2t$, and adding the results together, we get

$$u_2'(t) = \frac{1}{2}\sec^3 2t.$$

From the first equation in the above system we also obtain

$$u_1'(t) = -u_2'(t)\tan 2t = -\frac{1}{2}\sec^4 2t \sin 2t.$$

Integrating yields

$$u_1(t) = -\frac{1}{2}\int \sec^4 2t \sin 2t\, dt = -\frac{1}{2}\int \cos^{-4} 2t \sin 2t\, dt = -\frac{1}{12}\sec^3 2t,$$

$$u_2(t) = \frac{1}{2}\int \sec^3 2t\, dt = \frac{1}{8}\left(\sec 2t \tan 2t + \ln|\sec 2t + \tan 2t|\right).$$

Thus,

$$\begin{aligned}
v_p(t) &= -\frac{1}{12}\sec^3 2t \cos 2t + \frac{1}{8}\left(\sec 2t \tan 2t + \ln|\sec 2t + \tan 2t|\right)\sin 2t \\
&= -\frac{1}{12}\sec^2 2t + \frac{1}{8}\tan^2 2t + \frac{1}{8}\sin 2t \ln|\sec 2t + \tan 2t| \\
&= \frac{1}{24}\sec^2 2t - \frac{1}{8} + \frac{1}{8}\sin 2t \ln|\sec 2t + \tan 2t|,
\end{aligned}$$

and a general solution to the given equation is

$$v(t) = c_1\cos 2t + c_2\sin 2t + \frac{1}{24}\sec^2 2t - \frac{1}{8} + \frac{1}{8}\sin 2t \ln|\sec 2t + \tan 2t|.$$

**15.** The corresponding homogeneous equation is $y'' + y = 0$. Its auxiliary equation has the roots $r = \pm i$. Hence, a general solution to the homogeneous problem is given by

$$y_h(t) = c_1\cos t + c_2\sin t.$$

We will find a particular solution to the original equation by first finding a particular solution for each of two problems, one with the nonhomogeneous term $g_1(t) = 3\sec t$ and the other one with the nonhomogeneous term $g_2(t) = -t^2 + 1$. Then we will use the superposition principle to obtain a particular solution for the original equation. The term $3\sec t$ is not in a form that allows us to use the method of undetermined coefficients. Therefore, we will use the method of variation of parameters. To this end, let $y_1(t) = \cos t$ and $y_2(t) = \sin t$ (linearly independent solutions to the corresponding homogeneous problem). Then a particular solution $y_{p,1}$ to $y'' + y = 3\sec t$ has the form

$$y_{p,1}(t) = v_1(t)y_1(t) + v_2(t)y_2(t) = v_1(t)\cos t + v_2(t)\sin t,$$

where $v_1(t)$ and $v_2(t)$ are determined by the system

$$v_1' \cos t + v_2' \sin t = 0,$$

$$-v_1' \sin t + v_2' \cos t = 3 \sec t.$$

Multiplying the first equation by $\cos t$ and the second equation by $\sin t$ and subtracting the results, we get

$$v_1' = -3 \sec t \sin t = -3 \tan t.$$

Hence

$$v_1(t) = -3 \int \tan t \, dt = 3 \ln |\cos t| + C_1 \,.$$

To find $v_2'(t)$, we multiply the first equation of the above system by $\sin t$, the second by $\cos t$, and add the results to obtain

$$v_2' = 3 \sec t \cos t = 3 \qquad \Rightarrow \qquad v_2(t) = 3t + C_2 \,.$$

Therefore, for this first equation (with $g_1(t) = 3 \sec t$), by letting $C_1 = C_2 = 0$, we have a particular solution given by

$$y_{p,1}(t) = 3 \cos t \ln |\cos t| + 3t \sin t.$$

The nonhomogeneous term $g_2(t) = -t^2 + 1$ is of a form that allows us to use the method of undetermined coefficients. Thus, a particular solution to this nonhomogeneous equation will have the form

$$y_{p,2}(t) = A_2 t^2 + A_1 t + A_0 \quad \Rightarrow \quad y_{p,2}'(t) = 2A_2 t + A_1 \quad \Rightarrow \quad y_{p,2}''(t) = 2A_2 \,.$$

Plugging these expressions into the equation $y'' + y = -t^2 + 1$ yields

$$y_{p,2}'' + y_{p,2} = 2A_2 + A_2 t^2 + A_1 t + A_0 = A_2 t^2 + A_1 t + (2A_2 + A_0) = -t^2 + 1.$$

By equating coefficients, we obtain

$$A_2 = -1, \qquad A_1 = 0, \qquad 2A_2 + A_0 = 1 \quad \Rightarrow \quad A_0 = 3.$$

Therefore, we have

$$y_{p,2}(t) = -t^2 + 3.$$

By the superposition principle, we see that a particular solution to the original problem is given by

$$y_p(t) = y_{p,1}(t) + y_{p,2}(t) = 3\cos t \ln|\cos t| + 3t \sin t - t^2 + 3.$$

Combining this solution with the general solution to the homogeneous equation yields a general solution to the original differential equation,

$$y(t) = c_1 \cos t + c_2 \sin t - t^2 + 3 + 3t \sin t + 3\cos t \ln|\cos t|.$$

**17.** Multiplying the given equation by 2, we get

$$y'' + 4y = 2\tan 2t - e^t.$$

The nonhomogeneous term, $2\tan 2t - e^t$, can be written as a linear combination $2g_1(t) - g_2(t)$, where $g_1(t) = \tan 2t$ and $g_2(t) = e^t$. A particular solution to the equation

$$y'' + 4y = \tan 2t$$

is found in Problem 1, that is,

$$y_{p,1}(t) = -\frac{1}{4}\cos 2t \ln|\sec 2t + \tan 2t|.$$

A particular solution to

$$y'' + 4y = e^t$$

can be found using the method of undetermined coefficients. We look for $y_{p,2}$ of the form $y_{p,2}(t) = Ae^t$. Substitution yields

$$\left(Ae^t\right)'' + 4\left(Ae^t\right) = e^t \qquad \Rightarrow \qquad 5Ae^t = e^t \qquad \Rightarrow \qquad A = \frac{1}{5},$$

and so $y_{p,2} = (1/5)e^t$. By the superposition principle, a particular solution to the original equation is

$$y_p(t) = 2y_{p,1} - y_{p,2} = -\frac{1}{2}\cos 2t \ln|\sec 2t + \tan 2t| - \frac{1}{5}e^t.$$

Adding a general solution to the homogeneous equation, we get

$$y(t) = c_1 \cos 2t + c_2 \sin 2t - \frac{1}{2} \cos 2t \ln |\sec 2t + \tan 2t| - \frac{1}{5} e^t .$$

**19.** A general solution of the corresponding homogeneous equation is given by

$$y_h(t) = c_1 e^{-t} + c_2 e^t .$$

We will try to find a particular solution to the original nonhomogeneous equation of the form $y_p(t) = v_1(t)y_1(t) + v_2(t)y_2(t)$, where $y_1(t) = e^{-t}$ and $y_2(t) = e^t$. We apply formulas (10) on page 195 in the text, but replace indefinite integrals by definite integrals. Note that

$$y_1(t)y_2'(t) - y_1'(t)y_2(t) = e^{-x}e^x - \left(-e^{-x}\right)e^x = 2.$$

With $g(t) = 1/t$ and integration from 1 to $t$, formulas (10) yield

$$v_1(t) = \int_1^t \frac{-g(x)y_2(x)}{2}\, dx = -\frac{1}{2}\int_1^t \frac{e^x}{x}\, dx ,$$

$$v_2(t) = \int_1^t \frac{g(x)y_1(x)}{2}\, dx = \frac{1}{2}\int_1^t \frac{e^{-x}}{x}\, dx .$$

(Notice that we have chosen the lower limit of integration to be equal to 1 because the initial conditions are given at 1. We could have chosen any other value for the lower limit, but the choice of 1 will make the determination of the constants $c_1$ and $c_2$ easier.) Thus

$$y_p(t) = \frac{e^t}{2}\int_1^t \frac{e^{-x}}{x}\, dx - \frac{e^{-t}}{2}\int_1^t \frac{e^x}{x}\, dx ,$$

and so a general solution to the original differential equation is

$$y(t) = c_1 e^{-t} + c_2 e^t + \frac{e^t}{2}\int_1^t \frac{e^{-x}}{x}\, dx - \frac{e^{-t}}{2}\int_1^t \frac{e^x}{x}\, dx .$$

By plugging in the first initial condition (and using the fact that the integral of a function from $a$ to $a$ is zero which is why we have chosen the lower limit of integration to be the initial point, $t = 1$), we find that

$$y(1) = c_1 e^{-1} + c_2 e^1 = 0.$$

Differentiating $y(t)$ yields

$$y'(t) = -c_1 e^{-t} + c_2 e^t + \frac{e^t}{2}\int_1^t \frac{e^{-x}}{x}\,dx + \left(\frac{e^t}{2}\right)\left(\frac{e^{-t}}{t}\right) + \frac{e^{-t}}{2}\int_1^t \frac{e^x}{x}\,dx - \left(\frac{e^{-t}}{2}\right)\left(\frac{e^t}{t}\right),$$

where we have used the product rule and the fundamental theorem of calculus to differentiate the last two terms of $y(t)$. We now plug in the second initial condition into the equation we just found for $y'(t)$ to obtain

$$y'(1) = -c_1 e^{-1} + c_2 e^1 + \left(\frac{-e^{-1}}{2}\right)\left(\frac{e^1}{1}\right) + \left(\frac{e^1}{2}\right)\left(\frac{e^{-1}}{1}\right) = -c_1 e^{-1} + c_2 e^1 - \frac{1}{2} + \frac{1}{2} = -2.$$

Solving the system

$$c_1 e^{-1} + c_2 e^1 = 0,$$
$$-c_1 e^{-1} + c_2 e^1 = -2$$

yields $c_2 = -e^{-1}$ and $c_1 = e^1$. Therefore, the solution to our problem is given by

$$y(t) = e^{1-t} - e^{t-1} + \frac{e^t}{2}\int_1^t \frac{e^{-x}}{x}\,dx - \frac{e^{-t}}{2}\int_1^t \frac{e^x}{x}\,dx. \tag{4.8}$$

Simpson's rule is implemented on the software package provided free with the text (see also the discussion of the solution to Problem 25 in Exercises 2.3). Simpson's rule requires an even number of intervals, but we don't know how many are required to obtain the 2-place accuracy desired. We will compute the approximate value of $y(t)$ at $t = 2$ using 2, 4, 6, ... intervals for Simpson's rule until the approximate value changes by less than five in the third place. For $n = 2$, we divide $[1, 2]$ into 4 equal subintervals. Thus each interval will be of length $(2-1)/4 = 1/4$. Therefore the integrals are approximated by

$$\int_1^2 \frac{e^x}{x}\,dx \approx \frac{1}{12}\left[\frac{e^1}{1} + 4\frac{e^{1.25}}{1.25} + 2\frac{e^{1.5}}{1.5} + 4\frac{e^{1.75}}{1.75} + \frac{e^2}{2}\right] \approx 3.0592,$$

$$\int_1^2 \frac{e^{-x}}{x}\,dx \approx \frac{1}{12}\left[\frac{e^{-1}}{1} + 4\frac{e^{-1.25}}{1.25} + 2\frac{e^{-1.5}}{1.5} + 4\frac{e^{-1.75}}{1.75} + \frac{e^{-2}}{2}\right] \approx 0.1706.$$

223

Substituting these values into equation (4.8) we obtain

$$y(2) \approx e^{1-2} - e^{2-1} - \frac{e^{-2}}{2}(3.0592) + \frac{e^2}{2}(0.1706) = -1.9271.$$

Repeating these calculations for $n = 3$, 4, and 5 yields the approximations in Table 4-A.

**Table 4–A**: Successive approximations for $y(2)$ using Simpson's rule.

| Intervals | $y(2) \approx$ |
|---|---|
| 6 | −1.9275 |
| 8 | −1.9275 |
| 10 | −1.9275 |

Since these values do not change in the third place, we can expect that the first three places are accurate and we obtained an approximate solution of $y(2) = -1.93$.

**21.** A particular solution to the given equation has the form

$$y_p(t) = v_1(t)y_1(t) + v_2(t)y_2(t) = v_1(t)e^t + v_2(t)(t+1).$$

Since $y_1'(t) = e^t$, $y_2'(t) \equiv 1$, the system (9), with $a = a(t) = t$ and $g(t) = t^2$, becomes

$$v_1'(t)e^t + v_2'(t)(t+1) = 0,$$
$$v_1'(t)e^t + v_2'(t) = \frac{t^2}{t} = t.$$

Subtracting the second equation from the first one, we get

$$tv_2'(t) = -t \quad \Rightarrow \quad v_2'(t) = -1 \quad \Rightarrow \quad v_2(t) = -t.$$

Substituting $v_2'(t)$ into the first equation yields

$$v_1'(t)e^t - (t+1) = 0 \quad \Rightarrow \quad v_1'(t) = (t+1)e^{-t}$$
$$\Rightarrow \quad v_1(t) = \int (t+1)e^{-t}\,dt = -(t+1)e^{-t} + \int e^{-t}\,dt = -(t+2)e^{-t}.$$

Thus

$$y_p(t) = -(t+2)e^{-t}e^t - t(t+1) = -t^2 - 2t - 2.$$

(Note that $-2t - 2 = -2(t+1) = -2y_2(t)$ is a solution to the corresponding homogeneous equation. Thus, $-t^2 = y_p(t) + 2y_2(t)$ is another particular solution.)

**23.** We are seeking for a particular solution to the given equation of the form

$$y_p(t) = v_1(t)y_1(t) + v_2(t)y_2(t) = v_1(t)(5t-1) + v_2(t)e^{-5t}.$$

Since $y_1'(t) \equiv 5$, $y_2'(t) = -5e^{-5t}$, the system (9), with $a = a(t) = t$ and $g(t) = t^2 e^{-5t}$, becomes

$$v_1'(t)(5t-1) + v_2'(t)e^{-5t} = 0,$$
$$5v_1'(t) - 5v_2'(t)e^{-5t} = \frac{t^2 e^{-5t}}{t} = te^{-5t}.$$

Dividing the second equation by 5 and adding to the first equation yields

$$5tv_1'(t) = \frac{1}{5}te^{-5t} \quad \Rightarrow \quad v_1'(t) = \frac{1}{25}e^{-5t} \quad \Rightarrow \quad v_1(t) = -\frac{1}{125}e^{-5t}.$$

Substituting $v_1'(t)$ into the first equation, we get

$$\frac{1}{25}e^{-5t}(5t-1) + v_2'(t)e^{-5t} = 0 \quad \Rightarrow \quad v_2'(t) = -\frac{5t-1}{25} \quad \Rightarrow \quad v_2(t) = -\frac{t^2}{10} + \frac{t}{25}.$$

Thus

$$y_p(t) = -\frac{1}{125}e^{-5t}(5t-1) + \left(-\frac{t^2}{10} + \frac{t}{25}\right)e^{-5t} = \left(\frac{1}{125} - \frac{t^2}{10}\right)e^{-5t}.$$

(Since $(1/125)e^{-5t} = (1/125)y_2(t)$ is a solution to the corresponding homogeneous equation, the function $-(t^2/10)e^{-5t}$ is also a particular solution.)

**25.** A general solution to the corresponding homogeneous equation is

$$y_h(x) = c_1y_1(x) + c_2y_2(x) = x^{-1/2}\left(c_1 \cos x + c_2 \sin x\right).$$

To find a particular solution to the original equation, we apply the method of variation of parameters. To form the system (9) on page 195, we need $y_1'$ and $y_2'$. Applying the product rule, we get

$$y_1'(x) = -\frac{1}{2}x^{-3/2}\cos x - x^{-1/2}\sin x,$$

$$y_2'(x) = -\frac{1}{2} x^{-3/2} \sin x + x^{-1/2} \cos x.$$

Thus, functions $v_1(x)$ and $v_2(x)$ in a particular solution,

$$y_p(x) = v_1(x)y_1(x) + v_2(x)y_2(x),$$

satisfy the system

$$v_1' x^{-1/2} \cos x + v_2' x^{-1/2} \sin x = 0,$$
$$v_1'\left(-\frac{1}{2} x^{-3/2} \cos x - x^{-1/2} \sin x\right) + v_2'\left(-\frac{1}{2} x^{-3/2} \sin x + x^{-1/2} \cos x\right) = \frac{x^{5/2}}{x^2} = x^{1/2}.$$

From the first equation, we express $v_1' = -v_2' \tan x$ and substitute this expression into the second equation. After some algebra, the result simplifies to

$$v_2' = x \cos x \qquad \Rightarrow \qquad v_1' = -v_2' \tan x = -x \sin x.$$

Integrating, we get

$$v_1(x) = -\int x \sin x\, dx = x \cos x - \sin x + C_1,$$
$$v_2(x) = \int x \cos x\, dx = x \sin x + \cos x + C_2.$$

With $C_1 = C_2 = 0$,

$$y_p(x) = (x \cos x - \sin x)x^{-1/2}\cos x + (x \sin x + \cos x)x^{-1/2}\sin x = x^{1/2}.$$

Therefore, a general solution to the given nonhomogeneous Bessel equation is

$$y(t) = x^{1/2} + x^{-1/2}\left(c_1 \cos x + c_2 \sin x\right).$$

**EXERCISES 4.7:  Qualitative Considerations for Variable-Coefficient and Nonlinear Equations, page 208**

**1.** Let $Y(t) := y(-t)$. Then, using the chain rule, we get

$$\frac{dY}{dt} = y'(-t)\frac{d(-t)}{dt} = -y'(-t),$$

$$\frac{d^2Y}{dt^2} = \frac{d[-y'(-t)]}{dt} = -y''(-t)\frac{d(-t)}{dt} = y''(-t).$$

Therefore, denoting $-t = s$, we obtain

$$Y''(t) + tY(t) = y''(-t) + ty(-t) = y''(s) - sy(s) = 0.$$

**2.** Comparing the given equation with (13) on page 202 in the text, we conclude that

$$\text{inertia } m = 1, \qquad \text{damping } b = 0, \qquad \text{stiffness "}k" = -6y.$$

For $y > 0$, the stiffness "$k$" is negative, and it tends to reinforce the displacement. So, we should expect that the solutions $y(t)$ grow without bound.

**3.** As in Problem 2, this equation describes the motion of the mass-spring system with unit mass, no damping, and stiffness "$k$" $= -6y$. The initial displacement $y(0) = -1$ is negative as well as the initial velocity $y'(0) = -1$. So, starting from $t = 0$, $y(t)$ will decrease for a while. This will result increasing positive stiffness, $-6y$, i.e., "the spring will become stiffer and stiffer". Eventually, the spring will become so strong that the mass will stop and then go in the positive direction. While $y(t)$ is negative, the positive stiffness will force the mass to approach zero displacement point, $y = 0$. Thereafter, with $y(t) > 0$, the stiffness becomes negative, which means that the spring itself will push the mass further away from $y = 0$ in the positive direction with force, which increases with $y$. Thus, the curve $y(t)$ will increase unboundedly. Figure 4.23 confirms our prediction.

**5. (a)** Comparing the equation $y'' = 2y^3$ with equation (7) in Lemma 3, we conclude that $f(y) = 2y^3$, and so

$$F(y) = \int 2y^3 \, dy = \frac{1}{2}y^4 + C,$$

where $C$ is a constant. We can choose any particular value for $C$, say, $C = 0$. Thus $F(y) = (1/2)y^4$. Next, with constant $K = 0$ and sign "$-$" in front of the integral, equation (11) on page 201, becomes

$$t = -\int \frac{dy}{\sqrt{2(1/2)y^4}} = -\int y^{-2} dy = y^{-1} + c,$$

or, equivalently,

$$y = \frac{1}{t - c},$$

where $c$ is an arbitrary constant.

**(b)** A linear combination of $y_1(t) := 1/(t - c_1)$ and $y_2(t) := 1/(t - c_2)$,

$$C_1 y_1(t) + C_2 y_2(t) = \frac{C_1}{t - c_1} + \frac{C_2}{t - c_2} = \frac{(C_1 + C_2)t - (C_1 c_2 + C_2 c_1)}{(t - c_1)(t - c_2)},$$

is identically zero in a neighborhood of $t = 0$ if and only if $(C_1 + C_2)t - (C_1 c_2 + C_2 c_1) \equiv 0$. Thus the numerator must be the zero polynomial, i.e., $C_1$ and $C_2$ must satisfy

$$\begin{aligned} C_1 + C_2 &= 0, \\ C_1 c_2 + C_2 c_1 &= 0 \end{aligned} \qquad \Rightarrow \qquad \begin{aligned} C_2 &= -C_1, \\ C_1 (c_2 - c_1) &= 0. \end{aligned}$$

Since $c_1 \neq c_2$, the second equation implies that $C_1 = 0$, and then $C_2 = 0$ from the first equation. Thus, only the trivial linear combination of $y_1(t)$ and $y_2(t)$ vanishes identically around the origin, and so these functions are linearly independent.

**(c)** For any function of the form $y_c(t) := 1/(t - c)$, the equality

$$y_c'(t) = -\frac{1}{(t - c)^2} = -[y_c(t)]^2$$

holds for all $t \neq c$. In particular, at $t = 0$,

$$y_c'(0) = -[y_c(0)]^2.$$

(We assume that $c \neq 0$; otherwise, $t = 0$ is not in the domain.) Obviously, this equality fails for any positive initial velocity $y'(0)$, in particular, it is false for given data, $y(0) = 1$ and $y'(0) = 2$.

**6.** Rewriting given equation in the equivalent form $y'' = (-k/m)y$, we see that the function $f(y)$ in the energy integral lemma is $(-k/m)y$. So,

$$F(y) = \int \left(-\frac{k}{m} y\right) dy = -\frac{k}{2m} y^2 + C.$$

With $C = 0$, $F(y) = -[k/(2m)]y^2$, and the energy

$$E(t) = \frac{1}{2}[y'(t)]^2 - F[y(t)] = \frac{1}{2}[y'(t)]^2 - \left(-\frac{k}{2m}y^2\right) = \frac{1}{2}[y'(t)]^2 + \frac{k}{2m}y^2.$$

By the energy integral lemma,

$$\frac{1}{2}[y'(t)]^2 + \frac{k}{2m}y^2 = \text{const.}$$

Multiplying both sides by $2m$, we get the stated equation.

7. **(a)** Since, for a point moving along a circle of radius $\ell$, the magnitude $v$ of its linear velocity $\vec{v}$ and the angular velocity $\omega = d\theta/dt$ are connected by $v = \omega\ell = (d\theta/dt)\ell$, and the vector $\vec{v}$ is tangent to the circle (and so, perpendicular to the radius), we have

$$\text{angular momentum} = \ell \cdot mv = \ell \cdot m \cdot \frac{d\theta}{dt}\ell = m\ell^2\frac{d\theta}{dt}.$$

**(b)** From Figure 4.18, we see that the component of the gravitational force, $mg$, which is perpendicular to the level arm, has the magnitude $|mg\sin\theta|$ and is directed towards decreasing $\theta$. Thus,

$$\text{torque} = \ell \cdot (-mg\sin\theta) = -\ell mg\sin\theta.$$

**(c)** According to the Newton's law of rotational motion,

$$\text{torque} = \frac{d}{dt}(\text{angular momentum}) \quad \Rightarrow \quad -\ell mg\sin\theta = \frac{d}{dt}\left(m\ell^2\frac{d\theta}{dt}\right)$$

$$\Rightarrow \quad -\ell mg\sin\theta = m\ell^2\frac{d^2\theta}{dt^2} \quad \Rightarrow \quad \frac{d^2\theta}{dt^2} + \frac{g}{\ell}\sin\theta = 0.$$

9. According to Problem 8, with $\ell = g$, the function $\theta(t)$ satisfies the identity

$$\frac{(\theta')^2}{2} - \cos\theta = C = \text{const.} \tag{4.9}$$

Our first purpose is to determine the constant $C$. Let $t_a$ denote the moment when pendulum is in the apex point, i.e., $\theta(t_a) = \pi$. Since it doesn't cross the apex over, we also have $\theta'(t_a) = 0$. Substituting these two values into (4.9), we obtain

$$\frac{0^2}{2} - \cos\pi = C \quad \Rightarrow \quad C = 1.$$

Thus (4.9) becomes

$$\frac{(\theta')^2}{2} - \cos\theta = 1.$$

In particular, at the initial moment, $t = 0$,

$$\frac{[\theta'(0)]^2}{2} - \cos[\theta(0)] = 1.$$

Since $\theta(0) = 0$, we get

$$\frac{[\theta'(0)]^2}{2} - \cos 0 = 1 \qquad \Rightarrow \qquad [\theta'(0)]^2 = 4$$

$$\Rightarrow \qquad \theta'(0) = 2 \qquad \text{or} \qquad \theta'(0) = -2.$$

11. The "damping coefficient" in the Rayleigh equation is $b = (y')^2 - 1$. Thus, for low velocities $y'$, we have $b < 0$, and $b > 0$ for high velocities. Therefore, the low velocities are boosted, while high velocities are slowed, and so one should expect a limit cycle.

13. Qualitative features of solutions to Airy, Duffing, and van der Pol equations, are discussed after Example 3, in Examples 6 and 7, respectively. Comparing curves in Figure 4.26 with graphs depicted in Figures 4.13, 4.16, and 4.17, we conclude that the answers are

   (a) Airy;

   (b) Duffing;

   (c) van der Pol.

15. (a) Yes, because the "stiffness" $t^2$ is positive and no damping.

   (b) No, because of the negative "stiffness" $-t^2$.

   (c) Writing $y'' + y^5 = y'' + (y^4)y$, we conclude that the mass-spring model, corresponding to this equation, has positive "stiffness" $y^4$ and no damping. Thus the answer is "yes".

   (d) Here, the "stiffness" is $y^5$, which is negative for $y < 0$. So, "no".

   (e) Yes, because the "stiffness" $4 + 2\cos t \geq 2 > 0$ and no damping.

   (f) Since both the "damping" $t$ and the stiffness 1 are positive, all solutions are bounded.

**(g)** No, because the "stiffness", $-1$, is negative.

**17.** For the radius, $r(t)$, we have the initial value problem

$$r''(t) = -GMr^{-2}, \qquad r(0) = a, \qquad r'(0) = 0.$$

Thus, in the energy integral lemma, $f(r) = -GMr^{-2}$. Since

$$\int f(r)dr = \int \left(-GMr^{-2}\right) dr = GMR^{-1} + C,$$

we can take $F(r) = GMR^{-1}$, and the energy integral lemma yields

$$\frac{1}{2}\left[r'(t)\right]^2 - \frac{GM}{r(t)} = C_1 = \text{const.}$$

To find the constant $C_1$, we use the initial conditions.

$$C_1 = \frac{1}{2}\left[r'(0)\right]^2 - \frac{GM}{r(0)} = \frac{1}{2} \cdot 0^2 - \frac{GM}{a} = -\frac{GM}{a}.$$

Therefore, $r(t)$ satisfies

$$\frac{1}{2}\left[r'(t)\right]^2 - \frac{GM}{r(t)} = -\frac{GM}{a} \quad \Rightarrow \quad \frac{1}{2}\left(r'\right)^2 = \frac{GM}{r} - \frac{GM}{a} \quad \Rightarrow \quad r' = -\sqrt{\frac{2GM}{a}}\sqrt{\frac{a-r}{r}}.$$

(Remember, $r(t)$ is decreasing, and so $r'(t) < 0$.) Separating variables and integrating, we get

$$\int \sqrt{\frac{r}{a-r}}\, dr = \int \left(-\sqrt{\frac{2GM}{a}}\right) dt \Rightarrow a\left(\arctan\sqrt{\frac{r}{a-r}} - \frac{\sqrt{r(a-r)}}{a}\right) = -\sqrt{\frac{2GM}{a}}\, t + C_2.$$

We apply the initial condition, $r(0) = a$, once again to find the constant $C_2$. But this time we have to be careful because the argument of "arctan" function becomes infinite at $r = a$. So, we take the limit of both sides rather than making simple substitution.

$$\lim_{t\to+0} a\left(\arctan\sqrt{\frac{r(t)}{a-r(t)}} - \frac{\sqrt{r(t)[a-r(t)]}}{a}\right)$$

$$= a\left(\lim_{t\to+0}\arctan\sqrt{\frac{r(t)}{a-r(t)}} - \lim_{t\to+0}\frac{\sqrt{r(t)[a-r(t)]}}{a}\right) = a\left(\frac{\pi}{2} - 0\right) = a\frac{\pi}{2},$$

and, in the right-hand side,

$$\lim_{t \to +0} \left( -\sqrt{\frac{2GM}{a}} \, t + C_2 \right) = -\sqrt{\frac{2GM}{a}} \cdot 0 + C_2 = C_2.$$

Thus $C_2 = a\pi/2$ and $r(t)$ satisfies

$$a \left( \arctan \sqrt{\frac{r(t)}{a - r(t)}} - \frac{\sqrt{r(t)[a - r(t)]}}{a} \right) = -\sqrt{\frac{2GM}{a}} \, t + \frac{a\pi}{2}.$$

At the moment $t = T_0$, when Earth splashes into the sun, we have $r(T_0) = 0$. Substituting this condition into the last equation yields

$$a \left( \arctan \sqrt{\frac{0}{a - 0}} - \frac{\sqrt{0(a - 0)}}{a} \right) = -\sqrt{\frac{2GM}{a}} \, T_0 + \frac{a\pi}{2}$$

$$\Rightarrow \qquad 0 = -\sqrt{\frac{2GM}{a}} \, T_0 + \frac{a\pi}{2}$$

$$\Rightarrow \qquad T_0 = \frac{a\pi}{2} \sqrt{\frac{a}{2GM}} = \frac{\pi}{2\sqrt{2}} \sqrt{\frac{a^3}{GM}}.$$

Then the required ratio is

$$\frac{T_0}{T} = \frac{\pi}{2\sqrt{2}} \sqrt{\frac{a^3}{GM}} \Big/ 2\pi \sqrt{\frac{a^3}{GM}} = \frac{1}{4\sqrt{2}}.$$

## EXERCISES 4.8:   A Closer Look at Free Mechanical Vibrations, page 219

1. In this problem, we have undamped free vibration case governed by equation (2) on page 210 in the text. With $m = 3$ and $k = 48$, the equation becomes

$$3y'' + 48y = 0 \tag{4.10}$$

with the initial conditions $y(0) = -0.5$, $y'(0) = 2$.

The angular velocity of the motion is

$$\omega = \sqrt{\frac{k}{m}} = \sqrt{\frac{48}{3}} = 4.$$

It follows that

$$\text{period} = \frac{2\pi}{\omega} = \frac{2\pi}{4} = \frac{\pi}{2},$$

$$\text{natural frequency} = \frac{\omega}{2\pi} = \frac{2}{\pi}.$$

A general solution to (4.10), given in (4) on page 211 in the text, becomes

$$y(t) = C_1 \cos \omega t + C_2 \sin \omega t = C_1 \cos 4t + C_2 \sin 4t.$$

We find $C_1$ and $C_2$ from the initial conditions.

$$y(0) = (C_1 \cos 4t + C_2 \sin 4t)\big|_{t=0} = C_1 = -1/2,$$
$$y'(0) = (-4C_1 \sin 4t + 4C_2 \cos 4t)\big|_{t=0} = 4C_2 = 2$$

$$\Rightarrow \quad C_1 = -1/2,$$
$$C_2 = 1/2.$$

Thus, the solution to the initial value problem is

$$y(t) = -\frac{1}{2} \cos 4t + \frac{1}{2} \sin 4t = \frac{\sqrt{2}}{2} \sin\left(4t - \frac{\pi}{4}\right),$$

where we have used formulas (6) rewriting the solution in form (5), page 211 in the text. The amplitude of the motion therefore is $\sqrt{2}/2$.

Setting $y = 0$ in the above solution, we find values of $t$ when the mass passes through the point of equilibrium.

$$\frac{\sqrt{2}}{2} \sin\left(4t - \frac{\pi}{4}\right) = 0 \quad \Rightarrow \quad 4t - \frac{\pi}{4} = n\pi, \quad n = 0, 1, \ldots .$$

(Time $t$ is nonnegative.) The first moment when this happens, i.e., the smallest value of $t$, corresponds to $n = 0$. So,

$$4t - \frac{\pi}{4} = 0 \quad \Rightarrow \quad t = \frac{\pi}{16}.$$

3. The characteristic equation in this problem, $r^2 + br + 16 = 0$, has the roots

$$r = \frac{-b \pm \sqrt{b^2 - 64}}{2}. \tag{4.11}$$

Substituting given particular values of $b$ into (4.11), we find roots of the characteristic equation and solutions to the initial value problems in each case.

**b = 0.**

$$r = \frac{\pm\sqrt{-64}}{2} = \pm 4i.$$

A general solution has the form $y = C_1 \cos 4t + C_2 \sin 4t$. Constants $C_1$ and $C_2$ can be found from the initial conditions.

$$y(0) = (C_1 \cos 4t + C_2 \sin 4t)\big|_{t=0} = C_1 = 1,$$
$$y'(0) = (-4C_1 \sin 4t + 4C_2 \cos 4t)\big|_{t=0} = 4C_2 = 0 \qquad \Rightarrow \qquad \begin{matrix} C_1 = 1, \\ C_2 = 0 \end{matrix}$$

and so $y(t) = \cos 4t$.

**b = 6.**

$$r = \frac{-6 \pm \sqrt{36 - 64}}{2} = -3 \pm \sqrt{7}i.$$

A general solution has the form $y = (C_1 \cos\sqrt{7}t + C_2 \sin\sqrt{7}t)e^{-3t}$. For constants $C_1$ and $C_2$, we have the system

$$y(0) = \left(C_1 \cos\sqrt{7}t + C_2 \sin\sqrt{7}t\right)e^{-3t}\big|_{t=0} = C_1 = 1,$$
$$y'(0) = \left[(\sqrt{7}C_2 - 3C_1)\cos\sqrt{7}t - (\sqrt{7}C_1 + 3C_2)\sin\sqrt{7}t\right]e^{-3t}\big|_{t=0} = \sqrt{7}C_2 - 3C_1 = 0$$

$$\Rightarrow \quad \begin{matrix} C_1 = 1, \\ C_2 = 3/\sqrt{7}, \end{matrix}$$

and so

$$y(t) = \left[\cos\sqrt{7}t + \frac{3}{\sqrt{7}}\sin\sqrt{7}t\right]e^{-3t} = \frac{4}{\sqrt{7}}e^{-3t}\sin\left(\sqrt{7}t + \phi\right),$$

where $\phi = \arctan(\sqrt{7}/3) \approx 0.723$.

**b = 8.**

$$r = \frac{-8 \pm \sqrt{64 - 64}}{2} = -4.$$

Thus, $r = -4$ is a double root of the characteristic equation. So, a general solution has the form $y = (C_1 t + C_0)e^{-4t}$. For constants $C_1$ and $C_2$, we obtain the system

$$y(0) = (C_1 t + C_0)e^{-4t}\big|_{t=0} = C_0 = 1,$$
$$y'(0) = (-4C_1 t - 4C_0 + C_1)e^{-4t}\big|_{t=0} = C_1 - 4C_0 = 0 \qquad \Rightarrow \qquad \begin{matrix} C_0 = 1, \\ C_1 = 4, \end{matrix}$$

and so $y(t) = (4t + 1)e^{-4t}$.

$b = 10$.

$$r = \frac{-10 \pm \sqrt{100 - 64}}{2} = -5 \pm 3.$$

Thus, $r = -2, -8$, and a general solution is given by $y = C_1 e^{-2t} + C_2 e^{-8t}$. Initial conditions yield

$$y(0) = (C_1 e^{-2t} + C_2 e^{-8t}) \big|_{t=0} = C_1 + C_2 = 1,$$
$$y'(0) = (-2C_1 e^{-2t} - 8C_2 e^{-8t}) \big|_{t=0} = -2C_1 - 8C_2 = 0 \qquad \Rightarrow \qquad \begin{aligned} C_1 &= 4/3, \\ C_2 &= -1/3, \end{aligned}$$

and, therefore, $y(t) = (4/3)e^{-2t} - (1/3)e^{-8t}$ is the solution to the initial value problem.

The graphs of the solutions are depicted in Figures B.19–B.22 in the answers in the text.

5. The auxiliary equation associated with given differential equation is $r^2 + 10r + k = 0$, and its roots are $r = -5 \pm \sqrt{25 - k}$.

$k = 20$. In this case, $r = -5 \pm \sqrt{25 - 20} = -5 \pm \sqrt{5}$. Thus, a general solution is given by $y = C_1 e^{(-5+\sqrt{5})t} + C_2 e^{(-5-\sqrt{5})t}$. The initial conditions yield

$$y(0) = \left[ C_1 e^{(-5+\sqrt{5})t} + C_2 e^{(-5-\sqrt{5})t} \right]\Big|_{t=0} = C_1 + C_2 = 1,$$
$$y'(0) = \left[ (-5 + \sqrt{5})C_1 e^{(-5+\sqrt{5})t} + (-5 - \sqrt{5})C_2 e^{(-5-\sqrt{5})t} \right]\Big|_{t=0}$$
$$= (-5 + \sqrt{5})C_1 + (-5 - \sqrt{5})C_2 = 0$$

$$\Rightarrow \qquad \begin{aligned} C_1 &= \left(1 + \sqrt{5}\right)/2, \\ C_2 &= \left(1 - \sqrt{5}\right)/2, \end{aligned}$$

and, therefore, $y(t) = \left[\left(1 + \sqrt{5}\right)/2\right]e^{(-5+\sqrt{5})t} + \left[\left(1 - \sqrt{5}\right)/2\right]e^{(-5-\sqrt{5})t}$ is the solution to the initial value problem.

$k = 25$. Then $r = -5 \pm \sqrt{25 - 25} = -5$. Thus, $r = -5$ is a double root of the characteristic equation. So, a general solution has the form $y = (C_1 t + C_0)e^{-5t}$. For constants $C_1$ and $C_2$, using the initial conditions, we obtain the system

$$y(0) = (C_1 t + C_0) e^{-5t} \big|_{t=0} = C_0 = 1,$$
$$y'(0) = (-5C_1 t - 5C_0 + C_1) e^{-5t} \big|_{t=0} = C_1 - 5C_0 = 0 \qquad \Rightarrow \qquad \begin{aligned} C_0 &= 1, \\ C_1 &= 5, \end{aligned}$$

and so $y(t) = (5t + 1)e^{-5t}$.

$\boldsymbol{k = 30}$. In this case, $r = -5 \pm \sqrt{25 - 30} = -5 \pm \sqrt{5}i$. A general solution has the form $y = (C_1 \cos \sqrt{5}t + C_2 \sin \sqrt{5}t)e^{-5t}$. For constants $C_1$ and $C_2$, we have the system

$$y(0) = \left(C_1 \cos \sqrt{5}t + C_2 \sin \sqrt{5}t\right) e^{-5t} \big|_{t=0} = C_1 = 1,$$
$$y'(0) = \left[(\sqrt{5}C_2 - 5C_1) \cos \sqrt{5}t - (\sqrt{5}C_1 + 5C_2) \sin \sqrt{5}t\right] e^{-5t} \big|_{t=0} = \sqrt{5}C_2 - 5C_1 = 0$$

$$\Rightarrow \quad \begin{matrix} C_1 = 1, \\ C_2 = \sqrt{5}, \end{matrix}$$

and so

$$y(t) = \left[\cos \sqrt{5}t + \sqrt{5} \sin \sqrt{5}t\right] e^{-5t} = \sqrt{6}e^{-5t} \sin\left(\sqrt{5}t + \phi\right),$$

where $\phi = \arctan(1/\sqrt{5}) \approx 0.421$.

Graphs of the solutions for $k = 20$, $25$, and $30$ are shown in Figures B.23–B.25 in the answers in the text.

7. The motion of this mass-spring system is governed by equation (12) on page 213 in the text. With $m = 1/8$, $b = 2$, and $k = 16$ this equation becomes

$$\frac{1}{8} y'' + 2y' + 16y = 0, \tag{4.12}$$

and the initial conditions are $y(0) = -3/4$, $y'(0) = -2$. Since

$$b^2 - 4mk = 4 - 4(1/8)16 = -4 < 0,$$

we have a case of underdamped motion. A general solution to (4.12) is given in (16), that is, with $\alpha = -b/(2m) = -8$ and $\beta = (1/2m)\sqrt{4mk - b^2} = 8$, we have

$$y = (C_1 \cos 8t + C_2 \sin 8t) e^{-8t}.$$

Using the initial conditions, we find the constants $C_1$ and $C_2$.

$$y(0) = (C_1 \cos 8t + C_2 \sin 8t) e^{-8t} \big|_{t=0} = C_1 = -3/4,$$
$$y'(0) = 8 \left[(C_2 - C_1) \cos 8t - (C_2 + C_1) \sin 8t\right] e^{-8t} \big|_{t=0} = 8 (C_2 - C_1) = -2$$

$$\Rightarrow \quad \begin{matrix} C_1 = -3/4, \\ C_2 = -1, \end{matrix}$$

and so

$$y(t) = \left[ -\frac{3}{4} \cos 8t - \sin 8t \right] e^{-8t} = \frac{5}{4} e^{-8t} \sin(8t + \phi),$$

where $\tan \phi = (-3/4)/(-1) = 3/4$ and $\cos \phi = -1 < 0$. Thus,

$$\phi = \pi + \arctan(3/4) \approx 3.785.$$

The damping factor is $(5/4)e^{-8t}$, the quasiperiod is $P = 2\pi/8 = \pi/4$, and the quasifrequency is $1/P = 4/\pi$.

**9.** Substituting the values $m = 2$, $k = 40$, and $b = 8\sqrt{5}$ into equation (12) on page 213 in the text and using the initial conditions, we obtain the initial value problem

$$2\frac{d^2 y}{dt^2} + 8\sqrt{5}\frac{dy}{dt} + 40y = 0, \qquad y(0) = 0.1 \text{ (m)}, \quad y'(0) = 2 \text{ (m/sec)}.$$

The initial conditions are positive to reflect the fact that we have taken down to be positive in our coordinate system. The auxiliary equation for this system is

$$2r^2 + 8\sqrt{5}r + 40 = 0 \qquad \text{or} \qquad r^2 + 4\sqrt{5}r + 20 = 0.$$

This equation has a double root at $r = -2\sqrt{5}$. Therefore, this system is critically damped and the equation of motion has the form

$$y(t) = (C_1 + C_2 t)\, e^{-2\sqrt{5}t}.$$

To find the constants $C_1$ and $C_2$, we use the initial conditions $y(0) = 0.1$ and $y'(0) = 2$. Thus, we have

$$y(0) = 0.1 = C_1,$$
$$y'(0) = 2 = C_2 - 2\sqrt{5}C_1 \qquad \Rightarrow \qquad C_2 = 2 + 0.2\sqrt{5}.$$

From this we obtain

$$y(t) = \left[0.1 + \left(2 + 0.2\sqrt{5}\right) t\right] e^{-2\sqrt{5}t}.$$

The maximum displacement of the mass is found by determining the first time the velocity of the mass becomes zero. Therefore, we have

$$y'(t) = 0 = \left(2 + 0.2\sqrt{5}\right) e^{-2\sqrt{5}t} - 2\sqrt{5}\left[0.1 + \left(2 + 0.2\sqrt{5}\right) t\right] e^{-2\sqrt{5}t},$$

which gives

$$t = \frac{2}{2\sqrt{5}(2 + 0.2\sqrt{5})} = \frac{1}{\sqrt{5}(2 + 0.2\sqrt{5})}.$$

Thus the maximum displacement is

$$y\left[\frac{1}{\sqrt{5}(2 + 0.2\sqrt{5})}\right] = \left[0.1 + \left(2 + 0.2\sqrt{5}\right)\left(\frac{1}{\sqrt{5}(2 + 0.2\sqrt{5})}\right)\right] e^{-2\sqrt{5}/[\sqrt{5}(2+0.2\sqrt{5})]} \approx 0.242 \text{ (m)}.$$

**11.** The equation of the motion of this mass-spring system is

$$y'' + 0.2y' + 100y = 0, \qquad y(0) = 0, \quad y'(0) = 1.$$

Clearly, this is an underdamped motion because

$$b^2 - 4mk = (0.2)^2 - 4(1)(100) = -399.96 < 0.$$

So, we use use equation (16) on page 213 in the text for a general solution. With

$$\alpha = -\frac{b}{2m} = -\frac{0.2}{2} = -0.1 \quad \text{and} \quad \beta = \frac{1}{2m}\sqrt{4mk - b^2} = \frac{1}{2}\sqrt{399.96} = \sqrt{99.99},$$

equation (16) becomes

$$y(t) = \left(C_1 \cos\sqrt{99.99}\,t + C_2 \sin\sqrt{99.99}\,t\right) e^{-0.1t}.$$

From the initial condiions,

$$y(0) = \left(C_1 \cos\sqrt{99.99}\,t + C_2 \sin\sqrt{99.99}\,t\right) e^{-0.1t}\,\Big|_{t=0} = C_1 = 0,$$
$$y'(0) = \left[\left(\sqrt{99.99}\,C_2 - 0.1C_1\right)\cos\sqrt{99.99}\,t - \left(0.1C_2 + \sqrt{99.99}\,C_1\right)\sin\sqrt{99.99}\,t\right] e^{-0.1t}\,\Big|_{t=0}$$
$$= \sqrt{99.99}\,C_2 - 0.1C_1 = 1$$

$$\Rightarrow \qquad \begin{aligned} C_1 &= 0, \\ C_2 &= 1/\sqrt{99.99}\,. \end{aligned}$$

Therefore, the equation of motion is given by

$$y(t) = \frac{1}{\sqrt{99.99}} e^{-0.1t} \sin\sqrt{99.99}\,t\,.$$

The maximum displacement to the right occurs at the first point of local maximum of $y(t)$. The critical points of $y(t)$ are solutions to

$$y'(t) = \frac{e^{-0.1t}}{\sqrt{99.99}}\left(\sqrt{99.99}\cos\sqrt{99.99}\,t - 0.1\sin\sqrt{99.99}\,t\right) = 0$$

$$\Rightarrow \quad \sqrt{99.99}\cos\sqrt{99.99}\,t - 0.1\sin\sqrt{99.99}\,t = 0$$

$$\Rightarrow \quad \tan\sqrt{99.99}\,t = 10\sqrt{99.99} = \sqrt{9999}\,.$$

Solving for $t$, we conclude that the first point of local maximum is at

$$t = (1/\sqrt{99.99})\arctan\sqrt{9999} \approx 0.156\,\text{sec}.$$

**13.** In Example 3, the solution was found to be

$$y(t) = \sqrt{\frac{7}{12}}\, e^{-2t}\sin\left(2\sqrt{3}t + \phi\right), \tag{4.13}$$

where $\phi = \pi + \arctan(\sqrt{3}/2)$. Therefore, we have

$$y'(t) = -\sqrt{\frac{7}{3}}\, e^{-2t}\sin\left(2\sqrt{3}t + \phi\right) + \sqrt{7}\, e^{-2t}\cos\left(2\sqrt{3}t + \phi\right).$$

Thus, to find the relative extrema for $y(t)$, we set

$$y'(t) = -\sqrt{\frac{7}{3}}\, e^{-2t}\sin\left(2\sqrt{3}t + \phi\right) + \sqrt{7}\, e^{-2t}\cos\left(2\sqrt{3}t + \phi\right) = 0$$

$$\Rightarrow \quad \frac{\sin\left(2\sqrt{3}t + \phi\right)}{\cos\left(2\sqrt{3}t + \phi\right)} = \frac{\sqrt{7}}{\sqrt{7/3}} = \sqrt{3}$$

$$\Rightarrow \quad \tan\left(2\sqrt{3}t + \phi\right) = \sqrt{3}\,.$$

Since $\tan\theta = \sqrt{3}$ when $\theta = (\pi/3) + n\pi$, where $n$ is an integer, we see that the relative extrema will occur at the points $t_n$, where

$$2\sqrt{3}t_n + \phi = \frac{\pi}{3} + n\pi \qquad \Rightarrow \qquad t_n = \frac{(\pi/3) + n\pi - \phi}{2\sqrt{3}}\,.$$

# Chapter 4

By substituting $\pi + \arctan\left(\sqrt{3}/2\right)$ for $\phi$ in the last equation above and by requiring that $t$ be greater than zero, we obtain

$$t_n = \frac{(\pi/3) + (n-1)\pi - \arctan\left(\sqrt{3}/2\right)}{2\sqrt{3}}, \qquad n = 1, 2, 3, \ldots .$$

We see that the solution curve given by equation (4.13) above will touch the exponential curves $y(t) = \pm\left(\sqrt{7/12}\right)e^{-2t}$ when we have

$$\sqrt{\frac{7}{12}}\, e^{-2t} \sin\left(2\sqrt{3}t + \phi\right) = \pm\sqrt{\frac{7}{12}}\, e^{-2t},$$

where $\phi = \pi + \arctan\left(\sqrt{3}/2\right)$. This will occur when $\sin\left(2\sqrt{3}t + \phi\right) = \pm 1$. Since $\sin\theta = \pm 1$ when $\theta = (\pi/2) + m\pi$ for any integer $m$, we see that the times $T_m$, when the solution touches the exponential curves, satisfy

$$2\sqrt{3}T_m + \phi = \frac{\pi}{2} + m\pi \qquad \Rightarrow \qquad T_m = \frac{(\pi/2) + m\pi - \phi}{2\sqrt{3}},$$

where $\phi = \pi + \arctan\left(\sqrt{3}/2\right)$ and $m$ is an integer. Again requiring that $t$ be positive we see that $y(t)$ touches the exponential curve when

$$T_m = \frac{(\pi/2) + (m-1)\pi - \arctan\left(\sqrt{3}/2\right)}{2\sqrt{3}}, \qquad m = 1, 2, 3, \ldots .$$

From these facts it follows that, for $y(t)$ to be an extremum and, at the same time, touch the curves $y(t) = \pm\sqrt{7/12}\,e^{-2t}$, there must be integers $m$ and $n$ such that

$$\frac{(\pi/3) + n\pi - \arctan\left(\sqrt{3}/2\right)}{2\sqrt{3}} = \frac{(\pi/2) + m\pi - \arctan\left(\sqrt{3}/2\right)}{2\sqrt{3}}$$

$$\Rightarrow \quad \frac{\pi}{3} + n\pi = \frac{\pi}{2} + m\pi$$

$$\Rightarrow \quad n - m = \frac{1}{2} - \frac{1}{3} = \frac{1}{6} .$$

But, since $m$ and $n$ are integers, their difference is an integer and never $1/6$. Thus, the extrema of $y(t)$ do not occur on the exponential curves.

**15.** Since the exponential function is never zero, from the equation of motion (16) on page 213 in the text we conclude that the mass passes the equilibrium position, that is, $y(t) = 0$, if and only if

$$\sin(\omega t + \phi) = 0.$$

Therefore, the time between two successive crossings of the equilibrium position is $\pi/\omega$, which is a half of the quasiperiod $P$. So, we can find the quasiperiod $P$ by multiplying the time between two successive crossings of the equilibrium position by two. Whenever $P$ is computed, we can measure the displacement $y(t)$ at any moment $t$ (with $y(t) \neq 0$) and then at the moment $t + P$. Taking the quotient

$$\frac{y(t+P)}{y(t)} = \frac{Ae^{-(b/2m)(t+P)} \sin[\omega(t+P)+\phi]}{Ae^{-(b/2m)t} \sin(\omega t + \phi)} = e^{-(b/2m)P},$$

we can calculate the damping coefficient $b$ as

$$b = -\frac{2m \ln[y(t+P)/y(t)]}{P}.$$

**EXERCISES 4.9:   A Closer Look at Forced Mechanical Vibrations, page 227**

**1.** The frequency response curve (13) on page 223, with $m = 4$, $k = 1$, and $b = 2$, becomes

$$M(\gamma) = \frac{1}{\sqrt{(k - m\gamma^2)^2 + b^2\gamma^2}} = \frac{1}{\sqrt{(1 - 4\gamma^2)^2 + 4\gamma^2}}.$$

The graph of this function is shown in Figure B.26 in the answers in the text.

**3.** The auxiliary equation in this problem is $r^2 + 9 = 0$, which has roots $r = \pm 3i$. Thus, a general solution to the corresponding homogeneous equation has the form

$$y_h(t) = C_1 \cos 3t + C_2 \sin 3t.$$

We look for a particular solution to the original nonhomogeneous equation of the form

$$y_p(t) = t^s(A \cos 3t + B \sin 3t),$$

241

where we take $s = 1$ because $r = 3i$ is a simple root of the auxiliary equation. Computing the derivatives

$$y'(t) = A \cos 3t + B \sin 3t + t(-3A \sin 3t + 3B \cos 3t),$$

$$y''(t) = 6B \cos 3t - 6A \sin 3t + t(-9A \cos 3t - 9B \sin 3t),$$

and substituting $y(t)$ and $y''(t)$ into the original equation, we get

$$6B \cos 3t - 6A \sin 3t + t(-9A \cos 3t - 9B \sin 3t) + 9t(A \cos 3t + B \sin 3t) = 2 \cos 3t$$

$$\Rightarrow \qquad 6B \cos 3t - 6A \sin 3t = 2 \cos 3t \qquad \Rightarrow \qquad \begin{matrix} A = 0, \\ B = 1/3. \end{matrix}$$

So, $y_p(t) = (1/3)t \sin 3t$, and $y(t) = C_1 \cos 3t + C_2 \sin 3t + (1/3)t \sin 3t$ is a general solution. To satisfy the initial conditions, we solve

$$\begin{matrix} y(0) = C_1 = 1, \\ y'(0) = 3C_2 = 0 \end{matrix} \qquad \Rightarrow \qquad \begin{matrix} C_1 = 1, \\ C_2 = 0. \end{matrix}$$

So, the solution to the given initial value problem is

$$y(t) = \cos 3t + \frac{1}{3} t \sin 3t \,.$$

The graph of $y(t)$ is depicted in Figure B.27 in the answers section in the text.

5. (a) The corresponding homogeneous equation, $my'' + ky = 0$, is the equation of a simple harmonic motion, and so its general solution is given by

$$y_h(t) = C_1 \cos \omega t + C_2 \sin \omega t, \qquad \omega = \sqrt{k/m} \,.$$

Since $\gamma \neq \omega$, we look for a particular solution of the form

$$y_p(t) = A \cos \gamma t + B \sin \gamma t$$

$$\Rightarrow \qquad y_p'(t) = -A\gamma \sin \gamma t + B\gamma \cos \gamma t$$

$$\Rightarrow \qquad y_p''(t) = -A\gamma^2 \cos \gamma t - B\gamma^2 \sin \gamma t.$$

Substitution into the original equation yields

$$m\left(-A\gamma^2\cos\gamma t - B\gamma^2\sin\gamma t\right) + k\left(A\cos\gamma t + B\sin\gamma t\right) = F_0\cos\gamma t$$

$$\Rightarrow \qquad A\left(-m\gamma^2 + k\right)\cos\gamma t + B\left(-m\gamma^2 + k\right)\sin\gamma t = F_0\cos\gamma t$$

$$\Rightarrow \qquad \begin{aligned} A &= F_0/\left(k - m\gamma^2\right), \\ B &= 0 \end{aligned} \qquad \Rightarrow \qquad y_p(t) = \frac{F_0}{k - m\gamma^2}\cos\gamma t.$$

Therefore, a general solution to the original equation is

$$y(t) = C_1\cos\omega t + C_2\sin\omega t + \frac{F_0}{k - m\gamma^2}\cos\gamma t\,.$$

With the initial conditions, $y(0) = y'(0) = 0$, we get

$$\begin{aligned} y(0) &= C_1 + F_0/\left(k - m\gamma^2\right) = 0, \\ y'(0) &= \omega C_2 = 0 \end{aligned} \qquad \Rightarrow \qquad \begin{aligned} C_1 &= -F_0/\left(k - m\gamma^2\right), \\ C_2 &= 0. \end{aligned}$$

Therefore,

$$y(t) = -\frac{F_0}{k - m\gamma^2}\cos\omega t + \frac{F_0}{k - m\gamma^2}\cos\gamma t\,,$$

which can also be written in the form

$$y(t) = \frac{F_0}{k - m\gamma^2}\left(\cos\gamma t - \cos\omega t\right) = \frac{F_0}{m(\omega^2 - \gamma^2)}\left(\cos\gamma t - \cos\omega t\right)\,.$$

**(b)** Here one can apply the "difference-to-product" identity

$$\cos A - \cos B = 2\sin\left(\frac{B + A}{2}\right)\sin\left(\frac{B - A}{2}\right)$$

with $A = \gamma t$ and $B = \omega t$ to get

$$y(t) = \frac{2F_0}{m(\omega^2 - \gamma^2)}\sin\left(\frac{\omega + \gamma}{2}t\right)\sin\left(\frac{\omega - \gamma}{2}t\right)\,.$$

**(c)** For $F_0 = 32$, $m = 2$, $\omega = 9$, and $\gamma = 7$, the solution in part (b) becomes

$$y(t) = \frac{2(32)}{2(9^2 - 7^2)}\sin\left(\frac{9 + 7}{2}t\right)\sin\left(\frac{9 - 7}{2}t\right) = \sin 8t\sin t\,.$$

The graph of this function is shown in Figure B.28.

# Chapter 4

**7.** The auxiliary equation to equation (1) on page 220 in the text, $mr^2 + br + k = 0$, has roots

$$r = \frac{-b \pm \sqrt{b^2 - 4mk}}{2m},$$

which are both real ($b^2 > 4mk$) and negative because $\sqrt{b^2 - 4mk} < b$. Let

$$r_1 := \frac{-b - \sqrt{b^2 - 4mk}}{2m},$$

$$r_2 := \frac{-b + \sqrt{b^2 - 4mk}}{2m}.$$

Then a general solution to the homogeneous equation corresponding to (1) has the form

$$y_h(t) = c_1 e^{r_1 t} + c_2 e^{r_2 t}.$$

A particular solution to (1) is still given by (7) on page 221 in the text. Thus,

$$y(t) = c_1 e^{r_1 t} + c_2 e^{r_2 t} + \frac{F_0}{\sqrt{(k - m\gamma^2)^2 + b^2 \gamma^2}} \sin(\gamma t + \theta),$$

$\tan\theta = (k - m\gamma^2)/(b\gamma)$, is a general solution to the forced overdamped equation.

**9.** If a mass of $m = 8\,\text{kg}$ stretches the spring by $\ell = 1.96\,\text{m}$, then the spring stiffness must be

$$k = \frac{mg}{\ell} = \frac{8 \cdot 9.8}{1.96} = 40\,(\text{N/m}).$$

Substitution $m = 8$, $b = 3$, $k = 40$, and the external force $F(t) = \cos 2t$ into the equation (23) on page 226 in the text yields

$$8y'' + 3y' + 40y = \cos 2t.$$

The steady-state (a particular) solution to this equation is given in (6) and (7), page 221, that is,

$$
\begin{aligned}
y_p(t) &= \frac{F_0}{(k - m\gamma^2)^2 + b^2\gamma^2}\left\{(k - m\gamma^2)\cos\gamma t + b\gamma \sin\gamma t\right\} \\
&= \frac{1}{[40 - (8)(2)^2]^2 + (3)^2(2)^2}\left\{(40 - 8(2)^2)\cos 2t + (3)(2)\sin 2t\right\} \\
&= \frac{1}{100}\left\{8\cos 2t + 6\sin 2t\right\} = \frac{1}{10}\sin(2t + \theta),
\end{aligned}
$$

where $\theta = \arctan(8/6) \approx 0.927$.

**11.** First, we find the mass

$$m = \frac{8\,\text{lb}}{32\,\text{ft/sec}^2} = \frac{1}{4}\,\text{slug}.$$

Thus the equation (23), describing the motion, with $m = 1/4$, $b = 1$, $k = 10$, and the external force $F(t) = 2\cos 2t$ becomes

$$\frac{1}{4}\,y'' + y' + 10y = 2\cos 2t, \tag{4.14}$$

with the initial conditions are $y(0) = y'(0) = 0$. A general solution to the corresponding homogeneous equation is given in Section 4.8, formula (16). That is,

$$y_h(t) = e^{\alpha t}\left(C_1 \cos \beta t + C_2 \sin \beta t\right).$$

We compute

$$\alpha = -\frac{b}{2m} = -\frac{1}{2(1/4)} = -2 \quad \text{and} \quad \beta = \frac{1}{2(1/4)}\sqrt{4(1/4)(10) - 1^2} = 6.$$

So,

$$y_h(t) = e^{-2t}\left(C_1 \cos 6t + C_2 \sin 6t\right).$$

For a particular solution, we use formula (7), page 221 in the text.

$$
\begin{aligned}
y_p(t) &= \frac{F_0}{\sqrt{(k - m\gamma^2)^2 + b^2\gamma^2}}\,\sin(\gamma t + \theta) \\
&= \frac{2}{\sqrt{[10 - (1/4)(2)^2]^2 + (1)^2(2)^2}}\,\sin(2t + \theta) = \frac{2}{\sqrt{85}}\,\sin(2t + \theta),
\end{aligned}
$$

where $\theta = \arctan[(k - m\gamma^2)/(b\gamma)] = \arctan(9/2) \approx 1.352$. A general solution to (4.14) is then given by

$$y(t) = e^{-2t}\left(C_1 \cos 6t + C_2 \sin 6t\right) + \frac{2}{\sqrt{85}}\,\sin(2t + \theta).$$

From the initial conditions, we find

$$
\begin{aligned}
y(0) &= C_1 + (2/\sqrt{85})\sin\theta = 0, \\
y'(0) &= -2C_1 + 6C_2 + (4/\sqrt{85})\cos\theta = 0
\end{aligned}
$$

$$
\Rightarrow \quad
\begin{aligned}
C_1 &= -(2/\sqrt{85})\sin\theta = -18/85, \\
C_2 &= \left[C_1 - (2/\sqrt{85})\cos\theta\right]/3 = -22/255.
\end{aligned}
$$

$$\Rightarrow \qquad y(t) = e^{-2t}\left[-\frac{18}{85}\cos 6t - \frac{22}{255}\sin 6t\right] + \frac{2}{\sqrt{85}}\sin(2t + \theta).$$

The resonance frequency for the system is

$$\frac{\gamma_r}{2\pi} = \frac{\sqrt{(k/m) - (b^2)/(2m^2)}}{2\pi} = \frac{\sqrt{40 - 8}}{2\pi} = \frac{2\sqrt{2}}{\pi},$$

where we have used formula (15) on page 223 in the text for $\gamma_r$.

**13.** The mass attached to the spring is

$$m = \frac{32 \text{ lb}}{32 \text{ ft/sec}^2} = 1 \text{ slug}.$$

Thus the equation governing the motion, $my'' + by' + ky = F_{\text{ext}}$, with $m = 1$, $b = 2$, $k = 5$, and $F_{\text{ext}}(t) = 3\cos 4t$ becomes

$$y'' + 2y' + 5y = 3\cos 4t.$$

This is an underdamped motion because $b^2 - 4mk = (2)^2 - 4(1)(5) = -16 < 0$. For the steady-state solution of this equation we use formula (6) on page 221 in the text. Since $F_{\text{ext}}(t) = 3\cos 4t$, we have $F_0 = 3$, and $\gamma = 4$. Substituting $m$, $b$, $k$, $F_0$, and $\gamma$ into (6), we obtain

$$\begin{aligned} y_p(t) &= \frac{3}{[5 - (1)(4)^2]^2 + (2)^2(4)^2}\left\{[5 - (1)(4)^2]\cos 4t + (2)(4)\sin 4t\right\} \\ &= \frac{3}{185}(8\sin 4t - 11\cos 4t). \end{aligned}$$

## REVIEW PROBLEMS:  page 228

**1.** Solving the auxiliary equation, $r^2 + 8r - 9 = 0$, we find $r_1 = -9$, $r_2 = 1$. Thus a general solution is given by

$$y(t) = c_1 e^{r_1 t} + c_2 e^{r_2 t} = c_1 e^{-9t} + c_2 e^t.$$

**3.** The auxiliary equation, $4r^2 - 4r + 10 = 0$, has roots $r_{1,2} = (1 \pm 3i)/2$. Therefore a general solution is

$$y(t) = \left[c_1 \cos\left(\frac{3t}{2}\right) + c_2 \sin\left(\frac{3t}{2}\right)\right]e^{t/2}.$$

**5.** The roots of the auxiliary equation, $6r^2 - 11r + 3 = 0$, are $r_1 = 3/2$ and $r_2 = 1/3$. Thus,

$$y(t) = c_1 e^{r_1 t} + c_2 e^{r_2 t} = c_1 e^{3t/2} + c_2 e^{t/3}$$

is a general solution.

**7.** Solving the auxiliary equation, $36r^2 + 24r + 5 = 0$, we find

$$r = \frac{-24 \pm \sqrt{24^2 - 4(36)(5)}}{2(36)} = -\frac{1}{3} \pm \frac{1}{6}i.$$

Thus a general solution is given by

$$y(t) = \left[ c_1 \cos\left(\frac{t}{6}\right) + c_2 \sin\left(\frac{t}{6}\right) \right] e^{-t/3}.$$

**9.** The auxiliary equation, $16r^2 - 56r + 49 = (4r - 7)^2 = 0$, has a double root $r = 7/4$. Therefore, $e^{7t/4}$ and $te^{7t/4}$ are two linearly independent solutions, and a general solution is given by

$$y(t) = c_1 e^{7t/4} + c_2 t e^{7t/4} = (c_1 + c_2 t) e^{7t/4}.$$

**11.** This equation is a Cauchy-Euler equation. Using the approach discussed in Problem 38, Exercises 4.3, we make the substitution $t = e^s$ and obtain

$$\frac{dx}{ds} = \frac{dx}{dt}\frac{dt}{ds} = t\frac{dx}{dt},$$
$$\frac{d^2x}{ds^2} = \frac{d}{ds}\left(\frac{dx}{ds}\right) = \frac{dx}{ds} + t^2\frac{d^2x}{dt^2},$$
$$\Rightarrow \quad t^2\frac{d^2x}{dt^2} + 5x = \left(\frac{d^2x}{ds^2} - \frac{dx}{ds}\right) + 5x = \frac{d^2x}{ds^2} - \frac{dx}{ds} + 5x = 0.$$

The axiliary equation to this constant coefficient linear equation is $r^2 - r + 5 = 0$, which has roots

$$r = \frac{1 \pm \sqrt{1^2 - 4(1)(5)}}{2} = \frac{1 \pm \sqrt{19}}{2}.$$

Thus,

$$y(s) = e^{s/2}\left[ c_1 \cos\left(\frac{\sqrt{19}s}{2}\right) + c_2 \sin\left(\frac{\sqrt{19}s}{2}\right) \right]$$

is a general solution as a function of $s$. The back substitution, $s = \ln t$, yields

$$y(t) = t^{1/2} \left[ c_1 \cos \left( \frac{\sqrt{19}}{2} \ln t \right) + c_2 \sin \left( \frac{\sqrt{19}}{2} \ln t \right) \right].$$

**13.** The roots of the auxiliary equation, $r^2 + 16 = 0$, are $r = \pm 4i$. Thus a general solution to the corresponding homogeneous equation is given by

$$y_h(t) = c_1 \cos 4t + c_2 \sin 4t.$$

The method of undetermined coefficients suggests the form $y_p(t) = (A_1 t + A_0)e^t$ for a particular solution to the original equation. We compute

$$y_p'(t) = (A_1 t + A_0 + A_1)e^t, \qquad y_p''(t) = (A_1 t + A_0 + 2A_1)e^t$$

and substitute $y_p''(t)$ and $y_p(t)$ into the given equation. This yields

$$y_p'' + 16 y_p = \left[ (A_1 t + A_0 + 2A_1)e^t \right] + 16 \left[ (A_1 t + A_0)e^t \right] = te^t$$

$$\Rightarrow \quad (17A_1 t + 17A_0 + 2A_1) e^t = te^t \quad \Rightarrow \quad A_1 = \frac{1}{17}, A_0 = -\frac{2}{289}.$$

Therefore,

$$y_p(t) = \left( \frac{t}{17} - \frac{2}{289} \right) e^t$$

$$\Rightarrow \quad y(t) = y_h(t) + y_p(t) = c_1 \cos 4t + c_2 \sin 4t + \left( \frac{t}{17} - \frac{2}{289} \right) e^t.$$

**15.** This is a third order homogeneous linear differential equation with constant coefficients. Its auxiliary equation is $3r^3 + 10r^2 + 9r + 2 = 0$. Factoring yields

$$3r^3 + 10r^2 + 9r + 2 = (3r^3 + 3r^2) + (7r^2 + 7r) + (2r + 2) = (3r^2 + 7r + 2)(r + 1).$$

Thus the roots of the auxiliary equation are

$$r = -1 \quad \text{and} \quad r = \frac{-7 \pm \sqrt{7^2 - 4(3)(2)}}{6} = -2, -\frac{1}{3},$$

and a general solution is given by

$$y(t) = c_1 e^{-2t} + c_2 e^{-t} + c_3 e^{-t/3}.$$

**17.** To solve the auxiliary equation, $r^3 + 10r - 11 = 0$, we note that $r_1 = 1$ is a root. Dividing the polynomial $r^3 + 10r - 11$ by $r - 1$ we get

$$r^3 + 10r - 11 = (r-1)(r^2 + r + 11),$$

and so the other two roots are

$$r_{2,3} = \frac{-1 \pm \sqrt{1 - 4(1)(11)}}{2} = \frac{-1}{2} \pm \frac{\sqrt{43}}{2} i.$$

A general solution is then given by

$$y(t) = c_1 e^t + e^{-t/2} \left[ c_2 \cos\left(\frac{\sqrt{43}t}{2}\right) + c_3 \sin\left(\frac{\sqrt{43}t}{2}\right) \right].$$

**19.** By inspection, we find that $r = -3$ as a root of the auxiliary equation, $4r^3 + 8r^2 - 11r + 3 = 0$. Using, say, the long division, we get

$$4r^3 + 8r^2 - 11r + 3 = (r+3)(4r^2 - 4r + 1) = (r+3)(2r-1)^2.$$

Thus, in addition, $r = 1/2$ is a double root of the auxiliary equation. A general solution then has the form

$$y(t) = c_1 e^{-3t} + c_2 e^{t/2} + c_3 t e^{t/2}.$$

**21.** First, we solve the corresponding homogeneous equation,

$$y'' - 3y' + 7y = 0.$$

Since the roots of the auxiliary equation, $r^2 - 3r + 7 = 0$, are

$$r = \frac{3 \pm \sqrt{9 - 28}}{2} = \frac{3 \pm \sqrt{19}i}{2},$$

a general solution to the homogeneous equation is

$$y_h(t) = \left[ c_1 \cos\left(\frac{\sqrt{19}t}{2}\right) + c_2 \sin\left(\frac{\sqrt{19}t}{2}\right) \right] e^{3t/2}.$$

Chapter 4

We use the superposition principle to find a particular solution to the original nonhomogeneous equation.

A particular solution, $y_{p,1}(t)$ to $y'' - 3y' + 7y = 7t^2$ has the form

$$y_{p,1}(t) = A_2 t^2 + A_1 t + A_0.$$

Substitution yields

$$y''_{p,1} - 3y'_{p,1} + 7y_{p,1} = 2A_2 - 3(2A_2 t + A_1) + 7(A_2 t^2 + A_1 t + A_0) = 7t^2$$
$$\Rightarrow \quad (7A_2)t^2 + (7A_1 - 6A_2)t + (7A_0 - 3A_1 + 2A_2) = 7t^2$$

$$\begin{aligned} & 7A_2 = 7, & A_2 = 1, \\ \Rightarrow \quad & 7A_1 - 6A_2 = 0, & \Rightarrow \quad & A_1 = 6/7, \\ & 7A_0 - 3A_1 + 2A_2 = 0 & & A_0 = 4/49, \end{aligned}$$

and so

$$y_{p,1}(t) = t^2 + \frac{6}{7}t + \frac{4}{49}.$$

The other term in the right-hand side of the original equation is $e^t$. A particular solution to $y'' - 3y' + 7y = e^t$ has the form $y_{p,2}(t) = Ae^t$. Substitution yields

$$y''_{p,2} - 3y'_{p,2} + 7y_{p,2} = 5Ae^t = e^t \quad \Rightarrow \quad A = \frac{1}{5} \quad \Rightarrow \quad y_{p,2}(t) = \frac{1}{5}e^t.$$

By the superposition principle, a general solution to the original equation is

$$\begin{aligned} y(t) &= y_h(t) - y_{p,2}(t) + y_{p,1}(t) \\ &= \left[ c_1 \cos\left(\frac{\sqrt{19}t}{2}\right) + c_2 \sin\left(\frac{\sqrt{19}t}{2}\right) \right] e^{3t/2} - \frac{1}{5}e^t + t^2 + \frac{6}{7}t + \frac{4}{49}. \end{aligned}$$

23. The corresponding homogeneous equation in this problem is similar to that in Problem 13. Thus, $y_1(t) = \cos 4\theta$ and $y_2(t) = \sin 4\theta$ are its two linearly independent solutions, and a general solution is given by

$$y_h(\theta) = c_1 \cos 4\theta + c_2 \sin 4\theta.$$

For a particular solution to the original equation, we use the variation of parameters method. Letting

$$y_p(\theta) = v_1(\theta) \cos 4\theta + v_2(\theta) \sin 4\theta,$$

250

we get the following system for $v_1'$ and $v_2'$ (see (9) on page 195 in the text):

$$v_1'(\theta)\cos 4\theta + v_2'(\theta)\sin 4\theta = 0$$

$$-4v_1'(\theta)\sin 4\theta + 4v_2'(\theta)\cos 4\theta = \tan 4\theta.$$

Multiplying the first equation by $\sin 4\theta$ and the second equation by $(1/4)\cos 4\theta$, and adding the resulting equations together, we get

$$v_2'(\theta) = \frac{1}{4}\sin 4\theta \qquad \Rightarrow \qquad v_2 = -\frac{1}{16}\cos 4\theta + c_3.$$

From the first equation in the above system we also obtain

$$v_1'(\theta) = -v_2'(\theta)\tan 4\theta = -\frac{1}{4}\frac{\sin^2 4\theta}{\cos 4\theta} = -\frac{1}{4}(\sec 4\theta - \cos 4\theta)$$

$$\Rightarrow \qquad v_1(\theta) = -\frac{1}{4}\int(\sec 4\theta - \cos 4\theta)\,d\theta = -\frac{1}{16}\ln|\sec 4\theta + \tan 4\theta| + \frac{1}{16}\sin 4\theta + c_4.$$

Taking $c_3 = c_4 = 0$, we obtain

$$
\begin{aligned}
y_p(\theta) &= \left(-\frac{1}{16}\ln|\sec 4\theta + \tan 4\theta| + \frac{1}{16}\sin 4\theta\right)\cos 4\theta + \left(-\frac{1}{16}\cos\theta\right)\sin 4\theta \\
&= -\frac{1}{16}(\cos 4\theta)\ln|\sec 4\theta + \tan 4\theta|,
\end{aligned}
$$

and a general solution to the original equation is

$$y(\theta) = c_1\cos 4\theta + c_2\sin 4\theta - \frac{1}{16}(\cos 4\theta)\ln|\sec 4\theta + \tan 4\theta|.$$

**25.** Since the auxiliary equation, $4r^2 - 12r + 9 = (2r - 3)^2 = 0$, has a double root $r = 3/2$, a general solution to the corresponding homogeneous equation is

$$y_h(t) = c_1 e^{3t/2} + c_2 t e^{3t/2}.$$

By the superposition principle, a particular solution to the original equation has the form

$$y_p(t) = Ae^{5t} + Be^{3t}.$$

Substituting this expression into the given nonhomogeneous equation, we get

$$4y_p'' - 12y_p' + 9y_p = 4\left(25Ae^{5t} + 9Be^{3t}\right) - 12\left(5Ae^{5t} + 3Be^{3t}\right) + 9\left(Ae^{5t} + Be^{3t}\right)$$

Chapter 4

$$= 49Ae^{5t} + 9Be^{3t} = e^{5t} + e^{3t} \quad\Rightarrow\quad A = 1/49, \ B = 1/9.$$

Therefore, $y_p(t) = (1/49)e^{5t} + (1/9)e^{3t}$ and a general solution to the original equation is

$$y(t) = c_1 e^{3t/2} + c_2 t e^{3t/2} + \frac{1}{49} e^{5t} + \frac{1}{9} e^{3t}.$$

**27.** This is a Cauchy-Euler equation. Thus we make the substitution $x = e^t$ and get

$$x^2 \frac{d^2y}{dx^2} + 2x \frac{dy}{dx} - 2y = 6x^{-2} + 3x$$

$$\Rightarrow \quad \left( \frac{d^2y}{dt^2} - \frac{dy}{dt} \right) + 2\frac{dy}{dt} - 2y = 6(e^t)^{-2} + 3(e^t)$$

$$\Rightarrow \quad \frac{d^2y}{dt^2} + \frac{dy}{dt} - 2y = 6e^{-2t} + 3e^t. \tag{4.15}$$

The auxiliary equation, $r^2 + r - 2 = 0$, has the roots $r = -2, 1$. Therefore, a general solution to the corresponding homogeneous equation is

$$y_h(t) = c_1 e^t + c_2 e^{-2t}.$$

A particular solution to (4.15) has the form

$$y_p(t) = Ate^{-2t} + Bte^t.$$

(The factor $t$ appeared in both terms because $e^t$ and $e^{-2t}$ are both solutions to the homogeneous equation.) Differentiating, we find

$$y_p(t) = Ate^{-2t} + Bte^t$$
$$\Rightarrow \quad y_p'(t) = A(1 - 2t)e^{-2t} + B(t + 1)e^t$$
$$\Rightarrow \quad y_p''(t) = A(4t - 4)e^{-2t} + B(t + 2)e^t.$$

Substitution into (4.15) yields

$$-3Ae^{-2t} + 3Be^t = 6e^{-2t} + 3e^t \quad\Rightarrow\quad A = -2, \ B = 1.$$

Thus a general solution to (4.15) is given by

$$y(t) = y_h(t) + y_p(t) = c_1 e^t + c_2 e^{-2t} - 2te^{-2t} + te^t.$$

The back substitution $e^t = x$ (or $t = \ln x$) results

$$y(x) = c_1 x + c_2 x^{-2} - 2x^{-2} \ln x + x \ln x.$$

**29.** The roots of the auxiliary equation in this problem are

$$r = \frac{-4 \pm \sqrt{4^2 - 4(1)(7)}}{2} = -2 \pm \sqrt{3}i.$$

Therefore, a general solution is given by

$$y(t) = \left(c_1 \cos \sqrt{3}t + c_2 \sin \sqrt{3}t\right) e^{-2t}.$$

Substituting the initial conditions, we obtain

$$y(0) = \left(c_1 \cos \sqrt{3}t + c_2 \sin \sqrt{3}t\right) e^{-2t}\Big|_{t=0} = c_1 = 1,$$
$$y'(0) = \left[(-2c_1 + \sqrt{3}c_2) \cos \sqrt{3}t - (\sqrt{3}c_1 + 2c_2) \sin \sqrt{3}t\right] e^{-2t}\Big|_{t=0} = -2c_1 + \sqrt{3}c_2 = -2.$$

Solving this system yields $c_1 = 1$, $c_2 = 0$. The solution to the given initial value problem is

$$y(t) = e^{-2t} \cos \sqrt{3}t.$$

**31.** We solve the corresponding homogeneous equation. Its auxiliary equation, $r^2 - 2r + 10 = 0$, has the roots $r = 1 \pm 3i$. Thus

$$y_h(t) = (c_1 \cos 3t + c_2 \sin 3t) e^t$$

is a general solution.

Now, we apply the method of undetermined coefficients and look for a particular solution to the original nonhomogeneous equation of the form $y_p(t) = A \cos 3t + B \sin 3t$. Differentiating $y_p(t)$ twice, we obtain $y_p'(t) = -3A \sin 3t + 3B \cos 3t$, $y_p'' = -9A \cos 3t - 9B \sin 3t$ and substitute these expressions into the original equation. Thus we get

$$(-9A \cos 3t - 9B \sin 3t) - 2(-3A \sin 3t + 3B \cos 3t) + 10(A \cos 3t + B \sin 3t)$$
$$= 6 \cos 3t - \sin 3t$$

253

$$\Rightarrow \quad (A-6B)\cos 3t + (6A+B)\sin 3t = 6\cos 3t - \sin 3t$$

$$\Rightarrow \quad \begin{aligned} A-6B&=6,\\ 6A+B&=-1 \end{aligned} \quad \Rightarrow \quad \begin{aligned} A&=0,\\ B&=-1. \end{aligned}$$

So, $y_p(t) = -\sin 3t$, and $y(t) = (c_1\cos 3t + c_2\sin 3t)e^t - \sin 3t$ is a general solution to the given equation.

Next, we satisfy the initial conditions.

$$\begin{aligned} y(0)&=c_1=2,\\ y'(0)&=c_1+3c_2-3=-8 \end{aligned} \quad \Rightarrow \quad \begin{aligned} c_1&=2,\\ c_2&=-7/3. \end{aligned}$$

Hence, the answer is

$$y(t) = \left(2\cos 3t - \frac{7}{3}\sin 3t\right)e^t - \sin 3t.$$

**33.** The associated characteristic equation in this problem is $r^3 - 12r^2 + 27r + 40 = 0$, which is a third order equation. Using the rational root theorem, we look for its integer roots among the divisors of 40, which are $\pm 1$, $\pm 2$, $\pm 4$, $\pm 8$, $\pm 10$, $\pm 20$, and $\pm 40$. By inspection, $r=-1$ is a root. Dividing $r^3 - 12r^2 + 27r + 40$ by $r+1$, we get

$$r^3 - 12r^2 + 27r + 40 = (r^2 - 13r + 40)(r+1),$$

and so the other two roots of the auxiliary equation are the roots of $r^2 - 13r + 40 = 0$, which are $r=5$ and 8. Therefore, a general solution to the given equation is $y(t) = c_1e^{-t} + c_2e^{5t} + c_3e^{8t}$. We find the values of $c_1$, $c_2$, and $c_3$ from the initial conditions.

$$\begin{aligned} y(0)&=(c_1e^{-t}+c_2e^{5t}+c_3e^{8t})\big|_{t=0}=c_1+c_2+c_3=-3,\\ y'(0)&=(-c_1e^{-t}+5c_2e^{5t}+8c_3e^{8t})\big|_{t=0}=-c_1+5c_2+8c_3=-6,\\ y''(0)&=(c_1e^{-t}+25c_2e^{5t}+64c_3e^{8t})\big|_{t=0}=c_1+25c_2+64c_3=-12 \end{aligned} \quad \Rightarrow \quad \begin{aligned} c_1&=-1,\\ c_2&=-3,\\ c_3&=1. \end{aligned}$$

Therefore, $y(t) = -e^{-t} - 3e^{5t} + e^{8t}$ is the solution to the given initial value problem.

**35.** Since the roots of the auxiliary equation, $r^2 + 1 = 0$, are $r = \pm i$, the functions $y_1(\theta) = \cos\theta$ and $y_2(\theta) = \sin\theta$ are two linearly independent solutions to the corresponding homogeneous equation, and its general solution is given by

$$y_h(\theta) = c_1\cos\theta + c_2\sin\theta.$$

We apply the method of variation of parameters to find a particular solution to the original equation. We look for a particular solution of the form

$$y_p(\theta) = v_1(\theta)\cos\theta + v_2(\theta)\sin\theta,$$

where $v_1(\theta)$ and $v_2(\theta)$ satisfy the system (9), Section 4.6. That is,

$$v_1' \cos\theta + v_2' \sin\theta = 0,$$
$$-v_1' \sin\theta + v_2' \cos\theta = \sec\theta.$$

Multiplying the first equation by $\sin\theta$, the second equation by $\cos\theta$, and adding them together yield

$$v_2' \sin^2\theta + v_2' \cos^2\theta = \sec\theta\cos\theta \quad\Rightarrow\quad v_2' = 1 \quad\Rightarrow\quad v_2(\theta) = \theta.$$

From the first equation in the above system we also get

$$v_1' = -v_2'\tan\theta = -\tan\theta \quad\Rightarrow\quad v_1(\theta) = -\int \tan\theta\, d\theta = \ln|\cos\theta|,$$

where we have taken the zero integration constant. So,

$$y_p(\theta) = \cos\theta\ln|\cos\theta| + \theta\sin\theta,$$

and

$$y(\theta) = c_1\cos\theta + c_2\sin\theta + \cos\theta\ln|\cos\theta| + \theta\sin\theta$$

is a general solution to the original equation. Differentiating we find that

$$y'(\theta) = -c_1\sin\theta + c_2\cos\theta - \sin\theta\ln|\cos\theta| + \theta\cos\theta.$$

Substitution of $y(\theta)$ and $y'(\theta)$ into the initial conditions yields

$$y(0) = c_1 = 1,$$
$$y'(0) = c_2 = 2 \quad\Rightarrow\quad \begin{array}{l} c_1 = 1, \\ c_2 = 2, \end{array}$$

and so the answer is $y(\theta) = \cos\theta + 2\sin\theta + \cos\theta\ln|\cos\theta| + \theta\sin\theta.$

# Chapter 4

**37.** Comparing the given homogeneous equations with mass-spring oscillator equation (13) in Section 4.7,

$$[\text{inertia}]\, y'' + [\text{damping}]\, y' + [\text{stiffness}]\, y = 0,$$

we see that in equations (a) through (d) the damping coefficient is 0. So, the behavior, of solutions, as $t \to +\infty$, depends on the sign of the stiffness coefficient "$k$".

**(a)** "$k$" $= t^4 > 0$. This implies that all the solutions remain bounded as $t \to +\infty$.

**(b)** "$k$" $= -t^4 < 0$. The stiffness of the system is negative and increases unboundedly as $t \to +\infty$. It reinforces the displacement, $y(t)$, with magnitude increasing with time. Hence some solutions grow rapidly with time.

**(c)** "$k$" $= y^6 > 0$. Similarly to (a), we conclude that all the solutions are bounded.

**(d)** "$k$" $= y^7$. The function $f(y) = y^7$ is positive for positive $y$ and negative if $y$ is negative. Hence, we can expect that some of the solutions (say, ones satisfying negative initial conditions) are unbounded.

**(e)** "$k$" $= 3 + \sin t$. Since $|\sin t| \le 1$ for any $t$, we conclude that

$$\text{"}k\text{"} \ge 3 + (-1) = 2 > 0,$$

and all the solutions are bounded as $t \to +\infty$.

**(f)** Here there is positive damping "$b$" $= t^2$ increasing with time, which results an increasing drain of energy from the system, and positive constant stiffness $k = 1$. Thus all the solutions are bounded.

**(g)** Negative damping "$b$" $= -t^2$ increases (in absolute value) with time, which imparts energy to the system instead of draining it. Note that the stiffness $k = -1$ is also negative. Thus we should expect that some of the solutions increase unboundedly as $t \to +\infty$.

**39.** If a weight of $w = 32\,\text{lb}$ stretches the spring by $\ell = 6\,\text{in} = 0.5\,\text{ft}$, then the spring stiffness must be

$$k = \frac{w}{\ell} = \frac{32}{0.5} = 64\,(\text{lb/ft}).$$

Also, the mass $m$ of the weight is

$$m = \frac{w}{g} = \frac{32}{32} = 1 \text{ (slug)},$$

and the damping constant $b = 2\,\text{lb-sec/ft}$. The external force is given to be $F(t) = F_0 \cos \gamma t$ with $F_0 = 4$ and $\gamma = 8$.

Clearly, we have an underdamped motion because $b^2 - 4mk = 4 - 256 < 0$. So, we can use formula (6) in Section 4.9 for the steady-state solution. This yields

$$
\begin{aligned}
y_p(t) &= \frac{F_0}{(k - m\gamma^2)^2 + b^2\gamma^2} \left\{ (k - m\gamma^2) \cos \gamma t + b\gamma \sin \gamma t \right\} \\
&= \frac{4}{(64 - 8^2)^2 + 2^2 8^2} \left\{ (64 - 8^2) \cos 8t + (2)(8) \sin 8t \right\} = \frac{1}{4} \sin 8t .
\end{aligned}
$$

The resonant frequency for the system is $\gamma_r/(2\pi)$, where $\gamma_r$ is given in (15), Section 4.9. Applying this formula, we get

$$\text{resonant frequency} = \frac{1}{2\pi} \sqrt{\frac{k}{m} - \frac{b^2}{2m^2}} = \frac{1}{2\pi} \sqrt{\frac{64}{1} - \frac{2^2}{2(1^2)}} = \frac{\sqrt{62}}{2\pi} .$$

# CHAPTER 5: Introduction to Systems and Phase Plane Analysis

**EXERCISES 5.2:   Elimination Method for Systems, page 250**

**1.** Subtracting the second equation in the system from the first one, we eliminate $y$ and obtain

$$\begin{aligned} x' + y' &= & -2y, \\ y' &= & x - 2y \end{aligned} \qquad \Rightarrow \qquad x' = -x.$$

This equation is separable (also, it is linear). Separation yields

$$\frac{dx}{x} = -dt \qquad \Rightarrow \qquad \ln|x| = -t + C \qquad \Rightarrow \qquad x(t) = c_2 e^{-t}.$$

Substituting this solution into the second equation, we obtain an equation for $y$:

$$y' + 2y = x = c_2 e^{-t}.$$

This equation is a first order linear equation. Solving we obtain

$$\mu(t) = \exp\left(\int (2)dt\right) = e^{2t}$$

$$\Rightarrow \qquad e^{2t} y = \int \left(c_2 e^{-t}\right) e^{2t} dt = c_2 \int e^t dt = c_2 e^t + c_1$$

$$\Rightarrow \qquad y(t) = c_1 e^{-2t} + c_2 e^{-t}.$$

Therefore, a general solution is

$$x(t) = c_2 e^{-t}, \qquad y(t) = c_1 e^{-2t} + c_2 e^{-t}.$$

**3.** We eliminate $x$ by subtracting the second equation from the first equation. This yields

$$y' + 2y = 0 \qquad \Rightarrow \qquad \frac{dy}{y} = -2dt \qquad \Rightarrow \qquad \ln|y| = -2t + c \qquad \Rightarrow \qquad y(t) = c_2 e^{-2t}.$$

From the second equation we get

$$x' - y' = 0 \quad \Rightarrow \quad (x-y)' = 0 \quad \Rightarrow \quad x(t) - y(t) = c_1 \quad \Rightarrow \quad x(t) = c_1 + c_2 e^{-2t},$$

and a general solution is given by

$$x(t) = c_1 + c_2 e^{-2t}, \qquad y(t) = c_2 e^{-2t}.$$

5. Writing this system in operator notation yields the system

$$(D-1)[x] + D[y] = 5,$$
$$D[x] + (D+1)[y] = 1. \tag{5.1}$$

We will first eliminate the function $x(t)$, although we could proceed just as easily by eliminating the function $y(t)$. Thus, we apply the operator $D$ to the first equation and the operator $-(D-1)$ to the second equation to obtain

$$D(D-1)[x] + D^2[y] = D[5] = 0,$$
$$-(D-1)D[x] - (D-1)(D+1)[y] = -(D-1)[1] = 1.$$

Adding these two equations yields

$$\{D(D-1) - (D-1)D\}\,[x] + \{D^2 - (D^2-1)\}\,[y] = 1$$
$$\Rightarrow \quad 0 \cdot x + 1 \cdot y = 1 \quad \Rightarrow \quad y(t) = 1.$$

To find the function $x(t)$, we will eliminate $y$ from the system given in (5.1). Therefore, we multiply the first equation in (5.1) by $(D+1)$ and the second by $-D$ to obtain the system

$$(D+1)(D-1)[x] + (D+1)D[y] = (D+1)[5] = 5,$$
$$-D^2[x] - D(D+1)[y] = D[1] = 0.$$

By adding these two equations we obtain

$$\{(D^2-1) - D^2\}\,[x] = 5 \quad \Rightarrow \quad -x = 5 \quad \Rightarrow \quad x(t) = -5.$$

Therefore, this system of linear differential equation is solved by the functions

$$x(t) = -5 \quad \text{and} \quad y(t) = 1.$$

**7.** In order to eliminate $u$, we multiply the first equation by $(D-1)$, the second equation – by $(D+1)$, and subtract the results.

$$(D-1)\{(D+1)[u] - (D+1)[v]\} = (D-1)[e^t] = (e^t)' - e^t = 0,$$
$$(D+1)\{(D-1)[u] + (2D+1)[v]\} = (D+1)[5] = (5)' + 5 = 5$$

$$\Rightarrow \qquad (D^2-1)[u] - (D^2-1)[v] = 0,$$
$$(D^2-1)[u] + \{(D+1)(2D+1)\}[v] = 5$$

$$\Rightarrow \quad \{(D+1)(2D+1) + (D^2-1)\}[v] = 5 \quad \Rightarrow \quad \{D(D+1)\}[v] = \frac{5}{3}. \quad (5.2)$$

The corresponding homogeneous equation, $\{D(D+1)\}[v] = 0$, has the characteristic equation

$$r(r+1) = 0 \qquad \Rightarrow \qquad r = 0, -1,$$

and so its general solution is

$$v_h(t) = c_1 + c_2 e^{-t}.$$

Applying the method of undetermined coefficients, we look for a particular solution to (5.2) of the form $v_p(t) = ct^s$, where we choose $s = 1$ (because the homogeneous equation has constant solutions and does not have solutions of the form $ct$). Substitution $v = ct$ into (5.2) yields

$$\{D(D+1)\}[ct] = (D+1)[c] = c = \frac{5}{3} \qquad \Rightarrow \qquad v_p(t) = \frac{5}{3}t.$$

Therefore, a general solution to (5.2) is

$$v(t) = v_h(t) + v_p(t) = c_1 + c_2 e^{-t} + \frac{5}{3}t.$$

We now go back to the original system and subtract the second equation from the first one.

$$2u - (3D+2)[v] = e^t - 5$$

$$\Rightarrow \qquad u = \left(\frac{3}{2}D + 1\right)[v] + \frac{1}{2}e^t - \frac{5}{2}$$

$$\Rightarrow \qquad u = \frac{3}{2}\left(c_1 + c_2 e^{-t} + \frac{5}{3}t\right)' + \left(c_1 + c_2 e^{-t} + \frac{5}{3}t\right) + \frac{1}{2}e^t - \frac{5}{2}$$

$$\Rightarrow \qquad u(t) = c_1 - \frac{1}{2}c_2 e^{-t} + \frac{1}{2}e^t + \frac{5}{3}t.$$

Thus, a general solution to the given system is

$$u(t) = c_1 - \frac{1}{2}c_2 e^{-t} + \frac{1}{2}e^t + \frac{5}{3}t,$$

$$v(t) = c_1 + c_2 e^{-t} + \frac{5}{3}t.$$

**9.** Expressed in operator notation, this system becomes

$$(D+2)[x] + D[y] = 0,$$

$$(D-1)[x] + (D-1)[y] = \sin t.$$

In order to eliminate the function $y(t)$, we will apply the operator $(D-1)$ to the first equation above and the operator $-D$ to the second one. Thus, we have

$$(D-1)(D+2)[x] + (D-1)D[y] = (D-1)[0] = 0,$$

$$-D(D-1)[x] - D(D-1)[y] = -D[\sin t] = -\cos t.$$

Adding these two equations yields the differential equation involving the single function $x(t)$ given by

$$\left\{ (D^2 + D - 2) - (D^2 - D) \right\}[x] = -\cos t$$

$$\Rightarrow \qquad 2(D-1)[x] = -\cos t. \tag{5.3}$$

This is a linear first order differential equation with constant coefficients and so can be solved by the methods of Chapter 2. (See Section 2.3.) However, we will use the methods of Chapter 4. We see that the auxiliary equation associated with the corresponding homogeneous equation is given by $2(r-1) = 0$, which has the root $r = 1$. Thus, a general solution to the corresponding homogeneous equation is

$$x_h(t) = C_1 e^t.$$

We will use the method of undetermined coefficients to find a particular solution to the nonhomogeneous equation. To this end, we note that a particular solution to this differential equation will have the form

$$x_p(t) = A\cos t + B\sin t \qquad \Rightarrow \qquad x_p'(t) = -A\sin t + B\cos t.$$

Substituting these expressions into the nonhomogeneous equation given in (5.3) yields

$$2x'_p - 2x_p = 2(-A\sin t + B\cos t) - 2(A\cos t + B\sin t)$$
$$= (2B - 2A)\cos t + (-2A - 2B)\sin t = -\cos t.$$

By equating coefficients we obtain

$$2B - 2A = -1 \qquad \text{and} \qquad -2A - 2B = 0.$$

By solving these two equations simultaneously for $A$ and $B$, we see that

$$A = \frac{1}{4} \qquad \text{and} \qquad B = -\frac{1}{4}.$$

Thus, a particular solution to the nonhomogeneous equation given in (5.3) will be

$$x_p(t) = \frac{1}{4}\cos t - \frac{1}{4}\sin t$$

and a general solution to the nonhomogeneous equation (5.3) will be

$$x(t) = x_h(t) + x_p(t) = C_1 e^t + \frac{1}{4}\cos t - \frac{1}{4}\sin t.$$

We now must find a function $y(t)$. To do this, we subtract the second of the two differential equations in the system from the first to obtain

$$3x + y = -\sin t \qquad \Rightarrow \qquad y = -3x - \sin t.$$

Therefore, we see that

$$y(t) = -3\left[C_1 e^t + \frac{1}{4}\cos t - \frac{1}{4}\sin t\right] - \sin t$$
$$\Rightarrow \qquad y(t) = -3C_1 e^t - \frac{3}{4}\cos t - \frac{1}{4}\sin t.$$

Hence this system of differential equations has the general solution

$$x(t) = C_1 e^t + \frac{1}{4}\cos t - \frac{1}{4}\sin t \qquad \text{and} \qquad y(t) = -3C_1 e^t - \frac{3}{4}\cos t - \frac{1}{4}\sin t.$$

# Chapter 5

**11.** From the second equation, we obtain $u = -\left(D^2 + 2\right)[v]/2$. Substitution into the first equation eliminates $u$ and gives

$$\left(D^2 - 1\right)\left\{-\frac{1}{2}\left(D^2 + 2\right)[v]\right\} + 5v = e^t$$

$$\Rightarrow \qquad \left[\left(D^2 - 1\right)\left(D^2 + 2\right) - 10\right][v] = -2e^t$$

$$\Rightarrow \qquad \left(D^4 + D^2 - 12\right)[v] = -2e^t. \qquad\qquad (5.4)$$

Solving the characteristic equation, $r^4 + r^2 - 12 = 0$,

$$r^4 + r^2 - 12 = 0 \qquad \Rightarrow \qquad \left(r^2 + 4\right)\left(r^2 - 3\right) = 0 \qquad \Rightarrow \qquad r = \pm 2i, \pm\sqrt{3},$$

we conclude that a general solution to the corresponding homogeneous equation is

$$v_h(t) = c_1 \cos 2t + c_2 \sin 2t + c_3 e^{\sqrt{3}t} + c_4 e^{-\sqrt{3}t}.$$

A particular solution to (5.4) has the form $v_p(t) = ce^t$. Substitution yields

$$\left(D^4 + D^2 - 12\right)\left[ce^t\right] = ce^t + ce^t - 12ce^t = -10ce^t = -2e^t \qquad \Rightarrow \qquad c = \frac{1}{5}.$$

Therefore, $v = v_h + v_p = c_1 \cos 2t + c_2 \sin 2t + c_3 e^{\sqrt{3}t} + c_4 e^{-\sqrt{3}t} + e^t/5$ and

$$
\begin{aligned}
u &= -\frac{1}{2}\left(D^2 + 2\right)[v] = -\frac{1}{2}\left(c_1 \cos 2t + c_2 \sin 2t + c_3 e^{\sqrt{3}t} + c_4 e^{-\sqrt{3}t} + \frac{1}{5}e^t\right)'' \\
&\qquad\qquad -\left(c_1 \cos 2t + c_2 \sin 2t + c_3 e^{\sqrt{3}t} + c_4 e^{-\sqrt{3}t} + \frac{1}{5}e^t\right) \\
&= c_1 \cos 2t + c_2 \sin 2t - \frac{5}{2}c_3 e^{\sqrt{3}t} - \frac{5}{2}c_4 e^{-\sqrt{3}t} - \frac{3}{10}e^t.
\end{aligned}
$$

By replacing $(-5/2)c_3$ by $c_3$ and $(-5/2)c_4$ by $c_4$ we obtain the same answer as given in the text.

**13.** Expressing $x$ from the second equation and substituting the result into the first equation, we obtain

$$x = y' - y \qquad \Rightarrow \qquad \frac{d(y' - y)}{dt} = (y' - y) - 4y \qquad \Rightarrow \qquad y'' - 2y' + 5y = 0.$$

264

This homogeneous linear equation with constant coefficients has the characteristic equation $r^2 - 2r + 5 = 0$ with roots $r = 1 \pm 2i$. Thus a general solution is

$$y = c_1 e^t \cos 2t + c_2 e^t \sin 2t.$$

Therefore,

$$
\begin{aligned}
x &= \left(c_1 e^t \cos 2t + c_2 e^t \sin 2t\right)' - \left(c_1 e^t \cos 2t + c_2 e^t \sin 2t\right) \\
&= \left(c_1 e^t \cos 2t - 2c_1 e^t \sin 2t + c_2 e^t \sin 2t + 2c_2 e^t \cos 2t\right) - \left(c_1 e^t \cos 2t + c_2 e^t \sin 2t\right) \\
&= 2c_2 e^t \cos 2t - 2c_1 e^t \sin 2t.
\end{aligned}
$$

**15.** In operator form, the system becomes

$$
\begin{aligned}
-2z + (D - 5)[w] &= 5t, \\
(D - 4)[z] - 3w &= 17t.
\end{aligned}
$$

We multiply the first equation by 3, the second equation by $(D - 5)$, and add the resulting equations.

$$
\begin{aligned}
\{-6 + (D - 5)(D - 4)\}\,[z] &= 3(5t) + (D - 5)[17t] = -70t + 17 \\
\Rightarrow \quad \left(D^2 - 9D + 14\right)[z] &= -70t + 17.
\end{aligned}
$$

Solving the characteristic equation, $r^2 - 9r + 14 = 0$, we obtain $r = 2, 7$. Hence, a general solution to the corresponding homogeneous equation is $z_h(t) = c_1 e^{2t} + c_2 e^{7t}$. A particular solution has the form $z_p(t) = At + B$. Substitution yields

$$
\begin{aligned}
\left(D^2 - 9D + 14\right)[At + B] &= (At + B)'' - 9(At + B)' + 14(At + B) \\
&= 14At - 9A + 14B = -70t + 17
\end{aligned}
$$

$$
\Rightarrow \quad A = \frac{-70}{14} = -5, \quad B = \frac{17 + 9A}{14} = -2
$$

$$
\Rightarrow \quad z(t) = z_h(t) + z_p(t) = c_1 e^{2t} + c_2 e^{7t} - 5t - 2.
$$

We use now the second equation from the original system to find $w$.

$$
w = \frac{1}{3}\left(z' - 4z - 17t\right) = -\frac{2}{3}c_1 e^{2t} + c_2 e^{7t} + t + 1.
$$

Chapter 5

**17.** Expressed in operator notation, this system becomes

$$(D^2 + 5)[x] - 4[y] = 0,$$
$$-[x] + (D^2 + 2)[y] = 0.$$

In order to eliminate the function $x(t)$, we apply the operator $(D^2+5)$ to the second equation. Thus, we have

$$(D^2 + 5)[x] - 4[y] = 0,$$
$$-(D^2 + 5)[x] + (D^2 + 5)(D^2 + 2)[y] = 0.$$

Adding these two equations together yields the differential equation involving the single function $y(t)$ given by

$$\{(D^2 + 5)(D^2 + 2) - 4\}[y] = 0 \quad \Rightarrow \quad (D^4 + 7D^2 + 6)[y] = 0.$$

The auxiliary equation for this homogeneous equation, $r^4 + 7r^2 + 6 = (r^2 + 1)(r^2 + 6) = 0$, has roots $r = \pm i, \pm i\sqrt{6}$. Thus, a general solution is

$$y(t) = C_1 \sin t + C_2 \cos t + C_3 \sin \sqrt{6}t + C_4 \cos \sqrt{6}t.$$

We must now find a function $x(t)$ that satisfies the system of differential equations given in the problem. To do this we solve the second equation of the system of differential equations for $x(t)$ to obtain

$$x(t) = (D^2 + 2)[y].$$

Substituting the expression we found for $y(t)$, we see that

$$x(t) = -C_1 \sin t - C_2 \cos t - 6C_3 \sin \sqrt{6}t - 6C_4 \cos \sqrt{6}t$$
$$+2\left(C_1 \sin t + C_2 \cos t + C_3 \sin \sqrt{6}t + C_4 \cos \sqrt{6}t\right)$$
$$\Rightarrow \quad x(t) = C_1 \sin t + C_2 \cos t - 4C_3 \sin \sqrt{6}t - 4C_4 \cos \sqrt{6}t.$$

Hence this system of differential equations has the general solution

$$x(t) = C_1 \sin t + C_2 \cos t - 4C_3 \sin \sqrt{6}t - 4C_4 \cos \sqrt{6}t$$
$$y(t) = C_1 \sin t + C_2 \cos t + C_3 \sin \sqrt{6}t + C_4 \cos \sqrt{6}t.$$

**19.** From the first equation, we conclude that $y = x' - 4x$. Substitution into the second equation yields

$$(x' - 4x)' = -2x + (x' - 4x) \qquad \Rightarrow \qquad x'' - 5x' + 6x = 0.$$

The characteristic equation, $r^2 - 5r + 6 = 0$, has roots $r = 2, 3$, and so a general solution is

$$x(t) = c_1 e^{2t} + c_2 e^{3t}$$
$$\Rightarrow \qquad y(t) = \left(c_1 e^{2t} + c_2 e^{3t}\right)' - 4\left(c_1 e^{2t} + c_2 e^{3t}\right) = -2c_1 e^{2t} - c_2 e^{3t}.$$

We find constants $c_1$ and $c_2$ from the initial condition.

$$1 = x(0) = c_1 e^{2(0)} + c_2 e^{3(0)} = c_1 + c_2,$$
$$0 = y(0) = -2c_1 e^{2(0)} - c_2 e^{3(0)} = -2c_1 - c_2 \qquad \Rightarrow \qquad \begin{aligned} c_1 &= -1, \\ c_2 &= 2. \end{aligned}$$

Therefore, the answer to this problem is

$$x(t) = -e^{2t} + 2e^{3t}, \qquad y(t) = 2e^{2t} - 2e^{3t}.$$

**21.** To apply the elimination method, we write the system using operator notation:

$$\begin{aligned} D^2[x] - y &= 0, \\ -x + D^2[y] &= 0. \end{aligned} \tag{5.5}$$

Eliminating $y$ by applying $D^2$ to the first equation and adding to the second equation gives

$$\left(D^2 D^2 - 1\right)[x] = 0,$$

which reduces to

$$\left(D^4 - 1\right)[x] = 0. \tag{5.6}$$

The corresponding auxiliary equation, $r^4 - 1 = 0$, has roots $\pm 1, \pm i$. Thus, the general solution to (5.6) is given by

$$x(t) = C_1 e^t + C_2 e^{-t} + C_3 \cos t + C_4 \sin t. \tag{5.7}$$

Substituting $x(t)$ into the first equation in (5.5) yields

$$y(t) = x''(t) = C_1 e^t + C_2 e^{-t} - C_3 \cos t - C_4 \sin t. \tag{5.8}$$

# Chapter 5

We use initial conditions to determine constants $C_1$, $C_2$, $C_3$, and $C_4$. Differentiating (5.7) and (5.8), we get

$$
\begin{aligned}
3 &= x(0) = C_1 e^0 + C_2 e^{-0} + C_3 \cos 0 + C_4 \sin 0 = C_1 + C_2 + C_3, \\
1 &= x'(0) = C_1 e^0 - C_2 e^{-0} - C_3 \sin 0 + C_4 \cos 0 = C_1 - C_2 + C_4, \\
1 &= y(0) = C_1 e^0 + C_2 e^{-0} - C_3 \cos 0 - C_4 \sin 0 = C_1 + C_2 - C_3, \\
-1 &= y'(0) = C_1 e^0 - C_2 e^{-0} + C_3 \sin 0 - C_4 \cos 0 = C_1 - C_2 - C_4
\end{aligned}
$$

$$
\Rightarrow \quad
\begin{aligned}
C_1 + C_2 + C_3 &= 3, \\
C_1 - C_2 + C_4 &= 1, \\
C_1 + C_2 - C_3 &= 1, \\
C_1 - C_2 - C_4 &= -1.
\end{aligned}
$$

Solving we obtain $C_1 = C_2 = C_3 = C_4 = 1$. So, the desired solution is

$$
x(t) = e^t + e^{-t} + \cos t + \sin t,
$$
$$
y(t) = e^t + e^{-t} - \cos t - \sin t.
$$

**23.** We will attempt to solve this system by first eliminating the function $y(t)$. Thus, we multiply the first equation by $(D+2)$ and the second by $-(D-1)$. Therefore, we obtain

$$
(D+2)(D-1)[x] + (D+2)(D-1)D[y] = (D+2)\left[-3e^{-2t}\right] = 6e^{-2t} - 6e^{-2t} = 0,
$$
$$
-(D-1)(D+2)[x] - (D-1)(D+2)[y] = -(D-1)\left[3e^t\right] = -3e^t + 3e^t = 0.
$$

Adding these two equations yields

$$
0 \cdot x + 0 \cdot y = 0,
$$

which will be true for any two functions $x(t)$ and $y(t)$. (But not every pair of functions will satisfy this system of differential equations.) Thus, this is a degenerate system, and has infinitely many linearly independent solutions. To see if we can find these solutions, we will examine the system more closely. Notice that we could write this system as

$$
\begin{aligned}
(D-1)[x+y] &= -3e^{-2t}, \\
(D+2)[x+y] &= 3e^t.
\end{aligned}
$$

268

Therefore, let's try the substitution $z(t) = x(t) + y(t)$. We want a function $z(t)$ that satisfies the two equations

$$z'(t) - z(t) = -3e^{-2t} \quad \text{and} \quad z'(t) + 2z(t) = 3e^t, \tag{5.9}$$

simultaneously. We start by solving the first equation given in (5.9). This is a linear differential equation with constant coefficients which has the associated auxiliary equation $r - 1 = 0$. Hence, the solution to the corresponding homogeneous equation is

$$z_h(t) = Ce^t.$$

By the method of undetermined coefficients, we see that a particular solution will have the form

$$z_p(t) = Ae^{-2t} \quad \Rightarrow \quad z_p' = -2Ae^{-2t}.$$

Substituting these expressions into the first differential equation given in (5.9) yields

$$z_p'(t) - z_p(t) = -2Ae^{-2t} - Ae^{-2t} = -3Ae^{-2t} = -3e^{-2t} \quad \Rightarrow \quad A = 1.$$

Thus, the first equation given in (5.9) has the general solution

$$z(t) = Ce^t + e^{-2t}.$$

Now, substituting $z(t)$ into the second equation in (5.9) gives

$$Ce^t - 2e^{-2t} + 2\left(Ce^t + e^{-2t}\right) = 3e^t \quad \Rightarrow \quad 3Ce^t = 3e^t.$$

Hence, $C$ must be 1. Therefore, $z(t) = e^t + e^{-2t}$ is the only solution that satisfies both differential equations given in (5.9) simultaneously. Thus, any two differentiable functions that satisfy the equation $x(t) + y(t) = e^t + e^{-2t}$ will satisfy the original system.

**25.** Writing the system in operator form yields

$$\begin{aligned}
(D-1)[x] - 2y + z &= 0, \\
-x + D[y] - z &= 0, \\
-4x + 4y + (D-5)[z] &= 0.
\end{aligned}$$

# Chapter 5

We use the second equation to express $z$ in terms of $x$ and $y$.

$$z = -x + D[y]. \qquad (5.10)$$

Substituting this expression into the other two equations, we obtain

$$(D-1)[x] - 2y + (-x + D[y]) = 0,$$
$$-4x + 4y + (D-5)[-x + D[y]] = 0$$

$$\Rightarrow \qquad \begin{aligned} (D-2)[x] + (D-2)[y]) &= 0, \\ -(D-1)[x] + (D^2 - 5D + 4)[y] &= 0. \end{aligned} \qquad (5.11)$$

Now we eliminate $x$ by multiplying the first equation by $(D-1)$, the second equation – by $(D-2)$, and adding the results. This yields

$$\left\{(D-1)(D-2) + (D-2)(D^2 - 5D + 4)\right\}[y] = 0$$

$$\Rightarrow \quad \left\{(D-2)(D^2 - 4D + 3)\right\}[y] = 0 \quad \Rightarrow \quad \left\{(D-2)(D-1)(D-3)\right\}[y] = 0.$$

The roots of the characteristic equation, $(r-2)(r-1)(r-3) = 0$, are $r = 1, 2$, and $3$. Thus, a general solution for $y$ is

$$y = c_1 e^t + c_2 e^{2t} + c_3 e^{3t}.$$

With $h := x + y$, the first equation in (5.11) can be written in the form

$$(D-2)[h] = 0 \qquad \text{or} \qquad h' - 2h = 0,$$

which has a general solution $h = Ke^{2t}$. Therefore,

$$x = h - y = -c_1 e^t + (K - c_2)e^{2t} - c_3 e^{3t}.$$

To find $K$, we substitute the above solutions $x(t)$ and $y(t)$, with $c_1 = c_3 = 0$, into the second equation in (5.11). Thus we get

$$-(D-1)\left[(K - c_2)e^{2t}\right] + (D^2 - 5D + 4)\left[c_2 e^{2t}\right] = 0$$

$$\Rightarrow \quad -(K - c_2)e^{2t} + (4(c_2) - 5(2c_2) + 4(c_2))e^{2t} = 0$$

$$\Rightarrow \quad -K - c_2 = 0 \quad \Rightarrow \quad K = -c_2.$$

270

Hence,

$$x = -c_1 e^t - 2c_2 e^{2t} - c_3 e^{3t} .$$

Finally, we find $z$ using (5.10).

$$z = -\left(-c_1 e^t - 2c_2 e^{2t} - c_3 e^{3t}\right) + \left(c_1 e^t + c_2 e^{2t} + c_3 e^{3t}\right)' = 2c_1 e^t + 4c_2 e^{2t} + 4c_3 e^{3t} .$$

**27.** We eliminate $z$ by expressing

$$z = \frac{1}{4}\left(-x' + 4x\right) = -\frac{1}{4}(D-4)[x] \tag{5.12}$$

from the first equation and substituting (5.12) into the second and third equations. We obtain

$$2\left\{-\frac{1}{4}(D-4)[x]\right\} + (D-4)[y] = 0,$$

$$2x + 4y + D\left[-\frac{1}{4}(D-4)[x]\right] - 4\left\{-\frac{1}{4}(D-4)[x]\right\} = 0.$$

After some algebra, the above system simplifies to

$$-(D-4)[x] + 2(D-4)[y] = 0,$$

$$\left(D^2 - 8D + 8\right)[x] - 16y = 0.$$

We use the second equation to find that

$$y = \frac{1}{16}\left(D^2 - 8D + 8\right)[x]. \tag{5.13}$$

Then the first equation becomes

$$-(D-4)[x] + 2(D-4)\left[\frac{1}{16}\left(D^2 - 8D + 8\right)[x]\right] = 0$$

$$\Rightarrow \quad (D-4)\left\{-1 + \frac{1}{8}\left(D^2 - 8D + 8\right)\right\}[x] = 0 \quad \Rightarrow \quad (D-4)D(D-8)[x] = 0.$$

Solving the characteristic equation, we get $r = 0, 4$, and $8$; so

$$x = c_1 e^{8t} + c_2 e^{4t} + c_3 .$$

Chapter 5

Substitution of this solution into (5.12) and (5.13) yield

$$z = \frac{1}{4}(-x' + 4x) = -c_1 e^{8t} + c_3,$$

$$y = \frac{1}{16}(x'' - 8x' + 8x) = \frac{1}{2}\left(c_1 e^{8t} - c_2 e^{4t} + c_3\right).$$

**29.** We begin by expressing the system in operator notation

$$(D - \lambda)[x] + y = 0,$$
$$-3x + (D - 1)[y] = 0.$$

We eliminate $y$ by applying $(D - 1)$ to the first equation and subtracting the second equation from it. This gives

$$\{(D - 1)(D - \lambda) - (-3)\}[x] = 0$$

$$\Rightarrow \quad \{D^2 - (\lambda + 1)D + (\lambda + 3)\}[x] = 0. \tag{5.14}$$

Note that since the given system is homogeneous, $y(t)$ also satisfies this equation (compare (7) and (8) on page 247 of the text). So, we can investigate solutions $x(t)$ only. The auxiliary equation, $r^2 - (\lambda + 1)r + (\lambda + 3) = 0$, has roots

$$r_1 = \frac{(\lambda + 1) - \sqrt{\Delta}}{2}, \qquad r_2 = \frac{(\lambda + 1) + \sqrt{\Delta}}{2},$$

where the discriminant $\Delta := (\lambda + 1)^2 - 4(\lambda + 3)$. We consider two cases:

i) If $\lambda + 3 < 0$, i.e. $\lambda < -3$, then $\Delta > (\lambda + 1)^2$ and the root

$$r_2 > \frac{(\lambda + 1) + |\lambda + 1|}{2} = 0.$$

Therefore, the solution $x(t) = e^{r_2 t}$ is unbounded as $t \to +\infty$.

ii) If $\lambda + 3 \geq 0$, i.e. $\lambda \geq -3$, then $\Delta \leq (\lambda + 1)^2$. If $\Delta < 0$, then a fundamental solution set to (5.14) is

$$\left\{ e^{(\lambda+1)t/2} \cos\left(\frac{\sqrt{-\Delta}\, t}{2}\right), \ e^{(\lambda+1)t/2} \sin\left(\frac{\sqrt{-\Delta}\, t}{2}\right) \right\}. \tag{5.15}$$

If $\Delta \geq 0$, then $\sqrt{\Delta} < |\lambda + 1|$ and a fundamental solution set is

$$\begin{cases} \{e^{r_1 t}, e^{r_2 t}\}, & \text{if } \Delta > 0, \\ \{e^{r_1 t}, te^{r_1 t}\}, & \text{if } \Delta = 0, \end{cases} \tag{5.16}$$

where both roots $r_1$, $r_2$ are non-positive if and only if $\lambda \leq -1$. For $\lambda = -1$ we have $\Delta = (-1 + 1)^2 - 4(-1 + 3) < 0$, and we have a particular case of the fundamental solution set (5.15) (without exponential term) consisting of bounded functions. Finally, if $\lambda < -1$, then $r_1 < 0$, $r_2 \leq 0$, and all the functions listed in (5.15), (5.16) are bounded.

Any solution $x(t)$ is a linear combination of fundamental solutions and, therefore, all solutions $x(t)$ are bounded if and only if $-3 \leq \lambda \leq -1$.

**31.** Solving this problem, we follow the arguments described in Section 5.1, page 242 of the text, i.e., $x(t)$, the mass of salt in the tank A, and $y(t)$, the mass of salt in the tank B, satisfy the system

$$\frac{dx}{dt} = \text{input}_A - \text{output}_A,$$

$$\tag{5.17}$$

$$\frac{dy}{dt} = \text{input}_B - \text{output}_B,$$

with initial conditions $x(0) = 0$, $y(0) = 20$. It is important to notice that the volume of each tank stays at 100 L because the net flow rate into each tank is the same as the net outflow. Next we observe that "input$_A$" consists of the salt coming from outside, which is

$$0.2 \, \text{kg/L} \cdot 6 \, \text{L/min} = 1.2 \, \text{kg/min},$$

and the salt coming from the tank B, which is given by

$$\frac{y(t)}{100} \, \text{kg/L} \cdot 1 \, \text{L/min} = \frac{y(t)}{100} \, \text{kg/min}.$$

Thus,

$$\text{input}_A = \left[ 1.2 + \frac{y(t)}{100} \right] \, \text{kg/min}.$$

# Chapter 5

"output$_A$" consists of two flows: one is going out of the system and the other one is going to the tank B. So,

$$\text{output}_A = \frac{x(t)}{100}\,\text{kg/L} \cdot (4+3)\,\text{L/min} = \frac{7x(t)}{100}\,\text{kg/min},$$

and the first equation in (5.17) becomes

$$\frac{dx}{dt} = 1.2 + \frac{y}{100} - \frac{7x}{100}.$$

Similarly, the second equation in (5.17) can be written as

$$\frac{dy}{dt} = \frac{3x}{100} - \frac{3y}{100}.$$

Rewriting this system in the operator form, we obtain

$$
\begin{aligned}
(D+0.07)[x] - 0.01y &= 1.2\,, \\
-0.03x + (D+0.03)[y] &= 0\,.
\end{aligned}
\tag{5.18}
$$

Eliminating $y$ yields

$$\{(D+0.07)(D+0.03) - (-0.01)(-0.03)\}\,[x] = (D+0.03)[1.2] = 0.036\,,$$

which simplifies to

$$\left(D^2 + 0.1D + 0.0018\right)[x] = 0.036\,. \tag{5.19}$$

The auxiliary equation, $r^2 + 0.1r + 0.0018 = 0$, has roots

$$r_1 = -\frac{1}{20} - \sqrt{\frac{1}{400} - \frac{18}{10000}} = -\frac{1}{20} - \frac{\sqrt{7}}{100} = \frac{-5-\sqrt{7}}{100} \approx -0.0765\,,$$

$$r_2 = \frac{-5+\sqrt{7}}{100} \approx -0.0235\,.$$

Therefore, the general solution the corresponding homogeneous equation is

$$x_h(t) = C_1 e^{r_1 t} + C_2 e^{r_2 t}.$$

Since the nonhomogeneous term in (5.19) is a constant (0.036), we are looking for a particular solution of the form $x_p(t) = A = \text{const}$. Substituting into (5.19) yields

$$0.0018A = 0.036 \qquad \Rightarrow \qquad A = 20,$$

and the general solution, $x(t)$, is

$$x(t) = x_h(t) + x_p(t) = C_1 e^{r_1 t} + C_2 e^{r_2 t} + 20.$$

From the first equation in (5.18) we find

$$\begin{aligned}
y(t) &= 100 \cdot \{(D + 0.07)[x] - 1.2\} = 100 \frac{dx}{dt} + 7x(t) - 120 \\
&= 100 \left\{ r_1 C_1 e^{r_1 t} + r_2 C_2 e^{r_2 t} \right\} + 7 \left\{ C_1 e^{r_1 t} + C_2 e^{r_2 t} + 20 \right\} - 120 \\
&= \left( 2 - \sqrt{7} \right) C_1 e^{r_1 t} + \left( 2 + \sqrt{7} \right) C_2 e^{r_2 t} + 20.
\end{aligned}$$

The initial conditions imply

$$\begin{aligned}
0 &= x(0) = C_1 + C_2 + 20, \\
20 &= y(0) = \left( 2 - \sqrt{7} \right) C_1 + \left( 2 + \sqrt{7} \right) C_2 + 20
\end{aligned}$$

$$\Rightarrow \quad \begin{aligned}
C_1 + C_2 &= -20, \\
\left( 2 - \sqrt{7} \right) C_1 + \left( 2 + \sqrt{7} \right) C_2 &= 0
\end{aligned}$$

$$\Rightarrow \quad C_1 = - \left( 10 + \frac{20}{\sqrt{7}} \right), \qquad C_2 = - \left( 10 - \frac{20}{\sqrt{7}} \right).$$

Thus the solution to the problem is

$$x(t) = - \left( 10 + \frac{20}{\sqrt{7}} \right) e^{r_1 t} - \left( 10 - \frac{20}{\sqrt{7}} \right) e^{r_2 t} + 20 \text{ (kg)},$$

$$y(t) = \frac{30}{\sqrt{7}} e^{r_1 t} - \frac{30}{\sqrt{7}} e^{r_2 t} + 20 \text{ (kg)}.$$

**33.** Since no solution flows in or out of the system from the tank B, we conclude that the solution flows from the tank B to the tank A with the same rate as it does from A to B, that is, $1 \text{ L/min}$. Furthermore, the solution flows in and out of the tank A with the same rate, $4 \text{ L/min}$, and so the volume of the solution in the tank A (as well as in the tank B) remains constant, $100 \text{ L}$. Thus, with $x(t)$ and $y(t)$ denoting the amount of salt in the tanks A and B, respectively, the law "rate of change = input rate − output rate" becomes

*Tank* A:

$$x' = \left( 4 \text{ L/min} \cdot 0.2 \text{ kg/L} + 1 \text{ L/min} \cdot \frac{y}{100} \text{ kg/L} \right) - \frac{x}{100} \text{ kg/L} \cdot (1 \text{ L/min} + 4 \text{ L/min});$$

# Chapter 5

*Tank* B:

$$y' = 1\,\text{L/min} \cdot \frac{x}{100}\,\text{kg/L} - 1\,\text{L/min} \cdot \frac{y}{100}\,\text{kg/L}.$$

Hence, we obtain the system

$$x' = 0.8 - \frac{x}{20} + \frac{y}{100},$$
$$y' = \frac{x}{100} - \frac{y}{100}.$$

From the second equation, we find that $x = 100y' + y$. Substitution into the first equation yields

$$(100y' + y)' = 0.8 - \frac{100y' + y}{20} + \frac{y}{100}$$

$$\Rightarrow \qquad 100y'' + 6y' + \frac{1}{25}y = 0.8 \qquad \Rightarrow \qquad y'' + 0.06y' + 0.0004y = 0.008 . \quad (5.20)$$

The characteristic equation $r^2 + 0.06r + 0.0004 = 0$ of the corresponding homogeneous equation has roots

$$r = \frac{-0.06 \pm \sqrt{(0.06)^2 - 4(1)(0.0004)}}{2} = \frac{-3 \pm \sqrt{5}}{100},$$

and so

$$y_h(t) = c_1 e^{(-3-\sqrt{5})t/100} + c_2 e^{(-3+\sqrt{5})t/100}$$

is a general solution to the homogeneous equation. We now look for a particular solution of the form $y_p(t) = c$. Substitution into (5.20) gives

$$0.0004c = 0.008 \qquad \Rightarrow \qquad c = \frac{0.008}{0.0004} = 20.$$

Thus

$$y(t) = y_p(t) + y_h(t) = 20 + c_1 e^{(-3-\sqrt{5})t/100} + c_2 e^{(-3+\sqrt{5})t/100} \qquad (5.21)$$

is a general solution to (5.20). Then

$$x(t) = y + 100y' = 20 + (1 - 3 - \sqrt{5})c_1 e^{(-3-\sqrt{5})t/100} + (1 - 3 + \sqrt{5})c_2 e^{(-3+\sqrt{5})t/100}$$
$$= 20 - (2 + \sqrt{5})c_1 e^{(-3-\sqrt{5})t/100} + (-2 + \sqrt{5})c_2 e^{(-3+\sqrt{5})t/100}. \qquad (5.22)$$

Next, we use the initial condition, $x(0) = 0$, $y(0) = 20$, to find values of $c_1$ and $c_2$.

$$20 - (2 + \sqrt{5})c_1 + (-2 + \sqrt{5})c_2 = 0, \qquad \Rightarrow \qquad c_1 = 10/\sqrt{5},$$
$$20 + c_1 + c_2 = 20 \qquad\qquad\qquad\qquad\qquad c_2 = -10/\sqrt{5}.$$

With these values, the solution given in (5.21), (5.22) becomes

$$x(t) = 20 - \left(\frac{20 + 10\sqrt{5}}{\sqrt{5}}\right) e^{(-3 - \sqrt{5})t/100} + \left(\frac{20 - 10\sqrt{5}}{\sqrt{5}}\right) e^{(-3 + \sqrt{5})t/100},$$

$$y(t) = 20 + \left(\frac{10}{\sqrt{5}}\right) e^{(-3 - \sqrt{5})t/100} - \left(\frac{10}{\sqrt{5}}\right) e^{(-3 + \sqrt{5})t/100}.$$

**35.** Let $x(t)$ and $y(t)$ denote the temperatures at time $t$ in zones $A$ and $B$, respectively. Therefore, the rate of change of temperature in zone $A$ will be $x'(t)$ and in zone $B$ will be $y'(t)$. We can apply Newton's law of cooling to help us express these rates of change in an alternate manner. Thus, we observe that the rate of change of the temperature in zone $A$ due to the outside temperature is $k_1[100 - x(t)]$ and due to the temperature in zone $B$ is $k_2[y(t) - x(t)]$. Since the time constant for heat transfer between zone $A$ and the outside is 2 hrs $(= 1/k_1)$, we see that $k_1 = 1/2$. Similarly, we see that $1/k_2 = 4$ which implies that $k_2 = 1/4$. Therefore, since there is no heating or cooling source in zone $A$, we can write the equation for the rate of change of the temperature in the attic as

$$x'(t) = \frac{1}{2}[100 - x(t)] + \frac{1}{4}[y(t) - x(t)].$$

In the same way, we see that the rate of change of the temperature in zone $B$ due to the temperature of the attic is $k_3[x(t) - y(t)]$, where $1/k_3 = 4$; and the rate of change of the temperature in this zone due to the outside temperature is $k_4[100 - y(t)]$, where $1/k_4 = 4$. In this zone, however, we must consider the cooling due to the air conditioner. Since the heat capacity of zone $B$ is $(1/2)°$F per thousand Btu and the air conditioner has the cooling capacity of 24 thousand Btu per hr, we see that the air conditioner removes heat from this zone at the rate of $(1/2) \times 24° = 12°$ F/hr. (Since heat is *removed* from the house, this rate will be negative.) By combining these observations, we see that the rate of change of the temperature in zone $B$ is given by

$$y'(t) = -12 + \frac{1}{4}[x(t) - y(t)] + \frac{1}{4}[100 - y(t)].$$

# Chapter 5

By simplifying these equations, we observe that this cooling problem satisfies the system

$$4x'(t) + 3x(t) - y(t) = 200,$$
$$-x'(t) + 4y'(t) + 2y(t) = 52.$$

In operator notation, this system becomes

$$(4D + 3)[x] - [y] = 200,$$
$$-[x] + (4D + 2)[y] = 52.$$

Since we are interested in the temperature in the attic, $x(t)$, we will eliminate the function $y(t)$ from the system above by applying $(4D+2)$ to the first equation and adding the resulting equations to obtain

$$\{(4D + 2)(4D + 3) - 1\}[x] = (4D + 2)[200] + 52 = 452$$
$$\Rightarrow \quad \left(16D^2 + 20D + 5\right)[x] = 452. \tag{5.23}$$

This last equation is a linear equation with constant coefficients whose corresponding homogeneous equation has the associated auxiliary equation $16r^2 + 20r + 5 = 0$. By the quadratic formula, the roots to this auxiliary equation are

$$r_1 = \frac{-5 + \sqrt{5}}{8} \approx -0.345 \quad \text{and} \quad r_2 = \frac{-5 - \sqrt{5}}{8} \approx -0.905 \,.$$

Therefore, the homogeneous equation associated with this equation has a general solution given by

$$x_h(t) = c_1 e^{r_1 t} + c_2 e^{r_2 t},$$

where $r_1$ and $r_2$ are given above. By the method of undetermined coefficients, we observe that a particular solution to equation (5.23) will have the form

$$x_p(t) = A \quad \Rightarrow \quad x_p'(t) = 0 \quad \Rightarrow \quad x_p''(t) = 0.$$

Substituting these expressions into equation (5.23) yields

$$16x_p'' + 20x_p' + 5x_p = 5A = 452 \quad \Rightarrow \quad A = 90.4 \,.$$

278

Thus, a particular solution to the differential equation given in (5.23) is $x_p(t) = 90.4$ and the general solution to this equation will be

$$x(t) = c_1 e^{r_1 t} + c_2 e^{r_2 t} + 90.4 \,,$$

where $r_1 = (-5 + \sqrt{5})/8$ and $r_2 = (-5 - \sqrt{5})/8$. To determine the maximum temperature of the attic, we will assume that zones $A$ and $B$ have sufficiently cool initial temperatures. (So that, for example, $c_1$ and $c_2$ are negative.) Since $r_1$ and $r_2$ are negative, as $t$ goes to infinity, $c_1 e^{r_1 t}$ and $c_2 e^{r_2 t}$ each go to zero. Therefore, the maximum temperature that can be attained in the attic will be

$$\lim_{t \to \infty} x(t) = 90.4° \text{ F}.$$

**37.** In this problem, we combine the idea exploded in interconnected tanks problems,

$$\text{rate of change} = \text{rate in} - \text{rate out}, \tag{5.24}$$

with the Newton's law of cooling

$$\frac{dT}{dt} = K(T - M). \tag{5.25}$$

Let $x(t)$ and $y(t)$ denote temperatures in rooms A and B, respectively.

*Room A.* It gets temperature only from the heater with a rate

$$\text{rate in} = 80,000 \, \text{Btu/h} \cdot \frac{1/4°}{1000 \, \text{Btu}} = 20°/\text{h}.$$

Temperature goes out of the room A into the room B and outside with different coefficients of proportionality in (5.25): $K_1 = 1/2$ and $K_2 = 1/4$, respectively. Therefore,

$$
\begin{aligned}
\text{rate out} &= \text{rate into B} + \text{rate outside} \\
&= \frac{1}{2}(x - y) + \frac{1}{4}(x - 0) = \frac{3}{4}x - \frac{1}{2}y.
\end{aligned}
$$

Thus, (5.24) implies that

$$x' = 20 - \left( \frac{3}{4}x - \frac{1}{2}y \right) = 20 - \frac{3}{4}x + \frac{1}{2}y.$$

Chapter 5

*Room* B. Similarly, we obtain

$$y' = \left[1000 \cdot \frac{2}{1000} + \frac{1}{2}(x-y)\right] - \frac{1}{5}(y-0) = 2 + \frac{1}{2}x - \frac{7}{10}y.$$

Hence, the system governing the temperature exchange is

$$x' = 20 - (3/4)x + (1/2)y,$$
$$y' = 2 + (1/2)x - (7/10)y.$$

We find the critical points of this system by solving

$$\begin{aligned} 20 - (3/4)x + (1/2)y &= 0, \\ 2 + (1/2)x - (7/10)y &= 0 \end{aligned} \Rightarrow \begin{aligned} 3x - 2y &= 80, \\ -5x + 7y &= 20 \end{aligned} \Rightarrow \begin{aligned} x &= 600/11\,, \\ y &= 460/11\,. \end{aligned}$$

Therefore, $(600/11, 460/11)$ is the only critical point of the system. Analyzing the direction field, we conclude that $(600/11, 460/11)$ is an asymptotically stable node. Hence,

$$\lim_{t\to\infty} y(t) = \frac{460}{11} \approx 41.8°\text{F}.$$

(One can also find an explicit solution $y(t) = 460/11 + c_1 e^{r_1 t} + c_2 e^{r_2 t}$, where $r_1 < 0$, $r_2 < 0$, to conclude that $y(t) \to 460/11$ as $t \to \infty$.)

39. Let $y$ be an arbitrary function differentiable as many times as necessary. Note that, for a differential operator, say, $A$, $A[y]$ is a function, and so we can use commutative, associative, and distributive laws operating such functions.

(a) It is straightforward that

$$(A + B)[y] := A[y] + B[y] = B[y] + A[y] =: (B + A)[y].$$

To prove commutativity of the multiplication, we will use the linearity of the differential operator $D$, that is, $D[\alpha x + \beta y] = \alpha D[x] + \beta D[y]$ and the fact that $D^i D^j = D^{i+j} = D^j D^i$. For the latter,

$$\left(D^i D^j\right)[y] := D^i\left[D^j[y]\right] = \left(y^{(j)}\right)^{(i)} = y^{(i+j)} = \left(y^{(i)}\right)^{(j)} = D^j\left[D^i[y]\right] =: \left(D^j D^i\right)[y].$$

280

Thus we have

$$(AB)[y] := A\big[B[y]\big] = \left(\sum_{j=0}^{2} a_j D^j\right)\left[\left(\sum_{i=0}^{2} b_i D^i\right)[y]\right]$$

$$:= \left(\sum_{j=0}^{2} a_j D^j\right)\left[\sum_{i=0}^{2} b_i D^i[y]\right] := \sum_{j=0}^{2}\left\{a_j D^j\left[\sum_{i=0}^{2} b_i D^i[y]\right]\right\}$$

$$= \sum_{j=0}^{2}\sum_{i=0}^{2}\left(a_j D^j b_i D^i\right)[y] = \sum_{i=0}^{2}\sum_{j=0}^{2}\left(b_i D^i a_j D^j\right)[y]$$

$$= \sum_{i=0}^{2}\left\{b_i D^i\left[\sum_{j=0}^{2} a_j D^j[y]\right]\right\} =: \left(\sum_{i=0}^{2} b_i D^i\right)\left[\sum_{j=0}^{2} a_j D^j[y]\right]$$

$$=: \left(\sum_{i=0}^{2} b_i D^i\right)\left[\left(\sum_{j=0}^{2} a_j D^j\right)[y]\right] = B\big[A[y]\big] =: (BA)[y].$$

**(b)** We have

$$\{(A+B)+C\}[y] := (A+B)[y] + C[y] := (A[y] + B[y]) + C[y]$$

$$= A[y] + (B[y] + C[y]) =: A[y] + (B+C)[y] =: \{A+(B+C)\}[y]$$

and

$$\{(AB)C\}[y] := (AB)\big[C[y]\big] := A\Big[B\big[C[y]\big]\Big] =: A\big[(BC)[y]\big] =: \{A(BC)\}[y].$$

**(c)** Using the linearity of differential operators, we obtain

$$\{A(B+C)\}[y] := A\big[(B+C)[y]\big] := A\big[B[y] + C[y]\big]$$

$$= A\big[B[y]\big] + A\big[C[y]\big] =: (AB)[y] + (AC)[y] =: \{(AB)+(AC)\}[y].$$

**41.** As it was noticed in Example 2, we can treat a "polynomial" in $D$, that is, an expression of the form $p(D) = \sum_{i=0}^{n} a_i D^i$, as a regular polynomial, i.e., $p(r) = \sum_{i=0}^{n} a_i r^i$, while performing arithmetic operations. Hence, the factorization problem for $p(D)$ is equivalent to the factorization problem for $p(r)$, which is the same as finding its roots.

**(a)** $r = \dfrac{-3 \pm \sqrt{3^2 - 4(-4)}}{2} = \dfrac{-3 \pm 5}{2} = -4, 1 \quad \Rightarrow \quad D^2 + 3D - 4 = (D+4)(D-1).$

# Chapter 5

**(b)** $r = \dfrac{-1 \pm \sqrt{1^2 - 4(-6)}}{2} = \dfrac{-1 \pm 5}{2} = -3, 2 \quad \Rightarrow \quad D^2 + D - 6 = (D+3)(D-2)$.

**(c)** $r = \dfrac{-9 \pm \sqrt{9^2 - 4(-5)2}}{4} = \dfrac{-9 \pm 11}{4} = -5, 1/2 \quad \Rightarrow \quad 2D^2 + 9D - 5 = (D+5)(2D-1)$.

**(d)** $r = \pm\sqrt{2} \quad \Rightarrow \quad D^2 - 2 = (D + \sqrt{2})(D - \sqrt{2})$.

## EXERCISES 5.3: Solving Systems and Higher–Order Equations Numerically, page 261

**1.** We isolate $y''(t)$ first and obtain an equivalent equation

$$y''(t) = 3y(t) - ty'(t) + t^2 .$$

Denoting $x_1 := y$, $x_2 := y'$ we conclude that

$$x_1' = y' = x_2 ,$$
$$x_2' = (y')' = y'' = 3y - ty' + t^2 = 3x_1 - tx_2 + t^2 ,$$

with initial conditions $x_1(0) = y(0) = 3$, $x_2(0) = y'(0) = -6$. Therefore, given initial value problem is equivalent to

$$x_1' = x_2 ,$$
$$x_2' = 3x_1 - tx_2 + t^2 ,$$
$$x_1(0) = 3, \quad x_2(0) = -6.$$

**3.** Isolating $y^{(4)}(t)$, we get

$$y^{(4)}(t) = y^{(3)}(t) - 7y(t) + \cos t .$$

In this problem, we need four new variables – for $y(t)$, $y'(t)$, $y''(t)$, and $y^{(3)}(t)$. Thus we denote

$$x_1 = y, \qquad x_2 = y', \qquad x_3 = y'', \quad \text{and} \quad x_4 = y^{(3)} .$$

The initial conditions then become

$$x_1(0) = y(0) = 1, \ x_2(0) = y'(0) = 1, \ x_3(0) = y''(0) = 0, \ x_4(0) = y^{(3)}(0) = 2.$$

We have

$$x_1' = y' = x_2 ,$$

$$x_2' = (y')' = y'' = x_3,$$

$$x_3' = (y'')' = y^{(3)} = x_4,$$

$$x_4' = \left(y^{(3)}\right)' = y^{(4)} = y^{(3)} - 7y + \cos t = x_4 - 7x_1 + \cos t.$$

Hence, the required initial value problem for a system in normal form is

$$x_1' = x_2,$$

$$x_2' = x_3,$$

$$x_3' = x_4,$$

$$x_4' = x_4 - 7x_1 + \cos t,$$

$$x_1(0) = x_2(0) = 1, \quad x_3(0) = 0, \quad x_4(0) = 2.$$

**5.** First we express the given system as

$$x'' = x' - y + 2t,$$

$$y'' = x - y - 1.$$

Setting $x_1 = x$, $x_2 = x'$, $x_3 = y$, $x_4 = y'$ we obtain

$$
\begin{aligned}
x_1' &= x' = x_2, \\
x_2' &= x'' = x_2 - x_3 + 2t, \\
x_3' &= y' = x_4, \\
x_4' &= y'' = x_1 - x_3 - 1
\end{aligned}
\qquad \Rightarrow \qquad
\begin{aligned}
x_1' &= x_2, \\
x_2' &= x_2 - x_3 + 2t, \\
x_3' &= x_4, \\
x_4' &= x_1 - x_3 - 1
\end{aligned}
$$

with initial conditions $x_1(3) = 5$, $x_2(3) = 2$, $x_3(3) = 1$, and $x_4(3) = -1$.

**7.** In an equivalent form, we have a system

$$x''' = y + t,$$

$$y'' = \frac{2y - 2x'' + 1}{5}.$$

Setting

$$x_1 = x, \quad x_2 = x', \quad x_3 = x'', \quad x_4 = y, \quad x_5 = y',$$

Chapter 5

we obtain a system in normal form

$$x_1' = x_2 \, ,$$
$$x_2' = x_3 \, ,$$
$$x_3' = x_4 + t \, ,$$
$$x_4' = x_5 \, ,$$
$$x_5' = \frac{1}{5}\left(2x_4 - 2x_3 + 1\right)$$

with initial conditions

$$x_1(0) = x_2(0) = x_3(0) = 4, \quad x_4(0) = x_5(0) = 1.$$

9. To see how the improved Euler's method can be extended let's recall, from Section 3.6, the improved Euler's method (pages 127–128 of the text). For the initial value problem

$$x' = f(t, x), \qquad x(t_0) = x_0 \, ,$$

the recursive formulas for the improved Euler's method are

$$t_{n+1} = t_n + h,$$
$$x_{n+1} = x_n + \frac{h}{2}\left[f(t_n, x_n) + f(t_n + h, x_n + hf(t_n, x_n))\right],$$

where $h$ is the step size. Now suppose we want to approximate the solution $x_1(t)$, $x_2(t)$ to the system

$$x_1' = f_1(t, x_1, x_2) \qquad \text{and} \qquad x_2' = f_2(t, x_1, x_2),$$

that satisfies the initial conditions

$$x_1(t_0) = a_1, \qquad x_2(t_0) = a_2 \, .$$

Let $x_{1;n}$ and $x_{2;n}$ denote approximations to $x_1(t_n)$ and $x_2(t_n)$, respectively, where $t_n = t_0 + nh$ for $n = 0, 1, 2, \ldots$. The recursive formulas for the improved Euler's method are obtained by forming the vector analogue of the scalar formula. We obtain

$$t_{n+1} = t_n + h,$$

$$x_{1;n+1} = x_{1;n} + \frac{h}{2} \left[ f_1(t_n, x_{1;n}, x_{2;n}) \right.$$
$$+ f_1(t_n + h, x_{1;n} + h f_1(t_n, x_{1;n}, x_{2;n}), x_{2;n} + h f_2(t_n, x_{1;n}, x_{2;n})) \left. \right],$$
$$x_{2;n+1} = x_{2;n} + \frac{h}{2} \left[ f_2(t_n, x_{1;n}, x_{2;n}) \right.$$
$$+ f_2(t_n + h, x_{1;n} + h f_1(t_n, x_{1;n}, x_{2;n}), x_{2;n} + h f_2(t_n, x_{1;n}, x_{2;n})) \left. \right].$$

The approach can be used more generally for systems of $m$ equations in normal form.

Suppose we want to approximate the solution $x_1(t)$, $x_2(t)$, ..., $x_m(t)$ to the system

$$x_1' = f_1\left(t, x_1, x_2, \ldots, x_m\right),$$
$$x_2' = f_2\left(t, x_1, x_2, \ldots, x_m\right),$$
$$\vdots$$
$$x_m' = f_m\left(t, x_1, x_2, \ldots, x_m\right),$$

with the initial conditions

$$x_1(t_0) = a_1, \quad x_2(t_0) = a_2, \quad \ldots, \quad x_m(t_0) = a_m.$$

We adapt the recursive formulas above to obtain

$$t_{n+1} = t_n + h, \qquad n = 0, 1, 2, \ldots;$$
$$x_{1;n+1} = x_{1;n} + \frac{h}{2} \left[ f_1(t_n, x_{1;n}, x_{2;n}, \ldots, x_{m;n}) + f_1(t_n + h, x_{1;n} + h f_1(t_n, x_{1;n}, x_{2;n}, \ldots, x_{m;n}), \right.$$
$$\left. x_{2;n} + h f_2(t_n, x_{1;n}, x_{2;n}, \ldots, x_{m;n}), \ldots, x_{m;n} + h f_m(t_n, x_{1;n}, x_{2;n}, \ldots, x_{m;n})) \right],$$
$$x_{2;n+1} = x_{2;n} + \frac{h}{2} \left[ f_2(t_n, x_{1;n}, x_{2;n}, \ldots, x_{m;n}) + f_2(t_n + h, x_{1;n} + h f_1(t_n, x_{1;n}, x_{2;n}, \ldots, x_{m;n}), \right.$$
$$\left. x_{2;n} + h f_2(t_n, x_{1;n}, x_{2;n}, \ldots, x_{m;n}), \ldots, x_{m;n} + h f_m(t_n, x_{1;n}, x_{2;n}, \ldots, x_{m;n})) \right],$$
$$\vdots$$
$$x_{m;n+1} = x_{m;n} + \frac{h}{2} \left[ f_m(t_n, x_{1;n}, x_{2;n}, \ldots, x_{m;n}) + f_m(t_n + h, x_{1;n} + h f_1(t_n, x_{1;n}, x_{2;n}, \ldots, x_{m;n}), \right.$$
$$\left. x_{2;n} + h f_2(t_n, x_{1;n}, x_{2;n}, \ldots, x_{m;n}), \ldots, x_{m;n} + h f_m(t_n, x_{1;n}, x_{2;n}, \ldots, x_{m;n})) \right].$$

**11.** See the answer in the text.

# Chapter 5

**13.** See the answer in the text.

**15.** See the answer in the text.

**17.** Let $x_1 := u$ and $x_2 := v$, and denote the independent variable by $t$ (in order to be consistent with formulas in Section 5.3). In new notation, we have an initial value problem

$$x_1' = 3x_1 - 4x_2,$$
$$x_2' = 2x_1 - 3x_2,$$
$$x_1(0) = x_2(0) = 1$$

for a system in normal form. Here

$$f_1(t, x_1, x_2) = 3x_1 - 4x_2, \qquad f_2(t, x_1, x_2) = 2x_1 - 3x_2.$$

Thus formulas for $k_{i,j}$'s in vectorized Runge-Kutta algorithm become

$$k_{1,1} = h(3x_{1;n} - 4x_{2;n}),$$
$$k_{2,1} = h(2x_{1;n} - 3x_{2;n}),$$
$$k_{1,2} = h\left[3\left(x_{1;n} + \frac{k_{1,1}}{2}\right) - 4\left(x_{2;n} + \frac{k_{2,1}}{2}\right)\right],$$
$$k_{2,2} = h\left[2\left(x_{1;n} + \frac{k_{1,1}}{2}\right) - 3\left(x_{2;n} + \frac{k_{2,1}}{2}\right)\right],$$
$$k_{1,3} = h\left[3\left(x_{1;n} + \frac{k_{1,2}}{2}\right) - 4\left(x_{2;n} + \frac{k_{2,2}}{2}\right)\right],$$
$$k_{2,3} = h\left[2\left(x_{1;n} + \frac{k_{1,2}}{2}\right) - 3\left(x_{2;n} + \frac{k_{2,2}}{2}\right)\right],$$
$$k_{1,4} = h\left[3\left(x_{1;n} + k_{1,3}\right) - 4\left(x_{2;n} + k_{2,3}\right)\right],$$
$$k_{2,4} = h\left[2\left(x_{1;n} + k_{1,3}\right) - 3\left(x_{2;n} + k_{2,3}\right)\right].$$

With the inputs $t_0 = 0$, $x_{1;0} = x_{2;0} = 1$, and step size $h = 1$ we compute

$$k_{1,1} = h(3x_{1;0} - 4x_{2;0}) = 3(1) - 4(1) = -1,$$
$$k_{2,1} = h(2x_{1;0} - 3x_{2;0}) = 2(1) - 3(1) = -1,$$
$$k_{1,2} = h\left[3\left(x_{1;0} + \frac{k_{1,1}}{2}\right) - 4\left(x_{2;0} + \frac{k_{2,1}}{2}\right)\right] = 3\left(1 + \frac{-1}{2}\right) - 4\left(1 + \frac{-1}{2}\right) = -\frac{1}{2},$$

$$k_{2,2} = h\left[2\left(x_{1;0} + \frac{k_{1,1}}{2}\right) - 3\left(x_{2;0} + \frac{k_{2,1}}{2}\right)\right] = 2\left(1 + \frac{-1}{2}\right) - 3\left(1 + \frac{-1}{2}\right) = -\frac{1}{2},$$

$$k_{1,3} = h\left[3\left(x_{1;0} + \frac{k_{1,2}}{2}\right) - 4\left(x_{2;0} + \frac{k_{2,2}}{2}\right)\right] = 3\left(1 + \frac{-1/2}{2}\right) - 4\left(1 + \frac{-1/2}{2}\right) = -\frac{3}{4},$$

$$k_{2,3} = h\left[2\left(x_{1;0} + \frac{k_{1,2}}{2}\right) - 3\left(x_{2;0} + \frac{k_{2,2}}{2}\right)\right] = 2\left(1 + \frac{-1/2}{2}\right) - 3\left(1 + \frac{-1/2}{2}\right) = -\frac{3}{4},$$

$$k_{1,4} = h\left[3\left(x_{1;0} + k_{1,3}\right) - 4\left(x_{2;0} + k_{2,3}\right)\right] = 3\left(1 + \frac{-3}{4}\right) - 4\left(1 + \frac{-3}{4}\right) = -\frac{1}{4},$$

$$k_{2,4} = h\left[2\left(x_{1;0} + k_{1,3}\right) - 3\left(x_{2;0} + k_{2,3}\right)\right] = 2\left(1 + \frac{-3}{4}\right) - 3\left(1 + \frac{-3}{4}\right) = -\frac{1}{4}.$$

Using the recursive formulas, we find $t_1 = t_0 + h = 0 + 1 = 1$ and

$$x_{1;1} = x_{1;0} + \frac{1}{6}\left(k_{1,1} + 2k_{1,2} + 2k_{1,3} + k_{1,4}\right) = 1 + \frac{(-1) + 2(-1/2) + 2(-3/4) + (-1/4)}{6} = \frac{3}{8},$$

$$x_{2;1} = x_{2;0} + \frac{1}{6}\left(k_{2,1} + 2k_{2,2} + 2k_{2,3} + k_{2,4}\right) = 1 + \frac{(-1) + 2(-1/2) + 2(-3/4) + (-1/4)}{6} = \frac{3}{8}$$

as approximations to $x_1(1)$ and $x_2(1)$ with step $h = 1$.

We repeat the algorithm with $h = 2^{-m}$, $m = 1, 2, \dots$. The results of these computations are listed in Table 5-A.

Table 5–A: Approximations of the solution to Problem 17.

| $m$ | $h = 2^{-m}$ | $x_1(1; h)$ | $x_2(1; h)$ |
|---|---|---|---|
| 0 | 1.0 | 0.375 | 0.375 |
| 1 | 0.5 | 0.36817 | 0.36817 |
| 2 | 0.25 | 0.36789 | 0.36789 |

We stopped at $m = 2$, since

$$\left|x_1(1; 2^{-1}) - x_1(1; 2^{-2})\right| = \left|x_2(1; 2^{-1}) - x_2(1; 2^{-2})\right| = 0.36817 - 0.36789 = 0.00028 < 0.001.$$

Hence $u(1) = v(1) \approx 0.36789$.

# Chapter 5

**18.** For starting values we take $t_0 = 0$, $x_{0,1} = 10$, and $x_{0,2} = 15$, which are determined by the initial conditions. Here $h = 0.1$, and

$$f_1(t, x_1, x_2) = -(0.1)x_1 x_2 \,,$$

$$f_2(t, x_1, x_2) = -x_1 \,.$$

Now, using the definitions of $t_n$, $x_{i;n}$, $k_{i,1}$, $k_{i,2}$, $k_{i,3}$, and $k_{i,4}$ on page 258 of the text, we have

$$k_{1,1} = h f_1 \left( t_n, x_{1;n}, x_{2;n} \right) = -h(0.1) x_{1;n} x_{2;n} \,,$$

$$k_{2,1} = h f_2 \left( t_n, x_{1;n}, x_{2;n} \right) = -h x_{1;n} \,,$$

$$k_{1,2} = h f_1 \left( t_n + \frac{h}{2}, x_{1;n} + \frac{k_{1,1}}{2}, x_{2;n} + \frac{k_{2,1}}{2} \right) = -h(0.1) \left( x_{1;n} + \frac{k_{1,1}}{2} \right) \left( x_{2;n} + \frac{k_{2,1}}{2} \right) \,,$$

$$k_{2,2} = h f_2 \left( t_n + \frac{h}{2}, x_{1;n} + \frac{k_{1,1}}{2}, x_{2;n} + \frac{k_{2,1}}{2} \right) = -h \left( x_{1;n} + \frac{k_{1,1}}{2} \right) \,,$$

$$k_{1,3} = h f_1 \left( t_n + \frac{h}{2}, x_{1;n} + \frac{k_{1,2}}{2}, x_{2;n} + \frac{k_{2,2}}{2} \right) = -h(0.1) \left( x_{1;n} + \frac{k_{1,2}}{2} \right) \left( x_{2;n} + \frac{k_{2,2}}{2} \right) \,,$$

$$k_{2,3} = h f_2 \left( t_n + \frac{h}{2}, x_{1;n} + \frac{k_{1,2}}{2}, x_{2;n} + \frac{k_{2,2}}{2} \right) = -h \left( x_{1;n} + \frac{k_{1,2}}{2} \right) \,,$$

$$k_{1,4} = h f_1 \left( t_n + h, x_{1;n} + k_{1,3}, x_{2;n} + k_{2,3} \right) = -h(0.1) \left( x_{1;n} + k_{1,3} \right) \left( x_{2;n} + k_{2,3} \right) \,,$$

$$k_{2,4} = h f_2 \left( t_n + h, x_{1;n} + k_{1,3}, x_{2;n} + k_{2,3} \right) = -h \left( x_{1;n} + k_{1,3} \right) \,.$$

Using these values, we find

$$t_{n+1} = t_n + h = t_n + 0.1 \,,$$

$$x_{1;n+1} = x_{1;n} + \frac{1}{6} \left( k_{1,1} + 2k_{1,2} + 2k_{1,3} + k_{1,4} \right) \,,$$

$$x_{2;n+1} = x_{2;n} + \frac{1}{6} \left( k_{2,1} + 2k_{2,2} + 2k_{2,3} + k_{2,4} \right) \,.$$

In Table 5-B we give approximate values for $t_n$, $x_{1;n}$, and $x_{2;n}$.

From Table 5-B we see that the strength of the guerrilla troops, $x_1$, approaches zero, therefore with the combat effectiveness coefficients of 0.1 for guerrilla troops and 1 for conventional troops the conventional troops win.

**19.** See the answer in the text.

**Table 5–B**: Approximations of the solutions to Problem 18.

| $t_n$ | $x_{1;n} \approx$ | $x_{2;n} \approx$ |
|-------|-------------------|-------------------|
| 0     | 10                | 15                |
| 0.1   | 3.124             | 9.353             |
| 0.2   | 1.381             | 7.254             |
| 0.3   | 0.707             | 6.256             |
| 0.4   | 0.389             | 5.726             |
| 0.5   | 0.223             | 5.428             |

**21.** First, we convert given initial value problem to an initial value problem for a normal system. Let $x_1(t) = H(t)$, $x_2(t) = H'(t)$. Then $H''(t) = x_2'(t)$, $x_1(0) = H(0) = 0$, $x_2(0) = H'(0) = 0$, and we get

$$
\begin{aligned}
x_1' &= x_2\,, \\
60 - x_1 &= (77.7)x_2' + (19.42)x_2^2\,, \\
x_1(0) &= x_2(0) = 0
\end{aligned}
\qquad \Rightarrow \qquad
\begin{aligned}
x_1' &= x_2\,, \\
x_2' &= \left[60 - x_1 - (19.42)x_2^2\right]/77.7\,, \\
x_1(0) &= x_2(0) = 0.
\end{aligned}
$$

Thus $f_1(t, x_1, x_2) = x_2$, $f_2(t, x_1, x_2) = \left[60 - x_1 - (19.42)x_2^2\right]/77.7$, $t_0 = 0$, $x_{1;0} = 0$, and $x_{2;0} = 0$. With $h = 0.5$, we need $(5 - 0)/0.5 = 10$ steps to approximate the solution over the interval $[0, 5]$. Taking $n = 0$ in the vectorized Runge-Kutta algorithm, we approximate the solution at $t = 0.5$.

$$k_{1,1} = hx_{2;0} = 0.5(0) = 0,$$

$$k_{2,1} = h\left[60 - x_{1;0} - (19.42)x_{2;0}^2\right]/77.7 = 0.5\left[60 - (0) - (19.42)(0)^2\right]/77.7 = 0.38610\,,$$

$$k_{1,2} = h\left(x_{2;0} + \frac{k_{2,1}}{2}\right) = 0.5\left((0) + \frac{0.38610}{2}\right) = 0.09653\,,$$

$$k_{2,2} = h\left[60 - \left(x_{1;0} + \frac{k_{1,1}}{2}\right) - (19.42)\left(x_{2;0} + \frac{k_{2,1}}{2}\right)^2\right]/77.7 = 0.38144\,,$$

$$k_{1,3} = h\left(x_{2;0} + \frac{k_{2,2}}{2}\right) = 0.5\left((0) + \frac{0.38144}{2}\right) = 0.09536\,,$$

$$k_{2,3} = h \left[ 60 - \left( x_{1;0} + \frac{k_{1,2}}{2} \right) - (19.42) \left( x_{2;0} + \frac{k_{2,2}}{2} \right)^2 \right] /77.7 = 0.38124 \,,$$

$$k_{1,4} = h \left( x_{2;0} + k_{2,3} \right) = 0.5 \left( (0) + 0.38124 \right) = 0.19062 \,,$$

$$k_{2,4} = h \left[ 60 - (x_{1;0} + k_{1,3}) - (19.42)(x_{2;0} + k_{2,3})^2 \right] /77.7 = 0.36732 \,.$$

Using the recursive formulas, we find

$$t_1 = t_0 + h = 0 + 0.5 = 0.5$$

$$x_1(0.5) \approx x_{1;1} = x_{1;0} + \frac{1}{6} \left( k_{1,1} + 2k_{1,2} + 2k_{1,3} + k_{1,4} \right) = 0.09573 \,,$$

$$x_2(0.5) \approx x_{2;1} = x_{2;0} + \frac{1}{6} \left( k_{2,1} + 2k_{2,2} + 2k_{2,3} + k_{2,4} \right) = 0.37980 \,.$$

Next, we repeat the procedure with $n = 1, 2, \ldots, 9$. The results of these computations (the values of $x_{1;n}$ only) are presented in Table 5-C.

---

**Table 5–C**: Approximations of the solution to Problem 21.

| $n$ | $t_n$ | $x_{1;n} \approx H(t_n)$ | $n$ | $t_n$ | $x_{1;n} \approx H(t_n)$ |
|---|---|---|---|---|---|
| 0 | 0   | 0       | 6  | 3.0 | 2.75497 |
| 1 | 0.5 | 0.09573 | 7  | 3.5 | 3.52322 |
| 2 | 1.0 | 0.37389 | 8  | 4.0 | 4.31970 |
| 3 | 1.5 | 0.81045 | 9  | 4.5 | 5.13307 |
| 4 | 2.0 | 1.37361 | 10 | 5.0 | 5.95554 |
| 5 | 2.5 | 2.03111 |    |     |         |

---

**23.** Let $x_1 = y$ and $x_2 = y'$ to give the initial value problem

$$\begin{aligned} x_1' &= f_1(t, x_1, x_2) = x_2 \,, & x_1(0) &= a, \\ x_2' &= f_2(t, x_1, x_2) = -x_1 \left( 1 + rx_1^2 \right), & x_2(0) &= 0. \end{aligned}$$

Now, using the definitions of $t_n$, $x_{i;n}$, $k_{i,1}$, $k_{i,2}$, $k_{i,3}$, and $k_{i,4}$ on page 258 of the text, we have

$$k_{1,1} = h f_1 \left( t_n, x_{1;n}, x_{2;n} \right) = h x_{2;n} \,,$$

$$k_{2,1} = h f_2 \left( t_n, x_{1;n}, x_{2;n} \right) = -h x_{1;n} \left( 1 + r x_{1;n}^2 \right),$$

$$k_{1,2} = h f_1 \left( t_n + \frac{h}{2}, x_{1;n} + \frac{k_{1,1}}{2}, x_{2;n} + \frac{k_{2,1}}{2} \right) = h \left( x_{2;n} + \frac{k_{2,1}}{2} \right),$$

$$k_{2,2} = h f_2 \left( t_n + \frac{h}{2}, x_{1;n} + \frac{k_{1,1}}{2}, x_{2;n} + \frac{k_{2,1}}{2} \right) = -h \left( x_{1;n} + \frac{k_{1,1}}{2} \right) \left[ 1 + r \left( x_{1;n} + \frac{k_{1,1}}{2} \right)^2 \right],$$

$$k_{1,3} = h f_1 \left( t_n + \frac{h}{2}, x_{1;n} + \frac{k_{1,2}}{2}, x_{2;n} + \frac{k_{2,2}}{2} \right) = h \left( x_{2;n} + \frac{k_{2,2}}{2} \right),$$

$$k_{2,3} = h f_2 \left( t_n + \frac{h}{2}, x_{1;n} + \frac{k_{1,2}}{2}, x_{2;n} + \frac{k_{2,2}}{2} \right) = -h \left( x_{1;n} + \frac{k_{1,2}}{2} \right) \left[ 1 + r \left( x_{1;n} + \frac{k_{1,2}}{2} \right)^2 \right],$$

$$k_{1,4} = h f_1 \left( t_n + h, x_{1;n} + k_{1,3}, x_{2;n} + k_{2,3} \right) = h \left( x_{2;n} + k_{2,3} \right),$$

$$k_{2,4} = h f_2 \left( t_n + h, x_{1;n} + k_{1,3}, x_{2;n} + k_{2,3} \right) = -h \left( x_{1;n} + k_{1,3} \right) \left[ 1 + r \left( x_{1;n} + k_{1,3} \right)^2 \right].$$

Using these values, we find

$$t_{n+1} = t_n + h = t_n + 0.1,$$

$$x_{1;n+1} = x_{1;n} + \frac{1}{6} \left( k_{1,1} + 2 k_{1,2} + 2 k_{1,3} + k_{1,4} \right),$$

$$x_{2;n+1} = x_{2;n} + \frac{1}{6} \left( k_{2,1} + 2 k_{2,2} + 2 k_{2,3} + k_{2,4} \right).$$

In Table 5-D we give the approximate period for $r = 1$ and 2 with $a = 1$, 2 and 3, from this we see that the period varies as $r$ is varied or as $a$ is varied.

---

**Table 5–D**: Approximate period of the solution to Problem 23.

| $r$ | $a = 1$ | $a = 2$ | $a = 3$ |
|---|---|---|---|
| 1 | 4.8 | 3.3 | 2.3 |
| 2 | 4.0 | 2.4 | 1.7 |

---

**25.** With $x_1 = y$, $x_2 = y'$, and $x_3 = y''$, the initial value problem can be expressed as the system

$$\begin{aligned} x_1' &= x_2, & x_1(0) &= 1, \\ x_2' &= x_3, & x_2(0) &= 1, \\ x_3' &= t - x_3 - x_1^2, & x_3(0) &= 1. \end{aligned}$$

Chapter 5

Here

$$f_1(t, x_1, x_2, x_3) = x_2,$$
$$f_2(t, x_1, x_2, x_3) = x_3,$$
$$f_3(t, x_1, x_2, x_3) = t - x_3 - x_1^2.$$

Since we are computing the approximations for $c = 1$, the initial value for $h$ in Step 1 of the algorithm in Appendix E of the text is $h = (1-0)2^{-0} = 1$. The equations in Step 3 are

$$k_{1,1} = hf_1(t, x_1, x_2, x_3) = hx_2,$$

$$k_{2,1} = hf_2(t, x_1, x_2, x_3) = hx_3,$$

$$k_{3,1} = hf_3(t, x_1, x_2, x_3) = h(t - x_3 - x_1^2),$$

$$k_{1,2} = hf_1\left(t + \frac{h}{2}, x_1 + \frac{k_{1,1}}{2}, x_2 + \frac{k_{2,1}}{2}, x_3 + \frac{k_{3,1}}{2}\right) = h\left(x_2 + \frac{k_{2,1}}{2}\right),$$

$$k_{2,2} = hf_2\left(t + \frac{h}{2}, x_1 + \frac{k_{1,1}}{2}, x_2 + \frac{k_{2,1}}{2}, x_3 + \frac{k_{3,1}}{2}\right) = h\left(x_3 + \frac{k_{3,1}}{2}\right),$$

$$k_{3,2} = hf_3\left(t + \frac{h}{2}, x_1 + \frac{k_{1,1}}{2}, x_2 + \frac{k_{2,1}}{2}, x_3 + \frac{k_{3,1}}{2}\right) = h\left[t + \frac{h}{2} - x_3 - \frac{k_{3,1}}{2} - \left(x_1 + \frac{k_{1,1}}{2}\right)^2\right],$$

$$k_{1,3} = hf_1\left(t + \frac{h}{2}, x_1 + \frac{k_{1,2}}{2}, x_2 + \frac{k_{2,2}}{2}, x_3 + \frac{k_{3,2}}{2}\right) = h\left(x_2 + \frac{k_{2,2}}{2}\right),$$

$$k_{2,3} = hf_2\left(t + \frac{h}{2}, x_1 + \frac{k_{1,2}}{2}, x_2 + \frac{k_{2,2}}{2}, x_3 + \frac{k_{3,2}}{2}\right) = h\left(x_3 + \frac{k_{3,2}}{2}\right),$$

$$k_{3,3} = hf_3\left(t + \frac{h}{2}, x_1 + \frac{k_{1,2}}{2}, x_2 + \frac{k_{2,2}}{2}, x_3 + \frac{k_{3,2}}{2}\right) = h\left[t + \frac{h}{2} - x_3 - \frac{k_{3,2}}{2} - \left(x_1 + \frac{k_{1,2}}{2}\right)^2\right],$$

$$k_{1,4} = hf_1(t + h, x_1 + k_{1,3}, x_2 + k_{2,3}, x_3 + k_{3,3}) = h(x_2 + k_{2,3}),$$

$$k_{2,4} = hf_2(t + h, x_1 + k_{1,3}, x_2 + k_{2,3}, x_3 + k_{3,3}) = h(x_3 + k_{3,3}),$$

$$k_{3,4} = hf_3(t + h, x_1 + k_{1,3}, x_2 + k_{2,3}, x_3 + k_{3,3}) = h\left[t + h - x_3 - k_{3,3} - (x_1 + k_{1,3})^2\right].$$

Using the starting values $t_0 = 0$, $a_1 = 1$, $a_2 = 0$, and $a_3 = 1$, we obtain the first approximations

$$x_1(1; 1) = 1.29167,$$

$$x_2(1; 1) = 0.28125,$$

$$x_3(1; 1) = 0.03125.$$

Repeating the algorithm with $h = 2^{-1}$, $2^{-2}$, $2^{-3}$ we obtain the approximations in Table 5-E.

**Table 5–E**: Approximations of the Solution to Problem 25.

| $n$ | $h$ | $y(1) \approx x_1(1; 2^{-n})$ | $x_2(1; 2^{-n})$ | $x_3(1; 2^{-n})$ |
|---|---|---|---|---|
| 0 | 1.0 | 1.29167 | 0.28125 | 0.03125 |
| 1 | 0.5 | 1.26039 | 0.34509 | −0.06642 |
| 2 | 0.25 | 1.25960 | 0.34696 | −0.06957 |
| 3 | 0.125 | 1.25958 | 0.34704 | −0.06971 |

We stopped at $n = 3$ since

$$\left| \frac{x_1(1; 2^{-3}) - x_1(1; 2^{-2})}{x_1(1; 2^{-3})} \right| = \left| \frac{1.25958 - 1.25960}{1.25958} \right| = 0.00002 < 0.01,$$

$$\left| \frac{x_2(1; 2^{-3}) - x_2(1; 2^{-2})}{x_2(1; 2^{-3})} \right| = \left| \frac{0.34704 - 0.34696}{0.34704} \right| = 0.00023 < 0.01, \qquad \text{and}$$

$$\left| \frac{x_3(1; 2^{-3}) - x_3(1; 2^{-2})}{x_3(1; 2^{-3})} \right| = \left| \frac{-0.06971 + 0.06957}{-0.06971} \right| = 0.00201 < 0.01.$$

Hence

$$y(1) \approx x_1 \left(1; 2^{-3}\right) = 1.25958,$$

with tolerance $0.01$.

**27.** See the answer in the text.

**29.** See the answer in the text.

## EXERCISES 5.4: Introduction to the Phase Plane, page 274

**1.** Substitution of $x(t) = e^{3t}$, $y(t) = e^t$ into the system yields

$$\frac{dx}{dt} = \frac{d}{dt}\left(e^{3t}\right) = 3e^{3t} = 3\left(e^t\right)^3 = 3y^3,$$

$$\frac{dy}{dt} = \frac{d}{dt}\left(e^t\right) = e^t = y.$$

Thus, given pair of functions is a solution. To sketch the trajectory of this solution, we express $x$ as a function of $y$.

$$x = e^{3t} = \left(e^t\right)^3 = y^3 \qquad \text{for} \qquad y = e^t > 0.$$

Since $y = e^t$ is an increasing function, the flow arrows are directed away from the origin. See Figure B.29 in the answers of the text.

**3.** In this problem, $f(x,y) = x - y$, $g(x,y) = x^2 + y^2 - 1$. To find the critical point set, we solve the system

$$\begin{aligned} x - y &= 0, \\ x^2 + y^2 - 1 &= 0 \end{aligned} \quad \Rightarrow \quad \begin{aligned} x &= y, \\ x^2 + y^2 &= 1. \end{aligned}$$

Eliminating $y$ yields

$$2x^2 = 1 \quad \Rightarrow \quad x = \pm\frac{1}{\sqrt{2}}.$$

Substituting $x$ into the first equation, we find the corresponding value for $y$. Thus the critical points of the given system are $(1/\sqrt{2}, 1/\sqrt{2})$ and $(-1/\sqrt{2}, -1/\sqrt{2})$.

**5.** In this problem,

$$f(x,y) = x^2 - 2xy, \qquad g(x,y) = 3xy - y^2,$$

and so we find critical points by solving the system

$$\begin{aligned} x^2 - 2xy &= 0, \\ 3xy - y^2 &= 0 \end{aligned} \quad \Rightarrow \quad \begin{aligned} x(x - 2y) &= 0, \\ y(3x - y) &= 0. \end{aligned}$$

From the first equation we conclude that either $x = 0$ or $x = 2y$. Substituting these values into the second equation, we get

$$\begin{aligned} x = 0 &\quad \Rightarrow \quad y[3(0) - y] = 0 \quad \Rightarrow \quad -y^2 = 0 \quad \Rightarrow \quad y = 0; \\ x = 2y &\quad \Rightarrow \quad y[3(2y) - y] = 0 \quad \Rightarrow \quad 5y^2 = 0 \quad \Rightarrow \quad y = 0, \, x = 2(0) = 0. \end{aligned}$$

Therefore, $(0,0)$ is the only critical point.

**6.** We see by Definition 1 on page 266 of the text that we must solve the system of equations given by

$$y^2 - 3y + 2 = 0,$$
$$(x - 1)(y - 2) = 0.$$

By factoring the first equation above, we find that this system becomes

$$(y - 1)(y - 2) = 0,$$
$$(x - 1)(y - 2) = 0.$$

Thus, we observe that if $y = 2$ and $x$ is any constant, then the system of differential equations given in this problem will be satisfied. Therefore, one family of critical points is given by the line $y = 2$. If $y \neq 2$, then the system of equations above simplifies to $y - 1 = 0$, and $x - 1 = 0$. Hence, another critical point is the point $(1, 1)$.

**7.** Here $f(x, y) = y - 1$, $g(x, y) = e^{x+y}$. Thus the phase plane equation becomes

$$\frac{dy}{dx} = \frac{e^{x+y}}{y - 1} = \frac{e^x e^y}{y - 1}.$$

Separating variables yields

$$(y - 1)e^{-y}dy = e^x dx \qquad \Rightarrow \qquad \int (y - 1)e^{-y}dy = \int e^x dx$$

$$\Rightarrow \qquad -ye^{-y} + C = e^x \qquad \text{or} \qquad e^x + ye^{-y} = C.$$

**9.** The phase plane equation for this system is

$$\frac{dy}{dx} = \frac{g(x, y)}{f(x, y)} = \frac{e^x + y}{2y - x}.$$

We rewrite this equation in symmetric form,

$$-(e^x + y)\, dx + (2y - x)\, dy = 0,$$

and check it for exactness.

$$\frac{\partial M}{\partial y} = \frac{\partial}{\partial y}\left[-(e^x + y)\right] = -1,$$

$$\frac{\partial N}{\partial x} = \frac{\partial}{\partial x}(2y - x) = -1.$$

Therefore, the equation is exact. We have

$$F(x, y) = \int N(x, y)\, dy = \int (2y - x)\, dy = y^2 - xy + g(x);$$

$$M(x, y) = \frac{\partial}{\partial x} F(x, y) = \frac{\partial}{\partial x}\left(y^2 - xy + g(x)\right) = -y + g'(x) = -\left(e^x + y\right)$$

$$\Rightarrow \quad g'(x) = -e^x \quad \Rightarrow \quad g(x) = \int \left(-e^x\right) dx = -e^x.$$

Hence, a general solution to the phase plane equation is given implicitly by

$$F(x, y) = y^2 - xy - e^x = C \qquad \text{or} \qquad e^x + xy - y^2 = -C = c,$$

where $c$ is an arbitrary constant.

11. In this problem, $f(x, y) = 2y$ and $g(x, y) = 2x$. Therefore, the phase plane equation for given system is

$$\frac{dy}{dx} = \frac{2x}{2y} = \frac{x}{y}.$$

Separation variables and integration yield

$$y\, dy = x\, dx \qquad \Rightarrow \qquad \int y\, dy = \int x\, dx$$

$$\Rightarrow \qquad \frac{1}{2} y^2 = \frac{1}{2} x^2 + C \qquad \Rightarrow \qquad y^2 - x^2 = c.$$

Thus, the trajectories are hyperbolas if $c \neq 0$ and, for $c = 0$, the lines $y = \pm x$.

In the upper half-plane, $y > 0$, we have $x' = 2y > 0$ and, therefore, $x(t)$ increases. In the lower half-plane, $x' < 0$ and so $x(t)$ decreases. This implies that solutions flow from the left to the right in the upper half-plane and from the right to the left in the lower half-plane. See Figure B.30 in the text.

13. First, we will find the critical points of this system. Therefore, we solve the system

$$(y - x)(y - 1) = 0,$$
$$(x - y)(x - 1) = 0.$$

Notice that both of these equations will be satisfied if $y = x$. Thus, $x = C$ and $y = C$, for any fixed constant $C$, will be a solution to the given system of differential equations and one family of critical points is the line $y = x$. We also see that we have a critical point at the point $(1, 1)$. (This critical point is, of course, also on the line $y = x$.)

Next we will find the integral curves. Therefore, we must solve the first order differential equation given by

$$\frac{dy}{dx} = \frac{dy/dt}{dx/dt} = \frac{(x-y)(x-1)}{(y-x)(y-1)} \qquad \Rightarrow \qquad \frac{dy}{dx} = \frac{1-x}{y-1}.$$

We can solve this last differential equation by the method of separation of variables. Thus, we have

$$\int (y-1)dy = \int (1-x)dx$$

$$\Rightarrow \qquad \frac{y^2}{2} - y = x - \frac{x^2}{2} + C$$

$$\Rightarrow \qquad x^2 - 2x + y^2 - 2y = 2C.$$

By completing the square, we obtain

$$(x-1)^2 + (y-1)^2 = c,$$

where $c = 2C+2$. Therefore, the integral curves are concentric circles with centers at the point $(1, 1)$, including the critical point for the system of differential equations. The trajectories associated with the constants $c = 1$, $4$, and $9$, are sketched in Figure B.31 in the answers of the text.

Finally we will determine the flow along the trajectories. Notice that the variable $t$ imparts a flow to the trajectories of a solution to a system of differential equations in the same manner as the parameter $t$ imparts a direction to a curve written in parametric form. We will find this flow by determining the regions in the $xy$-plane where $x(t)$ is increasing (moving from left to right on each trajectory) and the regions where $x(t)$ is decreasing (moving from right to left on each trajectory). Therefore, we will use four cases to study the equation $dx/dt = (y-x)(y-1)$, the first equation in our system.

Case 1 : $y > x$ and $y < 1$. (This region is above the line $y = x$ but below the line $y = 1$.) In this case, $y - x > 0$ but $y - 1 < 0$. Thus, $dx/dt = (y - x)(y - 1) < 0$. Hence, $x(t)$ will be decreasing here. Therefore, the flow along the trajectories will be from right to left and so the movement is clockwise.

Case 2 : $y > x$ and $y > 1$. (This region is above the lines $y = x$ and $y = 1$.) In this case, we see that $y - x > 0$ and $y - 1 > 0$. Hence, $dx/dt = (y - x)(y - 1) > 0$. Thus, $x(t)$ will be increasing and the flow along the trajectories in this region will still be clockwise.

Case 3 : $y < x$ and $y < 1$. (This region is below the lines $y = x$ and $y = 1$.) In this case, $y - x < 0$ and $y - 1 < 0$. Thus, $dx/dt > 0$ and so $x(t)$ is increasing. Thus, the movement is from left to right and so the flow along the trajectories will be counterclockwise.

Case 4 : $y < x$ and $y > 1$. (This region is below the line $y = x$ but above the line $y = 1$.) In this case, $y - x < 0$ and $y - 1 > 0$. Thus, $dx/dt < 0$ and so $x(t)$ will be decreasing here. Therefore, the flow is from right to left and, thus, counterclockwise here also.

Therefore, above the line $y = x$ the flow is clockwise and below that line the flow is counter-clockwise. See Figure B.31 in the answers of the text.

15. From Definition 1 on page 266 of the text, we must solve the system of equations given by

$$2x + y + 3 = 0,$$
$$-3x - 2y - 4 = 0.$$

By eliminating $y$ in the first equation we obtain

$$x + 2 = 0$$

and by eliminating $x$ in the first equation we obtain

$$-y + 1 = 0.$$

Thus, we observe that $x = -2$ and $y = 1$ will satisfy both equations. Therefore $(-2, 1)$ is a critical point.

From Figure B.32 in the answers of the text we see that all solutions passing near the point $(-2, 1)$ do not stay close to it therefore the critical point $(-2, 1)$ is unstable.

**17.** For critical points, we solve the system

$$
\begin{aligned}
f(x,y) &= 0, \\
g(x,y) &= 0
\end{aligned}
\quad\Rightarrow\quad
\begin{aligned}
2x + 13y &= 0, \\
-x - 2y &= 0
\end{aligned}
\quad\Rightarrow\quad
\begin{aligned}
2(-2y) + 13y &= 0, \\
x &= 2y
\end{aligned}
\quad\Rightarrow\quad
\begin{aligned}
y &= 0, \\
x &= 0.
\end{aligned}
$$

Therefore, the system has just one critical point, $(0,0)$. The direction field is shown in Figure B.33 in the text. From this picture we conclude that $(0,0)$ is a center (stable).

**19.** We set $v = y'$. Then $y'' = (y')' = v'$ and so given equation is equivalent to the system

$$
\begin{aligned}
y' &= v, \\
v' - y &= 0
\end{aligned}
\quad\Rightarrow\quad
\begin{aligned}
y' &= v, \\
v' &= y.
\end{aligned}
$$

In this system, $f(y,v) = v$ and $g(y,v) = y$. For critical points we solve

$$
\begin{aligned}
f(y,v) = v &= 0, \\
g(y,v) = y &= 0
\end{aligned}
\quad\Rightarrow\quad
\begin{aligned}
y &= 0, \\
v &= 0
\end{aligned}
$$

and conclude that, in $yv$-plane, the system has only one critical point, $(0,0)$. In the upper half-plane, $y' = v > 0$ and, therefore, $y$ increases and solutions flow to the right; similarly, solutions flow to the left in the lower half-plane. See Figure B.34 in the answers of the text.

The phase plane equation for the system is

$$
\frac{dv}{dy} = \frac{dv/dx}{dy/dx} = \frac{y}{v} \quad\Rightarrow\quad v\,dv = y\,dy \quad\Rightarrow\quad v^2 - y^2 = c.
$$

Thus, the integral curves are hyperbolas for $c \neq 0$ and lines $v = \pm y$ for $c = 0$. On the line $v = -y$, the solutions flow into the critical point $(0,0)$, whereas solutions flow away from $(0,0)$ on $v = y$. So, $(0,0)$ is a saddle point (unstable).

**21.** First we convert the given equation into a system of first order equations involving the functions $y(t)$ and $v(t)$ by using the substitution

$$
v(t) = y'(t) \quad\Rightarrow\quad v'(t) = y''(t).
$$

Therefore, this equation becomes the system

$$
\begin{aligned}
y' &= v, \\
v' &= -y - y^5 = -y\left(1 + y^4\right).
\end{aligned}
$$

To find the critical points, we solve the system of equations given by $v = 0$ and $-y(1 + y^4) = 0$. This system is satisfied only when $v = 0$ and $y = 0$. Thus, the only critical point is the point $(0,0)$. To find the integral curves, we solve the first order equation given by

$$\frac{dv}{dy} = \frac{dv/dt}{dy/dt} = \frac{-y - y^5}{v}.$$

This is a separable equation and can be written as

$$v\, dv = \left(-y - y^5\right) dy \qquad \Rightarrow \qquad \frac{v^2}{2} = -\frac{y^2}{2} - \frac{y^6}{6} + C$$

$$\Rightarrow \qquad 3v^2 + 3y^2 + y^6 = c \qquad (c = 6C),$$

where we have integrated to obtain the second equation above. Therefore, the integral curves for this system are given by the equations $3v^2 + 3y^2 + y^6 = c$ for each positive constant $c$.

To determine the flow along the trajectories, we will examine the equation $dy/dt = v$. Thus, we see that

$$\frac{dy}{dt} > 0 \quad \text{when} \quad v > 0, \quad \text{and} \quad \frac{dy}{dt} < 0 \quad \text{when} \quad v < 0.$$

Therefore, $y$ will be increasing when $v > 0$ and decreasing when $v < 0$. Hence, above the $y$-axis the flow will be from left to right and below the $x$-axis the flow will be from right to left. Thus, the flow on these trajectories will be clockwise (Figure B.35 in the answers of the text). Thus $(0,0)$ is a center (stable).

**23.** With $v = y'$, $v' = y''$, the equation transforms to the system

$$\begin{aligned} y' &= v, \\ v' + y - y^4 &= 0 \end{aligned} \qquad \Rightarrow \qquad \begin{aligned} y' &= v, \\ v' &= y^4 - y. \end{aligned} \qquad (5.26)$$

Therefore, $f(y,v) = v$ and $g(y,v) = y^4 - y = y(y^3 - 1)$. We find critical points by solving

$$\begin{aligned} v &= 0, \\ y(y^3 - 1) &= 0 \end{aligned} \qquad \Rightarrow \qquad \begin{aligned} v &= 0, \\ y &= 0 \quad \text{or} \quad y = 1. \end{aligned}$$

Hence, system (5.26) has two critical points, $(0,0)$ and $(1,0)$.

In the upper half plane, $y' = v > 0$ and so solutions flow to the right; similarly, solutions flow to the left in the lower half-plane. See Figure B.36 in the text for the direction field. This figure indicates that $(0,0)$ is a stable critical point (center) whereas $(1,0)$ is a saddle point (unstable).

**25.** This system has two critical points, $(0,0)$ and $(1,0)$, which are solutions to the system

$$y = 0,$$
$$-x + x^3 = 0.$$

The direction field for this system is depicted in Figure B.37. From this figure we conclude that

**(a)** the solution passing through the point $(0.25, 0.25)$ flows around $(0,0)$ and thus is periodic;

**(b)** for the solution $(x(t), y(t))$ passing through the point $(2, 2)$, $y(t) \to \infty$ as $t \to \infty$, and so this solution is not periodic;

**(c)** the solution passing through the critical point $(1,0)$ is a constant (equilibrium) solution and so is periodic.

**27.** The direction field for given system is shown in Figure B.38 in the answers of the text. From the starting point, $(1,1)$, following the direction arrows the solution flows down and to the left, crosses the $x$-axis, has a turning point in the fourth quadrant, and then does to the left and up toward the critical point $(0,0)$. Thus we predict that, as $t \to \infty$, the solution $(x(t), y(t))$ approaches $(0,0)$.

**29. (a)** The phase plane equation for this system is

$$\frac{dy}{dx} = \frac{3y}{x}.$$

It is separable. Separating variables and integrating, we get

$$\frac{dy}{y} = \frac{3dx}{x} \quad \Rightarrow \quad \ln|y| = 3\ln|x| + C \quad \Rightarrow \quad y = cx^3.$$

So, integral curves are cubic curves. Since in the right half-plane $x' = x > 0$, in the left half-plane $x' < 0$, the solutions flow to the right in the right half-plane and to the left in the left half-plane. Solutions starting on the $y$-axis stay on it $(x' = 0)$; they flow up if the initial point is in the upper half-plane (because $y' = y > 0$) and flow down if the initial point in the lower half-plane. This matches the figure for unstable node.

(b) Solving the phase plane equation for this system, we get

$$\frac{dy}{dx} = \frac{-4x}{y} \quad \Rightarrow \quad y\,dy = -4x\,dx \quad \Rightarrow \quad y^2 + 4x^2 = C.$$

Thus the integral curves are ellipses. (Also, notice that the solutions flow along these ellipses in clockwise direction because $x$ increases in the upper half-plane and decreases in the lower half-plane.) Therefore, here we have a center (stable).

(c) Solving $-5x + 2y > 0$ and $x - 4y > 0$ we find that $x$ increases in the half-plane $y > 5x$ and decreases in the half-plane $y < 5x$, and $y$ increases in the half-plane $y < x/4$ and decreases in the half-plane $y > x/4$. This leads to the scheme ⟍⟋⟋⟍ for the solution's flows. Thus all solutions approach the critical point $(0,0)$, as $t \to \infty$, which corresponds to a stable node.

(d) An analysis, similar to that in (c), shows that all the solutions flow away from $(0,0)$. Among pictures shown in Figure 5.7, only the unstable node and the unstable spiral have this feature. Since the unstable node is the answer to (a), we have the unstable spiral in this case.

(e) The phase plane equation

$$\frac{dy}{dx} = \frac{4x - 3y}{5x - 3y},$$

has two linear solutions, $y = 2x$ and $y = 2x/3$. (One can find them by substituting $y = ax$ into the above phase plane equation and solving for $a$.) Solutions starting from a point on $y = 2x$ in the first quadrant, have $x' = 5x - 3(2x) = -x < 0$ and so flow toward $(0,0)$; similarly, solutions, starting from a point on this line in the third quadrant, have $x' = -x > 0$ and, again, flow to $(0,0)$. On the other line, $y = 2x/3$, the picture is opposite: in the first quadrant, $x' = 5x - 3(2x/3) = 3x > 0$, and $x' < 0$ in the third quadrant. Therefore, there are two lines, passing through the critical point $(0,0)$, such that solutions to the system flow into $(0,0)$ on one of them and flow away from $(0,0)$ on the other. This is the case of a saddle (unstable) point.

**(f)** The only remaining picture is the asymptotically stable spiral. (One can also get a diagram ⤢ for solution's flows with just one matching picture in Figure 5.7.)

**31. (a)** Setting $y' = v$ and so $y'' = v'$, we transform given equation to a first order system

$$\frac{dy}{dx} = v,$$
$$\frac{dv}{dx} = f(y).$$

**(b)** By the chain rule,

$$\frac{dv}{dy} = \frac{dv}{dx}\cdot\frac{dx}{dy} = \frac{dv}{dx}\bigg/\frac{dy}{dx} = \frac{f(y)}{v} \quad\Rightarrow\quad \frac{dv}{dy} = \frac{f(y)}{v}.$$

This equation is separable. Separation variables and integration yield

$$v\,dv = f(y)\,dy \quad\Rightarrow\quad \int v\,dv = \int f(y)\,dy$$

$$\Rightarrow\quad \frac{1}{2}v^2 = F(y) + K,$$

where $F(y)$ is an antiderivative of $f(y)$. Substituting back $v = y'$ gives the required.

**33.** Since $S(t)$ and $I(t)$ represent population and we cannot have a negative population, we are only interested in the first quadrant of the $SI$-plane.

**(a)** In order to find the trajectory corresponding to the initial conditions $I(0) = 1$ and $S(0) = 700$, we must solve the first order equation

$$\frac{dI}{dS} = \frac{dI/dt}{dS/dt} = \frac{aSI - bI}{-aSI} = -\frac{aS - b}{aS}$$

$$\Rightarrow\quad \frac{dI}{dS} = -1 + \frac{b}{a}\frac{1}{S}. \tag{5.27}$$

By integrating both sides of equation (5.27) with respect to $S$, we obtain the integral curves given by

$$I(S) = -S + \frac{b}{a}\ln S + C.$$

A sketch of this curve for $a = 0.003$ and $b = 0.5$ is shown in Figure B.39 in the answers of the text.

**(b)** From the sketch in Figure B.39 in the answers of the text we see that the peak number of infected people is 295.

**(c)** The peak number of infected people occurs when $dI/dS = 0$. From equation (5.27) we have

$$\frac{dI}{dS} = 0 = -1 + \frac{b}{a}\frac{1}{S}.$$

Solving for $S$ we obtain

$$S = \frac{b}{a} = \frac{0.5}{0.003} \approx 167 \text{ people.}$$

**35. (a)** We denote $v(t) = x'(t)$ to transform the equation

$$\frac{d^2x}{dt^2} = -x + \frac{1}{\lambda - x}$$

to an equivalent system of two first order differential equations, that is

$$\frac{dx}{dt} = v,$$
$$\frac{dv}{dt} = -x + \frac{1}{\lambda - x}.$$

**(b)** The phase plane equation in $xv$-plane for the system in (a) is

$$\frac{dv}{dx} = \frac{-x + 1/(\lambda - x)}{v}.$$

This equation is separable. Separating variables and integrating, we obtain

$$v\,dv = \left(-x + \frac{1}{\lambda - x}\right) dx \quad \Rightarrow \quad \int v\,dv = \int \left(-x + \frac{1}{\lambda - x}\right) dx$$

$$\Rightarrow \quad \frac{1}{2}v^2 = -\frac{1}{2}x^2 - \ln|\lambda - x| + C_1 \quad \Rightarrow \quad v^2 = C - x^2 - 2\ln|\lambda - x|$$

$$\Rightarrow \quad v = \pm\sqrt{C - x^2 - 2\ln(\lambda - x)}.$$

(The absolute value sign is not necessary because $x < \lambda$.)

**(c)** To find critical points for the system in (a), we solve

$$v = 0, \qquad \qquad v = 0, \qquad \qquad v = 0,$$
$$-x + \frac{1}{\lambda - x} = 0 \quad \Rightarrow \quad x^2 - \lambda x + 1 = 0 \quad \Rightarrow \quad x = \frac{\lambda \pm \sqrt{\lambda^2 - 4}}{2}.$$

For $0 < \lambda < 2$, $\lambda^2 - 4 < 0$ and so both roots are complex numbers. However, for $\lambda > 2$ there are two distinct real solutions,

$$x_1 = \frac{\lambda - \sqrt{\lambda^2 - 4}}{2} \qquad \text{and} \qquad x_2 = \frac{\lambda + \sqrt{\lambda^2 - 4}}{2},$$

and the critical points are

$$\left( \frac{\lambda - \sqrt{\lambda^2 - 4}}{2}, 0 \right) \qquad \text{and} \qquad \left( \frac{\lambda + \sqrt{\lambda^2 - 4}}{2}, 0 \right).$$

**(d)** The phase plane diagrams for $\lambda = 1$ and $\lambda = 3$ are shown in Figures B.40 and B.41 in the answers section of the text.

**(e)** From Figures B.40 we conclude that, for $\lambda = 1$, all solution curves approach the vertical line $x = 1 (= \lambda)$. This means that the bar is attracted to the magnet. The case $\lambda = 3$ is more complicated. The behavior of the bar depends on the initial displacement $x(0)$ and the initial velocity $v(0) = x'(0)$. From Figure B.41 we see that (with $v(0) = 0$) if $x(0)$ is small enough, then the bar will oscillate about the position $x = x_1$; if $x(0)$ is close enough to $\lambda$, then the bar will be attracted to the magnet. It is also possible that, with an appropriate combination of $x(0)$ and $v(0)$, the bar will come to rest at the saddle point $(x_2, 0)$.

**37.** **(a)** Denoting $y' = v$, we have $y'' = v'$, and (with $m = \mu = k = 1$) (16) can be written as a system

$$y' = v,$$

$$v' = -y + \begin{cases} y, & \text{if } |y| < 1, v = 0, \\ \text{sign}(y), & \text{if } |y| \geq 1, v = 0, \\ -\text{sign}(v), & \text{if } v \neq 0 \end{cases} = \begin{cases} 0, & \text{if } |y| < 1, v = 0, \\ -y + \text{sign}(y), & \text{if } |y| \geq 1, v = 0, \\ -y - \text{sign}(v), & \text{if } v \neq 0. \end{cases}$$

# Chapter 5

**(b)** The condition $v \neq 0$ corresponds to the third case in (5.28), i.e., the system has the form

$$y' = v,$$
$$v' = -y - \text{sign}(v).$$

The phase plane equation for this system is

$$\frac{dv}{dy} = \frac{dv/dt}{dy/dt} = \frac{-y - \text{sign}(v)}{v}.$$

We consider two cases.

1) $v > 0$. In this case $\text{sign}(v) = 1$ and we have

$$\frac{dv}{dy} = \frac{-y - 1}{v} \qquad \Rightarrow \qquad v\,dv = -(y+1)dy$$

$$\Rightarrow \qquad \int v\,dv = -\int (y+1)dy$$

$$\Rightarrow \qquad \frac{1}{2}v^2 = -\frac{1}{2}(y+1)^2 + C \qquad \Rightarrow \qquad v^2 + (y+1)^2 = c,$$

where $c = 2C$.

2) $v < 0$. In this case $\text{sign}(v) = -1$ and we have

$$\frac{dv}{dy} = \frac{-y + 1}{v} \qquad \Rightarrow \qquad v\,dv = -(y-1)dy$$

$$\Rightarrow \qquad \int v\,dv = -\int (y-1)dy$$

$$\Rightarrow \qquad \frac{1}{2}v^2 = -\frac{1}{2}(y-1)^2 + C \qquad \Rightarrow \qquad v^2 + (y-1)^2 = c.$$

**(c)** The equation $v^2 + (y+1)^2 = c$ defines a circle in the $yv$-plane centered at $(-1,0)$ and of the radius $\sqrt{c}$ if $c > 0$, and it is the empty set if $c < 0$. The condition $v > 0$ means that we have to take only the half of these circles lying in the upper half plane. Moreover, the first equation, $y' = v$, implies that trajectories flow from left to right. Similarly, in the lower half plane, $v < 0$, we have concentric semicircles $v^2 + (y-1)^2 = c$, $c \geq 0$, centered at $(1,0)$ and flowing from right to left.

**(d)** For the system found in (a),

$$f(y, v) = v,$$

$$g(y, v) = \begin{cases} 0, & \text{if } |y| < 1, \, v = 0, \\ -y + \text{sign}(y), & \text{if } |y| \geq 1, \, v = 0, \\ -y - \text{sign}(v), & \text{if } v \neq 0. \end{cases}$$

Since $f(y, v) = 0 \Leftrightarrow v = 0$ and

$$g(y, 0) = \begin{cases} 0, & \text{if } |y| < 1, \\ -y + \text{sign}(y), & \text{if } |y| \geq 1, \end{cases}$$

we consider two cases. If $y < 1$, then $g(y, 0) \equiv 0$. This means that any point of the interval $-1 < y < 1$ is a critical point. If $|y| \geq 1$, then $g(y, 0) = -y + \text{sign}(y)$ which is 0 if $y = \pm 1$. Thus the critical point set is the segment $v = 0$, $-1 \leq y \leq 1$.

**(e)** According to (c), the mass released at $(7.5, 0)$ goes in the lower half plane from right to left along a semicircle centered at $(1, 0)$. The radius of this semicircle is $7.5 - 1 = 6.5$, and its other end is $(1 - 6.5, 0) = (-5.5, 0)$. From this point, the mass goes from left to right in the upper half plane along the semicircle centered at $(-1, 0)$ and of the radius $-1 - (-5.5) = 4.5$, and comes to the point $(-1 + 4.5, 0) = (3.5, 0)$. Then the mass again goes from right to left in the lower half plane along the semicircle centered at $(1, 0)$ and of the radius $3.5 - 1 = 2.5$, and comes to the point $(1 - 2.5, 0) = (-1.5, 0)$. From this point, the mass goes in the upper half plane from left to right along the semicircle centered at $(-1, 0)$ and of the radius $-1 - (-1.5) = 0.5$, and comes to the point $(-1 + 0.5, 0) = (-0.5, 0)$. Here it comes to rest because $|-0.5| < 1$, and there is not a lower semicircle starting at this point. See the colored curve in Figure B.42 of the text.

## EXERCISES 5.5:  Coupled Mass-Spring Systems, page 284

**1.** For the mass $m_1$ there is only one force acting on it; that is the force due to the spring with constant $k_1$. This equals $-k_1(x - y)$. Hence, we get

$$m_1 x'' = -k_1(x - y).$$

# Chapter 5

For the mass $m_2$ there are two forces acting on it: the force due to the spring with constant $k_2$ is $-k_2 y$; and the force due to the spring with constant $k_1$ is $k_1(y - x)$. So we get

$$m_2 y'' = k_1(x - y) - k_2 y.$$

So the system is

$$m_1 x'' = k_1(y - x),$$
$$m_2 y'' = -k_1(y - x) - k_2 y,$$

or, in operator form,

$$\left(m_1 D^2 + k_1\right)[x] - k_1 y = 0,$$
$$-k_1 x + \left\{m_2 D^2 + (k_1 + k_2)\right\}[y] = 0.$$

With $m_1 = 1$, $m_2 = 2$, $k_1 = 4$, and $k_2 = 10/3$, we get

$$(D^2 + 4)[x] - 4y = 0,$$
$$-4x + (2D^2 + 22/3)[y] = 0, \tag{5.28}$$

with initial conditions:

$$x(0) = -1, \quad x'(0) = 0, \quad y(0) = 0, \quad y'(0) = 0.$$

Multiplying the second equation of the system given in (5.28) by 4, applying $(2D^2 + 22/3)$ to the first equation of this system, and adding the results, we get

$$(D^2 + 4)\left(2D^2 + \frac{22}{3}\right)[x] - 16x = 0$$

$$\Rightarrow \quad \left(2D^4 + \frac{46}{3}D^2 + \frac{40}{3}\right)[x] = 0$$

$$\Rightarrow \quad (3D^4 + 23D^2 + 20)[x] = 0.$$

The characteristic equation is

$$3r^4 + 23r^2 + 20 = 0,$$

which is a quadratic in $r^2$. So

$$r^2 = \frac{-23 \pm \sqrt{529 - 240}}{6} = \frac{-23 \pm 17}{6}.$$

Since $-20/3$ and $-1$ are negative, the roots of the characteristic equation are $\pm i\beta_1$ and $\pm i\beta_2$, where

$$\beta_1 = \sqrt{\frac{20}{3}}, \qquad \beta_2 = 1.$$

Hence

$$x(t) = c_1 \cos \beta_1 t + c_2 \sin \beta_1 t + c_3 \cos \beta_2 t + c_4 \sin \beta_2 t.$$

Solving the first equation of the system given in (5.28) for $y$, we get

$$y(t) = \frac{1}{4} \left(D^2 + 4\right)[x] = \frac{1}{4} \left[\left(-\beta_1^2 + 4\right) c_1 \cos \beta_1 t + \left(-\beta_1^2 + 4\right) c_2 \sin \beta_1 t \right.$$
$$\left. + \left(-\beta_2^2 + 4\right) c_3 \cos \beta_2 t + \left(-\beta_2^2 + 4\right) c_4 \sin \beta_2 t\right].$$

Next we substitute into the initial conditions. Setting $x(0) = -1$, $x'(0) = 0$ yields

$$-1 = c_1 + c_3,$$
$$0 = c_2 \beta_1 + c_4 \beta_2.$$

From the initial conditions $y(0) = 0$, $y'(0) = 0$, we get

$$0 = \frac{1}{4} \left[\left(-\beta_1^2 + 4\right) c_1 + \left(-\beta_2^2 + 4\right) c_3\right],$$
$$0 = \frac{1}{4} \left[\beta_1 \left(-\beta_1^2 + 4\right) c_2 + \beta_2 \left(-\beta_2^2 + 4\right) c_4\right].$$

The solution to the above system is

$$c_2 = c_4 = 0, \qquad c_1 = -\frac{9}{17}, \qquad c_3 = -\frac{8}{17},$$

which yields the solutions

$$x(t) = -\frac{9}{17} \cos \sqrt{\frac{20}{3}}\, t - \frac{8}{17} \cos t,$$
$$y(t) = \frac{6}{17} \cos \sqrt{\frac{20}{3}}\, t - \frac{6}{17} \cos t.$$

# Chapter 5

**3.** We define the displacements of masses from equilibrium, $x$, $y$, and $z$, as in Example 2. For each mass, there are two forces acting on it due to Hook's law.

For the mass on the left,

$$F_{11} = -kx \qquad \text{and} \qquad F_{12} = k(y - x);$$

for the mass in the middle,

$$F_{21} = -k(y - x) \qquad \text{and} \qquad F_{22} = k(z - y);$$

finally, for the mass on the right,

$$F_{31} = -k(z - y) \qquad \text{and} \qquad F_{32} = -kz.$$

Applying Newton's second law for each mass, we obtain the following system

$$mx'' = -kx + k(y - x),$$
$$my'' = -k(y - x) + k(z - y),$$
$$mz'' = -k(z - y) - kz,$$

or, in operator form,

$$\left(mD^2 + 2k\right)[x] - ky = 0,$$
$$-kx + \left(mD^2 + 2k\right)[y] - kz = 0,$$
$$-ky + \left(mD^2 + 2k\right)[z] = 0.$$

From the first equation, we express

$$y = \frac{1}{k}\left(mD^2 + 2k\right)[x] \tag{5.29}$$

and substitute this expression into the other two equations to get

$$-kx + \left(mD^2 + 2k\right)\left[\frac{1}{k}\left(mD^2 + 2k\right)[x]\right] - kz = 0,$$
$$-\left(mD^2 + 2k\right)[x] + \left(mD^2 + 2k\right)[z] = 0.$$

The first equation yields

$$z = -x + \left\{ \frac{1}{k} \left( mD^2 + 2k \right) \right\}^2 [x] = \left\{ \frac{1}{k^2} \left( mD^2 + 2k \right)^2 - 1 \right\} [x], \qquad (5.30)$$

and so

$$- \left( mD^2 + 2k \right) [x] + \left( mD^2 + 2k \right) \left[ \left\{ \frac{1}{k^2} \left( mD^2 + 2k \right)^2 - 1 \right\} [x] \right]$$

$$= \left( mD^2 + 2k \right) \left\{ \frac{1}{k^2} \left( mD^2 + 2k \right)^2 - 2 \right\} [x] = 0.$$

The characteristic equation for this homogeneous linear equation with constant coefficients is

$$\left( mr^2 + 2k \right) \left\{ \frac{1}{k^2} \left( mr^2 + 2k \right)^2 - 2 \right\} = 0,$$

which splits onto two equations,

$$mr^2 + 2k = 0 \qquad \Rightarrow \qquad r = \pm i \sqrt{\frac{2k}{m}} \qquad (5.31)$$

and

$$\frac{1}{k^2} \left( mr^2 + 2k \right)^2 - 2 = 0 \qquad \Rightarrow \qquad \left( mr^2 + 2k \right)^2 - 2k^2 = 0$$

$$\Rightarrow \qquad \left( mr^2 + 2k - \sqrt{2}k \right) \left( mr^2 + 2k + \sqrt{2}k \right) = 0$$

$$\Rightarrow \qquad r = \pm i \sqrt{\frac{(2 - \sqrt{2})k}{m}}, \qquad r = \pm i \sqrt{\frac{(2 + \sqrt{2})k}{m}}. \qquad (5.32)$$

Solutions (5.31) and (5.32) give normal frequences

$$\omega_1 = \frac{1}{2\pi} \sqrt{\frac{2k}{m}}, \qquad \omega_2 = \frac{1}{2\pi} \sqrt{\frac{(2 - \sqrt{2})k}{m}}, \qquad \omega_3 = \frac{1}{2\pi} \sqrt{\frac{(2 + \sqrt{2})k}{m}}.$$

Thus, a general solution $x(t)$ has the form $x(t) = x_1(t) + x_2(t) + x_3(t)$, where functions

$$x_j(t) = c_{1j} \cos(2\pi \omega_j t) + c_{2j} \sin(2\pi \omega_j t).$$

Note that $x_j$'s satisfy the following differential equations:

$$\left( mD^2 + 2k \right) [x_1] = 0,$$

Chapter 5

$$\left(mD^2 + 2k - \sqrt{2}k\right)[x_2] = 0, \tag{5.33}$$
$$\left(mD^2 + 2k + \sqrt{2}k\right)[x_3] = 0.$$

For normal modes, we find solutions $y_j(t)$ and $z_j(t)$, corresponding to $x_j$, $j = 1, 2$, and $3$ by using (5.29), (5.30), and identities (5.33).

$\omega_1$:

$$y_1 = \frac{1}{k}\left(mD^2 + 2k\right)[x_1] \equiv 0,$$
$$z_1 = \left\{\frac{1}{k}\left(mD^2 + 2k\right)^2 - 1\right\}[x_1] = -x_1;$$

$\omega_2$:

$$y_2 = \frac{1}{k}\left(mD^2 + 2k\right)[x_2] = \left\{\frac{1}{k}\left(mD^2 + 2k - \sqrt{2}k\right) + \sqrt{2}\right\}[x_2] = \sqrt{2}x_2,$$
$$z_2 = \left\{\frac{1}{k}\left(mD^2 + 2k\right)^2 - 1\right\}[x_2] = \left\{\left[\frac{1}{k}\left(mD^2 + 2k\right)^2 - 2\right] + 1\right\}[x_2] = x_2;$$

$\omega_3$:

$$y_3 = \frac{1}{k}\left(mD^2 + 2k\right)[x_3] = \left\{\frac{1}{k}\left(mD^2 + 2k + \sqrt{2}k\right) - \sqrt{2}\right\}[x_3] = -\sqrt{2}x_3,$$
$$z_3 = \left\{\frac{1}{k}\left(mD^2 + 2k\right)^2 - 1\right\}[x_3] = \left\{\left[\frac{1}{k}\left(mD^2 + 2k\right)^2 - 2\right] + 1\right\}[x_3] = x_3;$$

5. This spring system is similar to the system in Example 2 on page 282 of the text, except the middle spring has been replaced by a dashpot. We proceed as in Example 1. Let $x$ and $y$ represent the displacement of masses $m_1$ and $m_2$ to the right of their respective equilibrium positions. The mass $m_1$ has a force $F_1$ acting on its left side due to the left spring and a force $F_2$ acting on its right side due to the dashpot. Applying Hooke's law, we see that

$$F_1 = -k_1 x.$$

Assuming as we did in Section 4.1 that the damping force due to the dashpot is proportional to the magnitude of the velocity, but opposite in direction, we have

$$F_2 = b\left(y' - x'\right),$$

where $b$ is the damping constant. Notice that velocity of the arm of the dashpot is the difference between the velocities of mass $m_2$ and mass $m_1$. The mass $m_2$ has a force $F_3$ acting on its left side due to the dashpot and a force $F_4$ acting on its right side due to the right spring. Using similar arguments, we find

$$F_3 = -b\,(y' - x') \qquad \text{and} \qquad F_4 = -k_2 y.$$

Applying Newton's second law to each mass gives

$$m_1 x''(t) = F_1 + F_2 = -k_1 x(t) + b\,[y'(t) - x'(t)]\,,$$
$$m_2 y''(t) = F_3 + F_4 = -b\,[y'(t) - x'(t)] - k_2 y.$$

Plugging in the constants $m_1 = m_2 = 1$, $k_1 = k_2 = 1$, and $b = 1$, and simplifying yields

$$x''(t) + x'(t) + x(t) - y'(t) = 0,$$
$$-x'(t) + y''(t) + y'(t) + y(t) = 0. \tag{5.34}$$

The initial conditions for the system will be $y(0) = 0$ ($m_2$ is held in its equilibrium position), $x(0) = -2$ ($m_1$ is pushed to the left 2 ft), and $x'(0) = y'(0) = 0$ (the masses are simply released at time $t = 0$ with no additional velocity). In operator notation this system becomes

$$(D^2 + D + 1)\,[x] - D[y] = 0,$$
$$-D[x] + y''(t) + (D^2 + D + 1)\,[y] = 0.$$

By multiplying the first equation above by $D$ and the second by $(D^2 + D + 1)$ and adding the resulting equations, we can eliminate the function $y(t)$. Thus, we have

$$\left\{ (D^2 + D + 1)^2 - D^2 \right\} [x] = 0$$
$$\Rightarrow \qquad \left\{ [(D^2 + D + 1) - D] \cdot [(D^2 + D + 1) + D] \right\} [x] = 0$$
$$\Rightarrow \qquad \left\{ (D^2 + 1)\,(D + 1)^2 \right\} [x] = 0.$$

This last equation is a fourth order linear differential equation with constant coefficients whose associated auxiliary equation has roots $r = -1, -1, i$, and $-i$. Therefore, the solution to this differential equation is

$$x(t) = c_1 e^{-t} + c_2 t e^{-t} + c_3 \cos t + c_4 \sin t$$

$$\Rightarrow \quad x'(t) = (-c_1 + c_2)e^{-t} - c_2 t e^{-t} - c_3 \sin t + c_4 \cos t$$

$$\Rightarrow \quad x''(t) = (c_1 - 2c_2)e^{-t} + c_2 t e^{-t} - c_3 \cos t - c_4 \sin t.$$

To find $y(t)$, note that by the first equation of the system given in (5.34), we have

$$y'(t) = x''(t) + x'(t) + x(t).$$

Substituting $x(t)$, $x'(t)$, and $x''(t)$ into this equation yields

$$y'(t) = (c_1 - 2c_2)e^{-t} + c_2 t e^{-t} - c_3 \cos t - c_4 \sin t$$

$$+(-c_1 + c_2)e^{-t} - c_2 t e^{-t} - c_3 \sin t + c_4 \cos t + c_1 e^{-t} + c_2 t e^{-t} + c_3 \cos t + c_4 \sin t$$

$$\Rightarrow \quad y'(t) = (c_1 - c_2)e^{-t} + c_2 t e^{-t} - c_3 \sin t + c_4 \cos t.$$

By integrating both sides of this equation with respect to $t$, we obtain

$$y(t) = -(c_1 - c_2)e^{-t} - c_2 t e^{-t} - c_2 e^{-t} + c_3 \cos t + c_4 \sin t + c_5 \,,$$

where we have integrated $c_2 t e^{-t}$ by parts. Simplifying yields

$$y(t) = -c_1 e^{-t} - c_2 t e^{-t} + c_3 \cos t + c_4 \sin t + c_5 \,.$$

To determine the five constants, we will use the four initial conditions and the second equation in system (5.34). (We used the first equation to determine $y$). Substituting into the second equation in (5.34) gives

$$- \left[(-c_1 + c_2)e^{-t} - c_2 t e^{-t} - c_3 \sin t + c_4 \cos t\right]$$

$$+ \left[(-c_1 + 2c_2)e^{-t} - c_2 t e^{-t} - c_3 \cos t - c_4 \sin t\right]$$

$$+ \left[(c_1 - c_2)e^{-t} + c_2 t e^{-t} - c_3 \sin t + c_4 \cos t\right]$$

$$+ \left[-c_1 e^{-t} - c_2 t e^{-t} + c_3 \cos t + c_4 \sin t + c_5\right] = 0,$$

which reduces to $c_5 = 0$. Using the initial conditions and the fact that $c_5 = 0$, we see that

$$x(0) = c_1 + c_3 = -2, \qquad x'(0) = (-c_1 + c_2) + c_4 = 0,$$

$$y(0) = -c_1 + c_3 = 0, \qquad y'(0) = (c_1 - c_2) + c_4 = 0.$$

By solving these equations simultaneously, we find

$$c_1 = -1, \quad c_2 = -1, \quad c_3 = -1, \quad \text{and} \quad c_4 = 0.$$

Therefore, the solution to this spring-mass-dashpot system is

$$x(t) = -e^{-t} - te^{-t} - \cos t, \qquad y(t) = e^{-t} + te^{-t} - \cos t.$$

**7.** In operator notations,

$$\left(D^2 + 5\right)[x] - 2y = 0,$$

$$-2x + \left(D^2 + 2\right)[y] = 3 \sin 2t.$$

Multiplying the first equation by $\left(D^2 + 2\right)$ and the second equation by 2, and adding the results, we obtain

$$\left\{\left(D^2 + 2\right)\left(D^2 + 5\right) - 4\right\}[x] = 6 \sin 2t$$

$$\Rightarrow \qquad \left(D^4 + 7D^2 + 6\right)[x] = 6 \sin 2t$$

$$\Rightarrow \qquad \left(D^2 + 1\right)\left(D^2 + 6\right)[x] = 6 \sin 2t. \tag{5.35}$$

Since the characteristic equation, $(r^2 + 1)(r^2 + 6) = 0$, has the roots $r = \pm i$ and $r = \pm i\sqrt{6}$, a general solution to the corresponding homogeneous equation is given by

$$x_h(t) = c_1 \cos t + c_2 \sin t + c_3 \cos \sqrt{6}t + c_4 \sin \sqrt{6}t.$$

Due to the right-hand side in (5.35), a particular solution has the form

$$x_p(t) = A \cos 2t + B \sin 2t.$$

In order to simplify computations, we note that both functions, $\cos 2t$ and $\sin 2t$, and so $x_p(t)$, satisfy the differential equation $(D^2 + 4)[x] = 0$. Thus,

$$\left(D^2 + 1\right)\left(D^2 + 6\right)[x_h] = \left\{\left(D^2 + 4\right) - 3\right\}\left\{\left(D^2 + 4\right) + 2\right\}[x_h] = 2\left\{\left(D^2 + 4\right) - 3\right\}[x_h]$$

$$= -6x_h = -6A \cos 2t - 6B \sin 2t = 6 \sin 2t$$

$$\Rightarrow \qquad A = 0, \quad B = -1 \qquad \Rightarrow \qquad x_h(t) = -\sin 2t$$

and

$$x(t) = x_h(t) + x_p(t) = c_1 \cos t + c_2 \sin t + c_3 \cos \sqrt{6}t + c_4 \sin \sqrt{6}t - \sin 2t \,.$$

From the first equation in the original system, we have

$$
\begin{aligned}
y(t) \;&=\; \frac{1}{2}\left(x'' + 5x\right) \\
&=\; 2c_1 \cos t + 2c_2 \sin t - \frac{1}{2}c_3 \cos \sqrt{6}t - \frac{1}{2}c_4 \sin \sqrt{6}t - \frac{1}{2}\sin 2t \,.
\end{aligned}
$$

We determine constants $c_1$ and $c_3$ using the initial conditions $x(0) = 0$ and $y(0) = 1$.

$$
\begin{aligned}
0 &= x(0) = c_1 + c_3\,, \\
1 &= y(0) = 2c_1 - c_3/2
\end{aligned}
\quad\Rightarrow\quad
\begin{aligned}
c_3 &= -c_1\,, \\
2c_1 - (-c_1)/2 &= 1
\end{aligned}
\quad\Rightarrow\quad
\begin{aligned}
c_3 &= -2/5, \\
c_1 &= 2/5.
\end{aligned}
$$

To find $c_2$ and $c_4$, compute $x'(t)$ and $y'(t)$, evaluate these functions at $t = 0$, and use the other two initial conditions, $x'(0) = y'(0) = 0$. This yields

$$
\begin{aligned}
0 &= x'(0) = c_2 + \sqrt{6}c_4 - 2, \\
0 &= y'(0) = 2c_2 - \sqrt{6}c_4/2 - 1
\end{aligned}
\quad\Rightarrow\quad
\begin{aligned}
c_4 &= \sqrt{6}/5, \\
c_2 &= 4/5.
\end{aligned}
$$

Therefore, the required solution is

$$x(t) = \frac{2}{5}\cos t + \frac{4}{5}\sin t - \frac{2}{5}\cos \sqrt{6}t + \frac{\sqrt{6}}{5}\sin \sqrt{6}t - \sin 2t\,,$$

$$y(t) = \frac{4}{5}\cos t + \frac{8}{5}\sin t + \frac{1}{5}\cos \sqrt{6}t - \frac{\sqrt{6}}{10}\sin \sqrt{6}t - \frac{1}{2}\sin 2t\,.$$

**9.** Writing the equations of this system in operator form we obtain

$$\left\{mD^2 + \left(\frac{mg}{l} + k\right)\right\}[x_1] - kx_2 = 0,$$

$$-kx_1 + \left\{mD^2 + \left(\frac{mg}{l} + k\right)\right\}[x_2] = 0.$$

Applying $\{mD^2 + (mg/l + k)\}$ to the first equation, multiplying the second equation by $k$, and then adding, results in

$$\left\{\left[mD^2 + \left(\frac{mg}{l} + k\right)\right]^2 - k^2\right\}[x_1] = 0.$$

This equation has the auxiliary equation

$$\left(mr^2 + \frac{mg}{l} + k\right)^2 - k^2 = \left(mr^2 + \frac{mg}{l}\right)\left(mr^2 + \frac{mg}{l} + 2k\right) = 0$$

with roots $\pm i\sqrt{g/l}$ and $\pm i\sqrt{(g/l) + (2k/m)}$. As discussed on page 211 of the text $\sqrt{g/l}$ and $\sqrt{(g/l) + (2k/m)}$ are the normal angular frequencies. To find the normal frequencies we divide each one by $2\pi$ and obtain

$$\left(\frac{1}{2\pi}\right)\sqrt{\frac{g}{l}} \qquad \text{and} \qquad \left(\frac{1}{2\pi}\right)\sqrt{\frac{g}{l} + \frac{2k}{m}}\,.$$

## EXERCISES 5.6:   Electrical Circuits, page 291

1. In this problem, $R = 100\,\Omega$, $L = 4\,\text{H}$, $C = 0.01\,\text{F}$, and $E(t) = 20\,\text{V}$. Therefore, the equation (4) on page 287 of the text becomes

$$4\frac{d^2I}{dt^2} + 100\frac{dI}{dt} + 100I = \frac{d(20)}{dt} = 0 \qquad \Rightarrow \qquad \frac{d^2I}{dt^2} + 25\frac{dI}{dt} + 25I = 0.$$

The roots of the characteristic equation, $r^2 + 25r + 25 = 0$, are

$$r = \frac{-25 \pm \sqrt{(25)^2 - 4(25)(1)}}{2} = \frac{-25 \pm 5\sqrt{21}}{2}\,,$$

and so a general solution is

$$I(t) = c_1 e^{(-25-5\sqrt{21})t/2} + c_2 e^{(-25+5\sqrt{21})t/2}\,.$$

To determine constants $c_1$ and $c_2$, first we find the initial value $I'(0)$ using given $I(0) = 0$ and $q(0) = 4$. Substituting $t = 0$ into equation (3) on page 287 of the text (with $dq/dt$ replaced by $I(t)$), we obtain

$$L\frac{d[I(t)]}{dt} + RI(t) + \frac{1}{C}q(t) = E(t)$$

$$\Rightarrow \qquad 4I'(0) + 100(0) + \frac{1}{0.01}(4) = 20$$

$$\Rightarrow \qquad I'(0) = -95.$$

317

Thus, $I(t)$ satisfies $I(0) = 0$, $I'(0) = -95$. Next, we compute

$$I'(t) = \frac{c_1(-25 - 5\sqrt{21})}{2} e^{(-25-5\sqrt{21})t/2} + \frac{c_2(-25 + 5\sqrt{21})}{2} e^{(-25+5\sqrt{21})t/2},$$

substitute $t = 0$ into formulas for $I(t)$ and $I'(t)$, and obtain the system

$$\begin{aligned} 0 &= I(0) = c_1 + c_2, \\ -95 &= I'(0) = c_1(-25 - 5\sqrt{21})/2 + c_2(-25 + 5\sqrt{21})/2 \end{aligned} \quad \Rightarrow \quad \begin{aligned} c_1 &= 19/\sqrt{21}, \\ c_2 &= -19/\sqrt{21}. \end{aligned}$$

So, the solution is

$$I(t) = \frac{19}{\sqrt{21}} \left( e^{(-25-5\sqrt{21})t/2} - e^{(-25+5\sqrt{21})t/2} \right).$$

3. In this problem $L = 4$, $R = 120$, $C = (2200)^{-1}$, and $E(t) = 10\cos 20t$. Therefore, we see that $1/C = 2200$ and $E'(t) = -200\sin 20t$. By substituting these values into equation (4) on page 287 of the text, we obtain the equation

$$4\frac{d^2 I}{dt^2} + 120\frac{dI}{dt} + 2200I = -200\sin 20t.$$

By simplifying, we have

$$\frac{d^2 I}{dt^2} + 30\frac{dI}{dt} + 550I = -50\sin 20t. \tag{5.36}$$

The auxiliary equation associated with the homogeneous equation corresponding to (5.36) above is $r^2 + 30r + 550 = 0$. This equation has roots $r = -15 \pm 5\sqrt{13}i$. Therefore, the transient current, that is $I_h(t)$, is given by

$$I_h(t) = e^{-15t}\left[ C_1 \cos\left(5\sqrt{13}t\right) + C_2 \sin\left(5\sqrt{13}t\right)\right].$$

By the method of undetermined coefficients, a particular solution, $I_p(t)$, of equation (5.36) will be of the form $I_p(t) = t^s[A\cos 20t + B\sin 20t]$. Since neither $y(t) = \cos 20t$ nor $y(t) = \sin 20t$ is a solution to the homogeneous equation (that is the system is not at resonance), we can let $s = 0$ in $I_p(t)$. Thus, we see that $I_p(t)$, the steady-state current, has the form

$$I_p(t) = A\cos 20t + B\sin 20t.$$

To find the steady-state current, we must, therefore, find $A$ and $B$. To accomplish this, we observe that

$$I_p'(t) = -20A\sin 20t + 20B\cos 20t,$$

$$I_p''(t) = -400A\cos 20t - 400B\sin 20t.$$

Plugging these expressions into equation (5.36) yields

$$I_p''(t) + 30I_p'(t) + 550I(t) = -400A\cos 20t - 400B\sin 20t - 600A\sin 20t + 600B\cos 20t$$

$$+550A\cos 20t + 550B\sin 20t = -50\sin 20t$$

$$\Rightarrow \quad (150A + 600B)\cos 20t + (150B - 600A)\sin 20t = -50\sin 20t.$$

By equating coefficients we obtain the system of equations

$$15A + 60B = 0,$$
$$-60A + 15B = -5.$$

By solving these equations simultaneously for $A$ and $B$, we obtain $A = 4/51$ and $B = -1/51$. Thus, we have the steady-state current given by

$$I_p(t) = \frac{4}{51}\cos 20t - \frac{1}{51}\sin 20t.$$

As was observed on page 290 of the text, there is a correlation between the $RLC$ series circuits and mechanical vibration. Therefore, we can discuss the resonance frequency of the $RLC$ series circuit. To do so we associate the variable $L$ with $m$, $R$ with $b$, and $1/C$ with $k$. Thus, we see that the resonance frequency for an $RLC$ series circuit is given by $\gamma_r/(2\pi)$, where

$$\gamma_r = \sqrt{\frac{1}{CL} - \frac{R^2}{2L^2}},$$

provided that $R^2 < 2L/C$. For this problem

$$R^2 = 14,400 < 2L/C = 17,600.$$

Therefore, we can find the resonance frequency of this circuit. To do so we first find

$$\gamma_r = \sqrt{\frac{1}{CL} - \frac{R^2}{2L^2}} = \sqrt{\frac{2200}{4} - \frac{14400}{32}} = 10.$$

Hence the resonance frequency of this circuit is $10/(2\pi) = 5/\pi$.

# Chapter 5

**5.** In this problem, $C = 0.01\,\text{F}$, $L = 4\,\text{H}$, and $R = 10\,\Omega$. Hence, the equation governing the $RLC$ circuit is

$$4\frac{d^2 I}{dt^2} + 10\frac{dI}{dt} + \frac{1}{0.01}I = \frac{d}{dt}\left(E_0 \cos \gamma t\right) = -\frac{E_0 \gamma}{4} \sin \gamma t.$$

The frequency response curve $M(\gamma)$ for an $RLC$ curcuit is determined by

$$M(\gamma) = \frac{1}{\sqrt{[(1/C) - L\gamma^2]^2 + R^2\gamma^2}},$$

which comes from the comparison Table 5.3 on page 290 of the text and equation (13) in Section 4.9. Therefore

$$M(\gamma) = \frac{1}{\sqrt{[(1/0.01) - 4\gamma^2]^2 + (10)^2\gamma^2}} = \frac{1}{\sqrt{(100 - 4\gamma^2)^2 + 100\gamma^2}}.$$

The graph of this function is shown in Figure B.43 in the answers of the text. $M(\gamma)$ has its maximal value at the point $\gamma_0 = \sqrt{x_0}$, where $x_0$ is the point where the quadratic function $(100 - 4x)^2 + 100x$ attains its minimum (the first coordinate of the vertex). We find that

$$\gamma_0 = \sqrt{\frac{175}{8}} \qquad \text{and} \qquad M(\gamma_0) = \frac{2}{25\sqrt{15}} \approx 0.02.$$

**7.** This spring system satisfies the differential equation

$$7\frac{d^2 x}{dt^2} + 2\frac{dx}{dt} + 3x = 10\cos 10t.$$

Since we want to find an $RLC$ series circuit analog for the spring system with $R = 10$ ohms, we must find $L$, $1/C$, and $E(t)$ so that the differential equation

$$L\frac{d^2 q}{dt^2} + 10\frac{dq}{dt} + \frac{1}{C}q = E(t)$$

corresponds to the one above. Thus, we want $E(t) = 50\cos 10t$ volts, $L = 35$ henrys, and $C = 1/15$ farads.

**11.** For this electric network, there are three loops. Loop 1 is through a 10V battery, a 10$\Omega$ resistor, and a 20H inductor. Loop 2 is through a 10V battery, a 10$\Omega$ resistor, a 5$\Omega$ resistor, and a (1/30)F capacitor. Loop 3 is through a 5$\Omega$ resistor, a (1/30)F capacitor, and a 20H inductor.

320

Therefore, applying Kirchhoff's second law to this network yields the three equations given by

$$\text{Loop } 1: \quad 10I_1 + 20\frac{dI_2}{dt} = 10,$$

$$\text{Loop } 2: \quad 10I_1 + 5I_3 + 30q_3 = 10,$$

$$\text{Loop } 3: \quad 5I_3 + 30q_3 - 20\frac{dI_2}{dt} = 0.$$

Since the equation for Loop 2 minus the equation for Loop 1 yields the remaining equation, we will use the first and second equations above for our calculations. By examining a junction point, we see that we also have the equation $I_1 = I_2 + I_3$. Thus, we have $I_1' = I_2' + I_3'$. We begin by dividing the equation for Loop 1 by 10 and the equation for Loop 2 by 5. Differentiating the equation for Loop 2 yields the system

$$I_1 + 2\frac{dI_2}{dt} = 1,$$

$$2\frac{dI_1}{dt} + \frac{dI_3}{dt} + 6I_3 = 0,$$

where $I_3 = q_3'$. Since $I_1 = I_2 + I_3$ and $I_1' = I_2' + I_3'$, we can rewrite the system using operator notation in the form

$$(2D + 1)[I_2] + I_3 = 1,$$

$$(2D)[I_2] + (3D + 6)[I_3] = 0.$$

If we multiply the first equation above by $(3D + 6)$ and then subtract the second equation, we obtain

$$\{(3D + 6)(2D + 1) - 2D\}[I_2] = 6 \qquad \Rightarrow \qquad (6D^2 + 13D + 6)[I_2] = 6.$$

This last differential equation is a linear equation with constant coefficients whose associated equation, $6r^2 + 13r + 6 = 0$, has roots $-3/2, -2/3$. Therefore, the solution to the homogeneous equation corresponding to the equation above is given by

$$I_{2h}(t) = c_1 e^{-3t/2} + c_2 e^{-2t/3}.$$

By the method of undetermined coefficients, the form of a particular solution to the differential equation above will be $I_{2p}(t) = A$. By substituting this function into the differential equation,

Chapter 5

we see that a particular solution is given by

$$I_{2p}(t) = 1.$$

Thus, the current, $I_2$, will satisfy the equation

$$I_2(t) = c_1 e^{-3t/2} + c_2 e^{-2t/3} + 1.$$

As we noticed above, $I_3$ can now be found from the first equation

$$I_3(t) = -(2D+1)[I_2] + 1 = -2\left[-\frac{3}{2} c_1 e^{-3t/2} - \frac{2}{3} c_2 e^{-2t/3}\right] - \left[c_1 e^{-3t/2} + c_2 e^{-2t/3} + 1\right] + 1$$

$$\Rightarrow \quad I_3(t) = 2c_1 e^{-3t/2} + \frac{1}{3} c_2 e^{-2t/3}.$$

To find $I_1$, we will use the equation $I_1 = I_2 + I_3$. Therefore, we have

$$I_1(t) = c_1 e^{-3t/2} + c_2 e^{-2t/3} + 1 + 2c_1 e^{-3t/2} + \frac{1}{3} c_2 e^{-2t/3}$$

$$\Rightarrow \quad I_1(t) = 3c_1 e^{-3t/2} + \frac{4}{3} c_2 e^{-2t/3} + 1.$$

We will use the initial condition $I_2(0) = I_3(0) = 0$ to find the constants $c_1$ and $c_2$. Thus, we have

$$I_2(0) = c_1 + c_2 + 1 = 0 \quad \text{and} \quad I_3(0) = 2c_1 + \frac{1}{3} c_2 = 0.$$

Solving these two equations simultaneously yields $c_1 = 1/5$ and $c_2 = -6/5$. Therefore, the equations for the currents for this electric network are given by

$$I_1(t) = \frac{3}{5} e^{-3t/2} - \frac{8}{5} e^{-2t/3} + 1,$$

$$I_2(t) = \frac{1}{5} e^{-3t/2} - \frac{6}{5} e^{-2t/3} + 1,$$

$$I_3(t) = \frac{2}{5} e^{-3t/2} - \frac{2}{5} e^{-2t/3}.$$

**13.** In this problem, there are three loops. Loop 1 is through a 0.5 H inductor and a 1 Ω resistor. Loop 2 is through is through a 0.5 H inductor, a 0.5 F capacitor, and a voltage source supplying the voltage $\cos 3t$ V at time $t$. Loop 3 is through a 1 Ω resistor, a 0.5 F capacitor, and the voltage source. We apply Kirchhoff's voltage law, $E_L + E_R + E_C = E(t)$, to Loop 1 and Loop 2 to get two equations connecting currents in the network. (Similarly to Example 2 and Problem 11, there is no need to apply Kirchhoff's voltage law to Loop 3 because the resulting equation is just a linear combination of those for other two loops.)

Loop 1:

$$E_L + E_R = 0 \quad \Rightarrow \quad 0.5\frac{dI_1}{dt} + 1 \cdot I_2 = 0 \quad \Rightarrow \quad \frac{dI_1}{dt} + 2I_2 = 0. \qquad (5.37)$$

Loop 2:

$$E_L + E_C = \cos 3t \quad \Rightarrow \quad 0.5\frac{dI_1}{dt} + \frac{q_3}{0.5} = \cos 3t \quad \Rightarrow \quad \frac{dI_1}{dt} + 4q_3 = 2\cos 3t. \qquad (5.38)$$

Additionally, at joint points, by Kirchhoff's current law,

$$-I_1 + I_2 + I_3 = 0 \quad \Rightarrow \quad -I_1 + I_2 + \frac{dq_3}{dt} = 0. \qquad (5.39)$$

Putting (5.37)–(5.39) together yields the following system:

$$\frac{dI_1}{dt} + 2I_2 = 0,$$
$$\frac{dI_1}{dt} + 4q_3 = 2\cos 3t,$$
$$-I_1 + I_2 + \frac{dq_3}{dt} = 0$$

or, in operator form,

$$D[I_1] + 2I_2 = 0,$$
$$D[I_1] + 4q_3 = 2\cos 3t,$$
$$-I_1 + I_2 + D[q_3] = 0$$

with the initial condition $I_1(0) = I_2(0) = I_3(0) = 0$ ($I_3 = dq_3/dt$).

From the first equation, $I_2 = -(1/2)D[I_1]$, which (when substituted into the third equation) leads to the system

$$D[I_1] + 4q_3 = 2\cos 3t,$$
$$-(D+2)[I_1] + 2D[q_3] = 0.$$

Multiplying the first equation by $D$, the second equation – by 2, and subtracting the results, we eliminate $q_3$:

$$\{D^2 + 2(D+2)\}[I_1] = -6\sin 3t \qquad \Rightarrow \qquad (D^2 + 2D + 4)[I_1] = -6\sin 3t.$$

The roots of the characteristic equation, $r^2 + 2r + 4 = 0$, are $r = -1 \pm \sqrt{3}i$, and so a general solution to the corresponding homogeneous equation is

$$I_{1h} = C_1 e^{-t}\cos\sqrt{3}t + C_2 e^{-t}\sin\sqrt{3}t.$$

A particular solution has the form $I_{1p} = A\cos 3t + B\sin 3t$. Substitution into the equation yields

$$(-5A + 6B)\cos 3t + (-6A - 5B)\sin 3t = -6\sin 3t$$

$$\Rightarrow \qquad \begin{aligned} -5A + 6B &= 0, \\ -6A - 5B &= -6 \end{aligned} \qquad \Rightarrow \qquad \begin{aligned} A &= 36/61, \\ B &= 30/61. \end{aligned}$$

Therefore,

$$\begin{aligned} I_1 &= I_{1h} + I_{1p} \\ &= C_1 e^{-t}\cos\sqrt{3}t + C_2 e^{-t}\sin\sqrt{3}t + \frac{36}{61}\cos 3t + \frac{30}{61}\sin 3t. \end{aligned}$$

Substituting this solution into (5.37) we find that

$$\begin{aligned} I_2 &= -\frac{1}{2}\frac{dI_1}{dt} \\ &= \frac{C_1 - C_2\sqrt{3}}{2} e^{-t}\cos\sqrt{3}t + \frac{C_1\sqrt{3} + C_2}{2} e^{-t}\sin\sqrt{3}t - \frac{45}{61}\cos 3t + \frac{54}{61}\sin 3t. \end{aligned}$$

The initial condition, $I_1(0) = I_2(0) = 0$ yields

$$\begin{aligned} C_1 + 36/61 &= 0, \\ (C_1 - C_2\sqrt{3})/2 - 45/61 &= 0 \end{aligned} \qquad \Rightarrow \qquad \begin{aligned} C_1 &= -36/61, \\ C_2 &= -42\sqrt{3}/61. \end{aligned}$$

Thus

$$I_1 = -\frac{36}{61} e^{-t}\cos\sqrt{3}t - \frac{42\sqrt{3}}{61} e^{-t}\sin\sqrt{3}t + \frac{36}{61}\cos 3t + \frac{30}{61}\sin 3t,$$

$$I_2 = \frac{45}{61} e^{-t}\cos\sqrt{3}t - \frac{39\sqrt{3}}{61} e^{-t}\sin\sqrt{3}t - \frac{45}{61}\cos 3t + \frac{54}{61}\sin 3t,$$

$$I_3 = I_1 - I_2 = -\frac{81}{61} e^{-t}\cos\sqrt{3}t - \frac{3\sqrt{3}}{61} e^{-t}\sin\sqrt{3}t + \frac{81}{61}\cos 3t - \frac{24}{61}\sin 3t.$$

**EXERCISES 5.7:   Dynamical Systems, Poincarè Maps, and Chaos, page 301**

1. Let $\omega = 3/2$. Using system (3) on page 294 of the text with $A = F = 1$, $\phi = 0$, and $\omega = 3/2$, we define the Poincaré map

$$x_n = \sin(3\pi n) + \frac{1}{(9/4) - (4/4)} = \sin(3\pi n) + \frac{4}{5} = \frac{4}{5},$$

$$v_n = \frac{3}{2}\cos(3\pi n) = (-1)^n\frac{3}{2},$$

for $n = 0, 1, 2, \ldots$. Calculating the first few values of $(x_n, v_n)$, we find that they alternate between $(4/5, 3/2)$ and $(4/5, -3/2)$. Consequently, we can deduce that there is a subharmonic solution of period $4\pi$. Let $\omega = 3/5$. Using system (3) on page 294 of the text with $A = F = 1$, $\phi = 0$, and $\omega = 3/5$, we define the Poincaré map

$$x_n = \sin\left(\frac{6\pi n}{5}\right) + \frac{1}{(9/25) - 1} = \sin\left(\frac{6\pi n}{5}\right) - 1.5625,$$

$$v_n = \frac{3}{5}\cos\left(\frac{6\pi n}{5}\right) = (0.6)\cos\left(\frac{6\pi n}{5}\right),$$

for $n = 0, 1, 2, \ldots$. Calculating the first few values of $(x_n, v_n)$, we find that the Poincaré map cycles through the points

| | |
|---|---|
| $(-1.5625, 0.6)$, | $n = 0, 5, 10, \ldots$, |
| $(-2.1503, -0.4854)$, | $n = 1, 6, 11, \ldots$, |
| $(-0.6114, 0.1854)$, | $n = 2, 7, 12, \ldots$, |
| $(-2.5136, 0.1854)$, | $n = 3, 8, 13, \ldots$, |
| $(-0.9747, -0.4854)$, | $n = 4, 9, 14, \ldots$. |

Consequently, we can deduce that there is a subharmonic solution of period $10\pi$.

3. With $A = F = 1$, $\phi = 0$, $\omega = 1$, $b = -0.1$, and $\theta = 0$ (because $\tan\theta = (\omega^2 - 1)/b = 0$) the solution (5) to equation (4) becomes

$$x(t) = e^{0.05t}\sin\frac{\sqrt{3.99}}{2}t + 10\sin t.$$

Thus

$$v(t) = x'(t) = e^{0.05t}\left(0.05\sin\frac{\sqrt{3.99}}{2}t + \frac{\sqrt{3.99}}{2}\cos\frac{\sqrt{3.99}}{2}t\right) + 10\cos t$$

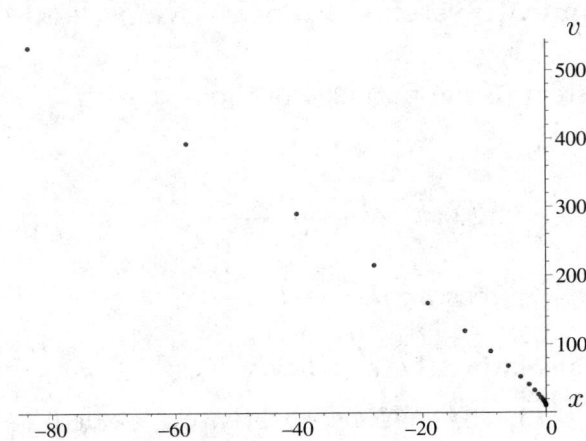

**Figure 5–A**: Poincaré section for Problem 3.

and, therefore,

$$x_n = x(2\pi n) \approx e^{0.1\pi n}\sin(1.997498\pi n),$$

$$v_n = v(2\pi n) \approx e^{0.1\pi n}\left(0.05\sin(1.997498\pi n) + 0.998749\cos(1.997498\pi n)\right) + 10.$$

The values of $x_n$ and $v_n$ for $n = 0, 1, \ldots, 20$ are listed in Table 5-F, and points $(x_n, v_n)$ are shown in Figure 5-A. When $n \to \infty$, the points $(x_n, v_n)$ become unbounded because of $e^{0.1\pi n}$ term.

5. We want to construct the Poincaré map using $t = 2\pi n$ for $x(t)$ given in equation (5) on page 295 of the text with $A = F = 1$, $\phi = 0$, $\omega = 1/3$, and $b = 0.22$. Since

$$\tan\theta = \frac{\omega^2 - 1}{b} = -4.040404,$$

we take $\theta = \tan^{-1}(-4.040404) = -1.328172$ and get

$$x_n = x(2\pi n) = e^{-0.22\pi n}\sin(0.629321\pi n) - (1.092050)\sin(1.328172),$$

$$v_n = x'(2\pi n) = -0.11e^{-0.22\pi n}\sin(0.629321\pi n) + (1.258642)e^{-0.22\pi n}\cos(0.629321\pi n)$$

$$+(1.092050)\cos(1.328172).$$

**Table 5–F**: Poincaré map for Problem 3.

| $n$ | $x_n$ | $v_n$ | $n$ | $x_n$ | $v_n$ |
|---|---|---|---|---|---|
| 0 | 0 | 10.998749 | 11 | −2.735915 | 41.387469 |
| 1 | −0.010761 | 11.366815 | 12 | −4.085318 | 52.925111 |
| 2 | −0.029466 | 11.870407 | 13 | −6.057783 | 68.700143 |
| 3 | −0.060511 | 12.559384 | 14 | −8.929255 | 90.267442 |
| 4 | −0.110453 | 13.501933 | 15 | −13.09442 | 119.75193 |
| 5 | −0.189009 | 14.791299 | 16 | −19.11674 | 160.05736 |
| 6 | −0.310494 | 16.554984 | 17 | −27.79923 | 215.15152 |
| 7 | −0.495883 | 18.967326 | 18 | −40.28442 | 290.45581 |
| 8 | −0.775786 | 22.266682 | 19 | −58.19561 | 393.37721 |
| 9 | −1.194692 | 26.778923 | 20 | −83.83579 | 534.03491 |
| 10 | −1.817047 | 32.949532 | | | |

In Table 5-G we have listed the first 21 values of the Poincaré map.

As $n$ gets large, we see that

$$x_n \approx -(1.092050)\sin(1.328172) \approx -1.060065,$$

$$v_n \approx (1.092050)\cos(1.328172) \approx 0.262366.$$

Hence, as $n \to \infty$, the Poincaré map approaches the point $(-1.060065, 0.262366)$.

**7.** Let $A$, $\phi$ and $A^*$, $\phi^*$ denote the values of constants $A$, $\phi$ in solution formula (2), corresponding to initial values $(x_0, v_0)$ and $(x_0^*, v_0^*)$, respectively.

(i) From recursive formulas (3) we conclude that

$$x_n - F/(\omega^2 - 1) = A\sin(2\pi\omega n + \phi),$$

$$v_n/\omega = A\cos(2\pi\omega n + \phi),$$

and so $(A, 2\pi\omega n + \phi)$ are polar coordinates of the point $(v_n/\omega, x_n - F/(\omega^2 - 1))$ in $vx$-plane. Similarly, $(A^*, 2\pi\omega n + \phi^*)$ represent polar coordinates of the point $(v_n^*/\omega, x_n^* - F/(\omega^2 - 1))$.

**Table 5–G**: Poincaré map for Problem 5.

| $n$ | $x_n$ | $v_n$ | $n$ | $x_n$ | $v_n$ |
|---|---|---|---|---|---|
| 0 | −1.060065 | 1.521008 | 11 | −1.059944 | 0.261743 |
| 1 | −0.599847 | 0.037456 | 12 | −1.060312 | 0.262444 |
| 2 | −1.242301 | 0.065170 | 13 | −1.059997 | 0.262491 |
| 3 | −1.103418 | 0.415707 | 14 | −1.060030 | 0.262297 |
| 4 | −0.997156 | 0.251142 | 15 | −1.060096 | 0.262362 |
| 5 | −1.074094 | 0.228322 | 16 | −1.060061 | 0.262385 |
| 6 | −1.070300 | 0.278664 | 17 | −1.060058 | 0.262360 |
| 7 | −1.052491 | 0.264458 | 18 | −1.060068 | 0.262364 |
| 8 | −1.060495 | 0.257447 | 19 | −1.060065 | 0.262369 |
| 9 | −1.061795 | 0.263789 | 20 | −1.060064 | 0.262366 |
| 10 | −1.059271 | 0.263037 | | | |

Therefore,

$$(v_n^*/\omega, x_n^* - F/(\omega^2 - 1)) \to (v_n/\omega, x_n - F/(\omega^2 - 1))$$

as $A^* \to A$ and $\phi^* \to \phi$ if $A \neq 0$ or as $A^* \to 0$ (regardless of $\phi^*$) if $A = 0$. Note that the convergence is uniform with respect to $n$. (One can easily see this from the distance formula in polar coordinates.) This is equivalent to

$$\begin{aligned} x_n^* - F/(\omega^2 - 1) &\to x_n - F/(\omega^2 - 1), \\ v_n^*/\omega &\to v_n/\omega \end{aligned} \qquad \Leftrightarrow \qquad \begin{aligned} x_n^* &\to x_n, \\ v_n^* &\to v_n \end{aligned}$$

uniformly with respect to $n$.

(ii) On the other hand, $A^*$ and $\phi^*$ satisfy

$$\begin{aligned} A^* \sin \phi^* + F/(\omega^2 - 1) &= x_0^*, \\ \omega A^* \cos \phi^* &= v_0^* \end{aligned} \qquad \Rightarrow \qquad \begin{aligned} A^* &= \sqrt{(x_0^* - F/(\omega^2 - 1))^2 + (v_0^*/\omega)^2}, \\ \cos \phi^* &= v_0^*/(\omega A^*). \end{aligned}$$

Therefore, $A^*$ is a continuous function of $(x_0^*, v_0^*)$ and so $A^* \to A$ as $(x_0^*, v_0^*) \to (x_0, v_0)$. If $(x_0, v_0)$ is such that $A \neq 0$, then $\phi^*$, as a function of $(x_0^*, v_0^*)$, is also continuous at $(x_0, v_0)$ and, therefore, $\phi^* \to \phi$ as $(x_0^*, v_0^*) \to (x_0, v_0)$.

Combining (i) and (ii) we conclude that

$$(x_n^*, v_n^*) \to (x_n, v_n) \qquad \text{as} \qquad (x_0^*, v_0^*) \to (x_0, v_0)$$

uniformly with respect to $n$. Thus, if $(x_0^*, v_0^*)$ is close to $(x_0, v_0)$, $(x_n^*, v_n^*)$ is close to $(x_n, v_n)$ for all $n$.

**9. (a)** When $x_0 = 1/7$, the doubling modulo 1 map gives

$$x_1 = \frac{2}{7} \,(\mathrm{mod}\,1) = \frac{2}{7}, \qquad\qquad x_2 = \frac{4}{7} \,(\mathrm{mod}\,1) = \frac{4}{7},$$

$$x_3 = \frac{8}{7} \,(\mathrm{mod}\,1) = \frac{1}{7}, \qquad\qquad x_4 = \frac{2}{7} \,(\mathrm{mod}\,1) = \frac{2}{7},$$

$$x_5 = \frac{4}{7} \,(\mathrm{mod}\,1) = \frac{4}{7}, \qquad\qquad x_6 = \frac{8}{7} \,(\mathrm{mod}\,1) = \frac{1}{7},$$

$$x_7 = \frac{2}{7} \,(\mathrm{mod}\,1) = \frac{2}{7}, \qquad\qquad \text{etc.}$$

This is the sequence $\left\{ \dfrac{1}{7}, \dfrac{2}{7}, \dfrac{4}{7}, \dfrac{1}{7}, \ldots \right\}$. For $x_0 = \dfrac{k}{7}$, $k = 2, \ldots, 6$, we obtain

$$\left\{ \frac{2}{7}, \frac{4}{7}, \frac{1}{7}, \frac{2}{7}, \ldots \right\}, \qquad \left\{ \frac{3}{7}, \frac{6}{7}, \frac{5}{7}, \frac{3}{7}, \ldots \right\},$$

$$\left\{ \frac{4}{7}, \frac{1}{7}, \frac{2}{7}, \frac{4}{7}, \ldots \right\}, \qquad \left\{ \frac{5}{7}, \frac{3}{7}, \frac{6}{7}, \frac{5}{7}, \ldots \right\},$$

$$\left\{ \frac{6}{7}, \frac{5}{7}, \frac{3}{7}, \frac{6}{7}, \ldots \right\}.$$

These sequences fall into two classes. The first has the repeating sequence $\overline{\dfrac{1}{7}, \dfrac{2}{7}, \dfrac{4}{7}}$ and the second has the repeating sequence $\overline{\dfrac{3}{7}, \dfrac{6}{7}, \dfrac{5}{7}}$.

**(c)** To see what happens, when $x_0 = \dfrac{k}{2^j}$, let's consider the special case when $x_0 = \dfrac{3}{2^2} = \dfrac{3}{4}$. Then,

$$x_1 = 2\left(\frac{3}{4}\right) (\mathrm{mod}\,1) = \frac{3}{2} \,(\mathrm{mod}\,1) = \frac{1}{2},$$

$$x_2 = 2\left(\frac{1}{2}\right)(\text{mod }1) = 1\,(\text{mod }1) = 0,$$

$$x_3 = 0,$$

$$x_4 = 0,$$

etc.

Observe that

$$x_2 = 2^2\left(\frac{3}{2^2}\right)(\text{mod }1) = 3\,(\text{mod }1) = 0.$$

In general,

$$x_j = 2^j\left(\frac{k}{2^j}\right)(\text{mod }1) = k\,(\text{mod }1) = 0.$$

Consequently, $x_n = 0$ for $n \geq j$.

**11. (a)** A general solution to equation (6) is given by $x(t) = x_h(t) + x_p(t)$, where

$$x_h(t) = Ae^{-0.11t}\sin\left(\sqrt{9879}t + \phi\right)$$

is the transient term (a general solution to the corresponding homogeneous equation) and

$$x_p(t) = \frac{1}{0.22}\sin t + \frac{1}{\sqrt{1 + 2(0.22)^2}}\sin\left(\sqrt{2}t + \psi\right), \quad \tan\psi = -\frac{1}{0.22\sqrt{2}},$$

is the steady-state term (a particular solution to (6)). ($x_p(t)$ can be found, say, by applying formula (7), Section 4.12, and using Superposition Principle of Section 4.7.) Differentiating $x(t)$ we get

$$v(t) = x'_h(t) + x'_p(t) = x'_h(t) + \frac{1}{0.22}\cos t + \frac{\sqrt{2}}{\sqrt{1 + 2(0.22)^2}}\cos\left(\sqrt{2}t + \psi\right).$$

The steady-state solution does not depend on initial values $x_0$ and $v_0$; these values affect only constants $A$ and $\phi$ in the transient part. But, as $t \to \infty$, $x_h(t)$ and $x'_h(t)$ tend to zero and so the values of $x(t)$ and $v(t)$ approach the values of $x_p(t)$ and $x'_p(t)$, respectively. Thus the limit set of points $(x(t), v(t))$ is the same as that of $(x_p(t), x'_p(t))$ which is independent of initial values.

**(b)** Substitution $t = 2\pi n$ into $x_p(t)$ and $x_p'(t)$ yields

$$x_n = x(2\pi n) = x_h(2\pi n) + \frac{1}{\sqrt{1 + 2(0.22)^2}} \sin\left(\sqrt{2}2\pi n + \psi\right),$$

$$v_n = v(2\pi n) = x_h'(2\pi n) + \frac{1}{0.22} + \frac{\sqrt{2}}{\sqrt{1 + 2(0.22)^2}} \cos\left(\sqrt{2}2\pi n + \psi\right).$$

As $n \to \infty$, $x_h(2\pi n) \to 0$ and $x_h'(2\pi n) \to 0$. Therefore, for $n$ large,

$$x_n \approx \frac{1}{\sqrt{1 + 2(0.22)^2}} \sin\left(\sqrt{2}2\pi n + \psi\right) = a \sin\left(2\sqrt{2}\pi n + \psi\right),$$

$$v_n \approx \frac{1}{0.22} + \frac{\sqrt{2}}{\sqrt{1 + 2(0.22)^2}} \cos\left(\sqrt{2}2\pi n + \psi\right) = c + \sqrt{2}a \cos\left(2\sqrt{2}\pi n + \psi\right).$$

**(c)** From part (b) we conclude that, for $n$ large

$$x_n^2 \approx a^2 \sin^2\left(2\sqrt{2}\pi n + \psi\right) \quad \text{and} \quad (v_n - c)^2 \approx 2a^2 \cos^2\left(2\sqrt{2}\pi n + \psi\right).$$

Dividing the latter by 2 and summing yields

$$x_n^2 + \frac{(v_n - c)^2}{2} \approx a^2 \left[\sin^2\left(2\sqrt{2}\pi n + \psi\right) + \cos^2\left(2\sqrt{2}\pi n + \psi\right)\right] = a^2,$$

and the error (coming from the transient part) tends to zero as $n \to \infty$. Thus any limiting point of the sequence $(x_n, v_n)$ satisfies the equation

$$x^2 + \frac{(v - c)^2}{2} = a^2,$$

which is an ellipse centered at $(0, c)$ with semiaxes $a$ and $a\sqrt{2}$.

## REVIEW PROBLEMS:  page 304

**1.** Expressing the system in the operator notation gives

$$D[x] + \left(D^2 + 1\right)[y] = 0,$$
$$D^2[x] + D[y] = 0.$$

# Chapter 5

Eliminating $x$ by applying $D$ to the first equation and subtracting the second equation from it yields

$$\{D(D^2+1) - D\}[y] = 0 \qquad \Rightarrow \qquad D^3[y] = 0.$$

Thus on integrating 3 times we get

$$y(t) = C_3 + C_2 t + C_1 t^2.$$

We substitute this solution into the first equation of given system to get

$$x' = -(y'' + y) = -[(2C_1) + (C_3 + C_2 t + C_1 t^2)] = -[(C_3 + 2C_1) + C_2 t + C_1 t^2].$$

Integrating we obtain

$$x(t) = -\int \left[(C_3 + 2C_1) + C_2 t + C_1 t^2\right] dt = C_4 - (C_3 + 2C_1)t - \frac{1}{2}C_2 t^2 - \frac{1}{3}C_1 t^3.$$

Thus the general solution of the given system is

$$x(t) = C_4 - (C_3 + 2C_1)t - \frac{1}{2}C_2 t^2 - \frac{1}{3}C_1 t^3,$$
$$y(t) = C_3 + C_2 t + C_1 t^2.$$

**3.** Writing the system in operator form yields

$$\begin{aligned}(2D-3)[x] - (D+1)[y] &= e^t, \\ (-4D+15)[x] + (3D-1)[y] &= e^{-t}.\end{aligned} \tag{5.40}$$

We eliminate $y$ by multiplying the first equation by $(3D-1)$, the second – by $(D+1)$, and summing the results.

$$\{(2D-3)(3D-1) + (-4D+15)(D+1)\}[x] = (3D-1)[e^t] + (D+1)[e^{-t}]$$
$$\Rightarrow \qquad (D^2+9)[x] = e^t.$$

Since the characterictic equation, $r^2 + 9 = 0$, has roots $r = \pm 3i$, a general solution to the corresponding homogeneous equation is

$$x_h(t) = c_1 \cos 3t + c_2 \sin 3t.$$

We look for a particular solution of the form $x_p(t) = Ae^t$. Substituting this function into the equation, we obtain

$$Ae^t + 9Ae^t = e^t \quad \Rightarrow \quad A = \frac{1}{10} \quad \Rightarrow \quad x_p(t) = \frac{e^t}{10},$$

and so

$$x(t) = x_h(t) + x_p(t) = c_1 \cos 3t + c_2 \sin 3t + \frac{e^t}{10}.$$

To find $y$, we multiply the first equation in (5.40) by 3 and add to the second equation. This yields

$$2(D+3)[x] - 4y = 3e^t + e^{-t}.$$

Thus

$$
\begin{aligned}
y &= \frac{1}{2}(D+3)[x] - \frac{3}{4}e^t - \frac{1}{4}e^{-t} \\
&= \frac{3(c_1 + c_2)}{2}\cos 3t - \frac{3(c_1 - c_2)}{2}\sin 3t - \frac{11}{20}e^t - \frac{1}{4}e^{-t}.
\end{aligned}
$$

5. Differentiating the second equation, we obtain $y'' = z'$. We eliminate $z$ from the first and the third equations by substituting $y'$ for $z$ and $y''$ for $z'$ into them:

$$
\begin{aligned}
x' &= y' - y, \\
y'' &= y' - x
\end{aligned}
\quad \Rightarrow \quad
\begin{aligned}
x' - y' + y &= 0, \\
y'' - y' + x &= 0
\end{aligned}
\tag{5.41}
$$

or, in operator notation,

$$
\begin{aligned}
D[x] - (D-1)[y] &= 0, \\
x + (D^2 - D)[y] &= 0.
\end{aligned}
$$

We eliminate $y$ by applying $D$ to the first equation and adding the result to the second equation:

$$\left\{ D^2[x] - D(D-1)[y] \right\} + \left\{ x + (D^2 - D)[y] \right\} = 0 \quad \Rightarrow \quad \left(D^2 + 1\right)[x] = 0.$$

This equation is the simple harmonic equation, and its general solution is given by

$$x(t) = C_1 \cos t + C_2 \sin t.$$

Chapter 5

Substituting $x(t)$ into the first equation of the system (5.41) yields

$$y' - y = -C_1 \sin t + C_2 \cos t. \tag{5.42}$$

The general solution to the corresponding homogeneous equation, $y' - y = 0$, is

$$y_h(t) = C_3 e^t.$$

We look for a particular solution to (5.42) of the form $y_p(t) = C_4 \cos t + C_5 \sin t$. Differentiating, we obtain $y_p'(t) = -C_4 \sin t + C_5 \cos t$. Thus the equation (5.42) becomes

$$
\begin{aligned}
-C_1 \sin t + C_2 \cos t = y_p' - y &= (-C_4 \sin t + C_5 \cos t) - (C_4 \cos t + C_5 \sin t) \\
&= (C_5 - C_4) \cos t - (C_5 + C_4) \sin t.
\end{aligned}
$$

Equating the coefficients yields

$$
\begin{aligned}
C_5 - C_4 &= C_2, \\
C_5 + C_4 &= C_1
\end{aligned} \tag{5.43}
$$

$$\Rightarrow \quad \text{(by adding the equations)} \quad 2C_5 = C_1 + C_2 \quad \Rightarrow \quad C_5 = \frac{C_1 + C_2}{2}.$$

From the second equation in (5.43), we find

$$C_4 = C_1 - C_5 = \frac{C_1 - C_2}{2}.$$

Therefore, the general solution to the equation (5.42) is

$$y(t) = y_h(t) + y_p(t) = C_3 e^t + \frac{C_1 - C_2}{2} \cos t + \frac{C_1 + C_2}{2} \sin t.$$

Finally, we find $z(t)$ from the second equation:

$$
\begin{aligned}
z(t) &= y'(t) = \left( C_3 e^t + \frac{C_1 - C_2}{2} \cos t + \frac{C_1 + C_2}{2} \sin t \right)' \\
&= C_3 e^t - \frac{C_1 - C_2}{2} \sin t + \frac{C_1 + C_2}{2} \cos t.
\end{aligned}
$$

Hence, the general solution to the given system is

$$x(t) = C_1 \cos t + C_2 \sin t,$$

$$y(t) = C_3 e^t + \frac{C_1 - C_2}{2} \cos t + \frac{C_1 + C_2}{2} \sin t,$$

$$z(t) = C_3 e^t - \frac{C_1 - C_2}{2} \sin t + \frac{C_1 + C_2}{2} \cos t.$$

To find constants $C_1$, $C_2$, and $C_3$, we use the initial conditions. So we get

$$0 = x(0) = C_1 \cos 0 + C_2 \sin 0 = C_1,$$

$$0 = y(0) = C_3 e^0 + \frac{C_1 - C_2}{2} \cos 0 + \frac{C_1 + C_2}{2} \sin 0 = C_3 + \frac{C_1 - C_2}{2},$$

$$2 = z(0) = C_3 e^0 - \frac{C_1 - C_2}{2} \sin 0 + \frac{C_1 + C_2}{2} \cos 0 = C_3 + \frac{C_1 + C_2}{2},$$

which simplifies to

$$C_1 = 0,$$

$$C_1 - C_2 + 2C_3 = 0,$$

$$C_1 + C_2 + 2C_3 = 4.$$

Solving we obtain $C_1 = 0$, $C_2 = 2$, $C_3 = 1$ and so

$$x(t) = 2 \sin t, \qquad y(t) = e^t - \cos t + \sin t, \qquad z(t) = e^t + \cos t + \sin t.$$

7. Let $x(t)$ and $y(t)$ denote the mass of salt in tanks A and B, respectively. The only difference between this problem and the problem in Section 5.1 is that a brine solution flows in tank A instead of pure water. This change affects the input rate for tank A only, adding

$$6\,\text{L/min} \times 0.2\,\text{kg/L} = 1.2\,\text{kg/min}$$

to the original $(y/12)\,$kg/min. Thus the system (1) on page 242 becomes

$$x' = -\frac{1}{3}x + \frac{1}{12}y + 1.2\,,$$

$$y' = \frac{1}{3}x - \frac{1}{3}y.$$

Following the solution in Section 5.1, we express $x = 3y' + y$ from the second equation and substitute it into the first equation.

$$(3y' + y)' = -\frac{1}{3}(3y' + y) + \frac{1}{12}y + 1.2 \quad \Rightarrow \quad 3y'' + 2y' + \frac{1}{4}y = 1.2\,.$$

# Chapter 5

A general solution to the corresponding homogeneous equation is given in (3) on page 243 of the text:

$$y_h(t) = c_1 e^{-t/2} + c_2 e^{-t/6}.$$

A particular solution has the form $y_p(t) \equiv C$, which results

$$3(C)'' + 2(C)' + \frac{1}{4}C = 1.2 \qquad \Rightarrow \qquad C = 4.8.$$

Therefore, $y_p(t) \equiv 4.8$, and a general solution to the system is

$$y(t) = y_h(t) + y_p(t) = c_1 e^{-t/2} + c_2 e^{-t/6} + 4.8,$$
$$x(t) = 3y'(t) + y(t) = -\frac{c_1}{2} e^{-t/2} + \frac{c_2}{2} e^{-t/6} + 4.8.$$

We find constants $c_1$ and $c_2$ from the initial conditions, $x(0) = 0.1$ and $y(0) = 0.3$. Substitution yields the system

$$-\frac{c_1}{2} + \frac{c_2}{2} + 4.8 = 0.1,$$
$$c_1 + c_2 + 4.8 = 0.3.$$

Solving, we obtain $c_1 = 49/20$, $c_2 = -139/20$, and so

$$x(t) = -\frac{49}{40} e^{-t/2} - \frac{139}{40} e^{-t/6} + 4.8,$$
$$y(t) = \frac{49}{20} e^{-t/2} - \frac{139}{20} e^{-t/6} + 4.8.$$

**9.** We first rewrite the given differential equation in an equivalent form as

$$y''' = \frac{1}{3}\left(5 + e^t y - 2y'\right).$$

Denoting $x_1(t) = y(t)$, $x_2(t) = y'(t)$, and $x_3(t) = y''(t)$, we conclude that

$$x_1' = y' = x_2,$$
$$x_2' = (y')' = y'' = x_3,$$
$$x_3' = (y'')' = y''' = \frac{1}{3}\left(5 + e^t x_1 - 2x_2\right),$$

that is,

$$x_1' = x_2,$$
$$x_2' = x_3,$$
$$x_3' = \frac{1}{3}\left(5 + e^t x_1 - 2x_2\right).$$

**11.** This system is equivalent to

$$x''' = t - y' - y'',$$
$$y''' = x' - x''.$$

Next, we introduce, as additional unknowns, derivatives of $x(t)$ and $y(t)$:

$$x_1(t) := x(t), \quad x_2(t) := x'(t), \quad x_3(t) := x''(t),$$
$$x_4(t) := y(t), \quad x_5(t) := y'(t), \quad x_6(t) := y''(t).$$

With new variables, the system becomes

$$x''' = (x'')' =: x_3' = t - y' - y'' =: t - x_5 - x_6,$$
$$y''' = (y'')' =: x_6' = x' - x'' =: x_2 - x_3.$$

Also, we have four new equations connecting $x_j$'s:

$$x_1' = x' =: x_2,$$
$$x_2' = (x')' = x'' =: x_3,$$
$$x_4' = y' =: x_5,$$
$$x_5' = (y')' = y'' =: x_6.$$

Therefore, the answer is

$$x_1' = x_2,$$
$$x_2' = x_3,$$
$$x_3' = t - x_5 - x_6,$$

$$x'_4 = x_5,$$

$$x'_5 = x_6,$$

$$x'_6 = x_2 - x_3.$$

**13.** With the notation used in (1) on page 264 of the text,

$$f(x,y) = 4 - 4y,$$

$$g(x,y) = -4x,$$

and the phase plane equation (see equation (2) on page 265 of the text) can be written as

$$\frac{dy}{dx} = \frac{g(x,y)}{f(x,y)} = \frac{-4x}{4 - 4y} = \frac{x}{y-1}.$$

This equation is separable. Separating variables yields

$$(y-1)\,dy = x\,dx \quad \Rightarrow \quad \int (y-1)\,dy = \int x\,dx \quad \Rightarrow \quad (y-1)^2 + C = x^2$$

or $x^2 - (y-1)^2 = C$, where $C$ is an arbitrary constant. We find the critical points by solving the system

$$\begin{aligned} f(x,y) = 4 - 4y = 0, \\ g(x,y) = -4x = 0 \end{aligned} \quad \Rightarrow \quad \begin{aligned} y = 1, \\ x = 0. \end{aligned}$$

So, $(0,1)$ is the unique critical point. For $y > 1$,

$$\frac{dx}{dt} = 4(1-y) < 0,$$

which implies that trajectories flow to the left. Similarly, for $y < 1$, trajectories flow to the right. Comparing the phase plane diagram with those given on Figure 5.12 on page 270 of the text, we conclude that the critical point $(0,1)$ is a saddle (unstable) point.

**15.** Some integral curves and the direction field for the given system are shown in Figure 5-B. Comparing this picture with Figure 5.12 on page 270 of the text, we conclude that the origin is an asymptotically stable spiral point.

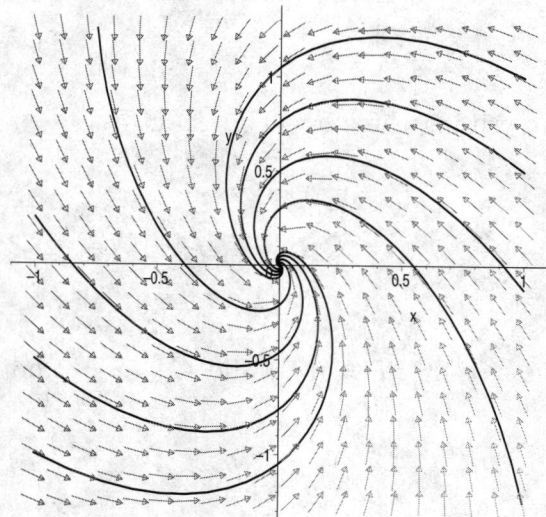

**Figure 5–B**: Integral curves and the direction field for Problem 15.

**17.** A trajectory is a path traced by an actual solution pair $(x(t), y(t))$ as $t$ increases; thus it is a directed (oriented) curve. An integral curve is the graph of a solution to the phase plane equation; it has no direction. All trajectories lie along (parts of) integral curves. A given integral curve can be the underlying point set for several different trajectories.

**19.** We apply Kirchhoff's voltage law to Loops 1 and 2.

Loop 1 contains a capacitor $C$ and a resistor $R_2$; note that the direction of the loop is opposite to that of $I_2$. Thus we have

$$\frac{q}{C} - R_2 I_2 = 0 \qquad \Rightarrow \qquad \frac{q}{C} = R_2 I_2,$$

where $q$ denotes the charge of the capacitor.

Loop 2 consists of an inductor $L$ and two resistors $R_1$ and $R_2$; note that the loop direction is opposite to the direction of $I_3$. Therefore,

$$R_2 I_2 - R_1 I_3 - L I_3' = 0 \qquad \Rightarrow \qquad R_2 I_2 = R_1 I_3 + L I_3'.$$

Chapter 5

For the top juncture, all the currents flow out, and the Kirchhoff's current law gives

$$-I_1 - I_2 - I_3 = 0 \qquad \Rightarrow \qquad I_1 + I_2 + I_3 = 0.$$

Therefore, the system, describing the current in $RLC$, is

$$\frac{q}{C} = R_2 I_2,$$
$$R_2 I_2 = R_1 I_3 + L I_3',$$
$$I_1 + I_2 + I_3 = 0.$$

With given data, $R_1 = R_2 = 1\,\Omega$, $L = 1\,\mathrm{H}$, and $C = 1\,\mathrm{F}$, and the relation $I_1 = dq/dt$, this system becomes

$$q = I_2,$$
$$I_2 = I_3 + I_3',$$
$$q' + I_2 + I_3 = 0.$$

Replacing in the last two equations $I_2$ by $q$, we get

$$I_3' + I_3 - q = 0,$$
$$q' + q + I_3 = 0.$$

We eliminate $q$ by substituting $q = I_3' + I_3$ into the second equation and obtain

$$I_3'' + 2I_3' + 2I_3 = 0.$$

The characteristic equation, $r^2 + 2r + 2 = 0$, has roots $r = -1 \pm i$ and so, a general solution to this homogeneous equation is $I_3 = e^{-t}(A\cos t + B\sin t)$. Thus

$$
\begin{aligned}
I_2 = q &= I_3' + I_3 \\
&= -e^{-t}(A\cos t + B\sin t) + e^{-t}(-A\sin t + B\cos t) + e^{-t}(A\cos t + B\sin t) \\
&= e^{-t}(B\cos t - A\sin t)
\end{aligned}
$$

and

$$
\begin{aligned}
I_1 = \frac{dq}{dt} &= -e^{-t}(B\cos t - A\sin t) + e^{-t}(-B\sin t - A\cos t) \\
&= e^{-t}[(A - B)\sin t - (A + B)\cos t].
\end{aligned}
$$

340

# CHAPTER 6: Theory of Higher Order Linear Differential Equations

**EXERCISES 6.1:** **Basic Theory of Linear Differential Equations, page 324**

**1.** Putting the equation in standard form,

$$y''' - \frac{3}{x} y' + \frac{e^x}{x} y = \frac{x^2 - 1}{x},$$

we find that

$$p_1(x) \equiv 0, \quad p_2(x) = -\frac{3}{x}, \quad p_3(x) = \frac{e^x}{x}, \quad \text{and} \quad q(x) = \frac{x^2 - 1}{x}.$$

Functions $p_2(x)$, $p_3(x)$, and $q(x)$ have only one point of discontinuity, $x = 0$, while $p_1(x)$ is continuous everywhere. Therefore, all these functions are continuous on $(-\infty, 0)$ and $(0, \infty)$. Since the initial point, $x_0 = 2$, belongs to $(-\infty, 0)$, Theorem 1 guarantees the existence of a unique solution to the given initial value problem on $(-\infty, 0)$.

**3.** For this problem, $p_1(x) = -1$, $p_2(x) = \sqrt{x - 1}$, and $g(x) = \tan x$. Note that $p_1(x)$ is continuous everywhere, $p_2(x)$ is continuous for $x \geq 1$, and $g(x)$ is continuous everywhere except at odd multiples of $\pi/2$. Therefore, these three functions are continuous simultaneously on the intervals

$$\left[1, \frac{\pi}{2}\right), \quad \left(\frac{\pi}{2}, \frac{3\pi}{2}\right), \quad \left(\frac{3\pi}{2}, \frac{5\pi}{2}\right), \dots.$$

Because 5, the initial point, is in the interval $(3\pi/2, 5\pi/2)$, Theorem 1 guarantees that we have a unique solution to the initial value problem on this interval.

**5.** Dividing the equation by $x\sqrt{x + 1}$, we obtain

$$y''' - \frac{1}{x\sqrt{x + 1}} y' + \frac{1}{\sqrt{x + 1}} y = 0.$$

# Chapter 6

Thus $p_1(x) \equiv 0$, $p_2(x) = 1/(x\sqrt{x+1})$, $p_3(x) = 1/\sqrt{x+1}$, and $g(x) \equiv 0$. Functions $p_1(x)$ and $q(x)$ are continuous on whole real line; $p_3(x)$ is defined and continuous for $x > -1$; $p_2(x)$ is defined and continuous for $x > -1$ and $x \neq 0$. Therefore, all these function is continuous on $(-1, 0)$ and $(0, \infty)$. The initial point lies on $(0, \infty)$, and so, by Theorem 1, the given initial value problem has a unique solution on $(0, \infty)$.

**7.** Assume that $c_1$, $c_2$, and $c_3$ are constants for which

$$c_1 e^{3x} + c_2 e^{5x} + c_3 e^{-x} \equiv 0 \quad \text{on} \quad (-\infty, \infty). \tag{6.1}$$

If we show that this is possible only if $c_1 = c_2 = c_3 = 0$, then linear independence will follow. Evaluating the linear combination in (6.1) at $x = 0$, $x = \ln 2$, and $x = -\ln 2$, we find that constants $c_1$, $c_2$, and $c_3$ satisfy

$$c_1 + c_2 + c_3 = 0,$$
$$8c_1 + 32c_2 + \frac{1}{2}c_3 = 0,$$
$$\frac{1}{8}c_1 + \frac{1}{32}c_2 + 2c_3 = 0.$$

This system is a homogeneous system of linear equations whose determinant

$$\begin{vmatrix} 1 & 1 & 1 \\ 8 & 32 & 1/2 \\ 1/8 & 1/32 & 2 \end{vmatrix} = \begin{vmatrix} 32 & 1/2 \\ 1/32 & 2 \end{vmatrix} - \begin{vmatrix} 8 & 1/2 \\ 1/8 & 2 \end{vmatrix} + \begin{vmatrix} 8 & 32 \\ 1/8 & 1/32 \end{vmatrix} = \frac{2827}{64} \neq 0.$$

Hence it has the unique trivial solution, that is, $c_1 = c_2 = c_3 = 0$.

**9.** Let $y_1 = \sin^2 x$, $y_2 = \cos^2 x$, and $y_3 = 1$. We want to find $c_1$, $c_2$, and $c_3$, not all zero, such that

$$c_1 y_1 + c_2 y_2 + c_3 y_3 = c_1 \sin^2 x + c_2 \cos^2 x + c_3 \cdot 1 = 0,$$

for all $x$ in the interval $(-\infty, \infty)$. Since $\sin^2 x + \cos^2 x = 1$ for all real numbers $x$, we can choose $c_1 = 1$, $c_2 = 1$, and $c_3 = -1$. Thus, these functions are linearly dependent.

**11.** Let $y_1 = x^{-1}$, $y_2 = x^{1/2}$, and $y_3 = x$. We want to find constants $c_1$, $c_2$, and $c_3$ such that

$$c_1 y_1 + c_2 y_2 + c_3 y_3 = c_1 x^{-1} + c_2 x^{1/2} + c_3 x = 0,$$

for all $x$ on the interval $(0, \infty)$. This equation must hold if $x = 1$, 4, or 9 (or any other values for $x$ in the interval $(0, \infty)$). By plugging these values for $x$ into the equation above, we see that $c_1$, $c_2$, and $c_3$ must satisfy the three equations

$$c_1 + c_2 + c_3 = 0,$$
$$\frac{c_1}{4} + 2c_2 + 4c_3 = 0,$$
$$\frac{c_1}{9} + 3c_2 + 9c_3 = 0.$$

Solving these three equations simultaneously yields $c_1 = c_2 = c_3 = 0$. Thus, the only way for $c_1 x^{-1} + c_2 x^{1/2} + c_3 x = 0$ for all $x$ on the interval $(0, \infty)$, is for $c_1 = c_2 = c_3 = 0$. Therefore, these three functions are linearly independent on $(0, \infty)$.

**13.** A linear combination, $c_1 x + c_2 x^2 + c_3 x^3 + c_4 x^4$, is a polynomial of degree at most four, and so, by the fundamental theorem of algebra, it cannot have more than four zeros unless it is the zero polynomial (that is, it has all zero coefficients). Thus, if this linear combination vanishes on *an interval*, then $c_1 = c_2 = c_3 = c_4 = 0$. Therefore, the functions $x$, $x^2$, $x^3$, and $x^4$ are linearly independent on any interval, in particular, on $(-\infty, \infty)$.

**15.** Since, by inspection, $r = 3$, $r = -1$, and $r = -4$ are the roots of the characteristic equation, $r^3 + 2r^2 - 11r - 12 = 0$, the functions $e^{3x}$, $e^{-x}$, and $e^{-4x}$ form a solution set. Next, we check that these functions are linearly independent by showing that their Wronskian is never zero.

$$W\left[e^{3x}, e^{-x}, e^{-4x}\right](x) = \begin{vmatrix} e^{3x} & e^{-x} & e^{-4x} \\ 3e^{3x} & -e^{-x} & -4e^{-4x} \\ 9e^{3x} & e^{-x} & 16e^{-4x} \end{vmatrix} = e^{3x}e^{-x}e^{-4x}\begin{vmatrix} 1 & 1 & 1 \\ 3 & -1 & -4 \\ 9 & 1 & 16 \end{vmatrix} = -84e^{-2x},$$

which does not vanish. Therefore, $\{e^{3x}, e^{-x}, e^{-4x}\}$ is a fundamental solution set and, by Theorem 4, a general solution to the given differential equation is

$$y = C_1 e^{3x} + C_2 e^{-x} + C_3 e^{-4x}.$$

**17.** Writing the given differential equation,

$$x^3 y''' - 3x^2 y'' + 6xy' - 6y = 0,$$

in standard form (17), we see that its coefficients, $-3/x$, $6/x^2$, and $-6/x^3$ are continuous on the specified interval, which is $x > 0$.

Next, substituting $x$, $x^2$, and $x^3$ into the differential equation, we verify that these functions are indeed solutions.

$$x^3 (x)''' - 3x^2 (x)'' + 6x(x)' - 6(x) = 0 - 0 + 6x - 6x = 0,$$
$$x^3 (x^2)''' - 3x^2 (x^2)'' + 6x(x^2)' - 6(x^2) = 0 - 6x^2 + 12x^2 - 6x^2 = 0,$$
$$x^3 (x^3)''' - 3x^2 (x^3)'' + 6x(x^3)' - 6(x^3) = 6x^3 - 18x^3 + 18x^3 - 6x^3 = 0.$$

Evaluating the Wronskian yields

$$W\left[x, x^2, x^3\right](x) = \begin{vmatrix} x & x^2 & x^3 \\ 1 & 2x & 3x^2 \\ 0 & 2 & 6x \end{vmatrix}$$

$$= x \begin{vmatrix} 2x & 3x^2 \\ 2 & 6x \end{vmatrix} - \begin{vmatrix} x^2 & x^3 \\ 2 & 6x \end{vmatrix} = x\left(6x^2\right) - \left(4x^3\right) = 2x^3.$$

Thus $W\left[x, x^2, x^3\right](x) \neq 0$ on $(0, \infty)$ and so $\{x, x^2, x^3\}$ is a fundamental solution set for the given differential equation. We involve Theorem 2 to conclude that

$$y = C_1 x + C_2 x^2 + C_3 x^3$$

is a general solution.

**19.** **(a)** Since $\{e^x, e^{-x}\cos 2x, e^{-x}\sin 2x, \}$ is a fundamental solution set for the associated homogeneous differential equation and since $y_p = x^2$ is a solution to the nonhomogeneous equation, by the superposition principle, we have a general solution given by

$$y(x) = C_1 e^x + C_2 e^{-x}\cos 2x + C_3 e^{-x}\sin 2x + x^2.$$

**(b)** To find the solution that satisfies the initial conditions, we must differentiate the general solution $y(x)$ twice with respect to $x$. Thus, we have

$$
\begin{aligned}
y'(x) &= C_1 e^x - C_2 e^{-x} \cos 2x - 2C_2 e^{-x} \sin 2x - C_3 e^{-x} \sin 2x + 2C_3 e^{-x} \cos 2x + 2x \\
&= C_1 e^x + (-C_2 + 2C_3)\, e^{-x} \cos 2x + (-2C_2 - C_3)\, e^{-x} \sin 2x + 2x\,, \\
y''(x) &= C_1 e^x + (C_2 - 2C_3)\, e^{-x} \cos 2x - 2\left(-C_2 + 2C_3\right) e^{-x} \sin 2x \\
&\qquad - \left(-2C_2 - C_3\right) e^{-x} \sin 2x + 2\left(-2C_2 - C_3\right) e^{-x} \cos 2x + 2 \\
&= C_1 e^x + (-3C_2 - 4C_3)\, e^{-x} \cos 2x + (4C_2 - 3C_3)\, e^{-x} \sin 2x + 2\,.
\end{aligned}
$$

Plugging the initial conditions into these formulas, yields the equations

$$
\begin{aligned}
y(0) &= C_1 + C_2 = -1, \\
y'(0) &= C_1 - C_2 + 2C_3 = 1, \\
y''(0) &= C_1 - 3C_2 - 4C_3 + 2 = -3.
\end{aligned}
$$

By solving these equations simultaneously, we obtain $C_1 = -1$, $C_2 = 0$, and $C_3 = 1$. Therefore, the solution to the initial value problem is given by

$$
y(x) = -e^x + e^{-x} \sin 2x + x^2.
$$

**21.** In the standard form, given equation becomes

$$
y''' + \frac{1}{x^2}\, y' - \frac{1}{x^3}\, y = \frac{3 - \ln x}{x^3}\,.
$$

Since its coefficients are continuous on $(0, \infty)$, we can apply Theorems 2 and 4 to conclude that a general solution to the corresponding homogeneous equation is

$$
y_h(x) = C_1 x + C_2 x \ln x + C_3 x (\ln x)^2
$$

and a general solution to the given nonhomogeneous equation is

$$
y(x) = y_p(x) + y_h(x) = \ln x + C_1 x + C_2 x \ln x + C_3 x (\ln x)^2\,.
$$

To satisfy the initial conditions, first we find

$$y'(x) = \frac{1}{x} + C_1 + C_2(\ln x + 1) + C_3\left[(\ln x)^2 + 2\ln x\right],$$

$$y''(x) = -\frac{1}{x^2} + \frac{C_2}{x} + C_3\left[\frac{2\ln x}{x} + \frac{2}{x}\right].$$

Substituting the initial conditions, $y(1) = 3$, $y'(1) = 3$, and $y''(1) = 0$, we get the system

$$
\begin{aligned}
3 &= y(1) = C_1, \\
3 &= y'(1) = 1 + C_1 + C_2, \\
0 &= y''(1) = -1 + C_2 + 2C_3
\end{aligned}
\qquad \Rightarrow \qquad
\begin{aligned}
C_1 &= 3, \\
C_1 + C_2 &= 2, \\
C_2 + 2C_3 &= 1
\end{aligned}
\qquad \Rightarrow \qquad
\begin{aligned}
C_1 &= 3, \\
C_2 &= -1, \\
C_3 &= 1.
\end{aligned}
$$

Thus,

$$y(x) = \ln x + 3x - x\ln x + x(\ln x)^2$$

is the desired solution.

**23.** Substituting $y_1(x) = \sin x$ and $y_2(x) = x$ into the given differential operator yields

$$L[\sin x] = (\sin x)''' + (sinx)' + x(\sin x) = -\cos x + \cos x + x\sin x = x\sin x,$$

$$L[x] = (x)''' + (x)' + x(x) = 0 + 1 + x^2 = x^2 + 1.$$

Note that $L[y]$ is a linear operator of the form (7). So, we can use the superposition principle.

**(a)** Since $2x\sin x - x^2 - 1 = 2(x\sin x) - (x^2 + 1)$, by the superposition principle,

$$y(x) = 2y_1(x) - y_2(x) = 2\sin x - x$$

is a solution to $L[y] = 2x\sin x - x^2 - 1$.

**(b)** We can express $4x^2 + 4 - 6x\sin x = 4(x^2 + 1) - 6(x\sin x)$. Hence,

$$y(x) = 4y_2(x) - 6y_1(x) = 4x - 6\sin x$$

is a solution to $L[y] = 4x^2 + 4 - 6x\sin x$.

**25.** Clearly, it is sufficient to prove (9) just for two functions, $y_1$ and $y_2$. Using the linear property of differentiation, we have

$$
\begin{aligned}
L\left[y_1 + y_2\right] &= \left[y_1 + y_2\right]^{(n)} + p_1\left[y_1 + y_2\right]^{(n-1)} + \cdots + p_n\left[y_1 + y_2\right] \\
&= \left[y_1^{(n)} + y_2^{(n)}\right] + p_1\left[y_1^{(n-1)} + y_2^{(n-1)}\right] + \cdots + p_n\left[y_1 + y_2\right] \\
&= \left[y_1^{(n)} + p_1 y_1^{(n-1)} + \cdots + p_n y_1\right] + \left[y_2^{(n)} + p_1 y_2^{(n-1)} + \cdots + p_n y_2\right] = L\left[y_1\right] + L\left[y_1\right].
\end{aligned}
$$

Next, we verify (10).

$$
\begin{aligned}
L\left[cy\right] &= \left[cy\right]^{(n)} + p_1\left[cy\right]^{(n-1)} + \cdots + p_n\left[cy\right] = cy^{(n)} + p_1 cy^{(n-1)} + \cdots + p_n cy \\
&= c\left[y^{(n)} + p_1 y^{(n-1)} + \cdots + p_n y\right] = cL\left[y\right].
\end{aligned}
$$

**27.** A linear combination

$$
c_0 + c_1 x + c_2 x^2 + \cdots + c_n x^n
$$

of the functions from the given set is a polynomial of degree at most $n$ and so, by the fundamental theorem of algebra, it cannot have more than $n$ zeros unless it is the zero polynomial, i.e., it has all zero coefficients. Thus, if this linear combination vanishes on a whole interval $(a, b)$, then it follows that $c_0 = c_1 = c_2 = \ldots = c_n = 0$. Therefore, the set of functions $\{1, x, x^2, \ldots, x^n\}$ is linearly independent on any interval $(a, b)$.

**29. (a)** Assuming that functions $f_1, f_2, \ldots, f_m$ are linearly dependent on $(-\infty, \infty)$, we can find their nontrivial linear combination vanishing identically on $(-\infty, \infty)$, i.e.,

$$
c_1 f_1 + c_2 f_2 + \cdots + c_m f_m \equiv 0 \qquad \text{on} \qquad (-\infty, \infty),
$$

where not all $c_j$'s are zeros. In particular, this linear combination vanishes on $(-1, 1)$, which contradicts the assumption that $f_1, f_2, \ldots, f_m$ are linearly independent on $(-1, 1)$.

**(b)** Let

$$
f_1(x) := |x - 1|, \qquad f_2(x) := x - 1.
$$

Chapter 6

On $(-1, 1)$ (even on $(-\infty, 1)$) we have $f_1(x) \equiv -f_2(x)$ or, equivalently, $f_1(x) + f_2(x) \equiv 0$ and so these functions are linearly dependent on $(-1, 1)$. However, their linear combination

$$c_1 f_1(x) + c_2 f_2(x) = \begin{cases} (c_2 - c_1)(x - 1), & x \le 1; \\ (c_1 + c_2)(x - 1), & x > 1 \end{cases}$$

cannot vanish identically on $(-\infty, \infty)$ unless $c_1 - c_2 = 0$ and $c_1 + c_2 = 0$, which implies $c_1 = c_2 = 0$.

**31.** **(a)** Linearity of differentiation and the product rule yield

$$y'(x) = (v(x)e^x)' = v'(x)e^x + v(x)(e^x)' = [v'(x) + v(x)]e^x,$$
$$y''(x) = [v'(x) + v(x)]'e^x + [v'(x) + v(x)](e^x)' = [v''(x) + 2v'(x) + v(x)]e^x,$$
$$y'''(x) = [v''(x) + 2v'(x) + v(x)]'e^x + [v''(x) + 2v'(x) + v(x)](e^x)'$$
$$= [v'''(x) + 3v''(x) + 3v'(x) + v(x)]e^x.$$

**(b)** Substituting $y$, $y'$, $y''$, and $y'''$ into the differential equation (32), we obtain

$$[v''' + 3v'' + 3v' + v]e^x - 2[v'' + 2v' + v]e^x - 5[v' + v]e^x + 6ve^x = 0$$
$$\Rightarrow \quad [(v''' + 3v'' + 3v' + v) - 2(v'' + 2v' + v) - 5(v' + v) + 6v]e^x = 0$$
$$\Rightarrow \quad v''' + v'' - 6v' = 0,$$

where we have used the fact that the function $e^x$ is never zero. Let $v' =: w$. Then $v'' = w'$, $v''' = w''$, and so the above equation becomes

$$w'' + w' - 6w = 0. \tag{6.2}$$

**(c)** The auxiliary equation for (6.2), $r^2 + r - 6 = 0$, has the roots $r = -3$ and $r = 2$. Therefore, a general solution to this differential equation is

$$w(x) = C_1 e^{-3x} + C_2 e^{2x},$$

where $C_1$ and $C_2$ are arbitrary constants. Choosing, say, $C_1 = -3$, $C_2 = 0$ and $C_1 = 0$, $C_2 = 2$, we find two linearly independent solutions,

$$w_1(x) = -3e^{-3x} \quad \text{and} \quad w_2(x) = 2e^{2x}.$$

Integration yields

$$v_1(x) = \int w_1(x)\,dx = \int \left(-3e^{-3x}\right) dx = e^{-3x},$$

$$v_2(x) = \int w_2(x)\,dx = \int \left(2e^{2x}\right) dx = e^{2x},$$

where we have chosen zero integration constants.

**(d)** With functions $v_1(x)$ and $v_2(x)$ obtained in (c), we have

$$y_1(x) = v_1(x)e^x = e^{-3x}e^x = e^{-2x}, \quad y_2(x) = v_2(x)e^x = e^{2x}e^x = e^{3x}.$$

To show that the functions $e^x$, $e^{-2x}$, and $e^{3x}$ are linearly independent on $(-\infty, \infty)$, we can use the approach similar to that in Problem 7. Alternatively, since these functions are solutions to the differential equation (32), one can apply Theorem 3, as we did in Problem 15. To this end,

$$W\left[e^x, e^{-2x}, e^{3x}\right](x) = \begin{vmatrix} e^x & e^{-2x} & e^{3x} \\ e^x & -2e^{-2x} & 3e^{3x} \\ e^x & 4e^{-2x} & 9e^{3x} \end{vmatrix} = e^x e^{-2x} e^{3x} \begin{vmatrix} 1 & 1 & 1 \\ 1 & -2 & 3 \\ 1 & 4 & 9 \end{vmatrix} = -30e^{2x} \neq 0$$

on $(-\infty, \infty)$ and so the functions $e^x$, $e^{-2x}$, and $e^{3x}$ are linearly independent on $(-\infty, \infty)$.

**33.** Let $y(x) = v(x)e^{2x}$. Differentiating $y(x)$, we obtain

$$y'(x) = [v'(x) + 2v(x)]\,e^{2x},$$

$$y''(x) = [v''(x) + 4v'(x) + 4v(x)]\,e^{2x},$$

$$y'''(x) = [v'''(x) + 6v''(x) + 12v'(x) + 8v(x)]\,e^{2x}.$$

Substituting these expressions into the given differential equation yields

$$[(v''' + 6v'' + 12v' + 8v) - 2\,(v'' + 4v' + 4v) + (v' + 2v) - (2v)]\,e^{2x} = 0$$

$$\Rightarrow \quad [v''' + 4v'' + 5v']\,e^{2x} = 0 \quad \Rightarrow \quad v''' + 4v'' + 5v' = 0.$$

With $w(x) := v'(x)$, the above equation becomes

$$w''(x) + 4w'(x) + 5w(x) = 0.$$

The roots of the auxiliary equation, $r^2 + 4r + 5 = 0$, for this second order equation are $r = -2 \pm i$. Therefore,

$$\{w_1(x), w_2(x)\} = \left\{e^{-2x}\cos x, e^{-2x}\sin x\right\}$$

form a fundamental solution set. Integrating, we get

$$v_1(x) = \int w_1(x) = \int e^{-2x}\cos x\, dx = \frac{e^{-2x}(\sin x - 2\cos x)}{5},$$

$$v_2(x) = \int w_2(x) = \int e^{-2x}\sin x\, dx = -\frac{e^{-2x}(2\sin x + \cos x)}{5},$$

where we have chosen integration constants to be zero. Thus, functions

$$f(x) = e^{2x},$$

$$y_1(x) = v_1(x)f(x) = \frac{e^{-2x}(\sin x - 2\cos x)}{5}e^{2x} = \frac{\sin x - 2\cos x}{5},$$

$$y_2(x) = v_2(x)f(x) = \frac{e^{-2x}(2\sin x + \cos x)}{5}e^{2x} = \frac{2\sin x + \cos x}{5}$$

are three linearly independent solutions to the given differential equation.

**35.** First, let us evaluate the Wronskian of the system $\{x, \sin x, \cos x\}$ to make sure that the result of Problem 34 can be applied.

$$W\left[x, \sin x, \cos x\right] = \begin{vmatrix} x & \sin x & \cos x \\ 1 & \cos x & -\sin x \\ 0 & -\sin x & -\cos x \end{vmatrix}$$

$$= x \begin{vmatrix} \cos x & -\sin x \\ -\sin x & -\cos x \end{vmatrix} - \begin{vmatrix} \sin x & \cos x \\ -\sin x & -\cos x \end{vmatrix}$$

$$= x\left(-\cos^2 x - \sin^2 x\right) - \left(-\sin x \cos x + \sin x \cos x\right) = -x.$$

Thus, $W\left[x, \sin x, \cos x\right] \neq 0$ on $(-\infty, 0)$ and $(0, \infty)$. Therefore, on either of these two intervals, $\{x, \sin x, \cos x\}$ is a fundamental solution set for the third order linear differential equation given in Problem 34. Expanding the determinant over its last column yields

$$\begin{vmatrix} x & \sin x & \cos x & y \\ 1 & \cos x & -\sin x & y' \\ 0 & -\sin x & -\cos x & y'' \\ 0 & -\cos x & \sin x & y''' \end{vmatrix} = y''' W[x, \sin x, \cos x] - y'' \begin{vmatrix} x & \sin x & \cos x \\ 1 & \cos x & -\sin x \\ 0 & -\cos x & \sin x \end{vmatrix}$$

$$+ y' \begin{vmatrix} x & \sin x & \cos x \\ 0 & -\sin x & -\cos x \\ 0 & -\cos x & \sin x \end{vmatrix} - y \begin{vmatrix} 1 & \cos x & -\sin x \\ 0 & -\sin x & -\cos x \\ 0 & -\cos x & \sin x \end{vmatrix}$$

$$= -xy''' - y'' \left[ x \begin{vmatrix} \cos x & -\sin x \\ -\cos x & \sin x \end{vmatrix} - \begin{vmatrix} \sin x & \cos x \\ -\cos x & \sin x \end{vmatrix} \right]$$

$$+ y'x \begin{vmatrix} -\sin x & -\cos x \\ -\cos x & \sin x \end{vmatrix} - y \begin{vmatrix} -\sin x & -\cos x \\ -\cos x & \sin x \end{vmatrix}$$

$$= -xy''' + y'' - xy' + y = 0.$$

**EXERCISES 6.2:  Homogeneous Linear Equations with Constant Coefficients, page 331**

**1.** The auxiliary equation

$$r^3 + 2r^2 - 8r = 0 \qquad \Rightarrow \qquad r\left(r^2 + 2r - 8\right) = r(r - 2)(r + 4) = 0$$

has the roots $r = 0$, 2, and $-4$. Thus a general solutions to the differential equation has the form

$$y = c_1 + c_2 e^{2x} + c_3 e^{-4x}.$$

**3.** The auxiliary equation for this problem is $6r^3 + 7r^2 - r - 2 = 0$. By inspection we see that $r = -1$ is a root to this equation and so we can factor it as follows

$$6r^3 + 7r^2 - r - 2 = (r + 1)(6r^2 + r - 2) = (r + 1)(3r + 2)(2r - 1) = 0.$$

Thus, we see that the roots to the auxiliary equation are $r = -1, -2/3$, and $1/2$. These roots are real and non-repeating. Therefore, a general solution to this problem is given by

$$z(x) = c_1 e^{-x} + c_2 e^{-2x/3} + c_3 e^{x/2}.$$

Chapter 6

**5.** We can factor the auxiliary equation, $r^3 + 3r^2 + 28r + 26 = 0$, as follows:

$$
\begin{aligned}
r^3 + 3r^2 + 28r + 26 &= (r^3 + r^2) + (2r^2 + 2r) + (26r + 26) \\
&= r^2(r+1) + 2r(r+1) + 26(r+1) = (r+1)(r^2 + 2r + 26) = 0.
\end{aligned}
$$

Thus either $r + 1 = 0 \Rightarrow r = -1$ or $r^2 + 2r + 26 = 0 \Rightarrow r = -1 \pm 5i$. Therefore, a general solution is given by

$$
y(x) = c_1 e^{-x} + c_2 e^{-x} \cos 5x + c_3 e^{-x} \sin 5x \, .
$$

**7.** Factoring the characteristic polynomial yields

$$
\begin{aligned}
2r^3 - r^2 - 10r - 7 &= (2r^3 + 2r^2) + (-3r^2 - 3r) + (-7r - 7) \\
&= 2r^2(r+1) - 3r(r+1) - 7(r+1) = (r+1)(2r^2 - 3r - 7).
\end{aligned}
$$

Thus the roots of the characteristic equation, $2r^3 - r^2 - 10r - 7 = 0$, are

$$
r + 1 = 0 \Rightarrow r = -1 \, ,
$$
$$
2r^2 - 3r - 7 = 0 \Rightarrow r = \frac{3 \pm \sqrt{3^2 - 4(2)(-7)}}{4} = \frac{3 \pm \sqrt{65}}{4} \, ,
$$

and a general solution is

$$
y(x) = c_1 e^{-x} + c_2 e^{(3+\sqrt{65})x/4} + c_3 e^{(3-\sqrt{65})x/4} \, .
$$

**9.** In the characteristic equation, $r^3 - 9r^2 + 27r - 27 = 0$, we recognize a complete cube, namely, $(r-3)^3 = 0$. Thus, it has just one root, $r = 3$, of multiplicity three. Therefore, a general solution to the given differential equation is given by

$$
u(x) = c_1 e^{3x} + c_2 x e^{3x} + c_3 x^2 e^{3x} \, .
$$

**11.** Since $r^4 + 4r^3 + 6r^2 + 4r + 1 = (r+1)^4$, the characteristic equation becomes $(r+1)^4 = 0$, and it has the root $r = -1$ of multiplicity four. Therefore, the functions $e^{-x}$, $xe^{-x}$, $x^2 e^{-x}$, and $x^3 e^{-x}$ form a fundamental solution set and a general solution to the given differential equation is

$$
y(x) = c_1 e^{-x} + c_2 x e^{-x} + c_3 x^2 e^{-x} + c_4 x^3 e^{-x} = \left( c_1 + c_2 x + c_3 x^2 + c_4 x^3 \right) e^{-x} \, .
$$

**13.** The auxiliary equation in this problem is $r^4 + 4r^2 + 4 = 0$. This can be factored as $(r^2 + 2)^2 = 0$. Therefore, this equation has roots $r = \sqrt{2}i, -\sqrt{2}i, \sqrt{2}i, -\sqrt{2}i$, which we see are repeated and complex. Therefore, a general solution to this problem is given by

$$y(x) = c_1 \cos\left(\sqrt{2}x\right) + c_2 x \cos\left(\sqrt{2}x\right) + c_3 \sin\left(\sqrt{2}x\right) + c_4 x \sin\left(\sqrt{2}x\right).$$

**15.** The roots to this auxiliary equation, $(r-1)^2(r+3)(r^2+2r+5)^2 = 0$, are

$$r = 1, 1, -3, -1 \pm 2i, -1 \pm 2i,$$

where we note that 1 and $-1 \pm 2i$ are repeated roots. Therefore, a general solution to the differential equation with the given auxiliary equation is

$$y(x) = c_1 e^x + c_2 x e^x + c_3 e^{-3x} + (c_4 + c_5 x)e^{-x}\cos 2x + (c_6 + c_7 x)e^{-x}\sin 2x.$$

**17.** From the differential operator, replacing $D$ by $r$, we obtain the characteristic equation

$$(r+4)(r-3)(r+2)^3(r^2+4r+5)^2 r^5 = 0,$$

whose roots

$$
\begin{array}{lcl}
r+4 = 0 & \Rightarrow & r = -4, \\
r-3 = 0 & \Rightarrow & r = 3, \\
(r+2)^3 = 0 & \Rightarrow & r = -2 \text{ of multiplicity 3}, \\
(r^2+4r+5)^2 = 0 & \Rightarrow & r = -2 \pm i \text{ of multiplicity 2}, \\
r^5 = 0 & \Rightarrow & r = 0 \text{ of multiplicity 5}.
\end{array}
$$

Therefore, a general solution is given by

$$y(x) = c_1 e^{-4x} + c_2 e^{3x} + \left(c_3 + c_4 x + c_5 x^2\right)e^{-2x} + (c_6 + c_7 x)e^{-2x}\cos x + (c_8 + c_9 x)e^{-2x}\sin x$$
$$+ c_{10} + c_{11}x + c_{12}x^2 + c_{13}x^3 + c_{14}x^4.$$

**19.** First, we find a general solution to the given equation. Solving the auxiliary equation,

$$r^3 - r^2 - 4r + 4 = (r^3 - r^2) - (4r - 4) = (r-1)(r^2 - 4) = (r-1)(r+2)(r-2) = 0,$$

Chapter 6

yields the roots $r = 1, -2$, and 2. Thus a general solution has the form

$$y(x) = c_1 e^x + c_2 e^{-2x} + c_3 e^{2x}.$$

Next, we find constants $c_1$, $c_2$, and $c_3$ such that the solution satisfies the initial conditions. Differentiating $y(x)$ and substituting the initial conditions, we obtain the system

$$y(0) = \left(c_1 e^x + c_2 e^{-2x} + c_3 e^{2x}\right)\big|_{x=0} = c_1 + c_2 + c_3 = -4,$$
$$y'(0) = \left(c_1 e^x - 2c_2 e^{-2x} + 2c_3 e^{2x}\right)\big|_{x=0} = c_1 - 2c_2 + 2c_3 = -1,$$
$$y''(0) = \left(c_1 e^x + 4c_2 e^{-2x} + 4c_3 e^{2x}\right)\big|_{x=0} = c_1 + 4c_2 + 4c_3 = -19.$$

Solving yields

$$c_1 = 1, \qquad c_2 = -2, \qquad c_3 = -3.$$

With these coefficients, the solution to the given initial problem is

$$y(x) = e^x - 2e^{-2x} - 3e^{2x}.$$

**21.** By inspection, $r = 2$ is a root of the characteristic equation, $r^3 - 4r^2 + 7r - 6 = 0$. Factoring yields

$$r^3 - 4r^2 + 7r - 6 = (r - 2)(r^2 - 2r + 3) = 0.$$

Therefore, the other two roots are the roots of $r^2 - 2r + 3 = 0$, which are $r = 1 \pm \sqrt{2}i$, and so a general solution to the given differential equation is given by

$$y(x) = c_1 e^{2x} + \left(c_2 \cos \sqrt{2}x + c_3 \sin \sqrt{2}x\right) e^x.$$

Differentiating, we obtain

$$y' = 2c_1 e^{2x} + \left[\left(c_2 + c_3\sqrt{2}\right)\cos \sqrt{2}x + \left(c_3 - c_2\sqrt{2}\right)\sin \sqrt{2}x\right] e^x,$$
$$y'' = 4c_1 e^{2x} + \left[\left(2c_3\sqrt{2} - c_2\right)\cos \sqrt{2}x - \left(2c_2\sqrt{2} + c_3\right)\sin \sqrt{2}x\right] e^x.$$

Hence, the initial conditions yield

$$\begin{aligned} y(0) &= c_1 + c_2 = 1, & c_1 &= 1, \\ y'(0) &= 2c_1 + c_2 + c_3\sqrt{2} = 0, & \Rightarrow \qquad c_2 &= 0, \\ y''(0) &= 4c_1 - c_2 + 2c_3\sqrt{2} = 0 & c_3 &= -\sqrt{2}. \end{aligned}$$

Substituting these constants into the general solution, we get the answer

$$y(x) = e^{2x} - \sqrt{2}e^x \sin\sqrt{2}x.$$

**23.** Rewriting the system in operator form yields

$$(D^3 - 1)[x] + (D+1)[y] = 0,$$
$$(D-1)[x] + y = 0.$$

Multiplying the second equation in this sytem by $(D+1)$ and subtracting the result from the first equation, we get

$$\{(D^3 - 1) - (D+1)(D-1)\}[x] = D^2(D-1)[x] = 0.$$

Since the roots of the characteristic equation, $r^2(r-1) = 0$ are $r = 0$ of multiplicity two and $r = 1$, a general solution $x(t)$ is given by

$$x(t) = c_1 + c_2 t + c_3 e^t.$$

From the second equation in the original system, we obtain

$$y(t) = x(t) - x'(t) = (c_1 + c_2 t + c_3 e^t) - (c_1 + c_2 t + c_3 e^t)' = (c_1 - c_2) + c_2 t.$$

**25.** A linear combination of the given functions

$$c_0 e^{rx} + c_1 x e^{rx} + c_2 x^2 e^{rx} + \cdots + c_{m-1}x^{m-1}e^{rx} = (c_0 + c_1 x + c_2 x^2 + \cdots + c_m x^m) e^{rx} \quad (6.3)$$

vanishes on an interval if and only if its polynomial factor, $c_0 + c_1 x + c_2 x^2 + \cdots + c_{m-1}x^{m-1}$, vanishes on this interval (the exponential factor, $e^{rx}$, is never zero). But, as we have proved in Problem 27, Section 6.1, the system of monomials $\{1, x, \ldots, x^n\}$ is linearly independent on any interval. Thus, the linear combination (6.3) vanishes on an inteval if and only if it has all zero coefficients, i.e., $c_0 = c_1 = \ldots = c_{m-1} = 0$. Therefore, the system $\{e^{rx}, xe^{rx}, \ldots, x^{m-1}e^{rx}\}$ is linearly independent on any interval, in particular, on $(-\infty, \infty)$.

# Chapter 6

**27.** Solving the auxiliary equation, $r^4 + 2r^3 - 3r^2 - r + (1/2) = 0$, using computer software yields the roots

$$r_1 = 1.119967680, \ r_2 = 0.2963247800, \ r_3 = -0.5202201098, \ r_4 = -2.896072350 \,.$$

Thus, all the roots are real and distinct. A general solution to the given equation is, therefore,

$$y(x) = c_1 e^{r_1 x} + c_2 e^{r_2 x} + c_3 e^{r_3 x} + c_4 e^{r_4 x} \approx c_1 e^{1.120x} + c_2 e^{0.296x} + c_3 e^{-0.520x} + c_4 e^{-2.896x} \,.$$

**29.** The auxiliary equation in this problem is $r^4 + 2r^3 + 4r^2 + 3r + 2 = 0$. Let

$$g(r) = r^4 + 2r^3 + 4r^2 + 3r + 2$$

$$\Rightarrow \qquad g'(r) = 4r^3 + 6r^2 + 8r + 3.$$

Then the Newton's recursion formula (2) in Appendix A of the text becomes

$$r_{n+1} = r_n - \frac{r_n^4 + 2r_n^3 + 4r_n^2 + 3r_n + 2}{4r_n^3 + 6r_n^2 + 8r_n + 3} \,.$$

With initial guess $r_0 = 1 + i$, this formula yields

$$r_1 = (1+i) - \frac{(1+i)^4 + 2(1+i)^3 + 4(1+i)^2 + 3(1+i) + 2}{4(1+i)^3 + 6(1+i)^2 + 8(1+i) + 3} \approx 0.481715 + 0.837327i \,,$$

$$r_2 = r_1 - \frac{r_1^4 + 2r_1^3 + 4r_1^2 + 3r_1 + 2}{4r_1^3 + 6r_1^2 + 8r_1 + 3} \approx 0.052833 + 0.763496i \,,$$

$$r_3 = r_2 - \frac{r_2^4 + 2r_2^3 + 4r_2^2 + 3r_2 + 2}{4r_2^3 + 6r_2^2 + 8r_2 + 3} \approx -0.284333 + 0.789859i \,,$$

$$\vdots$$

$$r_7 = r_6 - \frac{r_6^4 + 2r_6^3 + 4r_6^2 + 3r_6 + 2}{4r_6^3 + 6r_6^2 + 8r_6 + 3} \approx -0.500000 + 0.866025i \,,$$

$$r_8 = r_7 - \frac{r_7^4 + 2r_7^3 + 4r_7^2 + 3r_7 + 2}{4r_7^3 + 6r_7^2 + 8r_7 + 3} \approx -0.500000 + 0.866025i \,.$$

Therefore, first two roots of the auxiliary equation are

$$r \approx -0.5 + 0.866i \qquad \text{and} \qquad r = \overline{-0.5 + 0.866i} = -0.5 - 0.866i \,.$$

Similarly, we find other two roots. With the initial guess $r_0 = -1 - 2i$, we find that

$$r_1 = (-1 - 2i) - \frac{(-1-2i)^4 + 2(-1-2i)^3 + 4(-1-2i)^2 + 3(-1-2i) + 2}{4(-1-2i)^3 + 6(-1-2i)^2 + 8(-1-2i) + 3}$$
$$\approx -0.830703 - 1.652798i,$$

$\vdots$

$$r_6 \approx -0.499994 - 1.322875i,$$
$$r_7 \approx -0.500000 - 1.322876i,$$
$$r_8 \approx -0.500000 - 1.322876i.$$

Therefore, the other two roots are

$$r \approx -0.5 - 1.323i \qquad \text{and} \qquad r = \overline{-0.5 - 1.323i} = -0.5 + 1.323i.$$

Thus, the auxiliary equation has four complex roots, and a general solution to the given differential equation is given by

$$y(x) \approx c_1 e^{-0.5x}\cos(0.866x) + c_2 e^{-0.5x}\sin(0.866x) + c_3 e^{-0.5x}\cos(1.323x) + c_4 e^{-0.5x}\sin(1.323x).$$

**31. (a)** If we let $y(x) = x^r$, then we see that

$$\begin{aligned} y' &= rx^{r-1}, \\ y'' &= r(r-1)x^{r-2} = (r^2 - r)x^{r-2}, \\ y''' &= r(r-1)(r-2)x^{r-3} = (r^3 - 3r^2 + 2r)x^{r-3}. \end{aligned} \qquad (6.4)$$

Thus, if $y = x^r$ is a solution to this third order Cauchy-Euler equation, then we must have

$$x^3(r^3 - 3r^2 + 2r)x^{r-3} + x^2(r^2 - r)x^{r-2} - 2xrx^{r-1} + 2x^r = 0$$
$$\Rightarrow \quad (r^3 - 3r^2 + 2r)x^r + (r^2 - r)x^r - 2rx^r + 2x^r = 0$$
$$\Rightarrow \quad (r^3 - 2r^2 - r + 2)x^r = 0. \qquad (6.5)$$

Therefore, in order for $y = x^r$ to be a solution to the equation with $x > 0$, we must have $r^3 - 2r^2 - r + 2 = 0$. Factoring this equation yields

$$r^3 - 2r^2 - r + 2 = (r^3 - 2r^2) - (r - 2) = (r - 2)(r^2 - 1) = (r - 2)(r + 1)(r - 1) = 0.$$

# Chapter 6

Equation (6.5) will equal zero and, therefore, the differential equation will be satisfied for $r = \pm 1$ and $r = 2$. Thus, three solutions to the differential equation are $y = x$, $y = x^{-1}$, and $y = x^2$. Since these functions are linearly independent, they form a fundamental solution set.

**(b)** Let $y(x) = x^r$. In addition to (6.4), we need the fourth derivative of $y(x)$.

$$y^{(4)} = (y''')' = r(r-1)(r-2)(r-3)x^{r-4} = (r^4 - 6r^3 + 11r^2 - 6r)x^{r-4}.$$

Thus, if $y = x^r$ is a solution to this fourth order Cauchy-Euler equation, then we must have

$$x^4(r^4 - 6r^3 + 11r^2 - 6r)x^{r-4} + 6x^3(r^3 - 3r^2 + 2r)x^{r-3}$$
$$+ 2x^2(r^2 - r)x^{r-2} - 4xrx^{r-1} + 4x^r = 0$$
$$\Rightarrow \quad (r^4 - 6r^3 + 11r^2 - 6r)x^r + 6(r^3 - 3r^2 + 2r)x^r + 2(r^2 - r)x^r - 4rx^r + 4x^r = 0$$
$$\Rightarrow \quad (r^4 - 5r^2 + 4)x^r = 0. \tag{6.6}$$

Therefore, in order for $y = x^r$ to be a solution to the equation with $x > 0$, we must have $r^4 - 5r^2 + 4 = 0$. Factoring this equation yields

$$r^4 - 5r^2 + 4 = (r^2 - 4)(r^2 - 1) = (r-2)(r+2)(r-1)(r+1) = 0.$$

Equation (6.6) will be satisfied if $r = \pm 1, \pm 2$. Thus, four solutions to the differential equation are $y = x$, $y = x^{-1}$, $y = x^2$, and $y = x^{-2}$. These functions are linearly independent, and so form a fundamental solution set.

**(c)** Substituting $y = x^r$ into this differential equation yields

$$(r^3 - 3r^2 + 2r)x^r - 2(r^2 - r)x^r + 13rx^r - 13x^r = 0$$
$$\Rightarrow \quad (r^3 - 5r^2 + 17r - 13)x^r = 0.$$

Thus, in order for $y = x^r$ to be a solution to this differential equation with $x > 0$, we must have $r^3 - 5r^2 + 17r - 13 = 0$. By inspection we find that $r = 1$ is a root to this equation. Therefore, we can factor this equation as follows

$$(r-1)(r^2 - 4r + 13) = 0.$$

We find the remaining roots by using the quadratic formula. Thus, we obtain the roots $r = 1$, $2 \pm 3i$. From the root $r = 1$, we obtain the solution $y = x$. From the roots $r = 2 \pm 3i$, by applying the hint given in the problem, we see that a solution is given by

$$y(x) = x^{2+3i} = x^2 \left\{ \cos(3 \ln x) + i \sin(3 \ln x) \right\}.$$

Therefore, by Lemma 2 on page 172 of the text, we find that two real-valued solutions to this differential equation are $y(x) = x^2 \cos(3 \ln x)$ and $y(x) = x^2 \sin(3 \ln x)$. Since these functions and the function $y(x) = x$ are linearly independent, we obtain the fundamental solution set

$$\left\{ x, x^2 \cos(3 \ln x), x^2 \sin(3 \ln x) \right\}.$$

**33.** With suggested values of parameters $m_1 = m_2 = 1$, $k_1 = 3$, and $k_2 = 2$, the system (34)–(35) becomes

$$\begin{aligned} x'' + 5x - 2y &= 0, \\ y'' - 2x + 2y &= 0. \end{aligned} \qquad (6.7)$$

**(a)** Expressing $y = (x'' + 5x)/2$ from the first equation and substituting this expression into the second equation, we obtain

$$\frac{1}{2} (x'' + 5x)'' - 2x + (x'' + 5x) = 0$$

$$\Rightarrow \quad \left( x^{(4)} + 5x'' \right) - 4x + 2 \left( x'' + 5x \right) = 0$$

$$\Rightarrow \quad x^{(4)} + 7x'' + 6x = 0, \qquad (6.8)$$

as it is stated in (36).

**(b)** The characteristic equation corresponding to (6.8) is $r^4 + 7r^2 + 6 = 0$. This equation is of quadratic type. Substitution $s = r^2$ yields

$$s^2 + 7s + 6 = 0 \quad \Rightarrow \quad s = -1, -6.$$

Thus

$$r = \pm\sqrt{-1} = \pm i \quad \text{and} \quad r = \pm\sqrt{-6} = \pm i\sqrt{6},$$

and a general solution to (6.8) is given by

$$x(t) = c_1 \cos t + c_2 \sin t + c_3 \cos \sqrt{6}t + c_4 \sin \sqrt{6}t.$$

**(c)** As we have mentioned in (a), the first equation in (6.7) implies that $y = (x'' + 5x)/2$. Substituting the solution $x(t)$ yields

$$
\begin{aligned}
y(t) &= \frac{1}{2}\left[\left(c_1 \cos t + c_2 \sin t + c_3 \cos \sqrt{6}t + c_4 \sin \sqrt{6}t\right)'' \right. \\
&\qquad\qquad \left. +5\left(c_1 \cos t + c_2 \sin t + c_3 \cos \sqrt{6}t + c_4 \sin \sqrt{6}t\right)\right] \\
&= \frac{1}{2}\left[\left(-c_1 \cos t - c_2 \sin t - 6c_3 \cos \sqrt{6}t - 6c_4 \sin \sqrt{6}t\right)\right. \\
&\qquad\qquad \left. +5\left(c_1 \cos t + c_2 \sin t + c_3 \cos \sqrt{6}t + c_4 \sin \sqrt{6}t\right)\right] \\
&= 2c_1 \cos t + 2c_2 \sin t - \frac{c_3}{2}\cos \sqrt{6}t - \frac{c_4}{2}\sin \sqrt{6}t .
\end{aligned}
$$

**(d)** Initial conditions $x(0) = y(0) = 1$ and $x'(0) = y'(0) = 0$ imply the system of linear equations for $c_1$, $c_2$, $c_3$, and $c_4$. Namely,

$$
\begin{aligned}
x(0) &= c_1 + c_3 = 1, & c_1 &= 3/5, \\
y(0) &= 2c_1 - (c_3/2) = 1, & c_3 &= 2/5, \\
x'(0) &= c_2 + c_4\sqrt{6} = 0, \qquad\Rightarrow & c_2 &= 0, \\
y'(0) &= 2c_2 - (c_4\sqrt{6}/2) = 0 & c_4 &= 0.
\end{aligned}
$$

Thus, the solution to this initial value problem is

$$
x(t) = \frac{3}{5}\cos t + \frac{2}{5}\cos \sqrt{6}t , \qquad y(t) = \frac{6}{5}\cos t - \frac{1}{5}\cos \sqrt{6}t .
$$

**35.** Solving the characteristic equation yields

$$
EIr^4 - k = 0 \qquad\Rightarrow\qquad r^4 = \frac{k}{EI}
$$

$$
\Rightarrow\qquad r^2 = \sqrt{\frac{k}{EI}} \quad\text{or}\quad r^2 = -\sqrt{\frac{k}{EI}}
$$

$$
\Rightarrow\qquad r = \pm\sqrt[4]{\frac{k}{EI}} \quad\text{or}\quad r = \pm\sqrt[4]{-\frac{k}{EI}} = \pm i\sqrt[4]{\frac{k}{EI}} .
$$

The first two roots are real numbers, the other two are pure imaginary numbers. Therefore, a general solution to the vibrating beam equation is

$$
y(x) = C_1 e^{\sqrt[4]{k/(EI)}\,x} + C_2 e^{-\sqrt[4]{k/(EI)}\,x} + C_3 \sin\left(\sqrt[4]{\frac{k}{EI}}\,x\right) + C_4 \cos\left(\sqrt[4]{\frac{k}{EI}}\,x\right).
$$

Using the identities

$$e^{ax} = \cosh ax + \sinh ax, \qquad e^{-ax} = \cosh ax - \sinh ax,$$

we can express the solution in terms of hyperbolic and trigonometric functions as follows.

$$y(x) = C_1 e^{\sqrt{k/(EI)}x} + C_2 e^{-\sqrt{k/(EI)}x} + C_3 \sin\left(\sqrt[4]{\frac{k}{EI}}\,x\right) + C_4 \cos\left(\sqrt[4]{\frac{k}{EI}}\,x\right)$$

$$= C_1\left[\cosh\left(\sqrt[4]{\frac{k}{EI}}\,x\right) + \sinh\left(\sqrt[4]{\frac{k}{EI}}\,x\right)\right] + C_2\left[\cosh\left(\sqrt[4]{\frac{k}{EI}}\,x\right) - \sinh\left(\sqrt[4]{\frac{k}{EI}}\,x\right)\right]$$

$$+ C_3 \sin\left(\sqrt[4]{\frac{k}{EI}}\,x\right) + C_4 \cos\left(\sqrt[4]{\frac{k}{EI}}\,x\right)$$

$$= c_1 \cosh\left(\sqrt[4]{\frac{k}{EI}}\,x\right) + c_2 \sinh\left(\sqrt[4]{\frac{k}{EI}}\,x\right) + c_3 \sin\left(\sqrt[4]{\frac{k}{EI}}\,x\right) + c_4 \cos\left(\sqrt[4]{\frac{k}{EI}}\,x\right),$$

where $c_1 := C_1 + C_2$, $c_2 := C_1 - C_2$, $c_3 := C_3$, and $c_4 := C_4$ are arbitrary constants.

## EXERCISES 6.3: Undetermined Coefficients and the Annihilator Method, page 337

1. The corresponding homogeneous equation for this problem is $y''' - 2y'' - 5y' + 6y = 0$ which has the associated auxiliary equation given by $r^3 - 2r^2 - 5r + 6 = 0$. By inspection we see that $r = 1$ is a root to this equation. Therefore, this equation can be factored as follows

$$r^3 - 2r^2 - 5r + 6 = (r-1)(r^2 - r - 6) = (r-1)(r-3)(r+2) = 0.$$

Thus, the roots to the auxiliary equation are given by $r = 1$, $3$, and $-2$, and a general solution to the homogeneous equation is

$$y_h(x) = c_1 e^x + c_2 e^{3x} + c_3 e^{-2x}.$$

The nonhomogeneous term, $g(x) = e^x + x^2$, is the sum of an exponential term and a polynomial term. Therefore, according to Section 4.5, this equation has a particular solution of the form

$$y_p(x) = x^{s_1} C_1 e^x + x^{s_2}\left(C_2 + C_3 x + C_4 x^2\right).$$

Since $e^x$ is a solution to the associated homogeneous equation and $xe^x$ is not, we set $s_1 = 1$. Since none of the terms $x^2$, $x$, or 1 is a solution to the associated homogeneous equation, we set $s_2 = 0$. Thus, the form of a particular solution is

$$y_p(x) = C_1 x e^x + C_2 + C_3 x + C_4 x^2.$$

**3.** The associated homogeneous equation for this equation is $y''' + 3y'' - 4y = 0$. This equation has the corresponding auxiliary equation $y^3 + 3r^2 - 4 = 0$, which, by inspection, has $r = 1$ as one of its roots. Thus, the auxiliary equation can be factored as follows

$$(r-1)(r^2 + 4r + 4) = (r-1)(r+2)^2 = 0.$$

From this we see that the roots to the auxiliary equation are $r = 1, -2, -2$. Therefore, a general solution to the homogeneous equation is

$$y_h(x) = c_1 e^x + c_2 e^{-2x} + c_3 x e^{-2x}.$$

The nonhomogeneous term is $g(x) = e^{-2x}$. Therefore, a particular solution to the original differential equation has the form $y_p(x) = x^s c_1 e^{-2x}$. Since both $e^{-2x}$ and $xe^{-2x}$ are solutions to the associated homogeneous equation, we set $s = 2$. (Note that this means that $r = -2$ will be a root of multiplicity three of the auxiliary equation associated with the operator equation $A[L[y]](x) = 0$, where $A$ is an annihilator of the nonhomogeneous term $g(x) = e^{-2x}$ and $L$ is the linear operator $L := D^3 + 3D^2 - 4$.) Thus, the form of a particular solution to this equation is

$$y_p(x) = C_1 x^2 e^{-2x}.$$

**5.** In the solution to Problem 1, we determined that a general solution to the homogeneous differential equation associated with this problem is

$$y_h(x) = c_1 e^x + c_2 e^{3x} + c_3 e^{-2x},$$

and that a particular solution has the form

$$y_p(x) = C_1 x e^x + C_2 + C_3 x + C_4 x^2.$$

By differentiating $y_p(x)$, we find

$$y_p'(x) = C_1 xe^x + C_1 e^x + C_3 + 2C_4 x$$

$$\Rightarrow \quad y_p''(x) = C_1 xe^x + 2C_1 e^x + 2C_4$$

$$\Rightarrow \quad y_p'''(x) = C_1 xe^x + 3C_1 e^x.$$

Substituting these expressions into the original differential equation, we obtain

$$y_p'''(x) - 2y_p''(x) - 5y_p'(x) + 6y_p(x) = C_1 xe^x + 3C_1 e^x - 2C_1 xe^x - 4C_1 e^x - 4C_4$$

$$-5C_1 xe^x - 5C_1 e^x - 5C_3 - 10C_4 x + 6C_1 xe^x + 6C_2 + 6C_3 x + 6C_4 x^2 = e^x + x^2$$

$$\Rightarrow \quad -6C_1 e^x + (-4C_4 - 5C_3 + 6C_2) + (-10C_4 + 6C_3)x + 6C_4 x^2 = e^x + x^2.$$

Equating coefficients yields

$$-6C_1 = 1 \qquad \Rightarrow \quad C_1 = \frac{-1}{6},$$

$$6C_4 = 1 \qquad \Rightarrow \quad C_4 = \frac{1}{6},$$

$$-10C_4 + 6C_3 = 0 \qquad \Rightarrow \quad C_3 = \frac{10C_4}{6} = \frac{10}{36} = \frac{5}{18},$$

$$-4C_4 - 5C_3 + 6C_2 = 0 \qquad \Rightarrow \quad C_2 = \frac{4C_4 + 5C_3}{6} = \frac{4(1/6) + 5(5/18)}{6} = \frac{37}{108}.$$

Thus, a general solution to the nonhomogeneous equation is given by

$$y(x) = y_h(x) + y_p(x) = c_1 e^x + c_2 e^{3x} + c_3 e^{-2x} - \frac{1}{6} xe^x + \frac{1}{6} x^2 + \frac{5}{18} x + \frac{37}{108}.$$

**7.** In Problem 3, a general solution to the associated homogeneous equation was found to be

$$y_h(x) = c_1 e^x + c_2 e^{-2x} + c_3 xe^{-2x},$$

and the form of a particular solution to the nonhomogeneous equation was

$$y_p(x) = C_1 x^2 e^{-2x}.$$

363

Differentiating $y_p(x)$ yields

$$y_p'(x) = 2C_1 x e^{-2x} - 2C_1 x^2 e^{-2x} = 2C_1(x - x^2)e^{-2x}$$
$$\Rightarrow \quad y_p''(x) = -4C_1(x - x^2)e^{-2x} + 2C_1(1 - 2x)e^{-2x} = 2C_1(2x^2 - 4x + 1)e^{-2x}$$
$$\Rightarrow \quad y_p'''(x) = -4C_1(2x^2 - 4x + 1)e^{-2x} + 2C_1(4x - 4)e^{-2x} = 4C_1(-2x^2 + 6x - 3)e^{-2x} \, .$$

By substituting these expressions into the nonhomogeneous equation, we obtain

$$y_p'''(x) + 3y_p''(x) - 4y_p(x) = 4C_1(-2x^2 + 6x - 3)e^{-2x}$$
$$+ 6C_1(2x^2 - 4x + 1)e^{-2x} - 4C_1 x^2 e^{-2x} = e^{-2x}$$
$$\Rightarrow \quad -6C_1 e^{-2x} = e^{-2x} \, .$$

By equating coefficients, we see that $C_1 = -1/6$. Thus, a general solution to the nonhomogeneous differential equation is given by

$$y(x) = y_h(x) + y_p(x) = c_1 e^x + c_2 e^{-2x} + c_3 x e^{-2x} - \frac{1}{6} x^2 e^{-2x} \, .$$

9. Solving the auxiliary equation, $r^3 - 3r^2 + 3r - 1 = (r - 1)^3 = 0$, we find that $r = 1$ is its root of multiplicity three. Therefore, a general solution to the associated homogeneous equation is given by

$$y_h(x) = c_1 e^x + c_2 x e^x + c_3 x^2 e^x \, .$$

The nonhomogeneous term, $e^x$, suggests a particular solution of the form $y_p(x) = Ax^s e^x$, where we have to choose $s = 3$ since the root $r = 1$ of the auxiliary equation is of multiplicity three. Thus

$$y_p(x) = Ax^3 e^x \, .$$

Differentiating $y_p(x)$ yields

$$y_p'(x) = A\left(x^3 + 3x^2\right)e^x \, ,$$
$$y_p''(x) = A\left(x^3 + 6x^2 + 6x\right)e^x \, ,$$
$$y_p'''(x) = A\left(x^3 + 9x^2 + 18x + 6\right)e^x \, .$$

By substituting these expressions into the original equation, we obtain

$$y_p''' - 3y_p'' + 3y_p' - y = e^x$$

$$\Rightarrow \quad \left[A\left(x^3 + 9x^2 + 18x + 6\right)e^x\right] - 3\left[A\left(x^3 + 6x^2 + 6x\right)e^x\right]$$

$$+ 3\left[A\left(x^3 + 3x^2\right)e^x\right] - Ax^3e^x = e^x$$

$$\Rightarrow \quad 6Ae^x = e^x \qquad \Rightarrow \qquad A = \frac{1}{6},$$

and so $y_p(x) = x^3 e^x / 6$. A general solution to the given equation then has the form

$$y(x) = y_h(x) + y_p(x) = c_1 e^x + c_2 x e^x + c_3 x^2 e^x + \frac{1}{6}x^3 e^x.$$

**11.** The operator $D^5$, that is, the fifth derivative operator, annihilates any polynomial of degree at most four. In particular, $D^5$ annihilates the polynomial $x^4 - x^2 + 11$.

**13.** According to (i) on page 334 of the text, the operator $[D - (-7)] = (D + 7)$ annihilates the exponential function $e^{-7x}$.

**15.** The operator $(D-2)$ annihilates the function $f_1(x) := e^{2x}$ and the operator $(D-1)$ annihilates the function $f_2(x) := e^x$. Thus, the composition of these operators, namely, $(D-2)(D-1)$, annihilates both of these functions and so, by linearity, it annihilates their algebraic sum.

**17.** This function has the same form as the functions given in (iv) on page 334 of the text. Here we see that $\alpha = -1$, $\beta = 2$, and $m - 1 = 2$. Thus, the operator

$$\left[(D - \{-1\})^2 + 2^2\right]^3 = \left[(D + 1)^2 + 4\right]^3$$

annihilates this function.

**19.** Given function as a sum of two functions. The first term, $xe^{-2x}$, is of the type (ii) on the page 334 of the text with $m = 2$ and $r = -2$; so $[D - (-2)]^2 = (D + 2)^2$ annihilates this function. The second term, $xe^{-5x}\sin 3x$, is annihilated by

$$\left[(D - (-5))^2 + 3^2\right]^2 = \left[(D + 5)^2 + 9\right]^2$$

according to (iv). Therefore, the composition $[(D + 2)^2(D + 5)^2 + 9]^2$ annihilates the function $xe^{-2x} + xe^{-5x}\sin 3x$.

# Chapter 6

**21.** In operator form, the given equation can be written as

$$\left(D^2 - 5D + 6\right)[u] = \cos 2x + 1.$$

The function $g(x) = \cos 2x + 1$ is a sum of two functions: $\cos 2x$ is of the type (iii) on page 334 of the text with $\beta = 2$, and so it is innihilated by $(D^2 + 4)$; 1, as a constant, is annihilated by $D$. Therefore, the operator $D(D^2 + 4)$ innihilates the right-hand side, $g(x)$. Applying this operator to both sides of the differential equation given in this problem yields

$$D\left(D^2 + 4\right)\left(D^2 - 5D + 6\right)[u] = D\left(D^2 + 4\right)[\cos 2x + 1] = 0$$
$$\Rightarrow \quad D\left(D^2 + 4\right)(D - 3)(D - 2)[u] = 0.$$

This last equation has the associated auxiliary equation $r\left(r^2 + 4\right)(r - 3)(r - 2) = 0$, which has roots $r = 2, 3, 0, \pm 2i$. Thus, a general solution to the differential equation associated with this auxiliary equation is

$$u(x) = c_1 e^{2x} + c_2 e^{3x} + c_3 \cos 2x + c_4 \sin 2x + c_5 \,.$$

The homogeneous equation, $u'' - 5u' + 6u = 0$, associated with the original problem, has as its corresponding auxiliary equation $r^2 - 5r + 6 = (r - 2)(r - 3) = 0$. Therefore, the solution to the homogeneous equation associated with the original problem is $u_h(x) = c_1 e^{2x} + c_2 e^{3x}$. Since a general solution to this original problem is given by

$$u(x) = u_h(x) + u_p(x) = c_1 e^{2x} + c_2 e^{3x} + u_p(x)$$

and since $u(x)$ must be of the form

$$u(x) = c_1 e^{2x} + c_2 e^{3x} + c_3 \cos 2x + c_4 \sin 2x + c_5 \,,$$

we see that

$$u_p(x) = c_3 \cos 2x + c_4 \sin 2x + c_5 \,.$$

**23.** The function $g(x) = e^{3x} - x^2$ is annihilated by the operator $A := D^3(D - 3)$. Applying the operator $A$ to both sides of the differential equation given in this problem yields

$$A\left[y'' - 5y' + 6y\right] = A\left[e^{3x} - x^2\right] = 0$$

$$\Rightarrow \qquad D^3(D-3)(D^2-5D+6)[y] = D^3(D-3)^2(D-2)[y] = 0.$$

This last equation has the associated auxiliary equation

$$r^3(r-3)^2(r-2) = 0,$$

which has roots $r = 0, 0, 0, 3, 3, 2$. Thus, a general solution to the differential equation associated with this auxiliary equation is

$$y(x) = c_1 e^{2x} + c_2 e^{3x} + c_3 x e^{3x} + c_4 x^2 + c_5 x + c_6\,.$$

The homogeneous equation, $y'' - 5y' + 6y = 0$, associated with the original problem, is the same as in Problem 21 (with $u$ replaced by $y$). Therefore, the solution to the homogeneous equation associated with the original problem is $y_h(x) = c_1 e^{2x} + c_2 e^{3x}$. Since a general solution to this original problem is given by

$$y(x) = y_h(x) + y_p(x) = c_1 e^{2x} + c_2 e^{3x} + y_p(x)$$

and since $y(x)$ must be of the form

$$y(x) = c_1 e^{2x} + c_2 e^{3x} + c_3 x e^{3x} + c_4 x^2 + c_5 x + c_6\,,$$

we see that

$$y_p(x) = c_3 x e^{3x} + c_4 x^2 + c_5 x + c_6\,.$$

**25.** First, we rewrite the equation in operator form, that is,

$$\left(D^2 - 6D + 9\right)[y] = \sin 2x + x \qquad \Rightarrow \qquad (D-3)^2[y] = \sin 2x + x\,.$$

In this problem, the right-hand side is a sum of two functions. The first function, $\sin 2x$, is annihilated by $(D^2+4)$, and the operator $D^2$ annihilates the term $x$. Thus $A := D^2(D^2+4)$ annihilates the function $\sin 2x + x$. Applying this operator to the original equation (in operator form) yields

$$D^2(D^2+4)(D-3)^2[y] = D^2(D^2+4)[\sin 2x + x] = 0. \qquad (6.9)$$

# Chapter 6

This homogeneous equation has associated characteristic equation

$$r^2(r^2 + 4)(r - 3)^2 = 0$$

with roots $\pm 2i$, and double roots $r = 0$ and $r = 3$. Therefore, a general solution to (6.9) is given by

$$y(x) = c_1 e^{3x} + c_2 x e^{3x} + c_3 + c_4 x + c_5 \cos 2x + c_6 \sin 2x . \qquad (6.10)$$

Since the homogeneous equation, $(D - 3)^2[y] = 0$, which corresponds to the original equation, has a general solution $y_h(x) = c_1 e^{3x} + c_2 x e^{3x}$, the "tail" in (6.10) gives the form of a particular solution to the given equation.

**27.** Since

$$y'' + 2y' + 2y = \left(D^2 + 2D + 2\right)[y] = \left\{(D + 1)^2 + 1\right\}[y],$$

the auxiliary equation in this problm is $(r+1)^2 + 1 = 0$, whose roots are $r = -1 \pm i$. Therefore, a general solution to the homogeneous equation, corresponding to the original equation, is

$$y_h(x) = (c_1 \cos x + c_2 \sin x) e^{-x} .$$

Applying the operator $D^3\{(D+1)^2 + 1\}$ to the given equation, which annihilates its right-hand side, yields

$$D^3\left\{(D+1)^2 + 1\right\}\left\{(D+1)^2 + 1\right\}[y] = D^3\left\{(D+1)^2 + 1\right\}\left[e^{-x}\cos x + x^2\right] = 0$$

$$\Rightarrow \qquad D^3\left[(D+1)^2 + 1\right]^2[y] = 0. \qquad (6.11)$$

The corresponding auxiliary equation, $r^3[(r+1)^2 + 1]^2 = 0$ has a root $r = 0$ of multiplicity three and double roots $r = -1 \pm i$. Therefore, a general solution to (6.11) is given by

$$y(x) = (c_1 \cos x + c_2 \sin x) e^{-x} + (c_3 \cos x + c_4 \sin x) x e^{-x} + c_5 x^2 + c_6 x + c_7 .$$

Since $y(x) = y_h(x) + y_p(x)$, we conclude that

$$y_p(x) = (c_3 \cos x + c_4 \sin x) x e^{-x} + c_5 x^2 + c_6 x + c_7 .$$

**29.** In operator form, the equation becomes

$$\left(D^3 - 2D^2 + D\right)[z] = D(D-1)^2[z] = x - e^x.\tag{6.12}$$

Solving the corresponding auxiliary equation, $r(r-1)^2 = 0$, we find that $r = 0$, 1, and 1. Thus

$$z_h(x) = C_1 + C_2 e^x + C_3 x e^x$$

is a general solution to the homogeneous equation associated with the original equation. To annihilate the right-hand side in (6.12), we apply the operator $D^2(D-1)$ to this equation. Thus we obtain

$$D^2(D-1)D(D-1)^2[z] = D^2(D-1)\left[x - e^x\right] \quad \Rightarrow \quad D^3(D-1)^3 = 0.$$

Solving the corresponding auxiliary equation, $r^3(r-1)^3 = 0$, we see that $r = 0$ and $r = 1$ are its roots of multiplicity three. Hence, a general solution is given by

$$z(x) = c_1 + c_2 x + c_3 x^2 + c_4 e^x + c_5 x e^x + c_6 x^2 e^x.$$

This general solution, when compared with $z_h(x)$, gives

$$z_p(x) = c_2 x + c_3 x^2 + c_6 x^2 e^x.$$

**31.** Writing this equation in operator form yields

$$\left(D^3 + 2D^2 - 9D - 18\right)[y] = -18x^2 - 18x + 22.\tag{6.13}$$

Since,

$$D^3 + 2D^2 - 9D - 18 = D^2(D+2) - 9(D+2) = (D+2)\left(D^2 - 9\right) = (D+2)(D-3)(D+3),$$

(6.13) becomes

$$(D+2)(D-3)(D+3)[y] = -18x^2 - 18x + 22.$$

The auxiliary equation in this problem is $(r+2)(r-3)(r+3) = 0$ with roots $r = -2$, 3, and $-3$. Hence, a general solution to the corresponding homogeneous equation has the form

$$y_h(x) = c_1 e^{-2x} + c_2 e^{3x} + c_3 e^{-3x}.$$

# Chapter 6

Since the operator $D^3$ annihilates the nonhomogeneous term in the original equation and $r = 0$ is not a root of the auxiliary equation, we seek for a particular solution of the form

$$y_p(x) = C_0 x^2 + C_1 x + C_2.$$

Substituting $y_p$ into the given equation (for convenience, in operator form) yileds

$$\left(D^3 + 2D^2 - 9D - 18\right)\left[C_0 x^2 + C_1 x + C_2\right] = -18x^2 - 18x + 22$$

$$\Rightarrow \quad 0 + 2\left(2C_0\right) - 9\left[2C_0 x + C_1\right] - 18\left[C_0 x^2 + C_1 x + C_2\right] = -18x^2 - 18x + 22$$

$$\Rightarrow \quad -18C_0 x^2 + (-18C_1 - 18C_0)x + (-18C_2 - 9C_1 + 4C_0) = -18x^2 - 18x + 22.$$

Equating coefficients, we obtain the system

$$
\begin{aligned}
-18C_0 &= -18, \\
-18C_1 - 18C_0 &= -18, \\
-18C_2 - 9C_1 + 4C_0 &= 22
\end{aligned}
\qquad \Rightarrow \qquad
\begin{aligned}
C_0 &= 1, \\
C_1 &= 0, \\
C_2 &= -1.
\end{aligned}
$$

Thus, $y_p(x) = x^2 - 1$ and

$$y(x) = y_h(x) + y_p(x) = c_1 e^{-2x} + c_2 e^{3x} + c_3 e^{-3x} + x^2 - 1$$

is a general solution to the original nonhomogeneous equation. Next, we satisfy the initial conditions. Differentiation yields

$$y'(x) = -2c_1 e^{-2x} + 3c_2 e^{3x} - 3c_3 e^{-3x} + 2x,$$

$$y''(x) = 4c_1 e^{-2x} + 9c_2 e^{3x} + 9c_3 e^{-3x} + 2.$$

Therefore,

$$
\begin{aligned}
-2 = y(0) &= c_1 + c_2 + c_3 - 1, \\
-8 = y'(0) &= -2c_1 + 3c_2 - 3c_3, \\
-12 = y''(0) &= 4c_1 + 9c_2 + 9c_3 + 2
\end{aligned}
\qquad \Rightarrow \qquad
\begin{aligned}
c_1 + c_2 + c_3 &= -1, \\
-2c_1 + 3c_2 - 3c_3 &= -8, \\
4c_1 + 9c_2 + 9c_3 &= -14.
\end{aligned}
$$

Solving this system, we find that $c_1 = 1$, $c_2 = -2$, and $c_3 = 0$, and so

$$y(x) = e^{-2x} - 2e^{3x} + x^2 - 1$$

gives the solution to the given initial value problem.

**33.** Let us write given equation in operator form.

$$\left(D^3 - 2D^2 - 3D + 10\right)[y] = (34x - 16)e^{-2x} - 10x^2 + 6x + 34.$$

By inspection, $r = -2$ is a root of the characteristic equation, $r^3 - 2r^2 - 3r + 10 = 0$. Using, say, long division we find that

$$r^3 - 2r^2 - 3r + 10 = (r + 2)\left(r^2 - 4r + 5\right) = (r + 2)\left[(r - 2)^2 + 1\right]$$

and so the other two roots of the auxiliary equation are $r = 2 \pm i$. This gives a general solution to the corresponding homogeneous equation

$$y_h(x) = c_1 e^{-2x} + (c_2 \cos x + c_3 \sin x)\,e^{2x}.$$

According to the nonhomogeneous term, we look for a particular solution to the original equation of the form

$$y_p(x) = x\left(C_0 x + C_1\right)e^{-2x} + C_2 x^2 + C_3 x + C_4,$$

where the factor $x$ in the exponential term appears due to the fact that $r = -2$ is a root of the characteristic equation. Substituting $y_p(x)$ into the given equation and simplifying yield

$$\left(D^3 - 2D^2 - 3D + 10\right)[y_p(x)] = (34x - 16)e^{-2x} - 10x^2 + 6x + 34$$

$$\Rightarrow \quad (34C_0 x + 17C_1 - 16C_0)\,e^{-2x} + 10C_2 x^2 + (10C_3 - 6C_2)x$$

$$+10C_4 - 3C_3 - 4C_2 = (34x - 16)e^{-2x} - 10x^2 + 6x + 34.$$

Equating corresponding coefficients, we obtain the system

$$
\begin{aligned}
34C_0 &= 34, & \qquad C_0 &= 1, \\
17C_1 - 16C_0 &= -16, & C_1 &= 0, \\
10C_2 &= -10, & \Rightarrow \qquad C_2 &= -1, \\
10C_3 - 6C_2 &= 6, & C_3 &= 0, \\
10C_4 - 3C_3 - 4C_2 &= 34 & C_4 &= 3.
\end{aligned}
$$

Thus, $y_p(x) = x^2 e^{-2x} - x^2 + 3$ and

$$y(x) = y_h(x) + y_p(x) = c_1 e^{-2x} + (c_2 \cos x + c_3 \sin x)\,e^{2x} + x^2 e^{-2x} - x^2 + 3$$

is a general solution to the given nonhomogeneous equation. Next, we find constants $c_1$, $c_2$, and $c_3$ such that the initial conditions are satisfied. Differentiation yields

$$y'(x) = -2c_1 e^{-2x} + [(2c_2 + c_3)\cos x + (2c_3 - c_2)\sin x] e^{2x} + (2x - 2x^2)e^{-2x} - 2x,$$

$$y''(x) = 4c_1 e^{-2x} + [(3c_2 + 4c_3)\cos x + (3c_3 - 4c_2)\sin x] e^{2x} + (2 - 8x + 4x^2)e^{-2x} - 2.$$

Therefore,

$$
\begin{array}{lll}
3 = y(0) = c_1 + c_2 + 3, & & c_1 + c_2 = 0, \\
0 = y'(0) = -2c_1 + 2c_2 + c_3, & \Rightarrow & -2c_1 + 2c_2 + c_3 = 0, \\
0 = y''(0) = 4c_1 + 3c_2 + 4c_3 & & 4c_1 + 3c_2 + 4c_3 = 0.
\end{array}
$$

The solution of this homogeneous linear system is $c_1 = c_2 = c_3 = 0$. Hence, the answer is $y(x) = x^2 e^{-2x} - x^2 + 3$.

**35.** If $a_0 = 0$, then equation (4) becomes

$$a_n y^{(n)} + a_{n-1} y^{(n-1)} + \cdots + a_1 y' = f(x)$$

or, in operator form,

$$\left(a_n D^n + a_{n-1} D^{n-1} + \cdots + a_1 D\right)[y] = f(x)$$

$$\Rightarrow \quad D\left(a_n D^{n-1} + a_{n-1} D^{n-2} + \cdots + a_1\right)[y] = f(x). \tag{6.14}$$

Since the operator $D^{m+1}$ annihilates any polynomial $f(x) = b_m x^m + \cdots + b_0$, applying $D^{m+1}$ to both sides in (6.14) yields

$$D^{m+1} D\left(a_n D^{n-1} + a_{n-1} D^{n-2} + \cdots + a_1\right)[y] = D^{m+1}[f(x)] = 0$$

$$\Rightarrow \quad D^{m+2}\left(a_n D^{n-1} + a_{n-1} D^{n-2} + \cdots + a_1\right)[y] = 0. \tag{6.15}$$

The auxiliary equation, corresponding to this homogeneous equation is,

$$r^{m+2}\left(a_n r^{n-1} + a_{n-1} r^{n-2} + \cdots + a_1\right) = 0. \tag{6.16}$$

Since $a_1 \neq 0$,

$$\left.\left(a_n r^{n-1} + a_{n-1} r^{n-2} + \cdots + a_1\right)\right|_{r=0} = a_1 \neq 0,$$

which means that $r = 0$ is not a root of this polynomial. Thus, for the auxiliary equation (6.16), $r = 0$ is a root of exact multiplicity $m + 2$, and so a general solution to (6.15) is given by

$$y(x) = c_0 + c_1 x + \cdots + c_{m+1} x^{m+1} + Y(x), \tag{6.17}$$

where $Y(x)$, being associated with roots of $a_n r^{n-1} + a_{n-1} r^{n-2} + \cdots + a_1 = 0$, is a general solution to $(a_n D^{n-1} + a_{n-1} D^{n-2} + \cdots + a_1)[y] = 0$. (One can write down $Y(x)$ explicitly but there is no need in doing this.)

On the other hand, the auxiliary equation for the homogeneous equation, associated with (6.14), is $r(a_n r^{n-1} + a_{n-1} r^{n-2} + \cdots + a_1) = 0$, and $r = 0$ is its simple root. Hence, a general solution $y_h(x)$ to the homogeneous equation is given by

$$y_h(x) = c_0 + Y(x), \tag{6.18}$$

where $Y(x)$ is the same as in (6.17). Since $y(x) = y_h(x) + y_p(x)$, it follows from (6.17) and (6.18) that

$$y_p(x) = c_1 x + \cdots + c_{m+1} x^{m+1} = x\left(c_1 + \cdots + c_{m+1} x^m\right),$$

as stated.

**37.** Writing equation (4) in operator form yields

$$\left(a_n D^n + a_{n-1} D^{n-1} + \cdots + a_0\right)[y] = f(x). \tag{6.19}$$

The characteristic equation, corresponding to the associated homogeneous equation, is

$$a_n r^n + a_{n-1} r^{n-1} + \cdots + a_0 = 0. \tag{6.20}$$

Suppose that $r = \beta i$ is a root of (6.20) of multiplicity $s \geq 0$. ($s = 0$ means that $r = \beta i$ is *not* a root.) Then (6.20) can be factored as

$$a_n r^n + a_{n-1} r^{n-1} + \cdots + a_0 = \left(r^2 + \beta^2\right)^s \left(a_n r^{n-2s} + \cdots + a_0/\beta^{2s}\right) = 0$$

and so a general solution to the homogeneous equation is given by

$$y_h(x) = (c_1 \cos \beta x + c_2 \sin \beta x) + x(c_3 \cos \beta x + c_4 \sin \beta x)$$
$$+ \cdots + x^{s-1}(c_{2s-1} \cos \beta x + c_{2s} \sin \beta x) + Y(x), \tag{6.21}$$

373

## Chapter 6

where $Y(x)$ is the part of $y_h(x)$ corresponding to the roots of $a_n r^{n-2s} + \cdots + a_0/\beta^{2s} = 0$.

Since the operator $(D^2 + \beta^2)$ annihilates $f(x) = a\cos\beta x + b\sin\beta x$, applying this operator to both sides in (6.19), we obtain

$$(D^2 + \beta^2)\left(a_n D^n + a_{n-1}D^{n-1} + \cdots + a_0\right)[y] = (D^2 + \beta^2)[f(x)] = 0.$$

The corresponding auxiliary equation,

$$(r^2 + \beta^2)\left(a_n r^n + a_{n-1}r^{n-1} + \cdots + a_0\right) = 0 \quad \Rightarrow \quad (r^2 + \beta^2)^{s+1}\left(a_n r^{n-2s} + \cdots + a_0/\beta^{2s}\right) = 0$$

has $r = \beta i$ as its root of multiplicity $s + 1$. Therefore, a general solution to this equation is given by

$$y(x) = (c_1\cos\beta x + c_2\sin\beta x) + x(c_3\cos\beta x + c_4\sin\beta x)$$
$$+ \cdots + x^{s-1}(c_{2s-1}\cos\beta x + c_{2s}\sin\beta x) + x^s(c_{2s+1}\cos\beta x + c_{2s+2}\sin\beta x) + Y(x).$$

Since, $y(x) = y_h(x) + y_p(x)$, comparing $y(x)$ with $y_h(x)$ given in (6.21), we conclude that

$$y_p(x) = x^s(c_{2s+1}\cos\beta x + c_{2s+2}\sin\beta x).$$

All that remains is to note that, for any $m < s$, the functions $x^m\cos\beta x$ and $x^m\sin\beta x$ are presented in (6.21), meaning that they are solutions to the homogeneous equation corresponding to (6.19). Thus $s$ is the smallest number $m$ such that $x^m\cos\beta x$ and $x^m\sin\beta x$ are not solutions to the corresponding homogeneous equation.

**39.** Writing the system in operator form yields

$$(D^2 - 1)[x] + y = 0,$$
$$x + (D^2 - 1)[y] = e^{3t}.$$

Subtracting the first equation from the second equation multiplied by $(D^2 - 1)$, we get

$$\left\{(D^2 - 1)[x] + (D^2 - 1)^2[y]\right\} - \left\{(D^2 - 1)[x] + y\right\} = (D^2 - 1)\left[e^{3t}\right] - 0 = 8e^{3t}$$
$$\Rightarrow \quad \left\{(D^2 - 1)^2 - 1\right\}[y] = 8e^{3t} \quad \Rightarrow \quad D^2(D^2 - 2)[y] = 8e^{3t}. \tag{6.22}$$

374

The auxiliary equation, $r^2(r^2 - 2) = 0$, has roots $r = \pm\sqrt{2}$ and a double root $r = 0$. Hence,

$$y_h(t) = c_1 + c_2 t + c_3 e^{\sqrt{2}t} + c_4 e^{-\sqrt{2}t}$$

is a general solution to the homogeneous equation coresponding to (6.22). A particular solution to (6.22) has the form $y_p(t) = Ae^{3t}$. Substitution yields

$$D^2\left(D^2 - 2\right)\left[Ae^{3x}\right] = \left(D^4 - 2D^2\right)\left[Ae^{3x}\right] = 81Ae^{3x} - (2)9Ae^{3x} = 63Ae^{3x} = 8e^{3x}$$

$$\Rightarrow \quad y_p(t) = Ae^{3x} = \frac{8e^{3x}}{63},$$

and so

$$y(t) = y_p(t) + y_h(t) = \frac{8e^{3x}}{63} + c_1 + c_2 t + c_3 e^{\sqrt{2}t} + c_4 e^{-\sqrt{2}t}$$

is a general solution to (6.22). We find $x(t)$ from the second equation in the original system.

$$\begin{aligned} x(t) &= e^{3t} + y(t) - y''(t) \\ &= e^{3t} + \left(\frac{8e^{3x}}{63} + c_1 + c_2 t + c_3 e^{\sqrt{2}t} + c_4 e^{-\sqrt{2}t}\right) - \left(\frac{72e^{3x}}{63} + 2c_3 e^{\sqrt{2}t} + 2c_4 e^{-\sqrt{2}t}\right) \\ &= -\frac{e^{3x}}{63} + c_1 + c_2 t - c_3 e^{\sqrt{2}t} - c_4 e^{-\sqrt{2}t}. \end{aligned}$$

## EXERCISES 6.4:   Method of Variation of Parameters, page 341

1. To apply the method of variation of parameters, first we have to find a fundamental solution set for the corresponding homogeneous equation, which is

$$y''' - 3y'' + 4y = 0.$$

Factoring the auxiliary polynomial, $r^3 - 3r^2 + 4$, yields

$$r^3 - 3r^2 + 4 = \left(r^3 + r^2\right) - \left(4r^2 - 4\right) = r^2(r + 1) - 4(r - 1)(r + 1) = (r + 1)(r - 2)^2.$$

Therefore, $r = -1$, 2, and 2 are the roots of the auxiliary equation, and $y_1 = e^{-x}$, $y_2 = e^{2x}$, and $y_3 = xe^{2x}$ form a fundamental solution set. According to the variation of parameters method, we seek for a particular solution of the form

$$y_p(x) = v_1(x)y_1(x) + v_2(x)y_2(x) + v_3(x)y_3(x) = v_1(x)e^{-x} + v_2(x)e^{2x} + v_3(x)xe^{2x}.$$

To find functions $v_j$'s we need four determinants, the Wronskian $W[y_1, y_2, y_3](x)$ and $W_1(x)$, $W_2(x)$, and $W_3(x)$ given in (10) on page 340 of the text. Thus we compute

$$W\left[e^{-x}, e^{2x}, xe^{2x}\right](x) = \begin{vmatrix} e^{-x} & e^{2x} & xe^{2x} \\ -e^{-x} & 2e^{2x} & (1+2x)e^{2x} \\ e^{-x} & 4e^{2x} & (4+4x)e^{2x} \end{vmatrix} = e^{-x}e^{2x}e^{2x}\begin{vmatrix} 1 & 1 & x \\ -1 & 2 & 1+2x \\ 1 & 4 & 4+4x \end{vmatrix} = 9e^{3x},$$

$$W_1(x) = (-1)^{3-1}W\left[e^{2x}, xe^{2x}\right](x) = \begin{vmatrix} e^{2x} & xe^{2x} \\ 2e^{2x} & (1+2x)e^{2x} \end{vmatrix} = e^{4x},$$

$$W_2(x) = (-1)^{3-2}W\left[e^{-x}, xe^{2x}\right](x) = -\begin{vmatrix} e^{-x} & xe^{2x} \\ -e^{-x} & (1+2x)e^{2x} \end{vmatrix} = -(1+3x)e^{x},$$

$$W_3(x) = (-1)^{3-3}W\left[e^{-x}, e^{2x}\right](x) = \begin{vmatrix} e^{-x} & e^{2x} \\ -e^{-x} & 2e^{2x} \end{vmatrix} = 3e^{x}.$$

Substituting these expressions into the formula (11) for determining $v_j$'s, we obtain

$$v_1(x) = \int \frac{g(x)W_1(x)}{W[e^{-x}, e^{2x}, xe^{2x}]}\, dx = \int \frac{e^{2x}e^{4x}}{9e^{3x}}\, dx = \frac{1}{27}e^{3x},$$

$$v_2(x) = \int \frac{g(x)W_2(x)}{W[e^{-x}, e^{2x}, xe^{2x}]}\, dx = \int \frac{-e^{2x}(1+3x)e^{x}}{9e^{3x}}\, dx = -\frac{1}{9}\int (1+3x)\, dx = -\frac{x}{9} - \frac{x^2}{6},$$

$$v_3(x) = \int \frac{g(x)W_3(x)}{W[e^{-x}, e^{2x}, xe^{2x}]}\, dx = \int \frac{e^{2x}3e^{x}}{9e^{3x}}\, dx = \frac{x}{3},$$

where we have chosen zero integration constants. Then formula (12), page 340 of the text, gives a particular solution

$$y_p(x) = \frac{1}{27}e^{3x}e^{-x} - \left(\frac{x}{9} + \frac{x^2}{6}\right)e^{2x} + \frac{x}{3}xe^{2x} = \frac{1}{27}e^{2x} - \frac{xe^{2x}}{9} + \frac{x^2e^{2x}}{6}.$$

Note that the first two terms in $y_p(x)$ are solutions to the corresponding homogeneous equation. Thus, another (and simpler) answer is $y_p(x) = x^2e^{2x}/6$.

**3.** Let us find a fundamental solution set for the corresponding homogeneous equation,

$$z''' + 3z'' - 4z = 0.$$

Factoring the auxiliary polynomial, $r^3 + 3r^2 - 4$, yields

$$r^3 + 3r^2 - 4 = \left(r^3 - r^2\right) + \left(4r^2 - 4\right) = r^2(r-1) + 4(r+1)(r-1) = (r-1)(r+2)^2.$$

Therefore, $r = 1, -2$, and $-2$ are the roots of the auxiliary equation, and so the functions $z_1 = e^x$, $z_2 = e^{-2x}$, and $z_3 = xe^{-2x}$ form a fundamental solution set. A particular solution then has the form

$$z_p(x) = v_1(x)z_1(x) + v_2(x)z_2(x) + v_3(x)z_3(x) = v_1(x)e^x + v_2(x)e^{-2x} + v_3(x)xe^{-2x}. \quad (6.23)$$

To find functions $v_j$'s we need four determinants, the Wronskian $W[z_1, z_2, z_3](x)$ and $W_1(x)$, $W_2(x)$, and $W_3(x)$ given in (10) on page 340 of the text. Thus we compute

$$W[e^x, e^{-2x}, xe^{-2x}](x) = \begin{vmatrix} e^x & e^{-2x} & xe^{-2x} \\ e^x & -2e^{-2x} & (1-2x)e^{-2x} \\ e^x & 4e^{-2x} & (4x-4)e^{-2x} \end{vmatrix} = e^{-3x} \begin{vmatrix} 1 & 1 & x \\ 1 & -2 & 1-2x \\ 1 & 4 & 4x-4 \end{vmatrix} = 9e^{-3x},$$

$$W_1(x) = (-1)^{3-1}W[e^{-2x}, xe^{-2x}](x) = \begin{vmatrix} e^{-2x} & xe^{-2x} \\ -2e^{-2x} & (1-2x)e^{-2x} \end{vmatrix} = e^{-4x},$$

$$W_2(x) = (-1)^{3-2}W[e^x, xe^{-2x}](x) = -\begin{vmatrix} e^x & xe^{-2x} \\ e^x & (1-2x)e^{-2x} \end{vmatrix} = (3x-1)e^{-x},$$

$$W_3(x) = (-1)^{3-3}W[e^x, e^{-2x}](x) = \begin{vmatrix} e^x & e^{-2x} \\ e^x & -2e^{-2x} \end{vmatrix} = -3e^{-x}.$$

Substituting these expressions into the formula (11) on page 340 of the text, we obtain

$$v_1(x) = \int \frac{g(x)W_1(x)}{W[e^x, e^{-2x}, xe^{-2x}]}\, dx = \int \frac{e^{2x}e^{-4x}}{9e^{-3x}}\, dx = \frac{1}{9}\, e^x,$$

$$v_2(x) = \int \frac{g(x)W_2(x)}{W[e^x, e^{-2x}, xe^{-2x}]}\, dx = \int \frac{e^{2x}(3x-1)e^{-x}}{9e^{-3x}}\, dx$$

$$= \frac{1}{9}\int (3x-1)e^{4x}\, dx = \left(\frac{x}{12} - \frac{7}{144}\right)e^{4x},$$

$$v_3(x) = \int \frac{g(x)W_3(x)}{W[e^x, e^{-2x}, xe^{-2x}]}\, dx = \int \frac{e^{2x}(-3e^{-x})}{9e^{-3x}}\, dx = -\frac{1}{12}\, e^{4x}.$$

Substituting these expressions into (6.23) yields

$$z_p(x) = \frac{1}{9}\, e^x e^x + \left(\frac{x}{12} - \frac{7}{144}\right)e^{4x}e^{-2x} - \frac{1}{12}\, e^{4x}xe^{-2x} = \frac{1}{16}\, e^{2x}.$$

# Chapter 6

**5.** Since the nonhomogeneous term, $g(x) = \tan x$, is not a solution to a homogeneous linear differential equation with constant coefficients, we will find a particular solution by the method of variation of parameters. To do this, we must first find a fundamental solution set for the corresponding homogeneous equation, $y''' + y' = 0$. Its auxiliary equation is $r^3 + r = 0$, which factors as $r^3 + r = r(r^2 + 1)$. Thus, the roots to this auxiliary equation are $r = 0, \pm i$. Therefore, a fundamental solution set to the homogeneous equation is $\{1, \cos x, \sin x\}$ and

$$y_p(x) = v_1(x) + v_2(x)\cos x + v_3(x)\sin x.$$

To accomplish this, we must find the four determinants $W[1, \cos x, \sin x](x)$, $W_1(x)$, $W_2(x)$, $W_3(x)$. That is, we calculate

$$W[1, \cos x, \sin x](x) = \begin{vmatrix} 1 & \cos x & \sin x \\ 0 & -\sin x & \cos x \\ 0 & -\cos x & -\sin x \end{vmatrix} = \sin^2 x + \cos^2 x = 1,$$

$$W_1(x) = (-1)^{3-1} W[\cos x, \sin x](x) = \begin{vmatrix} \cos x & \sin x \\ -\sin x & \cos x \end{vmatrix} = (\cos^2 x + \sin^2 x) = 1,$$

$$W_2(x) = (-1)^{3-2} W[1, \sin x](x) = -\begin{vmatrix} 1 & \sin x \\ 0 & \cos x \end{vmatrix} = -\cos x,$$

$$W_3(x) = (-1)^{3-3} W[1, \cos x](x) = \begin{vmatrix} 1 & \cos x \\ 0 & -\sin x \end{vmatrix} = -\sin x.$$

By using formula (11) on page 340 of the text, we can now find $v_1(x)$, $v_2(x)$, and $v_3(x)$. Since $g(x) = \tan x$, we have (assuming that all constants of integration are zero)

$$v_1(x) = \int \frac{g(x)W_1(x)}{W[1, \cos x, \sin x](x)}\, dx = \int \tan x\, dx = \ln(\sec x),$$

$$v_2(x) = \int \frac{g(x)W_2(x)}{W[1, \cos x, \sin x](x)}\, dx = \int \tan x(-\cos x)\, dx = -\int \sin x\, dx = \cos x,$$

$$v_3(x) = \int \frac{g(x)W_3(x)}{W[1, \cos x, \sin x](x)}\, dx = \int \tan x(-\sin x)\, dx = -\int \frac{\sin^2 x}{\cos x}\, dx$$

$$= -\int \frac{1 - \cos^2 x}{\cos x}\, dx = \int (\cos x - \sec x)\, dx = \sin x - \ln(\sec x + \tan x).$$

378

Therefore, we have

$$y_p(x) = v_1(x) + v_2(x)\cos x + v_3(x)\sin x$$

$$= \ln(\sec x) + \cos^2 x + \sin^2 x - \sin x \ln(\sec x + \tan x)$$

$$\Rightarrow \quad y_p(x) = \ln(\sec x) - \sin x \ln(\sec x + \tan x) + 1.$$

Since $y \equiv 1$ is a solution to the homogeneous equation, we may choose

$$y_p(x) = \ln(\sec x) - \sin x \ln(\sec x + \tan x).$$

Note: We left the absolute value signs off $\ln(\sec x)$ and $\ln(\sec x + \tan x)$ because of the stated domain: $0 < x < \pi/2$.

**7.** First, we divide the differential equation by $x^3$ to obtain the standard form

$$y''' - 3x^{-1}y'' + 6x^{-2}y' - 6x^{-3}y = x^{-4}, \qquad x > 0,$$

from which we see that $g(x) = x^{-4}$. Given that $\{x, x^2, x^3\}$ is a fundamental solution set for the corresponding homogeneous equation, we are looking for a particular solution of the form

$$y_p(x) = v_1(x)x + v_3(x)x^2 + v_3(x)x^3. \tag{6.24}$$

Evaluating determinants $W[x, x^2, x^3](x)$, $W_1(x)$, $W_2(x)$, and $W_3(x)$ yileds

$$W[x, x^2, x^3](x) = \begin{vmatrix} x & x^2 & x^3 \\ 1 & 2x & 3x^2 \\ 0 & 2 & 6x \end{vmatrix} = x \begin{vmatrix} 2x & 3x^2 \\ 2 & 6x \end{vmatrix} - \begin{vmatrix} x^2 & x^3 \\ 2 & 6x \end{vmatrix} = 2x^3,$$

$$W_1(x) = (-1)^{3-1}W[x^2, x^3](x) = \begin{vmatrix} x^2 & x^3 \\ 2x & 3x^2 \end{vmatrix} = x^4,$$

$$W_2(x) = (-1)^{3-2}W[x, x^3](x) = -\begin{vmatrix} x & x^3 \\ 1 & 3x^2 \end{vmatrix} = -2x^3,$$

$$W_3(x) = (-1)^{3-3}W[x, x^2](x) = \begin{vmatrix} x & x^2 \\ 1 & 2x \end{vmatrix} = x^2.$$

So,

$$v_1(x) = \int \frac{g(x)W_1(x)}{W[x,x^2,x^3](x)}\, dx = \int \frac{x^{-4}x^4}{2x^3}\, dx = -\frac{1}{4x^2} + c_1,$$

$$v_2(x) = \int \frac{g(x)W_2(x)}{W[x,x^2,x^3](x)}\, dx = \int \frac{x^{-4}(-2x^3)}{2x^3}\, dx = \frac{1}{3x^3} + c_2,$$

$$v_3(x) = \int \frac{g(x)W_3(x)}{W[x,x^2,x^3](x)}\, dx = \int \frac{x^{-4}(x^2)}{2x^3}\, dx = -\frac{1}{8x^4} + c_3,$$

where $c_1$, $c_2$, and $c_3$ are constants of integration. Substitution back into (6.24) yields

$$y_p(x) = \left(-\frac{1}{4x^2} + c_1\right)x + \left(\frac{1}{3x^3} + c_2\right)x^2 + \left(-\frac{1}{8x^4} + c_3\right)x^3 = -\frac{1}{24x} + c_1 x + c_2 x^2 + c_3 x^3.$$

Since $\{x, x^2, x^3\}$ is a fundamental solution set for the homogeneous equation, taking $c_1$, $c_2$, and $c_3$ to be arbitrary constants, we obtain a general solution to the original nonhomogeneous equation. That is,

$$y(x) = -\frac{1}{24x} + c_1 x + c_2 x^2 + c_3 x^3.$$

9. To find a particular solution to the nonhomogeneous equation, we will use the method of variation of parameters. We must first calculate the four determinants $W[e^x, e^{-x}, e^{2x}](x)$, $W_1(x)$, $W_2(x)$, $W_3(x)$. Thus, we have

$$W[e^x, e^{-x}, e^{2x}](x) = \begin{vmatrix} e^x & e^{-x} & e^{2x} \\ e^x & -e^{-x} & 2e^{2x} \\ e^x & e^{-x} & 4e^{2x} \end{vmatrix} = -4e^{2x} + 2e^{2x} + e^{2x} + e^{2x} - 2e^{2x} - 4e^{2x} = -6e^{2x},$$

$$W_1(x) = \begin{vmatrix} 0 & e^{-x} & e^{2x} \\ 0 & -e^{-x} & 2e^{2x} \\ 1 & e^{-x} & 4e^{2x} \end{vmatrix} = (-1)^{3-1} \begin{vmatrix} e^{-x} & e^{2x} \\ -e^{-x} & 2e^{2x} \end{vmatrix} = 2e^x + e^x = 3e^x,$$

$$W_2(x) = \begin{vmatrix} e^x & 0 & e^{2x} \\ e^x & 0 & 2e^{2x} \\ e^x & 1 & 4e^{2x} \end{vmatrix} = (-1)^{3-2} \begin{vmatrix} e^x & e^{2x} \\ e^x & 2e^{2x} \end{vmatrix} = -\left(2e^{3x} - e^{3x}\right) = -e^{3x},$$

$$W_3(x) = \begin{vmatrix} e^x & e^{-x} & 0 \\ e^x & -e^{-x} & 0 \\ e^x & e^{-x} & 1 \end{vmatrix} = (-1)^{3-3} \begin{vmatrix} e^x & e^{-x} \\ e^x & -e^{-x} \end{vmatrix} = -1 - 1 = -2.$$

Therefore, according to formula (12) on page 340 of the text, a particular solution, $y_p(x)$, will be given by

$$y_p(x) = e^x \int \frac{3e^x g(x)}{-6e^{2x}}\,dx + e^{-x} \int \frac{-e^{3x} g(x)}{-6e^{2x}}\,dx + e^{2x} \int \frac{-2g(x)}{-6e^{2x}}\,dx$$

$$\Rightarrow \qquad y_p(x) = -\frac{1}{2} e^x \int e^{-x} g(x)\,dx + \frac{1}{6} e^{-x} \int e^x g(x)\,dx + \frac{1}{3} e^{2x} \int e^{-2x} g(x)\,dx.$$

**11.** First, we find a fundamental solution set to the corresponding homogeneous equation,

$$x^3 y''' - 3xy' + 3y = 0. \tag{6.25}$$

Here we involve the procedure of solving Cauchy-Euler equations discussed in Problem 38, Section 4.3. Thus, let $x = e^t$. Then $dx/dt = e^t = x$ and so the chain rule yields

$$\frac{dy}{dt} = \frac{dy}{dx}\frac{dx}{dt} = x\frac{dy}{dx},$$

$$\frac{d^2y}{dt^2} = \frac{d}{dt}\left(\frac{dy}{dt}\right) = \frac{d}{dx}\left(x\frac{dy}{dx}\right)\frac{dx}{dt} = \left[\frac{dy}{dx} + x\frac{d^2y}{dx^2}\right]x == x\frac{dy}{dx} + x^2\frac{d^2y}{dx^2} = \frac{dy}{dt} + x^2\frac{d^2y}{dx^2},$$

$$\Rightarrow \qquad x^2\frac{d^2y}{dx^2} = \frac{d^2y}{dt^2} - \frac{dy}{dt},$$

$$\frac{d^3y}{dt^3} = \frac{d}{dt}\left(\frac{d^2y}{dt^2}\right) = \frac{d}{dx}\left(x\frac{dy}{dx} + x^2\frac{d^2y}{dx^2}\right)\frac{dx}{dt} = \left[\frac{dy}{dx} + 3x\frac{d^2y}{dx^2} + x^2\frac{d^3y}{dx^3}\right]x$$

$$= x\frac{dy}{dx} + 3x^2\frac{d^2y}{dx^2} + x^3\frac{d^3y}{dx^3} = \frac{dy}{dt} + 3\left(\frac{d^2y}{dt^2} - \frac{dy}{dt}\right) + x^3\frac{d^3y}{dx^3} = 3\frac{d^2y}{dt^2} - 2\frac{dy}{dt} + x^3\frac{d^3y}{dx^3}$$

$$\Rightarrow \qquad x^3\frac{d^3y}{dx^3} = \frac{d^3y}{dt^3} - 3\frac{d^2y}{dt^2} + 2\frac{dy}{dt}.$$

Substituting these expressions into (6.25), we obtain

$$\left[\frac{d^3y}{dt^3} - 3\frac{d^2y}{dt^2} + 2\frac{dy}{dt}\right] - 3\left[\frac{dy}{dt}\right] + 3y = 0 \qquad \Rightarrow \qquad \frac{d^3y}{dt^3} - 3\frac{d^2y}{dt^2} - \frac{dy}{dt} + 3y = 0.$$

The auxiliary equation corresponding to this linear homogeneous equation with constant coefficients is

$$r^3 - 3r^2 - r + 3 = 0 \qquad \Rightarrow \qquad r^2(r-3) - (r-3) = 0 \qquad \Rightarrow \qquad (r-3)(r+1)(r-1) = 0,$$

# Chapter 6

whose roots are $r = 1, -1$, and 3. Therefore, the functions

$$y_1(t) = e^t, \qquad y_2(t) = e^{-t}, \quad \text{and} \quad y_3(t) = e^{3t}$$

form a fundamental solution set. Substituting back $e^t = x$ we find that

$$y_1(x) = e^t = x,$$
$$y_2(x) = e^{-t} = (e^t)^{-1} = x^{-1},$$
$$y_3(x) = e^{3t} = (e^t)^3 = x^3$$

form a fundamental solution set for the homogeneous equation (6.25). Next, we apply the variation of parameters to find a particular solution to the original equation. A particular solution has the form

$$y_p(x) = v_1(x)x + v_2(x)x^{-1} + v_3(x)x^3 . \tag{6.26}$$

To find functions $v_1(x)$, $v_2(x)$, and $v_3(x)$ we use formula (11) on page 340 of the text. We compute

$$W[x, x^{-1}, x^3](x) = \begin{vmatrix} x & x^{-1} & x^3 \\ 1 & -x^{-2} & 3x^2 \\ 0 & 2x^{-3} & 6x \end{vmatrix} = x \begin{vmatrix} -x^{-2} & 3x^2 \\ 2x^{-3} & 6x \end{vmatrix} - \begin{vmatrix} x^{-1} & x^3 \\ 2x^{-3} & 6x \end{vmatrix} = -16,$$

$$W_1(x) = (-1)^{3-1} W[x^{-1}, x^3](x) = \begin{vmatrix} x^{-1} & x^3 \\ -x^{-2} & 3x^2 \end{vmatrix} = 4x,$$

$$W_2(x) = (-1)^{3-2} W[x, x^3](x) = - \begin{vmatrix} x & x^3 \\ 1 & 3x^2 \end{vmatrix} = -2x^3,$$

$$W_3(x) = (-1)^{3-3} W[x, x^{-1}](x) = \begin{vmatrix} x & x^{-1} \\ 1 & -x^{-2} \end{vmatrix} = -2x^{-1}.$$

Also, writing the given equation in standard form,

$$y''' - \frac{3}{x^2} y' + \frac{3}{x^3} y = x \cos x,$$

we see that the nonhomogeneous term is $g(x) = x \cos x$. Thus, by (11),

$$v_1(x) = \int \frac{x \cos x (4x)}{-16} \, dx = -\frac{1}{4} \int x^2 \cos x \, dx = -\frac{1}{4} \left( x^2 \sin x + 2x \cos x - 2 \sin x \right) + c_1,$$

$$v_2(x) = \int \frac{x \cos x (-2x^3)}{-16}\, dx = \frac{1}{8} \int x^4 \cos x \, dx$$

$$= \frac{1}{8}\left(x^4 \sin x + 4x^3 \cos x - 12x^2 \sin x - 24x \cos x + 24 \sin x\right) + c_2,$$

$$v_3(x) = \int \frac{x \cos x (-2x^{-1})}{-16}\, dx = \frac{1}{8}\int \cos x\, dx = \frac{1}{8}\sin x + c_3,$$

where $c_1$, $c_2$, $c_3$ are constants of integration, and we have used integration by parts to evaluate $v_1(x)$ and $v_2(x)$. Substituting these functions into (6.26) and simplifying yields

$$y_p(x) = -\frac{\left(x^2 \sin x + 2x \cos x - 2\sin x\right)x}{4} + c_1 x$$

$$+ \frac{\left(x^4 \sin x + 4x^3 \cos x - 12x^2 \sin x - 24x \cos x + 24 \sin x\right)x^{-1}}{8} + c_2 x^{-1} + \frac{x^3 \sin x}{8} + c_3 x^3$$

$$= c_1 x + c_2 x^{-1} + c_3 x^3 - x \sin x - 3\cos x + 3x^{-1}\sin x.$$

If we allow $c_1$, $c_2$, and $c_3$ in the above formula to be arbitrary constants, we obtain a general solution to the original Cauchy-Euler equation. Thus, the answer is

$$y(x) = c_1 x + c_2 x^{-1} + c_3 x^3 - x\sin x - 3\cos x + 3x^{-1}\sin x.$$

**13.** Since

$$W_k(x) = \begin{vmatrix} y_1 & \cdots & y_{k-1} & 0 & y_{k+1} & \cdots & y_n \\ y_1' & \cdots & y_{k-1}' & 0 & y_{k+1}' & \cdots & y_n' \\ \vdots & & \vdots & \vdots & \vdots & & \vdots \\ y_1^{(n-2)} & \cdots & y_{k-1}^{(n-2)} & 0 & y_{k+1}^{(n-2)} & \cdots & y_n^{(n-2)} \\ y_1^{(n-1)} & \cdots & y_{k-1}^{(n-1)} & 1 & y_{k+1}^{(n-1)} & \cdots & y_n^{(n-1)} \end{vmatrix},$$

the $k$th column of this determinant consists of all zeros except the last entry, which is 1. Therefore, expanding $W_k(x)$ by the cofactors in the $k$th column, we get

$$W_k(x) = (0)C_{1,k} + (0)C_{2,k} + \cdots + (0)C_{n-1,n} + (1)C_{n,k}$$

$$= (1)(-1)^{n+k} \begin{vmatrix} y_1 & \cdots & y_{k-1} & y_{k+1} & \cdots & y_n \\ y_1' & \cdots & y_{k-1}' & y_{k+1}' & \cdots & y_n' \\ \vdots & & \vdots & \vdots & & \vdots \\ y_1^{(n-2)} & \cdots & y_{k-1}^{(n-2)} & y_{k+1}^{(n-2)} & \cdots & y_n^{(n-2)} \end{vmatrix}$$

$$= (-1)^{n+k} W\left[y_1, \ldots, y_{k-1}, y_{k+1}, \ldots, y_n\right](x).$$

Finally,

$$(-1)^{n+k} = (-1)^{(n-k)+(2k)} = (-1)^{n-k}.$$

## REVIEW PROBLEMS:  page 344

1. **(a)** In notation of Theorem 1, we have $p_1(x) \equiv 0$, $p_2(x) = -\ln x$, $p_3(x) = x$, $p_4(x) \equiv 2$, and $g(x) = \cos 3x$. All these functions, except $p_2(x)$, are continuous on $(-\infty, \infty)$, and $p_2(x)$ is defined and continuous on $(0, \infty)$. Thus, Theorem 1 guarantees the existence of a unique solution on $(0, \infty)$.

   **(b)** By dividing both sides of the given differential equation by $x^2 - 1$, we rewrite the equation in standard form, that is,

   $$y''' + \frac{\sin x}{x^2 - 1} y'' + \frac{\sqrt{x+4}}{x^2 - 1} y' + \frac{e^x}{x^2 - 1} y = \frac{x^2 + 3}{x^2 - 1}.$$

   Thus we see that

   $$p_1(x) = \frac{\sin x}{x^2 - 1}, \quad p_2(x) = \frac{\sqrt{x+4}}{x^2 - 1}, \quad p_3(x) = \frac{e^x}{x^2 - 1}, \quad \text{and} \quad g(x) = \frac{x^2 + 3}{x^2 - 1}.$$

   Functions $p_1(x)$, $p_3(x)$, and $g(x)$ are defined and continuous on $(-\infty, \infty)$ except $x = \pm 1$; $p_2(x)$ is defined and continuous on $\{x \geq -4, x \neq \pm 1\}$. Thus, the common domain for $p_1(x)$, $p_2(x)$, $p_3(x)$, and $g(x)$ is $\{x \geq -4, x \neq \pm 1\}$, and, in addition, these functions are continuous there. This set consists of three intervals,

   $$[-4, -1), \quad (-1, 1), \quad \text{and} \quad (1, \infty).$$

   Theorem 1 guarantees the existence of a unique solution on each of these intervals.

3. A linear combination,

   $$c_1 \sin x + c_2 x \sin x + c_3 x^2 \sin x + c_4 x^3 \sin x = \left(c_1 + c_2 x + c_3 x^2 + c_4 x^3\right) \sin x \qquad (6.27)$$

   vanishes identically on $(-\infty, \infty)$ if and only if the polynomial $c_1 + c_2 x + c_3 x^2 + c_4 x^3$ vanishes identically on $(-\infty, \infty)$. Since the number of real zeros of a polynomial does not exceed its degree, unless it's the zero polynomial, we conclude that the linear combination (6.27) vanishes identically on $(-\infty, \infty)$ if and only if $c_1 = c_2 = c_3 = c_4 = 0$. This means that the given functions are linearly independent on $(-\infty, \infty)$.

**5.** **(a)** Solving the auxiliary equation yields

$$(r+5)^2(r-2)^3(r^2+1)^2 = 0 \quad \Rightarrow \quad \begin{array}{l} (r+5)^2 = 0 \quad \text{or} \\ (r-2)^3 = 0 \quad \text{or} \\ (r^2+1)^2 = 0. \end{array}$$

Thus, the roots of the auxiliary equation are

$$r = -5 \quad \text{of multiplicity 2,}$$
$$r = 2 \quad \text{of multiplicity 3,}$$
$$r = \pm i \quad \text{of multiplicity 2.}$$

According to (22) on page 329 and (28) on page 330 of the text, the set of functions (assuming that $x$ is the independent variable)

$$e^{-5x}, \ xe^{-5x}, \ e^{2x}, \ xe^{2x}, \ x^2 e^{2x}, \ \cos x, \ x\cos x, \ \sin x, \ x\sin x$$

forms an independent solution set. Thus, a general solution is given by

$$c_1 e^{-5x} + c_2 xe^{-5x} + c_3 e^{2x} + c_4 xe^{2x} + c_5 x^2 e^{2x} + c_6 \cos x + c_7 x\cos x + c_8 \sin x + c_9 x\sin x.$$

**(b)** Solving the auxiliary equation yields

$$r^4(r-1)^2(r^2+2r+4)^2 = 0 \quad \Rightarrow \quad \begin{array}{l} r^4 = 0 \quad \text{or} \\ (r-1)^2 = 0 \quad \text{or} \\ (r^2+2r+4)^2 = 0. \end{array}$$

Thus, the roots of the auxiliary equation are

$$r = 0 \quad \text{of multiplicity 4,}$$
$$r = 1 \quad \text{of multiplicity 2,}$$
$$r = -1 \pm \sqrt{3}i \quad \text{of multiplicity 2.}$$

Using (22) on page 329 and (28) on page 330 of the text, we conclude that the set of functions (with $x$ as the independent variable)

$$1, \ x, \ x^2, \ x^3, \ e^x, \ xe^x, \ e^{-x}\cos\sqrt{3}x, \ xe^{-x}\cos\sqrt{3}x, \ \sin\sqrt{3}x, \ xe^{-x}\sin\sqrt{3}x$$

forms an independent solution set. A general solution is given then by

$$c_1 + c_2 x + c_3 x^2 + c_4 x^3 + c_5 e^x + c_6 xe^x + c_7 e^{-x}\cos\sqrt{3}x + c_8 xe^{-x}\cos\sqrt{3}x$$
$$+c_9\sin\sqrt{3}x + c_{10}xe^{-x}\sin\sqrt{3}x$$
$$= c_1 + c_2 x + c_3 x^2 + c_4 x^3 + (c_5 + c_6 x)e^x + (c_7 + c_8 x)e^{-x}\cos\sqrt{3}x$$
$$+(c_9 + c_{10}x)e^{-x}\sin\sqrt{3}x .$$

7. **(a)** $D^3$, since the third derivative of a quadratic polynomial is identically zero.

**(b)** The function $e^{3x} + x - 1$ is the sum of $e^{3x}$ and $x - 1$. The function $x - 1$ is annihilated by $D^2$, the second derivative operator, and, according to (i) on page 334 of the text, $(D-3)$ annihilates $e^{3x}$. Therefore, the composite operator

$$D^2(D - 3) = (D - 3)D^2$$

annihilates both functions and, hence, there sum.

**(c)** The function $x\sin 2x$ is of the form given in (iv) on page 334 of the text with $m = 2$, $\alpha = 0$, and $\beta = 2$. Thus, the operator

$$\left[(D - 0)^2 + 2^2\right]^2 = \left(D^2 + 4\right)^2$$

annihilates this function.

**(d)** We again use (iv) on page 334 of the text, this time with $m = 3$, $\alpha = -2$, and $\beta = 3$, to conclude that the given function is annihilated by

$$\left\{[D - (-2)]^2 + 3^2\right\}^3 = \left[(D + 2)^2 + 9\right]^3 .$$

**(e)** Representing the given function as a linear combination,

$$\left(x^2 - 2x\right) + \left(xe^{-x}\right) + (\sin 2x) - (\cos 3x),$$

we find an annihilator for each term. Thus, we have:

$x^2 - 2x$  is annihilated by $D^3$,

$xe^{-x}$      is annihilated by $[D - (-1)]^2 = (D + 1)^2$  (by (ii), page 334),

$\sin 2x$    is annihilated by $D^2 + 2^2 = D^2 + 4$        (by (iii), page 334),

$\cos 3x$    is annihilated by $D^2 + 3^2 = D^2 + 9$        (by (iii), page 334).

Therefore, the product $D^3(D + 1)^2(D^2 + 4)(D^2 + 9)$ annihilates the given function.

**9.** A general solution to the corresponding homogeneous equation,

$$x^3 y''' - 2x^2 y'' - 5xy' + 5y = 0,$$

is given by $y_h(x) = c_1 x + c_2 x^5 + c_3 x^{-1}$. We now apply the variation of parameters method described in Section 6.4, and seek for a particular solution to the original nonhomogeneous equation in the form

$$y_p(x) = v_1(x)x + v_2(x)x^5 + v_3(x)x^{-1}.$$

Since

$$(x)' = 1, \qquad (x)'' = 0,$$
$$(x^5)' = 5x^4, \qquad (x^5)'' = 20x^3,$$
$$(x^{-1})' = -x^{-2}, \quad (x^{-1})'' = 2x^{-3},$$

the Wronskian $W[x, x^5, x^{-1}](x)$ and determinants $W_k(x)$ given in (10) on page 340 of the text become

$$W[x, x^5, x^{-1}](x) = \begin{vmatrix} x & x^5 & x^{-1} \\ 1 & 5x^4 & -x^{-2} \\ 0 & 20x^3 & 2x^{-3} \end{vmatrix} = (x)\begin{vmatrix} 5x^4 & -x^{-2} \\ 20x^3 & 2x^{-3} \end{vmatrix} - (1)\begin{vmatrix} x^5 & x^{-1} \\ 20x^3 & 2x^{-3} \end{vmatrix}$$

$$= (x)(30x) - (-18x^2) = 48x^2,$$

$$W_1(x) = (-1)^{3-1}\begin{vmatrix} x^5 & x^{-1} \\ 5x^4 & -x^{-2} \end{vmatrix} = -6x^3,$$

$$W_2(x) = (-1)^{3-2} \begin{vmatrix} x & x^{-1} \\ 1 & -x^{-2} \end{vmatrix} = 2x^{-1},$$

$$W_3(x) = (-1)^{3-3} \begin{vmatrix} x & x^5 \\ 1 & 5x^4 \end{vmatrix} = 4x^5.$$

Now we divide both sides of the given equation by $x^3$ to obtain an equation in standard form, that is,

$$y''' - 2x^{-1}y'' - 5x^{-2}y' + 5x^{-3}y = x^{-5}.$$

Hence, the right-hand side, $g(x)$, in formula (1) on page 339 of the text equals to $x^{-5}$. Applying formula (11), page 340 of the text, yields

$$v_1(x) = \int \frac{x^{-5}(-6x^3)}{48x^2}\, dx = -\frac{1}{8} \int x^{-4}\, dx = \frac{1}{24} x^{-3},$$

$$v_2(x) = \int \frac{x^{-5}(2x^{-1})}{48x^2}\, dx = \frac{1}{24} \int x^{-8}\, dx = -\frac{1}{168} x^{-7},$$

$$v_3(x) = \int \frac{x^{-5}(4x^5)}{48x^2}\, dx = \frac{1}{12} \int x^{-2}\, dx = -\frac{1}{12} x^{-1}.$$

Therefore,

$$
\begin{aligned}
y_p(x) &= \left(\frac{1}{24} x^{-3}\right) x + \left(-\frac{1}{168} x^{-7}\right) x^5 + \left(-\frac{1}{12} x^{-1}\right) x^{-1} \\
&= \left(\frac{1}{24} - \frac{1}{168} - \frac{1}{12}\right) x^{-2} = -\frac{1}{21} x^{-2},
\end{aligned}
$$

and a general solution to the given equation is given by

$$y(x) = y_h(x) + y_p(x) = c_1 x + c_2 x^5 + c_3 x^{-1} - \frac{1}{21} x^{-2}.$$

# CHAPTER 7: Laplace Transforms

**EXERCISES 7.2:  Definition of the Laplace Transform, page 359**

**1.** For $s > 0$, using Definition 1 on page 351 and integration by parts, we compute

$$\mathcal{L}\{t\}(s) = \int_0^\infty e^{-st} t \, dt = \lim_{N \to \infty} \int_0^N e^{-st} t \, dt = \lim_{N \to \infty} \int_0^N t \, d\left(-\frac{e^{-st}}{s}\right)$$

$$= \lim_{N \to \infty}\left[-\frac{te^{-st}}{s}\Big|_0^N + \frac{1}{s}\int_0^N e^{-st}\, dt\right] = \lim_{N \to \infty}\left[-\frac{te^{-st}}{s}\Big|_0^N - \frac{e^{-st}}{s^2}\Big|_0^N\right]$$

$$= \lim_{N \to \infty}\left[-\frac{Ne^{-sN}}{s} + 0 - \frac{e^{-sN}}{s^2} + \frac{1}{s^2}\right] = \frac{1}{s^2}$$

because, for $s > 0$, $e^{-sN} \to 0$ and $Ne^{-sN} = N/e^{sN} \to 0$ as $N \to \infty$.

**3.** For $s > 6$, we have

$$\mathcal{L}\{t\}(s) = \int_0^\infty e^{-st} e^{6t}\, dt = \int_0^\infty e^{(6-s)t}\, dt = \lim_{N \to \infty}\int_0^N e^{(6-s)t}\, dt$$

$$= \lim_{N \to \infty}\left[\frac{e^{(6-s)t}}{6-s}\Big|_0^N\right] = \lim_{N \to \infty}\left[\frac{e^{(6-s)N}}{6-s} - \frac{1}{6-s}\right] = 0 - \frac{1}{6-s} = \frac{1}{s-6}.$$

**5.** For $s > 0$,

$$\mathcal{L}\{\cos 2t\}(s) = \int_0^\infty e^{-st}\cos 2t\, dt = \lim_{N \to \infty}\int_0^N e^{-st}\cos 2t\, dt$$

$$= \lim_{N \to \infty}\left[\frac{e^{-st}(-s\cos 2t + 2\sin 2t)}{s^2 + 4}\Big|_0^N\right]$$

$$= \lim_{N \to \infty}\left[\frac{e^{-sN}(-s\cos 2N + 2\sin 2N)}{s^2 + 4} - \frac{-s}{s^2 + 4}\right] = \frac{s}{s^2 + 4},$$

where we have used integration by parts to find an antiderivative of $e^{-st}\cos 2t$.

**7.** For $s > 2$,

$$\mathcal{L}\left\{e^{2t}\cos 3t\right\}(s) = \int_0^\infty e^{-st}e^{2t}\cos 3t\, dt = \int_0^\infty e^{(2-s)t}\cos 3t\, dt$$

$$= \lim_{N\to\infty}\left[\frac{e^{(2-s)t}\left((2-s)\cos 3t + 3\sin 3t\right)}{(2-s)^2+9}\bigg|_0^N\right]$$

$$= \lim_{N\to\infty}\frac{e^{(2-s)N}\left[(2-s)\cos 3N + 3\sin 3N\right] - (2-s)}{(2-s)^2+9} = \frac{s-2}{(s-2)^2+9}.$$

**9.** As in Example 4 on page 353 in the text, we first break the integral into separate parts. Thus,

$$\mathcal{L}\{f(t)\}(s) = \int_0^\infty e^{-st}f(t)\, dt = \int_0^2 e^{-st}\cdot 0\, dt + \int_2^\infty te^{-st}\, dt = \int_2^\infty te^{-st}\, dt.$$

An antiderivative of $te^{-st}$ was, in fact, obtained in Problem 1 using integration by parts. Thus, we have

$$\int_2^\infty te^{-st}\, dt = \lim_{N\to\infty}\left[\left(-\frac{te^{-st}}{s} - \frac{e^{-st}}{s^2}\right)\bigg|_2^N\right] = \lim_{N\to\infty}\left[-\frac{Ne^{-sN}}{s} - \frac{e^{-sN}}{s^2} + \frac{2e^{-2s}}{s} + \frac{e^{-2s}}{s^2}\right]$$

$$= \frac{2e^{-2s}}{s} + \frac{e^{-2s}}{s^2} = e^{-2s}\left(\frac{2}{s} + \frac{1}{s^2}\right) = e^{-2s}\left(\frac{2s+1}{s^2}\right).$$

**11.** In this problem, $f(t)$ is also a piecewise defined function. So, we split the integral and obtain

$$\mathcal{L}\{f(t)\}(s) = \int_0^\infty e^{-st}f(t)\, dt = \int_0^\pi e^{-st}\sin t\, dt + \int_\pi^\infty e^{-st}\cdot 0\, dt = \int_0^\pi e^{-st}\sin t\, dt$$

$$= \frac{e^{-st}\left(-s\sin t - \cos t\right)}{s^2+1}\bigg|_0^\pi = \frac{e^{-\pi s} - (-1)}{s^2+1} = \frac{e^{-\pi s} + 1}{s^2+1},$$

which is valid for all $s$.

**13.** By the linearity of the Laplace transform,

$$\mathcal{L}\left\{6e^{-3t} - t^2 + 2t - 8\right\}(s) = 6\mathcal{L}\left\{e^{-3t}\right\}(s) - \mathcal{L}\left\{t^2\right\}(s) + 2\mathcal{L}\{t\}(s) - 8\mathcal{L}\{1\}(s).$$

From Table 7.1 on page 358 in the text, we see that

$$\mathcal{L}\left\{e^{-3t}\right\}(s) = \frac{1}{s-(-3)} = \frac{1}{s+3}, \qquad s > -3;$$

$$\mathcal{L}\left\{t^2\right\}(s) = \frac{2!}{s^{2+1}} = \frac{2}{s^3}, \quad \mathcal{L}\left\{t\right\}(s) = \frac{1!}{s^{1+1}} = \frac{1}{s^2}, \quad \mathcal{L}\left\{1\right\}(s) = \frac{1}{s}, \quad s > 0.$$

Thus the formula

$$\mathcal{L}\left\{6e^{-3t} - t^2 + 2t - 8\right\}(s) = 6\frac{1}{s+3} - \frac{2}{s^3} + 2\frac{1}{s^2} - 8\frac{1}{s} = \frac{6}{s+3} - \frac{2}{s^3} + \frac{2}{s^2} - \frac{8}{s},$$

is valid for $s$ in the intersection of the sets $s > -3$ and $s > 0$, which is $s > 0$.

**15.** Using the linearity of Laplace transform and Table 7.1 on page 358 in the text, we get

$$
\begin{aligned}
\mathcal{L}\left\{t^3 - te^t + e^{4t}\cos t\right\}(s) &= \mathcal{L}\left\{t^3\right\}(s) - \mathcal{L}\left\{te^t\right\}(s) + \mathcal{L}\left\{e^{4t}\cos t\right\}(s) \\
&= \frac{3!}{s^{3+1}} - \frac{1!}{(s-1)^{1+1}} + \frac{s-4}{(s-4)^2 + 1^2} \\
&= \frac{6}{s^4} - \frac{1}{(s-1)^2} + \frac{s-4}{(s-4)^2 + 1},
\end{aligned}
$$

which is valid for $s > 4$.

**17.** Using the linearity of Laplace transform and Table 7.1 on page 358 in the text, we get

$$
\begin{aligned}
\mathcal{L}\left\{e^{3t}\sin 6t - t^3 + e^t\right\}(s) &= \mathcal{L}\left\{e^{3t}\sin 6t\right\}(s) - \mathcal{L}\left\{t^3\right\}(s) + \mathcal{L}\left\{e^t\right\}(s) \\
&= \frac{6}{(s-3)^2 + 6^2} - \frac{3!}{s^{3+1}} + \frac{1}{s-1} = \frac{6}{(s-3)^2 + 36} - \frac{6}{s^4} + \frac{1}{s-1},
\end{aligned}
$$

valid for $s > 3$.

**19.** For $s > 5$, we have

$$
\begin{aligned}
\mathcal{L}\left\{t^4 e^{5t} - e^t\cos\sqrt{7}t\right\}(s) &= \mathcal{L}\left\{t^4 e^{5t}\right\}(s) - \mathcal{L}\left\{e^t\cos\sqrt{7}t\right\}(s) \\
&= \frac{4!}{(s-5)^{4+1}} - \frac{s-1}{(s-1)^2 + (\sqrt{7})^2} = \frac{24}{(s-5)^5} - \frac{s-1}{(s-1)^2 + 7}.
\end{aligned}
$$

**21.** Since the function $g_1(t) \equiv 1$ is continuous on $(-\infty, \infty)$ and $f(t) = g_1(t)$ for $t$ in $[0, 1]$, we conclude that $f(t)$ is continuous on $[0, 1)$ and continuous from the left at $t = 1$. The function $g_2(t) \equiv (t-2)^2$ is also continuous on $(-\infty, \infty)$, and so $f(t)$ (which is the same as $g_2(t)$ on $(1, 10]$) is continuous on $(1, 10]$. Moreover,

$$\lim_{t \to 1^+} f(t) = \lim_{t \to 1^+} g_2(t) = g_2(1) = (1-2)^2 = 1 = f(1),$$

# Chapter 7

which implies that $f(t)$ is continuous from the right at $t = 1$. Thus $f(t)$ is continuous at $t = 1$ and, therefore, is continuous at any $t$ in $[0, 10]$.

**23.** All the functions involved in the definition of $f(t)$, that is, $g_1(t) \equiv 1$, $g_2(t) = t - 1$, and $g_3(t) = t^2 - 4$, are continuous on $(-\infty, \infty)$. So, $f(t)$, being a restriction of these functions, on $[0, 1)$, $(1, 3)$, and $(3, 10]$, respectively, is continuous on these three intervals. At points $t = 1$ and 3, $f(t)$ is not defined and so is not continuous. But one-sided limits

$$\lim_{t \to 1^-} f(t) = \lim_{t \to 1^-} g_1(t) = g_1(1) = 1,$$
$$\lim_{t \to 1^+} f(t) = \lim_{t \to 1^+} g_2(t) = g_2(1) = 0,$$
$$\lim_{t \to 3^-} f(t) = \lim_{t \to 3^-} g_2(t) = g_2(3) = 2,$$
$$\lim_{t \to 3^+} f(t) = \lim_{t \to 3^+} g_3(t) = g_3(3) = 5,$$

exist and pairwise different. Therefore, $f(t)$ has jump discontinuities at $t = 1$ and $t = 3$, and hence piecewise continuous on $[0, 10]$.

**25.** Given function is a rational function and, therefore, continuous on its domain, which is all reals except zeros of the denominator. Solving $t^2 + 7t + 10 = 0$, we conclude that the points of discontinuity of $f(t)$ are $t = -2$ and $t = -5$. These points are not in $[0, 10]$. So, $f(t)$ is continuous on $[0, 10]$.

**27.** Since

$$\lim_{t \to 0^+} f(t) = \lim_{t \to 0^+} \frac{1}{t} = \infty,$$

$f(t)$ has infinite discontinuity at $t = 0$, and so neither continuous nor piecewise continuous $[0, 10]$.

**29.** **(a)** First observe that $|t^3 \sin t| \le |t^3|$ for all $t$. Next, three applications of L'Hospital's rule show that

$$\lim_{t \to \infty} \frac{t^3}{e^{\alpha t}} = \lim_{t \to \infty} \frac{3t^2}{\alpha e^{\alpha t}} = \lim_{t \to \infty} \frac{6t}{\alpha^2 e^{\alpha t}} = \lim_{t \to \infty} \frac{6}{\alpha^3 e^{\alpha t}} = 0$$

for all $\alpha > 0$. Thus, fixed $\alpha > 0$, for some $T = T(\alpha) > 0$, we have $|t^3| < e^{\alpha t}$ for all $t > T$, and so

$$\left|t^3 \sin t\right| \le \left|t^3\right| < e^{\alpha t}, \qquad t > T.$$

Therefore, $t^3 \sin t$ is of exponential order $\alpha$, for any $\alpha > 0$.

**(b)** Clearly, for any $t$, $|f(t)| = 100e^{49t}$, and so Definition 3 is satisfied with $M = 100$, $\alpha = 49$, and any $T$. Hence, $f(t)$ is of exponential order 49.

**(c)** Since

$$\lim_{t\to\infty} \frac{f(t)}{e^{\alpha t}} = \lim_{t\to\infty} e^{t^3 - \alpha t} = \lim_{t\to\infty} e^{(t^2 - \alpha)t} = \infty,$$

we see that $f(t)$ grows faster than $e^{\alpha t}$ for any $\alpha$. Thus $f(t)$ is *not* of exponential order.

**(d)** Similarly to (a), for any $\alpha > 0$, we get

$$\lim_{t\to\infty} \frac{|t \ln t|}{e^{\alpha t}} = \lim_{t\to\infty} \frac{t \ln t}{e^{\alpha t}} = \lim_{t\to\infty} \frac{\ln t + 1}{\alpha e^{\alpha t}} = \lim_{t\to\infty} \frac{1/t}{\alpha^2 e^{\alpha t}} = 0,$$

and so $f(t)$ is of exponential order $\alpha$ for any positive $\alpha$.

**(e)** Since,

$$f(t) = \cosh\left(t^2\right) = \frac{e^{t^2} + e^{-t^2}}{2} > \frac{1}{2}\, e^{t^2}$$

and $e^{t^2}$ grows faster than $e^{\alpha t}$ for any fixed $\alpha$ (see page 357 in the text), we conclude that $\cosh\left(t^2\right)$ is *not* of exponential order.

**(f)** This function is bounded:

$$|f(t)| = \left|\frac{1}{t^2 + 1}\right| = fr1t^2 + 1 \le \frac{1}{0 + 1} = 1,$$

and so Definition 3 is satisfied with $M = 1$ and $\alpha = 0$. Hence, $f(t)$ is of exponential order 0.

**(g)** The function $\sin\left(t^2\right)$ is bounded, namely, $\left|\sin\left(t^2\right)\right| \le 1$. For any fixed $\beta > 0$, the limit of $t^4/e^{\beta t}$, as $t \to \infty$, is 0, which implies that $t^4 \le e^{\beta t}$ for all $t > T = T(\beta)$. Thus,

$$\left|\sin\left(t^2\right) + t^4 e^{6t}\right| \le 1 + e^{\beta t}e^{6t} = 2e^{\beta + 6t}.$$

This means that $f(t)$ is of exponential order $\alpha$ for any $\alpha > 6$.

**(h)** The function $3 + \cos 4t$ is bounded because

$$|3 + \cos 4t| \le 3 + |\cos 4t| \le 4.$$

Therefore, by the triangle inequality,

$$|f(t)| \ge \left|e^{t^2}\right| - |3 + \cos 4t| \ge e^{t^2} - 4,$$

and, therefore, for any fixed $\alpha$, $f(t)$ grows faster than $e^{\alpha t}$ (because $e^{t^2}$ does, and the other term is bounded). So, $f(t)$ is *not* of exponential order.

**(i)** Clearly, for any $t > 0$,

$$\frac{t^2}{t+1} = \frac{t}{t+1}\, t < (1)t = t.$$

Therefore,

$$e^{t^2/(t+1)} < e^t,$$

and Definition 3 holds with $M = 1$, $\alpha = 1$, and $T = 0$.

**(j)** Since, for any $x$, $-1 \le \sin x \le 1$, the given function is bounded. Indeed,

$$\left|\sin\left(e^{t^2}\right) + e^{\sin t}\right| \le \left|\sin\left(e^{t^2}\right)\right| + e^{\sin t} \le 1 + e$$

Thus it is of exponential order 0.

**31. (a)**

$$\mathcal{L}\left\{e^{(a+ib)t}\right\}(s) := \int_0^\infty e^{-st} e^{(a+ib)t}\, dt = \int_0^\infty e^{(a+ib-s)t}\, dt = \lim_{N\to\infty} \int_0^N e^{(a+ib-s)t}\, dt$$

$$= \lim_{N\to\infty}\left(\left.\frac{e^{(a+ib-s)t}}{a+ib-s}\right|_0^N\right) = \frac{1}{a+ib-s}\lim_{N\to\infty}\left(e^{(a-s+ib)N} - 1\right). \quad (7.1)$$

Since

$$e^{(a-s+ib)x} = e^{(a-s)x} e^{ibx},$$

where the first factor vanishes at $\infty$ if $a - s < 0$ while the second factor is a bounded ($\left|e^{ibx}\right| \equiv 1$) and periodic function, the limit in (7.1) exists if and only if $a - s < 0$. Assuming that $s > a$, we get

$$\frac{1}{a+ib-s}\lim_{N\to\infty}\left(e^{(a-s+ib)N} - 1\right) = \frac{1}{a+ib-s}(0-1) = \frac{1}{s-(a+ib)}.$$

**(b)** Note that $s - (a + ib) = (s - a) - ib$. Multiplying the result in (a) by the complex conjugate of the denominator, that is, $(s - a) + bi$, we get

$$\frac{1}{s - (a + ib)} = \frac{(s - a) + ib}{[(s - a) - ib] \cdot [(s - a) + ib]} = \frac{(s - a) + ib}{(s - a)^2 + b^2},$$

where we used the fact that, for any complex number $z$, $z\bar{z} = |z|^2$.

**(c)** From (a) and (b) we klnow that

$$\mathcal{L}\left\{e^{(a+ib)t}\right\}(s) = \frac{(s - a) + ib}{(s - a)^2 + b^2}.$$

Writing

$$\frac{(s - a) + ib}{(s - a)^2 + b^2} = \frac{s - a}{(s - a)^2 + b^2} + \frac{b}{(s - a)^2 + b^2}i,$$

we see that

$$\text{Re}\left[\mathcal{L}\left\{e^{(a+ib)t}\right\}(s)\right] = \text{Re}\left[\frac{s - a}{(s - a)^2 + b^2} + \frac{b}{(s - a)^2 + b^2}i\right] = \frac{s - a}{(s - a)^2 + b^2}, \quad (7.2)$$

$$\text{Im}\left[\mathcal{L}\left\{e^{(a+ib)t}\right\}(s)\right] = \text{Im}\left[\frac{s - a}{(s - a)^2 + b^2} + \frac{b}{(s - a)^2 + b^2}i\right] = \frac{b}{(s - a)^2 + b^2}. \quad (7.3)$$

On the other hand, by Euler's formulas,

$$\text{Re}\left[e^{-st}e^{(a+ib)t}\right] = e^{-st}\text{Re}\left[e^{at}(\cos bt + i\sin bt)\right] = e^{-st}e^{at}\cos bt$$

and so

$$\text{Re}\left[\mathcal{L}\left\{e^{(a+ib)t}\right\}(s)\right] = \text{Re}\left[\int_0^\infty e^{-st}e^{(a+ib)t}\,dt\right] = \text{Re}\left[\int_0^\infty e^{-s}e^{(a+ib)t}\,dt\right]$$

$$= \int_0^\infty \text{Re}\left[e^{-s}e^{(a+ib)t}\right]dt = \int_0^\infty e^{-st}e^{at}\cos bt\,dt = \mathcal{L}\left\{e^{at}\cos bt\right\}(s),$$

which together with (7.2) gives the last entry in Table 7.1. Similarly,

$$\text{Im}\left[\mathcal{L}\left\{e^{(a+ib)t}\right\}(s)\right] = \mathcal{L}\left\{e^{at}\sin bt\right\}(s),$$

and so (7.3) gives the Laplace transform of $e^{at}\sin bt$.

Chapter 7

**33.** Let $f(t)$ be a piecewise continuous function on $[a, b]$, and let a function $g(t)$ be continuous on $[a, b]$. At any point of continuity of $f(t)$, the function $(fg)(t)$ is continuous as the product of two continuous functions at this point. Suppose now that $c$ is a point of discontinuity of $f(t)$. Then one-sided limits

$$\lim_{t \to c^-} f(t) = L_- \quad \text{and} \quad \lim_{t \to c^+} f(t) = L_+$$

exist. At the same time, continuity of $g(t)$ yields

$$\lim_{t \to c^-} g(t) = \lim_{t \to c^+} g(t) = \lim_{t \to c} g(t) = g(c).$$

Thus, the product rule implies that one-sided limits

$$\lim_{t \to c^-} (fg)(t) = \lim_{t \to c^-} f(t) \cdot \lim_{t \to c^-} g(t) = L_- g(c)$$
$$\lim_{t \to c^+} (fg)(t) = \lim_{t \to c^+} f(t) \lim_{t \to c^+} g(t) = L_+ g(c)$$

exist. So, $fg$ has a jump (even removable if $g(c) = 0$) discontinuity at $t = c$.

Therefore, the product $(fg)(t)$ is continuous at any point on $[a, b]$ except possibly a finite number of points (namely, points of discontinuity of $f(t)$).

### EXERCISES 7.3: Properties of the Laplace Transform, page 365

**1.** Using the linearity of the Laplace transform we get

$$\mathcal{L}\left\{t^2 + e^t \sin 2t\right\}(s) = \mathcal{L}\left\{t^2\right\}(s) + \mathcal{L}\left\{e^t \sin 2t\right\}(s).$$

From Table 7.1 in Section 7.2 we know that

$$\mathcal{L}\left\{t^2\right\}(s) = \frac{2!}{s^3} = \frac{2}{s^3}, \quad \mathcal{L}\left\{e^t \sin 2t\right\}(s) = \frac{2}{(s-1)^2 + 2^2} = \frac{2}{(s-1)^2 + 4}.$$

Thus

$$\mathcal{L}\left\{t^2 + e^t \sin 2t\right\}(s) = \frac{2}{s^3} + \frac{2}{(s-1)^2 + 4}.$$

**3.** By the linearity of the Laplace transform,

$$\mathcal{L}\left\{e^{-t}\cos 3t + e^{6t} - 1\right\}(s) = \mathcal{L}\left\{e^{-t}\cos 3t\right\}(s) + \mathcal{L}\left\{e^{6t}\right\}(s) - \mathcal{L}\left\{1\right\}(s).$$

From Table 7.1 of the text we see that

$$\mathcal{L}\left\{e^{-t}\cos 3t\right\}(s) = \frac{s-(-1)}{[s-(-1)]^2 + 3^2} = \frac{s+1}{(s+1)^2 + 9}, \quad s > -1; \tag{7.4}$$

$$\mathcal{L}\left\{e^{6t}\right\}(s) = \frac{1}{s-6}, \quad s > 6; \tag{7.5}$$

$$\mathcal{L}\left\{1\right\}(s) = \frac{1}{s}, \quad s > 0. \tag{7.6}$$

Since (7.4), (7.5), and (7.6) all hold for $s > 6$, we see that our answer,

$$\mathcal{L}\left\{e^{-t}\cos 3t + e^{6t} - 1\right\}(s) = \frac{s+1}{(s+1)^2 + 9} + \frac{1}{s-6} - \frac{1}{s},$$

is valid for $s > 6$. Note that (7.4) and (7.5) could also be obtained from the Laplace transforms for $\cos 3t$ and 1, respectively, by applying the translation Theorem 3.

**5.** We use the linearity of the Laplace transform and Table 7.1 to get

$$\begin{aligned}
\mathcal{L}\left\{2t^2 e^{-t} - t + \cos 4t\right\}(s) &= 2\mathcal{L}\left\{t^2 e^{-t}\right\}(s) - \mathcal{L}\left\{t\right\}(s) + \mathcal{L}\left\{\cos 4t\right\}(s) \\
&= 2 \cdot \frac{2}{(s+1)^3} - \frac{1}{s^2} + \frac{s}{s^2 + 4^2} = \cdot\frac{4}{(s+1)^3} - \frac{1}{s^2} + \frac{s}{s^2 + 16},
\end{aligned}$$

which is valid for $s > 0$.

**7.** Since $(t-1)^4 = t^4 - 4t^3 + 6t^2 - 4t + 1$, we have from the linearity of the Laplace transform that

$$\mathcal{L}\left\{(t-1)^4\right\}(s) = \mathcal{L}\left\{t^4\right\}(s) - 4\mathcal{L}\left\{t^3\right\}(s) + 6\mathcal{L}\left\{t^2\right\}(s) - 4\mathcal{L}\left\{t\right\}(s) + \mathcal{L}\left\{1\right\}(s).$$

From Table 7.1 of the text, we get that, for $s > 0$,

$$\mathcal{L}\left\{t^4\right\}(s) = \frac{4!}{s^5} = \frac{24}{s^5},$$

$$\mathcal{L}\left\{t^3\right\}(s) = \frac{3!}{s^4} = \frac{6}{s^4},$$

# Chapter 7

$$\mathcal{L}\left\{t^2\right\}(s) = \frac{2!}{s^3} = \frac{2}{s^3},$$

$$\mathcal{L}\left\{t\right\}(s) = \frac{1!}{s^2} = \frac{1}{s^2},$$

$$\mathcal{L}\left\{1\right\}(s) = \frac{1}{s}.$$

Thus

$$\mathcal{L}\left\{(t-1)^4\right\}(s) = \frac{24}{s^5} - \frac{24}{s^4} + \frac{12}{s^3} - \frac{4}{s^2} + \frac{1}{s}, \quad s > 0.$$

**9.** Since

$$\mathcal{L}\left\{e^{-t}\sin 2t\right\}(s) = \frac{2}{(s+1)^2 + 4},$$

we use Theorem 6 to get

$$\mathcal{L}\left\{e^{-t}t\sin 2t\right\}(s) = \mathcal{L}\left\{t\left(e^{-t}\sin 2t\right)\right\}(s) = -\left[\mathcal{L}\left\{e^{-t}\sin 2t\right\}(s)\right]' = -\left[\frac{2}{(s+1)^2 + 4}\right]'$$

$$= -2(-1)\left[(s+1)^2 + 4\right]^{-2}\left[(s+1)^2 + 4\right]' = \frac{4(s+1)}{\left[(s+1)^2 + 4\right]^2}.$$

**11.** We use the definition of $\cosh x$ and the linear property of the Laplace transform.

$$\mathcal{L}\left\{\cosh bt\right\}(s) = \mathcal{L}\left\{\frac{e^{bt} + e^{-bt}}{2}\right\}(s)$$

$$= \frac{1}{2}\left[\mathcal{L}\left\{e^{bt}\right\}(s) + \mathcal{L}\left\{e^{-bt}\right\}(s)\right] = \frac{1}{2}\left[\frac{1}{s-b} + \frac{1}{s+b}\right] = \frac{s}{s^2 - b^2}.$$

**13.** In this problem, we need the trigonometric identity $\sin^2 t = (1 - \cos 2t)/2$ and the linearity of the Laplace transform.

$$\mathcal{L}\left\{\sin^2 t\right\}(s) = \mathcal{L}\left\{\frac{1 - \cos 2t}{2}\right\}(s)$$

$$= \frac{1}{2}\left[\mathcal{L}\left\{1\right\}(s) - \mathcal{L}\left\{\cos 2t\right\}(s)\right] = \frac{1}{2}\left[\frac{1}{s} - \frac{s}{s^2 + 4}\right] = \frac{2}{s(s^2 + 4)}.$$

**15.** From the trigonometric identity $\cos^2 t = (1 + \cos 2t)/2$, we find that

$$\cos^3 t = \cos t \cos^2 t = \frac{1}{2}\cos t + \frac{1}{2}\cos t \cos 2t.$$

Next we write

$$\cos t \cos 2t = \frac{1}{2}\left[\cos(2t + t) + \cos(2t - t)\right] = \frac{1}{2}\cos 3t + \frac{1}{2}\cos t.$$

Thus,

$$\cos^3 t = \frac{1}{2}\cos t + \frac{1}{4}\cos 3t + \frac{1}{4}\cos t = \frac{3}{4}\cos t + \frac{1}{4}\cos 3t.$$

We now use the linearity of the Laplace transform and Table 7.1 to find that

$$\mathcal{L}\left\{\cos^3 t\right\}(s) = \frac{3}{4}\mathcal{L}\left\{\cos t\right\}(s) + \frac{1}{4}\mathcal{L}\left\{\cos 3t\right\}(s) = \frac{3}{4}\frac{s}{s^2 + 1} + \frac{1}{4}\frac{s}{s^2 + 9},$$

which holds for $s > 0$.

**17.** Since $\sin A \sin B = [\cos(A - B) - \cos(A + B)]/2$, we get

$$
\begin{aligned}
\mathcal{L}\left\{\sin 2t \sin 5t\right\}(s) &= \mathcal{L}\left\{\frac{\cos 3t - \cos 7t}{2}\right\}(s) = \frac{1}{2}\left[\mathcal{L}\left\{\cos 3t\right\}(s) - \mathcal{L}\left\{\cos 7t\right\}(s)\right] \\
&= \frac{1}{2}\left[\frac{s}{s^2 + 9} - \frac{s}{s^2 + 49}\right] = \frac{20s}{(s^2 + 9)(s^2 + 49)}.
\end{aligned}
$$

**19.** Since $\sin A \cos B = [\sin(A + B) + \sin(A - B)]/2$, we get

$$
\begin{aligned}
\mathcal{L}\left\{\cos nt \sin mt\right\}(s) &= \mathcal{L}\left\{\frac{\sin[(m + n)t] + \sin[(m - n)t]}{2}\right\}(s) \\
&= \frac{1}{2}\frac{m + n}{s^2 + (m + n)^2} + \frac{1}{2}\frac{m - n}{s^2 + (m - n)^2}.
\end{aligned}
$$

**21.** By the translation property of the Laplace transform (Theorem 3),

$$\mathcal{L}\left\{e^{at}\cos bt\right\}(s) = \mathcal{L}\left\{\cos bt\right\}(s - a) = \left.\frac{u}{u^2 + b^2}\right|_{u=s-a} = \frac{s - a}{(s - a)^2 + b^2}.$$

**23.** Clearly,

$$(t \sin bt)' = (t)' \sin bt + t(\sin bt)' = \sin bt + bt \cos bt.$$

Therefore, using Theorem 4 and the entry 30, that is, $\mathcal{L}\left\{t \sin bt\right\}(s) = (2bs)/[(s^2 + b^2)^2]$, we obtain

$$
\begin{aligned}
\mathcal{L}\left\{\sin bt + bt \cos bt\right\}(s) &= \mathcal{L}\left\{(t \sin bt)'\right\}(s) = s\mathcal{L}\left\{t \sin bt\right\}(s) - (t \sin bt)\big|_{t=0} \\
&= \frac{s(2bs)}{(s^2 + b^2)^2} - 0 = \frac{2bs^2}{(s^2 + b^2)^2}.
\end{aligned}
$$

# Chapter 7

**25. (a)** By property (6) on page 363 of the text,

$$\mathcal{L}\left\{t\cos bt\right\}(s) = -\left[\mathcal{L}\left\{\cos bt\right\}(s)\right]' = -\left[\frac{s}{s^2+b^2}\right]' = \frac{s^2-b^2}{(s^2+b^2)^2}, \qquad s > 0.$$

**(b)** Again using the same property, we get

$$\begin{aligned}
\mathcal{L}\left\{t^2\cos bt\right\}(s) &= \mathcal{L}\left\{t(t\cos bt)\right\}(s) = -\left[\mathcal{L}\left\{t\cos bt\right\}(s)\right]' \\
&= -\left[\frac{s^2-b^2}{(s^2+b^2)^2}\right]' = \frac{2s^3-6sb^2}{(s^2+b^2)^3}, \qquad s > 0.
\end{aligned}$$

**27.** First observe that since $f(t)$ is piecewise continuous on $[0,\infty)$ and $f(t)/t$ approaches a finite limit as $t \to 0^+$, we conclude that $f(t)/t$ is also piecewise continuous on $[0,\infty)$. Next, since for $t \geq 1$ we have $|f(t)/t| \leq |f(t)|$, we see that $f(t)/t$ is of exponential order $\alpha$ since $f(t)$ is. These observations and Theorem 2 on page 357 of the text show that $\mathcal{L}\{f(t)/t\}$ exists. When the results of Problem 26 are applied to $f(t)/t$, we see that

$$\lim_{N\to\infty}\mathcal{L}\left\{\frac{f(t)}{t}\right\}(N) = 0.$$

By Theorem 6, we have that

$$F(s) = \int_0^\infty e^{-st}f(t)\,dt = \int_0^\infty \frac{te^{-st}f(t)}{t}\,dt = -\frac{d}{ds}\mathcal{L}\left\{\frac{f(t)}{t}\right\}(s).$$

Thus,

$$\begin{aligned}
\int_s^\infty F(u)\,du &= \int_s^\infty \left[-\frac{d}{du}\mathcal{L}\left\{\frac{f(t)}{t}\right\}(u)\right]du = \int_\infty^s \frac{d}{du}\mathcal{L}\left\{\frac{f(t)}{t}\right\}(u)\,du \\
&= \mathcal{L}\left\{\frac{f(t)}{t}\right\}(s) - \lim_{N\to\infty}\mathcal{L}\left\{\frac{f(t)}{t}\right\}(N) = \mathcal{L}\left\{\frac{f(t)}{t}\right\}(s).
\end{aligned}$$

**29.** From the linearity properties (2) and (3) on page 354 of the text we have

$$\mathcal{L}\left\{g(t)\right\}(s) = \mathcal{L}\left\{y''(t) + 6y'(t) + 10y(t)\right\}(s) = \mathcal{L}\left\{y''(t)\right\}(s) + 6\mathcal{L}\left\{y'(t)\right\}(s) + 10\mathcal{L}\left\{y(t)\right\}(s).$$

Next, applying properties (2) and (4) on pages 361 and 362 yields

$$\mathcal{L}\left\{g\right\}(s) = \left[s^2\mathcal{L}\left\{y\right\}(s) - sy(0) - y'(0)\right] + 6\left[s\mathcal{L}\left\{y\right\}(s) - y(0)\right] + 10\mathcal{L}\left\{y\right\}(s).$$

400

Keeping in mind the fact that all initial conditions are zero the above becomes

$$G(s) = \left(s^2 + 6s + 10\right)Y(s), \qquad \text{where} \qquad Y(s) = \mathcal{L}\{y\}(s).$$

Therefore, the transfer function $H(s)$ is given by

$$H(s) = \frac{Y(s)}{G(s)} = \frac{1}{s^2 + 6s + 10}.$$

**31.** Using Definition 1 of the Laplace transform in Section 7.2, we obtain

$$\mathcal{L}\{g(t)\}(s) = \int_0^\infty e^{-st}g(t)\,dt = \int_0^c (0)\,dt + \int_c^\infty e^{-st}f(t-c)\,dt = \left(t-c \to u,\ dt \to du\right)$$

$$= \int_0^\infty e^{-s(u+c)}f(u)\,du = e^{-cs}\int_0^\infty e^{-su}f(u)\,du = e^{-cs}\mathcal{L}\{f(t)\}(s).$$

**33.** The graphs of the function $f(t) = t$ and its translation $g(t)$ to the right by $c = 1$ are shown in Figure 7-A(a).

We use the result of Problem 31 to find $\mathcal{L}\{g(t)\}$.

$$\mathcal{L}\{g(t)\}(s) = e^{-(1)s}\mathcal{L}\{t\}(s) = \frac{e^{-s}}{s^2}.$$

**35.** The graphs of the function $f(t) = \sin t$ and its translation $g(t)$ to the right by $c = \pi/2$ units are shown in Figure 7-A(b).

We use the formula in Problem 31 to find $\mathcal{L}\{g(t)\}$.

$$\mathcal{L}\{g(t)\}(s) = e^{-(\pi/2)s}\mathcal{L}\{\sin t\}(s) = \frac{e^{-(\pi/2)s}}{s^2+1}.$$

**37.** Since $f'(t)$ is of exponential order on $[0,\infty)$, for some $\alpha, M > 0$, and $T > 0$,

$$|f'(t)| \le Me^{\alpha t}, \qquad \text{for all}\quad t \ge T. \tag{7.7}$$

On the other hand, piecewise continuity of $f'(t)$ on $[0,\infty)$ implies that $f'(t)$ is bounded on any finite interval, in particular, on $[0,T]$. That is,

$$|f'(t)| \le C, \qquad \text{for all}\quad t \text{ in } [0,T]. \tag{7.8}$$

401

Chapter 7

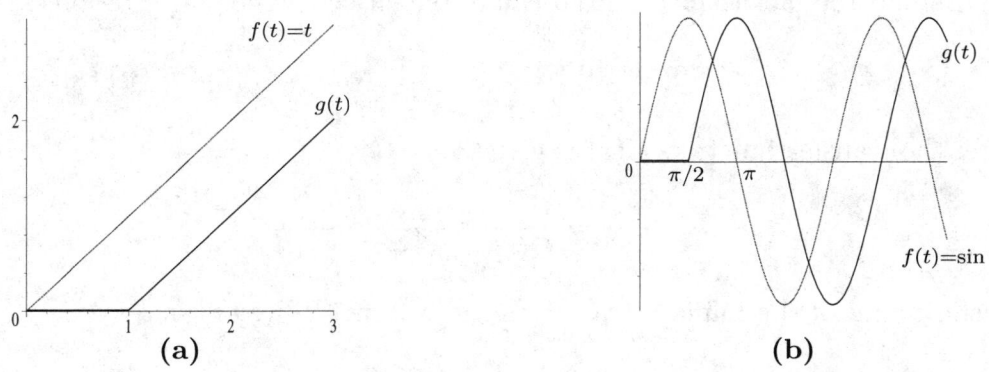

**Figure 7–A**: Graphs of functions in Problems 33 and 35.

From (7.7) and (7.8) it follows that, for $s > \alpha$,

$$\int_0^\infty e^{-st}|f'(t)|\,dt = \int_0^T e^{-st}|f'(t)|\,dt + \int_T^\infty e^{-st}|f'(t)|\,dt \leq C\int_0^T e^{-st}\,dt + M\int_T^\infty e^{-st}e^{\alpha t}\,dt$$

$$= \left.\frac{Ce^{-st}}{-s}\right|_0^T + \lim_{N\to\infty}\left[\left.\frac{Me^{(\alpha-s)t}}{\alpha-s}\right|_T^N\right] = \frac{C\left[1-e^{-sT}\right]}{s} + \frac{Me^{(\alpha-s)T}}{s-\alpha} \longrightarrow 0$$

as $s \to \infty$. Therefore, (7) yields

$$0 \leq |s\mathcal{L}\{f\}(s) - f(0)| = \left|\int_0^\infty e^{-st}f'(t)\,dt\right| \leq \int_0^\infty e^{-st}|f'(t)|\,dt \longrightarrow 0 \quad \text{as} \quad s \to \infty.$$

Hence, by the squeeze theorem,

$$\lim_{s\to\infty}|s\mathcal{L}\{f\}(s) - f(0)| = 0 \quad \Leftrightarrow \quad \lim_{s\to\infty}[s\mathcal{L}\{f\}(s) - f(0)] = 0 \quad \Leftrightarrow \quad \lim_{s\to\infty}s\mathcal{L}\{f\}(s) = f(0).$$

**EXERCISES 7.4: Inverse Laplace Transform, page 374**

**1.** From Table 7.1, the function $6/(s-1)^4 = (3!)/(s-1)^4$ is the Laplace transform of $e^{\alpha t}t^n$ with $\alpha = 1$ and $n = 3$. Therefore,

$$\mathcal{L}^{-1}\left\{\frac{6}{(s-1)^4}\right\}(t) = e^t t^3.$$

402

**3.** Writing

$$\frac{s+1}{s^2+2s+10} = \frac{s+1}{(s^2+2s+1)+9} = \frac{s+1}{(s+1)^2+3^2},$$

we see that this function is the Laplace transform of $e^{-t}\cos 3t$ (the last entry in Table 7.1 with $\alpha = -1$ and $b = 3$). Hence

$$\mathcal{L}^{-1}\left\{\frac{s+1}{s^2+2s+10}\right\}(t) = e^{-t}\cos 3t.$$

**5.** We complete the square in the denominator and use the linearity of the inverse Laplace transform to get

$$\mathcal{L}^{-1}\left\{\frac{1}{s^2+4s+8}\right\}(t) = \mathcal{L}^{-1}\left\{\frac{1}{(s+2)^2+2^2}\right\}(t) = \frac{1}{2}\mathcal{L}^{-1}\left\{\frac{2}{(s+2)^2+2^2}\right\}(t) = \frac{1}{2}e^{-2t}\sin 2t.$$

(See the Laplace transform formula for $e^{\alpha t}\sin bt$ in Table 7.1).

**7.** By completing the square in the denominator, we can rewrite $(2s+16)/(s^2+4s+13)$ as

$$\frac{2s+16}{s^2+4s+4+9} = \frac{2s+16}{(s+2)^2+3^2} = \frac{2(s+2)}{(s+2)^2+3^2} + \frac{4(3)}{(s+2)^2+3^2}.$$

Thus, by the linearity of the inverse Laplace transform,

$$\mathcal{L}^{-1}\left\{\frac{2s+16}{s^2+4s+13}\right\}(t) = 2\mathcal{L}^{-1}\left\{\frac{s+2}{(s+2)^2+3^2}\right\}(t) + 4\mathcal{L}^{-1}\left\{\frac{3}{(s+2)^2+3^2}\right\}(t)$$

$$= 2e^{-2t}\cos 3t + 4e^{-2t}\sin 3t.$$

**9.** We complete the square in the denominator, rewrite the given function as a sum of two entries in Table 7.1, and use the linearity of the inverse Laplace transform. This yields

$$\frac{3s-15}{2s^2-4s+10} = \frac{3}{2}\cdot\frac{s-5}{s^2-2s+5} = \frac{3}{2}\cdot\frac{(s-1)-4}{(s-1)^2+2^2} = \frac{(3/2)(s-1)}{(s-1)^2+2^2} - \frac{3(2)}{(s-1)^2+2^2}$$

$$\Rightarrow \quad \mathcal{L}^{-1}\left\{\frac{3s-15}{2s^2-4s+10}\right\} = \frac{3}{2}\mathcal{L}^{-1}\left\{\frac{s-1}{(s-1)^2+2^2}\right\} - 3\mathcal{L}^{-1}\left\{\frac{2}{(s-1)^2+2^2}\right\}$$

$$= \frac{3}{2}e^t\cos 2t - 3e^t\sin 2t.$$

**11.** In this problem, we use the partial fractions decomposition method. Since the denominator, $(s-1)(s+2)(s+5)$, is a product of three nonrepeated linear factors, the expansion has the form

$$\frac{s^2 - 26s - 47}{(s-1)(s+2)(s+5)} = \frac{A}{s-1} + \frac{B}{s+2} + \frac{C}{s+5}$$

$$= \frac{A(s+2)(s+5) + B(s-1)(s+5) + C(s-1)(s+2)}{(s-1)(s+2)(s+5)}.$$

Therefore,

$$s^2 - 26s - 47 = A(s+2)(s+5) + B(s-1)(s+5) + C(s-1)(s+2). \qquad (7.9)$$

Evaluating both sides of (7.9) for $s = 1$, $s = -2$, and $s = -5$, we find constants $A$, $B$, and $C$.

$$
\begin{aligned}
s = 1: \quad & (1)^2 - 26(1) - 47 = A(1+2)(1+5) && \Rightarrow && A = -4, \\
s = -2: \quad & (-2)^2 - 26(-2) - 47 = B(-2-1)(-2+5) && \Rightarrow && B = -1, \\
s = -5: \quad & (-5)^2 - 26(-5) - 47 = C(-5-1)(-5+2) && \Rightarrow && C = 6.
\end{aligned}
$$

Hence,

$$\frac{s^2 - 26s - 47}{(s-1)(s+2)(s+5)} = \frac{6}{s+5} - \frac{1}{s+2} - \frac{4}{s-1}.$$

**13.** The denominator has a simple linear factor, $s$, and a double linear factor, $s+1$. Thus, we look for the decomposition of the form

$$\frac{-2s^2 - 3s - 2}{s(s+1)^2} = \frac{A}{s} + \frac{B}{s+1} + \frac{C}{(s+1)^2} = \frac{A(s+1)^2 + Bs(s+1) + Cs}{s(s+1)^2},$$

which yields

$$-2s^2 - 3s - 2 = A(s+1)^2 + Bs(s+1) + Cs. \qquad (7.10)$$

Evaluating this equality for $s = 0$ and $s = -1$, we find $A$ and $C$, respectively.

$$
\begin{aligned}
s = 0: \quad & -2 = A(0+1)^2 && \Rightarrow && A = -2, \\
s = -1: \quad & -2(-1)^2 - 3(-1) - 2 = C(-1) && \Rightarrow && C = 1.
\end{aligned}
$$

To find $B$, we compare the coefficients at $s^2$ in both sides of (7.10).

$$-2 = A + B \qquad \Rightarrow \qquad B = -2 - A = 0.$$

Hence,

$$\frac{-2s^2 - 3s - 2}{s(s+1)^2} = \frac{1}{(s+1)^2} - \frac{2}{s}.$$

**15.** First, we complete the square in the quadratic $s^2 - 2s + 5$ to make sure that this polynomial is irreducible and to find the form of the decomposition. Since

$$s^2 - 2s + 5 = (s^2 - 2s + 1) + 4 = (s-1)^2 + 2^2,$$

we have

$$\frac{-8s - 2s^2 - 14}{(s+1)(s^2 - 2s + 5)} = \frac{A}{s+1} + \frac{B(s-1) + C(2)}{(s-1)^2 + 2^2} = \frac{A\left[(s-1)^2 + 4\right] + \left[B(s-1) + 2C\right](s+1)}{(s+1)\left[(s-1)^2 + 4\right]}$$

which implies that

$$-8s - 2s^2 - 14 = A\left[(s-1)^2 + 4\right] + \left[B(s-1) + 2C\right](s+1).$$

Taking $s = -1$, $s = 1$, and $s = 0$, we find $A$, $B$, and $C$, respectively.

$$
\begin{aligned}
s = -1: \quad & 8(-1) - 2(-1)^2 - 14 = A\left[(-1-1)^2 + 4\right] && \Rightarrow && A = -3, \\
s = 1: \quad & 8(1) - 2(1)^2 - 14 = A\left[(1-1)^2 + 4\right] + 2C(1+1) && \Rightarrow && C = 1, \\
s = 0: \quad & 8(0) - 2(0)^2 - 14 = A\left[(0-1)^2 + 4\right] + \left[B(0-1) + 2C\right](0+1) && \Rightarrow && B = 1,
\end{aligned}
$$

and so

$$\frac{-8s - 2s^2 - 14}{(s+1)(s^2 - 2s + 5)} = -\frac{3}{s+1} + \frac{(s-1) + 2}{(s-1)^2 + 4}.$$

**17.** First we need to completely factor the denominator. Since $s^2 + s - 6 = (s-2)(s+3)$, we have

$$\frac{3s+5}{s(s^2 + s - 6)} = \frac{3s+5}{s(s-2)(s+3)}.$$

Since the denominator has only nonrepeated linear factors, we can write

$$\frac{3s+5}{s(s-2)(s+3)} = \frac{A}{s} + \frac{B}{s-2} + \frac{C}{s+3}$$

for some choice of $A$, $B$ and $C$. Clearing fractions gives us

$$3s + 5 = A(s-2)(s+3) + Bs(s+3) + Cs(s-2).$$

With $s = 0$, this yields $5 = A(-2)(3)$ so that $A = -5/6$. With $s = 2$, we get $11 = B(2)(5)$ so that $B = 11/10$. Finally, $s = -3$ yields $-4 = C(-3)(-5)$ so that $C = -4/15$. Thus,

$$\frac{3s+5}{s(s^2+s-6)} = -\frac{5}{6s} + \frac{11}{10(s-2)} - \frac{4}{15(s+3)}.$$

**19.** First observe that the quadratic polynomial $s^2 + 2s + 2$ is irreducible because the discriminant $2^2 - 4(1)(2) = -4$ is negative. Since the denominator has one nonrepeated linear factor and one nonrepeated quadratic factor, we can write

$$\frac{1}{(s-3)(s^2+2s+2)} = \frac{1}{(s-3)[(s+1)^2+1]} = \frac{A}{s-3} + \frac{B(s+1)+C}{(s+1)^2+1},$$

where we have chosen a form which is more convenient for taking the inverse Laplace transform. Clearing fractions gives us

$$1 = A\left[(s+1)^2 + 1\right] + [B(s+1)+C](s-3). \qquad (7.11)$$

With $s = 3$, this yields $1 = 17A$ so that $A = 1/17$. Substituting $s = -1$, we see that $1 = A(1) + C(-4)$, or $C = (A-1)/4 = -4/17$. Finally, the coefficient $A+B$ at $s^2$ in the right-hand side of (7.11) must be the same as in the left-hand side, that is, 0. So $B = -A = -1/17$ and

$$\frac{1}{(s-3)(s^2+2s+2)} = \frac{1}{17}\left[\frac{1}{s-3} - \frac{s+1}{(s+1)^2+1} - \frac{4}{(s+1)^2+1}\right].$$

**21.** Since the denominator contains only nonrepeated linear factors, the partial fractions decomposition has the form

$$\frac{6s^2-13s+2}{s(s-1)(s-6)} = \frac{A}{s} + \frac{B}{s-1} + \frac{C}{s-6} = \frac{A(s-1)(s-6)+Bs(s-6)+Cs(s-1)}{s(s-1)(s-6)}.$$

Therefore,

$$6s^2 - 13s + 2 = A(s-1)(s-6) + Bs(s-6) + Cs(s-1).$$

Evaluating both sides of this equation for $s = 0$, $s = 1$, and $s = 6$, we find constants $A$, $B$, and $C$.

$$\begin{aligned}
s &= 0: & 2 &= 6A & &\Rightarrow & A &= 1/3, \\
s &= 1: & -5 &= -5B & &\Rightarrow & B &= 1, \\
s &= 6: & 140 &= 30C & &\Rightarrow & C &= 14/3.
\end{aligned}$$

Hence,

$$\frac{6s^2 - 13s + 2}{s(s-1)(s-6)} = \frac{1/3}{s} + \frac{1}{s-1} + \frac{14/3}{s-6}$$

and the linear property of the inverse Laplace transform yields

$$\mathcal{L}^{-1}\left\{\frac{6s^2 - 13s + 2}{s(s-1)(s-6)}\right\} = \frac{1}{3}\mathcal{L}^{-1}\left\{\frac{1}{s}\right\} + \mathcal{L}^{-1}\left\{\frac{1}{s-1}\right\} + \frac{14}{3}\mathcal{L}^{-1}\left\{\frac{1}{s-6}\right\} = \frac{1}{3} + e^t + \frac{14}{3}e^{6t}.$$

**23.** In this problem, the denominator of $F(s)$ has a simple linear factor, $s+1$, and a double linear factor, $s+3$. Thus, the decomposition is the form

$$\frac{5s^2 + 34s + 53}{(s+3)^2(s+1)} = \frac{A}{(s+3)^2} + \frac{B}{s+3} + \frac{C}{s+1} = \frac{A(s+1) + B(s+1)(s+3) + C(s+3)^2}{(s+3)^2(s+1)}.$$

Therefore, we must have

$$5s^2 + 34s + 53 = A(s+1) + B(s+1)(s+3) + C(s+3)^2.$$

Substitutions $s = -3$ and $s = -1$ yield values of $A$ and $C$, respectively.

$$s = -3: \quad -4 = -2A \quad \Rightarrow \quad A = 2,$$
$$s = -1: \quad 24 = 4C \quad \Rightarrow \quad C = 6.$$

To find $B$, we take, say, $s = 0$ and get

$$53 = A + 3B + 9C \quad \Rightarrow \quad B = \frac{53 - A - 9C}{3} = -1.$$

Hence,

$$\mathcal{L}^{-1}\left\{\frac{5s^2 + 34s + 53}{(s+3)^2(s+1)}\right\}(t) = 2\mathcal{L}^{-1}\left\{\frac{1}{(s+3)^2}\right\}(t) - \mathcal{L}^{-1}\left\{\frac{1}{s+3}\right\}(t) + 6\mathcal{L}^{-1}\left\{\frac{1}{s+1}\right\}(t)$$
$$= 2te^{-3t} - e^{-3t} + 6e^{-t}.$$

**25.** Observing that the quadratic $s^2 + 2s + 5 = (s+1)^2 + 2^2$ is irreducible, the partial fractions decomposition for $F(s)$ has the form

$$\frac{7s^2 + 23s + 30}{(s-2)(s^2 + 2s + 5)} = \frac{A}{s-2} + \frac{B(s+1) + C(2)}{(s+1)^2 + 2^2}.$$

# Chapter 7

Clearing fractions gives us

$$7s^2 + 23s + 30 = A\left[(s+1)^2 + 4\right] + \left[B(s+1) + C(2)\right](s-2).$$

With $s = 2$, this yields $104 = 13A$ so that $A = 8$; $s = -1$ gives $14 = A(4) + C(-6)$, or $C = 3$. Finally, the coefficient $A + B$ at $s^2$ in the right-hand side must match the one in the left-hand side, which is 7. So $B = 7 - A = -1$. Therefore,

$$\frac{7s^2 + 23s + 30}{(s-2)(s^2 + 2s + 5)} = \frac{8}{s-2} + \frac{-(s+1) + 3(2)}{(s+1)^2 + 2^2},$$

which yields

$$\mathcal{L}^{-1}\left\{\frac{7s^2 + 23s + 30}{(s-2)(s^2 + 2s + 5)}\right\} = 8\mathcal{L}^{-1}\left\{\frac{1}{s-2}\right\} - \mathcal{L}^{-1}\left\{\frac{s+1}{(s+1)^2 + 2^2}\right\} + 3\mathcal{L}^{-1}\left\{\frac{2}{(s+1)^2 + 2^2}\right\}$$

$$= 8e^{2t} - e^{-t}\cos 2t + 3e^{-t}\sin 2t.$$

**27.** First, we find $F(s)$.

$$F(s)\left(s^2 - 4\right) = \frac{5}{s+1} \quad \Rightarrow \quad F(s) = \frac{5}{(s+1)(s^2-4)} = \frac{5}{(s+1)(s-2)(s+2)}.$$

The partial fractions expansion yields

$$\frac{5}{(s+1)(s-2)(s+2)} = \frac{A}{s+1} + \frac{B}{s-2} + \frac{C}{s+2}.$$

Clearing fractions gives us

$$5 = A(s-2)(s+2) + B(s+1)(s+2) + C(s+1)(s-2).$$

With $s = -1$, $s = 2$, and $s = -2$ this yields $A = -5/3$, $B = 5/12$, and $C = 5/4$. So,

$$\mathcal{L}^{-1}\{F(s)\}(t) = -\frac{5}{3}\mathcal{L}^{-1}\left\{\frac{1}{s+1}\right\}(t) + \frac{5}{12}\mathcal{L}^{-1}\left\{\frac{1}{s-2}\right\}(t) + \frac{5}{4}\mathcal{L}^{-1}\left\{\frac{1}{s+2}\right\}(t)$$

$$= -\frac{5}{3}e^{-t} + \frac{5}{12}e^{2t} + \frac{5}{4}e^{-2t}.$$

**29.** Solving for $F(s)$ yields

$$F(s) = \frac{10s^2 + 12s + 14}{(s+2)(s^2 - 2s + 2)} = \frac{10s^2 + 12s + 14}{(s+2)[(s-1)^2 + 1]}.$$

Since, in the denominator, we have nonrepeated linear and quadratic factors, we seek for the decomposition

$$\frac{10s^2 + 12s + 14}{(s+2)[(s-1)^2+1]} = \frac{A}{s+2} + \frac{B(s-1)+C(1)}{(s-1)^2+1}.$$

Clearing fractions, we conclude that

$$10s^2 + 12s + 14 = A[(s-1)^2+1] + [B(s-1)+C](s+2).$$

Substitution $s = -2$ into this equation yields $30 = 10A$ or $A = 3$. With $s = 1$, we get $36 = A + 3C$ and so $C = (36-A)/3 = 11$. Finally, substitution $s = 0$ results $14 = 2A + 2(C-B)$ or $B = A + C - 7 = 7$. Now we apply the linearity of the inverse Laplace transform and obtain

$$\begin{aligned}
\mathcal{L}^{-1}\{F(s)\}(t) &= 3\mathcal{L}^{-1}\left\{\frac{1}{s+2}\right\}(t) + 7\mathcal{L}^{-1}\left\{\frac{s-1}{(s-1)^2+1}\right\}(t) + 11\mathcal{L}^{-1}\left\{\frac{1}{(s-1)^2+1}\right\}(t) \\
&= 3e^{-2t} + 7e^t\cos t + 11e^t\sin t.
\end{aligned}$$

**31.** Functions $f_1(t)$, $f_2(t)$, and $f_3(t)$ coincide for all $t$ in $[0,\infty)$ except a finite number of points. Since the Laplace transform a function is a definite integral, it does not depend on values of the function at finite number of points. Therefore, in (a), (b), and (c) we have one and the same answer, that is

$$\mathcal{L}\{f_1(t)\}(s) = \mathcal{L}\{f_2(t)\}(s) = \mathcal{L}\{f_3(t)\}(s) = \mathcal{L}\{t\}(s) = \frac{1}{s^2}.$$

By Definition 4, the inverse Laplace transform is a continuous function on $[0,\infty)$. $f_3(t) = t$ clearly satisfies this condition while $f_1(t)$ and $f_2(t)$ have removable discontinuities at $t = 2$ and $t = 1, 6$, respectively. Therefore,

$$\mathcal{L}^{-1}\left\{\frac{1}{s^2}\right\}(t) = f_3(t) = t.$$

**33.** We are looking for $\mathcal{L}^{-1}\{F(s)\}(t) = f(t)$. According to the formula given just before this problem,

$$f(t) = \frac{-1}{t}\mathcal{L}^{-1}\left\{\frac{dF}{ds}\right\}(t)$$

(take $n = 1$ in the formula). Since

$$F(s) = \ln\left(\frac{s+2}{s-5}\right) = \ln(s+2) - \ln(s-5),$$

we have

$$\frac{dF(s)}{ds} = \frac{d}{ds}\left(\ln(s+2) - \ln(s-5)\right) = \frac{1}{s+2} - \frac{1}{s-5}$$

$$\Rightarrow \quad \mathcal{L}^{-1}\left\{\frac{dF}{ds}\right\}(t) = \mathcal{L}^{-1}\left\{\frac{1}{s+2} - \frac{1}{s-5}\right\}(t) = e^{-2t} - e^{5t}$$

$$\Rightarrow \quad \mathcal{L}^{-1}\left\{F(s)\right\}(t) = \frac{-1}{t}\left(e^{-2t} - e^{5t}\right) = \frac{e^{5t} - e^{-2t}}{t}.$$

**35.** Taking the derivative of $F(s)$, we get

$$\frac{dF(s)}{ds} = \frac{d}{ds}\ln\frac{s^2+9}{s^2+1} = \frac{d}{ds}\left[\ln(s^2+9) - \ln(s^2+1)\right] = \frac{2s}{s^2+9} - \frac{2s}{s^2+1}.$$

So, using the linear property of the inverse Laplace transform, we obtain

$$\mathcal{L}^{-1}\left\{\frac{dF(s)}{ds}\right\}(t) = 2\mathcal{L}^{-1}\left\{\frac{s}{s^2+9}\right\}(t) - 2\mathcal{L}^{-1}\left\{\frac{s}{s^2+1}\right\}(t) = 2(\cos 3t - \cos t).$$

Thus

$$\mathcal{L}^{-1}\left\{F(s)\right\}(t) = \frac{-1}{t}\mathcal{L}^{-1}\left\{\frac{dF(s)}{ds}\right\}(t) = \frac{2(\cos t - \cos 3t)}{t}.$$

**37.** By the definition, both, $\mathcal{L}^{-1}\left\{F_1\right\}(t)$ and $\mathcal{L}^{-1}\left\{F_2\right\}(t)$, are continuous functions on $[0, \infty)$. Therefore, their sum, $\left(\mathcal{L}^{-1}\left\{F_1\right\} + \mathcal{L}^{-1}\left\{F_2\right\}\right)(t)$, is also continuous on $[0, \infty)$. Furthermore, the linearity of the Laplace transform yields

$$\mathcal{L}\left\{\left(\mathcal{L}^{-1}\left\{F_1\right\} + \mathcal{L}^{-1}\left\{F_2\right\}\right)\right\}(s) = \mathcal{L}\left\{\mathcal{L}^{-1}\left\{F_1\right\}\right\}(s) + \mathcal{L}\left\{\mathcal{L}^{-1}\left\{F_2\right\}\right\}(s) = F_1(s) + F_2(s).$$

Therefore, $\mathcal{L}^{-1}\left\{F_1\right\} + \mathcal{L}^{-1}\left\{F_2\right\}$ is a continuous function on $[0, \infty)$ whose Laplace transform is $F_1 + F_2$. By the definition of the inverse Laplace transform, this function is the inverse Laplace transform of $F_1 + F_2$, that is,

$$\mathcal{L}^{-1}\left\{F_1\right\}(t) + \mathcal{L}^{-1}\left\{F_2\right\}(t) = \mathcal{L}^{-1}\left\{F_1 + F_2\right\}(t),$$

and (3) in Theorem 7 is proved.

To show (4), we use the continuity of $\mathcal{L}^{-1}\{F\}$ to conclude that $c\mathcal{L}^{-1}\{F\}$ is a continuous function. Since the linearity of the Laplace transform yields

$$\mathcal{L}\{c\mathcal{L}^{-1}\{F\}\}(s) = c\mathcal{L}\{\mathcal{L}^{-1}\{F\}\}(s) = cF(s),$$

we have $c\mathcal{L}^{-1}\{F\}(t) = \mathcal{L}^{-1}\{cF\}(t)$.

**39.** In this problem, the denominator $Q(s) := s(s-1)(s+2)$ has only nonrepeated linear factors, and so the partial fractions decomposition has the form

$$F(s) := \frac{2s+1}{s(s-1)(s+2)} = \frac{A}{s} + \frac{B}{s-1} + \frac{C}{s+2}.$$

To find $A$, $B$, and $C$, we use the residue formula in Problem 38. This yields

$$A = \lim_{s \to 0} sF(s) = \lim_{s \to 0} \frac{2s+1}{(s-1)(s+2)} = \frac{2(0)+1}{(0-1)(0+2)} = -\frac{1}{2},$$

$$B = \lim_{s \to 1}(s-1)F(s) = \lim_{s \to 1} \frac{2s+1}{s(s+2)} = \frac{2(1)+1}{(1)(1+2)} = 1,$$

$$C = \lim_{s \to -2}(s+2)F(s) = \lim_{s \to 2} \frac{2s+1}{s(s-1)} = \frac{2(-2)+1}{(-2)(-2-1)} = -\frac{1}{2}.$$

Therefore,

$$\frac{2s+1}{s(s-1)(s+2)} = -\frac{1/2}{s} + \frac{1}{s-1} - \frac{1/2}{s+2}.$$

**41.** In notation of Problem 40,

$$P(s) = 3s^2 - 16s + 5, \qquad Q(s) = (s+1)(s-3)(s-2).$$

We can apply the Heaviside's expansion formula because $Q(s)$ has only nonrepeated linear factors. We need the values of $P(s)$ and $Q'(s)$ at the points $r_1 = -1$, $r_2 = 3$, and $r_3 = 2$. Using the product rule, we find that

$$Q'(s) = (s-3)(s-2) + (s+1)(s-2) + (s+1)(s-3),$$

and so

$$Q'(-1) = (-1-3)(-1-2) = 12, \quad Q'(3) = (3+1)(3-2) = 4, \quad Q'(2) = (2+1)(2-3) = -3.$$

Also, we compute

$$P(-1) = 24, \quad P(3) = -16, \quad P(2) = -15.$$

Therefore,

$$\mathcal{L}^{-1}\left\{\frac{3s^2 - 16s + 5}{(s+1)(s-3)(s-2)}\right\}(t) = \frac{P(-1)}{Q'(-1)}e^{(-1)t} + \frac{P(3)}{Q'(3)}e^{(3)t} + \frac{P(2)}{Q'(2)}e^{(2)t} = 2e^{-t} - 4e^{3t} + 5e^{2t}.$$

**43.** Since $s^2 - 2s + 5 = (s-1)^2 + 2^2$, we see that the denominator of $F(s)$ has nonrepeated linear factor $s+2$ and nonrepeated irreducible quadratic factor $s^2 - 2s + 5$ with $\alpha = 1$ and $\beta = 2$ (in notation of Problem 40). Thus the partial fractions decomposition has the form

$$F(s) = \frac{6s^2 + 28}{(s^2 - 2s + 5)(s+2)} = \frac{A(s-1) + 2B}{(s-1)^2 + 2^2} + \frac{C}{s+2}.$$

We find $C$ by applying the real residue formula derived in Problem 38.

$$C = \lim_{s \to -2} \frac{(s+2)(6s^2 + 28)}{(s^2 - 2s + 5)(s+2)} = \lim_{s \to -2} \frac{6s^2 + 28}{s^2 - 2s + 5} = \frac{52}{13} = 4.$$

Next, we use the complex residue formula given in Problem 42, to find $A$ and $B$. Since $\alpha = 1$ and $\beta = 2$, the formula becomes

$$2B + i2A = \lim_{s \to 1+2i} \frac{(s^2 - 2s + 5)(6s^2 + 28)}{(s^2 - 2s + 5)(s+2)} = \lim_{s \to 1+2i} \frac{6s^2 + 28}{s+2} = \frac{6(1+2i)^2 + 28}{(1+2i) + 2} = \frac{10 + 24i}{3 + 2i}.$$

Dividing we get

$$2B + i2A = \frac{(10 + 24i)(3 - 2i)}{(3 + 2i)(3 - 2i)} = \frac{78 + 52i}{13} = 6 + 4i.$$

Taking the real and imaginary parts yields

$$\begin{matrix} 2B = 6, \\ 2A = 4 \end{matrix} \quad \Rightarrow \quad \begin{matrix} B = 3, \\ A = 2. \end{matrix}$$

Therefore,

$$\frac{6s^2 + 28}{(s^2 - 2s + 5)(s+2)} = \frac{2(s-1) + 2(3)}{(s-1)^2 + 2^2} + \frac{4}{s+2}.$$

**EXERCISES 7.5:   Solving Initial Value Problems, page 383**

**1.** Let $Y(s) := \mathcal{L}\{y\}(s)$. Taking the Laplace transform of both sides of the given differential equation and using its linearity, we obtain

$$\mathcal{L}\{y''\}(s) - 2\mathcal{L}\{y'\}(s) + 5Y(s) = \mathcal{L}\{0\}(s) = 0. \tag{7.12}$$

We can express $\mathcal{L}\{y''\}(s)$ and $\mathcal{L}\{y'\}(s)$ in terms of $Y(s)$ using the initial conditions and Theorem 5 in Section 7.3.

$$\mathcal{L}\{y'\}(s) = sY(s) - y(0) = sY(s) - 2,$$
$$\mathcal{L}\{y''\}(s) = s^2Y(s) - sy(0) - y'(0) = s^2Y(s) - 2s - 4.$$

Substituting back into (7.12) and solving for $Y(s)$ yield

$$\left[s^2Y(s) - 2s - 4\right] - 2\left[sY(s) - 2\right] + 5Y(s) = 0$$
$$\Rightarrow \quad Y(s)\left(s^2 - 2s + 5\right) = 2s$$
$$\Rightarrow \quad Y(s) = \frac{2s}{s^2 - 2s + 5} = \frac{2s}{(s-1)^2 + 2^2} = \frac{2(s-1)}{(s-1)^2 + 2^2} + \frac{2}{(s-1)^2 + 2^2}.$$

Applying now the inverse Laplace transform to both sides, we obtain

$$y(t) = 2\mathcal{L}^{-1}\left\{\frac{s-1}{(s-1)^2 + 2^2}\right\}(t) + \mathcal{L}^{-1}\left\{\frac{2}{(s-1)^2 + 2^2}\right\}(t) = 2e^t\cos 2t + e^t\sin 2t.$$

**3.** Let $Y(s) := \mathcal{L}\{y\}(s)$. Taking the Laplace transform of both sides of the given differential equation, $y'' + 6y' + 9y = 0$, and using the linearity of the Laplace transform, we obtain

$$\mathcal{L}\{y''\}(s) + 6\mathcal{L}\{y'\}(s) + 9Y(s) = 0.$$

We use formula (4), page 362, to express $\mathcal{L}\{y''\}(s)$ and $\mathcal{L}\{y'\}(s)$ in terms of $Y(s)$.

$$\mathcal{L}\{y'\}(s) = sY(s) - y(0) = sY(s) + 1,$$
$$\mathcal{L}\{y''\}(s) = s^2Y(s) - sy(0) - y'(0) = s^2Y(s) + s - 6.$$

Therefore,

$$\left[s^2Y(s) + s - 6\right] + 6\left[sY(s) + 1\right] + 9Y(s) = 0$$

$$\Rightarrow \quad Y(s)\left(s^2 + 6s + 9\right) = -s$$

$$\Rightarrow \quad Y(s) = \frac{-s}{s^2 + 6s + 9} = \frac{-s}{(s+3)^2} = \frac{3}{(s+3)^2} - \frac{1}{s+3},$$

where the last equality comes from the partial fraction expansion of $-s/(s+3^2)$. We apply the inverse Laplace transform to both sides and use Table 7.1 to obtain

$$y(t) = 3\mathcal{L}^{-1}\left\{\frac{1}{(s+3)^2}\right\}(t) - \mathcal{L}^{-1}\left\{\frac{1}{s+3}\right\}(t) = 3te^{-3t} - e^{-3t}.$$

5. Let $W(s) = \mathcal{L}\{w\}(s)$. Then taking the Laplace transform of the equation and using linearity yield

$$\mathcal{L}\{w''\}(s) + W(s) = \mathcal{L}\{t^2 + 2\}(s) = \mathcal{L}\{t^2\}(s) + 2\mathcal{L}\{1\}(s) = \frac{2}{s^3} + \frac{2}{s}.$$

Since $\mathcal{L}\{w''\}(s) = s^2 W(s) - sw(0) - w'(0) = s^2 W(s) - s + 1$, we have

$$\left[s^2 W(s) - s + 1\right] + W(s) = \frac{2}{s^3} + \frac{2}{s}$$

$$\Rightarrow \quad \left(s^2 + 1\right)W(s) = s - 1 + \frac{2(s^2 + 1)}{s^3} \qquad \Rightarrow \qquad W(s) = \frac{s}{s^2+1} - \frac{1}{s^2+1} + \frac{2}{s^3}.$$

Now, taking the inverse Laplace transform, we obtain

$$w = \mathcal{L}^{-1}\left\{\frac{s}{s^2+1}\right\} - \mathcal{L}^{-1}\left\{\frac{1}{s^2+1}\right\} + \mathcal{L}^{-1}\left\{\frac{2}{s^3}\right\} = \cos t - \sin t + t^2.$$

7. Let $Y(s) := \mathcal{L}\{y\}(s)$. Using the initial conditions and Theorem 5 in Section 7.3 we can express $\mathcal{L}\{y''\}(s)$ and $\mathcal{L}\{y'\}(s)$ in terms of $Y(s)$, namely,

$$\mathcal{L}\{y'\}(s) = sY(s) - y(0) = sY(s) - 5,$$

$$\mathcal{L}\{y''\}(s) = s^2 Y(s) - sy(0) - y'(0) = s^2 Y(s) - 5s + 4.$$

Taking the Laplace transform of both sides of the given differential equation and using its linearity, we obtain

$$\mathcal{L}\{y'' - 7y' + 10y\}(s) = \mathcal{L}\{9\cos t + 7\sin t\}(s)$$

$$\Rightarrow \quad \left[s^2 Y(s) - 5s + 4\right] - 7\left[sY(s) - 5\right] + 10Y(s) = \frac{9s}{s^2+1} + \frac{7}{s^2+1}$$

$$\Rightarrow \quad \left(s^2 - 7s + 10\right) Y(s) = \frac{9s+7}{s^2+1} + 5s - 39 = \frac{5s^3 - 39s^2 + 14s - 32}{s^2+1}$$

$$\Rightarrow \quad Y(s) = \frac{9s+7}{s^2+1} + 5s - 39 = \frac{5s^3 - 39s^2 + 14s - 32}{(s^2+1)(s^2-7s+10)} = \frac{5s^3 - 39s^2 + 14s - 32}{(s^2+1)(s-5)(s-2)}.$$

The partial fractions decomposition of $Y(s)$ has the form

$$\frac{5s^3 - 39s^2 + 14s - 32}{(s^2+1)(s-5)(s-2)} = \frac{As+B}{s^2+1} + \frac{C}{s-5} + \frac{D}{s-2}.$$

Clearing fractions yields

$$5s^3 - 39s^2 + 14s - 32 = (As+B)(s-5)(s-2) + C(s^2+1)(s-2) + D(s^2+1)(s-5).$$

We substitute $s = 5$ and $s = 2$ to find $C$ and $D$, resprectively, and then $s = 0$ to find $B$.

$$
\begin{aligned}
s = 5: \quad -312 = 78C \qquad &\Rightarrow \qquad C = -4, \\
s = 2: \quad -120 = -15D \qquad &\Rightarrow \qquad D = 8, \\
s = 0: \quad -32 = 10B - 2C - 5D \qquad &\Rightarrow \qquad B = 0.
\end{aligned}
$$

Equating the coefficients at $s^3$, we also get $A + C + D = 5$, which implies that $A = 1$. Thus

$$Y(s) = \frac{s}{s^2+1} - \frac{4}{s-5} + \frac{8}{s-2} \qquad \Rightarrow \qquad y(t) = \mathcal{L}^{-1}\left\{Y(s)\right\}(t) = \cos t - 4e^{5t} + 8e^{2t}.$$

**9.** First, note that the initial conditions are given at $t = 1$. Thus, to use the method of Laplace transform, we make a shift in $t$ and move the initial conditions to $t = 0$.

$$z''(t) + 5z'(t) - 6z(t) = 21e^{t-1}$$

$$\Rightarrow \quad z''(t+1) + 5z'(t+1) - 6z(t+1) = 21e^{(t+1)-1} = 21e^{t}. \qquad (7.13)$$

Now, let $y(t) := z(t+1)$. Then the chain rule yields

$$y'(t) = z'(t+1)(t+1)' = z'(t+1),$$

$$y''(t) = [y'(t)]' = z''(t+1)(t+1)' = z''(t+1),$$

and (7.13) becomes

$$y''(t) + 5y'(t) - 6y(t) = 21e^{t} \qquad (7.14)$$

415

Chapter 7

with initial conditions

$$y(0) = z(0+1) = z(1) = -1, \qquad y'(0) = z'(0+1) = z'(1) = 9.$$

With $Y(s) := \mathcal{L}\{y(t)\}(s)$, we apply the Laplace transform to both sides of (7.14) and obtain

$$\mathcal{L}\{y''\}(s) + 5\mathcal{L}\{y'\}(s) - 6Y(s) = \mathcal{L}\{21e^t\}(s) = \frac{21}{s-1}. \qquad (7.15)$$

By Theorem 5, Section 7.3,

$$\mathcal{L}\{y'\}(s) = sY(s) - y(0) = sY(s) + 1,$$
$$\mathcal{L}\{y''\}(s) = s^2Y(s) - sy(0) - y'(0) = s^2Y(s) + s - 9.$$

Substituting these expressions back into (7.15) and solving for $Y(s)$ yield

$$[s^2Y(s) + s - 9] + 5[sY(s) + 1] - 6Y(s) = \frac{21}{s-1}$$

$$\Rightarrow \quad (s^2 + 5s - 6)Y(s) = \frac{21}{s-1} - s + 4 = \frac{-s^2 + 5s + 17}{s-1}$$

$$\Rightarrow \quad Y(s) = \frac{-s^2 + 5s + 17}{(s-1)(s^2+5s-6)} = \frac{-s^2+5s+17}{(s-1)(s-1)(s+6)} = \frac{-s^2+5s+17}{(s-1)^2(s+6)}.$$

The partial fractions decomposition for $Y(s)$ has the form

$$\frac{-s^2+5s+17}{(s-1)^2(s+6)} = \frac{A}{(s-1)^2} + \frac{B}{s-1} + \frac{C}{s+6}.$$

Clearing fractions yields

$$-s^2 + 5s + 17 = A(s+6) + B(s-1)(s+6) + C(s-1)^2.$$

Substitutions $s = 1$ and $s = -6$ give $A = 3$ and $C = -1$. Also, with $s = 0$, we have $17 = 6A - 6B + C$ or $B = 0$. Therefore,

$$Y(s) = \frac{3}{(s-1)^2} - \frac{1}{s+6} \quad \Rightarrow \quad y(t) = \mathcal{L}^{-1}\left\{\frac{3}{(s-1)^2} - \frac{1}{s+6}\right\}(t) = 3te^t - e^{-6t}.$$

Finally, shifting the argument back, we obtain

$$z(t) = y(t-1) = 3(t-1)e^{t-1} - e^{-6(t-1)}.$$

**11.** As in the previous problem (and in Example 3 in the text), we first need to shift the initial conditions to 0. If we set $v(t) = y(t+2)$, the initial value problem for $v(t)$ becomes

$$v''(t) - v(t) = (t+2) - 2 = t, \qquad v(0) = y(2) = 3, \ v'(0) = y'(2) = 0.$$

Taking the Laplace transform of both sides of this new differential equation gives us

$$\mathcal{L}\{v''\}(s) - \mathcal{L}\{v\}(s) = \mathcal{L}\{t\}(s) = \frac{1}{s^2}.$$

If we denote $V(s) := \mathcal{L}\{v\}(s)$ and express $\mathcal{L}\{v''\}(s)$ in terms of $V(s)$ using (4) in Section 4.3 (with $n = 2$), that is, $\mathcal{L}\{v''\}(s) = s^2V(s) - 3s$, we obtain

$$\left[s^2V(s) - 3s\right] - V(s) = \frac{1}{s^2}$$

$$\Rightarrow \quad V(s) = \frac{3s^3 + 1}{s^2(s^2 - 1)} = \frac{3s^3 + 1}{s^2(s+1)(s-1)} = -\frac{1}{s^2} + \frac{1}{s+1} + \frac{2}{s-1}.$$

Hence,

$$v(t) = \mathcal{L}^{-1}\{V(s)\}(t) = \mathcal{L}^{-1}\left\{-\frac{1}{s^2} + \frac{1}{s+1} + \frac{2}{s-1}\right\}(t) = -t + e^{-t} + 2e^t.$$

Since $v(t) = y(t+2)$, we have $y(t) = v(t-2)$ and so

$$y(t) = -(t-2) + e^{-(t-2)} + 2e^{t-2} = 2 - t + e^{2-t} + 2e^{t-2}.$$

**13.** To shift the initial conditions to $t = 0$, we make the substitution $x(t) := y(t + \pi/2)$ in the original equation and use the fact that

$$x'(t) := y'(t + \pi/2), \qquad x''(t) := y''(t + \pi/2).$$

This yields

$$y''(t) - y'(t) - 2y(t) = -8\cos t - 2\sin t$$
$$\Rightarrow \quad -8\cos\left(t + \frac{\pi}{2}\right) - 2\sin\left(t + \frac{\pi}{2}\right) = -8\cos\left(t + \frac{\pi}{2}\right) - 2\sin\left(t + \frac{\pi}{2}\right) = 8\sin t - 2\cos t$$
$$\Rightarrow \quad x''(t) - x'(t) - 2x(t) = 8\sin t - 2\cos t, \qquad x(0) = 1, \ x'(0) = 0.$$

Taking the Laplace transform of both sides in this last differential equation and using the fact that, with $X(s) := \mathcal{L}\{x\}(s)$,

$$\mathcal{L}\{x'\}(s) = sX(s) - 1 \quad \text{and} \quad \mathcal{L}\{x''\}(s) = s^2X(s) - s$$

(which comes from the initial conditions and (4) in Section 7.3), we obtain

$$[s^2X(s) - s] - [sX(s) - 1] - 2X(s) = \mathcal{L}\{8\sin t - 2\cos t\}(s) = \frac{8}{s^2+1} - \frac{2s}{s^2+1}$$

$$\Rightarrow \quad (s^2 - s - 2)X(s) = \frac{8 - 2s}{s^2+1} + s - 1 = \frac{s^3 - s^2 - s + 7}{s^2+1}$$

$$\Rightarrow \quad X(s) = \frac{s^3 - s^2 - s + 7}{(s^2+1)(s^2-s-2)} = \frac{s^3 - s^2 - s + 7}{(s^2+1)(s-2)(s+1)}.$$

We seek for the partial fractions decomposition of $X(s)$ in the form

$$\frac{s^3 - s^2 - s + 7}{(s^2+1)(s-2)(s+1)} = \frac{As + B}{s^2+1} + \frac{C}{(s-2)} + \frac{D}{s+1}.$$

Solving yields

$$A = \frac{7}{5}, \quad B = -\frac{11}{5}, \quad C = \frac{3}{5}, \quad D = -1.$$

Therefore,

$$X(s) = \frac{(7/5)s}{s^2+1} + \frac{(-11/5)}{s^2+1} + \frac{(3/5)}{(s-2)} - \frac{1}{s+1}$$

$$\Rightarrow \quad x(t) = \mathcal{L}^{-1}\{X(s)\}(t) = \frac{7}{5}\cos t - \frac{11}{5}\sin t + \frac{3}{5}e^{2t} - e^{-t}.$$

Finally, since $y(t) = x(t - \pi/2)$, we obtain the solution

$$y(t) = \frac{7}{5}\cos\left(t - \frac{\pi}{2}\right) - \frac{11}{5}\sin\left(t - \frac{\pi}{2}\right) + \frac{3}{5}e^{2(t-\pi/2)} - e^{-(t-\pi/2)}$$

$$= \frac{7}{5}\sin t + \frac{11}{5}\cos t + \frac{3}{5}e^{2t-\pi} - e^{(\pi/2)-t}$$

**15.** Taking the Laplace transform of $y'' - 3y' + 2y = \cos t$ and applying the linearity of the Laplace transform yields

$$\mathcal{L}\{y''\}(s) - 3\mathcal{L}\{y'\}(s) + 2\mathcal{L}\{y\}(s) = \mathcal{L}\{\cos t\}(s) = \frac{s}{s^2+1}. \tag{7.16}$$

If we put $Y(s) = \mathcal{L}\{y\}(s)$ and apply the property (4), page 362 of the text, we get

$$\mathcal{L}\{y'\}(s) = sY(s), \qquad \mathcal{L}\{y''\}(s) = s^2Y(s) + 1.$$

Substitution back into (7.16) yields

$$[s^2Y(s) + 1] - 3[sY(s)] + 2Y(s) = \frac{s}{s^2+1}$$

$$\Rightarrow \quad (s^2 - 3s + 2)Y(s) = \frac{s}{s^2+1} - 1 = \frac{-s^2+s-1}{s^2+1}$$

$$\Rightarrow \quad Y(s) = \frac{-s^2+s-1}{(s^2+1)(s^2-3s+2)} = \frac{-s^2+s-1}{(s^2+1)(s-1)(s-2)}.$$

**17.** With $Y(s) := \mathcal{L}\{y\}(s)$, we find that

$$\mathcal{L}\{y'\}(s) = sY(s) - y(0) = sY(s) - 1, \quad \mathcal{L}\{y''\}(s) = s^2Y(s) - sy(0) - y'(0) = s^2Y(s) - s,$$

and so the Laplace transform of both sides of the original equation yields

$$\mathcal{L}\{y'' + y' - y\}(s) = \mathcal{L}\{t^3\}(s)$$

$$\Rightarrow \quad [s^2Y(s) - s] + [sY(s) - 1] - Y(s) = \frac{6}{s^4}$$

$$\Rightarrow \quad Y(s) = \frac{1}{s^2+s-1}\left(\frac{6}{s^4} + s + 1\right) = \frac{s^5 + s^4 + 6}{s^4(s^2+s-1)}.$$

**19.** Let us denote $Y(s) := \mathcal{L}\{y\}(s)$. From the initial conditions and formula (4) on page 362 of the text we get

$$\mathcal{L}\{y'\}(s) = sY(s) - y(0) = sY(s) - 1, \quad \mathcal{L}\{y''\}(s) = s^2Y(s) - sy(0) - y'(0) = s^2Y(s) - s - 1.$$

The Laplace transform, applied to both sides of the given equation, yields

$$[s^2Y(s) - s - 1] + 5[sY(s) - 1] - Y(s) = \mathcal{L}\{e^t\}(s) - \mathcal{L}\{1\}(s) = \frac{1}{s-1} - \frac{1}{s} = \frac{1}{s(s-1)}$$

$$\Rightarrow \quad (s^2 + 5s - 1)Y(s) = \frac{1}{s(s-1)} + s + 6 = \frac{s^3 + 5s^2 - 6s + 1}{s(s-1)}$$

$$\Rightarrow \quad Y(s) = \frac{s^3 + 5s^2 - 6s + 1}{s(s-1)(s^2+5s-1)}.$$

# Chapter 7

**21.** Applying the Laplace transform to both sides of the given equation yields

$$\mathcal{L}\{y''\}(s) - 2\mathcal{L}\{y'\}(s) + \mathcal{L}\{t\}(s) = \mathcal{L}\{\cos t\}(s) - \mathcal{L}\{\sin t\}(s) = \frac{s-1}{s^2+1}.$$

If $\mathcal{L}\{y\}(s) =: Y(s)$, then it follows from the initial conditions and (4) on page 362 of the text that

$$\mathcal{L}\{y'\}(s) = sY(s) - 1, \quad \mathcal{L}\{y''\}(s) = s^2Y(s) - s - 3.$$

Therefore, $Y(s)$ satisfies

$$\left[s^2Y(s) - s - 3\right] - 2\left[sY(s) - 1\right] + Y(s) = \frac{s-1}{s^2+1}.$$

Solving for $Y(s)$ gives us

$$\left(s^2 - 2s + 1\right)Y(s) = \frac{s-1}{s^2+1} + s + 1 = \frac{s^3 + s^2 + 2s}{s^2+1}$$

$$\Rightarrow \quad Y(s) = \frac{s^3 + s^2 + 2s}{(s^2+1)(s^2 - 2s + 1)} = \frac{s^3 + s^2 + 2s}{(s^2+1)(s-1)^2}.$$

**23.** In this equation, the right-hand side is a piecewise defined function. Let us find its Laplace transform first.

$$\begin{aligned}
\mathcal{L}\{g(t)\}(s) &= \int_0^{\infty} e^{-st}g(t)\,dt = \int_0^2 e^{-st}t\,dt + \int_2^{\infty} e^{-st}5\,dt \\
&= \left.\frac{te^{-st}}{-s}\right|_0^2 - \int_0^2 \frac{e^{-st}}{-s}\,dt + \lim_{N\to\infty}\left.\frac{5e^{-st}}{-s}\right|_2^N \\
&= -\left[\frac{2e^{-2s}}{s}\right] - \left[\frac{e^{-2s}}{s^2} + \frac{1}{s^2}\right] + \frac{5e^{-2s}}{s} = \frac{1 + 3se^{-2s} - e^{-2s}}{s^2},
\end{aligned}$$

where we used integration by parts integrating $e^{-st}t$.

Using this formula and applying the Laplace transform to the given equation yields

$$\mathcal{L}\{y''\}(s) + 4\mathcal{L}\{y\}(s) = \mathcal{L}\{g(t)\}(s)$$

$$\Rightarrow \quad s^2\mathcal{L}\{y\}(s) + s + 4\mathcal{L}\{y\}(s) = \mathcal{L}\{g(t)\}(s)$$

$$\Rightarrow \quad \left(s^2 + 4\right)\mathcal{L}\{y\}(s) = \mathcal{L}\{g(t)\}(s) - s = \frac{-s^3 + 1 + 3se^{-2s} - e^{-2s}}{s^2}$$

$$\Rightarrow \quad \mathcal{L}\{y\}(s) = \frac{-s^3 + 1 + 3se^{-2s} - e^{-2s}}{s^2(s^2 + 4)}.$$

**25.** Taking the Laplace transform of $y''' - y'' + y' - y = 0$ and applying the linearity of the Laplace transform yields

$$\mathcal{L}\{y'''\}(s) - \mathcal{L}\{y''\}(s) + \mathcal{L}\{y'\}(s) - \mathcal{L}\{y\}(s) = \mathcal{L}\{0\}(s) = 0. \qquad (7.17)$$

If we denote $Y(s) := \mathcal{L}\{y\}(s)$ and and apply property (4) on page 362 of the text, we get

$$\mathcal{L}\{y'\}(s) = sY(s) - 1, \quad \mathcal{L}\{y''\}(s) = s^2Y(s) - s - 1, \quad LTy''' = s^3Y(s) - s^2 - s - 3.$$

Combining these equations with (7.17) gives us

$$\left[s^3Y(s) - s^2 - s - 3\right] - \left[s^2Y(s) - s - 1\right] + \left[sY(s) - 1\right] - Y(s) = 0$$
$$\Rightarrow \quad \left(s^3 - s^2 + s - 1\right)Y(s) = s^2 + 3$$
$$\Rightarrow \quad Y(s) = \frac{s^2 + 3}{s^3 - s^2 + s - 1} = \frac{s^2 + 3}{(s-1)(s^2+1)}.$$

Expanding $Y(s)$ by partial fractions results

$$Y(s) = \frac{2}{s-1} - \frac{s+1}{s^2+1} = \frac{2}{s-1} - \frac{s}{s^2+1} - \frac{1}{s^2+1}.$$

From Table 7.1 on page 358 of the text, we see that

$$y(t) = \mathcal{L}^{-1}\{Y(s)\}(t) = 2e^t - \cos t - \sin t.$$

**27.** Let $Y(s) := \mathcal{L}\{y\}(s)$. Then, by Theorem 5 in Section 7.3,

$$\mathcal{L}\{y'\}(s) = sY(s) - y(0) = sY(s) + 4,$$
$$\mathcal{L}\{y''\}(s) = s^2Y(s) - sy(0) - y'(0) = s^2Y(s) + 4s - 4,$$
$$\mathcal{L}\{y'''\}(s) = s^3Y(s) - s^2y(0) - sy'(0) - y''(0) = s^3Y(s) + 4s^2 - 4s + 2.$$

Using these equations and applying the Laplace transform to both sides of the given differential equation, we get

$$\left[s^3Y(s) + 4s^2 - 4s + 2\right] + 3\left[s^2Y(s) + 4s - 4\right] + 3\left[sY(s) + 4\right] + Y(s) = 0$$

$$\Rightarrow \qquad \left(s^3 + 3s^2 + 3s + 1\right) Y(s) + \left(4s^2 + 8s + 2\right) = 0$$

$$\Rightarrow \qquad Y(s) = -\frac{4s^2 + 8s + 2}{s^3 + 3s^2 + 3s + 1} = -\frac{4s^2 + 8s + 2}{(s+1)^3}.$$

Therefore, the partial fractions decomposition of $Y(s)$ has the form

$$-\frac{4s^2 + 8s + 2}{(s+1)^3} = \frac{A}{(s+1)^3} + \frac{B}{(s+1)^2} + \frac{C}{s+1} = \frac{A + B(s+1) + C(s+1)^2}{(s+1)^3}$$

$$\Rightarrow \qquad -(4s^2 + 8s + 2) = A + B(s+1) + C(s+1)^2.$$

Substitution $s = -1$ yields $A = 2$. Equating coefficients at $s^2$, we get $C = -4$. At last, substituting $s = 0$ we obtain

$$-2 = A + B + C \qquad \Rightarrow \qquad B = -2 - A - C = 0.$$

Therefore,

$$Y(s) = \frac{2}{(s+1)^3} + \frac{-4}{s+1} \qquad \Rightarrow \qquad y(t) = \mathcal{L}^{-1}\{Y\}(t) = t^2 e^{-t} - 4e^{-t} = \left(t^2 - 4\right) e^{-t}.$$

**29.** Using the initial conditions, $y(0) = a$ and $y'(0) = b$, and formula (4) on page 362 of the text, we conclude that

$$\mathcal{L}\{y'\}(s) = sY(s) - y(0) = sY(s) - a,$$

$$\mathcal{L}\{y''\}(s) = s^2 Y(s) - sy(0) - y'(0) = s^2 Y(s) - as - b,$$

where $Y(s) = \mathcal{L}\{y\}(s)$. Applying the Laplace transform to the original equation yields

$$\left[s^2 Y(s) - as - b\right] - 4\left[sY(s) - a\right] + 3Y(s) = \mathcal{L}\{0\}(s) = 0$$

$$\Rightarrow \qquad \left(s^2 - 4s + 3\right) Y(s) = as + b - 4a$$

$$\Rightarrow \qquad Y(s) = \frac{as + b - 4a}{s^2 - 4s + 3} = \frac{as + b - 4a}{(s-1)(s-3)} = \frac{A}{s-1} + \frac{B}{s-3}.$$

Solving for $A$ and $B$, we find that $A = (3a - b)/2$, $B = (b - a)/2$. Hence

$$Y(s) = \frac{(3a - b)/2}{s - 1} + \frac{(b - a)/2}{s - 3}$$

$$\Rightarrow \qquad y(t) = \mathcal{L}^{-1}\{Y\}(t) = \frac{3a - b}{2} \mathcal{L}^{-1}\left\{\frac{1}{s - 1}\right\}(t) + \frac{b - a}{2} \mathcal{L}^{-1}\left\{\frac{1}{s - 3}\right\}(t)$$

$$= \frac{3a - b}{2} e^t + \frac{b - a}{2} e^{3t}.$$

**31.** Similarly to Problem 29, we have

$$\mathcal{L}\{y'\}(s) = sY(s)-y(0) = sY(s)-a, \quad \mathcal{L}\{y''\}(s) = s^2Y(s)-sy(0)-y'(0) = s^2Y(s)-as-b,$$

with $Y(s) := \mathcal{L}\{y\}(s)$. Thus the Laplace transform of both sides of the the given equation yields

$$\mathcal{L}\{y'' + 2y' + 2y\}(s) = \mathcal{L}\{5\}(s)$$

$$\Rightarrow \quad [s^2Y(s) - as - b] + 2[sY(s) - a] + 2Y(s) = \frac{5}{s}$$

$$\Rightarrow \quad (s^2 + 2s + 2)Y(s) = \frac{5}{s} + as + 2a + b = \frac{as^2 + (2a+b)s + 5}{s}$$

$$\Rightarrow \quad Y(s) = \frac{as^2 + (2a+b)s + 5}{s(s^2 + 2s + 2)} = \frac{as^2 + (2a+b)s + 5}{s[(s+1)^2 + 1]}.$$

We seek for an expansion of $Y(s)$ of the form

$$\frac{as^2 + (2a+b)s + 5}{s[(s+1)^2 + 1]} = \frac{A}{s} + \frac{B(s+1)+C}{(s+1)^2 + 1}.$$

Clearing fractions, we obtain

$$as^2 + (2a+b)s + 5 = A\left[(s+1)^2 + 1\right] + [B(s+1) + C]s.$$

Substitutions $s = 0$ and $s = -1$ give us

$$s = 0: \quad 5 = 2A \qquad \Rightarrow \qquad A = 5/2,$$
$$s = -1: \quad 5 - a - b = A - C \Rightarrow \qquad C = A + a + b - 5 = a + b - 5/2.$$

To find $B$, we can compare coefficients at $s^2$:

$$a = A + B \qquad \Rightarrow \qquad B = a - A = a - 5/2.$$

So,

$$Y(s) = \frac{5/2}{s} + \frac{(a-5/2)(s+1)}{(s+1)^2 + 1} + \frac{a+b-5/2}{(s+1)^2 + 1}$$

$$\Rightarrow \quad y(t) = \mathcal{L}^{-1}\{Y\}(t) = \frac{5}{2} + \left(a - \frac{5}{2}\right)e^{-t}\cos t + \left(a + b - \frac{5}{2}\right)e^{-t}\sin t.$$

423

**33.** By Theorem 6 in Section 7.3,

$$\mathcal{L}\left\{t^2 y'(t)\right\}(s) = (-1)^2 \frac{d^2}{ds^2}\left[\mathcal{L}\left\{y'(t)\right\}(s)\right] = \frac{d^2}{ds^2}\left[\mathcal{L}\left\{y'(t)\right\}(s)\right]. \tag{7.18}$$

On the other hand, equation (4) on page 362 says that

$$\mathcal{L}\left\{y'(t)\right\}(s) = sY(s) - y(0), \qquad Y(s) := \mathcal{L}\left\{y\right\}(s).$$

Substitution back into (7.18) yields

$$
\begin{aligned}
\mathcal{L}\left\{t^2 y'(t)\right\}(s) &= \frac{d^2}{ds^2}\left[sY(s) - y(0)\right] = \frac{d}{ds}\left\{\frac{d}{ds}\left[sY(s) - y(0)\right]\right\} \\
&= \frac{d}{ds}\left[sY'(s) + Y(s)\right] = \left(sY''(s) + Y'(s)\right) + Y'(s) = sY''(s) + 2Y'(s).
\end{aligned}
$$

**35.** Taking the Laplace transform of $y'' + 3ty' - 6y = 1$ and applying the linearity of the Laplace transform yields

$$\mathcal{L}\left\{y''\right\}(s) + 3\mathcal{L}\left\{ty'\right\}(s) - 6\mathcal{L}\left\{y\right\}(s) = \mathcal{L}\left\{1\right\}(s) = \frac{1}{s}. \tag{7.19}$$

If we put $Y(s) = \mathcal{L}\left\{y\right\}(s)$ and apply property (4) on page 362 of the text with $n = 2$, we get

$$\mathcal{L}\left\{y''\right\}(s) = s^2 Y(s) - sy(0) - y'(0) = s^2 Y(s). \tag{7.20}$$

Furthermore, as it was shown in Example 4, Section 4.5,

$$\mathcal{L}\left\{ty'\right\}(s) = -sY'(s) - Y(s). \tag{7.21}$$

Substitution (7.20) and (7.21) back into (7.19) yields

$$
\begin{aligned}
& s^2 Y(s) + 3\left[-sY'(s) - Y(s)\right] - 6Y(s) = \frac{1}{s} \\
\Rightarrow \quad & -3sY'(s) + \left(s^2 - 9\right)Y(s) = \frac{1}{s} \\
\Rightarrow \quad & Y'(s) + \left(\frac{3}{s} - \frac{s}{3}\right)Y(s) = -\frac{1}{3s^2}.
\end{aligned}
$$

This is a first order linear differential equation in $Y(s)$, which can be solved by the techniques of Section 2.3. Namely, it has the integrating factor

$$\mu(s) = \exp\left[\int\left(\frac{3}{s} - \frac{s}{3}\right)ds\right] = \exp\left[3\ln s - \frac{s^2}{6}\right] = s^3 e^{-s^2/6}.$$

Thus

$$Y(s) = \frac{1}{\mu(s)} \int \mu(s) \left( -\frac{1}{3s^2} \right) ds = \frac{1}{s^3 e^{-s^2/6}} \int \frac{-s}{3} e^{-s^2/6} ds$$

$$= \frac{1}{s^3 e^{-s^2/6}} \left( e^{-s^2/6} + C \right) = \frac{1}{s^3} \left( 1 + C e^{s^2/6} \right).$$

Just as in Example 4 on page 380 of the text, $C$ must be zero in order to ensure that $Y(s) \to 0$ as $s \to \infty$. Thus $Y(s) = 1/s^3$, and from Table 7.1 on page 358 of the text we get

$$y(t) = \mathcal{L}^{-1} \left\{ \frac{1}{s^3} \right\} (t) = \frac{1}{2} \mathcal{L}^{-1} \left\{ \frac{2}{s^3} \right\} (t) = \frac{t^2}{2}.$$

**37.** We apply the Laplace transform to the given equation and obtain

$$\mathcal{L} \{ty''\} (s) - 2\mathcal{L} \{y'\} (s) + \mathcal{L} \{ty\} (s) = 0. \tag{7.22}$$

Using Theorem 5 (Section 7.3) and the initial conditions, we express $\mathcal{L} \{y''\} (s)$ and $\mathcal{L} \{y'\} (s)$ in terms of $Y(s) := \mathcal{L} \{y\} (s)$.

$$\mathcal{L} \{y'\} (s) = sY(s) - y(0) = sY(s) - 1, \tag{7.23}$$

$$\mathcal{L} \{y''\} (s) = s^2 Y(s) - sy(0) - y'(0) = s^2 Y(s) - s. \tag{7.24}$$

We now involve Theorem 6 in Section 7.3 to get

$$\mathcal{L} \{ty\} (s) = -\frac{d}{ds} \left[ \mathcal{L} \{y\} (s) \right] = -Y'(s). \tag{7.25}$$

Also, Theorem 6 and equation (7.24) yield

$$\mathcal{L} \{ty''\} (s) = -\frac{d}{ds} \left[ \mathcal{L} \{y''\} (s) \right] = -\frac{d}{ds} \left[ s^2 Y(s) - s \right] = 1 - 2sY(s) - s^2 Y'(s). \tag{7.26}$$

Substituting (7.23), (7.25), and (7.26) into (7.22), we obtain

$$\left[ 1 - 2sY(s) - s^2 Y'(s) \right] - 2 \left[ sY(s) - 1 \right] + \left[ -Y'(s) \right] = 0$$

$$\Rightarrow \quad - \left( s^2 + 1 \right) Y'(s) - 4sY(s) + 3 = 0$$

$$\Rightarrow \quad Y'(s) + \frac{4s}{s^2 + 1} Y(s) = \frac{3}{s^2 + 1}.$$

The integrating factor of this first order linear differential equation is

$$\mu(s) = \exp\left[\int \frac{4s}{s^2+1}\,ds\right] = \exp\left[2\ln\left(s^2+1\right)\right] = \left(s^2+1\right)^2.$$

Hence

$$Y(s) = \frac{1}{\mu(s)}\int \mu(s)\left(\frac{3}{s^2+1}\right)ds = \frac{1}{(s^2+1)^2}\int 3\left(s^2+1\right)ds$$

$$= \frac{1}{(s^2+1)^2}\left(s^3+3s+C\right) = \frac{(s^3+s)+(2s+C)}{(s^2+1)^2} = \frac{s}{s^2+1} + \frac{2s}{(s^2+1)^2} + \frac{C}{(s^2+1)^2},$$

where $C$ is an arbitrary constant. Therefore,

$$y(t) = \mathcal{L}^{-1}\{Y\}(t) = \mathcal{L}^{-1}\left\{\frac{s}{s^2+1}\right\}(t) + \mathcal{L}^{-1}\left\{\frac{2s}{(s^2+1)^2}\right\}(t) + \frac{C}{2}\mathcal{L}^{-1}\left\{\frac{2}{(s^2+1)^2}\right\}(t).$$

Using formulas (24), (29) and (30) on the inside back cover of the text, we finally get

$$y(t) = \cos t + t\sin t + c(\sin t - t\cos t),$$

where $c := C/2$ is an arbitrary constant.

**39.** Similarly to Example 5, we have the initial value problem (18), namely,

$$Iy''(t) = -ke(t), \qquad y(0) = 0, \quad y'(0) = 0,$$

for the model of the mechanism. This equation leads to equation (19) for the Laplace transforms $Y(s) := \mathcal{L}\{y(t)\}(s)$ and $E(s) := \mathcal{L}\{e(t)\}(s)$:

$$s^2 IY(s) = -kE(s). \tag{7.27}$$

But, this time, $e(t) = y(t) - a$ and so

$$E(s) = \mathcal{L}\{y(t) - a\}(s) = Y(s) - \frac{a}{s} \qquad \Rightarrow \qquad Y(s) = E(s) + \frac{a}{s}.$$

Substituting this relation into (7.27) yields

$$s^2 IE(s) + aIs = -kE(s) \qquad \Rightarrow \qquad E(s) = -\frac{-aIs}{s^2 I + k} = -\frac{as}{s^2 + (k/I)}.$$

Taking the inverse Laplace transform, we obtain

$$e(t) = \mathcal{L}^{-1}\{E(s)\}(t) = -a\mathcal{L}^{-1}\left\{\frac{s}{s^2 + (\sqrt{k/I})^2}\right\}(t) = -a\cos\left(\sqrt{k/I}\,t\right).$$

**41.** As in Problem 40, the differential equation modeling the automatic pilot is

$$Iy''(t) = -ke(t) - \mu e'(t), \qquad (7.28)$$

but now the error $e(t)$ is given by $e(t) = y(t) - at$.

Let $Y(s) := \mathcal{L}\{y(t)\}(s)$, $E(s) := \mathcal{L}\{e(t)\}(s)$. Notice that, as in Example 5 on page 382, we have $y(0) = y'(0) = 0$, and so $e(0) = 0$. Using these initial conditions and Theorem 5 in Section 7.3, we obtain

$$\mathcal{L}\{y''(t)\}(s) = s^2 Y(s) \qquad \text{and} \qquad \mathcal{L}\{e'(t)\}(s) = sE(s).$$

Applying the Laplace transform to both sides of (7.28) we then conclude that

$$I\mathcal{L}\{y''(t)\}(s) = -k\mathcal{L}\{e(t)\}(s) - \mu\mathcal{L}\{e'(t)\}(s)$$

$$\Rightarrow \qquad Is^2 Y(s) = -kE(s) - \mu sE(s) = -(k + \mu s)E(s). \qquad (7.29)$$

Since $e(t) = y(t) - at$,

$$E(s) = \mathcal{L}\{e(t)\}(s) = \mathcal{L}\{y(t) - at\}(s) = Y(s) - a\mathcal{L}\{t\}(s) = Y(s) - \frac{a}{s^2}$$

or $Y(s) = E(s) + a/s^2$. Substitution back into (7.29) yields

$$Is^2\left(E(s) + \frac{a}{s^2}\right) = -(k + \mu s)E(s)$$

$$\Rightarrow \qquad \left(Is^2 + \mu s + k\right)E(s) = -aI$$

$$\Rightarrow \qquad E(s) = \frac{-aI}{Is^2 + \mu s + k} = \frac{-a}{s^2 + (\mu/I)s + (k/I)}.$$

Completing the square in the denominator, we write $E(s)$ in the form suitable for inverse Laplace transform.

$$E(s) = \frac{-a}{[s + \mu/(2I)]^2 + (k/I) - \mu^2/(4I^2)}$$

$$= \frac{-a}{[s + \mu/(2I)]^2 + (4kI - \mu^2)/(4I^2)} = \frac{-2Ia}{\sqrt{4kI - \mu^2}} \frac{\sqrt{4kI - \mu^2}/(2I)}{[s + \mu/(2I)]^2 + (4kI - \mu^2)/(4I^2)}.$$

Chapter 7

Thus, using Table 7.1 on page 358 of the text, we find that

$$e(t) = \mathcal{L}^{-1}\left\{E(s)\right\}(t) = \frac{-2Ia}{\sqrt{4kI - \mu^2}}\, e^{-\mu t/(2I)} \sin\left[\frac{\sqrt{4kI - \mu^2}\,t}{2I}\right].$$

Compare this with Example 5 of the text and observe, how for moderate damping with $\mu < 2\sqrt{kI}$, the oscillations of Example 5 die out exponentially.

**EXERCISES 7.6:   Transforms of Discontinuous and Periodic Functions, page 395**

1. To find the Laplace transform of $g(t) = (t-1)^2 u(t-1)$ we apply formula (5) on page 387 of the text with $a = 1$ and $f(t) = t^2$. This yields

$$\mathcal{L}\left\{(t-1)^2 u(t-1)\right\}(s) = e^{-s}\mathcal{L}\left\{t^2\right\}(s) = \frac{2e^{-s}}{s^3}.$$

The graph of $g(t) = (t-1)^2 u(t-1)$ is shown in Figure 7-B(a).

3. The graph of the function $y = t^2 u(t-2)$ is shown in Figure 7-B(b). For this function, formula (8) on page 387 is more convenient. To apply the shifting property, we observe that $g(t) = t^2$ and $a = 2$. Hence

$$g(t+a) = g(t+2) = (t+2)^2 = t^2 + 4t + 4.$$

Now the Laplace transform of $g(t+2)$ is

$$\mathcal{L}\left\{t^2 + 4t + 4\right\}(s) = \mathcal{L}\left\{t^2\right\}(s) + 4\mathcal{L}\left\{t\right\}(s) + 4\mathcal{L}\left\{1\right\}(s) = \frac{2}{s^3} + \frac{4}{s^2} + \frac{4}{s}.$$

Hence, by formula (8), we have

$$\mathcal{L}\left\{t^2 u(t-2)\right\}(s) = e^{-2s}\mathcal{L}\left\{g(t+2)\right\}(s) = e^{-2s}\left(\frac{2}{s^3} + \frac{4}{s^2} + \frac{4}{s}\right) = \frac{e^{-2s}(4s^2 + 4s + 2)}{s^3}.$$

5. The function $g(t)$ equals zero until $t$ reaches 1, at which point $g(t)$ jumps to 2. We can express this jump by $(2-0)u(t-1)$. At $t = 2$ the function $g(t)$ jumps from the value 2 to the value 1. This can be expressed by adding the term $(1-2)u(t-2)$. Finally, the jump at $t = 3$ from 1 to 3 can be accomplished by the function $(3-1)u(t-3)$. Hence

$$g(t) = 0 + (2-0)u(t-1) + (1-2)u(t-2) + (3-1)u(t-3) = 2u(t-1) - u(t-2) + 2u(t-3)$$

428

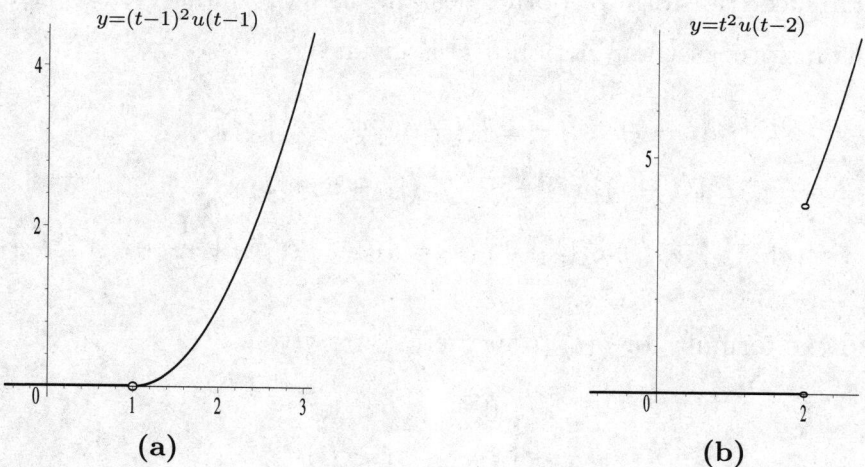

$y=(t-1)^2u(t-1)$

$y=t^2u(t-2)$

(a)

(b)

**Figure 7–B**: Graphs of functions in Problems 1 and 3.

and, by the linearity of the Laplace transform,

$$
\begin{aligned}
\mathcal{L}\left\{g(t)\right\}(s) &= 2\mathcal{L}\left\{u(t-1)\right\}(s) - \mathcal{L}\left\{u(t-2)\right\}(s) + 2\mathcal{L}\left\{u(t-3)\right\}(s) \\
&= 2\frac{e^{-s}}{s} - \frac{e^{-2s}}{s} + 2\frac{e^{-3s}}{s} \\
&= \frac{e^{-s} - e^{-2s} + 2e^{-3s}}{s}.
\end{aligned}
$$

**7.** Observe from the graph that $g(t)$ is given by

$$
\begin{cases}
0, & t < 1, \\
t, & 1 < t < 2, \\
1, & 2 < t.
\end{cases}
$$

The function $g(t)$ equals zero until $t$ reaches 1, at which point $g(t)$ jumps to the function $t$. We can express this jump by $tu(t-1)$. At $t = 2$ the function $g(t)$ jumps from the function $t$ to the value 1. This can be expressed by adding the term $(1-t)u(t-2)$. Hence

$$
g(t) = 0 + tu(t-1) + (1-t)u(t-2) = tu(t-1) - (t-1)u(t-2).
$$

429

# Chapter 7

Taking the Laplace transform of both sides and using formula (8) on page 387, we find that the Laplace transform of the function $g(t)$ is given by

$$
\begin{aligned}
\mathcal{L}\left\{g(t)\right\}(s) &= \mathcal{L}\left\{tu(t-1)\right\}(s) - \mathcal{L}\left\{(t-1)u(t-2)\right\}(s) \\
&= e^{-s}\mathcal{L}\left\{(t+1)\right\}(s) - e^{-2s}\mathcal{L}\left\{(t-1)+2\right\}(s) \\
&= \left(e^{-s} - e^{-2s}\right)\mathcal{L}\left\{t+1\right\}(s) = \left(e^{-s} - e^{-2s}\right)\left(\frac{1}{s^2} + \frac{1}{s}\right) = \frac{(e^{-s} - e^{-2s})(s+1)}{s^2}.
\end{aligned}
$$

**9.** First, we find the formula for $g(t)$ from the picture given.

$$
\begin{cases}
0, & t < 1, \\
t - 1, & 1 < t < 2, \\
3 - t, & 2 < t < 3, \\
0, & 3 < t.
\end{cases}
$$

Thus, this function jumps from 0 to $t-1$ at $t = 1$, from $t-1$ to $3-t$ at $t = 2$, and from $3-t$ to 0 at $t = 3$. Since the function $u(t-a)$ has the unit jump from 0 to 1 at $t = a$, we can express $g(t)$ as

$$
\begin{aligned}
g(t) &= [(t-1) - 0]u(t-1) + [(3-t) - (t-1)]u(t-2) + [0 - (3-t)]u(t-3) \\
&= (t-1)u(t-1) + (4-2t)u(t-2) + (t-3)u(t-3).
\end{aligned}
$$

Therefore,

$$
\begin{aligned}
\mathcal{L}\left\{g(t)\right\}(s) &= \mathcal{L}\left\{(t-1)u(t-1)\right\}(s) + \mathcal{L}\left\{(4-2t)u(t-2)\right\}(s) + \mathcal{L}\left\{(t-3)u(t-3)\right\}(s) \\
&= e^{-s}\mathcal{L}\left\{(t+1) - 1\right\}(s) + e^{-2s}\mathcal{L}\left\{4 - 2(t+2)\right\}(s) + e^{-3s}\mathcal{L}\left\{(t+3) - 3\right\}(s) \\
&= e^{-s}\mathcal{L}\left\{t\right\}(s) - 2e^{-2s}\mathcal{L}\left\{t\right\}(s) + e^{-3s}\mathcal{L}\left\{t\right\}(s) = \frac{e^{-s} - 2e^{-2s} + e^{-3s}}{s^2}.
\end{aligned}
$$

**11.** We use formula (6) on page 387 of the text with $a = 2$ and $F(s) = 1/(s-1)$. Since

$$
f(t) = \mathcal{L}^{-1}\left\{F(s)\right\}(t) = \mathcal{L}^{-1}\left\{\frac{1}{s-1}\right\}(t) = e^t \quad \Rightarrow \quad f(t-2) = e^{t-2},
$$

we get

$$
\mathcal{L}^{-1}\left\{\frac{e^{-2s}}{s-1}\right\}(t) = f(t-2)u(t-2) = e^{t-2}u(t-2).
$$

**13.** Using the linear property of the inverse Laplace transform, we obtain

$$\mathcal{L}^{-1}\left\{\frac{e^{-2s} - 3e^{-4s}}{s+2}\right\}(t) = \mathcal{L}^{-1}\left\{\frac{e^{-2s}}{s+2}\right\}(t) - 3\mathcal{L}^{-1}\left\{\frac{e^{-4s}}{s+2}\right\}(t).$$

To each term in the above equation, we can apply now formula (6), page 387 of the text with $F(s) = 1/(s+2)$ and $a = 2$ and $a = 4$, respectively. Since

$$f(t) := \mathcal{L}^{-1}\{F(s)\}(t) = \mathcal{L}^{-1}\{1/(s+2)\}(t) = e^{-2t},$$

we get

$$\mathcal{L}^{-1}\left\{\frac{e^{-2s}}{s+2}\right\}(t) - 3\mathcal{L}^{-1}\left\{\frac{e^{-4s}}{s+2}\right\}(t) = f(t-2)u(t-2) - 3f(t-4)u(t-4)$$
$$= e^{-2(t-2)}u(t-2) - 3e^{-2(t-4)}u(t-4).$$

**15.** Since

$$F(s) := \frac{s}{s^2+4s+5} = \frac{s}{(s+2)^2+1^2} = \frac{s+2}{(s+2)^2+1^2} - 2\frac{1}{(s+2)^2+1^2}$$
$$\Rightarrow \quad f(t) := \mathcal{L}^{-1}\{F(s)\}(t) = e^{-2t}(\cos t - 2\sin t),$$

applying Theorem 8 we get

$$\mathcal{L}^{-1}\left\{\frac{se^{-3s}}{s^2+4s+5}\right\}(t) = f(t-3)u(t-3) = e^{-2(t-3)}\left[\cos(t-3) - 2\sin(t-3)\right]u(t-3).$$

**17.** By partial fractions,

$$\frac{s-5}{(s+1)(s+2)} = -\frac{6}{s+1} + \frac{7}{s+2}$$

so that

$$\mathcal{L}^{-1}\left\{\frac{e^{-3s}(s-5)}{(s+1)(s+2)}\right\}(t) = -6\mathcal{L}^{-1}\left\{\frac{e^{-3s}}{s+1}\right\}(t) + 7\mathcal{L}^{-1}\left\{\frac{e^{-3s}}{s+2}\right\}(t)$$
$$= -6\mathcal{L}^{-1}\left\{\frac{1}{s+1}\right\}(t-3)u(t-3) + 7\mathcal{L}^{-1}\left\{\frac{1}{s+2}\right\}(t-3)u(t-3)$$
$$= \left[-6e^{-(t-3)} + 7e^{-2(t-3)}\right]u(t-3) = \left[7e^{6-2t} - 6e^{3-t}\right]u(t-3).$$

# Chapter 7

**19.** In this problem, we apply methods of Section 7.5 of solving initial value problems using the Laplace transform. Taking the Laplace transform of both sides of the given equation and using the linear property of the Laplace transform, we get

$$\mathcal{L}\{I''\}(s) + 2\mathcal{L}\{I'\}(s) + 2\mathcal{L}\{I\}(s) = \mathcal{L}\{g(t)\}(s). \tag{7.30}$$

Let us denote $\mathbf{I}(s) := \mathcal{L}\{I\}(s)$. By Theorem 5, Section 7.3,

$$\mathcal{L}\{I'\}(s) = s\mathbf{I}(s) - I(0) = s\mathbf{I}(s) - 10,$$
$$\mathcal{L}\{I''\}(s) = s^2\mathbf{I}(s) - sI(0) - I'(0) = s^2\mathbf{I}(s) - 10s. \tag{7.31}$$

To find the Laplace transform of $g(t)$, we express this function using the unit step function $u(t)$. Since $g(t)$ identically equals to 20 for $0 < t < 3\pi$, jumps from 20 to 0 at $t = 3\pi$ and then jumps from 0 to 20 at $t = 4\pi$, we can write

$$g(t) = 20 + (0 - 20)u(t - 3\pi) + (20 - 0)u(t - 4\pi) = 20 - 20u(t - 3\pi) + 20u(t - 4\pi).$$

Therefore,

$$\begin{aligned}
\mathcal{L}\{g(t)\}(s) &= \mathcal{L}\{20 - 20u(t - 3\pi) + 20u(t - 4\pi)\}(s) \\
&= 20\mathcal{L}\{1 - u(t - 3\pi) + u(t - 4\pi)\}(s) = 20\left(\frac{1}{s} - e^{-3\pi s} + e^{-4\pi s}\right).
\end{aligned}$$

Substituting this equation and (7.31) into (7.30) yields

$$\left[s^2\mathbf{I}(s) - 10s\right] + 2\left[s\mathbf{I}(s) - 10\right] + 2\mathbf{I}(s) = 20\left(\frac{1}{s} - \frac{e^{-3\pi s}}{s} + \frac{e^{-4\pi s}}{s}\right)$$

$$\Rightarrow \quad \mathbf{I}(s) = 10\frac{1}{s} + 20\frac{-e^{-3\pi s} + e^{-4\pi s}}{s[(s+1)^2 + 1]}. \tag{7.32}$$

Since $\mathcal{L}^{-1}\{1/s\}(t) = 1$ and

$$\begin{aligned}
\mathcal{L}^{-1}\left\{\frac{1}{s[(s+1)^2 + 1]}\right\}(t) &= \mathcal{L}^{-1}\left\{\frac{1}{2}\left[1s - \frac{s+1}{(s+1)^2 + 1} - \frac{1}{(s+1)^2 + 1}\right]\right\}(t) \\
&= \frac{1}{2}\left[1 - e^{-t}(\cos t + \sin t)\right],
\end{aligned}$$

applying the inverse Laplace transform to both sides of (7.32) yields

$$I(t) = \mathcal{L}^{-1}\left\{10\frac{1}{s} + 20\frac{-e^{-3\pi s}}{s[(s+1)^2 + 1]} + 20\frac{e^{-4\pi s}}{s[(s+1)^2 + 1]}\right\}(t)$$

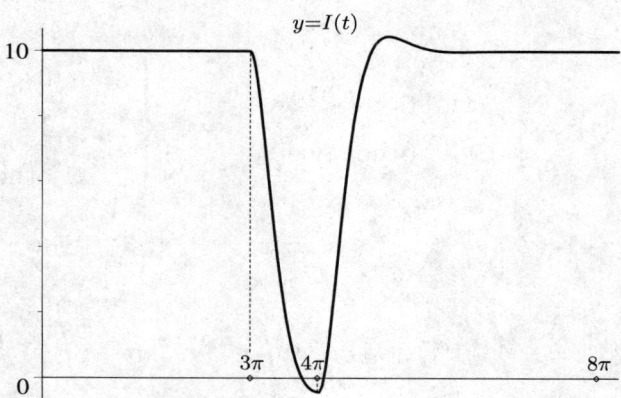

**Figure 7–C**: The graph of the function $y = I(t)$ in Problem 19.

$$
\begin{aligned}
&= 10 - 10u(t - 3\pi)\left[1 - e^{-(t-3\pi)}\left(\cos(t - 3\pi) + \sin(t - 3\pi)\right)\right] \\
&\qquad + 10u(t - 4\pi)\left[1 - e^{-(t-4\pi)}\left(\cos(t - 4\pi) + \sin(t - 4\pi)\right)\right] \\
&= 10 - 10u(t - 3\pi)\left[1 + e^{-(t-3\pi)}\left(\cos t + \sin t\right)\right] \\
&\qquad + 10u(t - 4\pi)\left[1 - e^{-(t-4\pi)}\left(\cos t + \sin t\right)\right].
\end{aligned}
$$

The graph of the solution, $y = I(t)$, $0 < t < 8\pi$, is depicted in Figure 7-C.

**21.** In the windowed version (11) of $f(t)$, $f_T(t) = t$ and $T = 2$. Thus

$$
\begin{aligned}
F_T(s) &:= \int_0^\infty e^{-st} f_T(t)\,dt = \int_0^2 e^{-st} t\,dt = -\left.\frac{te^{-st}}{s} - \frac{e^{-st}}{s^2}\right|_0^2 \\
&= -\frac{2e^{-2s}}{s} - \frac{e^{-2s}}{s^2} + \frac{1}{s^2} = \frac{1 - 2se^{-2s} - e^{-2s}}{s^2}.
\end{aligned}
$$

From Theorem 9 on page 391 of the text, we obtain

$$
\mathcal{L}\left\{f(t)\right\}(s) = \frac{F_T(s)}{1 - e^{-2s}} = \frac{1 - 2se^{-2s} - e^{-2s}}{s^2(1 - e^{-2s})}.
$$

The graph of the function $y = f(t)$ is given in Figure B.45 in the answers of the text.

**23.** We use formula (12) on page 391 of the text. With the period $T = 2$, the windowed version

433

Chapter 7

$f_T(t)$ of $f(t)$ is

$$f_T(t) = \begin{cases} f(t), & 0 < t < 2, \\ 0, & \text{otherwise} \end{cases} = \begin{cases} e^{-t}, & 0 < t < 1, \\ 1, & 1 < t < 2, \\ 0, & \text{otherwise.} \end{cases}$$

Therefore,

$$F_T(s) = \int_0^\infty e^{-st} f_T(t)\, dt = \int_0^1 e^{-st} e^{-t}\, dt + \int_1^2 e^{-st}\, dt$$

$$= \frac{e^{-(s+1)t}}{-(s+1)}\Big|_0^1 + \frac{e^{-st}}{-s}\Big|_1^2 = \frac{1 - e^{-(s+1)}}{s+1} + \frac{e^{-s} - e^{-2s}}{s}$$

and, by (12),

$$\mathcal{L}\{f(t)\}(s) = \frac{1}{1 - e^{-2s}}\left[\frac{1 - e^{-(s+1)}}{s+1} + \frac{e^{-s} - e^{-2s}}{s}\right].$$

The graph of $f(t)$ is shown in Figure B.46 in the answers of the text.

**25.** Similarly to Example 6 on page 392 of the text, $f(t)$ is a periodic function with period $T = 2a$, whose windowed version has the form

$$f_{2a}(t) = 1 - u(t - a), \qquad 0 < t < 2a.$$

Thus, using the linearity of the Laplace transform and formula (4) on page 386 for the Laplace transform of the unit step function, we have

$$F_{2a}(s) = \mathcal{L}\{f_{2a}(t)\}(s) = \mathcal{L}\{1\}(s) - \mathcal{L}\{u(t - a)\}(s) = \frac{1}{s} - \frac{e^{-as}}{s} = \frac{1 - e^{-as}}{s}.$$

Applying now Theorem 9 yields

$$\mathcal{L}\{f(t)\}(s) = \frac{1}{1 - e^{-2as}}\frac{1 - e^{-as}}{s} = \frac{1}{(1 - e^{-as})(1 + e^{-as})}\frac{1 - e^{-as}}{s} = \frac{1}{s(1 + e^{-as})}.$$

**27.** Observe that if we let

$$f_{2a}(t) = \begin{cases} f(t), & 0 < t < 2a, \\ 0, & \text{otherwise,} \end{cases}$$

434

denote the windowed version of $f(t)$, then from formula (12) on page 391 of the text we have

$$\mathcal{L}\left\{f(t)\right\}(s) = \frac{\mathcal{L}\left\{f_{2a}(t)\right\}(s)}{1 - e^{-2as}} = \frac{\mathcal{L}\left\{f_{2a}(t)\right\}(s)}{(1 - e^{-as})(1 + e^{-as})}.$$

Now

$$\begin{aligned}
f_{2a}(t) &= \frac{t}{a} + \left[\left(2 - \frac{t}{a}\right) - \frac{t}{a}\right] u(t - a) + \left[0 - \left(2 - \frac{t}{a}\right)\right] u(t - 2a) \\
&= \frac{t}{a} - \frac{2(t - a)u(t - a)}{a} + \frac{(t - 2a)u(t - 2a)}{a}.
\end{aligned}$$

Hence,

$$\begin{aligned}
\mathcal{L}\left\{f_{2a}(t)\right\}(s) &= \frac{1}{a}\mathcal{L}\left\{t\right\}(s) - \frac{2}{a}\mathcal{L}\left\{(t - a)u(t - a)\right\}(s) + \frac{1}{a}\mathcal{L}\left\{(t - 2a)u(t - 2a)\right\}(s) \\
&= \frac{1}{a}\frac{1}{s^2} - \frac{2}{a}\frac{e^{-as}}{s^2} + \frac{1}{a}\frac{e^{-as}}{s^2} = \frac{1}{as^2}\left(1 - 2e^{-as} + e^{-2as}\right) = \frac{(1 - e^{-as})^2}{as^2}
\end{aligned}$$

and

$$\mathcal{L}\left\{f(t)\right\}(s) = \frac{(1 - e^{-as})^2/(as^2)}{(1 - e^{-as})(1 + e^{-as})} = \frac{1 - e^{-as}}{as^2(1 + e^{-as})}.$$

**29.** Applying the Laplace transform to both sides of the given differential equation, we obtain

$$\mathcal{L}\left\{y''\right\}(s) + \mathcal{L}\left\{y\right\}(s) = \mathcal{L}\left\{u(t - 3)\right\}(s) = \frac{e^{-3s}}{s}.$$

Since

$$\mathcal{L}\left\{y''\right\}(s) = s^2\mathcal{L}\left\{y\right\}(s) - sy(0) - y'(0) = s^2\mathcal{L}\left\{y\right\}(s) - 1,$$

substitution yields

$$\begin{aligned}
&\left[s^2\mathcal{L}\left\{y\right\}(s) - 1\right] + \mathcal{L}\left\{y\right\}(s) = \frac{e^{-3s}}{s} \\
\Rightarrow \quad &\mathcal{L}\left\{y\right\}(s) = \frac{1}{s^2 + 1} + \frac{e^{-3s}}{s(s^2 + 1)} = \frac{1}{s^2 + 1} + e^{-3s}\left[\frac{1}{s} - \frac{s}{s^2 + 1}\right].
\end{aligned}$$

By formula (6) on page 387 of the text,

$$\mathcal{L}^{-1}\left\{e^{-3s}\left[\frac{1}{s} - \frac{s}{s^2 + 1}\right]\right\}(t) = \mathcal{L}^{-1}\left\{\frac{1}{s} - \frac{s}{s^2 + 1}\right\}(t - 3)u(t - 3) = [1 - \cos(t - 3)]u(t - 3).$$

Hence

$$y(t) = \mathcal{L}^{-1}\left\{\frac{1}{s^2 + 1} + e^{-3s}\left[\frac{1}{s} - \frac{s}{s^2 + 1}\right]\right\}(t) = \sin t + [1 - \cos(t - 3)]u(t - 3)$$

The graph of the solution is shown in Figure B.47 in the answers of the text.

# Chapter 7

**31.** We apply the Laplace transform to both sides of the differential equation and get

$$\mathcal{L}\{y''\}(s) + \mathcal{L}\{y\}(s) = \mathcal{L}\{t - (t-4)u(t-2)\}(s) = \frac{1}{s^2} - \mathcal{L}\{(t-4)u(t-2)\}(s). \quad (7.33)$$

Since $(t-4)u(t-2) = [(t-2) - 2]u(t-2)$, we can use formula (5) from Theorem 8 to find its Laplace transform. With $f(t) = t - 2$ and $a = 2$, this formula yields

$$\mathcal{L}\{(t-4)u(t-2)\}(s) = e^{-2s}\mathcal{L}\{t-2\}(s) = e^{-2s}\left[\frac{1}{s^2} - \frac{2}{s}\right].$$

Also,

$$\mathcal{L}\{y''\}(s) = s^2\mathcal{L}\{y\}(s) - sy(0) - y'(0) = s^2\mathcal{L}\{y\}(s) - 1.$$

Substitution back into (7.33) yields

$$\left[s^2\mathcal{L}\{y\}(s) - 1\right] + \mathcal{L}\{y\}(s) = \frac{1}{s^2} - e^{-2s}\left[\frac{1}{s^2} - \frac{2}{s}\right]$$

$$\Rightarrow \quad \mathcal{L}\{y\}(s) = \frac{1}{s^2} - e^{-2s}\frac{1 - 2s}{s^2(s^2+1)} = \frac{1}{s^2} - e^{-2s}\left[\frac{1}{s^2} - \frac{2}{s} + \frac{2s}{s^2+1} - \frac{1}{s^2+1}\right].$$

Applying now the inverse Laplace transform and using formula (6) on page 387 of the text, we obtain

$$
\begin{aligned}
y(t) &= \mathcal{L}^{-1}\left\{\frac{1}{s^2} - e^{-2s}\left[\frac{1}{s^2} - \frac{2}{s} + \frac{2s}{s^2+1} - \frac{1}{s^2+1}\right]\right\}(t) \\
&= t - \mathcal{L}^{-1}\left\{\frac{1}{s^2} - \frac{2}{s} + \frac{2s}{s^2+1} - \frac{1}{s^2+1}\right\}(t-2)u(t-2) \\
&= t - \left[(t-2) - 2 + 2\cos(t-2) - \sin(t-2)\right]u(t-2) \\
&= t + \left[4 - t + \sin(t-2) - 2\cos(t-2)\right]u(t-2).
\end{aligned}
$$

See Figure B.48 in the answers of the text.

**33.** By formula (4) on page 386 of the text,

$$\mathcal{L}\{u(t-2\pi) - u(t-4\pi)\}(s) = \frac{e^{-2\pi s}}{s} - \frac{e^{-4\pi s}}{s}.$$

Thus, taking the Laplace transform of $y'' + 2y' + 2y = u(t-2\pi) - u(t-4\pi)$ and applying the initial conditions $y(0) = y'(0)$ gives us

$$\left[s^2 Y(s) - s - 1\right] + 2\left[sY(s) - 1\right] + 2Y(s) = \frac{e^{-2\pi s} - e^{-4\pi s}}{s},$$

where $Y(s)$ is the Laplace transform of $y(t)$. Solving for $Y(s)$ yields

$$Y(s) = \frac{s+3}{s^2 + 2s + 2} + \frac{e^{-2\pi s} - e^{-4\pi s}}{s(s^2 + 2s + 2)}$$

$$= \frac{s+1}{(s+1)^2 + 1^2} + \frac{2(1)}{(s+1)^2 + 1^2} + \frac{e^{-2\pi s}}{s[(s+1)^2 + 1^2]} - \frac{e^{-4\pi s}}{s[(s+1)^2 + 1^2]}. \quad (7.34)$$

Since

$$\frac{1}{s[(s+1)^2 + 1^2]} = \frac{1}{2} \frac{(s^2 + 2s + 2) - (s^2 + 2s)}{s[(s+1)^2 + 1^2]} = \frac{1}{2}\left[\frac{1}{s} - \frac{s+1}{(s+1)^2 + 1^2} - \frac{1}{(s+1)^2 + 1^2}\right],$$

we have

$$\mathcal{L}^{-1}\left\{\frac{1}{s[(s+1)^2 + 1^2]}\right\}(t) = \mathcal{L}^{-1}\left\{\frac{1}{2}\left[\frac{1}{s} - \frac{s+1}{(s+1)^2 + 1^2} - \frac{1}{(s+1)^2 + 1^2}\right]\right\}(t)$$

$$= \frac{1}{2}\left[1 - e^{-t}\cos t - e^{-t}\sin t\right]$$

and, by formula (6) on page 387 of the text,

$$\mathcal{L}^{-1}\left\{\frac{e^{-2\pi s}}{s[(s+1)^2 + 1^2]}\right\}(t) = \frac{1}{2}\left[1 - e^{-(t-2\pi)}\cos(t - 2\pi) - e^{-(t-2\pi)}\sin(t - 2\pi)\right]u(t - 2\pi)$$

$$= \frac{1}{2}\left[1 - e^{2\pi-t}(\cos t + \sin t)\right]u(t - 2\pi)$$

$$\mathcal{L}^{-1}\left\{\frac{e^{-4\pi s}}{s[(s+1)^2 + 1^2]}\right\}(t) = \frac{1}{2}\left[1 - e^{-(t-4\pi)}\cos(t - 4\pi) - e^{-(t-4\pi)}\sin(t - 4\pi)\right]u(t - 4\pi)$$

$$= \frac{1}{2}\left[1 - e^{4\pi-t}(\cos t + \sin t)\right]u(t - 4\pi).$$

Finally, taking the inverse Laplace transform in (7.34) yields

$$y(t) = e^{-t}\cos t + 2e^{-t}\sin t + \frac{1}{2}\left[1 - e^{2\pi-t}(\cos t + \sin t)\right]u(t - 2\pi)$$

$$- \frac{1}{2}\left[1 - e^{4\pi-t}(\cos t + \sin t)\right]u(t - 4\pi).$$

**35.** We take the Laplace transform of the both sides of the given equation and obtain

$$\mathcal{L}\{z''\}(s) + 3\mathcal{L}\{z'\}(s) + 2\mathcal{L}\{z\}(s) = \mathcal{L}\{e^{-3t}u(t - 2)\}(s). \quad (7.35)$$

# Chapter 7

We use the initial conditions, $z(0) = 2$ and $z'(0) = -3$, and formula (4) from Section 7.3 to express $\mathcal{L}\{z'\}(s)$ and $\mathcal{L}\{z''\}(s)$ in terms of $Z(s) := \mathcal{L}\{z\}(s)$. That is,

$$\mathcal{L}\{z'\}(s) = sZ(s) - z(0) = sZ(s) - 2, \quad \mathcal{L}\{z''\}(s) = s^2 Z(s) - sz(0) - z'(0) = s^2 Z(s) - 2s + 3.$$

In the right-hand side of (7.35), we can use, say, the translation property of the Laplace transform (Theorem 3, Section 7.3) and the Laplace transform of the unit step function (formula (4), Section 7.6).

$$\mathcal{L}\{e^{-3t}u(t-2)\}(s) = \mathcal{L}\{u(t-2)\}(s+3) = \frac{e^{-2(s+3)}}{s+3}.$$

Therefore, (7.35) becomes

$$\left[s^2 Z(s) - 2s + 3\right] + 3\left[sZ(s) - 2\right] + 2Z(s) = \frac{e^{-2(s+3)}}{s+3}$$

$$\Rightarrow \quad \left(s^2 + 3s + 2\right) Z(s) = 2s + 3 + \frac{e^{-2(s+3)}}{s+3}$$

$$\Rightarrow \quad Z(s) = \frac{2s+3}{s^2 + 3s + 2} + e^{-2s-6}\frac{1}{(s+3)(s^2 + 3s + 2)}$$

$$= \frac{1}{s+1} + \frac{1}{s+2} + e^{-2s-6}\left[\frac{1/2}{s+3} - \frac{1}{s+2} + \frac{1/2}{s+1}\right].$$

Hence,

$$\begin{aligned}
z(t) &= \mathcal{L}^{-1}\left\{\frac{1}{s+1} + \frac{1}{s+2} + e^{-6}e^{-2s}\left[\frac{1/2}{s+3} - \frac{1}{s+2} + \frac{1/2}{s+1}\right]\right\}(t) \\
&= \mathcal{L}^{-1}\left\{\frac{1}{s+1}\right\}(t) + \mathcal{L}^{-1}\left\{\frac{1}{s+2}\right\}(t) \\
&\quad + \frac{e^{-6}}{2}\left[\mathcal{L}^{-1}\left\{\frac{1}{s+3}\right\} - 2\mathcal{L}^{-1}\left\{\frac{1}{s+2}\right\} + \mathcal{L}^{-1}\left\{\frac{1}{s+1}\right\}\right](t-2)u(t-2) \\
&= e^{-t} + e^{-2t} + \frac{e^{-6}}{2}\left[e^{-3(t-2)} - 2e^{-2(t-2)} + e^{-(t-2)}\right]u(t-2) \\
&= e^{-t} + e^{-2t} + \frac{1}{2}\left[e^{-3t} - 2e^{-2(t+1)} + e^{-(t+4)}\right]u(t-2).
\end{aligned}$$

**37.** Since

$$\mathcal{L}\{g(t)\}(s) = \int_0^\infty e^{-st}g(t)\,dt = \int_0^{2\pi} e^{-st}\sin t\,dt = \left.\frac{e^{-st}}{s^2+1}(-s\sin t - \cos t)\right|_0^{2\pi} = \frac{1 - e^{-2\pi s}}{s^2+1},$$

438

applying the Laplace transform to the original equation yields

$$\mathcal{L}\left\{y''\right\}(s) + 4\mathcal{L}\left\{y\right\}(s) = \mathcal{L}\left\{g(t)\right\}(s)$$

$$\Rightarrow \quad \left[s^2\mathcal{L}\left\{y\right\}(s) - s - 3\right] + 4\mathcal{L}\left\{y\right\}(s) = \frac{1 - e^{-2\pi s}}{s^2 + 1}$$

$$\Rightarrow \quad \mathcal{L}\left\{y\right\}(s) = \frac{s + 3}{s^2 + 4} + \frac{1}{(s^2 + 1)(s^2 + 4)} - \frac{e^{-2\pi s}}{(s^2 + 1)(s^2 + 4)}.$$

Using the partial fractions decomposition

$$\frac{1}{(s^2 + 1)(s^2 + 4)} = \frac{1}{3}\frac{(s^2 + 4) - (s^2 + 1)}{(s^2 + 1)(s^2 + 4)} = \frac{1}{3}\left[\frac{1}{s^2 + 1} - \frac{1}{6}\frac{2}{s^2 + 4}\right],$$

we conclude that

$$\mathcal{L}\left\{y\right\}(s) = \frac{s}{s^2 + 4} + \frac{4}{3}\frac{2}{s^2 + 4} + \frac{1}{3}\frac{1}{s^2 + 1} - e^{-2\pi s}\left[\frac{1}{3}\frac{1}{s^2 + 1} - \frac{1}{6}\frac{2}{s^2 + 4}\right]$$

and so

$$\begin{aligned}
y(t) &= \mathcal{L}^{-1}\left\{\frac{s}{s^2 + 4}\right\}(t) + \frac{4}{3}\mathcal{L}^{-1}\left\{\frac{2}{s^2 + 4}\right\}(t) + \mathcal{L}^{-1}\left\{\frac{1}{3}\frac{1}{s^2 + 1}\right\}(t) \\
&\qquad - \mathcal{L}^{-1}\left\{\frac{1}{3}\frac{1}{s^2 + 1} - \frac{1}{6}\frac{2}{s^2 + 4}\right\}(t - 2\pi)u(t - 2\pi) \\
&= \cos 2t + \frac{4}{3}\sin 2t + \frac{1}{3}\sin t - \left[\frac{1}{3}\sin(t - 2\pi) - \frac{1}{6}\sin 2(t - 2\pi)\right]u(t - 2\pi) \\
&= \cos 2t + \frac{4}{3}\sin 2t + \frac{1}{3}\sin t - \left[\frac{1}{3}\sin t - \frac{1}{6}\sin 2t\right]u(t - 2\pi) \\
&= \cos 2t + \frac{1}{3}\left[1 - u(t - 2\pi)\right]\sin t + \frac{1}{6}\left[8 + u(t - 2\pi)\right]\sin 2t.
\end{aligned}$$

**39.** We can express $g(t)$ using the unit step function as

$$g(t) = tu(t - 1) + (1 - t)u(t - 5) = [(t - 1) + 1]u(t - 1) - [(t - 5) + 4]u(t - 5).$$

Thus, formula (5) on page 387 of the text yields

$$\mathcal{L}\left\{g(t)\right\}(s) = e^{-s}\mathcal{L}\left\{t + 1\right\}(s) - e^{-5s}\mathcal{L}\left\{t + 4\right\}(s) = e^{-s}\left(\frac{1}{s^2} + \frac{1}{s}\right) - e^{-5s}\left(\frac{1}{s^2} + \frac{4}{s}\right).$$

Chapter 7

Let $Y(s) = \mathcal{L}\{y\}(s)$. Applying the Laplace transform to the given equation and using the initial conditions, we obtain

$$\mathcal{L}\{y''\}(s) + 5\mathcal{L}\{y'\}(s) + 6Y(s) = \mathcal{L}\{g(t)\}(s)$$

$$\Rightarrow \quad [s^2 Y(s) - 2] + 5[sY(s)] + 6Y(s) = \mathcal{L}\{g(t)\}(s)$$

$$\Rightarrow \quad (s^2 + 5s + 6)Y(s) = 2 + e^{-s}\left(\frac{1}{s^2} + \frac{1}{s}\right) - e^{-5s}\left(\frac{1}{s^2} + \frac{4}{s}\right)$$

$$\Rightarrow \quad Y(s) = \frac{2}{s^2 + 5s + 6} + e^{-s}\frac{s+1}{s^2(s^2+5s+6)} - e^{-5s}\frac{4s+1}{s^2(s^2+5s+6)}. \quad (7.36)$$

Using partial fractions decomposition, we can write

$$\frac{2}{s^2+5s+6} = \frac{2}{s+2} - \frac{2}{s+3},$$

$$\frac{s+1}{s^2(s^2+5s+6)} = \frac{1/36}{s} + \frac{1/6}{s^2} - \frac{1/4}{s+2} + \frac{2/9}{s+3},$$

$$\frac{4s+1}{s^2(s^2+5s+6)} = \frac{1/6}{s^2} + \frac{19/36}{s} - \frac{7/4}{s+2} + \frac{11/9}{s+3}.$$

Therefore,

$$\mathcal{L}^{-1}\left\{\frac{2}{s^2+5s+6}\right\}(t) = 2e^{-2t} - 2e^{-3t},$$

$$\mathcal{L}^{-1}\left\{\frac{s+1}{s^2(s^2+5s+6)}\right\}(t) = \frac{1}{36} + \frac{t}{6} - \frac{e^{-2t}}{4} + \frac{2e^{-3t}}{9},$$

$$\mathcal{L}^{-1}\left\{\frac{4s+1}{s^2(s^2+5s+6)}\right\}(t) = \frac{19}{36} + \frac{t}{6} - \frac{7e^{-2t}}{4} + \frac{11e^{-3t}}{9}.$$

Using these equations and taking the inverse Laplace transform in (7.36), we finally obtain

$$y(t) = 2e^{-2t} - 2e^{-3t} + \left[\frac{1}{36} + \frac{t-1}{6} - \frac{e^{-2(t-1)}}{4} + \frac{2e^{-3(t-1)}}{9}\right]u(t-1)$$

$$+ \left[\frac{19}{36} + \frac{t-5}{6} - \frac{7e^{-2(t-5)}}{4} + \frac{11e^{-3(t-5)}}{9}\right]u(t-5).$$

**41.** First observe that for $s > 0$, $T > 0$, we have $0 < e^{-Ts} < 1$ so that

$$\frac{1}{1-e^{-Ts}} = 1 + e^{-Ts} + e^{-2Ts} + e^{-3Ts} + \cdots \quad (7.37)$$

440

and the series converges for all $s > 0$. Thus,

$$\frac{1}{(s+\alpha)(1-e^{-Ts})} = \frac{1}{s+\alpha}\frac{1}{1-e^{-Ts}} = \frac{1}{s+\alpha}\left(1+e^{-Ts}+e^{-2Ts}+e^{-3Ts}+\cdots\right)$$

$$= \frac{1}{s+\alpha}+\frac{e^{-Ts}}{s+\alpha}+\frac{e^{-2Ts}}{s+\alpha}+\cdots,$$

and so

$$\mathcal{L}^{-1}\left\{\frac{1}{(s+\alpha)(1-e^{-Ts})}\right\}(t) = \mathcal{L}^{-1}\left\{\frac{1}{s+\alpha}+\frac{e^{-Ts}}{s+\alpha}+\frac{e^{-2Ts}}{s+\alpha}+\cdots\right\}(t). \qquad (7.38)$$

Taking for granted that the linearity of the inverse Laplace transform extends to the infinite sum in (7.38) and ignoring convergence questions yields

$$\mathcal{L}^{-1}\left\{\frac{1}{(s+\alpha)(1-e^{-Ts})}\right\} = \mathcal{L}^{-1}\left\{\frac{1}{s+\alpha}\right\}+\mathcal{L}^{-1}\left\{\frac{e^{-Ts}}{s+\alpha}\right\}+\mathcal{L}^{-1}\left\{\frac{e^{-2Ts}}{s+\alpha}\right\}+\cdots$$

$$= e^{-\alpha t}+e^{-\alpha(t-T)}u(t-T)+e^{-\alpha(t-2T)}u(t-2T)+\cdots$$

as claimed.

**43.** Using the expansion (7.37) obtained in Problem 41, we can represent $\mathcal{L}\{g\}(s)$ as

$$\mathcal{L}\{g\}(s) = \frac{\beta}{s^2+\beta^2}\frac{1}{1-e^{-Ts}} = \frac{\beta}{s^2+\beta^2}\left(1+e^{-Ts}+e^{-2Ts}+e^{-3Ts}+\cdots\right)$$

$$= \frac{\beta}{s^2+\beta^2}+e^{-Ts}\frac{\beta}{s^2+\beta^2}+e^{-2Ts}\frac{\beta}{s^2+\beta^2}+\cdots.$$

Since $\mathcal{L}^{-1}\{\beta/(s^2+\beta^2)\}(t) = \sin\beta t$, using the linearity of the inverse Laplace transform (extended to infinite series) and formula (6) in Theorem 8, we obtain

$$g(t) = \mathcal{L}^{-1}\left\{\frac{\beta}{s^2+\beta^2}\right\}(t)+\mathcal{L}^{-1}\left\{\frac{\beta}{s^2+\beta^2}\right\}(t-T)u(t-T)$$

$$+\mathcal{L}^{-1}\left\{\frac{\beta}{s^2+\beta^2}\right\}(t-2T)u(t-2T)+\cdots$$

$$= \sin\beta t+[\sin\beta(t-T)]u(t-T)+[\sin\beta(t-2T)]u(t-2T)+\cdots$$

as stated.

# Chapter 7

**45.** In order to apply the method of Laplace transform to given initial value problem, let us find $\mathcal{L}\{f\}(s)$ first. Since the period of $f(t)$ is $T = 1$ and $f(t) = e^t$ on $(0,1)$, the windowed version of $f(t)$ is

$$f_1(t) = \begin{cases} e^t, & 0 < t < 1, \\ 0, & \text{otherwise,} \end{cases}$$

and so

$$F_1(s) = \int_0^\infty e^{-st} f_1(t)\, dt = \int_0^1 e^{-st} e^t\, dt = \left.\frac{e^{(1-s)t}}{1-s}\right|_0^1 = \frac{1 - e^{1-s}}{s-1}.$$

Hence, Theorem 9 yields the following formula for $\mathcal{L}\{f\}(s)$:

$$\mathcal{L}\{f\}(s) = \frac{1 - e^{1-s}}{(s-1)(1 - e^{-s})}.$$

We can now apply the Laplace transform to the given differential equation and obtain

$$\mathcal{L}\{y''\}(s) + 3\mathcal{L}\{y'\}(s) + 2\mathcal{L}\{y\}(s) = \frac{1 - e^{1-s}}{(s-1)(1 - e^{-s})}$$

$$\Rightarrow \quad \left[s^2 \mathcal{L}\{y\}(s)\right] + 3\left[s\mathcal{L}\{y\}(s)\right] + 2\mathcal{L}\{y\}(s) = \frac{1 - e^{1-s}}{(s-1)(1 - e^{-s})}$$

$$\Rightarrow \quad \mathcal{L}\{y\}(s) = \frac{1 - e^{1-s}}{(s-1)(s^2 + 3s + 2)(1 - e^{-s})} = \frac{1 - e^{1-s}}{(s-1)(s+1)(s+2)(1 - e^{-s})}$$

$$\Rightarrow \quad \mathcal{L}\{y\}(s) = \frac{e}{(s-1)(s+1)(s+2)} + \frac{1 - e}{1 - e^{-s}} \frac{1}{(s-1)(s+1)(s+2)}.$$

Using the partial fractions decomposition

$$\frac{1}{(s-1)(s+1)(s+2)} = \frac{1/6}{s-1} - \frac{1/2}{s+1} + \frac{1/3}{s+2}$$

we find that

$$\mathcal{L}\{y\}(s) = \frac{e/6}{s-1} - \frac{e/2}{s+1} + \frac{e/3}{s+2} + \frac{1-e}{6}\frac{1}{(s-1)(1 - e^{-s})}$$

$$- \frac{1-e}{2}\frac{1}{(s+1)(1 - e^{-s})} + \frac{1-e}{3}\frac{1}{(s+2)(1 - e^{-s})}$$

$$\Rightarrow \quad y(t) = \frac{e}{6}e^t - \frac{e}{2}e^{-t} + \frac{e}{3}e^{-2t} + \frac{1-e}{6}\mathcal{L}^{-1}\left\{\frac{1}{(s-1)(1 - e^{-s})}\right\}(t)$$

$$- \frac{1-e}{2}\mathcal{L}^{-1}\left\{\frac{1}{(s+1)(1 - e^{-s})}\right\}(t) + \frac{1-e}{3}\mathcal{L}^{-1}\left\{\frac{1}{(s+2)(1 - e^{-s})}\right\}(t). \quad (7.39)$$

To each of the three inverse Laplace transforms in the above formula we can apply results of Problem 42(a) with $T = 1$ and $\alpha = -1$, 1, and 2, respectively. Thus, for $n < t < n + 1$, we have

$$\mathcal{L}^{-1}\left\{\frac{1}{(s-1)(1-e^{-s})}\right\}(t) = e^t\left[\frac{e^{-(n+1)}-1}{e^{-1}-1}\right],$$

$$\mathcal{L}^{-1}\left\{\frac{1}{(s+1)(1-e^{-s})}\right\}(t) = e^{-t}\left[\frac{e^{n+1}-1}{e-1}\right],$$

$$\mathcal{L}^{-1}\left\{\frac{1}{(s+2)(1-e^{-s})}\right\}(t) = e^{-2t}\left[\frac{e^{2(n+1)}-1}{e^2-1}\right].$$

Finally, substitution back into (7.39) yields

$$\begin{aligned}
y(t) &= \frac{e}{6}e^t - \frac{e}{2}e^{-t} + \frac{e}{3}e^{-2t} + \frac{1-e}{6}e^t\left[\frac{e^{-(n+1)}-1}{e^{-1}-1}\right] \\
&\qquad\qquad - \frac{1-e}{2}e^{-t}\left[\frac{e^{n+1}-1}{e-1}\right] + \frac{1-e}{3}e^{-2t}\left[\frac{e^{2(n+1)}-1}{e^2-1}\right] \\
&= \frac{e^{t-n}}{6} - \frac{e^{-t}(1+e-e^{n+1})}{2} + \frac{e^{-2t}(1+e+e^2-e^{2n+2})}{3(e+1)}.
\end{aligned}$$

**47.** Since

$$e^t = \sum_{k=0}^{\infty}\frac{t^k}{k!}$$

and

$$\mathcal{L}\left\{t^k\right\}(s) = \frac{k!}{s^{k+1}},$$

using the linearity of the Laplace transform we have

$$\mathcal{L}\left\{e^t\right\}(s) = \mathcal{L}\left\{\sum_{k=0}^{\infty}\frac{t^k}{k!}\right\}(s) = \sum_{k=0}^{\infty}\frac{\mathcal{L}\left\{t^k\right\}(s)}{k!} = \sum_{k=0}^{\infty}\frac{k!/s^{k+1}}{k!} = \frac{1}{s}\sum_{k=0}^{\infty}\left(\frac{1}{s}\right)^k. \qquad (7.40)$$

We can apply now the summation formula for geometric series, that is,

$$1 + x + x^2 + \cdots = \frac{1}{1-x},$$

which is valid for $|x| < 1$. With $x = 1/s$, $s > 1$, (7.40) yields

$$\mathcal{L}\left\{e^t\right\}(s) = \frac{1}{s}\frac{1}{1-(1/s)} = \frac{1}{s-1}.$$

# Chapter 7

**49.** Recall that the Taylor's series for $\cos t$ about $t = 0$ is

$$\cos t = 1 - \frac{t^2}{2!} + \frac{t^4}{4!} - \frac{t^6}{6!} + \cdots + (-1)^n \frac{t^{2n}}{(2n)!} + \cdots$$

so that

$$\frac{1 - \cos t}{t} = \frac{t}{2!} - \frac{t^3}{4!} + \frac{t^5}{6!} + \cdots + (-1)^{n+1} \frac{t^{2n-1}}{(2n)!} + \cdots .$$

Thus

$$\mathcal{L}\left\{\frac{1 - \cos t}{t}\right\}(s) = \frac{1}{2!}\mathcal{L}\left\{t\right\}(s) - \frac{1}{4!}\mathcal{L}\left\{t^3\right\}(s) + \cdots + \frac{(-1)^{n+1}}{(2n)!}\mathcal{L}\left\{t^{2n-1}\right\}(s) + \cdots$$

$$= \frac{1}{2}\frac{1}{s^2} - \frac{1}{4}\frac{1}{s^4} + \cdots + \frac{(-1)^{n+1}}{2n}\frac{1}{s^{2n}} + \cdots$$

$$= \sum_{n=1}^{\infty} \frac{(-1)^{n+1}}{2n}\frac{1}{s^{2n}} = \sum_{n=1}^{\infty} \frac{(-1)^{n+1}}{2ns^{2n}} .$$

To sum this series, recall that

$$\ln(1 - x) = -\sum_{n=1}^{\infty} \frac{x^n}{n} .$$

Hence,

$$\ln\left(1 + \frac{1}{s^2}\right) = -\sum_{n=1}^{\infty} \frac{(-1)^n}{ns^{2n}} = \sum_{n=1}^{\infty} \frac{(-1)^{n+1}}{ns^{2n}} .$$

Thus, we have

$$\frac{1}{2}\ln\left(1 + \frac{1}{s^2}\right) = \sum_{n=1}^{\infty} \frac{(-1)^{n+1}}{2ns^{2n}} = \mathcal{L}\left\{\frac{1 - \cos t}{t}\right\}(s) .$$

This formula can also be obtained by using the result of Problem 27 in Section 7.3 of the text.

**51.** We use formula (17) on page 394 of the text.

**(a)** With $r = -1/2$, (17) yields

$$\mathcal{L}\left\{t^{-1/2}\right\}(s) = \frac{\Gamma[(-1/2) + 1]}{s^{(-1/2)+1}} = \frac{\Gamma(1/2)}{s^{1/2}} = \frac{\sqrt{\pi}}{\sqrt{s}} = \sqrt{\frac{\pi}{s}} .$$

**(b)** This time, $r = 7/2$, and (17) becomes

$$\mathcal{L}\left\{t^{7/2}\right\}(s) = \frac{\Gamma[(7/2) + 1]}{s^{(7/2)+1}} = \frac{\Gamma(9/2)}{s^{9/2}} .$$

From the recursive formula (16) we find that

$$\Gamma\left(\frac{9}{2}\right) = \Gamma\left(\frac{7}{2}+1\right) = \frac{7}{2}\Gamma\left(\frac{7}{2}\right) = \frac{7}{2}\frac{5}{2}\Gamma\left(\frac{5}{2}\right) = \frac{7}{2}\frac{5}{2}\frac{3}{2}\Gamma\left(\frac{3}{2}\right) = \frac{7}{2}\frac{5}{2}\frac{3}{2}\frac{1}{2}\Gamma\left(\frac{1}{2}\right) = \frac{105\sqrt{\pi}}{16}.$$

Therefore,

$$\mathcal{L}\left\{t^{7/2}\right\}(s) = \frac{105\sqrt{\pi}}{16s^{9/2}}.$$

**53.** According to the definition (11) of the function $f_T(t)$, $f_T(t-kT) = 0$ if the point $t-kT$ does not belong to $(0,T)$. Therefore, fixed $t$, in the series (13) all the terms containing $f_T(t-kT)$ with $k$'s such that $t-kT \leq 0$ or $t-kT \geq T$ vanish. In the remaining terms, $k$ satisfies

$$0 < t - kT < T \qquad \Leftrightarrow \qquad \frac{t}{T} - 1 < k < \frac{t}{T}.$$

But, for any fixed $t$, there is at most one $k$ satisfying this condition.

**55.** Recall that

$$e^x = 1 + x + \frac{x^2}{2!} + \cdots + \frac{x^n}{n!} + \cdots.$$

Substituting $-1/s$ for $x$ above yields

$$e^{-1/s} = 1 - \frac{1}{s} + \frac{1}{2!s^2} - \frac{1}{3!s^3} + \cdots + \frac{(-1)^n}{n!s^n} + \cdots.$$

Thus, we have

$$s^{-1/2}e^{-1/s} = \frac{1}{s^{1/2}} - \frac{1}{s^{3/2}} + \frac{1}{2!s^{5/2}} + \cdots + \frac{(-1)^n}{n!s^{n+1/2}} + \cdots = \sum_{n=0}^{\infty} \frac{(-1)^n}{n!s^{n+1/2}}.$$

By Problem 52 of this section,

$$\mathcal{L}^{-1}\left\{\frac{1}{s^{n+(1/2)}}\right\}(t) = \frac{2^n t^{n-(1/2)}}{1 \cdot 3 \cdot 5 \cdots (2n-1)\sqrt{\pi}},$$

so that

$$\mathcal{L}^{-1}\left\{s^{-1/2}e^{-1/s}\right\}(t) = \mathcal{L}^{-1}\left\{\sum_{n=0}^{\infty} \frac{(-1)^n}{n!s^{n+1/2}}\right\}(t)$$

$$= \sum_{n=0}^{\infty} \frac{(-1)^n}{n!}\mathcal{L}^{-1}\left\{\frac{1}{s^{n+(1/2)}}\right\}(t) = \sum_{n=0}^{\infty} \frac{(-1)^n}{n!}\frac{2^n t^{n-(1/2)}}{1 \cdot 3 \cdot 5 \cdots (2n-1)\sqrt{\pi}}.$$

445

Multiplying the $n$th term by $[2 \cdot 4 \cdots (2n)]/[2 \cdot 4 \cdots (2n)]$, we obtain

$$
\begin{aligned}
\mathcal{L}^{-1}\left\{s^{-1/2}e^{-1/s}\right\}(t) &= \sum_{n=0}^{\infty} \frac{(-1)^n (2^n)^2 t^{n-(1/2)}}{(2n)!\sqrt{\pi}} = \sum_{n=0}^{\infty} \frac{(-1)^n (2^n)^2 t^n}{(2n)!\sqrt{\pi t}} \\
&= \left(\frac{1}{\sqrt{\pi t}}\right) \sum_{n=0}^{\infty} \frac{(-1)^n (2\sqrt{t})^{2n}}{(2n)!} = \left(\frac{1}{\sqrt{\pi t}}\right) \cos\left(2\sqrt{t}\right).
\end{aligned}
$$

**57.** Recall that the Maclaurin expansion of $\ln(1-x)$ is

$$
\ln(1-x) = -\sum_{n=1}^{\infty} \frac{x^n}{n},
$$

which converges for $|x| < 1$. Hence, substitution $-1/s^2$ for $x$ yields

$$
\ln\left(1 + \frac{1}{s^2}\right) = -\sum_{n=1}^{\infty} \frac{(-1)^n}{ns^{2n}} = \sum_{n=1}^{\infty} \frac{(-1)^{n+1}}{ns^{2n}}.
$$

Assuming that the inverse Laplace transform can be computed termwise, we obtain

$$
\mathcal{L}^{-1}\left\{\ln\left(1 + \frac{1}{s^2}\right)\right\} = \mathcal{L}^{-1}\left\{\sum_{n=1}^{\infty} \frac{(-1)^{n+1}}{ns^{2n}}\right\} = \sum_{n=1}^{\infty} \frac{(-1)^{n+1}}{n} \mathcal{L}^{-1}\left\{\frac{1}{s^{2n}}\right\}.
$$

From Table 7.1 in Section 7.2, $\mathcal{L}\left\{t^k\right\} = k!/s^{k+1}$, $k = 1, 2, \ldots$. Thus $\mathcal{L}^{-1}\left\{1/s^{k+1}\right\} = t^k/k!$. With $k = 2n - 1$, this yields

$$
\mathcal{L}^{-1}\left\{\frac{1}{s^{2n}}\right\}(t) = \frac{t^{2n-1}}{(2n-1)!}, \qquad n = 1, 2, \ldots
$$

and, therefore,

$$
\mathcal{L}^{-1}\left\{\ln\left(1 + \frac{1}{s^2}\right)\right\}(t) = \sum_{n=1}^{\infty} \frac{(-1)^{n+1}}{n} \frac{t^{2n-1}}{(2n-1)!} = -\frac{2}{t} \sum_{n=1}^{\infty} \frac{(-1)^n}{(2n)!} t^{2n}. \qquad (7.41)
$$

Since

$$
\cos t = \sum_{n=0}^{\infty} \frac{(-1)^n}{(2n)!} t^{2n} = 1 + \sum_{n=1}^{\infty} \frac{(-1)^n}{(2n)!} t^{2n},
$$

(7.41) implies that

$$
\mathcal{L}^{-1}\left\{\ln\left(1 + \frac{1}{s^2}\right)\right\}(t) = -\frac{2}{t}\left(\cos t - 1\right) = \frac{2(1 - \cos t)}{t}.
$$

**59.** Applying the Laplace transform to both sides of the original equation and using its linearity, we obtain

$$\mathcal{L}\{y''\}(s) - \mathcal{L}\{y\}(s) = \mathcal{L}\{G_3(t-1)\}(s). \tag{7.42}$$

Initial conditions, $y(0) = 0$ and $y'(0)=2$, and Theorem 5 in Section 7.3 imply that

$$\mathcal{L}\{y''\}(s) = s^2\mathcal{L}\{y\}(s) - sy(0) - y'(0) = s^2\mathcal{L}\{y\}(s) - 2.$$

In the right-hand side of (7.42), we can apply the result of Problem 58(c) with $a = 3$ and $b = 1$ to get

$$\mathcal{L}\{G_3(t-1)\}(s) = \frac{e^{-s} - e^{-4s}}{s}.$$

Thus (7.42) becomes

$$\left[s^2\mathcal{L}\{y\}(s) - 2\right] - \mathcal{L}\{y\}(s) = \frac{e^{-s} - e^{-4s}}{s}$$

$$\Rightarrow \quad \mathcal{L}\{y\}(s) = \frac{2}{s^2 - 1} + \frac{e^{-s} - e^{-4s}}{s(s^2 - 1)}.$$

Substituting partial fraction decompositions

$$\frac{2}{s^2 - 1} = \frac{1}{s - 1} - \frac{1}{s + 1}, \quad \frac{1}{s(s^2 - 1)} = \frac{1/2}{s - 1} + \frac{1/2}{s + 1} - \frac{1}{s}$$

yields

$$\mathcal{L}\{y\}(s) = \frac{1}{s - 1} - \frac{1}{s + 1} + (e^{-s} - e^{-4s})\left[\frac{1/2}{s - 1} + \frac{1/2}{s + 1} - \frac{1}{s}\right]$$

$$= \frac{1}{s - 1} - \frac{1}{s + 1} + e^{-s}\left[\frac{1/2}{s - 1} + \frac{1/2}{s + 1} - \frac{1}{s}\right] - e^{-4s}\left[\frac{1/2}{s - 1} + \frac{1/2}{s + 1} - \frac{1}{s}\right]. \tag{7.43}$$

Since

$$\mathcal{L}^{-1}\left\{\frac{1/2}{s - 1} + \frac{1/2}{s + 1} - \frac{1}{s}\right\}(t) = \frac{e^t + e^{-t} - 2}{2},$$

formula (6) on page 387 of the text gives us

$$\mathcal{L}^{-1}\left\{e^{-s}\left[\frac{1/2}{s - 1} + \frac{1/2}{s + 1} - \frac{1}{s}\right]\right\}(t) = \mathcal{L}^{-1}\left\{\frac{1/2}{s - 1} + \frac{1/2}{s + 1} - \frac{1}{s}\right\}(t - 1)u(t - 1)$$

$$= \frac{e^{t-1} + e^{1-t} - 2}{2}u(t - 1),$$

$$\mathcal{L}^{-1}\left\{e^{-4s}\left[\frac{1/2}{s-1}+\frac{1/2}{s+1}-\frac{1}{s}\right]\right\}(t)=\mathcal{L}^{-1}\left\{\frac{1/2}{s-1}+\frac{1/2}{s+1}-\frac{1}{s}\right\}(t-4)u(t-4)$$

$$=\frac{e^{t-4}+e^{4-t}-2}{2}\,u(t-4).$$

Taking the inverse Laplace transform in (7.43) yields

$$y(t)=e^t-e^{-t}+\frac{e^{t-1}+e^{1-t}-2}{2}\,u(t-1)-\frac{e^{t-4}+e^{4-t}-2}{2}\,u(t-4).$$

**61.** In this problem, we use the method of solving "mixing problems" discussed in Section 3.2. So, let $x(t)$ denote the mass of salt in the tank at time $t$ with $t=0$ denoting the moment when the process started. Thus, using the formula

$$\text{mass}=\text{volume}\times\text{concentration}\,,$$

we have the initial condition

$$x(0)=500\,(\text{L})\times0.2\,(\text{kg/L})=100\,(\text{kg}).$$

For the rate of change of $x(t)$, that is, $x'(t)$, we use then relation

$$x'(t)=\text{input rate}-\text{output rate}\,. \tag{7.44}$$

While the output rate (through the exit valve $C$) can be computed as

$$\text{output rate}=\frac{x(t)}{500}\,(\text{kg/L})\times12\,(\text{L/min})=\frac{3x(t)}{125}\,(\text{kg/min})$$

for all $t$, the input rate has different formulas for the first 10 minute and after that. Namely,

$$0<t<10\ (\text{valve }A):\quad \text{input rate}=12\,(\text{L/min})\times0.4\,(\text{kg/L})=4.8\,(\text{kg/min});$$

$$10<t\ (\text{valve }B):\quad \text{input rate}=12\,(\text{L/min})\times0.6\,(\text{kg/L})=7.2\,(\text{kg/min}).$$

In other words, the input rate is a function of $t$, which can be written as

$$\text{input rate}=g(t)=\begin{cases}4.8,&0<t<10,\\7.2,&10<t.\end{cases}$$

Using the unit step function, we can express $g(t) = 4.8 + 2.4u(t - 10)$ (kg/min). Therefore (7.44) becomes

$$x'(t) = g(t) - \frac{3x(t)}{125} \qquad \Rightarrow \qquad x'(t) + \frac{3}{125} x(t) = 4.8 + 2.4u(t - 10) \qquad (7.45)$$

with the initial condition $x(0) = 100$. Taking the Laplace transform of both sides yields

$$\mathcal{L}\{x'\}(s) + \frac{3}{125} \mathcal{L}\{x\}(s) = \mathcal{L}\{4.8 + 2.4u(t - 10)\}(s) = \frac{4.8}{s} + \frac{2.4e^{-10s}}{s}$$

$$\Rightarrow \qquad [s\mathcal{L}\{x\}(s) - 100] + \frac{3}{125} \mathcal{L}\{x\}(s) = \frac{4.8}{s} + \frac{2.4e^{-10s}}{s}$$

$$\Rightarrow \qquad \mathcal{L}\{x\}(s) = \frac{100s + 4.8}{s[s + (3/125)]} + \frac{2.4}{s[s + (3/125)]} e^{-10s}. \qquad (7.46)$$

Since

$$\frac{2.4}{s[s + (3/125)]} = 100 \left( \frac{1}{s} - \frac{1}{s + (3/125)} \right),$$

$$\frac{100s + 4.8}{s[s + (3/125)]} = 100 \left( \frac{2}{s} - \frac{1}{s + (3/125)} \right),$$

applying the inverse Laplace transform in (7.46), we get

$$x(t) = 100 \left( 2 - e^{-3t/125} \right) + 100 \left( 1 - e^{-3(t-10)/125} \right) u(t - 10).$$

Finally, dividing by the volume of the solution in the tank, which constantly equals to $500$ L, we conclude that

$$\text{concentration} = 0.4 - 0.2e^{-3t/125} + 0.2 \left( 1 - e^{-3(t-10)/125} \right) u(t - 10).$$

63. In this problem, the solution still enters the tank at the rate $12$ L/min, but leaves the tank at the rate only $6$ L/min. Thus, every minute, the volume of the solution in the tank increases by $12 - 6 = 6$ L. Therefore, the volume, as a function of $t$, is given by $500 + 6t$ and so

$$\text{output rate} = \frac{x(t)}{500 + 6t} \, (\text{kg/L}) \times 6 \, (\text{L/min}) = \frac{3x(t)}{250 + 3t} \, (\text{kg/min}).$$

Instead of equation (7.45) in Problem 61, we now have

$$x'(t) = g(t) - \frac{3x(t)}{250 + 3t} \qquad \Rightarrow \qquad (250 + 3t)x'(t) + 3x(t) = (250 + 3t)[48 + 24u(t - 10)].$$

449

Chapter 7

This equation has polynomial coefficients and can also be solved using the Laplace transform method. (See the discussion in Section 7.5, page 380, and Example 4.) But, as an intermediate step, one will obtain a first order linear differential equation for $\mathcal{L}\left\{x\right\}(s)$.

## EXERCISES 7.7:  Convolution, page 405

1. Let $Y(s) := \mathcal{L}\left\{y\right\}(s)$, $G(s) := \mathcal{L}\left\{g\right\}(s)$. Taking the Laplace transform of both sides of the given differential equation and using the linear property of the Laplace transform, we obtain

$$\mathcal{L}\left\{y''\right\}(s) - 2\mathcal{L}\left\{y'\right\}(s) + Y(s) = G(s).$$

The initial conditions and Theorem 5, Section 7.3, imply that

$$\mathcal{L}\left\{y'\right\}(s) = sY(s) + 1,$$
$$\mathcal{L}\left\{y''\right\}(s) = s^2Y(s) + s - 1.$$

Thus, substitution yields

$$\left[s^2Y(s) + s - 1\right] - 2\left[sY(s) + 1\right] + Y(s) = G(s)$$
$$\Rightarrow \quad \left(s^2 - 2s + 1\right)Y(s) = 3 - s + G(s)$$
$$\Rightarrow \quad Y(s) = \frac{3 - s}{s^2 - 2s + 1} + \frac{G(s)}{s^2 - 2s + 1} = \frac{2}{(s - 1)^2} - \frac{1}{s - 1} + \frac{G(s)}{(s - 1)^2}.$$

Taking now the inverse Laplace transform, we obtain

$$y(t) = 2\mathcal{L}^{-1}\left\{\frac{1}{(s - 1)^2}\right\}(t) - \mathcal{L}^{-1}\left\{\frac{1}{s - 1}\right\}(t) + \mathcal{L}^{-1}\left\{\frac{G(s)}{(s - 1)^2}\right\}(t).$$

Using Table 7.1, we find that

$$\mathcal{L}^{-1}\left\{\frac{1}{s - 1}\right\}(t) = e^t, \qquad \mathcal{L}^{-1}\left\{\frac{1}{(s - 1)^2}\right\}(t) = te^t,$$

and, by the convolution theorem,

$$\mathcal{L}^{-1}\left\{\frac{G(s)}{(s - 1)^2}\right\}(t) = \mathcal{L}^{-1}\left\{\frac{1}{(s - 1)^2}G(s)\right\}(t) = \left(te^t\right) * g(t) = \int_0^t (t - v)e^{t-v}g(v)\,dv.$$

Thus

$$y(t) = 2te^t - e^t + \int_0^t (t-v)e^{t-v}g(v)\,dv.$$

**3.** Taking the Laplace transform of $y'' + 4y' + 5y = g(t)$ and applying the initial conditions $y(0) = y'(0) = 1$ gives us

$$\left[s^2 Y(s) - s - 1\right] + 4\left[sY(s) - 1\right] + 5Y(s) = G(s),$$

where $Y(s) := \mathcal{L}\{y\}(s)$, $G(s) := \mathcal{L}\{g\}(s)$. Thus

$$Y(s) = \frac{s+5}{s^2+4s+5} + \frac{G(s)}{s^2+4s+5} = \frac{s+2}{(s+2)^2+1} + \frac{3}{(s+2)^2+1} + \frac{G(s)}{(s+2)^2+1}.$$

Taking the inverse Laplace transform of $Y(s)$ with the help of the convolution theorem yields

$$y(t) = e^{-2t}\cos t + 3e^{-2t}\sin t + \int_0^t e^{-2(t-v)}\sin(t-v)g(v)\,dv..$$

**5.** Since $\mathcal{L}^{-1}\{1/s\}(t) = 1$ and $\mathcal{L}^{-1}\{1/(s^2+1)\}(t) = \sin t$, writing

$$\frac{1}{s(s^2+1)} = \frac{1}{s}\cdot\frac{1}{s^2+1}$$

and using the convolution theorem, we obtain

$$\mathcal{L}^{-1}\left\{\frac{1}{s(s^2+1)}\right\}(t) = 1 * \sin t = \int_0^t \sin v\,dv = -\cos v\,\Big|_0^t = 1 - \cos t.$$

**7.** From Table 7.1, $\mathcal{L}^{-1}\{1/(s-a)\}(t) = e^{at}$. Therefore, using the linearity of the inverse Laplace transform and the convolution theorem, we have

$$\mathcal{L}^{-1}\left\{\frac{14}{(s+2)(s-5)}\right\}(t) = 14\mathcal{L}^{-1}\left\{\frac{1}{s+2}\cdot\frac{1}{s-5}\right\}(t) = 14e^{-2t} * e^{5t} = 14\int_0^t e^{-2(t-v)}e^{5v}\,dv$$

$$= 14e^{-2t}\int_0^t e^{7v}\,dv = 2e^{-2t}\left(e^{7t}-1\right) = 2\left(e^{5t}-e^{-2t}\right).$$

451

# Chapter 7

**9.** Since $s/(s^2+1)^2 = [s/(s^2+1)] \cdot [1/(s^2+1)]$ the convolution theorem tells us that

$$\mathcal{L}^{-1}\left\{\frac{s}{(s^2+1)^2}\right\}(t) = \mathcal{L}^{-1}\left\{\frac{s}{s^2+1} \cdot \frac{s}{s^2+1}\right\}(t) = \cos t * \sin t = \int_0^t \cos(t-v)\sin v\,dv.$$

Using the identity $\sin\alpha\cos\beta = [\sin(\alpha+\beta)+\sin(\alpha-\beta)]/2$, we get

$$\mathcal{L}^{-1}\left\{\frac{s}{(s^2+1)^2}\right\}(t) = \frac{1}{2}\int_0^t [\sin t + \sin(t-2v)]\,dv$$

$$= \frac{1}{2}\left(v\sin t + \frac{\cos(t-2v)}{2}\right)\Big|_0^t = \frac{t\sin t}{2}.$$

**11.** Using the hint, we can write

$$\frac{s}{(s-1)(s+2)} = \frac{1}{s+2} + \frac{1}{(s-1)(s+2)},$$

so that by the convolution theorem, Theorem 11 on page 400 of the text,

$$\mathcal{L}^{-1}\left\{\frac{s}{(s-1)(s+2)}\right\}(t) = \mathcal{L}^{-1}\left\{\frac{1}{s+2}\right\}(t) + \mathcal{L}^{-1}\left\{\frac{1}{(s-1)(s+2)}\right\}(t)$$

$$= e^{-2t} + e^t * e^{-2t} = e^{-2t} + \int_0^t e^{t-v}e^{-2v}\,dv$$

$$= e^{-2t} + e^t\int_0^t e^{-3v}\,dv = e^{-2t} - \frac{e^t}{3}\left(e^{-3t}-1\right) = \frac{2e^{-2t}}{3} + \frac{e^t}{3}.$$

**13.** Note that $f(t) = t * e^{3t}$. Hence, by (8) on page 400 of the text,

$$\mathcal{L}\{f(t)\}(s) = \mathcal{L}\{t\}(s)\mathcal{L}\{e^{3t}\}(s) = \frac{1}{s^2} \cdot \frac{1}{s-3} = \frac{1}{s^2(s-3)}.$$

**15.** Note that

$$\int_0^t y(v)\sin(t-v)\,dv = \sin t * y(t).$$

Let $Y(s) := \mathcal{L}\{y\}(s)$. Taking the Laplace transform of the original equation, we obtain

$$Y(s) + 3\mathcal{L}\{\sin t * y(t)\}(s) = \mathcal{L}\{t\}(s)$$

$$\Rightarrow \quad Y(s) + 3\mathcal{L}\{\sin t\}(s)Y(s) = \frac{1}{s^2} \qquad \Rightarrow \quad Y(s) + \frac{3}{s^2+1}Y(s) = \frac{1}{s^2}$$

$$\Rightarrow \quad Y(s) = \frac{s^2+1}{s^2(s^2+4)} = \frac{(1/4)}{s^2} + \frac{(3/8)2}{s^2+2^2}$$

$$\Rightarrow \quad y(t) = \mathcal{L}^{-1}\left\{\frac{(1/4)}{s^2} + \frac{(3/8)2}{s^2+2^2}\right\}(t) = \frac{t}{4} + \frac{3\sin 2t}{8}.$$

**17.** We use the convolution Theorem 11 to find the Laplace transform of the integral term.

$$\mathcal{L}\left\{\int_0^t (t-v)y(v)\,dv\right\}(s) = \mathcal{L}\{t*y(t)\}(s) = \mathcal{L}\{t\}(s)\mathcal{L}\{y(t)\}(s) = \frac{Y(s)}{s^2},$$

where $Y(s)$ denotes the Laplace transform of $y(t)$. Thus taking the Laplace transform of both sides of the given equation yields

$$Y(s) + \frac{Y(s)}{s^2} = \frac{1}{s} \quad \Rightarrow \quad Y(s) = \frac{s}{s^2+1} \quad \Rightarrow \quad y(t) = \mathcal{L}^{-1}\left\{\frac{s}{s^2+1}\right\}(t) = \cos t.$$

**19.** By the convolution theorem,

$$\mathcal{L}\left\{\int_0^t (t-v)^2 y(v)\,dv\right\}(s) = \mathcal{L}\{t^2 * y(t)\}(s) = \mathcal{L}\{t^2\}(s)\mathcal{L}\{y(t)\}(s) = \frac{2Y(s)}{s^3}.$$

Hence, applying the Laplace transform to the original equation yields

$$Y(s) + \frac{2Y(s)}{s^3} = \mathcal{L}\{t^3 + 3\}(s) = \frac{6}{s^4} + \frac{3}{s}$$

$$\Rightarrow \quad Y(s) = \frac{s^3}{s^3+2} \cdot \frac{6+3s^3}{s^4} = \frac{3}{s}$$

$$\Rightarrow \quad y(t) = \mathcal{L}^{-1}\left\{\frac{3}{s}\right\}(t) = 3.$$

**21.** As in Example 3 on page 402 of the text, we first rewrite the integro-differential equation as

$$y'(t) + y(t) - y(t) * \sin t = -\sin t, \qquad y(0) = 1. \tag{7.47}$$

We now take the Laplace transform of (7.47) to obtain

$$[sY(s) - 1] + Y(s) - \frac{1}{s^2+1}Y(s) = -\frac{1}{s^2+1},$$

where $Y(s) = \mathcal{L}\{y\}(s)$. Thus,

$$Y(s) = \frac{s^2}{s^3 + s^2 + s} = \frac{s}{s^2 + s + 1} = \frac{s}{(s+1/2)^2 + 3/4}$$

$$= \frac{s + 1/2}{(s+1/2)^2 + 3/4} - \frac{(1/\sqrt{3})(\sqrt{3}/2)}{(s+1/2)^2 + 3/4}.$$

Taking the inverse Laplace transform yields

$$y(t) = e^{-t/2} \cos\left(\frac{\sqrt{3}t}{2}\right) - \frac{1}{\sqrt{3}} e^{-t/2} \sin\left(\frac{\sqrt{3}t}{2}\right).$$

**23.** Taking the Laplace transform of the differential equation, and assuming zero initial conditions, we obtain

$$s^2 Y(s) + 9Y(s) = G(s),$$

where $Y = \mathcal{L}\{y\}$, $G = \mathcal{L}\{g\}$. Thus,

$$H(s) = \frac{Y(s)}{G(s)} = \frac{1}{s^2 + 9}.$$

The impulse response function is then

$$h(t) = \mathcal{L}^{-1}\{H(s)\}(t) = \mathcal{L}^{-1}\left\{\frac{1}{s^2 + 9}\right\}(t) = \frac{1}{3}\mathcal{L}^{-1}\left\{\frac{3}{s^2 + 3^2}\right\}(t) = \frac{\sin 3t}{3}.$$

To solve the initial value problem, we need the solution to the corresponding homogeneous problem. The auxiliary equation, $r^2 + 9 = 0$, has roots, $r = \pm 3i$. Thus, a general solution to the homogeneous equation is

$$y_h(t) = C_1 \cos 3t + C_2 \sin 3t.$$

Applying the initial conditions $y(0) = 2$ and $y'(0) = -3$, we obtain

$$2 = y(0) = (C_1 \cos 3t + C_2 \sin 3t)\big|_{t=0} = C_1,$$
$$-3 = y'(0) = (-3C_1 \sin 3t + 3C_2 \cos 3t\big|_{t=0} = 3C_2 \quad \Rightarrow \quad \begin{array}{l} C_1 = 2, \\ C_2 = -1. \end{array}$$

So

$$y_k(t) = 2\cos 3t - \sin 3t,$$

and the formula for the solution to the original initial value problem is

$$y = (h * g)(t) + y_k(t) = \frac{1}{3} \int_0^t g(v) \sin 3(t-v) \, dv + 2 \cos 3t - \sin 3t.$$

**25.** Taking the Laplace transform of both sides of the given equation and assuming zero initial conditions, we get

$$\mathcal{L}\{y'' - y' - 6y\}(s) = \mathcal{L}\{g(t)\}(s) \quad \Rightarrow \quad s^2 Y(s) - sY(s) - 6Y(s) = G(s).$$

Thus,

$$H(s) = \frac{Y(s)}{G(s)} = \frac{1}{s^2 - s - 6} = \frac{1}{(s-3)(s+2)}$$

is the transfer function. The impulse response function $h(t)$ is then given by

$$h(t) = \mathcal{L}^{-1}\left\{\frac{1}{(s-3)(s+2)}\right\}(t) = e^{3t} * e^{-2t} = \int_0^t e^{3(t-v)} e^{-2v} \, dv = e^{3t} \left.\frac{e^{-5v}}{-5}\right|_0^t = \frac{e^{3t} - e^{-2t}}{5}.$$

To solve the given initial value problem, we use Theorem 12. To this end, we need the solution $y_k(t)$ to the corresponding initial value problem for the homogeneous equation. That is,

$$y'' - y' - 6y = 0, \qquad y(0) = 1, \quad y'(0) = 8$$

(see (19) in the text). Applying the Laplace transform yields

$$\left[s^2 Y_k(s) - s - 8\right] - \left[sY_k(s) - 1\right] - 6Y_k(s) = 0$$

$$\Rightarrow \quad Y_k(s) = \frac{s+7}{s^2 - s - 6} = \frac{s+7}{(s-3)(s+2)} = \frac{2}{s-3} - \frac{1}{s+2}$$

$$\Rightarrow \quad y_k(t) = \mathcal{L}^{-1}\{Y_k(s)\}(t) = \mathcal{L}^{-1}\left\{\frac{2}{s-3} - \frac{1}{s+2}\right\}(t) = 2e^{3t} - e^{-2t}.$$

So,

$$y(t) = (h * g)(t) + y_k(t) = \frac{1}{5} \int_0^t \left[e^{3(t-v)} - e^{-2(t-v)}\right] g(v) \, dv + 2e^{3t} - e^{-2t}.$$

# Chapter 7

**27.** Taking the Laplace transform and assuming zero initial conditions, we find the transfer function $H(s)$.

$$s^2 Y(s) - 2sY(s) + 5Y(s) = G(s) \qquad \Rightarrow \qquad H(s) = \frac{Y(s)}{G(s)} = \frac{1}{s^2 - 2s + 5}.$$

Therefore, the impulse response function is

$$h(t) = \mathcal{L}^{-1}\left\{H(s)\right\}(t) = \mathcal{L}^{-1}\left\{\frac{1}{(s-1)^2 + 2^2}\right\}(t) = \frac{1}{2}\mathcal{L}^{-1}\left\{\frac{2}{(s-1)^2 + 2^2}\right\}(t) = \frac{1}{2}e^t \sin 2t.$$

Next, we find the solution $y_k(t)$ to the corresponding initial value problem for the homogeneous equation,

$$y'' - 2y' + 5y = 0, \qquad y(0) = 0, \quad y'(0) = 2.$$

Since the associated equation, $r^2 - 2r + 5 = 0$, has roots $r = 1 \pm 2i$, a general solution to the homogeneous equations is

$$y_h(t) = e^t \left(C_1 \cos 2t + C_2 \sin 2t\right).$$

We satisfy the initial conditions by solving

$$\begin{aligned} 0 &= y(0) = C_1 \\ 2 &= y'(0) = C_1 + 2C_2 \end{aligned} \qquad \Rightarrow \qquad \begin{aligned} C_1 &= 0, \\ C_2 &= 1. \end{aligned}$$

Hence, $y_k(t) = e^t \sin 2t$ and

$$y(t) = (h * g)(t) + y_k(t) = \frac{1}{2}\int\limits_0^t e^{t-v} \sin 2(t-v) g(v)\, dv + e^t \sin 2t$$

is the desired solution.

**29.** With given data, the initial value problem becomes

$$5I''(t) + 20I'(t) + \frac{1}{0.005}I(t) = e(t), \qquad I(0) = -1, \quad I'(0) = 8.$$

Using formula (15) on page 403 of the text, we find the transfer function

$$H(s) = \frac{1}{5s^2 + 20s + 200} = \frac{1}{5}\frac{1}{(s+2)^2 + 6^2}.$$

Therefore,

$$h(t) = \mathcal{L}^{-1}\left\{ \frac{1}{5} \frac{1}{(s+2)^2 + 6^2} \right\}(t) = \frac{1}{30} \mathcal{L}^{-1}\left\{ \frac{6}{(s+2)^2 + 6^2} \right\}(t) = \frac{1}{30} e^{-2t} \sin 6t.$$

Next, we consider the initial value problem

$$5I''(t) + 20I'(t) + 200I(t) = 0, \qquad I(0) = -1, \quad I'(0) = 8$$

for the corresponding homogeneous equation. Its characteristic equation, $5r^2 + 20r + 200 = 0$, has roots $r = -2 \pm 6i$, which yield a general solution

$$I_h(t) = e^{-2t}\left(C_1 \cos 6t + C_2 \sin 6t\right).$$

We find constants $C_1$ and $C_2$ so that the solution satisfies the initial conditions. Thus we have

$$\begin{aligned} -1 &= I(0) = C_1, \\ 8 &= I'(0) = -2C_1 + 6C_2 \end{aligned} \quad \Rightarrow \quad \begin{aligned} C_1 &= -1, \\ C_2 &= 1, \end{aligned}$$

and so $I_k(t) = e^{-2t}(\sin 6t - \cos 6t)$. Finally,

$$I(t) = h(t) * e(t) + I_k(t) = \frac{1}{30}\int_0^t e(v)e^{-2(t-v)}\sin 6(t-v)\,dv + e^{-2t}(\sin 6t - \cos 6t).$$

**31.** By the convolution theorem, we get

$$\mathcal{L}\{1 * 1 * 1\}(s) = \mathcal{L}\{1\}(s)\mathcal{L}\{1 * 1\}(s) = \mathcal{L}\{1\}(s)\mathcal{L}\{1\}(s)\mathcal{L}\{1\}(s) = \left(\frac{1}{s}\right)^3 = \frac{1}{s^3}.$$

Therefore, the definition of the inverse Laplace transform yields

$$1 * 1 * 1 = \mathcal{L}^{-1}\left\{\frac{1}{s^3}\right\}(t) = \frac{1}{2}\mathcal{L}^{-1}\left\{\frac{2}{s^3}\right\}(t) = \frac{1}{2}t^2.$$

**33.** Using the linear property of integrals, we have

$$\begin{aligned} f * (g + h) &= \int_0^t f(t-v)[g+h](v)\,dv = \int_0^t f(t-v)[g(v)+h(v)]\,dv \\ &= \int_0^t f(t-v)g(v)\,dv + \int_0^t f(t-v)h(v)\,dv = f * g + f * h. \end{aligned}$$

457

**35.** Since

$$\int_0^t f(v)\,dv = \int_0^t 1 \cdot f(v)\,dv = 1 * f(t),$$

we conclude that

$$\mathcal{L}\left\{\int_0^t f(v)\,dv\right\}(s) = \mathcal{L}\left\{1 * f(t)\right\}(s) = \mathcal{L}\left\{1\right\}(s)\mathcal{L}\left\{f(t)\right\}(s) = \frac{1}{s}F(s).$$

Hence, by the definition of the inverse Laplace transform,

$$\int_0^t f(v)\,dv = \mathcal{L}^{-1}\left\{\frac{1}{s}F(s)\right\}(t).$$

(Note that the integral in the left-hand side is a continuous function.)

**37.** Actually, this statement holds for any continuously differentiable function $h(t)$ on $[0,\infty)$ satisfying $h(0) = 0$. Indeed, first of all,

$$(h * g)(0) = \int_0^t h(t-v)g(v)\,dv\,\bigg|_{t=0} = \int_0^0 h(-v)g(v)\,dv = 0$$

since the interval of integration has zero length. Next, we apply the Leibniz's rule to find the derivative of $(h * g)(t)$.

$$(h * g)'(t) = \left(\int_0^t h(t-v)g(v)\,dv\right)' = \int_0^t \frac{\partial h(t-v)g(v)}{\partial t}\,dv + h(t-v)g(v)\,\bigg|_{v=t}$$

$$= \int_0^t h'(t-v)g(v)\,dv + h(0)g(t) = \int_0^t h'(t-v)g(v)\,dv$$

since $h(0) = 0$. Therefore,

$$(h * g)'(0) = \int_0^0 h'(-v)g(v)\,dv = 0,$$

again as a definite integral with equal limits of integration.

**EXERCISES 7.8:  Impulses and the Dirac Delta Function, page 412**

1. By equation (3) on page 407 of the text,

$$\int_{-\infty}^{\infty} (t^2 - 1)\boldsymbol{\delta}(t)\, dt = \left. (t^2 - 1)\right|_{t=0} = -1.$$

3. By equation (3) on page 407 of the text,

$$\int_{-\infty}^{\infty} (\sin 3t)\boldsymbol{\delta}\left(t - \frac{\pi}{2}\right) dt = \sin\left(3 \cdot \frac{\pi}{2}\right) = -1.$$

5. Formula (6) of the Laplace transform of the Dirac delta function yields

$$\int_{0}^{\infty} e^{-2t}\boldsymbol{\delta}(t - 1)\, dt = \mathcal{L}\left\{\boldsymbol{\delta}(t - 1)\right\}(2) = \left. e^{-s}\right|_{s=2} = e^{-2}.$$

7. Using the linearity of the Laplace transform and (6) on page 409 of the text, we get

$$\mathcal{L}\left\{\boldsymbol{\delta}(t - 1) - \boldsymbol{\delta}(t - 3)\right\}(s) = \mathcal{L}\left\{\boldsymbol{\delta}(t - 1)\right\}(s) - \mathcal{L}\left\{\boldsymbol{\delta}(t - 3)\right\}(s) = e^{-s} - e^{-3s}.$$

9. Since $\boldsymbol{\delta}(t - 1) = 0$ for $t < 1$,

$$\mathcal{L}\left\{t\boldsymbol{\delta}(t - 1)\right\}(s) := \int_{0}^{\infty} e^{-st} t\boldsymbol{\delta}(t - 1)\, dt = \int_{-\infty}^{\infty} e^{-st} t\boldsymbol{\delta}(t - 1)\, dt = \left. e^{-st}t\right|_{t=1} = e^{-s}$$

by equation (3) on page 407 of the text.

Another way to solve this problem is to use Theorem 6 inj Section 7.3. This yields

$$\mathcal{L}\left\{t\boldsymbol{\delta}(t - 1)\right\}(s) = -\frac{d}{ds}\mathcal{L}\left\{\boldsymbol{\delta}(t - 1)\right\}(s) = -\frac{d\left(e^{-s}\right)}{ds} = e^{-s}.$$

11. Since $\boldsymbol{\delta}(t - \pi) = 0$ for $t < \pi$, we use the definition of the Laplace transform and formula (3), page 407 of the text, to conclude that

$$\mathcal{L}\left\{(\sin t)\boldsymbol{\delta}(t - \pi)\right\}(s) := \int_{0}^{\infty} e^{-st}(\sin t)\boldsymbol{\delta}(t - \pi)\, dt = \int_{-\infty}^{\infty} e^{-st}(\sin t)\boldsymbol{\delta}(t - \pi)\, dt = e^{-\pi t}\sin \pi = 0.$$

# Chapter 7

**13.** Let $W(s) := \mathcal{L}\{w\}(s)$. Using the initial conditions and Theorem 5 in Section 7.3, we find that

$$\mathcal{L}\{w''\}(s) = s^2 W(s) - sw(0) - w'(0) = s^2 W(s).$$

Thus, applying the Laplace transform to both sides of the given equation yields

$$s^2 W(s) + W(s) = \mathcal{L}\{\delta(t-\pi)\}(s) = e^{-\pi s} \qquad \Rightarrow \qquad W(s) = \frac{e^{-\pi s}}{s^2+1}.$$

Taking the inverse Laplace transform of both sides of the last equation and using Theorem 8 in Section 7.6, we get

$$w(t) = \mathcal{L}^{-1}\left\{\frac{e^{-\pi s}}{s^2+1}\right\}(t) = \mathcal{L}^{-1}\left\{\frac{1}{s^2+1}\right\}(t-\pi)u(t-\pi) = \sin(t-\pi)u(t-\pi) = -(\sin t)u(t-\pi).$$

**15.** Let $Y := \mathcal{L}\{y\}$. Taking the Laplace transform of $y'' + 2y' - 3y = \delta(t-1) - \delta(t-2)$ and applying the initial conditions $y(0) = 2$, $y'(0) = -2$, we obtain

$$\left[s^2 Y(s) - 2s + 2\right] + 2\left[sY(s) - 2\right] - 3Y(s) = \mathcal{L}\{\delta(t-1) - \delta(t-2)\}(s) = e^{-s} - e^{-2s}$$

$$\Rightarrow \qquad Y(s) = \frac{2s+2+e^{-s}-e^{-2s}}{s^2+2s-3} = \frac{2s+2}{(s+3)(s-1)} + \frac{e^{-s}}{(s+3)(s-1)} - \frac{e^{-2s}}{(s+3)(s-1)}$$

$$= \frac{1}{s-1} + \frac{1}{s+3} + \frac{e^{-s}}{4}\left(\frac{1}{s-1} - \frac{1}{s+3}\right) - \frac{e^{-2s}}{4}\left(\frac{1}{s-1} - \frac{1}{s+3}\right),$$

so that by Theorem 8 on page 387 of the text we get

$$y(t) = e^t + e^{-3t} + \frac{1}{4}\left(e^{t-1} - e^{-3(t-1)}\right)u(t-1) - \frac{1}{4}\left(e^{t-2} - e^{-3(t-2)}\right)u(t-2).$$

**17.** Let $Y := \mathcal{L}\{y\}$. We use the initial conditions to find that

$$\mathcal{L}\{y''\}(s) = s^2 Y(s) - sy(0) - y'(0) = s^2 Y(s) - 2.$$

Thus taking the Laplace transform of both sides of the given equation and using formula (6) on page 409, we get

$$\left[s^2 Y(s) - 2\right] - Y(s) = 4\mathcal{L}\{\delta(t-2)\}(s) + \mathcal{L}\{t^2\}(s) = 4e^{-2s} + \frac{2}{s^3}$$

$$\Rightarrow \qquad Y(s) = \frac{4e^{-2s}}{s^2-1} + \frac{2(s^3+1)}{s^3(s^2-1)} = 2e^{-2s}\left(\frac{1}{s-1} - \frac{1}{s+1}\right) + \frac{2}{s-1} - \frac{2}{s^3} - \frac{2}{s}.$$

460

Now we can apply the inverse Laplace transform.

$$
\begin{aligned}
y(t) &= \mathcal{L}^{-1}\left\{2e^{-2s}\left(\frac{1}{s-1}-\frac{1}{s+1}\right)+\frac{2}{s-1}-\frac{2}{s^3}-\frac{2}{s}\right\}(t)\\
&= 2\left(\mathcal{L}^{-1}\left\{\frac{1}{s-1}\right\}-\mathcal{L}^{-1}\left\{\frac{1}{s+1}\right\}\right)(t-2)u(t-2)\\
&\qquad\qquad +2\mathcal{L}^{-1}\left\{\frac{1}{s-1}\right\}(t)-\mathcal{L}^{-1}\left\{\frac{2}{s^3}\right\}(t)-2\mathcal{L}^{-1}\left\{\frac{1}{s}\right\}(t)\\
&= 2\left(e^{t-2}-e^{2-t}\right)u(t-2)+2e^t-t^2-2.
\end{aligned}
$$

**19.** Let $W(s):=\mathcal{L}\{w\}(s)$. We apply the Laplace transform to the given equation and obtain

$$\mathcal{L}\{w''\}(s)+6\mathcal{L}\{w'\}(s)+5W(s)=\mathcal{L}\{e^t\boldsymbol{\delta}(t-1)\}(s). \tag{7.48}$$

From formula (4) on page 362 of the text we see that

$$
\begin{aligned}
\mathcal{L}\{w'\}(s) &= sW(s)-w(0)=sW(s),\\
\mathcal{L}\{w''\}(s) &= s^2W(s)-sw(0)-w'(0)=s^2W(s)-4.
\end{aligned} \tag{7.49}
$$

Also, the translation property (1), Section 7.3, of the Laplace transform yields

$$\mathcal{L}\{e^t\boldsymbol{\delta}(t-1)\}(s)=\mathcal{L}\{\boldsymbol{\delta}(t-1)\}(s-1)=e^{-(s-1)}=e^{1-s}. \tag{7.50}$$

Substituting (7.49) and (7.50) back into (7.48), we obtain

$$
\begin{aligned}
&\left[s^2W(s)-4\right]+6\left[sW(s)\right]+5W(s)=e^{1-s}\\
\Rightarrow\quad &W(s)=\frac{4+e^{1-s}}{s^2+6s+5}=\frac{4+e^{1-s}}{(s+1)(s+5)}=\frac{1}{s+1}-\frac{1}{s+5}+\frac{e}{4}e^{-s}\left(\frac{1}{s+1}-\frac{1}{s+5}\right).
\end{aligned}
$$

Finally, the inverse Laplace transform of both sides of this equation yields

$$w(t)=e^{-t}-e^{-5t}+\frac{e}{4}\left[e^{-(t-1)}-e^{-5(t-1)}\right]u(t-1).$$

**21.** We apply the Laplace transform to the given equation, solve the resulting equation for $\mathcal{L}\{y\}(s)$, and then use the inverse Laplace transforms. This yields

$$\mathcal{L}\{y''\}(s)+\mathcal{L}\{y\}(s)=\mathcal{L}\{\boldsymbol{\delta}(t-2\pi)\}(s)$$

$$\Rightarrow \quad \left[s^2\mathcal{L}\{y\}(s) - 1\right] + \mathcal{L}\{y\}(s) = e^{-2\pi s} \qquad \Rightarrow \qquad \mathcal{L}\{y\}(s) = \frac{1 + e^{-2\pi s}}{s^2 + 1}$$

$$\Rightarrow \quad y(t) = \mathcal{L}^{-1}\left\{\frac{1}{s^2+1}\right\}(t) + \mathcal{L}^{-1}\left\{\frac{1}{s^2+1}\right\}(t - 2\pi)u(t - 2\pi)$$

$$= \sin t + [\sin(t - 2\pi)]u(t - 2\pi) = [1 + u(t - 2\pi)]\sin t.$$

The graph of the solution is shown in Figure B.49 in the answers of the text.

**23.** The solution to the initial value problem

$$y'' + y = \delta(t - 2\pi), \qquad y(0) = 0, \quad y'(0) = 1$$

is given in Problem 21, that is

$$y_1(t) = [1 + u(t - 2\pi)]\sin t.$$

Thus, if $y_2(t)$ is the solution to the initial value problem

$$y'' + y = -\delta(t - \pi), \qquad y(0) = 0, \quad y'(0) = 0, \tag{7.51}$$

then, by the superposition principle (see Section 4.5), $y(t) = y_1(t) + y_2(t)$ is the desired solution. The Laplace transform of both sides in (7.51) yields

$$s^2\mathcal{L}\{y\}(s) + \mathcal{L}\{y\}(s) = -e^{-\pi s} \qquad \Rightarrow \qquad \mathcal{L}\{y\}(s) = -\frac{e^{-\pi s}}{s^2 + 1}$$

$$\Rightarrow \quad y_2(t) = -\mathcal{L}^{-1}\left\{\frac{1}{s^2+1}\right\}(t - \pi)u(t - \pi) = -[\sin(t - \pi)]u(t - \pi) = u(t - \pi)\sin t.$$

(We have used zero initial conditions to express $\mathcal{L}\{y''\}$ in terms of $\mathcal{L}\{y\}$.) Therefore, the answer is

$$y(t) = y_1(t) + y_2(t) = [1 + u(t - 2\pi)]\sin t + u(t - \pi)\sin t = [1 + u(t - \pi) + u(t - 2\pi)]\sin t.$$

The sketch of this curve is given in Figure B.50.

**25.** Taking the Laplace transform of $y'' + 4y' + 8y = \delta(t)$ with zero initial conditions yields

$$s^2Y(s) + 4sY(s) + 8Y(s) = \mathcal{L}\{\delta(t)\}(s) = 1.$$

Solving for $Y(s)$, we obtain

$$Y(s) = \frac{1}{s^2 + 4s + 8} = \frac{1}{(s+2)^2 + 4} = \frac{1}{2}\frac{2}{(s+2)^2 + 2^2}$$

so that

$$h(t) = \mathcal{L}^{-1}\left\{\frac{1}{2}\frac{2}{(s+2)^2 + 2^2}\right\}(t) = \frac{1}{2}e^{-2t}\sin 2t .$$

Notice that $H(s)$ for $y'' + 4y' + 8y = g(t)$ with $y(0) = y'(0) = 0$ is given by $H(s) = 1/(s^2 + 4s + 8)$, so that again

$$h(t) = \mathcal{L}^{-1}\left\{H(s)\right\}(t) = \frac{1}{2}e^{-2t}\sin 2t .$$

**27.** The Laplace transform of both sides of the given equation, with zero initial conditions and $g(t) = \boldsymbol{\delta}(t)$, gives us

$$s^2\mathcal{L}\{y\}(s) - 2s\mathcal{L}\{y\}(s) + 5\mathcal{L}\{y\}(s) = \mathcal{L}\{\boldsymbol{\delta}(t)\}(s)$$

$$\Rightarrow \quad \mathcal{L}\{y\}(s) = \frac{1}{s^2 - 2s + 5} = \frac{1}{(s-1)^2 + 2^2} .$$

The inverse Laplace transform now yields

$$h(t) = \mathcal{L}^{-1}\left\{\frac{1}{(s-1)^2 + 2^2}\right\}(t) = \frac{1}{2}\mathcal{L}^{-1}\left\{\frac{2}{(s-1)^2 + 2^2}\right\}(t) = \frac{1}{2}e^t\sin 2t .$$

**29.** We solve the given initial value problem to find the displacement $x(t)$. Let $X(s) := \mathcal{L}\{x\}(s)$. Applying the Laplace transform to the differential equation yields

$$\mathcal{L}\{x''\}(s) + 9X(s) = \mathcal{L}\left\{-3\boldsymbol{\delta}\left(t - \frac{\pi}{2}\right)\right\}(s) = -3e^{-\pi s/2} .$$

Since

$$\mathcal{L}\{x''\}(s) = s^2 X(s) - sx(0) - x'(0) = s^2 X(s) - s,$$

the above equation becomes

$$\left[s^2 X(s) - s\right] + 9X(s) = -3e^{-\pi s/2} \quad \Rightarrow \quad X(s) = \frac{s - 3e^{-\pi s/2}}{s^2 + 9} = \frac{s}{s^2 + 3^2} - e^{-\pi s/2}\frac{3}{s^2 + 3^2} .$$

Therefore,

$$x(t) = \mathcal{L}^{-1}\left\{\frac{s}{s^2 + 3^2} - e^{-\pi s/2}\frac{3}{s^2 + 3^2}\right\}(t)$$

**Chapter 7**

$$= \cos 3t - \left[\sin 3\left(t - \frac{\pi}{2}\right)\right] u\left(t - \frac{\pi}{2}\right) = \left[1 - u\left(t - \frac{\pi}{2}\right)\right]\cos 3t.$$

Since, for $t > \pi/2$, $u(t - \pi/2) \equiv 1$, we conclude that

$$x(t) \equiv 0 \quad \text{for} \quad t > \frac{\pi}{2}.$$

This means that the mass stops after the hit and remains in the equilibrium position thereafter.

**31.** By taking the Laplace transform of

$$ay'' + by' = cy = \boldsymbol{\delta}(t), \qquad y(0) = y'(0) = 0,$$

and solving for $Y := \mathcal{L}\{y\}$, we find that the transfer function is given by

$$H(s) = \frac{1}{as^2 + bs + c}.$$

If the roots of the polynomial $as^2 + bs + c$ are real and distinct, say $r_1$, $r_2$, then

$$H(s) = \frac{1}{(s - r_1)(s - r_2)} = \frac{1/(r_1 - r_2)}{s - r_1} - \frac{1/(r_1 - r_2)}{s - r_2}.$$

Thus

$$h(t) = \frac{1}{r_1 - r_2}\left(e^{r_1 t} - e^{r_2 t}\right)$$

and clearly $h(t)$ is bounded as $t \to \infty$ if and only if $r_1$ and $r_2$ are less than or equal to zero.

If the roots of $as^2 + bs + c$ are complex, then, by the quadratic formula, they are given by

$$-\frac{b}{2a} \pm \frac{\sqrt{4ac - b^2}}{2a} i$$

so that the real part of the roots is $-b/(2a)$. Now

$$H(s) = \frac{1}{as^2 + bs + c} = \frac{1}{a} \cdot \frac{1}{s^2 + (b/a)s + (c/a)} = \frac{1}{a} \cdot \frac{1}{[s + b/(2a)]^2 + (4ac - b^2)/(4a^2)}$$

$$= \frac{2}{\sqrt{4ac - b^2}} \cdot \frac{\sqrt{4ac - b^2}/(2a)}{[s + b/(2a)]^2 + [\sqrt{4ac - b^2}/(2a)]^2}$$

so that

$$h(t) = \frac{2}{\sqrt{4ac - b^2}} e^{-(b/2a)t} \sin\left(\frac{\sqrt{4ac - b^2}}{2a} t\right),$$

and again it is clear that $h(t)$ is bounded if and only if $-b/(2a)$, the real part of the roots of $as^2 + bs + c$, is less than or equal to zero.

**33.** Let a function $f(t)$ be defined on $(-\infty, \infty)$ and continuous in a neighborhood of the origin, $t = 0$. Since $\boldsymbol{\delta}(t) = 0$ for any $t \neq 0$, so does the product $f(t)\boldsymbol{\delta}(t)$. Therefore,

$$\int_{-\infty}^{\infty} f(t)\boldsymbol{\delta}(t)\, dt = \int_{-\varepsilon}^{\varepsilon} f(t)\boldsymbol{\delta}(t)\, dt \qquad \text{for any } \varepsilon > 0. \tag{7.52}$$

By the mean value theorem, for any $\varepsilon$ small enough (so that $f(t)$ is continuous on $(-\varepsilon, \varepsilon)$) there exists a point $\zeta_\varepsilon$ in $(-\varepsilon, \varepsilon)$ such that

$$\int_{-\varepsilon}^{\varepsilon} f(t)\boldsymbol{\delta}(t)\, dt = f(\zeta_\varepsilon) \int_{-\varepsilon}^{\varepsilon} \boldsymbol{\delta}(t)\, dt = f(\zeta_\varepsilon) \int_{-\infty}^{\infty} \boldsymbol{\delta}(t)\, dt = f(\zeta_\varepsilon).$$

Together with (7.52) this yields

$$\int_{-\infty}^{\infty} f(t)\boldsymbol{\delta}(t)\, dt = f(\zeta_\varepsilon), \qquad \text{for any } \varepsilon > 0.$$

Now we take limit, as $\varepsilon \to 0$, in both sides.

$$\lim_{\varepsilon \to 0} \left[ \int_{-\infty}^{\infty} f(t)\boldsymbol{\delta}(t)\, dt \right] = \lim_{\varepsilon \to 0} [f(\zeta_\varepsilon)].$$

Note that the integral in the left-hand side does not depend on $\varepsilon$, and so the limit equals to the integral itself. In the right-hand side, since $\zeta_\varepsilon$ belongs to $(-\varepsilon, \varepsilon)$, $\zeta_\varepsilon \to 0$ as $\varepsilon \to 0$, and the continuity of $f(t)$ implies that $f(\zeta_\varepsilon)$ converges to $f(0)$, as $\varepsilon \to 0$. Combining these observations, we get the required.

**35.** Following the hint, we solve the initial value problem

$$EIy^{(4)}(x) = L\boldsymbol{\delta}(x - \lambda), \qquad y(0) = y'(0) = 0,\ y''(0) = A,\ y'''(0) = B.$$

Using these initial conditions and Theorem 5 in Section 7.3 with $n = 4$, we obtain

$$\mathcal{L}\left\{y^{(4)}(x)\right\}(s) = s^4 \mathcal{L}\left\{y(x)\right\}(s) - sA - B,$$

# Chapter 7

and so the Laplace transform of the given equation yields

$$EI\left[s^4\mathcal{L}\left\{y(x)\right\}(s) - sA - B\right] = L\mathcal{L}\left\{\delta(x-\lambda)\right\}(s) = Le^{-\lambda s}.$$

Therefore,

$$\mathcal{L}\left\{y(x)\right\}(s) = \frac{L}{EI}\frac{e^{-\lambda s}}{s^4} + \frac{A}{s^3} + \frac{B}{s^4}$$

$$\Rightarrow\qquad y(x) = \mathcal{L}^{-1}\left\{\frac{L}{EI}\frac{e^{-\lambda s}}{s^4} + \frac{A}{s^3} + \frac{B}{s^4}\right\}(x)$$

$$= \frac{L}{EI3!}\mathcal{L}^{-1}\left\{\frac{3!}{s^4}\right\}(x-\lambda)u(x-\lambda) + \frac{A}{2!}\mathcal{L}^{-1}\left\{\frac{2!}{s^3}\right\}(x) + \frac{B}{3!}\mathcal{L}^{-1}\left\{\frac{3!}{s^4}\right\}(x)$$

$$= \frac{L}{6EI}(x-\lambda)^3u(x-\lambda) + \frac{A}{2}x^2 + \frac{B}{6}x^3. \tag{7.53}$$

Next, we are looking for $A$ and $B$ such that $y''(2\lambda) = y'''(2\lambda) = 0$. Note that, for $x > \lambda$, $u(x-\lambda) \equiv 1$ and so (7.53) becomes

$$y(x) = \frac{L}{6EI}(x-\lambda)^3 + \frac{A}{2}x^2 + \frac{B}{6}x^3.$$

Differentiating we get

$$y''(x) = \frac{L}{EI}(x-\lambda) + A + Bx \qquad\text{and}\qquad y'''(x) = \frac{L}{EI} + B.$$

Hence, $A$ and $B$ must satisfy

$$\begin{aligned}0 &= y''(2\lambda) = [L/(EI)](2\lambda - \lambda) + A + 2B\lambda, \\ 0 &= y'''(2\lambda) = L/(EI) + B\end{aligned}\qquad\Rightarrow\qquad \begin{aligned}A &= \lambda L/(EI), \\ B &= -L/(EI).\end{aligned}$$

Substitution back into (7.53) yields the solution

$$y(x) = \frac{L}{6EI}\left[(x-\lambda)^3u(x-\lambda) + 3\lambda x^2 - x^3\right].$$

## EXERCISES 7.9:   Solving Linear Systems with Laplace Transforms, page 416

1. Let $X(s) = \mathcal{L}\left\{x\right\}(s)$, $Y(s) = \mathcal{L}\left\{y\right\}(s)$. Applying the Laplace transform to both sides of the given equations yields

$$\begin{aligned}\mathcal{L}\left\{x'\right\}(s) &= 3X(s) - 2Y(s), \\ \mathcal{L}\left\{y'\right\}(s) &= 3Y(s) - 2X(s).\end{aligned} \tag{7.54}$$

Since
$$\mathcal{L}\{x'\}(s) = sX(s) - x(0) = sX(s) - 1,$$
$$\mathcal{L}\{y'\}(s) = sY(s) - y(0) = sY(s) - 1,$$

the system (7.54) becomes

$$sX(s) - 1 = 3X(s) - 2Y(s), \qquad \Rightarrow \qquad (s-3)X(s) + 2Y(s) = 1,$$
$$sY(s) - 1 = 3Y(s) - 2X(s) \qquad\qquad\qquad 2X(s) + (s-3)Y(s) = 1. \qquad (7.55)$$

Subtracting the second equation from the first equation yields

$$(s-5)X(s) + (5-s)Y(s) = 0 \qquad \Rightarrow \qquad X(s) = Y(s).$$

So, from the first equation in (7.55) we get

$$(s-3)X(s) + 2X(s) = 1 \quad \Rightarrow \quad X(s) = \frac{1}{s-1} \quad \Rightarrow \quad x(t) = \mathcal{L}^{-1}\left\{\frac{1}{s-1}\right\}(t) = e^t.$$

Since $Y(s) = X(s)$, $y(t) = x(t) = e^t$.

**3.** Let $Z(s) = \mathcal{L}\{z\}(s)$, $W(s) = \mathcal{L}\{w\}(s)$. Using the initial conditions we conclude that

$$\mathcal{L}\{z'\}(s) = sZ(s) - z(0) = sZ(s) - 1, \quad \mathcal{L}\{w'\}(s) = sW(s) - w(0) = sW(s).$$

Using these equations and taking the Laplace transform of the equations in the given system, we obtain

$$[sZ(s) - 1] + [sW(s)] = Z(s) - W(s), \qquad \Rightarrow \qquad (s-1)W(s) + (s+1)W(s) = 1,$$
$$sZ(s) - 1] - [sW(s)] = Z(s) - W(s) \qquad\qquad\qquad (s-1)W(s) - (s-1)W(s) = 1. \qquad (7.56)$$

Subtracting equations yields

$$2sW(s) = 0 \qquad \Rightarrow \qquad W(s) = 0 \qquad \Rightarrow \qquad w(t) = \mathcal{L}^{-1}\{0\}(t) \equiv 0.$$

Substituting $W(s)$ into either equation in (7.56), we obtain

$$(s-1)Z(s) = 1 \qquad \Rightarrow \qquad Z(s) = \frac{1}{s-1} \qquad \Rightarrow \qquad z(t) = \mathcal{L}^{-1}\left\{\frac{1}{s-1}\right\}(t) = e^t.$$

**5.** Denote $X(s) = \mathcal{L}\{x\}(s)$, $Y(s) = \mathcal{L}\{y\}(s)$. The Laplace transform of the given equations yields

$$\mathcal{L}\{x'\}(s) = Y(s) + \mathcal{L}\{\sin t\}(s),$$
$$\mathcal{L}\{y'\}(s) = X(s) + 2\mathcal{L}\{\cos t\}(s),$$

which becomes

$$sX(s) - 2 = Y(s) + 1/(s^2 + 1),$$
$$sY(s) = X(s) + 2s/(s^2 + 1) \qquad \Rightarrow \qquad \begin{aligned} sX(s) - Y(s) &= (2s^2 + 3)/(s^2 + 1), \\ -X(s) + sY(s) &= 2s/(s^2 + 1) \end{aligned}$$

after expressing $\mathcal{L}\{x'\}$ and $\mathcal{L}\{y'\}$ in terms of $X(s)$ and $Y(s)$. Multiplying the second equation by $s$ and adding the result to the first equation, we get

$$(s^2 - 1)Y(s) = \frac{4s^2 + 3}{s^2 + 1} \qquad \Rightarrow \qquad Y(s) = \frac{4s^2 + 3}{(s-1)(s+1)(s^2+1)}.$$

Since the partial fractions decomposition for $Y(s)$ is

$$\frac{4s^2 + 3}{(s-1)(s+1)(s^2+1)} = \frac{7/4}{s-1} - \frac{7/4}{s+1} + \frac{1/2}{s^2+1},$$

taking the inverse Laplace transform yields

$$y(t) = \mathcal{L}^{-1}\left\{\frac{7/4}{s-1} - \frac{7/4}{s+1} + \frac{1/2}{s^2+1}\right\}(t) = \frac{7}{4}e^t - \frac{7}{4}e^{-t} + \frac{1}{2}\sin t.$$

From the second equation in the original system,

$$x(t) = y' - 2\cos t = \frac{7}{4}e^t + \frac{7}{4}e^{-t} - \frac{3}{2}\cos t.$$

**7.** We will first write this system without using operator notation. Thus, we have

$$\begin{aligned} x' - 4x + 6y &= 9e^{-3t}, \\ x - y' + y &= 5e^{-3t}. \end{aligned} \tag{7.57}$$

By taking the Laplace transform of both sides of both of these differential equations and using the linearity of the Laplace transform, we obtain

$$\begin{aligned} \mathcal{L}\{x'\}(s) - 4X(s) + 6Y(s) &= 9/(s+3), \\ X(s) - \mathcal{L}\{y'\}(s) + Y(s) &= 5/(s+3), \end{aligned} \tag{7.58}$$

where $X(s)$ and $Y(s)$ are the Laplace transforms of $x(t)$ and $y(t)$, respectively. Using the initial conditions $x(0) = -9$ and $y(0) = 4$, we can express

$$\mathcal{L}\left\{x'\right\}(s) = sX(s) - x(0) = sX(s) + 9,$$
$$\mathcal{L}\left\{y'\right\}(s) = sY(s) - y(0) = sY(s) - 4.$$

Substituting these expressions into the system given in (7.58) and simplifying yields

$$(s-4)X(s) + 6Y(s) = -9 + \frac{9}{s+3} = \frac{-9s-18}{s+3},$$
$$X(s) + (-s+1)Y(s) = -4 + \frac{5}{s+3} = \frac{-4s-7}{s+3}.$$

By multiplying the second equation above by $-(s-4)$, adding the resulting equations, and simplifying, we obtain

$$\left(s^2 - 5s + 10\right)Y(s) = \frac{(4s+7)(s-4)}{s+3} + \frac{-9s-18}{s+3} = \frac{4s^2 - 18s - 46}{s+3}$$
$$\Rightarrow \quad Y(s) = \frac{4s^2 - 18s - 46}{(s+3)(s^2 - 5s + 10)}.$$

Note that the quadratic $s^2 - 5s + 10 = (s - 5/2)^2 + 15/4$ is irreducible. The partial fractions decomposition yields

$$
\begin{aligned}
Y(s) &= \frac{1}{17}\left[\frac{46s - 334}{(s-5/2)^2 + 15/4} + \frac{22}{s+3}\right] \\
&= \frac{1}{17}\left[46\left(\frac{s-5/2}{(s-5/2)^2+15/4}\right) - \frac{146\sqrt{15}}{5}\left(\frac{\sqrt{15}/2}{(s-5/2)^2+15/4}\right) + 22\,\frac{1}{s+3}\right],
\end{aligned}
$$

and so

$$y(t) = \mathcal{L}^{-1}\left\{Y(s)\right\}(t) = \frac{46}{17}e^{5t/2}\cos\left(\frac{\sqrt{15}t}{2}\right) - \frac{146\sqrt{15}}{85}e^{5t/2}\sin\left(\frac{\sqrt{15}t}{2}\right) + \frac{22}{17}e^{-3t}.$$

From the second equation in the system (7.57) above, we find that

$$
\begin{aligned}
x(t) &= 5e^{-3t} + y'(t) - y(t) = 5e^{-3t} + \frac{115}{17}e^{5t/2}\cos\left(\frac{\sqrt{15}t}{2}\right) \\
&\quad - \left(\frac{23\sqrt{15}}{17} + \frac{73\sqrt{15}}{17}\right)e^{5t/2}\sin\left(\frac{\sqrt{15}t}{2}\right) - \frac{219}{17}e^{5t/2}\cos\left(\frac{\sqrt{15}t}{2}\right) - \frac{66}{17}e^{-3t}
\end{aligned}
$$

$$= -\frac{150}{17} e^{5t/2} \cos\left(\frac{\sqrt{15}t}{2}\right) - \frac{334\sqrt{15}}{85} e^{5t/2} \sin\left(\frac{\sqrt{15}t}{2}\right) - \frac{3}{17} e^{-3t}.$$

**9.** Taking the Laplace transform of both sides of both of these differential equations yields the system

$$\mathcal{L}\{x''\}(s) + X(s) + 2\mathcal{L}\{y'\}(s) = 0,$$
$$-3\mathcal{L}\{x''\}(s) - 3X(s) + 2\mathcal{L}\{y''\}(s) + 4Y(s) = 0,$$

where $X(s) = \mathcal{L}\{x\}(s)$, $Y(s) = \mathcal{L}\{y\}(s)$. Using the initial conditions $x(0) = 2$, $x'(0) = -7$ and $y(0) = 4$, $y'(0) = -9$, we see that

$$\mathcal{L}\{x''\}(s) = s^2 X(s) - sx(0) - x'(0) = s^2 X(s) - 2s + 7,$$
$$\mathcal{L}\{y'\}(s) = sY(s) - y(0) = sY(s) - 4,$$
$$\mathcal{L}\{y''\}(s) = s^2 Y(s) - sy(0) - y'(0) = s^2 Y(s) - 4s + 9.$$

Substituting these expressions into the system given above yields

$$[s^2 X(s) - 2s + 7] + X(s) + 2[sY(s) - 4] = 0,$$
$$-3[s^2 X(s) - 2s + 7] - 3X(s) + 2[s^2 Y(s) - 4s + 9] + 4Y(s) = 0,$$

which simplifies to

$$(s^2 + 1)X(s) + 2sY(s) = 2s + 1,$$
$$-3(s^2 + 1)X(s) + 2(s^2 + 2)Y(s) = 2s + 3. \tag{7.59}$$

Multiplying the first equation by 3 and adding the two resulting equations eliminates the function $X(s)$. Thus, we obtain

$$(2s^2 + 6s + 4)Y(s) = 8s + 6 \quad \Rightarrow \quad Y(s) = \frac{4s + 3}{(s+2)(s+1)} = \frac{5}{s+2} - \frac{1}{s+1},$$

where we have factored the expression $2s^2 + 6s + 4$ and used the partial fractions expansion. Taking the inverse Laplace transform, we obtain

$$y(t) = \mathcal{L}^{-1}\{Y(s)\}(t) = 5\mathcal{L}^{-1}\left\{\frac{1}{s+2}\right\}(t) - \mathcal{L}^{-1}\left\{\frac{1}{s+1}\right\}(t) = 5e^{-2t} - e^{-t}.$$

To find the solution $x(t)$, we again examine the system given in (7.59) above. This time we will eliminate the function $Y(s)$ by multiplying the first equation by $s^2 + 2$ and the second equation by $-s$ and adding the resulting equations. Thus, we have

$$\left(s^2 + 3s + 2\right)\left(s^2 + 1\right)X(s) = 2s^3 - s^2 + s + 2$$

$$\Rightarrow \quad X(s) = \frac{2s^3 - s^2 + s + 2}{(s+2)(s+1)(s^2+1)}.$$

Expressing $X(s)$ in a partial fractions expansion, we find that

$$X(s) = \frac{4}{s+2} - \frac{1}{s+1} - \frac{s}{s^2+1}$$

and so

$$x(t) = \mathcal{L}^{-1}\left\{\frac{4}{s+2} - \frac{1}{s+1} - \frac{s}{s^2+1}\right\}(t) = 4e^{-2t} - e^{-t} - \cos t.$$

Hence, the solution to this initial value problem is

$$x(t) = 4e^{-2t} - e^{-t} - \cos t \quad \text{and} \quad y(t) = 5e^{-2t} - e^{-t}.$$

**11.** Since

$$\mathcal{L}\left\{x'\right\}(s) = sX(s) - x(0) = sX(s) \qquad \text{and}$$

$$\mathcal{L}\left\{y'\right\}(s) = sY(s) - y(0) = sY(s),$$

applying the Laplace transform to the given equations yields

$$sX(s) + Y(s) = \mathcal{L}\left\{1 - u(t-2)\right\}(s) = \frac{1}{s} - \frac{e^{-2s}}{s} = \frac{1 - e^{-2s}}{s},$$

$$X(s) + sY(s) = \mathcal{L}\left\{0\right\}(s) = 0.$$

From the second equation, $X(s) = -sY(s)$. Substituting this into the first equation, we eliminate $X(s)$ and obtain

$$-s^2Y(s) + Y(s) = \frac{1 - e^{-2s}}{s}$$

$$\Rightarrow \quad Y(s) = \frac{1 - e^{-2s}}{s(1 - s^2)} = \left(1 - e^{-2s}\right)\left(\frac{1}{s} - \frac{1/2}{s-1} - \frac{1/2}{s+1}\right).$$

Using now the linear property of the inverse Laplace transform and formula (6) on page 387, we get

$$y(t) \; = \; \mathcal{L}^{-1}\left\{\frac{1}{s} - \frac{1/2}{s-1} - \frac{1/2}{s+1}\right\}(t) - \mathcal{L}^{-1}\left\{\frac{1}{s} - \frac{1/2}{s-1} - \frac{1/2}{s+1}\right\}(t-2)u(t-2)$$

$$= 1 - \frac{e^t + e^{-t}}{2} - \left[1 - \frac{e^{t-2} + e^{-(t-2)}}{2}\right] u(t-2).$$

Since, from the second equation in the original system, $x = -y'$, we have

$$x(t) = -\left\{1 - \frac{e^t + e^{-t}}{2} - \left[1 - \frac{e^{t-2} + e^{-(t-2)}}{2}\right] u(t-2)\right\}$$

$$= \frac{e^t - e^{-t}}{2} - \left[\frac{e^{t-2} - e^{-(t-2)}}{2}\right] u(t-2).$$

**13.** Since, by formula (8) on page 387 of the text,

$$\mathcal{L}\left\{(\sin t)u(t-\pi)\right\}(s) = e^{-\pi s}\mathcal{L}\left\{\sin(t+\pi)\right\}(s) = e^{-\pi s}\mathcal{L}\left\{-\sin t\right\}(s) = -\frac{e^{-\pi s}}{s^2+1},$$

applying the Laplace transform to the given system yields

$$\mathcal{L}\left\{x'\right\}(s) - \mathcal{L}\left\{y'\right\}(s) = \mathcal{L}\left\{(\sin t)u(t-\pi)\right\}(s),$$
$$\mathcal{L}\left\{x\right\}(s) + \mathcal{L}\left\{y'\right\}(s) = \mathcal{L}\left\{0\right\}(s)$$

$$\Rightarrow \quad [sX(s) - 1] - [sY(s) - 1] = -\frac{e^{-\pi s}}{s^2+1},$$
$$X(s) + [sY(s) - 1] = 0,$$

where we have used the initial conditions, $x(0) = 1$ and $y(0) = 1$, and Theorem 4, Section 7.3, to express $\mathcal{L}\left\{x'\right\}(s)$ and $\mathcal{L}\left\{y'\right\}(s)$ in terms of $X(s) = \mathcal{L}\left\{x\right\}(s)$ and $Y(s) = \mathcal{L}\left\{y\right\}(s)$. The above system simplifies to

$$X(s) - Y(s) = -\frac{e^{-\pi s}}{s(s^2+1)},$$
$$X(s) + sY(s) = 1.$$

From the second equation, $X(s) = 1 - sY(s)$, and with this substitution the first equation becomes

$$1 - sY(s) - Y(s) = -\frac{e^{-\pi s}}{s(s^2+1)} \quad \Rightarrow \quad Y(s) = \left[1 + \frac{e^{-\pi s}}{s(s^2+1)}\right]\frac{1}{s+1} = \frac{1}{s+1} + \frac{e^{-\pi s}}{s(s+1)(s^2+1)}.$$

Using partial fractions we express

$$Y(s) = \frac{1}{s+1} + e^{-\pi s}\left[\frac{1}{s} - \frac{1/2}{s+1} - \frac{(1/2)s}{s^2+1} - \frac{1/2}{s^2+1}\right]$$

and so

$$y(t) = e^{-t} + \left[1 - \frac{1}{2}e^{-(t-\pi)} - \frac{1}{2}\cos(t-\pi) - \frac{1}{2}\sin(t-\pi)\right]u(t-\pi)$$

$$= e^{-t} + \left[1 - \frac{1}{2}e^{-(t-\pi)} + \frac{1}{2}\cos t + \frac{1}{2}\sin t\right]u(t-\pi).$$

Finally,

$$x(t) = -y'(t) = e^{-t} - \left[\frac{1}{2}e^{-(t-\pi)} - \frac{1}{2}\sin t + \frac{1}{2}\cos t\right]u(t-\pi).$$

**15.** First, note that the initial conditions are given at the point $t = 1$. Thus, for the Laplace transform method, we have to shift the argument to get zero initial point. Let us denote

$$u(t) := x(t+1) \qquad \text{and} \qquad v(t) := y(t+1).$$

The chain rule yields

$$u'(t) = x'(t+1)(t+1)' = x'(t+1), \quad v'(t) = y'(t+1)(t+1)' = y'(t+1).$$

In the original system, we substitute $t + 1$ for $t$ to get

$$x'(t+1) - 2y(t+1) = 2,$$
$$x'(t+1) + x(t+1) - y'(t+1) = (t+1)^2 + 2(t+1) - 1,$$

and make $u$ and $v$ substitution. This yields

$$u'(t) - 2v(t) = 2,$$
$$u'(t) + u(t) - v'(t) = (t+1)^2 + 2(t+1) - 1 = t^2 + 4t + 2$$

with initial conditions $u(0) = 1$, $v(0) = 0$. Taking the Laplace transform and using formula (2) on page 361 of the text, we obtain the system

$$[sU(s) - 1] - 2V(s) = \frac{2}{s},$$

$$[sU(s) - 1] + U(s) - sV(s) = \frac{2}{s^3} + \frac{4}{s^2} + \frac{2}{s},$$

where $U(s) = \mathcal{L}\{u\}(s)$, $V(s) = \mathcal{L}\{v\}(s)$. Expressing

$$U(s) = \frac{2V(s)}{s} + \frac{2}{s^2} + \frac{1}{s}$$

from the first equation and substituting this into the second equation, we obtain

$$\left[\frac{2}{s} + 2V(s)\right] + \left[\frac{2V(s)}{s} + \frac{2}{s^2} + \frac{1}{s}\right] - sV(s) = \frac{2}{s^3} + \frac{4}{s^2} + \frac{2}{s},$$

which yields

$$V(s) = \frac{1}{s^2} \qquad \Rightarrow \qquad U(s) = \frac{2}{s^3} + \frac{2}{s^2} + \frac{1}{s}.$$

Applying now inverse Laplace transforms yields

$$u(t) = t^2 + 2t + 1 = (t+1)^2, \qquad v(t) = \mathcal{L}^{-1}\left\{\frac{1}{s^2}\right\}(t) = t.$$

Finally,

$$x(t) = u(t-1) = t^2 \quad \text{and} \quad y(t) = v(t-1) = t - 1.$$

**17.** As in Problem 15, first we make a shift in $t$ to move the initial conditions to $t = 0$. Let

$$u(t) := x(t+2) \qquad \text{and} \qquad v(t) := y(t+2).$$

With $t$ replaced by $t + 2$, the original system becomes

$$x'(t+2) + x(t+2) - y'(t+2) = 2te^t,$$
$$x''(t+2) - x'(t+2) - 2y(t+2) = -e^t$$

or

$$u'(t) + u(t) - v'(t) = 2te^t, \qquad \text{with} \qquad \begin{aligned} u(0) &= 0, \\ u'(0) &= 1, \\ v(0) &= 1. \end{aligned}$$
$$u''(t) - u'(t) - 2v(t) = -e^t,$$

Applying the Laplace transform to these equations and expressing $\mathcal{L}\{u''\}$, $\mathcal{L}\{u'\}$, and $\mathcal{L}\{v'\}$ in terms of $U = \mathcal{L}\{u\}$ and $V = \mathcal{L}\{v\}$ (see formula (4) on page 362 of the text, we obtain

$$[sU(s)] + U(s) - [sV(s) - 1] = 2\mathcal{L}\{te^t\}(s) = \frac{2}{(s-1)^2},$$

$$\left[s^2U(s) - 1\right] - [sU(s)] - 2V(s) = -\frac{1}{s-1}.$$

We multiply the first equation by 2, the second equation by $s$, and subtract the resulting equations in order to eliminate $V(s)$. Thus we get

$$\left[s(s^2 - s) - 2(s + 1)\right]U(s) = s - \frac{s}{s-1} - \frac{4}{(s-1)^2} + 2$$

$$\Rightarrow \quad \left(s^3 - s^2 - 2s - 2\right)U(s) = \frac{s^3 - s^2 - 2s - 2}{(s-1)^2} \quad \Rightarrow \quad U(s) = \frac{1}{(s-1)^2}.$$

The inverse Laplace transform then yields

$$u(t) = \mathcal{L}^{-1}\left\{\frac{1}{(s-1)^2}\right\}(t) = te^t \quad \Rightarrow \quad x(t) = u(t-2) = (t-2)e^{t-2}.$$

We find $y(t)$ from the second equation in the original system.

$$y(t) = \frac{x''(t) - x'(t) + e^{t-2}}{2} = \frac{te^{t-2} - (t-1)e^{t-2} + e^{t-2}}{2} = e^{t-2}.$$

**19.** We first take the Laplace transform of both sides of all three of these equations and use the initial conditions to obtain a system of equations for the Laplace transforms of the solution functions:

$$sX(s) + 6 = 3X(s) + Y(s) - 2Z(s),$$
$$sY(s) - 2 = -X(s) + 2Y(s) + Z(s),$$
$$sZ(s) + 12 = 4X(s) + Y(s) - 3Z(s).$$

Simplifying yields

$$(s-3)X(s) - Y(s) + 2Z(s) = -6,$$
$$X(s) + (s-2)Y(s) - Z(s) = 2, \qquad (7.60)$$
$$-4X(s) - Y(s) + (s+3)Z(s) = -12.$$

To solve this system, we will use substitution to eliminate the function $Y(s)$. Therefore, we solve for $Y(s)$ in the first equation in (7.60) to obtain

$$Y(s) = (s-3)X(s) + 2Z(s) + 6.$$

Substituting this expression into the two remaining equations in (7.60) and simplifying yields

$$(s^2 - 5s + 7)X(s) + (2s - 5)Z(s) = -6s + 14,$$
$$-(s+1)X(s) + (s+1)Z(s) = -6. \qquad (7.61)$$

Next we will eliminate the function $X(s)$ from the system given in (7.61). To do this we can either multiply the first equation by $(s+1)$ and the second by $(s^2 - 5s + 7)$ and add, or we can solve the last equation given in (7.61) for $X(s)$ to obtain

$$X(s) = Z(s) + \frac{6}{s+1}, \qquad (7.62)$$

and substitute this into the first equation in (7.61). By either method we see that

$$Z(s) = \frac{-12s^2 + 38s - 28}{(s+1)(s^2 - 3s + 2)} = \frac{-12s^2 + 38s - 28}{(s+1)(s-2)(s-1)}.$$

Now, $Z(s)$ has the partial fraction expansion

$$Z(s) = \frac{-13}{s+1} + \frac{1}{s-1}.$$

Therefore, by taking inverse Laplace transforms of both sides of this equation, we obtain

$$z(t) = \mathcal{L}^{-1}\{Z(s)\}(t) = \mathcal{L}^{-1}\left\{\frac{-13}{s+1} + \frac{1}{s-1}\right\}(t) = -13e^{-t} + e^t.$$

To find $X(s)$, we will use equation (7.62) and the expression found above for $Z(s)$. Thus, we have

$$X(s) = Z(s) + \frac{6}{s+1} = \frac{-13}{s+1} + \frac{1}{s-1} + \frac{6}{s+1} = \frac{-7}{s+1} + \frac{1}{s-1}$$

$$\Rightarrow \quad x(t) = \mathcal{L}^{-1}\{X(s)\}(t) = \mathcal{L}^{-1}\left\{\frac{-7}{s+1} + \frac{1}{s-1}\right\}(t) = -7e^{-t} + e^t.$$

To find $y(t)$, we could substitute the expressions that we have already found for $X(s)$ and $Z(s)$ into the $Y(s) = (s-3)X(s) + 2Z(s) + 6$, which we found above, or we could return to the original system of differential equations and use $x(t)$ and $z(t)$ to solve for $y(t)$. For the latter method, we solve the first equation in the original system for $y(t)$ to obtain

$$\begin{aligned} y(t) &= x'(t) - 3x(t) + 2z(t) \\ &= 7e^{-t} + e^t + 21e^{-t} - 3e^t - 26e^{-t} + 2e^t = 2e^{-t}. \end{aligned}$$

Therefore, the solution to the initial value problem is

$$x(t) = -7e^{-t} + e^t, \qquad y(t) = 2e^{-t}, \qquad z(t) = -13e^{-t} + e^t.$$

**21.** We refer the reader to the discussion in Section 5.1 in obtaining the system (1) on page 242 of the text governing interconnected tanks. All the arguments provided remain in force except for the one affected by the new "valve condition", which the formula for the input rate for the tank A. In Section 5.1, just fresh water was pumped into the tank A and so there was no salt coming from outside of the system into the tank A . Now we have more complicated rule: the incoming liquid is fresh water for the first 5 min, but then it changes to a solution having a concentration 2 kg/L. This solution contributes additional

$$2\,(\text{kg/L}) \times 6\,(\text{L/min}) = 12\,(\text{kg/min})$$

to the input rate into the tank A. Thus, from the valve, we have

$$\begin{cases} 0, & t < 5, \\ 12, & t > 5 \end{cases} = 12u(t-5)\,(\text{kg/min})$$

of salt coming to the tank A. With this change, the system (1) in the text becomes

$$\begin{aligned} x' &= -x/3 + y/12 + 12u(t-5), \\ y' &= x/3 - y/3. \end{aligned} \tag{7.63}$$

Also, we have the initial conditions $x(0) = x_0 = 0$, $y(0) = y_0 = 4$. Let $X := \mathcal{L}\{x\}$ and $Y := \mathcal{L}\{y\}$. Taking the Laplace transform of both equations in the system above, we get

$$\mathcal{L}\{x'\}(s) = -\frac{1}{3}X(s) + \frac{1}{12}Y(s) + 12\mathcal{L}\{u(t-5)\}(s),$$

$$\mathcal{L}\{y'\}(s) = \frac{1}{3}X(s) - \frac{1}{3}Y(s).$$

Since $\mathcal{L}\{u(t-5)\}(s) = e^{-5s}/s$ and

$$\mathcal{L}\{x'\}(s) = sX(s) - x(0) = sX(s),$$

$$\mathcal{L}\{y'\}(s) = sY(s) - y(0) = sY(s) - 4,$$

we obtain

$$sX(s) = -\frac{1}{3}X(s) + \frac{1}{12}Y(s) + \frac{12e^{-5s}}{s},$$

$$sY(s) - 4 = \frac{1}{3}X(s) - \frac{1}{3}Y(s)$$

which simplifies to

$$4(3s+1)X(s) - Y(s) = \frac{144e^{-5s}}{s},$$

$$-X(s) + (3s+1)Y(s) = 12.$$

From the second equation in this system, we have $X(s) = (3s+1)Y(s) - 12$. Substitution into the first equation yields

$$4(3s+1)\left[(3s+1)Y(s) - 12\right] - Y(s) = \frac{144e^{-5s}}{s}$$

$$\Rightarrow \quad \left[4(3s+1)^2 - 1\right]Y(s) = 48(3s+1) + \frac{144e^{-5s}}{s}.$$

Note that

$$4(3s+1)^2 - 1 = \left[2(3s+1) + 1\right] \cdot \left[2(3s+1) - 1\right] = (6s+3)(6s+1) = 36\left(s + \frac{1}{2}\right)\left(s + \frac{1}{6}\right).$$

Therefore,

$$
\begin{aligned}
Y(s) &= \frac{4(3s+1)}{3(s+1/2)(s+1/6)} + \frac{4e^{-5s}}{s(s+1/2)(s+1/6)} \\
&= \frac{2}{(s+1/2)} + \frac{2}{(s+1/6)} + e^{-5s}\left[\frac{48}{s} + \frac{24}{s+1/2} - \frac{72}{s+1/6}\right],
\end{aligned}
$$

where we have applied the partial fractions decomposition. Taking the inverse Laplace transform and using Theorem 8 in Section 7.6 for the inverse Laplace transform of the term having the exponential factor, we get

$$
\begin{aligned}
y(t) &= 2\mathcal{L}^{-1}\left\{\frac{1}{(s+1/2)}\right\}(t) + 2\mathcal{L}^{-1}\left\{\frac{1}{(s+1/6)}\right\}(t) \\
&\quad + \left[48\mathcal{L}^{-1}\left\{\frac{1}{s}\right\} + 24\mathcal{L}^{-1}\left\{\frac{1}{s+1/2}\right\} - 72\mathcal{L}^{-1}\left\{\frac{1}{s+1/6}\right\}\right](t-5)u(t-5) \\
&= 2e^{-t/2} + 2e^{-t/6} + \left[48 + 24e^{-(t-5)/2} - 72e^{-(t-5)/6}\right]u(t-5).
\end{aligned}
$$

From the second equation in (7.63), after some algebra, we find $x(t)$.

$$x(t) = 3y'(t) + y = -e^{-t/2} + e^{-t/6} + \left[48 - 12e^{-(t-5)/2} - 36e^{-(t-5)/6}\right]u(t-5).$$

**23.** Recall that Kirchhoff's voltage law says that, in an electrical circuit consisting of an inductor of $L\,$H, a resistor of $R\,\Omega$, a capacitor of $C\,$F, and a voltage source of $E\,$V,

$$E_L + E_R + E_C = E, \tag{7.64}$$

where $E_L$, $E_R$, and $E_C$ denote the voltage drops across the inductor, resistor, and capacitor, respectively. These voltage grops are given by

$$E_L = L\frac{dI}{dt}, \qquad E_R := RI, \qquad E_C := \frac{q}{C}, \qquad (7.65)$$

where $I$ denotes the current passing through the correspondent element.

Also, Kirchhoff's current law states that the algebraic sum of currents passing through any point in an electrical network equals to zero.

The electrical network shown in Figure 7.28 consists of three closed circuits: loop 1 through the battery, $R_1 = 2\,\Omega$ resistor, $L_1 = 0.1\,\mathrm{H}$ inductor, and $L_2 = 0.2\,\mathrm{H}$ inductor; loop 2 through the inductor $L_1$ and $R_2 = 1\,\Omega$ resistor; loop 3 through the battery, resistors $R_1$ and $R_2$, and inductor $L_2$. We apply Kirchhoff's voltage law (7.64) to two of these loops, say, the loop 1 and the loop 2, and (since the equation obtained from Kirchhoff's voltage law for the third loop is a linear combination of the other two) Kirchhoff's current law to one of the junction points, say, the upper one. Thus, choosing the clockwise direction in the loops and using formulas (7.65), we obtain

Loop 1:

$$E_{R_1} + E_{L_1} + E_{L_2} = E \qquad \Rightarrow \qquad 2I_1 + 0.1I_3' + 0.2I_1' = 6;$$

Loop 2:

$$E_{L_1} + E_{R_2} = 0 \qquad \Rightarrow \qquad 0.1I_3' - I_2 = 0$$

with the negative sign due to the counterclockwise direction of the current $I_2$ in this loop;

Upper junction point:

$$I_1 - I_2 - I_3 = 0.$$

Therefore, we have the following system for the currents $I_1$, $I_2$, and $I_3$:

$$\begin{aligned} 2I_1 + 0.1I_3' + 0.2I_1' &= 6, \\ 0.1I_3' - I_2 &= 0, \\ I_1 - I_2 - I_3 &= 0 \end{aligned} \qquad (7.66)$$

479

with initial conditions $I_1(0) = I_2(0) = I_3(0) = 0$.

Let $\mathbf{I}_1(s) := \mathcal{L}\{I_1\}(s)$, $\mathbf{I}_2(s) := \mathcal{L}\{I_2\}(s)$, and $\mathbf{I}_3(s) := \mathcal{L}\{I_3\}(s)$. Using the initial conditions, we conclude that

$$\mathcal{L}\{I_1'\}(s) = s\mathbf{I}_1(s) - I_1(0) = s\mathbf{I}_1(s),$$
$$\mathcal{L}\{I_3'\}(s) = s\mathbf{I}_3(s) - I_3(0) = s\mathbf{I}_3(s).$$

Using these equations and taking the Laplace transform of the equations in (7.66), we come up with

$$(0.2s + 2)\mathbf{I}_1(s) + 0.1s\mathbf{I}_3(s) = \frac{6}{s},$$
$$0.1s\mathbf{I}_3(s) - \mathbf{I}_2(s) = 0,$$
$$\mathbf{I}_1(s) - \mathbf{I}_2(s) - \mathbf{I}_3(s) = 0$$

Expressing $\mathbf{I}_2(s) = 0.1s\mathbf{I}_3(s)$ from the second equation and substituting this into the third equation, we get

$$\mathbf{I}_1(s) - 0.1s\mathbf{I}_3(s) - \mathbf{I}_3(s) = 0 \qquad \Rightarrow \qquad \mathbf{I}_1(s) = (0.1s + 1)\mathbf{I}_3(s).$$

The latter, when substituted into the first equation, yields

$$(0.2s + 2)(0.1s + 1)\mathbf{I}_3(s) + 0.1s\mathbf{I}_3(s) = \frac{6}{s}$$

$$\Rightarrow \qquad \left[2(0.1s + 1)^2 + 0.1s\right]\mathbf{I}_3(s) = \frac{6}{s}$$

$$\Rightarrow \qquad \mathbf{I}_3(s) = \frac{6}{s[2(0.1s + 1)^2 + 0.1s]} = \frac{300}{s(s + 20)(s + 5)}.$$

We use the partial fractions decomposition to find that

$$\mathbf{I}_3(s) = \frac{3}{s} + \frac{1}{s + 20} - \frac{4}{s + 5}$$

and so

$$I_3(t) = \mathcal{L}^{-1}\left\{\frac{3}{s} + \frac{1}{s + 20} - \frac{4}{s + 5}\right\}(t) = 3 + e^{-20t} - 4e^{-5t}.$$

Now we can find $I_2(t)$ using the second equation in (7.66).

$$I_2(t) = 0.1I_3'(t) = 0.1\left(3 + e^{-20t} - 4e^{-5t}\right)' = -2e^{-20t} + 2e^{-5t}.$$

Finally, the third equation in (7.66) yields

$$I_1(t) = I_2(t) + I_3(t) = 3 - e^{-20t} - 2e^{-5t}.$$

## REVIEW PROBLEMS:   page 418

**1.** By the definition of Laplace transform,

$$\mathcal{L}\left\{f\right\}(s) = \int_0^\infty e^{-st} f(t)\, dt = \int_0^2 e^{-st}(3)\, dt + \int_2^\infty e^{-st}(6-t)\, dt.$$

For the first integral, we have

$$\int_0^2 e^{-st}(3)\, dt = \left.\frac{3e^{-st}}{-s}\right|_{t=0}^{t=2} = \frac{3(1-e^{-2s})}{s}.$$

The second integral is an improper integral. Using integration by parts, we obtain

$$
\begin{aligned}
\int_2^\infty e^{-st}(6-t)\, dt &= \lim_{M\to\infty} \int_2^M e^{-st}(6-t)\, dt = \lim_{M\to\infty}\left[ \left.(6-t)\frac{e^{-st}}{-s}\right|_{t=2}^{t=M} - \int_2^M \frac{e^{-st}}{-s}(-1)dt\right] \\
&= \lim_{M\to\infty}\left[ \frac{4e^{-2s}}{s} - \frac{(6-M)e^{-sM}}{s} + \left.\frac{e^{-st}}{s^2}\right|_{t=2}^{t=M}\right] \\
&= \lim_{M\to\infty}\left[ \frac{4e^{-2s}}{s} - \frac{(6-M)e^{-sM}}{s} + \frac{e^{-sM}}{s^2} - \frac{e^{-2s}}{s^2}\right] = \frac{4e^{-2s}}{s} - \frac{e^{-2s}}{s^2}.
\end{aligned}
$$

Thus

$$\mathcal{L}\left\{f\right\}(s) = \frac{3(1-e^{-2s})}{s} + \frac{4e^{-2s}}{s} - \frac{e^{-2s}}{s^2} = \frac{3}{s} + e^{-2s}\left(\frac{1}{s} - \frac{1}{s^2}\right).$$

**3.** From Table 7.1 on page 358 of the text, using the formula for the Laplace transform of $e^{at}t^n$ with $n = 2$ and $a = -9$, we get

$$\mathcal{L}\left\{t^2 e^{-9t}\right\}(s) = \frac{2!}{[s-(-9)]^3} = \frac{2}{(s+9)^3}.$$

**5.** We use the linearity of the Laplace transform and Table 7.1 to obtain

$$
\begin{aligned}
\mathcal{L}\left\{e^{2t} - t^3 + t^2 - \sin 5t\right\}(s) &= \mathcal{L}\left\{e^{2t}\right\}(s) - \mathcal{L}\left\{t^3\right\}(s) + \mathcal{L}\left\{t^2\right\}(s) - \mathcal{L}\left\{\sin 5t\right\}(s) \\
&= \frac{1}{s-2} - \frac{3!}{s^4} + \frac{2!}{s^3} - \frac{5}{s^2+5^2} = \frac{1}{s-2} - \frac{6}{s^4} + \frac{2}{s^3} - \frac{5}{s^2+25}.
\end{aligned}
$$

# Chapter 7

**7.** We apply Theorem 6 in Section 7.3 and obtain

$$\mathcal{L}\left\{t\cos 6t\right\}(s) = -\frac{d}{ds}\mathcal{L}\left\{\cos 6t\right\}(s) = -\frac{d}{ds}\left[\frac{s}{s^2+6^2}\right] = -\frac{(s^2+36)-s(2s)}{(s^2+36)^2} = \frac{s^2-36}{(s^2+36)^2}.$$

**9.** We apply formula (8), Section 7.6, on page 387 of the text and the linear property of the Laplace transform to get

$$
\begin{aligned}
\mathcal{L}\left\{t^2 u(t-4)\right\}(s) &= e^{-4s}\mathcal{L}\left\{(t+4)^2\right\}(s) = e^{-4s}\mathcal{L}\left\{t^2+8s+16\right\}(s) \\
&= e^{-4s}\left(\frac{2}{s^3}+\frac{8}{s^2}+\frac{16}{s}\right) = 2e^{-4s}\left(\frac{1}{s^3}+\frac{4}{s^2}+\frac{8}{s}\right).
\end{aligned}
$$

**11.** Using the linearity of the inverse Laplace transform and Table 7.1 we find

$$\mathcal{L}^{-1}\left\{\frac{7}{(s+3)^3}\right\}(t) = \frac{7}{2!}\mathcal{L}^{-1}\left\{\frac{2!}{[s-(-3)]^3}\right\}(t) = \frac{7}{2}t^2 e^{-3t}.$$

**13.** We apply partial fractions to find the inverse Laplace transform. Since the quadratic polynomial $s^2+4s+13 = (s+2)^2+3^2$ is irreducible, the partial fraction decomposition for the given function has the form

$$\frac{4s^2+13s+19}{(s-1)(s^2+4s+13)} = \frac{A}{s-1} + \frac{B(s+2)+C(3)}{(s+2)^2+3^2}.$$

Clearing fractions yields

$$4s^2+13s+19 = A[(s+2)^2+3^2] + [B(s+2)+C(3)](s-1).$$

With $s=1$, this gives $36 = 18A$ or $A = 2$. Substituting $s = -2$, we get

$$9 = 9A - 9C \qquad \Rightarrow \qquad C = A - 1 = 1.$$

Finally, with $s = 0$, we compute

$$19 = 13A + (2B+3C)(-1) \qquad \Rightarrow \qquad B = 2.$$

Thus

$$\frac{4s^2+13s+19}{(s-1)(s^2+4s+13)} = \frac{2}{s-1} + \frac{2(s+2)+(1)(3)}{(s+2)^2+3^2},$$

and so

$$\mathcal{L}^{-1}\left\{\frac{4s^2+13s+19}{(s-1)(s^2+4s+13)}\right\}(t) = 2\mathcal{L}^{-1}\left\{\frac{1}{s-1}\right\}(t)+2\mathcal{L}^{-1}\left\{\frac{s+2}{(s+2)^2+3^2}\right\}(t)$$

$$+\mathcal{L}^{-1}\left\{\frac{3}{(s+2)^2+3^2}\right\}(t)$$

$$= 2e^t+2e^{-2t}\cos 3t+e^{-2t}\sin 3t.$$

**15.** The partial fraction decomposition for the given function has the form

$$\frac{2s^2+3s-1}{(s+1)^2(s+2)} = \frac{A}{(s+1)^2}+\frac{B}{s+1}+\frac{C}{s+2} = \frac{A(s+2)+B(s+1)(s+2)+C(s+1)^2}{(s+1)^2(s+2)}.$$

Thus

$$2s^2+3s-1 = A(s+2)+B(s+1)(s+2)+C(s+1)^2.$$

We evaluate both sides of this equation at $s=-2,-1$, and 0. This yields

$$s=-2: \quad 2(-2)^2+3(-2)-1 = C(-2+1)^2 \;\Rightarrow\; C=1,$$
$$s=-1: \quad 2(-1)^2+3(-1)-1 = A(-1+2) \;\Rightarrow\; A=-2,$$
$$s=0: \quad -1 = 2A+2B+C \;\Rightarrow\; B=(-1-2A-C)/2=1.$$

Therefore,

$$\mathcal{L}^{-1}\left\{\frac{2s^2+3s-1}{(s+1)^2(s+2)}\right\}(t)=\mathcal{L}^{-1}\left\{\frac{-2}{(s+1)^2}+\frac{1}{s+1}+\frac{1}{s+2}\right\}(t)=-2te^{-t}+e^{-t}+e^{-2t}.$$

**17.** First we apply Theorem 8 in Section 7.6 to get

$$\mathcal{L}^{-1}\left\{\frac{e^{-2s}(4s+2)}{(s-1)(s+2)}\right\}(t)=\mathcal{L}^{-1}\left\{\frac{4s+2}{(s-1)(s+2)}\right\}(t-2)u(t-2). \qquad (7.67)$$

Applying partial fractions yields

$$\frac{4s+2}{(s-1)(s+2)}=\frac{2}{s-1}+\frac{2}{s+2} \;\Rightarrow\; \mathcal{L}^{-1}\left\{\frac{4s+2}{(s-1)(s+2)}\right\}(t)=2e^t+2e^{-2t}.$$

Therefore, it follows from (7.67) that

$$\mathcal{L}^{-1}\left\{\frac{e^{-2s}(4s+2)}{(s-1)(s+2)}\right\}(t)=\left[2e^{t-2}+2e^{-2(t-2)}\right]u(t-2)=\left(2e^{t-2}+2e^{4-2t}\right)u(t-2).$$

# Chapter 7

**19.** Applying the Laplace transform to both sides of the given equation and using the linearity of the Laplace transform yields

$$\mathcal{L}\{y'' - 7y' + 10y\}(s) = \mathcal{L}\{y''\}(s) - 7\mathcal{L}\{y'\}(s) + 10\mathcal{L}\{y\}(s) = 0. \qquad (7.68)$$

By Theorem 5 in Section 7.3,

$$\mathcal{L}\{y'\}(s) = s\mathcal{L}\{y\}(s) - y(0) = s\mathcal{L}\{y\}(s),$$
$$\mathcal{L}\{y''\}(s) = s^2\mathcal{L}\{y\}(s) - sy(0) - y'(0) = s^2\mathcal{L}\{y\}(s) + 3,$$

where we have used the initial conditions, $y(0) = 0$ and $y'(0) = -3$. Substituting these expressions into (7.68), we get

$$\left[s^2\mathcal{L}\{y\}(s) + 3\right] - 7\left[s\mathcal{L}\{y\}(s)\right] + 10\mathcal{L}\{y\}(s) = 0$$
$$\Rightarrow \quad (s^2 - 7s + 10)\mathcal{L}\{y\}(s) + 3 = 0$$
$$\Rightarrow \quad \mathcal{L}\{y\}(s) = \frac{-3}{s^2 - 7s + 10} = \frac{-3}{(s-2)(s-5)} = \frac{1}{s-2} - \frac{1}{s-5}.$$

Thus

$$y(t) = \mathcal{L}^{-1}\left\{\frac{1}{s-2} - \frac{1}{s-5}\right\}(t) = \mathcal{L}^{-1}\left\{\frac{1}{s-2}\right\}(t) - \mathcal{L}^{-1}\left\{\frac{1}{s-5}\right\}(t) = e^{2t} - e^{5t}.$$

**21.** Let $Y(s) := \mathcal{L}\{y\}(s)$. Taking the Laplace transform of the given equation and using properties of the Laplace transform, we obtain

$$\mathcal{L}\{y'' + 2y' + 2y\}(s) = \mathcal{L}\{t^2 + 4t\}(s) = \frac{2}{s^3} + \frac{4}{s^2} = \frac{2 + 4s}{s^3}.$$

Since

$$\mathcal{L}\{y'\}(s) = sY(s) - y(0) = sY(s), \qquad \mathcal{L}\{y''\}(s) = s^2Y(s) - sy(0) - y'(0) = s^2Y(s) + 1,$$

we have

$$\left[s^2Y(s) + 1\right] + 2\left[sY(s)\right] + 2Y(s) = \frac{2 + 4s}{s^3}$$
$$\Rightarrow \quad (s^2 + 2s + 2)Y(s) = \frac{2 + 4s}{s^3} - 1 = \frac{2 + 4s - s^3}{s^3}.$$

$$\Rightarrow \qquad Y(s) = \frac{2 + 4s - s^3}{s^3(s^2 + 2s + 2)} = \frac{2 + 4s - s^3}{s^3[(s+1)^2 + 1^2]}.$$

The partial fraction decomposition for $Y(s)$ has the form

$$\frac{2 + 4s - s^3}{s^3[(s+1)^2 + 1^2]} = \frac{A}{s^3} + \frac{B}{s^2} + \frac{C}{s} + \frac{D(s+1) + E(1)}{(s+1)^2 + 1^2}.$$

Clearing fractions, we obtain

$$2 + 4s - s^3 = A[(s+1)^2 + 1] + Bs[(s+1)^2 + 1] + Cs^2[(s+1)^2 + 1] + [D(s+1) + E]s^3.$$

Comparing coefficients at the corresponding power of $s$ in both sides of this equation yields

$$
\begin{aligned}
s^0: \quad & 2 = 2A & \Rightarrow \quad & A = 1, \\
s^1: \quad & 4 = 2A + 2B & \Rightarrow \quad & B = (4 - 2A)/2 = 1, \\
s^2: \quad & 0 = A + 2B + 2C & \Rightarrow \quad & C = -(A + 2B)/2 = -3/2, \\
s^4: \quad & 0 = C + D & \Rightarrow \quad & D = -C = 3/2, \\
s^3: \quad & -1 = B + 2C + D + E & \Rightarrow \quad & E = -1 - B - 2C - D = -1/2.
\end{aligned}
$$

Therefore,

$$Y(s) = \frac{1}{s^3} + \frac{1}{s^2} - \frac{3/2}{s} + \frac{(3/2)(s+1)}{(s+1)^2 + 1^2} - \frac{(1/2)(1)}{(s+1)^2 + 1^2}$$

$$\Rightarrow \qquad y(t) = \mathcal{L}^{-1}\{Y(s)\}(t) = \frac{t^2}{2} + t - \frac{3}{2} + \frac{3}{2}e^{-t}\cos t - \frac{1}{2}e^{-t}\sin t.$$

**23.** By formula (4) in Section 7.6,

$$\mathcal{L}\{u(t - 1)\}(s) = \frac{e^{-s}}{s}.$$

Thus, applying the Laplace transform to both sides of the given equation and using the initial conditions, we get

$$\mathcal{L}\{y'' + 3y' + 4y\}(s) = \frac{e^{-s}}{s}$$

$$\Rightarrow \qquad [s^2 Y(s) - 1] + 3[sY(s)] + 4Y(s) = \frac{e^{-s}}{s}$$

$$\Rightarrow \qquad Y(s) = \frac{1}{s^2 + 3s + 4} + \frac{e^{-s}}{s(s^2 + 3s + 4)}$$

# Chapter 7

$$\Rightarrow \qquad Y(s) = \frac{1}{(s+3/2)^2 + (\sqrt{7}/2)^2} + e^{-s}\frac{1}{s[(s+3/2)^2 + (\sqrt{7}/2)^2]},$$

where $Y(s) := \mathcal{L}\{y\}(s)$. To apply the inverse Laplace transform, we need the partial fraction decomposition of the last fraction above.

$$\frac{1}{s[(s+3/2)^2 + (\sqrt{7}/2)^2]} = \frac{A}{s} + \frac{B(s+3/2) + C(\sqrt{7}/2)}{(s+3/2)^2 + (\sqrt{7}/2)^2}.$$

Solving for $A$, $B$, and $C$ yields

$$A = \frac{1}{4}, \qquad B = -\frac{1}{4}, \qquad C = -\frac{3}{4\sqrt{7}}.$$

Therefore,

$$Y(s) = \frac{1}{(s+3/2)^2 + (\sqrt{7}/2)^2} + e^{-s}\left[\frac{1/4}{s} - \frac{(1/4)(s+3/2)}{(s+3/2)^2 + (\sqrt{7}/2)^2} - \frac{(3/4\sqrt{7})(\sqrt{7}/2)}{(s+3/2)^2 + (\sqrt{7}/2)^2}\right]$$

and the inverse Laplace transform gives

$$
\begin{aligned}
y(t) &= \mathcal{L}^{-1}\left\{\frac{1}{(s+3/2)^2 + (\sqrt{7}/2)^2}\right\}(t) \\
&\quad + \mathcal{L}^{-1}\left\{\frac{1/4}{s} - \frac{(1/4)(s+3/2)}{(s+3/2)^2 + (7/4)} - \frac{(3/4\sqrt{7})(\sqrt{7}/2)}{(s+3/2)^2 + (7/4)}\right\}(t-1)u(t-1) \\
&= \frac{2}{\sqrt{7}}e^{-3t/2}\sin\left(\frac{\sqrt{7}t}{2}\right) \\
&\quad + \left[\frac{1}{4} - \frac{1}{4}e^{-3(t-1)/2}\cos\left(\frac{\sqrt{7}(t-1)}{2}\right) - \frac{3}{4\sqrt{7}}e^{-3(t-1)/2}\sin\left(\frac{\sqrt{7}(t-1)}{2}\right)\right]u(t-1).
\end{aligned}
$$

**25.** Let $Y(s) := \mathcal{L}\{y\}(s)$. Then, from the initial conditions, we have

$$\mathcal{L}\{y'\}(s) = sY(s) - y(0) = sY(s), \qquad \mathcal{L}\{y''\}(s) = s^2Y(s) - sy(0) - y'(0) = s^2Y(s).$$

Moreover, Theorem 6 in Section 7.3 yields

$$\mathcal{L}\{ty'\}(s) = -\frac{d}{ds}\mathcal{L}\{y'\}(s) = -\frac{d}{ds}[sY(s)] = -sY'(s) - Y(s),$$

$$\mathcal{L}\{ty''\}(s) = -\frac{d}{ds}\mathcal{L}\{y''\}(s) = -\frac{d}{ds}[s^2Y(s)] = -s^2Y'(s) - 2sY(s).$$

486

Hence, applying the Laplace transform to the given equation and using the linearity of the Laplace transform, we obtain

$$\mathcal{L}\{ty'' + 2(t-1)y' - 2y\}(s) = \mathcal{L}\{ty''\}(s) + 2\mathcal{L}\{ty'\}(s) - 2\mathcal{L}\{y'\}(s) - 2\mathcal{L}\{y\}(s) = 0$$
$$\Rightarrow \quad [-s^2Y'(s) - 2sY(s)] + 2[-sY'(s) - Y(s)] - 2[sY(s)] - 2Y(s) = 0$$
$$\Rightarrow \quad -s(s+2)Y'(s) - 4(s+1)Y(s) = 0 \quad \Rightarrow \quad Y'(s) + \frac{4(s+1)}{s(s+2)}Y(s) = 0.$$

Separating variables and integrating yields

$$\frac{dY}{Y} = -\frac{4(s+1)}{s(s+2)}\,ds = -2\left(\frac{1}{s} + \frac{1}{s+2}\right)ds$$
$$\Rightarrow \quad \ln|Y| = -2(\ln|s| + \ln|s+2|) + C$$
$$\Rightarrow \quad Y(s) = \pm\frac{e^C}{s^2(s+2)^2} = \frac{c_1}{s^2(s+2)^2},$$

where $c_1 \neq 0$ is an arbitrary constant. Allowing $c_1 = 0$, we also get the solution $Y(s) \equiv 0$, which was lost in separation of variables. Thus

$$Y(s) = \frac{c_1}{s^2(s+2)^2} = \frac{c_1}{4}\left[\frac{1}{s^2} - \frac{1}{s} + \frac{1}{(s+2)^2} + \frac{1}{s+2}\right]$$

and so

$$y(t) = \mathcal{L}^{-1}\{Y(s)\}(t) = \frac{c_1}{4}\left(t - 1 + te^{-2t} + e^{-2t}\right) = c\left(t - 1 + te^{-2t} + e^{-2t}\right),$$

where $c = c_1/4$ is an arbitrary constant.

**27.** Note that the original equation can be written in the form

$$y(t) + t * y(t) = e^{-3t}.$$

Let $Y(s) := \mathcal{L}\{y\}(s)$. Applying the Laplace transform to both sides of this equation and using Theorem 11 in Section 7.7, we obtain

$$\mathcal{L}\{y(t) + t * y(t)\}(s) = Y(s) + \mathcal{L}\{t\}(s)Y(s) = \mathcal{L}\{e^{-3t}\}(s)$$
$$\Rightarrow \quad Y(s) + \frac{1}{s^2}Y(s) = \frac{1}{s+3} \quad \Rightarrow \quad Y(s) = \frac{s^2}{(s+3)(s^2+1)}.$$

The partial fraction decomposition for $Y(s)$ has the form

$$\frac{s^2}{(s+3)(s^2+1)} = \frac{A}{s+3} + \frac{Bs+C}{s^2+1} = \frac{A(s^2+1)+(Bs+C)(s+3)}{(s+3)(s^2+1)}.$$

Thus

$$s^2 = A(s^2+1)+(Bs+C)(s+3).$$

Evaluating both sides of this equation at $s = -3$, $0$, and $-2$ yields

$$\begin{array}{llll}
s = -3: & \Rightarrow & 9 = A(10) & \Rightarrow & A = 9/10, \\
s = 0: & \Rightarrow & 0 = A + 3C & \Rightarrow & C = -A/3 = -3/10, \\
s = -2: & \Rightarrow & 4 = 5A - 2B + C & \Rightarrow & B = (5A + C - 4)/2 = 1/10.
\end{array}$$

Therefore,

$$Y(s) = \frac{9/10}{s+3} + \frac{(1/10)s}{s^2+1} - \frac{3/10}{s^2+1}$$

$$\Rightarrow \quad y(t) = \mathcal{L}^{-1}\{Y(s)\}(t) = \frac{9}{10}e^{-3t} + \frac{1}{10}\cos t - \frac{3}{10}\sin t.$$

**29.** To find the transfer function, we use formula (15) on page 403 of the text. Comparing given equation with (14), we find that $a = 1$, $b = -5$, and $c = 6$. Thus (15) yields

$$H(s) = \frac{1}{as^2 + bs + c} = \frac{1}{s^2 - 5s + 6}.$$

The impulse response function $h(t)$ is defined as $\mathcal{L}^{-1}\{H\}(t)$. Using partial fractions, we see that

$$H(s) = \frac{1}{s^2 - 5s + 6} = \frac{1}{(s-3)(s-2)} = \frac{1}{s-3} - \frac{1}{s-2}$$

$$\Rightarrow \quad h(t) = \mathcal{L}^{-1}\left\{\frac{1}{s-3} - \frac{1}{s-2}\right\}(t) = e^{3t} - e^{2t}.$$

**31.** Let $X(s) := \mathcal{L}\{x\}(s)$, $Y(s) := \mathcal{L}\{y\}(s)$. Using the initial condition, we obtain

$$\mathcal{L}\{x'\}(s) = sX(s) - x(0) = sX(s), \qquad \mathcal{L}\{y'\}(s) = sY(s) - y(0) = sY(s).$$

Therefore, applying the Laplace transform to both sides of the equations in the given system yields

$$sX(s) + Y(s) = \mathcal{L}\{0\}(s) = 0,$$

$$X(s) + sY(s) = \mathcal{L}\{1 - u(t-2)\}(s) = \frac{1}{s} - \frac{e^{-2s}}{s} = \frac{1 - e^{-2s}}{s}.$$

Expressing $Y(s) = -sX(s)$ from the first equation and substituting this into the second equation, we eliminate $Y(s)$:

$$X(s) - s^2 X(s) = \frac{1 - e^{-2s}}{s}$$

$$\Rightarrow \quad X(s) = -\frac{1 - e^{-2s}}{s(s^2 - 1)} = -\frac{1 - e^{-2s}}{s(s-1)(s+1)}.$$

Since

$$-\frac{1}{s(s-1)(s+1)} = \frac{1}{s} - \frac{1/2}{s-1} - \frac{1/2}{s+1},$$

the inverse Laplace transform yields

$$
\begin{aligned}
x(t) &= \mathcal{L}^{-1}\left\{ (1 - e^{-2s}) \left( \frac{1}{s} - \frac{1/2}{s-1} - \frac{1/2}{s+1} \right) \right\}(t) \\
&= \mathcal{L}^{-1}\left\{ \frac{1}{s} - \frac{1/2}{s-1} - \frac{1/2}{s+1} \right\}(t) - \mathcal{L}^{-1}\left\{ \frac{1}{s} - \frac{1/2}{s-1} - \frac{1/2}{s+1} \right\}(t-2)u(t-2) \\
&= 1 - \frac{e^t + e^{-t}}{2} - \left[ 1 - \frac{e^{t-2} + e^{-(t-2)}}{2} \right] u(t-2).
\end{aligned}
$$

We now find $y(t)$ from the first equation in the original system.

$$y(t) = -x'(t) = \frac{e^t - e^{-t}}{2} - \frac{e^{t-2} - e^{-(t-2)}}{2} u(t-2).$$

# CHAPTER 8: Series Solutions of Differential Equations

**EXERCISES 8.1:   Introduction: The Taylor Polynomial Approximation, page 430**

1. To find Taylor approximations

$$y(0) + \frac{y'(0)}{1!}\,x + \frac{y''(0)}{2!}\,x^2 + \frac{y''(0)}{3!}\,x^3 + \cdots,$$

   we need the values of $y(0)$, $y'(0)$, $y''(0)$, etc. $y(0)$ is provided by the initial condition, $y(0) = 1$. Substituting $x = 0$ into the given differential equation,

$$y'(x) = x^2 + y(x)^2, \tag{8.1}$$

   we obtain

$$y'(0) = 0^2 + y(0)^2 = 0 + 1^2 = 1.$$

   Differentiating both sides of (8.1) yields

$$y''(x) = 2x + 2y(x)y'(x),$$

   and so

$$y''(0) = 2(0) + 2y(0)y'(0) = 0 + 2(1)(1) = 2.$$

   Hence

$$y(x) = 1 + \frac{1}{1!}\,x + \frac{2}{2!}\,x^2 + \cdots = 1 + x + x^2 + \cdots.$$

3. Using the initial condition, $y(0) = 0$ we substitute $x = 0$ and $y = 0$ into the given equation and find $y'(0)$.

$$y'(0) = \sin(0) + e^0 = 1.$$

To determine $y''(0)$, we differentiate the given equation with respect to $x$ and substitute $x = 0$, $y = 0$, and $y' = 1$ in the formula obtained:

$$y''(0) = (\sin y + e^x)' = (\sin y)' + (e^x)' = y' \cos y + e^x,$$

$$y''(0) = 1 \cdot \cos 0 + e^0 = 2.$$

Similarly, differentiating $y''(x)$ and substituting, we obtain

$$y''' = (y' \cos y + e^x)' = (y' \cos y)' + (e^x)' = y'' \cos y + (y')^2 (-\sin y) + e^x,$$

$$y'''(0) = y''(0) \cos 0 + (y'(0))^2 (-\sin y(0)) + e^0 = 2 \cos 0 + (1)^2 (-\sin 0) + 1 = 3.$$

Thus the first three nonzero terms in the Taylor polynomial approximations to the solution of the given initial value problem are

$$\begin{aligned} y(x) &= y(0) + \frac{y'(0)}{1!} x + \frac{y''(0)}{2!} x^2 + \frac{y'''(0)}{3!} x^3 + \cdots \\ &= 0 + \frac{1}{1} x + \frac{2}{2} x^2 + \frac{3}{6} x^3 + \cdots = x + x^2 + \frac{1}{2} x^3 + \cdots . \end{aligned}$$

5. We need the values of $x(0)$, $x'(0)$, $x''(0)$, etc. The first two are given by the initial conditions:

$$x(0) = 1, \qquad x'(0) = 0.$$

Writing the given equation in the form

$$x''(t) = -tx(t) \tag{8.2}$$

we find that

$$x''(0) = -0 \cdot x(0) = -0 \cdot 1 = 0.$$

Differentiating (8.2) and substituting $t = 0$ we conclude that

$$\begin{aligned} x'''(t) &= -\left[tx'(t) + x(t)\right] & \Rightarrow && x'''(0) &= -\left[0 \cdot x'(0) + x(0)\right] = -1, \\ x^{(4)}(t) &= -\left[tx''(t) + 2x'(t)\right] & \Rightarrow && x^{(4)}(0) &= -\left[0 \cdot x''(0) + 2x'(0)\right] = 0, \\ x^{(5)}(t) &= -\left[tx'''(t) + 3x''(t)\right] & \Rightarrow && x^{(5)}(0) &= -\left[0 \cdot x'''(0) + 3x''(0)\right] = 0, \\ x^{(6)}(t) &= -\left[tx^{(4)}(t) + 4x'''(t)\right] & \Rightarrow && x^{(6)}(0) &= -\left[0 \cdot x^{(4)}(0) + 4x'''(0)\right] = 4. \end{aligned}$$

Therefore,

$$x(t) = 1 - \frac{1}{3!} t^3 + \frac{4}{6!} t^6 + \cdots = 1 - \frac{t^3}{6} + \frac{t^6}{180} + \cdots .$$

**7.** We use the initial conditions to find $y''(0)$. Writing the given equation in the form

$$y''(\theta) = -y(\theta)^3 + \sin\theta$$

and substituting $\theta = 0$, $y(0) = 0$ we get

$$y''(0) = -y(0)^3 + \sin 0 = 0.$$

Differentiating the given equation we obtain

$$y''' = (y'')' = -\left(y^3\right)' + (\sin\theta)' = -3y^2y' + \cos\theta$$

$$\Rightarrow \quad y'''(0) = -3y(0)^2y'(0) + \cos 0 = -3(0)^2(0) + 1 = 1.$$

Similarly, we get

$$y^{(4)} = (y''')' = -3y^2y'' - 6y\left(y'\right)^2 - \sin\theta$$

$$\Rightarrow \quad y^{(4)}(0) = -3y(0)^2y''(0) - 6y(0)\left(y'(0)\right)^2 - \sin 0 = 0.$$

To simplify further computations we observe that since the Taylor expansion for $y(\theta)$ has the form

$$y(\theta) = \frac{1}{3!}\,\theta^3 + \cdots ,$$

then the Taylor expansion for $y(\theta)^3$ must begin with the term $(1/3!)^3\theta^9$, so that

$$\left.\left(y(\theta)^3\right)^{(k)}\right|_{\theta=0} = 0 \quad\text{for}\quad k = 0, 1, \ldots, 8\,.$$

Hence

$$y^{(5)} = -\left(y^3\right)^{(3)} - \cos\theta \quad\Rightarrow\quad y^{(5)}(0) = -\left.\left(y^3\right)^{(3)}\right|_{\theta=0} - \cos 0 = -1,$$

$$y^{(6)} = -\left(y^3\right)^{(4)} + \sin\theta \quad\Rightarrow\quad y^{(6)}(0) = -\left.\left(y^3\right)^{(4)}\right|_{\theta=0} - \sin 0 = 0,$$

$$y^{(7)} = -\left(y^3\right)^{(5)} + \cos\theta \quad\Rightarrow\quad y^{(7)}(0) = -\left.\left(y^3\right)^{(5)}\right|_{\theta=0} + \cos 0 = 1.$$

Thus, the first three nonzero terms of the Taylor approximations are

$$y(\theta) = \frac{1}{3!}\,\theta^3 - \frac{1}{5!}\,\theta^5 + \frac{1}{7!}\,\theta^7 + \cdots = \frac{1}{6}\,\theta^3 - \frac{1}{120}\,\theta^5 + \frac{1}{5040}\,\theta^7 + \cdots$$

# Chapter 8

**9. (a)** To construct $p_3(x)$ we need $f(1)$, $f'(1)$, $f''(1)$, and $f'''(1)$. Thus we have

$$
\begin{aligned}
f(x) &= \ln x & \Rightarrow & \quad f(1) = \ln 1 = 0, \\
f'(x) &= x^{-1} & \Rightarrow & \quad f'(1) = (1)^{-1} = 1, \\
f''(x) &= -x^{-2} & \Rightarrow & \quad f''(1) = -(1)^{-2} = -1, \\
f'''(x) &= 2x^{-3} & \Rightarrow & \quad f'''(1) = 2(1)^{-3} = 2,
\end{aligned}
$$

and so

$$
\begin{aligned}
p_3(x) &= 0 + \frac{1}{1!}(x-1) + \frac{-1}{2!}(x-1)^2 + \frac{2}{3!}(x-1)^3 \\
&= x - 1 - \frac{(x-1)^2}{2} + \frac{(x-1)^3}{3}.
\end{aligned}
$$

**(b)** To apply formula (6), we first compute

$$
f^{(4)}(x) = [f'''(x)]' = \left(2x^{-3}\right)' = -6x^{-4}.
$$

Thus, the error formula (6) yields

$$
\ln x - p_3(x) =: e_3(x) = \frac{f^{(4)}(\xi)}{4!}(x - x_0)^4 = \frac{-6\xi^{-4}}{24}(x-1)^4 = -\frac{(x-1)^4}{4\xi^4}
$$

$$
\Rightarrow \quad |\ln(1.5) - p_3(1.5)| = \left| -\frac{(1.5-1)^4}{4\xi^4} \right| = \frac{(0.5)^4}{4\xi^4}
$$

$$
\Rightarrow \quad |\ln(1.5) - p_3(1.5)| \le \frac{(0.5)^4}{4} = \frac{1}{64} = 0.015625,
$$

where we have used the fact $\xi > 1$.

**(c)** Direct calculations yield

$$
|\ln(1.5) - p_3(1.5)| \approx \left| 0.405465 - \left( 0.5 - \frac{(0.5)^2}{2} + \frac{(0.5)^3}{3} \right) \right| \approx 0.011202.
$$

**(d)** See Figure B.51 in the answers of the text.

**11.** First, we rewrite the given equation in the form

$$
y'' = -py' - qy + g.
$$

On the right-hand side of this equation, the function $y'$ is differentiable ($y''$ exists) and the functions $y$, $p$, $q$, and $g$ are differentiable (even twice). Thus we conclude that its left-hand side, $y''$, is differentiable being the product, sum, and difference of differentiable functions. Therefore, $y''' = (y'')'$ exists and is given by

$$y''' = (-py' - qy + g)' = -p'y' - py'' - q'y - qy' + g'.$$

Similarly, we conclude that the right-hand side of the equation above is a differentiable function since all the functions involved are differentiable (notice that we have just proved the differentiability of $y''$). Hence, $y'''$, its left-hand side is differentiable as well, i.e., $(y''')' = y^{(4)}$ does exist.

**13.** With form $k = r = A = 1$ and $\omega = 10$, the Duffing's equation becomes

$$y'' + y + y^3 = \cos 10t \qquad \text{or} \qquad y'' = -y - y^3 + \cos 10t.$$

Substituting the initial conditions, $y(0) = 0$ and $y'(0) = 1$ into the latter equation yields

$$y''(0) = -y(0) - y(0)^3 + \cos(10 \cdot 0) = -0 - (0)^3 + \cos 0 = 1.$$

Differentiating the given equation, we conclude that

$$y''' = \left(-y - y^3 + \cos 10t\right)' = -y' - 3y^2 y' - 10 \sin 10t,$$

which, at $t = 0$, gives

$$y'''(0) = -y'(0) - 3y(0)^2 y'(0) - 10 \sin(10 \cdot 0) = -1 - 3(0)^2(1) - 10 \sin 0 = -1.$$

Thus, the Taylor polynomial approximations to the solution of the given initial value problem are

$$y(t) = y(0) + \frac{y'(0)}{1!} t + \frac{y''(0)}{2!} t^2 + \frac{y'''(0)}{3!} t^3 + \cdots = t + \frac{1}{2} t^2 - \frac{1}{6} t^3 + \cdots.$$

**15.** For the Taylor polynomial $p_2(x)$, we need $y(0)$, $y'(0)$, and $y''(0)$. We already know $y(0)$ and $y'(0)$ from the initial conditions:

$$y(0) = 1 \qquad \text{and} \qquad y'(0) = 0.$$

Chapter 8

Expressing $y''(x)$ from the given equation yields

$$y''(x) = -\frac{2y'(x) + xy(x)}{x}.$$  (8.3)

The formal substitution of $x = 0$ in (8.3) gives "0/0"–indeterminate form. On the other hand, since the differentiability of a function implies its continuity, and we are given that $y(x)$ has derivatives of all orders at $x = 0$, we conclude that all the derivatives of $y(x)$ are continuous at $x = 0$. Therefore,

$$y''(0) = \lim_{x\to 0} y''(x),$$

and we can find the above limit by applying L'Hospital's rule. Namely,

$$\begin{aligned} y''(0) &= \lim_{x\to 0}\left[-\frac{2y'(x) + xy(x)}{x}\right] \\ &= -\lim_{x\to 0}\frac{[2y'(x) + xy(x)]'}{(x)'} = -\lim_{x\to 0}[2y''(x) + xy'(x) + y(x)], \end{aligned}$$

and the last limit can be found by substitution due to the continuity of $y(x)$ and its derivatives at $x = 0$. Hence,

$$y''(0) = -[2y''(0) + 0\cdot y'(0) + y(0)] = -2y''(0) - 1.$$

Solving for $y''(0)$ yields $y''(0) = -1/3$, and so

$$p_2(x) = y(0) + \frac{y'(0)}{1!}x + \frac{y''(0)}{2!}x^2 = 1 - \frac{x^2}{6}.$$

**EXERCISES 8.2:  Power Series and Analytic Functions, page 438**

**1.** Since $a_n = 2^{-n}/(n+1)$, the ratio test yields

$$\lim_{n\to\infty}\left|\frac{a_{n+1}}{a_n}\right| = \lim_{n\to\infty}\frac{2^{-(n+1)}/(n+2)}{2^{-n}/(n+1)} = \lim_{n\to\infty}\frac{2^{-1}(n+1)}{n+2} = \frac{1}{2} = L.$$

So, the radius of convergence is

$$\rho = \frac{1}{L} = 2.$$

In this power series, $x_0 = 1$. Hence, the endpoints of the interval of convergence are

$$x_1 = x_0 + \rho = 1 + 2 = 3,$$
$$x_2 = x_0 - \rho = 1 - 2 = -1.$$

At the point $x_1$, the series becomes

$$\sum_{n=0}^{\infty} \frac{2^{-n}}{n+1} (3-1)^n = \sum_{n=0}^{\infty} \frac{1}{n+1} = \infty$$

(harmonic series); at the point $x_2$ we have

$$\sum_{n=0}^{\infty} \frac{2^{-n}}{n+1} (-1-1)^n = \sum_{n=0}^{\infty} \frac{(-1)^n}{n+1} < \infty$$

by alternating series test. Therefore, the set of convergence is $[-1, 3)$.

**3.** We will use the ratio test given in Theorem 2 on page 432 of the text to find the radius of convergence for this power series. Since $a_n = n^2/2^n$, we see that

$$\frac{a_{n+1}}{a_n} = \frac{(n+1)^2/2^{n+1}}{n^2/2^n} = \frac{(n+1)^2}{2n^2}.$$

Therefore, we have

$$\lim_{n\to\infty} \left| \frac{a_{n+1}}{a_n} \right| = \lim_{n\to\infty} \left| \frac{(n+1)^2}{2n^2} \right| = \frac{1}{2} \lim_{n\to\infty} \frac{(n+1)^2}{n^2} = \frac{1}{2} \lim_{n\to\infty} \left( 1 + \frac{1}{n} \right)^2 = \frac{1}{2}.$$

Thus, the radius of convergence is $\rho = 2$. Hence, this power series converges absolutely for $|x+2| < 2$. That is, for

$$-2 < x + 2 < 2 \qquad \text{or} \qquad -4 < x < 0.$$

We must now check the end points of this interval. We first check the end point $-4$ or $x + 2 = -2$ which yields the series

$$\sum_{n=0}^{\infty} \frac{n^2(-2)^n}{2^n} = \sum_{n=0}^{\infty} (-1)^n n^2.$$

This series diverges since the $n$th term, $a_n = (-1)^n n^2$, does not approach zero as $n$ goes to infinity. (Recall that it is necessary for the $n$th term of a convergent series to approach zero

497

as $n$ goes to infinity. But this fact in itself does not prove that a series converges.) Next, we check the end point $x = 0$ or $x + 2 = 2$ which yields the series

$$\sum_{n=0}^{\infty} \frac{n^2 2^n}{2^n} = \sum_{n=0}^{\infty} n^2.$$

Again, as above, this series diverges. Therefore, this power series converges in the open interval $(-4, 0)$ and diverges outside of this interval.

5. With $a_n = 3/n^3$, the ratio test gives

$$L = \lim_{n \to \infty} \frac{3/(n+1)^3}{3/n^3} = \lim_{n \to \infty} \left(\frac{n}{n+1}\right)^3 = \left(\lim_{n \to \infty} \frac{n}{n+1}\right)^3 = 1.$$

Therefore, the radius of convergence is $\rho = 1/L = 1$. At the points $x_0 \pm \rho = 2 \pm 1$, that is, $x = 3$ and $x = 1$, we have the series

$$\sum_{n=0}^{\infty} \frac{3}{n^3} \qquad \text{and} \qquad \sum_{n=0}^{\infty} \frac{3(-1)^n}{n^3},$$

which are known to converge. Therefore, the set of convergence of the given series is the closed interval $[1, 3]$.

7. By writing

$$\sum_{k=0}^{\infty} a_{2k} x^{2k} = \sum_{k=0}^{\infty} a_{2k} \left(x^2\right)^k = \sum_{k=0}^{\infty} b_k z^k,$$

where $b_k := a_{2k}$ and $z := x^2$, we obtain a power series centered at the origin. The ratio test then yields the radius of convergence to be $1/L$, where

$$L = \lim_{k \to \infty} \left| \frac{b_{k+1}}{b_k} \right| = \lim_{k \to \infty} \left| \frac{a_{2(k+1)}}{a_{2k}} \right| = \lim_{k \to \infty} \left| \frac{a_{2k+2}}{a_{2k}} \right|.$$

So, the series $\sum_{k=0}^{\infty} b_k z^k$ converges for $|z| < 1/L$ and diverges for $|z| > 1/L$. Since $z = x^2$,

$$|z| < \frac{1}{L} \qquad \Leftrightarrow \qquad |x^2| < \frac{1}{L} \qquad \Leftrightarrow \qquad |x| < \frac{1}{\sqrt{L}}.$$

Hence, the original series converges for $|x| < 1/\sqrt{L}$ and diverges for $|x| > 1/\sqrt{L}$. By the definition, $1/\sqrt{L}$ is its radius of convergence.

The second statement can be proved in a similar way, since

$$\sum_{k=0}^{\infty} a_{2k+1} x^{2k+1} = x \sum_{k=0}^{\infty} a_{2k+1} \left(x^2\right)^k = x \sum_{k=0}^{\infty} b_k z^k ,$$

where $b_k := a_{2k+1}$ and $z := x^2$.

9. Since the addition of power series reduces to the addition of the coefficients at the corresponding powers of the variable, we make the following changes in indices of summation.

$$\begin{aligned} f(x): \quad n \to k \quad &\Rightarrow \quad f(x) = \textstyle\sum_{k=0}^{\infty} \left[1/(k+1)\right] x^k , \\ g(x): \quad n-1 \to k \quad &\Rightarrow \quad g(x) = \textstyle\sum_{k=0}^{\infty} 2^{-(k+1)} x^k . \end{aligned}$$

Therefore,

$$f(x) + g(x) = \sum_{k=0}^{\infty} \frac{1}{k+1}\, x^k + \sum_{k=0}^{\infty} 2^{-(k+1)} x^k = \sum_{k=0}^{\infty} \left[\frac{1}{k+1} + 2^{-k-1}\right] x^k .$$

11. We want to find the product $f(x)g(x)$ of the two series

$$f(x) = \sum_{n=0}^{\infty} \frac{x^n}{n!} = 1 + x + \frac{x^2}{2} + \frac{x^3}{6} + \frac{x^4}{24} + \cdots ,$$

and

$$g(x) = \sin x = \sum_{k=0}^{\infty} \left[\frac{(-1)^k}{(2k+1)!}\right] x^{2k+1} = x - \frac{x^3}{6} + \frac{x^5}{120} - \frac{x^7}{7!} + \cdots .$$

Therefore, we have

$$\begin{aligned} f(x)g(x) &= \left(1 + x + \frac{x^2}{2} + \frac{x^3}{6} + \frac{x^4}{24} + \cdots\right)\left(x - \frac{x^3}{6} + \frac{x^5}{120} - \frac{x^7}{7!} + \cdots\right) \\ &= x + x^2 + \left(\frac{1}{2} - \frac{1}{6}\right) x^3 + \left(\frac{1}{6} - \frac{1}{6}\right) x^4 + \left(\frac{1}{24} - \frac{1}{12} + \frac{1}{120}\right) x^5 + \cdots \\ &= x + x^2 + + \frac{1}{3}\, x^3 + \cdots . \end{aligned}$$

Note that since the radius of convergence for both of the given series is $\rho = \infty$, the expansion of the product $f(x)g(x)$ also converges for all values of $x$.

# Chapter 8

**13.** Using formula (6) on page 434 of the text, we obtain

$$
\begin{aligned}
f(x)g(x) &= \left[\sum_{n=0}^{\infty} \frac{(-1)^n}{n!}\, x^n\right]\left[\sum_{n=0}^{\infty} (-1)^n x^n\right] \\
&= \left(1 - x + \frac{1}{2}\,x^2 - \frac{1}{6}\,x^3 + \cdots\right)\left(1 - x + x^2 - x^3 + \cdots\right) \\
&= (1)(1) + \left[(1)(-1) + (-1)(1)\right]x + \left[(1)(1) + (-1)(-1) + \left(\frac{1}{2}\right)(1)\right]x^2 + \cdots \\
&= 1 - 2x + \frac{5}{2}\,x^2 + \cdots
\end{aligned}
$$

**15. (a)** Let $q(x) = \sum_{n=0}^{\infty} a_n x^n$. Multiplying both sides of the given equation by $\sum_{n=0}^{\infty} x^n/n!$, we obtain

$$
\left(\sum_{n=0}^{\infty} a_n x^n\right)\left(\sum_{n=0}^{\infty} \frac{1}{n!}\, x^n\right) = \sum_{n=0}^{\infty} \frac{1}{2^n}\, x^n .
$$

Thus, the right-hand side, $\sum_{n=0}^{\infty} x^n/2^n$, is the Cauchy product of $q(x)$ and $\sum_{n=0}^{\infty} x^n/n!$.

**(b)** With $c_n = 1/2^n$ and $b_n = 1/n!$, formula (6) on page 434 of the text yields:

$$
\begin{aligned}
n = 0: \quad & \frac{1}{2^0} = c_0 = a_0 b_0 = a_0 \cdot \frac{1}{0!} = a_0\,; \\
n = 1: \quad & \frac{1}{2^1} = c_1 = a_0 b_1 + a_1 b_0 = a_0 \cdot \frac{1}{1!} + a_1 \cdot \frac{1}{0!} = a_0 + a_1\,; \\
n = 2: \quad & \frac{1}{2^2} = c_2 = a_0 b_2 + a_1 b_1 + a_2 b_0 = a_0 \cdot \frac{1}{2!} + a_1 \cdot \frac{1}{1!} + a_2 \cdot \frac{1}{0!} = \frac{a_0}{2} + a_1 + a_2\,; \\
n = 3: \quad & \frac{1}{2^3} = c_3 = a_0 b_3 + a_1 b_2 + a_2 b_1 + a_3 b_0 = \frac{a_0}{6} + \frac{a_1}{2} + a_2 + a_3\,;
\end{aligned}
$$

etc.

**(c)** The system in (b) simplifies to

$$
\begin{aligned}
1 &= a_0\,, & a_0 &= 1\,, \\
1/2 &= a_0 + a_1\,, & a_1 &= 1/2 - a_0 = -1/2\,, \\
1/4 &= a_0/2 + a_1 + a_2\,, \quad \Rightarrow & a_2 &= 1/4 - a_0/2 - a_1 = 1/4\,, \\
1/8 &= a_0/6 + a_1/2 + a_2 + a_3\,, & a_3 &= 1/8 - a_0/6 - a_1/2 - a_2 = -1/24\,, \\
&\;\;\vdots & &\;\;\vdots
\end{aligned}
$$

Thus,

$$q(x) = 1 - \frac{1}{2}x + \frac{1}{4}x^2 - \frac{1}{24}x^3 + \cdots.$$

**17.** Since

$$\lim_{n\to\infty}\left|\frac{a_{n+1}}{a_n}\right| = \lim_{n\to\infty}\left|\frac{(-1)^{n+1}}{(-1)^n}\right| = \lim_{n\to\infty} 1 = 1,$$

by the ratio test, we find the radius of convergence of the given series to be $\rho = 1/1 = 1 > 0$. Therefore, Theorem 4 of page 434 of the text can be applied. This yields

$$\left[(1+x)^{-1}\right]' = \sum_{n=1}^{\infty}(-1)^n n x^{n-1} \quad \Rightarrow \quad -(1+x)^{-2} = \sum_{n=1}^{\infty}(-1)^n n x^{n-1},$$

and the radius of convergence of this series is also $\rho = 1$.

**19.** Here we will assume that this series has a positive radius of convergence. Thus, since we have

$$f(x) = \sum_{n=0}^{\infty} a_n x^n = a_0 + a_1 x + a_2 x^2 + a_3 x^3 + \cdots + a_n x^n + \cdots,$$

we can differentiate term by term to obtain

$$f'(x) = 0 + a_1 + a_2 2x + a_3 3x^2 + \cdots + a_n n x^{n-1} + \cdots = \sum_{n=1}^{\infty} a_n n x^{n-1}.$$

Note that the summation for $f(x)$ starts at zero while the summation for $f'(x)$ starts at one.

**21.** Using the ratio test, we find that the radius $\rho$ of convergence of the given series is

$$\rho = \frac{1}{\lim_{n\to\infty}|(-1)^{n+1}/(-1)^n|} = \frac{1}{1} = 1 > 0.$$

Thus, by Theorem 4 on page 434 of the text,

$$g(x) = \int_0^x f(t)\,dt = \int_0^x \left[\sum_{n=0}^{\infty}(-1)^n t^n\right] dt$$

$$= \sum_{n=0}^{\infty}(-1)^n \int_0^x t^n\,dt = \sum_{n=0}^{\infty}(-1)^n \frac{1}{n+1} t^{n+1}\Big|_0^x = \sum_{n=0}^{\infty}\frac{(-1)^n}{n+1}x^{n+1}.$$

On the other hand,

$$g(x) = \int\limits_0^x \frac{dt}{1+t} = \ln(1+t)\Big|_0^x = \ln(1+x), \quad x \in (-1,1).$$

**23.** Setting $k = n - 1$, we have $n = k + 1$. Note that $k = 0$ when $n = 1$. Hence, substitution into the given series yields

$$\sum_{n=1}^\infty na_n x^{n-1} = \sum_{k=0}^\infty (k+1)a_{k+1}x^k .$$

**25.** We let $n + 1 = k$ so that $n = k - 1$; when $n = 0$, then $k = 1$. Thus,

$$\sum_{n=0}^\infty a_n x^{n+1} = \sum_{k=1}^\infty a_{k-1}x^k .$$

**27.** Termwise multiplication yields

$$x^2 \sum_{n=0}^\infty n(n+1)a_n x^n = \sum_{n=0}^\infty n(n+1)a_n x^n x^2 = \sum_{n=0}^\infty n(n+1)a_n x^{n+2} .$$

Now we can shift the summation index by letting $k = n + 2$. Then we have $n = k - 2$, $n + 1 = k - 1$, $k = 2$ when $n = 0$, and so

$$\sum_{n=0}^\infty n(n+1)a_n x^{n+2} = \sum_{k=2}^\infty (k-2)(k-1)a_{k-2}x^k .$$

By replacing $k$ by $n$, we obtain the desired form.

**29.** We need to determine the $n$th derivative of $f(x)$ at the point $x = \pi$. Thus, we observe that

$$\begin{aligned}
f(x) = f^{(0)}(x) = \cos x \quad &\Rightarrow \quad f(\pi) = f^{(0)}(\pi) = \cos \pi = -1, \\
f'(x) = -\sin x \quad &\Rightarrow \quad f'(\pi) = -\sin \pi = 0, \\
f''(x) = -\cos x \quad &\Rightarrow \quad f''(\pi) = -\cos \pi = 1, \\
f'''(x) = \sin x \quad &\Rightarrow \quad f'''(\pi) = \sin \pi = 0, \\
f^{(4)}(x) = \cos x \quad &\Rightarrow \quad f^{(4)}(\pi) = \cos \pi = -1.
\end{aligned}$$

Since $f^{(4)}(x) = \cos x = f(x)$, the four derivatives given above will be repeated indefinitely. Thus, we see that $f^{(n)}(\pi) = 0$ if $n$ is odd and $f^{(n)}(\pi) = \pm 1$ if $n$ is even (where the signs alternate starting at $-1$ when $n = 0$). Therefore, the Taylor series for $f$ about the point $x_0 = \pi$ is given by

$$f(x) = -1 + 0 + \frac{1}{2!}(x-\pi)^2 + 0 - \frac{1}{4!}(x-\pi)^4 + \cdots + \frac{(-1)^{n+1}(x-\pi)^{2n}}{(2n)!} + \cdots$$

$$= \sum_{n=0}^{\infty} \frac{(-1)^{n+1}(x-\pi)^{2n}}{(2n)!}.$$

**31.** Writing

$$f(x) = \frac{1+x}{1-x} = \frac{(1-x)+2x}{1-x} = 1 + 2x\frac{1}{1-x},$$

we can use the power series expansion (3) on page 433 of the text (geometric series) to obtain the desired Taylor series. Thus we have

$$f(x) = 1 + 2x\frac{1}{1-x} = 1 + 2x\sum_{k=0}^{\infty} x^k = 1 + \sum_{k=0}^{\infty} 2x^{k+1}.$$

Shifting the summation index, that is, letting $k + 1 = n$, yields

$$f(x) = 1 + \sum_{k=0}^{\infty} 2x^{k+1} = 1 + \sum_{n=1}^{\infty} 2x^n.$$

**33.** Using the formula

$$c_j = \frac{f^{(j)}(x_0)}{j!}$$

for the coefficients of the Taylor series for $f(x)$ about $x_0$, we find

$$f(x_0) = x^3 + 3x - 4\,\big|_{x=1} = 0 \Rightarrow c_0 = 0,$$
$$f'(x_0) = 3x^2 + 3\,\big|_{x=1} = 6 \Rightarrow c_1 = 6/1! = 6,$$
$$f''(x_0) = 6x\,\big|_{x=1} = 6 \Rightarrow c_2 = 6/2! = 3,$$
$$f'''(x) \equiv 6 \Rightarrow c_3 = 6/3! = 1,$$
$$f^{(j)}(x) \equiv 0 \Rightarrow c_j = 0 \quad \text{for } j \geq 4.$$

Therefore,

$$x^3 + 3x - 4 = 6(x-1) + 3(x-1)^2 + (x-1)^3.$$

# Chapter 8

**35. (a)** We have

$$\frac{1}{x} = \frac{1}{1 + (x-1)} = \frac{1}{1-s}, \qquad \text{where} \quad s = -(x-1).$$

Since $1/(1-s) = \sum_{n=0}^{\infty} s^n$, the substitution $s = -(x-1)$ into both sides of this equality yields the expansion

$$\frac{1}{x} = \frac{1}{1-s} = \sum_{n=0}^{\infty} s^n = \sum_{n=0}^{\infty} [-(x-1)]^n = \sum_{n=0}^{\infty} (-1)^n (x-1)^n,$$

which is valid for

$$|s| = |x-1| < 1 \qquad \Rightarrow \qquad 0 < x < 2.$$

**(b)** Since the above series has positive radius of convergence $\rho = 1$, Theorem 4 on page 434 of the text can be applied. Hence, for $0 < x < 2$,

$$\ln x = \int_1^x \frac{1}{t}\, dt = \int_1^x \left[ \sum_{n=0}^{\infty} (-1)^n (t-1)^n \right] dt = \sum_{n=0}^{\infty} (-1)^n \int_1^x (t-1)^n\, dt$$

$$= \sum_{n=0}^{\infty} (-1)^n \frac{1}{n+1} (t-1)^{n+1} \Big|_1^x = \sum_{n=0}^{\infty} \frac{(-1)^n}{n+1} (x-1)^{n+1} = \sum_{k=1}^{\infty} \frac{(-1)^{k-1}}{k} (x-1)^k.$$

**37.** For $n = 0$, $f^{(0)}(0) := f(0) = 0$ by the definition of $f(x)$.

To find $f'(0)$, we use the definition of the derivative.

$$f'(0) = \lim_{x \to 0} \frac{f(x) - f(0)}{x - 0} = \lim_{x \to 0} \frac{e^{-1/x^2}}{x}. \qquad (8.4)$$

We compute left-hand and right-hand side limits by making the substitution $t = 1/x$. Note that $t \to +\infty$ when $x \to 0^+$ and $t \to -\infty$ when $x \to 0^-$. Thus we have

$$\lim_{x \to 0^{\pm}} \frac{e^{-1/x^2}}{x} = \lim_{t \to \pm\infty} te^{-t^2} = \lim_{t \to \pm\infty} \frac{t}{e^{t^2}} = \lim_{t \to \pm\infty} \frac{1}{2te^{t^2}} = 0,$$

where we applied L'Hospital's rule to the indeterminate form $\infty/\infty$. Therefore, the limit in (8.4) exists and equals 0. For any $x \neq 0$,

$$f'(x) = \left( e^{-1/x^2} \right)' = e^{-1/x^2} \left( -\frac{1}{x^2} \right)' = \frac{2}{x^3} e^{-1/x^2}.$$

Next, we proceed by induction. Assuming that, for some $n \geq 1$,

$$f^{(n)}(0) = 0 \quad \text{and} \quad f^{(n)}(x) = p\left(\frac{1}{x}\right) e^{-1/x^2}, \quad x \neq 0,$$

where $p(t)$ is a polynomial in $t$, we show that

$$f^{(n+1)}(0) = 0 \quad \text{and} \quad f^{(n+1)}(x) = q\left(\frac{1}{x}\right) e^{-1/x^2}, \quad x \neq 0,$$

where $q(t)$ is a polynomial in $t$. This will imply that $f^{(n)}(0) = 0$ for all $n \geq 0$.

Indeed, the substitution $t = 1/x$ in the one-sided limits yields

$$\lim_{x \to 0^{\pm}} \frac{f^{(n)}(x) - f^{(n)}(0)}{x - 0} = \lim_{x \to 0^{\pm}} \frac{p(1/x)e^{-1/x^2}}{x} = \lim_{t \to \pm\infty} \frac{tp(t)}{e^{t^2}} = \lim_{t \to \pm\infty} \frac{r(t)}{e^{t^2}},$$

where $r(t) = a_0 t^k + \cdots + a_k$ is a polynomial. Applying the L'Hospital's rule $k$ times, we obtain

$$\lim_{t \to \pm\infty} \frac{r(t)}{e^{t^2}} = \lim_{t \to \pm\infty} \frac{r'(t)}{\left(e^{t^2}\right)'} = \lim_{t \to \pm\infty} \frac{r'(t)}{2te^{t^2}}$$

$$= \lim_{t \to \pm\infty} \frac{r''(t)}{(4t^2 + 2)e^{t^2}} = \cdots = \lim_{t \to \pm\infty} \frac{k! a_0}{(2^k t^k + \cdots)e^{t^2}} = 0.$$

Since both one-sided limits exist and are equal, the regular limit exists and equals to the same number. That is,

$$f^{(n+1)}(0) = \lim_{x \to 0} \frac{f^{(n)}(x) - f^{(n)}(0)}{x - 0} = 0.$$

For any $x \neq 0$,

$$
\begin{aligned}
f^{(n+1)}(x) &= \left[ p\left(\frac{1}{x}\right) e^{-1/x^2} \right]' = \left[ p'\left(\frac{1}{x}\right) \left(\frac{1}{x}\right)' \right] e^{-1/x^2} + p\left(\frac{1}{x}\right) \left[ e^{-1/x^2} \left(-\frac{1}{x^2}\right)' \right] \\
&= \left[ -p'\left(\frac{1}{x}\right) \frac{1}{x^2} + p\left(\frac{1}{x}\right) \frac{2}{x^3} \right] e^{-1/x^2} = q\left(\frac{1}{x}\right) e^{-1/x^2},
\end{aligned}
$$

where $q(t) = -p'(t)t^2 + p(t)2t^3$.

## EXERCISES 8.3:   Power Series Solutions to Linear Differential Equations, page 449

**1.** Dividing the given equation by $(x + 1)$ yields

$$y'' - \frac{x^2}{x+1}\, y' + \frac{3}{x+1}\, y = 0.$$

Thus we see that

$$p(x) = -\frac{x^2}{x+1}, \qquad q(x) = \frac{3}{x+1}.$$

These are rational functions and so they are analytic everywhere except, perhaps, at zeros of their denominators. Solving $x + 1 = 0$, we find that $x = -1$, which is a point of infinite discontinuity for both functions. Consequently, $x = -1$ is the only singular point of the given equation.

**3.** Writing the equation in standard form yields

$$y'' + \frac{2}{\theta^2 - 2} y' + \frac{\sin\theta}{\theta^2 - 2} y = 0.$$

The coefficients

$$p(\theta) = \frac{2}{\theta^2 - 2} \qquad \text{and} \qquad q(\theta) = \frac{\sin\theta}{\theta^2 - 2}$$

are quotients of analytic functions, and so they are analytic everywhere except zeros $\theta = \pm\sqrt{2}$ of the denominator where they have infinite discontinuities. Hence, the given equation has two singular points, $\theta = \pm\sqrt{2}$.

**5.** In standard form, the equation becomes

$$x'' + \frac{t+1}{t^2 - t - 2} x' - \frac{t-2}{t^2 - t - 2} x = 0.$$

Hence

$$p(t) = \frac{t+1}{t^2 - t - 2} = \frac{t+1}{(t+1)(t-2)}, \qquad q(t) = -\frac{t-2}{t^2 - t - 2} = -\frac{t-2}{(t+1)(t-2)}.$$

The point $t = -1$ is a removable singularity for $p(t)$ since, for $t \neq -1$, we can cancel $(t+1)$-term in the numerator and denominator, and so $p(t)$ becomes analytic at $t = -1$ if we set

$$p(-1) := \lim_{t \to -1} p(t) = \lim_{t \to -1} \frac{1}{t-2} = -\frac{1}{3}.$$

At the point $t = 2$, $p(t)$ has infinite discontinuity. Thus $p(t)$ is analytic everywhere except $t = 2$. Similarly, $q(t)$ is analytic everywhere except $t = -1$. Therefore, the given equation has two singular points, $t = -1$ and $t = 2$.

**7.** In standard form, this equation becomes

$$y'' + \left(\frac{\cos x}{\sin x}\right) y = 0.$$

Thus, $p(x) = 0$ and, hence, is analytic everywhere. We also see that

$$q(x) = \frac{\cos x}{\sin x} = \cot x.$$

Note that $q(x)$ is the quotient of two functions ($\cos x$ and $\sin x$) that each have a power series expansion with a positive radius of convergence about each real number $x$. Thus, according to page 434 of the text, we see that $q(x)$ will also have a power series expansion with a positive radius of convergence about every real number $x$ as long as the denominator, $\sin x$, is not equal to zero. Since the cotangent function is $\pm\infty$ at integer multiples of $\pi$, we see that $q(x)$ is not defined and, therefore, not analytic at $n\pi$. Hence, the differential equation is singular only at the points $n\pi$, where $n$ is an integer.

**9.** Dividing the differential equation by $\sin\theta$, we get

$$y'' - \frac{\ln\theta}{\sin\theta} y = 0.$$

Thus, $p(\theta) \equiv 0$ and $q(\theta) = -\ln\theta/\sin\theta$. The function $q(\theta)$ is not defined for $\theta \le 0$ because of the logarithmic term and has infinite discontinuities at *positive* zeros of the denominator. Namely,

$$\sin\theta = 0 \quad \Rightarrow \quad \theta = k\pi, \quad k = 1, 2, 3, \dots .$$

At all other points $\theta$, $q(\theta)$ is analytic as a quotient of two analytic functions. Hence, the singular points of the given equation are

$$\theta \le 0 \quad \text{and} \quad \theta = k\pi, \quad k = 1, 2, 3, \dots .$$

**11.** The coefficient, $x + 2$, is a polynomial, and so it is analytic everywhere. Therefore, $x = 0$ is an ordinary point of the given equation. We seek a power series solution of the form

$$y(x) = \sum_{n=0}^{\infty} a_n x^n \quad \Rightarrow \quad y'(x) = \sum_{n=1}^{\infty} n a_n x^{n-1},$$

where we have applied Theorem 4 on page 434 of the text to find the power series expansion of $y'(x)$. We now substitute the power series for $y$ and $y'$ into the given differential equation and obtain

$$\sum_{n=1}^{\infty} n a_n x^{n-1} + (x+2) \sum_{n=0}^{\infty} a_n x^n = 0$$

$$\Rightarrow \quad \sum_{n=1}^{\infty} n a_n x^{n-1} + \sum_{n=0}^{\infty} 2 a_n x^n + \sum_{n=0}^{\infty} a_n x^{n+1} = 0. \qquad (8.5)$$

To sum these series, we make shifts in indices of summation so that they sum over the same power of $x$. In the first sum, we set $k = n - 1$ so that $n = k + 1$ and $k$ runs from 0 to $\infty$; in the second sum, we just replace $n$ by $k$; in the third sum, we let $k = n + 1$ and so $n = k - 1$, and the summation starts from 1. Thus the equation (8.5) becomes

$$\sum_{k=0}^{\infty} (k+1) a_{k+1} x^k + \sum_{k=0}^{\infty} 2 a_k x^k + \sum_{k=1}^{\infty} a_{k-1} x^k = 0$$

$$\Rightarrow \quad \left[ a_1 + \sum_{k=1}^{\infty} (k+1) a_{k+1} x^k \right] + \left[ 2a_0 + \sum_{k=1}^{\infty} 2 a_k x^k \right] + \sum_{k=1}^{\infty} a_{k-1} x^k = 0$$

$$\Rightarrow \quad (a_1 + 2a_0) + \sum_{k=1}^{\infty} \left[ (k+1) a_{k+1} + 2 a_k + a_{k-1} \right] x^k = 0.$$

For the power series on the left-hand side to be identically zero, we must have all zero coefficients. Hence,

$$a_1 + 2a_0 = 0 \quad \text{and} \quad (k+1) a_{k+1} + 2 a_k + a_{k-1} = 0 \quad \text{for all} \quad k \geq 1.$$

This yields

$$a_1 + 2a_0 = 0 \quad \Rightarrow \quad a_1 = -2a_0,$$
$$k = 1: \quad 2a_2 + 2a_1 + a_0 = 0 \quad \Rightarrow \quad a_2 = (-2a_1 - a_0)/2 = (4a_0 - a_0)/2 = 3a_0/2,$$
$$k = 2: \quad 3a_3 + 2a_2 + a_1 = 0 \quad \Rightarrow \quad a_3 = (-2a_2 - a_1)/3 = (-3a_0 + 2a_0)/3 = -a_0/3,$$
$$\vdots$$

Therefore,

$$y(x) = a_0 - 2a_0 x + \frac{3a_0}{2} x^2 - \frac{a_0}{3} x^3 + \cdots = a_0 \left( 1 - 2x + \frac{3x^2}{2} - \frac{x^3}{3} + \cdots \right),$$

where $a_0$ is an arbitrary constant (which is, actually, $y(0)$).

**13.** This equation has no singular points since the coefficients $p(x) \equiv 0$ and $q(x) = -x^2$ are analytic everywhere. So, let

$$z(x) = \sum_{k=0}^{\infty} a_k x^k \quad \Rightarrow \quad z'(x) = \sum_{k=1}^{\infty} k a_k x^{k-1} \quad \Rightarrow \quad z''(x) = \sum_{k=2}^{\infty} k(k-1) a_k x^{k-2} \,,$$

where we used Theorem 4 on page 434 of the text differentiating the series termwise. Substitution $z$ and $z''$ into the given equation yields

$$z'' - x^2 z = \sum_{k=2}^{\infty} k(k-1) a_k x^{k-2} - x^2 \sum_{k=0}^{\infty} a_k x^k = \sum_{k=2}^{\infty} k(k-1) a_k x^{k-2} - \sum_{k=0}^{\infty} a_k x^{k+2} \,.$$

We now shift indices of summation so that they sum over the same power of $x$. For the first sum, we substitute $n = k - 2$ so that $k = n + 2$, $k - 1 = n + 1$, and the summation starts from $n = 0$. In the second summation, we let $n = k + 2$ which yields $k = n - 2$ and $n = 2$ as the starting index. Thus we obtain

$$z'' - x^2 z = \sum_{n=0}^{\infty} (n+2)(n+1) a_{n+2} x^n - \sum_{n=2}^{\infty} a_{n-2} x^n \,.$$

Next step in writing the right-hand side as a single power series is to start both summations at the same point. To do this we observe that

$$\sum_{n=0}^{\infty} (n+2)(n+1) a_{n+2} x^n - \sum_{n=2}^{\infty} a_{n-2} x^n = 2a_2 + 6a_3 x + \sum_{n=2}^{\infty} (n+2)(n+1) a_{n+2} x^n - \sum_{n=2}^{\infty} a_{n-2} x^n$$

$$= 2a_2 + 6a_3 x + \sum_{n=2}^{\infty} \left[ (n+2)(n+1) a_{n+2} - a_{n-2} \right] x^n \,.$$

In order for this power series to equal zero, each coefficient must be zero. Therefore, we obtain

$$2a_2 = 0, \qquad 6a_3 = 0 \quad \text{and} \quad (n+2)(n+1) a_{n+2} - a_{n-2} = 0, \quad n \geq 2 \,.$$

From the first two equations we find that $a_2 = 0$ and $a_3 = 0$. Next we take $n = 2$ and $n = 3$ in the above recurrence relation and get

$$n = 2: \quad (4)(3) a_4 - a_0 = 0 \quad \Rightarrow \quad a_4 = a_0/12 \,,$$
$$n = 3: \quad (5)(4) a_5 - a_1 = 0 \quad \Rightarrow \quad a_5 = a_1/20 \,.$$

Hence,

$$z(x) = \sum_{k=0}^{\infty} a_k x^k = a_0 + a_1 x + (0)x^2 + (0)x^3 + \frac{a_0}{12} x^4 + \frac{a_1}{20} x^5 + \cdots$$

$$= a_0 \left( 1 + \frac{x^4}{12} + \cdots \right) + a_1 \left( x + \frac{x^5}{20} + \cdots \right).$$

**15.** Zero is an ordinary point for this equation since the functions $p(x) = x - 1$ and $q(x) = 1$ are both analytic everywhere and, hence, at the point $x = 0$. Thus, we can assume that the solution to this linear differential equation has a power series expansion with a positive radius of convergence about the point $x = 0$. That is, we assume that

$$y(x) = a_0 + a_1 x + a_2 x^2 + a_3 x^3 + \cdots = \sum_{n=0}^{\infty} a_n x^n.$$

In order to solve the differential equation we must find the coefficients $a_n$. To do this, we must substitute $y(x)$ and its derivatives into the given differential equation. Hence, we must find $y'(x)$ and $y''(x)$. Since $y(x)$ has a power series expansion with a positive radius of convergence about the point $x = 0$, we can find its derivative by differentiating term by term. We can similarly differentiate $y'(x)$ to find $y''(x)$. Thus, we have

$$y'(x) = 0 + a_1 + 2a_2 x + 3a_3 x^2 + \cdots = \sum_{n=1}^{\infty} n a_n x^{n-1}$$

$$\Rightarrow \quad y''(x) = 2a_2 + 6a_3 x + \cdots = \sum_{n=2}^{\infty} n(n-1) a_n x^{n-2}.$$

By substituting these expressions into the differential equation, we obtain

$$y'' + (x-1)y' + y = \sum_{n=2}^{\infty} n(n-1) a_n x^{n-2} + (x-1) \sum_{n=1}^{\infty} n a_n x^{n-1} + \sum_{n=0}^{\infty} a_n x^n = 0.$$

Simplifying yields

$$\sum_{n=2}^{\infty} n(n-1) a_n x^{n-2} + \sum_{n=1}^{\infty} n a_n x^n - \sum_{n=1}^{\infty} n a_n x^{n-1} + \sum_{n=0}^{\infty} a_n x^n = 0. \tag{8.6}$$

We want to be able to write the left-hand side of this equation as a single power series. This will allow us to find expressions for the coefficient of each power of $x$. Therefore, we first need to shift the indices in each power series above so that they sum over the same powers of $x$. Thus, we let $k = n - 2$ in the first summation and note that this means that $n = k + 2$ and that $k = 0$ when $n = 2$. This yields

$$\sum_{n=2}^{\infty} n(n-1)a_n x^{n-2} = \sum_{k=0}^{\infty} (k+2)(k+1)a_{k+2} x^k.$$

In the third power series, we let $k = n - 1$ which implies that $n = k + 1$ and $k = 0$ when $n = 1$. Thus, we see that

$$\sum_{n=1}^{\infty} n a_n x^{n-1} = \sum_{k=0}^{\infty} (k+1)a_{k+1} x^k.$$

For the second and last power series we need only to replace $n$ with $k$. Substituting all of these expressions into their appropriate places in equation (8.6) above yields

$$\sum_{k=0}^{\infty} (k+2)(k+1)a_{k+2} x^k + \sum_{k=1}^{\infty} k a_k x^k - \sum_{k=0}^{\infty} (k+1)a_{k+1} x^k + \sum_{k=0}^{\infty} a_k x^k = 0.$$

Our next step in writing the left-hand side as a single power series is to start all of the summations at the same point. To do this we observe that

$$\sum_{k=0}^{\infty} (k+2)(k+1)a_{k+2} x^k = (2)(1)a_2 x^0 + \sum_{k=1}^{\infty} (k+2)(k+1)a_{k+2} x^k,$$

$$\sum_{k=0}^{\infty} (k+1)a_{k+1} x^k = (1)a_1 x^0 + \sum_{k=1}^{\infty} (k+1)a_{k+1} x^k,$$

$$\sum_{k=0}^{\infty} a_k x^k = a_0 x^0 + \sum_{k=1}^{\infty} a_k x^k.$$

Thus, all of the summations now start at one. Therefore, we have

$$(2)(1)a_2 x^0 + \sum_{k=1}^{\infty} (k+2)(k+1)a_{k+2} x^k + \sum_{k=1}^{\infty} k a_k x^k$$

$$-(1)a_1 x^0 - \sum_{k=1}^{\infty} (k+1)a_{k+1} x^k + a_0 x^0 + \sum_{k=1}^{\infty} a_k x^k = 0$$

$$\Rightarrow \quad 2a_2 - a_1 + a_0 + \sum_{k=1}^{\infty} \left( (k+2)(k+1)a_{k+2} x^k + k a_k x^k - (k+1)a_{k+1} x^k + a_k x^k \right) = 0$$

$$\Rightarrow \qquad 2a_2 - a_1 + a_0 + \sum_{k=1}^{\infty} \left( (k+2)(k+1)a_{k+2} + (k+1)a_k - (k+1)a_{k+1} \right) x^k = 0.$$

In order for this power series to equal zero, each coefficient must be zero. Therefore, we obtain

$$2a_2 - a_1 + a_0 = 0 \qquad \Rightarrow \qquad a_2 = \frac{a_1 - a_0}{2},$$

and

$$(k+2)(k+1)a_{k+2} + (k+1)a_k - (k+1)a_{k+1} = 0, \qquad k \geq 1$$

$$\Rightarrow \qquad a_{k+2} = \frac{a_{k+1} - a_k}{k+2}, \qquad k \geq 1,$$

where we have canceled the factor $(k+1)$ from the recurrence relation, the last equation obtained above. *Note that in this recurrence relation we have solved for the coefficient with the largest subscript, namely $a_{k+2}$. Also, note that the first value for $k$ in the recurrence relation is the same as the first value for $k$ used in the summation notation.* By using the recurrence relation with $k = 1$, we find that

$$a_3 = \frac{a_2 - a_1}{3} = \frac{\dfrac{a_1 - a_0}{2} - a_1}{3} = \frac{-(a_1 + a_0)}{6},$$

where we have plugged in the expression for $a_2$ that we found above. By letting $k = 2$ in the recurrence equation, we obtain

$$a_4 = \frac{a_3 - a_2}{4} = \frac{\dfrac{-(a_1 + a_0)}{6} - \dfrac{a_1 - a_0}{2}}{4} = \frac{-2a_1 + a_0)}{12},$$

where we have plugged in the values for $a_2$ and $a_3$ found above. Continuing this process will allow us to find as many coefficients for the power series of the solution to the differential equation as we may want. Notice that the coefficients just found involve only the variables $a_0$ and $a_1$. From the recurrence equation, we see that this will be the case for all coefficients of the power series solution. Thus, $a_0$ and $a_1$ are arbitrary constants and these variables will be our arbitrary variables in the general solution. Hence, substituting the values for the coefficients that we found above into the solution

$$y(x) = \sum_{n=0}^{\infty} a_n x^n = a_0 + a_1 x + a_2 x^2 + a_3 x^3 + a_4 x^4 + \cdots,$$

yields the solution

$$
\begin{aligned}
y(x) &= a_0 + a_1 x + \frac{a_1 - a_0}{2} x^2 + \frac{-(a_1 + a_0)}{6} x^3 + \frac{-2a_1 + a_0}{12} x^4 + \cdots \\
&= a_0 \left( 1 - \frac{x^2}{2} - \frac{x^3}{6} + \frac{x^4}{12} + \cdots \right) + a_1 \left( x + \frac{x^2}{2} - \frac{x^3}{6} - \frac{x^4}{6} + \cdots \right).
\end{aligned}
$$

**19.** Since $x = 0$ is an ordinary point for the given equation, we seek for a power series expansion of a general solution of the form

$$
y(x) = \sum_{n=0}^{\infty} a_n x^n \qquad \Rightarrow \qquad y'(x) = \sum_{n=1}^{\infty} n a_n x^{n-1}.
$$

Substituting $y(x)$ and $y'(x)$ into the given equation, we obtain

$$
\sum_{n=1}^{\infty} n a_n x^{n-1} - 2x \sum_{n=0}^{\infty} a_n x^n = \sum_{n=1}^{\infty} n a_n x^{n-1} - \sum_{n=0}^{\infty} 2 a_n x^{n+1} = 0.
$$

We shift the indices of summations so that they sum over the same powers of $x$. In the first sum, we let $k = n - 1$. Then $n = k + 1$ and the summation starts from $k = 0$. In the second sum, let $k = n + 1$. Then $n = k - 1$ and $k = 1$ when $n = 0$. Thus we have

$$
\sum_{k=0}^{\infty} (k+1) a_{k+1} x^k - \sum_{k=1}^{\infty} 2 a_{k-1} x^k = a_1 + \sum_{k=1}^{\infty} [(k+1) a_{k+1} - 2 a_{k-1}] x^k = 0.
$$

In order for this power series to equal zero, each coefficient must be zero. That is,

$$
\begin{aligned}
&a_1 = 0, \\
&(k+1) a_{k+1} - 2 a_{k-1} = 0, \quad k \geq 1
\end{aligned}
\qquad \Rightarrow \qquad
\begin{aligned}
&a_1 = 0, \\
&a_{k+1} = 2 a_{k-1}/(k+1), \quad k \geq 1.
\end{aligned}
$$

Since $a_1 = 0$, it follows from this recurrence relation that all odd coefficients are zeros. Indeed,

$$
a_3 = \frac{2a_1}{3} = 0, \qquad a_5 = \frac{2a_3}{5} = 0, \qquad \text{etc.}
$$

For even coefficients, we have

$$
\begin{aligned}
k = 1: \quad & a_2 = 2a_0/2, \\
k = 3: \quad & a_4 = 2a_2/4 = 2[2a_0/2]/4 = 2^2 a_0/(2 \cdot 4), \\
k = 5: \quad & a_6 = 2a_4/6 = 2[2^2 a_0/(2 \cdot 4)]/6 = 2^3 a_0/(2 \cdot 4 \cdot 6), \\
& \vdots
\end{aligned}
$$

# Chapter 8

The pattern for the even coefficients is now apparent. Namely,

$$a_{2k} = \frac{2^k a_0}{2 \cdot 4 \cdots (2k)} = \frac{2^k a_0}{2^k (1 \cdot 2 \cdots k)} = \frac{a_0}{k!}, \qquad k = 1, 2, \ldots.$$

This formula remains correct for $k = 0$ as well with $0! := 1$. Thus

$$y(x) = \sum_{k=0}^{\infty} \frac{a_0}{k!} x^{2k} = a_0 \sum_{k=0}^{\infty} \frac{x^{2k}}{k!},$$

where $a_0$ is an arbitrary constant.

21. Since $x = 0$ is an ordinary point for this differential equation, we will assume that the solution has a power series expansion with a positive radius of convergence about the point $x = 0$. Thus, we have

$$y(x) = \sum_{n=0}^{\infty} a_n x^n \quad \Rightarrow \quad y'(x) = \sum_{n=1}^{\infty} n a_n x^{n-1} \quad \Rightarrow \quad y''(x) = \sum_{n=2}^{\infty} n(n-1) a_n x^{n-2}.$$

By plugging these expressions into the differential equation, we obtain

$$y'' - xy' + 4y = \sum_{n=2}^{\infty} n(n-1) a_n x^{n-2} - x \sum_{n=1}^{\infty} n a_n x^{n-1} + 4 \sum_{n=0}^{\infty} a_n x^n = 0$$

$$\Rightarrow \quad \sum_{n=2}^{\infty} n(n-1) a_n x^{n-2} - \sum_{n=1}^{\infty} n a_n x^n + \sum_{n=0}^{\infty} 4 a_n x^n = 0.$$

In order for each power series to sum over the same powers of $x$, we will shift the index in the first summation by letting $k = n - 2$, and we will let $k = n$ in the other two power series. Thus, we have

$$\sum_{k=0}^{\infty} (k+2)(k+1) a_{k+2} x^k - \sum_{k=1}^{\infty} k a_k x^k + \sum_{k=0}^{\infty} 4 a_k x^k = 0.$$

Next we want all of the summations to start at the same point. Therefore, we will take the first term in the first and last power series out of the summation sign. This yields

$$(2)(1) a_2 x^0 + \sum_{k=1}^{\infty} (k+2)(k+1) a_{k+2} x^k - \sum_{k=1}^{\infty} k a_k x^k + 4 a_0 x^0 + \sum_{k=1}^{\infty} 4 a_k x^k = 0$$

$$\Rightarrow \quad 2a_2 + 4a_0 + \sum_{k=1}^{\infty} (k+2)(k+1) a_{k+2} x^k - \sum_{k=1}^{\infty} k a_k x^k + \sum_{k=1}^{\infty} 4 a_k x^k = 0$$

514

$$\Rightarrow \qquad 2a_2 + 4a_0 + \sum_{k=1}^{\infty} \left[(k+2)(k+1)a_{k+2} + (-k+4)a_k\right] x^k = 0.$$

By setting each coefficient of the power series equal to zero, we see that

$$2a_2 + 4a_0 = 0 \qquad \Rightarrow \qquad a_2 = \frac{-4a_0}{2} = -2a_0\,,$$

$$(k+2)(k+1)a_{k+2} + (-k+4)a_k = 0 \qquad \Rightarrow \qquad a_{k+2} = \frac{(k-4)a_k}{(k+2)(k+1)}\,, \qquad k \geq 1,$$

where we have solved the recurrence equation, the last equation above, for $a_{k+2}$, the coefficient with the largest subscript. Thus, we have

$$k = 1 \qquad \Rightarrow \qquad a_3 = \frac{-3a_1}{3 \cdot 2} = \frac{-a_1}{2}\,,$$

$$k = 2 \qquad \Rightarrow \qquad a_4 = \frac{-2a_2}{4 \cdot 3} = \frac{(-2)(-4)a_0}{4 \cdot 3 \cdot 2} = \frac{a_0}{3}\,,$$

$$k = 3 \qquad \Rightarrow \qquad a_5 = \frac{-a_3}{5 \cdot 4} = \frac{(-3)(-1)a_1}{5 \cdot 4 \cdot 3 \cdot 2} = \frac{a_1}{40}\,,$$

$$k = 4 \qquad \Rightarrow \qquad a_6 = 0,$$

$$k = 5 \qquad \Rightarrow \qquad a_7 = \frac{a_5}{7 \cdot 6} = \frac{(-3)(-1)(1)a_1}{7 \cdot 6 \cdot 5 \cdot 4 \cdot 3 \cdot 2} = \frac{a_1}{560}\,,$$

$$k = 6 \qquad \Rightarrow \qquad a_8 = \frac{2a_6}{8 \cdot 7} = 0,$$

$$k = 7 \qquad \Rightarrow \qquad a_9 = \frac{3a_7}{9 \cdot 8} = \frac{(-3)(-1)(1)(3)a_1}{9!}\,,$$

$$k = 8 \qquad \Rightarrow \qquad a_{10} = \frac{4a_8}{10 \cdot 9} = 0,$$

$$k = 9 \qquad \Rightarrow \qquad a_{11} = \frac{5a_9}{11 \cdot 10} = \frac{(-3)(-1)(1)(3)(5)a_1}{11!}\,.$$

Now we can see a pattern starting to develop. (*Note that it is easier to determine sucha pattern if we consider specific coefficients that have not been multiplied out.*) We first note that $a_0$ and $a_1$ can be chosen arbitrarily. Next we notice that the coefficients with even subscripts larger than 4 are zero. We also see that the general formula for a coefficient with an odd subscript is given by

$$a_{2n+1} = \frac{(-3)(-1)(1) \cdots (2n-5)a_1}{(2n+1)!}\,.$$

Notice that this formula is also valid for $a_3$ and $a_5$. Substituting these expressions for the coefficients into the solution

$$y(x) = \sum_{n=0}^{\infty} a_n x^n = a_0 + a_1 x + a_2 x^2 + a_3 x^3 + a_4 x^4 + \cdots,$$

yields

$$
\begin{aligned}
y(x) &= a_0 + a_1 x - 2a_0 x^2 - \frac{a_1}{2} x^3 + \frac{a_0}{3} x^4 + \frac{a_1}{40} x^5 + \cdots \\
&\qquad\qquad\qquad\qquad + \frac{(-3)(-1)(1)\cdots(2n-5)a_1}{(2n+1)!} x^{2n+1} + \cdots \\
&= a_0 \left[ 1 - 2x^2 + \frac{x^4}{3} \right] + a_1 \left[ x - \frac{x^3}{2} + \frac{x^5}{40} + \cdots + \frac{(-3)(-1)(1)\cdots(2n-5)}{(2n+1)!} x^{2n+1} + \cdots \right] \\
&= a_0 \left[ 1 - 2x^2 + \frac{x^4}{3} \right] + a_1 \left[ x + \sum_{k=1}^{\infty} \frac{(-3)(-1)(1)\cdots(2k-5)}{(2k+1)!} x^{2k+1} \right].
\end{aligned}
$$

**29.** Since $x = 0$ is an ordinary point for this differential equation, we can assume that a solution to this problem is given by

$$y(x) = \sum_{n=0}^{\infty} a_n x^n \quad \Rightarrow \quad y'(x) = \sum_{n=1}^{\infty} n a_n x^{n-1} \quad \Rightarrow \quad y''(x) = \sum_{n=2}^{\infty} n(n-1) a_n x^{n-2}.$$

By substituting the initial conditions, $y(0) = 1$ and $y'(0) = -2$, into the first two equations above, we see that

$$y(0) = a_0 = 1, \quad \text{and} \quad y'(0) = a_1 = -2.$$

Next we will substitute the expressions found above for $y(x)$, $y'(x)$, and $y''(x)$ into the differential equation to obtain

$$y'' + y' - xy = \sum_{n=2}^{\infty} n(n-1) a_n x^{n-2} + \sum_{n=1}^{\infty} n a_n x^{n-1} - x \sum_{n=0}^{\infty} a_n x^n = 0$$

$$\Rightarrow \quad \sum_{n=2}^{\infty} n(n-1) a_n x^{n-2} + \sum_{n=1}^{\infty} n a_n x^{n-1} - \sum_{n=0}^{\infty} a_n x^{n+1} = 0.$$

By setting $k = n - 2$ in the first power series above, $k = n - 1$ in the second power series above, and $k = n + 1$ in the last power series, we can shift the indices so that $x$ is raised to the power $k$ in each power series. Thus, we obtain

$$\sum_{k=0}^{\infty}(k+2)(k+1)a_{k+2}x^k + \sum_{k=0}^{\infty}(k+1)a_{k+1}x^k - \sum_{k=1}^{\infty}a_{k-1}x^k = 0.$$

We can start all of the summations at the same point if we remove the first term from each of the first two power series above. Therefore, we have

$$(2)(1)a_2 + \sum_{k=1}^{\infty}(k+2)(k+1)a_{k+2}x^k + (1)a_1 + \sum_{k=1}^{\infty}(k+1)a_{k+1}x^k - \sum_{k=1}^{\infty}a_{k-1}x^k = 0$$

$$\Rightarrow \quad 2a_2 + a_1 + \sum_{k=1}^{\infty}\left[(k+2)(k+1)a_{k+2} + (k+1)a_{k+1} - a_{k-1}\right]x^k = 0.$$

By equating coefficients, we see that all of the coefficients of the terms in the power series above must be zero. Thus, we have

$$2a_2 + a_1 = 0 \quad \Rightarrow \quad a_2 = \frac{-a_1}{2},$$

$$(k+2)(k+1)a_{k+2} + (k+1)a_{k+1} - a_{k-1} = 0$$

$$\Rightarrow \quad a_{k+1} = \frac{a_{k-1} - (k+1)a_{k+1}}{(k+2)(k+1)}, \quad k \geq 1.$$

Thus, we see that

$$k = 1 \quad \Rightarrow \quad a_3 = \frac{a_0 - 2a_2}{3 \cdot 2} = \frac{a_0}{6} + \frac{a_1}{6}.$$

Using the fact that $a_0 = 1$ and $a_1 = -2$, which we found from the initial conditions, we calculate

$$a_2 = \frac{-(-2)}{2} = 1,$$

$$a_3 = \frac{1}{6} + \frac{-2}{6} = -\frac{1}{6}.$$

By substituting these coefficients, we obtain the cubic polynomial approximation

$$y(x) = 1 - 2x + x^2 - \frac{x^3}{6}.$$

The graphs of the linear, quadratic and cubic polynomial approximations are easily generated by using the software supplied with the text.

# Chapter 8

**31.** The point $x_0 = 0$ is an ordinary point for the given equation since $p(x) = 2x/(x^2 + 2)$ and $q(x) = 3/(x^2 + 2)$ are analytic at zero. Hence we can express a general solution in the form

$$y(x) = \sum_{n=0}^{\infty} a_n x^n.$$

Substituting this expansion into the given differential equation yields

$$(x^2 + 2) \sum_{n=2}^{\infty} n(n-1)a_n x^{n-2} + 2x \sum_{n=1}^{\infty} na_n x^{n-1} + 3 \sum_{n=0}^{\infty} a_n x^n = 0$$

$$\Rightarrow \quad \sum_{n=2}^{\infty} n(n-1)a_n x^n + \sum_{n=2}^{\infty} 2n(n-1)a_n x^{n-2} + \sum_{n=1}^{\infty} 2na_n x^n + \sum_{n=0}^{\infty} 3a_n x^n = 0.$$

To sum over like powers $x^k$, we put $k = n - 2$ into the second summation and $k = n$ into the other summations. This gives

$$\sum_{k=2}^{\infty} k(k-1)a_k x^k + \sum_{k=0}^{\infty} 2(k+2)(k+1)a_{k+2} x^k + \sum_{k=1}^{\infty} 2ka_k x^k + \sum_{k=0}^{\infty} 3a_k x^k = 0.$$

Next we separate the terms corresponding to $k = 0$ and $k = 1$ and combine the rest under one summation.

$$(4a_2 + 3a_0) + (12a_3 + 5a_1)x + \sum_{k=2}^{\infty} [k(k-1)a_k + 2(k+2)(k+1)a_{k+2} + 2ka_k + 3a_k] x^k = 0.$$

Setting the coefficients equal to zero and simplifying, we get

$$4a_2 + 3a_0 = 0,$$
$$12a_3 + 5a_1 = 0,$$
$$(k^2 + k + 3)a_k + 2(k+2)(k+1)a_{k+2} = 0, \qquad k \geq 2$$
$$a_2 = -3a_0/4,$$
$$\Rightarrow \qquad a_3 = -5a_1/12,$$
$$a_{k+2} = -(k^2 + k + 3)a_k/[2(k+2)(k+1)], \qquad k \geq 2.$$

From the initial conditions, we have

$$a_0 = y(0) = 1 \qquad \text{and} \qquad a_1 = y'(0) = 2.$$

Therefore,

$$a_2 = -3(1)/4 = -3/4,$$
$$a_3 = -5(2)/12 = -5/6,$$

and the cubic polynomial approximation for the solution is

$$y(x) = a_0 + a_1 x + x_2 x^2 + a_3 x^3 = 1 + 2x - \frac{3x^2}{4} - \frac{5x^3}{6}.$$

**33.** In Problem 7, Exercises 8.2 we showed that the radius of convergence of a power series $\sum_{n=0}^{\infty} a_{2n} x^{2n}$ is $\rho = 1/\sqrt{L}$, where

$$L = \lim_{n \to \infty} \left| \frac{a_{2(n+1)}}{a_{2n}} \right|.$$

In the series (13), $a_{2n} = (-1)^n/n!$ and so

$$L = \lim_{n \to \infty} \left| \frac{(-1)^{n+1}/(n+1)!}{(-1)^n/n!} \right| = \lim_{n \to \infty} \frac{1}{n+1} = 0.$$

Therefore, $\sqrt{L} = 0$ and $\rho = \infty$.

**35.** With the given values of parameters, we have an initial value problem

$$0.1q''(t) + \left(1 + \frac{t}{10}\right) q'(t) + \frac{1}{2} q(t) = 0, \qquad q(0) = 10, \quad q'(0) = 0.$$

Simplifying yields

$$q''(t) + (10 + t) q'(t) + 5q(t) = 0, \qquad q(0) = 10, \quad q'(0) = 0.$$

The point $t = 0$ is an ordinary point for this equation. Let $q(t) = \sum_{n=0}^{\infty} a_n t^n$ be the power series expansion of $q(t)$ about $t = 0$. Substituting this series into the above differential equation, we obtain

$$\sum_{n=2}^{\infty} n(n-1)a_n t^{n-2} + (10+t) \sum_{n=1}^{\infty} na_n t^{n-1} + 5 \sum_{n=0}^{\infty} a_n t^n = 0$$

$$\Rightarrow \quad \sum_{n=2}^{\infty} n(n-1)a_n t^{n-2} + \sum_{n=1}^{\infty} 10na_n t^{n-1} + \sum_{n=1}^{\infty} na_n t^n + \sum_{n=0}^{\infty} 5a_n t^n = 0.$$

# Chapter 8

Setting $k = n - 2$ in the first summation, $k = n - 1$ in the second summation, and $k = n$ in the last two summations, we obtain

$$\sum_{k=0}^{\infty}(k+2)(k+1)a_{k+2}t^k + \sum_{k=0}^{\infty}10(k+1)a_{k+1}t^k + \sum_{k=1}^{\infty}ka_k t^k + \sum_{k=0}^{\infty}5a_k t^k = 0.$$

Separating the terms corresponding to $k = 0$ and combining the rest under one sum yields

$$(2a_2 + 10a_1 + 5a_0) + \sum_{k=1}^{\infty}\left[(k+2)(k+1)a_{k+2} + 10(k+1)a_{k+1} + (k+5)a_k\right]t^k = 0.$$

Setting the coefficients equal to zero, we obtain the recurrence relations

$$2a_2 + 10a_1 + 5a_0 = 0,$$
$$(k+2)(k+1)a_{k+2} + 10(k+1)a_{k+1} + (k+5)a_k = 0, \qquad k \geq 1. \tag{8.7}$$

Next we use the initial conditions to find $a_0$ and $a_1$.

$$a_0 = q(0) = 10, \qquad a_1 = q'(0) = 0.$$

From the first equation in (8.7) we have

$$a_2 = \frac{-10a_1 - 5a_0}{2} = -25.$$

Taking $k = 1$ and $k = 2$ in the second equation in (8.7), we find $a_3$ and $a_4$.

$$k = 1: \quad 6a_3 + 20a_2 + 6a_1 = 0 \quad \Rightarrow \quad a_3 = -(20a_2 + 6a_1)/6 = 250/3,$$
$$k = 2: \quad 12a_4 + 30a_3 + 7a_2 = 0 \quad \Rightarrow \quad a_4 = -(30a_3 + 7a_2)/12 = -775/4.$$

Hence

$$q(t) = 10 + (0)t - 25t^2 + \frac{250t^3}{3} - \frac{775t^4}{4} + \cdots = 10 - 25t^2 + \frac{250t^3}{3} - \frac{775t^4}{4} + \cdots.$$

## EXERCISES 8.4: Equations with Analytic Coefficients, page 456

**3.** For this equation, $p(x) = 0$ and $q(x) = \dfrac{-3}{1 + x + x^2}$. Therefore, singular points will occur when

$$1 + x + x^2 = 0 \quad \Rightarrow \quad x = -\frac{1}{2} \pm \frac{\sqrt{3}}{2}i.$$

Thus, $x = 1$ is an ordinary point for this equation, and we can find a power series solution with a radius of convergence of at least the minimum of the distances between 1 and points $(-1/2) \pm (\sqrt{3}/2)i$, which, in fact, are equal. Recall that the distance between two complex numbers, $z_1 = a + bi$ and $z_2 = c + di$, is given by

$$\text{dist}\,(z_1, z_2) = \sqrt{(a - c)^2 + (b - d)^2}.$$

Thus, the distance between $(1 + 0 \cdot i)$ and $(-1/2) + (\sqrt{3}/2)i$ is

$$\sqrt{\left[1 - \left(-\frac{1}{2}\right)\right]^2 + \left[0 - \frac{\sqrt{3}}{2}\right]^2} = \sqrt{\frac{9}{4} + \frac{3}{4}} = \sqrt{3}.$$

Therefore, the radius of convergence for the power series solution of this differential equation about $x = 1$ will be at least $\rho = \sqrt{3}$.

9. We see that $x = 0$ and $x = 2$ are the only singular points for this differential equation and, thus, $x = 1$ is an ordinary point. Therefore, according to Theorem 5 on page 451 of the text, there exists a power series solution of this equation about the point $x = 1$ with a radius of convergence of at least one, the distance from 1 to either 0 or 2. That is, we have a general solution for this differential equation of the form

$$y(x) = \sum_{n=0}^{\infty} a_n (x - 1)^n,$$

which is convergent for all $x$ at least in the interval $(0, 2)$, the interval on which the inequality $|x - 1| < 1$ is satisfied. To find this solution we will proceed as in Example 3 on page 453 of the text. Thus, we make the substitution $t = x - 1$, which implies that $x = t + 1$. (Note that $dx/dt = 1$.) We then define a new function

$$Y(t) := y(t + 1) = y(x)$$
$$\Rightarrow \quad \frac{dY}{dt} = \left(\frac{dy}{dx}\right)\left(\frac{dx}{dt}\right) = \left(\frac{dy}{dx}\right) \cdot 1 = \frac{dy}{dx}$$
$$\Rightarrow \quad \frac{d^2Y}{dt^2} = \frac{d}{dt}\left(\frac{dY}{dt}\right) = \frac{d}{dt}\left(\frac{dy}{dx}\right) = \left(\frac{d^2y}{dx^2}\right)\left(\frac{dx}{dt}\right) = \frac{d^2y}{dx^2}.$$

521

Chapter 8

Hence, with the substitutions $t = x - 1$ and $Y(t) = y(t + 1)$, we transform the differential equation, $(x^2 - 2x)\,y''(x) + 2y(x) = 0$, into the differential equation

$$\left[(t + 1)^2 - 2(t + 1)\right] y''(t + 1) + 2y(t + 1) = 0$$
$$\Rightarrow \quad \left[(t + 1)^2 - 2(t + 1)\right] Y''(t) + 2Y(t) = 0$$
$$\Rightarrow \quad \left(t^2 - 1\right) Y''(t) + 2Y(t) = 0. \tag{8.8}$$

To find a general solution to (8.8), we first note that zero is an ordinary point of equation (8.8). Thus, we can assume that we have a power series solution of equation (8.8) of the form

$$Y(t) = \sum_{n=0}^{\infty} a_n t^n ,$$

which converges for all $t$ in $(-1, 1)$. (This means that $x = t + 1$ will be in the interval $(0, 2)$ as desired.) Substituting into equation (8.8) yields

$$\left(t^2 - 1\right) \sum_{n=2}^{\infty} n(n - 1)a_n t^{n-2} + 2 \sum_{n=0}^{\infty} a_n t^n = 0$$
$$\Rightarrow \quad \sum_{n=2}^{\infty} n(n - 1)a_n t^n - \sum_{n=2}^{\infty} n(n - 1)a_n t^{n-2} + \sum_{n=0}^{\infty} 2a_n t^n = 0.$$

Making the shift in the index, $k = n - 2$, in the second power series above and replacing $n$ with $k$ in the other two power series allows us to take each summation over the same power of $t$. This gives us

$$\sum_{k=2}^{\infty} k(k - 1)a_k t^k - \sum_{k=0}^{\infty} (k + 2)(k + 1)a_{k+2} t^k + \sum_{k=0}^{\infty} 2a_k t^k = 0.$$

In order to start all of these summations at the same point, we must take the first two terms out of the summation sign in the last two power series. Thus we have,

$$\sum_{k=2}^{\infty} k(k - 1)a_k t^k - (2)(1)a_2 - (3)(2)a_3 t - \sum_{k=2}^{\infty} (k + 2)(k + 1)a_{k+2} t^k$$
$$+ 2a_0 + 2a_1 t + \sum_{k=2}^{\infty} 2a_k t^k = 0$$

522

$$\Rightarrow \qquad 2a_0 - 2a_2 + (2a_1 - 6a_3)\,t + \sum_{k=2}^{\infty} \left[ k(k-1)a_k - (k+2)(k+1)a_{k+2} + 2a_k \right] t^k = 0.$$

For this power series to equal zero, each coefficient must be zero. Thus, we have

$$2a_0 - 2a_2 = 0 \qquad \Rightarrow \qquad a_2 = a_0\,, \qquad 2a_1 - 6a_3 = 0 \qquad \Rightarrow \qquad a_3 = \frac{a_1}{3}\,,$$

$$k(k-1)a_k - (k+2)(k+1)a_{k+2} + 2a_k = 0, \qquad k \geq 2$$

$$\Rightarrow \qquad a_{k+2} = \frac{k(k-1)a_k + 2a_k}{(k+2)(k+1)}\,, \quad k \geq 2 \qquad \Rightarrow \qquad a_{k+2} = \frac{(k^2 - k + 2)a_k}{(k+2)(k+1)}\,, \quad k \geq 2.$$

Therefore, we see that

$$k = 2 \qquad \Rightarrow \qquad a_4 = \frac{4a_2}{4 \cdot 3} = \frac{a_2}{3} = \frac{a_0}{3}\,,$$

$$k = 3 \qquad \Rightarrow \qquad a_5 = \frac{8a_3}{5 \cdot 4} = \frac{2a_1}{15}\,, \quad \text{etc.}$$

Plugging these values for the coefficients into the power series solution,

$$Y(t) = \sum_{n=0}^{\infty} a_n t^n = a_0 + a_1 t + a_2 t^2 + a_3 t^3 + a_4 t^4 + \cdots\,,$$

yields

$$Y(t) = a_0 + a_1 t + a_0 t^2 + \frac{a_1 t^3}{3} + \frac{a_0 t^4}{3} + \frac{2a_1 t^5}{15} + \cdots$$

$$\Rightarrow \qquad Y(t) = a_0 \left( 1 + t^2 + \frac{t^4}{3} + \cdots \right) + a_1 \left( t + \frac{t^3}{3} + \frac{2t^5}{15} + \cdots \right).$$

Lastly, we want to change back to the independent variable $x$. To do this, we recall that $Y(t) = y(t+1)$. Thus, if $t = x - 1$, then

$$Y(t) = Y(x - 1) = y\left([x-1] + 1\right) = y(x).$$

Thus, we replace $t$ with $x-1$ in the solution just found, and we obtain a power series expansion for a general solution in the independent variable $x$. Substituting, we have

$$y(x) = a_0 \left[ 1 + (x-1)^2 + \frac{1}{3}(x-1)^4 + \cdots \right] + a_1 \left[ (x-1) + \frac{1}{3}(x-1)^3 + \frac{2}{15}(x-1)^5 + \cdots \right].$$

# Chapter 8

**17.** Here $p(x) = 0$ and $q(x) = -\sin x$ both of which are analytic everywhere. Thus, $x = \pi$ is an ordinary point for this differential equation, and there are no singular points. Therefore, by Theorem 5 on page 451 of the text, we can assume that this equation has a general power series solution about the point $x = \pi$ with an infinite radius of convergence (i.e., $\rho = \infty$). That is, we assume that we have a solution to this differential equation given by

$$y(x) = \sum_{n=0}^{\infty} a_n(x - \pi)^n \qquad \left[ \Rightarrow \quad y'(x) = \sum_{n=1}^{\infty} na_n(x - \pi)^{n-1} \right],$$

which converges for all $x$. If we apply the initial conditions, $y(\pi) = 1$ and $y'(\pi) = 0$, we see that $a_0 = 1$ and $a_1 = 0$. To find a general solution of this differential equation, we will combine the methods of Example 3 and Example 4 on pages 453–455 of the text. Thus, we will first define a new function, $Y(t)$, using the transformation $t = x - \pi$. Thus, we define

$$Y(t) := y(t + \pi) = y(x).$$

Hence, by the chain rule (using the fact that $x = t + \pi$ which implies that $dx/dt = 1$), we have $dY/dt = (dy/dx)(dx/dt) = dy/dx$, and similarly $d^2Y/dt^2 = d^2y/dx^2$. We now solve the transformed differential equation

$$\frac{d^2Y}{dt^2} - \sin(t + \pi)Y(t) = 0 \qquad \Rightarrow \qquad \frac{d^2Y}{dt^2} + (\sin t)Y(t) = 0, \tag{8.9}$$

where we have used the fact that $\sin(t + \pi) = -\sin t$. When we have found the solution $Y(t)$, we will use the fact that $y(x) = Y(x - \pi)$ to obtain the solution to the original differential equation in terms of the independent variable $x$. Hence, we seek a power series solution to equation (8.9) of the form

$$Y(t) = \sum_{n=0}^{\infty} a_n t^n \quad \Rightarrow \quad Y'(t) = \sum_{n=1}^{\infty} na_n t^{n-1} \quad \Rightarrow \quad Y''(t) = \sum_{n=2}^{\infty} n(n-1)a_n t^{n-2}.$$

Since the initial conditions, $y(\pi) = 1$ and $y'(\pi) = 0$, transform into $Y(0) = 1$ and $Y'(0) = 0$, we must have

$$Y(0) = a_0 = 1 \qquad \text{and} \qquad Y'(0) = a_1 = 0.$$

524

Next we note that $q(t) = \sin t$ is an analytic function with a Maclaurin series given by

$$\sin t = \sum_{n=0}^{\infty} \frac{(-1)^n t^{2n+1}}{(2n+1)!} = t - \frac{t^3}{6} + \frac{t^5}{120} - \frac{t^7}{5040} + \cdots .$$

By substituting the expressions that we found for $Y(t)$, $Y''(t)$, and $\sin t$ into equation (8.9), we obtain

$$\sum_{n=2}^{\infty} n(n-1)a_n t^{n-2} + \left( t - \frac{t^3}{6} + \frac{t^5}{120} - \frac{t^7}{5040} + \cdots \right) \sum_{n=0}^{\infty} a_n t^n = 0.$$

Therefore, expanding this last equation (and explicitly showing only terms of up to order four), yields

$$\left( 2a_2 + 6a_3 t + 12a_4 t^2 + 20a_5 t^3 + 30a_6 t^4 + \cdots \right) + t \left( a_0 + a_1 t + a_2 t^2 + a_3 t^3 + \cdots \right)$$

$$- \frac{t^3}{6} \left( a_0 + a_1 t + \cdots \right) + \cdots = 0$$

$$\Rightarrow \quad \left( 2a_2 + 6a_3 t + 12a_4 t^2 + 20a_5 t^3 + 30a_6 t^4 + \cdots \right) + t \left( a_0 + a_1 t + a_2 t^2 + a_3 t^3 + \cdots \right)$$

$$+ \left( -\frac{a_0 t^3}{6} - \frac{a_1 t^4}{6} - \cdots \right) + \cdots = 0.$$

By grouping these terms according to their powers of $t$, we obtain

$$2a_2 + (6a_3 + a_0)\, t + (12a_4 + a_1)\, t^2 + \left( 20a_5 + a_2 - \frac{a_0}{6} \right) t^3 + \left( 30a_6 + a_3 - \frac{a_1}{6} \right) t^4 + \cdots = 0.$$

Setting these coefficients to zero and recalling that $a_0 = 1$ and $a_1 = 0$ yields the system of equations

$$2a_2 = 0 \qquad \Rightarrow \qquad a_2 = 0,$$

$$6a_3 + a_0 = 0 \qquad \Rightarrow \qquad a_3 = \frac{-a_0}{6} = \frac{-1}{6},$$

$$12a_4 + a_1 = 0 \qquad \Rightarrow \qquad a_4 = \frac{-a_1}{12} = 0,$$

$$20a_5 + a_2 - \frac{a_0}{6} = 0 \qquad \Rightarrow \qquad a_5 = \frac{\dfrac{a_0}{6} - a_2}{20} = \frac{\dfrac{1}{6}}{20} = \frac{1}{120},$$

$$30a_6 + a_3 - \frac{a_1}{6} = 0 \qquad \Rightarrow \qquad a_6 = \frac{\dfrac{a_1}{6} - a_3}{30} = \frac{0 + \dfrac{1}{6}}{30} = \frac{1}{180}.$$

Plugging these coefficients into the power series solution

$$Y(t) = \sum_{n=0}^{\infty} a_n t^n = a_0 + a_1 t + a_2 t^2 + \cdots,$$

yields the solution to equation (8.9):

$$Y(t) = 1 + 0 + 0 - \frac{t^3}{6} + 0 + \frac{t^5}{120} + \frac{t^6}{180} + \cdots = 1 - \frac{t^3}{6} + \frac{t^5}{120} + \frac{t^6}{180} + \cdots.$$

Lastly we want to find the solution to the original equation with the independent variable $x$. In order to do this, we recall that $t = x - \pi$ and $Y(x - \pi) = y(x)$. Therefore, by substituting these values into the equation above, we obtain the solution

$$y(x) = 1 - \frac{1}{6}(x - \pi)^3 + \frac{1}{120}(x - \pi)^5 + \frac{1}{180}(x - \pi)^6 + \cdots.$$

21. We assume that this differential equation has a power series solution with a positive radius of convergence about the point $x = 0$. This is reasonable because all of the coefficients and the forcing function $g(x) = \sin x$ are analytic everywhere. Thus, we assume that

$$y(x) = \sum_{n=0}^{\infty} a_n x^n \quad \Rightarrow \quad y'(x) = \sum_{n=1}^{\infty} n a_n x^{n-1}.$$

By substituting these expressions and the Maclaurin expansion for $\sin x$ into the differential equation, $y'(x) - xy(x) = \sin x$, we obtain

$$\sum_{n=1}^{\infty} n a_n x^{n-1} - x \sum_{n=0}^{\infty} a_n x^n = \sum_{n=0}^{\infty} (-1)^n \frac{x^{2n+1}}{(2n+1)!}.$$

In the first power series on the left, we make the shift $k = n - 1$. In the second power series on the left, we make the shift $k = n + 1$. Thus, we obtain

$$\sum_{k=0}^{\infty} (k+1) a_{k+1} x^k - \sum_{k=1}^{\infty} a_{k-1} x^k = \sum_{n=0}^{\infty} (-1)^n \frac{x^{2n+1}}{(2n+1)!}.$$

Separating out the first term of the first power series on the left yields

$$a_1 + \sum_{k=1}^{\infty} (k+1) a_{k+1} x^k - \sum_{k=1}^{\infty} a_{k-1} x^k = \sum_{n=0}^{\infty} (-1)^n \frac{x^{2n+1}}{(2n+1)!}$$

$$\Rightarrow \qquad a_1 + \sum_{k=1}^{\infty} \left[ (k+1)a_{k+1} - a_{k-1} \right] x^k = \sum_{n=0}^{\infty} (-1)^n \frac{x^{2n+1}}{(2n+1)!} \, .$$

Therefore, by expanding both of the power series, we have

$$a_1 + (2a_2 - a_0)\,x + (3a_3 - a_1)\,x^2 + (4a_4 - a_2)\,x^3 + (5a_5 - a_3)\,x^4$$
$$+ (6a_6 - a_4)\,x^5 + (7a_7 - a_5)\,x^6 + \cdots = x - \frac{x^3}{6} + \frac{x^5}{120} - \frac{x^7}{5040} + \cdots .$$

By equating the coefficients of like powers of $x$, we obtain

$$a_1 = 0,$$

$$2a_2 - a_0 = 1 \qquad \Rightarrow \qquad a_2 = \frac{a_0 + 1}{2},$$

$$3a_3 - a_1 = 0 \qquad \Rightarrow \qquad a_3 = \frac{a_1}{3} = 0,$$

$$4a_4 - a_2 = \frac{-1}{6} \qquad \Rightarrow \qquad a_4 = \frac{a_2 - 1/6}{4} = \frac{a_0}{8} + \frac{1}{12},$$

$$5a_5 - a_3 = 0 \qquad \Rightarrow \qquad a_5 = \frac{a_3}{5} = 0,$$

$$6a_6 - a_4 = \frac{1}{120} \qquad \Rightarrow \qquad a_6 = \frac{a_4 - 1/120}{6} = \frac{a_0}{48} + \frac{11}{720}.$$

Substituting these coefficients into the power series solution and noting that $a_0$ is an arbitrary number, yields

$$y(x) = \sum_{n=0}^{\infty} a_n x^n$$
$$= a_0 + 0 + \left( \frac{a_0}{2} + \frac{1}{2} \right) x^2 + 0 + \left( \frac{a_0}{8} + \frac{1}{12} \right) x^4 + 0 + \left( \frac{a_0}{48} + \frac{11}{720} \right) x^6 + \cdots$$
$$= a_0 \left[ 1 + \frac{1}{2}x^2 + \frac{1}{8}x^4 + \frac{1}{48}x^6 + \cdots \right] + \left[ \frac{1}{2}x^2 + \frac{1}{12}x^4 + \frac{11}{720}x^6 + \cdots \right].$$

**27.** Observe that $x = 0$ is an ordinary point for this differential equation. Therefore, we can assume that this equation has a power series solution about the point $x = 0$ with a positive

# Chapter 8

radius of convergence. Thus, we assume that

$$y(x) = \sum_{n=0}^{\infty} a_n x^n \quad \Rightarrow \quad y'(x) = \sum_{n=1}^{\infty} n a_n x^{n-1} \quad \Rightarrow \quad y''(x) = \sum_{n=2}^{\infty} n(n-1) a_n x^{n-2}.$$

The Maclaurin series for $\tan x$ is

$$\tan x = x + \frac{x^3}{3} + \frac{2x^5}{15} + \cdots,$$

which is given in the table on the inside front cover of the text. Substituting the expressions for $y(x)$, $y'(x)$, $y''(x)$, and the Maclaurin series for the function $\tan x$ into the differential equation, $(1 - x^2)y'' - y' + y = \tan x$, yields

$$(1 - x^2) \sum_{n=2}^{\infty} n(n-1) a_n x^{n-2} - \sum_{n=1}^{\infty} n a_n x^{n-1} + \sum_{n=0}^{\infty} a_n x^n = x + \frac{x^3}{3} + \frac{2x^5}{15} + \cdots$$

$$\Rightarrow \quad \sum_{n=2}^{\infty} n(n-1) a_n x^{n-2} - \sum_{n=2}^{\infty} n(n-1) a_n x^n - \sum_{n=1}^{\infty} n a_n x^{n-1} + \sum_{n=0}^{\infty} a_n x^n$$

$$= x + \frac{x^3}{3} + \frac{2x^5}{15} + \cdots.$$

By shifting the indices of the power series on the left-hand side of this equation, we obtain

$$\sum_{k=0}^{\infty} (k+2)(k+1) a_{k+2} x^k - \sum_{k=2}^{\infty} k(k-1) a_k x^k - \sum_{k=0}^{\infty} (k+1) a_{k+1} x^k + \sum_{k=0}^{\infty} a_k x^k = x + \frac{x^3}{3} + \frac{2x^5}{15} + \cdots.$$

Removing the first two terms from the summation notation in the first, third and fourth power series above yields

$$(2)(1)a_2 + (3)(2)a_3 x + \sum_{k=2}^{\infty} (k+2)(k+1) a_{k+2} x^k - \sum_{k=2}^{\infty} k(k-1) a_k x^k - (1)a_1 - (2)a_2 x$$

$$- \sum_{k=2}^{\infty} (k+1) a_{k+1} x^k + a_0 + a_1 x + \sum_{k=2}^{\infty} a_k x^k = x + \frac{x^3}{3} + \frac{2x^5}{15} + \cdots$$

$$\Rightarrow \quad (2a_2 - a_1 + a_0) + (6a_3 - 2a_2 + a_1)\, x$$

$$+ \sum_{k=2}^{\infty} \left[ (k+2)(k+1) a_{k+2} - k(k-1) a_k - (k+1) a_{k+1} + a_k \right] x^k = x + \frac{x^3}{3} + \frac{2x^5}{15} + \cdots.$$

By equating the coefficients of the two power series, we see that

$$2a_2 - a_1 + a_0 = 0 \qquad \Rightarrow \qquad a_2 = \frac{a_1 - a_0}{2},$$

$$6a_3 - 2a_2 + a_1 = 1 \qquad \Rightarrow \qquad a_3 = \frac{2a_2 - a_1 + 1}{6} = \frac{1 - a_0}{6},$$

$$4 \cdot 3a_4 - 2 \cdot 1a_2 - 3a_3 + a_2 = 0 \qquad \Rightarrow \qquad a_4 = \frac{a_2 + 3a_3}{12} = \frac{a_1 - 2a_0 + 1}{24}.$$

Therefore, noting that $a_0$ and $a_1$ are arbitrary, we can substitute these coefficients into the power series solution $y(x) = \sum_{n=0}^{\infty} a_n x^n = a_0 + a_1 x + a_2 x^2 + a_3 x^3 + a_4 x^4 + \cdots$ to obtain

$$y(x) = a_0 + a_1 x + \left( \frac{a_1}{2} - \frac{a_0}{2} \right) x^2 + \left( \frac{1}{6} - \frac{a_0}{6} \right) x^3 + \left( \frac{a_1}{24} - \frac{a_0}{12} + \frac{1}{24} \right) x^4 + \cdots$$

$$= a_0 \left( 1 - \frac{1}{2} x^2 - \frac{1}{6} x^3 - \frac{1}{12} x^4 + \cdots \right) + a_1 \left( x + \frac{1}{2} x^2 + \frac{1}{24} x^4 + \cdots \right)$$

$$+ \left( \frac{1}{6} x^3 + \frac{1}{24} x^4 + \cdots \right).$$

## EXERCISES 8.5:   Cauchy-Euler (Equidimensional) Equations Revisited, page 460

**5.** Notice that, since $x > 0$, we can multiply this differential equation by $x^2$ and rewrite it to obtain

$$x^2 \frac{d^2 y}{dx^2} - 5x \frac{dy}{dx} + 13y = 0.$$

We see that this is a Cauchy-Euler equation. Thus, we will assume that a solution has the form

$$y(x) = x^r \qquad \Rightarrow \qquad y'(x) = rx^{r-1} \qquad \Rightarrow \qquad y''(x) = r(r-1)x^{r-2}.$$

Substituting these expressions into the differential equation above yields

$$r(r-1)x^r - 5rx^r + 13x^r = 0$$

$$\Rightarrow \qquad \left( r^2 - 6r + 13 \right) x^r = 0 \qquad \Rightarrow \qquad r^2 - 6r + 13 = 0.$$

We obtained this last equation by using the assumption that $x > 0$. (We also could arrive at this equation by using equation (4) on page 458 of the text.) Using the quadratic formula, we

# Chapter 8

see that the roots to this equation are

$$r = \frac{6 \pm \sqrt{36 - 52}}{2} = 3 \pm 2i.$$

Therefore, using formulas (5) and (6) on page 458 of the text with complex conjugates roots (and using Euler's formula), we have two linearly independent solutions give by

$$y_1(x) = x^3 \cos(2 \ln x), \qquad y_2(x) = x^3 \sin(2 \ln x).$$

Hence the general solution to this equation is given by

$$y(x) = c_1 x^3 \cos(2 \ln x) + c_2 x^3 \sin(2 \ln x).$$

**7.** This equation is a third order Cauchy-Euler equation, and, thus, we will assume that a solution has the form $y(x) = x^r$. This implies that

$$y'(x) = rx^{r-1} \quad \Rightarrow \quad y''(x) = r(r-1)x^{r-2} \quad \Rightarrow \quad y'''(x) = r(r-1)(r-2)x^{r-3}.$$

By substituting these expressions into the differential equation, we obtain

$$[r(r-1)(r-2) + 4r(r-1) + 10r - 10]\, x^r = 0$$
$$\Rightarrow \quad [r^3 + r^2 + 8r - 10]\, x^r = 0 \quad \Rightarrow \quad r^3 + r^2 + 8r - 10 = 0.$$

By inspection we see that $r = 1$ is a root of this last equation. Thus, one solution to this differential equation will be given by $y_1(x) = x$ and we can factor the indicial equation above as follows:

$$(r-1)(r^2 + 2r + 10) = 0.$$

Therefore, using the quadratic formula, we see that the roots to this equation are $r = 1, -1 \pm 3i$. Thus, we can find two more linearly independent solutions to this equation by using Euler's formula as was done on page 458 of the text. Thus, three linearly independent solutions to this problem are given by

$$y_1(x) = x, \qquad y_2(x) = x^{-1} \cos(3 \ln x), \qquad y_3(x) = x^{-1} \sin(3 \ln x).$$

Hence, the general solution to this differential equation is

$$y(x) = c_1 x + c_2 x^{-1} \cos(3 \ln x) + c_3 x^{-1} \sin(3 \ln x).$$

**13.** We first must find two linearly independent solutions to the associated homogeneous equation. Since this is a Cauchy-Euler equation, we assume that there are solutions of the form

$$y(x) = x^r \quad \Rightarrow \quad y'(x) = rx^{r-1} \quad \Rightarrow \quad y''(x) = r(r-1)x^{r-2}.$$

Substituting these expressions into the associated homogeneous equation yields

$$[r(r-1) - 2r + 2]x^r = 0 \quad \Rightarrow \quad r^2 - 3r + 2 = 0 \quad \Rightarrow \quad (r-1)(r-2) = 0.$$

Thus, the roots to this indicial equation are $r = 1, 2$. Therefore, a general solution to the associated homogeneous equation is

$$y_h(x) = c_1 x + c_2 x^2.$$

For the variation of parameters method, let $y_1(x) = x$ and $y_2(x) = x^2$, and then assume that a particular solution has the form

$$y_p(x) = v_1(x)y_1(x) + v_2(x)y_2(x) = v_1(x)x + v_2(x)x^2.$$

In order to find $v_1(x)$ and $v_2(x)$, we would like to use formula (10) on page 195 of the text. To use equation (10), we must first find the Wronskian of $y_1$ and $y_2$. Thus, we compute

$$W[y_1, y_2](x) = y_1(x)y_2'(x) - y_2(x)y_1'(x) = 2x^2 - x^2 = x^2.$$

Next we must write the differential equation given in this problem in standard form. When we do this, we see that $g(x) = x^{-5/2}$. Therefore, by equation (10), we have

$$v_1(x) = \int \frac{-x^{-5/2}x^2}{x^2} \, dx = \int (-x^{-5/2}) dx = \frac{2}{3} x^{-3/2}$$

and

$$v_2(x) = \int \frac{x^{-5/2}x}{x^2} \, dx = \int x^{-7/2} dx = \frac{-2}{5} x^{-5/2}.$$

Thus, a particular solution is given by

$$y_p(x) = \left(\frac{2}{3} x^{-3/2}\right) x + \left(\frac{-2}{5} x^{-5/2}\right) x^2 = \frac{4}{15} x^{-1/2}.$$

Therefore, a general solution of the nonhomogeneous differential equation is given by

$$y(x) = y_h(x) + y_p(x) = c_1 x + c_2 x^2 + \frac{4}{15} x^{-1/2}.$$

# Chapter 8

**19. (a)** For this linear differential operator $L$, we have

$$
\begin{aligned}
L\left[x^r\right](x) &= x^3\left[r(r-1)(r-2)x^{r-3}\right] + x\left[rx^{r-1}\right] - x^r \\
&= r(r-1)(r-2)x^r + rx^r - x^r \\
&= \left(r^3 - 3r^2 + 3r - 1\right)x^r = (r-1)^3 x^r.
\end{aligned}
$$

**(b)** From part (a) above, we see that $r = 1$ is a root of multiplicity three of the indicial equation. Thus, we have one solution given by

$$
y_1(x) = x. \tag{8.10}
$$

To find two more linearly independent solutions, we use a method similar to that used in the text. By taking the partial derivative of $L\left[x^r\right](x) = (r-1)^3 x^r$ with respect to $r$, we have

$$
\begin{aligned}
\frac{\partial}{\partial r}\left\{L\left[x^r\right](x)\right\} &= \frac{\partial}{\partial r}\left\{(r-1)^3 x^r\right\} = 3(r-1)^2 x^r + (r-1)^3 x^r \ln x \\
\Rightarrow \quad \frac{\partial^2}{\partial r^2}\left\{L\left[x^r\right](x)\right\} &= \frac{\partial}{\partial r}\left\{3(r-1)^2 x^r + (r-1)^3 x^r \ln x\right\} \\
&= 6(r-1)x^r + 6(r-1)^2 x^r \ln x + (r-1)^3 x^r (\ln x)^2.
\end{aligned}
$$

Since $r - 1$ is a factor of every term in $\partial\left\{L\left[x^r\right](x)\right\}/\partial r$ and $\partial^2\left\{L\left[x^r\right](x)\right\}/\partial r^2$ above, we see that

$$
\left.\frac{\partial}{\partial r}\left\{L\left[x^r\right](x)\right\}\right|_{r=1} = 0, \tag{8.11}
$$

and

$$
\left.\frac{\partial^2}{\partial r^2}\left\{L\left[x^r\right](x)\right\}\right|_{r=1} = 0, \tag{8.12}
$$

We can use these facts to find the two solutions that we seek. In order to find a second solution, we would like an alternative form for

$$
\left.\frac{\partial\left\{L\left[x^r\right](x)\right\}}{\partial r}\right|_{r=1}.
$$

Using the fact that

$$
L[y](x) = x^3 y'''(x) + xy'(x) - y(x)
$$

532

and proceeding as in equation (9) on page 458 of the text with $w(r, x) = x^r$, we have

$$\frac{\partial}{\partial r} \{L[x^r](x)\} = \frac{\partial}{\partial r} \{L[w](x)\} = \frac{\partial}{\partial r} \left\{ x^3 \frac{\partial^3 w}{\partial x^3} + x \frac{\partial w}{\partial x} - w \right\}$$

$$= x^3 \frac{\partial^4 w}{\partial r \partial x^3} + x \frac{\partial^2 w}{\partial r \partial x} - \frac{\partial w}{\partial r} = x^3 \frac{\partial^4 w}{\partial x^3 \partial r} + x \frac{\partial^2 w}{\partial x \partial r} - \frac{\partial w}{\partial r}$$

$$= x^3 \frac{\partial^3}{\partial x^3} \left( \frac{\partial w}{\partial r} \right) + x \frac{\partial}{\partial x} \left( \frac{\partial w}{\partial r} \right) - \frac{\partial w}{\partial r} = L \left[ \frac{\partial w}{\partial r} \right](x),$$

where we are using the fact that mixed partials of $w(r, x)$ are equal. Therefore, combining this with equation (8.11) above yields

$$\frac{\partial}{\partial r} \{L[x^r](x)\} \bigg|_{r=1} L \left[ \frac{\partial x^r}{\partial r} \bigg|_{r=1} \right] = L \left[ x^r \ln x \big|_{r=1} \right] = L[x \ln x] = 0.$$

Thus, a second linearly independent solution is given by

$$y_2(x) = x \ln x.$$

To find a third solution, we will use equation (8.12) above. Hence, we would like to find an alternative form for $\partial^2 \{L[x^r](x)\} / \partial r^2$. To do this, we use the fact that

$$\frac{\partial}{\partial r} \{L[x^r](x)\} = x^3 \frac{\partial^4 w}{\partial r \partial x^3} + x \frac{\partial^2 w}{\partial r \partial x} - \frac{\partial w}{\partial r},$$

which we found above and the fact that mixed partial derivatives of $w(r, x)$ are equal. Thus, we have

$$\frac{\partial^2}{\partial r^2} \{L[x^r](x)\} = \frac{\partial}{\partial r} \left[ \frac{\partial}{\partial r} \{L[x^r](x)\} \right] = \frac{\partial}{\partial r} \left\{ x^3 \frac{\partial^4 w}{\partial r \partial x^3} + x \frac{\partial^2 w}{\partial r \partial x} - \frac{\partial w}{\partial r} \right\}$$

$$= x^3 \frac{\partial^5 w}{\partial r^2 \partial x^3} + x \frac{\partial^3 w}{\partial r^2 \partial x} - \frac{\partial^2 w}{\partial r^2} = x^3 \frac{\partial^5 w}{\partial x^3 \partial r^2} + x \frac{\partial^3 w}{\partial x \partial r^2} - \frac{\partial^2 w}{\partial r^2}$$

$$= x^3 \frac{\partial^3}{\partial x^3} \left( \frac{\partial^2 w}{\partial r^2} \right) + x \frac{\partial}{\partial x} \left( \frac{\partial^2 w}{\partial r^2} \right) - \frac{\partial^2 w}{\partial r^2} = L \left[ \frac{\partial^2 w}{\partial r^2} \right](x) = 0.$$

Therefore, combining this with equation (8.12) above yields

$$\frac{\partial^2}{\partial r^2} \{L[x^r](x)\} \bigg|_{r=1} = L \left[ \frac{\partial^2 (x^r)}{\partial r^2} \bigg|_{r=1} \right] = L \left[ x (\ln x)^2 \right] = 0,$$

where we have used the fact that $\partial^2 x^r / \partial r^2 = x^r (\ln x)^2$. Thus we see that another solution is

$$y_3(x) = x(\ln x)^2,$$

which, by inspection, is linearly independent from $y_1$ and $y_2$. Thus, a general solution to the differential equation is $y(x) = C_1 x + C_2 x \ln x + C_3 x (\ln x)^2$.

## EXERCISES 8.6: Method of Frobenius, page 472

**5.** By putting this equation in standard form, we see that

$$p(x) == -\frac{x-1}{(x^2-1)^2} = -\frac{x-1}{(x-1)^2(x+1)^2} = -\frac{1}{(x-1)(x+1)^2},$$

and

$$q(x) = \frac{3}{(x^2-1)^2} = \frac{3}{(x-1)^2(x+1)^2}.$$

Thus, $x = 1, -1$ are singular points of this equation. To check if $x = 1$ is regular, we note that

$$(x-1)p(x) = -\frac{1}{(x+1)^2} \quad \text{and} \quad (x-1)^2 q(x) = \frac{3}{(x+1)^2}.$$

These functions are analytic at $x = 1$. Therefore, $x = 1$ is a regular singular point for this differential equation. Next we check the singular point $x = -1$. Here

$$(x+1)p(x) = -\frac{1}{(x-1)(x+1)}$$

is not analytic at $x = -1$. Therefore, $x = -1$ is an irregular singular point for this differential equation.

**13.** By putting this equation in standard form, we see that

$$p(x) = \frac{x^2-4}{(x^2-x-2)^2} = \frac{(x-2)(x+2)}{(x-2)^2(x+1)^2} = \frac{x+2}{(x-2)(x+1)^2},$$

$$q(x) = \frac{-6x}{(x-2)^2(x+1)^2)}.$$

Thus, we have

$$(x-2)p(x) = \frac{x+2}{(x+1)^2} \quad \text{and} \quad (x-2)^2 q(x) = \frac{-6x}{(x+1)^2}.$$

Therefore, $x = 2$ is a regular singular point of this differential equation. We also observe that

$$\lim_{x \to 2}(x - 2)p(x) = \lim_{x \to 2} \frac{x + 2}{(x + 1)^2} = \frac{4}{9} = p_0 \,,$$

$$\lim_{x \to 2}(x - 2)^2 q(x) = -\lim_{x \to 2} \frac{6x}{(x + 1)^2} = -\frac{12}{9} = -\frac{4}{3} = q_0 \,.$$

Thus, we can use equation (16) on page 463 of the text to obtain the indicial equation

$$r(r - 1) + \frac{4r}{9} - \frac{4}{3} = 0 \quad \Rightarrow \quad r^2 - \frac{5r}{9} - \frac{4}{3} = 0.$$

By the quadratic formula, we see that the roots to this equation and, therefore, the exponents of the singularity $x = 2$, are given by

$$r_1 = \frac{5 + \sqrt{25 + 432}}{18} = \frac{5 + \sqrt{457}}{18} \,,$$

$$r_2 = \frac{5 - \sqrt{457}}{18} \,.$$

21. Here $p(x) = x^{-1}$ and $q(x) = 1$. This implies that $xp(x) = 1$ and $x^2 q(x) = x^2$. Therefore, we see that $x = 0$ is a regular singular point for this differential equation, and so we can use the method of Frobenius to find a solution to this problem. (Note also that $x = 0$ is the only singular point for this equation.) Thus, we will assume that this solution has the form

$$w(r, x) = x^r \sum_{n=0}^{\infty} a_n x^n = \sum_{n=0}^{\infty} a_n x^{n+r} \,.$$

We also notice that

$$p_0 = \lim_{x \to 0} xp(x) = \lim_{x \to 0} 1 = 1,$$

$$q_0 = \lim_{x \to 0} x^2 q(x) = \lim_{x \to 0} x^2 = 0.$$

Hence, we see that the indicial equation is given by

$$r(r - 1) + r = r^2 = 0.$$

This means that $r_1 = r_2 = 0$. Since $x = 0$ is the only singular point for this differential equation, we observe that the series solution $w(0, x)$ which we will find by the method of

Frobenius converges for all $x > 0$. To find the solution, we note that

$$w(r, x) = \sum_{n=0}^{\infty} a_n x^{n+r}$$

$$\Rightarrow \quad w'(r, x) = \sum_{n=0}^{\infty} (n+r)a_n x^{n+r-1}$$

$$\Rightarrow \quad w''(r, x) = \sum_{n=0}^{\infty} (n+r)(n+r-1)a_n x^{n+r-2}.$$

Notice that the power series for $w'$ and $w''$ start at $n = 0$. Substituting these expressions into the differential equation and simplifying yields

$$\sum_{n=0}^{\infty} (n+r)(n+r-1)a_n x^{n+r} + \sum_{n=0}^{\infty} (n+r)a_n x^{n+r} + \sum_{n=0}^{\infty} a_n x^{n+r+2} = 0.$$

Next we want each power series to sum over $x^{k+r}$. Thus, we let $k = n$ in the first and second power series and shift the index in the last power series by letting $k = n + 2$. Therefore, we have

$$\sum_{k=0}^{\infty} (k+r)(k+r-1)a_k x^{k+r} + \sum_{k=0}^{\infty} (k+r)a_k x^{k+r} + \sum_{k=2}^{\infty} a_{k-2} x^{k+r} = 0.$$

We will separate out the first two terms from the first two power series above so that we can start all of our power series at the same place. Thus, we have

$$(r-1)ra_0 x^r + r(1+r)a_1 x^{1+r} + \sum_{k=2}^{\infty} (k+r)(k+r-1)a_k x^{k+r}$$

$$+ ra_0 x^r + (1+r)a_1 x^{1+r} + \sum_{k=2}^{\infty} (k+r)a_k x^{k+r} + \sum_{k=2}^{\infty} a_{k-2} x^{k+r} = 0$$

$$\Rightarrow \quad [r(r-1) + r]a_0 x^r + [r(r+1) + (r+1)]a_1 x^{1+r}$$

$$+ \sum_{k=2}^{\infty} [(k+r)(k+r-1)a_k + (k+r)a_k + a_{k-2}] x^{k+r} = 0.$$

By equating coefficients and assuming that $a_0 \neq 0$, we obtain

$$r(r-1) + r = 0 \quad \text{(the indicial equation)},$$

$$[r(r+1) + (r+1)]a_1 = 0 \quad \Rightarrow \quad (r+1)^2 a_1 = 0,$$

and, for $k \geq 2$, the recurrence relation

$$(k+r)(k+r-1)a_k + (k+r)a_k + a_{k-2} = 0 \quad \Rightarrow \quad a_k = \frac{-a_{k-2}}{(k+r)^2}, \quad k \geq 2.$$

Using the fact (which we found from the indicial equation above) that $r_1 = 0$, we observe that $a_1 = 0$. Next, using the recurrence relation (and the fact that $r_1 = 0$), we see that

$$a_k = \frac{-a_{k-2}}{k^2}, \qquad k \geq 2.$$

Hence,

$$\begin{aligned}
k = 2 \quad &\Rightarrow \quad a_2 = \frac{-a_0}{4}, \\[2mm]
k = 3 \quad &\Rightarrow \quad a_3 = \frac{-a_1}{9} = 0, \\[2mm]
k = 4 \quad &\Rightarrow \quad a_4 = \frac{-a_2}{16} = \frac{-\frac{-a_0}{4}}{16} = \frac{a_0}{64}, \\[2mm]
k = 5 \quad &\Rightarrow \quad a_5 = \frac{-a_3}{25} = 0, \\[2mm]
k = 6 \quad &\Rightarrow \quad a_6 = \frac{-a_4}{36} = \frac{-\frac{a_0}{64}}{36} = -\frac{a_0}{2304}.
\end{aligned}$$

Substituting these coefficients into the solution

$$w(0,x) = \sum_{n=0}^{\infty} a_n x^n = a_0 + a_1 x + a_2 x^2 + a_3 x^3 + a_4 x^4 + a_5 x^5 + a_6 x^6 + \cdots,$$

we obtain the series solution for $x > 0$ given by

$$w(0,x) = a_0 \left[ 1 - \frac{1}{4} x^2 + \frac{1}{64} x^4 - \frac{1}{2304} x^6 + \cdots \right].$$

**25.** For this equation, we see that $xp(x) = x/2$ and $x^2 q(x) = -(x+3)/4$. Thus, $x = 0$ is a regular singular point for this equation and we can use the method of Frobenius to find a solution. To this end, we compute

$$\lim_{x \to 0} xp(x) = \lim_{x \to 0} \frac{x}{2} = 0, \qquad \text{and} \qquad \lim_{x \to 0} x^2 q(x) = \lim_{x \to 0} \frac{-(x+3)}{4} = \frac{-3}{4}.$$

# Chapter 8

Therefore, by equation (16) on page 463 of the text, the indicial equation is

$$r(r-1) - \frac{3}{4} = 0 \quad \Rightarrow \quad 4r^2 - 4r - 3 = 0 \quad \Rightarrow \quad (2r+1)(2r-3) = 0.$$

This indicial equation has roots $r_1 = 3/2$ and $r_2 = -1/2$. By the method of Frobenius, we can assume that a solution to this differential equation will have the form

$$w(r,x) = \sum_{n=0}^{\infty} a_n x^{n+r}$$

$$\Rightarrow \quad w'(r,x) = \sum_{n=0}^{\infty} (n+r) a_n x^{n+r-1}$$

$$\Rightarrow \quad w''(r,x) = \sum_{n=0}^{\infty} (n+r-1)(n+r) a_n x^{n+r-2},$$

where $r = r_1 = 3/2$. Since $x = 0$ is the only singular point for this equation, we see that the solution, $w(3/2, x)$, converges for all $x > 0$. The first step in finding this solution is to plug $w(r,x)$ and its first and second derivatives (which we have found above by term by term differentiation) into the differential equation. Thus, we obtain

$$\sum_{n=0}^{\infty} 4(n+r-1)(n+r) a_n x^{n+r} + \sum_{n=0}^{\infty} 2(n+r) a_n x^{n+r+1} - \sum_{n=0}^{\infty} a_n x^{n+r+1} - \sum_{n=0}^{\infty} 3 a_n x^{n+r} = 0.$$

By shifting indices, we can sum each power series over the same power of $x$, namely $x^{k+r}$. Thus, with the substitution $k = n$ in the first and last power series and the substitution $k = n+1$ in the two remaining power series, we obtain

$$\sum_{k=0}^{\infty} 4(k+r-1)(k+r) a_k x^{k+r} + \sum_{k=1}^{\infty} 2(k+r-1) a_{k-1} x^{k+r} - \sum_{k=1}^{\infty} a_{k-1} x^{k+r} - \sum_{k=0}^{\infty} 3 a_k x^{k+r} = 0.$$

Next removing the first term (the $k = 0$ term) from the first and last power series above and writing the result as a single power series yields

$$4(r-1)r a_0 x^r + \sum_{k=1}^{\infty} 4(k+r-1)(k+r) a_k x^{k+r} + \sum_{k=1}^{\infty} 2(k+r-1) a_{k-1} x^{k+r}$$

$$- \sum_{k=1}^{\infty} a_{k-1} x^{k+r} - 3 a_0 x^r - \sum_{k=1}^{\infty} 3 a_k x^{k+r} = 0$$

$$\Rightarrow \qquad [4(r-1)r - 3]\, a_0 x^r$$

$$+ \sum_{k=1}^{\infty} [4(k+r-1)(k+r)a_k + 2(k+r-1)a_{k-1} - a_{k-1} - 3a_k]\, x^{k+r} = 0.$$

By equating coefficients we see that each coefficient in the power series must be zero. Also we are assuming that $a_0 \neq 0$. Therefore, we have

$$4(r-1)r - 3 = 0, \qquad \text{(the indicial equation)},$$

$$4(k+r-1)(k+r)a_k + 2(k+r-1)a_{k-1} - a_{k-1} - 3a_k = 0, \qquad k \geq 1.$$

Thus, the recurrence equation is given by

$$a_k = \frac{(3 - 2k - 2r)a_{k-1}}{4(k+r-1)(k+r) - 3}, \qquad k \geq 1.$$

Therefore, for $r = r_1 = 3/2$, we have

$$a_k = \frac{-2k a_{k-1}}{4(k+1/2)(k+3/2) - 3}, \qquad k \geq 1 \qquad \Rightarrow \qquad a_k = \frac{-a_{k-1}}{2(k+2)}, \qquad k \geq 1.$$

Thus, we see that

$$k = 1 \qquad \Rightarrow \qquad a_1 = \frac{-a_0}{2 \cdot 3} = \frac{-a_0}{2^0 \cdot 3!},$$

$$k = 2 \qquad \Rightarrow \qquad a_2 = \frac{-a_1}{2 \cdot 4} = \frac{a_0}{2 \cdot 2 \cdot 3 \cdot 4} = \frac{a_0}{2^1 \cdot 4!},$$

$$k = 3 \qquad \Rightarrow \qquad a_3 = \frac{-a_2}{2 \cdot 5} = \frac{-a_0}{2^2 \cdot 5!},$$

$$k = 4 \qquad \Rightarrow \qquad a_4 = \frac{-a_3}{2 \cdot 6} = \frac{a_0}{2^3 \cdot 6!}.$$

Inspection of this sequence shows that we can write the $n$th coefficient, $a_n$, for $n \geq 1$ as

$$a_n = \frac{(-1)^n a_0}{2^{n-1}(n+2)!}.$$

Substituting these coefficients into the solution given by

$$w\left(\frac{3}{2}, x\right) = \sum_{n=0}^{\infty} a_n x^{n+(3/2)},$$

yields a power series solution for $x > 0$ given by

$$w\left(\frac{3}{2}, x\right) = a_0 x^{3/2} + a_0 \sum_{n=1}^{\infty} \frac{(-1)^n x^{n+(3/2)}}{2^{n-1}(n+2)!} .$$

But since substituting $n = 0$ into the general coefficient, $a_n$, yields $(-1)^0 a_0/(2^{-1}2!) = a_0$, the solution that we found above can be written as

$$w\left(\frac{3}{2}, x\right) = a_0 \sum_{n=0}^{\infty} \frac{(-1)^n x^{n+(3/2)}}{2^{n-1}(n+2)!} .$$

**27.** In this equation, we see that $p(x) = -1/x$ and $q(x) = -1$. Thus, the only singular point is $x = 0$. Since $xp(x) = -1$ and $x^2 q(x) = -x^2$, we see that $x = 0$ is a regular singular point for this equation and so we can use the method of Frobenius to find a solution to this equation. We also note that the solution that we find by this method will converge for all $x > 0$. To find this solution we observe that

$$p_0 = \lim_{x \to 0} xp(x) = \lim_{x \to 0}(-1) = -1 \quad \text{and} \quad q_0 = \lim_{x \to 0} x^2 q(x) = \lim_{x \to 0}(-x^2) = 0.$$

Thus, according to equation (16) on page 463 of the text, the indicial equation for the point $x = 0$ is

$$r(r-1) - r = 0 \quad \Rightarrow \quad r(r-2) = 0.$$

Therefore, the roots to the indicial equation are $r_1 = 2$, $r_2 = 0$. Hence, we will use the method of Frobenius to find the solution $w(2, x)$. If we let

$$w(r, x) = \sum_{n=0}^{\infty} a_n x^{n+r} ,$$

then

$$w'(r, x) = \sum_{n=0}^{\infty} (n+r)a_n x^{n+r-1} , \quad \text{and} \quad w''(r, x) = \sum_{n=0}^{\infty} (n+r-1)(n+r)a_n x^{n+r-2} .$$

By substituting these expressions into the differential equation and simplifying, we obtain

$$\sum_{n=0}^{\infty} (n+r-1)(n+r)a_n x^{n+r-1} - \sum_{n=0}^{\infty} (n+r)a_n x^{n+r-1} - \sum_{n=0}^{\infty} a_n x^{n+r+1} = 0.$$

Next we shift the indices by letting $k = n - 1$ in the first two power series above and $k = n + 1$ in the last power series above. Therefore, we have

$$\sum_{k=-1}^{\infty} (k+r)(k+r+1)a_{k+1}x^{k+r} - \sum_{k=-1}^{\infty} (k+r+1)a_{k+1}x^{k+r} - \sum_{k=1}^{\infty} a_{k-1}x^{k+r} = 0.$$

We can start all three of these summations at the same term, the $k = 1$ term, if we separate out the first two terms (the $k = -1$ and $k = 0$ terms) from the first two power series. Thus, we have

$$(r-1)ra_0x^{r-1} + r(r+1)a_1x^r + \sum_{k=1}^{\infty} (k+r)(k+r+1)a_{k+1}x^{k+r}$$

$$-ra_0x^{r-1} - (r+1)a_1x^r - \sum_{k=1}^{\infty} (k+r+1)a_{k+1}x^{k+r} - \sum_{k=1}^{\infty} a_{k-1}x^{k+r} = 0$$

$$\Rightarrow \quad [(r-1)r - r]a_0x^{r-1} + [r(r+1) - (r+1)]a_1x^r$$

$$+ \sum_{k=1}^{\infty} [(k+r)(k+r+1)a_{k+1} - (k+r+1)a_{k+1} - a_{k-1}]x^{k+r} = 0.$$

By equating coefficients and assuming that $a_0 \neq 0$, we obtain

$$r(r-1) - r = 0, \qquad \text{(the indicial equation)},$$
$$(r+1)(r-1)a_1 = 0, \tag{8.13}$$
$$(k+r)(k+r+1)a_{k+1} - (k+r+1)a_{k+1} - a_{k-1} = 0, \qquad k \geq 1,$$

where the last equation above is the recurrence relation. Simplifying this recurrence relation yields

$$a_{k+1} = \frac{a_{k-1}}{(k+r+1)(k+r-1)}, \qquad k \geq 1. \tag{8.14}$$

Next we let $r = r_1 = 2$ in equation (8.13) and in the recurrence relation, equation (8.14), to obtain

$$3a_1 = 0 \quad \Rightarrow \quad a_1 = 0,$$
$$a_{k+1} = \frac{a_{k-1}}{(k+3)(k+1)}, \qquad k \geq 1.$$

Thus, we have

$$k = 1 \quad \Rightarrow \quad a_2 = \frac{a_0}{4 \cdot 2}\,,$$

$$k = 2 \quad \Rightarrow \quad a_3 = \frac{a_1}{5 \cdot 3} = 0\,,$$

$$k = 3 \quad \Rightarrow \quad a_4 = \frac{a_2}{6 \cdot 4} = \frac{a_0}{6 \cdot 4 \cdot 4 \cdot 2} = \frac{a_0}{2^4 \cdot 3 \cdot 2 \cdot 2 \cdot 1 \cdot 1} = \frac{a_0}{2^4 \cdot 3! \cdot 2!}\,,$$

$$k = 4 \quad \Rightarrow \quad a_5 = \frac{a_3}{7 \cdot 5} = 0\,,$$

$$k = 5 \quad \Rightarrow \quad a_6 = \frac{a_4}{8 \cdot 6} = \frac{a_0}{8 \cdot 6 \cdot 2^4 \cdot 3! \cdot 2!} = \frac{a_0}{2^6 \cdot 4! \cdot 3!}\,.$$

By inspection we can now see that the coefficients of the power series solution $w(2, x)$ are

$$a_{2n-1} = 0$$

and

$$a_{2n} = \frac{a_0}{2^{2n} \cdot (n+1)! n!}\,,$$

for all $n \geq 1$. Thus, substituting these coefficients into the power series solution yields the solution

$$w(2, x) = a_0 \sum_{n=0}^{\infty} \frac{x^{2n+2}}{2^{2n} \cdot (n+1)! n!}\,.$$

**35.** In applying the method of Frobenius to this third order linear differential equation, we will seek a solution of the form

$$w(r, x) = \sum_{n=0}^{\infty} a_n x^{n+r}$$

$$\Rightarrow \quad w'(r, x) = \sum_{n=0}^{\infty} (n+r) a_n x^{n+r-1}$$

$$\Rightarrow \quad w''(r, x) = \sum_{n=0}^{\infty} (n+r-1)(n+r) a_n x^{n+r-2}$$

$$\Rightarrow \quad w'''(r, x) = \sum_{n=0}^{\infty} (n+r-2)(n+r-1)(n+r) a_n x^{n+r-3}\,,$$

where we have differentiated term by term. Substituting these expressions into the differential equation and simplifying yields

$$\sum_{n=0}^{\infty} 6(n+r-2)(n+r-1)(n+r)a_n x^{n+r} + \sum_{n=0}^{\infty} 13(n+r-1)(n+r)a_n x^{n+r}$$

$$+ \sum_{n=0}^{\infty}(n+r)a_n x^{n+r} + \sum_{n=0}^{\infty}(n+r)a_n x^{n+r+1} + \sum_{n=0}^{\infty} a_n x^{n+r+1} = 0.$$

By the shift of index $k = n+1$ in the last two power series above and the shift $k = n$ in all of the other power series, we obtain

$$\sum_{k=0}^{\infty} 6(k+r-2)(k+r-1)(k+r)a_k x^{k+r} + \sum_{k=0}^{\infty} 13(k+r-1)(k+r)a_k x^{k+r}$$

$$+ \sum_{k=0}^{\infty}(k+r)a_k x^{k+r} + \sum_{k=1}^{\infty}(k-1+r)a_{k-1} x^{k+r} + \sum_{k=1}^{\infty} a_{k-1} x^{k+r} = 0.$$

Next we remove the first term from each of the first three power series above so that all of these series start at $k = 1$. Thus, we have

$$6(r-2)(r-1)ra_0 x^r + \sum_{k=1}^{\infty} 6(k+r-2)(k+r-1)(k+r)a_k x^{k+r}$$

$$+13(r-1)ra_0 x^r + \sum_{k=1}^{\infty} 13(k+r-1)(k+r)a_k x^{k+r} + ra_0 x^r + \sum_{k=1}^{\infty}(k+r)a_k x^{k+r}$$

$$+ \sum_{k=1}^{\infty}(k-1+r)a_{k-1} x^{k+r} + \sum_{k=1}^{\infty} a_{k-1} x^{k+r} = 0$$

$$\Rightarrow \quad [6(r-2)(r-1)r + 13(r-1)r + r]a_0 x^r$$

$$+ \sum_{k=1}^{\infty}[6(k+r-2)(k+r-1)(k+r)a_k + 13(k+r-1)(k+r)a_k$$

$$+(k+r)a_k + (k-1+r)a_{k-1} + a_{k-1}]x^{k+r} = 0. \qquad (8.15)$$

If we assume that $a_0 \neq 0$ and set the coefficient of $x^r$ equal to zero, we find that the *indicial equation* is

$$6(r-2)(r-1)r + 13(r-1)r + r = 0 \quad \Rightarrow \quad r^2(6r-5) = 0.$$

Hence, the roots to the indicial equation are 0, 0, and 5/6. We will find the solution associated with the largest of these roots. That is, we will find $w(5/6, x)$. Also, from equation (8.15), we

Chapter 8

see that we have the recurrence relation

$$6(k+r-2)(k+r-1)(k+r)a_k + 13(k+r-1)(k+r)a_k$$
$$+(k+r)a_k + (k-1+r)a_{k-1} + a_{k-1} = 0, \qquad k \geq 1$$

$$\Rightarrow \quad a_k = \frac{-a_{k-1}}{6(k+r-2)(k+r-1) + 13(k+r-1) + 1}, \qquad k \geq 1.$$

If we assume that $r = 5/6$, then this recurrence relation simplifies to

$$a_k = \frac{-a_{k-1}}{k(6k+5)}, \qquad k \geq 1.$$

Therefore, we have

$$k = 1 \quad \Rightarrow \quad a_1 = \frac{-a_0}{11},$$
$$k = 2 \quad \Rightarrow \quad a_2 = \frac{-a_1}{34} = \frac{a_0}{374},$$
$$k = 3 \quad \Rightarrow \quad a_3 = \frac{-a_2}{69} = \frac{-a_0}{25,806}.$$

By substituting these coefficients into the solution $w(5/6, x) = \sum_{n=0}^{\infty} a_n x^{n+(5/6)}$, we obtain

$$w\left(\frac{5}{6}, x\right) = a_0\left(x^{5/6} - \frac{x^{11/6}}{11} + \frac{x^{17/6}}{374} - \frac{x^{23/6}}{25,806} + \cdots\right).$$

**41.** If we let $z = 1/x$ ($\Rightarrow dz/dx = -1/x^2$), then we can define a new function $Y(z)$ as

$$Y(z) := y\left(\frac{1}{z}\right) = y(x).$$

Thus, by the chain rule, we have

$$\frac{dy}{dx} = \frac{dY}{dx} = \left(\frac{dY}{dz}\right)\left(\frac{dz}{dx}\right) = \left(\frac{dY}{dz}\right)\left(-\frac{1}{x^2}\right) \qquad (8.16)$$

$$\Rightarrow \quad -x^2 \frac{dy}{dx} = \frac{dY}{dz}. \qquad (8.17)$$

Therefore, using the product rule and chain rule, we see that

$$\frac{d^2y}{dx^2} = \frac{d^2Y}{dx^2} = \frac{d}{dx}\left(\frac{dY}{dx}\right) = \frac{d}{dx}\left[\left(-\frac{1}{x^2}\right)\left(\frac{dY}{dz}\right)\right] \qquad \text{(by (8.16) above)}$$

$$= \frac{d}{dx}\left(-\frac{1}{x^2}\right) \times \left(\frac{dY}{dz}\right) + \left(-\frac{1}{x^2}\right) \times \frac{d}{dx}\left(\frac{dY}{dz}\right) \quad \text{(by product rule)}$$

$$= \left(\frac{2}{x^3}\right) \times \left(\frac{dY}{dz}\right) + \left(-\frac{1}{x^2}\right) \times \left[\left(\frac{d^2Y}{dz^2}\right)\left(\frac{dz}{dx}\right)\right] \quad \text{(by chain rule)}$$

$$= \left(\frac{2}{x^3}\right) \times \left(\frac{dY}{dz}\right) + \left(-\frac{1}{x^2}\right)^2 \times \left(\frac{d^2Y}{dz^2}\right) \quad \left(\text{since } \frac{dz}{dx} = -\frac{1}{x^2}\right)$$

$$= \frac{2}{x^3}\frac{dY}{dz} + \frac{1}{x^4}\frac{d^2Y}{dz^2}.$$

Hence, we have

$$x^3\frac{d^2y}{dx^2} = 2\frac{dY}{dz} + \frac{1}{x}\frac{d^2Y}{dz^2} = 2\frac{dY}{dz} + z\frac{d^2Y}{dz^2}. \tag{8.18}$$

By using the fact that $Y(z) = y(x)$ and equations (8.17) and (8.18) above, we can now transform the original differential equation into the differential equation

$$2\frac{dY}{dz} + z\frac{d^2Y}{dz^2} + \frac{dY}{dz} - Y = 0 \quad \Rightarrow \quad zY'' + 3Y' - Y = 0. \tag{8.19}$$

We will now solve this transformed differential equation. To this end, we first note that

$$p(z) = \frac{3}{z} \quad \Rightarrow \quad zp(z) = 3,$$

and

$$q(z)\frac{-1}{z} \quad \Rightarrow \quad z^2g(z) = -z.$$

Therefore, $z = 0$ is a regular singular point of this equation and so infinity is a regular singular point of the original equation.

To find a power series solution for equation (8.19), we first compute

$$p_0 = \lim_{z\to 0} zp(z) = 3 \quad \text{and} \quad q_0 = \lim_{z\to 0} z^2q(z) = 0.$$

Thus, the indicial equation for equation (8.19) is

$$r(r-1) + 3r = 0 \quad \Rightarrow \quad r(r+2) = 0.$$

Hence, this indicial equation has roots $r_1 = 0$ and $r_2 = -2$. We seek a solution of the form

$$w(r, z) = \sum_{n=0}^{\infty} a_n z^{n+r}.$$

Substituting this expression into equation (8.19) above yields

$$z \sum_{n=0}^{\infty} (n+r-1)(n+r)a_n z^{n+r-2} + 3\sum_{n=0}^{\infty}(n+r)a_n z^{n+r-1} - \sum_{n=0}^{\infty} a_n z^{n+r} = 0.$$

By simplifying, this equation becomes

$$\sum_{n=0}^{\infty} (n+r-1)(n+r)a_n z^{n+r-1} + \sum_{n=0}^{\infty} 3(n+r)a_n z^{n+r-1} - \sum_{n=0}^{\infty} a_n z^{n+r} = 0.$$

Making the shift of index $k = n - 1$ in the first two power series and $k = n$ in the last power series allows us to sum each power series over the same powers of $z$, namely $z^{k+r}$. Thus, we have

$$\sum_{k=-1}^{\infty}(k+r)(k+r+1)a_{k+1}z^{k+r} + \sum_{k=-1}^{\infty} 3(k+r+1)a_{k+1}z^{n+r} - \sum_{k=0}^{\infty} a_k z^{k+r} = 0.$$

By removing the first term from the first two power series above, we can write these three summations as a single power series. Therefore, we have

$$(r-1)ra_0 z^{r-1} + \sum_{k=0}^{\infty}(k+r)(k+r+1)a_{k+1}z^{k+r}$$

$$+3ra_0 z^{r-1} + \sum_{k=0}^{\infty} 3(k+r+1)a_{k+1}z^{n+r} - \sum_{k=0}^{\infty} a_k z^{k+r} = 0$$

$$\Rightarrow \quad [(r-1)r + 3r]\, a_0 z^{r-1} + \sum_{k=0}^{\infty} [(k+r)(k+r+1)a_{k+1} + 3(k+r+1)a_{k+1} - a_k]\, z^{k+r} = 0.$$

Equating coefficients and assuming that $a_0 \neq 0$ yields the indicial equation, $(r-1)r + 3r = 0$, and the recurrence relation

$$(k+r)(k+r+1)a_{k+1} + 3(k+r+1)a_{k+1} - a_k = 0, \qquad k \geq 0$$

$$\Rightarrow \quad a_{k+1} = \frac{a_k}{(k+r+1)(k+r+3)}, \qquad k \geq 0.$$

Thus, with $r = r_1 = 0$, we obtain the recurrence relation

$$a_{k+1} = \frac{a_k}{(k+1)(k+3)}, \qquad k \geq 3.$$

Since $a_0$ is an arbitrary number, we see from this recurrence equation that the next three coefficients are given by

$$k = 0 \quad \Rightarrow \quad a_1 = \frac{a_0}{3},$$
$$k = 1 \quad \Rightarrow \quad a_2 = \frac{a_1}{8} = \frac{a_0}{24},$$
$$k = 2 \quad \Rightarrow \quad a_3 = \frac{a_2}{15} = \frac{a_0}{360}.$$

Thus, from the method of Frobenius, we obtain a power series solution for equation (8.19) given by

$$Y(z) = w(0, z) = \sum_{n=0}^{\infty} a_n z^n = a_0 \left( 1 + \frac{1}{3} z + \frac{1}{24} z^2 + \frac{1}{360} z^3 + \cdots \right).$$

In order to find the solution of the original differential equation, we again make the substitution $z = 1/x$ and $Y(z) = Y(x^{-1}) = y(x)$. Therefore, in the solution found above, we replace the $z$'s with $1/x$ to obtain the solution given by

$$y(x) = Y\left(x^{-1}\right) = a_0 \left( 1 + \frac{1}{3} x^{-1} + \frac{1}{24} x^{-2} + \frac{1}{360} x^{-3} + \cdots \right).$$

**EXERCISES 8.7:  Finding a Second Linearly Independent Solution, page 482**

3. In Problem 21 of Exercises 8.6, we found one power series solution for this differential equation about the point $x = 0$ given by

$$y_1(x) = 1 - \frac{1}{4} x^2 + \frac{1}{64} x^4 - \frac{1}{2304} x^6 + \cdots,$$

where we let $a_0 = 1$. We also found that the roots to the indicial equation are $r_1 = r_2 = 0$. Thus, to find a second linearly independent solution about the regular singular point $x = 0$, we will use part (b) of Theorem 7 on page 475 of the text. Therefore, we see that this second linearly independent solution will have the form given by

$$y_2(x) = y_1(x) \ln x + \sum_{n=1}^{\infty} b_n x^n$$

$$\Rightarrow \quad y_2'(x) = y_1'(x) \ln x + x^{-1} y_1(x) + \sum_{n=1}^{\infty} n b_n x^{n-1}$$

Chapter 8

$$\Rightarrow \qquad y_2''(x) = y_1''(x)\ln x + 2x^{-1}y_1'(x) - x^{-2}y_1(x) + \sum_{n=1}^{\infty} n(n-1)b_n x^{n-2}.$$

Substituting these expressions into the differential equation yields

$$x^2\left\{ y_1''(x)\ln x + 2x^{-1}y_1'(x) - x^{-2}y_1(x) + \sum_{n=1}^{\infty} n(n-1)b_n x^{n-2}\right\}$$
$$+x\left\{ y_1'(x)\ln x + x^{-1}y_1(x) + \sum_{n=1}^{\infty} nb_n x^{n-1}\right\} + x^2\left\{ y_1(x)\ln x + \sum_{n=1}^{\infty} b_n x^{n}\right\} = 0,$$

which simplifies to

$$x^2 y_1''(x)\ln x + 2xy_1'(x) - y_1(x) + \sum_{n=1}^{\infty} n(n-1)b_n x^{n}$$
$$+xy_1'(x)\ln x + y_1(x) + \sum_{n=1}^{\infty} nb_n x^{n} + x^2 y_1(x)\ln x + \sum_{n=1}^{\infty} b_n x^{n+2} = 0,$$

$$\Rightarrow \qquad \left(x^2 y_1''(x) + xy_1'(x) + x^2 y_1(x)\right)\ln x + 2xy_1'(x)$$
$$+\sum_{n=1}^{\infty} n(n-1)b_n x^{n} + \sum_{n=1}^{\infty} nb_n x^{n} + \sum_{n=1}^{\infty} b_n x^{n+2} = 0.$$

Therefore, since $y_1(x)$ is a solution to the differential equation, the term in braces is zero and the above equation reduces to

$$2xy_1'(x) + \sum_{n=1}^{\infty} n(n-1)b_n x^{n} + \sum_{n=1}^{\infty} nb_n x^{n} + \sum_{n=1}^{\infty} b_n x^{n+2} = 0.$$

Next we make the substitution $k = n + 2$ in the last power series above and the substitution $k = n$ in the other two power series so that we can sum all three of the power series over the same power of $x$, namely $x^k$. Thus, we have

$$2xy_1'(x) + \sum_{k=1}^{\infty} k(k-1)b_k x^{k} + \sum_{k=1}^{\infty} kb_k x^{k} + \sum_{k=3}^{\infty} b_{k-2} x^{k} = 0.$$

By separating out the first two terms in the first two summations above and simplifying, we obtain

$$2xy_1'(x) + 0 + 2b_2 x^2 + \sum_{k=3}^{\infty} k(k-1)b_k x^{k} + b_1 x + 2b_2 x^2 + \sum_{k=3}^{\infty} kb_k x^{k} + \sum_{k=3}^{\infty} b_{k-2} x^{k} = 0$$

548

$$\Rightarrow \qquad 2xy_1'(x) + b_1 x + 4b_2 x^2 + \sum_{k=3}^{\infty} \left(k^2 b_k + b_{k-2}\right) x^k = 0. \qquad (8.20)$$

By differentiating the series for $y_1(x)$ term by term, we obtain

$$y_1'(x) = -\frac{1}{2}x + \frac{1}{16}x^3 - \frac{1}{384}x^5 + \cdots.$$

Thus, substituting this expression for $y_1'(x)$ into equation (8.20) above and simplifying yields

$$\left\{-x^2 + \frac{1}{8}x^4 - \frac{1}{192}x^6 + \cdots\right\} + b_1 x + 4b_2 x^2 + \sum_{k=3}^{\infty} \left(k^2 b_k + b_{k-2}\right) x^k = 0.$$

Therefore, by equating coefficients, we see that

$$b_1 = 0;$$

$$4b_2 - 1 = 0 \qquad \Rightarrow \qquad b_2 = \frac{1}{4};$$

$$9b_3 + b_1 = 0 \qquad \Rightarrow \qquad b_3 = 0;$$

$$\frac{1}{8} + 16b_4 + b_2 = 0 \qquad \Rightarrow \qquad b_4 = \frac{-3}{128};$$

$$25b_5 + b_3 = 0 \qquad \Rightarrow \qquad b_5 = 0;$$

$$\frac{-1}{192} + 36b_6 + b_4 = 0 \qquad \Rightarrow \qquad b_6 = \frac{11}{13,824}.$$

Substituting these coefficients into the solution

$$y_2(x) = y_1(x)\ln x + \sum_{n=1}^{\infty} b_n x^n,$$

yields

$$y_2(x) = y_1(x)\ln x + \frac{1}{4}x^2 - \frac{3}{128}x^4 + \frac{11}{13,824}x^6 + \cdots.$$

Thus, a general solution of this differential equation is given by

$$y(x) = c_1 y_1(x) + c_2 y_2(x),$$

where

$$y_1(x) = 1 - \frac{1}{4}x^2 + \frac{1}{64}x^4 - \frac{1}{2304}x^6 + \cdots,$$

$$y_2(x) = y_1(x)\ln x + \frac{1}{4}x^2 - \frac{3}{128}x^4 + \frac{11}{13,824}x^6 + \cdots.$$

# Chapter 8

**7.** In Problem 25 of Section 8.6, we found a solution to this differential equation about the regular singular point $x = 0$ given by

$$y_1(x) = \sum_{n=0}^{\infty} \frac{(-1)^n x^{n+(3/2)}}{2^{n-1}(n+2)!} = x^{3/2} - \frac{1}{6} x^{5/2} + \frac{1}{48} x^{7/2} + \cdots,$$

where we let $a_0 = 1$. We also found that the roots to the indicial equation for this problem are $r_1 = 3/2$ and $r_2 = -1/2$, and so $r_1 - r_2 = 2$. Thus, in order to find a second linearly independent solution about $x = 0$, we will use part (c) of Theorem 7 on page 475 of the text. Therefore, we will assume that this second solution has the form

$$y_2(x) = Cy_1(x) \ln x + \sum_{n=0}^{\infty} b_n x^{n-(1/2)}, \qquad b_0 \neq 0$$

$$\Rightarrow \quad y_2'(x) = Cy_1'(x) \ln x + C\frac{1}{x} y_1(x) + \sum_{n=0}^{\infty} \left(n - \frac{1}{2}\right) b_n x^{n-(3/2)}$$

$$\Rightarrow \quad y_2''(x) = Cy_1''(x) \ln x + 2C\frac{1}{x} y_1'(x) - C\frac{1}{x^2} y_1(x) + \sum_{n=0}^{\infty} \left(n - \frac{3}{2}\right)\left(n - \frac{1}{2}\right) b_n x^{n-(5/2)}.$$

Substituting these expressions into the differential equation yields

$$4x^2 \left[ Cy_1''(x) \ln x + 2C\frac{1}{x} y_1'(x) - C\frac{1}{x^2} y_1(x) + \sum_{n=0}^{\infty} \left(n - \frac{3}{2}\right)\left(n - \frac{1}{2}\right) b_n x^{n-(5/2)} \right]$$

$$+ 2x^2 \left[ Cy_1'(x) \ln x + C\frac{1}{x} y_1(x) + \sum_{n=0}^{\infty} \left(n - \frac{1}{2}\right) b_n x^{n-(3/2)} \right]$$

$$-(x+3) \left[ Cy_1(x) \ln x + \sum_{n=0}^{\infty} b_n x^{n-(1/2)} \right] = 0.$$

Multiplying through, we get

$$\left[ 4x^2 Cy_1''(x) \ln x + 8Cxy_1'(x) - 4Cy_1(x) + \sum_{n=0}^{\infty} 4\left(n - \frac{3}{2}\right)\left(n - \frac{1}{2}\right) b_n x^{n-(1/2)} \right]$$

$$+ \left[ 2x^2 Cy_1'(x) \ln x + 2Cxy_1(x) + \sum_{n=0}^{\infty} 2\left(n - \frac{1}{2}\right) b_n x^{n+(1/2)} \right]$$

$$- \left[ Cxy_1(x) \ln x + \sum_{n=0}^{\infty} b_n x^{n+(1/2)} + 3Cy_1(x) \ln x + \sum_{n=0}^{\infty} 3b_n x^{n-(1/2)} \right] = 0,$$

which simplifies to

$$C\left[4x^2y_1''(x) + 2x^2y_1'(x) - xy_1(x) - 3y_1(x)\right]\ln x + 8Cxy_1'(x) + 2C(x-2)y_1(x)$$

$$+ \sum_{n=0}^{\infty}(2n-3)(2n-1)b_nx^{n-(1/2)} + \sum_{n=0}^{\infty}(2n-1)b_nx^{n+(1/2)}$$

$$- \sum_{n=0}^{\infty}b_nx^{n+(1/2)} - \sum_{n=0}^{\infty}3b_nx^{n-(1/2)} = 0.$$

Since $y_1(x)$ is a solution to the differential equation, the term in brackets is zero. By shifting indices so that each power series is summed over the same power of $x$, we have

$$8Cxy_1'(x) + 2C(x-2)y_1(x) + \sum_{k=0}^{\infty}(2k-3)(2k-1)b_kx^{k-(1/2)}$$

$$+ \sum_{k=1}^{\infty}(2k-3)b_{k-1}x^{k-(1/2)} - \sum_{k=1}^{\infty}b_{k-1}x^{k-(1/2)} - \sum_{k=0}^{\infty}3b_kx^{k-(1/2)} = 0.$$

By writing all of these summations as a single power series (noting that the $k = 0$ term of the first and last summations add to zero), we obtain

$$8Cxy_1'(x) + 2C(x-2)y_1(x) + \sum_{k=0}^{\infty}(2k-3)(2k-1)b_kx^{k-(1/2)}$$

$$+ \sum_{k=1}^{\infty}\left[(2k-3)(2k-1)b_k + (2k-3)b_{k-1} - b_{k-1} - 3b_k\right]x^{k-(1/2)} = 0.$$

Substituting into this equation the expressions for $y_1(x)$ and $y_1'(x)$ given by

$$y_1(x) = \sum_{n=0}^{\infty}\frac{(-1)^n x^{n+(3/2)}}{2^{n-1}(n+2)!}, \qquad y_1'(x) = \sum_{n=0}^{\infty}\frac{(-1)^n[n+(3/2)]x^{n+(1/2)}}{2^{n-1}(n+2)!},$$

yields

$$\sum_{n=0}^{\infty}\frac{8C(-1)^n[n+(3/2)]x^{n+(3/2)}}{2^{n-1}(n+2)!} + \sum_{n=0}^{\infty}\frac{2C(-1)^n x^{n+(5/2)}}{2^{n-1}(n+2)!}$$

$$- \sum_{n=0}^{\infty}\frac{4C(-1)^n x^{n+(3/2)}}{2^{n-1}(n+2)!} + \sum_{k=1}^{\infty}\left[4k(k-2)b_k + 2(k-2)b_{k-1}\right]x^{k-(1/2)} = 0,$$

# Chapter 8

where we have simplified the expression inside the last summation. Combining the first and third power series yields

$$\sum_{n=0}^{\infty} \frac{8C(-1)^n(n+1)x^{n+(3/2)}}{2^{n-1}(n+2)!} + \sum_{n=0}^{\infty} \frac{2C(-1)^n x^{n+(5/2)}}{2^{n-1}(n+2)!}$$

$$+ \sum_{k=1}^{\infty} \left[4k(k-2)b_k + 2(k-2)b_{k-1}\right] x^{k-(1/2)} = 0, \quad (8.21)$$

By writing out the terms up to order $x^{7/2}$, we obtain

$$8C\left[x^{3/2} - \frac{1}{3}x^{5/2} + \frac{3}{16}x^{7/2} + \cdots\right] + 2C\left[x^{5/2} - \frac{1}{6}x^{7/2} + \cdots\right]$$

$$+ \left[(-4b_1 - 2b_0)x^{1/2} + (12b_3 + 2b_2)x^{5/2} + (32b_4 + 4b_3)x^{7/2} + \cdots\right] = 0.$$

Setting the coefficients equal to zero, yields

$$-4b_1 - 2b_0 = 0 \qquad\qquad \Rightarrow \qquad b_1 = -b_0/2;$$
$$8C = 0 \qquad\qquad \Rightarrow \qquad C = 0;$$
$$-(8/3)C + 2C + 12b_3 + 2b_2 = 0 \quad \Rightarrow \quad b_3 = -b_2/6;$$
$$(2/3)C - (1/3)C + 32b_4 + 4b_3 = 0 \quad \Rightarrow \quad b_4 = -b_3/8 = b_2/48.$$

From this we see that $b_0$ and $b_2$ are arbitrary constants and that $C = 0$. Also, since $C = 0$, we can use the last power series in (8.21) to obtain the recurrence equation $b_k = b_{k-1}/(2k)$. Thus, every coefficient after $b_4$ will depend only on $b_2$ (not on $b_0$). Substituting these coefficients into the solution,

$$y_2(x) = Cy_1(x)\ln x + \sum_{n=0}^{\infty} b_n x^{n-(1/2)},$$

yields

$$y_2(x) = b_0\left[x^{-1/2} - \frac{1}{2}x^{1/2}\right] + b_2\left[x^{3/2} - \frac{1}{6}x^{5/2} + \frac{1}{48}x^{7/2} + \cdots\right]$$

The expression in the brackets following $b_2$ is just the series expansion for $y_1(x)$. Hence, in order to obtain a second linearly independent solution, we must choose $b_0$ to be nonzero. Taking $b_0 = 1$ and $b_2 = 0$ gives

$$y_2(x) = x^{-1/2} - \frac{1}{2}x^{1/2}.$$

Therefore, a general solution is

$$y(x) = c_1 y_1(x) + c_2 y_2(x),$$

where

$$y_1(x) = x^{3/2} - \frac{1}{6} x^{5/2} + \frac{1}{48} x^{7/2} + \cdots \qquad \text{and} \qquad y_2(x) = x^{-1/2} - \frac{1}{2} x^{1/2} .$$

17. In Problem 35 of Section 8.6, we assumed that there exists a series solution to this problem of the form $w(r, x) = \sum_{n=0}^{\infty} a_n x^{n+r}$. This led to the equation (cf. equation (8.15), of the solution to Problem 35, Exercises 8.6)

$$r^2(6r - 5)a_0 x^r + \sum_{k=1}^{\infty} \left\{ (k+r)^2 [6(k+r) - 5]a_k + (k+r)a_{k-1} \right\} x^{k+r} = 0. \qquad (8.22)$$

From this we found the indicial equation $r^2(6r - 5) = 0$, which has roots $r = 0, 0, 5/6$. By using the root $5/6$, we found the solution $w(5/6, x)$. Hence one solution is

$$y_1(x) = x^{5/6} - \frac{x^{11/6}}{11} + \frac{x^{17/6}}{374} - \frac{x^{23/6}}{25,806} + \cdots ,$$

where we have chosen $a_0 = 1$ in $w(5/6, x)$. We now seek two more linearly independent solutions to this differential equation. To find a second linearly independent solution, we will use the root $r = 0$ and set the coefficients in equation (8.22) to zero to obtain the recurrence relation

$$k^2(6k - 5)a_k + ka_{k-1} = 0, \qquad k \geq 1.$$

Solving for $a_k$ in terms of $a_{k-1}$ gives

$$a_k = \frac{-a_{k-1}}{k(6k - 5)}, \qquad k \geq 1.$$

Thus, we have

$$k = 1 \qquad \Rightarrow \qquad a_1 = -a_0 ,$$

$$k = 2 \qquad \Rightarrow \qquad a_2 = \frac{-a_1}{14} = \frac{a_0}{14} ,$$

$$k = 3 \quad \Rightarrow \quad a_3 = \frac{-a_2}{39} = \frac{-a_0}{546},$$

$$k = 4 \quad \Rightarrow \quad a_4 = \frac{-a_3}{76} = \frac{a_0}{41,496},$$

$$k = 5 \quad \Rightarrow \quad a_5 = \frac{-a_4}{125} = \frac{-a_0}{5,187,000}.$$

Plugging these coefficients into the solution $w(0, x)$ and setting $a_0 = 1$ yields a second linearly independent solution

$$y_2(x) = 1 - x + \frac{1}{14}x^2 - \frac{1}{546}x^3 + \frac{1}{41,496}x^4 - \frac{1}{5,187,000}x^5 + \cdots.$$

To find a third linearly independent solution, we will use the repeated root $r = 0$ and assume that, as in the case of second order equations with repeated roots, the solution that we seek will have the form

$$y_3(x) = y_2(x)\ln x + \sum_{n=1}^{\infty} c_n x^n.$$

Since the first three derivatives of $y_3(x)$ are given by

$$y_3'(x) = y_2'(x)\ln x + x^{-1}y_2(x) + \sum_{n=1}^{\infty} nc_n x^{n-1},$$

$$y_3''(x) = y_2''(x)\ln x + 2x^{-1}y_2'(x) - x^{-2}y_2(x) + \sum_{n=1}^{\infty}(n-1)nc_n x^{n-2},$$

$$y_3'''(x) = y_2'''(x)\ln x + 3x^{-1}y_2''(x) - 3x^{-2}y_2'(x) + 2x^{-3}y_2(x) + \sum_{n=1}^{\infty}(n-2)(n-1)nc_n x^{n-3},$$

substituting $y_3(x)$ into the differential equation yields

$$6x^3 y'''(x) + 13x^2 y''(x) + (x + x^2)y'(x) + xy(x)$$

$$= 6x^3 \left[ y_2'''(x)\ln x + 3x^{-1}y_2''(x) - 3x^{-2}y_2'(x) + 2x^{-3}y_2(x) + \sum_{n=1}^{\infty}(n-2)(n-1)nc_n x^{n-3} \right]$$

$$+ 13x^2 \left[ y_2''(x)\ln x + 2x^{-1}y_2'(x) - x^{-2}y_2(x) + \sum_{n=1}^{\infty}(n-1)nc_n x^{n-2} \right]$$

$$+ (x + x^2)\left[ y_2'(x)\ln x + x^{-1}y_2(x) + \sum_{n=1}^{\infty} nc_n x^{n-1} \right] + x\left[ y_2(x)\ln x + \sum_{n=1}^{\infty} c_n x^n \right] = 0.$$

Since $y_2(x)$ is a solution to the given equation, this simplifies to

$$18x^2 y_2''(x) + 8xy_2'(x) + xy_2(x) + \sum_{n=1}^{\infty} 6(n-2)(n-1)nc_n x^n$$

$$+ \sum_{n=1}^{\infty} 13(n-1)nc_n x^n + \sum_{n=1}^{\infty} nc_n x^n + \sum_{n=1}^{\infty} nc_n x^{n+1} + \sum_{n=1}^{\infty} c_n x^{n+1} = 0.$$

By shifting indices and then starting all of the resulting power series at the same point, we can combine all of the summations above into a single power series. Thus, we have

$$18x^2 y_2''(x) + 8xy_2'(x) + xy_2(x)$$

$$+ c_1 x + \sum_{k=2}^{\infty} \left[6(k-2)(k-1)kc_k + 13(k-1)kc_k + kc_k + kc_{k-1}\right] x^k = 0. \qquad (8.23)$$

By computing $y_2'(x)$ and $y_2''(x)$, we obtain

$$y_2'(x) = -1 + \frac{1}{7} x - \frac{1}{182} x^2 + \frac{1}{10374} x^3 + \cdots,$$

$$y_2''(x) = \frac{1}{7} - \frac{1}{91} x + \frac{1}{3458} x^2 + \cdots.$$

By substituting these expressions into equation (8.23), we have

$$18x^2 \left(\frac{1}{7} - \frac{x}{91} + \frac{x^2}{3458} + \cdots\right) + 8x \left(-1 + \frac{x}{7} - \frac{x^2}{182} + \frac{x^3}{10374} + \cdots\right)$$

$$+ x \left(1 - x + \frac{x^2}{14} - \frac{x^3}{546} + \frac{x^4}{41,496} + \cdots\right) + c_1 x + \sum_{k=2}^{\infty} \left[(6k^3 - 5k^2)c_k + kc_{k-1}\right] x^k = 0.$$

Writing out the terms up to order $x^3$ we find

$$(-7 + c_1) x + \left(\frac{19}{7} + 28c_2 + 2c_1\right) x^2 + \left(-\frac{31}{182} + 117c_3 + 3c_2\right) x^3 + \cdots = 0.$$

By equating coefficients to zero, we obtain

$$-7 + c_1 = 0 \qquad \Rightarrow \qquad c_1 = 7;$$

$$19/7 + 28c_2 + 2c_1 = 0 \qquad \Rightarrow \qquad c_2 = -117/196;$$

$$-31/182 + 117c_3 + 3c_2 = 0 \quad \Rightarrow \qquad c_3 = 4997/298116.$$

Chapter 8

Therefore, plugging these coefficients into the expansion

$$y_3(x) = y_2(x)\ln x + \sum_{n=1}^{\infty} c_n x^n,$$

yields a third linearly independent solution is given by

$$y_3(x) = y_2(x)\ln x + 7x - \frac{117}{196}x^2 + \frac{4997}{298116}x^3 + \cdots.$$

Thus, a general solution is

$$y(x) = c_1 y_1(x) + c_2 y_2(x) + c_3 y_3(x),$$

where

$$y_1(x) = x^{5/6} - \frac{x^{11/6}}{11} + \frac{x^{17/6}}{374} - \frac{x^{23/6}}{25,806} + \cdots,$$

$$y_2(x) = 1 - x + \frac{x^2}{14} - \frac{x^3}{546} + \frac{x^4}{41,496} - \frac{x^5}{5,187,000} + \cdots,$$

$$y_3(x) = y_2(x)\ln x + 7x - \frac{117x^2}{196} + \frac{4997x^3}{298,116} + \cdots.$$

**23.** We will try to find a solution of the form

$$y(x) = \sum_{n=0}^{\infty} a_n x^{n+r}$$

$$\Rightarrow \quad y'(x) = \sum_{n=0}^{\infty} (n+r)a_n x^{n+r-1}$$

$$\Rightarrow \quad y''(x) = \sum_{n=0}^{\infty} (n+r)(n+r-1)a_n x^{n+r-2}.$$

Therefore, we substitute these expressions into the differential equation to obtain

$$x^2 y'' + y' - 2y = x^2 \sum_{n=0}^{\infty}(n+r)(n+r-1)a_n x^{n+r-2} + \sum_{n=0}^{\infty}(n+r)a_n x^{n+r-1} - 2\sum_{n=0}^{\infty} a_n x^{n+r} = 0$$

$$\Rightarrow \quad \sum_{k=0}^{\infty}(k+r)(k+r-1)a_k x^{k+r} + \sum_{k=-1}^{\infty}(k+r+1)a_{k+1}x^{k+r} - \sum_{k=0}^{\infty} 2a_k x^{k+r} = 0$$

$$\Rightarrow \quad ra_0 x^{r-1} + \sum_{k=0}^{\infty} \left[ (k+r)(k+r-1)a_k + (k+r+1)a_{k+1} - 2a_k \right] x^{k+r} = 0,$$

where we have changed all of the indices and the starting point for the second summation so that we could write these three power series as a single power series. By assuming that $a_0 \neq 0$ and $ra_0 x^{r-1} = 0$, we see that $r = 0$. Plugging $r = 0$ into the coefficients in the summation and noting that each of these coefficients must be zero yields the recurrence relation

$$k(k-1)a_k + (k+1)a_{k+1} - 2a_k = 0, \qquad k \geq 0$$

$$\Rightarrow \quad a_{k+1} = (2-k)a_k, \qquad k \geq 0.$$

Thus, we see that the coefficients of the solution are given by

$$k = 0 \quad \Rightarrow \quad a_1 = 2a_0 \, ; \quad k = 1 \quad \Rightarrow \quad a_2 = a_1 = 2a_0 \, ;$$

$$k = 2 \quad \Rightarrow \quad a_3 = 0 \, ; \quad k = 3 \quad \Rightarrow \quad a_4 = -a_3 = 0 \, .$$

Since each coefficient is a multiple of the previous coefficient, we see that $a_n = 0$ for $n \geq 3$. If we take $a_0 = 1$, then one solution is

$$y_1(x) = 1 + 2x + 2x^2 \, .$$

We will now use the reduction of order procedure described in Problem 31, Section 6.1, on page 326 of the text to find a second linearly independent solution. Thus we seek for a solution of the form

$$y(x) = y_1(x)v(x)$$

$$\Rightarrow \quad y'(x) = y_1'(x)v(x) + y_1(x)v'(x)$$

$$\Rightarrow \quad y''(x) = y_1''(x)v(x) + 2y_1'(x)v'(x) + y_1(x)v''(x).$$

Substituting $y(x)$, $y'(x)$, and $y''(x)$ into the given equation yields

$$\begin{aligned}
x^2 y'' + y' - 2y &= x^2 \left[ y_1''v + 2y_1'v' + y_1v'' \right] + \left[ y_1'v + y_1v' \right] - 2 \left[ y_1v \right] \\
&= \left[ x^2 y_1 \right] v'' + \left[ 2x^2 y_1' + y_1 \right] v' + \left[ x^2 y_1'' + y_1' - 2y_1 \right] v \\
&= \left[ x^2 y_1 \right] v'' + \left[ 2x^2 y_1' + y_1 \right] v' = 0
\end{aligned}$$

(since $y_1$ is a solution, the coefficient at $v$ equals to zero). With $w = v'$, the last equation becomes a first order separable equation which can be solved by methods of Section 2.2. Namely,

$$\left[x^2 y_1(x)\right] w'(x) + \left[2x^2 y_1'(x) + y_1(x)\right] w(x) = 0$$

$$\Rightarrow \quad \frac{dw}{w} = -\frac{2x^2 y_1'(x) + y_1(x)}{x^2 y_1(x)} \, dx = -\left(\frac{2y'(x)}{y_1(x)} + \frac{1}{x^2}\right) dx$$

$$\Rightarrow \quad \ln|w| = -\int \frac{2y'(x) dx}{y_1(x)} - \int \frac{dx}{x^2} = -2\ln|y_1(x)| + \frac{1}{x}$$

$$\Rightarrow \quad w(x) = \exp\left[-2\ln|y_1(x)| + \frac{1}{x}\right] = \frac{e^{1/x}}{[y_1(x)]^2}, \qquad (8.24)$$

where we have taken zero integration constant and positive function $w$. Since

$$[y_1(x)]^2 = 4x^4 + 8x^3 + 8x^2 + 4x + 1 \qquad \text{and}$$

$$e^{1/x} = 1 + x^{-1} + \frac{x^{-2}}{2} + \frac{x^{-3}}{6} + \frac{x^{-4}}{24} + \cdots$$

(we have used the Maclaurin expansion for $e^z$ with $z = 1/x$), performing long division with descending powers of $x$ in each polynomial, we see that

$$\frac{e^{1/x}}{[y_1(x)]^2} = \frac{1 + x^{-1} + \dfrac{x^{-2}}{2} + \dfrac{x^{-3}}{6} + \dfrac{x^{-4}}{24} + \cdots}{4x^4 + 8x^3 + 8x^2 + 4x + 1} = \frac{1}{4}x^{-4} - \frac{1}{4}x^{-5} + \frac{1}{8}x^{-6} + \cdots.$$

Therefore, (8.24) yields

$$v'(x) = w(x) = \frac{1}{4}x^{-4} - \frac{1}{4}x^{-5} + \frac{1}{8}x^{-6} + \cdots$$

$$\Rightarrow \quad v(x) = \int \left(\frac{1}{4}x^{-4} - \frac{1}{4}x^{-5} + \frac{1}{8}x^{-6} + \cdots\right) dx = -\frac{1}{12}x^{-3} + \frac{1}{16}x^{-4} - \frac{1}{40}x^{-5} + \cdots$$

and so

$$y(x) = y_1(x)v(x) = \left[1 + 2x + 2x^2\right]\left[-\frac{1}{12}x^{-3} + \frac{1}{16}x^{-4} - \frac{1}{40}x^{-5} + \cdots\right]$$

$$= -\frac{1}{6}x^{-1} - \frac{1}{24}x^{-2} - \frac{1}{120}x^{-3} + \cdots.$$

is a second linearly independent solution. Thus, a general solution to this differential equation is given by $y(x) = c_1 y_1(x) + c_2 y_2(x)$, where

$$y_1(x) = 1 + 2x + 2x^2 \qquad \text{and} \qquad y_2(x) = -\frac{1}{6}x^{-1} - \frac{1}{24}x^{-2} - \frac{1}{120}x^{-3} + \cdots.$$

**EXERCISES 8.8:** **Special Functions, page 493**

1. For this problem, we see that $\gamma = 1/2$, $\alpha + \beta + 1/4$, and $\alpha \times \beta = 2$. First we note that $\gamma$ is not an integer. Next, by solving in the last two equations above simultaneously for $\alpha$ and $\beta$, we see that either $\alpha = 1$ and $\beta = 1$ or $\alpha = 2$ and $\beta = 1$. Therefore, by assuming that $\alpha = 1$ and $\beta = 2$, equations (10) on page 485 and (17) on page 486 of the text yield the two solutions

$$y_1(x) = F\left(1, 2; \frac{1}{2}; x\right) \quad \text{and} \quad y_2(x) = x^{1/2} F\left(\frac{3}{2}, \frac{5}{2}; \frac{3}{2}; x\right).$$

Therefore, a general solution for this differential equation is given by

$$y(x) = c_1 F\left(1, 2; \frac{1}{2}; x\right) + c_2 x^{1/2} F\left(\frac{3}{2}, \frac{5}{2}; \frac{3}{2}; x\right).$$

Notice that

$$F(\alpha, \beta; \gamma; x) = 1 + \sum_{n=0}^{\infty} \frac{(\alpha)_n (\beta)_n}{n!(\gamma)_n} x^n = 1 + \sum_{n=0}^{\infty} \frac{(\beta)_n (\alpha)_n}{n!(\gamma)_n} x^n = F(\beta, \alpha; \gamma; x).$$

Therefore, letting $\alpha = 2$ and $\beta = 1$ yields an equivalent form of the same solution given by

$$y(x) = c_1 F\left(2, 1; \frac{1}{2}; x\right) + c_2 x^{1/2} F\left(\frac{5}{2}, \frac{3}{2}; \frac{3}{2}; x\right).$$

13. This equation can be written as

$$x^2 y'' + xy' + \left(x^2 - \frac{1}{4}\right) y = 0.$$

Thus, $\nu^2 = 1/4$ which implies that $\nu = 1/2$. Since this is not an integer (even though $2\nu$ is an integer), by the discussion on page 487 of the text, two linearly independent solutions to this problem are given by equations (25) and (26) also on page 487, that is

$$y_1(x) = J_{1/2}(x) = \sum_{n=0}^{\infty} \frac{(-1)^n}{n!\Gamma(3/2 + n)} \left(\frac{x}{2}\right)^{2n+1/2},$$

$$y_2(x) = J_{-1/2}(x) = \sum_{n=0}^{\infty} \frac{(-1)^n}{n!\Gamma(1/2 + n)} \left(\frac{x}{2}\right)^{2n-1/2}.$$

Therefore, a general solution to this differential equation is given by

$$y(x) = c_1 J_{1/2}(x) + c_2 J_{-1/2}(x).$$

# Chapter 8

**15.** In this problem $\nu = 1$. Thus, one solution to this differential equation is given by

$$y_1(x) = J_1(x) = \sum_{n=0}^{\infty} \frac{(-1)^n}{n!\,\Gamma(2+n)} \left(\frac{x}{2}\right)^{2n+1}.$$

By the discussion on page 487 of the text, $J_{-1}(x)$ and $J_1(x)$ are linearly dependent. Thus, $J_{-1}(x)$ will not be a second linearly independent solution for this problem. But, a second linearly independent solution will be given by equation (30) on page 488 of the text with $m = 1$. That is we have

$$y_2(x) = Y_1(x) = \lim_{\nu \to 1} \frac{\cos(\nu\pi) J_\nu(x) - J_{-\nu}(x)}{\sin(\nu\pi)}.$$

Therefore, a general solution to this differential equation is given by

$$y(x) = c_1 J_1(x) + c_2 Y_1(x).$$

**21.** Let $y(x) = x^\nu J_\nu(x)$. Then, by equation (31) on page 488 of the text, we have

$$y'(x) = x^\nu J_{\nu-1}(x).$$

Therefore, we see that

$$
\begin{aligned}
y''(x) &= D_x\left[y'(x)\right] = D_x\left[x^\nu J_{\nu-1}(x)\right] = D_x\left\{x\left[x^{\nu-1} J_{\nu-1}(x)\right]\right\} \\
&= x^{\nu-1} J_{\nu-1}(x) + x D_x\left[x^{\nu-1} J_{\nu-1}(x)\right] = x^{\nu-1} J_{\nu-1}(x) + x^\nu J_{\nu-2}(x).
\end{aligned}
$$

Notice that in order to take the last derivative above, we have again used equation (31) on page 488 of the text. By substituting these expressions into the left-hand side of the first differential equation given in the problem, we obtain

$$
\begin{aligned}
xy'' + (1-2\nu)y' + xy &= x\left[x^{\nu-1} J_{\nu-1}(x) + x^\nu J_{\nu-2}(x)\right] + (1-2\nu)\left[x^\nu J_{\nu-1}(x)\right] + x\left[x^\nu J_\nu(x)\right] \\
&= x^\nu J_{\nu-1}(x) + x^{\nu+1} J_{\nu-2}(x) + x^\nu J_{\nu-1}(x) - 2\nu x^\nu J_{\nu-1}(x) + x^{\nu+1} J_\nu(x). \quad (8.25)
\end{aligned}
$$

Notice that by equation (33) on page 488 of the text, we have

$$J_\nu(x) = \frac{2(\nu-1)}{x} J_{\nu-1}(x) - J_{\nu-2}(x).$$

560

$$\Rightarrow \qquad x^{\nu+1}J_\nu(x) = 2(\nu-1)x^\nu J_{\nu-1}(x) - x^{\nu+1}J_{\nu-2}(x).$$

Replacing $x^{\nu+1}J_\nu(x)$ in equation (8.25) with the above expression and simplifying yields

$$xy'' + (1-2\nu)y' + xy = x^\nu J_{\nu-1}(x) + x^{\nu+1}J_{\nu-2}(x) + x^\nu J_{\nu-1}(x)$$
$$-2\nu x^\nu J_{\nu-1}(x) + 2(\nu-1)x^\nu J_{\nu-1}(x) - x^{\nu+1}J_{\nu-2}(x) = 0.$$

Therefore, $y(x) = x^\nu J_\nu(x)$ is a solution to this type of differential equation.

In order to find a solution to the differential equation $xy'' - 2y' + xy = 0$, we observe that this equation is of the same type as the equation given above with

$$1 - 2\nu = -2 \qquad \Rightarrow \qquad \nu = \frac{3}{2}.$$

Thus, a solution to this equation will be

$$y(x) = x^{3/2}J_{3/2}(x) = x^{3/2}\sum_{n=0}^\infty \frac{(-1)^n}{n!\,\Gamma(5/2+n)}\left(\frac{x}{2}\right)^{2n+3/2}.$$

29. In Legendre polynomials, $n$ is a fixed nonnegative integer. Thus, in the first such polynomial, $n$ equals zero. Therefore, we see that $[n/2] = [0/2] = 0$ and, by equation (43) on page 491 of the text, we have

$$P_0(x) = 2^{-0}\frac{(-1)^0 0!}{0!0!0!}\,x^0 = 1.$$

Similarly, we have

$$n = 1 \quad \Rightarrow \quad \left[\frac{1}{2}\right] = 0 \quad \Rightarrow \quad P_1(x) = 2^{-1}\frac{(-1)^0 2!}{1!0!1!}\,x^1 = x,$$

$$n = 2 \quad \Rightarrow \quad \left[\frac{2}{2}\right] = 1 \quad \Rightarrow \quad P_2(x) = 2^{-2}\left(\frac{(-1)^0 4!}{2!0!2!}\,x^2 + \frac{(-1)^1 2!}{1!1!0!}\,x^0\right) = \frac{3x^2-1}{2},$$

$$n = 3 \quad \Rightarrow \quad \left[\frac{3}{2}\right] = 1 \quad \Rightarrow \quad P_3(x) = 2^{-3}\left(\frac{(-1)^0 6!}{3!0!3!}\,x^3 + \frac{(-1)^1 4!}{2!1!1!}\,x^1\right) = \frac{5x^3-3x}{2},$$

$$n = 4 \quad \Rightarrow \quad \left[\frac{4}{2}\right] = 2 \quad \Rightarrow \quad P_4(x) = 2^{-4}\left(\frac{(-1)^0 8!}{4!0!4!}\,x^4 + \frac{(-1)^1 6!}{3!1!2!}\,x^2 + \frac{(-1)^2 4!}{2!2!0!}\,x^0\right)$$
$$= \frac{35x^4 - 30x^2 + 3}{8}.$$

# Chapter 8

**37.** Since the Taylor series expansion of an analytic function $f(t)$ about $t = 0$ is given by

$$f(t) = \sum_{n=0}^{\infty} \frac{f^{(n)}(0)}{n!} t^n \,,$$

we see that $H(x)$ is just the $n$th derivative of $y(t) = e^{2tx - t^2}$ with respect to $t$ evaluated at the point $t = 0$ (treating $x$ as a fixed parameter). Therefore, we have

$$y(t) = e^{2tx - t^2} \qquad \Rightarrow \quad H_0(x) = y(0) = e^0 = 1,$$
$$y'(t) = (2x - 2t)e^{2tx - t^2} \qquad \Rightarrow \quad H_1(x) = y'(0) = 2xe^0 = 2x,$$
$$y''(t) = \left[-2 + (2x - 2t)^2\right] e^{2tx - t^2} \qquad \Rightarrow \quad H_2(x) = y''(0) = \left[-2 + (2x)^2\right] e^0 = 4x^2 - 2,$$
$$y'''(t) = \left[-6(2x - 2t) + (2x - 2t)^3\right] e^{2tx - t^2} \quad \Rightarrow \quad H_3(x) = y'''(0) = 8x^3 - 12x.$$

**39.** To find the first four Laguerre polynomials, we need to find the first four derivatives of the function $y(x) = x^n e^{-x}$. Therefore, we have

$$y^{(0)}(x) = x^n e^{-x} \,,$$
$$y'(x) = \left(nx^{n-1} - x^n\right) e^{-x} \,,$$
$$y''(x) = \left(n(n-1)x^{n-2} - 2nx^{n-1} + x^n\right) e^{-x} \,,$$
$$y'''(x) = \left(n(n-1)(n-2)x^{n-3} - 3n(n-1)x^{n-2} + 3nx^{n-1} - x^n\right) e^{-x} \,.$$

Substituting these expressions into Rodrigues's formula and plugging in the appropriate values of $n$ yields

$$L_0(x) = \frac{e^x}{0!} x^0 e^{-x} = 1,$$

$$L_1(x) = \frac{e^x}{1!} \left[1x^{1-1} - x^1\right] e^{-x} = 1 - x,$$

$$L_2(x) = \frac{e^x}{2!} \left[2(2-1)x^{2-2} - 2 \cdot 2x^{2-1} + x^2\right] e^{-x} = \frac{2 - 4x + x^2}{2} \,,$$

$$L_3(x) = \frac{e^x}{3!} \left[3(3-1)(3-2)x^{3-3} - 3 \cdot 3(3-1)x^{3-2} + 3 \cdot 3x^{3-1} - x^3\right] e^{-x}$$

$$= \frac{6 - 18x + 9x^2 - x^3}{6} \,.$$

**REVIEW PROBLEMS:  page 497**

**1. (a)** To construct the Taylor polynomials

$$p_n(x) = y(0) + \frac{y'(0)}{1!} x + \frac{y''(0)}{2!} x^2 + \cdots + \frac{y^{(n)}(0)}{n!} x^n$$

approximating the solution to the given initial value problem, we need $y(0)$, $y'(0)$, etc. $y(0)$ is provided by the initial condition, $y(0) = 1$. The value of $y'(0)$ can be deduced from the differential equation itself. We have

$$y'(0) = (0)y(0) - y(0)^2 = (0)(1) - (1)^2 = -1.$$

Differentiating both sides of the given equation, $y' = xy - y^2$, and substituting $x = 0$ into the resulting equation, we get

$$y'' = y + xy' - 2yy'$$
$$\Rightarrow \quad y''(0) = y(0) + (0)y'(0) - 2y(0)y'(0) = (1) + (0)(-1) - 2(1)(-1) = 3.$$

Differentiating once more yields

$$y''' = y' + y' + xy'' - 2y'y' - 2yy''$$
$$\Rightarrow \quad y'''(0) = (-1) + (-1) + (0)(3) - 2(-1)(-1) - 2(1)(3) = -10.$$

Thus,

$$p_3(x) = 1 + \frac{-1}{1!} x + \frac{3}{2!} x^2 + \frac{-10}{3!} x^3 = 1 - x + \frac{3x^2}{2} - \frac{5x^3}{3}.$$

**(b)** The values of $z(0)$ and $z'(0)$ are given. Namely, $z(0) = -1$ and $z'(0) = 1$. Substituting $x = 0$ into the given equation yields

$$z''(0) - (0)^3 z'(0) + (0)z(0)^2 = 0 \quad \Rightarrow \quad z''(0) = 0.$$

We now differentiate the given equation and evaluate the result at $x = 0$.

$$z''' - 3x^2 z' - x^3 z'' + z^2 + 2xzz' = 0$$

$$\Rightarrow \qquad z'''(0) = 3(0)^2 z'(0) + (0)^3 z''(0) - z(0)^2 - 2(0)z(0)z'(0) = -1.$$

One more differentiation yields

$$z^{(4)} - 6xz' - 3x^2 z'' - 3x^2 z'' - x^3 z''' + 2zz' + 2zz' + 2xz'z' + 2xzz'' = 0$$

$$\Rightarrow \qquad z^{(4)}(0) = -4z(0)z'(0) = 4.$$

Hence,

$$p_4(x) = -1 + \frac{1}{1!}x + \frac{0}{2!}x^2 + \frac{-1}{3!}x^3 + \frac{4}{4!}x^4 = -1 + x - \frac{x^3}{6} + \frac{x^4}{6}.$$

**3. (a)** Since both $p(x) = x^2$ and $q(x) = -2$ are analytic at $x = 0$, a general solution to the given equation is also analytic at this point. Thus, it has an expansion

$$y = \sum_{k=0}^{\infty} a_k x^k$$

$$\Rightarrow \qquad y' = \sum_{k=1}^{\infty} k a_k x^{k-1}$$

$$\Rightarrow \qquad y'' = \sum_{k=2}^{\infty} k(k-1) a_k x^{k-2}.$$

Substituting these expansions for $y$, $y'$, and $y''$ into the original equation yields

$$\sum_{k=2}^{\infty} k(k-1) a_k x^{k-2} + x^2 \sum_{k=1}^{\infty} k a_k x^{k-1} - 2 \sum_{k=0}^{\infty} a_k x^k = 0$$

$$\Rightarrow \qquad \sum_{k=2}^{\infty} k(k-1) a_k x^{k-2} + \sum_{k=1}^{\infty} k a_k x^{k+1} - \sum_{k=0}^{\infty} 2 a_k x^k = 0.$$

We now shift the indices of summation so that all three sums contain like powers $x^n$. In the first sum, we let $k - 2 = n$; in the second sum, let $k + 1 = n$; and let $k = n$ in the third sum. This yields

$$\sum_{n=0}^{\infty} (n+2)(n+1) a_{n+2} x^n + \sum_{n=2}^{\infty} (n-1) a_{n-1} x^n - \sum_{n=0}^{\infty} 2 a_n x^n = 0.$$

Separating the terms corresponding to $n = 0$ and $n = 1$, and combining the rest under one summation, we obtain

$$(2a_2 - 2a_0) + (6a_3 - 2a_1)\, x + \sum_{n=2}^{\infty} \left[ (n+2)(n+1) a_{n+2} + (n-1) a_{n-1} - 2 a_n \right] x^n = 0.$$

Therefore,

$$2a_2 - 2a_0 = 0,$$
$$6a_3 - 2a_1 = 0,$$
$$(n+2)(n+1)a_{n+2} + (n-1)a_{n-1} - 2a_n = 0, \quad n \geq 2.$$

This yields

$$a_2 = a_0, \qquad a_3 = \frac{a_1}{3}, \qquad \text{and} \qquad a_{n+2} = \frac{2a_n - (n-1)a_{n-1}}{(n+2)(n+1)}, \quad n \geq 2.$$

Hence,

$$y(x) = a_0 + a_1 x + a_2 x^2 + a_3 x^3 + \cdots = a_0 + a_1 x + a_0 x^2 + \frac{a_1}{3} x^3 + \cdots$$
$$= a_0 \left(1 + x^2 + \cdots\right) + a_1 \left(x + \frac{x^3}{3} + \cdots\right).$$

**5.** Clearly, $x = 2$ is an ordinary point for the given equation because $p(x) = x - 2$ and $q(x) = -1$ are analytic everywhere. Thus we seek for a solution of the form

$$w(x) = \sum_{k=0}^{\infty} a_k(x-2)^k.$$

Differentiating this power series yields

$$w'(x) = \sum_{k=1}^{\infty} ka_k(x-2)^{k-1} \qquad \text{and} \qquad w''(x) = \sum_{k=2}^{\infty} k(k-1)a_k(x-2)^{k-2}.$$

Therefore,

$$w'' + (x-2)w' - w = \sum_{k=2}^{\infty} k(k-1)a_k(x-2)^{k-2} + (x-2)\sum_{k=1}^{\infty} ka_k(x-2)^{k-1}$$
$$- \sum_{k=0}^{\infty} a_k(x-2)^k = 0$$
$$\Rightarrow \quad \sum_{k=2}^{\infty} k(k-1)a_k(x-2)^{k-2} + \sum_{k=1}^{\infty} ka_k(x-2)^k - \sum_{k=0}^{\infty} a_k(x-2)^k = 0.$$

Shifting the index of summation in the first sum yields

$$\sum_{n=0}^{\infty}(n+2)(n+1)a_{n+2}(x-2)^n + \sum_{n=1}^{\infty} na_n(x-2)^n - \sum_{n=0}^{\infty} a_n(x-2)^n = 0$$

$$\Rightarrow \quad \left[2a_2 + \sum_{n=1}^{\infty}(n+2)(n+1)a_{n+2}(x-2)^n\right] + \sum_{n=1}^{\infty}na_n(x-2)^n - \left[a_0 + \sum_{n=1}^{\infty}a_n(x-2)^n\right] = 0$$

$$\Rightarrow \quad (2a_2 - a_0) + \sum_{n=1}^{\infty}\left[(n+2)(n+1)a_{n+2} + na_n - a_n\right](x-2)^n = 0,$$

where we have separated the terms corresponding to $n = 0$ and collected the rest under one summation. In order that the above power series equals zero, it must have all zero coefficients. Thus,

$$2a_2 - a_0 = 0,$$
$$(n+2)(n+1)a_{n+2} + na_n - a_n = 0, \quad n \geq 1$$

$$\Rightarrow \quad \begin{aligned} a_2 &= a_0/2\,, \\ a_{n+2} &= (1-n)a_n/[(n+2)(n+1)]\,, \quad n \geq 1. \end{aligned}$$

For $n = 1$ and $n = 2$, the last equation gives $a_3 = 0$ and $a_4 = -a_2/12 = -a_0/24$. Therefore,

$$\begin{aligned} w(x) &= a_0 + a_1(x-2) + a_2(x-2)^2 + a_3(x-2)^3 + a_4(x-2)^4 + \cdots \\ &= a_0 + a_1(x-2) + \frac{a_0}{2}(x-2)^2 + (0)(x-2)^3 - \frac{1}{24}a_0(x-2)^4 + \cdots \\ &= a_0\left[1 + \frac{(x-2)^2}{2} - \frac{(x-2)^4}{24} + \cdots\right] + a_1(x-2). \end{aligned}$$

**7. (a)** The point $x = 0$ is a regular singular point for the given equation because

$$p(x) = \frac{-5x}{x^2} = -\frac{5}{x}\,, \qquad q(x) = \frac{9-x}{x^2}\,,$$

and the limits

$$p_0 = \lim_{x\to 0} xp(x) = \lim_{x\to 0}(-5) = -5,$$
$$q_0 = \lim_{x\to 0} x^2q(x) = \lim_{x\to 0}(9-x) = 9$$

exist. The indicial equation (3) on page 461 of the text becomes

$$r(r-1) + (-5)r + 9 = 0 \quad \Rightarrow \quad r^2 - 6r + 9 = 0 \quad \Rightarrow \quad (r-3)^2 = 0.$$

Hence, $r = 3$ is the exponent of the singularity $x = 0$, and a solution to the given differential equation has the form

$$y = x^3 \sum_{k=0}^{\infty} a_k x^k = \sum_{k=0}^{\infty} a_k x^{k+3} \,.$$

Substituting this power series into the given equation yields

$$x^2 \left( \sum_{k=0}^{\infty} a_k x^{k+3} \right)'' - 5x \left( \sum_{k=0}^{\infty} a_k x^{k+3} \right)' + (9 - x) \left( \sum_{k=0}^{\infty} a_k x^{k+3} \right) = 0$$

$$\Rightarrow \quad \sum_{k=0}^{\infty} (k+3)(k+2) a_k x^{k+3} - \sum_{k=0}^{\infty} 5(k+3) a_k x^{k+3} + (9 - x) \sum_{k=0}^{\infty} a_k x^{k+3} = 0$$

$$\Rightarrow \quad \sum_{k=0}^{\infty} \left[ (k+3)(k+2) - 5(k+3) + 9 \right] a_k x^{k+3} - \sum_{k=0}^{\infty} a_k x^{k+4} = 0$$

$$\Rightarrow \quad \sum_{k=0}^{\infty} k^2 a_k x^{k+3} - \sum_{k=0}^{\infty} a_k x^{k+4} = 0$$

$$\Rightarrow \quad \sum_{n=1}^{\infty} n^2 a_n x^{n+3} - \sum_{n=1}^{\infty} a_{n-1} x^{n+3} = 0$$

$$\Rightarrow \quad \sum_{n=1}^{\infty} \left( n^2 a_n - a_{n-1} \right) x^{n+3} = 0 \,.$$

Thus,

$$n^2 a_n - a_{n-1} = 0 \quad \text{or} \quad a_n = \frac{a_{n-1}}{n^2}, \quad n \geq 1.$$

This recurrence relation yields

$$n = 1: \quad a_1 = a_0/(1)^2 = a_0 \,,$$
$$n = 2: \quad a_2 = a_1/(2)^2 = a_0/4 \,,$$
$$n = 3: \quad a_3 = a_2/(3)^2 = (a_0/4)/9 = a_0/36 \,.$$

Therefore,

$$\begin{aligned} y(x) &= x^3 \left( a_0 + a_1 x + a_2 x^2 + a_3 x^3 + \cdots \right) \\ &= x^3 \left( a_0 + a_0 x + \frac{a_0}{4} x^2 + \frac{a_0}{36} x^3 + \cdots \right) = a_0 \left( x^3 + x^4 + \frac{x^5}{4} + \frac{x^6}{36} + \cdots \right) . \end{aligned}$$

# CHAPTER 9:  Matrix Methods for Linear Systems

**EXERCISES 9.1:  Introduction, page 507**

**3.** We start by expressing right-hand sides of all equations as dot products.

$$x + y + z = [1, 1, 1] \cdot [x, y, z], \quad 2z - x = [-1, 0, 2] \cdot [x, y, z], \quad 4y = [0, 4, 0] \cdot [x, y, z].$$

Thus, by definition of the product of a matrix and column vector, the matrix form is given by

$$\begin{bmatrix} x \\ y \\ z \end{bmatrix}' = \begin{bmatrix} 1 & 1 & 1 \\ -1 & 0 & 2 \\ 0 & 4 & 0 \end{bmatrix} \begin{bmatrix} x \\ y \\ z \end{bmatrix}.$$

**7.** First we have to express the second derivative, $y''$, as a first derivative in order to rewrite the equation as a first order system. Denoting $y'$ by $v$ we get

$$\begin{aligned} y' &= v, \\ mv' + bv + ky &= 0 \end{aligned} \qquad \text{or} \qquad \begin{aligned} y' &= v, \\ v' &= -\frac{k}{m} y - \frac{b}{m} v. \end{aligned}$$

Expressing the right-hand side of each equation as a dot product, we obtain

$$v = [0, 1] \cdot [y, v], \qquad -\frac{k}{m} y - \frac{b}{m} v = \left[ -\frac{k}{m}, -\frac{b}{m} \right] \cdot [y, v].$$

Thus, the matrix form of the system is

$$\begin{bmatrix} y \\ v \end{bmatrix}' = \begin{bmatrix} 0 & 1 \\ -k/m & -b/m \end{bmatrix} \begin{bmatrix} y \\ v \end{bmatrix}.$$

**11.** Introducing the auxiliary variables

$$x_1 = x, \quad x_2 = x', \quad x_3 = y, \quad x_4 = y',$$

# Chapter 9

we can rewrite the given system in normal form:

$$
\begin{aligned}
x_1' &= x_2 \\
x_3' &= x_4 \\
x_2' + 3x_1 + 2x_3 &= 0 \\
x_4' - 2x_1 &= 0
\end{aligned}
\qquad \text{or} \qquad
\begin{aligned}
x_1' &= x_2 \\
x_2' &= -3x_1 - 2x_3 \\
x_3' &= x_4 \\
x_4' &= 2x_1 \, .
\end{aligned}
$$

Since

$$
\begin{aligned}
x_2 &= [0,1,0,0] \cdot [x_1, x_2, x_3, x_4], & -3x_1 - 2x_3 &= [-3,0,-2,0] \cdot [x_1, x_2, x_3, x_4], \\
x_4 &= [0,0,0,1] \cdot [x_1, x_2, x_3, x_4], & 2x_1 &= [2,0,0,0] \cdot [x_1, x_2, x_3, x_4],
\end{aligned}
$$

the matrix is given by

$$
\begin{bmatrix} x_1 \\ x_2 \\ x_3 \\ x_4 \end{bmatrix}'
=
\begin{bmatrix}
0 & 1 & 0 & 0 \\
-3 & 0 & -2 & 0 \\
0 & 0 & 0 & 1 \\
2 & 0 & 0 & 0
\end{bmatrix}
\begin{bmatrix} x_1 \\ x_2 \\ x_3 \\ x_4 \end{bmatrix} .
$$

## EXERCISES 9.2: Review 1: Linear Algebraic Equations, page 512

**3.** By subtracting 2 times the first equation from the second, we eliminate $x_1$ from the latter. Similarly, $x_1$ is eliminated from the third equation by subtracting the first equation from it. So we get

$$
\begin{aligned}
x_1 + 2x_2 + x_3 &= -3, \\
-3x_3 &= 6, \\
x_2 - 3x_3 &= 6
\end{aligned}
\qquad
\begin{aligned}
\text{or} \\
\\
\text{(interchanging last two equations)}
\end{aligned}
\qquad
\begin{aligned}
x_1 + 2x_2 + x_3 &= -3, \\
x_2 - 3x_3 &= 6, \\
x_3 &= -2.
\end{aligned}
$$

The second unknown, $x_2$, can be eliminated from the first equation by subtracting 2 times the first one from it:

$$
\begin{aligned}
x_1 + 7x_3 &= -15, \\
x_2 - 3x_3 &= 6, \\
x_3 &= -2.
\end{aligned}
$$

Finally, we eliminate $x_3$ from the first two equations by adding $(-7)$ times and 3 times, respectively, the third equation. This gives

$$x_1 = -1,$$
$$x_2 = \phantom{-}0,$$
$$x_3 = -2.$$

**7.** Subtracting 3 times the first equation from the second equation yields

$$-x_1 + 3x_2 = 0,$$
$$0 = 0.$$

The last equation is trivially satisfied, so we ignore it. Thus, just one equation remains:

$$-x_1 + 3x_2 = 0 \quad \Rightarrow \quad x_1 = 3x_2.$$

Choosing $x_2$ as a free variable, we get $x_1 = 3s$, $x_2 = s$, where $s$ is any number.

**9.** We eliminate $x_1$ from the first equation by adding $(1-i)$ times the second equation to it:

$$[2 - (1+i)(1-i)]x_2 = 0,$$
$$-x_1 - (1+i)x_2 = 0.$$

Since $(1-i)(1+i) = 1^2 - i^2 = 1 - (-1) = 2$, we obtain

$$\begin{aligned}0 &= 0, \\ -x_1 - (1+i)x_2 &= 0\end{aligned} \quad \Rightarrow \quad x_2 = -\frac{1}{1+i}\,x_1 = \frac{-1+i}{2}\,x_1.$$

Assigning an arbitrary complex value to $x_1$, say $2s$, we see that the system has infinitely many solutions given by

$$x_1 = 2s, \qquad x_2 = (-1+i)s, \qquad \text{where } s \text{ is any complex number.}$$

**11.** It is slightly more convenient to put the last equation at the top:

$$\begin{aligned}-x_1 + x_2 + 5x_3 &= \phantom{-}0, \\ 2x_1 + \phantom{x_2 +} x_3 &= -1, \\ -3x_1 + x_2 + 4x_3 &= \phantom{-}1.\end{aligned}$$

# Chapter 9

We then eliminate $x_1$ from the second equation by adding 2 times the first one to it; and by subtracting 3 times the first equation from the third, we eliminate $x_1$ in the latter.

$$
\begin{aligned}
-x_1 + x_2 + 5x_3 &= 0, \\
-2x_2 - 11x_3 &= 1, \\
2x_2 + 11x_3 &= -1.
\end{aligned}
$$

To make the computations more convenient, we multiply the first equation by 2.

$$
\begin{aligned}
-2x_1 + 2x_2 + 10x_3 &= 0, \\
-2x_2 - 11x_3 &= 1, \\
2x_2 + 11x_3 &= -1.
\end{aligned}
$$

Now we add the second equation to each of the remaining, and obtain

$$
\begin{aligned}
-2x_1 \qquad - x_3 &= 1, \\
-2x_2 - 11x_3 &= 1, \\
0 &= 0
\end{aligned}
\qquad \text{or} \qquad
\begin{aligned}
-2x_1 \qquad - x_3 &= 1, \\
-2x_2 - 11x_3 &= 1.
\end{aligned}
$$

Choosing $x_3$ as free variable, i.e., $x_3 = s$, yields $x_1 = -(s+1)/2$, $x_2 = -(11s+1)/2$, $-\infty < s < \infty$.

**13.** The given system can be written in the equivalent form

$$
\begin{aligned}
(2-r)x_1 - 3x_2 &= 0, \\
x_1 - (2+r)x_2 &= 0.
\end{aligned}
$$

The variable $x_1$ can be eliminated from the first equation by subtracting $(2-r)$ times the second equation:

$$
\begin{aligned}
[-3 + (2-r)(2+r)]x_2 &= 0, \\
x_1 - (2+r)x_2 &= 0
\end{aligned}
\qquad \text{or} \qquad
\begin{aligned}
(1-r^2)x_2 &= 0, \\
x_1 - (2+r)x_2 &= 0.
\end{aligned}
$$

If $1 - r^2 \neq 0$, i.e., $r \neq \pm 1$, then the first equation implies $x_2 = 0$. Substituting this into the second equation, we get $x_1$. Thus, the given system has a unique (zero) solution for any $r \neq \pm 1$, in particular, for $r = 2$.

If $r = 1$ or $r = -1$, then the first equation in the latter system becomes trivial $0 = 0$, and the system degenerates to

$$x_1 - (2 + r)x_2 = 0 \quad \Rightarrow \quad x_1 = (2 + r)x_2.$$

Therefore, there are infinitely many solutions to the given system of the form

$$x_1 = (2 + r)s, \quad x_2 = s, \quad s \in (-\infty, \infty), \quad r = \pm 1.$$

In particular, for $r = 1$ we obtain

$$x_1 = 3s, \quad x_2 = s, \quad s \in (-\infty, \infty).$$

**EXERCISES 9.3: Review 2: Matrices and Vectors, page 521**

**5. (a)** $\mathbf{AB} = \begin{bmatrix} 1 & -2 \\ 2 & -3 \end{bmatrix} \begin{bmatrix} 1 & 0 \\ 1 & 1 \end{bmatrix} = \begin{bmatrix} 1-2 & 0-2 \\ 2-3 & 0-3 \end{bmatrix} = \begin{bmatrix} -1 & -2 \\ -1 & -3 \end{bmatrix}.$

**(b)** $\mathbf{AC} = \begin{bmatrix} 1 & -2 \\ 2 & -3 \end{bmatrix} \begin{bmatrix} -1 & 1 \\ 2 & 1 \end{bmatrix} = \begin{bmatrix} -1-4 & 1-2 \\ -2-6 & 2-3 \end{bmatrix} = \begin{bmatrix} -5 & -1 \\ -8 & -1 \end{bmatrix}.$

**(c)** By the Distributive Property of matrix multiplication given on page 515 of the text, we have

$$\mathbf{A}\,(\mathbf{B} + \mathbf{C}) = \mathbf{AB} + \mathbf{AC} = \begin{bmatrix} -1 & -2 \\ -1 & -3 \end{bmatrix} + \begin{bmatrix} -5 & -1 \\ -8 & -1 \end{bmatrix} = \begin{bmatrix} -6 & -3 \\ -9 & -4 \end{bmatrix}.$$

**13.** Authors note: We will use $R_i + cR_j \rightarrow R_k$ to denote the row operation "*add row i to c times row j and place the result into row k.*" We will use $cR_j \rightarrow R_k$ to denote the row operation "*multiply row j by c and place the result into row k.*"

As in Example 1 on page 517 of the text, we will perform row-reduction on the matrix $[\mathbf{A}|\mathbf{I}]$. Thus, we have

$$[\mathbf{A}|\mathbf{I}] = \begin{bmatrix} -2 & -1 & 1 & \big| & 1 & 0 & 0 \\ 2 & 1 & 0 & \big| & 0 & 1 & 0 \\ 3 & 1 & -1 & \big| & 0 & 0 & 1 \end{bmatrix}$$

$$R_2 + R_1 \to R_2$$
$$2R_3 + 3R_1 \to R_3$$

$$\begin{bmatrix} -2 & -1 & 1 & 1 & 0 & 0 \\ 0 & 0 & 1 & 1 & 1 & 0 \\ 0 & -1 & 1 & 3 & 0 & 2 \end{bmatrix}$$

$$R_1 - R_3 \to R_1$$

$$\begin{bmatrix} -2 & 0 & 0 & -2 & 0 & -2 \\ 0 & 0 & 1 & 1 & 1 & 0 \\ 0 & -1 & 1 & 3 & 0 & 2 \end{bmatrix}$$

$$-R_1/2 \to R_1$$
$$R_3 \to R_2$$
$$R_2 \to R_3$$

$$\begin{bmatrix} 1 & 0 & 0 & 1 & 0 & 1 \\ 0 & -1 & 1 & 3 & 0 & 2 \\ 0 & 0 & 1 & 1 & 1 & 0 \end{bmatrix}$$

$$-R_2 + R_3 \to R_2$$

$$\begin{bmatrix} 1 & 0 & 0 & 1 & 0 & 1 \\ 0 & 1 & 0 & -2 & 1 & -2 \\ 0 & 0 & 1 & 1 & 1 & 0 \end{bmatrix}.$$

Therefore, the inverse matrix is

$$\mathbf{A}^{-1} = \begin{bmatrix} 1 & 0 & 1 \\ -2 & 1 & -2 \\ 1 & 1 & 0 \end{bmatrix}.$$

To check the algebra, it's a good idea to multiply $\mathbf{A}$ by $\mathbf{A}^{-1}$ to verify that the product is the identity matrix.

19. Authors note: We will use $R_i + cR_j \to R_k$ to denote the row operation "*add row i to c times row j and place the result into row k.*" We will use $cR_j \to R_k$ to denote the row operation "*multiply row j by c and place the result into row k.*"

To find the inverse matrix $\mathbf{X}^{-1}(t)$, we will again use the method of Example 1 on page 517 of the text. Thus, we start with

$$[\mathbf{X}(t)|\mathbf{I}] = \begin{bmatrix} e^t & e^{-t} & e^{2t} & 1 & 0 & 0 \\ e^t & -e^{-t} & 2e^{2t} & 0 & 1 & 0 \\ e^t & e^{-t} & 4e^{2t} & 0 & 0 & 1 \end{bmatrix}$$

$$R_2 - R_1 \to R_2$$
$$R_3 - R_1 \to R_3$$
$$\begin{bmatrix} e^t & e^{-t} & e^{2t} & 1 & 0 & 0 \\ 0 & -2e^{-t} & e^{2t} & -1 & 1 & 0 \\ 0 & 0 & 3e^{2t} & -1 & 0 & 1 \end{bmatrix}$$

$$-R_2/2 \to R_2$$
$$R_3/3 \to R_3$$
$$\begin{bmatrix} e^t & e^{-t} & e^{2t} & 1 & 0 & 0 \\ 0 & e^{-t} & -e^{2t}/2 & 1/2 & -1/2 & 0 \\ 0 & 0 & e^{2t} & -1/3 & 0 & 1/3 \end{bmatrix}$$

$$R_1 - R_3 \to R_1$$
$$R_2 - R_3/2 \to R_2$$
$$\begin{bmatrix} e^t & e^{-t} & 0 & 4/3 & 0 & -1/3 \\ 0 & e^{-t} & 0 & 1/3 & -1/2 & 1/6 \\ 0 & 0 & e^{2t} & -1/3 & 0 & 1/3 \end{bmatrix}$$

$$R_1 - R_2 \to R_1$$
$$\begin{bmatrix} e^t & 0 & 0 & 1 & 1/2 & -1/2 \\ 0 & e^{-t} & 0 & 1/3 & -1/2 & 1/6 \\ 0 & 0 & e^{2t} & -1/3 & 0 & 1/3 \end{bmatrix}$$

$$e^{-t}R_1 \to R_1$$
$$e^t R_2 \to R_2$$
$$e^{-2t}R_3 \to R_3$$
$$\begin{bmatrix} 1 & 0 & 0 & e^{-t} & e^{-t}/2 & -e^{-t}/2 \\ 0 & 1 & 0 & e^t/3 & -e^t/2 & e^t/6 \\ 0 & 0 & 1 & -e^{-2t}/3 & 0 & e^{-2t}/3 \end{bmatrix}.$$

Thus, the inverse matrix $\mathbf{X}^{-1}(t)$ is given by the matrix

$$\mathbf{X}^{-1}(t) = \begin{bmatrix} e^{-t} & e^{-t}/2 & -e^{-t}/2 \\ e^t/3 & -e^t/2 & e^t/6 \\ -e^{-2t}/3 & 0 & e^{-2t}/3 \end{bmatrix}.$$

**23.** We will calculate this determinant by first finding its cofactor expansion about row 1. Therefore, we have

$$\begin{vmatrix} 1 & 0 & 0 \\ 3 & 1 & 2 \\ 1 & 5 & -2 \end{vmatrix} = (1)\begin{vmatrix} 1 & 2 \\ 5 & -2 \end{vmatrix} - 0 + 0 = -2 - 10 = -12.$$

**37.** We first calculate $\mathbf{X}'(t)$ by differentiating each entry of $\mathbf{X}(t)$. Therefore, we have

$$\mathbf{X}'(t) = \begin{bmatrix} 2e^{2t} & 3e^{3t} \\ -2e^{2t} & -6e^{3t} \end{bmatrix}.$$

575

Thus, substituting the matrix $\mathbf{X}(t)$ into the differential equation and performing matrix multiplication yields

$$\begin{bmatrix} 2e^{2t} & 3e^{3t} \\ -2e^{2t} & -6e^{3t} \end{bmatrix} = \begin{bmatrix} 1 & -1 \\ 2 & 4 \end{bmatrix} \begin{bmatrix} e^{2t} & e^{3t} \\ -e^{2t} & -2e^{3t} \end{bmatrix} = \begin{bmatrix} e^{2t} + e^{2t} & e^{3t} + 2e^{3t} \\ 2e^{2t} - 4e^{2t} & 2e^{3t} - 8e^{3t} \end{bmatrix}.$$

Since this equation is true, we see that $\mathbf{X}(t)$ does satisfy the given differential equation.

39. (a) To calculate $\int \mathbf{A}(t)\,dt$, we integrate each entry of $\mathbf{A}(t)$ to obtain

$$\int \mathbf{A}(t)\,dt = \begin{bmatrix} \int t\,dt & \int e^{t}dt \\ \int 1\,dt & \int e^{t}dt \end{bmatrix} = \begin{bmatrix} t^2/2 + c_1 & e^t + c_2 \\ t + c_3 & e^t + c_4 \end{bmatrix}.$$

(b) Taking the definite integral of each entry of $\mathbf{B}(t)$ yields

$$\int_0^1 \mathbf{B}(t)\,dt = \begin{bmatrix} \int_0^1 \cos t\,dt & -\int_0^1 \sin t\,dt \\ \int_0^1 \sin t\,dt & \int_0^1 \cos t\,dt \end{bmatrix} = \begin{bmatrix} \sin t\,|_0^1 & \cos t\,|_0^1 \\ -\cos t\,|_0^1 & \sin t\,|_0^1 \end{bmatrix} = \begin{bmatrix} \sin 1 & \cos 1 - 1 \\ 1 - \cos 1 & \sin 1 \end{bmatrix}.$$

(c) By the product rule on page 521 of the text, we see that

$$\frac{d}{dt}[\mathbf{A}(t)\mathbf{B}(t)] = \mathbf{A}(t)\mathbf{B}'(t) + \mathbf{A}'(t)\mathbf{B}(t).$$

Therefore, we first calculate $\mathbf{A}'(t)$ and $\mathbf{B}'(t)$ by differentiating each entry of $\mathbf{A}(t)$ and $\mathbf{B}(t)$, respectively, to obtain

$$\mathbf{A}'(t) = \begin{bmatrix} 1 & e^t \\ 0 & e^t \end{bmatrix} \quad \text{and} \quad \mathbf{B}'(t) = \begin{bmatrix} -\sin t & -\cos t \\ \cos t & -\sin t \end{bmatrix}.$$

Hence, by matrix multiplication we have

$$\frac{d}{dt}[\mathbf{A}(t)\mathbf{B}(t)] = \mathbf{A}(t)\mathbf{B}'(t) + \mathbf{A}'(t)\mathbf{B}(t)$$

$$= \begin{bmatrix} t & e^t \\ 1 & e^t \end{bmatrix}\begin{bmatrix} -\sin t & -\cos t \\ \cos t & -\sin t \end{bmatrix} + \begin{bmatrix} 1 & e^t \\ 0 & e^t \end{bmatrix}\begin{bmatrix} \cos t & -\sin t \\ \sin t & \cos t \end{bmatrix}$$

$$= \begin{bmatrix} e^t\cos t - t\sin t & -t\cos t - e^t\sin t \\ e^t\cos t - \sin t & -\cos t - e^t\sin t \end{bmatrix} + \begin{bmatrix} \cos t + e^t\sin t & e^t\cos t - \sin t \\ e^t\sin t & e^t\cos t \end{bmatrix}$$

$$= \begin{bmatrix} (1+e^t)\cos t + (e^t - t)\sin t & (e^t - t)\cos t - (e^t + 1)\sin t \\ e^t\cos t + (e^t - 1)\sin t & (e^t - 1)\cos t - e^t\sin t \end{bmatrix}.$$

**EXERCISES 9.4: Linear Systems in Normal Form, page 530**

1. To write this system in matrix form, we will define the vectors $\mathbf{x}(t) = \text{col}[x(t), y(t)]$ (which means that $\mathbf{x}'(t) = \text{col}[x'(t), y'(t)]$) and $\mathbf{f}(t) = \text{col}[t^2, e^t]$, and the matrix

$$\mathbf{A}(t) = \begin{bmatrix} 3 & -1 \\ -1 & 2 \end{bmatrix}.$$

Thus, this system becomes the equation in matrix form given by

$$\begin{bmatrix} x'(t) \\ y'(t) \end{bmatrix} = \begin{bmatrix} 3 & -1 \\ -1 & 2 \end{bmatrix} \begin{bmatrix} x(t) \\ y(t) \end{bmatrix} + \begin{bmatrix} t^2 \\ e^t \end{bmatrix}.$$

We can see that this equation is equivalent to the original system by performing matrix multiplication and addition to obtain the vector equation

$$\begin{bmatrix} x'(t) \\ y'(t) \end{bmatrix} = \begin{bmatrix} 3x(t) - y(t) \\ -x(t) + 2y(t) \end{bmatrix} + \begin{bmatrix} t^2 \\ e^t \end{bmatrix} = \begin{bmatrix} 3x(t) - y(t) + t^2 \\ -x(t) + 2y(t) + e^t \end{bmatrix}.$$

Since two vectors are equal only when their corresponding components are equal, we see that this vector equation implies that

$$x'(t) = 3x(t) - y(t) + t^2,$$
$$y'(t) = -x(t) + 2y(t) + e^t,$$

which is the original system.

5. This equation can be written as a first order system in normal form by using the substitutions $x_1(t) = y(t)$ and $x_2(t) = y'(t)$. With these substitutions this differential equation becomes the system

$$x_1'(t) = 0 \cdot x_1(t) + x_2(t),$$
$$x_2'(t) = 10x_1(t) + 3x_2(t) + \sin t.$$

We can then write this system as a matrix differential equation by defining the vectors $\mathbf{x}(t) = \text{col}[x_1(t), x_2(t)]$ (which means that $\mathbf{x}'(t) = \text{col}[x_1'(t), x_2'(t)]$), $\mathbf{f}(t) = \text{col}[0, \sin t]$, and the matrix

$$\mathbf{A} = \begin{bmatrix} 0 & 1 \\ 10 & 3 \end{bmatrix}.$$

Hence, the system above in normal form becomes the differential equation given in matrix form by

$$\begin{bmatrix} x_1'(t) \\ x_2'(t) \end{bmatrix} = \begin{bmatrix} 0 & 1 \\ 10 & 3 \end{bmatrix} \begin{bmatrix} x_1(t) \\ x_2(t) \end{bmatrix} + \begin{bmatrix} 0 \\ \sin t \end{bmatrix}.$$

(As in Problem 1 above, we can see that this equation in matrix form is equivalent to the system by performing matrix multiplication and addition and then noting that corresponding components of equal vectors are equal.)

7. This equation can be written as a first order system in normal form by using the substitutions $x_1(t) = w(t)$, $x_2(t) = w'(t)$, $x_3(t) = w''(t)$, and $x_4(t) = w'''(t)$. With these substitutions this differential equation becomes the system

$$\begin{aligned} x_1'(t) &= 0 \cdot x_1(t) + x_2(t) + 0 \cdot x_3(t) + 0 \cdot x_4(t), \\ x_2'(t) &= 0 \cdot x_1(t) + 0 \cdot x_2(t) + x_3(t) + 0 \cdot x_4(t), \\ x_3'(t) &= 0 \cdot x_1(t) + 0 \cdot x_2(t) + 0 \cdot x_3(t) + x_4(t), \\ x_4'(t) &= -x_1(t) + 0 \cdot x_2(t) + 0 \cdot x_3(t) + 0 \cdot x_4(t) + t^2 \,. \end{aligned}$$

We can then write this system as a matrix differential equation $\mathbf{x}' = \mathbf{Ax}$ by defining the vectors $\mathbf{x}(t) = \mathrm{col}[x_1(t), x_2(t), x_3(t), x_4(t)]$ (which means that $\mathbf{x}'(t) = \mathrm{col}[x_1'(t), x_2'(t), x_3'(t), x_4'(t)]$), $\mathbf{f}(t) = \mathrm{col}[0, 0, 0, t^2]$, and the matrix

$$\mathbf{A} = \begin{bmatrix} 0 & 1 & 0 & 0 \\ 0 & 0 & 1 & 0 \\ 0 & 0 & 0 & 1 \\ -1 & 0 & 0 & 0 \end{bmatrix}.$$

That is, the given fourth order differential equation is equivalent to the matrix system

$$\begin{bmatrix} x_1'(t) \\ x_2'(t) \\ x_3'(t) \\ x_4'(t) \end{bmatrix} = \begin{bmatrix} 0 & 1 & 0 & 0 \\ 0 & 0 & 1 & 0 \\ 0 & 0 & 0 & 1 \\ -1 & 0 & 0 & 0 \end{bmatrix} \begin{bmatrix} x_1(t) \\ x_2(t) \\ x_3(t) \\ x_4(t) \end{bmatrix} + \begin{bmatrix} 0 \\ 0 \\ 0 \\ t^2 \end{bmatrix}.$$

**17.** Notice that by scalar multiplication these vector functions can be written as

$$
\begin{bmatrix} e^{2t} \\ 0 \\ 5e^{2t} \end{bmatrix}, \quad
\begin{bmatrix} e^{2t} \\ e^{2t} \\ -e^{2t} \end{bmatrix}, \quad
\begin{bmatrix} 0 \\ e^{3t} \\ 0 \end{bmatrix}.
$$

Thus, as in Example 2 on page 526 of the text, we will prove that these vectors are linearly independent by showing that the only way that we can have

$$
c_1 \begin{bmatrix} e^{2t} \\ 0 \\ 5e^{2t} \end{bmatrix} + c_2 \begin{bmatrix} e^{2t} \\ e^{2t} \\ -e^{2t} \end{bmatrix} + c_3 \begin{bmatrix} 0 \\ e^{3t} \\ 0 \end{bmatrix} = \mathbf{0}
$$

for all $t$ in $(-\infty, \infty)$ is for $c_1 = c_2 = c_3 = 0$. Since the equation above must be true for all $t$, it must be true for $t = 0$. Thus, $c_1$, $c_2$, and $c_3$ must satisfy

$$
c_1 \begin{bmatrix} 1 \\ 0 \\ 5 \end{bmatrix} + c_2 \begin{bmatrix} 1 \\ 1 \\ -1 \end{bmatrix} + c_3 \begin{bmatrix} 0 \\ 1 \\ 0 \end{bmatrix} = \mathbf{0},
$$

which is equivalent to the system

$$
c_1 + c_2 = 0,
$$
$$
c_2 + c_3 = 0,
$$
$$
5c_1 - c_2 = 0.
$$

By solving the first and last of these equations simultaneously, we see that $c_1 = c_2 = 0$. Substituting these values into the second equation above yields $c_3 = 0$. Therefore, the original set of vectors must be linearly independent on the interval $(-\infty, \infty)$.

**21.** Since it is given that these vectors are solutions to the system $\mathbf{x}'(t) = \mathbf{A}\mathbf{x}(t)$, in order to determine whether they are linearly independent, we need only calculate their Wronskian. If their Wronskian is never zero, then these vectors are linearly independent and so form a fundamental solution set. If the Wronskian is identically zero, then the vectors are linearly dependent, and they do not form a fundamental solution set. Thus, we observe

$$
W\left[\mathbf{x}_1, \mathbf{x}_2, \mathbf{x}_3\right](t) = \begin{vmatrix} e^{-t} & e^{t} & e^{3t} \\ 2e^{-t} & 0 & -e^{3t} \\ e^{-t} & e^{t} & 2e^{3t} \end{vmatrix}
$$

579

$$= e^{-t} \begin{vmatrix} 0 & -e^{3t} \\ e^t & 2e^{3t} \end{vmatrix} - e^t \begin{vmatrix} 2e^{-t} & -e^{3t} \\ e^{-t} & 2e^{3t} \end{vmatrix} + e^{3t} \begin{vmatrix} 2e^{-t} & 0 \\ e^{-t} & e^t \end{vmatrix}$$

$$= e^{-t} \left(0 + e^{4t}\right) - e^t \left(4e^{2t} + e^{2t}\right) + e^{3t}(2 - 0) = -2e^{3t} \neq 0,$$

where we have used cofactors to calculate the determinant. Therefore, this set of vectors is linearly independent and so forms a fundamental solution set for the system. Thus, a fundamental matrix is given by

$$\mathbf{X}(t) = \begin{bmatrix} e^{-t} & e^t & e^{3t} \\ 2e^{-t} & 0 & -e^{3t} \\ e^{-t} & e^t & 2e^{3t} \end{bmatrix},$$

and a general solution of the system will be

$$\mathbf{x}(t) = \mathbf{X}(t)\mathbf{c} = c_1 \begin{bmatrix} e^{-t} \\ 2e^{-t} \\ e^{-t} \end{bmatrix} + c_2 \begin{bmatrix} e^t \\ 0 \\ e^t \end{bmatrix} + c_3 \begin{bmatrix} e^{3t} \\ -e^{3t} \\ 2e^{3t} \end{bmatrix}.$$

**27.** In order to show that $\mathbf{X}(t)$ is a fundamental matrix for the system, we must first show that each of its column vectors is a solution. Thus, we substitute each of the vectors

$$\mathbf{x}_1(t) = \begin{bmatrix} 6e^{-t} \\ -e^{-t} \\ -5e^{-t} \end{bmatrix}, \qquad \mathbf{x}_2(t) = \begin{bmatrix} -3e^{-2t} \\ e^{-2t} \\ e^{-2t} \end{bmatrix}, \qquad \mathbf{x}_3(t) = \begin{bmatrix} 2e^{3t} \\ e^{3t} \\ e^{3t} \end{bmatrix}$$

into the given system to obtain

$$\mathbf{A}\mathbf{x}_1(t) = \begin{bmatrix} 0 & 6 & 0 \\ 1 & 0 & 1 \\ 1 & 1 & 0 \end{bmatrix} \begin{bmatrix} 6e^{-t} \\ -e^{-t} \\ -5e^{-t} \end{bmatrix} = \begin{bmatrix} -6e^{-t} \\ e^{-t} \\ 5e^{-t} \end{bmatrix} = \mathbf{x}_1'(t),$$

$$\mathbf{A}\mathbf{x}_2(t) = \begin{bmatrix} 0 & 6 & 0 \\ 1 & 0 & 1 \\ 1 & 1 & 0 \end{bmatrix} \begin{bmatrix} -3e^{-2t} \\ e^{-2t} \\ e^{-2t} \end{bmatrix} = \begin{bmatrix} 6e^{-2t} \\ -2e^{-2t} \\ -2e^{-2t} \end{bmatrix} = \mathbf{x}_2'(t),$$

$$\mathbf{Ax}_3(t) = \begin{bmatrix} 0 & 6 & 0 \\ 1 & 0 & 1 \\ 1 & 1 & 0 \end{bmatrix} \begin{bmatrix} 2e^{3t} \\ e^{3t} \\ e^{3t} \end{bmatrix} = \begin{bmatrix} 6e^{3t} \\ 3e^{3t} \\ 3e^{3t} \end{bmatrix} = \mathbf{x}'_3(t).$$

Therefore, each column vector of $\mathbf{X}(t)$ is a solution to the system on $(-\infty, \infty)$.

Next we must show that these vectors are linearly independent. Since they are solutions to a differential equation in matrix form, it is enough to show that their Wronskian is never zero. Thus, we find

$$W(t) = \begin{vmatrix} 6e^{-t} & -3e^{-2t} & 2e^{3t} \\ -e^{-t} & e^{-2t} & e^{3t} \\ -5e^{-t} & e^{-2t} & e^{3t} \end{vmatrix}$$

$$= 6e^{-t} \begin{vmatrix} e^{-2t} & e^{3t} \\ e^{-2t} & e^{3t} \end{vmatrix} + 3e^{-2t} \begin{vmatrix} -e^{-t} & e^{3t} \\ -5e^{-t} & e^{3t} \end{vmatrix} + 2e^{3t} \begin{vmatrix} -e^{-t} & e^{-2t} \\ -5e^{-t} & e^{-2t} \end{vmatrix}$$

$$= 6e^{-t} \left( e^t - e^t \right) + 3e^{-2t} \left( -e^{2t} + 5e^{2t} \right) + 2e^{3t} \left( -e^{-3t} + 5e^{-3t} \right) = 20 \neq 0,$$

where we have used cofactors to calculate the determinant. Hence, these three vectors are linearly independent. Therefore, $\mathbf{X}(t)$ is a fundamental matrix for this system.

We will now find the inverse of the matrix $\mathbf{X}(t)$ by performing row-reduction on the matrix

$$[\mathbf{X}(t)|\mathbf{I}] \longrightarrow [\mathbf{I}|\mathbf{X}^{-1}(t)].$$

Thus, we have

$$[\mathbf{X}(t)|\mathbf{I}] = \begin{bmatrix} 6e^{-t} & -3e^{-2t} & 2e^{3t} & 1 & 0 & 0 \\ -e^{-t} & e^{-2t} & e^{3t} & 0 & 1 & 0 \\ -5e^{-t} & e^{-2t} & e^{3t} & 0 & 0 & 1 \end{bmatrix}$$

$$\begin{matrix} -R_2 \to R_1 \\ R_1 \to R_2 \end{matrix} \quad \begin{bmatrix} e^{-t} & -e^{-2t} & -e^{3t} & 0 & -1 & 0 \\ 6e^{-t} & -3e^{-2t} & 2e^{3t} & 1 & 0 & 0 \\ -5e^{-t} & e^{-2t} & e^{3t} & 0 & 0 & 1 \end{bmatrix}$$

$$\begin{matrix} R_2 - 6R_1 \to R_2 \\ R_3 + 5R_1 \to R_3 \end{matrix} \quad \begin{bmatrix} e^{-t} & -e^{-2t} & -e^{3t} & 0 & -1 & 0 \\ 0 & 3e^{-2t} & 8e^{3t} & 1 & 6 & 0 \\ 0 & -4e^{-2t} & -4e^{3t} & 0 & -5 & 1 \end{bmatrix}$$

Chapter 9

$$
\begin{array}{c}
-R_3/4 \to R_2 \\
R_2 \to R_3
\end{array}
\quad
\left[
\begin{array}{ccc|ccc}
e^{-t} & -e^{-2t} & -e^{3t} & 0 & -1 & 0 \\
0 & e^{-2t} & e^{3t} & 0 & 5/4 & -1/4 \\
0 & 3e^{-2t} & 8e^{3t} & 1 & 6 & 0
\end{array}
\right]
$$

$$
\begin{array}{c}
R_1 + R_2 \to R_1 \\
R_3 - 3R_2 \to R_3
\end{array}
\quad
\left[
\begin{array}{ccc|ccc}
e^{-t} & 0 & 0 & 0 & 1/4 & -1/4 \\
0 & e^{-2t} & e^{3t} & 0 & 5/4 & -1/4 \\
0 & 0 & 5e^{3t} & 1 & 9/4 & 3/4
\end{array}
\right]
$$

$$
\frac{1}{5} R_3 \to R_3
\quad
\left[
\begin{array}{ccc|ccc}
e^{-t} & 0 & 0 & 0 & 1/4 & -1/4 \\
0 & e^{-2t} & e^{3t} & 0 & 5/4 & -1/4 \\
0 & 0 & e^{3t} & 1/5 & 9/20 & 3/20
\end{array}
\right]
$$

$$
R_2 - R_3 \to R_2
\quad
\left[
\begin{array}{ccc|ccc}
e^{-t} & 0 & 0 & 0 & 1/4 & -1/4 \\
0 & e^{-2t} & 0 & -1/5 & 4/5 & -2/5 \\
0 & 0 & e^{3t} & 1/5 & 9/20 & 3/20
\end{array}
\right]
$$

$$
\begin{array}{c}
e^{t} R_1 \to R_1 \\
e^{2t} R_2 \to R_2 \\
e^{-3t} R_3 \to R_3
\end{array}
\quad
\left[
\begin{array}{ccc|ccc}
1 & 0 & 0 & 0 & e^{t}/4 & -e^{t}/4 \\
0 & 1 & 0 & -e^{2t}/5 & 4e^{2t}/5 & -2e^{2t}/5 \\
0 & 0 & 1 & e^{-3t}/5 & 9e^{-3t}/20 & 3e^{-3t}/20
\end{array}
\right].
$$

Therefore, we see that

$$
\mathbf{X}^{-1}(t) =
\left[
\begin{array}{ccc}
0 & e^{t}/4 & -e^{t}/4 \\
-e^{2t}/5 & 4e^{2t}/5 & -2e^{2t}/5 \\
e^{-3t}/5 & 9e^{-3t}/20 & 3e^{-3t}/20
\end{array}
\right].
$$

We now can use Problem 26 to find the solution to this differential equation for *any* initial value. For the initial value given here we note that $t_0 = 0$. Thus, substituting $t_0 = 0$ into the matrix $\mathbf{X}^{-1}(t)$ above yields

$$
\mathbf{X}^{-1}(0) =
\left[
\begin{array}{ccc}
0 & 1/4 & -1/4 \\
-1/5 & 4/5 & -2/5 \\
1/5 & 9/20 & 3/20
\end{array}
\right].
$$

Hence, we see that the solution to this problem is given by

$$
\mathbf{x}(t) = \mathbf{X}(t)\mathbf{X}^{-1}(0)\mathbf{x}(0)
$$

582

$$= \begin{bmatrix} 6e^{-t} & -3e^{-2t} & 2e^{3t} \\ -e^{-t} & e^{-2t} & e^{3t} \\ -5e^{-t} & e^{-2t} & e^{3t} \end{bmatrix} \begin{bmatrix} 0 & 1/4 & -1/4 \\ -1/5 & 4/5 & -2/5 \\ 1/5 & 9/20 & 3/20 \end{bmatrix} \begin{bmatrix} -1 \\ 0 \\ 1 \end{bmatrix}$$

$$= \begin{bmatrix} 6e^{-t} & -3e^{-2t} & 2e^{3t} \\ -e^{-t} & e^{-2t} & e^{3t} \\ -5e^{-t} & e^{-2t} & e^{3t} \end{bmatrix} \begin{bmatrix} -1/4 \\ -1/5 \\ -1/20 \end{bmatrix} = \begin{bmatrix} -(3/2)e^{-t} + (3/5)e^{-2t} - (1/10)e^{3t} \\ (1/4)e^{-t} - (1/5)e^{-2t} - (1/20)e^{3t} \\ (5/4)e^{-t} - (1/5)e^{-2t} - (1/20)e^{3t} \end{bmatrix} .$$

There are two short cuts that can be taken to solve the given problem. First, since we only need $\mathbf{X}^{-1}(0)$, it suffices to compute the inverse of $\mathbf{X}(0)$, not $\mathbf{X}(t)$. Second, by producing $\mathbf{X}^{-1}(t)$ we automatically know that $\det \mathbf{X}(0) \neq 0$ and hence $\mathbf{X}(t)$ is a fundamental matrix. Thus, it was not really necessary to compute the Wronskian.

**33.** Let $\phi(t)$ be an arbitrary solution to the system $\mathbf{x}'(t) = \mathbf{A}(t)\mathbf{x}(t)$ on the interval $I$. We want to find $\mathbf{c} = \mathrm{col}(c_1, c_2, \ldots, c_n)$ so that

$$\phi(t) = c_1\mathbf{x}_1(t) + c_2\mathbf{x}_2(t) + \cdots + c_n\mathbf{x}_n(t),$$

where $\mathbf{x}_1, \mathbf{x}_2, \ldots, \mathbf{x}_n$ are $n$ linearly independent solutions for this system. Since

$$c_1\mathbf{x}_1(t) + c_2\mathbf{x}_2(t) + \cdots + c_n\mathbf{x}_n(t) = \mathbf{X}(t)\mathbf{c},$$

where $\mathbf{X}(t)$ is the fundamental matrix whose columns are the vectors $\mathbf{x}_1, \mathbf{x}_2, \ldots, \mathbf{x}_n$, this equation can be written as

$$\phi(t) = \mathbf{X}(t)\mathbf{c} \tag{9.1}$$

Since $\mathbf{x}_1, \mathbf{x}_2, \ldots, \mathbf{x}_n$ are linearly independent solutions of the system $\mathbf{x}'(t) = \mathbf{A}(t)\mathbf{x}(t)$, their Wronskian is never zero. Therefore, as was discussed on page 528 of the text, $\mathbf{X}(t)$ has an inverse at each point in $I$. Thus, at $t_0$, a point in $I$, $\mathbf{X}^{-1}(t_0)$ exists and equation (9.1) becomes

$$\phi(t_0) = \mathbf{X}(t_0)\mathbf{c} \quad \Rightarrow \quad \mathbf{X}^{-1}(t_0)\phi(t_0) = \mathbf{X}^{-1}(t_0)\mathbf{X}(t_0)\mathbf{c} = \mathbf{c}.$$

Hence, if we define $\mathbf{c}_0$ to be the vector $\mathbf{c}_0 = \mathbf{X}^{-1}(t_0)\phi(t_0)$, then equation (9.1) is true at the point $t_0$ (i. e. $\phi(t_0) = \mathbf{X}(t_0)\mathbf{X}^{-1}(t_0)\phi(t_0)$). To see that, for this definition of $\mathbf{c}_0$, equation (9.1) is true for all $t$ in $I$ (and so this is the vector that we seek), notice that $\phi(t)$ and $\mathbf{X}(t)\mathbf{c}_0$

are both solutions to same initial value problem (with the initial value given at the point $t_0$). Therefore, by the uniqueness of solutions, Theorem 2 on page 525 of the text, these solutions must be equal on $I$, which means that $\phi(t) = \mathbf{X}(t)\mathbf{c}_0$ for all $t$ in $I$.

**EXERCISES 9.5: Homogeneous Linear Systems with Constant Coefficients, page 541**

**5.** The characteristic equation for this matrix is given by

$$|\mathbf{A} - r\mathbf{I}| = \begin{vmatrix} 1-r & 0 & 0 \\ 0 & -r & 2 \\ 0 & 2 & -r \end{vmatrix} = (1-r) \begin{vmatrix} -r & 2 \\ 2 & -r \end{vmatrix}$$

$$= (1-r)\left(r^2 - 4\right) = (1-r)(r-2)(r+2) = 0.$$

Thus, the eigenvalues of this matrix are $r = 1, 2, -2$. Substituting the eigenvalue $r = 1$, into equation $(\mathbf{A} - r\mathbf{I})\mathbf{u} = \mathbf{0}$ yields

$$(\mathbf{A} - \mathbf{I})\mathbf{u} = \begin{bmatrix} 0 & 0 & 0 \\ 0 & -1 & 2 \\ 0 & 2 & -1 \end{bmatrix} \begin{bmatrix} u_1 \\ u_2 \\ u_3 \end{bmatrix} = \begin{bmatrix} 0 \\ 0 \\ 0 \end{bmatrix}, \tag{9.2}$$

which is equivalent to the system

$$-u_2 + 2u_3 = 0,$$
$$2u_2 - u_3 = 0.$$

This system reduces to the system $u_2 = 0$, $u_3 = 0$, which does not assign any value to $u_1$. Thus, we can let $u_1$ be any value, say $u_1 = s$, and $u_2 = 0$, $u_3 = 0$ and the system given by (9.2) will be satisfied. From this we see that the eigenvectors associated with the eigenvalue $r = 1$ are given by

$$\mathbf{u}_1 = \mathrm{col}\,(u_1, u_2, u_3) = \mathrm{col}(s, 0, 0) = s\,\mathrm{col}(1, 0, 0).$$

For $r = 2$ we observe that the equation $(\mathbf{A} - r\mathbf{I})\mathbf{u} = \mathbf{0}$ becomes

$$(\mathbf{A} - 2\mathbf{I})\mathbf{u} = \begin{bmatrix} -1 & 0 & 0 \\ 0 & -2 & 2 \\ 0 & 2 & -2 \end{bmatrix} \begin{bmatrix} u_1 \\ u_2 \\ u_3 \end{bmatrix} = \begin{bmatrix} 0 \\ 0 \\ 0 \end{bmatrix},$$

whose corresponding system of equations reduces to $u_1 = 0$, $u_2 = u_3$. Therefore, we can pick $u_2$ to be any value, say $u_2 = s$ (which means that $u_3 = s$), and we find that the eigenvectors for this matrix associated with the eigenvalue $r = 2$ are given by

$$\mathbf{u}_2 = \text{col}\,(u_1, u_2, u_3) = \text{col}(0, s, s) = s\,\text{col}(0, 1, 1).$$

For $r = -2$, we solve the equation

$$(\mathbf{A} + 2\mathbf{I})\mathbf{u} = \begin{bmatrix} 3 & 0 & 0 \\ 0 & 2 & 2 \\ 0 & 2 & 2 \end{bmatrix} \begin{bmatrix} u_1 \\ u_2 \\ u_3 \end{bmatrix} = \begin{bmatrix} 0 \\ 0 \\ 0 \end{bmatrix},$$

which reduces to the system $u_1 = 0$, $u_2 = -u_3$. Hence, $u_3$ is arbitrary, and so we will let $u_3 = s$ (which means that $u_2 = -s$). Thus, solutions to this system and, therefore, eigenvectors for this matrix associated with the eigenvalue $r = -2$ are given by the vectors

$$\mathbf{u}_3 = \text{col}\,(u_1, u_2, u_3) = \text{col}(0, -s, s) = s\,\text{col}(0, -1, 1).$$

**13.** We must first find the eigenvalues and eigenvectors associated with the given matrix $\mathbf{A}$. Thus, we note that the characteristic equation for this matrix is given by

$$|\mathbf{A} - r\mathbf{I}| = \begin{vmatrix} 1 - r & 2 & 2 \\ 2 & -r & 3 \\ 2 & 3 & -r \end{vmatrix} = 0$$

$$\Rightarrow \quad (1-r)\begin{vmatrix} -r & 3 \\ 3 & -r \end{vmatrix} - 2\begin{vmatrix} 2 & 3 \\ 2 & -r \end{vmatrix} + 2\begin{vmatrix} 2 & -r \\ 2 & 3 \end{vmatrix} = 0$$

$$\Rightarrow \quad (1-r)\left(r^2 - 9\right) - 2(-2r - 6) + 2(6 + 2r) = (1-r)(r-2)(r+2) = 0$$

$$\Rightarrow \quad (r+3)[(1-r)(r-3)+8] = 0 \quad \Rightarrow \quad (r+3)(r-5)(r+1) = 0.$$

Therefore, the eigenvalues are $r = -3, -1, 5$. To find an eigenvector associated with the eigenvalue $r = -3$, we must find a vector $\mathbf{u} = \text{col}(u_1, u_2, u_3)$ which satisfies the equation $(\mathbf{A} + 3\mathbf{I})\mathbf{u} = \mathbf{0}$. Thus, we have

$$(\mathbf{A} + 3\mathbf{I})\mathbf{u} = \begin{bmatrix} 4 & 2 & 2 \\ 2 & 3 & 3 \\ 2 & 3 & 3 \end{bmatrix} \begin{bmatrix} u_1 \\ u_2 \\ u_3 \end{bmatrix} = \begin{bmatrix} 0 \\ 0 \\ 0 \end{bmatrix} \quad \Rightarrow \quad \begin{bmatrix} 2 & 0 & 0 \\ 0 & 1 & 1 \\ 0 & 0 & 0 \end{bmatrix} \begin{bmatrix} u_1 \\ u_2 \\ u_3 \end{bmatrix} = \begin{bmatrix} 0 \\ 0 \\ 0 \end{bmatrix},$$

where we have obtained the last equation above by using elementary row operations. This equation is equivalent to the system $u_1 = 0$, $u_2 = -u_3$. Hence, if we let $u_3$ have the arbitrary value $s_1$, then we see that, for the matrix $\mathbf{A}$, the eigenvectors associated with the eigenvalue $r = -3$ are given by

$$\mathbf{u} = \mathrm{col}\,(u_1, u_2, u_3) = \mathrm{col}\,(0, -s_1, s_1) = s_1\mathrm{col}(0, -1, 1).$$

Thus, if we choose $s_1 = 1$, then vector $\mathbf{u}_1 = \mathrm{col}(0, -1, 1)$ is one eigenvector associated with this eigenvalue. For the eigenvalue $r = -1$, we must find a vector $\mathbf{u}$ which satisfies the equation $(\mathbf{A} + \mathbf{I})\mathbf{u} = \mathbf{0}$. Thus, we see that

$$(\mathbf{A} + \mathbf{I})\mathbf{u} = \begin{bmatrix} 2 & 2 & 2 \\ 2 & 1 & 3 \\ 2 & 3 & 1 \end{bmatrix} \begin{bmatrix} u_1 \\ u_2 \\ u_3 \end{bmatrix} = \begin{bmatrix} 0 \\ 0 \\ 0 \end{bmatrix} \Rightarrow \begin{bmatrix} 1 & 2 & 0 \\ 0 & 1 & -1 \\ 0 & 0 & 0 \end{bmatrix} \begin{bmatrix} u_1 \\ u_2 \\ u_3 \end{bmatrix} = \begin{bmatrix} 0 \\ 0 \\ 0 \end{bmatrix},$$

which is equivalent to the system $u_1 = -2u_2$, $u_3 = u_2$. Therefore, if we let $u_2 = s_2$, then we see that vectors which satisfy the equation $(\mathbf{A} + \mathbf{I})\mathbf{u} = \mathbf{0}$ and, hence, eigenvectors for the matrix $\mathbf{A}$ associated with the eigenvalue $r = -1$ are given by

$$\mathbf{u} = \mathrm{col}\,(u_1, u_2, u_3) = \mathrm{col}\,(-2s_2, s_2, s_2) = s_2\mathrm{col}(-2, 1, 1).$$

By letting $s_2 = 1$, we find that one such vector will be the vector $\mathbf{u}_2 = \mathrm{col}(-2, 1, 1)$. In order to find an eigenvector associated with the eigenvalue $r = 5$, we will solve the equation $(\mathbf{A} - 5\mathbf{I})\mathbf{u} = \mathbf{0}$. Thus, we have

$$(\mathbf{A} - 5\mathbf{I})\mathbf{u} = \begin{bmatrix} -4 & 2 & 2 \\ 2 & -5 & 3 \\ 2 & 3 & -5 \end{bmatrix} \begin{bmatrix} u_1 \\ u_2 \\ u_3 \end{bmatrix} = \begin{bmatrix} 0 \\ 0 \\ 0 \end{bmatrix} \Rightarrow \begin{bmatrix} 1 & 0 & -1 \\ 0 & 1 & -1 \\ 0 & 0 & 0 \end{bmatrix} \begin{bmatrix} u_1 \\ u_2 \\ u_3 \end{bmatrix} = \begin{bmatrix} 0 \\ 0 \\ 0 \end{bmatrix},$$

which is equivalent to the system $u_1 = u_3$, $u_2 = u_3$. Thus, if we let $u_3 = s_3$, then, for the matrix $\mathbf{A}$, the eigenvectors associated with the eigenvalue $r = 5$ are given by

$$\mathbf{u} = \mathrm{col}\,(u_1, u_2, u_3) = \mathrm{col}\,(s_3, s_3, s_3) = s_3\mathrm{col}(1, 1, 1).$$

Hence, by letting $s_3 = 1$, we see that one such vector will be the vector $\mathbf{u}_3 = \text{col}(1, 1, 1)$. Therefore, by Corollary 1 on page 538 of the text, we see that a fundamental solution set for this equation is given by

$$\left\{ e^{-3t}\mathbf{u}_1, e^{-t}\mathbf{u}_2, e^{5t}\mathbf{u}_3 \right\}.$$

Thus, a general solution for this system is

$$\mathbf{x}(t) = c_1 e^{-3t}\mathbf{u}_1 + c_2 e^{-t}\mathbf{u}_2 + c_3 e^{5t}\mathbf{u}_3 = c_1 e^{-3t} \begin{bmatrix} 0 \\ -1 \\ 1 \end{bmatrix} + c_2 e^{-t} \begin{bmatrix} -2 \\ 1 \\ 1 \end{bmatrix} + c_3 e^{5t} \begin{bmatrix} 1 \\ 1 \\ 1 \end{bmatrix}.$$

**21.** A fundamental matrix for this system has three columns which are linearly independent solutions. Therefore, we will first find three such solutions. To this end, we will first find the eigenvalues for the matrix $\mathbf{A}$ by solving the characteristic equation given by

$$|\mathbf{A} - r\mathbf{I}| = \begin{vmatrix} -r & 1 & 0 \\ 0 & -r & 1 \\ 8 & -14 & 7-r \end{vmatrix} = 0$$

$$\Rightarrow \quad -r \begin{vmatrix} -r & 1 \\ -14 & 7-r \end{vmatrix} - \begin{vmatrix} 0 & 1 \\ 8 & 7-r \end{vmatrix} = 0$$

$$\Rightarrow \quad r^3 - 7r^2 + 14r - 8 = 0 \quad \Rightarrow \quad (r-1)(r-2)(r-4) = 0.$$

Hence, this matrix has three distinct eigenvalues, $r = 1, 2, 4$, and, according to Theorem 6 on page 538 of the text, the eigenvectors associated with these eigenvalues will be linearly independent. Thus, these eigenvectors will be used in finding the three linearly independent solutions which we seek. To find an eigenvector, $\mathbf{u} = \text{col}(u_1, u_2, u_3)$, associated with the eigenvalue $r = 1$, we will solve the equation $(\mathbf{A} - \mathbf{I})\mathbf{u} = 0$. Therefore, we have

$$(\mathbf{A} - \mathbf{I})\mathbf{u} = \begin{bmatrix} -1 & 1 & 0 \\ 0 & -1 & 1 \\ 8 & -14 & 6 \end{bmatrix} \begin{bmatrix} u_1 \\ u_2 \\ u_3 \end{bmatrix} = \begin{bmatrix} 0 \\ 0 \\ 0 \end{bmatrix} \quad \Rightarrow \quad \begin{bmatrix} -1 & 0 & 1 \\ 0 & -1 & 1 \\ 0 & 0 & 0 \end{bmatrix} \begin{bmatrix} u_1 \\ u_2 \\ u_3 \end{bmatrix} = \begin{bmatrix} 0 \\ 0 \\ 0 \end{bmatrix},$$

which is equivalent to the system $u_1 = u_3$, $u_2 = u_3$. Thus, by letting $u_3 = 1$ (which implies that $u_1 = u_2 = 1$), we find that one eigenvector associated with the eigenvalue $r = 1$ is given by the vector $\mathbf{u}_1 = \mathrm{col}(1, 1, 1)$. To find an eigenvector associated with the eigenvalue $r = 2$, we solve the equation

$$(\mathbf{A} - 2\mathbf{I})\mathbf{u} = \begin{bmatrix} -2 & 1 & 0 \\ 0 & -2 & 1 \\ 8 & -14 & 5 \end{bmatrix} \begin{bmatrix} u_1 \\ u_2 \\ u_3 \end{bmatrix} = \begin{bmatrix} 0 \\ 0 \\ 0 \end{bmatrix} \Rightarrow \begin{bmatrix} 4 & 0 & -1 \\ 0 & 2 & -1 \\ 0 & 0 & 0 \end{bmatrix} \begin{bmatrix} u_1 \\ u_2 \\ u_3 \end{bmatrix} = \begin{bmatrix} 0 \\ 0 \\ 0 \end{bmatrix},$$

which is equivalent to the system $4u_1 = u_3$, $2u_2 = u_3$. Hence, letting $u_3 = 4$ implies that $u_1 = 1$ and $u_2 = 2$. Therefore, one eigenvector associated with the eigenvalue $r = 2$ is the vector $\mathbf{u}_2 = \mathrm{col}(1, 2, 4)$. In order to find an eigenvector associated with the eigenvalue $r = 4$, we will solve the equation

$$(\mathbf{A} - 4\mathbf{I})\mathbf{u} = \begin{bmatrix} -4 & 1 & 0 \\ 0 & -4 & 1 \\ 8 & -14 & 3 \end{bmatrix} \begin{bmatrix} u_1 \\ u_2 \\ u_3 \end{bmatrix} = \begin{bmatrix} 0 \\ 0 \\ 0 \end{bmatrix} \Rightarrow \begin{bmatrix} 16 & 0 & -1 \\ 0 & 4 & -1 \\ 0 & 0 & 0 \end{bmatrix} \begin{bmatrix} u_1 \\ u_2 \\ u_3 \end{bmatrix} = \begin{bmatrix} 0 \\ 0 \\ 0 \end{bmatrix},$$

which is equivalent to the system $16u_1 = u_3$, $4u_2 = u_3$. Therefore, letting $u_3 = 16$ implies that $u_1 = 1$ and $u_2 = 4$. Thus, one eigenvector associated with the eigenvalue $r = 4$ is the vector $\mathbf{u}_3 = \mathrm{col}(1, 4, 16)$. Therefore, by Theorem 5 on page 536 of the text (or Corollary 1), we see that three linearly independent solutions of this system are given by $e^t\mathbf{u}_1$, $e^{2t}\mathbf{u}_2$, and $e^{4t}\mathbf{u}_3$. Thus, a fundamental matrix for this system will be the matrix

$$\begin{bmatrix} e^t & e^{2t} & e^{4t} \\ e^t & 2e^{2t} & 4e^{4t} \\ e^t & 4e^{2t} & 16e^{4t} \end{bmatrix}.$$

**33.** Since the coefficient matrix for this system is a $3 \times 3$ real symmetric matrix, by the discussion on page 540 of the text, we know that we can find three linearly independent eigenvectors for this matrix. Therefore, to find the solution to this initial value problem, we must first find three such eigenvectors. To do this we first find eigenvalues for this matrix. Therefore, we solve the characteristic equation given by

$$|\mathbf{A} - r\mathbf{I}| = \begin{vmatrix} 1 - r & -2 & 2 \\ -2 & 1 - r & -2 \\ 2 & -2 & 1 - r \end{vmatrix} = 0$$

$$\Rightarrow \quad (1-r)\begin{vmatrix} 1-r & -2 \\ -2 & 1-r \end{vmatrix} + 2\begin{vmatrix} -2 & -2 \\ 2 & 1-r \end{vmatrix} + 2\begin{vmatrix} -2 & 1-r \\ 2 & -2 \end{vmatrix} = 0$$

$$\Rightarrow \quad (1-r)\left[(1-r)^2 - 4\right] + 2\left[-2(1-r) + 4\right] + 2\left[4 - 2(1-r)\right] = 0$$

$$\Rightarrow \quad (1-r)(r-3)(r+1) + 8(r+1) = -(r+1)(r-5)(r+1) = 0.$$

Thus, the eigenvalues are $r = -1$ and $r = 5$, with $r = -1$ an eigenvalue of multiplicity two. In order to find an eigenvector associated with the eigenvalue $r = 5$, we solve the equation

$$(\mathbf{A} - 5\mathbf{I})\mathbf{u} = \begin{bmatrix} -4 & -2 & 2 \\ -2 & -4 & -2 \\ 2 & -2 & -4 \end{bmatrix}\begin{bmatrix} u_1 \\ u_2 \\ u_3 \end{bmatrix} = \begin{bmatrix} 0 \\ 0 \\ 0 \end{bmatrix} \Rightarrow \begin{bmatrix} 1 & 0 & -1 \\ 0 & 1 & 1 \\ 0 & 0 & 0 \end{bmatrix}\begin{bmatrix} u_1 \\ u_2 \\ u_3 \end{bmatrix} = \begin{bmatrix} 0 \\ 0 \\ 0 \end{bmatrix}.$$

This equation is equivalent to the system $u_1 = u_3$, $u_2 = -u_3$. Thus, if we let $u_3 = 1$, we see that for this coefficient matrix an eigenvector associated with the eigenvalue $r = 5$ is given by the vector $\mathbf{u}_1 = \text{col}(u_1, u_2, u_3) = \text{col}(1, -1, 1)$. We must now find two more linearly independent eigenvectors for this coefficient matrix. By the discussion above, these eigenvectors will be associated with the eigenvalue $r = 1$. Thus, we solve the equation

$$(\mathbf{A} + \mathbf{I})\mathbf{u} = \begin{bmatrix} 2 & -2 & 2 \\ -2 & 2 & -2 \\ 2 & -2 & 2 \end{bmatrix}\begin{bmatrix} u_1 \\ u_2 \\ u_3 \end{bmatrix} = \begin{bmatrix} 0 \\ 0 \\ 0 \end{bmatrix} \Rightarrow \begin{bmatrix} 1 & -1 & 1 \\ 0 & 0 & 0 \\ 0 & 0 & 0 \end{bmatrix}\begin{bmatrix} u_1 \\ u_2 \\ u_3 \end{bmatrix} = \begin{bmatrix} 0 \\ 0 \\ 0 \end{bmatrix}, \quad (9.3)$$

which is equivalent to the equation $u_1 - u_2 + u_3 = 0$. Therefore, if we arbitrarily assign the value $s$ to $u_2$ and $v$ to $u_3$, we see that $u_1 = s - v$, and solutions to equation (9.3) above will be given by

$$\mathbf{u} = \begin{bmatrix} s - v \\ s \\ v \end{bmatrix} = s\begin{bmatrix} 1 \\ 1 \\ 0 \end{bmatrix} + v\begin{bmatrix} -1 \\ 0 \\ 1 \end{bmatrix}.$$

By taking $s = 1$ and $v = 0$, we see that one solution to equation (9.3) will be the vector $\mathbf{u}_2 = \text{col}(1, 1, 0)$. Hence, this is one eigenvector for the coefficient matrix. Similarly, by letting $s = 0$ and $v = 1$, we find a second eigenvector will be the vector $\mathbf{u}_3 = \text{col}(-1, 0, 1)$. Since the eigenvectors $\mathbf{u}_1$, $\mathbf{u}_2$, and $\mathbf{u}_3$ are linearly independent, by Theorem 5 on page 536 of the text,

# Chapter 9

we see that a general solution for this system will be given by

$$\mathbf{x}(t) = c_1 e^{5t} \begin{bmatrix} 1 \\ -1 \\ 1 \end{bmatrix} + c_2 e^{-t} \begin{bmatrix} 1 \\ 1 \\ 0 \end{bmatrix} + c_3 e^{-t} \begin{bmatrix} -1 \\ 0 \\ 1 \end{bmatrix}.$$

To find a solution which satisfies the initial condition, we must solve the equation

$$\mathbf{x}(0) = c_1 \begin{bmatrix} 1 \\ -1 \\ 1 \end{bmatrix} + c_2 \begin{bmatrix} 1 \\ 1 \\ 0 \end{bmatrix} + c_3 \begin{bmatrix} -1 \\ 0 \\ 1 \end{bmatrix} \quad\Rightarrow\quad \begin{bmatrix} 1 & 1 & -1 \\ -1 & 1 & 0 \\ 1 & 0 & 1 \end{bmatrix} \begin{bmatrix} c_1 \\ c_2 \\ c_3 \end{bmatrix} = \begin{bmatrix} -2 \\ -3 \\ 2 \end{bmatrix}.$$

This equation can be solved by either using elementary row operations on the augmented matrix associated with this equation or by solving the system

$$c_1 + c_2 - c_3 = -2,$$
$$-c_1 + c_2 = -3,$$
$$c_1 + c_3 = 2.$$

By either method we find that $c_1 = 1$, $c_2 = -2$, and $c_3 = 1$. Therefore, the solution to this initial value problem is given by

$$\mathbf{x}(t) = e^{5t} \begin{bmatrix} 1 \\ -1 \\ 1 \end{bmatrix} - 2e^{-t} \begin{bmatrix} 1 \\ 1 \\ 0 \end{bmatrix} + e^{-t} \begin{bmatrix} -1 \\ 0 \\ 1 \end{bmatrix}$$

$$= \begin{bmatrix} e^{5t} - 2e^{-t} - e^{-t} \\ -e^{5t} - 2e^{-t} + 0 \\ e^{5t} + 0 + e^{-t} \end{bmatrix} = \begin{bmatrix} -3e^{-t} + e^{5t} \\ -2e^{-t} - e^{5t} \\ e^{-t} + e^{5t} \end{bmatrix}.$$

**37. (a)** In order to find the eigenvalues for the matrix $\mathbf{A}$, we will solve the characteristic equation

$$|\mathbf{A} - r\mathbf{I}| = \begin{vmatrix} 2-r & 1 & 6 \\ 0 & 2-r & 5 \\ 0 & 0 & 2-r \end{vmatrix} = 0 \quad\Rightarrow\quad (2-r)^3 = 0.$$

Thus, $r = 2$ is an eigenvalue of multiplicity three. To find the eigenvectors for the matrix $\mathbf{A}$ associated with this eigenvalue, we solve the equation

$$(\mathbf{A} - 2\mathbf{I})\mathbf{u} = \begin{bmatrix} 0 & 1 & 6 \\ 0 & 0 & 5 \\ 0 & 0 & 0 \end{bmatrix} \begin{bmatrix} u_1 \\ u_2 \\ u_3 \end{bmatrix} = \begin{bmatrix} 0 \\ 0 \\ 0 \end{bmatrix}.$$

This equation is equivalent to the system $u_2 = 0$, $u_3 = 0$. Therefore, we can assign $u_1$ to be any arbitrary value, say $u_1 = s$, and we find that the vector

$$\mathbf{u} = \mathrm{col}(u_1, u_2, u_3) = \mathrm{col}(s, 0, 0) = s\,\mathrm{col}(1, 0, 0)$$

will solve this equation and will, thus, be an eigenvector for the matrix $\mathbf{A}$. We also notice that the vectors $\mathbf{u} = s\,\mathrm{col}(1, 0, 0)$ are the only vectors that will solve this equation, and, hence, they will be the only eigenvectors for the matrix $\mathbf{A}$.

**(b)** By taking $s = 1$, we find that, for the matrix $\mathbf{A}$, one eigenvector associated with the eigenvalue $r = 2$ will be the vector $\mathbf{u}_1 = \mathrm{col}(1, 0, 0)$. Therefore, by the way eigenvalues and eigenvectors were defined (as was discussed in the text on page 533), we see that one solution to the system $\mathbf{x}' = \mathbf{A}\mathbf{x}$ will be given by the vector

$$\mathbf{x}_1(t) = e^{2t}\mathbf{u}_1 = e^{2t} \begin{bmatrix} 1 \\ 0 \\ 0 \end{bmatrix}.$$

**(c)** We know that $\mathbf{u}_1 = \mathrm{col}(1, 0, 0)$ is an eigenvector for the matrix $\mathbf{A}$ associated with the eigenvalue $r = 2$. Thus, $\mathbf{u}_1$ satisfies the equation

$$(\mathbf{A} - 2\mathbf{I})\mathbf{u}_1 = \mathbf{0} \qquad \Rightarrow \qquad \mathbf{A}\mathbf{u}_1 = 2\mathbf{u}_1. \tag{9.4}$$

We want to find a constant vector $\mathbf{u}_2 = \mathrm{col}(v_1, v_2, v_3)$ such that

$$\mathbf{x}_2(t) = te^{2t}\mathbf{u}_1 + e^{2t}\mathbf{u}_2$$

will be a second solution to the system $\mathbf{x}' = \mathbf{A}\mathbf{x}$. To do this, we will first show that $\mathbf{x}_2$ will satisfy the equation $\mathbf{x}' = \mathbf{A}\mathbf{x}$ if and only if the vector $\mathbf{u}_2$ satisfies the equation

$(\mathbf{A} - 2\mathbf{I})\mathbf{u}_2 = \mathbf{u}_1$. To this end, we find that

$$\mathbf{x}_2'(t) = 2te^{2t}\mathbf{u}_1 + e^{2t}\mathbf{u}_1 + 2e^{2t}\mathbf{u}_2 = 2te^{2t}\mathbf{u}_1 + e^{2t}\left(\mathbf{u}_1 + 2\mathbf{u}_2\right),$$

where we have used the fact that $\mathbf{u}_1$ and $\mathbf{u}_2$ are constant vectors. We also have

$$
\begin{aligned}
\mathbf{A}\mathbf{x}_2(t) &= \mathbf{A}\left(te^{2t}\mathbf{u}_1 + e^{2t}\mathbf{u}_2\right) \\
&= \mathbf{A}\left(te^{2t}\mathbf{u}_1\right) + \mathbf{A}\left(e^{2t}\mathbf{u}_2\right), && \text{distributive property of matrix multiplication} \\
&&& \text{(page 515 of the text)} \\
&= te^{2t}\left(\mathbf{A}\mathbf{u}_1\right) + e^{2t}\left(\mathbf{A}\mathbf{u}_2\right), && \text{associative property of matrix multiplication} \\
&&& \text{(page 515 of the text)} \\
&= 2te^{2t}\mathbf{u}_1 + e^{2t}\mathbf{A}\mathbf{u}_2, && \text{by equation (9.4) above.}
\end{aligned}
$$

Thus, if $\mathbf{x}_2(t)$ is to be a solution to the given system we, must have

$$
\begin{aligned}
&\mathbf{x}_2'(t) = \mathbf{A}\mathbf{x}_2(t) \\
\Rightarrow\quad & 2te^{2t}\mathbf{u}_1 + e^{2t}\left(\mathbf{u}_1 + 2\mathbf{u}_2\right) = 2te^{2t}\mathbf{u}_1 + e^{2t}\mathbf{A}\mathbf{u}_2 \\
\Rightarrow\quad & e^{2t}\left(\mathbf{u}_1 + 2\mathbf{u}_2\right) = e^{2t}\mathbf{A}\mathbf{u}_2 \,.
\end{aligned}
$$

By dividing both sides of this equation by the nonzero term $e^{2t}$, we obtain

$$\mathbf{u}_1 + 2\mathbf{u}_2 = \mathbf{A}\mathbf{u}_2 \quad \Rightarrow \quad (\mathbf{A} - 2\mathbf{I})\mathbf{u}_2 = \mathbf{u}_1 \,.$$

Since all of these steps are reversible, if a vector $\mathbf{u}_2$ satisfies this last equation, then $\mathbf{x}_2(t) = te^{2t}\mathbf{u}_1 + e^{2t}\mathbf{u}_2$ will be a solution to the system $\mathbf{x}' = \mathbf{A}\mathbf{x}$. Now we can use the formula $(\mathbf{A} - 2\mathbf{I})\mathbf{u}_2 = \mathbf{u}_1$ to find the vector $\mathbf{u}_2 = \text{col}(v_1, v_2, v_3)$. Hence, we solve the equation

$$(\mathbf{A} - 2\mathbf{I})\mathbf{u}_2 = \begin{bmatrix} 0 & 1 & 6 \\ 0 & 0 & 5 \\ 0 & 0 & 0 \end{bmatrix} \begin{bmatrix} v_1 \\ v_2 \\ v_3 \end{bmatrix} = \begin{bmatrix} 1 \\ 0 \\ 0 \end{bmatrix}.$$

This equation is equivalent to the system $v_2 + 6v_3 = 1$, $5v_3 = 0$, which implies that $v_2 = 1$, $v_3 = 0$. Therefore, the vector $\mathbf{u}_2 = \text{col}(0, 1, 0)$ will satisfy the equation $(\mathbf{A} - 2\mathbf{I})\mathbf{u}_2 = \mathbf{u}_1$ and, thus,

$$\mathbf{x}_2(t) = te^{2t} \begin{bmatrix} 1 \\ 0 \\ 0 \end{bmatrix} + e^{2t} \begin{bmatrix} 0 \\ 1 \\ 0 \end{bmatrix}.$$

will be a second solution to the given system. We can see by inspection $\mathbf{x}_2(t)$ and $\mathbf{x}_1(t) = e^{2t}\mathbf{u}_1$ are linearly independent.

**(d)** To find a third linearly independent solution to this system we will try to find a solution of the form $\mathbf{x}_3(t) = \dfrac{t^2}{2}e^{2t}\mathbf{u}_1 + te^{2t}\mathbf{u}_2 + e^{2t}\mathbf{u}_3$, where $\mathbf{u}_3$ is a constant vector that we must find, and $\mathbf{u}_1$ and $\mathbf{u}_2$ are the vectors that we found in parts (b) and (c), respectively. To find the vector $\mathbf{u}_3$, we will proceed as we did in part (c) above. We will first show that $\mathbf{x}_3(t)$ will be a solution to the given system if and only if the vector $\mathbf{u}_3$ satisfies the equation $(\mathbf{A} - 2\mathbf{I})\mathbf{u}_3 = \mathbf{u}_2$ . To do this we observe that

$$\mathbf{x}_3'(t) = te^{2t}\mathbf{u}_1 + t^2 e^{2t}\mathbf{u}_1 + e^{2t}\mathbf{u}_2 + 2te^{2t}\mathbf{u}_2 + 2e^{2t}\mathbf{u}_3 .$$

Also, using the facts that

$$(\mathbf{A} - 2\mathbf{I})\mathbf{u}_1 = \mathbf{0} \qquad \Rightarrow \qquad \mathbf{A}\mathbf{u}_1 = 2\mathbf{u}_1 \tag{9.5}$$

and

$$(\mathbf{A} - 2\mathbf{I})\mathbf{u}_2 = \mathbf{u}_1 \qquad \Rightarrow \qquad \mathbf{A}\mathbf{u}_2 = \mathbf{u}_1 + 2\mathbf{u}_2 , \tag{9.6}$$

we have

$$\begin{aligned}
\mathbf{A}\mathbf{x}_3(t) &= \mathbf{A}\left(\frac{t^2}{2}e^{2t}\mathbf{u}_1 + te^{2t}\mathbf{u}_2 + e^{2t}\mathbf{u}_3\right) \\
&= \mathbf{A}\left(\frac{t^2}{2}e^{2t}\mathbf{u}_1\right) + \mathbf{A}\left(te^{2t}\mathbf{u}_2\right) + +\mathbf{A}\left(e^{2t}\mathbf{u}_3\right), && \text{distributive property} \\
&= \frac{t^2}{2}e^{2t}\left(\mathbf{A}\mathbf{u}_1\right) + te^{2t}\left(\mathbf{A}\mathbf{u}_2\right) + e^{2t}\left(\mathbf{A}\mathbf{u}_3\right), && \text{associative property} \\
&= \frac{t^2}{2}e^{2t}\left(2\mathbf{u}_1\right) + te^{2t}\left(\mathbf{u}_1 + 2\mathbf{u}_2\right) + e^{2t}\mathbf{A}\mathbf{u}_3, && \text{equations (9.5) and (9.6)} \\
&= t^2 e^{2t}\mathbf{u}_1 + te^{2t}\mathbf{u}_1 + 2te^{2t}\mathbf{u}_2 + e^{2t}\mathbf{A}\mathbf{u}_3 .
\end{aligned}$$

Therefore, for $\mathbf{x}_3(t)$ to satisfy the given system, we must have

$$\mathbf{x}_3'(t) = \mathbf{A}\mathbf{x}_3(t)$$

$$\Rightarrow \quad te^{2t}\mathbf{u}_1 + t^2 e^{2t}\mathbf{u}_1 + e^{2t}\mathbf{u}_2 + 2te^{2t}\mathbf{u}_2 + 2e^{2t}\mathbf{u}_3 = t^2 e^{2t}\mathbf{u}_1 + te^{2t}\mathbf{u}_1 + 2te^{2t}\mathbf{u}_2 + e^{2t}\mathbf{A}\mathbf{u}_3$$

$$\Rightarrow \quad e^{2t}\mathbf{u}_2 + 2e^{2t}\mathbf{u}_3 = e^{2t}\mathbf{A}\mathbf{u}_3$$

$$\Rightarrow \quad \mathbf{u}_2 + 2\mathbf{u}_3 = \mathbf{A}\mathbf{u}_3$$

$$\Rightarrow \quad (\mathbf{A} - 2\mathbf{I})\mathbf{u}_3 = \mathbf{u}_2 .$$

Again since these steps are reversible, we see that, if a vector $\mathbf{u}_3$ satisfies the equation $(\mathbf{A} - 2\mathbf{I})\mathbf{u}_3 = \mathbf{u}_2$, then the vector

$$\mathbf{x}_3(t) = \frac{t^2}{2} e^{2t}\mathbf{u}_1 + te^{2t}\mathbf{u}_2 + e^{2t}\mathbf{u}_3$$

will be a third linearly independent solution to the given system. Thus, we can use this equation to find the vector $\mathbf{u}_3 = \text{col}(v_1, v_2, v_3)$. Hence, we solve

$$(\mathbf{A} - 2\mathbf{I})\mathbf{u}_3 = \begin{bmatrix} 0 & 1 & 6 \\ 0 & 0 & 5 \\ 0 & 0 & 0 \end{bmatrix} \begin{bmatrix} v_1 \\ v_2 \\ v_3 \end{bmatrix} = \begin{bmatrix} 0 \\ 1 \\ 0 \end{bmatrix}.$$

This equation is equivalent to the system $v_2 + 6v_3 = 0$, $5v_3 = 1$, which implies that $v_3 = 1/5$, $v_2 = -6/5$. Therefore, if we let $\mathbf{u}_3 = \text{col}(0, -6/5, 1/5)$, then

$$\mathbf{x}_3(t) = \frac{t^2}{2} e^{2t} \begin{bmatrix} 1 \\ 0 \\ 0 \end{bmatrix} + te^{2t} \begin{bmatrix} 0 \\ 1 \\ 0 \end{bmatrix} + e^{2t} \begin{bmatrix} 0 \\ -6/5 \\ 1/5 \end{bmatrix}$$

will be a third solution to the given system and we see by inspection that this solution is linearly independent from the solutions $\mathbf{x}_1(t)$ and $\mathbf{x}_2(t)$.

(e) Notice that

$$\begin{aligned} (\mathbf{A} - 2\mathbf{I})^3 \mathbf{u}_3 &= (\mathbf{A} - 2\mathbf{I})^2 [(\mathbf{A} - 2\mathbf{I})\mathbf{u}_3] \\ &= (\mathbf{A} - 2\mathbf{I})^2 \mathbf{u}_2 = (\mathbf{A} - 2\mathbf{I}) [(\mathbf{A} - 2\mathbf{I})\mathbf{u}_2] = (\mathbf{A} - 2\mathbf{I})\mathbf{u}_1 = \mathbf{0}. \end{aligned}$$

**43.** According to Problem 42, we will look for solutions of the form $\mathbf{x}(t) = t^r \mathbf{u}$, where $r$ is an eigenvalue for the coefficient matrix and $\mathbf{u}$ is an associated eigenvector. To find the eigenvalues for this matrix, we solve the equation

$$|\mathbf{A} - r\mathbf{I}| = \begin{vmatrix} 1-r & 3 \\ -1 & 5-r \end{vmatrix} = 0$$

$$\Rightarrow \quad (1-r)(5-r) + 3 = 0$$

$$\Rightarrow \quad r^2 - 6r + 8 = 0 \quad \Rightarrow \quad (r-2)(r-4) = 0.$$

Therefore, the coefficient matrix has the eigenvalues $r = 2, 4$. Since these are distinct eigenvalues, Theorem 6 on page 538 of the text assures us that their associated eigenvectors will be linearly independent. To find an eigenvector $\mathbf{u} = \mathrm{col}(u_1, u_2)$ associated with the eigenvalue $r = 2$, we solve the system

$$(\mathbf{A} - 2\mathbf{I})\mathbf{u} = \begin{bmatrix} -1 & 3 \\ -1 & 3 \end{bmatrix} \begin{bmatrix} u_1 \\ u_2 \end{bmatrix} = \begin{bmatrix} 0 \\ 0 \end{bmatrix},$$

which is equivalent to the equation $-u_1 + 3u_2 = 0$. Thus, if we let $u_2 = 1$ then, in order to satisfy this equation, we must have $u_1 = 3$. Hence, we see that the vector $\mathbf{u}_1 = \mathrm{col}(3, 1)$ will be an eigenvector for the coefficient matrix of the given system associated with the eigenvalue $r = 2$. Therefore, according to Problem 42, one solution to this system will be given by

$$\mathbf{x}_1(t) = t^2 \mathbf{u}_1 = t^2 \begin{bmatrix} 3 \\ 1 \end{bmatrix}.$$

To find an eigenvector associated with the eigenvalue $r = 4$, we solve the equation

$$(\mathbf{A} - 4\mathbf{I})\mathbf{u} = \begin{bmatrix} -3 & 3 \\ -1 & 1 \end{bmatrix} \begin{bmatrix} u_1 \\ u_2 \end{bmatrix} = \begin{bmatrix} 0 \\ 0 \end{bmatrix},$$

which is equivalent to the equation $u_1 = u_2$. Thus, if we let $u_2 = 1$, then we must have $u_1 = 1$ and so an eigenvector associated with the eigenvalue $r = 4$ will be given by the vector $\mathbf{u}_2 = \mathrm{col}(1, 1)$. Therefore, another solution to the given system will be

$$\mathbf{x}_2(t) = t^4 \mathbf{u}_2 = t^4 \begin{bmatrix} 1 \\ 1 \end{bmatrix}.$$

# Chapter 9

Clearly the solutions $\mathbf{x}_1(t)$ and $\mathbf{x}_2(t)$ are linearly independent. So the general solution to the given system with $t > 0$ will be

$$\mathbf{x}(t) = c_1 t^2 \begin{bmatrix} 3 \\ 1 \end{bmatrix} + c_2 t^4 \begin{bmatrix} 1 \\ 1 \end{bmatrix} = c_1 \begin{bmatrix} 3t^2 \\ t^2 \end{bmatrix} + c_2 \begin{bmatrix} t^4 \\ t^4 \end{bmatrix}.$$

**EXERCISES 9.6: Complex Eigenvalues, page 549**

**3.** To find the eigenvalues for the matrix $\mathbf{A}$, we solve the characteristic equation given by

$$|\mathbf{A} - r\mathbf{I}| = \begin{vmatrix} 1-r & 2 & -1 \\ 0 & 1-r & 1 \\ 0 & -1 & 1-r \end{vmatrix} = 0$$

$$\Rightarrow \quad (1-r) \begin{vmatrix} 1-r & 1 \\ -1 & 1-r \end{vmatrix} - 0 + 0 = 0$$

$$\Rightarrow \quad (1-r)\left[(1-r)^2 + 1\right] = (1-r)\left(r^2 - 2r + 2\right) = 0.$$

By this equation and the quadratic formula, we see that the roots to the characteristic equation and, therefore, the eigenvalues for the matrix $\mathbf{A}$ are $r = 1$, and $r = 1 \pm i$. To find an eigenvector $\mathbf{u} = \text{col}(u_1, u_2, u_3)$ associated with the real eigenvalue $r = 1$, we solve the system

$$(\mathbf{A} - \mathbf{I})\mathbf{u} = \begin{bmatrix} 0 & 2 & -1 \\ 0 & 0 & 1 \\ 0 & -1 & 0 \end{bmatrix} \begin{bmatrix} u_1 \\ u_2 \\ u_3 \end{bmatrix} = \begin{bmatrix} 0 \\ 0 \\ 0 \end{bmatrix},$$

which implies that $u_2 = 0$, $u_3 = 0$. Therefore, we can set $u_1$ arbitrarily to any value, say $u_1 = s$. Then the vectors

$$\mathbf{u} = \text{col}(u_1, u_2, u_3) = \text{col}(s, 0, 0) = s\,\text{col}(1, 0, 0)$$

will satisfy the above equation and, therefore, be eigenvectors for the matrix $\mathbf{A}$. Hence, if we set $s = 1$, we see that one eigenvector associated with the eigenvalue $r = 1$ will be the vector $\mathbf{u}_1 = \text{col}(1, 0, 0)$. Therefore, one solution to the given system will be

$$\mathbf{x}_1(t) = e^t \mathbf{u}_1 = e^t \begin{bmatrix} 1 \\ 0 \\ 0 \end{bmatrix}.$$

In order to find an eigenvector $\mathbf{z} = \text{col}(z_1, z_2, z_3)$ associated with the complex eigenvalue $r = 1 + i$, we solve the equation

$$[\mathbf{A} - (1+i)\mathbf{I}]\mathbf{z} = \begin{bmatrix} -i & 2 & -1 \\ 0 & -i & 1 \\ 0 & -1 & i \end{bmatrix} \begin{bmatrix} z_1 \\ z_2 \\ z_3 \end{bmatrix} = \begin{bmatrix} 0 \\ 0 \\ 0 \end{bmatrix}.$$

This equation is equivalent to the system

$$-iz_1 + 2z_2 - z_3 = 0 \quad \text{and} \quad -iz_2 + z_3 = 0.$$

Thus, if we let $z_2 = s$, then we see that $z_3 = is$ and

$$-iz_1 = -2z_2 + z_3 = -2s + is \quad \Rightarrow \quad (i)(-iz_1) = (i)(-2s + is)$$

$$\Rightarrow \quad z_1 = -2is - s = -s - 2is,$$

where we have used the fact that $i^2 = -1$. Hence, eigenvectors associated with the eigenvalue $r = 1+i$ will be $\mathbf{z} = s\text{col}(-1-2i, 1, i)$. By taking $s = 1$, we see that one eigenvector associated with this eigenvalue will be the vector

$$\mathbf{z}_1 = \begin{bmatrix} -1-2i \\ 1 \\ i \end{bmatrix} = \begin{bmatrix} -1 \\ 1 \\ 0 \end{bmatrix} + i\begin{bmatrix} -2 \\ 0 \\ 1 \end{bmatrix}.$$

Thus, by the notation on page 545 of the text, we have $\alpha = 1$, $\beta = 1$, $\mathbf{a} = \text{col}(-1, 1, 0)$, and $\mathbf{b} = \text{col}(-2, 0, 1)$. Therefore, according to formulas (6) and (7) on page 546 of the text, two more linearly independent solutions to the given system will be given by

$$\mathbf{x}_2(t) = (e^t \cos t)\mathbf{a} - (e^t \sin t)\mathbf{b} \quad \text{and} \quad \mathbf{x}_3(t) = (e^t \sin t)\mathbf{a} + (e^t \cos t)\mathbf{b}.$$

Hence, the general solution to the system given in this problem will be

$$\mathbf{x}(t) = c_1\mathbf{x}_2(t) + c_2\mathbf{x}_3(t) + c_3\mathbf{x}_1(t)$$

$$= c_1 e^t \cos t \begin{bmatrix} -1 \\ 1 \\ 0 \end{bmatrix} - c_1 e^t \sin t \begin{bmatrix} -2 \\ 0 \\ 1 \end{bmatrix} + c_2 e^t \sin t \begin{bmatrix} -1 \\ 1 \\ 0 \end{bmatrix} + c_2 e^t \cos t \begin{bmatrix} -2 \\ 0 \\ 1 \end{bmatrix} + c_3 e^t \begin{bmatrix} 1 \\ 0 \\ 0 \end{bmatrix}.$$

**7.** In order to find a fundamental matrix for this system, we must first find three linearly independent solutions. Thus, we seek the eigenvalues for the matrix $\mathbf{A}$ by solving the characteristic equation given by

$$|\mathbf{A} - r\mathbf{I}| = \begin{vmatrix} -r & 0 & 1 \\ 0 & -r & -1 \\ 0 & 1 & -r \end{vmatrix} = 0$$

$$\Rightarrow \quad -r \begin{vmatrix} -r & -1 \\ 1 & -r \end{vmatrix} - 0 + 0 = 0 \quad \Rightarrow \quad -r\left(r^2 + 1\right) = 0.$$

Hence, the eigenvalues for the matrix $\mathbf{A}$ will be $r = 0$ and $r = \pm i$. To find an eigenvector $\mathbf{u} = \mathrm{col}(u_1, u_2, u_3)$ associated with the real eigenvalue $r = 0$, we solve the equation

$$(\mathbf{A} - 0\mathbf{I})\mathbf{u} = \begin{bmatrix} 0 & 0 & 1 \\ 0 & 0 & -1 \\ 0 & 1 & 0 \end{bmatrix} \begin{bmatrix} u_1 \\ u_2 \\ u_3 \end{bmatrix} = \begin{bmatrix} 0 \\ 0 \\ 0 \end{bmatrix},$$

which is equivalent to the system $u_3 = 0$, $u_2 = 0$. Thus, if we let $u_1$ have the arbitrary value $u_1 = s$, then the vectors

$$\mathbf{u} = \mathrm{col}(u_1, u_2, u_3) = \mathrm{col}(s, 0, 0) = s\mathrm{col}(1, 0, 0)$$

will satisfy this equation and will, therefore, be eigenvectors for the matrix $\mathbf{A}$ associated with the eigenvalue $r = 0$. Hence, by letting $s = 1$, we find that one of these eigenvectors will be the vector $\mathbf{u} = \mathrm{col}(1, 0, 0)$. Thus, one solution to the given system will be

$$\mathbf{x}_1(t) = e^0 \mathbf{u} = \begin{bmatrix} 1 \\ 0 \\ 0 \end{bmatrix}.$$

To find two more linearly independent solutions for this system, we will first look for an eigenvector associated with the complex eigenvalue $r = i$. That is, we seek a vector, say, $\mathbf{z} = \mathrm{col}(z_1, z_2, z_3)$ which satisfies the equation

$$(\mathbf{A} - i\mathbf{I})\mathbf{z} = \begin{bmatrix} -i & 0 & 1 \\ 0 & -i & -1 \\ 0 & 1 & -i \end{bmatrix} \begin{bmatrix} z_1 \\ z_2 \\ z_3 \end{bmatrix} = \begin{bmatrix} 0 \\ 0 \\ 0 \end{bmatrix},$$

which is equivalent to the system

$$iz_1 = z_3 \qquad \text{and} \qquad iz_2 = -z_3 \, .$$

Thus, if we let $z_3$ be any arbitrary value, say $z_3 = is$, (which means that we must have $z_1 = s$ and $z_2 = -s$), then we see that the vectors, given by

$$\mathbf{z} = \text{col}(z_1, z_2, z_3) = \text{col}(s, -s, is) = s\,\text{col}(1, -1, i),$$

will be eigenvectors for the matrix $\mathbf{A}$ associated with the eigenvalue $r = i$. Therefore, by letting $s = 1$, we find that one of these eigenvectors will be the vector

$$\mathbf{z} = \begin{bmatrix} 1 \\ -1 \\ i \end{bmatrix} = \begin{bmatrix} 1 \\ -1 \\ 0 \end{bmatrix} + i \begin{bmatrix} 0 \\ 0 \\ 1 \end{bmatrix}.$$

From this, by the notation given on page 546 of the text, we see that $\alpha = 0$, $\beta = 1$, $\mathbf{a} = \text{col}(1, -1, 0)$, and $\mathbf{b} = \text{col}(0, 0, 1)$. Therefore, by formulas (6) and (7) on page 546 of the text, two more linearly independent solutions for this system will be

$$\mathbf{x}_2(t) = (\cos t)\mathbf{a} - (\sin t)\mathbf{b} = \begin{bmatrix} \cos t \\ -\cos t \\ 0 \end{bmatrix} - \begin{bmatrix} 0 \\ 0 \\ \sin t \end{bmatrix} = \begin{bmatrix} \cos t \\ -\cos t \\ \sin t \end{bmatrix}$$

and

$$\mathbf{x}_3(t) = (\sin t)\mathbf{a} + (\cos t)\mathbf{b} = \begin{bmatrix} \sin t \\ -\sin t \\ 0 \end{bmatrix} + \begin{bmatrix} 0 \\ 0 \\ \cos t \end{bmatrix} = \begin{bmatrix} \sin t \\ -\sin t \\ \cos t \end{bmatrix}.$$

Finally, since a fundamental matrix for the system given in this problem must have three columns which are linearly independent solutions of the system, we see that such a fundamental matrix will be given by the matrix

$$\mathbf{X}(t) = \begin{bmatrix} 1 & \cos t & \sin t \\ 0 & -\cos t & -\sin t \\ 0 & -\sin t & \cos t \end{bmatrix}.$$

Chapter 9

**17.** We will assume that $t > 0$. According to Problem 42 in Exercises 9.5, a solution to this Cauchy-Euler system will have the form $\mathbf{x}(t) = t^r \mathbf{u}$, where $r$ is an eigenvalue for the coefficient matrix of the system and $\mathbf{u}$ is an eigenvector associated with this eigenvalue. Therefore, we first must find the eigenvalues for this matrix by solving the characteristic equation given by

$$|\mathbf{A} - r\mathbf{I}| = \begin{vmatrix} -1-r & -1 & 0 \\ 2 & -1-r & 1 \\ 0 & 1 & -1-r \end{vmatrix} = 0$$

$$\Rightarrow \quad (-1-r)\begin{vmatrix} -1-r & 1 \\ 1 & -1-r \end{vmatrix} + \begin{vmatrix} 2 & 1 \\ 0 & -1-r \end{vmatrix} = 0$$

$$\Rightarrow \quad (-1-r)\left[(-1-r)^2 - 1\right] + 2(-1-r) = -(1+r)\left(r^2 + 2r + 2\right) = 0.$$

From this equation and by using the quadratic formula, we see that the eigenvalues for this coefficient matrix will be $r = -1, -1 \pm i$. The eigenvectors associated with the real eigenvalue $r = -1$ will be the vectors $\mathbf{u} = \mathrm{col}(u_1, u_2, u_3)$ which satisfy the equation

$$(\mathbf{A} + \mathbf{I})\mathbf{u} = \begin{bmatrix} 0 & -1 & 0 \\ 2 & 0 & 1 \\ 0 & 1 & 0 \end{bmatrix}\begin{bmatrix} u_1 \\ u_2 \\ u_3 \end{bmatrix} = \begin{bmatrix} 0 \\ 0 \\ 0 \end{bmatrix},$$

which is equivalent to the system $u_2 = 0$, $2u_1 + u_3 = 0$. Thus, by letting $u_1 = 1$ (which means that $u_3 = -2$), we see that the vector

$$\mathbf{u} = \mathrm{col}(u_1, u_2, u_3) = \mathrm{col}(1, 0, -2)$$

satisfies this equation and is, therefore, an eigenvector of the coefficient matrix associated with the eigenvalue $r = -1$. Hence, according to Problem 42 of Exercises 9.5, we see that a solution to this Cauchy-Euler system will be given by

$$\mathbf{x}_1(t) = t^{-1}\mathbf{u} = t^{-1}\begin{bmatrix} 1 \\ 0 \\ -2 \end{bmatrix} = \begin{bmatrix} t^{-1} \\ 0 \\ -2t^{-1} \end{bmatrix}.$$

To find the eigenvectors $\mathbf{z} = \text{col}(z_1, z_2, z_3)$ associated with the complex eigenvalue $r = -1 + i$, we solve the equation

$$(\mathbf{A} - (-1+i)\mathbf{I})\mathbf{z} = \begin{bmatrix} -i & -1 & 0 \\ 2 & -i & 1 \\ 0 & 1 & -i \end{bmatrix} \begin{bmatrix} z_1 \\ z_2 \\ z_3 \end{bmatrix} = \begin{bmatrix} 0 \\ 0 \\ 0 \end{bmatrix}$$

$$\Rightarrow \begin{bmatrix} -i & -1 & 0 \\ 0 & i & 1 \\ 0 & 0 & 0 \end{bmatrix} \begin{bmatrix} z_1 \\ z_2 \\ z_3 \end{bmatrix} = \begin{bmatrix} 0 \\ 0 \\ 0 \end{bmatrix},$$

which is equivalent to the system $-iz_1 - z_2 = 0$, $iz_2 + z_3 = 0$. Thus, if we let $z_1 = 1$, we must let $z_2 = -i$ and $z_3 = -1$ in order to satisfy this system. Therefore, one eigenvector for the coefficient matrix associated with the eigenvalue $r = -1+i$ will be the vector $\mathbf{z} = \text{col}(1, -i, -1)$ and another solution to this system will be $\mathbf{x}(t) = t^{-1+i}\mathbf{z}$. We would like to find real solutions to this problem. Therefore, we note that by Euler's formula we have

$$t^{-1+i} = t^{-1}t^i = t^{-1}e^{i\ln t} = t^{-1}[\cos(\ln t) + i\sin(\ln t)],$$

where we have made use of our assumption that $t > 0$. Hence, the solution that we have just found becomes

$$\begin{aligned} \mathbf{x}(t) &= t^{-1+i}\mathbf{z} = t^{-1}[\cos(\ln t) + i\sin(\ln t)]\mathbf{z} \\ &= t^{-1}[\cos(\ln t) + i\sin(\ln t)] \begin{bmatrix} 1 \\ -i \\ -1 \end{bmatrix} = \begin{bmatrix} t^{-1}\cos(\ln t) \\ t^{-1}\sin(\ln t) \\ -t^{-1}\cos(\ln t) \end{bmatrix} + i \begin{bmatrix} t^{-1}\sin(\ln t) \\ -t^{-1}\cos(\ln t) \\ -t^{-1}\sin(\ln t) \end{bmatrix}. \end{aligned}$$

Thus, by Lemma 2 (adapted to systems) on page 172 of the text we see that two more linearly independent solutions to this Cauchy-Euler system will be

$$\mathbf{x}_2(t) = \begin{bmatrix} t^{-1}\cos(\ln t) \\ t^{-1}\sin(\ln t) \\ -t^{-1}\cos(\ln t) \end{bmatrix} \quad \text{and} \quad \mathbf{x}_3(t) = \begin{bmatrix} t^{-1}\sin(\ln t) \\ -t^{-1}\cos(\ln t) \\ -t^{-1}\sin(\ln t) \end{bmatrix},$$

# Chapter 9

and, hence, a general solution will be given by

$$
\mathbf{x}(t) = c_1 \begin{bmatrix} t^{-1} \\ 0 \\ -2t^{-1} \end{bmatrix} + c_2 \begin{bmatrix} t^{-1}\cos(\ln t) \\ t^{-1}\sin(\ln t) \\ -t^{-1}\cos(\ln t) \end{bmatrix} + c_3 \begin{bmatrix} t^{-1}\sin(\ln t) \\ -t^{-1}\cos(\ln t) \\ -t^{-1}\sin(\ln t) \end{bmatrix}.
$$

## EXERCISES 9.7: Nonhomogeneous Linear Systems, page 555

**3.** We must first find the general solution to the corresponding homogeneous system. Therefore, we first find the eigenvalues for the coefficient matrix $\mathbf{A}$ by solving the characteristic equation given by

$$
|\mathbf{A} - r\mathbf{I}| = \begin{vmatrix} 1-r & -2 & 2 \\ -2 & 1-r & 2 \\ 2 & 2 & 1-r \end{vmatrix} = 0
$$

$$
\Rightarrow \quad (1-r)\begin{vmatrix} 1-r & 2 \\ 2 & 1-r \end{vmatrix} + 2\begin{vmatrix} -2 & 2 \\ 2 & 1-r \end{vmatrix} + 2\begin{vmatrix} -2 & 1-r \\ 2 & 2 \end{vmatrix} = 0
$$

$$
\Rightarrow \quad (1-r)\left[(1-r)^2 - 4\right] + 2\left[-2(1-r) - 4\right] + 2\left[-4 - 2(1-r)\right] = 0
$$

$$
\Rightarrow \quad (1-r)(r^2 - 2r - 3) + 4(2r - 6) = 0
$$

$$
\Rightarrow \quad (1-r)(r+1)(r-3) + 8(r-3) = (r-3)(r^2 - 9) = (r-3)(r-3)(r+3) = 0.
$$

Thus, the eigenvalues for the matrix $\mathbf{A}$ are $r = 3, -3$, where $r = 3$ is an eigenvalue of multiplicity two. Notice that, even though the matrix $\mathbf{A}$ has only two distinct eigenvalues, we are still guaranteed three linearly independent eigenvectors because $\mathbf{A}$ is a $3 \times 3$ real symmetric matrix. To find an eigenvector associated with the eigenvalue $r = -3$, we must find a vector $\mathbf{u} = \mathrm{col}(u_1, u_2, u_3)$ which satisfies the system

$$
(\mathbf{A} + 3\mathbf{I})\mathbf{u} = \begin{bmatrix} 4 & -2 & 2 \\ -2 & 4 & 2 \\ 2 & 2 & 4 \end{bmatrix}\begin{bmatrix} u_1 \\ u_2 \\ u_3 \end{bmatrix} = \begin{bmatrix} 0 \\ 0 \\ 0 \end{bmatrix} \Rightarrow \begin{bmatrix} 1 & 0 & 1 \\ 0 & 1 & 1 \\ 0 & 0 & 0 \end{bmatrix}\begin{bmatrix} u_1 \\ u_2 \\ u_3 \end{bmatrix} = \begin{bmatrix} 0 \\ 0 \\ 0 \end{bmatrix},
$$

which is equivalent to the system $u_1 + u_3 = 0$, $u_2 + u_3 = 0$. Hence, by letting $u_3 = -1$, we must have $u_1 = u_2 = 1$, and so the vector $\mathbf{u}_1 = \mathrm{col}(1, 1, -1)$ will then satisfy the above system.

Therefore, this vector is an eigenvector for the matrix $\mathbf{A}$ associated with the eigenvalue $r = -3$. Thus, one solution to the corresponding homogeneous system is given by

$$\mathbf{x}_1(t) = e^{-3t}\mathbf{u}_1 = e^{-3t}\begin{bmatrix} 1 \\ 1 \\ -1 \end{bmatrix}.$$

To find eigenvectors $\mathbf{u} = \text{col}(u_1, u_2, u_3)$ associated with the eigenvalue $r = 3$, we solve the equation given by

$$(\mathbf{A} - 3\mathbf{I})\mathbf{u} = \begin{bmatrix} -2 & -2 & 2 \\ -2 & -2 & 2 \\ 2 & 2 & -2 \end{bmatrix}\begin{bmatrix} u_1 \\ u_2 \\ u_3 \end{bmatrix} = \begin{bmatrix} 0 \\ 0 \\ 0 \end{bmatrix},$$

which is equivalent to the equation $u_1 + u_2 - u_3 = 0$. Thus, if we let $u_3 = s$ and $u_2 = v$, then we must have $u_1 = s - v$. Hence, solutions to the above equation and, therefore, eigenvectors for $\mathbf{A}$ associated with the eigenvalue $r = 3$ will be the vectors

$$\mathbf{u} = \begin{bmatrix} s - v \\ v \\ s \end{bmatrix} = s\begin{bmatrix} 1 \\ 0 \\ 1 \end{bmatrix} + v\begin{bmatrix} -1 \\ 1 \\ 0 \end{bmatrix},$$

where $s$ and $v$ are arbitrary scalars. Therefore, letting $s = 1$ and $v = 0$ yields the eigenvector $\mathbf{u}_2 = \text{col}(1, 0, 1)$. Similarly, by letting $s = 0$ and $v = 1$, we obtain the eigenvector $\mathbf{u}_3 = \text{col}(-1, 1, 0)$, which we can see by inspection is linearly independent from $\mathbf{u}_2$. Hence, two more solutions to the corresponding homogeneous system which are linearly independent from each other and from $\mathbf{x}_1(t)$ are given by

$$\mathbf{x}_2(t) = e^{3t}\mathbf{u}_2 = e^{3t}\begin{bmatrix} 1 \\ 0 \\ 1 \end{bmatrix} \quad \text{and} \quad \mathbf{x}_3(t) = e^{3t}\mathbf{u}_3 = e^{3t}\begin{bmatrix} -1 \\ 1 \\ 0 \end{bmatrix}.$$

Thus, the general solution to the corresponding homogeneous system will be

$$\mathbf{x}_h(t) = c_1 e^{-3t}\begin{bmatrix} 1 \\ 1 \\ -1 \end{bmatrix} + c_2 e^{3t}\begin{bmatrix} 1 \\ 0 \\ 1 \end{bmatrix} + c_3 e^{3t}\begin{bmatrix} -1 \\ 1 \\ 0 \end{bmatrix}.$$

Chapter 9

To find a particular solution to the nonhomogeneous system, we note that

$$\mathbf{f}(t) = \begin{bmatrix} 2e^t \\ 4e^t \\ -2e^t \end{bmatrix} = e^t \begin{bmatrix} 2 \\ 4 \\ -2 \end{bmatrix} = e^t \mathbf{g},$$

where $\mathbf{g} = \mathrm{col}(2, 4, -2)$. Therefore, we will assume that a particular solution to the nonhomogeneous system will have the form $\mathbf{x}_p(t) = e^t \mathbf{a}$, where $\mathbf{a} = \mathrm{col}(a_1, a_2, a_3)$ is a constant vector which must be determined. Hence, we see that $\mathbf{x}_p'(t) = e^t \mathbf{a}$. By substituting $\mathbf{x}_p(t)$ into the given system, we obtain

$$e^t \mathbf{a} = \mathbf{A}\mathbf{x}_p(t) + \mathbf{f}(t) = \mathbf{A}e^t \mathbf{a} + e^t \mathbf{g} = e^t \mathbf{A}\mathbf{a} + e^t \mathbf{g}.$$

Therefore, we have

$$e^t \mathbf{a} = e^t \mathbf{A}\mathbf{a} + e^t \mathbf{g} \quad \Rightarrow \quad \mathbf{a} = \mathbf{A}\mathbf{a} + \mathbf{g} \quad \Rightarrow \quad (\mathbf{I} - \mathbf{A})\mathbf{a} = \mathbf{g}$$

$$\Rightarrow \quad \begin{bmatrix} 0 & 2 & -2 \\ 2 & 0 & -2 \\ -2 & -2 & 0 \end{bmatrix} \begin{bmatrix} a_1 \\ a_2 \\ a_3 \end{bmatrix} = \begin{bmatrix} 2 \\ 4 \\ -2 \end{bmatrix}.$$

The last equation above can be solved by either performing elementary row operations on the augmented matrix or by solving the system

$$\begin{aligned} 2a_2 - 2a_3 &= 2, \\ 2a_1 - 2a_3 &= 4, \\ -2a_1 - 2a_2 &= -2. \end{aligned}$$

Either way, we obtain $a_1 = 1$, $a_2 = 0$, and $a_3 = -1$. Thus, a particular solution to the nonhomogeneous system will be given by

$$\mathbf{x}_p(t) = e^t \mathbf{a} = e^t \begin{bmatrix} 1 \\ 0 \\ -1 \end{bmatrix},$$

and so the general solution to the nonhomogeneous system will be

$$\mathbf{x}(t) = \mathbf{x}_h(t) + \mathbf{x}_p(t) = c_1 e^{-3t} \begin{bmatrix} 1 \\ 1 \\ -1 \end{bmatrix} + c_2 e^{3t} \begin{bmatrix} 1 \\ 0 \\ 1 \end{bmatrix} + c_3 e^{3t} \begin{bmatrix} -1 \\ 1 \\ 0 \end{bmatrix} + e^t \begin{bmatrix} 1 \\ 0 \\ -1 \end{bmatrix}.$$

**13.** We must first find a fundamental matrix for the corresponding homogeneous system $\mathbf{x}' = \mathbf{Ax}$. To this end, we first find the eigenvalues of the matrix $\mathbf{A}$ by solving the characteristic equation given by

$$|\mathbf{A} - r\mathbf{I}| = \begin{vmatrix} 2-r & 1 \\ -3 & -2-r \end{vmatrix} = 0 \quad \Rightarrow \quad (2-r)(-2-r)+3 = 0 \quad \Rightarrow \quad r^2 - 1 = 0 \,.$$

Thus, the eigenvalues of the coefficient matrix $\mathbf{A}$ are $r = \pm 1$. The eigenvectors associated with the eigenvalue $r = 1$ are the vectors $\mathbf{u} = \mathrm{col}(u_1, u_2)$ which satisfy the equation

$$(\mathbf{A} - \mathbf{I})\mathbf{u} = \begin{bmatrix} 1 & 1 \\ -3 & -3 \end{bmatrix} \begin{bmatrix} u_1 \\ u_2 \end{bmatrix} = \begin{bmatrix} 0 \\ 0 \end{bmatrix}.$$

This equation is equivalent to the equation $u_1 + u_2 = 0$. Therefore, if we let $u_1 = 1$, then we have $u_2 = -1$, so one eigenvector of the matrix $\mathbf{A}$ associated with the eigenvalue $r = 1$ is the vector $\mathbf{u}_1 = \mathrm{col}(1, -1)$. Hence, one solution of the corresponding homogeneous system is given by

$$\mathbf{x}_1(t) = e^t \mathbf{u}_1 = e^t \begin{bmatrix} 1 \\ -1 \end{bmatrix} = \begin{bmatrix} e^t \\ -e^t \end{bmatrix}.$$

To find an eigenvector associated with the eigenvalue $r = -1$, we solve the equation

$$(\mathbf{A} + \mathbf{I})\mathbf{u} = \begin{bmatrix} 3 & 1 \\ -3 & -1 \end{bmatrix} \begin{bmatrix} u_1 \\ u_2 \end{bmatrix} = \begin{bmatrix} 0 \\ 0 \end{bmatrix},$$

which is equivalent to the equation $3u_1 + u_2 = 0$. Since $u_1 = 1$ and $u_2 = -3$ satisfy this equation, one eigenvector for the matrix $\mathbf{A}$ associated with the eigenvalue $r = -1$ is the vector $\mathbf{u}_2 = \mathrm{col}(1, -3)$. Thus, another linearly independent solution of the corresponding homogeneous system is

$$\mathbf{x}_2(t) = e^{-t} \mathbf{u}_2 = e^{-t} \begin{bmatrix} 1 \\ -3 \end{bmatrix} = \begin{bmatrix} e^{-t} \\ -3e^{-t} \end{bmatrix}.$$

Hence, the general solution of the homogeneous system is given by

$$\mathbf{x}_h(t) = c_1 \begin{bmatrix} e^t \\ -e^t \end{bmatrix} + c_2 \begin{bmatrix} e^{-t} \\ -3e^{-t} \end{bmatrix},$$

and a fundamental matrix is

$$\mathbf{X}(t) = \begin{bmatrix} e^t & e^{-t} \\ -e^t & -3e^{-t} \end{bmatrix}.$$

To find the inverse matrix $\mathbf{X}^{-1}(t)$, we will perform row-reduction on the matrix $[\mathbf{X}(t)|\mathbf{I}]$. Thus, we have

$$[\mathbf{X}(t)|\mathbf{I}] = \begin{bmatrix} e^t & e^{-t} & 1 & 0 \\ -e^t & -3e^{-t} & 0 & 1 \end{bmatrix} \longrightarrow \begin{bmatrix} e^t & e^{-t} & 1 & 0 \\ 0 & -2e^{-t} & 1 & 1 \end{bmatrix}$$

$$\longrightarrow \begin{bmatrix} e^t & 0 & 3/2 & 1/2 \\ 0 & e^{-t} & -1/2 & -1/2 \end{bmatrix} \longrightarrow \begin{bmatrix} 1 & 0 & (3/2)e^{-t} & (1/2)e^{-t} \\ 0 & 1 & -(1/2)e^{-t} & -(1/2)e^{-t} \end{bmatrix}.$$

Therefore, we see that

$$\mathbf{X}^{-1}(t) = \begin{bmatrix} (3/2)e^{-t} & (1/2)e^{-t} \\ -(1/2)e^{-t} & -(1/2)e^{-t} \end{bmatrix}.$$

Hence, we have

$$\mathbf{X}^{-1}(t)\mathbf{f}(t) = \begin{bmatrix} (3/2)e^{-t} & (1/2)e^{-t} \\ -(1/2)e^{-t} & -(1/2)e^{-t} \end{bmatrix} \begin{bmatrix} 2e^t \\ 4e^t \end{bmatrix} = \begin{bmatrix} 5 \\ -3e^{2t} \end{bmatrix},$$

and so we have

$$\int \mathbf{X}^{-1}(t)\mathbf{f}(t)\,dt = \begin{bmatrix} \int (5)dt \\ -3\int e^{2t}dt \end{bmatrix} = \begin{bmatrix} 5t \\ -(3/2)e^{2t} \end{bmatrix},$$

where we have taken the constants of integration to be zero. Thus, by equation (8) on page 553 of the text, we see that

$$\mathbf{x}_p(t) = \begin{bmatrix} e^t & e^{-t} \\ -e^t & -3e^{-t} \end{bmatrix} \begin{bmatrix} 5t \\ -(3/2)e^{2t} \end{bmatrix} = \begin{bmatrix} 5te^t - (3/2)e^t \\ -5te^t + (9/2)e^t \end{bmatrix}.$$

Therefore, by adding $\mathbf{x}_h(t)$ and $\mathbf{x}_p(t)$ we obtain

$$\mathbf{x}(t) = c_1 \begin{bmatrix} e^t \\ -e^t \end{bmatrix} + c_2 \begin{bmatrix} e^{-t} \\ -3e^{-t} \end{bmatrix} + \begin{bmatrix} 5te^t - (3/2)e^t \\ -5te^t + (9/2)e^t \end{bmatrix}.$$

We remark that this answer is the same as the answer given in the text as can be seen by replacing $c_1$ by $c_1 + 9/4$.

**15.** We must first find a fundamental matrix for the associated homogeneous system. We will do this by finding the solutions derived from the eigenvalues and the associated eigenvectors for the coefficient matrix $\mathbf{A}$. Therefore, we find these eigenvalues by solving the characteristic equation given by

$$|\mathbf{A} - r\mathbf{I}| = \begin{vmatrix} -4 - r & 2 \\ 2 & -1 - r \end{vmatrix} = 0$$

$$\Rightarrow \quad (-4 - r)(-1 - r) - 4 = 0 \quad \Rightarrow \quad r^2 + 5r = 0.$$

Thus, the eigenvalues for the matrix $\mathbf{A}$ are $r = -5, 0$. An eigenvector for this matrix associated with the eigenvalue $r = 0$ is the vector $\mathbf{u} = \mathrm{col}(u_1, u_2)$ which satisfies the equation

$$\mathbf{Au} = \begin{bmatrix} -4 & 2 \\ 2 & -1 \end{bmatrix} \begin{bmatrix} u_1 \\ u_2 \end{bmatrix} = \begin{bmatrix} 0 \\ 0 \end{bmatrix}.$$

This equation is equivalent to the equation $2u_1 = u_2$. Therefore, if we let $u_1 = 1$ and $u_2 = 2$, then the vector $\mathbf{u}_1 = \mathrm{col}(1, 2)$ satisfies this equation and is, therefore, an eigenvector for the matrix $\mathbf{A}$ associated with the eigenvalue $r = 0$. Hence, one solution to the homogeneous system is given by

$$\mathbf{x}_1(t) = e^{(0)t}\mathbf{u}_1 = \begin{bmatrix} 1 \\ 2 \end{bmatrix}.$$

To find an eigenvector associated with the eigenvalue $r = -5$, we solve the equation

$$(\mathbf{A} + 5\mathbf{I})\mathbf{u} = \begin{bmatrix} 1 & 2 \\ 2 & 4 \end{bmatrix} \begin{bmatrix} u_1 \\ u_2 \end{bmatrix} = \begin{bmatrix} 0 \\ 0 \end{bmatrix},$$

which is equivalent to the equation $u_1 + 2u_2 = 0$. Thus, by letting $u_2 = 1$ and $u_1 = -2$, the vector $\mathbf{u}_2 = \mathrm{col}(u_1, u_2) = \mathrm{col}(-2, 1)$ satisfies this equation and is, therefore, an eigenvector for $\mathbf{A}$ associated with the eigenvalue $r = -5$. Hence, since the two eigenvalues of $\mathbf{A}$ are distinct, we see that another linearly independent solution to the corresponding homogeneous system is given by

$$\mathbf{x}_2(t) = e^{-5t}\mathbf{u}_2 = e^{-5t}\begin{bmatrix} -2 \\ 1 \end{bmatrix} = \begin{bmatrix} -2e^{-5t} \\ e^{-5t} \end{bmatrix}.$$

By combining these two solutions, we see that a general solution to the homogeneous system is

$$\mathbf{x}_h(t) = c_1 \begin{bmatrix} 1 \\ 2 \end{bmatrix} + c_2 \begin{bmatrix} -2e^{-5t} \\ e^{-5t} \end{bmatrix}$$

and a fundamental matrix for this system is the matrix

$$\mathbf{X}(t) = \begin{bmatrix} 1 & -2e^{-5t} \\ 2 & e^{-5t} \end{bmatrix}.$$

We will use equation (10) on page 553 of the text to find a particular solution to the nonhomogeneous system. Thus, we need to find the inverse matrix $\mathbf{X}^{-1}(t)$. This can be done, for example, by performing row-reduction on the matrix $[\mathbf{X}(t)|\mathbf{I}]$ to obtain the matrix $[\mathbf{I}|\mathbf{X}^{-1}(t)]$. In this way, we find that the required inverse matrix is given by

$$\mathbf{X}^{-1}(t) = \begin{bmatrix} 1/5 & 2/5 \\ -(2/5)e^{5t} & (1/5)e^{5t} \end{bmatrix}.$$

Therefore, we have

$$\mathbf{X}^{-1}(t)\mathbf{f}(t) = \begin{bmatrix} 1/5 & 2/5 \\ -(2/5)e^{5t} & (1/5)e^{5t} \end{bmatrix} \begin{bmatrix} t^{-1} \\ 4 + 2t^{-1} \end{bmatrix} = \begin{bmatrix} t^{-1} + (8/5) \\ (4/5)e^{5t} \end{bmatrix}.$$

From this we see that

$$\int \mathbf{X}^{-1}(t)\mathbf{f}(t)\, dt = \begin{bmatrix} \int [t^{-1} + (8/5)]\, dt \\ \int (4/5)e^{5t}\, dt \end{bmatrix} = \begin{bmatrix} \ln|t| + (8/5)t \\ (4/25)e^{5t} \end{bmatrix},$$

where we have taken the constants of integration to be zero. Hence, by equation (10) on page 553 of the text, we obtain

$$\mathbf{x}_p(t) = \mathbf{X}(t) \int \mathbf{X}^{-1}(t)\mathbf{f}(t)\, dt$$

$$= \begin{bmatrix} 1 & -2e^{-5t} \\ 2 & e^{-5t} \end{bmatrix} \begin{bmatrix} \ln|t| + (8/5)t \\ (4/25)e^{5t} \end{bmatrix} = \begin{bmatrix} \ln|t| + (8/5)t - (8/25) \\ 2\ln|t| + (16/5)t + (4/25) \end{bmatrix}.$$

Adding $\mathbf{x}_h(t)$ and $\mathbf{x}_p(t)$ yields the general solution to the nonhomogeneous system given by

$$\mathbf{x}(t) = c_1 \begin{bmatrix} 1 \\ 2 \end{bmatrix} + c_2 \begin{bmatrix} -2e^{-5t} \\ e^{-5t} \end{bmatrix} + \begin{bmatrix} \ln|t| + (8/5)t - (8/25) \\ 2\ln|t| + (16/5)t + (4/25) \end{bmatrix}.$$

**21.** We will find the solution to this initial value problem by using equation (13) on page 554 of the text. Therefore, we must first find a fundamental matrix for the associated homogeneous system. This means that we must find the eigenvalues and corresponding eigenvectors for the coefficient matrix of this system by solving the characteristic equation

$$|\mathbf{A} - r\mathbf{I}| = \begin{vmatrix} -r & 2 \\ -1 & 3-r \end{vmatrix}$$

$$\Rightarrow \quad -r(3-r) + 2 = 0 \quad \Rightarrow \quad r^2 - 3r + 2 = 0 \quad \Rightarrow \quad (r-2)(r-1) = 0.$$

Hence, $r = 1, 2$ are the eigenvalues for this matrix. To find an eigenvector $\mathbf{u} = \mathrm{col}(u_1, u_2)$ for this coefficient matrix associated with the eigenvalue $r = 1$, we solve the system

$$(\mathbf{A} - \mathbf{I})\mathbf{u} = \begin{bmatrix} -1 & 2 \\ -1 & 2 \end{bmatrix} \begin{bmatrix} u_1 \\ u_2 \end{bmatrix} = \begin{bmatrix} 0 \\ 0 \end{bmatrix}.$$

This system is equivalent to the equation $u_1 = 2u_2$. Thus, $u_1 = 2$ and $u_2 = 1$ is a set of values which satisfies this equation and, therefore, the vector $\mathbf{u}_1 = \mathrm{col}(2, 1)$ is an eigenvector for the coefficient matrix corresponding to the eigenvalue $r = 1$. Hence, one solution to the homogeneous system is given by

$$\mathbf{x}_1(t) = e^t \mathbf{u}_1 = e^t \begin{bmatrix} 2 \\ 1 \end{bmatrix} = \begin{bmatrix} 2e^t \\ e^t \end{bmatrix}.$$

Similarly, by solving the equation

$$(\mathbf{A} - 2\mathbf{I})\mathbf{u} = \begin{bmatrix} -2 & 2 \\ -1 & 1 \end{bmatrix} \begin{bmatrix} u_1 \\ u_2 \end{bmatrix} = \begin{bmatrix} 0 \\ 0 \end{bmatrix},$$

we find that one eigenvector for the coefficient matrix associated with the eigenvalue $r = 2$ is $\mathbf{u}_2 = \mathrm{col}(u_1, u_2) = \mathrm{col}(1, 1)$. Thus, another linearly independent solution to the associated homogeneous problem is given by

$$\mathbf{x}_2(t) = e^{2t} \mathbf{u}_2 = e^{2t} \begin{bmatrix} 1 \\ 1 \end{bmatrix} = \begin{bmatrix} e^{2t} \\ e^{2t} \end{bmatrix}.$$

609

# Chapter 9

By combining these two solutions, we obtain a general solution to the homogeneous system

$$\mathbf{x}_h(t) = c_1 \begin{bmatrix} 2e^t \\ e^t \end{bmatrix} + c_2 \begin{bmatrix} e^{2t} \\ e^{2t} \end{bmatrix},$$

and the fundamental matrix

$$\mathbf{X}(t) = \begin{bmatrix} 2e^t & e^{2t} \\ e^t & e^{2t} \end{bmatrix}.$$

In order to use equation (13) on page 554 of the text, we must also find the inverse of the fundamental matrix. One way of doing this is to perform row-reduction on the matrix $[\mathbf{X}(t)|\mathbf{I}]$ to obtain the matrix $[\mathbf{I}|\mathbf{X}^{-1}(t)]$. Thus, we find that

$$\mathbf{X}^{-1}(t) = \begin{bmatrix} e^{-t} & -e^{-t} \\ -e^{-2t} & 2e^{-2t} \end{bmatrix}.$$

From this we see that

$$\mathbf{X}^{-1}(s)\mathbf{f}(s) = \begin{bmatrix} e^{-s} & -e^{-s} \\ -e^{-2s} & 2e^{-2s} \end{bmatrix} \begin{bmatrix} e^s \\ -e^s \end{bmatrix} = \begin{bmatrix} 2 \\ -3e^{-s} \end{bmatrix}.$$

**(a)** Using the initial condition $\mathbf{x}(0) = \text{col}(5, 4)$, and $t_0 = 0$, we have

$$\mathbf{X}^{-1}(0) = \begin{bmatrix} 1 & -1 \\ -1 & 2 \end{bmatrix}.$$

Therefore

$$\int_{t_0}^{t} \mathbf{X}^{-1}(s)\mathbf{f}(s)\, ds = \int_{0}^{t} \mathbf{X}^{-1}(s)\mathbf{f}(s)\, ds = \begin{bmatrix} \int_0^t (2)ds \\ \int_0^t (-3e^{-s})\, ds \end{bmatrix} = \begin{bmatrix} 2t \\ 3e^{-t} - 3 \end{bmatrix},$$

from which it follows that

$$\mathbf{X}(t) \int_{t_0}^{t} \mathbf{X}^{-1}(s)\mathbf{f}(s)\, ds = \begin{bmatrix} 2e^t & e^{2t} \\ e^t & e^{2t} \end{bmatrix} \begin{bmatrix} 2t \\ 3e^{-t} - 3 \end{bmatrix} = \begin{bmatrix} 4te^t + 3e^t - 3e^{2t} \\ 2te^t + 3e^t - 3e^{2t} \end{bmatrix}.$$

We also find that

$$\mathbf{X}(t)\mathbf{X}^{-1}(t_0)\mathbf{x}_0 = \begin{bmatrix} 2e^t & e^{2t} \\ e^t & e^{2t} \end{bmatrix} \begin{bmatrix} 1 & -1 \\ -1 & 2 \end{bmatrix} \begin{bmatrix} 5 \\ 4 \end{bmatrix} = \begin{bmatrix} 2e^t & e^{2t} \\ e^t & e^{2t} \end{bmatrix} \begin{bmatrix} 1 \\ 3 \end{bmatrix} = \begin{bmatrix} 2e^t + 3e^{2t} \\ e^t + 3e^{2t} \end{bmatrix}.$$

Hence, by substituting these expressions into equation (13) on page 554 of the text, we obtain the solution to this initial value problem given by

$$\mathbf{x}(t) = \mathbf{X}(t)\mathbf{X}^{-1}(t_0)\mathbf{x}_0 + \mathbf{X}(t)\int_{t_0}^{t}\mathbf{X}^{-1}(s)\mathbf{f}(s)\,ds$$

$$= \begin{bmatrix} 2e^t + 3e^{2t} \\ e^t + 3e^{2t} \end{bmatrix} + \begin{bmatrix} 4te^t + 3e^t - 3e^{2t} \\ 2te^t + 3e^t - 3e^{2t} \end{bmatrix} = \begin{bmatrix} 4te^t + 5e^t \\ 2te^t + 4e^t \end{bmatrix}.$$

**(b)** Using the initial condition $\mathbf{x}(1) = \text{col}(0,1)$, and $t_0 = 1$, we have

$$\mathbf{X}^{-1}(1) = \begin{bmatrix} e^{-1} & -e^{-1} \\ -e^{-2} & 2e^{-2} \end{bmatrix}.$$

Therefore

$$\int_{t_0}^{t}\mathbf{X}^{-1}(s)\mathbf{f}(s)\,ds = \int_{1}^{t}\mathbf{X}^{-1}(s)\mathbf{f}(s)\,ds$$

$$= \begin{bmatrix} \int_1^t(2)ds \\ \int_1^t(-3e^{-s})\,ds \end{bmatrix} = \begin{bmatrix} 2t - 2 \\ 3e^{-t} - 3e^{-1} \end{bmatrix},$$

from which it follows that

$$\mathbf{X}(t)\int_{t_0}^{t}\mathbf{X}^{-1}(s)\mathbf{f}(s)\,ds = \begin{bmatrix} 2e^t & e^{2t} \\ e^t & e^{2t} \end{bmatrix}\begin{bmatrix} 2t - 2 \\ 3e^{-t} - 3e^{-1} \end{bmatrix}$$

$$= \begin{bmatrix} 4te^t - 4e^t + 3e^t - 3e^{2t-1} \\ 2te^t - 2e^t + 3e^t - 3e^{2t-1} \end{bmatrix} = \begin{bmatrix} 4te^t - e^t - 3e^{2t-1} \\ 2te^t + e^t - 3e^{2t-1} \end{bmatrix}.$$

We also find that

$$\mathbf{X}(t)\mathbf{X}^{-1}(t_0)\mathbf{x}_0 = \begin{bmatrix} 2e^t & e^{2t} \\ e^t & e^{2t} \end{bmatrix}\begin{bmatrix} e^{-1} & -e^{-1} \\ -e^{-2} & 2e^{-2} \end{bmatrix}\begin{bmatrix} 0 \\ 1 \end{bmatrix}$$

$$= \begin{bmatrix} 2e^t & e^{2t} \\ e^t & e^{2t} \end{bmatrix}\begin{bmatrix} -e^{-1} \\ 2e^{-2} \end{bmatrix} = \begin{bmatrix} -2e^{t-1} + 2e^{2t-2} \\ -e^{t-1} + 2e^{2t-2} \end{bmatrix}.$$

## Chapter 9

Hence, by substituting these expressions into equation (13) on page 554 of the text, we obtain the solution to this initial value problem given by

$$\mathbf{x}(t) = \mathbf{X}(t)\mathbf{X}^{-1}(t_0)\mathbf{x}_0 + \mathbf{X}(t)\int_{t_0}^{t}\mathbf{X}^{-1}(s)\mathbf{f}(s)\,ds$$

$$= \begin{bmatrix} -2e^{t-1} + 2e^{2t-2} \\ -e^{t-1} + 2e^{2t-2} \end{bmatrix} + \begin{bmatrix} 4te^t - e^t - 3e^{2t-1} \\ 2te^t + e^t - 3e^{2t-1} \end{bmatrix}$$

$$= \begin{bmatrix} -2e^{t-1} + 2e^{2t-2} + 4te^t - e^t - 3e^{2t-1} \\ -e^{t-1} + 2e^{2t-2} + 2te^t + e^t - 3e^{2t-1} \end{bmatrix}.$$

**(c)** Using the initial condition $\mathbf{x}(5) = \mathrm{col}(1,0)$, and $t_0 = 5$, we have

$$\mathbf{X}^{-1}(5) = \begin{bmatrix} e^{-5} & -e^{-5} \\ -e^{-10} & 2e^{-10} \end{bmatrix}.$$

Therefore

$$\int_{t_0}^{t}\mathbf{X}^{-1}(s)\mathbf{f}(s)\,ds = \int_{5}^{t}\mathbf{X}^{-1}(s)\mathbf{f}(s)\,ds = \begin{bmatrix} \int_5^t (2)ds \\ \int_5^t (-3e^{-s})\,ds \end{bmatrix} = \begin{bmatrix} 2t - 10 \\ 3e^{-t} - 3e^{-5} \end{bmatrix},$$

from which it follows that

$$\mathbf{X}(t)\int_{t_0}^{t}\mathbf{X}^{-1}(s)\mathbf{f}(s)\,ds = \begin{bmatrix} 2e^t & e^{2t} \\ e^t & e^{2t} \end{bmatrix}\begin{bmatrix} 2t - 10 \\ 3e^{-t} - 3e^{-5} \end{bmatrix}$$

$$= \begin{bmatrix} 4te^t - 20e^t + 3e^t - 3e^{2t-5} \\ 2te^t - 10e^t + 3e^t - 3e^{2t-5} \end{bmatrix} = \begin{bmatrix} 4te^t - 17e^t - 3e^{2t-5} \\ 2te^t - 7e^t - 3e^{2t-5} \end{bmatrix}.$$

We also find that

$$\mathbf{X}(t)\mathbf{X}^{-1}(t_0)\mathbf{x}_0 = \begin{bmatrix} 2e^t & e^{2t} \\ e^t & e^{2t} \end{bmatrix}\begin{bmatrix} e^{-5} & -e^{-5} \\ -e^{-10} & 2e^{-10} \end{bmatrix}\begin{bmatrix} 1 \\ 0 \end{bmatrix}$$

$$= \begin{bmatrix} 2e^t & e^{2t} \\ e^t & e^{2t} \end{bmatrix}\begin{bmatrix} e^{-5} \\ -e^{-10} \end{bmatrix} = \begin{bmatrix} 2e^{t-5} - e^{2t-10} \\ e^{t-5} - e^{2t-10} \end{bmatrix}.$$

Hence, by substituting these expressions into equation (13) on page 554 of the text, we obtain the solution to this initial value problem given by

$$\mathbf{x}(t) = \mathbf{X}(t)\mathbf{X}^{-1}(t_0)\mathbf{x}_0 + \mathbf{X}(t)\int_{t_0}^{t}\mathbf{X}^{-1}(s)\mathbf{f}(s)\,ds$$

$$= \begin{bmatrix} 2e^{t-5} - e^{2t-10} \\ e^{t-5} - e^{2t-10} \end{bmatrix} + \begin{bmatrix} 4te^t - 17e^t - 3e^{2t-5} \\ 2te^t - 7e^t - 3e^{2t-5} \end{bmatrix}$$

$$= \begin{bmatrix} 2e^{t-5} - e^{2t-10} + 4te^t - 17e^t - 3e^{2t-5} \\ e^{t-5} - e^{2t-10} + 2te^t - 7e^t - 3e^{2t-5} \end{bmatrix}.$$

**25. (a)** We will find a fundamental solutions set for the corresponding homogeneous system by deriving solutions using the eigenvalues and associated eigenvectors for the coefficient matrix. Therefore, we first solve the characteristic equation

$$|\mathbf{A} - r\mathbf{I}| = \begin{vmatrix} -r & 1 \\ -2 & 3-r \end{vmatrix} = 0$$

$$\Rightarrow \quad -r(3-r) + 2 = 0 \quad \Rightarrow \quad r^2 - 3r + 2 = 0 \quad \Rightarrow \quad (r-2)(r-1) = 0.$$

Therefore, we see that the eigenvalues for the coefficient matrix of this problem are $r = 1, 2$. Since these eigenvalues are distinct, the associated eigenvectors will be linearly independent, and so the solutions derived from these eigenvectors will also be linearly independent. We find an eigenvector for this matrix associated with the eigenvalue $r = 1$ by solving the equation

$$(\mathbf{A} - \mathbf{I})\mathbf{u} = \begin{bmatrix} -1 & 1 \\ -2 & 2 \end{bmatrix} \begin{bmatrix} u_1 \\ u_2 \end{bmatrix} = 0.$$

Since the vector $\mathbf{u}_1 = \mathrm{col}(u_1, u_2) = \mathrm{col}(1, 1)$ satisfies this equation, we see that this vector is one such eigenvector and so one solution to the homogeneous problem is given by

$$\mathbf{x}_1(t) = e^t\mathbf{u}_1 = e^t \begin{bmatrix} 1 \\ 1 \end{bmatrix}.$$

To find an eigenvector associated with the eigenvalue $r = 2$, we solve the equation

$$(\mathbf{A} - 2\mathbf{I})\mathbf{u} = \begin{bmatrix} -2 & 1 \\ -2 & 1 \end{bmatrix} \begin{bmatrix} u_1 \\ u_2 \end{bmatrix} = 0.$$

The vector $\mathbf{u}_2 = \text{col}(u_1, u_2) = \text{col}(1, 2)$ is one vector which satisfies this equation and so it is one eigenvector of the coefficient matrix associated with the eigenvalue $r = 2$. Thus, another linearly independent solution to the corresponding homogeneous problem is given by

$$\mathbf{x}_2(t) = e^{2t}\mathbf{u}_2 = e^{2t} \begin{bmatrix} 1 \\ 2 \end{bmatrix},$$

and a fundamental solution set for this homogeneous system is the set

$$\{e^t\mathbf{u}_1, e^{2t}\mathbf{u}_2\}, \qquad \text{where} \qquad \mathbf{u}_1 = \text{col}(1, 1) \quad \text{and} \quad \mathbf{u}_2 = \text{col}(1, 2).$$

**(b)** If we assume that $\mathbf{x}_p(t) = te^t\mathbf{a}$ for some constant vector $\mathbf{a} = \text{col}(a_1, a_2)$, then we have

$$\mathbf{x}_p'(t) = te^t\mathbf{a} + e^t\mathbf{a} = \begin{bmatrix} te^t a_1 \\ te^t a_2 \end{bmatrix} + \begin{bmatrix} e^t a_1 \\ e^t a_2 \end{bmatrix} = \begin{bmatrix} te^t a_1 + e^t a_1 \\ te^t a_2 + e^t a_2 \end{bmatrix}.$$

We also have

$$\begin{bmatrix} 0 & 1 \\ -2 & 3 \end{bmatrix} \mathbf{x}_p(t) + \mathbf{f}(t) = \begin{bmatrix} 0 & 1 \\ -2 & 3 \end{bmatrix} \begin{bmatrix} te^t a_1 \\ te^t a_2 \end{bmatrix} + \begin{bmatrix} e^t \\ 0 \end{bmatrix} = \begin{bmatrix} te^t a_2 + e^t \\ -2te^t a_1 + 3te^t a_2 \end{bmatrix}.$$

Thus, if $\mathbf{x}_p(t) = te^t\mathbf{a}$ is to satisfy this system, we must have

$$\begin{bmatrix} te^t a_1 + e^t a_1 \\ te^t a_2 + e^t a_2 \end{bmatrix} = \begin{bmatrix} te^t a_2 + e^t \\ -2te^t a_1 + 3te^t a_2 \end{bmatrix},$$

which means that

$$te^t a_1 + e^t a_1 = te^t a_2 + e^t,$$
$$te^t a_2 + e^t a_2 = -2te^t a_1 + 3te^t a_2.$$

By dividing out the term $e^t$ and equating coefficients, this system becomes the system

$$a_1 = a_2, \qquad\qquad a_1 = 1,$$
$$a_2 = -2a_1 + 3a_2, \quad a_2 = 0.$$

Since this set of equations implies that $1 = a_1 = a_2 = 0$, which is of course impossible, we see that this system has no solutions. Therefore, we cannot find a vector $\mathbf{a}$ for which $\mathbf{x}_p(t) = te^t\mathbf{a}$ is a particular solution to this problem.

**(c)** Assuming that

$$\mathbf{x}_p(t) = te^t\mathbf{a} + e^t\mathbf{b} = \begin{bmatrix} te^t a_1 \\ te^t a_2 \end{bmatrix} + \begin{bmatrix} e^t b_1 \\ e^t b_2 \end{bmatrix} = \begin{bmatrix} te^t a_1 + e^t b_1 \\ te^t a_2 + e^t b_2 \end{bmatrix},$$

where $\mathbf{a} = \mathrm{col}(a_1, a_2)$ and $\mathbf{b} = \mathrm{col}(b_1, b_2)$ are two constant vectors, implies that

$$\mathbf{x}_p'(t) = te^t\mathbf{a} + e^t\mathbf{a} + e^t\mathbf{b} = \begin{bmatrix} te^t a_1 + e^t a_1 + e^t b_1 \\ te^t a_2 + e^t a_2 + e^t a_2 \end{bmatrix}.$$

We also see that

$$\begin{bmatrix} 0 & 1 \\ -2 & 3 \end{bmatrix}\mathbf{x}_p(t) + \mathbf{f}(t) = \begin{bmatrix} 0 & 1 \\ -2 & 3 \end{bmatrix}\begin{bmatrix} te^t a_1 + e^t b_1 \\ te^t a_2 + e^t b_2 \end{bmatrix} + \begin{bmatrix} e^t \\ 0 \end{bmatrix}$$

$$= \begin{bmatrix} te^t a_2 + e^t b_2 + e^t \\ -2te^t a_1 - 2e^t b_1 + 3te^t a_2 + 3e^t b_2 \end{bmatrix}.$$

Thus, if $\mathbf{x}_p(t)$ is to satisfy this system, we must have

$$\begin{bmatrix} te^t a_1 + e^t a_1 + e^t b_1 \\ te^t a_2 + e^t a_2 + e^t b_2 \end{bmatrix} = \begin{bmatrix} te^t a_2 + e^t b_2 + e^t \\ -2te^t a_1 - 2e^t b_1 + 3te^t a_2 + 3e^t b_2 \end{bmatrix}, \tag{9.7}$$

which implies the system of equations given by

$$te^t a_1 + e^t a_1 + e^t b_1 = te^t a_2 + e^t b_2 + e^t,$$
$$te^t a_2 + e^t a_2 + e^t b_2 = -2te^t a_1 - 2e^t b_1 + 3te^t a_2 + 3e^t b_2.$$

Dividing each equation by $e^t$ and equating the coefficients in the resulting equations yields the system

$$\begin{aligned} a_1 &= a_2, & a_1 + b_1 &= b_2 + 1, \\ a_2 &= -2a_1 + 3a_2, & a_2 + b_2 &= -2b_1 + 3b_2. \end{aligned} \tag{9.8}$$

Taking the pair of equations on the right and simplifying yields the system

$$\begin{aligned} b_1 - b_2 &= 1 - a_1, \\ 2b_1 - 2b_2 &= -a_2. \end{aligned} \tag{9.9}$$

615

Chapter 9

By multiplying the first of these equations by 2, we obtain the system

$$2b_1 - 2b_2 = 2 - 2a_1 ,$$
$$2b_1 - 2b_2 = -a_2 ,$$

which when subtracted yields $2 - 2a_1 + a_2 = 0$. Applying the first equation in (9.8) (the equation $a_1 = a_2$) to this equation yields $a_1 = a_2 = 2$. By substituting these values for $a_1$ and $a_2$ into equation (9.9) above we see that both equations reduce to the equation

$$b_2 = b_1 + 1.$$

(Note also that the remaining equation in (9.8) reduces to the first equation in that set.) Thus, $b_1$ is free to be any value, say $b_1 = s$, and the set of values $a_1 = a_2 = 2$, $b_1 = s$, $b_2 = s + 1$, satisfies all of the equations given in (9.8) and, hence, the system given in (9.7). Therefore, particular solutions to the nonhomogeneous equation given in this problem are

$$\mathbf{x}_p(t) = te^t \begin{bmatrix} 2 \\ 2 \end{bmatrix} + e^t \begin{bmatrix} s \\ s+1 \end{bmatrix} = te^t \begin{bmatrix} 2 \\ 2 \end{bmatrix} + e^t \begin{bmatrix} 0 \\ 1 \end{bmatrix} + se^t \begin{bmatrix} 1 \\ 1 \end{bmatrix}.$$

But, since the vector $\mathbf{u} = e^t \mathrm{col}(1,1)$ is a solution to the corresponding homogeneous system, the last term can be incorporated into the solution $\mathbf{x}_h(t)$ and we obtain one particular solution to this problem given by

$$\mathbf{x}_p(t) = te^t \begin{bmatrix} 2 \\ 2 \end{bmatrix} + e^t \begin{bmatrix} 0 \\ 1 \end{bmatrix}.$$

(d) To find the general solution to the nonhomogeneous system given in this problem, we first form the solution to the corresponding homogeneous system using the fundamental solution set found in part (a). Thus, we have

$$\mathbf{x}_h(t) = c_1 e^t \begin{bmatrix} 1 \\ 1 \end{bmatrix} + c_2 e^{2t} \begin{bmatrix} 1 \\ 2 \end{bmatrix}.$$

By adding the solution found in part (c) to this solution, we obtain the general solution given by

$$\mathbf{x}(t) = c_1 e^t \begin{bmatrix} 1 \\ 1 \end{bmatrix} + c_2 e^{2t} \begin{bmatrix} 1 \\ 2 \end{bmatrix} + te^t \begin{bmatrix} 2 \\ 2 \end{bmatrix} + e^t \begin{bmatrix} 0 \\ 1 \end{bmatrix}.$$

## EXERCISES 9.8: The Matrix Exponential Function, page 566

3. **(a)** From the characteristic equation, $|\mathbf{A} - r\mathbf{I}| = 0$, we obtain

$$|\mathbf{A} - r\mathbf{I}| = \begin{vmatrix} 2-r & 1 & -1 \\ -3 & -1-r & 1 \\ 9 & 3 & -4-r \end{vmatrix} = 0$$

$$\Rightarrow \quad (2-r)\begin{vmatrix} -1-r & 1 \\ 3 & -4-r \end{vmatrix} - \begin{vmatrix} -3 & 1 \\ 9 & -4-r \end{vmatrix} + (-1)\begin{vmatrix} -3 & -1-r \\ 9 & 3 \end{vmatrix} = 0$$

$$\Rightarrow \quad (2-r)[(-1-r)(-4-r)-3] - [-3(-4-r)-9] - [-9-9(-1-r)] = 0$$

$$\Rightarrow \quad r^3 + 3r^2 + 3r + 1 = (r+1)^3 = 0.$$

Therefore, for the matrix $\mathbf{A}$, $r = -1$ is an eigenvalue of multiplicity three. Thus, by the Cayley-Hamilton theorem as stated on page 561 of the text, we have

$$(\mathbf{A} + \mathbf{I})^3 = \mathbf{0}$$

(so that $r = -1$ and $k = 3$).

**(b)** In order to find $e^{\mathbf{A}t}$, we first notice (as was done in the text on page 560) that

$$e^{\mathbf{A}t} = e^{[-\mathbf{I}+(\mathbf{A}+\mathbf{I})]t}, \quad \text{commutative and associative properties of matrix addition}$$
$$= e^{-\mathbf{I}t}e^{(\mathbf{A}+\mathbf{I})t}, \quad \text{property (d) on page 559 of the text [since } (\mathbf{A}+\mathbf{I})\mathbf{I} = \mathbf{I}(\mathbf{A}+\mathbf{I})]$$
$$= e^{-t}\mathbf{I}e^{(\mathbf{A}+\mathbf{I})t}, \quad \text{property (e) on page 559 of the text}$$
$$= e^{-t}e^{(\mathbf{A}+\mathbf{I})t}.$$

Therefore, to find $e^{\mathbf{A}t}$ we need only to find $e^{(\mathbf{A}+\mathbf{I})t}$ then multiply the resulting expression by $e^{-t}$. By formula (2) on page 558 of the text and using the fact that $(\mathbf{A} + \mathbf{I})^3 = \mathbf{0}$ (which implies that $(\mathbf{A} + \mathbf{I})^n = \mathbf{0}$ for $n \geq 3$), we have

$$e^{(\mathbf{A}+\mathbf{I})t} = \mathbf{I} + (\mathbf{A}+\mathbf{I})t + (\mathbf{A}+\mathbf{I})^2\left(\frac{t^2}{2}\right) + \cdots + (\mathbf{A}+\mathbf{I})^n\left(\frac{t^n}{n!}\right) + \cdots$$

$$= \mathbf{I} + (\mathbf{A}+\mathbf{I})t + (\mathbf{A}+\mathbf{I})^2\left(\frac{t^2}{2}\right). \tag{9.10}$$

617

Since

$$(\mathbf{A} + \mathbf{I})^2 = \begin{bmatrix} 3 & 1 & -1 \\ -3 & 0 & 1 \\ 9 & 3 & -3 \end{bmatrix} \begin{bmatrix} 3 & 1 & -1 \\ -3 & 0 & 1 \\ 9 & 3 & -3 \end{bmatrix} = \begin{bmatrix} -3 & 0 & 1 \\ 0 & 0 & 0 \\ -9 & 0 & 3 \end{bmatrix},$$

equation (9.10) becomes

$$e^{(\mathbf{A}+\mathbf{I})t} = \begin{bmatrix} 1 & 0 & 0 \\ 0 & 1 & 0 \\ 0 & 0 & 1 \end{bmatrix} + \begin{bmatrix} 3t & t & -t \\ -3t & 0 & t \\ 9t & 3t & -3t \end{bmatrix} + \begin{bmatrix} -3(t^2/2) & 0 & t^2/2 \\ 0 & 0 & 0 \\ -9(t^2/2) & 0 & 3(t^2/2) \end{bmatrix}$$

$$= \begin{bmatrix} 1 + 3t - 3t^2/2 & t & -t + t^2/2 \\ -3t & 1 & t \\ 9t - 9t^2/2 & 3t & 1 - 3t + 3t^2/2 \end{bmatrix}.$$

Hence, we have

$$e^{\mathbf{A}t} = e^{-t} \begin{bmatrix} 1 + 3t - 3t^2/2 & t & -t + t^2/2 \\ -3t & 1 & t \\ 9t - 9t^2/2 & 3t & 1 - 3t + 3t^2/2 \end{bmatrix}.$$

**9.** By equation (6) on page 562 of the text, we see that $e^{\mathbf{A}t} = \mathbf{X}(t)\mathbf{X}^{-1}(0)$, where $\mathbf{X}(t)$ is a fundamental matrix for the system $\mathbf{x}' = \mathbf{A}\mathbf{x}$. We will construct this fundamental matrix from three linearly independent solutions derived from the eigenvalues and associated eigenvectors for the matrix $\mathbf{A}$. Thus, we solve the characteristic equation

$$|\mathbf{A} - r\mathbf{I}| = \begin{vmatrix} -r & 1 & 0 \\ 0 & -r & 1 \\ 1 & -1 & 1-r \end{vmatrix} = 0$$

$$\Rightarrow \quad (-r) \begin{vmatrix} -r & 1 \\ -1 & 1-r \end{vmatrix} - \begin{vmatrix} 0 & 1 \\ 1 & 1-r \end{vmatrix} = 0$$

$$\Rightarrow \quad -r[-r(1-r) + 1] + 1 = -r^3 + r^2 - r + 1 = -(r-1)(r^2 + 1) = 0.$$

Therefore, the eigenvalues of the matrix $\mathbf{A}$ are $r = 1$ and $r = \pm i$. To find an eigenvector

$\mathbf{u} = \text{col}(u_1, u_2, u_3)$ associated with the eigenvalue $r = 1$, we solve the system

$$(\mathbf{A} - \mathbf{I})\mathbf{u} = \mathbf{0} \quad \Rightarrow \quad \begin{bmatrix} -1 & 1 & 0 \\ 0 & -1 & 1 \\ 1 & -1 & 0 \end{bmatrix}\begin{bmatrix} u_1 \\ u_2 \\ u_3 \end{bmatrix} = \begin{bmatrix} 0 \\ 0 \\ 0 \end{bmatrix} \quad \Rightarrow \quad \begin{bmatrix} -1 & 0 & 1 \\ 0 & -1 & 1 \\ 0 & 0 & 0 \end{bmatrix}\begin{bmatrix} u_1 \\ u_2 \\ u_3 \end{bmatrix} = \begin{bmatrix} 0 \\ 0 \\ 0 \end{bmatrix}.$$

This system is equivalent to the system $u_1 = u_3$, $u_2 = u_3$. Hence, $u_3$ is free to be any arbitrary value, say $u_3 = 1$. Then $u_1 = u_2 = 1$, and so the vector $\mathbf{u} = \text{col}(1, 1, 1)$ is an eigenvector associated with $r = 1$. Hence, one solution to the system $\mathbf{x}' = \mathbf{A}\mathbf{x}$ is given by

$$\mathbf{x}_1(t) = e^t\mathbf{u} = e^t\begin{bmatrix} 1 \\ 1 \\ 1 \end{bmatrix} = \begin{bmatrix} e^t \\ e^t \\ e^t \end{bmatrix}.$$

Since the eigenvalue $r = i$ is complex, we want to find two more linearly independent solutions for the system $\mathbf{x}' = \mathbf{A}\mathbf{x}$ derived from the eigenvectors associated with this eigenvalue. These eigenvectors, $\mathbf{z} = \text{col}(z_1, z_2, z_3)$, must satisfy the equation

$$(\mathbf{A} - i\mathbf{I})\mathbf{z} = \begin{bmatrix} -i & 1 & 0 \\ 0 & -i & 1 \\ 1 & -1 & 1-i \end{bmatrix}\begin{bmatrix} z_1 \\ z_2 \\ z_3 \end{bmatrix} = \begin{bmatrix} 0 \\ 0 \\ 0 \end{bmatrix},$$

which is equivalent to the system $z_1 = -z_3$, $z_2 = -iz_3$. Thus, one solution to this system is $z_3 = 1$, $z_1 = -1$, and $z_2 = -i$ and so one eigenvector for $\mathbf{A}$ associated with the eigenvalue $r = i$ is given by

$$\mathbf{z} = \begin{bmatrix} z_1 \\ z_2 \\ z_3 \end{bmatrix} = \begin{bmatrix} -1 \\ -i \\ 1 \end{bmatrix} = \begin{bmatrix} -1 \\ 0 \\ 1 \end{bmatrix} + i\begin{bmatrix} 0 \\ -1 \\ 0 \end{bmatrix}.$$

By the notation on page 546 of the text, this means that $\alpha = 0$, $\beta = 1$, $\mathbf{a} = \text{col}(-1, 0, 1)$ and $\mathbf{b} = \text{col}(0, -1, 0)$. Therefore, by equations (6) and (7) on page 546 of the text we see that two more linearly independent solutions to the system $\mathbf{x}' = \mathbf{A}\mathbf{x}$ are given by

$$\mathbf{x}_2(t) = e^{(0)t}(\cos t)\mathbf{a} - e^{(0)t}(\sin t)\mathbf{b} = \begin{bmatrix} -\cos t \\ 0 \\ \cos t \end{bmatrix} - \begin{bmatrix} 0 \\ -\sin t \\ 0 \end{bmatrix} = \begin{bmatrix} -\cos t \\ \sin t \\ \cos t \end{bmatrix},$$

$$\mathbf{x}_3(t) = e^{(0)t}(\sin t)\mathbf{a} + e^{(0)t}(\cos t)\mathbf{b} = \begin{bmatrix} -\sin t \\ 0 \\ \sin t \end{bmatrix} + \begin{bmatrix} 0 \\ -\cos t \\ 0 \end{bmatrix} = \begin{bmatrix} -\sin t \\ -\cos t \\ \sin t \end{bmatrix}.$$

Thus, a fundamental matrix for this system is

$$\mathbf{X}(t) = \begin{bmatrix} e^t & -\cos t & -\sin t \\ e^t & \sin t & -\cos t \\ e^t & \cos t & \sin t \end{bmatrix} \qquad \Rightarrow \qquad \mathbf{X}(0) = \begin{bmatrix} 1 & -1 & 0 \\ 1 & 0 & -1 \\ 1 & 1 & 0 \end{bmatrix}.$$

To find the inverse of the matrix $\mathbf{X}(0)$ we can, for example, perform row-reduction on the matrix $[\mathbf{X}(0)|\mathbf{I}]$ to obtain the matrix $[\mathbf{I}|\mathbf{X}^{-1}(0)]$. Thus, we see that

$$\mathbf{X}^{-1}(0) = \begin{bmatrix} 1/2 & 0 & 1/2 \\ -1/2 & 0 & 1/2 \\ 1/2 & -1 & 1/2 \end{bmatrix}.$$

Hence, we obtain

$$\begin{aligned} e^{\mathbf{A}t} = \mathbf{X}(t)\mathbf{X}^{-1}(0) &= \begin{bmatrix} e^t & -\cos t & -\sin t \\ e^t & \sin t & -\cos t \\ e^t & \cos t & \sin t \end{bmatrix} \begin{bmatrix} 1/2 & 0 & 1/2 \\ -1/2 & 0 & 1/2 \\ 1/2 & -1 & 1/2 \end{bmatrix} \\ &= \frac{1}{2} \begin{bmatrix} e^t + \cos t - \sin t & 2\sin t & e^t - \cos t - \sin t \\ e^t - \cos t - \sin t & 2\cos t & e^t - \cos t + \sin t \\ e^t - \cos t + \sin t & -2\sin t & e^t + \cos t + \sin t \end{bmatrix}. \end{aligned}$$

**11.** The first step in finding $e^{\mathbf{A}t}$ using a fundamental matrix for the system $\mathbf{x}' = \mathbf{A}\mathbf{x}$ is to find the eigenvalues for the matrix $\mathbf{A}$. Thus, we solve the characteristic equation

$$|\mathbf{A} - r\mathbf{I}| = \begin{vmatrix} 5 - r & -4 & 0 \\ 1 & -r & 2 \\ 0 & 2 & 5 - r \end{vmatrix} = 0$$

$$\Rightarrow \quad (5 - r) \begin{vmatrix} -r & 2 \\ 2 & 5 - r \end{vmatrix} + 4 \begin{vmatrix} 1 & 2 \\ 0 & 5 - r \end{vmatrix} = 0$$

$$\Rightarrow \qquad (5-r)[-r(5-r)-4] + 4(5-r) = -r(r-5)^2 = 0.$$

Therefore, the eigenvalues of $\mathbf{A}$ are $r = 0, 5$, with $r = 5$ an eigenvalue of multiplicity two. Next we must find the eigenvectors and generalized eigenvectors for the matrix $\mathbf{A}$ and from these vectors derive three linearly independent solutions of the system $\mathbf{x}' = \mathbf{Ax}$. To find the eigenvector associated with the eigenvalue $r = 0$, we solve the equation

$$\mathbf{Au} = \begin{bmatrix} 5 & -4 & 0 \\ 1 & 0 & 2 \\ 0 & 2 & 5 \end{bmatrix} \begin{bmatrix} u_1 \\ u_2 \\ u_3 \end{bmatrix} = \begin{bmatrix} 0 \\ 0 \\ 0 \end{bmatrix} \quad \Rightarrow \quad \begin{bmatrix} 1 & 0 & 2 \\ 0 & 2 & 5 \\ 0 & 0 & 0 \end{bmatrix} \begin{bmatrix} u_1 \\ u_2 \\ u_3 \end{bmatrix} = \begin{bmatrix} 0 \\ 0 \\ 0 \end{bmatrix}.$$

This equation is equivalent to the system $u_1 = -2u_3$, $2u_2 = -5u_3$ and one solution to this system is $u_3 = 2$, $u_1 = -4$, $u_2 = -5$. Therefore, one eigenvector of the matrix $\mathbf{A}$ associated with the eigenvalue $r = 0$ is given by the vector

$$\mathbf{u}_1 = \text{col}\,(u_1\,u_2\,u_3) = \text{col}(-4, -5, 2),$$

and so one solution to the system $\mathbf{x}' = \mathbf{Ax}$ is

$$\mathbf{x}_1(t) = e^0\mathbf{u}_1 = \begin{bmatrix} -4 \\ -5 \\ 2 \end{bmatrix}.$$

To find an eigenvector associated with the eigenvalue $r = 5$, we solve the equation

$$(\mathbf{A} - 5\mathbf{I})\mathbf{u} = \begin{bmatrix} 0 & -4 & 0 \\ 1 & -5 & 2 \\ 0 & 2 & 0 \end{bmatrix} \begin{bmatrix} u_1 \\ u_2 \\ u_3 \end{bmatrix} = \begin{bmatrix} 0 \\ 0 \\ 0 \end{bmatrix},$$

which is equivalent to the system $u_2 = 0$, $u_1 = -2u_3$. One solution to this system is $u_3 = 1$, $u_1 = -2$, $u_2 = 0$. Thus, one eigenvector of the matrix $\mathbf{A}$ associated with the eigenvalue $r = 5$ is the vector

$$\mathbf{u}_2 = \text{col}\,(u_1\,u_2\,u_3) = \text{col}(-2, 0, 1),$$

and so another linearly independent solution to the system $\mathbf{x}' = \mathbf{Ax}$ is given by

$$\mathbf{x}_2(t) = e^{5t}\mathbf{u}_2 = e^{5t} \begin{bmatrix} -2 \\ 0 \\ 1 \end{bmatrix} = \begin{bmatrix} -2e^{5t} \\ 0 \\ e^{5t} \end{bmatrix}.$$

Chapter 9

Since $r = 5$ is an eigenvalue of multiplicity two, we can find a generalized eigenvector (with $k = 2$) associated with the eigenvalue $r = 5$ which will be linearly independent from the vector $\mathbf{u}_2$ found above. Thus, we solve the equation

$$(\mathbf{A} - 5\mathbf{I})^2\mathbf{u} = \mathbf{0}. \tag{9.11}$$

Because

$$(\mathbf{A} - 5\mathbf{I})^2 = \begin{bmatrix} 0 & -4 & 0 \\ 1 & -5 & 2 \\ 0 & 2 & 0 \end{bmatrix}\begin{bmatrix} 0 & -4 & 0 \\ 1 & -5 & 2 \\ 0 & 2 & 0 \end{bmatrix} = \begin{bmatrix} -4 & 20 & -8 \\ -5 & 25 & -10 \\ 2 & -10 & 4 \end{bmatrix},$$

we see that equation (9.11) becomes

$$\begin{bmatrix} -4 & 20 & -8 \\ -5 & 25 & -10 \\ 2 & -10 & 4 \end{bmatrix}\begin{bmatrix} u_1 \\ u_2 \\ u_3 \end{bmatrix} = \begin{bmatrix} 0 \\ 0 \\ 0 \end{bmatrix} \Rightarrow \begin{bmatrix} -1 & 5 & -2 \\ 0 & 0 & 0 \\ 0 & 0 & 0 \end{bmatrix}\begin{bmatrix} u_1 \\ u_2 \\ u_3 \end{bmatrix} = \begin{bmatrix} 0 \\ 0 \\ 0 \end{bmatrix}.$$

This equation is equivalent to the equation

$$-u_1 + 5u_2 - 2u_3 = 0$$

and is, therefore, satisfied if we let $u_2 = s$, $u_3 = v$, and $u_1 = 5s - 2v$ for any values of $s$ and $v$. Hence, solutions to equation (9.11) are given by

$$\mathbf{u} = \begin{bmatrix} u_1 \\ u_2 \\ u_3 \end{bmatrix} = \begin{bmatrix} 5s - 2v \\ s \\ v \end{bmatrix} = s\begin{bmatrix} 5 \\ 1 \\ 0 \end{bmatrix} + v\begin{bmatrix} -2 \\ 0 \\ 1 \end{bmatrix}.$$

Notice that the vectors $v\mathrm{col}(-2, 0, 1)$ are the eigenvectors that we found above associated with the eigenvalue $r = 5$. Since we are looking for a vector which satisfies equation (9.11) and is linearly independent from this eigenvector we will choose $s = 1$ and $v = 0$. Thus, a generalized eigenvector for the matrix $\mathbf{A}$ associated with the eigenvalue $r = 5$ and linearly independent of the eigenvector $\mathbf{u}_2$ is given by

$$\mathbf{u}_3 = \mathrm{col}(5, 1, 0).$$

Hence, by formula (8) on page 563 of the text, we see that another linearly independent solution to the system $\mathbf{x}' = \mathbf{A}\mathbf{x}$ is given by

$$\mathbf{x}_3(t) = e^{\mathbf{A}t}\mathbf{u}_3 = e^{5t}\left[\mathbf{u}_3 + t(\mathbf{A} - 5\mathbf{I})\mathbf{u}_3\right]$$

$$= e^{5t}\begin{bmatrix} 5 \\ 1 \\ 0 \end{bmatrix} + te^{5t}\begin{bmatrix} 0 & -4 & 0 \\ 1 & -5 & 2 \\ 0 & 2 & 0 \end{bmatrix}\begin{bmatrix} 5 \\ 1 \\ 0 \end{bmatrix}$$

$$= e^{5t}\begin{bmatrix} 5 \\ 1 \\ 0 \end{bmatrix} + te^{5t}\begin{bmatrix} -4 \\ 0 \\ 2 \end{bmatrix} = \begin{bmatrix} 5e^{5t} - 4te^{5t} \\ e^{5t} \\ 2te^{5t} \end{bmatrix},$$

where we have used the fact that, by our choice of $\mathbf{u}_3$, $(\mathbf{A} - 5\mathbf{I})^2\mathbf{u}_3 = \mathbf{0}$ and so $(\mathbf{A} - 5\mathbf{I})^n\mathbf{u}_3 = \mathbf{0}$ for $n \geq 2$. (This is the reason why we used the generalized eigenvector to calculate $\mathbf{x}_3(t)$. The Cayley-Hamilton theorem, as given on page 561 of the text, states that $\mathbf{A}$ satisfies its characteristic equation, which in this case means that $\mathbf{A}(\mathbf{A} - 5\mathbf{I})^2 = \mathbf{0}$. However, we cannot assume from this fact that $(\mathbf{A} - 5\mathbf{I})^2 = 0$ because in matrix multiplication it is possible for two nonzero matrices to have a zero product.)

Our last step is to find a fundamental matrix for the system $\mathbf{x}' = \mathbf{A}\mathbf{x}$ using the linearly independent solutions found above and then to use this fundamental matrix to calculate $e^{\mathbf{A}t}$. Thus, from these three solutions we obtain the fundamental matrix given by

$$\mathbf{X}(t) = \begin{bmatrix} -4 & -2e^{5t} & 5e^{5t} - 4te^{5t} \\ -5 & 0 & e^{5t} \\ 2 & e^{5t} & 2te^{5t} \end{bmatrix} \quad \Rightarrow \quad \mathbf{X}(0) = \begin{bmatrix} -4 & -2 & 5 \\ -5 & 0 & 1 \\ 2 & 1 & 0 \end{bmatrix}.$$

We can find the inverse matrix $\mathbf{X}^{-1}(0)$ by (for example) performing row-reduction on the matrix $[\mathbf{X}(0)|\mathbf{I}]$ to obtain the matrix $[\mathbf{I}|\mathbf{X}^{-1}(0)]$. Thus, we find

$$\mathbf{X}^{-1}(0) = \frac{1}{25}\begin{bmatrix} 1 & -5 & 2 \\ -2 & 10 & 21 \\ 5 & 0 & 10 \end{bmatrix}.$$

Therefore, by formula (6) on page 562 of the text, we see that

$$e^{\mathbf{A}t} = \mathbf{X}(t)\mathbf{X}^{-1}(0) = \frac{1}{25}\begin{bmatrix} -4 & -2e^{5t} & 5e^{5t} - 4te^{5t} \\ -5 & 0 & e^{5t} \\ 2 & e^{5t} & 2te^{5t} \end{bmatrix}\begin{bmatrix} 1 & -5 & 2 \\ -2 & 10 & 21 \\ 5 & 0 & 10 \end{bmatrix}$$

$$= \frac{1}{25}\begin{bmatrix} -4 + 29e^{5t} - 20te^{5t} & 20 - 20e^{5t} & -8 + 8e^{5t} - 40te^{5t} \\ -5 + 5e^{5t} & 25 & -10 + 10e^{5t} \\ 2 - 2e^{5t} + 10te^{5t} & -10 + 10e^{5t} & 4 + 21e^{5t} + 20te^{5t} \end{bmatrix}.$$

**17.** We first calculate the eigenvalues for the matrix $\mathbf{A}$ by solving the characteristic equation

$$|\mathbf{A} - r\mathbf{I}| = \begin{vmatrix} -r & 1 & 0 \\ 0 & -r & 1 \\ -2 & -5 & -4 - r \end{vmatrix} = 0$$

$$\Rightarrow \quad (-r)\begin{vmatrix} -r & 1 \\ -5 & -4 - r \end{vmatrix} - \begin{vmatrix} 0 & 1 \\ -2 & -4 - r \end{vmatrix} = 0$$

$$\Rightarrow \quad -r[-r(-4 - r) + 5] - 2 = -\left(r^3 + 4r^2 + 5r + 2\right) = -(r + 1)^2(r + 2) = 0.$$

Thus, the eigenvalues for $\mathbf{A}$ are $r = -1, -2$, with $r = -1$ an eigenvalue of multiplicity two. To find an eigenvector $\mathbf{u} = \mathrm{col}(u_1, u_2, u_3)$ associated with the eigenvalue $r = -1$, we solve the equation

$$(\mathbf{A} + \mathbf{I})\mathbf{u} = \begin{bmatrix} 1 & 1 & 0 \\ 0 & 1 & 1 \\ -2 & -5 & -3 \end{bmatrix}\begin{bmatrix} u_1 \\ u_2 \\ u_3 \end{bmatrix} = \begin{bmatrix} 0 \\ 0 \\ 0 \end{bmatrix},$$

which is equivalent to the system $u_1 = u_3$, $u_2 = -u_3$. Therefore, by letting $u_3 = 1$ (so that $u_1 = 1$ and $u_2 = -1$), we see that one eigenvector for the matrix $\mathbf{A}$ associated with the eigenvalue $r = -1$ is the vector

$$\mathbf{u}_1 = \mathrm{col}(u_1, u_2, u_3) = \mathrm{col}(1, -1, 1).$$

Hence, one solution to the system $\mathbf{x}' = \mathbf{A}\mathbf{x}$ is given by

$$\mathbf{x}_1(t) = e^{-t}\mathbf{u}_1 = e^{-t}\begin{bmatrix} 1 \\ -1 \\ 1 \end{bmatrix}.$$

Since $r = -1$ is an eigenvalue of multiplicity two, we can find a generalized eigenvector associated with this eigenvalue (with $k = 2$) which will be linearly independent from the vector $\mathbf{u}_1$. To do this, we solve the equation

$$(\mathbf{A} + \mathbf{I})^2 \mathbf{u} = \mathbf{0}$$

$$\Rightarrow \begin{bmatrix} 1 & 1 & 0 \\ 0 & 1 & 1 \\ -2 & -5 & -3 \end{bmatrix} \begin{bmatrix} 1 & 1 & 0 \\ 0 & 1 & 1 \\ -2 & -5 & -3 \end{bmatrix} \begin{bmatrix} u_1 \\ u_2 \\ u_3 \end{bmatrix} = \begin{bmatrix} 0 \\ 0 \\ 0 \end{bmatrix}$$

$$\Rightarrow \begin{bmatrix} 1 & 2 & 1 \\ -2 & -4 & -2 \\ 4 & 8 & 4 \end{bmatrix} \begin{bmatrix} u_1 \\ u_2 \\ u_3 \end{bmatrix} = \begin{bmatrix} 0 \\ 0 \\ 0 \end{bmatrix} \quad \Rightarrow \quad \begin{bmatrix} 1 & 2 & 1 \\ 0 & 0 & 0 \\ 0 & 0 & 0 \end{bmatrix} \begin{bmatrix} u_1 \\ u_2 \\ u_3 \end{bmatrix} = \begin{bmatrix} 0 \\ 0 \\ 0 \end{bmatrix},$$

which is equivalent to the equation $u_1 + 2u_2 + u_3 = 0$. This equation will be satisfied if we let $u_3 = s$, $u_2 = v$, and $u_1 = -2v - s$ for any values of $s$ and $v$. Thus, generalized eigenvectors associated with the eigenvalue $r = -1$ are given by

$$\mathbf{u} = \begin{bmatrix} u_1 \\ u_2 \\ u_3 \end{bmatrix} = \begin{bmatrix} -2v - s \\ v \\ s \end{bmatrix} = s \begin{bmatrix} -1 \\ 0 \\ 1 \end{bmatrix} + v \begin{bmatrix} -2 \\ 1 \\ 0 \end{bmatrix}.$$

Hence, by letting $s = 2$ and $v = -1$, we find one such generalized eigenvector to be the vector

$$\mathbf{u}_2 = \mathrm{col}(0, -1, 2),$$

which we see by inspection is linearly independent from $\mathbf{u}_1$. Therefore, by equation (8) on page 563 of the text, we obtain a second linearly independent solution of the system $\mathbf{x}' = \mathbf{A}\mathbf{x}$ given by

$$\begin{aligned} \mathbf{x}_2(t) &= e^{\mathbf{A}t}\mathbf{u}_2 = e^{-t}\left[\mathbf{u}_2 + t(\mathbf{A} + \mathbf{I})\mathbf{u}_2\right] \\ &= e^{-t} \begin{bmatrix} 0 \\ -1 \\ 2 \end{bmatrix} + te^{-t} \begin{bmatrix} 1 & 1 & 0 \\ 0 & 1 & 1 \\ -2 & -5 & -3 \end{bmatrix} \begin{bmatrix} 0 \\ -1 \\ 2 \end{bmatrix} \end{aligned}$$

$$= e^{-t} \begin{bmatrix} 0 \\ -1 \\ 2 \end{bmatrix} + te^{-t} \begin{bmatrix} -1 \\ 1 \\ -1 \end{bmatrix} = e^{-t} \begin{bmatrix} -t \\ -1+t \\ 2-t \end{bmatrix}.$$

In order to obtain a third linearly independent solution to this system, we will find an eigenvector associated with the eigenvalue $r = -2$ by solving the equation

$$(\mathbf{A} + 2\mathbf{I})\mathbf{u} = \begin{bmatrix} 2 & 1 & 0 \\ 0 & 2 & 1 \\ -2 & -5 & -2 \end{bmatrix} \begin{bmatrix} u_1 \\ u_2 \\ u_3 \end{bmatrix} = \begin{bmatrix} 0 \\ 0 \\ 0 \end{bmatrix}.$$

This equation is equivalent to the system $2u_1 + u_2 = 0$, $2u_2 + u_3 = 0$. One solution to this system is given by $u_1 = 1$, $u_2 = -2$, and $u_3 = 4$. Thus, one eigenvector associated with the eigenvalue $r = -2$ is the vector

$$\mathbf{u}_3 = \text{col}(u_1, u_2, u_3) = \text{col}(1, -2, 4),$$

and another linearly independent solution to this system is given by

$$\mathbf{x}_3(t) = e^{-2t}\mathbf{u}_3 = e^{-2t} \begin{bmatrix} 1 \\ -2 \\ 4 \end{bmatrix}.$$

Hence, by combining the three linearly independent solutions that we have just found, we see that a general solution to this system is

$$\mathbf{x}(t) = c_1 e^{-t} \begin{bmatrix} 1 \\ -1 \\ 1 \end{bmatrix} + c_2 e^{-t} \begin{bmatrix} -t \\ -1+t \\ 2-t \end{bmatrix} + c_3 e^{-2t} \begin{bmatrix} 1 \\ -2 \\ 4 \end{bmatrix}.$$

**23.** In Problem 3, we found that

$$e^{\mathbf{A}t} = e^{-t} \begin{bmatrix} 1 + 3t - 3t^2/2 & t & -t + t^2/2 \\ -3t & 1 & t \\ 9t - 9t^2/2 & 3t & 1 - 3t + 3t^2/2 \end{bmatrix}.$$

In order to use the variation of parameters formula (equation (13) on page 565 of the text), we need to find expressions for $e^{\mathbf{A}t}\mathbf{x}_0$ and $\int_0^t e^{\mathbf{A}(t-s)}\mathbf{f}(s)\,ds$, where we have used the fact that $t_0 = 0$. Thus, we first notice that

$$\int_0^t e^{\mathbf{A}(t-s)}\mathbf{f}(s)\,ds = \int_0^t e^{\mathbf{A}t-\mathbf{A}s}\mathbf{f}(s)\,ds = e^{\mathbf{A}t}\int_0^t e^{-\mathbf{A}s}\mathbf{f}(s)\,ds\,.$$

Since $\mathbf{f}(s) = \mathrm{col}(0, s, 0)$, we observe that

$$e^{-\mathbf{A}s}\mathbf{f}(s) = e^s \begin{bmatrix} 1-3s-3s^2/2 & -s & s+s^2/2 \\ 3s & 1 & - \\ -9s-9s^2/2 & -3s & 1+3s+3s^2/2 \end{bmatrix} \begin{bmatrix} 0 \\ s \\ 0 \end{bmatrix}$$

$$= e^s \begin{bmatrix} -s^2 \\ s \\ -3s^2 \end{bmatrix} = \begin{bmatrix} -s^2 e^s \\ se^s \\ -3s^2 e^s \end{bmatrix}.$$

Therefore, we have

$$\int_0^t e^{\mathbf{A}(t-s)}\mathbf{f}(s)\,ds = e^{\mathbf{A}t}\int_0^t e^{-\mathbf{A}s}\mathbf{f}(s)\,ds$$

$$= e^{\mathbf{A}t} \begin{bmatrix} \int_0^t(-s^2 e^s)ds \\ \int_0^t(se^s)ds \\ \int_0^t(-3s^2 e^s)ds \end{bmatrix}$$

$$= e^{\mathbf{A}t} \begin{bmatrix} 2-e^t(t^2-2t+2) \\ 1+e^t(t-1) \\ 6-3e^t(t^2-2t+2) \end{bmatrix},$$

where we have used integration by parts to evaluate the three integrals above. Next, since $\mathbf{x}_0 = \mathrm{col}(0, 3, 0)$, we see that

$$e^{\mathbf{A}t}\mathbf{x}_0 = e^{-t} \begin{bmatrix} 1+3t-3t^2/2 & t & -t+t^2/2 \\ -3t & 1 & t \\ 9t-9t^2/2 & 3t & 1-3t+3t^2/2 \end{bmatrix} \begin{bmatrix} 0 \\ 3 \\ 0 \end{bmatrix} = e^{-t} \begin{bmatrix} 3t \\ 3 \\ 9t \end{bmatrix}.$$

# Chapter 9

Finally, substituting these expressions into the variation of parameters formula (13), page 565 of the text, yields

$$\mathbf{x}(t) = e^{\mathbf{A}t}\mathbf{x}_0 + \int_0^t e^{\mathbf{A}(t-s)}\mathbf{f}(s)\,ds$$

$$= e^{-t}\begin{bmatrix} 3t \\ 3 \\ 9t \end{bmatrix} + e^{\mathbf{A}t}\begin{bmatrix} 2 - e^t(t^2 - 2t + 2) \\ 1 + e^t(t - 1) \\ 6 - 3e^t(t^2 - 2t + 2) \end{bmatrix},$$

where $e^{\mathbf{A}t}$ is given above.

# CHAPTER 10: Partial Differential Equations

**5.** To find a general solution to this equation, we first observe that the auxiliary equation associated with the corresponding homogeneous equation is given by $r^2 - 1 = 0$. This equation has roots $r = \pm 1$. Thus, the solution to the corresponding homogeneous equation is given by

$$y_h(x) = C_1 e^x + C_2 e^{-x}.$$

By the method of undetermined coefficients, we see that the form of a particular solution to the nonhomogeneous equation is

$$y_p(x) = A + Bx,$$

where we have used the fact that neither $y = 1$ nor $y = x$ is a solution to the corresponding homogeneous equation. To find $A$ and $B$, we note that

$$y_p'(x) = B \qquad \text{and} \qquad y_p''(x) = 0.$$

By substituting these expressions into the original differential equation, we obtain

$$y_p''(x) - y_p(x) = -A - Bx = 1 - 2x.$$

By equating coefficients, we see that $A = -1$ and $B = 2$. Substituting these values into the equation for $y_p(x)$ yields

$$y_p(x) = -1 + 2x.$$

Thus, we see that

$$y(x) = y_h(x) + y_p(x) = C_1 e^x + C_2 e^{-x} - 1 + 2x.$$

Next we try to find $C_1$ and $C_2$ so that the solution $y(x)$ will satisfy the boundary conditions. That is, we want to find $C_1$ and $C_2$ satisfying

$$y(0) = C_1 + C_2 - 1 = 0 \quad \text{and} \quad y(1) = C_1 e + C_2 e^{-1} + 1 = 1 + e.$$

From the first equation we see that $C_2 = 1 - C_1$. Substituting this expression for $C_2$ into the second equation and simplifying yields

$$e - e^{-1} = C_1 \left( e - e^{-1} \right).$$

Thus, $C_1 = 1$ and $C_2 = 0$. Therefore,

$$y(x) = e^x - 1 + 2x$$

is the only solution to the boundary value problem.

13. First note that the auxiliary equation for this problem is $r^2 + \lambda = 0$. To find eigenvalues which yield nontrivial solutions we will consider the three cases: $\lambda < 0$, $\lambda = 0$, and $\lambda > 0$.

Case 1, $\lambda < 0$: In this case the roots to the auxiliary equation are $r = \pm\sqrt{-\lambda}$ (where we note that $-\lambda$ is a positive number). Therefore, a general solution to the differential equation $y'' + \lambda y = 0$ is given by

$$y(x) = C_1 e^{\sqrt{-\lambda}x} + C_2 e^{-\sqrt{-\lambda}x}.$$

In order to apply the boundary conditions we need to find $y'(x)$. Thus, we have

$$y'(x) = \sqrt{-\lambda}C_1 e^{\sqrt{-\lambda}x} - \sqrt{-\lambda}C_2 e^{-\sqrt{-\lambda}x}.$$

By applying the boundary conditions we obtain

$$y(0) - y'(0) = C_1 + C_2 - \sqrt{-\lambda}C_1 + \sqrt{-\lambda}C_2 = 0$$
$$\Rightarrow \quad \left(1 - \sqrt{-\lambda}\right)C_1 + \left(1 + \sqrt{-\lambda}\right)C_2 = 0,$$

and

$$y(\pi) = C_1 e^{\sqrt{-\lambda}\pi} + C_2 e^{-\sqrt{-\lambda}\pi} = 0 \quad \Rightarrow \quad C_2 = -C_1 e^{2\sqrt{-\lambda}\pi}.$$

By combining these expressions, we observe that

$$\left(1 - \sqrt{-\lambda}\right)C_1 - \left(1 + \sqrt{-\lambda}\right)C_1 e^{2\sqrt{-\lambda}\pi} = 0$$

$$\Rightarrow \quad C_1\left[\left(1 - \sqrt{-\lambda}\right) - \left(1 + \sqrt{-\lambda}\right)e^{2\sqrt{-\lambda}\pi}\right] = 0. \tag{10.1}$$

This last expression will be true if $C_1 = 0$ or if

$$e^{2\sqrt{-\lambda}\pi} = \frac{1 - \sqrt{-\lambda}}{1 + \sqrt{-\lambda}}.$$

But since $\sqrt{-\lambda} > 0$, we see that $e^{2\sqrt{-\lambda}\pi} > 1$ while $(1 - \sqrt{-\lambda})/(1 + \sqrt{-\lambda}) < 1$. Therefore, the only way that equation (10.1) can be true is for $C_1 = 0$. This means that $C_2$ must also equal zero and so in this case we have only the trivial solution.

Case 2, $\lambda = 0$: In this case we are solving the differential equation $y'' = 0$. This equation has a general solution given by .

$$y(x) = C_1 + C_2 x \quad \Rightarrow \quad y'(x) = C_2.$$

By applying the boundary conditions we obtain

$$y(0) - y'(0) = C_1 - C_2 = 0 \quad \text{and} \quad y(\pi) = C_1 + C_2\pi = 0.$$

Solving these equations simultaneously yields $C_1 = C_2 = 0$. Thus, we again find only the trivial solution.

Case 3, $\lambda > 0$: In this case the roots to the associated auxiliary equation are $r = \pm\sqrt{\lambda}i$. Therefore, the general solution is given by

$$y(x) = C_1 \cos\left(\sqrt{\lambda}x\right) + C_2 \sin\left(\sqrt{\lambda}x\right)$$

$$\Rightarrow \quad y'(x) = -\sqrt{\lambda}C_1 \sin\left(\sqrt{\lambda}x\right) + \sqrt{\lambda}C_2 \cos\left(\sqrt{\lambda}x\right).$$

By applying the boundary conditions, we obtain

$$y(0) - y'(0) = C_1 - \sqrt{\lambda}C_2 = 0 \quad \Rightarrow \quad C_1 = \sqrt{\lambda}C_2,$$

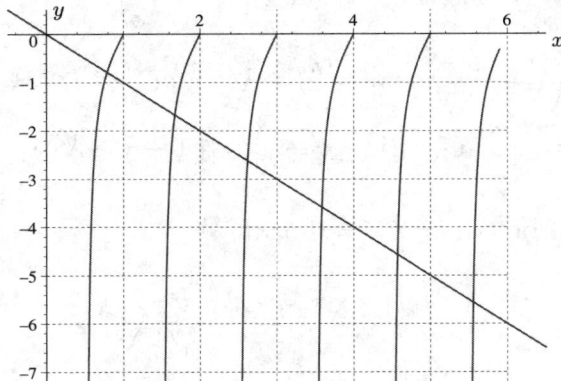

**Figure 10–A**: The intersection of the graphs $y = -x$ and $y = \tan(\pi x)$, $x > 0$.

and

$$y(\pi) = C_1 \cos\left(\sqrt{\lambda}\pi\right) + C_2 \sin\left(\sqrt{\lambda}\pi\right) = 0.$$

By combining these results, we obtain

$$C_2 \left[\sqrt{\lambda}\cos\left(\sqrt{\lambda}\pi\right) + \sin\left(\sqrt{\lambda}\pi\right)\right] = 0$$

Therefore, in order to obtain a solution other than the trivial solution, we must solve the equation

$$\sqrt{\lambda}\cos\left(\sqrt{\lambda}\pi\right) + \sin\left(\sqrt{\lambda}\pi\right) = 0.$$

By simplifying this equation becomes

$$\tan\left(\sqrt{\lambda}\pi\right) = -\sqrt{\lambda}.$$

To see that there exist values for $\lambda > 0$ which satisfy this equation, we examine the graphs of the equations $y = -x$ and $y = \tan(\pi x)$. For any values of $x > 0$ where these two graphs intersect, we set $\lambda = x^2$. These values for $\lambda$ will be the eigenvalues that we seek. From the graph in Figure 10-A, we see that there are (countably) infinitely many such eigenvalues. These values satisfy the equations

$$\tan\left(\sqrt{\lambda_n}\pi\right) + \sqrt{\lambda_n} = 0.$$

As $n$ becomes large, we can also see from the graph that these eigenvalues approach the square of odd multiples of $1/2$. That is,

$$\lambda_n \approx \frac{(2n-1)^2}{4},$$

when $n$ is large. Corresponding to the eigenvalue $\lambda_n$ we obtain the solutions

$$y_n(x) = C_{1n} \cos\left(\sqrt{\lambda_n}x\right) + C_{2n} \sin\left(\sqrt{\lambda_n}x\right) = \sqrt{\lambda_n}C_{2n} \cos\left(\sqrt{\lambda_n}x\right) + C_{2n} \sin\left(\sqrt{\lambda_n}x\right)$$

(since $C_{1n} = \sqrt{\lambda_n}C_{2n}$). Thus

$$y_n(x) = C_n\left[\sqrt{\lambda_n} \cos\left(\sqrt{\lambda_n}x\right) + \sin\left(\sqrt{\lambda_n}x\right)\right],$$

where $C_n$ is arbitrary.

**17.** We are solving the problem

$$\frac{\partial u(x,t)}{\partial t} = 3\frac{\partial^2 u(x,t)}{\partial t^2}, \qquad 0 < x < \pi, \quad t > 0,$$

$$u(0,t) = u(\pi,t) = 0, \qquad t > 0,$$

$$u(x,0) = \sin x - 7\sin 3x + \sin 5x.$$

A solution to this partial differential equation satisfying the first boundary condition is given in equation (11) on page 582 of the text. By letting $\beta = 3$ and $L = \pi$ in this equation we obtain the series

$$u(x,t) = \sum_{n=1}^{\infty} c_n e^{-3n^2 t} \sin nx. \tag{10.2}$$

To satisfy the initial condition, we let $t = 0$ in this equation and set the result equal to $\sin x - 7\sin 3x + \sin 5x$. This yields

$$u(x,t) = \sum_{n=1}^{\infty} c_n \sin nx = \sin x - 7\sin 3x + \sin 5x.$$

By equating the coefficients of the like terms, we see that $c_1 = 1$, $c_3 = -7$, $c_5 = 1$, and all other $c_n$'s are zero. Plugging these values into equation (10.2) gives the solution

$$\begin{aligned}
u(x,t) &= e^{-3(1)^2 t}\sin x - 7e^{-3(3)^2 t}\sin 3x + e^{-3(5)^2 t}\sin 5x \\
&= e^{-3t}\sin x - 7e^{-27t}\sin 3x + e^{-75t}\sin 5x.
\end{aligned}$$

# Chapter 10

**21.** By letting $\alpha = 3$ and $L = \pi$ in formula (24) on page 585 of the text, we see that the solution we want will have the form

$$u(x, t) = \sum_{n=1}^{\infty} [a_n \cos 3nt + b_n \sin 3nt] \sin nx. \tag{10.3}$$

Therefore, we see that

$$\frac{\partial u}{\partial t} = \sum_{n=1}^{\infty} [-3na_n \sin 3nt + 3nb_n \cos 3nt] \sin nx.$$

In order for the solution to satisfy the initial conditions, we must find $a_n$ and $b_n$ such that

$$u(x, 0) = \sum_{n=1}^{\infty} a_n \sin nx = 6 \sin 2x + 2 \sin 6x,$$

and

$$\frac{\partial u(x, 0)}{\partial t} = \sum_{n=1}^{\infty} 3nb_n \sin nx = 11 \sin 9x - 14 \sin 15x.$$

From the first condition, we observe that we must have a term for $n = 2, 6$ and for these terms we want $a_2 = 6$ and $a_6 = 2$. All of the other $a_n$'s must be zero. By comparing coefficients in the second condition, we see that we require

$$3(9)b_9 = 11 \quad \text{or} \quad b_9 = \frac{11}{27} \quad \text{and} \quad 3(15)b_{15} = -14 \quad \text{or} \quad b_{15} = -\frac{14}{45}.$$

We also see that all other values for $b_n$ must be zero. Therefore, by substituting these values into equation (10.3) above, we obtain the solution of the vibrating string problem with $\alpha = 3$, $L = \pi$ and $f(x)$ and $g(x)$ as given. This solution is given by

$$u(x, t) = 6 \cos(3 \cdot 2 \cdot t) \sin 2x + 2 \cos(3 \cdot 6 \cdot t) \sin 6x + \frac{11}{27} \sin(3 \cdot 9 \cdot t) \sin 9x - \frac{14}{45} \sin(3 \cdot 15 \cdot t) \sin 15x.$$

Or by simplifying, we obtain

$$u(x, t) = 6 \cos 6t \sin 2x + 2 \cos 18t \sin 6x + \frac{11}{27} \sin 27t \sin 9x - \frac{14}{45} \sin 45t \sin 15x.$$

**23.** We know from equation (11) on page 582 of the text that a formal solution to the heat flow problem is given by

$$u(x, t) = \sum_{n=1}^{\infty} c_n e^{-2(n\pi)^2 t} \sin n\pi x, \tag{10.4}$$

where we have made the substitutions $\beta = 2$ and $L = 1$. For this function to be a solution to the problem it must satisfy the initial condition $u(x,0) = f(x)$, $0 < x < 1$. Therefore, we let $t = 0$ in equation (10.4) above and set the result equal to $f(x)$ to obtain

$$u(x,0) = \sum_{n=1}^{\infty} c_n \sin n\pi x = \sum_{n=1}^{\infty} \frac{1}{n^2} \sin n\pi x.$$

By equating coefficients, we see that $c_n = n^{-2}$. Substituting these values of $c_n$ into equation (10.4) yields the solution

$$u(x,t) = \sum_{n=1}^{\infty} n^{-2} e^{-2(n\pi)^2 t} \sin n\pi x.$$

**EXERCISES 10.3:   Fourier Series, page 603**

5. Note that $f(-x) = e^x \cos(-3x) = e^x \cos 3x$. Since

$$f(-x) = e^x \cos 3x \neq e^{-x} \cos 3x = f(x)$$

unless $x = 0$ we see that this function is not even. Similarly since

$$f(-x) = e^x \cos 3x \neq -e^{-x} \cos 3x = -f(x),$$

this function is also not odd.

13. For this problem $T = 1$. Thus, by Definition 1 on page 594 of the text, the Fourier series for this function will be given by

$$\frac{a_0}{2} + \sum_{n=1}^{\infty} \left(a_n \cos n\pi x + b_n \sin n\pi x\right). \tag{10.5}$$

To compute $a_0$, we use equation (9) given in Definition 1 in the text noting that $\cos(0 \cdot \pi x) = 1$. Thus, we have

$$a_0 = \int_{-1}^{1} x^2 \, dx = \left.\frac{x^3}{3}\right|_{-1}^{1} = \frac{1}{3} - \frac{-1}{3} = \frac{2}{3}.$$

635

To find $a_n$ for $n = 1, 2, 3, \ldots$, we again use equation (9) on page 594 of the text. This yields

$$a_n = \int_{-1}^{1} x^2 \cos n\pi x \, dx = 2 \int_{0}^{1} x^2 \cos n\pi x \, dx,$$

where we have used the fact that $x^2 \cos n\pi x$ is an even function. Thus, using integration by parts twice, we obtain

$$
\begin{aligned}
a_n &= 2 \int_{0}^{1} x^2 \cos n\pi x \, dx = 2 \left[ x^2 \frac{\sin n\pi x}{n\pi} \Big|_{0}^{1} - \frac{2}{n\pi} \int_{0}^{1} x \sin n\pi x \, dx \right] \\
&= 2 \left[ \left( \frac{\sin n\pi}{n\pi} - 0 \right) - \frac{2}{n\pi} \left( -x \frac{\cos n\pi x}{n\pi} \Big|_{0}^{1} + \frac{1}{n\pi} \int_{0}^{1} \cos n\pi x \, dx \right) \right] \\
&= 2 \left[ 0 + \frac{2}{n^2 \pi^2} (\cos n\pi - 0) - \frac{2}{n^2 \pi^2} \left( \frac{1}{n\pi} \sin n\pi x \Big|_{0}^{1} \right) \right] \\
&= \frac{4}{n^2 \pi^2} (-1)^n - \frac{4}{n^3 \pi^3} (\sin n\pi - 0) = \frac{4}{n^2 \pi^2} (-1)^n .
\end{aligned}
$$

To calculate the $b_n$'s, note that since $x^2$ is even and $\sin n\pi x$ is odd, their product is odd (see Problem 7 in this section of the text). Since $x^2 \sin n\pi x$ is also continuous, by Theorem 1 on page 590 of the text, we have

$$b_n = \int_{-1}^{1} x^2 \sin n\pi x \, dx = 0 .$$

By plugging these coefficients into equation (10.5) above, we see that the Fourier series associated with $x^2$ is given by

$$\frac{1}{3} + \sum_{n=1}^{\infty} \frac{4}{n^2 \pi^2} (-1)^n \cos n\pi x .$$

**21.** We use Theorem 2 on page 600 of the text. Notice that $f(x) = x^2$ and $f'(x) = 2x$ are continuous on $[-1, 1]$. Thus, the Fourier series for $f$ converges to $f(x)$ for $-1 < x < 1$. Furthermore,

$$f\left(-1^{+}\right) = \lim_{x \to -1^{+}} x^2 = 1 \quad \text{and} \quad f\left(1^{-}\right) = \lim_{x \to 1^{-}} x^2 = 1 .$$

Hence,

$$\frac{1}{2}\left[f\left(-1^{+}\right)+f\left(1^{-}\right)\right]=\frac{1}{2}\left(1+1\right)=1,$$

and so, by Theorem 2, the sum of the Fourier series equals 1 when $x=\pm1$. Therefore, the Fourier series converges to

$$f(x)=x^{2} \qquad \text{for} \qquad -1 \le x \le 1.$$

Since the sum function must be periodic with period 2, the sum function is the 2-periodic extension of $f(x)$ which we can write as

$$g(x)=(x-2n)^{2}, \qquad 2n-1 \le x < 2n+1, \quad n=0,\pm1,\pm2,\dots .$$

**29.** To calculate the coefficients of this expansion we use formula (20) on page 599 of the text. Thus we have

$$c_{0}=\frac{\int_{-1}^{1} f(x)\,dx}{\|P_{0}\|^{2}}=\frac{0}{\|P_{0}\|^{2}}=0,$$

where we have used the fact that $f(x)$ is an odd function. To find $c_{1}$ we first calculate the denominator to be

$$\|P_{1}\|^{2}=\int_{-1}^{1} P_{1}^{2}(x)\,dx=\int_{-1}^{1} x^{2}\,dx=\left.\frac{x^{3}}{3}\right|_{-1}^{1}=\frac{2}{3}.$$

Therefore, we obtain

$$c_{1}=\frac{3}{2}\int_{-1}^{1} f(x)P_{1}(x)\,dx=\frac{3}{2}\,2\int_{0}^{1} x\,dx=\left.3\,\frac{x^{2}}{2}\right|_{0}^{1}=\frac{3}{2}.$$

Notice that in order to calculate the above integral, we used the fact that the product of the two odd functions $f(x)$ and $P_{1}(x)$ is even. To find $c_{2}$, we first observe that, since $f(x)$ is odd and $P_{2}(x)$ is even, their product is odd and so we have

$$\int_{-1}^{1} f(x)P_{2}(x)\,dx=0.$$

Hence

$$c_{2}=\frac{\int_{-1}^{1} f(x)P_{2}(x)\,dx}{\|P_{2}\|^{2}}=\frac{0}{\|P_{2}\|^{2}}=0.$$

# Chapter 10

**31.** We need to show that

$$\int_{-\infty}^{\infty} H_m(x)H_n(x)e^{-x^2}\,dx = 0,$$

for $m \neq n$, where $m, n = 0, 1, 2$. Therefore, we need to calculate several integrals. Let's begin with $m = 0$, $n = 2$. Here we see that

$$\int_{-\infty}^{\infty} H_0(x)H_2(x)e^{-x^2}\,dx = \int_{-\infty}^{\infty} \left(4x^2 - 2\right)e^{-x^2}\,dx$$

$$= \lim_{N\to\infty}\int_0^N \left(4x^2 - 2\right)e^{-x^2}\,dx + \lim_{M\to\infty}\int_{-M}^0 \left(4x^2 - 2\right)e^{-x^2}\,dx.$$

We will first calculate the indefinite integral using integration by parts with the substitution

$$u = x, \qquad dv = 2xe^{-x^2}\,dx$$
$$du = dx, \quad v = -e^{-x^2}.$$

That is we find

$$\int \left(4x^2 - 2\right)e^{-x^2}\,dx = 2\int 2x^2 e^{-x^2}\,dx - 2\int e^{-x^2}\,dx$$

$$= 2\left[-xe^{-x^2} + \int e^{-x^2}\,dx\right] - 2\int e^{-x^2}\,dx = -2xe^{-x^2} + C.$$

Substituting this result in for the integrals we are calculating and using L'Hospital's rule to find the limits, yields

$$\int_{-\infty}^{\infty} H_0(x)H_2(x)e^{-x^2}\,dx = \lim_{N\to\infty}\left(-2xe^{-x^2}\Big|_0^N\right) + \lim_{M\to\infty}\left(-2xe^{-x^2}\Big|_{-M}^0\right)$$

$$= \lim_{N\to\infty}\left(\frac{-2N}{e^{N^2}} + 0\right) + \lim_{M\to\infty}\left(0 - \frac{2M}{e^{M^2}}\right)$$

$$= -\lim_{N\to\infty}\frac{2N}{e^{N^2}} - \lim_{M\to\infty}\frac{2M}{e^{M^2}} = -0 - 0 = 0.$$

When $m = 0$, $n = 1$ and $m = 1$, $n = 2$, the integrals are, respectively,

$$\int_{-\infty}^{\infty} H_0(x)H_1(x)e^{-x^2}\,dx = \int_{-\infty}^{\infty} 2xe^{-x^2}\,dx$$

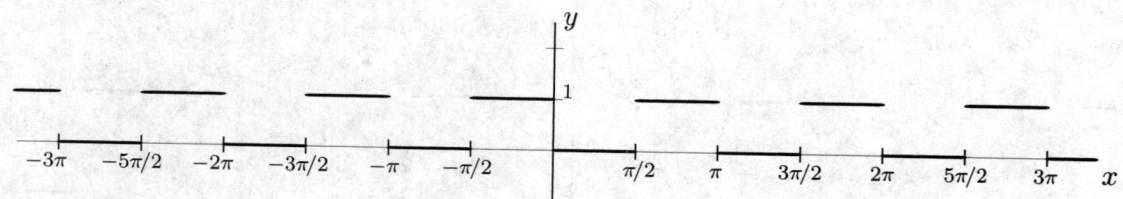

**Figure 10–B**: The graph of the $\pi$-periodic extension of $f$.

and

$$\int_{-\infty}^{\infty} H_1(x)H_2(x)e^{-x^2}\, dx = \int_{-\infty}^{\infty} 2x(4x^2 - 2)e^{-x^2}\, dx.$$

In each case the integrands are odd functions and hence their integrals over symmetric intervals of the form $(-N, N)$ are zero. Since it is easy to show that the above improper integrals are convergent, we get

$$\int_{-\infty}^{\infty} \cdots = \lim_{N\to\infty} \int_{-N}^{N} \cdots = \lim_{N\to\infty} 0 = 0.$$

Since we have shown that the 3 integrals above are all equal to zero, the first three Hermite polynomials are orthogonal.

## EXERCISES 10.4:   Fourier Cosine and Sine Series, page 611

3. **(a)** The $\pi$-periodic extension $\widetilde{f}(x)$ on the interval $(-\pi, \pi)$ is

$$\widetilde{f}(x) = \begin{cases} 0, & -\pi < x < -\pi/2, \\ 1, & -\pi/2 < x < 0, \\ 0, & 0 < x < \pi/2, \\ 1, & \pi/2 < x < \pi, \end{cases}$$

with $\widetilde{f}(x + 2\pi) = \widetilde{f}(x)$. The graph of this function is given in Figure 10-B.

**(b)** Using the formula on page 607 of the text, the odd $2\pi$-periodic extension $f_o$ on the

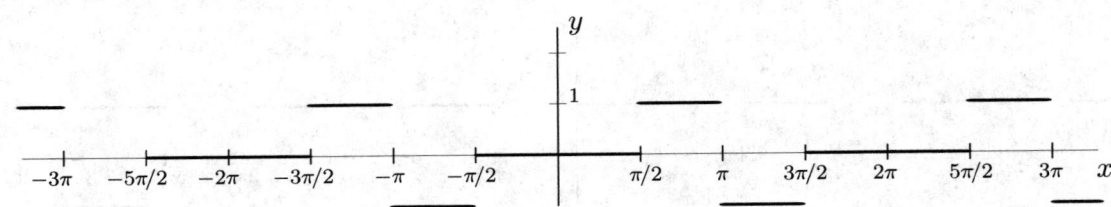

**Figure 10–C:** The graph of the odd $2\pi$-periodic extension of $f$.

interval $(-\pi, \pi)$ is

$$f_o(x) = \begin{cases} -f(-x), & -\pi < x < 0, \\ f(x), & 0 < x < \pi \end{cases} = \begin{cases} -1, & -\pi < x < -\pi/2, \\ 0, & -\pi/2 < x < 0, \\ 0, & 0 < x < \pi/2, \\ 1, & \pi/2 < x < \pi, \end{cases}$$

with $f_o(x + 2\pi) = f_o(x)$. The graph of $f_o(x)$ is given in Figure 10-C.

**(c)** Using the formula on page 608 of the text, the even $2\pi$-periodic extension $f_e$ on the interval $(-\pi, \pi)$ is

$$f_e(x) = \begin{cases} f(-x), & -\pi < x < 0, \\ f(x), & 0 < x < \pi \end{cases} = \begin{cases} 1, & -\pi < x < -\pi/2, \\ 0, & -\pi/2 < x < 0, \\ 0, & 0 < x < \pi/2, \\ 1, & \pi/2 < x < \pi, \end{cases}$$

with $f_e(x + 2\pi) = f_e(x)$. The graph of $f_e(x)$ is given in Figure 10-D.

**7.** Since $f$ is piecewise continuous on the interval $[0, \pi]$, we can use equation (6) in Definition 2 on page 609 of the text to calculate its Fourier sine series. In this problem $T = \pi$ and $f(x) = x^2$. Thus we have

$$f(x) = \sum_{n=1}^{\infty} b_n \sin nx, \qquad \text{with} \qquad b_n = \frac{2}{\pi} \int_0^{\pi} x^2 \sin nx \, dx .$$

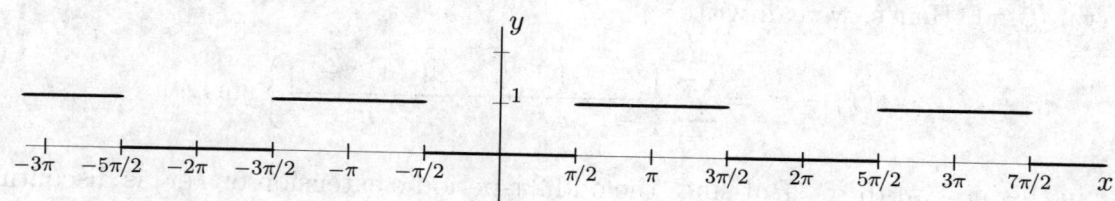

**Figure 10–D**: The graph of the even $2\pi$-periodic extension of $f$.

To calculate the coefficients, we use integration by parts twice to obtain

$$\frac{\pi}{2}b_n = \int_0^\pi x^2 \sin nx \, dx = -x^2 \frac{\cos nx}{n}\Big|_0^\pi + \frac{2}{n}\int_0^\pi x \cos nx \, dx$$

$$= -\frac{\pi^2 \cos n\pi}{n} + 0 + \frac{2}{n}\left[x\frac{\sin nx}{n}\Big|_0^\pi - \frac{1}{n}\int_0^\pi \sin nx \, dx\right]$$

$$= -\frac{\pi^2 \cos n\pi}{n} + \frac{2}{n}\left[0 - \frac{1}{n}\left(-\frac{\cos nx}{n}\Big|_0^\pi\right)\right]$$

$$= -\frac{\pi^2 \cos n\pi}{n} + \frac{2}{n^3}\left(\cos n\pi - \cos 0\right),$$

where $n = 1, 2, 3, \ldots$. Since $\cos n\pi = 1$ if $n$ is even and $\cos n\pi = -1$ if $n$ is odd for all $n = 1, 2, 3, \ldots$, we see that

$$\frac{\pi}{2}b_n = -\frac{\pi^2(-1)^n}{n} + \frac{2[(-1)^n - 1]}{n^3}.$$

Therefore, for $n = 1, 2, 3, \ldots$, we have

$$b_n = \frac{2\pi(-1)^{n+1}}{n} + \frac{4[(-1)^n - 1]}{\pi n^3}.$$

Substituting these coefficients into the Fourier sine series for $f(x) = x^2$, yields

$$\sum_{n=1}^\infty \left\{\frac{2\pi(-1)^{n+1}}{n} + \frac{4[(-1)^n - 1]}{\pi n^3}\right\} \sin nx.$$

Since $f(x) = x^2$ and $f\prime(x) = 2x$ are piecewise continuous on the interval $[0, \pi]$, Theorem 2 on page 600 of the text implies that this Fourier series converges pointwise to $f(x)$ on the interval $(0, \pi)$. Hence, we can write

$$f(x) = x^2 = \sum_{n=1}^{\infty} \left\{ \frac{2\pi(-1)^{n+1}}{n} + \frac{4[(-1)^n - 1]}{\pi n^3} \right\} \sin nx,$$

for $x$ in the interval $(0, \pi)$. But since the odd $2\pi$-periodic extension of $f(x)$ is discontinuous at odd multiples of $\pi$, the Gibbs' phenomenon (see Problem 39 on page 606 of the text) occurs around these points, and so the convergence of this Fourier sine series is not uniform on $(0, \pi)$.

13. Since $f(x) = e^x$ is piecewise continuous on the interval $[0, 1]$, we can use Definition 2 on page 609 of the text to find its Fourier cosine series. Therefore, we have

$$\frac{a_0}{2} + \sum_{n=1}^{\infty} a_n \cos n\pi x, \qquad \text{where} \qquad a_n = 2 \int_0^1 e^x \cos n\pi x \, dx.$$

Using the fact that $\cos 0 = 1$, we find the coefficient $a_0$ to be

$$a_0 = 2 \int_0^1 e^x \, dx = 2(e - 1).$$

We will use integration by parts twice (or the table of integrals on the inside cover of the text) to calculate the integrals in the remaining coefficients. This yields

$$\int e^x \cos n\pi x \, dx = \frac{e^x(\cos n\pi x + n\pi \sin n\pi x)}{1 + n^2\pi^2},$$

where $n = 1, 2, 3, \ldots$. Thus, the remaining coefficients are given by

$$a_n = 2 \int_0^1 e^x \cos n\pi x \, dx = \left. \frac{2e^x(\cos n\pi x + n\pi \sin n\pi x)}{1 + n^2\pi^2} \right|_0^2$$

$$= \frac{2e(\cos n\pi)}{1 + n^2\pi^2} - \frac{2e(1)}{1 + n^2\pi^2} = \frac{2[(-1)^n e - 1]}{1 + n^2\pi^2}, \qquad n = 1, 2, 3, \ldots,$$

where we have used the fact that $\cos n\pi = 1$ if $n$ is even and $\cos n\pi = -1$ if $n$ is odd. By substituting the above coefficients into the Fourier cosine series for $f$ given above, we obtain

$$e^x = e - 1 + 2 \sum_{n=1}^{\infty} \frac{(-1)^n e - 1}{1 + n^2\pi^2} \cos n\pi x,$$

for $0 < x < 1$. Note that we can say that $e^x$ for $0 < x < 1$ equals its Fourier cosine series because this series converges uniformly. To see this, first notice that the even $2\pi$-periodic extension of $f(x) = e^x$, $0 < x < 1$, is given by

$$f_e(x) = \begin{cases} e^{-x}, & -1 < x < 0, \\ e^x, & 0 < x < 1, \end{cases}$$

with $f_e(x+2\pi) = f_e(x)$. Since this extension is continuous on $(-\infty, \infty)$ and $f'_e(x)$ is piecewise continuous on $[-1, 1]$, Theorem 3 on page 601 of the text states that its Fourier series (which is the one we found above) converges uniformly to $f_e(x)$ on $[-1, 1]$ and so it converges uniformly to $f(x) = e^x$ on $(0, 1)$.

**17.** This problem is the same as the heat flow problem on page 580 of the text with $\beta = 5$, $L = \pi$ and $f(x) = 1 - \cos 2x$. Therefore, the formal solution to this problem is given in equations (11) and (12) on pages 582 and 583 of the text. Thus, the formal solution is

$$u(x, t) = \sum_{n=1}^{\infty} c_n e^{-5n^2 t} \sin nx \qquad 0 < x < \pi, \quad t > 0, \tag{10.6}$$

where

$$f(x) = 1 - \cos 2x = \sum_{n=1}^{\infty} c_n \sin nx.$$

Therefore, we must find the Fourier sine series for $1 - \cos 2x$. To do this, we can use equations (6) and (7) of Definition 2 on page 609 of the text. Hence, the coefficients are given by

$$c_n = \frac{2}{\pi} \int_0^\pi (1 - \cos 2x) \sin nx \, dx$$

$$= \frac{2}{\pi} \int_0^\pi \sin nx \, dx - \frac{2}{\pi} \int_0^\pi \cos 2x \sin nx \, dx, \qquad n = 1, 2, 3, \ldots.$$

Calculating the first integral above yields

$$\frac{2}{\pi} \int_0^\pi \sin nx \, dx = -\frac{2}{n\pi}(\cos n\pi - 1) = \frac{2}{n\pi}\left[1 - (-1)^n\right],$$

where we have used the fact that $\cos n\pi = 1$ if $n$ is even and $\cos n\pi = -1$ if $n$ is odd. To calculate the second integral, we use the fact that $2\cos\alpha\sin\beta = \sin(\beta - \alpha) + \sin(\beta + \alpha)$, to obtain

$$-\frac{2}{\pi}\int_0^\pi \cos 2x \sin nx\, dx = -\frac{1}{\pi}\left\{\int_0^\pi \sin[(n-2)x]\, dx + \int_0^\pi \sin[(n+2)x]\, dx\right\}$$

$$= \frac{1}{\pi(n-2)}\left\{\cos[(n-2)\pi] - 1\right\} + \frac{1}{\pi(n+2)}\left\{\cos[(n+2)\pi] - 1\right\}$$

$$= \frac{1}{\pi(n-2)}[(-1)^n - 1] + \frac{1}{\pi(n+2)}[(-1)^n - 1].$$

Combining these two integrals yields

$$c_n = \frac{2}{n\pi}[1 - (-1)^n] + \frac{1}{\pi(n-2)}[(-1)^n - 1] + \frac{1}{\pi(n+2)}[(-1)^n - 1]$$

$$= \begin{cases} 0, & \text{if } n \text{ is even,} \\ 4/(n\pi) - 2/[\pi(n-2)] - 2/[\pi(n+2)], & \text{if } n \text{ is odd,} \end{cases}$$

for $n = 1, 2, 3, \ldots$. Hence, we obtain the formal solution to this problem by substituting these coefficients into equation (10.6) above and setting $n = 2k - 1$. Therefore, we have

$$u(x,t) = \frac{2}{\pi}\sum_{k=1}^\infty \left[\frac{2}{2k-1} - \frac{1}{2k-3} - \frac{1}{2k+1}\right] e^{-5(2k-1)^2 t}\sin(2k-1)x.$$

**EXERCISES 10.5:   The Heat Equation, page 624**

**3.** If we let $\beta = 3$, $L = \pi$, and $f(x) = x$, we see that this problem has the same form as the problem in Example 1 on page 613 of the text. Therefore, we can find the formal solution to this problem by substituting these values into equation (14) on page 615 of the text. Hence, we have

$$u(x,t) = \sum_{n=0}^\infty c_n \cos e^{-3n^2 t}\cos nx, \qquad \text{where} \qquad f(x) = \sum_{n=0}^\infty c_n \cos nx. \qquad (10.7)$$

Thus, we must find the Fourier cosine series coefficients for $f(x) = x$, $0 < x < \pi$. (Note that the even $2\pi$-extension for $f(x) = x$, $0 < x < \pi$, which is given by

$$f_e(x) = \begin{cases} -x, & \text{for } -\pi < x < 0, \\ x, & \text{for } 0 < x < \pi, \end{cases}$$

with $f_e(x + 2\pi) = f_e(x)$, is continuous. Also note that its derivative is piecewise continuous on $[-\pi.\pi]$. Therefore, the Fourier series for this extension converges uniformly to $f_e$. This means that the equality sign in the second equation given in formula (10.7) above is justified for $0 < x < \pi$.) To find the required Fourier series coefficients, we use equations (4) and (5) given in Definition 2 on page 609 of the text. Hence, we have

$$x = \frac{a_0}{2} + \sum_{n=1}^{\infty} a_n \cos nx,$$

(so that $c_0 = a_0/2$ and $c_n = a_n$ for $n = 1, 2, 3, \ldots$) where

$$a_0 = \frac{2}{\pi} \int_0^{\pi} x \, dx = \frac{2}{\pi} \frac{x^2}{2} \Big|_0^{\pi} = \pi \quad \text{and} \quad a_n = \frac{2}{\pi} \int_0^{\pi} x \cos nx \, dx,$$

for $n = 1, 2, 3, \ldots$. To calculate the second integral above we use integration by parts to obtain

$$
\begin{aligned}
a_n &= \frac{2}{\pi} \int_0^{\pi} x \cos nx \, dx = \frac{2}{\pi} \left[ \frac{x}{n} \sin nx \Big|_0^{\pi} - \frac{1}{n} \int_0^{\pi} \sin nx \, dx \right] \\
&= \frac{2}{\pi} \left[ 0 - \frac{1}{n} \left( -\frac{\cos nx}{n} \Big|_0^{\pi} \right) \right] = \frac{2}{\pi n^2} (\cos n\pi - 1) = \frac{2}{\pi n^2} \left[ (-1)^n - 1 \right].
\end{aligned}
$$

Combining these results yields

$$
a_n = \begin{cases} \pi, & \text{if } n = 0, \\ -4/(\pi n^2), & \text{if } n \text{ is odd}, \\ 0, & \text{if } n \text{ is even and } n \neq 0, \end{cases}
$$

where $n = 0, 1, 2, \ldots$. The formal solution for this problem is, therefore, found by substituting these coefficients into the first equation given in formula (10.7) above. (Recall that $c_0 = a_0/2$ and $c_n = a_n$ for $n = 1, 2, 3, \ldots$.) Thus, we have

$$
\begin{aligned}
u(x, t) &= \frac{\pi}{2} e^{-0} \cos 0 - \sum_{k=0}^{\infty} \frac{4}{\pi(2k+1)^2} e^{-3(2k+1)^2 t} \cos(2k+1)x \\
&= \frac{\pi}{2} - \sum_{k=0}^{\infty} \frac{4}{\pi(2k+1)^2} e^{-3(2k+1)^2 t} \cos(2k+1)x
\end{aligned}
$$

# Chapter 10

**7.** This problem has nonhomogeneous boundary conditions and so has the same form as the problem in Example 2 on page 616 of the text. By comparing these two problems, we see that for this problem $\beta = 2$, $L = \pi$, $U_1 = 5$, $U_2 = 10$, and $f(x) = \sin 3x - \sin 5x$. To solve this problem, we assume that the solution consists of a steady state solution $v(x)$ and a transient solution $w(x, t)$. The steady state solution is given in equation (24) on page 617 of the text and is

$$v(x) = 5 + \frac{(10 - 5)x}{\pi} = 5 + \frac{5}{\pi} x .$$

The formal transient solution is given by equations (39) and (40) on page 619 of the text. By using these equations and making appropriate substitutions, we obtain

$$w(x, t) = \sum_{n=1}^{\infty} c_n e^{-2n^2 t} \sin nx , \qquad (10.8)$$

where the coefficients (the $c_n$'s) are given by

$$f(x) - v(x) = \sin 3x - \sin 5x - 5 - \frac{5}{\pi} x = \sum_{n=1}^{\infty} c_n \sin nx , \qquad 0 < x < \pi.$$

Therefore, we must find the Fourier sine series coefficients for the function $f(x) - v(x)$ for $0 < x < \pi$. Since the function $f(x) = \sin 3x - \sin 5x$ is already in the form of a sine series, we only need to find the Fourier sine series for $-v(x) = -5 - 5x/\pi$ and then add $\sin 3x - \sin 5x$ to this series. The resulting coefficients are the ones that we need. (Note that the Fourier sine series for $-5 - 5x/\pi$ will converge pointwise but not uniformly to $-5 - 5x/\pi$ for $0 < x < \pi$.) To find the desired Fourier series we use equations (6) and (7) in Definition 2 on page 609 of the text. Thus, with the appropriate substitutions, we have

$$-5 - \frac{5x}{\pi} = \sum_{n=1}^{\infty} b_n \sin nx , \qquad \text{where} \qquad b_n = \frac{2}{\pi} \int_0^{\pi} \left( -5 - \frac{5x}{\pi} \right) \sin nx \, dx .$$

To find the $b_n$'s, we will use integration by parts to obtain

$$b_n = -\frac{10}{\pi} \int_0^{\pi} \sin nx \, dx - \frac{10}{\pi^2} \int_0^{\pi} x \sin nx \, dx$$

646

$$= \frac{10}{n\pi}(\cos n\pi - 1) - \frac{10}{\pi^2}\left[-\frac{x}{n}\cos nx\Big|_0^\pi + \frac{1}{n}\int_0^\pi \cos nx\, dx\right]$$

$$= \frac{10}{n\pi}(\cos n\pi - 1) - \frac{10}{\pi^2}\left[-\frac{\pi}{n}\cos n\pi + 0\right]$$

$$= \frac{10}{n\pi}(2\cos n\pi - 1) = \frac{10}{n\pi}\left[2(-1)^n - 1\right], \qquad n = 1, 2, 3, \ldots .$$

Thus, the Fourier sine series for $\sin 3x - \sin 5x - 5 - 5x/\pi$ is given by

$$\sin 3x - \sin 5x - 5 - \frac{5x}{\pi} = \sin 3x - \sin 5x + \sum_{n=1}^{\infty} \frac{10}{n\pi}\left[2(-1)^n - 1\right]\sin nx$$

$$= \sin 3x - \sin 5x - \frac{30}{\pi}\sin x + \frac{10}{2\pi}\sin 2x - \frac{30}{3\pi}\sin 3x + \frac{10}{4\pi}\sin 4x$$

$$\qquad\qquad\qquad -\frac{30}{5\pi}\sin 5x + \sum_{n=6}^{\infty} \frac{10}{n\pi}\left[2(-1)^n - 1\right]\sin nx$$

$$= -\frac{30}{\pi}\sin x + \frac{5}{\pi}\sin 2x + \left(1 - \frac{10}{\pi}\right)\sin 3x + \frac{5}{2\pi}\sin 4x$$

$$\qquad\qquad -\left(1 + \frac{6}{\pi}\right)\sin 5x + \sum_{n=6}^{\infty} \frac{10}{n\pi}\left[2(-1)^n - 1\right]\sin nx .$$

We therefore obtain the formal transient solution by taking the coefficients from this Fourier series and substituting them in for the $c_n$ coefficients in equation (10.8) above. Thus, we find

$$w(x,t) = -\frac{30}{\pi}e^{-2(1)^2 t}\sin x + \frac{5}{\pi}e^{-2(2)^2 t}\sin 2x + \left(1 - \frac{10}{\pi}\right)e^{-2(3)^2 t}\sin 3x + \frac{5}{2\pi}e^{-2(4)^2 t}\sin 4x$$

$$\qquad -\left(1 + \frac{6}{\pi}\right)e^{-2(5)^2 t}\sin 5x + \sum_{n=6}^{\infty} \frac{10}{n\pi}\left[2(-1)^n - 1\right]e^{-2n^2 t}\sin nx ,$$

and so the formal solution to the original problem is given by

$$u(x,t) = v(x) + w(x,t)$$

$$= 5 + \frac{5x}{\pi} - \frac{30}{\pi}e^{-2t}\sin x + \frac{5}{\pi}e^{-8t}\sin 2x + \left(1 - \frac{10}{\pi}\right)e^{-18t}\sin 3x + \frac{5}{2\pi}e^{-32t}\sin 4x$$

$$\qquad -\left(1 + \frac{6}{\pi}\right)e^{-50t}\sin 5x + \sum_{n=6}^{\infty} \frac{10}{n\pi}\left[2(-1)^n - 1\right]e^{-2n^2 t}\sin nx .$$

647

# Chapter 10

**9.** Notice that this problem is a nonhomogeneous partial differential equation and has the same form as the problem given in Example 3 on page 618 of the text. By comparing these problems, we see that here $\beta = 1, P(x) = e^{-x}$, $L = \pi$, $U_1 = U_2 = 0$, and $f(x) = \sin 2x$. As in Example 3, we will assume that the solution is the sum of a steady state solution $v(x)$ and a transient solution $w(x, t)$. The steady state solution is the solution to the boundary value problem

$$v''(x) = -e^{-x}, \qquad 0 < x < \pi, \qquad v(0) = v(\pi) = 0.$$

Thus the steady state solution can be found either by solving this ODE or by substituting the appropriate values into equation (35) given on page 618 of the text. By either method we find

$$v(x) = \frac{e^{-\pi} - 1}{\pi} x - e^{-x} + 1.$$

The formal transient solution is then given by equations (39) and (40) on page 619 of the text. By making the appropriate substitutions into this equation, we obtain

$$w(x, t) = \sum_{n=1}^{\infty} c_n e^{-n^2 t} \sin nx, \tag{10.9}$$

where the $c_n$'s are given by

$$f(x) - v(x) = \sin 2x - \frac{e^{-\pi} - 1}{\pi} x + e^{-x} - 1 = \sum_{n=1}^{\infty} c_n \sin nx.$$

Hence, the problem is to find the Fourier sine coefficients for $f(x) - v(x)$. The first term, $f(x) = \sin 2x$, is already in the desired form. Therefore, the Fourier sine series for $f(x) - v(x)$ is

$$\sin 2x + \sum_{n=1}^{\infty} b_n \sin nx = b_1 \sin x + (b_2 + 1) \sin 2x + \sum_{n=3}^{\infty} b_n \sin nx,$$

where the $b_n$'s are the Fourier sine coefficients for $-v(x)$. This implies that if $n \neq 2$, then $c_n = b_n$ and if $n = 2$, then $c_n = b_n + 1$. The $b_n$ coefficients are given by equation (7) on page 609 of the text. Thus, we have

$$b_n = \frac{2}{\pi} \int_0^{\pi} \left[ -\frac{e^{-\pi} - 1}{\pi} x + e^{-x} - 1 \right] \sin nx \, dx$$

$$= \frac{2}{\pi}\left(-\frac{e^{-\pi}-1}{\pi}\right)\int_0^\pi x\sin nx\,dx + \frac{2}{\pi}\int_0^\pi e^{-x}\sin nx\,dx - \frac{2}{\pi}\int_0^\pi \sin nx\,dx .$$

We will calculate each integral separately. The first integral is found by using integration by parts. This yields

$$\frac{2}{\pi}\left(-\frac{e^{-\pi}-1}{\pi}\right)\int_0^\pi x\sin nx\,dx = \frac{-2(e^{-\pi}-1)}{\pi^2}\left[-\frac{x}{n}\cos nx\Big|_0^\pi + \frac{1}{n}\int_0^\pi \cos nx\,dx\right]$$

$$= \frac{-2(e^{-\pi}-1)}{\pi^2}\left[-\frac{\pi}{n}\cos n\pi + 0 + 0\right] = \frac{2(e^{-\pi}-1)}{n\pi}(-1)^n .$$

To find the second integral we use the table of integrals on the inside front cover of the text (or use integration by parts twice) to obtain

$$\frac{2}{\pi}\int_0^\pi e^{-x}\sin nx\,dx = \frac{2}{\pi}\left[\frac{-e^{-\pi}n\cos n\pi + n}{1+n^2}\right] = \frac{2n}{(1+n^2)\pi}\left[e^{-\pi}(-1)^{n+1}+1\right].$$

The last integral is found to be

$$-\frac{2}{\pi}\int_0^\pi \sin nx\,dx = \frac{2}{n\pi}\left[\cos n\pi - 1\right] = \frac{2}{n\pi}\left[(-1)^n - 1\right].$$

By combining all of these results, we find that the Fourier coefficients for $-v(x)$ are given by

$$b_n = \frac{2(e^{-\pi}-1)}{n\pi}(-1)^n + \frac{2n}{(1+n^2)\pi}\left[e^{-\pi}(-1)^{n+1}+1\right] + \frac{2}{n\pi}\left[(-1)^n-1\right].$$

Therefore, the coefficients for the formal transient solution are

$$c_n = \begin{cases} \dfrac{2(e^{-\pi}-1)}{n\pi}(-1)^n + \dfrac{2n}{(1+n^2)\pi}\left[e^{-\pi}(-1)^{n+1}+1\right] + \dfrac{2}{n\pi}\left[(-1)^n-1\right], & \text{if } n \neq 2, \\[4mm] \dfrac{e^{-\pi}-1}{\pi} + \dfrac{4}{5\pi}\left(1-e^{-\pi}\right)+1, & \text{if } n = 2. \end{cases}$$

Since the formal solution to the PDE given in this problem is the sum of its steady state solution and its transient solution, we find this final solution to be

$$u(x,t) = v(x) + w(x,t) = \frac{e^{-\pi}-1}{\pi}x - e^{-x} + 1 + \sum_{n=1}^\infty c_n e^{-n^2 t}\sin nx ,$$

where the $c_n$'s are given above.

**11.** Let $u(x,t) = X(x)T(t)$. Substituting $u(x,t) = X(x)T(t)$ into the PDE yields

$$T'(t)X(x) = 4X''(x)T(t) \qquad \Rightarrow \qquad \frac{T'(t)}{4T(t)} = \frac{X''(x)}{X(x)} = K,$$

where $K$ is a constant. Substituting the solution $u(x,t) = X(x)T(t)$ into the boundary conditions, we obtain

$$X'(0)T(t) = 0, \qquad X(\pi)T(t) = 0, \qquad t > 0.$$

Thus, we assume that $X'(0) = 0$ and $X(\pi) = 0$ since this allows the expressions above to be true for all $t > 0$ without implying that $u(x,t) \equiv 0$. Therefore, we have the two ODE's

$$\begin{aligned} X''(x) &= KX(x), \qquad 0 < x < \pi, \\ X'(0) &= X(\pi) = 0, \end{aligned} \tag{10.10}$$

and

$$T'(t) = 4KT(t), \qquad t > 0. \tag{10.11}$$

To solve boundary value problem (10.10), we will examine three cases.

Case 1: Assume $K = 0$. Now equation (10.10) becomes $X'' = 0$. The solution is $X(x) = ax+b$, where $a$ and $b$ are arbitrary constants. To find these constants we use the boundary conditions in (10.10). Thus, we have

$$X'(0) = a = 0 \qquad \Rightarrow \qquad a = 0 \qquad \Rightarrow \qquad X(x) = b,$$

and so

$$X(\pi) = b = 0 \qquad \Rightarrow \qquad b = 0.$$

Therefore, in this case we have only the trivial solution.

Case 2: Assume $K > 0$. In this case the auxiliary equation for equation (10.10) is $r^2 - K = 0$. The roots to this equation are $r = \pm\sqrt{K}$. Thus, the solution is

$$X(x) = C_1 e^{\sqrt{K}x} + C_2 e^{-\sqrt{K}x},$$

where $C_1$ and $C_2$ are arbitrary constants. To find these constants we again use the boundary conditions in (10.10). We first note that

$$X'(x) = C_1\sqrt{K}e^{\sqrt{K}x} - C_2\sqrt{K}e^{-\sqrt{K}x}.$$

Therefore,

$$X'(0) = C_1\sqrt{K} - C_2\sqrt{K} = 0 \quad \Rightarrow \quad C_1 = C_2 \quad \Rightarrow \quad X(x) = C_1\left(e^{\sqrt{K}x} + e^{-\sqrt{K}x}\right).$$

The other boundary condition implies that

$$X(\pi) = C_1\left(e^{\sqrt{K}\pi} + e^{-\sqrt{K}\pi}\right) = 0 \quad \Rightarrow \quad C_1\left(e^{2\sqrt{K}\pi} + 1\right) = 0.$$

The only way that the final equation above can be zero is for $C_1$ to be zero. Therefore, we again obtain only the trivial solution.

Case 3: Assume $K < 0$, so $-K > 0$. Then the auxiliary equation for equation (10.10) has the roots $r = \pm\sqrt{K} = \pm i\sqrt{-K}$. Therefore, the solution is

$$X(x) = C_1\sin\left(\sqrt{-K}x\right) + C_2\cos\left(\sqrt{-K}x\right)$$
$$\Rightarrow \quad X'(x) = C_1\sqrt{-K}\cos\left(\sqrt{-K}x\right) - C_2\sqrt{-K}\sin\left(\sqrt{-K}x\right).$$

Using the boundary condition $X'(0) = 0$, we obtain

$$0 = X'(0) = C_1\sqrt{-K}\cos 0 - C_2\sqrt{-K}\sin 0 = C_1\sqrt{-K} \quad \Rightarrow \quad C_1 = 0.$$

Hence, $X(x) = C_2\cos\left(\sqrt{-K}x\right)$. Applying the other boundary condition yields

$$0 = X(\pi) = C_2\cos\left(\sqrt{-K}\pi\right)$$
$$\Rightarrow \quad \sqrt{-K}\pi = (2n+1)\frac{\pi}{2} \quad \Rightarrow \quad K = -\frac{(2n+1)^2}{4}, \quad n = 0, 1, 2, \ldots.$$

Therefore, nontrivial solutions to problem (10.10) above are given by

$$X_n(x) = c_n\cos\left(\frac{2n+1}{2}x\right), \quad n = 0, 1, 2, \ldots.$$

Chapter 10

By substituting the values of $K$ into equation (10.11), we obtain

$$T'(t) = -(2n+1)^2 T(t), \qquad t > 0.$$

This is a separable differential equation, and we find

$$\frac{dT}{T} = -(2n+1)^2\, dt \qquad \Rightarrow \qquad \int \frac{dT}{T} = -(2n+1)^2 \int dt$$

$$\Rightarrow \qquad \ln|T| = -(2n+1)^2 t + A \qquad \Rightarrow \qquad T_n(t) = b_n e^{-(2n+1)^2 t}, \qquad n = 0, 1, 2, \dots,$$

(where $b_n = \pm e^A$). Hence, by the superposition principle (and since $u_n(x,t) = X_n(x)T_n(t)$), we see that the formal solution to the original PDE is

$$u(x,t) = \sum_{n=0}^{\infty} b_n e^{-(2n+1)^2 t} c_n \cos\left(\frac{2n+1}{2} x\right) = \sum_{n=0}^{\infty} a_n e^{-(2n+1)^2 t} \cos\left[\left(n+\frac{1}{2}\right)x\right], \qquad (10.12)$$

where $a_n = b_n c_n$. To find the $a_n$'s, we use the initial condition to obtain

$$u(x,0) = f(x) = \sum_{n=0}^{\infty} a_n \cos\left[\left(n+\frac{1}{2}\right)x\right]. \qquad (10.13)$$

Therefore, the formal solution to this PDE is given by equation (10.12), where the $a_n$'s are given by equation (10.13).

17. This problem is similar to the problem given in Example 4 on page 619 of the text with $\beta = 1$, $L = W = \pi$, and $f(x,y) = y$. The formal solution to this problem is given in equation (52) on page 621 of the text with its coefficients given on pages 621 and 622 in equations (54) and (55). By making appropriate substitutions in the first of these equations, we see that the formal solution to this problem is

$$u(x,y,t) = \sum_{m=0}^{\infty}\sum_{n=1}^{\infty} a_{mn} e^{-(m^2+n^2)t} \cos mx \sin ny. \qquad (10.14)$$

We can find the coefficients, $a_{0n}$, $n = 1, 2, 3, \dots$, by using equation (54) on page 621 of the text with the appropriate substitutions. This yields

$$a_{0n} = \frac{2}{\pi^2}\int_0^\pi\int_0^\pi y \sin ny \, dx \, dy = \frac{2}{\pi^2}\int_0^\pi y \sin ny \left[\int_0^\pi dx\right] dy$$

652

$$= \frac{2}{\pi} \int_0^\pi y \sin ny \, dy \qquad \text{(use integration by parts)}$$

$$= \frac{2}{\pi} \left[ -\frac{y}{n} \cos ny \Big|_0^\pi + \frac{1}{n} \int_0^\pi \cos ny \, dy \right]$$

$$= \frac{2}{\pi} \left[ -\frac{\pi}{n} \cos n\pi + \left( \frac{1}{n^2} \sin ny \Big|_0^\pi \right) \right] = \frac{2}{\pi} \left( -\frac{\pi}{n} \cos n\pi \right) = \frac{2}{n} (-1)^{n+1} .$$

We will use equation (55) on page 622 of the text to find the other coefficients. Thus for $m \geq 1$ and $n \geq 1$, we have

$$a_{mn} = \frac{4}{\pi^2} \int_0^\pi \int_0^\pi y \cos mx \sin ny \, dx \, dy$$

$$= \frac{4}{\pi^2} \int_0^\pi y \sin ny \left( \int_0^\pi \cos mx \, dx \right) dy = \frac{4}{\pi^2} \int_0^\pi y \sin ny(0) \, dy = 0.$$

The formal solution to this problem is found by substituting these coefficients into equation (10.14). To do this we first note that the coefficients for any terms containing $m \neq 0$ are zero. Hence, only terms containing $m = 0$ will appears in the summation. Therefore, the formal solution is given by

$$u(x, y, t) = \sum_{n=1}^\infty \frac{2}{n} (-1)^{n+1} e^{-n^2 t} \sin ny = 2 \sum_{n=1}^\infty \frac{(-1)^{n+1}}{n} e^{-n^2 t} \sin ny .$$

## EXERCISES 10.6:   The Wave Equation, page 636

1. This problem has the form of the problem given in equations (1)–(4) on page 625 of the text. Here, however, $\alpha = 1$, $L = 1$, $f(x) = x(1 - x)$, and $g(x) = \sin 7\pi x$. This problem is consistent because

$$f(0) = 0 = f(1), \qquad \text{and} \qquad g(0) = \sin 0 = 0 = \sin 7\pi = g(1).$$

The solution to this problem was derived in Section 10.2 of the text and given again in equation (5) on page 625 of the text. Making appropriate substitutions in equation (5) yields a formal

# Chapter 10

solution given by

$$u(x,t) = \sum_{n=1}^{\infty} [a_n \cos n\pi t + b_n \sin n\pi t] \sin n\pi x. \qquad (10.15)$$

To find the $a_n$'s we note that they are the Fourier sine coefficients for $x(1-x)$ and so are given by equation (7) on page 609 of the text. Thus, for $n = 1, 2, 3, \ldots$, we have

$$a_n = 2 \int_0^1 x(1-x) \sin n\pi x \, dx = 2 \left[ \int_0^1 x \sin n\pi x \, dx - \int_0^1 x^2 \sin n\pi x \, dx \right].$$

We will use integration by parts to calculate these two integrals. This yields

$$\int_0^1 x \sin n\pi x \, dx = -\frac{1}{n\pi} \cos n\pi = -\frac{1}{n\pi}(-1)^n$$

and

$$\int_0^1 x^2 \sin n\pi x \, dx = -\frac{1}{n\pi} \cos n\pi - \frac{2}{n^2\pi^2}\left(-\frac{1}{n\pi}\cos n\pi + \frac{1}{n\pi}\right) = -\frac{1}{n\pi}(-1)^n + \frac{2}{n^3\pi^3}[(-1)^n - 1].$$

Therefore, for $n = 1, 2, 3, \ldots$, we see that

$$a_n = 2\left\{ -\frac{1}{n\pi}(-1)^n + \frac{1}{n\pi}(-1)^n - \frac{2}{n^3\pi^3}[(-1)^n - 1] \right\} = -\frac{4}{n^3\pi^3}[(-1)^n - 1].$$

This can also be expressed as

$$a_n = \begin{cases} 0, & \text{if } n \text{ is even,} \\ 8/(n^3\pi^3), & \text{if } n \text{ is odd.} \end{cases}$$

The $b_n$'s were found in equation (7) on page 626. By making appropriate substitutions in this equations we have

$$\sin 7\pi x = \sum_{n=1}^{\infty} n\pi b_n \sin n\pi x.$$

From this we see that for $n = 7$

$$7\pi b_7 = 1 \qquad \Rightarrow \qquad b_7 = \frac{1}{7\pi},$$

654

and for all other $n$'s, $b_n = 0$. By substituting these coefficients into the formal solution given in equation (10.15) above, we obtain

$$u(x,t) = \frac{1}{7\pi} \sin 7\pi t \sin 7\pi x + \sum_{k=0}^{\infty} \frac{8}{[(2k+1)\pi]^3} \cos[(2k+1)\pi t] \sin[(2k+1)\pi x].$$

**5.** First we note that this problem is consistent because

$$g(0) = 0 = g(L) \qquad \text{and} \qquad f(0) = 0 = f(L).$$

The formal solution to this problem is given in equation (5) on page 625 of the text with the coefficients given in equations (6) and (7) on page 626. By equation (7), we see that

$$g(x) = 0 = \sum_{n=1}^{\infty} b_n \frac{n\pi\alpha}{L} \sin\left(\frac{n\pi x}{L}\right).$$

Thus, each term in this infinite series must be zero and so $b_n = 0$ for all $n$'s. Therefore, the formal solution given in equation (5) on page 625 of the text becomes

$$u(x,t) = \sum_{n=1}^{\infty} a_n \cos\left(\frac{n\pi\alpha t}{L}\right) \sin\left(\frac{n\pi x}{L}\right). \qquad (10.16)$$

To find the $a_n$'s we note that by equation (6) on page 626 of the text these coefficients are the Fourier sine coefficients for $f(x)$. Therefore, by using equation (7) on page 609 of the text, for $n = 1, 2, 3, \ldots$ we have

$$\begin{aligned}
a_n &= \frac{2}{L} \int_0^L f(x) \sin\left(\frac{n\pi x}{L}\right) dx = \frac{2}{L} \left[ \frac{h_0}{a} \int_0^a x \sin\left(\frac{n\pi x}{L}\right) dx + h_0 \int_a^L \frac{L-x}{L-a} \sin\left(\frac{n\pi x}{L}\right) dx \right] \\
&= \frac{2h_0}{L} \left[ \frac{1}{a} \int_0^a x \sin\left(\frac{n\pi x}{L}\right) dx + \frac{L}{L-a} \int_a^L \sin\left(\frac{n\pi x}{L}\right) dx - \frac{1}{L-a} \int_a^L x \sin\left(\frac{n\pi x}{L}\right) dx \right].
\end{aligned}$$

By using integration by parts, we find

$$\int x \sin\left(\frac{n\pi x}{L}\right) dx = -\frac{xL}{n\pi} \cos\left(\frac{n\pi x}{L}\right) + \frac{L^2}{n^2\pi^2} \sin\left(\frac{n\pi x}{L}\right).$$

Therefore, for $n = 1, 2, 3, \ldots$, the coefficients become

$$a_n = \frac{2h_0}{L} \left\{ \frac{1}{a} \left[ -\frac{aL}{n\pi} \cos\left(\frac{n\pi a}{L}\right) + \frac{L^2}{n^2\pi^2} \sin\left(\frac{n\pi a}{L}\right) \right] - \frac{L^2}{n\pi(L-a)} \left[ \cos n\pi - \cos\left(\frac{n\pi a}{L}\right) \right] \right.$$
$$\left. -\frac{1}{L-a} \left[ -\frac{L^2}{n\pi} \cos n\pi + \frac{aL}{n\pi} \cos\left(\frac{n\pi a}{L}\right) \right] + \frac{L^2}{n^2\pi^2} \left[ \sin n\pi - \sin\left(\frac{n\pi a}{L}\right) \right] \right\}.$$

After simplifying, this becomes

$$a_n = \frac{2h_0 L^2}{n^2\pi^2 a(L-a)} \sin\left(\frac{n\pi a}{L}\right), \qquad n = 1, 2, 3, \ldots.$$

By substituting this result into equation (10.16) above, we obtain the formal solution to this problem given by

$$u(x,t) = \frac{2h_0 L^2}{\pi^2 a(L-a)} \sum_{n=1}^{\infty} \frac{1}{n^2} \sin\left(\frac{n\pi a}{L}\right) \cos\left(\frac{n\pi a t}{L}\right) \sin\left(\frac{n\pi x}{L}\right).$$

7. If we let $\alpha = 1$, $h(x,t) = tx$, $L = \pi$, $f(x) = \sin x$, and $g(x) = 5\sin 2x - 3\sin 5x$, then we see that this problem has the same form as the problem given in Example 1 on page 627 of the text. The formal solution to the problem in Example 1 is given in equation (16) on page 628 of the text. Therefore, with the appropriate substitutions, the formal solution to this problem is

$$u(x,t) = \sum_{n=1}^{\infty} \left\{ a_n \cos nt + b_n \sin nt + \frac{1}{n} \int_0^t h_n(s) \sin[n(t-s)] \, ds \right\} \sin nx. \qquad (10.17)$$

The $a_n$'s are shown in equation (14) on page 628 of the text to satisfy

$$\sin x = \sum_{n=1}^{\infty} a_n \sin nx.$$

Thus, the only nonzero term in this infinite series is the term for $n = 1$. Therefore, we see that $a_1 = 1$ and $a_n = 0$ for $n \neq 1$. The $b_n$'s are given in equation (15) on page 628 of the text and so must satisfy

$$5\sin 2x - 3\sin 5x = \sum_{n=1}^{\infty} nb_n \sin nx,$$

which implies that

$$2b_2 = 5 \quad \Rightarrow \quad b_2 = \frac{5}{2} \quad \text{and} \quad 5b_5 = -3 \quad \Rightarrow \quad b_5 = -\frac{3}{5},$$

and $b_n = 0$ for all other values of $n$. To calculate the integral given in the formal solution we must first find the functions $h_n(t)$. To do this, we note that in Example 1, the functions $h_n(t)$, $n = 1, 2, \ldots$, are the Fourier sine coefficients for $h(x, t) = tx$ with $t$ fixed. These functions are given below equation (13) on page 628 of the text. (We will assume proper convergence of this series.) Thus, we have

$$h_n(t) = \frac{2}{\pi} \int_0^\pi tx \sin nx \, dx = \frac{2t}{\pi} \int_0^\pi x \sin nx \, dx$$

$$= \frac{2t}{\pi} \left[ -\frac{\pi}{n} \cos n\pi + 0 + \frac{1}{n^2} \sin n\pi - \sin 0 \right] = -\frac{2t}{\pi} \cos n\pi = \frac{2t}{\pi}(-1)^{n+1},$$

$n = 1, 2, 3, \ldots$, where we have used integration by parts to calculate this integral. Substituting this result into the integral in equation (10.17) above yields

$$\int_0^t h_n(s) \sin[n(t - s)] \, ds = \int_0^t \frac{2s}{\pi}(-1)^{n+1} \sin[n(t - s)] \, ds$$

$$= \frac{2(-1)^{n+1}}{n} \left[ \frac{t}{n} - \frac{\sin nt}{n^2} \right] = \frac{2(-1)^{n+1}}{n^3} (nt - \sin nt),$$

where $n = 1, 2, 3, \ldots$. By plugging the $a_n$'s, the $b_n$'s, and the result we just found into equation (10.17), we obtain the formal solution to this problem given by

$$u(x, t) = \cos t \sin x + \frac{5}{2} \sin 2t \sin 2x - \frac{3}{5} \sin 5t \sin 5x + \sum_{n=1}^\infty \frac{1}{n} \left[ \frac{2(-1)^{n+1}}{n^3} (nt - \sin nt) \right] \sin nx$$

$$= \cos t \sin x + \frac{5}{2} \sin 2t \sin 2x - \frac{3}{5} \sin 5t \sin 5x + 2 \sum_{n=1}^\infty \frac{(-1)^{n+1}}{n^3} \left( t - \frac{\sin nt}{n} \right) \sin nx.$$

**11.** We will assume that a solution to this problem has the form $u(x, t) = X(x)T(t)$. Substituting this expression into the partial differential equations yields

$$X(x)T''(t) + X(x)T'(t) + X(x)T(t) = \alpha^2 X''(x)T(t).$$

Dividing this equation by $\alpha^2 X(x)T(t)$ yields

$$\frac{T''(t) + T'(t) + T(t)}{\alpha^2 T(t)} = \frac{X''(x)}{X(x)}.$$

657

Chapter 10

Since these two expressions must be equal for all $x$ in $(0, L)$ **and** all $t > 0$, they can not vary. Therefore, they must both equal a constant, say $K$. This gives us the two ordinary differential equations

$$\frac{T''(t) + T'(t) + T(t)}{\alpha^2 T(t)} = K \quad \Rightarrow \quad T''(t) + T'(t) + \left(1 - \alpha^2 K\right) T(t) = 0 \qquad (10.18)$$

and

$$\frac{X''(x)}{X(x)} = K \quad \Rightarrow \quad X''(x) - KX(x) = 0. \qquad (10.19)$$

Substituting $u(x, t) = X(x)T(t)$ into the boundary conditions, $u(0, t) = u(L, t) = 0$, $t > 0$, we obtain

$$X(0)T(t) = 0 = X(L)T(t), \qquad t > 0.$$

Since we are seeking a nontrivial solution to the partial differential equation, we do not want $T(t) \equiv 0$. Therefore, for the above equation to be zero, we must have $X(0) = X(L) = 0$. Combining this fact with equation (10.19) above yields the boundary value problem given by

$$X''(x) - KX(x) = 0, \qquad \text{with} \qquad X(0) = X(L) = 0.$$

This problem was solved in Section 10.2 of the text. There we found that for $K = -(n\pi/L)^2$, $n = 1, 2, 3, \ldots$, we obtain nonzero solutions of the form

$$X_n(x) = A_n \sin\left(\frac{n\pi x}{L}\right), \qquad n = 1, 2, 3, \ldots. \qquad (10.20)$$

Plugging these values of $K$ into equation (10.18) above yields the family of linear ordinary differential equations with constant coefficients given by

$$T''(t) + T'(t) + \left(1 + \frac{\alpha^2 n^2 \pi^2}{L^2}\right) T(t) = 0, \qquad n = 1, 2, 3, \ldots. \qquad (10.21)$$

The auxiliary equations associated with these ODE's are

$$r^2 + r + \left(1 + \frac{\alpha^2 n^2 \pi^2}{L^2}\right) = 0.$$

By using the quadratic formula, we obtain the roots to these auxiliary equations. Thus, we have

$$r = \frac{-1 \pm \sqrt{1 - 4\left(1 + \frac{\alpha^2 n^2 \pi^2}{L^2}\right)}}{2} = -\frac{1}{2} \pm \frac{\sqrt{L^2 - 4L^2 - 4\alpha^2 n^2 \pi^2}}{2L}$$

658

$$= -\frac{1}{2} \pm \frac{\sqrt{3L^2 + 4\alpha^2 n^2 \pi^2}}{2L} i, \qquad n = 1, 2, 3, \ldots.$$

Hence, the solutions to the linear equations given in equation (10.21) above are

$$T_n(t) = e^{-t/2} \left[ B_n \cos\left( \frac{\sqrt{3L^2 + 4\alpha^2 n^2 \pi^2}}{2L} t \right) + C_n \sin\left( \frac{\sqrt{3L^2 + 4\alpha^2 n^2 \pi^2}}{2L} t \right) \right],$$

for $n = 1, 2, 3, \ldots$. By letting

$$\beta_n = \frac{\sqrt{3L^2 + 4\alpha^2 n^2 \pi^2}}{2L}, \tag{10.22}$$

for $n = 1, 2, 3, \ldots$, this family of solutions can be more easily written as

$$T_n(t) = e^{-t/2} \left[ B_n \cos \beta_n t + C_n \sin \beta_n t \right].$$

Substituting the solutions we have just found and the solutions given in equation (10.20) above into $u(x,t) = X(x)T(t)$, yields solutions to the original partial differential equation given by

$$u_n(x,t) = X_n(x) T_n(t) = A_n e^{-t/2} \left[ B_n \cos \beta_n t + C_n \sin \beta_n t \right] \sin\left( \frac{n\pi x}{L} \right), \qquad n = 1, 2, 3, \ldots.$$

By the superposition principle, we see that solutions to the PDE will have the form

$$u(x,t) = \sum_{n=1}^{\infty} e^{-t/2} \left[ a_n \cos \beta_n t + b_n \sin \beta_n t \right] \sin\left( \frac{n\pi x}{L} \right),$$

where $\beta_n$ is given in equation (10.22) above, $a_n = A_n B_n$, and $b_n = A_n C_n$. To find the coefficients $a_n$ and $b_n$, we use the initial conditions $u(x,0) = f(x)$ and $\partial u(x,0)/\partial t = 0$. Therefore, since

$$\frac{\partial u(x,t)}{\partial t} = \sum_{n=1}^{\infty} \left\{ (-1/2)\, e^{-t/2} \left[ a_n \cos \beta_n t + b_n \sin \beta_n t \right] \right.$$

$$\left. + e^{-t/2} \left[ -a_n \beta_n \sin \beta_n t + b_n \beta_n \cos \beta_n t \right] \right\} \sin\left( \frac{n\pi x}{L} \right),$$

we have

$$\frac{\partial u(x,0)}{\partial t} = 0 = \sum_{n=1}^{\infty} \left\{ -\frac{a_n}{2} + b_n \beta_n \right\} \sin\left( \frac{n\pi x}{L} \right).$$

Chapter 10

Hence, each term in this infinite series must be zero which implies that

$$-\frac{a_n}{2} + b_n\beta_n = 0 \quad \Rightarrow \quad b_n = \frac{a_n}{2\beta_n}, \quad n = 1, 2, 3, \ldots .$$

Thus, we can write

$$u(x,t) = \sum_{n=1}^{\infty} a_n e^{-t/2}\left[\cos\beta_n t + \frac{1}{2\beta_n}\sin\beta_n t\right]\sin\left(\frac{n\pi x}{L}\right), \tag{10.23}$$

where $\beta_n$ is given above in equation (10.22). To find the $a_n$'s, we use the remaining initial condition to obtain

$$u(x,0) = f(x) = \sum_{n=1}^{\infty} a_n \sin\left(\frac{n\pi x}{L}\right).$$

Therefore, the $a_n$'s are the Fourier sine coefficients of $f(x)$ and so satisfy

$$a_n = \frac{2}{L}\int_0^L f(x)\sin\left(\frac{n\pi x}{L}\right) dx . \tag{10.24}$$

Combining all of these results, we see that a formal solution to the telegraph problem is given by equation (10.23) where $\beta_n$ and $a_n$ are given in equation (10.22) and (10.24), respectively.

15. This problem has the form of the problem solved in Example 2 on page 631 of the text with $f(x) = g(x) = x$. There it was found that d'Alembert's formula given in equation (32) on page 631 of the text is a solution to this problem. By making the appropriate substitutions in this equation (and noting that $f(x+\alpha t) = x + \alpha t$ and $f(x-\alpha t) = x - \alpha t$), we obtain the solution

$$u(x,t) = \frac{1}{2}[(x+\alpha t)+(x-\alpha t)] + \frac{1}{2\alpha}\int_{x-\alpha t}^{x+\alpha t} s\,ds = x + \frac{1}{2\alpha}\left[\frac{s^2}{2}\Big|_{x-\alpha t}^{x+\alpha t}\right]$$

$$= x + \frac{1}{4\alpha}[(x+\alpha t)^2 - (x-\alpha t)^2] = x + \frac{1}{4\alpha}[4\alpha tx] = x + tx .$$

**EXERCISES 10.7: Laplace's Equation, page 649**

3. To solve this problem using separation of variables, we will assume that a solution has the form $u(x,y) = X(x)Y(y)$. Making this substitution into the partial differential equation yields

$$X''(x)Y(y) + X(x)Y''(y) = 0.$$

660

By dividing the above equation by $X(x)Y(y)$, we obtain

$$\frac{X''(x)}{X(x)} + \frac{Y''(y)}{Y(y)} = 0.$$

Since this equation must be true for $0 < x < \pi$ and $0 < y < \pi$, there must be a constant $K$ such that

$$\frac{X''(x)}{X(x)} = -\frac{Y''(y)}{Y(y)} = K, \qquad 0 < x < \pi, \quad \text{and} \quad 0 < y < \pi.$$

This leads to the two ordinary differential equations given by

$$X''(x) - KX(x) = 0 \tag{10.25}$$

and

$$Y''(y) + KY(y) = 0 \tag{10.26}$$

By making the substitution $u(x,y) = X(x)Y(y)$ into the first boundary conditions, that is, $u(0,y) = u(\pi,y) = 0$, we obtain

$$X(0)Y(y) = X(\pi)Y(y) = 0.$$

Since we do not want the trivial solution which would be obtained if we let $Y(y) \equiv 0$, these boundary conditions imply that

$$X(0) = X(\pi) = 0.$$

Combining these boundary conditions with equation (10.25) above yields the boundary value problem

$$X''(x) - KX(x) = 0, \qquad \text{with} \qquad X(0) = X(\pi) = 0.$$

To solve this problem, we will consider three cases.

Case 1: $K = 0$. For this case, the differential equation becomes $X''(x) = 0$, which has solutions $X(x) = A + Bx$. By applying the first of the boundary conditions, we obtain

$$X(0) = A = 0 \qquad \Rightarrow \qquad X(x) = Bx.$$

The second boundary condition yields

$$X(\pi) = B\pi = 0 \qquad \Rightarrow \qquad B = 0.$$

Chapter 10

Thus, in this case we obtain only the trivial solution.

Case 2: $K > 0$. In this case, the auxiliary equation associated with this differential equation is $r^2 - K = 0$, which has the real roots $r = \pm\sqrt{K}$. Thus, solutions to this problem are given by

$$X(x) = Ae^{\sqrt{K}x} + Be^{-\sqrt{K}x}.$$

Applying the boundary conditions yields

$$X(0) = A + B = 0 \quad \Rightarrow \quad A = -B \quad \Rightarrow \quad X(x) = -Be^{\sqrt{K}x} + Be^{-\sqrt{K}x}$$

and

$$X(\pi) = -Be^{\sqrt{K}\pi} + Be^{-\sqrt{K}\pi} = 0 \quad \Rightarrow \quad -B\left(e^{2\sqrt{K}\pi} - 1\right) = 0.$$

This last expression is true only if $K = 0$ or if $B = 0$. Since we are assuming that $K > 0$, we must have $B = 0$ which means that $A = -B = 0$. Therefore, in this case we again find only the trivial solution.

Case 3: $K < 0$. The auxiliary equation associated with the differential equation in this case has the complex valued roots $r = \pm\sqrt{-K}i$, (where $-K > 0$). Therefore, solutions to the ODE for this case are given by

$$X(x) = A\cos\left(\sqrt{-K}x\right) + B\sin\left(\sqrt{-K}x\right).$$

By applying the boundary conditions, we obtain

$$X(0) = A = 0 \quad \Rightarrow \quad X(x) = B\sin\left(\sqrt{-K}x\right)$$

and

$$X(\pi) = B\sin\left(\sqrt{-K}\pi\right) = 0 \quad \Rightarrow \quad \sqrt{-K} = n \quad \Rightarrow \quad K = -n^2, \quad n = 1, 2, 3, \ldots,$$

where we have assumed that $B \neq 0$ since this would lead to the trivial solution. Therefore, nontrivial solutions $X_n(x) = B_n\sin nx$ are obtained when $K = -n^2$, $n = 1, 2, 3\ldots$.

To solve the differential equation given in equation (10.26) above, we use these values for $K$. This yields the family of linear ordinary differential equations given by

$$Y''(y) - n^2 Y(y) = 0, \qquad n = 1, 2, 3, \ldots.$$

The auxiliary equations associated with these ODE's are $r^2 - n^2 = 0$, which have the real roots $r = \pm n$, $n = 1, 2, 3, \ldots$. Hence, the solutions to this family of differential equations are given by

$$Y_n(y) = C_n e^{ny} + D_n e^{-ny}, \qquad n = 1, 2, 3, \ldots.$$

With the substitutions $K_{1n} = C_n + D_n$ and $K_{2n} = C_n - D_n$, so that

$$C_n = \frac{K_{1n} + K_{2n}}{2}, \qquad \text{and} \qquad D_n = \frac{K_{1n} - K_{2n}}{2},$$

we see that these solutions can be written as

$$\begin{aligned} Y_n(y) &= \frac{K_{1n} + K_{2n}}{2} e^{ny} + \frac{K_{1n} - K_{2n}}{2} e^{-ny} \\ &= K_{1n} \frac{e^{ny} + e^{-ny}}{2} + K_{2n} \frac{e^{ny} - e^{-ny}}{2} = K_{1n} \cosh ny + K_{2n} \sinh ny. \end{aligned}$$

This last expression can in turn be written as

$$Y_n(y) = A_n \sinh(ny + E_n),$$

where $A_n = K_{2n}^2 - K_{1n}^2$ and $E_n = \tanh^{-1}(K_{1n}/K_{2n})$. (See Problem 18.)

The last boundary condition $u(x, \pi) = X(x)Y(\pi) = 0$ implies that $Y(\pi) = 0$ (since we do not want the trivial solution). Therefore, by substituting $\pi$ into the solutions just found, we obtain

$$Y_n(\pi) = A_n \sinh(n\pi + E_n).$$

Since we do not want $A_n = 0$, this implies that $\sinh(n\pi + E_n) = 0$. This will be true only if $n\pi + E_n = 0$ or in other words if $E_n = -n\pi$. Substituting these expressions for $E_n$ into the family of solutions we found for $Y(y)$, yields

$$Y_n(y) = A_n \sinh(ny - n\pi).$$

Therefore, substituting the solutions just found for $X(x)$ and $Y(y)$ into $u_n(x,y) = X_n(x)Y_n(y)$ we see that

$$u_n(x,y) = a_n \sin nx \sinh(ny - n\pi),$$

where $a_n = A_n B_n$. By the superposition principle, a formal solution to the original partial differential equation is given by

$$u(x,y) = \sum_{n=1}^{\infty} u_n(x,y) = \sum_{n=1}^{\infty} a_n \sin nx \sinh(ny - n\pi). \tag{10.27}$$

In order to find an expression for the coefficients $a_n$, we will apply the remaining boundary condition, $u(x,0) = f(x)$. From this condition, we obtain

$$u(x,0) = f(x) = \sum_{n=1}^{\infty} a_n \sin nx \sinh(-n\pi),$$

which implies that $a_n \sinh(-n\pi)$ are the coefficients of the Fourier sine series of $f(x)$. Therefore, by equation (7) on page 609 of the text, we see that (with $T = \pi$)

$$a_n \sinh(-n\pi) = \frac{2}{\pi} \int_0^\pi f(x) \sin nx \, dx \qquad \Rightarrow \qquad a_n = \frac{2}{\pi \sinh(-n\pi)} \int_0^\pi f(x) \sin nx \, dx.$$

Thus, a formal solution to this ODE is given in equation (10.27) with the $a_n$'s given by the equation above.

5. This problem has two nonhomogeneous boundary conditions, and, therefore, we will solve two PDE problems, one for each of these boundary conditions. These problems are

$$\frac{\partial^2 u}{\partial x^2} + \frac{\partial^2 u}{\partial y^2} = 0, \qquad 0 < x < \pi, \quad 0 < y < 1;$$

$$\frac{\partial u(0,y)}{\partial x} = \frac{\partial u(\pi, y)}{\partial x} = 0, \qquad 0 \le y \le 1,$$

$$u(x,0) = \cos x - \cos 3x, \qquad u(x,1) = 0, \qquad 0 \le x \le \pi,$$

and

$$\frac{\partial^2 u}{\partial x^2} + \frac{\partial^2 u}{\partial y^2} = 0, \qquad 0 < x < \pi, \quad 0 < y < 1;$$

$$\frac{\partial u(0,y)}{\partial x} = \frac{\partial u(\pi,y)}{\partial x} = 0, \qquad 0 \le y \le 1,$$
$$u(x,0) = 0, \qquad u(x,1) = \cos 2x, \qquad 0 \le x \le \pi.$$

If $u_1$ and $u_2$ are solutions to the first and second problems, respectively, then $u = u_1 + u_2$ will be a solution to the original problem. To see this notice that

$$\frac{\partial^2 u}{\partial x^2} + \frac{\partial^2 u}{\partial y^2} = \left(\frac{\partial^2 u_1}{\partial x^2} + \frac{\partial^2 u_2}{\partial x^2}\right) + \left(\frac{\partial^2 u_1}{\partial y^2} + \frac{\partial^2 u_2}{\partial y^2}\right)$$
$$= \left(\frac{\partial^2 u_1}{\partial x^2} + \frac{\partial^2 u_1}{\partial y^2}\right) + \left(\frac{\partial^2 u_2}{\partial x^2} + \frac{\partial^2 u_2}{\partial y^2}\right) = 0 + 0 = 0,$$
$$\frac{\partial u(0,y)}{\partial x} = \frac{\partial u_1(0,y)}{\partial x} + \frac{\partial u_2(0,y)}{\partial x} = 0 + 0 = 0,$$
$$\frac{\partial u(\pi,y)}{\partial x} = \frac{\partial u_1(\pi,y)}{\partial x} + \frac{\partial u_2(\pi,y)}{\partial x} = 0 + 0 = 0,$$
$$u(x,0) = u_1(x,0) + u_2(x,0) = \cos x - \cos 3x + 0 = \cos x - \cos 3x,$$
$$u(x,1) = u_1(x,1) + u_2(x,1) = 0 + \cos 2x = \cos 2x.$$

This is an application of the superposition principle.

The first of these two problems has the form of the problem given in Example 1 on page 639 of the text with $a = \pi$, $b = 1$, and $f(x) = \cos x - \cos 3x$. A formal solution to this problem is given in equation (10) on page 641 of the text. Thus, by making the appropriate substitutions, we find that a formal solution to the first problem is

$$u_1(x,y) = E_0(y-1) + \sum_{n=1}^{\infty} E_n \cos nx \sinh(ny - n).$$

To find the coefficients $E_n$, we use the nonhomogeneous boundary condition

$$u(x,0) = \cos x - \cos 3x.$$

Thus, we have

$$u_1(x,0) = \cos x - \cos 3x = -E_0 + \sum_{n=1}^{\infty} E_n \cos nx \sinh(-n).$$

Chapter 10

From this we see that for $n = 1$,

$$E_1 \sinh(-1) = 1 \quad \Rightarrow \quad E_1 = \frac{1}{\sinh(-1)}$$

and for $n = 3$,

$$E_3 \sinh(-3) = -1 \quad \Rightarrow \quad E_1 = \frac{-1}{\sinh(-3)}.$$

For all other values of $n$, $E_n = 0$. By substituting these values into the expression found above for $u_1$, we obtain the formal solution to the first of our two problems given by

$$u_1(x, y) = \frac{\cos x \sinh(y - 1)}{\sinh(-1)} - \frac{\cos 3x \sinh(3y - 3)}{\sinh(-3)}. \tag{10.28}$$

To solve the second of our problems, we note that, except for the last two boundary conditions, it is similar to the problem solved in Example 1 on page 639 of the text. As in that example, using the separation of variables technique, we find that the ODE

$$X''(x) - KX(x) = 0, \qquad X'(0) = X'(\pi) = 0,$$

has solutions $X_n(x) = a_n \cos nx$, when $K = -n^2$, $n = 1, 2, 3, \ldots$. By substituting these values for $K$ into the ODE

$$Y''(y) + KY(y) = 0,$$

we again find that a family solutions to this differential equation is given by

$$Y_0(y) = A_0 + B_0 y,$$
$$Y_n(y) = C_n \sinh\left[n \left(y + D_n\right)\right], \qquad n = 1, 2, 3 \ldots.$$

At this point, the problem we are solving differs from the example. The boundary condition $u(x, 0) = X(x)Y(0) = 0$, $0 \le x \le \pi$, implies that $Y(0) = 0$ (since we don't want the trivial solution). Therefore, applying this boundary condition to each of the solutions found above yields

$$Y_0(0) = A_0 + 0 = 0 \quad \Rightarrow \quad A_0 = 0,$$
$$Y_n(0) = C_n \sinh\left(nD_n\right) = 0 \quad \Rightarrow \quad D_n = 0,$$

where we have used the fact that $\sinh x = 0$ only when $x = 0$. By substituting these results into the solutions found above, we obtain

$$Y_0(y) = B_0 y,$$
$$Y_n(y) = C_n \sinh ny, \qquad n = 1, 2, 3 \ldots.$$

Combining these solutions with the solutions $X_n(x) = a_n \cos nx$ yields

$$u_{2,0}(x, y) = X_0(x)Y_0(y) = a_0 B_0 y \cos 0 = E_0 y,$$
$$u_{2,n}(x, y) = X_n(x)Y_n(y) = a_n C_n \cos nx \sinh ny = E_n \cos nx \sinh ny,$$

where $E_0 = a_0 B_0$ and $E_n = a_n C_n$. Thus, by the superposition principle, we find that a formal solution to the second problem is given by

$$u_2(x, y) = E_0 y + \sum_{n=1}^{\infty} E_n \cos nx \sinh ny.$$

By applying the last boundary condition of this second problem, namely $u(x, 1) = \cos 2x$, to these solutions, we see that

$$u_2(x, 1) = E_0 + \sum_{n=1}^{\infty} E_n \cos nx \sinh n = \cos 2x\,..$$

Therefore, when $n = 2$,

$$E_2 \sinh 2 = 1 \qquad \Rightarrow \qquad E_2 = \frac{1}{\sinh 2},$$

and for all other values of $n$, $E_n = 0$. By substituting these coefficients into the solution $u_2(x, y)$ that we found above, we obtain the formal solution to this second problem

$$u_2(x, y) = \frac{\cos 2x \sinh 2y}{\sinh 2}.$$

By the superposition principle (as noted at the beginning of this problem), a formal solution to the original partial differential equation is the sum of this solution and the solution given in equation (10.28). Thus, the solution that we seek is

$$u(x, y) = \frac{\cos x \sinh(y-1)}{\sinh(-1)} - \frac{\cos 3x \sinh(3y-3)}{\sinh(-3)} + \frac{\cos 2x \sinh 2y}{\sinh 2}.$$

# Chapter 10

**11.** In this problem, the technique of separation of variables, as in Example 2 on page 642 of the text, leads to the two ODE's

$$r^2 R''(r) + r R'(r) - \lambda R(r) = 0 \quad \text{and} \quad T''(\theta) + \lambda T(\theta) = 0.$$

Again, as in Example 2, we require the solution $u(r,\theta)$ to be continuous on its domain. Therefore, $T(\theta)$ must again be periodic with period $2\pi$. This implies that $T(-\pi) = T(\pi)$ and $T'(-\pi) = T'(\pi)$. Thus, as in Example 2, a family of solutions for the second ODE above which satisfies these periodic boundary conditions is

$$T_0(\theta) = B \quad \text{and} \quad T_n(\theta) = A_n \cos n\theta + B_n \sin n\theta, \quad n = 1, 2, 3, \ldots .$$

In solving this problem, it was found that $\lambda = n^2$, $n = 0, 1, 2 \ldots$. Again, as in Example 2, substituting these values for $\lambda$ into the first ODE above leads to the solutions

$$R_0(r) = C + D \ln r \quad \text{and} \quad R_n(r) = C_n r^n + D_n r^{-n}, \quad n = 1, 2, 3, \ldots .$$

Here, however, we are not concerned with what happens when $r = 0$. By our assumption that $u(r,\theta) = R(r)T(\theta)$, we see that solutions of the PDE given in this problem will have the form

$$u_0(r,\theta) = B(C + D \ln r) \quad \text{and} \quad u_n(r,\theta) = \left( C_n r^n + D_n r^{-n} \right) \left( A_n \cos n\theta + B_n \sin n\theta \right),$$

where $n = 1, 2, 3, \ldots$. Thus, by the superposition principle, we see that a formal solution to this Dirichlet problem is given by

$$u(r,\theta) = BC + BD \ln r + \sum_{n=1}^{\infty} \left( C_n r^n + D_n r^{-n} \right) \left( A_n \cos n\theta + B_n \sin n\theta \right),$$

or

$$u(r,\theta) = a + b \ln r + \sum_{n=1}^{\infty} \left[ \left( c_n r^n + e_n r^{-n} \right) \cos n\theta + \left( d_n r^n + f_n r^{-n} \right) \sin n\theta \right], \quad (10.29)$$

where $a = BC$, $b = BD$, $c_n = C_n A_n$, $e_n = D_n A_n$, $d_n = C_n B_n$, and $f_n = D_n B_n$. To find these coefficients, we apply the boundary conditions $u(1,\theta) = \sin 4\theta - \cos \theta$, and $u(2,\theta) = \sin \theta$, $-\pi \le \theta \le \pi$. From the first boundary condition, we see that

$$u(1,\theta) = a + \sum_{n=1}^{\infty} \left[ (c_n + e_n) \cos n\theta + (d_n + f_n) \sin n\theta \right] = \sin 4\theta - \cos \theta,$$

which implies that $a = 0$, $d_4 + f_4 = 1$, $c_1 + e_1 = -1$, and for all other values of $n$, $c_n + e_n = 0$ and $d_n + f_n = 0$. From the second boundary condition, we have

$$u(2, \theta) = a + b \ln 2 + \sum_{n=1}^{\infty} \left[ \left( c_n 2^n + e_n 2^{-n} \right) \cos n\theta + \left( d_n 2^n + f_n 2^{-n} \right) \sin n\theta \right] = \sin \theta,$$

which implies that $a = 0$, $b = 0$, $2d_1 + 2^{-1} f_1 = 1$, and for all other values of $n$, $2^n c_1 + 2^{-n} e_1 = 0$ and $2^n d_1 + 2^{-n} f_1 = 0$. By combining these results, we obtain $a = 0$, $b = 0$, and the three systems of two equations in two unknowns given by

$$\begin{aligned} d_4 + f_4 &= 1, \\ 2^4 d_4 + 2^{-4} f_4 &= 0 \end{aligned} \quad \text{and} \quad \begin{aligned} c_1 + e_1 &= -1, \\ 2c_1 + 2^{-1} e_1 &= 0 \end{aligned} \quad \text{and} \quad \begin{aligned} d_1 + f_1 &= 0, \\ 2d_1 + 2^{-1} f_1 &= 1, \end{aligned}$$

(where the first equation in each system was derived from the first boundary condition and the second equation in each system was derived from the second boundary condition), and for all other values of $n$, $c_n = 0$, $e_n = 0$, $d_n = 0$, $f_n = 0$. Solving each system of equations simultaneously yields

$$d_4 = -\frac{1}{255}, \qquad f_4 = -\frac{256}{255}, \qquad c_1 = \frac{1}{3}, \qquad e_1 = -\frac{4}{3}, \qquad d_1 = \frac{2}{3}, \qquad f_1 = -\frac{2}{3}.$$

By substituting these values for the coefficients into equation (10.29) above, we find that a solution to this Dirichlet problem is given by

$$u(r, \theta) = \left( \frac{1}{3} r - \frac{4}{3} r^{-1} \right) \cos \theta + \left( \frac{2}{3} r - \frac{2}{3} r^{-1} \right) \sin \theta + \left( -\frac{1}{255} r^4 - \frac{256}{255} r^{-4} \right) \sin 4\theta.$$

**15.** Here, as in Example 2 on page 642 of the text, the technique of separation of variables leads to the two ODE's given by

$$r^2 R''(r) + r R'(r) - \lambda R(r) = 0 \qquad \text{and} \qquad T''(\theta) + \lambda T(\theta) = 0.$$

Since we want to avoid the trivial solution, the boundary condition $u(r, 0) = R(r) T(0) = 0$ implies that $T(0) = 0$ and the boundary condition $u(r, \pi) = R(r) T(\pi) = 0$ implies that $T(\pi) = 0$. Therefore, we seek a nontrivial solution to the ODE

$$T''(\theta) + \lambda T(\theta) = 0, \qquad \text{with} \qquad T(0) = 0 \quad \text{and} \quad T(\pi) = 0. \tag{10.30}$$

# Chapter 10

To do this we will consider three cases for $\lambda$.

<u>Case 1: $\lambda = 0$.</u> This case leads to the differential equation $T''(\theta) = 0$, which has solutions $T(\theta) = A\theta + B$. Applying the first boundary condition yields $0 = T(0) = B$. Thus, $T(\theta) = A\theta$. The second boundary condition implies that $0 = T(\pi) = A\pi$. Hence, $A = 0$. Therefore, in this case we find only the trivial solution.

<u>Case 2: $\lambda < 0$.</u> In this case, the auxiliary equation associated with the linear differential equation given in equation (10.30) above is $r^2 + \lambda = 0$, which has the real roots $r = \pm\sqrt{-\lambda}$ (where $-\lambda > 0$). Thus, the solution to this differential equation has the form

$$T(\theta) = C_1 e^{\sqrt{-\lambda}\theta} + C_2 e^{-\sqrt{-\lambda}\theta}.$$

Applying the first boundary condition yields

$$0 = T(0) = C_1 + C_2 \quad \Rightarrow \quad C_1 = -C_2 \quad \Rightarrow \quad T(\theta) = -C_2 e^{\sqrt{-\lambda}\theta} + C_2 e^{-\sqrt{-\lambda}\theta}.$$

From the second boundary condition, we obtain

$$0 = T(\pi) = C_2\left(-e^{\sqrt{-\lambda}\pi} + e^{-\sqrt{-\lambda}\pi}\right) \quad \Rightarrow \quad C_2\left(e^{2\sqrt{-\lambda}\pi} - 1\right) = 0.$$

Since we are assuming that $\lambda < 0$, the only way that this last expression can be zero is for $C_2 = 0$. Thus, $C_1 = -C_2 = 0$ and we again obtain the trivial solution.

<u>Case 3: $\lambda > 0$.</u> In this case, the roots to the auxiliary equation associated with this differential equation are $r = \pm\sqrt{\lambda}i$. Therefore, the solution to the differential equation given in equation (10.30) is

$$T(\theta) = C_1 \sin\sqrt{\lambda}\theta + C_2 \cos\sqrt{\lambda}\theta.$$

From the boundary conditions, we see that

$$0 = T(0) = C_2 \quad \Rightarrow \quad T(\theta) = C_1 \sin\sqrt{\lambda}\theta,$$

and

$$0 = T(\pi) = C_1 \sin\sqrt{\lambda}\pi.$$

Since we do not want the trivial solution, this last boundary condition yields $\sin\sqrt{\lambda}\pi = 0$. This will be true if $\sqrt{\lambda} = n$ or, in other words, if $\lambda = n^2$, $n = 1, 2, 3, \ldots$. With these values for $\lambda$, we find nontrivial solution for the differential equation given in equation (10.30) above to be

$$T_n(\theta) = B_n \sin n\theta, \qquad n = 1, 2, 3, \ldots .$$

Substituting the values for $\lambda$ that we have just found into the differential equation

$$r^2 R''(r) + rR'(r) - \lambda R(r) = 0,$$

yields the ODE

$$r^2 R''(r) + rR'(r) - n^2 R(r) = 0, \qquad n = 1, 2, 3, \ldots .$$

This is the same Cauchy-Euler equation that was solved in Example 2 on page 642 of the text. There it was found that the solutions have the form

$$R_n(r) = C_n r^n + D_n r^{-n}, \qquad n = 1, 2, 3, \ldots .$$

Since we require that $u(r, \theta)$ to be bounded on its domain, we see that $u(r, \theta) = R(r)T(\theta)$ must be bounded about $r = 0$. This implies that $R(\theta)$ must be bounded. Therefore, $D_n = 0$ and so the solutions to this Cauchy-Euler equation are given by

$$R_n(r) = C_n r^n, \qquad n = 1, 2, 3, \ldots .$$

Since we have assumed that $u(r, \theta) = R(r)T(\theta)$, we see that formal solutions to the original partial differential equation are

$$u_n(r, \theta) = B_n C_n r^n \sin n\theta = c_n r^n \sin n\theta,$$

where $c_n = B_n C_n$. Therefore, by the superposition principle, we obtain the formal solutions to this Dirichlet problem

$$u(r, \theta) = \sum_{n=1}^{\infty} c_n r^n \sin n\theta .$$

The final boundary condition yields

$$u(1, \theta) = \sin 3\theta = \sum_{n=1}^{\infty} c_n \sin n\theta .$$

# Chapter 10

This implies that $c_3 = 1$ and for all other values of $n$, $c_n = 0$. Substituting these values for the coefficients into the formal solution found above, yields the solution to this Dirichlet problem on the half disk

$$u(r, \theta) = r^3 \sin 3\theta \,.$$

17. As in Example 2 on page 642 of the text, we solve this problem by separation of variables. There it was found that we must solve the two ordinary differential equations

$$r^2 R''(r) + r R'(r) - \lambda R(r) = 0, \tag{10.31}$$

and

$$T''(\theta) + \lambda T(\theta) = 0 \quad \text{with} \quad T(\pi) = T(n\pi) \quad \text{and} \quad T'(\pi) = T'(n\pi). \tag{10.32}$$

In Example 2, we found that when $\lambda = n^2$, $n = 0, 1, 2, \ldots$, the linear differential equation given in equation (10.32) has nontrivial solutions of the form

$$T_n(\theta) = A_n \cos n\theta + B_n \sin n\theta \,, \quad n = 0, 1, 2, \ldots \,,$$

and equation (10.31) has solutions of the form

$$R_0(r) = C + D \ln r \quad \text{and} \quad R_n(r) = C_n r^n + D_n r^{-n} \,, \quad n = 1, 2, 3, \ldots \,.$$

(Note that here we are not concerned with what happens to $u(r, \theta)$ around $r = 0$.) Thus, since we are assuming that $u(r, \theta) = R(r)T(\theta)$, we see that solutions to the original partial differential equation will be given by

$$u_0(r, \theta) = A_0(C + D \ln r) = a_0 + b_0 \ln r,$$

and

$$\begin{aligned} u_n(r, \theta) &= \left( C_n r^n + D_n r^{-n} \right) \left( A_n \cos n\theta + B_n \sin n\theta \right) \\ &= \left( a_n r^n + b_n r^{-n} \right) \cos n\theta + \left( c_n r^n + d_n r^{-n} \right) \sin n\theta \,, \end{aligned}$$

where $a_0 = A_0C$, $b_0 = A_0D$, $a_n = C_nA_n$, $b_n = D_nA_n$, $c_n = C_nB_n$, and $d_n = D_nB_n$. Thus, by the superposition principle, we see that a formal solution to the partial differential equation given in this problem will have the form

$$u(r, \theta) = a_0 + b_0 \ln r + \sum_{n=1}^{\infty} \left[ \left(a_n r^n + b_n r^{-n}\right) \cos n\theta + \left(c_n r^n + d_n r^{-n}\right) \sin n\theta \right]. \qquad (10.33)$$

By applying the first boundary condition, we obtain

$$u(1, \theta) = f(\theta) = a_0 + \sum_{n=1}^{\infty} \left[ (a_n + b_n) \cos n\theta + (c_n + d_n) \sin n\theta \right],$$

where we have used the fact that $\ln 1 = 0$. Comparing this equation with equation (8) on page 594 of the text, we see that $a_0$, $(a_n + b_n)$, and $(c_n + d_n)$ are the Fourier coefficients of $f(\theta)$ (with $T = \pi$). Therefore, by equations (9) and (10) on that same page we see that

$$a_0 = \frac{1}{2\pi} \int_{-\pi}^{\pi} f(\theta) \, d\theta,$$

$$a_n + b_n = \frac{1}{\pi} \int_{-\pi}^{\pi} f(\theta) \cos n\theta \, d\theta, \qquad (10.34)$$

$$c_n + d_n = \frac{1}{\pi} \int_{-\pi}^{\pi} f(\theta) \sin n\theta \, d\theta, \qquad n = 1, 2, 3 \ldots.$$

To apply the last boundary condition, we must find $\partial u / \partial r$. Hence, we find

$$\frac{\partial u(r, \theta)}{\partial r} = \frac{b_0}{r} + \sum_{n=1}^{\infty} \left[ \left(a_n n r^{n-1} - b_n n r^{-n-1}\right) \cos n\theta + \left(c_n n r^{n-1} - d_n n r^{-n-1}\right) \sin n\theta \right].$$

Applying the last boundary condition yields

$$\frac{\partial u(3, \theta)}{\partial r} = g(\theta) = \frac{b_0}{3} + \sum_{n=1}^{\infty} \left[ \left(a_n n 3^{n-1} - b_n n 3^{-n-1}\right) \cos n\theta + \left(c_n n 3^{n-1} - d_n n 3^{-n-1}\right) \sin n\theta \right].$$

Again by comparing this to equation (8) on page 594 of the text, we see that

$$\frac{b_0}{3}, \qquad \left(n 3^{n-1} a_n - n 3^{-n-1} b_n\right), \qquad \text{and} \qquad \left(n 3^{n-1} c_n - n 3^{-n-1} d_n\right)$$

are the Fourier coefficients of $g(\theta)$ (with $T = \pi$). Thus, by equations (9) and (10) on that same page of the text, we see that

$$b_0 = \frac{3}{2\pi} \int_{-\pi}^{\pi} g(\theta)\, d\theta\,,$$

$$n3^{n-1}a_n - n3^{-n-1}b_n = \frac{1}{\pi} \int_{-\pi}^{\pi} g(\theta) \cos n\theta\, d\theta\,, \tag{10.35}$$

$$n3^{n-1}c_n - n3^{-n-1}d_n = \frac{1}{\pi} \int_{-\pi}^{\pi} g(\theta) \sin n\theta\, d\theta\,, \qquad n = 1, 2, 3 \ldots .$$

Therefore, the formal solution to this partial differential equation will be given by equation (10.33) with the coefficients given by equations (10.34) and (10.35).

# CHAPTER 11: Eigenvalue Problems and Sturm-Liouville Equations

**EXERCISES 11.2:    Eigenvalues and Eigenfunctions, page 671**

1. The auxiliary equation for this problem is $r^2 + 2r + 26 = 0$, which has roots $r = -1 \pm 5i$. Hence a general solution to the differential equation $y'' + 2y' + 26y = 0$ is given by

$$y(x) = C_1 e^{-x} \cos 5x + C_2 e^{-x} \sin 5x.$$

We will now try to determine $C_1$ and $C_2$ so that the boundary conditions are satisfied. Setting $x = 0$ and $x = \pi$, we find

$$y(0) = C_1 = 1, \qquad y(\pi) = -C_1 e^{-\pi} = -e^{-\pi}.$$

Both boundary conditions yield the same result, $C_1 = 1$. Hence, there is a one parameter family of solutions,

$$y(x) = e^{-x} \cos 5x + C_2 e^{-x} \sin 5x.,$$

where $C_2$ is arbitrary.

13. First note that the auxiliary equation for this problem is $r^2 + \lambda = 0$. To find eigenvalues which yield nontrivial solutions we will consider the three cases $\lambda < 0$, $\lambda = 0$, and $\lambda > 0$.

Case 1. $\lambda < 0$: In this case the roots to the auxiliary equation are $\pm\sqrt{-\lambda}$ (where we note that $-\lambda$ is a positive number). Therefore, a general solution to the differential equation $y'' + \lambda y = 0$ is given by

$$y(x) = C_1 e^{\sqrt{-\lambda}x} + C_2 e^{-\sqrt{-\lambda}x}.$$

By applying the first boundary condition, we obtain

$$y(0) = C_1 + C_2 = 0 \qquad \Rightarrow \qquad C_2 = -C_1.$$

Thus

$$y(x) = C_1 \left( e^{\sqrt{-\lambda}x} - e^{-\sqrt{-\lambda}x} \right).$$

In order to apply the second boundary conditions, we need to find $y'(x)$. Thus, we have

$$y(x) = C_1\sqrt{-\lambda} \left( e^{\sqrt{-\lambda}x} + e^{-\sqrt{-\lambda}x} \right).$$

Thus

$$y(1) = C_1\sqrt{-\lambda} \left( e^{\sqrt{-\lambda}} + e^{-\sqrt{-\lambda}} \right) = 0. \tag{11.1}$$

Since $\sqrt{-\lambda} > 0$ and $e^{\sqrt{-\lambda}} + e^{-\sqrt{-\lambda}} \neq 0$, the only way that equation (11.1) can be true is for $C_1 = 0$. So in this case we have only the trivial solution. Thus, there are no eigenvalues for $\lambda < 0$.

Case 2. $\underline{\lambda = 0}$: In this case we are solving the differential equation $y'' = 0$. This equation has a general solution given by

$$y(x) = C_1 + C_2x \qquad \Rightarrow \qquad y'(x) = C_2.$$

By applying the boundary conditions, we obtain

$$y(0) = C_1 = 0 \qquad \text{and} \qquad y'(1) = C_1 = 0.$$

Thus $C_1 = C_2 = 0$, and zero is not an eigenvalue.

Case 3. $\underline{\lambda > 0}$: In this case the roots to the associated auxiliary equation are $r = \pm\sqrt{\lambda}i$. Therefore, the general solution is given by

$$y(x) = C_1 \cos\left(\sqrt{\lambda}x\right) + C_2 \sin\left(\sqrt{\lambda}x\right).$$

By applying the first boundary condition, we obtain

$$y(0) = C_1 = 0 \qquad \Rightarrow \qquad y(x) = C_2 \sin\left(\sqrt{\lambda}x\right).$$

In order to apply the second boundary conditions we need to find $y'(x)$. Thus, we have

$$y'(x) = C_2\sqrt{\lambda} \cos\left(\sqrt{\lambda}x\right),$$

and so

$$y'(1) = C_2 \sqrt{\lambda} \cos\left(\sqrt{\lambda}\right) = 0.$$

Therefore, in order to obtain a solution other than the trivial solution, we must have

$$\cos\left(\sqrt{\lambda}\right) = 0 \quad \Rightarrow \quad \sqrt{\lambda} = \left(n + \frac{1}{2}\right)\pi, \qquad n = 0, 1, 2, \ldots$$

$$\Rightarrow \quad \lambda_n = \left(n + \frac{1}{2}\right)^2 \pi^2, \qquad n = 0, 1, 2, \ldots.$$

For the eigenvalue $\lambda_n$, we have the corresponding eigenfunctions,

$$y_n(x) = C_n \sin\left[\left(n + \frac{1}{2}\right)\pi x\right], \qquad n = 0, 1, 2, \ldots,$$

where $C_n$ is an arbitrary nonzero constant.

**19.** The equation $(xy')' + \lambda x^{-1}y = 0$ can be rewritten as the Cauchy-Euler equation

$$x^2 y'' + xy' + \lambda y = 0, \qquad x > 0. \tag{11.2}$$

Substituting $y = x^r$ gives $r^2 + \lambda = 0$ as the auxiliary equation for (11.2). Again we will consider the three cases $\lambda < 0$, $\lambda = 0$, and $\lambda > 0$.

<u>Case 1. $\lambda < 0$:</u> Let $\lambda = -\mu^2$, for $\mu > 0$. The roots of the auxiliary equation are $r = \pm\mu$ and so a general solution to (11.2) is

$$y(x) = C_1 x^\mu + C_2 x^{-\mu}.$$

We first find $y'(x)$.

$$y'(x) = C_1 \mu x^{\mu-1} - C_2 \mu x^{-\mu-1} = \mu\left(C_1 x^{\mu-1} - C_2 x^{-\mu-1}\right).$$

Substituting into the first boundary condition gives

$$y'(1) = \mu\left(C_1 - C_2\right) = 0.$$

Since $\mu > 0$,

$$C_1 - C_2 = 0 \quad \Rightarrow \quad C_1 = C_2 \quad \Rightarrow \quad y(x) = C_1\left(x^\mu + x^{-\mu}\right).$$

Substituting this into the second condition yields

$$y\left(e^{\pi}\right) = C_1\left(e^{\mu\pi} + e^{-\mu\pi}\right) = 0. \tag{11.3}$$

Since $e^{\mu\pi} + e^{-\mu\pi} \neq 0$ the only way that equation (11.3) can be true is for $C_1 = 0$. So in this case we have only the trivial solution. Thus, there is no eigenvalue for $\lambda < 0$.

Case 2. $\lambda = 0$: In this case we are solving the differential equation $(xy')' = 0$. This equation can be solved as follows:

$$xy' = C_1 \quad \Rightarrow \quad y' = \frac{C_1}{x} \quad \Rightarrow \quad y(x) = C_2 + C_1 \ln x \,.$$

By applying the boundary conditions, we obtain

$$y'(1) = C_1 = 0 \quad \text{and} \quad y\left(e^{\pi}\right) = C_2 + C_1 \ln\left(e^{\pi}\right) = C_2 + C_1\pi = 0.$$

Solving these equations simultaneously yields $C_1 = C_2 = 0$. Thus, we again find only the trivial solution. Therefore, $\lambda = 0$ is not an eigenvalue.

Case 3. $\lambda > 0$: Let $\lambda = \mu^2$, for $\mu > 0$. The roots of the auxiliary equation are $r = \pm\mu i$ and so a general solution (11.2) is

$$y(x) = C_1 \cos\left(\mu \ln x\right) + C_2 \sin\left(\mu \ln x\right).$$

We next find $y\prime(x)$.

$$y'(x) = -C_1\left(\frac{\mu}{x}\right)\sin\left(\mu \ln x\right) + C_2\left(\frac{\mu}{x}\right)\cos\left(\mu \ln x\right).$$

By applying the first boundary condition, we obtain

$$y'(1) = C_2\mu = 0 \quad \Rightarrow \quad C_2 = 0.$$

Applying the second boundary condition, we obtain

$$y\left(e^{\pi}\right) = C_1 \cos\left(\mu \ln(e^{\pi})\right) = C_1 \cos\left(\mu\pi\right) = 0.$$

Therefore, in order to obtain a solution other than the trivial solution, we must have

$$\cos\left(\mu\pi\right) = 0 \quad \Rightarrow \quad \mu\pi = \left(n + \frac{1}{2}\right)\pi \quad n = 0, 1, 2, \ldots$$

$$\Rightarrow \qquad \mu = n + \frac{1}{2} \qquad \Rightarrow \qquad \lambda_n = \left(n + \frac{1}{2}\right)^2, \quad n = 0, 1, 2, \ldots.$$

Corresponding to the eigenvalues, $\lambda_n$'s, we have the eigenfunctions.

$$y_n(x) = C_n \cos\left[\left(n + \frac{1}{2}\right)\ln x\right], \qquad n = 0, 1, 2, \ldots,$$

where $C_n$ is an arbitrary nonzero constant.

**25.** As in Problem 13, the auxiliary equation for this problem is $r^2 + \lambda = 0$. To find eigenvalues which yield nontrivial solutions we will consider the three cases $\lambda < 0$, $\lambda = 0$, and $\lambda > 0$.

<u>Case 1. $\lambda < 0$:</u> The roots of the auxiliary equation are $r = \pm\sqrt{-\lambda}$ and so a general solution to the differential equation $y'' + \lambda y = 0$ is given by

$$y(x) = C_1 e^{\sqrt{-\lambda}x} + C_2 e^{-\sqrt{-\lambda}x}.$$

By applying the first boundary condition we obtain

$$y(0) = C_1 + C_2 = 0 \qquad \Rightarrow \qquad C_2 = -C_1.$$

Thus

$$y(x) = C_1\left(e^{\sqrt{-\lambda}x} - e^{-\sqrt{-\lambda}x}\right).$$

Applying the second boundary conditions yields

$$y\left(1 + \lambda^2\right) = C_1\left(e^{\sqrt{-\lambda}(1+\lambda^2)} - e^{-\sqrt{-\lambda}(1+\lambda^2)}\right) = 0.$$

Multiplying by $e^{\sqrt{-\lambda}(1+\lambda^2)}$ yields

$$C_1\left(e^{2\sqrt{-\lambda}(1+\lambda^2)} - 1\right) = 0.$$

Now either $C_1 = 0$ or

$$e^{2\sqrt{-\lambda}(1+\lambda^2)} = 1 \qquad \Rightarrow \qquad \sqrt{-\lambda}(1+\lambda^2) = 0 \qquad \Rightarrow \qquad \sqrt{-\lambda} = 0.$$

Since $\lambda < 0$, we must have $C_1 = 0$ and hence there are no eigenvalues for $\lambda < 0$.

# Chapter 11

**Case 2. $\lambda = 0$:** In this case we are solving the differential equation $y'' = 0$. This equation has a general solution given by

$$y(x) = C_1 + C_2 x.$$

By applying the boundary conditions, we obtain

$$y(0) = C_1 = 0 \quad \text{and} \quad y\left(1+\lambda^2\right) = C_1 + C_2\left(1+\lambda^2\right) = 0.$$

Solving these equations simultaneously yields $C_1 = C_2 = 0$. Thus, we find that is $\lambda = 0$ not an eigenvalue.

**Case 3. $\lambda > 0$:** The roots of the auxiliary equation are $r = \pm\sqrt{\lambda}i$ and so a general solution is

$$y(x) = C_1 \cos\left(\sqrt{\lambda}x\right) + C_2 \sin\left(\sqrt{\lambda}x\right).$$

Substituting in the first boundary condition yields

$$y(0) = C_1 \cos\left(\sqrt{\lambda}\cdot 0\right) + C_2 \sin\left(\sqrt{\lambda}\cdot 0\right) = C_1 = 0.$$

By applying the second boundary condition to $y(x) = C_2 \sin\left(\sqrt{\lambda}x\right)$, we obtain

$$y\left(1+\lambda^2\right) = C_2 \sin\left(\sqrt{\lambda}(1+\lambda^2)\right) = 0.$$

Therefore, in order to obtain a solution other than the trivial solution, we must have

$$\sin\left(\sqrt{\lambda}(1+\lambda^2)\right) = 0 \quad \Rightarrow \quad \sqrt{\lambda}(1+\lambda^2) = n\pi, \quad n = 1,2,3,\dots.$$

Hence choose the eigenvalues $\lambda_n$, $n = 1,2,3,\dots$, such that $\sqrt{\lambda_n}(1+\lambda_n^2) = n\pi$; and the corresponding eigenfunctions are

$$y_n(x) = C_n \sin\left(\sqrt{\lambda_n}x\right), \quad n = 1,2,3,\dots,$$

where the $C_n$'s are arbitrary nonzero constants.

**33. (a)** We assume that $u(x,t) = X(x)T(t)$. Then

$$u_{tt} = X(x)T''(t), \quad u_x = X'(x)T(t), \quad \text{and} \quad u_{xx} = X''(x)T(t).$$

Substituting these functions into $u_{tt} = u_{xx} + 2u_x$, we obtain

$$X(x)T''(t) = X''(x)T(t) + 2X'(x)T(t).$$

Separating variables yields

$$\frac{X''(x) + 2X'(x)}{X(x)} = -\lambda = \frac{T''(t)}{T(t)}, \qquad (11.4)$$

where $\lambda$ is some constant. The first equation in (11.4) gives

$$X''(x) + 2X'(x) + \lambda X(x) = 0.$$

Let's now consider the boundary conditions. From $u(0, t) = 0$ and $u(\pi, t) = 0$, $t > 0$, we conclude that

$$X(0)T(t) = 0 \qquad \text{and} \qquad X(\pi)T(t) = 0, \qquad t > 0.$$

Hence either $T(t) = 0$ for all $t > 0$, which implies $u(x, t) \equiv 0$, or

$$X(0) = X(\pi) = 0.$$

Ignoring the trivial solution $u(x, t) \equiv 0$, we obtain the boundary value problem

$$X''(x) + 2X'(x) + \lambda X(x) = 0, \qquad X(0) = X(\pi) = 0.$$

**(b)** The auxiliary equation for this problem, $r^2 + 2r + \lambda = 0$, has roots $r = -1 \pm \sqrt{1 - \lambda}$. To find eigenvalues which yield nontrivial solutions, we will consider the three cases $1 - \lambda < 0$, $1 - \lambda = 0$, and $1 - \lambda > 0$.

<u>Case 1, $1 - \lambda < 0$ ($\lambda > 1$)</u>: Let $\mu = \sqrt{-(1 - \lambda)} = \sqrt{\lambda - 1}$. In this case the roots to the auxiliary equation are $r = -1 \pm \mu i$ (where $\mu$ is a positive number). Therefore, a general solution to the differential equation is given by

$$X(x) = C_1 e^{-x} \cos \mu x + C_2 e^{-x} \sin \mu x.$$

By applying the boundary conditions, we obtain

$$X(0) = C_1 = 0 \qquad \text{and} \qquad X(\pi) = e^{-\pi} \left( C_1 \cos \mu \pi + C_2 \sin \mu \pi \right) = 0 \,.$$

Solving these equations simultaneously yields $C_1 = 0$ and $C_2 \sin \mu\pi = 0$. Therefore, in order to obtain a solution other than the trivial solution, we must have

$$\sin \mu\pi = 0 \qquad \Rightarrow \qquad \mu\pi = n\pi \qquad \Rightarrow \qquad \mu = n, \qquad n = 1, 2, 3, \dots .$$

Since $\mu = \sqrt{\lambda - 1}$,

$$\sqrt{\lambda - 1} = n \qquad \Rightarrow \qquad \lambda = n^2 + 1, \qquad n = 1, 2, 3, \dots .$$

Thus the eigenvalues are given by

$$\lambda_n = n^2 + 1, \qquad n = 1, 2, 3, \dots .$$

Corresponding to the eigenvalue $\lambda_n$, we obtain the solutions

$$X_n(x) = C_n e^{-x} \sin nx, \qquad n = 1, 2, 3, \dots ,$$

where $C_n \neq 0$ is arbitrary.

Case 2, $1 - \lambda = 0$ ($\lambda = 1$): In this case the associated auxiliary equation has double root $r = -1$. Therefore, the general solution is given by

$$X(x) = C_1 e^{-x} + C_2 x e^{-x}.$$

By applying the boundary conditions we obtain

$$X(0) = C_1 = 0 \qquad \text{and} \qquad X(\pi) = e^{-\pi} (C_1 + C_2 \pi) = 0.$$

Solving these equations simultaneously yields $C_1 = C_2 = 0$. So in this case we have only the trivial solution. Thus, $\lambda = 1$ is not an eigenvalue.

Case 3, $1 - \lambda > 0$ ($\lambda < 1$): Let $\mu = \sqrt{1 - \lambda}$. In this case the roots to the auxiliary equation are $r = -1 \pm \mu$ (where $\mu$ is a positive number). Therefore, a general solution to the differential equation is given by

$$X(x) = C_1 e^{(-1-\mu)x} + C_2 e^{(-1+\mu)x} .$$

By applying the first boundary condition we find

$$X(0) = C_1 + C_2 = 0 \qquad \Rightarrow \qquad C_2 = -C_1.$$

So we can express $X(x)$ as

$$X(x) = C_1 \left[ e^{(-1-\mu)x} - e^{(-1+\mu)x} \right].$$

Thus the second condition gives us

$$X(\pi) = C_1 \left[ e^{(-1-\mu)\pi} - e^{(-1+\mu)\pi} \right].$$

Since $e^{(-1-\mu)\pi} - e^{(-1+\mu)\pi} \neq 0$, $C_1 = 0$, and again in this case we have only the trivial solution. Thus, there are no eigenvalues for $\lambda < 1$.

Therefore, the eigenvalues are $\lambda_n = n^2 + 1$, $n = 1, 2, 3, \ldots$, with corresponding eigenfunctions $X_n(x) = C_n e^{-x} \sin nx$, $n = 1, 2, 3, \ldots$, where $C_n$ is an arbitrary nonzero constant.

## EXERCISES 11.3:  Regular Sturm-Liouville Boundary Value Problems, page 682

3. Here $A_2 = x(1 - x)$ and $A_1 = -2x$. Using formula (4) on page 673 of the text, we find

$$\mu(x) = \frac{1}{x(1-x)} e^{\int [A_1(x)/A_2(x)]dx} = \frac{1}{x(1-x)} e^{\int [-2x/x(1-x)]dx} = \frac{1}{x(1-x)} e^{-2\int dx/(1-x)}$$

$$= \frac{1}{x(1-x)} e^{2\ln(1-x)} = \frac{1}{x(1-x)}(1-x)^2 = \frac{1-x}{x}.$$

Multiplying the original equation by $\mu(x) = (1-x)/x$, we get

$$(1-x)^2 y''(x) - 2(1-x)y'(x) + \lambda \frac{1-x}{x} y(x) = 0$$

$$\Rightarrow \qquad [(1-x)^2 y'(x)]' + \lambda \frac{1-x}{x} y(x) = 0.$$

9. Here we consider the linear differential operator $L[y] := y'' + \lambda y$; $y(0) = -y(\pi)$, $y'(0) = -y'(\pi)$. We must show that

$$(u, L[v]) = (L[u], v),$$

where $u(x)$ and $v(x)$ are any functions in the domain of $L$. Now

$$(u, L[v]) = \int_0^\pi u(x)\left[v''(x) + \lambda v(x)\right] dx = \int_0^\pi u(x)v''(x)\, dx + \lambda \int_0^\pi u(x)v(x)\, dx$$

and

$$(L[u], v) = \int_0^\pi \left[u''(x) + \lambda u(x)\right] v(x)\, dx = \int_0^\pi u''(x)v(x)\, dx + \lambda \int_0^\pi u(x)v(x)dx.$$

Hence it suffices to show that $\int_0^\pi u(x)v''(x)\, dx = \int_0^\pi u''(x)v(x)\, dx$. To do this we start with $\int_0^\pi u''(x)v(x)\, dx$ and integrate by parts twice. Doing this we obtain

$$\int_0^\pi u''(x)v(x)\, dx = u'(x)v(x)\,\big|_0^\pi - u(x)v'(x)\,\big|_0^\pi + \int_0^\pi u(x)v''(x)\, dx.$$

Hence, we just need to show $u'(x)v(x)\,\big|_0^\pi - u(x)v'(x)\,\big|_0^\pi = 0$. Expanding gives

$$u'(x)v(x)\,\big|_0^\pi - u(x)v'(x)\,\big|_0^\pi = u'(\pi)v(\pi) - u'(0)v(0) - u(\pi)v'(\pi) + u(0)v'(0).$$

Since $u$ is in the domain of $L$, we have $u(0) = -u(\pi)$, and $u'(0) = -u'(\pi)$. Hence,

$$u'(x)v(x)\,\big|_0^\pi - u(x)v'(x)\,\big|_0^\pi = u'(\pi)\left[v(\pi) + v(0)\right] - u(\pi)\left[v'(\pi) + v'(0)\right].$$

But $v$ also lies in the domain of $L$ and hence $v(0) = -v(\pi)$ and $v'(0) = -v'(\pi)$. This makes the expressions in the brackets zero and we have $u'(x)v(x)\,\big|_0^\pi - u(x)v'(x)\,\big|_0^\pi = 0$.

Therefore, $L$ is selfadjoint.

**17.** In Problem 13 of Section 11.2, we found the eigenvalues to be

$$\lambda_n = \left(n + \frac{1}{2}\right)^2 \pi^2, \qquad n = 0, 1, 2, \ldots$$

with the corresponding eigenfunctions

$$y_n(x) = C_n \sin\left[\left(n + \frac{1}{2}\right)\pi x\right], \qquad n = 0, 1, 2, \ldots,$$

where $C_n$ is an arbitrary nonzero constant.

(a) We need only to choose the $C_n$ so that

$$\int_0^1 C_n^2 \sin^2 \left[ \left( n + \frac{1}{2} \right) \pi x \right] dx = 1.$$

We compute

$$\int_0^1 C_n^2 \sin^2 \left[ \left( n + \frac{1}{2} \right) \pi x \right] dx = \frac{1}{2} C_n^2 \int_0^1 \left( 1 - \cos \left[ (2n + 1) \pi x \right] \right) dx$$

$$= \frac{1}{2} C_n^2 \left( x - \frac{1}{(2n+1)\pi} \sin \left[ (2n+1)\pi x \right] \right) \Big|_0^1 = \frac{1}{2} C_n^2.$$

Hence, we can take $C_n = \sqrt{2}$ which gives

$$\left\{ \sqrt{2} \sin \left[ \left( n + \frac{1}{2} \right) \pi x \right] \right\}_{n=0}^{\infty},$$

as an orthonormal system of eigenfunctions.

(b) To obtain the eigenfunction expansion for $f(x) = x$, we use formula (25) on page 679 of the text. Thus,

$$c_n = \int_0^1 x\sqrt{2} \sin \left[ \left( n + \frac{1}{2} \right) \pi x \right] dx.$$

Using integration by parts with $u = \sqrt{2}x$ and $dv = \sin \left[ \left( n + \frac{1}{2} \right) \pi x \right] dx$, we find

$$c_n = \frac{-\sqrt{2}x \cos[(n + 1/2)\pi x]}{(n + 1/2)\pi} \Big|_0^1 + \int_0^1 \frac{\sqrt{2}x \cos[(n + 1/2)\pi x] \, dx}{(n + 1/2)\pi}$$

$$= \frac{-\sqrt{2} \cos[(n + 1/2)\pi]}{(n + 1/2)\pi} + \frac{\sqrt{2} \sin[(n + 1/2)\pi x]}{(n + 1/2)^2 \pi^2} \Big|_0^1$$

$$= 0 + \frac{\sqrt{2} \sin[(n + 1/2)\pi]}{(n + 1/2)^2 \pi^2} = \frac{(-1)^n \sqrt{2}}{(n + 1/2)^2 \pi^2}.$$

Therefore

$$x = \sum_{n=0}^{\infty} c_n \sqrt{2} \sin \left[ \left( n + \frac{1}{2} \right) \pi x \right] = \sum_{n=0}^{\infty} \frac{2(-1)^n}{(n + 1/2)^2 \pi^2} \sin \left[ \left( n + \frac{1}{2} \right) \pi x \right]$$

$$= \frac{8}{\pi^2} \sum_{n=0}^{\infty} \frac{(-1)^n}{(2n + 1)^2} \sin \left[ \left( n + \frac{1}{2} \right) \pi x \right].$$

# Chapter 11

**23.** In Problem 19 of Section 11.2, we found the eigenvalues

$$\lambda_n = \left(n + \frac{1}{2}\right)^2, \qquad n = 0, 1, 2, \ldots,$$

with the corresponding eigenfunctions

$$y_n(x) = C_n \cos\left[\left(n + \frac{1}{2}\right) \ln x\right], \qquad n = 0, 1, 2, \ldots,$$

where $C_n$ is an arbitrary nonzero constant.

**(a)** We need only to choose the $C_n$ so that

$$\int_1^{e^\pi} C_n^2 \cos^2\left[\left(n + \frac{1}{2}\right) \ln x\right] \frac{1}{x} \, dx = 1.$$

To compute, we let $u = \ln x$ and so $du = dx/x$. Substituting, we find

$$
\int_1^{e^\pi} C_n^2 \cos^2\left[\left(n + \frac{1}{2}\right) \ln x\right] \frac{1}{x} \, dx = C_n^2 \int_0^\pi \cos^2\left[\left(n + \frac{1}{2}\right) u\right] du
$$

$$
= \frac{1}{2} C_n^2 \int_0^\pi \{1 + \cos\left[(2n+1)u\right]\} \, du
$$

$$
= \frac{1}{2} C_n^2 \left(u + \frac{1}{2n+1} \sin\left[(2n+1)u\right]\right)\Bigg|_0^\pi = \frac{\pi}{2} C_n^2.
$$

Hence, we can take $C_n = \sqrt{2/\pi}$, which gives

$$\left\{\sqrt{\frac{2}{\pi}} \cos\left[\left(n + \frac{1}{2}\right) \ln x\right]\right\}_{n=0}^\infty,$$

as an orthonormal system of eigenfunctions.

**(b)** To obtain the eigenfunction expansion for $f(x) = x$, we use formula (25) on page 679 of the text. Thus, with $w(x) = x^{-1}$, we have

$$c_n = \int_1^{e^\pi} x \sqrt{\frac{2}{\pi}} \cos\left[\left(n + \frac{1}{2}\right) \ln x\right] x^{-1} dx.$$

Let $u = \ln x$. Then $du = dx/x$, and we have

$$
\begin{aligned}
c_n &= \sqrt{\frac{2}{\pi}} \int_0^\pi e^u \cos\left[\left(n + \frac{1}{2}\right)u\right] du \\
&= \sqrt{\frac{2}{\pi}} \left. \frac{e^u \cos[(n+1/2)u] + e^u(n+1/2)\sin[(n+1/2)u]}{1 + (n+1/2)^2} \right|_0^\pi \\
&= \sqrt{\frac{2}{\pi}} \frac{e^\pi(n+1/2)\sin[(n+1/2)\pi] - 1}{1 + (n+1/2)^2} = \sqrt{\frac{2}{\pi}} \frac{(-1)^n e^\pi(n+1/2) - 1}{1 + (n+1/2)^2}.
\end{aligned}
$$

Therefore,

$$
\begin{aligned}
x &= \sum_{n=0}^\infty c_n \sqrt{\frac{2}{\pi}} \cos\left[\left(n + \frac{1}{2}\right)\ln x\right] \\
&= \frac{2}{\pi} \sum_{n=0}^\infty \frac{(-1)^n e^\pi(n+1/2) - 1}{1 + (n+1/2)^2} \cos\left[\left(n + \frac{1}{2}\right)\ln x\right].
\end{aligned}
$$

## EXERCISES 11.4: Nonhomogeneous Boundary Value Problems and the Fredholm Alternative, page 692

**3.** Here our differential operator is given by

$$
L[y] = \left(1 + x^2\right) y'' + 2xy' + y.
$$

Substituting into the formula (3) page 684 of the text, we obtain

$$
\begin{aligned}
L^+[y] &= \left[(1 + x^2)y\right]'' - (2xy)' + y = \left[2xy + (1 + x^2)y'\right]' - 2y - 2xy' + y \\
&= 2y + 2xy' + 2xy' + (1 + x^2)y'' - 2y - 2xy' + y = (1 + x^2)y'' + 2xy' + y.
\end{aligned}
$$

**7.** Here our differential operator is given by

$$
L[y] = y'' - 2y' + 10y; \qquad y(0) = y(\pi) = 0.
$$

Hence

$$
L^+[v] = v'' + 2v' + 10v.
$$

687

# Chapter 11

To find the $D(L^+)$, we must have

$$P(u, v)(x)\,\big|_0^\pi = 0 \tag{11.5}$$

for all $u$ in $D(L)$ and $v$ in $D(L^+)$. Using formula (9) page 685 of the text for $P(u, v)$ with $A_1 = -2$ and $A_2 = 1$, we find

$$P(u, v) = -2uv - uv' + u'v.$$

Evaluating at $\pi$ and 0, condition (11.5) becomes

$$-2u(\pi)v(\pi) - u(\pi)v'(\pi) + u'(\pi)v(\pi) + 2u(0)v(0) + u(0)v'(0) - u'(0)v(0) = 0.$$

Since $u$ in $D(L)$, we know that $u(0) = u(\pi) = 0$. Thus the above equation becomes

$$u'(\pi)v(\pi) - u'(0)v(0) = 0.$$

Since $u'(\pi)$ and $u'(0)$ can take on any value, we must have $v(0) = v(\pi) = 0$ for this equation to hold for all $u$ in $D(L)$. Hence $D(L^+)$ consists of all function $v$ having continuous second derivatives on $[0, \pi]$ and satisfying the boundary condition

$$v(0) = v(\pi) = 0.$$

11. Here our differential operator is given by

$$L[y] = y'' + 6y' + 10y; \qquad y'(0) = y'(\pi) = 0.$$

Hence

$$L^+[v] = v'' - 6v' + 10v.$$

To find the $D(L^+)$, we must have

$$P(u, v)(x)\,\big|_0^\pi = 0 \tag{11.6}$$

for all $u$ in $D(L)$ and $v$ in $D(L^+)$. Again using formula (9) page 685 of the text for $P(u, v)$ with $A_1 = 6$ and $A_2 = 1$, we find

$$P(u, v) = 6uv - uv' + u'v.$$

Evaluating at $\pi$ and 0, condition (11.6) becomes

$$6u(\pi)v(\pi) - u(\pi)v'(\pi) + u'(\pi)v(\pi) - 6u(0)v(0) + u(0)v'(0) - u'(0)v(0) = 0.$$

Applying the boundary conditions $u'(0) = u'(\pi) = 0$ to the above equation yields

$$6u(\pi)v(\pi) - u(\pi)v'(\pi) - 6u(0)v(0) + u(0)v'(0) = 0$$

$$\Rightarrow \quad u(\pi)\left[6v(\pi) - v'(\pi)\right] - u(0)\left[6v(0) - v'(0)\right] = 0.$$

Since $u(\pi)$ and $u(0)$ can take on any value, we must have $6v(\pi) - v'(\pi) = 0$ and $6v(0) - v'(0) = 0$ in order for the equation to hold for all $u$ in $D(L)$. Therefore, the adjoint boundary value problem is

$$L^+[v] = v'' - 6v' + 10v; \qquad 6v(\pi) = v'(\pi) \quad \text{and} \quad 6v(0) = v'(0).$$

**17.** In Problem 7 we found the adjoint boundary value problem

$$L^+[v] = v'' + 2v' + 10v; \qquad v(0) = v(\pi) = 0. \tag{11.7}$$

The auxiliary equation for (11.7) is $r^2 + 2r + 10 = 0$, which has roots $r = -1 \pm 3i$. Hence a general solution to the differential equation in (11.7) is given by

$$y(x) = C_1 e^{-x} \cos 3x + C_2 e^{-x} \sin 3x.$$

Using the boundary conditions in (11.7) to determine $C_1$ and $C_2$, we find

$$y(0) = C_1 = 0 \quad \text{and} \quad y(\pi) = -C_1 e^{-\pi} = 0.$$

Thus $C_1 = 0$ and $C_2$ is arbitrary. Therefore, every solution to the adjoint problem (11.7) has the form

$$y(x) = C_2 e^{-x} \sin 3x.$$

It follows from the Fredholm alternative that if $h$ is continuous, then the nonhomogeneous problem has a solution if and only if

$$\int_0^\pi h(x) e^{-x} \sin 3x \, dx = 0.$$

# Chapter 11

**21.** In Problem 11 we found the adjoint boundary value problem

$$L^+[v] = v'' - 6v' + 10v; \qquad 6v(\pi) = v'(\pi) \quad \text{and} \quad 6v(0) = v'(0). \tag{11.8}$$

The auxiliary equation for (11.8) is $r^2 - 6r + 10 = 0$, which has roots $r = 3 \pm i$. Hence a general solution to the differential equation in (11.8) is given by

$$y(x) = C_1 e^{3x} \cos x + C_2 e^{3x} \sin x.$$

To apply the boundary conditions in (11.8), we first determine $y'(x)$.

$$y'(x) = 3C_1 e^{3x} \cos x - C_1 e^{3x} \sin x + 3C_2 e^{3x} \sin x + C_2 e^{3x} \cos x.$$

Applying the first condition, we have

$$-6C_1 e^{3\pi} = -3C_1 e^{3\pi} - C_2 e^{3\pi} \qquad \Rightarrow \qquad 3C_1 = C_2.$$

Applying the second condition, we have

$$6C_1 = 3C_1 + C_2 \qquad \Rightarrow \qquad 3C_1 = C_2.$$

Thus $C_2 = 3C_1$ where $C_1$ is arbitrary. Therefore, every solution to the adjoint problem (11.8) has the form

$$y(x) = C_1 e^{3x} (\cos x + 3 \sin x).$$

It follows from the Fredholm alternative that if $h$ is continuous, then the nonhomogeneous problem has a solution if and only if

$$\int_0^\pi h(x) e^{3x} (\cos x + 3 \sin x) \, dx = 0.$$

## EXERCISES 11.5:  Solution by Eigenfunction Expansion, page 698

**3.** In Example 1 on page 696 of the text we noted that the boundary value problem

$$y'' + \lambda y = 0; \qquad y(0) = 0, \quad y(\pi) = 0,$$

has eigenvalues $\lambda_n = n^2$, $n = 1, 2, 3, \ldots$, with corresponding eigenfunctions

$$\phi_n(x) = \sin nx, \qquad n = 1, 2, 3, \ldots .$$

Here $r(x) \equiv 1$, so we need to determine coefficients $\gamma_n$ such that

$$f(x) = \frac{f(x)}{r(x)} = \sum_{n=1}^{\infty} \gamma_n \sin nx = \sin 2x + \sin 8x.$$

Clearly $\gamma_2 = \gamma_8 = 1$ and the remaining $\gamma_n$'s are zero. Since $\mu = 4 = \lambda_2$ and $\gamma_2 = 1 \neq 0$ there is no solution to this problem.

**5.** In equation (18) on page 666 of the text we noted that the boundary value problem

$$y'' + \lambda y = 0; \qquad y'(0) = 0, \quad y'(\pi) = 0,$$

has eigenvalues $\lambda_n = n^2$, $n = 0, 1, 2, \ldots$, with corresponding eigenfunctions

$$\phi_n(x) = \cos nx, \qquad n = 0, 1, 2, \ldots .$$

Here $r(x) \equiv 1$, so we need to determine coefficients $\gamma_n$ such that

$$f(x) = \frac{f(x)}{r(x)} = \sum_{n=0}^{\infty} \gamma_n \cos nx = \cos 4x + \cos 7x.$$

Clearly $\gamma_4 = \gamma_7 = 1$ and the remaining $\gamma_n$'s are zero. Since $\mu = 1 = \lambda_1$ and $\gamma_1 = 0$,

$$(\mu - \lambda_1) c_1 - \gamma_1 = 0$$

is satisfied for any value of $c_1$. Calculating $c_4$ and $c_7$, we get

$$c_4 = \frac{\gamma_4}{\mu - \lambda_4} = \frac{1}{1 - 16} = -\frac{1}{15}$$

and

$$c_7 = \frac{\gamma_7}{\mu - \lambda_7} = \frac{1}{1 - 49} = -\frac{1}{48}.$$

Hence a one parameter family of solutions is

$$\phi(x) = \sum_{n=0}^{\infty} c_n \phi_n(x) = c_1 \cos x - \frac{1}{15} \cos 4x - \frac{1}{48} \cos 7x,$$

where $c_1$ is arbitrary.

9. We first find the eigenvalues and corresponding eigenfunctions for this problem. Note that the auxiliary equation for this problem is $r^2 + \lambda = 0$. To find eigenvalues which yield nontrivial solutions we will consider the three cases $\lambda < 0$, $\lambda = 0$, and $\lambda > 0$.

Case 1, $\lambda < 0$: Let $\mu = \sqrt{-\lambda}$, then the roots to the auxiliary equation are $r = \pm \mu$ and a general solution to the differential equation is given by

$$y(x) = C_1 \sinh \mu x + C_2 \cosh \mu x.$$

Since

$$y'(x) = C_1 \mu \cosh \mu x + C_2 \mu \sinh \mu x,$$

by applying the boundary conditions we obtain

$$y'(0) = C_1 \mu = 0 \qquad \text{and} \qquad y(\pi) = C_1 \sinh \mu \pi + C_2 \cosh \mu \pi = 0.$$

Hence $C_1 = 0$ and $y(\pi) = C_2 \cosh \mu \pi = 0$. Therefore $C_2 = 0$ and we find only the trivial solution.

Case 2, $\lambda = 0$: In this case the differential equation becomes $y'' = 0$. This equation has a general solution given by

$$y(x) = C_1 + C_2 x.$$

Since $y'(x) = C_2$, by applying the boundary conditions we obtain

$$y'(0) = C_2 = 0 \qquad \text{and} \qquad y(\pi) = C_1 + C_2 \pi = 0.$$

Solving these equations simultaneously yields $C_1 = C_2 = 0$. Thus, we again find only the trivial solution.

Case 3, $\lambda > 0$: Let $\lambda = \mu^2$, for $\mu > 0$. The roots of the auxiliary equation are $r = \pm \mu i$ and so a general solution is

$$y(x) = C_1 \cos \mu x + C_2 \sin \mu x.$$

Since

$$y'(x) = -C_1 \mu \sin \mu x + C_2 \mu \cos \mu x,$$

using the first boundary condition we find

$$y'(0) = -C_1\mu\sin(\mu\cdot 0) + C_2\mu\cos(\mu\cdot 0) = 0 \quad\Rightarrow\quad C_2\mu = 0 \quad\Rightarrow\quad C_2 = 0.$$

Thus substituting into the second boundary condition yields

$$y(\pi) = C_1\cos\mu\pi = 0.$$

Therefore, in order to obtain a solution other than the trivial solution, we must have

$$\cos\mu\pi = 0 \quad\Rightarrow\quad \mu = n + \frac{1}{2}, \quad n = 0, 1, 2, \dots.$$

Hence choose $\lambda_n = (n+1/2)^2$, $n = 0, 1, 2, \dots$, and

$$y_n(x) = C_n\cos\left[\left(n + \frac{1}{2}\right)x\right],$$

where the $C_n$'s are arbitrary nonzero constants.

Next we need to choose the $C_n$ so that

$$\int_0^\pi C_n^2 \cos^2\left[\left(n + \frac{1}{2}\right)x\right] dx = 1.$$

Computing we find

$$\int_0^\pi C_n^2 \cos^2\left[\left(n + \frac{1}{2}\right)x\right] dx = \frac{1}{2}C_n^2\int_0^\pi \{1 + \cos[(2n+1)x]\}\, dx$$

$$= \frac{1}{2}C_n^2\left\{x + \frac{1}{2n+1}\sin[(2n+1)x]\right\}\Big|_0^\pi = \frac{\pi}{2}C_n^2.$$

An orthonormal system of eigenfunctions is given when we take $C_n = \sqrt{2/\pi}$,

$$\left\{\sqrt{\frac{2}{\pi}}\cos\left[\left(n + \frac{1}{2}\right)x\right]\right\}_{n=0}^\infty.$$

Now $f(x)$ has the eigenfunction expansion

$$f(x) = \sum_{n=0}^\infty \gamma_n\sqrt{\frac{2}{\pi}}\cos\left[\left(n + \frac{1}{2}\right)x\right],$$

# Chapter 11

where

$$\gamma_n = \sqrt{\frac{2}{\pi}} \int_0^\pi f(x) \cos\left[\left(n + \frac{1}{2}\right) x\right] dx.$$

Therefore, with $\gamma_n$ as described above, the solution to the given boundary value problem has a formal expansion

$$\phi(x) = \sum_{n=0}^\infty \frac{\gamma_n}{1 - \lambda_n} \sqrt{\frac{2}{\pi}} \cos\left[\left(n + \frac{1}{2}\right) x\right] = \sum_{n=0}^\infty \frac{\gamma_n}{1 - (n + 1/2)^2} \sqrt{\frac{2}{\pi}} \cos\left[\left(n + \frac{1}{2}\right) x\right].$$

## EXERCISES 11.6:  Green's Functions, page 706

**1.** A general solution to the corresponding homogeneous equation, $y'' = 0$, is $y_h(x) = Ax + B$. Thus we seek for paricular solutions $z_1(x)$ and $z_2(x)$ of this form satisfying

$$\begin{aligned} z_1(0) &= 0, \\ z_2'(\pi) &= 0. \end{aligned} \tag{11.9}$$

The first equation yields

$$z_1(0) = B = 0.$$

Since $A$ is arbitrary, we choose $A = 1$ and so $z_1(x) = x$. Next, from the second equation in (11.9) we get

$$z_2'(\pi) = A = 0.$$

Taking $B = 1$, we obtain $z_2(x) = 1$.

With $p(x) \equiv 1$, we now compute

$$C = p(x)W\left[z_1, z_2\right](x) = (1)[(x)(0) - (1)(1)] = -1.$$

Thus, the Green's function is

$$G(x, s) = \begin{cases} -z_1(s)z_2(x)/C, & 0 \le s \le x, \\ -z_1(x)z_2(s)/C, & x \le s \le \pi \end{cases} = \begin{cases} s, & 0 \le s \le x, \\ x, & x \le s \le \pi. \end{cases}$$

694

**3.** A general solution to the homogeneous problem, $y'' = 0$, is $y_h(x) = Ax + B$, so $z_1(x)$ and $z_2(x)$ must be of this form. To get $z_1(x)$ we want to choose $A$ and $B$ so that

$$z_1(0) = B = 0.$$

Since $A$ is arbitrary, we can set it equal to 1 and $z_1(x) = x$. Next, to get $z_2(x)$ we need to choose $A$ and $B$ so that

$$z_2(\pi) + z_2'(\pi) = A\pi + B + A = 0.$$

Thus $B = -(1+\pi)A$. Taking $A = 1$, we get $z_2(x) = x - 1 - \pi$.

Now compute

$$C = p(x)W[z_1, z_2](x) = (1)[(x)(1) - (1)(x - 1 - \pi)] = 1 + \pi.$$

Thus, the Green's function is

$$G(x,s) = \begin{cases} -z_1(s)z_2(x)/C, & 0 \le s \le x, \\ -z_1(x)z_2(s)/C, & x \le s \le \pi \end{cases} = \begin{cases} \dfrac{-s(x-1-\pi)}{1+\pi}, & 0 \le s \le x, \\[2mm] \dfrac{-x(s-1-\pi)}{1+\pi}, & x \le s \le \pi. \end{cases}$$

**5.** The corresponding homogeneous differential equation, $y'' + 4y = 0$, has the characteristic equation $r^2 + 4 = 0$, whose roots are $r = \pm 2i$. Hence, a general solution to the homogeneous problem is given by

$$y_h(x) = C_1 \cos 2x + C_2 \sin 2x.$$

A solution $z_1(x)$ must satisfy the first boundary condition, $z_1(0) = 0$. Substitution yields

$$z_1(0) = C_1 \cos(2 \cdot 0) + C_2 \sin(2 \cdot 0) = 0 \quad \Rightarrow \quad C_1 = 0.$$

Setting $C_2 = 1$, we get $z_1(x) = \sin 2x$. For $z_2(x)$, we have to find constants $C_1$ and $C_2$ such that the second boundary condition is satisfied. Since

$$y_h'(x) = -2C_1 \sin 2x + 2C_2 \cos 2x,$$

we have

$$z_2'(\pi) = -2C_1\sin(2\pi) + 2C_2\cos(2\pi) = 2C_2 = 0 \qquad \Rightarrow \qquad C_2 = 0.$$

With $C_1 = 1$, $z_2(x) = \cos 2x$.

Next we find

$$C = p(x)W\left[z_1, z_2\right](x) = (1)[(\sin 2x)(-2\sin 2x) - (\cos 2x)(2\cos 2x)] = -2.$$

Thus, the Green's function in this problem is given by

$$G(x,s) = \begin{cases} -z_1(s)z_2(x)/C, & 0 \le s \le x, \\ -z_1(x)z_2(s)/C, & x \le s \le \pi \end{cases} = \begin{cases} (\sin 2s \cos 2x)/2, & 0 \le s \le x, \\ (\sin 2x \cos 2s)/2, & x \le s \le \pi. \end{cases}$$

13. In Problem 3 we found the Green's function for this boundary value problem. When $f(x) = x$, the solution is given by equation (16) on page 702 of the text. Substituting for $f(x)$ and $G(x,s)$ yields

$$y(x) = \int_a^b G(x,s)f(s)\,ds = \int_0^\pi G(x,s)s\,ds = \int_0^x \frac{-s^2(x-1-\pi)}{1+\pi}\,ds + \int_x^\pi \frac{-xs(s-1-\pi)}{1+\pi}\,ds.$$

Computing

$$\int_0^x \frac{-s^2(x-1-\pi)}{1+\pi}\,ds = -\frac{(x-1-\pi)}{1+\pi}\left(\frac{s^3}{3}\right)\Bigg|_{s=0}^x = -\frac{(x-1-\pi)}{1+\pi}\left(\frac{x^3}{3}\right) = -\frac{x^4}{3(1+\pi)} + \frac{x^3}{3},$$

$$\int_x^\pi \frac{-xs(s-1-\pi)}{1+\pi}\,ds = -\frac{x}{1+\pi}\left[\frac{s^3}{3} - \frac{(1+\pi)s^2}{2}\right]\Bigg|_{s=x}^\pi = -\frac{x}{1+\pi}\left[\frac{\pi^3}{3} - \frac{(1+\pi)\pi^2}{2}\right]$$

$$+\frac{x}{1+\pi}\left[\frac{x^3}{3} - \frac{(1+\pi)x^2}{2}\right] = -\frac{\pi^3 x}{3(1+\pi)} + \frac{\pi^2 x}{2} + \frac{x^4}{3(1+\pi)} - \frac{x^3}{2},$$

we finally get

$$\begin{aligned} y(x) &= \left[-\frac{x^4}{3(1+\pi)} + \frac{x^3}{3}\right] + \left[-\frac{\pi^3 x}{3(1+\pi)} + \frac{\pi^2 x}{2} + \frac{x^4}{3(1+\pi)} - \frac{x^3}{2}\right] \\ &= -\frac{x^3}{6} + \left[\frac{\pi^2}{2} - \frac{\pi^3}{3(1+\pi)}\right]x = -\frac{x^3}{6} + \frac{\pi^2(3+\pi)x}{6(1+\pi)}. \end{aligned}$$

**17.** A general solution to the corresponding homogeneous problem $y'' - y = 0$ is

$$y_h(x) = C_1 e^x + C_2 e^{-x}.$$

So $z_1(x)$ and $z_2(x)$ must be of this form. To get $z_1(x)$ we want to choose constants $C_1$ and $C_2$ so that

$$z_1(0) = C_1 e^0 + C_2 e^{-0} = C_1 + C_2 = 0.$$

Let $C_1 = 1$. Then $C_2 = -1$ and so $z_1(x) = e^x - e^{-x}$. Likewise, to get a $z_2(x)$, we find $C_1$ and $C_2$ so that

$$z_2(1) = C_1 e^1 + C_2 e^{-1} = 0 \qquad \Rightarrow \qquad C_2 = -C_1 e^2.$$

If we let $C_1 = 1$, then $C_2 = -e^2$. Hence $z_2(x) = e^x - e^2 e^{-x} = e^x - e^{2-x}$. We now compute

$$C = p(x) W[z_1, z_2](x) = (1) \left[ \left( e^x - e^{-x} \right) \left( e^x + e^{2-x} \right) - \left( e^x + e^{-x} \right) \left( e^x - e^{2-x} \right) \right] = 2e^2 - 2.$$

Thus, the Green's function is in this problem is

$$
G(x,s) = \begin{cases} -z_1(s) z_2(x)/C, & 0 \le s \le x, \\ -z_1(x) z_2(s)/C, & x \le s \le 1 \end{cases}
$$

$$
= \begin{cases} \left( e^s - e^{-s} \right) \left( e^x - e^{2-x} \right) / \left( 2 - 2e^2 \right), & 0 \le s \le x, \\ \left( e^x - e^{-x} \right) \left( e^s - e^{2-s} \right) / \left( 2 - 2e^2 \right), & x \le s \le 1. \end{cases}
$$

Here $f(x) = -x$. Using Green's function to solve the boundary value problem, we find

$$y(x) = \int_a^b G(x,s) f(s)\, ds = \int_0^x \frac{(e^s - e^{-s})(e^x - e^{2-x})(-s)}{2 - 2e^2}\, ds + \int_x^1 \frac{(e^x - e^{-x})(e^s - e^{2-s})(-s)}{2 - 2e^2}\, ds.$$

Computing integrals yields

$$\int_0^x \frac{(e^s - e^{-s})(e^x - e^{2-x})(-s)}{2 - 2e^2}\, ds = -\frac{e^x - e^{2-x}}{2 - 2e^2} \int_0^x \left( s e^s - s e^{-s} \right) ds$$

$$= -\frac{e^x - e^{2-x}}{2 - 2e^2} \left( s e^s - e^s + s e^{-s} + e^{-s} \right) \Big|_0^x$$

$$= -\frac{e^x - e^{2-x}}{2 - 2e^2} \left( x e^x - e^x + x e^{-x} + e^{-x} \right),$$

$$\int_x^1 \frac{(e^x - e^{-x})(e^s - e^{2-s})(-s)}{2 - 2e^2} \, ds = -\frac{e^x - e^{-x}}{2 - 2e^2} \int_x^1 \left(se^s - se^{2-s}\right) ds$$

$$= -\frac{e^x - e^{-x}}{2 - 2e^2} \left(se^s - e^s + se^{2-s} + e^{2-s}\right)\Big|_x^1$$

$$= -\frac{e^x - e^{-x}}{2 - 2e^2} \left[2e - \left(xe^x - e^x + xe^{2-x} + e^{2-x}\right)\right].$$

Thus

$$
\begin{aligned}
y(x) &= -\frac{e^x - e^{2-x}}{2 - 2e^2} \left(xe^x - e^x + xe^{-x} + e^{-x}\right) - \frac{e^x - e^{-x}}{2 - 2e^2}\left[2e - \left(xe^x - e^x + xe^{2-x} + e^{2-x}\right)\right] \\
&= \frac{-(e^x - e^{2-x})(xe^x - e^x + xe^{-x} + e^{-x}) - (e^x - e^{-x})(2e - xe^x + e^x - xe^{2-x} - e^{2-x})}{2 - 2e^2} \\
&= \frac{-2x + 2xe^2 - 2e^{1+x} + 2e^{1-x}}{2 - 2e^2} = -x + \frac{e^{1+x} - e^{1-x}}{e^2 - 1}.
\end{aligned}
$$

**25.** Substitution $y = x^r$ into the corresponding homogeneous Cauchy-Euler equation

$$x^2 y'' - 2xy' + 2y = 0,$$

we obtain the auxiliary equation

$$r(r - 1) - 2r + 2 = 0 \quad \text{or} \quad r^2 - 3r + 2 = (r - 1)(r - 2) = 0.$$

Hence a general solution to the corresponding homogeneous equation is

$$y_h(x) = C_1 x + C_2 x^2.$$

To get $z_1(x)$ we want to choose $C_1$ and $C_2$ so that

$$z_1(1) = C_1 + C_2 = 0 \quad \Rightarrow \quad C_2 = -C_1.$$

Let $C_1 = 1$, then $C_2 = -1$ and $z_1(x) = x - x^2$. Next we find $z_2(x)$ satisfying

$$z_2(2) = 2C_1 + 4C_2 = 0 \quad \Rightarrow \quad C_1 = -2C_2.$$

Hence, we let $C_2 = -1$, then $C_1 = 2$ and $z_2(x) = 2x - x^2$. Now compute (see the formula for $K(x,s)$ in Problem 22)

$$C(s) = A_2(s)W\left[z_1, z_2\right](s) = \left(s^2\right)\left[(s - s^2)(2 - 2s) - (1 - 2s)(2s - s^2)\right]$$

$$= \left(s^2\right)\left(2s - 4s^2 + 2s^3 - 2s + 5s^2 - 2s^3\right) = s^4,$$

$$K(x,s) = \begin{cases} -z_1(s)z_2(x)/C(s), & 1 \le s \le x, \\ -z_1(x)z_2(s)/C(s), & x \le s \le 2 \end{cases} = \begin{cases} -\dfrac{(s - s^2)(2x - x^2)}{s^4}, & 1 \le s \le x, \\ -\dfrac{(x - x^2)(2s - s^2)}{s^4}, & x \le s \le 2. \end{cases}$$

Simplifying yields

$$K(x,s) = \begin{cases} -x(2 - x)(s^{-3} - s^{-2}), & 1 \le s \le x, \\ -x(1 - x)(2s^{-3} - s^{-2}), & x \le s \le 2. \end{cases}$$

Hence, a solution to the boundary value problem with $f(x) = -x$ is

$$
\begin{aligned}
y(x) &= \int_a^b K(x,s)f(s)\,ds = \int_1^x K(x,s)f(s)\,ds + \int_x^2 K(x,s)f(s)\,ds \\
&= \int_1^x [-x(2 - x)(s^{-3} - s^{-2})](-s)\,ds + \int_x^2 [-x(1 - x)(2s^{-3} - s^{-2})](-s)\,ds \\
&= (2x - x^2)\int_1^x (s^{-2} - s^{-1})\,ds + (x - x^2)\int_x^2 (2s^{-2} - s^{-1})\,ds \\
&= (2x - x^2)\left(-s^{-1} - \ln s\right)\big|_1^x + (x - x^2)\left(-2s^{-1} - \ln s\right)\big|_x^2 \\
&= x^2 \ln 2 - x \ln 2 - x \ln x.
\end{aligned}
$$

**29.** Let $f(x) = \boldsymbol{\delta}(x - s)$. Let $H(x,s)$ be the solution to

$$\frac{\partial^4 H(x,s)}{\partial x^4} = -\boldsymbol{\delta}(x - s)$$

that satisfies the given boundary conditions, the jump condition

$$\lim_{x \to s^+} \frac{\partial^3 H(x,s)}{\partial x^3} - \lim_{x \to s^-} \frac{\partial^3 H(x,s)}{\partial x^3} = -1,$$

and $H$, $\partial H/\partial x$, $\partial^2 H/\partial x^2$ are continuous on the square $[0, \pi] \times [0, \pi]$. We begin by integrating to obtain

$$\frac{\partial^3 H(x,s)}{\partial x^3} = -u(x - s) + C_1,$$

where $u$ is the unit step function and $C_1$ is a constant. (Recall in Section 7.8 we observed that $u'(t-a) = \delta(t-a)$, at least formally.) $\partial^3 H/\partial x^3$ is not continuous along the line $x = s$, but it does satisfy the jump condition

$$\lim_{x \to s^+} \frac{\partial^3 H(x,s)}{\partial x^3} - \lim_{x \to s^-} \frac{\partial^3 H(x,s)}{\partial x^3} = \lim_{x \to s^+} [-u(x-s) + C_1] - \lim_{x \to s^-} [-u(x-s) + C_1]$$
$$= (-1 + C_1) - C_1 = -1.$$

We want $H(x,s)$ to satisfy the boundary condition $y'''(\pi) = 0$. So we solve

$$\frac{\partial^3 H}{\partial x^3}(\pi, s) = -u(\pi - s) + C_1 = -1 + C_1 = 0$$

to obtain $C_1 = 1$. Thus

$$\frac{\partial^3 H(x,s)}{\partial x^3} = -u(x-s) + 1.$$

We now integrate again with respect to $x$ to obtain

$$\frac{\partial^2 H(x,s)}{\partial x^2} = x - u(x-s)(x-s) + C_2.$$

(The reader should verify this is the antiderivative for $x \neq s$ by differentiating it.) We selected this particular form of the antiderivative because we need $\partial^2 H/\partial x^2$ to be continuous on $[0, \pi] \times [0, \pi]$. (The jump of $u(x-s)$ when $x-s$ is canceled by the vanishing of this term by the factor $(x-s)$.) Since

$$\lim_{x \to s} \frac{\partial^2 H(x,s)}{\partial x^2} = s + C_2,$$

we can define

$$\frac{\partial^2 H}{\partial x^2}(s,s) = s + C_2,$$

and we now have a continuous function. Next, we want $y''(\pi) = 0$. Solving we find

$$0 = \frac{\partial^2 H}{\partial x^2}(\pi, s) = \pi - u(\pi - s)(\pi - s) + C_2 = \pi - (\pi - s) + C_2 = s + C_2.$$

Thus, we find that $C_2 = -s$. Now,

$$\frac{\partial^2 H(x,s)}{\partial x^2} = (x-s) - u(x-s)(x-s).$$

We integrate with respect to $x$ again to get

$$\frac{\partial H(x,s)}{\partial x} = \frac{x^2}{2} - sx - u(x-s)\frac{(x-s)^2}{2} + C_3,$$

which is continuous on $[0,\pi] \times [0,\pi]$. We now want the boundary condition $y'(0) = 0$ satisfied. Solving, we obtain

$$0 = \frac{\partial H}{\partial x}(0,s) = -u(0-s)\frac{s^2}{2} + C_3 = C_3.$$

Hence,

$$\frac{\partial H(x,s)}{\partial x} = \frac{x^2}{2} - sx - u(x-s)\frac{(x-s)^2}{2}.$$

Integrating once more with respect to $x$, we have

$$H(x,s) = \frac{x^3}{6} - \frac{sx^2}{2} - u(x-s)\frac{(x-s)^3}{6} + C_4.$$

Now $H(x,s)$ is continuous on $[0,\pi] \times [0,\pi]$. We want $H(x,s)$ to satisfy the boundary condition $y(0) = 0$. Solving, we find

$$0 = H(0,s) = -u(0-s)\frac{(0-s)^3}{6} + C_4 = C_4.$$

Hence,

$$H(x,s) = \frac{x^3}{6} - \frac{sx^2}{2} - u(x-s)\frac{(x-s)^3}{6},$$

which we can rewrite in the form

$$H(x,s) = \begin{cases} \dfrac{s^2(s-3x)}{6}, & 0 \le s \le x, \\[2mm] \dfrac{x^2(x-3s)}{6}, & x \le s \le \pi. \end{cases}$$

## EXERCISES 11.7:   Singular Sturm-Liouville Boundary Value Problems, page 715

1. This is a typical singular Sturm-Liouville boundary value problem. Condition (ii) of Lemma 1 on page 710 of the main text holds since

$$\lim_{x \to 0^+} p(x) = \lim_{x \to 0^+} x = 0$$

and $y(x)$, $y'(x)$ remain bounded as $x \to 0^+$. Because

$$\lim_{x \to 1^-} p(x) = p(1) = 1$$

and $y(1) = 0$, the analogue of condition (i) of Lemma 1 holds at the right endpoint. Hence $L$ is selfadjoint.

The equation is Bessel's equation of order 2. On page 712 of the text, we observed that the solutions to this boundary value problem are given by

$$y_n(x) = c_n J_2(\alpha_{2n} x),$$

where $\sqrt{\mu_n} = \alpha_{2n}$ is the increasing sequence of real zeros of $J_2(x)$, that is, $J_2(\alpha_{2n}) = 0$.

Now to find an eigenfunction expansion for the given nonhomogeneous equation we compute the eigenfunction expansion for $f(x)/x$ (see page 694):

$$\frac{f(x)}{x} \sim \sum_{n=1}^{\infty} a_n J_2(\alpha_{2n} x),$$

where

$$a_n = \frac{\int_0^1 f(x) J_2(\alpha_{2n} x)\, dx}{\int_0^1 x J_2^2(\alpha_{2n} x)\, dx}, \qquad n = 1, 2, 3, \ldots.$$

Therefore,

$$y(x) = \sum_{n=1}^{\infty} \frac{a_n}{\mu - \alpha_{2n}^2} J_2(\alpha_{2n} x).$$

**3.** Again, this is a typical singular Sturm-Liouville boundary value problem. $L$ is selfadjoint since condition (ii) of Lemma 1 on page 710 of the main text holds at the left endpoint and the analogue of condition (i) holds at the right endpoint.

This is Bessel's equation of order 0. As we observed on page 712 of the text, $J_0(\sqrt{\mu} x)$ satisfies the boundary conditions at the origin. At the right endpoint, we want $J_0'(\sqrt{\mu}) = 0$. Now it follows from equation (32) on page 488 of the text, that the zeros of $J_0'$ and $J_1$ are the same. So if we let $\sqrt{\mu_n} = \alpha_{1n}$, the increasing sequence of zeros of $J_1$, then $J_0'(\alpha_{1n}) = 0$. Hence, the eigenfunctions are given by

$$y_n(x) = J_0(\alpha_{1n} x), \qquad n = 1, 2, 3, \ldots.$$

To find an eigenfunction expansion for the solution to the nonhomogeneous equation, we first expand $f(x)/x$ (see page 694):

$$\frac{f(x)}{x} \sim \sum_{n=1}^{\infty} b_n J_0\left(\alpha_{1n}x\right),$$

where

$$b_n = \frac{\int_0^1 f(x)J_0(\alpha_{1n}x)\,dx}{\int_0^1 xJ_0^2(\alpha_{1n}x)\,dx}, \qquad n = 1,2,3,\ldots.$$

Therefore,

$$y(x) = \sum_{n=1}^{\infty} \frac{b_n}{\mu - \alpha_{1n}^2} J_0\left(\alpha_{1n}x\right).$$

11. **(a)** Let $\phi(x)$ be an eigenfunction for

$$\frac{d}{dx}\left[x\frac{dy}{dx}\right] - \frac{\nu^2}{x}y + \lambda xy = 0.$$

Therefore,

$$\frac{d}{dx}\left[x\phi'(x)\right] - \frac{\nu^2}{x}\phi(x) + \lambda x\phi(x) = 0$$

$$\Rightarrow \quad \phi'(x) + x\phi''(x) - \frac{\nu^2}{x}\phi(x) + \lambda x\phi(x) = 0.$$

Multiplying both side by $\phi(x)$ and integrating both sides from 0 to 1, we obtain

$$\int_0^1 \phi(x)\phi'(x)\,dx + \int_0^1 x\phi(x)\phi''(x)\,dx - \int_0^1 \frac{\nu^2}{x}[\phi(x)]^2\,dx + \int_0^1 \lambda x[\phi(x)]^2\,dx = 0. \quad (11.10)$$

Now integrating by parts with $u = \phi(x)\phi'(x)$ and $dv = dx$, we have

$$\int_0^1 \phi(x)\phi'(x)\,dx = x\phi(x)\phi'(x)\,\Big|_0^1 - \int_0^1 x\left[\phi'(x)\phi'(x) + \phi(x)\phi''(x)\right]dx$$

$$= x\phi(x)\phi'(x)\,\Big|_0^1 - \int_0^1 x\left[\phi'(x)\right]^2dx - \int_0^1 x\phi(x)\phi''(x)\,dx.$$

703

Since $\phi(1) = 0$, we have

$$x\phi(x)\phi'(x) \Big|_0^1 = 0,$$

$$\int_0^1 \phi(x)\phi'(x)\,dx = -\int_0^1 x\,[\phi'(x)]^2\,dx - \int_0^1 x\phi(x)\phi''(x)\,dx.$$

Thus equation (11.10) reduces to

$$-\int_0^1 x\,[\phi'(x)]^2\,dx - \int_0^1 x\phi(x)\phi''(x)\,dx + \int_0^1 x\phi(x)\phi''(x)\,dx$$

$$-\nu^2 \int_0^1 x^{-1}[\phi(x)]^2\,dx + \lambda \int_0^1 x[\phi(x)]^2\,dx = 0$$

$$\Rightarrow \quad -\int_0^1 x\,[\phi'(x)]^2\,dx - \nu^2 \int_0^1 x^{-1}[\phi(x)]^2\,dx + \lambda \int_0^1 x[\phi(x)]^2\,dx = 0. \qquad (11.11)$$

(b) First note that each integrand in (11.11) is nonnegative on the interval $(0,1)$, hence each integral is nonnegative. Moreover, since $\phi(x)$ is an eigenfunction, it is a continuous function which is not the zero function. Hence, the second and third integrals are strictly positive. Thus, if $\nu > 0$, then $\lambda$ must be positive in order for the left-hand side of (11.11) to sum to zero.

(c) If $\nu = 0$, then only the first and third terms remain on the left hand side of equation (11.11). Since the first integral need only be nonnegative, we only need $\lambda$ to be nonnegative in order for equation (11.11) to be satisfied.

To show $\lambda = 0$ is not an eigenvalue, we solve Bessel's equation with $\nu = 0$, that is, we solve

$$xy'' + y' = 0,$$

which is the same as the Cauchy-Euler equation

$$x^2 y'' + xy' = 0.$$

Solving this Cauchy-Euler equation, we find a general solution

$$y(x) = c_1 + c_2 \ln x.$$

Since $\lim_{x \to 0^+} y(x) = -\infty$ if $c_2 \neq 0$, we take $c_2 = 0$. Now $y(x) = c_1$ satisfies the boundary condition (17) in the text. The right endpoint boundary condition (18) is $y(1) = 0$. So we want $0 = y(1) = c_1$. Hence the only solution to Bessel's equation of order 0 that satisfies the boundary conditions (17) and (18) is the trivial solution. Hence $\lambda = 0$ is not an eigenvalue.

## EXERCISES 11.8:   Oscillation and Comparison Theory, page 725

**5.** To apply the Sturm fundamental theorem to

$$y'' + (1 - e^x)\, y = 0, \qquad 0 < x < \infty, \tag{11.12}$$

we must find a $q(x)$ and a function $\phi(x)$ such that $q(x) \geq 1 - e^x$, $0 < x < \infty$, and $\phi(x)$ is a solution to

$$y'' + q(x)y = 0, \qquad 0 < x < \infty. \tag{11.13}$$

Because, for $x > 0$, $1 - e^x < 0$, we choose $q(x) \equiv 0$. Hence equation (11.13) becomes $y'' = 0$. The function $\phi(x) = x + 4$ is a nontrivial solution to this differential equation. Since $\phi(x) = x + 4$ does not have a zero for $x > 0$, any nontrivial solution to (11.12) can have at most one zero in $0 < x < \infty$. To use the Sturm fundamental theorem to show that any nontrivial solution to

$$y'' + (1 - e^x)\, y = 0, \qquad -\infty < x < 0, \tag{11.14}$$

has infinitely many zeros, we must find a $q(x)$ and a function $\phi(x)$ such that $q(x) \leq 1 - e^x$, $x < 0$, and $\phi(x)$ is a solution to

$$y'' + q(x)y = 0, \qquad -\infty < x < 0.$$

Because $1 - e^{-1} \approx 0.632$, we choose $q(x) \equiv 1/4$ and only consider the interval $(-\infty, -1)$. Hence, we obtain

$$y'' + \frac{1}{4}y = 0,$$

# Chapter 11

which has nontrivial solution $\phi(x) = \sin(x/2)$. Now the function $\phi(x)$ has infinitely many zeros in $(-\infty, -1)$ and between any two consecutive zeros of $\phi(x)$ any nontrivial solution to (11.14) must have a zero; hence any nontrivial solution to (11.14) will have infinitely many zeros in $(-\infty, -1)$.

9. First express

$$y'' + x^{-2}y' + \left(4 - e^{-x}\right)y = 0,$$

in Strum-Liouville form by multiplying by the integrating factor $e^{-1/x}$:

$$e^{-1/x}y'' + e^{-1/x}x^{-2}y' + e^{-1/x}\left(4 - e^{-x}\right)y = 0 \quad \Rightarrow \quad \left(e^{-1/x}y'\right)' + e^{-1/x}\left(4 - e^{-x}\right)y = 0.$$

Now when $x$ gets large, we have

$$\sqrt{\frac{p}{q}} \approx \sqrt{\frac{e^{-1/\text{large}}}{e^{-1/\text{large}}\left(4 - e^{-\text{large}}\right)}} \approx \sqrt{\frac{1}{(1)(4 - \text{small})}} \approx \sqrt{\frac{1}{4}} = \frac{1}{2}.$$

Hence, the distance between consecutive zeros is approximately $\pi/2$.

11. We apply Corollary 5 with $p(x) = 1 + x$, $q(x) = e^{-x}$, and $r(x) \equiv 1$ to a nontrivial solution on the interval $[0, 5]$. On this interval we have $p_M = 6$, $p_m = 1$, $q_M = 1$, $q_m = e^{-5}$, and $r_M = r_m = 1$. Therefore, for

$$\lambda > \max\left\{\frac{-q_M}{r_M}, \frac{-q_m}{r_m}, 0\right\} = 0,$$

the distance between two consecutive zeros of a nontrivial solution $\phi(x)$ to the given equation is bounded between

$$\pi\sqrt{\frac{p_m}{q_M + \lambda r_M}} = \pi\sqrt{\frac{1}{1 + \lambda}} \quad \text{and} \quad \pi\sqrt{\frac{p_M}{q_m + \lambda r_m}} = \pi\sqrt{\frac{6}{e^{-5} + \lambda}}.$$

# CHAPTER 12: Stability of Autonomous Systems

**EXERCISES 12.2:**   Linear Systems in the Plane, page 753

**3.** The characteristic equation for this system is $r^2 + 2r + 10 = 0$, which has roots $r = -1 \pm 3i$. Since the real part of each root is negative, the trajectories approach the origin, and the origin is an asymptotically stable spiral point.

**7.** The critical point is the solution to the system

$$-4x + 2y + 8 = 0,$$
$$x - 2y + 1 = 0.$$

Solving this system, we obtain the critical point $(3, 2)$. Now we use the change of variables

$$x = u + 3, \qquad y = v + 2,$$

to translate the critical point $(3, 2)$ to the origin $(0, 0)$. Substituting into the system of this problem and simplifying, we obtain a system of differential equations in $u$ and $v$:

$$\frac{du}{dt} = \frac{dx}{dt} = -4(u + 3) + 2(v + 2) + 8 = -4u + 2v,$$
$$\frac{dv}{dt} = \frac{dy}{dt} = (u + 3) - 2(v + 2) + 1 = u - 2v.$$

The characteristic equation for this system is $r^2 + 6r + 6 = 0$, which has roots $r = -3 \pm \sqrt{3}$. Since both roots are distinct and negative, the origin is an asymptotically stable improper node of the new system. Therefore, the critical point $(3, 2)$ is an asymptotically stable improper node of the original system.

**9.** The critical point is the solution to the system

$$2x + y + 9 = 0,$$
$$-5x - 2y - 22 = 0.$$

Solving this system, we obtain the critical point $(-4, -1)$. Now we use the change of variables

$$x = u - 4, \qquad y = v - 1,$$

to translate the critical point $(-4, -1)$ to the origin $(0, 0)$. Substituting into the system of this problem and simplifying, we obtain a system of differential equations in $u$ and $v$:

$$\frac{du}{dt} = \frac{dx}{dt} = 2(u - 4) + (v - 1) + 9 = 2u + v,$$

$$\frac{dv}{dt} = \frac{dy}{dt} = -5(u - 4) - 2(v - 1) - 22 = -5u - 2v.$$

The characteristic equation for this system is $r^2 + 1 = 0$, which has roots $r = \pm i$. Since both roots are distinct and pure imaginary, the origin is a stable center of the new system. Therefore, the critical point $(-4, -1)$ is a stable center of the original system.

15. The characteristic equation for this system is $r^2 + r - 12 = 0$, which has roots $r = -4$ and $r = 3$. Since the roots are real and have opposite signs, the origin is an unstable saddle point. To sketch the phase plane diagram, we must first determine two lines passing through the origin that correspond to the transformed axes. To find the transformed axes, we make the substitution $y = mx$ into

$$\frac{dy}{dx} = \frac{dy/dt}{dx/dt} = \frac{5x - 2y}{x + 2y}$$

to obtain

$$m = \frac{5x - 2mx}{x + 2mx}.$$

Solving for $m$ yields

$$m(x + 2mx) = 5x - 2mx \quad \Rightarrow \quad 2m^2 + 3m - 5 = 0 \quad \Rightarrow \quad m = -\frac{5}{2} \quad \text{or} \quad m = 1.$$

So $m = -5/2$ or $m = 1$. Hence, the two axes are $y = -5x/2$ and $y = x$. On the line $y = x$ one finds

$$\frac{dx}{dt} = 3x,$$

so the trajectories move away from the origin. On the line $y = -5x/2$ one finds

$$\frac{dy}{dt} = -4y,$$

so the trajectories move towards the origin. A phase plane diagram is given in Figure B.56 in the answers of the text.

**19.** The characteristic equation for this system is $(r+2)(r+2) = 0$ which has roots $r = -2, -2$. Since the roots are equal, real, and negative, the origin is an asymptotically stable point. To sketch the phase plane diagram, we determine the slope of the two lines passing through the origin that correspond to the transformed axes by substituting $y = mx$ into

$$\frac{dy}{dx} = \frac{dy/dt}{dx/dt} = \frac{-2y}{-2x+y}$$

to obtain

$$m = \frac{-2mx}{-2x+mx}.$$

Solving for $m$ yields

$$m(-2x+mx) = -2mx \quad \Rightarrow \quad m^2 = 0 \quad \Rightarrow \quad m = 0.$$

Since there is only one line ($y = 0$) through the origin that is a trajectory, the origin is an improper node. A phase plane diagram is given in Figure B.58 in the answers of the text.

## EXERCISES 12.3:    Almost Linear Systems, page 764

**5.** This system is almost linear since $ad - bc = (1)(-1) - (5)(-1) \neq 0$, and the functions $F(x, y) = G(x, y) = -y^2 = 0$ involve only high order terms in $y$. Since the characteristic equation for this system is $r^2 + 4 = 0$ which has pure imaginary roots $r = \pm 2i$, the origin is either a center or a spiral point and the stability is indeterminant.

**7.** To see that this system is almost linear, we first express $e^{x+y}$, $\cos x$, and $\cos y$ using their respective Maclaurin series. Hence, the system

$$\frac{dx}{dt} = e^{x+y} - \cos x,$$

$$\frac{dy}{dt} = \cos y + x - 1,$$

becomes

$$\frac{dx}{dt} = \left[1 + (x+y) + \frac{(x+y)^2}{2!} + \cdots\right] - \left[1 - \frac{x^2}{2!} + \cdots\right]$$

$$= x + y + \text{(higher orders)} = x + y + F(x,y),$$

$$\frac{dy}{dt} = \left[1 - \frac{y^2}{2!} + \cdots\right] + x - 1 = x + \text{(higher orders)} = x + G(x,y).$$

This system is almost linear since $ad - bc = (1)(0) - (1)(1) \neq 0$, and $F(x,y)$, $G(x,y)$ each only involve higher order forms in $x$ and $y$. The characteristic equation for this system is $r^2 - r - 1 = 0$ which has roots $r = (1 \pm \sqrt{5})/2$. Since these roots are real and have different signs the origin is an unstable saddle point.

9. The critical points for this system are the solutions to the pair of equations

$$16 - xy = 0,$$
$$x - y^3 = 0.$$

Solving the second equation for $x$ in terms of $y$ and substituting this into the first equation we obtain

$$16 - y^4 = 0$$

which has solutions $y = \pm 2$. Hence the critical points are $(8,2)$ and $(-8,-2)$.

We consider the critical point $(8,2)$. Using the change of variables $x = u + 8$ and $y = v + 2$, we obtain the system

$$\frac{du}{dt} = 16 - (u+8)(v+2),$$
$$\frac{dv}{dt} = (u+8) - (v+2)^3,$$

which simplifies to the almost linear system

$$\frac{du}{dt} = -2u - 8v - uv,$$
$$\frac{dv}{dt} = u - 12v - 6v^2 - v^3.$$

The characteristic equation for this system is $r^2 + 14r + 32 = 0$, which has the distinct negative roots $r = -7 \pm \sqrt{17}$. Hence $(8,2)$ is an improper node which is asymptotically stable.

Next we consider the critical point $(-8, -2)$. Using the change of variables $x = u - 8$ and $y = v - 2$, we obtain the system

$$\frac{du}{dt} = 16 - (u - 8)(v - 2),$$

$$\frac{dv}{dt} = (u - 8) - (v - 2)^3,$$

which simplifies to the almost linear system

$$\frac{du}{dt} = 2u + 8v - uv,$$

$$\frac{dv}{dt} = u - 12v + 6v^2 - v^3.$$

The characteristic equation for this system is $r^2 + 10r - 32 = 0$, which has the distinct roots $r = -5 \pm \sqrt{57}$. Since these roots are real and have different signs, $(-8, -2)$ is an unstable saddle point.

**13.** The critical points for this system are the solutions to the pair of equations

$$1 - xy = 0,$$

$$x - y^3 = 0.$$

Solving the second equation for $x$ in terms of $y$ and substituting this into the first equation we obtain

$$1 - y^4 = 0$$

which has solutions $y = \pm 1$. Hence the critical points are $(1, 1)$ and $(-1, -1)$.

We consider the critical point $(1, 1)$. Using the change of variables $x = u + 1$ and $y = v + 1$, we obtain the almost linear system

$$\frac{du}{dt} = 1 - (u + 1)(v + 1) = -u - v - uv,$$

$$\frac{dv}{dt} = (u + 1) - (v + 1)^3 = u - 3v - 3v^2 - v^3.$$

The characteristic equation for this system is $r^2 + 4r + 4 = 0$, which has the equal negative roots $r = -2$. Hence $(1, 1)$ is an improper or proper node or spiral point which is asymptotically stable.

Next we consider the critical point $(-1, -1)$. Using the change of variables $x = u - 1$ and $y = v - 1$, we obtain the almost linear system

$$\frac{du}{dt} = 1 - (u-1)(v-1) = u + v - uv,$$

$$\frac{dv}{dt} = (u-1) - (v-1)^3 = u - 3v + 3v^2 - v^3.$$

The characteristic equation for this system is $r^2 + 2r - 4 = 0$, which has roots $r = -1 \pm \sqrt{5}$. Since these roots are real and have different signs, $(-1, -1)$ is an unstable saddle point. A phase plane diagram is given in Figure B.59 in the answers of the text.

**21.** <u>Case 1: $h = 0$.</u> The critical points for this system are the solutions to the pair of equations

$$x(1 - 4x - y) = 0,$$
$$y(1 - 2y - 5x) = 0.$$

To solve this system, we first let $x = 0$, then $y(1 - 2y) = 0$. So $y = 0$ or $y = 1/2$.

When $y = 0$, we must have $x(1 - 4x) = 0$. So $x = 0$ or $x = 1/4$.

And if $x \neq 0$ and $y \neq 0$, we have the system

$$1 - 4x - y = 0,$$
$$1 - 2y - 5x = 0,$$

which has the solution $x = 1/3$, $y = -1/3$. Hence the critical points are $(0,0)$, $(0, 1/2)$, $(1/4, 0)$, and $(1/3, -1/3)$.

At the critical point $(0,0)$, the characteristic equation is $r^2 - 2r + 1 = 0$, which has equal positive roots $r = 1$. Hence $(0,0)$ is an improper or proper node or spiral point which is unstable. From Figure B.61 in the text, we see that $(0,0)$ is an improper node.

Next we consider the critical point $(0, 1/2)$. Using the change of variables $y = v + 1/2$ and $x = u$, we obtain the almost linear system

$$\frac{du}{dt} = u\left(1 - 4u - v - \frac{1}{2}\right) = \frac{1}{2}u - 4u^2 - uv,$$

$$\frac{dv}{dt} = \left(v + \frac{1}{2}\right)(1 - 2v - 1 - 5u) = -\frac{5}{2}u - v - 2v^2 - 5uv.$$

The characteristic equation for this system is $r^2 + (1/2)r - (1/2) = 0$, which has roots $r = 1/2$ and $r = -1$. Since these roots are real and have different signs, $(0, 1/2)$ is an unstable saddle point.

Now consider the critical point $(1/4, 0)$. Using the change of variables $x = u + 1/4$ and $y = v$, we obtain the almost linear system

$$\frac{du}{dt} = \left( u + \frac{1}{4} \right)(1 - 4u - 1 - v) = -u - \frac{1}{4}v - 4u^2 - uv,$$

$$\frac{dv}{dt} = v \left( 1 - 2v - 5u - \frac{5}{2} \right) = -\frac{1}{4}v - 2v^2 - 5uv.$$

The characteristic equation for this system is $r^2 + (5/4)r + (1/4) = 0$, which has roots $r = -1/4$ and $r = -1$. Since these roots are distinct and negative, $(1/4, 0)$ is an improper node which is asymptotically stable.

At the critical point $(1/3, -1/3)$, we use the change of variables $x = u + 1/3$ and $y = v - 1/3$ to obtain the almost linear system

$$\frac{du}{dt} = \left( u + \frac{1}{3} \right)\left( 1 - 4u - \frac{4}{3} - v + \frac{1}{3} \right) = -\frac{4}{3}u - \frac{1}{3}v - 4u^2 - uv,$$

$$\frac{dv}{dt} = \left( v - \frac{1}{3} \right)\left( 1 - 2v + \frac{2}{3} - 5u - \frac{5}{3} \right) = \frac{5}{3}u + \frac{2}{3}v - 2v^2 - 5uv.$$

The characteristic equation for this system is $r^2 + (2/3)r - (1/3) = 0$ which has roots $r = 1/3$ and $r = -1$. Again since these roots are real and have different signs, $(1/3, -1/3)$ is an unstable saddle point, but not of interest since $y < 0$. Species $x$ survives while species $y$ dies off. A phase plane diagram is given in Figure B.61 in the answers of the text.

Case 2: $h = 1/32$. The critical points for this system are the solutions to the pair of equations

$$x(1 - 4x - y) - \frac{1}{32} = 0,$$
$$y(1 - 2y - 5x) = 0.$$

To solve this system, we first set $y = 0$ and solve $x(1 - 4x) - 1/32 = 0$, which has solutions $x = (2 \pm \sqrt{2})/16$.

If $y \neq 0$, we have $1 - 2y - 5x = 0$. So $y = (1/2) - (5/2)x$. Substituting, we obtain

$$x\left[1 - 4x - \left(\frac{1}{2} - \frac{5}{2}x\right)\right] - \frac{1}{32} = 0.$$

Simplifying, we obtain

$$-\frac{3}{2}x^2 + \frac{1}{2}x - \frac{1}{32} = 0,$$

which has the solution $x = 1/4$ or $x = 1/12$. When $x = 1/4$, we have

$$y = \frac{1}{2} - \frac{5}{2}\left(\frac{1}{4}\right) = -\frac{1}{8}.$$

And when $x = 1/12$, we have

$$y = \frac{1}{2} - \frac{5}{2}\left(\frac{1}{12}\right) = \frac{7}{24}.$$

Hence the critical points are

$$\left(\frac{2-\sqrt{2}}{16}, 0\right), \qquad \left(\frac{2+\sqrt{2}}{16}, 0\right), \qquad \left(\frac{1}{4}, -\frac{1}{8}\right), \qquad \text{and} \qquad \left(\frac{1}{12}, \frac{7}{24}\right).$$

At the critical point $\left(\dfrac{2-\sqrt{2}}{16}, 0\right)$, we use the change of variables $x = u + \dfrac{2-\sqrt{2}}{16}$ and $y = v$ to obtain the almost linear system

$$\frac{du}{dt} = \left(u + \frac{2-\sqrt{2}}{16}\right)\left(1 - 4u - \frac{2-\sqrt{2}}{4} - v\right) - \frac{1}{32} = \frac{\sqrt{2}}{2}u - \frac{2-\sqrt{2}}{16}v - 4u^2 - uv,$$

$$\frac{dv}{dt} = v\left(1 - 2v - 5u - \frac{10-5\sqrt{2}}{16}\right) = \frac{6+5\sqrt{2}}{16}v - 2v^2 - 5uv.$$

The characteristic equation for this system is

$$\left(r - \frac{\sqrt{2}}{2}\right)\left(r - \frac{6+5\sqrt{2}}{16}\right) = 0,$$

which has distinct positive roots. Hence $\left(\dfrac{2-\sqrt{2}}{16}, 0\right)$ is an unstable improper node.

Now consider the critical point $\left( \dfrac{2+\sqrt{2}}{16}, 0 \right)$, where we use the change of variables $y = v$ and

$x = u + \dfrac{2+\sqrt{2}}{16}$ to obtain the almost linear system

$$\frac{du}{dt} = \left( u + \frac{2+\sqrt{2}}{16} \right)\left( 1 - 4u - \frac{2+\sqrt{2}}{4} - v \right) - \frac{1}{32} = -\frac{\sqrt{2}}{2}u - \frac{2+\sqrt{2}}{16}v - 4u^2 - uv,$$

$$\frac{dv}{dt} = v\left( 1 - 2v - 5u - \frac{10+5\sqrt{2}}{16} \right) = \frac{6-5\sqrt{2}}{16}v - 2v^2 - 5uv.$$

The characteristic equation for this system is

$$\left( r + \frac{\sqrt{2}}{2} \right)\left( r - \frac{6-5\sqrt{2}}{16} \right) = 0,$$

which has distinct negative roots. Hence $\left( \dfrac{2+\sqrt{2}}{16}, 0 \right)$ is an asymptotically stable improper node.

When the critical point is $(1/12, 7/24)$, the change of variables $x = u + 1/12$ and $y = v + 7/24$ leads to the almost linear system

$$\frac{du}{dt} = \left( u + \frac{1}{12} \right)\left( 1 - 4u - \frac{1}{3} - v - \frac{7}{24} \right) - \frac{1}{32} = \frac{1}{24}u - \frac{1}{12}v - 4u^2 - uv,$$

$$\frac{dv}{dt} = \left( v + \frac{7}{24} \right)\left( 1 - 2v - \frac{7}{12} - 5u - \frac{5}{12} \right) = -\frac{35}{24}u - \frac{7}{12}v - 2v^2 - 5uv.$$

The characteristic equation for this system is $r^2 + (13/24)r - (7/48) = 0$, which has roots $r = (-13 \pm \sqrt{505})/48$. Since these roots have opposite signs, $(1/12, 7/24)$ is an unstable saddle point.

And when the critical point is $(1/4, -1/8)$, the change of variables $x = u + 1/4$ and $y = v - 1/8$ leads to the almost linear system

$$\frac{du}{dt} = \left( u + \frac{1}{4} \right)\left( 1 - 4u - 1 - v + \frac{1}{8} \right) - \frac{1}{32} = -\frac{7}{8}u - \frac{1}{4}v - 4u^2 - uv,$$

$$\frac{dv}{dt} = \left( v - \frac{1}{8} \right)\left( 1 - 2v + \frac{1}{4} - 5u - \frac{5}{4} \right) = \frac{5}{8}u + \frac{1}{4}v - 2v^2 - 5uv.$$

# Chapter 12

The characteristic equation for this system is $r^2 + (5/8)r - (1/16) = 0$, which has roots $r = (-5 \pm \sqrt{41})/16$. Since these roots have opposite signs, $(1/4, -1/8)$ is an unstable saddle point. But since $y < 0$, this point is not of interest.

Hence, this is competitive exclusion; one species survives while the other dies off. A phase plane diagram is given in Figure B.62 in the answers of the text.

Case 3: $h = 5/32$. The critical points for this system are the solutions to the pair of equations

$$x(1 - 4x - y) - \frac{5}{32} = 0,$$
$$y(1 - 2y - 5x) = 0.$$

To solve this system, we first set $y = 0$ and solve

$$x(1 - 4x) - \frac{5}{32} = 0,$$

which has complex solutions. If $y \neq 0$, then we must have

$$1 - 2y - 5x = 0 \qquad \Rightarrow \qquad y = \frac{1}{2} - \frac{5}{2}x.$$

Substituting we obtain

$$x\left[1 - 4x - \left(\frac{1}{2} - \frac{5}{2}x\right)\right] - \frac{5}{32} = 0.$$

Simplifying, we obtain

$$-\frac{3}{2}x^2 + \frac{1}{2}x - \frac{5}{32} = 0,$$

which also has only complex solutions. Hence there are no critical points. The phase plane diagram shows that species $y$ survives while the $x$ dies off. A phase plane diagram is given in Figure B.63 in the answers of the text.

## EXERCISES 12.4:  Energy Methods, page 774

**3.** Here $g(x) = x^2/(x-1) = x + 1 + 1/(x-1)$. By integrating $g(x)$, we obtain the potential function

$$G(x) = \frac{x^2}{2} + x + \ln|x - 1| + C,$$

and so

$$E(x, v) = \frac{v^2}{2} + \frac{x^2}{2} + x + \ln|x - 1| + C.$$

Since $E(0, 0) = 0$ implies $C = 0$, let

$$E(x, v) = \frac{v^2}{2} + \frac{x^2}{2} + x + \ln|x - 1|.$$

Now, since we are interested in $E$ near the origin, we let $|x - 1| = 1 - x$ (because for $x$ near $0$, $x - 1 < 0$). Therefore,

$$E(x, v) = \frac{v^2}{2} + \frac{x^2}{2} + x + \ln(1 - x).$$

9. Here we have $g(x) = 2x^2 + x - 1$ and hence the potential function

$$G(x) = \frac{2x^3}{3} + \frac{x^2}{2} - x.$$

The local maxima and minima of $G(x)$ occur when $G'(x) = g(x) = 2x^2 + x - 1 = 0$. Thus the phase plane diagram has critical points at $(-1, 0)$ and $(1/2, 0)$. Since $G(x)$ has a strict local minimum at $x = 1/2$, the critical point $(1/2, 0)$ is a center. Furthermore, since $x = -1$ is strict local maximum, the critical point $(-1, 0)$ is a saddle point. A sketch of the potential plane and phase plane diagram is given in Figure B.65 in the answers of the text.

11. Here we have $g(x) = x/(x - 2) = 1 + 2/(x - 2)$ so the potential function is

$$G(x) = x + 2\ln|x - 2| = x + 2\ln(2 - x),$$

for $x$ near zero. Local maxima and minima of $G(x)$ occur when $G'(x) = g(x) = x/(x-2) = 0$. Thus the phase plane diagram has critical points at $(0, 0)$. Furthermore we note that $x = 2$ is not in the domain of $g(x)$ nor of $G(x)$. Now $G(x)$ has a strict local maximum at $x = 0$, hence the critical point $(0, 0)$ is a saddle point. A sketch of the potential plane and phase plane diagram for $x < 2$ is given in Figure B.66 in the answers of the text.

13. We first observe that $vh(x, v) = v^2 > 0$ for $v \neq 0$. Hence, the energy is continually decreasing along a trajectory. The level curves for the energy function

$$E(x, v) = \frac{v^2}{2} + \frac{x^2}{2} - \frac{x^4}{4}$$

# Chapter 12

are just the integral curves for Example 2(a) and are sketch in Figure 12.22 on page 770 of the text. The critical points for this damped system are the same as in the example and moreover, they are of the same type. The resulting phase plane is given in Figure B.67 in the answers of the text.

## EXERCISES 12.5: Lyapunov's Direct Method, page 782

**3.** We compute $\dot{V}(x, y)$ with $V(x, y) = x^2 + y^2$.

$$
\begin{aligned}
\dot{V}(x, y) &= V_x(x, y) f(x, y) + V_y(x, y) g(x, y) \\
&= 2x \left( y^2 + xy^2 - x^3 \right) + 2y \left( -xy + x^2 y - y^3 \right) \\
&= 4x^2 y^2 - 2x^4 - 2y^4 = -2 \left( x^2 - y^2 \right)^2 .
\end{aligned}
$$

According to Theorem 3, since $\dot{V}$ is negative semidefinite, $V$ is positive definite function, and $(0, 0)$ is an isolated critical point of the system, the origin is stable.

**5.** The origin is an isolated critical point for the system. Using the hint, we compute $\dot{V}(x, y)$ with $V(x, y) = x^2 - y^2$. Computing, we obtain

$$
\begin{aligned}
\dot{V}(x, y) &= V_x(x, y) f(x, y) + V_y(x, y) g(x, y) \\
&= 2x \left( 2x^3 \right) - 2y \left( 2x^2 y - y^3 \right) = 4x^4 - 4x^2 y^2 + 2y^2 = 2x^4 + \left( x^2 - y^2 \right)^2 ,
\end{aligned}
$$

which is positive definite. Now $V(0, 0) = 0$, and in every disk centered at the origin, $V$ is positive at some point (namely, those points where $|x| > |y|$). Therefore, by Theorem 4, the origin is unstable.

**7.** We compute $\dot{V}(x, y)$ with $V(x, y) = ax^4 + by^2$.

$$
\begin{aligned}
\dot{V}(x, y) &= V_x(x, y) f(x, y) + V_y(x, y) g(x, y) \\
&= 4ax^3 \left( 2y - x^3 \right) + 2by \left( -x^3 - y^5 \right) \\
&= 8ax^3 y - 4ax^6 - 2bx^3 y - 2by^6 .
\end{aligned}
$$

To eliminate the $x^3 y$ term, we let $a = 1$ and $b = 4$, then

$$\dot{V}(x, y) = -4x^6 - 8y^6,$$

and we get that $\dot{V}$ is negative definite. Since $V$ is positive definite and the origin is an isolated critical point, according to Theorem 3, the origin is asymptotically stable.

**11.** Here we set

$$y = \frac{dx}{dt} \qquad \Rightarrow \qquad \frac{dy}{dt} = \frac{d^2 x}{dt^2}.$$

Then, we obtain the system

$$\frac{dx}{dt} = y,$$
$$\frac{dy}{dt} = -\left(1 - y^2\right) y - x.$$

Clearly, the zero solution is a solution to this system. To apply Lyapunov's direct method, we try the positive definite function $V(x, y) = ax^2 + by^2$ and compute $\dot{V}$.

$$
\begin{aligned}
\dot{V}(x, y) &= V_x(x, y) f(x, y) + V_y(x, y) g(x, y) \\
&= 2ax\,(y) + 2by\left[-\left(1 - y^2\right) y - x\right] = 2axy - 2by^2 + 2by^4 - 2bxy.
\end{aligned}
$$

To eliminate the $xy$ terms, we choose $a = b = 1$, then

$$\dot{V}(x, y) = -2y^2 \left(1 - y^2\right).$$

Hence $\dot{V}$ is negative semidefinite for $|y| < 1$, so by Theorem 3, the origin is stable.

## EXERCISES 12.6:   Limit Cycles and Periodic Solutions, page 791

**5.** We compute $r\dfrac{dr}{dt}$:

$$
\begin{aligned}
r\frac{dr}{dt} &= x\frac{dx}{dt} + y\frac{dy}{dt} = x\left[x - y + x\left(r^3 - 4r^2 + 5r - 3\right)\right] + y\left[x + y + y\left(r^3 - 4r^2 + 5r - 3\right)\right] \\
&= x^2 - xy + x^2\left(r^3 - 4r^2 + 5r - 3\right) + xy + y^2 + y^2\left(r^3 - 4r^2 + 5r - 3\right) \\
&= r^2 + r^2\left(r^3 - 4r^2 + 5r - 3\right) = r^2\left(r^3 - 4r^2 + 5r - 2\right).
\end{aligned}
$$

Chapter 12

Hence

$$\frac{dr}{dt} = r\left(r^3 - 4r^2 + 5r - 2\right) = r(r-1)^2(r-2).$$

Now $dr/dt = 0$ when $r = 0, 1, 2$. The critical point is represented by $r = 0$, and when $r = 1$ or $2$, we have limit cycles of radius 1 and 2. When $r$ lies in $(0, 1)$, we have $dr/dt < 0$, so a trajectory in this region spirals into the origin. Therefore, the origin is an asymptotically stable spiral point. Now, when $r$ lies in $(1, 2)$, we again have $dr/dt < 0$, so a trajectory in this region spirals into the limit cycle $r = 1$. This tells us that $r = 1$ is a semistable limit cycle. Finally, when $r > 2$, $dr/dt > 0$, so a trajectory in this region spirals away from the limit cycle $r = 2$. Hence, $r = 2$ is an unstable limit cycle.

To find the direction of the trajectories, we compute $r^2 \dfrac{d\theta}{dt}$.

$$\begin{aligned}
r^2\frac{d\theta}{dt} &= x\frac{dy}{dt} - y\frac{dx}{dt} = x\left[x + y + y\left(r^3 - 4r^2 + 5r - 3\right)\right] - y\left[x - y + x\left(r^3 - 4r^2 + 5r - 3\right)\right] \\
&= x^2 + xy + xy\left(r^3 - 4r^2 + 5r - 3\right) - xy + y^2 - xy\left(r^3 - 4r^2 + 5r - 3\right) \\
&= x^2 + y^2 = r^2.
\end{aligned}$$

Hence $d\theta/dt = 1$, which tells us that the trajectories revolve counterclockwise about the origin. A phase plane diagram is given in Figure B.74 in the answers of the text.

**11.** We compute $r\, dr/dt$:

$$\begin{aligned}
r\frac{dr}{dt} &= x\frac{dx}{dt} + y\frac{dy}{dt} = x\left[y + x\sin\left(\frac{1}{r}\right)\right] + y\left[-x + y\sin\left(\frac{1}{r}\right)\right] \\
&= xy + x^2\sin\left(\frac{1}{r}\right) - xy + y^2\sin\left(\frac{1}{r}\right) = r^2\sin\left(\frac{1}{r}\right).
\end{aligned}$$

Hence,

$$\frac{dr}{dt} = r\sin\left(\frac{1}{r}\right),$$

and $dr/dt = 0$ when $r = 1/(n\pi)$, $n = 1, 2, \ldots$. Consequently, the origin $(r = 0)$ is not an isolated critical point. Observe that

$$\frac{dr}{dt} > 0 \quad \text{for} \quad \frac{1}{(2n+1)\pi} < r < \frac{1}{2n\pi},$$

$$\frac{dr}{dt} < 0 \quad \text{for} \quad \frac{1}{2n\pi} < r < \frac{1}{(2n-1)\pi}.$$

Thus, trajectories spiral into the limit cycles $r = 1/(2n\pi)$ and away from the limit cycles $r = 1/[(2n+1)\pi]$. To determine the direction of the spiral, we compute $r^2\, d\theta/dt$.

$$r^2\frac{d\theta}{dt} = x\frac{dy}{dt} - y\frac{dx}{dt} = x\left[-x + y\sin\left(\frac{1}{r}\right)\right] - y\left[y + x\sin\left(\frac{1}{r}\right)\right]$$

$$= -x^2 + xy\sin\left(\frac{1}{r}\right) - y^2 - xy\sin\left(\frac{1}{r}\right) = -r^2.$$

Hence $d\theta/dt = -1$, which tells us that the trajectories revolve clockwise about the origin. A phase plane diagram is given in Figure B.77 in the answers of the text.

**15.** We compute $f_x + g_y$ in order to apply Theorem 6. Thus

$$f_x(x,y) + g_y(x,y) = (-8 + 3x^2) + (-7 + 3y^2) = 3\left(x^2 + y^2 - 5\right),$$

which is less than 0 for the given domain. Hence, by Theorem 6, there are no nonconstant periodic solutions in the disk $x^2 + y^2 < 5$.

**19.** It is easily seen that $(0,0)$ is a critical point, however, it is not easily shown that it is the only critical point for this system. Using the Lyapunov function $V(x,y) = 2x^2 + y^2$, we compute $\dot{V}(x,y)$. Thus

$$\dot{V}(x,y) = V_x(x,y)\frac{dx}{dt} + V_y(x,y)\frac{dy}{dt}$$
$$= 4x\left(2x - y - 2x^3 - 3xy^2\right) + 2y\left(2x + 4y - 4y^3 - 2x^2y\right)$$
$$= 8x^2 - 8x^4 - 16x^2y^2 + 8y^2 - 8y^4 = 8\left(x^2 + y^2\right) - 8\left(x^2 + y^2\right)^2.$$

Therefore, $\dot{V}(x,y) < 0$ for $x^2 + y^2 > 1$ and $\dot{V}(x,y) > 0$ for $x^2 + y^2 < 1$. Let $C_1$ be the curve $2x^2 + y^2 = 1/2$, which lies inside $x^2 + y^2 = 1$, and let $C_2$ be the curve $2x^2 + y^2 = 3$, which lies outside $x^2 + y^2 = 1$. Now $\dot{V}(x,y) > 0$ on $C_1$ and $\dot{V}(x,y) < 0$ on $C_2$. Hence, we let $R$ be the region between the curves $C_1$ and $C_2$. Now, any trajectory that enters $R$ is contained in $R$. So by Theorem 7, the system has a nonconstant periodic solution in $R$.

Chapter 12

**25.** To apply Theorem 8, we check to see that all five conditions hold. Here we have $g(x) = x$ and $f(x) = x^2(x^2 - 1)$. Clearly, $f(x)$ is even, hence condition **(a)** holds. Now

$$F(x) = \int_0^x s^2\left(s^2 - 1\right) ds = \frac{x^5}{5} - \frac{x^3}{3}.$$

Hence $F(x) < 0$ for $0 < x < \sqrt{5/3}$ and $F(x) > 0$ for $x > \sqrt{5/3}$. Therefore, condition **(b)** holds. Furthermore, condition **(c)** holds since $F(x) \to +\infty$ as $x \to +\infty$, monotonically for $x > \sqrt{5/3}$. As stated above, $g(x) = x$ is an odd function with $g(x) > 0$ for $x > 0$, thus condition **(d)** holds. Finally, since

$$G(x) = \int_0^x s\, ds = \frac{x^2}{2},$$

we clearly have $G(x) \to +\infty$ as $x \to +\infty$, hence condition **(e)** holds. It follows from Theorem 8, that the Lienard equation has a unique nonconstant periodic solution.

**EXERCISES 12.7:   Stability of Higher-Dimensional Systems, page 798**

**5.** From the characteristic equation

$$-(r - 1)\left(r^2 + 1\right) = 0,$$

we find that the eigenvalues are 1, $\pm i$. Since at least one eigenvalue, 1, has a positive real part, the zero solution is unstable.

**9.** The characteristic equation is

$$\left(r^2 + 1\right)\left(r^2 + 1\right) = 0,$$

which has eigenvalues $\pm i$, $\pm i$. Next we determine the eigenspace for the eigenvalue $i$. Computing we find

$$\begin{vmatrix} i & -1 & -1 & 0 \\ 1 & i & 0 & -1 \\ 0 & 0 & i & -1 \\ 0 & 0 & 1 & i \end{vmatrix} \Rightarrow \begin{vmatrix} 1 & i & 0 & 0 \\ 0 & 0 & 1 & 0 \\ 0 & 0 & 0 & 1 \\ 0 & 0 & 0 & 0 \end{vmatrix}.$$

Hence the eigenspace is degenerate and by Problem 8(c) on page 798 of the text, the zero solution is unstable. Note: it can be shown that the eigenspace for the eigenvalue $-i$ is also degenerate.

**13.** To find the fundamental matrix for this system we first recall the Taylor series $e^x$, $\sin x$, and $\cos x$. These are

$$e^x = 1 + x + \frac{x^2}{2!} + \frac{x^3}{3!} + \cdots,$$

$$\sin x = x - \frac{x^3}{3!} + \frac{x^5}{5!} - \cdots,$$

$$\cos x = 1 - \frac{x^2}{2!} + \frac{x^4}{4!} - \cdots.$$

Hence

$$\frac{dx_1}{dt} = \left(1 - x_1 + \frac{x_1^2}{2!} - \cdots\right) + \left(1 - \frac{x_2^2}{2!} + \cdots\right) - 2 = -x_1 + \left(\frac{x_1^2}{2!} - \cdots\right) + \left(-\frac{x_2^2}{2!} + \cdots\right),$$

$$\frac{dx_2}{dt} = -x_2 + \left(x_3 - \frac{x_3^3}{3!} + \cdots\right) = -x_2 - x_3 + \left(-\frac{x_3^3}{3!} + \cdots\right),$$

$$\frac{dx_3}{dt} = 1 - \left[1 + (x_2 + x_3) + \frac{(x_2 + x_3)^2}{2!} + \cdots\right] = -x_2 - x_3 - \left[\frac{(x_2 + x_3)^2}{2!} + \cdots\right].$$

Thus,

$$\mathbf{A} = \begin{bmatrix} -1 & 0 & 0 \\ 0 & -1 & 1 \\ 0 & -1 & -1 \end{bmatrix}.$$

Calculating the eigenvalues, we have

$$|\mathbf{A} - r\mathbf{I}| = \begin{vmatrix} -1 - r & 0 & 0 \\ 0 & -1 - r & 1 \\ 0 & -1 & -1 - r \end{vmatrix} = 0.$$

Hence, the characteristic equation is $-(r+1)(r^2 + 2r + 2) = 0$. Therefore, the eigenvalues are $-1$, $-1 \pm i$. Since the real part of each is negative, the zero solution is asymptotically stable.

723

# Chapter 12

**15.** Solving for the critical points, we must have

$$-x_1 + 1 = 0,$$
$$-2x_1 - x_2 + 2x_3 - 4 = 0,$$
$$-3x_1 - 2x_2 - x_3 + 1 = 0.$$

Solving this system, we find that the only solution is $(1, -2, 2)$. We now use the change of variables

$$x_1 = u + 1, \qquad x_2 = v - 2, \qquad x_3 = w + 2$$

to translate the critical point to the origin. Substituting, we obtain the system

$$\frac{du}{dt} = -u,$$
$$\frac{dv}{dt} = -2u - v + 2w,$$
$$\frac{dw}{dt} = -3u - 2v - w.$$

Here **A** is given by

$$\mathbf{A} = \begin{bmatrix} -1 & 0 & 0 \\ -2 & -1 & 2 \\ -3 & -2 & -1 \end{bmatrix}.$$

Finding the characteristic equation, we have $-(r+1)(r^2 + 2r + 5) = 0$. Hence the eigenvalues are $-1$, $-1 \pm 2i$. Since each eigenvalue has a negative real part, the critical point $(1, -2, 2)$ is asymptotically stable.

# CHAPTER 13: Existence and Uniqueness Theory

**EXERCISES 13.1:   Introduction: Successive Approximations, page 812**

**1.** In this problem, $x_0 = 1$, $y_0 = y(x_0) = 4$, and $f(x, y) = x^2 - y$. Thus, applying formula (3) on page 807 of the text yields

$$y(x) = y_0 + \int_{x_0}^{x} f(t, y(t))\, dt = 4 + \int_{1}^{x} \left[t^2 - y(t)\right] dt = 4 + \int_{1}^{x} t^2\, dt - \int_{1}^{x} y(t)\, dt\,.$$

Since

$$\int_{1}^{x} t^2\, dt = \frac{t^3}{3}\bigg|_{1}^{x} = \frac{x^3}{3} - \frac{1}{3}\,,$$

the equation becomes

$$y(x) = 4 + \frac{x^3}{3} - \frac{1}{3} - \int_{1}^{x} y(t)\, dt = \frac{11}{3} + \frac{x^3}{3} - \int_{1}^{x} y(t)\, dt\,.$$

**3.** In the initial conditions, $x_0 = 1$ and $y_0 = -3$. Also, $f(x, y) = (y - x)^2 = y^2 - 2xy + x^2$. Therefore,

$$y(x) = y_0 + \int_{x_0}^{x} f(t, y(t))\, dt = -3 + \int_{1}^{x} \left(y^2(t) - 2ty(t) + t^2\right) dt\,.$$

Using the linear property of integrals, we find that

$$\int_{1}^{x} \left(y^2(t) - 2ty(t) + t^2\right) dt = \int_{1}^{x} y^2(t)\, dt - 2\int_{1}^{x} ty(t)\, dt + \int_{1}^{x} t^2\, dt$$

$$= \int_{1}^{x} \left[y^2(t) - 2ty(t)\right] dt + \frac{x^3}{3} - \frac{1}{3}\,,$$

we have

$$y(x) = \frac{x^3}{3} - \frac{10}{3} + \int_1^x y^2(t)\, dt - 2\int_1^x ty(t)\, dt. \tag{13.1}$$

Note that we can rewrite the last integral using integration by parts in terms of integrals of the function $y(x)$ alone. Namely,

$$\int_1^x ty(t)\, dt = t\int_1^t y(s)\, ds\bigg|_{t=1}^{t=x} - \int_1^x \int_1^t y(s)\, ds\, dt = x\int_1^x y(s)\, ds - \int_1^x \int_1^t y(s)\, ds\, dt$$

Thus, another form of the answer (13.1) is

$$y(x) = \frac{x^3}{3} - \frac{10}{3} + \int_1^x y^2(t)\, dt + x\int_1^x y(t)\, dt - \int_1^x \int_1^t y(s)\, ds\, dt\,.$$

**5.** In this problem, we have

$$g(x) = \frac{1}{2}\left(x + \frac{3}{x}\right).$$

Thus the recurrence formula (7) on page 807 of the text becomes

$$x_{n+1} = g(x_n) = \frac{1}{2}\left(x_n + \frac{3}{x_n}\right), \qquad n = 0, 1, \ldots.$$

With $x_0 = 3$ as an initial approximation, we compute

$$x_1 = \frac{1}{2}\left(x_0 + \frac{3}{x_0}\right) = \frac{1}{2}\left(3 + \frac{3}{3}\right) = 2.0\,, \qquad x_2 = \frac{1}{2}\left(x_1 + \frac{3}{x_1}\right) = \frac{1}{2}\left(2 + \frac{3}{2}\right) = 1.75\,,$$

and so on. The results of these computations is given in Table 13-A.

---

**Table 13–A:** Approximations for a solution of $x = \dfrac{1}{2}\left(x + \dfrac{3}{x}\right)$.

| | |
|---|---|
| $x_0 = 3.0$ | $x_3 = 1.732142857$ |
| $x_1 = 2.0$ | $x_4 = 1.732050810$ |
| $x_2 = 1.75$ | $x_5 = 1.732050808$ |

---

We stopped iterating after $x_5$ because $x_4 - x_5 < 10^{-8}$. Hence $x \approx 1.73205081$.

**7.** Since $g(x) = 1/(x^2 + 4)$, we have the recurrence formula

$$x_{n+1} = g(x_n) = \frac{1}{x_n^2 + 4}, \qquad n = 0, 1, \ldots$$

with an initial approximation $x_0 = 0.5$. Hence

$$x_1 = \frac{1}{x_0^2 + 4} = \frac{1}{(0.5)^2 + 4} = \frac{4}{17} \approx 0.2352941176,$$

$$x_2 = \frac{1}{x_1^2 + 4} \approx \frac{1}{(0.2352941176)^2 + 4} \approx 0.2465870307, \quad \text{etc.}$$

See Table 13-B. We stopped iterating after $x_7$ because the error $x_6 - x_7 < 10^{-9}$. Hence $x \approx 0.24626617$.

---

**Table 13–B**: Approximations for a solution of $x = \dfrac{1}{x^2 + 4}$.

| | |
|---|---|
| $x_0 = 0.5$ | $x_4 = 0.2462664586$ |
| $x_1 = 0.2352941176$ | $x_5 = 0.2462661636$ |
| $x_2 = 0.2465870307$ | $x_6 = 0.2462661724$ |
| $x_3 = 0.2462565820$ | $x_7 = 0.2462661721$ |

---

**9.** To start the method of successive substitutions, we observe that

$$g(x) = \left(\frac{5 - x}{3}\right)^{1/4}.$$

Therefore, according to equation (7) on page 807 of the text, we can find the next approximation from the previous one by using the recurrence relation

$$x_{n+1} = g(x_n) = \left(\frac{5 - x_n}{3}\right)^{1/4}.$$

We start the procedure at the point $x_0 = 1$. Thus, we obtain

$$x_1 = \left(\frac{5 - x_0}{3}\right)^{1/4} = \left(\frac{5 - 1}{3}\right)^{1/4} = \left(\frac{4}{3}\right)^{1/4} \approx 1.074569932,$$

Chapter 13

$$x_2 = \left(\frac{5-x_1}{3}\right)^{1/4} \approx \left(\frac{5-1.074569932}{3}\right)^{1/4} \approx 1.069526372\,,$$

$$x_3 = \left(\frac{5-x_2}{3}\right)^{1/4} \approx \left(\frac{5-1.069526372}{3}\right)^{1/4} \approx 1.069869749\,.$$

By continuing this process, we fill in Table 13-C below. Noticing that $x_7 - x_6 < 10^{-8}$, we stopped the procedure after seven steps. So, $x \approx 1.06984787$.

---

**Table 13–C**: Approximations for a solution of $x = \left(\frac{5-x}{3}\right)^{1/4}$.

| | |
|---|---|
| $x_0 = 1.0$ | $x_4 = 1.069846382$ |
| $x_1 = 1.074569932$ | $x_5 = 1.069847972$ |
| $x_2 = 1.069526372$ | $x_6 = 1.069847864$ |
| $x_3 = 1.069869749$ | $x_7 = 1.069847871$ |

---

11. First, we derive an integral equation corresponding to the given initial value problem. We have $f(x,y) = -y$, $x_0 = 0$, $y_0 = y(0) = 2$, and so the formula (3) on page 807 of the text yields

$$y(x) = 2 + \int_0^x [-y(t)]\,dt = 2 - \int_0^x y(t)\,dt\,.$$

Thus, Picard's recurrence formula (15) becomes

$$y_{n+1}(x) = 2 - \int_0^x y_n(t)\,dt, \qquad n = 0,1,\dots\,.$$

Starting with $y_0(x) \equiv y_0 = 2$, we compute

$$y_1(x) = 2 - \int_0^x y_0(t)\,dt = 2 - \int_0^x 2\,dt = 2 - 2t\,\Big|_{t=0}^{t=x} = 2 - 2x\,,$$

$$y_2(x) = 2 - \int_0^x y_1(t)\,dt = 2 - \int_0^x (2-2t)\,dt = 2 + (t-1)^2\,\Big|_{t=0}^{t=x} = 2 - 2x + x^2\,.$$

728

**13.** In this problem, $f(x,y) = 3x^2$, $x_0 = 1$, $y_0 = y(1) = 2$, and so Picard's iterations to the solution of the given initial value problem are given by

$$y_{n+1}(x) = 2 + \int_1^x \left(3t^2\right) dt = 2 + t^3 \Big|_{t=1}^{t=x} = x^3 + 1 \,.$$

Since the right-hand side does not depend on $n$, the sequence of iterations $y_k(x)$, $k = 1, 2, \ldots$, is a constant sequence. That is,

$$y_k(x) = x^3 + 1 \qquad \text{for any } k \geq 1.$$

In particular, $y_1(x) = y_2(x) = x^3 + 1$.

(In this connection, note the following. If it happens that one of the iterations, say, $y_k(x)$, obtained via (15) matches the exact solution to the integral equation (3), then all the subsequent iterations will give the same function $y_k(x)$. In other words, the sequence of iterations will become a constant sequence starting from its $k$th term. In the given problem, the first application of (15) gives the *exact* solution, $x^3 + 1$, to the original initial value problem and, hence, to the corresponding integral equation (3).)

**15.** We first write this differential equation as an integral equation. Integrating both sides from $x_0 = 0$ to $x$ and using the fact that $y(0) = 0$, we obtain

$$y(x) - y(0) = \int_0^x \left[y(t) - e^t\right] dt \qquad \Rightarrow \qquad y(x) = \int_0^x \left[y(t) - e^t\right] dt \,.$$

Hence, by equation (15) on page 811 of the text, the Picard iterations are given by

$$y_{n+1}(x) = \int_0^x \left[y_n(t) - e^t\right] dt \,.$$

Thus, starting with $y_0(x) \equiv y_0 = 0$, we calculate

$$y_1(x) = \int_0^x \left[y_0(t) - e^t\right] dt = -\int_0^x e^t dt = 1 - e^x \,,$$

729

$$y_2(x) = \int_0^x \left[ y_1(t) - e^t \right] dt = \int_0^x \left( 1 - 2e^t \right) dt = 1 - e^x = 2 + x - 2e^x \,.$$

**17.** First of all, remark that the function $f(x, y(x))$ in the integral equation (3), that is,

$$y(x) = y_0 + \int_{x_0}^x f(t, y(t)) \, dt \,,$$

is a continuous function as the composition of $f(x, y)$ and $y(x)$, which are both continuous by our assumption. Next, if $y(x)$ satisfies (3), then

$$y(x_0) = y_0 + \int_{x_0}^{x_0} f(t, y(t)) \, dt = y_0 \,,$$

because the integral term is zero as a definite integral of a continuous function with equal limits of integration. Therefore, $y(x)$ satisfies the initial condition in (1).

We recall that, by the fundamental theorem of calculus, if $g(x)$ is a continuous function on an interval $[a, b]$, then, for any fixed $c$ in $[a, b]$, the function $G(x) := \int_a^x g(t) \, dt$ is an antiderivative for $g(x)$ on $(a, b)$, i.e.,

$$G'(x) = \left( \int_a^x g(t) \, dt \right)' = g(x).$$

Thus,

$$y'(x) = \left( y_0 + \int_{x_0}^x f(t, y(t)) \, dt \right)' = f(t, y(t)) \, |_{t=x} = f(x, y(x)),$$

and so $y(x)$ satisfies the differential equation in (1).

**19.** The graphs of the functions $y = (x^2 + 1)/2$ and $y = x$ are sketched on the same coordinate axes in Figure 13-A.

By examining this figure, we see that these two graphs intersect only at $(1, 1)$. We can find this point by solving the equation

$$x = \frac{x^2 + 1}{2} \,,$$

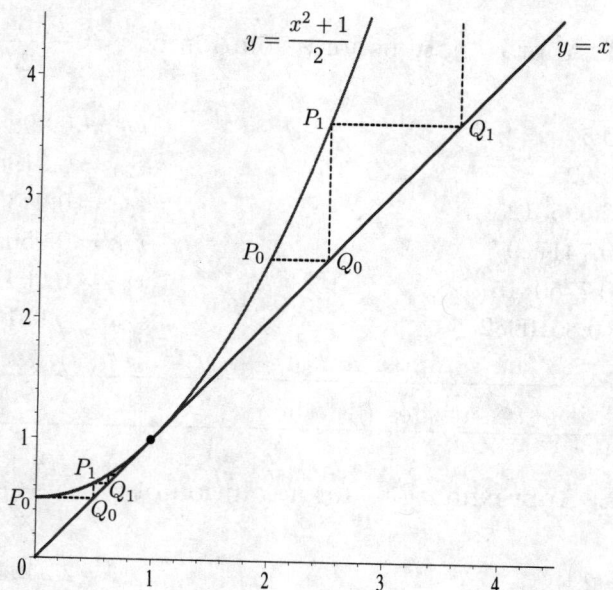

**Figure 13–A**: The method of successive substitution for the equation $x = \dfrac{x^2 + 1}{2}$.

for $x$. Thus, we have

$$2x = x^2 + 1 \quad \Rightarrow \quad x^2 - 2x + 1 = 0 \quad \Rightarrow \quad (x-1)^2 = 0 \quad \Rightarrow \quad x = 1.$$

Since $y = x$, the only intersection point is $(1, 1)$.

To approximate the solution to the equation $x = (x^2 + 1)/2$ using the method of successive substitutions, we use the recurrence relation

$$x_{n+1} = \frac{x_n^2 + 1}{2}.$$

Starting this method at $x_0 = 0$, we obtain the approximations given in Table 13-D. These approximations do appear to be approaching the solution $x = 1$.

However, if we start the process at the point $x = 2$, we obtain the approximations given in Table 13-E.

We observe that these approximations are getting larger and so do not seem to approach a fixed point. This also appears to be the case if we examine the pictorial representation for the

**Table 13–D**: Approximations for a solution of $x = \dfrac{x^2 + 1}{2}$ starting at $x_0 = 0$.

| | |
|---|---|
| $x_1 = 0.5$ | $x_{15} = 0.89859837$ |
| $x_2 = 0.625$ | $x_{20} = 0.91988745$ |
| $x_3 = 0.6953125$ | $x_{30} = 0.94337158$ |
| $x_4 = 0.7417297$ | $x_{40} = 0.95611749$ |
| $x_5 = 0.7750815$ | $x_{50} = 0.96414507$ |
| $x_{10} = 0.8610982$ | $x_{99} = 0.98102848$ |

**Table 13–E**: Approximations for a solution of $x = \dfrac{x^2 + 1}{2}$ starting at $x_0 = 2$.

| | |
|---|---|
| $x_1 = 2.5$ | $x_4 = 25.4946594$ |
| $x_2 = 3.625$ | $x_5 = 325.488829$ |
| $x_3 = 7.0703125$ | $x_6 = 52971.9891$ |

method of successive substitutions given in Figure 13-A. By plugging $x_0 = 0$ into the function $(x^2 + 1)/2$, we find $P_0$ to be the point $(0, 0.5)$. Then by moving parallel to the $x$-axis from the point $P_0$ to the line $y = x$, we observe that $Q_0$ is the point $(0.5, 0.5)$. Next, by moving parallel to the $y$-axis from the point $Q_0$ to the curve $y = (x^2 + 1)/2$, we find that $P_1$ is the point $(0.5, 0.625)$. Continuing this process moves us slowly in a step fashion to the point $(1, 1)$. However, if we start this process at $x_0 = 2$, we observe that this method moves us through larger and larger steps away from the point of intersection $(1, 1)$.

Note that for this equation, the movement of the method of successive substitutions is to the right. This is because the term $(x_n^2 + 1)/2$, in the recurrence relation, is increasing for $x > 0$. Thus, *the sequence of approximations $\{x_n\}$ is an increasing sequence*. Starting at a nonnegative point less than 1 moves us to the fixed point at $x = 1$, but starting at a point larger that 1 moves us to ever increasing values for our approximations and, therefore, away from the fixed point.

**EXERCISES 13.2:   Picard's Existence and Uniqueness Theorem, page 820**

**1.** In order to determine whether this sequence of functions converges uniformly, we find $\|y_n - y\|$. Since

$$y_n(x) - y(x) = \left(1 - \frac{x}{n}\right) - 1 = -\frac{x}{n},$$

we have

$$\|y_n - y\| = \max_{x \in [-1,1]} |y_n(x) - y(x)| = \max_{x \in [-1,1]} \frac{|x|}{n} = \frac{1}{n}.$$

Thus

$$\lim_{n \to \infty} \|y_n - y\| = \lim_{n \to \infty} \frac{1}{n} = 0$$

and $\{y_n(x)\}$ converges to $y(x)$ uniformly on $[-1, 1]$.

**3.** In order to determine whether this sequence of functions converges uniformly, we must find

$$\lim_{n \to \infty} \|y_n - y\|.$$

Therefore, we first compute

$$\|y_n - y\| = \|y_n\| = \max_{x \in [0,1]} \left| \frac{nx}{1 + n^2 x^2} \right| = \max_{x \in [0,1]} \frac{nx}{1 + n^2 x^2},$$

where we have removed the absolute value signs because the term $(nx)/(1 + n^2 x^2)$ is nonnegative when $x \in [0, 1]$. We will use calculus methods to obtain this maximum value. Thus, we differentiate the function $y_n(x) = (nx)/(1 + n^2 x^2)$ to obtain

$$y_n'(x) = \frac{n(1 - n^2 x^2)}{(1 + n^2 x^2)^2}.$$

Setting $y_n'(x)$ equal to zero and solving yields

$$n\left(1 - n^2 x^2\right) = 0 \quad \Rightarrow \quad n^2 x^2 = 1 \quad \Rightarrow \quad x = \pm \frac{1}{n}.$$

Since we are interested in the values of $x$ on the interval $[0, 1]$, we will only examine the critical point $x = 1/n$. By the first derivative test, we observe that the function $y_n(x)$ has a local maximum value at the point $x = 1/n$. At this point, we have

$$y_n\left(\frac{1}{n}\right) = \frac{n\left(n^{-1}\right)}{1 + n^2\left(n^{-1}\right)^2} = \frac{1}{2}.$$

Chapter 13

Computing

$$y_n(0) = \frac{n(0)}{1+n^2(0)^2} = 0,$$

$$y_n(1) = \frac{n(1)}{1+n^2(1)^2} = \frac{n}{1+n^2} < \frac{1}{n} \le \frac{1}{2} \quad \text{for} \quad n \ge 2,$$

we conclude that

$$\max_{x\in[0,1]} y_n(x) = \frac{1}{2}.$$

Therefore,

$$\lim_{n\to\infty} \|y_n - y\| = \lim_{n\to\infty} \frac{1}{2} = \frac{1}{2} \ne 0.$$

Thus, the given sequence of functions does *not* converge uniformly to the function $y(x) \equiv 0$ on the interval $[0,1]$.

This sequence of functions does, however, converge pointwise to the function $y(x) \equiv 0$ on the interval $[0,1]$. To see this, notice that for any fixed $x \in (0,1]$ we have

$$\lim_{n\to\infty} [y_n(x) - y(x)] = \lim_{n\to\infty} \frac{nx}{1+n^2x^2} = \lim_{n\to\infty} \frac{1}{2nx} = 0,$$

where we have found this limit by using L'Hospital's rule. At the point $x = 0$, we observe that

$$\lim_{n\to\infty} [y_n(0) - y(0)] = \lim_{n\to\infty} \frac{0}{1} = 0.$$

Thus, we have pointwise convergence but *not* uniform convergence. See Figure 13-B(a) for the graphs of functions $y_1(x)$, $y_{10}(x)$, $y_{30}(x)$, and $y_{90}(x)$.

5. We know (as was stated on page 433 of the text) that for all $x$ such that $|x| < 1$ the geometric series, $\sum_{k=0}^{\infty} x^k$, converges to the function $f(x) = 1/(1-x)$. Thus, for all $x \in [0,1/2]$, we have

$$\frac{1}{1-x} == 1 + x + x^2 + \cdots + x^k + \cdots = \sum_{k=0}^{\infty} x^k.$$

Therefore, we see that

$$\|y_n - y\| = \max_{x\in[0,1/2]} |y_n(x) - y(x)| = \max_{x\in[0,1/2]} \left| \sum_{k=0}^{n} x^k - \sum_{k=0}^{\infty} x^k \right| = \max_{x\in[0,1/2]} \sum_{k=n+1}^{\infty} x^k = \sum_{k=n+1}^{\infty} \left(\frac{1}{2}\right)^k$$

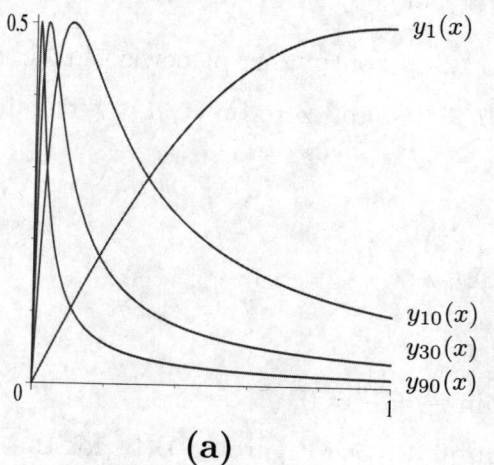

(a)

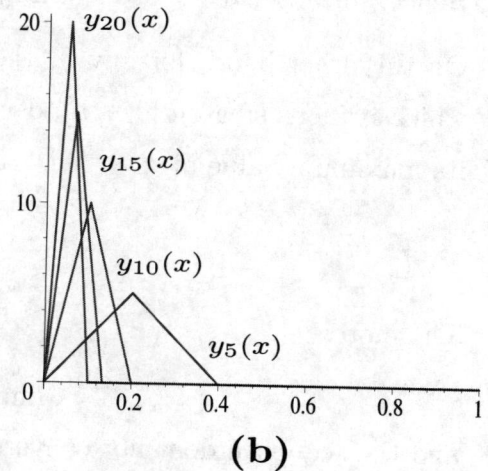

(b)

**Figure 13–B**: Graphs of functions in Problems 3 and 7.

and so

$$\lim_{n\to\infty} \|y_n - y\| = \lim_{n\to\infty} \left[ \sum_{k=n+1}^{\infty} \left(\frac{1}{2}\right)^k \right].$$

Since $\sum_{k=n+1}^{\infty}(1/2)^k$ is the tail end of a convergent series, its limit must be zero. Hence, we have

$$\lim_{n\to\infty} \|y_n - y\| = \lim_{n\to\infty} \left[ \sum_{k=n+1}^{\infty} \left(\frac{1}{2}\right)^k \right] = 0.$$

Therefore, the given sequence of functions converges uniformly to the function $y(x) = 1/(1-x)$ on the interval $[0, 1/2]$.

**7.** Let $x \in [0, 1]$ be fixed.

If $x = 0$, then $y_n(0) = n^2(0) = 0$ for any $n$ and so $\lim_{n\to\infty} y_n(0) = \lim_{n\to\infty} 0 = 0$.

For $x > 0$, let $N_x := [2/x] + 1$ with $[\cdot]$ denoting the interger part of a number. Then, for $n \geq N_x$, one has

$$n \geq \left[\frac{2}{x}\right] + 1 > \frac{2}{x} \qquad \Rightarrow \qquad x > \frac{2}{n}$$

and so, in evaluating $y_n(x)$, the third line in its definition must be used. This yields $y_n(x) = 0$ for all $n \geq N_x$, which implies that $\lim_{n\to\infty} y_n(x) = \lim_{n\to\infty} 0 = 0$.

Hence, for any fixed $x \in [0, 1]$, $\lim_{n \to \infty} y_n(x) = 0 = y(x)$.

On the other hand, for any $n$, the function $y_n(x)$ is a continuous piecewise linear function, which is increasing on $[0, 1/n]$, decreasing on $(1/n, 2/n)$, and zero on $[1/n, 1]$. Thus it attains its maximum value at $x = 1/n$, which is

$$y_n \left( \frac{1}{n} \right) = n^2 \left( \frac{1}{n} \right) = n.$$

Therefore,

$$\lim_{n \to \infty} \|y_n - y\| = \lim_{n \to \infty} \|y_n\| = \lim_{n \to \infty} n = \infty,$$

and the sequence does not converge uniformly on $[0, 1]$. See Figure 13-B(b) for the graphs of $y_5(x)$, $y_{10}(x)$, $y_{15}(x)$, and $y_{20}(x)$.

**9.** We need to find an $h > 0$ such that $h < \min \left( h_1, \alpha_1/M, 1/L \right)$. We are given that

$$R_1 = \{(x, y) : |x - 1| \leq 1, \ |y| \leq 1\} = \{(x, y) : 0 \leq x \leq 2, -1 \leq y \leq 1\},$$

and so $h_1 = 1$ and $\alpha_1 = 1$. Thus, we must find values for $M$ and $L$.

In order to find $M$, notice that, as was stated on page 816 of the text, we require that $M$ satisfy the condition

$$|f(x, y)| = |y^2 - x| \leq M,$$

for all $(x, y)$ in $R_1$. To find this upper bound for $|f(x, y)|$, we must find the maximum and the minimum values of $f(x, y)$ on $R_1$. (Since $f(x, y)$ is a continuous function on the closed and bounded region $R_1$, it will have a maximum and a minimum there.) We will use calculus methods to find this maximum and this minimum. Since the first partial derivatives of $f(x, y)$, given by

$$f_x(x, y) = -1, \quad \text{and} \quad f_y(x, y) = 2y,$$

are never both zero, the maximum and minimum must occur on the boundary of $R_1$. Notice that $R_1$ is bounded on the left by the line $x = 0$, on the right by the line $x = 2$, on the top by the line $y = 1$, and on the bottom by the line $y = -1$. Therefore, we will examine the behavior of $f(x, y)$ (and, thus, of $|f(x, y)|$) on each of these lines.

Case 1: On the left side of $R_1$ where $x = 0$, the function $f(x, y)$ becomes the function in the single variable $y$, given by

$$f(0, y) = F_1(y) = y^2 - 0 = y^2, \qquad y \in [-1, 1].$$

This function has a maximum at $y = \pm 1$ and a minimum at $y = 0$. Thus, on the left side of $R_1$ we see that $f$ reaches a maximum value of $f(0, \pm 1) = 1$ and a minimum value of $f(0, 0) = 0$.

Case 2: On the right side of $R_1$ where $x = 2$, the function $f(x, y)$ becomes the function in the single variable $y$, given by

$$f(2, y) = F_2(y) = y^2 - 2, \qquad y \in [-1, 1].$$

This function also has a maximum at $y = \pm 1$ and a minimum at $y = 0$. Thus, on the right side of $R_1$, the function $f(x, y)$ reaches a maximum value of $f(2, \pm 1) = -1$ and a minimum value of $f(2, 0) = -2$.

Case 3: On the top and bottom of $R_1$ where $y = \pm 1$, the function $f(x, y)$ becomes the function given by

$$f(x, \pm 1) = F_3(x) = (\pm 1)^2 - x = 1 - x, \qquad x \in [0, 2].$$

This function also has a maximum at $x = 0$ and a minimum at $x = 2$. Thus, on both the top and bottom of the region $R_1$, the function $f(x, y)$ reaches a maximum value of $f(0, \pm 1) = 1$ and a minimum value of $f(2, \pm 1) = -1$.

From the above cases we see that the maximum value of $f(x, y)$ is 1 and the minimum value is $-2$ on the boundary of $R_1$. Thus, we have $|f(x, y)| \leq 2$ for all $(x, y)$ in $R_1$. Hence, we choose $M = 2$.

To find $L$, we observe that $L$ is an upper bound for

$$\left| \frac{\partial f}{\partial y} \right| = |2y| = 2|y|,$$

on $R_1$. Since $y \in [-1, 1]$ in this region, we have $|y| \leq 1$. Hence, we see that

$$\left| \frac{\partial f}{\partial y} \right| = 2|y| \leq 2,$$

Chapter 13

for all $(x, y)$ in $R_1$. Therefore, we choose $L = 2$.

Now we can choose $h \geq 0$ such that

$$h < \min\left(h_1, \frac{\alpha_1}{M}, \frac{1}{L}\right) = \min\left(1, \frac{1}{2}\frac{1}{2}\right) = \frac{1}{2}.$$

Thus, Theorem 3 guarantees that the given initial value problem will have a unique solution on the interval $[1 - h, 1 + h]$, where $0 < h < 1/2$.

**11.** We are given that the recurrence relation for these approximations is $y_{n+1} = T[y_n]$. Using the definition of $T[y]$, we have

$$y_{n+1} = x^3 - x + 1 \int_0^x (u - x)y_n(u)\, du.$$

Thus, starting these approximations with $y_0(x) = x^3 - x + 1$, we obtain

$$
\begin{aligned}
y_1(x) &= x^3 - x + 1 + \int_0^x (u - x)y_0(u)\, du = x^3 - x + 1 + \int_0^x (u - x)\left[u^3 - u + 1\right] du \\
&= x^3 - x + 1 + \int_0^x (u^4 - u^2 + u - xu^3 + xu - x)\, du \\
&= x^3 - x + 1 + \left[\frac{x^5}{5} - \frac{x^3}{3} + \frac{x^2}{2} - \frac{x^5}{4} + \frac{x^3}{2} - x^2\right].
\end{aligned}
$$

By simplifying, we obtain

$$y_1(x) = -\frac{1}{20}x^5 + \frac{7}{6}x^3 - \frac{1}{2}x^2 - x + 1.$$

Substituting this result into the recurrence relation yields

$$
\begin{aligned}
y_2(x) &= x^3 - x + 1 \int_0^x (u - x)y_1(u)\, du \\
&= x^3 - x + 1 \int_0^x (u - x)\left[-\frac{1}{20}u^5 + \frac{7}{6}u^3 - \frac{1}{2}u^2 - u + 1\right] du
\end{aligned}
$$

$$= x^3 - x + 1 + \left[ -\frac{1}{140} x^7 + \frac{7}{30} x^5 - \frac{1}{8} x^4 - \frac{1}{3} x^3 + \frac{1}{2} x^2 \right.$$

$$\left. + \frac{1}{120} x^7 - \frac{7}{24} x^5 + \frac{1}{6} x^4 + \frac{1}{2} x^3 - x^2 \right].$$

When simplified, this yields

$$y_2(x) = \frac{1}{840} x^7 - \frac{7}{120} x^5 + \frac{1}{24} x^4 + \frac{7}{6} x^3 - \frac{1}{2} x^2 - x + 1.$$

**13.** Using properties of limits and the linear property of integrals, we can rewrite the statement that

$$\lim_{n \to \infty} \int_a^b y_n(x) \, dx = \int_a^b y(x) \, dx$$

in an equivalent form

$$\lim_{n \to \infty} \left[ \int_a^b y_n(x) - \int_a^b y(x) \, dx \right] = 0 \qquad \Leftrightarrow \qquad \lim_{n \to \infty} \int_a^b [y_n(x) - y(x)] \, dx = 0. \qquad (13.2)$$

The sequence $\{y_n\}$ converges uniformly to $y$ on $[a, b]$, which means, by the definition of uniform convergence, that

$$\|y_n - y\|_{C[a,b]} := \max_{x \in [a,b]} |y_n(x) - y(x)| \to 0 \quad \text{as} \quad n \to \infty.$$

Since

$$\left| \int_a^b [y_n(x) - y(x)] \, dx \right| \leq \int_a^b |y_n(x) - y(x)| \, dx \leq (b - a) \|y_n - y\|_{C[a,b]} \to 0$$

as $n \to \infty$, we conclude that

$$\lim_{n \to \infty} \left| \int_a^b [y_n(x) - y(x)] \, dx \right| = 0,$$

and (13.2) follows. (Recall that $\lim_{n \to \infty} a_n = 0$ if and only if $\lim_{n \to \infty} |a_n| = 0$.)

# Chapter 13

**15. (a)** In the given system,

$$x'(t) = -y^2(t), \quad x(0) = 0;$$
$$y'(t) = z(t), \quad y(0) = 1; \tag{13.3}$$
$$z'(t) = x(t)y(t), \quad z(0) = 0,$$

replacing $t$ by $s$, integrating the differential equations from $s = 0$ to $s = t$, and using the fundamental theorem of calculus we obtain

$$\int_0^t x'(s)\,ds = -\int_0^t y^2(s)\,ds; \qquad\qquad x(t) - x(0) = -\int_0^t y^2(s)\,ds;$$
$$\int_0^t y'(s)\,ds = \int_0^t z(s)\,ds; \qquad \Rightarrow \qquad y(t) - y(0) = \int_0^t z(s)\,ds;$$
$$\int_0^t z'(s)\,ds = \int_0^t x(s)y(s)\,ds \qquad\qquad z(t) - z(0) = \int_0^t x(s)y(s)\,ds.$$

By the initial conditions in (13.3), $x(0) = 0$, $y(0) = z(0) = 1$. Substituting these values into the above system yields

$$x(t) = -\int_0^t y^2(s)\,ds;$$
$$y(t) - 1 = \int_0^t z(s)\,ds; \tag{13.4}$$
$$z(t) - 1 = \int_0^t x(s)y(s)\,ds,$$

which is equivalent to the given system of integral equations. Thus, (13.3) implies (13.4). Conversely, differentiating equations in (13.4) and using the fundamental theorem of calculus (its part regarding integrals with variable upper bound), we conclude that solutions $x(t)$, $y(t)$, and $z(t)$ to (13.4) also satisfy differential equations in (13.3). Clearly,

$$x(0) = -\int_0^0 y^2(s)\,ds = 0;$$
$$y(0) - 1 = \int_0^0 z(s)\,ds = 0;$$
$$z(t) - 1 = \int_0^0 x(s)y(s)\,ds = 0,$$

and the initial conditions in (13.3) are satisfied. Therefore, (13.4) implies (13.3).

**(b)** With starting iterations $x_0(t) \equiv x(0) = 0$, $y_0(t) \equiv y(0) = 1$, and $z_0(t) \equiv z(0) = 1$, we compute $x_1(t)$, $y_1(t)$, and $z_1(t)$.

$$x_1(t) = -\int_0^t y_0^2(s)\, ds = -\int_0^t (1)^2\, ds = -t;$$

$$y_1(t) = 1 + \int_0^t z_0(s)\, ds = 1 + \int_0^t (1)\, ds = 1 + t;$$

$$z_1(t) = 1 + \int_0^t x_0(s) y_0(s)\, ds = 1 + \int_0^t (0)\, ds = 1.$$

Applying given recurrence formulas again yields

$$x_2(t) = -\int_0^t y_1^2(s)\, ds = -\int_0^t (1+s)^2\, ds = -(1+s)^3/3 \Big|_0^t = -t - t^2 - \frac{t^3}{3};$$

$$y_2(t) = 1 + \int_0^t z_1(s)\, ds = 1 + \int_0^t 1\, ds = 1 + t;$$

$$z_2(t) = 1 + \int_0^t x_1(s) y_1(s)\, ds = 1 - \int_0^t s(1+s)\, ds = 1 - (s^2/2 + s^3/3) \Big|_0^t = 1 - \frac{t^2}{2} - \frac{t^3}{3}.$$

## EXERCISES 13.3:  Existence of Solutions of Linear Equations, page 826

**1.** In this problem,

$$\mathbf{A}(t) = \begin{bmatrix} \cos t & \sqrt{t} \\ t^3 & -1 \end{bmatrix}, \qquad \mathbf{f}(t) = \begin{bmatrix} \tan t \\ e^t \end{bmatrix}.$$

In $\mathbf{A}(t)$, functions $\cos t$, $t^3$, and $-1$ are continuous on $(-\infty, \infty)$ while $\sqrt{t}$ is continuous on $[0, \infty)$. Therefore, $\mathbf{A}(t)$ is continuous on $[0, \infty)$. In $\mathbf{f}(t)$, the exponential function is continuous everywhere, but $\tan t$ has infinite discontinuities at $t = (k + 1/2)\pi$, $k = 0, \pm 1, \pm 2, \ldots$. The largest interval containing the initial point, $t = 2$, where $\tan t$ and, therefore, $\mathbf{f}(t)$, is continuous is $(\pi/2, 3\pi/2)$. Since $\mathbf{A}(t)$ is also continuous on $(\pi/2, 3\pi/2)$, by Theorem 6, given initial value problem has a unique solution on this interval.

**3.** By comparing this problem to the problem given in (14) on page 825 of the text, we see that in this case

$$p_1(t) = -\ln t, \qquad p_2(t) \equiv 0, \qquad p_3(t) = \tan t, \quad \text{and} \quad g(t) = e^{2t}.$$

# Chapter 13

We also observe that $t_0 = 1$. Thus, we must find an interval containing $t_0 = 1$ on which all of the functions $p_1(t)$, $p_2(t)$, $p_3(t)$, and $g(t)$ are simultaneously continuous. Therefore, we note that $p_2(t)$ and $g(t)$ are continuous everywhere; $p_1(t)$ is continuous on the interval $(0, \infty)$; and the interval which contains $t_0 = 1$ on which $p_3(t)$ is continuous is $(-\pi/2, \pi/2)$. Hence, these four functions are simultaneously continuous on the interval $(0, \pi/2)$ and this interval contains the point $t_0 = 1$. Therefore, Theorem 7 given on page 825 of the text guarantees that we will have a unique solution to this initial value problem on the whole interval $(0, \pi/2)$.

5. In this problem, we use Theorem 5. Since

$$\mathbf{f}(t, \mathbf{x}) = \begin{bmatrix} \sin x_2 \\ 3x_1 \end{bmatrix},$$

we have

$$\frac{\partial \mathbf{f}}{\partial x_1}(t, \mathbf{x}) = \begin{bmatrix} 0 \\ 3 \end{bmatrix}, \qquad \frac{\partial \mathbf{f}}{\partial x_2}(t, \mathbf{x}) = \begin{bmatrix} \cos x_2 \\ 0 \end{bmatrix}.$$

Vectors $\mathbf{f}$, $\partial \mathbf{f}/\partial x_1$, and $\partial \mathbf{f}/\partial x_2$ are continuous on

$$R = \{-\infty < t < \infty, -\infty < x_1 < \infty, -\infty < x_2 < \infty\}$$

(which is the whole space $\mathbb{R}^3$) since their components are. Moreover,

$$\left| \frac{\partial \mathbf{f}}{\partial x_1}(t, \mathbf{x}) \right| = 3, \qquad \left| \frac{\partial \mathbf{f}}{\partial x_2}(t, \mathbf{x}) \right| = |\cos x_2| \leq 1$$

for any $(t, \mathbf{x})$, and the condition (3) in Theorem 5 is satisfied with $L = 3$. Hence, given initial value problem has a unique solution on the whole real axis $-\infty < t < \infty$.

7. The equation

$$y'''(t) - (\sin t)y'(t) + e^{-t}y(t) = 0$$

is a linear homogeneous equation and, hence, has a trivial solution, $y(t) \equiv 0$. Clearly, this solution satisfies the initial conditions, $y(0) = y'(0) = y''(0) = 0$. All that remains to note is that the coefficients, $-\sin t$ and $e^{-t}$, are continuous on $(-\infty, \infty)$ and so, by Theorem 7, the solution $y \equiv 0$ is unique.

**EXERCISES 13.4:** Continuous Dependence of Solutions, page 832

**3.** To apply Theorem 9, we first determine the constant $L$ for $f(x, y) = e^{\cos y} + x^2$. To do this, we observe that

$$\frac{\partial f}{\partial y}(x, y) = -e^{\cos y} \sin y.$$

Now on any rectangle $R_0$, we have

$$\left| \frac{\partial f}{\partial y}(x, y) \right| = \left| -e^{\cos y} \sin y \right| = \left| e^{\cos y} \right| \, |\sin y| \leq e.$$

(More detailed analysis shows that this function attains its maximum at $y^* = (\sqrt{5} - 1)/2$, and this maximum equals to $1.4585\ldots$.) Thus, since $h = 1$, we have by Theorem 9,

$$|\phi(x, y_0) - \phi(x, \widetilde{y}_0)| \leq |y_0 - \widetilde{y}_0| \, e^e .$$

Since we are given that $|y_0 - \widetilde{y}_0| \leq 10^{-2}$, we obtain the result

$$|\phi(x, y_0) - \phi(x, \widetilde{y}_0)| \leq 10^{-2} e^e \approx 0.151543 .$$

**9.** We can use inequality (18) in Theorem 10 to obtain the bound, but first must determine the constant $L$ and the constant $\varepsilon$. Here $f(x, y) = \sin x + (1 + y^2)^{-1}$ and $F(x, y) = x + 1 - y^2$. Now,

$$\left| \frac{\partial f}{\partial y}(x, y) \right| = \left| \frac{2y}{(1 + y^2)^2} \right|$$

and

$$\left| \frac{\partial F}{\partial y}(x, y) \right| = |2y| \leq 2.$$

To find an upper bound for $|\partial f / \partial y|$ on $R_0$, we maximize $2y/(1 + y^2)^2$. Hence, we obtain

$$\left( \frac{2y}{(1 + y^2)^2} \right)' = \frac{2(1 + y^2)^2 - 2y \cdot 2(1 + y^2)2y}{(1 + y^2)^4} = \frac{2(1 + y^2) - 8y^2}{(1 + y^2)^3} = \frac{2 - 6y^2}{(1 + y^2)^3} .$$

Setting this equal to zero and solving for $y$, we obtain

$$\frac{2 - 6y^2}{(1 + y^2)^3} = 0 \quad \Rightarrow \quad 2 - 6y^2 = 0 \quad \Rightarrow \quad y = \pm \frac{1}{\sqrt{3}} .$$

# Chapter 13

Since $2y/(1+y^2)^2$ is odd, we need only use $y = 1/\sqrt{3}$. Thus

$$\left|\frac{\partial f}{\partial y}(x,y)\right| \le \frac{2/\sqrt{3}}{(1+1/3)^2} = \frac{3\sqrt{3}}{8},$$

and so $L = 3\sqrt{3}/8$. To obtain $\varepsilon$ we seek an upper bound for

$$|f(x,y) - F(x,y)| = \left|\sin x + \frac{1}{1+y^2} - x - 1 + y^2\right| \le |\sin x - x| + \left|\frac{1}{1+y^2} - 1 + y^2\right|.$$

Using Taylor's theorem with remainder we have

$$\sin x = x - \frac{x^3 \cos \xi}{3!},$$

where $0 \le \xi \le x$. Thus for $-1 \le x \le 1$ we obtain

$$|\sin x - x| = \left|x - \frac{x^3 \cos \xi}{3!} - x\right| = \frac{|x|^3 \cos \xi}{3!} \le \frac{1}{6}.$$

Applying Taylor's theorem with remainder to $1/(1+y^2) - 1 + y^2$, we obtain

$$g(y) = (1+y^2)^{-1} - 1 + y^2,$$
$$g'(y) = -2y(1+y^2)^{-2} + 2y,$$
$$g''(y) = -2(1+y^2)^{-2} + 2(1+y^2)^{-3}(2y)^2 + 2,$$
$$g'''(y) = 4(1+y^2)^{-3}(2y) - 6(1+y^2)^{-4}(2y)^3 + 2(1+y^2)^{-3}(8y).$$

Since $g(0) = g'(0) = g''(0) = 0$, we have

$$(1+y^2)^{-1} - 1 + y^2 = \frac{g'''(\xi)}{3!},$$

where $0 \le \xi \le y$. Thus, we obtain

$$\left|(1+y^2)^{-1} - 1 + y^2\right| = \left|\frac{g'''(\xi)}{3!}\right| \le \frac{8 + 48 + 16}{6} = 12.$$

Hence

$$|f(x,y) - F(x,y)| \le \frac{1}{6} + 12 = \frac{73}{6}.$$

It now follows from inequality (18) in Theorem 10 that

$$|\phi(x) - \psi(x)| \le \frac{73}{6} e^{3\sqrt{3}/8} \approx 23.294541,$$

for $x$ in $[-1, 1]$.